# Welfare Benefits Handbook

**27th edition**

Child Poverty Action Group

Child Poverty Action Group works on behalf of the more than one in four children in the UK growing up in poverty. It does not have to be like this. We use our understanding of what causes poverty and the impact it has on children's lives to campaign for policies that will prevent and solve poverty – for good. We provide training, advice and information to make sure hard-up families get the financial support they need. We also carry out high-profile legal work to establish and protect families' rights. If you are not already supporting us, please consider making a donation, or ask for details of our membership schemes, training courses and publications.

Published by Child Poverty Action Group
30 Micawber Street
London N1 7TB
Tel: 020 7837 7979
staff@cpag.org.uk
cpag.org.uk



A CIP record for this book is available from the British Library
ISBN: 978 1 915324 21 4
Child Poverty Action Group is a charity registered in England and Wales (registration number 294841) and in Scotland (registration number SC039339), and is a company limited by guarantee, registered in England (registration number 1993854). VAT number: 690 808117

Cover design by Colorido Studios
Internal design by Devious Designs
Typeset by DLxml, a division of RefineCatch Limited, Bungay, Suffolk
Content management system by Konnect Soft
Printed in the UK by CPI Group (UK) Ltd, Croydon CR0 4YY

# The authors

**Liam Bradford** is a freelance writer on welfare rights.

**Harriet Chaplin** is a welfare rights worker at CPAG.

**Lynsey Dalton** is a solicitor and freelance writer on welfare rights.

**Barbara Donegan** is a welfare rights worker at CPAG in Scotland.

**Moira Escreet** is a welfare rights worker at CPAG in Scotland.

**Carolyn George** is a freelance writer on welfare rights.

**Alison Gillies** is a welfare rights worker at CPAG in Scotland.

**Will Hadwen** is a freelance welfare rights worker for CPAG in Scotland and a freelance trainer.

**Henri Krishna** is a welfare rights worker at CPAG in Scotland.

**Susan Mitchell** is a welfare rights worker at CPAG.

**Simon Osborne** is a welfare rights worker at CPAG, based at CPAG in Scotland.

**Joanne Porter** is a welfare rights worker at CPAG in Scotland.

**Frances Ryan** is a welfare rights worker at CPAG in Scotland.

**Jon Shaw** is a welfare rights worker at CPAG in Scotland.

**Owen Stevens** is a welfare rights worker at CPAG.

**Jessica Strode** is judicial review project worker at CPAG.

**Carri Swann** is a welfare rights worker at CPAG.

**Angela Toal** is a welfare rights worker at CPAG in Scotland.

**Rebecca Walker** is an advice worker at Sheffield Citizens Advice and Law Centre and a freelance trainer and writer on welfare rights.

**Mark Willis** is a welfare rights worker at CPAG in Scotland.

# Acknowledgements

The authors would like to thank Liam Casey, Lizzie Flew, Barbara Gray, Claire Hall, Alison Lord, David Malcolm, Daniel Norris, Judith Paterson, Owen Polley, Louise Ross, Kelly Smith, Martin Williams, and Katie Wood at Maternity Action for their invaluable contribution.

Our thanks are also due to Simon Osborne, the book's content consultant.

We must acknowledge the efforts of the many authors of previous editions of the *National Welfare Benefits Handbook*, the *Rights Guide to Non-Means-Tested Benefits*, the *Jobseeker's Allowance Handbook* and the *Welfare Benefits and Tax Credits Handbook*, on which this book is based.

Thanks are also due to Nicola Johnston, Pauline Phillips and Kathy Proctor for editing and managing the production of the book, and to Kathleen Armstrong, Louise Heath, Anne Ketley and Sarah Warburton for proofreading the text. Particular thanks must go to Katherine Dawson and Anne Ketley for producing the index, and Bridget Rendell and Philippa Bradnock for managing the digital edition on CPAG Welfare Rights (cpag.org.uk/welfare-rights).

Your feedback is valuable and will help us improve future editions. Please complete the short survey at cpag.org.uk/handbook-survey.

**The law covered in this book was correct on 3 March 2025 and includes regulations laid up to this date.**

# Foreword

Welcome to the 2025/26 edition of the *Welfare Benefits Handbook*. As you may have noticed, tax credits have disappeared from the name of our flagship guide as they disappear from our social security system. The tax credit system, introduced in the first term of the New Labour government by Gordon Brown, played a significant role in reducing child poverty. By contrast, the last 15 years have seen numerous cuts and freezes to our social security system, so that now universal credit (UC) and child benefit are far too low, and child poverty is far too high.

Soon after the new UK government came in, it announced a Child Poverty Taskforce to draw up a new child poverty strategy. This will be published later in 2025, and the need could not be more urgent. This strategy is a huge opportunity to significantly reduce child poverty in the UK. It needs to be ambitious to match the scale of the challenge, and it needs to have targets to focus efforts.

Investment in our social security system must be central to the strategy. Tackling child poverty is a key role of a decent social security system of which we can all be proud. That includes ending the two-child limit, so that all children who need support receive it, and ending the benefit cap, which leaves families in very deep poverty. We also need an increase in adequacy across the board, the restoration of child benefit, and to ensure that families most at risk of poverty are able to access the social security system – which means, at a minimum, removing the 'no recourse to public funds' condition for families with children.

The strategy should also:

- address barriers to employment for parents who can work, and support these parents to get good jobs;
- improve parental leave entitlements and enable more flexible working;
- ensure there is enough secure, decent housing for families, and restore financial support for housing costs;
- address costs in the education system that can exclude some children from fully taking part in the school day;
- extend free school meals at least to children in families receiving UC, and ultimately make them a universal entitlement;
- increase affordable childcare and move towards universal access;
- invest in before- and after-school and holiday childcare;
- invest in preventative early years services that improve children's outcomes.

You can read our research on how to deliver a child poverty strategy at cpag.org.uk/childpovertystrategy.

We are very concerned about the new green paper, which sets out the biggest cut to disability benefits in a generation and undermines efforts to reduce poverty. The reforms will push children into poverty, and reduce living standards for many. The combined impact of more restrictive eligibility criteria and the reduced adequacy of disability benefits will mean some households will lose more than £100 a week. An increase in the UC standard allowance and more funding for employment support are welcome, as is the suggestion of a new contributory benefit. But these changes will not compensate for the devastating losses many families will face. If the government is serious about reducing child poverty and supporting sick and disabled people into work, it needs to invest in the social security system. Respond to the consultation before 30 June 2025 at gov.uk.

The UK government has also announced it will conduct a review of UC over the next year. We have published our priorities for reform of adequacy, the design of UC, and UC's relationship to work at cpag.org.uk/uc3steps.

Since taking office, the government has made some positive moves. We have long called for deductions that reduce a family's UC to be less severe. The government announced that households will pay back debts at a lower rate, with the deductions cap reduced from 25 per cent to 15 per cent of the UC standard allowance. One of the most common kinds of deduction is to pay back a new claim advance, which people take out to get through the five-week wait at the beginning of a UC claim. In our view, these advances should be non-repayable.

In addition, the government announced that the household support fund would be extended for another year. While welcome, we really need permanent ringfenced funding for local crisis support, alongside an adequately funded social security system that prevents people from reaching crisis point in the first place.

We also welcomed the changes to carer's allowance, which will allow carers to work up to 16 hours a week at the minimum wage. In previous years, the earnings threshold for carer's allowance hasn't kept track with minimum wage increases. This has resulted in carers having to either reduce their hours, or be subject to overpayments of carer's allowance that have then been clawed back.

We were also pleased to see the Scottish government's commitment to mitigate the two-child limit by 2026, which when added to the Scottish child payment represents a significant investment in supporting families and bringing down child poverty in Scotland. We need to see this same investment across the UK.

As the social security system continues to change, please share with us any issues that arise through our Early Warning System so we can continue to build our evidence of recurrent problems and advocate for change. Get in touch at cpag.org.uk/ews.

Thank you for your support for CPAG. We are here to help you do your vital work. See resources, information and advice at cpag.org.uk/welfare-rights.

Alison Garnham
Chief Executive, CPAG

# Contents


| | | |
|---|---|---|
| The authors | | iii |
| Acknowledgements | | iv |
| Foreword | | v |
| Abbreviations | | xii |
| Universal credit rates | | xiii |
| Means-tested benefit rates | | xiv |
| Non-means-tested benefit rates | | xvii |
| **Part 1** | **Introduction** | |
| | *Provides an overview of the benefits system and explains how to use this book to identify which benefits or statutory payments you can get and the amount you should receive. Read this part to understand how the information in the book is organised and how to find answers to specific questions about your entitlement.* | |
| Chapter 1 | How to use this book | 1 |
| **Part 2** | **Universal Credit** | |
| | *Covers the main rules for universal credit. Use this part if you are on a low income to check when you come under the universal credit system, whether you qualify for universal credit and to work out how much benefit you will get. It contains chapters on who can be included in your claim and on how your needs, housing costs, income and capital are calculated.* | |
| Chapter 2 | Transferring to universal credit | 19 |
| Chapter 3 | Universal credit | 35 |
| Chapter 4 | People included in your universal credit | 58 |
| Chapter 5 | The maximum amount | 66 |
| Chapter 6 | The housing costs element | 88 |
| Chapter 7 | Income | 124 |
| Chapter 8 | Capital | 149 |

3

**Part 3** **Other means-tested benefits**

***Explains the general rules for all the means-tested benefits, other than universal credit. Use this part if you are on a low income to check the main qualifying conditions. It contains chapters on who can be included in your claim, how your needs, income and capital are calculated, and the help you can get for certain housing costs. Use this part to check how much benefit you should get.***


| | | |
|---|---|---|
| Chapter 9 | Income-related employment and support allowance | 171 |
| Chapter 10 | Housing benefit | 181 |
| Chapter 11 | Pension credit | 238 |
| Chapter 12 | People included in your means-tested benefits | 254 |
| Chapter 13 | Applicable amounts | 265 |
| Chapter 14 | Help with ground rent, service charges and other housing costs | 286 |
| Chapter 15 | Housing benefit rent restrictions | 303 |
| Chapter 16 | Income: under pension age | 339 |
| Chapter 17 | Income: over pension age | 377 |
| Chapter 18 | Capital: under pension age | 398 |
| Chapter 19 | Capital: over pension age | 425 |


4

**Part 4** **Other benefits**

***Contains chapters on other benefits, statutory payments and additional help you may be able to get. Use this part to check whether you qualify for any of these benefits or payments, and for information on how to claim, the amount you may receive and how you are paid.***


| | | |
|---|---|---|
| Chapter 20 | Attendance allowance | 441 |
| Chapter 21 | Bereavement benefits | 453 |
| Chapter 22 | Carer's allowance | 471 |
| Chapter 23 | Child benefit and guardian's allowance | 487 |
| Chapter 24 | Disability living allowance | 511 |
| Chapter 25 | Discretionary housing payments | 548 |
| Chapter 26 | Contributory employment and support allowance | 555 |
| Chapter 27 | Health benefits | 573 |
| Chapter 28 | Industrial injuries benefits | 587 |
| Chapter 29 | New-style jobseeker's allowance | 610 |
| Chapter 30 | Maternity allowance | 629 |
| Chapter 31 | Personal independence payment | 645 |
| Chapter 32 | Retirement pensions | 687 |
| Chapter 33 | Social fund payments | 701 |
| Chapter 34 | Statutory maternity, adoption, paternity and other parental pay | 718 |
| Chapter 35 | Statutory sick pay | 746 |
| Chapter 36 | Other payments and support | 760 |

**Part 5** **Special benefit rules**

*Explains how particular circumstances, such as going into hospital, affect your entitlement to benefits and statutory payments. Use this part if any of the circumstances apply to you.*

| | | |
|---|---|---|
| Chapter 37 | Benefits for students | 791 |
| Chapter 38 | Benefits in hospital, care homes, prison and in other special circumstances | 816 |

**Part 6** **National insurance, work and work-related rules**

*Outlines the national insurance contribution conditions for contributory benefits and when you might qualify for national insurance credits, and explains the benefit rules on work and limited capability for work. Use this part to check whether you qualify for contributory benefits, to find out how work affects your benefit entitlement, what you may have do to prepare for and find work in order to get benefit, and what might happen if you do not do so.*

| | | |
|---|---|---|
| Chapter 39 | National insurance contributions | 857 |
| Chapter 40 | Work and benefits | 883 |
| Chapter 41 | Limited capability for work | 895 |
| Chapter 42 | Universal credit system work-related requirements | 934 |
| Chapter 43 | Universal credit system sanctions | 969 |

**Part 7** **Claiming benefits and getting paid**

*Gives general information on how to claim benefits and how you are paid, including details on the benefit cap, overpayments and hardship payments. Use this to check how to claim, how to get your claim backdated, and for what to do if your circumstances change, if you have been overpaid or if you have been accused of fraud.*

| | | |
|---|---|---|
| Chapter 44 | Claims | 1003 |
| Chapter 45 | Getting paid | 1017 |
| Chapter 46 | Hardship payments | 1050 |
| Chapter 47 | Overpayments | 1058 |
| Chapter 48 | Fraud and penalties | 1100 |

## Part 8 Getting a benefit decision changed

*Covers the different ways to challenge decisions, including appealing. Use this part if you are unhappy with a decision and want to know your rights and how to enforce them.*


| | | |
|---|---|---|
| Chapter 49 | Decisions | 1117 |
| Chapter 50 | Revisions and supersessions | 1128 |
| Chapter 51 | Appealing to the First-tier Tribunal | 1166 |
| Chapter 52 | Appealing to the Upper Tribunal and the courts | 1215 |
| Chapter 53 | Applying for judicial review | 1236 |
| Chapter 54 | Challenging decisions on statutory payments | 1249 |
| Chapter 55 | Complaints | 1260 |


## Part 9 Immigration and residence rules for benefits

*Explains how your immigration status affects your benefit entitlement in the UK and what happens if you go abroad. Use this part if you have come from abroad or are considering going abroad.*


| | | |
|---|---|---|
| Chapter 56 | Coming from abroad: immigration status | 1271 |
| Chapter 57 | Coming from abroad: residence rules | 1295 |
| Chapter 58 | Going abroad | 1368 |
| Chapter 59 | European Union co-ordination rules | 1388 |


## Part 10 Scottish social security benefits

*Contains information on the benefits which are part of the Scottish social security system. Use this part to check whether you can get a Scottish benefit, how to claim and what to do if you are unhappy with a determination.*


| | | |
|---|---|---|
| Chapter 60 | The Scottish social security system | 1417 |
| Chapter 61 | Adult disability payment | 1428 |
| Chapter 62 | Scottish child payment, Best Start grants and Best Start foods | 1451 |
| Chapter 63 | Carers' payments | 1467 |
| Chapter 64 | Child disability payment | 1483 |
| Chapter 65 | Funeral support payment | 1497 |
| Chapter 66 | Heating payments | 1505 |
| Chapter 67 | Pension age disability payment | 1512 |
| Chapter 68 | Claiming Scottish benefits and getting paid | 1521 |
| Chapter 69 | Determinations, redeterminations and appeals | 1533 |

## Appendices


| | | |
|---|---|---|
| Appendix 1 | Information and advice | 1571 |
| Appendix 2 | Useful publications | 1574 |
| Appendix 3 | Disability which puts a person at a disadvantage in getting a job | 1578 |
| Appendix 4 | Prescribed degrees of disablement | 1580 |
| Appendix 5 | Upper and lower earnings limits | 1583 |
| Appendix 6 | Minimum working conditions | 1584 |
| Appendix 7 | Abbreviations used in the notes | 1585 |

**Index** 1600

# Abbreviations

| | |
|---|---|
| AA | attendance allowance |
| ADP | adult disability payment |
| AFIP | armed forces independence payment |
| ARAP | Afghan Relocation and Assistance Policy |
| BRP | biometric residence permit |
| BSL | British Sign Language |
| CA | carer's allowance |
| CDP | child disability payment |
| CFCD | Counter Fraud, Compliance and Debt Directorate |
| CJEU | Court of Justice of the European Union |
| CRU | Compensation Recovery Unit |
| CSP | carer support payment |
| CTB | council tax benefit |
| CTC | child tax credit |
| DHP | discretionary housing payment |
| DLA | disability living allowance |
| DWP | Department for Work and Pensions |
| EEA | European Economic Area |
| EFTA | European Free Trade Association |
| ESA | employment and support allowance |
| EU | European Union |
| EUSS | European Union Settlement Scheme |
| EWC | expected week of childbirth |
| HB | housing benefit |
| HMCTS | HM Courts and Tribunals Service |
| HMRC | HM Revenue and Customs |
| IB | incapacity benefit |
| ICE | Independent Case Examiner |
| IIDB | industrial injuries disablement benefit |
| IS | income support |
| ISA | individual savings account |
| JSA | jobseeker's allowance |
| LES | scheme for locally employed staff in Afghanistan |
| MA | maternity allowance |
| MS | Medical Service |
| NI | national insurance |
| OISC | Office of the Immigration Services Commissioner |
| PADP | pension age disability payment |
| PAYE | pay as you earn |
| PC | pension credit |
| PHSO | Parliamentary and Health Service Ombudsman |
| PIP | personal independence payment |
| REA | reduced earning allowance |
| SADLA | Scottish adult disability living allowance |
| SAP | statutory adoption pay |
| SDA | severe disablement allowance |
| SDP | severe disability premium |
| SMP | statutory maternity pay |
| SNCP | statutory neonatal care pay |
| SPBP | statutory parental bereavement pay |
| SPP | statutory paternity pay |
| SSP | statutory sick pay |
| SSPP | statutory shared parental pay |
| SSS | Social Security Scotland |
| TFEU | Treaty on the Functioning of the European Union |
| UC | universal credit |
| UKVI | UK Visas and Immigration |
| VINCYP | Visual Impairment Network for Children and Young People |
| WTC | working tax credit |

# Universal credit rates

| Standard allowance | | £pm |
|---|---|---|
| Single | Under 25 | 316.98 |
| | 25 or over | 400.14 |
| Couple | Both under 25 | 497.55 |
| | One or both 25 or over | 628.10 |

| Elements | | |
|---|---|---|
| First child (if born before 6 April 2017) | | 339.00 |
| First child (if born on or after 6 April 2017), second child and each subsequent child who qualifies | | 292.81 |
| Disabled child addition | Lower rate | 158.76 |
| | Higher rate | 495.87 |
| Limited capability for work | | 158.76 |
| Limited capability for work-related activity | | 423.27 |
| Carer | | 201.68 |
| Childcare costs | One child | up to 1,031.88 |
| | Two or more children | up to 1,768.94 |
| | Percentage covered | 85% |
| Housing costs contribution | | 93.02 |
| Work allowance | UC includes a housing costs element | 411.00 |
| | UC does not include a housing costs element | 684.00 |
| Transitional severe disability premium element, see p27 | | |
| Transitional element, see p78 | | |

| Capital limits | Lower | Upper |
|---|---|---|
| | 6,000 | 16,000 |

Tariff income: £4.35 per £250 between lower and upper limits

# Means-tested benefit rates

## Income-related employment and support allowance

| | | Assessment phase | Main phase |
|---|---|---|---|
| **Personal allowances** | | *£pw* | *£pw* |
| Single | Under 25 | 72.90 | 92.05 |
| | 25 or over | 92.05 | 92.05 |
| Lone parent | 18 or over | 92.05 | 92.05 |
| Couple | One or both under 18 | 72.90–144.65 | 92.05–144.65 |
| | Both 18 or over | 144.65 | 144.65 |
| **Components** | | | |
| Work-related activity | | – | 36.55 |
| Support | | – | 48.50 |
| **Premiums** | | | |
| Carer | | 46.40 | 46.40 |
| Severe disability (one qualifies) | | 82.90 | 82.90 |
| Severe disability (two qualify) | | 165.80 | 165.80 |
| Enhanced disability | Single | 21.20 | 21.20 |
| | Couple | 30.25 | 30.25 |
| Pensioner | Couple, no component | 201.95 | – |
| | Couple, work-related activity component | – | 165.40 |
| | Couple, support component | – | 153.45 |
| **Capital limits** | | **Lower** | **Upper** |
| Standard | | 6,000 | 16,000 |
| Care homes | | 10,000 | 16,000 |

Tariff income: £1 per £250 between lower and upper limits

## Pension credit

### Guarantee credit

| | | |
|---|---|---|
| Standard minimum guarantee | Single | 227.10 |
| | Couple | 346.60 |
| Severe disability addition | One qualifies | 82.90 |
| | Two qualify | 165.80 |

| | | |
|---|---|---|
| Carer addition | | 46.40 |
| Child addition | Standard amount | 67.42 |
| | Standard amount for eldest child born before 6 April 2017 | 78.10 |
| | Disabled child increase | 36.54 |
| | Severely disabled child increase | 114.12 |
| **Savings credit** | | |
| Threshold | Single | 198.27 |
| | Couple | 314.34 |
| Maximum | Single | 17.30 |
| | Couple | 19.36 |
| **Capital disregard** | | |
| Standard/care homes | | 10,000 |
| No upper limit | | |
| Deemed income: £1 per £500 above disregard | | |

## Housing benefit

**Personal allowances**

| | | |
|---|---|---|
| Single | Under 25 | 72.90 |
| | Under 25 (on main phase ESA) | 92.05 |
| | 25 or over | 92.05 |
| Lone parent | Under 18 | 72.90 |
| | Under 18 (on main phase ESA) | 92.05 |
| | 18 or over | 92.05 |
| Couple | Both under 18 | 110.15 |
| | Both under 18 (claimant on main phase ESA) | 144.65 |
| | One or both 18 or over | 144.65 |
| Dependent children | Under 20 | 84.66 |
| Pension age (and claimant/partner not on income-related ESA or UC) | Single (reached pension age before 1 April 2021) | 244.40 |
| | Single (reached pension age on or after 1 April 2021) | 227.10 |
| | Couple (one or both reached pension age before 1 April 2021) | 366.00 |
| | Couple (both reached pension age on or after 1 April 2021) | 346.60 |

**Components**

| | | |
|---|---|---|
| Work-related activity | – | 36.55 |
| Support | – | 48.50 |

| **Premiums** | | |
|---|---|---|
| Carer | | 46.40 |
| Disability | Single | 43.20 |
| | Couple | 61.65 |
| Disabled child | | 81.37 |
| Enhanced disability | Single | 21.20 |
| | Couple | 30.25 |
| | Child | 32.75 |
| Severe disability | One qualifies | 82.90 |
| | Two qualify | 165.80 |
| Family | Ordinary rate | 19.48 |
| | Some lone parents | 22.20 |

| **Capital limits** | **Lower** | **Upper** |
|---|---|---|
| Standard | 6,000 | 16,000 |
| Care home or over pension age | 10,000 | 16,000 |

Tariff income: £1 per £250 between lower and upper limits;
£1 per £500 for those over pension age
No upper limit or tariff income for those on pension credit guarantee credit

## Social fund payments

| | | |
|---|---|---|
| Maternity grant | | 500.00 |
| Cold weather payment | | 25.00 |
| Winter fuel payment | Under 80 | 200.00 |
| (over pension age) | 80 or over | 300.00 |
| | Care home (under 80) | 100.00 |
| | Care home (80 or over) | 150.00 |

## Scotland-only payments

**Best Start grant**

| | | |
|---|---|---|
| Pregnancy and baby payment | | |
| | First child | 767.50 |
| | Any subsequent child | 383.75 |
| Early learning payment | | 319.80 |
| School-age payment | | 319.80 |
| **Scottish child payment** | | 27.15 |

# Non-means-tested benefit rates

| | £pw |
|---|---|
| **Attendance allowance** | |
| Higher rate | 110.40 |
| Lower rate | 73.90 |
| **Bereavement benefits** | |
| **Widowed parent's allowance/widowed mother's allowance** | 150.90 |
| **Bereavement support payment** | |
| **Higher rate** | |
| Lump sum | 3,500 |
| Monthly amount | 350.00 |
| **Standard rate** | |
| Lump sum | 2,500 |
| Monthly amount | 100.00 |
| **Carer's allowance** | 83.30 |
| **Child benefit** | |
| Only/eldest child | 26.05 |
| Other child(ren) | 17.25 |
| **Disability living allowance** | |
| **Care component** | |
| Highest rate | 110.40 |
| Middle rate | 73.90 |
| Lowest rate | 29.20 |
| **Mobility component** | |
| Higher rate | 77.05 |
| Lower rate | 29.20 |
| **Contributory employment and support allowance** | |
| **Assessment phase** | |
| Under 25 | 72.90 |
| 25 or over | 92.05 |
| **Main phase** | |
| 16 or over | 92.05 |
| Work-related activity component | 36.55 |
| Support component | 48.50 |

| | |
|---|---|
| **Guardian's allowance** | 22.10 |
| **Industrial injuries disablement benefit** | 20%: £45.06 to 100%: £225.30 |
| **New-style jobseeker's allowance** | |
| Under 25 | 72.90 |
| 25 or over | 92.05 |
| **Maternity allowance** | |
| Standard rate | 187.18 |
| **Personal independence payment** | |
| **Daily living component** | |
| Standard rate | 73.90 |
| Enhanced rate | 110.40 |
| **Mobility component** | |
| Standard rate | 29.20 |
| Enhanced rate | 77.05 |
| **Retirement pensions** | |
| State pension (full rate) | 230.25 |
| Category A | 176.45 |
| Category B (widow(er)/surviving civil partner) | 176.45 |
| Category B (spouse/civil partner) | 105.70 |
| Category D | 105.70 |
| **Severe disablement allowance** | 100.05 |
| Age addition (under 40) | 14.95 |
| Age addition (40–49) | 8.30 |
| Age addition (50–59) | 8.30 |
| Adult dependant | 49.20 |
| **Statutory maternity, adoption, paternity, shared parental, parental bereavement and neonatal care pay** | |
| Standard rate | 187.18 |
| **Statutory sick pay** | 118.75 |
| **National insurance contributions** | |
| Lower earnings limit | 125 |
| Primary threshold | 242 |
| Class 1 rate | 8% of £242 to £967 |
| Class 1 rate (above upper earnings limit) | 2% above £967 |
| Class 2 (voluntary) rate | 3.50 |

## Scotland-only payments

### Adult disability payment

**Daily living component**

| | |
|---|---|
| Standard rate | 73.90 |
| Enhanced rate | 110.40 |

**Mobility component**

| | |
|---|---|
| Standard rate | 29.20 |
| Enhanced rate | 77.05 |

### Child disability payment

**Care component**

| | |
|---|---|
| Highest rate | 110.40 |
| Middle rate | 73.90 |
| Lowest rate | 29.20 |

**Mobility component**

| | |
|---|---|
| Higher rate | 77.05 |
| Lower rate | 29.20 |

| | |
|---|---|
| **Carer support payment** | 83.80 |
| **Carer's allowance supplement** | 293.50 (June 2025) |
| | 293.50 (December 2025) |
| **Child winter heating payment** | 255.80 annual payment |
| **Winter heating payment** | 59.75 annual payment |
| **Young carer grant** | 390.25 annual payment |

# Part 1

# Introduction

# Chapter 1

# How to use this book

**This chapter covers:**


1. About this *Handbook* (below)
2. Using this *Handbook* (p4)
3. How this *Handbook* is organised (p6)
4. Finding out what you can get (p7)
5. Working out how much benefit you should receive (p14)
6. Finding information on challenging a decision (p15)


## 1. About this *Handbook*

This *Handbook* is the definitive guide to benefits and statutory payments, condensing a huge and complex area of law into a comprehensive and user-friendly book. It contains everything you need to know to understand your entitlement to benefits and statutory payments, and aims to answer any questions about your entitlement. The book explains how you claim and how much money you should get, how decisions are made and how to get them changed. It provides examples to illustrate how the rules work in practice and tactics to help you deal with common problems.

The book also helps you find the specific legislation, caselaw or official guidance relevant to the information contained in the text, should you need it. If you are an adviser, this *Handbook* is an essential tool, containing all you need to provide practical, effective and accurate advice.

***Updates and digital access***

This *Handbook* is published annually. It is updated throughout the year to reflect changes in legislation and new caselaw. These updates are published in CPAG's bi-monthly *Welfare Rights Bulletin* and are included in the online version of this *Handbook* on our digital platform CPAG Welfare Rights. This is a dedicated site for advisers where you can find our online handbooks, articles, benefit information and tools. See cpag.org.uk/welfare-rights for further information.

1

### Scope of this *Handbook*

The information in this *Handbook* applies to Great Britain.

#### Scotland

If you live in Scotland, some benefits and payments are different from those in England and Wales, as are some limited aspects of universal credit (UC). This is because the responsibility for certain benefits, and for certain aspects of UC, has been devolved to the Scottish Parliament. Social Security Scotland administers and pays benefits that come under the Scottish social security system, known in this *Handbook* as 'Scottish benefits'. Several Scottish benefits have been introduced, and others will be brought in in the future. See Chapter 60 for further information.

#### Northern Ireland

With some exceptions (such as child benefit and guardian's allowance), responsibility for social security is devolved to Northern Ireland. However, a principle of parity exists between Northern Ireland and Great Britain ensuring that, in most respects, the benefits described in this *Handbook* are available to people in Northern Ireland. Northern Ireland has its own benefits legislation, but the rules largely correspond to those in Great Britain. However, the administration and adjudicating bodies are often different and sometimes particular provisions in Northern Ireland are different.

## 2. Using this *Handbook*

There is lots of information in this *Handbook*, but you do not need to read it from cover to cover to find out about your benefit entitlement. If you are unfamiliar with the benefits system, a good place to start is the section in this chapter called 'Finding out what you can get' (see p7). This explains the best way to determine which benefits or statutory payments you qualify for and to establish how they interact with each other.

To find the answer to a particular question, or to understand the rules for a specific benefit, it should be easy to locate the information you need by using the detailed index or by using the individual benefit and statutory payment chapters as your starting point.

### Using the index

A simple way to find specific information in this book is to use the index. The index is designed to be detailed and intuitive to ensure you can easily locate the information you need.

- Use the entries in bold type, arranged alphabetically, to help you to find general information on a subject.

- Use the sub-entries under these, also arranged alphabetically, to find more specific information relevant to your search.
- Use the list at the start of the index to understand the abbreviations used.

For example, if you want to find information on how to claim attendance allowance, you can locate this either by looking up 'claims' and finding the 'AA' sub-heading underneath that or by looking up 'attendance allowance' and finding the 'claims' sub-heading underneath that.

## Using the individual benefit chapters

The chapters follow a common structure to help you easily find the information in them, and they refer you to other relevant information elsewhere in the book.

- Find the chapter about the particular benefit or statutory payment by using the contents list on pvii. Find the relevant part of the book and then locate the appropriate chapter in that part. To assist with this, tabs on the side of pages identify the number of the part you are in. The parts and chapters are also identified at the top of each page.
- Familiarise yourself with the standard way information is presented in these chapters (see p6). This will help you to locate information in the text easily. For example, if you want to know whether there are age limits for claiming a particular benefit, it is helpful to know that each chapter has a section called 'The rules about your age'.
- Alternatively, use the chapter contents at the start of each chapter to direct you to the likely section in the chapter to check. The section you are in within a chapter is identified at the top of the left-hand page.
- Follow any crossr eferences in the text to find any other relevant information in the book.

## Finding the law

To help you trace the source of the information in the text, references to the law (both legislation and caselaw) and guidance are given. It may be helpful to use these references, particularly if you are challenging a decision, as they provide the legal justification for the statements made in the text.

- Find the information in the book relevant to the issue you want to check and find the note for that information.
- Check the relevant note at the end of the chapter for the legal reference.
- Check Appendix 7 for an explanation of the abbreviations used in the references.
- See Appendices 1 and 2 for where to find the law and guidance online and for other useful sources of information.

The law referred to in this *Handbook* only applies in Great Britain. See p4 if you live in Northern Ireland.

1

# 3. How this *Handbook* is organised

The book is split into parts, and related chapters are grouped under these parts. A description of the information covered in each part, together with a list of chapters it contains, is included in the table of contents on pvii.

By developing a basic understanding of the purpose of each part, you can immediately identify where certain information will be in the book. For example, once you know that Part 9 covers the immigration and residence rules for benefits, you know to use this part if you need to check whether your immigration status affects your right to a particular benefit.

Similarly, the common structure of many of the chapters is designed to make it easier to find information in them.

## How the chapters are organised

To help you locate information easily, many of the *Handbook* chapters have a similar structure. Each chapter contains the following.

- **Chapter contents** to help you find the section you need.
- **Key facts** covering the key points about the information in the chapter. If the chapter is about a specific benefit or statutory payment, these include standard information, such as how work affects your entitlement, whether the benefit is means tested or non-means tested, whether you must have paid national insurance contributions to qualify and who administers your claim.
- **Endnotes** to the numbered references in the text. These are at the end of each chapter and, in most cases, cite the legal source of the information in the text.

In the chapters on specific benefits and statutory payments, the information is ordered in a similar way, usually under the following headings.

- **Who can get the particular benefit or statutory payment**: explains the qualifying conditions.
- **The rules about your age:** covers any relevant age limits.
- **People included in the claim:** who you can claim for or whether you must make a joint claim with someone else.
- **The amount of benefit:** the rules about how much money you should receive, with cross references to rules common to more than one benefit.
- **Special benefit rules:** to alert you when additional rules apply in particular circumstances – eg, if you are in hospital.
- **Claims and backdating:** how to claim, who should claim, the information you must provide, the date your claim is treated as having been made, whether your claim can be backdated, whether a claim for one benefit can be treated as a claim for another, and whether claims can be made in advance.
- **Getting paid:** how and when you are paid, and what to do if your circumstances change.

- **Tax, other benefits and the benefit cap:** whether the benefit or statutory payment is taxable, how it interacts with other benefits or statutory payments, and whether it is affected by rules on the benefit cap, plus signposts to other help you may get.

The text under these headings refers you to any other relevant information in the book which means you can answer almost any question you have on your entitlement by using the individual benefit or statutory payment chapter as a starting point.

## 4. Finding out what you can get

To find out about all the help you can get, it is important to check your entitlement in the following order.

- First, check whether you qualify for any non-means-tested benefits or statutory payments.
- Next, check your entitlement to means-tested benefits.
- Finally, check whether there is any other help available to you.

### Step 1: do you qualify for any non-means-tested benefits or statutory payments?

***What are non-means-tested benefits and statutory payments?***

A non-means-tested benefit is a benefit for which a detailed assessment of your income or capital is not needed to work out your entitlement. You may need to meet national insurance contribution conditions to qualify for some non-means-tested benefits ('contributory benefits') and you may qualify for others just because of your circumstances. Certain non-means-tested benefits ('earnings-replacement benefits') are intended to compensate you for loss of earnings. Your entitlement to non-means-tested benefits is not affected by any savings you have and only certain kinds of income affect your entitlement to some earnings-replacement benefits.

Statutory payments are payments an employer may be required to pay you if you are an employee and are not well enough for work or off work on maternity, paternity, adoption, shared parental, parental bereavement or neonatal care leave. Your entitlement to statutory payments depends on the level of your past earnings (and, for statutory shared parental pay, the past earnings of your partner), but it is not affected by any other income or savings you have.

Employment and support allowance (ESA) may be made up of a non-means-tested, contributory element (contributory ESA) and/or a means-tested element (income-related ESA). However, income-related ESA is being replaced by universal credit (UC), so new claims can now only be made for contributory ESA (but see p21). If you qualify for both elements, in effect, the means-tested element tops up the contributory element.

1

- Use the table below to see which non-means-tested benefits or statutory payments you may get. Check the benefits under all the circumstances that apply to you.
- Check which of these are earnings-replacement benefits (marked with an * in the table).
- Turn to the chapter on the benefits you are interested in, looking at any earnings-replacement benefits or statutory payments first. The chapters are arranged alphabetically in Part 4. The Scottish benefits are in Part 10.
- Check whether you meet the qualifying conditions for the benefit by looking at the section explaining who can get that benefit. Cross references take you to further details you may need to check.
- Look in the section 'Tax, other benefits and the benefits cap' for details of how the benefit may be affected by other benefits you already get or want to claim. Because of the overlapping benefit rules, certain non-means-tested benefits cannot be paid in full at the same time.
- If you think you qualify, use the section 'How to claim' for what to do next.

| *Your circumstances* | *Benefits you may get* | *Chapter* |
|---|---|---|
| Bereaved | Bereavement support payment* *or* | Chapter 21 |
| | Widowed parent's allowance* | Chapter 21 |
| | Statutory parental bereavement pay | Chapter 34 |
| Carer | In England and Wales, carer's allowance* | Chapter 22 |
| | In Scotland, carer support payment | Chapter 63 |
| | In Scotland, carer's allowance supplement** | Chapter 63 |
| Pregnant or have recently given birth | Statutory maternity pay | Chapter 34 |
| | Maternity allowance* | Chapter 30 |
| | Statutory shared parental pay | Chapter 34 |
| | Statutory neonatal care pay | Chapter 34 |
| | Child benefit | Chapter 23 |
| Recently adopted a child | Statutory adoption pay | Chapter 34 |
| | Statutory paternity pay | Chapter 34 |
| | Statutory shared parental pay | Chapter 34 |
| | Statutory neonatal care pay | Chapter 34 |
| | Child benefit | Chapter 23 |
| Father of a baby or partner of someone who has recently given birth or adopted a child | Statutory paternity pay | Chapter 34 |
| | Statutory shared parental pay | Chapter 34 |
| | Statutory neonatal care pay | Chapter 34 |
| Responsible for a child | Child benefit | Chapter 23 |
| | Guardian's allowance | Chapter 24 |
| | Statutory neonatal care pay | Chapter 34 |

| | | |
|---|---|---|
| Disabled (England and Wales) | Disability living allowance | Chapter 24 |
| | Personal independence payment | Chapter 31 |
| | Attendance allowance | Chapter 20 |
| | Industrial injuries benefits | Chapter 28 |
| Disabled (Scotland)*** | Child disability payment | Chapter 64 |
| | Scottish adult disability living allowance (for transferred claimants) | Chapter 60 |
| | Adult disability payment | Chapter 61 |
| | Pension age disability payment | Chapter 67 |
| | Industrial injuries benefits | Chapter 28 |
| Unfit for work | Contributory employment and support allowance* | Chapter 26 |
| | Statutory sick pay | Chapter 35 |
| | Industrial injuries benefits | Chapter 28 |
| Pensioner | State pension* | Chapter 32 |
| Unemployed and seeking work, or working part time and seeking more work | New-style jobseeker's allowance* | Chapter 29 |

* Earnings-replacement benefits
** Changes to benefits for carers in Scotland are expected by the end of 2025 (see p1467).
*** In Scotland, child disability payment has replaced disability living allowance. Existing claimants of personal independence payment and attendance allowance can continue to get those benefits until they are transferred to adult disability payment or pension age disability payment.

## Step 2: do you qualify for any means-tested benefits?

### *What are means-tested benefits?*

A means-tested benefit is one for which an assessment of your needs, income and capital is necessary to work out your entitlement. You only qualify for means-tested benefits if your (and your partner's) income and capital are not too high. The assessment of the amount you need to live on for means-tested benefits may increase if you get certain non-means-tested benefits.

Depending on your circumstances and when you made your claim, you may be entitled to a combination of non-means-tested benefits, a statutory payment and means-tested benefits, although you cannot qualify for certain means-tested benefits at the same time.

Universal credit (UC) has largely replaced other working-age means-tested benefits and tax credits (collectively known as 'legacy benefits'). Almost all awards of income support, income-based jobseeker's allowance and tax credits have now ended, as have many awards of working-age housing benefit (see p21). The DWP plans to end all remaining awards of income-related ESA and, except for people in 'specified' or 'temporary' accommodation, working-age housing benefit by March 2026 (see p23). This means that you cannot make a new claim for:

- income support; *or*
- income-based jobseeker's allowance; *or*
- income-related ESA (Chapter 9, but see p24); *or*
- if you or your partner are under pension age, housing benefit (except in very limited circumstances – see Chapter 10); *or*
- tax credits.

Instead, if you are under pension age (or if your partner is), you can claim UC. In very limited circumstances, you can get UC even if you (and if you are a member of a couple, your partner) are over pension age (see p22).

- If you (or your partner, if you have a partner) are under pension age and get income-related ESA (or income-related ESA and housing benefit); *and*
  - have received a letter (a 'migration notice') from the DWP telling you your income-related ESA is to end and inviting you to claim UC, see p25 for information on transferring to UC under the managed migration process; *or*
  - have not received a migration notice, check if you would be better off if you claimed UC. **Note:** once you have submitted a UC claim you cannot reclaim income-related ESA or working-age housing benefit, even if your claim for UC is unsuccessful or you are worse off on UC (the only exception is if you live in certain types of specified or temporary accommodation, when you can claim housing benefit as well as UC – see p183).
- If you (and if you have a partner, your partner) are pension age or over, or if neither you nor your partner get a legacy benefit, check the table below.
- Turn to the chapter(s) on the relevant benefit(s).
- Follow the procedure explained for checking non-means-tested benefits, by looking at the sections on who can get the benefit, 'Tax, other benefits and the benefit cap' and 'How to claim' in any relevant chapters.

| *Your circumstances* | *Benefit* | *Chapter* |
|---|---|---|
| You (and your partner, if you have a partner) are pension age or over* | Pension credit | Chapter 11 |
| You (and your partner, if you have a partner) are pension age or over and rent your home | Housing benefit | Chapter 10 |
| You (or your partner, if you have a partner) are under pension age | Universal credit** | Chapter 3 |

* If you are a member of a couple, both you and your partner usually must be pension age or over for you to qualify for pension credit or to make a new claim for housing benefit. For further details and exceptions, see p184 and p239. If you (and your partner, if you are in a couple) are pension age or over and have not claimed pension credit, then in very limited circumstances you may get UC (see p22).

** If you or your partner get a legacy benefit and have not received a migration notice, do not claim UC without first checking you will be better off transferring to UC (see above).

## Step 3: can you get any other help?

*What further help is there?*

If you are entitled to certain benefits, you may qualify for other benefits on that basis. These are called 'passported benefits'. Some of these passported benefits can also be awarded based on your other circumstances or age, or if you have a low income.

Other assistance may be available to people in certain circumstances and may be means tested – eg, council tax reduction.

Some types of passported benefits or other assistance are different in England, Wales and Scotland.

Entitlement to some of these payments is discretionary.

- Use the tables below to see the other help you may be able to get in your circumstances and to see whether the benefits you get help you qualify for any additional passported benefits.
- Use the relevant chapters to check whether you qualify for such help and, if you need to apply, how to do so (some are awarded automatically).
- Check whether you qualify for council tax reduction (see p761).
- Check Chapter 36 to see whether there are any other payments or other kinds of help you may be able to get.

| *Your circumstances* | *Benefits and other help you may get* | *Chapter* |
|---|---|---|
| Bereaved | In England and Wales, funeral expenses payment | Chapter 33 |
| | In England, children's funeral fund payment | Chapter 33 |
| | In Wales, help towards child funeral costs | Chapter 33 |
| | In Scotland, funeral support payment | Chapter 65 |
| Pregnant, recently given birth or adopted a child | In England and Wales, Sure Start maternity grant | Chapter 33 |
| | In Scotland, Best Start grant pregnancy and baby payment | Chapter 62 |
| | Health benefits | Chapter 27 |
| | In England and Wales, Healthy Start food | Chapter 36 |
| | In Scotland, Best Start foods | Chapter 62 |
| | Healthy Start vitamins (in Scotland, see p1464) | Chapter 36 |

1

| | | |
|---|---|---|
| Responsible for a child | In England and Wales, Sure Start maternity grant (if child is no more than 12 months old) | Chapter 33 |
| | In Scotland, Best Start grant pregnancy and baby payment, early learning payment or school-age payment | Chapter 62 |
| | In Scotland, Scottish child payment | Chapter 62 |
| | Free school lunches | Chapter 36 |
| | Health benefits for child | Chapter 27 |
| | In England and Wales, Healthy Start food | Chapter 36 |
| | In Scotland, Best Start foods | Chapter 62 |
| | Healthy Start vitamins (in Scotland, see p1464) | Chapter 36 |
| | In England and Wales, cold weather payment (in some circumstances) | Chapter 33 |
| | In Scotland, child winter heating payment (in some circumstances) | Chapter 66 |
| Disabled or unfit for work | In England and Wales, cold weather payment | Chapter 33 |
| | In Scotland, winter heating payment | Chapter 66 |
| | In Scotland, child winter heating payment | Chapter 66 |
| Carer | In Scotland, young carer grant | Chapter 63 |
| Preparing for or starting work | Flexible Support Fund | Chapter 36 |
| | For young people in Scotland, Job Start Payment | Chapter 60 |
| Pensioners | In England and Wales, winter fuel payment | Chapter 33 |
| | In England and Wales, cold weather payment | Chapter 33 |
| | In Scotland, winter heating payment | Chapter 66 |
| | In Scotland, pension age winter heating payment | Chapter 66 |
| | Health benefits | Chapter 27 |
| Aged 60 or over | Some health benefits | Chapter 27 |
| Own a home | Council tax reduction | Chapter 36 |
| | In England and Wales, discretionary reduction in council tax | Chapter 36 |
| Have a mortgage | Support for mortgage interest | Chapter 36 |
| Tenant | Council tax reduction | Chapter 36 |
| | Discretionary housing payment | Chapter 25 |

| | | |
|---|---|---|
| | In England and Wales, discretionary reduction in council tax | Chapter 36 |
| Not enough money to meet certain needs | Budgeting loan | Chapter 33 |
| | Budgeting advance of universal credit | Chapter 3 |
| | Health benefits | Chapter 27 |
| | Council tax reduction | Chapter 36 |
| | Other payments | Chapter 36 |

| *Passported benefit* | *Passports* |
|---|---|
| Free school lunches (p774)* | Some people on universal credit<br>Income-related employment and support allowance<br>Guarantee credit of pension credit (in England and Wales) |
| Health benefits (Chapter 27)** | Some people on universal credit<br>Income-related employment and support allowance<br>Guarantee credit of pension credit |
| Sure Start maternity grant, in England and Wales (p705) | Universal credit<br>Income-related employment and support allowance<br>Pension credit |
| Best Start grants, in Scotland (Chapter 62) | Universal credit<br>Income-related employment and support allowance<br>Housing benefit<br>Pension credit |
| Social fund funeral expenses payment, in England and Wales (p707) and funeral support payment, in Scotland (Chapter 65) | Universal credit<br>Income-related employment and support allowance<br>Housing benefit<br>Pension credit |
| Social fund cold weather payment, in England and Wales (p714) or winter heating payment, in Scotland (Chapter 66) | Some people on universal credit<br>Some people on income-related employment and support allowance<br>Pension credit |
| Social fund budgeting loan (p701) | Income-related employment and support allowance<br>Pension credit |

1

| | |
|---|---|
| Scottish child payment (Chapter 62) | Universal credit<br>Income-related employment and support allowance<br>Pension credit |

*Additionally, children in certain year groups are universally entitled to free school lunches and, in Scotland, children in funded early learning and childcare are entitled to a free meal. In Wales, children in local authority maintained primary schools are entitled to free school meals. In England and Wales, children may continue to qualify for free school lunches after entitlement to the passporting benefit ends. See p774 for further information and details of other circumstances in which children are entitled to free school lunches.

**Some health benefits are free for everyone in Scotland and Wales, and for people in England with certain conditions.

## 5. Working out how much benefit you should receive

***How much benefit will you get?***

The amount you get depends on which benefit you are claiming. Some non-means-tested benefits are paid at different rates depending on your circumstances. The amount of some contributory benefits may depend on your national insurance contribution record, and some (but not all) non-means-tested earnings-replacement benefits are affected by certain types of income. The amount of means-tested benefits you get always depends on your circumstances and involves a detailed assessment of your needs, income and capital. Tables of benefit rates for 2025/26 are on ppxiii–xix.

- Look at the chapters dealing with the benefit(s) you are interested in, checking the non-means-tested benefits and statutory payments chapters first. This is because any non-means-tested benefits you get may affect the amount of means-tested benefit you are entitled to.
- If you are not already getting the benefit, check you meet the entitlement conditions and then look at the section 'The amount of benefit'. Follow any relevant cross references for more detailed information about different aspects of the calculation.
- Check the section 'Tax, other benefits and the benefit cap' for additional information on how the benefit may be affected by other benefits you receive.
- If in doubt, use Appendix 1 for details of where you can get further help.

## 6. Finding information on challenging a decision

*Who makes decisions?*

The Department for Work and Pensions (DWP) is responsible for administering most benefits. HM Revenue and Customs (HMRC) is responsible for administering child benefit and guardian's allowance. HMRC also makes decisions on your national insurance contribution record and on your entitlement to statutory payments if you and your employer disagree. Social Security Scotland administers Scottish benefits. Local authorities administer housing benefit, council tax reduction schemes, certain education benefits and, except in Wales, local welfare assistance schemes (but in England, your local authority does not have to have a local welfare assistance scheme). The Welsh government is responsible for the Discretionary Assistance Fund for Wales.

HM Courts and Tribunals Service, which is part of the Ministry of Justice, is responsible for administering benefit appeals. The Scottish Courts and Tribunals Service administers appeals about Scottish benefits.

If you are unhappy with a decision that has been made on your claim, you can try to get it changed. The way you can challenge a decision and the procedures and time limits for doing so depend on the benefit concerned and on whether the decision you want to challenge is an initial decision on your claim or a decision that has been made following a revision, supersession, redetermination or appeal. Use the following steps if you are considering challenging a decision.

- First, check whether the decision is correct. See p4 for how to find answers to specific questions.
- If you think it is wrong, turn to the chapter on the benefit to which the decision relates and check the last bullet point in the key facts at the start of the chapter. This explains where to find information on challenging a decision relating to that benefit.
- Check the chapters in Part 8, or Chapter 69 for Scottish benefits, to find information on how you may be able to challenge the decision. For decisions relating to national insurance contributions, see p858. Check the information at the start of the chapter to be sure it is relevant to the benefit to which your challenge relates.
- Alternatively, look up 'challenging a decision' in the index. The sub-entries under it may help you to find the page number for the type of decision you want to challenge.

# Part 2

# Universal credit

# Chapter 2

# Transferring to universal credit

**This chapter covers:**

1. The universal credit system (below)
2. When you come under the universal credit system (p20)
3. Transferring to universal credit (p25)
4. Change of circumstances (p32)

**Key facts**

- Universal credit (UC) has been introduced for new claims from people who need means-tested benefit support because they have a low income.
- When you come under the UC system, UC replaces most other means-tested benefits and tax credits (called 'legacy' benefits) that you may have been getting.
- Many awards of legacy benefits have already been ended and replaced by UC.
- If you have not yet transferred to UC from legacy benefits, you can do so either by 'natural migration' (eg, by claiming UC after a change of circumstances) or by the DWP's 'managed migration' to UC process.
- The DWP aims to start the managed migration to UC process for people with remaining awards of legacy benefits during 2025.

## 1. The universal credit system

Universal credit (UC) combines means-tested support for adults under pension age and children into one benefit.

When you come under the UC system (see p20), UC replaces the following means-tested benefits and tax credits (known as 'legacy benefits'):

- income support;
- income-based jobseeker's allowance (JSA);
- income-related employment and support allowance (ESA);
- housing benefit (HB) for people of working age, except for specified or temporary accommodation (see p183);

- child tax credit;
- working tax credit.

UC does not replace pension credit (PC) or HB if you have reached pension age (see p239). However, if you are in a couple and you or your partner have reached pension age or are entitled to PC, you may come under the UC system in certain situations (see p23).

Even if you come under the UC system, you can still claim non-means-tested benefits. So, for example, you can still claim new-style JSA, new-style ESA, child benefit and carer's allowance, as well as UC.

New claims for legacy benefits are generally not possible (but see p21 for the limited exceptions). Existing awards of the legacy benefits continue for the time being, until they are transferred to claims for UC. You can transfer to UC:

- by 'natural migration' if you claim UC (see p25); *or*
- under the DWP's official 'managed migration' process (see p29).

When you come under the UC system, your existing legacy benefit award is terminated.

## 2. When you come under the universal credit system

In this *Handbook* we refer to you as 'coming under the UC system' when the universal credit (UC) rules apply to you. You come under the UC system when you make a claim for UC (if you are in a couple, you must usually claim UC jointly with your partner).[1] This includes where you claim UC under either the 'natural migration' or the 'managed migration' to UC processes (see p25). You are considered to have made a claim for UC at the point you submit your online UC claim form. Your entitlement to any of the legacy benefits you are still getting (see p19) stops if you claim UC. See p23 for how these benefits and tax credits are affected.

By April 2025, the DWP had started the managed migration process for many people with awards of legacy benefits. It aims to have begun managed migration for all remaining claimants by December 2025. To learn more about what has happened to legacy benefits, see p21.

You also come under the UC system if you make a new claim for jobseeker's allowance (JSA) or employment and support allowance (ESA). On a new claim, you can only get the contributory forms of these benefits, which the DWP refers to as 'new-style' JSA or ESA. If your income is low, you may be able to top up these benefits with UC.

Once you have claimed UC, you remain under the UC system – eg, you cannot return to income-related ESA.

## What has happened to legacy benefits?



Most awards of legacy benefits have now been replaced by UC. Some awards of income-related ESA and working-age housing benefit (HB) have not yet been replaced but are due to be, by coming under the managed migration to UC process, by December 2025. Awards of working-age HB in specified or temporary accommodation are not currently due to be replaced by UC.

The following legacy benefits have been replaced by UC:

- income support (IS);
- income-based JSA;
- child tax credit (CTC);
- working tax credit (WTC).

You cannot make a new claim for any of these (or renew an award of tax credits). If you had an award, generally that would have ended by April 2025, in most cases under the DWP's managed migration to UC process (but see p22 if you were getting tax credits and had reached pension age). In that process, the DWP would have sent you a notice that your legacy benefits were to end and invited you to claim UC (see p29).[2]

**Note**: some remaining awards of IS or income-based JSA may continue for a short time during 2025 because although the managed migration process had been started, it had not been completed by April 2025. The rules about the managed migration process on p29 will still be relevant in such cases.

For the main rules that applied to the legacy benefits, see the relevant chapter of the 2024/25 edition of this *Handbook*. Rules on transferring to UC from those benefits, including under the managed migration process, are in Chapter 2 of that edition.

If you were in a 'mixed-age' couple (ie, one of you had reached pension age but the other had not), you will usually have been told your legacy benefits were to end and invited to claim UC, under the managed migration to UC process. But in practice, that process did not apply if you were already entitled to pension credit (PC) in a mixed-age couple (see p239). In that situation, your PC can continue, as can your pension-age HB (see p184).[3] If you were getting tax credits, see below.

### Tax credits

Although you can no longer get tax credits, you can backdate a claim if you are a refugee who applied for asylum in the UK on or before 31 January 2019, and you contact HMRC after being granted refugee status (although you can still only be entitled up to 6 April 2025 – see p1291).

Some special rules apply to people of pension age who were getting tax credits.

2

If you were entitled to PC and tax credits, you did not come under the managed migration to UC process, but your tax credits will still have been brought to an end. The same applies if you were in a 'mixed-age' couple and already entitled to PC as well as tax credits.

For more on what will have happened, see the box below.

***Were you of pension age and getting tax credits?***

What happened depends on whether you were also entitled to PC.

**If you were also entitled to PC**, including if you were getting PC in a mixed-age couple, you did not come under the managed migration to UC process. Your PC can continue. But you would have been sent a tax credits 'closure notice' informing you that your tax credits were to end.[4] Your PC can be adjusted to include a child addition, and may include a transitional additional amount if you would have been worse off (see Chapter 11). You can still get pension-age HB.

**If you were *not* entitled to PC**, your tax credits ended under either the managed migration to UC process or via a tax credits 'closure notice' with an invitation to claim PC (see end of this box).

**If you, *and* your partner if you were a couple, were of pension age and entitled to WTC** (including if you got CTC and your WTC had been reduced to nil due to income), you came under the managed migration to UC process.[5] You would have been notified that your tax credits award was ending and invited to claim UC instead. If you transferred to UC in this way, some special rules apply to your UC:

- the basic condition for you to be under pension age is waived;
- if you have deferred a state pension, occupational or personal pension, this does not count as notional income for 12 assessment periods from the start of your UC claim;
- you are exempt from the benefit cap;
- if you get a transitional element in your UC, the usual rules on when you lose it (see p84) include where your earnings drop below the monthly equivalent of 16 hours a week at the minimum wage (not the level at which you are not subject to work-related requirements, as because of your age that does not apply anyway). However, this does not apply in the first 12 assessment periods of your UC award.

**If you were entitled to pension-age HB**, that would have ended (although if you get UC, despite your age you may still be entitled to working-age HB if you are in temporary or specified accommodation). You can get pension-age HB again if you stop being entitled to UC.

**If you were in a mixed-age couple and entitled to WTC and pension-age HB**, you would also have come under the managed migration process. However, the special UC rules above do not apply. Your pension-age HB would have ended (although if you get UC you may still be entitled to working-age HB if you are in temporary or specified accommodation). You can get pension-age HB again in certain circumstances (see p184).[6]

**If you, *and* your partner if you have one, were of pension age and entitled to CTC but not to WTC**, you did not come under the managed migration to UC process. Instead, you were sent a tax credits 'closure notice' informing you that your CTC was to end and inviting you to claim PC.[7] Your PC can be adjusted to include a child addition, and may include a transitional additional amount if you would have been worse off than when you were getting tax credits (see Chapter 11). You can still get pension-age HB. If you were in a mixed-age couple and entitled to CTC and pension-age HB, this would also have applied to you. You can still get pension-age HB.



## Income-related employment and support allowance and housing benefit

The legacy benefits income-related ESA and HB have started to be replaced by UC.

You cannot make a new claim for **income-related ESA**. Awards combined with CTC have already been replaced by UC, and remaining awards have started to be replaced. If you are still entitled to income-related ESA, that will end when you come under the managed migration to UC process, which is expected to be by December 2025 at the latest (see p29). You are still able to transfer to UC before that process applies – ie, by deciding to claim UC yourself and so transferring under the natural migration process (p25).

You cannot make a new claim for **working-age HB**, unless you live in specified or temporary accommodation (see p183). Awards of working-age HB combined with IS, income-based JSA and tax credits, or paid alone, have already ended (unless you are in specified or temporary accommodation, in which case your HB can continue). If you still have a current award combined with income-related ESA, that will end (again, unless you are in specified or temporary accommodation) when you come under the managed migration to UC process.

**Note:** if you are in a mixed-age couple, usually the only HB you were able to get was working-age HB, as you can only get pension-age HB in certain circumstances (see p182).

## How your legacy benefits are affected

The general rule is that if you claim UC you no longer qualify for:[8]

- **IS, income-based JSA, CTC and WTC.** These have all now been replaced by UC in most cases, even if you did not claim UC (see p21). Your IS or income-based JSA award continued or 'ran on' (as long as you would otherwise have remained entitled) for the first two weeks after the start of your UC award;
- **income-related ESA.** This is 'abolished' (replaced by UC) if you submit a new claim for UC, or for ESA or JSA. Your income-related ESA award continues or 'runs on' (as long as you would otherwise have remained entitled) for the first two weeks after the start of your UC award.[9] **Note:** when you come under the managed migration process (p29), your award will end, whether or not you claim UC;

- **working-age HB**, except for specified or temporary accommodation (see p183). Your HB award continues or 'runs on' (as long as you would otherwise have remained entitled, although you could argue that the rule does not actually require that) for the first two weeks after the start of your UC award.[10] **Note**: when you come under the managed migration process (p29), in most cases your award will end, whether or not you claim UC;
- **PC**. PC is not a legacy benefit being replaced by UC, but you cannot get PC and UC at the same time. You must be of pension age to get PC. A couple with only one partner who has reached pension age (a 'mixed-age couple') can get UC. They can choose to claim PC instead of UC only in certain circumstances (see p239). If you were getting tax credits and had reached pension age, your tax credit award will have ended by April 2025 and, depending on the facts, you may have been invited to claim UC or PC (see p21). If you come under the UC system as a single person but later become a member of a couple and your partner is entitled to PC, see p33.

The general rule is that if you claim UC when you are already getting income-related ESA or HB, your ESA or HB award stops and you cannot reclaim – it does not matter whether or not you are actually entitled to UC or if you withdraw your claim for UC.[11]

## New-style jobseeker's allowance and employment and support allowance

When JSA and contributory ESA are paid under the UC system, they are called 'new-style' JSA and 'new-style' ESA. These benefits are contributory benefits – ie, they depend on your national insurance contribution record. If you are on a low income, they can be topped up with UC. The rules about getting paid these benefits (eg, the rules on overpayments, claimant responsibilities and sanctions) are those that apply in the UC system. ESA still paid outside the UC system (whether it is income-related or contributory) is called 'old-style' ESA.

If you submit a new claim for UC, or JSA or ESA, you come under the UC system. You cannot then get income-related ESA because it is replaced by UC (and awards of income-based JSA have been replaced by UC). But you can still get new-style JSA and new-style ESA.[12]

You must claim UC if you need to top up your new-style JSA or ESA.

If you do not yet come under the UC system, you can still top up your old-style contributory ESA with income-related ESA, rather than UC. You do not need to make a new claim for ESA – your current award is adjusted.[13] Note, however, that income-related ESA is being replaced by UC under the managed migration process.

*Example*

Kyle gets contributory ESA. When he claimed it in 2017, he did not come under the UC system, so this is not new-style ESA. Kyle's income has now decreased. He can top up his contributory ESA with income-related ESA. He does not need to make a new claim – his current ESA award can be adjusted. However, the DWP tells Kyle that he must claim UC as a top-up. He refuses to do so and points out that his ESA is not 'new-style' ESA. The DWP checks this and adjusts his ESA award to include income-related ESA.

For some practical points about making a claim, see p619 for new-style JSA and p566 for new-style ESA.

## 3. Transferring to universal credit

If you are getting income-related employment and support allowance (ESA), including where you also get working-age housing benefit (HB), at some point you will transfer to universal credit (UC). The process of transferring to UC is known as 'migration'. You can transfer to UC:

- at any time, under 'natural migration' (see below); *or*
- when invited, under the DWP's 'managed migration' process (see p29). This process works by ending your income-related ESA and (in most cases) your working-age HB, and inviting you to claim UC instead. **Note:** awards of income support (IS), income-based jobseeker's allowance (JSA) and tax credits have already been transferred to UC under this process (see p21).

### Natural migration

You can transfer to UC at any time if you decide to submit a claim for UC – eg, after certain changes in your circumstances or because you believe you would be better off on UC. This is called 'natural migration' (for transferring to UC after the DWP starts you on the 'managed migration' process, see p29). Your entitlement to UC is not guaranteed. Remember that when you claim UC, any current awards of legacy benefits will stop (see p23) and you cannot return to them – it does not matter if you are not actually entitled to UC.

Natural migration can happen at any time, often after a change in your circumstances so you decide to claim UC or when you otherwise decide to make a claim for it. Some common examples are listed below.

- You have your first child. You may need to claim UC for means-tested support for your child.
- You move into a different local authority area and need help with your rent. Any previous HB award stops and you cannot usually make a new claim for HB, so you may need to claim UC. You can still get working-age HB in

temporary or specified accommodation (see p183), but you may also need to claim UC to cover your other needs. If you are in a 'mixed-aged' couple, you can only get pension-age HB in limited circumstances (see p184). If you move within the same local authority area, your HB award continues.[14]

- You believe you would be better off on UC and decide to make a claim for it. In general, being better off on UC is not likely when you are getting income-related ESA. Before you claim, check your potential entitlement and remember that a claim for UC stops your income-related ESA and you cannot return to it.

If you are severely disabled and have transferred to UC, see p27.

*Example*

Ellen gets income-related ESA and HB. She moves to a different flat. Because this is in the same local authority area, she does not need to make a new HB claim and both her HB and income-related ESA continue. Ellen moves again, this time to a property in a different local authority area. Her current HB claim comes to an end. Ellen is not in specified or temporary accommodation, so cannot make a new claim for HB. Instead, she claims UC. She has now transferred to UC via natural migration and her entitlement to income-related ESA ends, whether or not she is actually entitled to UC.

Note:

- A change in your circumstances does not, in itself, mean you transfer to UC. You must make a claim for UC for this to happen. Some claimants who do not yet come under the managed migration process have been wrongly told that they must claim UC, even though the change does not require them to claim UC. If this happens, do not claim UC unless you are sure you want to.
- Depending on your circumstances, you can be worse off after you transfer to UC via natural migration. There is no guarantee that your UC will be worth as much as your legacy benefits. Some claimants may be entitled to more on UC than on legacy benefits. This may be the case especially if you are working. But all will depend on your circumstances. Check your likely UC entitlement before claiming. Also remember to consider basic features of the UC system, such as online claiming (see p44) and the UC work-related requirements (see Chapter 42). Get advice if necessary. The DWP only provides transitional protection, meant to ensure you are not worse off on UC, if you transfer under the managed migration process (see p29).
- The Court of Appeal held that two claimants who had their legacy benefit incorrectly terminated by the DWP, and who then claimed UC but were worse off, had been subject to a violation of their human rights. The court said it was up to the government to provide a remedy[15] but the government has not changed the rules. Instead, compensation is likely to be offered in appropriate cases. If you are severely disabled, see p27.

## People who are severely disabled

If you transfer to UC via natural migration and you or your partner were entitled to the severe disability premium (SDP – see p275) in your (or your partner's) previous award of income-related ESA (or IS or income-based JSA, although those benefits have now been replaced by UC), you may be entitled to an additional amount of UC. This is called a 'transitional SDP element'. You may also be entitled to a transitional SDP element under the same rules if you transfer to UC via the managed migration process (see p29) but do not get transitional protection in the form of a 'transitional element' in your UC (see p78).[16] If you get a transitional element, the transitional SDP element does not apply.

**Note**: some of the rules refer to you having been entitled to IS, income-based JSA or child tax credit (CTC). By April 2025, these had been replaced by UC (see p21).

You are entitled to a transitional SDP element if:[17]

- you have not become part of a couple with someone already on UC; *and*
- within the month before your UC entitlement started, you were entitled (or you were part of a couple in which your partner was entitled) to income-related ESA (or IS or income-based JSA), and that included the severe disability premium; *and*
- you continued to satisfy the conditions for getting the severe disability premium up to and including the first day of your UC entitlement.

You cannot get a transitional SDP element amount if you were only entitled to HB, even if this included a severe disability premium.

The amount in the first monthly assessment period of your award (this may be subject to reduction in subsequent periods) is as follows.[18] **Note**: this amount applies to UC awards that start on or after 8 April 2025. Lower amounts applied in previous years.

***Transitional SDP element amount for awards starting on or after 8 April 2025***

| | |
|---|---|
| Single claimant, limited capability for work-related activity element included in UC | £143.37 |
| Single claimant, limited capability for work-related activity element not included in UC | £340.50 |
| Joint-claim couple, SDP was payable at the single rate (or couple rate but the £483.88 payment below does not apply), limited capability for work-related activity element included in UC | £143.37 |
| Joint-claim couple, SDP was payable at the single rate (or couple rate but the £483.88 payment below does not apply), limited capability for work-related activity element not included in UC | £340.50 |

| | |
|---|---|
| Joint-claim couple, SDP was payable at the couple rate and no one is getting (and entitled to) carer's allowance, carer support payment or the carer element of UC for either of you in your first UC monthly assessment period | £483.88 |

From 14 February 2024, the above amounts are increased by additional amounts where you were entitled to the SDP and were also getting another premium or premiums for disability in your legacy benefit – eg, the enhanced disability premium. To qualify for the additions, however, you must be entitled to a transitional SDP element. The DWP used powers allowing it to delay payments of UC, so as to include these additional amounts only where the UC award itself actually began on or after 14 February 2024. But if your UC began before then and your UC includes the transitional SDP premium in an assessment period that includes that date, at some point you should get the additions and arrears from 14 February 2024. The official intent is to begin introducing payments of these arrears early in 2025.[19] (For the period before 14 February 2024, see the note below.)

You can be entitled to more than one of these additions. You can get an addition where your UC includes a transitional SDP element (including where the element has been reduced to nil under the rules on p83) and within the month before your UC entitlement started you were also entitled (or you were part of a couple in which your partner was also entitled) to:[20]

- income-related ESA (or IS, or income-based JSA) that included an enhanced disability premium (see p273) and you continued to satisfy the conditions for that premium up to your first day of UC entitlement (the addition is £91.15 a month if you are a single claimant, £130.22 if you are a joint-claim couple);
- IS or income-based JSA that included a disability premium (see p272) and you continued to satisfy the conditions for that premium up to your first day of UC entitlement (the addition is £186.64 a month if you are a single claimant, £266.94 if you are a joint-claim couple);
- IS or income-based JSA that included a disabled child premium (see p271), or CTC that included a disabled child element at the low rate (see Chapter 62, section 2 of the 2024/25 edition of this *Handbook*), you continued to satisfy the conditions for that premium or element up to your first day of UC entitlement, and in your first UC assessment period from 14 February you are entitled to a disabled child addition to the UC child element at the low rate (see p271). The addition is £192.07 a month, whether you are a single claimant or a joint-claim couple.

Once you are entitled to a transitional SDP element under these rules, it continues to be included in your UC even if you stop satisfying the conditions for the severe disability premium. However, because your transitional SDP element is treated 'as if' it were a transitional element of UC, it can reduce or stop in the same way that the transitional element can – eg, if you start or stop being part of a couple (see p83).

Note:

- The transitional SDP element is treated 'as if' it were a 'transitional element' (which is the element that may be included under the managed migration process) and, when working out your UC, 'as if' it were part of your maximum amount of UC (see p40).[21]
- The transitional SDP element can continue but can also reduce ('erode') in your second or subsequent assessment period, or stop in the same way that a transitional element can (see p83). The element will erode over time.
- Before 14 February 2024, the amount of the transitional SDP element did not include the additions that apply from that date regarding the disability premium, enhanced disability premium, disabled child premium or the low rate of the child disability element in CTC. It has been held that, regarding people who qualified for the transitional SDP element, not also compensating them for the loss of the enhanced disability premium and the child disability element in CTC is unlawful.[22] The official intention is also to remedy that for the pre-14 February 2024 period. At the time of writing, it was understood that the DWP intended to make payments to cover the additions in that period by August 2025, although no new rules had been introduced. See CPAG's *Welfare Rights Bulletin* or the online version of this *Handbook* for updates.

## Managed migration

The DWP has been transferring people who are still getting legacy benefits to UC. When you are affected, the DWP writes to you to say that your legacy benefits are to end and invites you to make a claim for UC. This process is known as 'managed migration' to UC. There are no exemptions, although in practice the DWP has not been applying the managed migration process straight away in some cases – eg, in terminal illness or complex needs cases.

***Managed migration timetable***

**In 2023**, managed migration applied mainly to working-age people getting tax credits but no other legacy benefits.

**In 2024/25**, it was applied to people getting legacy benefits (including where combined with tax credits), with the exception of income-related ESA where that was not combined with CTC. From the summer of 2024, it was also applied to pension-age people getting tax credits. Most transfers under this process were due to be finished by April 2025 (in practice, some awards of IS and income-based JSA may continue for a short time after April while the process is completed). From September 2024, it started to be applied to people getting income-related ESA not combined with CTC. For what happened to the legacy benefits, see p21.

In **2025/26,** it is due to be applied to the remaining people getting income-related ESA (including where combined with HB) without CTC. The DWP aims to have started the process for all such people by December 2025, so that all awards have been ended and (where UC is awarded) replaced with UC by April 2026.[23]

If you are transferred to UC under the managed migration process and you would get less UC than the amount you were getting from your legacy benefits, you are entitled to a **transitional element** in your UC (see p78). If you are severely disabled and transfer under the managed migration process but are *not* entitled to a transitional element, you may still qualify for a **transitional SDP element** in your UC (see p27). The DWP refers to both of these elements as 'transitional protection', but they are different. **Note:** in 2025/26, the legacy benefits affected by this process will be remaining awards of income-related ESA and working-age HB. For a few remaining awards of IS or income-based JSA, the process may have started but not yet been completed by April 2025, but will be the same as described below.

The main rules and procedures are as follows.

- The DWP begins the managed migration process by sending you (and your partner, if you are in a couple) a 'migration notice'.[24] This tells you that your legacy benefit award is to end and invites you to make a claim for UC instead. Your legacy benefits will end even if you do not claim UC. Note that this notice has the heading 'Universal credit migration notice'; the DWP leaflet *Get Ready for Universal Credit* giving you information about the managed migration process is *not* a migration notice and receiving it does not involve you in managed migration.
- You become a 'notified person' when you are sent the migration notice.[25] The DWP can cancel your migration notice – eg, if it was sent in error or if this is considered necessary to protect your interests.[26]
- The migration notice lists a date by which you should make your UC claim 'in order to keep receiving financial support'. In the rules, this is called your 'deadline day'. The deadline day must be at least three months from the date of your migration notice (but you can be given less time than this if your previous migration notice was cancelled). This date can be extended if the DWP agrees that there is a good reason – eg, if you are unwell or need to arrange help to make your claim for UC.[27]
- If you claim UC on or before your deadline day, your legacy benefits will end. They will 'run on', or continue to be paid, for up to two weeks from your date of claim (see p23). If you do not claim UC by your deadline day, your legacy benefits will still end. They will 'run on', or continue to be paid, for two weeks after your deadline day.[28]
- To get a transitional element (ie, what the DWP calls 'transitional protection') in your UC, you must claim on or before a date which in the rules is called your

'final deadline'. This is a date one month (strictly speaking, one UC monthly assessment period) from your deadline day. If you claim after your deadline day but on or before your final deadline, you can still get a transitional element. You cannot get a transitional element if you claim after your final deadline.[29] If you claim UC after your deadline day but on or before your final deadline, your UC award automatically begins on your deadline day.[30]



You have made your claim for UC when you submit it – ie, in most cases, when you have completed and submitted the online claim form. This establishes the date of your claim (see p47). After you claim, you will likely be required to provide further information (eg, about your identity or income), usually at an interview (see p1009). If you do not provide the information within the time allowed (you should be given at least a month, but can be given longer), the DWP is likely to decide that you are not entitled to UC and say that your claim has been 'closed' (see p46). Although you can challenge this decision, unless it is changed you are not entitled to a transitional element, as you have been refused UC. If you make another claim before your final deadline and are awarded UC, the rules say that you cannot get a transitional element included,[31] although it is understood that the official intention is that you can still get a transitional element in this situation.

Your entitlement to your legacy benefits ends when you claim UC or, if you do not claim, on the day before your deadline day.[32] Your income-related ESA and HB 'run on' for the first two weeks of your UC claim, or for two weeks after your deadline day where you have not claimed UC, if you would otherwise have remained entitled (see p23) – ie, you can get paid both your UC and income-related ESA and HB for two weeks.

When you make your claim for UC, you are not automatically entitled – you must still satisfy the usual rules of entitlement (see Chapter 3). However, there are exceptions.[33]

- If you are a student when your legacy benefits end, you can get UC even if you are in full-time education – you do not have to satisfy the usual rule about not 'receiving education' (see p792). However, if you then stop getting UC and reclaim it, this exemption only applies again if you would qualify for either the transitional element (see p78) in your UC, or (if you were getting tax credits) the 'transitional capital disregard' (see the next bullet point).
- If you were entitled to tax credits when you claimed UC and had capital of over £16,000, the capital above £16,000 was ignored when calculating your entitlement to UC. This is called a 'transitional capital disregard' and can apply for up to 12 months, beginning with your first month on UC. Any capital between £6,000 and £16,000 produces assumed or 'tariff' income (see p149).
- If you were getting working tax credit as someone of pension age and transferred to UC via managed migration, see p21.

***Have you been sent a migration notice?***

If the DWP has sent you a migration notice, you are affected by managed migration. Note the following.

1. There is no choice about when you are affected. Get advice if you are worried or unsure.
2. If you need more time to claim UC than you have been given with the current deadline day (eg, because you are unwell or need help with the online claim), contact the DWP and explain this. If you are in a couple, check that the DWP is aware that the extension of time should apply to both of you. If you are getting tax credits jointly with your partner and they have a 'no recourse to public funds' restriction on their immigration leave, see the note on p1284.
3. If you are vulnerable because of your health, or have complex needs (eg, because you are homeless), the DWP should take account of that under its 'complex needs' procedures. If you think this has not happened, tell the DWP and ask that it does.
4. If your UC would be worth less than your legacy benefits, you should be protected by a transitional element in your UC, provided you claim UC within the time allowed and later supply any further information required. If you submit your claim for UC after your 'final deadline', you have not transferred to UC under the managed migration rules and are not entitled to this element.
5. If you submit your claim in time but fail to supply any further information that is required, the DWP is likely to regard this as a 'failed claim' and then say that your claim is 'closed'. This means that you have been refused UC. You can challenge the decision to 'close' your claim (see p46). You could try making another claim before your final deadline, but the DWP may still refuse to award you a transitional element.
6. If you have claimed UC but are in financial difficulty while waiting to be paid, you can apply for an advance (see p1023).

## 4. Change of circumstances

Generally, once you have transferred to universal credit (UC), you remain under the UC system. So, provided you continue to satisfy the rules of entitlement (see p36), you continue to get UC, even if your circumstances change – eg, you have a child or you become ill.[34] There are different rules for couples (see p33).

If you stop being entitled to UC, you cannot make a new claim for any of the legacy benefits (except for working-age HB if you are in temporary or specified accommodation – see p183). If you are in a 'mixed-age' couple and had been able to get pension-age housing benefit (HB) before being started on the migration to UC process, see p184. If your UC ended but you may now be entitled again, you must reapply for it, unless the rules about couples apply, or in some cases where your UC stopped due to your income (see p45). If it is less than six months since your award ended, you can reclaim by logging back into your online journal. This 'rapid reclaim' allows you to reclaim more quickly (see p45).

## Couples



If you were getting UC as a single person but then become part of a couple, you must report this change. You continue to come under the UC system as a couple with your new partner without making a new claim, and you continue to get UC, provided you still satisfy the basic rules.[35] See below if your new partner is getting pension credit (PC).

If your partner was not entitled to UC as a single person, any award they have of income-related employment and support allowance (ESA) or HB (except for specified or temporary accommodation) stops, and you are treated as claiming UC as a couple (the same applied if they were on income support, income-based jobseeker's allowance or tax credits).[36] If your partner was entitled to UC as a single person, you are entitled to UC as a couple without making a claim.[37]

*Example*

Ian has been entitled to UC as a single person since April 2023. He meets Jenna and moves in with her in July 2025. Jenna has been getting income-related ESA, together with HB. Ian and Jenna now come under the UC system as a couple. They satisfy the basic rules of entitlement for UC as a couple and are therefore entitled to UC without making a new claim. Jenna's awards of income-related ESA and HB end.

If your new partner is getting PC, you are treated as having made a joint claim for UC, and your partner's PC stops.[38] The PC stops from the date you became a couple, not the date of your joint claim for UC (the same applies regarding your partner's HB).[39] You do not need to make a new claim for UC. If only one of you is under pension age, you cannot usually make a new claim for PC, although there are exceptions (see p239).

If you were claiming UC as a couple but then separate from your partner, you must report the change. Both you and your ex-partner can stay on UC as single claimants without having to make new claims, and you both keep your existing UC assessment period (see p39 for what this is).[40]

*Example*

Padma and Mason were entitled to UC as joint claimants. They separate and Mason notifies the DWP that they are no longer a couple. Both Padma and Mason can be entitled to UC as single people and do not need to make new claims. The date they are paid their UC remains the same as when they were a couple.

# Notes



2. **When you come under the universal credit system**
   1 Art 3(3) and Sch 5 WRA(No.9)O, as applied in UC areas by subsequent commencement orders
   2 Regs 6A and 44 UC(TP) Regs; art 4 WRA(No.9)O
   3 paras 5.2-5.6 and 5.22 SS(SPAC)(A) Regs
   4 Reg 3 SS(SPAC)(A) Regs
   5 Reg 2 SS(SPAC)(A) Regs
   6 The Welfare Reform Act 2012 (Commencement No.31 and Savings and Transitional Provisions) (Amendment) Order 2024 No.604
   7 SS(SPAC)(A) Regs
   8 Regs 5, 6A, 8, 46 and 47 UC(TP) Regs
   9 Art 4 WRA(No.9)O; regs 46 and 47 UC(TP) Regs; reg 5 UC(MMP&MA) Regs
   10 Reg 8(2A) UC(TP) Regs
   11 Art 4 WRA(No.9)O; regs 6A and 8 UC(TP) Regs
   12 These benefits are not abolished under the UC system and can be claimed under the JSA Regs 2013 and the ESA Regs 2013
   13 *LH v SSWP (ESA)* [2014] UKUT 480 (AAC), reported as [2015] AACR 14

3. **Transferring to universal credit**
   14 Housing Benefit Circular A7/2018
   15 *R (on the application of TD, AD and Reynolds) v SSWP* [2020] EWCA Civ 618
   16 Sch 2 UC(TP) Regs, the rule about not being entitled to a transitional element is at para (7)
   17 Sch 2 UC(TP) Regs, as applied in awards from 27 January 2021, inserted by UC(TP)(SDP)A Regs
   18 Sch 2 para 5 UC(TP) Regs
   19 questions-statements.parliament.uk/written-questions/detail/2024-12-06/18471
   20 Sch 3 UC(TP) Regs
   21 Sch 2 paras 4, 5 and 6 UC(TP) Regs
   22 *FL v SSWP* [2024] UKUT 6 (AAC), applying (in a case about the enhanced disability premium) *R (on the application of) TP and AR (TP and AR No.3) v SSWP* [2022] EWHC 123 (Admin) and making it clear that tribunals are bound by it
   23 LA Welfare Direct 05/24
   24 Reg 44 UC(TP) Regs
   25 Reg 44(6) UC(TP) Regs
   26 Reg 44(5) UC(TP) Regs
   27 Regs 44(1)(b) and 45 UC(TP) Regs
   28 Reg 46(1) UC(TP) Regs
   29 Regs 46(4) and 48 UC(TP) Regs
   30 Reg 46(3) UC(TP) Regs
   31 Reg 57 UC(TP) Regs
   32 Regs 46, 48 and 49 UC(TP) Regs
   33 Regs 51 and 60 UC(TP) Regs

4. **Change of circumstances**
   34 A change does not automatically bring UC entitlement to an end, and instead the award can be adjusted to reflect the new circumstances
   35 Reg 9(7) and (8) UC,PIP,JSA&ESA(C&P) Regs
   36 Regs 5, 7 and 12A UC(TP) Regs; reg 9(8) UC,PIP,JSA&ESA(C&P) Regs
   37 Reg 9(7) UC,PIP,JSA&ESA(C&P) Regs; paras M4051-60 ADM
   38 Reg 9(8) UC,PIP,JSA&ESA(C&P) Regs; reg 5 UC(TP) Regs
   39 Regs 5(2)(b)(ii) and (iv) and 7(5)(c) UC(TP) Regs
   40 Reg 9(6) UC,PIP,JSA&ESA(C&P) Regs

# Chapter 3

# Universal credit

**This chapter covers:**


1. Who can get universal credit (p36)
2. The rules about your age (p37)
3. People included in the claim (p38)
4. The amount of benefit (p39)
5. Special benefit rules (p44)
6. Claims and backdating (p44)
7. Getting paid (p49)
8. Tax, other benefits and the benefit cap (p55)


## Key facts

- Universal credit (UC) is a benefit for people on a low income who are in or out of work.
- UC has replaced income support, income-based jobseeker's allowance, child tax credit and working tax credit. In 2025, it is due to replace remaining awards of income-related employment and support allowance and (in most cases) working-age housing benefit.
- UC is a means-tested benefit.
- You do not have to have paid national insurance contributions to qualify.
- UC can be paid in addition to non-means-tested benefits, but some of these are taken into account as income when calculating your UC.
- A benefit cap may be applied if the total amount of certain benefits you receive exceeds a specified amount, and your UC can be reduced.
- The DWP administers and pays UC.
- If you disagree with a UC decision, you can apply for a revision or supersession (see Chapter 50), or appeal against it (see Chapter 51). You must apply for a mandatory reconsideration before you can appeal.

2

# 1. Who can get universal credit

You qualify for universal credit (UC) if you (and your partner if you are in a couple):

- satisfy the '**basic conditions**' – ie:[1]
  - you are aged 18 or over and under pension age, with some exceptions – see p37. **Note:** some 16/17-year-olds can get UC (see p37); *and*
  - you are not 'receiving education', although there are some exceptions (see p37); *and*
  - you satisfy the 'habitual residence' and the 'right to reside' tests (see Chapter 57), and you are in, or treated as in, Great Britain (see Chapters 57 and 58); *and*
  - you are not a 'person subject to immigration control' (see p1272); *and*
  - usually, you have accepted a 'claimant commitment' (see p934). This is an agreement that you will meet certain requirements.[2] In particular, the claimant commitment includes the work-related requirements you normally must meet, which may include attending work-focused interviews, work preparation, work search and work availability; *and*
- satisfy the '**financial conditions**' – ie:[3]
  - your income is not too high; *and*
  - your savings and other capital are £16,000 or less. If you transferred to UC from tax credits under the 'managed migration' process and had capital of over £16,000, that excess capital is ignored for UC for up to 12 months (see p29).

## Couples

If you are a member of a couple (see p58), you must usually make a joint claim. Both of you must satisfy the above conditions of entitlement (and your income and capital are assessed jointly).[4]

Both of you do *not* need to meet all the basic conditions if one of you is:[5]

- over pension age; *or*
- 'receiving education' (but see below if one of you is aged 16 or 17).

If you are a member of a couple and one of you does not satisfy the conditions for UC, you may be able to claim as a single person. If so, your UC amounts are for a single person, but you still count as a couple and your income and capital are still assessed jointly. You can claim as a single person if your partner is:[6]

- aged 16 or 17 and is not someone who can get UC as an under-18-year-old (see p37 for who can); *or*
- not in (or treated as in) Great Britain, including if they failed the habitual residence or right to reside test (see Chapter 57); *or*
- a 'person subject to immigration control' (see p1272); *or*

- a prisoner or serving a sentence while detained in hospital, or is a member of a religious order and is fully maintained by the order.



You can also claim as a single person if you are in a polygamous marriage and:[7]
- your spouse is still married to someone else from an earlier marriage; *and*
- the other person in the earlier marriage still lives in the same household as your spouse.

### Receiving education

In general, you cannot claim UC if you are 'receiving education'. The basic rule is that if you are a qualifying young person (see p63) or undertaking full-time education, study or training, you are regarded as 'receiving education'.[8] There are exceptions – eg, if you have a child or a disability, are on a traineeship, or are without parental support. For full details, see Chapter 37. **Note:** if you are transferred to UC under the managed migration process (see p29), you can claim UC, even though you do not satisfy the basic rules because you are in full-time education (see p29).

If you are a member of a couple making a joint claim and one of you is receiving education (and so not eligible for UC) but the other is not, you may still be entitled to UC as a couple (see p36).

## 2. The rules about your age

In most cases, you (and your partner, if you are making a joint claim) must be 18 or over to claim universal credit (UC). However, some 16/17-year-olds can claim UC (see below).[9]

In most cases, you must be under pension age (see p689).[10] If you are in a couple, usually at least one of you must be under pension age. If one of you has reached pension age, this is called being in a 'mixed-age' couple. Some people of pension age can get UC if they have been transferred to UC from working tax credit under the managed migration process (see p21). **Note**: if you reach pension age while you are on UC, or you are in a mixed-age couple and the younger person also reaches pension age, your UC will 'run on' for the remainder of the monthly UC assessment period in which this change occurred.[11]

### 16/17-year-olds

You must normally be at least 18 years old to qualify for UC. If you are aged 16 or 17, you can get UC if one of the following applies.[12]
- You have limited capability for work, or you have a fit note, and you are waiting for a work capability assessment.

- You have 'regular and substantial caring responsibilities for a severely disabled person' – ie, you meet the conditions of entitlement to carer's allowance (CA) (see Chapter 22), or would do but for the fact that your earnings are too high.[13] This does not apply if you receive earnings from those caring responsibilities. You do not have to claim CA. If you are resident in Scotland or entitled to carer support payment, you are not required to meet the conditions of entitlement to CA. **Note:** you do not qualify under this rule if you were previously being looked after by a local authority (see p846).
- You are responsible for a child aged under 16 (see p64).
- Your partner is responsible for a child and satisfies the basic rules of entitlement for UC.
- You are pregnant and there are 11 weeks or fewer before the week your baby is due. **Note:** you do not qualify under this rule if you were previously being looked after by a local authority (see p846).
- You had a baby (or your baby was stillborn) not more than 15 weeks ago. **Note:** you do not qualify under this rule if you were previously being looked after by a local authority (see p846).
- You are without parental support (including support from someone acting in place of your parent – eg, a foster parent). For these purposes, you are treated as without parental support if you are not being looked after by a local authority, and:[14]
  - you are an orphan – ie, you do not have any parents; *or*
  - you live away from your parents because you are estranged from them (see p794 for the meaning) or there is a serious risk to your physical or mental health or you would experience significant harm if you lived with them; *or*
  - you live away from your parents and they are unable to support you financially because they have a 'physical or mental impairment', or they are in custody, or they are prohibited from entering Great Britain – eg, because of the Immigration Rules.

  **Note:** you do not qualify under this rule if you were previously being looked after by a local authority (see p846).

If you are a member of a couple and one of you is either 18 or over or satisfies the rules above, but the other does not, the one who is 18 or over or who satisfies the above rules can claim UC as a single person, but the other partner's income and capital are taken into account.[15]

## 3. **People included in the claim**

If you are single, you claim universal credit (UC) for yourself. If you are a member of a couple, you and your partner must usually make a joint claim for UC (see p45).[16] See p58 for who counts as a couple.

Your maximum amount (see Chapter 5), which forms part of the calculation of your benefit, includes elements for a child(ren) for whom you are responsible. **Note:** the number of children included in your maximum amount may be limited to two (see p68).

There are some situations in which you must show that you are 'responsible' for a child – eg:

- to take advantage of the special rules to help you meet the claimant responsibilities (see p938);
- so you can benefit from a 'work allowance' when calculating your UC entitlement (see p41);
- for some of the rules for the housing costs element (see Chapter 6).

You can count as responsible for any child under 16 and for any 'qualifying young person' (see p63 for who counts as a child).[17] You do not have to be the child's parent. For when you count as responsible for a child, see p64.

## 4. The amount of benefit

Universal credit (UC) is a means-tested benefit. The amount of UC you get depends on your needs (your 'maximum amount') and how much income and capital you (and your partner) have. If you are severely disabled and transferred to UC from your old means-tested benefit by natural migration (or by managed migration but are not entitled to a transitional element as part of that process), you may also get a transitional SDP element included in your UC. **Note:** you might get a reduced amount of UC if you are affected by the benefit cap – see p1025.

The amount you get is calculated over a monthly assessment period. As your income increases, your UC award is reduced.

***Assessment period***

The **'assessment period'** is one calendar month, beginning with the first date of entitlement to UC.[18] Each subsequent assessment period (ie, a calendar month) usually begins on the same day of the month, except if:

- the first day of entitlement to UC falls on the 31st of the month, in which case each assessment period begins on the last day of the month; *or*
- the first day of entitlement to UC falls on the 29th or 30th of the month, in which case each assessment period begins on the 29th or 30th. In February, it begins on the 27th (or in a leap year, on the 28th); *or*
- your entitlement has started before the actual date of claim because of the backdating rules, in which case the first assessment period begins on the first day of entitlement and ends on the day before the date of claim; *or*

– your first date of entitlement is changed, in which case the first assessment period is changed, but your other assessment periods still begin and end as they originally did.

2

*Examples*

Renata claims UC on 31 July. She is making a new claim as a single person. Her first monthly assessment period is from 31 July until 30 August inclusive. Her next assessment period begins on 31 August, and the one after that begins on 30 September.

Glenn claims UC on 7 November. His first assessment period is set to begin on 7 November, but he requests that his claim be backdated to 29 October as his disability meant he could not claim earlier, and this is accepted. Glenn's first assessment period now begins on 29 October and ends on 6 November; his second assessment period begins on 7 November, and all subsequent assessment periods begin on the seventh day of the month.

## Working out your universal credit

Your UC is worked out in the following way.

- **Step 1:** calculate your maximum amount. See Chapter 5 for details of this.
- **Step 2:** work out your earnings and check whether any can be ignored.
- **Step 3:** work out your other income and how much can be ignored.
- **Step 4:** calculate your total income.
- **Step 5:** calculate your UC entitlement.

### Step 1: calculate your maximum amount

Your maximum monthly UC is made up of the total of:[19]

- a standard allowance – for a single claimant or a couple (see p67);
- a child element for each child, with an increase for a disabled or severely disabled child (see p68). **Note:** the number of children you can get a child element for may be limited to two;
- a limited capability for work element, if you can still get it (see p71), or a limited capability for work-related activity element (p73) for an adult with ill health or disability. The limited capability for work element was abolished for new claims made on or after 3 April 2017 (see p71);
- a carer element for someone looking after a severely disabled person (see p75);
- a housing costs element for people paying rent or service charges (see Chapter 6). **Note:** you cannot get UC for help with your mortgage or loan for repairs and improvements. Instead, the DWP may offer you a loan to help meet your mortgage interest payments (see p764);
- a childcare costs element (see p76);
- a transitional element – if you transfer to UC under the managed migration process (see p29) and your UC is worth less than your legacy benefits (see p78);

- any transitional SDP element that you are entitled to after transferring to UC under the natural migration process (see p27).[20] The payment is treated 'as if' it is part of your maximum amount.



*Example*

Helen and Jason are a couple both aged over 25. They claim UC in May 2024. They have two children, both born after 6 April 2017. Helen works. Jason is ill and has limited capability for work and work-related activity. They do not have housing or childcare costs. Helen and Jason's maximum amount for UC is calculated as follows:

| | |
|---|---|
| Standard allowance | £628.10 |
| Child element (first child) | £292.81 |
| Child element (second child) | £292.81 |
| Limited capability for work-related activity element | £423.27 |
| **Total** | **£1,636.99** |

## Step 2: work out your earnings and how much can be ignored

See Chapter 7 for how to work out your earnings.

Once you have established your earnings, check whether any can be ignored when calculating your UC. This is done by comparing your earnings with a set amount, called a 'work allowance' (see below).

If your earnings do not exceed the work allowance, they are all ignored. If your earnings are more than your work allowance, 55 per cent of the excess is taken into account as income.[21] You are only entitled to a work allowance if certain circumstances apply. If no work allowance applies to you, 55 per cent of all your earnings are taken into account.

The way your earnings reduce the amount of your UC is sometimes called the **'taper'** – ie, the rate at which your UC tapers away as your earnings increase. As your earnings rise above any that are ignored, your UC reduces by 55 pence for every extra pound you earn.

### The work allowance

A work allowance only applies if you (or your partner) are responsible for a child or have limited capability for work.[22]

The amount of the allowance depends on whether your UC includes a housing costs element. Only one work allowance can apply.

**Note**: if you are entitled to UC but also get housing benefit (HB) because you are in temporary accommodation (which is not also 'exempt accommodation' – see p326, the meaning is the same as for HB), your UC is treated as if it includes a housing costs element.[23]

2

***Amount of the work allowance (per month)***

| | |
|---|---|
| Lower (UC includes a housing costs element) | £411 |
| Higher (UC does not include a housing costs element) | £684 |

***Examples***

Keira is a lone parent with a child aged six. She rents her home and is entitled to a housing costs element in her UC. She has a part-time job from which her earnings for UC over her assessment period are £490.

Because Keira has a child, a work allowance applies and so some of her earnings can be ignored. Keira's UC includes a housing costs element, so the lower work allowance of £411 applies. Her earnings exceed her work allowance by £79 (£490 – £411). 55 per cent of this excess is £43.45. Therefore £43.45 of Keira's monthly earnings is taken into account when calculating her UC.

Helen and Jason are a couple with two children. They are not entitled to a housing costs element. Helen has earnings from work. Jason is ill and has limited capability for work and work-related activity. Over their assessment period, Helen's earnings for UC are £1,200. Because they have children and also because Jason has limited capability for work, a work allowance applies, and some of Helen's earnings can be ignored. Their UC does not include a housing costs element, so a higher work allowance of £684 applies. Helen's earnings exceed the work allowance by £516 (£1,200 – £684). 55 per cent of this excess is £283.80. So £283.80 of Helen and Jason's monthly earnings is taken into account when calculating their UC.

## Step 3: work out your other income and how much can be ignored

See Chapter 7 for how to work out your other income and how much can be ignored.

If you have other income (eg, other benefits), unless it (or some of it) is ignored, it affects your UC by reducing it pound for pound. This is in addition to any reductions from your earnings.

### Income from capital

If you and your partner have more than £16,000 capital, you cannot get UC. An exception applies if you are transferred to UC from tax credits under the managed migration process (see p25). If your capital is more than £6,000 but £16,000 or less, you count as having an income of £4.35 a month for every £250, or part of £250, over £6,000.[24] This assumed monthly income is sometimes referred to as 'tariff income'.

For how to calculate your capital, including assumed monthly income, see Chapter 8.

### Step 4: calculate your total income

Add together the income that is to be taken into account under Steps 2 and 3.

### Step 5: calculate your universal credit entitlement

2

Deduct your total income to be taken into account (Step 4) from your maximum UC (Step 1).

**Note:** if you are not entitled to UC under these steps because your maximum UC does not yet include the limited capability for work-related activity element as you are still in the three-month waiting period (see p73), you are entitled to UC at the minimum amount of one pence.[25]

If you transferred to UC under natural migration and are entitled to a transitional SDP element (see p27), this is treated 'as if' it is part of your UC maximum amount.

***Example***

Helen and Jason are a couple both aged over 25, with two children. Helen works and earns £1,200 in their monthly assessment period. Jason is ill and has limited capability for work and work-related activity. He is entitled to new-style employment and support allowance (ESA) of £140.55 a week. For UC purposes, this is converted to a monthly figure of £609.05. They do not have housing costs or childcare costs included in their UC. They have savings of £5,000.

Their total income to be taken into account under Step 4 is £283.80 in earnings plus £609.05 new-style ESA during their monthly assessment period = £892.85

Their maximum UC under Step 1 = £1,636.99

Their monthly UC entitlement = £1,636.99 – £892.85 = £744.14

## Transitional protection

If you are transferred to UC under the managed migration process (see p29) and your UC maximum amount would be less than the amount you were getting on your legacy benefit, a 'transitional element' is included in your UC maximum amount (see p78). This is intended to ensure that you are not worse off at the point of transfer to UC.

Transitional protection only applies if you transfer to UC under the managed migration process. It does not apply if you claim UC after a transfer under the natural migration process (see p25). So you could find that if you claim UC under the natural migration process, it is worth less than the legacy benefit you were getting previously.

2

## 5. Special benefit rules

Special rules may apply if you:

- are 16/17-year-olds (see p37);
- are subject to immigration control (see p1272);
- have come from or are going abroad (see Chapters 57 and 58);
- are studying (see Chapter 37);
- are in prison or detention (see Chapter 38).

## 6. Claims and backdating

The general rules about claims and backdating are covered in Chapter 44. This section explains the specific rules that apply to universal credit (UC).

You can make a new claim for UC whenever you want. If you are still getting income-related employment and support allowance (ESA), at some point during 2025 you will come under the 'managed migration' to UC process (see p29), under which your income-related ESA award will end and you will be invited to claim UC instead. Claiming UC brings you under the UC system (see p20).

### Making a claim

Claims must usually be made online at universal-credit.service.gov.uk/start. You are asked to set up an online account and provide an email address, username, password and security questions.

If you need help claiming online, you can phone the UC helpline, free of charge, on 0800 328 5644 (textphone: 0800 328 1344; Welsh language: 0800 328 1744), Relay UK available, Monday to Friday 8am to 6pm. There is also a British Sign Language video relay service for making a claim. The DWP adviser can complete an online form on your behalf or arrange for you to be helped at your local job centre. Alternatively, your local Citizens Advice office can help you make a claim via the 'Help to claim' service (citizensadvice.org.uk/helptoclaim in England and Wales, cas.org.uk/helptoclaim in Scotland).

You can make a claim by phone instead, if the DWP allows it – ie, if you cannot use a computer or do not have access to one.[26] If so, although you are making a phone claim, in practice, the DWP fills in an online claim form for you so that you still have an online account. In exceptional circumstances, if you cannot use either a computer or a telephone, the DWP may make a home visit to help you claim, but you should not rely on this.

You can amend or withdraw your claim before a decision is made (see p1004). If you are in financial need while waiting to be paid, you may be able to get an advance payment of UC (see p1023).

If you were previously getting UC and it is less than six months since your award ended, you can reclaim by logging onto your online UC journal. This usually allows you to reclaim more quickly, and have the same assessment period as previously. If you are reclaiming after stopping work, you are only paid in full for the whole of the first assessment period if you reclaim within seven days of your job ending, although you can be allowed longer if you have a 'good reason' for not reclaiming within this time.[27]

**Note:** if you are getting income-related ESA or working-age housing benefit (HB), you should check your likely UC entitlement before deciding to claim UC (see p25). If instead you are transferring to UC under the managed migration process, some special rules about claiming UC apply (see p29). **Note:** this advice also applied if you were getting other legacy benefits, but by 2025 these had been replaced by UC in most cases (see p21).

## When you do not need to make a claim

You do not need to make a new claim (and you keep the same assessment period as before) if you have previously claimed UC and:[28]

- you were entitled to UC as a single claimant and are now part of a couple and your partner was also entitled to UC as a single claimant. Although you do not need to make a new joint claim, you must tell the DWP that you are now part of a couple; *or*
- you are now a member of a couple and either you or your partner (but not both of you) were entitled to UC as a single claimant and that award has now been terminated; *or*
- you were a member of a couple making a joint claim but have now ceased to be a couple. You must tell the DWP that you are now single or are a member of a new couple.

Also, where you have been refused UC or your award has been terminated, because (in either case) of having too much income, you can be treated as making a new claim without actually making a new claim, if the DWP decides that it should do this – eg, where it has enough information to make an award without a claim.[29] This applies for up to the next five of what would have been your monthly UC assessment periods after you were refused UC or had your award terminated. **Note:** the DWP may refer to you having a 'nil award' of UC in these circumstances. However, where your income is too high to qualify, there is no such thing in the law as a nil award of UC, and while this applies you do not have any entitlement to UC unless and until you make a successful claim.[30]

## Who should claim

If you are single, you claim on your own behalf as a single person. If you are a member of a couple, you must normally make a joint claim with your partner.[31] For when you count as a couple, see p38. If you are a member of a couple and one of you does not satisfy the conditions for UC, you can claim as a single person (although you still count as a couple and your income and capital are assessed jointly with your partner) in certain circumstances (see p36). The DWP treats your joint claim as one made by a single person.[32]

If you cannot manage your claim, another person can claim UC for you as your appointee (see p1005).[33]

## Information to support your claim

For the general information requirements that apply to all benefits, see p1006.

The DWP asks you to have certain information to hand when making your online claim. This includes:

- your bank, building society or credit union account details;
- the type of accommodation you have (eg, whether you are a private tenant, council tenant, housing association tenant or homeowner) and your landlord's details, if you have one;
- an email address and access to a phone;
- your national insurance (NI) number (if you do not have an NI number, you satisfy the NI number requirement if you have applied for one and the DWP has verified the information and evidence you provide – see p1007);
- information about your housing – eg, how much rent you pay;
- details of your income – eg, recent payslips and any other benefits;
- details of savings and any investments – eg, shares or a property that you rent to others;
- details of how much you pay for childcare if you want help with your childcare costs included in your UC;
- proof of your identity – eg, a driving licence, passport, debit or credit card, payslip or P60.

It is important that you provide any information required when you claim. Until you do, you may not count as having made a valid claim (see p1008). Your claim is valid if you provide the information requested on the online claim form.[34] In most cases, if you have completed the online form and submitted it, you will have made a valid claim.

You are then usually asked to provide further information or evidence, usually at an interview – eg, about your identity, or payslips, your rent agreement and bank statements. If you have a health condition that means that you cannot work, you can self-certify this for the first seven days. After that, you are usually asked to provide a fit note (ie, a medical certificate) from your doctor. Where necessary, you should be able to verify your identity using the gov.uk verifying service or, if you have a Government Gateway online account, using your credentials from that. The DWP will contact you if it needs to check any of the information you have already submitted. You may be asked to attend an interview at your local job centre.

If you do not comply with a request for further information, the DWP is likely to say that you have made a 'failed claim' and that your claim has been 'closed'. You should therefore comply if you can. If you cannot, tell the DWP in advance. If your claim is closed, you should be given a decision about this saying that you are not entitled to UC.



***Has your claim been closed?***

Do the following if you are told your claim has been closed.

1. If you can still access your online journal, use it to challenge the decision to close your claim – ie, that you are not entitled to UC. Download any documents and take screenshots of the decision to close your claim and your challenge to that decision, then make a new claim for UC as soon as possible. You will get a new online journal for your new claim, but may lose access to your old journal.
2. If you do not have access to your online journal, make a new claim for UC. You can then challenge the decision to close your claim on your new online journal.
3. There is nothing in the law about 'closing' a claim. What has actually happened is that the DWP has made a decision that you are not entitled to UC. The law does not say that you are not entitled to UC merely because you have not attended the interview.[35] So you may be able to argue that there is no basis for deciding that you were not entitled to UC. In any case, you must have been given at least a month to attend, or longer if considered reasonable.[36] If you have not attended an interview, the most common reason for a decision that you are not entitled to UC is because there is a doubt about your identity. If this is not in doubt (eg, if the DWP has accepted proof of your identity for your subsequent claim), you could argue that the decision to close your earlier claim should now be changed.

If you are working for an employer, the DWP uses a 'real-time information system' to obtain information about your earnings. Your employer is required to send information to HMRC every time your wages are paid.

You may also be asked to provide information after you are awarded UC, and if you fail to do so, your UC could be suspended or even terminated (see p1031).

## The date of your claim

The date of your claim is important as it determines when your entitlement to UC starts. This is not necessarily the date from when you are paid. For information about when payment of UC starts, see p49.

For an online claim, your date of claim is the date the DWP receives your online claim form.[37] If you had help from the DWP (or someone providing services to the DWP) with making your online claim before you claimed online, your date of claim is the date you notified the DWP that you needed help. **Note**:

the DWP does not accept that this applies if you get help from a Citizens Advice office.

If you are allowed to claim by phone, your date of claim is the date on which the claim is 'properly completed'. That is when you have given all the information the DWP requires on the phone.[38]

**Note:** if your claim is considered 'defective', you are given a month to correct the defects, or longer if considered reasonable. If you do, your claim is treated as having been made when you initially claimed.[39] In practice, very few online UC claims are defective because, without the required information on the online form, it is not possible to make the claim at all. Instead, your claim is valid if you have been able to submit the online claim form, although you are also usually then asked to provide further information or evidence to be entitled to UC (see p1009). If you were allowed to claim by phone, your claim is defective if you have not given all the information the DWP requires on the phone, but is valid once you have given that, and if you did that within the time allowed it should be treated as valid from the time when you started your claim.[40] Again, you may be asked to provide further information or evidence to be entitled to UC.

## Backdating your universal credit

UC can be backdated for a maximum of one month, but only in certain circumstances. If you make a joint claim, you and your partner must both satisfy one (or more) of these circumstances. **Note:** strictly speaking, it is the start of your UC award that is backdated, rather than the date of your claim. Your UC can be backdated if you could not reasonably be expected to have claimed earlier because:[41]

- you were previously getting income support, jobseeker's allowance, ESA, HB, child tax credit or working tax credit, and you were not notified that your entitlement was going to end before it did; *or*
- you have a disability (the rules do not define this); *or*
- you were unwell and this meant you could not claim on time, and you have supplied medical evidence showing that you were unwell; *or*
- you could not claim online because of a system failure or planned system maintenance, and you have now claimed on the first day that the system was working; *or*
- you made a joint claim for UC which was either turned down or awarded but later terminated because your partner did not accept their claimant commitment, but you have now ceased to be a couple and have reclaimed UC as a single person.

Backdating could apply, for example, where you lost entitlement to HB by having moved to a new local authority area (and so could not get HB again), but were not actually notified of that until later, when your new local authority told you that you had to claim UC instead.[42]

Consideration of whether you could not reasonably have been expected to apply earlier than you did should take account of all your circumstances – including, for example, language difficulties and whether you were aware of the possibility of claiming by phone.[43]

2

Request backdating as soon as you can. The online claim form does not ask if you want backdating, but you can still say that you want it by requesting this on your journal when you claim. In some cases, it may be that what you have said on your claim form (eg, about having a disability or being unwell in the period before you claim) constitutes an 'implied' claim for backdating.[44] You can still ask for backdating after your claim is decided, by requesting a revision (ie, mandatory reconsideration) of the decision on your UC entitlement – ie, when you get your first payment statement on your online journal.[45]

**Note:** if you are transferring to UC under the managed migration process (see p29), but you have missed the 'deadline day' allowed for making a claim for UC, you are treated as having claimed on that day if you claim by your 'final deadline'. You do not have to satisfy the bulleted points above.

If you might have qualified for benefit earlier, but did not claim because you were given the wrong information by the DWP or were misled by it, you could ask for compensation (see p1261) or complain to the Ombudsman (see p1266).

### If you claim the wrong benefit

There are no rules for when a claim for another benefit can be treated as a claim for UC. You should claim UC as soon as you can and, if necessary, ask for the claim to be backdated.

### Claiming in advance

If you claim UC when you are not yet entitled, but the DWP thinks you will be entitled within one month of the day you claimed, it can (but does not have to) make an advance award. If this applies, your claim is treated as having been made on the first day you are entitled to UC.[46] However, the DWP only accepts advance claims in very limited circumstances and currently does not specifiy any classes of case in which this will be done.[47]

## 7. Getting paid

The general rules on getting paid are covered in Chapter 45. This section explains the specific rules that apply to universal credit (UC).

***When is universal credit paid?***

You are normally paid within seven days of the end of an assessment period. UC is usually paid monthly, in arrears. If you live in Scotland, you can request that you be paid twice monthly.[48] If you find being paid monthly is difficult to budget for, you may be able to request more frequent payments under an 'alternative payment arrangement' (see p51).



Your award is assessed over an 'assessment period' of one calendar month, beginning from the date your entitlement starts (see p39).[49] UC should normally be paid direct into your account within seven days of the last day of the monthly assessment period or, if this is not possible, 'as soon as reasonably practicable' after that.[50] If you are getting UC as a single person and become a couple with someone else on UC, your new assessment period as a couple begins on the same day of each month as your old award ended, or that of your partner ended, whichever was earlier. If your new partner was not on UC, your new assessment period as a couple begins on the same day of the month as it did for your old award. If you were part of a couple on UC but are now single, your new assessment period begins on the same day of each month as it did for your old award.[51]

Your online UC journal should show when you will get your first payment of UC. In practice, you can expect to get your first payment about five weeks after claiming (although this may take longer in some cases). If you are in financial need in the meantime, or if there is a delay in subsequent payments, you may be able to get an advance payment of UC (see p1023). The advance must be repaid. Otherwise, you may be able to get help from your local authority (see p770).

Couples can decide which partner is paid. The DWP can decide that the other partner should be paid instead or can split the payments between you if it considers it to be in your interests, the interests of a child for whom you are responsible (see p64), or in the interests of a severely disabled person and your UC includes a carer element (see p75).[52] Couples with children making a new claim are guided to use the bank account of the main carer for their UC payments.

If you need a loan for an item you cannot afford, you can ask for a budgeting advance of UC (see p52).

Your UC can be paid in whole or in part to another person on your behalf, if the DWP considers this is necessary to protect your interests, or those of your partner, a child for whom you are responsible (see p64), or a severely disabled person and your UC includes a carer element (p75).[53]

The housing costs element to cover your rent is normally paid to you, rather than your landlord, unless paying your landlord would be in your interest. Official guidance says that your landlord can request that payment be made to them, and this will be granted automatically if your rent is over two months in arrears.[54] If you live in Scotland, you can request that payment be made direct to your landlord.[55] Otherwise, you may be able to request payment to your landlord under an 'alternative payment arrangement' (see p51).

**Note:**

- Deductions can be made from your UC to pay third parties (see p1033).

- Your UC might be paid at a reduced rate if you have been sanctioned (see Chapter 43) or committed a benefit offence (see p1111).
- For information on missing payments, see p1020. If you cannot get your UC payments because you have lost your bank card or you have forgotten your PIN, see p1019.
- If payment of your UC is delayed, see p1123. If you are waiting for a decision on your claim, or to be paid, you might be able to get an advance (see p1023). If you wish to complain about how your claim has been dealt with, or claim compensation, see Chapter 55.
- If payment of your UC is suspended, see p1031.
- If you are overpaid UC, you might have to repay it (see Chapter 47) and, in some circumstances, you may have to pay a penalty (see p1101). If you have been accused of fraud, see Chapter 48.
- If you are owed arrears of UC, these can be paid in instalments (see p1018).

## Alternative payment arrangements

If you find monthly payments difficult to budget for, or if having your UC housing costs element paid to you rather than to your landlord is leading to serious rent arrears, or if you need the payment of your UC to be split between you and your partner, it may be possible to have an alternative payment arrangement. **Note:** in Scotland, under the 'Scottish choices' scheme, you can ask for your UC to be paid twice monthly and/or for the housing element to be paid direct to your landlord. This is separate from alternative payment arrangements and cannot apply if those have already been applied to make similar arrangements.

Alternative payment arrangements are discretionary and there is no right of appeal against decisions about them, although you can ask the DWP to look at them again. You can request an alternative payment arrangement or the request can be made by someone else – eg, your landlord where you are in rent arrears (see the note below). It must be shown that you cannot manage the usual payment arrangement and, as a result, there is a risk of financial harm to you or someone in your family. According to government guidance, the following applies.[56]

- The DWP must be satisfied that alternative payment arrangements should apply, based on your inability to cope with usual payment and on your circumstances. For example, are you paying your bills on time? Can you manage a monthly budget? Are you used to managing money with your partner?
- Alternative payment arrangements are considered in the following order of priority:
  - paying rent (ie, the UC housing element) direct to your landlord to safeguard your home;
  - more frequent payment – ie, two payments a month, rather than just one. Exceptionally, more frequent payments can be considered;

  - splitting payment between the partners in a couple in specific situations – eg, if one partner is mismanaging the UC award or if there is domestic abuse.
- The DWP splits claimants into two tiers: tier one for those with circumstances with a 'high likely need' for alternative payment arrangements and tier two for those with 'less likely need'.
  **You are in tier one if you:**
  - have drug, alcohol and other addiction problems; *or*
  - have learning difficulties; *or*
  - have severe debt problems; *or*
  - are living in temporary or supported accommodation; *or*
  - are homeless; *or*
  - have experienced domestic abuse; *or*
  - have a mental health condition; *or*
  - are currently in rent arrears of at least two months' rent, or at threat of eviction or repossession; *or*
  - are aged 16 or 17, or have left local authority care; *or*
  - are a family with multiple and complex needs.

  **You are in tier two if you:**
  - have third-party deductions in place – eg, for utility arrears; *or*
  - are a refugee or asylum seeker; *or*
  - have a history of rent arrears; *or*
  - were previously homeless or living in supported accommodation; *or*
  - have a physical disability; *or*
  - have just left prison or hospital; *or*
  - are recently bereaved; *or*
  - have problems with language skills; *or*
  - are an ex-service person; *or*
  - are not in education, employment or training.

**Note:** a recent court decision has held that it is unlawful for an alternative payment arrangement to pay your housing element direct to your landlord to be introduced, without your first having been given the chance to comment – eg, to raise objections.[57] This decision may be appealed further. See CPAG's *Welfare Rights Bulletin* or the online version of this *Handbook* for updates.

## Budgeting advances

Budgeting advances are extra amounts of UC to help you with expenses – eg, buying essential furniture or household equipment, or expenses related to maternity or getting and keeping a job. Budgeting advances must be repaid, usually by deductions from future payments of your UC and usually over 12 months (24 for advances taken out from December 2024). They are discretionary. If you are refused a budgeting advance, you do not have a right to appeal against this decision.

If you are awarded a budgeting advance, the DWP must send you notice in writing that you will have it deducted from subsequent payments of your UC and that, if it is not deducted, you must otherwise repay it. The same rules apply to deductions from your UC that apply to the recovery of overpayments on p1073.

To get a budgeting advance:[58]

- you must apply for one; *and*
- you (or your partner if you are a couple) must be getting UC and (unless the expense is 'necessarily related' to employment) have been getting UC or income-related employment and support allowance (ESA) or pension credit (PC) for a continuous period of at least six months when the claim is made. (**Note:** this rule can also apply if you had been getting income support or income-based jobseeker's allowance but these have now been replaced by UC – see p21); *and*
- if you are single, your earnings from work must not exceed £2,600 in the period covered by the previous six complete monthly assessment periods. If you are a member of a couple, your joint earnings from work must not exceed £3,600 in this period. **Note:** if you are self-employed, your actual earned income is taken into account, not any assumed minimum income under the 'minimum income floor' (see p130); *and*
- there must be no outstanding budgeting advance (ie, which has not yet been recovered) paid to you (or your partner) and the DWP is satisfied that the budgeting advance can reasonably be expected to be recovered, taking into account all your debts and other liabilities.

The minimum amount of a budgeting advance is £100. The maximum payable is:

- if you are single and not responsible for a child, £348;
- if you are in a couple and not responsible for a child, £464;
- if you are responsible for a child and either single or in a couple, £812.

For when you are responsible for a child, see p258.

If your capital (or your joint capital if you are a couple) is over £1,000, the budgeting advance is reduced by the amount the capital exceeds £1,000. For how your capital is calculated, see Chapter 8.

## Change of circumstances

You must report changes in your circumstances that you have been told you must report, as well as any that you might reasonably be expected to know might affect your right to, the amount of, or the payment of, your benefit. You should do this as soon as possible. You are usually expected to report a change on your online UC journal. For official information on reporting a change, see gov.uk/universal-credit/changes-of-circumstances. See p1030 for further information.

If you become a member of a couple with someone who is not entitled to UC, their entitlement to income-related ESA and housing benefit (except for specified or temporary accommodation – see p183) ends (see p33).

If you are working and being taxed through PAYE (pay as you earn), the DWP should get information about changes in your earnings automatically from HMRC through the 'real-time information system'. However, if your employer has not reported your earnings, you should report them yourself. The DWP may specifically require you to do this.[59] Check with your employer that your earnings are being reported as you are paid. If you are self-employed, you must report your earnings every month.

When you notify the DWP of a change of circumstances, the decision on your UC is changed by a supersession of your UC award. This usually takes effect from the first day of the monthly assessment period in which the change occurred, or is expected to occur.[60] So a change that occurs part way through a monthly assessment period can be treated as having occurred on the first day of the period. However, note the following important exceptions.

- If you are single and the change is that you have reached pension age, or you are in a mixed-age couple and the younger person has now also reached pension age, the change takes effect from the start of the assessment period that follows the assessment period in which you (or the younger person in the couple) reached pension age.[61]
- If you are required by the DWP to report your earnings, you reported them when you were required to do so and your earnings decrease, the supersession takes effect from the first day of the assessment period in which the decrease occurred.[62]
- A change of circumstances which is advantageous to you is only backdated to the start of the assessment period in which it occurred if you report it before the end of that assessment period, unless the time allowed is extended. Otherwise, the change applies from the start of the assessment period in which you reported it. For full details, see p1152.
- Other exceptions may apply (see p1148).

***Examples***

Finn (30), a lone parent with one child (born after 6 April 2017), is entitled to maximum UC of £692.95 – ie, a standard allowance of £400.14, plus a child element of £292.81. His assessment period begins on 5 June. Halfway through this assessment period, Finn stops being responsible for a child as his son goes to live with his mother, and so Finn is no longer entitled to the child element. His maximum UC entitlement reduces to £400.14 a month. This change is not advantageous to Finn, but is backdated to the start of the assessment period – ie, to 5 June. This includes a period before he lost entitlement to the child element. However, Finn is not overpaid UC as he does not get paid until seven days after the end of the assessment period on 4 July. So Finn gets paid just £400.14 for the whole of the assessment period in which the change occurred.

Beth (26) is entitled to maximum UC of £400.14 a month (a standard allowance). Towards the end of her August monthly assessment period, she has a baby and her maximum UC entitlement increases by £292.81 as it now includes a child element. The change is advantageous to Beth. She reports the change before the end of the assessment period and it is backdated to the start of the assessment period – ie, including a period before she had her baby. When Beth gets paid (after the end of the assessment period in which the change occurred), she gets the additional £292.81 for the whole period. If Beth did not report the change until the start of her next assessment period, it may only have applied from the start of that period.



## 8. Tax, other benefits and the benefit cap

### Tax

Universal credit (UC) is not taxable.

### Means-tested benefits

The general rule is that if you claim UC, you come under the UC system and can no longer get income-related employment and support allowance (ESA). (UC has also replaced income support, income-based jobseeker's allowance (JSA) and tax credits – see p21.) You cannot qualify for housing benefit (HB), except if you live in specified or temporary accommodation (see p183).

If you are in a couple and claim UC, your partner's income-related ESA and HB stops and you get UC as a couple instead (see p32). If one (but not both) of you has reached pension age so that you are in a 'mixed-age couple', you cannot usually make a new claim for pension credit (PC) and must claim UC instead. You may still be able to claim PC in certain circumstances (see p239).

In Scotland, UC is a qualifying benefit for Scottish child payment (see p1452).

### Non-means-tested benefits

For the rules on entitlement to national insurance credits for people on UC, see p868.

When you come under the UC system (see p20):

- you can still claim new-style JSA or new-style contributory ESA. These are taken into account in full as income for UC (and so reduce your UC entitlement);
- you can claim other non-means-tested benefits at the same time as UC – eg, carer's allowance or (in Scotland) carer support payment, child benefit, personal independence payment or (in Scotland) adult disability payment, statutory sick pay and statutory maternity, adoption, paternity and shared parental pay;

- it can be worth claiming non-means-tested benefits. For example, if your child gets disability living allowance or child disability payment, you may be entitled to a disabled child addition (see p68).

2

For how non-means-tested benefits are treated when working out your income for UC, see Chapter 7.

## The benefit cap

UC is one of the specified benefits for the benefit cap. The benefit cap only applies if you are getting UC or HB. See p1025 for further information.

## Passports and other sources of help

If you are entitled to UC, you may also qualify for:

- health benefits such as free prescriptions (see Chapter 27);
- education benefits such as free school lunches (see p774);
- social fund payments (see Chapter 33) or, in Scotland, a Best Start grant (see p1452), funeral support payment (see Chapter 65) and winter heating payment (see Chapter 66);
- Healthy Start food and vitamins (see p771) or, in Scotland, Best Start foods (see p1455);
- help from your local welfare assistance scheme (see p770);
- council tax reduction (see p761).

# Notes

1. **Who can get universal credit**
 1 ss3 and 4 WRA 2012; reg 9 UC Regs
 2 s14 WRA 2012
 3 s5 WRA 2012
 4 ss3 and 4 WRA 2012
 5 Reg 3(2) UC Regs
 6 Reg 3(3) UC Regs
 7 Reg 3(4) UC Regs
 8 Reg 12 UC Regs

2. **The rules about your age**
 9 s4(3) WRA 2012; reg 8 UC Regs
 10 s4(4) WRA 2012
 11 Sch 1 para 26 UC,PIP,JSA&ESA(DA) Regs
 12 Reg 8(1) and (2) UC Regs
 13 Reg 30 UC Regs
 14 Reg 8(3) and (4) UC Regs
 15 Reg 3(3) UC Regs

3. **People included in the claim**
 16 s2 WRA 2012
 17 s10 WRA 2012

4. **The amount of benefit**
 18 Regs 21 and 21A UC Regs
 19 s8 WRA 2012
 20 Sch 2 para 4 UC(TP) Regs, as it applies to UC awards beginning on or after 27 January 2021
 21 Reg 22 UC Regs
 22 Reg 22 UC Regs
 23 Reg 5A UC(TP) Regs

24 Regs 18 and 72 UC Regs
25 Reg 28(7) UC Regs

6. **Claims and backdating**

26 Reg 8 UC,PIP,JSA&ESA(C&P) Regs
27 Regs 21(3C) and 22A UC Regs
28 Reg 9(6)-(8) UC,PIP,JSA&ESA(C&P) Regs; reg 21(3) UC Regs
29 Reg 32A UC,PIP,JSA&ESA(C&P) Regs
30 *Ipswich Borough Council v TP and SSWP* [2024] UKUT 117 (AAC)
31 s2 WRA 2012
32 Reg 9 UC,PIP,JSA&ESA(C&P) Regs
33 Reg 57 UC,PIP,JSA&ESA(C&P) Regs
34 Reg 8 UC,PIP,JSA&ESA(C&P) Regs
35 The DWP usually relies on reg 37 UC,PIP,JSA&ESA(C&P) Regs. However, this does not say anything about 'closing' a claim or not being entitled merely for failing to provide the evidence or information. See *PHC v SSWP* [2024] UKUT 340 (AAC).
36 Reg 37(3) UC,PIP,JSA&ESA(C&P) Regs
37 Reg 10 UC,PIP,JSA&ESA(C&P) Regs
38 Reg 10(1)(c) UC,PIP,JSA&ESA(C&P) Regs
39 Reg 10(2) UC,PIP,JSA&ESA(C&P) Regs
40 Regs 8(4)-(6) and 10(2) UC,PIP,JSA&ESA(C&P) Regs
41 Reg 26 UC,PIP,JSA&ESA(C&P) Regs
42 *CP v SSWP* [2020] UKUT 309 (AAC)
43 *CU v SSWP (UC)* [2024] UKUT 32 (AAC)
44 *WB v SSWP (UC)* [2022] UKUT 332 (AAC)
45 *SSWP v Miah* [2024] EWCA Civ 186; official guidance in ADM Memo 3/2023; see also cpag.org.uk/legal
46 s98 WRA 2012; reg 32 UC,PIP,JSA&ESA(C&P) Regs
47 para A2018 ADM

7. **Getting paid**

48 Reg 47 UC,PIP,JSA&ESA(C&P) Regs; The Universal Credit (Claims and Payments) (Scotland) Regulations 2017 No.227
49 s7 WRA 2012; reg 21 UC Regs
50 Reg 47(2) UC,PIP,JSA&ESA(C&P) Regs
51 Reg 21(3), (3A) and (3B) UC Regs
52 Reg 47(6) UC,PIP,JSA&ESA(C&P) Regs
53 Reg 58 UC,PIP,JSA&ESA(C&P) Regs
54 HB Circular A13/2013
55 The Universal Credit (Claims and Payments) (Scotland) Regulations 2017 No.227
56 DWP, *Alternative Payment Arrangements*, available at gov.uk
57 *Roberts v SSWP and Guinness Partnership Trust Ltd* [2025] EWHC 51 (Admin)
58 Regs 12-15 SS(PAB) Regs
59 Reg 61 UC Regs
60 Sch 1 para 20 UC,PIP,JSA&ESA(DA) Regs
61 Sch 1 para 26 UC,PIP,JSA&ESA(DA) Regs
62 Sch 1 para 22 UC,PIP,JSA&ESA(DA) Regs

2

# Chapter 4

# People included in your universal credit

**This chapter covers:**


1. Couples (below)
2. Children (p62)


This chapter covers the rules for universal credit (UC). For other means-tested benefits, see Chapter 12.

### Key facts

- Your partner and your children can be included in your UC.
- You count as a member of a 'couple' if you are married or in a civil partnership and are living with your partner in the same household. You also count as a couple if you are not married or in a civil partnership, but are living with your partner as if you are a married couple or civil partners.
- A child or 'qualifying young person' can be included as part of your family in your claim if you are responsible for them. They must normally live with you.
- You can continue to count as a couple, and children and young people can continue to be included in your UC, while you are living apart temporarily.

## 1. Couples

Your partner is included in your universal credit (UC) if you count as a 'couple' (you normally make a joint claim with your partner – see p45). You and your partner count as a couple if you are both aged 16 or over and you are:[1]

- married or civil partners and members of the same household; *or*
- not married or civil partners but 'living together as if' you are a married couple or civil partners.

### Spouse or civil partner

You can still be treated as part of a couple, even if you are married to someone else or in a civil partnership with someone else.[2]

There are special rules if you are polygamously married. If your spouse has another spouse from an earlier marriage and you all live in the same household, you can get UC as a single person.[3] You count as **polygamously married** if you are part of a marriage in which one of you is married to more than one person and your marriages took place in a country that permits polygamy (see also p460).[4]

You count as someone's **civil partner** if you have been registered as their civil partner.

## Living together as a married couple or civil partners

Even if you and your partner are not married or civil partners, you count as a couple if you are 'living together as if' you are a married couple or civil partners. We refer to this as 'cohabiting' in this *Handbook*. This applies to both different- and same-sex relationships.[5] The factors below are used as 'signposts' to determine whether or not you are cohabiting.[6] No one factor, in itself, is conclusive, as it is your overall relationship and your particular circumstances that are looked at.[7] The 'emotional aspect' of the relationship (your interdependence, devotion, love and affection) should also be considered.[8] Like your individual circumstances, this should not be regarded as conclusive. For example, if your partner stays with you for three nights or more a week, you should not automatically count as cohabiting.

***Are you cohabiting?***

1. Do you live in the same household? See below.
2. Do you have a sexual relationship? See below.
3. What are your financial arrangements? See p60.
4. Is your relationship stable? See p60.
5. Do you have children? See p60.
6. How do you appear in public? See p60.

### Living in the same household

If you live in the same household, you may be treated as cohabiting. For what counts as a 'household', see p60.

Even if you *do* share a household, you may not be cohabiting. It is essential to look at *why* two people are in the same household.[9] For example, if you are living in the same household for 'care, companionship and mutual convenience', you can argue that you are not cohabiting.[10]

### Being in a sexual relationship

In practice, a decision maker may not ask you about the existence of a sexual relationship, in which case they only have the information if you volunteer it. However, if you are appealing about whether you are a member of a couple, the

First-tier Tribunal should consider this and may ask you about it.[11] If you do not have a sexual relationship, you should say so (and perhaps offer to show your separate sleeping arrangements).

Having a sexual relationship is not sufficient, by itself, to prove you are cohabiting. If you have never had a sexual relationship, there is a strong (but not necessarily conclusive) presumption that you are not cohabiting.[12] A couple who abstain from a sexual relationship before marriage should not be counted as cohabiting until they are formally married.[13]

### Your financial arrangements

If one person is supported by the other or your household expenses are shared, this may be treated as evidence that you are cohabiting. However, it is important to consider how expenses are shared. There is a difference between, on the one hand, paying a fixed weekly contribution or rigidly sharing bills 50/50 (which does *not* suggest cohabitation) and, on the other hand, a common fund for income and expenditure (which might).

### A stable relationship

Marriage and civil partnership are expected to be stable and lasting and so an occasional or brief association should not be regarded as cohabitation. However, the fact that your relationship is stable does not make it cohabitation – eg, you can have a stable relationship as a landlord and lodger, but not be cohabiting.

The way you spend your time together, the activities you undertake together and the things you do for each other are relevant, so questions about how you spend your holidays and how you organise the shopping, the laundry and cleaning may be important.

### Children

If you have had a child together and live in the same household as the other parent, there is a strong (but not conclusive) presumption of cohabitation.

### Your appearance in public

Decision makers may check the electoral roll and claims for other benefits to see whether you present yourselves as a couple. If you do not have a committed, emotional, loving relationship that is publicly acknowledged, you can argue that you are not living together as a married couple or civil partners.[14]

## Households

The term 'household' is not defined. Whether you and another person should be treated as members of the same household is decided on the particular facts of your case.

A house or flat can contain a number of separate households and if one person has exclusive occupation of separate accommodation from another, they are not considered to be living in the same household. Physical presence is not, in itself, conclusive. There must be a 'particular kind of tie' binding two people together in a domestic establishment. So, for example, a husband and wife may live in separate households in the same care or nursing home.[15] For a couple to be in the same household, there must also be two or more people living together as a unit and having a reasonable level of independence and self-sufficiency. In one case, it was held that a married couple sharing a room in a residential home because they needed help organising their personal care and domestic activities were not self-sufficient and did not live in a domestic establishment, and therefore did not share a household.[16]

***Is there a separate household?***

If you think you should not be treated as a member of the same household as someone, check whether you can show that you maintain separate households. A separate household may exist if there:

- are independent arrangements for storing and cooking food or separate eating arrangements;
- are independent financial arrangements or separate commitments for housing costs;
- is no evidence of family life.

You cannot be a member of more than one household at the same time.[17] So if you are a member of one couple, you cannot also be treated as part of another. If two people maintain separate homes (ie, they each have a separate address where they usually live), they cannot share the same household.[18] Even if you have the right to occupy only part of a room, you may have your own household.[19]

If you are separated from your partner, but living under the same roof, you should not be treated as a couple if you are maintaining separate households. Any 'mere hope' of a reconciliation is not a 'reasonable expectation' if at least one partner has accepted that the relationship is at an end.[20]

**Note:** if you are still married or in a civil partnership, a shared attitude that the relationship is at an end may not be enough to show there is no shared household.[21]

## Couples living apart

**If you separate permanently** (ie, you do not intend to resume living with your partner), you no longer count as a couple.[22] When deciding whether you intend to resume living together or not, your intention must be 'unqualified' – ie, it must not depend on something over which you have no control, such as the right of entry to the UK being granted by the Home Office[23] or the offer of a suitable job.[24]

**If you and your partner are living apart temporarily**, you continue to count as a couple because you are still treated as members of the same household. If you were not living together in the same household before your time apart, you should not be regarded as living apart temporarily.[25] Your former household need not have been in the UK.[26]

However, **you no longer count as a couple** (and therefore claim as a single person) if you have been living apart (or expect to be living apart) for more than six months.[27] Only your income and capital are taken into account.

If either you or your partner go abroad, see p1372.

If your partner is in hospital, see p821. If they are in a care home, see p831. If your partner is a prisoner or serving a sentence while in hospital, see p839.

In any situation in which you still count as a couple but claim UC as a single person (see p36), your income and capital are still assessed jointly.[28]

## Challenging a decision that you are a couple

Your UC may be stopped or adjusted if the decision maker decides you are a member of a couple. If you disagree with a decision that you are a couple, you can apply for a revision or supersession (see Chapter 50), or appeal (see Chapter 51).

***How do you show that you are not a couple?***

1. Consider carefully what evidence to submit:
- if you are married or in a civil partnership, to show that you are not living in the same household as your spouse or civil partner;
- if you are not married or in a civil partnership, about each of the six questions on p59, the emotional aspect of your relationship and any other matters you consider relevant.

2. Provide evidence if the other person has another address (eg, a rent account and other household bills), receipts for board and lodging, statements from friends and relatives, or evidence of a formal separation, divorce proceedings or a dissolution application or order.

When you first claim, you must provide any information that is reasonably required to decide your claim.[29] A decision should then be made on all the available evidence.[30] However, if your UC award as a single person is stopped because it is alleged that you are part of a couple, the onus is on the decision maker to prove that you are.[31]

Although UC can continue to be paid to you as a couple, it will be affected – eg, because your alleged partner must also satisfy the basic conditions for UC and your income and capital are assessed jointly.

# 2. Children

A child may count as part of your family and be included in your universal credit (UC) if you or your partner are 'responsible' for them – ie, the child 'normally lives' with you (see p64).[32] You do not have to be the child's parent.

A child stops being included in your UC if you no longer fulfil these conditions or if they no longer count as a child.

If you are responsible for a child, you can get an additional amount (a child element) included in your UC. However, in most cases, you can only get child elements for a maximum of two children (see p68).

## Who counts as a child

A 'child' is someone who is:[33]

- aged under 16; *or*
- aged 16 or over but under 20 and counts as a 'qualifying young person' under the UC rules. This includes most young people studying for GCSEs or A levels or doing approved training. Specifically, it means someone who:[34]
  - is aged 16 but who has not reached 1 September following their 16th birthday; *or*
  - is aged 16–19 but who has not yet reached 1 September following their 19th birthday, and has been accepted for (or has enrolled on) approved training or non-advanced education at school or college, or another institution approved by the Secretary of State (see below). During term time, there must be more than 12 hours, on average, of tuition, practical work, supervised study or examinations a week. Meal breaks and unsupervised study are not included.

**Note:** a 19-year-old must have started (or been accepted for or enrolled on) the education or training before reaching 19 to count as a qualifying young person.

***Approved training and non-advanced education for universal credit***

**'Approved training'** is training that is approved by the DWP and provided under section 2(1) of the Employment and Training Act 1973 or section 2(3) of the Enterprise and New Towns (Scotland) Act 1990.

A course is **'non-advanced'** if it is below the level of 'advanced education'. Courses that count as advanced education include university degrees and other courses above GCSE, A level and Scottish National Qualifications above higher or advanced higher level.[35] See p489 for more examples of advanced and non-advanced courses.

## Who does not count as a child

A person does not count as a child if they are getting UC, income-related employment and support allowance (ESA), new-style jobseeker's allowance (JSA) or new-style ESA in their own right, and so do not count as a qualifying young person (see p488).[36]

2

## Responsibility for a child

A child is included in your UC if you are 'responsible' for them. You are responsible for a child if the child 'normally lives' with you.[37] When deciding whether a child lives with you, the DWP should consider the amount of time the child spends with you, as well as the nature of the support you provide.[38] **Note:** in practice, when deciding whether you are responsible for a child, the DWP checks to see whether you are entitled to child benefit for them. However, this is not the legal test of responsibility. In particular, the fact that you do not get child benefit for the child does *not* show that the child is not 'normally living' with you.

If the child normally lives with two (or more) people who are not a couple (eg, in the homes of separated parents), you are responsible if you have the main responsibility. In this situation, you can agree with the other person who this should be. The DWP can, however, decide otherwise or, if you cannot agree, decide which person has the main responsibility. Both the amount of time the child spends with you and the nature of the support you provide should be taken into account. It has been held that the rule giving responsibility for the child to the person regarded as having main responsibility is not unlawful discrimination against separated male parents who have shared care of the child.[39]

You cannot be treated as responsible for a child during any period in which they are:[40]

- being 'looked after by a local authority' (see below). However, that does not apply during planned short breaks in which the local authority temporarily looks after the child to provide respite care for you as the person who normally looks after them. It also does not apply, even if the child counts as being looked after by the local authority, while the child is living with you and you are their parent, or (except where you are a foster parent for the child) someone with parental responsibility for them, or if the child is placed with you for adoption;[41] *or*
- a prisoner; *or*
- temporarily absent from your household (see p60) and (for whatever reason) they have been, or are expected to be, absent for more than six months, including if this is for medical treatment abroad; *or*
- temporarily absent from your household and they have been, or are expected to be, absent from Great Britain for more than one month, unless it is under the same circumstances (medical treatment or death of a close relative) as those that apply to when you can get UC while absent (see p1371).

'Being looked after by a local authority' means being looked after by a local authority under specific legislation – ie, section 22 of the Children Act 1989, section 17(6) of the Children (Scotland) Act 1995 (this applies to some, although not all, kinship care arrangements) or section 74 of the Social Services and Well-being (Wales) Act 2014.[42] For example, if the local authority places the child with a foster parent, then usually nobody, including the foster parent, can count as responsible for them.

If UC is paid for a child, it cannot be split between parents if a child spends time equally between their two homes. The person who has main responsibility for the child has the child included in their UC.

2

## Notes

1. **Couples**
   1 s137(1) SSCBA 1992; CFC/7/1992; s39 WRA 2012
   2 R(SB) 8/85
   3 Reg 3(4) and (5) UC Regs
   4 Reg 3(5) UC Regs
   5 s39 WRA 2012
   6 *Crake and Butterworth v SBC* [1982] 1 All ER 498; [1981] 2 FLR 264 (QBD)
   7 R(SB) 17/81; R(G) 3/71; CIS/87/1993
   8 *PP v Basildon DC (HB)* [2013] UKUT 505 (AAC)
   9 *Crake and Butterworth v SBC* [1982] 1 All ER 498; [1981] 2 FLR 264 (QBD), quoted in R(SB) 35/85
   10 R(SB) 35/85
   11 CIS/87/1993; CIS/2559/2002; CIS/2074/2008
   12 CIS/87/1993
   13 CSB/150/1985
   14 *JP v SSWP (IS)* [2014] UKUT 17 (AAC)
   15 *Santos v Santos* [1972] 2 All ER 246; CIS/671/1992; CIS/81/1993
   16 CIS/4935/1997
   17 R(SB) 8/85
   18 R(SB) 4/83
   19 CSB/463/1986
   20 CIS/72/1994
   21 CIS/2900/1998
   22 Reg 3(6) UC Regs
   23 CIS/508/1992; CIS/13805/1996
   24 CIS/484/1993
   25 Reg 3(6) UC Regs; *Broxtowe BC v CS (HB)* [2014] UKUT 186 (AAC)
   26 CIS/508/1992
   27 Reg 3(6) UC Regs
   28 Reg 3(3) UC Regs
   29 Reg 37 UC,PIP,JSA&ESA(C&P) Regs
   30 CIS/317/1994
   31 R(I) 1/71

2. **Children**
   32 s10 WRA 2012; reg 4(2) UC Regs
   33 s40 WRA 2012; regs 2 and 5 UC Regs
   34 Reg 5 UC Regs
   35 Reg 12(3) UC Regs
   36 Reg 5(5) UC Regs
   37 Reg 4 UC Regs
   38 Reg 4 UC Regs; *MC v SSWP (UC)* [2018] UKUT 44 (AAC)
   39 *CD v SSWP* [2024] UKUT 256 (AAC)
   40 Reg 4(6) and (7) UC Regs
   41 Reg 4A UC Regs
   42 Reg 2, definition of 'looked after by a local authority', UC Regs

2

# Chapter 5

# The maximum amount

**This chapter covers:**


1. What is the maximum amount (below)
2. The standard allowance (p67)
3. Elements (p68)


## Key facts

- The maximum amount of universal credit (UC) is used, together with your income and capital, to calculate the amount of UC you are entitled to.
- The maximum amount is made up of a standard allowance plus, where applicable, one or more elements, depending on your circumstances – eg, if you have children.
- The elements that apply can include a transitional element to protect you from being worse off if you transfer to UC under the official 'managed migration' process.

## 1. What is the maximum amount

Your maximum universal credit (UC) is made up of the total of:

- a standard allowance, either for a single claimant or for a couple making a joint claim (see p67);
- a child element for each child, subject to a 'two-child limit' (exceptions may apply), with an increase for a disabled or severely disabled child (see p68);
- an element for an adult assessed as having limited capability for work and work-related activity (see p73). A separate element, abolished for new claimants, for someone assessed as just having limited capability for work can still be paid in some cases (see p71);
- a carer element for someone caring for a severely disabled person (see p75);
- a childcare costs element (see p76);
- a housing costs element for help with your rent or any service charges that you pay (see p78);

- a transitional element if you have transferred to UC under the 'managed migration' process and would otherwise be worse off than on legacy benefits (see p78). If you have transferred to UC under the natural migration process (or under the managed migration process but are not entitled to a transitional element) and you are entitled to a transitional SDP element as a result, this is treated as if it is part of your maximum amount (see p79). The DWP refers to both of these elements as 'transitional protection'.



### After a death

If any of the following people dies, your maximum amount of UC continues to be calculated as if that person had not died for the remainder of the monthly assessment period (see p39) in which the death occurs, and for the next two assessment periods:[1]

- your partner, if you have a joint UC claim with them (see p45);
- a child for whom you (or your partner in a joint claim) are responsible (see p68);
- a severely disabled person for whom you (or your partner in a joint claim) have regular and substantial caring responsibilities (see p75);
- someone who counts as a non-dependant for the housing costs element (see p103).

For example, if you have a joint claim and your partner dies, your maximum UC continues to include the couple rate of the standard allowance (and any element paid in respect of your partner) for the remainder of the assessment period in which they died, and for the next two assessment periods.

## 2. The standard allowance

A standard allowance is always included in your universal credit (UC) maximum amount. The amount depends on your age and whether you are claiming as a single person or making a joint claim with your partner.[2] See p45 for who counts as a couple, including when one of you is temporarily absent.

If you are making a joint claim with your partner and your partner dies, see p66.

**Note:** if one member of a couple does not satisfy the rules of entitlement for UC, the other partner may be able to claim as a single person (see p36). In this case, the standard allowance for a single claimant applies.

*Rates of standard allowance*

| | per month |
|---|---|
| **Single claimant** | |
| Under 25 | £316.98 |
| 25 or over | £400.14 |
| **Joint claimants** | |
| Both under 25 | £497.55 |
| One or both 25 or over | £628.10 |

2

# 3. Elements

## Child element

If you are responsible for a child or young person, you can get a child element included in your universal credit (UC) maximum amount. You are 'responsible' for a child who normally lives with you (see p64).[3] The child must either be aged under 16, or be aged 16–19 and a 'qualifying young person' for UC purposes (see p62).[4]

Before 6 April 2017, you got a child element for each child or young person you or your partner were responsible for. From 6 April 2017, a 'two-child limit' applies (see p69).

You may get a higher rate of the child element for the eldest or only child.[5] This was abolished from 6 April 2017, but continues to apply if your eldest or only child was born before that date.[6]

If a child is disabled, the child element is increased by a **'disabled child addition'**. You get the lower rate if the child is entitled to disability living allowance (DLA), Scottish adult disability living allowance (SADLA), child disability payment (CDP), personal independence payment (PIP) or adult disability payment (ADP). You get the higher rate instead if they are entitled to the DLA/SADLA/CDP care component at the highest rate, the daily living component of PIP/ADP at the enhanced rate, or if they are certified as severely sight impaired or blind by a consultant ophthalmologist.[7] The disabled child addition is still paid for a child, even if you cannot get a child element for them because of the two-child limit.[8]

If your child dies, see p67.

2

*Rates of child element*

| | *per month* |
|---|---|
| First child born before 6 April 2017 | £339.00 |
| Second child/all children born on or after 6 April 2017 | £292.81 |
| Disabled child addition | |
| Lower rate | £158.76 |
| Higher rate | £495.87 |

## The two-child limit

You cannot get an element for a child born on or after 6 April 2017 if you already have two or more other children included in your award, unless an exception applies (see p70). This is known as the 'two-child limit'.[9] You can always get an element for a child born before 6 April 2017.

The number and order of children (ie, whether a child is the first, second, third or subsequent child) is determined according to their dates of birth, so that the eldest child is regarded as the first.[10]

When establishing the number of children you have for this purpose, a child who is covered by either of the second or third exceptions starting below (ie, they are adopted or living with you under a 'non-parental care arrangement') is ignored. However, children who would be covered by any of the other exceptions (for example, a child conceived as a result of a non consensual conception) must count as your third or subsequent child for you to get an element for them. At the time of writing, this was subject to legal challenge.[11] See CPAG's *Welfare Rights Bulletin* or the online version of this *Handbook* for updates.

You can get an element for:

- any child born before 6 April 2017; *and*
- a child born on or after 6 April 2017 who is not counted as your third or subsequent child; *and*
- a third or subsequent child born on or after 6 April 2017 to whom an exception applies.

***Examples***

Mei has three children. One was born before 6 April 2017; the others were born on 6 May 2020 and 4 July 2022. No exceptions apply to the children. Mei gets a child element for two children: the child born before 6 April 2017 and the child born on 6 May 2020.

Sarah and Alex have four children. Two were born before 6 April 2017, two (Ella and Cole) after that date. Ella has been adopted by Sarah and Alex. They get child elements for three children: the two born before 6 April 2017, and one for Ella, as she is covered by an exception. Ella is not included when establishing how many children Sarah and Alex have, so Cole is counted as their third child. As Cole was born after 6 April 2017 and he is not covered by any of the exceptions, no child element is included for him.

The child element can become payable for a third child to whom the two-child limit has applied when an older child leaves the household (as you are no longer responsible for them), or when a young person leaves education (as they no longer qualify). In these situations, you should report the change as soon as possible to ensure you continue to receive the maximum two child elements.

### Exceptions

The two-child limit does not apply to the following children.[12]

- **A child born in a multiple birth**, other than the first born if you already have two or more children. So, if you have:
  - no older children, you get the child element for all children in a multiple birth;
  - one older child, you get the child element for all children in a multiple birth;
  - two or more older children, you get the child element for all but one of the children in a multiple birth.
- **A child living with you under a 'non-parental caring arrangement'.** This means they are either a child whose parent is aged under 16 and you are responsible for the parent, *or* that the child is living with you on a long-term basis because they are unable to live with their parents and you are caring for them as a family member or friend. You or your partner must not be the child's parent or step-parent and you must:
  - be named in a child arrangements order under section 8 of the Children Act 1989 or a residence order under Article 8 of the Children (Northern Ireland) Order 1995 as a person with whom the child is to live; *or*
  - be the appointed or special guardian, or be entitled to guardian's allowance, for the child; *or*
  - have a kinship care order under section 72(1) of the Children and Young People (Scotland) Act 2014, or parental responsibilities or rights under section 80 of the Adoption and Children (Scotland) Act 2007; *or*
  - continue to be responsible for the child if any of the above bullet points applied immediately before the child's 16th birthday; *or*
  - be caring for the child because otherwise it is likely they would be taken into the care of the local authority.
- **A child who is being adopted** by you from local authority care or who has been placed with you for adoption. This exception does not apply if:
  - you or your partner were the child's step-parent immediately before the adoption; *or*
  - you or your partner have been the child's parent (other than by adoption) at any other time; *or*
  - the child is being adopted direct from abroad.
- **A child who is likely to have been conceived as a result of rape, or in a controlling or coercive relationship** (a 'non-consensual conception'). You must not be living at the same address as the alleged perpetrator for this

exception to apply, even though you might have been living with that person at the time of conception. A 'controlling or coercive relationship' includes behaviour that causes you to fear, on at least two occasions, that violence will be used against you, or that causes you serious alarm or distress which has a substantial adverse effect on your day-to-day activities. You must provide evidence from an 'approved person' that you have had contact with them or another approved person about the rape or relationship. A list of 'approved persons' is in official guidance and includes healthcare professionals, social workers and approved organisations such as specialist rape charities.[13] Third-party evidence is not required if there has been a conviction for rape or coercive, controlling behaviour in the UK, or for a similar offence abroad, or if you have been awarded criminal injuries compensation after a sexual offence, physical abuse or mental injury, and it is likely that the offence or injury resulted in the conception. You can be treated as having provided evidence if you have already provided it to HMRC for child tax credit (CTC).

If you are the step-parent of the child but are no longer part of a couple with the child's parent, the exception can continue to apply if you are still responsible for the child, and the only reason for any breaks in your claim is your becoming single or part of a couple again.

## Limited capability for work element

The limited capability for work element was abolished for new claims from 3 April 2017.[14] You can no longer get the element if you are making a new claim for UC, unless you are covered by one of the exceptions in the bullet points below. If you (or your partner in a joint claim) are also entitled to the limited capability for work-related activity element (see p73), you receive that instead – you cannot get both elements. If you are also entitled to the carer element (see p75), usually the carer element is included instead of the limited capability for work element – but if you have a joint claim for UC, see below.

You can get the limited capability for work element if you (or your partner) are entitled to UC and have limited capability for work (see Chapter 41) and:[15]

- you were getting the element in your current award of UC (or had limited capability for work and were waiting for the element to be included in your UC) immediately before 3 April 2017; *or*
- you were getting the limited capability for work-related activity element in your current award of UC immediately before 3 April 2017 and on a reassessment it is decided that you are entitled to the limited capability for work element instead; *or*
- the decision that you had limited capability for work before 3 April 2017 is not made until after this date but you had supplied a medical certificate, including if the decision is made following a revision or an appeal; *or*

2

- you were entitled to employment and support allowance (ESA) or to national insurance (NI) credits for limited capability for work (see p867) immediately before 3 April 2017, and you remained entitled after this date until you claimed UC; *or*
- you claimed ESA before 3 April 2017 but the initial decision on your claim was changed following a revision or an appeal, and on or after 3 April 2017 your UC award needs to be changed to take account of this; *or*
- you were entitled to incapacity benefit, severe disablement allowance, income support (IS) 'on the grounds of disability' or NI credits for incapacity for work (see p867) immediately before 3 April 2017, and you remained entitled after this date until you claimed UC. Certain other conditions apply. If you are in this situation, get specialist advice.

There may be a three-month waiting period before the element can be included in your UC for the first time.[16] In practice, it is usually included straight away, because you are transferring to UC from ESA (see below).

**Note:** your entitlement to the element can continue if your UC stops and then starts again because you have become, or stopped being, a member of a couple, or if your UC stops because your income is too high but then starts again within six months. If you work and earn an amount at least equal to a certain earnings threshold, you may be reassessed (see p901).

If your partner was entitled to the element, but dies, see p66.

***Rate of limited capability for work element***

| | *per month* |
|---|---|
| Limited capability for work | £158.76 |

## Transfers to universal credit

If you transfer to UC from ESA (under either the 'natural migration' or the 'managed migration' process) and were entitled to the work-related activity component in your ESA (see p561) on the date you claimed UC, you are treated as having limited capability for work and the limited capability for work element can be included in your UC straight away.[17]

## Joint claims

If you are making a joint claim with your partner, only one limited capability for work element can be included, even if you both meet the conditions.[18]

If you were previously getting UC as a single person but then form a couple with someone who was not entitled to UC, but who was getting ESA that included the work-related activity component (see p561), the limited capability for work element is included in your joint UC award.[19]

If one of you satisfies the conditions for both the limited capability for work element and the carer element (see p75), usually the carer element is included in your maximum amount instead of the limited capability for work element. However, if you qualify for one of these elements and your partner qualifies for the other, both elements can be included.[20]

2

*Example*

Nathan and Dani have a joint claim for UC, made before 3 April 2017. They have a disabled son, Oliver. Nathan has limited capability for work. Dani is Oliver's carer and satisfies the conditions for the carer element. Both the limited capability for work element and the carer element were included in Nathan and Dani's UC award before 3 April 2017, and continue for as long as they remain entitled.

If Nathan were also a carer for Oliver, they could nominate Dani as the main carer so that both the limited capability for work and carer elements can continue to be paid.

## Limited capability for work-related activity element

A limited capability for work-related activity element is included in your maximum amount if you (or your partner in a joint claim) have been assessed as having limited capability for work-related activity.[21] If this applies to you, you are also regarded as having limited capability for work. For the assessment, see p914. **Note:** in some claims by 'mixed-age' couples, the DWP has refused to carry out an assessment of the pension-age member of the couple, simply because they have reached pension age. That is wrong, as the basic rule is that any UC claimant can be assessed, and the limited situations in which an assessment may not be carried out do not include reference to the claimant's age.[22]

If you are qualifying for the element for the first time, there is usually a three-month waiting period before it is included in your maximum amount. The three-month period begins on the day on which you provide a 'fit note' (medical certificate) or, where it would have been unreasonable to require you to have provided one, other evidence sufficient to show you had limited capability for work. This could be, for example, if you reported on your online journal that you were suffering from health problems affecting your ability to work and were not told you needed to get a fit note, but you later provide a backdated fit note.[23] In practice, you may have already provided a fit note (or other sufficient evidence) three months or more ago, in which case you will have already served the waiting period.[24] The element is then included from the beginning of the assessment period (see p39) that follows the assessment period in which the three months ended. The element can also be included straight away if you (or your partner in a joint claim):[25]

- are terminally ill; *or*

- were entitled to the element (or the limited capability for work element) immediately before your current UC award started and your previous UC award ended because you became a member of a couple or you stopped being a member of a couple; *or*
- were entitled to the element (or the limited capability for work element) and your previous UC award ended within the six months before your current award started, because your income was too high; *or*
- are entitled to an award of new-style ESA (ie, contributory ESA under the UC system) that includes the support component, or you were so entitled on the day before your UC started, the ESA has since stopped because of the rules on the duration of contributory ESA (see p564), but you now have limited capability for work-related activity again; *or*
- have limited capability for work for UC, but are then assessed as entitled to the limited capability for work-related activity element.

See also below if you transfer from ESA to UC or were only entitled to NI credits, or your ESA stopped due to your reaching pension age, and had limited capability for work-related activity.

If your award of UC immediately follows an 'extended period of sickness' on jobseeker's allowance (JSA) (see p614), the element can be included from the beginning of the assessment period that follows the period in which the three months ended, beginning with the first day of your extended period of sickness.[26]

If your partner is entitled to the element but dies, see p67.

If you also satisfy the conditions for the carer element (see p75), the limited capability for work-related activity element is paid instead. However, if you are in a couple, if one of you can qualify for the limited capability for work-related activity element and the other qualifies for the carer element, both elements can be included.[27]

***Rate of limited capability for work-related activity element***

| | *per month* |
|---|---|
| Limited capability for work-related activity | £423.27 |

## Transfers to universal credit

If you transfer to UC from ESA (under either the natural migration or the managed migration process) and were entitled to the support component in your ESA (see p560) on the date you claimed UC, you are treated as having limited capability for work-related activity and the element is included in your UC straight away.

The same applies if you were not entitled to ESA but, on the date you claimed UC, you were entitled to NI credits for limited capability for work and assessed as having limited capability for work-related activity (see p913).[28]

From 27 January 2025, the same can also apply if when you claimed UC you were no longer entitled to ESA because you had reached pension age, but had been on ESA and entitled to the support component. In that situation, if you claimed UC within a month of your ESA ending, and you would have remained entitled to ESA but for your reaching pension age, the element can be included in your UC straight away.[29] This change in the law was introduced following a decision that the rules before then breached the human rights of a pension-age claimant by not allowing the element to be included in her UC straight away.[30]

### Joint claims

If you are making a joint claim with your partner, only one limited capability for work-related activity element can be included, even if you both meet the conditions.[31]

If you were previously getting UC as a single person but then form a couple with someone who was not entitled to UC but was getting ESA that included the support component (see p560), the limited capability for work-related activity element is included in your joint UC award.[32]

## Carer element

A carer element is included in your maximum amount if you have 'regular and substantial' caring responsibilities for a severely disabled person.[33] This means that you satisfy, or would satisfy were it not for the level of your earnings, the conditions for carer's allowance (CA) (see p473). You do not need to have claimed CA. This also applies if you live in Scotland (or outside Great Britain but have a 'genuine and sufficient link' to Scotland). Additionally, in Scotland you count as having these caring responsibilities if you are entitled to carer support payment (CSP) (see p1467).

If you get the carer element, the person you care for cannot get a severe disability premium in their legacy benefits (see p275). You do not qualify for the carer element if you have any earnings from your caring responsibilities.[34] **Note:** if you are claiming as a single person and qualify for the limited capability for work-related activity element, you get that element instead of the carer element. But if you are in a couple, it may be possible for both elements to be included (see p73).

If you are claiming as a single person, only one carer element can be included, even if you care for more than one disabled person.

If you are making a joint claim, you can get two carer elements if both you and your partner satisfy the conditions, provided you are not caring for the same person. If you are caring for the same person, you can decide between you which partner should be entitled – eg, if it is necessary for your partner to be entitled to the carer element so that you can also get the limited capability for work or limited capability for work-related activity element. If you do not decide which one of you should be entitled to the carer element, that decision is made for you.[35] Similarly, if someone other than your partner is caring for the same person, only one of you can get CA, CSP or the carer element of UC for that care. You can decide between you who should be entitled.[36]

If the person you care for dies, the element should continue to be paid for a time (see p67). If the DWP fails to do this, it may be possible to challenge that on judicial review: ask your adviser to contact CPAG (see cpag.org.uk/jr for details).

***Rate of carer element***

| | *per month* |
|---|---|
| Carer | £201.68 |

## Childcare costs element

A childcare costs element is included in your maximum amount if you are working (or have an offer of work) and have paid childcare costs for 'relevant childcare' (see p77 for what this covers).

The amount of the element is 85 per cent of your childcare costs, up to a maximum of £1,031.88 a month for one child and £1,768.94 a month for two or more children.[37]

**Note:**

- If you have upfront childcare costs (eg, a deposit, retainer or fees) in advance of the childcare starting and you have started work or increased your working hours but have not yet received your first payment of UC that reflects those costs, your work coach can pay them direct to the childcare provider using the Flexible Support Fund (see p782). You can still receive the childcare costs element in respect of the same costs.[38] Other upfront childcare costs (eg, during the school holidays) can be met from a budgeting advance (see p52). If you get a budgeting advance, you can still get up to 85 per cent of the childcare costs (subject to the overall limits above) covered by the childcare costs element, once you have submitted a paid receipt.[39]
- If you are entitled to UC, you *cannot* also get tax-free childcare payments. See p779 for more details.

To get the childcare costs element, you must be in paid work (there are no minimum hours) or have an offer of paid work that is due to start before the end of your next UC monthly assessment period (see p39).[40] If you are in a couple, your partner must also be in paid work, unless they cannot provide childcare themselves because they have limited capability for work (see Chapter 41), or they are caring for a severely disabled person and get (or would be entitled to) CA (see p471), including in Scotland, or are entitled to CSP (see p1467), or they are temporarily absent from your household. **Note:** you stop counting as a couple if your partner is (or is expected to be) absent for more than six months.[41] If your partner is temporarily absent abroad, see p1370.

You are treated as still in paid work if you are getting statutory sick pay, statutory maternity pay, statutory adoption pay, statutory paternity pay, statutory shared parental pay, statutory parental bereavement pay, statutory neonatal care pay or maternity allowance. You are also treated as still in paid work if your work ended during your current assessment period or in the previous one.[42]

In addition, you must meet all the following conditions.[43]

- You have paid charges for 'relevant childcare' for a child for whom you are responsible – ie, the child normally lives with you. The rules require you to have already paid the charges, rather than just being liable to pay them. Regarding 'upfront' childcare costs, see the note above.
- The child is aged under 16 or has not reached the 1 September following their 16th birthday.
- The childcare is to enable you to do paid work (or enabled you to do paid work but that work has stopped).
- You report the charges to the DWP no later than the end of the monthly UC assessment period that follows the assessment period in which the charges were paid. You may be allowed to report them later than this under the same rules that apply to late notification of a change in circumstances (see p1153).

***Relevant childcare***

**'Relevant childcare'** means care for a child provided by the following.

**In England:**[44]

- a registered childcare provider – ie, someone registered with Ofsted under Part 3 of the Childcare Act 2006; *or*
- a school on school premises out of school hours (or at any time if the child has not reached compulsory school age); *or*
- an official domiciliary care provider – ie, registered with the Care Quality Commission.

**In Scotland:**[45]

- a registered childminder or similar provider of daycare – ie, registered as such under the Public Services Reform (Scotland) Act 2010; *or*
- a childcare agency under the Public Services Reform (Scotland) Act 2010; *or*
- a local authority registered to provide childminding or daycare under the Public Services Reform (Scotland) Act 2010.

**In Wales:**[46]

- a registered childminder or daycare provider – ie, registered under Part 2 of the Children and Families (Wales) Measure 2010; *or*
- someone providing daycare that would count for registration, were it not for the fact that it is provided in a care home, hospital, children's home, residential family centre or school; *or*
- someone providing childcare under a Welsh Senedd scheme for tax credit purposes or a home childcare approval scheme made by the Welsh Ministers; *or*

2

- out of school hours, a school on school premises or a local authority; *or*
- an official domiciliary care worker – ie, under the Domiciliary Care Agencies (Wales) Regulations 2004; *or*
- a foster parent (but not for the child who they are fostering) if, were it not for the fact that the child is too old, the childcare would count as registered childcare or daycare – ie, under Part 2 of the Children and Families (Wales) Measure 2010.

The following *does not count* as relevant childcare:[47]
- care provided by a 'close relative' of the child (ie, parent, parent-in-law, son, daughter, son-in-law, daughter-in-law, stepson, stepdaughter, stepbrother, stepsister and a partner of any of these) wholly or mainly in the child's home;[48]
- care provided by a foster parent, foster carer or kinship carer for a child who the person is fostering or looking after as a kinship carer.

***Rates of childcare costs element***

| | *per month* |
|---|---|
| Maximum for one child | £1,031.88 |
| Maximum for two or more children | £1,768.94 |

## Housing costs element

A housing costs element is included in your maximum amount for qualifying housing costs. Housing costs can be either rent or service charges. See Chapter 6 for when you are entitled and the amount of your housing costs element. **Note:** you cannot get a housing costs element for your mortgage interest payments or to repay a loan for repairs and improvements. Instead, the DWP may offer you a loan (see p764).

## Transitional element

If you transfer to UC under the managed migration process (see p29) and the amount of your UC would be less than the total amount of your legacy benefits (see p19), a transitional element is included in your UC.[49] This is intended to ensure that you are not worse off at the point you transfer to UC.

During 2025, the managed migration process is due to apply to remaining awards of income-related ESA and housing benefit (HB). Most awards of other legacy benefits (IS, income-based JSA and tax credits) have already been replaced by UC (see p21). If you have already gone through the managed migration process, you may already be getting a transitional element in your UC under the rules described below.

**Note:** you can only get a transitional element if you transfer to UC under the managed migration process (see p29). If you transfer under the natural migration process, or you do transfer under the managed migration process but do not get a transitional element, you may instead be entitled to a transitional SDP element. The DWP refers to both these elements as 'transitional protection'.

*Transitional SDP element*

- If you are severely disabled and transfer to UC under natural migration, or under managed migration but do not get a transitional element, you may instead be entitled to a 'transitional SDP element' (see p27). It is intended to compensate you for not having a severe disability element in your UC despite having had one in your legacy benefit. The transitional SDP element is not intended to ensure that you are not worse off on UC overall.
- The transitional SDP element is treated 'as if' it were part of your maximum amount of UC in working out your UC (see p39). So, it is included in your maximum amount.
- The transitional SDP element is also treated 'as if' it were a transitional element, so that it can be reduced or stopped in the same way that a transitional element can (see p83).

You *cannot* get a transitional element if:[50]

- you were claiming legacy benefits (see p19) as a couple, you transfer to UC under the managed migration process, but you claim UC as a single person (this includes where this is because although you have a partner they do not satisfy the UC conditions – see p36) or as a member of a different couple; *or*
- you were claiming legacy benefits as a single person, you transfer to UC under the managed migration process, but you are a couple for the purposes of UC (this includes where you have a partner but have claimed UC as a single person because they do not satisfy the UC conditions – see p36); *or*
- you were claiming legacy benefits as a member of a polygamous marriage, you transfer to UC under the managed migration process, but you claim UC as a single person or as a member of a couple; *or*
- for managed migration, it had been determined that you would have got a transitional element or, if you were transferring from tax credits, a 'transitional capital disregard' (see p29), but your claim for UC is refused. You cannot get a transitional element included in a later claim for UC, unless the reason you were not entitled to UC during managed migration was because your earnings (or in a joint claim, your and your partner's combined earnings) were too high.[51] In this case, if you reclaim UC and it starts within three months of the end of what would have been your first UC monthly assessment period, you can be entitled to a transitional element in your UC.

To get a transitional element, you must transfer to UC under the managed migration process. This means the DWP must have sent you a 'migration notice' informing you that you are affected by the process. You must then have made a 'qualifying claim' for UC – ie, you must have claimed on or before the 'final deadline'.[52] The final deadline is one month from the original 'deadline day' you are given by the DWP – eg, if your original deadline day is 14 August, your final deadline is 13 September.[53]

Even if you make your claim in time, you must usually provide further information at an interview. If you do not do so, the DWP regards this as a 'failed claim' and 'closes' your claim. This is actually a decision that you are not entitled to any UC at all, so you cannot get a transitional element. The rules seem to say that you cannot get a transitional element if you then reclaim, even if you do so before your final deadline, although it is not clear that this is the official intention.[54] If your claim is 'closed', you can challenge this decision (see p46).

To decide whether you are entitled to a transitional element, the DWP compares:[55]

- your 'total legacy amount'. This is the total amount of your legacy benefits based on the information held by DWP/HMRC on the day before your first day of UC entitlement, converted to a monthly amount. If you do not have an award of HB (or your award has been reduced to the minimum due to the benefit cap), and the benefit cap for UC would apply to you (see p1025) and your total entitlement to legacy benefits (excluding working tax credit – WTC) and benefits that count towards the UC benefit cap (including child benefit, contributory ESA and maternity allowance) exceeds the level of the cap, your total legacy amount is reduced. It is reduced by however much your benefits exceed the cap, minus (if you get the childcare element of WTC) your eligible WTC childcare costs, subject to the maximum that applies in your WTC childcare element (see p1382 of the 2024/25 edition of this *Handbook*); *and*
- your 'indicative UC amount'. This is the amount of UC you would get, based on your circumstances on the day before your first day of UC entitlement. The UC you would get is your maximum UC minus your relevant income – ie, the income that counts for UC (see Chapter 7). If your indicative UC amount is less than your total legacy amount, you get a transitional element to make up the difference between the two. If the benefit cap would apply to you (see p1025), your indicative UC amount is limited to the amount allowed by the benefit cap plus your childcare costs element.

## Calculating your indicative amount

- To calculate your indicative UC amount, the DWP makes certain assumptions which are set out in law.[56] If you went through managed migration from CTC, this will have included counting you as responsible for a child if you got CTC for that child. However, if your child was aged 19, your UC award may not have included a child element for them. Because of the way the indicative amount is calculated, that may not have been reflected in your transitional element – ie, so that you are worse off. Arguably, that is wrong.
- Your gross earnings are used, with a deduction applied for estimated tax and NI, then converted to a monthly amount. The DWP uses the earnings used to

calculate your legacy benefit. If you get income-related ESA and have earnings from permitted work (see p930), those earnings are all ignored in your ESA. However, in UC they are taken into account after applying a work allowance (see p41). It is understood that in calculating your indicative UC amount, the DWP will in practice take that UC approach, so your transitional element is higher and ensures that you are not worse off.[57]

- In practice, the DWP mainly uses the information from your awards of legacy benefits as currently held by the DWP and HMRC.[58] This can mean that some information (eg, in your UC claim form) is not used, even though it will be used in calculating your UC entitlement overall. For example, if you pay rent but do not get HB, no housing element is included in your indicative UC amount, even if your claim form includes that you pay rent and the element is therefore likely to be included in your UC award overall. (This could result in a bigger difference between your total legacy amount and your indicative UC amount, so that your transitional element is actually higher than might seem correct. See the note below.)
- The DWP can also use any further information and evidence (eg, from your UC claim form) if considered necessary.[59] For example, it may rely on your UC claim form to identify that you are a carer, or what capital you have, or if you have student income. See the note below.

**Note:** the way the DWP calculates the indicative UC amount has sometimes caused confusion. Remember that the transitional element is supposed to mean that your overall UC is not worth less than your legacy benefits at the point of your transfer to UC, and that the calculation can be challenged (see p84). See CPAG's *Welfare Rights Bulletin* or the online version of this *Handbook* for updates.

The weekly rate of your legacy benefits is converted to a monthly amount by multiplying it by 52 and dividing by 12.

## Calculating the transitional element

- If your indicative UC amount is the same as, or more than, your total legacy amount, you do not get a transitional element.
- If your indicative UC amount is less than your total legacy amount, but more than nil, you get a transitional element, worked out as the difference between your total legacy amount and your indicative UC amount.[60]
- If your indicative UC amount is nil, your transitional element is worked out differently, as follows.[61]
  - **Step 1:** calculate your total legacy amount.
  - **Step 2:** calculate the amount by which your relevant income exceeds your maximum UC used in calculating your UC indicative amount.

- **Step 3:** add together the figures in Step 1 and Step 2. This total is the amount of your transitional element.



*Examples*

Molly (26) is single and gets income-related ESA of £244.65 a week (including the enhanced disability and severe disability premiums and support component) and HB which covers her full rent of £225 a week. She is single. Molly has no earnings or other non-benefit income.

Molly also gets PIP, which is also ignored as income. The benefit cap does not apply because Molly gets PIP and the support component of ESA.

Molly's monthly total legacy amount is:

Income-related ESA: £1,060.15 (£244.65 x 52, divided by 12)

HB: £975 (£225 x 52, divided by 12)

Total = £2,035.15

**Note:** the total legacy amount does not include PIP.

Molly's monthly indicative UC amount is:

Standard allowance: £400.14

Limited capability for work-related activity component: £423.27

Housing costs element: £975

Total (maximum UC): £1,798.41

Indicative UC amount (the same as Molly's maximum UC as there is no relevant income to deduct) = £1,798.41

Molly's total legacy amount is higher than her indicative UC amount, so she is entitled to a transitional element.

The amount of Molly's transitional element is:

Total legacy amount (£2,035.15) *minus* indicative UC amount (£1,798.41) = £236.74

**Note:** because Molly will have a transitional element included in her UC, she cannot also be entitled to a transitional SDP element.

Eleanor (35) lives with her partner Taylor (33) and gets income-related ESA of £186.50 a week (including the enhanced disability and carer premiums and support component). Eleanor is entitled to PIP daily living component at the enhanced rate, and Taylor gets CA (£83.30 a week) as her carer. They own their home.

Taylor's CA will count as relevant income for their UC, but not the PIP. The benefit cap does not apply because Eleanor gets PIP and the support component and also because Taylor gets CA.

Eleanor and Taylor's monthly total legacy amount is:

Income-related ESA: £808.16 (£186.50 x 52, divided by 12)

Total: £808.16

**Note:** the total legacy amount does not include CA or PIP.

Eleanor and Taylor's monthly indicative UC amount is:
Standard allowance: £628.10
Carer element: £201.68
Limited capability for work-related activity component: £423.27
Total (maximum UC): £1,253.05
*minus* CA (relevant income): £360.97
Indicative UC amount= £892.08
**Note**: both the carer and limited capability for work-related activity elements are included, as Eleanor and Taylor are a couple and one satisfies the conditions for the carer element and the other satisfies the conditions for the limited capability for work-related activity element.

Eleanor and Taylor's total legacy amount is lower than their indicative UC amount, so they are not entitled to a transitional element.
**Note**: Eleanor and Taylor's overall UC will still be reduced by Taylor's CA.

## When the transitional element 'erodes' or stops

The amount of your transitional element is reduced over time by increases in your maximum UC. This is often referred to as 'erosion'. **Note:** erosion also applies, in the same way, to the transitional SDP element (see p27). In addition, certain changes of circumstances can mean that your transitional element stops outright.

### 'Erosion' of the transitional element

After your first monthly UC assessment period (but not before), the amount of your transitional element is reduced (or 'eroded') by any subsequent increase in the standard allowance or other elements included in your UC (including an element added for the first time), except for the childcare element.[62] This also applies to the transitional SDP element. Examples include where, after your first assessment period, the value of your other UC elements increases due to benefit uprating, or where your housing costs element goes up because of a rent increase. However, from 1 June 2025, erosion does not apply due to inclusion of the housing element in your UC where you had been getting HB in specified or temporary accommodation (see p183) in the month before the start of the UC assessment period in which the housing element was included.[63] The change in the law is due to a decision holding that the law before then breached the human rights of a claimant whose move from specified to standard rented accommodation resulted in the housing element immediately and completely eroding all of their transitional protection, leaving them worse off than they were on legacy benefits.[64] A more recent decision has held that the erosion of the transitional protection of a carer by the full amount of the limited capability for work-related activity element when she became entitled to that element in place of her carer element, leaving her worse off despite the increase in her needs, was also a breach of her human rights. The correct approach was to erode the transitional protection only by the difference between the claimant's carer element and the limited capability for work-related activity element, rather than by the full amount of the limited capability for work-related activity element.[65]

If your limited capability for work element is replaced by the limited capability for work-related activity element, your transitional element is reduced only by the difference between the limited capability for work element and the limited capability for work-related activity element – ie, it is not reduced by the full amount of the new limited capability for work-related activity element.[66]

Once erosion reduces your transitional element to nil, you do not get the transitional element again.

Further developments regarding the rules on erosion may follow. See CPAG's *Welfare Rights Bulletin* or the online version of this *Handbook* for updates.

### Losing the transitional element

Your entitlement to a transitional element ends if:[67]

- at the time of your UC claim, your earnings from work (or in a joint claim, your and your partner's combined earnings) were at least the single or (if you are a joint claimant) the couple threshold at which you are not subject to work search requirements (see p962 – you are treated as earning at that level if you are self-employed and the 'minimum income floor' is applied to you or would be but for the fact that you are in a 'start-up period'), but your earnings have now been below that threshold for three consecutive UC monthly assessment periods. Your entitlement to the element ends from the UC assessment period after the third of the assessment periods; *or*
- you originally claimed UC as a couple but you are now single, or you originally claimed UC as a single person but you are now part of a couple, unless because of your partner's circumstances you can still claim as a single person (see p36). Your entitlement to the element ends from the UC assessment period in which this occurs; *or*
- your UC comes to an end. In this case, you cannot get a transitional element in any future award of UC, unless your previous UC award ended because your earnings (or in a joint claim, your and your partner's combined earnings) increased so that your income was too high and your new UC award starts within three months of the end of what would have been your last UC monthly assessment period if your UC had not been terminated . In these circumstances, your new UC award includes the same transitional element as in your previous award, subject to the possibility that it may have reduced for the reasons above.

## Changing a decision about the transitional element

The transitional element is part of the calculation of your UC. You can challenge the decision on your entitlement to the element by requesting a revision (see

Chapter 50) or appealing against the decision on your UC entitlement – you must ask for a mandatory reconsideration first (see Chapter 51).

The rules say that the transitional element is based on your entitlement on your 'migration day' – ie, the day before your entitlement to UC started.[68]

However, rules also provide that the decision about your UC can still be revised or superseded if that information is now considered to be wrong because:[69]

- you (or your partner in a joint claim) misrepresented something; *or*
- you (or your partner in a joint claim) failed to report information you were required to report, and that failure was to your advantage; *or*
- there was an 'official error'. This means an error made by an officer of the DWP, HMRC, a local authority or a person employed by someone acting on behalf of these bodies. The rules on what counts as an official error are the same as what can count under the normal rules for revisions (see p1135).

Also, in some circumstances, rules provide that your transitional element can still be changed if, on or after your migration day, your legacy benefit award has been changed, following a request for a revision or supersession (or an appeal about that). So, for example, it may be that your UC transitional element can be increased to reflect that your legacy benefit award has now been changed to include a disability premium because, following a revision, you have been awarded PIP. However, the rule requires that you requested the revision or supersession of your legacy benefit *before* your migration day. So, the DWP might refuse to change your transitional element if you requested the revision or supersession of your legacy benefit *on or after* your migration day.[70] If you need more time to make the request before your migration day, ask the DWP for an extension.

**Note:** at the time of writing, it appeared that the DWP might change the transitional element (this could be to increase it or decrease it) in some other circumstances – eg, where you had claimed PIP before your migration day and that claim has now resulted in your being awarded PIP. See CPAG's *Welfare Rights Bulletin* or the online version of this *Handbook* for updates.

# Notes

2

1. **What is the maximum amount**
   1 Reg 37 UC Regs

2. **The standard allowance**
   2 Reg 36 UC Regs

3. **Elements**
   3 Reg 4 UC Regs
   4 Reg 24 UC Regs
   5 Reg 36 UC Regs
   6 Reg 43 UC(TP) Regs
   7 Reg 24 UC Regs
   8 s10(2) WRA 2012; reg 24(2) UC Regs
   9 s10(1A) WRA 2012; reg 24A UC Regs
   10 Reg 24B(1) UC Regs
   11 *R (LMN and EFG) v SSWP* [2024] EWHC 2577 (Admin) (decision awaited). See cpag.org.uk/non-consensual-conception-exception-ordering-rule
   12 Sch 12 UC Regs
   13 gov.uk/government/publications/support-for-a-child-conceived-without-your-consent
   14 s16 WRWA 2016
   15 Sch 2 Part 2 ESAUC(MA) Regs
   16 Reg 28 UC Regs, as applied by Sch 2 Part 2 ESAUC(MA) Regs
   17 Reg 19 UC(TP) Regs (as applied by ESAUC(MA) Regs); para M6192 ADM
   18 Reg 27(4) UC Regs (as applied by ESAUC(MA) Regs)
   19 Reg 19(1) and (3) UC(TP) Regs (as applied by ESAUC(MA) Regs)
   20 Reg 29(4) UC Regs (as applied by ESAUC(MA) Regs)
   21 Reg 27 UC Regs
   22 Regs 40 and 41 UC Regs
   23 *KS v SSWP* [2025] UKUT 15 (AAC)
   24 Reg 28 UC Regs; reg 2 SS(ME) Regs; para F5031 ADM.
   25 Reg 28 UC Regs
   26 Reg 20A UC(TP) Regs; para M6210 ADM
   27 Reg 29(4) UC Regs
   28 Regs 19, 20 and 21 UC(TP) Regs
   29 Reg 21(1)(a)(ii) UC(TP) Regs
   30 *PR v SSWP* [2023] UKUT 290 (AAC)
   31 Reg 27(4) UC Regs
   32 Reg 19(4) UC Regs
   33 Reg 29 UC Regs
   34 Regs 29 and 30 UC Regs
   35 Reg 29(2) and (3) UC Regs
   36 Reg 29(3) UC Regs; s70(7) SSCBA 1992
   37 Regs 34 and 36 UC Regs
   38 DWP, Universal Credit Guidance, *Flexible Support Fund*, v31.0, House of Commons library deposited papers, rightsnet.org.uk/resources/universal-credit-guidance
   39 House of Commons, *Hansard*, Written question 282562, answered 5 September 2019, questions-statements.parliament.uk
   40 Reg 32 UC Regs
   41 Reg 3(6) UC Regs
   42 Reg 32(2) UC Regs
   43 Reg 33 UC Regs
   44 Reg 35(2) UC Regs
   45 Reg 35(3) UC Regs
   46 Reg 35(4) UC Regs
   47 Reg 35(7) UC Regs
   48 Reg 2, definition of 'close relative', UC Regs
   49 Regs 50 and 52 UC(TP) Regs
   50 Regs 50 and 57 UC(TP) Regs
   51 Reg 57(2)(a) UC(TP) Regs
   52 Regs 48 and 50 UC(TP) Regs
   53 Reg 46(4) UC(TP) Regs
   54 Reg 57(1)(b) UC(TP) Regs; *Draft Universal Credit (Managed Migration) Regulations 2018: SSAC report and government statement*, November 2018, p14. You cannot get a transitional element if you are not entitled to an award of UC.
   55 Regs 52-54 UC(TP) Regs
   56 Reg 54(2) UC(TP) Regs
   57 There is no official guidance on this point, but DWP ministers and officials have stated that claimants doing permitted work would not be left worse off as a result of the way their earnings are treated: see 'Work, LCW and UC', *Welfare Rights Bulletin* 302 (Oct 2024)
   58 Under reg 54(7) UC(TP) Regs, the calculation is 'based on' information used for the total legacy amount – ie, that held for legacy benefits by DWP and HMRC

59 Reg 54(7) UC(TP) Regs allows the use of such further information or evidence as required by the DWP
60 Reg 55(1)(a) UC(TP) Regs
61 Reg 55(1)(b) UC(TP) Regs
62 Reg 55 UC(TP) Regs
63 Reg 55(5A) UC(TP) Regs
64 *SSWP v JA (UC)* [2024] UKUT 52 (AAC)
65 *SSWP v MJ* [2025] UKUT 35 (AAC); see also cpag.org.uk/legal
66 Reg 55 UC(TP) Regs
67 Regs 56 and 57 UC(TP) Regs
68 Regs 53(1) and 54(1) UC(TP) Regs
69 Reg 62(1)(a) UC(TP) Regs
70 Reg 62(1)(b) UC(TP) Regs

2

# Chapter 6

# The housing costs element

**This chapter covers:**


1. Who can get a housing costs element (p89)
2. The payment condition (p90)
3. The liability condition (p93)
4. The occupation condition (p97)
5. How the housing costs element is calculated: general rules (p101)
6. The housing costs element for private rented sector tenants (p110)
7. The housing costs element for social rented sector tenants (p114)
8. The housing costs element for owner-occupiers (p118)


## Key facts

- Your universal credit (UC) can include a housing costs element to help with rent and/or service charges.
- To receive the housing costs element, you must satisfy the payment, liability and occupation conditions.
- If you are a private tenant, the amount of rent used to calculate your housing costs element is based on a local housing allowance for a property with the number of bedrooms that you are allowed under the rules. This amount may be lower than the rent you actually pay.
- If you are a social rented sector tenant and your home has more bedrooms than you are allowed under the rules, your housing costs element is usually reduced by a percentage. This reduction is often called the 'bedroom tax'.
- If you are an owner-occupier (unless you have a shared ownership tenancy), you cannot get a housing costs element for your service charges if you (or your partner) have any earned income. Even if you have no earned income, you may not get a housing costs element during an initial waiting period.
- If your housing costs element does not cover your housing costs in full, you may be able to get extra financial assistance by applying for discretionary housing payments from your local authority (see Chapter 25).
- UC, including the housing costs element, is usually paid direct to you as a single monthly lump sum. You are responsible for paying your housing cost from this single payment. In some circumstances the DWP can make payments direct to a third party, such as your landlord, under alternative payment arrangements (see p51).

## 1. Who can get a housing costs element

Your universal credit (UC) maximum amount (see p66) can include a housing costs element if:[1]

- your accommodation is in Great Britain; *and*
- your accommodation is residential – ie, not for a business. If your accommodation is partly for a business and partly residential, you can get a housing costs element for the part that is residential; *and*
- you (or your partner, if you are a joint claimant) make rent payments (see p90) or service charge payments (see p92) that are eligible (the payment condition); *and*
- you (or your partner, if you are a joint claimant) are liable for the eligible rent or service charge payments, or are treated as liable (the liability condition) (see p93); *and*
- you normally occupy as your home the accommodation for which you make the eligible rent or service charge payments, or you are treated as doing so (the occupation condition) (see p97).

The accommodation can comprise the whole of a building or part of a building – eg, a flat in a block or a room in a shared house. You can get a housing costs element whether or not the accommodation comprises separate and self-contained premises.[2]

A housing costs element can include any of the eligible payments that you make. If you have a shared ownership tenancy (ie, you are buying part of your home and renting the rest), your housing costs element can include rent, as well as the service charge payments you make.[3]

Make sure you tell the DWP that you pay rent or service charges when you claim UC, so a housing costs element is included. If you are already getting UC and need to add your housing costs, request this via your online journal and notify a change of circumstances if relevant.

**Note:**

- You cannot get a housing costs element for help with your mortgage interest payments (or alternative finance payments). The DWP may offer you a loan for mortgage interest instead. See p764 for information.
- If a housing costs element is included in your UC maximum amount and you qualify for a work allowance, the lower work allowance applies and more of your earnings are taken into account (see p41).
- Your housing costs element is normally paid to you, but can be paid direct to your landlord (see p50). If your housing costs element is paid direct to your landlord and this is the total amount of UC to which you are entitled, you do not actually receive any UC, but you are still entitled to UC.

- If your housing benefit (HB) ends because you make a claim for UC, your HB entitlement can continue for two weeks ('HB run-on' – see p227). You do not have to pay HB run-on back, even if you qualify for a UC housing costs element for your rent for the same period. If your HB is being paid direct to your landlord, your HB run-on payments are usually also paid to them. If this happens, you can ask your landlord to pay you the HB run-on amount – eg, if you are up to date with your rent payments.

### When you cannot get a housing costs element

Your UC maximum amount *cannot* include a housing costs element if you:

- rent your accommodation and you are 16 or 17 and are, or have been, looked after by a local authority (see p846);[4] *or*
- are an owner-occupier (unless you have a shared ownership tenancy – ie, you are buying part of your home and renting the rest), during an assessment period in which you (or your partner) have any earned income (see p125), however much your earnings are.[5] This includes earnings from work you can do while claiming new-style employment and support allowance (ESA) or old-style contributory ESA (see p928) or from work of less than 16 hours a week you can do while claiming new-style jobseeker's allowance (see p887). The nature and duration of the work is not relevant – eg, it does not matter if your job is part time or temporary; *or*
- live in specified or temporary accommodation (see p91 for what counts), for the rent you pay for that accommodation.[6] You *can* get HB for the rent you pay in this accommodation.

## 2. The payment condition

You meet the payment condition for the housing costs element of universal credit (UC) if you make eligible rent payments (see below) and/or service charge payments (see p92).

### Rent payments

Eligible rent payments include the rent you pay to your landlord and can also include other types of payment. The eligible payments are:[7]

- rent; *and*
- payments for a licence or permission to occupy accommodation – eg, for bed and breakfast or a hostel. For houseboats, this can include continuous cruiser licence payments;[8] *and*
- mooring charges payable for a houseboat; *and*
- site rent for a caravan or mobile home (but not for a tent); *and*

- contributions made by a resident of a charity's almshouse towards its maintenance and the essential services in it. The almshouse must be run by a housing association.

2

When discussing UC, we use the term 'rent' to cover all of these payments.

## Payments that are not eligible

The following types of payments are *not* eligible rent payments:[9]

- ground rent (a payment that is often part of tenancies of more than 21 years);[10] *and*
- payments for a tent or its pitch; *and*
- payments for approved premises – eg, a bail or probation hostel; *and*
- payments made for specified or temporary accommodation. You *can* get housing benefit (HB) for these (see Chapter 10); *and*
- payments made for a care home; *and*
- mesne profits (or, in Scotland, violent profits). Check whether you are instead actually making payments for a licence or permission to occupy accommodation, which is an eligible rent payment.[11]

*Definitions*

**'Specified accommodation'** is:[12]

- accommodation provided by a relevant body to meet your need for, and where you get, care, support or supervision. The care, support or supervision does not have to be provided by the body providing the accommodation; *or*
- temporary accommodation (eg, a refuge) provided by a local authority or a relevant body for people who have left home because of domestic abuse (see p951 for what counts); *or*
- a local authority hostel for homeless people where you get care, support or supervision to assist you to be rehabilitated or resettled within the community; *or*
- 'exempt accommodation', such as specified types of supported accommodation (see p326 – the meaning is the same as for HB).

For these purposes, a 'relevant body' is a county council (in England) or a housing association, registered charity or voluntary organisation.

Your accommodation is **'temporary accommodation'** if you live in a specified type of homeless accommodation that does not count as 'exempt accommodation' (see p326 – the meaning is the same as for HB) and your rent is payable to a local authority or a provider of social housing (see p115 for the meaning).[13]

**'Care home'** means a care home (in England), a care home service (in Wales and Scotland) or an independent hospital.[14]

## Service charge payments

Eligible service charge payments are those which are:[15]

- for the costs of, or charges for, services or facilities that people occupying the accommodation benefit from or use – eg, communal cleaning, garden maintenance or communal stairways; *or*
- fairly attributable to the costs of, or charges for, services or facilities available with the accommodation that people occupying the accommodation may benefit from or use – eg, costs connected to providing laundry facilities.

The payments do not have to be separately identified – eg, in your tenancy agreement or lease. It does not matter if they are paid in addition to, or as part of, your rent, or if they are made under the same or a different agreement to that under which you occupy your home. However, if you live in social rented sector accommodation (eg, your landlord is a local authority or housing association) or you are an owner-occupier, there are extra conditions and the rules specify the charges that are eligible (see above).

### Payments that are not eligible

Service charge payments are *not* eligible and cannot be included in your housing costs element if:[16]

- the services or facilities to which the payments relate are for someone occupying a tent, approved premises (eg, a bail or probation hostel), a care home (see p91) or 'exempt accommodation' (see p326 – you may instead qualify for HB); *or*
- you have taken out a loan to make the payments, which is secured on your home. You may be able to get a loan from the DWP for help with the interest on the loan (see p764).

### Extra conditions for social rented sector tenants and owner-occupiers

If you live in social rented sector accommodation (see p115) or you are an owner-occupier, service charge payments are only eligible if you must pay them as a condition of occupying your accommodation – eg, as part of your tenancy agreement or lease and not as an optional extra.[17]

The costs and charges must be of a reasonable amount and for services and facilities that are reasonable to provide. They must fall into one or more of the following categories.[18]

- Category A: payments to maintain the general standard of accommodation – ie, for:
  - cleaning the outside of windows on the upper floors of a multi-storey building; *or*
  - if you have a shared ownership tenancy (ie, you are buying part of your home and renting the rest) or are an owner-occupier, internal or external

maintenance or repair of the accommodation. The payments must be separately identifiable.
- Category B: payments for the general upkeep of communal areas – ie, for the ongoing maintenance or cleaning of, and the supply of water, fuel or any other commodity to, internal or external areas (eg, laundry rooms, communal gardens and children's play areas).
- Category C: payments for basic communal services. These are payments for the provision, ongoing maintenance, cleaning or repair of basic services generally available to everyone living in the accommodation – eg, refuse collection, communal lifts, secure building access, fire alarm systems or wireless or television aerials to receive a service free of charge. Payments for someone employed to provide an eligible service (eg, a groundskeeper or caretaker), as well as the costs of managing and administering eligible services, are also included.[19]
- Category D: accommodation-specific charges. These must be for the use of essential items specific to the particular accommodation you occupy – eg, for furniture or domestic appliances.

However, payments are *not* eligible and cannot be included in your housing costs element if they are:[20]
- for services or facilities for which public funding is available, whether or not you are entitled to such funding; *or*
- connected to the use of an asset which will result in the transfer of that asset, or any interest in it – eg, payments for furniture and equipment that will eventually become yours; *or*
- for food, medical services or personal services (including personal laundry, cleaning or personal care services).

## 3. The liability condition

To qualify for a universal credit (UC) housing costs element, you (or your partner, if you are a joint claimant) must be liable to make eligible payments on a commercial basis or treated as liable to make the payments.[21] You count as liable if either you or your partner are liable. **Note:** sometimes you (or your partner) can be treated as *not* liable to make payments, even if you are (see p95).

In deciding whether your agreement is on a commercial basis, the DWP must look at the whole agreement and take all the circumstances into account. It is what you and your landlord have agreed, not what you or your landlord have later done or omitted to do, that is relevant.[22] The DWP should consider, among other things:[23]

2

- whether your agreement includes terms that are not legally enforceable – eg, if you do household chores. However, if you do chores in exchange for a lower rent, it could still be considered commercial;
- the rent you have agreed to pay; it does not have to be a market rent. Your agreement can count as commercial even if your landlord is not collecting the full contractual rent from you – eg, if it is not being met in full because of the way your housing costs element is calculated;
- your relationship to the person whom you are liable to pay. If they are a relative or close friend, or they provide you with care and support, this does not necessarily mean that your agreement is non-commercial (but see p95).

If you are jointly liable to make payments with someone, the way your housing costs element is calculated takes this into account. See p111 if you are a private tenant and p116 if you are a social rented sector tenant.

## Liability to pay rent

For you to be liable to pay rent, your agreement must be legally enforceable.[24] It is not enough if you only have a moral obligation, such as a promise to pay something whenever you can afford to do so. You can be liable to pay rent by yourself (solely liable) or you can be jointly liable to do so. You can count as liable to pay rent even if someone else has been paying it on your behalf, if you have already paid a sum of rent in advance, or if your landlord has failed to provide you with their address and so your rent is treated as not being due.[25]

***Does your agreement have to be in writing?***

If you have a written agreement with your landlord, this should establish that you are liable to pay rent, provided the liability is a genuine part of the agreement.[26]

Your agreement can be legally enforceable, even if it is not in writing, or is in writing but is not signed. The fact that you have made a firm promise to pay money to your landlord in return for occupying the property should be sufficient to show you are liable to pay rent and so allow you to qualify for a housing costs element.[27] There is nothing in the legislation that requires you to provide a tenancy agreement in order to prove liability for rent. If the DWP refuses to accept that you have a legal liability, you can challenge this decision, usually by requesting a mandatory reconsideration first and then lodging an appeal if the decision is not changed (see Chapter 51).

Even if the DWP accepts that your agreement is legally enforceable, it can still treat you as not liable to pay rent in specified situations (see p95).

## People treated as liable to make payments

You (or your partner) are treated as liable to make payments:[28]

- during rent-free periods;

- if a child or qualifying young person you (or your partner) are responsible for (see p64) is liable to make the payments; *or*
- if you are a member of a couple but you are awarded UC as a single person (except if you are in a polygamous marriage) and your partner is liable to make the payments. See p36 for when you are awarded UC as a single person; *or*
- if someone else is liable to make the payments but is not doing so (see below); *or*
- if payments are waived by the person to whom you are liable (eg, your landlord) as reasonable compensation for your carrying out reasonable repairs or redecoration that they would otherwise have had to carry out; *or*
- if someone else is liable to make the payments but is not doing so (see below).

### Another person is liable but is not paying

You (or your partner, if you are a joint claimant) are treated as liable to make payments if all of the following conditions are met:[29]

- the person who is liable for the payments is not making them; *and*
- you must make the payments yourself in order to continue to occupy the accommodation. You must have been living in that accommodation while the person who is liable was making the payments;[30] *and*
- it would be unreasonable to expect you to make other arrangements; *and*
- it is reasonable in all the circumstances to treat you as liable.

There are many situations where this may apply – including where:

- you have separated from your partner. **Note:** joint tenants are liable for the whole of the rent and do not need to be *treated as* liable (see p111 and p117);
- you have given up your home to live with and care for someone who has now gone into a care home or the liable person has died (you can be treated as liable for the payments on their home);
- the liable person ceases to qualify for a housing costs element because they have become a full-time student.

It does not matter whether or not the landlord is prepared to transfer the tenancy to you or wants to evict you. If the DWP refuses to treat you as liable, point out that the eligibility rules for the housing costs element and the rules for transferring tenancies are separate.[31] If you are refused the housing costs element, you can ask for a mandatory reconsideration of the decision, and then appeal if you remain unhappy with the outcome (see Chapter 51).

## People treated as not liable to make payments

You (or your partner) are treated as though you are *not* liable to make payments in the following situations.[32]

- You are liable to make the payments to someone who also lives in the accommodation, and who is:

  - your partner, or a child or qualifying young person you or your partner are responsible for (see p64); *or*
  - a close relative (see below) of yours or your partner, or of a child or qualifying young person for whom you or your partner are responsible.

  For example, this applies if you are living with, and pay rent to, your parents. If you are liable to pay service charge payments to the same person, you are also treated as not liable for those.
- You are liable to make the payments to a trustee of a trust or a company. This only applies if the trustees or beneficiaries of the trust, or the owners or directors of the company, include you, your partner or a qualifying young person (or in the case of trusts, a child) for whom you (or your partner) are responsible, or a close relative (see below) of any of these if the close relative lives in the accommodation with you. If you are liable to pay service charge payments to a trustee of the same trust (or of another trust whose trustees or beneficiaries include any of these people) or to the same company (or a company whose owners or directors include any of these people), you are also treated as not liable for those payments.
- The payments are for any amount of arrears for your accommodation, or for accommodation you occupied previously, that increase what you would otherwise be required to pay. This also applies to arrears payments for any other debt or unpaid charge.
- The DWP considers your liability to be 'contrived' (see below).
- You are treated as not liable to make service charge payments if you are liable to make them to someone who lives in your household (see p60 for the meaning), unless you also pay rent.

***Close relative***

A **'close relative'** is a parent, parent-in-law (including a civil partner's parent), son, daughter, son-in-law or daughter-in-law (including civil partners), sibling, step-parent (including a parent's civil partner), stepson or stepdaughter (including a civil partner's child), or the partners of any of these.[33] It also includes half-siblings.[34] Relations with in-laws or step-relatives are severed by divorce (or civil partnership dissolution) but arguably not by death – eg, stepchildren are still stepchildren after the death of their mother.

## Contrived agreements

You can be treated as not liable to make payments if your liability was 'contrived' to get the housing costs element included in your UC, or to increase the amount of your housing costs element.[35] This applies if either you or your landlord, or both, contrived the liability.[36] For your agreement to count as contrived, it must amount to an abuse, or taking improper advantage, of the UC scheme – ie, the main reason you entered into the agreement to make payments was to obtain or increase your UC housing costs element.[37] All the circumstances should be taken into account when deciding whether this is the case, including what the person you are liable to pay has to say. An agreement can count as contrived even if it was created with the best of motives.[38]



***Have you been told your agreement is contrived?***

'Contrived' is not defined in the rules. You can argue the following.

1. Your agreement should not count as contrived just because the person you are liable to pay is your parent, son or daughter or because you hope to be able to claim UC to help you with your rent – ie, if your main purpose is to get accommodation, not to obtain the UC housing costs element.[39]
2. You should not be regarded as having a contrived agreement just because you try to find out what payments can be covered by UC – eg, before moving in.
3. If your landlord deliberately charges high rents in order to have them paid by UC, you may be affected by this provision, even though you had no such intention yourself. Argue that a high rent, in itself, does not mean that the liability is contrived.[40]
4. If your landlord says you will be evicted if you cannot get the UC housing costs element, or get it increased, this suggests that the agreement is *not* contrived.[41]

**Note:** if the DWP says your agreement is contrived and does not include a housing costs element in your UC, you can ask for a mandatory reconsideration of the decision, and then appeal if you remain unhappy with the outcome (see Chapter 51).

## 4. The occupation condition

To qualify for the housing costs element of universal credit (UC), you must occupy the accommodation for which you make eligible payments as your home.[42] In some circumstances you are treated as occupying the accommodation while temporarily absent (see p100) or treated as *not* occupying the accommodation when you are (see p101). You cannot usually get a housing costs element for any accommodation other than that in which you normally live. However, there are special rules if you:

- have just moved into your home (see below); *or*
- are liable to make payments for more than one dwelling (see p98); *or*
- are in temporary accommodation while repairs are carried out on your home (see p99); *or*
- have left your previous home due to a fear of violence or abuse (see p99); *or*
- are temporarily absent from home (see p100).

### Moving home

If you have moved into new accommodation, you can be treated as having occupied it for up to one month before you moved in, provided you met the liability and payment conditions immediately before you moved in, and:[43]

- there was a delay in moving in, this was reasonable and necessary to enable the accommodation to be adapted to meet disability-related needs for you, your partner if you are a joint claimant, or a child or qualifying young person you (or your partner, if you are a joint claimant) are responsible for (see p64). The adaptations do not need to involve a change to the fabric or structure of the accommodation, but must be reasonably required and clearly connected to the needs.[44] The person with the disability must be getting the middle or highest rate of the disability living allowance or child disability payment care component, pension age disability payment, attendance allowance, armed forces independence payment, or the daily living component of personal independence payment or adult disability payment.
  **Note:** in these circumstances, you may also qualify for a housing costs element for your former home (see below), or for housing benefit (HB) for your former home (if it was specified or temporary accommodation – see p91); *or*
- you became liable to make payments for your new accommodation while you were a hospital inpatient or while you were living in a care home (see p91), or if you and your partner are joint claimants, while both of you are hospital inpatients or living in a care home.

## More than one home

You cannot usually be treated as occupying more than one dwelling as your home.[45] If you do occupy more than one dwelling, the DWP must consider all the circumstances to decide which you normally occupy as your home. **Note:** different rules apply if you are living away from your normal home because of a fear of domestic abuse (see p99).

You *can* be treated as occupying more than one dwelling as your home and get a housing costs element:

- for both your previous and your new home for up to one month if there was a delay in moving into your new home, this was reasonable and necessary to enable your new accommodation to be adapted to meet disability-related needs for you, your partner if you are a joint claimant, or a child or qualifying young person you (or your partner, if you are a joint claimant) are responsible for.[46] (The conditions are the same as those for moving home – see p97). This only applies if, immediately before you moved, you qualified for a UC housing costs element for your previous home and also met the payment and liability conditions (see p90 and p93) for your new home. **Note:** if you are only liable to make payments for your new home, you may qualify for a housing costs element for that accommodation for up to one month before you moved in (see p97);
- for two dwellings indefinitely if you have been housed in two dwellings by a provider of social housing (see p115) because of the number of children and qualifying young people who live with you.[47] You must normally occupy both

dwellings with the children or qualifying young people for whom you (or your partner, if you are a joint claimant) are responsible (see p64). You must meet the payment and liability conditions (see p90 and p93) for both dwellings.

## Temporary accommodation while repairs are carried out

If you have to move into temporary accommodation while essential repairs are carried out on your normal home, but you intend to return to that home, the following applies.[48]

- If you satisfy the payment and liability conditions for only one of the dwellings, you are treated as occupying it as your home. You get a housing costs element for the payments you make for that dwelling.
- If you satisfy the payment and liability conditions for both dwellings, you are only treated as occupying your normal home, even though you are not staying there currently. You get a housing costs element for the payments you make for your normal home.

**'Essential repairs'** means basic works rather than luxuries, but they need not be necessary to make the house habitable. Whether repairs count as 'essential' should be assessed taking account of your individual characteristics.[49]

## Fear of violence or abuse

Special rules apply for up to 12 months if you are living in accommodation other than your normal home and it is currently unreasonable to expect you to return to your normal home because of a reasonable fear of violence. You need not have experienced actual violence but you must fear violence in the home, or from a former partner, against you or any child or qualifying young person you are responsible for. Violence in your home includes violence by neighbours and hate crimes directed at your home. For these purposes, 'violence' is not defined but controlling or coercive behaviour, psychological, physical, sexual, financial or emotional abuse should count.[50] You must intend to return to your normal home.

If these rules apply:[51]

- you are treated as occupying both the accommodation you are living in *and* your normal home for up to 12 months if:
  - you satisfy the payment and liability conditions for both your current accommodation and your normal home; *and*
  - it is reasonable to include an amount for the payments for both dwellings in your housing costs element; *or*
- if you only satisfy the payment and liability conditions for one of the dwellings, you are treated as occupying that accommodation as your home if it is reasonable to include an amount for the payments for that accommodation in your housing costs element.

**Note:** if one of the homes is specified or temporary accommodation (eg, a refuge – see p91), you can qualify for HB for that accommodation and get a UC housing costs element for your other home.

In both cases, you are no longer treated as occupying your normal home when your absence has lasted, or is expected to last, longer than 12 months.[52] The decision whether or not your absence from home is expected to last longer than 12 months should initially be based on the circumstances on the date you leave your home.[53] If, at any time after that date, you no longer intend to return, or it becomes likely that you will be away from home for more than 12 months, your entitlement can be reconsidered.[54]

## Temporary absence from home

If you are only temporarily absent from your normal home, you continue to be treated as occupying it for up to six months, whatever the reason for your absence.[55] A new period of absence starts if you return home for even a short stay. A stay of at least 24 hours may be enough.[56] You can be treated as occupying your normal home for longer than six months if you have to live in other accommodation while repairs are being carried out on your normal home (see p99) or you are living away from home because of a fear of violence or abuse (see p99).

You can argue that you count as temporarily absent from home even if you have not yet stayed there – eg, you move in your furniture and belongings but then need to go into hospital.[57]

If you are a prisoner (see p839 – including if you are on temporary release), you can get a housing costs element for up to six months under this rule while you are temporarily absent from home, provided you were entitled to UC as a single person immediately before you became a prisoner, your UC included a housing costs element and you are not expected to be in custody for more than six months.[58] Note that prisoners are usually expected to serve only around half of their prison sentence in custody, with the remainder served 'on licence',[59] so if you receive a one-year sentence, you are not normally expected to be in custody for more than six months. If you are a member of a couple, your partner may instead be able to claim UC with a housing costs element in your absence.

**Note:**

- If you are temporarily absent from Great Britain for longer than a set period (from one to six months depending on the circumstances), your entitlement to UC may be affected (see p1371).
- If your partner, child or non-dependant (see p103) is temporarily absent from your home, this may affect how many bedrooms you are allowed when working out the amount of your housing costs element (see p107).

*When temporarily absent and treated as not occupying your home*

You are no longer treated as occupying your normal home when your absence has lasted, or is expected to last, longer than six months. The decision whether or not your absence from home is expected to last longer than six months should initially be based on the circumstances on the date you leave your home.[60] If, at any time after that date, you no longer intend to return home, or it becomes likely that you will be away from home for more than six months, your entitlement can be reconsidered.[61] If you initially told the DWP you were going to be away from home for more than six months, but realise that your absence will be shorter, it should also reconsider your entitlement.

2

## 5. How the housing costs element is calculated: general rules

This section covers the general rules for calculating the housing costs element. After applying these rules, there are different calculations to work out your housing costs element depending on whether you live in private rented accommodation (see p110), in social rented sector accommodation (see p115) or are an owner-occupier (see p118). If you live in a shared ownership property or have more than one home, see p102.

In all cases, to calculate your housing costs element you must first work out the monthly equivalent of your eligible rent or service charge payments (see p90 and p92), if these are paid other than calendar monthly. You must then work out:

- who counts as a member of your 'extended benefit unit' (broadly, the people who live with you – see p103); *and*
- the number of bedrooms you are allowed under the rules (known as the 'size criteria' – see p104); *and*
- whether a deduction must be made for any 'non-dependant' living with you (a 'housing costs contribution' – see p109).

*How do you work out monthly equivalents?*[62]

If you pay your rent or service charges:

– weekly, multiply by 52 and divide by 12;

– two-weekly, multiply by 26 and divide by 12;

– four-weekly, multiply by 13 and divide by 12;

– three-monthly, multiply by four and divide by 12;

– annually, divide by 12.

If you have a regular rent-free or service charge-free period, to work out the monthly equivalent divide the total payments you make over the year by 12 – eg, if you have four rent-free weeks each year and so only pay rent for 48 weeks, add together the 48 weeks payments and divide the total by 12.

2

Note:
- If you are a joint tenant, the housing costs element calculation takes this into account (see p111 for private rented accommodation and p116 for social rented accommodation).
- If a housing costs element is included in your universal credit (UC) maximum amount, you only get a lower work allowance, meaning that more of your earnings are taken into account when calculating your UC entitlement (see p41).
- If you have a shared ownership tenancy (ie, you are buying part of your home and renting the rest), your housing costs element can include amounts for the rent and service charge payments you make.[63] Your service charge payments are calculated as they would be for rent payments.

## If you have more than one home

Special rules for calculating your housing costs element apply if you qualify while occupying, or being treated as occupying, more than one dwelling.
- If you have been **housed in two dwellings** by a provider of social housing (see p115 for the meaning) because of the number of your children, your housing costs element is worked out using a single calculation.[64] All the eligible payments for both dwellings are taken into account, and you are treated as having the combined total number of bedrooms in both dwellings. Your housing costs element is calculated under the rules for social rented sector tenancies (see p115) if you pay rent to a social sector landlord for both dwellings. Otherwise, your housing costs element is calculated under the rules for private sector tenancies (see p110), in which case there is a special rule for working out your cap rent (see p112).
- If there was a delay in moving into your home because it was being **adapted for a disabled person** and you qualify for a housing costs element for both your old and your new accommodation (see p98), amounts are calculated for each home under the rules for social rented sector or private sector tenancies (as appropriate) and your housing costs element is the total of these.[65] However, housing costs contributions for a non-dependant (see p109) are only deducted from the rent payments for your old home.
- If you are living away from your normal home due to a **fear of violence or abuse** and are entitled to a housing costs element for both your current accommodation and your normal home (see p99), amounts are calculated for each home under the rules for social rented sector or private sector tenancies (as appropriate) and your housing costs element is the total of these. However, any housing costs contributions for non-dependants (see p109) are only deducted from the rent payments for the accommodation that you are determined as 'normally' occupying.[66]

## Extended benefit unit

Your extended benefit unit is relevant for working out how many bedrooms you are allowed under the rules (see p104). The members of your **'extended benefit unit'** are:[67]

- you; *and*
- your partner (if you are a joint claimant); *and*
- any child or qualifying young person you (or your partner, if you are a joint claimant) are responsible for (see p64); *and*
- any non-dependants (see below for who counts).

People can continue to count as members of your extended benefit unit during a temporary absence (see p100 and p107). You can continue to count as responsible for children or qualifying young people while they are absent from your household for a period (see p64).

### Who counts as a non-dependant

A **'non-dependant'** is a person who normally lives in your accommodation with you, other than your partner and any children or qualifying young people you are responsible for.[68] Examples of non-dependants are adult sons or daughters (and, generally, their children), or other adult relatives or friends who share your home. Someone who is only staying with you temporarily, or is only using your address as a postal address, does not count as a non-dependant. If you think the DWP has wrongly assumed that a person is (or is not) your non-dependant, you can ask for a mandatory reconsideration of the decision, and then appeal if you remain unhappy with the outcome (see Chapter 51). **Note:** some people do not count as non-dependants even if they normally live with you (see p104).

People only 'live in' your accommodation with you if they have their home with you and share some accommodation with you.[69] This includes sharing the kitchen (unless it is only used by someone else to prepare food for them).[70]

People only 'normally live' in your accommodation with you if they have been there long enough to regard your home as their normal home.[71] **Note:** for these purposes, someone can only have one normal home at a time.[72]

A number of factors should be considered to decide whether a person normally lives in your accommodation with you, including:

- the relationship between you;
- how much time the person spends at your address;
- where the person keeps clothes and personal belongings;
- whether the stay or absence from your address is temporary or permanent and, if the absence is temporary, how long the absence has lasted (see p107);
- whether the person has another place that could be regarded as home and if, for instance, rent is paid there or the person just travels around;

- a student's living arrangements while at university.[73]

No single factor on its own should be conclusive.

2

## People who are not non-dependants

Even if they normally live with you, the following people do *not* count as non-dependants and you are not allowed bedrooms for any of them under the rules (see below):

- a child or qualifying young person no one in your extended benefit unit (see p103) is treated as responsible for (see p64);
- your (or your partner's, if you are a joint claimant) foster children;
- someone to who you (or your partner, if you are a joint claimant) are liable to pay rent or service charges for, and any member of that person's household – eg, your resident landlord and family;
- someone who has already been treated as the non-dependant of another UC claimant, if the other claimant is also liable to pay rent or service charges for the accommodation you occupy. The other claimant is allowed a bedroom for that person, and a housing costs contribution (see p109) is only deducted from the other claimant's housing costs element, not yours;
- someone who is liable to pay rent or service charges on a commercial basis for the accommodation you occupy, whether this is to you (or your partner, if you are a joint claimant) or to another person – eg, your lodger or subtenant, or a joint tenant.

**Note:** your partner and any child or qualifying young person you or your partner are responsible for do not count as non-dependants.[74] However, you are allowed bedrooms for them if they count as members of your extended benefit unit.

## The number of bedrooms you are allowed

If you rent your home, to calculate your housing costs element you need to know how many bedrooms you are allowed under the rules (known as the 'size criteria'). You are only allowed a bedroom for someone who is a member of your extended benefit unit (see p103). 'Bedroom' is not defined, but see p108 for what may count.

You are allowed:[75]

- one bedroom for each of the following members of your extended benefit unit:
  - you (and your partner if you have one);
  - a qualifying young person you (or your partner, if you are a joint claimant) are responsible for (see p64);
  - each non-dependant aged at least 16 (see p103 for who counts). **Note:** you are entitled to one bedroom for each non-dependant, even if they are members of a couple;[76]
  - two children under 16 of the same gender;

  - two children under 10;
  - any other child under 16.

  **Note:** people who fit into more than one category are treated as being in the category that results in the lowest number of bedrooms; *and*
- one or more additional bedrooms in specified situations.



***Is there a limit to the number of bedrooms you are allowed?***

If you are a private tenant, the maximum number of bedrooms you are allowed, including any additional bedrooms, is four.[77] If you are a social rented sector tenant, there is no limit to the maximum number of bedrooms. In both cases, you can be 'allowed' more bedrooms than the number you actually have – ie, if you are over-occupying your home.[78]

A bedroom can be included for a person in your extended benefit unit who is temporarily absent from home (see p107). **Note:** you are not allowed a bedroom for anyone who is not part of your extended benefit unit because they are not a non-dependant (see p104).

***What if a member of your extended benefit unit dies?***

If your partner (if you were joint claimants), a child or qualifying young person you (or your partner) were responsible for (see p64), a non-dependant or a severely disabled person you were caring for dies, your UC continues to be calculated as if the person had not died for the assessment period in which the death occurred and the following two assessment periods. So if you are no longer allowed as many bedrooms under the rules, this does not affect your housing costs element until after the three assessment periods.[79]

## Additional bedrooms

In certain situations, you are allowed one or more additional bedrooms (but you are still subject to the overall cap of four bedrooms in private rented accommodation – see above).[80]

- **Non-resident carers.** You are allowed one additional bedroom for a non-resident carer, if you, any person in your extended benefit unit (see p103), or a child or young person in respect of whom you meet the 'foster parent condition' (see p106) need someone to stay overnight to provide care regularly, so long as overnight care has been arranged and is provided.[81] The person who is receiving the overnight care must receive pension age disability payment (PADP), attendance allowance (AA) (or equivalent benefits paid because of an injury at work or a war injury), the middle or highest rate of the disability living allowance (DLA), Scottish adult disability allowance (SADLA) or child disability payment (CDP) care component, the daily living component of personal independence payment (PIP) or adult disability payment (ADP), or

armed forces independence payment (AFIP).[82] Even if more than one person requires overnight care, only one additional bedroom is allowed.
- **Member of a couple who cannot share a bedroom.** Unless you are a member of a couple awarded UC as a single person (see p36), you are allowed one additional bedroom if you and your partner are not reasonably able to share a bedroom because of a disability. The disabled partner must be getting PADP, the higher rate of AA (or equivalent benefits paid because of an injury at work or a war injury), the middle or highest rate of the DLA/CDP care component, the daily living component of PIP/ADP, or AFIP.
- **Disabled child who cannot share a bedroom.** You are allowed one additional bedroom if you or any other person in your extended benefit unit (see p103) are responsible for a child under 16 who would normally be expected to share a bedroom under the rules, but cannot reasonably do so because of a disability. The child must be getting the middle or highest rate of the DLA/CDP care component. If more than one child qualifies, you are allowed as many additional bedrooms as you need to ensure that each child has their own bedroom.
- **Adoption, fostering and kinship carers.** You are allowed one additional bedroom if you (or your partner, if you are a joint claimant) meet the 'foster parent condition'. Only one additional bedroom is allowed even if you have more than one foster child, or if both you and your partner are foster parents or adopters.

You meet the **'foster parent condition'** if you have a child placed with you for adoption or you are a foster parent (in Scotland, this includes kinship carers of looked after children – see p64). If you are a foster parent, this applies even if you do not currently have a child placed with you, provided you have become an approved foster parent, or have fostered a child, within the last 12 months.

***Examples***

Scott and Tina have two daughters, aged 10 and 13, and two sons, aged 15 and 22. The 10-year-old daughter is severely disabled and is unable to share a bedroom because of this. Scott's parents live with them. They claim UC. They are allowed one bedroom for Scott and Tina, one bedroom for the daughters, one additional bedroom for their 10-year-old daughter due to her disability, two bedrooms for their sons and two bedrooms for Scott's parents. This is a total of seven bedrooms. They are private tenants, so the housing costs element calculation is based on a four-bedroom property – the maximum allowed. If they had been social rented sector tenants, their housing costs element would have been calculated based on a seven-bedroom property.

Luca is the foster parent of two sisters, aged 10 and 16. He has two sons, aged 10 and 12, one of whom is getting the middle rate of the DLA care component and cannot share a bedroom because of his disability. Luca is allowed one bedroom for himself, and would normally only be allowed one bedroom for his two sons. However, he is allowed one additional bedroom for his disabled son, and one additional bedroom because he is a foster parent. He is therefore allowed a total of four bedrooms for the purposes of calculating his UC housing costs element.

**Note:** the rules that allow additional bedrooms were amended in the past, following test cases. If you think you may have lost out, see pp98–99 of the 2020/21 edition of this *Handbook*.

## Temporary absence from home

When determining how many bedrooms you are allowed, a person can continue to be included in your extended benefit unit (see p103) while temporarily absent from your home.

**You (or your partner) continue to be included during:**[83]

- the one- to six-month period in which you (or your partner) continue to qualify for UC while temporarily absent from Great Britain (see p1371); *or*
- the first six months you are a prisoner (see p839), provided immediately before becoming a prisoner you were entitled to UC as a single person, you were getting a housing costs element and you are not expected to be in custody for more than six months; *or*
- during some other periods when you are temporarily away (see p99 and p100).

**Your children or qualifying young people continue to be included** if, immediately before the start of the period of absence, they were included in your extended benefit unit and you were getting a housing costs element. The children or qualifying young people are included:[84]

- during the first six months of their absence if they are:
  - being looked after by a local authority (see p846); *or*
  - a prisoner (see p839 – this includes if they are on temporary release), provided they are not expected to be in custody for more than six months; ***and***
  - immediately before the start of the period of absence, they were included in your extended benefit unit and you were getting a housing costs element;
- in any other case, for the period you continue to be treated as responsible for them while they are absent from your household (see p64).

**Your non-dependants continue to be included** if, immediately before the start of the period of absence, they were included in your extended benefit unit and, for the first three of the following bullet points, you were getting a housing costs element. They are included:[85]

- during the one- (or two-) month period in which they continue (or would have continued) to qualify for UC while temporarily absent from Great Britain (see p1371);
- during the first six months of their absence if they are:
  - temporarily absent from Great Britain to receive medical treatment or convalescence or to take their partner, child or a qualifying young person for medical treatment or convalescence (see p1371); *or*
  - a prisoner (see p839 – this includes if they are on temporary release), provided they are not expected to be in custody for more than six months;
- in any other case, for up to six months. However, they are no longer included if the absence lasts (or is expected to last) longer than six months;
- indefinitely, if they are your (or your partner's) son, daughter, stepson or stepdaughter and are a member of the armed forces away on operations.

## What counts as a bedroom

When working out the number of bedrooms you have in your home, you may need to consider what counts as a bedroom. For example, it may be advantageous for you to argue that a room is not a bedroom.

'Bedroom' is not defined in the rules. It is the ordinary meaning of the word that is relevant. It could be, for example, a lounge or living room, provided it contains a bed or is used for sleeping.[86]

The starting point is whether the room can be used as a bedroom – ie, a room is a bedroom if it is furnished and can be used for sleeping in. How a property is described by the landlord (eg, as a two- or three-bedroom house) or whether a room is designated as a bedroom may be relevant. However, the basis on which your rent is charged (eg, if your flat has two bedrooms but your landlord only charges the rent for a one-bedroom flat) is not relevant.[87]

You can try to argue that the DWP should not count a room in your home as a bedroom and therefore that your housing costs element should not be reduced (or reduced as much) under the rules on p115 (for social rented sector tenants). The DWP should, for example, take into account:[88]

- the size of the room (the dimensions and height) – eg, whether it can accommodate a single bed and somewhere to store clothes, whether it has a flat surface on which to place things safely, such as a glass of water, and whether there is space to dress and undress. If a room is too small, provide a measured plan and photographs if you can; *and*
- access to the room and whether it has adequate natural and electric lighting, heating, ventilation and privacy; *and*
- whether the room is safe to sleep in – eg, if it is contaminated with asbestos.

Suggest that your personal use of the room should also be considered (eg, if you have a disability and you use the room to store your equipment), as well as whether your home has been converted or adapted (eg, if two small bedrooms have been converted into one big bedroom, or if a bedroom has been redesignated). However, the DWP is likely to say that in deciding how many bedrooms there are in your home:

- it is the classification and description of the property when it is empty that is relevant and that this can only be changed if the property has been structurally altered with the approval of your landlord;[89]
- even if your home could be occupied in more than one way (eg, as either one- or two-bedroom), it can use the way your landlord designates the property to determine how many bedrooms it has.[90]

## Housing costs contributions

If your extended benefit unit includes a 'non-dependant' (see p103), a set deduction is usually made from your housing costs element.[91] This is because it is assumed that non-dependants make a contribution towards housing costs while living with you, whether or not they actually do so. For UC, the DWP calls these deductions 'housing costs contributions'. They may also be referred to as 'non-dependant deductions'. In some circumstances, no deductions are made. **Note:**

- If you are an owner-occupier, no such deduction is made from your service charge payments unless you have a shared ownership tenancy.
- A non-dependant can only be a member of the extended benefit unit of one UC claimant (or pair of joint claimants),[92] so a deduction is only made from that UC claimant's (or pair of joint claimants') housing costs element.
- No housing costs contribution (see below) is deducted from your housing costs element for anyone who is not a non-dependant (see p104).[93]

### When no deduction is made

No housing costs contribution is deducted for any of your non-dependants if you (or your partner, if you are a joint claimant):[94]

- get PADP, AA (or equivalent benefits paid because of an injury at work or a war injury), the middle or highest rate of the DLA/SADLA/CDP care component, the daily living component of PIP/ADP, or AFIP, or would receive it but for being in hospital; *or*
- are certified as severely sight impaired or blind by a consultant ophthalmologist.

No housing costs contribution is deducted for any non-dependant who is:[95]

- under 21 years old; *or*
- getting PADP, AA (or equivalent benefits paid because of an injury at work or a war injury), the middle or highest rate of the DLA care component, the daily living component of PIP/ADP, or AFIP, or who would receive it but for being in hospital; *or*
- getting carer's allowance or carer support payment; *or*
- getting pension credit; *or*
- a prisoner (see p839); *or*

2

- your (or your partner's, if you are a joint claimant) son, daughter, stepson or stepdaughter who is in the armed forces and is away on operations, but only if the person lived with you immediately before leaving, and intends to live with you at the end of the operations; *or*
- responsible for a child under five.

### The amount of the deduction

If a deduction must be made, it is made for every non-dependant who is a member of your extended benefit unit.[96] So if two of your non-dependants are members of a couple, two deductions are made. Each deduction is a fixed amount of £93.02 for the assessment period, irrespective of the non-dependant's income and what they pay you.[97]

## 6. The housing costs element for private rented sector tenants

If you are a private rented sector tenant, your housing costs element is calculated as follows.[98]

- **Step 1:** work out the monthly equivalent (see p101) of your core rent (see below). This is broadly the amount of eligible rent and service charges you must pay.
- **Step 2:** work out your cap rent (normally the local housing allowance for the category of dwelling that applies to you). This is the maximum amount of rent that can be included in your housing costs element (see p112). It may be lower than the rent you actually pay.
- **Step 3:** if your extended benefit unit (see p103) includes any non-dependants, deduct any housing costs contribution that applies (see p109) from the lowest of your core rent or your cap rent. What is left is the amount of your housing costs element. It can never be lower than nil.[99]

If you qualify for a housing costs element for more than one dwelling, special rules apply (see p102).

### Core rent

If you are solely liable or treated as liable (see p94) to make payments, your core rent is the total amount of all the eligible rent and service charge payments for which you satisfy the payment, liability and occupation conditions (see p90, p93 and p97) – ie, the amounts you actually pay – worked out as the monthly equivalent (see p101).[100]

### Jointly liable for payments

If you are jointly liable to make payments with someone, different rules apply. Your core rent is worked out using the following steps.[101]

- **Step 1:** work out the monthly equivalents (see p101) of the eligible rent and service charges for which you (and/or your partner) and any joint tenants are liable, for the whole of the dwelling.
- **Step 2:**
  - if the only people who are jointly liable are in the list of relevant family members below (eg, only you and your partner are liable), your core rent is the amount in Step 1; *or*
  - if one or more people in the list of relevant family members are jointly liable with one or more others who are not relevant family members (eg, you, your partner and a friend are joint tenants), divide the amount in Step 1 by the total number of people who are liable and multiply by the number of your relevant family members who are liable. This is your core rent. However, if the DWP is satisfied that it would be unreasonable to take this amount as your core rent, it must apportion the amount as it considers appropriate, taking into account the number of jointly liable people and the amount of the rent and service charges for which each is liable.

**Note:** if a joint tenant has left your home and is no longer paying rent, the housing costs element can be calculated on the basis that you are liable for the whole rent. This can apply, for example, where you have separated from a former partner. The DWP describes this as an 'untidy tenancy'.

***Relevant family members***

The **'relevant family members'** (the DWP calls them 'listed persons') are you, your partner and any child or qualifying young person you (or your partner, if you are a joint claimant) are responsible for (see p64).[102]

***Example***

Elma and her partner India are joint tenants of a two-bedroom private flat with a friend.

**Step 1:** the rent for the whole of the flat is £120 a week. The monthly equivalent is £120 x 52 ÷ 12 = £520

**Step 2:** Elma and India are jointly liable with a person who is not a relevant family member. Their core rent is therefore £520 ÷ 3 (the number of joint tenants) x 2 (the number of relevant family members) = £346.67 a month.

## Cap rent

Your cap rent is the maximum amount of rent that can be included in your housing costs element. It is normally the local housing allowance for the category

2

of dwelling that applies to you, in the area where you live.[103] This depends on how many bedrooms you are allowed under the rules (see p104), up to a maximum of four bedrooms. To work out which category of dwelling applies, see p113. For information about the local housing allowance rates, see p114.

**Note:**

- If your cap rent is higher than the amount of rent you pay, your housing costs element is calculated using your core rent (see p110).
- If your cap rent is lower than the amount of rent you must pay, you may be able to get extra financial assistance by applying for discretionary housing payments from your local authority (see Chapter 25).

If you have been housed in two dwellings by a provider of social housing (see p115 for the meaning), and you pay rent to a social sector landlord for one and rent to a private landlord for the other, your housing costs element is calculated under the rules for private sector tenancies. In this case, if the cap rents for the two dwellings are different (eg, because they are in different areas), the lowest amount at the time your housing costs element is first calculated is used.[104] Your housing costs element continues to be calculated on the basis of the cap rent for that dwelling until you move to other accommodation.

***Examples***

Irena is a joint tenant of a four-bedroom private flat with Leah, a friend. Irena's son, aged 27, lives with them. The rent for the flat is £1,000 a month, including eligible service charge payments. Irena claims universal credit (UC). Her extended benefit unit includes herself and her son, who counts as a non-dependant; Leah does not count as a non-dependant.

**Step 1:** Irena's core rent is £1,000 ÷ 2 x 1 = £500 a month.

**Step 2:** Irena's cap rent is the local housing allowance for two-bedroom accommodation. In her area, this is £400 a month. Her cap rent is lower than her core rent.

**Step 3:** Irena's housing costs element is therefore £400 (the cap rent) – £93.02 (housing costs contribution) = £306.98.

**Note:** if Leah also claims UC, her extended benefit unit does not include Irena's son as a non-dependant, so Leah's cap rent is the local housing allowance for the category of accommodation that applies to her. No housing costs contribution is deducted.

Abdur and Jahanara are a couple renting a two-bedroom private flat. They pay £150 a week. Their rent includes eligible service charges for the communal lift. Abdur's uncle Faisal and Faisal's 24-year-old son live with them. They are included in Abdur and Jahanara's extended benefit unit as non-dependants.

**Step 1:** Abdur and Jahanara's core rent is £150 x 52 ÷ 12 = £650 a month.

**Step 2:** their cap rent is the local housing allowance for three-bedroom accommodation (they are allowed one bedroom for themselves and one bedroom each for Faisal and his son). In their area, the local housing allowance rate for three-bedroom accommodation is £800 a month. Their core rent is lower than their cap rent.

**Step 3:** Abdur and Jahanara's extended benefit unit includes two non-dependants. Housing costs contributions of £93.02 x 2 = £186.04 are deducted. Their housing costs element is £650 (the core rent) – £186.04 (housing costs contributions) = £463.96.



## Categories of dwelling

The category of dwelling that applies to you depends on how many bedrooms you are allowed under the rules (see p104) and whether or not the one-bedroom shared accommodation category applies.

### One-bedroom shared accommodation

The one-bedroom shared accommodation category applies if you are a single person (or a member of a couple awarded UC as a single person – see p36), you are under 35 and you do not have any children or qualifying young people you are responsible for or non-dependants. This applies even if you do not live in shared accommodation.[105]

However, there are exceptions and this category of dwelling does *not* apply (even if you do live in shared accommodation) if:[106]

- you are under 35 and are getting attendance allowance, the middle or highest rate of the disability living allowance/child disability payment care component, the daily living component of personal independence payment/adult disability payment, or armed forces independence payment; *or*
- you are under 35 and meet the 'foster parent condition' (see p106); *or*
- you are at least 18 but under 25 and became a 'care leaver' under specified provisions before you were 18 (see p846);[107] *or*
- after you turned 16, you experienced or were threatened with domestic abuse by your partner, your former partner or a relative. See p951 for what counts as domestic abuse for these purposes. You must provide evidence from a registered healthcare professional, social worker, police officer, or another person acting in an official capacity – eg, your employer, a voluntary organisation or a charity; *or*
- you are under 35 and a competent authority (the Home Office) has determined that you have been the victim of modern slavery – ie, of trafficking in human beings, slavery, servitude or forced or compulsory labour; *or*
- you are under 35 and have lived in one or more hostels for homeless people for three months or more (this does not have to be continuous) and while living there you accepted support services to assist you in being rehabilitated or resettled in the community; *or*
- you are under 35 and are an offender subject to specific multi-agency public protection risk arrangements. It is understood that this applies if you are a level 2 or 3 offender.

**Note:** if one of the exceptions applies to you, the category of dwelling that applies is one-bedroom self-contained accommodation (see below).

*Definition*

For these purposes, **'relative'** means your (or your partner's or former partner's) parent, step-parent, son, daughter, stepson, stepdaughter, grandparent, grandchild. It also includes your (or your partner's or former partner's) sibling, uncle, aunt, niece, nephew or first cousin (whether full blood or half blood or by marriage or civil partnership).[108]

### One-bedroom self-contained accommodation

The one-bedroom self-contained accommodation category of dwelling applies if you are only allowed one bedroom under the rules (see p104) and the one-bedroom shared accommodation category (see p113) does not apply to you.[109]

If you are aged 35 or over (and you are single, not responsible for any children and have no non-dependants), it is understood that in practice the DWP applies this category of accommodation to you, even if you live in shared accommodation.

### Accommodation with two or more bedrooms

If you are allowed more than one bedroom under the rules, the category of dwelling that applies is that with the number of bedrooms you are allowed (see p104), up to a maximum of four.[110] It must be reasonable for you to occupy this category of accommodation, taking into account the number of people in your extended benefit unit (see p103).[111]

## Local housing allowance rates

Local housing allowance rates vary by area. They are based on the 30th percentile point of local market rents for assured tenancies in what is known as a 'broad rental market area', up to a maximum amount.[112]

See lha-direct.voa.gov.uk for the current local housing allowance rates in your area.

Local housing allowance rates are usually set annually, with changes taking effect from April. In 2025, local housing allowance rates have not increased and remain at the levels set in 2024 (see p311).[113]

# 7. The housing costs element for social rented sector tenants

How your housing costs element is calculated if you are a social rented sector tenant depends on whether you are solely or jointly liable for your rent and service charges. Your home is **'social rented sector accommodation'** if your landlord is a provider of social housing.

***Provider of social housing***

A **'provider of social housing'** is a local authority, a non-profit registered provider of social housing, a profit-making registered provider of social housing (if you have been housed in social housing) or a registered social landlord.[114]

Note:

- If you qualify for a housing costs element for more than one dwelling, special rules apply (see p102).
- Your housing costs element may be lower than as calculated below if the DWP thinks your rent or service charges are higher than is reasonable for a housing costs element to meet.[115] In this case, the DWP can apply to the rent officer. If the rent officer thinks that your landlord could reasonably have expected to get a lower amount of rent than what you pay, the lower amount is used to calculate your housing costs element, unless the DWP is satisfied that this is not appropriate. There is no right of appeal against this decision.[116]
- Your housing costs element can *never* be lower than nil.[117]
- If your rent or service charge payments have been reduced by a provider of social housing under a government-approved tenant incentive scheme, your rent and service charges are worked out as if no reduction had been made.[118]

## Solely liable to make payments

If you are solely liable to make rent (see p90) and service charge (see p92) payments, your housing costs element is worked out as follows.[119]

- **Step 1:** work out the monthly equivalents (see p101) of your eligible rent and service charges, and add these together.
- **Step 2:** from the total in Step 1, deduct any amount that is for the supply of a commodity – eg, for water or fuel.
- **Step 3:** work out the total number of bedrooms in your home and the number of bedrooms you are allowed under the rules (see p104). If you do not have more bedrooms than you are allowed, go to Step 5. If you have more bedrooms than you are allowed, go to Step 4.
- **Step 4:** apply the bedroom tax (see p117). Unless any of the circumstances in which no reduction is made apply, reduce the amount in Step 2 by:[120]
  - 14 per cent, if you have one bedroom too many; *or*
  - 25 per cent, if you have two or more bedrooms too many.
- **Step 5:** if your extended benefit unit (see p103) includes any non-dependants, deduct any housing costs contribution that applies (see p109).[121] The amount you have left is your housing costs element.

2

*Example*

Danielle rents a four-bedroom house from the local authority. She lives there with her 14-year-old daughter. Her rent is £125 a week. She has four rent-free weeks every year. Her extended benefit unit does not include any non-dependants.

**Step 1:** the monthly equivalent of her rent payments is £125 x 48 ÷ 12 = £500. Danielle does not have any service charge payments.

**Step 2:** the total payment is £500 a month.

**Step 3:** Danielle has four bedrooms in her home. She is only allowed two bedrooms under the rules: one bedroom for herself and one bedroom for her daughter, therefore Step 4 applies.

**Step 4:** she has two bedrooms too many. The amount in Step 2 must be reduced by 25 per cent. 25% x £500 = £125. £500 – £125 = £375

As Step 5 does not apply to Danielle, her housing costs element is £375 a month.

## Jointly liable to make payments

If you are jointly liable to make rent (see p90) and service charge (see p92) payments with someone (eg, you are a joint tenant), different rules apply.[122]

- **Step 1:** work out the monthly equivalents (see p101) of the eligible rent and service charges for which you and your joint tenant are liable, for the whole of the dwelling.
- **Step 2:** from the total in Step 1, deduct any amount that is for the supply of a commodity – eg, for water or fuel.
- **Step 3:** if the only people who are jointly liable are in the list of relevant family members on p111 (eg, you and your partner are the only joint tenants), go to Step 5. Otherwise, go to Step 4.
- **Step 4:** if you or one or more people in the list of relevant family members are jointly liable with one or more others who are not relevant family members (eg, you and a friend are joint tenants), divide the total rent and service charge payments by the total number of people who are liable and multiply by the number of your relevant family members who are liable. However, if the DWP is satisfied that it would be unreasonable to take this amount as your rent, it must apportion the amount as it considers appropriate, taking into account the number of jointly liable people and the amount of the rent and service charges for which each is liable. After calculating this figure, go straight to Step 7, as the bedroom tax does not apply to you.[123]
- **Step 5:** work out the total number of bedrooms in your home and the number of bedrooms you are allowed under the rules (see p104). If you have more bedrooms in your home than you are allowed under the rules, go to Step 6. Otherwise, go to Step 7.
- **Step 6:** apply the bedroom tax (see below). Unless any of the circumstances in which no reduction is made apply, reduce the amount in Step 2 by:[124]

  - 14 per cent, if you have one bedroom too many; *or*
  - 25 per cent, if you have two or more bedrooms too many.
- **Step 7:** if your extended benefit unit (see p103) includes any non-dependants, deduct any housing costs contribution that applies (see p109).[125] The amount you have left is your housing costs element.



**Note:** if a joint tenant has left your home and is no longer paying rent, the housing costs element can be calculated on the basis that you are liable for the whole rent. This can apply, for example, where you have separated from a former partner. The DWP describes this as an 'untidy tenancy'.

***Example***

Curtis, his partner and a friend are joint tenants of a three-bedroom housing association flat. The rent is £180 a week.

The monthly equivalent of the rent payments is £180 x 52 ÷ 12 = £780 a month.

They do not have any service charge payments.

The total payment is therefore £780 a month.

Curtis and his partner are relevant family members. The amount that can be included in their housing costs element is therefore £780 ÷ 3 (the number of joint tenants) x 2 (the number of relevant family members) = £520 a month.

Their extended benefit unit does not include any non-dependants. The housing costs element is therefore £520 a month.

## The bedroom tax

If you are a social rented sector tenant and you have more bedrooms in your home than you are allowed under the rules (see p104), a reduction is usually made when calculating your universal credit housing costs element.[126] This is often referred to as the 'bedroom tax'. The DWP refers to this as the 'under-occupation charge' or the 'removal of the spare room subsidy'. 'Bedroom' is not defined. See p108 for what may count.

If your housing costs element is reduced by the bedroom tax, you may be able to get discretionary housing payments from your local authority to help you pay your rent (see Chapter 25).

No reduction can be made under these rules if:

- you are a **joint tenant with someone other than your partner** (see Step 4 on p116); *or*
- you have a **shared ownership tenancy**;[127] *or*
- you live in a dwelling adapted for you under a **'sanctuary scheme'** – ie, a scheme that provides enhanced security measures to enable households at risk of domestic abuse to remain safely in their homes. This applies if:[128]
  - the scheme is operated by a local authority, a registered social landlord (in Wales or Scotland) or a registered provider of social housing (in England).

For information about registered providers of social housing in England, see gov.uk/guidance/lists-of-registered-social-housing-providers-and-regulatory-judgements. For details about registered social landlords in Wales, see gov.wales/registered-social-landlords. For the details in Scotland, see housingregulator.gov.scot; *and*

- you or a member of your extended benefit unit (see p103) have experienced or been threatened with domestic abuse (see p951 for what counts) by a partner, a former partner or a relative; *and*
- you or the member of your extended benefit unit are not living at the same address as the perpetrator unless that person is a qualifying young person and is a dependant of a member of your extended benefit unit; *and*
- you provide relevant evidence from a healthcare professional, a police officer, a registered social worker, an employer or trade union representative or a public, voluntary or charitable body.

For these purposes, 'relative' has the meaning defined on p114.[129]

## 8. The housing costs element for owner-occupiers

If you are an owner-occupier, you may get a housing costs element if you satisfy the payment, liability and occupation conditions for service charges for your accommodation (see p92).[130]

You cannot get a housing costs element to cover mortgage interest or other loans secured on the property. However, the DWP may offer you a loan for this (see p764). You should seek independent advice before accepting a loan.

The housing costs element is calculated as follows.[131]

- **Step 1:** work out the amount of each eligible service charge payment.
- **Step 2:** work out the period for which each payment is payable, and if payments are made other than calendar monthly, work out the monthly equivalent (see p101).
- **Step 3:** add together all the monthly amounts for different eligible service charges. This is the amount of your housing costs element.

**Note:**

- You cannot get a housing costs element (other than for rent and service charges if you have a shared ownership tenancy – see below[132]) if you (or your partner) have any earned income, however much your earnings are.[133] This includes earnings from work you can do while claiming new-style employment and support allowance (ESA – see p928) or from work of less than 16 hours a week you can do while claiming new-style jobseeker's allowance (JSA – see p887).

- If you have a shared ownership tenancy (ie, you are buying part of your home and renting the rest), your housing costs element can also include an amount for your rent. In this case, your service charge payments are not calculated under these rules. They are calculated as for rented accommodation.[134] See p110 if you live in private rented accommodation and p115 if you live in social rented sector accommodation.
- You may only qualify for a housing costs element after a waiting period.



## The waiting period

If you are an owner-occupier, a housing costs element for service charge payments cannot usually be included until after a waiting period of nine consecutive assessment periods.[135] The DWP may also call this a 'qualifying period'.

The waiting period runs from when:[136]

- you have a new award of universal credit (UC) that would otherwise include a housing costs element under these rules – ie, you claim UC for the first time or claim after a break in your entitlement to UC; *or*
- you requalify for a housing costs element for service charge payments after it had previously ceased to be included in your UC award for any reason – eg, due to earnings from a temporary job.

If you cease to qualify for a housing costs element for service charge payments for any reason during a waiting period, it stops running. A new waiting period starts again from the beginning under whichever of the above rules apply.[137]

***Example***

Zhen, who is unemployed and has no income, makes a claim for UC. She is an owner-occupier, pays eligible service charge payments for the cleaning of the common areas in her block of flats and for a concierge service, and (but for having to serve a waiting period) qualifies for a housing costs element. She waits nine consecutive assessment periods, then a housing costs element for service charge payments is included in her UC from the 10th assessment period. Zhen gets a part-time temporary job, so she no longer qualifies for a housing costs element as an owner-occupier because she has earned income, although her entitlement to UC continues. When her job ends, a housing costs element will be included again, once she has been getting UC for a further nine consecutive assessment periods.

There are no waiting period rules for rent payments. Therefore, if you have a shared ownership tenancy (ie, you are buying part of your home and renting the rest), your housing costs element can include the rent and all service charge payments you make straight away, without a waiting period.

## Exceptions

There are limited exceptions to the general waiting period rule.

- If you are entitled to new-style JSA or ESA, immediately before your award of UC starts, any period when you were only getting one of those benefits may count towards your waiting period.[138]
- If you (or your partner or a former partner) were entitled to income support (IS), income-based JSA or income-related ESA in the month before the date you claimed (or were treated as claiming) UC (or you would have been entitled but for your entitlement ending because the benefit was abolished):[139]
  - if your (or your partner's or former partner's) IS/JSA/ESA included help with housing costs (see Chapter 14), you do not have to serve a waiting period; *or*
  - if your (or your partner's or your former partner's) IS/JSA/ESA did not yet include help with housing costs because you were serving a waiting period, your UC waiting period is 273 days, minus the number of days you were entitled to IS/JSA/ESA (including the time you were treated as entitled under specified linking rules, as well as any time between the date the IS/JSA/ESA ended and the date you are awarded UC).
- If an award of UC made while you were a joint claimant ended because you ceased to be a couple, you were joint owner-occupiers, you occupy the same home you occupied with your former partner and have been awarded UC as a single person:[140]
  - if a housing costs element was not yet included in your joint award of UC, any assessment period (or part of an assessment period) in respect of which you had been getting UC counts towards the waiting period for your new UC award. For example, if you and your former partner had been getting UC for 45 days, a housing costs element can be included once you have been getting UC for nine assessment periods, minus 45 days;
  - if a housing costs element was included in your joint award of UC, you do not have to serve another waiting period.

  This can also apply to your former partner – ie, if your former partner continues to occupy the same accommodation and claims, and is awarded, UC.

# Notes

**1. Who can get a housing costs element**

1 s11 WRA 2012; reg 25 UC Regs
2 s11(2)(c) WRA 2012
3 Reg 26(4)-(6) UC Regs
4 Reg 8(4) and Sch 4 para 4 UC Regs
5 Reg 26(5) and Sch 5 para 4 UC Regs
6 Sch 1 para 3(h) and (i) UC Regs

2. **The payment condition**
7 Reg 25(2)(a) and Sch 1 para 2 UC Regs
8 *AB v LB Camden (HB)* [2020] UKUT 158 (AAC)
9 Sch 1 para 3 UC Regs
10 s2 *Leasehold Reform (Ground Rent) Act 2022: Guidance for leaseholders, landlords and managing agents*
11 data.parliament.uk/DepositedPapers/Files/DEP2024-0673/040_Claimants_without_having_a_tenancy_V3.0.pdf
12 Sch 1 para 3A UC Regs
13 Sch 1 para 3B UC Regs
14 Sch 1 para 1 UC Regs
15 Reg 25(2)(c) and Sch 1 para 7(1), (2) and (4) UC Regs
16 Sch 1 para 7(1) and (3) UC Regs; reg 2 and Sch 1 para 5(2) LMI Regs
17 Sch 1 para 8(3) UC Regs
18 Sch 1 para 8(4) and (5) UC Regs
19 para F2074 ADM
20 Sch 1 para 8(6) UC Regs; paras F2076-F2077 ADM

3. **The liability condition**
21 Reg 25(3) UC Regs
22 R(H) 1/03; *Warwick DC v SSWP and CH (HB)* [2020] UKUT 240 (AAC)
23 *R v Poole BC ex parte Ross* [1995] 28 HLR 351 (QBD); CH/1076/2002; CH/296/2004; CH/1097/2004
24 *R v Rugby BC HBRB ex parte Harrison* [1994] 28 HLR 36 (QBD); CH/2959/2006
25 CH/3579/2003; CH/257/2005; see response to Freedom of Information request 'Guidance on housing element on universal credit when rent is paid in advance', 30 October 2023 on whatdotheyknow.com (ref FOI2023 78549)
26 R(H) 3/03
27 *R v Poole BC ex parte Ross* [1995] 28 HLR 351 (QBD); *R v Warrington BC ex parte Williams* [1997] 29 HLR 872 (QBD)
28 Reg 25(3) and Sch 2 paras 1-4 UC Regs
29 Sch 2 para 2 UC Regs
30 *ZD v LB Hillingdon (HB)* [2021] UKUT 305 (AAC)
31 paras A3/3.140-141 GM
32 Sch 2 paras 5-10 UC Regs
33 Reg 2 UC Regs
34 *Bristol City Council v JKT* [2016] UKUT 517 (AAC)
35 Sch 2 para 10 UC Regs
36 para F2142 ADM
37 *R v Solihull MBC ex parte Simpson* [1995] 1 FLR 140 (CA); CH/39/2007
38 CH/2258/2004
39 *R v Sutton LBC HBRB ex parte Keegan* [1992] 27 HLR 92 (QBD)
40 *R v Manchester City Council ex parte Baragrove Properties Ltd* [1991] 23 HLR 337 (QBD); *R v Gloucestershire County Council ex parte Victoria Dadds* [1996] EWHC Admin 311; CH/39/2007
41 *R v Sutton LBC HBRB ex parte Keegan* [1992] 27 HLR 92 (QBD)

4. **The occupation condition**
42 Reg 25(4) and Sch 3 paras 1(1) and 2 UC Regs
43 Sch 3 paras 7 and 8 UC Regs
44 *Bury MBC v DC (HB)* [2011] UKUT 43 (AAC); *R (Mahmoudi) v LB Lewisham and Another* [2014] EWCA Civ 284, reported as [2014] AACR 14
45 Sch 3 para 1(2)-(4) UC Regs
46 Sch 3 para 5 UC Regs
47 Sch 3 para 4 UC Regs
48 Sch 3 paras 3 and 9(2) UC Regs
49 R(SB) 10/81; *SH v LB Southwark* [2023] UKUT 198 (AAC)
50 See the definitions of domestic violence/abuse for other purposes in reg 98(4) UC Regs and ss1 and 2 Domestic Abuse Act 2021; see also DWP, *Help Available From the Department for Work and Pensions for People who are Victims of Domestic Violence and Abuse*, updated 16 April 2024, available on gov.uk
51 Sch 3 paras 6 and 9(3) UC Regs
52 Sch 3 para 9(3) UC Regs
53 CH/1237/2004
54 CH/3893/2004
55 Sch 3 para 9 UC Regs
56 *R v Penwith DC ex parte Burt* [1990] 22 HLR 292 (QBD)
57 R(H) 9/05
58 Regs 2 and 19(1)(b), (2) and (3) UC Regs; paras E3040-E3042 ADM
59 sentencingcouncil.org.uk/sentencing-and-the-council/types-of-sentence/determinate-prison-sentences
60 CH/1237/2004
61 CH/3893/2004

5. **How the housing costs element is calculated: general rules**
62 Schs 4 para 7 and 5 para 13 UC Regs
63 Reg 26(4)-(6) UC Regs
64 Sch 4 para 17 UC Regs
65 Sch 4 para 18 UC Regs
66 Sch 4 para 19 UC Regs
67 Sch 4 paras 1, definitions of 'renters' and 'joint renters', and 9(1) UC Regs

68 Sch 4 para 9(2) UC Regs
69 *AM v SSWP (IS)* [2011] UKUT 387 (AAC)
70 CSIS/185/1995
71 CIS/14850/1996
72 *JP v Bournemouth BC (HB)* [2018] UKUT 75 (AAC)
73 *RR v SSWP (UC)* [2024] UKUT 261 (AAC), paras 32 and 33
74 Sch 4 para 9(2)(a), (b) and (g) UC Regs
75 Sch 4 paras 2, 8 and 10 UC Regs
76 DWP, Universal Credit Guidance, 'The size criteria for renters', v7.0, House of Commons library deposited papers, rightsnet.org.uk/resources/universal-credit-guidance
77 Sch 4 para 26 UC Regs
78 DWP, Universal Credit Guidance, 'The size criteria for renters', v7.0, House of Commons library deposited papers, rightsnet.org.uk/resources/universal-credit-guidance
79 Reg 37 UC Regs
80 Reg 2 and Sch 4 paras 2, 10, 12 and 26 UC Regs
81 *SM v SSWP* [2023] UKUT 176 (AAC)
82 Reg 2, definition of 'attendance allowance', and Sch 4 para 12(3) UC Regs
83 Sch 3 paras 3, 6 and 9 and Sch 4 para 11(3) UC Regs
84 Sch 4 para 11(2) UC Regs
85 Sch 4 para 11(4)-(6) UC Regs
86 *Bolton MBC v BF (HB)* [2014] UKUT 48 (AAC)
87 *CB v Manchester City Council and SSWP (HB)* [2015] UKUT 556 (AAC)
88 *SSWP v Nelson and Nelson* [2014] UKUT 525 (AAC), reported as [2015] AACR 21; *Stevenage BC v ML (HB)* [2016] UKUT 164 (AAC); *M v SSWP* [2017] UKUT 443 (AAC); *E v Bristol City Council* [2018] UKUT 287 (AAC)
89 *SSWP v the City of Glasgow Council and IB* [2017] CSIH 35, reported as [2017] AACR 29
90 *SSWP v RR (HB)* [2018] UKUT 180 (AAC)
91 Sch 4 paras 13, 22 and 33 UC Regs
92 Sch 4 para 9(2)(f) UC Regs
93 Sch 4 paras 9(2) and 13 UC Regs
94 Sch 4 para 15 UC Regs
95 Sch 4 para 16 UC Regs
96 Sch 4 para 13 UC Regs
97 Sch 4 para 14(1) UC Regs

6. **The housing costs element for private rented sector tenants**

98 Reg 26(2) and Sch 4 para 22 UC Regs
99 Sch 4 para 14(3) UC Regs
100 Sch 4 paras 3(1), 6, 7 and 23 UC Regs
101 Reg 26(2) and Sch 4 paras 3(1), 6, 7 and 24 UC Regs
102 Sch 4 para 2 UC Regs, definition of 'listed persons'
103 Sch 4 paras 25(1), (2) and (5) and 26 UC Regs
104 Sch 4 para 25(3) and (4) UC Regs
105 Sch 4 paras 2, 27 and 28 UC Regs; Sch 1 para 1(a) RO(UCF)O
106 Sch 4 para 29 UC Regs
107 Sch 4 para 29(2) UC Regs
108 Sch 4 para 2 UC Regs
109 Sch 4 paras 8 and 25(2) UC Regs; Sch 1 para 1(b) RO(UCF)O
110 Sch 4 paras 8, 25(2) and 26 UC Regs; Sch 1 para 1(c)-(e) RO(UCF)O
111 Sch 4 para 8(1) UC Regs
112 Sch 4 para 25(2) and (5) UC Regs; arts 3 and 4 and Sch 1 RO(UCF)O; art 4 The Rent Officers (Housing Benefit and Universal Credit Functions) (Amendment) Order 2024 No.11
113 Art 4 The Rent Officers (Housing Benefit and Universal Credit Functions) (Modification) Order 2025 No.5

7. **The housing costs element for social rented sector tenants**

114 Schs 3 para 4(3) and 4 para 2 UC Regs
115 Sch 4 para 32 UC Regs
116 Sch 3 para 6 UC,PIP,JSA&ESA(D&A) Regs
117 Sch 4 para 14(3) UC Regs
118 Sch 4 para 32A UC Regs
119 Sch 4 paras 3, 6, 30-34 and 36 UC Regs
120 Sch 4 paras 34 and 36 UC Regs
121 Sch 4 para 33 UC Regs
122 Sch 4 paras 3, 6, 30-32, 35 and 36 UC Regs
123 Sch 4 para 35(4) UC Regs; data.parliament.uk/DepositedPapers/Files/DEP2024-0673/095_Joint_tenancies_V8.0.pdf
124 Sch 4 para 36 UC Regs
125 Sch 4 para 33 UC Regs
126 Sch 4 paras 2 and 30 UC Regs
127 Sch 4 para 36(5) UC Regs
128 Reg 98(4) and Sch 4 paras 2 and 36(6) UC Regs
129 Sch 4 para 2 UC Regs

8. **The housing costs element for owner-occupiers**

130 Reg 26(3) UC Regs
131 Sch 5 para 13 UC Regs
132 Reg 26(4)-(6) and Sch 5 para 4(3) UC Regs

133 Sch 5 para 4 UC Regs
134 Reg 26(4)-(6) UC Regs
135 Sch 5 para 5(1) UC Regs
136 Sch 5 para 5(1) and (2) UC Regs
137 Sch 5 para 5(3) UC Regs
138 Reg 2, definitions of 'JSA' and 'ESA', and Sch 5 para 6 UC Regs
139 Reg 29 UC(TP) Regs
140 Sch 5 paras 1(2) and 7 UC Regs

2

# Chapter 7

# Income

**This chapter covers:**


1. Whose income counts (below)
2. What counts as income (p125)
3. Earnings (p125)
4. Other income (p136)
5. Notional income (p142)
6. Working out monthly income (p144)


### Key facts

- Your entitlement to universal credit (UC) and how much you get depends on your income.
- Your own income counts and, if you are a member of a couple, your partner's income also counts.
- Your earnings from employment and self-employment are taken into account on a monthly basis over each assessment period.
- If earnings from self-employment are low, your UC award may be assessed on more earnings than you get, called the 'minimum income floor'.
- Certain other kinds of income are also taken into account.

## 1. Whose income counts

If you are single, only your own income counts when working out your universal credit (UC) award.[1]

Couples usually make a joint claim, and your UC award is worked out using both your income and your partner's income.[2]

There are some situations in which one member of a couple qualifies for UC, but the other does not – eg, in certain circumstances, if your partner is under 18, does not meet residence tests, is out of the country or is in prison (see p36). In these cases, you make a single claim. You do not get any amount for your partner in your UC award, but your partner's income (and capital) is still added to yours when working out how much UC you get.[3]

Children's income is ignored.[4]

2

# 2. What counts as income

The amount of universal credit (UC) you are entitled to depends on how much income you have.

**'Income'** for UC means:[5]

- earnings from employment (see p126) and self-employment (see p128) or any other paid work;[6] *and*
- certain other income:[7]
  - certain benefits (see p137);
  - maintenance for you or your partner, but not for a child (see p138);
  - student loans and grants. See p795 for how much of the loan counts and which grants are ignored;
  - certain income from employment and training schemes (see p138);
  - occupational and personal pensions and annuities (see p139);
  - certain insurance payments (see p139);
  - income from a trust (see p140 for which types are ignored);
  - income you are assumed to have from savings and other capital (see p140);
  - sports awards from UK Sport (see p141);
  - miscellaneous income (see p141);
  - capital that is treated as income (see below).

In some situations, you may be treated as having income you do not actually have. This is called 'notional income' (see p142). If a type of income is not specified in the rules as being included for UC, it is ignored and does not affect your award. See p142 for some examples of income that is ignored.

## Income or capital?

Any amounts that are paid regularly and refer to a specific period are treated as income, not as capital.[8] This is the case even if payments might otherwise be regarded as capital or as part capital – eg, payments under an annuity are treated as income.

If you have a lump sum that is payable by instalments (eg, an investment bond that allows regular withdrawals), each instalment is treated as income while any instalments outstanding, together with any other capital you have, is above £16,000. Once the amount of any instalments outstanding, together with any other capital you have, is below this limit, each instalment is treated as capital.[9]

# 3. Earnings

**'Earned income'** means any profit or remuneration from employment, self-employment or any other paid work.[10] Paid work means any work done for payment or in expectation of payment, and does not include voluntary work where the only payment is for expenses.[11] How earnings are assessed depends on whether you are employed (see below) or self-employed (see p128).

## Employed earnings

Universal credit (UC) is assessed each month. To work out the amount of earnings from employment to take into account in the assessment, do the following.

- Check whether the payment counts as earnings (see below).
- Work out your monthly earnings for the assessment period (see p144).
- Calculate your net earnings for the assessment period (see p127).

If you also have self-employed earnings, these are worked out (see p128) and added to your monthly employed earnings to give your total earned income. To work out how your earnings affect your UC award, check whether you have a work allowance (see p41). The work allowance is deducted from your earnings and 55 per cent of what is left is taken into account as income in your UC award. If you do not have a work allowance, 55 per cent of your total earnings is taken into account. See p41 for more about how your earnings affect your UC award.

### What counts as earnings

**'Earnings'** means 'remuneration or profits derived from... employment'. Employed earnings are received under an employment contract ('contract of service'), which may be written, verbal or implied, or in an 'office' such as local councillors.[12] Earnings include:[13]

- wages and overtime pay;
- tips, bonuses and commission;
- fees;
- holiday pay;
- statutory sick pay or other sick pay from your employer;
- statutory maternity pay, statutory adoption pay, statutory paternity pay, statutory shared parental pay, statutory parental bereavement pay, statutory neonatal care pay or other pay from your employer while you are on maternity, adoption, paternity or parental leave;
- any refund of income tax or national insurance (NI) contributions from HMRC for a tax year when you were in paid work or from an employer.[14] This includes tax from unearned income. A refund of income tax from self-employment counts as self-employed earnings (see p128);
- an equal pay settlement – eg, through a 'single status' agreement.[15]

The DWP usually gets information on your earnings from the records your employer sends to HMRC each time you are paid (see p145). So what counts for earnings for UC is usually what is recorded on PAYE (pay as you earn) records and is defined in terms of what counts as taxable income. However, there are differences and not all kinds of taxable income count for UC purposes. For how earnings are treated if you are involved in a trade dispute, see p891.



### What does not count as earnings

Types of income not taken into account as earnings for UC include the following (some of which are taxable):[16]

- expenses incurred 'wholly, exclusively and necessarily' in the course of your employment;[17]
- certain taxable and tax-exempt expenses and allowances – eg, mileage allowance or homeworkers' additional expenses (eg, listed on HMRC Form P11D from your employer);[18]
- expenses if you are a service user being consulted about provision of services by certain public bodies. A fee for participation counts as earnings;[19]
- benefits in kind – eg, a salary sacrifice scheme, non-cash vouchers (eg, for childcare), living accommodation connected with work, cars and car fuel benefits, parking or meals;[20]
- allowances for special types of employment – eg, certain armed forces allowances, free coal to miners or allowances in lieu of coal, and offshore oil and gas workers' travel, subsistence and accommodation allowances.[21]

### Payments when you stop work

Your final earnings when you stop work are taken into account in the assessment period in which they are paid (even if they are paid late).[22] This includes arrears of pay, pay in lieu of notice and accrued holiday pay.[23] The following lump-sum payments are taken into account as capital:[24]

- statutory and contractual redundancy pay;
- employment tribunal awards for unfair dismissal;
- payments under settlement agreements for loss of future earnings (but payments for historic losses count as earnings) or injury to feelings (but payments for personal injury are disregarded as capital – see p159).[25]

### Working out net earnings

From your monthly earnings for the assessment period, deduct the following payments you make in that period:[26]

- income tax; *and*
- class 1 NI contributions; *and*
- any contribution you make towards a personal or occupational pension scheme. If you pay contributions through your employer, your payslips should show your wages after the contributions have been deducted, so there is no further deduction to make.

Also deduct any charity payments made under a payroll giving scheme.

## Self-employed earnings

UC is assessed each month. You can have self-employed earnings even if you are not in 'gainful self-employment' (see p132).[27] To work out the amount of your self-employed earnings to take into account in the assessment, do the following.[28]

- Work out your actual receipts for the assessment period (see below).
- Deduct any permitted expenses from your receipts (see p129).
- From the result (or your share of it, if you are in a business partnership), deduct any payment made in the assessment period for income tax and NI contributions. If the result is negative, there is a loss and the amount of your self-employed earnings is nil (but set minimum earnings may apply – see p130).
- Deduct any contributions made by you to a personal or occupational pension (but not if these have already been deducted from your employed earnings). If the result is negative, the amount of your self-employed earnings is nil (but set minimum earnings may apply – see p130).
- Deduct any unused losses carried forward from earlier assessment periods, starting from the earliest (see p130).
- Check whether the amount worked out as above (adding any earnings from employment) is above a set minimum level of earnings (see p130).

### Receipts from self-employment

The starting point to work out how much self-employed earnings are taken into account is the actual amount of receipts into the business in the assessment period – eg, sales, takings and payment for work.[29] Include:[30]

- any refund of income tax, VAT or NI contributions for the self-employment;
- receipts in kind – ie, the value of the goods or service you provided for which you accepted payment in kind;[31]
- sale of business assets (if previously deducted from earnings for UC as an expense). If you stop using an asset for the business but do not sell it, the market value counts as a receipt.

***Do you have income from social media?***

The DWP views income received from the following online activity as self-employed income, and you are expected to report it:[32]

– advertisements;
– gifts;
– partnering with brands;
– paid promotional content;
– streaming contracts;
– selling your own products.

You may also report any permitted expenses for this work.

2

## Permitted expenses

Expenses must be reasonable and 'wholly and exclusively' incurred for the purposes of your business.[33] Reasonable expenses may include:[34]

- regular costs – eg, rent, utilities, insurance and wages;
- stock purchase;
- stationery and advertising;
- repairs of business assets;
- transport (but see below for flat-rate deductions);
- equipment purchase and hire;
- up to £41 repayment of interest on a loan – eg, for an overdraft or credit card;
- VAT.

These are just examples. The deduction allowed is usually the actual amount of permitted expenses paid in the assessment period. However, there are flat-rate deductions for the use of a vehicle that you can choose to include instead of the actual expense of buying and using the vehicle:[35]

- for a motorcycle, 24 pence a mile;
- for a car, van or other vehicle, 45 pence a mile for the first 833 miles, then 25 pence a mile after that (for a car, you must use this rate rather than the actual expense).

If an expense has been incurred partly for business and partly for private purposes, it can be apportioned and the part that is identifiably for business deducted.[36] There are set deductions for the following.[37]

- If you use your own home for 'income-generating activities' for the business, instead of deducting actual expenses, there is a flat-rate deduction that depends on the number of hours completed in the assessment period. Income-generating activities include providing services to customers, business administration, sales and marketing, but do not include being on call.[38] The deduction is:
  - £10 for work of at least 25 hours up to 50 hours in the month; *or*
  - £18 for work of more than 50 hours up to 100 hours in the month; *or*
  - £26 for more than 100 hours' work in the month.
- If you live in premises that you use mainly for your business, deduct an amount from the expenses relating to the premises, depending on the number of people living there:
  - £350 if you live alone; *or*
  - £500 if you live with one other person; *or*
  - £650 if you live with two or more other people.

***Example***

Gabrielle runs a guest house. She and her partner live in the guest house. Gabrielle works out her expenses as £1,500 for the monthly assessment period for the whole house. She finds it difficult to say which expenses are for the business. Instead of apportioning expenses for business and personal use, she deducts £500 from the £1,500 for the whole house. The expenses allowed are £1,000.



## Offsetting losses

If your receipts in an assessment period are less than your expenses, income tax and NI contributions (but not adding pension contributions), this amount is a loss. A loss from a previous assessment period is deducted from the next assessment period in which there is a profit. The loss is deducted from your self-employed earnings worked out as above after tax, NI contributions and pension contributions are deducted. If there is not enough profit to use up the whole loss, the amount left over (the 'unused loss') is carried forward.[39] If there are unused losses to apply from more than one assessment period, these are deducted in order, starting with the earliest. Losses from a previous UC award are offset against profits in a new award if the break in your claims is no more than six months. However, losses from months between awards cannot be offset unless you have made a UC claim for those months.

***Example***

Daisy is a self-employed gardener. Business is slow in the winter. For the assessment periods ending:

- 28 February, she receives £300 cash from customers, pays £600 for new equipment, has travel expenses of £100, pays no tax or NI and pays £50 into her pension. Her self-employed earnings are nil and she has a loss of £400 (£300 – £600 – £100);
- 28 March, she receives £300 cash from customers, has travel expenses of £100, pays no tax or NI and pays £50 into her pension. Before offsetting her losses, her self-employed earnings are £150 (£300 – £100 – £50). She uses up £150 of her £400 loss from the previous month, giving self-employed earnings of nil and leaving £250 unused losses to carry forward;
- 28 April, she receives £1,700 cash from customers, has travel expenses of £200, pays no tax or NI and pays £50 into her pension. Before offsetting her losses, her self-employed earnings are £1,450 (£1,700 – £200 – £50). She uses up the remaining £250 unused losses, giving self-employed earnings of £1,200.

(In February and March, when Daisy's earnings are below the set minimum, she is in a 'start-up period' so the 'minimum income floor' does not apply.)

## Minimum level of earnings

If your main work is self-employment but your earnings are low, your UC may be assessed on higher earnings than you have. This is called the **'minimum income floor'** and is generally at the level of the national minimum wage for the number of hours the DWP expects you to work – usually 35 hours a week. This applies if:[40]

- you are in 'gainful self-employment' (see p132); *and*
- you are not in a 'start-up' period (see p133); *and*
- you would be subject to all work-related requirements were it not for having the minimum income floor applied. (Having the minimum income floor applied means no work-related requirements can be imposed on you.) If you are not subject to any work-related requirements (for a reason other than having the minimum income floor applied), or just subject to work-focused interviews or work preparation, your actual earnings from self-employment are taken into account, however low they are.

**If you are single** and the minimum income floor applies to you, your earnings are treated as being at the individual earnings threshold in any assessed income period in which your earned income from self-employment, together with any earnings from employment, is below this level.[41] The individual earnings threshold is the same threshold used to decide your work-related requirements (see p955), with a notional amount for tax and NI contributions deducted.

***Example***

Omari has a window cleaning business. He is single. For the current assessment period, he declares earnings of £1,000. The DWP works out Omari's minimum income floor to be £1,626 a month (35 hours a week x £12.21 x 52 ÷ 12 rounded down, less estimated £225 for notional tax and NI contributions). Omari's UC award for the assessment period is worked out on earnings of £1,626.

**If you are in a couple** and the minimum income floor applies to you, your combined earnings for the UC assessment are usually your partner's earnings added to the minimum income floor for you.

***Example***

Kathryn and Lenni are a couple. Kathryn has a dog grooming business and Lenni is a care worker. Kathryn declares self-employed earnings of £400 for the assessment period and Lenni's earnings are £1,500. The DWP works out Kathryn's minimum income floor to be £1,626 a month (35 hours a week x £12.21 x 52 ÷ 12 rounded down, less estimated £225 for notional tax and NI contributions). Their UC award is worked out on earnings of £3,126 (£1,626 for Kathryn and £1,500 for Lenni).

However, a couple cannot be treated as having combined earnings of more than a certain amount. This amount is the same as the joint earnings threshold for couples used to decide if there are any work-related requirements to fulfil (see p955), but with a notional amount for tax and NI contributions deducted.[42]

- If your actual combined earnings are above the joint earnings threshold, your actual earnings count in the UC assessment, with no minimum income floor.
- If your actual combined earnings (ie, ignoring the minimum income floor) are below the joint earnings threshold in any assessed income period, your earnings are treated as being the individual earnings threshold (see p955) less:
  - a notional amount for tax and NI contributions; *and*
  - an amount to ensure that, when added to your partner's earnings, you are not treated as having more than the joint earnings threshold.

If you are a couple but claiming as a single person (eg, because your partner is a 'person subject to immigration control'), the minimum income floor does not apply to your partner's self-employed earnings. Instead, your partner's actual earnings are combined with yours.

***Example***

Marie and Adeel are a couple. Adeel is a self-employed builder and Marie works part time in a shop. They have a two-year-old child and Marie is the 'responsible carer'. Adeel declares earnings of £1,100 and Marie £900. The DWP works out Adeel's minimum income floor to be £1,626 a month (35 hours a week x £12.21 x 52 ÷ 12 rounded down, less estimated £225 for tax and NI contributions).

Adeel and Marie's actual combined earnings are £2,000 (£1,100 + £900).

This is below their joint earnings threshold of £2,472 (£1,626 for Adeel plus £846 for Marie (16 hours a week x £12.21 x 52 ÷ 12 rounded down, with no tax or NI contribution deduction at this earnings level)).

Adding Adeel's minimum income floor to Marie's actual earnings gives £2,526 (£1,626 + £900). This is £54 above their joint earnings threshold of £2,472, so Adeel is treated as having earnings of £1,572 (£1,626 – £54). This is because Marie is earning £54 more than her earnings threshold for her expected hours.

### Gainful self-employment

When you claim UC or when you tell the DWP that you are self-employed, you are asked to attend a 'gateway' interview if you must meet all the work-related requirements. You are asked to bring evidence that you are in 'gainful self-employment'. This means that:[43]

- the self-employment is your main employment – ie, it is your only employment or, if you also work for an employer, you normally spend more hours on, or have more earnings from, your self-employment; *and*
- your earnings count as self-employed earnings – ie, they are not employed earnings and are from carrying out a 'trade, profession or vocation'.[44] If it is not clear whether you are employed or self-employed, the DWP may look at a number of factors, including whether you pay your own tax, whether your work is supervised and whether you can decide your own hours;[45] *and*

- your self-employment is 'organised, developed, regular and carried on in expectation of profit' – eg, whether you work for financial gain, how many hours you do, whether you have a business plan or have taken steps to get work, what work is arranged, whether you are registered as self-employed with HMRC and whether you advertise your business.[46]

2

### *Self-employment and sickness*

The DWP may decide that you are in gainful self-employment even though you are off sick and unable to do any work, or you currently have no income at all from your business. The DWP views short-term illness (such as colds, flu, strains and sprains) as part of the normal pattern of self-employment which you should plan for, and does not change your expected hours or minimum income floor.[47] If it is a long-term condition (or develops into one), and you provide medical evidence, your expected hours can be reduced to a level that is reasonable, thereby reducing the minimum income floor. This can mean, if appropriate, reducing expected hours to nil and the minimum income floor to zero for a temporary period, while you are still considered to be in gainful self-employment. For a long-term health condition which means you cannot continue your business and it is unclear when you will be able to take it up again, you may be considered to be no longer in gainful self-employment, so the minimum income floor cannot apply.

If you disagree with a decision to apply a minimum income floor, you can ask for a revision and then appeal. You may be able to argue, for example, that your self-employment is no longer organised or regular and you no longer have an expectation of profit. Bear in mind that business assets can only be disregarded for a limited time (see p406). If you are off sick and your weekly earnings are below 16 times the hourly rate of the minimum wage (see Appendix 6), send the DWP medical certificates so that it can assess whether you have limited capability for work.[48] See p901 for how your earnings affect this assessment. If you are found to have limited capability for work, only your actual earnings should be taken into account, because you should no longer be subject to all the work-related requirements (see p130).

Once the DWP decides you are in gainful self-employment, you normally have a start-up period before the minimum income floor applies (see below)

If you are not in gainful self-employment, you must still report your earnings, and these are taken into account in your UC award, but no minimum income floor is applied.

#### Start-up period

If you are self-employed, you may have 12 months, called the 'start-up period', in which the minimum income floor does not apply and your UC is worked out on your actual earnings, however low they are.[49]

The start-up period runs from the beginning of the assessment period in which the DWP decides you are in gainful self-employment. It does not only apply to new businesses. However, if you have ever had the minimum income floor applied to that self-employment before, it applies again without a start-up period. You are expected to take active steps to increase your earnings to the level of your individual earnings threshold – ie, the level that means you no longer have to meet work-related requirements (see p955). The DWP can end the start-up period if it decides you are not doing this or are no longer in gainful self-employment.

The start-up period continues to run even if your UC stops and starts during the year.[50] Although you can only have one start-up period for the same self-employment, if you begin different self-employment, you can have a new start-up period provided more than five years have passed since the start of the earlier period.

## Running your business as a sole trader, partner or limited company

You are self-employed if you run your business as a sole trader or in a partnership. Your self-employed earnings are worked out as normal (see p128), and business assets are ignored as capital (see p157).

If, instead of being a sole trader, you run your business through a company, your income and capital are worked out in the same way as for a sole trader or partnership if you have a similar level of control in the company to that of a sole trader or a partner (but see below if the company is a property business).[51] For example, you may have your own limited company and be a director of the company. You may also be an employee of your limited company and receive dividends as a shareholder. This means that:[52]

- earnings you receive as a director or employee are taken into account as 'employed earnings'. These are usually paid through PAYE and reported to the DWP by HMRC through the 'real-time information' system;
- self-employed earnings are taken into account worked out in the usual way based on receipts into the business, deducting earnings paid to you as a director or employee as 'permitted expenses' (see p129). You should report self-employed earnings each month on your UC account;
- if this is your main employment, you count as being in 'gainful self-employment' and can be treated as having earnings at the minimum income floor if your earnings from self-employment and employment as a director or employee added together are below this level (see p130);
- the value of shares is disregarded as capital, and dividends are not taken into account as income (because income from capital that is disregarded is not in the list of income that is taken into account – see p141). Exceptionally, dividends could in reality be earnings and counted as such;[53]
- you are treated as owning the business assets or a proportion of the assets in a partnership. However, company assets used only for the business are

disregarded as capital while you are engaged in any work for the company – eg, you are not a sleeping partner doing no work in the business.[54]

A company with rental income from property in the UK or abroad is a 'property business' and treated differently from the rules above.[55] If your control of the company is like that of a sole trader or partner, the value of your shares is disregarded as capital. However, the business assets, including the property's value, count as yours and are not normally disregarded. The company's income is not treated as your self-employed earnings. Assets are only disregarded if the company is classed as 'carrying on a trade' – eg, running a hotel or bed and breakfast may be a trade, whereas letting flats may not be.[56]

The rules above do not apply if you are mainly employed under off-payroll arrangements (IR35) through an intermediary company.[57]

## Surplus earnings from employment and self-employment

If you earn above a certain threshold and your UC stops, a 'surplus earnings' amount may be carried over to a new UC claim if you claim again within six months. This applies if:[58]

- your earnings (and your partner's earnings, if you are a couple) in the assessment period in which your UC ended were above the 'relevant threshold'. Your actual self-employed earnings are included, not the minimum income floor; *and*
- you make a new claim, or the DWP treats you as claiming,[59] within six months of your previous UC entitlement – ie, the start of the new assessment period is within six months of the end of the previous one; *and*
- you have not been entitled to UC since the end of your previous award, and neither has your partner in a joint claim; *and*
- you have not experienced domestic violence or abuse in the last six months or in the six months before your previous UC ended – see p951).

The 'relevant threshold' is:

- £2,500; *plus*
- any work allowance to which you are entitled; *plus*
- maximum UC (see p66) less any income you have other than earnings, multiplied by 100 and divided by 55 (this gives the point at which your UC is reduced to nil by earnings).

The amount above this threshold is your surplus earnings. **Note:** the £2,500 figure may decrease to £300 from April 2026.[60]

If you have surplus earnings included in a new claim for UC, the amount of your award may be reduced in the first month, or you may get no UC. The amount of surplus earnings is recalculated each time you claim over the six months by adding your actual earnings to the surplus from the last claim. Any amount above the relevant threshold becomes the new surplus, which is again added to your actual earnings the next time you claim. This means that if your actual earnings drop below the relevant threshold and you make a new claim, the surplus goes down. If the first reclaim is unsuccessful, you can claim again in the following month(s) until you become entitled. Once the six-month period is over, any remaining surplus is ignored.

Normally, to become entitled to UC again without delay, you should claim as soon as your earnings are below the relevant threshold because the surplus does not decrease until a claim is actually made. However, in practice, the DWP usually treats you as making a claim on the first day of each assessment period after your entitlement ended for up to five months, so surplus earnings can decrease each month until your UC award can start again automatically.[61] Bear in mind that the surplus can also increase if you claim or are treated as claiming again when your earnings are still above the threshold.

If you separate from your partner, any surplus earnings from a previous joint claim are usually shared equally in a new single claim, but if an equal share is not reasonable, ask the DWP to change it.

***Examples***

Laura and Leo claimed UC jointly when Leo had to stop work because of ill health. Laura works part time and earns £600 a month. Their maximum UC as a couple with a housing costs element is £1,000 a month. Leo has now been dismissed from employment. His final earnings of £8,000, including pay in lieu of notice and holiday pay, are paid in May and their UC award ends.

- The relevant threshold is £4,318.18 (£1,000 maximum UC x 100 ÷ 55 = £1,818 + £2,500). Surplus earnings are therefore £4,281.82 (£8,600 actual earnings minus the relevant threshold of £4,318.18).
- In June, their income is still above maximum UC so it is too high for an award of UC (£4,281.82 surplus earnings plus £600 Laura's earnings = £4,881.82 x 55 per cent = £2,685). Surplus earnings of £563.64 (£4,881.82 minus the relevant threshold of £4,318.18) are carried forward.
- In July, their income is now below their maximum UC of £1,000 (£563.64 surplus earnings plus £600 Laura's earnings = £1,163.64 x 55 per cent = £640). They are awarded UC of £360 (£1,000 maximum UC minus £640 earnings). There are no more surplus earnings to carry forward.

## 4. **Other income**

Only certain specified types of income, other than earnings, are taken into account for universal credit (UC). These are listed on p125 and explained in more detail below. This kind of income reduces your UC pound for pound. Any other income is ignored.

## Benefits

Some benefits are taken into account as income; others are disregarded.

### Benefits that are taken into account

The following benefits count in full:[62]

- carer's allowance (CA) – but not CA supplement in Scotland;
- carer support payment (in Scotland);
- employment and support allowance (ESA);
- industrial injuries benefits, except constant attendance allowance and exceptionally severe disablement allowance, which are disregarded;
- jobseeker's allowance (JSA);
- maternity allowance;
- retirement pensions;
- severe disablement allowance;
- widow's pension and widowed parent's allowance;
- foreign social security benefits and state retirement pensions that are similar to those listed above;[63]
- an overpayment of income support (IS), income-based JSA (not joint-claim JSA), income-related ESA or housing benefit (HB) if you are not entitled to that benefit and the overpayment falls within a UC assessment period.[64]

Statutory sick pay, statutory maternity pay, statutory adoption pay, statutory paternity pay, statutory shared parental pay, statutory parental bereavement pay and statutory neonatal care pay are treated as earnings and so may benefit from the work allowance.

### Benefits that are not taken into account

All other benefits are ignored – eg:

- adult disability payment (in Scotland);
- armed forces independence payment;
- attendance allowance;
- bereavement support payment;
- Best Start grant (in Scotland);
- CA supplement (in Scotland);
- child benefit;
- child disability payment (in Scotland);
- child winter heating payment (in Scotland);
- disability living allowance;
- funeral support payment (in Scotland);

- guaranteed income payment and surviving guaranteed income payment under the Armed Forces Compensation Scheme;
- guardian's allowance;
- HB if you are in specified or temporary accommodation (see p183);
- industrial injuries constant attendance allowance and exceptionally severe disablement allowance;
- pension age disability payment (in Scotland);
- pension age winter heating payment (in Scotland)
- personal independence payment;
- Scottish adult disability living allowance;
- Scottish child payment;
- short-term assistance (in Scotland);
- social fund payments;
- two-week run-on of IS, income-based JSA and income-related ESA (see p23);
- war disablement pension;
- war widow's, widower's or surviving civil partner's pensions;
- winter heating payment (in Scotland);
- young carer grant (in Scotland).

## Maintenance payments

Maintenance for a child is ignored completely.

Any maintenance for you or your partner made by your or your partner's spouse/civil partner or former spouse/civil partner under a court order or a maintenance agreement counts in full as income.

If a former partner makes payments direct to a third party (eg, your mortgage lender), this should not count as your income.[65] However, if there is income available to you that you choose not to access, you may be treated as having it under the 'notional income' rules (see p142).

If you *pay* maintenance to a former partner or a child not living with you, your payments are not disregarded when working out your income for UC.

## Student loans and grants

For the special rules on the treatment of student loans, grants and other student support, see Chapter 37.

## Employment and training schemes

The following payments from employment or training programmes under section 2 of the Employment and Training Act 1973 or section 2 of the Enterprise and New Towns (Scotland) Act 1990 are taken into account:[66]

- those made as a substitute for UC – eg, a training allowance;

- those intended for certain living costs. Payments for food, ordinary clothing or footwear, fuel, rent or other housing costs, including council tax, are all taken into account.



All other payments are disregarded – eg, travel expenses, childcare expenses and special needs payments.

## Occupational and personal pensions and annuities

The following income is taken into account:[67]

- an occupational pension;
- income from a personal pension;
- income from a retirement annuity contract (including an annuity purchased for you or transferred to you on divorce);
- payments from a former employer for early retirement on the grounds of ill health or disability, unless this was under a court order or settlement of a claim;
- an overseas pension;
- a Civil List Act pension;
- payment under an equity release scheme. This provides regular payments from a loan secured on your home;
- payments from the Financial Assistance Scheme and periodic payments from the Pension Protection Fund (these help some people with underfunded occupational schemes whose employer has gone out of business).

See p144 if you are over pension age and have not drawn your pension. If you are under pension age, UC is not affected if you choose not to draw a pension

DWP guidance says that the full amount should be taken into account before any deduction for income tax.[68] Income from an annuity is taken into account, except income from an annuity bought from personal injury compensation, which is ignored.[69] An annuity is usually when you pay a lump sum to an insurance company, often on retirement, with the capital built up in your personal pension, which then pays you an income for the rest of your life. It may also be through a home income plan where the annuity is bought with a loan secured on the home.

## Insurance payments

Payments under a policy to insure against the risk of losing income due to illness, accident or redundancy are taken into account in full.[70] Mortgage payment protection insurance policies or any equivalent payments are not taken into account. If your insurance policy contains an amount for mortgage protection (sometimes called a 'mixed income protection policy'), this amount should be disregarded.[71]

## Trusts, personal injury payments and special compensation schemes

2

Income from a trust is taken into account, whether it is a discretionary trust or other type of trust, unless it is set up from personal injury compensation.[72] For more about how income and capital in a trust is treated, see p153.

If you get an amount awarded to you because of a personal injury (see p160), it can be disregarded in certain circumstances.[73]

- If you receive the compensation in regular payments, they are disregarded as income.
- If the compensation is in a trust, both the capital value of the trust and any income from it are ignored. For more about how payments from personal injury trusts are treated, see p159.
- If the compensation was used to buy an annuity, payments under the annuity are ignored.
- If the compensation is administered by the court on your behalf or can only be used by direction of the court, the capital is ignored, and regular payments are disregarded as income.
- If the compensation is not used in one of the above ways, it is disregarded as capital for 12 months. This gives you a chance to put it in a trust or buy an annuity.

Regular payments from specified compensation schemes are disregarded as income and lump sums are disregarded indefinitely – eg, from infected blood schemes (see p159).

## Income from capital

If you have capital over £16,000, you are not entitled to UC. If your capital is below this level, it can affect the amount of income taken into account. This is either because you have actual income from the capital, such as income from a trust, or because it is assumed that the capital gives you a certain amount of income.

### Assumed monthly income from capital

If your capital is over £6,000 but not more than £16,000, you are treated as having some income from it. This 'assumed monthly income', often called 'tariff income', is set at the rate of £4.35 a month for every £250, or part of £250, between £6,000.01 and £16,000.[74]

***Example***

Andrea and Matteo have savings of £7,000. This is above the £6,000 limit, so they are treated as having an income of £17.40 a month from their savings (4 x £4.35).

Some capital is disregarded when working out how much capital you have (see p150 and p154). You are not treated as having an assumed monthly income from disregarded capital.[75]

2

## Rental and other income from capital

If your capital is treated as giving you tariff income, any actual income you have from the same capital is treated as part of your capital from the day it is due to be paid to you.[76] For example, if you own a property other than the home in which you live, rent is taken into account not as income but as capital and added to the capital value of the property itself (see also p142). However, if the property's value can be disregarded (see p154), there is no tariff income, which means the rental income is also ignored.[77] Normally, renting out property is not classed as 'carrying on a trade' so rental income is not self-employed earnings.[78]

*Example*

Bashir owns a flat that he rents out for £1,000 a month, which he uses to pay the mortgage. He does not live in the flat himself so the rent he gets does not count as income for UC but is added to his capital. The flat is valued at £100,000 (after deducting 10 per cent for expenses of sale), but only £7,000 counts as capital once his outstanding mortgage is deducted. He has an assumed income of £34.80 (£7,000 + £1,000 = £8,000, £4.35 for each £250 above £6,000 is 8 x £4.35 = £34.80).

Actual income from an annuity and from a trust is taken into account, unless the income is disregarded because the annuity or trust is from personal injury compensation (see p139 and p140). In these two cases, the capital is not treated as giving you any assumed monthly income.[79] See p140 for how trusts are treated.

## Sports awards

A sports award from UK Sport out of National Lottery funds for living expenses is taken into account. This covers food, ordinary clothing and footwear, fuel, rent, housing costs and council tax for you, your partner or dependent child.[80] Amounts for anything else are ignored – eg, sportswear

## Specified miscellaneous income

Miscellaneous income taken into account is unearned income that is taxable under the HMRC 'sweep-up' provisions in Part 5 of the Income Tax (Trading and Other Income) Act 2005 – eg:[81]

- copyright royalties;
- income from films and sound recordings;
- income from estates in administration.

## Other income

Only income specified in the rules and described above can affect your UC. Any other kind of income is ignored – eg:

- adoption allowances, fostering allowances, child arrangement order payments and kinship care payments. Foster carers for children and young people are not treated as self-employed for UC, and therefore do not need to report their fostering allowances and fees as self-employed earnings. However, paid carers of adults (shared lives carers) are treated as self-employed and must declare payments and expenses;[82]
- local welfare assistance (see p770), including household support fund payments and 'thank you' payments under the Homes for Ukraine scheme;
- mortgage protection policy payments;
- payments to third parties – eg, if a relative pays your phone bill for you;
- rental income from a room you let in your own home.[83] This is because actual income that comes from capital that is disregarded (the value of the home you live in is disregarded) is not in the list of income that is taken into account. If you are a tenant and rent out a spare room to a subtenant or boarder, the rent is ignored, but see p109 if it is not a commercial arrangement – eg, they are a friend or relative.[84] However, if you rent out a property that you do not live in, the capital value of that property is taken into account and the rent is treated as capital, not as income. This is because actual income that comes from capital that is *not* disregarded is generally treated as capital (see p141);
- strike pay from a trade union (see p891);[85]
- support from a charity;
- voluntary payments – eg, if a relative gives you regular money. However, if it is voluntary maintenance for you (rather than for a child, which is always ignored) from a separated or former spouse or civil partner, this is taken into account.

# 5. Notional income

In some circumstances, you can be treated as having income you do not actually have. This is called 'notional income'. You may be treated as having notional income if:

- you deliberately reduce your earnings in order to claim, or increase the amount of, universal credit (UC); *or*
- you work free of charge or for less than the going rate; *or*
- you fail to apply for available income.

## Deliberately getting rid of income

If you deliberately reduce your earnings from employment or self-employment in order to claim UC or increase the amount you get, you are treated as though you still have that income.[86] In particular, this applies if you got UC, or more UC, and the DWP believes this was a foreseeable result and was what you intended. Even if your employer has arranged for you to lose income, you may still be treated as though you had the income if you or your employer intended you to get UC, or more UC, by doing so.

This rule does not apply to other kinds of income, but there is a similar rule about failing to apply for income that is available to you (see below).

## Cheap or unpaid labour

If you are doing work free of charge or for less than the going rate (eg, you are working for a relative), you are treated as though you had earnings that would be reasonable for that work.[87] The comparison is with what the pay would be for similar work in the same location.

You are not treated as having more income than you receive for that work if:[88]

- the person cannot afford to pay you, or pay you more; *or*
- you work for a charitable or voluntary organisation or as a volunteer, and it is accepted that it is reasonable for you to give your services free of charge or at less than the going rate; *or*
- you are on a government-approved employment or training programme; *or*
- you are a service user who is being consulted about the provision of services by certain public bodies.

## Failing to apply for income

If you fail to apply for income that would be available to you if you applied for it, you are treated as having that income.[89]

However, you cannot be treated as having another benefit that you have not applied for, with the exception of retirement pension.

If you are over pension age (ie, you are getting UC because your partner is under pension age), you may be treated as having pension income even though you have not applied for it. If you are under pension age, you can choose not to apply for pension income without your UC award being affected (see below).

This rule does not apply to earnings from employment or self-employment.

### Deferring a state pension

If you are over pension age and defer your state pension, retirement pension, graduated retirement benefit or any shared additional pension paid on divorce, you are treated as having that income for UC. However, a deferred or unclaimed pension does not count as notional income for 12 assessment periods if you are over pension age and were previously entitled to working tax credit (WTC) and claimed UC under managed migration.[90]

The amount that counts is the pension to which you would expect to be entitled, less any overlapping benefit you get – eg, carer's allowance. To account for the time it can take to process claims, you are only treated as having this income from the date you could expect to get it were you to make a claim.

### Leaving funds in an occupational or personal pension

Although you can usually choose to take some or all of your occupational or personal pension from age 55, your UC is not affected if you do not, unless you are over pension age.[91]

If you are over pension age, the following applies:

- You are treated as having income from an occupational pension you have elected to defer beyond the scheme's retirement age,[92] as though you had claimed it. The time it might take to process it is taken into account, and any overlapping benefit is deducted.
- If you have a defined contribution occupational or personal pension, you are generally expected to buy an annuity or take the equivalent income that would be payable through an annuity.[93] If you leave funds in your pension pot, you are treated as having notional income based on the annuity those funds could yield. If you take one or more lump sums from your pension pot, these count as capital and notional income is worked out based on what is left in your pension pot.

However, a deferred or unclaimed pension does not count as notional income for 12 assessment periods if you are over pension age and were previously entitled to WTC and claimed UC under managed migration.[94]

See p139 for how pension payments are treated.

## 6. Working out monthly income

Universal credit (UC) is paid in arrears for the previous monthly assessment period (see p39). Awards are worked out month by month. Your award is then adjusted as your earnings or other income increase or decrease, but always for a whole assessment period.[95] UC awards are not adjusted for income changes part way through the monthly assessment period. See p53 for reporting changes in your earnings and when this affects your award.

**Note:** if you transfer to UC under 'managed migration' (see p29), when calculating the 'transitional element', the DWP may make certain assumptions about your earnings and other income instead of following the usual rules for working out how much income to take into account (see p80).

## Earnings

When you first claim, the DWP can make a decision on whether you qualify for UC based on an estimate of your earnings.[96] At the end of the first assessment period, your award is based on your actual earnings instead.[97]

The amount of earnings used to work out your UC award for each assessment period is based on the actual amount you received in that assessment period.[98] There is no averaging from one month to the next.

***Wage cycles***

You may find that two lots of monthly wages fall into one assessment period – eg, in a month when you are paid early because the usual payday falls on a weekend. To avoid your UC payments changing, the two payments of wages can be allocated over two assessment periods.[99] This should happen automatically.[100]

However, if you are paid weekly, fortnightly or four-weekly, your regular pay is not reallocated when an 'extra' payday falls in an assessment period. Your UC reduces or ends in these months. If your UC ends, reclaim in the following month if your UC award does not start up again automatically.

**Note:** cases about four-weekly and fortnightly payments that were appealed have held that the DWP is correct to take pay into account when it is actually paid, even if that means counting two (or more) lots of pay in one assessment period or that wages are too low in other months to be exempt from the benefit cap.[101]

**If you are employed**, your employer must report your earnings to HMRC every time you are paid. This is called 'real-time information'. Usually, the employed earnings figure used in the UC assessment is taken from the amount in the report(s) received by the DWP in that assessment period.[102] If your employer is late in paying you, the payment counts when it is reported, not when it was due to be paid to you.[103] However, if your employer is late in reporting earnings to HMRC, the DWP can take the payment into account in the assessment period in which you received it instead of when it was reported.[104]

Instead of using a real-time information report, the DWP must decide the amount of earnings using other evidence if:[105]

- the DWP thinks your employer is unlikely to provide an accurate report on time;
- no information is received from HMRC in an assessment period – eg, because your employer has not sent a report to HMRC or HMRC has not passed it on;
- the information in the report is wrong.

If you think the DWP has used the wrong earnings figure or the real-time information report is wrong, send any evidence you have of the correct amount (eg, wage slips or bank statements) and ask for a formal decision. You can then ask for a revision and appeal.[106] However, unless the DWP thinks it is a failure or mistake, if no real-time information report is received, you are simply treated as having no earnings for that assessment period.

**If you are self-employed**, you must report your earnings every month. Your UC award is based on the actual amount received in the assessment period and the actual amounts paid – eg, tax and expenses. How to work out your earnings for the assessment period is explained on p128.

If you are asked to self-report, you must act quickly in order for your earnings to be taken into account in the same assessment period as you received them. If you report late, the DWP can treat your earnings as received in that later period. If you fail to provide information or evidence, payment of your UC may be suspended (see p1031).

## Other income

Any other income you have that is not earnings is worked out as a monthly amount – eg:[107]

- multiply weekly payments by 52 and divide by 12;
- multiply fortnightly payments by 26 and divide by 12;
- multiply payments for four weeks by 13 and divide by 12;
- multiply payments for three months by four and divide by 12;
- a payment of income for a whole year is divided by 12.

If your income varies and there is a cycle that can be identified, take one cycle and convert this into a monthly amount. If there is no cycle to the income, it is worked out by taking three months of income, or another period if that would give a more accurate picture, and calculating an average monthly amount.

**Note:** there are different rules for working out student income (see p795).

***Example***

Lennon gets new-style employment and support allowance (ESA) of £184.10 every two weeks. The amount of ESA taken into account in his UC award is £398.88 (£184.10 x 26 ÷ 12).

If you start or stop getting any unearned income, the amount taken into account is worked out over the number of days for which the income is paid in that assessment period. For example, if ESA of £184.10 a fortnight is awarded from 18 November (giving a monthly amount of £398.88) and your assessment period runs from 29 October to 28 November, the amount taken into account for that period is £144.25 (£398.88 x 12 ÷ 365 x 11 days).

# Notes

1. **Whose income counts**
   1 s8(4)(a) WRA 2012
   2 s8(4)(b) and Sch 1 para 4(5) WRA 2012; reg 22(1) UC Regs
   3 Regs 3(3) and (6) and 22(3) UC Regs
   4 Because ss5 and 8 WRA 2012 only count income of a 'claimant' or 'joint claimants'

2. **What counts as income**
   5 s8(3) WRA 2012
   6 Reg 52 UC Regs
   7 Reg 66 UC Regs
   8 Reg 46(3) UC Regs
   9 Reg 46(4) UC Regs; para H5102 ADM

3. **Earnings**
   10 Reg 52 UC Regs
   11 Reg 2 UC Regs
   12 para H3006 ADM
   13 Reg 55(2), (4) and (4A) UC Regs; HMRC, *Employment Income Manual*, para 00520
   14 *SK and DK v SSWP (UC)* [2023] UKUT 21 (AAC), reported as [2023] AACR 5
   15 *Minter v Kingston upon Hull City Council and Potter v SSWP* [2011] EWCA Civ 1155; HMRC, *Employment Income Manual*, para 02530
   16 Reg 55(2) and (3)(a) UC Regs
   17 Part 5 Ch 2 and s336 IT(EP)A 2003
   18 Part 4 IT(EP)A 2003
   19 Regs 53(2) and 55(3)(b) UC Regs; para H3164 ADM
   20 Part 3 Chs 2-11 and Part 4 Ch 6 IT(EP)A 2003
   21 Part 4 Ch 8 IT(EP)A 2003
   22 Reg 54(1) UC Regs; *NM v SSWP* [2021] UKUT 46 (AAC)
   23 Reg 55(2) UC Regs; *RMcE v Department for Communities (UC)* [2021] NI Com 59. These are 'general earnings' under s7(3) IT(EP)A 2003 – see HMRC, *Employment Income Manual*, paras 12850 and 13874 for non-contractual pay in lieu of notice.
   24 Reg 55(2) UC Regs. These come under s401 IT(EP)A 2003 or not otherwise taxable, and are therefore not 'general earnings' under s7(3) – see HMRC, *Employment Income Manual*, paras 12960, 12965 and 13005.
   25 *DR v SSWP* [2024] UKUT 196 (AAC)
   26 Reg 55(5) UC Regs
   27 para H4010 ADM
   28 Reg 57 UC Regs
   29 Regs 54 and 57(3) UC Regs
   30 Reg 57(4) and (5) UC Regs
   31 para H4184 ADM
   32 Universal Credit Guidance, *Self-employed earnings*, v15.0, House of Commons library deposited papers, rightsnet.org.uk/resources/universal-credit-guidance
   33 Reg 58(1) UC Regs
   34 Reg 58(2) and (3) UC Regs; para H4214 ADM
   35 Reg 59(2) UC Regs
   36 Reg 58(1)(b) UC Regs
   37 Reg 59(3) and (4) UC Regs
   38 para H4241 ADM
   39 Reg 57A UC Regs
   40 Reg 62(1) and (5) UC Regs
   41 Reg 62(2) and (4) UC Regs
   42 Reg 62(3) and (4) UC Regs
   43 Reg 64 UC Regs
   44 Reg 57(1) UC Regs
   45 para H4016 ADM
   46 para H4050 ADM
   47 Universal Credit Guidance, *Periods of sickness and self-employment*, v8.0, House of Commons library deposited papers, rightsnet.org.uk/index.php/resources/universal-credit-guidance
   48 Guidance says gainfully self-employed claimants can be referred for a work capability assessment: Universal Credit Guidance, *Periods of sickness and self-employment*, v8.0, House of Commons library deposited papers, rightsnet.org.uk/index.php/resources/universal-credit-guidance
   49 Reg 63 UC Regs
   50 para H4102 (Example 2) ADM
   51 Reg 77(1) UC Regs
   52 Reg 77(2) to (4) UC Regs
   53 *HMRC v PA Holdings Ltd* [2011] EWCA Civ 1414
   54 R(IS) 13/93; R(IS) 14/98
   55 Reg 77(1), (2) and (6) UC Regs

56 The distinction between carrying on a trade and a property business is complex. See, for example, *RM v Sefton Council (HB)* [2016] UKUT 357 (AAC), reported as [2017] AACR 5 and HMRC, *Property Income Manual,* para 4300.
57 Reg 77(5) UC Regs
58 Reg 54A UC Regs
59 Reg 32A UC,PIP,JSA&ESA(C&P) Regs
60 Secretary of State determination under reg 5 The Universal Credit (Surpluses and Self-employed Losses) (Digital Service) Amendment Regulations 2015 No.345; Autumn Budget 2024, para 5.135
61 Reg 32A UC,PIP,JSA&ESA(C&P) Regs; Universal Credit Guidance, *Claim closure*, v25.0, House of Commons library deposited papers, rightsnet.org.uk/resources/universal-credit-guidance

4. **Other income**
62 Reg 66(1)(a) and (b) UC Regs; reg 25(1) UC(TP) Regs
63 *LR v SSWP (UC)* [2022] UKUT 65 (AAC)
64 Reg 10 UC(TP) Regs
65 Because there is no rule to treat payments to a third party as yours
66 Reg 66(1)(f) UC Regs
67 Regs 66(1)(la) and 67 UC Regs; reg 16 SPC Regs
68 para H5004 ADM
69 Reg 66(1)(i) UC Regs
70 Reg 66(1)(h) UC Regs
71 para H5086 ADM
72 Reg 66(1)(j) UC Regs
73 Reg 75 UC Regs
74 Reg 72(1) UC Regs
75 Reg 72(2) UC Regs
76 Reg 72(3) UC Regs
77 Regs 66 and 72 UC Regs
78 HMRC, *Property Income Manual,* para 4300 has examples of letting activity constituting a trade
79 Reg 72(2) UC Regs
80 Reg 66(1)(g) UC Regs
81 Reg 66(1)(m) UC Regs; Part 5 IT(TOI)A 2005
82 Universal Credit guidance, *Self-employed earnings,* v15.0, House of Commons library deposited papers, rightsnet.org.uk/index.php/resources/universal-credit-guidance
83 para H5112 ADM
84 para H5112 ADM
85 HMRC, *Employment Income Manual,* para 06500

5. **Notional income**
86 Reg 60(1) and (2) UC Regs
87 Reg 60(3) UC Regs
88 Reg 60(4) UC Regs
89 Reg 74 UC Regs
90 Reg 60B UC(TP) Regs
91 Parliamentary answer UIN 19835,12 December 2024, questions-statements.parliament.uk/written-questions/detail/2024-12-12/19835
92 Reg 74(4) UC Regs; reg 18(1D) SPC Regs; *BRG v SSWP (SPC)* [2014] UKUT 246 (AAC)
93 para H5172 ADM
94 Reg 60B UC(TP) Regs

6. **Working out monthly income**
95 Sch 1 paras 20-30 UC,PIP,JSA&ESA(DA) Regs
96 Reg 54(2)(a) UC Regs
97 para H3011 ADM
98 Reg 54 UC Regs
99 Reg 61(6) UC Regs
100 DWP, *Touchbase*, 27 August 2021
101 *LG v SSWP (UC)* [2021] UKUT 121 (AAC); *Pantellerisco and others v SSWP* [2021] EWCA Civ 1454; *SSWP v LM* [2023] UKUT 72 (AAC)
102 Reg 61(2)(a) UC Regs
103 *NM v SSWP* [2021] UKUT 46 (AAC)
104 Reg 61(5) UC Regs
105 Reg 61 UC Regs
106 Reg 41 UC,PIP,JSA&ESA(DA) Regs
107 Reg 73 UC Regs

# Chapter 8

# Capital

**This chapter covers:**

1. The capital limits (below)
2. Whose capital counts (p151)
3. What counts as capital (p151)
4. Disregarded capital (p154)
5. Deliberately getting rid of capital (p161)
6. How capital is valued (p164)

### Key facts

- Capital includes savings, investments, property and lump-sum payments.
- Some kinds of capital are ignored when working out your universal credit (UC) – eg, the value of the home in which you live.
- If you have more than £16,000 capital, you are not entitled to UC. However, there is a temporary exception for some people who moved to UC from tax credits.
- If you have capital above a certain amount, your UC is affected, because this is assumed to give you a certain monthly income.
- If you deliberately get rid of capital in order to get more UC, you are treated as still having it.

## 1. The capital limits

There is a lower and upper capital limit.[1]

- The lower limit is £6,000.
- The upper limit is £16,000.

If you have less than £6,000 of capital, this does not affect your benefit. If you have over £16,000 of capital, you are not entitled to universal credit (UC) (but see p150 for a temporary exception if you moved from tax credits to UC). If you have between £6,000.01 and £16,000, you may be entitled to benefit, but it is assumed that you have some income from your capital.

This assumed monthly income, often called 'tariff income' (see p140), is £4.35 a month for every £250, or part of £250, of your capital between £6,000.01 and £16,000.

When working out the value of your capital, some is disregarded (see p154). You may be treated as having capital which you do not actually have (see p161).

*Example*

Jacqueline has £7,100 savings. She is assumed to have £21.75 a month income from her savings (5 x £4.35).

## Temporary disregard after a move from tax credits to universal credit

If you were getting tax credits and had over £16,000 of capital immediately before becoming entitled to UC through 'managed migration' (see p29), the amount above £16,000 is disregarded.[2] This is called the 'transitional capital disregard'. Your UC award takes into account an assumed monthly income of £174 from your capital between £6,000 and £16,000.

The disregard lasts for up to 12 monthly assessment periods. It ends if your capital drops below £16,000 and in any of the circumstances in which someone loses a UC transitional element (see p84).[3] If your UC award ends because of earnings, the transitional capital disregard continues to apply in your next award if it begins within three months of the end of the assessment period in which your UC terminated.[4] The gap in entitlement does not count towards the maximum 12-month disregard.

*Example*

Tasie had £20,000 savings on 4 June 2024 when her child tax credit stopped and she started getting UC through managed migration. Her UC award is worked out assuming she has £174 a month income from savings (40 x £4.35) up to £16,000 and the rest of her savings are disregarded. A year later, she has had no breaks in her UC entitlement and has £19,000 savings. Without the transitional capital disregard, her capital is now over the limit and her UC ends on 4 June 2025.

To stay entitled to UC after the transitional capital disregard ends, you could consider reducing your capital to below £16,000 by repaying a debt or mortgage, but if you spend it on goods or services, you could be treated as still having it (see p161).

## 2. Whose capital counts

If you are a member of a couple (see p58), you must usually make a joint claim for universal credit (UC) and your partner's capital is added to yours when working out your entitlement (see p36).[5]

In the limited circumstances when you must make a single claim for UC despite being a member of a couple (see p36), your partner's capital (and income) is still added to yours.[6]

Your child's capital is not taken into account and does not affect your benefit.[7]

If savings or capital are in your name, it is usually assumed to be your capital. However, you may be able to show that although it is in your name, it is not your capital and you are holding it on trust for someone else – eg, a child.[8] If someone else is holding savings or capital on trust for you, even though it is not in your name, it still counts as your capital (see p152).

If savings or capital are in joint names, see p164.

## 3. What counts as capital

All your capital is taken into account, unless it is disregarded (see p154) or treated as income (see p125).

The term 'capital' is not defined. In general, it means lump-sum or one-off payments, rather than a series of payments – eg, it includes savings, property and statutory redundancy payments.[9]

Capital payments can usually be distinguished from income because they are not payable for any specified period and are not part of a regular series of payments (although capital can be paid by instalments).[10]

**Note:** some capital is treated as income (see p125) and some income is treated as capital (see p153).

### Savings

Your savings generally count as capital – eg, cash you have at home, premium bonds, shares, unit trusts and money in a bank or building society account, including in an ISA or Help to Buy ISA. The amount in an ISA usually all counts as your capital, even if you are saving for a deposit on a home or intend to use it to pay off your mortgage. However, 25 per cent of a Lifetime ISA is ignored if you are aged under 60 – ie, the government bonus.[11] If you can provide evidence to the DWP that your mortgage lender has an equitable charge on an ISA which you took out at the same time as your mortgage, the DWP may deduct the charge from the value of the ISA.[12] An ISA in your name is always your capital, so you cannot claim to be holding it on trust for someone else (eg, a child).[13]

2

If you have put aside money to pay bills, this is still counted as your capital.[14] If your savings are just below the capital limit, you could pay bills by monthly direct debit or use a budget account to keep your capital below the limit.

Income not spent by the end of the assessment period after the one in which you received it is treated as your capital.[15]

Cryptoassets (also known as cryptocurrencies – eg, bitcoin) or virtual assets are treated as capital in the same way as other investments. You are expected to provide a screenshot of your cryptoassets wallet that shows the current value.[16]

## Fixed-term investments

Fixed-term investments count as capital. However, if an investment is currently unobtainable, it may have little or no value. If you can convert the investment into a form that lets you access it, sell your interest, or raise a loan through a reputable bank using the asset as security, the amount you can get for it counts.

## Property and land

Any property or land you own counts as capital. Many types of property are disregarded (see p154). If there is doubt about who owns the property, see below.

## Ownership of capital and loans

Usually, it is clear when capital belongs to you and should be taken into account. However, it may be less clear if you are holding money for someone else or if you have been given a loan which you are expected to repay.

A loan to you usually counts as money you possess and therefore counts as capital. However, you can argue that a loan, money or other assets you hold for someone else should be disregarded if it is:

- a loan granted on condition that you only use the interest, but do not touch the capital because the capital element has never been at your disposal;[17] *or*
- money you have been given to be used for a particular purpose on condition that it must be returned if not used in that way;[18] *or*
- property you have bought on behalf of someone else who is paying the mortgage;[19] *or*
- money held in your bank account on behalf of another person, which is to be returned to them at a future date;[20] *or*
- savings from someone else's benefit paid to you as an 'appointee' – eg, your child's disability living allowance;[21] *or*
- a loan, which you are under an immediate obligation to repay;[22] *or*
- your asset but you have expressed a clear intention that it is for someone else's benefit and renounced its use for yourself;[23] *or*
- some property and you lead someone to believe that you are transferring your interest in it to them but fail to do so (eg, it is never properly conveyed) and that person acts on the belief that they own it (eg, they spend money on

repairs). You can argue the asset has been transferred and you are like a trustee.[24] This is called **'proprietary estoppel'**.



If you lend money to someone, it could still count as your 'notional capital' (see p161), depending on your reasons for lending it. You usually have a legal right to be repaid and this, in itself, could have a capital value (although the value would normally be less than the amount loaned, and could be nil if you have no expectation of getting the money back).[25]

## Trusts

Capital in a non-discretionary trust is taken into account because you can obtain the capital at any time. If this takes you over the £16,000 capital limit, you are not entitled to UC. However, if your capital is between £6,000.01 and £16,000, you are not treated as having an assumed monthly income from the capital.[26] Capital in a discretionary trust does not normally count as your capital because payments are at the discretion of the trustee and you cannot demand payment.[27]

There is no difference between a discretionary and non-discretionary trust in the way that payments to you from the trust are treated. In either case, they are taken into account. Generally, regular payments for a particular period are treated as income, and a lump sum is treated as capital.[28] If trustees of a discretionary trust choose to pay your bills direct or buy you something that is disregarded (eg, because it is a personal possession), this should not affect your benefit.

If the trust is from money for a personal injury to you or your partner, the rules are more generous (see p159).

**Note:** putting money in a discretionary trust has the advantage of the value of the trust itself being disregarded. However, if you transfer money into a trust in order to get more benefit, it can still count as yours under the notional capital rules (see p161).

## Money held by your solicitor

Money held by your solicitor normally counts as your capital. This includes compensation payments (but see p159 for when payments for personal injury are disregarded).[29] If you have had legal aid and your solicitor is holding money back while working out the statutory charge to be deducted for legal costs, it does not count as your capital.[30]

## Income treated as capital

Unless the capital is disregarded or does not give you an assumed monthly income, actual income from capital (eg, interest on your savings, share dividends or rent from a property that is not your home) is treated as capital from the day it is due to be paid.[31] This avoids any double counting of income from capital that is also treated as giving you an assumed monthly income (see p140).

2

*Example*

Bradley has £6,800 savings, which gives him interest of £8 a month. His UC assessment takes into account an assumed monthly income from his savings of £17.40 (£4.35 a month for each £250, or part of £250, above the £6,000 lower capital limit). The actual £8 interest is added to his capital.

# 4. Disregarded capital

## Your home

If you own the home in which you live, its value is ignored.[32] This disregard can continue to apply if you are temporarily away from home.[33]

If you own more than one property, only the one you occupy is disregarded under this rule.[34]

Exceptionally, two separate properties can be regarded as a single home, as though one were an annexe of the other, if you personally (rather than a member of your family) normally occupy both properties.[35] This is more likely if you have a large family, but you could argue that it should apply if neither property on its own meets your family's needs – eg, if you are a carer living between two properties.[36]

Your home can include croft land and smallholdings if they cannot be sold separately.[37]

### When the value of the property is disregarded

The value of the property can be disregarded, even if you do not normally live in it, in the following circumstances.

- **If you have left your former home following a relationship breakdown**, the value of the property is ignored for six months from the date you left or longer if it is reasonable to do so. It may also be disregarded for longer if any of the steps listed below are taken. If it is occupied by your former partner who is a lone parent, its value is ignored for as long as they live there.[38]
- **If you have sought legal advice or have started legal proceedings to occupy property as your home**, its value is ignored for six months from the date you first took either of these steps.[39] The six months can be extended if it is reasonable to do so.
- **If you are taking reasonable steps to dispose of a property**, its value is ignored for six months from the date you first took such steps (which may be before you claim benefit).[40] Advertising at an unrealistic sale price does not

count as 'reasonable', but placing the property with an estate agent or contacting a possible buyer should,[41] as might taking ancillary proceedings to resolve financial issues in a divorce.[42] The disregard can continue beyond six months, even for years – eg, if a court orders that a former matrimonial home should not be sold until the children are grown up.[43] Taking a property off the market and putting it on again does not necessarily begin a new six-month period, but it may do if the second attempt to sell is quite separate.[44]



- **If you are carrying out essential repairs or alterations which are needed so that you can occupy a property as your home**, the value of the property is ignored for six months from the date you began the repairs.[45] 'Steps' may include applying for planning permission or a grant or loan to make the property habitable, employing an architect or finding someone to do the work.[46] If you cannot move into the property within that period because the work is not finished, its value can be disregarded for as long as is necessary to allow the work to be carried out.
- **If you have acquired a property and intend to live in it as your home but have not yet moved in,** its value is ignored for six months from the date you acquired it, or for longer if that is reasonable.[47]
- **If you sell your home and intend to use the proceeds to buy another home,** the capital is ignored for six months from the date you received the money.[48] This also applies even if you do not own your home but, for a price, you surrender your tenancy rights to a landlord.[49] If you need longer to complete a purchase, your capital can continue to be ignored if it is reasonable to do so. You do not need to have decided within the six months to buy a particular property. It is sufficient if you intend to use the proceeds to buy some other home within the six-month (or extended) period,[50] although your 'intention' must involve more than a mere 'hope' or 'aspiration'.[51] There must be an element of 'certainty' that you may be able to show by evidence of a practical commitment to another purchase, although this need not involve any binding obligation.[52] If you intend to use only part of the proceeds to buy another home, only that part is disregarded even if, for example, you have put the rest of the money aside to renovate your new home.[53]
- **If your home is damaged or you lose it altogether**, an insurance policy payment is ignored for six months from the date it is received, or longer if it is reasonable to do so.[54]
- **If you have taken out a loan or been given money for the express purpose of essential repairs or alterations to your home,** it is ignored for six months, or longer if it is reasonable to do so.[55] If it is a condition of the loan that it must be returned if the improvements are not carried out, you could argue that it should be ignored altogether.[56]
- **If you have deposited money with a housing association as a condition of occupying your home**, this is ignored indefinitely.[57] If money that was deposited for this purpose is now to be used to buy another home, this is

ignored for six months, or longer if reasonable, in order to allow you to complete the purchase.[58]

- **Grants made to buy a home** are ignored for six months, or longer if it is reasonable to do so.[59]



When considering whether it is reasonable to extend the disregard period, all the circumstances should be considered – eg, your personal circumstances, any efforts made by you to use, or dispose of, the home[60] and the general state of the property market. In practice, periods of around 18 months are not considered unusual.

**Note:** it is possible for property to be ignored under more than one of the above paragraphs together or in succession.[61]

Rent that you receive from property which is disregarded is ignored (see p141).

## The home of a partner, former partner or relative

The value of a home is ignored if it is occupied as the home of:[62]

- a close relative who is over pension age or has limited capability for work; *or*
- your former partner from whom you are not estranged but you are living apart (so are not treated as still living together or living in the same household for universal credit (UC) purposes) – eg, if one of you is living in a care home; *or*
- your former partner from whom you are estranged and who is a lone parent. If your former partner is not a lone parent, the value of the home is ignored for six months for UC from the date you ceased to live in the home.

***Definitions***

**'Close relative'** includes a parent, son, daughter, step-parent, stepson, stepdaughter, parent-in-law, son-in-law, daughter-in-law, sibling, or a partner of any of these people.[63] It also includes half-siblings and adopted children.[64]

You are **'estranged'** if you are living apart because your relationship has broken down, even if the separation is amicable.[65]

**'Lone parent'** is not defined. You could argue for a broad definition – eg, including shared care arrangements and irrespective of which parent receives child benefit.

## Personal possessions

All personal possessions, including jewellery, furniture or cars, are ignored.[66] A personal possession has been defined as any physical asset not used for business purposes, other than land.[67] However, a home you own but do not live in is not usually considered a personal possession and counts as capital (see p154). Personal possessions are not ignored if you have bought them in order to be able to claim or get more benefit. In this case, the sale value, rather than the purchase price, is counted as actual capital and the difference is treated as notional capital (see p161).[68]

An insurance payment for damage to, or the loss of, any personal possessions, which is to be used for their repair or replacement, is ignored for six months, or longer if reasonable.[69]



## Business assets

If you are self-employed, your business assets are ignored for as long as you continue to work in that business.[70] Business assets include items like machinery, vehicles, fixtures and cash in the bank.[71] See p134 if you run your business through a company rather than as a sole trader or partnership.

If you cannot work because you are sick or incapacitated, the assets are disregarded for six months from when you stopped work if you can reasonably expect to work in the business again when you recover, or for longer if reasonable in the circumstances.[72]

If you stop working in the business, you are allowed six months (or longer if reasonable) to sell these assets without their value affecting your UC, provided you are taking reasonable steps to sell them.[73]

If the purchase value of an asset was deducted as an expense from your earnings and you later sell or stop using the asset for the business, the sale price (or market value if you were to sell) is treated as a receipt when working out your earnings (see p128).[74]

Assets may be used partly for business and partly for private use. They are disregarded if used 'wholly or mainly' for the business.[75] For example, arguably, the value of a car would be disregarded if you used it for the business more than half the time, and for personal use the rest of the time. Personal and business assets can be difficult to tell apart – eg, if you do not have a separate business account. The test is whether the assets are 'part of the fund employed and risked in the business'.[76]

The business must be one in which you are 'carrying on a trade, profession or vocation'. Letting properties is not usually classed as carrying on a trade, so the value of property that you rent out is not ignored as a business asset.[77]

## Personal pension schemes

The value of the right to receive an occupational or personal pension is ignored.[78] The value of a fund held in a personal pension scheme is also ignored as capital.[79] Although you can usually choose to take some, or all, of your occupational or personal pension at age 55, your UC is not affected if you do not. Any regular withdrawals count in full as unearned income, and lump sum withdrawals count as capital. However, if you are over pension age, you are usually expected to take your pension and are treated as having a notional income if you do not take it all (see p144).

2

## Insurance policy and annuity surrender values

The surrender value currently held in a life assurance policy is ignored.[80] Some investments include an element of life insurance – eg, endowment policies. If the policy terms include how the payment on death is calculated, the whole investment is ignored.[81] However, you cannot choose to put money in such an investment in order to increase your benefit entitlement, because you are likely to be caught by the notional capital rule if you do (see p161).

## Benefits

### Arrears of benefits and tax credits

Arrears of the following benefits and tax credits, and any compensation you get for late payment of these, are ignored for 12 months from when you receive them, or longer in some cases of arrears of £5,000 or more (see below):[82]

- UC;
- any benefit that is ignored as income for UC (see p137);
- income support (IS), income-based jobseeker's allowance (JSA), income-related employment and support allowance (ESA), housing benefit (HB), child tax credit (CTC) and working tax credit (WTC);
- compensation for lost or delayed new-style ESA because of a DWP error;[83]
- maternity allowance if you received the arrears either during the current UC award or while you were getting IS, income-based JSA, income-related ESA, HB, pension credit (PC), CTC or WTC, they were disregarded in that award and you became entitled to UC within a month of that award ending.

Arrears of £5,000 or more continue to be ignored beyond 12 months to the end of the UC award in which you received them if they are:

- paid to compensate for an official error or error of law and they would be disregarded from an award of another means-tested benefit under the rules described on p408 or p432;
- compensation for lost or delayed new-style ESA because of a DWP error.[84]

In either of the two bullets above, if the arrears were ignored in an earlier award of IS, income-based JSA, income-related ESA, HB, PC, CTC or WTC, they continue to be ignored in a UC award that starts within a month of the earlier award ending.

***Example***

Evan is on income-related ESA. On 1 May 2025, he gets a payment of £12,000 arrears of ESA due to him because of an official error. In June 2025, he claims UC and his ESA ends. The £12,000 arrears continue to be disregarded in his UC for as long as the award continues.

**Note**: although arrears are ignored as capital, you may have been paid more UC or other means-tested benefit than you would have been entitled to if benefit had been paid on time. The DWP may deduct the difference from the arrears of the delayed benefit. Otherwise, if the arrears are not reduced, the overpayment is recoverable (see p1062).

### Other benefits and payments

- The initial lump sum of bereavement support payment is ignored for 12 months from the date you receive it. Arrears of monthly payments to a surviving cohabiting partner whose partner died before 9 February 2023 are ignored for 12 months from the date you receive them.[85]
- Widowed parent's allowance arrears that include a period before 9 February 2023 paid to a surviving cohabiting partner are ignored for 12 months from the date you receive them.[86] Although ignored as capital, the arrears can also count as income for the period they cover and reduce entitlement to any UC or other means-tested benefit paid in the same period. The DWP can recover the overpayment from you or deduct it from the arrears (see p1062).
- Social fund payments and, in Scotland, Best Start grant and funeral support payment, are ignored for 12 months from the date you receive them.[87]
- Young carer grant winter heating payment, pension age winter heating payment and child winter heating payment (in Scotland) are ignored for 52 weeks from the date you receive them.[88]
- Any 'transitional SDP amount' of UC (see p27) paid as a lump sum in a UC award that started before 27 January 2021 is ignored for 12 months from the date of payment or until your award ends, if this is longer.[89]
- Cost of living payments are disregarded indefinitely.[90] These were payments of up to £650 in 2022/23 and £900 in 2023/24 if you were entitled to UC or other means-tested benefits, and an additional £150 in 2022/23 and 2023/24 if you were entitled to a disability benefit. These payments are disregarded from your capital for as long as they remain unspent.[91]

## Personal injury payments and special compensation schemes

If you have money in a trust or annuity from a personal injury to you, the value of the trust and any income from the trust or annuity is disregarded. A lump sum from the trust or annuity is, however, taken into account as capital.[92] It should not affect your UC if the trustees give you regular, or even annual, payments, pay your bills instead of giving you a lump sum or buy you something that would be disregarded because it is a personal possession – eg, furniture or a car. If an award is administered by a court (eg, the Court of Protection), its value and income from it is also disregarded. A payment for personal injury to you that is not in a trust is disregarded for 12 months from the date it is paid to you. If the personal injury is to your partner and they have since died, you cannot carry over the remainder of the 12-month disregard, or if the payment is in a trust, it is no longer ignored.[93]

2

***Definitions***

**'Personal injury'** includes not only accidental and criminal injuries, but also any disease and injury as a result of a disease.[94] An employment tribunal award or settlement for psychiatric injury counts as personal injury but not an award for injury to feelings.[95]

**'Sum awarded'** includes any amounts as a result of personal injury – eg, for loss of earnings.[96]

**'Trust'**. Any money in a trust 'derived from' compensation for personal injury to you is disregarded irrespective of the type of trust.[97]

Personal injury payments include compensation from the Criminal Injuries Compensation Scheme.[98]

## Special compensation schemes

Lump-sum payments of capital you receive from specific schemes and certain schemes approved by the government are ignored indefinitely, including:[99]

- the National Emergencies Trust;
- the Windrush Compensation Scheme;
- the Child Migrants Trust (for children subjected to migration programmes before 1971);
- the Victims of Overseas Terrorism Compensation Scheme;
- payments for historic institutional child abuse in the UK;
- payments from an infected blood scheme;
- payments, including from court settlements, for people affected by the 2017 fire at Grenfell Tower;
- Post Office compensation payments for Horizon system failings;
- vaccine damage payments under the Vaccine Damage Payments Act 1979;
- payments from the Ministry of Defence's LGBT Financial Recognition Scheme;
- victims' payments under the Troubles Permanent Disablement Payment Scheme.[100]

Regular payments from these schemes are ignored as income.

If you have other capital and a disregarded payment in the same account, it should be accepted that money is withdrawn from the other capital before the disregarded payment, unless evidence shows otherwise.[101]

## Funeral plan payments

The value of any funeral plan contract is ignored indefinitely.[102] A funeral plan contract is a contract under which:

- you make payments to another person to ensure you are provided with a funeral; *and*
- the sole purpose of the plan is to provide a funeral.



### Social services and community care payments

The following payments from a local authority are ignored for 12 months:[103]

- payments for children, young people and families made under: sections 17, 23B, 23C or 24A of the Children Act 1989; section 12 of the Social Work (Scotland) Act 1968; sections 29 or 30 of the Children (Scotland) Act 1995; or sections 37, 38, 109, 110, 114 or 115 of the Social Services and Well-being (Wales) Act 2014;
- payments to meet welfare needs related to old age or disability, unless they are for certain living expenses (eg, food, fuel, clothing, footwear, rent, housing costs or council tax) for you, your partner or dependent child;
- local welfare assistance (see p770) to meet an immediate short-term need or establish or maintain a settled home in certain circumstances. These include household support fund payments and 'thank you' payments under the Homes for Ukraine scheme.

See p891 if you or your partner are involved in a trade dispute.

### Miscellaneous payments

The following payments are disregarded:

- 20 per cent of money in a tax-free childcare account (see p779);[104]
- any payments made to holders of the Victoria or George Cross.[105]

## 5. Deliberately getting rid of capital

If you deliberately get rid of capital in order to claim or increase your universal credit (UC), you are treated as still having it.[106] This is called 'notional capital'. Notional capital counts in the same way as the capital you do have.

You are not treated as having deprived yourself of capital if:[107]

- you pay off or reduce a debt which you owe; *or*
- you pay for goods or services, if the purchase was reasonable in the circumstances of your case.

**Note:** if you are treated as having notional capital, a 'diminishing notional capital rule' (see p163) may be applied so that the value of the notional capital you are treated as having is considered to reduce over time.

2

## Paying off debts and bankruptcy

You are not treated as having deprived yourself of capital if you repay or reduce a debt that you owe – eg, you could repay a credit card debt, mortgage, overdraft or loan. It does not matter if the terms of the debt allow you to repay later. However, you may be asked for evidence that you owed the debt, so if you repay a loan from a family member, it may be harder to show that the debt existed.

If you are declared bankrupt, you cannot spend your capital without court approval and cannot usually be considered to have deprived yourself of it if you do. Capital you have (but cannot spend) does not count for benefit purposes from the date of the bankruptcy order.[108] However, if you deliberately go bankrupt or do not take reasonable steps to discharge the bankruptcy in order to get benefit, your capital can still count as notional capital.

## Paying for goods and services

If you spend money on goods and services, you are not treated as having deprived yourself of capital if the purchase was reasonable. There is no list of items that are allowed or excluded – it depends on the circumstances. However, you are less likely to be caught by this rule if you spend money on day-to-day necessities or replacing household goods, and more likely to be caught if you choose to buy something like an expensive holiday.

## Intention to claim or increase universal credit

If you have spent your capital in some way other than paying off a debt or paying for goods and services that are regarded as reasonable, you are only treated as having deprived yourself of capital if you intended to claim UC or increase the amount of UC.

Relevant factors include the following.

- At the time you used your capital, how much choice did you have in spending the money in the way you did?[109]
- How long was it before you needed to claim UC? The longer it was, the less likely it is that you spent the capital in order to get UC. However, there is no set safe period after which you can claim UC without the DWP considering whether you have deliberately deprived yourself of capital.[110]
- Were you mentally capable at the time?[111]

You should not be treated as having deprived yourself of capital if:

- you did not know about the capital limit for UC – you cannot have an intention to get more UC if you do not know about the capital rules. If you are already familiar with the benefit system (eg, you have claimed benefit before and had official information about the capital rules), this is evidence that you did know about the capital limits;[112] *or*

- you told the DWP what you planned to do with your capital and were told that it would not affect your UC. If you went ahead and spent the money the way you said you would, you cannot be said to have intended to get more UC by doing so.[113]



If you use up your resources, you may have more than one motive for doing so. Even if qualifying for benefit is only a less significant motive for your actions and the main motive is something different (eg, ensuring your home is in good condition by spending capital on repairs and improvements), you may still be considered to have deprived yourself of a resource in order to get benefit.[114]

You can deprive yourself of capital, even if you receive another resource in return.[115] For example, if you buy a car so that you can get more benefit, your actual capital includes the value of the car, and the difference between that and the purchase price is treated as notional capital.[116]

## The diminishing notional capital rule

If you have deliberately deprived yourself of capital, the value of your notional capital is assumed to reduce over time. This is known as the 'diminishing notional capital rule'.

The notional capital amount is not fixed, but reduces over time at a set rate, as follows.

If you are treated as having notional capital of:[117]

- over £16,000 and your UC entitlement stops, in the following month the amount of UC you would have received but for the notional capital is deducted from the amount of notional capital;
- between £6,000 and £16,000, in the following assessment period the amount of the assumed income from that notional capital is deducted from the amount of notional capital.

Notional capital is reduced in the same way in each subsequent month.

Notional capital is added to any actual capital you may have. This may reduce your UC award because of the amount of assumed monthly income from capital included in the assessment (see p140), or end it altogether.

If your UC stops altogether, make a fresh claim when you think you might become entitled. Ask the DWP to tell you how long it will be before a new claim might succeed. If you have both actual and notional capital, you may need to spend your actual capital to meet your living expenses.

# 6. How capital is valued

2

## Market value

Your capital is valued at its current market or surrender value.[118] This means the amount of money you could raise by selling it or raising a loan against it. This is the price that a willing buyer would pay to a willing seller on a particular date.[119] So if an asset is difficult or impossible to realise, its market value should be heavily discounted or even nil.[120]

If you cannot legally dispose of capital (eg, because of a restraint order), the market value is nil.[121]

In the case of a house, an estate agent's figure for a quick sale is a more appropriate valuation than the district valuer's figure for a sale within three months.[122]

It is not uncommon for an unrealistic assessment to be made of the value of your capital. If you disagree with the decision, you could ask for a revision or appeal (see Chapters 50 and 51).

## Expenses of sale

If there would be expenses involved in selling your capital, 10 per cent is deducted from its value (before any debts are deducted) for the cost of sale.[123]

## Debts

Deductions are made from the gross value of your capital for any debt or mortgage secured on it.[124] If a creditor (eg, a bank) holds the land certificate to your property as security for a loan and has registered notice of its deposit at the Land Registry, this counts as a debt secured on your property.[125] If a single mortgage is secured on a house and land, and the value of the house is disregarded for benefit purposes, the whole of the mortgage can be deducted when calculating the value of the land.[126]

If you have debts that are not secured against your capital (eg, tax liabilities), these cannot be offset against the value of your capital.[127] However, once you have repaid your debts, your capital may be reduced. **Note:** you can still be treated as having the capital if you deliberately get rid of it in order to get benefit (see p161).

If you have an overdrawn bank account and have savings in another account with the same bank, the amount of the overdraft should be deducted from your savings if the terms of the accounts allow the bank to make these transfers.[128]

## Jointly owned capital

If you own any capital asset (except as a partner in a company – see p134) with someone else under a 'joint tenancy', you are treated as owning an equal share of the asset with the other owner(s) – eg, if you own the asset with one other person, you are each treated as having a 50 per cent share of it.[129] This applies regardless of whether the capital asset is in the UK or abroad. See p166 for the rules that apply to assets abroad.[130]

This does not apply if you jointly own the capital asset as 'tenants in common'.[131] In this case, your actual share in the asset is valued.

*Joint tenancies and tenancies in common*

With a **'joint tenancy'**, each co-owner owns the whole of the capital asset 'jointly and severally'. If one of the joint tenants were to die, their interest in the asset would pass automatically to the other joint tenant(s). With a **'tenancy in common'**, each co-owner owns a discrete share in the asset. This share can be passed on in their will by the person who has died to whoever they choose.

If you have a joint tenancy, the value of your deemed share is calculated in the same way as your actual capital. However, it is only the value of your deemed share looked at in isolation that counts, and this is usually worth less than the same proportion of the value of the whole asset. For example, if the asset is a house, the value of any deemed share may be very small or even worthless, particularly if the house is occupied and there is a possibility that the sale of the property cannot be forced. This is because even a willing buyer could not be expected to pay much for an asset they would have difficulty making use of.[132] However, a value may be placed on a part share when the other joint owner does not wish to sell, as there may be a market for investors in such shares.[133] Whether a sale can be forced depends on individual circumstances. For example, a court may be more likely to order a sale of property left jointly in a will with no restrictions on use.[134] Valuations should take into account legal costs and the length of time it could take to gain possession of the property.[135] A valuation should set out details of the valuer's expertise (where relevant), describe the property in sufficient detail to show that all factors relevant to its value have been taken into account, state any assumptions on which it is based and explain what the market is for that type of sale.[136] You may need to challenge any decision (see Chapters 50 and 51) based on an inadequate valuation.

## Treatment of assets after a relationship breakdown

When partners separate, assets, such as a former home or bank account, may be in joint or sole names. If, for instance, a bank account is in joint names, you and your former partner are treated as having a 50 per cent share each under the rules on jointly held capital. On the other hand, a former partner may have a right to some, or all, of an asset that is in your sole name – eg, they may have deposited most of the money in a bank account in your name. If this is established, you may be treated as not entitled to the whole of the account but as holding part of it as trustee for your former partner.[137] If an asset such as the matrimonial home belongs to your former partner and you have no share in it, you cannot be treated as having any interest in it under the Matrimonial Causes Act 1973 unless you take divorce or separation proceedings and get a property order.[138]

## Shares

Shares are valued at their current market value less 10 per cent for the cost of sale, and after deducting any 'lien' held by brokers for sums owed for purchase or commission.[139] Market value can be worked out from the listed share price. If a more exact value is needed (eg, because your capital is close to the limit), DWP guidance says it should be calculated by taking the lowest and highest share prices for the day (from uk.finance.yahoo.com) and using the lowest price plus a quarter of the difference between the two.[140] Fluctuations in price between routine reviews of your award are normally ignored.

## Unit trusts

Unit trusts are valued on the basis of the bid price quoted in newspapers. No deduction is allowed for the cost of sale because this is already included in the bid price.[141]

## The right to receive a payment in the future

The value of any such right is its market value – what a willing buyer will pay to a willing seller.[142] For something which is not yet realisable, this may be very small.

## Overseas assets

If you have assets abroad and there are no exchange controls or other prohibitions to prevent you transferring your capital to the UK, your assets are valued at their current market or surrender value in that country.[143]

If you are not allowed to transfer your capital, you are treated as having capital equal to the amount that a willing buyer in this country would give for those assets (which might not be very much).[144]

Deduct 10 per cent for any expenses of sale, any debts or mortgage secured on the assets and any charges for converting the payment into sterling.[145]

# Notes

2

**1. The capital limits**

1 Regs 18 and 72 UC Regs
2 Reg 51 UC(TP) Regs
3 Regs 51(3) and 56 UC(TP) Regs
4 Reg 57 UC(TP) Regs

**2. Whose capital counts**

5 s5(2) WRA 2012
6 Reg 18(2) UC Regs
7 para H1077 ADM
8 para H1074 ADM

**3. What counts as capital**

9 para H1020 ADM
10 *R v SBC ex parte Singer* [1973] 1 WLR 713 (cited in CH/412/2007); reg 46(3) UC Regs
11 para H1659 ADM
12 para H1658 ADM
13 para H1658 ADM
14 R(IS) 3/93
15 para H1050 ADM
16 Universal Credit Guidance, *Treatment of capital*, v16.0, House of Commons library deposited papers, rightsnet.org.uk/resources/universal-credit-guidance
17 R(SB) 12/86
18 *Barclays Bank v Quistclose Investments Ltd* [1970] AC 567; R(SB) 49/83; R(SB) 53/83; R(SB) 1/85; *MW v SSWP (JSA)* [2016] UKUT 469 (AAC), reported as [2017] AACR 15
19 R(SB) 49/83
20 R(SB) 12/86; for how this works in Scotland, see *JK v SSWP (JSA)* [2010] UKUT 437 (AAC), reported as [2011] AACR 26; *DF v SSWP* [2015] UKUT 611 (AAC)
21 *MC v SSWP (IS)* [2015] UKUT 600 (AAC)
22 CIS/2287/2008
23 R(IS) 1/90; CSIS/639/2006
24 R(SB) 23/85; CSIS/639/2006
25 *JC v SSWP* [2009] UKUT 22 (AAC)
26 Reg 72(2) UC Regs
27 *Gartside v Inland Revenue Commissioners* [1968] 1 All ER 121; [1968] AC 553; *LG v SSWP (ESA)* [2019] UKUT 220 (AAC)
28 Regs 46, 48 and 66(1)(j) UC Regs
29 *Thomas v CAO*, appendix to R(SB) 17/87
30 CIS/984/2002
31 Reg 72(3) UC Regs

**4. Disregarded capital**

32 Sch 10 para 1 UC Regs
33 para H2038 ADM
34 Schs 3 para 1(1) and 10 para 1(2) UC Regs
35 R(JSA) 9/03; R(SB) 10/89
36 *MM v SSWP (IS)* [2012] UKUT 358 (AAC); para H2040 ADM
37 Sch 3 paras 1(4) and 2 UC Regs; para H2039 ADM
38 Reg 48(2) and Sch 10 para 5 UC Regs
39 Reg 48(2) and Sch 10 para 4(1)(b) and (2) UC Regs
40 Sch 10 para 6 UC Regs
41 R(SB) 32/83
42 R(IS) 5/05
43 Reg 48(2) UC Regs
44 *SP v SSWP* [2009] UKUT 255 (AAC)
45 Reg 48(2) and Sch 10 para 4(1)(c) UC Regs
46 *R v LB Tower Hamlets Review Board ex parte Kapur*, 12 June 2000, unreported
47 Reg 48(2) and Sch 10 para 4(1)(a) UC Regs
48 Reg 48(2) and Sch 10 para 13(a) UC Regs
49 R(IS) 6/95
50 R(IS) 7/01
51 CIS/685/1992
52 CIS/8475/1995; CIS/15984/1996
53 R(SB) 14/85
54 Reg 48(2) and Sch 10 para 14 UC Regs
55 Reg 48(2) and Sch 10 para 15 UC Regs
56 *Barclays Bank v Quistclose Investments Ltd* [1970] AC 567; CSB/975/1985
57 Sch 10 para 12 UC Regs
58 Reg 48(2) and Sch 10 para 13(b) UC Regs
59 Reg 48(2) and Sch 10 para 13(c) UC Regs
60 CIS/4757/2003
61 CIS/6908/1995
62 Sch 10 paras 2, 3 and 5 UC Regs
63 Reg 2 UC Regs
64 CSB/209/1986; CSB/1149/1986; R(SB) 22/87
65 R(IS) 5/05; CH/3777/2007

66 Reg 46(2) UC Regs
67 R(H) 7/08
68 CIS/494/1990; R(IS) 8/04; para H1895 ADM
69 Reg 48(2) and Sch 10 para 14 UC Regs
70 Sch 10 para 7 UC Regs
71 para H2022 ADM
72 Reg 48(2) and Sch 10 para 8(b) UC Regs
73 Reg 48(2) and Sch 10 para 8(a) UC Regs
74 Reg 57(5) UC Regs
75 Sch 10 para 7 UC Regs
76 R(SB) 4/85
77 HMRC, *Property Income Manual*, para 4300
78 Sch 10 para 10 UC Regs
79 para H5174 ADM
80 Sch 10 para 9 UC Regs
81 R(IS) 7/98
82 Sch 10 para 18 UC Regs; regs 10B and 10C UC(TP) Regs
83 In practice, this applies to new-style ESA but arguably applies to old-style ESA because of how 'contributory ESA' in reg 10C UC(TP) Regs is defined in reg 2.
84 Regs 10A and 10C UC(TP) Regs
85 Sch 10 para 20 UC Regs
86 Sch 10 para 18ZA UC Regs
87 Sch 10 paras 16, 21 and 22 UC Regs
88 Sch 10 paras 23 and 24 UC Regs
89 Sch 2 para 7 UC(TP) Regs; reg 3 UC(TP)(SDP)A Regs
90 s8 SS(AP)A 2022; s8 SS(AP)A 2023
91 para H1767 ADM
92 Reg 75 UC Regs
93 R(IS) 3/03
94 R(SB) 2/89; *KQ v SSWP (IS)* [2011] UKUT 102 (AAC), reported as [2011] AACR 43
95 *DR v SSWP (UC)* [2024] UKUT 196 (AAC)
96 R(IS) 15/96
97 *Q v SSWP (JSA)* [2020] UKUT 49 (AAC)
98 para H2028 ADM
99 Reg 76 UC Regs; para H2051 ADM
100 Reg 26 VP Regs
101 para H2054 ADM
102 Sch 10 para 11 UC Regs
103 Sch 10 paras 17 and 18A UC Regs
104 para H1156 ADM
105 Sch 10 para 19 UC Regs

5. **Deliberately getting rid of capital**
106 Reg 50(1) and (2) UC Regs
107 Reg 50(2) UC Regs
108 *KS v SSWP* [2009] UKUT 122 (AAC), reported as [2010] AACR 3
109 R(SB) 12/91; para H1832 ADM
110 CIS/264/1989; R(IS) 7/98
111 para H1830 ADM
112 R(SB) 9/91; R(SB) 12/91
113 *LH v SSWP (IS)* [2014] UKUT 60 (AAC); para H1842 ADM
114 R(SB) 38/85; R(IS) 1/91; R(H) 1/06
115 R(SB) 40/85
116 R(IS) 8/04
117 Reg 50(3) UC Regs

6. **How capital is valued**
118 Reg 49(1) UC Regs
119 R(SB) 57/83; R(SB) 6/84
120 R(SB) 18/83
121 *CS v SSWP* [2014] UKUT 518 (AAC)
122 R(SB) 6/84
123 Reg 49(1) UC Regs
124 Reg 49(1)(b) UC Regs
125 CIS/255/1989
126 R(SB) 27/84
127 R(SB) 2/83; R(SB) 31/83
128 *JRL v SSWP (JSA)* [2011] UKUT 63 (AAC), reported as [2011] AACR 30
129 Reg 47 UC Regs
130 CIS/2575/1997
131 *Hourigan v SSWP* [2002] EWCA Civ 1890, reported as R(IS) 4/03
132 CIS/15936/1996; CIS/263/1997; CIS/3283/1997 (joint decision); R(IS) 26/95
133 *JM v Eastleigh BC (HB)* [2016] UKUT 464 (AAC)
134 *JM v Eastleigh BC (HB)* [2016] UKUT 464 (AAC)
135 R(IS) 3/96
136 R(JSA) 1/02; *Reigate and Banstead BC v GB (HB)* [2018] UKUT 225 (AAC)
137 R(IS) 2/93
138 R(IS) 1/03
139 Reg 49 UC Regs
140 paras H1660-65 ADM
141 para H1673 ADM
142 *Peters v CAO*, appendix to R(SB) 3/89
143 Reg 49(2)(a) UC Regs
144 Reg 49(2)(b) UC Regs
145 Reg 49(3) UC Regs

# Part 3

# Other means-tested benefits

# Chapter 9

# Income-related employment and support allowance

3

**This chapter covers:**


1. Who can get income-related employment and support allowance (p172)
2. The rules about your age (p173)
3. People included in the award (p174)
4. The amount of benefit (p174)
5. Work-related requirements (p176)
6. Special benefit rules (p178)
7. Claims and backdating (p178)
8. Getting paid (p178)
9. Tax, other benefits and the benefit cap (p179)


## Key facts

- Employment and support allowance (ESA) is a benefit for people who are unable to work because of illness or disability (known as having 'limited capability for work') and who are not entitled to statutory sick pay.
- Whether you have limited capability for work is assessed by a test called the work capability assessment.
- There are two types of ESA: **contributory ESA**, which is not means tested (but can be affected by certain pensions), and **income-related ESA**, which is means tested.
- You cannot make a new claim for income-related ESA. If you already get it, your award can continue but the DWP aims to replace it with universal credit (UC) by starting you on the managed migration to UC process at some point.
- You do not have to have paid national insurance contributions to qualify for income-related ESA.
- ESA is administered and paid by the DWP.
- If you disagree with an ESA decision, you can apply for a revision or supersession (see Chapter 50), or appeal against it (see Chapter 51). You must apply for a mandatory reconsideration before you can appeal (for ESA there is an exception to this, if you would be entitled to ESA pending the appeal). All parts of the decision may be looked at.

3

***Continuing entitlement to income-related ESA***

If you are already entitled to income-related ESA, you can continue to qualify until:

– you are affected by the managed migration process, and either you claim UC or, if you have not yet claimed UC, you reach your 'deadline day'. The DWP intends to start the process for everyone still getting income-related ESA by December 2025 (see p29); *or*

– you claim UC. **Note:** when you make a new claim for UC, your income-related ESA entitlement can continue for two weeks. See p178 for information about income-related ESA run-on; *or*

– you become a member of a couple and your partner is getting UC.

## 1. Who can get income-related employment and support allowance

You qualify for employment and support allowance (ESA) if you:[1]

- have 'limited capability for work' (see p895); *and*
- are aged 16 or over, but under pension age (see p239); *and*
- are in Great Britain (see Chapter 58 if you go abroad); *and*
- are not entitled in your own right to statutory sick pay; *and*
- are not doing any work (except work you can do while claiming – see p928).

The above conditions apply to both income-related and contributory ESA. To qualify for income-related ESA, you must also satisfy extra rules (see p173).

You may qualify for income-related ESA even if you do not qualify for contributory ESA. You may qualify for both income-related ESA and contributory ESA.

***Old-style and new-style employment and support allowance***

Your ESA (both income-related and contributory) is called 'old-style' ESA. However, if you come under the universal credit (UC) system (see p20), you cannot get income-related ESA because it is replaced by UC. You can still get contributory ESA under the UC system, but in that case it is called 'new-style' ESA.

**Note:** you cannot make a new claim for income-related ESA. But if you are already entitled to contributory ESA and do not come under the universal credit (UC) system, you may be able to top this up with income-related ESA without having to make a new claim (see p24).

Some ESA claimants (but not those in the 'support group' – see p560) can be required to undertake work-related requirements (see p176).

### Extra rules for income-related employment and support allowance

You qualify for income-related ESA if, in addition to satisfying the basic rules of entitlement to ESA on p172:[2]

- your income (see Chapter 16) is less than your applicable amount (see Chapter 13); *and*
- your capital (see Chapter 18) is not over £16,000;[3] *and*
- you are not entitled to pension credit (PC); *and*
- your partner, if you are in a couple (see p254), is not engaged in full-time paid work (p883) or treated as being in full-time paid work (p886); *and*
- your partner is not entitled to income-related ESA or PC in their own right; *and*
- you are not 'receiving education', unless you are entitled to disability living allowance, scottish adult disability living allowance, child disability payment, personal independence payment, adult disability payment or armed forces independence payment, in which case you can still qualify for income-related ESA;[4] *and*
- you are not a 'person subject to immigration control' (see p1272);[5] *and*
- you satisfy the 'right to reside' and 'habitual residence' tests (see Chapter 57).[6]

***Education***

You are in **'education'** if you are a 'qualifying young person' (eg, you are under 20 and in full-time, non-advanced education or approved training – see p488) or if you are on a course classed as full time (see p798).[7] Get advice if you are unsure.

### Disqualification from benefit

You can be disqualified from receiving ESA for up to six weeks (or have your benefit paid at a reduced rate if you are in 'hardship') in the circumstances described on p557. The rules are the same for both income-related ESA and contributory ESA.

However, the rules for income-related ESA are different from those for contributory ESA if you are:

- absent from Great Britain (see p1380), *or*
- a prisoner or detained in legal custody (see p840).

## 2. The rules about your age

You must be aged at least 16, but under pension age (see p690). It is your age as the claimant that is relevant, not the age of your partner.[8]

3

## 3. People included in the award

If you are single, you get income-related employment and support allowance (ESA) for yourself.

If you are a member of a couple (see p254 for who counts), one of you (the person who claimed it) can get income-related ESA for both of you. The applicable amount that forms part of the calculation of your benefit includes a personal allowance for a couple and can include premiums based on both your and your partner's circumstances. When your benefit is worked out, your partner's income and capital are usually added to yours. Whichever one of you gets ESA, the other may qualify for national insurance (NI) credits in order to protect their NI record (see Chapter 39).

ESA does not include amounts for children. However, there are some situations in which you must show that you are responsible for a child who is living in your household – eg:

- to be exempt from compulsory work-related interviews and activity (see p176);
- for help with housing costs if you are an owner-occupier (see p289 and p295).

You do not have to be the child's parent. For who counts as a child, see p259. For when you count as responsible for a child and when they count as living in your household, see pp260–61.

## 4. The amount of benefit

The amount of income-related employment and support allowance (ESA) you get depends on your needs (your applicable amount) and how much income and capital you have. For the calculation, see below.

**Note:**

- If you are appealing against a decision that you do not have limited capability for work and you get ESA pending the outcome of your appeal (see p925), you are only paid at the 'assessment phase' (see p559) rate – ie, you do not get an additional component.
- You are entitled to just one award of ESA, but this may be made up of both old-style contributory ESA and income-related ESA.[9] If you are entitled to both, the total amount of ESA payable is the same amount as your income-related ESA, but is made up of contributory ESA topped up with income-related ESA.

### Calculating income-related employment and support allowance

Income-related ESA is worked out as follows.

3

### Step 1: calculate your applicable amount

Your applicable amount consists of:

- in all cases:
  - **a personal allowance** (see p266). Your personal allowance is paid at a lower rate if you are under 25; *and*
  - **premiums** for any special needs (see p270);
- **a support component**, if you are assessed as having limited capability for work-related activity (see p560 – the rules are the same as for contributory ESA). If you are not assessed as having limited capability for work-related activity, you may still be entitled to **a work-related activity component**, but only if your claim started before its abolition in April 2017 (see p561 – the rules are the same as for contributory ESA);
- **a 'transitional addition'** if you were transferred to ESA from incapacity benefit, severe disablement allowance or income support (IS) on grounds of disability, and were entitled to income-related ESA as part of the transfer (eg, because your ESA would have been less than your IS, or on transfer your contributory ESA should have been topped up with income-related ESA). Although your ESA can continue to include a transitional addition, it is reduced by increases in your ESA.

You cannot get help with your mortgage interest costs in your income-related ESA applicable amount. Instead, you may be able to get a loan from the DWP (see p764).

For more details on applicable amounts, see Chapter 13.

### Step 2: calculate your income

This is the amount you have coming in each week from, for instance, other benefits, part-time earnings and maintenance (see Chapter 16). If you have capital over £6,000 (£10,000 if you live in a care home), it also includes your tariff income (see p360).

### Step 3: deduct income from applicable amount

If your income is less than your applicable amount, your income-related ESA equals the difference between the two. If your income is the same as or more than your applicable amount, you are not entitled to ESA.

***Example***

Luke (35) is getting income-related ESA. He lives with his wife, Maeve (27). Maeve works 10 hours a week and earns £120 a week. Luke is assessed as being entitled to a support component.

**Main phase**
Applicable amount = £223.40 a week (personal allowance of £144.65 for a couple both aged 18 or over *plus* an enhanced disability premium (at the couple rate) of £30.25 *plus* a support component of £48.50)
Income to be taken into account (£20 earnings disregard applies) = £100
Luke's income-related ESA is £223.40 *minus* £100 = £123.40



**Note:** earnings you receive for 'permitted work' (see p928) are disregarded when calculating the amount of your income-related ESA.

Your ESA may be reduced if:

- you do not comply with work-related requirements that have been applied to you – see below. **Note:** these requirements do not apply if you are in the support group for ESA; *or*
- you are disqualified from ESA but are in 'hardship' (see p557 – the rules are the same as for contributory ESA); *or*
- you have committed a benefit offence (see p1111).

## 5. Work-related requirements

### Work-related interviews and activity

If you are getting old-style employment and support allowance (ESA) (either income-related or contributory), the DWP can require you to take part in work-focused interviews. This only applies if you are in the work-related activity group (see p561). Rules also allow your partner to be required to take part in interviews.

If you are not required to attend an interview, you can still take part in work-related schemes on a voluntary basis. Interviews may be arranged throughout the time you are on benefits, but can be waived or deferred if they are not appropriate or unlikely to be helpful.

At the interview, you discuss job opportunities, education, training and rehabilitation with the interviewer. You are not required to take action based on the discussions.

Some exemptions apply, including for lone parents responsible for a child under one.[10] You also need not have an interview as the partner of a claimant if you or your partner are responsible for a child under one.[11]

If you (or your partner) do not take part, you could be given a sanction and your benefit could be paid at a reduced rate. Taking part involves attending the interview, participating in discussions, and may involve completing an action plan. You do not have to look for work. There is no right of appeal about work-focused interviews, but you can complain. Reasonable adjustments must be made if you have a disability. For further details of the interviews, including exemptions, see Chapter 48 of the 2021/22 edition of this *Handbook*.

Unless you are exempt or in the support group, if you get old-style ESA (either income-related or contributory) you may also be required to undertake 'work-related activity'. If the DWP decides that you are required to do so, it must notify you in a written action plan telling you what you have to do.[12] You can ask for your action plan to be reconsidered, and a written decision must be issued.[13] Any requirement must be reasonable, taking into account your circumstances.[14] **'Work-related activity'** is any activity which makes it more likely that you will get a job or remain in work.[15] You may be required to undertake work-related activity if you are required to take part in work-focused interviews – ie, you are in the work-related activity group, rather than the 'support group' for ESA (see p561).[16]

If you fail to take part in work-related activity without good cause, you may be given a sanction. However, this does not apply to employment support schemes delivered by or for the Scottish government (eg, as part of Fair Start Scotland), because they are voluntary.

You cannot be required to apply for jobs or to undertake work. Although you can be asked to do work experience, this is voluntary.[17]

If you are the lone parent of a child under 13, you can only be required to undertake work-related activity during your child's normal school hours.[18]

## Exemptions

You cannot be required to undertake work-related activity if:[19]

- you are a lone parent who is responsible for a child under three who is a member of your household (see p260 and p261); *or*
- you are exempt from the requirement to take part in work-focused interviews; *or*
- you are entitled to carer's allowance, or your income-related ESA includes a carer premium (p279).

## Sanctions

You can be sanctioned for failing to take part in work-focused interviews or activity (for the different rules that apply to new-style ESA, see Chapter 43).

You can be given a sanction if, without good cause:

- you (or, in some cases, your partner) fail to take part in a work-focused interview; *or*
- you fail to take part in work-related activity when required to do so.

You should be given at least five days to show you have good cause before any decision to impose a sanction is made.[20] For more detail about these sanctions, see Chapter 49 of the 2021/22 edition of this *Handbook*.

3

## 6. Special benefit rules

Special rules may apply if you:

- are subject to immigration control (see p1272);
- have come from abroad (see Chapter 57) or are going abroad (see Chapter 58);
- are living in a care home or similar accommodation, or people in prison or detention (see Chapter 38).

## 7. Claims and backdating

You cannot make a new claim for income-related employment and support allowance (ESA). For the specific rules that applied to income-related ESA, see pp166–68 of the 2020/21 edition of this *Handbook*.

## 8. Getting paid

As income-related and contributory employment and support allowance (ESA) are two types of the same benefit, the rules described on p568 on getting paid contributory ESA also apply to income-related ESA.

You may be asked to provide information after you are awarded ESA, and if you fail to do so, your ESA could be suspended or even terminated (see p1031).

For when your income-related ESA may be paid at a reduced rate, see p175.

### Income-related employment and support allowance run-on

If you are getting income-related ESA and make a new claim for universal credit (UC), your income-related ESA entitlement continues for two weeks (called a 'run-on payment'), as long as you would otherwise have remained entitled.[21] You do not have to make a claim for a run-on payment. It should be made automatically. You do not have to pay back a run-on payment and it does not count as a specified benefit for the benefit cap (see p1025).[22]

### Change of circumstances

You must report changes in your circumstances that you have been told to report, as well as any that you might reasonably be expected to know might affect your right to, the amount of or the payment of your benefit. You should do this as soon as possible, preferably in writing. See p1030 for further information.

**Note:** if you become a member of a couple with someone entitled to UC, your entitlement to income-related ESA ends (see p33).

# 9. Tax, other benefits and the benefit cap

## Tax

Income-related employment and support allowance (ESA) is not taxable.[23]

## Means-tested benefits

If you are entitled to income-related ESA, it is an automatic passport to maximum housing benefit (HB). If you are not entitled to HB already, you must make a separate claim (if you still can). In Scotland, income-related ESA is a qualifying benefit for Scottish child payment (see p1459).

## Non-means-tested benefits

You can be entitled to income-related ESA and old-style contributory ESA at the same time.

While you are on income-related ESA, you get national insurance credits for limited capability for work (see p865).

You are not entitled to ESA if you are entitled to statutory sick pay.[24]

Most non-means-tested benefits are taken into account as income when working out the amount of income-related ESA you get. However:

- attendance allowance, pension age disability payment, disability living allowance, child disability payment, Scottish adult disability living allowance, personal independence payment, adult disability payment, guardian's allowance and child benefit are not taken into account;
- it can still be worth claiming non-means-tested benefits. If you or your partner qualify for certain of these, you also qualify for certain premiums and therefore a higher rate of income-related ESA.

If your partner is entitled to new-style JSA, you can get ESA. Your partner's JSA is taken into account when assessing your income for income-related ESA.

## The benefit cap

ESA is one of the specified benefits for the benefit cap. However, the benefit cap does *not* apply if you or your partner receive ESA which includes a support component. In other cases, it only applies if you are getting universal credit or HB. See p1025 for further information.

## Passports and other sources of help

If you are entitled to income-related ESA, you also qualify for health benefits (see Chapter 27) and education benefits such as free school lunches (see p774). You may also qualify for social fund payments (see Chapter 33) or, in Scotland, a Best

Start grant (see p1451) or a funeral support payment (see Chapter 65). You may also qualify for Scottish child payment (see p1452). You may be entitled to a council tax reduction (see p761).

## Financial help on starting work

If you stop getting income-related ESA because you or your partner start work, or your partner's earnings or hours increase, you may be able to get housing costs run-on if you have had those included (see p299) or a mortgage interest run-on if you have been getting a loan for your mortgage interest payments (see p769), or extended payments of HB if you pay rent (see p224). Your local authority may also provide extended help with council tax. See p781 for information about other financial help you may get.

# Notes

1. **Who can get income-related employment and support allowance**
   1 ss1 and 20(1) WRA 2007; reg 40(1) ESA Regs
   2 Sch 1 para 6 WRA 2007
   3 Reg 110 ESA Regs
   4 Reg 18 ESA Regs; Schs 1 para 2 and 2 para 2 ESA(TP)(EA)(No.2) Regs
   5 s115 IAA 1999
   6 Reg 70 and Sch 5 para 11 ESA Regs
   7 Regs 14-17 ESA Regs

2. **The rules about your age**
   8 s1 WRA 2007

4. **The amount of benefit**
   9 s6 WRA 2007

5. **Work-related requirements**
   10 Reg 54(2) ESA Regs
   11 Reg 7 SS(JPIP) Regs
   12 Reg 5 ESA(WRA) Regs
   13 Reg 7 ESA(WRA) Regs
   14 Reg 3(4)(a) ESA(WRA) Regs
   15 s13(7) and (8) WRA 2007
   16 s13 WRA 2007; reg 3 ESA(WRA) Regs
   17 para 53073 DMG
   18 Reg 3(5) ESA(WRA) Regs
   19 Reg 3(2) ESA(WRA) Regs
   20 *DL v SSWP (JSA)* [2013] UKUT 295 (AAC)

8. **Getting paid**
   21 Reg 5 UC(MMP&MA) Regs
   22 Reg 8B UC(TP) Regs

9. **Tax, other benefits and the benefit cap**
   23 s677 IT(EP)A 2003
   24 s20 WRA 2007

# Chapter 10

# Housing benefit

3

**This chapter covers:**


1. Who can get housing benefit (p182)
2. The rules about your age (p196)
3. People included in the award (p198)
4. The amount of benefit (p199)
5. Special benefit rules (p211)
6. Claims and backdating (p211)
7. Getting paid (p221)
8. Tax, other benefits and the benefit cap (p231)


## Key facts

- Housing benefit (HB) is a benefit for people on a low income who pay rent.
- You may qualify for HB under two separate sets of rules – 'working-age HB' or 'pension-age HB'.
- You can only make a new claim for working-age HB in limited circumstances. In most cases, if you are under pension age, you can get help with your rent by claiming universal credit (UC) and including your housing costs.
- The amount of rent used to calculate the HB you get may be restricted, so HB does not necessarily meet the full amount of rent you must pay.
- HB is a means-tested benefit.
- You do not need to have paid national insurance contributions to qualify.
- You can qualify for HB whether you are in or out of work.
- If you need extra financial assistance to meet your housing costs, you can claim discretionary housing payments to top up your HB (see Chapter 25).
- A benefit cap may be applied if the total amount of certain benefits you receive exceeds a specified amount and your HB can be reduced.
- HB is administered and paid by local authorities, although it is a national scheme and the rules are mainly determined by DWP regulations.
- If you disagree with an HB decision, you can apply for a revision or a supersession (see Chapter 50), or appeal against it (see Chapter 51). You do *not* have to apply for a mandatory reconsideration before you can appeal.

***New claims for, and continuing entitlement to, housing benefit***

If you are at least pension age, or if you are a member of a couple and both of you are at least pension age, you can make a new claim for pension-age HB. In all other cases (ie, if you are under pension age or if you are a member of a 'mixed-age couple'), you can only make a **new claim** for HB in limited circumstances. See p183 for further information.

If you are already entitled to HB, you can continue to qualify:

- until you claim UC or you become a member of a couple with a partner who is getting UC (see p23 and p33). **Note:** in both cases, you continue to qualify for HB, even if you are entitled to UC, if the HB is for 'specified' or 'temporary' accommodation (see p183); *or*
- until you and your partner are affected by the managed migration transfer process, that is, you are notified by the DWP that your HB will end and are invited to claim UC. See p29 for further information; *or*
- for two weeks after you become entitled to UC (called 'HB run-on' – see p227).

At some point, the DWP will amend the pension credit (PC) rules to include help with rent. It will then transfer existing pension-age HB claims to PC. See CPAG's *Welfare Rights Bulletin* or the online version of this *Handbook* for updates.

# 1. Who can get housing benefit

You qualify for housing benefit (HB) if:[1]

- your income is low enough (see p199 and Chapter 16 (for 'working-age HB') or Chapter 17 (for 'pension-age HB')); *and*
- your capital is worth £16,000 or less (unless you or your partner are getting the guarantee credit of pension credit (PC) – see Chapter 18 (for working-age HB) or Chapter 19 (for pension-age HB);[2] *and*
- the payments you make can be met by HB (see p185); *and*
- you or your partner count as liable to pay rent (see p186); *and*
- the payments you make are for the home in which you normally live (see p190) or you are only temporarily absent from it; *and*
- you satisfy the 'right to reside' and the 'habitual residence' tests (see Chapter 57); *and*
- you are not a 'person subject to immigration control' (see p1272). There are exceptions to this rule.

There are two sets of HB rules. You can qualify for what is known as **working-age HB** or for **pension-age HB**. See p197 to find out which rules apply to you. **Note:** if you are a member of a **'mixed-age couple'** (ie, one of you is at least pension age – see p690 – but not the other), you may qualify for working-age HB instead of pension-age HB, even though one of you is at least pension age. In some cases, if you are, or become, a mixed-age couple, your entitlement to HB can end and you need to claim universal credit (UC) for help with your rent (see p197).

## Who can make a new claim for housing benefit

You can only make a new claim for working-age HB (see p197) for 'specified accommodation' or 'temporary accommodation'.[3] You can get HB for your rent even if you are also getting UC.

You can make a new claim for pension-age HB (see p197) if you (and if you are in a couple, you *and* your partner) are at least pension age (see p690).[4] **Note:** if you are a UC claimant and reach pension age (see p690), you can make a new claim for HB (and PC) during your last UC assessment period. Your entitlement to HB can then start from the date you reach pension age, even if you are still getting UC.[5]

If you are a member of a mixed-age couple (ie, only one of you is at least pension age), you cannot normally make a new claim for HB unless it is for specified accommodation or temporary accommodation, but see p184 for the exceptions.

If you cannot make a new claim for HB you can make a claim for UC for help with your rent.

**Note:** if there is a break in your entitlement to HB (eg, you move to a new home in a different local authority area), you can only make a new claim for HB if the rules above, or the rules below that allow claims by mixed-age couples, apply.

### *Specified and temporary accommodation*

**'Specified accommodation'** is:[6]

- accommodation provided by a 'relevant body' to meet your need for, and where you get, care, support or supervision – eg, supported accommodation for vulnerable young people or for those affected by a mental health condition or substance abuse; *or*
- temporary accommodation provided by a local authority or a relevant body because you have left your home due to domestic violence or abuse – eg, a refuge. For what counts, see p951. The rules are the same as for UC; *or*
- a local authority hostel for homeless people where you get care, support or supervision to assist you to be rehabilitated or resettled within the community; *or*
- 'exempt accommodation' (certain types of supported accommodation – see p326).

For these purposes, a **'relevant body'** is a housing association, registered charity or voluntary organisation or, in England, a county council.

Your accommodation is **'temporary accommodation'** if you live in a defined type of homeless accommodation that does not count as exempt accommodation (see p326) and your rent is payable to a local authority or a 'provider of social housing' (see p202).[7]

## Mixed-age couples

You cannot normally make a new claim for HB if you are a member of a mixed-age couple – ie, if one of you is at least pension age but not the other. If you cannot claim HB under these rules, check whether you can under any of the rules on p183. If you cannot make a new claim for HB under any of the rules, you can make a claim for UC.



There are exceptions and you *can* make a new claim for pension-age HB, even if you are member of a mixed-age couple, if:[8]

- you had reached pension age by 14 May 2019, you were entitled to pension-age HB (see p197) or PC (or both) on that date and have been entitled to some pension-age HB or PC continuously since that date as part of the same mixed-age couple. **Note:** if you were getting tax credits but were not getting PC, you may have been sent a letter by the DWP inviting you to claim PC or UC (see p29). If you were invited to claim UC and your HB award ended, the rule above continues to apply and you can claim HB again, even though your continuous entitlement ended. However, you must claim within the following time periods.
  - If you claimed UC before the deadline you were given and were awarded UC and your UC award later ended, you must claim HB within three months starting on the day after the day your UC award ended.
  - If you did not claim UC, or claimed before the deadline you were given but were not entitled to UC, you must claim HB within three months starting on the day after the day your HB award ended.

  In both cases, you must satisfy all the rules for getting HB on the day you claim HB; *or*
- you are a member of a couple and you are at least pension age and are not entitled to UC either as a single claimant or jointly with your partner because:
  - your partner:
    - has been (or is expected to be) absent from home for more than six months, so you are no longer treated as a couple; *or*
    - is aged 16 or 17 and cannot get UC (see p37 for who can); *or*
    - is a 'person subject to immigration control' (see p1272); *or*
    - is not in (or treated as in) Great Britain, including if your partner has failed the habitual residence test or right to reside test (see Chapter 57); *or*
    - is a prisoner or serving a sentence while detained in hospital; *or*
    - is a member of a religious order and is fully maintained by the order; *or*
  - you are in a polygamous marriage in specified circumstances.

  In this case, you can claim pension-age HB as a single person; *or*
- you are in a polygamous marriage but are treated as a couple with one of your partners and both of you are at least pension age. In this case, you or the other member of the couple can claim pension-age HB.

Note:
- If you become a member of a mixed-age couple while you are entitled to HB, in some situations, your entitlement to HB can end and in some it can continue (see p197).
- If you were getting UC jointly with your partner as a member of a mixed-age couple, you are no longer a couple and you are at least pension age, you can claim and qualify for pension-age HB from the first day of the UC assessment period in which you stopped being a couple.[9]



## Payments that can be met by housing benefit

HB can meet any of the following types of payment.[10] In this *Handbook*, we refer to any of these payments as 'rent'. The payment must be in return for your occupation of the home.

- Rent paid in respect of a tenancy. This can include rent or ground rent payable in respect of a lease of 21 years or less.[11] If your lease is for longer than 21 years, the rent or ground rent may be met by PC or income-related employment and support allowance (ESA) (see p287).
- Payments in respect of a licence or other permission to occupy premises – eg, if you are a lodger or live in bed and breakfast accommodation. For houseboats, this can include continuous cruiser licence payments.[12]
- 'Mesne profits' (in Scotland, 'violent profits'), including payments made if you remain in occupation when a tenancy has been ended.
- Other payments for the use and occupation of premises. This does not include boat licence and mooring permit fees if you live in a houseboat, but see above.[13]
- Payments for eligible service charges (see p205).
- Rent, including mooring charges, for a houseboat.
- Site rent for a caravan or mobile home (but not a tent, although this may be met by PC or income-related ESA – see p287).
- Rent paid on a garage or land (unless used for business purposes). Either you must be making a reasonable effort to end your liability for it or you cannot rent your home without it.[14]
- Contributions made by a resident of a charity's almshouse.
- Payments made under a rental purchase agreement under which the purchase price is paid in more than one instalment and you do not finally own your home until all, or an agreed part of, the purchase price has been paid.
- In Scotland, payments in respect of croft land.

## Payments that cannot be met by housing benefit

HB cannot meet any of the following types of payments – ie, payments made:[15]

- by an owner or under a long tenancy (ie, you own your accommodation or have a lease of more than 21 years), unless you have a shared ownership tenancy (ie, you are only buying a share of your home). In this case, you can

get HB for the rent or eligible service charges you pay. You are treated as the owner of the property if you have the right to sell it, even though you may not be able to do so without the consent of other joint owners;[16]
- for a dwelling owned (or part owned) by your partner;
- by a Crown tenant;
- for a dwelling let by a housing association under a co-ownership scheme under which you receive a payment related to the value of the accommodation when you leave;
- under a hire purchase (eg, for the purchase of a mobile home), credit sale or a conditional sale agreement except to the extent that it is in respect of land.

In some of the above situations, the payments may be met by PC or income-related ESA instead. See Chapter 14 for further information.

Note:
- HB cannot meet payments if you are getting income-related ESA for these.[17]
- If you live in a care home, you cannot usually get HB for the rent you pay to the home (see p832).

## Liability to pay rent

To qualify for HB you must count as liable to pay rent. You count as liable if either you or your partner are liable.[18] You can be treated as liable even if you are not (see p187). You can be treated as not liable even if you are (or can be treated as) liable (see p187). If you pay your rent in advance, you are treated as liable to pay it, even if you paid it before claiming HB.[19] You can be liable to pay rent by yourself or you can be jointly liable to do so (see p189).

For you to be liable to pay rent, your agreement must be legally enforceable.[20] It is not enough if you only have a moral obligation, such as a promise to pay something whenever you can afford to do so. You can count as liable to pay rent even if someone else has been paying it on your behalf.[21]

### *Does your agreement have to be in writing?*

If you have a written agreement with your landlord, this should establish that you are liable to pay rent, provided the liability is a genuine part of the agreement.[22]

Your agreement can be legally enforceable even if it is not in writing. The fact that you have made a firm promise to pay money to your landlord in return for your occupation of the property should be sufficient to show you are liable to pay rent and so allow you to qualify for HB.[23] If the local authority refuses to accept that you have a legal liability, apply for a revision or appeal (see Chapters 50 and 51).

**Note:** if you are under 18, you can be liable to pay rent and can qualify for HB. If you are under 16, there may be a question about whether you have a legally enforceable liability for rent.

## People treated as liable to pay rent

You are treated as liable to pay rent if:[24]

- you have to pay rent to continue to live in your home because the liable person is not doing so; *and*
  - you are the former partner of the liable person; *or*
  - you are not the former partner of the liable person and it is reasonable to treat you as liable.[25] It must be reasonable in all of the circumstances and in light of the overall purpose of the HB scheme.[26]

  You must have been living in the home while the liable person was paying the rent.[27]

  It does not matter whether or not the landlord is prepared to transfer the tenancy to you or wants to evict you.[28] If the local authority refuses your HB claim, point out that the eligibility rules for HB and for transferring tenancies are separate, and apply for a revision or appeal; *or*
- your landlord allows you a rent-free period as compensation for carrying out repairs or redecoration (for a maximum of eight benefit weeks in a rent-free period). If you expect the work to last longer, arrange with your landlord to schedule the work in periods of eight weeks or less, separated by at least one complete benefit week in which you resume paying rent; *or*
- you are the partner of a full-time student who is treated as not liable to pay rent (see below) and therefore cannot qualify for HB. This means you can qualify for HB even if your partner cannot. See p801 for information about students who can qualify for HB.

Even if you fall into one of these categories, in certain circumstances, you can still be treated as not liable to pay rent and so not entitled to HB.

## People treated as not liable to pay rent

Even if you or your partner are liable to pay rent, in the following situations you can be treated as though you are not liable and cannot qualify for HB.[29]

- You are a full-time student. This does *not* apply if you are getting pension-age HB (see p197) or if you are a student who can qualify for HB (see p802) and you are getting working-age HB (see p197).
- You do not satisfy the habitual residence test (see p1300).
- You are a member of, and are fully maintained by, a religious order.[30]
- You are living in a care home or an independent hospital (but see p832).[31]
- You pay rent to someone who also lives in the dwelling and is your (or your partner's) close relative (see p189 for who counts).[32] Your landlord may be regarded as living in your dwelling if you share some accommodation, other than a bathroom, toilet, hall or passageway.[33] It does not matter if you use the accommodation at different times or if you pay to use it.[34]
- Your agreement to pay rent is not on a commercial basis.[35] It is what you and your landlord have agreed, not what you or your landlord have later done or

omitted to do, that is relevant.[36] In deciding whether or not your agreement is commercial, the local authority must look at the whole agreement, taking all the circumstances into account. It must consider, among other things:[37]

– whether your agreement includes terms that are not legally enforceable;
– the rent you must pay under the agreement. It does not have to be a market rent. Paying a low rent does not necessarily mean your agreement is not commercial – eg, if you do chores in exchange for a lower rent. Your agreement can count as commercial even if your landlord is not collecting the full contractual rent from you;
– your relationship to your landlord. However, just because your landlord is a relative or close friend, or provides you with care and support, does not mean that your agreement is non-commercial.

- You are renting from:[38]
  – any ex-partner of yours and the home is your former joint home with that ex-partner; *or*
  – any ex-partner of your partner and the home is your partner's former joint home with that ex-partner.
- You or your partner are responsible for a child (under 16) of a person who is your landlord.[39] This only applies if the child is included in your HB award.
- You or your partner, or an ex-partner or close relative of either of you, who lives with you, is:[40]
  – a director or employee of a company which is your landlord; *or*
  – a trustee or beneficiary of a trust which is your landlord.

  This rule does not apply if you can show the arrangement was not intended to take advantage of the HB scheme (see p189).
- You are renting accommodation from a trustee of a trust, of which your (or your partner's) child (under 16) is a beneficiary.
- You were previously the non-dependant (see p207) of someone who lived, and continues to live, in the accommodation. This rule does not apply if you can show that the agreement was not created to 'take advantage of the HB scheme' (see p189).[41]
- You or your current partner previously owned, or had a long tenancy in (ie, a lease of more than 21 years), the accommodation and fewer than five years have passed since you last owned it (or the long tenancy ceased).[42]

  This rule does not apply if you can show that you could not have continued to occupy the accommodation without giving up ownership (or the long tenancy) – eg, the lender was seeking possession of your home. Whether you were legally or practically compelled to give up ownership or the long tenancy is relevant, but your motivation for doing so is not.[43] You do not have to be in immediate danger of having to leave your home for this exception to apply.[44] You may need to show that you have taken steps to explore alternatives.[45]

- You or your partner are employed by your landlord and are occupying your accommodation as a condition of employment. This should not apply if you continue to live in the accommodation after ceasing employment.
- If none of the above apply, the local authority considers that your liability to pay rent has been created to take advantage of the HB scheme (see below).

*Close relatives*

A **'close relative'** is a parent, parent-in-law (including a civil partner's parent), son, son-in-law (including a son's civil partner), daughter, daughter-in-law (including a daughter's civil partner), sibling, step-parent (including a parent's civil partner), stepson (including a civil partner's son), stepdaughter (including a civil partner's daughter), or the partners of any of these.[46] It also includes half-siblings.[47] Relations with in-laws or steprelatives are severed by divorce (or civil partnership dissolution) but arguably not by death – eg, stepchildren are still stepchildren after the death of their mother.[48]

### Agreements taking advantage of the housing benefit scheme

For your agreement to count as taking advantage of the HB scheme, it must amount to an abuse of the scheme or to taking improper advantage of it. This only applies if the agreement gives you an advantage – eg, it increases the amount of HB to which you would otherwise be entitled.[49]

It must be shown that the main reason you entered into the agreement was to obtain HB.[50] All the circumstances should be considered, including what your landlord has to say.[51] An agreement can count as taking advantage of the HB scheme even if it was created from the best motives.[52] Bear the following in mind.

- You should *not* be seen as taking advantage of the HB scheme just because:
  - your landlord is your parent[53] or another close relative; *or*
  - you hope to be able to claim HB to help you with your rent – ie, if your main purpose is to get accommodation, not to obtain HB;[54] *or*
  - you researched what rent can be covered by HB before moving in.
- If you are a tenant of a landlord who deliberately charges high rents in order to have them paid by HB, you may be affected by this provision, even though you had no such intention yourself. Argue that a high rent, in itself, does not mean that the liability takes advantage of the HB scheme.[55]
- If your landlord says you will be evicted if you cannot get HB, this suggests that the agreement does *not* take advantage of the HB scheme.[56]

You can appeal if the local authority says your agreement is taking advantage of the HB scheme and that you are not entitled to HB.

## Joint liability

If you are a member of a couple (see p254) and are jointly liable for the rent, only one of you can qualify for HB.[57]

How a group of single people living together and paying rent to their landlord is treated depends on how many of you are liable under the agreement. If all, or some, of you have joint liability for the rent, you can each make a separate claim and be paid HB on your share (unless the local authority thinks the joint tenancy has been created to take advantage of the HB scheme). If you live in shared accommodation with people other than your partner and children included in your claim, and are jointly liable for the rent with them, see p203 for how this affects the calculation of your benefit – ie, how your 'eligible rent' is apportioned between you.

## Occupying accommodation as your home

HB is paid for your 'normal home' – this is the home in which you and your partner and any children included in your award (see p258) normally live.[58] You cannot usually be paid for any other home. However, there are special rules if you:

- have just moved into your home (see below);
- are temporarily absent from home (see p191);
- are liable to pay rent on more than one home (see p195);
- are in certain other situations (see p196).

If you occupy more than one property or room as your home (eg, because you have a large family and rent adjacent flats, or have a live-in carer and rent two adjacent rooms in shared accommodation), you can argue that both properties or rooms count as part of your home – ie, that you only have one home.[59]

If you have to live in an approved bail or probation hostel or are a prisoner on temporary release, you are treated as not occupying the accommodation in which you are staying.[60] You cannot qualify for HB for any rent you pay for the hostel, but you may be able to qualify for HB for your normal home. See p191 for the rules on temporary absence from home.

### Moving home

If you have just moved into your home but were liable to pay rent before moving in, you can get HB on your new home for up to four weeks before you moved in. You only qualify if the delay in moving was reasonable and:[61]

- you were waiting for a payment from a local welfare assistance scheme or a social fund payment for a need connected with the move – eg, removal expenses or to help you set up home. This only applies if:
  - you have a child aged five or under living with you; *or*
  - you are getting pension-age HB; *or*
  - you are getting working-age HB and you qualify for a disability, severe disability or disabled child premium, or a support component, or you or your partner are a member of the 'work-related activity group' (see p561); *or*
- you were waiting for adaptations to be finished to meet needs you, your partner or a child included in your award (see p258) have because of a

disability. The adaptations do not have to involve a change to the structure of the dwelling, but must be reasonably required and have a clear connection to the disability needs;[62] *or*
- you became liable to make payments on your new home while you were a hospital patient or in residential accommodation (see p194 for the meaning).

Before moving, you must either have notified the local authority of the move or have claimed HB (if you still can – see p183). You can claim HB in advance (see p218). If you have given up your previous home and have no other home, you can argue that the date you move in is the date you move your furniture and belongings in.[63] Your HB is not paid until you move in. If an earlier claim for HB you made before you moved in was turned down, you must claim again (if you still can) within four weeks of moving to qualify.

**Note:** if you must pay rent for your old home as well as your new accommodation, you can only get HB for one of these unless you are covered by the rules described on p195.[64]

### If you are not liable to pay rent for your new accommodation

If you move and are not liable to pay rent in your new accommodation (eg, if you are now staying with a relative or are in prison or hospital and you cannot get HB while temporarily absent from home), you can get HB for up to four weeks for your former home if you:[65]
- were liable for rent on it immediately before moving and continue to be liable – eg, because you have to give notice to your landlord; *and*
- could not reasonably have avoided liability for rent on your former home.

## Temporary absence from home

If you are temporarily absent from your normal home, you can qualify for HB for a period, provided you have not rented out your home and intend to return to it.[66] The length of time you can be away depends on the circumstances and whether you are absent from home in or outside Great Britain. You can argue that you count as temporarily absent from your home even if you have not yet stayed there – eg, you move your furniture and belongings in, but then have to go into hospital.[67] **Note:** you can claim and qualify for HB while you are temporarily absent from home, even if you were not getting HB before you left.

You can get HB while you are absent from your normal home for up to:
- **13 weeks**, whatever the reason for your absence (see p192); *or*
- **52 weeks**, if you are in any of the situations described on p192.

The period can be shorter if you are, or have been, absent from Great Britain (see p194).

The number of weeks runs from the date you leave home.[68] The day you leave home is included, but not the day you return home.[69] If, for example, you have been away from home for 10 weeks and then have grounds to continue to get HB for 52 weeks, you only get HB for the balance: 42 weeks. A new period of absence starts if you return home for even a short stay. A stay of at least 24 hours may be enough.[70] **Note:** if you are a prisoner on temporary release, you continue to be treated as absent from home.[71]

The local authority may use these rules to decide:

- if someone living with you who is temporarily absent from home (eg, a student who is away during term time) is a non-dependant (see p207);[72] *or*
- whether your partner, or a child or young person included in your award, counts as occupying your home.

3

***Will you be away from home temporarily?***

1. Let the local authority know that you will be absent from your normal home and the reason for this, as well as if you will be absent from Great Britain, preferably before you leave. Make it clear that your absence will be temporary and that you are unlikely to be away for longer than the period allowed.
2. Your intention to return, and whether or not you are unlikely to be away for longer than the period allowed, should be based initially on the circumstances on the date you leave your home, unless you are in residential accommodation for a trial period.[73]
3. If, at any time after you leave your home, you no longer intend to return or it becomes likely that you will be away from home (or absent from Great Britain) for longer than the period allowed, inform the local authority of this change in your circumstances to avoid an overpayment. In this case, the local authority can reconsider your entitlement.[74] If you initially told the local authority you would be away from home for more than the period allowed, but realise that your absence will now be shorter, it should also reconsider your entitlement.

### Housing benefit for up to 13 weeks

You can get HB for up to 13 weeks while you are absent from your normal home and you are in Great Britain.[75] It does not matter why you are away from home. You must be unlikely to be away for more than 13 weeks. Within the 13-week period, you can be absent from Great Britain for up to four weeks. The four-week period can be extended to up to eight weeks in limited cases (see p194).

### Housing benefit for up to 52 weeks

You can get HB for up to 52 weeks if you are unlikely to be away from your normal home for longer than this (or, in exceptional circumstances, unlikely to be away for substantially longer than this) in the situations listed below.[76] Within the 52-week period, you can be absent from Great Britain for up to four or 26 weeks at a time as the case may be (see p193 and p194). The four-week period can be extended to up to eight weeks in limited cases.

You can get HB for up to 52 weeks if you are absent from your normal home in the following circumstances.[77] Within the 52-week period, you can get HB while you are temporarily absent from Great Britain for up to 26 weeks (see p194).

- You are **resident in a hospital or similar institution** as a patient. You cannot get HB after you have been resident in hospital for 52 weeks, even if this is because you have a serious mental illness. **Note:** a new period of absence starts if you return home for even a short stay.[78]
- You, your partner or a 'dependent child' under 16 are **undergoing medical treatment or 'medically approved' convalescence**, other than in residential accommodation. Dependent child is not defined in the rules, so could include children who are not included in your claim.
- You are **receiving 'medically approved' care** (ie, certified by a medical practitioner), other than in residential accommodation.
- You are away from home because of a **fear of violence** in your home or from a former partner, or a child or 'qualifying young person' previously included in your claim. 'Violence' is not defined for these purposes, but argue that fear of controlling behaviour or psychological, physical, sexual, financial and emotional abuse counts.[79] You need not have experienced actual violence. Violence in your home includes violence by neighbours and hate crimes directed at your home. See p195 if you need to claim for two homes and p196 if you do not intend to return to your former home.

You can also get HB for up to 52 weeks if you are absent from your normal home in the following circumstances.[80] Within the 52-week period, you can get HB while you are temporarily absent from Great Britain for up to four weeks (see p194).

- You are a **remand prisoner** held in custody pending trial or sentence. Once you are sentenced, you no longer qualify for HB under this rule, but may still qualify under the 13-week rule on p192. The 13 weeks run from the date you were first in prison, so any time you spend in prison awaiting trial or sentence counts towards the 13 weeks. **Note:** you are treated as still in custody if you are on temporary release.[81]
- You must live in an approved hostel or at an address away from your normal home as a **condition of bail**.
- You are **providing medically approved care** – ie, certified by a medical practitioner.
- You are **caring for a child** under 16 whose parent or guardian is away from home receiving medically approved care or medical treatment.
- You are **undertaking a training course**.
- You are a **student**. You must not come into the first category under 'Other situations' on p196, or be entitled to HB on two homes (see p195).
- You are in residential accommodation for **short-term or respite care**.

3

***Definitions***[82]

**'Residential accommodation'** means a care home, an independent hospital or an Abbeyfield home. It also means an establishment managed or provided by a body incorporated by Royal Charter or constituted by an Act of Parliament, other than a local social services authority.

A **'training course'** is a course of training or instruction provided by or on behalf of, or approved by, a government department, the Secretary of State, Skills Development Scotland, Scottish Enterprise or Highlands and Islands Enterprise.

### Trial period in residential accommodation

You can get HB for up to 13 weeks while you are in Great Britain in residential accommodation (see above) for a trial period to see whether it suits your needs.[83] When you enter the accommodation, you must intend to return home if it is not suitable.[84] If the accommodation does not suit your needs, you can have further 13-week trial periods in other accommodation and get HB for further 13-week periods, provided you are not away from home for more than 52 weeks in total.

### Absence from Great Britain

You can get HB while you are temporarily absent from Great Britain for up to:

- **four weeks,** whatever the reason.[85] You must be unlikely to be away for longer than four weeks; *or*
- **eight weeks,** if you are temporarily absent from Great Britain in connection with the death of your partner or a child or young person included in your award (see p258), or the death of your or your partner's or child's or young person's close relative (see p189) and the local authority thinks it is unreasonable to expect you to return to Great Britain within four weeks; *or*
- **four or 26 weeks,** in the situations in which you can get HB while absent from home for up to 52 weeks (see p192). You must be unlikely to be away for longer than this (or, in exceptional circumstances, unlikely to be away for substantially longer than this);[86] *or*
- **26 weeks,** while you are absent from Great Britain as a member of the armed forces posted overseas, a mariner or a continental shelf worker. You must be unlikely to be away for longer than 26 weeks.[87]

The number of weeks runs from the first day of absence from Great Britain.[88] The 13 or 52 weeks you are allowed to be absent from home *in* Great Britain continue to run during any period you are absent from Great Britain.[89] When you return to Great Britain, if you are still away from your normal home, you can continue getting HB for the remainder (if any) of the allowed 13- or 52-week period. However, if your HB ceased because you were no longer treated as occupying your normal home (eg, because you had been absent from Great Britain too long), you cannot qualify for HB until you return home.[90]

*Examples*

Matthew visits his daughter in London for a week before going on a three-week holiday to France. He lets the local authority know this and also that he plans to visit his sister in Manchester for two weeks on the way home. He can be absent from home for up to 13 weeks and absent from Great Britain for up to four weeks within that period. He gets HB for 1 + 3 + 2 = 6 weeks while he is temporarily absent from home.

Martina travels to Canada to visit her grandson for two weeks. At the end of the second week, she notifies the local authority that she intends to stay a further three weeks. She is no longer treated as occupying her normal home because she is going to be absent from Great Britain for longer than four weeks. She therefore only gets HB for two weeks.

Yu Ling goes on a training course in York. She notifies the local authority that she will be away from home for 20 weeks. During the 20-week course, she will be on a placement in France for two weeks. Yu Ling therefore continues to get HB for the 20-week period she is away from home (18 weeks in Great Britain and two weeks outside Great Britain).

## Housing benefit for more than one home

You can usually only get HB for one home. **Note:** if you occupy more than one property as a home (eg, you rent adjacent flats because you have a large family or two adjacent rooms in shared accommodation because you have a live-in carer), you can argue that you only have one home.[91]

If you occupy two homes, you can get HB:

- **for up to four weeks** for your new and your old home, if:[92]
  - you have moved into the new home and you could not reasonably avoid having to pay rent on your old home.[93] The local authority must consider the reasons why you had to move quickly – eg, if you were forced to move quickly to take advantage of better accommodation, you may not have been able to avoid leaving without giving notice; *or*
  - a move was delayed while you were adapting your new home to meet needs you, your partner or a child included in your award have because of disability. You can get HB on both homes for the four weeks prior to the date you move. The adaptations do not have to involve a change to the structure of the dwelling, but must be reasonably required and have a clear connection to the disability needs;[94]
- **for up to 52 weeks** for a temporary home and your normal home, if you have left your normal home because of a fear of violence in that home or from a former partner, or a child or qualifying young person previously included in your award. See p193 for what counts as violence. You must intend to return

to your normal home, and it must be reasonable for you to receive payments for both homes. The payments can be either HB or UC. For example, if your temporary home counts as specified accommodation or temporary accommodation (see p183), you can get HB for it, and HB (or a UC housing costs element) for the rent you pay for your normal home;[95]

- **indefinitely** for your two normal homes, if:[96]
  - you are a member of a couple and you or your partner are a student eligible for HB (see p802) or are on a training course (see p194 for the meaning), it is necessary for you to live apart and it is reasonable for you to receive HB for both homes; *or*
  - the local authority has housed you in more than one home because your family is large.

3

### Other situations

If you have left your home because of a **fear of violence** in your home or from a former partner, or a child or qualifying young person previously included in your award (see p193 for what counts as violence) and you do not intend to return, you can get HB for four weeks for your former home.[97] You can only get HB for your former home if your liability to pay rent was unavoidable – eg, you should have given your landlord notice, but had to leave in a hurry.

**If you have two homes**, and you are only liable to pay for one of them, you are treated as occupying the home for which you pay and therefore get HB for that home, even when you are not there. You cannot get HB under this rule if you pay rent for both homes, or if you pay rent for one and a mortgage on the other. You get HB for the home for which you pay if:[98]

- you are a single claimant or a lone parent, and you are either a student eligible for HB (see p802) or on a training course (see p194), and you live in one home during periods of study or training and another home at other times – eg, for vacations; *or*
- you had to move into temporary accommodation for essential repairs to be carried out on your main home.[99] **'Essential repairs'** means basic works rather than luxuries, but they need not be crucial to making the house habitable.[100]

## 2. The rules about your age

There are no lower or upper age limits for qualifying for housing benefit (HB). However, if you are a single claimant under 35 and are living in private rented accommodation, the amount of your rent is usually restricted – ie, the amount of rent that can be met by HB is based on that for shared accommodation (see Chapter 15).

If you are under 16, there may be a question about whether you have a legally enforceable liability for rent (see p186). If you are 16 or 17 and are being, or have been, looked after by a local authority, you cannot usually qualify for HB. See p846 for further information.

## Working-age or pension-age housing benefit

You can qualify for HB under two different sets of rules – ie, for 'working-age HB' or 'pension-age HB'.[101] Which rules apply usually depends on your (and your partner's) age, but see below if you are a member of a 'mixed-age couple' – ie, one of you is at least pension age but not the other.

You can qualify for **working-age HB** if:[102]

- you are not yet pension age; *or*
- you are at least pension age but you or your partner are on income-related employment and support allowance (ESA) or universal credit (UC).[103]

You do *not* have to be getting UC or income-related ESA to qualify for working-age HB.

You can qualify for **pension-age HB** if:[104]

- you are at least pension age; *and*
- neither you nor your partner are on income-related ESA or UC.[105]

You do *not* have to be getting pension credit (PC) to qualify for pension-age HB.

Most of the rules are the same, but there are some differences. For example, if you get pension-age HB, your applicable amount is higher than for working-age HB and the income and capital rules are more generous. Pension-age HB can be backdated for up to three months, but working-age HB can only be backdated for up to one month.

### Mixed-age couples

If you are a member of a mixed-age couple – ie, one of you is at least pension age but not the other:

- since 15 May 2019, you can only make a new claim for HB and for PC in limited circumstances (see p183 and p239). You may have to claim UC (or working-age HB if you still can) instead of pension-age HB, even though one of you is at least pension age;
- in some situations, your HB entitlement can end. If your entitlement to both HB and PC ends, you can claim UC.

#### When housing benefit ends if you are a member of a mixed-age couple

Your entitlement to HB can end if you are, or become, a member of a mixed-age couple, if your entitlement to pension-age HB as a member of that couple would otherwise start on or after 15 May 2019 (but see p184 if you were entitled to pension-age HB or PC before that date and p29 if you were getting tax credits and were sent a UC managed migration notice). Your entitlement to HB ends:[106]

- when you become a member of a mixed-age couple. This applies if you were not a member of a mixed-age couple when you were awarded HB – eg, because you were getting working-age or pension-age HB as a single person; *or*
- when you reach pension age so you are now a member of a mixed-age couple, if you were getting working-age HB while you and your partner were both under pension age; *or*
- if you are pension age, are a member of a mixed-age couple and are getting working-age HB because you (or your partner) are on UC or your partner is on income-related ESA, when entitlement to that benefit ends.

Your HB entitlement ends on the date the change takes effect under the HB rules (see p230).

**Note:** your entitlement to HB does *not* end, even if you are a member of a mixed-age couple, if:
- the HB is for 'specified' or 'temporary' accommodation' (see p183);[107] *or*
- you are not yet pension age, are getting working-age HB and are on income-related ESA when your partner reaches pension age.

***Examples***

Rangan and Janelle are a couple, both under pension age. Rangan has been getting working-age HB while in low-paid work. When he reaches pension age, his HB entitlement ends. He cannot make a new claim for pension-age HB because he is now a member of a mixed-age couple. He and Janelle can make a joint claim for UC.

Aoife is getting pension-age HB. She and her partner Gethin decide to live together. Gethin is not yet pension age. Aoife's HB entitlement ends. She and Gethin can make a joint claim for UC.

May and Ellie are a couple. May gets working-age HB and income-related ESA. When Ellie reaches pension age, May's entitlement to HB and income-related ESA continues, even though she is now a member of a mixed-age couple. May gets a full-time job so is no longer entitled to income-related ESA. Her entitlement to working-age HB therefore also ends. She and Ellie can make a joint claim for UC.

## 3. **People included in the award**

You get housing benefit (HB) for yourself. However, if you are a member of a couple, only one of you can qualify for HB. You or your partner get HB for you both. Your applicable amount includes a personal allowance for a couple and can include premiums and components based on both your and your partner's circumstances. When your benefit is worked out, your partner's income and capital are usually added to yours. See p254 for who counts as a couple.

There are some situations in which you must show that you are responsible for a child who is living in your household – eg:

- so your applicable amount can include allowances and premiums for them;
- to show you are a lone parent so you can benefit from a higher earnings disregard (see p348 and p383);
- to qualify for a disregard of earnings for childcare costs (see p350 and p384);
- for some of the rules about the size of accommodation or the number of bedrooms you are allowed that affect your 'maximum HB' (see Chapter 15).

See p259 for who counts as a child (this includes some qualifying young people). You do not have to be the child's parent. For when you count as responsible for a child, and when a child counts as living in your household, see p260.

## 4. The amount of benefit

The amount of housing benefit (HB) you get depends on:

- your applicable amount (see Chapter 13). This is made up of personal allowances, as well as premiums and components based on your circumstances and possibly a transitional addition;
- your 'maximum HB' (see p201);
- if you are not on the guarantee credit of pension credit (PC), income-related employment and support allowance (ESA) or universal credit (UC), how much:
  - capital you have (see p200 and Chapter 18 (for working-age HB) or Chapter 19 (for pension-age HB)); *and*
  - income you have (see p200 and Chapter 16 (for working-age HB) or Chapter 17 (for pension-age HB)).

For how to calculate HB, if you are on a means-tested benefit, see p200, and if you are *not* on a means-tested benefit, see p200.

You may qualify for a higher rate of HB, or if you do not qualify currently, you may qualify for HB (if you can still make a new claim – see p183):

- when the benefit rates go up; *or*
- if you (or your partner or a child included in your award) become entitled to another benefit (a 'qualifying benefit' – see p219); *or*
- if you or your partner reach pension age (see p690). If you qualify for pension-age HB (see p197), your applicable amount is higher and the income and capital rules are also more generous.

If you need help with the costs of your housing in addition to the HB you get, you may qualify for discretionary housing payments (see Chapter 25).

**Note:** you may get a reduced amount of HB if you are affected by the benefit cap (see p1025) or your HB is restricted because of a benefit offence (see p1111).

## If you are on a means-tested benefit

3

Being on the guarantee credit of PC, income-related ESA or UC is an automatic passport to maximum HB because all of your income and capital are ignored.[108] The amount of HB you get is always your maximum HB (see p201 for how to work this out).

For these purposes, you are treated as being on:[109]

- income-related ESA when it is payable to you and also when you satisfy the conditions of entitlement but are not being paid it because you are disqualified for one of the reasons on p173;
- UC on any day you are entitled to it, whether or not it is being paid to you. You must be entitled to some UC; what the DWP may call a 'nil award' of UC does not necessarily count.[110]

*Example*

Ralph and his partner are the joint housing association tenants of a two-bedroom flat. Ralph's aunt lives with them and counts as a non-dependant. They pay rent of £150 a week. Ralph gets income-related ESA. Ralph's aunt, aged 45, gets UC. Ralph gets working-age HB. None of the rent restriction rules apply, so no reduction to the rent is made and the amount of rent that can be covered (the 'eligible rent' – see p202) is £150 a week. Ralph's maximum HB is therefore £130.35 a week (£150 *minus* a non-dependant deduction of £19.65 – see p207).

Because he gets income-related ESA, Ralph's HB is £130.35 a week.

## If you are not on a means-tested benefit

If you are not on the guarantee credit of PC, income-related ESA or UC, follow the steps below to calculate your HB.[111]

- **Step 1:** check that your capital is not too high (see Chapter 18 for working-age HB or Chapter 19 for pension-age HB).
- **Step 2:** work out your maximum HB (see p201).
- **Step 3:** work out your applicable amount (see Chapter 13).
- **Step 4:** work out your income (see Chapter 16 (for working-age HB) or Chapter 17 (for pension-age HB), but also p806 if you are a student and p378 if you are getting the savings credit of PC).
- **Step 5:** calculate HB.
  - **If your income is less than or equal to your applicable amount,** HB equals your maximum HB.

- **If your income is greater than your applicable amount**, work out the difference. HB equals your maximum HB minus 65 per cent of the difference between your income and your applicable amount.

*Examples*

Huw (45) and Anna (46) are a couple who are joint private tenants of a two-bedroom flat. They pay £160 rent a week. Huw is unemployed. Anna works 21 hours a week and is paid £201.75 a week after deductions of tax and national insurance (NI) contributions. Anna gets working-age HB. A rent restriction is applied and so the amount of rent that can be covered (her eligible rent – see p202) is £120 a week.

The couple have no non-dependants. Therefore Anna's maximum HB (see below) is £120 a week. Her applicable amount is £144.65 (the standard rate for a couple if one member is at least 18).

Income to be taken into account is £191.75 of Anna's earnings a week (because £10 of her earnings are disregarded – see p349).

The difference between her income and her applicable amount is £47.10 a week (£191.75 – £144.65).

65% x £47.10 = £30.62 a week.

Anna's HB is therefore £120 (maximum HB) – £30.62 = £89.38 a week.

Brian (75) lives alone and gets pension-age HB. He receives an 'old' retirement pension (see Chapter 32) of £176.45 a week. His weekly income from his private pension is £70. His total weekly income is therefore £246.45 (£176.45 + £70). He is a sole tenant of his one-bedroom council flat. His rent of £125 a week includes his heating and hot water. No reduction is made under any rent restriction rules, but deductions are made for heating and hot water so his eligible rent (see p202) is £85.65 a week (£125 – £35.25 and £4.10). Therefore his maximum HB is £85.65 because he has no non-dependants.

His applicable amount is £244.40 (adult personal allowance for a single person who reached pension age before 1 April 2021).

The difference between his income and his applicable amount is £2.05 (£246.45 – £244.40).

65% x £2.05 = £1.33 a week.

Brian's HB is therefore £85.65 – £1.33 = £84.32 a week.

## Maximum housing benefit

To calculate your HB, you need to know the maximum amount of HB you can get. Your maximum HB is worked out as follows.[112]

- **Step 1:** work out the amount of your rent that can be covered by HB (your eligible rent) on a weekly basis. Unless you have any non-dependants for whom a deduction must be made (see p207), this is your maximum HB.

- **Step 2:** if you have any non-dependants for whom a deduction must be made, your maximum HB is the figure in Step 1, minus the non-dependant deduction(s) (see p207). This is because it is assumed non-dependants make a contribution towards your outgoings, whether or not they do so.

*Example*

Ceallach, Stacey and their adult son live in a two-bedroom flat rented from the local authority. Ceallach is the sole tenant. The rent is £100 a week. This does not include any service charges. Their son earns £250 a week gross.

The amount of rent that can be covered (eligible rent) is £100

*Minus* non-dependant deduction = £45.15

**Maximum HB** = £54.85

## Eligible rent

The amount of your rent that can be covered by HB is called your eligible rent. This is not necessarily the rent you pay to your landlord. You need to know your eligible rent to work out your maximum HB.

Your eligible rent is:[113]

- if any of the rent restriction schemes apply to you, the amount to which your rent is restricted under those rules (known as your 'maximum rent'). See Chapter 15 for details of all the schemes, which one (if any) applies to you and how your rent may be restricted; *or*
- if none of the rent restriction rules apply to you, the amount of rent you must pay your landlord (your contractual rent) minus any ineligible charges (see p203). The local authority has general powers to decrease your eligible rent to an amount it considers appropriate (but see p307).

If your rent has been reduced by a 'provider of social housing' under a government-approved tenant incentive scheme, your eligible rent is worked out as if no reduction had been made.[114] A **'provider of social housing'** is a local authority, a non-profit registered provider of social housing, a profit-making registered provider of social housing (if you have been housed in social housing) or a registered social landlord.

**Note:**

- If you are a single claimant under 35 living in private rented accommodation, the amount of your rent is usually restricted – ie, the amount of rent that can be met by HB is based on that for shared accommodation (see Chapter 15).
- If the rent you pay covers both residential and other accommodation (eg, for business use), your HB only covers the rent you pay for the residential accommodation.[115] You cannot get HB for any part of your accommodation that is used exclusively for business purposes.
- You cannot get HB for rent supplements charged to clear your rent arrears.[116]

## Calculating your weekly eligible rent

HB is always paid for a specific benefit week – a period of seven consecutive days beginning with a Monday and ending on a Sunday.[117] If you pay rent at different intervals (eg, monthly or daily), the amount must be converted to a weekly figure before HB can be calculated.[118]

### Rent-free periods

If you have a regular rent-free period (eg, you only pay rent 48 weeks a year), you get no HB during your rent-free period. Your applicable amount, weekly income, non-dependant deductions, the set deductions for meals and fuel charges and the minimum amount payable (but not your eligible rent) are adjusted.[119] This is to ensure that you do not lose or gain benefit by ignoring your circumstances in the weeks that you do not pay rent.

This does not apply if your landlord has temporarily waived the rent in return for your doing repairs (see p187).

## If you live in shared accommodation

Unless the local housing allowance or social sector rent restriction rules apply to you (see p307 and p313), if you share accommodation with people other than your partner and children included in your award and are jointly liable for the rent with them (see p189), the local authority apportions your eligible rent between you. If the rent includes any ineligible service charges, these are apportioned between you on the same basis. If only one of you is liable for the rent, that person is treated as the tenant and the other(s) may count as a non-dependant(s) (see p207).

To work out how to apportion your eligible rent, the local authority considers the number of jointly liable people in the property and the proportion of the rent actually paid by each liable person.[120] It should also consider other relevant circumstances. In some circumstances, it could be appropriate to apportion the whole rent to you, even if you are jointly liable.[121]

*Example*

Sophia and her sister rent a two-bedroom housing association flat. They are joint tenants and pay rent of £100 a week and this is the eligible rent. Sophia claims pension-age HB. The eligible rent is apportioned between her and her sister. Sophia's HB is based on £50 (£100 ÷ two).

## Ineligible charges

The local authority normally deducts ineligible charges when it works out the amount of your eligible rent. **Note:** if your rent is restricted under the local housing allowance rules (see p307), or the rules for hostels, houseboats, mobile homes, caravans and boarders (see p317), an adjustment for ineligible charges is made in this process.

Ineligible charges include:

- water charges for your personal use. Water charges in respect of communal areas (eg, in supported or sheltered accommodation) are eligible;[122] *and*
- most fuel charges; *and*
- some service charges (see p206), including charges for meals.

3

***Communal areas***

**'Communal areas'** include access areas like halls and passageways, but not rooms in common use, except those in sheltered accommodation – eg, a shared dining room.[123]

## Fuel charges

Fuel charges are ineligible unless they are for communal areas (see p205).[124] If your fuel charge is:

- specified on your rent book or is readily identifiable from your agreement with your landlord, the full amount of the charge is ineligible.[125] However, if your fuel charge is considered to be unrealistically low, a flat-rate amount is ineligible instead (see below). This is also the case if your total fuel charge is specified but contains an unknown amount for communal areas;
- not readily identifiable, a flat-rate amount is ineligible. The amounts are:[126]

| | |
|---|---|
| **If you and your family occupy more than one room:** | |
| For heating (other than hot water) | £35.25 |
| For hot water | £4.10 |
| For lighting | £2.85 |
| For cooking | £4.10 |
| **If you and your family occupy one room only:** | |
| For heating alone, or heating combined with either hot water or lighting or both | £21.10 |
| For cooking | £4.10 |

The above amounts are added together if fuel is supplied for more than one purpose. If you live in shared accommodation and are a joint tenant with people other than your partner and children included in your award, all the amounts may be apportioned according to your share of the rent (see p203).

The local authority must notify you if flat-rate fuel amounts have been used in calculating your HB. It must explain that if you can produce evidence from which the actual or approximate amount of your fuel charge can be estimated, the flat-rate amounts may be varied accordingly.

***Do you occupy one room only?***

The lower amounts apply if the accommodation you and your partner and children occupy comprises one room only. This is not defined, but the decision maker may say this means that if you only occupy one room but share the use of other rooms (such as a communal lounge), the higher amounts apply.[127] Argue that bathrooms, toilets and shared kitchens are not rooms you occupy. If you are forced to live in one room because the other room(s) in your accommodation are, in practice, unfit to live in (eg, because of severe mould or dampness), argue that the lower amounts apply.



### Fuel for communal areas

If you pay a service charge for fuel in communal areas and that charge is separately identified, it may be included as part of your eligible rent.[128] If you pay a charge for the provision of a heating system (eg, regular boiler maintenance), this is also eligible if the amount is separately identified from any other fuel charge you pay.[129]

## Service charges

Service charges are only covered by HB if payment is a condition of occupying the accommodation rather than an optional extra. Eligible and ineligible charges are listed below. If the local authority regards any of the eligible charges as excessive, it estimates a reasonable amount given the cost of comparable services.

### Eligible services

The following services are eligible for HB:[130]

- services for the provision of adequate accommodation. These include some warden and caretaker services, and water charges for communal areas (see p204) – eg, in supported or sheltered accommodation, gardens, children's play areas, lifts, entryphones, communal telephone costs, portering and rubbish removal. TV and radio relay charges are covered – eg, satellite or cable, including free-to-view UK channels; *and*
- laundry facilities (eg, a laundry room in an apartment block), but not charges for the provision of personal laundry; *and*
- furniture and household equipment, but not if there is an agreement that the furniture will eventually become yours; *and*
- cleaning of the outside of windows if you or a member of your household cannot clean them yourself, and cleaning of rooms and windows in communal areas, unless your local authority, a county council in England or the Welsh Ministers pays for these.

3

### Ineligible services

The following services are not eligible for HB:[131]

- food, including prepared meals (see below);
- sports facilities;
- TV rental, licence and subscription fees (but see p205);
- transport;
- personal laundry service;
- provision of an emergency alarm system;
- medical expenses;
- nursing and personal care;
- counselling and other support services;
- any other charge not connected with the provision of adequate accommodation and not specifically included in the list of eligible charges on p205.

It is the amount of the charge specified in your rent agreement that is not eligible for HB, although local authorities can substitute their own estimate if they consider the amount to be unreasonably low.[132] If the amount is not specified in your rent agreement, the local authority estimates how much is fairly attributable to the service, given the cost of comparable services.[133]

If your housing costs include an amount for meals, set amounts are ineligible regardless of the actual cost.[134] The amounts are:

| | |
|---|---|
| **If at least three meals a day are provided:** | |
| For the claimant, partner and each child aged 16 or over included in the award | £35.95 |
| For each child aged under 16 included in the award | £18.25 |
| **If breakfast only is provided:** | |
| For the claimant, partner and each child included in the award | £4.35 |
| **In all other cases (part board):** | |
| For the claimant, partner and each child aged 16 or over included in the award | £24.00 |
| For each child aged under 16 included in the award | £12.00 |

Children only count as having reached the age of 16 on the first Monday in September following their 16th birthday.

The standard amounts are also ineligible for everyone who has meals paid for by you – eg, a non-dependant.[135]

### Support services in supported accommodation

If you live in supported accommodation, HB can help with your rent. However, HB is not available for the support services provided with your accommodation.

Instead, the local authority funds these (eg, via your landlord or a voluntary organisation) and you may be charged for them.

## Deductions for non-dependants

If people other than your partner and children included in your award normally live with you they may count as non-dependants and a set deduction is usually made from your eligible rent when your maximum HB is calculated (see p201).[136] This is because it is assumed non-dependants contribute towards your outgoings, whether or not they do so. Examples of non-dependants are adult sons or daughters, elderly relatives or friends who share your home.

### Who counts as a non-dependant

People only count as your non-dependants if they normally live with you.[137] So, for example, someone who is only staying with you temporarily but normally lives elsewhere, or is homeless and is only using your address as a postal address, should not count as a non-dependant. If you think the local authority wrongly assumes that a person is your non-dependant, ask for a revision or appeal (see Chapters 50 and 51). **Note:** some people do not count as non-dependants even if they normally live with you (see p208).

People only **'live with you'** if they have their home with you and share some accommodation with you.[138] If they only share a bathroom, toilet or a communal area such as a hall, passageway or room in common use in sheltered accommodation, they do not count as living with you. If other areas of the house are shared (including the kitchen, unless it is only used by someone else to prepare the person's food[139]), the person counts as living with you. This is the case even if you only use them at different times, provided you have a shared right to use them and live in the same household (see p262 for the meaning of 'household').[140] A person who is separately liable to pay rent to your landlord does not count as living with you for these purposes.

People should only count as **'normally'** living with you if they have been there long enough to regard your home as their normal home.[141] Factors to be taken into account include:[142]

- the relationship between you;
- how much time the person spends at your address;
- where the person:
  - has post sent;
  - is registered to vote or with a GP or dentist;
  - registered a mobile phone;
  - keeps clothes and personal belongings;
- if the person has a pet, where it is kept;
- whether their stay or absence from your address is temporary or permanent. The temporary absence rules on p191 may be used to work this out;[143]

- whether the person has another place that could be regarded as home and if, for instance, the person pays rent or water charges there, or just travels around.

### People who do not count as non-dependants

The following people do *not* count as non-dependants, and no non-dependant deduction is made for them, even if they normally live with you:[144]

3

- your partner;
- a child or 'qualifying young person' included in your award;
- a child or qualifying young person living with you who does not count as a member of your household (see p261) – eg, a foster child;
- someone who is staying with you but whose normal home is elsewhere. **Note:** for these purposes, someone can only have one normal home at a time;[145]
- someone who is employed by a charitable or voluntary organisation as a resident carer for you or your partner. This applies if a charge is made for the services, paid by you or a public body on your behalf;
- any person, or a member of that person's household, to whom you or your partner are liable to pay rent on a commercial basis – eg, a resident landlord;
- someone who jointly occupies your home and is either the joint owner with you or your partner or is liable with you or your partner to make payments in respect of occupying it. You do not jointly occupy the home with someone unless you made a joint agreement with your landlord to do so. The mere fact that you live in the same home does not make you joint occupiers;[146]
- someone who is liable to pay rent on a commercial basis to you or your partner – eg, your tenants or lodgers. However, although no non-dependant deduction can be made for that person, the rent paid can count as your income (see p358 and p387).

**Note:** if people come within the last three categories above, they *do* count as non-dependants if they are treated as not liable for rent under the rules explained on pp187–89 (other than if they are students or have failed the 'habitual residence test').[147]

## When a non-dependant deduction is not made

No deduction is made for any of your non-dependants if either you or your partner:[148]

- are certified as severely sight impaired or blind by a consultant ophthalmologist (or are within 28 weeks of ceasing to be certified); *or*
- receive attendance allowance (AA) (or equivalent benefits paid because of injury at work or a war injury), pension age disability payment (PADP), the care component of disability living allowance (DLA), Scottish adult disability living allowance (SADLA) or child disability payment (CDP), the daily living component of personal independence payment (PIP) or adult disability payment (ADP) or armed forces independence payment (AFIP).

If deductions must be made, no deduction is made for any non-dependant who is:[149]

- under 18 years old;
- under 25 and;
  - entitled to UC and does not have any earned income; *or*
  - on income-related ESA that does not include the support component and the non-dependant has not been placed in the work-related activity group (see p561).

  Someone can be treated as being on income-related ESA for these purposes (see p200);
- on PC;
- staying with you temporarily but whose normal home is elsewhere;
- receiving a training allowance in connection with youth training under specified provisions;[150]
- a full-time student (see Chapter 37). For working-age HB, this only applies during the student's period of study, or unless the student is in full-time paid work, during the summer vacation. 'Full-time student' is not defined for pension-age HB;
- a member of the armed or reserved forces who usually lives with you and is away on operations, irrespective of the length of the absence;
- in hospital for more than 52 weeks. Separate stays in hospital which are not more than 28 days apart are added together when calculating the 52 weeks;
- in prison.



## The amount of the deductions

If you have non-dependants living with you who are 18 or over, and for whom a deduction must be made, when working out your maximum HB, a fixed amount is deducted from your eligible rent (see p201), whatever they pay you. A deduction is made for every non-dependant living in your household, except in the case of a non-dependant couple (see p210).

Unless your non-dependant is in full-time paid work, a £19.65 deduction is made each week. If your non-dependant is in full-time paid work, the amount of the deduction depends on the person's weekly gross income as follows.[151]

| *Income bands* | *Deduction* |
|---|---|
| Aged 18 or over and in full-time paid work with a weekly gross income of: | |
| £577 or more | £126.65 |
| £463–£576.99 | £115.45 |
| £348–£462.99 | £101.35 |
| £266–£347.99 | £62.00 |
| £183–£265.99 | £45.15 |
| All others (for whom a deduction is made) | £19.65 |

3

The rules on full-time paid work are in Chapter 40. **Note:**

- A non-dependant who is not in (or is treated as not being in) full-time paid work does not attract the higher levels of deduction even if weekly gross income is £183 or more.
- People on (or treated as being on) income-related ESA (see p200) for more than three days in a benefit week do not count as being in full-time paid work in that week.[152] This means the lower deduction (£19.65) is made (or, in some cases, no deduction).

Gross income includes wages before tax and NI are deducted, plus any other income the non-dependant has (apart from AA (or equivalent benefits paid because of injury at work or a war injury), PADP, DLA/SADLA/CDP, PIP/ADP and AFIP). Also ignored are payments from specified trusts and schemes established to compensate people, including victims of medical and other errors, institutional child abuse, emergencies, disasters and acts of terrorism.[153]

***Do you know your non-dependant's income?***

If you do not know your non-dependant's income, ask the local authority to consider the circumstances – eg, if your non-dependant is doing a job which is normally very low paid. The local authority should not assume the worst – eg, that your non-dependant earns the highest amount. It should assess the likely level of income on the evidence available.[154]

### Non-dependant couples

Only one deduction is made for a couple (or the members of a polygamous marriage) who are non-dependants. The deduction made is the highest that would have been made if they were treated as individuals.[155] To decide which income band applies (see p209), their joint income counts, even if only one of them is in full-time work.[156]

### Non-dependants of joint occupiers

If you share a non-dependant with any other joint occupiers, the deduction is divided between you, taking into account the proportion of housing costs paid by each of you.[157] If the person is a non-dependant of only one of you, the full deduction is made from that person's benefit. No apportionment is made between the members of a couple (or polygamous marriage).

### If you are getting pension-age HB

If you are getting pension-age HB (see p197) and a non-dependant moves in with you (so a deduction should be made), or there has been a change of circumstances in respect of a non-dependant (so a higher deduction should be made), the effect of this can be delayed for 26 weeks.[158]

### Your non-dependant's income or capital is more than yours

Normally, a non-dependant's income is only relevant when deciding which non-dependant deduction applies. However, unless you are on the guarantee credit of PC, or are on or treated as on income-related ESA (see p200), your HB entitlement is assessed based on your non-dependant's income *and* capital rather than your own if:[159]

- the non-dependant's income and capital are both greater than yours; *and*
- the local authority is satisfied you have made an arrangement with your non-dependant to 'take advantage of the HB scheme' (see p189).

Any income and capital normally treated as belonging to you are completely ignored, but the rest of the HB calculation proceeds as normal.

## 5. Special benefit rules

Special rules may apply if you:

- are 16/17-year-olds previously looked after by a local authority (see p846);
- have come from or are going abroad (see Chapters 56, 57 and 58);
- are studying (see Chapter 37);
- are in hospital, living in a care home or similar accommodation, or in prison (see Chapter 38).

## 6. Claims and backdating

To be entitled to housing benefit (HB), you must make a claim for it.[160] Claim as soon as you think you may be entitled to it or you may lose benefit. The rules about backdating are explained on p216.

You must make a separate application for discretionary housing payments to the local authority (see Chapter 25).

### Making a claim

A claim for HB must normally be made in writing on a properly completed claim form.[161] Check your local authority's website to find out where to get a claim form. The local authority can treat any written document (eg, a letter) as a claim, provided the information and evidence you provide is sufficient. **Note:** if you make a claim for pension credit (PC), you can claim HB at the same time (see p212).

It is always best to claim HB in writing if you can. Keep a copy in case queries arise. However, you may also be able to claim:

- by phone if:
  - your local authority has a number for this purpose.[162] If the local authority provides a written statement of your circumstances, you must approve this statement for your claim to be valid. **Note:** even if you cannot claim by phone, if you call to ask to be sent a claim form and you return it within one month, your written claim is backdated to the date of your call (see p215); *or*
  - you claim PC by phone;
- online or by email, if your local authority has authorised it.[163]



### If you claim pension credit

If you make a claim for PC by phone, your HB claim may be completed at the same time.[164] The DWP takes your details and sends you a statement of your circumstances to check, sign and return to the DWP, along with evidence to support your claim. It forwards your HB claim to the local authority. You can claim HB by calling the DWP (using the number specified) at any time before a decision is made on your PC claim. If the local authority or DWP provides a written statement of your circumstances, you must approve this for your claim to be valid. If you claim HB in this way, keep a copy and chase your claim up with the local authority to ensure they have received it. **Note:** this rule also applies if you can still make a claim for HB (see p183) and you claim contributory employment and support allowance (ESA) or new-style jobseeker's allowance (JSA).

If you are providing information or evidence that is required or notifying a change of circumstances to the DWP in connection with your PC award – eg, by phone – you can claim HB in the same manner as you reported the change to the DWP, if it agrees. You must claim HB before a decision is made on your PC award.[165] **Note:** this rule also applies if you can still make a new claim for HB (see p183) and you have an award of ESA or JSA.

### Making sure your claim is valid

If possible, your claim for HB should be accompanied by all the information and evidence needed to assess it.[166] Your claim is 'defective' if you:

- do not complete your claim form properly or you claim in writing, but not on the claim form (eg, by letter or email), and do not provide sufficient information and evidence; *or*
- claim by phone and do not provide all the information required during the call.

It is very important that you provide any information or evidence required. Until you do, your claim may be defective and you may not count as having made a valid claim. However, you should not delay your claim just because you do not have all the evidence ready to send immediately.

### Correcting a defective claim

If your claim is defective, you can correct it. If you have:[167]

- not completed the claim form properly, the local authority can return it to you to do so. However, if you sent or gave your claim form to the DWP, it can ask you to provide the local authority with information needed to complete the form; *or*
- claimed in writing, but not on the claim form (eg, by letter or email), the local authority can send you a claim form to complete properly; *or*
- claimed by phone to:
  - the local authority, the local authority must give you an opportunity to provide the information required; *or*
  - the DWP, it can give you an opportunity to provide the information required. However, if the DWP does not do so, the local authority *must* give you an opportunity to provide the information, unless it thinks it already has sufficient information. If it does, your claim is treated as though it was received on the date of your original claim.

If you return the form completed properly or provide the information or evidence within one month of the last time you were told your claim is defective, your claim is treated as though it was received on the date of your original claim.[168] The local authority can allow you longer than one month if it thinks this reasonable.

If your claim is defective and it is not accepted as valid, you should be given a decision saying so. You can appeal against the decision (see Chapter 51).

## Amending or withdrawing your claim

**You may amend your claim** (this includes asking for your claim to be backdated) at any time before a decision on it is made. You can do this by writing to the local authority, by phone to the local authority or the DWP on the specified number or by any other manner the local authority or DWP decides or accepts.[169] Amendments are treated as though they were part of your original claim.

**You may withdraw your claim** at any time before a decision is made on it.[170] You must do this by writing to the local authority or, if you made your claim by phone to the local authority, by phone to the local authority. A notice to withdraw your claim takes effect from the day it is received.

## Where to claim

If you claim in writing, you must usually send or give your HB claim to the local authority's designated office for the receipt of HB claims.[171] The address is usually on the claim form or a notice accompanying it. It is always best to send or give your claim direct to the local authority and it may speed up your claim if you do so. However, you can also send or give your claim to:[172]

- if you or your partner are making a claim for PC (or JSA or ESA), your DWP office. The DWP must usually forward it to the local authority within two working days of receiving it, or as soon as practicable after. If you claim HB in this way, keep a copy and chase your claim up with the local authority to ensure they have received it;[173] *or*

- a county council office, if your local authority has arranged for claims to be received there; *or*
- if you are at least pension age, any **'authorised office'** – ie, an office nominated by the DWP and authorised by the local authority for receiving HB claims.

3

Keep a copy of your claim form wherever possible. Ask for confirmation that you have delivered it to the relevant office.

## Who should claim

If you are a single person or a lone parent, you claim HB on your own behalf. If you are a member of a couple, only one of you can claim; you can decide between you who should do so. If you cannot agree, the local authority decides.[174]

***Who should you choose to make the claim?***

If you are a member of a couple, the choice of claimant may affect the amount of HB you receive – eg, if one of you is a full-time student and not eligible for HB (see p801) or if one of you is getting ESA and the other is getting personal independence payment. However, if you are considering changing the award to your partner's name, check whether a new claim is possible (see p183) and also whether this could result in your becoming subject to harsher rent restriction rules (see Chapter 15) or losing entitlement to any premiums or components (see Chapter 13).

### Appointees

If you cannot manage your claim, the local authority must accept a claim made by someone formally appointed to act legally on your behalf.[175] If no one has been formally appointed, the local authority can decide to make someone aged over 18 an appointee who can act on your behalf. For the purpose of the claim, appointees have the same rights and are responsible for carrying out the same duties as though they were the claimant.

You can write to ask to be an appointee. If you no longer want to be an appointee, you can resign after giving four weeks' notice. The local authority may terminate any appointment at any time.[176] If someone is given a formal legal appointment, that person automatically takes over from the person appointed by the local authority.[177]

## Information to support your claim

When you claim HB, you must:

- satisfy the national insurance (NI) number requirement (see below), unless you live in a hostel.[178] If you are a member of a couple, your partner must also usually satisfy this requirement; *and*
- provide proof of your identity, if required; *and*
- provide information and evidence required with the claim. Until you do, you may not count as having made a valid claim. Correct any defects as soon as possible or your date of claim may be affected.



If you or your partner are getting JSA, and have notified the DWP that you (or your partner) have started work, the DWP can ask you to provide the local authority with any information or evidence it needs to decide whether you continue to be entitled to HB.[179] This only applies if, as a result of the change, entitlement to JSA will end or the amount of new-style JSA will reduce.

The local authority may ask you to provide information *after* you are awarded HB to determine whether you are still entitled to HB. You must supply this within one month, or longer if the local authority thinks this is reasonable.[180] If you do not, your HB could be suspended or even terminated (see p1031). **Note:** you must actually have been notified; proof of posting to your last known address is not sufficient.[181]

### The national insurance number requirement

For how you (and your partner) can satisfy the NI number requirement, and for when your partner is exempt, see p1007. The rules are the same as for other benefits. However, note the following.

- You do not have to satisfy the NI number requirement if you live in a hostel.[182]
- If you have claimed HB with a claim for PC and the DWP has accepted that you satisfy the NI number requirement, the local authority can accept that you also satisfy it for HB purposes.[183]

## The date of your claim

The date of your claim is important because it determines when your entitlement to HB starts. This is not necessarily the date from when you are paid. For information about when entitlement to HB starts, see p220.

Your date of claim is not necessarily the date the local authority receives it. It can be an earlier date.

Your date of claim is usually the earliest of:[184]

- the date you first notify a designated office, DWP office or authorised office (see p214) (or county council office, if the local authority has arranged for claims to be received there) that you want to claim HB, provided a properly completed claim is received in one of those offices within one month. The one-month period can be extended if the local authority thinks it is reasonable; *or*

- the date your valid claim is received by the designated office, DWP office or authorised office (or county council office, if the local authority has arranged for claims to be received there).



There are exceptions to the above rules.[185]

- If you or your partner have successfully claimed the guarantee credit of PC and your HB claim is made within one month of that claim being received by the DWP, your claim is treated as having been made on the first day of entitlement to that benefit. For example, if your claim for the guarantee credit of PC is backdated, and your claim for HB was made two weeks after your PC claim was received by the DWP, your date of claim for HB purposes is the date to which your PC claim is backdated.[186]
- If you are awarded universal credit (UC) and you claim HB within one month of your UC claim or, if you are someone who does not have to make a claim for UC, within one month of being notified that you were awarded UC, your HB claim is treated as having been made on the first day of entitlement to UC.
- If you or your partner are on the guarantee credit of PC, income-related ESA or UC, have just become liable to pay rent for your home and your HB claim reaches the local authority's designated office or DWP office within one month of your becoming liable, your claim is treated as having been made on the date that you first became liable to pay rent.
- If you have separated from your partner or your partner has died, and your partner was entitled to HB on the date this happened, your claim is treated as having been made on the date of the separation or death if you claim within one month.

You must make sure your claim is valid. If it is defective, you are given a short time to correct the defects (see p213). If you do, your claim is treated as having been made when you initially claimed.

## Backdating your claim

It is very important to claim in time. Even if your claim is backdated, the arrears of HB that you can get are limited.

- A claim for pension-age HB can be backdated for up to three months. You do not have to show a good reason for your late claim (see p217).
- A claim for working-age HB (only allowed in limited cases – see p183) can be backdated for up to one month. You must show a good reason for your late claim (called 'good cause' – see p218).

For backdated HB to be considered, you must ask for HB for a past period. Do this as soon as possible, preferably at the same time as your claim for HB. Any backdated HB is calculated based on your circumstances and the HB rules as they were over the backdating period.

If you would have been entitled to HB for an earlier period than the backdating rules allow, you could:

- ask for an 'any time' revision if there are grounds (see p1135);
- ask for compensation from the local authority if you were given wrong information or misled by it (see p1261);
- complain to the Ombudsman (see p1267).

If you only qualify for HB when a 'qualifying benefit' is awarded, see p219 for when your claim may be backdated further.

### Three months' backdating

A claim for pension-age HB (see p197) can be backdated for up to three months.[187] This applies whatever the reasons were for your delay in claiming and, even if you do not ask for HB for a past period, until some time after you make your claim for HB. You only need to show that you qualified for HB during that period.

You can get backdated HB for the three months before the date of your HB claim (see p215) – eg, the date your claim was received or the date you notified the local authority that you wanted to claim HB.[188] However, if you or your partner successfully claimed the guarantee credit of PC and your claim for HB is received within one month of your PC claim being received by the DWP, your entitlement to HB cannot begin earlier than three months before your claim for PC was made (or treated as having been made).

### One month's backdating

A claim for working-age HB (see p197) can be backdated for up to one month.[189]

You must show that you qualified for HB during the period *and* prove you had a continuous good reason (called good cause) for failing to claim or to ask for backdated HB. You can only get backdated HB from the latest of:[190]

- **date one:** the day from which you had continuous good cause for your late claim; *or*
- **date two:** the day one month before your date of claim. Your date of claim is not necessarily the date the local authority receives it. It can be an earlier date (see p215); *or*
- **date three:** the day one month before you asked for backdated HB.

***Example***

Siobhan, aged 41, lives in supported accommodation (called 'specified accommodation'). She claimed working-age HB on 7 May 2025. After getting advice, she asked for backdated HB on 16 May 2025.

The local authority accepts that she had a continuous good cause for her late claim from 24 February 2025.

Date one = 24 February 2025.

Date two = 7 April 2025. This is the day one month before her date of claim for HB.

Date three = 16 April 2025. This is the day one month before she asked for backdated HB.

Siobhan gets backdated HB from 16 April 2025, the latest of the three relevant dates.



If you are claiming HB after a previous entitlement ended, as well as asking for backdated HB, you should see whether you can challenge the local authority's decision to end your entitlement to HB (see Chapters 50 and 51).

You count as having **'good cause'** for your late claim if you can show there is something that would probably have caused a reasonable person of your age and experience to act (or fail to act) as you did, taking all the circumstances into account (including your state of health and the information which you received and which you might have obtained).[191] The more reasonable your behaviour in not claiming earlier given your circumstances, the more likely it is that you have a good cause.[192] If you have a mental health problem that makes you act unreasonably, this must be borne in mind.[193] If you have difficulty communicating in English or understanding documents, or have little knowledge of the benefits system, this should be taken into account, but these are not usually considered a good cause in themselves.[194] For examples of what may be good cause for a late claim, see p210 of the 2020/21 edition of this *Handbook*.

## If you claim the wrong benefit

There are no rules that allow a claim for another benefit to be treated as a claim for HB.

## Claiming in advance

You can claim HB in advance if you become liable for rent for the first time but cannot move into your accommodation until after your liability begins. You must claim HB as soon as you are liable for rent. Once you move in, you may be able to receive HB for the four weeks before moving in (see p190).

If you are not entitled to HB now, the local authority can treat your claim as having been made in the benefit week immediately before you are first entitled, unless the reason you do not qualify straight away is because you fail the 'habitual residence test' (see p1300). This applies if you will become entitled:[195]

- within 13 weeks of claiming working-age HB or 17 weeks of claiming pension-age HB; *or*
- within 17 weeks of claiming either type of HB if you or your partner will be pension age (see p690) within 17 weeks.

If this happens, you do not need to make a further claim later.

## Housing benefit after an award of a qualifying benefit

You may not be entitled to HB currently, but would be once you, your partner or a child or 'qualifying young person' included in your claim become entitled to a qualifying benefit (eg, a disability benefit or carer's allowance), because you then qualify for premiums or components. Alternatively, you may be entitled to a higher rate of benefit once the qualifying benefit is awarded. If you are already entitled to HB when the qualifying benefit is awarded, see p1137, p1147 and p1157.



***Do you only qualify for housing benefit when a qualifying benefit is awarded?***

If you only qualify for HB when a qualifying benefit is awarded, the rules operate in an unfair way so you should do the following.

1. Claim HB (if you still can) while waiting to hear about the claim for a qualifying benefit.
2. If you do not qualify for HB, ask the local authority to wait to make a decision on your HB claim until the award of the qualifying benefit is made (known as 'stockpiling' your claim). You may have to persuade the local authority that it can do so. If the local authority refuses, argue that its failure to delay making a decision on your claim was an 'error of law' and that there are grounds for an any time revision (see p1135).[196]
3. If you are refused HB but are then awarded a qualifying benefit, claim again and ask for your claim to be backdated. If you need to, argue that you have a good cause for your late claim (see p218).
4. If you lose benefit because of how the rules operate, ask your local authority for compensation to cover the period before your fresh HB claim.

## Notice of the decision

Once the local authority has all the information and evidence required, it must make a decision on your claim for HB within 14 days or as soon as 'reasonably practicable'.[197] If you are a 'person affected by the decision', you must be notified of it by the local authority without delay or as soon as reasonably practicable.[198] In all other cases (eg, if a decision is made following a change in your circumstances), you (and other people affected by the decision) must be notified within 14 days or as soon as reasonably practicable. You can request reasons for a decision. Your request must be in writing and it must be signed by you.[199]

***Person affected by a decision***

You are a person affected by a decision if you are:[200]

- a claimant; *or*
- someone acting for a claimant who is unable to act for themself – eg, an appointee; *or*
- someone from whom the local authority decides to recover an overpayment (including a landlord); *or*
- a landlord or agent if the decision concerns whether or not to make a direct payment of HB to you.[201]

## Information a decision notice should contain

If the decision is one you can appeal (see p1172), you must be informed of:[202]

- your right to appeal against the decision; *and*
- your right to a written statement of reasons for the decision (if this is not already included – see p1125. The rules are the same as for other benefits.)



The other information that must be provided varies with the particular circumstances of your case and includes the following.[203]

- The normal weekly amount of HB to which you are entitled, including the amount of any deductions for non-dependants and fuel. You must be told why fuel deductions have been made and that they can be varied if you provide evidence of the actual amount involved.
- The amount of your rent that can be covered by HB (your weekly 'eligible rent' – see p202).
- If you are a private tenant, the day your HB will be paid and whether payment will be made weekly or monthly.
- The date on which your entitlement starts (see below).
- In some cases, how your applicable amount is calculated, how your income has been assessed and the amount of capital the local authority has taken into account. If the income and capital of a non-dependant has been used instead of yours to calculate your HB (see p211), you must be informed of this and the reasons why.
- If your claim was:
  - successful, your duty to notify the local authority of any change in circumstances which may affect your entitlement and the kinds of changes that should be reported;
  - unsuccessful, a statement explaining exactly why you are not entitled.
- If it has been decided to pay your HB direct to your landlord, information saying how much is to be paid to your landlord and when payments will start.

## When your entitlement starts

Your entitlement to HB starts:[204]

- if you become liable for rent for the first time (for a home you have moved into), in the week your claim is made or is treated as having been made, from the Monday of that week. This includes if you become liable for daily payments in a hostel or accommodation provided by the local authority on a short-term lease or because you are homeless. This means that your HB starts on the same day your liability to pay rent actually begins;[205] *or*
- in all other cases, from the Monday following your date of claim, or following the date from when you are treated as claiming if your claim is backdated or you claim in advance.

## 7. Getting paid

How housing benefit (HB) is paid depends on whether you are the tenant of the local authority responsible for paying HB or a private or housing association tenant. If you cannot act for yourself, payment can be made to someone acting on your behalf (see p222). In some circumstances, payment can be made direct to your landlord (see p222). No HB is payable if the amount would be less than 50 pence a week.[206]



***When is housing benefit paid?***

You are normally paid in arrears at intervals of a week, two weeks, four weeks or a month, depending on when your rent is usually due. HB can also be paid at longer intervals if you agree.[207] If you are a private or housing association tenant, the local authority can pay your HB weekly to avoid an overpayment or if you are liable to pay rent weekly and it is in your interests for HB to be paid weekly.

Different rules apply if HB is paid direct to your landlord.[208]

**Note:**

- Your HB might be paid at a reduced rate if you have been sanctioned for a benefit offence (see p1111).
- If payment of your HB is delayed, see p228. You might be able to get a 'payment on account'. If you wish to complain about how your claim has been dealt with or claim compensation, see Chapter 55.
- If payment of your HB is suspended, see p1031.
- If you are overpaid HB, you might have to repay it (see Chapter 47) and, in some circumstances, you might have to pay a penalty (see p1101). If you have been accused of fraud, see Chapter 48.

### How your benefit is paid

**If your landlord is the local authority** responsible for paying HB, your HB is paid as a reduction in your rent. This is called a 'rent rebate'.[209]

**If you are a private or housing association tenant**, you receive HB in the form of a 'rent allowance'.[210] If you live in a caravan, mobile home or houseboat, this applies even if you are also liable to pay a local authority – eg, for site or mooring fees. HB is normally paid to you, although, in some cases, it may be paid direct to your landlord or to someone acting on your behalf.

**Note:** if your rent allowance is:

- less than £1 a week, the local authority can pay your HB up to six months in arrears;[211]
- more than £2 a week, you can insist on two-weekly payments, unless HB is paid direct to your landlord.[212]

The local authority has the discretion to pay you by whatever method it chooses, but, in doing so, it must consider your 'reasonable needs and convenience'.[213]

If the local authority refuses to replace a payment which has never arrived, seek legal advice. You could write to the local authority and threaten to sue in the county court (sheriff court in Scotland).

3

## Payment to someone acting on your behalf

If an appointee or someone legally empowered to act for you has claimed HB on your behalf, that person can also receive the HB payments.[214]

If you can manage your HB for yourself, you can still nominate an agent to receive or collect it for you. To do this, you must make a written request to the local authority. Anyone you nominate must be aged 18 or over.[215]

If a claimant dies, any unpaid HB may be paid to a personal representative or, if there is none, to the next of kin aged 16 or over.[216] A written application must be received by the local authority within 12 months of the claimant's death. The local authority may allow longer. If HB was being paid to the landlord before the claimant's death, the local authority can pay any outstanding HB to the landlord to clear the remaining rent due.

## Payment direct to a landlord

Your HB can be paid direct to your landlord (or the person you pay rent to) but only in specified circumstances. Your landlord could contact the local authority about this.[217] The local authority can suspend payment while it makes enquiries about who should be paid your HB.[218] If the local authority has concerns about your landlord, see p223.

If you have just claimed HB or the local authority has carried out a supersession of your award, and the local authority thinks you have not already paid your rent and that it would be in the interests of the 'efficient administration' of HB, it can make the first payment to your landlord.[219]

Both you and your landlord should be notified if HB is to be paid to your landlord. If it is *not* in your interests to have HB paid direct to your landlord, it is worth trying to persuade the local authority to withhold it rather than paying it to your landlord. Get advice before you do so.

### When payment must be made to your landlord

The local authority *must* pay your HB, including payments on account (see p228), direct to your landlord (or the person you pay rent to), if:[220]

- you or your partner are getting pension credit (PC), or for working-age HB, jobseeker's allowance (JSA) or employment and support allowance (ESA) and the DWP has decided to pay part of that benefit to your landlord for arrears (see p1035); *or*
- you have rent arrears equivalent to eight weeks' rent or more, unless you can show that it is in your overriding interest not to make direct payments.[221]

Compulsory direct payments stop once your arrears have been reduced to less than eight weeks' rent. The local authority may then choose to continue direct payments on a discretionary basis.

#### Payment to your landlord on a discretionary basis

The local authority may pay your HB direct to your landlord (or the person you pay rent to):

- if the local housing allowance rent restriction rules do *not* apply to you (see p307):[222]
  - if you have requested or agreed to direct payments; *or*
  - without your agreement, if it decides that direct payments are in your or your family's best interests. You do not have to have any of your family living with you for payment to be made to your landlord under this rule;[223]
- if the local housing allowance rent restriction rules apply to you (see p307), if the local authority:[224]
  - thinks you are likely to have difficulty managing your own financial affairs or that it is improbable that you will pay your rent. The local authority can make direct payments (for a maximum of eight weeks) while it considers the situation; *or*
  - thinks it will help you to secure or keep accommodation. **Note:** the government intends that this should only apply if the rent is at a level you can afford; *or*
  - has already made direct payments to your landlord during your current award of HB in any of the situations when direct payments must be made;
- whether or not the local housing allowance rent restriction rules apply to you, without your agreement if you have left the address for which you were getting HB and there are rent arrears. In this case, direct payments of any unpaid HB due in respect of that accommodation can be made, up to the total of the outstanding arrears.[225] If your landlord retained your tenancy deposit to cover any of the rent arrears, the local authority should consider this. It should also deduct any amounts you could offset against what you would owe if your landlord were to take you to court to recover the rent arrears – eg, an amount you paid for repairs that were your landlord's responsibility.[226]

#### When the local authority has concerns about a landlord

The local authority may refuse to make direct payments if it is not satisfied that your landlord is a 'fit and proper person'.[227] However, direct payments may still be made if the local authority is satisfied it is in your or your family's best interests.[228] If the local authority decides not to make payments to your landlord, it can make payments to you (including sending you a cheque payable to the landlord) or to a trusted third party, such as a social worker or solicitor.[229]

## Continuing payments

Your HB can continue to be paid at the same rate, even though your entitlement might otherwise have changed.

- When your entitlement to:
  - income-related ESA ends because you or your partner are moving on to PC, you may be able to continue to receive HB at the same rate for four weeks (see below); *or*
  - income-related or contributory ESA or severe disablement allowance (SDA) ends because you or your partner start work or increase your hours or earnings, you may be entitled to extended payments of HB (see below);

  **Note:** this rule also applied if your entitlement to income support (IS) or income-based JSA ended for the reasons described above.
- If you are getting HB when you make a new claim for universal credit (UC), your HB may continue for two weeks (called 'HB run-on' – see p227).

### Continuing payments on claiming pension credit

To avoid problems caused by delays in reassessing your HB when you move from income-related ESA on to PC, you can receive pension-age HB for a period, normally at the same rate as the HB you were getting before. Your 'maximum HB' (see p201) is recalculated if your rent increases or there is a change in the non-dependant deductions (see p207) that should be made.[230] **Note:** this rule also applied if you moved from IS or income-based JSA on to PC. Although this rule does not apply if you transfer to PC from UC, instead you can claim pension-age HB during your last UC assessment period, and qualify for HB from the date you reach pension age.[231]

You qualify for continuing payments if:[232]

- your partner has claimed PC and the DWP has certified this; *or*
- your income-related ESA ceased because you reached pension age (see p690). The DWP must certify this and that you are required to claim, or have claimed, PC (or are treated as having done so).

You get continuing payments for:[233]

- four weeks from the day after your income-related ESA ceases; *or*
- if the four-week period ends other than on a Sunday, until the Sunday after the end of the four-week period.

### Extended payments of housing benefit

If you or your partner are on income-related or contributory ESA or SDA and your entitlement ends because you (or your partner) start work or increase your hours or pay, you may be entitled to continue to receive the same amount of HB as you did before your entitlement to one of those benefits ended, for up to four weeks. These are called extended payments of HB.

You do not have to claim extended payments of HB. They should be paid automatically.[234] However, your local authority needs to know that your or your partner's entitlement to ESA or SDA has ceased, so you must notify it.

If you want to get an extended payments decision changed, you can apply for a revision or supersession or appeal (see Chapters 50 and 51).



### Who can get extended payments

You qualify for extended payments of HB if you are getting HB, you (or your partner) started work (including self-employed work) or increased your hours or pay, and:[235]

- you are getting working-age HB (see p197) and your (or your partner's) entitlement to income-related ESA ended.[236] You (or your partner) must have been entitled to, and in receipt of, IS, new-style, income-based or joint-claim JSA or income-related ESA, or a combination of these, for at least 26 weeks; *or*
- your (or your partner's) entitlement to contributory ESA or SDA ended, and:[237]
  - you (or your partner) were not entitled to or in receipt of income-related ESA; *and*
  - if you are getting pension-age HB, you are not in receipt of PC; *and*
  - you (or your partner) had been continuously entitled to, and in receipt of, contributory ESA or SDA, or a combination of these, for at least 26 weeks.

In both cases, the work, or increase in earnings or hours, must be expected to last at least five weeks.

***Do you need to report the change in your circumstances?***

1. If you are getting ESA or SDA and you start work or your hours or pay change, you must report this to the DWP. The end of your entitlement to these benefits is also a change in your circumstances that you must report to the local authority (see p228). Report the change as soon as possible.
2. If you do not report the end of your entitlement to ESA or SDA to the local authority, your entitlement to extended payments of HB is not affected, but this could result in an overpayment of HB after the extended payment period.
3. You could be entitled to a higher rate of HB than you were before your entitlement to ESA or SDA ended.

If you move home, you can still qualify for extended payments of HB, provided the day you moved was in the same week, or the week before, you or your partner started work or increased your hours or pay.[238] See below for how the amount of the extended payments can be affected.

### The amount of the extended payments and how long they last

Extended payments of HB are paid for four weeks unless:[239]

- any of the weeks count as rent-free periods (see p203); *or*
- your liability to pay rent ceases altogether within the four weeks.

3

If you claim UC during the four-week period, your entitlement to HB can still continue for two weeks (called HB run-on – see p227). However, your entitlement can end at the end of the four-week period, if this is sooner, if you would no longer be entitled to HB after the end of that period.

The weekly amount of your extended payments (unless you move into local authority accommodation in a different local authority area – see below) is the higher of the amount of HB:[240]

- you got in the last (non-rent-free) week before your entitlement to ESA or SDA ended; *or*
- to which you would be entitled based on your new circumstances; *or*
- to which your partner would be entitled if your partner claimed.

However, if the benefit cap is, or was, applied (see p1025), it is the amount of HB you would have got if it did not apply – ie, the amount before any reduction.[241]

Always report any changes in your circumstances during the four-week period to ensure the weekly amount you get is the highest of the above amounts.[242]

***Example***

Matilda is a housing association tenant to whom none of the rent restriction rules apply. She has a non-dependant. She gets working-age HB. Her rent is £125 a week. She was getting HB of £79.85 in the week before her entitlement to income-related ESA ceased, because a non-dependant deduction of £45.15 was made. Her weekly HB entitlement based on her new circumstances is £35.37. Her extended payments are therefore £79.85 a week. In the second week of the four-week period, Matilda's non-dependant moves out. Her weekly entitlement based on her circumstances is now £80.52 (£35.37 + £45.15), because a non-dependant deduction is no longer made. Her extended payments are now £80.52 for the remainder of the four-week period. This is also Matilda's HB entitlement from the end of the period.

You may qualify for extended payments of HB for two homes (see p195). However, if your liability to pay rent for either of these ceases within the four-week period, the amount of your extended payments is reduced by the amount of HB payable for that home.[243]

If you were being paid discretionary housing payments (see Chapter 25), ask for these to continue for the extended payment period.

If you move into local authority accommodation in a different local authority area, the weekly amount of your extended payments of HB is the amount of HB you got in the last (non-rent-free) week before your entitlement to ESA or SDA ended – ie, the amount you got at your old address.[244] The extended payments can be paid to you or to the new local authority landlord. If you or your partner can claim HB at your new address, the amount you or your partner get is reduced by the weekly amount of the extended payments. The effect is that, if your new HB entitlement is higher, your extended payments are 'topped up'.

If you move house in any other circumstances (eg, to privately rented or housing association accommodation, or within the same local authority area), your extended payments are worked out under the normal rules. If you also qualify for HB at your new address, it does not appear that the local authority can reduce the amount of HB you get by the weekly amount of your extended payments.[245]

### Ongoing entitlement to housing benefit

Your entitlement to HB continues until at least the end of the extended payment period.[246] It can continue after that if you qualify under the normal HB rules, but at the weekly rate based on your new circumstances. You do not have to make a fresh claim. Your HB entitlement is continuous.

**Note:** unless you move to local authority accommodation in a different local authority area, if your partner claims HB, this cannot be paid to your partner while you are getting extended payments of HB.[247]

## Housing benefit run-on

If you are getting HB and make a new claim for UC, your HB entitlement continues for two weeks (called a run-on or transitional HB payment), as long as you would otherwise remain entitled (but you can try to argue that the rules do not require this).[248] You do not have to claim a run-on payment. It should be made automatically. You do not have to pay a run-on payment back, even if you qualify for a UC housing costs element for your rent for the same period. HB run-on counts as a specified benefit for the benefit cap (see p1025).

If your HB is being paid direct to your landlord, your run-on payment is usually also paid to your landlord. If this happens, you should ask your landlord to pay you the HB run-on – eg, if you are up to date with your rent payments.

**Note:**

- You are treated as entitled to UC during the two-week run-on period, even if no decision has been made on your UC claim.[249] UC is a passport to maximum HB (see p200). However, if you claimed UC because you were sent a 'migration notice' under the managed migration process (see p29), the amount of your HB run-on is the amount of HB to which you were entitled on the first day of the two-week run-on period.[250]
- Your entitlement to HB can continue indefinitely if this is for 'specified' or 'temporary' accommodation (see p183).
- The benefit cap is not applied to your HB if you get UC.[251]

3

## Delays and complaints

The local authority must make a decision on your claim, tell you in writing what the decision is, and pay you any HB to which you are entitled within 14 days or, if that is not reasonably practicable, as soon as possible after that.[252] If you consider a delay to be unreasonable, make a complaint (see p1265). In serious cases, judicial review may be an option (see Chapter 53).

### Payments on account

If you are a private or housing association tenant and the local authority has not been able to assess your HB within the required period, the local authority must normally make a payment on account (sometimes called an interim payment) while your claim is being sorted out.[253] The local authority should automatically do this. You should not have to request a payment on account, but check with the local authority to ensure it is going to make one.[254] Bear the following in mind.

- Payments on account are not discretionary. The local authority *must* pay you an amount that it considers reasonable.
- Payments on account can only be refused if it is clear that you will not be entitled to HB, or the reason for the delay is that you have been asked for information or evidence in support of your claim and you have failed, without a good reason, to provide it (see p215).[255] If the delay has been caused by a third party (eg, the rent officer, your bank or employer), this does not affect your right to a payment on account.
- The local authority must notify you of the amount of a payment on account and that it can recover any overpayment which occurs if your actual HB entitlement is different from the payment.[256]
- If your payment on account is less than your actual entitlement, your future HB can be adjusted to take account of the underpayment.[257]
- If the local authority has not made a payment on account, complain.

## Change of circumstances

You must report any change in your circumstances which you may reasonably be expected to know may affect your right to, the amount of or payment of your HB.[258] You should do this promptly to the office handling your claim. The local authority must tell you in writing about the changes you must report.[259] There may be a number of changes which the local authority requires you to report, depending on the particular circumstances of your case. **Note:** if you are getting PC, you only have to report specified changes (see p229).

If you do not report a change promptly, any resulting overpayment may be recoverable from you (see Chapter 47) and, in some circumstances, you may have to pay a penalty (see p1101). If you are considered to have acted knowingly or dishonestly, you may also be guilty of an offence (see Chapter 48). **Note:**

- It is important to report changes to the right department, not to other parts of the local authority such as social services.[260]
- If your benefit is paid to someone else on your behalf, the duty to report any relevant changes also extends to that person.[261]

If in doubt, always report changes in circumstances even if you think they may not affect your entitlement to HB. If you think that the local authority might not have taken a change into account, you should check with it.



### How to report a change of circumstances

It is always best to report a change in your circumstances in writing (eg, in a letter) and keep a copy. However, you can also report a change to the local authority:[262]

- by phone (unless the local authority says you must report it in writing), if your local authority has published a number for this purpose or allows you to claim HB by phone; *or*
- electronically (eg, by email), if your local authority authorises it.[263]

You may report a change in your circumstances to the DWP, instead of the local authority, if the DWP has provided a number for this purpose and:[264]

- you or your partner are getting JSA; *and*
- the change of circumstances is that you or your partner have started work; *and*
- as a result of the change, entitlement to JSA will end or the amount will reduce.

If the change is a death, there is a special rule (sometimes called 'Tell Us Once').[265] Check whether your local authority provides this service.

### Changes you must report if you get pension credit

If you get PC, the only changes you must report to the local authority are:[266]

- any change to your tenancy, apart from changes in your rent if you are a local authority tenant; *and*
- any changes affecting the residence or income of a non-dependant who normally lives with you; *and*
- any absence from your home which is, or is likely to be, for more than 13 weeks (more than four weeks if you are absent from Great Britain); *and*
- if you are only getting the savings credit of PC:[267]
  - changes affecting a child under 16 who lives with you that could affect how much HB you get. You need not report changes in the child's age; *and*
  - any changes to your capital that do, or could, take it above £16,000; *and*
  - any changes in the income or capital of a non-dependant, if your HB has been assessed on the basis of this instead of your own (see p211), and whether the non-dependant has stopped, or resumed, living with you; *and*
  - any changes in the income or capital of your partner that have not been taken into account since the determination of your PC award, and whether your partner has stopped, or resumed, living with you.

You must report other changes affecting your PC claim to the DWP. Relevant changes should then be passed to the local authority by the DWP.

## Changes you must report if you do not get pension credit

The changes you must report if you are getting PC, listed on p229, are all changes that could affect your right to, the amount of or payment of your HB. So they are also changes you must report if you are *not* getting PC. Examples of other types of change you must report if you do not get PC include changes to:

- your family income or capital;
- the number of boarders you have or the payments made by them;
- your status – eg, marriage, civil partnership, cohabitation or separation.

However, you do *not* have to report:[268]

- any change in your age, or that of your partner or child(ren) or your non-dependant(s). **Note:** you *do* have to report any change that results in a child or young person no longer being included in your award (see p258);
- if you are on income-related ESA, any changes that affect the amount of that benefit. **Note:** you *do* have to report entitlement to income-related ESA ending. Do not assume that the DWP does this on your behalf.

## When changes in circumstances take effect

In most cases, a change takes effect from the Monday after it occurred.[269] This applies whether or not a decision is advantageous to you. However, if you are liable to pay rent on a daily basis (eg, in a hostel) and the change means you are no longer entitled to HB, it takes effect on the day it occurs.[270]

### Exceptions

There are a number of exceptions to the general rule described above, which include the following.[271]

- If the change is one you are required to notify to the local authority, it is advantageous to you and you fail to notify the change within the one-month time limit (or any longer period allowed by the local authority – see p1153), the date of notification is usually treated as if this is the date the change occurred. This means you lose out if you report the change late.
- If you are getting pension-age HB and either a non-dependant comes to live with you or there is a change so that a higher non-dependant deduction should be made, the effect of this can be delayed for 26 weeks.
- If you are entitled to HB (but not UC) when you become a member of a couple with someone getting UC and your new partner moves in with you, unless your HB is for specified accommodation or temporary accommodation (see p183) or you are at least pension age and are getting pension-age HB, your entitlement to HB ends on the day before the date you are jointly entitled to UC with your new partner, or the day before the date you would have been

entitled had you met all the financial conditions for UC.[272] **Note:** if you move in with your new partner, or you are at least pension age and are getting pension-age HB, your HB entitlement ends under the normal HB rules.[273]

## 8. Tax, other benefits and the benefit cap

### Tax

Housing benefit (HB) is not taxable.

### Means-tested benefits

If you are entitled to HB, entitlement to the guarantee credit of pension credit, universal credit (UC) or income-related employment and support allowance is an automatic passport to 'maximum HB' (see p201) because all your income and capital are ignored.

### Non-means-tested benefits

Most non-means-tested benefits are taken into account as income when working out the amount of HB you get. However:

- attendance allowance, disability living allowance, personal independence payment, guardian's allowance and child benefit and certain Scottish benefits (ie, adult disability payment, Scottish adult disability living allowance, pension age disability payment, child disability payment, carer support payment, carer's allowance supplement, child winter heating payment, young carer grant and Scottish short-term assistance) are not taken into account;
- it can still be worth claiming non-means-tested benefits, even if they are taken into account. If you, your partner or your child(ren) qualify for certain of these, you also qualify for certain premiums and components (see Chapter 13) and, potentially, a higher rate of HB. If you think you may qualify, get advice to see whether you would be better off.

You may only qualify for HB once you or your partner, or a child or 'qualifying young person' included in your award, are awarded another benefit (known as a 'qualifying benefit'). You may be entitled to a higher rate of HB once the qualifying benefit is awarded (see p219).

### The benefit cap

HB is one of the specified benefits for the benefit cap (but HB for 'specified accommodation' – see p183 for what counts – is ignored). The benefit cap only applies if you are getting HB or UC. See p1025 for further information.

## Passports and other sources of help

If you have been awarded HB, you may qualify for discretionary housing payments (see Chapter 25) or council tax reduction (see p761). You may qualify for a social fund funeral expenses payment (see p707) or (in Scotland) a funeral support payment (see Chapter 65). In Scotland, you may qualify for Best Start foods or a Best Start grant (see Chapter 62).



## Financial help on starting work

You may be entitled to extended payments of HB (see p224). Your local authority may also offer extended help with council tax. See p781 for information about other financial help you may get.

# Notes

1. **Who can get housing benefit**

1 s130 SSCBA 1992; s115 IAA 1999; reg 10 HB Regs; reg 10 HB(SPC) Regs
2 Reg 26 HB(SPC) Regs
3 Reg 6A(1) and (2) UC(TP) Regs
4 Reg 6A(4) UC(TP) Regs
5 Regs 5(2)(c) and 6A(3) UC(TP) Regs
6 Reg 2(1) UC(TP) Regs; reg 98(4) and Sch 1 para 3A UC Regs
7 Reg 2(1) UC(TP) Regs; Sch 1 para 3B UC Regs
8 Reg 6A(5) UC(TP) Regs; arts 2(3), 4 and 7 WRA(No.31)O
9 Art 7(2)(b) and (3)(b) WRA(No.31)O
10 Regs 11(1) and 12(1) HB Regs; regs 11(1) and 12(1) HB(SPC) Regs
11 CH/3110/2003; R(H) 3/07
12 *AB v LB Camden (HB)* [2020] UKUT 158 (AAC)
13 R(H) 9/08; *Kirklees MBC v JM (HB)* [2018] UKUT 219 (AAC)
14 Reg 2(4)(a) HB Regs; reg 2(4)(a) HB(SPC) Regs
15 Regs 11(2) and 12(2) HB Regs; reg 12(2) HB(SPC) Regs
16 Reg 2(1) HB Regs and reg 2(1) HB(SPC) Regs, definition of 'long tenancy' and 'owner'; CH/2258/2004; *Burton v New Forest DC* [2004] EWCA Civ 1510, reported as R(H) 7/05; R(H) 3/07; CH/3586/2005; R(H) 8/07; *CR v Wycombe DC* [2009] UKUT 19 (AAC); *GN v Sevenoaks BC (HB)* [2016] UKUT 271 (AAC); *BC v (1) Liverpool City Council (2) SSWP* [2020] UKUT 28 (AAC)
17 Reg 11(2) HB Regs
18 Reg 8(1)(a) and (b) HB Regs; reg 8(1)(a) and (b) HB(SPC) Regs
19 Reg 8(2) HB Regs; reg 8(2) HB(SPC) Regs
20 *R v Sheffield HBRB ex parte Smith* and *R v Rugby BC HBRB ex parte Harrison* [1994] 28 HLR 36 (QBD); CH/2959/2006
21 CH/257/2005
22 R(H) 3/03
23 *R v Poole BC ex parte Ross* [1995] 28 HLR 351 (QBD) CO-3127-93; *R v Warrington BC ex parte Peter S Williams* [1997] EWHC 78 (Admin), 29 HLR 872 (QBD)
24 Reg 8(1)(c)-(e) HB Regs; reg 8(1)(c)-(e) HB(SPC) Regs; *ZD v LB of Hillingdon (HB)* [2021] UKUT 305 (AAC)
25 CSHB/606/2005

26 *FK v Wandsworth BC (HB)* [2016] UKUT 570 (AAC); *Babergh DC v GW (HB)* [2017] UKUT 40 (AAC)
27 *ZD v LB Hillingdon (HB)* [2021] UKUT 305 (AAC)
28 paras A3/3.140-41 GM
29 Regs 9, 10 and 56 HB Regs; regs 9 and 10 HB(SPC) Regs
30 *Scott v SSWP* [2011] EWCA Civ 103
31 Reg 9(4) HB Regs; reg 9(4) HB(SPC) Regs; CH/1326/2004; CH/1328/2004
32 CH/542/2006; R(H) 5/06 decided that the rule did not conflict with the Human Rights Act
33 Reg 3(4) HB Regs; reg 3(4) HB(SPC) Regs; R(H) 5/06; CPC/1446/2008; *RK v SSWP* [2008] UKUT 34 (AAC)
34 *Thamesdown BC v Goonery* [1995] 1 CLY 2600
35 R(H) 1/03; CH/1171/2002; CH/2899/2005
36 R(H) 1/03; *Warwick DC v SSWP and CH (HB)* [2020] UKUT 240 (AAC)
37 Reg 9(2) HB Regs; reg 9(2) HB(SPC) Regs; *R v Poole BC ex parte Ross* [1995] 28 HLR 351 (QBD) CO-3127-93; CH/1076/2002; CH/296/2004; CH/1097/2004; paras A3/3.258-65 GM
38 *DH v Kirklees MBC and SSWP (HB)* [2011] UKUT 301 (AAC), reported as [2012] AACR 16; *LB Bexley v KM* [2017] UKUT 354 (AAC)
39 *R (Tucker) v Secretary of State* [2001] EWCA Civ 1646. The court decided that the rule did not conflict with the Human Rights Act; *South Lanarkshire Council v DG* [2018] UKUT 417 (AAC); para A3/3.269 GM
40 Reg 9(3) HB Regs; reg 9(3) HB(SPC) Regs; *SD v LB Brent* [2009] UKUT 7 (AAC)
41 Reg 9(3) HB Regs; reg 9(3) HB(SPC) Regs
42 Reg 2(1) HB Regs; reg 2(1), definition of 'owner' and 'long tenancy', HB(SPC) Regs; CH/1278/2002; R(H) 6/04; *MH v Wirral MBC* [2009] UKUT 60 (AAC); *Bradford MDC v MRC (HB)* [2010] UKUT 315 (AAC); *Nottingham CC v CJ (HB)* [2011] UKUT 392 (AAC); *GN v Sevenoaks BC (HB)* [2016] UKUT 271 (AAC)
43 CH/3853/2001; CH/396/2002; R(H) 6/07; *KH v Sheffield CC* [2008] UKUT 11 (AAC)
44 *RS v Fife Council and SSWP* [2018] UKUT 322 (AAC)
45 *CH v Wakefield DC* [2009] UKUT 20 (AAC)
46 Reg 2(1) HB Regs; reg 2(1) HB(SPC) Regs
47 R(SB) 22/87; *Bristol City Council v JKT (HB)* [2016] UKUT 517 (AAC)
48 paras A3/3.243-45 GM
49 *MP v Sutton LBC (HB)* [2021] UKUT 193 (AAC)
50 *R v Solihull MBC ex parte Simpson* [1995] 1 FLR 140 (CA); CH/39/2007
51 *R (Mackay) v Barking and Dagenham HBRB* [2001] EWHC 234 (Admin)
52 CH/2258/2004
53 *R (Mackay) v Barking and Dagenham HBRB* [2001] EWHC 234 (Admin)
54 *R v Sutton LBC HBRB ex parte Keegan* [1992] 27 HLR 92 (QBD)
55 *R v Manchester CC ex parte Baragrove Properties Ltd* [1991] 23 HLR 337 (QBD); *R v Gloucestershire CC ex parte Victoria Dadds* [1996], EWHC Admin 311, 29 HLR 700 (QBD); CH/39/2007
56 *R v Poole BC ex parte Ross* [1995] 28 HLR 351 (QBD) CO-3127-93
57 s134(2) SSCBA 1992; reg 82(1) HB Regs; reg 63(1) HB(SPC) Regs
58 s130(1) SSCBA 1992; reg 7(1) and (2) HB Regs; reg 7(1) and (2) HB(SPC) Regs
59 R(H) 5/09; *Birmingham City Council v IB* [2009] UKUT 116 (AAC)
60 Reg 7(5), (14) and (15)(c) HB Regs; reg 7(5), (14) and (15)(c) HB(SPC) Regs
61 Regs 2(1) and 7(8) HB Regs; regs 2(1) and 7(8) HB(SPC) Regs
62 *Bury MBC v DC (HB)* [2011] UKUT 43 (AAC); *R (Mahmoudi) v LB Lewisham and Another* [2014] EWCA Civ 284
63 R(H) 9/05
64 CH/2201/2002
65 Reg 7(7) HB Regs; reg 7(7) HB(SPC) Regs; para A3/3.430 GM
66 Reg 7(11)(b) and (c), (13)(a) and (b), (13D)(a) and (b), (13G)(a) and (b), (16)(a)-(c) and (18) HB Regs; reg 7(11)(b) and (c), (13)(a) and (b), (13D)(a) and (b), (13G)(a) and (b), (16)(a)-(c) and (18) HB(SPC) Regs
67 R(H) 9/05
68 Reg 7(13) and (17) HB Regs; reg 7(13) and (17) HB(SPC) Regs
69 *KdeS v Camden LB (HB)* [2011] UKUT 457 (AAC)
70 *R v Penwith DC ex parte Burt* [1990] 22 HLR 292 (QBD); para A3/3.460 GM
71 Reg 7(14) and (15)(a) HB Regs; reg 7(14) and (15)(a) HB(SPC) Regs
72 R(H) 8/09; *SK v South Hams DC (HB)* [2010] UKUT 129 (AAC), reported as [2010] AACR 40

3

73 CH/1237/2004
74 CH/3893/2004
75 Reg 7(13) HB Regs; reg 7(13) HB(SPC) Regs
76 Reg 7(16)(d)(i) and (17) HB Regs; reg 7(16)(d)(i) and (17) HB(SPC) Regs
77 Reg 7(16)(c)(ii), (iii), (vii) and (x) HB Regs; reg 7(16)(c)(ii), (iii), (vii) and (x) HB(SPC) Regs
78 *Obrey and Others v SSWP* [2013] EWCA Civ 1584
79 Reg 2(1) HB Regs and reg 98(4) UC Regs, definition of 'domestic violence'; gov.uk/government/publications/domestic-violence-and-abuse-help-from-dwp
80 Reg 7(16)(c)(i), (iv)-(vi), (viii)-(ix) and (16A) HB Regs; reg 7(16)(c)(i), (iv)-(vi), (viii)-(ix) and (16A) HB(SPC) Regs
81 Reg 7(14) and (15)(b) HB Regs; reg 7(14) and (15)(b) HB(SPC) Regs; CSH/499/2006
82 Reg 7(18) HB Regs; reg 7(18) HB(SPC) Regs
83 Reg 7(11) and (12) HB Regs; reg 7(11) and (12) HB(SPC) Regs
84 *SSWP v Selby DC and Bowman* [2006] EWCA Civ 271, reported as R(H) 4/06
85 Reg 7(13C)-(13E) HB Regs; reg 7(13C)-(13E) HB(SPC) Regs
86 Reg 7(16)(d)(ii) and (iii), (17C) and (17D) HB Regs; reg 7(16)(d)(ii) and (iii), (17C) and (17D) HB(SPC) Regs
87 Reg 7(13F), (13G) and (18) HB Regs; reg 7(13F), (13G) and (18) HB(SPC) Regs
88 Reg 7(13D), (13G), (17C) and (17D) HB Regs; reg 7(13D), (13G), (17C) and (17D) HB(SPC) Regs; *Slough BC v PK* [2019] UKUT 128 (AAC)
89 Reg 7(13A) and (17A) HB Regs; reg 7(13A) and (17A) HB(SPC) Regs
90 Reg 7(13B) and (17B) HB Regs; reg 7(13B) and (17B) HB(SPC) Regs
91 R(H) 5/09; *Birmingham City Council v IB* [2009] UKUT 116 (AAC)
92 Reg 7(6)(d) and (e) HB Regs; reg 7(6)(d) and (e) HB(SPC) Regs
93 CH/1911/2006
94 *R (Mahmoudi) v LB Lewisham and Another* [2014] EWCA Civ 284
95 Reg 7(6)(a) HB Regs; reg 7(6)(a) HB(SPC) Regs
96 Reg 7(6)(b) and (c) HB Regs; reg 7(6)(b) and (c) HB(SPC) Regs
97 Reg 7(10) HB Regs; reg 7(10) HB(SPC) Regs
98 Reg 7(3) and (4) HB Regs; reg 7(3) and (4) HB(SPC) Regs
99 *SH v LB Southwark* [2023] UKUT 198 (AAC)
100 R(SB) 10/81

2. **The rules about your age**

101 For working-age HB, see the HB Regs. For pension-age HB, see the HB(SPC) Regs.
102 Reg 5 HB Regs
103 Reg 2(3A) and (3B) HB Regs; *Ipswich BC v TD & SSWP (HB)* [2024] UKUT 117 (AAC)
104 Reg 5 HB(SPC) Regs
105 Reg 2(3A) HB(SPC) Regs; *Ipswich BC v TD & SSWP (HB)* [2024] UKUT 117 (AAC)
106 Art 6 WRA(No.31)O
107 Art 6(4) WRA(No.31)O

4. **The amount of benefit**

108 s130(3) SSCBA 1992; Schs 4 para 12, 5 para 4, and 6 para 5 HB Regs; reg 26 HB(SPC) Regs; *R v Penwith DC ex parte Menear* [1991] 24 HLR 120 (QBD); *R v South Ribble BC ex parte Benjamin Hamilton* [2000] 33 HLR 104 (CA); *DF v LB Waltham Forest (HB)* [2017] UKUT 306 (AAC)
109 Reg 2(3), (3A) and (3B) HB Regs; reg 2(3) and (3A) HB(SPC) Regs; *SMcH v Perth and Kinross Council (HB)* [2015] UKUT 126 (AAC)
110 *Ipswich BC v TD and SSWP* [2024] UKUT 118 (AAC)
111 s130(3) SSCBA 1992; reg 71 HB Regs; reg 51 HB(SPC) Regs
112 Reg 70 HB Regs; reg 50 HB(SPC) Regs
113 Regs 12B(2), 12BA(2), 12C(2) and 12D(2) HB Regs; regs 12B(2), 12C(2) and 12D(2) HB(SPC) Regs; regs 12(3) HB Regs and HB(SPC) Regs, as set out in Sch 3 para 5(1) HB&CTB(CP) Regs
114 Reg 12(2A) and (2B) HB Regs; reg 12(2A) and (2B) HB(SPC) Regs; reg 12(6A) and (6B) HB Regs and HB(SPC) Regs, as set out in Sch 3 para 5(1) HB&CTB(CP) Regs
115 Regs 12B(3) and 12C(2) HB Regs; regs 12B(3) and 12C(2) HB(SPC) Regs; reg 12(4) HB Regs and HB(SPC) Regs, as set out in Sch 3 para 5 HB&CTB(CP) Regs
116 Reg 11(3) HB Regs; reg 11(2) HB(SPC) Regs
117 Reg 2(1) HB Regs; reg 2(1) HB(SPC) Regs
118 Reg 80 HB Regs; reg 61 HB(SPC) Regs
119 Reg 81(3) and Sch 1 para 7(2) HB Regs; reg 62(3) and Sch 1 para 7(2) HB(SPC) Regs

120 Regs 12B(4) and 12C(2) HB Regs; regs 12B(4) and 12C(2) HB(SPC) Regs; reg 12(5) HB Regs and HB(SPC) Regs, as set out in Sch 3 para 5 HB&CTB(CP) Regs; CH/3376/2002; *R (Naghshbandi) v Camden LBC* [2002] EWCA Civ 1038
121 CH/3376/2002
122 Reg 12B(2) HB Regs; reg 12B(2) HB(SPC) Regs; reg 12(3) HB Regs and HB(SPC) Regs, as set out in Sch 3 para 5 HB&CTB(CP) Regs; *R v Bristol City Council ex parte Jacobs* [1999] 32 HLR 82 (QBD); *Liverpool City Council v (1) NM, (2) WD (HB)* [2015] UKUT 532 (AAC), reported as [2016] AACR 19
123 Sch 1 para 8 HB Regs; Sch 1 para 8 HB(SPC) Regs. For the meaning of 'sheltered accommodation', see *Oxford City Council v Basey* [2012] EWCA Civ 115, reported as [2012] AACR 38.
124 Sch 1 para 5 HB Regs; Sch 1 para 5 HB(SPC) Regs
125 Sch 1 para 6(1) HB Regs; Sch 1 para 6(1) HB(SPC) Regs
126 Sch 1 para 6(2) and (3) HB Regs; Sch 1 para 6(2) and (3) HB(SPC) Regs
127 paras A4/4.912-13 GM
128 Sch 1 paras 5 and 6(1)(b) HB Regs; Sch 1 paras 5 and 6(1)(b) HB(SPC) Regs
129 Sch 1 para 8 HB Regs; Sch 1 para 8 HB(SPC) Regs
130 Sch 1 para 1(a)(ii)-(iv) and (b) HB Regs; Sch 1 para 1(a)(ii)-(iv) and (b) HB(SPC) Regs; para A4/4.730 GM; *CP and Others v Aylesbury Vale DC v SSWP (HB)* [2011] UKUT 22 (AAC); *Liverpool City Council v (1) NM, (2) WD (HB)* [2015] UKUT 532 (AAC), reported as [2016] AACR 19
131 Reg 12B(2)(b) and Sch 1 para 1 HB Regs; reg 12B(2)(b) and Sch 1 para 1 HB(SPC) Regs; reg 12(3)(b) HB Regs and HB(SPC) Regs, as set out in Sch 3 para 5 HB&CTB(CP) Regs
132 Reg 12B(2)(c) and Sch 1 para 3(2) HB Regs; reg 12B(2)(c) and Sch 1 para 3(2) HB(SPC) Regs; reg 12(3)(c) HB Regs and HB(SPC) Regs, as set out in Sch 3 para 5 HB&CTB(CP) Regs
133 Sch 1 para 3 HB Regs; Sch 1 para 3 HB(SPC) Regs
134 Sch 1 paras 1(a)(i) and 2(1) HB Regs; Sch 1 paras 1(a)(i) and 2(1) HB(SPC) Regs
135 Sch 1 para 2(6) and (7) HB Regs; Sch 1 para 2(6) and (7) HB(SPC) Regs
136 Reg 70 HB Regs; reg 50 HB(SPC) Regs
137 Reg 3(1) HB Regs; reg 3(1) HB(SPC) Regs
138 Reg 3(4) and Sch 1 para 8 HB Regs; reg 3(4) and Sch 1 para 8 HB(SPC) Regs; CPC/1446/2008; *AM v SSWP (IS)* [2011] UKUT 387 (AAC)
139 CSIS/185/1995
140 *Thamesdown BC v Goonery* [1995] 1 CLY 2600 (CA); *RK v SSWP* [2008] UKUT 34 (AAC)
141 CIS/14850/1996
142 para A5/5.521 GM; *RR v SSWP (UC)* [2024] UKUT 261 (AAC)
143 R(H) 8/09; *SK v South Hams DC (HB)* [2010] UKUT 129 (AAC), reported as [2010] AACR 40
144 Reg 3(2) HB Regs; reg 3(2) HB(SPC) Regs
145 *JP v Bournemouth BC (HB)* [2018] UKUT 75 (AAC), reported as [2018] AACR 30
146 *R v Chesterfield BC ex parte Fullwood* [1993] 26 HLR 126
147 Reg 3(3) HB Regs; reg 3(3) HB(SPC) Regs
148 Regs 2(1), definition of 'attendance allowance', and 74(6) HB Regs; regs 2(1), definition of 'attendance allowance', and 55(6) HB(SPC) Regs
149 Reg 74(1), (7), (8) and (10) HB Regs; reg 55(1), (7)-(9) HB(SPC) Regs
150 s2 ETA 1973; s2 Enterprise and New Towns (Scotland) Act 1990
151 Reg 74(1) and (2) HB Regs; reg 55(1) and (2) HB(SPC) Regs
152 Reg 6(6) HB Regs; reg 6(6) HB(SPC) Regs
153 Reg 74(9) HB Regs; reg 55(10) HB(SPC) Regs
154 CH/48/2006
155 Reg 74(3) HB Regs; reg 55(3) HB(SPC) Regs
156 Reg 74(4) HB Regs; reg 55(4) HB(SPC) Regs
157 Reg 74(5) HB Regs; reg 55(5) HB(SPC) Regs
158 Reg 59(10)-(13) HB(SPC) Regs
159 Reg 26 HB Regs; reg 24 HB(SPC) Regs

6. **Claims and backdating**
160 s1 SSAA 1992
161 Reg 83(1), (2) and (9) HB Regs; reg 64(2), (3) and (10) HB(SPC) Regs
162 Reg 83(4A) and (4B) HB Regs; reg 64(5A) and (5C) HB(SPC) Regs
163 Reg 83A and Sch 11 HB Regs; reg 64A and Sch 10 HB(SPC) Regs
164 Reg 83(4AA), (4AB) and (4BA) HB Regs; reg 64(5B), (5BA) and (5CA) HB(SPC) Regs

165 Reg 83(4AC)-(4AE) HB Regs; reg 64(5BB)-(5BD) HB(SPC) Regs; Explanatory Memorandum to SI 2008 No.2299
166 Reg 83(1), (4C), (6) and (9) HB Regs; reg 64(2), (5D), (7) and (10) HB(SPC) Regs
167 Reg 83(4D), (4DA), (7) and (7A) HB Regs; reg 64(5E), (5EA), (8) and (8A) HB(SPC) Regs
168 Reg 83(4E), (4F), (8) and (8A) HB Regs; reg 64(5F), (5G), (9) and (9A) HB(SPC) Regs
169 Reg 87(1) and (3) HB Regs; reg 68(1) and (3) HB(SPC) Regs
170 Reg 87(4)-(6) HB Regs; reg 68(4)-(6) HB(SPC) Regs
171 Reg 83(4)(b) HB Regs; reg 64(5)(b) HB(SPC) Regs
172 Regs 2, definition of 'appropriate DWP office', and 83(4)(a), (f) and (g) and (13) HB Regs; regs 2, definition of 'appropriate DWP office', and 64(5)(a), (f) and (g) and (14) HB(SPC) Regs
173 Reg 83(4)(c) HB Regs; reg 64(5)(c) HB(SPC) Regs
174 Reg 82(1) HB Regs; reg 63(1) HB(SPC) Regs; CH/2995/2006
175 Reg 82(2), (3), (5) and (6) HB Regs; reg 63(2), (3), (5) and (6) HB(SPC) Regs
176 Reg 82(4) HB Regs; reg 63(4) HB(SPC) Regs
177 Reg 82(4)(c) HB Regs; reg 63(4)(c) HB(SPC) Regs
178 s1(1A)-(1C) SSAA 1992
179 Reg 86(1A) HB Regs; reg 67(1A) HB(SPC) Regs; *CH v Plymouth City Council and DE* [2018] UKUT 215 (AAC)
180 Reg 86(1) HB Regs; reg 67(1) HB(SPC) Regs
181 *AA v LB Hounslow* [2008] UKUT 13 (AAC)
182 Reg 4(1)(a) HB Regs; reg 4(1)(a) HB(SPC) Regs
183 para A1/1.300 GM
184 Reg 83(5)(d) and (e) HB Regs; reg 64(6)(d) and (e) HB(SPC) Regs
185 Reg 83(5)(a)-(c) and (5A) HB Regs; reg 64(6)(a)-(c) HB(SPC) Regs
186 *Leicester City Council v LG* [2009] UKUT 155 (AAC)
187 Reg 64(1) HB(SPC) Regs
188 Regs 57 and 64(1), (1A) and (6) HB(SPC) Regs; *Leicester City Council v LG* [2009] UKUT 155 (AAC)
189 Reg 83(12) HB Regs
190 Reg 83(12A) HB Regs
191 R(S) 2/63 (T); CH/2659/2002; CH/474/2002; CH/393/2003; A2/Annex A GM
192 *UH v LB Islington (HB)* [2010] UKUT 64 (AAC)
193 CH/474/2002
194 R(G) 1/75
195 Reg 83(10) and (11) HB Regs; reg 64(11) and (12) HB(SPC) Regs
196 CG/1479/1999; CIS/217/1999
197 Reg 89 HB Regs; reg 70 HB(SPC) Regs
198 Reg 90 HB Regs; reg 71 HB(SPC) Regs; reg 10 HB&CTB(DA) Regs
199 Reg 90(2) HB Regs; reg 71(2) HB(SPC) Regs; reg 10 HB&CTB(DA) Regs
200 Reg 3 HB&CTB(DA) Regs
201 CH/180/2006
202 Reg 10(1) HB&CTB(DA) Regs
203 Sch 9 paras 9-15 HB Regs; Sch 8 paras 9-15 HB(SPC) Regs; reg 10(1) HB&CTB(DA) Regs
204 Reg 76 HB Regs; reg 57 HB(SPC) Regs; R(H) 9/07; *SL v Renfrewshire Council (HB)* [2014] UKUT 411 (AAC)
205 Regs 2(1), definition of 'benefit week', and 80(2), (3)(a), (4) and (8) HB Regs; regs 2(1), definition of 'benefit week', and 61(2), (3)(a), (4) and (8) HB(SPC) Regs

7. **Getting paid**

206 Reg 75 HB Regs; reg 56 HB(SPC) Regs
207 Reg 92(1) and (6) HB Regs; reg 73(1) and (6) HB(SPC) Regs
208 Reg 92(3) and (4) HB Regs; reg 73(3) and (4) HB(SPC) Regs
209 s134(1A) SSAA 1992
210 s134(1B) SSAA 1992; regs 91A and 94(1) HB Regs; regs 72A and 75(1) HB(SPC) Regs
211 Reg 91(2) HB Regs; reg 72(2) HB(SPC) Regs
212 Reg 92(5) HB Regs; reg 73(5) HB(SPC) Regs
213 Reg 91(1)(b) HB Regs; reg 72(1)(b) HB(SPC) Regs; para A6/6.120 GM
214 Reg 94(2) HB Regs; reg 75(2) HB(SPC) Regs
215 Reg 94(3) HB Regs; reg 75(3) HB(SPC) Regs
216 Reg 97 HB Regs; reg 78 HB(SPC) Regs
217 *R v Haringey LBC ex parte Azad Ayub* [1992] 25 HLR 566 (QBD)
218 R(H) 1/08
219 Reg 96(2) HB Regs; reg 77(2) HB(SPC) Regs
220 Reg 95 HB Regs; reg 76 HB(SPC) Regs; Sch 9 SS(C&P) Regs; *R v Haringey LBC ex parte Azad Ayub* [1992] 25 HLR 566 (QBD)

221 CH 3244/2007; *ST v Sunderland City Council (HB)* [2019] UKUT 33 (AAC), reported as [2019] AACR 20
222 Reg 96(1)(a) and (b) and (3A)(a) HB Regs; reg 77(1)(a) and (b) and (3A)(a) HB(SPC) Regs
223 *DLT v Eastleigh BC (HB)* [2014] UKUT 242 (AAC)
224 Regs 95(2A) and 96(3A)(b) HB Regs; regs 76(2A) and 77(3A)(b) HB(SPC) Regs
225 Regs 95(2A) and 96(1)(c) HB Regs; regs 76(2A) and 77(1)(c) HB(SPC) Regs
226 *E v Dacorum BC & M* [2017] UKUT 93 (AAC)
227 Regs 95(3) and 96(3) HB Regs; regs 76(3) and 77(3) HB(SPC) Regs
228 Reg 96(3) HB Regs; reg 77(3) HB(SPC) Regs
229 para A6/6.212 GM
230 Reg 54(6) HB(SPC) Regs
231 Reg 5(2)(c) UC(TP) Regs
232 Reg 54(1) and (2) HB(SPC) Regs
233 Regs 2(1), definition of 'benefit week', and 54(3)-(5) HB(SPC) Regs
234 s32(4) WRA 2007
235 ss32-34 WRA 2007
236 Reg 72 HB Regs
237 Reg 73 HB Regs; reg 53 HB(SPC) Regs
238 Regs 72(4) and 73(2) HB Regs; reg 53(2) HB(SPC) Regs; CH/1762/2004
239 Regs 72A, 72B(6), 73A and 73B(6) HB Regs; regs 53A and 53B(6) HB(SPC) Regs
240 Regs 72B and 73B HB Regs; regs 52 and 53B HB(SPC) Regs
241 Regs 72E and 73E HB Regs
242 Regs 72D(2) and 73D(2) HB Regs; regs 52 and 53D(2) HB(SPC) Regs
243 Regs 72B(5) and 73B(5) HB Regs; reg 53B(5) HB(SPC) Regs
244 Regs 72C and 73C HB Regs; regs 52 and 53C HB(SPC) Regs
245 s34(3) WRA 2007; reg 2(1) HB Regs; reg 2(1), definitions of 'mover' and 'second authority', HB(SPC) Regs
246 s32(1), (2) and (13) WRA 2007; regs 72D and 73D HB Regs; reg 53D HB(SPC) Regs
247 Regs 72B(7) and 73B(7) HB Regs; regs 52(3) and 53B(7) HB(SPC) Regs
248 Regs 8(2A), 8A, 44 and 46(1)(a) UC(TP) Regs
249 Reg 8A(a) UC(TP) Regs
250 Reg 8A(c) UC(TP) Regs
251 Reg 75F(1)(g) HB Regs
252 Regs 89(2), 90(1) and 91(3) HB Regs; regs 70(2), 71(1) and 72(3) HB(SPC) Regs
253 Reg 93(1) HB Regs; reg 74(1) HB(SPC) Regs
254 *R v Haringey LBC ex parte Azad Ayub* [1992] 25 HLR 566 (QBD)
255 Reg 93(1) HB Regs; reg 74(1) HB(SPC) Regs; *R v Haringey LBC ex parte Azad Ayub* [1992] 25 HLR 566 (QBD)
256 Reg 93(2) HB Regs; reg 74(2) HB(SPC) Regs
257 Reg 93(3) HB Regs; reg 74(3) HB(SPC) Regs
258 Reg 88(1) HB Regs; reg 69(1) HB(SPC) Regs; reg 4 SS(NCC) Regs
259 Regs 86(3) and 90 and Sch 9 paras 9(1)(g) and 10(a) HB Regs; regs 67(3) and 71 and Sch 8 paras 9(1)(g) and 10(a) HB(SPC) Regs
260 Regs 2(1), 86(3) and 88(1) HB Regs; regs 2(1), 67(3) and 69(1) HB(SPC) Regs
261 Reg 88(1) HB Regs; reg 69(1) HB(SPC) Regs
262 Reg 88(1) HB Regs; reg 69(1) HB(SPC) Regs
263 Reg 88A and Sch 11 HB Regs; reg 69A and Sch 10 HB(SPC) Regs
264 Reg 88(6) HB Regs; reg 69(9) HB(SPC) Regs
265 Reg 88ZA HB Regs; reg 69ZA HB(SPC) Regs; gov.uk/after-a-death/organisations-you-need-to-contact-and-tell-us-once
266 Reg 69(6)-(8) HB(SPC) Regs
267 Reg 69(7) HB(SPC) Regs
268 Reg 88(1), (3) and (4) HB Regs; reg 69(1), (3) and (4) HB(SPC) Regs
269 Regs 2(1), definition of 'benefit week', and 79(1) HB Regs; regs 2(1), definition of 'benefit week', and 59(1) HB(SPC) Regs; reg 8(2) HB&CTB(DA) Regs
270 Reg 79(8) HB Regs; reg 59(8) HB(SPC) Regs
271 Reg 79(2)-(10) HB Regs; regs 59(2)-(13) and 60 HB(SPC) Regs; regs 7(2)(o) and 8(14D) HB&CTB(DA) Regs
272 Regs 5(2)(a) and 7 UC(TP) Regs
273 Regs 5(2) and 7(5)(b) and (c) UC(TP) Regs

3

# Chapter 11

# Pension credit

**This chapter covers:**


1. Who can get pension credit (p239)
2. The rules about your age (p239)
3. People included in the claim (p240)
4. The amount of pension credit (p241)
5. Special benefit rules (p246)
6. Claims and backdating (p246)
7. Getting paid (p249)
8. Tax, other benefits and the benefit cap (p251)


## Key facts

- Pension credit (PC) is a benefit for people on a low income who are at least pension age.
- There are two types of PC: **guarantee credit**, which ensures a minimum level of income, and **savings credit**. You can be entitled to either guarantee credit or savings credit or to both.
- PC is a means-tested benefit.
- PC can include additional amounts for severe disability, carers, for a child or qualifying young person you are responsible for, and for some types of housing costs.
- You do not have to have paid national insurance contributions to qualify.
- You can qualify for PC whether you are in or out of work.
- PC is administered and paid by the Pension Service, which is part of the DWP.
- If you disagree with a PC decision, you can apply for a revision or supersession (see Chapter 50), or appeal against it (see Chapter 51). You must apply for a mandatory reconsideration before you can appeal.

# 1. Who can get pension credit

## Guarantee credit

You qualify for the guarantee credit of pension credit (PC) if:[1]

- you are at least pension age (see p690). If you have a partner and make a new claim for PC, both of you must usually be pension age.[2] There are exceptions (see p240); *and*
- you are not a 'person subject to immigration control' (see p1272), although there are exceptions to this rule (see p1280);[3] *and*
- you are in Great Britain (except for periods of temporary absence – see p1375) and satisfy the 'habitual residence' and 'right to reside' tests (see Chapter 57);[4] *and*
- your partner (if you have one) is not entitled to PC;[5] *and*
- your income is below a certain amount (known as the 'appropriate minimum guarantee' – see p241).[6]



## Savings credit

You qualify for the savings credit of PC if:[7]

- either:
  - you and your partner (if you have one) reached pension age (see p690) before 6 April 2016; *or*
  - you or your partner reached pension age before 6 April 2016, you were entitled to savings credit on 6 April 2016 and you have remained entitled to it;[8] *and*
- you are in Great Britain (except for periods of temporary absence – see p1375) and satisfy the habitual residence and right to reside tests (see Chapter 57);[9] *and*
- your partner (if you have one) is not entitled to PC;[10] *and*
- you are not a 'person subject to immigration control', although there are exceptions to this rule (see p1280);[11] *and*
- your qualifying income exceeds the savings credit threshold, but is not so high that it removes all savings credit entitlement (see p245).[12]

# 2. The rules about your age

You must have reached pension age – ie, the minimum qualifying age for state retirement pension.[13] The pension age for both men and women is currently 66 years.[14] It is due to start increasing again from 2026. When you reach pension age depends on your date of birth.

To check your pension age, see gov.uk/state-pension-age.

If you are a member of a couple and you are at least pension age but your partner is not (called a 'mixed-age couple' in this *Handbook*), you cannot usually qualify for pension credit (PC).[15] You and your partner may be able to claim universal credit (UC) instead.

There are exceptions to this rule. If you are a member of a mixed-age couple, you can continue to qualify for PC if, on 14 May 2019 as part of the same couple, you were entitled to:[16]

3

- PC; *or*
- pension-age housing benefit (HB) (see p182); *or*
- both PC and pension-age HB.

You continue to qualify for PC provided you have been continuously entitled to PC or pension-age HB or both, as part of the same mixed-age couple. You can make a new claim for PC, provided you are entitled to pension-age HB on this basis and have been since 14 May 2019. You can also claim PC and/or reclaim pension-age HB if your pension-age HB ended because you were subject to the managed migration to UC process, as long as you claim within three months beginning with the day after pension-age HB or UC terminates.[17]

If you are in a mixed-age couple, you have reached pension age and your partner cannot claim UC because they do not satisfy certain UC conditions, you can instead get PC (and pension-age HB) as a single person, either until the reason your partner cannot claim UC no longer applies or until they reach pension age.[18] This situation can arise if your partner:

- does not satisfy the habitual residence test (see Chapter 57), or is a 'person subject to immigration control' (see p1272); *or*
- is a prisoner, or is detained in hospital serving a prison sentence (see p836); *or*
- is a member of a religious order and fully maintained by it; *or*
- is absent from Great Britain for more than the permitted period (normally one month although there are exceptions – see p1372); *or*
- is under 18, and not someone who can claim UC when 16/17 (see p37).

If the partner under pension age is temporarily absent from the household and is, or is expected to be, absent for more than six months, the person who has reached pension age can claim PC (and pension-age HB) as a single person until the end of the absence, as you are no longer treated as a couple for UC.[19]

## 3. People included in the claim

If you are single, you claim pension credit (PC) for yourself. If you are a member of a couple (see p254) and both you and your partner are pension age, either of you can claim PC for you both. If only one of you is pension age, see above.

The 'appropriate minimum guarantee' that forms part of the PC calculation includes an allowance for a couple and can include additional amounts based on your and your partner's circumstances, including child-related amounts if you are responsible for a child or qualifying young person. When the amount of your PC is worked out, your partner's income and capital are usually added to yours.

If you are claiming PC but your partner has not yet reached pension age, they may qualify for national insurance (NI) credits to protect their NI record depending on their other circumstances (see p865).



## 4. The amount of pension credit

The amount of pension credit (PC) you get depends on whether you claim as a single person or as a member of a couple, whether you are responsible for any children or qualifying young people, and whether you have a severe disability, caring responsibilities or eligible housing costs. The maximum amount of guarantee credit you could receive is reduced by your income (subject to any applicable disregards). Savings credit entitlement is based on the amount of your pension(s) and certain other income (see p245).

For general information on income and capital, see Chapters 17 and 19. For information on qualifying income for savings credit, see p245.

### Guarantee credit

Your maximum amount of guarantee credit is known as the 'appropriate minimum guarantee'.[20] It is made up of:

- the standard minimum guarantee; *and*
- if applicable, additional amounts.

### Standard minimum guarantee

If you do not have any additional needs (see below), you receive an award of PC which ensures that your weekly income is brought up to a standard minimum guarantee level, depending on your circumstances.

| *Amount of standard minimum guarantee* | |
|---|---|
| Single person[21] | £227.10 |
| Couple[22] | £346.60 |
| Each additional spouse in a polygamous marriage[23] | £119.50 |

### Additional amounts

If you have certain additional needs, are responsible for children or qualifying young people, or have certain housing costs, an additional amount(s) is added to the standard minimum guarantee. There may also be a 'transitional additional amount' to ensure you are not worse off when moving onto PC from tax credits, income support (IS), income-based jobseeker's allowance (JSA) or income-related employment and support allowance (ESA).

You can get amounts for a child or qualifying young person you are responsible for included in your PC.[24] For who is a child or qualifying young person for PC purposes, see p259, and for more information on being responsible for them, see p261.

3

*Additional amounts*

| | | |
|---|---|---|
| **Severe disability**[25] | | |
| The qualifying rules are broadly the same as for the severe disability premium (see p275). | £82.90 | £165.80 (if both partners qualify) |
| **Carer**[26] | | |
| The qualifying rules are the same as for the carer premium (see p279). | £46.40 | £92.80 (if both partners qualify) |
| **Children** (see p258).[27] | | |
| First child born before 6 April 2017 | £78.10 | Additional £36.54 for disability, or £114.12 for severe disability |
| Each subsequent child | £67.42 | |
| **Housing costs**[28] | See below | |
| **Transitional**[29] | See below | |

#### Housing costs

You can get certain housing costs included in your PC (see Chapter 14). These can cover certain service charges, ground rent for a lease of more than 21 years and payments for tent fees. **Note**: you cannot get an amount in your PC for the costs of your mortgage interest payments or for a loan for repairs and improvements. Instead, the DWP may offer you a loan (see p764).

#### Transitional amounts if you were previously on IS, income-based JSA or income-related ESA

If you were in receipt of IS, income-based JSA or income-related ESA immediately before you first became entitled to PC, to ensure you are not worse off by moving onto PC, your appropriate minimum guarantee may include a transitional amount.[30] The transitional amount reduces over time by any increase in your appropriate minimum guarantee and stops when you or your partner are no longer entitled to PC (disregarding any break in entitlement of less than eight weeks).[31]

#### Transitional amount if you were previously on child tax credit

If you were of pension age (including if you were in a 'protected mixed-age couple' – see p184) and getting child tax credit (CTC), and you were not entitled to working tax credit (WTC) or you were but you already got PC, you should have been sent a 'tax credit closure notice' about the ending of your CTC at some point in 2024/25.[32] This invited you to claim PC, or, if you were already getting PC, explained that your CTC was ending and you would start to get amounts for children included in your PC instead. If you already got PC, or if you claimed it after the notice was issued but on or before the deadline in the notice (or on or before the last day of a month beginning with the deadline day), your appropriate minimum guarantee may include a 'transitional additional amount'.[33] If you were already claiming PC, you did not need to do anything. If you were not already claiming PC and you did not claim on or before the deadline, your CTC ended the day before the deadline day. If you claimed PC on or before the deadline day, CTC ended the day before your claim.[34] You cannot backdate your PC to a date on which you were still entitled to tax credits.[35]

The transitional additional amount is usually the difference between your weekly entitlement to CTC (calculated using a daily rate multiplied by seven) plus any existing PC entitlement (if already getting it) on the last day of your entitlement to tax credits, and an 'indicative amount' of PC calculated according to your circumstances on the same day, including amounts for your children.[36] The DWP will assume you are responsible for a child or qualifying young person if you get the child element of CTC for them. For more information about CTC, including how it was calculated, see the 2024/25 edition of this *Handbook*. However, if the guarantee credit in your indicative PC is nil (because your income is greater than your appropriate minimum guarantee), then the transitional amount is your weekly CTC entitlement plus your excess income (the amount of your income above your appropriate minimum guarantee), minus maximum savings credit (if your indicative PC amount includes savings credit or would include it if your income did not reduce it to nil).

If, when the tax credit notice was issued, you had already deferred a state pension (see p688), occupational or personal pension, this will not count as income for 52 weeks from the date your PC award began (this does not apply if you already got PC when you were sent a tax credit closure notice).[37] This disregard is applied to your actual and indicative PC.

The transitional additional amount reduces as your appropriate minimum guarantee (see p241) rises – eg, with any increase in rates or a new additional amount.[38] It stops completely when it reduces to nil, if your relationship status for PC purposes changes (see p254), or if you are no longer responsible for any of the children and/or qualifying young people you were responsible for when your tax credit closure notice was issued (see p260).

## When your appropriate minimum guarantee may be reduced

Your appropriate minimum guarantee may be reduced in certain circumstances. The most important of these are if:[39]

- you are a couple and one of you is a 'person subject to immigration control' (see p1286);
- you are a prisoner (see p840). In this case, your appropriate minimum guarantee is nil, unless you are on remand;
- your partner is abroad (see p1375);
- you are a member of and fully maintained by a religious order. In this case, your appropriate minimum guarantee is nil.

## The guarantee credit calculation

### Step 1: calculate your appropriate minimum guarantee

Your appropriate minimum guarantee comprises:

- the standard minimum guarantee for you and your partner, if you have one (see p241); *plus*
- additional amounts for any special needs and/or certain housing costs (see p241).

### Step 2: calculate your income

This is the amount you have coming in each week – eg, from benefits (including state retirement pensions), private pensions and earnings.[40] Not all income counts (eg, personal independence payment (PIP), adult disability payment, disability living allowance, Scottish adult disability living allowance, child disability payment, attendance allowance (AA), pension age disability payment and child benefit are disregarded in full) and some income can be disregarded. See Chapter 17 for details. If you have more than £10,000 of capital, you are treated as having income of £1 for every £500 (or part thereof) over £10,000.[41]

### Step 3: deduct income from appropriate minimum guarantee

The amount of your guarantee credit is your appropriate minimum guarantee less any relevant income you have.[42] If your income is above the appropriate minimum guarantee, you do not qualify for any guarantee credit.

***Examples***

Connie (76) is single. She gets AA. She lives alone and no one gets carer's allowance, carer support payment or the universal credit (UC) carer element for looking after her. She lives in rented accommodation.

Her appropriate minimum guarantee is:

| | |
|---|---|
| Standard minimum guarantee (single person rate) | £227.10 |
| Severe disability additional amount | £82.90 |
| **Total** | **£310** |

Her weekly income is her basic state pension of £176.45. AA is ignored as income.

Connie is therefore entitled to £133.55 guarantee credit to bring her total income up to £310. She is also entitled to maximum pension-age housing benefit and any other passported benefits that may apply.

Lani (74) and Kekoa (78) are a couple. Their daughter Jaclyn (44) lives with them and gets UC. Lani gets the enhanced rate of the daily living component of PIP and Kekoa gets AA. Their appropriate minimum guarantee is £346.60.
Their joint weekly income for calculating PC is £384.33, made up of basic state pension of £286.33 (Lani £109.88 and Kekoa £176.45), occupational pension of £95 and £3 deemed income from £11,500 savings. PIP and AA are ignored as income.
They are not entitled to any guarantee credit because their income exceeds their appropriate minimum guarantee of £346.60. Their appropriate minimum guarantee does not include a severe disability addition because Jaclyn lives with them. However, they may be entitled to savings credit.

3

## Savings credit

You can only get savings credit if:

- you and your partner (if you have one) both reached pension age (see p690) before 6 April 2016; *or*
- either you or your partner reached pension age before 6 April 2016, and on that date you had an existing award of savings credit and you have remained entitled to it since then.[43]

In addition, the amount of your qualifying income must be above the savings credit threshold,[44] and if not entitled to guarantee credit, your excess income must not be so high that it wipes out savings credit.

| *Savings credit threshold* | |
|---|---|
| Single person | £198.27 |
| Couple | £314.34 |

**'Qualifying income'** for this purpose is all the income that counts for guarantee credit (see Chapter 17) except:[45]

- incapacity benefit;
- new-style ESA;
- new-style JSA;
- severe disablement allowance;
- maternity allowance;
- maintenance payments for you, or your partner, from a spouse or former spouse.

The amount of savings credit you are entitled to is calculated by taking 60 per cent of your qualifying income above the savings credit threshold. This is then capped, if needed, to a maximum figure, known as **'maximum savings credit'**.[46]

If you are entitled to the guarantee credit of PC, this will be your savings credit award and will be added to your overall PC entitlement. If you are not entitled to guarantee credit because your income is too high, this figure will be reduced (and may be wiped out), by 40 per cent of your excess income above your appropriate minimum guarantee.

***Maximum savings credit***

| | |
|---|---|
| Single person | £17.30 |
| Couple | £19.36 |

***Example***

Bert (82) lives alone. He has weekly qualifying income of £256 made up of his state pension and occupational pension. He does not qualify for any additional amounts, and does not get guarantee credit because his income exceeds the standard minimum guarantee. His income is more than the savings credit threshold and exceeds it by £57.73 (£256 – £198.27). 60 per cent of this is £34.64. This is capped to maximum savings credit for a single person of £17.30. His excess income above his appropriate minimum guarantee is £28.90 (£227.10 – £256). 40 per cent is £11.56. His savings credit entitlement is £17.30 – £11.56 = £5.74 per week. Although this is a small award, it will entitle Bert to some passported help (see p252).

To calculate savings credit, follow the steps above or use the calculator at gov.uk/pension-credit-calculator.

## 5. **Special benefit rules**

Special rules may apply if you:

- are subject to immigration control (see p1272);
- have come from or are going abroad (see Chapters 57 and 58);
- are in hospital or living in a care home or similar accommodation, or in prison or detention (see Chapter 38).

## 6. **Claims and backdating**

The general rules about claims and backdating are covered in Chapter 44. This section explains the specific rules that apply to pension credit (PC).

### Making a claim

A claim can be made:[47]

- online at gov.uk/pension-credit/how-to-claim. The online service states that you must have already claimed your state pension; *or*

- by phoning the Pension Service on 0800 99 1234 (textphone: 0800 169 0133; Relay UK and BSL relay services are available) between 8am and 6pm, Monday to Friday; *or*
- in writing on the approved form (Form PC1), although the Pension Service usually prefers you to claim online or by phone if you can. You ask for the form by calling the number above or print a copy from gov.uk/pension-credit/how-to-claim. Local authority housing benefit (HB) offices and some other 'alternative offices' (see p1004) may also provide the form. However, if you send in the form without first indicating your intention to claim (see p248), your date of claim will be affected.



You must provide any information or evidence required (see below). In certain circumstances, the DWP may accept a written application not on the approved form. You can amend or withdraw your claim before a decision is made (see p1004). If there is a delay in dealing with your claim, you may be able to get a short-term advance of benefit (see p1023).

## Who should claim

If you are a single person, you must claim on your own behalf. If you are a member of a couple, you must choose which one of you claims for you both (see p254). If you cannot agree who should claim, a decision maker decides.[48]

You can swap who claims, provided you both agree. It may be worthwhile doing so – eg, if one of you is about to go abroad.

If you cannot manage your claim, another person can claim PC for you as your appointee (see p1005).

## Information to support your claim

For the general information requirements that apply to all benefits, see p1006.

It is important you provide any information required when you claim. Until you do, you may not count as having made a valid claim (see p1008). Correct any defects as soon as possible or your date of claim may be affected.

When you claim, you are asked about your circumstances, including details of any income and savings, children you are responsible for, and any housing costs you or your partner have. You must include details of any personal pension scheme to which you belong or retirement anunity contract you hold.[49] If further information or evidence is needed, see below for when your claim begins.

Once your claim has been decided, you are sent a letter detailing the amount of any award, and the information on which it is based. You are asked to check this and report any omissions or changes.

Even if your claim is valid, you may be asked to supply further information to support your claim (see p1009). You may also be asked to provide further information after you are awarded PC. If you fail to do so, your benefit may be suspended or even terminated (see p1031).

## The date of your claim

The date of your claim is important as it determines when your entitlement to PC starts. This is not necessarily the date from which you are paid. For information about when payment of PC starts, see p249.

3

Your date of claim (unless the backdating rules apply) is:[50]

- the date your claim, properly completed with all the required information and evidence, is received at the appropriate office (the DWP, local authority HB office or county council office); *or*
- the date you notify the appropriate office of your intention to claim, so long as you submit a properly completed claim with all the required information and evidence within one month of this date.

You must make sure your claim is valid. If it is 'defective', you are given one month (or longer if considered reasonable) to correct the defects (see p1008). If you do, your claim is treated as having been made when you initially claimed.[51] If you are making an advance claim for PC before you have reached pension age and your claim is defective, you may correct it at any time before the end of the advance period.[52] In this case, the one-month time limit to supply required information or evidence runs from the day following the end of the advance period.[53]

### Backdating your claim

It is important that you claim in time because PC can only be backdated for up to three months. Your claim can be backdated if you satisfy the qualifying conditions over the period for which you require backdating – you do not have to show why your claim was late.[54] If you want your claim to be backdated, it is important that you ask – claims are not automatically backdated. If you claim by phone, you should be asked about the date from when you want your claim to start.

If you claim backdated PC within three months of being awarded a qualifying benefit and an earlier PC claim was refused because you did not get a qualifying benefit (see p1012) at that time, your PC can be backdated to the date of your earlier PC claim or the date when the qualifying benefit was first payable, whichever is later.[55] You must make an initial claim for PC before you hear about the 'qualifying benefit' to take advantage of this rule, and the qualifying benefit claim must be made no later than 10 working days after the initial PC claim. At the time of writing, carer support payment is not a qualifying benefit. If you are affected by this, get advice. For general rules on backdating, see p1011.

There is an exception to the PC backdating rules if you claimed because you had received a tax credit closure notice. You cannot backdate to a day on which you were still entitled to tax credits.[56]

### Claiming in advance

PC can be claimed up to four months before you qualify, whether this is before you reach pension age and you know you will be entitled then *or* after you reach pension age when you know you will have a future entitlement – eg, because of a drop in income.[57] The date of your claim is the date on which you qualify. You cannot make an advance claim if the reason you do not qualify straight away is because you fail the habitual residence test (see p1301).



### Claiming universal credit and reaching pension age

If you were claiming universal credit (UC) immediately before becoming entitled to PC, you should receive a full month's UC for the assessment period during which you or your partner reach pension age. Any PC or HB you receive should be ignored for the UC payment. Similarly, any UC payment should be ignored for the new PC award.[58]

## 7. Getting paid

The general rules on getting paid are in Chapter 45. This section explains the specific rules that apply to pension credit (PC).

***When is pension credit paid?***

| | *Qualifying age on or after 6 April 2010* | *Qualifying age before 6 April 2010* |
|---|---|---|
| *When is PC paid?* | The day you are paid depends on your national insurance number (see p1020).[59] | Monday, or the same day as your retirement pension is paid.[60] |
| *How often is PC paid?* | Weekly, fortnightly or four-weekly in arrears. | Weekly in advance, unless you are paid by direct credit transfer when it is paid in arrears.[61]<br>If you were entitled to income support immediately before 6 October 2003 and paid in arrears, PC is also paid in arrears.[62] |

If you are entitled to less than 10 pence a week, you are not paid PC, unless you are receiving another social security benefit that can be paid with PC.[63] You still have an underlying entitlement which allows you to get passported help if applicable (see p252). If your entitlement is less than £1 a week, a decision maker can decide to pay you quarterly in arrears.

There may be a delay between the date of your claim and the date PC becomes payable. This is because entitlement does not normally start until the first day of the benefit week following the start of the award.[64] A benefit week is the week in respect of which PC is payable in your case. There are exceptions to this rule for people moving to PC from other means-tested benefits.[65]

3

Note:

- Deductions can be made from your PC to pay to third parties (see p1033).
- Your PC might be paid at a reduced rate if you have been sanctioned for a benefit offence (see p1111).
- If a decision about your PC is delayed, see p1123. If you are waiting for a decision on your claim, or to be paid, you may be able to get a short-term advance (see p1023). If you wish to complain about how your claim has been dealt with, or claim compensation, see Chapter 55.
- If payment of your PC is suspended, see p1031.
- If you are overpaid PC, you might have to repay it (see Chapter 47) and, in some circumstances, you may have to pay a penalty (see p1101). If you have been accused of fraud, see Chapter 48.
- If you are owed arrears of PC, these can be paid in instalments if you agree (see p1018).

## Change of circumstances

You must report changes in your circumstances you have been told to report, as well as any that you might reasonably be expected to know might affect your right to benefit, including the amount and payment. You should do this as soon as possible, preferably in writing. See p1030 for further information.

If you reached pension age before 6 April 2016 and have been informed you do not have to report certain changes to your income for an indefinite period, called an 'assessed income period', see below.

If there has been a relevant change of circumstances, a decision maker looks at your claim again and makes a new decision. To find out when the new decision takes effect, see p1148.

If you become a member of a 'mixed-age couple' (see p240), your entitlement to PC usually stops. You and your partner may be able to claim universal credit instead.

### When your pension credit is adjusted

If you are paid in advance, your PC is usually adjusted from the day the change occurs or is expected to occur, if this is the day you are paid benefit. If it is not, your PC is usually adjusted from the start of the next benefit week. If you are paid in arrears, your PC is usually adjusted from the first day of the benefit week in which the change occurs or is expected to occur. However, there are a few exceptions to these general rules.[66]

## Assessed income period

An 'assessed income period' is a period during which you are not required to report any changes in certain types of your income, known as 'retirement provision'.[67] This only applies to you if you were already getting PC before 6 April 2016 and are still in an assessed income period which started before that date. No new assessed income periods have been set since then. For details of what is included in retirement provision, see the 2015/16 edition of this *Handbook*.

All other changes (including changes to other income) that affect your PC entitlement must be reported to the DWP as soon as they occur. During the assessed income period, your PC entitlement may change due to 'deemed increases in retirement provision' – eg, periodic increases in an occupational pension. See the 2015/16 edition of this *Handbook* for details.

Before 6 April 2016, an assessed income period could be set for a fixed period, usually five years or, if you were 75 or over, for an indefinite period.[68] All fixed-period assessed income periods have now ended. If an assessed income period has been set for an indefinite period, it only comes to an end if:[69]

- you become a member of a couple; *or*
- you cease to be a member of a couple; *or*
- your partner reaches the age of 65; *or*
- you are no longer entitled to PC; *or*
- you are single and go to live in a care home on a permanent basis; *or*
- payments of retirement provision due to you stop temporarily or are less than the amount due, and your PC award is superseded as a result.

# 8. Tax, other benefits and the benefit cap

## Tax

Pension credit (PC) is not taxable.

## Means-tested benefits

If you are entitled to PC, the following applies.

- An award of guarantee credit is an automatic passport to maximum pension-age housing benefit (HB).[70] If you are only entitled to savings credit, your pension-age HB claim is calculated using the Pension Service's assessment of your income and capital. In both cases, if you are not already entitled to pension-age HB, you must make a separate claim.

- If you get guarantee credit, the £16,000 limit on your capital does not apply for pension-age HB.[71] It does apply if you only receive savings credit.
- In Scotland, PC is a qualifying benefit for Scottish child payment (see p1459).

## Non-means-tested benefits



Some non-means-tested benefits are taken into account as income when calculating entitlement to PC. Others have a £10 disregard and some are disregarded entirely. See Chapter 17 for details.

Qualifying for certain non-means-tested benefits can help you qualify for more PC. For example, if you qualify for carer's allowance or carer support payment, even if it is not payable to you because of the overlapping benefit rules, you are entitled to a carer addition in your appropriate minimum guarantee.

## The benefit cap

PC is *not* one of the specified benefits for the benefit cap. The benefit cap does not apply when you are over pension age, whether you claim PC or not.

## Passports and other sources of help

If you are entitled to PC, you may also be eligible for:

- a Christmas bonus (see p783);
- health benefits, if you are getting the guarantee credit (see Chapter 27);
- Healthy Start food (see Chapter 36) or, in Scotland, Best Start foods (see Chapter 62);
- free school lunches in England and Wales, if you are getting the guarantee credit (see p774). In Scotland, local councils have discretion to award free school lunches if you are on PC;[72]
- social fund payments (see Chapter 33) or, in Scotland, a Best Start grant (see p1452) or funeral support payment (see Chapter 65);
- in England and Wales, the winter fuel payment (see p715) and a cold weather payment (see p714), or in Scotland, a winter heating payment (see p1505). Also in Scotland, PC may affect your entitlement to pension age winter heating payment (see p1507);
- council tax reduction from your local authority (see p761);
- a Warm Home Discount (see p781);
- home insulation grants and discretionary grants from the local authority towards the cost of home improvements (see p782).

# Notes

1. **Who can get pension credit**
1 ss1 and 2 SPCA 2002
2 ss1(6) and 4(1A) SPCA 2002
3 s4(2) SPCA 2002
4 s1(2)(a) SPCA 2002; regs 2 and 3 SPC Regs
5 s4(1) SPCA 2002
6 s2(1) SPCA 2002; reg 6 SPC Regs
7 s3 SPCA 2002
8 s3 SPCA 2002, as amended by PA 2014; reg 7A SPC Regs
9 s1(2)(a) SPCA 2002; regs 2-4 SPC Regs
10 s4(1) SPCA 2002
11 s4(2) SPCA 2002
12 s3(2)-(4) SPCA 2002

2. **The rules about your age**
13 s1(6) SPCA 2002
14 s126 and Sch 4 PA 1995
15 s4(1A) SPCA 2002
16 Art 4 WRA(No.31)O; HB Circular A9/2019 (10 July 2019)
17 Art 4(3) WRA(No.31)O as amended by SI 2024/604
18 Art 7 WRA(No.31)O; Vol 13, para 77150 DMG; HB Circular A9/2019, paras 15-17
19 Reg 5(3)-(5) SPC Regs

4. **The amount of pension credit**
20 s2(3) SPCA 2002
21 Reg 6(1)(b) SPC Regs
22 Reg 6(1)(a) SPC Regs
23 Reg 6 and Sch III para 1(5) SPC Regs
24 Regs 6(6)(d) and Sch IIA SPC Regs
25 Reg 6(4) and (5) SPC Regs
26 Reg 6(6)(a) SPC Regs
27 Reg 6(6)(d) and Sch IIA SPC Regs
28 Reg 6(6)(c) and Sch II SPC Regs
29 Reg 6(6)(b) and (6)(e) SPC Regs
30 Reg 6(6)(b) and Sch I para 6 SPC Regs
31 Sch I para 6(8) and (9) SPC Regs
32 Art 3A WRA(No.32)O
33 Regs 6(6)(e) and Sch IIB para 2 SPC Regs
34 Art 3B WRA(No.32)O
35 Reg 5 SS(SPAC)(A) Regs
36 Sch IIB paras 3-6 SPC Regs
37 Reg 18(5A) SPC Regs
38 Sch IIB para 7 SPC Regs
39 Regs 5 and 6(2) and (3) SPC Regs
40 s15 SPCA 2002; regs 14-24 SPC Regs
41 Reg 15(6) SPC Regs
42 s2(2) SPCA 2002
43 s3(1) SPCA 2002; reg 7A SPC Regs
44 Reg 7(2) SPC Regs
45 Reg 9 SPC Regs
46 s3(7) SPCA 2002; reg 7(1)(a) SPC Regs

6. **Claims and backdating**
47 Regs 4ZC and 4D SS(C&P) Regs
48 Reg 4D(7) SS(C&P) Regs
49 Reg 7(4) SS(C&P) Regs
50 Regs 4D and 4F SS(C&P) Regs
51 Reg 4D(6D), (6E), (10) and (11) SS(C&P) Regs
52 Regs 4D(12) and 4E(3) SS(C&P) Regs
53 Reg 7(1C) SS(C&P) Regs
54 Reg 19(2) and (3) SS(C&P) Regs
55 Reg 6(16) and (18) SS(C&P) Regs
56 Reg 5(1) SS(SPAC)(A) Regs
57 Regs 4E and 13D SS(C&P) Regs
58 Reg 5(2)(c) UC(TP) Regs; reg 66 UC Regs; reg 15(1)(za) SPC Regs

7. **Getting paid**
59 Reg 26BA SS(C&P) Regs
60 Reg 26B SS(C&P) Regs
61 Regs 21(3) and 26B(4) SS(C&P) Regs
62 Reg 36(6) SPC(CTMP) Regs
63 Reg 13 SPC Regs
64 Reg 16A(1) and (4) SS(C&P) Regs
65 Reg 16A(2) SS(C&P) Regs; reg 5(2)-(4) SS(SPAC)(A) Regs
66 Reg 7 and Sch 3B SS&CS(DA) Regs
67 ss6-10 SPCA 2002; regs 10-12 SPC Regs
68 s9(1) SPCA 2002
69 s9(4) SPCA 2002; reg 12 SPC Regs

8. **Tax, other benefits and the benefit cap**
70 Reg 26 HB(SPC) Regs
71 Reg 26 HB(SPC) Regs
72 'Good Practice Principles for School Meal Debt Management', Convention of Scottish Local Authorities, 2023, cosla.gov.uk/__data/assets/pdf_file/0029/41798/Good-Practice-Principles-for-School-Meal-Debt-Management.pdf

3

# Chapter 12

# People included in your means-tested benefits

**This chapter covers:**


1. Couples (below)
2. Children (p258)
3. Households (p262)


This chapter covers the rules for means-tested benefits other than universal credit (UC). For UC, see Chapter 4.

### Key facts

- Your partner and, in some cases, your children can be included in your means-tested benefit.
- You count as a member of a 'couple' if you are married or in a civil partnership and are living with your partner in the same household. You also count as a couple if you are not married or in a civil partnership, but are living with your partner as if you are a married couple or civil partners.
- A child or 'qualifying young person' can be included as part of your family if you are responsible for them. They must also live in your household.
- You can continue to count as a couple, and children and young people can continue to be included in your means-tested benefit, while you are living apart temporarily.

## 1. Couples

Your partner is included in your means-tested benefit if you count as a 'couple'. You and your partner count as a couple if you are both 16 or over and you are:[1]

- married or civil partners and members of the same household; *or*
- not married or civil partners but 'living together as if' you are a married couple or civil partners.

For when you count as living in the same 'household', see p262. For pension credit (PC) only, if your partner is a 'person subject to immigration control' (see p1272), you are treated as *not* being members of the same household and so do not count as a couple.[2]

**Note**: income support and income-based jobseeker's allowance have been replaced by universal credit (see p21). The rules about couples in this chapter used to apply to those benefits in the same way that they apply to income-related employment and support allowance (ESA).



## Spouse or civil partner

You can still be treated as part of a couple, even if you are married to someone else or in a civil partnership with someone else.[3]

There are special rules if you are polygamously married.[4] You count as **polygamously married** if you are part of a marriage in which one of you is married to more than one person and your marriages took place in a country that permits polygamy (see also p460).[5] For ESA only, you and all your partners must also be living in the same household (see p262).

You count as someone's **civil partner** if you have been registered as their civil partner.

## Living together as a married couple or civil partners

Even if you and your partner are not married or civil partners, you count as a couple if you are 'living together as if' you are a married couple or civil partners. We refer to this as 'cohabiting' in this *Handbook*. This applies to both different- and same-sex relationships.[6]

If you are getting income-related ESA, usually the local authority should not make a separate decision about whether you are cohabiting when considering your entitlement to housing benefit (HB).[7] However, if the local authority thinks that the benefit award on which your HB claim is based is fraudulent, it can decide that you are not entitled to HB.[8] If you have not been awarded income-related ESA or PC, the local authority must consider whether you are cohabiting and may reach a different conclusion from that of the DWP.[9]

The factors below are used as 'signposts' to determine whether or not you are cohabiting.[10] No one factor, in itself, is conclusive, as it is your overall relationship and your particular circumstances that are looked at.[11] The 'emotional aspect' of the relationship (your interdependence, devotion, love and affection) should also be considered.[12] Like your individual circumstances, this should not be regarded as conclusive. For example, if your partner stays with you for three nights or more a week, you should not automatically be treated as cohabiting.

***Are you cohabiting?***

1. Do you live in the same household? See p256.
2. Do you have a sexual relationship? See p256.
3. What are your financial arrangements? See p256.

4. Is your relationship stable? See below.
5. Do you have children? See p257.
6. How do you appear in public? See p257.

3

## Living in the same household

If you live in the same household, you may be treated as cohabiting. For what counts as a 'household', see p262.

Even if you *do* share a household, you may not be cohabiting. It is essential to look at *why* two people are in the same household.[13] For example, if you are living in the same household for 'care, companionship and mutual convenience', you can argue that you are not cohabiting.[14]

## Being in a sexual relationship

In practice, a decision maker may not ask you about the existence of a sexual relationship, in which case they only have the information if you volunteer it. However, if you are appealing about whether you are a member of a couple, the First-tier Tribunal should consider this and may ask you about it.[15] If you do not have a sexual relationship, you should say so (and perhaps offer to show your separate sleeping arrangements).

Having a sexual relationship is not sufficient, by itself, to prove you are cohabiting. If you have never had a sexual relationship, there is a strong (but not necessarily conclusive) presumption that you are not cohabiting.[16] A couple who abstain from a sexual relationship before marriage should not be counted as cohabiting until they are formally married.[17]

## Your financial arrangements

If one person is supported by the other or your household expenses are shared, this may be treated as evidence that you are cohabiting. However, it is important to consider how expenses are shared. There is a difference between, on the one hand, paying a fixed weekly contribution or rigidly sharing bills 50/50 (which does *not* suggest cohabitation) and, on the other hand, a common fund for income and expenditure (which might).

## A stable relationship

Marriage and civil partnership are expected to be stable and lasting and so an occasional or brief association should not be regarded as cohabitation. However, the fact that your relationship is stable does not make it cohabitation – eg, you can have a stable relationship as a landlord and lodger, but not be cohabiting.

The way you spend your time together, the activities you undertake together and the things you do for each other are relevant, so questions about how you spend your holidays and how you organise the shopping, the laundry and cleaning may be important.

### Children

If you have had a child together and live in the same household as the other parent, there is a strong (but not conclusive) presumption of cohabitation.

### Your appearance in public

Decision makers may check the electoral roll and awards of other benefits to see whether you present yourselves as a couple. If you do not have a committed, emotional, loving relationship that is publicly acknowledged, you can argue that you are not living together as a married couple or civil partners.[18]



## Couples living apart

**If you separate permanently** (ie, you do not intend to resume living with your partner), you no longer count as a couple.[19] When deciding whether you intend to resume living together or not, your intention must be 'unqualified' – ie, it must not depend on something over which you have no control, such as the right of entry to the UK being granted by the Home Office[20] or the offer of a suitable job.[21]

**If you and your partner are living apart temporarily**, you continue to count as a couple because you are still treated as members of the same household (but see below). If you were not living together in the same household before your time apart, you should not be regarded as living apart temporarily.[22] Your former household need not have been in the UK.[23]

However, even if you and your partner are only living apart temporarily, **you no longer count as a couple if:**

- **for income-related ESA, PC and HB**, you are likely to be separated for more than 52 weeks. However, you still count as a couple if you are unlikely to be separated for 'substantially' longer than 52 weeks and there are exceptional circumstances, such as a stay in hospital or having no control over the length of the absence;[24]
- **for income-related ESA and PC:**[25]
  - either of you is in custody;
  - either of you is released on temporary licence from prison;
  - either of you is detained in a high security psychiatric hospital (in Scotland, a 'state hospital') under the mental health provisions;
  - either of you is staying permanently in a care home, an Abbeyfield Home or an independent hospital;
  - you are abroad and do not qualify for benefit while temporarily absent from Great Britain. For when you qualify while temporarily absent and for when your partner is abroad, see p1380 (for income-related ESA) and p1375 (for PC).

If you and your partner continue to count as a couple while you are temporarily living apart, your partner's income and capital continue to be taken into account. However, in certain situations, your benefit is calculated in a different way (see p833 for care homes and p842 for approved bail or probation hostels).

3

## Challenging a decision that you are a couple

Your benefit may be stopped or adjusted if the decision maker decides you are a member of a couple. If you disagree with a decision that you are a couple, you can apply for a revision or supersession (see Chapter 50), or appeal (see Chapter 51).

***How do you show that you are not a couple?***

1. Consider carefully what evidence to submit:
– if you are married or in a civil partnership, to show that you are not living in the same household;
– if you are not married or in a civil partnership, about each of the six questions on p255, the emotional aspect of your relationship and any other matters you consider relevant.
2. Provide evidence if the other person has another address (eg, a rent account and other household bills), receipts for board and lodging, statements from friends and relatives, or evidence of a formal separation, divorce proceedings or a dissolution application or order.

If your benefit as a single person is stopped or adjusted because it is alleged that you are a couple, the onus is on the decision maker to prove that you are.[26]

If your benefit is stopped because it is decided that you are a couple, challenge the decision.

## 2. Children

A child may count as part of your family for your means-tested benefit. However, you can only get additional amounts in your benefit for a child in certain circumstances. You do not have to be the child's parent.

**Note:** income support and income-based jobseeker's allowance have been replaced by universal credit (UC) (see p21). The rules about children for those benefits were very similar to those for income-related employment and support allowance (ESA), but there were some differences. See Chapter 16 of the 2024/25 edition of this *Handbook*.

**For income-related ESA and housing benefit (HB)**, a child is part of your family for benefit purposes (although you do not necessarily get additional amounts for them) if:[27]

- you or your partner are 'responsible' for the child (see p260); *and*
- the child is living in your 'household' (see p261).

**For the guarantee credit of pension credit (PC)**, a child is part of your family if you are 'responsible' for the child (see p261).[28] **Note:** the rules also require you not to have an award of tax credits, although tax credits have been replaced by UC (see p21).

A child stops being part of your family for your benefit if you no longer fulfil the above conditions or if they no longer count as a child (see below).

If a child is part of your family for benefit purposes, you can get an additional amount for them included in your HB and your PC.

**Note:** usually, you only get additional amounts in your benefit for a maximum of two children. For more information, see p268. However, this does not apply to PC or to pension-age HB. If an amount for children can be included in your PC or pension-age HB, you get an additional amount for each child that qualifies.

3

ESA does not include additional amounts for children.[29]

## Who counts as a child

**For income-related ESA and HB,** a 'child' is someone who is:[30]

- aged under 16; *or*
- aged 16 or over but under 20 and counts as a 'qualifying young person' for child benefit purposes. This includes, for example, most young people who are at school or college full time studying for GCSEs or A levels (or equivalent), or who are doing approved training. See p488 for who counts as a qualifying young person. A young person can continue to count as a child after they have left school or training until the 'terminal date' (see p491) or the end of the child benefit 'extension period' (see p490).

A 19-year-old must have started (or been accepted for or enrolled on) the education or training before reaching 19 to count as a qualifying young person.

**For PC,** a 'child' is someone who is:[31]

- aged under 16; *or*
- aged 16 or over but under 20 and a 'qualifying young person' for PC.

A 'qualifying young person' for PC includes most young people studying for GCSEs or A levels or who are doing approved training. Specifically, it means someone who is:[32]

- aged 16 but who has not reached 1 September following their 16th birthday; *or*
- aged 16–19 but who has not reached 1 September following their 19th birthday, and has been accepted for (or has enrolled on) approved training or non-advanced education at school or college, or another institution approved by the Secretary of State (see below). During term time there must be more than 12 hours, on average, of tuition, practical work, supervised study or examinations a week. Meal breaks and unsupervised study are not included.

***Approved training and non-advanced education for pension credit***

**'Approved training'** is training that is approved by the DWP and provided under section 2(1) of the Employment and Training Act 1973 or section 2(3) of the Enterprise and New Towns (Scotland) Act 1990.

A course is **'non-advanced'** if it is below the level of 'advanced education'. Courses that count as advanced education include university degrees and other courses above GCSE, A level and Scottish National Qualifications above higher or advanced higher level.[33] See p489 for more examples of advanced and non-advanced courses.

## 3 Who does not count as a child

**For income-related ESA and HB**, a person does *not* count as a child if:[34]

- they are getting certain benefits in their own right and so do not count as a qualifying young person (see p496); *or*
- they are excluded from entitlement to HB because they are aged 16 or 17, have left local authority care on or after 1 October 2001, and certain other conditions apply (see p846).

**For PC**, a person does not count as a child if they are getting UC, ESA (contributory or income-related), or new-style JSA in their own right.[35]

## Responsibility for a child

**For income-related ESA and HB**, a child is included in your benefit if you are 'responsible' for them and they are living in your 'household'.

- **You are treated as responsible for a child for ESA** if the child 'usually lives' with you. This is not defined in the rules.[36]
- **You are treated as responsible for a child for HB** if the child is 'normally living' with you.[37] This means that they spend more time with you than with anyone else.[38] If it is unclear in whose household the child lives, or if they spend an equal amount of time with two parents in different homes (this may not mean literally three and a half days with each parent[39]), you are treated as having responsibility if:[40]
  - you get child benefit for the child (see Chapter 23); *or*
  - no one gets child benefit, but you have applied for it; *or*
  - no one has applied for child benefit, or both of you have applied, but you appear to have the most responsibility.

  **Note:** a 'substantial minority carer' (someone with shared care of the child and who has the child with them for at least 104 nights a year) cannot be regarded as responsible for a child for HB.[41]

In these rules, it is only necessary to look at who gets child benefit when it is unclear in whose household the child *normally* lives or if they spend and equal amount of time with parents in different homes.

A child can only be the responsibility of one person in any week for HB.[42] The rules for ESA do not expressly say this but, in any case, a person can only be responsible for a child if they usually live with them.

If benefit is paid for a child, it cannot be split between parents if a child spends their time equally between their two homes.

**For PC**, a child is included if you are 'responsible' for them. You are responsible for a child if they 'normally live with' you.[43] This includes considering the amount of time they spend with you as welll as the nature of the support you provide.[44] If the child normally lives with two (or more) people who are not a couple (eg, in the homes of separated parents), you are responsible if you have the main responsibility. In this situation, you can agree with the other person who this should be. The DWP can, however, decide otherwise or, if you cannot agree, decide which person has the main responsibility.



You cannot be treated as responsible for a child during any period in which they are:[45]

- looked after by a local authority (including being placed with a foster parent), except during planned short breaks in local authority care to provide respite care for the person who normally looks after the child or where they are placed with someone who has parental responsibility for them; *or*
- a prisoner; *or*
- temporarily absent but in Great Britain, and they have been, or are expected to be, absent for more than 52 weeks, unless there are 'exceptional circumstances' (eg, they are in hospital) and the absence is unlikely to be substantially more than 52 weeks; *or*
- temporarily absent from Great Britain and they have been, or are expected to be, absent from Great Britain for more than four weeks, unless it is for the death of a close relative or medical treatment, when the period of absence may be, respectively, eight weeks or 26 weeks (see p1375).

## Living in the same household

In addition to being responsible for a child, for ESA and HB a child is only included if they are a member of the same household. If you count as responsible for a child, they are usually treated as a member of your household, despite any temporary absence. For exceptions to the rule, see below. For what 'household' means, see p262. The requirement for the child to be a member of your household does not apply to PC (but the child must normally be living with you).

### When a child does not count as a member of your household

A child does *not* count as a member of your household if:[46]

- **for ESA and HB**, they are not living with you and:
  - they have no intention of resuming living with you; *or*
  - they are likely to be absent for more than 52 weeks, unless there are exceptional circumstances, such as being in hospital, or if you have no control over the length of absence and it is unlikely to be substantially longer than 52 weeks; *or*

3

- they are being fostered by you or your partner following a formal placement by social services. This does not apply if you are fostering privately or if social services has made a less formal arrangement for the child to live with you; *or*
- they are living with you or your partner prior to adoption and have been placed by social services or an adoption agency; *or*
- they are boarded out with you or your partner, whether or not with a view to adoption; *or*
- they have been placed with someone else prior to adoption; *or*
- they are in the care of, or being looked after by, the local authority and not living with you. However, the child counts as a member of your household on the days when they come home – eg, for the weekend or a holiday.[47] Make sure you tell the decision maker in good time. For HB, your child counts as a member of the household for all that week, whether they return for all or only part of it;[48]

- **for ESA only**, they are not living with you and:
  - they have been in hospital or in a local authority home for more than 12 weeks and have not been in regular contact with you or other members of your household. The 12 weeks run from the date they went into hospital or the home;[49] *or*
  - they are in custody. **Note:** they can still be included in your award for any periods they spend at home;[50] *or*
  - they have been abroad for more than 26 weeks to get medical treatment.[51] The 26-week period runs from the day the child went abroad.

## 3. Households

The term 'household' is not defined. Whether you and another person should be treated as members of the same household is decided on the particular facts of your case. For pension credit only, if your partner is a 'person subject to immigration control' (see p1272), you are treated as *not* being members of the same household and so do not count as a couple.[52]

A house or flat can contain a number of separate households and if one person has exclusive occupation of separate accommodation from another, they are not considered to be living in the same household. Physical presence is not, in itself, conclusive. There must be a 'particular kind of tie' binding two people together in a domestic establishment. So, for example, a husband and wife may live in separate households in the same care or nursing home.[53] For a couple to be in the same household, there must also be two or more people living together as a unit and having a reasonable level of independence and self-sufficiency. In one case, it was held that a married couple sharing a room in a residential home because they needed help organising their personal care and domestic activities were not self-sufficient and did not live in a domestic establishment, and therefore did not share a household.[54]

***Is there a separate household?***

If you think you should not be treated as a member of the same household as someone, check whether you can show that you maintain separate households. A separate household may exist if there:

- are independent arrangements for storing and cooking food or separate eating arrangements;
- are independent financial arrangements or separate commitments for housing costs;
- is no evidence of family life.

You cannot be a member of more than one household at the same time.[55] So if you are a member of one couple, you cannot also be treated as part of another. If two people maintain separate homes (ie, they each have separate addresses where they usually live), they cannot share the same household.[56] Even if you have the right to occupy only part of a room, you may have your own household.[57]

If you are separated from your partner, but living under the same roof, you should not be treated as a couple if you are maintaining separate households. Any 'mere hope' of a reconciliation is not a 'reasonable expectation' if at least one partner has accepted that the relationship is at an end.[58]

**Note:** if you are still married or in a civil partnership, a shared attitude that the relationship is at an end may not be enough to show there is no shared household.[59]

# Notes

1. **Couples**

1 s137(1) SSCBA 1992; CFC/7/1992
**ESA** Sch 1 para 6(5) WRA 2007; reg 2(1) ESA Regs
**PC** s17(1) SPCA 2002; reg 1(2) SPC Regs
**HB** Reg 2(1) HB Regs; reg 2(1) HB(SPC) Regs

2 Reg 5(1)(h) SPC Regs

3 R(SB) 8/85

4 **ESA** Regs 68 and 83 ESA Regs
**PC** Reg 8 and Sch 3 SPC Regs
**HB** Regs 23 and 25 HB Regs; regs 22 and 23 HB(SPC) Regs

5 **ESA** Reg 2(1) ESA Regs
**PC** s12 SPCA 2002
**HB** Reg 2(1) HB Regs; reg 2(1) HB(SPC) Regs

6 **ESA** Sch 1 para 6(6) WRA 2007; reg 2(1) ESA Regs
**PC** s17(1A) SPCA 2002; reg 1(2) SPC Regs
**HB** Reg 2(1) HB Regs; reg 2(1) HB(SPC) Regs; s137(1A) SSCBA 1992
7 *R v Penwith DC HBRB ex parte Menear* [1991] 24 HLR 115 (QBD). However, *AM v Chelmsford BC (HB)* [2013] UKUT 245 (AAC) suggests that this only applies to the assessment of income and capital, and not to cohabitation questions.
8 *R v South Ribble BC HBRB ex parte Hamilton* [2000] 33 HLR 102 (CA)
9 CH/4014/2007
10 *Crake and Butterworth v SBC* [1982] 1 All ER 498; [1981] 2 FLR 264 (QBD)
11 R(SB) 17/81; R(G) 3/71; CIS/87/1993
12 *PP v Basildon DC (HB)* [2013] UKUT 505 (AAC)
13 *Crake and Butterworth v SBC* [1982] 1 All ER 498; [1981] 2 FLR 264 (QBD), quoted in R(SB) 35/85
14 R(SB) 35/85
15 CIS/87/1993; CIS/2559/2002; CIS/2074/2008
16 CIS/87/1993
17 CSB/150/1985
18 *JP v SSWP (IS)* [2014] UKUT 17 (AAC)
19 **ESA** Reg 156(3)(a) ESA Regs
**PC** Reg 5(1)(a)(i) SPC Regs
**HB** Reg 21(2)(a) HB Regs; reg 21(2)(a) HB(SPC) Regs
20 CIS/508/1992; CIS/13805/1996
21 CIS/484/1993
22 **ESA** Reg 156(2) ESA Regs
**PC** Reg 5(2) SPC Regs
**HB** Reg 21(1) HB Regs; reg 21(1) HB(SPC) Regs
**All** *Broxtowe BC v CS (HB)* [2014] UKUT 186 (AAC)
23 CIS/508/1992
24 **ESA** Reg 156(3) ESA Regs
**PC** Reg 5(1)(a) SPC Regs
**HB** Reg 21(2) HB Regs; reg 21(2) HB(SPC) Regs
25 **ESA** Reg 156(4) ESA Regs. This wrongly refers to Chapter 4, but correctly refers to the rules on temporary absence from Great Britain.
**PC** Reg 5(1)(b)-(d) and (f) SPC Regs
26 R(I) 1/71

2. **Children**
27 **ESA** Reg 2(1), definition of 'family', ESA Regs
**ESA/HB** s137 SSCBA 1992
28 Reg 6 and Sch IIA SPC Regs
29 Reg 1 SS(WTCCTC)(CA) Regs
30 **ESA** Reg 2(1) ESA Regs
**HB** Reg 19 HB Regs; reg 19 HB(SPC) Regs; s137 SSCBA 1992
31 Reg 4A and Sch IIA SPC Regs
32 Reg 4A and Sch IIA SPC Regs
33 Reg 4A SPC Regs
34 **ESA** Reg 2(1), definition of 'young person', ESA Regs
**HB** Reg 19(2) HB Regs; reg 19(2) HB(SPC) Regs
35 Reg 4A SPC Regs
36 Reg 156(10) ESA Regs
37 Reg 20(1) HB Regs; reg 20(1) HB(SPC) Regs
38 CFC/1537/1995
39 CFC/1537/1995
40 Reg 20(2) HB Regs; reg 20(2) HB(SPC) Regs
41 *JD v SSWP and LB Richmond upon Thames (HB)* [2013] UKUT 642 (AAC); *JB v SSWP and Basingstoke and Deane BC (HB)* [2014] UKUT 223 (AAC)
42 Reg 20(3) HB Regs; reg 20(3) HB(SPC) Regs
43 Sch IIA para 3 SPC Regs
44 Sch IIA para 3(3) and (4) SPC Regs; reg 4 UC Regs; *MC v SSWP (UC)* [2018] UKUT 44 (AAC) was about UC but arguably should also apply to PC
45 Sch IIA paras 4-8 SPC Regs
46 **ESA** Reg 156 ESA Regs
**HB** Reg 21 HB Regs; reg 21 HB(SPC) Regs
47 Reg 156(8) ESA Regs
48 Reg 21(5) HB Regs; reg 21(5) HB(SPC) Regs
49 Reg 156(6)(c) ESA Regs
50 Reg 156(6)(h) and (8) ESA Regs
51 Reg 156(6)(a) and (b) ESA Regs

3. **Households**
52 Reg 5(1)(h) SPC Regs
53 *Santos v Santos* [1972] 2 All ER 246; CIS/671/1992; CIS/81/1993
54 CIS/4935/1997
55 R(SB) 8/85
56 R(SB) 4/83
57 CSB/463/1986
58 CIS/72/1994
59 CIS/2900/1998

# Chapter 13

# Applicable amounts

3

**This chapter covers:**

1. What are applicable amounts (below)
2. Personal allowances (p266)
3. Premiums and additional amounts (p270)
4. Components (p281)

### Key facts

- Applicable amounts are used in some means-tested benefits to calculate the amount of benefit to which you are entitled.
- Applicable amounts apply in income-related employment and support allowance and housing benefit. They also used to apply in income support and income-based jobseeker's allowance, although those benefits have now been replaced by universal credit.
- There are additional amounts in the guarantee credit of pension credit for people who are severely disabled, carers or people who have a child, which are similar to the premiums included in applicable amounts.
- Applicable amounts are made up of personal allowances, premiums, certain housing costs and, in some cases, components. You may have one or more of these included.

## 1. What are applicable amounts

Your applicable amount for income-related employment and support allowance (ESA) is the amount you are expected to live on each week. Your applicable amount for housing benefit (HB) is the amount used to calculate how much help you need with your rent. Pension credit (PC) has similar rules for the calculation of 'additional amounts'.

**Note**: applicable amounts also used to apply for income support (IS) and income-based jobseeker's allowance (JSA), but in most cases, those benefits have now been replaced by universal credit (see p21). For how applicable amounts used to apply for IS and income-based JSA, see the 2024/25 edition of this *Handbook*.

### What is included in your applicable amount

Your applicable amount is made up of:

- **personal allowances**: the amount the law says you need for living expenses (see below). PC has a 'standard minimum guarantee' (see p241);
- **premiums (or in PC, additional amounts)**: the amount given for certain extra needs you, your partner or children may have (see p270);
- **a support or work-related activity component** in income-related ESA and, in some circumstances, in HB (see p281);
- certain **housing costs** in income-related ESA and PC (see p287).

***Can you get allowances and premiums for children?***

You can get allowances and premiums for children in your HB (see p268 and p270), but not in your income-related ESA. You can get an additional amount for children as part of the guarantee credit of PC (see p270).

## 2. Personal allowances

The amount of your personal allowance in income-related employment and support allowance (ESA) and housing benefit (HB) depends on your age and whether you are claiming as a single person or a couple. You also get an allowance for each child included in your HB.

**Note:** personal allowances also applied in your income support (IS) or income-based jobseeker's allowance (JSA), before they were replaced by universal credit (see p21). For how personal allowances applied to your IS or JSA, see the 2024/25 edition of this *Handbook*.

If you are polygamously married (see p254), you receive an extra amount for each additional spouse in your household.[1]

### Rates of personal allowances for people aged 18 or over

**Note:** some 16/17-year-olds may also be entitled to these rates (see p267).

If you have been getting working-age HB (see p197) and this continues even though you are now a member of a 'mixed-age couple' (ie, if one of you is at least pension age, but not the other) (see p197), your personal allowance remains as for working-age HB, even though one of you has reached pension age.

| *Income-related ESA/working-age HB* | |
|---|---|
| **Single claimant:** | |
| Aged 18–24 | £72.90 |
| Aged 25 or over | £92.05 |
| Aged 18 or over and ESA includes (or would include) a support component or claimant in work-related activity group (ESA/working-age HB only) | £92.05 |
| **Lone parent:** | |
| Aged 18 or over | £92.05 |
| **Couple:** | |
| Both aged 18 or over | £144.65 |
| One aged under 18 (some ESA cases only and all HB cases) | £144.65 |
| One aged under 18 (other ESA cases): | |
| *either* | £92.05 |
| *or* | £72.90 |
| **Polygamous marriages (each additional qualifying spouse):** | |
| Partner aged 18 or over | £52.60 |
| | |
| *Pension-age HB* | |
| **Single claimant:** | |
| Reached pension age before 1 April 2021 | £244.40 |
| Reached pension age on or after 1 April 2021 | £227.10 |
| **Lone parent** | £244.40 |
| **Couple:** | |
| One or both pension age or over (one or both reached pension age before 1 April 2021) | £366.00 |
| Both pension age or over (both reached pension age on or after 1 April 2021) | £346.60 |
| **Polygamous marriages (each additional qualifying spouse):** | |
| One or more spouse(s) pension age or over (one or more reached pension age before 1 April 2021) | £121.60 |
| All spouses pension age or over (all reached pension age on or after 1 April 2021) | £119.50 |

## Rates of personal allowances for 16/17-year-olds

- For income-related ESA:
  - you get £72.90; *or*
  - if your ESA includes the support component or if you are in the work-related activity group, you get £92.05; *or*

- if you are in a couple (unless one of the circumstances below applies) and your partner is also under 18, the same amounts as above (£72.90 or £92.05) apply.

- For HB:
  - if you are single (including if you are a lone parent), you get the same rate as 18–24-year-olds – ie, £72.90; *or*
  - if you are entitled to ESA and qualify for the support component or you are in the work-related activity group (see p281), you get £92.05; *or*
  - if you are in a couple and your partner is also under 18, you get £110.15. If your partner is aged 18 or over, or if you are entitled to ESA and either get the support component or are in the work-related activity group, you get £144.65.

  For this purpose, you count as qualifying for an ESA component even if your actual award of ESA is nil – eg, because you are only entitled to national insurance contribution credits.

Most 16/17-year-olds who have previously been looked after by a local authority cannot claim HB (see p846).

### Young couples in special circumstances

**Note:** the following rules apply to income-related ESA only.[2]

If you are a member of a young couple (where at least one of you is aged 16–17), you are entitled to a personal allowance for a couple at a higher rate in certain circumstances. The main circumstance in which this applies is where you are both aged 16–17 and one of you is responsible for a child. Another is where both of you would qualify for income-related ESA if you were not in a couple. For full details, see Chapter 17 of the 2022/23 edition of this *Handbook*.

The higher rate is £144.65, where at least one of you is aged 16–17.

## Personal allowances for children

Personal allowances for children are included in your HB applicable amount. Income-related ESA does *not* include personal allowances for children. Although there is no personal allowance for a child as part of pension credit (PC), you may be entitled to an additional amount in your guarantee credit of PC (see p270).

For when children are included in your award and for who counts as a child, see p258. Your child's income and capital do not affect the amount of HB or ESA to which you are entitled.

### The two-child limit

You get one personal allowance in your HB applicable amount for each child. However, for working-age HB, you cannot get a personal allowance for a third or subsequent child born on or after 6 April 2017, unless an exception applies (see below). This is known as the 'two-child limit'. Also, you do not get a personal allowance for a third or subsequent child who becomes part of your award (eg, the child of a new partner) on or after 6 April 2017 or is in a new claim made on or after that date, unless an exception applies. **Note:** the two-child limit applies only to working-age HB, and not to pension-age HB (see p197).

The limit applies to children for whom you or your partner are responsible and who are living in your household (see p260).[3]

If you already had a personal allowance for a third or subsequent child included in your HB on 5 April 2017, you continue to get a personal allowance for the child while that award continues.

A personal allowance can become payable for a third child who is born on or after 6 April 2017 and to whom this limit applies if an older child leaves the household (so that you are no longer responsible for them) or if a young person leaves education (so that they no longer qualify). In these situations, you should report the change as soon as possible to continue getting the maximum two personal allowances.

#### Exceptions

An exception applies, and so a personal allowance is payable in your working-age HB, to the following children – ie, the 'two-child limit' does not apply to them.

- A child living with you and being adopted by you from local authority care, or living with you under a 'non-parental caring arrangement'. This used to mean the same as it did in child tax credit (CTC), but now is likely to mean the same as it does for universal credit (UC) (see p70). It was required that for an exception to apply to a child in your HB, it had to have applied in your CTC. See CPAG's *Welfare Rights Bulletin* or the online version of this *Handbook* for updates. When establishing how many children you have for the two-child limit, a child to whom this exception applies is ignored. (It was required that for an exception to apply to a child in your HB, it had to have applied in your CTC – again, check CPAG's *Welfare Rights Bulletin* or the online version of this *Handbook* for updates.) So, you can get an element for any such child, plus up to two more children, plus any further (third or subsequent) children to whom an exception also applies.
- A child born in a multiple birth, other than the first born if you already have two or more children.
- A child likely to have been conceived as a result of rape or in a controlling or coercive relationship and you are not living with the alleged perpetrator. This is likely to mean the same as it does for UC (see p70) – see CPAG's *Welfare Rights Bulletin* or the online version of this *Handbook* for updates.

### Rate of personal allowance for children

There is one rate of personal allowance for children who are included in your award: £84.66. You get one personal allowance for each child.

# 3. Premiums and additional amounts

Premiums are added to your personal allowance. They are intended to help with the extra expenses you have due to your age, having a disability and, in some circumstances, having children. Some premiums are not included in some of the means-tested benefits. Pension credit (PC) has additional amounts for severe disability, carers and children.

**Note:** if you or your partner are entitled to pension-age housing benefit (HB) (see p197), your HB can only include the family, disabled child, enhanced disability for a child, severe disability and carer premiums.[4] In these circumstances, your HB cannot include a disability premium. There are no pensioner premiums in either pension-age or working-age HB.

See p280 for information about backdating premiums. See p280 for the premium rates and for which premiums can be paid in addition to other premiums.

## Premiums and additional amounts for children

Certain premiums can be included in your HB applicable amount if you have children included in your claim. These are the family premium, disabled child premium and the child rate of the enhanced disability premium. Income-related employment and support allowance (ESA) does not include these premiums.

For who counts as a child and when children are included in your claim, see p258. Your child's income and capital do not affect the amount of your HB or ESA.

You can qualify for an additional amount for a child in the guarantee credit of PC if you are responsible for the child (see p258).[5] You get an additional amount for each child who qualifies. The weekly standard amount of the addition is £67.42 for each child born on or after 6 April 2017, or £78.10 for your eldest child only, if they were born before that date. If the child is entitled to disability living allowance (DLA), child disability payment (CDP), personal independence payment (PIP) or adult disability payment (ADP), the standard amount is increased by £36.54. However, if they are entitled to the highest rate of the care component of DLA/CDP or the enhanced rate of the daily living component of PIP/ADP, or they are certified as severely sight impaired or blind by a consultant ophthalmologist, the standard rate is instead increased by £114.12.

If your child dies, you can continue to get the additional amount for up to eight weeks after their death (or until they would have reached 20 years old, if that is earlier).

## Family premium

**Note:** the familiy premium was abolished for new claims from 1 May 2016 for HB. If a child was included before 1 May 2016, you continue to get the premium, provided you still have a child included and you do not make a new claim for HB on or after that date.[6] The family premium cannot be included in income-related ESA.

This premium could also have been included in your income support (IS) or income-based jobseeker's allowance (JSA), in some circumstances, before they were replaced by universal credit (UC) (see p21). For how this premium could have applied to your IS or income-based JSA, see the 2024/25 edition of this *Handbook*.



You may be entitled to a family premium in your HB if at least one child is included. Only one family premium can be included, irrespective of how many children you have.[7] The premium can be paid even if you are not the child's parent.

If your child is looked after by a local authority or is in custody for part of the week, the family premium is affected in the same way as the disabled child premium (see below).

## Disabled child premium

You are entitled to a disabled child premium in your HB for each child included who gets any rate of DLA, CDP, PIP, ADP (where they count as a 'qualifying young person' for child benefit purposes – see p488, and are still part of your family for benefit purposes – see p258) or armed forces independence payment (AFIP) if they are at least 16, or extra-statutory payments to compensate for non-payment of DLA/CDP or PIP/ADP, or they are blind.[8] A disabled child premium can still be included for a third or subsequent child, even if you do not get a personal allowance for them because of the 'two-child limit' (see p268).

This premium could also have been included in your IS or income-based JSA, before they were replaced by UC (see p21). For how this premium could have applied to your IS or income-based JSA, see the 2024/25 edition of this *Handbook*.

A child is treated as blind if they are certified as severely sight impaired or blind by a consultant ophthalmologist and for the first 28 weeks after they have ceased to be certified as such on regaining their sight.[9] If DLA/CDP or PIP/ADP stops because the child has gone into hospital, see p823.

If a child who is being looked after by a local authority or who is in custody comes home for part of a week, you can still get the full premium in your HB if the child is part of your household for any part of the week, provided the local authority thinks this is reasonable, given how often and for how long the child is at home with you.[10]

### If your child dies

If your child dies, you may be able to continue receiving the disabled child premium for eight weeks if:[11]

- you get child benefit for the child following their death (see p506); *and*

- you were getting the disabled child premium for that child in your applicable amount immediately before their death.

## Disability premium

You may be entitled to a disability premium in HB. Income-related ESA does not include a disability premium.

This premium could also have been included in your IS or income-based JSA, before they were replaced by UC (see p21). For how this premium could have applied to your IS or income-based JSA, see the 2024/25 edition of this *Handbook*.

There is a single rate or, if you are in a couple and at least one of you qualifies, a couple rate.

You qualify for a disability premium if one of the following qualifying conditions applies, and none of the exclusions apply (see p273).[12] The person who satisfies the qualifying condition must be under pension age (see p689).

- You (or your partner) are getting a qualifying benefit. These are:[13]
  - attendance allowance (AA), pension age disability payment (PADP), DLA, PIP, ADP, AFIP or an equivalent benefit paid to meet attendance needs because of an injury at work (see Chapter 28) or a war injury;[14] *or*
  - AA, PADP, DLA, PIP or ADP if you (or your partner) were getting one of these benefits, but payment was suspended when one of you became a hospital patient;[15] *or*
  - war pensioner's mobility supplement; *or*
  - severe disablement allowance (SDA); *or*
  - an NHS mobility scooter or private car (for you or your partner) because of a disability;[16] *or*
  - extra-statutory payments to compensate you or your partner for not getting any of the above benefits.[17]

  Once you qualify for the disability premium, you or your partner are treated as still getting a qualifying benefit if you no longer receive it because of the overlapping benefit rules (see p1021).[18]
- You (or your partner) are certified as severely sight impaired or blind by a consultant ophthalmologist. If you (or your partner) regain your sight, you still qualify for 28 weeks after you stop being certified.

### If you undertake training

If you go on a government training course or receive a training allowance, you keep the disability premium even though you may stop receiving one of the qualifying benefits, or cease to be entitled to statutory sick pay during the course, provided you continue to be entitled to HB. After the course, the premium continues if you are getting a qualifying benefit or remain incapable of work.[19]

### Exclusions

You cannot get a disability premium in your HB if:

- you have, or are treated as having, limited capability for work.[20] This applies even if you would otherwise qualify for the premium – eg, if you (or your partner) get DLA, PIP or are certified as blind or severely sight impaired. If your partner is the HB claimant and does not have (and is not treated as having) limited capability for work, the disability premium can be included;[21] *or*
- you get pension-age HB (see p197).



***Do you have limited capability for work?***

1. If you claim ESA or national insurance credits on the basis of limited capability for work and you are a member of a couple, it may be beneficial for your partner to be the HB claimant instead of you so the disability premium can be included in your applicable amount.
2. If you have (or are treated as having) limited capability for work, although you cannot qualify for a disability premium, you may qualify for either the support or work-related activity component in your applicable amount, although this is not normally until after the ESA 'assessment phase' has ended. **Note:** the work-related activity component was abolished for new claims from 3 April 2017.
3. If your partner has limited capability for work but you do not, you can still qualify for the disability premium, which is paid at the couple rate. However, if the disability premium is awarded, you cannot qualify for a support or work-related activity component in your applicable amount.

## Enhanced disability premium

The enhanced disability premium can be included in your income-related ESA and HB in respect of disabled adults and, for HB only, disabled children.[22]

This premium could also have been included in your IS or income-based JSA, before they were replaced by UC (see p21). For how this premium could have applied to your IS or income-based JSA, see the 2024/25 edition of this *Handbook*.

Regarding **disabled adults**, you are entitled to an enhanced disability premium (at the single rate, or if you are in a couple, the couple rate) in your income-related ESA and HB if:

- you or your partner receive the highest rate of the DLA or Scottish adult disability living allowance (SADLA) care component, the enhanced rate of the daily living component of PIP/ADP, or AFIP. If it is your partner who satisfies this, they must be under pension age; *or*
- for income-related ESA, you qualify for the support component (see p560); *or*
- for HB, the decision maker has determined that you have, or can be treated as having, limited capability for work-related activity (see p914).

This premium can be paid in addition to both the disability and severe disability premiums (see p280). For more details of the premiums with which the enhanced disability premium can be paid, see p280.

The person who qualifies for the premium must usually be under pension age (see p689). For HB, if you are single and you reach pension age, you are paid the higher personal allowance (as part of pension-age HB) instead. If you are in a mixed-age couple (ie, one of you has reached pension age and the other has not) and you continue getting working-age HB (see p197), you are treated as both still under pension age and can continue to get the premium. For income-related ESA, if you are in a mixed-age couple and you remain entitled to the benefit, you are paid a pensioner premium instead.

Regarding **disabled children**, for HB, you qualify for one enhanced disability premium for each child included in your claim who gets the highest rate of the DLA/CDP care component, the enhanced rate of the daily living component of PIP/ADP, or AFIP.

An enhanced disability premium can still be included for a third or subsequent child, even if you do not get a personal allowance for them because of the 'two-child limit' (see p268).

Income-related ESA does not include the child rate of this premium (although you can qualify for the adult rate).

In most cases, you (or your partner or child) are treated as receiving the highest rate of the DLA/CDP care component or the enhanced rate of the daily living component of PIP/ADP during any period when DLA, CDP, PIP or ADP is suspended while you/they are in hospital. However, some people who have been in hospital for more than 52 weeks or, in some cases, if their partner has, cannot qualify (see p822).

## Pensioner premiums

A pensioner premium can be included in your income-related ESA. HB does not include a pensioner premium – you get a higher personal allowance instead.

This premium, and in some cases a higher pensioner premium, could also have been included in your IS or income-based JSA before they were replaced by UC (see p21). For how this could have applied, see the 2024/25 edition of this *Handbook*.

You qualify for a pensioner premium in your income-related ESA if your partner has reached pension age (see p689).

The pensioner premium is paid at a single or couple rate. The couple rate of the premium is included in your applicable amount even though only one partner fulfils the condition. The rate of the pensioner premium in income-related ESA also depends on whether or not you are entitled to the support component or are in the work-related activity group (see p282).

## Severe disability premium and severe disability addition

A severe disability premium can be included in your income-related ESA or HB. A severe disability addition can be included in your PC.

This premium could also have been included in your IS or income-based JSA, before they were replaced by UC (see p21). For how this premium could have applied to your IS or income-based JSA, see the 2024/25 edition of this *Handbook*.



You qualify for a severe disability premium (or for a severe disability addition in the guarantee credit of PC) if *all* the following apply to you.[23]

- You receive a 'qualifying benefit' (see p276). If you are a couple for income-related ESA or HB, your partner must also be getting a qualifying benefit, or be certified as severely sight impaired or blind by a consultant ophthalmologist (or treated as certified because it is no more than 28 weeks since they stopped being certified).[24] For PC, both of you must be getting a qualifying benefit or one must be getting a qualifying benefit and the other certified as severely sight impaired or blind or treated as certified. For PC only, either partner can be the claimant.[25] If you are a member of a couple, you and your partner are treated as getting any of these benefits while one or both of you are in hospital, but only if you are not claiming the premium or additional amount for severe disability on the basis that your partner (or you, for PC) is certified as severely sight impaired or blind or treated as certified.[26] For income-related ESA and HB, the benefit must be paid for you or your partner. Receipt of benefit for someone else (eg, a child) does not count.[27] It is probably intended that the same rule should apply to PC.
- You do not have a non-dependant aged 18 or over (eg, an adult son or daughter) 'normally residing with you' (see p277). It does not matter whose house it is.[28] Someone is only counted as residing with you if you share accommodation, apart from a bathroom, lavatory or a communal area such as a hall, passageway or a room in common use in sheltered accommodation. If they are separately liable to pay for the accommodation, they do not count as residing with you.[29]
- No one gets carer's allowance (CA), carer support payment (CSP – see Chapter 63) or the UC carer element for looking after you or, if you are a couple, no one gets CA/CSP or the UC carer element for both of you (but see p821 if one or both of you go into hospital). If you are a member of a couple and someone gets CA/CSP or the carer element for one (but not both) of you, but you are both disabled, you can get the severe disability premium at the single person's rate. Only actual receipt of CA/CSP counts (except if it is not paid because of the loss of benefit rules – see p1111).[30] No account is taken of any underlying entitlement to CA/CSP if it is awarded but not paid because of the overlapping benefit rules, or of any extra-statutory payments to compensate for it not being paid. Similarly, no account is taken of any backdated payments or arrears of CA, CSP or of the carer element.[31] Argue that no account should also be taken

of any overpaid CA, CSP or carer element and that, if you have been denied the premium because of a CA/CSP or carer element overpayment, it should be repaid to you.

***Receiving a qualifying benefit***

A **'qualifying benefit'** is either AA, PADP, the middle or highest rate of the DLA/SADLA care component, the daily living component of PIP, ADP, AFIP, constant attendance allowance or exceptionally severe disablement allowance (or the equivalent war pension). You are **'treated as receiving'** a qualifying benefit if you receive an extra-statutory payment to compensate you for not receiving that benefit.[32]

3

## Couples

You get the couple rate if both you and your partner get a qualifying benefit and no one gets CA, CSP or the carer element of UC for either of you. If CA, CSP or the carer element of UC is paid for one of you, or if your partner does not get a qualifying benefit but is certified as severely sight impaired or blind by a consultant ophthalmologist (or treated as certified), you get the single person's rate. In polygamous marriages, the single person's rate is awarded for each eligible spouse who gets a qualifying benefit while CA, CSP or the carer element of UC is not paid.

**Note:**

- You and/or your partner are treated as getting a qualifying benefit, even though it has stopped being paid because you/your partner have been in hospital for more than four weeks, but the severe disability premium is paid at the single person's rate only. Similarly, for income-related ESA and HB, if you are a couple, a person who is caring for you or your partner is treated as receiving CA, CSP or the carer element of UC even though they are no longer getting it because the person for whom they care has been in hospital for more than four weeks.[33]
- For couples on income-related ESA only, if you or your partner temporarily move into a care home, you still count as a couple but your applicable amount is calculated in a different way (see p833).[34] If your applicable amount is calculated as if you and your partner were single claimants, this means that if the person who stays at home gets a qualifying benefit, a severe disability premium is included in the applicable amount of that person.
- For PC, if you or your partner temporarily move into a care home, you still count as a couple if you have not been apart for substantially more than 52 weeks (see p832). So, once the partner in the care home loses their AA, PADP or DLA care component, no severe disability premium can be paid for either of you, even if the partner at home gets a qualifying benefit, unless the partner in the care home is certified as severely sight impaired or blind (or treated as certified).

## Who is not a non-dependant

Non-dependants are adults living with you who are not included in your benefit award (eg, an adult son or daughter, or a parent), but who are regarded as being able to contribute towards your household costs.

The following people who live with you do *not* count as non-dependants.[35]

**For income-related ESA, HB and PC:**

- anyone aged under 18;
- anyone else who receives a qualifying benefit for the severe disability premium (see p275);[36]
- anyone who is certified as severely sight impaired or blind by a consultant ophthalmologist (or treated as certified);[37]
- anyone staying in your home who normally lives elsewhere. It may be relevant to consider things like why the residence started, how long it has continued and your relationship;[38]
- any person (and, for income-related ESA and PC only, their partner) employed by a charitable or voluntary body as a resident carer for you or your partner if you pay a charge for that service (even if the charge is only nominal).[39] **Note:** these rules do not apply to a live-in carer employed directly by you (even if, for example, you are paying them from direct payments made to you by social services for that purpose).

**For income-related ESA and HB:**

- any member of your 'family' (see p278 for who counts). This may include any child or qualifying young person under the age of 20 (see p258) as well as your partner, although your partner must be getting a qualifying benefit (or would be if not in hospital) or be certified as severely sight impaired or blind, for you to get the severe disability premium (see p275);
- any child or qualifying young person who is living with you but who is not a member of your household (see p261).[40]

**For income-related ESA and PC:**

- any person (or their partner) who jointly occupies (see p278) your home and is either the co-owner with you or your partner, or jointly liable with you or your partner to make payments to a landlord for occupying it. Close relatives (see p278), however, *do* count as non-dependants *unless* the co-ownership or joint liability to make payments to a landlord existed either before 11 April 1988 or by the time you or your partner first moved in;
- any person (or any member of their household) who is liable to pay you or your partner on a commercial basis (see p278) for occupying the dwelling (eg, tenants or licensees), unless they are a close relative of you or your partner;
- any person (or any member of their household) to whom you or your partner are liable to make payments on a commercial basis for occupying the dwelling, unless they are a close relative of you or your partner;

- if someone comes to live with you to look after you (or your partner) and has not lived with you before, your severe disability premium or amount for severe disability remains in payment for the first 12 weeks after the carer moves in, even if they would otherwise count as a non-dependant.[41] After that, you lose the premium or the amount for severe disability. The carer should then consider claiming CA or CSP.

3

For PC:

- any child or qualifying young person.[42] This is defined in the same way as for UC (see p63).

For HB:[43]

- any person who jointly occupies your home and is either the co-owner with you or your partner, or liable with you or your partner to make payments for occupying it. A joint occupier who was a non-dependant at any time within the previous eight weeks counts as a non-dependant if the local authority thinks that the change of arrangements was created to take advantage of the HB scheme;
- any person who is liable to pay you or your partner on a commercial basis for occupying the dwelling, unless they are a close relative of yours or your partner, or if the local authority thinks that the rent or other agreement has been created to take advantage of the HB scheme (but this cannot apply if the person was otherwise liable to pay rent for the accommodation at any time during the eight weeks before the agreement was made);
- any person, or any member of their household, to whom you or your partner are liable to make payments for your accommodation on a commercial basis, unless they are a close relative of you or your partner.

***Definitions***

**'Close relative'** is a parent, parent-in-law (including a civil partner's parent), son, son-in-law (including a son's civil partner), daughter, daughter-in-law (including a daughter's civil partner), sibling, step-parent (including a parent's civil partner), stepson (including a civil partner's son), stepdaughter (including a civil partner's daughter), or the partners of any of these.[44]

**'Member of the family'** means your partner and any child who lives in your household and for whom you or your partner count as 'responsible' (see p260).[45]

**'Jointly occupies'** is a legal relationship involving occupation by two or more people (whether as owner-occupiers, tenants or licensees) with the same legal right.[46] It does not exist if people merely have equal access to different parts of the premises.

**'Commercial basis'** has no legal meaning, and there is no requirement for there to be an intention to make a profit.[47] The reasonableness of the charge should be judged just against the cost of occupying the dwelling, not taking into account the additional costs of

providing food, clothing and care.[48] A useful, but not conclusive, test to apply is to consider whether the same arrangement might have been entered into with a lodger.[49]
**'Liability'** means a legal or contractual liability. The arrangements need not be in writing.[50]

## Carer premium and carer addition



A carer premium can be included in your income-related ESA or HB. A carer addition can be included in your PC.

This premium could also have been included in your IS or income-based JSA, before they were replaced by UC (see p21). For how this premium could have applied to your IS or income-based JSA, see the 2024/25 edition of this *Handbook*.

You qualify for a carer premium or a carer addition in PC, if you or your partner are entitled to CA (see Chapter 22 ) or CSP (see Chapter 63).[51]

You are entitled to CA/CSP even if (having claimed it) you do not receive it because of the overlapping benefit rules (see p1021) – eg, you get contributory ESA or retirement pension instead.

If the person you or your partner are getting CA/CSP for dies, or you or your partner stop being entitled to CA/CSP for another reason, your entitlement to a carer premium or carer addition continues for a further eight weeks. The eight-week period runs from the Sunday after the death (or from the date of the death, if the death occurs on a Sunday). In other cases, it runs from the date entitlement to CA/CSP stops.[52]

A double-rate premium is awarded if both you and your partner satisfy the conditions for it.

***Should you claim carer's allowance/carer support payment?***

1. Before claiming CA/CSP, consider how your claim affects the entitlement to the severe disability premium or severe disability addition of the disabled person for whom you care (see p275).
2. Any backdated award of CA/CSP does not affect a disabled person's entitlement to the severe disability premium or severe disability addition.[53] You may be able to take advantage of this rule so that you are paid CA/CSP or the carer premium/addition for the same period in which the disabled person has already received a severe disability premium or a severe disability addition.
3. Although the severe disability premium or severe disability addition is not payable throughout any period during which a carer is receiving CA/CSP, if you are a carer and it is later decided that you have been overpaid CA/CSP, the disabled person should ask for the decision refusing the severe disability premium or addition to be revised. You must be both entitled to *and* in receipt of CA/CSP for the severe disability premium/addition not to be payable.[54]
4. Other than for HB, if payment of CA/CSP stops, the severe disability premium/addition can be backdated to the date the CA/CSP stopped.[55]

5. Even if you do not claim CA/CSP, if you get UC and your award includes a carer element (see p75), the disabled person for whom you care cannot get the severe disability premium or severe disability addition.

## Payment and rates of premiums

3

*Rates of premiums*

The following premiums can be paid in addition to any other premium, except that the enhanced disability premium cannot be paid in addition to the pensioner premium.[56]

| | |
|---|---|
| **Family premium** | £19.48 |
| **Disabled child premium** | £81.37 |
| (for each qualifying child) | |
| **Severe disability premium** | |
| Single (or one partner in couple qualifies) | £82.90 |
| Couple (both partners qualify) | £165.80 |
| **Carer premium** | |
| Single (or one partner in couple qualifies) | £46.40 |
| Couple (both partners qualify) | £92.80 |
| **Enhanced disability premium** | |
| Child (for each qualifying child) | £32.75 |
| Single | £21.20 |
| Couple (one or both partners qualify) | £30.25 |

Only one of the following premiums can be paid. If you qualify for more than one, you get the highest.[57]

| | |
|---|---|
| **Disability premium** | |
| Single | £43.20 |
| Couple | £61.65 |
| **Pensioner premium for income-related ESA** | |
| Entitled to support component, couple | £153.45 |
| Entitled to work-related activity component, couple | £165.40 |
| Not entitled to either component, couple | £201.95 |

**Note:** you may be entitled to a lone parent increase in the HB family premium if you were entitled to it on 5 April 1998.[58] See p793 of the 2011/12 edition of this *Handbook*.

## Backdating premiums

To qualify for the disability, enhanced disability, pensioner, severe disability, disabled child or carer premium, you or your partner or child must usually be awarded a 'qualifying benefit' for each premium. The date you can begin to get your premium may depend on when your qualifying benefit is awarded. However, because of the time it may take to deal with your claim for the qualifying benefit, or if your claim is backdated (see p1011) or initially refused but awarded some time later after a revision (see p1130), supersession (see p1143) or appeal (see p1166), you may not get your premium straight away and you may have to apply for it to be backdated.



### If you are already getting benefit

If you are still getting income-related ESA, or get HB or PC, you should ask for your award of this benefit either to be revised or superseded and for your premium to be backdated to the date from which the qualifying benefit is awarded, or to when you first got (or claimed) ESA, HB or PC, if that is later. There is no limit to the period for which arrears can be paid to you.[59]

### If you were refused benefit or lost entitlement

If you were refused or lost your entitlement to income-related ESA or HB and you are later awarded a qualifying benefit, you can no longer get income-related ESA or, in most cases, HB (but see below) and must now claim UC instead. If you lost entitlement but should have been entitled to a premium while you were entitled, you may still be able to get arrears for the period before your entitlement ended. For when you can still make a new claim for HB, see p21.

New claims for PC can still be made after the award of a qualifying benefit. See p248 for the rules on backdating.

If you lose your HB because you lose entitlement to a qualifying benefit, the decision ending your HB can be revised if the qualifying benefit is reinstated. Your HB can be fully backdated in this situation, although if you have claimed UC in the meantime any arrears will only be up to the date you claimed UC. You must tell the local authority that your qualifying benefit has been reinstated, but you do not need to make a fresh claim for HB.[60]

## 4. Components

Your applicable amount for income-related employment and support allowance (ESA) and, in certain circumstances, housing benefit (HB) may include either:[61]

- a support component (see p282); *or*
- if you can still get it, a work-related activity component (see p282).

You cannot be awarded both components at the same time.

You can qualify for one of these components in your HB if either you or your partner meet the conditions for it and have limited capability for work. If you qualify for one component and your partner qualifies for the other, the component for which *you* qualify is awarded.[62]

To qualify for a component in income-related ESA, you must meet the conditions yourself – ie, as the claimant. You cannot qualify based on your partner's limited capability for work alone.

Note:

- You cannot start to qualify for a component in your HB applicable amount if you have reached pension age (see p689), unless you or your partner are on income-related ESA or universal credit (UC).
- For HB, provided either you or your partner satisfy the conditions for the component and have limited capability for work, it does not matter if ESA is not paid, or if your entitlement to ESA has stopped because of the rules on how long you can be paid contributory ESA.
- For income-related ESA, if you or your partner have been receiving free treatment as a hospital inpatient continuously for more than 52 weeks, you cannot qualify for either component.[63]

## Support component

To qualify for a support component in income-related ESA, you must meet the conditions described on p560.

You qualify for a support component in your HB if:[64]

- you or your partner have been awarded ESA and you are entitled to the support component (see p560), or you have been refused ESA but you would have been entitled to the component had you been entitled to ESA; *and*
- you are not entitled to a disability premium (p272); *and*
- either you or your partner have limited capability for work-related activity (see p914).

## Work-related activity component

The work-related activity component was abolished for new claims from 3 April 2017. For who can still get a work-related activity component in ESA, see p561.

You can still get a work-related activity component in your HB if:[65]

- you or your partner have been awarded ESA and are entitled to the work-related activity component (see p561), or you have been refused ESA but you would have been entitled to the component had you been entitled to ESA; *and*
- you are not entitled to a disability premium (p272); *and*
- the decision maker has determined that you or your partner have, or can be treated as having, limited capability for work (see p895).

**Note:** you keep the maximum work-related activity component in your HB even if you lose it in ESA because of a sanction.[66] The full amount of ESA continues to be taken into account as your income.

## Rates of components

| *Rates of components*[67] | |
|---|---|
| Support component | £48.50 |
| Work-related activity component | £36.55 |



There is no higher rate paid for couples.

## Backdating components

Your entitlement to either the support or work-related activity component in your ESA normally starts once the 'assessment phase' has ended (see p559). If your assessment phase ends later than 13 weeks after you claim, your entitlement to a component can be backdated to the beginning of the 14th week of your claim.[68] If you make a claim, or request a revision or supersession of your entitlement expressly on the grounds of being terminally ill (see p562 – the rules are the same as for contributory ESA), you do not have to wait for the assessment phase to end to qualify for the support component, but can qualify either from the date of your claim, or from the date on which you became terminally ill if that is later.[69]

If you are getting HB and you become entitled to a support or work-related activity component, you qualify for that component in your applicable amount from the Monday on or after your entitlement to the component began. If your HB entitlement starts after the date your entitlement to the component began, you qualify for the component in your HB applicable amount from the date your entitlement to HB began.[70]

If you only become entitled to HB once a component is awarded to you, you should claim (or reclaim) HB as promptly as you can, as you can only get a maximum of one month's backdating (see p216). **Note:** in most cases, you cannot now make a new claim for HB and must claim UC instead. See p182 for when you can make a new claim for HB. Claiming UC brings you under the UC system (see p20).

# Notes

3

## 2. Personal allowances

1 **ESA** Reg 68(1)(b) ESA Regs
**HB** Reg 23(b) HB Regs; Sch 3 para 1 HB(SPC) Regs
2 Sch 4 para 1(3) ESA Regs
3 Regs 5, 6 and 9 The Social Security (Restrictions on Amounts for Children and Qualifying Young Persons) (Amendment) Regulations 2017 No.376; reg 22 HB Regs; reg 22 HB(SPC) Regs

## 3. Premiums and additional amounts

4 Sch 3 paras 3 and 6-9 HB(SPC) Regs
5 Reg 6(6)(d) and Sch IIA SPC Regs
6 Reg 4 The Housing Benefit (Abolition of the Family Premium and date of claim) (Amendment) Regulations 2015 No.1857
7 Sch 3 para 3 HB Regs; Sch 3 para 3 HB(SPC) Regs
8 Sch 3 paras 16 and 20(7) HB Regs; Sch 3 paras 8 and 12(3) HB(SPC) Regs
9 Sch 3 paras 13(1)(a)(v) and (2) and 16(c) HB Regs; Sch 3 para 8(b) HB(SPC) Regs
10 Reg 21(4) and (5) HB Regs; reg 21(4) and (5) HB(SPC) Regs
11 Sch 3 para 16 HB Regs; Sch 3 para 8 HB(SPC) Regs
12 Sch 3 para 12 HB Regs
13 Sch 3 para 13(1)(a)(i) HB Regs
14 Reg 2(1), definition of 'attendance allowance', HB Regs
15 Sch 3 para 13(1)(a)(iii) HB Regs
16 Sch 3 para 13(1)(a)(iv) HB Regs
17 Sch 3 para 18 HB Regs
18 Sch 3 para 7(1)(a) HB Regs
19 Sch 3 paras 7(1)(b) and 13(5) HB Regs
20 The rules only refer to the 'claimant'
21 Sch 3 para 13(9) HB Regs
22 **ESA** Sch 4 para 7 ESA Regs
**HB** Sch 3 para 15 HB Regs; Sch 3 para 7 HB(SPC) Regs
23 **ESA** Sch 4 para 6 ESA Regs
**PC** Reg 6(4) and Sch 1 paras 1 and 2 SPC Regs
**HB** Sch 3 para 14 HB Regs; Sch 3 para 6 HB(SPC) Regs
24 **ESA** Sch 4 para 6(3) and (9) ESA Regs
**HB** Sch 3 para 14(3) HB Regs; Sch 3 para 6(3) HB(SPC) Regs
25 Sch 1 para 11(b) and (c) SPC Regs
26 **ESA** Sch 4 para 6(5)(a) ESA Regs
**PC** Sch 1 para 1(2)(b) SPC Regs
**HB** Sch 3 para 14(5) HB Regs; Sch 3 para 6(7) HB(SPC) Regs
27 **ESA** Sch 4 para 10 ESA Regs
**HB** Sch 3 para 19 HB Regs; Sch 3 para 11 HB(SPC) Regs
See also R(IS) 10/94, upheld in *Rider v CAO* [1996] *The Times*, 30 January (CA).
28 *Bate v CAO* [1996] 2 All ER 790 (HL), reported as R(IS) 12/96
29 **ESA** Reg 71(6) ESA Regs
**HB** Reg 3(4) HB Regs; Sch 3 para 6(7) HB(SPC) Regs
30 **ESA** Sch 4 para 6(2)(a)(iii) and (b) ESA Regs
**PC** Sch 1 para 1(1)(a)(iii) SPC Regs
**HB** Sch 3 para 14(2)(a)(iii) and (b) HB Regs; Sch 3 para 6(2)(a)(iii) and (b) HB(SPC) Regs
31 **ESA** Sch 4 para 6(6) ESA Regs
**PC** Sch 1 para 2(c) SPC Regs
**HB** Sch 3 para 14(6) HB Regs; Sch 3 para 6(8) HB(SPC) Regs
32 **ESA** Sch 4 para 9 ESA Regs
**PC** Sch 1 para 1(2)(a)(ii) SPC Regs
**HB** Sch 3 para 18 HB Regs; Sch 3 para 10 HB(SPC) Regs
33 **ESA** Sch 4 para 6(5) ESA Regs
**PC** Reg 6(5) and Sch 1 para 1(2)(b) SPC Regs
**HB** Sch 3 para 14(5) HB Regs; Sch 3 para 6(7) HB(SPC) Regs
34 Reg 156 and Sch 5 para 4 ESA Regs
35 **ESA** Reg 71 and Sch 4 para 6 ESA Regs
**PC** Sch 1 para 2 SPC Regs
**HB** Reg 3 HB Regs; reg 3 HB(SPC) Regs
36 **ESA** Sch 4 para 6(4)(a) ESA Regs
**PC** Sch 1 para 2(2)(a) SPC Regs
**HB** Sch 3 para 13(4) HB Regs; Sch 3 para 6(6) HB(SPC) Regs
37 **ESA** Sch 4 para 6(4)(c) and (9) ESA Regs
**PC** Sch 1 para 2(2)(b) and (c) SPC Regs
**HB** Sch 3 para 14(4)(b) HB Regs; Sch 3 para 6(6)(b) HB(SPC) Regs
38 CIS/14850/1996, para 10

39 **ESA** Reg 71(2)(c) and (d) ESA Regs
**PC** Sch 1 para 2(d) and (e) SPC Regs
**HB** Reg 3(2)(f) HB Regs; reg 3(2)(f) HB(SPC) Regs
40 **ESA** Reg 71(2)(b) ESA Regs
**HB** Reg 3(2)(c) HB Regs; reg 3(2)(c) HB(SPC) Regs
41 **ESA** Sch 4 para 6(4)(b) and (7) ESA Regs
**PC** Sch 1 para 2(3) and (4) SPC Regs
42 Sch 1 para 2(2)(f) SPC Regs
43 Regs 3 and 9(1) HB Regs; regs 3 and 9(1) HB(SPC) Regs
44 **ESA** Reg 2(1) ESA Regs
**HB** Reg 2(1) HB Regs; reg 2(1) HB(SPC) Regs
**All** Definition of 'close relative'
45 **HB** s137(1) SSCBA 1992
**ESA** Reg 2(1) ESA Regs
46 *Bate v CAO* [1996] 2 All ER 790 (HL), reported as R(IS) 12/96
47 R(IS) 11/98, tribunal of commissioners
48 CIS/754/1991; R(IS) 11/98, para 12
49 R(IS) 11/98, para 8
50 CIS/754/1991
51 **ESA** Sch 4 para 8 ESA Regs
**PC** Reg 6(6)(a) and Sch 1 para 4 SPC Regs
**HB** Sch 3 para 17 HB Regs; Sch 3 para 9 HB(SPC) Regs
52 **ESA** Sch 4 para 8(2)-(4) ESA Regs
**PC** Sch 1 para 4(2) and (3) SPC Regs
**HB** Sch 3 paras 7 and 17(3) and (4) HB Regs; Sch 3 paras 5 and 9(3) HB(SPC) Regs
53 **ESA** Sch 4 para 6(6) ESA Regs
**PC** Sch 1 para 1(2)(c) SPC Regs
**HB** Sch 3 para 14(6) HB Regs; Sch 3 para 6(8) HB(SPC) Regs
54 **ESA** Sch 4 para 6(2)(a)(iii) and (b) ESA Regs
**PC** Sch 1 para 1(1)(ii), (b) and (c)(iv) SPC Regs
**HB** Sch 3 para 14(2)(a)(iii) and (b) HB Regs; Sch 3 para 6(2)(a)(iii) and (b) HB(SPC) Regs
55 Reg 7(2)(bc) SS&CS(DA) Regs
56 **ESA** Sch 4 para 3 ESA Regs
**HB** Sch 3 para 6 HB Regs
57 Sch 3 para 5 HB Regs
58 Sch 3 para 3 HB Regs
59 **ESA** Regs 3(7) and 6(2)(e) SS&CS(DA) Regs
**HB** Regs 4(7B) and 7(2)(i) HB&CTB(DA) Regs
60 Reg 4(7C) HB&CTB(DA) Regs

4. **Components**

61 **ESA** s4(2), (4) and (5) WRA 2007
**HB** Reg 22 and Sch 3 paras 21-24 HB Regs
62 Sch 3 para 22(2) HB Regs
63 Reg 69(2) and Sch 5 para 13 ESA Regs
64 Sch 3 paras 22 and 24 HB Regs
65 Sch 3 para 23 HB Regs; Sch 2 Part 1 ESAUC(MA) Regs
66 Because there is no provision to remove it in these circumstances
67 **ESA** Sch 4 paras 12 and 13 ESA Regs
**HB** Sch 3 paras 25 and 26 HB Regs
68 Regs 6(2)(r) and 7(38) SS&CS(DA) Regs
69 Reg 7(1)(a) ESA Regs; regs 3(9)(c), 6(2)(a) and 7(2)(be) SS&CS(DA) Regs
70 Regs 4(7B), 7(2)(o) and 8(14D) HB&CTB(DA) Regs

# Chapter 14

3

# Help with ground rent, service charges and other housing costs

**This chapter covers:**


1. Who can get help with housing costs (p287)
2. Which housing costs can be met (p287)
3. The amount of housing costs (p289)
4. Liability to pay housing costs (p294)
5. Occupying accommodation as your home (p294)
6. Housing costs run-on (p299)


If you are an owner-occupier or a long leaseholder, this chapter covers the rules for help with ground rent, service charges and certain other housing costs that can be included in your pension credit (PC) or income-related employment and support allowance (ESA). It does not cover the rules on help with these costs for universal credit (UC) or for help with your rent with UC or housing benefit (see Chapters 6 and 10). It does not cover DWP loans for mortgage interest (see p764).

## Key facts

- If you are entitled to PC or income-related ESA and you own or are buying your home or you are a long leaseholder, your benefit can include help with a variety of housing costs, such as ground rent and service charges.
- Your benefit cannot include help with your mortgage or other loans – eg, for repairs or improvements. Instead, the DWP may offer you a loan.

The rules in this chapter applied if you were entitled to income support or income-based jobseeker's allowance. If you need advice about housing costs that could be included with these benefits, see Chapter 18 in the 2023/2024 edition of this *Handbook*.

**Note:** if you have (or take out) a loan to pay for any of these repairs and improvements, you may be offered a loan by the DWP to help with the interest (see p764). Get independent financial advice before you accept this.

## 3. The amount of housing costs



Once you have worked out which housing costs your benefit can meet, calculate the amount that is included in your pension credit (PC) appropriate minimum guarantee (see p241) or income-related employment and support allowance (ESA) applicable amount (see Chapter 13). This is the weekly charge for the housing costs that can be included in your benefit.[15] If your home is used for both business and residential purposes, only the housing costs for the part you live in are included.[16] **Note:**

- From your weekly qualifying housing costs remember to deduct any charges that are not eligible – eg, fuel charges.
- You may also have a deduction made for other people living in your home (known as non-dependants – see below).

***How do you work out weekly equivalents?***

If you pay your housing costs annually or irregularly or over 53 weeks, the weekly amount is worked out by dividing what is payable for the year by 52.[17]

***Example***

Dean is the owner-occupier of a two-bedroom flat. He does not have a mortgage. His brother, who is on contributory ESA, lives with him. Dean is getting PC. He pays ground rent of £936 a year and a qualifying service charge of £8.50 a week for caretaker services.

**Step 1:** £936 ÷ 52 = £18 a week for ground rent + £8.50 a week for service charges = £26.50 a week housing costs.

**Step 2:** the weekly non-dependant deduction (see below) for Dean's brother is £19.65. £26.50 – £19.65 = £6.85 a week help with housing costs.

Even if your housing costs have been waived because you or your partner, or, for ESA only, a child or qualifying young person included in your award, have paid for repairs or redecoration that are not your responsibility, you can still get PC or income-related ESA for them for up to eight weeks.[18]

**Note:** you may only get a share of the housing costs if you share liability or are treated as liable because you share the costs with someone (see p294).

### Deductions for non-dependants

If other people normally live with you in your home who are not part of your family for benefit purposes (called 'non-dependants'), a set deduction is usually made from the amount you get for housing costs.[19] This is because non-dependants are assumed to contribute towards your outgoings, whether or not they do so. Examples of non-dependants are adult sons or daughters or older relatives who share your home. For who counts as a non-dependant, see p207 – the rules are the same as for housing benefit (HB).

The DWP may use the rules on p296 to decide that someone is only temporarily absent from your home, and so still counts as a non-dependant.[20]

If you think the DWP has wrongly assumed that a person is normally living with you, ask for a revision or appeal (see Chapters 50 and 51).

## People who are not non-dependants

The following people do not count as non-dependants, even if they normally live with you, and no deduction is made, although any rent or lodging charges paid by them to you affect the amount of your PC (see p387) or income-related ESA (see p358).[21]

- Your partner and:
  - for PC, anyone under 20 for whom you or your partner are responsible ('responsible' is not defined in the rules); *or*
  - for ESA, any child or qualifying young person included in your award (see p258) or who lives with you but does not count as a member of your household (see p261) – eg, a foster child or a child placed with you prior to adoption.
- Someone who is liable to pay you or your partner on a commercial basis in order to live in your home (eg, a subtenant, licensee or boarder), along with other members of that person's household. This does not apply if the person is your or your partner's close relative (see p294 for who counts). A low charge does not necessarily mean that the arrangement is not commercial. You do not have to make a profit. An arrangement between friends can be commercial.
- For ESA only, someone other than a close relative (see p294) to whom you, or your partner, are liable to make payments on a commercial basis (eg, as a subtenant, licensee or boarder) in order to live in the property. Other members of the person you pay's household also do not count as your non-dependants.
- Someone who jointly occupies your home and is a co-owner or joint tenant with you or your partner. Your joint occupier's partner is also not a non-dependant. For ESA only, close relatives (see p294) who jointly occupy your home are treated as non-dependants unless they had joint liability before 11 April 1988 or joint liability existed on or before the date you first lived in the property (or your partner did, if your partner is the joint owner/tenant). However, a non-dependant deduction is not made for them even though they are non-dependants (see p291).
- Someone who is employed by a charitable or voluntary organisation as a resident carer for you, or your partner, and who you pay for that service (even if the charge is nominal) and the carer's partner who also lives in your home.

## When a deduction is not made

No deduction is made for any of your non-dependants if either you or your partner:[22]

- are certified as severely sight impaired or blind by a consultant ophthalmologist (or are within 28 weeks of ceasing to be certified); *or*
- get attendance allowance (AA) (or equivalent benefits paid because of injury at work or a war injury), pension age disability payment (PADP), the care component of disability living allowance (DLA) or Scottish adult disability living allowance (SADLA), the daily living component of personal independence payment (PIP) or adult disability payment (ADP), or armed forces independence payment (AFIP), or for income-related ESA only, the care component of child disability payment (CDP).



No deduction is made for a non-dependant:[23]

- who is 16 or 17 years old; *or*
- who is staying with you but whose normal home is elsewhere. This is not just about the amount of time the person spends living at any one address; all relevant factors should be taken into account.[24] For these purposes, someone can only have one normal home at a time;[25] *or*
- for whom a deduction is already being made from your HB; *or*
- who is getting PC; *or*
- who is under 25 years old and:
  - entitled to universal credit (UC) and does not have any earned income; *or*
  - getting income-related ESA while still in the assessment phase (see p559).

  **Note:** this also applied while an under 25-year old was getting income support (IS) or income-based jobseeker's allowance (JSA); *or*
- who gets a training allowance in connection with youth training under specific provisions;[26] *or*
- who is a full-time student. For ESA, this only applies during the student's period of study (see Chapter 37) or, so long as the student is not in full-time paid work, during the summer vacation; *or*
- who is not living with you at present because they:
  - have been in hospital for more than 52 weeks. Separate stays in hospital which are not more than 28 days apart are added together when calculating the 52 weeks;
  - are a prisoner. See p839. The definition is the same as for UC; *or*
- for ESA only, who is a close relative (see p294) and a co-owner or joint tenant with you, or your partner. For PC, no deduction is made because co-owners and joint tenants do not count as non-dependants, even if they are close relatives.

## The amount of the deduction

A fixed amount is deducted from the housing costs included in your benefit. A deduction is usually made for each non-dependant in your home. If you also have a support for mortgage interest (SMI) loan from the DWP (see p764), the deduction is apportioned between the help you get with housing costs and your loan payments. **Note:** if the deduction is higher than the amount of housing costs that can otherwise be included, no housing costs are included in your benefit.

3

The deduction is calculated as follows.[27]

- **Step 1:** work out the weekly amount of housing costs that can be included in your benefit (see p289). If you have an SMI loan from the DWP (see p764), add the weekly amount of your loan payments to the amount of housing costs that can be included in your benefit.
- **Step 2:** work out the total amount of non-dependant deductions (see p293). Remember that a deduction is generally made for each of your non-dependants. If you do *not* have an SMI loan from the DWP, the amount in this step is the non-dependant deduction made from your housing costs and you do not need to go on to Steps 3 and 4.
- **Step 3:** if you have an SMI loan from the DWP, divide the weekly amount of your loan payments by the total from Step 1. Multiply the result by the total amount of non-dependant deductions in Step 2.
- **Step 4:** work out the difference between the amounts in Step 2 and Step 3. If you have an SMI loan from the DWP, this is the non-dependant deduction made from your housing costs.

***Examples***

Keira is getting PC. She owns her flat and pays ground rent of £2,002 a year and a service charge of £30 a week. Her sister, aged 45, lives with her and earns £250 a week. Keira does not have an SMI loan from the DWP.

**Step 1:** the weekly amount of housing costs that can be included in Keira's PC is £38.50 (£2,002 ÷ 52) + £30 = £68.50.

**Step 2:** the weekly non-dependant deduction for her sister is £45.15. As Keira does not have an SMI loan, this is the non-dependant deduction. Her PC housing costs are £23.35 (£68.50 – £45.15).

Joel is the owner-occupier of a three-bedroom flat. He has been getting income-related ESA for several years. He pays a mortgage, has an SMI loan and gets weekly loan payments of £121.90 a week. He pays ground rent of £18 a week and qualifying service charges of £10 a week. Two friends live with him. One is on new-style JSA. The other is in low-paid full-time work and earns £190 a week (gross).

**Step 1:** the weekly amount of housing costs is £28 (£18 + £10).
£28 + £121.90 (weekly loan payment) = £149.90

**Step 2:** the weekly non-dependant deduction for the friend on new-style JSA is £19.65 and for the friend in low-paid work is £45.15. The total amount of non-dependant deductions is £64.80 (£19.65 + £45.15).

**Step 3:** £121.90 (loan payment) divided by £149.90 (the total in Step 1) x £64.80 (the total non-dependant deductions) = £52.69

**Step 4:** the non-dependant deduction to be made from Joel's housing costs is £12.11 (£64.80 – £52.69).

So Joel's income-related ESA includes housing costs of £15.89 a week (£28 – £12.11). A non-dependant deduction of £52.69 is made from his loan payments.



### The deductions

If the non-dependant is not in full-time paid work, a deduction of £19.65 is made for each week.

For non-dependants in full-time paid work, the amount of the deduction depends on their gross weekly income.[28] The amounts are the same as for HB (see p209).

The rules on full-time paid work are covered in Chapter 40. **Note:**

- A non-dependant who is not in (or is treated as not in) full-time paid work does not attract the higher level of deduction even if the gross weekly income is £183 or more.
- For PC, if non-dependants were getting IS or income-based JSA for more than three days in a benefit week, they did not count as being in full-time paid work in that week.[29] This meant the lower deduction was made (or, in some cases, no deduction was made).

Gross income includes wages before tax and national insurance are deducted, plus any other income the non-dependant has, but not AA (or equivalent benefits paid because of injury at work or a war injury), PADP, DLA, SADLA, PIP, ADP and AFIP. Also ignored are payments from specified trusts and schemes established to compensate people, including victims of medical and other errors, of institutional child abuse, emergencies, disasters and acts of terrorism and, for PC only, payments in kind, or for income-related ESA, CDP.[30] If you do not know your non-dependant's income, see p210. The issues are the same as for HB.

A deduction is made for each non-dependant in your home. However, if you have a non-dependant couple and a non-dependant deduction applies to both members, only one deduction is made – the highest applicable.[31] The couple's joint income counts.

If you are a joint occupier with someone other than your partner, any deductions are shared proportionally between you and the other joint occupier(s).[32]

# 4. Liability to pay housing costs

You count as liable to pay housing costs if:[33]

- either you, or your partner, are liable to pay them. However, you do not count as liable to pay housing costs if you pay these to someone who is a member of your household (see p262 for the meaning of 'household'). If you or your partner share liability, you might only get help with your share; *or*
- you share the costs with other members of your household in specified circumstances (see below). You might only get help with your share; *or*
- someone else is liable to pay them but is not paying, so you have to meet the cost yourself to continue to live in your home. You must show that it is reasonable in all the circumstances for you to pay instead – eg, if you have given up your home to live with and care for someone who has now gone into a care home, or if you have separated from your partner (even if you have not lived in the home continuously since your partner left[34]).

## Shared liability

If you share the housing costs with someone else, you count as liable to pay them (even if you are not legally liable) if:[35]

- you share the costs with other members of your household and none of them are your or your partner's 'close relatives'; *and*
- at least one of those with whom you share is liable; *and*
- it is reasonable in all the circumstances to treat you as sharing responsibility for the costs.

You might only get help with your share.[36] However, if the other person is not paying their share, you can argue that you should get help with the full amount.

### *Close relative*

**'Close relative'** means a parent, parent-in-law (including a civil partner's parent), son, son-in-law (including a son's civil partner), daughter, daughter-in-law (including a daughter's civil partner), sibling (including half-siblings), step-parent (including a parent's civil partner), stepson (including a civil partner's son) or stepdaughter (including a civil partner's daughter), or the partners of any of these. Adopted children cease to be related to their birth family on adoption and become the relatives of the adoptive family.[37]

# 5. Occupying accommodation as your home

You can get help with housing costs for the home in which you normally live.[38] You cannot usually be paid for any other home. Even if you are liable to pay housing costs for a property, if you have no immediate intention of living there, you cannot get help with the costs.[39] You can argue that a home can consist of more than one building if you occupy more than one dwelling – eg, because your family is too large for one.[40]

> ***Your home***
> Your **'home'** is defined as the building, or part of the building, in which you live. This includes any garage, garden, outbuildings and other premises and land which it is not reasonable or practicable to sell separately.[41]



## Moving home

If you have just moved into your home but were liable to pay housing costs before moving in, your pension credit (PC) or income-related employment and support allowance (ESA) can include help with the costs for up to four weeks if your delay in moving was reasonable. You must have claimed PC or income-related ESA before moving in.

You must satisfy one of the following conditions.[42]

- You were waiting for adaptations to be finished to meet your or your partner's disability needs or those of:
  - for PC, someone under 20 for whom you or your partner is responsible ('responsible' is not defined in the rules); *or*
  - for ESA, a child or qualifying young person included in your award (see p258)

  The adaptations do not need to involve a change to the fabric or structure of the dwelling, but must be reasonably required and have a clear connection to the disability.[43]
- You became responsible for the housing costs while you were in hospital or a similar institution, or you were in a care home or an independent hospital (or, for ESA only, in an Abbeyfield home).
- You were waiting for local welfare assistance or a social fund payment for a need connected with the move – eg, for removal expenses or items to help you set up home.[44] In addition, for ESA only you must:
  - have a child aged five or under living with you; *or*
  - qualify for a severe disability or pensioner premium; *or*
  - be getting main phase ESA.

  For ESA, this also applied if you were getting child tax credit which included an element for a disabled or severely disabled child.

The amount for housing costs is not actually included in your benefit until you move in. If the earlier PC claim you made before you moved was turned down, you must claim again within four weeks of moving in to qualify. You can no longer make a new claim for income-related ESA, so if your initial claim was turned down, you need to claim universal credit.

## Temporary absence from home

3

If you are temporarily absent from home but are still entitled to PC or income-related ESA, have not rented out your home and intend to return, help with your housing costs continues to be paid for a period. You can argue that you count as temporarily absent even if you have not yet stayed there – eg, you move your furniture and belongings in but then have to go into hospital.[45]

You can get help with housing costs for up to:

- **13 weeks** while you are away, whatever the reason. You must be unlikely to be away for longer than this;[46]
- **52 weeks** if you are in one of the groups on p297. You must be unlikely to be away for longer than this (or, in exceptional circumstances, unlikely to be away for substantially longer than this).[47]

The 13 and 52 weeks both run from the date you leave home. The day you leave home is included, but not the day you return home.[48] If, for example, you have been away from home for 10 weeks and then have grounds to continue to get help with housing costs for 52 weeks, you only get this for the balance: 42 weeks. However, a new period of absence starts if you return home even for a short stay – eg, a day or a weekend.[49]

**Note:** your entitlement to benefit may be affected if you are outside Great Britain (see Chapter 58).

***Are you going to be away from home for a period?***

1. You must let the DWP know about your absence from home, preferably before you go away.
2. Make it clear that your absence is temporary and how long you are likely to be away.
3. Your intention to return, and whether or not you are unlikely to be away for longer than 13/52 weeks, is considered initially based on the circumstances on the date you leave your home, unless you are in a care home or independent hospital (or, for ESA, an Abbeyfield home) for a trial period (see p297).[50] If at any time after that date, you no longer intend to return or it becomes likely that you will be away from home for more than the 13/52 weeks, your entitlement to help with housing costs can be reconsidered.[51] If you initially told the DWP you were going to be away from home for more than 13/52 weeks, but realise that your absence will now be shorter, it should also reconsider your entitlement.

If you have someone living with you who is temporarily absent (eg, a student who is away during term time), the DWP may use these rules to decide whether the person is a non-dependant (see p289).[52]

If you have to live in **temporary accommodation while essential repairs are done** to your normal home and you only have to pay housing costs for one of the homes, your PC or income-related ESA includes help with the housing costs for that home.[53] This is not subject to the normal limits on temporary absence from home.[54] If you have to pay for both homes, you may be able to get help with housing costs for both for up to four weeks (see p298). However, after the four weeks, you are only paid for one home – your normal home if you are unlikely to be away for more than 13/52 weeks, or your temporary home if you will be away for longer.



## Housing costs for up to 52 weeks

You can get help with your housing costs for up to 13 weeks if you are in a care home or an independent hospital (or, for ESA only, an Abbeyfield home) for a trial period to see if it suits your needs.[55] On the date you enter the accommodation, you must intend to return home if it is not suitable.[56] If the accommodation does not suit your needs, you can have further trial periods in other homes and your housing costs met for further 13-week periods, as long as you are not away from home for more than 52 weeks in total.

You can get help with your housing costs for up to 52 weeks if you are unlikely to be away for longer than this (or, in exceptional circumstances, unlikely to be away for substantially longer than this) in the following situations.[57] There must be some causal link between your absence from home and being in one of these situations.[58]

- You are resident in a hospital or a similar institution as a patient. You cannot get help with housing costs after you have been resident in hospital for 52 weeks even if this is because you are seriously mentally ill. However, a new period of absence starts if you return home even for a short stay.[59]
- You are receiving care (approved by a doctor) in the UK or abroad, or you, your partner or, for PC, a dependant under 20, or for ESA, a dependent child, are receiving medical treatment or convalescing in the UK or abroad (approved by a doctor). This cannot be in a care home or an independent hospital or for ESA, an Abbeyfield home.
- You are attending a specified 'training course' in the UK or abroad.
- You are required to live in an approved hostel or an address away from your normal home as a condition of bail.
- You are in prison on remand pending trial or sentence. You can argue that this applies even if you are simultaneously serving another sentence.[60] Once you are sentenced, you are no longer entitled to help with housing costs in PC or ESA.
- You are in a care home or an independent hospital, or, for ESA an Abbeyfield home, for short-term or respite care.
- You are providing care for someone living in the UK or abroad (approved by a doctor).

- You are, for PC caring for someone under 20, or for ESA caring for a child under 16, whose parent or guardian is receiving medical treatment or care (approved by a doctor) away from home.
- You are away from home because of a fear of violence (see below if you need to claim for two homes and for what counts as violence).
- You are a full-time student[61] and:
  - living apart from your partner but cannot get help with housing costs for two homes; *or*
  - a single claimant or a lone parent who is liable to pay housing costs on both a term-time and a home address.

## Housing costs for more than one home

In most cases, you can only get help with the housing costs for one home. If you occupy more than one dwelling as a home (eg, because you have a large family), you can argue that you only have one home.[62]

If you have to pay housing costs for two homes, you *can* get PC or income-related ESA for both:[63]

- **for up to four weeks** if you have moved into a new home and cannot avoid having to pay for the other one as well;[64]
- **indefinitely** if you left your home because of a fear of violence. Argue that fear of controlling behaviour or of psychological, physical, sexual, financial and emotional abuse counts.[65] Provided you left home because of this and are still away from home because of this, it does not matter if you were away from home for some other reason during this period – eg, because you were in prison.[66] You must show that it is reasonable for you to get payment for two homes. So, if you do not intend to return home or someone else is paying the housing costs, you might not get PC or income-related ESA for both homes.
  'Violence' means violence against you and not caused by you.[67] For the purpose of these rules, it must be fear of violence:[68]
  - in your home. Fear of a racist attack should be covered, provided the attack would take place in your home. Remember that your garden and garage, for example, count (see p295); *or*
  - from a former partner; *or*
  - for PC, from a close relative (see p294 for who counts); *or*
  - for ESA, from a child or qualifying young person who is no longer included in your award;
- **indefinitely** if you are a member of a couple and you or your partner are a full-time student or on a training course and living away from your home. You have to show that it is reasonable for you to get payment for two homes.

If you have to live away from your normal home because you or your partner are a full-time student or on a specified training course:[69]

- if you are in a couple and have to live apart, you can get help with housing costs for both of your homes if it is reasonable for you to get help with both;
- if you are a single person or lone parent and must pay housing costs for *either* your normal home *or* your term-time accommodation but not both, you can get help with housing costs for the home for which you pay.



If none of the above applies, you may only get help with your usual home for up to 52 weeks during a temporary absence (see p296).[70]

If you have been getting help with housing costs for your term-time accommodation and you stop living there during a vacation, you cannot continue to get this unless you are away because you are in hospital.[71]

**Note:** if you have to live in temporary accommodation while essential repairs are done to your normal home and you only have to pay for housing costs for one of the homes (see p297).

## 6. Housing costs run-on

When you (or your partner) return to work or increase your hours and so count as being in full-time paid work, you no longer qualify for income-related employment and support allowance (ESA). However, if you qualify for housing costs run-on, you are paid income support (IS) for your housing costs for the first four weeks after you go into full-time paid work, even though the benefit you were getting was income-related ESA. **Note:**

- Housing costs run-on is paid automatically – you do not need to claim it.[72] However, you must let the DWP know you are starting full-time paid work.
- Housing costs run-on is a payment of IS. Therefore:
  - it is not taxable; *and*
  - it is included in the benefit cap (see p1025); *and*
  - you might get health benefits (see Chapter 27) and education benefits, such as free school lunches (see p774).

### Who can get housing costs run-on

You qualify for housing costs run-on if:[73]

- you or your partner take up a new job or increase your weekly hours of work and so count as being in full-time paid work under the IS rules (see p956 of the 2024/25 edition of this *Handbook*). You must expect the work to last for at least five weeks; *and*
- throughout the 26 weeks before the day you count as being in full-time paid work, you or your partner were receiving IS, income-based jobseeker's allowance (JSA) or income-related ESA. Periods when you were receiving housing costs run-on do not count towards the 26 weeks;[74] *and*

- on the day before you or your partner started the work, your income-related ESA (or if you were still getting it, IS or income-based JSA) applicable amount included help with any of the types of housing costs that can be met (see p287) and you or your partner still count as liable to pay them (see p294).

If you qualify, you are paid IS for the housing costs for the first four weeks of full-time paid work.[75] If you claim universal credit during that period, your entitlement to housing costs run-on can still continue for two weeks, or if sooner, until the end of the four-week period.[76]

## The amount of housing costs run-on

You are paid the lowest of:[77]

- the weekly amount of IS, income-based JSA or income-related ESA for housing costs that you were getting immediately before you or your partner took up full-time paid work; *or*
- your or your partner's IS, income-based JSA or income-related ESA entitlement in the week before you took up full-time paid work (or the amount to which you would have been entitled had you not been getting a training allowance).

Your earnings from the full-time paid work and any other income you get are disregarded.[78] All of your capital is also disregarded.[79]

Your housing costs run-on can be adjusted if specified changes occur.[80]

# Notes

1. **Who can get help with housing costs**

1 **ESA** Regs 67(1)(c) and 69(1)(d) and Sch 6 para 1 ESA Regs
**PC** Reg 6(6)(c) and Sch 2 para 1 SPC Regs

2. **Which housing costs can be met**

2 **ESA** Sch 6 para 18(1) ESA Regs
**PC** Sch 2 para 13(1) SPC Regs
**Both** s1 Rentcharges Act 1977

3 CH/3110/2003; R(H) 3/07

4 **ESA** Reg 2(1) ESA Regs; paras 44422-4 DMG
**PC** Sch 2 para 13(6)(a) SPC Regs; paras 7939-41 DMG

5 **ESA** Sch 6 para 18(5) ESA Regs
**PC** Sch 2 para 13(5) SPC Regs

6 **ESA** Sch 6 para 7 ESA Regs
**PC** Sch 2 para 6 SPC Regs

7 **ESA** Sch 6 para 18(2) ESA Regs
**PC** Sch 2 para 13(2) SPC Regs

8 **ESA** Sch 6 para 18(2)(b) ESA Regs
**PC** Sch 2 para 13(2)(b) SPC Regs

9 R(IS) 4/91; CIS/1460/1995; CIS/15036/1996

10 R(IS) 4/92; R(IS) 19/93

11 CIS/4/1988

12 **ESA** Sch 6 para 18(2)(c) and (6) ESA Regs
**PC** Sch 2 para 13(2)(c) and (7) SPC Regs
**Both** CIS/15036/1996; CIS/488/2008

13 *KW v SSWP (IS)* [2012] UKUT 180 (AAC)
14 **ESA** Sch 6 para 1(3) and (4) ESA Regs
**PC** Sch 2 para 1 (3) SPC Regs

3. **The amount of housing costs**

15 **ESA** Sch 6 para 18(1) ESA Regs
**PC** Sch 2 para 13(1) SPC Regs
16 **ESA** Sch 6 para 7 ESA Regs
**PC** Sch 2 para 6 SPC Regs
17 **ESA** Sch 6 para 18(3) ESA Regs
**PC** Sch 2 para 13(3) SPC Regs
18 **ESA** Sch 6 para 18(4) ESA Regs
**PC** Sch 2 para 13(4) SPC Regs
19 **ESA** Reg 71 and Sch 6 para 19 ESA Regs
**PC** Sch 2 paras 1(4)-(9) and 14 SPC Regs
20 R(H) 8/09; *SK v South Hams DC (HB)* [2010] UKUT 129 (AAC), reported as [2010] AACR 40
21 **ESA** Reg 71 ESA Regs
**PC** Sch 2 para 1(4)-(7) SPC Regs
22 **ESA** Sch 6 para 19(6) ESA Regs
**PC** Sch 2 para 14(6) SPC Regs
23 **ESA** Sch 6 para 19(7) ESA Regs
**PC** Sch 2 para 14(7) SPC Regs
24 *RR v SSWP (UC)* [2024] UKUT 261 (AAC)
25 *JP v Bournemouth BC (HB)* [2018] UKUT 75 (AAC), reported as [2018] AACR 30
26 Made under s2 ETA 1973 or s2 Enterprise and New Towns (Scotland) Act 1990 or by the Secretary of State for people enlisted in HM forces for any special term of service specified in regulations
27 **ESA** Sch 6 para 19(2A) ESA Regs
**PC** Sch 2 para 14(2A) SPC Regs
**Both** Reg 14 LMI Regs
28 **ESA** Sch 6 para 19(1) and (2) ESA Regs
**PC** Sch 2 para 14(1) and (2) SPC Regs
**Both** Reg 14 LMI Regs
29 Sch 2 para 2(6) SPC Regs
30 **ESA** Sch 6 para 19(8) ESA Regs
**PC** Sch 2 para 14(8) SPC Regs
31 **ESA** Sch 6 para 19(3) and (4) ESA Regs
**PC** Sch 2 para 14(3) and (4) SPC Regs
32 **ESA** Sch 6 para 19(5) ESA Regs
**PC** Sch 2 para 14(5) SPC Regs

4. **Liability to pay housing costs**

33 **ESA** Sch 6 para 4 ESA Regs
**PC** Sch 2 para 3 SPC Regs
34 *Ewens v Secretary of State for Social Security*, reported as R(IS) 8/01; *FK v Wandsworth BC (HB)* [2016] UKUT 570 (AAC); *Babergh DC v GW (HB)* [2017] UKUT 40 (AAC)
35 **ESA** Sch 6 para 4(c) ESA Regs
**PC** Sch 2 para 3(c) SPC Regs
36 **ESA** Sch 6 para 7(5) ESA Regs
**PC** Sch 2 para 6(5) SPC Regs
37 **ESA** Reg 2(1) ESA Regs
**PC** Reg 1(2) SPC Regs
**Both** R(SB) 22/87

5. **Occupying accommodation as your home**

38 **ESA** Sch 6 para 5(1) ESA Regs
**PC** Sch 2 para 4(1) SPC Regs
39 CIS/297/1994; *PJ v SSWP (SPC)* [2014] UKUT 152 (AAC)
40 *SSWP v Mohamed Miah,* reported as R(JSA) 9/03; R(H) 5/09
41 **ESA** Reg 2(1) ESA Regs
**PC** Reg 1(2) SPC Regs
**Both** Definition of 'dwelling occupied as the home', s137(1) SSCBA 1992 and reg 2(1), definition of 'dwelling', ESA Regs
42 **ESA** Sch 6 para 5(7) and (13) ESA Regs
**PC** Sch 2 para 4(7) SPC Regs
43 *R (Mahmoudi) v LB Lewisham and Another* [2014] EWCA Civ 284, [2013] UKUT 26 AAC, reported as [2014] AACR 14
44 **ESA** Reg 2(1) ESA Regs
**PC** Reg 1(2) SPC Regs
**Both** Definition of 'local welfare provision'
45 R(H) 9/05
46 **ESA** Sch 6 para 5(10) ESA Regs
**PC** Sch 2 para 4(10) SPC Regs
47 **ESA** Sch 6 para 5(11)-(13) ESA Regs
**PC** Sch 2 para 4(11)-(13) SPC Regs
48 *KdeS v Camden LB (HB)* [2011] UKUT 457 (AAC)
49 *R v Penwith DC ex parte Burt* [1990] 22 HLR 292 (QBD)
50 CH/1237/2004
51 CH/3893/2004
52 R(H) 8/09; *SK v South Hams DC (HB)* [2010] UKUT 129 (AAC), reported as [2010] AACR 40; *RR v SSWP (UC)* [2024] UKUT 261 (AAC)
53 **ESA** Sch 6 para 5(5) ESA Regs
**PC** Sch 2 para 4(5) SPC Regs
54 CIS/719/1994
55 **ESA** Sch 6 para 5(8) and (9) ESA Regs
**PC** Sch 2 para 4(8) and (9) SPC Regs
56 *SSWP v Selby DC and Bowman* [2006] EWCA Civ 271, reported as R(H) 4/06
57 **ESA** Sch 6 para 5(11)-(13) ESA Regs
**PC** Sch 2 para 4(11)-(13) SPC Regs
58 *Torbay BC v RF* [2010] UKUT 7 (AAC), reported as [2010] AACR 26
59 *Obrey and Others v SSWP* [2013] EWCA Civ 1584

60 *MR v Bournemouth BC (HB)* [2011] UKUT 284 (AAC)
61 **ESA** Regs 2(1) and 131 ESA Regs
**PC** Reg 1(2) SPC Regs; reg 61(1) IS Regs
62 R(H) 5/09
63 **ESA** Sch 6 para 5(6) ESA Regs
**PC** Sch 2 para 4(6) SPC Regs
64 CH/1911/2006
65 See the definition of 'domestic violence' in reg 2(1) HB Regs, reg 98(4) UC Regs and gov.uk/government/publications/domestic-violence-and-abuse-help-from-dwp
66 CIS/543/1993
67 CIS/339/1993
68 **ESA** Sch 6 para 5(6)(a) ESA Regs
**PC** Sch 2 para 4(6)(a) SPC Regs
69 **ESA** Regs 2(1) and 131 and Sch 6 para 5(6)(b) ESA Regs
**PC** Reg 1(2) and Sch 2 para 4(6)(b) SPC Regs; reg 61(1) IS Regs
70 **ESA** Sch 6 para 5(11)(c)(viii) ESA Regs
**PC** Sch 2 para 4(11)(c)(viii) SPC Regs
71 **ESA** Sch 6 para 5(4) ESA Regs
**PC** Sch 2 para 4(4) SPC Regs

6. **Housing costs run-on**
72 Reg 3(h) SS(C&P) Regs
73 Reg 6(5) and (8) IS Regs
74 Reg 6(7) IS Regs
75 Reg 6(6) and Sch 1B para 9A IS Regs
76 Regs 8(2A) and 46(1) UC(TP) Regs
77 Sch 7 para 19A(1) IS Regs
78 Schs 8 para 15C and 9 para 74 IS Regs
79 Sch 10 para 62 IS Regs
80 Sch 7 para 19A(2) and (3) IS Regs

# Chapter 15

# Housing benefit rent restrictions

3

**This chapter covers:**


1. How to use this chapter (below)
2. The local housing allowance rules (p307)
3. The social sector rules: the 'bedroom tax' (p313)
4. Hostels, houseboats, mobile homes, caravans and boarders (p317)
5. Exempt accommodation and claimants: the old scheme rules (p322)
6. Common rules (p327)
7. Delaying a rent restriction (p333)
8. Challenging a rent restriction (p334)


This chapter covers the rent restriction rules for housing benefit (HB). The rent restriction rules for the universal credit housing costs element are covered in Chapter 6.

## Key facts

- If you are a private tenant, your HB may be based on a rent lower than the one you are liable to pay if it is restricted under one of three rent restriction schemes.
- If you are a local authority or housing association tenant and your home has more bedrooms than the rules allow, the rent used to calculate your HB may be restricted under the social sector rent restriction rules (often called the 'bedroom tax'). In exceptional cases, some housing association tenants have their rent restricted under one of the schemes that apply to private tenants.
- If your rent is restricted, you may be able to get discretionary housing payments from your local authority to help with any shortfall.

## 1. How to use this chapter

Your housing benefit (HB) might not cover the full amount of rent you have to pay. This is because, in many cases, the local authority must reduce the rent it uses to calculate your HB by applying what is known as a 'rent restriction'. This *Handbook* refers to the result as your 'maximum rent'.

***How does 'maximum rent' affect your housing benefit calculation?***

The maximum amount of HB you can get (your 'maximum HB' – see p201) is your 'eligible rent' minus any non-dependant deductions that must be made. If any of the rent restriction schemes apply, your 'eligible rent' is your 'maximum rent'.



There are four possible rent restriction schemes:

- the local housing allowance rules;
- the social sector rules, often called the 'bedroom tax';
- the rules for those living in hostels, houseboats, mobile homes or caravans or who are boarders;
- the rules that apply if you live in what is known as 'exempt accommodation' or you are an 'exempt claimant' – called the 'old scheme' rules in this chapter.

The scheme that applies to you depends on the type of tenancy you have and the type of accommodation you occupy. You should therefore do the following.

- **Step 1**: work out which rent restriction scheme, if any, applies to you. **Note:** your tenancy may be excluded from some or all of the schemes (see p306).
- **Step 2:** go to the relevant section in this chapter for the rules that affect your HB award.

For the common rules that apply to more than one scheme, see p327. To find out if you can get a rent restriction delayed, see p333, or challenge a rent restriction decision, see p334.

## Which rent restriction rules apply

To check which scheme applies to you, if:

- you are a private tenant, see p305;
- you are a housing association tenant, see p305;
- you are a local authority tenant, see p305.

**Note:** if you are a private or housing association tenant, your tenancy may be excluded from some or all of the rent restriction schemes (see p306). If none of the rent restriction schemes apply to you, see p307.

***Are you thinking of moving home or will there be a break in your entitlement?***

If you are getting HB and are considering a move, or there will be a break in your entitlement to HB and you can still make a new claim (see p183), check whether the rent restriction rules that will apply in your new situation will be more or less favourable to you. In some cases, you can check the rent figure that will be used to calculate your HB.

## If you are a private tenant

If your tenancy is not excluded (see p306), the local housing allowance rules on p307 apply in most cases. However, there are exceptions. If:

- you live in a specified type of temporary or supported accommodation (called 'exempt accommodation') or you have been getting HB since 1 January 1996 usually for the same property, the old scheme rules on p322 apply; *or*
- your rent includes board and attendance, or you live in a hostel, houseboat, mobile home or caravan, the rules that use rent officer determinations on p317 apply. These rules *may* also apply in other situations if the local authority considers your rent to be unreasonably high or your accommodation to be unreasonably large.



## If you are a housing association tenant

If your tenancy is not excluded (see p306) and neither you nor your partner are at least pension age (see p690), the social sector rules (often called the 'bedroom tax') on p313 apply in most cases. However, there are exceptions. If:

- you live in a specified type of temporary or supported accommodation (called 'exempt accommodation') or you have been getting HB since 1 January 1996 usually for the same property, the old scheme rules on p322 apply; *or*
- your rent includes board and attendance, or you live in a hostel, houseboat, mobile home or caravan, the rules that use rent officer determinations on p317 apply. These rules *may* also apply in other situations if the local authority considers your rent to be unreasonably high or your accommodation to be unreasonably large; *or*
- if your landlord is not a registered social landlord (in Wales or Scotland) or is not a registered provider of social housing (in England), the local housing allowance rules apply (see p307).

***Registered social landlords and providers of social housing***

For information about registered providers of social housing in England, see gov.uk/guidance/lists-of-registered-social-housing-providers-and-regulatory-judgements. For information about registered social landlords in Wales, see gov.wales/registered-social-landlords, and for the details in Scotland, see housingregulator.gov.scot.

## If you are a local authority tenant

If you are getting working-age HB (see p197), the social sector rules on p313 (often called the 'bedroom tax') usually apply, but there are a number of exceptions (see p313). The social sector rules do *not* apply if you or your partner are at least pension age (see p690). **Note:** if you are at least pension age and you have been getting HB since 1 January 1996 usually for the same property, in exceptional cases, the old scheme rules on p322 may apply.

## When your tenancy is excluded

If you have what is known as an 'excluded tenancy', and you are:

- a private tenant, none of the rent restriction schemes apply to you; *or*
- a housing association tenant, none of the rent restriction schemes apply to you unless your landlord is a registered housing association (see below). If this is the case, the social sector rules on p313 may apply.

The following are excluded tenancies.[1]

- A regulated or protected tenancy – ie, a tenancy entered into before 15 January 1989 or, in Scotland, 2 January 1989.
- A tenancy in an approved bail or probation hostel. However, if you are required to live in such a hostel, you cannot qualify for HB towards the rent you pay to the hostel (see p190).
- A former local authority or new town letting which has been transferred to a new owner. Your tenancy is not excluded if there has been a rent increase since the transfer and:
  - the local authority considers your rent to be unreasonably high; *or*
  - if the transfer took place before 7 October 2002, the local authority considers your accommodation to be unreasonably large.

  If your tenancy is *not* excluded under this rule, the rent restriction rules that apply to hostels, houseboats, mobile homes, caravans and boarders on p317 apply, even if you do not live in one of those types of accommodation.
- A shared ownership tenancy – ie, you are buying part of your home and renting the rest. However, your tenancy is *not* excluded under this rule if your shared ownership tenancy is with a private landlord, in which case the local housing allowance rules on p307 apply.
- A letting by a registered housing association, by a county council (if you live in a caravan or mobile home provided on a travellers' site[2]) or for a caravan, mobile home or houseboat (if you are also liable to make payments to a local authority – eg, for site or mooring fees). Your tenancy is not excluded if:
  - the local authority considers your rent to be unreasonably high; *or*
  - you are getting pension-age HB (see p197) and the local authority considers your accommodation to be unreasonably large.

  If your tenancy is *not* excluded under this rule, the rent restriction rules that apply to hostels, houseboats, mobile homes, caravans and boarders on p317 apply, even if you do not live in one of those types of accommodation.

***Registered housing association***

A 'registered housing association' is a private registered provider of social housing (in England), a housing association registered in a register maintained by the Welsh Ministers (in Wales), a housing association registered by the Scottish Ministers (in Scotland) or a registered social landlord (in Wales or Scotland).[3] **Note:** in England, if the provider is profit making, a registered housing association tenancy is only an excluded tenancy if the housing is available at a rent below the market rate.

### If none of the rent restriction rules apply

Even if none of the rent restriction rules apply to you (eg, you have an excluded tenancy), the local authority still has discretion to decrease the amount of rent it uses to calculate your HB to an amount it considers 'appropriate'.[4] It should have evidence which justifies doing so and must use its discretion properly. All the circumstances should be taken into account, including your health and finances, the special housing-related needs of anyone occupying your home and whether alternative accommodation is available to HB claimants.[5] Local authorities should rarely use their powers to decrease your HB in this way. If your HB is reduced under this rule, apply for a revision or appeal (see Chapters 50 and 51).

***Has the local authority used rent officer determinations to calculate your HB?***

The local authority may say that it can use its discretion to decrease the amount of rent used to calculate your HB, even though it has already restricted your rent under the rules that use rent officer determinations (see p317).[6] If this happens, argue that discretion should only be used in this way if none of the rent restriction rules apply.[7]

## 2. The local housing allowance rules

If the local housing allowance rules apply, they determine the amount of rent used to calculate your housing benefit (HB) – called your 'maximum rent' in this *Handbook*.[8] Your maximum rent may be lower than the rent you must pay to your landlord. **Note:** these rules do *not* apply if you have an excluded tenancy (see p306).

The local housing allowance rules apply if you move to a new home while you are entitled to HB or you make a new claim for HB (if you still can), and you are:[9]

- a private tenant. This includes if you have a shared ownership tenancy with a private landlord. **Note:** there are exceptions and other rules may instead apply (see p305);
- a housing association tenant, but only if your landlord is *not* a registered social landlord (in Wales or Scotland) or a registered provider of social housing (in England). **Note:** if this is not the case, other rules may instead apply (see p305).

## How your rent is restricted

Under the local housing allowance rules, your '**maximum rent**' is the lower of:[10]

- the local housing allowance that applies to you (see below); *or*
- your 'cap rent'.



*Cap rent*

Your '**cap rent**' is the rent you are liable (or treated as liable) to pay for your home (including service charges).[11] If you share your accommodation with anyone other than your partner and you are jointly liable for the rent with that person, the local authority apportions the cap rent between you. **Note:** the local authority may say it has general discretion to decrease your cap rent to an amount it considers appropriate under the rules for those where none of the rent restriction rules apply (see p307).[12]

Note:

- If you share accommodation and are jointly liable for the rent (eg, you are joint tenants) with someone other than your partner (or a child included in your award), and you are not members of the same household, your maximum rent is the lower of the local housing allowance that applies to you personally or your cap rent – ie, it is based on your share of the rent.
- A rent restriction can be delayed in specified circumstances (see p333).
- You may be able to challenge a rent restriction (see p334).

*Examples*

Rio (28) shares a privately rented house with four friends. Rio gets HB. The appropriate local housing allowance for him is that for one-bedroom shared accommodation: £80 a week. The rent for the house is £300 a week. His cap rent is £60 (£300 ÷ 5). This is lower than the local housing allowance, so Rio's maximum rent is £60 a week.

Sue and her partner have a joint tenancy of a private flat. Sue's cousin lodges with them. Sue gets HB. The appropriate local housing allowance for her is that for two-bedroom accommodation: £150 a week. The rent for the flat, and therefore the cap rent, is £210 a week. Sue's cousin is not a joint tenant so the cap rent is not apportioned. The cap rent is higher than the local housing allowance, so Sue's maximum rent is £150 a week.

## Which local housing allowance applies

The local housing allowance that applies to you depends on the area in which you live and the category of dwelling that applies to you (see p309). The category of dwelling is based on the number of bedrooms you are allowed under the rules (known as the '**size criteria**'), not the number of bedrooms in the dwelling.

## The number of bedrooms you are allowed

You are allowed (up to a maximum of four bedrooms):[13]

- one bedroom for each of the following 'occupiers' (see p329) who is a member of your household (see p262), each coming only into the first category that is applicable:
  - a 'member of a couple who cannot share a bedroom' (see p331 for who counts);
  - the partner of a 'member of a couple who cannot share a bedroom';[14]
  - a couple (see p254 for who counts);
  - a person aged 16 or over;
  - a 'child who cannot share a bedroom' (see p332 for who counts);
  - two children under 16 of the same sex;
  - two children under 10;
  - a child under 16; *and*
- one or two additional bedrooms if specified people need overnight care or if you (or your partner) are a 'qualifying parent or carer' – eg, a fostering, adoption or kinship carer (see p329).

**Note:** you are only allowed a bedroom for a 'child who cannot share a bedroom' or a 'member of a couple who cannot share a bedroom' if you have a bedroom in your home that is additional to those you would be allowed if the child or the member of the couple *were* able to share a bedroom. 'Bedroom' is not defined, but see p330 for what may count.

You cannot argue that a category is not applicable if there is no room in your home large enough to accommodate the people in that category.[15]

***Examples***

Calum and AJ have two sons, both under age 10. AJ's nephew, aged 20, lives with them. Calum is allowed three bedrooms under the rules: one for Calum and AJ, one for the two sons and one for the nephew.

Kwame (40) lives with his father in the same household. They are joint tenants. He is allowed two bedrooms under the rules, even though he is getting HB as a single person.

Stephen is the foster parent of two children. His non-dependent son, aged 24, lives with him. He is allowed three bedrooms under the rules: one for Stephen, one for his son and one additional room because he is a 'qualifying parent or carer'.

## Categories of dwelling

The category of dwelling that applies to you depends on how many bedrooms you are allowed and whether or not you are living in shared accommodation.

3

### One-bedroom shared accommodation

Unless you (or your partner) qualify for a severe disability premium (see Chapter 13), the one-bedroom shared accommodation category of dwelling applies if you are only allowed one bedroom under the rules and:[16]

- you are under 35 and are a 'young individual', even if you do not live in shared accommodation. See p328 for who counts as a young individual and for who does *not* count. This category does *not* apply if you have a non-dependant living with you (see p207); *or*
- you (and your partner) live in shared accommodation. You count as living in shared accommodation if you do not have the exclusive use of at least two rooms, or the exclusive use of one room as well as the exclusive use of a bathroom, a toilet and a kitchen or facilities for cooking. This category does *not* apply if:[17]
  - you (or your partner) are under the age of 25 and:
    - were provided with accommodation by the local authority under specified provisions. **Note:** in some cases, you cannot qualify for HB if you are being, or were previously, looked after by a local authority (see p846); *or*
    - were looked after by (in the care of), or under the supervision of, a local authority under specific legal provisions after you turned 16; *or*
    - ceased to be subject to a compulsory supervision order under section 83 of the Children's Hearings (Scotland) Act 2011 which had continued after you turned 16. There are exceptions.

**Note:** if you are only allowed one bedroom under the rules and the rules above do not apply to you, your HB should be based on the local housing allowance for one-bedroom self-contained accommodation.[18]

### One-bedroom self-contained accommodation

The one-bedroom self-contained accommodation category of dwelling applies if you are allowed one bedroom under the rules (see p309).[19] You must have:

- the exclusive use of at least two rooms; *or*
- the exclusive use of one room as well as the exclusive use of a bathroom, a toilet and a kitchen or facilities for cooking.

**Note:** unless you qualify for the severe disability premium, this category does not apply to you if you are a 'young individual' (see p328) and you do not have a non-dependant living with you. Instead, the one-bedroom shared accommodation category applies.

You have the 'exclusive use' of a room if you have the legal right to exclude others from the room.[20]

*Room*

**'Room'** means a bedroom or a 'room suitable for living in', other than one you share with someone who is not a member of your household, a non-dependant or someone who pays rent to you or your partner.[21]



**Dwellings with two or more bedrooms**

If you are allowed more than one bedroom under the rules, the category of dwelling that applies is that for a dwelling with the number of bedrooms you are allowed (see p309), up to a maximum of four.[22] So this category applies, for example, if you are a lone parent or a member of a couple with children, you have a non-dependant living with you, you are a 'person who requires overnight care', someone who lives with you is a 'member of a couple who cannot share a bedroom', you are a 'qualifying parent or carer', or you are a joint tenant with someone other than your partner who is a member of your household.

## Local housing allowance rates

Local housing allowances for each category of dwelling are usually set by the rent officer annually on the last working day of January, to take effect the following 1 April. From April 2025 to April 2026 this is the allowance set by the rent officer on 31 January 2024. This was the lowest of two figures:[23]

- the amount of rent at the 30th percentile point of local market rents for assured tenancies for each category of dwelling in what is known as a 'broad rental market area'; *or*
- for the specified categories of dwelling below, the amount listed.

| *Category of dwelling* | *Maximum local housing allowance* |
|---|---|
| One-bedroom shared accommodation | £331.39 |
| One-bedroom self-contained accommodation | £331.39 |
| Two-bedroom accommodation | £412.86 |
| Three-bedroom accommodation | £497.10 |
| Four-bedroom accommodation | £704.22 |

**Note:** if the rent officer set a local housing allowance for a category of dwelling that was lower than it was on 31 March 2020, the local housing allowance is that which applied for that category on 31 March 2020.[24]

See lha-direct.voa.gov.uk for the current rates in your area.

3

## How long the restriction applies

The amount of your restricted rent (your 'maximum rent') is based on the local housing allowance that applies to you when your award of HB is assessed. Your HB is based on this amount until the next time the local authority assesses your award.[25] This is usually only annually (on 1 April), even if the amount of the local housing allowance changes. When the local authority reassesses your award, it uses the local housing allowance that then applies. Some changes of circumstance can lead to an earlier reassessment – ie, if:[26]

- there is a change in the category of dwelling that applies to you (see p309) – ie, you are allowed more or fewer bedrooms because, for instance, someone has moved in with you or has moved out, or your child has reached age 16 and is allowed a bedroom under the rules; *or*
- your partner or a child included in your award (see p258) (or a relative of yours or your partner who lives in the same accommodation as you without a separate right to do so) dies. **Note:** see p333 to find out if a restriction can be delayed; *or*
- there is a change that affects the amount of your cap rent (see p308) – eg, the rent you pay goes up or down; *or*
- you move to a new home.

Your maximum rent is then based on the local housing allowance that applies on the date of the change.[27]

### *Example*

Ada rents a three-bedroom house from a private landlord. She pays £170 a week rent. This is her cap rent. She has one son, aged seven. The local housing allowance that applies is that for a dwelling with two bedrooms. When her HB award is assessed, this is £105. Ada's maximum rent is £105 because this is lower than her cap rent.

Ada's sister comes to live with her. As there has been a change in the category of dwelling that applies to Ada (this is now a dwelling with three bedrooms), the local authority reassesses her HB award. The local housing allowance for a dwelling with three bedrooms is now £158. Ada's maximum rent is now £158 because this is still lower than her cap rent.

## If you are considering renting accommodation

If you are getting HB and the local housing allowance rules apply, you may wish to find out the rent figure that will be used when your HB award is reassessed (usually annually). If you are considering renting accommodation, the local housing allowance rules apply, and you can still make a new claim for HB (see p183), you may want to find out the rent figure that will be used to calculate it.

Check which category of dwelling applies to you (see p309) and work out the local housing allowance that applies to you. Then check the amount of that local housing allowance in your area at lha-direct.voa.gov.uk.

## 3. The social sector rules: the 'bedroom tax'



The social sector rules usually apply if you are getting 'working-age HB' and are a local authority or housing association tenant living in accommodation with more bedrooms than you are allowed under the rules (known as the 'size criteria' – see p316).[28] There are exceptions (see below). The social sector rules are commonly referred to as the 'bedroom tax', or by the DWP as the 'removal of the spare room subsidy' or the 'under-occupation charge'.

If the social sector rules apply, they determine the amount of rent used to calculate your housing benefit (HB) – called your 'maximum rent' in this *Handbook*.[29] Your maximum rent may be lower than the rent you must pay. **Note:** these rules *only* apply for calculating 'working-age HB', not 'pension-age HB'.

If you live in Scotland and these rules apply, you should automatically be entitled to a discretionary housing payment. See Chapter 25.

### When the social sector rules do not apply

There are exceptions and your rent *cannot* be restricted under the social sector rules if:[30]

- you are getting pension-age HB (see p197); *or*
- you are getting working-age HB (see p197), you are a member of a couple and you or your partner are at least pension age; *or*
- any of the other rent restriction rules described in this chapter apply. See p307, p317 and p322; *or*
- you are a housing association tenant and your tenancy is one of the excluded tenancies listed on p306 (other than the last one), unless your landlord is a registered housing association (see p306); *or*
- you live in a dwelling adapted under a 'sanctuary scheme' (see below); *or*
- you have a shared ownership tenancy – ie, you are buying part of your home and renting the rest; *or*
- your rent is for mooring charges for a houseboat or for identifiable payments for caravan or mobile home site fees;[31] *or*
- you live in specified types of temporary accommodation for homeless people provided by a local authority or a registered housing association (see p306).

#### Sanctuary schemes

Your rent *cannot* be restricted under the social sector rules if you live in a dwelling adapted under a **'sanctuary scheme'** – ie, a scheme that provides enhanced security measures to enable households at risk of domestic abuse to remain safely in their homes. This applies if:[32]

- the scheme is operated by a local authority, a registered social landlord (in Wales or Scotland) or a registered provider of social housing (in England). See p305 for information about registered providers of social housing and registered social landlords; *and*
- you or a member of your household have experienced or been threatened with domestic violence (this includes domestic abuse – see p328 for what counts) by a partner, a former partner or a relative; *and*
- you (or the member of your household) are not living at the same address as the partner, former partner or relative unless that person is a young person who is a dependant of a member of your household; *and*
- you provide relevant evidence from a healthcare professional, a police officer, a registered social worker, an employer or trade union representative or a public, voluntary or charitable body.

For these purposes, 'relative' means the victim's (or the victim's partner's or former partner's) parent, step-parent, son, daughter, stepchild, grandparent or grandchild. It also includes the victim's (or the victim's partner's or former partner's) sibling, uncle, aunt, niece, nephew or first cousin (whether full blood or half blood or by marriage or civil partnership).

## How your rent is restricted

The way your rent is restricted depends on whether you are a sole tenant or a joint tenant with your partner only (see below), or you are a joint tenant with someone other than your partner (see p315). **Note:**

- No matter how many bedrooms you have, if the social sector rules do not apply to you (see p313), your rent *cannot* be restricted under these rules.
- A restriction can be delayed in specified circumstances (see p333).
- You may be able to challenge a rent restriction (see p334).

### If you are a sole tenant or a joint tenant with your partner only

If you are the only person liable for the rent for your home (or you are jointly liable, but only with your partner), your 'maximum rent' is determined under the following steps.[33]

- **Step 1:** work out the number of bedrooms in your home. 'Bedroom' is not defined, but see p330 for what may count.
- **Step 2:** work out how many bedrooms you are allowed under the rules for all the people who occupy your home (see p316).
- **Step 3:** calculate the amount of your 'eligible rent' (see p202) as if your rent were not restricted. This is the contractual rent for the whole dwelling minus any ineligible charges – eg, for fuel or services. If the number of bedrooms in

Step 1 is the same as or lower than the number in Step 2, this is your maximum rent – ie, your rent is *not* restricted.

- **Step 4:** if the number of bedrooms in Step 1 is more than the number in Step 2, reduce the amount in Step 3 by:
  - 14 per cent if you have one too many bedrooms; *or*
  - 25 per cent if you have at least two too many bedrooms.

  This reduced amount is your maximum rent. If it appears to the local authority that the amount in Step 4 is still too high to be met by HB, it has a general discretion to restrict your maximum rent further.[34]



***Example***

Delyth and her partner rent a two-bedroom flat from a housing association. Their rent is £140 a week. Delyth gets HB.

**Step 1**: there are two bedrooms in their home.

**Step 2**: Delyth is only allowed one bedroom under the rules (see p316).

**Step 3**: the amount of the 'eligible rent' as if her rent were not restricted is £140 a week.

**Step 4**: because there is one more bedroom than the number allowed in Step 2, the amount in Step 3 is reduced by 14 per cent.

14% x £140 = £19.60. Delyth's maximum rent is restricted to £120.40 (£140 – £19.60).

## If you are a joint tenant

If you (and your partner) are liable for the rent with at least one other person (eg, you are a joint tenant with someone other than your partner), follow the steps above. However, the local authority apportions the amount in Step 3 or Step 4 (as the case may be) between you, taking all the circumstances into account, including the number of people and the proportion of rent each pays.[35]

***Example***

Jess and Pat are joint tenants of a four-bedroom council house. They are not a couple. Their rent is £210 a week. Jess pays £140 and Pat pays £70. Jess is an approved foster parent. Pat gets HB.

**Step 1**: the number of bedrooms in Pat's home is four.

**Step 2**: he is allowed three bedrooms under the rules: one for himself, one for Jess and an additional room because Jess counts as a 'qualifying parent or carer'.

**Step 3**: the amount of the rent that can be covered by HB (the 'eligible rent') is £210.

**Step 4**: because Pat has one more bedroom than the number allowed in Step 2, the amount in Step 3 is reduced by 14 per cent. 14% x £210 = £29.40

£210 – £29.40 = £180.60.

Pat pays one-third of the rent, and the local authority apportions the maximum rent accordingly. One-third of £180.60 = £60.20.

Pat's maximum rent is £60.20.

**Note:** if Jess is also getting HB, her maximum rent would be two-thirds of £180.60 = £120.40. If Jess is getting UC, see p116.

## The number of bedrooms you are allowed



Under the rules (the 'size criteria'), you are allowed:[36]

- one bedroom for each of the following 'occupiers' (see p329), each coming only into the first category that is applicable:
  - a 'member of a couple who cannot share a bedroom' (see p331 for who counts);
  - the partner of a 'member of a couple who cannot share a bedroom';[37]
  - a couple (see p254 for who counts);
  - a person aged 16 or over;
  - a 'child who cannot share a bedroom' (see p332 for who counts);
  - two children under 16 of the same sex;
  - two children under 10;
  - a child under 16; *and*
- one or more additional bedrooms if specified people need overnight care or if you (or your partner) are a 'qualifying parent or carer' – eg, a fostering, adoption or kinship carer (see p329).

You cannot argue that a category is not applicable if there is no room in your home large enough to accommodate the people in that category.[38]

Unlike the local housing allowance rules, there is no maximum number of bedrooms.

***Examples***

David lives with his wife and child in a four-bedroom council house. He gets HB. David gets the daily living component of personal independence payment and is a 'member of a couple who cannot share a bedroom'. David is therefore allowed three bedrooms under the rules: one for himself, one for his wife and one for his child. He has one too many bedrooms and his rent is restricted.

Lee, an approved foster parent, shares a three-bedroom council house with his mother and father. His foster daughter lives with them. Lee and his father are joint tenants. Lee gets HB. Lee is allowed two bedrooms under the rules: one for him and one for his mother and father. However, he is allowed one additional bedroom because he is a 'qualifying parent or carer'. So he is allowed a total of three bedrooms. For the purposes of the social sector rules, he does not have too many bedrooms and his rent is not restricted.

# 4. Hostels, houseboats, mobile homes, caravans and boarders

If you live in certain types of accommodation, the local authority uses 'determinations' made by the rent officer (see p319) to restrict the amount of rent it uses to calculate your housing benefit (HB) – called your 'maximum rent' in this *Handbook*. These are sometimes called the local reference rent rules. Your 'maximum rent' is usually the lowest of the rent officer's determinations, even if the rent you pay is higher.[39] **Note:** these rules do not apply if you have an excluded tenancy (see p306).

These rules apply if:[40]

- you live in a hostel, houseboat, mobile home or caravan; *or*
- your rent includes board and attendance – eg, you are a boarder or live in a hotel or guest house.

**Note:** if you have been getting HB continuously since before 7 April 2008, these rules may still apply if you live in other types of accommodation – eg, if you rent a private house or flat. See p398 of the 2019/20 edition of this *Handbook*.

In rare cases, these rules also apply if:

- your landlord is a registered housing association (see p306), or a county council (if you live in a caravan or mobile home provided on a travellers' site[41]), or you are renting a caravan, mobile home or houseboat (and you are also liable to make payments to a local authority – eg, for the site or mooring fees). However, they only apply if the local authority considers your rent to be unreasonably high (or, in some cases, your accommodation to be unreasonably large). Otherwise, you have an 'excluded tenancy' (see p306); *or*
- your tenancy was a local authority or new town letting, but it has been transferred to a new owner. However, they only apply if there has been a rent increase since the transfer and:
  - the local authority considers your rent to be unreasonably high; *or*
  - if the transfer took place before 7 October 2002, the local authority considers your accommodation to be unreasonably large.

  Otherwise, you have an 'excluded tenancy' (see p306).

## How your rent is restricted

Under these rules, the local authority asks the rent officer to make determinations about the rent for your home and uses these to establish the amount of your **'maximum rent'**. The determinations include:

- a 'claim-related rent', based on the size of your accommodation and the rent you pay (see p320); *and*
- a 'local reference rent', based on average rents for specific types of accommodation in the area in which you live (see p321); *and*

- a 'single room rent', based on average rents for shared accommodation in your area (see p321).

Your maximum rent is then either:[42]
- the lowest of the claim-related rent or the local reference rent; *or*
- if you are a 'young individual' (see p328), the lowest of the single room rent or the claim-related rent (minus any payments for meals), but only if you do not qualify for a severe disability premium (see p275) or you do not have any non-dependants living with you (see p207).

3

***Example***
A couple rent a three-bedroom mobile home with a living room and separate dining room. They pay rent of £120 a week. The rent officer decides that the accommodation is too big and that the rent is too high, so determines a claim-related rent of £90 and a local reference rent of £80. Their maximum rent is therefore £80 a week.

**Note:**
- Your maximum rent only covers the rent you pay for residential accommodation.
- If you are in shared accommodation, your maximum rent can be apportioned between you and the people you share with.[43]
- A rent restriction can be delayed in specified circumstances (see p333).
- If you have been continuously entitled to, and in receipt of, HB for the same property since 5 October 1997, your maximum rent is the local reference rent plus half the difference between the local reference rent and the claim-related rent.[44]
- If you are considering renting accommodation, the local reference rent rules apply and you are likely to claim HB (if you still can – see p183), you can apply to the local authority for a pre-tenancy determination to find out the rent that will be used to calculate it (see p322).
- The local authority is likely to say it has general discretion to decrease your maximum rent to an amount it considers appropriate (but see p307).[45]
- You may be able to challenge a rent restriction (see p334).

## When the local authority must apply to the rent officer

The local authority must apply to the rent officer for determinations if you move to a new home while you are entitled to HB, or if the last reference to the rent officer was made in respect of your home at least 52 weeks ago.[46] It must also apply if:
- there has been a specified change in circumstances since the rent officer's last determinations (see p319); *or*
- you make a new claim for HB (if you still can); *or*

- your HB was being restricted under the local housing allowance rules on p307, but these no longer apply – eg, if the home you rent was sold to a housing association and the rules that use rent officer determinations now apply instead.

**Note:** the local authority *cannot* apply to the rent officer in specified situations.[47] This means that in some cases a determination made for a previous tenant may be valid for your HB award.



### Specified changes in circumstances

The local authority must apply to the rent officer if there has been one of the following changes in circumstances since a rent officer's determination.[48]

- The number of occupiers has changed (except in a hostel). Argue that this should *not* apply if someone who normally lives with you is only away temporarily.[49]
- There has been a substantial change in the condition of the dwelling or the terms of the tenancy (other than a term relating to the rent).
- There has been an increase in the rent under a term of the tenancy, unless the previous determination was a significantly high, size-related or exceptionally high rent determination (see p320).[50]
- A size-related rent determination was made and a child living with you has reached the age of 10 or 16, or there has since been a change in the composition of the household – eg, someone has moved in or moved out, but not if the person is your (or your partner's) son, daughter, stepson or stepdaughter who usually lives with you, who is in the armed forces away on (or who has returned home from) operations.
- The size of accommodation you are allowed under the rules is affected because:
  - you or your partner, a person who occupies your dwelling as a home, or a child or young person in respect of whom you or your partner are a 'qualifying parent or carer' (eg, your foster child) become, or cease to be, a 'person who requires overnight care' (see p332); *or*
  - you or your partner become or cease to be a 'qualifying parent or carer' (see p333); *or*
  - a child becomes, or stops being, a 'child who cannot share a bedroom' (see p332); *or*
  - a person occupying your dwelling as a home becomes, or stops being, a 'member of a couple who cannot share a bedroom' (see p331).

## The rent officer's determinations about your rent

The rent officer makes 'determinations' about the rent for your home, comparing it with the rent for other private sector tenancies in the area (the 'claim-related rent' – see p320). The rent officer also makes determinations that indicate the average rents for specific types of accommodation (the 'local reference rent' and the 'single room rent' – see p321).

## The claim-related rent

The **'claim-related rent'** is the lowest of the determinations below or, if no such determination is made, the rent you are supposed to pay.[51]

3

*The determinations*

A **'significantly high rent determination'** is made if your rent is significantly higher than that paid for similar tenancies and dwellings in the immediate area around your home.[52]

An **'exceptionally high rent determination'** is made if the rent officer considers the 'rent payable' for your home to be exceptionally high.[53]

A **'size-related rent determination'** is made if your accommodation is larger than you are allowed under the rules.[54] **Note:** if you are a single person under 35 and are a 'young individual' (see p328), the rent officer must also identify a single room rent (see p321).

### The size of accommodation you are allowed

To work out the size of accommodation you are allowed under the rules (known as the 'size criteria'), the rent officer allows you:

- one bedroom or 'room suitable for living in' for each of the following 'occupiers' (see p329), each coming only into the first category for which they are eligible:[55]
  - a 'member of a couple who cannot share a bedroom' (see p331 for who counts);
  - the partner of a 'member of a couple who cannot share a bedroom';[56]
  - a couple (see p254 for who counts);
  - a person aged 16 or over;
  - a 'child who cannot share a bedroom' (see p332 for who counts);
  - two children under 16 of the same sex;
  - two children under 10;
  - a child under 16; *and*
- one or two additional bedrooms (or 'rooms suitable for living in') if specified people need overnight care or if you (or your partner) are a 'qualifying parent or carer' — eg, a fostering, adoption or kinship carer (see p329).

Note:

- You are only allowed a bedroom for a 'child who cannot share a bedroom' or a 'member of a couple who cannot share a bedroom' if you have a bedroom in your home that is additional to those you would be allowed if the child or the member of the couple *were* able to share a bedroom. 'Bedroom' is not defined, but see p330 for what may count.

- Unlike the local housing allowance rules, there is no maximum number of bedrooms.

You are also allowed the following number of **'rooms suitable for living in'** – eg, a living room or dining room.

| *Number of occupiers* | *Number of rooms* |
|---|---|
| Fewer than four | One |
| Four to six | Two |
| Seven or more | Three |

If any of the rooms in your home are not suitable for living in (eg, because of their size or lack of ventilation), argue that they should be ignored.

***Example***

Alicia and Cole have three children: two sons, aged 12 and 14, and a daughter, aged 17. Under the rules, they are allowed one room for themselves, one for their sons and one for their daughter – three bedrooms, as well as two other 'rooms suitable for living in'. They are therefore allowed five rooms, as well as a kitchen, bathroom and toilet.

## The local reference rent and single room rent

The rent officer makes determinations that indicate the average rents for specific types of accommodation in a 'broad rental market area'.

***The determinations***

**The 'local reference rent'** is the midpoint of 'reasonable market rents' for assured tenancies in the broad rental market area appropriate to the size of property in which you live (or the size you are allowed – see p320).[57]

**The 'single room rent'** is the midpoint of 'reasonable market rents' for assured tenancies in the broad rental market area in which the tenant has exclusive use of one bedroom only, and other than that only shares a living room, kitchen, toilet and bathroom, and makes no payment for board and attendance.[58] **Note:** it is only used to calculate your HB if you are under 35 and are a 'young individual' (see p328 for who counts and who does *not* count). Your 'maximum rent' (see p317) is based on the single room rent unless you qualify for a severe disability premium as part of your applicable amount (see Chapter 13) or you have a non-dependant living with you (see p207).[59]

## Service charges

The local authority notifies the rent officer of the amount of rent you are supposed to pay, whether this includes service charges and the amount of the charges that can and cannot be met by HB (see p205).[60] The claim-related rent (see p320) does not include ineligible charges unless you live in one-room accommodation and the landlord provides substantial board and attendance. In this case, the claim-related rent and local reference rent (though not the single room rent) include charges for meals.[61]

3

### How long the restriction applies

Once your maximum rent is set, your HB is paid on the basis of this until the next time the local authority applies to the rent officer for determinations about the rent for your home (usually annually). However, if you negotiate with your landlord and a new rent is agreed which is lower than the maximum rent, your HB is recalculated using your new rent.[62]

### If you are considering renting accommodation

If you are considering renting accommodation, the rules that use rent officer determinations apply and you are likely to claim HB (if you still can – see p183), you might want to find out the rent figure that will be used to calculate it. In this case, you can apply for a **pre-tenancy determination.**[63] You can also apply if you are already receiving HB and your tenancy is due for renewal, but your tenancy agreement must have started at least 11 months before you apply.[64]

Note:

- You must apply in writing on the form approved by your local authority. Both you and your prospective landlord must sign it.[65]
- A pre-tenancy determination is usually valid for a year.[66] So, if someone else applied for a pre-tenancy determination for your accommodation in the previous 12 months, it also applies to you.
- You cannot appeal against a pre-tenancy determination. However, if you accept the tenancy and claim HB, you can ask for it to be redetermined. If you subsequently negotiate a lower rent with your landlord which is lower than your 'maximum rent', your HB is recalculated using your new rent.[67]

## 5. Exempt accommodation and claimants: the old scheme rules

More generous rent restriction rules (called the 'old scheme' rules in this *Handbook*) apply if you are getting housing benefit (HB) and you:

- live in specified types of temporary or supported accommodation, known as **'exempt accommodation'** (see p326), whenever you started living there – eg, even if this was recently; *or*

- have been getting HB since 1 January 1996, usually for the same property – ie, if you are an **'exempt claimant'** (see p326).

These rules are sometimes called the 'pre-January 1996 rules'.

If these rules apply, they determine the amount of rent used to calculate your HB – called your 'maximum rent' in this *Handbook*. This amount may be lower than the rent you must pay.

**Note:** you cannot usually qualify for HB if you come under the universal credit (UC) system (see p20). However, if you live in 'exempt accommodation', the help you get with your rent for this is not provided in UC. Instead, you can claim HB for the rent you pay and the old scheme rules apply.

## How your rent is restricted

Under the old scheme rules, your **maximum rent** is either:

- your contractual rent minus ineligible charges (see p203). It only covers the rent you pay for residential accommodation. If you are in shared accommodation, the rent is apportioned between you and the people with whom you share;[68] *or*
- if the local authority decides your rent should be restricted because your accommodation is unreasonably large (see below) or your rent is unreasonably high (see p324), the amount it considers appropriate.[69]

If the local authority restricts your rent, it must take into account the cost of suitable alternative accommodation (see p324) and other circumstances that are reasonably relevant to the decision – eg, pregnancy, the difficulty of finding other suitable accommodation and whether it would have to rehouse you if you had to move.[70] It should not be unduly influenced by the amount of subsidy it is paid by the government, but can take this into account when deciding on a reasonable level of rent. Your maximum rent cannot be reduced below the amount of rent payable for suitable alternative accommodation.[71]

**Note:**

- If you are in a protected group (see p325), your rent cannot be restricted unless suitable cheaper alternative accommodation is available and it is reasonable to expect you to move.
- A rent restriction can be delayed in some circumstances (see p333).
- You may be able to challenge a rent restriction (see p334).

### Is your accommodation unreasonably large?

Your accommodation counts as unreasonably large if it is larger than what is reasonably needed for you and anyone else who occupies the accommodation.[72] This should include whether you need additional space – eg, because you or someone who lives with you has a disability, or someone who lives elsewhere visits you regularly. When deciding whether your home is unreasonably large, the local authority must take account of suitable alternative accommodation (see below) occupied by other households of the same size.[73]

## Is your rent unreasonably high?

3

Your rent (including service charges and licence fees) counts as unreasonably high if it is too high compared with that for suitable alternative accommodation (see below) elsewhere.[74] In making the comparison, the local authority:

- must consider the full range of rents that could be paid for such accommodation and not just the cheapest;[75] *and*
- can consider subsidised rents (eg, by public funding) even if your rent is not subsidised.[76]

If your rent is within the range or just above it, the local authority may find it difficult to justify finding your rent to be unreasonably high.[77]

**Note:** when deciding whether your rent is unreasonably high, the local authority may ask a rent officer to assess what a reasonable rent for your property would be, but the figures are not binding. The local authority (not the rent officer) must decide whether your rent is unreasonably high, using different criteria from that used by the rent officer.[78]

## Suitable alternative accommodation

'Suitable alternative accommodation' must be suitable for the age and health of all the people that the local authority must take into account, having regard to the nature of the accommodation and the facilities available.[79] The local authority must consider these factors, even if you do not raise your housing needs yourself.[80]

It is not sufficient for the local authority simply to show that cheaper or smaller alternative accommodation exists. When comparing your home with 'alternative accommodation' the local authority:

- cannot just compare homes with the same number of bedrooms. It must try to establish what other facilities are available;[81]
- must compare your home with other properties offering the same security of tenure – eg, if you have an assured tenancy, the local authority cannot rely on comparisons with accommodation that is let on an assured shorthold tenancy, or with council or housing association properties;[82]
- does not have to exclude properties you cannot take because the landlord wants a deposit you cannot afford.[83] However, if you are in a 'protected group', you might be able to argue that the accommodation is not available to you (see p325);
- should not make comparisons with other parts of the country where accommodation costs differ widely from local ones, but it may compare your property with one in a less expensive area within the same city.[84]

## Are you in a protected group?

You are in a 'protected group' if any of the people the local authority must take into account:[85]

- are at least pension age (see p690); *or*
- satisfy any of the tests for having limited capability for work (see Chapter 41) or being incapable of work (see p683 of the 2013/14 edition of this *Handbook*);[86] *or*
- have a child (including a 'qualifying young person') living with them for whom they are responsible (see p260).

### *Who must the local authority take into account?*

The local authority must take into account:[87]

- you; *and*
- your partner; *and*
- any child(ren), including qualifying young people, included in your award (see p258); *and*
- any of your (or your partner's) relatives (see p334 for who counts) who live in the same dwelling as you without a separate right to do so.

Even if the local authority decides that your rent or the size of your accommodation is unreasonable, if you are in a protected group, your rent can only be restricted if:[88]

- suitable cheaper alternative accommodation (see p324) is available to you. It is only 'available' if the local authority proves that it exists and is available to you. The local authority must:
  - have sufficient evidence to show there is an active housing market with accommodation of a suitable type, rent and location for you, but it does not need to refer to specific properties;[89] *and*
  - take into account personal factors, such as whether you can afford to pay a deposit.[90] The local authority may produce a list of properties that it says are available to you. If they are not available because of your personal circumstances, try to show why;[91] *and*
- it is reasonable to expect you to move. The local authority must take into account the effects of a move on:[92]
  - your ability to retain your job; *and*
  - the education of any child or young person living with you. In considering this, the local authority must justify any decision that it is reasonable to make the child travel to, or move, school.[93]

  The local authority may say that it does not need to consider any other factors, such as your health.[94] However, if there are good reasons why you cannot move other than those listed above, try to argue that alternative accommodation cannot be suitable.[95]

## Exempt accommodation

The old scheme rules apply to you if you live in what is known as 'exempt accommodation', whenever you started living there – eg, even if this was recently.

Your accommodation is exempt accommodation if it is:[96]

- temporary accommodation (resettlement places) for people without a settled way of life, funded by the government; *or*
- accommodation provided by a housing association, non-metropolitan county council, registered charity or voluntary organisation and that body, or a person acting on its behalf, also provides you with care, support or supervision.[97] You must need the care, support or supervision and it must be more than a token or minimal amount.[98] Even if the care, support or supervision your landlord provides duplicates other provisions (eg, in a local authority care plan), you can still count as living in exempt accommodation.[99] **Note:** if the person (or body) providing the care, support or supervision has a contract with the local authority to provide these, but is not providing the accommodation, the decision maker is likely to say it is not exempt accommodation.[100]

## Exempt claimants: getting housing benefit since 1 January 1996

The old scheme rules also apply to you if you are what is known as an 'exempt claimant' – ie, you are a private tenant (or, in exceptional cases, a local authority or housing association tenant – see p327) and you:[101]

- have been continuously entitled to and in receipt of HB since 1 January 1996; *and*
- continue to occupy the same property as your home (except if you are forced to move because fire, flood or natural catastrophe makes it uninhabitable).

If you can still make a new claim for HB (see p183), provided that, when you make it, you are *not* someone to whom the local housing allowance rules would now apply (see p307):[102]

- breaks in your HB claim of up to four weeks are ignored; *and*
- an exemption can be transferred to you if you claim HB because:
  - an exempt claimant dies and you are that person's relative (see p334 for who counts) or a member of that person's family occupying the same accommodation without a separate right to do so. You must continue to occupy the same property and claim within four weeks of the death; *or*
  - your partner (who was exempt) has been detained in custody and is not entitled to HB under the temporary absence rules (see p191). You must continue to occupy the same property and claim within four weeks of the detention; *or*
  - your partner (who was exempt) has left the dwelling and you claim within four weeks of the date your partner left.

The exemption can only be transferred if the exempt claimant was getting HB at the time of death (or leaving the dwelling).[103] If it cannot be transferred, other rent restriction rules may apply when you make a new HB claim (if you still can).

### If you are a local authority or housing association tenant

You cannot count as an exempt claimant if you are a local authority or registered housing association tenant (see p306) unless:[104]

- you (or your partner) are at least pension age (see p690); *or*
- the old scheme rules applied to you on or before 31 March 2013 – ie, using these rules, the local authority:
  - restricted your rent; *or*
  - decided that your accommodation was too large or your rent was too high, but did not restrict your rent because the rules for those in a protected group applied (see p325), or the restriction was delayed for either of the reasons on p333.

### If your rent increases

If your landlord increases your rent while you are entitled to HB, the local authority cannot increase the amount of your rent that can be covered by HB (your 'eligible rent' – see p202) by the full amount of the increase if it decides that the increase is:[105]

- unreasonably high compared with increases in suitable alternative accommodation (see p324). The local authority must consider the amount of the increase, as well as the amount of your previous rent and what your rent will be, and compare it with the rent in the suitable alternative accommodation.[106] It should also consider, for example, the quality of the accommodation, your age and state of health, whether you would have to move if the increase is not met and how a move would affect you;[107] *or*
- unreasonable because there has been an increase within the preceding 12 months.

If the local authority considers a rent increase to be unreasonable, it may refuse to meet all of that increase or meet only so much of it as it considers appropriate. If your rent has been increased for the second time in under 12 months but is still below the market level for suitable alternative accommodation, or the increase reflects improvements made to your accommodation, argue for the full amount to be allowed.

## 6. Common rules

Some terms are the same for some or all of the rent restriction rules. These are covered in this section and are referred to above where relevant.

## Young individuals

3

If you are a 'young individual', your maximum rent is based on the local housing allowance for one-bedroom shared accommodation (under the local housing allowance rules) or the single room rent (under the rules for hostels, houseboats, mobile homes, caravans and boarders). In general, you count as a 'young individual' if you are a single claimant under 35, but there are a number of exceptions. You do *not* count as a young individual if:[108]

- your landlord is a registered housing association (see p306); *or*
- you are under the age of 25 and:
  - were looked after by (in the care of), or under the supervision of, a local authority under specific legal provisions after you turned 16 or were provided with accommodation by the local authority under specific provisions; *or*
  - ceased to be subject to a compulsory supervision order under section 83 of the Children's Hearings (Scotland) Act 2011 which continued after you turned 16. **Note:** there are exceptions; *or*
- you are a 'person who requires overnight care' (see p332 for who counts); *or*
- you are a 'qualifying parent or carer' (see p333 for who counts); *or*
- after you turned 16, you experienced or were threatened with domestic violence by your partner, former partner or a relative. You must provide evidence from a registered healthcare professional, social worker, police officer or another person acting in an official capacity – eg, your employer, a voluntary organisation or a charity; *or*
- a competent authority – eg, the Home Office – has determined that you have been the victim of modern slavery (ie, of trafficking in human beings, slavery, servitude or forced or compulsory labour); *or*
- you are at least 16 but under 35 and have lived in one or more hostels for homeless people for three months or more (this does not have to be continuous) and while living in such a hostel you accepted support services to assist you in being rehabilitated or resettled in the community; *or*
- you are at least 25 but under 35 and are an offender subject to specific multi-agency public protection management arrangements. It is understood that this applies if you are a level 2 or 3 offender.[109]

***Definitions***[110]

'**Domestic violence**' means any incident, or pattern of incidents, of controlling behaviour, coercive behaviour, violence or abuse, including but not limited to psychological, physical, sexual, emotional or financial abuse, regardless of the gender or sexuality of the victim.

For these purposes, '**relative**' means your or your partner's or former partner's parent step-parent, son, daughter, stepson, stepdaughter, grandparent or grandchild. It also includes your (or your partner's or former partner's) sibling, uncle, aunt, niece, nephew or first cousin (whether full blood or half blood or by marriage or civil partnership).

## Occupiers

An **'occupier'** is:[111]

- for the local housing allowance and the social sector rules, you and anyone else living in the dwelling who the local authority is satisfied occupies your dwelling as a home. For the local housing allowance rules only, a joint tenant who is not a member of your household (see p262) does not count as an occupier; *and*
- for the rules that use rent officer determinations, anyone the local authority includes on the form used to refer your tenancy to the rent officer.



Also included are your (or your partner's) son, daughter, stepson or stepdaughter who is in the armed forces deployed on operations and who was your non-dependant (see p207) before being deployed, provided they intend to return to your home.[112]

'Occupiers' can therefore include not only your partner and children, but also other people – eg, a joint tenant (but for the local housing allowance rules, only if the joint tenant is a member of your household), a non-dependant or a live-in carer.[113] You can argue that people are 'occupiers' if they normally live with you, but are temporarily away.[114] The local authority may use the temporary absence rules described on p191 to decide whether someone counts as occupying your home.

**Note:**

- A foster child or child placed with you for adoption under specified provisions does not count as an occupier.[115] However, you may qualify for an additional bedroom (see below) if you or your partner are a 'qualifying parent or carer' or if the child is a 'person who requires overnight care'.
- If you share the care of a child, the child is considered to be occupying the home of one person – the person with whom the child normally lives.[116]

## Additional bedrooms

In addition to the number of bedrooms (or for the rules that use rent officer determinations (see p317), 'rooms suitable for living in') allowed for the occupiers in your home, you are allowed one additional bedroom in the following situations. If both apply, you are allowed two.[117]

- **Non-resident carers.** If you (or your partner), a person who occupies your dwelling as a home (eg, your child or a non-dependant) or a child or young person in respect of whom you or your partner are a 'qualifying parent or carer' (eg, your foster child) are a 'person who requires overnight care' (see p332 for who counts), you are allowed one additional bedroom for a non-resident carer. Even if more than one person requires overnight care, only one additional bedroom is allowed.

- **Fostering, adoption and kinship carers.** If you (or your partner) are a 'qualifying parent or carer' (ie, certain foster parents and people with whom a child has been placed for adoption – see p333 for who counts), you are allowed one additional bedroom. Even if you (or your partner) have more than one foster child or child placed with you for adoption, only one additional bedroom is allowed.



If the social sector rules apply and you are jointly liable for the rent with someone other than your partner (eg, a joint tenant), you are also allowed an additional bedroom for that person if the person (or the person's partner) is a 'person who requires overnight care' or a 'qualifying parent or carer'.[118] You are allowed two additional bedrooms if both conditions are satisfied.

**Note:**

- The rules that allow additional bedrooms were amended in the past following test cases. If you think you may have lost out, see pp98–99 of the 2020/21 edition of this *Handbook*.
- Even if your dwelling has been adapted under a 'sanctuary scheme', you are not allowed additional rooms. However, if the social sector rules apply, your rent cannot be restricted (see p313).

## What counts as a bedroom

When working out the number of bedrooms in your home, you may need to consider what counts as a bedroom. For example, you may need to argue that a room is a bedroom, or it may be more advantageous for you to argue that a room is not a bedroom.

***What is a bedroom?***

'Bedroom' is not defined in the rules. It is the ordinary meaning of the word that is relevant. It could be, for example, a lounge or living room, provided it contains a bed or is used for sleeping.[119] The starting point is whether the room can be used as a bedroom – ie, a room is a bedroom if it is furnished and can be used for sleeping in.

How a property is described by the landlord (eg, as a two- or three-bedroom house) or whether a room is designated as a bedroom may be relevant. However, the basis on which your rent is charged (eg, if your flat has two bedrooms but your landlord only charges the rent for a one-bedroom flat) is not relevant.[120]

You may want to argue that the local authority should not count a room in your home as a bedroom and therefore that your housing benefit should not be reduced (or reduced as much) under the rent restriction rules. In deciding whether a room is a bedroom, the local authority should, for example, take into account:[121]

- the size of the room (the dimensions and height) – eg, whether it can accommodate a single bed and somewhere to store clothes and whether it has

a flat surface on which to place things safely, such as a glass of water, and whether there is space to dress and undress. If a room is too small, provide a measured plan and photographs if you can; *and*
- access to the room and whether it has adequate natural and electric lighting, heating, ventilation and privacy; *and*
- whether the room is safe to sleep in – eg, it is not safe if it is contaminated with asbestos.

Suggest your personal use of the room should also be taken into account (eg, if you use the room to store equipment you need because of a severe disability), as well as whether your home has been converted or adapted – eg, if two small bedrooms have been converted into one big bedroom, or if a bedroom has been redesignated. However, the local authority is likely to say that in deciding how many bedrooms there are in your home:
- it is the classification and description of the property when it is empty that is relevant and that the classification can only be changed if the property has been structurally altered with the approval of your landlord;[122]
- even if your home could be used in more than one way (eg, as either a one- or two-bedroom property), the local authority can use the way your landlord designates the property to determine how many bedrooms it has.[123]

## Couples who cannot share a bedroom

If you and your partner, or the members of any couple occupying your dwelling as a home (eg, your non-dependants), cannot share a bedroom, you are allowed an additional room under the size criteria. To count as a 'couple who cannot share a bedroom':[124]
- the person who cannot share must be getting attendance allowance (AA) or pension age disability payment (PADP), the middle or highest rate of disability living allowance (DLA)/Scottish adult disability living allowance (SADLA)/ child disability payment (CDP) care component, the daily living component of personal independence payment (PIP)/adult disability payment (ADP), or armed forces independence payment (AFIP); *and*
- the local authority must be satisfied that the person cannot reasonably share a bedroom with the other member of the couple because of the disability.

Note:
- Under the local housing allowance rules and the rules that use rent officer determinations, you are only allowed an additional room if you have a bedroom in your home additional to those you would be allowed if the couple were able to share a bedroom (see p309 and p320).
- Before 1 April 2017, a bedroom might not have been allowed (when it should have been) for a disabled member of a couple who cannot share a bedroom.

You can still apply for a revision on grounds of official error if you were affected and think you should have been allowed an additional bedroom.[125]

## Child who cannot share a bedroom

You are allowed an additional room for a 'child who cannot share a bedroom' under the size criteria. To count as a 'child who cannot share a bedroom':[126]

- the child must be under 16 and must be entitled to the middle or highest rate of DLA/CDP care component, whether or not it is being paid; *and*
- the local authority must be satisfied that the child cannot reasonably share a bedroom with another child under 16 because of the disability.

Note:

- Under the local housing allowance rules and the rules that use rent officer determinations, you are only allowed an additional room if you have a bedroom in your home additional to those you would be allowed if the child were able to share a bedroom (see p309 and p320).
- Before 4 December 2013, a bedroom might not have been allowed (when it should have been) for a severely disabled child who cannot share a bedroom. You can still apply for a revision on grounds of official error if you were affected and think you should have been allowed a bedroom for a disabled child.[127]

## Person who requires overnight care

If you (or your partner), a person who occupies your dwelling as a home (eg, your child or a non-dependant) or a child or young person in respect of whom you or your partner are a 'qualifying parent or carer' (eg, your foster child) are a 'person who requires overnight care', you are allowed an additional room under the size criteria. Under the social sector rules, you are also allowed an additional bedroom for someone who is jointly liable for the rent with you if that person (or their partner) is a 'person who requires overnight care'.

A 'person who requires overnight care' is someone who:[128]

- is getting AA, PADP, the middle or highest rate of DLA/SADLA/CDP care component, the daily living component of PIP/ADP or AFIP; *or*
- has (or if the person is a child, you have) provided the local authority with sufficient certificates, documents, information or evidence to satisfy it that overnight care is required.

In addition, arrangements must have been made for one or more people who do not live with you to provide overnight care and to stay overnight regularly in your home for this purpose. You must satisfy the local authority that this care is reasonably required. The carer does not necessarily have to stay overnight on the majority of nights, but the care must be needed sufficiently often and steadily enough that a bedroom has to be available for the carer.[129] The carer must be provided with the use of a bedroom additional to those used by other people who live with you. 'Bedroom' is not defined, but see p330 for what might count.

**Note:** a person can count as a 'person who requires overnight care' while away from your home, provided they can be treated as occupying it – eg, while temporarily absent (see p191).

### Qualifying parent or carer



If you (or your partner) are a 'qualifying parent or carer', you are allowed one additional bedroom under the size criteria. Under the social sector rules, you are also allowed an additional bedroom for someone who is jointly liable for the rent with you if that person (or that person's partner) is a 'qualifying parent or carer'.

You count as a 'qualifying parent or carer' if:[130]

- a child has been placed (or in Scotland, boarded out) with you under specified provisions – eg, prior to adoption or as a foster parent; *or*
- you are an approved foster parent (in Scotland, this includes approved foster and kinship carers). This applies even if you do not currently have a child placed with you, provided you have become an approved foster parent, or have fostered a child, within the last 52 weeks.

To come within the definition, you must have a bedroom in your home that is additional to those used by the other people living in your home. 'Bedroom' is not defined, but see p330 for what might count.

You do not count as a qualifying parent or carer if you provide accommodation for a disabled person under an adult placement scheme. However, you can argue that you should still be allowed an additional bedroom.[131]

## 7. Delaying a rent restriction

A rent restriction can be delayed:

- for up to 12 months, if a member of your family (or any of your or your partner's relatives who lived in the same accommodation as you without a separate right to do so) dies and you still live there (temporary absences of up to 13 weeks are allowed);[132] *or*
- for up to 13 weeks, if you, or a member of your family (or any of your or your partner's relatives who live in the same dwelling as you without a separate right to do so) could meet the costs of the dwelling when you took them on (this could include other bills as well as the rent). This only applies if neither you nor your partner were entitled to housing benefit (HB) in the 52 weeks before your current award of HB.[133]

Under the local housing allowance and social sector rent restriction rules, the amount of your rent that can be covered by your HB (your 'eligible rent' – see p202) can change before the end of the 12-month/13-week period if, as calculated under these rules, it is now the same or higher, or you move to a new home or another member of your family (or relative) dies.[134]

***Family members and relatives***[135]

**'Family'** means you, your partner and any child or qualifying young person for whom you or your partner are responsible and who lives in your household.

**'Relative'** means a close relative (see p189 for who counts) or a grandparent, grandchild, uncle, aunt, nephew or niece.

***Example***

Ryan lives in a private three-bedroom flat with his wife and their 30-year-old son. They pay rent of £225 a week. Until her recent death, Ryan's sister lived with them. Ryan's rent was being restricted to the local housing allowance for a three-bedroom property (£190).

When he notifies the local authority of the death of his sister, his rent is restricted to the local housing allowance for a two-bedroom property (£150). However, the decrease is delayed for 12 months from the date of his sister's death.

Ryan gets pension credit and HB. Before his sister's death, his HB was £170.35 a week (£190 *minus* a non-dependant deduction of £19.65).

For 12 months from his sister's date of death, his HB is £190 a week.

## 8. Challenging a rent restriction

If you disagree with the local authority's decision to apply a rent restriction (eg, if you think the rules do not apply in your case, or the wrong rules have been applied) or with the factual basis on which the decision was made (eg, you are a 'person who requires overnight care' or a 'member of a couple who cannot share a bedroom' and you should have been allowed more bedrooms under the rules or a room in your home should not count as a bedroom), you can ask for a revision or appeal (see Chapters 50 and 51).[136] However, if the local housing allowance rules apply, you cannot appeal against the amount of the local housing allowance.

If the rules that use rent officer determinations apply (see p317), you:

- cannot appeal against a rent officer's determination, but the local authority can ask for it to be redetermined.[137] This might reduce your maximum rent (and the local authority might restrict your rent further), so consider your position carefully – you could end up with less housing benefit (HB). For details of the rules, see p414 of the 2019/20 edition of this *Handbook*;
- can appeal against local authority decisions about your award of HB which involve rent officer determinations – ie, you can challenge the factual basis on

which the rent officer made a determination, such as whether you are a 'young individual' or whether someone occupies accommodation with you.[138] If you are in doubt, you may want to appeal *and* ask for a redetermination.



# Notes

1. **How to use this chapter**

1 Regs 13C(5)(a) and (c) and 14(2)(b) and Sch 2 paras 3-13 HB Regs; regs 13C(5)(a) and (c) and 14(2)(b) and Sch 2 paras 3-13 HB(SPC) Regs
2 The law refers to 'gypsies and travellers': Sch 2 para 3 HB Regs; Sch 2 para 3 HB(SPC) Regs
3 Reg 2(1) and Sch 2 para 3(1A) HB Regs; reg 2(1) and Sch 2 para 3(1A) HB(SPC) Regs
4 Reg 12B(6) HB Regs; reg 12B(6) HB(SPC) Regs
5 *R (on the application of Laali) v Westminster Housing Benefit Review Board* [2000] QBD CO/1845/2000, [2002] HLR 179; *R v Macclesfield BC HBRB ex parte Temsamani* [1999] EWHC Admin 168, unreported (QBD); A4 Annex B GM
6 Reg 12C(2) and (3) HB Regs; reg 12C(2) HB(SPC) Regs; *DC v LB Bromley (HB)* [2018] UKUT 416 (AAC)
7 *AA v Chesterfield BC* [2011] UKUT 156 (AAC)

2. **The local housing allowance rules**

8 Reg 12D(2)(a) HB Regs; reg 12D(2)(a) HB(SPC) Regs
9 Reg 13C(1), (2)(a)-(c) and (5) HB Regs; reg 13C(1), (2)(a)-(c) and (5) HB(SPC) Regs
10 Reg 13D(1) and (5) HB Regs; reg 13D(1) and (5) HB(SPC) Regs
11 Reg 13D(4) and (12) HB Regs; reg 13D(4) and (12) HB(SPC) Regs
12 *DC v LB Bromley (HB)* [2018] UKUT 416 (AAC)
13 Reg 13D(2)(c) and (3) HB Regs; reg 13D(2)(c) and (3) HB(SPC) Regs
14 Reg 2(6) HB Regs; reg 2(7) HB(SPC) Regs
15 *SSWP v Hockley and Nuneaton and Bedworth BC* [2019] EWCA Civ 1080
16 Reg 13D(2)(a) HB Regs; reg 13D(2)(a) HB(SPC) Regs
17 Regs 2(1), definition of 'young individual', (b)-(f) and (i) and 13D(2)(a) HB Regs; reg 13D(2)(a) and (12) HB(SPC) Regs
18 Ch 2 paras 2.060-2.061 *Local Housing Allowance Guidance Manual*
19 Reg 13D(2)(b) HB Regs; reg 13D(2)(b) HB(SPC) Regs
20 *JS v SSWP and Cheshire West and Chester BC (HB)* [2014] UKUT 36 (AAC), reported as [2014] AACR 26
21 Reg 13D(2)(b) HB Regs; reg 13D(2)(b) HB(SPC) Regs
22 Reg 13D(2)(c) HB Regs; reg 13D(2)(c) HB(SPC) Regs
23 Reg 13D(1) HB Regs; reg 13D(1) HB(SPC) Regs; art 4B(2A) and (2B) and Sch 3B RO(HBF)O; art 4B(2A) and (2B) and Sch 3B RO(HBF)(S)O; The Rent Oficers (Housing Benefit and Universal Credit Functions) (Modification) Order 2025 No.5
24 Sch 3B para 3A RO(HBF)O; Sch 3B para 3A RO(HBF)(S)O
25 Regs 12D(2) and 13C(3) HB Regs; regs 12D(2) and 13C(3) HB(SPC) Regs
26 Regs 2, definition of 'linked person', 12D(2)(b) and 13C(2)(d) HB Regs; regs 2, definition of 'linked person', 12D(2)(b) and 13C(2)(d) HB(SPC) Regs
27 Reg 13D(1) and (12), definition of 'relevant date', HB Regs; reg 13D(1) and (12), definition of 'relevant date', HB(SPC) Regs

3. **The social sector rules: the 'bedroom tax'**

28 Reg A13(1) HB Regs
29 Reg 12BA HB Regs
30 Regs 2(1), definition of 'registered housing association', and A13(1)-(5) HB Regs
31 *FT v Perth and Kinross Council and SSWP (HB)* [2019] UKUT 43 (AAC)
32 Regs 2(1), definition of 'domestic violence', 12(2B) and A13(2)(f) and (5) HB Regs
33 Reg B13(2) HB Regs
34 Reg B13(4) HB Regs
35 Reg B13(2)(c) HB Regs
36 Reg B13(5) and (8) HB Regs
37 Reg 2(6) HB Regs
38 *SSWP v Hockley and Nuneaton and Bedworth BC* [2019] EWCA Civ 1080

4. **Hostels, houseboats, mobile homes, caravans and boarders**

39 Reg 12C HB Regs; reg 12C HB(SPC) Regs
40 Regs 13(1), 13C(5)(a)-(e) and (6) and 14(1) HB Regs; regs 13(1), 13C(5)(a)-(e) and (6) and 14(1) HB(SPC) Regs
41 The law refers to 'gypsies and travellers': Sch 2 para 3 HB Regs; Sch 2 para 3 HB(SPC) Regs
42 Reg 13(2), (3), (5) and (6) HB Regs; reg 13(2), (3), (5) and (6) HB(SPC) Regs
43 Reg 12C(2) and (3) HB Regs; reg 12C(2) HB(SPC) Regs
44 Reg 13(4) HB Regs; reg 13(4) HB(SPC) Regs; Sch 3 para 8 HB&CTB(CP) Regs
45 *DC v LB Bromley (HB)* [2018] UKUT 416 (AAC)
46 Reg 14(1) and (8) HB Regs; reg 14(1) and (8) HB(SPC) Regs
47 Reg 14(2)(a) and (7) and Sch 2 para 2(1) and (2) HB Regs; reg 14(2)(a) and (7) and Sch 2 para 2(1) and (2) HB(SPC) Regs
48 Reg 14(1) and (8) and Sch 2 para 2(3)(a)-(d) and (f)-(h) and (4) HB Regs; reg 14(1) and (8) and Sch 2 para 2(3)(a)-(g) and (4) HB(SPC) Regs
49 R(H) 8/09; *SK v South Hams DC (HB)* [2010] UKUT 129 (AAC), reported as [2010] AACR 40
50 CH/1556/2006; CH/3590/2007
51 Sch 1 para 6 RO(HBF)O; Sch 1 para 6 RO(HBF)(S)O
52 Sch 1 para 1 RO(HBF)O; Sch 1 para 1 RO(HBF)(S)O
53 Sch 1 para 3 RO(HBF)O; Sch 1 para 3 RO(HBF)(S)O
54 Sch 1 paras 1(4) and 2 RO(HBF)O; Sch 1 paras 1(4) and 2 RO(HBF)(S)O
55 Sch 2 para 1 RO(HBF)O; Sch 2 para 1 RO(HBF)(S)O
56 Reg 2(6) HB Regs; reg 2(7) HB(SPC) Regs
57 Sch 1 paras 4 and 9(2) RO(HBF)O; Sch 1 paras 4 and 9(2) RO(HBF)(S)O
58 Sch 1 para 5 RO(HBF)O; Sch 1 para 5 RO(HBF)(S)O
59 Reg 13(5) and (6) HB Regs
60 Reg 114A(6) and (8)(a) HB Regs; reg 95A(6) and (8)(a) HB(SPC) Regs
61 Sch 1 paras 5(2)(c) and 7(1) RO(HBF)O; Sch 1 paras 5(2)(c) and 7(1) RO(HBF)(S)O
62 Reg 13ZB(1) HB Regs; reg 13ZB(1) HB(SPC) Regs
63 Reg 14(1)(e) and (2) HB Regs; reg 14(1)(e) and (2) HB(SPC) Regs
64 Reg 14(8), definition of 'prospective occupier', HB Regs; reg 14(8), definition of 'prospective occupier', HB(SPC) Regs
65 Reg 14(1)(e) and (8), definition of 'specified matters', HB Regs; reg 14(1)(e) and (8), definition of 'specified matters', HB(SPC) Regs
66 Sch 2 para 2(2)(b) HB Regs; Sch 2 para 2(2)(b) HB(SPC) Regs
67 Reg 13ZB(2)-(4) HB Regs; reg 13ZB(2)-(4) HB(SPC) Regs

5. **Exempt accommodation and claimants: the old scheme rules**

68 Reg 12(3)-(5) HB Regs and reg 12(3)-(5) HB(SPC) Regs, as set out in Sch 3 para 5(1) HB&CTB(CP) Regs
69 Reg 13(3) HB Regs and reg 13(3) HB(SPC) Regs, as set out in Sch 3 para 5(2) HB&CTB(CP) Regs
70 *R v City of Westminster HBRB ex parte Mehanne* [2001] UKHL 11
71 *R v Brent LBC HBRB ex parte Connery* [1989] 22 HLR 40 (QBD)
72 *R v LB of Kensington and Chelsea ex parte Pirie* [1997] EWHC Admin 331, unreported (QBD)
73 Reg 13(3)(a) HB Regs and reg 13(3)(a) HB(SPC) Regs, as set out in Sch 3 para 5(2) HB&CTB(CP) Regs
74 Reg 13(3)(b) HB Regs and reg 13(3)(b) HB(SPC) Regs, as set out in Sch 3 para 5(2) HB&CTB(CP) Regs; *R v Beverley DC HBRB ex parte Hare* [1995] 27 HLR 637 (QBD); *R v Kensington and Chelsea RBC ex parte Abou-Jaoude*, 10 May 1996, unreported (QBD); CH/2704/2011

75 *Macleod v Banff and Buchan District HBRB* [1988] SLT 753 (CS); *Malcolm v Tweedale District HBRB* [1994] SLT 1212 (CS); CH/4970/2002
76 *Birmingham City Council v SSWP and Others* [2016] EWCA Civ 1211
77 *R v Kensington and Chelsea RBC ex parte Abou-Jaoude*, 10 May 1996, unreported (QBD); *R v Coventry City Council ex parte Waite*, 7 July 1995, unreported (QBD)
78 *R v Kensington and Chelsea RBC HBRB ex parte Sheikh*, 14 January 1996, unreported (QBD)
79 Reg 13(9) HB Regs and reg 13(9) HB(SPC) Regs, as set out in Sch 3 para 5(2) HB&CTB(CP) Regs
80 R(H) 2/05
81 *R v Lambeth LBC HBRB ex parte Harrington, Howell and Glynn*, 22 November 1996, unreported (QBD)
82 Reg 13(9)(a) HB Regs and reg 13(9)(a) HB(SPC) Regs, as set out in Sch 3 para 5(2) HB&CTB(CP) Regs; *R v LB of Kensington and Chelsea ex parte Pirie* [1997] EWHC Admin 331, unreported (QBD); *Coventry CC ex parte Waite*, 7 July 1995, unreported (QBD)
83 *R v Waltham Forest LBC ex parte Holder* [1996] 29 HLR 71 (QBD); *R v Slough BC ex parte Green*, 15 November 1996, EWHC Admin 238, unreported (QBD)
84 *R v Waltham Forest LBC ex parte Holder* [1996] 29 HLR 71 (QBD); *R v Kensington and Chelsea RBC HBRB ex parte Sheikh*, 14 January 1996, unreported (QBD)
85 Reg 13(4) HB Regs and reg 13(4) HB(SPC) Regs, as set out in Sch 3 para 5(2) HB&CTB(CP) Regs
86 R(H) 3/06
87 Reg 13(10) and (11) HB Regs and reg 13(10) and (11) HB(SPC) Regs, as set out in Sch 3 para 5(2) HB&CTB(CP) Regs
88 Reg 13(4) HB Regs and reg 13(4) HB(SPC) Regs, as set out in Sch 3 para 5(2) HB&CTB(CP) Regs
89 *R v Housing Benefit Review Board for East Devon DC ex parte Gibson and Gibson* [1993] EWCA 25 HLR 487 (QBD); CH/4306/2003
90 *R v Waltham Forest LBC ex parte Holder* [1996] 29 HLR 71 (QBD)
91 *R v Oadby and Wigston DC ex parte Dickman* [1995] 28 HLR 806 (QBD)
92 Reg 13(9)(b) HB Regs and reg 13(9)(b) HB(SPC) Regs, as set out in Sch 3 para 5(2) HB&CTB(CP) Regs
93 *R v Kensington and Chelsea RBC HBRB ex parte Sheikh*, 14 January 1996, unreported (QBD)
94 *R v Kensington and Chelsea RBC HBRB ex parte Carney* [1996] EWCA Admin 62, Crown Office Digest 124 (QBD)
95 *R v LB Camden HBRB ex parte W* [1999] EWHC Admin 818, unreported (QBD); *R v Westminster CC HBRB ex parte Pallas* [1997] unreported (QBD)
96 Reg 13C(5)(b) HB Regs; reg 13C(5)(b) HB(SPC) Regs; Sch 3 para 4(1)(b) and (10) HB&CTB(CP) Regs; CH/1289/2007
97 R(H) 7/07; R(H) 4/09; CH/3900/2005; CH/2726/2008; *East Hertfordshire DC v KT* [2009] UKUT 12 (AAC); *Bristol City Council v AW* [2009] UKUT 109 (AAC)
98 R(H) 7/07; CH/1289/2007; *Salford CC v PF* [2009] UKUT 150 (AAC)
99 *MMcF v Sefton BC (HB)* [2016] UKUT 403 (AAC)
100 R(H) 2/07
101 Sch 3 para 4(1)(a), (2), (3) and (4) HB&CTB(CP) Regs
102 Reg 13C HB Regs; reg 13C HB(SPC) Regs; Sch 3 para 4(2)(a) and (b), (5), (6), (9) and (10) HB&CTB(CP) Regs
103 Sch 3 para 4(10), definition of 'previous beneficiary', HB&CTB(CP) Regs
104 Reg 2(1), definition of 'registered housing association', HB Regs; Sch 3 para 4(2)(aa) HB&CTB(CP) Regs
105 Reg 13ZA HB Regs and reg 13ZA HB(SPC) Regs, as set out in Sch 3 para 5(3) HB&CTB(CP) Regs
106 *BM v Cheshire West and Cheshire Council* [2009] UKUT 162 (AAC)
107 CH/2214/2003

6. **Common rules**

108 Reg 2(1) and (1A)-(1C), definitions of 'domestic violence' and 'young individual', HB Regs
109 gov.uk/government/publications/multi-agency-public-protection-arrangements-mappa-guidance
110 Reg 2(1) HB Regs
111 Regs B13(5) and 13D(12) HB Regs; reg 13D(12) HB(SPC) Regs; art 2(1) RO(HBF)O; art 2(1) RO(HBF)(S)O
112 Regs B13(8) and 13D(12) and Sch 2 para 2(4) HB Regs; reg 13D(12) and Sch 2 para 2(4) HB(SPC) Regs
113 *AA v Chesterfield BC and SSWP (HB)* [2011] UKUT 156 (AAC)
114 R(H) 8/09; *SK v South Hams DC (HB)* [2010] UKUT 129 (AAC), reported as [2010] AACR 40

115 Reg 21(3) HB Regs; reg 21(3) HB(SPC) Regs
116 *R v Swale BC HBRB ex parte Marchant* [1999] EWCA QBCOF 99 0071 4, [2000] 1 FLR 246; *R (Cotton and Others) v SSWP and New Forest DC and Others* [2014] EWHC 3437 (Admin); *PC v SSWP (HB)* [2014] UKUT 467 (AAC); *MR v North Tyneside Council and SSWP* [2015] UKUT 34 (AAC); *SSWP v MM and Northumberland CC* [2015] UKUT 624 (AAC)
117 Regs B13(6)(a) and (b), (7)(a) and (9)(a), (b) and (e) and 13D(3A) and (3B) HB Regs; reg 13D(3A) and (3B) HB(SPC) Regs; Sch 2 paras 1A and 1B RO(HBF)O; Sch 2 paras 1A and 1B RO(HBF)(S)O
118 Reg B13(6)(ab) and (b), (7) and (9)(c) and (d) HB Regs
119 *Bolton MBC v BF (HB)* [2014] UKUT 48 (AAC)
120 *CB v Manchester City Council and SSWP (HB)* [2015] UKUT 556 (AAC)
121 *SSWP v Nelson and Nelson* [2014] UKUT 525 (AAC), reported as [2015] AACR 21; *Stevenage BC v ML (HB)* [2016] UKUT 164 (AAC); *M v SSWP* [2017] UKUT 443 (AAC); *Nuneaton and Bedworth BC v RH and SSWP* [2017] UKUT 471 (AAC), reported as [2019] AACR 27; *E v Bristol City Council* [2018] UKUT 287 (AAC)
122 *SSWP v the City of Glasgow Council and IB* [2017] CSIH 35, reported as [2017] AACR 38
123 *SSWP v RR (HB)* [2018] UKUT 180 (AAC)
124 Reg 2(1) HB Regs; reg 2(1) HB(SPC) Regs
125 *R (Carmichael) v SSWP and R (Rutherford) v SSWP* [2016] UKSC 58
126 Reg 2(1) HB Regs; reg 2(1) HB(SPC) Regs
127 *Burnip v Birmingham City Council and Others* [2012] EWCA Civ 629
128 Reg 2(1) HB Regs; reg 2(1) HB(SPC) Regs
129 *SD v Eastleigh BC (HB)* [2014] UKUT 325 (AAC)
130 Reg 2(1) HB Regs; reg 2(1) HB(SPC) Regs
131 *SSWP v PE and Bolton MBC* [2017] UKUT 393 (AAC)

7. **Delaying a rent restriction**

132 Regs 2(1), definitions of 'reckonable rent' and 'linked person', 12BA(3)-(5), 12D(3), (4) and (8) and 13ZA(1) and (2) HB Regs; regs 2(1), definitions of 'reckonable rent' and 'linked person', 12D(3), (4) and (8) and 13ZA(1) and (2) HB(SPC) Regs; reg 13(5) HB Regs and reg 13(5) HB(SPC) Regs, as set out in Sch 3 para 5(2) HB&CTB(CP) Regs
133 Regs 12BA(6)-(8), 12D(5), (6) and (8) and 13ZA(3) and (4) HB Regs; regs 12D(5), (6) and (8) and 13ZA(3) and (4) HB(SPC) Regs; reg 13(7) and (8) HB Regs and reg 13(7) and (8) HB(SPC) Regs, as set out in Sch 3 para 5(2) HB&CTB(CP) Regs
134 Regs 12BA(5) and (8) and 12D(7) HB Regs; reg 12D(7) HB(SPC) Regs
135 Reg 2(1) HB Regs; reg 2(1) HB(SPC) Regs

8. **Challenging a rent restriction**

136 *LB Bexley v LD (HB)* [2010] UKUT 79 (AAC); *SK v South Hams DC (HB)* [2010] UKUT 129 (AAC), reported as [2010] AACR 40
137 Regs 15, 16 and 17 HB Regs; regs 15, 16 and 17 HB(SPC) Regs
138 *SK v South Hams DC (HB)* [2010] UKUT 129 (AAC), reported as [2010] AACR 40; *LB Bexley v LD (HB)* [2010] UKUT 79 (AAC)

# Chapter 16

# Income: under pension age

3

**This chapter covers:**


1. Whose income counts (below)
2. What counts as income (p340)
3. Earnings (p340)
4. Other income (p352)
5. Notional income (p365)
6. Working out weekly income (p368)


This chapter explains the rules for working out your weekly income for income-related employment and support allowance (ESA) and working-age housing benefit (HB). The rules on how earnings are calculated also apply to your (but not your partner's) earnings for contributory ESA and new-style jobseeker's allowance. For pension credit and pension-age HB rules if you and your partner are over pension age, see Chapter 17. If you are in a couple and one of you is over pension age but not the other, see p197 for whether the working-age or pension-age HB rules apply. For universal credit (UC), see Chapter 7.

## Key facts

- Your entitlement to income-related ESA and working-age HB and the amount you get depend on how much income you have.
- Your own income counts and, if you are a member of a couple, your partner's income also counts.
- Some income may be completely or partly ignored, or it may count in full.
- Some income may be treated as capital and some capital treated as income.
- If you get income-related ESA (or UC), you are entitled to maximum HB, so you do not need to work out your income again for HB.

## 1. Whose income counts

Your income counts and, if you are a member of a couple (see p254), your partner's income also counts.[1] The income of your dependent children does not affect your means-tested benefits.[2]

**Note:** if you or your partner are getting income-related employment and support allowance (or universal credit), all your (and your partner's) income is ignored for housing benefit.[3]

3

## 2. What counts as income

All income is taken into account for income-related employment and support allowance (ESA) unless it is specifically ignored (or 'disregarded').

If you get income-related ESA (or universal credit), all your income is ignored for housing benefit (HB).[4] Otherwise, all income is taken into account for HB, other than income that is specifically disregarded.

Income only counts if it is paid to you for your own use. It may not count if you cannot prevent it being paid to a third party (eg, paying maintenance under an attachment of earnings order), although other payments for you made to a third party might count (see p366).[5]

Income is converted into a weekly amount (see p368).

### Income or capital

Payments of income are normally made in respect of a specified period and form part of a regular series of payments.[6] However, sometimes a one-off payment can be income depending on what it is paid for – eg, a settlement for underpaid wages under equal pay legislation.[7] Some income is treated as capital (see p402) and some capital is treated as income (see p360).

## 3. Earnings

How earnings are treated depends on whether you are employed (see below) or self-employed (see p345). In both cases, some of your earnings can be disregarded (see p347).

### Employed earnings

This section explains how any earnings received by you or your partner are treated. The same rules apply to your (but not your partner's) earnings if you are claiming contributory employment and support allowance (ESA – see p930) or new-style jobseeker's allowance (JSA – see p616), with some differences which are noted.

To work out how earnings are taken into account, do the following.

- Check whether the payments count as earnings (see p341). In some cases, payments are treated as capital, as income other than earnings, or ignored altogether.

- Calculate your net earnings (see p342 and p346).
- Work out your weekly net earnings (see p368).
- For ESA, check whether this is work you are allowed to do while claiming (see p928). For 'permitted work', work out whether this is within the 'permitted work' limit (see p930). If you are within the permitted work limit, all your earnings are disregarded. If you exceed the permitted work limit, you are not entitled to ESA. If you are the partner of the income-related ESA claimant, the permitted work limit does not apply to you, and your weekly net earnings are taken into account after the appropriate disregard.
- For housing benefit (HB) or partner of the income-related ESA claimant, deduct the appropriate weekly earnings disregard (see p347).
- Work out the date from when earnings are taken into account (see p371). For income-related employment and support allowance (ESA), also work out the period covered by the earnings (see p368). Usually, a payment counts from the date it is due to be paid and for the length of time it has been paid – eg, a month's wages count for a month, starting from the day they are due, at the weekly rate as calculated.

There are special rules for how payments affect benefit when you leave a job (see p343).

## What counts as earnings

**'Earnings'** means 'any remuneration or profit derived from ... employment'. This includes:[8]

- wages and overtime pay;
- any bonus or commission (including tips);
- holiday pay (but see p343 if your job ends or you are off work);
- for HB, any statutory sick pay (SSP) or contractual sick pay;
- statutory maternity pay (SMP), statutory adoption pay (SAP), statutory paternity pay (SPP), statutory shared parental pay (SSPP), statutory parental bereavement pay (SPBP), statutory neonatal care pay (SNCP) or any other payment made to you by your employer while you are on maternity, adoption, paternity, shared parental or parental bereavement leave.[9] For new-style JSA and income-related ESA, all such pay is treated as 'other income' rather than earnings (and therefore does not reduce your new-style JSA) and is counted in full less any tax, class 1 national insurance (NI) contributions and half of any pension contributions;[10]
- any payments made by your employer for expenses not 'wholly, exclusively and necessarily' incurred in carrying out your job, including any travel expenses to and from work, and any payments made to you for caring for your child or partner;

- a retainer (eg, payments during the school holidays if you work for the school meals service[11]) or a guarantee payment – eg, if you are working short time or laid off;[12]
- certain compensation payments in respect of the termination of your employment, including employment tribunal awards and pay in lieu of notice. See p343 for the way these are treated when you stop work. For income-related ESA, compensatory refunds of contributions to an occupational scheme[13] are not treated as earnings;
- an equal pay settlement – eg, through a 'single-status agreement';[14]
- any payment of a non-cash voucher which is liable for class 1 NI contributions.[15] Non-cash vouchers that are not liable for contributions are classed as payments in kind (see below).[16]

## What does not count as earnings

Examples of payments not counted as earnings include the following.

- Payments in kind (eg, petrol) are ignored,[17] although they may be counted as 'notional income' (see p367).[18] Non-cash vouchers that are not liable for class 1 NI contributions (eg, certain childcare and charitable vouchers) are treated as payments in kind and are disregarded.[19]
- Payments towards expenses that are 'wholly, exclusively and necessarily' incurred during the course of your work, such as travelling expenses, are ignored.[20] Any expenditure for both business and private use should be apportioned as appropriate (and any determination by HMRC normally followed).[21]
- If you are a local councillor, travelling expenses and subsistence payments are (and basic allowances may be[22]) ignored as expenses 'wholly, exclusively and necessarily' incurred in your work.
- Earnings payable abroad which cannot be brought into the UK (eg, because of exchange control regulations) are ignored.[23]
- Any occupational pension[24] counts as 'other income', not earnings, and the net amount is taken into account in full.[25] See p617 (and p562) for the occupational pension rules for new-style JSA (and contributory ESA).

## Calculating net earnings from employment

Both your 'gross' earnings and 'net' earnings must be calculated.

### Gross and net earnings

**'Gross earnings'** means the amount of earnings received from your employer less deductions for any expenses wholly, necessarily and exclusively incurred by you to carry out your duties.[26] See p341 for what counts as earnings.

**'Net earnings'** means your gross earnings less any deductions made for:[27]

– income tax; *and*

– class 1 NI contributions; *and*

- half of any contribution you make towards a personal or occupational pension scheme; *and*
- an amount you have agreed to give up under a vaild 'salary sacrifice' scheme in exchange for your employer's agreement to make a payment in kind – eg, an employer contribution towards an occupational pension scheme.[28]



For HB, if your earnings are estimated, the amount of tax and NI contributions you would expect to pay on those earnings is also estimated. This amount, plus half of any pension contribution you are paying, is then deducted.[29]

For HB, the local authority has the discretion to ignore changes in tax or NI contributions for up to 30 benefit weeks – eg, if April tax changes are not reflected in your actual income until several months later.[30]

## Payments when you stop work

If you were getting benefit while working, your final earnings are generally taken into account. If you stop work and are not already getting benefit, see p344.

### You were getting benefit when working

If your job ends and you were getting benefit while you were in work, any payments made to you when that job ends are taken into account as earnings as follows.[31]

- Final earnings are taken into account as normal (including wages, bonuses and expenses that count as earnings).
- For income-related ESA and HB, pay in lieu of notice is taken into account; for income-related ESA, final earnings are taken into account first, followed by pay in lieu of notice.
- Contractual redundancy pay, ex gratia payments and other types of compensation (other than employment tribunal awards) above the level of entitlement to statutory redundancy pay:
  - are treated as capital for income-related ESA, if you work out your notice or get full pay in lieu of notice. Otherwise, they are taken into account as earnings for one week only;
  - together with pay in lieu of notice, are treated as earnings for new-style JSA, up until the end of the fixed-term contract, if you had one, or until the end of the notice period (sometimes longer if the employer says it covers a longer period). For JSA, if none of the payment covers pay in lieu of notice or early termination of a fixed-term contract, the total of these payments covers a standard number of weeks arrived at by dividing the payment by the weekly maximum statutory redundancy payment (£719) if this is shorter than the notice period;
  - are treated as capital for HB, except any amount representing loss of income, which is taken into account as earnings.

The weeks the payments count for start after the period covered by final earnings and any pay in lieu of notice.



- Holiday pay normally counts as earnings. However, it counts as capital if your contract provides for it to be payable more than four weeks after employment ends. For new-style JSA and income-related ESA, it counts for the number of weeks covered by the holiday pay (not the number of working weeks[32]) starting after the period covered by other payments listed in the above three bullet points.
- An employment tribunal award (eg, for unfair dismissal) is taken into account as earnings.
- Arrears of sick, maternity, adoption, paternity and other parental pay count as earnings for HB, and as 'other income', rather than earnings, for new-style JSA and income-related ESA.[33]
- Statutory redundancy payments are treated as capital.

*Example*

Fiona has been getting HB in temporary accommodation while working part time. She finishes work on 16 July and is given £180, made up of £100 final wages and £80 holiday pay. The £180 wages and holiday pay are taken into account as normal for HB, deducting the earnings disregard.

### Your job ends before benefit starts

If you stop work before you claim contributory ESA, any final payments from your job are ignored. For income-related ESA, see p415 of the 2018/19 edition of this *Handbook*.

If your employment ends before your entitlement to new-style JSA or HB begins, any payments that count as earnings (see p341), including wages, holiday pay (but see below) and pay in lieu of notice, are ignored as income for that benefit, except for the payments below.[34]

The following payments are taken into account.

- A retainer counts as earnings.
- If you were in full-time paid work (see p883), certain employment tribunal awards (and out-of-court settlements) count as earnings, including compensation because of unfair dismissal.[35] If you were in part-time work, these are ignored for HB, but count for JSA.
- Guarantee payments for workless days or while suspended on medical or maternity grounds count as earnings, including when awarded by an employment tribunal.[36]
- Arrears of statutory or contractual sick, maternity, adoption, paternity, shared parental and parental bereavement pay and lump-sum advance payments are taken into account for JSA as income, without any earnings disregard, from

when they are paid for the same length of time covered by the arrears. They are ignored for HB.[37]

- Statutory redundancy pay counts as capital.[38]
- Contractual redundancy pay (deducting an amount for your statutory entitlement) is ignored completely for new-style JSA.[39] For HB, it counts as capital.[40]
- Some redundancy schemes make periodic payments after leaving work. These are treated as income other than earnings.[41]
- Ex gratia payments and other kinds of compensation (other than employment tribunal awards) are treated in the same way as contractual redundancy pay.
- Holiday pay is usually ignored. However, if your job ends, it counts as capital if your contract provides for it to be payable more than four weeks after termination of employment.[42]

If you stop work before your benefit begins but your employment has not ended (eg, you go on sick leave or maternity leave), statutory and contractual sick, maternity, adoption, paternity and other parental pay are taken into account as income without any earnings disregard for new-style JSA.[43] For HB, they count as earnings with the usual disregard.[44] If holiday pay is due to be paid more than four weeks after you stopped work, it is treated as capital (unless, for JSA, you are involved in a trade dispute). It is ignored if it is due to be paid less than four weeks after you stop work.[45] All other payments that count as earnings are ignored, except for a retainer or guarantee payments for workless days or for medical or maternity suspension.[46] If you are suspended from work, any earnings are taken into account as normal.

***Example***

Kaley has had to leave her home and job because of domestic abuse. She leaves her full-time job on 31 May with one month's wages and three days' holiday pay. Both are due to be paid on 31 May. She moves into temporary accommodation and claims HB after her job ends. Her final wages and holiday pay are ignored. She is entitled to HB from 1 June.

**Note:** if you were getting HB while working and after your job has ended you made a fresh claim for JSA, your final earnings are taken into account for HB (see p343), but disregarded for JSA.

## Self-employed earnings

This section explains how any earnings from self-employment received by you or your partner are treated. The same rules apply to your (but not your partner's) earnings if you are claiming new-style JSA.

To work out how earnings are taken into account, do the following.

- Calculate net earnings (see below).
- Work out your average earnings (see below).
- Deduct the appropriate weekly earnings disregard (see p347).

## Calculating net earnings

3

Your **'net profit'** must be worked out. This is your self-employed earnings minus:[47]

- reasonable expenses (see below); *and*
- income tax and NI contributions; *and*
- half of any premium paid for a personal pension scheme which is eligible for tax relief.

Drawings from capital do not count as income, whether or not the business is in profit.[48] If you receive payments for board and lodging, these do not count as earnings,[49] but as other income (less any disregards – see p358).

### Reasonable expenses

Expenses must be reasonable and 'wholly and exclusively' incurred for your business.[50] If a car or phone, for example, is used partly for business and partly for private purposes, the costs of it can be apportioned, and the amount attributable to business use can be deducted.[51]

**Reasonable expenses include:**[52]

- repayments of capital on loans for replacing equipment and machinery;
- interest on a loan taken out for the purposes of the business;
- excess of VAT paid over VAT received.

**Reasonable expenses do not include:**[53]

- any capital expenditure;
- depreciation;[54]
- any loss incurred before the beginning of the current period being used to work out average earnings (see below). If the business makes a loss, the net profit is nil;[55]
- capital repayments on loans taken out for business purposes;
- business entertainment expenses;
- for HB, debts (other than proven bad debts) – but the expenses of recovering debt can be deducted.

## Working out average earnings from self-employment

For new-style JSA and income-related ESA, the weekly amount is the average of earnings:[56]

- over a one-year period (in practice, usually the last year for which accounts are available);[57] *or*
- over a more appropriate period if you have recently taken up self-employment, there has been a change that will affect your business, or for any other reason

if a different period may enable your income and expenditure to be calculated more accurately.

For HB, your weekly earnings are averaged over an 'appropriate' period (usually based on your last year's trading accounts), which must not be longer than a year.[58]

For all benefits, if your earnings are royalties, copyright payments or payments under the Public Lending Right scheme, the amount of earnings is divided by the weekly amount of benefit that would be payable if you had not received this income plus the amount that would be disregarded from those earnings (for income-related ESA, the amount of benefit that would be payable includes any contributory ESA).[59] For new-style JSA and income-related ESA, you are not entitled to benefit for the resulting number of weeks. For HB, earnings are taken into account for the resulting number of weeks.

If you stop doing self-employed work, any earnings from that work are disregarded except for royalties and copyright and Public Lending Right scheme payments.[60]

### Childminders

In practice, childminders are always treated as self-employed. Your net profit is deemed to be one-third of your earnings less income tax, your NI contributions and half of personal pension scheme contributions (see p346).[61] The rest of your earnings are completely ignored.

## Disregarded earnings

Some of your earnings from employment or self-employment are disregarded and do not affect your benefit. The amount of the disregard depends on your circumstances. For the amount of disregarded earnings for new-style JSA, see p616.

- For HB, there is an additional disregard depending on the hours you work, a childcare costs disregard and a permitted work disregard.
- For income-related ESA, earnings from 'permitted work' are disregarded, or £20 a week is disregarded from certain other work or partner's earnings.

### Disregards for income-related employment and support allowance

#### Permitted work disregard

- All your earnings from 'permitted work' (see p930) are disregarded. (Only £20 can be disregarded from self-employed earnings from royalties, copyright payments or Public Lending Right scheme payments.)[62]
- If your earnings are less than the permitted work limit, up to £20 of what is left can be disregarded from your partner's earnings.[63]

**Note:** your earnings from any permitted work (for both contributory and income-related ESA) are assessed in the same way as that described in this chapter.[64] See p562 for how a councillor's allowance is assessed.

### £20 disregard

£20 of your earnings (including those of your partner) is disregarded if:[65]

- you are doing work you may do while getting ESA (see p928), but only if it is:
  - as a councillor; *or*
  - as a disability member of the First-tier Tribunal; *or*
  - during an emergency to protect someone or to prevent serious damage to property or livestock; *or*
  - while receiving assistance in pursuing self-employment under a government scheme; *or*
- your partner is in part-time employment of under 24 hours a week (but if you are doing permitted work, see p347); *or*
- your partner is working, but does not count as being in full-time paid work because they:
  - are childminding in their home; *or*
  - are a carer under the rules for who could qualify for income support (see p235 of the 2024/25 edition of this *Handbook*); *or*
  - are an auxiliary coastguard, part-time firefighter, part-time member of a lifeboat crew or member of the reserve forces; *or*
  - are working as a councillor; *or*
  - would not qualify for JSA because they have been involved in a trade dispute (see p891), or it is the first 15 days following their return to work after being involved in a trade dispute; *or*
  - are working in any of the cases listed on p884.

## Disregards for housing benefit

### £25 disregard

Lone parents on HB have £25 of their earnings ignored.[66] **Note:** if you get income-related ESA (or UC), all your earnings are disregarded for HB, so this £25 disregard does not apply.

### £20 disregard

£20 of your earnings (including those of your partner) is disregarded if:

- you or your partner qualify for a disability premium (see p272);[67] *or*
- you or your partner qualify for a severe disability premium (see p275), the support component or work-related activity component (see p282), or you are in the 'work-related activity group' (see p561);[68] *or*
- you or your partner qualify for a carer premium (see p279). The disregard applies to the carer's earnings. If both partners in a couple get the carer premium, £20 is disregarded from their combined earnings. If you are the carer

and the claimant, and your earnings are less than £20, up to £10 of the disregard can be used on your partner's earnings (or all of what is left of it if your partner's earnings are from one of the services listed in the next bullet point) – but the total disregard cannot be more than £20;[69] *or*
- you or your partner are an auxiliary coastguard, part-time firefighter, part-time member of a lifeboat crew or member of the reserve forces.[70] If you earn less than £20 for doing any of these services, you can use up to £5 (up to £10, if you have a partner) of the disregard on another job[71] or on a partner's earnings from another job.[72]

If you qualify under more than one category, you still have a maximum of only £20 of your earnings disregarded.

#### Basic £5 or £10 disregard

If you do not qualify for a £25 or £20 disregard or the permitted work disregard (see below), £5 of your earnings is disregarded if you are single. For couples, £10 of your total earnings is disregarded – whether or not you are both working.[73]

### Permitted work disregard for housing benefit

If you or your partner are doing 'permitted work' (see p930) and getting contributory ESA, severe disablement allowance (SDA) or NI credits for limited capability for work or incapacity, your earnings from permitted work are also disregarded for HB.[74] This is instead of the usual disregard of £5, £10, £20 or £25.

If your earnings from permitted work are less than the limit, you can use up the rest:
- on your partner's earnings, up to a maximum of £20 or up to the limit if they are also doing permitted work, but there is only one disregard between you; *or*
- on your own earnings from other work. See p928 for other work you may do while getting one of these benefits. If you are a lone parent, you can also top up the disregard on earnings from other work to £25.

### Additional disregard for housing benefit

For HB only, whichever earnings disregard applies is increased by £17.10 if:[75]
- you or your partner are aged 25 or over and work 30 hours or more a week on average; *or*
- you or your partner work 16 hours or more a week on average and you have a child who is part of your family for benefit purposes (see p258), or your HB includes the family premium (see p270); *or*
- you are a lone parent and work 16 hours or more a week on average; *or*
- you or your partner work 16 hours or more a week on average and your HB includes a disability premium (see p272), the support component or work-related activity component (see p281), or you are in the 'work-related activity group' (see p561). For couples, the partner for whom the premium/component

is awarded or who is in the work-related activity group must be working 16 hours or more a week on average.

The additional earnings disregard does not apply if your total earnings are less than the total of £17.10 plus any earnings disregard and childcare costs disregard (see below).

**Note:** only one additional disregard is allowed from your (or your partner's) earnings.

***Example***

Cara and Rose are a couple in temporary accommodation with one child aged eight. Cara gets contributory ESA and HB. Rose works part time for 16 hours a week, earning £192. The amount of Rose's earnings taken into account for HB is £154.90 a week. From her £192 wages, £20 is disregarded because Cara is in the work-related activity group, and £17.10 is disregarded because they have a child and Rose works sufficient hours for the additional disregard.

## Childcare costs disregard for housing benefit

For HB, up to £175 a week for one child, or up to £300 a week for two or more children, can be deducted from your (or your partner's) earnings (from employment or self-employment) for childcare costs if you are:[76]

- a lone parent working 16 hours or more a week; *or*
- a couple and both of you work 16 hours or more a week, or one of you works 16 hours or more a week and the other is 'incapacitated' (see p352), or is in hospital or prison.

The most that can be deducted for one child is £175, even if you pay more. For more than one child, £300 is the maximum, even if you pay more or have to pay for more than two children.

It is not necessary for the childcare to be provided only while you are at work, nor for it to be work-related, and there is no requirement for the charges to be reasonable.

You can still get this disregard for childcare costs if you are off work sick, although for lone parents it stops after 28 weeks (see p351).

The childcare costs disregard only applies to charges you pay for certain types of childcare provided for any child(ren) in your family under the age of 15 (or 16 if your child is disabled – see p351). A child is not treated as having reached the age of 15/16 until the day before the first Monday in September following their 15th/16th birthday.[77]

*Disabled child*

A child is defined as **'disabled'** if they are:[78]

– in receipt of disability living allowance (DLA), child disability payment (CDP), personal independence payment (PIP), adult disability payment (ADP) or armed forces independence payment (AFIP); *or*

– certified as severely sight impaired or blind by a consultant ophthalmologist, or stopped being certified before the first Monday in September following their 16th birthday, but no more than one year and 28 weeks before then.



The childcare must be provided:[79]

- by a registered childminder or other registered childcare provider (such as a nursery or local authority daycare service); *or*
- out of school hours for children between the ages of eight and 15/16, by a school on school premises or a local authority – eg, an out-of-hours or holiday play scheme.

You cannot include charges for care provided by a relative of the child in the child's own home even if the relative is a registered childminder, nor charges paid by you to your partner or by your partner to you for a child in your family. You can include charges for childcare outside the child's home provided by a relative other than your partner if they are a registered childminder. The registered childminder could be a former partner who may be the child's parent. Charges for compulsory education do not count.

If you or your partner are on maternity, adoption, paternity, shared parental, parental bereavement or neonatal care leave, you are treated as working, and so can get the childcare disregard if you (or your partner):[80]

- were working in the week immediately before the leave began; *and*
- are entitled to SMP, SAP, SPP, SSPP, SPBP, SNCP (see Chapter 34) or maternity allowance (MA) (see Chapter 30).

You are no longer treated as working and so cannot get the childcare costs disregard when:

- the maternity, adoption, paternity, shared parental, parental bereavement or neonatal care leave ends; *or*
- you or your partner stop getting SMP, SAP, SPP, SSPP, SPBP, SNCP or MA.

You can get the childcare costs disregard for the new child in your family while you are still on parental leave.

### Childcare costs and ill health or disability

You can still have a childcare costs disregard while off work sick for the first 28 weeks while you are getting SSP, ESA or NI credits for limited capability for work, provided you were working at least 16 hours a week immediately before you started getting one of these benefits.[81]

After 28 weeks, lone parents who are off work sick can no longer get a childcare costs disregard, but couples can do so (before or after 28 weeks) if one works 16 hours or more a week and the other is treated as 'incapacitated'.

3

*Incapacitated*

You (or your partner) are treated as **'incapacitated'** if:[82]

- you get ESA which includes a support or work-related activity component, or SDA; *or*
- you get attendance allowance, pension age disability payment, Scottish adult disability living allowance, DLA/CDP, PIP/ADP, AFIP or constant attendance allowance (or an equivalent award under the war pensions or industrial injuries schemes), or you would receive one of these benefits but for the fact that you (or your partner) are in hospital; *or*
- you have an NHS-provided wheelchair, mobility scooter or similar vehicle; *or*
- your HB includes a disability premium, support component or work-related activity component for the incapacitated person's incapacity or limited capability for work, or that person is in the work-related activity group (see p561); *or*
- you (but not your partner) have been treated as having limited capability for work or as incapable of work for a continuous period of 196 days or more (disregarding any break of up to 84 or 56 days respectively).

### Calculating childcare costs

The costs to be taken into account are estimated over whatever period, not exceeding a year, will give the best estimate of the average weekly charge based on information provided by the childminder or care provider.

## 4. **Other income**

As well as income from earnings, most other forms of income are taken into account in full, less any tax due. To work out the weekly income to take into account, check whether the payment can be disregarded (in part or in full), deduct any tax due and work out the weekly amount (see p368). Where a taxable benefit or other unearned income is not taxed at source and you have not yet had a tax assessment, ask HMRC for a forecast of the tax due on that income. Otherwise, the DWP calculates how much tax to deduct.[83]

For housing benefit (HB), the local authority has discretion to ignore changes in tax rates for up to 30 weeks – eg, where April changes are not reflected in your income until later.[84]

## Benefits

### Benefits that are taken into account

The following count in full:

- carer's allowance (CA) – but not CA supplement in Scotland;[85]
- carer support payment (CSP) (in Scotland);
- child's payment under the Armed Forces Compensation Scheme (but if it is paid for a dependent child, it is usually ignored);
- new-style jobseeker's allowance (JSA);
- contributory employment and support allowance (ESA). If ESA is paid at a reduced rate because of a sanction, it is still the full rate that counts;[86]
- severe disablement allowance;
- industrial injuries benefits, except constant attendance allowance and exceptionally severe disablement allowance, which are disregarded;
- maternity allowance;
- retirement pensions;
- statutory sick pay, statutory maternity pay, statutory adoption pay, statutory paternity pay, statutory shared parental pay, statutory parental bereavement pay and statutory neonatal care pay count for income-related ESA only, less any class 1 NI contributions and half of any pension contributions and any tax.[87] These are treated as earnings for HB and therefore may benefit from an earnings disregard (see p347);[88]
- widow's pension.

### Benefits that are not taken into account

The following are ignored completely:

- adult disability payment (ADP – in Scotland);[89]
- armed forces independence payment;[90]
- attendance allowance (AA);[91]
- bereavement support payment;[92]
- Best Start grants (in Scotland);[93]
- CA supplement (in Scotland);[94]
- child benefit;[95]
- child disability payment (in Scotland);[96]
- Christmas bonus;[97]
- constant attendance allowance, exceptionally severe disablement allowance or severe disablement occupational allowance paid because of an injury at work or a war injury;[98]
- disability living allowance (DLA);[99]
- funeral support payment (in Scotland);[100]
- guardian's allowance;[101]
- HB;[102]

- universal credit (UC), and income-related ESA are ignored for HB.[103] There are special HB rules for these (see p200);
- mobility supplement under the War Pension Scheme;[104]
- pension age disability payment (in Scotland);
- personal independence payment (PIP);[105]
- Scottish adult disability living allowance (SADLA);
- Scottish child payment;[106]
- short-term assistance (in Scotland);[107]
- any extra-statutory payment made to you to compensate for non-payment of IS, income-based JSA, income-related ESA, UC, mobility supplement, AA, DLA, PIP or (except for HB) ADP;[108]
- social fund payments.[109] They are also disregarded as capital indefinitely;[110]
- any supplementary payments to war widows, widowers or surviving civil partners for pre-1973 service;[111]
- any payment made by the DWP to compensate for the loss of HB;[112]
- any payment in consequence of a reduction in liability for council tax, including from a council tax reduction scheme.[113]

## Benefits that are partly taken into account

The following benefits have £10 ignored (or more for HB – see below):[114]

- widowed parent's allowance (£15 is disregarded for HB);[115]
- war disablement pension;[116]
- guaranteed income payment and survivor's guaranteed income payment under the Armed Forces Compensation Scheme (or if another pension reduces the payment to below £10, ignore the remainder from the pension);
- war widow's, widower's or surviving civil partner's pension;
- an extra-statutory payment made instead of the above pensions;
- similar payments made by another country;
- a pension from any government paid to the victims of Nazi persecution.[117]

Even if you have more than two payments which attract a £10 disregard, only £20 in all can be ignored.[118] However, the £10 disregard allowed on the above payments is in addition to the total disregard of any mobility supplement or attendance allowance (ie, constant attendance allowance, exceptionally severe disablement allowance and severe disablement occupational allowance) paid as part of a war disablement pension.

The £10 disregard may overlap with other disregards, such as on student loans and access funds (see p809 and p812), when a combined maximum of £20 is allowed.

Local authorities may have discretionary local schemes to increase the £10 disregard on war disablement pension, war widow's or widower's pension, and the guaranteed income payment and survivor's guaranteed income payment in your HB. Most increase the disregard or ignore the full amount, so check your local scheme.[119]

### Benefit delays

Problems can arise if a decision maker tries to take into account a benefit you are not receiving (such as CA or CSP) because it has been delayed. In such a case, the benefit should not be treated as income you have. For income-related ESA, you should get your full benefit, and the DWP deducts the difference from the arrears of the delayed benefit when it is eventually awarded.[120]

For the treatment of payments of arrears of certain benefits and tax credits, see p408.

### Benefit deductions and overpayments

If any deductions are being taken from your benefit (eg, for an overpayment, rent or bills), the full amount of benefit is taken into account before the deduction is taken off.[121]

## Maintenance payments

If you get **child maintenance** for a child who is a member of your family, it is all ignored if it is made by the child's parent (who is not your partner) or by another 'liable relative' (see below).[122] Child maintenance payments include:

- any payment made voluntarily;
- payments under a court order or consent order;
- child support maintenance (assessed by the Child Maintenance Service);
- in Scotland, payments under a registered maintenance agreement.

**Note:** arrears of regular child support maintenance should be treated as income for a past period. Arrears are ignored as income if, for HB, they cover a period since 27 October 2008 or, for other benefits, since 12 April 2010. Before that, arrears may mean that you have been overpaid benefit, although some overpaid benefits can be deducted from arrears before you get them.[123]

### Other kinds of maintenance

If you get another kind of maintenance payment from a former partner (eg, maintenance for yourself):[124]

- £15 is ignored for HB if a child is part of your family for benefit purposes (see p258) or a family premium included in your HB. If you get maintenance from more than one person, only £15 of the total is ignored;
- for income-related ESA, it is regarded as a 'liable relative' payment and usually counts in full.

***Liable relative***

A **'liable relative'** is:[125]

– a spouse, civil partner, former spouse or civil partner; *or*

- a parent of a child who is a member of your family; *or*
- someone who can reasonably be treated as the child's father because of the financial support they make.



For income-related ESA, any payment from a liable relative other than child maintenance is taken into account in full as income, whether it is paid regularly or as a lump sum, with some exceptions as follows.[126]

- Payments made direct to someone else and not to you (ie, to a third party) are taken into account as maintenance if they are for certain normal living expenses (food, clothing, footwear), for certain bills (fuel, council tax, water charges), for rent met by HB or for housing costs met by ESA (such as service charges). Payments for other expenses, such as mortgage repayments paid direct to the mortgage lender or TV licence payments paid direct, are ignored.[127] This means it can be better for you if your ex-partner pays these other kinds of expenses direct rather than to you. If you use your maintenance payments to pay the mortgage yourself, it is taken into account as your income, so you will get less benefit.
- Payments in kind, such as food, holidays and clothing, are ignored (except if you are involved in a trade dispute).
- Gifts (eg, birthday and Christmas presents) of up to £250 in total in any period of 52 weeks are not taken into account as maintenance, but may count as capital.
- If you have already spent a payment before the DWP makes its decision about the effect on your benefit, the payment is ignored, provided you did not deliberately get rid of the money in order to claim or increase your benefit. The issues are the same as the deprivation of income/capital rule on p413.
- A payment from a disposition of property because of divorce, separation, nullity or dissolution of a civil partnership is not taken into account as maintenance (so is not treated as income), but usually counts as capital. This applies, for example, if your former partner buys out your interest in a home so you get a lump-sum settlement instead of a share of the property itself.[128]
- Payments for a child who is not a member of your household (eg, a child looked after by a local authority and not living with you, or a child in custody) do not count as maintenance. They should be ignored if you spend the money on the child, but count as income if you keep the money or spend it on yourself.[129]
- A payment made after the liable relative has died no longer counts as maintenance (so is not automatically treated as income), but is still taken into account as income or capital under the normal rules.

If you get payments towards maintenance from someone who is not a liable relative (eg, a grandparent), this usually counts as a voluntary payment and is ignored (see below).

### If you pay maintenance

If you *pay* maintenance to a former partner or a child not living with you, your payments are not disregarded for the purpose of calculating your income for any benefits.[130] See p417 if part of a personal or occupational pension is paid to a former partner.



## Student loans and grants

For the special rules on the treatment of student loans, grants and other types of student support, see Chapter 37.

## Adoption, fostering and similar payments

The following payments are disregarded:[131]

- an adoption allowance, unless, in Scotland and Wales,[132] it is paid for a child who is not a member of your family (eg, before the adoption order has been granted), in which case any amount you spend on the child is disregarded and any you keep for yourself is taken into account;
- a fostering allowance while a child is placed with you by a local authority directly or through an independent fostering agency[133] or a voluntary organisation under specific legal provisions.[134] In these fostering arrangements, the child does not count as a member of your family (see p261). If the fostering arrangement is a private one, any money you receive from the child's parent(s) is counted as maintenance (see p355);
- a child arrangements order allowance paid by a local authority (in England and Wales) for a child who is a member of your family. Any payments made by the birth parents count as maintenance (see p355);
- kinship care payments (in Scotland) made under specific legislation;[135]
- a special guardianship allowance (in England and Wales) paid for a child who is a member of your family.

## Charitable, voluntary and personal injury payments

If you receive regular charitable or voluntary payments or certain personal injury payments, they are disregarded as income.[136] If you receive irregular charitable or voluntary payments, they are treated as capital but are unlikely to affect your benefit unless they take your capital above the limit.[137] Single lump sum payments from specified compensation schemes are disregarded indefinitely and other payments may be disregarded as income – eg, from an infected blood scheme (see p410).

Payments from a former partner or the parent of your child are treated as maintenance (see p355). See also p366 for payments made to someone else on your behalf, p364 for payments disregarded under miscellaneous income and p410 for lump sum personal injury payments.

***Definitions***

A **'voluntary payment'** is one given without getting anything back in return.[138]

**'Personal injury payments'** are:[139]

- payments from a trust fund set up out of money paid because of any personal injury to you;
- payments under an annuity purchased either under an agreement or court order set up because of any personal injury to you, or from money paid because of any personal injury to you;
- payments you get under an agreement or court order because of any personal injury to you. This does not include an occupational pension – eg, if you have retired early because of personal injury.[140]

## Income from tenants and lodgers

How income from tenants is treated depends on whether or not you live in the same property.

### Lettings without board

If you let out any rooms in your home to tenants, subtenants or licensees under a formal contractual arrangement, £20 of your weekly charge for each tenant, subtenant or licensee (and their family) is ignored.[141] The balance counts as income.

If someone shares your home under an informal arrangement, any payment they make to you for living and accommodation costs is ignored,[142] but a non-dependant deduction may be made from any HB or housing costs paid with income-related ESA (see p207 and p289).

### Boarders

If you have any boarders on a commercial basis in your own home, and the boarder or any member of their family is not a close relative of yours, the first £20 of the weekly charge is ignored and half of any balance remaining is then taken into account as your income.[143] For HB, this applies even if the boarder is a close relative and it is not a commercial arrangement. However, a non-dependant deduction may be made for them (see p207). This disregard applies for each boarder you have. The charge must normally include at least some meals.[144]

**Note:** if you let part of your home, any income left after applying the above disregards which is intended to be used to meet any housing costs of your own which are not met by income-related ESA or HB, may also be disregarded (see p362).[145]

### Tenants in other properties

If you have a freehold interest in a property other than your home and you let it out, the rent is normally treated as capital.[146] This rule also applies if you have a leasehold interest in another property which you are subletting. The full rent counts initially (as well as the capital value of the property itself) but if you spend some on a debt that is immediately repayable (eg, a monthly mortgage payment) after a period (eg, a month for monthly paid rent), only what remains continues to count as capital. If you spend it on something else to deliberately increase your benefit, the notional capital rules could treat you as still having the money (see p413).[147]

The rent is treated as income if the property you let is in one of the categories where the capital value is disregarded (see p403). In this case, the expenses listed below are deducted from the income. Check if you might be better off claiming universal credit (UC). For UC, rental income is disregarded altogether if the property's capital value is disregarded.

## Income from capital

In general, actual income generated from capital (eg, interest on savings) is ignored as income.[148] It counts as capital from the date you are due to receive it.[149] However, income derived from the following categories of disregarded capital (see p403) is treated as income:[150]

- your home;
- your former home, if you are estranged, divorced or your civil partnership has ended;
- property which you have acquired for occupation as your home, but you have not yet been able to move into;
- property which you intend to occupy as your home, but which needs essential repairs or alterations;
- property occupied wholly or partly by a partner or relative of any member of your family who has reached pension age or who is incapacitated;
- property occupied by your former partner, unless you are estranged, divorced or your civil partnership has ended;
- property for sale;
- property which you are taking legal steps to obtain to occupy as your home;
- your business assets;
- a trust of personal injury compensation.

Some expenses are deducted from this income. Income from property (other than your current home) is ignored up to the amount of the total mortgage repayments (ie, capital and interest, and any payments that are a condition of the mortgage, such as insurance or an endowment policy),[151] council tax and water charges paid in respect of the property for the same period over which the income is received.[152]

## Tariff income from capital

If your capital is over a certain level, you are treated as having an assumed income from it, called your **'tariff income'**. You are assumed to have an income of £1 a week for every £250, or part of £250, by which your capital exceeds £6,000 but does not exceed £16,000.[153]

If you are in a care home or similar accommodation (see p399), tariff income applies between £10,000 and £16,000.

## Capital that counts as income

The following capital is treated as income:

- instalments of capital outstanding when you claim benefit, if they would bring you over the capital limit. The outstanding instalments count as income by spreading them over the number of weeks between each instalment;[154]
- any payment from an annuity[155] (see p361 for when this is disregarded);
- periodic payments made under an agreement or court order for any personal injury to you (see p357 for when these are disregarded);[156]
- some lump sums from liable relatives (see p355).

**Note:** capital counted as income cannot also be treated as producing a tariff income (see above).[157]

Sometimes, you may find that withdrawals from a capital sum are treated as income.[158] This is most likely if the sum was intended to help cover living expenses over a particular period – eg, a bank loan taken out by a student.

## Income tax refunds

Pay as you earn (PAYE) refunds and self-employment tax refunds are treated as capital.[159]

## Income from employment and training programmes

Payments from employment or training programmes under section 2 of the Employment and Training Act 1973 or section 2 of the Enterprise and New Towns (Scotland) Act 1990 are treated as follows.[160]

**The following payments are taken into account:**

- a training allowance; *and*
- payments intended for certain living costs while you are participating in a scheme to enhance your employment prospects. Payments for food, ordinary clothing or footwear, fuel, rent met by HB, housing costs met by income-related ESA, council tax or water charges are all taken into account.

**All other payments are disregarded** – eg:
- travel expenses;
- childcare expenses;
- special needs payments;
- expenses for participating in a specified scheme for assisting people to obtain employment.[161]

For ESA, any payment for expenses incurred in complying with a requirement to undertake work-related activity (see p176) is ignored.[162]



## Occupational and personal pensions and annuities

Although you can usually choose to take some, or all, of your occupational or personal pension from age 55, your benefit is not affected if you do not – ie, there is no notional income or capital assumed. Any regular withdrawals from your pension pot or pension income you take count in full as income. If you take a lump sum, this counts as capital, and notional capital rules can apply to how you spend it (see p413).[163] If your partner has reached pension age and chooses not to take income from an occupational or personal pension, you are treated as having notional income. If you (or your partner) have reached pension age, see also p389.

Discretionary payments from a hardship fund are not regarded as an occupational pension, but are treated as charitable or voluntary payments (see p357).[164]

Payments from an annuity count in full unless:
- the annuity is set up with money paid because of personal injury to you, or under an agreement or court order because of personal injury to you (see p357); *or*
- the annuity is set up with money from a home income plan, in which case income from the annuity equal to the interest payable on the loan with which the annuity was bought is ignored if:[165]
  - you used at least 90 per cent of the loan made to you to buy the annuity; *and*
  - the annuity will end when you and your partner die; *and*
  - you or your partner are responsible for paying the interest on the loan; *and*
  - you (if you took out the loan), or your partner (if they did), were at least 65 at the time the loan was made; *and*
  - the loan is secured on a property which you or your partner own or in which you have an interest, and the property on which the loan is secured is your home, or that of your partner.

  If the interest on the loan is payable after income tax has been deducted, it is an amount equal to the net interest payment that is disregarded. Otherwise, it is the gross amount of the interest payment.

## Mortgage and insurance payments

For income-related ESA only, ignore:

- payments you receive under a mortgage insurance policy which you use to maintain mortgage payments;[166]
- provided you have not already used mortgage protection insurance payments for the same purpose, any money you receive which is given, and which you use, to make the following payments:[167]
  - payments due on a secured loan that does not qualify for a DWP support for mortgage interest (SMI) loan (see p764);
  - capital payments and interest payments on a loan that qualifies for a DWP SMI loan, but which are not met by the DWP loan;
  - service charges and other eligible housing costs that are not met by the help you get with housing costs in your benefit (see Chapter 14);
- payments of premiums on an insurance policy which you took out to insure against the risk of not being able to make the payments in the above three categories, and premiums on a buildings insurance policy;
- payment of any rent that is not covered by HB (see Chapter 10);
- payment of the part of your accommodation charge in a care home that exceeds that payable by a local authority.

***Example***

Roshan is on income-related ESA. He is an owner-occupier with a mortgage. He gets a DWP SMI loan, which pays £300 a month towards his interest payments of £400 a month. He still has to pay £100 a month mortgage interest, £200 a month capital repayments and £30 a month premiums on his buildings insurance, which totals £330. He receives £360 a month from an income protection insurance policy. Of this, £330 is ignored and £30 a month counts as his income.

If you are using maintenance from a former partner or parent of your child (but not child maintenance, which is disregarded whatever you use it for) to pay these costs, it may be taken into account as a 'liable relative payment', unless it is paid direct to someone else – eg, a lender (see p355).

For HB only, payments you receive under an insurance policy to insure against the risk of being unable to maintain payments on a loan secured on your home are ignored. However, anything you get above the total of the following counts as your income:[168]

- the amount you use to maintain your payments; *and*
- any premium you pay for the policy; *and*
- any premium for an insurance policy to insure against loss or damage to your home.

Payments you receive under an insurance policy to insure against the risk of being unable to maintain hire purchase or similar payments or other loan payments (eg, credit card debts) are also ignored. However, anything you get above the amount you use to make your payments and the premium for the policy counts as your income.[169]



## Social services, community care and other payments

**The following payments are ignored:**

- local welfare assistance to meet an immediate short-term need or establish or maintain a settled home in certain circumstances (see p770). These include household support fund payments and 'thank you' payments under the Homes for Ukraine scheme;[170]
- payments from a local authority for children, families and people in need, made under section 17 of the Children Act 1989, section 12 of the Social Work (Scotland) Act 1968, section 22 of the Children (Scotland) Act 1995 or sections 37 or 38 of the Social Services and Well-being (Wales) Act 2014;[171]
- payments from a local authority for young people who were previously looked after by the local authority, paid under sections 23B or 24A of the Children Act 1989, section 30 of the Children (Scotland) Act 1995 or sections 109, 110, 114 or 115 of the Social Services and Well-being (Wales) Act 2014. A payment under section 23C of the Children Act 1989 is also ignored as the young person's income and as yours if the young person passes it to you, they were in your care, are still living with you and are aged 18 or over – eg, under 'staying put' arrangements. In Scotland, this applies to payments under sections 26A and 29 of the Children (Scotland) Act 1995 and includes young people aged 16 or over in 'continuing care';[172]
- direct payments to you under an education, health and care plan for a child with special educational needs (paid in England);[173]
- any community care or healthcare direct payments. Local authorities or the NHS pay these to disabled people or carers to buy their own services instead of providing services direct. A direct payment is not ignored as the income of the person you pay for services, even if this is your partner;[174]
- any payment you or your partner receive for looking after someone who is temporarily in your care if it is paid under community care arrangements by the NHS, local authority, voluntary organisation or the person being looked after.[175] Any HB paid to you by a local authority for that person is not ignored, although see p358 for other possible disregards;
- payments from a local authority for support services to help you live independently (eg, under the Supporting People programme, often called 'housing-related support') are ignored indefinitely;[176]
- if you live in a care home and a local authority arranged your place, local authority payments towards your fees are ignored for income-related ESA. If a

local authority did not arrange your place, any payment intended and used for your maintenance is fully disregarded if it is a voluntary or charitable payment, and partly disregarded if not – up to the difference between the care home fees and your applicable amount;[177]

- a lump-sum payment from a local authority to enable you to make adaptations to your home for a disabled child. This is treated as capital and ignored.[178]

3

## Miscellaneous income

**The following income is ignored:**

- any discretionary housing payments paid by a local authority;[179]
- education maintenance allowances (paid in Scotland and Wales) and 16 to 19 bursary fund payments (paid in England).[180] These are paid to some young people staying on at school or other non-advanced education;
- any payment to cover your expenses if you are working as an unpaid volunteer or working unpaid for a charity or voluntary organisation;[181]
- payments in kind.[182] These may include food, fuel, cigarettes,[183] clothing, holidays, gifts, accommodation, transport or nursery education vouchers. Cash in lieu of concessionary coal to former British Coal workers counts in full.[184] However, see p365 for the rules on notional income and p341 for the rules on non-cash vouchers paid as earnings. Items for essential living needs provided by the Home Office to an asylum-seeking partner are ignored for income-related ESA;
- a payment (other than a training allowance) to a disabled person under the Disabled Persons (Employment) Act 1944 to assist them to obtain or retain employment;[185]
- any payments, other than for loss of earnings or a benefit, made to jurors or witnesses for attending court;[186]
- Victoria Cross or George Cross payments or similar awards;[187]
- income paid outside the UK which cannot be transferred here;[188]
- if income is paid in another currency, any bank charges for converting the payment into sterling;[189]
- fares to hospital and refunds for prescription or dental charges;[190]
- payments instead of milk tokens and vitamins, or instead of Healthy Start;[191]
- payments to assist with prison visits;[192]
- for HB, if you make a parental contribution to a student's grant or loan, an equal amount of any 'unearned' income you have for the period the grant or loan is paid. If your unearned income does not cover the contribution, the balance can be disregarded from your earnings;[193]
- a sports award made by UK Sport from National Lottery funds for living expenses is taken into account. This covers food, ordinary clothing or footwear, fuel, council tax, water charges and rent (less any non-dependant deductions) for which HB could be payable or housing costs that could be met by income-

related ESA. Payments for anything else are ignored – eg, sportswear and dietary supplements to enhance performance;[194]

- any payment for expenses if you are being consulted as a service user by the DWP or a health, care or housing body that provides statutory services (expenses do not count as earnings either).[195]



## 5. Notional income

In certain circumstances, you may be treated as having income, even if you do not possess it or if you have used it up.

### Deliberately getting rid of income

If you deliberately get rid of income in order to claim or increase your benefit, you are treated as though you still receive that income.[196] The basic issues involved are the same as those for deliberately getting rid of capital (see p413). **Note:** the rule only applies if your intention was to gain benefit for yourself or your partner. It should not apply if, for example, you stop claiming carer's allowance (CA) solely to allow the cared-for person to get a severe disability premium unless it is your partner (see p275).[197] However, if you do not claim a benefit which would clearly be paid if you did, it may be argued that you have failed to apply for income (see below).

You are not automatically treated as having the income if you claim universal credit (UC) instead, although the income could be considered under the UC rules (see p143).

### Failing to apply for income

If you fail to apply for income you are entitled to without having to fulfil further conditions, you are treated as having it from the date you could have obtained it.[198]

This does *not* include, for example, income from:

- a discretionary trust;
- a trust set up from money paid as a result of a personal injury;
- funds administered by a court as a result of a personal injury;
- a rehabilitation allowance made under the Employment and Training Act 1973;
- jobseeker's allowance and employment and support allowance (for ESA only);
- if you are under pension age (see p239), a personal or occupational pension scheme or payments from the Pension Protection Fund. However, if you or your partner have reached pension age and choose not to take your full pension, you are treated as having an income.[199]

It must be certain that the income or benefits would be paid if you were to apply. For example, it may be difficult for the DWP to establish that there was 'no doubt' that CA would be paid to you if you have chosen not to claim it because of the effect on the benefit of the person you are caring for (see p275).[200]

As soon as you apply or make a claim, the rule ceases to apply.[201]



## Income due to you that has not been paid

For income-related ESA only, you are treated as possessing any income that is owing to you – eg:[202]

- wages that are legally due to you, but are not paid;
- an occupational pension payment that is due but has not been received, unless the pension scheme has insufficient funds.[203]

This rule should not apply if:

- any social security benefit has been delayed; *or*
- you are waiting for a late payment of a government training allowance or a benefit from a European Economic Area country; *or*
- money is due to you from a discretionary trust or a trust set up from money paid as a result of a personal injury; *or*
- you are owed earnings when your job has ended because of redundancy but these have not been paid to you.[204]

The income must be due to *you* (or your family) and for your own benefit.[205]

### Unpaid wages

For income-related ESA only, if you have wages due to you, but you do not yet know the exact amount or you have no proof of what they will be, you are treated as having a wage similar to that normally paid for that type of work in that area.[206] If your wages cannot be estimated, you may qualify for a short-term advance (see p1023).[207] For how wages are estimated for housing benefit, see p370.

## Income paid to someone else on your behalf

If money is paid to someone on your behalf (eg, a landlord for your rent), this can count as notional income.[208] If so, it is still subject to the usual disregards that would apply if it were actual income – eg, a voluntary or charitable payment of income is ignored whether it is paid direct to you or to someone else on your behalf. See p416 for a description of these third-party rules – they are the same as those for notional capital.

Income in kind given to a third party for you is ignored (eg, a food parcel used to prepare meals for you). However, money given to someone who uses it to buy you goods or services counts as notional income under the usual rules.

## Income paid to you for someone else

If you or your partner get a payment for someone not in the 'family' (eg, a relative living with you), it counts as your income if you keep any of it yourself or spend it on yourself or your partner unless it is, for example:[209]

- from a specified infected blood scheme (see p410);
- income in kind – eg, a food parcel given to you to make meals for someone else.



## Cheap or unpaid labour

If you are helping another person or an organisation by doing work that would normally be paid, or be paid a higher wage, you are deemed to receive a wage similar to that normally paid for that kind of job in that area.[210]

The burden of proving that your work is something for which an employer would pay, and what the comparable wages are, lies with the decision maker in the DWP or local authority.[211]

The rule does not apply if:[212]

- you are on an unpaid approved work placement or work experience; *or*
- you are on a government employment or training programme with no training allowance, or only travel or meals expenses; *or*
- you can show that the person (including a limited company[213]) cannot, in fact, afford to pay, or afford to pay more; *or*
- you work for a charitable or voluntary organisation or as a volunteer, and it is accepted that it is reasonable for you to give your services free of charge.[214]

Sometimes it may also be reasonable to do a job free of charge from a sense of community duty, particularly if the job would otherwise remain undone and there would be no financial profit to an employer.[215]

If you are caring for a sick or disabled relative, it is usually accepted that it is reasonable to do this free of charge rather than expecting them to pay you from benefits. However, if you need to show that it is reasonable, you should take into account, for instance:[216]

- how much care you give and what other care options there are;
- your housing arrangements;
- whether you gave up work to care;
- the risk of your losing entitlement to CA if you were paid, or to a social services assessment of your needs;
- whether your relative would actually pay you.

# 6. Working out weekly income

## Income-related employment and support allowance

To work out your weekly income for income-related employment and support allowance (ESA), you should do the following.



- Work out the period covered by the income (see below).
- Establish the date from when to start taking the income into account (see below).
- Convert the income into a weekly amount if necessary (see p369). There are special rules on variable income, payments for less than a week and overlapping payments.

These rules apply to earnings from employment and to income other than earnings. These rules also apply to your (but not your partner's) earnings if you are claiming new-style jobseeker's allowance (JSA). See p346 for how self-employed earnings are assessed.

### Period covered by a payment

- If a payment of income is made for an identifiable period, it is taken into account for a period of equal length.[217] For example, a week's part-time earnings are taken into account for a week. If you are paid monthly, the payments are taken into account for the number of weeks between the date you are treated as having been paid and the date you are next due to be paid.
- If the payment does not relate to a particular period, the amount of the payment is divided by the amount of the weekly income-related ESA to which you would otherwise be entitled. If part of the payment should be disregarded, the amount of income-related ESA is increased by the appropriate disregard. The result of this calculation is the number of weeks that you are not entitled to income-related ESA.[218] **Note**: if your benefit is stopped, you cannot make a new claim. If you claim universal credit (UC) instead, the payment is assessed under UC rules.
- Payments made on leaving a job, if not ignored, are taken into account for a forward period (see p343).

### Date from when a payment counts

The date from when a payment of earnings and/or other income counts depends on when it was due to be paid. If it was due to be paid before you claimed new-style JSA or income-related ESA, it counts from the date on which it was due to be paid.[219] Otherwise, it is treated as having been paid on the first day of the benefit week in which it is due, or on the first day of the first benefit week after that in which it is practicable to take it into account.[220]

Payments of UC, new-style JSA, ESA and maternity allowance (MA) are treated as paid on a daily basis for each day for which they are paid.[221]

*Benefit week*

The **'benefit week'** for ESA, although this may vary, is normally the seven days ending with the day allocated to you according to your national insurance number (also your payday).[222] The benefit week for HB is the seven days starting on a Monday.[223]



The date a payment is due may be different from the date of actual payment. Earnings are due on the employee's normal payday. If the contract of employment does not reveal the date of due payment and there is no evidence to indicate otherwise, the date the payment was received should be taken as the date it was due.[224] If your contract of employment is terminated without proper notice, outstanding wages, wages in hand, holiday pay and any pay in lieu of notice are due on the last day of employment and are treated as having been paid on that day, even if this does not happen (although these are usually disregarded).[225]

If you receive compensation (eg, in a sex discrimination equal pay case), the relevant date is probably the date when the earnings in question were due to be paid,[226] not when the compensation was awarded.[227]

For the treatment of payments at the end of a job, see p343.

## Converting income into a weekly amount

To convert income to a weekly amount:

- if the payment is for less than a week, it is treated as the weekly amount;
- if the payment is for a month, multiply by 12 and divide by 52;
- multiply a payment for three months by four and divide by 52;
- divide a payment for a year by 52;
- for any other period, divide the payment by the number of days in the period then multiply by seven.

If you work on certain days but are paid monthly, it is necessary to decide whether the payment is for the days worked or for the whole month. This generally depends on the terms of your contract of employment,[228] but may depend on how your employer has arranged to make payments to you.[229]

### Variable income

If your income fluctuates or your earnings vary because you do not work every week, your weekly income may be averaged over the cycle if there is an identifiable one or, if there is not, over five weeks, or over another period if this would be more accurate.[230] If the cycle involves periods when you do no work, those periods are included in the cycle, but not other absences – eg, holidays or sickness.

3

#### Part weeks

- If you are paid for a period of a week or more and only part of it is counted in a particular benefit week (see p369), multiply the whole payment by the number of days it covers in the benefit week, then divide the result by the total number of days covered by the payment.[231]
- If any payment of MA falls partly into the benefit week, only the amount paid for those days is taken into account. For any payment of JSA or ESA, the amount taken into account is the weekly amount multiplied by the number of days in the part week and divided by seven.[232]

#### Overlapping payments

If you have regularly received a certain kind of payment of income from one source and in a particular benefit week (see p369) you receive that payment and another of the same kind from the same source (eg, if your employer first pays you sick pay in arrears and this then overlaps with a payment in advance), the maximum amount to be taken into account is the one paid first.[233]

This does not apply if the second payment was due to be taken into account in another week, but the overlapping week is the first in which it could practically be counted (see p368).

## Housing benefit

To assess your current normal weekly income for HB, you should do the following.

- Average your earnings over a past period (see below for earnings from employment and p346 for self-employed earnings).
- Estimate income other than earnings (see p352 for what income counts) by looking at an appropriate period of up to 52 weeks. The period chosen must give an accurate assessment of your income.[234]
- Convert earnings from employment and income other than earnings into a weekly amount if necessary:
  - count a payment for less than a week as the weekly amount;
  - multiply a monthly payment by 12 and divide by 52;
  - for other periods, divide the payment by the number of days in the period then multiply by seven.
- Deduct the appropriate earnings disregard(s) (see p347).
- Work out the date from when the income is taken into account (see p371).

### Averaging earnings

For HB, earnings as an employee are usually averaged out over the previous:[235]

- five weeks if you are paid weekly; *or*
- two months if you are paid monthly.

If your earnings vary, or if there is likely to be, or has recently been, a change (eg, you usually do overtime but have not done so recently, or you are about to get a pay rise), the local authority may average them over a different period if this is likely to give a more accurate picture of what you are going to earn.[236]

If you are on strike, the local authority should not take into account your pre-strike earnings and average them out over the strike period.[237]

If you have only just started work and your earnings cannot be averaged over the normal period (ie, five weeks or two months), an estimate is made, based on any earnings you have been paid so far if these are likely to reflect your future average wage. If you have not yet been paid or your initial earnings do not represent what you will normally earn, your employer must provide an estimate of your average weekly earnings.[238] If you start work after having been on certain benefits, you may get four weeks' extended payments of HB at the same amount (see p224). If your earnings change during your award, your new weekly average figure is estimated based on what you are likely to earn over whatever period (up to 52 weeks) best allows an accurate estimate.[239] If averaging does not result in a weekly figure, the amount is converted (see p370).



### Date from when a payment counts

The average weekly earnings from employment are taken into account for HB from the start of a new claim or from the first day of the benefit week (see p369) after you start work if you are already getting HB. If average weekly earnings change, the new amount counts from the date of change, even if you are not paid until later.[240]

Other benefits are taken into account for the period they are paid for.[241]

## Notes

1 **Whose income counts**

1 **HB** s136(1) SSCBA 1992
**ESA** Sch 1 para 6(2) WRA 2007; reg 83 ESA Regs

2 **ESA** Reg 83(2) ESA Regs
**HB** Reg 25(3) HB Regs

3 Schs 4 para 12 and 5 para 4 HB Regs

2. **What counts as income**

4 Schs 4 para 12 and 5 para 4 HB Regs

5 R(IS) 4/01; see *BL v SSWP (SPC)* [2018] UKUT 4 (AAC) for the meaning of income

6 *R v SBC ex parte Singer* [1973] 1 WLR 713 (cited in CH/412/2007)

7 *Minter v Kingston Upon Hull City Council and Potter v SSWP* [2011] EWCA Civ 1155

3. **Earnings**

8 **JSA** Reg 58(1) JSA Regs 2013
**ESA** Reg 95(1) ESA Regs; reg 80(1) ESA Regs 2013
**HB** Reg 35(1) HB Regs
**All** R(SB) 21/86

9 Reg 35(1)(i)-(j) HB Regs

10 **JSA** Reg 58(2)(c) JSA Regs 2013
**ESA** Regs 95(2)(b) and 104(8) and Sch 8 paras 1 and 4 ESA Regs; reg 80(2)(b) ESA Regs 2013
11 **JSA** Reg 58(1)(d) JSA Regs 2013
**ESA** Reg 95(1)(e) ESA Regs; reg 80(1)(e) ESA Regs 2013
**HB** Reg 35(1)(e) HB Regs
12 R(IS) 9/95
13 **JSA** Reg 67(4)(d) JSA Regs 2013
**ESA** Reg 95(4), definition of 'compensation', ESA Regs; reg 80(4) ESA Regs 2013
14 *Minter v Kingston Upon Hull City Council and Potter v SSWP* [2011] EWCA Civ 1155
15 **JSA** Reg 58(1)(i) JSA Regs 2013
**ESA** Reg 95(1)(k) ESA Regs; reg 80(1)(k) ESA Regs 2013
**HB** Reg 35(1)(k) HB Regs
16 **JSA** Reg 58(3) JSA Regs 2013
**ESA** Reg 95(3) ESA Regs; reg 80(3) ESA Regs 2013
**HB** Reg 35(3) HB Regs
17 **JSA** Reg 58(2)(a) JSA Regs 2013
**ESA** Reg 95(2)(a) and Sch 8 para 22 ESA Regs; reg 80(2)(a) ESA Regs 2013
**HB** Reg 35(2)(a) and Sch 5 para 23 HB Regs
18 CIS/11482/1995
19 para 26096 DMG
20 **JSA** Reg 58(2)(d) JSA Regs 2013
**ESA** Reg 95(2)(c) ESA Regs; reg 80(2)(c) ESA Regs 2013
**HB** Reg 35(2)(b) HB Regs
21 R(FIS) 4/85; R(FC) 1/91; R(IS) 13/91
22 CIS/77/1993; CIS/89/1989
23 **JSA** Sch para 9 JSA Regs 2013
**ESA** Sch 7 para 9 ESA Regs
**HB** Sch 4 para 13 HB Regs
24 **JSA** Reg 58(2)(e) JSA Regs 2013
**ESA** Reg 95(2)(d) ESA Regs; reg 80(2)(d) ESA Regs 2013
**HB** Reg 35(2)(c) HB Regs
25 **ESA** Reg 104(8) and Sch 8 para 1 ESA Regs
**HB** Reg 40(10) and Sch 5 para 1 HB Regs
26 *Parsons v Hogg* [1985] 2 All ER 897 (CA), appendix to R(FIS) 4/85
27 **JSA** Reg 59(1) and (3) JSA Regs 2013
**ESA** Reg 96(3) ESA Regs; reg 81(2) ESA Regs 2013
**HB** Reg 36(3) HB Regs
28 *SSWP v NC (ESA)* [2024] UKUT 251
29 Regs 29(2) and 36(6) HB Regs
30 Reg 34 HB Regs; para BW2.34 GM
31 **JSA** Reg 58 JSA Regs 2013
**ESA** Reg 95 ESA Regs
**HB** Reg 35 HB Regs
32 R(JSA) 1/06
33 **JSA** Reg 58(2)(c) JSA Regs 2013
**ESA** Regs 95(2)(b) and 104(8) ESA Regs
34 **JSA** Sch paras 1(1)(a) and (2) and 2 JSA Regs 2013
**HB** Sch 4 paras 1(b) and 2(b)(i) HB Regs
35 **JSA** Reg 58(1)(f) JSA Regs 2013
**HB** Reg 35(1)(g) HB Regs
36 **JSA** Sch paras 1(1)(a), (2)(a)(ii), (2)(b)(ii) and 2 JSA Regs 2013
**HB** Sch 4 paras 1(b)(i)(bb), (b)(ii)(bb) and 2 HB Regs
37 **JSA** Reg 58(2)(c) JSA Regs 2013
**HB** Reg 35(1)(I)-(j) HB Regs
38 **JSA** Reg 58(2)(f) JSA Regs 2013
**HB** Because not listed as earnings in reg 35 HB Regs
39 Regs 98(1)(b), (3) and 104(4) and Sch 6 para 1(1) JSA Regs
40 **JSA** Reg 58(1)(b) and Sch paras 1(1)(a) and 2 JSA Regs 2013
**HB** Reg 35 HB Regs
**Both** CJSA/82/98
41 **JSA** Regs 98(2)(b) and 103(6)(a) JSA Regs; reg 58(2)(b) JSA Regs 2013
**HB** Reg 35(1)(b) HB Regs
42 **JSA** Regs 98(1)(c) and 110(3) JSA Regs; reg 58(1)(c) JSA Regs 2013
**HB** Regs 35(1)(d) and 46(3) HB Regs
43 **JSA** Reg 58(2)(c) JSA Regs 2013
**ESA** Regs 95(2)(b) and 104(8) ESA Regs
44 Reg 35(1)(i)-(j) and Sch 4 paras 1(c) and 2(b)(ii) HB Regs
45 **JSA** Reg 58(1)(c) and Sch paras 1(1)(b) and 2 JSA Regs 2013
**ESA** Regs 95(1)(d) and 112(3) and Sch 7 paras 1(1)(b) and 2 ESA Regs
**HB** Regs 35(1)(d) and 46(3) and Sch 4 paras 1(c) and 2(b)(ii) HB Regs
46 **JSA** Sch paras 1(1)(b) and 2 JSA Regs 2013
**ESA** Sch 7 paras 1(1)(b) and 2 ESA Regs
**HB** Sch 4 paras 1(c) and 2(b)(ii) HB Regs
47 **JSA** Regs 60(1) and 61(3) JSA Regs 2013
**ESA** Regs 97(1) and 98(3) ESA Regs; regs 82(1) and 83(2) ESA Regs 2013
**HB** Regs 37 and 38(3) HB Regs
48 *AR v Bradford MDC* [2008] UKUT 30 (AAC), reported as R(H) 6/09
49 **JSA** Reg 60(2)(a) JSA Regs 2013
**ESA** Reg 97(2)(a) ESA Regs; reg 82(2)(a) ESA Regs 2013
**HB** Sch 5 para 42 HB Regs

50 **JSA** Reg 61(3) and (7) JSA Regs 2013
**ESA** Reg 98(3)(a), (4), (7) and (8)(a) ESA Regs; reg 83(2)(a), (3), (6) and (7)(a) ESA Regs 2013
**HB** Reg 38(3)(a), (4), (7) and (8)(a) HB Regs
51 R(IS) 13/91; R(FC) 1/91; CFC/26/1989
52 **JSA** Reg 61(6) and (8) JSA Regs 2013
**ESA** Reg 98(6) and (8)(b) ESA Regs; reg 83(5) and (7)(b) ESA Regs 2013
**HB** Reg 38(6) and (8)(b) HB Regs
53 **JSA** Reg 61(5) and (7) JSA Regs 2013
**ESA** Reg 98(5) ESA Regs; reg 83(4) ESA Regs 2013
**HB** Reg 38(5) HB Regs
54 *SSWP v SK (CA)* [2013] UKUT 12 (AAC), reported as [2014] AACR 24
55 CFC/836/1995
56 **JSA** Regs 55 and 61(10) JSA Regs 2013
**ESA** Regs 92 and 98(10) ESA Regs; regs 77 and 83(9) ESA Regs 2013
57 para 27054 DMG, but see *GM v SSWP (JSA)* [2010] UKUT 221 (AAC), reported as [2011] AACR 9
58 Regs 30(1) and 33(2) HB Regs
59 **JSA** Reg 55(2) JSA Regs 2013
**ESA** Reg 92(2) ESA Regs
**HB** Reg 37(3) and (4) HB Regs
60 **JSA** Sch para 4 JSA Regs 2013
**ESA** Sch 7 para 4 ESA Regs
**HB** Sch 4 para 2A HB Regs
61 **JSA** Reg 61(9) JSA Regs 2013
**ESA** Reg 98(9) ESA Regs; reg 83(8) ESA Regs 2013
**HB** Reg 38(9) HB Regs
62 Sch 7 paras 5 and 5A ESA Regs
63 Sch 7 para 6 ESA Regs
64 Reg 88 ESA Regs; reg 39(5) ESA Regs 2013
65 Sch 7 paras 7 and 14 ESA Regs
66 Sch 4 para 4 HB Regs
67 Sch 4 para 3(2) HB Regs
68 Sch 4 para 3(2) HB Regs
69 Sch 4 paras 5 and 6 HB Regs
70 Sch 4 para 8(1) HB Regs
71 Sch 4 para 9 HB Regs
72 Sch 4 para 8(2)(b) HB Regs
73 Sch 4 paras 7 and 10 HB Regs
74 Sch 4 para 10A HB Regs
75 Sch 4 para 17 HB Regs
76 Regs 27(1)(c) and 28 HB Regs; reg 30(1)(c) HB(SPC) Regs
77 Reg 28(6) HB Regs; reg 31(6) HB(SPC) Regs
78 Reg 28(13) HB Regs; reg 31(13) HB(SPC) Regs
79 Reg 28(6)-(8) HB Regs; reg 31(6)-(8) HB(SPC) Regs
80 Reg 28(14) HB Regs; reg 31(14) HB(SPC) Regs
81 Reg 28(2)-(4) HB Regs; reg 31(2)-(4) HB(SPC) Regs
82 Reg 28(11), (12) and (12A) HB Regs; reg 31(11), (12) and (12A) HB(SPC) Regs

4. **Other income**

83 R(IS) 4/05
84 Reg 34 HB Regs; BW2.34 GM
85 **ESA** Sch 8 para 69 ESA Regs
**HB** Sch 5 para 68 HB Regs
86 Reg 40(5A) HB Regs
87 Reg 95(2) and Sch 8 para 4 ESA Regs
88 Reg 35(1)(i) HB Regs
89 **ESA** Sch 8 paras 8 and 11 ESA Regs
**HB** Sch 5 para 73 HB Regs
90 **ESA** Sch 8 para 66 ESA Regs
**HB** Sch 5 para 6 HB Regs
91 **ESA** Sch 8 para 11 ESA Regs
**HB** Sch 5 para 9 HB Regs
92 **ESA** Sch 8 para 68 ESA Regs
**HB** Sch 5 para 67 HB Regs
93 **ESA** Sch 8 para 70 ESA Regs
**HB** Sch 5 para 69 HB Regs
94 **ESA** Sch 8 para 69 ESA Regs
**HB** Sch 5 para 68 HB Regs
95 **ESA** Sch 8 para 7(2) ESA Regs
**HB** Sch 5 para 65 HB Regs
96 **ESA** Sch 8 para 71 ESA Regs
**HB** Sch 5 para 73 HB Regs
97 **ESA** Sch 8 para 37 ESA Regs
**HB** Sch 5 para 32 HB Regs
98 **ESA** Sch 8 para 11 ESA Regs
**HB** Sch 5 paras 6 and 9 HB Regs
99 **ESA** Sch 8 paras 8 and 11 ESA Regs
**HB** Sch 5 para 6 HB Regs
100 **ESA** Sch 8 para 71 ESA Regs
**HB** Sch 5 para 70 HB Regs
101 **ESA** Sch 8 para 6 ESA Regs
**HB** Sch 5 para 50 HB Regs
102 **ESA** Sch 8 paras 64 ESA Regs
**HB** Sch 5 HB Regs
103 Sch 5 para 4 HB Regs
104 **ESA** Sch 8 para 10 ESA Regs
**HB** Sch 5 para 8 HB Regs
105 **ESA** Sch 8 paras 8 and 11 ESA Regs
**HB** Sch 5 para 6 HB Regs
106 **ESA** Sch 8 para 72 ESA Regs
**HB** Sch 5 para 71 HB Regs
107 **ESA** Sch 8 para 73 ESA Regs
**HB** Sch 5 para 72 HB Regs
108 **ESA** Sch 8 paras 9 and 10 ESA Regs
**HB** Sch 5 paras 7 and 8 HB Regs
109 **ESA** Sch 8 para 35 ESA Regs
**HB** Sch 5 para 31 HB Regs
110 **ESA** Sch 9 para 23 ESA Regs
**HB** Sch 6 para 20 HB Regs

3

111 **ESA** Sch 8 paras 49, 51 and 52 ESA Regs
**HB** Sch 5 paras 53-55 HB Regs
112 **ESA** Sch 8 para 42 ESA Regs
**HB** Sch 5 para 36 HB Regs
113 **ESA** Sch 8 para 44 ESA Regs
**HB** Sch 5 para 41 HB Regs
114 **ESA** Sch 8 para 17 ESA Regs
**HB** Sch 5 para 15 HB Regs; Sch Part 2 HB&CTB(WPD) Regs
115 **ESA** Sch 8 para 17 ESA Regs
**HB** Sch 5 para 15 HB Regs; Sch Part 2 HB&CTB(WPD) Regs
116 Sch 5 para 16 HB Regs
117 *MN v (1) Bury Council (2) SSWP (HB)* [2014] UKUT 187 (AAC)
118 **ESA** Sch 8 para 39 ESA Regs
**HB** Sch 5 para 34 HB Regs
119 s134(8) SSAA 1992; HB&CTB(WPD) Regs
120 s74(2) SSAA 1992; reg 17 CA(CSP)(S) Regs
121 **ESA** Reg 104(1) and (3) ESA Regs
**HB** Reg 40(1) and (5) HB Regs
122 **ESA** Sch 8 para 60 ESA Regs
**HB** Sch 5 para 47A HB Regs
123 *KW v Lancaster City Council v SSWP (HB)* [2011] UKUT 266 (AAC); s74A SSAA 1992
124 Sch 5 para 47 HB Regs
125 Reg 119 ESA Regs
126 Regs 119 and 120 ESA Regs
127 Reg 107(3)(c) ESA Regs
128 R(SB) 1/89
129 Reg 107(4) ESA Regs
130 CIS/683/1993
131 **ESA** Sch 8 paras 26 and 28 ESA Regs
**HB** Sch 5 paras 25 and 26 HB Regs
132 **ESA** Reg 107(4) ESA Regs
**HB** Reg 42(6)(c) HB Regs
**Both** Vol 9 Ch 51 para 51215 DMG
133 *Hillingdon LBC v EB* [2021] UKUT 208 (AAC)
134 Under ss22C(2) or 59(1)(a) Children Act 1989, s81(2) Social Services and Well-being (Wales) Act 2014 or s26 Children (Scotland) Act 1995 or regs 33 or 51 Looked After Children (Scotland) Regulations 2009 No.210.
135 Under s73 Children and Young People (Scotland) Act 2014, s22 Children (Scotland) Act 1995, reg 33 Looked After Children (Scotland) Regulations 2009 or s50 Children Act 1975
136 **ESA** Sch 8 para 16 ESA Regs
**HB** Sch 5 para 14 HB Regs
137 **ESA** Reg 112(7) ESA Regs
**HB** Reg 46(6) HB Regs
138 R(H) 5/05 explains the difference between a loan and a voluntary payment
139 **ESA** Sch 8 para 16(3) ESA Regs
**HB** Sch 5 para 14 HB Regs
140 *Malekout v SSWP* [2010] EWCA Civ 162, reported as [2010] AACR 28
141 **ESA** Sch 8 para 20 ESA Regs
**HB** Sch 5 para 22 HB Regs
142 **ESA** Sch 8 para 19 ESA Regs
**HB** Sch 5 para 21 HB Regs
143 **ESA** Sch 8 para 21 ESA Regs
**HB** Sch 5 para 42 HB Regs
144 **ESA** Reg 2(1), definition of 'board and lodging', ESA Regs
**HB** Sch 5 para 42(2), definition of 'board and lodging accommodation', HB Regs
145 CIS/13059/1996
146 **ESA** Reg 112(4) ESA Regs
**HB** Reg 46(4) HB Regs
**Both** *CAO v Palfrey and Others, The Times*, 17 February 1995; R(IS) 26/95
147 CIS/563/1991
148 **ESA** Sch 8 para 23(1) ESA Regs
**HB** Sch 5 para 17(1) HB Regs
149 **ESA** Reg 112(4) ESA Regs
**HB** Reg 46(4) HB Regs
150 **ESA** Sch 8 para 23(2) ESA Regs
**HB** Sch 5 para 17(1) HB Regs
151 CFC/13/1993
152 **ESA** Sch 8 para 23(2) and (3) ESA Regs
**HB** Sch 5 para 17(2) HB Regs
153 **ESA** Reg 118 ESA Regs
**HB** Reg 52 HB Regs
154 **ESA** Reg 91(2) ESA Regs
**HB** Reg 33 HB Regs
155 **ESA** Reg 105(2) ESA Regs
**HB** Reg 41(2) HB Regs
156 **ESA** Reg 105(5) ESA Regs
**HB** Reg 41(5) HB Regs
157 **ESA** Sch 9 para 25 ESA Regs
**HB** Sch 6 para 22 HB Regs
158 *R v SBC ex parte Singer* [1973] 1 All ER 931; *R v Oxford County Council ex parte Jack* [1984] 17 HLR 419; *R v West Dorset DC ex parte Poupard* [1988] 20 HLR 295
159 **ESA** Reg 112(2) ESA Regs
**HB** Reg 46(2) HB Regs
160 **ESA** Sch 8 para 15 ESA Regs
**HB** Sch 5 para 13 HB Regs
161 **ESA** Sch 8 para 1A ESA Regs
**HB** Sch 5 paras A2 and A3 HB Regs
162 Sch 8 para 15A ESA Regs
163 Vol 5 Ch 28 para 28627 DMG
164 Vol 5 Ch 28 para 28090 DMG

165 **ESA** Reg 105(2) and Sch 8 para 18 ESA Regs
**HB** Reg 41(2) HB Regs
166 **ESA** Sch 8 para 31 ESA Regs
167 **ESA** Sch 8 para 32 ESA Regs
**All** R(IS) 13/01
168 Sch 5 para 29 HB Regs
169 **ESA** Sch 8 para 33 ESA Regs
**HB** Sch 5 para 29 HB Regs
170 Memo ADM 13/22; Explanatory Memorandum to The Universal Credit (Local Welfare Provision Disregard) (Amendment) Regulations 2022 No.448
171 **ESA** Sch 8 para 30 ESA Regs
**HB** Sch 5 para 28 HB Regs
172 **ESA** Sch 8 para 30(2) and (3) ESA Regs
**HB** Sch 5 para 28A HB Regs
173 **ESA** Sch 8 para 67 ESA Regs
**HB** Sch 5 para 66 HB Regs
174 **ESA** Sch 8 para 53 ESA Regs
**HB** Sch 5 para 57 HB Regs
**Both** *Casewell v SSWP* [2008] EWCA Civ 524, reported as R(IS) 7/08
175 **ESA** Sch 8 para 29 ESA Regs
**HB** Sch 5 para 27 HB Regs
176 **ESA** Sch 8 para 63 ESA Regs
**HB** Sch 5 para 63 HB Regs
177 Sch 8 paras 16, 34 and 56 ESA Regs
178 **ESA** Sch 9 para 12(b) ESA Regs
**HB** Sch 6 para 10(b) HB Regs
179 **ESA** Sch 8 para 62 ESA Regs
**HB** Sch 5 para 62 HB Regs
180 **ESA** Sch 8 para 13 ESA Regs
**HB** Sch 5 para 11 HB Regs
181 **ESA** Sch 8 para 2 ESA Regs
**HB** Sch 5 para 2 HB Regs
182 **ESA** Sch 8 para 22 ESA Regs
**HB** Sch 5 para 23 HB Regs
183 BW2 Annex B para 13 GM
184 para 28102 DMG
185 **ESA** Sch 8 para 48 ESA Regs
**HB** Sch 5 para 49 HB Regs
186 **ESA** Sch 8 para 43 ESA Regs
**HB** Sch 5 para 39 HB Regs
187 **ESA** Sch 8 para 12 ESA Regs
**HB** Sch 5 para 10 HB Regs
188 **ESA** Sch 8 para 24 ESA Regs
**HB** Sch 5 para 24 HB Regs
189 **ESA** Sch 8 para 25 ESA Regs
**HB** Sch 5 para 33 HB Regs
190 **ESA** Sch 8 para 45 ESA Regs
**HB** Sch 5 para 44 HB Regs
191 **ESA** Sch 8 para 46 ESA Regs
**HB** Sch 5 para 45 HB Regs
192 **ESA** Sch 8 para 47 ESA Regs
**HB** Sch 5 para 46 HB Regs
193 Schs 4 para 11 and 5 paras 19 and 20 HB Regs
194 **ESA** Sch 8 para 57 ESA Regs
**HB** Sch 5 para 59 HB Regs
195 **ESA** Sch 8 para 2A ESA Regs
**HB** Sch 5 para 2A HB Regs

5. **Notional income**

196 **ESA** Reg 106(1) ESA Regs
**HB** Reg 42(1) HB Regs
197 paras 28608-16 DMG; see also CIS/15052/1996
198 **ESA** Reg 106(2) ESA Regs
**HB** Reg 42(2) HB Regs
199 Reg 106(3) and (4) ESA Regs
200 Vol 9 Ch 51 paras 51516-28 DMG
201 CIS/16271/1996
202 Reg 107(1) ESA Regs
203 Reg 107(2)(a) and (b) ESA Regs
204 Reg 107(2)(c) ESA Regs
205 CIS/15052/1996, para 10
206 Reg 108(1) ESA Regs
207 Reg 2 SS(PAOR) Regs
208 **ESA** Reg 107(3) ESA Regs
**HB** Reg 42(6)(b) HB Regs
209 **ESA** Reg 107(4) and (5) ESA Regs
**HB** Reg 42(6)(c) and (7) HB Regs
210 **ESA** Reg 108(3) ESA Regs
**HB** Reg 42(9) HB Regs
211 R(SB) 13/86
212 **ESA** Reg 108(4) ESA Regs
**HB** Reg 42(10) HB Regs
213 R(SB) 13/86
214 **ESA** Reg 108(4)(a) ESA Regs
**HB** Reg 42(10)(a) HB Regs
215 CIS/147/1993
216 *Sharrock v CAO*, 26 March 1991 (CA); CIS/93/1991; CIS/422/1992; CIS/701/1994

6. **Working out weekly income**

217 **JSA** Reg 54(2) JSA Regs 2013
**ESA** Reg 91(2) ESA Regs; reg 76(2) ESA Regs 2013
218 **JSA** Reg 54(2)(c) JSA Regs 2013
**ESA** Reg 91(2)(c) ESA Regs; reg 76(2)(c) ESA Regs 2013
219 **JSA** Reg 56(a) JSA Regs 2013
**ESA** Reg 93(1)(a) ESA Regs; reg 78(a) ESA Regs 2013
220 **JSA** Reg 56(b) JSA Regs 2013
**ESA** Reg 93(1)(b) ESA Regs; reg 78(b) ESA Regs 2013
221 Reg 93(2) ESA Regs
222 **JSA** reg 2(2) JSA Regs 2013
**ESA** Reg 2(1) ESA Regs; reg 2 ESA Regs 2013
223 Reg 2 HB Regs

3

224 R(SB) 33/83
225 R(SB) 22/84; R(SB) 11/85
226 CIS/590/1993
227 Arguably, the acceptance in *Minter v Kingston Upon Hull City Council and Potter v SSWP* [2011] EWCA Civ 1155 that if a payment is income, it is attributed to a past period, takes precedence over the contrary reasoning in *SSWP v JP (JSA)* [2010] UKUT 90 (AAC)
228 R(IS) 3/93
229 R(IS) 10/95
230 **JSA** Reg 57(5) JSA Regs 2013
**ESA** Reg 94(6) ESA Regs; reg 79(5)(b) ESA Regs 2013
231 **JSA** Reg 57(2) and (3) JSA Regs 2013
**ESA** Reg 94(2) and (3) ESA Regs; reg 79(2) and (3) ESA Regs 2013
232 Reg 94(4) ESA Regs
233 **JSA** Reg 57(4) and Sch para 8 JSA Regs 2013
**ESA** Reg 94(5) and Sch 7 para 8 ESA Regs; reg 79(4) ESA Regs 2013
234 Reg 31 HB Regs
235 Reg 29(1)(a) HB Regs
236 Reg 29(1)(b) HB Regs; para BW2/W2.53 GM
237 *R v HBRB of LB Ealing ex parte Saville* [1986] 18 HLR 349
238 Reg 29(2) HB Regs
239 Reg 29(3) HB Regs
240 Reg 29A HB Regs
241 Reg 31(2) HB Regs

# Chapter 17

# Income: over pension age

3

**This chapter covers:**


1. Whose income counts (below)
2. What counts as income (p378)
3. Earnings (p379)
4. Other income (p385)
5. Notional income (p391)
6. Working out weekly income (p393)


This chapter explains the rules for working out your weekly income for pension credit (PC) and for pension-age housing benefit (HB) if you and your partner are over pension age and neither of you are on income-related employment and support allowance (ESA) or universal credit (UC). See Chapter 16 for the rules for income-related ESA and for working-age HB if you and your partner are under pension age. If you are in a couple and one of you is over pension age but not the other, see p197 for whether the working-age or pension-age HB rules apply. See Chapter 7 for the rules for UC.

**Note:** whenever HB is referred to in this chapter, this only applies to the pension-age rules.

## Key facts

- Your entitlement to PC and pension-age HB and the amount you get depends on how much income you have.
- Your own income counts and, if you are a member of a couple, your partner's income also counts.
- Some income may be completely or partly ignored, or it may count in full.
- If you get the guarantee credit of PC, you are entitled to maximum HB, so you do not need to work out your income again for HB.

## 1. Whose income counts

If you are a member of a couple (see p254), your partner's income is added to yours.[1]

The income of a dependent child does not affect pension credit or housing benefit.[2]

## 2. What counts as income

3

### Pension credit

For pension credit (PC), **'income'** means:[3]

- earnings (see p379 and p381);
- certain benefits, including state retirement pensions and war pensions (see p385);
- maintenance (see p387);
- income from tenants and lodgers (see p387);
- income from capital (see p388);
- other specified miscellaneous income, including occupational and personal pensions (see p389);
- notional income (see p391);
- any income paid in lieu of the above.

For each type of income, some income is taken into account and some is ignored (or disregarded) in the assessment of PC. If the rules do not specify a type of income as being included in the assessment, it is ignored and does not affect your benefit.

For the rules on qualifying income for the savings credit and the 'assessed income period', see Chapter 11.

### Housing benefit

How your income affects your entitlement to housing benefit (HB) depends on whether you are getting PC and, if so, which type of PC.

#### If you get pension credit guarantee credit

If you (or your partner) get the guarantee credit of PC, all your (and your partner's) income is ignored.[4] This is because entitlement to guarantee credit of PC acts as a passport to maximum HB.

#### If you get pension credit savings credit

If you (or your partner) only get the savings credit of PC, your income for HB purposes is the income (and capital) figure used by the DWP to work out your PC, plus:[5]

- the amount of savings credit of PC; *and*
- any income (and capital) of your partner which was not taken into account in the PC calculation;

*minus:*[6]
- an amount disregarded from your earnings for childcare charges (see p384);
- the higher amount disregarded from your earnings if you:
  - are a lone parent (see p383);
  - are paid maintenance (see p387);
- any additional full-time earnings disregard (see p384);
- any earnings disregarded from 'permitted work' (see p383);
- any discretionary increase to the £10 disregard for war pensions, and war widows' and widowers' pensions (see p387).



### If you do not get pension credit

If you or your partner are over pension age (see p239) and do not get the guarantee or savings credit of PC (or universal credit or income-related employment and support allowance), income is defined in the same way as for PC (see p378).[7] Some income is taken into account and some disregarded, but the rules are not always the same as for PC. The differences are explained in the relevant sections below.

## Net weekly income

The income that is taken into account is the amount after deducting any tax or national insurance (NI) contributions.[8]

For HB, the local authority may ignore changes (eg, Budget changes) in tax or NI contributions for up to 30 benefit weeks. When the changes are eventually taken into account, you are not treated as having been underpaid or overpaid benefit during the period of the delay.[9]

Once you have worked out what income should be taken into account, this is converted into a weekly amount (see p393) and the total taken into account in the benefit assessment. See p394 for the date from which a payment is counted. Chapters 10 and 11 explain how income affects the amount of HB or PC you get.

# 3. Earnings

How earnings are treated depends on whether you are an employed earner (see below) or are self-employed (see p381). In both cases, some of your earnings can be disregarded (see p382).

## Employed earnings

### What counts as earnings

**'Earnings'** means 'any remuneration or profit derived from... employment'.

This includes:[10]
- wages and overtime pay;
- any bonus or commission (including tips);

- holiday pay – but this is ignored if your employment ends before your pension credit (PC) or housing benefit (HB) entitlement starts;
- statutory sick pay and contractual sick pay,[11] statutory maternity pay, statutory adoption pay, statutory paternity pay, statutory shared parental pay, statutory parental bereavement pay, statutory neonatal care pay or any other payment made to you by your employer while you are on maternity leave;[12]
- any payments made by your employer for expenses not 'wholly, exclusively and necessarily' incurred in carrying out your job, such as travel expenses to and from work, and payments made to you for looking after members of your family;
- pay in lieu of notice, or pay in lieu of remuneration except for periodic payments following redundancy. However, all earnings, including pay in lieu, are ignored if your employment ends before your PC or HB entitlement starts;
- a retainer fee (eg, payment during the school holidays if you work for the school meals service[13]) or a guarantee payment;[14]
- an equal pay settlement – eg, through a 'single status agreement';[15]
- any payment of a non-cash voucher which is liable for class 1 national insurance (NI) contributions.[16] Non-cash vouchers that are not liable for contributions (eg, certain childcare and charitable vouchers) are classed as payments in kind and ignored.[17]

## What does not count as earnings

Examples of payments not counted as earnings include the following.

- Payments in kind (eg, petrol) are ignored.[18]
- Payments towards expenses that are 'wholly, exclusively and necessarily' incurred, such as travelling expenses during the course of your work, are ignored.[19]
- If you are a local councillor, travelling expenses and subsistence payments are (and basic allowances may be[20]) ignored as expenses 'wholly, exclusively and necessarily' incurred in your work.
- If your earnings are paid in another currency, any bank charges for converting them into sterling are deducted before taking them into account.[21]
- The net amount of any occupational pension,[22] although not counted as earnings, counts as other income and is taken into account in full.[23]
- Any compensation payments made by an employment tribunal for unfair dismissal or unlawful discrimination do not count as earnings.[24]

## Calculating net earnings from employment

Both your gross earnings and net earnings must be calculated. It is your net earnings that are taken into account in the assessment. See p393 for how earnings are converted into a weekly amount.

*Gross and net earnings*

**'Gross earnings'** means the amount of earnings received from your employer less deductions for any expenses wholly, necessarily and exclusively incurred by you to carry out your duties.[25] See p379 for what counts as earnings and examples of expenses that can be deducted.

**'Net earnings'** means your gross earnings less any deductions made for:[26]

- income tax; *and*
- class 1 NI contributions; *and*
- half of any contribution you make towards a personal or occupational pension scheme.

If your earnings are estimated for HB, the amount of tax and NI you would expect to pay on those earnings is estimated and deducted, together with half of any pension contributions you are paying.[27]

### Payments when you stop work

Redundancy payments are treated as capital.[28]

If you leave a job before you claim HB or PC, any earnings should be disregarded as income except certain copyright royalties, and payments for patents, trademarks or under the Public Lending Right scheme.[29]

If you are already getting HB or PC when you leave your job, your earnings are not disregarded for that benefit.

For PC, any final payment is treated as having been paid on the date your next regular payment of earnings would have been paid and taken into account for the same period, unless the final payment is higher than the normal amount. If it is higher, work out over how many normal payment periods it counts – eg, if the final payment is between two and three times as much as normal, it counts over three payment periods.[30]

*Example*

Merrin has been getting PC and working part time. She earns £120 a week, paid on a Friday. She finishes work on Wednesday 7 August and on that day is given £130, made up of £90 final wages and £40 holiday pay. This £130 is treated as having been paid on Friday 9 August and taken into account for two weeks: £120 in the first week and the remaining £10 in the second week.

## Self-employed earnings

### Calculating net earnings

Your **'net profit'** over the period before your claim must be worked out. This is your self-employed earnings minus:[31]

- reasonable expenses (see p346 – the rules are the same as those for people under pension age, except that expenses relating to debts are not excluded); *and*
- income tax and NI contributions; *and*
- half of any premium paid in respect of a personal pension scheme which is eligible for tax relief.[32] You must supply certain information about the scheme or annuity contract to the DWP or local authority, if requested.[33]

3

If you receive payments for board and lodging charges, these do not count as earnings, but as other income (less any disregards – see p388).[34]

### Working out average earnings from self-employment

The weekly amount is the average of earnings:[35]

- over a period of one year (in practice, normally the last year for which accounts are available); *or*
- over a more appropriate period if you have recently taken up self-employment or there has been a change which will affect your business.

### Childminders

In practice, childminders are always treated as self-employed. Your net profit is deemed to be one-third of your earnings less income tax, NI contributions and half of certain pension contributions.[36] The rest of your earnings are completely ignored.

## Disregarded earnings

Some of your earnings from employment or self-employment are disregarded and do not affect your PC or HB. The amount depends on your circumstances. For HB, there is also an additional disregard depending on the hours you work, a childcare costs disregard and a permitted work disregard.

### Pension credit

#### £20 disregard

£20 of your earnings (including those of your partner) is disregarded if:

- you are a lone parent;[37] *or*
- you or your partner qualify for an additional amount of PC for being a carer (see p279). If both of you qualify, only £20 is disregarded in total;[38] *or*
- you or your partner are in receipt of:[39]
  - employment and support allowance (ESA) or severe disablement allowance (SDA); *or*
  - attendance allowance (AA), disability living allowance (DLA), Scottish adult disability living allowance (SADLA), personal independence payment (PIP), adult disability payment (ADP), pension age disability payment (PADP), armed forces independence payment (AFIP) or a mobility supplement; *or*

- you or your partner are certified as severely sight impaired or blind by a consultant ophthalmologist;[40] *or*
- you or your partner previously had a £20 earnings disregard in your income support, income-based jobseeker's allowance or income-related ESA and that benefit ended no more than eight weeks before PC entitlement began (the disregard ends if you have a break in employment of more than eight weeks) or, immediately before reaching pension age, there was a £20 disregard in your PC because you or your partner were getting incapacity benefit or SDA. You cannot get this disregard if you have more than an eight-week break in your PC claim;[41] *or*
- you or your partner are an auxiliary coastguard, a part-time firefighter, part-time member of a lifeboat crew or member of the reserve forces.[42] If your earnings are less than £20 a week, what is left over can be disregarded from your, or your partner's, earnings from any other employment.

**Note:** if you qualify under more than one category, you still have a maximum of £20 of your earnings disregarded.

#### Basic £5 or £10 disregard

If you do not qualify for a £20 disregard, £5 of your earnings is disregarded if you are single. If you claim as a member of a couple, £10 of your total income is disregarded, whether or not you are both working.[43]

### Housing benefit

#### Permitted work disregard

For HB only, any earnings from 'permitted work' are disregarded if you or your partner are doing 'permitted work' in the circumstances described on p349.[44]

#### £25 disregard

Lone parents on HB have £25 of their earnings ignored.[45]

#### £20 disregard

£20 of your earnings is disregarded if:

- you or your partner qualify for a carer premium. If both of you qualify, only £20 is disregarded in total;[46] *or*
- you or your partner are in receipt of:[47]
  - ESA with a work-related activity or support component or SDA; *or*
  - AA, DLA, SADLA, PIP, ADP (in practice[48]), PADP, AFIP or a mobility supplement; *or*
- you or your partner are certified as severely sight impaired or blind by a consultant ophthalmologist;[49] *or*
- you or your partner have (or are treated as having) limited capability for work and the assessment phase has ended;[50] *or*

- you or your partner are (or are treated as) incapable of work and have been for a continuous period of 364 days (196 days if you are terminally ill);[51] *or*
- you or your partner had a £20 earnings disregard in your HB or council tax benefit (CTB) in the eight weeks before you or your partner reached pension age. You cannot get this disregard if you have more than an eight-week break in your employment or in your HB claim (or previously, CTB claim);[52] *or*
- you or your partner are an auxiliary coastguard, a part-time firefighter, part-time member of a lifeboat crew or in the reserve forces. If your earnings are less than £20 a week, what is left can be disregarded from your or your partner's earnings from other employment.[53]

**Note:** if you qualify under more than one category, you still have a maximum of £20 of your earnings disregarded.

#### Basic £5 or £10 disregard

If you do not qualify for a £25 or £20 disregard, or a permitted work disregard, £5 of your earnings is disregarded if you are single. If you claim as a member of a couple, £10 of your total income is disregarded, whether or not you are both working.[54]

#### Additional disregard

For HB only, whichever earnings disregard applies is increased by £17.10 if:[55]

- you or your partner work 30 hours or more a week on average; *or*
- you or your partner work 16 hours or more a week on average and you have a child who is part of your family for benefit purposes (see p258) or your HB includes the family premium (see p270); *or*
- you are a lone parent and work 16 hours or more a week on average; *or*
- you or your partner work 16 hours or more a week on average and one or both of you get ESA which includes a support or work-related activity component, SDA, AA, DLA, SADLA, PIP, ADP (in practice[56]), PADP, AFIP, a mobility supplement or you are certified as severely sight impaired or blind by a consultant ophthalmologist or have been incapable of work for 364 days (196 days if terminally ill). For couples, the partner who is disabled is the one who must be working 16 hours or more a week on average.

The additional earnings disregard does not apply if your total earnings are less than the total of £17.10, plus any earnings disregard and childcare costs disregard.

**Note:** only one additional disregard is allowed from your (or your partner's) earnings.

#### Childcare costs disregard

For HB only, up to £175 a week for one child, or up to £300 a week for two or more children, can be deducted from your (or your partner's) earnings (from employment or self-employment) for childcare costs in certain circumstances.[57] The rules are the same as those for people under pension age (see p350), except you can also have a childcare costs disregard if you are a couple and one of you works 16 hours or more a week and the other is aged 80 or over. There is no childcare costs disregard for PC.

3

## 4. Other income

### Benefits

Some benefits are taken into account as income; others are disregarded, either in full or partly.

#### Benefits that are taken into account

The following benefits are taken into account:[58]

- widow's pension;
- carer's allowance (CA) – but not CA supplement in Scotland;
- carer support payment (in Scotland);
- a war orphan's pension, dependant's allowance or payment under the Armed Forces Compensation Scheme for someone whose parent died and who is still eligible as an adult because of disability;[59]
- new-style jobseeker's allowance;
- severe disablement allowance;
- contributory employment and support allowance (ESA). If ESA is paid at a reduced rate because of a sanction, the full rate still counts;[60]
- industrial injuries benefits, except constant attendance allowance and exceptionally severe disablement allowance, which are disregarded;
- maternity allowance;
- retirement pensions;
- statutory sick pay, statutory maternity pay, statutory adoption pay, statutory paternity pay, statutory shared parental pay, statutory parental bereavement pay and statutory neonatal care pay. These are treated as earnings and may benefit from an earnings disregard (see p382);[61]
- foreign social security benefits which are similar to the benefits listed above.[62]

#### Benefits that are not taken into account

The following benefits are ignored completely:[63]

- adult disability payment (in Scotland);
- armed forces independence payment;
- attendance allowance (AA);
- bereavement support payment;
- Best Start grant (in Scotland);

3

- CA supplement (in Scotland);
- child benefit;
- child disability payment (in Scotland);
- child winter heating payment (in Scotland);
- Christmas bonus (see p783);
- constant attendance allowance, exceptionally severe disablement allowance or severe disablement occupational allowance paid because of an injury at work or a war injury;
- disability living allowance;
- funeral support payment (in Scotland);
- guardian's allowance;
- HB;
- mobility supplement under the War Pension Scheme;
- pension age disability payment (in Scotland);
- pension age winter heating payment (in Scotland);
- personal independence payment;
- Scottish adult disability living allowance;
- Scottish child payment;
- short-term assistance (in Scotland);
- social fund payments;
- supplementary payments to pre-1973 war widows or widowers;
- universal credit;
- winter heating payment (in Scotland);
- young carer grant (in Scotland).

### Benefits that are partly taken into account

For HB only, £15 of widowed parent's allowance is ignored.[64]

The following benefits have £10 ignored (or more for HB – see below):

- for PC only, widowed parent's allowance;[65]
- war disablement pension;[66]
- guaranteed income payment and survivor's guaranteed income payment under the Armed Forces Compensation Scheme (if reduced to under £10 by another pension, the remainder is disregarded from the pension);[67]
- war widow's, widower's or surviving civil partner's pension;[68]
- an extra-statutory payment made instead of the above pensions;[69]
- similar payments made by another country;[70]
- a pension from any government paid to the victims of Nazi persecution.[71]

The £10 disregard allowed on the above war pensions is in addition to the total disregard of any mobility supplement or attendance allowance (ie, constant attendance allowance, exceptionally severe disablement allowance and severe disablement occupational allowance) paid as part of a war disablement pension.

Local authorities may have discretionary local schemes to increase the £10 disregard on a war disablement, war widow's, widower's or surviving civil partner's pension and on the guaranteed income payment and survivor's guaranteed income payment in your HB.[72] Most increase the disregard or ignore the full amount, so check your local scheme.

### Benefit delays

If you have made a claim for benefit but have not yet been paid, the benefit should not be treated as income you have. For PC, you should get your full benefit and the DWP deducts the difference from arrears of the delayed benefit when it is awarded.[73]

For the treatment of payments of arrears of certain benefits, see p432.

### Benefit deductions and overpayments

If any deductions are being taken from a benefit (eg, for an overpayment, rent or bills), the full amount of benefit is taken into account before taking off the deduction.[74]

## Maintenance payments

**For PC**, any maintenance payments for you or your partner made by your (or your partner's) spouse/civil partner or former spouse/civil partner count in full as income. Maintenance for a child is ignored completely.[75]

**For HB**, if you have a child who is part of your family for benefit purposes (see p258) or have a family premium included in your HB, £15 of any maintenance payments for you or your partner made by your (or your partner's) spouse/civil partner or former spouse/civil partner is disregarded.[76] If you receive maintenance from more than one person, only £15 of the total is disregarded. Other kinds of maintenance (eg, for a child) do not count as income and are ignored completely.[77]

If you *pay* maintenance to a former partner or a child not living with you, your payments are not disregarded for the purpose of calculating your income for PC or HB.[78] See p393 if part of a personal or occupational pension is paid to a former partner.

## Income from tenants and lodgers

How income from tenants is treated depends on whether or not you live in the same property.

### Lettings without board

If you own or are the tenant of your home, and you rent out a room(s) under an agreement, £20 of your weekly charge for each person is ignored. The balance is taken into account.[79]

If someone shares your home under an informal arrangement and is not paying rent under an agreement, any money they pay is ignored,[80] but a non-dependant deduction may be made from any HB or housing costs paid with PC (see p207 and p289).

## Boarders

If you have a boarder in your own home, the first £20 a week of the amount they pay you is ignored and half of any balance remaining is taken into account as your income.[81] For PC, this does not apply if the boarder is a close relative (see p294) or the arrangement is not commercial.[82] Instead, the whole payment is ignored but there could be a non-dependant deduction from any housing costs paid with PC.[83] For HB, a non-dependant deduction could apply on top of this disregard if the boarder is a close relative or the arrangement is not commercial.[84]

This disregard applies for each boarder you have. The charge must normally include at least some meals.[85] If you have a business partner, even though your gross income includes just your share of the weekly charge to boarders, you still get the full disregard of £20 plus half the excess for each boarder.[86]

## Tenants in other properties

Rent from a property other than your home is not taken into account as income.[87] Instead, the value of the property counts as capital and is treated as producing a 'tariff income' (see below). If the property's value can be disregarded (see p428), both the rent and the capital value are ignored (there is no tariff income).[88]

# Income from capital

The general rule is that capital (unless it is disregarded) is assumed to provide a set rate of income – called 'deemed income' (often called 'tariff income') (see below). *Actual* income generated from capital is ignored as income, except from the types of capital listed below.[89] In these cases, any actual income (but no deemed income) is taken into account.[90] **Note:** for HB, it is only taken into account if the total capital listed below is worth more than £10,000.[91]

Actual income from the following capital is taken into account:

- the value of the right to receive a payment in the future of:
  - income under a life interest or life rent;
  - rent, unless you only have a reversionary (ie, future) interest in the property. For the way the actual rent is treated, see p387;
  - the surrender value or income under an annuity;
- property held in a trust, but not charitable trusts or trusts set up out of payments from personal injury to you or your partner. Income from a discretionary trust can be ignored in some circumstances (see p390).

There are no rules that treat capital of any kind as though it were income.

## Deemed income from capital

**For PC**, if you have capital above £10,000, you are treated as having an assumed income of £1 a week for every £500, or part of £500, by which your capital exceeds £10,000.[92] This is called 'deemed income'. There is no upper capital limit.

**For HB**, the following applies.

- If you or your partner are getting the guarantee credit of PC, all your (and your partner's) capital is ignored.[93]
- In any other case, there is a capital limit of £16,000.[94] If you have capital above £10,000, you are treated as having an assumed income of £1 a week for every £500, or part of £500, of capital between £10,000.01 and £16,000.[95]



**For PC and HB**, you are not treated as having any deemed income on capital that is disregarded (see p428).[96]

***Example***

Bruce (72) has savings of £12,000. Deemed income of £4 a week is taken into account. Any interest from the savings is ignored as income.

## Occupational and personal pensions

The following income is taken into account:[97]

- an occupational pension;
- income from a personal pension;
- income from a retirement annuity contract, including an annuity purchased for you or transferred to you on divorce;
- payments from a former employer for early retirement on the grounds of ill health or disability, unless this was under a court order or settlement of a claim;[98]
- an overseas pension;
- a Civil List Act pension;[99]
- payment under an equity release scheme.[100] This provides regular payments from a loan secured on your home. For some home income plans where you buy an annuity, interest on the loan can be disregarded (see p390);
- payments from the Financial Assistance Scheme and periodic payments from the Pension Protection Fund (these help some people with underfunded occupational schemes whose employer has gone out of business).

Some charitable trusts provide discretionary income to people retired from specific occupations. This is ignored for PC and HB.[101]

### Occupational and personal pension options

If you have a defined contribution occupational or personal pension (a 'money purchase' pension), for benefit purposes you are generally expected to buy an annuity or take the equivalent income that would be payable through an annuity. Income from an annuity is taken into account. Income that you draw direct from your pension pot is compared to the amount you could get from an annuity and whichever amount is higher is taken into account.[102]

If you also take a lump sum, this counts as your capital.[103] **Note:** if you choose to take a lump sum and spend it in the hope of increasing benefit entitlement, you are likely to be caught by the rules on deprivation of capital (see p413).

If you leave some, or all, of the funds in your pension pot, you are treated as having notional income, usually based on the annuity those funds could yield (see p392).

If you are below pension age, the rules are different (see p361).

## Specified miscellaneous income

Any income from copyright royalties and payments for patents, trademarks or under the Public Lending Right scheme are counted in full. Add the payments to your earnings (if any), if you are the first owner of the copyright or patent or author of the book, and deduct the appropriate earnings disregards on p382.[104]

The following income is ignored:

- income paid outside the UK which cannot be transferred here;[105]
- if income is paid in another currency, any bank charges for converting the payment into sterling;[106]
- income from an annuity is normally taken into account. However, an amount equal to the interest payable on the loan with which the annuity was bought is ignored if:[107]
  - you used at least 90 per cent of the loan made to you to buy the annuity; *and*
  - the annuity will end when you and your partner die; *and*
  - you or your partner are responsible for paying the interest on the loan; *and*
  - you (if you took out the loan) or your partner (if your partner did) were at least 65 or higher pension age at the time the loan was made; *and*
  - the loan is secured on a property that you or your partner own or have an interest in, and the property on which the loan is secured is your home or your partner's home.

  If the interest on the loan is payable after income tax has been deducted, it is an amount equal to the net interest payment that is disregarded, otherwise it is the gross amount of the interest payment;
- any discretionary payment made to you by trustees is ignored altogether, except if the payment is for the purpose of:
  - obtaining food, ordinary clothing or footwear, or household fuel. School uniforms and sportswear are examples of clothing and footwear that are not ordinary; *or*

- paying rent, council tax or water charges for which you or your partner (if any) are liable. 'Rent' means eligible rent for HB purposes, less any non-dependant deductions; *or*
- meeting housing costs which could be met by PC.

In this case, £20 of the payment is disregarded or, if the payment is less than £20, the whole of the payment is disregarded.[108] If this disregard overlaps with certain other disregards (eg, certain war pensions), a combined maximum of £20 is allowed.[109] **Note:** this is a weekly disregard, so payments spread over different or successive benefit weeks attract a £20 disregard for each week;

- periodic payments made to you or your partner under an agreement entered into in settlement of a claim for any injury to you or your partner;[110]
- any payment ordered by a court to be made to you or your partner because of an accident, injury or disease you or your partner (or, for HB only, your child) have.[111]



### Other income

Only income that is specified in the rules can affect your benefit (see p378). Any other kind of income is ignored – eg:

- local welfare assistance (see p770), including household support fund payments and 'thank you' payments under the Homes for Ukraine scheme;[112]
- student loans and grants.[113] For HB only, see p364 if you make a parental contribution to a student's grant or loan or towards your under-25-year-old child's expenses in advanced education;
- adoption allowances, fostering allowances, child arrangements order payments and kinship care payments;[114]
- charitable and voluntary payments are not taken into account as income, so if a charity or a person gives you voluntary payments, these do not reduce your benefit. **Note:** maintenance payments can affect your benefit (see p387);
- payments for expenses if you are being consulted as a service user by certain public bodies. Other payments count as earnings but, if you choose not to take them or have them paid to someone else on your behalf, they do not count as your notional income;[115]
- victims' payments under the Victims of Overseas Terrorism Compensation Scheme.[116]

## 5. Notional income

In certain circumstances, you may be treated as having income that you do not possess.

**Note:** if you are working but earning less than the going rate, you are not treated as though your wages are higher than those you get, as you are for other means-tested benefits (see p367).

## Deliberately getting rid of income



If you deliberately get rid of income in order to claim or increase your benefit, you are treated as though you were still in receipt of that income.[117] The basic issues involved are the same as those for deliberately getting rid of capital (see p435). **Note:** this rule can only apply if your intention was to gain benefit for *yourself* (or your partner). It should not apply if, for example, you stop claiming carer's allowance (CA) solely to allow the cared-for person to get a severe disability premium in their benefit (see p275).[118]

If you give up income you get from a small occupational or personal pension to take a lump sum instead, you could be caught by this rule. However, if this is a 'trivial commutation lump sum', you are not treated as still having that income (although the capital counts). There are similar sounding lump sums (eg, 'trivial commutation lump-sum death benefit' which is paid to a dependant), which do not have this protection, so get advice from your pension provider.[119]

## Failing to apply for pension income

Sometimes you can be treated as having pension income, even though you have not applied for it.[120]

### Deferring a state pension

If you defer your state pension, category A or B pension, graduated retirement benefit or any shared additional pension paid on divorce, you are *not* treated as having that income for housing benefit (HB) before you claim it. However, you are treated as having that income for pension credit (PC). However, for PC, a deferred or unclaimed pension is not treated as notional income for 52 weeks if you were previously entitled to child tax credit and claimed PC after receiving a tax credits closure notice by or within one month of the deadline specified.[121]

The amount that counts for PC is the pension to which you would expect to be entitled were you to claim, less any overlapping benefit you get – eg, CA. If you have a choice of taking a lump sum instead of extra pension income, the amount is based on your taking the lump-sum option (there is no lump-sum choice when claiming a deferred post-April 2016 state pension). To account for the time it can take to process claims, you are only treated as having this income from the date you could expect to get it were you to make a claim.

For both PC and HB, you are treated as having any amount of category C or D pension and age addition to which you might expect to be entitled if you were to claim. For PC, any overlapping benefit you get is deducted.

### Leaving funds in an occupational or personal pension

You are treated as having any income from an occupational pension you have elected to defer beyond the scheme's retirement age,[122] as though you had claimed it. For PC, the time it might take to process it is taken into account and any overlapping benefit is deducted. If you have a defined contribution occupational or personal pension, for benefit purposes you are generally expected to buy an annuity or take the equivalent income that would be payable through an annuity. However, for PC, a deferred or unclaimed pension is not treated as notional income for 52 weeks if you were previously entitled to child tax credit and claimed PC by or within one month of the deadline specified on your tax credits closure notice.[123]



If you leave funds in your pension pot, this is disregarded as capital, but you are treated as having notional income based on the annuity those funds could yield.[124] If you take one or more lump sums from your pension pot, these count as capital and notional income is worked out on what is left in your pension pot. See p389 for how pension payments are treated.

### Income paid to someone else on your behalf

Any money that counts as income and is paid to someone on your behalf is normally treated as being yours and is then either taken into account or ignored as income under the rules described in this chapter. The exception is for payments of income made under an occupational or personal pension scheme (or, for HB only, from the Pension Protection Fund) if you or your partner are bankrupt (or, in Scotland, the subject of a sequestration order). In this case, if the payment is made to the trustee or other person acting on your creditors' behalf and you (and your partner) have no income other than the payment made, it is not treated as being yours.[125]

If you have had a judicial separation rather than a divorce so that usual pension-splitting arrangements are not available, and a court has ordered you to pay part of your pension to your former partner, you could argue this does not count as yours.[126] However, if you pay maintenance from your pension under an agreement out of court, this income is likely to still count as yours.[127]

---

## 6. Working out weekly income

To work out your weekly income, you should do the following.

- Work out whether income is taken into account, or fully or partly disregarded (see p377).
- If income varies, work out an average income (see p394).
- Convert the income into a weekly amount if necessary (see p394).
- Add any deemed weekly income from capital (see p389).

## Averaging income

If your earnings vary because you do not work the same hours every week, your weekly income may be averaged over the cycle, if there is an identifiable one.[128] If you do not work a recognisable cycle or your income fluctuates, your income is worked out based on:[129]

- the last two payments before your claim was made or treated as made (or, where applicable, before your claim was superseded) if those payments are at least one month apart; *or*
- the last four payments before your claim was made or treated as made (or, where applicable, before your claim was superseded) if the last two payments are less than a month apart; *or*
- calculating (or estimating for housing benefit – HB) any other payments that would give a more accurate figure for your average weekly income.

In all cases, if the cycle involves periods when you do no work, these are included in the cycle, but not other absences – eg, holidays or sickness.

The payment is treated as if made for a period of a year if you are entitled to:[130]

- royalties or other sums for the use of any copyright, patent or trademark; *or*
- payments for any book registered under the Public Lending Right 1982 scheme; *or*
- payments made on an occasional basis.

## Converting income into a weekly amount

Pension credit (PC) and HB are calculated on a weekly basis, so your earnings and other income have to be converted into a weekly amount if necessary. The following rules apply to income from employment and other income.[131] For income from self-employment, see p381.

- If the payment is for less than a week, it is treated as the weekly amount.
- If the payment is for a month, multiply by 12 and divide by 52.
- Multiply a payment for three months by four and divide by 52.
- Divide a payment for a year by 52.
- Multiply payments for any other periods by seven and divide by the number of days in the period.

## Date from when a payment counts

The general rule for PC is that benefits are treated as having been paid on the last day of the PC 'benefit week' in which the benefit is payable, but on the first day if the benefit is paid in advance.[132] Some benefits are treated slightly differently. New-style jobseeker's allowance, contributory employment and support allowance and maternity allowance are treated as having been paid on the day that benefit is payable. For HB, benefits are taken into account over the period for which they are payable.[133]

For other types of income, for PC, the general rule is that income counts from the date it is paid for the length of time it has been paid – eg, a month's occupational pension paid on 10 November counts from 10 November to 9 December.[134]

For HB, weekly earnings are taken into account from the start of a new claim or from the first day of the 'benefit week' after you start work. If average weekly earnings change, the new amount counts from the date of change, even if you are not paid until later.[135]



*Benefit week*

For PC, a **'benefit week'** is the seven days ending on the day PC is payable if paid in arrears, or starting on that day if paid in advance.[136]

For HB, a **'benefit week'** is the seven days starting on a Monday.[137]

# Notes

1. **Whose income counts**
 1 **PC** s5 SPCA 2002
 **HB** s136(1) SSCBA 1992
 2 Reg 23(3) HB(SPC) Regs

2. **What counts as income**
 3 s15 SPCA 2002; reg 15 SPC Regs
 4 Regs 25 and 26 HB(SPC) Regs
 5 Reg 27(4) HB(SPC) Regs
 6 Reg 27(4) HB(SPC) Regs
 7 Reg 29 HB(SPC) Regs
 8 **PC** Reg 17(10) SPC Regs
 **HB** Reg 33(12) HB(SPC) Regs
 9 Reg 34 HB(SPC) Regs

3. **Earnings**
 10 **PC** Reg 17A(2) SPC Regs
 **HB** Reg 35(1) HB(SPC) Regs
 11 **PC** Reg 17A(h) and (k) SPC Regs
 **HB** Reg 35(1)(h) and (k) HB(SPC) Regs
 12 **PC** Reg 17A(h)-(k) SPC Regs
 **HB** Reg 35(1)(h)-(k) HB(SPC) Regs
 13 **PC** Reg 17A(2)(e) SPC Regs
 **HB** Reg 35(1)(e) HB(SPC) Regs
 14 R(IS) 9/95
 15 *Minter v Kingston Upon Hull City Council and Potter v SSWP* [2011] EWCA Civ 1155
 16 **PC** Reg 17A(2)(g) SPC Regs
 **HB** Reg 35(1)(g) HB(SPC) Regs
 17 **PC** Reg 17A(4) SPC Regs
 **HB** Reg 35(3) HB(SPC) Regs
 18 **PC** Reg 17A(3)(a) SPC Regs
 **HB** Reg 35(2)(a) HB(SPC) Regs
 19 **PC** Reg 17A(3)(b) SPC Regs
 **HB** Reg 35(2)(b) HB(SPC) Regs
 20 CIS/77/1993; CIS/89/1989
 21 **PC** Sch 6 para 7 SPC Regs
 **HB** Sch 4 para 10 HB(SPC) Regs
 22 **PC** Reg 17A(3)(c) SPC Regs
 **HB** Reg 35(2)(c) HB(SPC) Regs
 23 **PC** s15(1)(c) SPCA 2002
 **HB** Reg 29(1)(c) HB(SPC) Regs
 24 **PC** Reg 17A(3)(e) SPC Regs
 **HB** Reg 35(2)(e) HB(SPC) Regs
 25 *Parsons v Hogg* [1985] 2 All ER 897 (CA), appendix to R(FIS) 4/85
 26 **PC** Regs 17(10) and 17A(4A) SPC Regs
 **HB** Reg 36(2) and (4) HB(SPC) Regs
 27 Reg 36(5) HB(SPC) Regs
 28 para 86162 DMG

29 **PC** Sch 6 para 6 SPC Regs
**HB** Sch 4 para 8 HB(SPC) Regs
30 Reg 17ZA SPC Regs
31 **PC** Reg 17B(5) SPC Regs; reg 13(1) and (4) SSB(CE) Regs
**HB** Reg 39(1)-(3) HB(SPC) Regs
32 **PC** Reg 17B(1) SPC Regs; regs 2 and 13(4) SSB(CE) Regs
**HB** Regs 2(1) and 39(2) and (11) HB(SPC) Regs
33 **PC** Reg 32(3) SS(C&P) Regs
**HB** Reg 67(5) HB(SPC) Regs
34 **PC** Reg 17B(4)(b) SPC Regs; reg 12(2) SSB(CE) Regs
**HB** Reg 38(2)(a) HB(SPC) Regs
35 **PC** Reg 17B SPC Regs; reg 11(1) SSB(CE) Regs
**HB** Reg 37(1) HB(SPC) Regs
36 **PC** Reg 17B(5)(b) SPC Regs; reg 13(10) SSB(CE) Regs
**HB** Reg 39(8) HB(SPC) Regs
37 Sch 6 para 1 SPC Regs
38 Sch 6 paras 3 and 4A SPC Regs
39 Sch 6 para 4(1)(a) SPC Regs
40 Sch 6 para 4(1)(b) SPC Regs
41 Sch 6 para 4(2)-(4) SPC Regs
42 Sch 6 para 2 SPC Regs
43 **PC** Sch 6 para 5 SPC Regs
**HB** Sch 4 para 7 HB(SPC) Regs
44 Sch 4 para 5A HB(SPC) Regs
45 Sch 4 para 2 HB(SPC) Regs
46 Sch 4 para 4 HB(SPC) Regs
47 Sch 4 para 5(1)(a) HB(SPC) Regs
48 ADP is not listed in regulations but the official intention is generally to treat ADP the same as PIP; LA Welfare Direct 2/22
49 Sch 4 para 5(1)(b) HB(SPC) Regs
50 Sch 4 para 5(1)(d) HB(SPC) Regs
51 Sch 4 para 5(1)(c) HB(SPC) Regs
52 Sch 4 para 5(2) HB(SPC) Regs
53 Sch 4 para 3 HB(SPC) Regs
54 **PC** Sch 6 para 5 SPC Regs
**HB** Sch 4 para 7 HB(SPC) Regs
55 Sch 4 para 9 HB(SPC) Regs
56 ADP is not listed in regulations but the official intention is generally to treat ADP the same as PIP; LA Welfare Direct 2/22
57 Reg 30(1)(c) HB(SPC) Regs

4. **Other income**

58 **PC** s15(1)(b) and (e) SPCA 2002; reg 15(1) SPC Regs
**HB** Reg 29(1)(b) and (j) HB(SPC) Regs
59 **PC** Reg 15(5)(a) and (ab) SPC Regs
**HB** Reg 29(1)(h) and (l) HB(SPC) Regs
60 **PC** Reg 15(3) SPC Regs
**HB** Reg 29(3) HB(SPC) Regs
61 **PC** Reg 17A(2)(h)-(j) SPC Regs
**HB** Reg 35(1)(h)-(j) HB(SPC) Regs
62 **PC** Reg 15(2) SPC Regs
**HB** Reg 29(1)(k) HB(SPC) Regs
63 **PC** s15 SPCA 2002; reg 15(1) and Sch 4 paras 2-6 SPC Regs
**HB** Reg 29(1) and Sch 5 paras 2-6 HB(SPC) Regs
64 Sch 5 paras 7 and 8 HB(SPC) Regs
65 Sch 4 paras 7 and 7A SPC Regs
66 **PC** Sch 4 para 1(a) SPC Regs
**HB** Sch 5 para 1(a) HB(SPC) Regs; Sch Part 1 HB&CTB(WPD) Regs
67 **PC** Sch 4 para 1(cc) SPC Regs
**HB** Sch 5 para 1(d) HB(SPC) Regs
68 **PC** Sch 4 para 1(b), (ba) and (c) SPC Regs
**HB** Sch 5 para 1(b) and (c) HB(SPC) Regs; Sch Part 1 HB&CTB(WPD) Regs
69 **PC** Sch 4 para 1(d) SPC Regs
**HB** Sch 5 para 1(e) HB(SPC) Regs
70 **PC** Sch 4 para 1(e) SPC Regs
**HB** Sch 5 para 1(f) HB(SPC) Regs
71 **PC** Sch 4 para 1(f) SPC Regs
**HB** Sch 5 para 1(g) HB(SPC) Regs
**Both** *MN v (1) Bury Council (2) SSWP (HB)* [2014] UKUT 187 (AAC)
72 ss134(8) and 139(6) SSAA 1992; *R v South Hams DC ex parte Ash* [1999] EWHC Admin 418
73 s74(2) SSAA 1992; reg 17 CA(CSP)(S) Regs
74 **PC** Reg 15(3) SPC Regs
**HB** Reg 29(3) HB(SPC) Regs
75 Reg 15(5)(d) SPC Regs
76 Sch 5 para 20 HB(SPC) Regs
77 Reg 29(1)(o) HB(SPC) Regs
78 CIS/683/1993
79 **PC** Sch 4 para 9 SPC Regs
**HB** Sch 5 para 10 HB(SPC) Regs
80 **PC** Income from capital under s15(1)(i) SPCA 2002 would count, but is ignored under regs 15(6) and 17(8), Sch 5 para 1A and Sch 4 para 18 SPC Regs
**HB** Reg 29(1)(i) HB(SPC) Regs
81 **PC** Sch 4 para 8 SPC Regs
**HB** Sch 5 para 9 HB(SPC) Regs
82 Reg 1(2), definition of 'board and lodging accommodation', SPC Regs
83 Sch 4 para 18 SPC Regs
84 Reg 2(1), definition of 'board and lodging accommodation', HB(SPC) Regs
85 **PC** Reg 1(2), definition of 'board and lodging accommodation', SPC Regs
**HB** Reg 2(1), definition of 'board and lodging accommodation', HB(SPC) Regs

86 CIS/521/2002
87 **PC** s15(1)(i) SPCA 2002; Sch 4 para 18 SPC Regs
**HB** Reg 29(1)(i) and Sch 5 para 22 HB(SPC) Regs
88 **PC** Reg 17(8) SPC Regs
**HB** Regs 29(1)(i) and 44(2) HB(SPC) Regs
89 **PC** Sch 4 para 18 SPC Regs
**HB** Sch 5 para 22 HB(SPC) Regs
90 **PC** s15(1)(i) SPCA 2002; reg 15(6) and Sch 4 para 18 SPC Regs
**HB** Reg 29(1)(i) HB(SPC) Regs
91 Sch 5 para 24 HB(SPC) Regs
92 s15(2) SPCA 2002; reg 15(6) SPC Regs
93 Regs 25 and 26 HB(SPC) Regs
94 Reg 43 HB(SPC) Regs
95 Reg 29(2) HB(SPC) Regs
96 **PC** Regs 15(6) and 17(8) SPC Regs
**HB** Regs 29(2) and 44(2) HB(SPC) Regs
97 **PC** ss15(1)(c) and 16(1) SPCA 2002; reg 16 SPC Regs
**HB** Reg 29(1)(c) HB(SPC) Regs
98 **PC** Reg 16 SPC Regs
**HB** Reg 29(1)(s) HB(SPC) Regs
99 **PC** Reg 16 SPC Regs
**HB** Reg 29(1)(t) HB(SPC) Regs
100 **PC** Reg 16 SPC Regs
**HB** Reg 29(1)(w) HB(SPC) Regs
101 para 85139 DMG
102 **PC** Reg 18(2)-(10) SPC Regs; para 85460 DMG
**HB** Reg 41(4)-(8) HB(SPC) Regs
103 para 85457 DMG
104 **PC** Reg 17(9) SPC Regs
**HB** Reg 33(8) HB(SPC) Regs
105 **PC** Sch 4 para 15 SPC Regs
**HB** Sch 5 para 16 HB(SPC) Regs
106 **PC** Sch 4 para 16 SPC Regs
**HB** Sch 5 para 17 HB(SPC) Regs
107 **PC** Sch 4 para 10 SPC Regs
**HB** Sch 5 para 11 HB(SPC) Regs
108 **PC** Sch 4 para 11 SPC Regs
**HB** Sch 5 para 12 HB(SPC) Regs
109 **PC** Sch 4 para 11(3)(b) SPC Regs
**HB** Sch 5 para 12(3) HB(SPC) Regs
110 **PC** Sch 4 para 14 SPC Regs
**HB** Sch 5 para 15 HB(SPC) Regs
111 **PC** Sch 4 para 13 SPC Regs
**HB** Sch 5 para 14 HB(SPC) Regs
112 Memo ADM 13/22; Explanatory Memorandum to The Universal Credit (Local Welfare Provision Disregard) (Amendment) Regulations 2022 No.448
113 The rules do not include grants and loans in the definition of 'income'
114 **PC** s15 SPCA 2002; regs 15 and 17B(4) SPC Regs
**HB** Regs 29 and 38(2) HB(SPC) Regs
115 **PC** Regs 17A(3)(f), 18(7A) and 24(2) SPC Regs
**HB** Regs 35(2)(f), 41(8C) and 42(3) HB(SPC) Regs
116 Reg 26 VP Regs

5. **Notional income**

117 **PC** Reg 18(6)-(8B) SPC Regs
**HB** Reg 41(8)-(8BD) HB(SPC) Regs
118 paras 28608-16 DMG; see also CIS/15052/1996
119 **PC** Reg 18(9) SPC Regs
**HB** Reg 41(11) HB(SPC) Regs
120 **PC** Reg 18(1)-(5) SPC Regs
**HB** Reg 41(1)-(7) HB(SPC) Regs
121 Reg 18(5A) SPC Regs
122 para 85453 DMG; *BRG v SSWP (SPC)* [2014] UKUT 246 (AAC)
123 Reg 18(5A) SPC Regs
124 **PC** Reg 18(2)-(5) SPC Regs; para 85456 DMG; *SSWP v Goulding* [2019] EWCA Civ 839
**HB** Reg 41(4)-(8) HB(SPC) Regs
125 **PC** Reg 24 SPC Regs
**HB** Reg 42 HB(SPC) Regs
126 CH/1672/2007
127 *BL v SSWP (SPC)* [2018] UKUT 4 (AAC)

6. **Working out weekly income**

128 **PC** Reg 17(2)(b)(i) SPC Regs
**HB** Reg 33(2)(b)(i) HB(SPC) Regs
129 **PC** Reg 17(2)(b)(ii) SPC Regs
**HB** Reg 33(2)(b)(ii) HB(SPC) Regs
130 **PC** Reg 17(4) SPC Regs
**HB** Reg 33(4) HB(SPC) Regs
131 **PC** Reg 17(1) SPC Regs
**HB** Reg 33(1) HB(SPC) Regs
132 Reg 13B SPC Regs
133 Reg 33(6) HB(SPC) Regs
134 R(PC) 3/08; *PS v SSWP (SPC)* [2016] UKUT 21 (AAC)
135 Reg 33(2A) and (3A) HB(SPC) Regs
136 Reg 1(2) SPC Regs
137 Reg 2 HB(SPC) Regs

# Chapter 18

# Capital: under pension age

3

**This chapter covers:**


1. The capital limits (p399)
2. Whose capital counts (p399)
3. What counts as capital (p400)
4. Disregarded capital (p403)
5. Notional capital (p413)
6. How capital is valued (p418)


This chapter explains how capital affects your entitlement to income-related employment and support allowance (ESA). It also applies to working-age housing benefit (HB) rules if you and your partner are under pension age. Chapter 19 explains the rules for pension credit and for pension-age HB rules if you and your partner are over pension age. If you are in a couple and one of you is over pension age but not the other, see p197 for whether the working-age or pension-age HB rules apply. For universal credit, see Chapter 8.

## Key facts

- If you have more than £16,000 capital, you are not entitled to income-related ESA or working-age HB.
- If you have capital above a lower limit of £6,000 (higher if you live in a care home), your benefit is affected because it is assumed that your capital gives you some income – often called 'tariff income'.
- Some kinds of capital are ignored when working out your benefit – eg, the value of the home in which you live.
- Getting income-related ESA means you always get the maximum amount of HB, so there is no need to work out your capital again for HB.
- If you deliberately get rid of capital in order to get more benefit, you are treated as still having it. This is called 'notional capital'.

## 1. The capital limits

There is a lower and upper limit.[1]

- The lower limit is £6,000.
- The upper limit is £16,000.

If you have over £16,000 of capital, you are not entitled to benefit. The first £6,000 is ignored and does not affect your weekly benefit. If you have between £6,000.01 and £16,000, you may be entitled to benefit, but it is assumed that you have some income from your capital. This is known as **'tariff income'**.

This tariff income (see p360) is assumed to be £1 a week for every £250, or part of £250, of your capital between £6,000.01 and £16,000.

If you live in a care home, see below.

When working out the value of your capital, some capital is disregarded (see p403). You may also be treated as having some capital which you do not actually have (see p413).

***Example***

Michael gets income-related employment and support allowance (ESA). He has £6,900 in savings. He is assumed to have tariff income of £4 a week.

### Care homes

If you live permanently in a care home (see p832):

- the lower limit is £10,000,
- the upper limit is £16,000.

Tariff income starts above £10,000.

***Example***

Glenn gets income-related ESA. He has £8,100 in savings. He is assumed to have tariff income of £9 a week. Glenn moves permanently into a care home. Because his savings are below the £10,000 limit, they are now disregarded entirely. A few months later he sells his home and gets £80,000. As a result, he is no longer entitled to income-related ESA

## 2. Whose capital counts

If you are a member of a couple (see p254), your partner's capital is added to yours.[2]

Your child's capital is not added to yours and does not affect your benefit.[3]

3

# 3. What counts as capital

All your capital is taken into account, unless it is specifically ignored (or 'disregarded') (see p403) or is treated as income (see p360).

The term 'capital' is not defined. Generally, it means lump-sum or one-off payments rather than a series of payments – eg, it includes savings, property and statutory redundancy payments.[4]

Capital payments can normally be distinguished from income because they are not payable for any specified period and are not part of a regular series of payments (although capital can be paid by instalments).[5]

**Note:** some capital is treated as income (see p360) and some income is treated as capital (see p402).

## Savings

Your savings generally count as capital – eg, cash you have at home, premium bonds, shares, unit trusts and money in a bank account or building society.

If you have put aside money to pay bills, this is still counted as your capital.[6] If your savings are just below the capital limit, you could pay bills by monthly direct debit or use a budget account to keep your capital below the limit.

Savings from past employed earnings and other income (including benefits – see p408) are treated as capital after the period for which the income was paid has lapsed – eg, a weekly payment of child benefit becomes capital a week after it is paid and a monthly occupational pension becomes capital after a month.[7] Beyond that, employed earnings continue to be treated as income until deductions for tax, national insurance and pension contributions have been made.[8]

## Fixed-term investments

Capital held in fixed-term investments counts. However, if it is currently unobtainable, it may have little or no value. If you can convert the investment into a form that lets you access it, sell your interest, or raise a loan through a reputable bank using the asset as security, the amount you can get for it counts.

## Property and land

Any property or land that you own counts as capital. Many types of property are disregarded (see p403). If there is doubt about who owns the property, see below.

## Loans and ownership of capital

Usually, it is clear when capital belongs to you and should be taken into account. However, it may be less clear if you are holding money for someone else or if you have been given a loan which you are expected to repay.

A loan to you usually counts as money you possess and therefore counts as capital. However, you can argue that a loan, money or other asset you hold for someone else should be disregarded if it is:

- a loan granted on condition that you only use the interest, but do not touch the capital because the capital element has never been at your disposal;[9]
- money you have been paid to be used for a particular purpose on condition that the money must be returned if not used in that way;[10]
- property you have bought on behalf of someone else who is paying the mortgage;[11]
- money held in your bank account on behalf of another person, which is to be returned to them at a future date;[12]
- savings from someone else's benefit paid to you as an appointee – eg, your child's disability living allowance;[13]
- a loan and when you get it, you are under an immediate obligation to repay it;[14]
- your own asset but you have expressed a clear intention that it is for someone else's benefit and renounced its use for yourself;[15]
- your interest in a property and you lead someone to believe that you are transferring it to them but fail to do so (eg, it is never properly conveyed) and that person acts on the belief that they own it (eg, they spend money on repairs). You can argue the asset has been transferred and you are like a trustee.[16] This is called **'proprietary estoppel'**.



If you lend money to someone, it could still count as your notional capital (see p413), depending on your reasons for lending it. You usually have a legal right to be repaid and this, in itself, could have a capital value, although the value would normally be less than the amount loaned, and could be nil if you have no expectation of getting the money back.[17]

## Trusts

A trust is a way of owning any asset such as money, a house or shares. A 'trustee' looks after the capital and owns the legal title. The trustee uses the capital for the benefit of someone else (the 'beneficiary'). If you are a trustee, the capital is not yours to use for yourself unless you are also a beneficiary.

Whether your money is in a discretionary or non-discretionary trust can make a difference to how your benefits are affected.

Payments made from:

- a discretionary trust count as income or capital depending on the nature of the payment.[18] Capital payments are taken into account in full, but income from the trust is generally treated as a voluntary payment and is ignored.[19] The trust asset itself does not normally count as your capital because payments are at the discretion of the trustees and you cannot demand payment (of either income

or capital).[20] To be a discretionary trust, the trust's terms must give trustees discretion over not just when to pay but also whether to make payments at all;[21]
- a non-discretionary trust count in full as capital, whatever the nature of the payment.[22] The trust asset itself also counts as your capital, because in a non-discretionary trust you can obtain the asset from the trustee at any time. For under-18-year-olds who have no right to payment (16 in Scotland, or older if the trust specifies), the value of the trust asset may have a current value which is less than the whole amount;
- a trust set up from money for a personal injury to you or your partner are treated more generously (see p410).

Trustees may have a discretion to use such funds to purchase items that would normally be disregarded as capital, such as personal possessions (eg, a wheelchair, car or new furniture) or to arrange payments that would normally be disregarded as income – eg, ineligible housing costs. Similarly, they may have discretion to clear debts or pay for a holiday, leisure items or educational or medical needs. See p357 for the treatment of voluntary payments, and p366 for the treatment of payments made to third parties.

**Note:**
- Putting money in a discretionary trust has the advantage of the value of the trust itself being disregarded. However, if you transfer money into a trust in order to get more benefit, it can still count as yours under the notional capital rules (see p413).
- Capital in a non-discretionary trust is taken into account. If this takes you over the £16,000 capital limit, you are not entitled to benefit.

## Money held by your solicitor

Money held by your solicitor normally counts as your capital. This includes compensation payments (but see p410 for when payments for personal injury are disregarded).[23] If you have had legal aid and your solicitor is holding money back while working out the statutory charge to be deducted for legal costs, it does not count as your capital.[24]

## Income treated as capital

Certain payments that appear to be income are treated as capital. These are:[25]
- income from capital – eg, interest on a bank account, share dividends and income from property let to tenants (see p358). However, the following count as income, not capital:
  - income from the first five disregarded property bullet points on p403;
  - trust funds administered by a court (see p410);

- income from the home of a partner, former partner or relative in the circumstances described on p405;
- income from the home in which you normally live;
- income from business assets or personal injury trusts;

- a lump sum or 'bounty' paid to you not more than once a year as a part-time firefighter, part-time member of a lifeboat crew, auxiliary coastguard or member of the reserve forces. If paid more often, it counts as earnings;
- the following payments:
  - an advance of earnings or loan from your employer;
  - holiday pay which is not payable until more than four weeks after your employment ends or is interrupted;
  - income tax refunds;
  - irregular (one-off) charitable or voluntary payments;
- for income-related employment and support allowance only, a discharge grant paid on release from prison;
- for housing benefit only, any arrears of child tax credit or working tax credit.[26]

# 4. Disregarded capital

## Your home

If you own the home in which you normally live, its value is ignored.[27]

*Your home*

Your **'home'** includes any garage, garden, outbuildings and land belonging to the property, together with any premises that you do not occupy as your home but which it is impractical or unreasonable to sell separately – eg, croft land.[28]

This disregard applies to any home in which you are treated as normally living – eg, because you are only temporarily living away from it (see p296). If you own more than one property, only the one that you normally occupy is disregarded under this rule.[29]

Exceptionally, two separate properties can be regarded as a single home as though one was an annexe of the other, if you personally (rather than a member of your family) normally occupy both properties.[30] This is most likely to be the case for a large family, but other situations are possible where neither property on its own caters for a family's needs – eg, if there is a carer living between two properties.[31]

### When the value of the property is disregarded

The value of the property can be disregarded, even if you do not normally live in it, in the following circumstances.

3

- **If you have left your former home following a relationship breakdown,** the property's value is ignored for 26 weeks from the date you left. It may also be disregarded for longer if any of the steps below are taken. If it is occupied by your former partner who is a lone parent, its value is ignored for as long as they live there.[32]
- **If you have sought legal advice or have started legal proceedings to occupy the property as your home,** its value is ignored for 26 weeks from the date you first took either of these steps.[33] The 26 weeks can be extended if it is reasonable to do so.
- **If you are taking reasonable steps to dispose of a property,** its value is ignored for 26 weeks from the date you first took such steps (which may be before you claim benefit).[34] The steps you take must be 'reasonable'. Advertising at an unrealistic sale price does not count, but placing the property with an estate agent or contacting a possible buyer should,[35] as might taking ancillary proceedings to resolve financial issues in a divorce.[36] The disregard can continue beyond 26 weeks, even for years if it is reasonable – eg, if a court orders that the former matrimonial home should not be sold until the children are grown up. Taking a property off the market and putting it on again does not necessarily begin a new 26-week period, but it may do if the second attempt to sell is quite separate.[37]
- **If you are carrying out essential repairs or alterations which are needed so that you can occupy a property as your home,** the property's value is ignored for 26 weeks from the date you first began to take steps to carry them out.[38] 'Steps' may include applying for planning permission or a grant or loan to make the property habitable, employing an architect or finding someone to do the work.[39] If you cannot move into the property within that period because the work is not finished, its value can be disregarded for as long as is necessary to allow the work to be carried out.
- **If you have acquired a property and intend to live there as your home but have not yet moved in,** its value is ignored if you intend to live there within 26 weeks of acquiring it.[40] If you cannot move in by then, the value can be ignored for as long as seems reasonable.
- **If you sell your home and intend to use the proceeds to buy another home,** the capital is ignored for 26 weeks from the date of the sale.[41] This also applies even if you do not own your home but, for a price, you surrender your tenancy rights to a landlord.[42] If you need longer to complete a purchase, your capital can continue to be ignored if it is reasonable to do so. You do not need to have decided within the 26 weeks to buy a particular property. It is sufficient if you intend to use the proceeds to buy another home within the 26-week (or extended) period,[43] although your 'intention' must involve more than a mere 'hope' or 'aspiration'.[44] There must be an element of 'certainty' that you may be able to show by evidence of a practical commitment to another purchase, although this need not involve any binding obligation.[45] If you intend to use

only part of the proceeds to buy another home, only that part is disregarded even if, for example, you have put the rest of the money aside to renovate your new home.[46]

- **If your home is damaged or you lose it altogether**, any payment in consequence of that, including compensation, which is to be used for its repair, or for acquiring another home, is ignored for 26 weeks, or longer if it is reasonable to do so.
- **If you have taken out a loan or been given money for the express purpose of essential repairs or improvements to your home**, it is ignored for 26 weeks, or longer if it is reasonable to do so.[47] If it is a condition of the loan that it must be returned if the improvements are not carried out, you should argue that it should be ignored altogether.[48]
- **If you have deposited money with a housing association as a condition of occupying your home**, this is ignored indefinitely.[49] If money that was deposited for this purpose is now to be used to buy another home, this is ignored for 26 weeks, or longer if reasonable, in order to allow you to complete the purchase.[50]
- **Grants made to buy a home** are ignored for up to 26 weeks if made to local authority tenants to buy a home or do repairs or alterations to it. They can be ignored for longer, if reasonable, to allow completion of the purchase or the repairs/alterations. **Note:** the repairs or alterations must be required to make the property fit for occupation as your home.[51]

When considering whether it is reasonable to extend the period during which time the property's value is disregarded, all the circumstances should be considered – eg, your personal circumstances, any efforts made by you to use or dispose of the home[52] and the general state of the property market. In practice, periods of around 18 months are not considered unusual.

**Note:** it is possible for property to be ignored under more than one of the above paragraphs together or in succession.[53]

Some income generated from property which is disregarded is ignored (see p359).

## The home of a partner, former partner or relative

The value of a home (see p403) is ignored if it is occupied as the home of:[54]

- someone over pension age (see p239), or who has limited capability for work or is incapacitated (see p406), who is:
  - a relative of yours or of your partner or dependent child; *or*
  - your spouse or civil partner, provided you are still treated as living in the same household (see p254), or your cohabitee, provided you are still treated as living together as a married couple (see p255); *or*

- your former partner from whom you are not estranged but you are living apart (and are therefore not treated as still living together or as living in the same household) – eg, if one of you is living in a care home; *or*
- your former partner from whom you are estranged and who is a lone parent. If your former partner is not a lone parent, the value of the home is ignored for 26 weeks from the date you ceased to live in the home.

3

***Definitions***

**'Incapacitated'** is not defined, but guidance suggests it includes anyone who is getting employment and support allowance (ESA), statutory sick pay, attendance allowance (AA) or disability living allowance (DLA) or who would qualify because of their health condition or disability.[55] It may also include anyone who is getting personal independence payment (PIP), adult disability payment (ADP), Scottish adult disability living allowance (SADLA); pension age disability payment (PADP) or universal credit (UC) who has limited capability for work or limited capability for work-related activity. However, you should argue for a broader interpretation, if necessary.

**'Relative'** is a parent, son, daughter, step-parent, stepson, stepdaughter, parent-in-law, son-in-law, daughter-in-law, sibling, or a partner of any of these people, half-sibling, adopted child, grandparent or grandchild, uncle, aunt, nephew or niece.[56]

You are **'estranged'** if you are living apart because your relationship has broken down, even if the separation is amicable.[57]

## Personal possessions

All personal possessions, including jewellery, furniture or a car, are ignored.[58] A personal possession has been defined as any physical asset not used for business purposes, other than land.[59] For example, in one case, a static caravan on a non-residential site was treated as a personal possession. However, a home that you own but do not live in is not normally a personal possession and does count as capital (see p403). Personal possessions are not ignored if you have bought them in order to be able to claim or get more benefit. In this case, the sale value, rather than the purchase price, is counted as actual capital and the difference is treated as notional capital (see p413).[60]

Compensation for damage to, or the loss of, any personal possessions, which is to be used for their repair or replacement, is ignored for six months, or longer if reasonable.[61]

### Business assets

If you are self-employed, your business assets are ignored for as long as you continue to work in that business.[62]

If you cannot work because you are sick or incapacitated, the assets are disregarded for 26 weeks from the date of claim if you intend to work in the business again when you are able, or for longer if reasonable in the circumstances.[63]

If you stop working in the business, you are allowed a reasonable time to sell these assets without their value affecting your benefit.

It is sometimes difficult to distinguish between personal and business assets. The test is whether the assets are 'part of the fund employed and risked in the business'.[64]



### Running your business as a sole trader, partner or limited company

If you run your business as a sole trader or in a partnership, you are self-employed and business assets are ignored as capital (see above).

If you run your business through a company, you are treated as though you were a sole trader or in a partnership if you have a similar level of control in the company to that of a sole trader or a partner. For example, you may be a director of your own limited company. You are treated as owning the business assets, or a proportion of the assets in a partnership, and the assets are ignored while you are engaged in any work for the company. Instead of the value of any shares you hold being taken into account as capital as they normally would, the value of shares is disregarded.

For income-related ESA, the DWP must treat your capital this way, but for HB, the local authority has discretion about whether to apply these rules to treat you as though you were a sole trader or in a partnership when you run your business through a company.[65]

## Personal pension schemes

The value of a fund held in a personal pension scheme is ignored as capital.[66] The value of the right to receive an occupational or personal pension is also ignored. However, if your partner is over pension age and chooses not to take income from the pension, you are treated as having notional income (see p361).

## Insurance policy and annuity surrender values

The surrender value of a life assurance policy is ignored.[67] Some investments include an element of life insurance – eg, endowment policies. If the policy terms include how the payment on death is calculated, the whole investment is ignored.[68] However, you cannot choose to put money into such an investment in order to increase your benefit entitlement, because you are likely to be caught by the notional capital rule if you do (see p413).

The surrender value of any annuity is also ignored,[69] as is the value of the right to receive any payment under an annuity. Any payment under the annuity counts as income[70] (but see p361 for when this is ignored).

3

## Future interest in property

A future interest in most kinds of property is ignored.[71] A **'future interest'** is one which will only revert to you, or become yours for the first time, when some future event occurs – eg, where someone else has a life interest in a fund and you are only entitled to it after that person has died.

However, this does not include a freehold or leasehold interest in property which has been let *by you* to tenants. If you did not let the property to the tenant (eg, because the tenancy was entered into before you bought the property), your interest in the property should be ignored as a future interest in the normal way.

## The right to receive a payment in the future

If you know that you will receive a payment in the future and you could sell your right to it at any time, it has a market value and therefore constitutes an actual capital resource. The value of this is ignored if it is a right to receive:[72]

- income under a life interest or, in Scotland, a life rent; *or*
- an occupational or personal pension; *or*
- any rent if you are not the freeholder or leaseholder. Any actual income which this right generates for you and which is not disregarded as income can be taken into account as income; *or*
- any payment under an annuity (see p361). Any actual income generated by this right and which is not disregarded as income can be taken into account as income; *or*
- any earnings or income that is ignored because it is frozen abroad; *or*
- any outstanding instalments if capital is being paid by instalments; *or*
- any payment under a trust fund set up with money paid because of a personal injury to you or your partner.

### Benefits

#### Arrears of benefits and tax credits

Arrears of the following are ignored for 52 weeks after you receive them, or longer in some cases where there has been official error or an error of law (see p409):[73]

- AA;
- ADP (in Scotland);
- armed forces independence payment;
- bereavement support payment;
- child disability payment (in Scotland);
- child tax credit;
- DLA;
- discretionary housing payments;
- income-related ESA;
- housing benefit (HB);
- income support;

- income-based jobseeker's allowance;
- maternity allowance;
- mobility supplement;
- PADP (in Scotland);
- pension age winter heating payment (in Scotland)
- PIP;
- Scottish child payment;
- SADLA;
- short-term assistance (in Scotland);
- UC;
- working tax credit;
- concessionary payments instead of any of the above;
- for HB only, compensation for lost or delayed (new-style) contributory ESA because of a DWP error.



If the arrears are £5,000 or more and are paid to compensate for an official error (see p1135) or an error of law, they are ignored until the end of your (or your partner's) award. If you or your partner move to UC, they continue to be ignored for the whole of this next and any subsequent award(s) if there is no gap between awards.[74]

**Note:** although arrears are ignored as capital, you may have been paid more income-related ESA or HB than you would have been entitled to if benefit had been paid on time. Usually, the DWP deducts the difference from the arrears of the delayed benefit. Otherwise, if the arrears are not reduced, the overpayment is recoverable from you (see p1062). For HB, the overpayment is not deducted from the arrears but may be recoverable (see p1078).

## Other benefits and payments

The following are ignored for 52 weeks from the date you receive them, or indefinitely where specified:

- initial lump sum of bereavement support payment and, for a surviving cohabiting partner whose partner died before 9 February 2023, arrears of monthly payments;[75]
- widowed parent's allowance arrears, that include a period before 9 February 2023, paid to a surviving cohabiting partner.[76] Although ignored as capital, the arrears can also count as income for the period they cover and reduce entitlement to means-tested benefits paid in the same period. The DWP can deduct the difference from the arrears or recover the overpayment from you;
- social fund payments (ignored indefinitely);[77]
- Best Start grant (in Scotland) (ignored indefinitely);[78]
- child winter heating payment (in Scotland) (ignored indefinitely);[79]
- fares to hospital, and payments for prescriptions and dental charges;[80]
- funeral support payment (in Scotland) (ignored indefinitely);[81]

- payments in lieu of Healthy Start or Best Start foods prepaid card;[82]
- payments to assist prison visits;[83]
- certain payments to war widows, widowers and surviving civil partners;[84]
- winter heating payment (in Scotland) (ignored indefinitely);[85]
- young carer grant (in Scotland) (ignored indefinitely);[86]
- any payments by the Secretary of State to compensate for the loss of entitlement to HB (ignored indefinitely);[87]
- cost of living payments are disregarded indefinitely.[88] These were additional payments of up to £650 in 2022/23 and £900 in 2023/24 for people on means-tested benefits and an additional £150 in 2022/23 and 2023/24 for people on disability benefits. These amounts are disregarded from your capital for as long as they remain unspent.[89]

## Charitable, personal injury and other compensation payments

- **Charitable payments.** If a charity gives you a one-off grant, it counts as capital and affects your benefit if it takes your capital above the limit. Any payment in kind, such as food or clothing, by a charity is ignored.[90]
- **Personal injury payments.** If you have money in a trust from a personal injury to you, the value of the trust and any income from it is disregarded.[91] A lump sum from the trust is taken into account as capital. It should not affect your benefit if the trustees give you regular or even annual payments, pay your bills or, instead of giving you a lump sum, buy you something that would be disregarded because it is a personal possession – eg furniture or a car.

  If an award for damages for personal injury to you is administered by a court (eg, the Court of Protection), its value and income from it is also disregarded.[92] This also applies if the court-administered fund is for children to compensate for the death of a parent.

  If you have just received a payment for personal injury to you, it is disregarded for 52 weeks from when you receive it.[93] This gives you time to put it into a trust or annuity before your benefit is affected. There is no 52-week disregard for another payment for the same injury, but it is disregarded as soon as it is in a trust.

  If the personal injury is to your partner, there is a 52-week disregard for the initial payment and the value of a trust is disregarded, but not income from the trust or annuity. If your partner has since died, you cannot carry over the remainder of the 52-week disregard, or if the payment is in a trust, it is no longer ignored.[94]

Personal injury payments include compensation from the Criminal Injuries Compensation Scheme.[95]

***Definitions***

**'Personal injury'** includes not only accidental and criminal injuries, but also any disease and injury as a result of a disease.[96]

Payments include any amounts in consequence of personal injury – eg, for loss of earnings.[97]

**'Trust'**. Any money in a trust 'derived from' compensation for personal injury to you is disregarded irrespective of the type of trust.[98]



- **Special compensation schemes.** Any single lump sum payment of capital you receive from certain special schemes is disregarded indefinitely, including:[99]
  - the National Emergencies Trust;
  - the Windrush Compensation Scheme;
  - the Child Migrants Trust (for children subjected to migration programmes before 1971);
  - the Victims of Overseas Terrorism Compensation Scheme;
  - schemes to make child abuse payments for historic institutional child abuse in the UK;
  - payments from an infected blood scheme;
  - for people affected by the 2017 fire at Grenfell Tower;
  - Post Office compensation payments for Horizon system failings;
  - vaccine damage payments under the Vaccine Damage Payments Act 1979;
  - payments from the Ministry of Defence's LGBT Financial Recognition Scheme;
  - victims' payments under the Troubles Permanent Disablement Payment Scheme.[100]

  For schemes that make regular payments, these are disregarded as income.[101] For most of the schemes, money from your partner's payments is ignored indefinitely, or for two years from your child's payments if they have no partner or dependent child.[102]

If you have other capital and a disregarded payment in the same account, it should be accepted that money is withdrawn from the other capital before the disregarded payment, unless evidence shows otherwise.[103]

## Social services, community care and other payments

The following payments from a local authority are ignored indefinitely:[104]

- payments for children and families made under section 17 of the Children Act 1989, section 12 of the Social Work (Scotland) Act 1968 or, for HB, section 22 of the Children (Scotland) Act 1995 and sections 37 and 38 of the Social Services and Well-being (Wales) Act 2014;

- payments to young people who have previously been looked after by the local authority made under sections 23B or 24A of the Children Act 1989, section 30 of the Children (Scotland) Act 1995 or sections 109, 110, 114 or 115 of the Social Services and Well-being (Wales) Act 2014. A payment under section 23C of the Children Act 1989 is also ignored as the young person's capital, and as yours if they pass it to you, they were in your care, and are still living with you and are aged 18 or over – eg, under 'staying put' arrangements. In Scotland, this applies to payments under sections 26A and 29 of the Children (Scotland) Act 1995 and includes young people aged 16 or over in 'continuing care'.

See p891 if you or your partner are involved in a trade dispute.

Also ignored indefinitely are:

- local welfare assistance to meet an immediate short-term need or establish or maintain a settled home in certain circumstances (see p770). These include household support fund payments and 'thank you' payments under the Homes for Ukraine Scheme;[105]
- community care or healthcare direct payments;[106]
- education, health and care plan payments, paid in England for a child with special educational needs;[107]
- payments from a local authority for support services to help you live independently (eg, under the Supporting People programme, often called 'housing-related support');[108]
- special guardianship allowances, payable in England and Wales;[109]
- kinship care payments, payable in Scotland;[110]
- payments under sections 2, 3 or 4 of the Adoption and Children Act 2002.[111]

## Employment and training programme payments

Some payments are ignored for 52 weeks from the date they are received:[112]

- payment for travel or other expenses from a specified scheme for assisting people to obtain employment;
- for income-related ESA, payment for travel or other expenses for undertaking required work-related activity;
- payment under section 2 of the Employment and Training Act 1973 or section 2 of the Enterprise and New Towns (Scotland) Act 1990.

Payments to disabled people under the Disabled Persons (Employment) Act 1944 (other than a training allowance) to assist with employment, or local authority payments to assist blind homeworkers, are ignored indefinitely.[113]

For when employment and training programme payments are treated as notional income and notional capital, see p366 and p416.

## Miscellaneous payments

The following payments are disregarded:

- a sports award made by the UK Sport National Lottery funds, except for any part of the award which is made for ordinary living expenses (see p364). It is disregarded for 26 weeks;[114]
- an education maintenance allowance or a 16 to 19 bursary fund payment are ignored indefinitely;[115]
- for income-related ESA, any payments made to jurors or witnesses for attending at court, except for payments for loss of earnings or benefit;[116]
- refunds of council tax liability (ignored for 52 weeks from the date you receive the arrears);[117]
- 20 per cent of money in a tax-free childcare account (see p779);[118]
- any payments made to holders of the Victoria or George Cross.[119]



# 5. Notional capital

In certain circumstances, you are treated as having capital that you do not have. This is called **'notional capital'**.[120] There is a similar rule for notional income (see p365). Notional capital counts in the same way as the capital you do have.

You may be treated as having notional capital if:

- you deliberately deprive yourself of capital in order to claim or increase benefit (see below); *or*
- you fail to apply for capital which is available to you (see p416); *or*
- someone makes a payment of capital to a third party on your behalf or on behalf of a member of your family (see p416); *or*
- you (or a member of your family) receive a payment of capital on behalf of a third party and you (or the member of your family) use or keep the capital (see p417); *or*
- you are running a business through a company instead of as a sole trader or a partner (see p407).

**Note:** if you are treated as having notional capital because you have deliberately deprived yourself of capital in order to claim or increase benefit, a 'diminishing notional capital rule' (see p415) may be applied so that the value of the notional capital you are treated as having is considered to reduce over time.

## Deliberately getting rid of capital

If you deliberately get rid of capital in order to claim or increase your benefit, you are treated as still having it.[121] The same applies if your partner got rid of capital, even if they did so before you became a couple.[122] You are likely to be affected by this rule if, at the time of using up your money, you knew that you might qualify for benefit (or more benefit), or qualify more quickly as a result. You should not be affected if you knew nothing about the effect of using up your capital (eg, you did not know about the capital limit for claiming benefit)[123] or if you have been using up your capital at a rate which is reasonable in the circumstances. This is because you cannot have the intention if you do not know about the capital rules.[124] Knowledge of capital limits can be inferred from a reasonable familiarity with the benefit system as a claimant,[125] but if you fail to make enquiries about the capital limit, this does not constitute an intention to secure benefit.

In practice, arguing successfully that you have not deprived yourself of capital to get or increase benefit may depend on whether you can show that you would have spent the money in the way you did (eg, to pay off debts or reduce your mortgage) regardless of the effect on your benefit entitlement. If this is unclear, the burden of proving that you did it to get benefit lies with the decision maker.

### Your intentions

Even if you did know about the capital limits, it still has to be shown that you intended to obtain, retain or increase your benefit.[126] For example, in one case, a claimant faced repossession of his home and transferred ownership to his daughter (who he feared would otherwise be made homeless), despite having been warned by DWP staff that he would be disqualified from benefit if he did so. It was held that, under the circumstances, he had not disposed of the property with the intention of gaining benefit.[127] The longer the period that has elapsed since the disposal of the capital, the less likely it is for the purpose of obtaining benefit.[128] However, no matter how long it has been since you may have disposed of an asset, there is no set 'safe' period after which benefit can be claimed without the need for further enquiry.[129]

If you use up your resources, you may have more than one motive for doing so. Even if qualifying for benefit is only a lesser motive for your actions and the main motive is something different (eg, ensuring your home is in good condition by spending capital on repairs and improvements), you may still be considered to have deprived yourself of a resource in order to gain benefit.[130]

The test is not what the money has been spent on, but your intention behind the expenditure. However, examples of the kinds of expenditure that could be caught by this rule are expensive holidays and putting money in trust.[131] **Note:** for income-related employment and support allowance (ESA), putting money in trust for yourself does not constitute deprivation if the capital came from compensation paid for a personal injury.[132]

You can deprive yourself of capital, even if you receive another resource in return.[133] For example, if you buy a car so that you can get more benefit, your actual capital includes the value of the car, and the difference between that and the purchase price is treated as notional capital.[134]

## Paying off debts and bankruptcy

If you pay off a debt that you are legally required to repay immediately, you may not be counted as having deprived yourself of capital in order to gain benefit.[135] It is the facts of your case that are important: if you paid off an immediately repayable debt when you thought it would not be recalled for some time, you might be considered to have deprived yourself of money in order to get benefit. However, even if you pay off a debt that you are not legally required to repay immediately, the decision maker must still prove that you did so in order to get benefit.[136] Get advice about whether you would be better off claiming universal credit (UC) instead. For UC, paying off a debt does not count as deprivation of capital (see p162).

If you are declared bankrupt, you cannot spend your capital without court approval and cannot usually be held to have deprived yourself of it if you do. Capital you have (but cannot spend) does not count for benefit purposes from the date of the bankruptcy order.[137] However, if you deliberately go bankrupt or do not take reasonable steps to discharge the bankruptcy in order to get benefit, your capital can still count as notional capital.

## How notional capital is calculated

Notional capital is generally calculated in the same way as actual capital and the same disregards usually apply (see p403).[138] However, you may not be able to rely on the 26-week (or longer) disregard you would otherwise be allowed to take steps to dispose of a property (see p403), even if the new owner is trying to sell it (but there is conflicting caselaw on this).[139]

**Note:** you should continue to get maximum HB if you are still entitled to some income-related ESA after intentionally depriving yourself of capital.[140]

## The diminishing notional capital rule

The diminishing notional capital rule provides a way of working out how the value of your notional capital may be treated as reducing over time. It only applies if you have deliberately deprived yourself of capital.[141]

It applies from the first week after the week in which it is decided that notional capital is to be taken into account.

- If your benefit is reduced because of tariff income from your notional capital, that capital is diminished by the amount of the reduction each week. For example, if your notional capital is £6,750 (and you have no other capital), giving a tariff income of £3 a week, the reduction is £3 a week until it reaches £6,500, when it will be £2 and so on. For HB, the amount of your notional capital is also reduced by the amount of income-related ESA you would have had if no notional capital had been taken into account.
- If you have both actual and notional capital, you may have to use your actual capital to meet your living expenses. There is no reason why this should affect the amount by which your notional capital is diminished, even if this

effectively results in double counting. Any reduction in your actual capital should be taken into account in calculating any tariff income arising from your combined actual and notional capital, unless you have spent it at such a rate and in such a way that it raises questions of intent, when you may find that the notional capital rules are applied all over again.

- If your benefit award has ended because of notional capital, the amount of notional capital reduces over time. Once it has reduced to a point when a fresh claim might succeed, you cannot make a new claim for income-related ESA and can only claim HB in limited circumstances (see p21). Instead, you can claim UC. See p494 of the 2018/19 edition of this *Handbook* for how notional capital is reduced for these benefits. **Note:** you are not automatically treated as having the notional capital in a UC claim. If you wish to claim UC, you should do so without delay in order to have the capital considered again under the UC rules (see p161).

## Failing to apply for capital

You are expected to apply for any capital that is due to you – eg, if money is held by a court which could be released if you applied, or an unclaimed premium bond win. If you would get capital if you applied for it, you are treated as having that capital.[142]

You are only treated as having such capital from the date you could obtain it. This rule does not apply if you do not apply for:

- capital from a discretionary trust; *or*
- capital from a trust (or fund administered by a court) set up from money paid as a result of a personal injury; *or*
- capital from a personal pension scheme or, if you are under pension age (see p239), from an occupational pension scheme or a payment from the Pension Protection Fund; *or*
- a loan which you could only get if you gave your home or other disregarded capital (see p403) as security.

## Capital payments made to a third party on your behalf

If someone pays an amount to a third party (eg, a fuel company or a building society) for you or your partner (or a child for HB), this may count as your capital. It counts if the payment is to cover:[143]

- certain normal living expenses – ie, food, household fuel, council tax, water charges or ordinary clothing or footwear. School uniforms and sportswear are not ordinary clothing,[144] nor are special shoes needed because of a disability.[145] Payments made, for instance, for food or clothes for you or your partner count as yours. However, since a child's capital is not counted as belonging to you, a payment to, for example, a clothes shop for your child should count as the child's notional capital and not yours, and, in most cases, is ignored; *or*

- rent which could be met by HB (less any non-dependant deductions); *or*
- for income-related ESA only, housing costs which could be met by income-related ESA.

Payments to a third party do *not* count as yours if they are:[146]
- for other kinds of expenses (eg, a TV licence or mortgage repayments), unless they come from a benefit or pension (see below); *or*
- from a specified infected blood scheme (see p411) or certain other specified compensation schemes; *or*
- for participating in a specified scheme for assisting people to obtain employment.



Payments from an occupational or personal pension scheme or from the Pension Protection Fund to a third party count as yours regardless of whether or not the payments are used, or intended to be used, for ordinary living expenses.[147] They are disregarded if:
- you (or your partner) are bankrupt (or in Scotland, the subject of a sequestration order), the payment is made to the trustee or other person acting on your creditors' behalf and you and your partner (or your family for HB) have no income other than the payment made;[148] *or*
- the payments do not support you financially and therefore do not reduce or remove your need to be supported by income-related ESA or HB – eg, deductions from an occupational pension made under an attachment of earnings order to a former partner.[149] If you have had a judicial separation, rather than divorce, so the usual pension-splitting arrangements are not available, and a court has ordered you to pay part of your pension to your former partner, you could argue that this does not count as yours.[150]

For income-related ESA only, payments *derived* from certain social security benefits (including war disablement pensions, war widows' pensions and Armed Forces Compensation Scheme payments) and paid to a third party count:[151]
- as yours, if you are entitled to the benefit; *and*
- as your partner's, if they are entitled to the benefit.

For income-related ESA, there are different rules if you could be liable to pay maintenance (see p355).

## Capital payments made to you for a third party

If you or your partner get a payment for someone not in your family (eg, a relative), it only counts as yours if it is kept or used by you.[152] For HB, the same also applies to payments received by a member of your family for someone not in the family. Payments from a specified infected blood scheme or certain other specified compensation schemes (see p411), or a specified scheme for assisting people to obtain employment, do not count at all. Payments from pension schemes paid for a third party are disregarded in the same circumstances as described on p416.

## 6. How capital is valued

### Market value

Your capital is valued at its current market or surrender value.[153] This means the amount of money you could raise by selling it or raising a loan against it. This is the price that a willing buyer would pay to a willing seller on a particular date.[154] So if an asset is difficult or impossible to realise, its market value should be heavily discounted or even nil.[155]

If you cannot legally dispose of capital (eg, because of a restraint order), the market value is nil.[156]

In the case of a house, an estate agent's figure for a quick sale is a more appropriate valuation than the district valuer's figure for a sale within three months.[157]

It is not uncommon for an unrealistic assessment to be made of the value of your capital. If you disagree with the decision, you could ask for a revision or appeal (see Chapters 50 and 51).

### Expenses of sale

If there would be expenses involved in selling your capital, 10 per cent is deducted from its value (before any debts are deducted) for the cost of sale.[158]

### Debts

Deductions are made from the gross value of your capital for any debt or mortgage secured on it.[159] If a creditor (eg, a bank) holds the land certificate to your property as security for a loan and has registered notice of its deposit at the Land Registry, this counts as a debt secured on your property.[160] If a single mortgage is secured on a house and land, and the value of the house is disregarded for benefit purposes, the whole of the mortgage can be deducted when calculating the value of the land.[161]

If you have debts that are not secured against your capital (eg, tax liabilities), these cannot be offset against the value of your capital.[162] However, once you have repaid your debts, your capital may be reduced. **Note:** you can still be treated as having the capital if you deliberately get rid of it in order to get benefit (see p413).

If you have an overdrawn bank account and have savings in another account with the same bank, the amount of the overdraft should be deducted from your savings if the terms of the accounts allow the bank to make these transfers.[163]

## Jointly owned capital

If you own any capital asset (except as a partner in a company – see p407) with someone else under a 'joint tenancy', you are treated as owning an equal share of the asset with the other owner(s) – eg, if you own the asset with one other person, you are each treated as having a 50 per cent share of it.[164] This applies regardless of whether the capital asset is in the UK or abroad. See p420 for the rules that apply to assets abroad.[165]



This does not apply if you jointly own the capital asset as 'tenants in common'.[166] In this case, your actual share in the asset is valued.

### *Joint tenancies and tenancies in common*

With a **'joint tenancy'**, each co-owner owns the whole of the capital asset 'jointly and severally'. If one of the joint tenants were to die, their interest in the asset would pass automatically to the other joint tenant(s).

With a **'tenancy in common'**, each co-owner owns a discrete share in the asset. This share can be passed on in their will by the person who has died to whoever they choose.

If you have a joint tenancy, the value of your deemed share is calculated in the same way as your actual capital. However, it is only the value of your deemed share looked at in isolation that counts, and this will usually be worth less than the same proportion of the value of the whole asset. For example, if the asset is a house, the value of any deemed share may be very small or even worthless, particularly if the house is occupied and there is a possibility that the sale of the property cannot be forced. This is because even a willing buyer could not be expected to pay much for an asset they would have difficulty making use of.[167] However, a value may be placed on a part share when the other joint owner does not wish to sell, as there may be a market for investors for such shares.[168] Whether a sale can be forced depends on individual circumstances. For example, a court may be more likely to order a sale of property left jointly in a will with no restrictions on use.[169] Valuations should take into account legal costs and the length of time it could take to gain possession of the property.[170] A valuation should set out details of the valuer's expertise (where relevant), describe the property in sufficient detail to show that all factors relevant to its value have been taken into account, state any assumptions on which it is based and explain what the market is for that type of sale.[171] You may need to challenge any decision (see Chapters 50 and 51) based on an inadequate valuation.

## Treatment of assets after a relationship breakdown

When partners separate, assets, such as a former home or bank account, may be in joint or sole names. If, for instance, a bank account is in joint names, you and your former partner are treated as having a 50 per cent share each under the rules on jointly held capital (see p419). On the other hand, a former partner may have a right to some, or all, of an asset that is in your sole name – eg, they may have deposited most of the money in a bank account in your name. If this is established, you may be treated as not entitled to the whole of the account but as holding part of it as trustee for your former partner.[172] If an asset such as the matrimonial home belongs to your former partner and you have no share in it, you cannot be treated as having any interest in it under the Matrimonial Causes Act 1973 unless you take divorce or separation proceedings and get a property order.[173]

3

## Shares

Shares are valued at their current market value less 10 per cent for the cost of sale, and after deducting any 'lien' held by brokers for sums owed for purchase or commission.[174] Market value can be worked out from the listed share price. If a more exact value is needed (eg, because your capital is close to the limit), DWP guidance says it should be calculated by taking the lowest and highest share prices for the day (from uk.finance.yahoo.com) and using the lowest price plus a quarter of the difference between the two.[175] Fluctuations in price between routine reviews of your award are normally ignored. If you have a minority holding of shares in a company, the value of the shares should be based on what you could realise on them, and not by valuing the entire share capital of the company and attributing to you an amount calculated according to the proportion of shares held.[176]

## Unit trusts

Unit trusts are valued on the basis of the bid price quoted in newspapers. No deduction is allowed for the cost of sale because this is already included in the bid price.[177]

## The right to receive a payment in the future

The value of any such right that is not ignored (see p408) is its market value – what a willing buyer will pay to a willing seller.[178] For something which is not yet realisable, this may be very small.

## Overseas assets

If you have assets abroad and there are no exchange controls or other prohibitions to prevent you transferring your capital to the UK, your assets are valued at their current market or surrender value in that country.[179]

If you are not allowed to transfer your capital, you are treated as having capital equal to the amount that a willing buyer in this country would give (which might not be very much).[180] Deduct 10 per cent for any expenses of sale, any debts or mortgage secured on the assets and any charges for converting the payment into sterling.[181]

# Notes



1. **The capital limits**
   1 **ESA** Regs 110 and 118 ESA Regs
   **HB** Regs 43 and 52 HB Regs

2. **Whose capital counts**
   2 **ESA** Sch 1 para 6(2) WRA 2007
   **HB** s136(1) SSCBA 1992
   3 **ESA** Reg 83(2) ESA Regs
   **HB** Reg 25(3) HB Regs

3. **What counts as capital**
   4 para BW1.71 GM; Vol 5 Ch 29 para 29020 DMG
   5 *R v SBC ex parte Singer* [1973] 1 WLR 713 (cited in CH/412/2007)
   6 R(IS) 3/93
   7 R(IS) 3/93 para 22
   8 R(SB) 2/83; R(SB) 35/83; R(IS) 3/93
   9 R(SB) 12/86
   10 *Barclays Bank v Quistclose Investments Ltd* [1970] AC 567; R(SB) 49/83; R(SB) 53/83; R(SB) 1/85; *MW v SSWP (JSA)* [2016] UKUT 469 (AAC), reported as [2017] AACR 15
   11 R(SB) 49/83
   12 R(SB) 12/86; for how this works in Scotland, see *JK v SSWP (JSA)* [2010] UKUT 437 (AAC), reported as [2011] AACR 26; *DF v SSWP* [2015] UKUT 611 (AAC)
   13 *MC v SSWP (IS)* [2015] UKUT 600 (AAC)
   14 CIS/2287/2008
   15 R(IS) 1/90; CSIS/639/2006
   16 R(SB) 23/85; CSIS/639/2006
   17 *JC v SSWP* [2009] UKUT 22 (AAC)
   18 CIS/25/1989
   19 **ESA** Sch 8 para 16 ESA Regs
   **HB** Sch 5 para 14 HB Regs
   **Both** Vol 5 Ch 29 para 29239 DMG; *SM v SSWP* [2020] UKUT 265 (AAC)
   20 *Gartside v Inland Revenue Commissioners* [1968] 1 All ER 121; [1968] AC 553
   21 *LG v SSWP (ESA)* [2019] UKUT 220 (AAC), reported as [2020] AACR 5
   22 **ESA** Reg 112(4) ESA Regs
   **HB** Reg 46(4) HB Regs
   23 *Thomas v CAO*, appendix to R(SB) 17/87
   24 CIS/984/2002
   25 **ESA** Reg 112 ESA Regs
   **HB** Reg 46 HB Regs
   26 Reg 46(9) HB Regs

4. **Disregarded capital**
   27 **ESA** Sch 9 para 1 ESA Regs
   **HB** Sch 6 para 1 HB Regs
   28 **ESA** Reg 2(1), definition of 'dwelling occupied as the home', ESA Regs
   **HB** Sch 6 para 1 HB Regs
   29 **ESA** Sch 9 para 1 ESA Regs
   **HB** Sch 6 para 1 HB Regs
   30 R(JSA) 9/03; R(SB) 10/89
   31 *MM v SSWP (IS)* [2012] UKUT 358 (AAC)
   32 **ESA** Sch 9 para 5 ESA Regs
   **HB** Sch 6 para 25 HB Regs
   33 **ESA** Sch 9 para 7 ESA Regs
   **HB** Sch 6 para 27 HB Regs
   34 **ESA** Sch 9 para 6 ESA Regs
   **HB** Sch 6 para 26 HB Regs
   **Both** CIS/6908/1995; R(IS) 4/97
   35 R(SB) 32/83
   36 R(IS) 5/05
   37 *SP v SSWP* [2009] UKUT 255 (AAC)
   38 **ESA** Sch 9 para 8 ESA Regs
   **HB** Sch 6 para 28 HB Regs
   39 *R v LB Tower Hamlets Review Board ex parte Kapur*, 12 June 2000, unreported
   40 **ESA** Sch 9 para 2 ESA Regs
   **HB** Sch 6 para 2 HB Regs
   41 **ESA** Sch 9 para 3 ESA Regs
   **HB** Sch 6 para 3 HB Regs
   42 R(IS) 6/95
   43 R(IS) 7/01
   44 CIS/685/1992
   45 CIS/8475/1995; CIS/15984/1996
   46 R(SB) 14/85

47 **ESA** Sch 9 para 12(b) ESA Regs
**HB** Sch 6 para 10(b) HB Regs
48 *Barclays Bank v Quistclose Investments Ltd* [1970] AC 567; CSB/975/1985
49 **ESA** Sch 9 para 13(a) ESA Regs
**HB** Sch 6 para 11(a) HB Regs
50 **ESA** Sch 9 para 13(b) ESA Regs
**HB** Sch 6 para 11(b) HB Regs
51 **ESA** Sch 9 para 36 ESA Regs
**HB** Sch 6 para 38 HB Regs
52 CIS/4757/2003
53 CIS/6908/1995
54 **ESA** Sch 9 paras 4 and 5 ESA Regs
**HB** Sch 6 paras 4 and 25 HB Regs
55 **HB** BW1/Annex A/A1.01 GM
**ESA** Vol 9 Ch 52 para 52435 DMG
56 **ESA** Reg 2(1) ESA Regs
**HB** Reg 2(1) HB Regs
**Both** CSB/209/1986; CSB/1149/1986; R(SB) 22/87
57 R(IS) 5/05; CH/3777/2007; *Bristol City Council v SJP (HB)* [2019] UKUT 360 (AAC)
58 **ESA** Sch 9 para 14 ESA Regs
**HB** Sch 6 para 12 HB Regs
59 R(H) 7/08
60 CIS/494/1990; R(IS) 8/04
61 **ESA** Sch 9 para 12(a) ESA Regs
**HB** Sch 6 para 10(a) HB Regs
62 **ESA** Sch 9 para 10(1) ESA Regs
**HB** Sch 6 para 8(1) HB Regs
63 **ESA** Sch 9 para 10(2) ESA Regs
**HB** Sch 6 para 8(2) HB Regs
64 R(SB) 4/85
65 Reg 49(5) HB Regs; *CA v Hastings BC* [2022] UKUT 57 (AAC)
66 **ESA** Sch 9 paras 28 and 29 ESA Regs
**HB** Sch 6 para 32 HB Regs
67 **ESA** Sch 9 para 20 ESA Regs
**HB** Sch 6 para 17 HB Regs
68 R(IS) 7/98
69 **ESA** Sch 9 para 15 ESA Regs
**HB** Sch 6 para 13 HB Regs
70 **ESA** Reg 105(2) ESA Regs
**HB** Reg 41(2) HB Regs
**Both** *Beattie v Secretary of State for Social Security* [2001] EWCA Civ 498, upholding CIS/114/1999, reported as R(IS) 10/01
71 **ESA** Sch 9 para 9 ESA Regs
**HB** Sch 6 para 7 HB Regs
72 **ESA** Sch 9 paras 15, 16, 18, 19, 21, 28 and 30 ESA Regs
**HB** Sch 6 paras 13-16, 18, 31 and 33 HB Regs
73 **ESA** Sch 9 para 11 ESA Regs
**HB** Sch 6 paras 9 and 9A HB Regs
74 **ESA** Sch 9 para 11(2) ESA Regs
**HB** Sch 6 para 9(2) HB Regs
75 **ESA** Sch 9 para 60 ESA Regs
**HB** Sch 6 para 62 HB Regs
76 **ESA** Sch 9 para 11A ESA Regs
**HB** Sch 6 para 9A HB Regs
77 **ESA** Sch 9 para 23 ESA Regs
**HB** Sch 6 para 20 HB Regs
78 **ESA** Sch 9 para 63 ESA Regs
**HB** Sch 6 para 65 HB Regs
79 **ESA** Sch 9 para 66 ESA Regs
**HB** Sch 6 para 68 HB Regs
80 **ESA** Sch 9 para 37 ESA Regs
**HB** Sch 6 para 40 HB Regs
81 **ESA** Sch 9 para 64 ESA Regs
**HB** Sch 6 para 66 HB Regs
82 **ESA** Sch 9 para 38 ESA Regs
**HB** Sch 6 para 41 HB Regs
83 **ESA** Sch 9 para 39 ESA Regs
**HB** Sch 6 para 42 HB Regs
84 **ESA** Sch 9 para 40 ESA Regs
**HB** Sch 6 para 39 HB Regs
85 **ESA** Sch 9 para 66 ESA Regs
**HB** Sch 6 para 68 HB Regs
86 **ESA** Sch 9 para 65 ESA Regs
**HB** Sch 6 para 67 HB Regs
87 **ESA** Sch 9 para 33 ESA Regs
**HB** Sch 6 para 30 HB Regs
88 s8 SS(AP)A 2023
89 para 52780 DMG
90 **ESA** Sch 9 para 31 ESA Regs
**HB** Sch 6 para 34 HB Regs
91 **ESA** Schs 8 para 16 and 9 para 16 ESA Regs
**HB** Schs 5 para 14 and 6 para 14 HB Regs
**Both** *R v ex parte Singer* [1973] 1 WLR 713
92 **ESA** Schs 8 paras 16 and 23, and 9 paras 43 and 44 ESA Regs
**HB** Schs 5 paras 14 and 17, and 6 paras 45 and 46 HB Regs
93 **ESA** Sch 9 para 17 ESA Regs
**HB** Sch 6 para 14A HB Regs
94 R(IS) 3/03
95 Vol 9 Ch 52 para 52415 DMG
96 R(SB) 2/89; *KQ v SSWP (IS)* [2011] UKUT 102 (AAC), reported as [2011] AACR 43
97 R(IS) 15/96
98 *Q v SSWP (JSA)* 2020 UKUT 49 (AAC)
99 **ESA** Sch 9 paras 27, 50. 53, 54 and 61 ESA Regs
**HB** Sch 6 paras 24, 54, 55, 56 and 63 HB Regs
**Both** Vol 9 Ch 52 para 52447 DMG
100 Reg 26 VP Regs

101 **ESA** Sch 8 para 41 ESA Regs
**HB** Sch 5 para 35 HB Regs
**Both** Vol 9 Ch 51 para 51341 DMG
102 Vol 9 Ch 52 para 52484 DMG
103 Vol 9 Ch 52 para 52445 DMG
104 **ESA** Sch 9 para 22 ESA Regs
**HB** Sch 6 para 19 HB Regs
105 **ESA** Sch 9 para 23A ESA Regs
**HB** Sch 6 para 20A HB
**Both** Explanatory Memorandum to The Universal Credit (Local Welfare Provision Disregard) (Amendment) Regulations 2022 No.448
106 **ESA** Sch 9 para 56 ESA Regs
**HB** Sch 6 para 58 HB Regs
107 **ESA** Sch 9 para 59 ESA Regs
**HB** Sch 6 para 61 HB Regs
108 **ESA** Sch 9 para 55 ESA Regs
**HB** Sch 6 para 57 HB Regs
109 **ESA** Sch 9 para 58 ESA Regs
**HB** Sch 6 para 60 HB Regs
110 **ESA** Sch 9 para 62 ESA Regs
**HB** Sch 6 para 64 HB Regs
111 **ESA** Sch 9 para 57 ESA Regs
**HB** Sch 6 para 59 HB Regs
112 **ESA** Sch 9 paras 1A, 32 and 32A ESA Regs
**HB** Sch 6 paras A2, A3 and 35 HB Regs
113 **ESA** Sch 9 paras 41 and 42 ESA Regs
**HB** Sch 6 paras 43 and 44 HB Regs
114 **ESA** Sch 9 para 47 ESA Regs
**HB** Sch 6 para 50 HB Regs
115 **ESA** Sch 9 para 52 ESA Regs
**HB** Sch 6 para 51 HB Regs
116 **ESA** Sch 9 para 34 ESA Regs
117 **ESA** Sch 9 para 35 ESA Regs
**HB** Sch 6 para 37 HB Regs
118 H1156 ADM
119 **ESA** Sch 9 para 45 ESA Regs
**HB** Sch 6 para 47 HB Regs

5. **Notional capital**

120 **ESA** Reg 115(8) ESA Regs
**HB** Reg 49(6) HB Regs
121 **ESA** Reg 115(1) ESA Regs
**HB** Reg 49(1) HB Regs
122 R(IS) 7/07
123 CIS/124/1990; CSB/1198/1989
124 CIS/124/1990
125 R(SB) 9/91
126 CIS/40/1989
127 CIS/621/1991. See also CJSA/3937/2002 and *LH v SSWP (IS)* [2014] UKUT 60 (AAC)
128 CIS/264/1989
129 R(IS) 7/98, para 12(3)
130 R(SB) 38/85; R(IS) 1/91; R(H) 1/06
131 para BW1.714 GM
132 Reg 115(1)(a) ESA Regs
133 R(SB) 40/85
134 R(IS) 8/04
135 R(SB) 12/91; *Verna Jones v SSWP* [2003] EWCA Civ 964; *VW v SSWP (IS)* [2015] UKUT 51 (AAC), reported as [2015] AACR 39
136 CIS/2627/1995; *Verna Jones v SSWP* [2003] EWCA Civ 964
137 *KS v SSWP* [2009] UKUT 122 (AAC), reported as [2010] AACR 3
138 **ESA** Reg 115(8) ESA Regs
**HB** Reg 49(7) HB Regs
139 CIS/30/1993, but other commissioners have taken a different view (see, for example, CIS/25/1990 and CIS/81/1991)
140 para BW1.831 GM
141 **ESA** Reg 116(1) ESA Regs
**HB** Reg 49(1) HB Regs
142 **ESA** Reg 115(2) ESA Regs
**HB** Reg 49(2) HB Regs
143 **ESA** Regs 2(1) and 115(3)(c) ESA Regs
**HB** Reg 49(3)(a) and (7) HB Regs
144 **ESA** Reg 2(1) ESA Regs
**HB** Reg 49(7)(b) HB Regs
145 Vol 9 Ch 52 para 52860 DMG
146 **ESA** Reg 115(3)(c), (5)(a) and (ba) ESA Regs
**HB** Reg 49(3)(b), (4)(a), (bb) and (bc) HB Regs
147 **ESA** Reg 115(3)(b) ESA Regs
**HB** Reg 49(3)(a) HB Regs
148 **ESA** Reg 115(5)(c) ESA Regs
**HB** Reg 49(4)(c) HB Regs
149 R(IS) 4/01
150 CH/1672/2007
151 **ESA** Reg 115(3)(a) ESA Regs
152 **ESA** Reg 115(4) ESA Regs
**HB** Reg 49(3)(c) HB Regs

6. **How capital is valued**

153 **ESA** Reg 113 ESA Regs
**HB** Reg 47(a) HB Regs
154 R(SB) 57/83; R(SB) 6/84
155 R(SB) 18/83
156 *CS v SSWP* [2014] UKUT 518 (AAC)
157 R(SB) 6/84
158 **ESA** Reg 113(a) ESA Regs
**HB** Reg 47(a) HB Regs
159 **ESA** Reg 113(b) ESA Regs
**HB** Reg 47(b) HB Regs
160 CIS/255/1989
161 R(SB) 27/84
162 R(SB) 2/83; R(SB) 31/83
163 *JRL v SSWP (JSA)* [2011] UKUT 63 (AAC), reported as [2011] AACR 30

164 **ESA** Reg 117 ESA Regs
**HB** Reg 51 HB Regs
165 CIS/2575/1997
166 *Hourigan v SSWP* [2002] EWCA 1890, reported as R(IS) 4/03
167 CIS/15936/1996; CIS/263/1997; CIS/3283/1997 (joint decision); R(IS) 26/95
168 *JM v Eastleigh BC (HB)* [2016] UKUT 464 (AAC)
169 *JM v Eastleigh BC (HB)* [2016] UKUT 464 (AAC)
170 R(IS) 3/96
171 R(JSA) 1/02; CH/1953/2003; *Reigate and Banstead BC v GB* [2018] UKUT 225 (AAC)
172 R(IS) 2/93
173 R(IS) 1/03
174 **ESA** Reg 113 ESA Regs
**HB** Reg 47(a) HB Regs
175 R(IS) 18/95; Vol 9 Ch 52 paras 52666-71 DMG
176 R(SB) 18/83; R(IS) 2/90
177 **ESA** Vol 9 Ch 52 para 52681 DMG
**HB** BW1/1.530 GM
178 *Peters v CAO* (appendix to R(SB) 3/89)
179 **ESA** Reg 114(a) ESA Regs
**HB** Reg 48(a) HB Regs
180 **ESA** Reg 114(b) ESA Regs
**HB** Reg 48(b) HB Regs
181 **ESA** Sch 9 para 26 ESA Regs
**HB** Sch 6 para 23 HB Regs

# Chapter 19

# Capital: over pension age

**This chapter covers:**


1. The capital limits (p426)
2. Whose capital counts (p427)
3. What counts as capital (p427)
4. Disregarded capital (p428)
5. Deliberately getting rid of capital (p435)
6. How capital is valued (p436)


This chapter explains how capital affects your entitlement to pension credit (PC). It also applies to pension-age housing benefit (HB) if you and your partner are over pension age and neither of you are on income-related employment and support allowance (ESA) or universal credit (UC). If you get income-related ESA or UC, your capital is ignored for HB. Chapter 18 explains the rules for income-related ESA and for working-age HB if you and your partner are under pension age. If you are in a couple and one of you is over pension age but not the other, see p197 for whether the working-age or pension-age HB rules apply. Chapter 8 explains the rules for UC.

Whenever HB is referred to in this chapter, this only applies to the rules for people over pension age. The law refers to the qualifying age for PC rather than pension age, but since December 2018, this has been the same as pension age.

## Key facts

- There is no upper capital limit for PC.
- Generally, you are not eligible for pension-age HB if your total capital is over £16,000. However, if you get the guarantee credit of PC, there is no capital limit for HB because all your capital is ignored.
- If you have capital over £10,000, this affects the amount of PC or HB you get because it is assumed that your capital gives you some income – called 'deemed income'.
- Capital includes your and your partner's savings, investments and property. Some kinds of capital are ignored when working out your PC or HB – eg, the value of the home in which you live.
- If you deliberately get rid of capital in order to get more benefit, you are treated as still having it.

# 1. The capital limits

## Pension credit

There is no upper capital limit for pension credit (PC) beyond which you are excluded from benefit. There is, however, a lower limit of £10,000.

3

Capital of £10,000 or less is ignored. If you have capital above £10,000, you are treated as having a deemed income (sometimes called 'tariff income') of £1 for every £500, or part of £500, by which your capital exceeds £10,000.[1]

## Housing benefit

There is a lower and upper limit.[2]

- The lower capital limit is £10,000.
- The upper limit is £16,000.

The first £10,000 of your capital is ignored. If you have capital above £10,000, you are treated as having a deemed income of £1 for every £500, or part of £500, by which your capital exceeds that amount.[3] If you have over £16,000, you are not entitled to housing benefit (HB) unless you get the guarantee credit of PC, in which case all your and your partner's capital (and income) is ignored for HB.[4] This is because entitlement to PC guarantee credit acts as a passport to maximum HB. Because PC has no upper capital limit, you can get maximum HB even with capital above £16,000.

If you get the savings credit of PC, but not the guarantee credit, the following applies.[5]

- Your capital for HB purposes is the capital figure worked out by the DWP for your PC. This is modified to include any capital belonging to your partner which was not taken into account in the PC calculation.
- During an 'assessed income period' (see p251), an increase in your capital does not affect your PC savings credit, but may affect HB. If capital increases above £16,000 (worked out by the local authority under the HB rules), you are no longer entitled to HB. If your capital increases but is still less than £16,000, the local authority must continue to use the DWP's capital figure.

***Example***

Grace (85) is a widow. She has a state pension and a personal pension. She gets HB and the savings credit of PC, but not the guarantee credit. Her PC award letter shows that she has an assessed income period. When she inherits £20,000, her HB stops, but her PC is not affected unless the assessed income period ends because of a change in her circumstances.

## 2. Whose capital counts

If you are a member of a couple, your partner's capital is added to yours.

## 3. What counts as capital



All your capital is taken into account, unless it is specifically ignored (or 'disregarded') (see p428).

The term 'capital' is not defined. Generally, it means lump-sum or one-off payments rather than a series of payments – eg, savings, investments and property.[6] Capital payments can normally be distinguished from income because they are not payable for any specified period and are not part of a regular series of payments (although capital can be paid by instalments).[7]

### Savings

Your savings generally count as capital – eg, cash you have at home, premium bonds, stocks and shares, unit trusts and money in a bank account.

Savings from past income (including benefits – see p432) are treated as capital after the period for which the income was paid has lapsed. If you have put aside money to pay bills, this is still counted as your capital.[8] If your savings are just below the capital limit, you could pay bills by monthly direct debit or use a budget account to keep your capital below the limit.

### Fixed-term investments

Capital held in fixed-term investments counts. However, if it is currently unobtainable, it may have little or no value. If you can convert the investment into a form that lets you access it, sell your interest, or raise a loan through a reputable bank using the asset as security, the amount you can get for it counts. If it takes time to produce evidence about the nature and value of the investment, you may be able to get a short-term advance of pension credit (see p1023) or a payment on account of housing benefit (see p228).[9]

### Property and land

Any property or land that you own counts as capital. Many types of property are disregarded (see p429). If there is doubt about who owns the property, see p401.

### Loans

A loan to you usually counts as money you possess and counts as capital. However, in some limited circumstances, you can argue that a loan should be disregarded (see p400). If you lend someone money, see p400.

### Trusts

Money or property held in a trust for you or your partner is ignored when working out whether you have any deemed income from capital (see p388). You are not assumed to have a fixed income from the trust.[10] This applies to both discretionary and non-discretionary trusts. However, payments actually made from the trust can be taken into account. If made regularly, payments are treated as income. For discretionary trusts, regular payments are either disregarded in full or in part (see p390). If payments are not made regularly, they are taken into account as capital.

3

The rules are different if the trust is set up from personal injury payments (see p434). Payments made from certain charitable trusts are specifically ignored (see p434).

### Money held by your solicitor

Money held by your solicitor normally counts as your capital. This includes compensation payments (but see p434 for when payments for personal injury are disregarded).[11] If you have had legal aid and your solicitor is holding money back while working out the statutory charge to be deducted for legal costs, it does not count as your capital.[12]

## 4. Disregarded capital

### Your home

If you own the home you normally live in, its value is ignored.[13]

***Your home***

Your **'home'** includes any garage, garden, outbuildings and land belonging to the property, together with any premises that you do not occupy as your home but which it is impractical or unreasonable to sell separately – eg, croft land.[14]

This disregard applies to any home in which you are treated as normally living – eg, because you are only temporarily living away from it (see p296). However, if you own more than one property, only the value of the one normally occupied is disregarded under this rule.[15] Exceptionally, two separate properties can be regarded as a single home, as though one was an annexe of the other, if you personally (rather than a member of your family) normally occupy both.[16] This is most likely to be the case for a large family, but other situations are possible where neither property on its own caters for a family's needs – eg, if there is a carer living between two properties.[17]

## When the value of the property is disregarded

The value of the property can be disregarded, even if you do not normally live in it, in the following circumstances.

- **If you have left your former home following a relationship breakdown,** the property's value is ignored for 26 weeks from the date you left. It may also be disregarded for longer if any of the steps below are taken. If it is occupied by your former partner who is a lone parent, its value is ignored for as long as they live there.[18]
- **If you have sought legal advice or have started legal proceedings to occupy the property as your home,** its value is ignored for 26 weeks from the date you first took either of these steps.[19] The 26 weeks can be extended, if it is reasonable to do so.
- **If you are taking reasonable steps to dispose of any property,** its value is ignored for 26 weeks from the date you first took such steps (which may start before you claimed benefit) or longer if it is reasonable in the circumstances.[20] See p404 for more details.
- **If you are carrying out essential repairs or alterations which are needed so that you can occupy a property as your home,** the value of the property is ignored for 26 weeks from the date you first began to take steps to carry them out or longer if necessary.[21] See p404 for more details.
- **If you have acquired a property to occupy as your home but have not yet moved in,** its value is ignored if you intend to live there within 26 weeks of acquiring it.[22] If you cannot move in by then, the property's value can be ignored for as long as seems reasonable.
- **Any amounts paid to you or deposited in your name for the sole purpose of buying a home for you to live in or carrying out essential repairs or alterations to your home or the home you intend to occupy** are ignored for a year from the date you were paid them.[23] This includes money from the sale of a home that you earmark to buy another place to live in.[24] For pension credit (PC), if there is an assessed income period (p251) that extends beyond the year's disregard, the rules provide for the disregard to last until the end of that period.
- **Any compensation paid under an insurance policy for loss or damage to your home** is ignored for a year from the date it is paid to you.[25] For PC, if there is an assessed income period, it can be disregarded until the end of that period in the same way as explained in the bullet point above.

When considering whether it is reasonable to increase the period during which time the value of your property is disregarded, all the circumstances should be considered – eg, your personal circumstances, any efforts made by you to use or dispose of the home[26] and the general state of the property market. In practice, periods of around 18 months are not considered unusual.

Note: it is possible for the value of the property to be ignored under more than one of the above paragraphs together or in succession.[27]

## The home of a former partner or relative

The value of a home (see p428) is ignored if it is occupied wholly or partly as the home of:[28]

3

- a relative of yours or of your partner (see p406 for who this includes) who is over pension age (see p239) or who is incapacitated (see below);[29] *or*
- your former partner from whom you are not estranged, divorced or out of a civil partnership – eg, if one of you is living in a care home; *or*
- your former partner from whom you are estranged, divorced or out of a civil partnership if they are a lone parent. If your former partner is not a lone parent, the value of the home is ignored for 26 weeks from the date you ceased to live in the home.[30]

***Definitions***

**'Incapacitated'** is not defined, but guidance suggests it includes anyone who is getting employment and support allowance (ESA), statutory sick pay (SSP), attendance allowance (AA) or disability living allowance (DLA), or a similar benefit, or who would qualify because of their health condition or disability.[31]

It may also include anyone getting personal independence payment (PIP), adult disability payment (ADP), Scottish adult disability living allowance (SADLA), pension age disability payment (PADP) or universal credit (UC) who has limited capability for work or limited capability for work-related activity. However, you should argue for a broader interpretation, if necessary.

You are **'estranged'** if you are living apart because your relationship has broken down, even if the separation is amicable.[32]

## Personal possessions

All personal possessions, including items such as jewellery, furniture or a car, are ignored.[33] A personal possession has been defined as any physical asset not used for business purposes, other than land.[34] A home that you own but do not live in is not a personal possession, but counts as capital (see p388).

Compensation paid under an insurance policy for damage to, or loss of, your personal possessions is ignored for a year from the date you were paid the compensation or, for PC only, until the end of the assessed income period (if there is one) if that is longer.[35]

## Business assets

If you are self-employed, your business assets are ignored for as long as you continue to work in that business.[36] If you cannot work because of physical or mental illness, but intend to work in the business when you are able, the disregard operates for 26 weeks from the date of claim, or for longer if reasonable in the circumstances.[37] For more about this, see p406.

If you run your business as a sole trader or in a partnership, you are self-employed and business assets are ignored as capital as above. If you run your business through a company, you are treated as though you were a sole trader or in a partnership if you have a similar level of control in the company to that of a sole trader or partner. For example, you may be a director of your own limited company. You are treated as owning the business assets and they are ignored as capital while you are engaged in any work for the company. Instead of the value of any shares you hold being taken into account as they normally would, the value of shares is disregarded.[38]



## Insurance policy and annuity surrender values

The surrender value of any life assurance policy is ignored.[39] Some investments include an element of life insurance – eg, endowment policies. If the policy terms include how the payment on death is calculated, the whole investment is ignored.[40] However, you cannot choose to put money into such an investment in order to increase your benefit entitlement, because you are likely to be caught by the notional capital rule if you do (see p435).

The surrender value of any annuity is also ignored for the purposes of the deemed income rule (see p388). Any actual income the surrender value generates for you, and which is not disregarded as income, can be taken into account as income.[41] Any payment under the annuity counts as income (but see p390 for when this is ignored).[42]

## Future interests in property

A future interest in most kinds of property is ignored.[43] A **'future interest'** is one which will only revert to you, or become yours for the first time, when some future event occurs. However, this does not include a freehold or leasehold interest in property that you have let to tenants. If you did not let the property to the tenant (eg, because the tenancy was entered into before you bought the property), your interest should be ignored as a future interest.

## The right to receive a payment in the future

If you know you will receive a payment in the future and you could sell your right to that payment at any time, it has a market value and therefore constitutes an actual capital resource. The value of this is ignored if it is a right to receive:[44]

- income under a life interest or, in Scotland, a life rent; *or*
- an occupational or personal pension; *or*
- any rent if you are not the freeholder or leaseholder; *or*
- any payment under an annuity.

3

## Benefits

### Arrears of benefits

Arrears of specified benefits are ignored as capital:[45]

- for one year after you receive them; *or*
- for PC, if there is an assessed income period that extends beyond the year's disregard (p251), the rules provide for the disregard to last until the end of that period. However, it is not clear how this applies in all cases. For example, it does not apply if your PC entitlement or assessed income period began only after the year's disregard had expired.[46] Arguably, it should apply in other cases where there is an assessed income period;[47] *or*
- for the remainder of the PC or housing benefit (HB) award if the arrears are £5,000 or more and are paid to compensate for an official error or an error of law, and which you received in full since becoming entitled to PC or HB. If you got the compensation before then, it is still disregarded if your current award follows immediately from a previous award of income support (IS), income-based jobseeker's allowance (JSA), income-related ESA, UC, HB or council tax benefit (CTB) (or PC, for current awards of HB) in which the compensation was disregarded, or it is still being disregarded in an award of one of those benefits.

The '**specified benefits**' are:

- armed forces independence payment;
- AA, PADP, constant attendance allowance and exceptionally severe disablement allowance;
- ADP (in Scotland);
- bereavement support payment;
- Best Start grant (in Scotland);
- child disability payment (in Scotland);
- child tax credit;
- child winter heating payment (in Scotland) (for HB, it is ignored indefinitely);
- CTB;
- DLA;
- funeral support payment (in Scotland);
- income-related ESA;
- HB;
- IS;
- income-based JSA;
- maternity allowance;
- PC;
- pension age winter heating payment (in Scotland) (for HB, it is ignored indefinitely);
- PIP;
- SADLA;

- Scottish child payment;
- short-term assistance (in Scotland);
- social fund payments (including winter fuel payments);
- UC;
- winter heating payment (in Scotland) (for HB, it is ignored indefinitely);
- young carer grant (in Scotland) (for HB, it is ignored indefinitely);
- for PC only, child benefit;
- for HB only, working tax credit and discretionary housing payments;
- concessionary payments (ie, compensation) made instead of any of the above benefits or payments made in lieu of any of these benefits;
- compensation for lost or delayed new-style ESA because of a DWP error.



**Note**: although arrears are ignored as capital, you may have been paid more PC or HB than you would have been entitled to if benefit had been paid on time. For PC, the DWP usually deducts the difference from the arrears of the delayed benefit. Otherwise, if the arrears are not reduced, the overpayment is recoverable from you (see p1062). For HB, the overpayment may be recoverable (see p1078).

### Other benefits and payments

The following payments are ignored for one year (or, for PC, to the end of the assessed income period) from when you get them:[48]

- refunds of council tax liability, including from a council tax reduction scheme;
- arrears of a supplementary pension to war widows, widowers or surviving civil partners for pre-1973 service.

The initial lump sum of bereavement support payment and, for a surviving cohabiting partner whose partner died before 9 February 2023, arrears of monthly payments are ignored for 52 weeks from when you get the payment.[49] Widowed parent's allowance arrears, that include a period before 9 February 2023, paid to a surviving cohabiting partner are ignored for 52 weeks from when you get the payment.[50] Although ignored as capital, the arrears of widowed parent's allowance can also count as income for the period they cover and reduce entitlement to PC or HB paid in the same period. The DWP can deduct overpaid PC from the arrears or recover the overpayment of PC or HB from you. Lump-sum state retirement pension, if you deferred your pension and chose a lump sum rather than increased income, is ignored indefinitely.[51]

Cost of living payments are disregarded indefinitely.[52] These were additional payments of up to £650 in 2022/23, £900 in 2023/24 for people on means-tested benefits and an additional £150 in 2022/23 and 2023/24 for people on disability benefits. These amounts are disregarded from your capital for as long as they remain unspent.[53]

## Personal injury and other compensation payments

- **Personal injury payments.** Any money paid because of a personal injury to you or your partner is ignored, whether or not it has been placed in a trust.[54] Neither deemed income (see p388) nor actual income from the fund is taken into account.[55] If the personal injury was to your partner and they have since died, the capital value is no longer ignored.[56] If an award for damages for personal injury to you or your partner is administered by a court (eg, the Court of Protection), its value, and income and capital from it, are disregarded.[57] 'Personal injury' includes not only accidental and criminal injury (including from the Criminal Injuries Compensation Scheme[58]) but also any disease and injury as a result of a disease.[59]
- **Special compensation schemes.** Any payment of capital (or income) from specific schemes is disregarded indefinitely, including:[60]
  - the National Emergencies Trust;
  - the Windrush Compensation Scheme;
  - the Child Migrants Trust (for children subjected to migration programmes before 1971);
  - the Victims of Overseas Terrorism Compensation Scheme;
  - schemes to make child abuse payments for historic institutional child abuse in the UK;
  - payments from an infected blood scheme;
  - for people affected by the 2017 fire at Grenfell Tower;
  - Post Office compensation payments for Horizon system failings;
  - vaccine damage payments under the Vaccine Damage Payments Act 1979;
  - payments from the Ministry of Defence's LGBT Financial Recognition Scheme;
  - victims' payments under the Troubles Permanent Disablement Payment Scheme.[61]

  For most of the schemes, money from your partner's payments is ignored indefinitely, or for two years from your child's payments if they have no partner or dependent child.

If you have other capital and a disregarded payment in the same account, it should be accepted that money is withdrawn from the other capital before the disregarded payment, unless evidence shows otherwise.

## Funeral plan payments

The value of any funeral plan contract is ignored indefinitely.[62]

A funeral plan contract is a contract under which:

- you make at least one payment to another person; *and*
- that person undertakes to ensure you are provided with a funeral; *and*
- the sole purpose of the plan is to ensure you are provided with a funeral.

### Social services, community care and other payments

The following payments are ignored for one year (or for PC, to the end of the assessed income period) from when you get the payments:[63]

- local welfare assistance payments (see p770). These include household support fund payments and 'thank you' payments under the Homes for Ukraine Scheme;
- payments from a local authority for support services to help you live independently – eg, under the Supporting People programme, sometimes called 'housing-related support'.



Ignored indefinitely are:[64]

- community care or healthcare direct payments;
- payments from a local authority to a young person in Scotland aged 16 or over in 'continuing care' or passed to you by the young person if they still live with you and were in your care;
- for HB, direct payments under an education, health and care plan, paid in England for a child with special educational needs.

## 5. Deliberately getting rid of capital

If you deliberately get rid of capital in order to claim or increase benefit, you are treated as still having it (see p413). This is called **'notional capital'**.[65]

You are not treated as having deprived yourself of capital if:[66]

- you pay off or reduce a debt which you owe; *or*
- you pay for goods or services if the purchase of those goods or services was reasonable in the circumstances of your case.

Notional capital counts in the same way as capital you do have, except that a 'diminishing notional capital rule' may be applied so that the value of the notional capital you are treated as having is considered to reduce over time.

### The diminishing notional capital rule

The diminishing notional capital rule applies if you are treated as having notional capital because of depriving yourself of capital.

If you are getting pension credit (PC), the amount of the notional capital goes down each week by the extra PC you are losing because of the notional capital – eg, through having 'deemed income' taken into account.[67] For example, if your notional capital is £11,000, you have £2 a week less PC because of deemed income (see p389), so £2 a week is deducted from the notional capital until it reaches £10,500, when it will be £1 a week.

If you are not getting any PC, notional capital goes down, not just by the amount of PC you would have had, but also by any additional housing benefit (HB) you would have had if notional capital had not been taken into account. Ask the DWP for a forecast of when it is worth claiming again. If in doubt, you can claim every 26 weeks (but not more often).

For HB, the same rule applies to reduce your notional capital except that, not only is it reduced by the amount of HB you are losing because of the notional capital, but it is also reduced by any PC you would have been entitled to (or income-related employment and support allowance), whether or not you are currently getting HB.[68]



## 6. How capital is valued

There are a number of issues to consider when valuing capital.

- **Market value.** Capital is valued at its current market or surrender value,[69] which could be very low if it is difficult to sell. See p418 for more information.
- **Expenses of sale.** If there would be expenses involved in selling your capital, 10 per cent is deducted from its value for the cost of sale.[70]
- **Debts.** Deductions are made from the gross value of your capital for any debt or mortgage secured on it.[71] For more information, see p418.
- **Capital that is jointly owned under a joint tenancy.** If you jointly own any capital asset (except as a partner in a company, when the rules explained on p430 apply instead) under a joint tenancy, you are treated as owning an equal share of the asset with all other owners.[72] For example, if two of you own the asset, you are each treated as having a 50 per cent share of it. This rule does not apply, however, if you jointly own the capital asset as 'tenants in common'.[73] For more information, see p419.
- **Treatment of assets after a relationship breakdown.** There are no specific rules about this, but there is some guidance and caselaw (see p419).
- **Shares** are valued at their current market value, less 10 per cent for the cost of sale and after deducting any 'lien' held by brokers for sums owed for the cost of their acquisition and any commission.[74] See p420 for more details.
- **Unit trusts** are valued on the basis of the bid price quoted in newspapers. No deduction is allowed for the cost of sale because this is already included in the bid price.[75]
- **The right to receive a payment in the future.** The value that is not ignored (see p431) is its market value – ie, what a willing buyer would pay to a willing seller.[76] For something which is not yet realisable, this may be very small.
- **Overseas assets.** If you have assets abroad, and there are no exchange controls or other prohibitions that would prevent you transferring your capital to this country, your assets are valued at their current market or surrender value in that country.[77] If you are not allowed to transfer your capital, you are treated as

having capital equal to the amount that a willing buyer in this country would give (which might not be very much).[78] Deduct 10 per cent for any expenses of sale, any debts or mortgage secured on the assets and any charges for converting the payment into sterling.[79]

- **Payments in other currencies.** Any payment in a currency other than sterling is taken into account after deducting banking charges or commission payable on conversion.[80]



# Notes

1. **The capital limits**
1 s15(2) SPCA 2002; reg 15(6) SPC Regs
2 Reg 43 HB(SPC) Regs
3 Reg 29(2) HB(SPC) Regs
4 Reg 26 HB(SPC) Regs
5 Reg 27 HB(SPC) Regs

3. **What counts as capital**
6 BP1/P1.71 GM
7 *R v SBC ex parte Singer* [1973] 1 WLR 713 (cited in CH/412/2007)
8 R(IS) 3/93; R(PC) 3/08
9 **PC** Reg 2 SS(PAOR) Regs
**HB** Reg 74(1) HB(SPC) Regs
10 **PC** Sch 5 para 28 SPC Regs
**HB** Sch 6 para 30 HB(SPC) Regs
11 *Thomas v CAO*, appendix to R(SB) 17/87
12 CIS/984/2002

4. **Disregarded capital**
13 **PC** Sch 5 para 1A SPC Regs
**HB** Sch 6 para 26 HB(SPC) Regs
14 **PC** Reg 1(2), definition of 'dwelling occupied as the home', SPC Regs
**HB** Reg 2(1), definition of 'dwelling occupied as the home', HB(SPC) Regs
15 **PC** Sch 5 para 1A SPC Regs
**HB** Sch 6 para 26 HB(SPC) Regs
16 R(JSA) 9/03; R(SB) 10/89
17 *MM v SSWP (IS)* [2012] UKUT 358 (AAC)
18 **PC** Sch 5 para 6(1) SPC Regs
**HB** Sch 6 para 6(1) HB(SPC) Regs
19 **PC** Sch 5 para 2 SPC Regs
**HB** Sch 6 para 2 HB(SPC) Regs
20 **PC** Sch 5 para 7 SPC Regs
**HB** Sch 6 para 7 HB(SPC) Regs
**Both** CIS/6908/1995; R(IS) 4/97
21 **PC** Sch 5 para 3 SPC Regs
**HB** Sch 6 para 3 HB(SPC) Regs
22 **PC** Sch 5 para 1 SPC Regs
**HB** Sch 6 para 1 HB(SPC) Regs
23 **PC** Sch 5 paras 17 and 19 SPC Regs
**HB** Sch 6 paras 18 and 20 HB(SPC) Regs
24 *DG v SSWP (SPC)* [2010] UKUT 241 (AAC); DWP, *A Detailed Guide to Pension Credit for Advisers and Others*, PC10S, September 2024
25 **PC** Sch 5 paras 17 and 18 SPC Regs
**HB** Sch 6 paras 18 and 19 HB(SPC) Regs
26 CIS/4757/2003
27 CIS/6908/1995
28 **PC** Sch 5 para 4 SPC Regs
**HB** Sch 6 para 4 HB(SPC) Regs
29 **PC** Reg 1(2), definition of 'close relative', SPC Regs
**HB** Reg 2(1), definition of 'close relative', HB(SPC) Regs
30 **PC** Sch 5 para 6 SPC Regs
**HB** Sch 6 para 6 HB(SPC) Regs
31 **PC** para 84444 DMG
**HB** para BP1, Annex A1.01 GM
32 R(IS) 5/05; CPC/683/2007; *Bristol City Council v SJP (HB)* [2019] UKUT 360 (AAC)
33 **PC** Sch 5 para 8 SPC Regs
**HB** Sch 6 para 8 HB(SPC) Regs
34 R(H) 7/08
35 **PC** Sch 5 paras 17 and 18 SPC Regs
**HB** Sch 6 paras 18 and 19 HB(SPC) Regs
36 **PC** Sch 5 para 9 SPC Regs
**HB** Sch 6 para 9 HB(SPC) Regs
37 **PC** Sch 5 para 9A SPC Regs
**HB** Sch 6 para 10 HB(SPC) Regs

38 **PC** Reg 21(3) and (4) SPC Regs
**HB** Reg 47(3) and (4) HB(SPC) Regs
39 **PC** Sch 5 para 10 SPC Regs
**HB** Sch 6 para 11 HB(SPC) Regs
40 R(IS) 7/98
41 **PC** Sch 5 para 26 SPC Regs
**HB** Sch 6 para 29 HB Regs
42 **PC** s15(1)(d) SPCA 2002
**HB** Reg 29(1)(d) HB(SPC) Regs
**Both** R(IS) 10/01
43 **PC** Sch 5 para 5 SPC Regs
**HB** Sch 6 para 5 HB(SPC) Regs
44 **PC** Sch 5 paras 22 and 24-26 SPC Regs
**HB** Sch 6 paras 24 and 27-29 HB(SPC) Regs
45 **PC** Sch 5 paras 17, 20 and 20A SPC Regs
**HB** Sch 6 paras 18, 21, 22, 26J and 26K HB(SPC) Regs
46 *DG v SSWP (SPC)* [2010] UKUT 241 (AAC)
47 But see CPC/206/2005 and CPC/1928/2005, which suggest that an assessed income period could be reduced on revision in some cases
48 **PC** Sch 5 paras 20(1)(f) and 20B SPC Regs
**HB** Sch 6 paras 26B and 26E HB(SPC) Regs
49 **PC** Sch 5 para 23E SPC Regs
**HB** Sch 6 para 26H HB(SPC) Regs
50 **PC** Sch 5 para 20AA SPC Regs
**HB** Sch 6 para 22A HB(SPC) Regs
51 **PC** Sch 5 paras 23A and 23AA SPC Regs
**HB** Sch 6 paras 26A and 26AA HB(SPC) Regs
52 s8 SS(AP)A 2023
53 para 84016 DMG
54 **PC** Sch 5 para 16(1) SPC Regs
**HB** Sch 6 para 17(1) HB(SPC) Regs
55 **PC** Regs 15(6) and 17(8) and Schs 4 para 18 and 5 para 16 SPC Regs
**HB** Regs 29(1)(i) and (2) and 44(2) and Sch 6 para 17 HB(SPC) Regs
56 R(IS) 3/03
57 **PC** Schs 4 paras 13 and 14, and 5 para 16(2) SPC Regs
**HB** Schs 5 paras 14 and 15, and 6 para 17(2) HB(SPC) Regs
58 para BP1.160 GM; para 29414 DMG
59 R(SB) 2/89
60 **PC** Sch 5 paras 12-15 SPC Regs
**HB** Sch 6 paras 13-16 HB(SPC) Regs
**Both** para 84475 DMG
61 Reg 26 VP Regs
62 **PC** Sch 5 para 11 SPC Regs
**HB** Sch 6 para 12 HB(SPC) Regs
63 **PC** Sch 5 paras 17 and 20(1)(d) and (e) SPC Regs
**HB** Sch 6 paras 18 and 21(1)(e) and (f) HB(SPC) Regs
**Both** Explanatory Memorandum to The Universal Credit (Local Welfare Provision Disregard) (Amendment) Regulations 2022 No.448
64 **PC** Sch 5 paras 23C and 23D SPC Regs
**HB** Sch 6 paras 26D, 26F and 26G HB(SPC) Regs

5. **Deliberately getting rid of capital**

65 **PC** Reg 21 SPC Regs
**HB** Reg 47 HB(SPC) Regs
66 **PC** Reg 21(2) SPC Regs
**HB** Reg 47(2) HB(SPC) Regs
67 Reg 22 SPC Regs
68 Reg 48 HB(SPC) Regs

6. **How capital is valued**

69 **PC** Reg 19(a) SPC Regs
**HB** Reg 45(a) HB(SPC) Regs
70 **PC** Reg 19(a) SPC Regs
**HB** Reg 45(a) HB(SPC) Regs
71 **PC** Reg 19(b) SPC Regs
**HB** Reg 45(b) HB(SPC) Regs
72 **PC** Reg 23 SPC Regs
**HB** Reg 49 HB(SPC) Regs
73 R(IS) 4/03
74 **PC** Reg 19(a) SPC Regs
**HB** Reg 45(a) HB(SPC) Regs
75 **PC** para 84772 DMG
**HB** para BP1 P1.530 GM
76 *Peters v CAO* (appendix to R(SB) 3/89)
77 **PC** Reg 20(a) SPC Regs
**HB** Reg 46(a) HB(SPC) Regs
78 **PC** Reg 20 SPC Regs
**HB** Reg 46(b) HB(SPC) Regs
79 **PC** Sch 5 para 21 SPC Regs
**HB** Sch 6 para 23 HB(SPC) Regs
80 **PC** Sch 5 para 21 SPC Regs
**HB** Sch 6 para 23 HB(SPC) Regs

# Part 4

# Other benefits

# Chapter 20

# Attendance allowance

**This chapter covers:**


1. Who can get attendance allowance (p442)
2. The rules about your age (p443)
3. People included in the claim (p443)
4. The amount of benefit (p444)
5. Special benefit rules (p444)
6. Claims and backdating (p445)
7. Getting paid (p449)
8. Tax, other benefits and the benefit cap (p450)


## Key facts

- Attendance allowance (AA) is a benefit for people with disabilities or long-term health problems who have attention or supervision needs and who are pension age or over when they claim.
- AA is paid at one of two rates, depending on your needs.
- AA is a non means-tested benefit.
- You do not have to have paid national insurance contributions to qualify.
- You can get AA whether or not you work.
- AA can be paid in addition to most other benefits and is disregarded as income for means-tested benefits.
- AA is administered and paid by the DWP.
- If you disagree with an AA decision, you can apply for a revision or supersession (see Chapter 50), or appeal against it (see Chapter 51). You must apply for a mandatory reconsideration before you can appeal.
- AA usually stops being paid if you are in hospital or residential care for more than 28 days.

***Scotland***

AA for people living in Scotland is being replaced by pension age disability payment (PADP) (see Chapter 67). The eligibility rules and rates of payment are similar to those for AA. Social Security Scotland is responsible for administering and paying PADP.

# 1. Who can get attendance allowance

You can get attendance allowance (AA) if:[1]

- you are pension age or over (see below); *and*
- you satisfy the disability conditions (see below); *and*
- unless terminally ill, you have satisfied the disability conditions for at least six months (sometimes called the 'qualifying period' condition); *and*
- you are not entitled to personal independence payment (see Chapter 31), adult disability payment (see Chapter 61) or the care component of disability living allowance (DLA) (see Chapter 24); *and*
- you satisfy the residence conditions (see p1347); *and*
- you are not a 'person subject to immigration control', although there are exceptions to this (see p1272).

## The disability conditions

AA is paid at a lower or higher rate, depending on your attention and supervision needs.[2] You get the **lower rate** of AA if you satisfy one of the daytime disability conditions *or* one of the night-time disability conditions. You may also get the lower rate of AA if you undergo renal dialysis (see p444).

You get the **higher rate** of AA if you satisfy one of the daytime disability conditions *and* one of the night-time disability conditions. You also get the higher rate of AA if you are terminally ill (see p444).

***Daytime disability conditions***

You are so severely disabled, physically or mentally, that throughout the day you need:[3]

– frequent attention from another person in connection with your bodily functions; *or*

– continual supervision in order to avoid substantial danger to yourself or others.

***Night-time disability conditions***

You are so severely disabled, physically or mentally, that at night you need:[4]

– prolonged or repeated attention from another person in connection with your bodily functions; *or*

– another person to be awake for a prolonged period or at frequent intervals to watch over you in order to avoid substantial danger to yourself or others.

The daytime and night-time disability conditions are the same as those for the middle and highest rates of the care component of DLA (see p519). You can argue that DLA caselaw about the meaning of these conditions ought to be followed in your AA case – including caselaw about the meanings of 'attention', 'supervision' and 'bodily functions'.

## 2. The rules about your age

You can only claim attendance allowance (AA) if you have reached pension age.[5] Pension age is currently 66. Between 2026 and 2028 it will rise to 67 (see p690).

If you are approaching pension age and have problems with daily living or mobility, it may be better to claim personal independence payment (PIP) or adult disability payment (ADP) now rather than waiting to claim AA. PIP and ADP can be more generous because they have a mobility component in addition to a daily living component.



### If you are getting another disability benefit and reach pension age

If you are getting PIP, ADP or disability living allowance (DLA) when you reach pension age, you can continue getting that benefit and do not need to claim AA instead.

This means that you can continue to receive a PIP, DLA or ADP mobility component after you reach pension age. You can also start getting the mobility component of PIP after reaching pension age in certain circumstances (see p667).

You cannot get AA at the same time as PIP, ADP or the care component of DLA, but if you are over pension age and have an award of only the mobility component of DLA, you can claim AA in addition to it. In practice, however, this is likely to lead to a reassessment of your DLA instead or may trigger a move from DLA to PIP (see p526).

If you have reached pension age and need to renew or change a DLA, PIP or ADP award, or have had an award of DLA, PIP or ADP which ended within the last 12 months and want to reclaim that benefit instead of starting a fresh AA claim, see p526 for DLA, p667 for PIP and p1434 for ADP.

## 3. People included in the claim

You claim attendance allowance (AA) for yourself. If you have a partner, one or both of you can get AA depending on your individual needs.

## 4. The amount of benefit

Attendance allowance is paid at one of two weekly rates:[6]

- the lower rate is £73.90;
- the higher rate is £110.40.

# 5. Special benefit rules

Special rules may apply if you:

- get renal dialysis (see below);
- are terminally ill (see below);
- are subject to immigration control (see p1269);
- have come from or are going abroad (see Chapters 57, 58 and 59);
- are in hospital or a hospice, staying in a care home or similar accommodation, or in prison or detention (see Chapter 38).

4

## Renal dialysis

If you are undergoing renal dialysis, you may be automatically entitled to the lower rate of attendance allowance (AA).[7]

This applies if you have treatment regularly for two or more sessions a week. The dialysis must normally require the attendance or supervision of another person. If you dialyse in hospital as an outpatient, these special rules only apply if you do so without help from any member of staff. Others who dialyse in hospital do not qualify, but can still count these spells of hospital dialysis towards the six-month 'qualifying period' (see p442).

Even if you do not qualify for AA under this route, you may qualify under the ordinary conditions.

## Terminal illness

You are regarded as **'terminally ill'** for the purposes of AA if you have a progressive disease and can reasonably be expected to die within 12 months as a result.[8] This does not mean that it must be more likely than not that you will die within this period, but rather that your doctor would not be surprised were you to die within 12 months.[9]

If you are classed as terminally ill, you are automatically entitled to the higher rate of AA. This is paid straight away without you having to serve the six-month qualifying period.[10]

Claims in respect of terminal illness are referred to as 'claims under the special rules'. See p446 for how to make a special rules claim.

# 6. Claims and backdating

The general rules about claims and backdating are covered in Chapter 44. This section explains the specific rules that apply to attendance allowance (AA).

## Making a claim

You must make a claim for AA in writing. It is normally best to request the claim form (AA1) from the AA helpline, because this means the form will be date-stamped with the date you called. This secures your date of claim (see p447). Keep a record of the date you called in case the DWP fails to date-stamp your form.

4

### *Forms*

Form AA1 is available from the AA helpline on 0800 731 0122 (textphone: 0800 731 0317; Relay UK and BSL relay services are available).

When you call, the DWP may complete a checklist to assess your 'potential benefit entitlement'. This is not part of the claim process and you should always be sent a claim form.

Claim forms are also available from Citizens Advice and other advice agencies, and there is a PDF version of the form that you can fill in digitally and then print at gov.uk/attendance-allowance/how-to-claim.

These forms are not date-stamped. If you choose one of these options, send the completed form as soon as possible because your date of claim will be the date the DWP receives it (see p447).

It is usually best to send the completed form to Freepost DWP Attendance Allowance (all on one line; you do not need a postcode or a stamp). You can also take or send it to any other DWP office, and may be able to take or send it to an 'alternative office' (see p1004). In certain circumstances, the DWP may accept a written application which is not on the approved form.[11]

An online claim system for AA is planned but does not exist at the time of writing.[12]

### *Completing the claim form*

The success of an AA claim can depend on how thoroughly you have completed the claim form, so try to include a detailed description of how you manage to carry out each activity. It is a good idea to use extra sheets of paper to provide enough detail about your needs because there is limited space to do so on the form. Keep a copy of your claim form in case queries arise. There are useful tips on completing the form in the disability living allowance (DLA) chapter (see pp534–38). Although those pages focus on DLA for children, the disability conditions for the middle and highest rate care components of DLA are the same as the conditions for AA. There is no mobility component for AA but problems you have with walking may still be relevant to your AA claim if they mean that you need attention or supervision – eg, if you need help to avoid falling because you are unsteady on your feet.

You must provide any information or evidence required (see below). You can amend or withdraw your claim before a decision is made (see p1004).

## People who are classed as terminally ill

The AA claims process is different if you are classed as being terminally ill (see p444). You should explain that the claim is on the grounds of terminal illness when making it. It is usually best to request a claim form by phone to protect your date of claim. You must provide Form SR1, completed by your GP, consultant or specialist nurse, detailing your medical condition.

**Note:** Form DS1500 is still accepted by the DWP to evidence terminal illness although it has been replaced by Form SR1.[13]

You usually need to return the AA claim form as well as the SR1, but do not need to fill in the parts of the claim form relating to your care needs.

After receiving your SR1, the DWP usually makes a fast-tracked decision to award you AA, but may contact your healthcare professionals first for further information. If the DWP decides you do not meet the special rules, you can claim AA in the normal way and/or request a mandatory reconsideration of the decision.

## Who should claim

You normally claim AA for yourself. If you cannot manage your claim, another person can claim AA for you as your 'appointee' (see p1005).

Someone else can make a claim on behalf of a terminally ill person without their knowledge or permission.[14] They can also apply for a revision or supersession, or lodge an appeal, on the same basis.

## Information to support your claim

For the general information requirements that apply to all benefits, see p1006.

It is important that you provide any information required when you claim. Until you do, you may not count as having made a valid claim (see p1008). Provide any missing information as soon as possible or your date of claim may be affected. See p537 for the evidence you may want to provide to help support your claim.

Even if you have provided all that was required when you claimed, you may be asked to provide further information (see p1009).

You may also be asked to provide further information *after* you are awarded AA. If you fail to do so, your AA could be suspended, or even terminated (see p1031).

## The date of your claim

The date of your claim is important as it determines when your entitlement to AA starts. This is not necessarily the date from when you are paid. For information about when payment of AA starts, see p449.

The date of your claim is generally the date your *request* for a claim pack is received by the DWP or alternative office (see p1004) – eg, the date you phoned to request a claim form. This applies provided you return the properly completed form within six weeks of the date of your request.[15] The DWP can extend the six-week deadline if it considers that it is reasonable, so if you return the form late, explain why.[16]

If the DWP has issued a form without date-stamping it, attach a covering letter to the form explaining when and where it was issued and ask to be paid from that date or from six weeks before you sent it in.[17]

If you are using a downloaded form or a blank one issued by an advice agency, it will not have a date-stamp on it and your date of claim is the date the completed form is received by the DWP.

You must make sure your claim is valid. If it is 'defective', you are given a short time to correct the defects (see p1009). If you do, your claim is treated as having been made when you initially claimed.[18]

### Backdating your claim

It is important to claim as soon as you think you may qualify. A claim for AA *cannot* be backdated.[19]

If you might have qualified for benefit earlier but did not claim because you were given the wrong information or were misled by the DWP, you could make a complaint and ask for compensation (see p1261).

### If you claim the wrong benefit

A claim for DLA or personal independence payment can be treated as a claim for AA and vice versa, if it appears to the DWP that you are not entitled to the benefit you claimed. A claim for an increase of industrial injuries disablement benefit if constant attendance is needed can be treated as a claim for AA and vice versa (see p1013).[20]

### Claiming in advance

A claim for AA can be made in advance, before you have satisfied the six-month 'qualifying period' (see p442) or any other qualifying condition, provided you claim no more than six months before you will qualify.[21] In this scenario, the date of your claim is the date on which you meet all the qualifying conditions. If you want to claim in advance, make this clear when you claim or the DWP may not consider it.

## Renewal claims

If you have a fixed-term award of AA (see p449) and you want to continue getting the benefit at the end of that period, you must make a renewal claim. You should be sent a new claim form up to six months before the fixed term is due to end. Take note of your award end date and, if you do not receive a renewal pack six months beforehand, contact the DWP to make a new claim yourself. It is important that you return your completed claim form well before the award expires, as no backdating is possible.

4

The DWP normally treats a renewal claim as a new claim, beginning on the day after your old award ends.[22] However, it may use the information you give in the renewal claim to revise or supersede your existing award, in which case your entitlement may be changed from an earlier date.[23]

If your AA award has ended, you can reclaim the same rate within two years without having to serve the standard six-month qualifying period again.[24]

## How your claim is dealt with

The DWP can award AA based on your claim form alone, but may choose to contact someone you have named on the form for more information. It is a good idea to include details of all the people who know and understand your needs, including medical professionals, carers, social workers, close family and friends. You may also decide to enclose written evidence from them. If the DWP cannot obtain sufficient information, it may also arrange for you to be given a medical examination by a healthcare professional acting on behalf of the DWP, who may visit you at home. This is very unusual in practice. If you refuse a medical examination without good cause, the DWP must decide your claim against you.[25]

The DWP may phone you to ask for further information. If you do not want to be phoned, state this clearly on the claim form.

You may get a decision on a new claim for AA within 40 working days. Claims made under the special rules (see p444) should be decided more quickly. If you disagree with the decision, you can ask for a revision and then appeal (see Chapters 50 and 51).

If you challenge an AA decision, you may receive a 'decision explanation call' from the DWP. This does not affect your right to continue with a revision request and/or appeal.

See p537 for suggestions about the evidence you can use to support a claim, revision or appeal.

# 7. Getting paid

The general rules on getting paid are covered in Chapter 45. This section explains the specific rules that apply to attendance allowance (AA).

***When is attendance allowance paid?***

You are normally paid on a Monday, but the DWP can vary the payday. AA is normally paid every four weeks in arrears. Alternatively, AA can be paid at shorter or longer intervals in arrears, or weekly in advance.[26]

If you leave hospital or a care home and expect to return there within 28 days, AA can be paid at a daily rate for days at home.[27]

Note:

- If you get other DWP benefits, AA may be paid in a single payment with them instead – eg, with retirement pension.
- Even if you have been sanctioned for a benefit offence (see p1111), you must be paid your AA.
- If payment of your AA is delayed, see p1123. If you wish to complain about how your claim has been dealt with, or claim compensation, see Chapter 55.
- If payment of your AA is suspended, see p1031.
- If you have been overpaid AA, you may have to repay it (see Chapter 47) and, in some circumstances, you may have to pay a penalty (see p1101). If you have been accused of fraud, see Chapter 48.
- If you are owed arrears of AA, these can be paid in instalments (see p1018).

## Length of awards

An award of AA can be made for a fixed period or indefinitely.[28] The length of an award depends on how long the DWP estimates your current needs may last. Whatever the length of an award, the DWP can reduce or stop it at any time if there are grounds for revision or supersession (see Chapter 50).

There is no legal minimum length for an award.[29] If you think benefit should be awarded for longer, perhaps because your condition is such that your care needs will not decrease, you can consider asking for a revision (see p1130). However, if you challenge the length of your award, the rate of your award will also be reconsidered.

Awards under the special rules (see p444) are normally made for a fixed period of three years.

## Change of circumstances

You must report changes in your circumstances that you have been told to report, as well as any that you may reasonably be expected to know may affect your right to, the amount of or payment of your benefit. You should do this as soon as possible, preferably in writing. See p1030 for further information. It is usually best to get independent advice before reporting a change in your health that you think may affect your entitlement to AA.

If your condition deteriorates so that you become eligible for the higher rate, the higher rate can be paid from the day you become eligible, provided you tell the DWP no later than a month after completing the six-month qualifying period. If you do not report a change of circumstances within the month, it may be sufficient to do so within 13 months if there were special circumstances that meant it was not practical to report the change earlier.[30] If payment of (but not entitlement to) AA has stopped (eg, while you are in hospital or a care home), still notify the DWP of a deterioration so that the correct rate is paid when payment resumes.

If your condition improves so that you do not qualify for the higher rate or you lose benefit altogether, the new decision usually takes effect from the date you tell the DWP of the improvement, or from the date of the decision if the DWP made it without your asking.[31] It only takes effect from an earlier date (and causes an overpayment) if you should have realised earlier that the change should have been reported. It is accepted that it is difficult for claimants to realise when a gradual improvement begins to affect benefit entitlement.[32]

## 8. **Tax, other benefits and the benefit cap**

### Tax

Attendance allowance (AA) is not taxable.[33]

### Means-tested benefits

AA is not taken into account as income when calculating any of the means-tested benefits. AA is paid on top of these, and if you or your partner get AA, this can increase the amount of means-tested benefit you get (or mean that you qualify for means-tested benefits for the first time).

You may qualify for one or more of the following extra amounts:

- a limited capability for work-related activity element included in your universal credit (UC) if you are entitled to AA, as you are treated as having limited capability for work-related activity (see p917);
- a severe disability premium (see p275) included in your income-related employment and support allowance (ESA) if your partner gets AA and you meet the other conditions for this premium;
- a severe disability premium included in your housing benefit (HB), or an addition for severe disability included in the guarantee credit of pension credit

(PC), if you get AA and meet the other conditions for this premium or addition (see p275).

No housing costs contributions from a non-dependant are taken into account when calculating your UC housing costs element if you, your partner or the non-dependant get AA, or would get it but for being in hospital (see p109). If you or your partner get AA, non-dependant deductions are not made from your HB (see p208), or from any housing costs included in income-related ESA or the guarantee credit of PC (see p291).



## Non-means-tested benefits

AA may be paid in addition to any other non-means-tested benefits, except that:

- it 'overlaps' with armed forces independence payment (see p779) and constant attendance allowance under the industrial injuries scheme (see p600) or war pensions scheme.[34] See p1021 for details of the overlapping benefit rules; *and*
- you cannot claim AA if you are entitled to personal independence payment, adult disability payment, or the care component of disability living allowance.[35]

If you get AA and someone regularly looks after you, that person may be entitled to carer's allowance (CA) (see Chapter 22) or carer support payment (see p1467), and they (or their partner if claiming as a couple) may also get a carer element in UC (see p75), a carer premium in income-related ESA or HB, or a carer addition in the guarantee credit of PC (see p279). However, your entitlement to a severe disability premium (or severe disability additional amount) can be affected if they get CA or a carer element in UC, so always get advice before encouraging them to claim.

A young person aged 16, 17 or 18 living in Scotland who cannot get CA may be able to get a young carer grant for looking after you (see Chapter 63).

## The benefit cap

AA is *not* one of the specified benefits for the benefit cap. The benefit cap does *not* apply if you or your partner get AA even if it is not paid because the person entitled is in hospital or a care home. The benefit cap also does *not* apply if you do not get AA, but you (and your partner, if you have one) are over pension age. See p1025 for further information.

## Passports and other sources of help

You qualify for a Christmas bonus if you get AA at any rate (see p783). You may qualify for council tax reduction (see p761).

If any member of your household gets AA at any rate, you may get a grant for help with insulation and other energy efficiency measures in your home (see p782).

# Notes

4

1. **Who can get attendance allowance**
   1 ss64, 65 and 66 SSCBA 1992; reg 2 SS(AA) Regs
   2 s65(3) SSCBA 1992
   3 s64(2) SSCBA 1992
   4 s64(3) SSCBA 1992

2. **The rules about your age**
   5 s64(1) SSCBA 1992

4. **The amount of benefit**
   6 Sch 4 Part III SSCBA 1992

5. **Special benefit rules**
   7 s65(2) SSCBA 1992; reg 5 SS(AA) Regs
   8 s66(2)(a) SSCBA 1992
   9 DWP, *The 'Special Rules': how the benefit system supports people nearing the end of life*, September 2024
   10 s66(1) SSCBA 1992

6. **Claims and backdating**
   11 Reg 4(1) SS(C&P) Regs
   12 DWP, *DWP Digital Services: product design (retirement, bereavement and care)*, April 2022
   13 DWP, *The 'Special Rules': how the benefit system supports people nearing the end of life*, September 2024
   14 s66(2)(b) SSCBA 1992; regs 3(9)(b), 6(6)(c) and 25(b) SS&CS(DA) Regs
   15 Reg 6(8), (8A) and (9) SS(C&P) Regs
   16 Reg 6(9) SS(C&P) Regs; *SN v SSWP (PIP)* [2018] UKUT 210 (AAC) – although decided on similar rules for PIP, this case considers circumstances that may be reasonable and the discussion is relevant for AA claims
   17 Reg 6(8A) SS(C&P) Regs
   18 Reg 6(1)(b) SS(C&P) Regs
   19 s65(4) SSCBA 1992. For example, see *JW v DfC* [2024] NICom 12
   20 Reg 9(1) and Sch 1 SS(C&P) Regs; reg 25(3) and (4) UC,PIP,JSA&ESA(C&P) Regs
   21 s65(6) SSCBA 1992
   22 Reg 13C SS(C&P) Regs
   23 CDLA/14895/1996
   24 s65(1)(b) SSCBA 1992; reg 3 SS(AA) Regs
   25 s19(3) SSA 1998

7. **Getting paid**
   26 Reg 22 and Sch 6 SS(C&P) Regs
   27 Reg 25 SS(C&P) Regs
   28 s65(1)(a) SSCBA 1992
   29 R(DLA) 11/02
   30 Regs 7(9)(b) and 8 SS&CS(DA) Regs
   31 s10(5) SSA 1998
   32 Reg 7(2)(c) SS&CS(DA) Regs; *RD v SSWP (DLA)* [2011] UKUT 95 (AAC); *DC v SSWP (DLA)* [2011] UKUT 336 (AAC)

8. **Tax, other benefits and the benefit cap**
   33 s677 IT(EP)A 2003
   34 Sch 1 paras 5 and 5a SS(OB) Regs
   35 s64(1) and (1A) SSCBA 1992

# Chapter 21

# Bereavement benefits

**This chapter covers:**


1. Bereavement support payment (p454)
2. Widowed parent's allowance (p456)
3. Definitions (p458)
4. Special benefit rules (p461)
5. Claims and backdating (p462)
6. Getting paid (p465)
7. Tax, other benefits and the benefit cap (p467)


## Key facts

- Bereavement benefits are paid to widows, widowers, surviving civil partners and surviving cohabiting partners with children or who are pregnant. **Note:** this chapter refers to surviving cohabiting partners with children as 'cohabiting partners'. If your spouse, civil partner or cohabiting partner died on or after 6 April 2017, the relevant bereavement benefit is **bereavement support payment**. If they died before this date, and you have dependent children, you may be able to get **widowed parent's allowance**.
- To qualify for all bereavement benefits, your late spouse, civil partner or cohabiting partner must have either satisfied the national insurance contribution conditions or, except surviving cohabiting partners claiming widowed parent's allowance, have been an 'employed earner' and died as a result of an industrial accident or disease.
- You must be under pension age to qualify for bereavement benefits.
- Bereavement benefits are non-means-tested benefits.
- You can get bereavement benefits whether you are in or out of work.
- Beginning a new relationship may affect your entitlement.
- Bereavement benefits are administered and paid by the DWP.
- If you disagree with a bereavement benefit decision, you can apply for a revision or a supersession (see Chapter 50), or appeal against it (see Chapter 51). You must apply for a mandatory reconsideration before you can appeal.

**Note:** before 9 February 2023, surviving cohabiting partners were not able to claim bereavement benefits. However, as a result of two successful court cases,[1] the law was changed to allow cohabiting partners with children to claim these benefits.[2] As well as satisfying the usual entitlement conditions, you must have been living with your partner when they died and have been entitled to the relevant benefit at the time of their death. Special backdating rules applied between 9 February 2023 and 8 November 2024, which meant that if your partner died before 9 February 2023 and you satisfied the conditions on or after 30 August 2018, you could get additional backdating: see Chapter 25 of the 2024/25 edition of this *Handbook* for more information on this. The normal backdating rules apply from 8 November 2024.



# 1. Bereavement support payment

Bereavement support payment is a benefit for people whose spouse, civil partner or cohabiting partner died on or after 6 April 2017. It comprises monthly payments, payable for a maximum period of 18 months, and a lump-sum payment in the first month.

## Who can get bereavement support payment

You can get bereavement support payment if:[3]

- you are a widow, widower, surviving civil partner or surviving cohabiting partner with dependent children; *and*
- your spouse, civil partner or cohabiting partner died on or after 6 April 2017; *and*
- your late spouse, civil partner or cohabiting partner either:
  - satisfied the national insurance (NI) contribution conditions (see p878); *or*
  - was an 'employed earner' and died as a result of an industrial injury or disease (see p461); *and*
- you are under pension age; *and*
- you satisfy the residence condition (see p1345).

**Note:** the law changed on 9 February 2023 to allow cohabiting partners with dependent children or who are pregnant to claim bereavement support payment. Surviving cohabiting partners without dependent children are not eligible for bereavement support payment.

A court decision has held that the requirement that your late spouse or civil partner satisfied the NI conditions is unlawful if, because of disability, they could not work (and so could never make NI contributions) throughout their working life.[4] Get advice if you are in this situation.

### Time limits

To get bereavement support payment for the maximum 18-month period, you must claim within three months of the date your spouse, civil partner or cohabiting partner died (see p464). To get the initial lump-sum payment, you must claim within 12 months of their death.[5]

## The rules about your age

There is no lower age limit for bereavement support payment.

Bereavement support payment cannot be paid if you are pension age or over, but you may qualify for state pension (see p688) or a survivor's inherited state pension instead (see p693).



## People included in the claim

You claim bereavement support payment for yourself. You cannot get an increase for a new partner or for your children. If you have dependent children, you are, however, paid the higher rate of bereavement support payment.[6]

## The amount of bereavement support payment

There are two rates of bereavement support payment – a standard rate and a higher rate. You get the higher rate if:[7]

- you were pregnant when your spouse, civil partner or cohabiting partner died; *or*
- you were entitled to child benefit when your spouse, civil partner or cohabiting partner died, *or*
- since your spouse, civil partner or cohabiting partner died, you have become entitled to child benefit for a child or qualifying young person who was residing with you or your late spouse, civil partner or cohabiting partner immediately before they died. This applies even if you subsequently cease to be entitled to child benefit for that child or qualifying young person. **Note:** if you are awarded the standard rate of bereavement support payment because you do not yet receive child benefit, if child benefit is later awarded, your bereavement support payment can be increased on revision or supersession and arrears paid for the same length of time under the qualifying benefit rules (see p1157).

If your cohabiting partner has died, because you are only entitled to bereavement support payment if you have dependent children, you are only entitled to the higher rate.

***Rates of bereavement support payment*** [8]

| | *Standard rate* | *Higher rate* |
|---|---|---|
| Initial lump sum | £2,500 | £3,500 |
| Monthly amount | £100 | £350 |

### Starting a new relationship

If you start cohabiting with a new partner, enter into a new civil partnership or remarry, this does not affect your entitlement to bereavement support payment.[9]

## 2. Widowed parent's allowance

4

Widowed parent's allowance is a benefit for people whose spouse, civil partner or cohabiting partner died before 6 April 2017. However, as a surviving cohabiting partner you are only eligible if you met the entitlement conditions listed below on or after 30 August 2018. It comprises fortnightly payments, payable for as long as you meet the conditions of entitlement.

### Who can get widowed parent's allowance

You can get widowed parent's allowance if:[10]

- you are a widow, widower, surviving civil partner or surviving cohabiting partner; *and*
- your spouse, civil partner or cohabiting partner died before 6 April 2017; *and*
- your late spouse, civil partner or cohabiting partner either:
  - satisfied the national insurance (NI) contribution conditions (see p879); *or*
  - for spouses and civil partners only, was an 'employed earner' and died as the result of an industrial injury or disease (see p461); *and*
- you are under pension age; *and*
- you are entitled to child benefit for at least one 'eligible child'.

**Note**: the law changed on 9 February 2023 to allow cohabiting partners who satisfied the entitlement conditions on or after 30 August 2018 to claim widowed parent's allowance (see p457).

#### Eligible child

A 'child' means both a 'child' and a 'qualifying young person' (see p488 for the definitions). An 'eligible child' is someone who:[11]

- is your and your late spouse's/civil partner's/cohabiting partner's child; *or*
- *you* were entitled to child benefit for and you were residing with your late spouse, civil partner or cohabiting partner immediately before they died – ie, even if the child is not your late spouse's/civil partner's/cohabiting partner's child; *or*
- your late spouse, civil partner or cohabiting partner immediately before they died was entitled to child benefit for – ie, even if the child is not your child.

### Treated as entitled to child benefit

- You still count as entitled to child benefit if it has been awarded to you, but you have elected for it not to be paid to avoid the high-income child benefit charge (see p507).
- You or your late spouse or civil partner can be treated as entitled to child benefit if you would have been entitled to it had you claimed it and had the child in question not been abroad.[12] **Note**: this rule does not apply to cohabiting partners.
- If you are not already getting child benefit for the eligible child, you need to claim it.



### Treated as residing with your spouse or civil partner

**Note**: the following rules do not apply to cohabiting partners.

- If you and your spouse or civil partner were living apart at the time of their death, you can still be considered to have been residing with them if your separation was only intended to be temporary.[13] This depends on the facts of your case.[14]
- If you have been widowed before or survived a previous civil partner, and this meant that you were left to care for dependent children, you can qualify for widowed parent's allowance on the basis of the death of your most recent spouse or civil partner, even if you were not residing with them when they died.[15]

### Time limit

Provided you meet all the conditions of entitlement on p456, there is no time limit for claiming widowed parent's allowance after the death of your spouse, civil partner or cohabiting partner (but see below). It then remains payable until you no longer meet one of these conditions – eg, your child is no longer an eligible child because of their age. **Note**: if it is your cohabiting partner who has died, you must have met the entitlement conditions on or after 30 August 2018. If you had ceased to meet the conditions by this date, you are not entitled to widowed parent's allowance.

## The rules about your age

There is no lower age limit for widowed parent's allowance. Widowed parent's allowance cannot be paid if you are pension age or over, but you may qualify for state pension (see p688) or a survivor's inherited state pension instead (see p693).

## People included in the claim

You claim widowed parent's allowance for yourself. You cannot claim widowed parent's allowance if you have a new partner (see p458). New claims do not include an increase for your children.

### The amount of widowed parent's allowance

Widowed parent's allowance is made up of:

- a basic allowance. The full weekly rate is £150.90, but it may be paid at a reduced rate if your late spouse's, civil partner's or cohabiting partner's NI contribution record was incomplete (see below); *and*
- an additional earnings-related payment based on your late spouse's, civil partner's or cohabiting partner's earnings under the additional state pension scheme, if their NI contribution record qualifies you for this (see p879). You may be entitled to this even if their contribution record is not sufficient for you to qualify for basic widowed parent's allowance.[16]



#### Reduction if your late spouse, civil partner or cohabiting partner had an incomplete contribution record

If your late spouse, civil partner or cohabiting partner had an incomplete NI contribution record, the amount of widowed parent's allowance you receive is reduced proportionately.[17] You may be able to increase your entitlement to widowed parent's allowance by paying voluntary NI contributions on your spouse's, civil partner's or cohabiting partner's behalf, even though they died. Contact HMRC (tel: 0300 200 3500; textphone: 0300 200 3519; Relay UK service available) about this. See p864 for further details and for the time limits for making such payments.

### Starting a new relationship

Entitlement to widowed parent's allowance ends if you remarry, enter into a new civil partnership or a new cohabiting partnership.[18] You cannot requalify for it, even if you subsequently get divorced, if your civil partnership is dissolved or if you stop cohabiting with your partner. The exception to this is if you are a surviving spouse or civil partner and you began cohabiting with a new partner before 9 February 2023, in which case your widowed parent's allowance is suspended but can be reinstated if you later separate.[19]

## 3. Definitions

### Widows, widowers, surviving civil partners and surviving cohabiting partners

To get bereavement benefits, you must be a widow, widower, surviving civil partner or surviving cohabiting partner. To be entitled to bereavement benefits, you must have been married to your spouse (in a same-sex or opposite-sex marriage), in a civil partnership with your partner or in a cohabiting partnership at the date of your partner's death. The marriage or civil partnership must have been valid under UK law, but see below. A **'cohabiting partnership'** is defined as a couple who are not married to, or civil partners of, each other but are 'living together as if they were married' or in a civil partnership.[20] There is no minimum amount of time you must have been cohabiting with your partner; it is enough that you were cohabiting at the time of their death.[21]

## Marriage 'by cohabitation with habit and repute'

In Scotland,[22] you can count as a widow or widower if you were married by 'cohabitation with habit and repute', even if you did not go through a wedding ceremony, provided your cohabitation began before 4 May 2006.[23] For this to apply, your relationship must have been like that of a husband and wife and more than simply living together – there must have been something about it which meant it could be inferred that you and your partner consented to marriage and that nothing existed that would have prevented a valid marriage taking place – eg, one of you being married to someone else.[24] In addition, your relationship must have been such that other people generally believed you were married.[25] If you are pregnant or have dependent children and it is not accepted that you counted as married under this rule, you may be entitled to bereavement benefits as a cohabiting partner instead.



## If you have more than one bereavement

If, following the death of your spouse, civil partner or cohabiting partner, you remarry or form a new civil partnership or cohabiting partnership, and your new spouse, civil partner or cohabiting partner then dies, your entitlement to bereavement benefits depends on the national insurance (NI) contribution record of your most recent spouse, civil partner or cohabiting partner.

## Invalid marriages

A **void** marriage or civil partnership (ie, one in which at least one of the partners was not eligible to marry or form a civil partnership) is invalid. From a legal point of view, it is treated as if it never existed.[26] In England and Wales, a **voidable** marriage or civil partnership is treated as having been valid until a decree absolute of annulment is pronounced.[27] Questions about the validity of marriages or civil partnerships are decided by a special unit at the DWP. If a question arises about the validity of your marriage or civil partnership, get advice from a family law specialist. Arguably, if your marriage or civil partnership is void, you may be entitled to bereavement benefits as a cohabiting partner instead (if you either have dependent children or are pregnant).

## Separation, divorce and dissolution

If you were divorced when your former spouse died, your civil partnership had been dissolved when your former civil partner died, or you had separated from your cohabiting partner when they died, you are not a widow, widower, surviving civil partner or surviving cohabiting partner.

A divorce only becomes effective when the decree absolute is pronounced (a decree of divorce, in Scotland), and a civil partnership is dissolved when a final dissolution order is issued (a decree of dissolution, in Scotland). If you were in the process of obtaining a divorce or of dissolving your civil partnership, but your spouse or civil partner died before it was finalised, you are still a widow, widower or surviving civil partner (and so may be entitled to bereavement benefits). This is the case even if you were judicially separated.



### Polygamous marriages

If your marriage was polygamous, you are not usually entitled to bereavement benefits following the death of your spouse because, generally, the law in England, Wales and Scotland does not treat you as legally married unless your marriage is a monogamous one.[28]

**Note:**

- If your marriage was *previously* polygamous rather than actually polygamous when your spouse died (eg, if any other spouse had already died), you can qualify.
- A marriage is only considered polygamous if the law of the country where the marriage takes place permits either party to have another wife or husband.[29]
- Whether your marriage is considered polygamous depends on whether you were your spouse's first wife or husband, and on where you and your spouse were 'domiciled' at the time of your marriage and any subsequent marriage. In general terms, 'domicile' means the country in which you have chosen to make your permanent home.[30] In particular, no one domiciled in England or Wales can contract a polygamous marriage anywhere in the world even if the local law allows it.[31]
- If you are the surviving partner but your marriage is considered to have been polygamous and you are refused benefit, depending on the facts of your case (in particular, where the facts suggest that your marriage was actually monogamous), you may be able to argue that you should still be entitled under human rights rules.[32] Seek advice.

***Example***

At the time of their wedding, Muneeba and Shaheen were domiciled in Pakistan and were married under Islamic law. After the wedding, they came to live in England, made their permanent home here and had no intention of returning to live in Pakistan at any time. Later, Shaheen returned temporarily to Pakistan and married a second wife. As Shaheen was domiciled in England rather than Pakistan at the time of the second marriage, English law does not recognise the second marriage and therefore regards Muneeba as Shaheen's only wife. Provided she meets the other entitlement conditions, Muneeba is entitled to bereavement benefits.[33] If Shaheen had reacquired domicile in Pakistan at the time of his second marriage, and his second wife was still alive, both marriages would be polygamous, and neither wife could claim bereavement benefits.[34]

### Cohabitation

'**Cohabiting**' means living with someone as if you are a married couple. Deciding whether or not you are cohabiting may not be straightforward. For further information, see p255.

If the DWP refuses you widowed parent's allowance because it believes you are cohabiting with a new partner and you do not agree, you can challenge its decision (see Chapters 50 and 51).



### Industrial accident or disease

The meaning of 'industrial accident or disease' is discussed on p589 and p593. To qualify for bereavement benefits, the industrial accident or disease must have been a cause of your late spouse's, civil partner's or cohabiting partner's death, but it need not have been a direct cause or the only cause.[35] Your late spouse, civil partner or cohabiting partner must have been an 'employed earner' – ie, an employee, not self-employed (see p859).[36] If your cohabiting partner died from an industrial accident or disease, you are only eligible for bereavement support payment, not widowed parent's allowance. This means you are not entitled to bereavement benefits if your partner died from an industrial accident or disease before 6 April 2017, unless they satisfied the NI contributions condition.

## 4. Special benefit rules

Special rules may apply to:

- widows whose husbands died before 9 April 2001 (see below);
- people who have obtained a gender recognition certificate (see p462);
- surviving cohabiting partners with children whose partner died before 9 February 2023 (see p462);
- people who are going abroad (see Chapter 58);
- people in prison or detention (see Chapter 38).

### Widows whose husbands died before 9 April 2001

If you are a widow whose husband died before 9 April 2001, you are not entitled to bereavement benefits. You may still be getting widow's pension or widowed mother's allowance, although the latter is unlikely because given the time that has passed you will probably no longer be responsible for an eligible child. For more information on these older widows' benefits see p536 of the 2022/23 edition of this *Handbook*.

### People who have obtained a gender recognition certificate

If you annulled or dissolved an existing marriage or civil partnership in order to obtain a full gender recognition certificate (which, before 10 December 2014 in England and Wales and 16 December 2014 in Scotland, you had to do),[37] you are not entitled to bereavement benefits on the basis of your ex-spouse's or ex-civil partner's national insurance contribution record, if they subsequently die.

If you are getting widow's pension when a full gender recognition certificate is issued, any entitlement ends. Widowed mother's allowance also ends, but you can qualify for widowed parent's allowance instead.[38]

4

### Surviving cohabiting partners with children whose partner died before 9 February 2023

If your cohabiting partner died before 9 February 2023 *and* you satisfied the entitlement conditions on any day between 30 August 2018 and 8 February 2023 *and* you claimed the relevant bereavement benefit between 9 February 2023 and 8 November 2024, special backdating rules applied. In some cases, arrears were paid from the date your partner died. From 9 November 2024, the normal backdating rules apply, both if your partner died before 9 February 2023 (which will only apply to widowed parent's allowance) or afterwards. See Chapter 25 of the 2024/25 edition of this *Handbook* for more information.

## 5. Claims and backdating

The general rules about claims and backdating are covered in Chapter 44. This section explains the specific rules that apply to bereavement benefits.

### Making a claim

Claim bereavement support payment or widowed parent's allowance:

- by phoning the DWP's Bereavement Service on 0800 151 2012 (Welsh language: 0800 731 0453; textphone: 0800 731 0464; Relay UK and British Sign Language services are available). After giving information by phone, you are sent a statement to approve, sign and return; *or*
- in writing, usually on the approved form.

***Forms***

Form BSP1 is the approved form for bereavement support payment. You can also claim online at gov.uk/bereavement-support-payment/how-to-claim.

There are two forms for widowed parent's allowance: Form BB1 is the approved form for spouses and civil partners; Form BB2 is the approved form for cohabiting partners.

When you register the death, you are usually given a Certificate of Registration of Death. If you complete the form on the certificate and send it to the DWP, you should be sent the correct bereavement benefit form. Alternatively, you can request a form from DWP's Bereavement Service on the number above or apply online at gov.uk.

You must provide any information or evidence required (see below).

If there is a delay in dealing with your claim, you may be able to get a short-term advance of benefit (see p1023).

## Who should claim

You must normally claim bereavement benefits yourself. If you cannot manage your claim, another person can claim bereavement benefits for you as your appointee (see p1005).

## Information to support your claim

For the general information requirements that apply to all benefits, see p1006.

It is important that you provide any information required when you claim. Until you do, you may not count as having made a valid claim (see p1008). Correct any defects as soon as possible or your date of claim may be affected.

You are normally also expected to provide proof of your spouse's, civil partner's or cohabiting partner's death. If you have reported the death to a local DWP office under the 'Tell Us Once' arrangements (see p1030), you are given a reference number, which you can use as proof of death when you make a claim through the Bereavement Service.

Alternatively, when you register the death you get a death certificate, which can be provided as proof. If you do not have proof that your spouse, civil partner or cohabiting partner has died, see p464.

You are also usually expected to provide your marriage or civil partnership certificate.[39] Caselaw has provided guidance on assessing evidence from countries where reliable documentary proof of life events, such as marriage, may not be available.[40]

Evidencing cohabitation may be more difficult than evidencing a marriage or civil partnership, particularly if your partner died a long time ago. You should provide any information that shows a shared address – eg, utility bills, bank statements or tenancy agreements. The DWP also checks its records. If there is insufficient evidence to show cohabitation, the DWP should accept your declaration that you were living together at the time of your partner's death.[41]

Even if you have provided all that was required when you claimed, you may be asked to provide further information to support your claim (see p1009). You may be asked to provide information after you are awarded bereavement benefits. If you fail to do so, your benefit may be suspended or even terminated (see p1031).

## The date of your claim

The date of your claim determines when your entitlement to bereavement support payment (including the lump sum) or widowed parent's allowance starts. This is not necessarily the date from when you are paid. For information about when payment of a bereavement benefit starts, see p465.

The date of your claim is normally the date of your call, if you claim by phone, or the date your written or online claim is received.[42]

You must make sure your claim is valid. If it is 'defective', you are given a short time to correct the defects (see p1009). If you do, your claim is treated as having been made when you initially claimed.[43]



### Backdating your claim

If your spouse, civil partner or cohabiting partner dies, **bereavement support payment** is automatically backdated to the date of their death, provided you claim within three months of the date of their death.[44]

Your bereavement support payment award ends 18 months after your spouse, civil partner or cohabiting partner died,[45] so you should claim within three months of the date of their death to receive the maximum 18-month award.

If you claim more than three months after the date of their death, your claim is automatically backdated for three months.[46] Because of this, you can claim bereavement support payment up until 21 months after your spouse, civil partner or cohabiting partner dies, but you will not receive the maximum award.[47]

***Examples***

Rachel's civil partner died on 20 August 2024. She claimed bereavement support payment on 4 February 2025. It is paid for the period 4 November 2024 to 20 February 2026. The length of her award is limited to approximately 15.5 months.

Hugh's wife died on 10 July 2023. He claimed bereavement support payment on 28 March 2025. It is paid for the period 28 December 2024 to 10 January 2025. The length of his award is limited to two weeks. He also misses out on the initial lump-sum payment.

Payment of **widowed parent's allowance** can be backdated for up to three months before the date you claim,[48] provided you satisfy the qualifying conditions over that period. You do not need to show reasons why your claim is late.

If you might have qualified for benefit earlier but did not claim because you were given the wrong information or were misled by the DWP, you could make a complaint and seek compensation (see Chapter 55).

#### If there is a delay in hearing or uncertainty about a death

If you did not find out straight away that your spouse or civil partner had died, but you find out within 12 months of the death, you can apply for bereavement support payment within 12 months of becoming aware of the death, and request that it be backdated to the date of death.[49]

If it is presumed that your spouse or civil partner has died, but this has not been established for certain, you can ask the DWP to make a decision that they died (or are likely to have died) on a particular date. You should provide the information and evidence that has led you to presume they died.

If the DWP decides they died *before* 6 April 2017, you can then claim widowed parent's allowance within 12 months of the date of that decision and have it backdated to the date the DWP has decided your late spouse or civil partner died.[50]

**Note:** you are not entitled to bereavement benefits under this rule if it is your cohabiting partner, rather than your spouse or civil partner, who has died.



These are also the only circumstances in which you may still qualify for the other two 'old' bereavement benefits (bereavement allowance and/or a bereavement payment). See Chapter 24 of the 2017/18 edition of this *Handbook* for more information about these benefits.

If the DWP decides they died *on or after* 6 April 2017, you can claim bereavement support payment within 12 months of the date of that decision and have it backdated to the presumed date of death.

### If you claim the wrong benefit

The decision maker can treat a claim for state pension as a claim for widowed parent's allowance and vice versa.[51] A claim for bereavement support payment can be treated as a claim for widowed parent's allowance and vice versa. See p1013 for details of interchanging claims in this way.

### Claiming in advance

You can claim bereavement benefits up to three months before you expect to qualify. In most circumstances, you will not know of your need to claim benefit in advance, but this may be relevant if, for example, you know that you will no longer be cohabiting.[52] The date of your claim is the date on which you qualify.

## 6. Getting paid

The general rules on getting paid are covered in Chapter 45. This section explains the specific rules that apply to bereavement benefits.

***When are bereavement benefits paid?***

Bereavement support payment is paid monthly in arrears, on the same day of the month as the date of death of your spouse, civil partner or cohabiting partner. In months when it cannot be paid on this day because it falls on the 29th, 30th or 31st, it is paid on the last day of the month.[53]

Widowed parent's allowance is normally paid fortnightly, in arrears.

Bereavement support payment and widowed parent's allowance are daily benefits. Payments can be made for part periods at the beginning and end of claims. Part payments are calculated using the daily rate.

**Note:**

- Your widowed parent's allowance might be paid at a reduced rate in certain circumstances (see p458).
- You may not be paid bereavement benefit if you have received a sanction for a benefit offence (see p1111).
- If payment of your bereavement benefit is delayed, see p1123. If you are waiting for a decision on your claim, or to be paid, you might be able to get a short-term advance (see p1023). If you wish to complain about how your claim has been dealt with, or claim compensation, see Chapter 55.
- If payment of your bereavement benefit is suspended, see p1031.
- If you are overpaid a bereavement benefit, you might have to repay it (see Chapter 47) and, in some circumstances, you may have to pay a penalty (see p1101). If you have been accused of fraud, see Chapter 48.
- If you are owed arrears of a bereavement benefit, these can be paid in instalments (see p1018).

## Priority between claimants

The general rule is that only one person can be awarded a bereavement benefit for the same death,[54] but there is an exception regarding the period before 9 February 2023, for which see Chapter 25 of the 2024/25 edition of this *Handbook*. The general rule where there are two or more people who could be entitled (which is now possible following the change in the rules for cohabiting partners) is that the person who was living in the same household as the deceased at the time of their death is entitled to bereavement benefits.[55]

In the more limited situations where two or more people were living with the deceased at the time of their death, there is an order of priority.[56]

- If you were married/in a civil partnership with the person who has died, and you are either pregnant or get child benefit, you have priority.
- If no one was married/in a civil partnership with the deceased, and you are either pregnant or get child benefit, you have priority.
- If more than one of you is pregnant or gets child benefit, if you have been a member of the household for longer than the other person(s), you have priority.
- If both, or all, of you had been members of the same household for the same amount of time, and more than one of you is either pregnant or gets child benefit, the DWP decides who has priority.

## Change of circumstances

You must report changes in your circumstances that you have been told to report, as well as any that you might reasonably be expected to know might affect your right to, the amount of, or the payment of, your benefit. You should do this as soon as possible, preferably in writing. See p1030 for further information.

If a change of circumstances affects your entitlement to widowed parent's allowance, before your benefit can be stopped or adjusted, the decision maker should first revise or supersede the earlier decision on your entitlement (see Chapter 50).[57] For when a new decision takes effect, see p1150.



# 7. Tax, other benefits and the benefit cap

## Tax

**Bereavement support payment** is not taxable.[58] **Widowed parent's allowance** is taxable.[59]

## Means-tested benefits

The initial lump sum of **bereavement support payment** counts as capital for all means-tested benefits, but it is disregarded for up to 52 weeks (or, for universal credit (UC), 12 months). The monthly payments count as income, but are disregarded for all means-tested benefits, including UC.[60]

**Widowed parent's allowance** counts as income for means-tested benefits. However:

- £10 of your weekly widowed parent's allowance is disregarded when calculating your entitlement to income-related employment and support allowance (ESA)[61] and pension credit (PC);[62]
- an increase in your widowed parent's allowance for a child is disregarded when calculating your entitlement to income-related ESA and PC;
- £15 of your weekly widowed parent's allowance is disregarded when calculating your entitlement to housing benefit (HB).[63] However, if you are getting the savings credit (and not the guarantee credit) of PC, the income used to calculate your HB is that used by the DWP to calculate your entitlement to PC (which includes only a £10 disregard from your widowed parent's allowance – see p378).

There are no equivalent widowed parent's allowance disregards for UC.[64] For information about how arrears of bereavement support payment and widowed parent's allowance for cohabiting partners are treated for means-tested benefits, see Chapter 25 of the 2024/25 edition of this *Handbook*.

If your partner was entitled to HB when they died, this ends. You can now only make a new claim for HB in limited circumstances (see p183). If you can make a new HB claim and you claim within a month of your partner's death, your HB claim can be treated as having been made on the date your partner died (see p215). In some circumstances, it can be backdated further (see p216). If you cannot make a new HB claim, you can claim UC (see Chapter 3).

## Non-means-tested benefits

Bereavement support payment is not an overlapping benefit – apart from widow's pension and widowed parent's allowance, you can be paid it at the same time as any of the benefits listed on p1021. However, widowed parent's allowance is affected by the overlapping benefit rules (see p1021).

4

Once you reach pension age, your entitlement to bereavement benefits stops. However, you may qualify for state pension (see p688) or a survivor's inherited state pension instead (see p693).

If your bereavement benefit stops before you reach pension age, you may qualify for national insurance credits following bereavement for new-style ESA and new-style JSA (see p873).[65]

## The benefit cap

Bereavement support payment is *not* one of the specified benefits for the benefit cap.[66] However, widowed parent's allowance is a specified benefit for the benefit cap.[67] It only applies if you are getting UC or HB. Fifteen pounds of your weekly widowed parent's allowance is ignored if the cap is applied through your HB. See p1025 for further information.

## Passports and other sources of help

If you are entitled to widowed parent's allowance, you are also entitled to a Christmas bonus (see p783).

In some circumstances, you may qualify for a social fund funeral expenses payment (see p707). In Scotland, you may qualify for a funeral support payment (see Chapter 65).

If your child has died, you may qualify for a payment from the children's funeral fund in England or a £500 payment towards funeral costs in Wales (see p708). If your child has died and you are an employee, you may be entitled to statutory parental bereavement pay (see p724).

If you have low income and capital, you may be entitled to UC (see Chapter 3) and/or council tax reduction (see p761). In limited circumstances, you may be entitled to HB (see Chapter 10).

For advice about what to do after someone dies, see gov.uk. In Scotland, see also the online Scottish government leaflet '*What to Do After a Death in Scotland*', available at gov.scot.

# Notes

1 *McLaughlin, Re Judicial Review (Northern Ireland)* [2018] UKSC 48; *Jackson and others v SSWP* [2020] EWHC 183
2 BB(R)O

1. **Bereavement support payment**
3 s30 PA 2014
4 *Jwanczuk v SSWP* [2023] EWCA Civ 1156
5 Reg 3(2) and (5) BSP Regs
6 Reg 4 BSP Regs
7 Reg 4 BSP Regs
8 Reg 3(1)-(6) BSP Regs
9 House of Commons, *Hansard,* Written statement HCWS409, 12 January 2017, para 5, at questions-statements.parliament.uk

2. **Widowed parent's allowance**
10 ss39A and 60(2) and (3) SSCBA 1992
11 s39A(3) SSCBA 1992
12 Reg 16ZA(1)(a) SS(WB&RP) Regs
13 Reg 2(4) SSB(PRT) Regs
14 CIS/1059/2014
15 Reg 16ZA(2) SS(WB&RP) Regs
16 Reg 6(2) SS(WB&RP) Regs
17 Reg 6 SS(WB&RP) Regs
18 s39A(4), (4A) and (4B) SSCBA 1992
19 ADM Memo 9-23: *Change to Underlying Entitlement Conditions for Widowed Parent's Allowance due to the Introduction of the Bereavement Benefits (Remedial) Order 2023*

3. **Definitions**
20 s30(6B) PA 2014; s39A(7) SSCBA 1992
21 House of Commons, *Hansard*, col 4, 24 January 2023
22 But see *CAO v Bath* [1999] EWCA Civ 3008 (CA), reported as R(G) 1/00; R(G) 2/70
23 R(G) 5/83; s3 Family Law (Scotland) Act 2006; The Family Law (Scotland) Act 2006 (Commencement, Transitional Provisions and Savings) Order 2006 No.212
24 R(G) 1/71
25 CSG/7/1995; CSG/681/2003; but see also CSG/648/2007
26 R(G) 2/63
27 R(G) 1/73
28 *Hyde v Hyde* [1866]; reg 2 SSFA(PM) Regs
29 Reg 1(2) SSFA(PM) Regs
30 R(S) 2/92
31 s11(3) MCA 1973
32 *NA v SSWP (BB)* [2019] UKUT 144 (AAC). The facts included a religious marriage recognised in Pakistan but not recognised in England and Wales, where the late spouse had only ever lived with one other spouse.
33 R(G) 1/95
34 R(G) 1/93; R(P) 2/06
35 CI/142/1949; R(I) 14/51
36 ss2(a) and 60(2) SSCBA 1992

4. **Special benefit rules**
37 s4 GRA 2004
38 Sch 5 paras 3-5 GRA 2004

5. **Claims and backdating**
39 Reg 7(1) SS(C&P) Regs
40 CP/4062/2004; see also CP/891/2008 and *AR v SSWP* [2012] UKUT 467 (AAC)
41 Letter from Viscount Younger of Leckie to Lord Davies of Brixton and Baroness Sherlock, 2 February 2023, depositedpapers.parliament.uk/depositedpaper/2284993/files
42 Reg 6(1) and (1ZA) SS(C&P) Regs
43 Regs 4(7), (7ZA), (8), (12) and (13) and 6(1) SS(C&P) Regs
44 Reg 2(2)(a) BSP Regs
45 Reg 2(3) BSP Regs
46 Reg 2(2)(b) BSP Regs
47 Reg 2(2)(b)(ii) BSP Regs
48 Reg 19(2) SS(C&P) Regs
49 ss1(2) and 3(1)(b)(ii) and (2)(b) SSAA 1992; s8 SSA 1998; CG/7235/95, para 13
50 ss1(2) and 3(1)(b)(i), (2)(a) and (3) SSAA 1992; s8 SSA 1998; CG/7235/95, para 14
51 Reg 9(1) and Sch 1 Part 1 SS(C&P) Regs
52 Reg 13 SS(C&P) Regs

6. **Getting paid**
53 Reg 3 BSP Regs
54 s30(1A) PA 2014; s39A(3A) SSCBA 1992
55 s30(1C) PA 2014; s39A(3C) SSCBA 1992

4

56 s30(1D) PA 2014; s39A(3D) SSCBA 1992
57 Reg 17 SS(C&P) Regs

7. **Tax, other benefits and the benefit cap**

58 s677 IT(EP)A 2003
59 ss577-79 and 676 IT(EP)A 2003
60 **UC** Reg 66 UC Regs
**ESA** Sch 8 para 68 ESA Regs
**HB** Sch 5 para 67 HB Regs
61 Sch 8 para 17(i) ESA Regs
62 Sch IV para 7 SPC Regs
63 Reg 40 and Sch 5 para 16 HB Regs; reg 29 and Sch 5 para 7 HB(SPC) Regs
64 Regs 22 and 66 UC Regs
65 Reg 8C SS(Cr) Regs
66 s96 WRA 2012
67 Reg 79 UC Regs; regs 75A, 75C and 75G HB Regs

# Chapter 22

# Carer's allowance

**This chapter covers:**


1. Who can get carer's allowance (p472)
2. The rules about your age (p479)
3. People included in the claim (p479)
4. The amount of benefit (p479)
5. Special benefit rules (p480)
6. Claims and backdating (p480)
7. Getting paid (p482)
8. Tax, other benefits and the benefit cap (p483)


4

## Key facts

- Carer's allowance (CA) is paid to people who care for someone who is severely disabled.
- CA is a non-means-tested benefit.
- You do not have to have paid national insurance contributions to qualify.
- You can qualify for CA whether you are in or out of work, but you must not earn more than £196 a week.
- CA can be paid in addition to other benefits, but the overlapping benefit rules may apply. CA counts as income, but you may be entitled to an additional amount in your means-tested benefits if you get CA.
- CA is administered and paid by the DWP's Carer's Allowance Unit.
- If you disagree with a CA decision, you can apply for a revision or a supersession (see Chapter 50), or appeal against it (see Chapter 51). You must apply for a mandatory reconsideration before you can appeal.

***Carers' payments in Scotland***

A new benefit called carer support payment (CSP) has replaced CA for new claims in Scotland (see p1467). If you currently get CA and live in Scotland, you will automatically be moved to CSP without having to make a new claim. If you currently get CA and subsequently move to Scotland, you will need to make an application for CSP (see p1474). CSP is administered by Social Security Scotland. See Chapter 63 for details of carers' payments in Scotland.

Carer's allowance supplement is an additional amount paid to claimants in Scotland who receive CA or CSP on a particular date (see p1476).

If you live in Scotland and your leave to remain is subject to a 'no recourse to public funds' condition (see p1276) but you are in an exempt group who can claim CA or CSP (see p1282), get immigration advice before claiming.

# 1. Who can get carer's allowance

You qualify for carer's allowance (CA) if:[1]

- you are caring for a severely disabled person (see below). You do not have to be the person's relative, nor do you have to live with them; *and*
- the care you give is regular and substantial (see p473); *and*
- you are not gainfully employed, which means you earn £196 or less a week (see p473); *and*
- you are not in full-time education (see p804); *and*
- you are over compulsory school age (see p479);[2] *and*
- you are, in most cases, not a 'person subject to immigration control' (see p1272); *and*
- you satisfy the residence conditions (see p1347).

***Severely disabled person***

In this chapter, a **'severely disabled person'** is someone who is paid attendance allowance (AA), the highest or middle rate of the care component of disability living allowance (DLA) or child disability payment (CDP), either rate of the daily living component of personal independence payment (PIP) or adult disability payment (ADP), armed forces independence payment or constant attendance allowance of £90.20 a week or more paid with an industrial injuries benefit or war disablement pension (see p600).[3]

Note:

- Only one person can get CA and/or the carer's element in universal credit for caring for the same disabled person. If more than one person qualifies, notify the DWP in writing signed by all those who qualify which of you should be entitled to CA. If you cannot agree, the DWP decides[4] (see p1469 for competing claims in Scotland).
- Even if you care for two or more disabled people, you can only qualify for one award of CA for the same day.[5]
- The consent of the person for whom you care is not required for you to claim and be awarded CA.[6]
- If the person for whom you care has a severe disability premium/addition included in their benefits, their entitlement can be affected if you claim CA (see p483).

## Regularly and substantially caring

To qualify for CA, you must be 'regularly and substantially' caring for a severely disabled person. You satisfy this requirement during any week in which you are (or are likely to be) engaged in caring for them for 35 hours or more.[7] A week runs from Sunday to Saturday.[8] Caring can include supervision as well as assistance. If time is spent preparing for the disabled person to come to stay with you or clearing up after the visit, this can also count towards the 35 hours.[9]

Note:

- You cannot average the hours if you provide care for more than 35 hours in some weeks and fewer than 35 in others.[10] You must be caring for at least 35 hours in each week of your award.
- If you are caring for two or more disabled people, you can only qualify for CA if you are caring for at least one of them for 35 hours or more a week.[11] You cannot add together the hours you are caring for both/all of them to make up the 35.



### Breaks from caring

You can take a temporary break from caring and continue to qualify for CA. This applies if you have been providing care for at least 35 hours a week in 22 of the last 26 weeks, or for at least 14 of the last 26 weeks if either you or the disabled person were in hospital (or a similar institution). Weeks before you claimed CA can be counted. This means you can have a four-week break from caring in any period of six months, or a 12-week break if one of you was in hospital or in a similar institution (see p817 for what counts) for at least eight of those weeks.[12]

CA stops if the AA, DLA/CDP, PIP/ADP or constant attendance allowance of the person for whom you are caring stops because they are in hospital or in a similar institution (see p818).[13]

### If the person receiving care dies

If the person you care for dies, you continue to be entitled to CA for a further eight weeks, provided you satisfy the other qualifying conditions. The eight weeks run from the Sunday following the death, or from the day of the death if this was a Sunday.[14] You are not entitled if payment of the person's PIP/ADP, DLA/CDP or AA had stopped because they had been in hospital or a care home for more than 28 days when they died (see p818 and p826).

## Gainfully employed

You cannot qualify for CA if you are gainfully employed. You count as gainfully employed in a week (and cannot qualify for CA in that week) if your earnings from employment and/or self-employment in the previous week were more than £196.[15] If you are aged at least 21, this means you can earn just over 16 times the National Minimum Wage (see p1584). In the future, the DWP hopes to reduce overpayments by sending a text message to claimants when their earnings exceed the threshold.[16] Your earnings are ignored if you are working during a period when you are not actually caring for the severely disabled person – eg, because they are in hospital or you are on a four-week break from caring (see p473).[17]

## Earnings from employment

To work out how earnings from employment affect your entitlement to CA:

- check whether the payment counts as earnings (see below) and whether it can be disregarded (see p478);
- work out your weekly net earnings (see p475);
- work out the date from when your earnings count and the period they cover (see p476).

### What counts as earnings

For employees, '**earnings**' means 'any remuneration or profit derived from... employment'. The main type of income which counts as earnings is therefore your wages. The following are also included:[18]

- any bonus or commission (including tips);
- holiday pay (but not if it is payable more than four weeks after a job ends or is interrupted);
- compensation for unfair dismissal and certain other types of compensation under the Employment Rights Act 1996 or under trade union legislation;
- an equal pay settlement;[19]
- any payments made by an employer for expenses not 'wholly, exclusively and necessarily' incurred in carrying out the job, including any travel expenses to and from work, and any payments made to you for the cost of arranging care for members of your family;
- a retainer (eg, paid during the school holidays to people who work for the school meals service) or a guarantee payment;
- statutory and/or contractual sick, maternity, adoption, paternity, shared parental, parental bereavement pay and neonatal care pay in respect of children born on or after 6 April 2025 (see p725);
- certain payments at the end of a job (see p475).

This list is not exhaustive and other payments from employment may also count as earnings.[20]

It is the pay you actually receive that is taken into account, rather than what you are legally entitled to,[21] so if you receive less than the national minimum or living wage, it is this lesser amount that counts as earnings.

### What does not count as earnings

The following are examples of payments that *do not* count as earnings:

- periodic payments made as part of a redundancy scheme;[22]

- occupational pension payments;[23]
- payments made by your employer, or you if you are not reimbursed by your employer, towards expenses that are 'wholly, exclusively and necessarily' incurred in the performance of employment, such as travelling expenses during the course of work;[24]
- payments relating to expenses incurred for participating in a service user consultation.[25]

See p478 for information on earnings disregards.



### Payments when you stop work

If you stop work before you claim CA, your final earnings generally do not affect your benefit. Provided your entitlement begins after the employment ends, the following are disregarded:[26]

- final wages, paid or due, including bonuses, commission, tips and expenses that count as earnings;
- holiday pay;
- pay in lieu of notice;
- pay in lieu of remuneration – eg, a loss of earnings payment to a councillor;
- statutory or contractual redundancy pay and other compensation payments (other than from an employment tribunal complaint).

Certain payments after your employment ends *are* taken into account:[27]

- occupational or personal pension payments, unless you are over pension age and they are paid on retirement;
- statutory or contractual maternity, adoption, paternity, shared parental, parental bereavement or sick pay, and neonatal care pay in respect of children born on or after 6 April 2025 (see p725);
- an employment tribunal award or settlement of a complaint to a tribunal or court – eg, compensation for unfair dismissal;
- a retainer.

If you are already entitled to CA when a job ends, any final earnings at the end of that employment are not disregarded.

### Calculating net earnings from employment

'Earnings' are net earnings. '**Net earnings**' are gross earnings less any deductions made for income tax, class 1 national insurance (NI) contributions and half of any contribution made towards a personal or occupational pension scheme.[28] It is the amount of weekly earnings that is important; monthly earnings are multiplied by 12 and divided by 52 to arrive at a weekly figure.[29] If payment is for a period of less than a week, it is treated as a payment for a week.[30]

If your earnings fluctuate, your weekly earnings may be averaged as follows.[31]

- If you have a regular pattern of work, your weekly earnings are averaged over one complete 'cycle' of work. This includes periods when no work is done if this forms part of your regular pattern of work – eg, if you regularly work three weeks on and one week off, your earnings are averaged over four weeks.
- In any other case, your earnings are averaged over five weeks, or whatever other period enables the average weekly earnings to be assessed more accurately.

If the DWP refuses to calculate your earnings by way of an average, you can appeal (see Chapter 51).[32]

4

### The date from when earnings from employment are counted

Earnings are usually treated as having been received on the first day of the benefit week in which they are due to be paid.[33]

The date that a payment is due may differ from the date of actual payment. Earnings are due on your normal payday. If the contract of employment does not say when the payment is due and there is no evidence to suggest differently, the date the payment was received should be taken as the date it was due.[34] If a contract of employment is terminated without proper notice, outstanding wages, wages in hand, holiday pay and any pay in lieu of notice are due on the last day of employment and are treated as paid on that day, even if this does not happen. See p478 for when payments are disregarded. If an employment tribunal awards compensation for loss of earnings (eg, for being dismissed in circumstances constituting sex discrimination, or an equal pay settlement), there is disagreement about whether the relevant date is the date when the earnings were due to be paid, or when the compensation was awarded.

***Benefit week***

The '**benefit week**' is the seven days corresponding to the week for which CA is paid.[35]

### The period covered by earnings from employment

Earnings count for a future period starting from the above date. The length of that period is worked out as follows.[36]

- If a payment is made for a particular period, it is taken into account for the number of benefit weeks corresponding to that period. For example, a week's part-time earnings are taken into account for a week. For monthly payments, earnings are taken into account for the number of weeks between the date they are treated as paid and the date the next monthly earnings are treated as paid. If a payment is for a particular period but is a one-off payment (eg, holiday pay on leaving a job if the final payments count – see p475), it is taken into account for the number of weeks from the date it is due to the date the next normal monthly earnings would be treated as paid.[37]

- One-off payments that are not for a specific period are divided by the relevant earnings limit (£196) plus one penny and any disregard that applies to your earnings to work out the number of weeks for which you will not get benefit.
- If two payments of different types of earnings are made (eg, wages and holiday pay) and the periods worked out as above overlap, they are taken into account consecutively.[38]

## Earnings from self-employment

Weekly earnings from self-employment (including any allowance from a DWP scheme to assist with a business[39]) are averaged over a year unless:[40]

- you have recently become self-employed; *or*
- there has been a change that is likely to affect the normal pattern of the business.

In either case, earnings are averaged over whatever other period the decision maker considers will give the most accurate figure. This means that when you first claim CA, you should provide an up-to-date set of accounts.

For royalties or similar payments (eg, from copyrights), the period for which these payments count is calculated in a similar way to that for payments made to employees for unspecified periods.[41]

See below for how earnings of childminders, members of a partnership or share fishermen are calculated. Otherwise, the net profit from self-employment is used.

**'Net profit'** is calculated by taking the earnings from self-employment over the period and deducting:[42]

- expenses incurred during the period wholly and exclusively for the purposes of the business. For example, if a car or phone is used partly for business and partly for private purposes, the costs of it can be apportioned and the amount attributable to business use can be deducted.[43] Certain expenses cannot be deducted, including business entertainment, repayment of capital on a business loan, capital expenditure and depreciation, and providing board and lodging or renting a room in your home; *and*
- income tax and NI contributions;[44] *and*
- half of any contributions made during the period towards a personal pension scheme or retirement annuity contract.

Childminders are always treated as self-employed and your net profit is deemed to be one-third of your earnings from childminding less income tax, NI contributions and half of certain pension contributions.[45] The rest of your earnings are completely ignored.

For members of a partnership or share fishermen, the relevant share of the net profit is used, and expenses incurred wholly and exclusively for the business are deducted before calculating the share of the profits. After that, income tax, NI contributions and half of any premiums paid into a personal pension or under a retirement annuity contract are deducted from the share.[46]

## Notional earnings

You are treated as having 'notional earnings' if it is not possible to work out your actual earnings from employment or self-employment when your claim is decided.[47] This may apply if, for example, the job is new and pay depends on performance, or it is a new business and there is no way of calculating the profits of that business. If so, the notional earnings are an amount that is considered reasonable, taking into account the number of hours worked and the earnings paid for comparable work in the area.

Estimates of the appropriate deductions for income tax and NI contributions and half of any occupational or personal pension contributions are deducted from notional earnings, as are any earnings disregards and, if relevant, care charges and childcare costs you incur as a result of caring for the severely disabled person (see below).[48]

## Disregarded earnings

Some income, which might otherwise be classed as earnings, is specifically disregarded and does not affect your CA entitlement. The same earnings disregards apply whether the earnings are from employment or self-employment.

When calculating earnings, the cost of looking after the person you care for, up to a maximum amount, can be deducted from your earnings. If you are getting CA and, because of your work, you have to pay for someone (other than a close relative) to look after the severely disabled person for whom you care (or to look after a child under 16 for whom you or your partner are getting child benefit), these care costs can be deducted when your earnings are calculated (in addition to any disregarded earnings).[49] The maximum deduction is 50 per cent of the figure which would otherwise be your net earnings. Any disregarded income is deducted from your net earnings before calculating the 50 per cent figure.

***Close relative***

**'Close relative'** means a parent, son, daughter, brother, sister or partner (see p254) of you or the severely disabled person for whom you care.

In addition, the following amounts can be disregarded from your earnings:[50]

- any payment made to you by someone who normally lives with you on an informal or non-contractual basis as part of their contribution towards shared living expenses;
- the first £20 a week of any income for renting out room(s) in your home;

- the first £20 of any income you receive each week for providing board and lodging in your home and 50 per cent of any amount over £20. This disregard applies to each person who lodges with you;
- payments from a local authority or voluntary organisation for fostering or accommodating a child under formal arrangements;
- payments from a health authority, clinical commissioning group, local authority or voluntary organisation for providing temporary care. There is no set time after which care is no longer temporary;[51]
- income tax refunds;
- if you are an employee, any loan or advance of earnings from your employer;
- certain 'bounty' payments made to part-time firefighters, auxiliary coastguards, members of the reserve armed forces and part-time lifeboat crews;
- unless you are abroad yourself, earnings payable abroad which cannot be brought into Great Britain and any bank charges for converting earnings paid in another currency into sterling.



## 2. The rules about your age

You can claim carer's allowance (CA) if you are aged over compulsory school age.[52] In England and Wales, this is the last Friday in June if you will have turned 16 by the end of the summer holidays. In Scotland, it is either 31 May or the first day of the Christmas holidays depending when your birthday falls. There is no upper age limit. However, because of the overlapping benefit rules, if you receive a state pension you may not be paid CA, even if you qualify (see p1021). Even if you are not paid CA, you may qualify for a carer element in your universal credit (see p75), a carer premium in your means-tested benefits or a carer addition in pension credit (see p279). If you are aged 16 to 18 and live in Scotland, you may be able to get a young carer grant (see p1476).

## 3. People included in the claim

You claim carer's allowance (CA) for yourself. You cannot claim any increase in your CA for child or adult dependants.

## 4. The amount of benefit

Carer's allowance is paid at a weekly rate of £83.30.[53]

## 5. Special benefit rules

Special rules may apply if you:
- are subject to immigration control (see p1272);
- have come from or are going abroad (see Chapters 57, 58 and 59);
- or the person you are caring for, are in hospital or prison, or the person you are caring for is in a care home or similar accommodation (see Chapter 38).



## 6. Claims and backdating

The general rules on claims and backdating are covered in Chapter 44. This section explains the specific rules that apply to carer's allowance (CA).

If you are claiming a means-tested benefit, see p483 before claiming CA. It is not always advisable for you to claim CA because of its effect on your other benefits (and possibly those of the person for whom you care). You do not have to claim CA to get the carer element in universal credit (see p75).

### Making a claim

You can apply for CA online at gov.uk/carers-allowance/how-to-claim.

If you are unable to apply online, you can download Form DS700 (or DS700SP if you get a state pension) from gov.uk/government/publications/carers-allowance-claim-form, or request it by phoning the Carer's Allowance Unit (0800 731 0207; textphone 731 0317, Relay UK and BSL relay services are available). Post your completed form to the Carer's Allowance Unit, Mail Handling Site A, Wolverhampton WV98 2AB. You may also be able to make your claim by taking or sending it to an 'alternative office' (see p1004).

Keep a copy of your claim form in case queries arise.

You must provide any information or evidence required (see p481). In certain circumstances, the DWP may accept a written application not on the approved form.[54] You can amend or withdraw your claim before a decision is made (see p1004). If there is a delay in making a claim, you may be able to get a short-term advance of benefit (see p1023).

### Who should claim

You must normally claim CA on your own behalf. However, if you cannot manage your claim, another person can claim CA for you as your appointee (see p1005).

Before claiming, you should be aware of how CA affects your entitlement to means-tested benefits and the means-tested benefit entitlement of the person you care for (see p483).

## Information to support your claim

For the general information requirements that apply to all benefits, see p1006.

It is important that you provide any information required when you claim. Until you do, you may not count as having made a valid claim (see p1008). Correct any defects as soon as possible or your date of claim may be affected.

Even if your claim is valid, you may be asked to provide further information to support your claim (see p1009). You may also be asked to provide information after you are awarded CA and if you fail to do so, your CA could be suspended, or even terminated (see p1031).



## The date of your claim

The date of your claim is important as it determines when your entitlement to CA starts. This is not necessarily the date from when you are paid. For information about when payment of CA starts, see p482.

Your date of claim is usually the date on which your completed claim form is received by the DWP or a designated alternative office (see p1004).[55] If you submit your claim online, your date of claim is usually the date it is received, although a decision maker has the discretion to treat it as having been received on an earlier or later date than this.[56]

You must make sure your claim is valid. If it is 'defective', you are given a short time to correct the defects (see p1009). If you do, your claim is treated as having been made when you initially claimed.[57]

### Backdating your claim

It is important to claim in time. A claim for CA can usually only be backdated for a maximum of three months.[58] You must satisfy the qualifying conditions over that period. You do not have to show any reasons why your claim was late. The claim form asks you the date from which you want the claim to start: put the date you want your claim backdated to.

Your claim can be backdated for more than three months in the following situations.[59]

- If you claim CA within three months of a decision to award a 'qualifying benefit' to the person for whom you care (including a decision made by the First-tier Tribunal, the Upper Tribunal or a court), your CA is backdated to the first day of the benefit week in which the qualifying benefit is payable. However, if the decision awarding the qualifying benefit was made following a renewal claim when a fixed period award has ended or is due to end, your CA is only backdated to the first day of the benefit week in which the renewal award became payable.
- Your CA stopped because the qualifying benefit of the person for whom you care was reduced or stopped. This includes if a fixed-term award for the qualifying benefit came to an end or if payment of attendance allowance (AA),

disability living allowance (DLA), child disability payment (CDP), personal independence payment (PIP) or adult disability payment (ADP) stopped because the person for whom you care went into hospital, a care home or other similar accommodation. If you make a further claim within three months of the decision to reinstate the qualifying benefit, or of payment starting again, your CA is backdated to the date your earlier claim ended or the date from when the qualifying benefit was reawarded or became payable again, whichever is later.

4

***Qualifying benefit***

A **'qualifying benefit'** is AA, the middle or highest rate of the DLA/CDP care component, either rate of the daily living component of PIP/ADP, armed forces independence payment or constant attendance allowance.

If you might have qualified for benefit earlier but did not claim because you were given the wrong information or were misled by the DWP, you could ask for compensation (see p1261) or complain to the Ombudsman (see p1266).

### Claiming in advance

You can claim CA up to three months before you qualify.[60] This gives the DWP time to ensure you receive benefit as soon as you are entitled. The date of your claim is the date on which you qualify. The decision maker can award benefit from a future date if they believe you will satisfy all the CA qualifying conditions on that date. You should consider claiming in advance – eg, if you currently earn more than £196 a week, but you plan to stop work or reduce your hours.

## 7. Getting paid

The general rules on getting paid are covered in Chapter 45. This section explains the specific rules that apply to carer's allowance (CA).

***When is carer's allowance paid?***

You are paid on a Monday (or Wednesday if the person for whom you care receives constant attendance allowance with an industrial injuries benefit or war pension).[61] CA is paid weekly in advance or four-weekly in arrears (up to 13-weekly in arrears if you agree).[62]

Payments normally run from the first payday after the date of your claim, unless the date of your claim is on your payday, when they run from that day.

Note:
- CA awards are usually made for an indefinite period, but can be made for a fixed period – eg, if a change of circumstances is expected.[63]
- Deductions can be made from your CA to repay certain loans (see p1039) and, in some cases, to pay child support maintenance (see p1038).
- You might not be paid CA if you have been sanctioned for a benefit offence (see p1111).
- If payment of your CA is delayed, see p1123. If you are waiting for a decision on your claim, or to be paid, you might be able to get a short-term advance (see p1023). If you wish to complain about how your claim has been dealt with, or claim compensation, see Chapter 55.
- If payment of your CA is suspended, see p1031.
- If you are overpaid CA, you might have to repay it (see Chapter 47) and, in some circumstances, you might have to pay a penalty (see p1101). If you have been accused of fraud, see Chapter 48.
- If you are owed arrears of CA, these can be paid in instalments (see p1018).

### Change of circumstances

You must report changes in your circumstances that you have been told to report, as well as any that you might reasonably be expected to know might affect your right to, the amount of, or the payment of, your benefit. This includes for example, if the person you are caring for dies, and you are still caring for another severely disabled person. You should tell the DWP as soon as possible, preferably in writing. See p1030 for further information. You can also notify your change of circumstances at gov.uk/carers-allowance.[64]

**Note:** if the person that you are caring for dies, but you are still caring for another severely disabled person, notify Carer's Allowance of the death and that you are caring for another person.

When there has been a relevant change of circumstances, a decision maker looks at your claim again and makes a new decision. To find out the date from which the new decision takes effect, see p1150.

## 8. Tax, other benefits and the benefit cap

### Tax

Carer's allowance (CA) is taxable.[65]

### Means-tested benefits

Before you claim CA, consider how your claim may affect your universal credit (UC) entitlement and the benefits of the person you care for.

Your claim for CA may mean:

- you get a carer element included in your UC (see p75);
- if you get a UC transitional element and subsequently become entitled to a new carer element, your UC transitional element will be reduced by the amount of the carer element (see p83);
- if you receive UC, you are not required to undertake any work-related requirements. This also applies if you would qualify for CA but for the fact you are earning more than £196 a week (see p952).



Your claim for CA may affect the benefits of the person you care for:

- if your CA starts from an earlier date (see p481) including a period when the person you care for was receiving income support (IS), income-related employment and support allowance (ESA), income-based jobseeker's allowance (JSA), or housing benefit (HB) including a severe disability premium, their entitlement to the severe disability premium in that period may be affected (see p275);
- if, because of your CA claim, the person you care for is not entitled to a severe disability premium in their IS, JSA or ESA on the date they claim UC under natural migration, their entitlement to a UC transitional SDP element may be affected[66] (see p27). If, however, they claimed UC under 'managed migration' on a date before you claim CA, the amount of their UC transitional element may not be affected[67] (see p84);
- if the person you care for receives pension credit (PC) including a severe disability addition, their entitlement to that addition will be affected (see p275).

Bear in mind that the severe disability premium/addition/UC transitional SDP element (see p280) is likely to be worth more than CA and/or the UC carer element (see p40).

## Income

CA counts in full as income for all means-tested benefits.

CA counts as 'qualifying income' for the savings credit of PC (see p245).

**Note:** for means-tested benefits other than UC, if you choose not to claim CA or give up your CA award, you can be treated as if you receive CA if the DWP decides that you deliberately failed to apply for it or deprived yourself of it to qualify for, or increase your entitlement to, benefit for yourself or your family (see p365 and p391).

## The amount of means-tested benefits

If you are getting UC and:

- you are a member of a couple, you can get a childcare costs element in your UC if one of you is in paid work and the other is not in paid work, is unable to provide childcare and qualifies for CA;

- you (or your partner) qualify for CA, or would do but for the fact that your (or their) earnings are higher than £196 a week, a carer element is included in your UC maximum amount. However, if you:
  - are a single claimant with 'limited capability for work-related activity', your UC includes a limited capability for work-related activity element instead of a carer element;
  - are a member of a couple, the limited capability for work-related activity element (or limited capability for work element if you are still entitled to it) and the carer element can only both be included in your UC if they are awarded to different people who meet the conditions.

  You may need to work out how you would be better off financially.



If you received CA (or were entitled to it but did not receive it because of the overlapping benefit rules – see p1021), so a carer premium/additional amount was included in your IS, income-based JSA, income-related ESA, PC and HB when you claimed UC, this may affect your transitional UC element (see p78).

## Non-means-tested benefits

For each week you receive CA, you can get national insurance credits (see p871).

CA is subject to the overlapping benefit rules, which means that you may not be paid CA in full if another earnings-replacement benefit (eg, state pension) is paid to you (see p1021).

## The benefit cap

CA is *not* one of the specified benefits for the benefit cap.[68] If you receive CA (or you would receive it but for the overlapping benefit rules), you are exempt from the cap. See p1025 for further information.

## Passports and other sources of help

If you get CA (or would get it but for the overlapping benefit rules), you are entitled to a Christmas bonus (see p783). You may be able to get help, support and services from your local authority – ask for a carer's assessment. If you have a low income, you may be entitled to council tax reduction (see p761).

# Notes

1. **Who can get carer's allowance**
   1 s70 SSCBA 1992; reg 9(1) SS(ICA) Regs
   2 *SSWP v BC (CA)* [2023] UKUT 10 (AAC)
   3 s70(2) SSCBA 1992; reg 3 SS(ICA) Regs; para 2(a) Part V Sch 4 SSCBA 1992
   4 s70(7), (7A) and (7ZA) SSCBA 1992; reg 7(1) SS(ICA) Regs; DMG 60026
   5 s70(7) SSCBA 1992
   6 *SSWP v GK* [2023] UKUT 273 (AAC)
   7 Reg 4(1) SS(ICA) Regs
   8 s122 SSCBA 1992
   9 CG/6/1990
   10 R(G) 3/91
   11 Reg 4(1A) SS(ICA) Regs
   12 Reg 4(2) SS(ICA) Regs
   13 *SSWP v Pridding* [2002] EWCA Civ 306
   14 s70(1A) SSCBA 1992
   15 Reg 8(1) SS(ICA) Regs
   16 *Hansard*, Volume 754, col 16, 7 October 2024
   17 Reg 8(2) SS(ICA) Regs
   18 Reg 9 SSB(CE) Regs
   19 *Minter v Kingston Upon Hull CC and Potter v SSWP* [2011] EWCA Civ 1155
   20 R(IS) 9/95; CIS/743/1992
   21 R(IB) 7/03
   22 Reg 9(1)(b) SSB(CE) Regs
   23 Reg 2(1) SSB(CE) Regs
   24 Reg 9(3)(a) SSB(CE) Regs; *Parsons v Hogg* [1985] 2 All ER 897 (CA), appendix to R(FIS) 4/85 as cited by R(IS) 16/93
   25 Reg 9(3)(b) SSB(CE) Regs
   26 Sch 1 para 12 SSB(CE) Regs
   27 Sch 1 para 12(2) SSB(CE) Regs
   28 Reg 10(4) SSB(CE) Regs; DMG para 15380
   29 Regs 6(1) and 8(1)(b)(i) SSB(CE) Regs
   30 Reg 8(1)(a) SSB(CE) Regs
   31 Reg 8(3) SSB(CE) Regs
   32 *KR v SSWP (CA)* [2023] UKUT 202 (AAC), para 19
   33 Reg 7(b) SSB(CE) Regs
   34 R(SB) 33/83
   35 Reg 2(1) SSB(CE) Regs
   36 Reg 6(2) SSB(CE) Regs
   37 *Cotton v SSWP* [2009] EWCA Civ 1333, reported as [2010] AACR 17
   38 Reg 6(3) SSB(CE) Regs; *Cotton v SSWP* [2009] EWCA Civ 1333, reported as [2010] AACR 17
   39 Reg 12(1) SSB(CE) Regs
   40 Reg 11(1) SSB(CE) Regs
   41 Reg 11(2) SSB(CE) Regs
   42 Reg 13(1)(a) and (b), (4) and (5) SSB(CE) Regs
   43 R(IS) 13/91; R(FC) 1/91
   44 See also reg 14 SSB(CE) Regs
   45 Regs 13(10) and 14 SSB(CE) Regs
   46 Reg 13(1)(b) and (5) SSB(CE) Regs
   47 Reg 4(1) and (3) SSB(CE) Regs
   48 Regs 3(2) and 10(3) and Sch 1 and 3 SSB(CE) Regs
   49 Regs 10(3) and 13(3) and Sch 3 SSB(CE) Regs
   50 Sch 1 SSB(CE) Regs
   51 CG/1752/2006

2. **The rules about your age**
   52 s70(3) SSCBA 1992 read with *SSWP v BC (CA)* [2023] UKUT 10 (AAC). For details of compulsory school age, see gov.uk/know-when-you-can-leave-school

4. **The amount of benefit**
   53 Sch 4 SSCBA 1992

6. **Claims and backdating**
   54 Reg 4(1) SS(C&P) Regs
   55 Reg 6(1)(a) and (1ZA) SS(C&P) Regs
   56 Reg 4ZC and Sch 9ZC para 4(1) and (2) SS(C&P) Regs
   57 Reg 6(1)(b) SS(C&P) Regs
   58 Reg 19 SS(C&P) Regs
   59 Reg 6(16)-(22), (33) and (34) SS(C&P) Regs
   60 Reg 13 SS(C&P) Regs

7. **Getting paid**
   61 Reg 22(3) and Sch 6 SS(C&P) Regs
   62 Reg 22(1) SS(C&P) Regs
   63 Reg 17 SS(C&P) Regs
   64 Reg 32ZA SS(C&P) Regs

8. **Tax, other benefits and the benefit cap**
   65 ss660, 661 and 676 IT(EP)A 2003
   66 Para 3(b) Sch 2 UC(TP) Regs
   67 Reg 62 UC(TP) Regs
   68 Reg 83(1)(i) and (j) UC Regs

# Chapter 23

# Child benefit and guardian's allowance

4

**This chapter covers:**


1. Who can get child benefit (p488)
2. Who can get guardian's allowance (p496)
3. The rules about your age (p498)
4. People included in the claim (p498)
5. The amount of benefit (p499)
6. Special benefit rules (p499)
7. Claims and backdating (p501)
8. Getting paid (p504)
9. Tax, other benefits and the benefit cap (p507)


## Key facts

- You may be entitled to child benefit if you are responsible for a child or qualifying young person. You need not be the child's parent.
- You may be entitled to guardian's allowance if you are responsible for a child or qualifying young person and one or both of the child's parents have died. Usually, you must *not* be the child's parent.
- Child benefit and guardian's allowance are non-means-tested benefits.
- You do not need to have paid national insurance contributions to qualify.
- You can qualify whether you are in or out of work.
- If your or your partner's income is over £60,000 a year, one of you may be liable to pay more tax if you get child benefit. Guardian's allowance is not taxable.
- Child benefit and guardian's allowance are administered and paid by HMRC.
- If you disagree with a decision, you can apply for a revision or a supersession (see Chapter 50), or appeal against it (see Chapter 51). You must apply for a mandatory reconsideration before you can appeal.

# 1. Who can get child benefit

**Note:** in this chapter, the term 'child' is generally used to refer to both a child and a 'qualifying young person'.

You qualify for child benefit for a child if:[1]

- they are a child or qualifying young person (see below); *and*
- you are responsible for the child (see p492); *and*
- you have priority over other claimants (see p493); *and*
- you are not a 'person subject to immigration control' (see p1272); *and*
- you and the child satisfy the residence conditions (see p1346).

4

In some circumstances, even if you meet these conditions, you cannot get child benefit (see p495). If a child you get child benefit for dies, see p506.

**Note:** guardian's allowance is a separate benefit, but you must usually get child benefit to qualify. For who can get guardian's allowance, see p496.

## Who counts as a child

Anyone aged under 16 counts as a **child.**[2] You can also get child benefit for a child aged 16 or over if they count as a qualifying young person.

## Who is a qualifying young person

A '**qualifying young person**' is someone aged 16, 17, 18 or 19 who is:[3]

- not in 'relevant education' or training, but only until 31 August (or, if born on 31 August, 1 September)[4] after their 16th birthday; *or*
- 16 or 17, not in *any* education or training, and in an 'extension period' (see p490); *or*
- undertaking, or enrolled or accepted on, a qualifying type of education (see p489) or 'approved training' (see p490); *or*
- not in relevant education or approved training and it is before the 'terminal date' (see p491).

See p495 for when you cannot get child benefit for a qualifying young person.

***Relevant education***

**'Relevant education'** is defined as education that is full time and not advanced, so any 'full-time, non-advanced education' (see p489) counts as relevant education.

A child counts as a qualifying young person until none of the above situations apply.[5] If child benefit for a child stops because they are not a qualifying young person, but they later meet the conditions again, you can make a new claim. See p491 if there is a temporary interruption in meeting the conditions.

## Education

A child under 20 counts as a qualifying young person if they:[6]

- are in full-time, non-advanced education (see below), which they started, or were enrolled or accepted on, before turning 19; *or*
- receive 'appropriate full-time education' in England (see p490), which they started, or were enrolled or accepted on, before turning 19; *or*
- were previously in one of these types of education, and are enrolled or accepted on another such course.



The education must not be provided as a result of the child's employment or because of an office they hold. See p491 if your child's education is interrupted.

**Note:**

- If a child leaves education before age 20, they may still count as a qualifying young person (see p488).
- HMRC sometimes treats a child who starts a course of full-time, non-advanced education while aged 19 as having begun the course before turning 19 if they have been in full-time, non-advanced education *continuously* since before turning 19. This means they count as a qualifying young person during the course, even if they were not enrolled or accepted on it before turning 19.

***Examples of non-advanced and advanced courses of education***[7]

| *Non-advanced courses* | *Advanced courses* |
|---|---|
| GCSEs, AS, A and T levels | A university degree |
| NVQ and SVQ level 3 and below | NVQ or SVQ level 4 or above |
| Scottish National Qualifications (up to Higher or Advanced Higher level) | HND or HNC |
| International Baccalaureate | Diploma of Higher Education |
| BTEC and OCR Nationals | A teaching qualification |

### Full-time, non-advanced education

To count as 'full-time, non-advanced education', a child's course must normally be provided at a school or college.[8] If a child is educated elsewhere (eg, at home), this also counts if either they were being educated in this way before the age of 16 or they have a statement of special educational needs that assesses home education as suitable for their needs.[9] HMRC must approve these kinds of education.[10]

To count as full time, the course must be for an average of over 12 hours a week during term time, including tuition, supervised study,[11] exams and practical work, but not meal breaks and unsupervised study.[12]

### Appropriate full-time education

To count as 'appropriate full-time education', the education must be suitable for the child, taking into account their age, ability and aptitude and any special educational needs. It cannot be an advanced course.[13]

It does not matter where the education takes place, provided it is in England. If the education is provided at home, it is treated as full time. Education which is not provided at a school is treated as full time if it is a tailored activity designed to enable the child to stay in education or training, or if it lasts at least 540 hours a year and was developed by a college, higher education institution or training provider to meet the child's needs.[14]

4

## Approved training

**Note:** in England, there is no approved training.[15] Check whether a child's training counts as 'appropriate full-time education' instead (see above).

A child under 20 counts as a qualifying young person if they:[16]

- are doing approved training, which they started, or were enrolled or accepted on, before turning 19; *or*
- were in full-time, non-advanced education or approved training, and are now enrolled or accepted on approved training.

*Approved training*

**'Approved training'** includes:[17]

– in Scotland, No One Left Behind;

– in Wales, Traineeships, Foundation Apprenticeships or Jobs Growth Wales+.

The training must not be paid or provided under a contract of employment (but see p491).

See p491 if a child's training is interrupted. If a child leaves approved training before turning 20, they may still count as a qualifying young person (see p488).

## The extension period

If a child is 16 or 17, they continue to count as a qualifying young person during an **extension period** if:[18]

- they are not in any kind of education or training; *and*
- they are registered as available for work, education or training with a careers service or a specified body; *and*
- they are not in remunerative work (see p496); *and*
- you were entitled to child benefit for them immediately before the extension period started; *and*
- you apply online at gov.uk/government/publications/child-benefit-apply-for-extension-ch299 within three months of the date your child's education or training finished. Sign in using your Government Gateway account.[19]

The extension period begins on the Monday after the child's education or training ends and lasts for 20 weeks. If a child turns 18 during the extension period, child benefit ends unless they count as a qualifying young person on another ground (see p488).

If a child's extension period is interrupted, see below.

## The terminal date rule

If a child leaves qualifying education (see p489) or approved training (see p490) before reaching 20, they count as a qualifying young person until:[20]

- the terminal date if this is a Sunday, or the Sunday after the terminal date (see below); *or*
- if earlier, the Sunday of the week in which they turn 20, or the day before their 20th birthday if they turn 20 on a Monday.

A child does not count as a qualifying young person under this rule if they are in remunerative work (see p496).

***Terminal date***

The **'terminal date'** is the first of the following dates that falls after the date a child left education or training:

- the last day in February; *or*
- 31 May; *or*
- 31 August; *or*
- 30 November.

**Note:**

- If a child has left education but returns to sit an exam for a previous course, they are treated as still being in education until the date of the last exam for which they were entered before leaving education.[21]
- A child who has completed Highers or Advanced Highers in Scotland is treated as being in education until a comparable course in England or Wales ends, if this is later.[22]
- A child cannot count as a qualifying young person while in education or training provided as a part of a job. If they are under 20, it is arguable that they count as a qualifying young person from the date they leave such a course until the terminal date, as this rule does not exclude people whose course is provided as part of a job.

## Interruptions

If there is a break in a child's satisfying the conditions to be a qualifying young person, this is ignored:[23]

- for up to six months (whether the interruption began before or after the child turned 16) if it is 'reasonable' in the circumstances; *or*
- indefinitely if it is caused by the child's physical or mental illness or disability, and the length of the interruption is 'reasonable' in the circumstances.

This means a child still counts as a qualifying young person during the interruption. HMRC states that this only applies if there is an interruption during a course of education or training, but it arguably also applies to 16/17-year-olds during the extension period.

4

However, an interruption cannot be ignored if, immediately afterwards, the child starts or is likely to start:[24]

- a training course which is not approved training; *or*
- a course of advanced education; *or*
- education connected to their employment.

## Responsible for a child

You are only entitled to child benefit for a child you are responsible for. You count as responsible for a child in any week in which:[25]

- the child is living with you (see below); *or*
- you contribute to the cost of supporting the child (see p493).

### A child living with you

To count as living with a child, you must share both a home and 'a settled course of daily living'.[26] This is not the same as 'residing together' or 'presence under the same roof'.[27] A child may be living with you even while they are away. There are special rules if a child is looked after by a local authority (see p499).

#### Living apart

If a child used to live with you, but is now absent, they are treated as still living with you if you have not lived apart for more than 56 days in the last 16 weeks.[28] Days a child is absent are ignored if the child is away *only* to:[29]

- receive education or training (HMRC states that this must be full-time education or approved training); *or*
- stay in certain types of residential accommodation because of their disability, or because their health would be 'significantly impaired or further impaired' if they did not stay there (but see below); *or*
- receive inpatient treatment in a hospital or similar institution (but see below).

In the latter two situations above, a maximum of 12 consecutive weeks' absence can be ignored, unless you regularly incur expenditure for the child, in which case the absence can be ignored indefinitely.[30] If you make visits, or give the child pocket money, this rule should be satisfied. Periods in hospital or residential accommodation separated by 28 days or less are treated as one when calculating the 12 weeks.

Even if a child is not living with you, you may still qualify for child benefit for them if you contribute to the cost of supporting them.

See p1376 if your child is abroad.

*Example*

Lily's son was in hospital for 18 weeks. She regularly took him food and comics. On being discharged, he stayed with his aunt for a month, then returned home. Lily is entitled to child benefit while her son is away from home. He is treated as still living with her while in hospital as she regularly incurred expenditure for him. He also counts as still living with her while staying with his aunt, as he was not absent from home for more than 56 days in the previous 16 weeks – the period in hospital is ignored when calculating the 56 days.

### Contributing to the cost of supporting a child

If a child does not live with you, you can still qualify for child benefit if you contribute to the cost of supporting the child. You must contribute at least the amount of child benefit that would be paid for the child (see p499).[31]

**Note:**

- Contributions need not be regular, but must total the amount of child benefit you would qualify for during the period being considered.[32]
- Payments in kind rather than cash may be counted.[33]
- If you live with your spouse or civil partner, any contribution made by one of you can be treated as a contribution by the other.[34]
- If you and another person(s) each contribute less than the amount of child benefit for the child, but your total contributions are at least the amount of child benefit payable, one of you is treated as contributing the whole sum. If you disagree with who this should be, HMRC decides. If you are awarded child benefit on this basis, you alone must then contribute at least the amount of child benefit paid for the child to remain entitled.[35]

## Priority between claimants

More than one person can potentially qualify for child benefit for the same child – eg, if they live with one parent and are maintained by the other or there is a shared care arrangement. Only one person can be awarded child benefit for a child, so there is an order of priority for who gets child benefit if two or more people make a claim.[36]

If two or more people have claimed child benefit for the same child and would qualify for it, the following order of priority applies.[37]

- If you live with the child, you have priority over someone contributing to the cost of supporting them.

- If you are a woman, you have priority over your *male* spouse or civil partner if you reside together (see p495).
- If you are the child's parent (including a step-parent, adoptive parent and someone with legal parental responsibility),[38] you have priority over a non-parent.
- If you are the child's mother or stepmother and are *not* married or in a civil partnership with a man, you have priority over the other parent if you reside together (see p495).
- In any other case, the person agreed between you and the other claimant has priority. If there is no agreement, HMRC chooses who has priority. You cannot appeal against HMRC's choice (but see p1173).[39]



If your claim takes priority over an existing claim, child benefit continues to be paid on the existing claim for the three weeks following the week in which you claim, unless the other claimant withdraws their claim or their child benefit entitlement ends.[40] Even if your claim has priority, you cannot usually receive child benefit for a period before you made your claim if it has already been paid to someone else for the same child (but see p505).

If you have claimed child benefit and want someone who has equal or lower priority to you to receive it, contact the Child Benefit Office (see p501).[41]

Consider conceding priority to your partner if you spend time abroad, as child benefit usually ends if you have been abroad for more than eight (or sometimes 12) weeks (see p1376).

## Separation and the priority rules

Problems can arise if there are competing child benefit claims from recently separated parents. Even if a child only lives with one parent, they may also be treated as still living with the other parent for a period (usually 56 days) under the rules described on p492. If you are in this situation and a child lives with you but is still treated as living with their other parent, both of you are potentially entitled to child benefit for the child. If neither of you withdraws your claim, the priority rules apply (see p493). In practice, this means that if you are the child's mother, your claim usually takes priority for 56 days after you separate permanently, whoever the child lives with. However, if you are the child's father and got child benefit before you separated, your claim has priority for three weeks after the week the mother claims.[42]

**Note:** if your ex-partner was getting child benefit when you made your competing claim, see p505.

***Do you share your child's care with their other parent?***

Separated parents may both potentially be entitled to child benefit. If you disagree with who should receive it, HMRC decides who should be paid. This usually involves looking at who has the greater responsibility of care. Consider the following questions when deciding how best to present your case to HMRC.

1. How many hours each week do you each care for the child?
2. What are the terms of any court orders? Do they reflect the actual care arrangements, and does the other parent pay you child support maintenance?
3. Where are the child's possessions kept?
4. At which address is the child registered with services, such as school and their doctor?
5. What contributions do each of you make to the cost of bringing up the child? (This may not be conclusive if the resources of one parent are greater than the other.)
6. What impact might the decision have on each parent?[43]
7. Are there other children of the same relationship? In one case involving two parents with almost equal responsibility for their two children, the High Court held that it was reasonable for HMRC to decide that each parent should get child benefit for one child.[44]

These are just examples of the issues to consider – each case depends on its circumstances.

If HMRC refuses your child benefit claim because child benefit is already in payment to your ex-partner for the same child without considering the factors above[45] or HMRC delays in deciding such a claim, you may be able to challenge this by judicial review (see Chapter 53).

### Residing together

It may be important to decide whether you and another person are treated as 'residing together'[46] if you both claim child benefit for the same child (see p493). If you are married, in a civil partnership or a child's parent, you and your spouse/civil partner/the other parent are treated as residing together if your absence from each other:[47]

- is not likely to be permanent (even if you have never lived together);[48] *or*
- is solely because one of you is in hospital, or in a similar institution for people with mental health problems, whether this is temporary or permanent.

It is also possible to be absent from one another while living under the same roof – eg, if you are maintaining separate households.[49]

## When you cannot get child benefit

Even if you meet all the entitlement conditions, you cannot get child benefit if:[50]

- you are the child's spouse, civil partner or partner; *or*
- the child is married, in a civil partnership or living with their partner as if they were married or civil partners[51] unless:
  - the child's spouse, civil partner or partner is in full-time, non-advanced education or approved training; *or*
  - the child and their spouse or civil partner are not residing together (see above – the definition is the same); *or*

- in some circumstances, the child is in remunerative work (see below); *or*
- the child is aged 16 or over and receiving universal credit; *or*
- the child has spent more than eight consecutive weeks (but see p499):
  - in prison or other custody; *or*
  - being looked after by a local authority.

### 16–19-year-olds who work

If a child is aged 16 or over and counts as a qualifying young person under the terminal date rule (see p491) or is in an extension period (see p490), you cannot get child benefit for them if they are in remunerative work – ie, they work for 24 hours or more a week in expectation of payment.[52]

4

If a child is under 16 or a qualifying young person on any other ground (see p488), any work they do should not affect your child benefit.

## 2. Who can get guardian's allowance

You qualify for guardian's allowance for a child or qualifying young person (see p488 for who counts – the rules are the same as for child benefit) if:[53]

- you are entitled to, or treated as entitled to, child benefit for them (see below); *and*
- they are an 'eligible child' (see p497) and either:
  - live with you, or are treated as living with you (see p492); *or*
  - you contribute to the cost of providing for them (see p498); *and*
- the residence conditions are satisfied (see p1346); *and*
- you are not the child's parent (but see p498).

If a child for whom you get guardian's allowance dies, see p506.

### Entitled to child benefit

To get guardian's allowance for a child, you must normally be entitled to child benefit for them (see p488). You are treated as entitled to child benefit if:[54]

- you elect not to be paid your entitlement to avoid the high-income child benefit charge (see p507); *or*
- you live with your spouse and they are entitled to child benefit for the child; *or*
- you live in Great Britain and you would be entitled to child benefit for the child were you (or your spouse or civil partner, if you live with them) not getting a family benefit from another country.

You are treated as entitled to child benefit the week before your entitlement begins, so guardian's allowance can start on the same day as child benefit.[55]

## Eligible child

A child is an **'eligible child'** if the child's parents (or adoptive parents):[56]

- have both died (or the child was adopted by one person who has now died); *or*
- were not married or in a civil partnership, the mother has died and the father is unknown (but see p498 if the child has been adopted); *or*
- are divorced or their civil partnership has been dissolved, one parent has died and when they died, the other parent did not have custody of, and was not maintaining, the child, and neither arrangement was required by a court order or child support calculation.



A child is also an eligible child if one of the child's parents (or adoptive parents) has died, and:[57]

- when they died the other parent was missing and cannot be found; *or*
- the other parent is in prison or detained in hospital by a court order (but see below).

### Missing parents

If one of a child's parents has died, you may qualify for guardian's allowance if, at the date of the death, you did not know the other parent's whereabouts. Since then, you must have been unable to discover their whereabouts, despite making all reasonable efforts to do so – eg, by asking known relatives and friends and checking old addresses.[58] You may not have to make such efforts if there is a risk that you or the child might experience harm or undue distress if you try to trace the missing parent – eg, if they are a threat to your, or the child's, physical safety or emotional wellbeing.[59]

If you have had contact with the other parent since the death (but before the decision on the claim), you cannot get guardian's allowance, as their whereabouts are known.[60] This may apply even if the contact was only brief (eg, at the funeral), and if the surviving parent later disappears.

If there has been no contact, but you can communicate with the surviving parent somehow, this is probably sufficient to show that their whereabouts are known.[61] 'Whereabouts' is not the same as an address, so showing that you do not know their address may not be enough to qualify for guardian's allowance if you have some details of where they live, work or can often be found. However, if you only know that the surviving parent is in a large urban area, you can argue that their whereabouts are unknown.

### Prison sentences

If one of a child's parents has died and the other is in prison, you are only entitled to guardian's allowance if the surviving parent is:[62]

- serving a sentence of imprisonment or detention of at least two years (whether that sentence started before or after the date of death); *or*
- detained in hospital by order of a court under specified legislation.

There are detailed rules about what counts as imprisonment or detention and for calculating whether the length of a sentence amounts to two years, so get advice if you are affected.[63] Guardian's allowance is reduced if the parent in prison contributes to the cost of providing for the child.[64]

### Contributing to the cost of providing for a child

To qualify for guardian's allowance for a child who does not live with you, you must contribute at least the amount of child benefit a week to the cost of providing for them. This must be in addition to any contribution you make to qualify for child benefit for the child (see p493).[65]

4

When calculating whether you contribute at least the amount of child benefit, include contributions made by your spouse or civil partner if you live together. If you do not currently make contributions, you are treated as doing so if you state in writing that you will once you are awarded guardian's allowance. Any decision to award you guardian's allowance on this basis is revised if you do not make the contributions.[66]

### Parents, adoptive parents and step-parents

You cannot qualify for guardian's allowance for a child if you are the child's parent, unless one of the following exceptions applies.[67]

- If a child is adopted, their adoptive parents count as parents, so if you are the child's biological parent you can claim guardian's allowance (if the qualifying conditions are met).[68]
- If you have adopted a child, you can continue to get guardian's allowance if you were entitled to it immediately before the adoption.
- HMRC says that if you are a child's step-parent, you do not count as a parent for guardian's allowance and can get guardian's allowance for your stepchild.[69]

## 3. The rules about your age

If you claim child benefit or guardian's allowance, there is no upper or lower age limit to be entitled.

## 4. People included in the claim

You claim child benefit for each child for whom you are responsible. You claim guardian's allowance for each eligible child (see p497).

## 5. The amount of benefit

Child benefit and guardian's allowance are paid at the following weekly rates.[70]

| | £pw |
|---|---|
| Child benefit: eldest eligible child | 26.05 |
| Child benefit: other children (each) | 17.25 |
| Guardian's allowance | 22.10 |



The higher rate of child benefit is paid for the eldest (or only) child in a family.[71] If you live with your partner and both of you receive child benefit for a child from a previous relationship, the higher rate is only paid to the person who has the eldest child.[72]

## 6. Special benefit rules

Special rules may apply if:

- a child is being looked after by a local authority, or is in prison or detention;
- you or the child have come from, or are going, abroad (see Chapters 56, 57, 58 and 59);
- you are in prison or detention (see Chapter 38).

### Your child is being looked after by a local authority, or is in prison or detention

**Note:** the rules in this section prevent you from getting guardian's allowance for an 'eligible child' (see p497) if your child benefit for that child stops.

Special rules apply if a child is:[73]

- looked after by a local authority, is provided with or placed in accommodation under certain legislation and some of the cost of the child's accommodation or maintenance is met by local authority or public funds (but see p500); *or*
- subject to a compulsory supervision order and lives in residential accommodation under certain legislation; *or*
- in prison or other detention (such as a detention centre or young offenders' institution) as a result of criminal proceedings or non-payment of a penalty imposed on conviction.

If any of these circumstances apply to a child and have done so for at least one day a week in the last eight consecutive weeks, your child benefit entitlement for them ends, unless the child 'ordinarily' lives with you throughout at least one whole day each week (even if they are not actually at home in that particular week).[74] A **'day'** runs from midnight to midnight, so, in practice, they must ordinarily stay with you for two nights during a week for you to qualify.[75] A **'week'** means seven days beginning with a Monday.[76]

After the first eight weeks' absence, even if the child does not ordinarily live with you for at least one day a week, you can still get child benefit when the child stays with you for a week or more.[77]

**Note:**

- Even if a child ordinarily lives with you or comes to stay with you for over a week, if the local authority is making certain payments you may still not qualify for child benefit (see below).
- If a child stops being looked after by a local authority, stops being subject to a supervision order or stops being in prison for at least a week (ie, from Monday to Sunday), but is later in one of those situations again, the eight-week period restarts.
- You can still get child benefit for a child who is looked after by a local authority if the child is placed in residential accommodation because they have a disability or because the child's health would be impaired were they not in the accommodation (see p492).[78]
- If a child is detained in a hospital or similar institution because of mental health problems, the child is only treated as being in prison if they were moved there from prison or detention and the expected release date under the child's sentence has not passed. Otherwise, you can continue to get child benefit, provided you meet the normal qualifying conditions.[79]
- If a child was in custody but is not sentenced to imprisonment or detention, you should be paid child benefit for them for the period of their detention.[80]

## Fostering, adoption and kinship care

If you are a foster carer, a kinship carer or are adopting a child, payments you get from the local authority may affect your child benefit. In many situations, child benefit entitlement is not affected, but it is in the following circumstances.

- *You* cannot get child benefit for a child if a local authority has arranged for them to be placed with you under a placement, or a looking-after or fostering arrangement, and the local authority pays for the child's accommodation or maintenance under section 22C(10) of the Children Act 1989, regulation 33 of the Looked After Children (Scotland) Regulations 2009 or section 81(13) of the Social Services and Well-being (Wales) Act 2014.[81]
- *No one* can get child benefit for a child if the child has been placed with prospective adopters and a local authority pays for the child's accommodation or maintenance under the above provisions.[82]

If the situations above do not apply, the normal rules on entitlement apply, including the rules on children being looked after by a local authority described on p499 (and the exceptions to these rules described on p500).

Your entitlement to child benefit is not affected if you look after a child under private fostering arrangements.

## 7. Claims and backdating



The general rules about claims and backdating are covered in Chapter 44. This section explains the specific rules for child benefit and guardian's allowance.

### Making a claim

You should make a claim for child benefit online (you need to be registered with the Government Gateway to submit the claim form this way[83]). If you cannot claim online, you can download the claim form or contact HMRC by phone (you may need to try more than once to be put through to an adviser) and then post your application to HMRC.[84] HMRC says that if you sign in with your Government Gateway account to claim online[85] you may be paid quicker. If you already receive child benefit, you can amend your details, including to notify HMRC of an additional child, online, via the HMRC app,[86] by post or phone.

**Note:** if you cannot get an appointment to register the birth before the child is three months old, you can apply for child benefit, but you will not receive the payments until you inform HMRC that the birth has been registered.

You must usually get child benefit to be able to get guardian's allowance, but you must make a separate claim. You should make a claim for guardian's allowance in writing to the Guardian's Allowance Unit at the Child Benefit Office.

***Forms***

For child benefit, claim online at gov.uk/child-benefit/how-to-claim or follow the link in the HMRC app. If you cannot do so, download Form CH2 (and CH2 (CS) for additional children) from gov.uk/government/publications/claim-child-benefit-if-you-cannot-claim-online or, if you cannot do so, get the forms by calling the Child Benefit Office.

For guardian's allowance, use Form BG1, which you can get by calling the Guardian's Allowance Unit (part of the Child Benefit Office) or downloading it from gov.uk/guardians-allowance/how-to-claim. **Note:** if you download either form, although you can still fill it in in your browser, you must then print, sign and send the form by post rather than submit it online.[87]

The postal address for enquiries is: HMRC – Child Benefit Office, PO Box 1, Newcastle upon Tyne NE88 1AA. If your letter is about guardian's allowance, you should write 'Guardian's Allowance Unit' at the start of the address. The address is different if you are sending a claim by post, and is written on the claim form. You can also contact HMRC by phone:

- child benefit helpline: 0300 200 3100; Welsh language: 0300 200 1900; Relay UK service available;
- guardian's allowance helpline: 0300 322 9080.

Keep a copy of your claim form in case queries arise.

You must provide any information or evidence required (see below). You can amend or withdraw your claim before a decision is made (see p1004). If there is a delay in deciding your claim, you can ask for an interim payment (see p505).



## Who should claim

You make your own claim for child benefit and guardian's allowance. If you cannot manage your claim, another person can claim for you as your appointee (see p1005).

If someone else also claims child benefit for the same child, you can only get child benefit for that child if your claim has priority (see p493).

If you are a woman and live with your *male* spouse or civil partner, you are entitled to child benefit[88] and guardian's allowance[89] rather than him. However, it can be paid to either of you, unless you ask for him not to be paid by written notice to the Child Benefit Office,[90] and for guardian's allowance by also using the approved form.[91]

**Note:** to receive child benefit for a second or subsequent child, you need to notify HMRC within one month of becoming responsible for them (this can be extended for up to 13 months in specified circumstances – see p1153).[92] To notify HMRC online or via the HMRC app, select 'Make a Claim' and then 'Add a child to an existing claim', or if you cannot do so, contact HMRC by post or phone (see above).

## Information to support your claim

For the general information requirements that apply to all benefits, see p1006.

It is important that you provide any information required when you claim. Until you do, you may not count as having made a valid claim (see p1008). Correct any defects as soon as possible or your date of claim may be affected.

HMRC can require you to supply information and evidence considered reasonable and usually asks to see your child's birth or adoption certificate when you claim child benefit, unless:

- child benefit has already been paid for the child (to you or someone else); *or*
- the child was born in Great Britain and the birth has been registered. In this case, you must give details from the birth certificate – the system number in England and Wales or the district, year and entry number in Scotland.

If you cannot register the birth before the child is three months old, you can apply for child benefit and then inform HMRC when the birth has been registered to start being paid.

If your child was born abroad, HMRC requires the child's passport or travel documents used to enter the UK.

If you claim guardian's allowance, you must usually provide the child's birth certificate, together with the death certificates of the child's parent(s) and an adoption certificate, if relevant to your claim.

From 7 April 2025, if you are under 16 when you claim child benefit, you do not need to have, or to have applied for, a national insurance number.[93]



Send any documents that you must provide to the Child Benefit Office (using the address on the claim form). Original documents should usually be returned to you within four weeks. If you are being supported by British Red Cross, Scottish Refugee Council or as part of a resettlement scheme and get help from a DWP resettlement coach, HMRC says you can instead have your documents verified by the Jobcentre.[94]

Even if you have provided all that was required when you claimed, you may be asked to provide further information to support your claim (see p1009). You may also be asked to provide information after you are awarded benefit. If you fail to do so, your benefit could be suspended or even terminated (see p1031).

## The date of your claim

The date of your claim is important as it determines when your entitlement to child benefit and guardian's allowance starts. This is not necessarily the date from which you are paid. For information about when payment starts, see p504.

Your date of claim is normally the date on which your claim form is received at the Child Benefit Office.[95]

You must make sure your claim is valid. If it is 'defective', you are given a short time to correct the defect (see p1009). If you do, your claim is treated as having been made when you initially claimed.[96]

### Backdating your claim

It is important to claim in time. A claim for child benefit or guardian's allowance can normally only be backdated for up to three months.[97] If you cannot register the birth before the child is three months old, you can apply before registering in order to be paid from the date of birth. Payments start once you have informed HMRC that the registration has been done. There are special rules if you are getting benefit and move between Great Britain and Northern Ireland (see p1291). You do not have to show why your claim was late, but you should explain when you want your claim to start. However, if someone else has an award of child benefit for the same child, see p505.

If you might have been entitled to child benefit or guardian's allowance earlier but did not claim as you were given the wrong information or misled by the DWP or HMRC, you could ask for compensation or complain to the Ombudsman (see Chapter 55).

### If you claim the wrong benefit

A claim for guardian's allowance can also be treated as a claim for child benefit for the same child and vice versa.[98] See p1013 for further information.

### Claiming in advance

If you do not qualify for child benefit or guardian's allowance when you claim but will do within three months of that date, the decision maker can make an advance award and treat your date of claim as the date on which you first qualify.[99]

## 8. Getting paid

The general rules on getting paid are covered in Chapter 44. This section explains the specific rules for child benefit and guardian's allowance.

***When is your benefit paid?***

You are usually paid on a Monday (or on a Tuesday), although HMRC can choose any day of the week as your payday. Benefit is usually paid four-weekly for three weeks in arrears and one week in advance.

Child benefit and guardian's allowance are weekly benefits. You must normally meet the entitlement conditions at the start of a week (ie, midnight between Sunday and Monday) to be entitled to benefit for that week.[100] Payment begins from the Monday after the date of your claim (see p503) or, if the date of your claim is a Monday, from that date.[101] See p505 if someone else has been getting child benefit for the child.

You can be paid weekly if:[102]

- you are a lone parent; *or*
- you or your partner get universal credit, income-related employment and support allowance or pension credit; *or*
- HMRC is satisfied that a four-weekly payment 'is causing hardship'.

Your guardian's allowance is always paid at the same time as your child benefit, if you are entitled to both.[103]

Child benefit and guardian's allowance cannot be paid for less than a week. If your entitlement ends, payment continues up to the end of that week.

Your benefit is awarded for an indefinite period unless this would be inappropriate – eg, if a change is expected in the near future.[104]

Note:
- Your benefit can be paid to someone else if this is needed to protect your interests or the interests of the child.[105]
- Even if you have been sanctioned for a benefit offence (see p1111), you must be paid child benefit and guardian's allowance.
- If your payment of child benefit or guardian's allowance is delayed (see p1123), you might be able to get an interim payment (see below). If you want to complain about how your claim has been dealt with, or claim compensation, see Chapter 55.
- If payment of child benefit or guardian's allowance is suspended, see p1031.
- If you are overpaid benefit, you might have to repay it (see Chapter 47) and, in some circumstances, you may have to pay a penalty (see p1101). If you have been accused of fraud, see Chapter 48.



## Interim payments

If your claim for child benefit or guardian's allowance is delayed, you can ask HMRC for an interim payment. HMRC does not make an interim payment if you have an appeal pending. An interim payment can be made if it seems that you may be entitled to benefit and:[106]
- there is a delay in your making a claim; *or*
- you have claimed, but not in the correct way – eg, you have filled in the form incorrectly; *or*
- you have claimed correctly, but the claim cannot be dealt with immediately; *or*
- you have been awarded benefit, but it cannot be paid immediately, other than by an interim payment.

Note:
- There is no right of appeal against a refusal of an interim payment. See the note on p1024 – but HMRC must change the decision, not the DWP.
- An interim payment can be deducted from any later payment of benefit. If it is more than your actual entitlement, the overpayment can be recovered. You should be notified of this in advance.[107]

## If someone else has been getting child benefit for the child

If you claim child benefit for a child and someone else is already getting child benefit for that child, you are only entitled if your claim has priority over the existing claimant's claim (see p493). If so, your benefit starts from the fourth week after the week in which you claim, unless the existing claimant withdraws their claim before then or stops getting child benefit for another reason.

Even if your claim has priority, if child benefit has already been paid to someone else for the same child for a period before you claimed, you can only get child benefit for the period before you claimed if:[108]

- a decision maker (or the First-tier or Upper Tribunal) has decided that the child benefit paid is recoverable because the other person failed to disclose, or misrepresented, a material fact (see p1064) and no appeal against that decision has been made within the time limit. **Note:** if you appeal against a decision refusing your claim under this rule, the tribunal cannot decide that the other person was not entitled for a period before you claimed;[109] *or*
- a decision has been made that the other person was not entitled to child benefit, and the other person has voluntarily repaid the child benefit for that period.

These rules usually prevent you from getting guardian's allowance for a child if someone else gets child benefit for them (as you must usually be entitled to child benefit to qualify for guardian's allowance – see p496).

## Change of circumstances

You must report any change in your circumstances that you are told to report, as well as any that you might reasonably be expected to know might affect your right to, the amount of, or the payment of your benefit. You should do this as soon as possible, preferably in writing.

You can amend your details, including to notify HMRC of responsibility for an additional child, online at at gov.uk/report-changes-child-benefit, via the HMRC app,[110] by post or phone.[111] See p1030 for further information.

If there has been a relevant change of circumstances, HMRC looks at your claim again and makes a new decision. For when the new decision takes effect, see p1150.

### If a child dies

If you were getting child benefit for a child who then dies, your benefit is paid for the next eight weeks, or until the Monday after the child would have turned 20, if that is sooner. If your partner got child benefit for the child and also dies, you are entitled to benefit for the eight-week period if you were living together when your partner died.[112]

If a child is born and dies in the same week, you can get child benefit for this eight-week period if you satisfied the entitlement conditions during that week.[113]

These rules allow you to also get guardian's allowance for a child during a period after the child dies, provided the child continues to count as an eligible child. You do not need to satisfy the conditions about living together or providing for the child's needs (see p496).[114]

## 9. Tax, other benefits and the benefit cap

### Tax

Guardian's allowance is not taxable.[115]

If your (or your partner's) 'adjusted net income' in a tax year is over £60,000, you are liable to pay tax on your 'taxable child benefit' for that year. This is called the 'high-income child benefit charge'. For this rule, income is counted on an individual basis – ie, it is *not* the combined income of you and your partner.

Your 'taxable child benefit' includes child benefit for any week that starts in the tax year which is paid to:[116]

- you; *or*
- your partner (but only for weeks when you were partners); *or*
- someone who gets child benefit for a child who lives with you, but not with them (but only if neither that person nor their partner is liable for the charge themselves).

If both you and your partner have income over £60,000, whoever has the highest income is liable for the charge. If you are liable for the charge, you must declare this to HMRC by giving details of your income on a self-assessment tax form within the time limit to do so. See gov.uk/child-benefit-tax-charge for further details.

**Note:**[117]

- The high-income child benefit charge is 1 per cent of your taxable child benefit for each complete £200 of income you have over £60,000 in a tax year. If your income is over £80,000, the charge equals the total amount of taxable child benefit.
- Child benefit awarded after a child dies is not included in your taxable child benefit.

### Electing not to be paid child benefit

To avoid liability for the high-income child benefit charge, you (or your partner, if your partner is the claimant) can ask HMRC not to pay child benefit. HMRC may not agree to this – eg, if deductions are being made from child benefit to recover an overpayment.[118]

If you elect not to be paid (rather than not claiming child benefit, or ending your claim), your entitlement to child benefit continues. This means that you (or someone with whom you live or who cares for your child) may still qualify for national insurance (NI) credits (see p868 and p870). You can also qualify for guardian's allowance if the child is an eligible child (see p497), or other benefits such as more generous bereavement benefits (see Chapter 21). For these reasons, consider claiming child benefit, even if you do not want it to be paid.

After electing not to receive child benefit, you have up to two years after the end of the tax year to ask for child benefit to be paid for that year if you realise that your child benefit would have been more than the charge.

## Means-tested benefits

If you get child benefit or guardian's allowance:

- means-tested benefits can be paid in addition to them;
- they are ignored when calculating your entitlement to universal credit (UC), income-related employment and support allowance, pension credit and housing benefit (HB).[119]



## Non-means-tested benefits

Increases in non-means-tested benefits for dependent children were abolished in 2003, but some people still get them. You cannot get both guardian's allowance and an increase for the same child.[120] If you still get an increase for a child, it is reduced if you also get the higher rate of child benefit (£26.05) for that child (see p1023).[121]

If you get child benefit for a child aged under 12, you (or, in some circumstances, someone who resides with you or cares for the child) can qualify for NI credits (see p868 and p870).

Your entitlement to any other non-means-tested benefit is not affected by getting child benefit or guardian's allowance.

## The benefit cap

Child benefit is one of the specified benefits for the benefit cap. It only applies if you are getting UC or HB. You are exempt from the benefit cap if you get guardian's allowance.[122] See p1025 for further information.

## Other sources of help

If your income is low, you may be entitled to a council tax reduction (see p761). You may be eligible for free school lunches for your child (see p774).

In Scotland, you may be entitled to an additional Scottish child payment (see Chapter 62).

Children and young people under 19 may qualify for health benefits (see Chapter 27). Young people aged 16 to 19 in non-advanced education may qualify for financial help with their studies (see p776).

# Notes

## 1. Who can get child benefit

1 ss141-47 SSCBA 1992; s115 IAA 1999
2 s142(1) SSCBA 1992
3 s142(2) SSCBA 1992; regs 2-7 CB Regs
4 If a child turns 16 on 31 August, HMRC states that they are only a qualifying young person up to and including that day but, arguably, this is not correct: compare para 07030 CBTM with reg 4(3) CB Regs
5 Reg 2(2) CB Regs
6 Reg 3 CB Regs
7 Reg 1(3) CB Regs
8 Reg 3(2)(a)(i) CB Regs
9 Reg 3(3) CB Regs
10 Reg 3(2)(a)(ii) CB Regs
11 'Supervised' study requires the close proximity of a teacher or tutor to enforce discipline, and provide encouragement and help: R(F) 1/93, but see also *Flemming v SSWP* [2002] EWCA Civ 641 (reported as R(G) 2/02) and *SSWP v Deane* [2010] EWCA Civ 699
12 Reg 1(3) CB Regs
13 Reg 3(2)(ab) CB Regs; s4 Education and Skills Act 2008
14 s4 Education and Skills Act 2008; reg 3 The Duty to Participate in Education or Training (Miscellaneous Provisions) Regulations 2013 No.1205
15 para 07024 CBTM
16 Reg 3(2)(c) and (d) and (4) CB Regs
17 Reg 1(3) CB Regs
18 Reg 5 CB Regs
19 gov.uk/personal-tax-account
20 Reg 7 CB Regs
21 Reg 7(2)(2.1) CB Regs
22 Reg 7(2)(1.3) CB Regs
23 Reg 6(2) and (3) CB Regs
24 Reg 6(4) CB Regs
25 s143 SSCBA 1992
26 R(F) 2/81
27 R(F) 2/79 as referenced by para 06020 CBTM
28 s143(2) SSCBA 1992
29 s143(3) SSCBA 1992; reg 9 CB Regs; para 06040 CBTM
30 s143(3)(b) and (c) and (4) SSCBA 1992; reg 10 CB Regs
31 s143(1)(b) SSCBA 1992
32 *RK v HMRC (CHB)* [2015] UKUT 357 (AAC), reported as [2016] AACR 4
33 para 06080 CBTM
34 Reg 11(4) CB Regs
35 Reg 11 CB Regs
36 s144(3) and Sch 10 SSCBA 1992
37 s13(1) SSAA 1992 and Sch 10 SSCBA 1992
38 s147(3) SSCBA 1992; R(F) 1/08
39 Sch 2 para 4 SSA 1998
40 Sch 10 para 1 SSCBA 1992
41 Regs 14 and 15 CB Regs
42 CF/1771/2003
43 *Geraldine Murphy's application* [2023] NIKB 119
44 *R (on the application of) Ford v Board of Inland Revenue* [2005] EWHC 1109 (Admin); see also *R (on the application of) Chester v Secretary of State for Social Security* [2001] EWHC 1119 (Admin)
45 *Geraldine Murphy's application* [2023] NIKB 119
46 Or 'residing with' each other – see *Grove v Insurance Officer*, reported as an appendix to R(F) 4/85
47 s147(4) SSCBA 1992; regs 1(3) and 34 CB Regs
48 R(F) 4/85
49 R(F) 2/81, citing R(F) 2/79
50 Sch 9 SSCBA 1992; regs 8, 12, 13 and 16 CB Regs
51 But see *KW v HMRC (CB)* [2011] UKUT 489 (AAC)
52 Regs 1(3), 5(2)(c) and 7(3) CB Regs

## 2. Who can get guardian's allowance

53 ss77 and 122(5) SSCBA 1992
54 s122(4) and (5) SSCBA 1992; reg 4A SSB(Dep) Regs
55 Reg 4A(1)(b) and (3) SSB(Dep) Regs
56 s77(2)(a) and (8)(a) SSCBA 1992; regs 3-6 GA(Gen) Regs
57 s77(2)(b) and (c) and (8) SSCBA 1992; reg 7 GA(Gen) Regs
58 s77(2)(b) SSCBA 1992
59 para 12090 CBTM
60 CG/60/1992
61 CG/60/1992; CF/2735/2003
62 Reg 7 GA(Gen) Regs
63 Reg 7 GA(Gen) Regs; para 12050 CBTM

64 s77(8)(c) SSCBA 1992; reg 8 GA(Gen) Regs
65 ss77(6)(b) and 143(1)(b) SSCBA 1992
66 Reg 5 SSB(Dep) Regs
67 s77(10) and (11) SSCBA 1992; regs 4 and 6(2) GA(Gen) Regs
68 R(G) 4/83(T) (appendix) as referenced by para 12020 CBTM
69 para 12010 CBTM; and s147(3) SSCBA 1992 only treats a step-parent as a parent for child benefit purposes, but see also R(F) 1/08 which suggests that anyone with parental responsibility is likely to count as a parent

5. **The amount of benefit**
70 Reg 2(1) CB(R) Regs; Sch 4 Part III para 5 SSCBA 1992
71 Reg 2(1) CB(R) Regs
72 Reg 2(2) CB(R) Regs

6. **Special benefit rules**
73 s147(2) and Sch 9 para 1 SSCBA 1992; regs 16-19 CB Regs
74 Reg 16(1)(b)(iv) and (2) CB Regs
75 R(F) 3/85 as referenced by para 08061 CBTM
76 s147(1) SSCBA 1992
77 Reg 16(1)(b)(i)-(iii) CB Regs
78 Regs 9 and 18(b) CB Regs
79 Reg 17(2)-(5) CB Regs
80 Regs 1(3) and 17(1) CB Regs
81 Reg 16(3) CB Regs
82 Reg 16(4) and (5) CB Regs

7. **Claims and backdating**
83 gov.uk/personal-tax-account
84 gov.uk/child-benefit/how-to-claim
85 gov.uk/log-in-register-hmrc-online-services
86 gov.uk/guidance/download-the-hmrc-app
87 Reg 5 CB&GA(Admin) Regs
88 s144(3) and Sch 10 para 3 SSCBA 1992
89 s77(9) SSCBA 1992
90 Reg 15 CB Regs; para 08050 CBTM
91 Reg 10 GA Regs; para 12080 CBTM
92 Regs 16 and 17 CB&GA(DA) Regs
93 Child Benefit and Guardian's Allowance (Miscellaneous Amendments) Regulations 2025 No.207
94 Email from HMRC to CPAG, 27 January 2025
95 Reg 5 CB&GA(Admin) Regs
96 Reg 10 CB&GA(Admin) Regs
97 Reg 6 CB&GA(Admin) Regs
98 Reg 11 CB&GA(Admin) Regs
99 Reg 12 CB&GA(Admin) Regs

8. **Getting paid**
100 s147(2) SSCBA 1992
101 Reg 13 CB&GA(Admin) Regs
102 Regs 18 and 19 CB&GA(Admin) Regs
103 Reg 18(4) CB&GA(Admin) Regs
104 Reg 15 CB&GA(Admin) Regs
105 Reg 33 CB&GA(Admin) Regs
106 Reg 22 CB&GA(Admin) Regs; para 03070 CBTM
107 Regs 22(3), 41 and 42 CB&GA(Admin) Regs
108 Sch 10 para 1 SSCBA 1992; s13(2) SSAA 1992; reg 38 CB Regs; CF/2826/2007
109 *CB v HMRC and AE (CHB)* [2016] UKUT 506 (AAC)
110 gov.uk/guidance/download-the-hmrc-app
111 gov.uk/government/organisations/hm-revenue-customs/contact/child-benefit
112 s145A SSCBA 1992; reg 20 CB Regs
113 s145A(3) SSCBA 1992
114 s145A(4) SSCBA 1992

9. **Tax, other benefits and the benefit cap**
115 s677 IT(EP)A 2003
116 ss681B, 681D and 681H IT(EP)A 2003
117 ss681C, 681E and 681H IT(EP)A 2003; Spring Budget 2024
118 s13A SSAA 1992; see also HMRC, *Elections Not to Receive Child Benefit*, 2012, gov.uk/government/publications/elections-not-to-receive-child-benefit
119 **UC** Reg 66 UC Regs
**ESA** Sch 8 para 7(2) ESA Regs
**PC** Regs 9 and 15(1)(j) SPC Regs
**HB** Sch 5 para 65 HB Regs; regs 27 and 29 HB(SPC) Regs
120 Reg 7(4) SS(OB) Regs
121 Reg 8 SS(OB) Regs
122 **UC** Reg 83(1)(k) UC Regs
**HB** Reg 75F(1)(i) HB Regs

# Chapter 24

# Disability living allowance

4

**This chapter covers:**


1. Disability living allowance mobility component (p512)
2. Disability living allowance care component (p519)
3. The rules about your age (p526)
4. People included in the claim (p529)
5. The amount of benefit (p529)
6. Special benefit rules (p530)
7. Claims and backdating (p530)
8. Getting paid (p538)
9. Tax, other benefits and the benefit cap (p541)


**Note:** new claims for disability living allowance (DLA) can only be made for children under 16. This chapter therefore covers the DLA rules for children. There are still some adults who get DLA, because they claimed it before the introduction of personal independence payment. There are important differences between the DLA rules for adults and those for children. See p526, and Chapter 27 of the 2015/16 edition of this *Handbook*, for details of the rules for adults.

## Key facts

- DLA is a benefit for people with disabilities or long-term health problems, who need help getting around and/or who need supervision or attention.
- Some adults who claimed DLA in the past continue to receive it, but you can only make a new DLA claim for a child under 16.
- DLA has a care component and a mobility component. You can get either one or both of the components. Each component has different rates.
- DLA is a non-means-tested benefit.
- You can get DLA whether you are in or out of work.
- You do not have to have paid national insurance contributions to get DLA.
- DLA can be paid in addition to other benefits and is disregarded as income for means-tested benefits.
- DLA is administered and paid by the DWP.
- If you disagree with a DLA decision, you can apply for a revision or a supersession (see Chapter 50), or appeal against it (see Chapter 51). You must apply for a mandatory reconsideration before you can appeal.

- You cannot make a new DLA claim for a child under 16 who lives in Scotland. Instead, you should claim child disability payment (CDP – see Chapter 64). The Scottish government has transferred all existing child DLA claimants in Scotland to CDP.

# 1. Disability living allowance mobility component



Disability living allowance (DLA) mobility component is for children under 16 who have a limited ability to walk or get around. This can be for a range of reasons. The mobility component can be paid at a lower or higher rate.

See p535 for tips on answering the mobility questions on the DLA claim form.

## Who can get the mobility component

A child can get DLA mobility component if they:[1]

- satisfy the residence conditions (see p1347); *and*
- are not a 'person subject to immigration control', although there are some exceptions (see p1272); *and*
- are aged three or over (five or over for the lower rate), under 16, and not living in Scotland when you claim (see p526); *and*
- satisfy the 'disability conditions' for either the higher rate (see above) or the lower rate (see p517); *and*
- unless terminally ill (see p530), have satisfied the disability conditions throughout the three months immediately before the award begins and are likely to continue to satisfy them for the next six months (the 'required period' condition; see p533 if reclaiming); *and*
- are likely to be able to 'benefit from enhanced facilities for locomotion'.

***To benefit from enhanced facilities for locomotion***

To get the DLA mobility component, a child must be able to make outdoor journeys from time to time, even if they have to be carried to a car for a ride.[2] It is not essential that they are interested in or enjoy going out, provided it would be beneficial for them to do so.

## Disability conditions for the higher rate mobility component

A child aged three or over can get the higher rate mobility component if they:[3]

- have a disability from a physical cause that means they are unable, or virtually unable, to walk (see p513); *or*
- were born without feet or are a double amputee (see p515); *or*
- are both blind and deaf (see p515); *or*

- are blind or severely visually impaired (see p515); *or*
- have a 'severe mental impairment', have 'severe behavioural problems' and qualify for the highest rate of the DLA care component (see p516).

## 'Unable or virtually unable to walk'

A child can get the higher rate if they have a disability from a physical cause that means:[4]

- they are unable to walk; *or*
- their ability to walk outdoors is so limited in terms of the distance, speed, length of time or the manner in which they can make progress on foot without severe discomfort that they are virtually unable to walk; *or*
- the exertion required to walk would constitute a danger to their life or be likely to lead to a serious deterioration in their health.

4

Personal circumstances, such as the location of the child's home, should not be taken into account. It is not, for instance, relevant if they live a long way from the nearest bus stop,[5] or if they cannot use public transport.

### Physical disability

A child's inability, or virtual inability, to walk must arise from their physical condition.[6] There can be a physical cause (eg, pain or dizziness), even without a medically diagnosed origin. It does not matter if the original cause was mental, provided a current physical impairment affects their walking. For example, if a child's walking is impaired by weakness due to anorexia nervosa, the cause is physical.[7] Myalgic encephalomyelitis (ME), or chronic fatigue syndrome, should be accepted as having a physical origin unless there is evidence that any mobility restrictions are purely psychological.[8] A child's discomfort from chronic diarrhoea might make them virtually unable to walk.[9] Inability to make progress on foot because of developmental conditions may qualify if the cause is physical – eg, Down's syndrome or autism are both accepted as physical disorders of development of the brain.[10]

### Unable to walk

A child is unable to walk if they cannot move their body along by alternate, weight-bearing steps of the feet.[11]

### Prostheses, aids and medication

Entitlement is usually based on a child's ability to walk with any prosthesis or artificial aid they use, or that would be suitable for them. However, if they have no feet, they qualify automatically even if they can mobilise with a prosthesis or artificial aid (see p515).[12]

They may not qualify if they are able to walk with crutches. However, if they have one leg and no artificial limb suitable to use, they are regarded as 'unable to walk', even if they can get around on crutches.[13]

Any medication the child normally and reasonably uses is taken into account – eg, it may not be practical to carry a bulky nebuliser.[14] Their walking should be assessed as they are now, not how they might be after any treatment.[15]

### Outdoors

The test is how a child copes with the terrain and environment normally encountered outdoors. Take into account any problems they have with balance on uneven pavements/roads, or if their condition is made worse by wind or rain.[16] Walking indoors is not necessarily an indication of ability to walk outdoors.[17]



### Distance

The law does not specify a distance to use when determining a child's inability to walk. In practice, they may be refused benefit if you tick on the claim form that they can walk more than 50 metres. However, their walking speed, the time it takes to cover the distance and the manner of walking are also relevant, so give details about these on the form. Taking more than a minute to walk 50 metres is slow, so if an older child cannot walk this fast without severe discomfort, say so.[18]

### Without severe discomfort

Any walking that a child can do only with severe discomfort should be ignored when considering whether they are virtually unable to walk.[19] Their discomfort does not need to amount to 'severe pain or distress'.[20] If, when walking, they feel severe discomfort (eg, pain or breathlessness brought on by walking), make this clear.[21] They may be able to walk a distance without severe discomfort, a further distance that causes severe discomfort, and then have to stop altogether. The test is how far they can walk before going any further causes severe discomfort. You should state this distance on the claim form, rather than how far they can walk before actually having to stop. If they can walk further without severe discomfort after a brief rest, this could be taken into account.[22]

If a child is in severe discomfort before they start to walk, even if the pain gets no worse, they should count as being virtually unable to walk, provided their disability affects the physical act of walking.[23] They do not count as being virtually unable to walk if something unconnected with walking (eg, a skin condition relating to sunlight) causes the discomfort.[24]

### The exertion required to walk

A child can get the higher rate mobility component if the exertion required to walk endangers their health. If the deterioration in health is sudden, you must show that they would never recover, or recovery would take a significant period of time (eg, 12 months) or would require some form of medical intervention. So, a child with ME who needs a few days' rest after walking would not satisfy this test.[25] As a child's difficulties with walking must be connected with physical exertion and not mental exertion, the fact that walking may cause a child stress, or lead to a deterioration in mental health, does not count.[26]

## People without feet

A child can get the higher rate mobility component if they do not have feet or legs (missing from the ankle or above). They are automatically treated as being unable to walk,[27] even if they can walk with prostheses.

## Blind and deaf

A child can get the higher rate mobility component if:[28]

- the degree of disablement resulting from their loss of vision is 100 per cent; *and*
- the degree of disablement resulting from their loss of hearing is 80 per cent on a scale where 100 per cent represents absolute deafness; *and*
- the combined effect of the blindness and deafness means that they are unable to walk to any intended or required destination while outdoors without the help of another person.

The regulations do not specify how to assess the degree of disablement, but caselaw suggests that the industrial injury provisions should be used (see p595).[29] So 100 per cent disablement through 'loss of vision' means 'loss of sight to such an extent as to render the claimant unable to perform any work for which eyesight is essential'.[30] This is the definition used when someone is registered as severely sight impaired (blind). However, whether or not a child is registered, or the outcome of visual acuity and visual fields tests, is not conclusive of whether they satisfy this condition.

If a child's level of hearing loss, averaged between both ears at 1, 2 and 3 kHz, is at least 87 decibels, they satisfy the 80 per cent disablement test.[31] They may have to undertake a hearing test. The test takes into account any hearing aid they use or could reasonably be expected to use.[32]

## Blind or severely visually impaired

A child can get the higher rate mobility component if they have been certified blind or severely sight impaired and have combined visual acuity in both eyes on the Snellen scale, while using appropriate corrective lenses if necessary, of:[33]

- less than 3/60; *or*
- 3/60 or more, but less than 6/60, if they have a complete loss of peripheral vision and a central visual field of no more than 10 degrees.

'Appropriate' corrective lenses are lenses that the child can wear without discomfort.[34] The test has to be met by both eyes – an average cannot be used if their level of vision in one eye is worse than the other.[35]

The Snellen test is taken indoors. This may be discriminatory.[36] If a child does not qualify according to the Snellen scale but their vision is significantly worse outdoors, get specialist advice.

## Severe mental impairment and behavioural problems

A child can get the higher rate mobility component if they:[37]

- have a 'severe mental impairment' – ie, arrested development, or incomplete physical development, of the brain, which results in severe impairment of intelligence and social functioning; *and*
- display severe behavioural problems – ie, the child:
  - exhibits extreme disruptive behaviour; *and*
  - regularly requires someone else to intervene and physically restrain them to prevent them causing injury to themselves or others or damage to property; *and*
  - is so unpredictable that another person has to be present and watching over them whenever they are awake;[38] *and*
- qualify for the highest rate of the DLA care component (see p519).

4

If a child does not meet all the above conditions, they might still get the higher rate mobility component because a disability prevents them from walking effectively, so that they are virtually unable to walk (see p513).[39]

### Arrested or incomplete development

The DWP acknowledges that there is no precise age at which an individual's brain stops developing, and decision makers must take this into account when assessing 'arrested or incomplete development'.[40] As a result of the arrested or incomplete brain development, there must also be a severe impairment of intelligence and of social functioning.[41]

### Severe impairment of intelligence and social functioning

An IQ of 55 or less is generally accepted as a 'severe impairment of intelligence'. However, using a crude measure of intelligence based on IQ alone is not appropriate. Some children may have a higher IQ but be unable to apply it practically.[42] A child's 'useful intelligence' (eg, their 'degree of judgement in relation to everyday living', including factors such as sense of danger) should be taken into account.[43] For example, an autistic child with no awareness of danger may have severely impaired intelligence even if their IQ is over 55, and language and communication skills assessment may be particularly important in considering a child's social functioning.[44] Whether a child has 'severe impairment of intelligence and social functioning' should, therefore, be treated as a single test and all the evidence considered as a whole.

### Physical restraint

Physical restraint may involve as little as a hand on the arm. You do not need to show that any force is used.[45] However, if the presence of someone who watches over a child is enough on its own to prevent them from causing injury to themselves or others or damage to property, or a specially adapted environment allows them to be safely left alone, they may not pass the test. The DWP should not focus only on how the child is outdoors or in a structured safe environment, and must consider their need for, and the nature of, intervention in all environments.[46] There is no definition in the law of how often intervention has to be needed before it can be said to be 'regularly' required. The DWP should consider the facts as a whole and decide if the behaviour occurs regularly according to the ordinary meaning of the word.[47] Behaviour does not have to be violent to be classed as 'disruptive'.[48] Involuntary behaviour, such as falls due to seizures, can be classed as 'disruptive'.[49]



## Disability condition for the lower rate mobility component

A child aged five or over can get the lower rate mobility component if they are 'so severely disabled physically or mentally' that they cannot get around outdoors 'without guidance or supervision from another person most of the time'.[50]

Any ability they may have to use familar routes without guidance or supervision should be ignored.[51] Getting the lower rate mobility component is based on the child's need for supervision or guidance, rather than any physical difficulty they have walking that may mean they can get the higher rate.[52]

### The 'additional requirements' test

You must show that a child requires guidance or supervision and also that either:[53]

- they require substantially more guidance or supervision than children of their age in 'normal' physical and mental health; *or*
- children of the same age in 'normal' physical and mental health would not require such guidance or supervision.

The fact that all young children require some guidance or supervision outdoors is not the point. If a child needs a substantially greater amount or a different type of guidance or supervision, compared to what is normally needed by children of a similar age, they should qualify.[54] For example, a child with a visual impairment or learning disability may need an adult to hold, guide or watch over them in situations in which most children of a similar age would only require someone to accompany them. Similarly, a young deaf child may need someone to stay within touching distance, whereas a hearing child would not.[55]

See p534 for tips on how to describe a child's needs on the claim form.

### Supervision

'Supervision' can be precautionary. For example, it can be monitoring a child's physical, mental or emotional state in case they need more assistance to continue walking, or monitoring the route ahead for obstacles/dangers or places/situations which might upset them. Supervision can also be active, such as encouraging or cajoling a child, or distracting them from fears[56] or possibly alarming situations.[57]

Unlike the 'continual supervision' condition for the DLA care component, the child does not need to require supervision to prevent 'substantial danger'.[58] If they get the care component because they require continual supervision, they may also get the lower rate mobility component.[59] However, this is not automatic; their eligibility must be assessed on the mobility criteria alone.[60]

The supervision does not need to improve the child's walking ability, but should enable them to 'take advantage of the faculty of walking'. It is enough that supervision helps, even if it does not remove risks completely or if the child does not always respond well to the person providing it.

Likewise, it is enough if they need to have supervision (eg, to provide help in the event of seizures),[61] even though they have no difficulty getting about.[62]

### Guidance

'Guidance' can mean physically leading or directing a child, but can also mean giving verbal instructions, suggestions or persuasion, helping to avoid obstacles or places that upset them, or leading or persuading a child when they become disorientated or are anxious. Even if a companion only intervenes occasionally, they could still be guiding 'most of the time' if a child would otherwise not know when to change direction. If a child has a visual impairment, they may need guidance to follow directions, avoid obstacles or cross roads (even if they use a guide dog or cane). If they are deaf and their main method of communication is sign language, they may require guidance in unfamiliar places if they are unable to ask for directions. However, an older child may not qualify if they can study maps, read street signs or communicate with passers by.[63]

### Fear and anxiety

A child can get the lower rate mobility component because of a mental as well as a physical disablement. If they have an anxiety disorder and need an escort's help to overcome fear of going outside, they are likely to satisfy the 'guidance or supervision' requirement.[64] There is conflicting caselaw, but if no amount of reassurance can persuade them to go outside, they may not qualify.[65] If they can just manage a walk into their garden, this could be enough to qualify.[66]

Any fear or anxiety that stops a child going out alone must be a symptom of mental disability in order to count. Fear and anxiety arising from a physical disability, such as a fear of having to cope with incontinence while alone, is not sufficient, although they may still have a physical need for supervision.[67] If their physical disability causes such fear or anxiety that they can be said to be mentally disabled, they may qualify.

## 2. Disability living allowance care component

Disability living allowance (DLA) care component is for children under 16 who have attention or supervision needs. It can be paid at a lowest, middle or highest rate.

See p534 for tips on completing the DLA claim form.



### Who can get the care component

A child can get the DLA care component if they:[68]

- satisfy the residence conditions (see p1347); *and*
- are not a 'person subject to immigration control', although there are some exceptions (see p1272); *and*
- are under 16 and not living in Scotland when you claim (see p526); *and*
- are not in residential care (see p826); *and*
- satisfy the disability conditions for the lowest, middle or highest rate of the care component (see below); *and*
- unless terminally ill (see p530), have satisfied the disability conditions throughout the three months immediately before the award begins and are likely to continue to satisfy them for the next six months (the 'required period' condition; see p533 if reclaiming).

### The disability conditions

A child can get the **lowest rate care component** if they are so severely disabled, physically or mentally, that they require attention from another person for a significant portion of the day (whether during a single period or a number of periods) in connection with their bodily functions (see p523).[69]

A child can get the **middle rate care component** if they:

- satisfy one of the daytime disability conditions *or* one of the night-time disability conditions;[70] *or*
- undergo renal dialysis (in certain circumstances – see p530).[71]

A child can get the **highest rate care component** if they:

- satisfy one of the daytime disability conditions *and* one of the night-time disability conditions;[72] *or*
- are terminally ill (see p530).[73]

***Daytime disability conditions***

A child is so severely disabled, physically or mentally, that they require:[74]

– frequent attention from another person throughout the day in connection with their bodily functions (see p521); *or*

– continual supervision throughout the day in order to avoid substantial danger to themselves or others (see p524).

4

***Night-time disability conditions***

A child is so severely disabled, physically or mentally, that they require:[75]

– prolonged or repeated attention from another person at night in connection with their bodily functions (see p521); *or*

– another person to be awake at night for a prolonged period or at frequent intervals to watch over them in order to avoid substantial danger to themselves or others (see p526).

## The 'additional requirements' test

You must show not only that a child requires attention or supervision, but also that either:[76]

- the child has attention or supervision requirements 'substantially in excess of the normal requirements' of a child of the same age; *or*
- the child has substantial attention or supervision requirements which younger children in 'normal' physical and mental health may also have, but which children of the same age and in 'normal' physical and mental health would not have.

This extra test does not apply if you are claiming DLA care component for a child who is terminally ill (see p530).[77]

The fact that all young children require assistance throughout the day is not the point. If a child needs substantially more, or a different type of, assistance, compared to that normally required by a child of the same age, they should qualify.[78] See p534 for tips on how to describe a child's needs on the claim form.

## 'So severely disabled physically or mentally'

To get the care component, a child must be 'so severely disabled physically or mentally' that they need attention or supervision. They do not need to have a specific medical condition. What is important is that they are so disabled that they have care needs.[79] However, medical evidence can still be important to establish that they are disabled and what their care needs are.[80]

Problems sometimes arise if, for example, a child has behavioural problems or a developmental delay that have not been attributed to a disability. The test here is whether a child has the physical or mental power to control the behaviour.[81]

## Interpreting the conditions

### 'Requires'

You must show that a child 'requires' attention or supervision from another person. The test is what is 'reasonably required' rather than what is 'medically required'.[82] For example, if an incontinent child needs help changing bedding, this help should count as 'reasonably required', even if not actually required to protect their skin. All younger children may have difficulty with bladder or bowel control from time to time, so in this example, the attention required must be substantially more than, or different from, the attention normally needed by children of the same age.



#### Reasonably requires attention

Attention must be 'reasonably required to enable' a child 'as far as reasonably possible to live a normal life'. Having a social life, recreation and cultural activities are part of normal life. If a child is blind, it is reasonable for you to read to them or guide them during social outings. Similarly, if a child has learning disabilities, it is reasonable to help them to travel to, or take part in, social and recreational pursuits. A child's age and interests should be taken into account when deciding what is reasonable.[83]

#### Reasonably requires supervision

The requirement for supervision need only be reasonable. Most risks can be avoided by staying in a chair all day, but that may be totally unreasonable.[84] A child cannot be expected to avoid every risk of harm (eg, any situation in which they might fall) in order to avoid the need for them to have supervision.[85]

When considering a child's need for continual supervision (see p524), you can argue that the fact that supervision is provided shows it is needed. Bear in mind that the supervision must be substantially more than, or different from, the supervision a child the same age might normally require.

### Refusing medical treatment

Refusing medical treatment for a child may affect whether or not they can get the care component. If treatment offered by their doctor would remove the need for help, the attention or supervision a child gets may not be reasonably required. However, it may not be 'reasonably appropriate' for you to agree to the treatment – eg, because of the risks or side effects.[86] Attention or supervision should be accepted as reasonable if you refuse invasive surgery for a child.[87]

### Attention

**'Attention'** is 'a service of a close and intimate nature... involving personal contact carried out in the presence of the disabled person'.[88] For example, helping a child to drink counts, but carrying the drink to where they are sitting does not.[89] Although attention must usually involve personal contact, it need not be *physical* contact. Contact established by spoken word may count if, for example, a child is blind.[90] Thus, reading, describing or giving verbal instructions can be attention.

Similarly, if a child needs to be cajoled or stimulated to do routine tasks, they may require attention in the form of active stimulation.[91] Spoken reassurance can count if it must be given in the physical presence of a child. Bear in mind that the attention must be substantially more than, or different from, the attention a child the same age might normally require.

Attention from professionals should be included when considering the total amount of attention a child requires.[92]



### Bodily functions

The attention a child requires must be in connection with **'bodily functions'** – ie, the normal action of any organ of the body, or a number of organs acting together. Examples of bodily functions include breathing, dressing, drinking, eating, eliminating waste products, getting into or out of bed, hearing, seeing, sitting, sleeping, walking and functions of the brain.[93] Attention is in connection with bodily functions if it is a substitute way of providing what the function would, were it not impaired.[94] For example, guiding a visually impaired child so that they are able to walk outside should be treated as attention with the bodily function of 'seeing' rather than 'walking'. A guide assists with 'seeing' by acting 'as the eyes'. Similarly, help to push a child who uses a wheelchair should be treated as attention.[95]

### Attention or supervision?

**'Attention'** involves a service of an 'active nature'.[96] **'Supervision'** is passive and 'may be precautionary or anticipatory, yet never result in intervention'.[97] Where supervision does lead to intervention, it becomes attention, so the two categories can overlap. If a child needs to be supervised because they are likely to fall and injure themselves, they receive attention when a carer gives them a steadying hand or warns of an obstacle.[98] If attention is frequent, a child can get the middle rate care component, even if the supervision is not 'continual' throughout the day. Sometimes an act can be both supervision and attention. It is, therefore, important to emphasise the full extent of a child's needs without trying to fit them neatly into either category at the expense of leaving things out.

### Communication

Communication involves several bodily functions, including functions of the brain (eg, language processing or comprehension) and senses (eg, hearing). You need to identify which bodily function is impaired and what attention is needed from another person in connection with that function.[99] If a child is profoundly deaf, they may need an interpreter,[100] or extra effort may be required to initiate a two-way conversation.[101]

Explaining written information to a child with poor literacy skills as a result of deafness[102] or a learning disability may also qualify.[103]

#### Domestic duties

Although attention must normally be given in a child's presence, a period of attention can include incidental activities that could be done without them. If a carer strips a soiled bed at night, the extra tasks of wringing out the sheets or hanging them up to dry could count as attention if done on the spot, as would cleaning a soiled carpet in the event of incontinence.[104] Taking the washing away or doing the cleaning at a different time does not qualify as attention.

Domestic tasks performed by a carer outside a child's presence do not normally count as attention.[105] There is conflicting caselaw on whether helping an older child do domestic tasks that children of the same age might normally do for themselves is attention that is reasonably required.[106] Helping a child who has a visual impairment to tidy up around the house is assistance with the bodily function of 'seeing' and can count as attention.[107] Similarly, helping a child with a learning disability to go shopping for clothes may include attention to help them communicate their requirements. Argue that if an older child can learn to tidy up at home or shop for themselves, this is part of what constitutes a 'normal life' (see p521).[108]

#### Help looking after children

If an older child is a parent, help to enable them to look after their children can also count as attention.[109] For example, lifting or holding a baby for feeding is a sufficiently intimate service.[110] It will help if you can identify the bodily function in connection with which the child needs attention. Similarly, assistance to take part in outdoor activities with their children allows a young parent to lead a normal social life.[111] However, while help provided to a disabled young parent may count as attention, help given directly to their child does not.[112]

#### Special diets

Attention generally only counts if it needs to be given in a child's physical presence, so it is often difficult to include help with food preparation. Arguably, this type of help may count if it is part of a broader sequence of care tasks. For example, the various parts of the process of regulating a younger diabetic child's blood sugar levels, some of which require personal contact and some not, should all be treated as attention because they are integral elements of an overall regime.[113] A child with a learning disability or an eating disorder might need similar help to eat properly.

### 'Attention... for a significant portion of the day'

A child can get the lowest rate care component if they need attention for a 'significant portion of the day'.[114] This can be attention for either one period or a number of periods – eg, they could need help with activities connected with getting up at the beginning of the day and with activities connected with going to bed at the end of the day, but otherwise not need extra help. Help at night does not count for the lowest rate.[115]

'A significant portion of the day' is often taken to mean an hour or thereabouts.[116] However, if a child's carer spends less time than that in total but has to give help for a number of short periods, that might qualify.[117]

If a carer has little time available or the help they give is in spells of particularly concentrated activity, less than an hour's help may be enough. Factors like the amount, importance or effect of the attention may be taken into account.[118]

4

## Frequent attention throughout the day

A child satisfies the 'daytime attention' condition if they need frequent attention throughout the day.[119] Frequency refers to the number and pattern of times attention is needed over a period of time, and should be considered as a whole.[120] A child may still qualify even if the times when attention is needed are not spread evenly throughout the day.[121] The aggregate amount of time taken up is not relevant. So it is possible for a child to need help frequently for a short period each time, and so get the middle rate care component, even if the total amount of time may not be regarded as a 'significant portion of the day', and so they might not get the lowest rate.[122]

If a child only needs help at the beginning and end of the day, this is unlikely to be accepted as frequent. Help with toileting (eg, to reach the toilet, use a commode or deal with zips) or help to walk inside the house are both examples of activities that most children usually engage in frequently.

## Continual supervision throughout the day

A child satisfies the 'daytime supervision' condition if they require another person to provide 'continual supervision' throughout the day to avoid the risk of substantial danger to the child or to others.[123] Supervision can be precautionary and anticipatory. It does not necessarily involve direct intervention. The supervision test has four aspects.[124]

- **There must be a substantial danger to a child or someone else as a result of their medical condition.** What is a 'substantial danger' must be decided on the facts of each case. For example, if a child falls and loses consciousness (eg, due to seizures), they would not be able to do anything to save themselves from injury and so this is more likely to be a 'substantial danger' than if other children fall but only sustain minor bruises.
- **The substantial danger must be one which it is reasonable to guard against.** The test is not whether harm is more likely than not to occur, but whether there is a real possibility that cannot be ignored of harm occurring.[125] This involves weighing the likelihood of the risk and the seriousness of the potential consequences. For example, the consequences of a child running out onto the

road could be dire, even though such an incident may be rare.[126] So, in a case like this, it can be argued that the child reasonably requires continual supervision.[127] In assessing the likelihood of danger, the DWP must look at what has happened in the past as well as what may happen.[128]

- **There must be a need for the supervision.** What counts is the level of supervision a child 'reasonably requires' (see p521). It is not necessary that supervision makes it impossible for harm to occur. The correct approach is to decide whether supervision would result in 'a real reduction in the risk of harm'.[129]
- **The supervision must be continual.** This does not mean 'continuing without interruption'. However, supervision which is required only occasionally or spasmodically is insufficient.[130] The fact that a child may need less supervision in a safe structured environment, such as school, does not mean that continual supervision is not required.[131] If it is unavoidable that a child is left alone for a period, they can still qualify if you can show that they are at risk during this time. A child who is liable to seizures without warning may need continual supervision.[132] Even if they have warning of seizures, they may require continual supervision if they suffer from prolonged periods of confusion, or need monitoring to make sure they come out of the seizure safely.[133]

Bear in mind that the supervision a child requires must be substantially more than, or different from, the supervision normally needed by children of the same age (see p520).

## Night and day

'Night' is 'that period of inactivity' which begins when 'the household... closes down for the night'.[134] 'Night' is normally assumed to be the period beginning at around 11pm and ending around 7am.[135] The pattern of activities of each household needs to be taken into account. If a carer stays up late to help a child but would otherwise go to bed earlier, that should count as night care.[136] Similarly, if a carer gets up early in the morning to help a child rather than rise later with the rest of the household, that should count as night care.[137] The definition of 'night' for a child is the same as for an adult, so that help given to a child in the evening before the adults have gone to bed counts only towards satisfying the day condition even if the child is in bed.[138]

## Prolonged or repeated attention at night

A child satisfies the 'night-time attention' condition if the attention a child needs during the night is either prolonged or repeated.[139] There is no clear definition of **'prolonged'**. An assumption that 20 minutes is prolonged has been accepted as a reasonable starting point, but shorter periods should also be considered.[140] **'Repeated'** simply means twice or more.[141] There is no requirement that attention should be needed 'most of the time' – eg, on more than half the nights in a week. A broad overall judgement of a child's needs should be made.[142]

Sleeping is a 'bodily function', so soothing a child back to sleep is attention.[143] The fact that difficulty sleeping may not be a direct result of the child's disability does not matter. It is the attention the child reasonably requires, beyond what other children of their age might need, that must be considered. Attention may also be needed with communication or other bodily functions to help a child get back to sleep.[144]



### Watching over at night

A child satisfies the night-time supervision condition if they need someone to be awake to watch over them at night to avoid the risk of substantial danger to themself or others.[145] The person watching over a child must be awake for a 'prolonged period' or 'at frequent intervals'. A 'prolonged period' may mean 20 minutes or more.[146] 'At frequent intervals' is more than twice. The frequent intervals need not be spread throughout the night, but can be concentrated in one part of it.[147]

## 3. The rules about your age

### Children

New claims for disability living allowance (DLA) can only be made for children under 16. **Note:** children in Scotland must claim child disability payment rather than DLA (see p512).

The higher rate mobility component can be paid from age three onwards and the lower rate mobility component from age five.[148] The three months before the child reaches this age can form the qualifying period (see p512), enabling payment to be made from their birthday.

There is no lower age limit for DLA care component. However, a baby must meet the qualifying conditions for three months before DLA becomes payable, unless they are terminally ill.[149]

See p527 for what happens to a child's DLA when they turn 16.

### Adults

Historically, DLA was awarded to adults as well as children. Some adults still get DLA but it has been replaced by personal independence payment (PIP – see Chapter 31) for most working-age people.

If you are an adult who gets DLA and you turned 65 on or before 8 April 2013, you can continue to receive DLA for as long as you meet the qualifying conditions.[150] You can continue to make renewal claims and/or seek a different rate of DLA, although you may not be able to start getting the mobility component or a higher rate of it once you are 65.[151] If you are an adult who gets DLA and you were under 65 on 8 April 2013, you may in future be asked to transfer to PIP.

**Note:** if you are an adult who gets DLA and you live in or are moving to Scotland, see p1419.

## Transferring from disability living allowance to personal independence payment

### Transferring to personal independence payment as an adult

Anyone who is 16 or over, was under 65 on 8 April 2013 and still gets DLA may be invited to claim PIP at some point. At the time of writing, this 'migration' process has been put on hold for many claimants until 2028 but you will still be invited to claim PIP if you get DLA and turn 16 (see below), or as an adult if your fixed-term DLA award expires or you report a relevant change in your circumstances (unless the change is that you are leaving Great Britain).[152] Always check letters about your DLA carefully to see whether you have been told to claim PIP.

If you are getting DLA and are over pension age when you are told to claim PIP, you are assessed for PIP as if you were under pension age and so you will have access to all the components and rates of PIP.[153] If you are not then awarded any rate of PIP, your claim should be treated as a claim for attendance allowance (AA).[154]

If you are 16 or over (and were under 65 on 8 April 2013), you can choose to claim PIP, even if you have not been sent a letter telling you to do so.[155]

***Should you claim personal independence payment?***

1. If you have received a letter saying that you must claim PIP, you should do so straight away or you risk your DLA award ending.
2. If you get DLA and have *not* been told to claim PIP, get specialist advice before claiming PIP, to help you decide whether it is a good idea. This is because the entitlement conditions for PIP are different from those for DLA and you may not qualify. If you claim PIP, your DLA award ends. Once you have claimed PIP, usually you cannot change your mind.[156]
3. If you already get the higher rate mobility component and highest rate care component of DLA and have not been told to claim PIP, a claim for PIP has no prospect of increasing your income. The DWP should advise you not to proceed with a claim for PIP (unless your condition has improved).[157]

### Transferring to personal independence payment on reaching age 16

If you are claiming DLA for a child, they will normally be invited to claim PIP when they reach 16 and their DLA will end.[158] The DWP will normally write to explain this to you when the child is 15 years and seven months old. It will send a further letter when the child is 15 years and 10 months old, and will write again when the child is 16 to invite them to claim PIP. If a child gets DLA while a hospital inpatient, they are exempt from the transfer to PIP while in hospital. This exemption applies even if you report a relevant change in their circumstances (eg, that their care needs have changed) while they are in hospital.[159]

If your child is about to turn 16 and their award of DLA for either component is for a fixed term that is due to end on the day before their 16th birthday or within the following six months, the DWP will extend the award until the day before they turn 17 or, if earlier, the day their DLA ends under the rules on transferring to PIP.[160] These extensions are to give them time to claim PIP and have a decision made on entitlement.



If your child gets DLA under the 'special rules' on the basis of terminal illness (see p530), they will only be invited to claim PIP when their current award expires.[161]

Always check letters about DLA carefully to see whether your child has been asked to claim PIP.

### Claims for personal independence payment

If a young person receives a written invitation to claim PIP, it must state that they have 28 days to make a claim and tell them how to do so. The time limit can be extended if the DWP thinks it reasonable to do so.[162] The letter must also tell the young person that, if they do not claim PIP, their DLA award will end and when this will happen.[163]

The young person should claim PIP, following the instructions in the letter, as soon as possible, because their DLA award will end whether they claim PIP or not. If necessary, you can make the claim on a young person's behalf as their appointee (see p1005). The DWP should ask you about this before the young person reaches 16 (see p532).

If a young person does not claim PIP within the time allowed, their DLA award is suspended from their next payment day. They must be sent a letter explaining that their award has been suspended and will be terminated if they do not claim PIP within 28 days of the date on which it was suspended. If they do then make a claim, their award of DLA is reinstated until a PIP decision is made. If they still do not claim PIP, their DLA award ends from the date it was suspended.[164] If this happens, they should make a new claim for PIP if they satisfy the rules of entitlement (see p646).

If a young person claims PIP, DLA usually ends four weeks after the first DLA payday following the PIP decision. This applies whether the young person is awarded PIP or not.[165] There can be a different end date for DLA if PIP is initially refused but awarded following a mandatory reconsideration request or appeal.[166] The young person must be notified in writing of the end date of the DLA award and the start date of any PIP award.[167]

If a young person gets DLA and has been invited to claim PIP or is in the process of claiming PIP and they notify the DWP of a change of circumstances that may affect their entitlement to DLA, this is treated as a report of a change of circumstances for PIP instead.[168]

See p671 for details of the assessment process once a young person claims PIP.

If a young person does not provide information needed to assess their entitlement to PIP (see p671) and does not have a good reason (see p675), their PIP claim will be refused. If this happens, their DLA award ends 14 days after the first DLA payday following the decision refusing their PIP claim.[169] If they win an appeal against the decision that they do not have good reason, their DLA award should be reinstated until a decision on their PIP claim is made.[170] If they are subsequently awarded PIP, it starts from the day after their DLA award ends.[171]



The qualifying conditions for PIP have some similarities to those for DLA, but are also significantly different. See Chapter 31 for details. It is possible that a young person claiming PIP on turning 16 will be awarded a different rate of PIP from the rate of DLA they previously received. If this happens, they should get advice and consider seeking a revision and then appealing. Although the qualifying conditions are different, the evidence used to make the previous DLA award may address the same needs for help with daily living and mobility as are relevant to the PIP conditions. The DWP (and the First-tier Tribunal on appeal) should consider this evidence where relevant.[172]

If a young person's DLA entitles your household to a car through the Motability scheme (see p543) and the young person is not awarded the enhanced rate mobility component of PIP when they transfer from DLA, you will no longer be able to continue in the Motability scheme. Contact Motability for details of support and transitional payments available.

***Adults***

The rules in this section apply to adult DLA claimants as well as to children reaching 16. If you are an adult DLA claimant, these rules apply whether you choose to claim PIP or you are notified that your DLA will stop and you are invited to claim PIP.[173]

## 4. **People included in the claim**

You claim disability living allowance for a child under 16.

## 5. **The amount of benefit**

Disability living allowance (DLA) mobility component is paid at one of two weekly rates:[174]

- the lower rate is £29.20;

- the higher rate is £77.05.

DLA care component is paid at one of three weekly rates:[175]

- the lowest rate is £29.20;
- the middle rate is £73.90;
- the highest rate is £110.40.

## 6. Special benefit rules

4

Special rules may apply to children:

- having renal dialysis (see below);
- who are classed as being terminally ill (see below);
- subject to immigration control (see p1269);
- who have come from or are going abroad (see Chapters 57, 58 and 59);
- in hospital or a hospice or living in a care home or similar accommodation, or in a young offenders' institution or other form of detention (see Chapter 38).

### Renal dialysis

If a child is having renal dialysis, special rules may allow them to get the middle rate of disability living allowance (DLA) care component.[176] The rules are the same as for attendance allowance (AA) (see p444).

### Terminal illness

A child is regarded as 'terminally ill' for the purposes of DLA if they have a progressive disease from which their death can reasonably be expected within 12 months.[177] This does not mean that it must be more likely than not that they will die within this period, but rather that their doctor would not be surprised were they to die within 12 months.[178] They are automatically treated as satisfying the conditions for the highest rate of the DLA care component and do not need to satisfy the three-month qualifying period.[179]

They do not automatically get the DLA mobility component. They must satisfy the usual disability conditions (except the three-month qualifying period) and be likely to continue to satisfy them for the next six months or for the rest of their life if this is shorter.[180]

Claims for children who are classed as terminally ill are referred to as 'claims under the special rules' (see p531).

## 7. Claims and backdating

The general rules about claims and backdating are covered in Chapter 44. This section explains the specific rules that apply to disability living allowance (DLA).

## Making a claim

You must make a claim for DLA in writing. You should do this by completing the approved claim form (DLA1 Child). It is best to request a form from the DLA helpline. The DWP may complete a checklist to assess a child's 'potential benefit entitlement'. This is not part of the claim process and you should always be sent a claim form. It is best to send the completed form to the address on it (Freepost DWP DLA Child). You can also take or send it to any other DWP office, and may be able to take or send it to an 'alternative office' (see p1004).



*Forms*

Form DLA1 Child is available from the DLA helpline on 0800 121 4600, textphone: 0800 121 4523 (Relay UK and BSL relay services available).

The form should be date-stamped by the DWP. You have six weeks from the date of your request to return it. If you return it within this time, the date you requested it will be treated as your date of claim.[181] Keep a record of the date you asked for it in case this does not happen.

Claim forms are also available from Citizens Advice or other advice agencies, and gov.uk has a version of the form that you can fill in online and then print. These forms are not date-stamped. If you choose one of these options, send in the completed form as soon as possible as your date of claim is the date your completed form is received by the DWP (see p532).

**Note:** the success of a DLA claim can often depend on how thoroughly you have completed the form. Include all the relevant information and use extra pages if necessary. Keep a copy of the form in case queries arise. For tips on completing the form, see p534.

You must provide any information or evidence required. In certain circumstances, the DWP may accept a written application which is not on the approved form (see p1009).[182] You can amend or withdraw the claim before a decision is made (see p1004).

Claims for children classed as terminally ill are made in a different way.

### Claiming for a child classed as terminally ill

If your child is classed as being terminally ill (see p530), you must tick the box on the claim form to say you are claiming under the 'special rules'.[183] In addition to the claim form you must provide Form SR1, completed by the child's GP, consultant or specialist nurse, detailing their medical condition. **Note:** Form DS1500 is still accepted by the DWP to evidence terminal illness though it has been replaced by Form SR1.[184] You do not need to fill in the parts of the claim form relating to the child's need for personal care, as they will automatically be awarded the highest rate of the care component, but if you also wish to claim the mobility component for them, you must answer the mobility-related questions on the claim form.

## Who should claim

A claim for a child under 16 is made by an appointee (see p1005). This is usually the child's parent. We use 'you' throughout this chapter to refer to the appointee who is claiming on behalf of a child.

Before a child reaches 16, the DWP should ask whether they will continue to need an appointee or will be able to handle their own benefits claims.[185] See p527 for how personal independence payment (PIP) affects DLA for a child when they turn 16.



## Information to support your claim

For the general information requirements that apply to all benefits, see p1006.

It is important that you provide any information required when you claim. Until you do, you may not count as having made a valid claim (see p1008). Provide any missing information as soon as possible or your date of claim may be affected. **Note:** for DLA, there is no requirement to provide a national insurance number for a child under 16.

For suggestions about evidence you might want to provide when completing the claim form, see p534.

Even if you have provided all that was required when you claimed, you may be asked to provide further information to support the claim (see p1009). You may be asked to provide information after DLA is awarded, and if you fail to do so, DLA could be suspended or even terminated (see p1031).

## The date of your claim

The date of a DLA claim is important as it determines when a child's entitlement to DLA starts. This is not necessarily the date from when DLA is paid. For information about when payment of DLA starts, see p538.

The date of claim is the date your request for a claim pack is received by the DWP or an 'alternative office' (see p1004), provided you return the properly completed form within six weeks of the date of your request.[186]

If the DWP has issued a form without date-stamping it, attach a covering letter to the form explaining when and where it was issued and ask to be paid from that date or six weeks before you sent it in.[187] The DWP can extend the six-week deadline if it considers that it is reasonable, so if you return the form late, explain why.[188]

If you are using a downloaded claim form or a blank one issued by an advice agency, your date of claim is the date the DWP receives your completed form.

You must make sure the claim is valid. If it is 'defective', you are given a short time to correct the defects (see p1009). If you do, the claim is treated as having been made when you initially claimed.[189]

### Backdating your claim

It is very important to claim in time. A claim for DLA *cannot* be backdated.[190]

If a child might have qualified for benefit earlier but you did not claim because you were given the wrong information or were misled by the DWP, you could make a complaint and ask for compensation (see p1261).



### If you claim the wrong benefit

If you claim attendance allowance (AA) or PIP by mistake for a child under 16 instead of DLA, the claim for AA or PIP can be treated as a claim for DLA, and vice versa (see p1013).[191]

### Claiming in advance

A claim for DLA can be made before a child has satisfied the three-month qualifying period[192] or any other qualifying condition. Provided you claim no more than three months before they would qualify for DLA, a decision can be made on the claim in advance of their date of entitlement. The date of the claim is the date on which the child qualifies. If you want to claim in advance, make this clear when you claim or the DWP might not consider it.

## Renewal claims

If a child has a fixed-term award of DLA (see p539) and they need to continue getting the benefit at the end of that period, you must make a renewal claim. You should be sent a renewal claim form (DLA1A Child) up to six months before the fixed term is due to end. Take note of the award end date and, if you do not receive a renewal pack six months beforehand, contact the DWP to make a new claim yourself. It is important that you return your completed renewal claim form well before the award expires, as no backdating is possible.

The DWP normally treats a renewal claim as a new claim beginning on the day after an award ends.[193] However, the information you give in the renewal claim may be used to revise or supersede the child's existing award, in which case their entitlement may be changed from an earlier date.[194]

On a renewal claim, a child does not have to serve the three-month qualifying period again, provided they meet all the other qualifying conditions for the rate previously received. The last three months of the previous award is treated as the qualifying period.[195] If they qualify for a different rate when you reclaim, they *do* have to show they have met the qualifying conditions for three months.

When a child approaches age 16, they are usually required to claim PIP, rather than make a renewal claim for DLA (see p527).

See p527 for how the introduction of PIP affects adults who get DLA .

## Completing the claim form

The DLA claim form is long and asks about different aspects of a child's mobility problems and supervision and attention needs. If you find it difficult to complete the form, the DWP can help you by phone or, in some circumstances, send a visiting officer to your home. Most advice agencies can also help. The following tips should help you fill in the form as fully as possible.

- **Give as much detail as you can.** Fill in all the relevant pages and use extra sheets of paper to explain the child's difficulties in full. If the same difficulties apply on more than one page, repeat the information or refer back to earlier in the form. The same help may count towards both the care component and the mobility component – eg, if a child needs attention to deal safely with seizures, this may help satisfy the conditions for the care component and may also mean they need guidance and supervision when walking outdoors.[196] Do not worry if a lot of the questions do not apply to the child. The information you give in just one section could be enough for them to get DLA. There is space to include details of people who know about their difficulties. Include carers and support workers, as well as medical professionals. There is also a statement to be completed by someone who knows the child. If their doctor or hospital fills this in, they should not charge for this.[197] If you do not have anyone who can complete it, leave it blank.
- **Aids and adaptions.** The form asks about those the child uses or has been assessed for. If the DWP thinks that a child can use a particular aid or adaptation, it may decide the child does not need attention or supervision. Therefore, try to explain how useful any equipment actually is, the help the child needs to use it and whether they still need extra help from another person in spite of the equipment. If, for instance, you have had a bath rail fitted, but they still find it very difficult to climb in or out of a bath, explain this. If a child uses picture cards to communicate, explain the amount of help they need to use them, and how long this takes to communicate effectively compared to communication with a non-disabled child.
- **Frequency, variability and duration.** You are asked throughout the form to estimate how long the child needs help for, and how often. Explain:
  - how long they need help for, to show that they need attention for a 'significant portion of the day' (see p523) or 'prolonged' attention at night (see p525);
  - how often they need help, to show that they need 'frequent attention throughout the day' (see p524) or watching over 'repeatedly' during the night (see p526);
  - how many days a week they need help, to establish their overall needs, particularly if they have a variable or fluctuating condition. If the child's condition does not vary but they only receive all the help they need on certain days, say that they need help seven days a week. It is the help needed,

not the help they get, that counts. If they only have problems a few days a week, they may still get DLA. It is not simply comparing the number of 'good' versus 'bad' days.[198] Explain fully the help they need on 'bad' days, but include the help needed on 'good' days for an overall picture.

- **Mobility.** See p513 and p517 and the tactics on p537 for how to describe a child's walking ability or the help they need getting about outdoors. Children can only qualify for DLA mobility component from age three, but problems with getting around may also indicate care or supervision needs, so explain these mobility problems even if the child is younger than three. It can be difficult to explain how a disabled child requires 'substantially more' guidance or supervision outdoors in order to qualify for the lower rate mobility component (see p517). Most young children do not go out, at least in unfamiliar places, on their own. However, a child with a sensory impairment or learning disability may require much more direct or close supervision than a non-disabled child.[199] A child may normally be allowed to walk in the presence of an adult, but a disabled child may require an adult to hold or guide them. Also, even a familiar route may be hazardous to a child whose sight is impaired. It may help to make comparisons with siblings or classmates. An older child with attention deficit disorder may need to be accompanied to school or to local shops, whereas other children might be allowed to go alone.[200]
- **Extra attention, supervision or guidance.** When explaining a child's 'extra' requirements, bear in mind that they must be 'substantially in excess' of those required by a child of the same age who does not have a disability (see p517 and p520). It may be either the extra time you devote or the degree of attention, supervision or guidance a child requires.[201] The fact that it may not be unusual for some children of the same age to require similar assistance is irrelevant. The comparison should be with an 'average child' the same age – ie, a child of average intelligence whose behaviour is neither particularly good nor challenging.[202] Disabled children may need extra help to develop daily living skills, language and social skills. For example, babies with sensory impairments may require more physical stimulation to aid parental bonding and develop communication skills. A child with a disability might need intensive help with eating, rather than be expected to eat unaided or only need certain foods cut up. Similarly, a child with a disability may need supervision to avoid dangers that children would usually be expected to deal with themselves by their age. A child with a disability may need help to use toys, may need to be coaxed to explore their environment and may develop these skills later than other children. Consider also whether certain activities are more difficult for the child than usual – eg, if they cause them pain, or make them dizzy, tired or breathless. If they take a long time to perform particular tasks, explain this. Also say if they are not able to perform a particular activity adequately – eg, if they cannot bend to reach their feet when washing.

- **Sensory impairments.** There are sections on help with seeing, hearing, speaking and communication. The specific needs of deaf children or blind children can be described here. Blind children may need extra help with lots of daily activities. Explain the help required throughout the form. For example, they may need someone to tell them if they have stains on their clothes or if their hands are clean – you should explain these problems in the 'dressing' and 'washing' sections and not just in the 'seeing' section. The help a child with a sensory impairment needs to undertake social and leisure activities should also be explained.
- **Communicating.** Deaf children whose first language is British Sign Language may need help to understand or communicate in written or spoken English. Blind children will not only need help to understand written information, but may also need help to learn braille. Children with learning difficulties may need help to express themselves, understand other people or follow instructions or warnings.
- **Mental disabilities.** In the sections on help with communication and on supervision during the day, mention any problems caused by anxiety, intrusive thoughts or anger, or learning difficulties. Remember that a child who needs encouraging or prompting to do things can get DLA, as well as a child who needs physical help with them. If they need assistance to undertake social or leisure activities, information about that help may also fit in the form's mobility section. At the end of the form is a page to 'tell us anything else you think we should know'. It often helps to summarise mental health problems here and explain any other attention or supervision needs the child has.
- **About the child's development.** Describing the extra care or supervision that a child needs compared to others is extremely important. If you are not sure when a child should normally be crawling, walking, speaking, playing with others, understanding instructions, using the toilet independently, feeding themselves, and so on, ask your health visitor or GP. For example, most children pick up and eat food by 8–12 months. Therefore, if you are still feeding a child after 12 months, you are providing attention that a non-disabled child of the same age would not need. It often helps to make comparisons with other children you know. When completing renewal forms, always describe all the child's needs even if you think the DWP already knows about them. Bear in mind that, if you do not mention something, the DWP may suppose that the child no longer needs the same help as they did when they were younger.
- **Children of nursery or school age.** Children who have a disability, particularly those with sensory impairments or learning disabilities, usually require extra help with learning and school work. This should be explained, as well as other help (eg, help going to the toilet) that they may need at school or nursery. Extra help in the classroom or with homework due to special educational needs can count towards a child's attention needs, as cognition is a bodily

function of the brain (see p521).[203] Straightforward teaching would probably not be sufficiently intimate to qualify,[204] but additional help (eg, because of dyslexia) may count.[205]

### *What evidence should you provide?*

When making a claim, and especially when preparing for an appeal, ensure that you have as much evidence as possible to support what you say about the child in the claim form. This can include any of the following.

**Evidence that you provide about your knowledge of the child**



**About their care needs.** Often the easiest way for the DWP or First-tier Tribunal to get a picture of a child's care needs and their pattern is for you to keep a diary for a week or a month, to record variations in their condition and the help they need. This can be particularly useful if they have unpredictable care needs or experience irregular events, such as seizures or falls, which mean that they need extra supervision. Usually this is best presented as a table. You can also ask other carers, friends or family members to keep a diary or write letters in support of the claim or appeal.

**About their walking ability.** Walk outdoors with the child to measure the distance they can walk without severe discomfort, then write a description of the time it takes to walk this far. It may help to give an example of the distance – eg, 'They can walk past five houses – about 40 metres.'

Describe the terrain. Is it rough or uneven? Are there steps or slopes which present them with problems?

Explain what sort of discomfort they experience (eg, pain or breathlessness) and how it changes as they walk.

Describe their manner of walking – eg, they may have problems with balance, or may walk with a limp, drag their feet or shuffle.

Say if the child needs to stop to rest. Try to explain how far they can walk before they need to stop, and for how long they need to rest. Bear in mind that if they can walk a further distance without severe discomfort after a brief rest, it is the total distance that counts.

You can use the 'Directions' function on Google Maps to measure distances.

Go somewhere unfamiliar with the child and note down all the difficulties the child has and the guidance they need.

**Evidence from third parties**

You can send photocopies of any reports with the claim form.

**Doctors' reports.** These could be reports already provided by specialists to the child's GP. Often hospital doctors will send copies of reports they write to the child's parent/guardian. Ask the GP for copies of any reports you do not have from the child's medical records. Alternatively, ask the GP or specialist to write a specific letter for the child's claim or appeal. The doctor may charge for this. It is not usually worth providing hospital appointment letters and other routine documents which do not comment on the child's diagnosis, treatment or disability, but it may be if the letter is your only evidence of a referral. The

DWP may request a specific report from the child's GP. It can help to make an appointment to discuss with the GP beforehand the child's day-to-day problems.

**Reports from other medical professionals.** Reports from health visitors, physiotherapists, psychiatric and other specialist nurses and occupational therapists can often provide more detailed information about a child's disability and how it affects their day-to-day life than reports from doctors, who only discuss symptoms and treatment. If you know a report has been produced but you do not have a copy, ask the child's GP to print it from their medical records.

**Social services and educational reports.** If a child has had a social care needs assessment, statement of special educational needs or other care or support plan, this may provide useful supporting evidence of the extra help they need.

**DWP medical services assessments.** The DWP's decisions can be based on reports by doctors or other healthcare professionals acting on behalf of the DWP. These should not necessarily be preferred to your own or your GP's evidence. You should examine any report carefully and explain why any unhelpful findings or assessments are wrong. If, however, the assessment report supports your claim, you should highlight this.

### How a claim is dealt with

DLA can be awarded on the basis of the claim form alone, but the DWP may contact someone you named on the form for more information. It is a good idea to include details of all the medical professionals and other people who know and understand the child's needs and, if possible, enclose evidence from them.

The DWP may phone you to ask for further information. If you do not want to be phoned, write this clearly on the claim form.

If the DWP cannot get sufficient information, it may also arrange for the child to be given a medical examination by a healthcare professional acting on behalf of the DWP, who will sometimes visit them at home.

If you (or an older child) refuse a medical examination 'without good cause', the claim is likely to be refused.[206]

The DWP aims to deal with new claims for DLA within 40 working days.[207] Claims made under the special rules (see p530) should be decided more quickly. If you disagree with the decision, you can ask for a revision and then appeal (see Chapters 50 and 51) on behalf of the child. See p537 for suggestions about the evidence you can use to support a claim, revision or appeal.

## 8. Getting paid

The general rules on getting paid are covered in Chapter 45. This section explains the specific rules that apply to disability living allowance (DLA).

As DLA is claimed for a child under the age of 16, it is usually paid to an adult with whom they are living. The DWP appoints the adult (an appointee) to act on the child's behalf. The appointee is normally the child's parent.[208]

DLA can continue to be paid to the appointee in some circumstances when the child and appointee are not living together, including during a temporary separation of up to 12 weeks, or when the child is absent at a boarding school or in residential care (although other rules may mean that payment stops in such circumstances – see Chapter 38). DLA ceases to be paid to the appointee immediately when the child is in the care of a local authority or any similar arrangement, unless it is not intended to last for more than 12 weeks.[209]



***When is disability living allowance paid?***

DLA is normally paid on a Wednesday, but the DWP can vary the payday.[210] It is usually paid every four weeks in arrears. However:

- DLA can be paid at shorter intervals in individual cases;[211]
- DLA for children classed as terminally ill, paid under the 'special rules', can be paid weekly.

If the child leaves a care home and expects to return there within 28 days, DLA can be paid at a daily rate for days at home.[212]

Note:

- The higher rate of the DLA mobility component can be paid direct to Motability if you have use of a car through the scheme (see p543).
- Even if you have been sanctioned for a benefit offence (see p1111), you must be paid DLA.
- If payment of DLA is delayed, see p1123. If you wish to complain about how a claim has been dealt with, or claim compensation, see Chapter 55.
- If payment of a child's DLA is suspended, see p1031. If you have been overpaid DLA, you might have to repay it (see Chapter 47) and, in some circumstances, you may have to pay a penalty (see p1101). If you have been accused of fraud, see Chapter 48.
- If you are owed arrears of DLA, these can be paid in instalments (see p1018).

## Length of awards

An award of DLA can be made for a fixed period or indefinitely.[213] An award's length depends on how long the DWP estimates the child's current needs may last.

Awards are usually made for at least six months because of the requirement that a child should satisfy the disability conditions for the next six months. However, there is no legal minimum length for an award.[214] If you think benefit should be awarded for longer than it has been, perhaps because the child's condition is such that their care or mobility needs will not decrease, consider asking for a revision (see p1130). Bear in mind that if you challenge the length of an award, the rate of the award can also be reconsidered. Whatever the length of an award, the DWP can reduce or stop it at any time if these are grounds for revision or supersession (see Chapter 50).

If an award is for a fixed period, you will be invited to make a renewal claim up to six months before the award runs out (see p533).

A 'special rules' award (see p530) on the basis of terminal illness is normally made for three years.

4

Although DLA has two components, there can only be a single DLA award, consisting of one or both components. If a child has an award of both components, they must be aligned to end on the same day even if they started at different times.[215]

See p527 for how personal independence payment affects DLA when a child reaches 16 (even if they currently have an indefinite award of DLA).

## Change of circumstances

You must report any change in a child's circumstances that you have been told you must report, as well as any that you might reasonably be expected to know might affect their right to, the amount of, or payment of DLA. You should do this as soon as possible, preferably in writing. See p1030 for further information. It is usually best to get independent advice before reporting a change in a child's health that you think might affect their entitlement to DLA.

If a child's condition deteriorates so that they become eligible for a higher rate or another component, the higher rate or additional component can be paid from the day they become eligible, provided you tell the DWP no later than a month after they complete the three-month qualifying period. If you do not report a change of circumstances within the month, it may be sufficient to do so within 13 months if there were 'special circumstances' that meant it was not practical to report the change earlier.[216] If payment of (but not entitlement to) DLA has stopped (eg, while a child is in a care home), still notify the DWP of any change so that the correct rate is paid when payment resumes.

If a child's condition improves so that they should drop down a rate, lose a component or lose benefit altogether, the new decision normally takes effect from the date you tell the DWP of the improvement, or from the date of the decision if the DWP changed it without your asking.[217] It only takes effect from an earlier date (and causes an overpayment) if you should have realised earlier that the change should have been reported. It is accepted that it may be difficult to realise when a gradual improvement begins to affect benefit entitlement.[218]

*Moving to or from Scotland*

If a child who gets DLA and lives in another part of the UK moves to Scotland, they should notify the DWP.[219] At the time of writing, a child in this situation will then be transferred to child disability payment (CDP – see Chapter 64) automatically without having to make a claim. The rules may change in the course of 2025/26, meaning that automatic transfer will no longer be possible and a new claim for CDP will be required.[220] See CPAG's *Welfare Rights Bulletin* or the online edition of this *Handbook* for updates. DLA can continue for a maximum of 13 weeks after a move to Scotland.[221] If a child who lives in Scotland and gets CDP moves to another part of the UK, they continue to be treated as resident in Scotland and entitled to CDP for 13 weeks to allow them time to claim DLA.[222] The DLA claim form includes questions to identify anyone who has recently moved from Scotland to England or Wales and who gets, or is waiting on a decision on a claim for, CDP.



## 9. Tax, other benefits and the benefit cap

### Tax

Disability living allowance (DLA) is not taxable.[223]

### Means-tested benefits

DLA for a child is not taken into account as income when calculating any of the means-tested benefits for a person who has responsibility for the child. DLA is paid on top of these and getting DLA can increase the amount of them.

If you are responsible for a child who is entitled to DLA, you may as a result qualify for one or more of the following extra amounts:

- a disabled child addition in your universal credit (UC) (see p68). This is paid at the higher rate if they are entitled to the highest rate care component. **Note:** the disabled child addition is included for the child even if the child element is not received because of the 'two-child limit' (see p68);
- a disabled child premium (see p271) in your housing benefit (HB). If they get the highest rate care component, your HB also includes an enhanced disability premium (see p273).

If you or your partner receive DLA, you may as a result qualify for one or more of the following extra amounts:

- a limited capability for work-related activity element in your UC if you or your partner are entitled to the highest rate of the DLA care component and are aged 66 or over (see p918). Alternatively, your UC may include a limited capability for work element if you or your partner are entitled to DLA, but not

the highest rate of the care component, and are 66 or over, in some circumstances (see p71 and p897);
- a disability premium (see p272) in your HB , unless you have reached pension age;
- an enhanced disability premium (see p273) in your income-related employment and support allowance (ESA) and HB if you or your partner are entitled to the highest rate DLA care component and are under pension age;
- a severe disability premium/addition in your income-related ESA, the guarantee credit of pension credit (PC) and HB, if you receive the highest or middle rate care component and meet the other conditions for that premium/ addition (see p275).



No housing costs contributions from a non-dependant are taken into account when calculating your UC housing costs element if you, your partner or the non-dependant get the DLA middle or highest rate care component, or would get it but for being in hospital (see p109). If you or your partner get any rate of the DLA care component, non-dependant deductions are *not* made from any housing costs covered by your HB (see p208), or from any housing costs included in your income-related ESA or the guarantee credit of PC (see p291).

## Non-means-tested benefits

You can get DLA in addition to any other non-means-tested benefits, except that:
- you cannot be paid both DLA and personal independence payment;
- you cannot be entitled to both DLA and child disability payment;[224]
- DLA overlaps with armed forces independence payment;[225]
- DLA care component overlaps with attendance allowance and constant attendance allowance under the industrial injuries scheme (see p600) or war pensions scheme (see p779);[226]
- DLA mobility component overlaps with the war pensioners' mobility supplement payable under the war pensions scheme (see p779).[227]

See p1021 for details of the overlapping benefits rules.

A person who regularly looks after a child or adult who gets the highest or middle rate care component may be entitled to carer's allowance (CA) (see Chapter 22) or carer support payment (CSP) (see p1467), and they (or their partner if claiming as a couple) may also get a carer element in UC (see p75), a carer premium in income-related ESA or HB, or a carer addition in the guarantee credit of PC (see p279). However, if you are an adult and your carer gets CA or CSP or a carer element in UC, it may affect your entitlement to a severe disability premium (or additional amount), so always get advice.

A young person aged 16, 17 or 18 living in Scotland who cannot get CA or CSP may be able to get a young carer grant for looking after you (see p1476).

## The benefit cap

DLA is *not* one of the specified benefits for the benefit cap. The benefit cap does *not* apply if you, your partner or child get DLA, even if it is not paid because the person entitled is in hospital or a care home. In other cases, it only applies if you are getting UC or HB. See p1025 for further information.

## Passports and other sources of help

You qualify for a Christmas bonus if you receive DLA at any rate (see p783). If you are on a low income, you may be entitled to council tax reduction (see p761).

If you get the higher rate mobility component, you or your carer can be exempt from paying road tax on a car used solely by, or for, you. Contact the DLA helpline (see p531) for an exemption certificate. You may be able to get a provisional driving licence from age 16 instead of 17.

If you get the higher rate mobility component, you should qualify for the blue badge scheme of parking concessions. Contact your local authority.

If any member of your household receives DLA at any rate, you can get a grant for help with insulation and other energy efficiency measures in your home (see p782) and may be entitled to other benefits, such as concessionary travel.

### Motability

Motability is a charity that runs a scheme to help you lease or buy a car if you receive (or a child for whom you are responsible receives) the higher rate of DLA mobility component for 12 months or more (see p512). DLA mobility component is paid direct to Motability.[228] You may also have to make extra payments. For further details, phone 0300 456 4566 or visit motability.co.uk.

# Notes

1. **Disability living allowance mobility component**
   1 ss71(6) and 73 SSCBA 1992
   2 CM/5/1986; *BP v SSWP* [2009] UKUT 90 (AAC)
   3 s73 SSCBA 1992; reg 12(1)(b) SS(DLA) Regs
   4 Reg 12(1)(a) SS(DLA) Regs
   5 R(M) 3/78
   6 Reg 12(1)(a) SS(DLA) Regs; R(M) 2/78; R(DLA) 4/06
   7 CDLA/1525/2008
   8 CDLA/2822/1999; CDLA/4329/2001
   9 *MMF v SSWP (DLA)* [2012] UKUT 312 (AAC)
   10 R(M) 3/86; CSDLA/202/2007; CDLA/3839/2007; *DM v SSWP (DLA)* [2010] UKUT 375 (AAC)
   11 R(M) 2/89; CDLA/97/2001; *Sandhu v SSWP* [2010] EWCA Civ 962
   12 Reg 12(1)(b) and (4) SS(DLA) Regs
   13 R(M) 2/89
   14 CDLA/3188/2002; *HJ v SSWP (DLA)* [2010] UKUT 307 (AAC)

15 R(M) 1/95; CSDLA/171/1998
16 CM/208/1989
17 *JK v SSWP (DLA)* [2010] UKUT 197 (AAC)
18 CDLA/1389/1997; CDLA/2195/2008
19 R(M) 1/81
20 R(M) 2/92
21 R(M) 1/83
22 CM/267/93; CDLA/608/1994; R(DLA) 4/03
23 R(DLA) 4/04
24 *Hewitt and Diment v CAO*, 29 June 1998, reported as R(DLA) 6/99
25 R(M) 1/98; CDLA/3941/2005 interpreted 'exertion' to mean the activity of walking 'however slight the exertion'
26 *KS v SSWP (DLA)* [2013] UKUT 390 (AAC)
27 Reg 12(1)(b) SS(DLA) Regs
28 Reg 12(2) and (3) SS(DLA) Regs
29 R(DLA) 3/95
30 Sch 2 SS(GB) Regs; *GB v SSWP (DLA)* [2016] UKUT 566 (AAC)
31 Reg 34(2) and Sch 3 Parts II and III SS(IIPD) Regs
32 Reg 12(2)(b) SS(DLA) Regs
33 s73(1AB) SSCBA 1992; reg 12(1A) SS(DLA) Regs
34 *NC v SSWP (DLA)* [2012] UKUT 384 (AAC)
35 *SSWP v IK (DLA)* [2014] UKUT 174 (AAC)
36 *SSWP v YR (DLA)* [2014] UKUT 80 (AAC)
37 s73(3) SSCBA 1992; reg 12(5) and (6) SS(DLA) Regs
38 *JH v SSWP (DLA)* [2010] UKUT 456 (AAC); *AH v SSWP (DLA)* [2012] UKUT 387 (AAC); *SSWP v MG (DLA)* [2012] UKUT 429 (AAC)
39 R(M) 3/86; CSDLA/202/2007
40 *N McM v SSWP (DLA)* [2014] UKUT 312 (AAC); para 61353 DMG
41 R(DLA) 3/98; *MP v SSWP (DLA)* [2014] UKUT 426 (AAC)
42 *M (a child) v CAO*, 29 October 1999, reported as R(DLA) 1/00
43 CDLA/95/1995; *DM v SSWP (DLA)* [2015] UKUT 87 (AAC); *EC (by SC) v SSWP (DLA)* [2017] UKUT 391 (AAC)
44 CDLA/3215/2001; *CD v SSWP (DLA)* [2013] UKUT 68 (AAC); *MP v SSWP (DLA)* [2014] UKUT 426 (AAC)
45 CDLA/2054/1998
46 R(DLA) 7/02; R(DLA) 9/02; CDLA/3244/2001; CDLA/2955/2008; *SSWP v DM (DLA)* [2010] UKUT 318 (AAC); *SSWP v MG (DLA)* [2012] UKUT 429 (AAC); see also paras 61381-61384 DMG
47 *XTC v SSWP (DLA)* [2020] UKUT 342 (AAC); *CC v DfC (DLA)* [2024] NICom18, a Northern Ireland case likely to be persuasive in Great Britain
48 *XTC v SSWP (DLA)* [2020] UKUT 342 (AAC)
49 *TV v SSWP (DLA)* [2013] UKUT 364 (AAC)
50 s73(1)(d) SSCBA 1992. See also DWP, *Medical guidance for DLA decision makers (child cases): staff guide*, July 2024.
51 s73(1)(d) SSCBA 1992
52 CDLA/42/1994
53 s73(4A) SSCBA 1992
54 *BM v SSWP (DLA)* [2015] UKUT 18 (AAC); *KC-M S (by EC) v SSWP (DLA)* [2015] UKUT 284 (AAC)
55 CDLA/2268/1999
56 R(DLA) 3/04
57 CDLA/42/1994
58 CDLA/42/1994
59 CDLA/42/1994; CDLA/3360/1995; CSDLA/591/1997; CDLA/2643/1998
60 R(DLA) 4/01
61 R(DLA) 6/05
62 R(DLA) 4/01
63 R(DLA) 4/01
64 CDLA/42/1994; R(DLA) 3/04
65 CDLA/2364/1995 and *KH v SSWP (DLA)* [2015] UKUT 8 (AAC), but see CDLA/42/1994
66 CDLA/2142/2005
67 Reg 12(7) and (8) SS(DLA) Regs; R(DLA) 3/04; CDLA/2409/2003; R(DLA) 6/05; *SSWP v DC (DLA)* [2011] UKUT 235 (AAC)

2. **Disability living allowance care component**

68 ss71(6) and 72 SSCBA 1992
69 s72(1)(a) and (4)(c) SSCBA 1992
70 s72(4)(b) SSCBA 1992
71 Reg 7 SS(DLA) Regs
72 s72(4)(a) SSCBA 1992
73 s72(5) SSCBA 1992
74 s72(1)(b) SSCBA 1992
75 s72(1)(c) SSCBA 1992
76 s72(1A)(b) SSCBA 1992
77 s72(5) SSCBA 1992
78 R(DLA) 1/05; *BM v SSWP (DLA)* [2015] UKUT 18 (AAC), reported as [2015] AACR 29
79 R(DLA) 3/06, tribunal of commissioners. See also DWP, *Medical guidance for DLA decision makers (child cases): staff guide*, July 2024, available at gov.uk.
80 CDLA/4475/04
81 R(DLA) 3/06, tribunal of commissioners

82 R(A) 3/86; *Mallinson v Secretary of State for Social Security*, 21 April 1994 (HL), reported as R(A) 3/94
83 *Secretary of State for Social Security v Fairey (aka Halliday)*, 21 May 1997 (HL), reported as R(A) 2/98; see also para 61107 DMG
84 R(A) 3/89
85 R(A) 5/90
86 CDLA/3925/1997; *HJ v SSWP (DLA)* [2010] UKUT 307 (AAC)
87 R(DLA) 10/02
88 Reg 10C SS(DLA) Regs; *R v National Insurance Commissioner ex parte Secretary of State for Social Services* [1981] 1 WLR 1017 (CA), also reported as R(A) 2/80
89 R(A) 1/06
90 *Mallinson v Secretary of State for Social Security*, 21 April 1994 (HL), reported as R(A) 3/94
91 CA/177/1988; CDLA/14696/1996; R(DLA) 1/07, tribunal of commissioners
92 paras 61105 and 61535 DMG
93 R(DLA) 1/07, tribunal of commissioners; see also para 61101 DMG
94 *Mallinson v Secretary of State for Social Security*, 21 April 1994 (HL), reported as R(A) 3/94
95 *SJ v SSWP (DLA)* [2014] UKUT 222 (AAC)
96 R(A) 3/74
97 R(A) 2/75
98 CA/86/1987
99 R(DLA) 1/07, tribunal of commissioners
100 *R v Social Security Commissioner ex parte Butler*, February 1984, unreported; *Secretary of State for Social Security v Fairey (aka Halliday)*, 21 May 1997 (HL), reported as R(A) 2/98
101 *Secretary of State for Social Security v Fairey (aka Halliday)*, 21 May 1997 (HL), reported as R(A) 2/98; R(DLA) 1/02; R(DLA) 2/02; R(DLA) 3/02; *SSWP v PV (DLA)* [2010] UKUT 33 (AAC)
102 R(DLA) 2/02
103 CDLA/3607/2001
104 *Cockburn v CAO and Another*, 21 May 1997 (HL), reported as R(A) 2/98; *Ramsden v SSWP*, 31 January 2003 (CA), reported as R(DLA) 2/03; *KH (by CH) v SSWP (DLA)* [2022] UKUT 303 (AAC)
105 *R v National Insurance Commissioner ex parte Secretary of State for Social Services* [1981] 1 WLR 1017 (CA), reported as R(A) 2/80
106 CDLA/267/1994, CDLA/11652/1995, CDLA/3711/1995, CDLA/12381/1996, CDLA/16996/1996, CDLA/16129/1996 and CDLA/4352/1999 are useful, but conflict with CSDLA/281/1996 and CSDLA/314/1997
107 CDLA/267/1994
108 *Secretary of State for Social Security v Fairey (aka Halliday)*, 21 May 1997 (HL), reported as R(A) 2/98
109 CDLA/16129/1996, CDLA/16996/1996 and CDLA/4352/1999 are useful, but conflict with CSDLA/314/1997
110 CDLA/4352/1999 and CDLA/5216/1998, the latter being more restrictive
111 CDLA/4352/1999
112 CDLA/5216/1998
113 R(DLA) 1/98
114 s72(1)(a)(i) SSCBA 1992
115 R(DLA) 8/02
116 CDLA/58/1993
117 CSDLA/29/1994
118 *Ramsden v SSWP*, 31 January 2003 (CA), reported as R(DLA) 2/03; *SO v SSWP (DLA)* [2019] UKUT 272 (AAC)
119 s72(1)(b)(i) SSCBA 1992
120 R(DLA) 5/05
121 CA/140/1985
122 *AB v SSWP (DLA)* [2015] UKUT 522 (AAC)
123 s72(1)(b)(ii) SSCBA 1992
124 R(A) 1/83
125 *RJ, GMcL and CS v SSWP (PIP)* [2017] UKUT 105 (AAC), reported as [2017] AACR 32. Although this case relates to PIP, the same arguments about the likelihood of harm occurring and the need for supervision to prevent it also apply to DLA.
126 CA/15/1979, approved in R(A) 1/83
127 R(A) 2/89
128 CA/33/1984
129 R(A) 3/92
130 R(A) 1/73
131 *CP v SSWP (DLA)* [2013] UKUT 230 (AAC)
132 *Moran v Secretary of State for Social Services, The Times*, 14 March 1987 (CA), reported as R(A) 1/88
133 R(A) 5/81
134 *R v National Insurance Commissioner ex parte Secretary of State for Social Services* [1974] 1 WLR 1290 (DC), reported as R(A) 4/74
135 R(A) 1/04
136 CDLA/2852/2002
137 CDLA/997/2003; *LB v SSWP (DLA)* [2018] UKUT 445 (AAC)

138 R(A) 1/78
139 s72(1)(c)(i) SSCBA 1992
140 R(DLA) 5/05
141 R(DLA) 5/05
142 *AD v SSWP (DLA)* [2017] UKUT 29 (AAC)
143 R(A) 3/78
144 *ES (by CS, appointee) v SSWP (DLA)* [2020] UKUT 10 (AAC)
145 s72(1)(c)(ii) SSCBA 1992
146 Vol 10 Ch 61 para 61165 DMG
147 Vol 10 Ch 61 para 61164 DMG



3. **The rules about your age**
148 s73(1A) SSCBA 1992
149 s72(2) and (5) SSCBA 1992
150 Reg 4(1)(a) PIP(TP) Regs
151 Reg 3 and Sch 1 SS(DLA) Regs
152 Reg 3(5) and (6) PIP(TP) Regs
153 Reg 27 PIP(TP) Regs
154 DWP, *Personal Independence Payment Handbook*, September 2024, under 'DLA claimants who have turned 65 after 8 April 2013', available at gov.uk
155 Reg 4 PIP(TP) Regs
156 Regs 12, 13 and 15 PIP(TP) Regs
157 DWP, *Personal Independence Payment Handbook,* September 2024, under 'Choosing to claim PIP before invited to do so by DWP', available at gov.uk
158 Reg 3(3) PIP(TP) Regs
159 Reg 3(4A) and (5B) PIP(TP) Regs
160 Reg 18 PIP(TP) Regs
161 Reg 3(4) PIP(TP) Regs; DWP, *Personal Independence Payment Handbook*, September 2024, under 'PIP and existing DLA special rules claimants', available at gov.uk
162 Reg 8(4) PIP(TP) Regs
163 Regs 3 and 7 PIP(TP) Regs
164 Regs 9, 10, 11 and 17 PIP(TP) Regs
165 Reg 17(1)(b)(ii) and (3) PIP(TP) Regs
166 Regs 13(1) and 17(2)(b) PIP(TP) Regs; *SR v SSWP (PIP)* [2024] UKUT 308 (AAC)
167 Reg 17(1) and (3) PIP(TP) Regs
168 Reg 20 PIP(TP) Regs
169 Reg 13(1) PIP(TP) Regs
170 *OM v SSWP (PIP)* [2017] UKUT 458 (AAC)
171 Regs 13(2) and 17(2)(b) PIP(TP) Regs
172 R(M) 1/96; *CH and KN v SSWP (PIP)* [2018] UKUT 330 (AAC); *CH (by TH) v SSWP (PIP)* [2020] UKUT 70 (AAC)
173 Reg 12 PIP(TP) Regs

5. **The amount of benefit**
174 Reg 4(2) SS(DLA) Regs
175 Reg 4(1) SS(DLA) Regs

6. **Special benefit rules**
176 Reg 7 SS(DLA) Regs
177 ss66(2)(a) and 72(5) SSCBA 1992
178 DWP, *The 'Special Rules': how the benefit system supports people nearing the end of life,* September 2024, available at gov.uk
179 s72(5) SSCBA 1992
180 s73(9)(b)(ii) and (12) SSCBA 1992

7. **Claims and backdating**
181 Reg 6(8), (8A) and (9) SS(C&P) Regs
182 Reg 4(1) SS(C&P) Regs
183 ss72(5) and 73(12) SSCBA 1992; regs 3(9)(b) and 6(6)(c) SS&CS(DA) Regs
184 DWP, *The 'Special Rules': how the benefit system supports people nearing the end of life,* September 2024, available at gov.uk
185 For the process of moving from an appointee for a child getting DLA to one for a person aged 16 or over claiming PIP, see regs 28 and 29 PIP(TP) Regs and *P v SSWP (PIP)* [2018] UKUT 359 (AAC)
186 Reg 6(8), (8A) and (9) SS(C&P) Regs
187 Reg 6(8A) SS(C&P) Regs
188 Reg 6(9) SS(C&P) Regs; *SNN v SSWP (PIP)* [2018] UKUT 210 (AAC) - although decided on similar rules for PIP, this case considers circumstances that may be reasonable and the discussion is relevant for DLA claims
189 Reg 6(1)(b) SS(C&P) Regs
190 s76(1) SSCBA 1992
191 Reg 9(1) and Sch 1 SS(C&P) Regs; reg 25(3) and (4) UC,PIP,JSA&ESA (C&P) Regs
192 Reg 13A(1) SS(C&P) Regs
193 Reg 13C SS(C&P) Regs
194 CDLA/14895/1996
195 Regs 6 and 11 SS(DLA) Regs
196 R(DLA) 4/01; CDLA/333/2005; *DN v SSWP (DLA)* [2016] UKUT 233 (AAC)
197 DWP, *DWP Medical (Factual) Reports: a guide to completion,* September 2024
198 R(A) 2/74; see also *Moyna v SSWP,* 31 July 2003 (HL), reported as R(DLA) 7/03; *DJ v SSWP (DLA)* [2016] UKUT 169 (AAC)
199 CDLA/2268/1999
200 CDLA/4806/2002
201 CSDLA/76/1998
202 CA/92/1992; *DJ v SSWP (DLA)* [2016] UKUT 169 (AAC)
203 *SSWP v Hughes (a minor)*, reported as R(DLA) 1/04
204 CDLA/1983/2006
205 *KM v SSWP (DLA)* [2013] UKUT 159 (AAC), reported as [2014] AACR 2

206 s19(3) SSA 1998
207 House of Commons, *Hansard*, Written question UIN 9516, answered 24 October 2024, available at questions-statements.parliament.uk

8. **Getting paid**
208 Reg 43 SS(C&P) Regs
209 Reg 43 SS(C&P) Regs
210 Reg 22(3) and Sch 6 SS(C&P) Regs
211 Reg 22 SS(C&P) Regs
212 Reg 25 SS(C&P) Regs
213 s71(3) SSCBA 1992
214 R(DLA) 11/02
215 s71(3) SSCBA 1992; CDLA/2887/2008
216 Regs 7(9) and 8 SS&CS(DA) Regs
217 s10(5) SSA 1998
218 Reg 7(2)(c) SS&CS(DA) Regs; *RD v SSWP (DLA)* [2011] UKUT 95 (AAC); *DC v SSWP (DLA)* [2011] UKUT 336 (AAC)
219 SSS, *Child Disability Payment decision making guide: when an individual in receipt of DLAC moves to Scotland*, January 2025, available at socialsecurity.gov.scot
220 Reg 7 SS(CPCTMA)(S) Regs
221 Reg 2ZA SS(DLA) Regs
222 Regs 35 and 36 DACYP(S) Regs

9. **Tax, other benefits and the benefit cap**
223 s677 IT(EP)A 2003
224 s71(7) SSCBA 1992
225 Art 24C The Armed Forces and Reserve Forces (Compensation Scheme) Order 2011 No.517
226 Sch 1 para 5 SS(OB) Regs
227 Reg 42(1)(b)(ii) SS(C&P) Regs
228 Regs 44, 45 and 46 SS(C&P) Regs

# Chapter 25

# Discretionary housing payments

4

**This chapter covers:**

1. Who can get discretionary housing payments (below)
2. The rules about your age (p550)
3. People included in the claim (p551)
4. The amount of discretionary housing payments (p551)
5. Claims, decisions and getting paid (p552)
6. Tax, other benefits and the benefit cap (p553)

## Key facts

- You must be entitled to help with your rent in universal credit (UC) or housing benefit (HB) to get discretionary housing payments (DHPs).
- DHPs are administered and paid by your local authority. They can be made if you need help to meet your housing costs – eg, because your UC or HB does not cover your full rent due to a restriction, or due to deductions for non-dependants, or you are affected by the benefit cap.
- DHPs can be made for lump-sum payments – eg, for rent in advance or a deposit for a new home, or if you have removal expenses.
- Payments are discretionary. They are paid from a cash-limited budget allocated to your local authority.
- In Scotland, the Scottish government has committed to fully fund DHPs to any eligible person affected by the 'bedroom tax' or benefit cap.
- You cannot appeal against a DHP decision, but you can ask the local authority for a review, complain, escalate a complaint to an ombudsman or seek judicial review.

## 1. Who can get discretionary housing payments

A local authority can pay you discretionary housing payments (DHPs) if you are entitled to:[1]

- universal credit (UC) and your maximum amount includes a housing costs element for rent (see Chapter 6), or (in England and Wales only) would include one but for the fact that you live in specified or temporary accommodation (see p91 for what counts); *or*
- housing benefit (HB) (see Chapter 10).

You must also appear to the local authority to require financial assistance, in addition to the benefit to which you are already entitled, in order to meet your 'housing costs'. Housing costs are not defined in the rules. You can get DHPs even if your benefit is being paid direct to your landlord.

4

### *When can discretionary housing payments be made?*

Examples of when DHPs can be made include:[2]

- if your UC or HB award is reduced due to:
  - the benefit cap (see p1025) or the social sector rent restriction rules (the 'bedroom tax') (see p115 and p313). See below if you are in Scotland; *or*
  - any of the other rent restriction rules in Chapter 6 or Chapter 15; *or*
  - the 'two-child limit' (see p69 and p268); *or*
  - a non-dependant deduction (see p109 and p207); *or*
- lump-sum payments for rent in advance, deposits or removal expenses; *or*
- where you have to pay housing costs for two homes but only get UC or HB for one of them.

The decision to award you a DHP is always discretionary, so you are not guaranteed to get one in the circumstances listed above (but see below if you are in Scotland). You may also get a DHP in other circumstances where you need financial assistance to meet your housing costs.

Official guidance suggests local authorities may wish to prioritise certain groups, including those escaping domestic abuse, care leavers under 35 and where a disabled person is a member of your household.[3] In Scotland, the guidance also suggests DHPs be used to tackle and reduce child poverty by targeting payments at six priority family types at greatest risk, and in circumstances where families might be under additional financial pressure.[4]

The local authority has the discretion *whether* to pay you, the *amount* to pay you (within certain limits) and over what *period* to pay you.[5] The rules do not limit the length of time over which DHPs can be paid, so this can be indefinite.

In Scotland, the Scottish government funds DHPs to fully mitigate the 'bedroom tax' and benefit cap, so if you apply to your local authority for a DHP for a loss of benefit due to the bedroom tax or benefit cap, you should receive one.[6]

DWP guidance to local authorities in England and Wales is at gov.uk/government/publications/discretionary-housing-payments-guidance-manual.

The Scottish government DHP guidance to local authorities is at gov.scot/publications/scottish-discretionary-housing-payment-guidance-manual/documents.

## When discretionary housing payments cannot be made

DHPs cannot be made to you if you need financial assistance as a consequence of any of the following:[7]



- (England and Wales only) ineligible service charges for UC or HB (see p92 and p203);
- water and sewerage charges;
- liability for council tax. Instead, you may be able to get help from your local authority's council tax reduction scheme (see p761);
- your rent payments increasing to cover arrears of rent, service charges or other unpaid charges. In Scotland, an application for a backdated DHP can be considered to cover rent arrears for the same period;[8]
- your benefit (eg, employment and support allowance (ESA)) being reduced due to your refusal to take part in a work-focused interview;
- your UC or jobseeker's allowance (JSA) being paid at a reduced (or nil) rate because of a sanction under specified rules;
- any of your benefits being suspended;
- a reduction of your benefit due to recovery of an overpayment of HB or council tax benefit, or reduction of your UC due to recovery of an overpayment of UC, JSA or ESA;
- your benefit being restricted due to a benefit offence (see p1111). **Note:** DWP guidance to local authorities in England and Wales wrongly suggests this applies if you are in breach of a community service order.

**Note:** in Scotland, if the fifth, sixth, seventh or ninth bullet point above applies, you can still get a DHP where the need arises due to immediate 'exceptional circumstances or exceptional events' such as a medical crisis or bereavement.[9]

# 2. The rules about your age

There are no lower or upper age limits for discretionary housing payments. However, you must be entitled to universal credit (UC) that includes (or, in England and Wales, would include) a housing costs element for rent, or to housing benefit (HB), to qualify and therefore must meet the age rules for UC and HB (see p37 and p196).

## 3. People included in the claim

You claim discretionary housing payments for yourself. However, the circumstances and needs of your children and your partner, as well as your own, should be considered when deciding whether you can be paid and how much you can get.

## 4. The amount of discretionary housing payments

Discretionary housing payments (DHPs) are normally paid in weekly amounts. The local authority can decide how much and for how long to pay you and from when to backdate your payments.[10] In Scotland, guidance states that DHPs can be backdated for up to 12 months for any reason, and for longer if exceptional circumstances apply and the budget allows. However, DHPs can only be paid for periods during which you are (or were) entitled to universal credit (UC) and your maximum amount includes (or, in England and Wales, would include) a housing costs element for rent, or you are (or were) entitled to housing benefit (HB).

In England and Wales, you cannot be paid more than:[11]

- if you are entitled to UC and your DHPs are calculated as a monthly amount, the amount of housing costs element for rent as calculated for your maximum amount (see Chapter 6), or if you are in specified or temporary accommodation (see p91), the amount of your rent and service charges; *or*
- if you are entitled to HB and your DHPs are calculated as a weekly amount, the amount of your rent and other payments that HB can meet (see p185), not including any amounts paid for ineligible service charges and rent-free periods.

In Scotland, you cannot usually be paid more than the amount of rent you are liable for.[12] However, if you get a DHP because you are subject to the benefit cap, the amount can include other reasonable costs connected with housing, such as utility bills and service charges, up to the full amount you are capped.[13]

Any UC for your housing costs or HB you have already received (or will receive) for the period may be deducted when calculating the amount of DHP you are paid.[14]

There is no restriction on the amount of one-off payments. Larger amounts (eg, for rent in advance, a rent deposit or removal expenses) can therefore be paid by a lump sum.

**Note:**

- In deciding whether to pay you DHPs and, if so, how much to pay you, the local authority can look at what income and capital you have. However, in England and Wales, it cannot take disability living allowance (DLA) mobility component into account.[15] You can also argue that it should not take attendance allowance, pension age disability payment, DLA care component, personal independence payment, adult disability payment, child disability payment or Scottish adult DLA into account, based on the purpose of such payments and what they are already being used for.[16] In Scotland, guidance says that whether such payments are taken into account depends on your other circumstances.[17]

- If you need additional help with housing costs because there is a shortfall between your UC or HB and the rent you are liable to pay, ensure the local authority knows this, particularly if you are getting UC, as it may not already have this information.
- If you need help with your housing costs because your UC award has been reduced due to the or 'two-child limit' or (in England and Wales only) benefit cap, and that reduction is more than the maximum amounts above, any DHP can only help you up to that maximum amount allowed.

## 5. Claims, decisions and getting paid

Ask your local authority how to claim discretionary housing payments (DHPs). It can accept a claim from you or someone acting on your behalf. You must be entitled to universal credit that includes (or, in England and Wales, would include) a housing costs element for rent, or to housing benefit. Your local authority decides what 'form or manner' your claim should take – eg, in writing or by other means.[18] In Scotland, you may not need to make a claim if you are entitled due to being affected by the 'bedroom tax' or benefit cap, but if you think you are entitled and have not yet received a DHP, make a claim rather than wait for the local authority to pay you.[19]

You must provide grounds for your claim and any other information the local authority specifies.[20] Provide any evidence that shows why you need DHPs – eg, a financial statement and proof of any disability or medical condition affecting you or the people who live with you.

**Note:**

- If you want your claim to be backdated, tell the local authority.
- You must be given written notice of the local authority's decision on your claim and the reasons for its decision as soon as is 'reasonably practicable'.[21] In Scotland, you should also be told how to challenge the decision.[22]
- The local authority can pay you or, if reasonable, someone else – eg, your landlord.[23]
- It is your duty to report to the local authority any change in your circumstances that may be relevant to payment of your DHPs continuing.[24]
- In Scotland, if you made an application or requested a review before the new scheme came into force on 1 April 2024 and it has not yet been decided, or a

decision is made about such an application or review, it is now decided under the new scheme.[25]

### Getting a decision changed

You do not have a right to appeal against a DHP decision. However, you can ask the local authority to review its decision.[26] You are entitled to written notice of, and reasons for, the review decision as soon as is reasonably practicable.[27] If you are unhappy with a review decision, you can complain (see p1265). You may be able to challenge a review decision by judicial review (see Chapter 53). If the local authority's decision involves maladministration (error or wrongdoing), you can also complain to the Ombudsman (see p1267).



## 6. Tax, other benefits and the benefit cap

Discretionary housing payments (DHPs) are not taxable.

If you get DHPs:

- they are disregarded as income and capital for all means-tested benefits;[28]
- in England and Wales, you may also qualify for a discretionary reduction in your council tax bill (see p761).[29] Ensure you claim both this and DHPs, if relevant, to avoid missing out.

DHPs are *not* one of the specified benefits for the benefit cap.

## Notes

1. **Who can get discretionary housing payments**

1 **EW** s69 CSPSSA 2000; reg 2(1) DFA Regs
**S** Exception 6 para F1, Part 2 Sch 5 SA 1998; s88 SS(S)A 2018

2 **EW** *DHP Guidance Manual,* 31 May 2022, paras 8, 9, 18 and 28
**S** *SDHP Guidance Manual,* 27 March 2024, paras 3, 5, 6, 10 and 16

3 **EW** *DHP Guidance Manual,* 31 May 2022, paras 59 and 60
**S** *SDHP Guidance Manual,* 27 March 2024, para 28.2

4 *SDHP Guidance Manual,* 27 March 2024, paras 28.3 and 28.4

5 **EW** Reg 2(2) DFA Regs
**S** s91(2)(a) SS(S)A 2018; *SDHP Guidance Manual,* 27 March 2024, paras 2, 8 and 9

6 *SDHP Guidance Manual,* 27 March 2024, paras 2.3, 5 and 6

7 **EW** Reg 3 DFA Regs
**S** s89(2) and (4) SS(S)A 2018; *SDHP Guidance Manual,* 27 March 2024, paras 7 and 30-32

8 *SDHP Guidance Manual*, 27 March 2024, para 31
9 s88(3) SS(S)A 2018; *SDHP Guidance Manual*, 27 March 2024, paras 7.4 and 32.2

4. **The amount of discretionary housing payments**
10 **EW** Reg 5 DFA Regs
**S** s91(2)(a) SS(S)A 2018; *SDHP Guidance Manual*, 27 March 2024, paras 8, 9 and 11
11 Reg 4 DFA Regs
12 s91(2)(a) SS(S)A 2018; *SDHP Guidance Manual*, 27 March 2024, para 8
13 *SDHP Guidance Manual*, 27 March 2024, paras 3.2, 6.6 and 8.2
14 *R (Gargett) v Lambeth LB* [2008] EWCA Civ 1450. *SDHP Guidance Manual*, 27 March 2024, para 8.3 – but para 33 notes that this caselaw is not binding on the new scheme, but is highly persuasive.
15 *R (Hardy) v Sandwell MBC* [2015] EWHC 890 (Admin)
16 *DHP Guidance Manual*, 31 May 2022, para 26
17 *SDHP Guidance Manual*, 27 March 2024, para 14.2 (but at para 33 notes that while *R (Hardy) v Sandwell MBC* [2015] EWHC 890 (Admin) is not binding on the new scheme, it may be held to be highly persuasive)

5. **Claims, decisions and getting paid**
18 **EW** Reg 6(1)(a) DFA Regs
**S** s91(2)(b) SS(S)A 2018
19 *SDHP Guidance Manual*, 27 March 2024, para 13.1
20 **EW** Reg 7 DFA Regs
**S** s91(2)(c)(i) SS(S)A 2018; *SDHP Guidance Manual*, 27 March 2024, para 14.1
21 **EW** Reg 6(3) DFA Regs
**S** *SDHP Guidance Manual*, 27 March 2024, para 17
22 *SDHP Guidance Manual*, 27 March 2024, para 18.1
23 **EW** Reg 6(2) DFA Regs
**S** s88(4) SS(S)A 2018; *SDHP Guidance Manual*, 27 March 2024, para 20
24 **EW** Reg 7(b) DFA Regs
**S** *SDHP Guidance Manual*, 27 March 2024, para 21
25 Reg 3 The Social Security (Scotland) Act 2018 (Commencement No.10 and Transitional Provision) Regulations 2024 No.57
26 **EW** Reg 8 DFA Regs
**S** s91(2)(b) and (c) SS(S)A 2018; *SDHP Guidance Manual*, 27 March 2024, para 18
27 **EW** Reg 6(3) DFA Regs
**S** s91(2)(c)(i) SS(S)A 2018; *SDHP Guidance Manual*, 27 March 2024, para 18.4

6. **Tax, other benefits and the benefit cap**
28 **UC** Reg 66 UC Regs
**ESA** Schs 8 para 62 and 9 para 11(1)(c) ESA Regs
**PC** Reg 15 SPC Regs
**HB** Schs 5 para 62 and 6 para 9(1)(d) HB Regs; reg 29 and Sch 6 para 21(2)(k) HB(SPC) Regs
29 s13A(1)(c) LGFA 1992

# Chapter 26

# Contributory employment and support allowance

4

**This chapter covers:**


1. Who can get contributory employment and support allowance (p556)
2. The rules about your age (p558)
3. People included in the claim (p558)
4. The amount of benefit (p558)
5. Special benefit rules (p565)
6. Claims and backdating (p565)
7. Getting paid (p568)
8. Tax, other benefits and the benefit cap (p570)


## Key facts

- Employment and support allowance (ESA) is a benefit for people who have 'limited capability for work' (ie, they are unable to work because of illness or disability) and who are not entitled to statutory sick pay.
- Limited capability for work is assessed by a test called the work capability assessment.
- There are two types of ESA: **contributory ESA**, which is generally not means tested (but can be affected by certain pensions and councillor's allowance), and **income-related ESA**, which is means tested. Contributory ESA paid under the universal credit (UC) system is called 'new-style' ESA; contributory ESA paid outside the UC system is called 'old-style' ESA. If you make a new claim, or claim UC, you come under the UC system and any contributory ESA you are entitled to is new-style ESA.
- To qualify for contributory ESA, you must have paid sufficient national insurance contributions.
- In some cases, contributory ESA is paid for a maximum of 365 days.
- You may be able to get your new-style ESA topped up with UC or (if you have not yet come under the UC system) get your old-style contributory ESA topped up with income-related ESA.
- ESA is administered and paid by the DWP.

- If you disagree with an ESA decision, you can apply for a revision or supersession (see Chapter 50), or appeal against it (see Chapter 51). You must apply for a mandatory reconsideration before you can appeal (for ESA there is an exception to this requirement, where you would be entitled to ESA pending the appeal). All parts of the decision may be looked at.

## 1. Who can get contributory employment and support allowance

4

You qualify for employment and support allowance (ESA) if you:[1]

- have 'limited capability for work' (see p895); *and*
- are aged 16 or over, but under pension age (see p690); *and*
- are in Great Britain (see Chapters 58 and 59 if you go abroad); *and*
- are not entitled to statutory sick pay or new-style jobseeker's allowance (JSA); *and*
- are not engaged in any work, whether it is paid or unpaid, unless it is work you are allowed to do while claiming (called 'permitted work' – see p930).

In addition to the above, you must satisfy the extra rules that apply to contributory ESA on p557.

***Do you come under the universal credit system?***

New claims for contributory ESA are only possible under the universal credit (UC) system. This is called **'new-style' ESA**. If you make a new claim for ESA, you come under the UC system (see p24). You must usually accept a 'claimant commitment' (see p934). However, if you already get ESA and have not yet come under the UC system, your ESA is called **'old-style' ESA**. If you are still getting old-style income-related ESA, that could be adjusted to also include contributory ESA without the need for a new claim, although qualifying for it will be difficult due to the national insurance (NI) contribution conditions (see p875). Note that if you are still getting income-related ESA, you will come under the managed migration to UC process at some point in 2025 (see p29).

You are not usually entitled to ESA for the first seven days of your claim (see p928). However, you may be able to get a short-term advance of ESA paid to you during this waiting period (p1023). You cannot get ESA and certain other benefits at the same time (see p570).

***Incapacity benefit and severe disablement allowance***

Contributory ESA has, in most cases, replaced awards of two older non-means-tested benefits paid for people unable to work because of ill health. These benefits were incapacity benefit (IB) and severe disablement allowance (SDA). If you were already entitled to SDA and reached pension age before 6 April 2014, you can continue to receive it. For more details, see p563.

## Extra rules for contributory employment and support allowance

As well as satisfying the basic rules for ESA above, you qualify for contributory ESA if:[2]

- you satisfy the NI contribution conditions (see p875); *or*
- you were getting IB or SDA and you have been transferred to contributory ESA (see p563); *or*
- you satisfied the conditions for ESA in youth and you remain entitled.

### Employment and support allowance in youth

ESA in youth was abolished for new claimants from 1 May 2012.[3] For details of the rules, see Chapter 10 of the 2012/13 edition of this *Handbook*.

If you lose entitlement to ESA in youth because you have received it for a year, but have still got limited capability for work and are put in the 'support group' (see p561) because your condition has worsened, you can requalify for contributory ESA without having to satisfy the NI contribution conditions.[4]

## Disqualification from benefit

You can be disqualified from receiving ESA for up to six weeks if you:[5]

- have 'limited capability for work' because of your own misconduct (but not, for example, if this is due to pregnancy or a sexually transmitted disease); *or*
- have failed without 'good cause' to accept medical treatment (excluding vaccination, inoculation or major surgery) recommended by a doctor treating you and which would be likely to overcome your limited capability for work; *or*
- have failed without 'good cause' to stop engaging in behaviour that would 'retard' your recovery; *or*
- are absent from your home without telling the DWP where you may be found without 'good cause'.

'Good cause' is not defined.

You are not disqualified if you inform the DWP of your circumstances and you are considered to be in hardship – ie, if you are:[6]

- pregnant, or a member of your family is pregnant; *or*
- a single claimant aged under 18, or a member of a couple and both of you are under 18; *or*

- responsible (or your partner is responsible) for a child who lives with you. This does not apply to new-style ESA; *or*
- entitled (or your partner is entitled) to attendance allowance (AA), pension age disability payment (PADP), the middle or highest rate of the care component of disability living allowance (DLA), Scottish adult disability living allowance (SADLA) or child disability payment (CDP), the daily living component of personal independence payment (PIP) or adult disability payment (ADP), or armed forces independence payment (AFIP); *or*
- waiting (or your partner is waiting) for a decision on a claim for AA, PADP, DLA, CDP, PIP, ADP or AFIP; *or*
- caring (or your partner is caring) for someone who is entitled to AA, PADP, the middle or highest rate care component of DLA/CDP, the daily living component of PIP/ADP or AFIP (or who is waiting for a decision on a claim for AA, PADP, DLA/SADLA/CDP, PIP/ADP or AFIP); *or*
- your partner is at least pension age (see p689); *or*
- at risk of hardship (or a member of your family is at risk) if ESA is not paid to you, including if there is a 'substantial risk' that you will not have sufficient essential items such as food, clothing and heating.

In any of the above situations, your ESA is paid at a reduced rate. You get 80 per cent of your basic allowance (or if you still get income-related ESA, 80 per cent of your personal allowance – see p266).[7]

You can also be disqualified from receiving contributory ESA during any period in which you are:

- absent from Great Britain (see p1380); *or*
- a prisoner or detained in legal custody (see Chapter 38).

## 2. The rules about your age

You must be aged at least 16, but under pension age (see p690).

## 3. People included in the claim

You claim contributory employment and support allowance for yourself. You cannot claim any increases for your partner or children.

## 4. The amount of benefit

During an initial 'assessment phase' (see p559), you are usually paid just a basic amount of contributory employment and support allowance (ESA). After the assessment phase, in the 'main phase' you may also get an additional component. You can get either a 'support component' (see p560) or (in certain cases only) a 'work-related activity component' (see p561). **Note:** the work-related activity component was abolished for new claimants from 3 April 2017. For who can still get the component, see p561.

There are no increases in contributory ESA for other adults or children.

Your contributory ESA may be reduced if:

- you get a pension or a councillor's allowance (see p562); *or*
- you are in the work-related activity group (see p561) and you do not comply with requirements to attend work-focused interviews and carry out work-related activity (see Chapter 42 for new-style ESA, or, if you have not yet come under the UC system, p176 for old-style ESA). *or*
- you have been given a sanction because you have committed a benefit offence (see p1111).



**Note:**

- If you are appealing against a decision that you do not have limited capability for work and get ESA pending your appeal being heard (see p925), you are paid at the assessment phase rate – ie, you get the basic allowance only.
- You may also be entitled to UC, if you come under the UC system (see p20). If you do, your new-style ESA is topped up by your UC. If you have not yet not come under the UC system, your old-style contributory ESA can still be topped up by income-related ESA.

## The assessment phase

When you are first entitled to ESA, you are in an 'assessment phase' until a decision is made on your limited capability for work. You usually just get a basic allowance of contributory ESA, the amount of which depends on your age. Your ESA does not usually include an additional component (but see p562 for when a component can be included in the assessment phase).

The assessment phase lasts for at least 13 weeks. If, after 13 weeks, the DWP has not decided whether you have limited capability for work (eg, because it has not yet completed the work capability assessment – see Chapter 41), the assessment phase continues until the DWP has made its decision.[8] If you are claiming new-style ESA immediately after an 'extended period of sickness' on new-style jobseeker's allowance (JSA – see p614), the 13-week period starts on the first day of the period of sickness.

If the assessment phase lasts longer than 13 weeks, if you are awarded an additional component, it is backdated to the 14th week of your claim.[9]

If you are appealing against a decision that you do not have limited capability for work and are getting ESA pending your appeal (see p925), the assessment phase does not usually end until the First-tier Tribunal has made its decision.

However, if you experience a new condition or your condition significantly worsens before your appeal is heard, a new determination on your limited capability for work can be made and it is possible for the assessment phase to end.[10]

It is possible for your assessment phase to begin on the first day of a period of previous entitlement to ESA, so that some, or all, of the 13 weeks are treated as already served.[11] This happens if your current period of limited capability for work is linked to a previous one (see p928) in which you were entitled to ESA for less than 13 weeks. In these circumstances, your assessment phase ends when your combined entitlement from the previous and current ESA awards amounts to 13 weeks, unless the DWP has not yet completed your assessment, in which case it does not end until the DWP has made its decision.

If you were on new-style JSA during an 'extended period of sickness' (see p614), this counts as time when you had a previous entitlement to ESA.

## Calculating your contributory employment and support allowance

Contributory ESA is worked out as follows.

- Add together the basic allowance and the amount of any component to which you are entitled.
  - In the 'assessment phase', you are normally only entitled to a basic allowance.[12] This is £72.90 if you are under 25 or £92.05 if you are 25 or over. In some circumstances, such as if you are terminally ill, you may also be entitled to either a support component (see below) or a work-related activity component (see p561).
  - In the 'main phase', you are entitled to a basic allowance of £92.05, irrespective of your age. If you qualify, you can also get a support component of £48.50 a week. If you do not qualify for this, you may still be entitled to a work-related activity component of £36.55 a week, although that component was abolished for new claimants from 2017.
- Deduct from this sum an amount for certain pension payments or for a councillor's allowance, if applicable (see p562).
- Add any transitional addition to which you are entitled if you have been transferred to ESA from incapacity benefit (IB) or severe disablement allowance (SDA) (see p563).[13]

### Support component

The support component can be included in your entitlement to both contributory and income-related ESA.[14]

In most cases, you are entitled to the support component if:

- the assessment phase (see p559) has ended (but see p562); *and*

- as well as having limited capability for work, you are also assessed as having 'limited capability for work-related activity' (see p913).

*The support group*

If you are assessed or treated as having limited capability for work-related activity, the DWP describes you as being in the '**support group**'.

If you are in the support group, you need not take part in work-focused interviews or associated activity as a condition of getting benefit.[15]

The DWP decides whether or not you have limited capability for work-related activity as part of the work capability assessment (see p896). If you disagree with the DWP's decision, you can ask for a mandatory reconsideration, and then appeal if you remain unhappy with the outcome. But if the DWP has decided that you do not have limited capability for work (ie, you have 'failed' the work capability assessment) and so are not entitled to ESA, you may be able to appeal straight away, without first applying for a mandatory reconsideration (see p924). If you appeal and the First-tier Tribunal finds that you have limited capability for work, it should also consider whether you have limited capability for work-related activity.[16]

## Work-related activity component

The work-related activity component was abolished for new claimants from 3 April 2017.[17] You can no longer get the component if you are making a new claim.

You can still get the work-related activity component after 3 April 2017 in certain circumstances where you claimed ESA before that date, or you were transferred from IB or SDA to contributory ESA, or from income support (IS) to income-related ESA.[18] See Chapter 30 of the 2023/24 edition of this *Handbook* for full details.

*The work-related activity group*

If you are *assessed* under the work capability assessment as having limited capability for work, but not for work-related activity (see Chapter 41), the DWP describes you as being in the '**work-related activity group**'. This is the case even if you cannot get the work-related activity component. The DWP also describes you as being in the work-related activity group if you are *treated* as having limited capability for work (see p896), except if you are waiting for your work capability assessment to be carried out or if you are appealing.[19]

If you can get it, the work-related activity component can be included in both contributory and (if you still get it) income-related ESA if:[20]

- the assessment phase (see p559) has ended (but see below); *and*
- you are not assessed as having 'limited capability for work-related activity' (see p913) – ie, you are not entitled to the support component; *and*
- you comply with the requirement to attend work-focused interviews and associated activity.

You may be required to take part in work-focused interviews and undertake work-related activity (see Chapter 42 for new-style ESA or, if you have not yet come under the UC system, p176 for old-style contributory ESA).



## Who can get a component in the assessment phase

You are entitled to the support component (or the work-related activity component, if you can still get it) during the assessment phase if:[21]

- you have requalified for contributory ESA after having previously lost it because of the rules on how long it can be paid (see p564) and now satisfy the conditions for the support component; *or*
- you are terminally ill (ie, you have a progressive disease, as a result of which your death can reasonably be expected within 12 months) and have either claimed ESA on these grounds, or asked for a revision or supersession and have said that you are terminally ill. In this case, you qualify for the support component automatically and it is included straight away; *or*
- your period of limited capability for work is linked under the 12-week linking rule (see p928) to an earlier period in which you were entitled to ESA, you were entitled to a component in this earlier claim and it did not end because you were found to be fit for work – ie, you did not fail the work capability assessment. In this case, the component can be included straight away; *or*
- your period of limited capability for work is linked under the 12-week linking rule (see p928) to an earlier period in which you were entitled to ESA, you were entitled to a component or that award lasted 13 weeks or longer, and it ended either because you failed the work capability assessment or before you could be assessed. In this case, you can only get the component again once you have been assessed as passing the work capability assessment, although it is dated from the start of your second award.

## Deductions for pension payments and councillor's allowance

A deduction is made from your contributory ESA if you receive certain pension payments of over £85 a week and/or if you are a local councillor and your net allowances are more than £195.50 a week.[22]

**Pension payments** taken into account for contributory ESA are periodic payments made under:[23]

- any personal, occupational or public service pension scheme;

- any permanent health insurance policy arranged by your employer that provides payments in connection with ill health or disability after your employment ends. However, if you contributed more than 50 per cent of the pension premiums, the amount you receive from this kind of pension is ignored;
- the Pension Protection Fund and the Financial Assistance Scheme.

If the total amount of the gross pension payments you receive is more than £85 a week, your contributory ESA is reduced by half the pension payments above £85.

Other types of pension payments (including one-off lump-sum payments) are ignored. The following types of payment are also ignored:[24]

- any part of your pension paid direct to an ex-spouse or ex-civil partner by the pension scheme trustees under a court order (although the DWP may not accept this);[25]
- any payments you receive as a result of the death of the pension holder;
- any shortfall in your pension if it cannot be paid in full because the pension scheme is in deficit or has insufficient funds;
- payments under a pension scheme for death as a result of military or war service under section 639(2) of the Income Tax (Earnings and Pensions) Act 2003, or a guaranteed income payment.

**Note:** if you were transferred from IB to ESA (see below) and your pension payment was ignored immediately before the transfer, it continues to be ignored in your ESA.[26]

**If you are a local councillor** and your net allowances are more than £195.50 a week, your contributory ESA is reduced by the amount by which the net allowances exceed £195.50.[27]

## Transfers to employment and support allowance

Most people who were getting IB, SDA or IS on the grounds of disability on 27 October 2008 had their claim transferred to a claim for ESA. If you were transferred from IB or SDA to contributory ESA but it would have been less than your IB or SDA, you were entitled to the difference as a transitional addition. But, as ESA is a single benefit, you may also have been entitled to income-related ESA if your income and capital were low enough. If you got a transitional addition, it is reduced by subsequent increases in your ESA. For more details, see Chapter 31 of the 2016/17 edition of this *Handbook*.

The transfer process did not apply to people who reached pension age before 6 April 2014. If you were getting SDA and reached pension age before 6 April 2014, you can continue to get SDA so long as you continue to meet the qualifying conditions. See Chapter 4 of the 2000/01 edition of this *Handbook* for the qualifying conditions for SDA.

## Duration of contributory employment and support allowance

Contributory ESA is usually only paid for a **maximum of 365 days**. But you can be paid it for longer because any time while you have limited capability for work-related activity (p913) and are entitled to the support component (ie, you are in the 'support group') is ignored when caclulating the 365-day period. Once you have received contributory ESA for a year and have not been in the support group for that time, you lose your entitlement to contributory ESA. The following applies.[28]

4

- Time spent in the assessment phase is taken into account when calculating the 365-day period, except if you were assessed as having limited capability for work-related activity (p913) and put in the support group.
- If you are appealing about not being in the support group, days when you get ESA while you are appealing are taken into account when calculating the 365-day period. This time is then ignored if your appeal is successful.
- If you were transferred from IB or SDA to contributory ESA, your 365-day period is calculated from the date your award was converted to contributory ESA.

You can requalify for contributory ESA if:[29]

- you remain assessed or treated as having limited capability for work, and you are also assessed as having limited capability for work-related activity for the support component (see p913) – ie, you are put in the support group; *or*
- the tax years used to decide whether you satisfy the national insurance (NI) contribution conditions (see p875) include at least one year which is later than the last of the relevant tax years which applied to your previous entitlement, and you satisfy the NI contribution conditions again. If you continue to have limited capability for work and still get income-related ESA, under the linking rules (p928), the tax years remain the same as those that applied to your previous entitlement, so you cannot requalify in this way. However, if you have a break in your ESA entitlement altogether (ie, of both contributory and income-related ESA) of more than 12 weeks (including if you get UC during the break), you start a new period of limited capability for work and the linking rules do not apply.[30]

***Example***

Sadio (24) has worked since leaving school and has a full NI contribution record, but in July 2024 had to leave his job because of ill health and claimed new-style ESA. He is not assessed as being in the ESA support group.

ESA during assessment phase = £72.90 (basic allowance for someone aged under 25)

ESA during main phase = £92.05

Because Sadio is not in the support group, his award of contributory ESA, which began in July 20243, is limited to 365 days.

The relevant tax years for the NI contribution conditions for the July 20243 claim are 2021/22 and 2022/23.

After a year of payment, Sadio's new-style ESA stops on 1 July 2025. His condition has not changed and he still does not qualify for the support component. He still has limited capability for work. As his ESA has stopped completely (ie, he is not entitled to income-related ESA either), after 12 weeks Sadio may requalify for new-style ESA. This is because when he makes a new claim for ESA he starts a new period of limited capability for work which does not link to his previous one. One of the relevant tax years that applies to the new claim (2023/24) is later than the years that applied to Sadio's previous claim. However, he must still satisfy the NI contribution conditions again using the new relevant tax years.

4

## 5. Special benefit rules

Special rules may apply if you:

- are subject to immigration control (employment and support allowance in youth only) (see p1272);
- are going abroad (see Chapter 58);
- are in prison or detention (see Chapter 38).

## 6. Claims and backdating

The general rules about claims and backdating are covered in Chapter 44. This section explains the specific rules that apply to contributory employment and support allowance (ESA). Most new claims for contributory ESA can now only be for new-style ESA – ie, under the UC system.

Sometimes, you must attend a medical examination to assess whether you have limited capability for work (p896) or limited capability for work-related activity (p913). Also, unless you are in the 'support group' (see p560), you may be required to attend compulsory work-focused interviews and, in some cases, carry out work-related activity.

If you are appealing against a decision that you do not have limited capability for work, you do not need to make a new claim for ESA to get ESA pending your appeal, although you must submit a fit note.[31] For when ESA can be paid pending an appeal, see p925.

**Note:** if you are refused contributory ESA because you do not meet the national insurance (NI) contribution conditions, in some cases, it may be worth claiming at a later date that falls in a different benefit year (see p875).

## Making a claim

ESA paid under the UC system is called 'new-style' ESA. This applies to most new claims. For when you come under the UC system (which includes where you make a new claim for ESA), see p20.

You can start a claim for new-style ESA:[32]

- online at gov.uk/employment-support-allowance/how-to-claim; *or*
- if you cannot claim online, or if you are claiming for someone as their appointee, by phone on 0800 055 6688 (textphone: 0800 328 1344; Relay UK and BSL relay services are also available).[33] Say that you wish to claim 'new-style' contributory ESA.

4

If you have not yet come under the UC system, you may be able to get 'old-style' contributory ESA instead. But this will be very unusual, as you need to be getting income-related ESA already and then satisfy the NI contribution conditions for having that award changed so as also to include contributory ESA, without the need for a new claim. Similarly, you cannot usually start getting income-related ESA now (as if you are making a new claim you must claim UC instead). But if you are already getting old-style contributory ESA, you may be able to top that up with income-related ESA without needing a new claim. Contact Jobcentre Plus about this.

If you want to claim UC to top up your new-style ESA, you must do this separately.

You must provide information or evidence as required (see p620). You can amend or withdraw your claim before a decision is made (see p1004). If there is a delay in deciding your claim, you may be able to get a short-term advance (see p1023).

## Who should claim

You claim contributory ESA on your own behalf. However, if you cannot manage your claim, another person can claim ESA for you as your appointee (see p1005).

## If you are employed

If you are employed, you should normally be paid statutory sick pay (SSP) (see Chapter 35) for the first 28 weeks of your limited capability for work. If your employer thinks that you are not entitled to SSP, or if your entitlement to SSP has run out, it should complete and give you Form SSP1. To get contributory ESA, you then need to make a claim for it – ie, for new-style ESA. **Note:** claiming ESA will mean that you come under the UC system (see p20). You are normally expected to include Form SSP1 and a fit note with your claim. If your employer refuses you SSP on the grounds that you are not entitled to it, your claim for ESA can be backdated to the date of your SSP claim (see p568). If you disagree with your employer's decision not to pay SSP, you can refer the matter to HMRC (see

Chapter 54), but do not delay claiming ESA. If you have asked HMRC to decide whether you are entitled to SSP, tell the DWP this when you claim ESA.

## Information to support your claim

For the general information requirements that apply to all benefits, see p1006.

It is important that you provide any information required when you claim. Until you do, you may not count as having made a valid claim (see p1008). Correct any defects as soon as possible or your date of claim may be affected.

The DWP may ask you to provide information, including:

- your NI number;
- a fit note (sometimes also called a 'sick note') – this is a medical certificate from your doctor or other registered healthcare professional (ie, a registered nurse, occupational therapist, pharmacist or physiotherapist);
- your GP's address and phone number;
- your contact phone number (if you have one);
- your bank account details;
- details of your employer (if you have one);
- details of other money you are getting, such as benefits, pensions or health insurance payments, including the date your SSP ends, if you are claiming it.

For the first seven days of your limited capability for work, the DWP should accept a self-certificate as medical evidence. After seven days, usually you must provide a fit note. If it is unreasonable to expect you to provide this, the DWP can accept other evidence if that is sufficient.[34]

The DWP may refer you for a medical assessment. If you do not attend the medical without good cause, your claim can be refused.[35]

You may be asked to provide further information to support your claim (see p1009). You may also be asked to provide information after you are awarded ESA and, if you fail to do so, your ESA could be suspended or even terminated (see p1031).

## The date of your claim

The date of your claim is important as it determines when your entitlement to ESA starts (subject to the rules on waiting days – see p569). This is not necessarily the date from when you are paid. For when payment of ESA starts, see p568.

Unless it is backdated, the date of your claim' is usually the date of your online claim is received or, if you are allowed to claim by phone, your phone call. If you have notified the DWP of an intention to claim and your properly completed claim is made within a month (or longer if allowed), the date of your claim is the date you notified your intention to claim.[36]

You must make sure your claim is valid. If it is 'defective', you are given a short time to correct the defects (see p1008 and p1009). If you do, your claim is treated as having been made when you initially claimed.[37]

### Backdating your claim

Your claim can be backdated for up to three months before the day you actually claim – ie, for time during this period when you were entitled to ESA. You should state from which date you are claiming in that period and ask for it to be backdated. You do not need special reasons for backdating.[38]

4

### If you claim the wrong benefit

If your employer has decided that you are not entitled to SSP and you claim ESA within three months of being notified in writing of this, your ESA claim is treated as having been made on the date of your SSP claim.[39]

A claim for maternity allowance (MA) can be treated as a claim for ESA and vice versa.[40] If your MA claim is accepted as a claim for ESA, your ESA can be backdated for up to three months before the date you claimed MA if you satisfy the qualifying conditions during that period (see p1013).

### Claiming in advance

You can claim ESA up to three months before the date on which you qualify for it.[41] The date of your claim is the date on which you qualify.

## Starting work when your claim ends

If you start work, you may be able to benefit from the rules for linking periods of limited capability for work should you fall sick again later (see p928). If this is the case, provided you claim ESA again within a 12-week linking period, you get the same amount of ESA you previously received.

# 7. Getting paid

The general rules on getting paid are covered in Chapter 45. This section explains the specific rules that apply to both contributory and income-related employment and support allowance (ESA).

***When is employment and support allowance paid?***

The day you are paid depends on your national insurance number (see p1020).[42] ESA is usually paid fortnightly in arrears, although it can be paid at different intervals, including at a daily rate of one-seventh of the weekly amount.[43]

ESA is a weekly benefit, although in some cases it can be paid for a part week.[44]

Note:
- Your contributory ESA might be paid at a reduced rate in some circumstances (see p559).
- Deductions can be made from your ESA to pay to third parties (see p1033).
- You might not be paid ESA, or it might be paid at a reduced rate, if you have been sanctioned for a benefit offence (see p1111).
- If payment of your ESA is delayed, see p1123. If you are waiting for a decision on your claim, or to be paid, you might be able to get a short-term advance (see p1023). If you wish to complain about how your claim has been dealt with, or claim compensation, see Chapter 55.
- If payment of your ESA is suspended, see p1031. This includes if you have failed to supply evidence of your limited capability for work.
- If you are overpaid ESA, you might have to repay it (see Chapter 47) and, in some circumstances, you may have to pay a penalty (see p1101). If you have been accused of fraud, see Chapter 48.
- If you are owed arrears of ESA, these can be paid in instalments (see p1018).



## Change of circumstances

You must report changes in your circumstances that you have been told you must report, as well as any that you might reasonably be expected to know might affect your right to, the amount of, or the payment of your benefit. You should do this as soon as possible, preferably in writing. See p1030 for further information.

Your ESA is usually adjusted from the beginning of the week in which the change of circumstances takes effect.[45] However, there are exceptions – eg, if you have notified the DWP that you are terminally ill or if you have failed to notify it of a change about your limited capability for work (see p1148).[46]

## Waiting days

You are not entitled to ESA for seven 'waiting days' at the beginning of your period of limited capability for work (see p928 – note that if your period of lmited capability for work is linked to an earlier one, you do not have to serve further waiting days).[47] Waiting days do not apply if:
- your entitlement to ESA starts within 12 weeks of your entitlement to pension credit, jobseeker's allowance (JSA), carer's allowance, statutory sick pay or maternity allowance coming to an end (income support (IS) is also included, but note that most awards of IS – and also income-based JSA – have now been replaced by UC – see p21); *or*
- you have requalified for contributory ESA on the basis of being put in the support group (see p561), having previously lost entitlement because of the rules on how long you can be paid contributory ESA (see p564); *or*
- you are terminally ill; *or*

- you have been discharged from the armed forces and three or more days before the discharge were days of sickness absence.

You may be able to get a short-term advance before your first payment is due (see p1023).

## 8. Tax, other benefits and the benefit cap



### Tax

Contributory employment and support allowance (ESA), including ESA in youth, is taxable.[48] If you were transferred from incapacity benefit (IB) or severe disablement allowance (SDA) to contributory ESA, your contributory ESA is still taxable, even if your IB/SDA was not.

### Means-tested benefits

If you are entitled to contributory ESA:

- it counts as income for means-tested benefits if you do not get income-related ESA;
- if you come under the universal credit (UC) system (see p20), you may be entitled to UC to top up your new-style ESA;
- if you do not yet come under the UC system and you get old-style contributory ESA, you may be entitled to income-related ESA to top it up, without making a new claim (see p24);
- you may be entitled to an additional component as part of your housing benefit (HB) (see p281).

You can get new-style ESA at the same time as UC.

### Non-means-tested benefits

While you are on contributory ESA, you may be entitled to national insurance credits for limited capability for work (see p865).

Contributory ESA is affected by the rules on overlapping benefits (see p1021), which means that you may not be paid it in full if another earnings-replacement benefit is paid to you.

You are not entitled to ESA if you are entitled to statutory sick pay.[49] You can continue to get contributory ESA if you then get statutory maternity pay (SMP), statutory adoption pay (SAP), statutory paternity pay (SPP), statutory parental bereavement pay (SPBP) or statutory neonatal care pay (SNCP). You can get contributory ESA and statutory shared parental pay (SSPP) if the amount of the SSPP is less than the amount of ESA. Your ESA is reduced by the amount of the SMP, SAP, SSPP or SNCP you get.[50]

You cannot get new-style ESA and new-style JSA in your own right at the same time. If your partner is entitled to new-style JSA, you can still get new-style ESA.

## The benefit cap

ESA is one of the specified benefits for the benefit cap. However, the benefit cap does not apply if you or your partner receive ESA which includes a support component. In other cases, it only applies if you are getting UC or HB. See p1025 for further information.



## Passports and other sources of help

If you receive contributory ESA, you may be eligible for:

- a Christmas bonus (see p783);
- health benefits such as free prescriptions (see Chapter 27);
- education benefits such as free school lunches (see p774);
- council tax reduction (see p761).

## Financial help on starting work

If you stop getting contributory ESA because you start work, you may be able to get extended payments of HB if you pay rent (see p224). Your local authority may provide extended help with council tax. See p781 for information about other financial help you may get.

# Notes

1. **Who can get contributory employment and support allowance**
   1 ss1 and 20(1) WRA 2007; reg 40(1) and (7) ESA Regs; reg 37(1) and (8) ESA Regs 2013
   2 Sch 1 paras 1-4 WRA 2007
   3 s53 WRA 2012; s1(3A) WRA 2007
   4 s52 WRA 2012
   5 s18 WRA 2007; reg 157 ESA Regs; reg 93 ESA Regs 2013
   6 Regs 157(3) and 158 ESA Regs; reg 94 ESA Regs 2013
   7 Sch 5 para 14 ESA Regs; reg 63 ESA Regs 2013

4. **The amount of benefit**
   8 s24(2) WRA 2007; reg 4 ESA Regs; reg 5 ESA Regs 2013
   9 Reg 7(38) SS&CS(DA) Regs; reg 35(7) UC,PIP,JSA&ESA(DA) Regs
   10 Regs 5, 6 and 87 ESA Regs 2013
   11 Reg 5 ESA Regs; reg 6 ESA Regs 2013
   12 s2(1)(a) WRA 2007; regs 7 and 67(2) and Sch 4 para 1(1)(b) and (c) ESA Regs; regs 7 and 62(1) ESA Regs 2013
   13 s2(2) and (3) WRA 2007; reg 67(2) and (3) and Sch 4 paras 1(a), 12 and 13 ESA Regs; Sch 2 para 12 ESA(TP)(EA)(No.2) Regs
   14 ss2(2) and 4(4) WRA 2007

15 Reg 54 ESA Regs; ss11 and 11D WRA 2007
16 *PM v SSWP (ESA)* [2012] UKUT 188 (AAC)
17 s15 WRWA 2016
18 Sch 2 Part 1 ESAUC(MA) Regs
19 Reg 2 IS Regs; reg 1 JSA Regs; reg 1 SPC Regs; reg 2 HB Regs; reg 2 HB(SPC) Regs; reg 1 SFCWP Regs
20 ss2(3) and 4(5) WRA 2007
21 Reg 7 ESA Regs; reg 7 ESA Regs 2013
22 Regs 72-79 ESA Regs; regs 64-72 ESA Regs 2013
23 s3 WRA 2007; regs 72, 72A and 74 ESA Regs; regs 64, 65 and 67 ESA Regs 2013
24 Reg 75 ESA Regs; reg 68 ESA Regs 2013
25 R(IB) 1/04 applied this to IB, but it is not followed by the DWP for ESA
26 Schs 1 para 11 and 2 para 14 ESA(TP)(EA)(No.2) Regs
27 Regs 76(1), 79 and 94(1) ESA Regs; regs 69, 72 and 79 ESA Regs 2013
28 ss51 and 52 WRA 2012; ss1A and 1B WRA 2007
29 ss1A and 1B WRA 2007
30 para 41847 DMG; para V2045 ADM

6. **Claims and backdating**
31 Reg 3(j) SS(C&P) Regs; reg 7 ESA Regs 2013
32 Regs 13 and 15 UC,PIP,JSA&ESA(C&P) Regs
33 gov.uk/how-to-claim-new-style-esa
34 Regs 2 and 5 SS(ME) Regs
35 s19 SSA 1998; reg 23 ESA Regs
36 Reg 6(1F) SS(C&P) Regs; regs 14 and 16 UC,PIP,JSA&ESA(C&P) Regs
37 Regs 4G(5) and 4H(6) and (7) SS(C&P) Regs; regs 13(5) and 15(4) UC,PIP,JSA&ESA(C&P) Regs
38 Reg 19 and Sch 4 para 16 SS(C&P) Regs; reg 28 UC,PIP,JSA&ESA(C&P) Regs
39 Reg 10(1A) SS(C&P) Regs; reg 17 UC,PIP,JSA&ESA(C&P) Regs
40 Reg 9 and Sch 1 SS(C&P) Regs; reg 25 UC,PIP,JSA&ESA(C&P) Regs
41 Reg 13(9) SS(C&P) Regs; reg 34 UC,PIP,JSA&ESA(C&P) Regs

7. **Getting paid**
42 Reg 26C(2) SS(C&P) Regs; reg 51 UC,PIP,JSA&ESA(C&P) Regs
43 Reg 26C SS(C&P) Regs; reg 51(5) UC,PIP,JSA&ESA(C&P) Regs
44 para 46011 DMG
45 Reg 7(2)(a) and Sch 3C SS&CS(DA) Regs; reg 35 and Sch 1 para 1 UC,PIP,JSA&ESA(C&P) Regs
46 Reg 7(2) and (25) and Sch 3C SS&CS(DA) Regs; reg 35 and Sch 1 paras 6 and 9 UC,PIP,JSA&ESA(C&P) Regs
47 Reg 144 ESA Regs; reg 85 ESA Regs 2013

8. **Tax, other benefits and the benefit cap**
48 ss658(4) and 661(1) IT(EP)A 2003
49 s20 WRA 2007
50 Regs 80-82BB ESA Regs; regs 73-75B ESA Regs 2013

# Chapter 27

# Health benefits

**This chapter covers:**


1. Who can get health benefits (below)
2. Prescriptions (p578)
3. Dental treatment and dentures (p579)
4. Sight tests and glasses (p580)
5. Wigs and fabric supports (p581)
6. Fares to receive NHS treatment (p581)
7. Claims and refunds (p582)


### Key facts

- Health benefits help with the costs of NHS prescriptions, dental treatment, sight tests and glasses, wigs and fabric supports, and fares to receive NHS treatment.
- Some people are exempt from charges and can get full help with NHS costs and fares. Others qualify for full or partial help in specific situations or if their income and capital are below a certain amount (known as the low income scheme).
- Health benefits are administered by the NHS Business Services Authority

## 1. Who can get health benefits

Although the NHS generally provides free healthcare, there are fixed charges for some items and services such as prescriptions, dental treatment, sight tests and glasses, and wigs and fabric supports. You may also have fares to pay to get to hospital or another establishment for NHS treatment. However, you may qualify for full help with the charges and fares (ie, you may get the items or services free of charge) or you may get partial help (ie, you get a reduction).

In some cases, you must make a claim (see p582). If you pay for an item or service that you could have received free or at a reduced cost, you can apply for a refund (see p584).

## Full help

You get full help with charges and fares if you:

- are in an exempt group; *or*
- satisfy specific conditions, depending on the item or service. See p578 for prescriptions, p579 for dental treatment and dentures, p580 for sight tests and glasses, p581 for wigs and fabric supports and p581 for fares to receive NHS treatment; *or*
- get full help with health costs under the low income scheme (see p575). If you do not qualify for full help with health costs, you may qualify for partial help under the low income scheme.



## Exempt groups

You qualify for full help with charges and fares if you are in an exempt group. You are in an exempt group if:[1]

- you, or a member of your family (see p575 for who counts), get any of the following qualifying benefits:
  - universal credit (UC). In the assessment period (see p39) before the health cost was incurred, you (or you and your partner together) must either have:
    - no earnings; *or*
    - earnings no greater than £435 (or £935, if you have limited capability for work, limited capability for work-related activity, or if the child element is included in your UC); *or*
  - income-related employment and support allowance (ESA) or the guarantee credit of pension credit (PC); *or*
- you, or a member of your family, are an asylum seeker who gets asylum support (see p1289). Dependants for whom you are claiming asylum support count as members of your family; *or*
- you are aged 16 or 17 and you get support from a local authority after being looked after (in Scotland, getting support under section 29(1) of the Children (Scotland) Act 1995 after leaving care). This does not appear in the regulations for sight tests in England and Wales or for vouchers for glasses and contact lenses in England, but NHS booklet *Help with Health Costs* (HC11) states you are entitled to full help with health costs under the low income scheme.

Even if you are not in one of the exempt groups, note the following.

- If you are a war disablement pensioner, you may qualify for free prescriptions, wigs and fabric supports. You may also be able to claim money back for dental treatment, sight tests, glasses or contact lenses or fares to hospital. You must have a valid war pension exemption certificate, and must need the items or treatment, or to travel, because of your war disability. See p583 for where to claim.
- If you are a hospital inpatient, all medication and NHS treatment is provided free (including glasses and contact lenses if prescribed through the hospital

eye service). If you are an outpatient or are at a walk-in centre, medication taken and treatment given while you are in the hospital or walk-in centre are also provided without charge (but you may be charged for dentures and bridges).

*Member of the family*

**'Family'** means you and your partner and any child or qualifying young person included in your claim for the qualifying benefit.

4

## Partial help

If you do not qualify for full help with charges and fares, you may still qualify for partial help under the low income scheme.

## The low income scheme

You and members of your family (see above for who counts) may be entitled to full or partial help with NHS charges under the low income scheme, even if you do not qualify for full help on other grounds. You must make a claim (see p582). The low income scheme is administered by the NHS Business Services Authority.

You (and members of your family) qualify for full help if:

- you have capital of less than £16,000 (or if you live permanently in a care home, less than £23,250 in England and Scotland, or £24,000 in Wales).[2] Your capital is calculated in a *similar* way as for income-related ESA (see Chapter 16); *and*
- your income (see p577) does not exceed your 'requirements' (see p576) by more than 50 per cent of the current cost of an English prescription.[3] If your income exceeds your requirements by more than this amount, see below to find out whether you qualify for partial help with charges.

If you are entitled to full help, you are issued with an HC2 certificate. If you are entitled to partial help, you are issued with an HC3 certificate. See p583 for more information.

### Partial help with items and services

If you do not qualify for full help with NHS charges, you (and members of your family) may qualify for partial help with these under the low income scheme. You may get:[4]

- reduced-cost dental treatment (including check-ups) and appliances (including dentures); *and*
- reduced-cost sight tests in England and Wales (eye tests are free in Scotland[5]). There is no set charge for sight tests, so it is worth shopping around if you are not entitled to a free test; *and*
- vouchers towards the cost of glasses and contact lenses; *and*

- in England, reduced-cost wigs and fabric supports (these are free in Wales and Scotland); *and*
- partial help with fares to receive NHS treatment.

**Note:** in England, you cannot qualify for reduced-cost prescriptions under the low income scheme, only free prescriptions. If you cannot qualify for free prescriptions, see p579 for information about prepayment certificates. In Wales and Scotland, prescriptions are free.

You are expected to pay up to a set amount towards the charges. The set amount is:[6]

- for dental charges and charges for wigs and fabric supports, three times the amount by which your income exceeds your requirements (your 'excess income');
- for glasses or lenses, twice the amount of your excess income;
- for a sight test or fares to receive NHS treatment, the amount of your excess income.

***Example***

Bill's income exceeds his requirements by £6, so he cannot qualify for full help under the low income scheme. However, he may get partial help. He has to pay the first £18 of dental charges and charges for wigs and fabric supports, the first £6 of the cost of a sight test, the first £12 towards the cost of glasses and lenses and the first £6 of his fares to receive NHS treatment. If he lives in England, he must pay the full cost of prescriptions.

## Calculating your requirements

Your 'requirements' are similar to the ESA applicable amount (see Chapter 13). The most significant elements and differences are set out below. There are no reductions in the applicable amounts of people who are subject to immigration control or who are not habitually resident in the UK, or for students, people engaged in a trade dispute or people without accommodation.

Your requirements are made up of the following elements.[7]

- **Personal allowance(s):**

| | |
|---|---|
| Single person aged under 25 | £72.90 |
| Single person aged under 25, entitled to ESA work-related activity or support component, or incapable of work for at least 28 weeks starting on or after 27 October 2008 | £92.05 |
| Single person aged 25–59 or lone parent aged under 60 | £92.05 |
| Single person or lone parent aged 60 or over | £227.10 |
| Couples, both partners aged under 60 | £144.65 |
| Couples, one or both partners aged 60 or over | £346.60 |

- **Premiums:** the disability, enhanced disability, severe disability and carer premiums are added to your requirements if you would qualify for them (see p270).
  A disability premium can also be included if you or your partner have been incapable of work for 28 weeks. It can also be included if you (or your partner) have been awarded ESA which includes a work-related activity or support component, or if you (or they) have been getting ESA for at least 28 weeks. You (and your partner) must be under 60.
  If you are a single claimant or a lone parent, the amount of the disability premium is increased to £48.50 if you qualify for an ESA support component or if you are getting the middle or highest rate care component of disability living allowance (DLA) or Scottish adult disability living allowance (SADLA), either rate of the daily living component of personal independence payment (PIP) or adult disability payment (ADP), or armed forces independence payment (AFIP), and have been getting ESA or have been incapable of work, for at least 28 weeks.
  An enhanced disability premium can be included if you (or your partner) are getting the DLA/SADLA highest rate care component, the enhanced rate of the daily living component of PIP/ADP, AFIP or ESA which includes a support component. You (and your partner) must be under 60.
- **Weekly council tax.**
- **Weekly rent *less* any housing benefit** (HB) and any non-dependant deductions. Deductions for fuel and ineligible service charges are made in accordance with the HB rules.
- **Weekly mortgage interest and capital payments on loans** secured on a home, to buy a home or to adapt a home for the special needs of a disabled person, and payments on an endowment policy relating to the purchase of a home. Some other housing costs can be included. Deductions are made for non-dependants.

If you live permanently in a care home, your requirements are your weekly accommodation charge, including meals and services, and a personal expenses allowance. If your place is being funded by a local authority (fully or in part), you are exempt from some charges.

## Calculating your income

Your income is calculated in a similar way as as for income-related ESA (see Chapter 16), with modifications. These include the following.[8]

- Your income is normally taken into account in the week in which it is paid. If you are affected by a trade dispute, your normal earnings are taken into account.
- You are entitled to an earnings disregard of £20 if you get a disability premium (see p272), or if you or your partner are aged 60 or over.

- If you (or your partner) are doing permitted work while claiming ESA (see p930), the amount of earnings that can be disregarded is the same as for income-related ESA (see p347). If you *and* your partner are both doing permitted work, the disregard is applied to your joint income.
- The full amount of your (or your partner's) contributory ESA is taken into account, even if it is paid at a reduced rate because you failed to take part in a work-focused interview. This does not appear to apply to new-style ESA (see p555), so the amount received should be taken into account.
- Regular liable relative payments (see p355) count as weekly income. Irregular payments are averaged over the 13 weeks before your claim. Lump-sum payments are treated as capital.
- Student loans and grants are divided by 52, unless you are in your final year or are doing a one-year course, in which case the loan is divided by the number of weeks you are studying. The £10 disregard from student loans only applies if you are eligible for a premium, you receive an allowance because of deafness, or you are not a student but your partner is. In addition, in England and Wales, sums in excess of a specified amount of a maintenance grant and certain loans paid to Scottish students studying in England or Wales are disregarded. Also, if a voluntary payment is taken into account, up to £20 of it is disregarded.
- If you live permanently in residential or nursing care:
  - in Wales, no tariff income from any capital is taken into account;
  - in England and Scotland, the lower threshold for tariff income is £14,250.

  Remember that if your place is being funded by a local authority (in full or in part), you are exempt from some charges.
- The savings credit of PC is ignored as income.

## 2. Prescriptions

Prescriptions are free in Wales and Scotland. You qualify for free prescriptions in England (and you can get an English prescription free in Wales and Scotland) if:[9]

- you are in one of the exempt groups listed on p574; *or*
- you qualify under the low income scheme (see p575); *or*
- you are aged 60 or over; *or*
- you are aged under 16, or you are under 19 and in full-time education; *or*
- you are pregnant or have given birth in the last 12 months; *or*
- you are a permanent resident in a care home and your place is partly or wholly funded by a local authority; *or*
- you are prescribed or given specific medicines for a pandemic disease; *or*
- you are in prison or a young offenders' institution or other secure accommodation (or were given the prescription while you were); *or*
- you are detained under the Immigration Act 1971 or section 62 of the Nationality, Immigration and Asylum Act 2002; *or*

- you have:
  - a continuing physical disability, which prevents you going out without the help of another person;
  - epilepsy requiring continuous anticonvulsive therapy;
  - a permanent fistula, including a caecostomy, ileostomy, laryngostomy or colostomy, needing continuous surgical dressing or an appliance;
  - diabetes mellitus (except where treatment is by diet alone);
  - diabetes insipidus and other forms of hypopituitarism;
  - myxoedema;
  - hypoparathyroidism;
  - forms of hypoadrenalism (including Addison's disease), for which specific substitution therapy is essential;
  - myasthenia gravis;
  - cancer, for which you are undergoing treatment, or if you are receiving treatment for the effects of cancer or cancer treatment.



If you have any of the conditions listed in the last bullet point, ask your GP for Form FP92A to apply for a medical exemption certificate, which you should present when you collect your prescription. Medical exemption certificates are valid for no more than five years.

If you are exempt from NHS charges because you are pregnant or have given birth in the last 12 months, ask your midwife, health visitor or GP for a maternity exemption form, which can be issued online straight away or by post.

## Prepayment certificates

In England, you can save money by buying a prepayment certificate if you are not exempt from charges and need more than three prescription items in three months or 11 items in a year.

Apply on Form FP95, online at www.nhsbsa.nhs.uk/help-nhs-prescription-costs/prescription-prepayment-certificates, at registered chemists, by phone (0300 330 1341) or by post.

You can claim a refund in certain circumstances – eg, if you buy a prepayment certificate and then qualify for free prescriptions.

In England, a HRT prepayment certificate (HRT PPC) allows you to pay a one-off charge equivalent to two single prescription charges for all HRT prescriptions for a year. You can apply for the HRT PPC online.[10]

# 3. Dental treatment and dentures

NHS dental check-ups are free in Scotland. In England, Wales and Scotland, you qualify for free NHS dental treatment (including check-ups) and appliances (including dentures) if, when your treatment is arranged or charges are made:[11]

- you are in one of the exempt groups listed on p574; *or*
- you qualify under the low income scheme (see p575); *or*
- you are under 18, or you are under 19 and in full-time education; *or*
- in Wales, for free check-ups only, you are under 25 or are 60 or over; *or*
- you are pregnant or have given birth within the last 12 months; *or*
- you are a permanent resident in a care home and your place is being partly or wholly funded by a local authority; *or*
- in England and Wales, you are in prison or a young offenders' institution; *or*
- you are a patient of the community dental service (available if you have difficulty getting treatment because of a disability or for other reasons – contact your health authority for details) or an NHS hospital dental service. **Note:** there may be a charge for dentures and bridges; *or*
- in Scotland, you are starting a course of dental treatment before the age of 26.

4

## 4. **Sight tests and glasses**

### Free sight tests

NHS sight tests are free in Scotland. In England and Wales, you qualify for a free NHS sight test if:[12]

- you are in one of the exempt groups listed on p574; *or*
- you qualify under the low income scheme (see p575); *or*
- you are aged 60 or over; *or*
- you are under 16, or you are under 19 and in full-time education; *or*
- you are registered blind or partially sighted; *or*
- you have been prescribed complex or powerful lenses; *or*
- you have been diagnosed as having diabetes or glaucoma or are at risk of getting glaucoma; *or*
- you are aged 40 or over and are the parent, sibling or child of someone with glaucoma; *or*
- you are a patient of the hospital eye service; *or*
- in England, you are on leave from prison or a young offenders' institution.

### Vouchers for glasses and contact lenses

If you are given a prescription for glasses following an eye test, you may be entitled to a voucher that you can use to buy glasses or contact lenses if you need these for the first time or because your previous ones have worn out through fair wear and tear, or your new prescription differs from your old one. You qualify if:[13]

- you are in one of the exempt groups listed on p574; *or*
- you qualify under the low income scheme (see p575); *or*
- you are under 16, or under 19 and in full-time education; *or*

- you are a hospital eye service patient needing frequent changes of glasses or contact lenses; *or*
- you have been prescribed complex or powerful lenses; *or*
- in England, you are on leave from prison or a young offenders' institution.

In addition, you may be entitled to a voucher when your glasses or lenses need to be replaced or repaired if, because of illness (illness or disability in Scotland), you have lost or damaged them and the cost of repair or replacement is not covered by insurance or warranty. This only applies if:[14]

- you are under 16, or under 19 and in full-time education. **Note:** the requirement for the loss or damage to have been caused by illness (illness or disability in Scotland) does not apply to children under 16 and, in England, to young people under 18 who were previously looked after by a local authority;[15] *or*
- you or a member of your family (see p575 for who counts) are covered by the first bullet point listed under 'Exempt groups' on p574; *or*
- you qualify under the low income scheme (see p575); *or*
- you have been prescribed complex or powerful lenses.

You can redeem the voucher at any supplier when you buy your glasses or contact lenses (or have glasses repaired). Vouchers are, however, only valid for two years.[16] Vouchers might not cover the full cost of the glasses or lenses you choose to buy. Prices vary; you may need to shop around if you do not want to pay the extra cost.

## 5. Wigs and fabric supports

Wigs and fabric supports are free in Scotland and Wales. You qualify for free wigs and fabric supports in England if:[17]

- you are in one of the exempt groups listed on p574; *or*
- you qualify under the low income scheme (see p575); *or*
- you are a hospital inpatient; *or*
- you are aged under 16, or under 19 and in full-time education; *or*
- you are a permanent resident in a care home and your place is being partly or wholly funded by a local authority; *or*
- you are in prison or a young offenders' institution or are detained under the Immigration Act 1971 or section 62 of the Nationality, Immigration and Asylum Act 2002.

## 6. Fares to receive NHS treatment

You qualify for full help with your fares to attend a hospital or any other establishment for NHS treatment or services if:[18]

- you are in one of the exempt groups listed on p574; *or*
- you qualify under the low income scheme (see p575); *or*
- you are a permanent resident in a care home and a local authority is partly or wholly funding your place; *or*
- you live in the Isles of Scilly or the Scottish Islands or Highlands and have to travel more than a specified distance. Special rules, including maximum costs, apply.[19]

4

A companion's travel expenses can also be covered – eg, if your child is attending a hospital and you need to accompany them, or if you need to be accompanied for medical reasons. You get help with the cost of travelling by the cheapest means of transport that is reasonable and, in Scotland, if necessary, the cost of overnight accommodation. This usually means standard-class public transport. If you must travel by car or taxi, you should be paid a mileage allowance, road and toll charges and unavoidable parking charges, or taxi fares. In Scotland, if you are the parent, primary carer or sibling under 18 of a child or young person under 18 in hospital, you can apply to the Young Patients Family Fund for help with costs of travel, food or accommodation, regardless of your income or benefits.[20]

Claim at the place where you receive NHS treatment. You may be able to request payment in advance of travel if this is necessary.

Travel expenses can be covered if you are travelling abroad to receive NHS treatment if the means and cost of travel, as well as any requirements for a companion, have been agreed in advance with the health service body that has arranged the treatment. In England and Wales, you are entitled to payment for travel to and from the airport, ferry port or international train station if you are in one of the above groups. You are also entitled to payment or repayment of onward travelling expenses to the treatment centre, whether or not you come into one of the above groups. In Scotland, the rules do not specify what can be covered.

## 7. Claims and refunds

In some situations, you do not have to make a claim for help with charges.

- If you are exempt on the grounds of your age, receipt of a qualifying benefit or because you are a full-time student aged under 19, complete the back of the prescription form (if required), or complete the appropriate form at your dentist, optician or hospital. See below if you get universal credit (UC).
- If you are an asylum seeker receiving asylum support, an HC2 certificate is issued by the Home Office. For advice, call Migrant Help (0808 801 0503).
- If you are exempt because you are pregnant or have given birth in the last 12 months, you need an exemption certificate. Ask your doctor, midwife or health visitor for a form.

- If you are entitled to free prescriptions because you have one of the conditions listed on p578, you need an exemption certificate. Apply on Form FP92A, which you can get from your GP.

In other cases, you must make a claim.

**Note:** if you are a war disablement pensioner, contact the Veterans UK helpline on 0808 191 4218 or see gov.uk/guidance/war-pension-scheme-wps.

## Claiming if you get universal credit

If you are unsure whether you are entitled to help with health costs because you do not know how much you earned in your last complete assessment period before the day you apply for help with health costs, check your online journal or call the UC helpline (tel: 0800 328 5644). If you cannot get a figure for your last month's earned income and you think it might exceed the threshold, you should pay the relevant charge and ask for a refund form at the same time. For prescription charges, you cannot get the refund form (Form FP57) at a later stage.

## Claiming under the low income scheme

You must make a claim to get full or partial help with charges and fares under the low income scheme. This includes if you are an asylum seeker but you are not receiving asylum support. If you *are* receiving asylum support, see p582. This also includes if you are exempt because you live in a care home or you are aged 16 or 17 and were previously looked after by a local authority.

Claim on Form HC1. If you have less than £6,000 capital, you can usually claim online or download a form at www.nhsbsa.nhs.uk/nhs-low-income-scheme or request a form by calling 0300 330 1343 (England), 0345 603 1108 (Wales) or 0131 275 6386 (Scotland). Another person can apply on your behalf if you cannot act for yourself.

If you live in a care home or you are aged 16 or 17 and were previously looked after by a local authority, you can use a shorter Form HC1(SC).

### Getting a certificate and when it expires

If you qualify for:

- full help, you are sent an HC2 certificate;
- partial help, you are sent an HC3 certificate which tells you the contribution you must make towards the charges.

Certificates are normally valid for 12 months. However, they are valid for:[21]

- five years if you are a single person aged 65 or over, or one of a couple, one aged 60 or over and the other aged 65 or over. This only applies if you do not receive earnings, or payments from an occupational pension, a personal pension or an annuity, and you do not have a dependent child or young person as a member of your household; *or*

- six months from the date of claim if you are receiving asylum support; *or*
- until the end of your course or the start of the next academic year if you are a full-time student.

Make a repeat claim on Form HC1 shortly before the expiry date. If you have a five-year certificate, you must notify the issuing authority of any changes in your family or household composition. In other cases, changes of circumstances (eg, starting work and increases in income) do not affect the validity of a certificate. However, if the change could result in increased help (eg, your income has *decreased*), you can reapply for a fresh assessment before the certificate expires.

4

## Overpayments and fraud

If you receive help to which you were not entitled, you can be issued with a penalty notice requiring you to pay the charge you should have paid plus a penalty, unless you can show that you did not act 'wrongfully' or with 'any lack of care'. The penalty can be increased if you do not pay it within 28 days, and court proceedings can be taken to recover the debt. Anyone wrongly claiming help with charges on your behalf can be liable to pay a penalty charge. You can also be prosecuted if you obtain help based on a false statement or representation.[22]

## Delays and complaints

For general queries or to make an informal complaint, phone 0300 330 1343. If you are unhappy with the decision on your claim or how it has been dealt with, or there are delays in obtaining a certificate, you can make a formal complaint by phone, in writing or email to the NHS Business Services Authority. See www.nhsbsa.nhs.uk/contact-us/complaints. If necessary, you could pay for the treatment or items you need and, after the outcome of your complaint, try to obtain a refund.

## Refunds

If you pay for an item or service that you could have got free or at reduced cost, you can apply for a refund. Do this within three months of paying the charge, although the time limit can sometimes be extended if you can show good cause for applying late – eg, you were ill.[23]

Apply for a refund of a prescription charge (in England) on Form FP57, which you must obtain when you pay, as one cannot be supplied later. For other items and services, apply on the relevant Form HC5 specific to that item/service, available to download at www.nhsbsa.nhs.uk or by calling 0300 330 1343 (England), 0345 603 1108 (Wales) or 0131 275 6386 (Scotland). You must submit a receipt or other documents to show that you have paid the charge. If you need an HC2 or HC3 certificate and have not applied for one, send a Form HC1 with your application for a refund.

# Notes

## 1. Who can get health benefits

1 **E** Regs 2-5 NHS(TERC) Regs; reg 3 POS Regs; reg 8 NHS(OCP) Regs 2013
**S** Regs 2-4 NHS(TERC)(S) Regs; regs 3 and 8 NHS(OCP)(S) Regs
**W** Regs 2-5 NHS(TERC)(W) Regs; reg 13 NHS(GOS) Regs; regs 3 and 8 NHS(OCP) Regs

2 **E** Sch 1 Table A NHS(TERC) Regs
**S** Sch Part 1 NHS(TERC)(S) Regs
**W** Sch 1 Table A NHS(TERC)(W) Regs

3 **E** Reg 5(2)(e) and (f) NHS(TERC) Regs; reg 3(2)(c) and (d) POS Regs; regs 3(2) and 8(3)(b) and (c) NHS(OCP) Regs 2013
**S** Reg 4(2)(c) and (d) NHS(TERC)(S) Regs; regs 3(2) and 8(3)(e) and (f) NHS(OCP)(S) Regs
**W** Reg 5(2)(e) NHS(TERC)(W) Regs; reg 13(2)(e) and (f) NHS(GOS) Regs; regs 3(2) and 8(3)(e) and (f) NHS(OCP) Regs

4 **E** Reg 6 NHS(TERC) Regs; regs 3 and 8 NHS(OCP) Regs 2013
**S** Reg 5 NHS(TERC)(S) Regs; regs 3 and 8 NHS(OCP)(S) Regs
**W** Reg 6 NHS(TERC)(W) Regs; regs 3 and 8 NHS(OCP) Regs

5 s13 Smoking, Health and Social Care (Scotland) Act 2005

6 **E** Reg 6 NHS(TERC) Regs; regs 7, 15 and 20 NHS(OCP) Regs 2013
**S** Reg 5 NHS(TERC)(S) Regs; regs 14 and 19 NHS(OCP)(S) Regs
**W** Reg 6 NHS(TERC)(W) Regs; regs 7, 14 and 19 NHS(OCP) Regs

7 **E** Reg 17 and Sch 1 Table B NHS(TERC) Regs
**S** Reg 8 and Sch Part 2 NHS(TERC)(S) Regs
**W** Reg 16 and Sch 1 Table B NHS(TERC)(W) Regs

8 **E** Reg 16 and Sch 1 Table A NHS(TERC) Regs
**S** Reg 8 and Sch Part 1 NHS(TERC)(S) Regs
**W** Reg 15 and Sch 1 Table A NHS(TERC)(W) Regs

## 2. Prescriptions

9 **E** Regs 10-13 NHS(CDA) Regs; regs 4 and 5 NHS(TERC) Regs
**S** Regs 3 and 4 NHS(FP&CDA)(S) Regs
**W** Regs 3, 4 and 8 NHS(FP&CDA)(W) Regs; regs 4 and 5 NHS(TERC)(W) Regs

10 health-charge-exemptions.nhsbsa.nhs.uk/buy-hrt-ppc

## 3. Dental treatment and dentures

11 **E** s177 NHSA 2006; regs 3 and 7 and Sch 5 NHS(DC) Regs; regs 4 and 5 NHS(TERC) Regs
**S** Sch 11 NHS(S)A 1978; reg 5 and Sch 2 NHS(DC)(S) Regs; regs 3 and 4 NHS(TERC)(S) Regs
**W** s126 NHS(W)A 2006; regs 3 and 7 and Sch 5 NHS(DC)(W) Regs; regs 4 and 5 NHS(TERC)(W) Regs

## 4. Sight tests and glasses

12 **E** Reg 3 POS Regs; regs 3 and 8 NHS(OCP) Regs 2013
**W** Reg 13 NHS(GOS) Regs; regs 3 and 8 NHS(OCP) Regs

13 **E** Regs 8 and 9 NHS(OCP) Regs 2013
**S** Regs 8 and 9 NHS(OCP)(S) Regs
**W** Regs 8 and 9 NHS(OCP) Regs

14 **E** Regs 8 and 16 NHS(OCP) Regs 2013
**S** Regs 8 and 15 NHS(OCP)(S) Regs
**W** Regs 8 and 15 NHS(OCP) Regs

15 **E** Reg 16(3) NHS(OCP) Regs 2013
**S** Reg 15(1) NHS(OCP)(S) Regs
**W** Reg 15(1) NHS(OCP) Regs

16 **E** Reg 12(1) NHS(OCP) Regs 2013
**S** Reg 12(1) NHS(OCP)(S) Regs
**W** Reg 12(1) NHS(OCP) Regs

## 5. Wigs and fabric supports

17 **E** Regs 10,11 and 12 NHS(CDA) Regs; regs 4 and 5 NHS(TERC) Regs
**S** Regs 3 and 4 NHS(FP&CDA)(S) Regs
**W** Regs 3, 4 and 8 NHS(FP&CDA)(W) Regs

6. **Fares to receive NHS treatment**

18 **E** s183(a) NHSA 2006; regs 3 and 5 NHS(TERC) Regs
**S** s75A(1)(b) NHS(S)A 1978; regs 3 and 4 NHS(TERC)(S) Regs
**W** s131(a) NHS(W)A 2006; regs 3 and 5 NHS(TERC)(W) Regs

19 **E** Reg 9 NHS(TERC) Regs
**S** Reg 7 NHS(TERC)(S) Regs

20 mygov.scot/young-patients-family-fund

7. **Claims and refunds**

21 **E** Reg 8 NHS(TERC) Regs
**S** Reg 10 NHS(TERC)(S) Regs
**W** Reg 8 NHS(TERC)(W) Regs

22 **E** ss193 and 194 NHSA 2006
**S** ss99ZA and 99ZB NHS(S)A 1978
**W** ss141 and 142 NHS(W)A 2006

23 **E** Reg 11 NHS(TERC) Regs; reg 18 NHS(CDA) Regs; regs 6 and 24 NHS(OCP) Regs 2013
**S** Reg 11 NHS(TERC)(S) Regs; reg 5 NHS(FP&CDA)(S) Regs; reg 20 NHS(OCP)(S) Regs
**W** Reg 10 NHS(TERC)(W) Regs; regs 3(10) and 11A NHS(FP&CDA)(W) Regs; regs 6 and 20 NHS(OCP) Regs

# Chapter 28

# Industrial injuries benefits

**This chapter covers:**


1. Who can get industrial injuries benefits (below)
2. Industrial injuries disablement benefit (p599)
3. Reduced earnings allowance (p601)
4. Retirement allowance (p602)
5. Special benefit rules (p603)
6. Claims and backdating (p603)
7. Getting paid (p605)
8. Tax, other benefits and the benefit cap (p606)


4

## Key facts

- Industrial injuries benefits are paid if you are disabled as a result of an accident at work or a disease caused by your job (but not if this is self-employment).
- The main industrial injuries benefit is **disablement benefit**, but you may also qualify for **reduced earnings allowance** or **retirement allowance**.
- All industrial injuries benefits are non-means-tested benefits.
- You do not have to have paid national insurance contributions to qualify.
- You can qualify whether you are in or out of work.
- Industrial injuries benefits are administered and paid by the DWP.
- If you disagree with an industrial injuries benefit decision, you can apply for a revision or a supersession (see Chapter 50), or appeal against it (see Chapter 51). You must apply for a mandatory reconsideration before you can appeal.

***Future changes***

In Scotland, industrial injuries benefits will be replaced by employment injury assistance. Social Security Scotland will be responsible for administering and paying this and existing industrial injuries disablement benefits in Scotland (see p1418).

## 1. Who can get industrial injuries benefits

You can qualify for industrial injuries benefits if you satisfy the **'industrial injury condition'** – ie:[1]

- you have had a 'personal injury' in an 'industrial accident' (see p589) or you have a 'prescribed industrial disease' (see p593); *and*
- at the time of the injury you were an employed earner (see below); *and*
- as a result of that accident or disease, you have had a 'loss of faculty' (see p595); *and*
- as a result of that 'loss of faculty', you are 'disabled'.

Industrial injuries benefits include industrial injuries disablement benefit, reduced earnings allowance (REA) and retirement allowance. You can only qualify for REA or retirement allowance if your accident, or in the case of a prescribed industrial disease, the onset of that disease (see p601), occurred before 1 October 1990.[2]

If you have been injured by your work, you may also have the right to sue your employer. Legal help may be available and you may be able to get a free consultation with a solicitor. Your right to compensation from your employer is separate from your rights to benefit under the industrial injuries scheme (although your compensation may be reduced if you have received benefits from the DWP – see p1043).

## Employed earners

You can only get industrial injuries benefits if you were an 'employed earner' (see p859) and your accident or disease was caused by your employment.[3] If you are self-employed, you are excluded from the scheme.

If you pay, or ought to pay, class 1 national insurance (NI) contributions (see p860) as an employed earner, you can qualify for industrial injuries benefits. This includes if you pay class 1 (and, in the case of volunteer development workers, class 2 – see p861) contributions while abroad.[4] You can also qualify if your earnings are too low to pay contributions.

Certain workers are treated as employed earners – eg, apprentices, agency workers, taxi drivers, office cleaners and various others.[5] You can also be treated as an employed earner if you participate in a government course or training scheme which forms part of a mandatory work scheme. The person or organisation providing the training is treated as the employer for the purposes of making a claim.[6]

You are treated as *not* being an employed earner if:[7]

- you are employed by your spouse or civil partner and either your employment is not for the purpose of their business or profession (eg, if your partner employs you as their carer) or your earnings are normally below the lower earnings limit (see p860); *or*
- you are employed by a close relative (parent, step-parent, grandparent, son, daughter, stepchild, brother, sister, half-brother or half-sister) in a private house where you both live, and your employment is not for your relative's trade or business carried out there; *or*

- you are a member of, or a civilian employed by, visiting armed forces, unless (in the case of a civilian employee) you are normally resident in the UK.

If you were not lawfully employed in the work in which you had the accident or contracted the disease that gave rise to your claim for benefit, you can still be treated as an employed earner. This is at the DWP's discretion.[8]

## Personal injury

Personal injury includes the obvious, such as broken legs or arms, but also covers the less obvious, such as strains and psychological injury.[9] An assault at work causing slight physical injury may cause a far greater psychological injury – eg, resulting in agoraphobia. The question is whether or not you have experienced a physiological or psychological change for the worse. It is not enough just to be in pain if the pain is merely a symptom of an existing condition and does not make that condition substantially worse.[10] The damage must be to you or part of you. Dislocation of an artificial hip joint counts as a personal injury,[11] but damage to a pair of spectacles does not.[12]



## Accident

The term 'accident' has been defined as an unlooked-for mishap or occurrence.[13] However, an accident need only be unexpected from your point of view.[14] It does not matter if an expert could have predicted it. If you do a heavy or dangerous job where accidents are common, a resulting injury is just as much an accident as if your job is sedentary and comparatively safe. A heart attack can be an injury, but there needs to be some external event or series of events causing it, such as heavy lifting or work-related stress.[15] Deliberate acts by third parties can be accidents – eg, assaults on security workers or staff in shops and hospitals.[16]

An accident is 'industrial' if you can show a connection with your work. This connection is established if the accident arose 'out of and in the course of your employment'.[17] It is not only industrial workers who can have 'industrial accidents'; all employees can. For example, if you are an office worker and you trip over boxes of office supplies left in front of a door and injure yourself, this should count as an 'industrial accident'. There need not be a dramatic event; any accident sustained while doing your job can qualify – eg, spilling a hot drink and scalding yourself. Mental trauma following an interview could count as an industrial accident.[18]

### Accident or process?

Benefit is payable for an 'accident', but not for a 'process' (unless it causes a 'prescribed disease' – see p593). Falling from a ladder and breaking your leg is an accident, but developing back pain as the result of years of heavy manual work is a process, as is breathing in dust over many years.[19] However, sometimes a series of events over a period of time can be treated as an accident for benefit purposes.[20]

The cumulative effect of a series of incidents can also result in an accident.[21] Your claim for benefit should not be refused simply because you cannot identify which incidents caused the injury.[22]

*Example*

Scott's job is trimming excess plastic from electrical cables with clippers. A particularly rigid batch comes through and each cut requires greater strength. Over two or three days he suffers a strain injury in his hand. The series of cuts constitute a series of accidents that meets the definition.



It is easier to establish the series of events as an accident if the period of time is fairly short,[23] or if it is noticed at an identifiable moment.[24] An accident is proved if you can establish that an identifiable occurrence must have happened, even if it is impossible to prove when.[25]

## In the course of employment

The accident must arise 'in the course of employment'.

Generally, when you arrive at your employer's workplace and are on its private property, you are 'in the course of your employment'. You do not have to have clocked in or have reported to your workplace. If you arrive early (eg, to get ready for work or to have a meal in the canteen),[26] you are covered, unless you arrive early for your own convenience.[27] You are probably covered during breaks from working if you remain on the employer's property,[28] but probably not if you go elsewhere. So if, during a tea break, you go to a local shop to buy a snack, you are outside the course of your employment.[29] If you are allowed to have a snack either at home or at work while still on duty, you are covered.[30]

While at work, most activities are considered to be in the course of employment.[31] Chatting[32] or attending union meetings,[33] for example, are 'reasonably incidental' to the employment, provided they are not done in breach of instructions.[34] Even if you were doing something in breach of instructions, you may still be covered if:

- the accident would have been taken as arising out of, and in the course of, your employment if you had not been acting in breach of those instructions; *and*
- what you were doing was for the purposes of, or in connection with, your employment.[35]

*Example*

Nina works in a paper factory where there is an absolute ban on riding on the load of a forklift truck. She is seen riding on the load, falls off and is injured. Usually, she would not be covered, but she saw the load was slipping and rode on the truck to hold it on. This was done for the purposes of her employment and so on this occasion she is covered.

Even if you are at home, depending on your contract, you may be covered.[36] You may be covered when you are off on sick leave, if you are engaged in contractual duties.[37]

*Example*

While on sick leave with stress, Remy is seen relaxing in the park by a former colleague he had reported for theft. He is assaulted and his jaw is broken. This is an industrial accident arising *out of* his employment (see p592) but not in the course of it, as he was not engaged in any contractual duties or any activities related to his work at the time of the assault.

4

In making your claim (see p603) or arguing your case at an appeal (see Chapter 51), consider all aspects of your employment, including the wording of your contract and the degree of flexibility in the arrangements between you and your employer.[38]

## Accidents while travelling

You are not in the course of your employment (see p590) during ordinary journeys to and from work, unless you are travelling on transport operated by or on behalf of your employer, or arranged by your employer, and not being operated in the ordinary course of a public transport service.[39]

Many employees have no set place of work – eg, lorry drivers, home helps, fuel company employees. Lorry drivers are at work when driving their lorries, but gas company workers travelling direct from home to their first job of the day are not always in the course of employment (see p590), even if driving a company van. It depends on the circumstances, including the rules for the use of the van.[40] In one case, a home help was found to be in the course of her employment travelling between jobs, but not going to the first job or from the last. This is because she became engaged in her employment once she started at the first job and remained engaged until the end of the day.[41]

Some employees with no fixed hours of work may be regarded as covered from the moment of leaving home.[42] So, you can be treated as being at your place of work while attending a meeting at a site where you do not work.[43] You must look at all the factors when deciding whether or not you were in the course of your employment. For example, a police officer who had to travel about 40 miles from home to a training course was in the course of his employment while travelling.[44] Provided you go reasonably directly, with no marked deviation from a proper route, and do not embark on activities unrelated to the journey, you may be covered.

One important factor in deciding whether you are in the course of your employment is whether you receive wages for travelling.[45] However, if you receive a flat-rate travelling allowance as compensation for having to work at a workplace other than your normal base, this may not be enough to make your journey to your alternative workplace part of your work.[46]

## Arising out of employment

As well as arising in the course of your employment (see p590), the accident (see p589) must arise 'out of' your employment, so that in some way the employment contributed to it. For example, the fact that you suffered a detached retina at work is not sufficient to show it arose 'out of' the employment, but medical evidence which shows that it was caused by sudden head movements while inspecting a production line enables you to establish that an industrial accident (see p589) took place. An unexplained fracture while walking at work is not an industrial accident,[47] but it is if you slip and the fracture occurs while you are falling. You are covered even if you are more susceptible to injury because, for example, your bones are brittle[48] or your eyesight is poor.

*Example*

Ewan, a farm worker, suffers sudden pain in the groin while doing his normal job of digging. It is found that a previous hernia, which had been surgically repaired, has given way. The DWP says that this could have happened at any time and so did not arise 'out of' the employment. Ewan's doctor says it could have happened at any time but probably did so at that time because of the heavy digging. The First-tier Tribunal awards him benefit.

An accident also arises out of your employment if it arises in the course of employment (see p590) and it is caused by:[49]

- another person's misconduct, 'skylarking' or negligence; *or*
- the behaviour or presence of an animal (including a bird, fish or insect); *or*
- your being struck by any object or by lightning.

In all cases, you must not have contributed to the accident by your conduct, either outside your employment or by any act 'not incidental to' the employment. (This involves looking at what you are employed to do, then at whether you were discharging a duty when the accident occurred, or whether what you were doing was reasonably incidental to that duty.) If you are skylarking at work and are injured as a result, for example, this is not incidental to your employment. If you act to deter someone else from doing so, however, this does not take you out of the course of your employment.[50]

An accident is deemed to arise out of, and in the course of, your employment if you are helping people in an emergency or trying to save property at or near where you are employed.[51]

## Prescribed industrial disease

It is not sufficient simply to have a medical diagnosis that you have a particular disease.[52] It must be on a list of diseases[53] known to have a link to a particular 'prescribed' occupation (see below).[54] The prescribed diseases are set out in regulations, and each one is identified by a letter followed by a number. For example, A12 is carpal tunnel syndrome and D1 is pneumoconiosis. Each prescribed disease has a statutory definition and you must fit within that. The complete list can be found in the DWP guidance.[55] From time to time, new diseases are added. You cannot claim benefit for a disease for any period before it was added to the list.

4

If the DWP accepts that you have a prescribed industrial disease, other diseases which result from it are included when assessing your 'loss of faculty' and disablement.[56] See p595 for how your disablement is assessed.

### Prescribed occupations

Different diseases are 'prescribed' for specific types of jobs because particular jobs have different health risks. To qualify for benefit on grounds of a prescribed industrial disease, you must have a disease which is on the list and prove that:

- you have worked in one or more of the jobs for which that disease is prescribed ('prescribed occupations'); *and*
- your job caused the disease.

If the DWP refuses to accept that you have worked in a prescribed occupation, you should obtain advice, preferably from your trade union or an advice agency. An expert's report may help to prove your case.

### Time limits

For most prescribed diseases, you do not have to have worked in a prescribed occupation for any minimum length of time. You can also claim at any time, even if it is many years since you worked in that occupation. However, there are exceptions to these general rules. For example, if you have occupational deafness (prescribed disease A10), you must have worked in a prescribed occupation for 10 years and claim within five years of having done so.[57] If you have occupational asthma (prescribed disease D7), you must claim within 10 years of working in a prescribed occupation.[58] If you have cataracts (prescribed disease A2), you must have worked in a prescribed occupation for five years or more in aggregate.[59] The DWP guidance lists relevant time limits or qualifying periods for other prescribed diseases.[60]

### Cause

For some diseases, unless the contrary can be proved, it is assumed that, if you have the disease within a particular interval (one, two, six or 12 months, depending on the disease) of working in the prescribed occupation (see above), the occupation caused it.[61] With other diseases, there is a presumption that a specific type of occupation caused them, regardless of when you last worked in that occupation.[62] There are also diseases where no assumed link exists (eg, dermatitis – prescribed disease D5), and you must establish the link 'on a balance of probabilities' – ie, that there is more likely a connection than not.[63] The DWP investigates the connection issue, and you may need to ask your GP or consultant for a report linking the disease to your occupation. DWP guidance says that, for some prescribed diseases, barring exceptional circumstances, the presumption that the disease was caused by the occupation should be automatic.[64]

4

There are different time conditions for carpal tunnel syndrome (prescribed disease A12[65]) in respect of some prescribed occupations, tuberculosis (prescribed disease B5[66]), pneumoconiosis (prescribed disease D1[67]) and, for some prescribed occupations, certain cancers of the urinary tract (prescribed disease C23[68]).

*Examples*

Ellen has been a farm worker for 10 years and has developed osteoarthritis of the hip (prescribed disease A13). She also broke her hip on a climbing holiday three years ago. The climbing accident does not alter the presumption that her prescribed disease was caused by her occupation.

Callum is a legal clerk who works for several hours a day typing on a computer keyboard. He develops typist's cramp (task-specific focal dystonia: prescribed disease A4) and is unable to continue using keyboards. His claim for benefit is rejected because he has not shown, on the balance of probabilities, that his work caused the condition. The decision maker points out that he has a computer at home which he uses every evening and at weekends for gaming. Callum successfully appeals the decision: he produces evidence that he uses a virtual reality headset and controllers at home along with a report from his physiotherapist stating that this activity is unlikely to cause his symptoms.

## Onset and recrudescence

The **'onset'** (date of starting) of a prescribed disease is taken as the date you first had a relevant 'loss of faculty' (see p595). In deafness cases, it is the later of either the date you first experienced the loss of faculty or the date you successfully claimed benefit.[69] For Dupuytren's contracture (prescribed disease A15), the date of onset is the date that the contracture stage of the disease is reached.[70]

In diseases other than deafness, asthma and respiratory conditions, you can improve and then worsen again. It is important to know whether it is a **'recrudescence'** (fresh outbreak of the existing disease) or a completely new attack. The first is deemed to be a continuation of the existing prescribed disease;[71] with the second, you have to wait 15 weeks before disablement benefit can be claimed. If a further attack starts during a current period of assessment, it is assumed to be a recrudescence unless proved otherwise.

## Loss of faculty and disablement

In addition to showing the link between your injury or disease and your occupation, you must also establish that you have had a 'loss of faculty' and are 'disabled'.

**'Loss of faculty'** is the damage or impairment of part of the body or mind caused by the industrial accident or disease. **'Disability'** is the inability to do something as a result of that damage or impairment. The total of all of your disabilities, taken together, amount to a **'disablement'**. This disablement is expressed as a percentage.

In assessing your disablement, the DWP considers three questions.

- Has the relevant industrial accident (see p589) or prescribed disease (see p593) resulted in a loss of faculty (see below)?
- What is the extent of disablement resulting from a loss of faculty (this is expressed as a percentage – see below)?
- What period is to be taken into account by the assessment (see p598)?

### A loss of faculty

A 'loss of faculty' is an 'impairment of the proper functioning of part of the body or mind'[72] caused by an accident or disease. A 'loss of faculty' is not the same as disablement. It includes disfigurement, even if the disfigurement is not accompanied by a loss of physical faculty.[73] A decision that there has been a personal injury resulting from an industrial accident (see p589) does not prevent the DWP or First-tier Tribunal from finding that there is no loss of faculty.[74]

### The extent of disablement

The extent of your disablement is assessed on a percentage basis. To qualify for disablement benefit (see p599), generally you must reach a threshold of at least 14 per cent disablement. However, a finding of at least 1 per cent may permit a claim for REA (see p601).

Any assessment between 14 and 19 per cent is treated as being 20 per cent.[75] If the total disablement from all industrial accidents and diseases is more than 20 per cent, it is rounded to the nearest multiple of 10 per cent, with multiples of 5 per cent or more being rounded upwards.[76] For example, an assessment of 22 per cent is rounded down to 20 per cent and an assessment of 25 per cent is rounded up to 30 per cent.

Your disablement is assessed by comparing you with a person of the same age and sex whose physical and mental condition is 'normal'.[77] Any other personal circumstances (eg, where you live or the proximity of your home to a bus stop) are not taken into account.

***What happens at the assessment?***

It is important that you are straightforward with the examining healthcare professional. There are checks to establish that your symptoms are consistent with the injury, and that your movements are consistent with the disablement you claim you have. How you walk, sit and how you undress (if relevant) are also considered. Ensure that the examiner is aware of all the things that you now cannot do due to your injury or disease.

Some assessments of disablement are set out in regulations.[78] These are known as 'prescribed degrees of disablement' and include various amputations (eg, loss of a hand or a leg) and degrees of hearing loss (see Appendix 4). However, even in these cases, the DWP must take into account the real disablement resulting from an injury and increase or decrease the figure to arrive at a reasonable assessment[79] – eg, the loss of a right hand is more disabling for a right-handed person than for a left-handed person. The full extent of your disablement caused by the injury must be taken into account. A further disablement or condition which arises at a later date, but which can be shown to be caused by the industrial accident or disease, must be included in the assessment.[80]

Diffuse mesothelioma causing impaired functioning of the pleura, pericardium or peritoneum automatically has an assessment of 100 per cent disablement.[81]

When there is no prescribed degree of disablement, reference may be made to the prescribed percentages to help with the assessment.[82] Although you may suggest that your assessment should be a particular percentage, the DWP makes its own judgement.[83]

### Offsets if your disability has more than one cause

If a disability is congenital or arose before an industrial one, it is deducted from the total disablement.[84] The reduction is often called the 'offset'. Mistakes are sometimes made because the DWP incorrectly offsets for medical conditions that have not caused any disability.

*Examples*

Ivy loses a hand, which would normally be 60 per cent, but she had previously lost the index finger. So 14 per cent is deducted, leaving 46 per cent (rounded up to 50 per cent).

Lucy has a back injury as a result of an industrial accident. The DWP has reduced her assessment by 5 per cent on the grounds of a pre-existing disability of which she knew nothing. Many people have spines that are slightly curved as a result of lifting things. The DWP may have looked at an x-ray, correctly considered that her curved spine was not due to the relevant accident and then incorrectly reduced her assessment.

In the second example, the DWP should have considered whether the pre-existing loss of faculty (see p595), the curved spine, actually had (or would have) led to disablement that would have occurred regardless of the industrial accident. It should have considered, among other things, whether the loss of faculty led to disablement before the industrial accident occurred. There is no physical disablement if you do not have any pain or restriction of movement and it is therefore wrong to reduce your assessment unless there is a good reason for deciding that disablement would have arisen during the period of assessment even if the industrial accident had not occurred.

In the second example, depending on the medical opinion:

- there may be no offset; *or*
- it may be appropriate to make a life award (see p598) with some uniform offset over the whole period in respect of any future back problems Lucy is likely to have; *or*
- it may be appropriate to make a stepped assessment, making no offset initially but bringing one in at some future date, or applying different levels of offset for different parts of the period covered by the award.[85]



No reduction is made if your injury is one for which the regulations award 100 per cent and this is considered a reasonable assessment for the industrial accident.[86]

The DWP should also bear in mind that, even if you had a pre-existing problem which caused a disability, the accident may worsen the effects of it, as well as cause a new problem. In such a case, the assessment should reflect the increase in the original problem as well as the new disability.[87]

If another disability arose after an industrial accident, the DWP must first assess the disablement arising from the industrial injury. If it is less than 11 per cent, any disability from the other cause is ignored. If it is more than 11 per cent, any extra disablement caused by the effect of the industrial injury on the other disability is added.[88]

***Examples***

David loses a little finger in an industrial accident and is assessed as 7 per cent disabled as a result. He then loses the other fingers of that hand in a non-industrial accident. He continues to be assessed as 7 per cent disabled because of the industrial accident.

Travis loses the middle, ring and little fingers of one hand in an industrial accident and is assessed as 30 per cent disabled as a result. He then loses the index finger of that hand in a non-industrial accident. His total disablement is now 50 per cent. But loss of the index finger only would have been 14 per cent. The disablement resulting from his industrial accident may therefore be reassessed at 36 per cent (50 per cent *minus* 14 per cent), which is rounded up to 40 per cent.

### Two or more industrial accidents or diseases

If you have more than one industrial accident, the percentages of disablement (see p595 and Appendix 4) can be added together and may entitle you to benefit, even if neither accident would do so on its own. If you have two or more industrial accidents, you may end up in a situation where the second or later accident is made worse by the interaction with the effect of the previous accident(s). Your most recent assessment should include an increase for any such interaction.[89] This also applies if an industrial disease (see p593) interacts with the effects of an industrial accident.

*Example*

Ambika has a fall at work and seriously injures her left leg. She receives a life assessment of 10 per cent. Years later, she has a further fall and seriously injures the other leg. She is assessed as 10 per cent disabled for that accident, with a further 5 per cent for the extra disability she has as a result of the interaction between the two injuries. The total of 25 per cent is rounded up, resulting in payment of a 30 per cent pension.

There are special rules if you have pneumoconiosis. They allow for certain conditions to be taken into account in order to increase the assessment, even though these conditions did not arise from the pneumoconiosis. Any effect of tuberculosis is assessed with the effects of the pneumoconiosis.[90] If your disability is assessed at 50 per cent because of the pneumoconiosis, any additional disability because of chronic obstructive pulmonary disease is added.[91] If you have made such a claim for pneumoconiosis, you cannot then make a separate claim for chronic obstructive pulmonary disease.[92]

## The period covered by the assessment

The DWP or First-tier Tribunal decides how long you will likely be affected by a relevant loss of faculty and how long you have already been affected (see p595). Percentage assessments are usually made for six months, or for one or two years, or are given for life,[93] but definite dates must be given.

An assessment is either final or provisional.[94] You get a provisional assessment when there is doubt about what will happen in the future, and you are automatically called for another assessment at the end of the period.[95] Life assessments are final.

If you are given a final assessment for a fixed period, this means that the DWP believes you will no longer be affected by your accident or disease by the end of that period. If you think that the effects of the accident or disease will last for longer, consider an appeal against that assessment (see Chapter 51).

If your condition deteriorates during a period of assessment, or if you still have a disability at the end of a period for which you have been given a final assessment, you should apply for a supersession (see p1143).

An assessment of disablement for occupational deafness is for life.[96]

## 2. Industrial injuries disablement benefit

The main benefit linked to industrial accidents and diseases is industrial injuries disablement benefit (IIDB). You may qualify for additional amounts of benefit paid along with or as increases to IIDB. These are:

- constant attendance allowance (see p600);
- exceptionally severe disablement allowance (see p601);
- reduced earnings allowance (see p601).[97]



### Who can get industrial injuries disablement benefit

You can qualify for IIDB if:[98]

- you satisfy the industrial injury condition (see p587) as a result of one or more industrial accidents (see p589) or prescribed diseases (see p593); *and*
- your resulting disablement is assessed as being at least 14 per cent (1 per cent in the case of pneumoconiosis, byssinosis and diffuse mesothelioma) (see p595 and Appendix 4); *and*
- 90 days (excluding Sundays) have elapsed since the date of the accident or of the onset of the prescribed disease or injury (if you have mesothelioma, you can be paid without serving this waiting period).

#### Disqualification

You may be disqualified for up to six weeks if you do not provide the required information, notify changes in your circumstances, or do not have a medical examination or treatment. You cannot, however, be disqualified for refusing to have an operation, unless it is a minor one.[99]

### The rules about your age

There are no specific age rules or requirement to have paid national insurance contributions. You must simply be under a contract of employment. Therefore, a child who is working is covered, as well as a person over pension age.

### People included in the claim

You claim IIDB for yourself. You cannot claim any increases for an adult or your child(ren) unless you are getting unemployability supplement (abolished for new claims after 5 April 1987).

### The amount of benefit

The amount of benefit you get depends on the extent of your disablement.[100] See p595 for how this is assessed.

| *Extent of disablement* | *£ per week* |
|---|---|
| 100% | 225.30 |
| 90% | 202.77 |
| 80% | 180.24 |
| 70% | 157.71 |
| 60% | 135.18 |
| 50% | 112.65 |
| 40% | 90.12 |
| 30% | 67.59 |
| 11%–20% | 45.06 |

4

IIDB can be paid if the assessment of your disablement is at least 14 per cent,[101] except in the cases of pneumoconiosis, byssinosis and diffuse mesothelioma, when it must be at least 1 per cent.[102] Before 1 October 1986, IIDB was paid for an assessment of disablement of at least 1 per cent. The old rules are still in force for claims made before this date.[103] If you are getting a payment as a result of such a small percentage assessment, see p176 of the 17th edition of CPAG's *Rights Guide to Non-Means-Tested Benefits*.

You may be able to get an increase of benefit.

## Increases of industrial injuries disablement benefit

You get increased IIDB if you qualify for constant attendance allowance or exceptionally severe disablement allowance.

### Constant attendance allowance

You qualify for constant attendance allowance if:[104]

- you are entitled to IIDB based on a degree of disablement assessed at 100 per cent; *and*
- you require constant attendance as a result of the relevant loss of faculty (see p595).

Disablement as a result of pre-1948 industrial accidents and diseases, war injuries and injuries incurred while on police or fire duty may be taken into account in considering the degree of your disablement.

The amount you get depends on your disability and the amount of attendance you need.[105]

- The higher weekly rate of £180.40 is paid if you are 'so exceptionally severely disabled as to be entirely, or almost entirely dependent on (constant) attendance for the necessities of life and [are] likely to remain so dependent for a prolonged period and the attendance so required is whole-time'.
- The lower weekly rate of £90.20 is paid if you are 'to a substantial extent dependent on (constant) attendance for the necessities of life, and [are] likely

to remain so dependent for a prolonged period'. This amount can be increased to as much as £135.30 a week if 'the extent of such attendance is greater by reason of the beneficiary's exceptionally severe disablement'. If attendance is part time only, the amount payable is 'such sum as may be reasonable in the circumstances' (usually £45.10 a week).

Some people will be better off claiming disability living allowance, personal independence payment or attendance allowance instead, where this is paid at a higher rate.



#### Exceptionally severe disablement allowance

This is paid at the weekly rate of £90.20 if you are entitled to constant attendance allowance (or would be if you were not in hospital) at the higher or intermediate rate, and you are likely to remain so permanently.[106]

## 3. Reduced earnings allowance

Reduced earnings allowance (REA) is available if you had an accident or started to have a disease before 1 October 1990. A successful first claim can still be made now if you had an accident or disease before this date.

The amount of REA you get depends on whether your current earnings, or earnings in a job which it is considered you could do, are less than the current earnings in your previous 'regular occupation'. This involves looking at your work history and the content of your job, rather than at your job title.

See Chapter 32 of the 2015/16 edition of this *Handbook* for the qualifying conditions for REA.

### Who is still entitled to reduced earnings allowance

You qualify for REA if:[107]

- you satisfy the industrial injury condition (see p587) because of an industrial accident (see p589) before 1 October 1990 or an industrial disease (see p593), the onset of which was before that date (see p594); *and*
- your resulting disablement is assessed as being at least 1 per cent (see p595 and Appendix 4); *and*
- as a result of a relevant loss of faculty, either:
  - you are incapable and likely to remain permanently incapable of following your regular occupation and are incapable of following employment of an equivalent standard which is suitable in your case; *or*
  - you are, and have been at all times since the end of the 90-day qualifying period for industrial injuries disablement benefit (IIDB), incapable of following your regular occupation or employment of an equivalent standard

which is suitable in your case. (If you did return to your former, regular occupation – eg, to see whether you could carry on – this will not necessarily prevent a later claim for REA from succeeding.[108])

***Date of onset before October 1990?***

If the disease you suffer from was added to the list of prescribed industrial diseases on or after 10 October 1990, you will not qualify for REA in respect of it, even if the date of onset was before this date. In some cases, the definition of a prescribed disease on the list of industrial diseases can be 'extended', meaning that the qualifying criteria have been widened since it was first added to the list. If you suffer from a disease which is classified as a prescribed industrial disease on the basis of such extended criteria, and the extension occurred on or after 10 October 1994, then you cannot get REA in respect of that disease, regardless of the date of onset.[109]

For more details, see p695 of the 2015/16 edition of this *Handbook*.

### The amount of benefit

The amount of REA you get is the amount by which your current earnings, or earnings in a job which it is considered you could do, are less than the current earnings in your previous regular occupation (see p697 of the 2015/16 edition of this *Handbook*).[110]

The maximum amount you can receive for any one award is £90.12 a week.[111] The total you can receive from IIDB and REA (whether for one or more awards) is 140 per cent of the standard rate of IIDB.[112] If you were over pension age and retired before 6 April 1987, your allowance is reduced if it would otherwise mean you would be receiving more than 100 per cent of the standard rate of IIDB.[113] If you qualified for REA and were retired or treated as retired on either 10 April 1988 or 9 April 1989, you continue to receive the allowance at the same 'frozen' rate. Its value therefore erodes over time.

## 4. Retirement allowance

Retirement allowance is a reduced rate of reduced earnings allowance (REA – see p601) for people over pension age, paid for life. Your REA does not stop simply because you have reached pension age. However, it can continue until you give up regular employment.

You qualify for retirement allowance if:[114]

- you are over pension age (see p690);
- you have given up regular employment;

- you were entitled to REA at a rate of at least £2 a week (in total, if you had more than one award) immediately before you gave up regular employment;
- you are not entitled to REA.

You can only get one award of retirement allowance, even if you had more than one award of REA.[115]

The amount of retirement allowance you get is £22.53 a week or 25 per cent of the amount of REA you were receiving, whichever is the lower. There are no increases for dependants.



## 5. Special benefit rules

Special rules may apply if you:
- are going abroad (see Chapters 58 and 59);
- are in prison or detention (see Chapter 38).

## 6. Claims and backdating

The general rules about claims and backdating are covered in Chapter 44. This section explains the specific rules that apply to industrial injuries benefits.

### Making a claim

You should usually claim industrial injuries benefits in writing.[116] You do not have to make a claim for retirement allowance.[117]

The notes you get with the claim form tell you where you should send your completed claim form. Keep a copy of your claim in case queries arise.

*Forms*

There are different forms depending on the benefit claimed and whether you are claiming for an accident or a disease. You can download the IIDB form from gov.uk/industrial-injuries-disablement-benefit/how-to-claim or phone to request a form (0800 121 8379; textphone: 0800 169 0314; Relay UK service available). You need to request the REA form by phone (0800 121 8379; textphone: 0800 169 0314; Relay UK service available).

You must provide any information or evidence required. In certain circumstances, the DWP may accept a written application not on the approved form.[118] You can amend or withdraw your claim before a decision is made (see p1004).

## Who should claim

You claim for yourself. If you cannot manage your claim, another person can for you as your appointee (see p1005).

## Information to support your claim

For the general information requirements that apply to all benefits, see p1006.

It is important that you provide any information required when you claim. Until you do, you may not count as having made a valid claim (see p1008). Correct any defects as soon as possible or your date of claim may be affected.

Even if your claim is valid, you may be asked to provide further information to support your claim (see p1009). You may also be asked to provide information after you are awarded industrial injuries benefits, and if you fail to do so, your benefit could be suspended, or even terminated (see p1031).

## The date of your claim

The date of your claim is important, as it determines when your entitlement to industrial injuries benefits starts. This is not necessarily the date from when you are paid. For information about when payment of benefit starts, see p605.

The date of your claim is the date it is received at the industrial injuries disablement benefit (IIDB) centre.

You must make sure your claim is valid. If it is 'defective', you are given a short time to correct the defects (see p1009). If you do, your claim is treated as having been made when you initially claimed.[119]

### Backdating your claim

It is important to claim in time. Your claim can be backdated for up to three months if you satisfy the qualifying conditions over that period. You do not have to show any reasons why your claim was late. The rules on backdating are covered on p1012.

If you might have qualified for benefit earlier but did not claim because you were given the wrong information or were misled by the DWP, ask for compensation (see p1261) or complain to the Ombudsman (see p1266).

### If you claim the wrong benefit

In some circumstances, it is possible for a claim for one benefit to be treated as a claim for a different benefit (see p1013). However, for industrial injuries benefits it is only possible to 'interchange' constant attendance allowance with DLA and AA.[120]

### Claiming in advance

You can make an advance claim for IIDB if you have had an accident or have a prescribed disease and you are within the 90-day waiting period. The date of your claim is the date on which you qualify. Otherwise it is not possible to claim industrial injuries benefits in advance.

## Renewal claims

Assessments can be provisional or final, and for a limited period or for life. A provisional assessment means that the DWP considers that your medical condition has not yet settled down, and may get worse or better. At the end of a provisional assessment, you are invited to be re-examined. A final assessment means that the DWP believes that your condition has settled down and your case is dealt with once and for all. At the end of a period of award, you must therefore apply for a renewal of benefit.

If you get IIDB for a particular disease, you may recover at some point but subsequently have a further attack. If there is a continuation (or recrudescence) of the old disease, you do not have to wait 90 days before becoming entitled to IIDB.



# 7. Getting paid

The general rules on getting paid are covered in Chapter 45. This section explains the specific rules that apply to industrial injuries benefits.

***When are industrial injuries benefits paid?***

You are paid on a Wednesday,[121] weekly in advance or four weeks in arrears.[122]

**Note:**

- You might not be paid your industrial injuries benefit if you have been sanctioned for a benefit offence (see p1111).
- If payment of your industrial injuries benefit is delayed, see p1123. If you are waiting for a decision on your claim, or to be paid, you may be able to get a short-term advance (see p1023). If you wish to complain about how your claim has been dealt with, or claim compensation, see Chapter 55.
- If payment of your industrial injuries benefit is suspended, see p1031.
- If you are overpaid industrial injuries benefit, you may have to repay it (see Chapter 47) and, in some circumstances, you may have to pay a penalty (see p1101). If you have been accused of fraud, see Chapter 48.
- If you are owed arrears of industrial injuries benefit, these can be paid in instalments (see p1018).

## Change of circumstances

You must report any change of circumstances that you have been told you must report, as well as any that you might reasonably be expected to know might affect your right to, the amount of, or the payment of your benefit. You should do this as soon as possible, preferably in writing. See p1030 for further information.

## 8. Tax, other benefits and the benefit cap

### Tax

Industrial injuries benefits are not taxable.[123]

4

### Means-tested benefits

Industrial injuries disablement benefit (IIDB), reduced earnings allowance (REA) and retirement allowance are taken into account in full for all the means-tested benefits. Constant attendance allowance and exceptionally severe disablement allowance are disregarded.

### Non-means-tested benefits

In general, the overlapping benefits rule does not apply to industrial injuries benefits, apart from constant attendance allowance (see p1021). It is possible, for example, to get full disablement benefit as well as full employment and support allowance.

Carer's allowance (see Chapter 22) or carer support payment (see p1467) may be paid to someone who is 'regularly and substantially caring' for you while you are getting constant attendance allowance (see p600).[124]

If your spouse or civil partner died as a result of an industrial accident or disease, you may qualify for a bereavement benefit even though the national insurance contribution conditions are not satisfied (see Chapter 21).[125]

### The benefit cap

Industrial injuries benefits are *not* specified benefits for the benefit cap. It does *not* apply if you or your partner get IIDB, REA or retirement allowance.

### Passports and other sources of help

You qualify for a Christmas bonus if you get disablement benefit, but only if it includes unemployability supplement or constant attendance allowance (see p783).

In addition to IIDB, you may be able to get a one-off lump sum payment if:

- you have pneumoconiosis (including asbestosis, silicosis and kaolinosis), byssinosis, diffuse mesothelioma, diffuse pleural thickening, or primary carcinoma of the lung if accompanied by asbestosis or diffuse pleural thickening; *and*

- you are unable, or unlikely to be able, to get compensation from your employer (eg, they have ceased trading).

You should claim without delay, at the same time that you claim IIDB (see p603). Dependants of someone who met the above conditions and has since died may also be able to claim. Claims should be made within one year of diagnosis, or, for a dependant's claim, within one year of death.

If you have contracted an asbestos or dust-related disease, you should seek expert advice on benefits and compensation straight away. For example, you may qualify for a lump sum under the Diffuse Mesothelioma Scheme 2008 if you have contracted this disease, even if you were not exposed to asbestos as an employee, or under the Diffuse Mesothelioma Payment Scheme, if you did contract the disease as an employee. Dependants can also claim under these schemes but any award is likely to be lower than for a claim started before death.

Time limits apply, but in some instances may be extended if there is good cause. All these lump sum payments may be deducted from any compensation awarded for personal injury (see p1043).

4

# Notes

1. **Who can get industrial injuries benefits**

1 ss94 and 103 SSCBA 1992
2 Sch 7 para 11(1) SSCBA 1992, reg 14A SS(IIPD) Regs
3 ss94(1) and 108(1) SSCBA 1992
4 Reg 10C(5) and (6) SSB(PA) Regs
5 Regs 2, 4 and 6 SS(EEEIIP) Regs; *Uber BV and others (Appellants) v Aslam and others (Respondents)* [2021] UKSC 5; *Addison Lee Ltd v Lange and others* [2021] EWCA Civ 594
6 Regs 2 and 3 IIB(ETSC) Regs; s95A SSCBA 1992
7 Reg 3 SS(EEEIIP) Regs
8 s97 SSCBA 1992
9 R(I) 49/52
10 R(I) 1/76
11 R(I) 5/81
12 R(I) 1/82
13 *Fenton v Thorley* [1903] AC 443 (HL)
14 CI/123/1949
15 *Jones v Secretary of State for Social Services* [1972] AC 944 (HL), also reported as an appendix to R(I) 3/69; *SSWP v Scullion* [2010] EWCA Civ 310
16 *Trim Joint District School Board of Management v Kelly* [1914] AC 667 (HL)
17 s94(1) SSCBA 1992
18 CI/105/1998; CI/142/2006
19 *Roberts v Dorothea Slate Quarries Co Ltd* [1948] 2 All ER 201 (HL)
20 R(I) 24/54; R(I) 43/55
21 CI/3370/1999
22 *Mullen v SSWP* [2002] Session Case 251; SLT 149; SCLR 475; *Greens Weekly Digest* 3-121, IH (2DIV)
23 R(I) 43/61; R(I) 4/62
24 R(I) 18/54
25 CI/159/1950
26 *R v National Insurance Commissioner ex parte East* [1976] ICR 206 (DC), also reported as an appendix to R(I) 16/75
27 R(I) 1/59; R(I) 45/55

28 *R v Industrial Injuries Commissioner ex parte AEU* [1966] 2 QB 31 (CA), also reported as an appendix to R(I) 4/66
29 R(I) 10/81
30 *R v National Insurance Commissioner ex parte Reed* (DC), reported as an appendix to R(I) 7/80
31 s94(3) SSCBA 1992
32 R(I) 46/53
33 R(I) 9/57
34 *R v Industrial Injuries Commissioner ex parte AEU* [1966] 2 QB 31 (CA), also reported as an appendix to R(I) 4/66
35 s29(6)(b) SSA 1998; CI/210/1950
36 R(I) 64/51
37 R(I) 1/99
38 *Nancollas v Insurance Officer* [1985] 1 All ER 833 (CA), also reported as an appendix to R(I) 7/85
39 s99 SSCBA 1992
40 R(I) 1/88
41 R(I) 12/75
42 R(I) 4/70
43 R(I) 1/93
44 *Nancollas v Insurance Officer* [1985] 1 All ER 833 (CA); *Ball v Insurance Officer* [1985] 1 All ER 833 (CA); both also reported as an appendix to R(I) 7/85
45 *Smith v Stages* [1989] 2 WLR 529 (HL)
46 R(I) 1/91
47 R(I) 6/82
48 R(I) 12/52
49 s101 SSCBA 1992
50 R(I) 3/67
51 s100 SSCBA 1992
52 R(I) 3/03
53 Sch 1 SS(IIPD) Regs
54 Reg 2 SS(IIPD) Regs
55 DWP, *Industrial Injuries Disablement Benefits: technical guidance*, Appendix 1, gov.uk/government/publications/industrial-injuries-disablement-benefits-technical-guidance
56 Reg 3 SS(IIPD) Regs
57 Regs 2(c) and 25 SS(IIPD) Regs
58 Reg 36 SS(IIPD) Regs
59 Reg 2(e) SS(IIPD) Regs
60 DWP, *Industrial Injuries Disablement Benefits: technical guidance*, Appendix 1, gov.uk/government/publications/industrial-injuries-disablement-benefits-technical-guidance
61 Reg 4(1), (4) and (5) SS(IIPD) Regs
62 Reg 4(2) and (6) SS(IIPD) Regs
63 Reg 4(1) SS(IIPD) Regs
64 Appendix 7 Ch 67 DMG
65 Reg 4(5) SS(IIPD) Regs
66 Reg 4(3) SS(IIPD) Regs
67 Reg 4(7) SS(IIPD) Regs
68 Reg 4(6) SS(IIPD) Regs
69 Reg 6(2)(c) SS(IIPD) Regs
70 *DR v SSWP (II)* [2021] UKUT 191 (AAC)
71 Reg 7 SS(IIPD) Regs
72 *Jones v Secretary of State for Social Services* [1972] AC 944 (HL), also reported as an appendix to R(I) 3/69
73 CI/499/2000; s122(1) SSCBA 1992
74 s30 SSA 1998
75 s103(3) SSCBA 1992
76 s103(2) and (3) SSCBA 1992; regs 15A and 15B SS(IIPD) Regs
77 Sch 6 para 1 SSCBA 1992
78 Sch 2 SS(GB) Regs; Sch 3 SS(IIPD) Regs
79 Reg 11(6) SS(GB) Regs
80 *JL and DO v SSWP (II)* [2011] UKUT 294 (AAC), reported as [2012] AACR 15
81 Reg 20A SS(IIPD) Regs
82 Reg 11(8) SS(GB) Regs; R(I) 5/95; R(I) 1/04
83 CI/636/1993. In some cases, it may be an error of law to arrive at a different figure without giving reasons for this (para 10).
84 Reg 11(3) SS(GB) Regs
85 CI/34/1993
86 Reg 11(7) SS(GB) Regs
87 R(I) 3/91
88 Reg 11(4) SS(GB) Regs
89 R(I) 3/91
90 Reg 21 SS(IIPD) Regs
91 Reg 22 SS(IIPD) Regs
92 Reg 2(d) SS(IIPD) Regs; para 67943 DMG
93 Sch 6 para 6 SSCBA 1992
94 Sch 6 para 7 SSCBA 1992
95 Sch 6 para 6(2)(b) SSCBA 1992
96 Reg 29 SS(IIPD) Regs

### 2. Industrial injuries disablement benefit

97 s94(2) SSCBA 1992
98 ss94, 103 and 108 SSCBA 1992
99 Reg 40 SS(GB) Regs
100 Sch 4 SSCBA 1992
101 s103(1) SSCBA 1992
102 Reg 20(1) SS (IIPD) Regs
103 Sch 7 para 9(1)(a) SSCBA 1992; reg 14 SS(II&D)MP Regs
104 s104 SSCBA 1992
105 s104 SSCBA 1992; reg 19 SS(GB) Regs
106 s105 SSCBA 1992

### 3. Reduced earnings allowance

107 Sch 7 paras 11 and 12(1), (2) and (7) SSCBA 1992; SS(II)REA Regs
108 *SSWP v RD (II)* [2017] UKUT 481 (AAC)
109 Reg 14A SS(IIPD) Regs

110 Sch 7 para 11(10) SSCBA 1992
111 Regs 2 and 3 SS(II)(REA) Regs; Sch 7 para 11(13) SSCBA 1992
112 Sch 7 para 11(10) SSCBA 1992
113 Sch 7 para 11(11) SSCBA 1992

4. **Retirement allowance**
114 Sch 7 para 13 SSCBA 1992
115 *TA v SSWP (II)* [2010] UKUT 101 (AAC)

6. **Claims and backdating**
116 Reg 4(1) SS(C&P) Regs
117 Reg 3(e) SS(C&P) Regs
118 Reg 4(1) SS(C&P) Regs
119 Reg 6(1)(b) SS(C&P) Regs
120 Sch 1 Part 1 SS(C&P) Regs

7. **Getting paid**
121 Sch 6 para 3 SS(C&P) Regs
122 Reg 22 SS(C&P) Regs

8. **Tax, other benefits and the benefit cap**
123 s677 IT(EP)A 2003
124 Regs 14, 17 and 21 SS(IB)(T) Regs
125 s60(2) and (3) SSCBA 1992

# Chapter 29

# New-style jobseeker's allowance

4

**This chapter covers:**


1. Who can get new-style jobseeker's allowance (p611)
2. The rules about your age (p615)
3. People included in the award (p615)
4. The amount of benefit (p616)
5. Special benefit rules (p618)
6. Claims and backdating (p619)
7. Getting paid (p625)
8. Tax, other benefits and the benefit cap (p626)


## Key facts

- Jobseeker's allowance (JSA) is a benefit for people who are looking for work.
- Contribution-based JSA is called new-style JSA.
- New-style JSA is a non-means-tested benefit, but it can be affected by earnings and certain pension payments.
- You must have paid sufficient national insurance contributions.
- You cannot qualify for JSA if you count as being in full-time paid work.
- You must normally be fit for work and meet work-related requirements.
- You may be able to get your new-style JSA topped up with universal credit.
- If you are given a sanction (see Chapter 43), your JSA may be paid at a reduced or nil rate.
- JSA is administered and paid by the DWP.
- If you disagree with a JSA decision, you can apply for a revision or a supersession (see Chapter 50), or appeal against it (see Chapter 51). You must apply for a mandatory reconsideration before you can appeal.

## 1. Who can get new-style jobseeker's allowance

You qualify for new-style jobseeker's allowance (JSA) if you:[1]

- accept a claimant commitment (see p934); *and*
- are not in full-time paid work (see p613); *and*
- do not have limited capability for work. However, in certain circumstances, if you are sick or have gone abroad for NHS hospital treatment, you can still get new-style JSA (see p613); *and*
- are not in relevant education (see p805); *and*
- are below pension age (see p690); *and*
- are in Great Britain. New-style JSA can continue to be paid in limited circumstances while you are temporarily away (see p1381). For changes due to the UK leaving the European Union, see p1390.

These are the main conditions for getting new-style JSA.

As well as meeting the main conditions, you must also:[2]

- satisfy the contribution conditions (see p875). This depends on your record of national insurance (NI) contributions and credits in the two tax years (6 April to 5 April) immediately before the benefit year (the calendar year) in which your jobseeking period begins (or in which a period linked to a jobseeking period begins, if earlier); *and*
- not have earnings from work above a prescribed amount (see p616).

In addition, you can be required to meet work-related requirements. These are work-focused interviews, work preparation, work search and work availability.[3] You can be given a sanction if you fail to meet them. See Chapters 42 and 43 for details.

### Jobseeking periods

A **'jobseeking period'** is the period during which you meet the main conditions for getting new-style JSA.[4] Your jobseeking period is relevant for several reasons, including whether you satisfy the contribution conditions. You are not usually entitled to new-style JSA for the first seven days of your jobseeking period. These are known as 'waiting days' (see p626).

In some cases, two or more jobseeking periods can be joined together and treated as if they were one period.

Two jobseeking periods are treated as linked if they are separated by one or any combination of the following:[5]

- any period of no more than 12 weeks; *or*
- a period during which you are doing jury service; *or*
- a 'linked period' (see p612); *or*

- any period of no more than 12 weeks which comes between two linked periods or between a jobseeking period and a linked period.

***What does not count as part of a jobseeking period***

The following do not count as part of a jobseeking period:[6]

- days for which you do not claim (or are not treated as claiming) JSA; *and*
- a period for which you claimed backdated benefit which has been refused; *and*
- any week (Sunday to Saturday) for which you are not entitled to JSA because you were involved in a trade dispute (see p891) for all or part of that week; *and*
- days on which you are not entitled to JSA because you have not provided your NI number (see p1007).

In all cases, JSA could include days/periods/weeks when you were entitled to income-based JSA, for which see previous editions of this *Handbook*.

4

## Linked periods

A **'linked period'** is any period during which you:[7]

- have, or are treated as having, limited capability for work (see Chapter 41); *or*
- are incapable of work or treated as incapable of work (see p683 of the 2013/14 edition of this *Handbook*); *or*
- are entitled to maternity allowance; *or*
- are undergoing training for which a training allowance is payable; *or*
- are entitled to carer's allowance or carer support payment, but only if this allows you to get new-style JSA when you would not otherwise satisfy the contribution conditions.

You cannot argue that taking time out of work to look after children is a linked period for these purposes.[8]

## How jobseeking periods and linked periods work

When a new jobseeking period is linked to a previous jobseeking period or a linked period, this means that:

- the question of whether you satisfy the NI contribution conditions for new-style JSA is decided by looking at your situation at the beginning of the first jobseeking period (or the beginning of a period linked to a jobseeking period, if earlier) and not at the beginning of your current claim. For example, if you claim JSA immediately after a period of limited capability for work, the contribution test is applied using the date on which you first had limited capability for work;[9]
- if you make a fresh claim for JSA but your jobseeking period links with a previous one, you do not have to serve any waiting days (see p626);

- if the jobseeking periods together (not including any linked periods) are longer than 182 days, you cannot get any more new-style JSA (see p618).

*Example*

Ramses was working full time until he was injured in a car accident on 5 November 2024 and claimed employment and support allowance (ESA). On 28 April 2025, he is fit for work and claims new-style JSA. Because the period during which he had limited capability for work links to his current jobseeking period (see the rules for linked periods on p612), he must have sufficient NI contributions in the two tax years before 2024 (the relevant benefit year) – ie, he must meet the contribution conditions for JSA as at 5 November 2024 rather than 28 April 2025.



## Full-time paid work

You cannot usually qualify for new-style JSA if you are in full-time paid work. This means 16 hours or more each week.[10] All the rules on work are covered in Chapter 40. See p887 for new-style JSA.

In some situations, you are treated as *not* being in full-time work even if you work 16 hours or more, and in others, you are treated as being in full-time work when you are not (see p884). See p885 for how your hours are calculated and p884 for what counts as paid work.

## Limited capability for work

To qualify for new-style JSA, usually you must not have limited capability for work.[11] See Chapter 41 for the test that decides this. If your health improves and you claim JSA, you may be asked to provide medical evidence that you no longer have limited capability for work. There are special rules that may help you meet the work-related requirements (see p946). In all cases, you must still show that you are available for work if you are ill or have a disability.

### Qualifying for new-style jobseeker's allowance while sick

Even if you have limited capability for work, you can be treated as *not* having limited capability for work:

- during a short period of up to two weeks (see p614); *or*
- during an extended period of up to 13 weeks (see p614); *or*
- while you are temporarily absent from Great Britain for NHS hospital treatment under certain provisions (see p615).

In all cases, you can continue to qualify for JSA if the *only* reason why you would not otherwise do so is that you cannot work because of ill health.[12]

You are *not* allowed a two-week period of sickness, or an 'extended period of sickness' if you:[13]

- state in writing that you are going to claim (or have claimed) universal credit (UC) or ESA; *or*
- were getting statutory sick pay (SSP) in the eight weeks before you were sick, or (for two-week periods of sickness) if the period of sickness follows immediately after an extended period of sickness. Instead, you can claim benefit on the basis of having limited capability for work without having to serve any ESA 'waiting days' (see p569); *or*
- are temporarily absent from Great Britain for NHS treatment. Instead, you may qualify for JSA under the rules on p615.



**Note:** if you are only going to be unable to work for a short time, it may be better to continue on new-style JSA than to claim UC or ESA. Get advice if you are unsure. Take the following into account.

- Switching from new-style JSA to ESA and then back again when you are no longer sick means you must make a succession of benefit claims. You could be without income while these are being processed.
- You can only receive new-style JSA for 182 days in any jobseeking period (see p618). If you qualify for contributory ESA, it is paid indefinitely if you are in the support group. Otherwise, it is paid for 365 days (see p564).

### Two-week periods of sickness

You are allowed up to two two-week periods of sickness in a jobseeking period (see p611) or, if your jobseeking period has lasted more than 12 months, in any successive 12-month period.[14] You must make a written declaration that you have been unfit for work from a specific date or for a specific period on a form available from the Jobcentre Plus office.[15] If you continue to qualify for new-style JSA, you do not normally have to meet a work search requirement and a special rule helps you meet the work availability requirement (see p959).[16]

If you are sick for longer than these rules allow, you may be able to qualify for new-style JSA during an extended period of sickness (see below). Otherwise, you may instead qualify for ESA for the time you are unable to work, and UC to top this up if relevant.

**Note:** the two-week periods do not include any period when you qualify for an extended period of sickness.[17]

### Extended periods of sickness

You are allowed an 'extended period of sickness' if you state that you:[18]

- have been, or expect to be, unable to work for more than two weeks, but not for more than 13 weeks; *or*
- have already been unable to work for two two-week periods of sickness under the rules described above and you have been, or expect to be, unable to work for two weeks or less.

You must satisfy the DWP that you cannot work by providing evidence as required. This includes a medical certificate from a healthcare professional.

You are treated as not having limited capability for work for up to 13 weeks from the first day you are sick, or until you are no longer sick if this is sooner.[19] You are only allowed one extended period of sickness in the 12 months that start on the first day of sickness.[20]

If you are sick for longer than these rules allow, you can claim UC or ESA for the time you are unable to work.

You do not have to meet a work search requirement if the DWP is satisfied that it would be unreasonable to require you to comply with one, and special rules help you meet the work availability requirement if the DWP is satisfied it would be unreasonable to apply the normal rules.[21]



### NHS treatment abroad

You are treated as not having limited capability for work if you are temporarily absent from Great Britain to get NHS hospital treatment under certain provisions.[22] You can claim for an indefinite period. This does not apply if you stated in writing before the period of absence began that you claimed ESA immediately before the beginning of the period.

You must make a written declaration that you will be unfit for work from a specific date or for a specific period on a form available from the Jobcentre Plus office.[23]

You do not have to meet a work search requirement and a special rule helps you meet the work availability requirement.[24]

## 2. The rules about your age

There is no minimum age for entitlement to new-style jobseeker's allowance (JSA). However, in practice, because you can only qualify if you satisfy the national insurance contribution conditions, you are unlikely to qualify before you are 18. You cannot qualify for new-style JSA if you are pension age or over (see p690).

## 3. People included in the award

You get new-style jobseeker's allowance for yourself. You cannot get any increases for your partner or children.

# 4. The amount of benefit

New-style jobseeker's allowance (JSA) is paid at the following weekly rates.[25]

| *Age of claimant* | *£pw* |
|---|---|
| Under 25 | 72.90 |
| 25 or over | 92.05 |

4

These amounts are reduced penny for penny if you receive certain pension payments of more than £50 in any week or any part-time earnings. For more on how these types of income affect new-style JSA, see below and p617. Any other income you receive does *not* affect your new-style JSA (but see p1021 for the rules on overlapping benefits). Any capital you have and the income and capital of your partner and children do not affect your new-style JSA, but may affect any means-tested benefits you (or your partner) get.

**Note:**

- New-style JSA is only paid for a limited period (see p618).
- You may qualify for universal credit to top up your new-style JSA if you satisfy the means test.
- Your JSA may be paid at a reduced (or nil) rate if you are given a sanction (see Chapter 43) or if you have committed a benefit offence (see p1111).

## Deductions for earnings

You cannot qualify for new-style JSA if you are in full-time paid work, so it is your earnings from part-time work that affect your entitlement.[26] The rules on the following are the same as for income-related employment and support allowance:

- what counts as earnings (p341);
- calculating net earnings from employment (p342);
- payments when you stop work (p343);
- calculating net earnings from self-employment (p346);
- working out average earnings from self-employment (p346);
- childminders (p347);
- how weekly earnings from employment are assessed (p368).

There are different rules on how your earnings affect your new-style JSA.

### How earnings affect your new-style jobseeker's allowance

Your new-style JSA is reduced by the full amount of any earnings you receive over a disregarded amount.[27] Normally £5 a week of your earnings is disregarded. However, if you are an auxiliary coastguard, a part-time firefighter, a part-time member of a lifeboat crew or a member of the reserve forces, £20 a week is disregarded.[28] If you earn less than £20 for doing any of these services, you can use up to £5 of the disregard on earnings from another job.

You are not entitled to new-style JSA for any week in which your earnings exceed a prescribed amount.[29] However, the days in any week when your earnings exceed this amount do not count towards your maximum 182 days of new-style JSA (see p618). The prescribed amount is not the same for everyone. It is calculated by adding together the amount of the relevant earnings disregard and the rate of new-style JSA paid to someone your age (see p616), and then deducting one penny.



### *Example*

Claire (35) is entitled to new-style JSA of £92.05 a week. She works part time and her net earnings are £45 a week. Her earnings disregard is £5 a week. Claire therefore gets £52.05 new-style JSA a week (£92.05 – £40). Applying the formula: (£92.05 + £5) – £0.01 = £97.04. So if Claire were to earn more than £97.04 a week, she would not be entitled to new-style JSA.

## Deductions for pension payments

Certain pension payments you receive may affect your new-style JSA.[30] The gross amount of your pension payments is taken into account (ie, the amount before tax is deducted), and this is converted into a weekly amount.[31] A pension payment is counted from the first day of the benefit week in which the payment is made to you.[32] £50 of your weekly pension payments (or if you get more than one pension, of the total of your weekly pension payments) is disregarded, and your new-style JSA is reduced by the remainder.[33] If your pension increases while you are on new-style JSA, the change should be taken into account from the first day of the benefit week in which the increase is paid.[34]

Any pension payments you receive because of the death of a person who was a member of a pension scheme are ignored.[35] For example, if your late partner was a member of a scheme, any payment made to you following your partner's death does not affect your new-style JSA.

### *Example*

Patrick claims new-style JSA and is entitled from Wednesday 16 April 2025. His benefit week begins on a Friday. He starts receiving a personal pension of £68 a week from Monday 21 April 2025. £18 a week (£68 – £50) is deducted from his new-style JSA from the benefit week starting Friday 18 April 2025.

Note:
- The amount of your pension payments, or a combination of earnings and pension payments, may mean that you are not paid any new-style JSA. However, unless your earnings also exceed the prescribed amount (see p616), you remain *entitled* to new-style JSA (provided you also satisfy the other conditions for getting it).
- Any day on which you are entitled to JSA (even if it is not paid) counts towards your 182 days' entitlement to new-style JSA.

## Duration of new-style jobseeker's allowance

You cannot receive more than 182 days of new-style JSA in any jobseeking period (see p611) or in two or more jobseeking periods if your entitlement is based on national insurance (NI) contributions in the same two contribution years.[36]

You can have another 182 days of new-style JSA for a later claim if:[37]
- you satisfy the contribution conditions; *and*
- at least one of the two contribution years used to decide whether you satisfy the contribution conditions is later than the second contribution year used to decide your previous entitlement. This can only apply if you are in a later jobseeking period than the one during which you exhausted your entitlement to new-style JSA.

### Days that count towards the 182-day total

Each day for which you are entitled to new-style JSA, even if you are not paid, counts. This includes days when the amount you are paid has been reduced to nil because you are getting a pension or a combination of pension and earnings.

Days on which you are *not* entitled to new-style JSA can also count. This applies to days within a jobseeking period on which you are not entitled to new-style JSA because it is not payable either because you have been given a sanction or because you have committed a benefit offence, so long as you satisfy the contribution conditions for JSA.

Days on which you are not entitled to JSA and which do *not* count include:
- waiting days (see p626); *and*
- days in any benefit week in which you are not entitled to new-style JSA because you earn more than the prescribed amount (see p616) – but see above if you have been given a sanction.

# 5. Special benefit rules

Special rules may apply if you:
- have come from or are going abroad (see Chapters 56, 57, 58 and 59);

- are studying (see Chapter 37);
- are involved in a trade dispute (see p891).

# 6. Claims and backdating

The general rules about claims and backdating are covered in Chapter 44. This section explains the specific rules that apply to new-style jobseeker's allowance (JSA).

**Note:** in rare cases, it may be beneficial for you to delay your claim for new-style JSA so that you can draw on a different year's record of national insurance (NI) contributions.

JSA claims are dealt with by DWP decision makers (see p1118) and work coaches (see p935).



## Making a claim

You can start your claim for new-style JSA:[38]

- online at gov.uk/guidance/new-style-jobseekers-allowance#how-to-claim (if you are aged 18 or over); *or*
- if you cannot claim online (eg, because you are under 18, need help to claim or need to be sent communications in braille, large print or by audio CD), by phoning Jobcentre Plus on 0800 055 6688 (Welsh language: 0800 012 1888; textphone: 0800 023 4888; Relay UK and BSL relay services are available). Say that you want to claim new-style JSA.

If you cannot do either, and you are not required to attend an initial interview (see p620), you can claim by completing a paper claim form approved by the DWP.[39] Get advice if you cannot claim online or by phone, or find this difficult, and the Jobcentre Plus office tells you that you cannot start your claim in any other way. **Note:** you can make initial contact with the DWP by phone or letter to say you want to claim. The date of your initial contact is important because it usually determines the date on which your claim is treated as having been made (see p621).

If you claim online, you get a text or email to confirm your claim has been submitted. The DWP then contacts you within 14 days of your claim to arrange for you to complete your claim at an initial interview.[40]

You may be sent or given a form to complete about the work you will be looking for and how you intend to go about getting it. The information you give forms the basis of your claimant commitment.

If you want to claim universal credit to top up your new-style JSA, you must do this separately.

You must provide any information or evidence required. You can amend or withdraw your claim before a decision is made (see p1004). If there is a delay in deciding your claim, you may be able to get a short-term advance (see p1023).

### Claiming national insurance credits

If you do not get new-style JSA but want to claim NI credits for unemployment, see p866.

## Who should claim



You claim new-style JSA on your own behalf. If you cannot manage your claim, another person can claim for you as your appointee (see p1005).

## Information to support your claim

For the general information requirements that apply to all benefits, see p1006. In addition, for new-style JSA, the DWP asks you to provide your bank account details or those of a family member or trusted friend, employment details for the past six months, including your employer's contact details and the dates you worked for the employer, and if you have a private pension, a statement letter.

It is important that you provide any information required when you claim. Until you do, you may not count as having made a valid claim (see p1008).

Correct any defects as soon as possible or your date of claim may be affected.

You may be asked to provide further information to support your initial claim (see p1009), or after you are awarded JSA. If you fail to do so, your JSA could be suspended, or even terminated (see p1031).

### The initial interview

For your new-style JSA claim to be valid, you must usually attend and participate in an initial interview with a work coach at a Jobcentre Plus office. The DWP contacts you within 14 days of your claim to arrange this.[41] If you do not attend the interview:

- at the right time or place, your date of claim is affected (see p622);
- at all (and the DWP does not waive the requirement to do so), you have not made a valid claim and so do not qualify for new-style JSA.

If you must attend the Jobcentre Plus office and this means being away from home for too long, arrangements can be made for your interview to be carried out elsewhere. You can take someone with you to the interview.

You are asked to bring your P45 if you have one, and to provide one photographic proof of identity (eg, your passport or driving licence), one other proof of identity (eg, a P60 or savings book) and one proof of your address (eg, a recent utility bill or payslip). Make sure you take any required documents to the initial interview.

If you have been sent a claim form, complete it before your interview. If you do not provide all the evidence and information required, your interview might not go ahead.

### At the interview

At the interview:

- you are asked questions to confirm your identity;
- you are told what is expected from you while you are receiving JSA;
- you and your work coach discuss what work you are looking for, what you need to do to find it and how many hours you need to spend each week looking for it;
- a claimant commitment is drawn up for you to sign. It should take account of your health, your home responsibilities and how much help you need to get to work;
- you may be referred to a job vacancy immediately. However, a claimant commitment should still be completed to establish your entitlement in case you do not get the job.

The interview also covers what you were doing before you became unemployed and why you left your previous job. If the person who interviews you thinks that you may have left voluntarily or been dismissed for misconduct, your case is referred to a decision maker who will probably make further enquiries to decide whether to give you a sanction.

## The date of your claim

The date of your claim is important as it determines when your entitlement to new-style JSA starts (subject to the rules on 'waiting days' – see p626).[42] This is not necessarily the date from when you are paid.

In all cases, you must supply a properly completed claim (on a form, online or by phone, with all the information and evidence required). Your date of claim is not necessarily the date the DWP receives it. It can be an earlier date. It depends on whether or not you must attend an initial interview.

- If you must attend an initial interview (see p620), your date of claim is the date you first contact the Jobcentre Plus office, so long as you attend your initial interview at the time specified by the DWP and by that time a properly completed claim is, or has been, provided.[43] The DWP can extend the time you have to provide or make a properly completed claim up to one month after the date of first contact. This is discretionary, so provide your claim as required if possible.
- If you are not required to attend an initial interview, your date of claim is the earliest of:[44]

- the date you first contact the Jobcentre Plus office, so long as a properly completed claim is provided within one month of your first contact or a longer period that the DWP thinks is reasonable; *or*
- the date on which a properly completed claim is received at the Jobcentre Plus office; *or*
- if you are notified that your claim is defective and you supply all the information required within one month of this, or a longer period that the DWP thinks is reasonable, the date your claim is received.



### If you fail to attend the initial interview or provide a properly completed claim

If you fail to attend your initial interview at the time specified by the DWP, or you fail to provide a properly completed claim by the interview date and cannot show a good reason for this (called 'good cause'), the rules above do not apply. Instead, so long as a properly completed claim is provided, your date of claim is the date you eventually go to the Jobcentre Plus office or provide a properly completed claim.[45] Your entitlement to new-style JSA cannot start until that date.

Good cause is not defined. All relevant circumstances must be considered. These may relate to your abilities or external factors. The general test is whether some factor would probably cause a reasonable person of your age and experience to act, or fail to act, as you did.

### Backdating your claim

It is important to claim in time. A claim for new-style JSA can only be backdated for up to one or three months in limited circumstances.

If you want your claim to be backdated:

- it is always best to state this clearly when you claim. Explain why you are claiming late and provide evidence or information that backs this up if you can. Even if you did not ask for backdating when you made your claim, argue that backdating must still be considered;[46]
- explain why there was no one else who could have helped you to claim, if relevant. However, if a person has been formally appointed by a court or the DWP to act on your behalf, your appointee (see p1005), not you, must show that it was not reasonable to claim sooner.[47] If someone is informally acting on your behalf, you must show that it was reasonable for you to delegate responsibility for your claim and that you took care to ensure that the person helping you claimed properly.[48]

**Note:** if you might have qualified for new-style JSA earlier but did not claim because you were given the wrong information or were misled by the DWP, you could ask for compensation (see p1261) or complain to the Ombudsman (see p1266).

### One month's backdating

Your claim must be backdated for up to one month if one or more of the following applies (or has applied), and because of this, you could not reasonably have been expected to make your claim any earlier.[49]

- The office where you were supposed to claim was closed (eg, because of a strike) and there were no other arrangements for claims to be made.
- You could not get to the DWP office because there were difficulties with the type of transport you normally use and there was no reasonable alternative.
- There were adverse postal conditions (eg, bad weather or a postal strike) or the post office failed to act under its agreement to deliver under-stamped mail to the DWP.
- You could not make an online claim for JSA because the DWP's computer system was not working.[50]
- You stopped getting contributory employment and support allowance, but were not informed before your entitlement ceased, so you could not claim new-style JSA in time.
- In the month before you claimed JSA:
  - you separated from your partner; *or*
  - a close relative of yours died. **'Close relative'** means your partner, parent, son, daughter or sibling.
- You could not notify the DWP by phone of your intention to claim because the phone lines to the office were busy or not working.



### Three months' backdating

Your claim must be backdated for up to three months if one or more of the following applies (or has applied), and because of this, you could not reasonably have been expected to make your claim any earlier.[51] If more than one reason applies, the combined effect of all of them must be considered in deciding whether it was reasonable for you to claim earlier.[52]

- You were given information by an officer of the DWP and, as a result, thought your claim would not succeed. **'Information'** includes general information produced by the DWP and placed on government websites. It does not have to be tailored to your circumstances or involve personal communication between you and an officer.[53] The information that is relevant includes if:
  - you were given incorrect information or the wrong claim form and this led you to claim the wrong benefit;
  - someone with authority to act on your behalf was given incorrect information;[54]
  - you were told your claim would not be accepted;[55]
  - you were told you did not have to fill in a claim form;[56]
  - the refusal of, or failure to respond to, an earlier claim for the same or a different benefit led you to believe that you were not entitled;[57]

- the information was incomplete and had not included advice on claiming when it should have done.[58]

'**Officer**' includes anyone carrying out public functions at the benefit office – eg, a security guard.[59] It does not matter if the information you received was correct or reasonable on the basis of any information that you gave to the officer about your circumstances, provided the officer's advice caused you to think that a claim would fail.[60] If you have been misled, misinformed or given insufficient advice by an officer of the DWP, explain how and when this happened and, if possible, give the name and a description of the officer concerned.

4

- You were given advice in writing by Citizens Advice or another advice service, a solicitor or other professional adviser (eg, an accountant), a medical practitioner or a local authority and, as a result, thought your claim would not succeed. '**Advice in writing**' includes leaflets, emails or information on a website, provided it is directed at claimants in your position. It is not enough for your adviser to record a note of verbal advice unless you are provided with a copy.[61] However, your claim should be backdated if you are given written confirmation of advice that was originally given to you orally, provided this is done before the decision maker decides whether you are entitled to backdating.[62]
- You could not get to the DWP office because of bad weather.
- It was not 'reasonably practicable' for you to seek help from anyone else to make your claim, and:
  - you have learning, language or literacy difficulties, or you are deaf or blind; *or*
  - you were caring for someone who is sick or disabled; *or*
  - you were dealing with a domestic emergency that affected you. Serious circumstances that affect your home or household and mean you need to take immediate action should count. This could include a situation involving a bereavement.[63]

It is whether it is reasonably practicable for you to seek help, not whether it is reasonably practicable for another person to proactively offer help to you.[64] The DWP should consider all the circumstances.

## If you claim the wrong benefit

There are no rules that allow a claim for another benefit to be treated as a claim for new-style JSA.

## Claiming in advance

If you do not qualify for new-style JSA from the date of your claim, but will do so within the next three months, it can be awarded from the first date on which you qualify.[65] This gives the DWP time to ensure you receive benefit as soon as you are entitled. Let the DWP know you want to claim in advance when you claim and at your initial interview. You might have to persuade the DWP that it can accept a claim in advance.

## 7. Getting paid

The general rules on getting paid are covered in Chapter 45. This section explains the specific rules that apply to new-style jobseeker's allowance (JSA).

***When is new-style jobseeker's allowance paid?***

New-style JSA is normally paid fortnightly in arrears.[66]

4

New-style JSA is a weekly benefit, although in some cases it can be paid for part weeks.[67] Most questions about entitlement and payment are decided in relation to a particular **'benefit week'** – ie, the period of seven days ending on the day of the week allocated to you according to your national insurance (NI) number.[68]

If you are entitled to less than 10 pence a week, you are not paid at all,[69] but you are still eligible for NI credits (see p866). If you are entitled to less than £1 a week, the DWP can decide to pay you at longer intervals of not more than 13 weeks.[70]

**Note:**

- Deductions can sometimes be made from your new-style JSA to pay to third parties (see pp1033–39).
- Your new-style JSA might be paid at a reduced (or nil) rate if you have been sanctioned for a benefit offence (see p1111) or for other reasons (see Chapter 43).
- If payment of your JSA is delayed, see p1123. If you are waiting for a decision on your claim, or to be paid, you may be able to get a short-term advance (see p1023). If you wish to complain about how your claim has been dealt with, or claim compensation, see Chapter 55.
- If payment of your JSA is suspended, see p1031.
- If you are overpaid new-style JSA, you might have to repay it (see Chapter 47) and, in some circumstances, you may have to pay a penalty (see p1101). If you have been accused of fraud, see Chapter 48.
- If you are owed arrears of new-style JSA, these can be paid in instalments (see p1018).

### After you are awarded new-style jobseeker's allowance

Once you have been awarded new-style JSA, to continue to receive it, you must meet work-related requirements. This includes attending and participating in regular interviews. You can be given a sanction if you fail to do so. See Chapter 42 for the requirements after you are awarded new-style JSA, and Chapter 43 for information about sanctions.

## Change of circumstances

You must report changes in your circumstances that you have been told you must report, as well as any that you might reasonably be expected to know might affect your right to, the amount of, or the payment of, your benefit, including any that are likely to occur. You should do this as soon as possible, preferably in writing. See p1030 for further information.



When there has been a relevant change of circumstances, a decision maker looks at your claim again and makes a new decision.

As a general rule, your new-style JSA is adjusted from the first day of the benefit week in which the change occurs or is expected to do so.[71] There are several exceptions to this rule.[72] In particular, if a decision is to your advantage, but you failed to notify the DWP of a change within the time limit (normally one month, but this can be extended – see p1153), your new-style JSA is adjusted from the first day of the benefit week in which you notified the change.

## Waiting days

You are not entitled to new-style JSA for the first seven 'waiting days' in any jobseeking period (see p611) unless:[73]

- your claim is linked to a previous claim for JSA, so both are treated as part of the same jobseeking period. The JSA could be income-based JSA, for which see previous editions of this *Handbook*; or
- you were entitled to income support, employment and support allowance (ESA), carer's allowance or carer support payment in the 12 weeks before you became entitled to JSA.

In addition, you do not have to serve any waiting days if you swap from an award of contributory ESA to a claim for new-style JSA.[74]

You may be able to get a short-term advance before your first payment of new-style JSA is due (see p1023).

# 8. Tax, other benefits and the benefit cap

## Tax

New-style jobseeker's allowance (JSA) is taxable.[75] The tax is not deducted while new-style JSA is being paid, but reduces the refund you would otherwise receive through pay as you earn (PAYE) when you return to work. Any tax refunds of PAYE payments are paid to you at the end of the tax year to which they relate. Any other tax refund is paid only when you stop getting JSA.

## Means-tested benefits

New-style JSA counts as income for means-tested benefits. However, if you (or your partner) get universal credit (UC), pension credit or income-related employment and support allowance (ESA), new-style JSA is ignored for housing benefit (HB) purposes.

If you need more income, you (and your partner) may be able to claim UC to top up your new-style JSA. If you have a partner, your partner may be able to claim other benefits.



## Non-means-tested benefits

While you are on new-style JSA, you are entitled to national insurance credits (see p866). New-style JSA is affected by the overlapping benefit rules (see p1021).

## The benefit cap

New-style JSA is one of the specified benefits for the benefit cap. It only applies if you are getting UC or HB. See p1025 for further information.

## Other sources of help

If you (or your partner) are entitled to UC or income-related ESA in addition to new-style JSA, you may also qualify for other sources of help. See the chapters on those benefits for further information. If you are not entitled to one of those benefits, you may qualify for health benefits under the low income scheme (see p575). Whether or not you are entitled to one of those benefits, you may qualify for council tax reduction (see p761). You may also qualify for help from your local welfare assistance scheme (see p770).

## Financial help on starting work

See p781 for information about other financial help you might get.

# Notes

1. **Who can get new-style jobseeker's allowance**
   1 s1 JSA 1995
   2 s2 JSA 1995
   3 ss6-6I JSA 1995
   4 Reg 37(1) JSA Regs 2013
   5 Reg 39 JSA Regs 2013
   6 Reg 37(2) JSA Regs 2013
   7 Reg 39(2) and (4) JSA Regs 2013

8 *LE v SSWP* [2009] UKUT 166 (AAC). The judge decided that the rule indirectly discriminated against women but that the discrimination was justified.
9 s2(1) and (4) JSA 1995
10 Reg 42 JSA Regs 2013
11 s1(2)(f) JSA 1995
12 Regs 46(1)(c), 46A(1)(d) and 47(1)(d) JSA Regs 2013
13 Regs 46(1), (4)-(6) and 46A(1)(e) and (6) JSA Regs 2013
14 Reg 46(1) and (3) JSA Regs 2013
15 Reg 46(2) JSA Regs 2013
16 Reg 16(5) JSA Regs 2013
17 Reg 46(7) JSA Regs 2013
18 Reg 46A(1), (3) and (3A) JSA Regs 2013
19 Reg 46A(4) JSA Regs 2013
20 Reg 46A(5) JSA Regs 2013
21 Reg 16A JSA Regs 2013
22 Reg 47 JSA Regs 2013
23 Reg 47(2) JSA Regs 2013
24 Reg 16(3)(b)(iii) JSA Regs 2013

4. **The amount of benefit**

25 s4(1) and (2) JSA 1995; reg 49 JSA Regs 2013
26 s4(1) JSA 1995; regs 50 and 53-63 JSA Regs 2013
27 s4(1)(b) JSA 1995; reg 50 JSA Regs 2013
28 Regs 59(2) and 61(2) and Sch JSA Regs 2013
29 s2(1)(c) JSA 1995; reg 48 JSA Regs 2013
30 ss4(1) and 35(1) JSA 1995; R(JSA) 1/01
31 Reg 51 JSA Regs 2013; R(U) 8/83
32 Reg 51(2) JSA Regs 2013
33 Reg 51(1) JSA Regs 2013
34 Reg 51(3) JSA Regs 2013
35 Reg 51(4) JSA Regs 2013
36 s5(1) JSA 1995
37 s5(2) JSA 1995

6. **Claims and backdating**

38 Regs 3 and 23 and Sch 2 UC,PIP,JSA&ESA(C&P) Regs; gov.uk/guidance/new-style-jobseekers-allowance
39 Reg 21 UC,PIP,JSA&ESA(C&P) Regs
40 Reg 19 UC,PIP,JSA&ESA(C&P) Regs
41 Reg 19 UC,PIP,JSA&ESA(C&P) Regs
42 Reg 29(1) UC,PIP,JSA&ESA(C&P) Regs
43 Reg 20 UC,PIP,JSA&ESA(C&P) Regs
44 Regs 21, 22 and 24 UC,PIP,JSA&ESA(C&P) Regs
45 Reg 20(2) UC,PIP,JSA&ESA(C&P) Regs
46 *AM v SSWP (UC)* [2022] UKUT 242 (AAC)
47 R(SB) 17/83
48 R(P) 2/85
49 Reg 29(4) and (5) UC,PIP,JSA&ESA(C&P) Regs
50 *NK v SSWP (UC)* [2023] UKUT 65 (AAC)
51 Reg 29(2) and (3) UC,PIP,JSA&ESA(C&P) Regs
52 CIS/2484/1999
53 *SSWP v PG (JSA)* [2015] UKUT 616 (AAC), but see also *S K-G v SSWP (JSA)* [2014] UKUT 430 (AAC), which earlier came to the opposite conclusion, holding that 'information' must be tailored to your circumstances in some way
54 CJSA/4573/1999
55 CJSA/4066/1998
56 CIS/610/1998
57 R(IS) 3/01; CIS/4490/1998
58 CJSA/0580/2003
59 CIS/610/1998
60 CIS/3994/1998; CSIS/815/2004
61 CIS/5430/1999
62 CJSA/1136/1998
63 *PE v SSWP (JSA)* [2024] UKUT 424 (AAC)
64 CIS/2057/1998
65 Reg 34 UC,PIP,JSA&ESA(C&P) Regs

7. **Getting paid**

66 Reg 52 UC,PIP,JSA&ESA(C&P) Regs
67 s1(3) and Sch 1 para 5 JSA 1995; reg 64 JSA Regs 2013
68 Reg 2(2) JSA Regs 2013
69 Reg 52 JSA Regs 2013
70 Reg 52(3) UC,PIP,JSA&ESA(C&P) Regs
71 Reg 35 and Sch 1 UC,PIP,JSA&ESA(DA) Regs
72 Reg 35 and Sch 1 Part 1 UC,PIP,JSA&ESA(DA) Regs
73 Sch 1 para 4 JSA 1995; reg 36 JSA Regs 2013
74 Reg 48(5) UC,PIP,JSA&ESA(DA) Regs

8. **Tax, other benefits and the benefit cap**

75 ss671-75 IT(EP)A 2003

# Chapter 30

# Maternity allowance

**This chapter covers:**


1. Who can get maternity allowance (p630)
2. The rules about your age (p636)
3. People included in the claim (p637)
4. The amount of benefit (p637)
5. Special benefit rules (p638)
6. Claims and backdating (p638)
7. Getting paid (p641)
8. Tax, other benefits and the benefit cap (p642)


## Key facts

- If you are pregnant or have recently given birth and are not entitled to statutory maternity pay, you may qualify for maternity allowance (MA).
- MA is a non-means-tested benefit.
- You can qualify for MA whether you are in or out of work, but to qualify you must have recently been employed or self-employed or have helped your spouse or civil partner with their business.
- You do not need to have paid national insurance (NI) contributions to qualify although, in some circumstances, your entitlement may depend on your spouse's or civil partner's NI contribution record and if you are self-employed, your NI contribution record may affect the amount of MA you receive.
- MA is affected by the overlapping benefit rules, so you may not be able to get MA and another earnings-replacement benefit at the same time.
- If you work while claiming MA, you may be disqualified from getting MA for a period.
- MA is administered and paid by the DWP.
- If you disagree with a decision on MA, you can apply for a revision or supersession (see Chapter 50), or appeal against it (see Chapter 51). You must apply for a mandatory reconsideration before you can appeal.

# 1. Who can get maternity allowance

You qualify for maternity allowance (MA) if:[1]

- you are pregnant or have recently given birth; *and*
- you are not entitled to statutory maternity pay (SMP) for the same pregnancy or birth; *and one of the following two bullet points applies*
- you qualify on the basis of your own employment or self-employment. To qualify on this basis:
  - you must have been employed or self-employed in at least 26 weeks in your test period (see p631). This is called the 'employment condition' (see p631); *and*
  - your average weekly earnings in 13 weeks of your test period (or, if you are self-employed, the average weekly earnings you are treated as having) must have been at least £30 a week. This is called the 'earnings condition' (see p632); *and*
  - you must be within your 39-week 'maternity allowance period' (MA period – see p633); *or*
- you qualify on the basis of having helped your spouse or civil partner with their self-employment. To qualify on this basis:
  - your spouse or civil partner must have been a self-employed earner in at least 26 weeks in your test period and they must either have paid or be treated as having paid class 2 national insurance (NI) contributions for those 26 weeks (if necessary, they can voluntarily pay class 2 contributions early to help you meet this condition and can apply for a refund if it is later determined that they would have met the condition for being treated as having paid them – see p862);[2] *and*
  - for at least part of each of those 26 weeks you must have taken part in, or assisted, your spouse or civil partner with their self-employment, but not have been employed by, or in partnership with, them; *and*
  - you must be within your 14-week 'qualifying period' (see p634); *and*
  - you must not qualify for MA on the basis of your own employment or self-employment.

If you qualify for MA on the basis of your own employment or self-employment, your MA can be paid over a longer period and may be paid at a higher weekly rate than if you qualify for MA on the basis of having helped your spouse or civil partner with their self-employment.

Provided you meet the above conditions, you can qualify for MA even if you are no longer employed or self-employed, or helping your spouse or civil partner with their self-employment.

You may be disqualified from receiving MA if you work or fail to attend a medical examination (see p635). If you have a miscarriage or your baby dies, see p638.

**Note:**
- Whether or not you qualify for MA, also check your entitlement to employment and support allowance (see p642).
- If you get SMP (or if you would have got SMP but for having reduced your maternity pay period in connection with a claim for shared parental leave or statutory shared parental pay (SSPP – see Chapter 34)), you cannot receive MA for the same week for the same baby, even if you have more than one job or have been self-employed as well as employed.[3]

4

***Definitions***

Your **'expected week of childbirth'** (EWC) is the week, starting on a Sunday, in which your baby is due to be born.

Your **'test period'** is the 66 weeks immediately before your EWC. For the dates of your test period, use the maternity allowance test period calculator at gov.uk/government/publications/maternity-allowance-claim-form.

## Employment condition

To qualify for MA on the basis of your employment or self-employment, you must have been employed or self-employed for at least 26 weeks in your test period.[4] If you are employed or self-employed for part of a week, the whole of that week counts. The 26 weeks do not need to be consecutive and you do not need to have been in the same job for the whole period. You need only show that you have been employed and/or self-employed for any part of each of the 26 weeks. For MA, a week starts on a Sunday and to count as employed or self-employed you must be an employed or self-employed earner (see p859).

See p638 if you have worked abroad.

**Note:**
- If you are an agency worker or have a zero-hour contract and you have a contract of employment, or a contract to provide services, you count as employed whether or not you are provided with work in a particular week.[5]
- When you become self-employed, you are normally required to register with HMRC for NI and tax purposes. If you delay registering, the DWP may consider the date on which you registered as the date your self-employment started, rather than the date you became a self-employed earner. If, as a consequence, the DWP decides you do not meet the employment condition for MA, get advice.

- Even if you do not meet the employment condition, you may still qualify for MA if you have helped your spouse or civil partner with their self-employment (see p630).

***Example***

Fay's baby is due on Saturday 28 June 2025.

Fay's EWC begins on Sunday 22 June 2025 and her 66-week test period runs from Sunday 17 March 2024 to Saturday 21 June 2025. In this period, Fay was a self-employed earner from Tuesday 7 May 2024 until Thursday 25 July 2024 and was employed from Wednesday 8 January 2025 until Friday 11 April 2025. As the weeks in which she is employed or self-employed for part of a week count as a full week, the weeks in which she started and ended her self-employment and employment count, and Fay meets the 26-week employment condition.

## Earnings condition

To qualify for MA on the basis of your employment or self-employment, your average weekly earnings in 13 weeks of your test period (or, if you are self-employed, the average weekly earnings you are treated as having – see below) must be at least £30 a week. This is known as the 'MA threshold'. For how earnings are averaged, see p637.[6]

**Note:** even if you do not meet this earnings condition, you may still qualify for MA if you have helped your spouse or civil partner with their self-employment (see p630).

### Earnings from employment

If you are employed, your gross earnings are used to calculate your average weekly earnings. What counts as earnings is the same as for SMP (see p729).[7] If you get a backdated pay rise for the period over which your earnings are averaged, this is included in the calculation.[8]

### Earnings from self-employment

The amount you actually earn from self-employment is not taken into account. Instead, you are treated as earning a certain amount based on whether or not you have paid, or are treated as having paid, class 2 NI contributions, and this figure is used to calculate your average weekly earnings. For each week:[9]

- for which you have paid, or are treated as having paid, a class 2 NI contribution, you are treated as having earnings of an amount 90 per cent of which is equal to the maximum amount of MA that can be paid for that week. In 2025/26, this is £207.98;[10]
- for which you could have paid a class 2 contribution but have not done so, and have not been treated as having paid a class 2 contribution, you are treated as having earnings of £30 a week – ie, equal to the MA threshold.

For tax years from 6 April 2024, there is no longer any requirement to pay class 2 contributions. However, you are treated as having paid them if your annual taxable profits for the tax year are at least equal to the 'small profits threshold' (see p861).

For the tax year 2023/24, you had to pay class 2 contributions if your taxable profits were above the 'lower profits threshold' for the year. If your annual taxable profits were less than this but were at least equal to the small profits threshold, you are treated as having paid them. For the amounts of these thresholds, see gov.uk/government/publications/rates-and-allowances-national-insurance-contributions.

You can choose to pay class 2 contributions voluntarily for weeks when you are self-employed and are not treated as having paid them and, prior to 6 April 2024, when you were not required to pay them.

**Note:** your annual taxable profits are calculated after the end of the tax year through the income tax self-assessment procedure. This means the question of whether you can be treated as having paid class 2 contributions for weeks of self-employment in a tax year may not be decided until 31 January after the end of the tax year. You may benefit from paying class 2 contributions before this, on a voluntary basis (see p862), if this is necessary to help you meet the condition in the first bullet point and qualify for a higher rate of MA (see p637).[11] If you then find that the amount of your taxable profits means you meet the condition for being treated as having paid class 2 contributions without needing to have paid them, you can apply for a refund, but should do so by 31 January after the end of the tax year.

## Maternity allowance period

MA awarded on the basis of your employment or self-employment can only be paid for weeks in your MA period.[12] This is a period of 39 consecutive weeks that normally starts on the day your maternity pay period would have begun had you been entitled to SMP (see p719). However:[13]

- if you are not employed or self-employed at the beginning of the 11th week before your EWC (see p631), your MA period starts from the beginning of that week (but if your baby was born before this, it starts from the day after the birth); *and*
- if you are not entitled to MA during the 11th week before your EWC, but you become entitled to it before your baby is born (perhaps because you then meet the earnings or employment condition), provided you have stopped work, the earliest day on which your MA period can start is the day you become entitled to MA, and the latest it can start is the day after the birth.

## Reducing your maternity allowance period and statutory shared parental pay

If you get MA on the basis of your own employment or self-employment (rather than on the basis that you help your spouse or civil partner with their self-employment), you can end your MA period early so that the father of your child or your partner can qualify for SSPP from their employer (see p722) and/or shared parental leave from work. If they meet the qualifying conditions, they can then get SSPP for the number of weeks of MA that you have chosen to give up.

To reduce your MA period in this way, you must give the DWP office dealing with your claim a 'curtailment notification' stating the date you want your MA period to end (called your 'curtailment date'). This should be submitted at least eight weeks before your curtailment date (although the DWP has discretion to accept less notice than this).[14] Your curtailment date must fall at least two weeks after the birth of your baby (or four weeks after it, if you are employed in premises that come within the definitions of a 'factory') and at least one week before what would have been the last day of your MA period. It is advisable to give a curtailment notification in writing, although the DWP cannot insist on this.

Think carefully before giving up your MA in this way, as it is only possible to cancel a curtailment notification if you do so before your curtailment date and:[15]

- you gave the curtailment notification before your child was born, and inform the DWP that you want to cancel it within six weeks of the birth (but you can subsequently give another curtailment notification); *or*
- your partner has died and you inform the DWP that you want to cancel the curtailment notification within a reasonable time after the death and provide the date of death.

## 14-week qualifying period

MA awarded on the basis that you have helped your spouse or civil partner with their self-employment can be paid for a maximum of 14 consecutive weeks, called the **'qualifying period'**. Your qualifying period starts:[16]

- if you stopped working with your spouse or civil partner before the beginning of the 11th week before your EWC, on the first day of the 11th week before your EWC;
- if you stopped working with your spouse or civil partner during or after the 11th week before your EWC (but before the day your baby is born), on the day after you stop work. Once you have reached the fourth week before your EWC, this applies even if you just refrain from working with your spouse or civil partner (eg, because you are unwell), if this is at least in part because of your pregnancy or childbirth;
- otherwise, on the day after you have your baby.

**'Stopping work'** either means stopping permanently or until after the birth.

**Note:** if you are not entitled to MA during the 11th week before your EWC but you become entitled to it before your baby is born, provided you have stopped working with your spouse or civil partner, the earliest day your 14-week qualifying period can start is the day you become entitled to MA and the latest is the day after the birth.[17]

## Disqualification from maternity allowance

In some circumstances, you can be disqualified from MA if you work or you fail to attend a medical examination. You can challenge the DWP's decision to disqualify you from MA, including its decision on the length of the disqualification period (see Chapters 50 and 51).

4

### If you work

The DWP can disqualify you from receiving MA if:[18]

- you are entitled to MA on the basis of your own employment or self-employment (see p630) and you work for more than 10 days during your MA period. The disqualification must be for no longer than is reasonable given the circumstances, but must be for at least the number of days you worked in excess of the 10 days. Both employed and self-employed work counts and the 10 days do not need to be consecutive. If you work for part of a day, it counts as a full day. If you work for 10 days or fewer, your MA is unaffected, even if you are paid for that work; *or*
- you are entitled to MA on the basis of helping with your spouse or civil partner's self-employment (see p630) and you do *any* work during your 14-week qualifying period. This applies if the work is helping your spouse or partner with their business, or if it is work you do as an employee or as a self-employed earner. The disqualification must be for no longer than is reasonable given the circumstances, but must be for at least the number of days you worked.

It is important to tell the DWP of work that you do, including the dates you have worked and whether your pattern of work is different from the pattern you had before you started your maternity leave.

***Example***

Before going on maternity leave, Saira, who is self-employed, worked full time. She qualifies for MA of £187.18 a week (because she was treated as having paid class 2 NI contributions for 13 weeks in her test period) but while on maternity leave still does small amounts of administrative work, such as responding to enquiries with information about when she will return to work after her maternity leave. She also took on a contract that meant she worked for three hours a day on a total of 16 days, working two days a week over an eight-week period. The DWP decides that the small amounts of administrative work she does, which are minimal and necessary to maintain her business while she is on leave, can be ignored. However, each of the days on which she worked for three hours count as a full day of work. Although the first 10 such days do not affect her entitlement to MA, the other six do. As she was previously working full time, the DWP decides that it is reasonable to disqualify her from MA for only two days a week in the latter three weeks of the contracted work, and deducts £53.48 from her weekly MA in those weeks (two-sevenths of £187.18).[19]

4

**Note:**

- If you are employed and on maternity leave, working for your employer for more than 10 days also may affect your continued entitlement to leave. If you do not want your maternity leave to end, get employment advice before agreeing to such work.
- If you have been disqualified from MA because you have returned to work and have worked for more than 10 days, provided you have not brought your MA period to an end by submitting a curtailment notification (see p634) you may be able to get MA again if you stop work and are still within your MA period. If you are employed and your maternity leave has ended because of your return to work, this could be during a period when you are on sick leave or when you take shared parental leave.

### If you fail to attend a medical

You are disqualified from receiving MA if, before the birth of your baby, you fail to attend a medical examination without good cause. For this to apply, you must have been given written notice of the examination at least three days beforehand by the DWP or someone acting on its behalf. The DWP can disqualify you for as long as is reasonable given the circumstances, but the disqualification cannot start until the day of the missed examination and cannot continue once you have given birth.[20]

Whether or not you have good cause for failing to attend depends on your circumstances.

## 2. The rules about your age

There are no upper or lower age limits for receiving maternity allowance.

## 3. People included in the claim

You claim maternity allowance (MA) just for yourself. You cannot claim any additional MA for a partner or children.

## 4. The amount of benefit

| *Type of maternity allowance* | *Maximum period of payment* | *Weekly amount* |
|---|---|---|
| Entitlement arising from your own employment or self-employment (see p630) | 39 weeks | £187.18 or 90 per cent of your average weekly earnings, whichever is less[21] |
| Entitlement arising from helping your spouse or civil partner with their self-employment (see p630) | 14 weeks | £27.00[22] |

No additional maternity allowance is paid for multiple births (ie, when you give birth to more than one baby as part of the same pregnancy).

### Calculating average weekly earnings

If you qualify for maternity allowance (MA) on the basis of your own employment or self-employment, your average weekly earnings are used to determine both whether you meet the earnings condition (see p632) and the amount of MA you get. They are calculated as follows.[23]

- If, for at least 13 weeks in your 66-week test period, you either have paid class 2 national insurance contributions as a self-employed person or are treated as having paid them (see p861), no calculation is needed – you automatically qualify for the maximum weekly amount of MA of £187.18 a week.
- Otherwise, add together your earnings (this includes your earnings from employment (see p632) and/or the earnings you are treated as having from self-employment – see p632) in the 13 weeks in your 66-week test period when your earnings are highest and divide the total by 13. If you have more than one job, the earnings from all your jobs, including earnings you are treated as having from self-employment, are counted.

In both cases, the 13 weeks do not need to be consecutive. If you are not paid weekly, work out your weekly earnings by dividing the payments you receive by the nearest number of weeks in the period for which they are paid.[24]

## 5. Special benefit rules

Special rules may apply if:

- your baby is stillborn or dies (see below);
- you have been employed abroad (see below);
- you are going abroad (see Chapters 58 and 59);
- you in prison or detention (see Chapter 38).

4

### Miscarriages, stillbirths and neonatal deaths

If you satisfy the usual qualifying conditions (see p630), you can get maternity allowance (MA) if:[25]

- after 24 weeks of pregnancy, your baby is stillborn (if your baby is stillborn before this, you cannot qualify for MA but you may qualify for other benefits – see p7 or seek advice); *or*
- your baby is born alive but then dies (even if this happens before 24 weeks of pregnancy).

### People who have been employed abroad

If, following a period of employment abroad, you have returned to Great Britain and you remained ordinarily resident in Great Britain while you were away, you may be able to rely on your employment abroad to satisfy the employment and earnings conditions for MA.[26]

In addition, in some circumstances, you may be able to rely on periods you have worked in a European Economic Area country to qualify for MA (see p1354).

## 6. Claims and backdating

The general rules about claims and backdating are covered in Chapter 44. This section explains the specific rules that apply to maternity allowance (MA).

If you are (or have recently been) employed, you may be entitled to statutory maternity pay (SMP – see Chapter 34) from your employer (or ex-employer) instead of MA. If you were employed in the 15th week before your expected week of childbirth (EWC), the DWP expects you to have applied for SMP. If your employer has decided you are not entitled to SMP, it should give you Form SMP1 explaining why and you should send this to the DWP to support your claim for MA. If you disagree with your employer's decision, or your employer fails to give you a decision, also ask HMRC to make a decision on your entitlement to SMP (see Chapter 54).

## Making a claim

A claim for MA must be made in writing, normally on the approved form (although the DWP decision maker may accept a written application not on the approved form).[27]

*Forms*

The approved form is Form MA1, which you can get from gov.uk/maternity-allowance/how-to-claim. Alternatively, you can get a paper copy of the form sent to you by ordering one online at secure.dwp.gov.uk/ask-for-a-maternity-allowance-claim-form or by phoning the Jobcentre Plus national contact centre (0800 055 6688; textphone: 0800 023 4888; Relay UK and BSL relay services available).



Keep a copy of your claim in case queries arise. Your claim will only be accepted if it is received after the 15th week before your EWC.[28]

You must provide any information or evidence required (see below). You can amend or withdraw your claim before a decision is made (see p1004). If there is a delay in deciding your claim or you are waiting to be paid, you may be able to get a short-term advance of benefit (see p1023).

## Who should claim

You must normally claim MA for yourself. If you cannot manage your claim, another person can claim MA for you as your appointee (see p1005).

## Information to support your claim

For the general information requirements that apply to all benefits, see p1006.

It is important that you provide any information required when you claim. Until you do, you may not count as having made a valid claim (see p1008). Correct any defects as soon as possible as your date of claim may be affected.

For MA, the DWP also expects you to provide:

- Form MAT B1 from your doctor or a registered midwife, giving the expected date of birth of your child and, if you are claiming MA after your baby is born, giving the date of the baby's birth.[29] Form MAT B1 is not accepted as evidence of your EWC if it is issued before the 20th week before your EWC. If you cannot obtain Form MAT B1, other evidence can be accepted, if it is sufficient, such as a letter on headed notepaper from your GP or midwife giving the information requested on Form MAT B1;
- if you have been employed:
  - payslips or other written proof of your earnings (providing payslips or proof for the 13 weeks during your test period in which your earnings were highest may mean you get more MA – see p637); *and*

- Form SMP1 from any employer for whom you worked during the 15th week before your EWC.

  Do not delay claiming MA because you are waiting for your SMP1 or evidence of your earnings; you can send these later;
- if you are claiming MA on the basis that you help your spouse or civil partner with their self-employment, your marriage or civil partnership certificate.

4

Even if you have provided all that was required when you claimed, you may be asked to provide further information to support your claim (see p1009). You may also be asked to provide information after you are awarded MA. If you fail to do so, your MA could be suspended, and subsequently terminated (see p1031).

## The date of your claim

The date of your claim is important as it can determine when your entitlement to MA starts. This is not necessarily the date from when you are paid. For information about when payment of MA starts, see p641.

The date of your claim is normally the date it is received at a DWP office.[30]

You must make sure your claim is valid. If it is 'defective', you are given a short time to correct the defect (see p1009). If you do, your claim is treated as having been made when you initially claimed.[31]

### Backdating your claim

A claim for MA can be backdated for up to three months if you satisfy the qualifying conditions over that period. You do not have to show any reasons why your claim was late.[32]

If you might have qualified for benefit earlier but did not claim because you were given the wrong information or were misled by the DWP, you could ask for compensation (see p1261) or complain to the Independent Case Examiner or to the Ombudsman (see p1262 and p1266).

If you claimed employment and support allowance (ESA) instead of MA, or if you have been refused SMP, see below.

### If you claim the wrong benefit

A claim for ESA may also be treated as a claim for MA and vice versa (see p1013).[33]

If your employer (or former employer) has decided that you are not entitled to SMP and you claim MA within three months of being notified of your employer's decision in writing, your claim for MA is treated as having been made either on the date you gave your employer notice of when you wanted the maternity pay period to start or at the beginning of the 14th week before your EWC, whichever is later.[34]

## Claiming in advance

You cannot make a claim for MA until after the 15th week before your EWC (ie, until week 26 of pregnancy), but you should claim as soon as possible after that.[35] However, if you qualify on the basis of your own employment or self-employment, it may be worth waiting a few weeks before claiming if this means you will have higher average earnings, and these would increase the amount of your MA.



# 7. Getting paid

The general rules on getting paid are covered in Chapter 45. This section explains the specific rules that apply to maternity allowance (MA).

***When is maternity allowance paid?***

The day you are paid depends on your national insurance number (see p1020). MA is normally paid fortnightly or four-weekly in arrears.[36]

If you have claimed in time and are entitled to MA, payment normally runs from the first day of your MA period (see p633) or 14-week 'qualifying period' (see p634) until that period ends. To calculate the amount of MA due for a period of less than a week, use the daily rate of MA, which is one-seventh of the weekly amount.[37]

**Note:**

- In some circumstances, you can be disqualified from receiving MA (see p635).
- Even if you have been sanctioned for a benefit offence (see p1111), you must be paid your MA.
- If payment of your MA is delayed, see p1123. If you are waiting for a decision on your claim, or to be paid, you might be able to get a short-term advance (see p1023). If you wish to complain about how your claim has been dealt with, or claim compensation, see Chapter 55.
- If payment of your MA is suspended, see p1031.
- If you are overpaid MA, you might have to repay it (see Chapter 47) and, in some circumstances, you may have to pay a penalty (see p1101). If you have been accused of fraud, see Chapter 48.
- If you are owed arrears of MA, these can be paid in instalments (see p1018).

## Change of circumstances

You must report any change in your circumstances that you have been told you must report, as well as any that you may reasonably be expected to know may affect your right to, the amount of, or the payment of, your benefit. You should do this as soon as possible, preferably in writing. See p1030 for further information.

If the change affects your entitlement to MA, a decision maker looks at your claim again and makes a new decision (see p1143). The date from which the new decision takes effect depends on whether or not it is advantageous to you and whether you reported the change in time (see p1150).

## 8. Tax, other benefits and the benefit cap

### Tax

Maternity allowance (MA) is not taxable.[38]

### Means-tested benefits

If you are entitled to MA:

- you may also qualify for universal credit (UC – see Chapter 3). If you or your partner are getting a legacy benefit (see p19), seek advice before claiming UC (but see p29 if the DWP has invited you to claim UC under the 'managed migration' process);
- the MA you get is taken into account in full as income when calculating your entitlement to UC, income-related employment and support allowance, the guarantee credit of pension credit and housing benefit (HB). However, any arrears of MA paid on the basis of your own employment or self-employment may be ignored as capital for these benefits for a certain period (see p158, p408 and p432).

### Non-means-tested benefits

MA is affected by the overlapping benefit rules (see p1021).

For details of how your entitlement to MA affects your entitlement to statutory sick pay, see p754.

If you get MA on the basis of your own employment or self-employment, reducing your MA period may allow the father of your baby or your partner to get statutory shared parental pay and/or shared parental leave (see Chapter 34).

For details of your entitlement to national insurance credits when you get MA, see p867.

Because a claim for MA can be treated as a claim for ESA (see p1013), if you claim MA but do not qualify for it, the DWP also considers your entitlement to ESA. You can be treated as having 'limited capability for work' for a period before and after the birth if you have submitted a Form MAT B1 (or similar evidence of your expected week of childbirth) to the DWP, or if, because of your pregnancy, there is a serious risk to your or your baby's health if you work (see p898).

If you qualify for both MA and contributory ESA, you cannot receive both benefits in full because of the overlapping benefit rules. If you qualify for both, you normally get the higher benefit. In some circumstances, contributory ESA may be more than your MA entitlement. You can be treated as having limited capability for work if you are pregnant and you are entitled to MA (see p898).

## The benefit cap

MA is one of the specified benefits for the benefit cap. It only applies if you are getting UC or HB. See p1025 for further information.

4

## Other sources of help

For details of whether you may qualify for:

- a Sure Start maternity grant if you live in England or Wales, see p705, or, if you live in Scotland, a Best Start grant pregnancy and baby payment, see p1453;
- Scottish child payment if you live in Scotland, see p1452;
- certain health benefits, see Chapter 27;
- Healthy Start food and vitamins, see p771, or, if you live in Scotland, Best Start foods, see p1455;
- council tax reduction, see p761;
- help with childcare costs, see p777.

# Notes

1. **Who can get maternity allowance**
 1 ss35(1) and (2) and 35B(1), (2) and (4) SSCBA 1992
 2 Reg 90ZA SS(Con) Regs
 3 ss35(1)(d) and (3E) and 35B(1)(d) SSCBA 1992
 4 s35(1)(b) SSCBA 1992
 5 para 62516 DMG
 6 ss35(1)(c) and (6A) and 35A(4) SSCBA 1992
 7 s35A(4)(a) SSCBA 1992; reg 2 SS(MatA)(E) Regs
 8 Reg 6(2) SS(MatA)(E) Regs
 9 Reg 3 SS(MatA)(E) Regs
 10 s35A(5)(c), (5A) and (5B) SSCBA 1992; reg 5 SS(MatA)(E) Regs
 11 Reg 90ZA SS(Con) Regs
 12 ss35(2) and 165 SSCBA 1992; reg 2(2) SMP Regs
 13 ss35(2) and 165 SSCBA 1992; reg 2 SMP Regs, reg 3 SS(MatA) Regs
 14 Regs 3-5 MA(C) Regs
 15 Reg 6 MA(C) Regs
 16 s35B(4)-(8) SSCBA 1992
 17 Reg 3(2B) and (2C) SS(MatA) Regs
 18 Reg 2(1)-(4) SS(MatA) Regs
 19 paras 62592-9 DMG
 20 Reg 2(7) and (8) SS(MatA) Regs

4. **The amount of benefit**
 21 ss35(1) and 35A SSCBA 1992
 22 ss35(6A) and 35B(3) and (10) SSCBA 1992

23 Regs 4 and 6 SS(MatA)(E) Regs
24 Reg 6(3) SS(MatA)(E) Regs

5. **Special benefit rules**
25 ss35(6) and 35B(10) SSCBA 1992
26 SS(MatA)(WA) Regs

6. **Claims and backdating**
27 Reg 4(1) SS(C&P) Regs
28 Reg 14(1) SS(C&P) Regs
29 Reg 2(3) SS(ME) Regs
30 Reg 6(1) SS(C&P) Regs
31 Regs 4(7) and (7ZA) and 6(1) SS(C&P) Regs
32 Reg 19(2) SS(C&P) Regs
33 Regs 9 and 11 and Sch 1 Part I SS(C&P) Regs; regs 18 and 25 UC,PIP,JSA&ESA(C&P) Regs
34 Reg 10(3) and (4) SS(C&P) Regs
35 Reg 14 SS(C&P) Regs

7. **Getting paid**
36 Reg 24 SS(C&P) Regs
37 s35(5) SSCBA 1992

8. **Tax, other benefits and the benefit cap**
38 s677 IT(EP)A 2003

# Chapter 31

# Personal independence payment

4

**This chapter covers:**


1. Who can get personal independence payment (p646)
2. The rules about your age (p667)
3. People included in the claim (p669)
4. The amount of benefit (p669)
5. Special benefit rules (p669)
6. Claims and backdating (p670)
7. Getting paid (p677)
8. Tax, other benefits and the benefit cap (p679)


## Key facts

- Personal independence payment (PIP) is a benefit for adults with a disability or long-term health problem who have difficulty with day-to-day tasks, moving around or going out.
- PIP is normally awarded to working-age adults but can sometimes be paid after pension age (see p667).
- PIP has two components, daily living and mobility, each of which is paid at a standard or an enhanced rate. You can qualify for one or both components.
- PIP is a non-means-tested benefit.
- You do not have to have paid national insurance contributions to qualify.
- You can get PIP whether or not you work.
- PIP can be paid in addition to other benefits and is disregarded as income for means-tested benefits.
- PIP is administered and paid by the DWP.
- If you disagree with a PIP decision, you can apply for a revision or a supersession (see Chapter 50), or appeal against it (see Chapter 51). You must apply for a mandatory reconsideration before you can appeal.

**Note:** PIP in Scotland is being replaced by adult disability payment (ADP). You can no longer make a new PIP claim if you live in Scotland. The Scottish government aims to transfer all PIP claimants in Scotland to ADP by the end of 2025, though this may change. See Chapter 61 for more information.

# 1. Who can get personal independence payment

You can get personal independence payment (PIP) if you:
- meet the age rules (see p667); *and*
- are not a 'person subject to immigration control' (see Chapter 56); *and*
- meet the residence conditions (see p1347); *and*
- meet the disability conditions for the daily living component, the mobility component or both (see below); *and*
- meet the required period condition (see p666), unless you are terminally ill.

4

If you meet these criteria but live in Scotland, see Chapter 61.

If you are getting disability living allowance (DLA), see p527 to help you decide whether to claim PIP.

## The disability conditions

Your entitlement to PIP is assessed using a points-based test. You 'score' points based on how your physical or mental condition affects your ability to undertake specific daily living (see p647) and mobility activities (see p660).[1] Each activity has a list of statements ('descriptors') that describe different difficulties you may have with completing the activity – eg, whether you need physical help from another person.

Points are awarded based on what help you reasonably need, not what help you actually get.[2] You should be assessed for your ability to perform activities while living a 'normal' daily life. You should not lose points if you can manage to perform certain activities, but only by adopting a significantly sheltered or altered lifestyle – eg, going out only at certain times, or avoiding all noisy environments.[3] See p664 if your difficulties vary on different days.

It is your difficulties with the specified activities that count, not your ability or inability to perform other activities in your daily life. While inferences might be drawn from your ability to perform non-PIP activities (eg, working, caring for children or driving a car), these must be genuinely comparable and questions should be asked about what you need to do when.[4]

Your difficulties must be due to your 'physical or mental condition',[5] but this does not mean you need a specific medical diagnosis.[6] However, there must be a physical or mental cause of your difficulty with carrying out a particular activity.[7] For example, if you are illiterate, you cannot score points for this reason unless you have a condition that affects your ability to learn to read.[8] Drug or alcohol dependency counts as a mental condition.[9] You should also score points for difficulties that are a side effect of medication you must take to treat a physical or mental condition.

You get points for one descriptor per activity – the one that best describes your difficulties. If more than one descriptor applies, see p665.

The points you score for each activity relevant to a component are added together. You qualify for a component at:[10]

- the standard rate if you score 8 points or more; *or*
- the enhanced rate if you score 12 points or more.

You automatically qualify for the enhanced rate of the daily living component if you are classed as terminally ill (see p669).

## The daily living activities

There are 10 daily living activities.

The points you score for each activity depend on the amount and type of help you need. You do not score any points if you can manage an activity 'unaided'. This means without 'supervision', 'prompting' or 'assistance', and without using an 'aid or appliance'.[11] If your difficulties vary, see p664.

The highest scoring descriptor for most activities applies if you cannot undertake the activity at all, even with these kinds of help. It arguably also applies if you need so much help with an activity that someone else effectively does it for you.[12]

### *Assistance, supervision and prompting*[13]

**'Assistance'** means 'physical intervention by another person and does not include speech'. It is help to carry out an activity and does not include someone doing the whole activity for you.[14] It does not include giving verbal instructions, which counts as 'prompting'.

**'Supervision'** means 'the continuous presence of another person for the purpose of ensuring [your] safety'. You must need supervision throughout the activity. You need supervision if there is a 'real risk' of harm while carrying out the activity, considering both the likelihood and seriousness of the harm.[15] This means that you may still score points even if you would not come to any harm most days if left unsupervised. **Note**: this interpretation was not previously accepted. The DWP is reviewing some PIP decisions made since 9 March 2017 to check they are in line with this interpretation.[16] Get advice if you think that you should have scored more points.

The risk does not need to be caused by doing the activity; it is enough that you need continuous supervision to carry it out (see p663).[17] If someone is also supervising other people at the same time, you can still satisfy a supervision descriptor.[18]

**'Prompting'** means 'reminding, encouraging or explaining by another person'. You can score points for needing prompting even if you can sometimes manage unaided when there is a specific or urgent need to undertake the activity.[19] The person prompting you does not always need to be in your presence, so prompting by phone (or, arguably, someone leaving you notes or reminders)[20] can allow you to score points if you need this to be able to carry out an activity.

For how your ability to carry out the activities with these kinds of help is assessed, see p663.

You qualify for the enhanced rate of the daily living component if you are classed as terminally ill (see p669), even if you have no problems with any of the activities.

## Aids and appliances

4

You score points for most of the daily living activities if you do not need help from another person, but need an 'aid or appliance' to carry out the activity. You must need to use it because of your physical or mental condition. An aid or appliance means 'any device which improves, provides or replaces [your] impaired mental or physical function; and includes a prosthesis'.[21] Some examples are an artificial leg, bone-anchored hearing aid,[22] walking stick, wheelchair, modified cutlery needed because of your disability, or adaptations to your home like grab rails in the bathroom or a shower seat. It is unlikely to include surgical implants like hip replacements, retinal implants and heart valves.[23]

An aid or appliance can be something you need to use before you can manage an activity – eg, to warm up your hands, improving your manual dexterity.

An aid or appliance that you do *not* use is still taken into account if you could 'reasonably be expected' to use it to manage the activity.[24]

***Could you use an aid or appliance?***

When you could reasonably be expected to use an aid or appliance is not set out in the regulations. Some factors that may be relevant to whether it is reasonable for you to use an aid or appliance include whether:

- you have been advised to use it by a medical professional; ***and***
- it is available to you (this might include affordability if the NHS does not provide it); *and*
- it is practical for you to use it – eg, whether you can store it in your home.

If you are assessed as needing an aid or appliance to manage an activity and you think this is not reasonable, try to get evidence to show that you cannot use it, it is not affordable or practical, or you still need help from someone despite using it.

The aid need not be something that only disabled people use, or specifically designed to help with the task that you need it for. However, it will not normally be seen as an aid or appliance if it is widely used in the same way by people who do not have your difficulties.[25] For example, many people sit down to dress, so you will not score points for needing to do this if you are otherwise able to dress unaided. However, if you need an aid to perform an essential part of the activity (eg, to lean on a shelf or use a crutch to stand up while dressing), you should score points.[26]

Your ability to use reasonable alternatives may mean that you are assessed as managing an activity 'unaided'. However, any alternatives that significantly restrict your choices arguably still count as aids.[27]

*Examples*

Adam wears slip-on shoes because his arthritis means it takes him more than twice as long to tie his shoelaces as it used to. He can manage all his other clothing unaided. As slip-on shoes are a reasonable alternative, Adam can dress and undress unaided.

Brian has severely restricted motor function following a stroke. He must wear slip-on shoes to manage alone. To dress within a reasonable time, he must also wear loose-fitting clothing, including trousers with elasticated waistbands. The types of clothes that Brian must wear to dress without help are sufficiently limited so they amount to using aids to dress, even though someone without Brian's difficulties may also choose to wear them.



## Activity 1: preparing food

| *Descriptors* | *Points* |
|---|---|
| a. Can prepare and cook a simple meal unaided. | 0 |
| b. Needs to use an aid or appliance to be able to either prepare or cook a simple meal. | 2 |
| c. Cannot cook a simple meal using a conventional cooker but is able to do so using a microwave. | 2 |
| d. Needs prompting to be able to either prepare or cook a simple meal. | 2 |
| e. Needs supervision or assistance to either prepare or cook a simple meal. | 4 |
| f. Cannot prepare and cook food. | 8 |

*Definitions*[28]

**'Simple meal'** means a cooked one-course meal for one using fresh ingredients.

**'Prepare'**, in the context of food, means make food ready for cooking or eating.

**'Cook'** means heat food at or above waist height. (This means that difficulty bending down to use a low oven is not relevant.)[29]

See also the definitions common to all the daily living activities on p647. For what counts as being able to carry out an activity, see p663.

This is an objective test of your ability to manage the tasks involved in preparing ingredients and cooking a reasonable range of simple meals. It takes no account of your specific dietary needs,[30] religious beliefs or cultural preferences.[31] Similarly, the impact of things such as childcare responsibilities or family size on your ability to prepare a meal is not relevant.[32]

Descriptor 1c only looks at whether you can *cook* using a microwave but your ability to *prepare* the ingredients for a simple meal must also be considered.[33] To 'prepare' food, you must be able to peel and chop vegetables.[34] If you must use pre-prepared vegetables, you score points for needing assistance to prepare or cook a meal, unless you could prepare them with an aid or appliance. Aids to help you prepare and cook food could include specialist cooking utensils or a spiked chopping board. Lever arm taps and lightweight pans are less likely to be accepted as aids,[35] and a perching stool arguably does not count as an aid unless your condition means you can only stand for very short periods.[36]

If you cannot read, tell the time or use timers because of your condition (eg, a learning difficulty), this is relevant to whether you score points for this activity. However, you do not automatically score any points due to reading difficulties, as it is possible to cook without being able to read.[37]

It is arguable that you satisfy descriptor 1f if you cannot prepare or cook food, no matter how much help you get, even though you can manage the other tasks unaided.[38]

## Activity 2: taking nutrition

| *Descriptors* | *Points* |
|---|---|
| a. Can take nutrition unaided. | 0 |
| b. Needs:<br>(i) to use an aid or appliance to be able to take nutrition; *or*<br>(ii) supervision to be able to take nutrition; *or*<br>(iii) assistance to be able to cut up food. | 2 |
| c. Needs a therapeutic source to be able to take nutrition. | 2 |
| d. Needs prompting to be able to take nutrition. | 4 |
| e. Needs assistance to be able to manage a therapeutic source to take nutrition. | 6 |
| f. Cannot convey food and drink to their mouth and needs another person to do so. | 10 |

*Definitions*[39]

**'Take nutrition'** means cut food into pieces, convey food and drink to one's mouth, chew and swallow food and drink, or take nutrition using a therapeutic source.

**'Therapeutic source'** means parenteral or enteral tube feeding using a rate-limiting device such as a delivery system or feed pump.

See also the definitions common to all the daily living activities on p647. For what counts as being able to carry out an activity, see p663.

This activity focuses on the mechanical actions involved in eating and drinking (or using a therapeutic source), so the nutritious quality of what you consume is not relevant.[40] However, if your condition means that you need prompting to eat at all,[41] or your condition means that you need to eat lots of calories and you need prompting to eat enough, you can satisfy descriptor 2d.[42] You can also arguably satisfy 2b or d if you require supervision or prompting to stop eating, so you only take nutrition for as often as is reasonably required and not for any longer.[43]

You must be able to manage every aspect of taking nutrition without a therapeutic source to manage this activity unaided, so difficulty safely swallowing solid foods can potentially allow you to score points for this activity due to the choking risk.[44]



Specially designed cutlery (eg, 'easy-grip') counts as an aid for this activity. An aid or appliance that helps you either to cut *or* convey *or* chew *or* swallow food can satisfy descriptor 2b.[45]

If you spill so much food that you need to change your clothes after eating, this is arguably not taking nutrition to an acceptable standard. Unless an aid or appliance, such as an adapted cup or cutlery, helps to cut up your food or prompting from someone else means you can manage this, you should satisfy descriptor 2f.

If you need help to set up or put away therapeutic feeding equipment due to your condition, you should satisfy descriptor 2e, even if you do not need help to use it once it has been set up. If you use such equipment overnight, you count as using it on two days for the purpose of deciding how many points you score, if your needs vary on different days (see p664).[46]

## Activity 3: managing therapy or monitoring a health condition

| *Descriptors* | *Points* |
|---|---|
| a. Either:<br>(i) does not receive medication or therapy or need to monitor a health condition; *or*<br>(ii) can manage medication or therapy or monitor a health condition unaided. | 0 |
| b. Needs any one or more of the following:<br>(i) to use an aid or appliance to be able to manage medication;<br>(ii) supervision, prompting or assistance to be able to manage medication;<br>(iii) supervision, prompting or assistance to be able to monitor a health condition. | 1 |
| c. Needs supervision, prompting or assistance to be able to manage therapy that takes no more than 3.5 hours a week. | 2 |
| d. Needs supervision, prompting or assistance to be able to manage therapy that takes more than 3.5 but no more than 7 hours a week. | 4 |
| e. Needs supervision, prompting or assistance to be able to manage therapy that takes more than 7 but no more than 14 hours a week. | 6 |

| | |
|---|---|
| f. Needs supervision, prompting or assistance to be able to manage therapy that takes more than 14 hours a week. | 8 |

*Definitions*[47]

**'Manage medication'** means take medication, where a failure to do so is likely to result in a deterioration in your health.

**'Medication'** means medication to be taken at home, which is prescribed or recommended by a registered doctor, nurse or pharmacist.

**'Monitor a health condition'** means detect significant changes in your condition which are likely to lead to a deterioration in your health, and take action advised by a registered doctor, registered nurse, or health professional who is regulated by the Health Professions Council,[48] without which your health is likely to deteriorate.

**'Manage therapy'** means undertake therapy, where a failure to do so is likely to result in a deterioration in your health.

**'Therapy'** means therapy undertaken at home prescribed or recommended by a registered doctor, nurse or pharmacist, or health professional regulated by the Health Professions Council. It does not include taking or applying, or otherwise receiving or administering, medication (whether orally, topically or by any other means), or any action which falls within the definition of 'monitor a health condition'.[49]

See also the definitions common to all the daily living activities on p647. For what counts as being able to carry out an activity, see p663.

Examples of therapy include needing help with dialysis, fitting bandages[50] (including compression stockings[51]), undertaking specialist massage treatment at home or managing a special diet.[52] You cannot score points for help with therapy if a specific descriptor in another activity describes exactly the same kind of help.[53] For example, needing assistance to self-catheterise scores points under Activity 5,[54] and needing assistance to take nutrition using a therapeutic device scores points under Activity 2.[55] However, needing supervision or prompting with these things may arguably score you points for Activity 3.[56]

General supervision provided in supported accommodation is not therapy.[57] Smoking cessation treatment and weight loss counselling do not count as therapy if there is no evidence that smoking or obesity are making your condition worse.[58] It is arguable that if you need help with exercises to *improve* some aspect of how your condition affects you or to make you more comfortable, your health would deteriorate without it, and so it counts as therapy.[59]

As your need for therapy will itself result from your condition, you do not need to show that your condition is connected to the specific help that you need with it, just that you need help.[60] When deciding which descriptor is satisfied, the amount of time you need help with therapy is relevant, not the length of time the therapy takes.[61] The help you need to set up a machine you use for therapy (eg, a TENS machine) counts, even if you can manage unaided once it has been set up.[62]

As the descriptors about therapy refer to the amount of help you need during 'a week', you should not be excluded by the rule on fluctuating conditions (see p664) if you only need help with therapy on a minority of days.

Monitoring your health condition could include someone checking on how you are – eg, if you have schizophrenia which is normally controlled by medication.

Aids and appliances to help you manage medication could include a dosette box to organise pills if you are forgetful due to your condition, or a specialist device to help you inject yourself if you have difficulty with manual dexterity. However, an inhaler or syringe does not count as an aid, as it is a way of delivering medication, not something you need to use to help you manage your medication independently.[63]

**Note:** the DWP is looking again at some decisions made after 28 November 2016 which concern medication and monitoring, or diet as therapy.[64] Get advice if you think you should have scored more points for this activity.

4

## Activity 4: washing and bathing

| *Descriptors* | *Points* |
|---|---|
| a. Can wash and bathe unaided. | 0 |
| b. Needs to use an aid or appliance to be able to wash or bathe. | 2 |
| c. Needs supervision or prompting to be able to wash or bathe. | 2 |
| d. Needs assistance to be able to wash either their hair or body below the waist. | 2 |
| e. Needs assistance to be able to get in or out of a bath or shower. | 3 |
| f. Needs assistance to be able to wash their body between the shoulders and waist. | 4 |
| g. Cannot wash and bathe at all and needs another person to wash their entire body. | 8 |

*Definitions*[65]

'**Bathing**' includes getting into or out of an unadapted bath or shower.

See also the definitions common to all the daily living activities on p647. For what counts as being able to carry out an activity, see p663.

A bath seat counts as an aid for this activity.[66] If you cannot get into an unadapted bath without help, you satisfy descriptor 4e, even if you have a wet room at home, so you never need to do this.[67]

If you are at risk if you bathe alone, whether you need supervision depends on the seriousness of the harm and how likely it is (see p647). You should not be expected to reduce the time you spend in the bath or shower to avoid the risk.[68]

If you must remove your hearing aid or cochlear implant processor to shower or bathe and could not hear a standard fire or smoke alarm or someone breaking into your home without it, you should satisfy either descriptor 4b or 4c.[69] **Note:** the DWP is looking again at some decisions made after 21 August 2020 which concern taking out a hearing aid or cochlear implant to wash or bathe. Get advice if you think you should have scored more points for this activity.[70]

To wash to an acceptable standard, you should be clean (and, arguably, dry)[71] when you have finished. If it takes you a long time to wash and bathe without help, you can argue that you need assistance.

4

If you can only motivate yourself to have a bath or shower if you have something important to do that day, it is arguable that you still need prompting to wash or bathe because you would not manage this unprompted on a normal day.[72]

## Activity 5: managing toilet needs or incontinence

| *Descriptors* | *Points* |
|---|---|
| a. Can manage toilet needs or incontinence unaided. | 0 |
| b. Needs to use an aid or appliance to be able to manage toilet needs or incontinence. | 2 |
| c. Needs supervision or prompting to be able to manage toilet needs. | 2 |
| d. Needs assistance to be able to manage toilet needs. | 4 |
| e. Needs assistance to be able to manage incontinence of either bladder or bowel. | 6 |
| f. Needs assistance to be able to manage incontinence of both bladder and bowel. | 8 |

*Definitions*[73]

**'Manage incontinence'** means manage involuntary evacuation of the bowel or bladder, including use a collecting device or self-catheterisation, and clean oneself afterwards.

**'Toilet needs'** means getting on and off an unadapted toilet, evacuating the bladder and bowel, and cleaning oneself afterwards.

See also the definitions common to all the daily living activities on p647. For what counts as being able to carry out an activity, see p663.

Even if you only have difficulty with one of the three things included in the definition of 'toilet needs' above, you can still score points for this activity.[74] However, you must have difficulty with an aspect of the activity as defined, so following a strict hygiene regime to avoid infections does not mean that you score points, unless your ability to do one of these three things is affected by your condition.[75] If you manage incontinence independently but not 'to an acceptable standard' or 'within a reasonable time period' (see p663), you should score points for needing assistance.[76]

Examples of aids and appliances include a raised toilet seat, grab rails near the toilet,[77] a stoma and colostomy bag,[78] incontinence pads,[79] or a shower head used to clean yourself.[80] If it is reasonable for you to use incontinence pads most days (including using pads overnight) as a precaution, you satisfy descriptor 5b, even if you are only actually incontinent on a minority of days,[81] or do not actually use pads.[82] A commode can count as an aid for this activity, but only if part of the reason you must use it is that your condition means you have difficulty with toilet needs or incontinence (not if you solely use it because of mobility problems, for example).[83] You score more points if you need help from someone else to use one of these things – eg, assistance to change a stoma bag.[84]

Difficulty dressing and undressing to use the toilet does not allow you to score points for this activity.[85]



## Activity 6: dressing and undressing

| *Descriptors* | *Points* |
|---|---|
| a. Can dress and undress unaided. | 0 |
| b. Needs to use an aid or appliance to be able to dress or undress. | 2 |
| c. Needs either: (i) prompting to be able to dress, undress or determine appropriate circumstances for remaining clothed; *or* (ii) prompting or assistance to be able to select appropriate clothing. | 2 |
| d. Needs assistance to be able to dress or undress their lower body. | 2 |
| e. Needs assistance to be able to dress or undress their upper body. | 4 |
| f. Cannot dress or undress at all. | 8 |

***Definitions***[86]

**'Dress and undress'** includes put on and take off socks and shoes.

See also the definitions common to all the daily living activities on p647. For what counts as being able to carry out an activity, see p663.

You can score points if you only have difficulty with either dressing or undressing. Similarly, you can score points if you struggle with either socks or shoes.[87]

If you must wear them due to your condition, clothes that are easier to manage, such as slip-on shoes, cardigans rather than jumpers or items with zips rather than buttons, may count as aids to help you dress, depending on how much your choices are restricted by your condition(s).[88] If you only need one of these things (eg, your only difficulty is with tying shoelaces), you may still be assessed as able to dress and undress unaided (see p648).[89]

If you must sit down to dress or undress, this does not count as needing an aid or appliance.[90] However, if you then need to use an aid (eg, a crutch) to get up and finish dressing (eg, to pull trousers fully into position and do them up), you may satisfy descriptor 6b.[91]

Selecting appropriate clothing includes choosing the right clothes for the weather, and also not reusing dirty clothes.[92] If you take a long time to choose clothes due to your condition (eg, because you have body dysmorphia and choosing clothes could be traumatic), you may satisfy descriptor 6c.[93]



## Activity 7: communicating verbally

| *Descriptors* | *Points* |
|---|---|
| a. Can express and understand verbal information unaided. | 0 |
| b. Needs to use an aid or appliance to be able to speak or hear. | 2 |
| c. Needs communication support to be able to express or understand complex verbal information. | 4 |
| d. Needs communication support to be able to express or understand basic verbal information. | 8 |
| e. Cannot express or understand verbal information at all even with communication support. | 12 |

*Definitions*[94]

**'Basic verbal information'** means information in your native language conveyed verbally in a simple sentence.

**'Complex verbal information'** means information in your native language conveyed verbally in either more than one sentence or one complicated sentence.

**'Communication support'** means support from someone trained or experienced in communicating with people with specific communication needs, including interpreting verbal information into a non-verbal form and vice versa.

See also the definitions common to all the daily living activities on p647. For what counts as being able to carry out an activity, see p663.

If you have problems speaking English because you have never learned the language, this does not count. If strangers find it hard to understand you (due to your condition affecting your speech, rather than your accent), you may be assessed as needing help to communicate to an acceptable standard and within a reasonable time.

Your ability to read, write or send text messages is not relevant, but if you use writing to communicate in the absence of speech (eg, pen and paper or a text-to-audio device), you may satisfy descriptor 7b.[95] The ability to lip read is not used to conclude that you can understand speech – ie, your lip-reading ability will be disregarded and you can still score points.[96] If you have difficulty using a phone or understanding speech in a noisy environment due to your condition, you may score points.[97]

The definition of 'communication support' includes both someone with specialist training, like a British Sign Language interpreter, and someone who does not have specialist training but who is experienced in helping you to communicate, such as a family member.[98] How many points you score for needing communication support depends on whether you need help with even a single simple sentence (8 points), or whether you can manage this but need help with anything more complicated (4 points).

You are unlikely to score points if you cannot speak, hear or understand speech in certain social situations (eg, because of a mental health condition like anxiety), but can do so in other social settings or with people you know well.[99] You may instead score points for difficulties engaging with people (Activity 9).

4

## Activity 8: reading and understanding signs, symbols and words

| *Descriptors* | *Points* |
|---|---|
| a. Can read and understand basic and complex written information either unaided or using spectacles or contact lenses. | 0 |
| b. Needs to use an aid or appliance, other than spectacles or contact lenses, to be able to read or understand either basic or complex written information. | 2 |
| c. Needs prompting to be able to read or understand complex written information. | 2 |
| d. Needs prompting to be able to read or understand basic written information. | 4 |
| e. Cannot read or understand signs, symbols or words at all. | 8 |

*Definitions*[100]

**'Basic written information'** means signs, symbols and dates written or printed in standard size text in your native language.

**'Complex written information'** means more than one sentence of written or printed standard size text in your native language.

**'Read'** includes read signs, symbols and words, but does not include read braille. (The exclusion of braille from the definition means that if you have no effective sight at all, you are treated as unable to read.)

See also the definitions common to all the daily living activities on p647. For what counts as being able to carry out an activity, see p663.

If your ability to read is affected so that you satisfy a descriptor at certain times of the day, you should score points even if you can read unaided at other times.[101]

Similarly, it is arguable that you should be assessed as needing an aid or appliance to read (rather than someone to help) only if you can read both outside and inside using aids.

As stated in the descriptors, glasses and contact lenses do not count as aids or appliances, so you cannot score points under this activity if glasses or contact lenses enable you to read effectively. If you can read to the standard required with one eye (including using glasses), then a problem with your other eye does not mean you score points.[102]

If your mental or cognitive impairment means you need help to understand the meaning of written information, you should score points for this activity. If you have never learned to read in English, you only score points for this activity if this is because of a physical or mental condition.[103] While the standard of reading required is low, to satisfy descriptor 8d (rather than 8e), you must be able to quickly read and understand some words without any help.[104]

## Activity 9: engaging with other people face to face

| *Descriptors* | *Points* |
|---|---|
| a. Can engage with other people unaided. | 0 |
| b. Needs prompting to be able to engage with other people. | 2 |
| c. Needs social support to be able to engage with other people. | 4 |
| d. Cannot engage with other people due to such engagement causing either: (i) overwhelming psychological distress to the claimant; *or* (ii) the claimant to exhibit behaviour which would result in a substantial risk of harm to the claimant or another person. | 8 |

***Definitions***[105]

**'Psychological distress'** means distress related to an enduring mental health condition or an intellectual or cognitive impairment.

**'Social support'** means support from a person trained or experienced in assisting people to engage in social situations.

See also the definitions common to all the daily living activities on p647. For what counts as being able to carry out an activity, see p663.

This activity looks at your ability to interact with individuals or small groups,[106] and in social situations.[107] You can score points despite being able to engage with people you know (eg, family and friends) or people you must interact with for a specific and limited purpose (eg, health professionals or the tribunal).[108]

'Engage with other people' means to 'interact with others in a contextually and socially appropriate manner', 'understand body language' and 'establish relationships'.[109] All three factors should be considered.[110] The test is whether you can engage with adults generally, not just with particular groups of people, such as women or young people.[111] Both mental and physical conditions are relevant to this activity – eg, a visual impairment may affect your ability to understand body language.[112]

'Establish relationships' does not refer to any particular type of relationship, but means something more than just the ability to respond to questions.[113] Even if you undertake social activities (eg, going to a pub[114] or visiting a shopping centre to make a purchase[115]), you may still score points for this activity if you cannot engage with other people and establish a relationship without help, or if the social activities you can cope with alone are very specific and limited by your condition.[116] While the descriptors distinguish between 'prompting' and 'social support', there is some overlap between them.

The person prompting you does not always need to be physically present.

'Social support' does not need to be provided by a professional. It could come from someone else – eg, a family member or friend who has significant experience of supporting you.[117] Social support does not have to be provided at the time of the activity or immediately beforehand. If, for example, you have monthly counselling sessions, and this support is necessary for you to engage with other people, you are likely to satisfy descriptor 9c.[118]

If you cannot engage with other people at all, this must be for one of the reasons mentioned in descriptor 9d for you to satisfy it.[119]

**Note**: the DWP's interpretation of this activity used to be less generous. It is contacting claimants who get PIP (or who have been refused it since 6 April 2016) who might score more points for this activity.[120] Get advice if you think you would have scored more points for this activity or been entitled to PIP, but your need for social support was not properly taken into account.

### Activity 10. making budgeting decisions

| *Descriptors* | *Points* |
|---|---|
| a. Can manage complex budgeting decisions unaided. | 0 |
| b. Needs prompting or assistance to be able to make complex budgeting decisions. | 2 |
| c. Needs prompting or assistance to be able to make simple budgeting decisions. | 4 |
| d. Cannot make any budgeting decisions at all. | 6 |

*Definitions*[121]

**'Complex budgeting decisions'** involve calculating household and personal budgets, managing and paying bills and planning future purchases.

**'Simple budgeting decisions'** involve calculating the cost of goods and calculating change required after a purchase.

See also the definitions common to all the daily living activities on p647. For what counts as being able to carry out an activity, see p663.

The descriptors assess difficulty making decisions because of your physical or mental condition. Poor money management skills unrelated to your condition are not relevant. However, if your condition means that you are very impulsive, you can satisfy descriptor 10b if this prevents you from budgeting effectively.[122] You can score points whatever your 'intellect', as motivation and other factors can prevent you from completing an activity unaided.[123]

4

You only satisfy a descriptor (as opposed to a higher-scoring one) if you can make *all* of the types of decisions that form part of the relevant definition. So, if you cannot manage a household budget at all due to your condition, you should be assessed as unable to make 'complex budgeting decisions' even if you can pay bills by yourself or with some help.[124]

It is unlikely that you will be awarded points for this activity based solely on a physical condition.[125] However, if you have difficulty making decisions due to a physical condition (eg, you have a visual impairment and need someone to read information repeatedly to be able to make a decision), you may arguably satisfy descriptor 10b.[126]

## The mobility activities

There are two mobility activities in the assessment.

For how your ability to carry out an activity is assessed, see p663.

For which descriptor you satisfy if your difficulties vary, see p664.

### Activity 1: planning and following journeys

| *Descriptors* | *Points* |
|---|---|
| a. Can plan and follow the route of a journey unaided. | 0 |
| b. Needs prompting to be able to undertake any journey to avoid overwhelming psychological distress to the claimant. | 4 |
| c. Cannot plan the route of a journey. | 8 |
| d. Cannot follow the route of an unfamiliar journey without another person, assistance dog or orientation aid. | 10 |
| e. Cannot undertake any journey because it would cause overwhelming psychological distress to the claimant. | 10 |
| f. Cannot follow the route of a familiar journey without another person, an assistance dog or an orientation aid. | 12 |

*Definitions*[127]

**'Assistance dog'** means a dog trained to guide or assist a person with a sensory impairment.

**'Orientation aid'** means a specialist aid designed to assist disabled people to follow a route safely. A standard satnav does not count as an orientation aid, although one designed or modified for disabled people might.[128]

**'Prompting'** means reminding, encouraging or explaining by another person.

**'Psychological distress'** means distress related to an enduring mental health condition or an intellectual or cognitive impairment.

**'Unaided'** means without the use of an aid or appliance, or supervision, prompting or assistance.



If you need prompting to leave the house as the thought of going out causes overwhelming psychological distress, you can satisfy descriptor 1b even if once you start a journey you do not need to be accompanied by someone else;[129] prompting by phone is arguably sufficient.[130] Arguably, you can satisfy descriptor 1b or 1e if you need prompting to, or cannot, go out during part of a day if your 'lifestyle is restricted to more than a trivial extent'.[131]

The use of the words 'follow the route' means that you can satisfy descriptors 1d and 1f if you need someone to help you get to your destination (this could include help to navigate, supervision to keep you safe, or help to deal with unexpected diversions), but not if you only need help to communicate with people you meet during a journey.[132] It is possible to satisfy descriptor 1d or 1f if you sometimes manage a specific journey alone, as long as you generally need one of the kinds of help described.[133]

If you can manage part of a journey (eg, in your car) by yourself, you can still score points if you need someone else with you at the start or end of the journey.[134] Your ability to manage a range of journeys using different types of transport (and not just a short or local journey) should be considered.[135] However, to score points for this activity, your difficulties must be due to a mental, cognitive or sensory impairment and not purely physical difficulties with managing different kinds of transport.[136]

You can only satisfy descriptors 1d and 1f due to anxiety if you need someone with you to avoid *overwhelming* psychological distress.[137] That person does not need to be taking action to help you if their presence alone is enough to relieve the distress.[138]

DWP guidance suggests that if you satisfy descriptor 1e as you cannot leave the house at all on the majority of days, you cannot also satisfy descriptor 1f.[139] This is arguably not correct (eg, if you also have a visual impairment and would need a guide dog if you were able to go out), but the Upper Tribunal has held that if you satisfy descriptor 1e, whether you also satisfy descriptor 1f should be decided without taking account of any psychological distress that you experience.[140]

## Activity 2: moving around

| *Descriptors* | *Points* |
|---|---|
| a. Can stand and then move more than 200 metres, either aided or unaided. | 0 |
| b. Can stand and then move more than 50 metres but no more than 200 metres, either aided or unaided. | 4 |
| c. Can stand and then move unaided more than 20 metres but no more than 50 metres. | 8 |
| d. Can stand and then move using an aid or appliance more than 20 metres but no more than 50 metres. | 10 |
| e. Can stand and then move more than one metre but no more than 20 metres, either aided or unaided. | 12 |
| f. Cannot, either aided or unaided:<br>(i) stand; *or*<br>(ii) move more than one metre. | 12 |

*Definitions*[141]

**'Aided'** means with the use of an aid or appliance, or supervision, prompting or assistance. (See also the definitions of these terms on p647 and p648.)

**'Stand'** means stand upright with at least one biological foot on the ground. (This means that double amputees are treated as unable to stand and satisfy descriptor 2f.)

**'Unaided'** means without the use of an aid or appliance, or supervision, prompting or assistance.

This activity looks at your ability to 'stand and then move', so any movement you can manage using a wheelchair is ignored. The descriptors assess your ability on the usual surfaces you might encounter outdoors, including your ability to manage kerbs but not flights of steps or steep slopes.[142]

If you can manage more than 50 metres using an aid or appliance or with help, you can only satisfy descriptor 2a or 2b, even if you can only manage less than 50 metres unaided.[143]

You do not need to be able to manage the distance mentioned in one go, as brief stops do not mean that you cannot move this distance.[144] However, the length and duration of any stops are relevant to whether you can move that distance repeatedly and within a reasonable time period. The DWP guidance suggests a reasonable time period for this activity is 30 metres per minute.[145] If you can move a particular distance 'within a reasonable time period', the fact that you can only move slowly is not relevant to whether you are managing the activity to an acceptable standard.[146] However, pain,[147] dizziness, breathlessness and any risk to your health if you walk too far[148] are all relevant to whether you can move to an acceptable standard (or safely).

If moving around causes you significant pain, its impact on how far you can walk can be considered, even if the pain has no known physical cause.[149] However, if your physical difficulties walking are caused by psychological distress, this is considered under Activity 1 instead.[150]

The points you score for this activity should take account of how often you want to go out but cannot due to your condition (as long as this is reasonable).[151]

## Can you carry out an activity?

You must be able to manage an activity safely, to an acceptable standard, repeatedly and within a reasonable time period to complete it. If you cannot, for example, complete an activity safely even with prompting, then you must be awarded a higher scoring descriptor.[152]

- **Safely.** This means 'in a manner unlikely to cause harm to [you] or to another person, either during or after completion of the activity'. There must be a real possibility of harm occurring that cannot be ignored, considering both the likelihood and severity of harm. A severe consequence that is relativity unlikely to happen is still relevant[153] – eg, an absence of accidents does not necessarily mean you can perform an activity safely.[154] You should also not be expected to restrict how you carry out an activity (eg, how long you shower for) in order to do it safely.[155] If you have seizures or other symptoms that come on suddenly, this may make certain activities unsafe. Whether this is accepted is likely to depend on whether you get any warning signs and what you can do to make yourself safe during the warning period.[156]
  **Note**: the way that 'safely' is understood has changed as the result of an Upper Tribunal decision and the DWP is looking again at decisions made since 9 March 2017.[157] Get advice if you think that your ability to perform activities 'safely' has not been properly assessed.
- **To an acceptable standard.** This is not defined in the regulations, and what it means is closely linked to the activity in question. What is an acceptable standard will depend to an extent on your experience of doing the activity, making the test a subjective one.[158] The level of pain you experience when managing an activity is one factor that should be considered[159] You may live with constant pain and therefore be able to cope better than another person without the same pain. However, this does not mean you can complete an activity to an acceptable standard – eg, walking despite pain is arguably not walking to an acceptable standard[160] and the same argument could be made for the rest of the activities.[161]
- **Repeatedly.** This means 'as often as the activity being assessed is reasonably required to be completed'. This means that if you have problems with an activity at some point during a day, you should satisfy a scoring descriptor on that day.[162] In considering how often you 'reasonably' need to undertake an activity, your own choices should generally be respected.[163]

- **Within a reasonable time period.** This means 'no more than twice as long as the maximum period that a person without a physical or mental condition which limits that person's ability to carry out the activity in question would normally take to complete that activity'. Time you spend thinking about the activity (eg, choosing clothes) can be taken into account if the hesitation is due to your condition.[164]

4

When considering the disability conditions, you should read these four factors into each descriptor. For example, descriptor 1a ('can prepare and cook a simple meal unaided') should be read as 'can *safely, repeatedly, to an acceptable standard and within a reasonable time period* prepare and cook a simple meal unaided'.

The four factors should be considered separately. For example, if you can manage the activity 'within a reasonable time period', the fact that you are doing it slowly is not relevant to the question of whether you can manage 'to an acceptable standard'.[165]

These definitions still leave a lot of discretion to the DWP. If you think you have not been given enough points because of this rule, you can ask for a mandatory reconsideration and then appeal. Explain which factor means that the descriptor you were awarded does not apply, and which descriptor you think you satisfy instead.

***Example***

Beth has a condition that means she is impatient and has a limited perception of danger. Having a friend prompt her while she prepares and cooks food does not allow her to manage this activity *safely*. Even using a microwave leaves her at risk of harm from preparing vegetables with knives or eating undercooked food. However, having a friend supervise and physically assist Beth does keep her safe. She therefore satisfies descriptor 1e.

## Fluctuating conditions

If a scoring descriptor applies to you at some point in a day (ie, 24 hours, starting from midnight), you should be accepted as satisfying it on that day, unless the amount of help you need is so minimal that it can be ignored.[166]

***Example***

Craig has a visual impairment, which causes him difficulty in poor light. After dark, he needs another person with him to be able to follow the route of an unfamiliar journey. During daylight hours, he can often follow journeys by himself. Craig should satisfy descriptor 1d in the planning and following journeys activity.

Which descriptor you are awarded for an activity also depends on how your condition affects you on different days. You are normally assessed over a one-year period starting from three months before you claim PIP and ending nine months after, or starting from the date your condition starts to affect you if that is later.[167] If you reclaim PIP after a gap and the 'special rule' on p666 applies, the assessment looks at the last three months of your previous award and the nine months from the date of your new claim.[168]

The descriptor for which you score points is decided as follows.[169]

- If only one descriptor in the activity applies to you on over 50 per cent of the days in the one-year period described above, that descriptor is used.
- If two or more descriptors each apply to you on over 50 per cent of the days in the period, the one that scores the most points is used.
- If neither of the above bullet points applies, but the number of days on which you satisfy two or more scoring descriptors totals more than 50 per cent of the days, the scoring descriptor that applies most often is used. If two descriptors apply on the same number of days, the highest scoring one is used.



The one-year period described above is also known as the 'required period'. See p666.

***Example***

Aisha makes a new claim for PIP on 3 May 2025. She has arthritis, which has affected her ability to dress for more than three months, so the period considered is from 3 February 2025 to 3 February 2026 (three months before the date she claimed and nine months after that date). Her condition is not deteriorating, but it affects her differently on different days. About two days a week (or 104 days a year), she can dress and undress unaided. Three days a week (or 156 days a year), she manages to dress using loose clothes with no buttons, slip-on shoes and a grabber to help with her socks. On a further two days a week (104 days a year), she also needs assistance from a family member to dress her upper body. The third bullet point above applies, as no single descriptor is satisfied on over half the days. Aisha satisfies descriptor 6b as she meets one or other of the scoring descriptors on over half of the days, and this descriptor applies most often.

It can be very difficult to decide which descriptors you satisfy if your condition fluctuates. It may be helpful for you to keep a diary over several weeks to help explain how your condition affects you.

When calculating which descriptor you should satisfy under this rule, it is important to think about how the effects of your condition vary, bearing in mind that you may not need to attempt some activities every day. For example, if your mental health condition means you can only go out or make budgeting decisions on good days, a couple of times a week, you can score points for these activities even if you manage to do them on good days. Similarly, the fact that you can sometimes manage activities if there is a specific reason why you must do so does not mean that you need no prompting to manage them on other days.[170]

**Note:** if you have more than one fluctuating condition and these affect your ability to manage a particular activity independently of each other, you may be affected on more than half of the days in the period considered, even if each condition only affects you on a minority of days.[171]

## The required period condition

4

Unless you are classed as terminally ill (see p669), you can only get PIP if you satisfy the 'required period condition'.[172] This normally means that you must be expected to meet the disability conditions for over one year in total. The required period condition consists of two separate periods (the 'past period' and the 'prospective period').[173]

If it is likely that you have met the disability conditions for three months ('the past period') on the date when you claim PIP, it can be awarded from that date. You must also be likely to continue to meet the conditions for at least another nine months from that date ('the prospective period').

If you do not satisfy the past period condition when you claim, a PIP award can be made starting from a date up to three months after the date your claim is decided, if you will satisfy both parts of the required period condition on that date.[174]

For how the required period condition affects an ongoing award of PIP, see p679.

**Note:**

- A special rule applies if:
  - you used to get PIP; *and*
  - your award ended less than two years ago (one year if you are aged 66 or over); *and*
  - you make a new claim based on the same condition(s) or a new condition that developed as a result of a previous one.

  In this situation, if you met the disability conditions for a component at a particular rate during the last three months of your previous award, you qualify for the same component from the date of your new claim, if your needs are expected to last for at least nine months from that date.[175]
- If you claim PIP and either you get DLA and are being transferred to PIP (see p527) or your DLA award ended under two years ago (one year if you are 66 or over), you do not have to satisfy the past period test. You must still satisfy the prospective period test.[176]

## 2. The rules about your age

You must be 16 or over to claim personal independence payment (PIP).[177]

The upper age limit for making a new PIP claim is normally the day before you reach pension age (currently 66).[178] If you are 66 or over and wish to claim a disability benefit and none of the exceptions below apply, see Chapter 20.

***Future changes***

The upper age limit to claim PIP will increase to 67 as the pension age rises between May 2026 and March 2028 (see p690).

There are several qualifications to the upper age limit.

- If you were under 65 on 8 April 2013 and either you are entitled to disability living allowance (DLA) or your entitlement ended less than a year ago, you can claim PIP even if you are 66 or over.[179] See p527 if you get DLA and are thinking about claiming PIP.
- If you claimed PIP when you were under 66, an award can be made to you.[180]
- If you are entitled to PIP when you turn 66, your award continues to its end date if you still meet the entitlement conditions.[181]
- Your PIP award can be revised or superseded after you turn 66. This includes awarding or increasing the daily living component (see Chapter 50).[182]
- If your PIP award has a fixed end date, you can make a renewal claim up to six months before this date, even if you are 66 or over (see p678). Also, if you have been entitled to PIP (or adult disability payment in Scotland), you can reclaim PIP within one year of your previous award ending, even if you are now 66 or over. Your new claim must be for the same disability or health condition(s) as your former award, or a new condition that has developed as a result of the original one(s).[183]

**Note:** in the latter two situations above, your entitlement to the mobility component is restricted (see below).

### Mobility component for older people

There is a general rule that you cannot get the mobility component of PIP after you turn 66. There are many exceptions.

You can usually get the mobility component when you are 66 or over in all of the following situations.

- You are entitled to the mobility component when you turn 66 and continue to meet the entitlement conditions.[184]
- Before turning 66, you claim PIP, ask for a supersession of your existing PIP award because of a change of circumstances, or the DWP takes action with a

view to superseding your award (eg, issues an award review form in response to a perceived change of circumstances), but the new decision on your entitlement is only made after you turn 66.[185]

**Note:** this may not apply where the DWP has only initiated a scheduled award review. However, if in the review form you state that your needs have changed, this may then be interpreted as a supersession request.

- You have requested revision of, or appealed against, a decision that was made before you turned 66, but you do not get a new decision (eg, the appeal is not heard) until after you have turned 66.[186]
- You are 66 or over, you have an existing award of PIP/adult disability payment including the mobility component or have had such an award at any point within the last year, you continue to meet the entitlement conditions due to the same health condition(s) or a new condition that has developed as a result of the original one(s), and you make a new PIP claim (including a renewal claim). In this situation, you cannot start getting the enhanced rate if your previous award only included the standard rate.[187]
- You are 66 or over, you have an existing award of PIP including the mobility component (or the mobility component stopped less than a year ago), and:[188]
  - your PIP award is superseded because of a change of circumstances which happened after you reached pension age; *or*
  - your PIP award is superseded because the DWP has received further medical evidence (usually an assessment report) and the second bullet point above does not apply; *or*
  - in Scotland,[189] your PIP award is superseded due to receipt of a new official medical report after you reach 66.

To get the same rate you had previously, you must continue to meet the entitlement conditions due to substantially the same health condition(s). If you previously got the enhanced rate, you can now get the standard rate even if your mobility needs result from a new condition. If your existing award only includes the standard rate, you cannot start getting the enhanced rate. **Note:** the rules described above about your PIP award being superseded were different before 30 November 2020 regarding not being able to start getting the enhanced rate. Before that date, if you were of pension age and getting the standard rate of the mobility component and had not reported a change in your circumstances, but the DWP had received a new medical assessment report showing you were entitled to an increase, then the DWP should have increased your award. If it did not, you may still be able to get the enhanced rate awarded, but you will need to ask the DWP for that. See gov.uk/guidance/apply-for-your-pip-claim-to-be-looked-at-if-your-mobility-award-was-not-increased-because-you-reached-state-pension-age.

**Note:** there may be other grounds to supersede your PIP award (see p1143). It is only if your award is superseded after you turn 66 for one of the reasons above that your entitlement to the mobility component is restricted.[190]

- You were under 65 on 8 April 2013 and either you have an existing DLA award and you are claiming PIP as part of the transfer process (see p527), or your DLA award ended less than a year ago and you are making a new PIP claim. In either situation, you can be awarded the standard or the enhanced rate of the mobility component of PIP, regardless of your age and whether your DLA award included a mobility component.[191]



## 3. People included in the claim

You claim personal independence payment (PIP) as an individual. If you have a partner, one or both of you can get PIP depending on your individual needs.

## 4. The amount of benefit

The daily living component of personal independence payment (PIP) is paid at one of two weekly rates:[192]
- the standard rate is £73.90;
- the enhanced rate is £110.40.

The mobility component of PIP is paid at one of two weekly rates:[193]
- the standard rate is £29.20;
- the enhanced rate is £77.05.

## 5. Special benefit rules

Special rules may apply if you:
- are classed as terminally ill (see below);
- have come from, or are going, abroad (see Chapters 56, 57, 58 and 59);
- are in hospital or living in a care home or similar accommodation, or in prison or detention (see Chapter 38).

### Terminal illness

For personal independence payment (PIP), you are classed as 'terminally ill' if you have a progressive disease from which your death can reasonably be expected within 12 months. If you claim PIP and you are classed as terminally ill, you are automatically entitled to the enhanced rate of the daily living component. You must still satisfy the disability conditions in order to get the mobility component (see p660), but you do not need to satisfy the required period condition (see p666).[194] If you are classed as terminally ill, it does not matter how long you have lived in Great Britain.[195] However, there are other residence tests that you must satisfy (see p1347).

Claims made in the last 12 months of life are referred to as 'special rules' claims and the claim process is different (see p671). If you want to claim PIP, or you are requesting a revision or supersession, on the basis of being terminally ill, you should expressly state this.[196] Someone else can claim PIP on behalf of a terminally ill person without their knowledge or authority.[197]

4

## 6. Claims and backdating

The general rules about claims are covered in Chapter 44. This section explains the specific rules that apply to personal independence payment (PIP).

**Note:** if you get disability living allowance (DLA) and have received a letter telling you to claim PIP, you should do so straight away, as your DLA award will end. If you get DLA and have *not* been sent a letter telling you to claim PIP, get specialist advice about whether you should ask to switch now (see p527).

### Making a claim

It is usually best to claim PIP by phone. Contact the **PIP claims line** on 0800 917 2222 (textphone: 0800 917 7777; Relay UK and BSL relay services available). If you cannot claim by these methods, you can ask to be sent Form PIP1.[198] You may also be able to apply online (see below).

***Forms***

Form PIP1 is available from the PIP claims line.

If you cannot use the phone and there is no one to help you, write asking for a claim form to Personal Independence Payment New Claims, Post Handling Site B, Wolverhampton WV99 1AH. This will delay your date of claim.

If you need to submit your claim form by email as your condition means that you cannot claim by phone or in writing, you should be able to request an email address to send your claim to.[199]

Online claims for PIP are now possible, although initially only in some areas. Check if you are eligible at apply-for-pip.dwp.gov.uk/eligibility/check-if-eligible. You cannot make an online claim if you are terminally ill.[200] Online claims involve completing both a PIP1 and PIP2 online, with no phone call to the DWP necessary. Online claims are not the same as receiving a digital PIP2 by email.

You must provide any information or evidence required (see p571). You can amend or withdraw your claim before a decision is made (see p1004).

If you get PIP already and your award ends within the next year, see p678.

### People classed as terminally ill

The PIP claims process is different if you are classed as terminally ill (see p669). You should explain that the claim is on the grounds of terminal illness when making it. You must provide Form SR1, completed by your GP, consultant or specialist nurse or doctor, detailing your medical condition. **Note:** Form DS1500 should still be accepted by the DWP to evidence terminal illness, though it has been replaced by Form SR1.[201]

If you are terminally ill, you are asked questions about your mobility needs as part of the claim. You are not asked to complete a separate questionnaire or attend a consultation.[202]

Someone else can claim PIP on behalf of a terminally ill person without their knowledge or authority.[203] If you have claimed PIP on someone else's behalf, you can also ask for a revision or supersession (see p1128) and appeal against a decision without their knowledge or authority.[204]

## Who should claim

You must normally make a claim for PIP yourself. If you cannot manage your claim, another person can claim PIP for you as your appointee (see p1005). Someone else can also claim PIP for a person who is terminally ill (see above).

## Information to support your claim

For the general information requirements that apply to all benefits, see p1006.

It is important that you provide any information required when you claim. Until you do, you may not count as having made a valid claim (see p1008). Correct any defects as soon as possible or your date of claim may be affected.

You do not need to have a national insurance (NI) number to start a claim for PIP.[205]

Once you have claimed, there is a separate assessment process.

Even if your claim is valid, you may be asked to provide further information to support your claim (see p1009). You may also be asked to provide information after you are awarded PIP and, if you fail to do so, your PIP could be suspended or even terminated (see p1031).

### The assessment process

**Note:** this assessment process does not apply if you are terminally ill (see above).

If you claim PIP and meet the basic entitlement conditions (see p646), you are assessed to see whether you meet the disability conditions (see p646) and the required period condition (see p666). You are also assessed in this way if your PIP award is being reviewed (see p678) or you report a change in your circumstances (see p679). The assessment process can include requirements to:[206]

- provide information or evidence (normally in the form of a questionnaire about how you manage daily living and mobility activities); *and*
- attend a consultation with a health professional.

### The questionnaire

You are sent a questionnaire which asks about your condition(s), any treatment you receive, and how you may manage the daily living and mobility activities. Different questionnaires are generally used for new claims (Form PIP2) and to review existing PIP awards (Form AR1). Both are available in paper or digital form (the latter emailed as either a PDF to complete or a link to an online PIP2). Some people can also complete the entire PIP claim online (see p670).

4

**Note:** the DWP is testing a new, six-page 'light-touch' review form (Form AR2). This form is for claimants who are usually on 10-year PIP awards whose conditions are high level, unlikely to change or only get worse, or who are around or over state pension age. These are claimants who would not usually be expected to have an in-person assessment at review.[207] If you have a query about an existing PIP claim, contact the PIP helpline on 0800 121 4433 (textphone: 0800 121 4493; Relay UK and BSL relay available – see gov.uk/disability-benefits-helpline).

You can request the questionnaire in an alternative format (eg, large print, braille or British Sign Language) by contacting the PIP helpline. If your request is refused, you can complain (see p1260), but you should try to return the questionnaire you have if you can, as otherwise, your claim may be refused.

The DWP must receive your completed questionnaire within one month of the day it was sent to you. If you need longer (eg, because you need help to complete it), you must ask the DWP for an extension as soon as possible. You will be allowed the extension if the request is considered reasonable.[208] If you do not return the questionnaire (or other information requested about the disability conditions) without good reason (see p675), a 'negative determination' is made, and your claim is refused (or your existing award ends).[209]

The questionnaire asks for the contact details of the health professionals who best know how your condition affects you. Even when it has these details, the DWP does not usually contact them to ask for evidence about your health. It is generally your responsibility to provide any relevant medical evidence.

Form PIP2 also asks whether you need help to attend an assessment. The review form (AR1) asks for similar information as the PIP2 form but in a more condensed way. It asks whether you can complete the activity safely, and whether you need help from another person or to use aids. It then asks why and when those needs began.

***How you should complete the questionnaire***

1. If you are finding the form difficult, many advice agencies can help you to complete it.
2. If someone else has to fill in the questionnaire for you, or you can only to do so slowly or with pain, explain this in the questionnaire.

3. Read the activities list on pp647–63 to get an idea of what the DWP needs to know about each activity. Remember that many terms in the assessment have special definitions – eg, 'cook' means to heat food at or above waist height.
4. It may help to draft your answers first before filling in the form.
5. For each activity, explain whether you can do things 'safely', 'repeatedly', 'to an acceptable standard' and 'within a reasonable time period' (see p663).
6. Explain whether you have better and worse days. You may need different help with an activity on different days or at different times of day. If so, explain how often you need each kind of help, as this is relevant to the points you score (see p664).
7. List any aids or appliances (see p648) that you need to help you complete an activity, and any problems you have using them.
8. When describing how your condition affects you, it is useful to give real-life examples – eg, a time when you needed prompting or were unable to complete an activity 'safely'.
9. Use pp647–63 to work out your likely score. Your answers should not be exaggerated, but check that you have not underestimated any of your problems and have given all the details you can.
10. If you can, ask someone who knows you well to check that your answers fully explain your difficulties.
11. Ensure to mention all your symptoms and all side effects of medication. If you do not take any medication, state why. Absence of medication does not mean your health condition is not severe as you may not take medication due to its side effects or you may refuse to take medication due to poor compliance.[210] You can explain this in the additional information section at the end of the form.
12. If you have other information relevant to your difficulties with daily living or mobility activities, send a copy with the questionnaire, marked with your name and NI number. This could include a report from an occupational therapist or consultant, information from your GP, a support worker or carer, or a statement from a friend or family member. Ensure the evidence is helpful by checking how closely it relates to the activities in the assessment. Evidence that confirms the severity of your condition may also be useful – eg, x-rays, test results or a Certificate of Vision Impairment.
13. If you have had a previous award of DLA, you can ask the DWP to consider evidence from your DLA claim when making a decision on your PIP claim. You might also ask the DWP to look at evidence from a work capability assessment (see Chapter 41).
14. If you can, make a copy of the completed questionnaire before returning it to the DWP, and keep a copy of any extra information that you send with it. You may wish to send your form by recorded delivery, but you do not need to. If you send the form at the post office, you can ask for free proof of postage.

The DWP sends your completed questionnaire to a health professional, who decides what other evidence they think is needed. This may include requiring you to take part in a consultation.

### The consultation

You can be required to take part in a consultation with a health professional to assess whether you satisfy the disability conditions (even if you already have a PIP award). The DWP publishes a guide to carrying out assessments for health professionals.[211]

Four private companies carry out the consultations on behalf of the DWP, depending on where you live. They will contact you to explain what you need to do.

- Maximum UK Services Ltd covers the North of England and Scotland.
- Capita Business Services covers the Midlands, Wales and Northern Ireland.
- Serco covers South West England.
- Ingeus UK Ltd covers South East England, London and East Anglia.

4

It is possible that a health professional will prepare a report without a consultation.[212]

Consultations can be held in person or by telephone or video call. You must normally be sent written notice of the date and time of the consultation (and, if in person, where it will be) at least seven days in advance. This rule does *not* apply if you accept less notice or notice by phone.[213]

You should not be asked to travel for more than 90 minutes on public transport to get to an in-person consultation.[214]

#### *Recordings of consultations*

The assessment provider can audio record your telephone or in-person assessment. You must request this in advance. You can also, or alternatively, make your own audio recording. Video recordings are not permitted.[215]

You can ask for someone else to take part in the consultation to support you, and they can also give information to the health professional. The health professional asks you questions about how you manage the different daily living and mobility activities.

#### *What you should do at the consultation*

1. In advance, read the activities list on pp647–63 to get an idea of what the assessor needs to know about each activity.
2. Explain as much as possible about how you are affected by your condition(s). For each activity you talk about, explain whether you can do things 'safely', 'repeatedly', 'to an acceptable standard' and 'within a reasonable time period' (see p663).
3. If you need to take extra medication to take part in the consultation, explain this and also what you can and cannot do taking your normal dose.
4. If you have good and bad days, ensure that you explain this and how your needs are different on a bad day. This is especially important if you are assessed on a better day.

5. If you are not fluent in English, it is vital that someone who can interpret for you takes part. Contact the assessment provider as soon as possible if you need an interpreter.
6. The assessment report can also include informal observations of your behaviour – eg, whether you can take part without support, and (for face-to-face consultations) your demeanour, how far you appear to be able to walk and whether you travelled to the assessment centre alone.



If you must take part in an in-person consultation, it is usually in an assessment centre but you can ask for it to take place at your home. You should try to provide medical evidence explaining why you cannot attend an assessment centre (but should not be required to pay for evidence).[216] If your request is refused and you do not attend, your claim may be refused.

**If you fail to complete part of the assessment process**

If you return a questionnaire late or do not take part in a consultation, and the DWP does not accept that you had good reason for the failure, it makes a 'negative determination'. This results in a new PIP claim being refused[217] or an existing award being superseded and removed from the date of the decision (see p1144).[218]

If the DWP makes a negative determination, you can ask for a mandatory reconsideration (see p1168), and appeal if the decision is not changed. You should also get advice about making a new claim in case your challenge is not successful.

Check carefully any letters that you received about the assessment process. It may be arguable that the information sent to you was not sufficient to make you aware of the requirement to return the questionnaire or take part in the consultation.[219]

***Good reason***

In deciding whether you have **'good reason'**, the DWP must consider the state of your health and the nature of your disability, along with any other reasons why you did not do what was required.[220] Guidance suggests several other things *may* amount to good reason, including domestic emergencies and not having received notifications.[221] The guidance suggests that telling the assessment provider what has happened as soon as possible is relevant to whether you have good reason or not. You should contact the assessment provider as soon as you can to explain why you cannot (or did not) take part in a consultation. Guidance to health professionals suggests that a negative determination should not be made if you have a mental or cognitive impairment and do not return a questionnaire, so if you have this kind of condition, you should explain any effect it had on your ability to return it.[222]

You should try to get supporting evidence – eg, confirmation of postal problems at your address, or medical evidence of the impact of the request to take part in a consultation on your condition. The unsuitability of the location where you were required to take part in a consultation can be a good reason for not attending it.[223]

## The date of your claim

The date of your claim is important as it determines when your entitlement to PIP starts. For information about when *payment* of PIP starts, see p677.

Your date of claim differs depending on how you make the initial claim.

- If you claim by phone, your date of claim is usually the date of your call to the PIP new claims line. If you phone to request a PIP1 form, the date of claim is the date you made the phone request.
- If you make an online claim, the date of claim is the date you submit the PIP1 section.
- If you write to the DWP asking for a PIP1 form to be sent to you, the date of claim is the date the DWP receive this request.



These dates only apply as long as the DWP receives your properly completed form within one month, or longer if reasonable.[224]

If you try to start a PIP claim by phone but the call handler incorrectly tells you that you are not eligible (eg, because they do not accept that you are exempt from the 'past presence test' – see p1347) and fails to take your claim, the date of the call should nonetheless be treated as your date of claim if you submit a paper claim form within one month, or longer if reasonable.[225]

You must make sure your claim is valid. If it is 'defective', you are given a short time to correct the defects (see p1008). If you do, your claim is treated as having been made when you initially claimed.[226]

### Backdating your claim

You cannot backdate a claim for PIP.[227]

If you might have qualified for PIP sooner but did not claim because you were given the wrong information or misled by the DWP, you could pursue a complaint, asking for compensation (see Chapter 55).

### If you claim the wrong benefit

A claim for DLA or attendance allowance can be treated as a claim for PIP and vice versa.[228] In both cases, this only applies if the DWP thinks you are not entitled to the benefit you actually claimed. See p1013 for further information.

### Claiming in advance

You can claim PIP in advance if you do not satisfy the entitlement conditions but will do so within three months of the date your claim is decided.[229] This may be relevant if you do not satisfy the required period condition (see p666) when you first claim. In this situation, the date you first qualify is your date of claim. If you want to claim in advance, make this clear when you claim or the DWP might not consider it.

If you already get PIP, you can make a renewal claim up to six months before your award ends (see p678).

# 7. Getting paid

The general rules on getting paid are in Chapter 45. This section explains the specific rules that apply to personal independence payment (PIP).

***When is personal independence payment paid?***

PIP is usually paid on the same day of the week as the decision was made on your claim, but this can be changed by the DWP. PIP is usually paid every four weeks in arrears, or if you are terminally ill, weekly in advance.[230]

Payment of PIP starts after a decision has been made on your claim.



Note:

- The enhanced rate of the mobility component can be paid direct to Motability (see p681) if you are buying or leasing a car through the scheme.[231]
- Payment of PIP may be made to someone else on your behalf (eg, an appointee) if this is needed to protect your interests.[232]
- Even if you have been sanctioned for a benefit offence (see p1111), you must be paid PIP.
- If payment of your PIP is delayed, see p1123. If you wish to complain about how your claim has been dealt with, or claim compensation, see Chapter 55.
- If payment of your PIP is suspended, see p1031.
- If you are overpaid PIP, you may have to repay it (see Chapter 47) and, in some circumstances, you may have to pay a penalty (see p1101). If you have been accused of fraud, see Chapter 48.
- If you are owed arrears of PIP, these can be paid either in a lump sum or in instalments (see p1018).

## Length of awards

PIP is normally awarded for a fixed period – eg, two or five years. The length of award depends on how likely it is that your needs will change over time. You are normally awarded PIP for three years if you are terminally ill.[233]

An indefinite award can be made if a fixed-term award would be inappropriate.[234] Most indefinite awards are reviewed every 10 years, to check they are still correct.[235] The DWP is testing a short review form (AR2) for some claimants with these 10-year awards (see p672).

If you think that you should have been given a longer award, you can ask for a mandatory reconsideration (see p1130), and appeal if the decision is not changed.[236] If you do this, the amount of your benefit may also be reconsidered.

**Note:** your entitlement to PIP can be reassessed at any time, regardless of the stated length of your award.[237] If your award is coming to an end, see p678.

## Reviews and renewal claims

If you already get PIP, you can make a renewal claim up to six months before your award ends.[238] However, you may not need to do this, as your award may be reviewed by the DWP one year before it ends.[239] The DWP's operational guidance states that all awards longer than two years will be subject to review in this way, and awards for two years or less may also have a review scheduled, but this is at the decision maker's discretion.[240]

If your award is not reviewed, the DWP should contact you around three months before it ends to remind you to make a new claim. You do *not* need to wait to be contacted to make a new claim.

4

**Note:** if no decision is made on a renewal claim or review before the end of your award, your PIP may stop and other benefits may also be affected. At the time of writing, the DWP is operating a temporary policy of extending PIP awards automatically by 12 months when a review is due but has not yet been completed.[241]

***Is your personal independence payment award ending?***

If you are awarded PIP for a fixed period, you may be referred for a review a year before your award ends. Your award letter should say whether your award will be reviewed,[242] or you can contact the PIP helpline (tel: 0800 121 4433; textphone: 0800 121 4493) to check.

The process of reviewing your award is similar to the assessment process for new claims (see p671). Return the questionnaire as soon as possible and take part in any consultation, otherwise a negative determination may be made, ending your PIP award (see p675). A decision maker then decides whether to carry out a supersession (see p1143). A supersession decision could extend, change or remove your PIP award.

If your award is due to end in less than six months and the DWP has not contacted you, you may wish either to make a renewal claim or to request a supersession (see p1143) to make sure you get a decision before your award ends. Get advice about the possible impact on your current award.

If there is a delay in getting a decision, or you are unsure what is happening, call the PIP helpline. If you are told that your award is likely to end before an assessment can be carried out, make a complaint (see Chapter 55). If you have been told your PIP award has been automatically extended by 12 months, but your condition has significantly changed, call the PIP helpline to ask for your review to be prioritised.

## Administrative exercises

The DWP is undertaking several PIP administrative exercises, also called legal entitlements and administrative practices (LEAP) reviews.[243] These reviews involve large numbers of PIP decisions being looked at again because there has been a new understanding of the law after an Upper Tribunal or higher court decision. See p653, p654 and p659. Get advice if you receive a letter saying that an earlier decision about your entitlement to PIP has been looked at again or if you have not heard from the DWP but think you should be included in a LEAP exercise.

### Change of circumstances

**Note:** a change of circumstances is not just a change in the level of your needs. It can also include that your needs are now expected to last beyond the end date of your award.[244] If your award is due to end in less than one year, see p678.

You must report any changes in your circumstances that you have been told you must report, as well as any that you might reasonably be expected to know might affect your right to, the amount of, or the payment of, PIP. If a change means you can no longer meet the nine-month required period condition for PIP (see p666), you should report it.[245] It is usually best to get independent advice before reporting a change in your health that you think might affect your entitlement to PIP.

You should report any changes in your circumstances as soon as possible, preferably in writing. See p1030 for further information.

If a payment of PIP has stopped but entitlement has continued (eg, because you are in hospital, a care home or prison – see Chapter 38), still notify the DWP of any changes so the correct rate is paid when payment resumes.

If there has been a relevant change of circumstances, a decision maker looks at your award again and makes a new decision. To find out the date from which the new decision takes effect, see p1148.

If you get PIP, already live in Scotland and plan to report a change of circumstances, see p1445. If you get PIP and plan to move to Scotland, see p1444.

## 8. Tax, other benefits and the benefit cap

### Tax

Personal independence payment (PIP) is not taxable.[246]

### Means-tested benefits

PIP is not taken into account as income when calculating means-tested benefits, and is paid in addition to them. Getting PIP can increase the amount of means-tested benefit you get by making you eligible for certain additions, premiums and components.

If you or your partner are entitled to PIP, you may qualify for:

- a limited capability for work-related activity element in your universal credit (UC) if you or your partner are entitled to the enhanced rate of the PIP daily

living component and are aged 66 or over (see p918). Alternatively, your UC may include a limited capability for work element if you or your partner are entitled to PIP but not the enhanced rate of the daily living component, and are 66 or over, in some circumstances (see p71 and p897);
- a disability premium in housing benefit (HB) if you are under 66 (see p272);
- an enhanced disability premium in income-related employment and support allowance (ESA) or HB if you or your partner are entitled to the enhanced rate of the daily living component and are under 66 (see p273);
- a severe disability premium/addition in income-related ESA, the guarantee credit of pension credit (PC) or HB if you or your partner receive the daily living component and meet other conditions (see p275).

If your child is entitled to PIP and still counts as part of your household (even if you do not get a basic amount for them because of the 'two-child limit'), you may qualify for:
- a disabled child addition in UC, paid at a higher rate if they are entitled to the enhanced rate of the daily living component (see p68);
- a disabled child premium in HB (see p271);
- an enhanced disability premium in HB if they are entitled to the enhanced rate of the daily living component (see p273);
- an additional amount in your PC paid at a higher rate if they are entitled to the enhanced rate of the daily living component (see p270).

If you or your partner receive the daily living component, non-dependant deductions are not made from your HB (see p207), or from any housing costs included in your income-related ESA or the guarantee credit of PC (see p289).

No housing costs contributions from a non-dependant are taken into account when calculating your UC housing costs element if you, your partner or the non-dependant receive the PIP daily living component, or are entitled to it but payment is suspended as you are in hospital (see p109).

## Non-means-tested benefits

PIP may be paid in addition to any other non-means-tested benefits. However, exceptions include:
- you are not entitled to PIP while you are entitled to adult disability payment or child disability payment;[247]
- if you are entitled to PIP, you cannot claim disability living allowance[248] or attendance allowance;[249]
- PIP overlaps with some war pension payments for constant attendance or mobility, and armed forces independence payment (see p779);[250]
- PIP daily living component overlaps with constant attendance allowance under the industrial injuries scheme (see p600);[251]

- PIP mobility component is not paid if you get a grant for a vehicle from the NHS, military or other public funds.[252]

If you get the daily living component of PIP and someone regularly looks after you, that person may be entitled to carer's allowance (CA) (see Chapter 22) or carer support payment (see p1467) and they may also get a carer element in UC (see p75), a carer premium in income-related ESA or HB, or a carer addition in the guarantee credit of PC (see p279). However, any severe disability premium/ addition you get will stop if they get CA or the carer element of UC, so always get advice. If you receive a transitional SDP element within your UC, this is unaffected by someone claiming CA or someone receiving the carer element of UC (see p27).

If you get the daily living component, a young person living in Scotland may be able to get a young carer grant for looking after you (see p1476).

## The benefit cap

PIP is *not* one of the specified benefits for the benefit cap.

## Passports and other sources of help

You qualify for a Christmas bonus if you get PIP (see p783).

If you get PIP, you may be entitled to a blue badge parking concession or a concessionary travel card. Contact your local authority for more information.

If you receive the PIP mobility component and you or your carer have a car used only by you or for you, your road tax may be reduced. See the details at gov.uk/financial-help-disabled/vehicles-and-transport.

### Motability

Motability is a charity that runs a scheme to help you lease or buy a car, scooter or powered wheelchair. You are eligible if you get the enhanced rate of the PIP mobility component and have 12 months or more left to run on your award.

If you use the scheme, your PIP mobility component is paid direct to Motability rather than to you.[253] You may also have to make extra payments for the vehicle. For further information, see motability.co.uk.

# Notes

1. **Who can get personal independence payment**

1 ss77-80 WRA 2012; Part 2 and Sch 1 SS(PIP) Regs
2 *MB v SSWP (PIP)* [2016] UKUT 250 (AAC)
3 *PM v SSWP (PIP)* [2017] UKUT 154 (AAC); *EG v SSWP (PIP)* [2017] UKUT 101 (AAC)
4 *JM v SSWP (PIP)* [2024] UKUT 283 (AAC); *AE v SSWP* [2024] UKUT 381 (AAC)
5 ss78-79 WRA 2012
6 *MR v SSWP (PIP)* [2017] UKUT 86 (AAC); *PW by his appointee v SSWP* [2023] UKUT 121 (AAC)
7 *TK v SSWP (PIP)* [2020] UKUT 22 (AAC), reported as [2020] AACR 18
8 *KP v SSWP (PIP)* [2017] UKUT 30 (AAC)
9 *SD v SSWP (PIP)* [2017] UKUT 310 (AAC); *DE v SSWP (PIP)* [2021] UKUT 226 (AAC)
10 Regs 5 and 6 SS(PIP) Regs
11 Sch 1 Part 1 SS(PIP) Regs
12 *JT v SSWP (PIP)* [2018] UKUT 101 (AAC); *CP v SSWP (PIP)* [2018] UKUT 5 (AAC)
13 Sch 1 Part 1 SS(PIP) Regs
14 *SSWP v GM (PIP)* [2017] UKUT 268 (AAC)
15 *RJ, GMcL and CS v SSWP v RJ (PIP)* [2017] UKUT 105 (AAC), reported as [2017] AACR 32
16 DWP, *Safety and Supervision: changes to PIP law from 9 March 2017*, 26 November 2024, gov.uk/government/publications/personal-independence-payment-changes/safety-and-supervision-changes-to-pip-law-from-9-march-2017
17 *SSWP v IM (PIP)* [2015] UKUT 680 (AAC)
18 *LB v SSWP (PIP)* [2017] UKUT 436 (AAC)
19 *GG v SSWP (PIP)* [2016] UKUT 194 (AAC); *PM v SSWP (PIP)* [2017] UKUT 502 (AAC)
20 *SSWP v MMcK* [2017] CSIH 57. The Supreme Court made no comment on this suggestion in the appeal against this decision (*SSWP v MM (Scotland)* [2019] UKSC 34, reported as [2019] AACR 26).
21 Reg 2 SS(PIP) Regs
22 *AB v SSWP* [2024] UKUT 376 (AAC)
23 *MR v SSWP (PIP)* [2017] UKUT 86 (AAC), although the comments were not strictly necessary to the decision in that case
24 Reg 4(2) SS(PIP) Regs
25 *CW v SSWP (PIP)* [2016] UKUT 197 (AAC), reported as [2016] AACR 44; *NA v SSWP (PIP)* [2015] UKUT 572 (AAC); *AP v SSWP (PIP)* [2016] UKUT 501 (AAC)
26 *MR v SSWP (PIP)* [2019] UKUT 293 (AAC)
27 *PE v SSWP (PIP)* [2015] UKUT 309 (AAC), reported as [2016] AACR 10; *JM v SSWP (PIP)* [2016] UKUT 542 (AAC)
28 Sch 1 Part 1 SS(PIP) Regs
29 *RH v SSWP (PIP)* [2015] UKUT 281 (AAC)
30 *SSWP v KJ (PIP)* [2017] UKUT 358 (AAC)
31 *ZI v SSWP (PIP)* [2016] UKUT 572 (AAC), reported as [2018] AACR 1
32 *SC v SSWP (PIP)* [2017] UKUT 317 (AAC)
33 *AI v SSWP (PIP)* [2016] UKUT 322 (AAC)
34 *LC v SSWP (PIP)* [2016] UKUT 150 (AAC)
35 *GB v SSWP (PIP)* [2015] UKUT 546 (AAC) – however the DWP may not accept this interpretation: see *AP v SSWP (PIP)* [2016] UKUT 501 (AAC); *YW (deceased) by MM v SSWP (PIP)* [2017] UKUT 42 (AAC)
36 *DR v SSWP (PIP)* [2018] UKUT 209 (AAC), but see also *EG v SSWP (PIP)* [2015] 275 UKUT (AAC), which came to the opposite view
37 *SSWP v DT (PIP)* [2017] UKUT 272 (AAC)
38 *AI v SSWP (PIP)* [2016] UKUT 322 (AAC)
39 Sch 1 Part 1 SS(PIP) Regs
40 *MM and BJ v SSWP (PIP)* [2016] UKUT 490 (AAC), reported as [2017] AACR 17
41 *JW v SSWP (PIP)* [2018] UKUT 169 (AAC)
42 *TK v SSWP (PIP)* [2020] UKUT 22 (AAC), reported as [2020] AACR 18
43 *SO v SSWP (PIP)* [2023] UKUT 56 (AAC)
44 *PA v SSWP (PIP)* [2019] UKUT 270 (AAC)
45 *CB v SSWP (PIP)* [2022] UKUT 100 (AAC)
46 *SSWP v KS (PIP)* [2018] UKUT 102 (AAC)
47 Sch 1 Part 1 SS(PIP) Regs
48 Now called the Health and Care Professions Council
49 *CK v SSWP (PIP)*; *JM v SSWP (PIP)* [2022] UKUT 122 (AAC)
50 *PM v SSWP (PIP)* [2018] UKUT 138 (AAC)
51 *CF v SSWP (PIP)* [2024] UKUT 224 (AAC)

52 *SSWP v LB (PIP)* [2016] UKUT 530 (AAC). The DWP interprets this aspect of the decision as still applying to the current definition of 'therapy' - see DWP, *Special Diet as Therapy: changes to PIP law from 28 November 2016*, 26 November 2024, gov.uk/government/publications/personal-independence-payment-changes.
53 *KM v SSWP (PIP)* [2018] UKUT 296 (AAC)
54 *AS v SSWP (PIP)* [2017] UKUT 104 (AAC), reported as [2017] AACR 31
55 *SSWP v TMcl (PIP)* [2016] UKUT 574 (AAC)
56 *SSWP v KS (PIP)* [2018] UKUT 102 (AAC); *EK v Department for Communities (PIP)* [2024] NICom52
57 *DC v SSWP (PIP)* [2016] UKUT 11 (AAC)
58 *AH v SSWP (PIP)* [2016] UKUT 276 (AAC)
59 *MM v SSWP (PIP)* [2018] UKUT 193 (AAC), but note that the point was not finally decided
60 *TK v SSWP (PIP)* [2020] UKUT 22 (AAC), reported as [2020] AACR 18
61 *MF v SSWP (PIP)* [2015] UKUT 554 (AAC), reported as [2016] AACR 20
62 *RH v SSWP (PIP)* [2015] UKUT 281 (AAC)
63 *RB v SSWP (PIP)* [2016] UKUT 556 (AAC)
64 DWP, *Changes to PIP law from 28 November 2016 to 15 March 2017*, 26 November 2024, available at gov.uk
65 Sch 1 Part 1 SS(PIP) Regs
66 *AP v SSWP (PIP)* [2016] UKUT 501 (AAC)
67 *SP v SSWP (PIP)* [2016] UKUT 190 (AAC), reported as [2016] AACR 43
68 *SH v SSWP (PIP)* [2018] UKUT 251 (AAC); *RJ, GMcL and CS v SSWP v RJ (PIP)* [2017] UKUT 105 (AAC), reported as [2017] AACR 32
69 *KT and SH v SSWP (PIP)* [2020] UKUT 252 (AAC)
70 DWP, *Risk and Safety: changes to PIP law from 21 August 2020*, 26 November 2024, available at gov.uk
71 *MB v SSWP (PIP)* [2018] UKUT 139 (AAC)
72 *GG v SSWP (PIP)* [2016] UKUT 194 (AAC)
73 Sch 1 Part 1 SS(PIP) Regs
74 *GW v SSWP (PIP)* [2015] UKUT 570 (AAC)
75 *DA v SSWP (PIP)* [2019] UKUT 320 (AAC)
76 *MS v SSWP* [2024] UKUT 185 (AAC)
77 *FK v SSWP (PIP)* [2017] UKUT 375 (AAC)
78 *JM v SSWP (PIP)* [2016] UKUT 296 (AAC)
79 *BS v SSWP (PIP)* [2016] UKUT 456 (AAC)
80 *GW v SSWP (PIP)* [2015] UKUT 570 (AAC)
81 *SSWP v NH (PIP)* [2017] UKUT 258 (AAC)
82 *KO v SSWP (PIP)* [2018] UKUT 78 (AAC)
83 *KW v SSWP (PIP)* [2017] UKUT 54 (AAC)
84 *SH v Department for Communities (PIP)* [2024] NICom 46
85 *GP v SSWP (PIP)* [2015] UKUT 498 (AAC)
86 Sch 1 Part 1 SS(PIP) Regs
87 *JM v SSWP (PIP)* [2016] UKUT 542 (AAC)
88 *PE v SSWP (PIP)* [2015] UKUT 309 (AAC), reported as [2016] AACR 10
89 *JM v SSWP (PIP)* [2016] UKUT 542 (AAC)
90 *CW v SSWP (PIP)* [2016] UKUT 197 (AAC), reported as [2016] AACR 44; *AP v SSWP (PIP)* [2016] UKUT 501 (AAC)
91 *MR v SSWP (PIP)* [2019] UKUT 293 (AAC)
92 *DP v SSWP (PIP)* [2017] UKUT 156 (AAC)
93 *ML v SSWP (PIP)* [2017] UKUT 171 (AAC)
94 Sch 1 Part 1 SS(PIP) Regs
95 *BM v DfC (PIP)* [2019] NICom 33, reported as [2020] AACR 15 and therefore persuasive while not binding outside of Northern Ireland
96 *P v SSWP (PIP)* [2018] UKUT 376 (AAC)
97 *EG v SSWP (PIP)* [2017] UKUT 101 (AAC)
98 *TC v SSWP (PIP)* [2016] UKUT 550 (AAC)
99 *SSWP v AS (PIP)* [2017] UKUT 454 (AAC); *GJ v SSWP (PIP)* [2016] UKUT 8 (AAC)
100 Sch 1 Part 1 SS(PIP) Regs
101 *TR v SSWP (PIP)* [2015] UKUT 626 (AAC), reported as [2016] AACR 23
102 *MR v SSWP (PIP)* [2017] UKUT 86 (AAC)
103 *KP v SSWP (PIP)* [2017] UKUT 30 (AAC)
104 *SE v SSWP (PIP)* [2021] UKUT 1 (AAC)
105 Sch 1 Part 1 SS(PIP) Regs
106 *SM v SSWP (PIP)* [2019] UKUT 292 (AAC); *AM v SSWP (PIP)* [2017] UKUT 7 (AAC)
107 *DV v SSWP (PIP)* [2017] UKUT 244 (AAC); *SF v SSWP (PIP)* [2016] UKUT 543 (AAC)
108 *PM v SSWP (PIP)* [2017] UKUT 154 (AAC)
109 Sch 1 Part 1 SS(PIP) Regs; *SF v SSWP (PIP)* [2016] UKUT 543 (AAC); *SSWP v AM (PIP)* [2015] UKUT 215 (AAC). Both decisions held that the definition of 'engage socially' applies to the words 'engage with other people' in the descriptors.
110 *HA v SSWP (PIP)* [2018] UKUT 56 (AAC); *KW v SSWP (PIP)* [2024] UKUT 410 (AAC)
111 *HA v SSWP (PIP)* [2018] UKUT 56 (AAC); *RC v SSWP (PIP)* [2017] UKUT 352 (AAC)
112 *DV v SSWP (PIP)* [2017] UKUT 244 (AAC)
113 *RC v SSWP (PIP)* [2017] UKUT 352 (AAC)
114 *HJ v SSWP* (PIP) [2016] UKUT 487 (AAC)
115 *TC v DfC (PIP)* [2024] NICom30
116 *AC v SSWP (PIP)* [2021] UKUT 216 (AAC)
117 *SSWP v MM (Scotland)* [2019] UKSC 34, reported as [2019] AACR 26; *SL v SSWP (PIP)* [2016] UKUT 147 (AAC)

118 *SSWP v MM (Scotland)* [2019] UKSC 34, reported as [2019] AACR 26, as interpreted by the DWP in para 9 ('Example 3') of ADM Memo 22/20: *PIP Daily Living Activity 9 - effect of Supreme Court judgement*
119 *JT v SSWP (PIP)* [2020] UKUT 186 (AAC)
120 DWP, *Social support, changes to PIP law from 6 April 2016*, 26 November 2024, available at gov.uk
121 Sch 1 Part 1 SS(PIP) Regs
122 *DP v SSWP (PIP)* [2017] UKUT 156 (AAC)
123 *PR v SSWP (PIP)* [2015] UKUT 584 (AAC); *JW v SSWP (PIP)* [2018] UKUT 169 (AAC)
124 *SE v SSWP (PIP)* [2021] UKUT 1 (AAC)
125 *RB v SSWP (PIP)* [2016] UKUT 393 (AAC)
126 *SSWP v LB (PIP)* [2016] UKUT 530 (AAC)
127 Sch 1 Part 1 SS(PIP) Regs
128 *SSWP v NF (PIP)* [2017] UKUT 480 (AAC)
129 *AA v SSWP (PIP)* [2018] UKUT 339 (AAC)
130 The definition of 'prompting' does not require the physical presence of the person who is prompting you
131 *TR v SSWP (PIP)* [2015] UKUT 626 (AAC), reported as [2016] AACR 23; *PM v SSWP (PIP)* [2017] UKUT 154 (AAC); *AA v SSWP (PIP)* [2018] UKUT 339 (AAC). Note that PIP AG Part 2 suggests that this argument may not be accepted, although it does suggest that only being able to go out in darkness is not managing this activity to an acceptable standard.
132 *MH v SSWP (PIP)* [2016] UKUT 531 (AAC), reported as [2018] AACR 12
133 *AA v SSWP (PIP)* [2018] UKUT 339 (AAC)
134 *JB v SSWP (PIP)* [2019] UKUT 203 (AAC); *SB v SSWP (PIP)* [2019] UKUT 274 (AAC)
135 *MC v SSWP (PIP)* [2019] UKUT 264 (AAC); *SSWP v IV (PIP)* [2016] UKUT 420 (AAC)
136 *HO'H v SSWP (PIP)* [2020] UKUT 135 (AAC)
137 *MH v SSWP (PIP)* [2016] UKUT 531 (AAC), reported as [2018] AACR 12
138 *AA v SSWP (PIP)* [2018] UKUT 339 (AAC)
139 PIP AG Part 2
140 *MH v SSWP (PIP)* [2016] UKUT 531 (AAC), reported as [2018] AACR 12
141 Sch 1 Part 1 SS(PIP) Regs
142 *DT v SSWP (PIP)* [2016] UKUT 240 (AAC)
143 *AP v SSWP (PIP)* [2016] UKUT 501 (AAC), but note that *KL v SSWP (PIP)* [2015] UKUT 612 (AAC) came to a different conclusion and interprets the law more generously
144 *KN v SSWP (PIP)* [2016] UKUT 261 (AAC); *TF v SSWP (PIP)* [2015] UKUT 661 (AAC)
145 PIP AG Part 2 para 2.2.27
146 *KL v SSWP (PIP)* [2016] UKUT 545 (AAC)
147 *LH v SSWP (PIP)* [2018] UKUT 57 (AAC); *PS v SSWP (PIP)* [2016] UKUT 536 (AAC); *LB v SSWP (PIP)* [2024] UKUT 338 (AAC)
148 *CM v SSWP (PIP)* [2020] UKUT 259 (AAC)
149 *NK v SSWP (PIP)* [2016] UKUT 146 (AAC)
150 *MH v SSWP (PIP)* [2016] UKUT 531 (AAC), reported as [2018] AACR 12
151 *PM v SSWP (PIP)* [2017] UKUT 154 (AAC); *BM v SSWP (PIP)* [2017] UKUT 486 (AAC)
152 Reg 4(2A) and (4) SS(PIP) Regs
153 *RJ, GMcL and CS v SSWP v RJ (PIP)* [2017] UKUT 105 (AAC), reported as [2017] AACR 32
154 *NH v SSWP* [2024] UKUT 173 (AAC)
155 *SH v SSWP (PIP)* [2018] UKUT 251 (AAC)
156 *AM v SSWP (PIP)* [2024] UKUT 289 (AAC)
157 DWP *Safety and supervision: changes to PIP law from 9 March 2017*, 26 November 2024, available at gov.uk
158 *PA v SSWP (PIP)* [2019] UKUT 270 (AAC); *PM v SSWP (PIP)* [2017] UKUT 154 (AAC)
159 *PS v SSWP (PIP)* [2016] UKUT 326 (AAC)
160 *LB v SSWP (PIP)* [2024] UKUT 338 (AAC)
161 *KW vSSWP (PIP)* [2024] UKUT 410 (AAC)
162 *TR v SSWP (PIP)* [2015] UKUT 626 (AAC), reported as [2016] AACR 23
163 *PM v SSWP (PIP)* [2017] UKUT 154 (AAC)
164 *ML v SSWP (PIP)* [2017] UKUT 171 (AAC)
165 *KL v SSWP (PIP)* [2016] UKUT 545 (AAC)
166 *TR v SSWP (PIP)* [2015] UKUT 626 (AAC), reported as [2016] AACR 23. This is essentially a question of whether an activity can be undertaken 'repeatedly'.
167 Regs 2, 7(3) and 14 SS(PIP) Regs; reg 24 PIP(TP) Regs; *AB v SSWP (PIP)* [2017] UKUT 217 (AAC)
168 Regs 2, 7(3) and 15 SS(PIP) Regs
169 Reg 7 SS(PIP) Regs
170 *GG v SSWP (PIP)* [2016] UKUT 194 (AAC)
171 *AK v SSWP (PIP)* [2015] UKUT 620 (AAC)
172 ss81 and 82 WRA 2012; regs 12-14 SS(PIP) Regs
173 *AH v SSWP (PIP)* [2016] UKUT 541 (AAC)
174 Reg 33(1) UC,PIP,JSA&ESA(C&P) Regs
175 Regs 15 and 26 SS(PIP) Regs
176 Reg 23 PIP(TP) Regs; *AH v SSWP (PIP)* [2016] UKUT 541 (AAC)

2. **The rules about your age**

177 Reg 5 PIP(TP) Regs
178 s83 WRA 2012

179 Reg 27 PIP(TP) Regs
180 Reg 25(b) SS(PIP) Regs
181 Reg 25(a) SS(PIP) Regs
182 Reg 27 SS(PIP) Regs
183 Regs 15 and 26 SS(PIP) Regs
184 Reg 25(a) SS(PIP) Regs
185 Reg 25(b) SS(PIP) Regs; reg 23 and Sch 1 paras 15 and 18 UC,PIP,JSA&ESA(DA) Regs
186 s9(3) SSA 1998
187 Regs 15 and 26 SS(PIP) Regs
188 Reg 27 SS(PIP) Regs
189 The Social Security (Personal Independence Payment) Amendment (Scotland) Regulations 2020 No.340
190 *MH v SSWP (PIP)* [2020] UKUT 185 (AAC)
191 Reg 27 PIP(TP) Regs. The definitions of 'previous award' and 'component' in reg 2 SS(PIP) Regs mean that regs 15 and 26 of those regulations only apply to people who have had a previous PIP award.

4. **The amount of benefit**

192 Reg 24(1) SS(PIP) Regs
193 Reg 24(2) SS(PIP) Regs

5. **Special benefit rules**

194 s82(2), (3) and (4) WRA 2012
195 Reg 21 SS(PIP) Regs
196 s82(1)(b) WRA 2012; regs 5(2)(c) and 23(2) UC,PIP,JSA&ESA(DA) Regs
197 s82(5) WRA 2012

6. **Claims and backdating**

198 Reg 11(1) UC,PIP,JSA&ESA(C&P) Regs; DWP, *PIP Handbook*, November 2024, gov.uk/government/publications/personal-independence-payment-fact-sheets
199 House of Commons, *Hansard*, Written question 121453, answered 18 January 2018, available at questions-statements.parliament.uk
200 gov.uk/pip/claiming-end-of-life
201 DWP, *The 'Special Rules': how the benefit system supports people nearing the end of life*, November 2024, available at gov.uk
202 DWP, *PIP Handbook*, November 2024, gov.uk/government/publications/personal-independence-payment-fact-sheets
203 s82(5) WRA 2012
204 Reg 49(c) UC,PIP,JSA&ESA(DA) Regs
205 para A2148 ADM
206 s80 WRA 2012; regs 8 and 9 SS(PIP) Regs
207 DWP, *PIP Handbook*, November 2024, gov.uk/government/publications/personal-independence-payment-fact-sheets/pip-handbook#assessment-providers
208 Reg 8(1) and (2) SS(PIP) Regs
209 Reg 8(3) SS(PIP) Regs
210 PIP AG Part 1 para 1.3.36
211 PIP AG, gov.uk/government/publications/personal-independence-payment-assessment-guide-for-assessment-providers
212 Reg 9(1) SS(PIP) Regs says that you 'may' be required to attend a consultation
213 Regs 9(1)(a)-(b), 9(3)(a)-(b) and 9(4) SS(PIP) Regs
214 DWP, *PIP Handbook*, November 2024, gov.uk/government/publications/personal-independence-payment-fact-sheets/pip-handbook
215 PIP AG, paras 1.6.58-64
216 PIP AG, paras 1.6.72-76
217 s80(4)-(6) WRA 2012; regs 8(3) and 9(2) SS(PIP) Regs
218 Reg 26(2) UC,PIP,JSA&ESA(DA) Regs; *KB v SSWP (PIP)* [2016] UKUT 537 (AAC)
219 *IR v SSWP (PIP)* [2019] UKUT 374 (AAC)
220 Reg 10 SS(PIP) Regs
221 Ch P6 ADM
222 PIP AG, para 1.1.7
223 *OM v SSWP (PIP)* [2017] UKUT 458 (AAC); *TC v SSWP (PIP) (No.2)* [2018] UKUT 286 (AAC)
224 Reg 12(1)(c) UC,PIP,JSA&ESA(C&P) Regs
225 Reg 12(1)(c) UC,PIP,JSA&ESA(C&P) Regs: the call was notification of your intention to claim
226 Regs 11(6) and 12 UC,PIP,JSA&ESA(C&P) Regs
227 Reg 27 UC,PIP,JSA&ESA(C&P) Regs
228 Reg 25(3) and (4) UC,PIP,JSA&ESA(C&P) Regs
229 Reg 33(1) UC,PIP,JSA&ESA(C&P) Regs

7. **Getting paid**

230 Regs 48 and 49 UC,PIP,JSA&ESA(C&P) Regs
231 Reg 62 UC,PIP,JSA&ESA(C&P) Regs
232 Reg 58(2) UC,PIP,JSA&ESA(C&P) Regs
233 para P2079 ADM
234 s88(2) and (3) WRA 2012. See also *DT v DfC (PIP)* [2021] NICom54, while not binding outside of Northern Ireland.
235 para P2062 ADM
236 *RS v SSWP (PIP)* [2016] UKUT 85 (AAC); *GT v SSWP (PIP)* [2019] UKUT 30 (AAC)

237 Reg 11 SS(PIP) Regs
238 Reg 33(2) UC,PIP,JSA&ESA(C&P) Regs
239 para P2063 ADM
240 DWP, *Setting an Award Period,* data.parliament.uk/DepositedPapers/Files/DEP2018-1113/UIN_174062_-_Award_period_guidance_10.10.18.pdf
241 DWP, 'Personal independence payment extension exercise for claims awaiting review', in *LA Welfare Direct 9/2022*, 10 October 2022, gov.uk/government/publications/la-welfare-direct-bulletins-2022/la-welfare-direct-92022
242 gov.uk/pip/when-your-pip-claim-is-reviewed
243 gov.uk/government/publications/personal-independence-payment-changes
244 *PH v SSWP (DLA)* [2013] UKUT 268 (AAC). While this was a DLA case, it is strongly arguable that the reasoning also applies to fixed-term awards of PIP.
245 Reg 14(b) SS(PIP) Regs; *BM v SSWP (PIP)* [2017] UKUT 486 (AAC)

8. **Tax, other benefits and the benefit cap**
246 s677(1) IT(EP)A 2003
247 s77(4) WRA 2012
248 Reg 22(1) PIP(TP) Regs
249 s64(1) and (1A) SSCBA 1992
250 Sch 1 paras 5 and 5a SS(OB) Regs; reg 61 UC,PIP,JSA&ESA(C&P) Regs
251 Sch 1 para 5 SS(OB) Regs
252 Reg 61 UC,PIP,JSA&ESA(C&P) Regs
253 Regs 62, 63 and 64 UC,PIP,JSA&ESA(C&P) Regs

# Chapter 32

# Retirement pensions

4

**This chapter covers:**


1. Who can get state pension (p688)
2. The rules about your age (p689)
3. People included in the claim (p690)
4. The amount of benefit (p690)
5. Special benefit rules (p695)
6. Claims and backdating (p695)
7. Getting paid (p698)
8. Tax, other benefits and the benefit cap (p699)


This chapter covers the rules that apply to people who reach pension age on or after 6 April 2016 and who are eligible for the new state retirement pension, known as 'state pension'. People who reached pension age before 6 April 2016, including those who had already claimed their state retirement pension and those who had deferred claiming it, continue on the previous retirement pension scheme. In this chapter, these pensions are referred to as 'old' retirement pensions. For more details about these, see the 2015/16 edition of this *Handbook*.

## Key facts

- State pension is a non-means-tested, contributory benefit, paid to people who reach pension age on or after 6 April 2016.
- State pension is an individual pension based solely on your own national insurance contributions (although there are some limited exceptions).
- You can qualify whether you are in or out of work.
- State pension is affected by the overlapping benefit rules.
- State pension is administered and paid by the Pension Service, which is part of the DWP.
- If you reached pension age before 6 April 2016, you cannot get state pension, but you may be entitled to an 'old' retirement pension instead.
- If you disagree with a decision on your state pension, you can apply for a revision or a supersession (see Chapter 50), or appeal against it (see Chapter 51). You must apply for a mandatory reconsideration before you can appeal.

# 1. Who can get state pension

You can get state pension if you reach pension age (see p690) on or after 6 April 2016. Whether you qualify and the amount you receive depends on your national insurance (NI) contribution record. Your NI record of contributions and credits before 6 April 2016 forms your 'starting amount'. The starting amount will be either the amount you would have got under the old retirement pension rules, or the amount you would have got if the new state pension rules had always existed, whichever is higher. If your starting amount is less than the current full state pension, the Pension Service will also look at your NI record after 5 April 2016 up to when you reached pension age to see if you had any qualifying years during this period. If you do, each year will increase your state pension payment, but you cannot be paid more than the full rate.[1] If you have qualifying years from before 6 April 2016, your state pension is paid at the transitional rate (see p691). This may be more or less than, or the same as, the full rate. You normally need at least 10 qualifying years to receive any state pension.[2] See Chapter 39 for details of the contribution conditions for state pension.

***Did you reach pension age before 6 April 2016?***

If you reached pension age before 6 April 2016, you cannot claim state pension. However, you may be entitled to an 'old' retirement pension – ie, a category A, category B or category D retirement pension. This applies even if you reached pension age before 6 April 2016 but deferred claiming your retirement pension until after that date.

The rules for 'old' retirement pensions are not explained in detail in this chapter. See Chapter 36 of the 2015/16 edition of this *Handbook* for full details.

You are not automatically paid state pension when you reach pension age. You must make a claim, unless you are a widow in certain situations (see p696). If you do not claim, you are treated as having deferred your state pension (see below).

You do not have to retire from work if you reach pension age and claim state pension. If you decide to carry on working, your earnings do not reduce the state pension you receive and you no longer pay NI contributions. However, the amount of tax you pay may increase because state pension is taxable.

There are some groups of claimants to whom special rules apply (see p695).

## Deferring your state pension

Once you reach pension age, you can choose to defer your entitlement to state pension. In return, you later become entitled to a higher rate of pension. **Note:** you do not have the option of taking a taxable lump-sum payment plus interest.

You can defer your state pension by simply not claiming it when you reach pension age. If you are already claiming, you can choose to stop getting it to get more later on, but you can only do this once. To stop claiming, you must notify the Pension Service by phone or in writing.[3] Your claim will be stopped immediately unless you specify a different date within the next 28 days of your letter or phone call.[4] You can cancel the deferment at any time by making a claim for state pension, and can backdate that cancellation by up to 12 months.[5]

Your state pension is increased by 1 per cent for every nine weeks you defer.[6] For example, if you defer your pension for one year, it increases by approximately 5.8 per cent, which increases a full state pension by approximately £13.35 a week. You are not entitled to any increase unless you defer your pension for long enough to earn an increase of at least 1 per cent – ie, a minimum of nine weeks.[7]

The increase is calculated on the amount you would have received immediately before the end of the deferral period if you had not deferred claiming. If your entitlement changes during the deferral period (eg, because you become entitled to an inherited amount on the death of your spouse or civil partner – see p693), the calculation takes this into account so that it is based on the rates of pension to which you would have been entitled throughout the deferral period.[8]

You do not receive an increase in state pension for any whole week in the period of deferral in which:[9]

- you get carer's allowance, carer support payment, incapacity benefit, severe disablement allowance, unemployability supplement, widow's pension or widowed mother's allowance, or your spouse, civil partner or anyone you are residing with is getting an increase in any of these benefits for you; *or*
- you would have been disqualified from receiving state pension because you were a prisoner; *or*
- you or your partner get pension credit, universal credit or income-related employment and support allowance.

If you die either while deferring your state pension or after you have started to receive your state pension, your deferral increase is not inheritable.

If you are going to live abroad and have deferred your state pension, see p695.

## 2. The rules about your age

State pension can be claimed when you reach pension age if this is on or after 6 April 2016. An advance claim can be made up to four months before you become entitled (see p695). If you reached pension age before this date, you may be entitled to an 'old' retirement pension instead (see Chapter 36 of the 2015/16 edition of this *Handbook*).

*Pension age*

Pension age for men and women has been the same since November 2018.

Between 2026 and 2028, it will rise to 67.[10] A person born after 5 October 1954 but before 6 April 1960 will reach pension age at 66. A person born between 6 April 1960 and 5 March 1961 will reach pension age at up to 66 years and 11 months, depending on their date of birth. Someone born after 5 March 1961 but before 6 April 1977 will reach pension age at 67.[11] Men and women born after 5 April 1977 are expected to be affected by an increase in pension age to 68. This change is due to take place between 2044 and 2046.[12]

You can check when you will reach pension age using the official calculator at gov.uk/state-pension-age.

4

## 3. People included in the claim

You claim state pension for yourself. You do not get an increase in your state pension for an adult dependant or any children.

## 4. The amount of benefit

The full weekly rate of state pension is £230.25. In addition, you may receive a higher pension if you defer your entitlement to state pension (see p688). Some people may receive a transitional rate of state pension that is higher than £230.25 (see p691). You can request a forecast estimating your state pension entitlement from the Future Pension Centre by phone on 0800 731 0175 (textphone: 0800 731 0176), by writing to the Pension Service or at gov.uk/check-state-pension.

*The amount of 'old' retirement pensions*

If you reached pension age before 6 April 2016, you cannot get state pension but may instead be entitled to an 'old' retirement pension.

**Category A retirement pension** is paid at a weekly rate of £176.45.

**Category B retirement pension for a spouse or civil partner** is paid at a weekly rate of £105.70.

**Category B retirement pension for a widow, widower or surviving civil partner** is paid at a weekly rate of £176.45.

**Category D retirement pension** is paid at a weekly rate of £105.70

The above amounts are the full rates. You get a reduced rate if you have not paid or been credited with sufficient national insurance (NI) contributions to qualify for the full rate.

If you receive one of these retirement pensions, you receive an age addition of 25 pence a week if you are over 80.

Depending on which pension you are entitled to, you may also receive:

- graduated retirement benefit, based on earnings between 1961 and 1975;
- an additional state pension, based on earnings after 5 April 1978;
- a higher pension if entitlement was deferred;
- an amount equivalent to the age-related addition to long-term incapacity benefit if you received this within eight weeks of reaching pension age (see p690). If you have an additional state pension, this amount is offset against it;
- an increase for a child (see p690).

See Chapter 36 of the 2015/16 edition of this *Handbook* for full details of when you may be entitled to these additional amounts.



State pension is an individual pension based solely on your own contributions (except in the circumstances described below) – ie, you cannot count the contributions of your spouse or civil partner towards your pension. If your spouse or civil partner reached pension age before 6 April 2016, they may be entitled to an 'old' retirement pension based on your NI contributions up to 5 April 2016.

You must have at least 10 qualifying years (see p874) to receive any state pension.[13] If you do not have the required qualifying years for the full state pension, you get a reduced rate. This is calculated by multiplying 1/35th of the full rate by the number of qualifying years. For example, if you have 17 qualifying years, you receive a state pension of £111.84 a week (17 x £230.25 ÷ 35). Only people whose qualifying years are all from 2016/17 onwards have their state pension calculated this way.

For many years, people will likely have a mix of contributions made before and after 6 April 2016. NI contributions and credits for years before 6 April 2016 count towards your state pension. There are transitional rules that aim to ensure that anyone reaching pension age after this date receives at least the same level of entitlement as they would have done under the 'old' retirement pension scheme based on their own NI contributions.

There are transitional provisions for:

- people who have paid, been treated as having paid, or been credited with contributions for tax years before the introduction of state pension (see below); *and*
- women who before 1977 elected to pay a reduced rate of contributions (see p692); *and*
- inheriting entitlement from a late spouse or civil partner who had made contributions for tax years before the introduction of state pension (see p693).

## Transitional rate of state pension

If you have qualifying years (see p874) before 6 April 2016, the amount of your state pension is worked out to ensure that your 'starting amount' is at least as much as you would have received under the 'old' retirement pension rules.[14] You must have at least 10 qualifying years to receive a transitional rate of state pension.[15]

Your 'starting amount' is the higher of:

- your entitlement to 'old' retirement pension. This takes account of your entitlement to basic category A retirement pension, additional pension and graduated retirement benefit. See Chapter 36 of the 2015/16 edition of this *Handbook*; and
- your entitlement under the new state pension rules as if they had applied throughout your working life.



In each case, a deduction is made if you were contracted out from the additional state pension scheme.

If you are entitled to a substantial amount of additional pension, your starting amount may be higher than the full rate of state pension. If so, the difference between your starting amount and the full rate is called your 'protected payment'. Your protected payment is paid on top of your full state pension and is increased each year in line with inflation. Your transitional rate of state pension up to the level of the full state pension is increased each year at the same rate as the state pension.[16] Any further qualifying years you have do not add more to your state pension.

If your starting amount is lower than the full state pension, you can add additional qualifying years up to the amount needed to qualify for a full-rate state pension or until you reach pension age, whichever is first. You may wish to do this even if you already have more than 35 qualifying years – eg, if, despite having more than 35 qualifying years, you do not qualify for the full rate because a deduction has been applied to reflect contracting out.[17] You may be able to pay NI contributions to fill in gaps in your record (see Chapter 39). Each qualifying year on your NI record adds 1/35th of the full amount (about £6.58 a week) to your state pension.

## Women who paid reduced-rate contributions

Before 1977, married women and widows could opt out of gaining entitlement to retirement pension in their own right by electing to pay reduced-rate NI contributions (see Chapter 39). Their entitlement to retirement pension was based on the contributions of their spouse.

State pension is based on an individual's own contribution record, but there are special transitional rules for women who reach pension age on or after 6 April 2016 and who have paid reduced-rate contributions. These apply if you still had the right to pay reduced-rate NI contributions at the start of the period of 35 years ending in the tax year before you reach pension age – ie, if you reached pension age in May 2016, you had a 'reduced-rate election' in force at the beginning of the 1981/82 tax year.

If you have any qualifying years from having paid or been credited with sufficient NI contributions in some tax years before 2016/17, there is an alternative calculation if this would be more beneficial than the transitional rate to which you would otherwise be entitled. This is at least equivalent to the combination of:[18]

- the standard rate of basic 'old' retirement pension based on the NI contributions of a spouse or civil partner (£105.70 if you are married or in a civil partnership and your spouse or civil partner has also reached state pension age, or £176.45 if you are widowed, divorced or if your civil partnership is dissolved); *and*
- any additional pension to which you are entitled based on your own contribution record.

If you have no qualifying years from before 6 April 2016, you receive a transitional rate of state pension equivalent to the full category B retirement pension if both you and your spouse have reached pension age, or to the full category A retirement pension if you are no longer married or in a civil partnership.[19]

**Note**: the DWP is contacting some married women, widows and women aged over 80 who were underpaid state pension. See gov.uk/government/publications/state-pension-underpayments-progress-on-cases-reviewed-to-30-september-2024.

## Widows, widowers and surviving civil partners

If you reach pension age on or after 6 April 2016, there are transitional rules that may allow you to qualify for an amount of state pension (known as a 'survivor's inherited state pension') based on the additional pension that your late spouse or civil partner would have been entitled to under the 'old' retirement pension scheme. This only applies if you were married or in a civil partnership before 6 April 2016 and your spouse or civil partner died while you were married or civil partners. If you were under pension age when they died, and you remarry or enter a new civil partnership before you reach pension age, you do not qualify.[20]

If your spouse or civil partner reached pension age, or died below pension age, before 6 April 2016, you may be entitled to an inherited amount based on the amount of additional pension you would have been entitled to under the 'old' category B retirement pension rules.[21]

You may be entitled to an inherited amount of half of the difference between your spouse or civil partner's transitional rate and the full rate of state pension, if:[22]

- they reached pension age, or died below pension age, on or after 6 April 2016; *and*
- they were entitled to the transitional rate of state pension immediately before they died (or would have been if they had reached pension age before they died or on the same day as you reached pension age); *and*

- their transitional rate was, or would have been, more than the full rate of state pension.

Your survivor's pension is paid in addition to any state pension or transitional rate of state pension (including one paid to women who elected to pay reduced-rate NI contributions – see p692).

You do not lose this amount if you marry or form a civil partnership again after reaching pension age. However, as this new marriage or civil partnership takes place after 6 April 2016, you cannot get an inherited amount from your new spouse/civil partner if they subsequently die, even if this would have been a higher amount.

**Note:** if you reached pension age before 6 April 2016 and your spouse or civil partner dies after this date, you may still qualify for a category B retirement pension based on their contributions in the tax years before the tax year beginning 6 April 2016. See Chapter 36 of the 2015/16 edition of this *Handbook* for more details. This applies whether or not they reached pension age before 6 April 2016.

For how your entitlement to bereavement benefits affects entitlement to state pension, see Chapter 21.

## Inheriting a deferred 'old' retirement pension

You may inherit an amount of state pension equivalent to an inherited deferred amount of 'old' retirement pension if:[23]

- your spouse or civil partner reached pension age before 6 April 2016; *and*
- they had either claimed their 'old' retirement pension and were receiving a weekly increase from having deferred it, or were still deferring their 'old' retirement pension when they died; *and*
- at the time of their death, you were over pension age or, if you were under pension age, you had not remarried or entered a new civil partnership before reaching pension age.

If your spouse or civil partner was deferring their 'old' retirement pension when they died and had deferred it for at least 12 months, you can choose to claim this amount as a lump sum or as a weekly state pension (a 'widowed person's or surviving civil partner's lump sum or pension'). If you do not make a choice within three months of being notified by the DWP of your right to do so (or a longer period if the DWP allows this), you are paid a lump sum. In certain circumstances, you can change your mind, provided you do so within three months of making a choice.[24] If your spouse or civil partner was already getting their 'old' retirement pension or they had deferred it for less than 12 months, you receive the inherited deferral payment as an extra weekly amount.

These rules mean you have the same options as you would have had under the old retirement pension system, so it applies regardless of when you reach pension age.

### Inherited graduated retirement benefit

You may be entitled to an amount of inherited survivor's state pension based on the graduated retirement benefit entitlement of your late spouse or civil partner. This is based on graduated contributions they may have paid between 1961 and 1975. You can choose a lump sum or a weekly amount if they had deferred their entitlement to graduated retirement benefit for at least 12 months at the time of their death.[25]

## 5. Special benefit rules



Special rules may apply if you:
- have come from or are going abroad (see below);
- are in prison or detention (see Chapter 38).

### People coming from or going abroad

If you have lived elsewhere than the UK during your working life, your state pension may be affected – eg, it may be paid at a reduced rate. However, reciprocal arrangements with many countries may help you qualify for a full pension. If you have worked in a European Economic Area (EEA) state, you may benefit from the European Union (EU) co-ordination rules (see Chapter 59). If these rules cover you, your employment in an EEA state and contributions paid there can count towards your overall national insurance contribution record used to determine your entitlement to state pension (see p1406). If the EU co-ordination rules do not cover you, you may be able to benefit from other agreements (see p1297).

If you go to live abroad, your state pension can be paid in any other country. However, unless you move to live in an EEA state, Switzerland, Gibraltar or a country with which the UK has a reciprocal agreement for pensions, you are not entitled to uprating increases, so the amount of pension you receive is frozen at the rate at which it was paid when you went abroad. Similarly, if you claim a deferred pension abroad, the uprating increases that occurred while you were abroad are ignored when calculating both the deferral increase and rate payable.[26]

## 6. Claims and backdating

The general rules about claims and backdating are covered in Chapter 44. This section explains the specific rules that apply to state pensions.

### Making a claim

You must usually make a claim for state pension (but see p696 if you are a widow). You should get a letter no later than two months before you reach pension age, telling you to make a claim online or call for a claim form. Call the helpline if you do not receive this before reaching pension age.

A claim for state pension can be made:[27]

- online at gov.uk/get-state-pension if you have been sent an invitation code. If you have not received a letter with an invitation code, you can request this online; *or*
- in writing. Call the helpline (0800 731 7898; textphone: 0800 731 7339; Relay UK and BSL relay services are available) to ask for a claim form and send it to Pension Service 8, Post Handling Site B, Wolverhampton WV98 1AF. You may be able to make your claim by taking or sending it to an alternative office (see p1004).



If you make a claim for state pension, your pension should be calculated under the rules (including the various transitional rules) as they apply to you. You do not need to identify and claim for the different elements that apply to you.

You must provide any information or evidence required (see p697). In certain circumstances, the DWP may accept a written application not on the approved form.[28] You can amend or withdraw your claim before a decision is made (see p1004). If there is a delay in making a claim, you may be able to get a short-term advance of benefit (see p1023). If you are in financial hardship, it can help to mention it to see if the claim can be processed quicker.

## If you are a widow

If you are a widow, you do not need to make a claim for state pension if either:[29]

- you are getting widowed mother's allowance immediately before you reach pension age; *or*
- you are getting a widow's pension immediately before you reach pension age.

You must make a claim for state pension if you want to start receiving it before your widow's pension or widowed mother's allowance stops. If your widow's pension or widowed mother's allowance includes additional state pension, you receive this as an extra amount on top of your state pension, provided you do not remarry or form a new civil partnership before you reach pension age. If your state pension, plus any inherited amount, is less than your widow's pension or widowed mother's allowance, you are paid the difference until those benefits come to an end.

If you make a claim for state pension, your pension should be calculated under the rules (including the various transitional rules) as they apply to you. You do not need to identify and claim for the different elements that apply to you.[30]

## Who should claim

You must normally claim state pension on your own behalf. However, if you cannot manage your claim, another person can claim state pension for you as your appointee (see p1005).

## Information to support your claim

For the general information requirements that apply to all benefits, see p1006.

It is important to provide any information required when you claim. Until you do, you may not count as having made a valid claim (see p1008). Correct any defects as soon as possible or your date of claim may be affected.



When you claim state pension, you must prove you have reached pension age. For most people, it is sufficient to produce your birth certificate, but problems can occur if you were born in a country which did not have a formal system of registering births. Other evidence that can prove your birth date includes:

- passport or identity card; *or*
- school, health or army records; *or*
- statements from people who know you.

Even if you have provided all that was required when you claimed, you may be asked to provide further information to support your claim (see p1009). You may also be asked to provide information after you are awarded state pension and if you fail to do so, your state pension could be suspended or even terminated (see p1031).

## The date of your claim

The date of your claim is important as it determines when your entitlement to state pension starts. This is not necessarily the date from when you are paid. For information about when payment of state pension starts, see p698.

The date of your claim is the date your written or online claim, properly completed with all the required evidence and information, is received at the Pension Service or other designated office.

You must make sure your claim is valid. If it is not, you are given a short time to correct the defects (see p1008). Your claim is then treated as having been made when you initially claimed.[31]

### Backdating your claim

It is important to claim in time, because the maximum period for backdating is 12 months. You cannot backdate your claim for any period before the date you would have first become entitled to state pension.[32] You do not have to show any reason why your claim is late. The rules on backdating are covered on p1011.

If you claim more than 12 months after you became entitled to state pension, you are treated as having deferred your entitlement. You can still request that your claim is backdated but you should consider the impact on your deferral amount when requesting backdating. If you backdate your claim, it reduces the amount of time you deferred claiming your pension, which reduces the amount of your weekly increase. You may also owe tax if you had other taxable income during the backdated period. Weigh up the financial implications of your options when considering backdating – if necessary, get advice.

If you might have qualified for state pension earlier but did not claim because you were given the wrong information or were misled by the DWP, you could ask for compensation (see p1261) or complain to the Ombudsman (see p1266).



### If you claim the wrong benefit

If you have claimed the wrong benefit, in certain circumstances, your claim can be interchanged with another benefit.[33] For state pension, this interchange is only possible with bereavement benefits. If you claim state pension on the wrong form (eg, you complete a claim form for 'old' retirement pension), it is likely to be treated as a valid claim if the form is properly completed.[34]

### Claiming in advance

Claims for state pension (including a claim where you have deferred your entitlement – see p688) can be made up to four months in advance.[35] You should take advantage of this, as it can take a long time to sort out your contribution record. The date of your claim is the date on which you qualify.

## 7. Getting paid

The general rules on getting paid are covered in Chapter 45. This section explains the specific rules that apply to state pension. **Note:** rules on payment of 'old' retirement pension are very similar to rules on payment of state pension. See p781 of the 2015/16 edition of this *Handbook*.

***When is state pension paid?***

The day you are paid depends on your national insurance number (see p1020).[36] State pension is normally paid weekly, fortnightly or four-weekly in arrears. It can be paid every 13 weeks if you agree, or at longer intervals of up to a year if the DWP directs, and you are entitled to less than £5 a week.[37]

State pension is payable from the date on which you reach pension age. If this is a day other than your payday, part-week payments are made.

**Note:**

- Deductions can be made from your state pension to pay third parties (see p1033).

- Even if you have been sanctioned for a benefit offence (see p1111), you must be paid your state pension.
- If payment of your state pension is delayed, see p1123. If you are waiting for a decision on your claim, or to be paid, you may be able to get a short-term advance (see p1023). If you wish to complain about how your claim has been dealt with, or claim compensation, see Chapter 55.
- If payment of your state pension is suspended, see p1031.
- If you are overpaid state pension, you may have to repay it (see Chapter 47) and, in some circumstances, you may have to pay a penalty (see p1101). If you have been accused of fraud, see Chapter 48.
- If you are owed arrears of state pension, these can be paid in instalments (see p1018).



### Change of circumstances

You must report changes in your circumstances that you have been told you must report, as well as any that you might reasonably be expected to know might affect your right to, the amount of, or the payment of, your state pension. You should do this as soon as possible, preferably in writing. See p1030 for further information.

## 8. Tax, other benefits and the benefit cap

### Tax

State pension (and 'old' retirement pension) is taxable.[38] This includes inheritable lump-sum payments of deferred 'old' retirement pension and graduated retirement benefit.[39]

### Means-tested benefits

State pension (and 'old' retirement pension) is taken fully into account for means-tested benefits, but pensioners receive a higher rate of some means-tested benefits.

You may qualify for pension credit to top up your state pension income (see p239).

### Non-means-tested benefits

State pension (and 'old' retirement pension) is affected by the overlapping benefit rules (see p1021).

### The benefit cap

State pension (and 'old' retirement pension) is *not* a specified benefit for the benefit cap.[40] The benefit cap does not apply when you are over pension age, whether you claim your state pension or not. However, if you have a partner under pension age and they are claiming universal credit, the benefit cap may apply. See p1025 for further information.

## Passports and other sources of help

You qualify for a Christmas bonus (see p783) if you receive state pension (or 'old' retirement pension).[41] People aged 60 or over qualify for free prescriptions and eye tests regardless of their income. If you are on a low income, you may be entitled to council tax reduction (see p761).



# Notes

1. **Who can get state pension**
   1 s4 PA 2014; reg 13(1) SP Regs
   2 s2(3) PA 2014
   3 Reg 7 SP Regs
   4 Reg 8 SP Regs
   5 Reg 9 SP Regs
   6 s17(4) PA 2014; reg 10 SP Regs
   7 s17(2) PA 2014
   8 Reg 12A SP Regs
   9 Reg 11 SP Regs

2. **The rules about your age**
   10 s126 and Sch 4 PA 1995; s26 PA 2014
   11 DMG Memo 18/14
   12 *State Pension Age Review 2023*, DWP policy paper, 30 March 2023

4. **The amount of benefit**
   13 s3(2) PA 2014
   14 s5 and Sch 1 PA 2014
   15 s4 PA 2014; reg 13(2) SP Regs
   16 Sch 2 PA 2014; ss148AC and 151A SSAA 1992
   17 PA 2014, Explanatory Notes, para 61
   18 s11 and Sch 6 PA 2014
   19 s12 and Sch 7 PA 2014
   20 s7 and Schs 3 and 4 PA 2014
   21 Sch 3 paras 2-4 PA 2014
   22 Sch 3 paras 5-8 PA 2014
   23 s8 PA 2014
   24 ss8 and 9 PA 2014; regs 4-6 SP Regs
   25 s10 PA 2014; regs 15-20 SP Regs

5. **Special benefit rules**
   26 ss18(3) and 20 PA 2014; s179 SSAA 1992; regs 21-23 SP Regs

6. **Claims and backdating**
   27 Regs 4 and 4ZC SS(C&P) Regs
   28 Reg 4(1) SS(C&P) Regs
   29 Reg 3(d) SS(C&P) Regs
   30 Reg 3(ja) SS(C&P) Regs
   31 Reg 6(1)(b) SS(C&P) Regs
   32 Reg 19(1) and Sch 4 SS(C&P) Regs
   33 Reg 9(1) and Sch 1 SS(C&P) Regs
   34 Reg 4(1) SS(C&P) Regs
   35 Regs 15 and 15B(2) SS(C&P) Regs

7. **Getting paid**
   36 Reg 22CA(4) SS(C&P) Regs
   37 Reg 22CA(2) and (3) SS(C&P) Regs

8. **Tax, other benefits and the benefit cap**
   38 s577(2)(za) IT(EP)A 2003
   39 s8(4B) Finance (No.2) Act 2005
   40 s96(11)(za) WRA 2012
   41 s150(2) SSCBA 1992

# Chapter 33

# Social fund payments

**This chapter covers:**


1. Budgeting loans (below)
2. Sure Start maternity grants (p705)
3. Funeral expenses payments (p707)
4. Cold weather payments (p714)
5. Winter fuel payments (p715)
6. Tax, other benefits and the benefit cap (p716)


4

## Key facts

- The social fund provides one-off loans and payments for specific expenses or circumstances.
- **Budgeting loans** are interest-free loans. **Sure Start maternity grants, funeral expenses payments, cold weather payments** and **winter fuel payments** are non-repayable.
- Social fund loans and payments are administered and paid by the DWP. Some are replaced in Scotland by payments made by Social Security Scotland.
- If you disagree with a budgeting loan decision, there is an internal review system and then a further review to the Independent Case Examiner.
- If you disagree with a decision on a Sure Start maternity grant, funeral expenses payment, cold weather payment or winter fuel payment, you can apply for a revision (see Chapter 50), or appeal against it (see Chapter 51). You must apply for a mandatory reconsideration before you can appeal.

## 1. **Budgeting loans**

Budgeting loans are available in England, Wales and Scotland. To be eligible, you must satisfy all the following conditions. **Note:** if you come under the universal credit (UC) system (see p20), you cannot apply for a budgeting loan and must apply for a budgeting advance of your UC payments instead (see p52).

- **You must be in receipt of a 'qualifying benefit'** when your budgeting loan application is determined.[1] Qualifying benefits are: income-related employment and support allowance (ESA) and pension credit (PC) (guarantee or savings credit). Payments on account and hardship payments are included. You are treated as being in receipt of a qualifying benefit if it is being paid to you, or to an appointee on your behalf. You are eligible if you receive a backdated award of a qualifying benefit, covering the date your application was determined. **Note:** you are not 'in receipt of' a qualifying benefit if your partner or another member of your family is the claimant.[2]

- **You and/or your partner, between you, must have been receiving a qualifying benefit throughout the 26 weeks before the date your application is determined**, disregarding any number of breaks of 28 days or less.[3] If you are in receipt of PC, any time when you were in receipt of UC can count when calculating the 26 weeks and any breaks of up to one calendar month are ignored. A period covered by a payment of arrears should count, as should any benefit received while in Northern Ireland. The waiting days at the start of a claim for ESA (see p569) do not count. More than one partner could help you satisfy the qualifying period.
- **You must not have too much capital.**[4] Any budgeting loan award is reduced by the amount of capital you have over £1,000 (£2,000 if you or your partner are aged 63 or over). For how your capital is calculated, see Chapter 18 for income-related ESA and Chapter 19 for PC. Payments made from the Family Fund to you, your partner or child, and refugee integration loans are ignored. Capital held by your children should be disregarded.
- **You, or your partner, must not be involved in a trade dispute** (see p891).[5]
- **You must not be a 'person subject to immigration control'** (there are exceptions to this rule) – see p1272.
- **The loan must be for one or more of the following categories of allowable expenses**, the need for which occurs in the UK:[6]
  - furniture and household equipment;
  - clothing and footwear;
  - maternity expenses;
  - funeral expenses;
  - rent in advance and/or removal expenses to secure accommodation;
  - improvement, maintenance and security of the home;
  - travelling expenses;
  - expenses associated with seeking or re-entering work;
  - hire purchase and other debts for any of the above items.

  You must tick the category of expense for which you need the loan on the application form. You do not have to specify the items you need – eg, a bed or a winter coat.
- **The loan must be a minimum of £100.**[7] You must state how much you are asking for on your application form. You cannot be awarded more than the maximum amount.
- **You must be likely to be able to repay the loan** (see p704).[8]

The maximum amount you can be awarded is:
- £348 if you are a single person; *or*
- £464 if you have a partner; *or*
- £812 if you or your partner claim child benefit.

You may get less, depending on the amount you requested and the capital rules. Any loan may also be reduced by the amount of any other social fund debt you or your partner have. You cannot be liable to repay more than £1,500 in total.



## Applying and getting paid

Apply online at gov.uk/budgeting-help-benefits, or in writing on Form SF500, available from gov.uk or your local job centre. A written application in some other form may be accepted although this is not guaranteed. An application can be made on your behalf by your appointee or by another person, provided you give your written consent.[9]

If you apply by post, you should receive a written decision within 21 days. If you apply online, you can choose to receive the decision by text or email, which should be received within seven days. If you take this option, you can accept the loan online, and payment will be made more quickly.

Your application is treated as having been made on the day DWP receives it.[10] If your application was incomplete and you complied with a request for additional information, it is treated as having been made on the day it was originally received.

Loans are generally paid in the same way as your qualifying benefit.

## Challenging a decision

You should receive a written decision within seven days (if you applied online) or 21 days (if you applied by post), with an explanation if it has been refused or partly refused, together with a notification of your right to request a review.

If you want to challenge the decision, you can ask for a review which will be carried out by a different decision maker. However, a decision is only likely to be changed if it is based on incorrect information about your circumstances or if the amount you are allowed to borrow has increased.

You must apply for a review of a decision by writing to the office where the decision was made within 28 days of the date the decision was issued to you.[11] Your application must include your grounds for requesting a review.[12] If someone makes an application on your behalf, it must be accompanied by your written permission (unless the person is your appointee – see p1005).[13]

Late applications can be accepted for special reasons.[14] Special reasons are not defined, but submitting a new application may be quicker if you cannot apply in time.

If a decision is not wholly revised in your favour, the reviewing officer must phone or write to you to explain why and ask further questions if necessary.

If you are still unhappy with the decision, you can ask the Independent Case Examiner (see p1262) to carry out a second-tier review.[15] Do this in writing within 28 days, although the time limit may be extended for special reasons.

## Repayments

4

All loans must be repaid to the DWP.[16]

The decision maker may give you more than one option for repaying a loan, depending on whether you have any other outstanding social fund loans and your other financial commitments. They may offer an option of a higher loan with an increased repayment rate, but you cannot be asked to repay at a rate higher than 20 per cent of your income-related applicable amount or PC appropriate minimum guarantee plus any child benefit you receive. The loan must be repaid within 104 weeks.

The details of the loan offer and repayment terms are included in the decision. You have 14 days from the date the decision was sent to return the declaration agreeing to one of the offers made to you. This time limit can be extended for special reasons.[17]

### Methods of repayment

Budgeting loans are usually recovered by direct deductions from your benefit, although you can make a payment at any time to pay off all or part of the debt. Deductions can only be made from the following benefits:[18]

- bereavement benefits (except bereavement support payment);
- carer's allowance;
- disablement benefit, reduced earnings allowance and industrial death benefit;
- ESA (contributory or income-related);
- incapacity benefit;
- maternity allowance;
- PC;
- retirement pensions;
- severe disablement allowance;
- UC.

A loan can be recovered from:[19]

- you (the applicant) or the person who the loan was for;
- your partner, if you are living together as a couple (see p254);
- a person who is liable to maintain either the person who made the application or the person on whose behalf it was made.

### Rescheduling repayment terms

You cannot request a review of a decision relating to repayment terms or recovery. If you have accepted a loan, however, and the repayment terms are causing hardship (eg, because your financial situation has deteriorated), you can ask the DWP to reschedule the loan to reduce the weekly repayment.

## 2. Sure Start maternity grants



Sure Start maternity grants are available in England and Wales. If you live in Scotland, you may instead qualify for a Best Start grant (see Chapter 62).

You qualify for a Sure Start maternity grant if you satisfy all the following conditions.

- **You or your partner have been awarded one of the following qualifying benefits** (including payments on account and hardship payments) in respect of the day you claim a maternity grant:[20]
  - universal credit;
  - income-related employment and support allowance;
  - pension credit (guarantee or savings credit).

  You are treated as receiving one of these benefits if you are entitled to a DWP loan for help with your mortgage interest (see p764), even if you are not actually entitled to the benefit. You are eligible if you receive a backdated award of a qualifying benefit covering the date you claim a maternity grant. If you are waiting for a decision on a claim for a qualifying benefit, the DWP may defer making a decision on your maternity grant claim until the qualifying benefit claim has been decided. If your maternity grant claim is refused while you are waiting for a decision on a qualifying benefit, you should reclaim a maternity grant within three months of being awarded the qualifying benefit. **Note:** if you do not claim a maternity grant within the time limits (see p706), a backdated award of a qualifying benefit does not qualify you for a grant. If you are not entitled to a qualifying benefit in your own right because you are under 16 (or under 20 and and not entitled to the qualifying benefit because you are in education – see Chapter 37), a member of your family can claim a maternity grant for you if they are getting a qualifying benefit in respect of you.
- **You live in England or Wales.**[21]
- **One of the following applies:**[22]
  - you or a member of your family are pregnant or have given birth in the last six months (including stillbirth after 24 weeks of pregnancy);
  - you are the parent (but not the mother and not the mother's partner) of a child who is less than 12 months old, or you are responsible for that parent, and you are responsible for the child;
  - you are the guardian of a child who is less than 12 months old;

  - you or your partner have a child who is less than 12 months old placed with you for adoption and you are responsible for the child;
  - you have adopted a child who is less than 12 months old under a recognised adoption which takes place outside the UK;
  - you or your partner have been granted a child arrangements order, parental order (following a surrogate pregnancy) or adoption order for a child who is less than 12 months old.

  In the last five cases, you are entitled to a payment even if one has already been made to the birth mother or a member of her family.[23]
- **No other member of your family is under 16 at the time of claim** (excluding any child you adopted or became responsible for as a kinship carer or foster carer, provided they were over 12 months old when you became responsible for them). However, a grant can be awarded for each child of a multiple birth, but the number of grants is reduced if there are other children in the family who are under 16. For example, if you give birth to triplets and already have one or more children under 16 in the family (and none of them are multiple births) two grants are awarded, or if you already have twins, you are awarded one grant. If you are under 20 and another member of your family claims for you, the grant is payable, provided you do not have other children under 16.[24] If you are a refugee, you can be entitled in respect of your first child born in the UK, even if you have another child or children from before you came to the UK.[25] This also applies if you have come to the UK from Afghanistan or Ukraine and are covered by the rule exempting you from the habitual residence and past presence tests (see p1348).[26]
- **You or your partner are not involved in a trade dispute** (see p891), unless specified circumstances apply.[27]
- **You claim within the time limits** (see 706).
- **You are not a 'person subject to immigration control'** (there are exceptions to this rule) – see p1272.

'Partner' means, where you count as being in a couple, your partner in that couple. 'Family' means you, your partner if you have one, and any children in your household. Couples, children and households are defined as they are for mean-tested benefits (see Chapter 12).

## The amount

You are entitled to a grant of £500 for each qualifying child or expected qualifying child.[28] The payment is not affected by any capital you have and is not repayable.

## Claiming and getting paid

Claim on Form SF100, which you can get from your local Jobcentre Plus office or gov.uk/sure-start-maternity-grant/how-to-claim or by phoning the Sure Start

Maternity Grant helpline (0800 169 0140; textphone 0800 169 0286; Relay UK and British Sign Language services also available).

There are strict time limits for claiming. You can claim a maternity grant from 11 weeks before the first day of your expected week of childbirth until six months after the actual date of the birth. If you adopt a child, have a child arrangements order for a child or have a child by a surrogate mother, you can claim up to six months following the date of the adoption, child arrangements order or parental order, provided the child is under 12 months when the claim is made. You cannot make a successful claim outside these time limits.[29]



Your date of claim is normally the date the DWP receives your form.[30] If you make a written claim in some other way, you should be sent the appropriate form to complete. If you return it within one month, or a longer period if the DWP considers this reasonable, your date of claim is the date the DWP received your initial application.[31] See p705 for when your claim can be backdated if you are subsequently awarded a qualifying benefit.

If you are overpaid a maternity grant, you may have to repay it (see Chapter 47), and in some circumstances, you may have to pay a penalty (see p1101).

## 3. Funeral expenses payments

Funeral expenses payments are available in England and Wales. If you live in Scotland, you may instead qualify for a funeral support payment (see Chapter 65).

You qualify for a funeral expenses payment if you satisfy all the following conditions.

- **You or your partner have been awarded one of the following qualifying benefits** (including payments on account and hardship payments) in respect of the day you claim a funeral expenses payment:[32]
  - universal credit;
  - income-related employment and support allowance;
  - housing benefit (HB);
  - pension credit (guarantee or savings credit).

  You are treated as receiving one of these benefits if you are entitled to a DWP loan for help with your mortgage interest (see p764), even if you are not actually entitled to the benefit. You are eligible if you receive a backdated award of a qualifying benefit which covers the date you claim a funeral expenses payment. If you are waiting for a decision on a claim for a qualifying benefit, the DWP may defer making a decision on a claim for a funeral expenses payment until the qualifying benefit claim has been decided. If your claim for a funeral expenses payment is refused while you are waiting for a decision on a qualifying benefit claim, reclaim it within three months of being awarded the qualifying benefit. **Note:** if you do not claim a funeral expenses payment within the time limit, a backdated award of a qualifying benefit does not qualify you for a grant.

- **You live in England or Wales.**[33]
- **You or your partner are in one of the categories of eligible people** listed below who can be treated as responsible for the funeral expenses.
- **You or your partner accept responsibility for funeral expenses** (see p711).[34] If you are claiming as a close relative or close friend, it must also be reasonable for you to accept responsibility.
- **The funeral takes place in the UK** – see p711 for exceptions for European Economic Area (EEA) nationals.[35]
- **A social fund funeral payment has not already been made in respect of the person who has died** (but the amount of a previous award can be revised up to the maximum allowed under the rules).[36]
- **The person who died was 'ordinarily resident' in the UK** (see p1299).[37]
- **You are not a 'person subject to immigration control'** (there are exceptions to this rule) – see p1272.
- **You claim within the time limits** (see p713).

In England, there is also a **children's funeral fund payment.**[38] This is available for the funeral of a child aged under 18 or a stillborn child born after the 24th week of pregnancy (although, in practice, fees are not always charged). The payment covers reasonable burial or cremation fees and reasonable associated expenses, including a coffin or casket, but not costs exclusively related to religious requirements. The payment is available for all such funerals and does not depend on low income, entitlement to benefit or on satisfying residence conditions. No children's funeral fund payment can be made if a funeral expenses payment has already been paid to cover the same items. In most cases, the application is made by the person providing the funeral – eg, the funeral director. In Wales, there is a £500 payment towards the cost of a child's funeral (also local and community council burial and cremation fees for children under 18 are waived). This is understood to be in addition to the funeral expenses payment from the social fund.

## Eligible people

You are only eligible for a funeral expenses payment if you or your partner are in one of the following groups of people who can be treated as responsible for the funeral costs.[39]

- You were the partner of the person when they died.
- The deceased was a child for whom you were responsible when they died, and there is no absent parent, or there is an absent parent, but they (or their partner) were getting a qualifying benefit (see p707) when the child died. If there is an absent parent who was not getting a qualifying benefit when the

child died, you may qualify for a payment as a close relative of the child. If the deceased was a stillborn child, you are eligible for a funeral expenses payment if you were the parent or the parent's partner – it does not matter whether there is an absent parent.
- You were a parent, son or daughter of the person who died and it is reasonable for you to accept responsibility for the funeral expenses (see p711), and you are not excluded by the rules below.
- You were a close relative or a close friend of the person who died, and it is reasonable for you to accept responsibility for the funeral expenses (see p711), and you are not excluded by the rules below.



*Definitions*[40]

**'Child'** has the same meaning as it does for means-tested benefits (see p258). You are 'responsible' for a child if you get, or could get, child benefit for them (see p260).

**'Stillborn child'** means a child born dead after 24 weeks of pregnancy.

**'Absent parent'** means a parent of a deceased child, where the child:
– was not living in that parent's household at the date of death; *and*
– was living with another person who was responsible for them.

**'Close relative'** means parent, parent-in-law, son, son-in-law, daughter, daughter-in-law, step parent, stepson, stepson-in-law, stepdaughter, stepdaughter-in-law, brother, brother-in-law, sister, sister-in-law.

**'Close friend'** is not defined in the law. It can include a relative who is not a close relative – eg, a grandparent or grandchild.[41]

**'Partner'** means, where you count as being in a couple, your partner in that couple: that is defined as it is for means-tested benefits (see p254). You also count as a partner, however, if you were living in a care home when the person died and:[42]
– you and your spouse or civil partner were living in the same home; *or*
– you were a member of a couple before one or both of you moved into the home.

This rule is designed to enable a surviving partner to claim a funeral expenses payment if one or both partners were in a home at the date of death.

## Exclusion of certain close relatives and friends

If you claim as a close relative or close friend of the person who died (see p711), you cannot get a funeral expenses payment if:
- the person who died had a partner (unless that partner died before the funeral without claiming a funeral payment);[43] *or*
- the deceased was a child or stillborn child and a responsible person or parent can claim a funeral payment under the above rules;[44] *or*
- there is (other than you) a parent, son or daughter of the person who died, unless they are:[45]
  - under the age of 18; *or*

- aged 18 or 19 and count as a qualifying young person for child benefit purposes (see p488); *or*
- getting (or their partner gets) a qualifying benefit (see p707); *or*
- estranged from the deceased when they died ('estranged' is not defined); *or*
- a student aged 18 on a full-time course of advanced education (eg, A levels, Scottish national qualification at higher or advanced level, HNDs, degree level or above), or aged 19 to pension age on any full-time course; *or*
- a member of a religious order which fully maintains them; *or*
- a prisoner (including in youth custody or a remand centre) who (or whose partner) was getting a qualifying benefit immediately before being detained; *or*
- resident in a care establishment and the costs are met in whole or in part by a local authority; *or*
- an inpatient receiving free treatment in a hospital or similar institution and they (or their partner) received a qualifying benefit immediately before becoming a patient; *or*
- an asylum seeker receiving asylum support from the Home Office or a local authority; *or*
- ordinarily resident (see p1299) outside the UK; *or*

- there is a close relative of the deceased who was in *closer contact* with the deceased than you were, taking into account the nature and extent of such contact;[46] *or*
- there is a close relative of the deceased who was in *equally close contact* with the deceased as you were and who (or whose partner) is not getting a qualifying benefit (see p707).[47]

**Note:** the last two bullet points do not apply if the close relative was under 18 when the person died, or was a student, member of a religious order, prisoner, inpatient or asylum seeker as set out above, or was ordinarily resident outside the UK.[48]

If you are refused payment on this ground, the DWP (not you) must establish whether there is another close relative who is not getting a qualifying benefit.[49]

***Examples***

Shirley is not entitled to a funeral expenses payment because, although she looked after her brother for many years before he died, he had a son who is not getting a qualifying benefit (see p707). Although the son rarely saw his father, they were not estranged.

Trevor is entitled to a funeral expenses payment when his close friend Miles dies because, although Miles had two surviving close relatives, a son and a sister-in-law, the son is getting HB, and Trevor was in closer contact with Miles than either of them were.

## Accepting responsibility for funeral costs

To qualify for a funeral payment, you or your partner must accept responsibility for funeral expenses.[50] This means you must be liable to pay the funeral costs, even if you do not make the arrangements.[51]

If the funeral director's account or contract is in your name, you should normally be treated as having accepted responsibility. If it is in someone else's name (or another person has paid the bill), you can still be responsible if:

- they are acting as your agent – eg, because you are too distressed to act on your own behalf;[52] *or*
- they transfer liability to you, before full payment, with the consent of the funeral director.[53]



If you are a close relative (see p709) or close friend of the person who died, it must also be reasonable for you to accept responsibility for the funeral expenses, in the light of the nature and extent of your contact with them.[54] In one case, it was held reasonable for a person to have accepted responsibility for his father's funeral even though he had not seen him for 24 years.[55]

## European Economic Area nationals

These rules only apply if you have protected rights from 1 January 2021 (see p1390).

You can get a funeral expenses payment for a funeral that takes place in any member state of the EEA or Switzerland (see p1389) if:[56]

- you are a worker or self-employed, or you retain that status; *or*
- you are a member of the family of a worker – ie:
  - their spouse or civil partner; *or*
  - the worker's/spouse's/civil partner's child, grandchild or other descendant who is either under 21 or dependent; *or*
  - a dependent relative of the worker, spouse or civil partner in the ascending line – eg, a parent or grandparent; *or*
- you have a permanent right to reside in the UK.

If you have been refused a payment for a funeral that took place in an EEA state and you satisfied the above rules, you should ask for a revision (see p1135).

## The amount

You are entitled to a payment that is sufficient to cover:[57]

- the necessary costs of purchasing a new burial plot and necessary burial fees, including any medical references or other required documents. The burial of ashes following cremation is not, however, covered; *and*
- the necessary cremation fees, including medical references, certificates and removing a pacemaker (restricted to £20 if not carried out by a doctor); *and*

- the costs of documentation necessary for the release of the assets of the person who died; *and*
- the reasonable cost of transport for the portion of journeys in excess of 80 kilometres (50 miles), undertaken to:
  - transport the body within the UK to a funeral director's premises or to a place of rest; *and*
  - transport the coffin and bearers in a hearse and the mourners in another vehicle from the funeral director's premises or place of rest to the funeral. The cost of this plus burial in an existing plot cannot exceed the cost of such transport plus the purchase and burial costs of a new plot;[58] *and*
- the necessary expenses of one return journey for the responsible person to arrange or attend the funeral. The maximum allowed is the cost of a return journey from home to where the burial or cremation costs are incurred; *and*
- up to £1,000 for any other funeral expenses – eg, funeral director's fees, religious costs, flowers and other transport costs.

Note:
- The cost of any items or services provided under a prepaid funeral plan or equivalent arrangement cannot be met. Expenses not covered by the plan can be met if they fall into the above categories, but the maximum allowed under the last category is restricted to £120.[59]
- Costs relating to religious requirements cannot be included in the amount allowed for burial and transport.[60]
- Where there is more than one ceremony for the deceased, payment can only be awarded for the event that encompasses the final disposal of the body.[61] Where a body has not been recovered, payment can be made for a service equivalent to a burial or cremation.

If the amount awarded does not cover your funeral expenses, you may be able to claim a budgeting loan (see p701).

## Deductions from awards

The following are deducted from an award of a funeral expenses payment:[62]
- the assets of the person who died, which are available to you or a member of your family (this means your partner if you have one, and any children in your household, defined as for means-tested benefits – see Chapter 12) without probate or letters of administration. However, if you have a joint account with the person who died, those assets become yours at the point of death and cannot be deducted.[63] Assets at the date of death count, even if you have spent or distributed them before your claim for a funeral payment.[64] However, arrears of most benefits payable to the deceased at the date of death are excluded from the assets;[65]

- a lump sum legally due to you or a member of your family from an insurance policy, occupational pension scheme, burial club or equivalent source on the person's death;
- a funeral grant paid by the government for a war disablement pensioner;
- an amount paid or payable under a prepaid funeral plan or equivalent arrangement (whether or not the plan was fully paid).

Any capital you have apart from the above does not affect the amount of the funeral payment.



## Claiming and getting paid

Claim by phoning the Bereavement Service helpline on 0800 151 2012 (textphone 0800 731 0464; Relay UK and British Sign Language services also available). You can also claim by post using the claim Form SF200, available via gov.uk/funeral-payments/how-to-claim, or from your local Jobcentre Plus office.

There are strict time limits for claiming. You can claim at any time from the date of death to up to six months after the date of the funeral.[66] There is no provision for late claims.

When completing the form, bear in mind the rules about accepting responsibility for the funeral expenses and your contact with the person who died.

Your date of claim is normally the date the form is received by the DWP or when you make your telephone claim.[67] If you do not complete form SF200 properly or apply in writing but not on the form, you should be sent the form to complete or correct. If you submit it within one month (or a longer period if the DWP considers this reasonable), your claim is treated as having been made on the date you originally applied.[68] See p707 for when your claim can be backdated if you are subsequently awarded a qualifying benefit.

Payment is normally made direct to the funeral director, unless you have already paid the bill.[69]

If you are overpaid a funeral expenses payment, you may have to repay it (see Chapter 47), and, in some circumstances, you may have to pay a penalty (see p1101). However, see below for recovery from the estate of the person who died.

## Recovery from the estate

The DWP is entitled to recover funeral expenses payments from the estate of the person who died and usually attempts to do so.[70] Funeral expenses are a first charge on the estate and have priority over anything else (although there may be insufficient assets for full repayment).[71]

4

# 4. Cold weather payments

Cold weather payments are available in England and Wales. If you live in Scotland, you may instead be entitled to a winter heating payment (see p1505).

You qualify for a cold weather payment if you satisfy all the following conditions.

- **There is a period of cold weather** in the area where you have your usual home. This is defined as seven consecutive days during which your designated local weather site either forecasts or records a temperature at or below zero degrees celsius.[72]
- **You have been awarded pension credit** (guarantee or savings credit) for at least one day during the period of cold weather. **You also qualify if you have been awarded universal credit (UC), or income-related employment and support allowance (ESA)** for at least one day during the period of cold weather[73] and:
  - your UC includes an increase for a disabled or severely disabled child, or you have been assessed as having, or are treated as having, limited capability for work or limited capability for work-related activity, and you are not in employment or gainful self-employment during the period of cold weather or on the day it is forecast; *or*
  - your income-related ESA applicable amount includes the pensioner premium, severe disability premium or enhanced disability premium, or you have been assessed as having, or are treated as having, limited capability for work or limited capability for work-related activity; *or*
  - you are responsible for a child under five (if you get UC, this only applies if you are not in work or self-employment during the period of cold weather or on the day it is forecast).

  You are treated as receiving one of the above benefits if you are entitled to a DWP loan for help with your mortgage interest (see p764), even if you are not actually entitled to the benefit.
- **You are not living in a care home, independent hospital or Abbeyfield Home** unless you are responsible for a child under five.[74]
- **You are not a 'person subject to immigration control'** (there are exceptions to this rule) – see p1272.

## The amount

£25 is paid for each week of cold weather.[75]

## Claiming and getting paid

You do not claim a cold weather payment. The DWP should automatically pay you if you qualify. However, if you are in receipt of ESA and have a baby, or a child under five comes to live with you, you should notify the DWP to ensure you get a payment automatically. Your district DWP should publicise when there are periods of cold weather in your area. If you do not receive payment and you think you are entitled, submit a written claim and ask for a written decision. A payment cannot be made more than 26 weeks from the last day of the winter period (1 November to 31 March) in which the cold weather period fell.[76] If you are overpaid a cold weather payment, you might have to repay it (see Chapter 47), and, in some circumstances, you may have to pay a penalty (see p1101).



## 5. Winter fuel payments

Winter fuel payments are available in England and Wales. If you live in Scotland, you may instead qualify for a pension age winter fuel payment (see Chapter 66). In Scotland, child winter heating payment is also payable for some disabled children and young people (see p1506).

You qualify for a winter fuel payment if you satisfy all the following conditions.[77]

- **You have reached pension age** in the 'qualifying week'.
- **In respect of any day within the qualifying week, you are ordinarily resident in England or Wales** (see p1299) **or you are habitually resident in a specific European Economic Area (EEA) country and satisfy other requirements** (see p1357).
- **In respect of any day within the qualifying week, you (or your partner if you are in a couple) are entitled to a qualifying benefit** (pension credit, income-related employment and support allowance or universal credit, or a benefit equivalent to one of these where you are habitually resident in a specific EEA country).
- **You claim in time** (see p716), if a claim is required.
- **You are not excluded from a payment under the rules below.**

*The qualifying week*

The **'qualifying week'** is the week beginning on the third Monday in September.

### Who cannot get a winter fuel payment

You are excluded from entitlement to a payment if, throughout the qualifying week:[78]

- you are serving a custodial sentence; *or*
- you have been receiving free inpatient treatment for more than 52 weeks in a hospital or similar institution (see p817); *or*
- you are living in residential care and have been for at least 12 weeks; *or*

- you are a 'person subject to immigration control' (there are exceptions) – see p1272.

*Living in residential care*

You count as **'living in residential care'** if you are living in a care home (ie, an independent home which is registered or exempt from registration, or a local authority home which provides board) or independent hospital throughout the qualifying week and the 12 preceding weeks, disregarding temporary absences.

4

### The amount

Subject to the rules below, you are entitled to a winter fuel payment of:[79]

- £200 if you are aged between pension age and 79 (inclusive) in the qualifying week (see p715); *or*
- £300 if you (or your partner, if you are in a couple) are aged 80 or over in the qualifying week.

### Claiming and getting paid

Most people get the winter fuel payment automatically. DWP records of your circumstances can be used to show that you are entitled without you having to claim.[80]

Most people who do need to claim live abroad. If you need to claim, you must claim a winter fuel payment on or before 31 March following the qualifying week.[81] To ensure you receive your payment before Christmas, submit your claim before the qualifying week. Contact the winter fuel payment centre on 0800 731 0160 (Relay UK and British Sign Language services also available) or download a claim form from gov.uk/winter-fuel-payment. For more information see gov.uk/winter-fuel-payment/if-you-live-abroad.

You should get a written decision.

The government aims to make payments between mid-November and Christmas.

## 6. Tax, other benefits and the benefit cap

Social fund loans and payments are not taxable.

They are disregarded as income and capital for means-tested benefits, and do not affect entitlement to non-means-tested benefits.

Social fund loans and payments are *not* specified benefits for the benefit cap.

# Notes

1. **Budgeting loans**
   1 Dir 8 BLG
   2 *R v SFI ex parte Davey*, 19 October 1998 (HC), unreported
   3 Dir 8 BLG
   4 Dir 9 BLG
   5 Dir 8 BLG
   6 Dir 2 BLG
   7 Dir 53 BLG
   8 Dir 11 BLG
   9 Reg 4 SF(AM) Regs
   10 Reg 5 SF(AM) Regs
   11 Reg 2(1)(a) and (2)(a) SF(AR) Regs
   12 Reg 2(4) SF(AR) Regs
   13 Reg 2(6) SF(AR) Regs
   14 Reg 2(3) SF(AR) Regs
   15 para 132 Part 4 BLG
   16 s78(1) SSAA 1992
   17 Reg 6(3) and (4) SF(AM) Regs
   18 Reg 3 SF(RDB) Regs
   19 s78(3) SSAA 1992

2. **Sure Start maternity grants**
   20 Reg 5(2) SFM&FE Regs
   21 Reg 5(6) SFM&FE Regs
   22 Reg 5(3) SFM&FE Regs
   23 Reg 3A SFM&FE Regs
   24 Reg 5A SFM&FE Regs
   25 *SK and LL v SSWP* [2020] UKUT 145 (AAC)
   26 Reg 5A(8) SFM&FE Regs
   27 Reg 6 SFM&FE Regs
   28 Reg 5(1) SFM&FE Regs
   29 Reg 19 and Sch 4 para 8 SS(C&P) Regs
   30 Reg 6(1)(a) SS(C&P) Regs
   31 Regs 4(7) and 6(1)(b) SS(C&P) Regs

3. **Funeral expenses payments**
   32 Reg 7(3) and (4) SFM&FE Regs
   33 Reg 7(9A) SFM&FE Regs
   34 Reg 7(7) SFM&FE Regs
   35 Reg 7(9)(a) and (b) SFM&FE Regs
   36 Reg 4(1) and (2) SFM&FE Regs
   37 Reg 7(5) SFM&FE Regs
   38 The Social Fund (Children's Funeral Fund for England) Regulations 2019 No.1064
   39 Reg 7(8)(a)-(e) SFM&FE Regs
   40 Reg 3(1) SFM&FE Regs
   41 CIS/788/2003
   42 Reg 3(2) SFM&FE Regs
   43 Regs 7(8)(e) and 8(4) SFM&FE Regs
   44 Reg 7(8)(e) SFM&FE Regs; R(IS) 7/04
   45 Reg 8(1) and (2) SFM&FE Regs
   46 Reg 8(7)(a) SFM&FE Regs
   47 Reg 8(7)(b) SFM&FE Regs
   48 Reg 8(8) SFM&FE Regs
   49 *Kerr v Department for Social Development (NI)* [2004] All ER(D) 65, reported as [2004] UKHL 23
   50 Reg 7(7) SFM&FE Regs
   51 CSB/488/1982
   52 CIS/12344/1996; R(IS) 6/98
   53 CIS/85/1991
   54 Reg 7(8)(e) SFM&FE Regs
   55 CIS/12783/1996
   56 Reg 7(10) SFM&FE Regs
   57 Reg 9(1), (2) and (3) SFM&FE Regs
   58 Reg 9(8) SFM&FE Regs
   59 Reg 9(10) SFM&FE Regs
   60 Reg 9(7) SFM&FE Regs
   61 *JEC v SSWP* [2021] UKUT 243 (AAC); ADM Memo 17/21; DMG Memo 12/21
   62 Reg 10(1) SFM&FE Regs
   63 Vol 7 Ch 39 para 39404 DMG
   64 R(IS) 14/91
   65 Reg 10(1A) SFM&FE Regs
   66 Sch 4 para 9 SS(C&P) Regs
   67 Reg 6(1)(a) SS(C&P) Regs
   68 Regs 4(7) and 6(1)(b) SS(C&P) Regs
   69 Reg 35(2) SS(C&P) Regs
   70 s78(4) SSAA 1992; CIS/616/1990
   71 R(SB) 18/84

4. **Cold weather payments**
   72 Reg 2(1) and (2) SFCWP Regs
   73 Reg 1A(2), (3) and (6) SFCWP Regs
   74 Reg 1A(4) SFCWP Regs
   75 Reg 3 SFCWP Regs
   76 Reg 2(6) SFCWP Regs

5. **Winter fuel payments**
   77 Reg 2 SFWFP Regs
   78 Reg 4 SFWFP Regs
   79 Regs 2 and 3 SFWFP Regs
   80 Reg 5 SFWFP Regs
   81 Reg 4(1)(c) SFWFP Regs

4

# Chapter 34

# Statutory maternity, adoption, paternity and other parental pay

**This chapter covers:**

1. Who can get a payment (p719)
2. The rules about your age (p733)
3. People included in the claim (p733)
4. The amount of benefit (p733)
5. Special benefit rules (p734)
6. Claims (p737)
7. Getting paid (p738)
8. Tax, other benefits and the benefit cap (p739)

## Key facts

- Statutory maternity pay (SMP), statutory adoption pay (SAP), statutory paternity pay (SPP) and statutory shared parental pay (SSPP) are payments made to certain employees by their employers for the birth or adoption of a child.
- Statutory parental bereavement pay (SPBP) is a payment made to certain employees by their employers following the death of a child or a stillbirth.
- Statutory neonatal care pay (SNCP) is a payment made by employers to certain employees while they are absent from work while caring for a child who is or was receiving neonatal care.
- SMP, SAP, SPP, SSPP, SPBP and SNCP are not means tested, although they have employment and earnings conditions.
- You do not need to intend to return to work to qualify for SMP, SAP, SPP, SSPP, SPBP or SNCP, and you do not have to repay any of these payments if you do not return.
- You may be entitled to more maternity, adoption, paternity, shared parental pay or pay in connection with a parental bereavement or a child's neonatal care under your employment contract.

- If you disagree with your employer's decision on your entitlement, or if your employer has failed to make a decision, you can challenge this (see Chapter 54).

*Future changes*

The government has introduced an Employment Rights Bill which will extend rights to paternity leave to new employees, introduce wider bereavement leave (to cover other specified close bereavements) and allow paternity leave to be taken after shared parental leave. It is expected that most of these changes will not come into force before 2026.



# 1. Who can get a payment

## Statutory maternity pay

You qualify for statutory maternity pay (SMP) from your employer if you are pregnant or have recently given birth and:

- you have been continuously employed by the same employer for at least 26 weeks (see p727) by the end of the week which is 15 weeks before the week in which your baby is due (the 'expected week of childbirth' – EWC);[1] *and*
- your average gross weekly earnings are at least the 'lower earnings limit' (£125 a week in 2025/26). Your earnings are looked at over a 'relevant period' which depends on the EWC (see p729);[2] *and*
- you are in the 'maternity pay period' (see below);[3] *and*
- you give your employer at least 28 days' notice of the date you want payment of your SMP to start, unless this is not reasonably practicable (see p737),[4] and Form MAT B1 from your doctor or midwife confirming the expected date of birth (this can be submitted later if needed).[5]

If you do not qualify for SMP, you may be able to get maternity allowance (MA) instead (see Chapter 30).

## The maternity pay period

SMP is paid for up to 39 consecutive weeks. You can usually choose to start to receive SMP at any point between 11 weeks before your baby is due and the day after your baby is born. However, if you have to stop work earlier than planned, your maternity pay period may begin earlier than the date given in your notice to your employer in the following circumstances.[6]

- If your baby is born early, your maternity pay period begins the day after. You should let your employer know as soon as you can (if possible, within 28 days). Your employer can ask you to confirm this in writing.[7]
- If you are off work because of your pregnancy on a day within four weeks of your EWC, your SMP starts the day after.

- If you leave your job, see p734.

You may decide to reduce your maternity pay period – eg, if this would allow the father of the child/your partner to claim statutory shared parental leave and/or pay (see p722). There are statutory limits on how early your employer can allow you to return to work if you are an employee.

## Statutory adoption pay

4

You qualify for statutory adoption pay (SAP) from your employer if you are adopting a child under UK law and:

- you have been continuously employed by the same employer for at least 26 weeks (see p727) by the end of the week in which you are notified that you have been matched with a child for adoption;[8] *and*
- your average gross weekly earnings are at least the 'lower earnings limit' (£125 a week in 2025/26). Your earnings are looked at over a 'relevant period', which depends on the date you are matched with a child – see p729;[9] *and*
- you are in the 'adoption pay period' (see below);[10] *and*
- you give your employer at least 28 days' notice of when you want payments of SAP to start, unless this is not reasonably practicable (see p737) (you can give a start date which relates to the day of placement – ie, without specifying an actual date), the 'matching certificate' from the adoption agency confirming the placement date and the date you were notified of it, and a declaration that you want to receive SAP rather than statutory paternity pay (SPP).[11] Your employer can request that you give notice in writing.

**Note:** you will usually be better off claiming SAP rather than SPP, as it is paid for longer.

If you are jointly adopting a child, only one of you can claim SAP. You should consider the amount payable when making this decision (see p733). The person who is not claiming SAP may be able to claim SPP (adoption) – see below.

See p736 if you are adopting a child from abroad.

### The adoption pay period

SAP is paid for up to 39 consecutive weeks. You can choose to start to receive SAP, at the earliest, 14 days before the day you expect the child to be placed with you and, at the latest, on the date of placement (or the day after if you are at work that day). You need to inform your employer when the child is actually placed with you if you asked for your SAP to start on that day or the following day.[12]

You may decide to reduce the adoption pay period – eg, if this would allow your partner to claim statutory shared parental leave and/or pay (see p722).

The adoption pay period ends early if the child is not placed with you, or if the adoption ends because the child dies or they are returned to the adoption agency.[13] In these circumstances, payment of SAP continues for eight weeks, then stops.

## Statutory paternity pay

You qualify for SPP from your employer if you are taking time off work to care for a child or to support your partner, and you satisfy the conditions below. You can be:

- the child's father, if you expect to have responsibility for their upbringing; *or*
- the partner of the child's mother, if you expect to share the main responsibility for the child's upbringing with her;[14] *or*
- the person adopting a child; *or*
- the adopter's partner, if you expect to share the main responsibility for the child's upbringing with them.[15]



**Note:** you may have a choice between SAP and SPP if you are adopting with your partner. Bear in mind that SAP can be worth more to begin with, depending on your earnings, and has a longer maximum pay period (see p733).

You qualify for SPP if:

- you have been continuously employed by the same employer for at least 26 weeks (see p727):
  - by the end of the week which is 15 weeks before the week the baby is due (the 'EWC');[16] *or*
  - by the end of the week in which you (and/or your partner) are notified that you have been matched with a child for adoption;[17] *and*
- you continue to be employed by the same employer up to and including the day of the birth or adoption placement;[18]
- your average gross weekly earnings are at least the 'lower earnings limit' (£125 a week in 2025/26). Your earnings are looked at over a 'relevant period' which depends on the EWC or the date you are matched with a child for adoption (see p729);[19] *and*
- you are in the 'paternity pay period' (see p722);[20] *and either*
  - at least 15 weeks in advance of the EWC (unless not reasonably practicable – see p737), you notify your employer of the due date. At least 28 days before the EWC (or 28 days before your SPP start date, if you have asked for your SPP to start later), unless this time limit is not reasonably practicable (see p737), you must also give notice of the week/s when you want your SPP to be paid and provide a declaration that you are entitled to claim. You must make this declaration each time you give notice (if giving it separately for different weeks);[21] *or*
  - within seven days of notification of the adoption match (unless not reasonably practicable – see p737), you notify your employer of the date of notification of the match, the date you expect the child to be placed for

adoption, the week/s when you want your SPP to be paid (you can give a date which relates to the day of placement – ie, without specifying an actual date) and provide a declaration that you are entitled to claim.[22]

You cannot be paid SPP at the same time as statutory shared parental pay (SSPP), nor if you have already taken SSPP for the same birth/adoption.

### The paternity pay period

SPP is paid for a maximum of two weeks. The earliest SPP can be paid is the child's date of birth or the date of the child's placement for adoption, and the latest is 52 weeks after that date or, if the child is born early, 52 weeks from the first day of the EWC.[23] For SPP for a birth, you can choose whether you want SPP to start on the day the child is born, the following day or a specified number of days after the birth. In this case, you must inform your employer of the date the child is born as soon as you can after the birth. Alternatively, you can request that SPP starts on a specific date so long as this is after the first day of the EWC. In this case, you only need to let the employer know if the child has not arrived by the date you specified, as this will have to be changed.[24]

For SPP for an adoption, you can choose whether you want SPP to start on the day the child is placed with you and your partner, the following day or a specified number of days after the placement. In this case, you must inform your employer when the child is placed with you as soon as you can. Alternatively, you can request that SPP starts on a specific date as long as this is later than the expected date of placement. In this case, you only need to let your employer know if the child has not been placed with you by the date you have asked SPP to start, as this will have to be changed.[25]

You can choose for SPP to be paid for one week, two weeks, or for two non-consecutive weeks.[26] You can give notice for both weeks at the same time, or separately.

## Statutory shared parental pay

You may qualify for SSPP from your employer if your partner has chosen to give up her SMP or maternity allowance (MA), or their SAP, early.

You may also qualify if you have recently given birth or adopted a child and you choose to give up your SMP or SAP early. You might choose to do this because the rules on when SSPP can be paid are more flexible and it could allow you to return to work for a longer period than would otherwise be possible without losing your right to more paid leave. If you are doing this as a mother/adopter, bear in mind that SMP/SAP is worth more than SSPP for the first six weeks. Your employer may also offer enhanced maternity or adoption pay, making it more financially viable to remain on maternity or adoption leave.

Note:
- SMP, SAP or MA must have been paid for at least two weeks before it can be given up early.[27]
- If you or your partner change your mind about swapping to SSPP, any 'curtailment' (ie, early ending) of SMP, SAP or MA can be cancelled if the curtailment notice was given before the birth and it is cancelled within six weeks of the birth or (for birth or adoption) your partner dies and you cancel the curtailment of your SMP, SAP or MA within a reasonable period after the death.[28] You cannot cancel curtailment in an adoption situation unless your partner dies. However, even if you are not able to cancel curtailment, your SAP will not end unless you/your partner are entitled to SSPP.



You qualify for SSPP if:
- you have been continuously employed by the same employer for at least 26 weeks (see p727) by the end of either the week that is 15 weeks before the week the baby is due (the EWC)[29] or when you (and/or your partner) are notified that you have been matched with a child for adoption.[30] You must also continue in this employment at least until the week before your SSPP starts; *and*
- your average gross weekly earnings are at least the 'lower earnings limit' (£125 a week in 2025/26). Your earnings are looked at over a relevant period which depends on the EWC or the date you are matched with a child for adoption (see p729);[31] *and*
- you are in the 'shared parental pay period' (see p724);[32] *and*
- your partner has sent a 'curtailment notice' to their employer at least eight weeks before they want payment of SMP, SAP or MA to stop,[33] or you have sent your employer a curtailment notice if you want your own SMP or SAP to stop[34] and you have given your employer:
  - at least eight weeks' notice of the date you want payments of SSPP to start; *and*
  - notification of the baby's due date, the date of birth or the date of the adoption placement; *and*
  - confirmation of the total number of weeks and the period(s) for which you intend to claim SSPP and you intend to care for the child during this period; *and*
  - a declaration from your partner giving their details and confirming that they consent to your claiming SSPP and that you will share the main responsibility for the care of the child with them, and a declaration from you, confirming that you are entitled to claim. To ensure you provide all the information required in these declarations, it is recommended that you use the official forms (see p737).[35]

If you are the mother or the SAP claimant and you want to claim SSPP, your partner in the application (this can be the father of the child, your spouse, civil partner or your partner who lives with you and the child) must:[36]

- have the main responsibility for the child (apart from you); *and*
- have been employed for 26 weeks in the 66 weeks before the EWC or before the week you are notified that you have been matched with a child for adoption; *and*
- have average weekly earnings of at least £30 in 13 of those 66 weeks.



### The shared parental pay period

When you or your partner give notice that you wish to 'curtail' your SMP, SAP or MA (after it has been paid for at least two weeks), SSPP is payable for the remaining number of weeks in the 39-week period. If both you and your partner qualify for SSPP, and you both intend to claim it, you can share the available weeks of SSPP between you in whatever proportion you choose. If you are going to do this, you must both give at least eight weeks' notice of your intention to take SSPP. You can get SSPP for the same or different weeks. Alternatively, either one of you can get all the available weeks of SSPP.

The weeks of SSPP can be paid over one continuous period or over a number of shorter periods (if your employer agrees to this). It cannot be paid for any day falling after the child's first birthday, or after the first anniversary of their adoption placement. You can give your employer notice of your intention to take SSPP and then follow this up with notice of specific periods of SSPP (and leave) you wish to book, or do both of these at the same time (see p737), but you must usually give at least eight weeks' notice before any period of SSPP.

## Statutory parental bereavement pay

Statutory parental bereavement pay (SPBP) is paid for up to two weeks to employees who meet certain conditions in respect of the death of a child or a stillbirth. You qualify for SPBP if a child under 18 dies or is stillborn after 24 weeks of pregnancy (see p735) and you:[37]

- are a bereaved parent; *and*
- have been continuously employed by the same employer for at least 26 weeks (see p727) ending with the week immediately before the week in which the child died, and continue to be employed by that employer from that point to the day of the child's death; *and*
- have average gross weekly earnings of at least the 'lower earnings limit' (£125 in 2025/26). Your earnings are looked at over a 'relevant period', which depends on the week in which the death occurred (see p729); *and*
- give your employer notice of the week or weeks you want the payment to be made.

A **'bereaved parent'** includes all legal parents (including adoptive parents), natural (biological) parents whose children have been adopted and the adopter was required to allow them to be in contact with the child, legal parents and intended parents (who have applied for, or intend to apply for, a parental order in respect of a child under a surrogacy arrangement).[38]

You are also a bereaved parent if you had day-to-day responsibility for the child, and they were living in your own home for at least four weeks ending with the day the child died. However, you are not a parent if an actual parent of the child, or someone else who had responsibility for the child, is also living in the premises where the child is cared for. You are also not a parent if you are entitled to receive any remuneration in respect of the care of the child. Remuneration means payment for work that you do, whether in cash or kind, but some payments do not count – eg, a fostering allowance paid by a local authority. Remuneration also does not include benefits you may receive for the child such as child benefit, child tax credit or universal credit. 4

The partner of a bereaved parent is also entitled to SPBP if they meet the other conditions. A **'partner'** means someone who lives with the parent and the child in an enduring family relationship and is not a close relative of the parent.[39]

You must give your employer notice of the SPBP you want to take. The maximum number of weeks of SPBP for the death of one child is two (however, you can be entitled to SPBP in respect of more than one child[40]). You can choose to be paid for either one week or two, or you can take two separate weeks at different times. SPBP can only be paid within 56 weeks beginning with the date of the child's death.[41] You are supposed to give notice of at least 28 days before the first day for which you want to receive SPBP, but if this is not reasonably practicable, you should give it as soon as you can do so.[42]

With your notice, you should include the following in writing:[43]

- the name of the person claiming SPBP; *and*
- the date of the child's death; *and*
- a declaration that you meet one of the conditions for being a bereaved parent – eg, you are the child's parent or the partner of a bereaved parent.

If you later change your mind about your weeks of SPBP, you can withdraw your notice. You must give notice to withdraw no later than the first day of a week of SPBP if you were going to be taking it within 56 days of the child's death, and at least a week before a week of SPBP if you were going to be taking it later than that.[44]

## Statutory neonatal care pay

You qualify for statutory neonatal care pay (SNCP) if:[45]

- you have a prescribed parental or personal relationship with a child born on or after 6 April 2025 who is receiving, or has received, neonatal care; *and*

- that care continues for at least seven days beginning with the day after the care starts; *and*
- you satisfy the continuous employment rule (see p727); *and*
- you satisfy the earnings condition (see p729); *and*
- you give your employer notice of the week or weeks you want the payment to be made.

Neonatal care must start within the 28 days beginning the day after the child's birth.[46] Parents can take a maximum of 12 weeks of pay and a minimum of one week, to be taken within the first 68 weeks of a baby's birth.[47] A parent is entitled to one week of SNCP for every period of seven days during which the child receives uninterrupted neonatal care.[48]

Neonatal care includes:[49]

- medical care received in hospital; *or*
- medical care received elsewhere after being discharged as a hospital inpatient, where the care is under the direction of a consultant and includes monitoring and visits from healthcare professionals arranged by the hospital; *or*
- palliative or end of life care.

You satisfy the parental or personal relationship condition if you are:[50]

- a parent; *or*
- a partner of the child's mother; *or*
- an intended parent (you have or expect to be granted a parental order, see p736); *or*
- an adopter, prospective adopter (see p736) or an overseas adopter (see p736); *or*
- the partner of any of the adopters in the previous bullet point.

You must have or expect to have responsibility for the upbringing of the child, and if you are a partner of the mother/adopter, this must be the main responsibility (apart from that of your partner). SNCP may be available to each person covered by these rules.

While the child is in neonatal care, and for seven days after the day this stops, the weeks of pay do not have to be consecutive. After this period, only one week or consecutive weeks may be taken.[51]

You and your employer can mutually agree that no notice is required for you to take SNCP. Otherwise, you must give notice (in writing if your employer requires it). If you are taking pay for weeks before the end of the seven days after the day the child stops receiving neonatal care, you are supposed to give notice within 28 days of the beginning of your SNCP (ie, you can give notice after it has begun). If you are taking SNCP after that, you are supposed to give notice no later than 15 days before the beginning of a one-week period of SNCP, and no later than 28 days before two or more consecutive weeks. If it is not reasonably practicable to give notice within these times, you should give notice as soon as you can do so.[52]

The notice should include:

- the name of the person claiming SNCP;
- the date of the child's birth, or, if you are an adopter, the date of their placement with you or entry into Great Britain to live with you;
- the date that the child started to receive neonatal care (or each date if there has been more than one occasion);
- if neonatal care has already ended, the date the child ceased to receive it;
- a declaration that you cared or intend to care for the child during weeks of SNCP;
- a declaration that you meet the parental or personal relationship conditions.



If a child stops receiving neonatal care after you have given notice, you must let your employer know when this happened as soon as reasonably practicable. If you change your mind about SNCP to be taken more than seven days after the child leaves neonatal care, you can withdraw your notice in writing, giving at least 15 days' notice before the period of SNCP starts for one week of SNCP and 28 days' notice for two or more consecutive weeks.

## Continuous employment

To satisfy the continuous employment rule, you must have been employed by an employer who was liable to pay employer's national insurance (NI) contributions for you, or would have been if your earnings had been high enough (see p860) or you had been older (if you are under 16).[53] For the statutory payments in this chapter, you usually need to have been employed for 26 weeks by the end of the week which is 15 weeks before the EWC (see p719); for adoption, by the date you (and/or your partner) are notified that you have been matched with a child; or for the death of a child, by the end of the week before the week in which your child died. For SNCP, if you are not entitled to SMP, SPP or SAP for the same child, you can still satisfy the 26-week continuous employment rule for SNCP if you have been employed for 26 weeks by the end of the week before the week in which the neonatal care starts.[54]

Any work, even for only part of a week, counts as a week of work. A week for SMP, SAP, SPP, SSPP, SPBP or SNCP usually runs from Sunday to Saturday, so you need to check which week the date falls into and count backwards. For SPP, you must also continue to be employed by the same employer up to and including the day the child is born or placed for adoption.[55] For SSPP and SNCP, you must also continue to be employed by the same employer until the week immediately before any period of SSPP or SNCP begins.[56]

If you are an 'employed earner' for NI purposes (see p859), you normally count as an employee.[57] If you are employed under a contract of apprenticeship, you count as an employee.[58] Agency workers count, if someone is liable to pay employer's NI contributions, so if you have been employed by the same agency for long enough, you may qualify. Your employer may be an umbrella company rather than the agency itself.[59] Company directors who are paid a salary also count, so if you are a director of your own company, you may be liable to pay yourself statutory payments.

You need not have a written contract of employment to count as an employee.

Periods of employment in a European Economic Area country may count towards your period of continuous employment if you were employed by the same employer in Great Britain in the 15th week before your EWC, the week you were notified that you had been matched with a child for adoption, or, for the death of a child, the week immediately before the week in which your child died.[60] In addition, if you were working outside Great Britain but your employer was liable to pay class 1 NI on your earnings, then your period of employment may count.

Even if you are an employee, you may not be entitled to SMP, SAP, SPP or SSPP if your employer is based outside Great Britain (see p1385). See p1385 if you are employed abroad.

If the baby is born early (in or before the 15th week before your EWC), you satisfy the 26-week continuous employment rule if you would have been employed for 26 weeks by the end of the week 15 weeks before the EWC (for SMP, SPP, SSPP or SNCP for a birth).[61]

For SMP, if you are employed for only part of the 15th week before your EWC, the whole week still counts towards your continuous employment. For SAP, the same applies if you are employed for only part of the week in which you received notification that you have been matched with a child. For SMP, SAP, SPP, SSPP, SPBP and SNCP, if you have been employed for each of the 26 weeks needed (but no more), the first of those 26 weeks does not need to be a complete week. For the purposes of counting the weeks, the first week starts on the first day of your employment and ends at midnight on the following Saturday (or ends at midnight on the start date if you started employment on a Saturday).[62]

## Breaks in employment

If you return to work for the same employer following a break in your employment, certain weeks when you were not employed can still count towards your 26 weeks' continuous employment. These include weeks in which you were:[63]

- incapable of work because of sickness or injury; *or*
- absent because your employer temporarily had no work to offer you – eg, you are an agency worker and the agency was unable to find you work in any particular week; *or*

- absent from work, but because of an arrangement or custom, you are regarded as continuing in employment – eg, if you are a teacher employed on a term-by-term contract.

**Note:** the above rules are only relevant when there is a *break* in your employment with your employer. So, for example, sickness absence should count towards your continuous employment if you remain employed by your employer while off sick, as should absence because of adoption, paternity, shared parental, parental bereavement, neonatal care or parental leave.

For SMP only, if you have gaps between contracts with the same employer of no more than 26 weeks during which you are absent from work wholly or partly because of pregnancy, and you are employed both before and after your baby is born but not while you are off work due to childbirth, the weeks in between the contracts can still count towards your continuous employment.[64]



If your employer offers contracts of up to 26 weeks, at least twice a year, to people who have worked there before, and you are absent from work due to pregnancy (for SMP), disease or disability, you do not need to return to work to benefit from these rules.[65]

If your employment is legally transferred from one employer to another, your employment is unbroken.[66] If you have been reinstated or re-engaged following an unfair dismissal claim, any period between your dismissal and your reinstatement or re-engagement counts towards your 26 weeks' continuous employment.[67] If you have been dismissed without being reinstated or re-engaged, see p734.

If being on strike has affected the weeks which count towards your continuous employment, see p892.

## Earnings

### What counts as earnings

As well as your gross wages, bonuses and any overtime pay you receive during the relevant period, your earnings include payments such as:[68]

- other statutory payments;
- arrears of pay following reinstatement or re-engagement in your job or a continuation of your contract of employment under the Employment Rights Act 1996.

Certain payments (eg, some payments in kind) are ignored.[69]

### How earnings are averaged

For births, earnings are averaged over a 'relevant period' ending with the last normal payday which falls either in or before the 15th week before the EWC, and going back to the day after the last normal payday which fell at least eight weeks before that – ie, roughly 23 weeks before the baby is due. For SMP, gov.uk has a table of dates which can also be used for SPP, SSPP and SNCP for births. For adoptions, the relevant period ends with the last normal payday that falls in or before the week you are notified of being matched with a child for adoption, and goes back to the day after the last normal payday which falls at least eight weeks before that. For the death of a child, the relevant period ends with the last normal payday which falls before the first day of the week in which the child dies, and goes back to the day after the last normal payday which falls at least eight weeks before that. In the case of a stillbirth, you may also be entitled to SMP (see p735). For SNCP, the relevant period if you are not entitled to SMP, SPP or SAP for the child is the eight weeks ending with the week before the week in which the neonatal care starts.

The earnings in the relevant period rule is always used, even if you are underpaid or overpaid in this period (but see below if your pay rises).

A week for SMP, SPP, SAP, SSPP, SPBP and SNCP runs from a Sunday to Saturday. If you are paid at intervals of one or more calendar months, weekly earnings are calculated by dividing earnings received in the relevant period by the number of calendar months in that period (to the nearest whole number), multiplying by 12 and dividing by 52.[70] If you are not paid monthly or weekly, or there is not an exact number of weeks in the relevant period that applies to you, your weekly earnings are calculated by taking the total of your earnings in the relevant period, dividing by the number of days in the relevant period and multiplying by seven.

## Pay rises

**For SMP**, if you are awarded a pay rise that affects your wages for any part of the period from the first day of your 'relevant period' until the last day of your statutory maternity leave, your employer should reassess your average earnings during the relevant period as if your earnings for each of the weeks in that period had included the pay increase, and pay any arrears of SMP due to you. This is the case, even if the pay rise did not happen until after the relevant period.[71] If you become entitled to SMP as a result of the pay rise, your employer should deduct any payments of MA that you may have received for the same period from the SMP you are owed.[72]

**For SAP, SPP, SSPP, SPBP** and **SNCP**, only a backdated pay rise that is paid in respect of the relevant period used to calculate your SAP, SPP, SSPP, SPBP or SNCP will lead to your employer recalculating the average and paying any arrears of SAP, SPP, SSPP, SPBP or SNCP due to you.[73]

## The lower earnings limit

For births, the lower earnings limit used is the one in force at the end of the 15th week before the EWC. For adoptions, the lower earnings limit used is the one in force at the end of the week in which you or the adopter are notified of being matched with the child for adoption. For deaths, the lower earnings limit is the one in force at the end of the week immediately before the week in which the child dies. For the tax year 2025/26, the lower earnings limit is £125 a week. See Appendix 5 for the amounts for other years.

## Working while getting statutory payments for the birth, adoption or death of a child

Your entitlement to SMP, SAP, SPP, SSPP, SPBP or SNCP is not affected by any work you do on a self-employed basis. However, your entitlement may be affected if you work for an employer.



### Working for the employer who is paying you

You can do up to 10 'keeping in touch' days' work for the employer who pays you SMP or SAP, and up to 20 for SSPP, without your entitlement to these payments being affected. However, if you do any work for that employer in excess of these 10/20 days, you lose a week's payment for every week in which you do that further work.[74] **Note:** HMRC seems to interpret the rules about 'keeping in touch' days for SSPP as meaning that, if you work for 20 days or more, your SSPP ends altogether. Arguably, this is incorrect and can be challenged. Get specialist advice if you are affected.

If you do any work during the paternity pay period for an employer who is paying you SPP, that employer is not liable to pay you SPP for the week in which you work.[75] If you do any work during the parental bereavement pay or neonatal care pay period for an employer who is paying you SPBP or SNCP, that employer is not liable to pay you SPBP or SNCP for the week in which you work.[76]

These rules apply even if you are working for the employer under a new contract which did not exist before your maternity, paternity or adoption pay period began.

For SMP, if you return to work for your employer but you are then off sick during what would otherwise be your maternity pay period, you are not entitled to statutory sick pay (SSP). Instead, you can get SMP for each week in which you are off for a whole week. This does not apply if you have curtailed your maternity pay period and you are past the curtailment date (see p723), when you would be able to get SSP as usual. If you had returned to work before giving a curtailment notice, any additional weeks' SMP you are paid while off work sick are ignored when calculating the number of weeks for which SSPP can be paid.[77] This may allow you or your partner to book SSPP.

### Working for more than one employer who is liable to pay you

If you work for more than one employer and you meet the conditions of entitlement to SMP (see p719), SAP (see p720), SPP (see p721), SPBP (see p724) or SNCP (see p725) in respect of the work you do for each, you can get SMP, SAP, SPP, SPBP or SNCP from each job. However, if your earnings from any of your jobs are aggregated when calculating your liability to pay NI contributions, the jobs are counted as one and the amount your employers must pay is apportioned between them.

If more than one employer is liable to pay you SMP, SAP, SPP, SPBP or SNCP, unless the payments are just one award apportioned between them, any work you do for one of them does not affect your entitlement to SMP, SAP, SPP, SPBP or SNCP from the other.

If more than one employer is liable to pay you SSPP, you do not need to be on shared parental leave from all your jobs at the same time. The number of weeks of SSPP you can get from each employer is calculated without looking at how many weeks of SSPP you get from any other employer. However, *all* the weeks you get SSPP, from any employer, are counted when calculating the number of weeks of SSPP which would be left for your partner to take. There is no double counting of the same week(s) though, so if you get SSPP from more than one employer for one week, that week is only counted once, meaning you may be better off claiming SSPP from all your liable employers for the same weeks if your partner intends to take some SSPP as well.[78]

## Working for another employer

If you work for another employer who is not liable to pay you SMP, SAP, SPP, SSPP, SPBP or SNCP, this usually brings your statutory payments to an end early.[79] This means that if you start working for a new employer, your SMP, SAP, SPP, SSPP, SPBP or SNCP comes to an end. However, there are three exceptions.

- For SMP, if the work is done before your baby is born, your entitlement to SMP is unaffected.[80]
- For SPP, being employed by a new employer does not stop your former employer from being liable for one or two weeks of SPP, if you meet the conditions and have given the correct notice. However, you must not work for your new employer in a week of SPP, or you lose SPP for that week. You may need to seek advice about getting time off from your new employer, or arrange to take your SPP before you start working for them.[81]
- Your SMP, SAP, SPP, SSPP, SPBP or SNCP is not affected by any work you do for an employer who is not liable to pay you SMP, SAP, SPP, SSPP, SPBP or SNCP if you also worked for that employer in:
  - the 15th week before the EWC, for SMP, SPP (birth), SSPP (birth) and SNCP (if you are entitled to SMP or SPP for the birth); *or*
  - the week in which you or the adopter were notified that you had been matched with a child for adoption, for SAP, SPP (adoption) and SNCP (if you are entitled to SAP or SPP for the adoption); *or*
  - the 15th week before the expected week of the child's placement for adoption, for SSPP (adoption); *or*
  - for SBPB, the week immediately before the week of the child's death; *or*
  - for SNCP only, the week immediately before the one in which the neonatal care starts, if you are not entitled to SMP, SAP or SPP for the child.[82]

If you work for an employer who is not liable to pay you, and for whom you did not work in the relevant week, you must notify the employer who is paying you within seven days of the first day on which you do the work. It is advisable to inform your employer in writing. For SAP, SPP, SSPP, SPBP and SNCP, your employer has the right to request the information in writing.[83]

## 2. The rules about your age

There are no upper or lower age limits for statutory maternity pay, statutory adoption pay, statutory paternity pay, statutory shared parental pay, statutory parental bereavement pay or statutory neonatal care pay.



## 3. People included in the claim

You claim statutory maternity pay, statutory adoption pay, statutory paternity pay, statutory shared parental pay, statutory parental bereavement pay or statutory neonatal care pay for yourself. You cannot claim any increase for your partner or children.

## 4. The amount of benefit

| | *Maximum period of payment* | *Gross amount* |
|---|---|---|
| Statutory maternity pay and statutory adoption pay | 39 weeks | First six weeks: 90% of average weekly earnings<br>Remaining 33 weeks: Lesser of £187.18 or 90% of average weekly earnings |
| Statutory paternity pay | Two weeks | Lesser of £187.18 or 90% of average weekly earnings |
| Statutory shared parental pay | 37 weeks | Lesser of £187.18 or 90% of average weekly earnings |
| Statutory parental bereavement pay | Two weeks | Lesser of £187.18 or 90% of average weekly earnings |

| Statutory neonatal care pay | 12 weeks | Lesser of £187.18 or 90% of average weekly earnings |
|---|---|---|

If you meet the conditions of entitlement with more than one employer, see p731.

4

## 5. Special benefit rules

Special rules may apply to:

- people who give up their job or who have been dismissed (see below);
- stillbirths, multiple births or adoption (see p735);
- people who have adopted a child from abroad (see p736);
- foster parents approved as adopters (see p736);
- people whose baby is born with the help of a surrogate (see p736);
- people in prison or detention (see p836);
- people who are abroad or going abroad (see Chapter 58);
- people involved in a trade dispute (see p892).

### If you give up your job or are dismissed

Your employer is still liable to pay you statutory maternity pay (SMP), statutory adoption pay (SAP), statutory paternity pay (SPP), statutory shared parental pay (SSPP), statutory parental bereavement pay (SPBP) or statutory neonatal care pay (SNCP) if:

- you give up your job or are dismissed after you start receiving your statutory payments (but see p1258 if your employer is insolvent);[84] *or*
- your employer dismisses you at any time, provided HMRC or an employment tribunal finds this was 'solely or mainly' to avoid paying SMP, SAP, SPP, SSPP, SPBP or SNCP, and you had been employed by that employer for at least eight continuous weeks. In this situation, the amount you are paid for SMP, SAP, SPP, SPBP or SNCP is calculated using your average earnings during the eight-week period ending with the last day in respect of which you are paid.[85] For the amount of SSPP, your average earnings are calculated over the period ending on the last day you are paid and going back to the day after the last payday which falls at least eight weeks before that;[86] *or*
- you satisfy the qualifying conditions and your job ends for any reason at any time after:
  - **for SMP**, the beginning of the 15th week before the expected week of childbirth (EWC);[87] *or*

- **for SAP**, the beginning of the week in which you were notified of being matched with a child for adoption;[88] *or*
- **for SPP**, the day on which the child is born,[89] or placed for adoption;[90] *or*
- **for SSPP**, the beginning of the week in which your period of SSPP starts;[91] *or*
- **for SPBP**, the day on which the child dies;[92] *or*
- **for SNCP**, the beginning of the week in which your period of SNCP starts.[93]

If you qualify for SMP but your job ends before your maternity pay period was due to start, your SMP starts at the beginning of the 11th week before the EWC or, if your job ends after this, on the day after you finish work, unless your baby is born before these dates (in which case it begins the day after the birth).[94]

If you qualify for SAP but your job ends before your adoption pay period was due to start, it starts 14 days before the expected date of placement or, if your job ends after this, on the day after you finish work, unless your child is placed with you before this (in which case it begins on the date of placement).[95]

If you are dismissed while pregnant or in connection with maternity, adoption, paternity, shared parental, parental bereavement or neonatal care leave or pay, get advice about your employment rights urgently.

## Stillbirths, deaths, multiple births and adoptions

If your baby is stillborn after 24 weeks' pregnancy, SMP and SPP are payable in the same way as for a live birth, so if you have a stillbirth certificate, you can qualify.[96] If the baby is stillborn before you have completed 24 full weeks of pregnancy, this is treated as a miscarriage, and SMP and SPP are not payable. You may, however, qualify for statutory sick pay (SSP), employment and support allowance or universal credit. It may be possible to argue that a week for the purposes of this rule means seven days and not the Sunday to Saturday definition used for the employment or earnings conditions (see p730).[97] You should get advice if you are close to 24 weeks and miss out due to the way the weeks are counted.

If the baby is born alive but then dies (even after only a moment), this is a live birth and you can get SMP or SPP, even if it happens before 24 weeks of pregnancy. However, SSPP can only be paid if the child's death occurs after you have given notice to your employer of your intention to claim SSPP. SPP must be taken within eight weeks, unless you had already given notice before the death.[98]

You may be entitled to SPBP as well as SMP, SPP or SSPP. You can take this in addition (but not at the same time) as long as you do so within 56 weeks of the stillbirth, and give the required notice (see p725). The 'relevant period' for averaging earnings is different for the death of a child (see p729), but if you are already on SMP when your baby is stillborn, you will usually qualify for SPBP as well, unless your SMP is very low. If you were on SSP in the period before a stillbirth, you may not qualify for SPBP but could still qualify for SMP.

If you do qualify for both SMP and SPBP, remember that SMP has to be taken immediately after the stillbirth (unless SMP has already started). SPBP will need to be taken at some point after the SMP ends, but this does not have to be immediately afterwards (as long as it is within the 56-week period), and you will need to give your employer separate notice for this. SPP must be taken within eight weeks, unless you have already given notice.

If you have accrued entitlement to SNCP and the child dies, their placement for adoption with you is disrupted, or a parental order does not proceed, you do not have to meet the conditions of caring for the child during weeks of SNCP.[99]

No additional SMP, SAP, SPP or SSPP is payable if you or your partner give birth to more than one baby, or have more than one child placed with you for adoption, unless this happens as part of a different adoption arrangement.[100] You are entitled to SPBP in respect of each child if you satisfy the conditions in respect of the death of more than one child.[101]



## If you are adopting a child from abroad

If you are adopting a child from abroad, you may be entitled to SAP, SPP, SSPP or SNCP. To qualify, you must still satisfy the usual rules of entitlement (see p720, p721 and p722), but with certain modifications.[102] Although you must have 'official notification' that you have been approved for adoption from the UK authorities (sometimes called a 'certificate of eligibility and suitability to adopt'), you will not have been matched with a child for adoption by UK authorities under UK law, and so you will not be able to provide the date of placement or the date of notification of being matched for adoption. You should therefore use Form SC6 (for SAP) or Form SC5 (for SPP), available from gov.uk, to apply for SAP or SPP from your employer for an overseas adoption. There is currently no official form for SSPP or SNCP.

## Foster parents approved as adopters

In England, if you are a local authority foster parent who has been approved as a prospective adopter and you are fostering the child in the meantime (sometimes called a 'fostering for adoption' placement), you may qualify for SAP, SPP or SSPP before the actual adoption.[103] For SBPB and SNCP, this applies in both England and Wales.[104]

## If your baby is born with the help of a surrogate

If you have had a child with the help of a surrogate mother, you may qualify for SAP, SPP, SSPP, SPBP or SNCP if:[105]

- you have obtained a parental order from the court; *or*
- on the date of the child's birth you intend to apply for a parental order from the court within six months of the baby's birth, and you expect your application to be successful.

If this applies, your entitlement to SAP, SPP and SSPP can start from the due date, the date of birth of the child or afterwards. If you do not apply for a parental order within the time limit, your application is unsuccessful (and you cannot reapply or appeal). If the child dies, you can only take your SPP within an eight-week period of the time limit expiring, your application being refused or the child's death, unless you had already given notice for a later date.[106]

## 6. Claims

### Making a claim

You do not need to complete a claim form to qualify for statutory maternity pay (SMP), statutory adoption pay (SAP), statutory paternity pay (SPP), statutory shared parental pay (SSPP), statutory parental bereavement pay (SPBP) or statutory neonatal care pay (SNCP), but you must give your employer the required notice and evidence within the relevant time limit. However, for SSPP, it is advisable to use forms, available via gov.uk/shared-parental-leave-and-pay, to ensure you provide all the information and evidence needed.

Notification sent to your employer in a properly addressed and prepaid letter is treated as having been given on the day it is posted.[107] For SMP, SAP, SPP and SPBP, you should provide notice in writing and supply evidence at the same time, if you are able to do so, or as soon as possible afterwards. For SSPP, you can send notice and information to your employer electronically, if your employer has agreed to this. For SNCP, you and your employer can agree to waive the notice requirement.[108] If this is not agreed, you must provide notice in writing if your employer requests it.[109]

*Time limits*

You must give your employer notice of when you want your SMP, SAP, SPP, SSPP, SPBP or SNCP to start within the time limits specified for each benefit 'or as soon as reasonably practicable after that'. Depending on the payment, you may also need to notify your employer separately when the payment needs to start – eg, because your baby arrives early, or because you have asked for your payment to start when the baby arrives. There is also a time limit for providing required information and/or evidence, which is usually the same as the time limit to give notice. However, for SMP, you must provide evidence to your employer (usually your Form MAT B1 or the baby's birth certificate) by the end of the third week of the maternity pay period (see p719). Where you have good cause for not meeting this time limit, you must provide the evidence by the end of the 13th week of the maternity pay period.[110] For SNCP, if notice is required, the time limits depend on when the SNCP is taken (see p726).

The terms 'good cause' and 'reasonably practicable' are not defined – you must show that any delay was reasonable, given your circumstances. If you miss a time limit, your employer may not pay you. If you think your employer's decision is wrong, you can challenge it (see Chapter 54).

If your employer has its own maternity, adoption, paternity, shared parental, payparental bereavement or neonatal care pay scheme, the notice requirements for this scheme may be different. Check this with your employer.

### Who should claim

If you are entitled to SMP, SAP, SPP, SSPP, SPBP or SNCP but are not well enough to deal with your claims, HMRC can appoint someone else to act for you.[111] This person must apply in writing to be your appointee (see p1005). For further information, contact the HMRC national insurance helpline (tel: 0300 200 3500; textphone: 0300 200 3519).

### If you claim the wrong benefit

In some circumstances where you claim statutory sick pay but you are close to your due date, your employer may be able to start your maternity leave and pay you SMP instead (see p740).

You may get a claim for maternity allowance backdated if your employer has informed you that you are not entitled to SMP (see p640).

## 7. Getting paid

Statutory maternity pay (SMP), statutory adoption pay (SAP), statutory paternity pay (SPP), statutory shared parental pay (SSPP), statutory parental bereavement pay (SPBP) and statutory neonatal care pay (SNCP) are usually paid by your employer in the same way and at the same intervals as your normal wages or salary.[112]

**Note:**

- If you are also entitled to contractual maternity, adoption, paternity, shared parental, parental bereavement or neonatal care pay (or any other contractual remuneration) from your employer for the same period, SMP, SAP, SPP, SSPP, SPBP or SNCP may be offset against it or may form part of your payments.[113]
- Your employer cannot pay you SMP, SAP, SPP, SSPP, SPBP or SNCP by making a payment in kind, or by providing board and lodging, or by providing a service or some other facility.[114]
- If you become entitled to SMP because of a pay rise, your employer can deduct any maternity allowance (MA) you received for the same period from the SMP you are owed.[115]

- If your entitlement has been decided by a decision maker from HMRC, or by the First-tier or Upper Tribunal, your employer may be required to pay you within a certain time limit (see p1257). If your employer cannot or will not pay you, see p1258 for when payment can be made by HMRC.
- The rules on overpayments described in Chapter 47 do not apply to SMP, SAP, SPP, SSPP, SPBP or SNCP. If your employer tells you that you have been overpaid SMP, SAP, SPP, SSPP, SPBP or SNCP, get advice on your entitlement. You may also need debt advice. If your employer decides you have been paid SMP in error, consider claiming MA. You may be able to get this backdated (see p640).
- If your employer becomes insolvent, see p1258.
- For SAP, SPP, SSPP, SPBP or SNCP, HMRC, not your employer, pays you if you are entitled for a period after you were imprisoned or detained, or if you were subsequently released without charge, found not guilty or given a non-custodial sentence (see p837).[116]



### Change of circumstances

You must keep your employer informed of any change of circumstances that may affect your entitlement, such as if you start work for someone else while your employer is paying you SMP, SAP, SPP, SSPP, SPBP or SNCP. For SSPP, you must inform your employer if the person getting SMP, MA or SAP decides to cancel curtailment of these payments (see p723) and continue to receive SMP, MA or SAP, as this means you will not qualify for SSPP. For SNCP, you must inform your employer if the child leaves neonatal care after you have given notice to take SNCP.

If you qualify for SMP, SAP, SPP, SSPP, SPBP or SNCP, your entitlement is not affected if you go abroad.

## 8. Tax, other benefits and the benefit cap

### Tax

Statutory maternity pay (SMP), statutory adoption pay (SAP), statutory paternity pay (SPP), statutory shared parental pay (SSPP), statutory parental bereavement pay (SPBP) and statutory neonatal care pay (SNCP) are treated as earnings, and you pay tax and national insurance (NI) contributions as appropriate.[117]

### Means-tested benefits

**If you come under the universal credit (UC) system** (see p20), you may qualify for UC as well as SMP, SAP, SPP, SSPP, SPBP and SNCP.

For UC and contributory employment and support allowance (ESA), in some circumstances you can be treated as having limited capability for work-related activity while pregnant (see p917).

When calculating your entitlement to means-tested benefits, SMP, SAP, SPP, SSPP, SPBP and SNCP are:

- treated as employed earnings for UC;
- treated in full as income for income-related ESA;
- treated as earnings for housing benefit (HB) and pension credit. You may be able to get an allowance for certain childcare charges deducted from your earnings when calculating your entitlement to HB.



## Non-means-tested benefits

Provided you do not have limited capability for work and are not treated as having limited capability for work (but see p611), you may qualify for new-style JSA while getting SMP, SAP, SPP, SSPP, SPBP or SNCP. As you must accept a claimant commitment to qualify for JSA, get advice before claiming if you are still employed – the DWP may contact your employer and this may jeopardise your employment.

You cannot get statutory sick pay (SSP) when you are receiving SMP. If you are off work with a pregnancy-related illness (or an existing condition made worse by your pregnancy) in the four weeks before the expected week of childbirth, your employer can start your maternity leave (even if it is sooner than you had planned) and pay you SMP rather than SSP. It cannot do this if your illness is *not* pregnancy related.

You cannot receive SAP, SPP, SSPP, SPBP or SNCP for any week in which you are entitled to SSP.[118]

If you get SMP, you cannot also get maternity allowance (MA) for the same period in respect of the same pregnancy.[119]

If you are getting SMP, SAP, SPP, SSPP, SPBP or SNCP, you may qualify for NI credits (see p873). It may be important to claim credits in order to protect your future entitlement to contributory benefits, such as state pension. However, you will not need them if your SMP, SAP, SPP, SSPP, SPBP or SNCP is at least the lower earnings limit.

### Contributory employment and support allowance

You can qualify for contributory ESA as well as SPP if you satisfy the conditions for contributory ESA during your paternity pay period.

You can also qualify for contributory ESA while you are getting SMP, SAP, SSPP or SNCP if you satisfy the NI contribution conditions and had limited capability for work (or you could be treated as having limited capability for work) on the day before your statutory payments started.[120] However, your contributory ESA is reduced by the amount of SMP, SAP, SSPP or SNCP you receive for the same week.

In some circumstances, if you are in hospital, you can be treated as having limited capability for work (see p917). If you have a high-risk pregnancy, you may be treated as having limited capability for work-related activity (see p917).

## The benefit cap

SMP, SAP, SPP, SSPP, SPBP and SNCP are *not* specified benefits for the benefit cap.

## Other sources of help

For details of:

- a Sure Start maternity grant, see p705, or, if you live in Scotland, a Best Start grant pregnancy and baby payment, see p1453. You do not have to be a person who has given birth to a child to qualify for these grants;
- funeral expenses payments and other financial help specific to the cost of children's funerals if you live in England or Wales, see p707, or if you live in Scotland, a funeral support payment, see Chapter 65;
- free prescriptions, help with fares to receive NHS treament and free NHS dental treatment, see Chapter 27;
- Healthy Start food vouchers and vitamins, see p771, or, in Scotland, the Best Start foods scheme, see p1455;
- tax-free childcare, see p779.

# Notes

1. **Who can get a payment**
 1 s164(2)(a) SSCBA 1992
 2 s164(2)(b) SSCBA 1992
 3 s165 SSCBA 1992; reg 2 SMP Regs
 4 s164(4) and (5) SSCBA 1992
 5 Reg 22 SMP Regs
 6 Reg 2 SMP Regs
 7 Reg 23 SMP Regs
 8 s171ZL(2)(b) and (3) SSCBA 1992
 9 ss171ZL(2)(d) and 171ZS(6)-(8) SSCBA 1992
 10 s171ZN(2) SSCBA 1992; reg 21 SPPSAP(G) Regs
 11 s171ZL(6) and (7) SSCBA 1992; regs 23 and 24 SPPSAP(G) Regs
 12 Regs 21 and 23 SPPSAP(G) Regs
 13 Reg 22 SPPSAP(G) Regs
 14 s171ZA(2)(a) SSCBA 1992; reg 4 SPPSAP(G) Regs
 15 s171ZB(2)(a) SSCBA 1992; reg 11 SPPSAP(G) Regs
 16 s171ZA(2)(b) and (3) SSCBA 1992
 17 s171ZB(2)(b) and (3) SSCBA 1992
 18 ss171ZA(2)(d) and 171ZB(2)(d) SSCBA 1992
 19 **Father/mother's partner**
 ss171ZA(2)(c) and 171ZJ(6)-(8) SSCBA 1992
 **Adopter/adopter's partner**
 ss171ZB(2)(c) and 171ZJ(6)-(8) SSCBA 1992

**Notes**

20 **Father/mother's partner** s171ZE(2) SSCBA 1992; reg 6 SPPSAP(G) Regs
**Adopter/adopter's partner** s171ZE(2) SSCBA 1992; reg 12 SPPSAP(G) Regs
21 s171ZC(1) and (3)(c) SSCBA 1992; reg 6B SPPSAP(G) Regs
22 s171ZC(1) and (3)(c) SSCBA 1992; reg 12B SPPSAP(G) Regs
23 Regs 6A and 12A SPPSAP(G) Regs
24 Regs 6 and 7 SPP(SAP)(G) Regs
25 Regs 12(1) and 13 SPPSAP(G) Regs
26 Regs 6(2) and 12(2) SPPSAP(G) Regs
27 Regs 7(2)(b), (3) and (6) and 12(2)(c) and (5) SMP&SAP(C) Regs
28 **SMP and SAP** Regs 8 and 13 SMP&SAP(C) Regs
**MA** Reg 6 MA(C) Regs
29 **Father/mother's partner** s171ZU(4)(d) and (g) SSCBA 1992; reg 30 SSPP(G) Regs
**Mother** s171ZU(2)(c) and (f) SSCBA 1992; reg 30 SSPP(G) Regs
30 **Adopter** s171ZV(2)(c) and (f) SSCBA 1992; reg 31 SSPP(G) Regs
**Adopter's partner** s171ZV(4)(d) and (g) SSCBA 1992; reg 31 SSPP(G) Regs
31 **Father/mother's partner** ss171ZU(4)(f) and 171ZZ4(6)-(8) SSCBA 1992; reg 30 SSPP(G) Regs
**Mother** ss171ZU(2)(e) and 171ZZ4(6)-(8) SSCBA 1992; reg 30 SSPP(G) Regs
**Adopter** ss171ZV(2)(e) and 171ZZ4(6)-(8) SSCBA 1992; reg 31 SSPP(G) Regs
**Adopter's partner** ss171ZV(4)(f) and 171ZZ4(6)-(8) SSCBA 1992; reg 31 SSPP(G) Regs
32 **Father/mother's partner/mother** Reg 10 SSPP(G) Regs
**Adopter/adopter's partner** Reg 22 SSPP(G) Regs
33 **Father/mother's partner** Regs 5 and 7 SMP&SAP(C) Regs
**Adopter's partner** Regs 10 and 12 SMP&SAP(C) Regs
34 **Mother** Regs 4 and 7 SMP&SAP(C) Regs
**Adopter** Regs 9 and 12 SMP&SAP(C) Regs
35 **Father/mother's partner** ss171ZU(4)(j)-(p) and 171ZW(1)(b) SSCBA 1992; reg 7 SSPP(G) Regs
**Adopter's partner** ss171ZV(4)(j)-(p) and 171ZW(1)(b) SSCBA 1992; reg 20 SSPP(G) Regs
**Mother** ss171ZU(2)(i)-(o) and 171ZW(1)(b) SSCBA 1992; reg 6 SSPP(G) Regs
**Adopter** ss171ZV(2)(i)-(o) and 171ZW(1)(b) SSCBA 1992; reg 19 SSPP(G) Regs
36 Regs 4(1) and (3), 17(1) and (3) and 29 SSPP(G) Regs
37 ss171ZZ6 and 171ZZ7 SSCBA 1992
38 Reg 4 SPBP(G) Regs
39 Reg 4(1)(g) and (8)(b), (c) and (d) SPBP(G) Regs
40 s171ZZ6(6) SSCBA 1992
41 Reg 7 SPBP(G) Regs
42 Reg 8(1) SPBP(G) Regs
43 Reg 8(2), (3), (4) and (5) SPBP(G) Regs
44 Reg 8(6), (7), (8) and (9) SPBP(G) Regs
45 s171ZZ16 and s171ZZ17 SSCBA 1992, as inserted by Sch Neonatal (Leave and Pay) Act 2023; reg 2 SNCP(G) Regs (draft)
46 s171ZZ16(4) SSCBA 1992; reg 4 SNCP(G) Regs (draft)
47 s171ZZ19(2) to (5) SSCBA 1992; reg 10 SNCP(G) Regs (draft)
48 Reg 7 SNCP(G) Regs (draft)
49 Reg 4 SNCP(G) Regs (draft)
50 Reg 5 SNCP(G) Regs (draft)
51 Regs 3 and 9 SNCP(G) Regs (draft)
52 Reg 11 SNCP(G) Regs (draft)
53 **SMP** s171(1) SSCBA 1992; reg 17 SMP Regs
**SAP&SPP** ss171ZJ(1) and (2) and 171ZS(1) and (2) SSCBA 1992; reg 32 SPPSAP(G) Regs
**SSPP** s171ZZ4(1) SSCBA 1992; reg 33 SSPP(G) Regs
**SPBP** s171ZZ8(1) SSCBA 1992; reg 11 SPBP(G) Regs
**SNCP** s171ZZ18(1) SSCBA 1992; reg 14 SNCP(G) Regs (draft)
54 s171ZZ16(6)(e) SSCBA 1992
55 ss171ZA(2)(d) and 1717ZB(2)(d) SSCBA 1992
56 Regs 30(1)(c) and 31(1)(c) SSPP(G) Regs; s171ZZ16(3) SSCBA 1992; reg 15 SNCP(G) Regs (draft)
57 **SMP** Reg 17 SMP Regs
**SAP&SPP** Reg 32 SPPSAP(G) Regs
**SSPP** Reg 33 SSPP(G) Regs
**SPBP** Reg 11 SPBP(G) Regs
**SNCP** Reg 14 SNCP(G) Regs (draft)

58 **SMP** Reg 17(2) SMP Regs
**SAP&SPP** Reg 32 SPPSAP(G) Regs
**SSPP** Reg 33(4) SSPP(G) Regs
**SPBP** Reg 114) SPBP(G) Regs
**SNCP** Reg 14(4) SNCP(G) Regs (draft)
59 See HMRC guidance at gov.uk/guidance/working-through-an-umbrella-company#how-an-umbrella-company-works
60 **SMP** Regs 2 and 5 SMP(PAM) Regs
**SAP&SPP** Regs 3, 5 and 6 SPPSAP(PAM) Regs
**SSPP** Regs 5 and 7 SSPP(PAM) Regs
**SPBP** Regs 5 and 7 SPBP(PAM) Regs
**SNCP** Regs 5 and 7 SNCP(PAM) Regs
61 **SMP** Reg 4(2)(a) SMP Regs
**SAP&SPP** Reg 5(a) SPPSAP(G) Regs
**SSPP** Reg 30(2) and (3) SSPP(G) Regs
**SNCP** Reg 24(2) SNCP(G) Regs (draft)
62 **SMP** Reg 16A SMP Regs
**SAP&SPP** Reg 35A(2) SPPSAP(G) Regs
**SSPP** Reg 30(1B) SSPP(G) Regs
**SPBP** Reg 15 SPBP(G) Regs
**SNCP** Reg 19 SNCP(G) Regs (draft)
63 **SMP** Reg 11 SMP Regs
**SAP&SPP** Reg 33 SPPSAP(G) Regs
**SSPP** Reg 34 SSPP(G) Regs
**SPBP** Reg 12 SPBP(G) Regs
**SNCP** Reg 16 SNCP(G) Regs (draft)
64 Reg 11(1)(d) and (3) SMP Regs
65 **SMP** Reg 11(3A) SMP Regs
**SAP&SPP** Reg 33(3) SPPSAP(G) Regs
**SSPP** Reg 34(4) SSPP(G) Regs
**SPBP** Reg 12(4) SPBP(G) Regs
**SNCP** Reg 16(4) SNCP(G) Regs (draft)
66 **SMP** Reg 14 SMP Regs
**SAP&SPP** Reg 36 SPPSAP(G) Regs
**SSPP** Reg 37 SSPP(G) Regs
**SPBP** Reg 16 SPBP(G) Regs
**SNCP** Reg 20 SNCP(G) Regs (draft)
67 **SMP** Reg 12 SMP Regs
**SAP&SPP** Reg 34 SPPSAP(G) Regs
**SSPP** Reg 35 SSPP(G) Regs
**SPBP** Reg 13 SPBP(G) Regs
**SNCP** Reg 17 SNCP(G) Regs (draft)
68 **SMP** Reg 20 SMP Regs
**SAP&SPP** Reg 39 SPPSAP(G) Regs
**SSPP** Reg 32(7) and (8) SSPP(G) Regs
**SPBP** Reg 19 SPBP(G) Regs
**SNCP** Reg 23 SNCP(G) Regs (draft)
69 **SMP** Reg 20(2)(a) SMP Regs
**SAP&SPP** Reg 39(2)(a) SPPSAP(G) Regs
**SSPP** Reg 32(7)(a) SSPP(G) Regs
**SPBP** Reg 19(2) SPBP(G) Regs
**SNCP** Reg 23(2) SNCP(G) Regs (draft)
70 **SMP** Reg 21(5) SMP Regs
**SAP&SPP** Reg 40(5) SPPSAP(G) Regs
**SSPP** Reg 32(4) SSPP(G) Regs
**SPBP** Reg 19(6) SPBP(G) Regs
**SNCP** Reg 23(6) SNCP(G) Regs (draft)
71 Reg 21(7) SMP Regs
72 Reg 21B SMP Regs
73 **SAP&SPP** Reg 40(7) SPPSAP(G) Regs
**SSPP** Reg 32(6) SSPP(G) Regs
**SPBP** Reg 19(8) SPBP(G) Regs
**SNCP** Reg 23(8) SNCP(G) Regs (draft)
74 **SMP** s165(4) and (5) SSCBA 1992; reg 9A SMP Regs
**SAP** s171ZN(3) and (4) SSCBA 1992; reg 27A SPPSAP(G) Regs
**SSPP** Regs 4(2)(g), 5(2)(e), 12, 15, 17(2)(g), 18(2)(e), 24 and 27 SSPP(G) Regs
75 s171ZE(5) and (6) SSCBA 1992
76 **SPBP** s171ZZ9(6) SSCBA 1992
**SNCP** s171ZZ19(6) SSCBA 1992
77 Regs 10(1)(a)(i) and 22(1)(a)(i) SSPP(G) Regs
78 ss171ZU(2)(n) and (o) and (4)(o) and (p) and 171ZV(2)(n) and (o) and (4)(o) and (p) SSCBA 1992; regs 10(7) and (8) and 22(5) and (6) SSPP(G) Regs
79 **SMP** s165(6) SSCBA 1992; reg 8(2) SMP Regs
**SAP** s171ZN(5) SSCBA 1992; reg 26(1) SPPSAP(G) Regs
**SPP** s171ZE(7) SSCBA 1992;
**SSPP** ss171ZU(2)(n) and (4)(o), 171ZV(2)(n) and (4)(o) and 171ZY(4) SSCBA 1992, regs 12, 15, 24 and 27 SSPP(G) Regs
**SSBP** s171ZZ9(8) SSCBA 1992; reg 10 SPBP(G) Regs
**SNCP** s171ZZ19(8) SSCBA 1992
80 s165(6) SSCBA 1992
81 Reg 17 SPPSAP(G) Regs
82 **SMP** Reg 8(1) SMP Regs
**SAP** Reg 25 SPPSAP(G) Regs
**SPP** Regs 10 and 16 SPPSAP(G) Regs
**SSPP** Regs 12, 15, 24 and 27 SSPP(G) Regs
**SPBP** Reg 10 SPBP(G) Regs
**SNCP** Reg 13 SNCP(G) Regs (draft)
83 **SMP** Reg 24 SMP Regs
**SAP** Reg 26(2) and (3) SPPSAP(G) Regs
**SPP** Reg 17 SPPSAP(G) Regs
**SSPP** Regs 12(2) and (3) and 24(2) and (3) SSPP(G) Regs
**SPBP** Reg 10 (2) and (3) SPBP(G) Regs
**SNCP** Reg 13(2) and (3) SNCP(G) Regs (draft)

4

5. **Special benefit rules**

84 **SMP** s164(2)(a) and (3) SSCBA 1992
**SAP** s171ZM SSCBA 1992
**SPP** s171ZD SSCBA 1992
**SSPP** s171ZX SSCBA 1992
**SPBP** s171ZZ8 SSCBA 1992
**SNCP** s171ZZ18 SSCBA 1992

85 **SMP** s164(8) SSCBA 1992; reg 3(1) SMP Regs
**SAP** s171ZM(2) SSCBA 1992; reg 30 SPPSAP(G) Regs
**SPP** s171ZD(2) SSCBA 1992; reg 20 SPPSAP(G) Regs
**SPBP** s1717ZZ8(2) SSCBA 1992; Reg 22 SPBP(G) Regs
**SNCP** s171ZZ(2) SSCBA 1992; Reg 27 SNCP(G) Regs (draft)

86 s171ZX(2) SSCBA 1992; reg 42 SSPP(G) Regs

87 s164(2)(a) SSCBA 1992

88 s171ZL(2)(b) and (3) SSCBA 1992

89 s171ZA(2)(b) and (d) SSCBA 1992

90 s171ZB(2)(b) and (d) SSCBA 1992

91 Regs 30(2)(a) and (c) and 31(2)(a) and (c) SSPP(G) Regs

92 s171ZZ6(2)(e) SSCBA 1992

93 Reg 15 SNCP(G) Regs (draft)

94 s165(2) SSCBA 1992; reg 2(3) and (5) SMP Regs

95 Reg 29 SPPSAP(G) Regs

96 ss171(1) and 171ZA(5) SSCBA 1992

97 para 62025 DMG. This guidance relates to MA but it is arguable that a similar approach could be taken for SMP.

98 Reg 16A SPPSAP(G) Regs

99 Reg 6 and Sch SNCP(G) Regs (draft)

100 **SMP** s171(1) SSCBA 1992
**SAP** s171ZL(5) SSCBA 1992
**SPP** ss171ZA(4) and 171ZB(6) SSCBA 1992
**SSPP** ss171ZU(16) and 171ZV(16) SSCBA 1992

101 s171ZZ6(6) SSCBA 1992

102 SSCBA(AAO) Regs; SPP(A)&SAP(AO)(No.2) Regs; The Statutory Shared Parental Pay (Adoption from Overseas) Regulations 2014 No.3093; reg 5, definition of 'overseas adopter', SNCP(G) Regs (draft)

103 Reg 2(2)(c) and (d), (3) and (4) SPPSAP(G) Regs; reg 2 SSPP(G) Regs

104 Regs 3 and 4 SBPB(G) Regs; reg 5 SNCP(G) Regs (draft)

105 **SPP&SAP** SSCBA(APOC) Regs and SPPSAP(POPA) Regs amend SSCBA 1992 and the SPPSAP(G) Regs for parental order cases
**SSPP** SSCBA(APOC) Regs and SSPP(POC) Regs amend SSCBA 1992 and the SSPP(G) Regs for parental order cases
**SPBP** Regs 3 and 4(1)(e) SPBP(G) Regs
**SNCP** Reg 5 SNCP(G) Regs (draft)

106 Reg 14A SPPSAP(POPA) Regs

6. **Claims**

107 **SMP** Regs 22(4) and 23(3) SMP Regs
**SAP&SPP** Reg 47 SPPSAP(G) Regs
**SSPP** Reg 49(3)(b) SSPP(G) Regs

108 Reg 11(11) SNCP(G) Regs (draft)

109 s171ZZ17(3) SSCBA 1992

110 Reg 22(3) SMP Regs

111 **SMP** Reg 31 SMP Regs
**SAP&SPP** Reg 46 SPPSAP(G) Regs
**SSPP** Reg 48 SSPP(G) Regs
**SPBP** Reg 28 SPBP(G) Regs
**SNCP** Reg 32 SNCP(G) Regs (draft)

7. **Getting paid**

112 **SMP** Reg 27 SMP Regs
**SAP&SPP** Reg 41 SPPSAP(G) Regs
**SSPP** Reg 43 SSPP(G) Regs
**SPBP** Reg 23 SPBP(G) Regs
**SNCP** Reg 28 SNCP(G) Regs (draft)

113 **SMP** Sch 13 para 3 SSCBA 1992
**SAP** s171ZP(5) SSCBA 1992
**SPP** s171ZG(2) SSCBA 1992
**SSPP** s171ZZ1 SSCBA 1992
**SPBP** s171ZZ11 SSCBA 1992; reg 21 SPBP(G) Regs
**SNCP** s171ZZ21 SSCBA 1992; reg 26 SNCP(G) Regs (draft)

114 **SMP** Reg 27 SMP Regs
**SAP&SPP** Reg 41 SPPSAP(G) Regs
**SSPP** Reg 43 SSPP(G) Regs
**SPBP** Reg 23 SPBP(G) Regs
**SNCP** Reg 28 SNCP(G) Regs (draft)

115 Reg 21B SMP Regs

116 **SAP&SPP** Reg 44 SPPSAP(G) Regs
**SSPP** Reg 46 SSPP(G) Regs
**SPBP** Reg 26 SPBP(G) Regs
**SNCP** Reg 30 SNCP(G) Regs (draft)

8. **Tax, other benefits and the benefit cap**

117 s4(1)(a)(ii)-(viii) SSCBA 1992
118 **SAP** Reg 27(1)(a) SPPSAP(G) Regs
**SPP** Reg 18(a) SPPSAP(G) Regs
**SSPP** Regs 14(1)(a) and 26(1)(a) SSPP(G) Regs
**SPBP** Reg 9(1)(a) SPBP(G) Regs
**SNCP** Reg 12 SNCP(G) Regs (draft)
119 s35(1)(d) SSCBA 1992
120 s20(2)-(5), (6) and (7) WRA 2007; regs 80, 81, 82A, 82B ESA Regs; regs 73, 74, 75A and 75B ESA Regs 2013

# Chapter 35

# Statutory sick pay



**This chapter covers:**


1. Who can get statutory sick pay (p747)
2. The rules about your age (p752)
3. People included in the claim (p752)
4. The amount of benefit (p752)
5. Special benefit rules (p753)
6. Claims and backdating (p754)
7. Getting paid (p757)
8. Tax, other benefits and the benefit cap (p758)


## Key facts

- Statutory sick pay (SSP) is paid by employers to certain employees who are unfit for work.
- SSP can be paid for up to 28 weeks.
- SSP is a non-means-tested benefit.
- Your entitlement to SSP is not based on your national insurance contribution record, but your usual earnings must be above a certain amount to qualify.
- If you qualify, SSP is the minimum amount your employer should pay while you are sick. You may also be entitled to occupational sick pay under your contract.
- If you disagree with your employer's decision on your entitlement to SSP, or if your employer has failed to make a decision, you can challenge this (see Chapter 54).

***Future changes***

The government plans to make changes to SSP, including removing the requirement to earn at least the lower earnings limit and removing waiting days.[1] The rate of SSP will also change so that for some low earners it is a certain percentage of earnings or the current SSP flat rate, whichever is lower. It is unknown when these changes will come into force, but it may not be before 2026.

See CPAG's *Welfare Rights Bulletin* or the online version of this *Handbook* for updates.

# 1. Who can get statutory sick pay

You qualify for statutory sick pay (SSP) if:[2]
- you are an employee (see below); *and*
- you are incapable of work (see below); *and*
- you are within a period of incapacity for work (see p748); *and*
- you are within your period of entitlement to SSP (see p749); *and*
- the day is a qualifying day (see p751); *and*
- your normal earnings are at least the lower earnings limit for national insurance (NI) contributions (see p750).



There are some groups of people to whom special rules apply (see p753). Certain people do not qualify for SSP (see p749). See below if your employer has dismissed you solely or mainly to avoid paying SSP.

## Employees

To be entitled to SSP, you must be an employee. If you count as an 'employed earner' for NI purposes (you are liable to pay class 1 NI contributions, or would be if you earned enough – see p859), or you would do so but for being under 16, you normally count as an employee for SSP purposes – eg, you may count as an employee if you are an agency worker.

You do not have to have a written contract of employment. Your right to SSP cannot be taken away by any agreement, whether you sign it or not.[3] If your employer dismisses you to avoid paying SSP, see below.

Even if you are an employee, you are treated as if you are not (and so your employer does not have to pay you SSP) if your employer is:[4]
- not resident and not present in Great Britain, and does not have a place of business in Great Britain (and is not treated as having one); *or*
- exempt from social security legislation because of an international treaty.

### Dismissal from work

If your employer dismisses you during your period of entitlement to SSP solely or mainly to avoid paying you SSP, it is still liable to pay you SSP. In these circumstances, your employer is liable to pay you SSP until either your period of entitlement to SSP ends or until your contract would have ended had you not been dismissed, whichever occurs first.[5] If your employer dismisses you for any other reason, you are not normally entitled to SSP from that employer once your contract ends.

## Incapable of work

To qualify for SSP, you must be 'incapable of work'. This has a specific meaning for SSP. To be incapable of work for SSP purposes, you must be:[6]

- incapable of doing work that you could reasonably be expected to do under the terms of your contract because you have a specific illness, or a physical or mental disability; *or*
- treated as incapable of such work (see below).

Usually, after seven days of absence, you need to provide evidence of your incapacity for work (see p756). It is up to your employer to decide whether it accepts that you are incapable of work. If it does not, it does not pay you SSP, although you can challenge its decision. Your employer may consult its own medical adviser (if it has one) or your doctor (with your permission). If your employer refuses to pay you SSP, you can ask HMRC to make a decision (see Chapter 54).



## Treated as incapable of work

Even if you are not actually incapable of work, your employer may treat you as incapable of work if:[7]

- you have been officially excluded or prevented from working because you have (or it is suspected that you have) an infection, disease or contamination detailed under public health legislation, or you have been in contact with someone who has; *or*
- you are under medical care in connection with a specific illness or physical or mental disability; *and*
  - a doctor has stated that you should not work as a precautionary measure or to convalesce; *and*
  - you do not go in to work for your employer.

If you are incapable of work for just part of a day, you must be treated as incapable of work for the whole day provided you do not do any work on that day. If you are a shift worker and you are incapable of work for part of a day but you do some work on that day, you should still be treated as incapable of work for the whole day if you only finish a shift that began the day before and you do not do any work on a shift that starts on that day and ends the next.

## Period of incapacity for work

For SSP to be paid, you must be within a 'period of incapacity for work'.[8] This is defined as four or more consecutive days of incapacity for work. This means that you can only qualify for SSP if you are incapable of work for at least four days in a row. Every day of the week (including Sunday) counts, even if it is not a day on which you would normally work. Days of incapacity for work that fall before or after the period covered by your contract can still be included in your period of incapacity for work (but see p751 if you have not yet started work).

Two or more periods of incapacity for work are 'linked' and treated as a single period if they are separated by eight weeks or less.

## Period of entitlement to statutory sick pay

You only qualify for SSP if you are within 'a period of entitlement'. In certain circumstances, a period of entitlement cannot arise so you do not qualify for SSP.

### When entitlement to statutory sick pay starts

A period of entitlement normally starts on the first day of your period of incapacity for work, unless your contract of employment starts either during your period of incapacity for work or between two periods separated by eight weeks or less (if you have not yet started working for your employer, see p751).[9]



### When entitlement to statutory sick pay ends

A period of entitlement to SSP ends (and so your SSP stops) if:[10]

- your period of incapacity for work ends; *or*
- you reach your maximum 28 weeks' entitlement to SSP from a particular employer in that period of entitlement (see p753); *or*
- your contract of employment ends, including where you leave your job (unless it has been brought to an end by your employer solely or mainly to avoid paying SSP – see p747); *or*
- in some circumstances, you are pregnant or have just had a baby (see p754); *or*
- you reach the third anniversary of the start of that period of entitlement without a break in linked periods of incapacity for work; *or*
- you are in prison or detained in legal custody (see p837).

Two or more periods of incapacity for work separated by eight weeks or less are linked and treated as a single period.[11] It may therefore be possible for you to have a period of entitlement which lasts for three years and not to have exhausted your 28 weeks' entitlement to SSP over that period.

If you have received your maximum 28 weeks' entitlement to SSP from a particular employer and you are still incapable of work, see p753.

If your employer stops paying you SSP because it decides your period of entitlement has ended, see p756.

### When statutory sick pay is not paid

In certain circumstances, a period of entitlement to SSP cannot arise. As a result, you do not qualify for any SSP during your period of incapacity for work.

A period of entitlement cannot arise if:[12]

- your normal weekly earnings are below the lower earnings limit (see p750); *or*
- at some time in the 85 days before the date on which your period of entitlement would have begun, you were entitled to employment and support allowance (ESA) or you would have been entitled had you met the contribution conditions. For this to apply, you must have claimed ESA (or made a claim for another benefit that was treated as a claim for ESA). If you have limited

capability for work, you may qualify for universal credit (UC) and/or ESA instead of SSP; *or*

- at the time when your period of entitlement would have begun there is a strike at your workplace (but see p892); *or*
- you have not yet started work under your contract of employment (but see p751 if you had an earlier contract with the same employer); *or*
- you are in prison or legal custody (see p837); *or*
- at the time when your period of entitlement would have begun, you were entitled to statutory maternity pay (SMP) or, in some circumstances, maternity allowance (see p754); *or*
- you are within the period immediately before or after you give birth (see p754).

4

If your employer decides not to pay you SSP on any of the above grounds, see p756.

**People with low earnings**

You cannot get SSP if your 'normal weekly earnings' are less than the lower earnings limit for NI contributions (£125 a week in 2025/26 – see p860).

Your **'normal weekly earnings'** are calculated by averaging your gross earnings from your employer (ie, before tax and NI contributions are deducted) over the period between:[13]

- your last normal payday before your period of entitlement to SSP began (see below); *and*
- the day after the last normal payday that falls at least eight weeks before this.

Only payments actually made in this period (including the last normal payday before entitlement began, but not including the one at least eight weeks before that) count, even if, in theory, you should have been paid more.[14] However, if your employer has unlawfully withheld *all* of your wages for the period, you should not be excluded from entitlement to SSP only because you have low earnings.[15]

If you are paid every one or more calendar months, your average earnings are calculated by dividing your earnings over the above period by the number of calendar months in the period (to the nearest whole number), multiplying by 12 and dividing by 52. If you are paid at other intervals and the period is not an exact number of weeks, the average is calculated by dividing your earnings by the number of days in the above period and multiplying by seven.

As well as your wages, your gross earnings include payments such as:[16]

- SSP, SMP, statutory adoption pay, statutory paternity pay, statutory shared parental pay, statutory parental bereavement pay and statutory neonatal care pay;
- contractual or occupational maternity pay;

- arrears of pay following reinstatement or re-engagement in your job or a continuation of a contract of employment under particular legislation.

Certain payments (eg, some payments in kind) are ignored.[17]

If you have not been employed long enough to have been paid wages over this eight-week period, your normal weekly earnings are calculated in reference to the period for which you have actually received earnings, or the earnings you are entitled to for a week's work.[18]

See p753 if you have more than one job.



### People who have not yet started work

If you have agreed to work for an employer but have not started work when your period of incapacity for work begins, you are not entitled to SSP from that employer for any day during your period of incapacity for work (so will not be entitled to SSP even from the date you were due to start work). However, you are entitled to SSP if you previously worked for them and there are eight weeks or less between the date your new contract starts and the date your last contract with the employer ended.[19] You do not have to have written contracts for this to apply.

## Qualifying days

You can only be entitled to SSP for 'qualifying days'. SSP is generally not paid for your first three qualifying days, which are known as 'waiting days' (see p752).[20]

Qualifying days are usually the days of the week on which you usually work. Other days may be selected as qualifying days by agreement between you and your employer if they would better reflect your contract of employment – eg, if you work a complicated shift pattern. If you have this type of agreement, a week begins on Sunday and there must be a minimum of one qualifying day in each week.[21]

If you and your employer cannot agree which days are qualifying days, they are presumed to be:[22]

- the days on which it is agreed that you are 'required to work'; *or*
- Wednesday, if it is agreed that you are not required to work on any day in that week – eg, offshore oil workers, who may work two weeks 'on' and then two weeks 'off'; *or*
- if you cannot agree about which days you are or are not required to work, every day in the week, except days on which you and your employer agree that no employee works.

'Required to work' means required by the terms of your contract of employment. Days when you can choose whether to work (eg, voluntary overtime) do not count.[23]

### Waiting days

SSP is not paid for the first three qualifying days in a period of entitlement.[24] These are called **'waiting days'** and, as they must be qualifying days, they are not necessarily the first three days of your sickness.

If your period of incapacity for work can be linked to an earlier one in your period of entitlement with the same employer (see p748), any waiting days you served in the earlier linked period(s) do not have to be served again and you can get SSP from your first qualifying day in your present one.



## 2. The rules about your age

There are no lower or upper age limits for entitlement to statutory sick pay.

## 3. People included in the claim

You claim statutory sick pay for yourself. You cannot claim any increases for your partner or child(ren).

## 4. The amount of benefit

Statutory sick pay (SSP) is payable at a rate of £118.75 a week. The weekly amount of SSP is the same irrespective of how many hours you normally work for your employer each week when you are not sick.[25]

SSP is a daily benefit. It can be paid for periods of less than a week. The daily rate is calculated by dividing the weekly amount by the number of qualifying days you have in that week. A week for these purposes runs from Sunday to Saturday.

***Example***

Evie works in a shop four days a week (Wednesday to Saturday). These are her qualifying days. After injuring her hand, she is incapable of work for just over two weeks. In the week of her injury, she works on Wednesday and is off sick for the rest of the week. Her period of entitlement to SSP begins on Thursday, the first day of her absence, but she is not entitled to SSP for that week as the first three qualifying days in her period of entitlement (Thursday to Saturday) are waiting days. As she is incapable of work for all her qualifying days in the next week, she gets £118.75 SSP. The following week, she is off sick on Wednesday, Thursday and Friday and returns to work on Saturday. She receives £89.06 SSP (£118.75 divided by her four qualifying days to give a daily rate paid for three days).

## People with more than one job

If you cannot work, you are entitled to SSP from any job for which you fulfil the qualifying conditions. So you can get payments of SSP from two different employers or payments for more than one contract with the same employer – eg, if you are both a daytime teacher and an evening tutor with a local authority. However, if your earnings from any of your different jobs are added together when calculating your liability to pay class 1 national insurance contributions (which usually means you contribute less than if they had been treated separately), you can only receive a total of £118.75 a week in SSP from those jobs. In these circumstances, your employers' liability to pay you SSP is apportioned by agreement between them or, if they cannot agree, in proportion to their share of your combined earnings.[26]



It is possible for you to be unable to work on one contract and be entitled to SSP, but be able to work on a different contract – eg, if you perform different tasks for each.

## Maximum entitlement to statutory sick pay

You are entitled to a maximum of 28 weeks of SSP from a particular employer in any one period of entitlement (see p749) – ie, 28 times the weekly rate of SSP.[27]

Once you have reached your maximum 28 weeks' entitlement with a particular employer, you cannot qualify for SSP again from that employer for the same contract until your current period of incapacity for work ends and a new one arises. Previous periods of incapacity for work are linked to your current one and treated as one period if they are separated by eight weeks or less.[28] However, see p749 if you claimed employment and support allowance (ESA) in the intervening period.

If you are still incapable of work after you have received your 28-week entitlement to SSP, consider claiming new-style contributory ESA and/or universal credit (UC) if you are not already claiming it (see Chapters 3 and 26). Note that claiming ESA or UC brings you under the UC system (see p20).

# 5. Special benefit rules

Special rules may apply if you:

- are going abroad (see p1384);
- are pregnant or have recently given birth (see p754);
- are involved in a trade dispute (see p891) or are in prison or detention (see p836).

### Women who are pregnant or who have recently given birth

If you are entitled to statutory maternity pay (SMP – see p719), you cannot get statutory sick pay (SSP) during the maternity pay period. If you are entitled to maternity allowance (MA) on the basis of your own employment or self-employment (see p630), you cannot get SSP during the MA period.[29] Within the limits set out on p633 and p719 (unless your baby is born early), you can choose when your maternity pay or MA period begins. So, for example, your employer cannot insist that you claim SMP or MA at the earliest possible date in order to limit the period for which it has to pay SSP.

4

Even if you are not entitled to SMP or MA, or if you are entitled to MA on the basis that you have helped your spouse or civil partner with their self-employment (see p630):[30]

- you cannot get SSP (because a period of entitlement cannot arise) if your period of incapacity for work started at some time during the 18 weeks which run from the first of the following dates:
  - the beginning of the week in which you had your baby (but see below); *or*
  - if you are incapable of work either wholly or partly because of your pregnancy on a day that falls in the four weeks before your 'expected week of childbirth' (EWC), the beginning of the week that contains the first such day;
- if SSP is already being paid to you (because your period of entitlement started before the above period, or because your incapacity for work was not initially linked to your pregnancy), it stops from the first of the following dates:[31]
  - the first day falling on or after the beginning of the fourth week before your EWC when you are incapable of work wholly or partly because of your pregnancy; *or*
  - the date on which you have your baby.

For the above purposes, a week begins on a Sunday. If your baby is stillborn before you have completed 24 weeks of pregnancy, you qualify for SSP if you satisfy the other conditions of entitlement.

## 6. Claims and backdating

To qualify for statutory sick pay (SSP), you must notify your employer of your incapacity for work, rather than notifying the DWP or HMRC.

### Making a claim

Inform your employer that you are sick (note the time limits on p755). Your employer should then decide whether you are entitled to SSP. You do not need to complete a claim form.

## Telling your employer that you are sick

Your employer can decide the time limit within which you should report your sickness absence and how you should report it. Your employer must take reasonable steps to inform you of what you need to do when you are absent due to sickness. However, for SSP purposes, your employer cannot insist that you report your sickness:[32]

- earlier than the first qualifying day (which is not necessarily your first day of sickness – see p751), or by a specific time on the first qualifying day (but they can require notice at some point during that day); *or*
- personally; *or*
- by providing medical evidence; *or*
- more than once a week; *or*
- on a printed form or other document provided by your employer.

### Time limits

The following time limits apply for notifying your employer.[33]

- You must report your incapacity for work within the time limit set by your employer, if it has taken reasonable steps to inform you of this (unless it requires you to give notice earlier than the first qualifying day).
- If your employer has not taken reasonable steps to inform you, or it has made no arrangements about the notification required, you must report your incapacity for work in writing on or before the seventh day after your first qualifying day (see p751).
- This seven-day time limit, or your employer's time limit, can be extended by one month if you have good cause for the delay. What is 'good cause' is not defined in the regulations, but you must show that your delay was reasonable given the circumstances.
- If it is not practical for you to inform your employer within that time, the time limit can be extended further, provided you have notified it as soon as is reasonably practicable and at the latest on or before the 91st day after your first qualifying day.

Notice sent in a properly addressed prepaid letter is treated as being given on the day it was posted. If you do not notify your employer of your absence within the above time limits, you can still be entitled to SSP (and qualify for a total of 28 weeks' payment in your period of entitlement if you are off work for that long), but your entitlement starts from a later date.[34]

## Information to support your claim

Your employer can require you to provide 'such information as may reasonably be required' to determine your claim for SSP.[35]

## Medical evidence

For the first seven days of your incapacity for work you are only required to provide a self-certificate as evidence of your incapacity for work. Your employer cannot insist on your obtaining a fit note – ie, medical certificate from your doctor.[36]

After the first seven days, employers usually expect you to provide a fit note from a doctor or other registered 'healthcare professional' (a registered nurse, occupational therapist, pharmacist or physiotherapist).[37] On the fit note, your doctor or healthcare professional can state either that you are not fit for work, or that you 'may be fit for work taking account of the following advice'. These statements are not related to your specific job. If your doctor or healthcare professional thinks you may be fit for some work, they can include a description of the effects of your condition on your ability to work and specify whether they think you may benefit from a phased return to work, altered hours, amended duties or workplace adaptations to facilitate your return to work.[38] If you provide other information (eg, a statement from an osteopath or chiropractor), this can be accepted if your employer considers it sufficient.[39] Whatever type of medical information you provide, it is up to your employer to decide whether or not to accept it. See Chapter 54 if you want to challenge your employer's decision.

## Who should claim

Where possible, you should notify your employer of your incapacity for work. If that is not possible, someone else could do so on your behalf. If your employer does not accept that and it cannot be resolved with your employer, the HMRC disputes team could be contacted (see Chapter 54).

## If you claim the wrong benefit

A claim for another benefit cannot be treated as a claim for SSP. However, if you have notified your employer of your sickness but you are not entitled to SSP, you may be able to get a claim for employment and support allowance (ESA) backdated more than the usual three months (see p568).

## Backdating your entitlement

To qualify for SSP, you must notify your employer of your sickness (see p755). Even if you have not notified your employer promptly, your entitlement can still be backdated if you do so within the time limits on p755.

## If statutory sick pay ends or is refused

If your employer decides that you are not entitled to SSP or stops paying you, it should provide you with a statement (usually on Form SSP1) within certain time limits, giving you the reasons for its decision.[40] If you disagree with your employer's decision, see Chapter 54 for how to challenge it.

Whether or not you agree with your employer's decision, you should consider claiming other benefits. If you are not well enough to work, consider claiming new-style ESA and/or universal credit (UC) (see Chapters 3 and 26). Claiming ESA or UC brings you under the UC system (see p19). Get advice if necessary. The DWP usually asks HMRC to make a decision on your entitlement to SSP before it makes a decision on your claim for ESA.



## 7. Getting paid

Statutory sick pay (SSP) is usually paid in the same way and at the same intervals as your wages or salary.

SSP is a daily benefit, so if you qualify for it, it can be paid for periods of less than a week. See p752 for the way the daily rate is calculated.

**Note:**

- If you are entitled to contractual sick pay from your employer at the same time as SSP, SSP forms part of your contractual sick pay.[41]
- Your employer cannot pay you SSP by making a payment in kind or by providing board and lodging, a service or other facilities.[42]
- Deductions that can be made from your wages (eg, union subscriptions) can also be made from your SSP.[43]
- If your entitlement to SSP has been decided by HMRC or by the First-tier Tribunal or Upper Tribunal, your employer may be required to pay your SSP within a certain time limit (see p1257).
- If your employer cannot or will not pay you, see p1258 for details of when HMRC can pay SSP.
- The rules on overpayments and recovery of overpaid benefit described in Chapter 47 do not apply to SSP. If your employer pays you SSP and later decides that you were not entitled to it, it may attempt to recover the overpaid sum by deducting it from your wages. Get advice if this happens. If your employer decides that you have been overpaid SSP in error, consider claiming employment and support allowance. You may be able to get your claim backdated (see p568).

### Change of circumstances

Notify your employer of any change in your circumstances that may affect your entitlement to SSP.

# 8. Tax, other benefits and the benefit cap

## Tax

Statutory sick pay (SSP) is treated like any other earnings. You pay tax and, depending on the amount of your earnings in the same week, national insurance (NI) contributions by pay as you earn (PAYE) in the normal way.[44]

## Means-tested benefits

4

You (and your partner) may be able to claim universal credit (UC) as well as SSP or, if you are already getting UC, you may be entitled to more UC.

For the purpose of qualifying for help with the cost of childcare in your UC, you can be treated as still in paid work while getting SSP (see p76).

When calculating your entitlement to means-tested benefits, SSP is:

- treated as employed earnings for UC. It is your net earnings that are taken into account (see p127);
- treated as earnings for pension credit and housing benefit (HB). It is your net earnings that are taken into account (see Chapters 16 and 17). If you get SSP, an allowance for certain childcare charges may be deducted from your earnings when calculating your entitlement to HB (see p350).

## Non-means-tested benefits

If you are getting SSP, you cannot get:[45]

- employment and support allowance; *or*
- statutory adoption pay (SAP); *or*
- statutory paternity pay (SPP); *or*
- statutory shared parental pay (SSPP); *or*
- statutory parental bereavement pay (SPBP); *or*
- statutory neonatal care pay (SNCP).

You cannot qualify for SSP during your maternity pay period or, if your entitlement is based on your own employment or self-employment, during your maternity allowance (MA) period (see p633).[46] If you get MA on the basis of your spouse's or partner's employment or self-employment, see p754.

SSP may affect your entitlement to some non-means-tested benefits. SSP counts towards the earnings condition for MA, statutory maternity pay, SAP, SPP, SSPP, SPBP and SNCP. SSP counts as earnings for carer's allowance, carer support payment and reduced earnings allowance.

SSP does not affect your entitlement to other non-means-tested benefits.

Unless you have other earnings, such as occupational sick pay, you do not have to pay NI contributions while on SSP as the weekly rate of SSP is below the NI lower earnings limit. Instead, you are entitled to class 1 NI credits (see p867).[47]

## The benefit cap

SSP is *not* one of the specified benefits for the benefit cap.

## Other sources of help

If you are on a low income, you may be entitled to certain health benefits (see Chapter 27). You may be entitled to council tax reduction (see p761).



# Notes

1 ss8 and 9 Employment Rights Bill

1. **Who can get statutory sick pay**
2 ss151-154 SSCBA 1992
3 s151(2) SSCBA 1992
4 Reg 16(2) SSP Regs
5 Reg 4 SSP Regs
6 s151(4) SSCBA 1992
7 Reg 2 and Sch 1 SSP Regs
8 s152 SSCBA 1992
9 s153(2), (7) and (8) SSCBA 1992
10 ss153(2) and (12) and 155 SSCBA 1992; reg 3(1), (3) and (4) SSP Regs
11 s152(3) SSCBA 1992
12 s153(3) and Sch 11 SSCBA 1992; reg 3 SSP Regs
13 s163(2) SSCBA 1992; regs 17 and 19 SSP Regs
14 Sch 11 para 2(c) SSCBA 1992; reg 19 SSP Regs
15 *Seaton v HMRC* [2011] UKUT 297 (TCC)
16 Reg 17 SSP Regs
17 Reg 17(2) SSP Regs
18 Reg 19(7) and (8) SSP Regs
19 Sch 11 para 6 SSCBA 1992
20 ss154 and 155(1) SSCBA 1992
21 s154(3) SSCBA 1992
22 Reg 5(2) and (3) SSP Regs
23 R(SSP) 1/85
24 s155(1) SSCBA 1992

4. **The amount of benefit**
25 s157 SSCBA 1992
26 Regs 20 and 21 SSP Regs
27 s155(2)-(4) SSCBA 1992
28 s152(3) SSCBA 1992

5. **Special benefit rules**
29 s153(2)(d) and (12) SSCBA 1992
30 Reg 3(5) SSP Regs
31 Reg 3(4) SSP Regs

6. **Claims and backdating**
32 Reg 7(1), (4) and (5) SSP Regs
33 Reg 7(1)-(3) SSP Regs
34 s156 SSCBA 1992
35 s14(1) SSAA 1992
36 Reg 2(2) SSP(ME) Regs
37 Reg 1(2), definition of 'healthcare professional', and reg 2(1)(a) SSP(ME) Regs
38 Sch 1 SSP(ME) Regs
39 Reg 2(1) SSP(ME) Regs
40 Reg 15 SSP Regs

7. **Getting paid**
41 Sch 12 para 2 SSCBA 1992
42 Reg 8 SSP Regs
43 s151(3) SSCBA 1992

8. **Tax, other benefits and the benefit cap**
44 s4(1) SSCBA 1992
45 s20(1) WRA 2007; regs 18 and 27 SPPSAP(G) Regs; regs 14(1)(a) and 26(1)(a) SSPP(G) Regs; reg 9(1)(a) SPBP(G) Regs; reg 12(1)(a) SNCP(G) Regs (draft)
46 s153(2)(d) and (12) SSCBA 1992
47 Reg 8B(2)(a)(iii) SS(Cr) Regs

# Chapter 36

# Other payments and support

4

**This chapter covers:**

1. Council tax reduction (p761)
2. Support for mortgage interest loans (p764)
3. Local welfare assistance schemes (p770)
4. Healthy Start food and vitamins (p771)
5. Education benefits (p774)
6. Help with childcare costs (p777)
7. Payments for former members of the armed forces (p779)
8. Financial help when preparing for and starting work (p781)
9. Warm Home Discount (p781)
10. Help to Save (p782)
11. Other financial help (p782)

In addition to the support described in this chapter, you may qualify for discretionary housing payments (see Chapter 25), a hardship payment during a sanction (see Chapter 46), a social fund payment (see Chapter 33) or a benefit advance (see p1023).

## Key facts

- You may be able to get other payments and support in addition to your benefits. For some of these, you must be receiving a qualifying benefit.
- You may be able to get financial help from your local authority – eg, your council tax may be reduced, you may qualify for help under its welfare assistance scheme or your child may be able to get free school lunches.
- If you are an owner-occupier and getting universal credit or another means-tested benefit, you may be offered a loan from the DWP to help with your mortgage interest payments.
- If you are pregnant or a parent, you may be able to get a Healthy Start or Best Start Foods payment card for milk, fruit and vegetables, and free vitamins.
- You can get free childcare, or help with childcare costs, in certain circumstances.
- You may qualify for extra payments if you have an illness or disability due to serving in the armed forces.
- Other sources of financial help are available.

# 1. Council tax reduction

If you need help to pay your council tax, you may be able to get a reduction under your local authority's council tax reduction scheme. In some areas, this is known as council tax support or rebate.

**Note:**

- A council tax reduction is *not* a social security benefit and the general benefit rules in this *Handbook* do not apply.
- As well as, or instead of, a council tax reduction, you may qualify for a **council tax discount** (eg, a 25 per cent discount if you are the only resident) or a **council tax exemption** (eg, if only students occupy the dwelling), which is not means tested and depends on your circumstances. For further information, see CPAG's *Council Tax Handbook*.



In England and Wales, local authorities can devise their own local council tax reduction schemes that must meet minimum requirements. In Wales, if a local authority does not adopt its own scheme, a default scheme applies. Check with your local authority whether it has its own local scheme or the default scheme applies. Scotland has a national scheme administered by local authorities.[1]

Check with your local authority whether you qualify for a council tax reduction. Ensure the rules are being applied correctly in your case. If your local authority has adopted its own scheme, check that it meets the minimum requirements. **Note:**

- You may be able to get extended help for a period if you take up paid work, more paid work or better-paid work.
- In England and Scotland, but not in Wales, there is an alternative maximum council tax reduction (known as 'second adult rebate') designed to help you if you share your home with anyone on a low income.
- In Scotland, if your property is in council tax bands E to H, you may be entitled to additional council tax reduction if your income is below a certain level.

***Can you get a discretionary reduction from your local authority?***

In England and Wales, in addition to its council tax reduction scheme, your local authority has a discretionary power to reduce your council tax bill.[2] Local authorities can reduce the council tax payable in individual circumstances (eg, if you are in financial hardship) and in group cases (eg, during a local emergency, such as flooding). Apply for a discretionary reduction in writing, stating that you are applying for a reduction under section 13A of the Local Government Finance Act 1992, and provide any supporting evidence. If the local authority refuses, you can appeal against its decision to a valuation tribunal.

## Common rules for all applicants

The following basic conditions apply in England, Wales and Scotland for all applicants, whether you are under or over pension age.

- You must be liable for council tax on the dwelling in which you are a resident.[3]
- You must not be a 'person subject to immigration control' (see p1272) and you must satisfy the habitual residence test (see p1301).[4]
- In England, you must make an application for council tax reduction.[5] In Scotland, you must usually make an application, but some local authorities treat you as having applied if you have made a claim for universal credit (UC).[6] Check whether your local authority does this. In Wales, you must usually make an application for council tax reduction, but if you submit a claim for UC you are automatically treated as having applied.[7]
- You can apply for council tax reduction in writing. You can also apply by phone or online if your local authority allows this. If your claim is defective, you must be notified and given at least one month to correct it.
  - If you or your partner have been awarded UC or pension credit (PC) and apply for council tax reduction within one month of applying for that benefit, the date of your application is the date of your benefit claim.
  - If you or your partner are on UC, income-related employment and support allowance (ESA) or PC and apply for council tax reduction within one month of becoming liable to pay council tax for the first time, the date of your application is the date you became liable for council tax.
- Council tax reduction is generally applied by reducing your council tax bill.
- If you disagree with a council tax reduction decision, you can appeal, initially to the local authority. Appeals must be in writing and made within one month of your being sent the decision in Wales or within two months in Scotland. There are no formal time limits for appeals in England.
- If you are not satisfied with the outcome of the appeal, you can make a further appeal to a valuation tribunal (in England and Wales) or the local taxation chamber of the First-tier Tribunal (in Scotland). In England and Wales, you must appeal within two months of the date of the local authority's response. In Scotland, you must appeal within 42 days of the date of the response.[8]

## Common rules for applicants over pension age

The following rules apply in England, Wales and Scotland for applicants of pension age or over. These rules apply if your partner is under pension age, but they do not apply if you or your partner are entitled to UC or income-related ESA.[9]

- If you or your partner are getting the guarantee credit of PC, you are entitled to the maximum council tax reduction, which is 100 per cent of your council tax liability less any non-dependant deductions.
- If neither you nor your partner are getting the guarantee credit of PC, and you have capital over £16,000, you cannot qualify for council tax reduction.

Capital under £10,000 is ignored. If you have capital between £10,000 and £16,000, a tariff income is counted of £1 a week for every £500, or part of £500, over £10,000.
- If you are not getting PC, your applicable amount, income and capital are calculated in a broadly equivalent way to housing benefit (HB) (see Chapters 13, 17 and 19).
- If your income is below your applicable amount, you are entitled to the maximum council tax reduction, which is 100 per cent of your council tax liability less any non-dependant deductions.
- If your income is above your applicable amount, your maximum council tax reduction is reduced by 20 per cent of your excess income.
- A non-dependant deduction may be made for another adult living in your home. The rules for who counts as a non-dependant and when a deduction is made are the same as for HB (see p207), but the amounts are different.
- Your application can be backdated for three months.



## If you are under pension age

### England

The support for working-age people varies from one local authority to another. Some of the main features or the minimum requirements of council tax reduction schemes for people under pension age in England are as follows.[10]
- The capital limit may be less than £16,000.
- If you get income-related ESA, you are entitled to the maximum council tax reduction, but this may be less than 100 per cent of your council tax liability, so you may be required to make a minimum payment.
- Your local authority may set rules to allow your application to be backdated, but is not obliged to do so.
- Your local authority must make a decision within 14 days of receiving your properly completed application, or as soon as is reasonable.

### Wales

Some of the main features of the minimum requirements and the default scheme in Wales for working-age people are as follows.[11]
- You cannot qualify for council tax reduction if you have capital over £16,000. Capital under £6,000 is ignored. If you have capital between £6,000 and £16,000, a tariff income is counted of £1 a week for every £250, or part of £250, over £6,000.
- If you get income-related ESA, you are entitled to maximum council tax reduction, which is 100 per cent of your council tax liability less any non-dependant deductions.
- If you get UC, your applicable amount is your maximum UC, and your income is the figure used by the DWP plus the amount of UC payable. Monthly

amounts are converted to weekly amounts by multiplying by 12 and dividing by 52.

- If you do not get UC, your applicable amount is calculated in a similar way as for means-tested benefits, but all personal allowances and premiums have increased in line with inflation since 2013, even if the equivalent allowances in social security payments have been frozen.
- If your income is below your applicable amount, you are entitled to maximum council tax reduction, which is 100 per cent of your council tax liability less any non-dependant deductions.
- If your income is more than your applicable amount, your maximum council tax reduction is reduced by 20 per cent of your excess income.
- Your application may be backdated for up to three months if you had continuous good cause for not applying earlier.



### Scotland

Some of the main features of the working-age council tax reduction scheme in Scotland are as follows.[12]

- You cannot qualify for council tax reduction if you have capital over £16,000. Capital under £6,000 is ignored. If you have capital between £6,000 and £16,000, a tariff income is counted of £1 a week for every £250, or part of £250, over £6,000.
- There is no two-child limit, and the amount for each child is higher than the child element in UC.
- If your income is below your applicable amount, you are entitled to maximum council tax reduction, which is 100 per cent of your council tax liability.
- If your income is more than your applicable amount, your maximum council tax reduction is reduced by 20 per cent of your excess income.
- Your application may be backdated for up to six months if you had continuous good cause for not applying earlier.
- Arrears of council tax are not recoverable if they are due to an official error that overpaid your council tax reduction.

## 2. Support for mortgage interest loans

If you have a mortgage, the DWP may offer you loan payments to help with the interest payments. You are only eligible for the offer of a loan if you are entitled to universal credit (UC), income-related employment and support allowance (ESA) or pension credit (PC). The DWP calls these support for mortgage interest (SMI) loans.

If you accept a loan for your mortgage interest, regular payments are made, usually direct to your lender.[13] Payments are made monthly (for UC) or four-weekly (for income-related ESA or PC). The amount of each loan payment is calculated using a formula and is not necessarily what you have to pay (see p767).

### *Getting advice*

It is vital to get independent legal and financial advice (eg, from a financial adviser or solicitor) before accepting an SMI loan from the DWP. **Note:** the information about the loan you get from the DWP or its agent (currently in a phone call from Serco) is *not* independent advice.



**Note:**
- An SMI loan is *not* a social security benefit.
- You normally have to repay the loan (see p769). There are exceptions.
- A charge on your property (a standard security in Scotland) is made in favour of the DWP. This enables the DWP to recover what you owe it, if there is sufficient equity in your property.
- The DWP adds interest to the total amount you owe until the earliest of the date the loan is paid back (or written off), or you have died (or until both you and your partner have died) or, in some cases, you are sent a statement of what you owe the DWP so you can repay in full. The rate of interest charged by the DWP is set out in the rules and is 1.1 per cent at the time of writing (see gov.uk/support-for-mortgage-interest/repaying-your-loan).[14]

Even though an SMI loan is not a benefit, if you disagree with a decision about a loan, you can apply for a revision or a supersession, or appeal against the decision under the rules that apply to benefits.[15] You must apply for a mandatory reconsideration before you can appeal. See Chapters 50 and 51.

**Note:** if you have other housing costs (eg, ground rent or service charges), help with these may be included in your UC, income-related ESA or PC. See Chapter 6 for UC and Chapter 14 for the other means-tested benefits.

## Who can get a support for mortgage interest loan

You can get an SMI loan if:[16]
- you are entitled to UC; *or*
- you are entitled (or treated as entitled) to income-related ESA or PC. You are treated as entitled to one of these benefits if you have claimed it and you are not entitled solely because your income is the same as, or more than, your applicable amount (your standard minimum guarantee for PC), but is less than this amount plus the weekly loan payments you would receive if you were entitled.

You must also meet the following conditions:

- your loan qualifies (see below); *and*
- you (or your partner) count as liable to pay your loan (see below); *and*
- your loan is for the home in which you normally live (see p767); *and*
- the DWP offers you an SMI loan and you accept the offer. You (and your partner) must sign and return the loan agreement. You must also create a legal charge (in England and Wales) or a standard security (in Scotland) in favour of the DWP. If you have a partner and both of you are the legal owners of your home, you must both do this. If only one of you is the legal owner, the other must give their written consent.



The DWP must provide you with specified information within the six months before you accept an SMI loan.[17] This includes a summary of the terms and conditions of the DWP loan agreement and information about where you and your partner can get further information and independent legal and financial advice about the loan. A third party may provide the information on the DWP's behalf. Currently, the third party is Serco. The DWP says this information will be provided by phone. **Note:** this information is *not* independent advice.

## Which loans qualify

Depending on which benefit you are entitled to, the SMI loan can cover:[18]

- for UC, interest payments on a loan that is secured on the accommodation you occupy, or are treated as occupying, as a home (see p97), whatever the purpose of the loan; *and*
- for income-related ESA or PC, mortgages and other loans for house purchase and loans used to pay for specified repairs and improvements or to meet a service charge for these. The types of repairs and improvements are those on p288 that are excluded from help with housing costs; *and*
- for UC or PC, 'alternative finance payments' – ie, payments made under alternative finance arrangements to enable you to acquire an interest in the accommodation you occupy, or are treated as occupying, as a home (see p767), such as a Sharia-compliant mortgage.

The rules for the loans that qualify are broadly the same as for the housing costs rules before 6 April 2018. See the 2017/18 edition of this *Handbook* for details. For UC, see pp488–89 and for income-related ESA and PC, see pp46–52.

## Liability for payments

To get an SMI loan, you or your partner must be liable (or treated as liable) to make payments on a qualifying loan.[19] **Note:** in specified situations, you or your partner can be treated as *not* liable to make payments even if you are, including (for UC) if the DWP considers the liability to be contrived.[20]

For UC, the rules for who counts as liable for payments are broadly the same as for the housing costs rules before 6 April 2018. See pp490–94 of the 2017/18 edition of this *Handbook*. For income-related ESA and PC, the rules for who counts as liable are broadly the same as for the housing costs rules in Chapter 14 (see p294).

**Note:** if you are jointly liable to make payments with someone other than your partner, you are only treated as liable for the proportion of the payments for which you (and your partner) are responsible.[21]

## Occupying the accommodation as a home

To get an SMI loan, you must normally occupy the accommodation as your home.[22] You cannot usually get an SMI loan for any other home. However, there are special rules if you:[23]

- have just moved into your home;
- are liable to make payments for more than one dwelling, including if you have left your home because of a fear of domestic violence;
- are temporarily absent from home, including if you are away from home because of a fear of domestic violence;
- are in temporary accommodation while repairs are carried out on your home;
- (for income-related ESA and PC only) are a student or on a training course.

For UC, the rules on occupying accommodation are broadly the same as for the housing costs rules before 6 April 2018. See pp494–98 of the 2017/18 edition of this *Handbook*. For income-related ESA and PC, the rules on occupying accommodation are broadly the same as for the housing costs rules in Chapter 14 (see p294).

# The amount of loan payments

If you accept an SMI loan, regular payments are usually made direct to your lender. Your monthly (for UC) or four-weekly (for income-related ESA or PC) loan payments are worked out by applying a standard percentage rate to the amount you owe to your lender, subject to an upper limit, and dividing by 12 or 52 as relevant.[24] Any income above your applicable amount (for income-related ESA) or appropriate minimum guarantee (for PC) or any unearned income above your maximum amount (for UC) is deducted. Also deducted is the amount of any payment you get under a mortgage protection insurance policy.

The standard rate is the average mortgage rate published by the Bank of England and it changes when the published rate varies by 0.5 percentage points or more.[25] At the time of writing, the rate is 3.66 per cent. The current rate is confirmed at gov.uk/support-for-mortgage-interest/what-youll-get.

**Note:** even if there is a reduction in the amount you owe your lender, your regular loan payments are usually only recalculated annually, on the anniversary of the date you started getting them.[26]

If the amount you owe your lender is more than an upper limit, your loan payments are usually calculated using the upper limit.[27] The upper limit is usually £200,000 if you are entitled to UC or income-related ESA.

If you are entitled to PC, the upper limit is usually £100,000. However, if you are entitled to income-related ESA with an upper limit of £200,000 and you then claim PC within 12 weeks, the £200,000 upper limit continues to apply.[28]

### Deductions for non-dependants

4

No non-dependant deductions or housing costs contributions are deducted from loan payments if you get UC. If you are entitled to income-related ESA or PC, a set deduction is made from your weekly loan payments for people who normally live with you in your home who are not part of your family for benefit purposes (called 'non-dependants').[29] The rules for who counts as a non-dependant, and when a deduction is made, are broadly the same as for the housing costs rules in Chapter 14 (see pp289–91). To calculate the deduction amount, see p292. If you have other housing costs (eg, ground rent or service charges, see p288) and help with these is included in your benefit, the non-dependant deduction is apportioned between the help you get with housing costs and your loan payments.

## When loan payments start and end

Once you have accepted an SMI loan, your regular loan payments start:[30]

- if you are entitled to PC, from your first date of entitlement to PC (there is no waiting period); *or*
- if you are entitled to UC as a couple and one of you was a PC claimant receiving loan payments in the month before your UC award started, from your first date of entitlement to UC (there is no waiting period); *or*
- otherwise, if you are entitled to UC, from the first day of the first assessment period after an initial waiting period of three consecutive assessment periods in which you are entitled to UC. If you were getting loan payments while entitled to (or treated as entitled to) income support, income-based jobseeker's allowance or income-related ESA and claimed UC within one month of that award ending, you do not have to serve the waiting period again for UC; *or*
- from a later start date if you request it.

Loan payments are always made in arrears. Once loan payments start, you can ask to stop getting them at any time. Loan payments end if:[31]

- you are no longer entitled to UC. If you become entitled to UC again within six months, you can qualify for loan payments without the three-month waiting period; *or*
- you are no longer entitled (or treated as entitled) to income-related ESA or PC. If you were getting loan payments because you were entitled to PC, and you

become entitled to UC as part of a couple, you can get loan payments without the three-month waiting period; *or*

- you are no longer liable (or treated as liable) to pay your loan; *or*
- you are no longer occupying (or treated as occupying) your home; *or*
- your SMI loan agreement ends in accordance with its terms.

Check whether you must repay your SMI loan interest (see below).

## Mortgage interest run-on

When you (or your partner) begin work or increase your hours and so count as being in full-time paid work, you no longer qualify for income-related ESA and therefore no longer qualify for an SMI loan. However, if you qualify for mortgage interest run-on, your weekly loan payments continue to be paid for the first four weeks after you go into full-time paid work. The payments are made to you directly instead of to your lender.[32] **Note:** you do not have to make a claim to qualify for mortgage interest run-on; it is paid automatically. However, you must let the DWP know you are starting full-time paid work. The rules are broadly the same as they were before 6 April 2018. See pp474–75 of the 2017/18 edition of this *Handbook*.

## Repaying the loan

The amount of your loan (ie, the total of all the loan payments you have received) and any interest you owe the DWP must normally be repaid in full in any of the following situations.[33]

- You sell your home (although if you have bought a new home, you can request that a loan balance be transferred to your new home).[34]
- Ownership of your home is transferred, assigned or otherwise disposed of. This does not apply if this is to:
  - you, following your partner's death, or your partner, following your death, provided you or your partner live in the home; *or*
  - you, from a former spouse or civil partner under a court order or an agreement for maintenance, provided you live in the home.
- You die or, if you have a partner and they are the owner, they die or, if you are both owners, both of you die (but note the exceptions immediately above).

In the first two situations, repayment is made from the proceeds of the sale, transfer or assignment. In the third situation, repayment is made from the person's estate.

Interest is charged on the amount of loan payments at the average gilt rate published by the Office for Budget Responsibility (at the time of writing, 4.1 per cent) and is set for six-month periods starting on 1 January and 1 July.[35] Check the current rate at gov.uk/support-for-mortgage-interest/repaying-your-loan.

You can repay some, or all, of what you owe before any of the above situations occur, provided you pay at least £100 at a time. **Note:** if your home is transferred, assigned or otherwise disposed of at less than the market value, it is treated as if this happened at market value for the purposes of the repayment rules.[36]

**Note:** if the DWP has a legal charge (in England or Wales) or a standard security (in Scotland) on your home and there is not enough equity to cover the amount you owe, repayment is limited to the amount that is available after other prior ranking charges or securities (eg, your outstanding mortgage) have been paid.[37] This means that if there is insufficient left, or nothing left, after repayment of the prior rankings, any remaining SMI loan interest and any interest you owe the DWP are written off and are considered to be fully repaid.



## 3. Local welfare assistance schemes

Help may be available under local welfare assistance schemes set up by your local authority (in England) or by the devolved administrations (the Discretionary Assistance Fund in Wales and the Scottish Welfare Fund in Scotland). The DWP may refer to this as 'local welfare provision'.

You may qualify if you need help, for example:

- with immediate short-term needs in a crisis – eg, if you do not have sufficient resources, or you need help with expenses in an emergency or as a result of a fire or flood in your home;
- to establish yourself in the community following a stay in institutional or residential accommodation, or to help you remain in the community;
- to set up a home in the community as part of a planned resettlement programme – eg, the Afghan Resettlement Programme;
- to ease exceptional pressure on your family;
- to enable you to care for a prisoner or young offender on temporary release;
- with certain travel expenses – eg, to visit someone in hospital, to attend a funeral, to ease a domestic crisis, to visit a child living with their other parent or to move to suitable accommodation.

In England, the local scheme is at your local authority's discretion (and it may not have one). Check with your local authority to find out what help is available, whether you qualify and how to apply.

In Wales, the Discretionary Assistance Fund offers non-repayable emergency assistance payments and individual assistance payments.

The Scottish Welfare Fund provides community care grants and crisis grants. Local authorities have some discretion about how they operate the fund in their area but they must also follow statutory guidance.[38] You should apply to your local authority.

# 4. Healthy Start food and vitamins

In England and Wales, if you qualify for Healthy Start food and vitamins, you get free vitamins as well as a payment card that can be used to buy specified types of food.

In Scotland, there is a Best Start foods scheme (see p1455).

## Healthy Start food

If you qualify for Healthy Start food, you:[39]

- get a payment card credited with £4.25 or more a week (see p772) that can be used at any shop that sells Healthy Start food and accepts Mastercard; *or*
- get a cash payment of the same value if you cannot use the card within a reasonable distance of your home.

*Healthy Start food*

**'Healthy Start food'** means liquid cow's milk and cow's milk-based infant formula, fresh, frozen or canned fruit, vegetables and pulses including loose, pre-packed, whole, sliced, chopped or mixed fruit or vegetables (but not to which fat, salt, sugar, flavouring or any other ingredients have been added).[40] Some shops that sell food, but not a range of Healthy Start foods, are unable to accept Healthy Start card payments.

### Who can claim

You qualify for a Healthy Start payment card if:[41]

- **you are at least 10 weeks pregnant** and you are:
  - 18 or over and are entitled to (or are a partner or member of the family of someone who is entitled to) a qualifying benefit (see p772);
  - under 18, whether or not you are entitled to a qualifying benefit (but not if you are excluded from these because you are a 'person subject to immigration control' – see p1272); *or*
- **you are a mother** who has parental responsibility for a child under one and:
  - you are 16 or over and entitled to (or you are a partner or member of the family of someone who is entitled to) a qualifying benefit. If you are entitled to universal credit (UC) or pension credit (PC), your child must be under one year old. For other benefits, your child must be under one or it must be less than a year since their expected date of birth. This means you can continue to qualify for credits on your card for a period after your child is one – ie, if they were born prematurely; *or*
  - it is less than four months since your baby's expected date of birth and you have not yet notified Healthy Start that they were born. You must have been entitled to a qualifying benefit before your baby was born. This allows your entitlement to continue until you notify the birth. Once you do, you can

then qualify under the rule above (if you are 16 or over). **Note:** as long as you provided the notification within the four-month period, you can also get extra credit on your card for your child from their date of birth.

If you qualify for more than one child under this rule (eg, you have twins), you get a credit on your card for each. If you do not have parental responsibility but would otherwise qualify, your child qualifies instead of you;[42]

- **you are responsible for a child under four** who is a member of your family. You or a member of the family must be entitled to a qualifying benefit; *or*
- **you are responsible for a child under four** who is a British citizen, you have no recourse to public funds due to your immigration status (see p1276) and your monthly earned income is no more than £408.[43]

4

The **qualifying benefits** are:[44]

- UC, if during the last complete assessment period or the assessment period before that, you (and your partner) have no earnings, or earned no more than £408. If you stop being entitled to UC or your earnings exceed the £408 threshold, you continue to qualify for Healthy Start food vouchers for a further eight weeks after the last complete assessment period;
- PC;
- income-related employment and support allowance (ESA) – a qualifying benefit during pregnancy only.

***Definitions***

**'Parental responsibility'** means parental responsibility as defined in section 3(1) of the Children Act 1989 (in England or Wales).[45]

**'Family'** means a person and their partner and any child or qualifying young person who is a member of their household and for whom they or their partner count as being responsible.[46] So, for example, if you are not entitled to a qualifying benefit but are included in your mother's or father's claim for one of these, you can qualify for Healthy Start. To count as the member of a family of someone entitled to UC, they must be responsible for you under the UC rules (see p260) and must also satisfy the £408 earnings rule described above.

If you are an asylum seeker receiving asylum support, you get an extra amount to help you buy healthy food if you are pregnant or have a child under three.

## The amount of credit

Each week you get £4.25 credited on your card for each of your children aged between one and four, £8.50 for each of your children under one (or within one year of their expected date of birth), plus £4.25 if you are pregnant.

The sums for those receiving asylum support can be higher – see gov.uk/asylum-support/what-youll-get.

*Example*

Leela is 17 weeks pregnant. She has three children: twin girls aged two and a boy aged seven. She is getting UC, has no earnings and does not have a partner. She qualifies for a £4.25 credit because she is more than 10 weeks pregnant. Her twins each qualify for a £4.25 credit as they are under four. Her son does not qualify for a credit. Leela gets £12.75 credited to her card each week. When the baby is born, Leela will be entitled to an £8.50 credit for a child under one, plus a £4.25 credit for each of the twins aged under four, so she will get £17 credited to her card each week.



### Claims

You must make a claim for Healthy Start and must provide specified information and evidence.[47] You can claim:

- if you get UC, online at healthystart.nhs.uk/how-to-apply;
- if you get another qualifying benefit, or you are pregnant and under 18, by email to healthystart@nhsbsa.nhs.uk or by phone on 0300 330 7010;
- if you are not getting a qualifying benefit because you have no recourse to public funds, but your child is a British citizen, request an application form by email to healthystartclaim@dhsc.gov.uk.

If you are getting Healthy Start while you are pregnant and then inform Healthy Start of your baby's birth by phone while they are under four months old, you can get extra credits for them from their date of birth.[48] You may need to make a claim for UC (or add them to your existing UC claim) to ensure that you continue to qualify for Healthy Start. You are still entitled to Healthy Start for a child even if a child element is not payable in UC because of the 'two-child limit'.

If you do not get credits on your payment card to which you think you are entitled, or have any other problems, contact the Healthy Start Issuing Unit on 0300 330 7010 or using the online form at healthystart.nhs.uk/contact-us.

## Healthy Start vitamins

If you qualify for a Healthy Start payment card, you also qualify for Healthy Start vitamins.[49] Vitamin drops are available for children under four, and adult vitamins are available to mothers during pregnancy and until their child's first birthday. Ask your health professional what the local arrangements are for getting these.

You need to show your Healthy Start payment card to collect the vitamins.[50]

For information on vitamins for pregnant women, breastfeeding mothers and children in Scotland, see p1464.

4

# 5. Education benefits

Financial help is available from your local authority if you are in school or are a student, or if you have children in school or college.

## Free school lunches

Children are entitled to free school lunches if their families get:[51]

- universal credit (UC). In Scotland, you and your partner must not have earnings of more than £850 in the UC assessment period before your application. In England and Wales, your and your partner's combined earnings must not exceed the following (only one need apply):
  - £616.67 in the UC assessment period immediately before the date you claim free school lunches; *or*
  - £1,233.34 in total in the two UC assessment periods immediately before the date you claim free school lunches; *or*
  - £1,850 in total in the three UC assessment periods immediately before the date you claim free school lunches;
- income-related employment and support allowance (ESA);[52]
- in England and Wales only, the guarantee credit of pension credit (PC). In Scotland, free school meals may be offered to families receiving the guarantee credit of PC on a discretionary basis.[53]

**Note:** pupils entitled to free school lunches on 31 March 2022 in England or on 31 December 2023 in Wales, or who become entitled to free school lunches via UC after those dates, continue to be entitled until they finish the phase of education (eg, primary or secondary school) that they were in on 31 March 2022 (England) or 31 December 2023 (Wales), whether or not their households continue to get UC.[54] In England, guidance states that any child gaining eligibility for free school meals after 1 March 2018 will be protected against losing free school meals until March 2025 and then until the end of their phase of education.[55]

Also entitled are:

- 16–18-year-olds getting the above benefits in their own right;
- families who have an asylum claim and are receiving asylum support;
- some families with no recourse to public funds or no immigration status, or with some other similar restrictions (eg, with pre-settled status but not accepted as having a qualifying right to reside – see p1307) in England, provided the annual income of a family able to work with one child is less than £22,700 (in London, £31,200) or with two or more children is less than £26,300 (in London, £34,800). In Wales and Scotland, free school meals are extended to these families at the local authority's discretion;[56]

- all children in funded early learning and childcare in Scotland, who can get a free meal which can be breakfast, lunch or dinner.[57]

***Universal free school meals***

**England**: free school lunches are provided to all children in reception, year 1 and year 2.

**Wales**: all primary school children are eligible for free school breakfasts and free school lunches.[58]

**Scotland**: free school lunches are provided to all Primary 1–5 pupils. The Scottish government plans to expand free school lunches to all Primary 6–7 pupils in receipt of Scottish child payment during 2025/26.[59]



## School transport, school clothes, activities and equipment

Local authorities must provide **free transport to school** for pupils aged five to 16 if it is considered necessary to enable the pupil to get to the 'nearest suitable school'. This applies if the pupil lives more than a set distance from that school. However, if there is no safe walking route, a pupil must be given free transport no matter how far away they live from the nearest suitable school. Free school transport must also be provided to pupils with special educational needs and to those whose parents are on a low income – ie, if they qualify for free school lunches.

Local authorities can give **grants for school uniforms and other school clothes**. Each authority determines its own eligibility rules. In Scotland, there are national minimum amounts: you will get at least £120 for a child of primary school age and at least £150 for a child of secondary school age (see mygov.scot/clothing-grants). Some school governing bodies or parents' associations also provide help with school clothing.

In Wales, the School Essentials Grant can help cover the costs of school uniform, **school activities** like learning a musical instrument, and **school equipment** like PE kit, pens, pencils and school bag (see gov.wales/school-essentials-grant-help-school-costs). At the time of writing, the School Essentials Grant scheme is due to end on 31 May 2025.

## Free milk for children

Children under five are entitled to 189–200 millilitres of free milk on each day they are looked after for two hours or more:

- in local authority daycare; *or*
- by a registered childminder or daycare provider; *or*
- in a school, playcentre or workplace nursery which is exempt from registration.

Children under one are allowed fresh milk or infant formula.

In England and Wales, this milk is provided by the Welfare Food Scheme.[60] In Scotland, it is provided by the Milk and Healthy Snack Scheme, which also offers a non-dairy alternative and a healthy snack.[61]

Older schoolchildren may also be provided with free milk, and where it is provided in England and Wales, it should be free for children entitled to free school meals on grounds of low income.[62]

## Free period products

Free period products are available in schools and colleges. In England, if you are in school or aged under 19 in non-advanced education, you should be able to access free period products when you need them. If you are aged 19 or over, you can access free period products if you are continuing on a course you began before 19 or have an education, health and care plan.[63] In Wales, every school and college provides free period products.[64] In Scotland, education authorities are required to make period products available to all school pupils and education providers must do the same for students at college or university.[65]

## Education maintenance allowance and 16 to 19 bursaries

**An education maintenance allowance** is a means-tested payment for young people who stay on in non-advanced education and who live in Wales or Scotland. Payments are made direct to the young person and are conditional on regular course attendance. The young person gets a weekly allowance (of £40 in Wales and £30 in Scotland) during term time. For further details, see studentfinancewales.co.uk or mygov.scot/ema.

**The 16 to 19 bursaries** are payments for young people aged 16 to 19 who stay on in further education or training in England. These are available through the school, college or training provider. Certain young people in need (eg, young people in care, care leavers, young people without parental support who get UC, or those who get UC or ESA and either disability living allowance or personal independence payment) can get the maximum bursary. Discretionary bursaries are available to those in financial difficulty. See gov.uk/1619-bursary-fund for further information.

Neither payment counts as income for any benefits the parent or child may be getting. They are also not affected by any income the young person has from part-time work.

To find out what help is available, contact your local authority or your college or university, or see gov.uk/student-finance.

## 6. Help with childcare costs

### Free early education and childcare

Preschool children are entitled to a certain number of free hours of registered childcare, depending on their age and your circumstances. You may also be able to get help with childcare costs through universal credit (UC) (see p76) for extra hours that are not covered by this free provision, and for childcare for other age groups. The free childcare available differs in each country of the UK.

**Note:** free childcare may not start immediately when your child reaches the qualifying age. Term dates and the date you start a new job or return to work may affect when you can get free childcare. See the individual schemes for details.



#### England

From the age of **nine months**, your child is entitled to 570 hours a year of free childcare (equal to 15 hours a week for 38 weeks) if you are in work and earning within set limits (see p778).[66]

Your child is also entitled to this free childcare place at the age of **two** if:[67]

- you get UC, and your and your partner's combined earnings do not exceed the following (only one need apply):
  - £1,283.34 in the previous assessment period; *or*
  - £2,556.67 in total in the previous two assessment periods; *or*
  - £3,850 in total in the previous three assessment periods; *or*
- you get income-related employment and support allowance (ESA); *or*
- you get the guarantee credit of pension credit (PC); *or*
- you get asylum support from the Home Office; *or*
- your child is looked after by a local authority; *or*
- your child has left care under an adoption order, special guardianship order or child arrangements order; *or*
- your child has a statement of special educational needs or an education, health and care plan; *or*
- your child gets disability living allowance.

At the ages of **three and four**, your child is entitled to 570 hours a year of free childcare (equal to 15 hours a week for 38 weeks), regardless of your income and whether you are in work or not.[68]

Your child is entitled to 1,140 hours a year of free childcare (equal to 30 hours a week for 38 weeks) at the ages of three and four if you are in work and earning within set limits (see p778).[69]

For more information and how to apply, see childcarechoices.gov.uk.

**Note:** under current plans, the 30-hour entitlement for children of eligible working parents will be extended to all children aged nine months to four years from September 2025.[70]

***Earnings rules for working parents***[71]

To qualify for free childcare hours because you are working, you must usually expect to earn at least the amount of the minimum wage at 16 hours a week over the next three months, and no more than £100,000 a year. If you have a partner, you must usually both be working within these individual limits. You can still qualify if one of you works and the other gets carer's allowance (CA) or the carer element of UC, gets ESA or has limited capability for work. You are still treated as in work while you are getting maternity, adoption, paternity, shared parental or other parental payments (see Chapter 34).

## Wales

Your child may be entitled to free childcare and other support at the age of **two or three** under the Flying Start scheme in some areas of Wales. See your local council's Family Information Service for more information.[72]

At the ages of **three and four**, all children are entitled to a minimum of 10 hours a week free early education for 48 weeks of the year, known as Foundation Phase nursery.[73] Your child may also be entitled to up to 30 hours a week childcare for 48 weeks of the year at the ages of three and four if you are in work and earning within set limits, known as the Childcare Offer for Wales. You must usually be earning at least the amount of the minimum wage at 16 hours a week and less than £100,000 a year. If you have a partner, you must usually both be working within these individual limits. You are still treated as in work if you are on statutory leave.[74] The exact amount of childcare you can get depends on your local authority.

## Scotland

At the age of **two**, your child is entitled to 1,140 hours a year of free early education and childcare (around 30 hours a week during term time) if you get:[75]

- UC with earnings no more than £850 in the assessment period before you apply;[76] *or*
- income-related ESA; *or*
- incapacity benefit or severe disablement allowance; *or*
- PC; *or*
- asylum support provided under Part VI of the Immigration and Asylum Act 1999.

Once they are eligible, your child remains entitled to free childcare even if you stop receiving these benefits. Your child also qualifies for 1,140 hours of free childcare from the age of two if they are looked after by the local authority or are the subject of a kinship care order.

At the ages of **three and four**, your child is entitled to 1,140 hours a year of free childcare, regardless of your income and whether you are in work or not.[77]

### Tax-free childcare

Tax-free childcare is a government scheme to help middle and higher income parents with the cost of childcare. Parents of children aged under 12 (under 17, if they are disabled) can apply.[78]

The government tops up each payment of 80 pence you make into an online childcare account by 20 pence. The maximum annual top-up for each child in qualifying childcare is £2,000 (£4,000 for each disabled child). Payments from the account are debited to a registered childcare provider.

Payments can be made up until 1 September after the child's 11th birthday (16th birthday, if they are disabled). There is no limit on how many children you can make payments for.

You (and your partner) must usually both be working and each earning at least 16 times the minimum wage for your age, and your individual earnings must not be expected to exceed £100,000 a year each. One of a couple does not have to be in work if they get CA, carer support payment, contributory ESA or credits for limited capability for work.[79]

**Note:** you cannot be in the tax-free childcare scheme and still get UC.[80] The government may introduce rules that mean you lose all your UC entitlement if you register for the scheme. If you are considering tax-free childcare, you should therefore check whether or not you will be better off. In most cases, you will be better off continuing to claim UC. If you are in any doubt, get advice.

For more information, see childcarechoices.gov.uk.

## 7. Payments for former members of the armed forces

If you are a former member of the armed forces, you can claim under the following schemes, administered by the Ministry of Defence.

You can qualify for **war pension disablement benefits** if you have ill health or a disablement caused by service before 6 April 2005.[81] The degree of your disablement is assessed on a percentage scale (100 per cent disablement qualifies for the maximum award). If you are assessed at 20 per cent or more, you receive a pension, and if you are assessed at under 20 per cent, you get a lump sum (gratuity). You can also qualify for a number of supplementary allowances. Two of these are particularly important.

- **Constant attendance allowance.** You qualify for this if your disablement is assessed at 80 per cent or more, and because of your disablement you require 'constant attendance'.[82] This has the same meaning as either 'attention' or 'supervision' for attendance allowance (AA) or the disability living allowance (DLA) care component (see p521). The allowance is paid at four different rates depending on the number of hours for which you require constant attendance and whether this is in the daytime or at night. If you claim AA, pension age disability payment (PADP), DLA care component or the daily living component of either personal independence payment (PIP) or adult disability payment (ADP), any constant attendance allowance to which you are entitled is deducted from these benefits.[83] **Note:** the top two rates of constant attendance allowance are considerably more than the highest rates of AA/PADP, DLA care component or PIP/ADP daily living component.
- **Mobility supplement.** You qualify for this if your disablement is assessed at 40 per cent or more, and because of your disablement your ability to walk is lost or significantly impaired.[84] This is, in effect, the same test as for the higher rate of the mobility component of DLA. There is a single rate of benefit currently worth £86.00 a week. If you claim the mobility component of DLA, child disability payment (CDP), PIP or ADP, any mobility supplement to which you are entitled is deducted from your DLA, CDP, PIP or ADP entitlement.[85] **Note:** unlike DLA, CDP, PIP and ADP, there is no upper age limit for claiming mobility supplement.

You can qualify for help under the **Armed Forces Compensation Scheme** if you have ill health or a disablement caused by service on or after 6 April 2005.[86] The main benefit is a lump-sum payment. To qualify, you must have had an injury or ill health that comes within one of the specified 'descriptors'. Each descriptor is assigned to a 'tariff level', running from 1 (the most severe) to 15, which determines the amount payable. If you receive an award within tariff levels 1–11, you also qualify for a 'guaranteed income payment', calculated as a percentage of your salary on the day your service in the armed forces ended. Awards are at 30, 50, 75 or 100 per cent, depending on your tariff level.

**Armed forces independence payment** is payable to those entitled to a guaranteed income payment under the Armed Forces Compensation Scheme at the 50 per cent rate or more.[87] It is payable at a rate equivalent to the total of the enhanced rates of both the daily living and mobility components of PIP.

For more information, see gov.uk/government/organisations/veterans-uk or call Veterans UK on 0808 191 4218.

## 8. Financial help when preparing for and starting work

### Flexible Support Fund

You may be able to get some financial support from the Flexible Support Fund, administered by Jobcentre Plus, to help your transition into work after a period of time on benefit – eg, for childcare costs, travel expenses and new clothes for interviews, and training course fees. You are expected to fund travel costs for fortnightly work search interviews yourself, but travelling expenses for additional appointments can be refunded.[88] Payments are discretionary. The Flexible Support Fund can be used more widely for upfront childcare costs before you receive your first wage. Check with your Jobcentre Plus office or employment scheme or programme provider to see what is available. Do this before you start work, because you may have to apply before your job starts or within a short period of starting it.



### Travel discount card

If you are looking for work, you may be eligible for a Jobcentre Plus travel discount card, which entitles you to a 50 per cent reduction on selected rail fares, and on other public transport in some areas. This is available if you have been unemployed and claiming universal credit or jobseeker's allowance for three to nine months if you are aged under 25, or three to 12 months if you are aged 25 or over. You may also qualify if you are claiming other benefits and are 'actively engaged' with a Jobcentre Plus adviser.[89] Some information is available at gov.uk/government/publications/support-to-help-with-the-cost-of-transport.

### Scottish Job Start Payment

In Scotland, you may qualify for a Job Start Payment towards the costs of starting a new job (see p1419).

## 9. Warm Home Discount

You may qualify for a one-off annual discount of £150 on your energy bill under the Warm Home Discount scheme if you get the guarantee credit of pension credit, or you are on a low income and get other qualifying means-tested benefits and meet your energy supplier's criteria. For further information, visit gov.uk/the-warm-home-discount-scheme. This does not affect your entitlement to a cold weather payment (see p714), a winter fuel payment (see p715) or any of the heating payments in Scotland (see Chapter 66).

## 10. Help to Save

Help to Save is a UK-wide government scheme offering a top-up to working people on low incomes who open a new type of savings account and pay into it regularly. To be eligible, you must be getting universal credit (UC) with earnings of at least £846.56 a month (the monthly equivalent of 16 hours a week at the national living wage).[90]

Help to Save accounts last for four years. You can pay in up to £50 a month. After two years, the government will pay a bonus of 50 per cent of your highest balance, and again at the end of the four years. The government bonus is disregarded as capital for UC and other means-tested benefits. Your account can remain open, and you can keep paying into it and receive bonuses, even if you are no longer entitled to the benefit that made you eligible to open it. Help to Save is administered by HMRC. You can withdraw money at any time, but it will affect the amount of your bonus. You can close your account at any time, but if you close your account early, you will not get a bonus and cannot open another account.

See gov.uk/get-help-savings-low-income for more information.

## 11. Other financial help

This *Handbook* focuses on information about social security benefits. However, there is other financial help, or help in kind, to which you may be entitled.

See the *Disability Rights Handbook*, published by Disability Rights UK, for help for those with care needs.

### Food banks

If you are experiencing severe financial hardship (eg, caused by debt or benefit delays), you may be able to get vouchers for food which can be redeemed at a food bank. Vouchers are available from frontline care professionals such as doctors and social workers. Jobcentre Plus staff may also give out vouchers. You can find further information and contact details for many food banks at trussell.org.uk or foodaidnetwork.org.uk/our-members or by contacting your local authority.

You may be able to get help with food or meals through local community groups which are part of the FareShare network. See more information at fareshare.org.uk.

### Repairs, improvements and energy efficiency

Your local authority may be able to provide you with a grant to help with the cost of improving your home. The main types of grants available are:

- home improvement grants; *and*
- disabled facilities grants.

You may also be able to get:

- assistance from a home improvement agency (a local not-for-profit organisation) to repair, improve, maintain or adapt your home, sometimes called 'care and repair' or 'staying put' schemes, or with small repairs, safety checks and odd jobs from a handyperson service. For information see, foundations.uk.com (England), careandrepair.org.uk (Wales) or careandrepairscotland.co.uk (Scotland);
- a grant for help with insulation and other energy efficiency measures in your home. Different schemes operate in England, Wales and Scotland. For further information, visit energysavingtrust.org.uk. See CPAG's *Fuel Rights Handbook*.



## Special funds for sick or disabled people

A range of help is available if you have an illness or disability to assist with things like paying for care services in your own home, equipment, holidays, furniture and transport needs. There is extra financial assistance available if you have haemophilia or HIV contracted via haemophilia treatment. Grants are also available for practical support to help you do your job – eg, to pay for specialist equipment and travel.

For more information, see the *Disability Rights Handbook*, published by Disability Rights UK.

## Help from social services

Local authority social services departments have statutory duties to provide a range of practical and financial help to families, children, young people, older people, disabled people, carers and asylum seekers.

## Charities

There are charities that provide various types of financial help to people in need. Your local authority social services department or local advice centre may know of appropriate charities that could assist you, or you can consult publications, such as *A Guide to Grants for Individuals in Need* and the *Charities Digest*, in your local library. Turn2us has details of charities that can provide financial help on its website turn2us.org.uk, and for many of them you can apply for support directly from there.

## Christmas bonus

You qualify for a Christmas bonus of £10 if you are entitled (or treated as being entitled) to any of the qualifying benefits for at least part of the 'relevant week' (even if the benefit is paid later). The relevant week is usually the week beginning with the first Monday in December.[91]

*Qualifying benefits*[92]

Adult disability payment; armed forces independence payment; attendance allowance; carer's allowance; carer support payment; child disability payment; disability living allowance; contributory employment and support allowance which includes either the support or the work-related activity component; long-term incapacity benefit; industrial death benefit for widows or widowers; industrial injuries disablement benefit (if it includes unemployability supplement or constant attendance allowance); pension age disability payment; pension credit (PC); personal independence payment; Scottish adult disability living allowance; severe disablement allowance; state retirement pension; war disablement pension (if it includes the mobility supplement, constant attendance allowance or unemployability supplement, or if you are at least pension age – see p690); war widow's or surviving civil partner's pension; and widowed parent's allowance.

You may also qualify for an extra bonus for your partner (a further £10) if they have not received a bonus in their own right, and:[93]

- you are both at least pension age (see p690) and you are entitled, or may be treated as entitled, to an increase in one of the qualifying benefits in respect of them; *or*
- you are both at least pension age and the only qualifying benefit you get is PC.

The bonus is not taxable and has no effect on other benefits.

It is paid automatically. However, you should contact the DWP within a year if you have not obtained your bonus, otherwise your right is lost.[94]

# Notes

1. **Council tax reduction**

1 ss13A and 80 LGFA 1992
**E** CTRS(DS)E Regs; CTRS(PR)E Regs
**W** CTRS(DS)W Regs; CTRSPR(W) Regs
**S** CTR(S) Regs; CTR(SPC)S Regs

2 s13A(1)(c) LGFA 1992

3 ss13A(1) and 80 LGFA 1992

4 **E** Regs 12 and 13 CTRS(PR)E Regs
**W** Regs 28 and 29 CTRSPR(W) Regs
**S** Regs 16 and 19 CTR(S) Regs; regs 16 and 19 CTR(SPC)S Regs

5 **E** Sch 7 para 1 CTRS(PR)E Regs
**S** Regs 22-30 CTR(S) Regs; regs 61-68 CTR(SPC)S Regs

6 Reg 24 CTR(S) Regs

7 Sch 12 paras 1-7 CTRSPR(W) Regs; reg 11 The Council Tax Reduction Schemes (Prescribed Requirements and Default Scheme) (Miscellaneous Amendments) (Wales) Regulations 2025 No.59
8 **E** Sch 7 para 8 CTRS(PR)E Regs
**W** Sch 12 paras 8-10 CTRSPR(W) Regs
**S** Regs 93-94 CTR(S) Regs; regs 70A-70B CTR(SPC)S Regs
9 **E** Reg 3 CTRS(PR)E Regs
**W** Reg 3 CTRSPR(W) Regs
**S** Reg 12 CTR(SPC)S Regs
10 CTRS(PR)E Regs
11 CTRSPR(W) Regs
12 CTR(S) Regs

2. **Support for mortgage interest loans**
13 Reg 17 LMI Regs
14 Reg 15 LMI Regs
15 s8(3)(bc) SSA 1998
16 Regs 2(1) and (aa), 3, 4 and 5 LMI Regs
17 Regs 5(2)(d) and 6 LMI Regs
18 Regs 2 and 3(2)(a) and Sch 1 LMI Regs
19 Reg 3(2)(b) and Sch 2 LMI Regs
20 Sch 2 paras 3 and 6 LMI Regs
21 Reg 3(3) LMI Regs
22 Reg 3(2)(c) and Sch 3 LMI Regs
23 Sch 3 paras 4-10 and 13-18 LMI Regs
24 Regs 2(1), 7, 11, 12, 13 and 14A LMI Regs
25 Reg 13 LMI Regs
26 Regs 2(1), 11(4) and (5) and 12(4) and (5) LMI Regs; reg 7(12B) SS&CS(DA) Regs
27 Regs 11(1), (2) and (3) and 12(1) and (2) LMI Regs
28 Reg 11(2) LMI Regs; 'modified rules' is defined in reg 2 by reference to the Social Security (Housing Costs Special Arrangements) (Amendment and Modification) Regulations 2008 No.3195. These do not specify UC but the information on gov.uk/support-for-mortgage-interest/what-youll-get says the higher limit applies when moving from other benefits to PC.
29 Reg 14 LMI Regs
30 Regs 2, definition of 'qualifying period', 8 and 21 LMI Regs
31 Reg 9(1)-(3) and (8) LMI Regs
32 Reg 9(4)-(6) LMI Regs
33 Reg 16 LMI Regs
34 Reg 16A LMI Regs
35 Reg 15 LMI Regs
36 Reg 16(7) LMI Regs
37 Reg 16(4), (5) and (6) LMI Regs

3. **Local welfare assistance schemes**
38 Welfare Funds (Scotland) Act 2015; The Welfare Funds (Scotland) Regulations 2016 No.107; Scottish government, *Scottish Welfare Fund: statutory guidance – March 2021*, available at gov.scot

4. **Healthy Start food and vitamins**
39 Regs 5(2) and 8 HSS&WF(A) Regs
40 Regs 2(1) and 5(1) and Sch 3 HSS&WF(A) Regs; HSS(DHSF)(W) Regs
41 Reg 3 HSS&WF(A) Regs
42 Reg 3(5) HSS&WF(A) Regs
43 healthystart.nhs.uk/how-to-apply
44 Reg 3(8)-(11) HSS&WF(A) Regs
45 Reg 2(1) HSS&WF(A) Regs
46 Reg 2(1) HSS&WF(A) Regs
47 Reg 4 and Sch 2 HSS&WF(A) Regs
48 Reg 4(2) HSS&WF(A) Regs
49 Reg 3 HSS&WF(A) Regs
50 Reg 8A HSS&WF(A) Regs

5. **Education benefits**
51 **E** s512ZB Education Act 1996; Free School Lunches and Milk, and School and Early Years Finance (Amendments Relating to Universal Credit) (England) Regulations 2018 No.148
**W** s512ZB Education Act 1996; The Free School Lunches and Milk (Universal Credit) (Wales) Order 2019 No.187 (W.47)
**S** s53(7) and (8) Education (Scotland) Act 1980; reg 4A The Education (School Lunches) (Scotland) Regulations 2009 No.178
52 In England only, rules providing for this seem to have been removed from 31 March 2022 – see the Welfare Reform Act 2012 (Commencement No.30 and Transitory Provisions) Order 2018 No.145. However, in practice, free school lunches in this context have continued: see gov.uk/apply-free-school-meals.
53 COSLA, *Good Practice Principles for School Meal Debt Management*, available at cosla.gov.uk
54 Art 3 Welfare Reform Act 2012 (Commencement No.30 and Transitory Provisions) Order 2018 No.145; art 3 The Free School Lunches and Milk (Universal Credit) (Wales) Order 2019 No.187
55 gov.uk/government/publications/free-school-meals-guidance-for-schools-and-local-authorities

56 **E** Department for Education, *Providing Free School Meals to Families with No Recourse to Public Funds*, October 2024
**W** Welsh government, *No Recourse to Public Funds (NRPF): guidance*, March 2023, gov.wales/no-recourse-public-funds-nrpf-guidance-html
**S** See mygov.scot/school-meals
57 The Education (School Lunches) (Scotland) Regulations 2015 No.269; mygov.scot/school-meals
58 s88 School Standards and Organisation (Wales) Act 2013; Welsh government, *Universal Primary Free School Meals*, gov.wales/universal-primary-free-school-meals-upfsm
59 Scottish Budget 2025/26
60 Reg 18 WF Regs
61 The Milk and Healthy Snack Scheme (Scotland) Regulations 2021 No.82
62 **E&W** s512ZB Education Act 1996
**S** s53 Education (Scotland) Act 1980
63 Department of Education, *Period Product Scheme for Schools and Colleges in England*, 7 September 2023
64 Welsh government press release, 15 February 2023, gov.wales/period-products-are-not-luxury-and-access-them-even-more-important-during-cost-living-crisis-vows
65 s2 Period Products (Free Provision) (Scotland) Act 2021

6. **Help with childcare costs**
66 Reg 2(5)(b) The Childcare (Free of Charge for Working Parents) (England) (Amendment and Transitional Provision) Regulations 2023 No.1330
67 Reg 1(2), definition of 'eligible child', The Local Authority (Duty to Secure Early Years Provision Free of Charge) Regulations 2014 No.2147; The Local Authority (Duty to Secure Early Years Provision Free of Charge) (Amendment) Regulations 2018 No.146
68 Reg 3 The Local Authority (Duty to Secure Early Years Provision Free of Charge) Regulations 2014 No.2147
69 Reg 44 The Childcare (Free of Charge for Working Parents) (England) Regulations 2022 No.1134
70 Reg 2(8) The Childcare (Free of Charge for Working Parents) (England) (Amendment and Transitional Provision) Regulations 2023 No.1330
71 Regs 14-18 The Childcare (Free of Charge for Working Parents) (England) Regulations 2022 No.1134
72 gov.wales/get-help-flying-start
73 gov.wales/sites/default/files/publications/2019-03/foundation-phase-nursery-guide-for-parents-and-carers.pdf
74 gov.wales/childcare-3-and-4-year-olds
75 The Provision of Early Learning and Childcare (Specified Children) (Scotland) Order 2014 No.196
76 The Provision of Early Learning and Childcare (Specified Children) (Scotland) Amendment Order 2024 No.73
77 The Provision of Early Learning and Childcare (Specified Children) (Scotland) Order 2014 No.196
78 childcarechoices.gov.uk
79 Childcare Payments (Eligibility) Regulations 2015 No.448
80 ss30 and 31 Childcare Payments Act 2014

7. **Payments for former members of the armed forces**
81 The Naval, Military and Air Forces Etc. (Disablement and Death) Service Pensions Order 2006 No.606
82 Reg 8 The Naval, Military and Air Forces Etc. (Disablement and Death) Service Pensions Order 2006 No.606
83 **AA, DLA and PIP** Reg 6 SS(OB) Regs
**PADP** Reg 26(3) DAOP(S) Regs
**ADP** Reg 34(4) DAWAP(S) Regs
84 Reg 20 The Naval, Military and Air Forces Etc. (Disablement and Death) Service Pensions Order 2006 No.606
85 **DLA** Reg 42(1) SS(C&P) Regs
**CDP** Reg 23(6) DACYP(S) Regs
**PIP** Reg 61(1) UC,PIP,JSA&ESA(C&P) Regs
**ADP** Reg 34(6) DAWAP(S) Regs
86 The Armed Forces and Reserve Forces (Compensation Scheme) Order 2011 No.517
87 Regs 24A-24F The Armed Forces and Reserve Forces (Compensation Scheme) Order 2011 No.517

8. **Financial help when preparing for and starting work**
88 DWP, Universal Credit Guidance, *Flexible Support Fund*, v31.1, House of Commons library deposited papers, rightsnet.org.uk/resources/universal-credit-guidance
89 See response to Freedom of Information request 'Job Centre Discount Card', 2 August 2015 on whatdotheyknow.com

10. **Help to Save**
90 The Savings (Government Contributions) Act 2017; The Help-to-Save Accounts Regulations 2018 No.87

11. **Other financial help**
91 ss148(1), 149(1) and 150(4) SSCBA 1992
92 ss149(4) and 150(1) SSCBA 1992
93 ss148(2) and (5) and 150(2) SSCBA 1992
94 Reg 38 SS(C&P) Regs

# Part 5

# Special benefit rules

# Chapter 37

# Benefits for students

**This chapter covers:**


1. Universal credit (p792)
2. Employment and support allowance (p797)
3. Housing benefit (p801)
4. Other benefits (p804)
5. Student income and means-tested benefits (p806)


England, Scotland and Wales have separate education systems with different student funding.

This chapter covers only those benefits which are potentially affected if you are studying.

## Key facts

- If you are a part-time student, your benefits are not usually affected by your studying, although there are extra conditions to meet for jobseeker's allowance and, for some students, universal credit.
- Most full-time students are excluded from claiming means-tested benefits. There are some exceptions, including for parents, disabled students and some young people on further education courses.
- Even if you can claim means-tested benefits, most student funding for living costs counts as income and reduces or stops your benefit.
- If you are a full-time student and are taking time out from your course but have not abandoned it completely, you still count as a student and cannot usually claim benefits, but there are some exceptions.
- Certain benefits, including maternity allowance, statutory sick pay, child benefit, disability living allowance, child disability payment, personal independence payment and adult disability payment, have no special eligibility rules for full-time students, so you can claim these in the same way as anyone else.

# 1. Universal credit

For more information about when you come under the universal credit (UC) system, see p20.

Undertaking a course of study (the law refers to this as 'receiving education') may mean that you are not eligible for UC, unless you are in one of the groups of people for whom an exception is made (see p793). In general, these are students with children, some disabled students and young students in non-advanced education who have no parental support.

There is an exception for full-time students who are managed migrated to UC, which allows them to be eligible for UC where they would not normally be eligible (see p29).

5

## Receiving education

If you are receiving education, in most cases you are not eligible for UC.[1] There are exceptions (see p793).

You are 'receiving education' if you are:[2]

- undertaking a full-time course of advanced education. This is education above the level of advanced NVQ, AS/A level or a Scottish national qualification (higher or advanced higher), and includes degree-level or postgraduate-level courses and HNDs; *or*
- undertaking another full-time course of study or training for which a loan or grant is provided for your maintenance.

In addition, you are treated as receiving education if:

- you are a 'qualifying young person'. You must be enrolled on, or accepted on, a course of non-advanced education or approved training of more than 12 hours a week, and you must have been enrolled on, accepted on or have started the course before you turned 19. You can continue to be a qualifying young person until 31 August after your 19th birthday (see p63).[3] A qualifying young person on a 'relevant training scheme' is not treated as receiving education. This includes someone on a traineeship[4] or on certain courses or schemes of work or voluntary work preparation. If you have left education, you are still a qualifying young person until 31 August after your 16th birthday; *or*
- none of the above three bullet points apply, but you are on a course that is not compatible with your work-related requirements (see p794).[5]

You count as receiving education from the day you start, to the last day of your course, or sooner if you abandon it or are dismissed from it.[6]

Whether a course is 'full time' is a question of fact and relates to the course and not the student. Generally, what the educational establishment says is conclusive, but there may be exceptions, such as if a student has exemptions from part of the course.[7]

If you are undertaking a part of a modular course (one that consists of two or more modules, and your college or university requires you to successfully complete a specific number of modules before it considers you to have completed the course), you count as undertaking it for the period beginning on the day that part of the course starts, and ending on the last day on which you are registered with your college or university as attending or undertaking that part of your course. This includes any vacations, unless that vacation follows the last day on which you are required to attend or undertake your course, or on such earlier date that you finally abandon or are dismissed from that part of the course.[8]

If you have failed examinations or failed to complete a module, any period in which you undertake the course to retake those examinations or modules is classed as part of the course and you are treated as undertaking a course (even if your college or university registers you as a part-time student during your resit period).[9]

5

## Who is entitled to universal credit while receiving education

You are eligible for UC while receiving education (although at least some of your student funding may count as income) if you are:[10]

- under 21 on a non-advanced course (or you are aged 21 and turned 21 on the course) and are 'without parental support' (see below); *or*
- responsible for a child or qualifying young person (p62); *or*
- a single foster parent; *or*
- a member of a couple, both of you are full-time students and one of you is responsible for a child or is a foster parent; *or*
- assessed as having or treated as having limited capability for work for UC (see p895) and you also get attendance allowance, pension age disability payment, disability living allowance, child disability payment, personal independence payment or adult disability payment. It must have been decided that you have limited capability for work before the date you start receiving education; *or*
- over pension age (see p239); *or*
- a student with a partner who is not a student, or who is a student but would be entitled to UC themself while receiving education;[11] *or*
- waiting to return to your course after taking time out because of illness or caring responsibilities (see p797).[12]

### *Without parental support*

**'Without parental support'** means you are not looked after by a local authority and you:[13]

– have no parent; *or*

– cannot live with your parents because you are estranged from them, or because there is a serious risk to your physical or mental health, or you would suffer significant harm if you lived with them; *or*

– are living away from your parents, and they cannot support you financially because they are ill or disabled, in prison or not allowed to enter Britain.

**'Parent'** includes a person acting in place of a parent.

A **'person acting in place of a parent'** can include a local authority or voluntary organisation if you are being cared for by them, or foster carers, but only until you leave care.[14] It does not include a person who is your sponsor under the Immigration Rules.[15] This depends on the facts but, for example, living with a friend's parents does not necessarily mean they are acting as your parent.[16]

**'Estrangement'** implies emotional disharmony,[17] where you have no desire to have any prolonged contact with your parents or they feel similarly towards you. It is possible to be estranged even though your parents are providing some financial support or you still have some contact with them. If you are being cared for by a local authority, it is also possible to be estranged from the local authority. If you are, you could qualify for UC if you have to live away from accommodation provided by a local authority.[18]

5

## When someone else can claim for you

If you cannot get UC yourself, someone may be able to claim for you if you are a 'qualifying young person' – ie, generally, if you are under 20 and in non-advanced education (see p62 and p259).

## Your work-related requirements

Most people claiming UC have work-related requirements as a condition of getting benefit, which may involve undertaking work-related activity or looking for work (see p938). You have no work-related requirements if you are receiving education and are eligible for UC (unless you are only eligible under the last bullet point above – waiting to return to your course) and you are:[19]

- under 21 (or 21 and you turned 21 on your course) in non-advanced education and 'without parental support' (see p793); *or*
- in receipt of student income which is taken into account for UC – ie, a student loan or a maintenance grant (see p795). For English- or Welsh-funded students, if your student income is a postgraduate loan, this only applies if your course is full time. **Note:** you may have work-related requirements over the summer vacation, when student income is ignored.

**Note:** even if you do not fit into one of the above groups, you may have no work-related requirements under the general rules – eg, if you are responsible for a child under one or if you are severely disabled (see p950).

If you are receiving education but do not get a loan or grant, you may therefore be subject to all work-related requirements, and must be available for and actively seeking work (see p959). This is more likely to be the case if you are in non-advanced education or on some postgraduate courses.

## Studying part time

If you are on a part-time course, you may still be treated as receiving education if the course is not compatible with your work-related requirements.[20] So if you are subject to all work-related requirements, you must show that you meet these despite being on a part-time course. In some cases, it may be possible to argue that the course should be seen as 'voluntary work preparation' and therefore reduce your work search requirements (see p941).[21]

If you are on a part-time course that is accepted as compatible with your work-related requirements, you can get UC.

## How student income affects universal credit

If you (or your partner) have any student income, it may count as income for UC.[22] You are counted as having student income if you are undertaking a course and have a student loan or grant in respect of that course.[23]

5

### Grants

The term 'grant' means an educational grant or award. It does not include a grant paid to someone under 21 in non-advanced education to enable them to finish a course.[24] This means that education maintenance allowance payments and 16 to 19 bursary fund payments do not count as student income. Access or discretionary fund payments are likely to count as student income (as an 'educational grant'), unless they can be disregarded under the rules below (although note that one-off payments count as capital rather than income).

**If you get a grant but do not get a loan**, the grant income is taken into account for UC. Certain amounts of your grant are disregarded as your income if they are:[25]

- for tuition fees or exams;
- in respect of your disability;
- for extra costs of residential study away from your usual place of study during term time;
- to pay for the costs of your normal home (if you live somewhere else during your course), unless your UC meets these;
- for the maintenance of someone who is not included in your UC claim;
- for books, equipment, course travel costs or childcare costs.

**If you get a grant and also get a loan** and your grant is paid for the same period, it is completely disregarded unless it is for the maintenance of someone who is part of your UC claim (eg, a partner or a child) or for rent payments that are met by UC.[26]

### Student loans

Student loans for maintenance count as income if you could get a loan by taking 'reasonable steps', even if you choose not to apply for one.[27] If you do not have a loan because of 'principled and conscientious' objections to taking one out, you may be able to argue that you should not be treated as having a loan as taking one out would not be a 'reasonable step' for you, but much will depend on the facts in your case.[28] The maximum loan you could be entitled to (or 30 per cent of the maximum for a postgraduate master's degree or doctoral loan in England or Wales[29]) is taken into account as income.

This is the case even if the loan is reduced by an assessed parental (or partner) contribution, or if a grant replaces part of the loan. However, if you are eligible for a special support element as part of your maintenance loan in England, this is disregarded, as it is paid for books, travel, equipment and childcare.[30] You may need to get a statement from Student Finance England explaining your entitlement. The special support loan in Scotland is disregarded in the same way as the special support element of the loan in England.[31]

5

The Welsh government learning grant is taken into account as income, as it is a grant replacing part of the loan.[32]

Tuition fee loans are ignored. Note that if you need to use your maintenance loan to pay your tuition fees, your maintenance loan still counts as income.[33]

## Calculating student income

UC is paid for an assessment period of one month (see p49). Student income counts as income in assessment periods that fall during the course, as well as in the assessment period in which the course, and any subsequent year of the course, begins.[34] Student income is ignored in the assessment period during which the end of the course or the start of the long vacation falls. The long vacation is the longest holiday, lasting at least a month, in a course which is at least two years long. Student income is also ignored in any other assessment period that falls completely within the long vacation.[35]

In each assessment period, £110 of student income is disregarded for anyone with student income.

To work out how much of your student income is taken into account.

- **Step 1:** calculate your annual loan or grant or, if the course lasts for less than a year, the amount of loan or grant for the course.
- **Step 2:** work out how many assessment periods apply for that year, or for the course if it is less than a year long.
- **Step 3:** divide the amount from Step 1 by the number of assessment periods in Step 2.
- **Step 4:** deduct £110.

***Example***

Georgianna gets a student loan of £11,658 in total. This includes a special support element of £4,327, which is disregarded, leaving £7,331. Year one of her course runs from 23 September 2024 to 9 May 2025. Her assessment periods run from the 20th of the month to the 19th of the following month. Her loan counts as income for seven assessment periods.

£7,331 ÷ 7 = £1,047.29

£1,047.29 – £110 = £937.29

Georgianna's UC is calculated on student income of £937.29 a month from 20 September 2024 to 19 April 2025.

## Taking time out from your course

During a temporary absence from your course, you usually still count as receiving education, so the student rules apply. Therefore, if you take time out because you have to resit exams or you are ill, you still count as receiving education and are only eligible for UC if you are in one of the eligible groups (see p793) – eg, you are a parent.

You do not count as receiving education and can claim UC if you have taken time out from your course because of illness or caring responsibilities, you have now recovered or your caring responsibilities have ended, you are not eligible for a grant or student loan and you are waiting to return to your course.[36] Your institution must have agreed to your taking time out, and you must have recovered from your illness or your caring responsibilities must have ended within the last year.

If you leave your course completely, you no longer count as receiving education, so the normal UC rules apply. Student income is taken into account up to the end of the assessment period before the one in which you leave the course.

If you take time out of a modular course, which amounts to time out of 'a part' of such a course, it may be argued that you do not count as undertaking a course during that period.[37]

## Giving up your course

If you abandon or are dismissed from your course, you no longer count as receiving education. You can then claim UC in the normal way (see p36).[38]

# 2. Employment and support allowance

Whether you can qualify for employment and support allowance (ESA) while studying full time depends on the type of ESA.

You can qualify for **contributory ESA** as a full-time or part-time student (see p557).

You cannot qualify for **income-related ESA** if you are receiving education unless you are getting disability living allowance (DLA), child disability payment

(CDP), personal independence payment (PIP), adult disability payment (ADP) or armed forces independence payment (AFIP) (see below). You may be able to qualify if you are studying part time (see p801).

**Note:** in certain circumstances, if you are attending a training course and are paid a training allowance, you cannot qualify for ESA because you do not count as having limited capability for work (see p901).[39]

You are treated as a student until either the last day of your course or until you abandon or are dismissed from it.[40] The 'last day of the course' is the date on which the last day of the final academic year is officially scheduled to fall.[41]

## Who is entitled to income-related employment and support allowance

5

You cannot make a new claim for income-related ESA (see p21).

However, if you currently get contributory ESA and do not come under the universal credit (UC) system (see p20), you can also qualify for income-related ESA if your income is low enough.

If you are receiving education, you can only qualify for income-related ESA if you are getting DLA, CDP, PIP, ADP or AFIP.[42] This usually applies for the duration of your course, including vacations. See p800 if you have finished studying.

For income-related ESA, you count as 'receiving education' if you are:

- a 'qualifying young person' for child benefit purposes (see p488), but not if you are on a traineeship;[43] *or*
- undertaking a 'course of study'.[44] The DWP may refer to you as a 'full-time student'. A course of study includes a sandwich course (see p799), but does not include a traineeship.

**Note:**

- The term 'full-time student' is used in the rest of this section to refer to someone who is receiving education for income-related ESA purposes.
- Unless you are a 'qualifying young person' for child benefit purposes, if you qualify for income-related ESA as a full-time student because you are getting DLA, CDP, PIP, ADP or AFIP, you automatically count as having limited capability for work (see p896).[45]

### Full-time student

**In England and Wales,** your course counts as full time and you are treated as a full-time student if:[46]

- it is fully or partly funded by the Secretary of State under section 14 of the Education Act 2002 or section 100 of the Apprenticeships, Skills, Children and Learning Act 2009, or by the Welsh government, and your personal 'learning agreement' involves more than 16 hours of guided learning each week. Courses include academic or vocational courses leading to a recognised qualification. The Secretary of State and the Welsh government also fund basic literacy and numeracy courses, English as a Second or Other Language (ESOL) programmes, Access and similar courses that prepare you to move on to qualification-bearing courses, and courses developing independent living skills for people with learning difficulties. The number of guided learning hours you do each week is set out in your learning agreement. This is signed by the college. The DWP uses this agreement to decide whether or not you are on a full-time course;[47] *or*

- it is not funded by the Secretary of State under section 14 of the Education Act 2002 or section 100 of the Apprenticeships, Skills, Children and Learning Act 2009, or the Welsh government, and is a 'full-time course of study'.

**In Scotland**, your course counts as full time and you are treated as being a full-time student if:[48]

- it is totally or partly funded by the Scottish Ministers at a college of further education, is not higher education *and* your personal learning document states that your course:
  - involves more than 16 hours a week of classroom-based or workshop-based programmed learning under the guidance of a teacher; *or*
  - involves more than 21 hours' study a week, 16 hours or less of which involve classroom-based or workshop-based programmed learning, and the rest of which involve using structured learning packages with the help of a teacher.

  Your learning document sets out the number of hours of 'learning' you do each week. This is signed by the college. The DWP uses this document to decide whether or not you are on a full-time course; *or*
- it is a course of higher education which is funded wholly or in part by the Scottish Ministers and is a full-time course of study; *or*
- it is not funded by the Scottish Ministers and is a full-time course of study.

5

### Sandwich courses

A course is a 'sandwich course' if it consists of alternate periods of full-time study at your educational institution and periods of industrial, professional or work experience organised so that, taking the course as a whole, you attend the periods of full-time study for an average of at least 18 weeks in each year.[49] This does not apply if it is a course of initial teacher training. If your periods of full-time study and work experience alternate within any week of your course, the days of full-time study are aggregated with each other and with any weeks of full-time study to determine the number of weeks of full-time study in each year.

Work experience includes periods of employment abroad for modern language students whose course is at least half composed of modern language study.

### Health-related courses

If you attend a health-related course for which you are entitled to receive an NHS bursary, you are treated as a full-time or part-time student as appropriate and not an employee.[50]

### Modular courses

A modular course consists of two or more modules, and your college or university requires you to successfully complete a specific number of modules before it considers you to have completed the course.[51] You are treated as a full-time student if you are currently attending part of a modular course that would be classed as a full-time course.[52] You are treated as a full-time student for the period beginning on the day your course is defined as a full-time course and ending on the last day on which you are registered with your college or university as attending or undertaking that part of your course. This includes any vacations, unless that vacation follows the last day you are required to attend or undertake your course, or on such earlier date that you finally abandon or are dismissed from that part of the course.[53]



If you have failed examinations or failed to complete a module, any period you attend or undertake the course to retake those examinations or modules is classed as part of the full-time course and you are treated as a full-time student (even if your college or university registers you as a part-time student during your resit period).[54]

Because the rules do not define what is a full-time course, unless funded by the Secretary of State under section 14 of the Education Act 2002 or section 100 of the Apprenticeships, Skills, Children and Learning Act 2009, by the Welsh government or by the Scottish Ministers (see p799), you may be able to argue that you are not attending a full-time course, regardless of your attendance, if your course is not defined as full time or part time by your college or university.[55]

**Note:** if you take time out of a complete 'part' of a modular course, you may not count as undertaking a course during this time.[56]

## Maintaining two homes

If you are a full-time student and qualify for income-related ESA, you may be entitled to help with the costs of more than one home if you have to live away from your normal home to attend a course. For further details, see p298.

## When you stop being a full-time student

Once you stop being a full-time student, you may be able to get income-related ESA (see Chapter 9). However, bear the following in mind.

- If you were a 'qualifying young person' for child benefit purposes (eg, you were under 20 and on a full-time course of non-advanced education – see p488), you continue to count as a qualifying young person for a period after your education or training ends – eg, if you have enrolled on another course or during the child benefit 'extension period' (see p490). While you continue to be treated as a qualifying young person, you can only qualify for income-related ESA if you are receiving DLA, CDP, PIP, ADP or AFIP. If you cannot qualify for ESA in your own right, your parents may be able to continue to claim child benefit and UC for you.

- If you counted as a full-time student other than because you were a 'qualifying young person' for child benefit purposes (see p488), you continue to be treated as a full-time student until the last day of your course, or until you abandon the course or are dismissed from it.

### Studying part time

You can qualify for income-related ESA if you do not count as a full-time student under the rules described on p798.

### When someone else can claim for you

If you are under 20, a 'qualifying young person' for child benefit purposes (see p488) and cannot qualify for ESA because you are 'receiving full-time education' (see p797) or are a full-time student (see p798), someone else may be able to qualify for child benefit and UC if they are treated as 'responsible' for you.

5

### How student income affects employment and support allowance

There are special rules for assessing your income from your student grant, loan or other types of student support (see p806). The normal rules for assessing your other income and capital apply (see Chapters 16 and 18).

## 3. Housing benefit

You cannot usually make a new claim for housing benefit (HB) (but see p21 for the exceptions).

**Note:** if you are eligible for HB, and you (and any partner) have reached pension age, the student rules for HB do not apply and there are no restrictions on your studying and qualifying for HB.[57] However, if you are pension age and your partner is not, the student rules do apply (unless you have transitional protection as a mixed-age couple – see p196).

Whether you can get HB depends on whether you are classed as a full-time or a part-time student. The rules for deciding whether you are a full-time student are similar to those for employment and support allowance (ESA) (see p798), except that there is no separate rule in HB if you are a 'qualifying young person'.

If you are a full-time student, you cannot usually qualify for HB, but there are some exceptions (see p802).

You are treated as a student until either the last day of your course or until you abandon or are dismissed from it.[58] The 'last day of the course' is the date on which the last day of the final academic year is officially scheduled to fall.[59]

## Full-time students who are entitled to housing benefit

You can qualify for HB (although new claims cannot usually be made, and most student funding counts as income) if:[60]

- you are on universal credit (UC) (except if your UC includes an amount for housing costs (see Chapter 6)) or income-related ESA; *or*
- you are under 21, not following a course of higher education (higher education includes degree courses, teacher training, HND, HNC and postgraduate courses), or are aged 21 and you reached that age while on such a course and are still on it, or you are a child or a 'qualifying young person' for child benefit purposes (see p488); *or*
- you and your partner are both full-time students and either or both of you are responsible for a child or qualifying young person (see p488); *or*
- you are a lone parent responsible for a dependent child or qualifying young person aged under 20 (see p488); *or*
- you are a lone foster carer and the child has been formally placed with you; *or*
- you meet the conditions for the disability premium (see p272). You cannot qualify for a disability premium if you have limited capability for work; *or*
- you have been (or have been treated as) incapable of work (see p683 of the 2013/14 edition of this *Handbook*) for 196 days (28 weeks); *or*
- you have had (or have been treated as having) limited capability for work (see p895) for 196 days (28 weeks) and you continue to have it. Two or more periods are joined to form a single period if they are separated by 12 weeks or less. **Note:** claims from 27 October 2008 are assessed under these rules rather than the incapacity for work rules in the bullet point above, unless, broadly, you already get incapacity benefit; *or*
- you meet the conditions for the severe disability premium (see p275); *or*
- you qualify for a disabled students' allowance because you are deaf; *or*
- you are waiting to go back to your course, having taken approved time out because of an illness or caring responsibility and this has now ended.

**Note**: even if you are a full-time student who comes into one of the above groups, you cannot qualify for HB if the circumstances under either of the two headings below apply to you.

### Being away from your term-time accommodation

Even if you are a full-time student who can qualify for HB, if your main reason for occupying your home is to enable you to attend your course, you cannot qualify for HB on that home for any full week when you are absent from it outside your period of study (see p807).[61]

This rule does not apply if:

- you are away from home because you are in hospital;[62] *or*
- the main reason for occupying your home is *not* to enable you to attend your course but for some other purpose – eg, to provide a home for your children or

for yourself because you do not have a home elsewhere to live when you are not attending your course. If this applies, any absences outside your period of study are dealt with under the temporary absence rules (see p191).

### Accommodation rented from an educational establishment

If you are a full-time student who can qualify for HB (see p802), you can usually get HB even if you rent your accommodation from your educational establishment.[63] If you are a part-time student, this rule applies if you could qualify for HB if you were treated as a full-time student.

You cannot, however, get HB if you are a:

- full-time student waiting to go back to your course, having taken approved time out because of illness or caring responsibilities and your illness or caring responsibilities have not yet ended; *or*
- part-time student whose only basis of entitlement to HB if you were a full-time student would be that you are receiving income-related ESA.

The above two exceptions do not apply if:

- your educational establishment itself rents the accommodation from a third party other than on a long lease or where the third party is an education authority providing the accommodation as part of its functions; *or*
- the accommodation is owned by a separate legal body – eg, a company established to build halls of residence.

You cannot get HB if the local authority decides that your educational establishment has arranged for your accommodation to be provided by a person or body other than itself to take advantage of the HB scheme.

### Maintaining two homes

The rules about claiming HB for two homes are explained on p195. If you are one of a couple and receive HB for two homes, the assessment of HB for each home is based on your joint income and your applicable amount as a couple.

## Part-time students

You may be able to qualify for HB if you are studying part time. The rules for deciding whether you are a part-time student are similar to the rules for ESA (see p798), except that there is no separate rule in HB if you are a qualifying young person.

## Partners of students

If your partner is not a student, they can qualify for HB if they meet the qualifying conditions.[64] The claim is assessed in the normal way, except that the rules about being away from term-time accommodation (see p802) apply to your partner's claim.[65] Additionally, the special rules for assessing any income you receive from a grant, loan and other types of student support apply (see p806).

### How student income affects housing benefit

If you or your partner are on UC or income-related ESA, you are entitled to maximum HB (see p201).

If you are not on UC or income-related ESA but you or your partner are eligible for HB, your entitlement is calculated in the same way as for other claimants (see Chapters 16 and 18), except that there are special rules for assessing the amount of your income from grants, loans and other types of student support (see p806). **Note:** for courses lasting more than one year, in many cases loans and grants are not counted as income over the summer vacation. You may find therefore that your HB entitlement is higher over this period, and that you need to check that your entitlement is reviewed at that time.

5

### Payments

Students are covered by all the normal rules on the administration and payment of HB (see Chapter 10). However, there is a provision that can apply specifically to students. The local authority may decide to pay a rent allowance once each term, although students have the same right as other claimants to insist on fortnightly payments if their entitlement is more than £2 a week.[66]

## 4. Other benefits

### Carer's allowance

You cannot qualify for carer's allowance (CA) (see Chapter 22) if you are in full-time education.[67] Usually, if the university, college or school describes the course as full time, you are regarded as being in full-time education, although there may be exceptions – eg, if you are exempted from parts of the course.[68] So the actual hours you attend may not be crucial. However, if you are attending for 21 hours a week or more (as specified by the institution), you are treated as being in full-time education. When calculating the 21 hours, include only hours spent in 'supervised study'. Ignore any time spent on meal breaks or unsupervised study undertaken on or off the premises of the educational establishment.[69]

If you have left school, but have not yet reached compulsory school leaving age, you cannot get CA until after your compulsory school leaving age.[70]

You are treated as still being in full-time education during vacations and any temporary interruption of the course, but not if you have abandoned the course or been dismissed from it. If an interruption is not temporary (eg, if you have agreed with your institution to take a whole year out of your course), you may be able to claim CA.[71]

**Note:** if you cannot get CA because you are a full-time student, you cannot get a carer element in universal credit (UC) (if you are eligible for UC while studying).

*Supervised study*

**'Supervised study'** does not depend on whether your supervisor (ie, teacher, tutor, lecturer) is present with you.[72] If your study is directed to your course of education and the curriculum of your course and it is undertaken to meet the reasonable requirements of your course, it normally counts as supervised study. It counts regardless of whether that study is undertaken on or off the premises of the educational institution you attend.

**'Unsupervised study'** means work beyond the reasonable requirements of your course.

In assessing your hours of attendance, evidence from your educational institution about the amount of time you are expected to study to complete your course is important.



## Carer support payment

In Scotland, you claim carer support payment (CSP) instead of CA (see p1468). You can usually qualify for CSP if you are a student, but may not be eligible if you are aged 16–19 on a non-advanced course of 'full-time education' or approved training, or under 20 and being provided with 'appropriate full-time education' in England (see p490).[73] Those aged 16–19 in non-advanced full-time education are not excluded from CSP if they are someone who would qualify for UC while receiving education (except if the reason they would qualify is that they are waiting to return to their course after taking time out due to illness or caring responsibilities (see p793)).[74]

'Full-time education' is education undertaken in pursuit of a course, where the average time spent during term time in receiving tuition, engaging in practical work, supervised study or taking examinations exceeds 21 hours a week, ignoring meal breaks and unsupervised study time (see definitions above for CA).

## New-style jobseeker's allowance

Students who are in relevant education cannot claim new-style jobseeker's allowance (JSA). You are in relevant education if you are:[75]

- a qualifying young person (see p63) (unless you are on a traineeship); *or*
- on a full-time course of advanced education; *or*
- on another full-time course for which a loan or grant is provided for your maintenance (or would be available upon application); *or*
- on a course which is not compatible with your work-related requirements.

**Note:** if you are in relevant education, you can only claim new-style JSA if you took time out because of illness or caring responsibilities and in the past year you have recovered or the caring responsibilities have ended, you are not eligible for a student loan or grant and you are waiting to rejoin your course.

### National insurance credits

You may be able to receive national insurance credits (see Chapter 39) for a tax year in which you were on a full-time course.

## 5. Student income and means-tested benefits

The rules in this section apply to income-related employment and support allowance (ESA) and housing benefit (HB). They apply if you are a part-time or a full-time student. If you are claiming universal credit (UC), see p795.



There are many types of financial support available for students, paid as either grants or loans. Some types of grant or loan are available to all students who meet the entitlement conditions. Others are available on a discretionary basis. The support varies depending on whether you live in England, Wales or Scotland. For more information, see gov.uk/student-finance, studentfinancewales.co.uk, studentinformation.gov.scot or CPAG's *Benefits for Students in Scotland Handbook* (available free at cpag.org.uk/handbooks).

If you (or your partner) are a student, some of your (or your partner's) income from your grant, loan and certain other forms of student support is taken into account when calculating the amount of your benefit.[76] Your other income and capital are dealt with under the normal rules (see Chapters 16 and 18).

**Note:** the DWP has issued guidance to decision makers on how student support should be treated. Often this guidance only covers some of the benefits to which this section refers. For example, guidance may have been issued for HB purposes, but no equivalent guidance has been issued for ESA. In addition, the legislation and guidance may not cover all sources of student support across the UK, particularly as new sources of support are introduced.

- This section applies to support available to new students for the 2024/25 academic year. For how grants and loans are treated for students who started their course in previous academic years, see the previous editions of this *Handbook*.
- Grant and loan income do not affect your new-style jobseeker's allowance, contributory ESA or carer support payment.
- Any student income you have from a grant or loan is not taken into account as income if you are claiming HB and you are getting income-related ESA or UC.[77]

### Grants

Student grants include any kind of educational grant or award, bursary (such as those paid by the NHS for certain health-related courses), scholarship, studentship, exhibition or supplementary allowance.[78] Payments from access funds (see p812), education maintenance allowances or similar payments are not treated as grants.

Some grants are ignored as income (see p808) and others are taken into account. When calculating income from a grant, certain amounts can be disregarded.

If you are assessed as entitled to a parental or partner's contribution to your grant, it counts as income, whether or not it has been paid to you.[79] However, only the amount of contribution you actually receive counts if, for ESA, you are a lone parent, or a full-time student who gets disability living allowance (DLA), child disability payment (CDP), personal independence payment (PIP) or adult disability payment (ADP).

## Calculating grant income

Your grant income is apportioned:[80]

- if it is payable for your period of study (unless you are attending a sandwich course), over the number of benefit weeks in your period of study; *or*
- if it is payable for a period other than your period of study, over the number of benefit weeks in the period for which the grant is payable.



In most cases, the former applies and your grant income is assessed over a period starting from the 'benefit week' which coincides with (or immediately follows) the first day of your 'period of study' (see below) and ending with the benefit week, the last day of which coincides with (or immediately precedes) the last day of your period of study. In this context, 'benefit week' means the week for which benefit is paid.[81]

This means your grant income is apportioned over the number of complete benefit weeks in your period of study. Any part weeks at the beginning or end of that period are ignored.

### *Period of study*

'**Period of study**' means:[82]

- for a course of one year or less, from the start of the course to the last day of the course;
- for a course of more than one year, in the first and subsequent years (but not the final year), from the start of the course or the start of the year of the course to:
  - if the grant is payable for a period of 12 months, the day before the start of the next year of the course; *or*
  - in any other case, the day before the start of your normal summer vacation;
- in the final year of a course lasting more than one year, from the start of the final year of the course to the last day of the course.

Dependants' grants are taken into account over the same period as the student loan if you have a student loan or you are eligible for one.[83]

If you are attending a sandwich course, your grant income is taken into account over a different period. Any periods spent on placement or work experience in your period of study are excluded and your grant is apportioned over the remaining benefit weeks in your period of study. **Note:** this only applies if your grant is payable for your period of study. If your grant is payable for a different period, it is taken into account over the number of benefit weeks in the period for which it is payable.

## Grant income that is ignored

The following grant income is ignored:[84]

- any allowance for tuition and examination fees;
- disabled students' allowance;
- any allowance to meet the cost of residential study away from your normal educational establishment during term time;
- any allowance for the cost of your normal home (away from college) but, for ESA, only up to the amount of your rent that is not met by HB;
- any amount for a partner or child living abroad;
- any amount for the childcare costs of a dependent child;
- any amount for the cost of books and equipment;
- any amount for travel costs related to course attendance;
- parents' learning allowance;
- Welsh government learning grant for further education students;
- special support payment in Wales;[85]
- if you have been required to contribute to your own grant (eg, because you have other income, such as maintenance), an amount equivalent to that contribution is disregarded.[86] In the case of a couple, the amount of any contribution that one member has been assessed to pay to their partner who is a student is disregarded from the non-student's income;[87]
- an education maintenance allowance, 16 to 19 bursary or similar payments, including a Care to Learn payment;[88]
- higher education bursary for care leavers in England.

In addition to the above amounts, the following fixed sums are ignored.[89] These disregards apply only to the grant you receive for your period of study and not to any supplementary allowances you may be paid during the long vacation.[90]

- A fixed amount of £390 for books and equipment (2024/25 academic year). If your grant includes a specific amount to cover the cost of books and equipment, that amount is ignored in addition to this fixed amount.
- A fixed amount of £303 for the cost of travel (2024/25 academic year). If your grant includes a specific amount to cover the cost of travel expenses for attending your course, that amount is ignored in addition to this fixed amount. If your actual travel costs are higher than any sum specified in your grant for travel (which is ignored under the rules above) plus this fixed amount, the additional costs are not ignored and are taken into account.[91]

Note:

- If you also receive a student loan, the fixed amounts for books and equipment and for travel are not disregarded when calculating your grant income, but are disregarded from your loan income instead (see below).
- For these purposes, the 2024/25 academic year began on 1 August 2024 if your period of study (see p807) began in August 2024. If your period of study began on or after 1 September 2024, the fixed sums apply from that date.

## Loans

Student loans are treated as income, but certain amounts can be disregarded. **Note:** some supplementary allowances paid under the student loan provisions are paid as non-repayable grants and are treated as grant income (see p806).



### Calculating income from a student loan

How your, or your partner's, student loan is treated depends on whether your course lasts for one year or less, or for a longer period (see p811).[92]

The maximum amount of available loan is taken into account as income, even if you do not apply for a loan or for the maximum amount.[93] If you do not have a loan because of 'principled and conscientious' objections to taking one out, you may be able to argue that you should not be treated as having a loan as taking one out would not be a 'reasonable step' for you, but much will depend on the facts in your case.[94] If you get a postgraduate master's degree or doctoral degree loan in England or Wales, 30 per cent of the maximum is taken into account.[95] However, for ESA only, if you do not get a loan while you are taking time out because of ill health, there is no assumed loan taken into account.[96] The special support element in a maintenance loan for full-time undergraduate students in England is ignored as income[97] – you may need to get a statement from Student Finance England showing the breakdown of your loan entitlement. The special support loan in Scotland is disregarded in the same way as the special support element of the loan in England.[98]

You are treated as having a parental or partner's contribution to your loan and this is taken into account as income, whether or not it has been paid to you. However, only the amount of contribution you actually receive counts if, for ESA, you are a full-time student who gets DLA, CDP, PIP or ADP (see p798).[99]

A student loan for maintenance and a supplementary allowance paid to a student on a Postgraduate Certificate in Education course are treated in the same way as student loans and supplementary allowances for undergraduate students.

If you are on a health-related course funded by the NHS, only the lower maximum loan rate should be taken into account.

### Loan income that is ignored

The following are ignored.

- Loans paid for tuition fees (known as a 'fee loan' or a 'fee contribution loan').[100]

- If you have been required to make a contribution to your own loan (eg, because you have other income, such as maintenance), an amount equivalent to that contribution is disregarded as income.[101]
- In the case of a couple, the amount of any contribution that one member has been assessed to pay to their partner who is a student is disregarded from the non-student's income.[102]

Also ignored is a fixed amount of:[103]
- £390 for the cost of books and equipment (2024/25 academic year); *and*
- £303 for the cost of travel (2024/25 academic year).

5

**Note:** for these purposes, the 2024/25 academic year began on 1 August 2024 if your period of study (see p807) began in August 2024. If your period of study began on or after 1 September 2024, the fixed sums apply from that date.

£10 a week is ignored for each week in the period over which your loan income is taken into account (see below). This amount may overlap with other disregards applied to certain war pensions (see p354) and access funds (see p812). A combined maximum sum of £20 a week can be ignored.

## The period over which loan income is taken into account

Loan income is apportioned over a period of 'benefit weeks'.

The first benefit week may fall before the start of your actual academic year and the last benefit week may fall either before or after the last day of your academic year (academic years vary between educational institutions). This may mean your benefit is recalculated several times depending on when your actual academic year falls in relation to the relevant benefit weeks. You must make a new claim (if you still can) or check that your entitlement is revised at these times.

### *Academic year*

The rules give a definition of an 'academic year' for the purposes of calculating student loan income. This definition may be different from the actual academic year of the educational institution you attend. **'Academic year'** means a period of 12 months beginning on 1 January, 1 April, 1 July or 1 September, according to whether your course begins in the winter, the spring, the summer or the autumn respectively. If you are required to begin attending your course during August or September and to continue attending through the autumn, the academic year of your course is treated as beginning in the autumn rather than the summer – ie, from 1 September.[104]

If you are required to start attending your course in August, or your course is for less than one academic year, the period begins with the benefit week, the first day of which coincides with, or immediately follows, the first day of the course.[105]

If your academic year does not start on 1 September, your loan payable for that academic year is apportioned equally between the benefit weeks in the period beginning with the benefit week, the first day of which coincides with, or immediately follows, the first day of that academic year and ending with the benefit week, the last day of which coincides with, or immediately precedes, the last day of that academic year. Excluded from that are any benefit weeks falling entirely within the quarter during which, in the decision maker's opinion, your longest vacation falls.[106]

*Quarters*

**'Quarter'** means one of the periods from 1 January to 31 March, 1 April to 30 June, 1 July to 31 August, or 1 September to 31 December.[107]

In the first, or only, year of your course, your loan income (calculated under the rules below) is ignored for each benefit week that falls before the start of your 'period of study' (the first day of the first term). This is because you cannot be treated as a student until you actually start your course.[108]

**A course lasting for one academic year or less**

Your loan is apportioned over the benefit weeks beginning with the benefit week, the first day of which coincides with, or immediately follows, the first day of the 'academic year' (or, if a course begins in August, from the first day of the first benefit week on or after the first day of the course) and ending with the benefit week, the last day of which coincides with, or immediately follows, the last day of the course.

**A course lasting for more than one academic year**

Unless it is your final year, your loan is apportioned over the period from the earlier of:

- the first day of the first benefit week in September; *or*
- the first benefit week, the first day of which coincides with, or immediately follows, the first day of the autumn term.

It is taken into account until the last day of the benefit week that coincides with, or immediately precedes, the last day of June.

**Final year of a course**

Your loan is taken into account over the period beginning with either:

- if the final academic year starts on 1 September, the benefit week, the first day of which coincides with, or immediately follows, the earlier of 1 September or the first day of the autumn term; *or*

- the benefit week, the first day of which coincides with, or immediately follows, the first day of the academic year.

It is taken into account until the benefit week, the last day of which coincides with, or immediately precedes, the last day of the course.

### Income from other types of loan

Any financial support you receive in the form of a loan (other than a student loan), including a loan received from an overseas source, does not count as a student loan or a grant.[109] It is taken into account as 'other income' (see p352).

## Discretionary funds and other payments

Access funds (which include the discretionary learner support funds available to some students in further education, any discretionary hardship funds offered by higher education institutions in England or Wales, the 16 to 19 bursary fund in England and discretionary funds in Scotland) are administered by colleges and universities.[110] Individual educational institutions may call all or part of these funds by other names – eg, access bursary, mature students' bursary, and childcare support. Payments from access funds should be distinguished from payments with similar names from other sources – eg, hardship loans.

How a payment from access funds is treated depends on whether it is paid as a single lump sum, in instalments or to bridge the period before you start your course or receive a student loan payment.

### A single lump-sum payment

A single lump-sum payment is treated as capital, but is disregarded for 52 weeks if the payment is intended for, and used for, any items, expenses or charges which you or your partner may incur (other than 'daily living expenses').[111] However, if the payment is intended for but not used for these items, expenses or charges, it is immediately taken into account as capital. A single lump-sum payment made for daily living expenses counts as capital immediately.

*Daily living expenses*

'**Daily living expenses**' are:

– food;

– ordinary clothing or footwear – ie, for normal daily use, but not including school uniforms or any that are used solely for sporting activities;

– household fuel, council tax and water charges,

– for ESA only, rent for which HB is payable;

– for HB, your 'eligible rent', minus any non-dependant deductions;

– for ESA only, housing costs met by income-related ESA.

### Payments made in instalments

Payments made in instalments are treated as income, but are disregarded in full.[112] However, if the payment is intended and used for daily living expenses, it is taken into account as income for each week it is intended to cover, except for the first £20 a week, which is disregarded. This amount may overlap with other disregards applied to certain war pensions (see p354) and student loans (see p809). A combined maximum sum of £20 a week can be ignored.

### Payments before course starts or student loan received

A payment (whether paid as a single payment or in instalments) is ignored, even if it is for 'daily living expenses', if it is made:[113]

- on or after whichever is the earlier of 1 September or the first day of your course, if it is intended to bridge the period before you receive your student loan; *or*
- before the first day of your course, if it is made in anticipation of your becoming a student.



### Other sources of income intended to cover study costs

If you receive a payment from any source other than a grant or student loan, which is intended to cover items or expenses that would be ignored when calculating grant income, the payment made from that other source is also ignored.[114] You must show that the payment is necessary for you to be able to attend the course. Any sum paid which is not necessary (or is likely to exceed the sum necessary) for you to attend the course counts as income. For example, if your grant or student loan does not cover all your tuition fees, any money received from another source, such as a parent, intended to make up the difference, is ignored as income. However, if the amount you receive is greater than is likely to be necessary to pay the difference, the amount above that sum counts as income.

## Once you have completed your course

For ESA only, any grant income, student loan or assessed contribution made by a parent or spouse/civil partner as part of the loan or grant that you received no longer counts as income once you have completed your course.[115] It should also be ignored as income for HB once you have completed the course.

Any student financial support you have left once you have completed your course counts as capital (see Chapter 18), as there are no provisions to disregard it under the rules about capital.

# Notes

1. **Universal credit**
 1 s4(1)(d) WRA 2012
 2 Reg 12 UC Regs
 3 Reg 5 UC Regs
 4 para H6035 ADM
 5 Reg 12(4) UC Regs
 6 Reg 13 UC Regs
 7 *BK v SSWP* [2022] UKUT 73 (AAC)
 8 Reg 13(1)(b), (2) and (3) UC Regs
 9 Reg 13(2)(a) UC Regs
 10 Reg 14 UC Regs
 11 Reg 3(2)(b) UC Regs
 12 Reg 13(4) UC Regs
 13 Reg 8(3) UC Regs
 14 CIS/11766/1996
 15 R(IS) 9/94
 16 *NP v SSWP* [2009] UKUT 243 (AAC)
 17 R(SB) 2/87
 18 CIS/11441/1995
 19 Reg 89 UC Regs
 20 Reg 12(4) UC Regs
 21 Reg 95(4) UC Regs
 22 Regs 68-71 UC Regs
 23 Reg 68(1) UC Regs
 24 Reg 68(7) UC Regs
 25 Reg 70 UC Regs
 26 Reg 68(3) UC Regs
 27 Reg 68(7) UC Regs
 28 *IB v Gravesham BC and SSWP (HB)* [2023] UKUT 193 (AAC). This is an HB case but should apply equally in UC.
 29 Reg 69(1A) UC Regs
 30 para H6131 ADM
 31 gov.scot/news/increasing-financial-support-for-scottish-students
 32 *SO v SSWP* [2024] UKUT 305 (AAC)
 33 *SSWP v AD* [2023] UKUT 272 (AAC)
 34 Reg 68(1) UC Regs
 35 Reg 68(7) UC Regs
 36 Reg 13(4) UC Regs
 37 *RVS v SSWP* [2019] UKUT 102 (AAC)
 38 Reg 13 UC Regs

2. **Employment and support allowance**
 39 Reg 32(2) and (3) ESA Regs
 40 **ESA** Reg 2(1), definition of 'period of study', ESA Regs
 **HB** Reg 53(2)(b) HB Regs
 41 **ESA** Reg 131(1), definition of 'last day of the course', ESA Regs
 **HB** Reg 53(1), definition of 'last day of the course', HB Regs
 42 Sch 1 para 6(1)(g) WRA 2007; reg 18 ESA Regs
 43 Reg 15 ESA Regs
 44 Reg 14 ESA Regs
 45 Regs 14 and 33(2) ESA Regs
 46 **ESA** Reg 131(1) definition of 'full-time student', ESA Regs
 **HB** Reg 53(1), definition of 'full-time course of study', HB Regs
 47 para 41578 DMG
 48 **ESA** Reg 131(1), definition of 'full-time student', ESA Regs
 **HB** Reg 53(1), definitions of 'full-time course of study' and 'higher education', HB Regs
 49 **ESA** Reg 131(1), definition of 'sandwich course', ESA Regs
 **HB** Reg 53(1), definition of 'sandwich course', HB Regs
 50 R(IS) 19/98
 51 **ESA** Reg 131(4) ESA Regs
 **HB** Reg 53(4) HB Regs
 52 **ESA** Reg 131(2)(a) ESA Regs
 **HB** Reg 53(2)(a) HB Regs
 53 **ESA** Reg 131(3)(b) ESA Regs
 **HB** Reg 53(3)(b) HB Regs
 54 **ESA** Reg 131(3)(a) ESA Regs
 **HB** Reg 53(3)(a) HB Regs
 55 R(IS) 15/98; R(IS) 7/99; CJSA/836/1998; R(IS)1/00; *Chief Adjudication Officer v Webber* [1997] 4 All ER 274
 56 *RVS v SSWP* [2019] UKUT 102 (AAC)

3. **Housing benefit**
 57 There are no student rules in the HB(SPC) Regs
 58 Reg 53(2)(b) HB Regs
 59 Reg 53(1), definition of 'last day of the course', HB Regs
 60 Reg 56(2) HB Regs
 61 Reg 55(1) HB Regs
 62 Reg 55(2) HB Regs
 63 Reg 57 HB Regs
 64 Reg 8(1)(e) HB Regs
 65 Reg 58 HB Regs
 66 Reg 92(7) HB Regs

4. **Other benefits**

67 Reg 5 SS(ICA) Regs
68 *SSWP v Deane* [2010] EWCA Civ 699
69 Reg 5(2) SS(ICA) Regs
70 *SSWP v BC (CA)* [2023] UKUT 10 (AAC)
71 *SM v SSWP* [2016] UKUT 406 (AAC)
72 R(G) 2/02
73 Reg 13(1) CA(CSP)(S) Regs
74 Regs 1(3) and 13(2) and (3) CA(CSP)(S) Regs; The Carer Support Payment (Amendment) (Scotland) Regulations 2024 SSI No.173
75 Reg 45 JSA Regs 2013

5. **Student income and means-tested benefits**

76 **ESA** Reg 131, definition of 'full-time student', ESA Regs
**HB** Reg 53(1), definition of 'student' and 'course of study', HB Regs
77 Sch 5 para 4 HB Regs
78 **ESA** Reg 131(1), definition of 'grant', ESA Regs
**HB** Reg 53(1), definition of 'grant', HB Regs
79 **ESA** Reg 131(1), definition of 'grant income', ESA Regs
**HB** Reg 53(1), definition of 'grant income', HB Regs
80 **ESA** Reg 132(4) ESA Regs
**HB** Reg 59(5) HB Regs
81 Sch 7 para 4 SS(C&P) Regs
82 **ESA** Reg 131(1), definition of 'period of study', ESA Regs
**HB** Reg 53, definition of 'period of study', HB Regs
83 **ESA** Reg 132(6) ESA Regs
**HB** Reg 59(7) HB Regs
84 **ESA** Reg 132(2) and (3) ESA Regs
**HB** Reg 59(2) and (3) HB Regs
85 **ESA** para 51951 DMG
**HB** paras C2/2.170-73 GM
86 **ESA** Reg 141 ESA Regs
**HB** Reg 67 HB Regs
87 **ESA** Reg 140 ESA Regs
**HB** Reg 66 HB Regs
88 **ESA** Schs 8 para 13 and 9 para 52 ESA Regs
**HB** Schs 5 para 11 and 6 para 51 HB Regs
89 **ESA** Reg 132(3) ESA Regs
**HB** Reg 59(3) HB Regs
90 CIS/91/1994
91 R(IS) 7/95
92 **ESA** Reg 131(1), definition of 'student loan', ESA Regs
**HB** Reg 53(1), definition of 'student loan', HB Regs
93 **ESA** Reg 137(4) and (5) ESA Regs
**HB** Reg 64(3) and (4) HB Regs
94 *IB v Gravesham BC and SSWP (HB)* [2023] UKUT 193 (AAC)
95 **ESA** Reg 137(5A) ESA Regs
**HB** Reg 64(4A) HB Regs
96 Reg 137(4A) ESA Regs
97 **ESA** Reg 139A ESA Regs; para 51953 DMG
**HB** Reg 64B HB Regs
98 **ESA** Reg 139A ESA Regs
**HB** Reg 64B HB Regs
99 Reg 137(5) ESA Regs
100 **ESA** Reg 139 ESA Regs
**HB** Reg 64A HB Regs
101 **ESA** Reg 141 ESA Regs
**HB** Reg 67 HB Regs
102 **ESA** Reg 140 ESA Regs
**HB** Reg 66 HB Regs
103 **ESA** Reg 137(3) and (6) ESA Regs
**HB** Reg 64(2) and (5) HB Regs
104 **ESA** Reg 131(1), definition of 'academic year', ESA Regs
**HB** Reg 53(1), definition of 'academic year', HB Regs
105 **ESA** Reg 137(3)(a) ESA Regs
**HB** Reg 64(2)(a) HB Regs
106 **ESA** Reg 137(3)(b) ESA Regs
**HB** Reg 64(2)(b) HB Regs
107 **ESA** Regs 104(6) and 137(3)(c) ESA Regs
**HB** Reg 64(2)(b) HB Regs
**Both** The Education (Student Support) (No.2) Regulations 2008 No.1582
108 CIS/3734/2004
109 R(IS) 16/95
110 **ESA** Reg 131(1), definition of 'access funds', ESA Regs
**HB** Reg 53(1), definition of 'access funds', HB Regs
111 **ESA** Regs 2(1) and 142(3) ESA Regs
**HB** Regs 2(1) and 68(3) and (4) HB Regs
112 **ESA** Regs 2(1) and 138 ESA Regs
**HB** Regs 2(1) and 65 HB Regs
113 **ESA** Reg 138(4) ESA Regs
**HB** Reg 65(5) HB Regs
114 **ESA** Reg 136(1) ESA Regs
**HB** Reg 63 HB Regs
115 Sch 8 paras 15 and 54 ESA Regs

# Chapter 38

# Benefits in hospital, care homes, prison and in other special circumstances

5

**This chapter covers:**

1. Hospital patients (below)
2. People in care homes and similar accommodation (p826)
3. Prisoners (p836)
4. 16/17-year-old care leavers (p846)
5. People without accommodation (p847)

### Key facts

- Your benefit entitlement may be affected if you (or your partner, child or non-dependant) go into hospital, a care home or prison. It may also be affected if you are without accommodation, or if you are aged 16 or 17 and were previously looked after by a local authority.
- Some benefits are not payable, or are payable at a reduced rate, either immediately or after a specified period.
- You should always notify the relevant benefit authority as soon as possible if any of the above circumstances apply, or cease to apply, to avoid being overpaid or underpaid.

## 1. Hospital patients

Some benefits are affected after you, your partner or child have been a patient in a hospital, or in an institution similiar to a hospital, for a period of time. In some cases, benefit is no longer paid. In other cases, it is paid at a reduced rate.

See p825 for information on paying for your normal home while you are a patient.

You can arrange for someone else to access your benefit while you are a patient (see p1019). If you cannot manage your claim, someone else can act as your appointee (see p1005).

Always inform the DWP, HMRC, Social Security Scotland (SSS) and/or the local authority as soon as you can if your benefits may be affected by the rules described below, to avoid being overpaid or underpaid.

## Who counts as a patient

For most benefits other than personal independence payment (PIP), adult disability payment (ADP), pension age disability payment (PADP) and Scottish adult disability living allowance (SADLA), you count as a 'patient' if you are being maintained free of charge while undergoing medical or other treatment as an inpatient in a hospital or 'similar institution'. The treatment must be provided and funded under NHS legislation, or in a hospital or similar institution which is maintained or administered by the Defence Council.[1] You do not count as a patient if you are getting treatment as a private patient, you are meeting the cost of your treatment in a private hospital or the local authority has organised the placement.[2] Hospital patient is not defined for child disability payment (CDP): no definition is needed as being a hosptial patient does not affect payment (see p818).

For PIP, ADP, PADP, and SADLA, you count as a 'patient' if you are undergoing medical or other treatment as an inpatient at a hospital or 'similar institution' and any of the costs of your treatment, accommodation and any related services are paid for 'out of public funds'. The costs count as being paid for 'out of public funds' where you are being provided with medical or other treatment under NHS legislation, or you are in a hospital or similar institution which is maintained or administered by the Defence Council. You do not count as a patient for PIP, ADP, PADP or SADLA if you are getting treatment as a private patient or meeting the cost of your treatment in a private hospital.[3]

*Definitions*

**'Hospitals'** include all NHS hospitals, armed forces hospitals and special hospitals such as Broadmoor, Rampton and the State Hospital in Scotland. Prison hospital wings do not count as hospitals.[4]

A **'similar institution'** to a hospital is not defined in the law, but can include some care homes (see below), and rehabilitation units that provide medical or nursing care.[5]

**'Medical or other treatment'** is treatment by a doctor, dentist or professionally qualified or trained nurse, or by someone under the supervision of such a person.[6]

If you are in a care home and receiving medical or nursing care that is more than 'incidental and ancillary' to your other care needs, the NHS is responsible for meeting your care home costs in full. In this situation, you count as a patient. For PIP, ADP, PADP or SADLA if you are in a care home which is deemed to be a 'similar institution' to a hospital (ie, because you are provided with medical or nursing care), you count as a patient if the NHS is paying for any of your care, treatment, accommodation or related services.[7]

**Note:** if you are detained in hospital while serving a sentence of imprisonment under certain provisions, you may be treated as a prisoner rather than a patient for benefit purposes (see p841).

### The days on which you count as a patient

You count as a patient from the day after the day you enter hospital (or a similar institution) up to and including:

- for attendance allowance (AA), PADP, disability living allowance (DLA), PIP, ADP and SADLA, the day before the day you leave (unless, for PIP only, you go straight into a care home or prison, in which case you count as a patient up to and including the day you leave hospital);[8] *or*
- for other benefits where the issue is relevant, the day you leave.[9]

5

*Example*

Laurie gets PIP and employment and support allowance (ESA). She is admitted to hospital on 1 January. She is discharged on 21 January.

For PIP, she counts as a patient from 2 January up to and including 20 January = 19 days.

For ESA, she counts as a patient from 2 January up to and including 21 January = 20 days.

## Disability benefits

If you are under 18 when you go into hospital, you continue to be paid DLA, PIP, CDP or ADP regardless of how long you are in hospital, even if you turn 18 while you are still a hospital inpatient.[10] This applies whether or not you were entitled to DLA, PIP, CDP or ADP when you went into hospital, so if you were under 18 when you became a patient, you can claim DLA, PIP, CDP or ADP while you are in hospital and if it is awarded, you will be paid it. If you are under 16 and were entitled to DLA when you went into hospital, you can continue to get DLA after age 16 (and have your DLA renewed) while you remain in hospital – you do not have to claim PIP.[11] If you are getting CDP, are terminally ill and you are a hospital patient, you can keep getting CDP after you reach 18, without any upper age limit. Otherwise, you can keep getting it up to your 19th birthday if you have claimed ADP and you are waiting for a decision.[12]

If you are 18 or over when you become a hospital patient, you are not paid AA, PADP, DLA, PIP, ADP or SADLA after being a patient for 28 days.[13] Even if your payment of AA, PADP, DLA, PIP, ADP or SADLA stops because of these rules, your *entitlement* continues. This means that payment can begin again following your discharge from hospital without you having to make a new claim. Payment of AA, PADP, DLA, PIP, ADP and SADLA can be at a daily rate if you are expected to be readmitted within 28 days.[14]

There is a 28-day 'linking rule' which means that:[15]

- different periods spent as a patient separated by 28 days or fewer are linked together and treated as one period;
- for AA, DLA and PIP, periods spent as a resident in a care home (or, for PIP, as a prisoner) link with periods spent as a patient if they are 28 days or fewer apart. For ADP, PADP and SADLA, periods spent in a care home or as a prisoner only link with periods spent as a patient if you transfer directly from one place to the other.

***Example***

Patrick is claiming AA. He goes into hospital for an operation on 16 July and is discharged on 30 July. He counts as a patient from 17 July up to and including 29 July = 13 days. His AA is not affected by his stay in hospital.

Patrick has to go back into hospital for further treatment on 10 August. He counts as a patient again from 11 August. As there are fewer than 28 days between his discharge and readmission, the two spells in hospital are linked. When he has been a patient for a further 15 days, he cannot be paid AA.

Note:

- If you are terminally ill, you can be paid AA, PADP, DLA, CDP, PIP, ADP or SADLA while you are in a hospice.[16] This applies unless the hospice is an NHS hospital (see p828).
- If you are awarded AA, PADP, DLA, PIP or ADP while you are a patient, and you were 18 or over when admitted to hospital, payment cannot begin until you are discharged.[17]
- You can continue to be paid the mobility component of DLA while you are a patient if you have been a patient since 31 July 1995 (other than if you are detained under the Mental Health Act). You are paid at the lower rate (even if you would otherwise qualify for the higher rate). This transitional protection ends if you cease being a patient for more than 28 consecutive days. This continues to apply if you live in Scotland and you are transferred to SADLA (see p1422).[18]
- You continue to be exempt from the benefit cap (see p1025) even if you or your partner are no longer receiving AA, PADP, DLA, PIP or ADP after being a patient for 28 days.[19]
- If you live in Scotland and are being transferred to ADP from PIP or DLA, you are paid ADP for 28 days after the transfer, even if your PIP/DLA has already stopped being paid because you have been in hospital for more than 28 days.[20]

## Carer's allowance and carer support payment

You no longer qualify for carer's allowance (CA) or carer support payment (CSP) if the person you care for no longer receives AA, PADP, DLA, PIP, ADP or SADLA –

5

ie, if they are aged 18 or over and have been a patient for 28 days. If the person you care for is discharged and payment of AA, PADP, the DLA or SADLA care component or the daily living component of PIP or ADP resumes, you should reclaim CA if you satisfy the rules for entitlement. Your claim can be backdated to the date from when AA, PADP, DLA, PIP, ADP or SADLA is payable again, provided you reclaim CA within three months of that date.[21] If your CSP has stopped for this reason and the person you care for is discharged and payment of AA, PADP, the DLA or SADLA care component or the daily living component of PIP or ADP resumes, SSS should make a determination on your CSP entitlement with you needing to make a claim, providing the break has lasted no longer than 26 weeks.[22] If you notify SSS within 13 weeks of becoming entitled to CSP again, the CSP can be backdated to the date you became entitled to it again. This 13-week period can be extended if you have good reason for notifying the change late.[23] If it is over 26 weeks, you should reclaim CSP.

A temporary break in caring does not necessarily affect your CA (see p473) or CSP (see p1468), including if you (or the person you care for) are a hospital patient. You can remain entitled to CA or CSP during a temporary break (or breaks) of up to four weeks in any period of 26 weeks. You can remain entitled to CA or CSP for up to 12 weeks if you or the person you care for have been in hospital for at least eight of those 12 weeks.[24] This can be useful if you (or the person you care for) are going in and out of hospital. However, if the person you care for is 18 or over when admitted into hospital, has been a patient for 28 days and is therefore no longer receiving AA, PADP, DLA, PIP, ADP or SADLA (see p818), your entitlement to CA or CSP ends, even though you have not yet had a temporary break of 12 weeks.

## Universal credit

Your universal credit (UC) is not usually affected until you (or your partner or child) have been in hospital for more than six months. However, you are no longer entitled to a carer element if the AA, PADP, DLA, PIP , ADP or SADLA of the person you care for stops because they are 18 or over when admitted and have been in hospital for more than 28 days.[25] See p825 for information on paying for your usual home.

### Single claimants

You can continue to get UC while you are in hospital. However, the housing costs element stops if your stay in hospital exceeds, or is expected to exceed, six months.[26] If you receive a loan from the DWP to help you with your mortgage interest, payments stop if your stay in hospital exceeds, or is expected to exceed, six months.[27] **Note:** when calculating the six-month period, there is no 'linking rule' joining two or more periods in hospital.

### Couples

You and your partner continue to count as a couple for UC while one of you is temporarily absent from the household, including when one of you is in hospital. You must continue to make a joint claim with your partner and UC is paid as usual. If the partner who is not in hospital is working, you may qualify for a childcare costs element (see p76). If the absence exceeds, or is expected to exceed, six months, you no longer count as a couple.[28] **Note:** when calculating the six-month period, there is no 'linking rule' joining two or more periods in hospital.

If you no longer count as a couple:

- you can no longer make a joint claim for UC;
- the calculation of your benefit no longer includes amounts for your partner;
- notify the DWP as you may both have to reclaim UC as single people.

### Children

A child continues to be included in your UC claim while temporarily absent from your household because they are in hospital. However, a child is no longer included in your claim if the absence exceeds, or is expected to exceed, six months.[29] **Note:** when calculating the six-month period, there is no 'linking rule' joining two or more periods in hospital.

If your child is no longer included in your claim:

- the calculation of your benefit no longer includes amounts for them;
- your work allowance (see p41) and the work-related requirements you must meet may change (see Chapter 42).

## Other means-tested benefits

If you are getting income-related ESA, housing benefit (HB) or pension credit (PC) when you go into hospital, these benefits can often continue, although the amount to which you are entitled might change (see below). See p820 for how UC is affected. See p825 about paying for your usual home.

### If your, or your partner's, disability benefit stops

If payment of your (or your partner's) AA, PADP, DLA, PIP/ADP or SADLA stops because you (or your partner) are 18 or over when you (or your partner) go into hospital and you (or your partner) have been in hospital for 28 days, the severe disability premium included in your income-related ESA or HB or the severe disability addition in your PC is affected.

- If you are single, you are no longer entitled to the severe disability premium in your income-related ESA or HB, or to the PC severe disability addition.
- If you are a member of a couple, you (or your partner) are treated as getting AA, PADP, DLA, PIP/ADP or SADLA if the only reason it is not being paid is because you (or your partner) are a patient. This means that you continue to get the severe disability premium/addition in your means-tested benefit. However, it is paid at the single rate instead of the couple rate.[30] For the purposes of

entitlement to the severe disability premium/addition, your carer or your partner's carer still counts as getting CA, CSP or the carer element of UC, even if it has stopped because you (or your partner) have been an inpatient for more than 28 days.[31]

Entitlement to the disability premium in HB, the enhanced disability premium in income-related ESA and HB are not affected when payment of AA, PADP, DLA, PIP/ADP or SADLA stops after 28 days.[32] However, these premiums can be affected if you (or your partner) are a patient for 52 weeks (see below).

For HB, if you are a member of a couple, a deduction for childcare charges can be made from earnings if one of you is in full-time paid work and the other is in hospital (see p350 and p384).

5

### If your carer's allowance or carer support payment stops

You no longer qualify for CA or CSP when payment of the AA, PADP, DLA, PIP, ADP or SADLA of the person you are caring for stops. In this situation, the carer premium in your income-related ESA and HB or the carer addition in PC can continue to be paid for eight weeks after your entitlement to CA or CSP stops (see p279). After this, you are no longer entitled to a carer premium or addition. If your CA or CSP stops because *you* are a patient, the person you were caring for may become entitled to the severe disability premium or addition (see p275 for the severe disability premium).

### Pension credit child amounts

If you get PC which includes an amount for a child (see p258), the amount for the child can continue while they are in hospital – providing the hospital stay is not expected to exceed, or has not exceeded, 52 weeks or, in exceptional circumstances, it is unlikely to be substantially more than 52 weeks.[33] There is no 'linking rule' in this provision. This means that if your child is discharged from hospital and is then readmitted, a new period as a patient starts.

### If a hospital stay lasts for more than 52 weeks

You still count as a couple for ESA, PC and HB while you and your partner are temporarily apart. However, you no longer count as a couple if you are likely to be separated for more than 52 weeks or, in exceptional circumstances (including a stay in hospital), not substantially more than 52 weeks.[34] If you no longer count as a couple, you are each treated as a single claimant (or lone parent) for these benefits.

If your child has been in hospital for more than 52 weeks, they may no longer count as living with you (see p261) and no longer be included in your claim.

**Note:**
- HB and help with your housing costs may no longer be payable once you have been away from home for 52 weeks – eg, if you live alone. For information about paying for your usual home while you are a patient, see p825.
- If you have a non-dependant living with you and they have been a patient for 52 weeks, non-dependant deductions made for them stop (see p825).[35]

The rate of income-related ESA may be lower if you (or your partner) have been a patient continuously for more than 52 weeks, because you are no longer entitled to certain premiums (see below). You may have already lost the severe disability and carer premiums (see p821). The calculation of HB may also be affected if you are not 'passported' to the maximum amount.

There are no 'linking rules' with these provisions. This means that if you are discharged from hospital and are then readmitted, a new period as a patient starts and you can again be entitled to income-related ESA, PC or HB premiums at the rate you were getting before your hospital admission. If you have completely lost your entitlement to income-related ESA or HB, you are likely to have to claim UC instead (see p19).

#### Premiums and components: single claimants and lone parents

If you are a single claimant or a lone parent and have been a patient for more than 52 weeks, the enhanced disability premium and work-related activity component or support component are no longer included in your income-related ESA.

#### Premiums and components: couples

If you are a member of a couple and:
- both you and your partner have been a patient for more than 52 weeks, but you still count as a couple:[36]
  - the enhanced disability premium is not included in your income-related ESA. **Note:** the pensioner premium is included in your income-related ESA if you or your partner qualify;
  - the work-related activity component and the support component are not included in your income-related ESA;
- one of you has been a patient for more than 52 weeks, but you still count as a couple, you are paid the normal rate of income-related ESA. Premiums may be affected by changes to other benefits (see p822).[37]

#### Premiums: children

If your child is a patient (or you are), they may no longer be included in your claim if they no longer count as living with you (see p258). In this case, you can no longer get allowances and premiums for the child in your HB. If the child *is* still included in your claim, you continue to be entitled to the normal HB premiums, including the disabled child and enhanced disability premiums –

these are not affected if you or your child have been a patient for more than 52 weeks.[38]

## Other benefits

### Child benefit

Your entitlement to child benefit can be affected if your child is not living with you. However, periods of up to 84 days when your child is receiving inpatient treatment in a hospital or similar institution are ignored. If your child has been in hospital for 84 days or longer, you remain entitled to child benefit if:

- you are regularly incurring expenditure in respect of the child; *or*
- you are contributing at least the amount of child benefit to the cost of supporting the child.

5

See p492 for details of these rules.

### Contributory employment and support allowance

You are not entitled to a work-related activity or support component in your contributory ESA once you have been a patient continuously for more than 52 weeks.[39]

### New-style jobseeker's allowance

You cannot qualify for new-style JSA if you have limited capability for work (see p613). You must also meet work-related requirements (see p938). If you cannot satisfy these conditions because you are in hospital, you may need to claim a different benefit such as UC or ESA instead. You can continue to get JSA:[40]

- for up to 13 weeks during a period of sickness; *or*
- indefinitely, if you are absent from Great Britain for NHS hospital treatment.

In these circumstances, you are treated as not having limited capability for work and as satisfying the wok-related requirements for JSA (see p613).

### Winter fuel payment

You are not entitled to a winter fuel payment if you have been a patient for 52 weeks or more immediately before the qualifying week (see p715).[41] It is expected that this rule will also apply to pension age winter heating payment in Scotland (see p1507).

### Scottish child payment

You continue to get Scottish child payment while the child is in hospital or while you are in hospital, provided you continue to satisfy the normal conditions of entitlement (see p1452).

## Paying for your usual home

The benefit you can get to help pay for your usual home may be affected while you, or your partner, child or non-dependant, are temporarily in hospital (whether as an NHS or private patient). **Note:** if you leave your home permanently, you are no longer entitled to benefit for it.

- You can get a UC housing costs element for up to six months, provided your absence from home does not exceed (or is not expected to exceed) six months (see p100).[42] If you are on UC and are getting a DWP loan to help pay your mortgage interest, payments stop if you have been absent for six months (or if your absence is likely to exceed six months).[43]
- You can get HB or help with your housing costs (service charges and ground rent for owner-occupiers) with your income-related ESA or PC, provided you have not been absent (or are not likely to be absent) from home for more than 52 weeks or, in exceptional circumstances, not substantially longer than 52 weeks (see p191 and p296), you intend to return home and you do not sub-let it.[44] You can get HB or help with housing costs for a maximum of 52 weeks. If you are on income-related ESA or PC and you get a DWP loan to help with your mortgage interest, you can continue to get this provided you have not been absent (or are not likely to be absent) for more than 52 weeks or, in exceptional circumstances, not substantially longer than 52 weeks. You can continue to get the DWP loan for a maximum of 52 weeks.[45]

**Note:**

- Another person (eg, your partner) might be able to qualify for these benefits (or for the DWP loan to help pay mortgage interest – see p766) instead of you if they are (or can be treated as) liable to pay the rent or housing costs (see p93, p186 and p294).
- There are no 'linking rules' with these provisions. This means that if a new period as a patient starts, you can again be entitled to HB or an amount in your UC, income-related ESA or PC – eg, if you are discharged from hospital and then are readmitted.
- For HB, you can be treated as occupying, but temporarily absent from, a new dwelling, even if you have not yet stayed there, if you move your furniture and belongings in but cannot move in yourself – eg, because you are in hospital .[46]

### Partners, children and non-dependants

If your partner, child or non-dependant is away from home because they are in hospital, this could affect the amount of your HB or housing costs paid with your UC, income-related ESA or PC. This could apply, for example, if they no longer count as living with you or, for UC, they no longer count as a member of your 'extended benefit unit' (see p103). Bear the following in mind.

- If you live in rented accommodation, you may no longer be allowed the same number of bedrooms under the size criteria (see p309, p316, p320 and p104) and your UC or HB may be reduced. For UC, this only applies if your partner, child or non-dependant is absent (or expected to be absent) from home for more than six months.[47]

- If your non-dependant is absent, check whether a deduction for housing costs contributions or a non-dependant deduction should still be made for them (see p207, p289 and p109).

## 2. People in care homes and similar accommodation

5

Most benefits are paid as normal if you live in a care home or similar type of accommodation. However, some benefits are no longer payable and some may be paid at a reduced rate. The benefits affected are covered below through to p834, but see p492 for how your child benefit could be affected if you or your child are resident in a care home.

Always inform the DWP, HMRC, Social Security Scotland (SSS) and/or the local authority promptly if your benefits may be affected by the rules described in this section, to avoid being overpaid or underpaid.

***Care homes and similar accommodation***

This *Handbook* does not cover all the different kinds of care homes and similar accommodation and the funding arrangements for people living in them. The rules covered below mainly apply to homes which provide you with accommodation and personal and/or nursing care. They do not apply to other types of supported or sheltered accommodation, even if you receive personal care services from your local authority social services department (social work department in Scotland). Some homes are run by the NHS, some by local authorities and some are independent.

If your care home is funded by the NHS, you may count as a 'patient' in a hospital or similar institution, in which case the rules on p816 apply to you.

### Disability benefits

You cannot usually be paid the following benefits once you have been a resident in a care home for 28 days if any of the 'costs of any qualifying services' provided for you are met out of public or local funds:[48]

- attendance allowance (AA);
- pension age disability payment (PADP);
- care component of disability living allowance (DLA) or child disability payment (CDP);
- daily living component of personal independence payment (PIP) or adult disability payment (ADP);

- Scottish adult disabilty living allowance (SADLA).

Until then, AA, PADP, the DLA/CDP/SADLA care component and the PIP/ADP daily living component are paid as normal. See p828 for exceptions to these rules.

***Care homes, qualifying services and specified provisions***

For these purposes, a '**care home**' is an establishment that provides you with accommodation as well as nursing or personal care.[49]

'**Qualifying services**' are the costs of accommodation, board and personal care.[50] For AA and DLA, the 'costs of any qualifying services' do *not* include the cost of:[51]

- domiciliary services (including personal care) provided in a private dwelling;
- improvements to, or furniture/equipment provided for, a private dwelling because of a disabled person's needs, or for a care home, for which a grant/payment was made out of public funds, except if the grant/payment is of a regular or repeated nature;
- social and recreational activities outside the care home;
- buying or running a motor vehicle used in connection with any qualifying service provided in the care home.

For AA, DLA and PIP, the 'qualifying services' only count as such if they are provided under 'specified provisions'. The '**specified provisions**' are:[52]

- Part III of the National Assistance Act 1948, sections 59 and 59A of the Social Work (Scotland) Act 1968, the Mental Health (Care and Treatment) (Scotland) Act 2003, the Community Care and Health (Scotland) Act 2002, the Mental Health Act 1983, section 57 of the Health and Social Care Act 2001, Part 1 of the Care Act 2014 and Part 4 of the Social Services and Well-being (Wales) Act 2014; *or*
- any other Acts relating to people with disabilities or (in the case of DLA and PIP only) young people, education or training – eg, in some special residential schools.

In most cases, a local authority pays for the services in a care home under one of these provisions, but it is always worth checking. Local authorities also have powers to provide accommodation under housing legislation and the Local Government Act 1972, in which case AA, DLA and PIP are not affected.[53] **Note:** the First-tier Tribunal can decide that your placement is being funded under a different legal power than the one the local authority has stated.[54]

**Note:**

- The mobility component of DLA, PIP, CDP, ADP, armed forces independence payment and SADLA are paid as normal however long you are a resident in a care home.
- If your entitlement to AA, PADP, the DLA/CDP care component or PIP/ADP daily living component begins while you are in a care home, you cannot be paid for days when you count as resident in the care home (including the first 28 days).[55]

- Entitlement to AA, PADP, DLA/CDP, PIP/ADP or SADLA continues while you are in a care home, even after payment stops. This means that payment can begin again when you are no longer resident in a care home.
- You continue to be exempt from the benefit cap (see p1025), even if you or your partner or child are no longer receiving AA, PADP, DLA/CDP, PIP/ADP or SADLA after being resident in a care home for 28 days.[56]
- If the NHS provides nursing services in a care home and your nursing needs are more than 'merely incidental and ancillary' to other care needs, you may be treated as a 'patient' for AA, DLA and PIP purposes (see p817).[57]
- If you think the DWP or SSS has refused payment of AA, PADP, DLA, CDP, PIP, ADP or SADLA wrongly, you can appeal (see Chapters 51 and 69). You must first apply for a mandatory reconsideration (or redetermination for CDP, ADP, PADP and SADLA) .
- If you live in Scotland and you are transferred from PIP to ADP, you are paid ADP daily living component for 28 days after the transfer even if your PIP daily living component or DLA care component has already stopped because you have been in a care home for more than 28 days.[58]

5

## Exceptions

There are exceptions to the rules. You can be paid AA, PADP, the DLA/CDP/SADLA care component and the PIP/ADP daily living component after you have been resident in a care home for 28 days if:

- for AA, DLA and PIP, you are terminally ill and are in a hospice, provided the DWP has been informed that you are terminally ill. In most cases, the DWP must be informed in writing.[59] This applies unless the hospice is an NHS hospital; *or*
- for CDP, you are in a hospice;[60] *or*
- for ADP, PADP or SADLA, you are in a hospice, which is not an NHS hospital, and you have a terminal illness;[61] *or*
- for DLA and PIP only, you are a student and the cost of your accommodation is wholly or partly met from a student grant or loan, or from a grant made to educational institutions under specified legislation;[62] *or*
- you are under 16 (for DLA and CDP) and being looked after by a local authority, or aged 16 or 17 (for DLA, CDP, PIP and ADP) and you are receiving services from your local authority because of your disability or health, but only if you have been placed by the local authority in a private dwelling with a family, a relative or some other suitable person;[63] *or*
- for DLA, CDP, PIP and ADP, your accommodation is outside the UK and a local authority is meeting the costs of any qualifying services under specified legislation relating to education – eg, at the Higashi School;[64] *or*
- you are 'self-funding'.

## If you are self-funding

You can continue to be paid AA, PADP, the DLA/CDP/SADLA care component and the PIP/ADP daily living component if you are meeting the whole cost of all the 'qualifying services' either from your own resources, or with the help of another person or a charity – known as 'self-funding'.[65] This applies whether you are in an independent or local authority home. **Note:** in Scotland, if you receive free personal care from the local authority, you do **not** count as self-funding.

You count as self-funding even if:

- you are claiming benefits, such as universal credit (UC), employment and support allowance (ESA), pension credit (PC), AA, DLA, CDP, PIP, ADP or SADLA; *or*
- a local authority has arranged and contracted to pay for your placement, provided you are paying the whole cost of all the 'qualifying services'; *or*
- a local authority is temporarily funding your placement while you sell a property (eg, your former home), or if you have entered into what is known as a 'deferred payment agreement'. You must be liable and able to repay the local authority in full when the property is sold, or when payment under the deferred agreement falls due. This is known as 'retrospective self-funding'.[66]

5

### *Are you likely to become self-funding?*

If you move into a care home and are initially receiving help with the fees from the local authority, the DWP should suspend payment of your AA, DLA or PIP if you are likely to become self-funding in the future – eg, if you are only getting local authority help while you sell your former home, or your capital is likely to increase above the limit of the local authority's means test. When you repay the local authority and become self-funding, payment can resume and any arrears can be paid to you. If the DWP terminated payment of your AA, DLA or PIP and refuses to pay you arrears when you become self-funding, you can argue that the decision to terminate payment should be revised on the grounds of 'official error'.[67] We expect this principle to apply to CDP, ADP, PADP and SADLA.

## Days on which you count as being resident in a care home

The general rule is that you count as resident in a care home from the day after you enter until the day before you leave.[68] However, for AA, PADP, DLA/CDP and ADP, if you are a patient in a hospital or similar institution (or, for ADP, PADP or SADLA, a prisoner) and enter a care home, you count as a resident in the care home from the day you enter the care home.[69]

For AA and DLA, if you transfer from a care home to a hospital or similar institution, or for PIP, if you transfer from a care home to hospital, a similar institution or to prison, the last day you count as resident in a care home is the day on which you transfer. For ADP, PADP or SADLA, you stop counting as a resident in a care home the day before you transfer to hospital, a similar institution or prison. For CDP, if you transfer from a care home to prison, you stop counting as a resident in a care home the day before you transfer.[70]

There is a 28-day 'linking rule'. This means that different periods as a resident in a care home separated by 28 days or fewer link together to calculate the 28 days when you can continue to be paid AA/PADP, the DLA/CDP/SADLA care component or the PIP/ADP daily living component.[71] For AA, DLA and PIP, periods spent as a patient in a hospital or similar institution (or, for PIP, as a prisoner) also count towards the 28-day limit on payment if they are separated by 28 days or fewer from periods when you are resident in a care home in the circumstances described above. For ADP, PADP and SADLA, periods in a care home only link with periods spent in hospital or as a prisoner if you transfer directly from one place to the other. A period in hospital if you were under 18 when you were admitted does not count.[72]



It can be important to plan periods of respite care in the light of the linking rules so that you can continue to be paid AA, PADP, the DLA/CDP/SADLA care component or the PIP/ADP daily living component for as long as possible. This can also enable your carer to keep their carer's allowance (CA) or carer support payment (CSP).

## How other benefits are affected

If payment of AA, PADP, the DLA/CDP/SADLA care component or the PIP/ADP daily living component stops, CA/CSP is affected in the same way as for hospital patients (see p819). The carer premium, paid with income-related ESA and housing benefit (HB), and the carer addition paid with PC, can continue to be paid for eight weeks after CA/CSP stops (see p279).[73] The UC carer element stops as soon as the relevant disability benefit stops because you no longer satisfy the conditions of entitlement for CA/CSP.[74]

Once payment of AA, PADP, the DLA/SADLA care component or the PIP/ADP daily living component stops because you have been resident in a care home for 28 days, you are no longer entitled to the severe disability premium or addition paid with income-related ESA, HB and PC. In addition, you may no longer be entitled to the disability or enhanced disability premium if the only reason you qualified was because you were receiving AA, PADP, DLA/SADLA care component or PIP/ADP daily living component.

Note:

- For income-related ESA if you only live in a care home for part of the week and are entitled to DLA/ADP/PIP when you are staying elsewhere, you can be paid, for example, the severe disability and enhanced disability premiums when you are staying away from the care home from the date the change occurs (or is expected to occur).[75]
- For ESA only, you qualify for the enhanced disability premium if you are getting the ESA support component, even if you are not receiving the DLA care component or PIP/ADP daily living component.

- If you are still being paid AA, PADP, DLA care component or PIP/ADP daily living component (eg, because you have not yet been in a care home for 28 days), you may be entitled to a severe disability premium, even if you were not before – eg, if you are no longer treated as living with a non-dependant or a partner.

## Universal credit

You cannot get the UC housing costs element for the rent you pay to your care home.[76] If you are in a care home, the lower capital threshold for the tariff income rule remains £6,000 (see p149), unlike in benefits such as income-related ESA and HB for people under pension age, where the lower capital threshold increases if you are resident in a care home (see p833).

*Care home*

A **'care home'** means:[77]

- a care home (a care home service in Scotland) as defined in section 3 of the Care Standards Act 2000, paragraph 2 of Schedule 12 to the Public Services Reform (Scotland) Act 2010 or Part I of the Regulation and Inspection of Social Care (Wales) Act 2016. If the home comes within the definition, it counts as a care home even if it also has some other function, such as an educational institution;[78]
- an independent hospital (an independent healthcare service in Scotland) as defined in section 275 of the National Health Service Act 2006 (in England) other than a health service hospital, section 2 of the Care Standards Act 2000 (in Wales) or section 10F(1)(a) and (b) of the National Health Service (Scotland) Act 1978 (in Scotland).

Get advice if you are unsure whether you live in a care home within this definition.

### Single claimants

You can continue to get UC while in a care home. The housing costs element for your normal home can continue if your stay in a care home is temporary. However, the housing costs element stops if your stay in a care home exceeds, or is expected to exceed, six months.[79] If your stay is temporary and you receive a loan from the DWP to help with your mortgage interest, payments stop if your stay in a care home exceeds, or is expected to exceed, six months.[80]

### Couples

You and your partner continue to count as a couple while one of you is temporarily absent from the household, including when one of you is in a care home. You must continue to make a joint claim and UC is paid as normal. If the person who is not living in a care home is working, you may qualify for the childcare costs element (see p76). However, if the absence is permanent or it exceeds, or is likely to exceed, six months, you no longer count as a couple.[81] If you no longer count as a couple:

- you can no longer make a joint claim for UC;
- the calculation of your benefit no longer includes amounts for your partner;
- you should notify the DWP as you may both have to reclaim UC as single claimants.

### Children

A child continues to be included in your claim while temporarily absent from your household because they are in a care home. While the child is still included in your UC claim, you still get the child element for them and any disabled child element, even if the relevant disability benefit has stopped being paid.[82] However, they are no longer included in your claim if the absence exceeds, or is expected to exceed, six months.[83] If your child is 'looked after' by the local authority (see p64) and living in a care home, they are no longer included in your claim, unless it is just for a period of respite.[84] If your child is no longer included in your claim:

- the calculation of your benefit no longer includes amounts for them;
- the work-related requirements you must meet may change (see Chapter 42).

## Other means-tested benefits

How your income-related ESA, PC and HB are affected depends on whether you (or your partner or child) are temporarily or permanently living in a care home. If you are in a care home (on either basis), these benefits are generally calculated in the usual way, although if payment of your AA, PADP, DLA/CDP/SADLA care component or PIP/ADP daily living component stops, you may no longer be entitled to certain premiums (see p830). For information about paying for your usual home, see p834.

For the definition of 'care home', see p831. The meaning is the same as for UC, except it also includes an Abbeyfield home.

**Note:**

- If you have a partner, you may no longer count as a couple if you (or your partner) are resident in a care home. If your child is resident in a care home, they may no longer be included in your claim (see p833).
- For PC, if you have an 'assessed income period' (see p251), it ends if you do not have a partner and are permanently provided with accommodation in a care home (other than in an Abbeyfield home). This means your income may be reassessed.[85]

### Housing benefit for your care home

You cannot usually get HB for the rent you pay to your care home.[86] For these purposes, a care home does *not* include an Abbeyfield home. There are exceptions if you were entitled to HB for your care home when the rules changed at various times in the past and you have transitional protection.[87]

**Note:** if you are living with an approved carer under the adult placement scheme (often called 'shared lives schemes'), the normal conditions of entitlement to HB apply and you may be able to get HB.[88]

## Tariff income from savings

For income-related ESA and, if you and your partner are under pension age, for HB, if you are permanently resident in a care home, the threshold for calculating your tariff income from any capital is increased to £10,000 (see p399), instead of £6,000. This also applies if you live in Polish resettlement accommodation (certain care homes for Polish people who came to the UK as refugees after the second world war). Some temporary absences from the care home or resettlement accommodation are ignored.[89] For HB, the £10,000 threshold is only relevant (and only applies) in the limited situations in which you can get HB while living in a care home. For PC (and pension-age HB), the threshold is always £10,000 (see p426).



## Partners and children

- If you or your partner permanently move into a care home (for PC only, other than to an Abbeyfield home), you no longer count as a couple.[90] This also applies if you and your partner are both in care homes permanently, even if you are in the same home and the same room.[91] If you do not count as a couple, your benefit and your partner's is calculated as if you were single claimants.
- If you or your partner move into a care home temporarily, you still count as a couple if you intend to live together again. This only applies if you are unlikely to be apart for more than 52 weeks or your time apart is longer than 52 weeks, but there are exceptional circumstances and the time apart is unlikely to be substantially longer than 52 weeks.[92] If you still count as a couple:
  - your PC and HB continue to be assessed under the normal rules. This means that, once the person in the care home stops getting AA, PADP, the DLA/SADLA care component or the PIP/ADP daily living component, no severe disability premium (or additional amount) for either of you can be included in your applicable amount unless you can receive it on the basis that the person who is in the care home is severely sight impaired or blind (see p275);
  - your applicable amount for income-related ESA is calculated in a special way. You receive the amount for two single claimants if this is higher than the amount you receive as a couple. This can include the severe disability premium in respect of either or both of you as if you were single claimants, even if you are not normally entitled to it at home.[93]

If child benefit stops because your child lives in a care home or is being looked after by a local authority, this may affect whether they are included in your claim (see p258). If your child is no longer included, you can no longer get a personal allowance and premiums for them in your HB. Entitlement to premiums for your child is also affected if they are no longer paid DLA/CDP or PIP/ADP.

**Pension credit child amounts**

When a child is in a care home, what happens to the child amount included in PC depends on whether the child is looked after by the local authority. If the child is not looked after by the local authority, the amount for them can continue while they are in a care home providing the stay is not expected to exceed, or has not exceeded, 52 weeks or, in exceptional circumstances, the stay is unlikely to be substantially more than 52 weeks.[94] The child addition and any extra amount that you may get if the child has a disability (see p270) continues during a temporary absence even if their DLA, CDP or PIP has stopped being paid.[95] There is no 'linking rule' in this provision. This means that if the child comes home from a care home and then goes back in, a new period in a care home starts. If they are in a care home and count as 'looked after' by the local authority, you no longer get the child amount in your PC unless it is a 'planned short break' (respite).[96]

## Social fund payments

Some social fund payments are affected if you are in a care home. You cannot get:

- a cold weather payment (see p714) if you are in a care home (see p826) or Polish resettlement accommodation, unless you are responsible for a child under five;[97]
- a winter fuel payment (see p715) if you have been in a care home or Polish resettlement accommodation for at least 12 weeks immediately before the qualifying week (see p715).[98]

## Child winter heating payment and winter heating payment

You remain entitled to the Scottish child winter heating payment (see p1506) even if your child's DLA/CDP care component or PIP/ADP daily living component has stopped being paid because they have been in a care home for more than 28 days.[99] Entitlement to winter heating payment (see p1505) is not affected by being in a care home.[100]

## Scottish child payment

You can continue to get Scottish child payment while the child is in a care home, or while you are in a care home, provided you continue to satisfy the conditions of entitlement (see p1452).

## Paying for your usual home

The benefit you can get to help pay for your usual home may be affected while you, or your partner, child or non-dependant, are temporarily in a care home.

**Note:** if you leave your home permanently (eg, you become a permanent resident in a care home), you are no longer entitled to benefit for it.

If you are temporarily away from home, you can qualify for:

- UC housing costs element for up to six months, provided your absence from home does not exceed (or is not expected to exceed) six months (see p100). If you are on UC and are getting a DWP loan to help pay your mortgage interest, payments stop if you have been absent for six months (or your absence is likely to exceed six months);[101]
- HB, or help with your housing costs (service charges and ground rent for owner-occupiers) in your income-related ESA or PC, for up to 52 weeks, provided your absence from home does not exceed (or is not likely to exceed) 52 weeks, you intend to return to your home and you do not sub-let it. In exceptional circumstances, the absence may be expected to be longer than 52 weeks, provided it is not likely to last substantially longer than 52 weeks. HB or housing costs are still only payable for a maximum of 52 weeks (see p191 and p296). If you are on income-related ESA or PC and you get a DWP loan to help with your mortgage interest, these same rules apply. The loan is still only payable for a maximum of 52 weeks.[102]



Note:

- Another person (eg, your partner) might be able to qualify for these benefits (or for the DWP loan to help with mortgage interest – see p766) instead of you if they are (or can be treated as) liable to pay the rent or housing costs (see p94, p186 and p294).
- There are no 'linking rules' with these provisions. This means that, if a new period in a care home starts, you can continue to get HB or an amount in your UC, income-related ESA or PC.
- For HB, you can be treated as occupying, but temporarily absent from, a new dwelling, even if you have not yet stayed there, if you move in your furniture and belongings but cannot move in yourself – eg, because you are in hospital or a care home on a temporary basis.[103]
- There are special rules if you are a temporary resident in a care home for a trial period. If you intend to return home, you can get HB and help with your housing costs in your income-related ESA and PC for up to 13 weeks for each trial period (in different care homes), subject to an overall maximum of 52 weeks (see p191 and p296).[104] This does not apply to UC.

## Partners, children and non-dependants

If your partner, child or non-dependant is away from home because they are in a care home, this could affect the amount of your HB or housing costs paid with your UC, income-related ESA or PC. This could apply, for example, if they no longer count as living with you or, for UC, they no longer count as a member of your 'extended benefit unit' (see p103). Bear the following in mind.

- If you live in rented accommodation, you may no longer be allowed the same number of bedrooms under the size criteria (see p309, p316, p320 and p104) and your UC or HB may be reduced. For UC, this only applies if your partner, child or non-dependant is absent (or expected to be absent) from home for more than six months.[105]
- If your non-dependant is absent, check whether a deduction for housing costs contributions or a non-dependant deduction should still be made for them (see p207, p289 and p109).

## 3. Prisoners

Most benefits are affected if you are a prisoner. Some are not payable, some are suspended and some are only payable for a temporary period. There are also issues to consider if you are given an alternative sentence to prison.

Always inform the DWP, HMRC, Social Security Scotland and/or the local authority as soon as you, or a member of your family, enter or leave prison to avoid any underpayment or overpayment of benefit. If you are being held on remand and are then sentenced, notify the benefit authorities as soon as you are remanded and again when you are sentenced.

### Non-means-tested benefits

You are disqualified from getting most non-means-tested benefits while you are a prisoner. For statutory sick pay (SSP), statutory maternity pay (SMP), statutory adoption pay (SAP), statutory paternity pay (SPP), statutory shared parental pay (SSPP), statutory parental bereavement pay (SPBP) and statutory neonatal care pay (SNCP), see p837. For other non-means-tested benefits, see p837. In some cases, payment of your benefit is only suspended pending the outcome of your trial or sentencing (see p838). For benefits that are payable, see p838.

***Prisoners***

You count as a **'prisoner'** for **non-means-tested benefits** if you are in prison or detained in legal custody.[106] This includes if you are remanded in custody awaiting trial or sentencing as well as if you are serving a custodial sentence. You do not count as a prisoner if you are on bail or living in approved premises (eg, a bail or probation hostel), or if you are released on parole, on licence or under a home detention curfew (electronic tagging).

See p841 if you are detained in a hospital or similar institution as a person with a mental disorder.

## Statutory sick, maternity, adoption, paternity and other parental pay

If you are a prisoner you:[107]

- are not entitled to SSP. If you are getting SSP, your entitlement ends;
- cannot be paid SMP. Even if you are then released from prison during the maternity pay period, you do not get SMP for the rest of that period. If you cannot be paid SMP, check whether you can be paid maternity allowance (MA) (see p629) instead on your release from prison;
- cannot be paid SAP, SPP, SSPP, SPBP or SNCP for the time you are a prisoner, unless you are subsequently released without charge or after being found not guilty, or you are convicted but do not receive a custodial sentence. If one of these applies, you should receive arrears for the period you were detained and payment should also resume for any period of entitlement after your release.



## Other non-means-tested benefits

If you are a prisoner, you cannot be paid **attendance allowance** (AA), **bereavement benefits**, **disability living allowance** (DLA), **carer's allowance** (CA), **contributory employment and support allowance** (ESA), **MA**, **reduced earnings allowance** (REA), **retirement allowance**, **retirement pensions** or **severe disablement allowance** (SDA).[108] Pending trial or sentencing, these benefits are only suspended, meaning you may be owed arrears if you do not receive a prison sentence (see p838).

You are paid **personal independence payment** (PIP), **adult disability payment** (ADP), **pension age disability payment** (PADP) or **Scottish adult disability living allowance** (SADLA) for the first 28 days that you count as a prisoner, whatever the outcome of the proceedings against you.[109] However, this does not apply if you are awarded PIP, ADP or PADP while you are a prisoner, in which case you are not paid PIP, PADP or, if you are 18 or over, ADP until your release from prison.[110] If you are aged 16 or 17, ADP mobility component can be paid while you are in prison, including if you are awarded it after becoming a prisoner.[111] There is a 'linking rule' for PIP, ADP, PADP and SADLA which means that different periods spent as a prisoner separated by one year or less are linked together and treated as one period.[112] Periods spent in a care home or hospital are also linked with periods spent as a prisoner (see p818 and p829).

If you live in Scotland and you are transferred from PIP/DLA to ADP or from AA to PADP, you will be paid ADP or PADP for 28 days after the transfer even if your PIP/DLA/AA has already stopped being paid.[113]

If you live in Scotland, you are transferred from DLA to SADLA and you have already been a prisoner for more than 28 days, you will not be paid SADLA while you remain a prisoner. If you have been a prisoner for less than 28 days when SADLA is awarded, you will receive payment for the days remaining in the 28 days period.[114]

If you get **child disability payment** (CDP), you continue to be paid the care component for the first 28 days that you are a prisoner and you continue to be paid the mobility component during any period when you are a prisoner including if it is awarded after you become a prisoner.[115]

If you get **new-style jobseeker's allowance** (JSA), you cannot meet the work-related requirements for JSA while you are in prison. In addition, you are treated as not having met the work availability requirement if you are on temporary release under specified provisions.[116] However, you may be able to satisfy the DWP that you should not have to meet a work search requirement during temporary police detention (legal custody in Scotland).

For non-means-tested benefits payable while you are a prisoner, see below.

### Benefits that are suspended

5

If you are a remand prisoner awaiting trial or sentence, payment of contributory ESA, SDA, AA, DLA, CA, MA, REA, retirement pensions, retirement allowance and bereavement benefits is suspended pending the outcome. If you subsequently receive a sentence of imprisonment or detention (including a suspended sentence), you are not paid the benefits for the whole period you are in prison.[117]

If you do not receive a sentence of imprisonment or detention, or your conviction is quashed, full arrears of any of the benefits that have been withheld are payable when you are released.[118] Arrears are only payable if the normal conditions of entitlement for benefit were met while you were a remand prisoner. For contributory ESA, you are treated as not having limited capability for work once you have been disqualified as a prisoner for six weeks.[119] This rule does not apply if contributory ESA is suspended and subsequently reinstated because you do not receive a custodial sentence, because you are not actually 'disqualified' in this situation.[120]

### Benefits payable

You are entitled to **industrial injuries disablement benefit** (but not any of the increases on p600) for periods when you are a prisoner. However, you are not paid until you are released and you can only get a maximum of 12 months' arrears.[121] If you are in prison for more than a year, you should be paid for the 12-month period which gives you the most benefit.[122] You are entitled to full arrears for any period you were on remand, provided you are not subsequently sentenced to imprisonment or detention.[123]

You are entitled to **child benefit** and **guardian's allowance**:[124]

- while you are a prisoner. You must continue to be 'responsible' for the child (see p492). If you are in prison for some time, you may want to arrange for child benefit to be paid to the person looking after your child;
- while your child is a prisoner, but entitlement to child benefit usually ends after eight weeks.[125] There are exceptions to the rules (see p499). Full arrears are payable at the end of any remand period if your child is not sentenced to imprisonment or detention. Once entitlement to child benefit ends, entitlement to guardian's allowance in respect of the child also ends.

**Note:** if child benefit stops because your child is a prisoner, this may affect whether you can get personal allowances and premiums for them with your housing benefit (HB).

You are entitled to carer support payment (CSP) while you are a prisoner providing you satisfy the rules that allow you to get CSP during a temporary break in care (see p1469).[126]

## Universal credit

If you are a single person and you become a prisoner, you can get the housing costs element in your UC for up to six months. To be entitled, you must have been getting the housing costs element immediately before you were a prisoner, and certain other conditions apply (see p844).[127] You do not get any other elements of UC.[128]

5

*Prisoners*

You count as a '**prisoner**' if you are:[129]

- detained in custody (eg, in prison or a young offenders' institution) awaiting trial or sentence (on remand) or following a sentence of imprisonment; *or*
- on temporary release under specific provisions (this does not include parole licence).

If your partner or a child included in your claim is a prisoner, see below. If you have a non-dependant who is a prisoner, no deduction is made from your housing costs element (see p109), but you no longer qualify for a bedroom for them in the size criteria if they are expected to be a prisoner for more than six months (see p107).[130]

### Couples

If one of you is a prisoner, or is serving a prison sentence while detained in hospital, the other partner is treated as claiming UC as a single claimant.[131] Provided you still count as a couple, your and your partner's income and capital are still assessed jointly, but your UC amount is that for a single person.[132] If the partner who is not a prisoner is working, you may qualify for a childcare costs element (see p76). In any case, if the absence from the household exceeds, or is expected to exceed, six months, you no longer count as a couple.[133] The amount of your housing costs element for your rent may be affected (see p845).

### Children

While your child is a prisoner, they are not included in your claim (see p62).[134] If your child is no longer included in your claim:

- the calculation of your benefit no longer includes amounts for them;
- the amount of your housing costs element for your rent may be affected (see p845);

- the work allowance which applies to you (see p41) and work-related requirements you must meet may change if, for example, you no longer have a dependent child living with you (see Chapter 42).

## Other means-tested benefits

For ESA, PC and HB, see p839 for when you count as a prisoner.[135]

You do not count as a prisoner if you are detained in hospital under specific mental health provisions (but see p841 if you received a prison sentence as a result of a criminal conviction). Check whether your benefit is affected by the special rules for hospital patients instead (see p821). In addition, you do not count as a prisoner if you are:

- released on licence or parole; *or*
- on bail or living in approved premises – eg, a bail or probation hostel; *or*
- released under a home detention curfew (electronic tagging).



If you are a prisoner:

- income-related ESA and PC guarantee credit usually stop immediately. The only exception to this is if you get income-related ESA or PC guarantee credit which includes an amount for housing costs (service charges and ground rent for owner-occupiers – see p286). In this situation, you can get the benefit for up to 52 weeks while you are detained in custody awaiting trial or sentence, but you only get your housing costs paid. If you have continued to be entitled to one of these benefits (because you get housing costs), it will stop once you have been sentenced;[136]
- you can continue to qualify for HB for a limited period (see p844);
- you cannot get any savings credit of PC.[137]

If you have a non-dependant who is a prisoner, no non-dependant deduction is made for them.[138] However, for HB you may no longer qualify for a bedroom for them after a period. See p207 and p289 for further information about non-dependant deductions.

### Partners and children

If you have a partner and one of you is a prisoner:

- you no longer count as a couple for income-related ESA or PC;[139]
- you continue to count as a couple for HB, provided you intend to live together again and the prisoner is unlikely to be away for substantially longer than 52 weeks.[140] If the partner who is not a prisoner is working, they may be able to have childcare costs deducted from their earnings (see p350 and p384).[141]

If you no longer count as a couple, the partner who is *not* a prisoner may be able to claim benefit as a single person.

If child benefit stops because your child is a prisoner, they may no longer be included in your claim for HB, in which case your entitlement to a personal allowance and premiums for them might be affected.

If you get PC which includes an amount for a child (see p258), the amount for the child stops if they become a prisoner.[142]

## Social fund payments

You cannot get a winter fuel payment if you are serving a custodial sentence (see p715). You cannot get other social fund payments if you are not getting a qualifying benefit (see Chapter 33).[143]

## If you are detained under mental health legislation



Special rules apply for non-means-tested benefits (other than new-style JSA, SSP, SMP, SAP, SPP, SSPP, SNCP, CDP, ADP, SADLA and CSP) and for UC, income-related ESA and PC if, although you received a prison sentence as a result of a criminal conviction, you are currently detained in a hospital or similar institution as a person with a mental disorder under sections 45A or 47 of the Mental Health Act 1983, section 59A of the Criminal Procedure (Scotland) Act 1995 or section 136 of the Mental Health (Care and Treatment) (Scotland) Act 2003. This applies if you are:[144]

- ordered to be detained in hospital by a court after you are convicted, where the court specifies a length of sentence; *or*
- sent to prison, but later transferred to hospital by order.

If this applies, although you are a hospital patient, you are treated as a prisoner for the above benefits, but only until you would have been entitled to be released under your original sentence or, if you are held under an indeterminate sentence (eg, you are a life prisoner), until your release is authorised.[145] After that, if you are still in hospital, your benefit might be affected under the rules that apply to hospital patients (see p816).

**Note:** if you are detained in a hospital or similar institution under provisions other than those listed above (eg, you were convicted of a criminal offence but were ordered to be detained in hospital under a provision other than those specified above), you may be paid non-means-tested benefits, or you may qualify for UC, income-related ESA or PC. Check whether your benefit is affected under the rules that apply to hospital patients (see p816).

## Community sentences

You do not count as a prisoner if you have been given a community sentence that involves punishment or supervision in the community. However, bear the following in mind.

- There might be a question about whether you satisfy the work-related requirements for UC or JSA. However, guidance suggests that any restrictions caused by a community sentence or order should be taken into account when setting a work search requirement.[146]
- If you undertake basic skills training and are treated as a full-time student, this may affect your entitlement to benefits (see Chapter 37).

## If you are on bail or living in approved premises

Your non-means-tested benefits are paid as normal if you are on bail or living in approved premises (eg, a bail or probation hostel) or other accommodation as a condition of bail. However, special rules can apply for means-tested benefits.

**For UC**, you and your partner continue to count as a couple while one of you is temporarily absent from the household. You must continue to make a joint claim and UC is paid as normal. However, if the absence exceeds, or is expected to exceed, six months, you no longer count as a couple.[147] If you no longer count as a couple, you can no longer make a joint claim for UC and the calculation of your benefit no longer includes amounts for your partner. Each partner must make a claim for UC as a single person if appropriate.

**For income-related ESA, PC and HB**, if you have a partner and are temporarily separated because one of you is living away from home, you still count as a couple if you intend to live together again, but only if you are unlikely to be apart for more than 52 weeks or, in exceptional circumstances, not substantially longer than 52 weeks.[148] For income-related ESA only, if one of you is living in an approved bail or probation hostel, your applicable amount is calculated in a special way – at either the single rate for each of you added together or the couple rate, whichever is greater.[149]

If you are required to live away from home in an approved bail or probation hostel or another address that you are bailed to:

- you cannot get the UC housing costs element for the hostel.[150] You can get the housing costs element for your normal home for up to six months, provided you are not expected to be away for longer;[151]
- you cannot get HB for the rent you pay for the hostel;[152]
- you can continue to get HB and help with your housing costs in income-related ESA or PC for your normal home for up to 52 weeks, provided you intend to return home and you are unlikely to be away for longer than this (or, in exceptional circumstances, not substantially longer than this);[153]
- you can get a DWP loan for your mortgage interest on your normal home for up to six months (UC) or 52 weeks (other benefits), provided you are not expected to be away for longer than this and you continue to satisfy the other conditions of entitlement.[154]

If you are no longer entitled to the UC housing costs element or HB for your normal home (or the DWP loan to help with mortgage interest – see p766), these can be paid to another person if they are (or can be treated as) liable (see p93, p294 and p186).

## Benefits on release

If you are **temporarily released** (on temporary licence), you no longer count as a prisoner for non-means-tested benefits. You still count as a prisoner for means-tested benefits (unless you are released on parole licence).

When you are **permanently released**, you should claim any benefits to which you are entitled as soon as possible. The prison gives you a discharge form that can help you prove your identity. You may also be interviewed by a DWP liaison officer before you leave prison, who should point out which benefits you might be able to claim.

- As UC is generally paid in arrears, you may need to apply for a UC advance (see p1023).
- If you are an offender who is subject to multi-agency risk management arrangements, you are exempt from the private sector rent restriction rules for single claimants under 35 (see p113).
- You may receive a discharge grant from the Prison Service, which counts as capital for income-related ESA.[155] The rules do not say how it should be treated for UC, PC or HB.
- If you are released without being sentenced to imprisonment or detention, you should receive any arrears of your non-means-tested benefits that were suspended (see p838).
- If you are released following the quashing of a conviction, you are entitled to national insurance credits for the period you were imprisoned or detained (see p873).



## Help with travelling expenses

The Help with Prison Visits scheme can help a partner or close relative (or another person if they are your only visitor) with the cost of visiting you in prison, or the cost of someone bringing your children to visit you. They must be getting 'qualifying income'.

Claim online at gov.uk/help-with-prison visits or contact Help with Prison Visits, PO Box 17594, Birmingham B2 2QP (tel: 0300 063 2100). You can also email HelpwithPrisonVisits@justice.gov.uk.

*Qualifying income*

**'Qualifying income'** is UC, income-related ESA and PC, and health benefits on low-income grounds. If your qualifying benefit is UC, your income must be below a specified level.

If you live on Orkney, Shetland or the Western Isles, see sps-additional-support.form.service.justice.gov.uk for the additional help you may get with prision vists.

## Paying for your usual home

The benefit you can get to help pay for your normal home may be affected while you, or your partner, child or non-dependant, are temporarily in prison. **Note:** if you leave your home permanently, you are no longer entitled to benefit for it.

### Universal credit housing costs

If you are a prisoner, whether awaiting trial or sentence or serving a custodial sentence, you can continue to qualify for a UC housing costs element for your normal home for up to six months.[156] However, you can only qualify following a sentence of imprisonment if you have not been sentenced to a term that is expected to go beyond the six-month period. The six-month period includes any time you have already been in prison before being sentenced – eg, if you were remanded in custody.[157] You can only get the housing costs element if you were entitled to it immediately before becoming a prisoner.[158] You must have been entitled to UC for at least one assessment period before becoming a prisoner.[159] If you are on UC and get a DWP loan for your mortgage interest, payments may continue for up to six months, provided your absence is not expected to last for more than six months.[160]

The UC housing costs element (or the DWP loan to help with mortgage interest – see p766) can be paid to another person (eg, your partner) if they are (or can be treated as) liable to pay the rent or housing costs (see p94).

### Housing benefit and other means-tested benefits

While you are detained in custody awaiting trial or sentence, you can get HB and help with your housing costs (service charges and ground rent for owner-occupiers) paid with income-related ESA or PC for your normal home for up to 52 weeks, provided you intend to return home, you are unlikely to be away for longer than this (or, in exceptional circumstances, unlikely to be away for substantially longer than this) and you do not sub-let your home.[161]

If you get a DWP loan for your mortgage interest and you are on a benefit other than UC, payments may continue while you are detained in custody awaiting trial or sentence for up to 52 weeks, provided you intend to return home, you are unlikely to be away for longer than this (or in exceptional circumstances, unlikely to be away for substantially longer than this) and you do not sub-let your home.[162]

If you are serving a custodial sentence, you can get HB for up to 13 weeks, provided you are unlikely to be away from your normal home for longer than this – ie, you are serving a short sentence.[163] The 13 weeks run from the date you were first in prison and include any time you spend in prison awaiting trial or sentence.[164] If you are serving a sentence of more than 13 weeks, you may still be entitled to HB, provided you are likely to spend no more than 13 weeks in prison – eg, you may be released early on a home detention curfew (electronic tagging).

If you are on temporary release under specific provisions, you continue to be treated as a prisoner.[165] This means that, even if you return home, you are still treated as if you are away from home.

In this situation, if you are a convicted prisoner, you are not entitled to income-related ESA or PC and cannot get help with your housing costs.

For HB, you are still treated as if you are away from home and these periods count towards the 13/52 weeks for which HB may be payable.[166]

When calculating how long you have been absent from home for HB, the day you go into prison is counted as a day of absence but the day you return home is not.[167]

**Note:**

- You should report any change in your circumstances as soon as possible – ie, when you are remanded in custody, begin a custodial sentence or are being released from custody.
- If you do not qualify for HB for 52 or 13 weeks under the rules described above, you may be able to continue to get HB for a former home for up to four benefit weeks if you are still liable to pay rent for it, and you could not reasonably have avoided this liability – eg, because your tenancy agreement required you to give notice.[168]
- HB and housing costs paid with income-related ESA or PC can be paid to another person (eg, your partner) if they are (or can be treated as) liable to pay the rent or housing costs (see p294, p93 and p186). There is a similar rule for mortgage interest loans.[169]

## Partners, children and non-dependants

If your partner, child or non-dependant is away from home because they are in prison, this could affect the amount of your HB or housing costs paid with your UC, income-related ESA or PC. This could apply, for example, if they no longer count as living with you or, for UC, they no longer count as a member of your 'extended benefit unit' (see p103). Bear the following in mind.

- If you live in rented accommodation, you may no longer be allowed the same number of bedrooms under the size criteria (see p309, p316, p320 and p104) and your UC or HB may be reduced. For UC, this only applies if your partner, child or non-dependant is absent (or expected to be absent) from home for more than six months.[170]
- If your non-dependant is absent, check whether a deduction for housing costs contributions or a non-dependant deduction should still be made for them (see p207, p289 and p109).

5

# 4. 16/17-year-old care leavers

You cannot usually qualify for universal credit (UC) or housing benefit (HB) if you are aged 16 or 17 and count as a 'care leaver' for these purposes (although there are exceptions – see p847[171]). Entitlement to other benefits is not affected by being a care leaver.

Being a care leaver means that you were previously 'looked after' by the local authority and certain other conditions apply. Your local authority must assess and meet your needs for maintenance, accommodation and support. In addition, you cannot be treated as a child member of the family of a person claiming income-related employment and support allowance (ESA) or HB. So, for example, they cannot get allowances and premiums for you with their HB.[172]

5

*Being looked after*

Being **'looked after'** means, for example, that you were subject to a care, supervision or permanence order, or provided with accommodation by the local authority under specified legal provisions.

Note:

- If you are *currently* being looked after by a local authority:
  - for UC purposes, you generally cannot be treated as the responsibility of a person, so, for example, they cannot get child elements for you in their UC. However, there are exceptions to this (see p64);[173]
  - for pension credit (PC) purposes, you generally cannot be treated as the responsibility of a person, so, for example, they cannot get child elements for you in their PC. However, there are exceptions to this (see p260);[174]
  - you cannot be included as a child in another person's claim for HB if you are not living with them (see Chapter 12);
  - a person cannot usually qualify for child benefit for you (see p495).
- If you are aged 16 or 17 and *currently* being looked after by a local authority, you cannot qualify for UC unless any of the exceptions on p847 apply.[175]
- Local DWP and social services offices should liaise to quickly resolve any disputes about who is responsible for supporting you. If you are refused both benefit and social services support, get specialist advice.

## Who is excluded from universal credit

Unless one of the exceptions on p847 applies, you are excluded from UC as a care leaver if you are no longer looked after by the local authority, you are aged 16 or 17 and:[176]

- you were looked after by a local authority (and, in Scotland, were provided with accommodation) for at least 13 weeks (or, in Scotland, three months). The 13-week/three-month period must have started after your 14th birthday and, in England and Wales, ended after you turn 16. In Scotland, you must have been looked after and accommodated for at least three months since your 14th birthday and have been looked after, but not necessarily accommodated, by the local authority at or beyond your 16th birthday. The local authority must be obliged to provide you with aftercare services; *or*

- in Scotland, you are in a 'continuing care' placement under section 26A of the Children (Scotland) Act 1995, you were being looked after and accommodated for at least three months since your 14th birthday and were looked after, but not necessarily accommodated, by the local authority at or beyond your 16th birthday; *or*
- in England or Wales, you are not subject to a care order, but you were in hospital, or detained in a remand centre or a young offenders' or similar institution when you became 16 and, immediately before you were in hospital or detained, you were being looked after by a local authority (in Wales, accommodated) for at least 13 weeks since your 14th birthday.



The 13 weeks or three months do not have to be continuous. Some pre-planned short-term placements, after which you return to the care of your parent, or person acting as your parent, do not count towards the 13 weeks or three months. In Scotland, any period when you have been placed with a member of your family does not count towards the three months.[177] 'Member of family' is not defined but we understand it to mean a person who has parental rights/responsibilities for you and so would not normally include a kinship carer, unless that person had been granted parental rights. This means that if, for example, you were looked after by the local authority and placed with a kinship carer for at least three months since your 14th birthday, and you were still looked after at or beyond your 16th birthday, you are normally excluded from UC while you are under 18.

**Note:** in England and Wales, you are not excluded from UC if you have been in a family placement (ie, living with your parent, someone with parental responsibility for you or someone who had a child arrangements order for you before you were looked after) for at least six months (unless the placement has broken down).[178]

### Who is not excluded from universal credit

Even if you fall within the definition of care leaver, you can get UC if you (or your partner) are responsible for a child or if you have limited capability for work.[179] However, you cannot get the housing costs element for your rent.[180]

## 5. People without accommodation

Entitlement to non-means-tested benefits, universal credit (UC) and pension credit (PC) is unaffected if you do not have accommodation. However, income-related employment and support allowance (ESA) may be paid at a reduced rate (see p849). If you do not have accommodation, you may need support from the job centre to ensure you satisfy the jobseeking conditions for new-style jobseeker's allowance (JSA) or the claimant responsibilities for UC.

If you become homeless and have no money, you can apply for a budgeting advance or a short-term advance (see p52 and p1023). It is possible to get help at any time in an emergency. You may also be able to claim local welfare assistance (see p770).

If you are homeless, the local authority may have a duty to assist you with accommodation or advice. A child or young person may be entitled to help from social services.

5

**Note:**

- If you are at least 16, have been living in a homeless hostel for at least three months and have accepted rehabilitation or resettlement support, you are exempt from the private sector rent restriction rules in housing benefit and UC for single people under 35 (see p113 and p328). The three-month period does not need to be continuous.[181]
- You can qualify for help with payments for a tent and its pitch (if that is your home) with income-related ESA and PC (see p287). You cannot get a UC housing costs element for rent payments you make for a tent or the site on which a tent stands.[182]

## Jobseeking conditions and claimant responsibilities

Even if you are homeless, to qualify for UC (and new-style JSA and ESA if you come under the UC system), you must accept a claimant commitment and, to avoid being sanctioned, meet your work-related requirements (see Chapter 42).

Being homeless may reduce your prospects of finding work, but personal circumstances that reduce your chances of being employed should not prevent you from getting UC or new-style JSA. You can be available for work even if you do not have accommodation.

**Note:**

- The fact that you are homeless should be taken into account when deciding whether you satisfy the work search requirements. UC guidance states that your work coach should carefully consider how homelessness and any other complex needs affect you and can tailor or temporarily switch off work search requirements.[183]
- The DWP can agree deductions from your expected hours of work search for time you spend dealing with a domestic emergency or other temporary circumstances, which can include homelessness. Work search and work availability requirements can also be suspended.[184] See p943.

## Income-related employment and support allowance

The amount of your income-related ESA may be lower than normal if you are a person 'without accommodation'.[185] You get the personal allowance for you (and your partner, if you have one) and any additional component in income-related ESA that you are entitled to, but you do not get any premiums.[186] **Note:** there are no special rules about the amount of UC payable if you do not have accommodation.

Having no fixed address is *not* the same as being 'without accommodation'. If you have accommodation, but are staying in different places on different nights (eg, with different friends or relatives), your income-related ESA should be paid as normal.[187]

*Accommodation*

'**Accommodation**' is not defined in the rules and should be interpreted widely and flexibly. The DWP says that, to count as having accommodation, you must have 'an effective shelter from the elements which is capable of being heated, in which occupants can sit, lie down, cook and eat, and which is reasonably suited for continuous occupation. The site of the accommodation may alter from day to day, but it is still accommodation if the structure is habitable.'[188]

Examples include tents, caravans, mobile homes and other substantial shelters. The DWP is likely to say that cardboard boxes, bus shelters, sleeping bags and cars do not qualify.[189]

**Note:** if you are temporarily absent from the accommodation you normally occupy as your home, even if you are living a lifestyle as though you have no accommodation (eg, you are sleeping rough), you should be treated as having accommodation.[190]

# Notes

1. **Hospital patients**

1 Reg 2(4) SS(HIP) Regs; reg 6 SS(AA) Regs; regs 8 and 12A SS(DLA) Regs

2 paras 18021 and 18059 DMG; R(DLA) 2/06

3 **PIP** s86(2) and (3) WRA 2012; reg 29(2) SS(PIP) Regs; para P3012 ADM
**ADP** Reg 28 DAWAP(S) Regs;
**PADP** Reg 20 DAOP(S) Regs
**SADLA** Reg 23 DA(SADLA) Regs

4 paras 18028-33 and 18041 DMG; para P3001 ADM; SSS DMG, *Effect of time spent in care homes, hospitals or similar institutions*

5 *White v CAO, The Times*, 2 August 1993, reported as R(IS) 18/94; *Botchett v CAO, The Times*, 8 May 1996, 2 CCLR 121 (CA); *R v North and East Devon Health Authority ex parte Coughlan* [1999] 2 CCLR 285; R(DLA) 2/06
6 *SSWP v Slavin* [2011] EWCA Civ 1515, reported as [2012] AACR 30
7 paras 18060-63 DMG; s86(2) and (3) WRA 2012; reg 29(2) SS(PIP) Regs; para P3062 ADM; reg 28(4) DAWAP(S) Regs; reg 20(4) DAOP(S) Regs; reg 23(4) DA(SADLA) Regs
8 **AA** Reg 6(2A) SS(AA) Regs
**DLA** Regs 8(2A) and 12A(2A) SS(DLA) Regs
**PIP** Reg 32(2) SS(PIP) Regs
**ADP** Reg 31(2) DAWAP(S) Regs
**PADP** Reg 23(2) DAOP(S) Regs
**SADLA** Reg 26(2) DA(SADLA) Regs
9 Reg 2(5) SS(HIP) Regs
10 **DLA** Reg 8(2B) SS(DLA) Regs
**PIP** Reg 29(3) SS(PIP) Regs
**CDP** Reg 21 DACYP(S) Regs
**ADP** Reg 28(1) and (5) DAWAP(S) Regs
11 Regs 2, 3(4A) and (5B) and 19 PIP(TP) Regs
12 Reg 4 DACYP(S) Regs
13 **AA** Reg 8(4) SS(AA) Regs
**DLA** Regs 10(6) and (7) and 12B(9A) and (12) SS(DLA) Regs
**PIP** Reg 30(3) and (4) SS(PIP) Regs
**ADP** Reg 28(2) DAWAP(S) Regs
**PADP** Reg 20(2) DAOP(S) Regs
**SADLA** Reg 23(2) DA(SADLA) Regs
14 **AA/DLA** Reg 25 SS(C&P) Regs
**PIP** Reg 50 UC,PIP,JSA&ESA(C&P) Regs
**ADP** Reg 34(3) DAWAP(S) Regs
**PADP** Reg 26(2) DAOP(S) Regs
**SADLA** Reg 29(3) DA(SADLA) Regs
15 **AA** Reg 8(2) SS(AA) Regs
**DLA** Regs 10(5) and 12B(3) SS(DLA) Regs
**PIP** Reg 32(4) and (5) SS(PIP) Regs
**ADP** Regs 28(3) and 31(5) and (6) DAWAP(S) Regs
**PADP** Regs 20(3) and 23(5) and (6) DAOP(S) Regs
**SADLA** Regs 23(3) and 26(5) and (6) DA(SADLA) Regs
16 **AA** Reg 8(4) and (5) SS(AA) Regs
**DLA** Regs 10(6) and (7) and 12B(9A) and (12) SS(DLA) Regs
**PIP** Reg 30(3) and (4) SS(PIP) Regs
**ADP** Reg 29 DAWAP(S) Regs
**PADP** Reg 21 DAOP(S) Regs
**SADLA** Reg 24 DA(SADLA) Regs
17 **AA** Reg 8(3) SS(AA) Regs
**DLA** Regs 10(3) and 12B(2) SS(DLA) Regs
**PIP** Reg 30(2) SS(PIP) Regs
**ADP** Reg 32(2)(b) DAWAP(S) Regs
**PADP** Reg 24(2)(b) DAOP(S) Regs
18 Regs 12B(4)-(6) and 12C SS(DLA) Regs; reg 27(7) DA(SADLA) Regs
19 Reg 75F(1)(f) HB Regs; reg 83(1)(h) UC Regs
20 Sch 2 para 14 DAWAP(S) Regs; reg 10(c) DAWAP(TPMA)(S) Regs
21 Reg 6(19)-(21) SS(C&P) Regs
22 Reg 23(2) CA(CSP)(S) Regs
23 Reg 23(9) CA(CSP)(S) Regs
24 **CA** Reg 4(2) SS(ICA) Regs
**CSP** Reg 40 CA(CSP)(S) Regs
25 Regs 29(1) and 30 UC Regs
26 Sch 3 para 9 UC Regs
27 Sch 3 para 18 LMI Regs
28 s39 WRA 2012; reg 3(6) UC Regs
29 s10 WRA 2012; reg 4(7) UC Regs
30 **ESA** Sch 4 paras 6(2)(b) and (5)(a) and (c) and 11(2(b) ESA Regs
**HB** Sch 3 paras 14(2)(b) and (5)(a) and (c) and 20(6)(b) HB Regs; Sch 3 paras 6(2)(b) and (7)(a) and (c) and 12(b) HB(SPC) Regs
**PC** Reg 6(5)(b) and Sch 1 para 1(1)(b) and (2)(b) and (ba) SPC Regs
31 **ESA** Sch 4 para 6(2)(b) and (5)(b) ESA Regs
**HB** Sch 3 para 14(2)(b) and (5)(b) HB Regs; Sch 3 para 6(2)(b) and (7)(b) HB(SPC) Regs
32 **ESA** Sch 4 para 7 ESA Regs
**HB** Sch 3 paras 13(1)(a)(iii) and 15(1) HB Regs; Sch 3 para 7 HB(SPC) Regs
33 Reg 6 and Sch IIA para 6 SPC Regs
34 **ESA** Reg 156(1)-(3) ESA Regs
**PC** Reg 5(1)(a) SPC Regs
**HB** Reg 21(1) and (2) HB Regs; reg 21(1) and (2) HB(SPC) Regs
35 Reg 74(7)(f) HB Regs; reg 55(7)(f) HB(SPC) Regs
36 Schs 4 para 7(2)(b) and 5 para 13 ESA Regs
37 Schs 4 paras 5, 6, 7 and 5 para 13 ESA Regs
38 Sch 3 paras 15(1) and 16(a) HB Regs; Sch 3 paras 7 and 8(a) HB(SPC) Regs
39 Sch 5 para 13 ESA Regs; reg 63(1) ESA Regs 2013
40 Regs 46A(1), (3) and (3A) and 47 JSA Regs 2013; regs 55ZA(1), (3) and (3A) and 55A JSA Regs
41 Reg 4(1)(a)(iii) SFWFP Regs
42 Sch 3 para 9 UC Regs

43 Sch 3 para 18 LMI Regs
44 **ESA** Sch 6 para 5(11) ESA Regs
**PC** Sch II para 4(11) SPC Regs
**HB** Reg 7(16) HB Regs; reg 7(16) HB(SPC) Regs
45 Sch 3 para 10 LMI Regs
46 R(H) 9/05
47 Sch 4 para 11 UC Regs

2. **People in care homes and similar accommodation**

48 **AA/DLA** ss67(2) and 72(8) SSCBA 1992; regs 7 and 8(1) SS(AA) Regs; regs 9 and 10(1) SS(DLA) Regs
**PIP** s85 WRA 2012; regs 28 and 30(1) SS(PIP) Regs
**CDP** Reg 17(2) DACYP(S) Regs
**ADP** Reg 27(2) DAWAP(S) Regs
**PADP** Reg 19(2) DAOP(S) Regs
**SADLA** Reg 22(2) DA(SADLA) Regs
49 ss67(3) and 72(9) SSCBA 1992; s85(3) WRA 2012; reg 2 DACYP(S) Regs; reg 2 DAWAP(S) Regs; reg 2 DAOP(S) Regs; reg 2 DA(SADLA) Regs
50 **AA/DLA** ss67(4) and 72(10) SSCBA 1992
**PIP** s85(4) WRA 2012
**CDP** Reg 2 DACYP(S) Regs
**ADP** Reg 2 DAWAP(S) Regs, as amended by SSI 2022 No.217
**PADP** Reg 2 DAOP(S) Regs
**SADLA** Reg 2 DA(SADLA) Regs
51 Reg 7(3) SS(AA) Regs; reg 9(6) SS(DLA) Regs
52 **AA** Reg 7(2) SS(AA) Regs
**DLA** Reg 9(2) SS(DLA) Regs
**PIP** Reg 28(2)-(4) SS(PIP) Regs
53 CDLA/1465/1998; CDLA/2127/2000
54 **CA**/2985/1997
55 **AA** Reg 8(3) SS(AA) Regs
**DLA** Reg 10(3) SS(DLA) Regs
**PIP** Reg 30(2) SS(PIP) Regs
**CDP** Reg 20 DACYP(S) Regs
**ADP** Reg 32(1) and (2)(a) DAWAP(S) Regs
**PADP** Reg 24(1) and (2)(a) DAOP(S) Regs
56 **UC** Reg 83(1)(h) UC Regs
**HB** Reg 75F(1)(f) HB Regs
57 R(DLA) 2/06
58 Sch 2 para 14 DAWAP(S) Regs; reg 10(c) DAWAP(TPMA)(S) Regs
59 **AA** Reg 8(4) and (5) SS(AA) Regs
**DLA** Reg 10(6) and (7) SS(DLA) Regs
**PIP** Reg 30(3) SS(PIP) Regs
60 Reg 21 DACYP(S) Regs
61 **ADP** Reg 29 DAWAP(S) Regs
**PADP** Reg 24 DAOP(S) Regs
**SADLA** Reg 24 DA(SADLA) Regs
62 **DLA** Reg 9(3) SS(DLA) Regs
**PIP** Reg 28(2)(f) SS(PIP) Regs
63 **DLA** Reg 9(4)(a) and (b) and (5) SS(DLA) Regs
**PIP** Reg 28(3)(a) and (4) SS(PIP) Regs
**CDP** Reg 17(5)(b) DACYP(S) Regs
**ADP** Reg 27(5)(a) DAWAP(S) Regs
64 **DLA** Reg 9(4)(c) SS(DLA) Regs
**PIP** Reg 28(3)(b) SS(PIP) Regs
**CDP** Reg 17(5)(b) DACYP(S) Regs
**ADP** Reg 27(5)(b) DAWAP(S) Regs
65 **AA** Reg 8(6) SS(AA) Regs
**DLA** Reg 10(8) SS(DLA) Regs
**PIP** Reg 30(5) SS(PIP) Regs
**CDP** Reg 17(4) DACYP(S) Regs
**ADP** Reg 27(4) DAWAP(S) Regs
**PADP** Reg 19(4) DAOP(S) Regs
**SADLA** Reg 22(4) DA(SADLA) Regs
*Steane v CAO and Secretary of State*, 24 July 1996, reported as R(A) 3/96
66 R(A) 1/02; CA/3800/2006; *CAO v Creighton and Others* [1999] NICA 13, reported as R 1/00 (AA); *SSWP v DA* [2009] UKUT 214 (AAC)
67 *SSWP v JL (DLA)* [2011] UKUT 293 (AAC); Vol 10 Ch 61 para 61751 DMG; para P3049 ADM
68 **AA** Reg 7(4) SS(AA) Regs
**DLA** Reg 9(7) SS(DLA) Regs
**PIP** Reg 32(1) and (2) SS(PIP) Regs
**CDP** Reg 19 DACYP(S) Regs
**ADP** Reg 31 DAWAP(S) Regs
**PADP** Reg 23 DAOP(S) Regs
**SADLA** Reg 26(2) DA(SADLA) Regs
69 **AA** Reg 7(5) SS(AA) Regs
**DLA** Reg 9(8) SS(DLA) Regs
**CDP** Reg 19(4) DACYP(S) Regs
**ADP** Reg 31(5) DAWAP(S) Regs
**PADP** Reg 23(5) DAOP(S) Regs
70 **AA** Reg 7(6) SS(AA) Regs
**DLA** Reg 9(9) SS(DLA) Regs
**PIP** Reg 32(3) SS(PIP) Regs
**CDP** Reg 19(5) DACYP(S) Regs
**ADP** Reg 31(5) DAWAP(S) Regs
**PADP** Reg 23(5) DAOP(S) Regs
71 **AA** Reg 8(2) SS(AA) Regs
**DLA** Reg 10(5) SS(DLA) Regs
**PIP** Reg 32(4) SS(PIP) Regs
**CDP** Reg 17(3) DACYP(S) Regs
**ADP** Reg 27(3) DAWAP(S) Regs
**PADP** Reg 19(30 DAOP(S) Regs
**SADLA** Reg 22(3) DA(SADLA) Regs

72 **AA** Reg 8(2)(b) SS(AA) Regs
**DLA** Reg 10(5)(b) SS(DLA) Regs
**PIP** Reg 32(4) and (5) SS(PIP) Regs
**ADP** Reg 31(5) DAWAP(S) Regs
**PADP** Reg 23(5) DAOP(S) Regs
**SADLA** Reg 26(5) DA(SADLA) Regs
73 **ESA** Sch 4 para 8(4) ESA Regs
**PC** Sch 1 para 4 SPC Regs
**HB** Sch 3 para 17(2) HB Regs; Sch 3 para 9(2) HB(SPC) Regs
74 Regs 29(1) and 30 UC Regs
75 Sch 3C para 3(f) and (g) SS&CS(DA) Regs
76 Sch 1 para 3(d) UC Regs
77 Sch 1 para 1 UC Regs
78 *SA v SSWP (IS)* [2010] UKUT 345 (AAC), reported as [2011] AACR 16
79 Sch 3 para 9 UC Regs
80 Sch 3 para 18 LMI Regs
81 s39 WRA 2012; reg 3(6) UC Regs
82 Reg 24(2) UC Regs
83 s10 WRA 2012; reg 4(7) UC Regs
84 Regs 4 and 4A UC Regs
85 Reg 12(c) SPC Regs
86 Reg 9(1)(k) HB Regs; reg 9(1)(k) HB(SPC) Regs
87 Sch 3 para 9 HB&CTB(CP) Regs
88 HB guidance manual para 4.385
89 **ESA** Reg 118(2), (3) and (4) ESA Regs
**HB** Reg 52(3)-(5), (8) and (9) HB Regs
90 **ESA** Reg 156(4)(d) ESA Regs
**PC** Reg 5(1)(b) SPC Regs
**HB** Reg 21(2) HB Regs; reg 21(2) HB(SPC) Regs
91 Appendix to CIS/4934/1997; CIS/4965/1997; CIS/5232/1997; CIS/3767/1997
92 **ESA** Reg 156(1)-(3) ESA Regs
**PC** Reg 5(1)(a) SPC Regs
**HB** Reg 21(1) and (2) HB Regs; reg 21(1) and (2) HB(SPC) Regs
93 Sch 5 paras 4 and 5 ESA Regs; CIS/1544/2001
94 Reg 6 and Sch IIA para 6 SPC Regs
95 Sch IIA para 9 SPC Regs
96 Sch IIA para 4 SPC Regs
97 Reg 1A(4) and (5) SFCWP Regs
98 Reg 4(1)(a)(v) SFWFP Regs
99 Reg 4(2) WHACYP(S) Regs
100 Reg 4 WHA(LI)(S) Regs
101 Sch 3 para 18(1) LMI Regs
102 Sch 3 para 10 LMI Regs
103 R(H) 9/05
104 **ESA** Sch 6 para 5(8)-(12) ESA Regs
**PC** Sch 2 para 4(8)-(12) SPC Regs
**HB** Reg 7(11)-(13), (16) and (17) HB Regs; reg 7(11)-(13), (16) and (17) HB(SPC) Regs
105 Sch 4 para 11 UC Regs

3. **Prisoners**

106 **ESA** s18(4)(b) WRA 2007
**PIP** s87 WRA 2012
**Statutory payments** Reg 3(1) and (2) SSP Regs; reg 9 SMP Regs; regs 18(c) and 27(1)(c) SPPSAP(G) Regs; regs 14 and 26 SSPP(G) Regs
**Other benefits** s113(1)(b) and Sch 9 para 1 SSCBA 1992; reg 2(9) and (10) SS(GB) Regs; reg 10(2)(d) and Sch 2 para 7(b)(ii) SSB(Dep) Regs; R(S) 8/79
**ADP** Reg 2 DAWAP(S) Regs
**CDP** Reg 2 DACYP(S) Regs
**CSP** Reg 2 CA(CSP)(S) Regs
107 Reg 3(1) and (2) SSP Regs; reg 9 SMP Regs; regs 18 and 27(1)(c) and (2) SPPSAP(G) Regs; regs 14 and 26 SSPP(G) Regs; reg 9(1)(c) and (2) SPBP(G) Regs; reg 12(1)(c) and (2) SNCP(G) Regs (draft)
108 **ESA** s18(4)(b) WRA 2007; reg 160 ESA Regs; reg 96 ESA Regs 2013
**Other benefits** s113(1)(b) SSCBA 1992; reg 2 SS(GB) Regs; s19 PA 2014; regs 2 and 3 SP Regs
109 **PIP** s87 WRA 2012; reg 31(1) SS(PIP) Regs
**ADP** Reg 30 DAWAP(S) Regs
**PADP** Reg 22 DAOP(S) Regs
**SADLA** Reg 25 DA(SADLA) Regs
110 **PIP** Reg 31(2) SS(PIP) Regs
**ADP** Reg 32(2)(c) DAWAP(S) Regs
**PADP** Reg 24(2)(c) DAOP(S) Regs
111 Regs 3(3)(b) and 32(2)(c)(ii) DAWAP(S) Regs
112 **PIP** Reg 32(1) and (5) SS(PIP) Regs
**ADP** Reg 30(4) DAWAP(S) Regs
**PADP** Reg 22(4) DAOP(S) Regs
**SADLA** Reg 25(4) DA(SADLA) Regs
113 **ADP** Sch 2 para 14 DAWAP(S) Regs; reg 10(c) DAWAP(TPMA(S) Regs
**PADP** Sch para 12 DAOP(S) Regs
114 Reg 27 DA(SADLA) Regs
115 Reg 18 DACYP(S) Regs
116 Reg 13(1)(b) JSA Regs 2013
117 **ESA** Reg 160(1), (2) and (5)(c) ESA Regs; reg 96(1), (2) and (6)(c) ESA Regs 2013
**Other benefits** Reg 2(2) and (8)(c) SS(GB) Regs; reg 14 SS(ICA) Regs; s19 PA 2014; regs 2 and 3 SP Regs
**All** R(S) 1/71
118 **ESA** Reg 161 ESA Regs; reg 97 ESA Regs 2013
**Other benefits** Reg 3 SS(GB) Regs; reg 14 SS(ICA) Regs
119 Reg 159(1) ESA Regs; reg 95 ESA Regs 2013

120 Reg 160 ESA Regs; reg 96 ESA Regs 2013
121 Regs 2(6) and (7) and 3(1) SS(GB) Regs
122 Reg 2(7) SS(GB) Regs; para 12091 DMG
123 Reg 2(2) and (7) SS(GB) Regs
124 **CB** s113(1)(b) SSCBA 1992. Child benefit is not in Parts 2-5 of that Act.
**GA** Reg 2(5) SS(GB) Regs
125 Sch 9 para 1(a) SSCBA 1992; regs 16 and 17 CB Regs
126 Reg 40 CA(CSP)(S) Regs
127 Reg 19 UC Regs
128 This is the policy intention as reflected in ADM E3030 and 3040. Reg 19 UC Regs states that 'entitlement to UC cannot arise' where the claimant is a prisoner. This wording suggests new claims to UC are prevented, as opposed to existing claims being affected.
129 Reg 2 UC Regs
130 Sch 4 paras 11 and 16(2)(h) UC Regs
131 Reg 3(3)(c) UC Regs
132 Regs 18, 22(3) and 36(3) UC Regs
133 s39 WRA 2012; reg 3(6) UC Regs
134 Reg 4(6)(b) UC Regs
135 **ESA** Reg 69(2) ESA Regs
**PC** Reg 1(2) SPC Regs
**HB** Reg 7(14) and (16)(c)(i) HB Regs; reg 7(14) and (16)(c)(i) HB(SPC) Regs
136 **ESA** Schs 5 para 3 and 6 para 5(11) and (12) ESA Regs
**PC** Reg 6(2)(a), (3), (6)(c), (7), (9) and (10) SPC Regs
137 Reg 7(3) SPC Regs
138 **ESA** Sch 6 para 19(7)(g) ESA Regs
**PC** Sch 2 para 14(7)(e) SPC Regs
**HB** Reg 74(7)(f) HB Regs; reg 55(7)(f) HB(SPC) Regs
139 **ESA** Reg 156(4) ESA Regs
**PC** Reg 5(1)(c)(ii) and (iii) SPC Regs
140 Reg 21(2) HB Regs; reg 21(2) HB(SPC) Regs
141 Reg 28 HB Regs; reg 31 HB(SPC) Regs
142 Sch IIA para 5 SPC Regs
143 *Stewart v SSWP* [2011] EWCA Civ 907 decided that the exclusion of prisoners from entitlement to a funeral expenses payment did not breach the HRA 1998
144 **UC** Reg 19(1)(c) and (4) UC Regs
**ESA** Regs 69(3)-(5) and 160(3)-(4A) and Sch 5 para 12 ESA Regs; reg 96(3)-(5) ESA Regs 2013
**PC** Reg 8 and Sch 3 para 2 SPC Regs
**PIP** Reg 31(3) and (4) SS(PIP) Regs
**Other benefits** Reg 2(3), (4) and (4A) SS(GB) Regs
**All** CSS/239/2007; *JB v SSWP (IS)* [2010] UKUT 263 (AAC)
145 **UC** Reg 19(1)(c) and (4) UC Regs
**ESA** Regs 69(3)-(5) and 160(3)-(4A) and Sch 5 para 12 ESA Regs; reg 96(3)-(5) ESA Regs 2013
**PC** Reg 8 and Sch 3 para 2 SPC Regs
**PIP** Reg 31(3) and (4) SS(PIP) Regs
**Other benefits** Reg 2(3)-(4A) SS(GB) Regs
**All** CSS/239/2007; *JB v SSWP (IS)* [2010] UKUT 263 (AAC)
146 paras J3086 and R4086 ADM
147 s39 WRA 2012; reg 3(6) UC Regs
148 **ESA** Reg 156(3) ESA Regs
**PC** Reg 5(1)(a) SPC Regs
**HB** Reg 21(1) and (2) HB Regs; reg 21(1) and (2) HB(SPC) Regs
149 Sch 5 para 4(a)(v) ESA Regs
150 Schs 1 paras 1 and 3(c) and 3 para 1(1) UC Regs
151 Sch 3 para 9 UC Regs
152 Reg 7(5) HB Regs; reg 7(5) HB(SPC) Regs
153 **ESA** Sch 6 para 5(11)(c)(i) and (12) ESA Regs
**PC** Sch 2 para 4(11)(c)(i) and (12) SPC Regs
**HB** Reg 7(16)(c)(i) and (17) HB Regs; reg 7(16)(c)(i) and (17) HB(SPC) Regs
154 Sch 3 paras 10(2)(c) and 18 LMI Regs
155 Reg 112(6) ESA Regs
156 Reg 19(2) and (3) UC Regs
157 Reg 19(2)(b) UC Regs
158 Reg 19(2)(a) UC Regs
159 *SSWP v AH (UC)* [2023] UKUT 274 (AAC)
160 Sch 3 para 18 LMI Regs
161 **ESA** Schs 5 para 3 and 6 para 5(11) and (12) ESA Regs
**PC** Reg 6(2)(a), (3), (6)(c), (7), (9) and (10) and Sch 2 para 4(11) and (12) SPC Regs
**HB** Reg 7(16)(c)(i) and (17) HB Regs; reg 7(16)(c)(i) and (17) HB(SPC) Regs
162 Sch 3 para 10(1) and (2) LMI Regs
163 Reg 7(13) HB Regs; reg 7(13) HB(SPC) Regs
164 CSH/499/2006
165 **UC** Reg 2(1) UC Regs
**ESA** Reg 69(2) and Sch 5 para 3(a) ESA Regs
**PC** Regs 1(2) and 6 SPC Regs
166 Reg 7(14) and (15) HB Regs; reg 7(14) and (15) HB(SPC) Regs; R(IS) 17/93
167 *KdeS v Camden LB (HB)* [2011] UKUT 457 (AAC)
168 Reg 7(7) HB Regs; reg 7(7) HB(SPC) Regs; Ch A3, paras 3.430-32 GM
169 Sch 2 para 2 LMI Regs
170 Sch 4 para 11 UC Regs

4. **16/17-year-old care leavers**

171 **UC** Reg 8(1), (2) and (4) UC Regs
**HB** ss6 and 8(6) C(LC)A 2000; C(LC)SSB(S) Regs
172 **ESA** Reg 2(1), definition of 'young person', ESA Regs
**HB** Reg 19(2)(c) HB Regs; reg 19(2)(c) HB(SPC) Regs
173 Regs 4(6)(a) and 4A UC Regs
174 Sch IIA para 4 SPC Regs
175 Reg 8(1) and (4) UC Regs
176 Reg 8(2) and (4) UC Regs
177 Reg 8(4)(b) UC Regs. 'Member of your family' is not defined. Arguably, the intention is to exclude periods of time when you are living with a person who has parental responsibilities for you.
178 Reg 3(5) and (6) CL(E) Regs; reg 4(4)-(6) C(LC)(W) Regs
179 Reg 8(1) and (2) UC Regs
180 Sch 4 para 4 UC Regs

5. **People without accommodation**

181 **UC** Sch 4 para 29(4) UC Regs
**HB** Reg 2(1), definition of 'young individual', HB Regs
182 Sch 1 paras 1 and 3(b) UC Regs
183 DWP, *Universal Credit Guidance, Homelessness and at risk of homelessness*, House of Commons library deposited papers, available at rightsnet.org.uk/resources/universal-credit-guidance
184 **UC** Reg 95(2) UC Regs
**JSA** Reg 12(2) and (3) JSA Regs 2013
185 This rule was challenged under the HRA 1998, but the court decided the rules did not conflict with it: *R (RJM) v SSWP* [2008] UKHL 63
186 Sch 5 para 1 ESA Regs
187 paras 24157 and 54157 DMG
188 paras 24158-59 and 54158-59 DMG
189 paras 24159-60 and 54159-60 DMG; R(IS) 23/98
190 para 24162 and para 54162 DMG

# Part 6

# National insurance, work and work-related rules

# Chapter 39

# National insurance contributions

**This chapter covers:**

1. National insurance contributions and contributory benefits (below)
2. Paid national insurance contributions (p858)
3. National insurance credits (p865)
4. Contribution conditions for benefits (p874)

6

This chapter explains the national insurance (NI) contribution rules relevant to contributory benefits. For details of the NI number requirement that applies to most benefits, see p1007.

## Key facts

- Entitlement to some benefits, called 'contributory' benefits, and sometimes the amount paid, depends on your NI contribution record. For some benefits, it depends on the contribution record of your spouse or civil partner, or your late spouse, civil partner or cohabiting partner.
- If you are employed or self-employed, you may be liable to pay NI contributions. If you are not liable to pay contributions, in some circumstances, you can be awarded NI credits, or you may be able to pay contributions voluntarily.
- There are different types of NI contributions (called 'classes'). Not all classes of NI contributions or all types of NI credits count for all contributory benefits.
- HMRC collects NI contributions.

## 1. National insurance contributions and contributory benefits

Your national insurance (NI) contribution record is based on the NI contributions you have paid, or the NI credits you have received, for each tax year – ie, 6 April to 5 April.

Benefits that have NI contribution conditions are known as '**contributory benefits**'. They, are:

- new-style jobseeker's allowance;
- contributory employment and support allowance (either old-style or new-style – see Chapter 26);
- bereavement support payment and widowed parent's allowance;
- state pension and 'old' (ie, category A and B) retirement pensions.

Entitlement to contributory benefits normally depends on NI contribution conditions being met. For the detailed rules, see pp874–79.

In some circumstances, you may be liable to pay NI contributions. If you are not, to help you meet the contribution conditions for some contributory benefits, you may either be credited with earnings or with contributions, or you can sometimes choose to pay contributions. For details of NI credits, see p865.

6

**Note:** if you are self-employed, your entitlement to maternity allowance (MA) and the amount you receive may be affected by whether you have paid class 2 NI contributions (see p632). For you to qualify for MA on the basis that you help your spouse or civil partner with their self-employment, they must meet conditions relating to class 2 NI contributions (see p630).

### How decisions are made

Most decisions on NI contributions are made by an officer of HMRC. Appeals against such decisions can be decided by an HMRC review or a tribunal that considers tax appeals.[1] The process is similar to appealing against an HMRC decision on entitlement to a statutory payment (see p1252).

Decisions relating to entitlement to NI credits are made either by HMRC or the DWP, depending on the type of NI credit. If you disagree with a decision on your entitlement, you can apply for a revision or supersession (see Chapter 50), or appeal against it (see Chapter 51). You must apply for a mandatory reconsideration before you can appeal. Your appeal is decided by a social security tribunal.[2]

---

## 2. **Paid national insurance contributions**

There are seven different types ('classes') of paid national insurance (NI) contributions.[3] Classes 1, 2 and 3 can help you to qualify for contributory benefits, but only class 1 contributions count for *all* contributory benefits. Class 3A contributions, which could only be paid if you reached pension age before 6 April 2016, count towards entitlement to additional state pension (see p782 of the 2015/16 edition of this *Handbook* for details).

If you are an employed earner, you may be liable for class 1 contributions, depending on the amount you earn. If you are a self-employed earner, you may be liable for class 4 contributions), unless your profits are low or you are exempt from payment. If you are not liable to pay contributions, you may choose to pay class 2 (if self-employed) or class 3 contributions voluntarily, known as 'voluntary contributions'.

| *Class of contribution* | *Payable by* | *Giving entitlement to* |
|---|---|---|
| Class 1 | Employed earners and their employers | All benefits with contribution conditions |
| Class 1A and 1B | Employers of employed earners | No benefits |
| Class 2 | Self-employed earners (voluntary contributors) | All benefits with contribution conditions, except new-style jobseeker's allowance (JSA) |
| Class 3 | Voluntary contributors | State pension, category A and B retirement pensions and widowed parent's allowance |
| Class 3A | Voluntary contributors | An amount (a 'unit') of additional state pension |
| Class 4 | Self-employed earners | No benefits |

## The rules about your age

- You are not liable for class 1 contributions if you are under 16 or over pension age (see p690).[4]
- You cannot pay class 3 contributions if you are under 16 (and sometimes if you are 17 or 18) or for the tax year in which you reach pension age or any subsequent tax year.[5]

## Employed earners and self-employed earners

Your liability to pay class 1 or 4 NI contributions depends on whether you are an employed or self-employed earner.[6] It is normally clear whether you are employed or self-employed. If there is a dispute, it usually concerns whether you are employed under a *contract of service* (in which case, you are an employee) or a *contract for services* (in which case, you are self-employed).[7] **Note:**

- To be an employed or self-employed earner, you must be 'gainfully employed'.
- Office holders, including people in elective office, who receive earnings are classed as employed earners. Office holders include judges, registrars of births, marriages and deaths and most company directors. (If you are a company director and pay yourself a wage from which class 1 NI contributions are deducted, this may help you to claim both statutory payments and contributory benefits. You need to register as an employer.)
- Certain people are deemed to be employed earners. These include office cleaners, many agency workers and people employed by their spouse or civil partner for the purposes of their spouse's or civil partner's employment.[8]

- Examiners, moderators and invigilators are deemed to be self-employed.[9]
- If you have two or more jobs, it is possible to be both employed and self-employed.
- You do not have to pay NI contributions on earnings from certain kinds of employment – eg, if you are employed by your spouse or civil partner and it is not for the purpose of their employment, or if you are employed in your home by a close relative who lives with you and the job is not for a trade or business that is carried out there.[10]

### More than one job

If you are employed as an employed earner in more than one job, the basic rule is that your liability to pay class 1 contributions is calculated for each job as if the other(s) did not exist, although the total you pay is subject to a maximum.[11] There are some exceptions – eg, if you have two different jobs for the same employer or employers who carry on business with each other. In this situation, earnings from these jobs are normally added together to stop employers avoiding liability and your NI contributions are based on your total earnings.[12]



## Class 1 contributions

Class 1 contributions have two elements: primary contributions (paid by employed earners) and secondary contributions (paid by employers).[13]

The amount of primary class 1 contributions you pay depends on the amount you earn in relation to the upper and lower earnings limit for the tax year, and the amount of that year's 'primary threshold'. See Appendix 5 for the earnings limits and the primary threshold.

If your earnings are equal to or below the primary threshold, you do not have to pay NI contributions on them. If they are between the lower earnings limit and the primary threshold, you are treated as if you had paid class 1 NI contributions on those earnings.[14]

If you earn more than the primary threshold, you are liable to pay class 1 contributions at a percentage of your earnings between the primary threshold and upper earnings limit, plus a further percentage of the earnings you have above the upper earnings limit (see p1583).[15] If you are a married woman or widow with reduced liability for contributions (see p862), you pay lower class 1 contributions.[16]

For the current contribution rates, see gov.uk/national-insurance-rates-letters.

Your employer is responsible for deducting your contributions from your earnings and paying them with its own contributions to HMRC.[17] If your employer has failed to pay your contributions to HMRC, you are treated as though they had been paid, unless you have been negligent or consented to or connived in that arrangement.[18]

## Class 2 contributions

**Compulsory class 2** contributions were abolished from the 2024/25 tax year.[19] Before then, you had to pay class 2 contributions in a tax year in which you were a self-employed earner (see p859) unless your taxable profits in that year were either below the 'small profits threshold', or between that threshold and the 'lower profits threshold', or you were exempt from payment. From 6 April 2024, these compulsory class 2 contributions are abolished. Although compulsory class 2 contributions have been abolished, provided you are a self-employed earner, you may still choose to pay **voluntary class 2** contributions to protect or improve your NI contribution record (see p864).[20] You may wish to do this, for example, to ensure you have sufficient contributions for contributory benefits, including retirement pension, if your profits are below the small profits threshold.

The small profits threshold for 2025/26 is £6,845, and the lower profits threshold is £12,570. You do not have to pay class 2 contributions even if your profits exceed £12,750. In this situation, you continue to receive access to contributory benefits, including the state pension by being treated as having paid class 2 contributions.[21] If your profits do not exceed the lower profits threshold but are at or above the small profits threshold, you will continue to be treated as having paid class 2 contributions for benefit.[22] If your profits are below the small profits threshold, you can still choose to pay voluntary class 2 contributions.

The main grounds for being exempt from compulsory payment (ie, before 2024/25) were that you received certain benefits – eg, maternity allowance (MA) or employment and support allowance (ESA) for the week to which the contribution relates, or carer's allowance for at least part of that week.[23]

Class 2 contributions are payable at a flat rate.[24] The current and previous year's rates are:

| | |
|---|---|
| 2025/26 | £3.50 a week |
| 2024/25 | £3.45 a week |

**Note:**

- The self-assessment procedure was not used to collect class 2 contributions in tax years before 2015/16. For details, see the 2014/15 edition of this *Handbook*.
- Married women and widows with reduced liability for contributions (see p862) cannot pay for class 2 contributions voluntarily.[25]
- Volunteer development workers employed abroad and share fishermen can, if they wish, pay class 2 contributions at special rates, which count towards contribution-based JSA, unlike other class 2 contributions.[26]

## Class 2 contributions and maternity allowance

You can voluntarily pay class 2 contributions early to increase your entitlement to MA (see p633), or your spouse or civil partner can pay them early to enable you to qualify for MA if you help with their self-employment (see p630). In either situation, the contributions may be paid at any time from the week to which they relate. See above for when you are treated as having paid class 2 contributions.

If you employ yourself (eg, as a company director) and pay yourself a wage, you should check to see whether you are liable for class 1 contributions, as you may be able to claim statutory maternity pay instead.

## Class 3 contributions

Payment of class 3 contributions is voluntary.[27] They only give entitlement to state pension, category A and B retirement pensions and widowed parent's allowance.[28] To help you decide whether to pay class 3 contributions, see p864.

Class 3 contributions are paid at a flat rate. The current and previous year's rates are:[29]

| | |
|---|---|
| 2025/26 | £17.75 a week |
| 2024/25 | £17.45 a week |

## Class 3A contributions

Class 3A contributions were voluntary contributions for people reaching pension age before April 2016. See the 2016/17 edition of this *Handbook*.

## Reduced liability for married women and widows

Women who were married or widowed on 6 April 1977 could choose to pay reduced class 1 or no class 2 contributions, provided they applied to do so before 12 May 1977.[30]

If you 'elected' to pay at this reduced rate, you can continue to do so until you either apply to pay the full rate again (called 'revoking an election') or until the right to pay reduced contributions is automatically lost.[31] These reduced-rate contributions do not help you build up entitlement to contributory benefits.

If you have paid reduced-rate NI contributions and reach pension age on or after 6 April 2016, see p692 for how your state pension may be calculated. If you reached pension age before 6 April 2016 and you do not qualify for a retirement pension based on your own contributions, you may qualify for a category B retirement pension instead. See Chapter 36 of the 2015/16 edition of this *Handbook* for details.

To pay the full rate again, complete the form in HMRC leaflet CF9 for married women or CF9A for widows.[32]

## Coming from abroad and going abroad

The rules on liability for NI contributions when you have come to the UK from abroad, or if you go abroad, are complex. In particular, the rules described below may not apply if you are covered by the European Union co-ordination rules (see p1392) or if you move from or to a country which has a reciprocal agreement with the UK (see p1297). In some circumstances, contributions paid in other countries count towards British benefits. In particular, this may apply if you have paid contributions in the European Economic Area (see p1388). You may also be entitled to benefits from other countries while you are in this country.

**If you have come from abroad** and are employed or self-employed in Great Britain, you may be liable for class 1 or 4 contributions.[33] If you are self-employed but not liable to pay contributions, you may be able to pay class 2 contributions voluntarily. If you are not liable to pay contributions, you can choose to pay class 3 contributions if you are resident (see p1299) in Great Britain throughout the course of the tax year in respect of which you wish to pay contributions and, in some circumstances, even if you have not been resident for the whole tax year.[34]

6

**If you are abroad** working as an employee and your employer has a place of business in Britain, in some circumstances, for the first year, you must still pay class 1 contributions. If you are not liable or are no longer liable to pay class 1 contributions, it may be worth paying class 3 contributions (see p864).[35]

If you are self-employed outside Great Britain, you may pay class 2 contributions if you wish, provided you were employed or self-employed immediately before you left Britain and either:

- you have been resident in Great Britain for a continuous period of at least three years at some time in the past; *or*
- you have paid contributions producing an earnings factor of at least 52 times the lower earnings limit in each of three years in the past. Each set of 52 flat-rate contributions paid before April 1975 counts as satisfying that condition in respect of one year.[36]

Certain volunteer development workers who are employed abroad may also be allowed to pay class 2 contributions.[37]

Normally, class 3 contributions may be paid while you are abroad if you satisfy either of the conditions allowing you to pay class 2 contributions (but you do not need to have been employed or self-employed before you left Britain or while abroad). You may also pay them if you paid class 1 contributions for the first year you were employed abroad.[38]

For information on payment of NI contributions while abroad, see gov.uk/national-insurance-if-you-go-abroad or call the HMRC helpline (tel: 0300 200 3500 or from abroad: +44 191 203 7010; textphone: 0300 200 3519).

Northern Ireland and Isle of Man contributions count towards British benefits.

## Improving your contribution record

If there are years for which you do not have a full contribution record, it may be beneficial to pay voluntary contributions: either voluntary class 2 contributions (see p861) or class 3 contributions (see p862). Before paying voluntary contributions in respect of a tax year, check whether you qualify for NI credits in that year. (In any event, you are not entitled to pay class 3 contributions if you would instead be entitled to class 3 credits – see p865.[39]) You can check your NI record online, or get details for requesting an NI statement by phone or post, via gov.uk/check-national-insurance-record.

If it is more than 30 days before you reach pension age, you can also request a state pension statement to help you decide whether to pay voluntary contributions. You can do this online or by post: see gov.uk/check-state-pension. If you are within 30 days of pension age, contact the Future Pension Centre helpline for details of your state pension (tel: 0800 731 0175; textphone: 0800 731 0176 (Welsh language 0800 731 0456); Relay UK and British Sign Language services also available).

6

***Should you make voluntary contributions?***

1. Both class 2 and 3 contributions may help you qualify for state pension or for a higher rate of state pension. Class 2 contributions also count for contributory ESA.
2. Class 2 contributions count for bereavement support payment; class 3 contributions and NI credits do not.
3. Both class 2 and 3 contributions count for widowed parent's allowance.
4. Voluntary contributions may be paid on behalf of a contributor after their death, provided they are paid no later than they would have been allowed to pay them.[40]
5. Consider the cost of paying voluntary contributions and compare this to the additional amount of benefit that might be awarded.
6. Class 2 and 3 contributions paid late do not always count for benefit purposes.
7. If you have overpaid contributions for a particular year or have paid voluntary contributions in error, you may be able to get a refund.
8. Get advice before paying voluntary contributions for years in which you have paid contributions abroad. In some cases, these can count towards British benefits (see p863).
9. If in doubt about paying the contributions, get advice.

## Late payment of contributions

Payments of class 1, 2 or 3 NI contributions are considered late if they are paid after the date on which they are due to be paid.

If you are liable for class 1 contributions, your employer is responsible for paying them to HMRC. If your employer failed to pay these or has paid them late, you are treated as if the contributions had been paid (usually on the date they were due to be paid), unless you have been negligent or consented to, or connived in, the failure to pay.[41]

Class 2 contributions are due on 31 January after the end of the tax year for which they are paid. Class 3 contributions are due 42 days after the end of the tax year for which they are paid.[42]

Contributions paid after these dates normally cannot help you to qualify for contributory benefits for any period falling before the date you pay them. They can usually only count towards your benefit entitlement for the period from the date they have been paid if:[43]

- for class 1 contributions, they were paid by the end of the second tax year after the tax year for which the contributions are paid; *or*
- for class 2 or 3 contributions, they are paid by the end of the sixth tax year after the tax year in which you are liable to pay them or, if they are voluntary contributions, in which you are entitled to pay them (although special rules apply if you make late payments of class 2 contributions through PAYE (pay as you earn)); *or*
- for class 3 contributions (for any tax year in which, for at least six months, you were a full-time apprentice, in full-time education or training or a prisoner, and for the year before and after such a year in which you met this condition but for less than six months), they are paid by the end of the sixth complete tax year after the end of a period of education, apprenticeship or imprisonment.

6

Even if paid within these time limits, class 2 contributions paid late cannot count for the second contribution condition for new-style JSA and contributory ESA until six weeks after they have been paid.[44] This also applies to class 1 contributions paid after the start of the relevant benefit year, unless they can be treated as paid earlier in the circumstances described above.

In limited circumstances (in particular where the lateness was due to 'ignorance or error' of the person supposed to pay but that is not considered due to failure to exercise 'due care and diligence'), contributions paid after the above time limits can still count for benefit purposes.[45]

## 3. National insurance credits

In some circumstances, you can be 'credited' with earnings (sometimes known as class 1 credits) or with class 3 contributions. Credits can help you satisfy:

- the second contribution condition for benefits with two contribution conditions – ie, new-style jobseeker's allowance (JSA), contributory employment and support allowance (ESA) (including new-style ESA) and, if your spouse or civil partner died before 6 April 2017, widowed parent's allowance; *and*
- the contribution conditions for retirement pensions (see p866).

Not all types of credits count for all these contributory benefits, although many class 1 credits do. Class 3 credits count for widowed parent's allowance and state pension. They also count for category A and B retirement pensions.

**Note:**

- You can only receive sufficient credits in any tax year to meet the contribution condition for that year.[46]
- Some credits are awarded automatically; others you must claim. To help you decide whether to claim credits or to see whether you have been awarded credits, you can check your national insurance (NI) contribution record at gov.uk/check-national-insurance-record or you can apply for a statement of your NI record at tax.service.gov.uk/shortforms/form/NIStatement or by phone.
- Credits cannot help you satisfy the first contribution condition for benefits with two contribution conditions, or qualify for bereavement support payment, which has a single contribution condition.
- If you are a married woman with reduced liability for contributions (see p862), you can only qualify for credits for universal credit (UC) (see p868), for certain parents and carers (see p868), for family members providing childcare (see p870), for official error (see below), starting credits (but see p871) or credits following bereavement (see p873). You are not entitled to other types of credits.
- Some people were credited with earnings for the tax years from 1993/94 to 2007/08 following an official error arising from discrepancies between the DWP and HMRC computer systems.[47] These credits were awarded automatically. See the 2009/10 edition of this *Handbook*.

Enquiries about credits can be made to the NI helpline (tel: 0300 200 3500; textphone: 0300 200 3519), or by writing to HMRC (see p864).

## Retirement pensions and credits

If you reach pension age on or after 6 April 2016, you may qualify for state pension. If you reached pension age before this date, you may qualify for category A or B retirement pension.

Most types of credits (including class 3 credits) can help you meet the contribution conditions for these benefits, and help determine the amount you receive.

For transitional rate state pension (see p691), most kinds of credits for tax years before 6 April 2016 can be taken into account when calculating your 'starting amount'.

## Credits for unemployment

These credits can help you meet the contribution conditions for all contributory benefits (see p857), except bereavement support payment.

If you are entitled to UC and do not receive any new-style JSA, these credits do not apply. However, you can get credits for UC (see p868).

You can be credited with earnings equal to the lower earnings limit for either:[48]

- each complete week (ie, the seven days from Sunday to Saturday) for which you receive JSA (or for which you would have received JSA but for the loss of benefit for benefit offences rules – see p1111); *or*
- each complete week in which you are not entitled to UC (to be entitled, you normally must have claimed it) but for which you satisfy, or can be treated as satisfying, the following qualifying conditions for JSA – ie, you:
  - are not engaged in full-time paid work (see p883); *and*
  - are not in relevant education (see p805); *and*
  - do not have limited capability for work (see Chapter 41); *and*
  - are under pension age; *and*
  - satisfy the work-related requirements (see p938), or you would have satisfied them in that week but for having limited capability for work (see p613) or being incapable of work for part of the week.

6

Credits for unemployment are awarded automatically if you get new-style JSA. Otherwise, you must apply in writing to Jobcentre Plus, either on the first day for which you are claiming them or within a reasonable time after that. You must provide the DWP with the evidence it requires to show that you satisfy the conditions. Even if you are not entitled to JSA, it can be important to continue to sign on at the Jobcentre Plus office in order to get credits for unemployment and protect your right to contributory benefits.

However, you do not get credits for weeks in which:[49]

- you would not have been entitled to JSA (whether or not you actually claimed it) because you are involved in a trade dispute; *or*
- your JSA is reduced (or not paid) because you have been sanctioned. See p970 for when this may apply.

## Credits for limited capability for work or incapacity for work

These credits can help you meet the contribution conditions for all contributory benefits, except bereavement support payment.

You can be credited with earnings equal to the lower earnings limit for each complete week during which you either:[50]

- are entitled to statutory sick pay (SSP); *or*
- have limited capability for work; *or*
- would have had limited capability for work for contributory ESA, had you been entitled to it (even if the reason you are not entitled to contributory ESA is because of the 365-day limit – see p564) or would have had limited capability for work had you claimed ESA or maternity allowance (MA) in time; *or*

- were incapable of work or could be treated as such, or you would have been had you made a claim for incapacity benefit (IB) or MA. For information on incapacity for work, see p683 of the 2013/14 edition of this *Handbook*.

You cannot qualify for these credits for weeks you are entitled to UC (you must have claimed it), unless you are also entitled to ESA, SSP, MA, IB or severe disablement allowance in those weeks. You also cannot qualify for these credits for days you were treated as not having limited capability for work (see p901) or not being incapable of work (or days on which you would have been, had you otherwise been entitled to ESA or IB).

These credits are awarded automatically if you get ESA or MA. You can apply for ESA, even if you are not entitled to the benefit, and maintain a 'credits only' claim for limited capability for work (but see p20 on coming under the UC system as a result of claiming ESA). To apply for credits because you get SSP, write to HMRC (see p864). In other circumstances, you must apply to Jobcentre Plus. Unless the credits are awarded automatically, you must apply for them before the end of the benefit year (ie, by the first Saturday in January – see p876) following the tax year in which you are entitled to the credit. This time limit can be extended if it is considered reasonable to do so, given your circumstances.

6

## Credits for universal credit

These credits can help you meet the contribution conditions for widowed parent's allowance and state pension. They also count for category A and B retirement pensions. They are awarded automatically.

If you are entitled to UC for at least part of a week, you can be credited with a class 3 contribution for that week.[51]

If you are not entitled to UC because your income and/or capital is too high and you are looking for work or have limited capability for work, you should consider applying for credits for unemployment (see p866) or limited capability for work (see p867).

## Credits for certain parents and carers

These credits can help you meet the contribution conditions for widowed parent's allowance and state pension. They also count for category A and B retirement pensions.

You can be credited with a class 3 contribution for each week which falls after 6 April 2010 if:

- for any part of the week, you are awarded child benefit for a child under the age of 12;[52] *or*
- you reside with someone who, for any part of the week, is awarded child benefit for a child aged under 12 and:
  - you share responsibility with that person for a child under 12; *and*

- in the tax year to which the credit relates, the person awarded child benefit has paid or been credited with NI contributions with an earnings factor of more than 52 times that year's lower earnings limit (see Appendix 5). In calculating this, any credits they get on the basis of the child benefit award are ignored.[53]

**Note**: in this situation, for weeks from 6 April 2016, the rules on when you qualify for a class 3 credit for state pension are different and indicate only that you must be the partner of someone who gets child benefit for a child, you must reside with your partner and you both must share the responsibility for the child. The rules do not expressly state that the child must be under 12 (although your partner still must have paid, or been credited with, sufficient NI contributions);[54] *or*

- in that week you are caring for someone for at least 20 hours, or for more than one person for a total of at least 20 hours and:[55]
  - the person(s) for whom you care is entitled to a qualifying benefit (see below); *or*
  - the decision maker considers that the level of care provided is appropriate.

  You can continue to qualify for these credits for 12 weeks after the week in which you stop satisfying this condition – this allows you to have breaks in caring of up to 12 weeks without losing credits; *or*
- for any part of the week, you are an approved foster parent or foster carer (including a kinship carer in Scotland);[56] *or*
- the week falls in the 12 weeks:[57]
  - before the date you become entitled to carer's allowance (CA) or carer support payment (CSP); *or*
  - following the week you stop being entitled to CA (unless you already qualify for credits for CA or CSP for that week – see p871).

### *Qualifying benefit*

A **'qualifying benefit'** includes the daily living components of personal independence payment and adult disability payment, attendance allowance, pension age disability payment, the middle or highest rate of disability living allowance and Scottish adult disability living allowance care component, child disability payment care component, armed forces independence payment, constant attendance allowance in respect of an industrial or war disablement and certain payments under the Pneumoconiosis, Byssinosis and Miscellaneous Diseases Benefit Scheme or Workmen's Compensation (Supplementation) Scheme.[58]

Unless you are entitled because you are awarded child benefit for a child under 12, in most circumstances, you must be ordinarily resident in Great Britain and not in prison or legal custody to qualify for these credits.[59]

If you get child benefit, CA or CSP, the credits are awarded automatically. If you qualify because you are caring for someone for at least 20 hours, apply to the DWP using a carer's credit application form (Form CC1). Otherwise, apply to HMRC on Form CF411A. Both forms are available at gov.uk. Your application must be received before the end of the tax year following the tax year to which the credits relate. This time limit can be extended if the DWP or HMRC considers it reasonable in the circumstances.[60]

**Note:** you can qualify for these credits on the basis of an award of child benefit even if you (or the person with whom you reside) have elected not to receive the child benefit because of the high-income child benefit charge (see p507).

### Credits for home responsibilities protection

Home responsibilities protection, which helped a contributor satisfy the contribution conditions for widowed parent's allowance and category A or B retirement pension, was abolished on 6 April 2010 and was replaced with NI credits for certain parents and carers (see p868). For details, see p973 of the 2021/22 edition of this *Handbook*.

6

## Credits for family members providing childcare

If you do not qualify for credits as a parent or a carer (see p868), these credits can help you meet the contribution conditions for widowed parent's allowance and state pension. They also count for category A retirement pension if you reached pension age on or after 6 April 2012 and for category B retirement pension in certain circumstances. See the 2015/16 edition of this *Handbook* for details.

From 6 April 2011, you can be credited with a class 3 contribution for each week during which you provide childcare for a child aged under 12, if:[61]

- you are a specified 'family member' of the child (you do not need to be a blood relative and many ex-family members count – see p871); *and*
- someone has been awarded child benefit for the child for that week and, in the tax year in which that falls, their contribution record is sufficient for the year to count as a qualifying year for state pension (see p879). In calculating this, any credits they get on the grounds of receiving child benefit for a child under 12 are ignored; *and*
- you are ordinarily resident in Great Britain (see p1299).

There is no set number of hours for which you must care for the child to qualify. Only one person can qualify for these credits for a particular week for the same child(ren) covered by a child benefit award. The credits are in respect of the child benefit award, and not per child. However, if childcare is shared, it may be possible for someone else to get credits for different weeks in a tax year.

You must apply to HMRC for these credits after the end of the tax year in question. There is no time limit for claiming.[62] Use Form CA9176 (for specified adult childcare credits), available at gov.uk/guidance/apply-for-specified-adult-childcare-credits.

**Note:** if you satisfy the qualifying conditions, you can still get these credits, even if the person entitled to child benefit elects not to receive it because of the high-income child benefit charge (see p507).

*Family member*

You count as a **'family member'** if you are:[63]

- the child's parent (from 6 April 2016 for state pension, this only applies if you are their non-resident parent, but see p868 if you reside together), grandparent, great- or great-great-grandparent, sibling, aunt or uncle (including if you are an adopted, step- or half-sibling of the child or of the child's parent);
- a spouse or civil partner, or former spouse or civil partner, of any of the above relatives, or their son or daughter;
- a partner or former partner of any of the above (including, for instance, a former partner of a former spouse of one of the above relatives), or their son or daughter;
- the child's niece, nephew or first cousin;
- a spouse, civil partner or partner (or former spouse, civil partner or partner) of the child's first cousin.

A 'partner' is someone with whom the relative lives as if they were married or civil partners.

## Credits for carer's allowance or carer support payment

These credits can help you meet the contribution conditions for all contributory benefits, except bereavement support payment. They are awarded automatically.

You can be credited with earnings equal to the lower earnings limit for each week in which you receive CA (see Chapter 22) or CSP (see Chapter 63), or would receive it but for the loss of benefit for benefit offences rules (see p1111).[64] You also receive credits if the only reason why you do not receive CA is because you are receiving widowed parent's allowance, bereavement allowance or a widow's benefit instead. **Note:** this does not apply to bereavement support payment, as you receive both CA and bereavement support payment at the same time.

If you are caring for someone but are not entitled to these credits, you may qualify for credits for certain carers (see p868).

## Starting credits

These credits can help you meet the contribution conditions for widowed parent's allowance. They also count for category A and B retirement pensions and for calculating the transitional rate of state pension (see p880). They are awarded automatically.

You can receive class 3 credits for the tax years in which you reach the age of 16, 17 and 18 if you would otherwise have had an insufficient contribution record for those years to count towards the contribution conditions for the above benefits.[65]

However, for category A and B retirement pensions (and for calculating the transitional rate of state pension), you could only qualify for these credits:

- for tax years falling before 6 April 2010; *and*
- if you had to make an application for an NI number to be allocated to you, if your application for an NI number was made before 6 April 2010.

No credits were made under this provision for years before 6 April 1975.

## Education and training credits

For the purpose of qualifying for new-style JSA and contributory ESA, you can be credited with earnings equal to the lower earnings limit for either one of the two complete tax years that fall before the relevant benefit year (see p876) if:

- for any part of those tax years you were on:[66]
  - a course of full-time training, including training to acquire occupational or vocational skills (or, if you are disabled, a part-time course of at least 15 hours a week); *or*
  - a course of full-time education; *or*
  - an apprenticeship; *and*
- in the other tax year in which you must satisfy the second contribution condition for the benefit (see p877), you have an earnings factor of 50 times the lower earnings limit without relying on this provision; *and*
- you were at least 18 (or you reached 18) in the tax year in question; *and*
- you were under 21 when the course or apprenticeship started; *and*
- your course of education, training or apprenticeship has finished.

You can receive credits which count for all contributory benefits (except bereavement support payment) for each week in which you are undertaking a training course approved by a DWP decision maker if:[67]

- in that week you were not entitled to UC – but see p868 for credits if you were entitled to UC. To be entitled to UC, you normally must have claimed it; *and*
- the training is full time (or at least 15 hours a week if you are disabled) or it is an introductory course; *and*
- the training is not part of your job; *and*
- the training is intended to last for one year or less (except in certain circumstances if it is a course for disabled people); *and*
- you were 18 or over at the beginning of the tax year in which the week falls.

If Jobcentre Plus arranged the course, you get the credits automatically. Otherwise, you must apply by writing to HMRC (see p864).

## Credits for statutory maternity, adoption, paternity, shared parental, parental bereavement pay and neonatal care pay

These credits can help you meet the contribution conditions for all contributory benefits, except bereavement support payment.

You can be credited with earnings equal to the lower earnings limit for each week for which you receive these statutory payments.[68]

To apply for these credits, write to HMRC (see p864). Your application must be received before the end of the benefit year (see p876) following the tax year in which the week falls, but this time limit may be extended if reasonable to do so.

## Credits for jury service

These credits can help you meet the contribution conditions for all contributory benefits, except bereavement support payment.

You are entitled to be credited with earnings equal to the lower earnings limit for each week after 6 April 1988 during which you spend at least part of the week on jury service, unless you are self-employed in that week.[69]

To apply for these credits, write to HMRC (see p864). Your application must be received before the end of the benefit year (see p876) following the tax year in which the week falls (or such further period as is reasonable).

## Credits following bereavement

These credits help you meet the contribution conditions for new-style JSA and contributory ESA. They are awarded automatically.

If you were entitled to bereavement payment, widowed parent's allowance or bereavement allowance, you can be credited with sufficient earnings for each year up to and including the one in which your entitlement to any of those benefits stopped, to enable you to satisfy the second contribution condition for new-style JSA or contributory ESA.[70]

For the purpose of satisfying the second contribution condition for contributory ESA, you are also entitled to credits for each year up to and including the one in which your entitlement to widow's allowance (abolished in April 1988) or widowed mother's allowance ended.[71]

## Credits for tax credits

Tax credits have now been replaced by UC (see p21). For rules on NI credits for getting tax credits, see Chapter 43 of the 2024/25 edition of this *Handbook*.

## Credits for a quashed conviction

These credits can help you meet the contribution conditions for all contributory benefits, except bereavement support payment.

If you were imprisoned or detained in legal custody after being convicted of an offence, and that conviction has since been quashed, you can be credited with earnings for each week during at least part of which you were imprisoned or detained.[72]

To apply for these credits, write to HMRC (see p864).

## Credits for service families

These credits can help you meet the contribution conditions for all contributory benefits, except bereavement support payment.

From 6 April 2010, you can be credited with earnings equal to that year's lower earnings limit for each week during any part of which you were:[73]

- the spouse or civil partner of a member of the armed forces (or someone treated as such for the purpose of occupying accommodation); *and*
- accompanying, or were treated as accompanying, them on an assignment outside the UK.

6

You must usually apply for these class 1 credits on the approved form (Form MODCA1, available at gov.uk) once you have a confirmed date for the end of the overseas posting and before the end of the tax year following the tax year in which the overseas assignment ended. This time limit can be extended if it is reasonable, given your circumstances.

The decision maker has discretion to accept an application made before you receive confirmation of the end date of the overseas assignment. If your application is accepted, you can be awarded credits for the period before your application, but you must make a further application under these rules for credits for any subsequent period.

Alternatively, to help you meet the contribution conditions for state pension only, you can be credited with a class 3 contribution for each week in any tax year from 6 April 1975 in which, for at least part of the week, you meet the above conditions, provided the member of the armed forces you were accompanying had paid or been credited with sufficient NI contributions for that year to count as a qualifying year (see p879).[74] In this situation, you must normally apply for the credits on the approved form. There is an online form at gov.uk. Applications can only be made for a past period.

**Note:** in respect of years from 6 April 2010, claim the class 1 credits if you satisfy the conditions for them, as they count towards the contribution conditions for more benefits – the class 3 credits only count for state pension.

# 4. Contribution conditions for benefits

Entitlement to contributory benefits normally depends on the national insurance (NI) contribution conditions being met.

- **For state pension**, your entitlement is based on your own NI contribution record. However, in some cases, for the transitional rate of state pension, the amount you receive depends on the contribution record of your spouse or civil partner (or your late or former spouse or civil partner) (see p691).
- **For new-style jobseeker's allowance (JSA) and contributory employment and support allowance (ESA) (including new-style ESA)**, your entitlement is based on your own NI contribution record (unless you qualify for contributory ESA without needing to satisfy the contribution conditions).
- **For bereavement support payment and widowed parent's allowance**, the relevant 'contributor' is your late spouse, civil partner or (except for the standard rate of bereavement support payment) your cohabiting partner.

You may be credited with earnings or contributions to fill gaps in your contribution record (see p865).

NI contributions normally cannot count for benefit purposes until after they have been paid (if they are paid late, see p864). However, in some circumstances, your entitlement to benefit, or the amount of benefit you are entitled to, may depend on class 2 or 3 contributions which you have not yet paid because the due date for their payment has not been reached (see p864). In this situation, provided you pay the contributions by the due date, they can be treated as having been paid earlier.[75] If you claimed benefit before paying the contributions, once you have paid them the earlier decision on your claim can be revised to take account of the contributions.[76] This may not apply if you are late in notifying HMRC of your self-employment.

If you reached pension age before 6 April 2016, see the 2015/16 edition of this *Handbook* for the contribution conditions for category A and B retirement pensions. The contribution conditions for bereavement payment, bereavement allowance, incapacity benefit (IB) and widow's pension are covered in previous editions of this *Handbook*.

It may be possible for you to rely on the contributions you have paid in other European Economic Area states to qualify for contributory benefits (see p1388).

If you are a woman who has paid reduced-rate NI contributions, see p692 for how your state pension is calculated.

## Jobseeker's allowance and employment and support allowance

New-style JSA and contributory ESA (either old-style or new-style – see Chapter 26) have two contribution conditions relating to the two complete tax years falling immediately before the 'relevant benefit year'. If you claim in 2025, you must satisfy the contribution conditions for the 2022/23 and 2023/24 tax years.

***Tax and relevant benefit years***

A **'tax year'** runs from 6 April to 5 April the following year.

A **'benefit year'** is almost the same as a calendar year and runs from the first Sunday in January.[77]

The **'relevant benefit year'** is usually the calendar year during which you meet the entitlement conditions and submit a claim for new-style JSA or contributory ESA. However:

- for new-style JSA, if it is earlier than the year in which you make your claim, the relevant benefit year is the benefit year in which a period that is linked to the current jobseeking period began (see p611);
- for contributory ESA, if you otherwise would not meet the contribution conditions for contributory ESA, your relevant benefit year can be any benefit year which includes any part of your current period of limited capability for work (or any part of any period(s) of limited capability for work that can be linked to your current period – see p928). **Note:** a period of limited capability for work cannot include a period before the three-month time limit for backdating an ESA claim.[78]

6

## When the contribution conditions do not apply

You can qualify for contributory ESA without having to satisfy the contribution conditions if your contributory ESA ended because you had received it for 365 days in the circumstances described on p564, you continued to have (or be treated as having) limited capability for work after your entitlement ended and you now have, or are treated as having, limited capability for work-related activity (see p913).[79] In this situation, you can qualify for contributory ESA again without satisfing the contribution conditions. If you previously claimed incapacity benefit or severe disablement benefit, different rules may allow you to claim ESA without meeting the contribution conditions in the relevant year (see p980 of the 2021/22 edition of this *Handbook*).

## The first condition: paid contributions

You must have paid, or be treated as having paid, at least 26 weeks' contributions on earnings at the lower earnings limit in one of the last two complete tax years immediately before the relevant benefit year.[80]

***Lower earnings limits***

| | |
|---|---|
| 2022/23 | £123 |
| 2023/24 | £123 |
| 2024/25 | £123 |
| 2025/26 | £125 |

*Example*

If Billie makes a claim in 2025, she meets the first condition if she earned at least £123 a week for 26 weeks between 6 April 2022 and 5 April 2023, or at least £123 a week for 26 weeks between 6 April 2023 and 5 April 2024.

Note:

- The 26 weeks do not need to be consecutive but must fall in a single tax year.
- For new-style JSA, only class 1 contributions count towards meeting this condition (unless you are a share fisherman or volunteer development worker, when special class 2 contributions also count). For ESA, both class 1 and class 2 contributions count.[81]

### When the first condition is relaxed

In some situations, the first contribution condition is relaxed so that sufficient contributions paid in *any* one tax year are enough to satisfy the condition, provided they were paid, or treated as paid, before the week for which you are claiming the benefit.

For new-style JSA and contributory ESA, this applies if you were entitled to credits for service families (see p874) in at least one week in the tax year before the relevant benefit year (see p876).[82]

For contributory ESA, it also applies if you:[83]

- were entitled to carer's allowance or carer support payment in the last complete tax year before the relevant benefit year (even if it was not paid because of the overlapping benefit rules – see p1021); *or*
- were entitled to NI credits for a quashed conviction at some time in any tax year before the relevant benefit year (or you would have been entitled to such credits had you claimed them); *or*
- were in full-time paid work for more than two years immediately before your period of limited capability for work began and you were entitled to working tax credit which included a disabled worker or severe disability element (see Chapter 15 of the 2024/25 edition of this *Handbook*).

## The second condition: paid or credited contributions

You must have paid, or be treated as having paid or received NI credits amounting to, contributions on earnings of at least 50 times the lower earnings limit in each of the two complete tax years immediately before the relevant benefit year.[84]

*Example*

If Tasso makes a claim in 2025, he meets the second condition if he paid (or is treated as having paid or received credits amounting to) contributions on total earnings of at least £6,150 (50 x £123) in 2022/23, and in 2023/24.

Note:

- Only certain NI credits count towards meeting this condition – eg, credited class 3 contributions do not count (see pp865–74).
- To count, any paid contributions must be class 1 contributions (or special class 2 contributions – see p861) for new-style JSA, or class 1 or 2 contributions for contributory ESA.[85]
- To satisfy this condition with NI credits, you must have been awarded them for at least 50 weeks during each of the two years.

### The timing of your claim

In rare cases, delaying a claim for new-style JSA may be beneficial so that you can draw on a different year's contribution record. This is because the 'relevant tax years' in which you must meet the contribution conditions depend on the benefit year (see p875) in which your jobseeking period starts. In particular, if you claim before the first Sunday in January, this may mean that your benefit year is actually the previous calendar year. Any day for which you do not claim does not count as part of your jobseeking period (see p611),[86] so it is easy to postpone when that period begins. However, if you claim and are refused benefit because the contribution conditions are not satisfied, your jobseeking period will have started. You must then normally wait for more than 12 weeks to make a fresh claim. The 12-week gap breaks the jobseeking period.

The situation is different for contributory ESA. If your claim for contributory ESA is refused only because you do not meet the contribution conditions, in some cases, it can be worth making a later claim that falls in a different benefit year (see p876).

***Example***

Kit lives with her partner who works full time. Kit was self-employed and paid class 2 NI contributions throughout the tax years 2022/23 and 2023/24 (in the tax year 2021/22 she did not pay NI contributions or get NI credits). In December 2024, she became ill and claimed contributory ESA (ie, new-style ESA) for the first time. The relevant benefit year was 2024, and the two complete tax years that fall before that are 2021/22 and 2022/23. Having no contributions or credits for 2021/22, Kit was refused contributory ESA. If she claims again in the 2025 benefit year, the contributions she paid in 2022/23 and 2023/24 are counted and she may qualify for contributory ESA. The rules allow 2025 to count as her relevant benefit year because part of her period of limited capability for work falls in that year.

## Bereavement support payment

To satisfy the contribution condition for bereavement support payment, your late spouse, civil partner or cohabiting partner must have paid NI contributions on earnings of at least 25 times that year's lower earnings limit – eg, £3,125 in 2025/26: 25 x £125.

This condition must be met in any one tax year in your late spouse's, civil partner's or cohabiting partner's working life, but only class 1 or 2 NI contributions count (see p985 in the 2021/22 edition of this *Handbook* for the meaning of 'working life').[87]

## Widowed parent's allowance

There are two contribution conditions for widowed parent's allowance. See Chapter 21 for details of the other entitlement rules.

Your late spouse, civil partner or cohabiting partner must have satisfied the contribution conditions.[88] The first is that in any one tax year before they died, they must have paid NI contributions (class 1, 2 or 3) on earnings of at least that year's lower earnings limit. This is deemed to be satisfied in certain situations, including where they were getting ESA or long-term IB in the year in which they died or the preceding year.

The second condition is that, to be entitled to the maximum rate of widowed parent's allowance, during their working life for a required number of tax years, your late spouse, civil partner or cohabiting partner paid NI contributions or received NI credits on earnings of at least 52 times that year's lower earnings limit. The required number of years will depend on the length of their working life.

For further details of the contribution conditions, see p984 of the 2021/22 edition of this *Handbook*.

## Retirement pensions

If you reached pension age before 6 April 2016, you are not entitled to state pension but may be entitled to category A or B retirement pension instead.[89] For the NI contribution conditions for category A and B retirement pensions, see the 2015/16 edition of this *Handbook*.

### State pension

If you reach pension age on or after 6 April 2016 (ie, if you are a woman born on or after 6 April 1953 or a man born on or after 6 April 1951), you may be entitled to state pension (see Chapter 32).

Your entitlement to state pension and the amount you receive depends on the number of NI qualifying years you have.

*Qualifying years*[90]

A **'qualifying year'** is a tax year in your working life in which you have paid class 1, 2 or 3 NI contributions or received NI credits which, in total, produced an earnings factor of at least 52 times that year's lower earnings limit – eg, £6,500 in 2025/26: 52 x £125. Most, but not all, kinds of NI credits can be counted. For tax years before 6 April 1978, contributions or credits must have been paid on earnings of at least 50 times that year's lower earnings limit for the year to count as a qualifying year.[91]

To qualify for state pension, you must have at least 10 qualifying years (but see below if you paid a reduced rate of NI contributions as a married woman).[92]

If one of your qualifying years is a tax year before 6 April 2016, your entitlement to state pension is calculated at the transitional rate (see below).[93]

Note:

- If you have paid reduced-rate NI contributions as a married woman or widow and your election to pay at a reduced rate was in force at the start of the 35-year period which ends in the tax year before you reach pension age, you do not need to have 10 qualifying years to qualify for state pension.[94] See p692 for how your entitlement is calculated.
- If your spouse or civil partner has died, you may qualify for an amount of state pension based on their contribution record. See p693 for details.

6

### The transitional rate of state pension

If at least one of your qualifying years falls before 6 April 2016, your entitlement to state pension is initially assessed at a transitional rate. The amount you receive depends on your 'starting amount' as well as subsequent qualifying years if needed. See p691 for how the transitional rate is calculated.

# Notes

1. **National insurance contributions and contributory benefits**
   1 s11 SSC(TF)A 1999; Part III SSC(DA) Regs; arts 6(c)(i) and 7 The First-tier Tribunal and Upper Tribunal (Chambers) Order 2010 No.2655
   2 Sch 3 para 17 SSA 1998; s17 SSC(TF)A 1999; arts 2-4 The National Insurance Contribution Credits (Transfer of Functions) Order 2009 No.1377

2. **Paid national insurance contributions**
   3 s1(2) SSCBA 1992
   4 ss6(1) and (3) and 11(7) SSCBA 1992
   5 s13 SSCBA 1992; regs 48(1) and 49(1)(f) and (2A)-(2C) SS(Con) Regs
   6 s2(1) SSCBA 1992
   7 *Ready Mix Concrete South East Ltd v Ministry of Pensions and National Insurance* [1968] 2 QB 497 (QBD); *Global Plant v Secretary of State for Health and Social Security* [1971] 3 All ER 385 (QBD)
   8 Sch 1 paras 1 SS(CatE) Regs
   9 Sch 1 paras 6 SS(CatE) Regs
   10 Sch 1 paras 7-12 SS(CatE) Regs
   11 Regs 13, 14, 15 and 21 SS(Con) Regs
   12 Sch 1 para 1 SSCBA 1992; regs 13, 14, 15 and 21 SS(Con) Regs
   13 ss6 and 7 SSCBA 1992
   14 ss6 and 6A SSCBA 1992
   15 s8 SSCBA 1992

16 Reg 131 SS(Con) Regs
17 Sch 1 para 3 SSCBA 1992
18 Reg 60 SS(Con) Regs
19 s3 National Insurance Contributions (Reduction in Rates) Act 2023
20 s11(6) SSCBA 1992; reg 43 SS(Con) Regs
21 s11(5A) and (5B) SSCBA 1992
22 s11(5A) and (5B) SSCBA 1992
23 s11 SSCBA 1992; reg 43 SS(Con) Regs
24 s11 SSCBA 1992
25 Reg 127(1) SS(Con) Regs
26 Regs 125, 149, 151 and 152 SS(Con) Regs
27 s13 SSCBA 1992
28 s14 SSCBA 1992; reg 49 SS(Con) Regs
29 s13(1) SSCBA 1992
30 Reg 127 SS(Con) Regs
31 Regs 128(1) and 130 SS(Con) Regs
32 Available from gov.uk/reduced-national-insurance-married-women
33 ss2(1), 6 and 11 SSCBA 1992; reg 145(1)(a), (c), (d) and (2) SS(Con) Regs
34 Reg 145(1) (e) SS(Con) Regs
35 Reg 146 SS(Con) Regs
36 Regs 147 and 148 SS(Con) Regs
37 Regs 149 and 151 SS(Con) Regs
38 Regs 146(2)(b), 147 and 148 SS(Con) Regs
39 Regs 43(3), 48 and 49 SS(Con) Regs
40 Reg 62 SS(Con) Regs
41 Reg 60 SS(Con) Regs; reg 5 SS(CTCNIN) Regs
42 Reg 1(2) SS(CTCNIN) Regs
43 Reg 4 SS(CTCNIN) Regs; reg 48(3)(b) SS(Con) Regs
44 Reg 4(7) and (8) SS(CTCNIN) Regs
45 Regs 50 and 61 SS(Con) Regs; regs 4(11), 5A, 6, 6A and 6B SS(CTCNIN) Regs

3. **National insurance credits**

46 Reg 3 SS(Cr) Regs; reg 25(2) SP Regs
47 Regs 8D, 8E and 8F SS(Cr) Regs
48 Reg 8A SS(Cr) Regs; regs 26 and 29 SP Regs
49 Reg 8A(5) SS(Cr) Regs; regs 26 and 29 SP Regs
50 Reg 8B SS(Cr) Regs; regs 26 and 29 SP Regs
51 Reg 8G SS(Cr) Regs; regs 26 and 31 SP Regs
52 s23A(2) and (3)(a) SSCBA 1992; regs 27 and 34(1)(a) SP Regs
53 s23A(2) and (3)(c) SSCBA 1992; regs 2, 5(1)(a), 6 and 9 SS(CCPC) Regs; reg 27 SP Regs
54 Reg 34(1)(b) and (2)-(4) SP Regs
55 s23A(2) and (3)(c) SSCBA 1992; regs 5(1)(b) and 7(1)(c) SS(CCPC) Regs; regs 27, 37(1) and (2)(a) and 38(1)(c) SP Regs
56 s23A(2) and (3)(b) SSCBA 1992; reg 4 SS(CCPC) Regs; reg 36 SP Regs
57 Reg 7 SS(CCPC) Regs; reg 38(1)(a) and (b) and (2) SP Regs
58 Reg 2 SS(CCPC) Regs; reg 37(4) SP Regs
59 Reg 8 SS(CCPC) Regs; regs 34(2), 36(1) and 37(3) SP Regs
60 Regs 9-12 SS(CCPC) Regs; regs 34(2)(e), 36(3), 37(5) and (6) and 39(a) SP Regs
61 Reg 9F SS(Cr) Regs; regs 26 and 35 SP Regs
62 Reg 9F(8) SS(Cr) Regs; reg 39(b) SP Regs
63 Sch SS(Cr) Regs; reg 35(6)-(8) SP Regs
64 Reg 7A SS(Cr) Regs; regs 26 and 29 SP Regs
65 Reg 4 SS(Cr) Regs; reg 26 SP Regs
66 Reg 8 SS(Cr) Regs
67 Reg 7 SS(Cr) Regs; regs 26 and 29 SP Regs
68 Reg 9C SS(Cr) Regs; regs 26 and 29 SP Regs
69 Reg 9B SS(Cr) Regs; regs 26 and 29 SP Regs
70 Reg 8C SS(Cr) Regs
71 Reg 3(1)(b) SSB(MW&WSP) Regs
72 Reg 9D SS(Cr) Regs; regs 26 and 29 SP Regs
73 Reg 9E SS(Cr) Regs; regs 26 and 29 SP Regs
74 Regs 28 and 33 SP Regs

4. **Contribution conditions for benefits**

75 Regs 7(1) and 7A SS(CTCNIN) Regs
76 Reg 3(8J) and (8K) SS&CS(DA) Regs
77 s21(6) SSCBA 1992; s2(4) JSA 1995; Sch 1 para 3 WRA 2007
78 Sch 1 para 3(1)(f) WRA 2007
79 s1B WRA 2007; Sch 2 paras 2 and 15 ESA(TP)(EA)(No.2) Regs
80 **JSA** ss1(2)(d) and 2(1)(a) JSA 1995
**ESA** Sch 1 para 1 WRA 2007
81 **JSA** ss1(2)(d) and 2 JSA 1995; regs 34, 69 and 75 JSA Regs 2013
**ESA** Sch 1 para 1 WRA 2007; reg 7A ESA Regs; reg 8 ESA Regs 2013
82 Reg 8(2)(ca) ESA Regs; reg 35 JSA Regs 2013; reg 9(2)(d) ESA Regs 2013
83 Reg 8 ESA Regs; reg 9 ESA Regs 2013
84 **JSA** ss1(2)(d) and 2(1)(b) JSA 1995
**ESA** Sch 1 para 2 WRA 2007
85 s2 JSA 1995; Sch 1 para 2 WRA 2007; regs 69 and 75 JSA Regs 2013
86 Reg 37(2)(a) JSA Regs 2013
87 s31 PA 2014

88 Sch 3 para 5 SSCBA 1992
89 s1 PA 2014
90 s2(4) PA 2014
91 s4(4) and (5) PA 2014
92 Reg 13 SP Regs
93 s4(1)(c) PA 2014
94 s11(1) PA 2014

# Chapter 40

# Work and benefits

**This chapter covers:**

1. Paid work, full-time paid work and hours (below)
2. How work affects universal credit (p886)
3. How work affects new-style jobseeker's allowance and means-tested benefits benefits (p887)
4. How work affects non-means-tested benefits (p890)
5. People involved in trade disputes (p891)



This chapter explains which benefits you can receive while you are in paid work. It also examines how benefits are affected when a partner or somebody else living with you works.

This chapter does not explain how earnings affect the calculation of benefits. For these rules, see the relevant chapter in this *Handbook* for each specific benefit.

### Key facts

- You can qualify for universal credit if you or your partner are in paid work, whether it is part time or full time.
- You cannot usually get new-style jobseeker's allowance if you are in full-time paid work.
- You cannot usually get income-related employment and support allowance if you are working, or if your partner is in full-time paid work.
- You can qualify for housing benefit and pension credit while working.
- Entitlement to some non-means-tested benefits benefits is affected by work.
- Your benefits might be affected if you are (or a member of your household is) involved in a trade dispute.

## 1. Paid work, full-time paid work and hours

### Universal credit

For universal credit (UC), **'paid work'** means work for which you are paid, or which you do in expectation of payment, even if you never receive any. The work may be part time or full time. This applies both to employed earners and to self-employed people. Paid work does not include volunteering or pro-bono work for which you are not paid or are only paid expenses.[1] 'Full-time work' and 'hours' are not defined for UC purposes.

## New-style jobseeker's allowance and means-tested benefits

The following benefits have definitions about what is work and how your hours are calculated:

- new-style jobseeker's allowance (JSA);
- income-related employment and support allowance (ESA);
- pension credit (PC);
- housing benefit (HB).

The rules about these benefits are described below. For non-means-tested benefits other than new-style JSA, see section 4 of this chapter.

6

**Note**: usually, you cannot get income-related ESA if you do *any* work, with some exceptions (see p928). In practice, if you get income-related ESA, the detailed rules described below usually apply to your partner's work. You also cannot usually get contributory ESA if you do any work (see p890).

### Paid work

The rules about 'paid work' have been interpreted in older caselaw. This caselaw, as summarised here, is still likely to apply to the current rules.

**'Paid work'** is work for which you are paid, or which you do in expectation of payment, even if you never actually receive any.[2] Whether or not you are in paid work should be decided at the time the work is done, not later with hindsight.[3] An expectation of payment needs to be realistic and not just a hope or desire to make money.[4] Payment includes payment in kind, such as meals, accommodation or produce.[5]

If you are self-employed, the DWP counts drawings from your business to meet living expenses (in cash or in kind) as payment for work, unless the drawings are from the business capital.[6] If you simply invest in a business and do not help to run it, you are not treated as self-employed.[7] If your business is not yet, or has stopped being, profitable, this may raise questions about whether you are really working in expectation of payment.[8]

### Full-time paid work

There are specific rules for new-style JSA, income-related ESA, PC and HB about what counts as 'full-time paid work', also called 'remunerative work', and how that affects the benefit: see section 3 of this chapter.

Some rules apply to income-related ESA and new-style JSA only. You (or, for income-related ESA, just your partner and non-dependant) are not treated as being in full-time paid work if you (or they) are:[9]

- working on a training scheme and being paid a training allowance under specific provisions; *or*
- volunteering or working pro bono, other than for a relative, and receiving no payment or only expenses; *or*
- caring for someone who is staying with you but is not normally a member of your household, and receiving payments from a health authority, local authority or voluntary organisation, or from the person concerned under section 26(3A) of the National Assistance Act 1948, for caring for them; *or*
- a foster carer (or, in Scotland only, a kinship carer) receiving a payment from a local authority or voluntary organisation for a child you are looking after; *or*
- working as a part-time firefighter, auxiliary coastguard, member of the Army Reserve or other reserve forces, or member of a lifeboat crew; *or*
- performing duties as a local authority councillor; *or*
- engaged in an activity for which you receive, or expect to receive, an award from a UK sports council and no other payment; *or*
- a student doing work in connection with your course;[10] *or*
- on maternity, adoption, paternity or other parental leave, or absent from work due to sickness, even if you normally work 16/24 hours or more each week.[11]



## Hours

The hours you are classed as working generally include:

- all hours actually worked for (or in expectation of) payment; *and*
- hours from all jobs; *and*
- overtime that you do routinely.

For new-style JSA and income-related ESA only, paid lunch hours and breaks count towards your total hours.[12]

If you are self-employed, generally your hours include all those necessary to run your business. This includes time spent producing or selling goods or providing services for which you are paid, but can also include time spent on other tasks such as visiting potential customers, providing estimates, advertising, bookkeeping, buying, cleaning and doing research.[13] The decision maker should accept your account of what is necessary to run your business unless there is a reason for doubt.[14] Note that some of the initial unpaid work necessary to set up a business may not count as hours of paid work.[15] During periods when you are not in work, or if you have ceased trading, you should not count as being in work.[16]

### Fluctuating hours

If your (or your partner's or your non-dependant's) hours fluctuate, there are rules on how they should be averaged.

- **Regular pattern of work.** If there is a regular pattern of work (a 'work cycle'), the average hours worked throughout that cycle are used. For example, if you regularly work three weeks and then have one week off, your hours are averaged over the four-week period (the work cycle).[17] For weeks when you are on paid holiday, off sick, on maternity, adoption, paternity or other parental leave, or absent from work without a good reason, the hours you would otherwise have worked are included when calculating your average hours.[18]

- **If there is no regular pattern of work.** If there is no recognisable work cycle, your hours are calculated using the average over the five weeks immediately before the date of claim (or supersession), or the average over a different period if this would give a more representative figure.[19] If you are self-employed, this may well be an accounting year.
- **No work pattern yet established.** This may be the case in a new job. In this instance, your hours are calculated as the number (or average number) of hours you are expected to work each week.[20] Once you have more evidence about your average hours, the decision can be revised or superseded.
- **Seasonal or term-time only work.** If your (or your partner's or non-dependant's) work is casual or intermittent, you can usually argue that your hours should only count during the period when you are actually working. For example, if you are a seasonal worker who only works in the summer, you can argue that you should not be treated as working the same hours throughout the rest of the year.[21]

  However, this may not be the case for PC or HB if you have a recognisable year-long work cycle, with periods when you do not work. In this situation, the average number of hours you work is calculated across your year-long work cycle. This figure determines whether you count as being in full-time paid work, even during your non-working, non-paid periods.[22] This is known as the 'term-time only' worker rule. It affects people who work in schools and colleges, and may also affect those doing other seasonal jobs.

## 2. How work affects universal credit

You can qualify for universal credit (UC) whether or not you, your partner or anybody else in your household does paid work. This applies to employed earners and self-employed people.

However, any earnings may reduce your UC entitlement to nil. See Chapter 7 for how earned income affects the amount of your UC.

Some elements of UC also have eligibility rules based on work status.

- You cannot get the housing costs element of UC for payments you make as an owner-occupier if you or your partner have any earnings, no matter how low these are (although if you have a shared ownership tenancy, you might still be entitled regarding your rental payments – see p90).
- You can usually only get the childcare costs element of UC if you are working, have an offer of work, or your work very recently ended (see p76).[23]

You are treated as being in work or receiving earned income if you are getting statutory sick pay, statutory maternity, adoption, paternity or other parental pay, or (for childcare costs only) maternity allowance.[24] See p883 for what else counts as paid work for UC.

Work can also affect deductions being made from your UC for third-party debts (see p1035). Certain deductions should stop when your earnings (or, if you have a partner, your combined earnings) equal or exceed your work allowance for three monthly assessment periods.

Work can determine whether your UC award will be subject to the benefit cap (see p1025).

## 3. How work affects new-style jobseeker's allowance and means-tested benefits



The following benefits have rules about how hours of work affect entitlement:

- new-style jobseeker's allowance (JSA);
- income-related employment and support allowance (ESA);
- pension credit (PC);
- housing benefit (HB).

The rules for these benefits are described below. For non-means-tested benefits other than new-style JSA, see section 4 of this chapter.

Except where otherwise stated, the rules in this section apply to both employed and self-employed people.

**Note:** having a non-dependant who is in full-time paid work does not affect your eligibility for the following benefits, but for income-related ESA, PC and HB, it may lead to higher non-dependant deductions (see p292 and p209). Your non-dependant generally counts as being in full-time paid work if they work 16 hours or more a week.[25] See p885 for how hours are calculated.

### New-style jobseeker's allowance

You cannot usually get new-style JSA if you are in full-time paid work.[26] This means 16 hours or more a week.[27]

See p885 for how hours are calculated. Hours spent as an unpaid carer for someone entitled to a disability benefit (eg, attendance allowance or pension age disability payment, PIP or adult disability payment, DLA or child disability payment) are ignored.[28]

You can *also* be treated as in full-time paid work if you are:

- absent from full-time paid work without a good reason;[29] *or*
- no longer in full-time paid work but still within the period covered by certain holiday pay or payments in lieu.[30] See also p343.

You are *not* treated as being in full-time paid work if you are:

- in any of the categories on p884; *or*
- on work experience or participating in a specified scheme for helping people into work.

Even if you are eligible for new-style JSA, any part-time earnings may reduce your entitlement to nil (see p616).

## Income-related employment and support allowance

You cannot usually get income-related ESA if:

- you do any work (with some limited exceptions – see p928);[31] *or*
- your partner does full-time paid work.

**Note:** you also cannot usually get contributory ESA if you do any work (see p890).

Your partner is generally regarded as being in full-time paid work if they work 24 hours or more a week.[32] See p885 for how hours are calculated.

Your partner or your non-dependant can *also* be treated as being in full-time paid work if they:

- normally work full time, but are on holiday and intend to resume work once the holiday is over.[33] They can argue that they only count as being on holiday if they are paid for it;[34] *or*
- are absent from full-time paid work without a good reason.[35]

You or your partner can also be treated as working if you have stopped work (in your partner's case, full-time paid work) but are still within the period covered by certain holiday pay or payments in lieu.[36] See also p343.

Your partner or your non-dependant is *not* treated as being in full-time paid work if they:

- fall into any of the categories on p884; *or*
- work as a childminder in their own home.[37]

Even if you are eligible for income-related ESA, your partner's earnings may reduce your entitlement to nil. See Chapter 16 for how earned income affects the amount of your ESA.

## Pension credit

You can qualify for PC whether or not you, your partner, or anybody else in your household does paid work. However, any earnings may reduce your PC entitlement to nil. See Chapter 17 for how earned income affects the amount of your PC.

If a non-dependant counts as being in full-time paid work, this can affect non-dependant deductions from PC. Your non-dependant generally counts as being in full-time work when working 16 hours or more a week.[38] See p885 for how hours are calculated. For PC, the 'term-time only' worker rule can apply (see p886) and the calculation of hours does not include paid breaks like lunch or tea breaks.[39]

Your non-dependant can *also* be treated as in full-time paid work if they:[40]

- normally work full time, but are on holiday and intend to resume work once the holiday is over. They can argue that they only count as being on holiday if they are paid for it;[41] *or*
- are absent from full-time paid work without a good reason.

Your non-dependant is *not* treated as being in full-time paid work if they are:[42]

- on maternity, adoption, paternity or other parental leave, or absent from work because of sickness; *or*
- getting a sports award from a UK sports council and no other payment.

## Housing benefit

You can qualify for HB whether or not you, your partner, or anybody else in your household does paid work.

However, work can affect the calculation of your HB. Work status, including whether you count as in full time or 'remunerative' work, determines whether you get an additional earnings disregard or childcare costs disregard, and can affect the rate of any non-dependant deductions (see p209, p349 and p384). Beyond this, any earnings may reduce your HB entitlement to nil. See Chapters 16 and 17 for how earned income affects the amount of your HB. See also p1028, which describes the effect that work can have on the benefit cap.

For HB, you, your partner or your non-dependant generally count as being in full-time, 'remunerative' work if you are working 16 hours or more a week.[43] See p885 for how hours are calculated. The 'term-time only' worker rule can apply (see p886).

You, your partner or your non-dependant can *also* be treated as in full-time paid work if you (or they) are:[44]

- normally in full-time work, but currently on holiday and intending to resume work once the holiday is over. You can argue that you only count as being on holiday if you are paid for it;[45] *or*
- absent from full-time paid work without a good reason.

You, your partner or your non-dependant are *not* treated as being in full-time paid work if you (or they) are:[46]

- on maternity, adoption, paternity or other parental leave, or absent from work because of sickness. However, this rule does not apply for the purposes of the childcare costs disregard (see p350 and p384); *or*

- getting income-related ESA for more than three days in the relevant benefit week; *or*
- getting a sports award from a UK sports council and no other payment.

# 4. How work affects non-means-tested benefits

New-style jobseeker's allowance has specific rules: see sections 1 and 3 of this chapter. Some other non-means-tested benefits also have rules about work. These are summarised below.

| *Benefit* | *Work-related eligibility rules* |
|---|---|
| Bereavement benefits (see Chapter 21) | Your deceased partner must have either satisfied national insurance (NI) conditions or been an employed earner who died as a result of industrial injury or disease. You can be eligible for these benefits whether or not you work. |
| Carer's allowance (see Chapter 22) and carer support payment (see Chapter 63) | You cannot qualify if you earn more than £196 a week each week (see p473 for how this is calculated). The person you care for can be in or out of work. |
| Child benefit (see Chapter 23) | You cannot claim for certain 16–19-year-olds who do paid work for 24 hours or more a week (see p496). |
| Contributory (including new-style) employment and support allowance (see Chapter 26) | You cannot qualify while working,[47] with limited exceptions (see p928). |
| Industrial injuries benefits (see Chapter 28) | You must have been an employed earner when you had an accident or contracted a disease. |
| Maternity allowance (see Chapter 30) | You must satisfy an employment condition in order to qualify (see p631). |
| Statutory sick pay (SSP) (see Chapter 35) | You are only eligible if you meet employment conditions (see p747). Self-employed people cannot claim SSP. |
| Statutory maternity, adoption, paternity, and other parental pay (see Chapter 34) | You are only eligible if you meet employment conditions (see pp719–32). Self-employed people do not qualify. |

Whether you are an employed earner or self-employed also affects your NI contributions (see Chapter 39).

## 5. People involved in trade disputes

Trade dispute law is complex. If there is any doubt about whether you are involved in a trade dispute, get specialist employment advice.

### Universal credit

For universal credit (UC), the definition of 'trade dispute' is the same as it is in employment law.[48] You remain entitled to UC if you are involved in a trade dispute, and remain eligible for advances if you meet the usual eligibility criteria. However, if you (or your partner) have withdrawn your labour in support of a trade dispute, you are treated as having the same earnings you would have otherwise. This applies unless your contract of employment has been terminated.[49] Any strike pay you receive (eg, from your trade union) does not count as income.[50] You should not be sanctioned for taking part in a trade dispute.[51]

### Other benefits

#### New-style jobseeker's allowance

For new-style jobseeker's allowance (JSA), a 'trade dispute' means any dispute between fellow employees, or between employees and employers, connected with terms or conditions of employment, or the employment or non-employment of anyone.[52]

You are not entitled to new-style JSA, including hardship payments, for a week in which on any day you are involved in a trade dispute.[53] Weeks when you are not entitled to new-style JSA do not count as part of your jobseeking period (see p611), meaning that they do not count towards your 182-day entitlement.[54]

You should not be sanctioned on JSA for taking part in a trade dispute.[55]

#### Income-related employment and support allowance, pension credit and housing benefit

There are no rules that reduce the amount of your income-related employment and support allowance (ESA), pension credit (PC) or housing benefit (HB) if you or your partner are involved in a trade dispute. However, your earnings can be reassessed and averaged differently to take account of the reduction in earnings (see p370 for working-age HB, p394 for pension-age HB, p369 for income-related ESA and p394 for PC).

For income-related ESA, your partner is treated as not being in full-time paid work if they are involved in a trade dispute and for the first 15 days following their return to work.[56]

### Non-dependants

Non-dependant deductions made from your income-related ESA or PC housing costs, and from HB, are usually higher if your non-dependant is in full-time paid work. However, if your non-dependant is involved in a trade dispute, this may mean that the non-dependant deduction should be reduced. See p209 and p292 for further information.

## Benefits paid to you by your employer

### Statutory sick pay

You can generally continue to qualify for statutory sick pay (SSP) if you were already entitled to it when a trade dispute began. You cannot qualify if you become incapable of work *during* a stoppage of work caused by a trade dispute, unless you can prove that you did not have a direct interest in the dispute on or before that date.[57] If you are disqualified from getting SSP on this basis, you are not entitled at any point during your period of sickness, even if the trade dispute ends. You may, however, qualify for ESA. 'Stoppage of work' and 'trade dispute' are not defined in the SSP rules. However, an overtime ban or working to grade does not count as a stoppage of work.[58]

6

### Statutory maternity, adoption, paternity, shared parental, parental bereavement and neonatal care pay

To qualify for these types of statutory parental pay, you must have been employed for a continuous period of at least 26 weeks ending on a specified date (see p728). Any week in which you are not working because of a trade dispute does not break your continuity of employment for this purpose. However, unless you can prove that at no time did you have a direct interest in the trade dispute:[59]

- any such week does not count towards the total of 26 weeks' employment; *and*
- if you are dismissed during the stoppage of work, your continuity of employment ends on the day you stopped work.

## Social fund payments

Involvement in a trade dispute does not affect your entitlement to a DWP funeral expenses payment, cold weather payment or winter fuel payment, to a funeral support payment in Scotland, or to payments from the Scottish Welfare Fund. You cannot, however, qualify for a DWP budgeting loan if you or your partner are involved in a trade dispute.[60]

The rules about whether you count as being involved in a trade dispute are largely the same as for JSA (see p891).

You do not count as being involved in a trade dispute during a period when you are incapable of work, or from the sixth week before the week you are due to have a baby to the end of the seventh week after the week the baby is born.[61]

## Sure Start and Best Start schemes

If you or your partner are involved in a trade dispute, your entitlement to a Sure Start maternity grant is not affected if your 'qualifying benefit' is UC, income-related ESA or PC.

In Scotland, so long as you remain entitled to a qualifying benefit, your entitlement to Best Start grants and food is not affected (see Chapter 62).[62]

# Notes

1. **Paid work, full-time paid work and hours**
   1 Reg 2, definition of 'paid work', UC Regs
   2 R(IS) 5/95; *Fiore v CAO*, 20 June 1995; para R2210 ADM (for new-style JSA); paras 41272 and 41316 DMG (for income-related ESA)
   3 *CAO v Ellis* [1995] (CA), reported as R(IS)22/95; CTC/626/2001
   4 R(IS) 1/93
   5 CFC/33/1993; R(FIS) 1/83
   6 para 41333 DMG
   7 CIS/649/1992
   8 *CAO v Ellis* [1995] (CA), reported as R(IS)22/95; CIS/434/1994
   9 **JSA** Reg 44 JSA Regs 2013
   **ESA** Reg 43 and Sch 6 para 2(6) and (8) ESA Regs
   10 R(FIS) 1/86; CDWA/1/1992
   11 **JSA** Reg 43(1) JSA Regs 2013
   **ESA** Reg 43(3) and Sch 6 para 2(5) ESA Regs
   12 **JSA** Reg 42(3)(a) JSA Regs 2013
   **ESA** Regs 42(2) and 45(9) and Sch 6 para 2(7) ESA Regs
   13 para 4153 DMG; R(FIS) 6/85; *Kazantzis v CAO* [1999], reported as R(IS) 13/99
   14 para 20267 DMG
   15 *Kevin Smith v CAO* [1994] (CA), reported as R(IS) 21/95
   16 R(JSA) 1/09; *GM v SSWP (JSA)* [2010] UKUT 221 (AAC), reported as [2012] AACR 9; *Saunderson v SSWP* [2012] ScotCS CSIH 10
   17 **JSA** Reg 42(2)(b)(i) JSA Regs 2013
   **ESA** Regs 42(2) and 45(8)(b)(i) and Sch 6 para 2(2)(a) ESA Regs
   **PC** Sch 2 para 2(2)(a) SPC Regs
   **HB** Reg 6(2)(a) HB Regs; reg 6(2)(a) HB(SPC) Regs
   18 R(JSA) 5/03
   19 **JSA** Reg 42(2)(b)(ii) JSA Regs 2013
   **ESA** Regs 42(2) and 45(8)(b)(ii) and Sch 6 para 2(2)(b) ESA Regs
   **PC** Sch 2 para 2(2)(b) SPC Regs
   **HB** Reg 6(2)(b) HB Regs; reg 6(2)(b) HB(SPC) Regs
   **All** para 4131 DMG; CFC/2963/2001; *NS v SSWP (IS)* [2015] UKUT 423 (AAC)
   20 **JSA** Reg 42(2)(a) JSA Regs 2013
   **ESA** Regs 42(2) and 45(8)(a) and Sch 6 para 2(3) ESA Regs
   **PC** Sch 2 para 2(4) SPC Regs
   **HB** Reg 6(4) HB Regs; reg 6(4) HB(SPC) Regs
   21 R(JSA)1/07; *Saunderson v SSWP* [2012] ScotCS CSIH 10
   22 **PC** Sch 2 para 2(3) SPC Regs
   **HB** Reg 6(3) HB Regs; reg 6(3) HB(SPC) Regs
   **All** *Stafford and Banks v CAO* [2001] UKHL 33, reported as R(IS) 15/01

2. **How work affects universal credit**
   23 Reg 32 UC Regs
   24 Regs 32(2)(b) and 55 and Sch 5 para 4 UC Regs

### 3. How work affects new-style jobseeker's allowance and means-tested benefits

25 **ESA** Sch 6 para 2(1) ESA Regs
**PC** Sch 2 para 2(1) SPC Regs
**HB** Reg 6(1) HB Regs; reg 6(1) HB(SPC) Regs
26 s1(2)(3) JSA 1995
27 Reg 42 JSA Regs 2013
28 Reg 42(3)c) JSA Regs 2013
29 Reg 43(1) JSA Regs 2013
30 Reg 43(2) and (3) JSA Regs 2013
31 Sch 1 para 6(1)(e) WRA 2007; regs 40 and 41 ESA Regs
32 Reg 42(1) ESA Regs
33 Reg 42(3) and Sch 6 para 2(4) ESA Regs
34 R(JSA) 5/03; para 41384 DMG
35 Reg 42(3) and Sch 6 para 2(4) ESA Regs
36 Regs 41(2) and (3) and 42(4) and (5) ESA Regs
37 Reg 43(1)(a) ESA Regs
38 Sch 2 para 2(1) SPC Regs
39 Vol 13 Ch 78 App 5, paras 47 and 81 DMG
40 Sch 2 para 2(5) SPC Regs
41 R(JSA) 5/03; Vol 13, Ch 78 App 2, para 73 DMG
42 Sch 2 para 2(7)-(8) SPC Regs
43 Reg 6(1) HB Regs; reg 6(1) HB(SPC) Regs
44 Reg 6(5) HB Regs; reg 6(5) HB(SPC) Regs
45 R(JSA) 5/03; para 20309 DMG
46 Reg 6(7)-(8) HB Regs; reg 6(6)-(8) HB(SPC) Regs

### 4. How work affects non-means-tested benefits

47 Reg 37 ESA Regs 2013

### 5. People involved in trade disputes

48 Reg 2, definition of 'trade dispute' (as defined in s244 of the Trade Union and Labour Relations (Consolidation) Act 1992), UC Regs
49 Reg 56 UC Regs
50 Reg 66 UC Regs
51 Reg 113(1) UC Regs
52 s35(1), definition of 'trade dispute', JSA 1995
53 ss14 and 35(1), definition of 'week', JSA 1995
54 Reg 37(2)(d) JSA Regs 2013
55 Reg 28(1)(d) JSA Regs 2013
56 Reg 43(2)(b) ESA Regs
57 Sch 11 paras 2(g) and 7 SSCBA 1992
58 R(SSP) 1/86
59 **SMP** Reg 13 SMP Regs
**SAP/SPP** Reg 35 SPPSAP(G) Regs
**SSPP** Reg 36 SSPP(G) Regs
**SPBP** Reg 14 SPBP(G) Regs
**SNCP** Reg 18 SNCP(G) Regs (draft)
60 SF Dir 8(1)(b)
61 s126(1) and (2) SSCBA 1992; s14 JSA 1995; reg 171 JSA Regs; reg 3 SFM&FE Regs; SF Dir 8
62 Regs 3(1) and 6 SFM&FE Regs; s126 SSCBA 1992; s14 JSA 1995

# Chapter 41

# Limited capability for work

**This chapter covers:**


1. The work capability assessment (p896)
2. Challenging a decision (p923)
3. Periods of limited capability for work (p928)
4. Work you can do while claiming employment and support allowance (p928)


6

## Key facts

- If you are unable to work because of illness or disability, you may be entitled to benefit and national insurance credits on the basis of having 'limited capability for work'. The main benefits this affects are universal credit (UC) and employment and support allowance.
- Whether or not you have limited capability for work is assessed by the 'work capability assessment'. This also tests whether you have 'limited capability for work-related activity'. If so, you are not required to attend work-focused interviews or prepare to return to work, and are entitled to a higher amount of benefit.
- If you work, you may be regarded as not having limited capability for work or work-related activity.
- If you disagree with the decision about your limited capability for work or work-related activity, you can apply for a revision or supersession (see Chapter 50), or appeal against it (see Chapter 51).

***Future changes***

The work capability assessment is to be abolished in 2028. Benefit entitlement will then no longer depend on limited capability for work or for work-related activity. Instead, a 'health element' in UC will depend on entitlement to personal independence payment (PIP). Details, including of arrangements in Scotland where PIP is replaced by adult disability payment, were not available at time of writing. See CPAG's *Welfare Rights Bulletin* or the online version of this *Handbook* for updates.

# 1. The work capability assessment

The work capability assessment is a test used by the DWP to decide whether:

- you have 'limited capability for work' – ie, whether you can get benefit on the basis of being unable to work because of your health condition; *and*
- you have 'limited capability for work-related activity' – ie, whether your health condition is so severe that, in addition to being unable to work, you are not required to engage in activities such as attending interviews about looking for work or retraining.

The assessment is used to decide whether you can get extra amounts included in your universal credit (UC) and your work-related responsibilities if you come under the UC system. It is also used to decide your entitlement to employment and support allowance (ESA).

6

The work capability assessment is also used to decide whether you are entitled to national insurance (NI) credits for limited capability for work (see Chapter 39) and whether you can still get a work-related activity component in your housing benefit (HB) (see p281). **Note:** this component was abolished for new claims from 3 April 2017. For NI credits and HB, whether you have limited capability for work is decided under the rules for ESA.

You satisfy the work capability assessment if you score sufficient points (see p902) or you do not but an exceptional circumstance applies (see p900). You also satisfy the test without actually undergoing the assessment if you are treated as having limited capability for work (see below). In some circumstances, you can be treated as not having limited capability for work even though you have passed the assessment (see p901).

**Note:** for UC, there are limited circumstances in which a work capability assessment may not be carried out. These are where you are treated as not having limited capability for work because you have previously failed the assessment (either for UC or new-style ESA) or where you work and earn at or above a certain threshold, and no exceptions apply. See p901 for details.

## Treated as having limited capability for work

You are automatically treated as having limited capability for work (without undergoing the work capability assessment) in certain circumstances. In other circumstances, you may be treated as having limited capability for work because of your health.[1]

### Universal credit

You are automatically treated as having limited capability for work for UC if:

- you have already been assessed as having limited capability for work for new-style ESA – ie, contributory ESA paid under the UC system;[2] *or*

- you are transferring to UC from old-style ESA and before claiming UC you were assessed or treated as having limited capability for work for ESA (in this situation, if you are a student, you are treated as having limited capability for work from *before* the date you started receiving education, so that you can get UC while in education);[3] *or*
- you were entitled to NI contribution credits for limited capability for work when you claimed UC (this can include where your ESA stopped before you claimed UC, for a reason other than it being found that you did not have limited capability for work);[4] *or*
- you had been getting ESA but that stopped when you reached pension age, you claim UC (eg, as part of a mixed-age couple) within a month of your ESA ending and you would have remained entitled to ESA but for reaching pension age;[5] *or*
- you are treated as having limited capability for work-related activity for UC (see p917) – eg, because you are terminally ill, receiving treatment for cancer or are pregnant.



You are treated as having limited capability for work for UC because of your health if:[6]

- you are at least pension age (see p689) and get disability living allowance (DLA), Scottish adult disaility living allowance (SADLA), personal independence payment (PIP) or adult disability payment (ADP); *or*
- you have been given official notice not to work because of being in contact with an infectious disease; *or*
- you are an inpatient in hospital where you have been medically advised to stay for at least 24 hours, or are recovering from treatment as an inpatient (and the DWP is satisfied that your condition remains sufficiently serious), including if you are attending a residential rehabilitation programme for drug or alcohol addiction; *or*
- you are receiving plasmapheresis, regular weekly treatment for haemodialysis for chronic renal failure, or regular weekly treatment for total parenteral nutrition for gross impairment of enteric function, or are recovering from such treatment.

**Note:** unlike for ESA, there is no UC rule that treats you as having limited capability for work while you are waiting for the work capability assessment to be carried out. However, the bullet points above might still apply to you in either of those situations.

***Are you transferring to universal credit from employment and support allowance?***

If you were getting ESA but then claim UC, you are automatically treated as having limited capability for work. However, the DWP may wrongly overlook this rule and insist that you have to be assessed again. If this affects you, note the following.

1. Point out the rule and insist that you should be treated as having limited capability for work for UC. If necessary, challenge the decision on your UC entitlement.
2. The DWP may say that it needs to check that you were getting ESA – complain if this is taking a long time. Ultimately, an unreasonably long delay might be challenged by judicial review (see p1268).
3. If you were getting the support component in your ESA (or NI credits for limited capability for work-related activity), the limited capability for work-related activity element should be included in your UC from your first monthly assessment period.[7]
4. If you were getting the work-related activity component in your ESA, the limited capability for work element should be included in your UC from your first monthly assessment period.[8]
5. Remember that, despite these rules, the DWP can still apply the work capability assessment to you again in the future.

## Employment and support allowance

You are automatically treated as having limited capability for work for ESA if:[9]

- you are waiting for an assessment or (in some circumstances) an appeal (see p899); *or*
- you satisfy one of the eating and drinking descriptors for limited capability for work-related activity (see p913); *or*
- you are entitled to statutory sick pay; *or*
- for income-related ESA only, you are in education, you are not a 'qualifying young person' (see p488) and you get income-related ESA because you receive DLA, SADLA, PIP, ADP or armed forces independence payment (AFIP);[10] *or*
- for contributory ESA only, you get UC and have been assessed as having limited capability for work for UC.[11]

You are treated as having limited capability for work because of your health for ESA if:[12]

- you are pregnant or have recently given birth, you are not entitled to maternity allowance (MA) or statutory maternity pay, you have a medical certificate giving the expected or actual date of birth, and you are within the period beginning with the first day of the sixth week before the expected week of childbirth (or the actual day of childbirth if earlier) and ending on the 14th day after you have the baby; *or*
- you are pregnant and entitled to MA; *or*

- you are pregnant and there is a serious risk to your health or your baby's health if you do not refrain from work; *or*
- you are terminally ill – ie, your death can reasonably be expected within 12 months; *or*
- you are receiving chemotherapy or radiotherapy treatment for cancer, recovering from such treatment or are likely to receive such treatment within six months from the date the DWP determines whether or not you pass the work capability assessment; *or*
- you have been given official notice not to work because of being in contact with an infectious disease; *or*
- you are an inpatient in hospital where you have been medically advised to stay for at least 24 hours, or are recovering from treatment as an inpatient (and the DWP is satisfied that your condition remains sufficiently serious), including if you are attending a residential programme of rehabilitation for drug or alcohol addiction; *or*
- you are receiving plasmapheresis, regular weekly treatment for haemodialysis for chronic renal failure, or regular weekly treatment for total parenteral nutrition for gross impairment of enteric function, or are recovering from such treatment. The DWP must be satisfied that you should continue to be treated as having limited capability for work. In the first week of such treatment, you must be receiving it or recovering from it for at least two days. You continue to be treated as having limited capability for work if your treatment later goes down to one day a week. However, you cannot get income-related ESA in any week in which you work (apart from work you can do while claiming – see p928), although you can claim contributory ESA for the days of treatment and recovery.[13]

#### If you are waiting for an assessment or you are appealing

You are treated as having limited capability for work if:[14]

- you are applying for ESA and have provided a current fit note (ie, a medical certificate), but the work capability assessment has not yet been carried out. You can get ESA while waiting for your assessment. However, this does not apply if you are reclaiming ESA after having failed the work capability assessment, unless your condition has significantly worsened or you have a new health condition. Your condition has significantly worsened if it is considered that you would now be likely to pass the work capability assessment;[15] *or*
- you are appealing against a decision that you have failed the work capability assessment (ie, you were found not to have limited capability for work) and you have submitted a fit note. However, unless your current claim for ESA was made before 30 March 2015, this only applies if:
  - this is the first time you have failed the work capability assessment; *or*

- this is the first time you have failed the work capability assessment since a previous decision that you satisfied it (see p925); *or*

- you are reclaiming ESA and have provided a current fit note after being treated as failing the work capability assessment because you failed to return the ESA50 questionnaire or failed to attend the medical. You can get ESA while waiting for your assessment. However, this only applies if:
  - you have now returned the questionnaire; *or*
  - it is more than six months since the decision treating you as not having limited capability for work; *or*
  - your condition has significantly worsened. Your condition has significantly worsened if it is considered that you would now be likely to pass the work capability assessment;[16] *or*
  - you have a new health condition.

6

***Examples***

Emily had back pain and so applied for new-style ESA (ie, contributory ESA under the UC system), but failed the work capability assessment. Later, she develops depression and reclaims ESA, supplying a fit note. The DWP accepts that Emily has a new condition, and so treats her as having limited capability for work and pays her ESA while a new work capability assessment is arranged.

Manish claims new-style ESA but fails the work capability assessment. He decides to apply for ESA again a month later. The DWP does not consider that his condition has significantly worsened or that he has a new health condition, so he is not treated as having limited capability for work, and is not paid ESA before getting a decision on his new claim.

## Exceptional circumstances

If you have been assessed under the work capability assessment but do not score sufficient points to have limited capability for work, you are treated as doing so for UC and ESA if:[17]

- you have an uncontrolled or uncontrollable life-threatening disease, and there is medical evidence to show this. There must be reasonable cause for the disease not to be controllable by a recognised therapeutic procedure; *or*
- because of your illness, there would be a 'substantial risk' to the mental or physical health of any person were you to be found not to have limited capability for work. The 'substantial risk' could arise from the sort of work you may be expected to do, or from the journey to or from work, although it is not necessary to go into the detail of individual job descriptions or potential jobseeker's agreements. The risk may also arise from the journey to or from a job interview or attendance at the job centre.[18] However, this exceptional circumstance does not apply if the risk could be significantly reduced by

reasonable adjustments in your workplace, or by your taking medication prescribed by your doctor.

## Treated as not having limited capability for work

### Universal credit

For UC, you are treated as *not* having limited capability for work if:[19]

- you have previously failed the work capability assessment, either for UC or for new-style ESA. The DWP does not reassess you unless the decision was made in ignorance of, or based on a mistake about, a material fact, or there has been a relevant change in your condition; *or*
- you do not return the UC50 questionnaire (see p920) or you do not attend the medical (see p921), and do not have good reason (see p921) for this; *or*
- you work, none of the exceptions in the bullet points below apply and your earnings are at or above a certain threshold. This is the level of earnings you would be paid for 16 hours' work a week at the 'national living wage' (ie, national minimum wage for people aged 21 and over), converted to a monthly amount – ie, in 2025/26 earnings at or above £846.56 a month.[20]

You can work and earn above this threshold without automatically being treated as not having limited capability for work if:

- you are entitled to attendance allowance (AA), pension age disability payment, DLA, SADLA, child disability payment, PIP, ADP or AFIP (but the DWP may still apply the work capability assessment to you); *or*
- you have already been assessed as scoring sufficient points to have limited capability for work or limited capability for work-related activity (see p913) for UC or new-style ESA (but the DWP may still reapply the work capability assessment to you); *or*
- you have not been assessed, or have but not scored sufficient points, but are treated under the UC system as having limited capability for work, or for work-related activity, because of your health (see p896 and p913), or because an exceptional circumstance applies (see p900). The DWP cannot now apply the work capability assessment, but could still reconsider whether you should still be treated as having limited capability for work or work-related activity.

***Are you transferring to universal credit from employment and support allowance?***

If you were getting ESA and doing 'permitted work' (see p930), but then claim UC, it is not clear whether the rules about work described above should apply to you. Bear in mind the following.

1. UC does not have a permitted work rule, but there is no general rule that prevents you from having limited capability for work if you are doing some work.
2. In many situations, your earnings from permitted work will be below the earnings threshold, you are getting PIP or DLA, or you are treated as having limited capability for work (or for work-related activity) because of your health or because an exceptional circumstance applies. In these situations, you are *not* automatically treated as not having limited capability for work.
3. The DWP usually accepts that you have limited capability for work at the point you transfer from ESA to UC, but it may consider reapplying the work capability assessment to you.



## Employment and support allowance

For ESA, you are treated as *not* having limited capability for work, even if you have been assessed as satisfying the work capability assessment, if you:

- do not return the ESA50 questionnaire (see p920) or attend the medical (see p921) while the work capability assessment applies to you, and you do not have good cause (see p920 and p922); *or*
- do any work, except certain work you can do while claiming (see p928);[21] *or*
- are disqualified from receiving contributory ESA (even if you are not already entitled to it) for more than six weeks because you are a prisoner. If this applies, but you are entitled to income-related ESA (ie, pending trial, or sentence following conviction), you are only treated as not having limited capability for work after your entitlement has ended;[22] *or*
- attend a training course and receive a training allowance or premium, unless your ESA claim is for a period beginning after you stopped attending the course, or if the training allowance or premium was only for travelling or meal expenses;[23] *or*
- are (or were) a member of the armed forces and the day in question is a day of sickness absence from duty.[24]

## Scoring points

The assessment does not take into account actual jobs, your education or training, or any language or literacy problems. It is a test of your ability to perform certain activities, taking account of a 'specific bodily disease or disablement' or a 'specific mental illness or disablement', and the direct results of medical treatment (from a registered doctor) for these.[25]

There are two lists of activities: one physical (see below), one mental (see p909). Under each activity, there is a further list of statements, called 'descriptors', which describe different levels of difficulty in carrying out the activity. Attached to each descriptor is a points score. You are awarded the highest scoring descriptor in each activity that applies to you.

For the physical activities, this takes into account your ability when wearing or using any aid, appliance or prosthesis that you normally wear or use, or any aid or appliance that you could reasonably be expected to wear or use.[26]

To score enough points to satisfy the test, you must score a total of 15 points or more. The points can be scored in one or more activities, and scores from the physical and mental activities can be combined. For example, you can score nine points in the physical test and six points in the mental test.

## Good days and bad days, pain and tiredness

Generally, what counts is your capability as it is 'most of the time'. If you cannot repeat an activity with a reasonable degree of regularity, you should be considered unable to perform it. The following points apply.

- Your ability to perform an activity with some degree of repetition should be considered and a 'broad-brush' approach applied, rather than just a day-by-day approach.[27]
- A descriptor should apply to you if you cannot perform the activity most of the time. The severity of your condition, the frequency of your good and bad days and the unpredictability of the bad days are all relevant.[28]
- If you have long periods of remission, you may be considered capable of work during these periods. This depends on the severity of your condition and on the length of your periods of ill health and your periods of remission.[29]
- Pain, fatigue and the increasing difficulty you may have in performing an activity on a repeated basis compared with someone in good health should be taken into account.[30] 'Pain' may include nausea and dizziness.[31]
- Any risk to your health in performing an activity should be considered, particularly if carrying it out is against medical advice. If the risk is sufficiently serious, you may be considered incapable of the activity.[32]

## Physical disabilities

To score points in the physical test, your incapacity must arise from a 'specific bodily disease or disablement'.[33]

### Activity 1: mobilising

Mobilising unaided by another person with or without a walking stick, manual wheelchair or other aid if such aid is normally used, or could reasonably be worn or used

| *Descriptors* | *Points* |
|---|---|
| a. Cannot, unaided by another person, either:<br>(i) mobilise more than 50 metres on level ground without stopping in order to avoid significant discomfort or exhaustion; *or*<br>(ii) repeatedly mobilise 50 metres within a reasonable timescale because of significant discomfort or exhaustion. | 15 |
| b. Cannot, unaided by another person, mount or descend two steps even with the support of a handrail. | 9 |
| c. Cannot, unaided by another person, either:<br>(i) mobilise more than 100 metres on level ground without stopping in order to avoid significant discomfort or exhaustion; *or*<br>(ii) repeatedly mobilise 100 metres within a reasonable timescale because of significant discomfort or exhaustion. | 9 |
| d. Cannot, unaided by another person, either:<br>(i) mobilise more than 200 metres on level ground without stopping in order to avoid significant discomfort or exhaustion; *or*<br>(ii) repeatedly mobilise 200 metres within a reasonable timescale because of significant discomfort or exhaustion. | 6 |
| e. None of the above applies. | 0 |

Your ability to use a walking stick or manual wheelchair (but not an electric one) or another aid can be taken into account if you usually use one or could 'reasonably' use one. Issues such as your ability to propel and handle a manual wheelchair and whether one is medically suitable for you should be taken into account.[34] Official guidance stresses the importance of considering things like fatigue and breathlessness.[35] **Note**: if descriptor 1(a) applies, you also have limited capability for work-related activity (see p913).

### Activity 2: standing and sitting

Standing and sitting

| *Descriptors* | *Points* |
|---|---|
| a. Cannot move between one seated position and another seated position located next to one another without receiving physical assistance from another person. | 15 |
| b. Cannot, for the majority of the time, remain at a work station, either: (i) standing unassisted by another person (even if free to move around); *or* (ii) sitting (even in an adjustable chair); *or* (iii) a combination of (i) and (ii), for more than 30 minutes, before needing to move away in order to avoid significant discomfort or exhaustion. | 9 |
| c. Cannot, for the majority of the time, remain at a work station: (i) standing unassisted by another person (even if free to move around); *or* (ii) sitting (even in an adjustable chair); *or* (iii) a combination of (i) and (ii), for more than an hour before needing to move away in order to avoid significant discomfort or exhaustion. | 6 |
| d. None of the above applies. | 0 |

Official guidance says that in transferring from one seated position to another, it is reasonable to take into account a transfer board, but not something more specialised, such as a hoist. Your ability to stand does not require you to stand absolutely still, but you must have at least one hand free, so if you need two crutches to stand, this would not count as ability to stand.[36] **Note:** if descriptor 2(a) applies, you also have limited capability for work-related activity (see p913).

### Activity 3: reaching

Reaching

| *Descriptors* | *Points* |
|---|---|
| a. Cannot raise either arm as if to put something in the top pocket of a coat or jacket. | 15 |
| b. Cannot raise either arm to top of head as if to put on a hat. | 9 |
| c. Cannot raise either arm above head height as if to reach for something. | 6 |
| d. None of the above applies. | 0 |

This activity is about your ability to reach with either arm above waist height. It is not a test of your ability to use your hands or fingers.[37] **Note:** if descriptor 3(a) applies, you also have limited capability for work-related activity (see p913).

### Activity 4: picking up, moving and transferring things

| Picking up and moving or transferring by the use of the upper body and arms | |
|---|---|
| ***Descriptors*** | ***Points*** |
| a. Cannot pick up and move a 0.5 litre carton full of liquid. | 15 |
| b. Cannot pick up and move a one litre carton full of liquid. | 9 |
| c. Cannot transfer a light but bulky object such as an empty cardboard box. | 6 |
| d. None of the above applies. | 0 |

This activity is about picking up and moving specified objects, but is not a test of your ability to carry them. Problems with your shoulders, neck or back, as well as with your arms, should be taken into account.[38] It may be that you can transfer a bulky cardboard box with just one arm, but this will depend on all the circumstances of your condition.[39] **Note:** if descriptor 4(a) applies, you also have limited capability for work-related activity (see p913).

6

### Activity 5: manual dexterity

| Manual dexterity | |
|---|---|
| ***Descriptors*** | ***Points*** |
| a. Cannot press a button (such as a telephone keypad) with either hand or cannot turn the pages of a book with either hand. | 15 |
| b. Cannot pick up a £1 coin or equivalent with either hand. | 15 |
| c. Cannot use a pen or pencil to make a meaningful mark with either hand. | 9 |
| d. Cannot single-handedly use a suitable keyboard or mouse. | 9 |
| e. None of the above applies. | 0 |

This activity is about your hand and wrist function with work-related tasks, such as using a keypad or a computer keyboard or mouse. It is not a test of your computer literacy. A 'meaningful mark' can be something simple such as a signature or tick.[40] Official guidance says that to score points for inability to use a suitable keyboard or mouse, you must be unable to use both the keyboard and mouse. However, there is a conflict in the caselaw about this, and you may be able to argue that your inability to use one of them means you should score points.[41] **Note:** if descriptor 5(a) applies, you also have limited capability for work-related activity (see p913).

### Activity 6: making yourself understood

Making self understood through speaking, writing, typing, or other means which are normally or could reasonably be used, unaided by another person

| *Descriptors* | *Points* |
|---|---|
| a. Cannot convey a simple message, such as the presence of a hazard. | 15 |
| b. Has significant difficulty conveying a simple message to strangers. | 15 |
| c. Has some difficulty conveying a simple message to strangers. | 6 |
| d. None of the above applies. | 0 |

This activity is about expressing yourself to be understood, but is not restricted to speech. Official guidance mentions brain injury, motor neurone disease, Parkinson's disease and stroke are among possible relevant conditions. If you have communication problems arising from a panic disorder or chronic fatigue syndrome, the guidance suggests scoring points under the mental health assessment instead if your problems are 'purely due to mental health problems'.[42] **Note:** if descriptor 6(a) applies, you also have limited capability for work-related activity (see p913).

### Activity 7: understanding communication

Understanding communication by:
(i) verbal means (such as hearing or lip reading) alone;
(ii) non-verbal means (such as reading 16-point print or braille) alone; *or*
(iii) a combination of (i) and (ii),
using any aid that is normally or could reasonably be used, unaided by another person.

| *Descriptors* | *Points* |
|---|---|
| a. Cannot understand a simple message, such as the location of a fire escape, due to sensory impairment. | 15 |
| b. Has significant difficulty understanding a simple message from a stranger due to sensory impairment. | 15 |
| c. Has some difficulty understanding a simple message from a stranger due to sensory impairment. | 6 |
| d. None of the above applies. | 0 |

You may score points in this activity if you have a hearing impairment, a visual impairment or both a hearing and a visual impairment, which means you have problems understanding simple communication. Your ability is assessed taking account of things like hearing aids, braille and large print communication. You may score points if you have problems understanding either spoken or written communication – you do not need to have problems with both.[43] **Note:** if descriptor 7(a) applies, you also have limited capability for work-related activity (see p913).

### Activity 8: navigation and maintaining safety

Navigation and maintaining safety using a guide dog or other aid if either or both are normally or could reasonably be used

| *Descriptors* | *Points* |
|---|---|
| a. Unable to navigate around familiar surroundings, without being accompanied by another person, due to sensory impairment. | 15 |
| b. Cannot safely complete a potentially hazardous task such as crossing the road, without being accompanied by another person, due to sensory impairment. | 15 |
| c. Unable to navigate around unfamiliar surroundings, without being accompanied by another person, due to sensory impairment. | 9 |
| d. None of the above applies. | 0 |

This is a test of your ability to get about safely if you have a 'sensory impairment'. This usually means impaired sight or hearing, but could include impairment of other senses, or possibly if you have serious balance problems due to Meniere's disease.[44] Your ability is assessed taking into account your guide dog or other aid if it is normally used or if it could reasonably be used. This usually means used by you or people in your situation, acting reasonably in all the circumstances.[45] Official guidance says that you are not assessed as using a guide dog unless you actually have one, and that GPS devices are not considered.[46]

### Activity 9: incontinence

Absence or loss of control while conscious leading to extensive evacuation of the bowel and/or bladder, other than enuresis (bedwetting), despite the wearing or use of any aids or adaptations which are normally or could reasonably be worn or used

| *Descriptors* | *Points* |
|---|---|
| a. At least once a month experiences:<br>(i) loss of control leading to extensive evacuation of the bowel and/or voiding of the bladder; *or*<br>(ii) substantial leakage of the contents of a collecting device, sufficient to require cleaning and a change in clothing. | 15 |
| b. The majority of the time is at risk of loss of control leading to extensive evacuation of the bowel and/or voiding of the bladder, sufficient to require cleaning and a change in clothing, if not able to reach a toilet quickly. | 6 |
| c. Neither of the above applies. | 0 |

This activity is about managing incontinence. Because 'extensive' evacuation of the bowel or bladder is referred to, minor leakage or dribbling do not count. Incontinence that occurs while you are asleep or having a fit or seizure is not covered.[47] The test is meant to deal with issues of personal dignity, so if you have an incontinence problem and because of mobility problems you are unable to reach a toilet before you lose control, you score points, provided this is frequent enough.[48] **Note:** to be assessed as also having limited capability for work-related activity on this activity, you must lose control at least once a week (see p913).

### Activity 10: consciousness during waking moments

Consciousness during waking moments

| *Descriptors* | *Points* |
|---|---|
| a. At least once a week, has an involuntary episode of lost or altered consciousness resulting in significantly disrupted awareness or concentration. | 15 |
| b. At least once a month, has an involuntary episode of lost or altered consciousness resulting in significantly disrupted awareness or concentration. | 6 |
| c. Neither of the above applies. | 0 |

This activity is about involuntary lost or altered consciousness that results in 'significantly disrupted awareness or concentration'. Because it is in the context of 'during waking moments', it is about problems that occur when you are normally awake. 'Altered' consciousness is regarded as a 'definite clouding of mental faculties resulting in loss of control of thoughts or action'.[49] Official guidance says that dizziness or vertigo are not relevant, unless it is in the context of an epileptic or similar seizure.[50]

## Mental disabilities

To score points in the mental disabilities test, your incapacity must arise from a 'specific mental illness or disablement'.[51] See CPAG's *Mental Health and Benefits Handbook* for more information about the mental health descriptors.

### Activity 11: learning tasks

Learning tasks

| *Descriptors* | *Points* |
|---|---|
| a. Cannot learn how to complete a simple task, such as setting an alarm clock. | 15 |
| b. Cannot learn anything beyond a simple task, such as setting an alarm clock. | 9 |
| c. Cannot learn anything beyond a moderately complex task, such as the steps involved in operating a washing machine to clean clothes. | 6 |
| d. None of the above applies. | 0 |

This is about your ability to learn new tasks – but note that the specified tasks are just examples. If you cannot repeat a task or have to be shown how to do it again, you have not learned it. Official guidance mentions learning disability, organic brain disorders, including stroke, and receptive dysphasia among possible relevant conditions.[52] **Note:** if descriptor 11(a) applies, you also have limited capability for work-related activity (see p913).

### Activity 12: awareness of everyday hazards

Awareness of everyday hazards (such as boiling water or sharp objects)

| *Descriptors* | *Points* |
|---|---|
| a. Reduced awareness of everyday hazards leads to a significant risk of:<br>(i) injury to self or others; *or*<br>(ii) damage to property or possessions,<br>such that the claimant requires supervision for the majority of the time to maintain safety. | 15 |
| b. Reduced awareness of everyday hazards leads to a significant risk of:<br>(i) injury to self or others; *or*<br>(ii) damage to property or possessions,<br>such that the claimant frequently requires supervision to maintain safety. | 9 |
| c. Reduced awareness of everyday hazards leads to a significant risk of:<br>(i) injury to self or others; *or*<br>(ii) damage to property or possessions,<br>such that the claimant occasionally requires supervision to maintain safety. | 6 |
| d. None of the above applies. | 0 |

This activity is about your ability to recognise risks from common hazards, such as boiling water or sharp objects. A wide range of conditions could be relevant here: learning difficulties or conditions affecting concentration, including the detrimental effects of medication, or from brain injury or other neurological conditions affecting self-awareness. It may also apply if you have a severe depressive illness or a psychotic disorder and, as a result, have a significant reduction in your attention and concentration, although the official guidance says it is unlikely to apply to anxiety disorders.[53] **Note:** if descriptor 12(a) applies, you also have limited capability for work-related activity (see p913).

### Activity 13: initiating and completing personal action

Initiating and completing personal action (which means planning, organisation, problem-solving, prioritising or switching tasks)

| *Descriptors* | *Points* |
|---|---|
| a. Cannot, due to impaired mental function, reliably initiate or complete at least two sequential personal actions. | 15 |
| b. Cannot, due to impaired mental function, reliably initiate or complete at least two sequential personal actions for the majority of the time. | 9 |
| c. Frequently cannot, due to impaired mental function, reliably initiate or complete at least two sequential personal actions. | 6 |
| d. None of the above applies. | 0 |

The 'personal action' is about planning, organisation, problem-solving, prioritising and switching tasks. There is no definition of 'personal action' and a common sense approach should be taken, including things like cooking, dressing, washing and brushing your teeth, planning a simple meal, and dealing with finances and appointments.[54] You must be able to carry out the personal action 'reliably'. In one case, someone with obsessive compulsive disorder who took an excessive amount of time to complete at least two actions was found not to be able to 'reliably' complete them.[55] **Note:** if descriptor 13(a) applies, you also have limited capability for work-related activity (see p913).

### Activity 14: coping with change

Coping with change

| *Descriptors* | *Points* |
|---|---|
| a. Cannot cope with any change to the extent that day-to-day life cannot be managed. | 15 |
| b. Cannot cope with minor planned change (such as a prearranged change to the routine time scheduled for a lunch break), to the extent that, overall, day-to-day life is made significantly more difficult. | 9 |
| c. Cannot cope with minor unplanned change (such as the timing of an appointment on the day it is due to occur), to the extent that, overall, day-to-day life is made significantly more difficult. | 6 |
| d. None of the above applies. | 0 |

Official guidance says that this activity is about your ability to deal with changes in routine. Possible relevant conditions include moderate/severe learning disability, autistic spectrum disorder, brain injury, obsessive compulsive disorder, severe anxiety or psychotic illness.[56] Inability to cope could be indicated by a number of responses, including stress reactions and the need for another person to intervene.[57] **Note:** if descriptor 14(a) applies, you also have limited capability for work-related activity (see p913).

### Activity 15: getting about

Getting about

| *Descriptors* | *Points* |
|---|---|
| a. Cannot get to any place outside the claimant's home with which the claimant is familiar. | 15 |
| b. Is unable to get to a specified place with which the claimant is familiar, without being accompanied by another person. | 9 |
| c. Is unable to get to a specified place with which the claimant is unfamiliar without being accompanied by another person. | 6 |
| d. None of the above applies. | 0 |

6

This activity is about your ability to go out without being helped by someone else. It takes account of problems from conditions like learning difficulties, severe anxiety and agoraphobia, rather than physical health problems which are considered in Activities 1 and 8. For ESA, use of a mobile phone app should not be taken into account.[58] Strictly speaking, that does not also apply for UC, but in any case, you may be able to argue that an app does not mean that you do not need to be accompanied by another person.

### Activity 16: coping with social engagement

Coping with social engagement due to cognitive impairment or mental disorder

| *Descriptors* | *Points* |
|---|---|
| a. Engagement in social contact is always precluded due to difficulty relating to others or significant distress experienced by the claimant. | 15 |
| b. Engagement in social contact with someone unfamiliar to the claimant is always precluded due to difficulty relating to others or significant distress experienced by the claimant. | 9 |
| c. Engagement in social contact with someone unfamiliar to the claimant is not possible for the majority of the time due to difficulty relating to others or significant distress experienced by the claimant. | 6 |
| d. None of the above applies. | 0 |

The problems taken into account in this activity are those arising from 'cognitive impairment or mental disorder'. To score points, your social engagement must be restricted due to 'difficulty relating to others or significant distress'. Autism could be relevant here, but so could other conditions – eg, anxiety, depression and personality disorder. The activity is supposed to test your ability to engage with others in a working environment, so it should not be limited to socialising but should include things like reciprocity, give and take, initiation and response.[59] **Note:** if descriptor 16(a) applies, you also have limited capability for work-related activity (see below).

### Activity 17: appropriateness of behaviour with other people

Appropriateness of behaviour with other people, due to cognitive impairment or mental disorder

| *Descriptors* | *Points* |
|---|---|
| a. Has, on a daily basis, uncontrollable episodes of aggressive or disinhibited behaviour that would be unreasonable in any workplace. | 15 |
| b. Frequently has uncontrollable episodes of aggressive or disinhibited behaviour that would be unreasonable in any workplace. | 15 |
| c. Occasionally has uncontrollable episodes of aggressive or disinhibited behaviour that would be unreasonable in any workplace. | 9 |
| d. None of the above applies. | 0 |

This activity considers problems due to 'cognitive impairment or mental disorder'. Merely being disinhibited or angry is not enough. Alcohol abuse, for example, does not count by itself, but if you are assessed as having alcohol (or drug) dependency, or a condition like autism or psychotic illness, the consequences for your behaviour may count.[60] All the descriptors look at whether you have 'uncontrollable episodes of aggressive or disinhibited behaviour which would be unreasonable in any workplace'. The behaviour could be physical but also verbal – eg, serious verbal aggression.[61] **Note:** if descriptor 17(a) applies, you also have limited capability for work-related activity (see below).

## Limited capability for work-related activity

The work capability assessment includes an assessment of whether you have 'limited capability for work-related activity'. This is to decide whether your disability is so severe or your health is so poor that, in addition to not being able to work, you cannot be expected to do things like attend work-focused interviews or retraining. For UC, if you have limited capability for work-related activity, you are said to have 'limited capability for work and work-related activity'.[62]

The test decides whether you are entitled to a limited capability for work-related activity element in your UC (see p73) and whether you are in the 'support group' for ESA (see p560). If you have claimed HB as well as ESA, it is used to decide whether you are entitled to a support component in your HB (see p282).

You may automatically count as having limited capability for work-related activity, or you may be required to complete a questionnaire and/or attend a medical. If you do not return the questionnaire or take part in the medical and do not have 'good reason' ('good cause' for ESA), you are treated as not having limited capability for work-related activity.

When deciding whether you have good reason/good cause, the DWP must take into account:[63]

- whether you were outside Great Britain at the time you were notified;
- your state of health;
- the nature of any disability you have;
- any other matter it thinks appropriate.

## Assessing limited capability for work-related activity

To have limited capability for work-related activity, your mental or physical condition must be such that one or more statements (or 'descriptors') describing a severe limitation in certain activities could be applied to you.

6

A descriptor applies if it applies to you for the majority of the time(s) you try to do the activity described. You are assessed wearing any prosthesis that you are normally fitted with or wear, and/or using any aid or appliance that you normally wear or use, or could reasonably be expected to wear or use.[64]

Some descriptors are about physical incapacity. To have them applied to you, your incapacity must arise from 'a specific bodily disease or disablement'. Other descriptors are about mental incapacity. To have them applied to you, your incapacity must arise from 'a specific mental illness or disablement'.[65]

The DWP may retest you to find out whether there has been a relevant change of circumstances, to see whether a previous finding was wrong or mistaken, or (for ESA only) if it has been three months or more since your last test.[66]

You may be required to complete a questionnaire and/or attend a medical examination.

| Activity | Descriptors |
|---|---|
| 1. Mobilising unaided by another person with or without a walking stick, manual wheelchair or other aid if such aid is normally, or could reasonably be, worn or used. | Cannot either:<br>(a) mobilise more than 50 metres on level ground without stopping in order to avoid significant discomfort or exhaustion; *or*<br>(b) repeatedly mobilise 50 metres within a reasonable timescale because of significant discomfort or exhaustion. |
| 2. Transferring from one seated position to another. | Cannot move between one seated position and another seated position located next to one another without receiving physical assistance from another person. |
| 3. Reaching. | Cannot raise either arm as if to put something in the top pocket of a coat or jacket. |
| 4. Picking up and moving or transferring by the use of the upper body and arms (excluding standing, sitting, bending or kneeling and all other activities specified in this Schedule). | Cannot pick up and move a 0.5 litre carton full of liquid. |
| 5. Manual dexterity. | Cannot press a button (such as a telephone keypad) with either hand or cannot turn the pages of a book with either hand. |
| 6. Making self understood through speaking, writing, typing, or other means which are normally, or could reasonably be, used unaided by another person. | Cannot convey a simple message, such as the presence of a hazard. |
| 7. Understanding communication by:<br>(i) verbal means (such as hearing or lip reading) alone; *or*<br>(ii) non-verbal means (such as reading 16-point print or braille) alone; *or*<br>(iii) a combination of (i) and (ii),<br>using any aid that is normally, or could reasonably be, used unaided by another person. | Cannot understand a simple message, such as the location of a fire escape, due to sensory impairment. |

| | |
|---|---|
| 8. Absence or loss of control while conscious leading to extensive evacuation of the bowel and/or voiding of the bladder, other than enuresis (bedwetting), despite the wearing or use of any aids or adaptations which are normally, or could reasonably be, worn or used. | At least once a week experiences:<br>(a) loss of control leading to extensive evacuation of the bowel and/or voiding of the bladder; *or*<br>(b) substantial leakage of the contents of a collecting device,<br>sufficient to require the individual to clean themselves and change clothing. |
| 9. Learning tasks. | Cannot learn how to complete a simple task, such as setting an alarm clock, due to cognitive impairment or mental disorder. |
| 10. Awareness of hazard. | Reduced awareness of everyday hazards, due to cognitive impairment or mental disorder, leads to a significant risk of:<br>(a) injury to self or others; *or*<br>(b) damage to property or possessions,<br>such that the claimant requires supervision for the majority of the time to maintain safety. |
| 11. Initiating and completing personal action (which means planning, organisation, problem-solving, prioritising or switching tasks). | Cannot, due to impaired mental function, reliably initiate or complete at least two sequential personal actions. |
| 12. Coping with change. | Cannot cope with any change, due to cognitive impairment or mental disorder, to the extent that day-to-day life cannot be managed. |
| 13. Coping with social engagement, due to cognitive impairment or mental disorder. | Engagement in social contact is always precluded due to difficulty relating to others or significant distress experienced by the claimant. |
| 14. Appropriateness of behaviour with other people, due to cognitive impairment or mental disorder. | Has, on a daily basis, uncontrollable episodes of aggressive or disinhibited behaviour that would be unreasonable in any workplace. |

| | |
|---|---|
| 15. Conveying food or drink to the mouth. | (a) Cannot convey food or drink to the claimant's own mouth without receiving physical assistance from someone else; *or*<br>(b) Cannot convey food or drink to the claimant's own mouth without repeatedly stopping or experiencing breathlessness or severe discomfort; *or*<br>(c) Cannot convey food or drink to the claimant's own mouth without receiving regular prompting given by someone else in the claimant's physical presence; *or*<br>(d) Owing to a severe disorder of mood or behaviour, fails to convey food or drink to the claimant's own mouth without receiving:<br>(i) physical assistance from someone else; *or*<br>(ii) regular prompting given by someone else in the claimant's presence. |
| 16. Chewing or swallowing food or drink. | (a) Cannot chew or swallow food or drink; *or*<br>(b) Cannot chew or swallow food or drink without repeatedly stopping, experiencing breathlessness or severe discomfort; *or*<br>(c) Cannot chew or swallow food or drink without repeatedly receiving regular prompting given by someone else in the claimant's presence; *or*<br>(d) Owing to a severe disorder of mood or behaviour, fails to:<br>(i) chew or swallow food or drink; *or*<br>(ii) chew or swallow food or drink without regular prompting given by someone else in the claimant's presence. |

## Treated as having limited capability for work-related activity

You are treated as having limited capability for work-related activity because of your health if:[67]

- you have a terminal illness – ie, your death can reasonably be expected within 12 months; *or*

- you are receiving chemotherapy or radiotherapy treatment for cancer, or are recovering from that treatment, or you are likely to receive such treatment within six months from the date the DWP determines whether or not you have limited capability for work-related activity. In any of these circumstances, the DWP must be satisfied that you have limited capability for work-related activity. When deciding this, the decision maker should take into account the medical evidence to see if your cancer treatment has side effects which are likely to limit your ability to carry out work-related activity;[68] *or*
- because of a specific disease or disablement, there would be a 'substantial risk' to your mental or physical health or to the mental or physical health of someone else if you were found not to have limited capability for work-related activity (if you appeal about this rule, the appeal tribunal should have a list of the types of work-related activity available in your area, indicating the most and least difficult, and which activities the DWP says you can do without substantial risk);[69] *or*
- you are pregnant and there would be a serious risk of damage to your health or to your baby's health if you do not refrain from work-related activity and, for UC only, from work; *or*
- for UC only, you have reached pension age (see p239) and are entitled to AA, the highest rate of the DLA/SADLA care component or the enhanced rate of the PIP/ADP daily living component; *or*
- for UC only, on the date you claimed UC, you were entitled to old-style ESA and were assessed or treated as having limited capability for work-related activity for ESA – ie, you were entitled to the support component. The limited capability for work-related activity element should be included in your UC from your first monthly assessment period;[70] *or*
- for UC only, on the date you claimed UC, you were entitled to NI credits for limited capability for work and had been assessed as, or treated as having, limited capability for work-related activity (this can include where you had stopped being entitled to ESA for a reason other than it being found that you no longer had limited capability for work). The limited capability for work-related activity element should be included in your UC from your first monthly assessment period;[71] *or*
- for UC only, on the date you claimed UC you were not entitled to ESA, but had been getting ESA and assessed or treated as having limited capability for work-related activity, your ESA ended due to you reaching pension age and you claim UC (eg, as part of a mixed-age couple) within a month of your ESA ending, and you would have remained entitled to ESA but for reaching pension age;[72] *or*
- for new-style ESA only, you are currently entitled to UC and have already been assessed as having limited capability for work and work-related activity.[73]

See p73 for when the limited capability for work-related activity element is included.

***Are you transferring to universal credit from employment and support allowance?***

If you were getting ESA and were assessed as having limited capability for work-related activity, but then claim UC, you automatically have limited capability for work-related activity.[74] However, the DWP may wrongly overlook this rule and insist that you have to be assessed again. If this affects you, note the following.

1. Point out the rule and insist that you should be automatically treated as having limited capability for work-related activity for UC. If necessary, challenge the decision on your UC entitlement.
2. The DWP may say that it needs to check that you were getting ESA – complain if this takes a long time. Ultimately, an unreasonably long delay might be challenged by judicial review (see p1268).
3. The limited capability for work-related activity element should be included in your UC from your first monthly assessment period.
4. Remember that, despite these rules, the DWP can still apply the work capability assessment to you again.

6

## The work capability assessment process

For UC, you are usually sent a questionnaire (UC50) to complete. You may also be required to take part in a medical assessment. However, a decision can be made without a questionnaire or a medical if it is considered that there is enough other information.[75] For ESA, the information provided with your claim (including, where required, a fit note (medical certificate) from your doctor or other registered 'healthcare professional' – ie, a registered nurse, occupational therapist, pharmacist or physiotherapist) is considered. Unless you are treated as having limited capability for work (see p896), you are usually sent a questionnaire (ESA50) to complete. You may also be required to take part in a medical assessment. However, a decision can be made without a questionnaire or a medical if it is considered that there is enough other information.[76]

Medical assessments are carried out (by a doctor or other 'approved healthcare professional') on behalf of the DWP medical service by the Health Assessment Advisory Service. For official information about the assessment, such as having an audio recording of your medical, using an interpreter and the location of assessment centres, see chdauk.co.uk. For advice about the questionnaire and medical, see p920 and p921.

***In-person, telephone and video assessments***

- Medical assessments can be carried out in-person at an assessment centre, or by telephone or video call. In practice, many are now carried out by telephone or video call.
- If a telephone or video assessment is arranged, but you fail to attend or take part in it without good cause, as with an in-person assessment, you are regarded as not having limited capability for work (see p921).
- If a telephone or video assessment is not considered suitable for you, there may be a delay until an in-person assessment can be arranged. However, remember that a decision can be made without an assessment if there is enough other information.

There are no rules on how often you are reassessed. Usually, this is decided by the DWP medical service. If you are assessed as having limited capability for work-related activity (see p913), have a 'severe, lifelong' disability or condition and are 'unlikely to ever be able to move into work', you will not be reassessed.[77]

6

## The questionnaire

Unless it is already accepted that you have limited capability for work or are treated as having limited capability for work, you are usually sent a questionnaire (UC50 or ESA50) to complete.

***How do you complete the questionnaire?***

1. Read the notes on the form before answering the questions. It may be helpful to draft your answers on a separate sheet of paper first.
2. If someone has to complete the questionnaire for you, or if you can only do so yourself slowly or with pain, explain this.
3. Make sure to list all your symptoms. If you have to appeal, the First-tier Tribunal may be less likely to believe you have symptoms if you did not mention them on the questionnaire. Ask someone who knows you well to check your answers.
4. If you have good and bad days, explain this. If possible, give a rough estimate of how often you could perform the activity and how often you could not.
5. Compare the draft of your answers with the list beginning on p903 and work out your score. Your answers should not be exaggerated, but check that you have not underestimated any of your problems and have given all the details you can.
6. If you have difficulties with English or reading and writing, get independent help before you submit the form.
7. If someone has helped you fill out the form, include their details at the end where the form asks about this.
8. Always make a copy of your questionnaire with your answers before returning it.

You have four weeks from the date the questionnaire is sent to complete and return it. A reminder must be sent to you at least three weeks after the questionnaire was sent. You must then be given a further week from the date the reminder was sent to return the questionnaire. If you still do not return it in time, you are treated as not having limited capability for work, unless you can show that you had a good reason (for ESA, good cause) for not returning it on time.[78]

***Good cause and good reason***

When deciding whether you have **'good cause'**, the DWP must consider all the circumstances, including whether you were outside Great Britain at the relevant time, your state of health and the nature of your disability.[79] There is no equivalent rule for deciding whether you have **'good reason'** for UC, but in practice the same issues should be considered.

If you are late in completing and returning the questionnaire, do so as soon as you can and explain why you were late. If your benefit stops because you are considered not to have had good reason/cause, but you think you did, consider challenging the decision (see p923). You should also make a fresh claim for benefit – but note that if you are not already under the UC system, a new claim for UC or ESA will bring you under the UC system (see p20). You can appeal if the DWP decides you did not have a good reason/cause (see Chapter 57).

'Complex needs' or 'safeguarding' procedures apply if you are considered to be vulnerable – eg, if you have a serious mental health condition. These procedures are not a legal requirement but involve extra checks before treating you as not having limited capability for work. If you think you are vulnerable, ask whether the procedures were considered and seek advice.

On receiving your completed questionnaire, the DWP considers whether you should be treated as having limited capability for work or whether you clearly score enough points to satisfy the test. If neither of these applies, a medical examination is arranged.

## Medical assessments

You may be required to attend and take part in a medical assessment as part of the work capability assessment. **Note**: in-person assessments are being reintroduced in some cases, but you may be asked to take part in a telephone or video assessment instead (see p919). Bear in mind the following.

- If you fail to attend and take part in a medical assessment without a good reason (for ESA, good cause), you are treated as not having limited capability for work.
- If you cannot attend or take part in the medical, contact your assessment centre immediately to explain why and ask for another appointment.
- If you have an in-person appointment but are too ill to travel, ask to be examined at home.

- If you have an in-person medical, you can claim your travel expenses for going to the medical. If you have to attend by taxi or minicab, you cannot claim for your fares unless your assessment centre agrees to this before you travel.
- You can have a friend or adviser at the medical with you. They can take notes.
- The medical examiner considers the information on your questionnaire, what you tell them, and your appearance and behaviour during the assessment.

To complete the medical report, the medical examiner asks about your condition and assesses whether, in their opinion, you have limited capability for work. They consider your abilities in each of the specific areas of activity.

The medical examiner asks about your typical day and uses the information to assess your ability to perform the activities in the work capability assessment. Tell the examiner about things like good and bad days and what medication you are taking. The examiner then completes a report (a UC85 or ESA85), indicating which descriptors they think apply to you, and sends it to the DWP.

6

### Failing to attend a medical assessment

If you do not attend and take part in a medical examination without a good reason (good cause for ESA), you are treated as not having limited capability for work – ie, you fail the work capability assessment. You must have been sent notice of the date and time of the medical at least seven days beforehand, unless you agreed to accept less notice than this.[80]

#### *Good reason and good cause*

When deciding whether you have **'good cause'** for ESA, the DWP must consider all the circumstances, including those that apply to the questionnaire (see p920). 'Good cause' may also include being too ill or distressed on the day of the medical, or wishing to be examined by someone of the same sex and this was not possible.

In practice, the same sort of things should be taken into account when deciding whether you have **'good reason'** for UC.

If your benefit stops because you are considered not to have good reason/cause for failing to attend and take part in the medical, but you think you did, consider challenging the decision (see p923). You can also make a fresh claim for benefit, but note that a new claim for UC or ESA will bring you under the UC system (see p20). If the DWP does not accept that you had good cause/reason, consider appealing (see Chapter 51).

'Complex needs' or 'safeguarding' procedures apply if you are considered to be 'vulnerable' – eg, if you have a serious mental health condition. These procedures are not a legal requirement but involve extra checks before treating you as not having limited capability for work. If you think you are vulnerable, ask whether the procedures were considered, and seek advice.

### The decision

The decision on whether or not you have limited capability for work is made by a DWP decision maker. The decision maker can disagree with the medical report, although in practice, this is unusual. The medical examiner includes in the medical report a suggested date when the work capability assessment should be applied to you again in order to retest your capability. You cannot appeal about how often you are retested.

If the decision maker does not consider that you have limited capability for work, you may still be entitled to some UC if your claim was for UC. If your claim was for ESA, you are not entitled to ESA. If you have been getting ESA, your award is revised or superseded (see Chapter 50) and your benefit is stopped.

## 2. Challenging a decision



You can challenge a decision by applying for a revision or supersession (see Chapter 50) or appealing (see Chapter 51). You must usually apply for a mandatory reconsideration before you can appeal. However, in an employment and support allowance (ESA) case where you are challenging a decision that you do not have limited capability for work, if you would be entitled to get ESA while appealing (see p925), you can appeal immediately.[81]

Initially, the DWP makes a 'determination' on your limited capability for work.[82] The determination should then be incorporated into a decision about your entitlement to benefit or national insurance (NI) credits for limited capability for work. You only have a right of appeal once this is included in a decision.[83]

Appeals are considered by the First-tier Tribunal, which must include a medically qualified person (see p1198). The tribunal does not have to follow either the UC85 or ESA85 medical report or the DWP's decision.

When you appeal against a decision, the whole decision can be looked at again if it is considered right to do so. So, the tribunal may decide to look at an aspect of the decision that you are happy with and do not want changed. This could result in losing some or even all of your entitlement. The tribunal should warn you if it wants to look at an aspect of the decision that you do not want changed.

***Are you appealing?***

1. Get advice from one of the organisations listed in Appendix 1.
2. Remember that there are only certain circumstances in which you can work and still be regarded as having limited capability for work (see p896). If you work while you are appealing, you may lose entitlement to benefit, even if you eventually win your appeal.
3. Request a copy of the medical evidence that the DWP holds on your file. If you appeal, a copy of the medical report should be included in the appeal papers that the DWP sends to you and HM Courts and Tribunals Service.

4. Request a hearing of your appeal (ie, rather than a decision just based on the papers). This will give the tribunal the opportunity to hear from you first-hand about how your condition affects you and what happened at the medical examination.
5. Discuss your limited capability for work with your own doctor (or other registered healthcare professional). In practice, winning an appeal can be difficult if your GP or consultant does not support you.
6. Get medical evidence to support your appeal, if you can – eg, from your GP or consultant. It is more helpful if they comment on the issues in your appeal rather than just setting out your diagnosis and treatment. Check whether your doctor insists on charging you. Your doctor can provide your medical records without charging, although this evidence is sometimes not as useful as evidence commenting on the things at issue in your appeal.
7. If you cannot get medical evidence, consider using previous medical reports if you passed the work capability assessment and getting evidence from other sources – eg, a community nurse or an occupational therapist. You could ask the tribunal to obtain further medical evidence, although, in practice, it may refuse.[84]
8. The tribunal should make a decision based on all the evidence – medical and non-medical. If necessary, point out that it can prefer your own or your doctor's evidence to that of the medical examiner.[85]
9. DWP medical reports may have inconsistencies or errors in them. The tribunal must deal with any discrepancies and take these into account when considering the weight to be given to different sources of evidence.[86]
10. The tribunal cannot carry out its own medical examination of you.[87] However, be aware that it may observe your conduct in the room – eg, how you walk or sit.
11. Consider asking a person who lives with you or knows you well to attend the hearing to describe your day-to-day problems.
12. Take a list of any medication you are taking to the hearing.

## Getting benefit while challenging a decision

If you have claimed **universal credit (UC)**, you can continue to get UC while your request for a mandatory reconsideration is being considered and while your appeal is pending.

If you have been refused **ESA** because you have failed the work capability assessment, you cannot get ESA while your request for a mandatory reconsideration is being considered. However, if you could get ESA while appealing (see p925) then the requirement for you to have a mandatory reconsideration before you can appeal does not apply, so you can appeal straight away.[88] If you cannot get ESA, you may be able to get UC instead (see p927). However, a claim for UC brings you under the UC system (see p20). That means you can no longer get income-related ESA (or other means-tested benefits), even if your challenge of the ESA decision is successful.

If you submit a new claim for ESA or jobseeker's allowance (JSA), you can no longer get income-related ESA, even if your challenge to the refusal of your ESA is successful.

Once you have appealed, you may be able to get ESA while your appeal is pending (see below) – you do not need to make a new claim. This is usually the best option, if you are able to get ESA. You cannot get income-related ESA pending your appeal if you have claimed UC or JSA and so have come under the UC system. Getting ESA pending your appeal does *not* mean that you come under the UC system, as it does not require a new claim to be made.[89]

*Example*

Jamal was getting income-related ESA, but this stops when he fails the work capability assessment. Jamal decides to challenge the decision and to claim UC. As he has claimed UC, he now comes under the UC system.

Jamal appeals against the decision on his failure of the work capability assessment, and gets UC while his ESA appeal is pending. Jamal's appeal is eventually successful, but he remains on UC and does not go back to income-related ESA. If Jamal had not claimed UC, once he appealed, he may have been able to get income-related ESA pending his appeal instead of having to claim UC.

6

## Getting employment and support allowance while appealing

If you can appeal against a decision that you do not have limited capability for work for ESA and it is the first such decision you have had, or the first since a previous decision that you have limited capability for work, then once you have appealed and you have submitted a medical certificate, you can get ESA until the First-tier Tribunal makes its decision.[90] You cannot get ESA pending an appeal if you are being *treated as* not having limited capability for work because you did not return the questionnaire or attend the medical (see p920 and p922). **Note**: if you are still getting income-related ESA, at some point during 2025, you will come under the DWP's managed migration to UC process (see p29), which will bring your income-related ESA entitlement to an end.

Once you have appealed, the government has said that your ESA pending an appeal can cover the period when your request for a mandatory reconsideration was being considered.[91]

However, you cannot get ESA pending an appeal if the decision that you do not have limited capability for work is the second, or a subsequent, such decision you have had in a row and the decision you are appealing against is about a claim made on or after 30 March 2015.

*Examples*

Mina claims new-style ESA (ie, contributory ESA under the UC system) in June 2025. She is found not to have limited capability for work – ie, she fails the work capability assessment. Mina would be entitled to ESA while appealing (in her case, this is because it is the first time she has failed the work capability assessment), so she appeals straight away and sends in a medical certificate. Mina gets ESA pending the appeal.

Matt is still getting income-related ESA, as he has not yet come under the managed migration process. When he first claimed income-related ESA (in 2017), he was found not to have limited capability for work (ie, he failed the work capability assessment), but he appealed and successfully challenged this and so he was paid ESA. In May 2025, Matt has another work capability assessment and fails it. Matt would be entitled to ESA while appealing, as although this is not the first time he has failed the work capability assessment, it is the first time since the tribunal decided that in fact he had passed it. So Matt does not need to have a mandatory reconsideration before he can appeal. Matt appeals again and sends in a medical certificate. He does not claim UC. Matt gets income-related ESA pending the appeal.

If you have limited capability for work, but are appealing about whether or not you should be put in the support group, you remain entitled to ESA while your request for a mandatory reconsideration is being considered and while your appeal is pending. However, the amount you are paid does not include the support component.

**Note:**

- To get ESA pending an appeal, you must continue to submit fit notes (ie, medical certificates). You do not need to make a new claim for ESA.[92]
- ESA pending an appeal does not include an additional component, although it can include any premiums and housing costs to which you are entitled.[93]
- You are treated as having limited capability for work while you are appealing, so the DWP does not usually assess you in this period. However, if you develop a new condition or your condition significantly worsens, the DWP can assess you again. If it determines that you have limited capability for work, you can get ESA in the normal way (including either of the additional components) from that point on. The First-tier Tribunal still considers your appeal for the period up until then. Even if the DWP determines that you do not have limited capability for work, you remain entitled to ESA pending the appeal.[94]
- If your appeal is successful, the original decision about your limited capability for work is changed so that you are entitled to ESA (although this does not apply to income-related ESA from the point you claimed UC or JSA, if that is what you did). Your ESA continues in the normal way, and you can qualify for an additional component.

- If your appeal is successful but the DWP considers that your condition improved while the appeal was pending, it may decide that you do not have limited capability for work now.[95] You can appeal against this decision, and should be able to get ESA pending the appeal again.[96]
- If you lose your appeal, the original decision that you do not have limited capability for work is not changed. From the week after the week in which the First-tier Tribunal notifies the DWP of its decision, the DWP treats you as not having had limited capability for work while you were getting ESA pending your appeal.[97] Your entitlement to ESA therefore stops, although you keep the ESA that was paid to you pending the appeal. Although you can appeal against the decision to treat you as not having limited capability for work, the prospect of success is likely to be limited, as the rules allow the DWP to do this when you have lost your appeal.[98]

### Getting jobseeker's allowance while challenging a decision

If you submit a new claim for new-style JSA, you will come under the UC system. You cannot then get income-related ESA, even if your challenge is successful.



### Getting universal credit while challenging a decision

Generally, you can get UC while challenging a decision. If you make a new claim for UC, you will come under the UC system (see p20) and cannot get income-related ESA again.

You can get UC while waiting for your request for a mandatory reconsideration to be considered and once you have appealed. You may still be able to get new-style contributory ESA or new-style JSA under the UC system. You may be subject to work-related requirements while you are appealing (see Chapter 42). If your challenge is successful, your UC can then include a limited capability for work element, if you can still get it, or a limited capability for work-related activity element if that applies.[99] If your challenge is unsuccessful, you may still be able to get UC, but will not be entitled to a limited capability for work or limited capability for work-related activity element.

## If your condition worsens

**For UC**, once there has been a decision that you do not have limited capability for work, there is no further work capability assessment, unless there is evidence to suggest that the decision was made in ignorance of, or based on a mistake about, a material fact, or there has been a relevant change in circumstances regarding your condition.[100]

**For ESA**, if your condition has significantly worsened since the decision, or you have a new condition, and you are not already getting ESA pending the appeal, you could make a new claim for ESA – but see the note below. In this situation, you should be treated as having limited capability for work until a new work capability assessment is carried out (see p896).

**Note:** if you make a new claim for ESA, you come under the UC system, if you have not already done so. If you come under the UC system, you cannot get income-related ESA. You can get UC instead. You may still be able to get new-style contributory ESA.

If you are already getting ESA pending the appeal, you could inform the DWP and ask it to make a determination on your limited capability for work. If the DWP thinks that you still fail the work capability assessment, your entitlement to ESA after the appeal has been decided could be affected, even if you win your appeal.

## 3. Periods of limited capability for work

A 'period of limited capability for work' for employment and support allowance (ESA) generally means a period in which you have, or are treated as having, limited capability for work. It does not include any period not covered by your claim for ESA.[101] However, see the linking rules below. There are no rules on periods of limited capability for work for universal credit.

### Linking rules

Different periods of limited capability for work can be joined or 'linked' to form one continuous period for ESA. The effect is that you are treated as having had limited capability for work throughout the whole of the linked period. Different periods are linked if they are not more than 12 weeks apart.[102]

If periods of limited capability for work are linked, it means that:

- the question of whether or not you satisfy the national insurance contribution conditions for contributory ESA may be decided at the beginning of the first period (see p875);[103]
- you do not have to serve further 'waiting days' (see p569) before becoming entitled to ESA because you have already served them;
- you may get one of the additional ESA components straight away, or once you have been reassessed as passing the work capability assessment;
- for the purposes of the rules on housing costs, certain linking rules apply.

## 4. Work you can do while claiming employment and support allowance

The general rule is that you cannot work and be entitled to employment and support allowance (ESA) at the same time.[104] With certain exceptions (see p929), in any week in which you work (paid or unpaid), you are not entitled to ESA and you are automatically treated as not having limited capability for work, even if it has previously been decided that you do.[105]

However, you are only treated as not entitled to ESA on the actual days that you work, rather than the whole week, if you work:

- during the first week of your claim; *or*
- during the last week in which you had limited capability for work or were treated as having limited capability for work.[106]

It is arguable that work that is so minimal that it can be regarded as trivial or negligible should be ignored.[107]

You can do certain work without automatically being treated as not having limited capability for work. For how earnings from this may affect income-related ESA, see p347. **Note:** earnings under the 'permitted work' rules (see p930) that are under the relevant earnings limit are ignored for ESA (but see the Note on p930 about universal credit (UC)).

You can do the following:[108]

- work as a local councillor;
- work (for a maximum of one day or two half days a week) as a member of the First-tier Tribunal if you have been appointed because of your experience of disability issues;
- domestic work (eg, cooking and cleaning) in your own home;
- caring for a relative;
- caring for another person living with you under specific legislation relating to accommodating children or temporarily caring for someone else if you are paid for this;
- caring for someone provided with 'continuing care' by a local authority under section 26A of the Children (Scotland) Act 1995, where you get payments for that;
- work you do to protect someone or prevent serious damage to property or livestock during an emergency;
- work done while receiving assistance in pursuing self-employment under section 2 of the Employment and Training Act 1973 or section 2 of the Enterprise and New Towns (Scotland) Act 1990 (test-trading);
- voluntary work that is not for a relative, provided the only payment you receive is to cover your reasonable expenses and it is considered reasonable for you to work free of charge;
- work done in the course of a work placement (unpaid work experience with an employer), approved in writing by the DWP before the placement starts;
- for contributory ESA, any work you do in a week in which you are treated as having limited capability for work because you are receiving plasmapheresis, regular weekly treatment for haemodialysis for chronic renal failure, regular

weekly treatment for total parenteral nutrition, or are recovering from such treatment (see p898);[109]
- 'permitted work' (see below).

*Relatives*

A **'relative'** is a grandparent, grandchild, uncle, aunt, nephew or niece, and includes **'close relatives'** – ie, parent, parent-in-law, son, son-in-law, daughter, daughter-in-law, step-parent, stepson, stepdaughter, sibling, or the partner of any of these.

**Note:** you can work and still be entitled to UC. However, if you earn more than a set monthly amount from work, you may be treated as not having limited capability for work or the DWP may reassess you (see p901). If you are doing permitted work for contributory ESA and also claiming UC, for UC your earnings from that work are treated in the same way as any other earnings from work (see p125).

6

## Permitted work

'Permitted work' (sometimes called 'exempt' work) is work of any kind, which you can do while on ESA:[110]

- as part of a treatment programme done under medical supervision while you are in hospital or regularly attending hospital as an outpatient, provided you do not earn more than £195.50 a week; *or*
- for an unlimited period, provided you do not earn more than £20 a week. This is called the 'permitted work lower limit'; *or*
- for an unlimited period, provided you do not earn more than £195.50 a week and you are in 'supported work' (sometimes called 'supervised work'); *or*
- for an unlimited period, where you work on average fewer than 16 hours a week and in any week you do not earn more than £195.50 a week. This is called the 'permitted work higher limit'. For how your hours are calculated, see p885.

*Supported work*

**'Supported work'** is work which is supervised by someone employed by a public or local authority, or by a voluntary organisation or community interest company, whose job it is to find work for disabled people. This could include work in a sheltered workshop or with help from social services. The DWP usually says you need not have the person working alongside you, although the support should be ongoing and regular. Where possible, check in advance that the DWP agrees that the work counts as supported work.

If your earnings in any week are higher than the relevant limit, you are not entitled to ESA for that week.[111] Your earnings are worked out for this purpose in the same way as for income-related ESA (see p340), except that only your own earnings count, not those of your partner. Only your earnings count, not any other kind of income.

Although there are no special rules, you must inform the DWP, in advance if possible, about any permitted work you do. The DWP asks you to complete Form PW1, available at gov.uk/government/publications/employment-and-support-allowance-permitted-work-form. If the particular activities you carry out in your work suggest that your limited capability for work may have changed, the DWP might reassess this.

# Notes



1. **The work capability assessment**

1 **UC** Reg 39 and Schs 8 and 9 UC Regs
**ESA** Regs 20, 25 and 26 ESA Regs; regs 16, 22 and 26 ESA Regs 2013
2 Reg 39(1)(a) UC Regs
3 Reg 19(2) UC(TP) Regs
4 Reg 21(1)(a)(i) UC(TP) Regs; *JW v SSWP (UC)* [2022] UKUT 117 (AAC)
5 Reg 21(1)(a)(ii) UC(TP) Regs
6 Reg 39(6) and Sch 8 UC Regs
7 Reg 19(4) UC(TP) Regs
8 Reg 19(2) UC(TP) Regs, with savings regarding pre-April 2017 as in the ESAUC(MA) Regs
9 Regs 20, 25, 26 and 32A ESA Regs; regs 16, 22, 26 and 28 ESA Regs 2013
10 Reg 33(2) ESA Regs
11 Reg 16(1)(h) ESA Regs 2013
12 Regs 20, 25, 26, 33 and 35 ESA Regs; regs 16, 21 and 22 ESA Regs 2013
13 Regs 26, 44 and 46 ESA Regs; regs 22, 38 and 40 ESA Regs 2013
14 Reg 30 ESA Regs; reg 26 ESA Regs 2013
15 *EI v SSWP (ESA)* [2016] UKUT 397 (AAC)
16 *EI v SSWP (ESA)* [2016] UKUT 397 (AAC)
17 **UC** Sch 8 paras 4 and 5 UC Regs
**ESA** Reg 29 ESA Regs; reg 25 ESA Regs 2013
18 *Charlton v SSWP* [2009] EWCA Civ 42; *JW v SSWP* [2011] UKUT 416 (AAC); *ET v SSWP (UC)* [2021] UKUT 47 (AAC)
19 Regs 41, 43 and 44 UC Regs
20 Reg 41(2) and (3) UC Regs
21 Reg 44 ESA Regs; reg 37 ESA Regs 2013
22 Reg 159 ESA Regs; reg 95 ESA Regs 2013
23 Reg 32(2) and (3) ESA Regs; reg 27(2) and (3) ESA Regs 2013
24 Reg 32(1) ESA Regs; reg 27(1) ESA Regs 2013
25 **UC** Regs 39 and 42 UC Regs
**ESA** Reg 19 ESA Regs; reg 15 ESA Regs 2013
26 **UC** Reg 42(2) UC Regs
**ESA** Reg 19(4) ESA Regs; reg 15(4) ESA Regs 2013
27 *AF v SSWP (ESA)* [2011] UKUT 61 (AAC), *SAG v Department for Social Development (ESA)* [2011] NICom171
28 CIB/14534/1996
29 CIB/2620/2000
30 CIB/14587/1996; CIB/14722/1996; CIB/13161/1996; CIB/13508/1996
31 CIB/14722/1996
32 CSIB/12/1996
33 **UC** Reg 39(4) and Sch 6 UC Regs
**ESA** Reg 19(5) and Sch 2 ESA Regs; reg 15(5) and Sch 2 ESA Regs 2013
34 *SI v SSWP (ESA)* [2014] UKUT 308 (AAC), reported as [2015] AACR 5; *AR v SSWP (ESA)* [2013] UKUT 417 (AAC)
35 *WCA Handbook*, para 3.2.2
36 *WCA Handbook*, para 3.2.3
37 *WCA Handbook*, para 3.2.4

38 *TO'B v SSWP (ESA)* [2011] UKUT 461 (AAC); *AG v SSWP (ESA)* [2018] UKUT 137 (AAC)
39 *KH v SSWP (ESA)* [2014] UKUT 455 (AAC)
40 *SSWP v LH (ESA)* [2017] UKUT 475 (AAC)
41 *WCA Handbook*, para 3.2.6; *CL v SSWP (ESA)* [2013] UKUT 434 (AAC) holds that inability to use keyboard or a mouse is sufficient; *DG v SSWP (ESA)* [2014] UKUT 100 (AAC) holds that inability to use both is required
42 *WCA Handbook*, para 3.2.8
43 *WCA Handbook*, para 3.2.9
44 *SSWP v AI (rule 17) (ESA)* [2017] UKUT 346 (AAC)
45 CIB/14499/1996
46 *WCA Handbook*, para 3.2.7
47 *WCA Handbook*, para 3.2.10
48 *EM v SSWP (ESA)* [2014] UKUT 34 (AAC)
49 *CB v SSWP (ESA)* [2015] UKUT 287 (AAC)
50 *WCA Handbook*, para 3.2.11
51 **UC** Reg 39(4) and Sch 6 UC Regs
**ESA** Reg 19(5) and Sch 2 ESA Regs; reg 15(5) and Sch 2 ESA Regs 2013
52 *WCA Handbook*, para 3.5.2
53 *WCA Handbook*, para 3.5.3
54 *MP v SSWP (ESA)* [2015] UKUT 458 (AAC); *WCA Handbook*, para 3.5.4
55 *MW v SSWP (ESA)* [2014] UKUT 112 (AAC)
56 *WCA Handbook*, para 3.5.5
57 *GV v SSWP (ESA)* [2013] UKUT 405 (AAC)
58 *WCA Handbook*, para 3.5.6; *TM v SSWP (ESA)* [2018] UKUT 9 (AAC)
59 *JC v SSWP (ESA)* [2014] UKUT 352 (AAC), reported as [2015] AACR 6
60 *WCA Handbook*, para 3.5.8; *DR v SSWP (ESA)* [2014] UKUT 188 (AAC), reported as [2014] AACR 38
61 *WC v SSWP (ESA)* [2014] UKUT 363
62 Reg 40 UC Regs
63 Reg 39 ESA Regs; reg 36 ESA Regs 2013
64 **UC** Reg 42(2) UC Regs
**ESA** Reg 34(3) ESA Regs; reg 30(3) ESA Regs 2013
65 **UC** Reg 40(3) UC Regs
**ESA** Reg 34(6) ESA Regs; reg 30(6) ESA Regs 2013
66 **UC** Reg 41 UC Regs
**ESA** Reg 34 ESA Regs; reg 30 ESA Regs 2013
67 **UC** Sch 9 UC Regs
**ESA** Reg 35 ESA Regs; reg 31 ESA Regs 2013
68 paras 42050-52 and 42680 DMG
69 *KS v SSWP (UC)* [2021] UKUT 132 (AAC)
70 Reg 19(4) UC(TP) Regs
71 Reg 21 UC(TP) Regs; *JW v SSWP (UC)* [2022] UKUT 117 (AAC)
72 Reg 21(1)(a)(ii) UC(TP) Regs
73 Reg 31 ESA Regs 2013
74 Reg 19(4) UC(TP) Regs
75 Regs 43 and 44 UC Regs
76 Regs 21 and 23 ESA Regs; regs 17 and 19 ESA Regs 2013
77 DWP, *Employment and Support Allowance and Universal Credit: changes to the work capability assessment from 29 September 2017*, September 2017
78 **UC** Reg 43 UC Regs
**ESA** Reg 22 ESA Regs; reg 18 ESA Regs 2013
79 Reg 24 ESA Regs; reg 18 ESA Regs 2013
80 **UC** Reg 44 UC Regs
**ESA** Reg 23 ESA Regs; reg 19 ESA Regs 2013

2. **Challenging a decision**

81 *R (Connor) v SSWP* [2020] EWHC 1999 (Admin); para A3014; para 03012 DMG
82 **UC** Reg 39 UC Regs
**ESA** Reg 19 ESA Regs; reg 15 ESA Regs 2013
83 para 06041 DMG
84 s20 SSA 1998; R(S) 3/84
85 CIB/407/1998; CIB/1149/1998; R(M) 1/93; CIB/3074/2003
86 CIB/511/2005
87 s20(3) SSA 1998
88 *R (Connor) v SSWP* [2020] EWHC 1999 (Admin); Official guidance in para A3014 ADM and para 03012 DMG
89 Reg 3(j) SS(C&P) Regs
90 Reg 30(1) and (3) ESA Regs; reg 26(1) and (3) ESA Regs 2013
91 House of Commons, *Hansard*, Written answers, 16 December 2013, col 486W
92 Reg 30(3) ESA Regs; reg 26(3) ESA Regs 2013; reg 3(j) SS(C&P) Regs; reg 7 UC,PIP,JSA&ESA(C&P) Regs
93 Reg 5(4) ESA Regs; reg 6(5) ESA Regs 2013 provides that the assessment phase applies, pending the First-tier Tribunal's decision
94 Reg 147A(2) and (4) ESA Regs; reg 87(2) and (4) ESA Regs 2013
95 Reg 147A(6) and (7) ESA Regs; reg 87(7) and (8) ESA Regs 2013
96 This is because the DWP will have made a determination that you do not have limited capability for work, and not merely treated you as not having limited capability for work, so reg 30(3) ESA Regs and reg 26(3) ESA Regs 2013 should apply

97 Reg 147A(5) ESA Regs; reg 87(5) ESA Regs 2013
98 Reg 3(j) SS(C&P) Regs; Memo DMG 33/10, para 52; reg 7 UC,PIP,JSA&ESA(C&P) Regs
99 Art 24 WRA(No.9)O
100 Reg 41(4) UC Regs

3. **Periods of limited capability for work**
101 Reg 2, definition of 'period of limited capability for work', ESA Regs
102 Regs 2 and 145 ESA Regs; regs 2 and 86 ESA Regs 2013
103 Sch 1 paras 1-3 WRA 2007

4. **Work you can do while claiming employment and support allowance**
104 Reg 40 ESA Regs; reg 37 ESA Regs 2013
105 Regs 40 and 44 ESA Regs; regs 37 and 38 ESA Regs 2013
106 Reg 40(4) ESA Regs; reg 37(4) ESA Regs 2013
107 CIB/5298/1997; CIB/6777/1999
108 Regs 40 and 45 ESA Regs; regs 37 and 39 ESA Regs 2013
109 Reg 46 ESA Regs; reg 40 ESA Regs 2013
110 Reg 45 ESA Regs; reg 39 ESA Regs 2013
111 Regs 40(1) and (2)(f) and 45 ESA Regs; regs 37(2)(f) and 39 ESA Regs 2013

# Chapter 42

# Universal credit system work-related requirements

**This chapter covers:**


1. The claimant commitment (below)
2. The work-related requirements (p938)
3. Which requirements apply (p948)


6

This chapter covers your responsibilities if you come under the universal credit (UC) system (see p20), whether you are getting UC, jobseeker's allowance (JSA) or employment and support allowance (ESA). The DWP calls JSA or ESA under the UC system 'new-style' JSA and ESA. If you do not come under the UC system, you may have responsibilities in connection with JSA or ESA (the DWP may refer to these as 'old-style' JSA or ESA). For details, see the 2024/25 edition of this *Handbook*.

## Key facts

- If you come under the UC system, to qualify for UC, new-style JSA or new-style ESA, you must usually accept a claimant commitment.
- You may have to meet some or all of the work-related requirements, which are conditions connected to finding work or getting ready to find work. These are: work-focused interviews, work preparation, work search and work availability.
- If you do not meet the work-related requirements which apply to you, you may be given a sanction. Your benefit is then paid at a reduced or nil rate (see Chapter 43). However, you may qualify for UC hardship payments (see Chapter 46).

## 1. The claimant commitment

A claimant commitment is a record of your responsibilities connected to your benefit award.[1] If you come under the universal credit (UC) system (see p20), you must usually accept a claimant commitment to qualify for UC, new-style jobseeker's allowance (JSA) and new-style employment and support allowance

(ESA).[2] If you are claiming UC jointly with your partner, both of you must usually accept a claimant commitment.[3] If you are required to accept one and do not do so, you are not entitled to UC, JSA or ESA.

You *can* qualify for UC, new-style JSA or new-style ESA without accepting a claimant commitment if the DWP considers that you cannot accept one because you lack the capacity to do so, or there are exceptional circumstances which mean it would be unreasonable to expect you to accept one at the moment[4] – eg, you are likely to be in hospital for several weeks or there is a domestic emergency. For UC and new-style ESA, you do not have to accept a claimant commitment if you are terminally ill – ie, due to a progressive disease, your death can reasonably be expected within 12 months.[5] If you lack capacity, the DWP may refer your claim to see whether an appointee is needed (see p1005). Your appointee cannot accept a claimant commitment on your behalf.[6] If you already have an appointee, this may indicate that you lack capacity, and the requirement to accept a claimant commitment may be waived.[7]

A claimant commitment must include:[8]

- the main work-related requirements you must meet (see p948). This may not include all the specific work-related actions you are required to meet; *and*
- any other information the DWP thinks is appropriate to include – eg, the consequences of failing to carry out work-related requirements if applicable.

**Note:**

- Specific work-related requirement actions may be stated elsewhere (eg, on your online journal if you have one), and not only in the commitments section. If so, it should always be made clear what you have to do and what are the consequences of not doing it.[9]
- Even if you do not have to meet any work-related requirements, your claimant commitment explains your other responsibilities – eg, to report changes in your circumstances.

***Work coaches***

Job centre staff who support and interview you if you are claiming benefits under the UC system are called **'work coaches'**. Your work coach draws up your claimant commitment and discusses your responsibilities with you. Decisions about what you must do to meet your work-related responsibilities cannot be changed by a revision, supersession or an appeal, but you can negotiate, ask for a second opinion or a review or ask to speak to a manager. If necessary, you can complain. You may be interviewed over the phone or in person at a job centre. Your work coach may also contact you via your online account if you have one.

## Accepting your claimant commitment

You must accept the most up-to-date version of your claimant commitment using the method specified by the DWP. This could be online, by phone or in writing.[10] Be sure to use the method specified or you may not count as accepting the claimant commitment. For example, even if you have attended a commitments meeting, you may still need to accept your claimant commitment via your online journal.

If no work-related requirements are to be imposed on you (see p950), or you only have to participate in work-focused interviews (see p956), your first claimant commitment is usually accepted as part of the normal claims process.[11] Otherwise, your first claimant commitment is drawn up by your work coach for you to accept after a discussion (which usually takes place at a commitments meeting).

Your claimant commitment should be tailored to your circumstances,[12] so ensure that you inform your work coach of any problems you may have in meeting work-related requirements and that any limitations you are allowed (see p946) are put on record.

6

**Note:**

- If you refuse to accept a claimant commitment, you should be offered a 'cooling off' period specified by the DWP. Guidance states that this will be a maximum of up to seven days in which to reconsider.[13]
- If you are not happy with your claimant commitment, you may be able to get it reviewed (see p937).

If you accept your claimant commitment within the time the DWP has specified, you are usually treated as accepting it on the date of your claim (or any date to which your claim has been backdated).[14] If you are awarded UC or ESA without making a claim (see p45), you are treated as accepting it on the first day of the first assessment period (for UC) or the first benefit week (for ESA) of your benefit award. You can request a second opinion (also known as a review) on whether the requirements in your commitment are reasonable before you accept them.[15]

The time within which you must accept your claimant commitment (including one that has been updated) can be extended if:

- for UC and JSA, you ask the DWP to review any action that it has been proposed you take as a work search or work availability requirement, or whether there should be any limitations on these requirements;[16]
- for ESA, you ask for an extension.[17]

The DWP must be satisfied that your request is reasonable. Be careful not to miss any time limits specified by the DWP for accepting your claimant commitment as this may result in your claim being refused or your award terminated. Even if you are not happy with your claimant commitment, it may be better to agree to it and make it clear that you will comply. You can then ask for a review (see p937).

Remember that if you are claiming with a partner, you must usually both accept a claimant commitment and, if you do not do so, your claim may be refused or your award terminated.

*Risk of 'claim closure'*

Your claim may be refused (the DWP is likely to refer to your claim being 'closed') because you have failed to attend or participate in your first commitments meeting. You should contact the DWP as soon as possible to avoid your claim being refused in this way and explain any additional needs you have. Otherwise, your claim may be refused on the day after the appointment. If you have additional needs (eg, English is not your first language, or you have literacy difficulties or a disability), your claim should not be refused immediately, and the DWP may contact you to rebook your appointment.[18] The DWP may refer to your additional needs as 'complex needs'. Let it know about your circumstances as soon as possible (even if this is after the meeting) if you think this should apply to you.[19] If your claim is 'closed', this is a refusal to award you benefit (eg, UC) and you can ask for a written explanation of the decision. You should be advised of your right to challenge the decision by mandatory reconsideration and appeal.[20] You should also consider submitting a new claim in the meantime.

If you already have an award, it should not end because you fail to participate in a commitments review meeting (see below) you are required to attend. However, you may be sanctioned if you do not have a good reason for your failure to participate.[21] If you refuse to or fail to accept new commitments which have been drawn up and sent to you (which may be done with or without a meeting) and exceptional circumstances do not apply (see p935), your award may end. You must be informed of the consequences of not accepting your new commitments. The DWP may refer to this as 'claim closure' too, but in any case, it is a decision to end your entitlement and you can request a mandatory reconsideration and appeal if necessary. To avoid a sanction, you should comply with the work-related requirements in your previous claimant commitment if you can.

6

## Reviewing your claimant commitment

Your claimant commitment can be reviewed and updated as the DWP thinks fit.[22] This is done on an ongoing basis to record any changes to the expectations placed on you and the consequences for failing to comply with them. A review may, but does not have to, involve an interview with you – eg, if you are working and an interview would involve time off work, it may not be reasonable to expect you to participate.

Guidance suggests your claimant commitment should be reviewed after any change in your circumstances.[23] You can also ask for your claimant commitment to be reviewed and updated at any time. The DWP may refer to this as a 'request for a second opinion', and may restrict the number of times you can ask for one.[24]

See p936 for when the time for accepting your claimant commitment can be extended if you ask for a review.

If a review is carried out, make it clear that you intend to do everything possible to comply with the work-related requirements. Keep a record of what you have done and any reasons you have for not being able to comply fully. If you do not accept a new claimant commitment which has been sent to you, your award may end (see p937), unless there were circumstances which made it unreasonable for you to accept (see p935).

You cannot appeal a decision about your claimant commitment. If you think a decision is unreasonable, you can complain and continue to negotiate. If negotiation and complaint are unsuccessful, get advice about a possible claim for judicial review (see Chapter 53). If you are an adviser, you may be able to send a judicial review pre-action letter yourself (see p1242). You can challenge a decision to end your award (including when the DWP calls this 'claim closure' – see p937) by mandatory reconsideration and appeal.



## 2. The work-related requirements

If you come under the universal credit (UC) system (see p20), you may have to meet work-related requirements, sometimes even if you are in paid work.[25] There are some situations when no work-related requirements can be imposed on you (see p950). See pp948–64 for which (if any) requirements may apply.

If you do not meet the requirements, you continue to be entitled to benefit, but you may be given a sanction and your benefit may be paid at a reduced or nil rate (see Chapter 43). For information on avoiding a sanction, see p970. **Note:** if you are entitled to UC and also to new-style jobseeker's allowance (JSA) or employment and support allowance (ESA), you only need to meet one set of work-related requirements – those for UC.[26]

The work-related requirements are:

- work-focused interviews (see p939); *and*
- work preparation (see p940); *and*
- work search (UC and JSA only – see p941); *and*
- work availability (UC and JSA only – see p945).

**Note:** you may also have to attend other interviews connected to the work-related requirements while you are entitled to UC, new-style JSA or new-style ESA (see p948).

Your work-related requirements and the specific actions you must take may be set out in your claimant commitment or may be notified to you in some other way.[27] You should not be sanctioned if the DWP has not given you proper notification of a requirement that allows you to understand what you must do and the consequences of not complying.[28]

## Work-focused interviews

If a work-focused interview requirement is imposed on you, you must take part in one or more interviews relating to work or work preparation.[29] The main purpose of a work-focused interview is to make it more likely that you will find work (or more or better paid work if you are already working). You may also have to participate in other interviews for any purpose connected to the work-related requirements (see p948). Participation includes attending in the way specified by the DWP, whether in person or by phone. However, if you are not very late for an interview, you may still have participated, depending on all the circumstances of the interview.[30]

The DWP tells you how, when and where a work-focused interview will take place. It should also tell you the reason for the interview, in basic terms, and the consequences of failing to participate.[31] If the DWP does not clarify the type of interview and the consequences of non-compliance, you should not be sanctioned if you fail to attend or participate, as the DWP has not imposed a valid work-related requirement.[32]

There is no legal minimum or maximum frequency for work-focused interviews. However, guidance may suggest a minimum – eg, every three months for the responsible carer (see p953) of a one-year-old, every month for the responsible carer of a two-year-old.[33]

A work-focused interview may:[34]

- assess your prospects for obtaining or remaining in work (and/or, for UC, more or better paid work);
- assist or encourage you to obtain or remain in work (and/or, for UC, more or better paid work);
- identify activities you can undertake and opportunities for training, education or rehabilitation that will make it more likely that you will obtain or remain in work (and/or, for UC, more or better paid work);
- identify current or future work opportunities that are relevant to you;
- if you are claiming UC, decide whether you are in gainful self-employment (see p132) and, if so, whether you qualify for a start-up period during which the minimum income floor does not apply (see p130).

**Note**: your interview will usually be carried out over the phone or in person at a job centre. You do not have a choice about how the interview is carried out, but you should inform the DWP if you have any particular needs – eg, you have literacy difficulties, English is not your first language, or you are disabled. You should be offered a home visit or telephone interview, if appropriate. If the DWP insists on an interview that is not appropriate (eg, because it is not accessible to you), you can complain. If you have to attend the job centre, you are required to fund your travel costs yourself, but you may be able to get discounted fares (see p781). If the frequency of in-person interviews is causing you financial hardship, you should talk to your work coach and complain if necessary. If you cannot attend an interview for any reason, contact the DWP and explain why as soon as you can and in writing if possible – eg, on your journal.

## Work preparation

If a work preparation requirement is imposed on you, you must take 'particular action' specified by the DWP that makes it more likely that you will obtain paid work, more paid work or better paid work.[35]

### *Particular action*

**'Particular action'** can include attending a skills assessment, improving personal presentation, participating in training or an employment programme, undertaking work experience or a work placement, and developing a business plan.[36] Employment programmes may be delivered by organisations contracted by the DWP, and vary depending on where you live. If you have limited capability for work, work preparation can include participating in assessments and interviews to gather information and discuss what might enable you to improve your capability for work. Voluntary employability support may also be available. The DWP must make it clear if you are required to participate in any work preparation activity, and explain the consequences if you fail to participate. **Note:** employment programmes provided by or for the Scottish government are voluntary, and you cannot be sanctioned if you do not participate.[37] Work placement trials should not be mandatory unless you are in the all work-related requirements group (see p959).

6

### If you have a disability

Your health condition or disability should always be considered when deciding what you must do as work preparation, including any adjustments you need. It does not matter whether you have limited capability for work or not.[38]

If you have a disability or health condition that affects the work you can do, you may be able to get specialist support via the job centre. For further information, see gov.uk/looking-for-work-if-disabled. You should make sure you are clear about what is voluntary and what counts as specified work preparation. You cannot be sanctioned if you fail to participate in an employment support scheme provided by or for the Scottish government.

### If you are aged under 25

If you are 16 to 24 years old, unemployed and must meet all the work-related requirements for UC (see p959), you may be offered a variety of options of work preparation, depending on where you live. If you are 16 to 19 and referred to training to help you gain skills needed to find work (or more or better paid work), this does not prevent you from receiving UC.[39] If you are offered a job via an employment scheme and have earned income, then your UC will be affected by your earnings in the usual way (see p41).

Participation in employment schemes for young people may be a work preparation requirement. However, if your work preparation requirement is temporarily suspended, you should not be referred to one.[40] If you do not have to meet all the work-related requirements, you may still be able to voluntarily participate in employment schemes.

If you choose to take part in employment support services provided by or for the Scottish government, these are voluntary, and you cannot be sanctioned if you do not participate. You should be clearly informed of anything that is compulsory and the consequences of not taking part should be explained.

## Work search

If a work search requirement is imposed on you, you are expected to take 'all reasonable action' to obtain paid work, more paid work or better paid work. You must also take any 'particular action' specified by the DWP for the same purpose.[41] You may be able to agree restrictions about the type of work, location and/or hours that you are expected to apply for (see p946).

*Particular action*

**'Particular action'** can include carrying out work searches, applying for jobs, creating and maintaining an online profile, registering with an employment agency and seeking references.[42] The DWP can specify the amount of time you must spend doing any 'particular action'.

**Note:** if you are told to apply for a particular job vacancy, you are treated as failing to meet the work search requirement if you are offered an interview for the vacancy and do not participate.[43]

### All reasonable action

In general, 'reasonable action' means you are expected to look for work, regardless of its type or the salary. However, certain limitations can apply to the work you are available for and seeking to do (see p946).

To count as taking 'all reasonable action' to find paid work, more paid work or better paid work, you must take action that gives you the best prospects of obtaining work. If you are unemployed, this usually includes making job applications. You must normally spend a specified number of hours in each week seeking work – ie:[44]

- at least the weekly number of hours you are expected to work (your 'expected hours' – see p942), minus any deductions the DWP allows (see p943); *or*
- fewer hours than your 'expected hours', provided the DWP is satisfied that you have taken all reasonable action. For example, if you have been offered a job to

start the following week, you may have completed all reasonable action despite spending fewer than your expected hours searching for work. Alternatively, you may have an unavoidable situation which prevents you from spending more hours on your work search.[45] You should make sure the DWP is aware of any particular circumstances that affect your work search.

**Your expected hours**

You are normally expected to spend 35 hours a week looking for work (your 'expected hours'). However, in practice, you may not have to look for more work or pay if your earnings are at or above the administrative earnings threshold (see p962). A lower number of expected hours applies in some cases. This is the number that the DWP thinks is:[46]

- for UC, compatible with your caring responsibilities, if you are a 'responsible carer' (see p953) of a child who has not yet reached compulsory school age – ie, aged three or four. The DWP says that the maximum expected hours in this situation is 30 hours a week, but could be lower (eg, because of travel to and from a childcare provider), and should be compatible with your caring responsibilities, including the availability of childcare;[47]
- compatible with your child's normal school hours (including travelling time to and from school), if you are a 'responsible carer' (or, for JSA only, a 'responsible foster carer') for a child under 13. For UC, your child must have reached compulsory school age. The DWP says that the maximum expected hours in this situation is 30 hours a week, but could be lower (eg, because of travel to and from school if you take your child there and/or pick them up), and should be compatible with the child's normal school hours, taking into account the availability of childcare.[48] 'Responsible foster carer' is not defined, but it should apply if you are a 'responsible foster parent' (see p953);
- compatible with your caring responsibilities, if you are a 'relevant carer', a 'responsible carer' (for UC, for a child aged 13 or over) or a 'responsible foster parent' (see p953 for the definitions), and the DWP is satisfied that you have reasonable prospects of obtaining paid work, more paid work or better paid work;
- reasonable in the light of your 'physical or mental impairment'. Expected hours must be reduced if your health condition affects what you are able to do.

If you think your expected hours are too high given your health, disability or caring responsibilities, you can negotiate with your work coach and ask for a review (see p937). Make it clear that you will comply with your current hours if at all possible. You cannot appeal a decision about your expected hours of work search. If negotiation is unsuccessful, you can complain, but get advice first if possible. If negotiation and complaining are not successful, get advice about a possible judicial review pre-action letter. If you are an adviser, you may be able to send a letter yourself (see p1242).[49] Keep a record of the requests you make to vary your expected hours (eg, by asking via your online journal and taking a screenshot), even if they are not changed.

The DWP can agree deductions from your expected hours of work search for the time you spend:[50]

- carrying out paid work; *or*
- carrying out voluntary work. You can do as much voluntary work as you wish, but this can only ever count towards 50 per cent of your expected hours; *or*
- carrying out a work preparation requirement or 'voluntary work preparation' – ie, action that you agree with the DWP to take on a voluntary basis to make it more likely you will obtain paid work, more work or better paid work; *or*
- dealing with temporary childcare responsibilities, a domestic emergency, funeral arrangements or other temporary circumstances. You should not be sanctioned if you temporarily reduce your work search hours because of this type of unavoidable circumstance,[51] but you should try to agree this with your work coach or inform the DWP as soon as possible. In some cases, your work coach could suspend your work search requirement completely for a temporary period (see p964).

6

***Examples***

Claudia is getting new-style JSA. She is looking for shop work. To get relevant experience, she volunteers in a charity shop for 10 hours a week. Her expected hours are 35 hours a week. However, she need only spend 25 hours a week looking for work because the DWP agrees to deduct the 10 hours she is doing voluntary work.

Alec and Lamar are joint UC claimants. Alec spends a lot of time caring for Lamar who has a long-term condition and currently gets personal independence payment mobility component only (no daily living component). All of the work-related requirements are imposed on Alec. No work-related requirements are imposed on Lamar because he has limited capability for work-related activity. Alec counts as a relevant carer (see p953) and his expected hours are 25 hours a week (the hours the DWP is satisfied are compatible with his caring responsibilities – there is no specific guidance on Alec's situation). He is therefore meant to look for work for 25 hours a week.

**Proving you are searching for work**

Always keep careful records of the steps you take to find work or get more hours/pay. Your work coach should agree with you how you will evidence your work search, and the DWP may require you to confirm and verify what you have done.[52]

***How do you prove you are searching for work?***

1. Check your claimant commitment to ensure you understand what the DWP expects you to do each week. You must be able to give details of the action you have taken (eg, at an interview with your work coach), so it is vital that you keep a record of your attempts to get a job. However, the DWP should accept that it is not always possible to provide evidence of your work search – eg, employers do not always respond and some of your work search may be by face-to-face conversations, which you cannot prove took place.[53]

2. Make a note every time you do anything that may count as work search. Include the dates and times, who you spoke to and what was said. You should do this online if you have been asked to do so as part of your UC journal.

3. Keep copies of any letters or emails you send, of any advertisements you reply to and any job applications you make. If you deliver your CV or a job application by hand, ask for a receipt as proof. Make notes of job searches you do online, including when you use the government's online 'Find a job' service. Take screenshots of relevant activity if your job search is mainly recorded online.

6

4. Tell the DWP if you face particular barriers in searching for work and recording the steps you have taken – eg, if you have difficulty reading or writing, using a computer or with the English language. You should still try to present proof of your work search – eg, by getting a friend or relative to help you compile your record of jobseeking steps. The DWP should consider what is reasonable for you in the light of all your circumstances and consider whether you need additional support.[54]

5. Sometimes, your activities to seek work may be looked at more intensively than usual, possibly over several previous weeks, so ensure they are always sufficient. Do not rely on the fact that your activities have so far not been challenged by the job centre.

6. The 'Find a job' service shows the jobs that have been suggested for you and the jobs for which you have applied. The DWP may ask you to allow it to access your account to check on what you have been doing. Although using 'Find a job' is not a requirement of UC or JSA, if you do not use it the DWP may decide that you are not taking 'all reasonable action'.

7. If the DWP has suggested jobs that you have not applied for, your work coach may question whether you meet the work search requirement. It is therefore best to follow up suggestions from your work coach, even if you think they are not appropriate. If you do not meet the requirements of a job (eg, it requires a driving licence and you do not have one), you should point this out to your work coach and could also consider a complaint, but it is still best to apply to avoid a sanction. You may also be matched with a vacancy by your work coach and supported within a particular job. Again, it is best to participate to avoid a sanction, but consider a complaint if the job is not appropriate. If you are sanctioned for not accepting or for leaving a vacancy you have been matched with, you can ask for a mandatory reconsideration and appeal if necessary (see p997).

## Work availability

If a work availability requirement is imposed on you, you must be able and willing immediately to:[55]

- take up paid work, more paid work or better paid work; *and*
- attend an interview in connection with obtaining paid work, more paid work or better paid work.

You may be able to limit the work you are available for and seeking to do. See p946 for further information.

**Note:** for JSA, you are treated as *not* meeting the work availability requirement if you are a prisoner on temporary release under specified provisions, so you cannot claim JSA (see p838).[56]

### Able and willing to take up work or attend an interview immediately

You must usually be immediately willing and able to attend an interview offered to you in connection with obtaining paid work.[57] It must be lawful for you to work in Great Britain. There must be nothing to prevent you from receiving offers of interviews or job offers (eg, because you are away from home for a short time), and nothing to prevent you from acting on them straight away, with the following exceptions. You are allowed:[58]

- **up to one week** to take up work if you are doing voluntary work, if the DWP is satisfied you need longer;
- **up to one month** to take up work if you are a 'responsible carer' or a 'relevant carer' (see p953 for the definitions), if the DWP is satisfied you need longer, taking into account alternative care arrangements;
- **until after your notice period** has passed if you are working and you have a duty under employment law or under the terms of your contract to give your employer notice that you are leaving work.

In all the situations above, you can also be given **up to 48 hours' notice to attend an interview** in connection with obtaining work. If you are employed, you may be required to find more or better paid work unless you earn enough (see p962). However, if you cannot arrange to attend an interview due to your existing work, you should argue that it is not reasonable for you to risk losing this.

Even if no work search requirement can be imposed on you for a period, you must be able and willing to take up paid work or attend an interview immediately once the circumstances that exempt you from the work search requirement no longer apply (see p959). In some cases, the DWP might think this is reasonable *before* the circumstances that exempt you from looking for work no longer apply, or that it is reasonable for you to attend an interview even when it is unreasonable for you to be able to take up paid work.[59]

### Holidays

You are not allowed a holiday from work search and work availability in UC or JSA under the UC system. If you go away, you must continue to meet your work-related requirements, including being contactable and being able to return to attend an interview or start a job, unless your work coach has agreed that these requirements are suspended. You should also ensure you are aware of the rules on being away from your normal home for the housing element (see p100), and being away from Great Britain (see p1371), to avoid losing your UC.

## Limitations on availability and search for work

You can limit the work you are available for and seeking to do, provided the DWP is satisfied that certain conditions apply. You can limit:[60]

- the type of work and rate of pay (see below);
- the number of hours a week, or the times, you can work (see below);
- the location of the work (see p947).

6

You may be able to agree limits on your availability for either an indefinite or a limited period.

### The type of work and rate of pay

You can limit the type of work and/or rate of pay in the following circumstances.[61]

- If you have previously done work of a particular type and/or at a particular rate of pay, you can limit your work search and availability to work of a similar type and/or rate of pay for a maximum of four weeks from your date of claim (or, if you were exempt from work-related requirements while getting UC because you had sufficient earnings, from the date you cease paid work if this is later). The DWP must be satisfied that you have a reasonable prospect of getting work despite the limitation. Ensure you understand when the period starts and ends.
- If you have a 'physical or mental impairment' that has a substantial adverse effect on your ability to do work of a particular type or in particular locations, you do not have to be available for or look for such work. You do not have to show that you have a reasonable prospect of getting work.

If you need to limit the type of work you look for because of sincerely held beliefs (eg, on religious or conscientious grounds), you may be able to negotiate this. You must show your job expectations are realistic and achieveable despite this restriction.[62]

### The number of hours

You are normally expected to search for work for at least 35 hours a week (see p942 for the rules about your 'expected hours' of work search). If you are a 'relevant carer' or a 'responsible carer' (see p953 for the definitions), or you have a 'physical or mental impairment', your expected hours may be lower and, in this situation, the hours you are expected to search for work and to be available for work are the same.[63]

There may be times when you have taken 'all reasonable action' (see p941) to find work even though your hours of work search are lower than the expected number, providing you can show what you have done gives you the best prospects of finding work.[64]

## The location of the work

In some circumstances, you can limit the location of the work you must search for and be available to do.[65] Help may be available from the Flexible Support Fund with travel costs to interviews or when starting work (see p781).

### Travel time

You need only be available for, and to look for, work in locations that are no more than 90 minutes travel time from your home in either direction. When looking at travel time, the DWP should consider the frequency of public transport and any disability or health condition you have, which may mean travelling independently takes you longer. Your ability to travel may also be affected by your caring responsibilities. If you have a health condition, caring responsibilities or other issues which affect your ability to travel or to find work, your expected travel to work time and location should be limited to take account of these.[66] If you are the responsible carer of a child under 13, the need for travel time to and from school or childcare should be taken into account. If you have a physical or mental impairment or you are a responsible carer of a child under 13, you do not need to show that you have a reasonable prospect of finding work despite your travel restrictions. If you are not the responsible carer but are a 'relevant carer' of a child under 13 (see p953), you can negotiate a shorter expected travel time based on your circumstances if you can show that you still have a reasonable prospect of work.



### Location

If you have a physical or mental impairment that has a substantial adverse effect on your ability to do work in particular locations (eg, you cannot manage stairs), you do not have to be available for work or to look for work in those locations.[67]

## The effect of the rules on minimum working conditions

The rules about minimum working conditions (see Appendix 6) can affect your claim for UC or JSA if you are looking for work. You can insist that you are only available for work that meets these conditions (ie, that you will not accept a job if the terms do not comply with the legal requirements) – eg, if an employer is offering a job at less than the minimum wage. The DWP says that you can be sanctioned for failing to apply for a zero-hour contract. However, you should not be sanctioned if a zero-hour contract employer reduces your hours because you took work elsewhere or where the hours offered restrict your ability to increase your earnings with other employers.[68] You should consider a complaint if you are told to apply for a job without guaranteed hours which is inappropriate for your circumstances (eg, because you have childcare responsibilities) and you may have good reason if you fail to apply for or accept such a job (see p994).

## Other interviews

The DWP can require you to participate in an interview for any purpose connected to any of the work-related requirements – ie, to:[69]

- impose a work-related requirement on you; *or*
- verify that you have complied with a work-related requirement; *or*
- assist you to comply with a work-related requirement.

At the interviews, you may be asked to provide evidence and information. You may also be asked to report any changes in your circumstances that are relevant to your work-related requirements and your compliance with them. You must be informed of an interview and made aware of the consequences of failing to attend and take part (you cannot be sanctioned for failing to attend or participate unless you received proper notification).[70] This can be provided in a written document (letter or claimant commitment), online (eg, via your UC journal), face to face or by text, email or phone. The DWP should record how and when you were notified and what you were told to do.[71] As with work-focused interviews, you do not have a choice about how your interview is carried out (but see p939).

# 3. Which requirements apply

Many people must meet *all* the work-related requirements (see p959). However:

- in some cases, no work-related requirements at all can be imposed on you (see p950); *or*
- you may only have to meet a work-focused interview requirement (see p956); *or*
- you may only have to meet a work-focused interview and a work preparation requirement (see p957); *or*
- you may not have to meet a work search or a work availability requirement for a period (see p959).

**Note:** if you are entitled to universal credit (UC) and also to new-style jobseeker's allowance (JSA) or employment and support allowance (ESA), you must only meet one set of work-related requirements – those for UC.[72]

Your work-related requirements depend on your circumstances. If you are responsible for a child, your work-related requirements usually depend on their age, and if you are in a couple, whether you are the 'responsible carer' (see p953). You cannot appeal a decision about which work-related responsibilities apply to you, so if you think they are unreasonable or incorrect, you should negotiate with your work coach and, if necessary, complain. Where negotiation and complaint are not successful, you should seek advice about the possibility of a judicial review pre-action letter. If you are an adviser, you can consider sending a pre-action letter yourself (see p1242).[73] To avoid a sanction, make it clear that you will comply with your work-related responsibilities in the meantime. Keep a record of your attempts to negotiate and/or complain. If you are sanctioned, you can appeal this decision (see p997) – eg, because your work-related requirements were not reasonable. You must ask for a mandatory reconsideration first, but you can do this at any time (there is no time limit for requesting a revision of sanction decisions).

***Which work-related requirements apply?***

| *Your circumstances* | *Work-related requirement* |
|---|---|
| Sick or disabled with limited capability for work-related activity (see p954)<br>Looking after a child under one or caring for someone with a disability (see p952)<br>Recent experience of domestic abuse (see p951)<br>On UC and earning a sufficient amount (see p954)<br>At least pension age (see p956)<br>In some circumstances, in education (see p956) | No work-related requirements. You do not have to look for work, be available for work or participate in activity or conversations about preparing for work or improving your skills. However, you must usually still agree a claimant commitment (see p934), and you must report changes in your circumstances. |
| Looking after a child aged one<br>On ESA as a lone parent with a child aged at least one but under three<br>Foster parent or 'friend and family carer' for a child over one and under 16 (see p956) | Work-focused interviews only (see p956). |
| Looking after a child aged two (see p957)<br>Limited capability for work (see p957) | Work preparation (see p940), work-focused interviews (see p939) and other interviews connected to the work-related requirements (see p948). |

| | |
|---|---|
| All other claimants (see p959) | All the work-related requirements apply if you are not in any of the above groups. This could include some people with responsibility for children aged three or over, some disabled people, some students and some people in work. Your expected hours of work search are up to your work coach but may depend on your circumstances, including the age of your children if you are a responsible carer (see p942). However, you may be able to restrict your availability for work and the type of work you have to look for (see p946). |
| Temporary circumstances | Even if you would usually have all work-related requirements, there may be temporary circumstances when the work search and work availability requirements do not apply to you, including if you are sick (see p959), bereaved or have experienced domestic abuse (see p961), are earning a sufficient amount (see p962) and in other temporary circumstances (see p963). |

## No work-related requirements

No work-related requirements *at all* can be imposed on you if:

- you have recently experienced domestic violence or abuse (see p951); *or*
- for UC and new-style ESA (or if you are getting *both* new-style JSA *and* UC), you fit into a specified group – ie, you are:
  - looking after children or have other caring responsibilities (see p952);
  - sick or disabled (see p954);
  - for UC only, in work and earning enough (see p954);
  - in other specified situations (see p956).

If your situation changes so that you are covered by the above, any requirements already imposed cease to have effect.[74] It is important to report changes as soon as possible to make sure the DWP is aware of this.

## Domestic violence or abuse

If you notify the DWP that you have experienced, or been threatened with, domestic violence or abuse from a person who is your partner, your former partner or a family member, and you satisfy specified conditions, all work-related requirements that have been imposed on you cease to have effect for 13 consecutive weeks from the date of notification.[75] In addition, no new work-related requirements can be imposed on you during this period. For UC, if, but for the domestic abuse rules, you would have to meet all the work-related requirements and you are the 'responsible carer' of a child under 16 (see p953), no work availability or work search requirements can be imposed for a further 13 consecutive weeks (ie, for 26 weeks in total), although you could be required to attend work-focused interviews and/or engage in work preparation after the first 13 weeks.[76] The guidance goes further and suggests that work-related support is voluntary even after the first 13 weeks. For responsible carers of children who do not have to meet all the work-related requirements, the guidance suggests no work-related requirements at all should apply for 26 weeks.[77]

You must satisfy all the following conditions.

- This rule must not have applied to you on any earlier occasion in the 12 months before you notify the DWP.
- An incident of domestic abuse (or threat of domestic abuse) must have taken place within the six months before you notify the DWP.
- When you notify the DWP, you must not be living at the same address as the person who was abusive or threatened you with abuse. However, if you are still at the same address, the DWP can consider suspending your work search and work availability on the grounds of a domestic emergency (see p964).[78]
- As soon as possible, and no later than one month after you notify the DWP, you must provide evidence from a person acting in an official capacity that shows that your circumstances are consistent with those of a person who has experienced, or been threatened with, domestic violence or abuse in the six months before you notified the DWP, and that you have made contact with the person acting in an official capacity about an incident that occurred in that six-month period.

### *Domestic violence or abuse*[79]

**'Domestic abuse'** means any incident or incidents of physical or sexual abuse, violent or threatening behaviour, controlling behaviour, coercive behaviour, psychological, emotional, economic or other abuse, regardless of gender or sexuality. Economic abuse can include financial abuse and any abuse which has an adverse effect on you being able to acquire, use or maintain money or other property, or which has an adverse effect on you being able to obtain goods and services. The abuse may have been directed towards another person and still be an experience or threat of domestic abuse – eg, if your child has experienced abuse.

**'Partner'**, for the purposes of domestic abuse only, includes: your spouse/civil partner or former spouse/civil partner, someone you have agreed to marry or civilly partner (even if that agreement has terminated), someone who has, or used to have, a parental relationship to a child at the same time as you (as a legal parent or with parental responsibility), or someone with whom you have had an intimate personal relationship. It does not matter if you have never lived with the partner/former partner.

**'Family member'** for these purposes means: parent, step-parent, child, stepchild, grandparent, grandchild, sibling, uncle, aunt, niece, nephew, first cousin. It includes half-siblings, aunts, cousins, nieces, nephews and cousins, and relatives via marriage or civil partnership (whether current or former).

A **'person acting in an official capacity'** means a healthcare professional, a police officer, a registered social worker, your employer or your trade union representative. It also means any public, voluntary or charitable body with which you have had direct contact in connection with domestic abuse.

6

### Looking after children and other caring responsibilities

If you are getting UC or new-style ESA, no work-related requirements can be imposed on you if:[80]

- for UC, you are the 'responsible carer' (see p953) of a child under one; *or*
- for ESA, you are not a member of a couple and you are responsible for a child under one – eg, you are a lone parent. The rules do not define when you count as responsible for a child; *or*
- you are the 'responsible foster parent' (see p953) of a child under one; *or*
- you are an 'adopter' (see p953) and it is not more than 12 months (for UC) or 52 weeks (for ESA) since your child was placed with you for adoption. You can elect for the 12 months (or 52 weeks) to start in the 14 days before your child was expected to be placed with you; *or*
- you are pregnant and your baby is due in 11 or fewer weeks; *or*
- you had a baby not more than 15 weeks ago (including if this was a stillbirth); *or*
- you have regular and substantial caring responsibilities for a severely disabled person (see p954); *or*
- you have caring responsibilities for one or more severely disabled people for at least 35 hours a week, but do not satisfy the qualifying conditions for carer's allowance (CA) or have entitlement to carer support payment (CSP) (see p954). For UC, this only applies if the DWP is satisfied that it is unreasonable for you to meet a work search requirement and a work availability requirement, even if these are limited.

### *Definitions*

You are a **'responsible carer'**:[81]

- for UC, if you are a single person, or a member of a couple claiming as a single person, who is responsible for a child under 16 (see p64) – eg, you are a lone parent, or you claim as a single person because your partner does not meet the basic conditions of UC;
- for JSA and ESA, if you are the only person responsible for a child under 16.

If you are a member of a couple and you are joint claimants, you are a responsible carer for UC if you or your partner (for JSA and ESA, you *and* your partner) are responsible for a child under 16 and you and your partner have nominated you as being responsible for the child. Only one of you can be nominated. You do not have to be the child's parent. The nomination applies to all the children you or your partner are responsible for. It can only be changed once in the 12 months after the nomination or if there has been a change of circumstances which the DWP considers relevant. If the DWP does not allow you to change a nomination, get advice. You cannot appeal a decision about who the responsible carer is. The other member of a couple may be a 'relevant carer', or, if you have a disabled child, may have 'regular and substantial caring responsibilities' (see p954).

You are a **'relevant carer'** if:[82]

- you are the parent of a child, have caring responsibilities for them but are not the 'responsible carer'; *or*
- you have caring responsibilities for someone who has a 'physical or mental impairment' (and for JSA only, the impairment means they need such care). However, if you care for a disabled person on attendance allowance (AA), pension age disability payment (PADP), Scottish adult disability living allowance (SADLA), disability living allowance (DLA), child disability payment (CDP), personal independence payment (PIP) or adult disability payment (ADP), you may have regular and substantial caring responsibilities (see p954).

You are a **'responsible foster parent'** if you are the child's only foster parent or, if you are a member of a couple who are both foster parents, you and your partner have nominated you as the 'responsible foster parent'.[83] Only one of you can be nominated. The nomination applies to all the children for whom you or your partner are responsible. It can only be changed once in the 12 months after the nomination or if there has been a relevant change of circumstances.

You are an **'adopter'** if you have been matched with a child by an adoption agency and you are, or are intended to be, the 'responsible carer' of the child.[84] This does not apply if you are the child's foster parent or close relative.

A person is **'severely disabled'** if they are someone to whom AA, PADP, the highest or middle rate of DLA/SADLA/CDP care component, the daily living component of PIP, the daily living component of ADP, armed forces independence payment or constant attendance allowance under the industrial or war disablement schemes (see p600) is payable.[85]

You have '**regular and substantial caring responsibilities**' if you satisfy the qualifying conditions for CA (see Chapter 22), or you would do but for the fact that your earnings are higher than allowed for CA (currently £196 a week – see p473).[86] However, you must not receive any earnings at all from your caring responsibilities. You do not have to be getting CA. If you live in Scotland, the same rules apply even if, in practice, you cannot make a new claim for CA due to its replacement by CSP. If you are entitled to CSP, you have regular and substantial caring responsibilities. If you are not covered by these rules, you may still be a 'relevant carer', which may reduce your work-related requirements (see p953 and p946).

6

## Sick and disabled people

If you are getting UC or new-style ESA, no work-related requirements can be imposed on you if:[87]

- you have both limited capability for work and limited capability for work-related activity – ie, you are in the support group for ESA and/or have limited capability for work-related activity for UC, including if you have transferred to UC from ESA in the support group or while getting national insurance (NI) credits with limited capability for work-related activity status (see Chapter 41); *or*
- you are entitled to ESA only, but it is paid at a nil rate – eg, because you are getting an occupational pension.

## You are earning enough

If you are getting UC, no work-related requirements at all can be imposed on you if you are:[88]

- a single claimant, or a member of a couple, and your own average monthly earnings are at least your individual earnings threshold (see p955); *or*
- a member of a couple and your combined average monthly earnings are at least your joint earnings threshold (see p955). No work-related requirements can be imposed on you even if you are not working but your partner earns enough to meet this threshold;[89] *or*
- self-employed and are treated as having a minimum earnings level (see p130); *or*
- an apprentice and your average monthly earnings are at least the amount you would be paid at the rate of the national minimum wage (see Appendix 6) for 30 hours work (or, if lower, for your weekly 'expected hours' – see p942).

Your monthly earnings are calculated using your gross actual or estimated earned income in the current assessment period – ie, before income tax, NI contributions and pension contributions have been deducted.[90] If your earnings fluctuate, these are averaged over one cycle of work or, if there is no cycle, over three months or the period that enables the average to be worked out more accurately. The DWP can disregard earnings from employment that has ended if this enables it to determine your monthly earnings more accurately. This means that if you are no longer working and receive a final payment of wages, the DWP can decide that you must meet work-related requirements, but does not have to.

**Note:** usually, if you are getting UC and you or your partner earn a certain amount each month (excluding self-employed earnings) – called the 'administrative earnings threshold' – you are not expected to look for more work (see p962). The DWP may refer to this as being in the 'light touch' regime.

### Earnings thresholds

- **To work out your individual earnings threshold**, multiply the amount you would earn at the hourly rate of the national minimum wage by the relevant number of hours for you (see below). Multiply this amount by 52 and divide it by 12.[91]
- **To work out your joint earnings threshold if you are a member of a couple**, work out the sum of your and your partner's individual earnings thresholds and add these together.[92] However, if you are claiming as a single person because your partner does not meet the UC conditions (see p36), your joint earnings threshold is the sum of your individual threshold and the amount someone would be paid at the rate of the minimum wage for 35 hours work (multiplied by 52 and divided by 12).

Fractions of a pound are ignored.[93]

For your individual threshold, the relevant hours are:[94]

- the hours you are expected to work each week (your 'expected hours') – usually 35 a week. A lower number of hours can apply (see p942); *or*
- 16 hours a week, if (but for your earnings reaching the threshold) you would otherwise be someone who only has to meet a work-focused interview requirement (see p956) or a work-focused interview requirement and a work preparation requirement (see p957).

***Example***

Tejan and Adaku are joint UC claimants in their 40s. They have three children, the youngest of whom is of compulsory school age and under 13. They agree that Adaku should be the 'responsible carer'. Tejan's 'expected hours' are 35 a week. The DWP agrees that Adaku's 'expected hours' are 30 a week as these are compatible with their youngest child's school hours (see p942).

Tejan works 30 hours a week and earns £2,400 a month.

35 hours x £12.21 = £427.35

£427.35 x 52 ÷ 12 = £1,851.85

His individual earnings threshold is £1,851.

Adaku works 15 hours a week and earns £860 a month.

30 hours x £12.21 = £366.30

366.30 x 52 ÷ 12 = £1,587.30

Her individual earnings threshold is £1,587.

Their joint earnings threshold is therefore £1,851 + £1,587 = £3,438

Their joint earnings (£3,260) do not exceed their joint earnings threshold. Tejan has no work-related requirements but Adaku is in the all work-related requirements group. However, as the couple earn more than the couple administrative earnings threshold (see p962), Adaku is not currently expected to look for more earnings or hours.

### Other situations – pension-age claimants and claimants in education

If you are getting UC or new-style ESA, no work-related requirements can be imposed on you if:[95]

- for UC, you are at least pension age; *or*
- you are in full-time, non-advanced education or training and you have no parental support (see p38). For ESA, this also applies if you have been enrolled or accepted for the education or training. For both UC and ESA, you must be under 21, or be aged 21 and have reached that age while on the course; *or*
- for UC, you are eligible for UC while receiving education (see p793) and you have student income (see p795) for your course which is taken into account when calculating your UC. If your student income is a postgraduate master's or doctoral degree loan, this only applies if your course is full time.

6

## Work-focused interview requirement only

If you are in the work-focused interview 'regime', you are required to participate in interviews to discuss work and consider steps to prepare for it, but all action other than participating in the interviews is voluntary.

A work-focused interview requirement, and no other work-related requirements, can be imposed on you if you are getting UC or new-style ESA and:[96]

- for UC, you are the 'responsible carer' (see p953) of a child aged one; *or*
- for ESA, you are a single person who is responsible for a child aged at least one but under three; *or*
- you are a foster parent, and you:
  - are the 'responsible foster parent' (see p953) of a:
    - child aged at least one but under 16; *or*
    - qualifying young person (see p259). The DWP must be satisfied that the young person has care needs which make it unreasonable for you to have to meet a work search requirement or a work availability requirement even if these were limited (for UC), or a work preparation requirement (for ESA); *or*
  - are not the 'responsible foster parent' (see p953) of a child under 16 or a qualifying young person, but the DWP is satisfied that the child or young

person has care needs which make it unreasonable for you to have to meet a work search requirement or a work availability requirement even if these were limited (for UC), or a work preparation requirement (for ESA); *or*
  - do not have a child or qualifying young person placed with you currently, but intend to have one placed with you, and within the past eight weeks:
    - for UC, you have been in any of the situations described above applying to foster parents; *or*
    - for ESA, you have been the 'responsible foster parent' of a child aged at least one but under 16; *or*
- you have become a 'friend or family carer' (see below) for a child under 16 in the past 12 months, and you are their 'responsible carer' (see p953).

**Note:** no work-related requirements can be imposed on you if your child is under one and you are the 'responsible foster parent', or for UC, the 'responsible carer', or for ESA, a single person who is responsible for the child (see p952).

***Friend or family carer***[97]

You are a **'friend or family carer'** if you are responsible for a child under 16 but are not their parent or step-parent. You must be taking care of the child because:

- they have no parents, or have parents who are unable to care for them. For when you count as responsible for a child for UC, see p64. 'Responsible for a child' is not defined in the ESA rules; *or*
- it is likely that they would otherwise be looked after by a local authority because there are concerns about their welfare.

If you have been getting UC or ESA on the basis that you have to meet additional work-related requirements but you now fit into one of the groups above, any requirements previously imposed on you cease to apply.[98]

If you have young children, your work-focused interviews should be arranged taking childcare availability into account. You should be told that you can rearrange your interview if you have a good reason why you cannot attend – eg, childcare, social services or medical appointments.[99]

## Work-focused interview and work preparation requirement only

If a work-focused interview requirement *and* a work preparation requirement (but no other work-related requirements) can be imposed on you, you are only expected to prepare for a move into paid work, more paid work or better paid work – eg, by participating in a training or employment scheme. You do not have to look for work or be available for work.

For UC, this requirement applies if you are the 'responsible carer' (see p953) of a child aged two. It also applies if you are entitled to new-style ESA or UC and you have limited capability for work (see Chapter 41).[100] You do not automatically count as having limited capability for work until this has been decided in a work capability assessment (see p896 for some exceptions). If you are providing medical evidence (usually fit notes), guidance states that after 28 days you should be referred for a work capability assessment if this has not already been done.[101] Apart from the first 14 days (during which the DWP may have to suspend your work search and work availability requirement – see p959), the DWP has discretion about which work-related requirements to apply until you have a decision about your limited capability for work (see p960). Any work search requirements must take your condition(s) into account. Your work coach may agree voluntary, tailored commitments with you during this time, but can still set mandatory commitments as well if appropriate. They must make clear what you have to do to avoid being sanctioned, and what is voluntary. However, if you are someone who can be treated as having limited capability for work (see p896), guidance says you must not be required to look for work while awaiting a work capability assessment outcome. If you are someone who can be treated as having limited capability for work-related activity (see p917), guidance says that all work-related requirements should be switched off.[102]

***Do you have limited capability for work?***

If you have a limited capability for work decision, make sure your work coach knows how your illness affects what you can do and ask them to use their discretion in deciding which requirements to impose on you. If you are on ESA and have been found to have limited capability for work, or you were on ESA in the work-related activity group or had NI credits for limited capability for work when you claimed UC, and there has been no subsequent decision finding you capable of work, that limited capability for work decision applies to your UC.[103] You may have to point this out to your work coach.

If you have limited capability for work, reasonable adjustments for your health needs must be offered when carrying out work-focused interviews (eg, offering phone interviews where appropriate) and in determining what you should do to prepare for work. Your work coach may agree voluntary, tailored commitments with you, but can still decide to set mandatory commitments as well.[104]

If you are the responsible carer of a child aged two, interviews must be accommodated around childcare availability and you should only be expected to carry out mandatory work preparation when another responsible adult is looking after your child(ren).[105]

Note:

- In some situations (eg, if you are in the ESA 'support group'), no work-related requirements at all can be imposed on you (see p950).

- If you have been getting UC on the basis that you have to meet other work-related requirements, but you are now in one of the above groups, any requirements previously imposed cease to apply.[106]

## All work-related requirements

If you do not come into any of the other work-related requirement groups (see p949) and none of the temporary circumstances apply to you (see below), the DWP *must* impose a work search requirement and a work availability requirement on you for UC and JSA. It can also impose a work-focused interview requirement or a work preparation requirement, or both, and is likely to do so.[107] **Note:** if you are getting ESA, a work search and work availability requirement can *never* be imposed on you.

You may be in the all work-related requirements group even though you are working (see p954 for the level of earnings you and/or your partner need to have for no work-related requirements). In this case, the DWP may refer to your requirements as 'in-work conditionality'. If you and/or your partner are earning below a certain amount (see p962), your in-work conditionality may include having to look for more work or pay.

If you think you should have been covered by any of the exceptions, but have been told you must meet all the requirements, or if your work-related requirements are unreasonable given your circumstances, you should consider negotiating with your work coach, requesting a review (see p937) and complaining if necessary. You cannot appeal against your work-related requirements, but if negotiation and complaint are not successful, get advice about a possible claim for judicial review (see Chapter 53). If you are an adviser, you may be able to send a judicial review pre-action letter yourself (see p1242). If you are given a sanction for failing to meet a requirement, you can appeal. You must apply for a mandatory reconsideration first, but there is no time limit on doing this (even if the sanction has now finished).

### No work search or work availability requirement for a period

If you are getting UC or new-style JSA or both, a work search and a work availability requirement cannot be imposed on you for a period (but you may have to meet other work-related requirements) in a number of situations.

**Note:** for ESA, a work search or work availability requirement can *never* be imposed on you.

#### Sick and disabled people

If you are getting UC or new-style JSA, a work search requirement cannot be imposed on you for specified periods if you are unfit for work. This usually applies for a maximum of 14 days and no more than twice in any 12-month period.[108] For the first seven days, you must provide a declaration that you are unfit for work. For any further days, you must provide a fit note (for UC only, this only applies if

6

requested by the DWP). However, if you have previously failed a work capability assessment while under the UC system, or you have been treated as not having limited capability for work for UC because you failed to provide information or attend an assessment, the DWP can decide not to suspend your work search requirement. This should only apply if you are unfit for work because of the same condition (or substantially the same condition) and you are not being referred to a new work capability assessment.[109]

In several situations, the DWP has discretion whether or not to impose a work search requirement. This applies:[110]

- for UC, if you are unfit more than twice, or for longer than 14 days, and the DWP thinks it would be unreasonable to require you to meet a work search requirement even if it were limited. This could apply, for example, if you are waiting for a work capability assessment. If it is not possible to meet even limited requirements such as participating in work-focused interviews, or your requirements do not reflect your condition, you should negotiate with your work coach and complain if necessary;
- for UC and JSA, if you have failed a previous work capability assessment or were treated as not having limited capability for work, and your medical evidence shows that you currently have the same, or substantially the same, condition as you had before those decisions were made. Even if the DWP does not refer you for a new work capability assessment, it can decide that it is unreasonable to require you to meet a limited work search requirement. However, it does not have to do so. This means you can be expected to meet a limited work search requirement even though you are unwell or disabled – eg, while you are appealing a work capability assessment outcome. You should negotiate with your work coach and complain if it is not possible for you to meet your requirements and/or it affects your health;
- for JSA, if you are allowed an 'extended period of sickness' of up to 13 weeks under the rules described on p614 and the DWP thinks it would be unreasonable to require you to meet a work search requirement. If you are sick for longer than 13 weeks, you can no longer claim JSA.

You must provide a fit note. For UC only, this only applies if requested by the DWP after the first seven days of sickness.

For the work availability requirement, you only need to be both willing and able to take up work and to attend an interview for UC when the above circumstances no longer apply or, for JSA, when the period of sickness has ended.[111] However, if the DWP thinks it is reasonable to require you to attend an interview, you must be able and willing to attend one before the period of sickness has ended.

You cannot appeal against your work-related requirements but if negotiation, asking for a review (see p937) and complaining are not successful, get advice about a possible judicial review (see Chapter 53). If you are an adviser, you may be able to send a judicial review pre-action letter yourself (see p1242). Keep a record of everything you do to try to change your work-related requirements and explain clearly why you think they are unreasonable if this is the case.

If you continue to provide fit notes for UC, guidance says that the DWP should refer you for a work capability assessment from day 29 of your sickness or declared disability, if it has not already done so.[112] While you are waiting for the assessment, your work coach may agree voluntary commitments with you, as well as any mandatory ones considered appropriate.[113] You can request a second opinion if your work-related requirements are not reasonable (see p937). Guidance says that if you can be treated as having limited capability for work-related activity, all work-related requirements should be switched off.[114]

If you have failed a work capability assessment, it may not be possible to be referred for a further work capability assessment (see p927). However, the DWP should still take your condition into account when putting together your work-related requirements. It can take into account medical evidence to do so (this applies whether or not you are challenging the decision that you are capable of work).



### Bereavement and domestic violence and abuse

If you are getting UC or new-style JSA, a work search requirement cannot be imposed on you if it is less than six months since the death of your partner or a child under 16 (or, for UC only, a 'qualifying young person').[115] You or your partner must have been responsible for the child or qualifying young person, or you must have been the child's parent. For when you count as responsible for a child for UC, see p64. 'Responsible for a child' is not defined in the JSA rules.

For UC only, a work search requirement cannot be imposed on you if you are the 'responsible carer' of a child under 16 (see p953), and there has been a 'significant disruption' in your normal childcare responsibilities because in the last 24 months:[116]

- a parent, sister or brother, or a person who was the previous responsible carer, of the child has died; *or*
- any person who normally lived in the same accommodation as the child has died. The person does not have to have been a relative or carer. They must have been living in the accommodation at the time of their death, and must not be liable to make payments for the accommodation on a commercial basis; *or*
- the child has experienced or witnessed a violent or abusive incident. This does not apply if you are the perpetrator of that violence or abuse. Violence and abuse are not defined, but incidents of physical or emotional, financial and other non-physical abuse should count, as long as this has significantly disrupted your childcare responsibilities. The violence or abuse does not have to have happened within the child's home, and the perpetrator does not have to be a family member or anyone known to you or the child.

The suspension of the work search requirement can apply for one month in each of the four consecutive six-month periods after the event occurs, beginning on a date specified by the DWP after you have notified it of the circumstances, and provided that the DWP is satisfied that the circumstances apply.[117] If the death affecting the child is that of your partner, another child or a qualifying young person, and the rules described above apply, or if *you* have experienced domestic abuse and the rules on p951 apply, the month runs at the same time as any period you have been allowed under those rules – ie, you do not get any extra time.

For the work availability requirement, you only need to be willing and able to take up work and attend an interview once the circumstances no longer apply.[118]

#### You have sufficient earnings from employment

If you are getting UC, a work search requirement cannot usually be imposed on you, but you can legally be required to meet other work-related requirements if:[119]

- your employed earnings (see p126) are at least £952 a month. This applies whether you are single or in a couple, based on your own employed earnings; *or*
- you are in a couple and your joint employed earnings (see p126) are at least £1,534 a month. It does not matter if you have no earnings yourself.

6

**Note:** the amounts above are based on 18 hours a week at the national minimum wage for those aged 21 and over (individual), and 29 hours a week at the national minimum wage for those 21 and over (couple). It does not matter how old you actually are. These rules only apply to people who would otherwise have to look for work and be available for work.

Your gross earnings in the current assessment period are calculated or estimated before deductions for tax, NI or pension contributions. However, if your earnings fluctuate, they can be averaged over your cycle of work, over three months, or over any other period allowing an accurate monthly average to be calculated.[120] The DWP may decide to ignore earnings you receive from a job which has finished. Self-employed earnings do not count.

The DWP calls these earnings levels the 'administrative earnings threshold' and may refer to people in the all work-related requirements group with these earnings as being in the 'light touch' regime.[121]

It is possible to be randomly selected for an 'in-work pilot scheme' even though you are in the 'light touch' regime. If this happens, you can be required to look for more work, hours or pay. You must be informed of your selection in writing. There are certain circumstances in which you must not be selected – eg, where you are unfit for work for longer than 14 days.[122]

**Note:** if your monthly earnings are above your individual or joint earnings threshold (the 'conditionality earnings threshold'), no work-related requirements can be imposed on you (see p954), so this rule only applies if your monthly employed earnings are at least at the level of the relevant administrative earnings threshold, but lower than the relevant conditionality earnings threshold.

*Example*

Erin (27) is working part time. Her gross pay is £970 a month. Under the UC rules, she is expected to work 35 hours a week.

35 x £12.21 = £427.35

£427.35 x 52 ÷ 12 = £1,851.85.

Her individual conditionality earnings threshold is therefore £1,851. Although she is not exempt from all the work-related requirements, because her pay is more than £952 a month, a work search requirement cannot be imposed on her unless she is selected for an in-work pilot scheme.

For the work availability requirement, you only need to be willing and able to take up work and attend an interview once the circumstances no longer apply – ie, once your earnings reduce to below the relevant limit.[123] For work-focused interviews and work preparation, although you could legally be required to participate, support from a work coach and work preparation are currently voluntary. Any activities you agree to would be voluntary and guidance says you cannot be sanctioned for failing to complete them.[124]

6

## Other temporary circumstances

If you are getting UC or new-style JSA, a work search requirement cannot be imposed on you if:[125]

- you are attending a court or tribunal as a witness or party to the proceedings; *or*
- you qualify for UC or JSA while you are temporarily absent from Great Britain (see p1381 and p1371) because you are:
  - receiving, or taking your child under 16 (or, for UC only, your partner or a qualifying young person) for, medical treatment or, for UC only, convalescence or care; *or*
  - for JSA only, attending a job interview; *or*
- you are receiving and participating in a course of treatment for alcohol or drug addiction and have been for no more than six months; *or*
- you are under police protection while a witness in a criminal investigation or proceedings, and have been for no more than three months; *or*
- for UC only, you are a prisoner (see p839); *or*
- for UC, you are carrying out a 'public duty'. This is not defined, but should include being on jury service, crewing a lifeboat or carrying out duties as a volunteer firefighter or special constable.[126] For JSA, see p964.

For the work availability requirement, you only need to be willing and able to take up work and attend an interview once the circumstances no longer apply.[127]

If the DWP is satisfied that it would be unreasonable for you to have to meet a work search requirement even if this were limited, a work search requirement cannot be imposed on you if:[128]

- for JSA only, you are carrying out a public duty; *or*
- you are carrying out a work preparation requirement (see p940) or 'voluntary work preparation' – ie, action agreed with the DWP that makes it more likely that you will get paid work; *or*
- you have temporary childcare responsibilities; *or*
- there are other temporary circumstances. These could include anything that makes it unreasonable for you to seek work – eg, becoming homeless, caring for a relative, or a flood, fire or other disaster at your home. For UC, dealing with domestic emergencies and funeral arrangements are specifically included, but other situations may also make it unreasonable – eg, moving house or a child's exclusion from school.[129]



For the work availability requirement, if you fall under the bullet points above, you only need to be willing and able to both take up work and/or attend an interview when the circumstances no longer apply.[130] However, for UC, if the DWP thinks it is reasonable to require you to attend an interview, you must be able and willing to do so before the circumstances cease to apply. The DWP may decide that it is reasonable to require you to attend an interview, but not to require you to be willing and able to take up paid work immediately.

If any of the temporary circumstances apply to you, you should explain why you are not currently able to look for work and make sure that there is a record of your circumstances. You may be able to argue you should not be sanctioned if temporary circumstances applied and the DWP did not consider suspending your work search requirement.[131]

# Notes

**1. The claimant commitment**

1 **UC** s14(1) WRA 2012
**JSA** s6A(1) JSA 1995
**ESA** s11A(1) WRA 2007

2 **UC** s4(1)(e) WRA 2012
**JSA** s1(2)(b) JSA 1995
**ESA** s1(3)(aa) WRA 2007

3 s3(2) WRA 2012

4 **UC** Reg 16 UC Regs
**JSA** Reg 8 JSA Regs 2013
**ESA** Reg 45 ESA Regs 2013

5 **UC** Reg 16(2) UC Regs
**ESA** Reg 45(2) ESA Regs

6 See also DWP, Universal Credit Guidance, *Appointees, personal acting bodies and corporate acting bodies*, v14.0.0 and *Claimant commitment – overview*, v13.0, House of Commons library deposited papers, rightsnet.org.uk/resources/universal-credit-guidance
7 paras J1021-2 ADM indicate all the evidence should be considered first. Guidance to other DWP staff indicates the requirement is waived in all appointee cases, see Universal Credit Guidance, *Claimant commitment – overview*, v13.0, House of Commons library deposited papers, rightsnet.org.uk/resources/universal-credit-guidance.
8 **UC** s14(4) WRA 2012
**JSA** s6A(4) JSA 1995
**ESA** s11A(4) WRA 2007
9 *JB v SSWP (UC)* [2018] UKUT 360 (AAC)
10 **UC** s14(5) WRA 2012; reg 15 UC Regs
**JSA** s6A(5) JSA 1995; reg 7 JSA Regs 2013
**ESA** s11A(5) WRA 2007; reg 44 ESA Regs 2013
11 para J1011 ADM
12 DWP, Universal Credit Guidance, *Building the claimant commitment*, v14.0, House of Commons library deposited papers, rightsnet.org.uk/resources/universal-credit-guidance
13 para J1010 ADM
14 **UC** Reg 15(1) and (2) UC Regs
**JSA** Reg 7(1) JSA Regs 2013
**ESA** Reg 44(1) and (2) ESA Regs 2013
15 DWP, Universal Credit Guidance, *Claimant commitment not accepted*, v7.0, House of Commons library deposited papers, rightsnet.org.uk/resources/universal-credit-guidance
16 **UC** Reg 15(3) UC Regs
**JSA** Reg 7(2) JSA Regs 2013
17 Reg 44(3) ESA Regs 2013
18 DWP, Universal Credit Guidance, *Fail to attend*, v24.0, House of Commons deposited papers, rightsnet.org.uk/resources/universal-credit-guidance
19 DWP, Universal Credit Guidance, *Complex Needs Overview*, v20.0, House of Commons deposited papers, rightsnet.org.uk/resources/universal-credit-guidance
20 You may be able to challenge the decision by arguing that you accepted your default claimant commitment when you made your UC claim and this has not yet been replaced by a personalised commitment, so the DWP cannot show that you do not meet the basic conditions of UC
21 *FO v SSWP (UC)* [2022] UKUT 56 (AAC); para J1036 ADM
22 **UC** s14(2) WRA 2012
**JSA** s6A(2) JSA 1995
**ESA** s11A(2) WRA 2007
23 DWP, Universal Credit Guidance, *Claimant commitment - overview*, v13.0, House of Commons library deposited papers, rightsnet.org.uk/resources/universal-credit-guidance
24 DWP, Universal Credit Guidance, *Claimant commitment not accepted*, v7.0, House of Commons library deposited papers, rightsnet.org.uk/resources/universal-credit-guidance

2. **The work-related requirements**
25 **UC** s13 WRA 2012
**JSA** ss6 and 6F JSA 1995
**ESA** s11 WRA 2007
26 **JSA** Reg 5(2) JSA Regs 2013
**ESA** Reg 42(2) ESA Regs 2013
27 **UC** s24(4) WRA 2012
**ESA** s11H(4) WRA 2007
**JSA** s6H(4) JSA 1995
28 *JB v SSWP* [2018] UKUT 360 (AAC)
29 **UC** s15 WRA 2012
**JSA** s6B JSA 1995
**ESA** s11B WRA 2007
30 *SA v SSWP (JSA)* [2015] UKUT 454 (AAC)
31 para J3031 ADM; failing to do this may mean no valid work-related requirement has been imposed: see *JB v SSWP (UC)* [2018] 360 (AAC)
32 *KG v SSWP (UC)* [2020] UKUT 307 (AAC)
33 DWP, Universal Credit Guidance, *Work-focused interview regime*, v11.0, and *Work preparation regime*, v21.0, House of Commons deposited papers, rightsnet.org.uk/resources/universal-credit-guidance
34 **UC** Regs 87 and 93 UC Regs
**JSA** Reg 10 JSA Regs 2013
**ESA** Reg 46 ESA Regs 2013
35 **UC** s16(1) and (2) WRA 2012
**JSA** s6C(1) and (2) JSA 1995
**ESA** s11C(1) and (2) WRA 2007
36 **UC** s16(3)-(6) WRA 2012
**JSA** s6C(3) JSA 1995
**ESA** s11C(3)-(6) WRA 2007

37 See, for example, DWP, Universal Credit Guidance, *Fair Start Scotland programme*, v11.0, House of Commons deposited papers, rightsnet.org.uk/resources/universal-credit-guidance
38 DWP, Universal Credit Guidance, *Work preparation regime*, v21.0, House of Commons library deposited papers, rightsnet.org.uk/resources/universal-credit-guidance
39 Reg 12(1B) UC Regs
40 DWP, Universal Credit Guidance, *Youth offer*, v8.0, House of Commons deposited papers, rightsnet.org.uk/resources/universal-credit-guidance
41 **UC** s17(1) WRA 2012
**JSA** s6D(1) JSA 1995
42 **UC** s17(2) and (3) WRA 2012
**JSA** s6D(2) and (3) JSA 1995
43 **UC** Reg 94 UC Regs
**JSA** Reg 11 JSA Regs 2013
44 **UC** Reg 95(1) UC Regs
**JSA** Reg 12(1) JSA Regs 2013
45 *RR v SSWP (UC)* [2017] UKUT 459 (AAC)
46 **UC** Reg 88 UC Regs
**JSA** Reg 9 JSA Regs 2013
47 Reg 88(2)(aa) UC Regs; DWP, Universal Credit Guidance, *Hours of work-related activity*, v12.0, House of Commons library deposited papers, rightsnet.org.uk/resources/universal-credit-guidance
48 Reg 88(2)(b) UC Regs; DWP, Universal Credit Guidance, *Hours of work-related activity*, v12.0, House of Commons library deposited papers, rightsnet.org.uk/resources/universal-credit-guidance
49 cpag.org.uk/judicial-review-template-letters-uc
50 **UC** Reg 95(2)-(4) UC Regs
**JSA** Regs 4(1) and 12(2) and (3) JSA Regs 2013
51 *RR v SSWP (UC)* [2017] UKUT 459 (AAC)
52 **UC** s23(3) WRA 2012
**JSA** s6G(3) JSA 1995
DWP, Universal Credit Guidance, *Intensive work search regime*, v30.0, House of Commons deposited papers, rightsnet.org.uk/resources/universal-credit-guidance
53 para J3103 ADM
54 paras J3253-57 ADM
55 **UC** s18(1) and (2) WRA 2012; regs 87 and 96(1) UC Regs
**JSA** s6E(1) and (2) JSA 1995; regs 3(7) and 13(1) JSA Regs 2013
56 Reg 13(1)(b) JSA Regs 2013
57 **UC** Reg 96(1) UC Regs
**JSA** Reg 13(1)(a) JSA Regs 2013
58 **UC** Reg 96(2)-(5) UC Regs
**JSA** Regs 2 and 13(2)-(5) JSA Regs 2013
59 Reg 99(5B) UC Regs
60 **UC** s17(4) and (5) WRA 2012
**JSA** s6D(4) and (5) JSA 1995
61 **UC** Reg 97(4)-(6) UC Regs
**JSA** Reg 14(3) and (4) JSA Regs 2013
62 DWP, Universal Credit Guidance, *Job goals and competing for vacancies*, v5.0, House of Commons library deposited papers, rightsnet.org.uk/resources/universal-credit-guidance
63 **UC** Reg 97(2) UC Regs
**JSA** Reg 14(5) JSA Regs 2013
64 **UC** Reg 95 (1) UC Regs
**JSA** Reg 12(1) JSA Regs 2013
65 **UC** Reg 97(3) and (6) UC Regs
**JSA** Reg 14(2) and (4) JSA Regs 2013
66 DWP, Universal Credit Guidance, *Work-related requirements for claimants with children* and *Building the claimant commitment*, v14.0, House of Commons library deposited papers, rightsnet.org.uk/resources/universal-credit-guidance
67 **UC** Reg 97(6) UC Regs
**JSA** Reg 14(4) UC Regs
68 para K2301 ADM
69 **UC** s23 WRA 2012
**JSA** s6G JSA 1995
**ESA** s11G WRA 2007
70 para K1171 ADM; *JB v SSWP (UC)* [2018] UKUT 360 (AAC); *KG v SSWP (UC)* [2020] UKUT 307 (AAC)
71 Note to para J3001 ADM

3. **Which requirements apply**
72 **JSA** Reg 5(2) JSA Regs 2013
**ESA** Reg 42(2) ESA Regs 2013
73 cpag.org.uk/judicial-review-template-letters-uc
74 **UC** s19(5) WRA 2012
**JSA** Reg 15(1)(a) JSA Regs 2013
**ESA** s11D(3) WRA 2007
75 **UC** Reg 98 UC Regs
**JSA** Regs 5 and 15 JSA Regs 2013
**ESA** Reg 49 ESA Regs 2013
Although not supported by guidance, it is arguable that abuse or fear of abuse from a family member under 16 is 'domestic violence' under the regulations.
76 Reg 98(1A) UC Regs

77 DWP, Universal Credit Guidance, *Domestic abuse*, v26.0, House of Commons library deposited papers, rightsnet.org.uk/resources/universal-credit-guidance
78 DWP, Universal Credit Guidance, *Domestic abuse*, v26.0, House of Commons library deposited papers, rightsnet.org.uk/resources/universal-credit-guidance
79 The DWP is using the cross-governmental definition of domestic violence and abuse under the Domestic Abuse Act 2021; DWP, *'Help available from the Department for Work and Pensions for people who are victims of domestic violence and abuse'*, updated 16 April 2024, available on gov.uk; ss1 and 2 Domestic Abuse Act 2021; DWP, Universal Credit Guidance, *Domestic abuse*, v26.0, House of Commons library deposited papers, rightsnet.org.uk/resources/universal-credit-guidance. The UC (reg 98(4) UC Regs), JSA (reg 15(4) and (5) JSA Regs 2013) and ESA (reg 49(4) and (5) Regs 2013) regulations have not been amended at the time of writing, but give a wide definition of 'domestic violence'. You should rely on the definition which covers you.
80 **UC** s19(2)(b) and (c) WRA 2012; reg 89(1)(b), (c), (d) and (f) UC Regs
**JSA** Reg 5 JSA Regs 2013
**ESA** s11D(2)(b) and (c) WRA 2007; reg 47(1)(a), (b), (c), (f) and (g) ESA Regs 2013
81 **UC** s19(6) WRA 2012; reg 86 UC Regs
**JSA** Reg 4 JSA Regs 2013
**ESA** Reg 41 ESA Regs 2013
82 **UC** Reg 85 UC Regs
**JSA** Reg 4(1) JSA Regs 2013
83 **UC** Regs 85 and 86 UC Regs
**JSA** Reg 4 JSA Regs 2013
**ESA** Reg 41 ESA Regs 2013
84 **UC** Reg 89(3) UC Regs
**ESA** Reg 47(5) ESA Regs 2013
85 **UC** Reg 89(2) UC Regs
**ESA** Reg 47(5) ESA Regs 2013
86 **UC** Reg 30 UC Regs
**ESA** Reg 47(2) and (3) ESA Regs 2013
87 **UC** s19(2)(a) WRA 2012
**ESA** s11D(2)(a) WRA 2007; reg 47(1)(e) ESA Regs 2013
88 Reg 90 UC Regs
89 Reg 90(3)(a) UC Regs
90 Reg 90(6) UC Regs
91 Reg 90(2) UC Regs
92 Reg 90(3) UC Regs
93 Reg 6(1A) UC Regs
94 Regs 88 and 90(2) UC Regs
95 **UC** s19 WRA 2012; regs 68(7), definition of 'postgraduate loan', and 89(1)(a), (da) and (e), (4) and (5) UC Regs
**ESA** s11D WRA 2007; reg 47(1)(d) ESA Regs 2013
96 **UC** s20 WRA 2012; reg 91 UC Regs
**ESA** s11E WRA 2007; reg 48 ESA Regs 2013
97 **UC** Reg 91(3) UC Regs
**ESA** Reg 48(3) ESA Regs 2013
98 **UC** s20(3) WRA 2012
**ESA** s11E(3) WRA 2007
99 DWP, Universal Credit Guidance, *Work-focused interview regime*, v.11.0, House of Commons library deposited papers, rightsnet.org.uk/universal-credit-guidance
100 **UC** s21 WRA 2012
**ESA** s11F WRA 2007
101 DWP, Universal Credit Guidance, *Health conditions and disabilities – day 1 to day 29*, House of Commons library deposited papers, rightsnet.org.uk/resources/universal-credit-guidance
102 DWP, *Universal Credit Guidance, Health conditions and disabilities – day 1 to day 29*, House of Commons library deposited papers, rightsnet.org.uk/resources/universal-credit-guidance
103 Regs 19 and 21 UC(TP) Regs; reg 39(1)(a) UC Regs
104 DWP, Universal Credit Guidance, *Work preparation regime*, v21.0, House of Commons library deposited papers, rightsnet.org.uk/resources/universal-credit-guidance
105 DWP, Universal Credit Guidance, *Work preparation regime*, v21.0, House of Commons library deposited papers, rightsnet.org.uk/resources/universal-credit-guidance
106 s21(4) WRA 2012
107 **UC** s22 WRA 2012
**JSA** s6F JSA 1995
108 **UC** Reg 99(1)(a) and (4) UC Regs
**JSA** Reg 16(1)(a) and (5) JSA Regs 2013
109 **UC** Reg 99(4ZA) and (4ZB) UC Regs
**JSA** Reg 16(5A) and (5B) JSA Regs 2013
110 **UC** Reg 99(5)(c) and (d) UC Regs
**JSA** Regs 16(5B) and 16A(1) and (2) JSA Regs 2013

111 **UC** Reg 99 (1)(b), (2B), (2C), (5A) and (5B) UC Regs
**JSA** Regs 16 (1)(b) and 16A(4)-(6) JSA Regs 2013
112 DWP, Universal Credit Guidance, *Health conditions and disabilities – day 1 to day 29*, House of Commons library deposited papers, rightsnet.org.uk/resources/universal-credit-guidance
113 DWP, Universal Credit Guidance, *Work-related requirements and ongoing contact in the health journey*, House of Commons library deposited papers, rightsnet.org.uk/resources/universal-credit-guidance
114 DWP, Universal Credit Guidance, *Treated as having LCWRA and day 1 WCA referrals*, House of Commons library deposited papers, rightsnet.org.uk/resources/universal-credit-guidance
115 **UC** Reg 99(1) and (3)(d) UC Regs
**JSA** Reg 16(3)(c) JSA Regs 2013
116 Reg 99(1) and (4A) UC Regs
117 Reg 99(4B) and (4C) UC Regs
118 **UC** Reg 99(1)(b) UC Regs
**JSA** Reg 16(1)(b) JSA Regs 2013
119 Regs 6(1A) and 99(1), (6) and (6A) UC Regs
120 Reg 2, definition of 'monthly earnings', and reg 90(6), UC Regs
121 DWP, *Universal Credit Guidance, Light touch regime*, v10.0, House of Commons library deposited papers, rightsnet.org.uk/resources/universal-credit-guidance. If you do not have to look for work for other reasons, such as being the main carer of a child aged one or two, the DWP does not regard you as in 'light touch' and may require you to participate in work-focused interviews because you are in the work-focused interview or work preparation 'regime'.
122 The Universal Credit (Work-Related Requirements) In Work Pilot Scheme and Amendment Regulations 2015 No.89, as amended by SI 2025 No.168
123 Reg 99(1)(b) UC Regs
124 DWP, Universal Credit Guidance, *Light touch regime*, v10.0, House of Commons library deposited papers, rightsnet.org.uk/resources/universal-credit-guidance
125 **UC** Reg 99(1) and (3)(a)-(c) and (e)-(g) UC Regs
**JSA** Reg 16(1), (3)(a), (b), (d) and (e) and (4) JSA Regs 2013
126 para J3208 ADM
127 **UC** Reg 99(1)(b) UC Regs
**JSA** Reg 16(1)(b) JSA Regs 2013
128 **UC** Reg 99(2A) and (5)(a) and (b) UC Regs
**JSA** Reg 16(1) and (4) JSA Regs 2013
129 paras J3068-72 ADM
130 **UC** Reg 99(2B), (2C), (5A) and (5B) UC Regs
**JSA** Reg 16(1)(b) JSA Regs 2013
131 *RR v SSWP (UC)* [2017] UKUT 459 (AAC)

# Chapter 43

# Universal credit system sanctions

**This chapter covers:**


1. When you can be sanctioned (p970)
2. How your benefit is reduced (p979)
3. The sanction period (p983)
4. Good reasons for your actions (p989)
5. Sanction decisions (p995)
6. Challenging a sanction decision (p997)


6

The rules on sanctions in this chapter apply if you come under the universal credit (UC) system, whether you are getting UC, jobseeker's allowance (JSA) or employment and support allowance (ESA) (see p20). JSA or ESA under the UC system are called new-style JSA and new-style ESA. If you claim JSA, that is only payable under the UC system. If you get ESA but you do not yet come under the UC system (ie, you get old-style ESA), see p176.

## Key facts

- If you are getting UC or new-style JSA or new-style ESA and you do not meet your work-related requirements, you may be given a sanction.
- If you are given a sanction, your benefit is paid at a reduced (or sometimes nil) rate for a period.
- Whether or not you can be sanctioned, and for how long, depends on what you have done, or failed to do, in relation to your work-related requirements.
- It is always better to avoid a sanction if you can. If a sanction decision is made, consider challenging it. If a sanction is applied, you may still be able to avoid it if you can show that you have a good reason for your actions.
- You may qualify for hardship payments if you have been given a sanction.
- You can apply for a revision or supersession (see Chapter 50), or appeal (see Chapter 51) against a sanction decision. You must apply for a mandatory reconsideration before you can appeal.

# 1. When you can be sanctioned

You can be given a sanction if you do not meet the work-related requirements you have as a condition of getting universal credit (UC) and, if you come under the UC system (see p20), new-style jobseeker's allowance (JSA) and new-style employment and support allowance (ESA). See Chapter 42 for the work-related requirements.

You cannot be sanctioned if you do not have any work-related requirements, including if you are in the 'support group' for ESA (see p950). In practice, most sanctions are applied in UC, and sanctions in ESA and JSA are very uncommon.

***What can you do to avoid a sanction?***

1. Talk to your work coach if you think that any work-related activity you are being asked to do is unreasonable. Explain why it is unreasonable – eg, because of your health or caring responsibilities. You should keep a record (a note of the date, time and what was said) of your attempts to negotiate with your work coach, as this could be important if you have to show you had a good reason at a later date. Unreasonable claimant commitments could, depending on the facts of your case, be the subject of judicial review (see Chapter 53).

2. If there is a possibility that you will be given a sanction, give full details of your side of the story. Use this chapter to work out what information and evidence you should provide. Ensure the DWP is aware of any needs that make it difficult for you to fulfil your work-related requirements.

3. If you must show you had a good reason for what you did or did not do, explain your reasons fully and in time. See pp989–95 for what may (or may not) count.

4. If you left or were dismissed from a job and it appears there may have been misconduct or that you left voluntarily without a good reason, your former employer is asked for a statement. You should be given an adequate chance to comment on what it says. Your remarks may be passed to your employer for further comments. Make sure you explain why you disagree with an allegation or why you had a good reason for leaving your job. If you are going to an employment tribunal (eg, to claim unfair dismissal), say so. Discuss your reply with whoever is advising you on this, as you may be asked questions at the employment tribunal hearing by your former employer about what you have said.

5. If you refused to apply for or accept a job, what the potential employer says might be taken into account. Explain what enquiries you made about the nature of the job and your reasons for not applying for or accepting it. For example, if you assumed the employer would not make adjustments but you did not ask it about this, you may not have a good reason.

6. If you are taking part in a training scheme or employment programme, it is probably the provider who raises doubts about your compliance or attendance. Before a sanction is imposed, you should be given an adequate chance to comment on any statements made against you. Bear in mind that even if the scheme or programme provider is satisfied that

you have done what was required of you or that you had a good reason for failing to do so, the DWP may reach a different conclusion.

7. Information, queries or declarations you send to the DWP can be posted on your online journal, if you have one. If you cannot post on your journal or do not have one, you should communicate with the DWP in any way accessible to you – eg, by phone or in person. In any case, keep a record of all your interactions with the DWP, irrespective of how they take place – eg, by taking a screenshot of messages on your journal.

If you are given a sanction, your UC, new-style JSA or ESA is paid at a reduced (or nil) rate during a set 'sanction period'. There are four levels of sanctions (see below). The amount of the benefit reduction and the length of the sanction period depend on which work-related requirement you failed to meet. Special rules apply to the length of the sanction period if you are aged 16 or 17.

If you are entitled to UC, the reduction in your benefit is applied to your UC, even if the sanction was in respect of your JSA or ESA claim. See p982 for information about applying a sanction to another benefit if your circumstances change. The days in your sanction period count towards your days of entitlement to new-style JSA or new-style ESA, even if you are not actually paid any benefit. For example, if you are entitled to 365 days of new-style ESA and are sanctioned for 14 days, you only receive it for 351 days.

| *Work-related requirement* | *Level of sanction* |
|---|---|
| Failing to apply for or to accept paid work (UC and JSA only) | High |
| Ceasing paid work or losing pay for specified reasons (UC and JSA only) | High |
| Failing to be available for paid work or to take all reasonable action to get paid work (UC and JSA only) | Medium |
| Failing to meet a work-focused interview requirement (where other requirements also apply) | Low |
| Failing to meet a requirement connected to a work-related requirement | Low |
| Failing to meet a work preparation requirement | Low |
| Failing to take a particular action to get paid work (UC and JSA only) | Low |
| Failing to meet a work-related interview requirement (where no other requirements apply) (UC and ESA only) | Lowest |

We refer to things that can lead to a sanction (eg, leaving work voluntarily) as 'sanctionable actions'. The DWP may refer to the cause of a sanction as a 'sanctionable failure'.[1]

In some cases, you cannot be given a sanction if you can show you had a good reason for your actions (see p989). You may be able to get UC hardship payments (including if you are getting JSA or ESA) if you have been sanctioned.

If you disagree with a sanction decision, see p997 for information about challenging it.

**Note:** different rules apply if you have been given a sanction because of a benefit offence (see p1111).

## High level sanctions

If you are getting UC or new-style JSA, you can be given a high level sanction if you are in the 'all work-related requirements group' (see p959) and you:[2]

- fail to apply for a particular vacancy or accept an offer of paid work without a good reason (see below); *or*
- cease paid work or lose pay voluntarily without a good reason or because of misconduct (see p973); *or*
- fail to take part in a prescribed work placement.

6

### Failing to apply for or to accept paid work

You can be given a high level UC or new-style JSA sanction if, without a good reason:[3]

- you are told to apply for a particular vacancy for paid work and you do not do so, or you fail to take up paid work when it is offered to you (see p945). **Note:** if the vacancy was available because of a strike, you cannot be given a sanction;[4] *or*
- you failed to take up an offer of paid work before you claimed UC (or JSA). For UC, you must be subject to all the work-related requirements (see p959) when you are awarded UC. For both UC and JSA, no reduction in your benefit can be made if the number of days between the date you failed to take up the offer and your date of claim for UC (or JSA) is more than the sanction period that would otherwise apply.[5]

*Paid work*

**'Paid work'** for these purposes means work done for payment or for which you expect to be paid.[6]

The DWP might treat you as having refused to apply for or accept paid work if you do not arrive on time, go to the wrong place, ask an employer for unreasonable conditions or behave in such a way as to put off a prospective employer.[7] It is not a good reason to refuse paid work or fail to apply for it because you are not sure of the effect on your benefits.[8]

**Note:**

- You only have to be available for work and to look for work in locations that are no more than 90 minutes from your home.[9] You may find it difficult to show you have a good reason if your travel time is shorter than this, but if you have agreed (or tried to agree) a shorter travel to work time with your work coach, you should make this clear when you challenge the sanction (see p947).
- You may be able to show that you have a good reason for refusing a job (or applying for one) if you have previously done work of a particular type or at a particular rate of pay, you have been allowed to limit your work search to looking for work of a similar type or rate of pay (see p946), or you have agreed other limitations on the sort of work you are available for, and you refuse a job that does not meet these conditions.
- The DWP says that if you are getting UC and you refuse to accept a job with a zero-hour contract without a good reason, you can be given a sanction if the contract allows you to take up work with other employers that will lift your earnings above your individual earnings threshold (see p955). However, you should not be given a sanction if the contract restricts your ability to increase your earnings with other employers.[10] Exclusivity clauses are unenforceable in law,[11] but DWP guidance suggests that such a requirement from a potential employer could mean you cannot be required to take up the job – eg, if the hours offered restrict your flexibility to increase your earnings with other employers, you should not be sanctioned for refusing.[12] You are likely to be asked for proof that your employer would prevent you from doing other work, but a contract does not necessarily have to be in writing. If you are reluctant to take a zero-hour contract because of fluctuating earnings which would make it difficult for you to budget, make your work coach aware of this and get independent advice.

6

## Ceasing paid work or losing pay

Unless any of the exceptions on p974 apply, you can be given a high level UC or new-style JSA sanction if you cease paid work or lose pay:[13]

- 'voluntarily' (see p975) and without a good reason (see p991). You have not left work voluntarily if there is a genuine redundancy situation or your contract of employment ends, even if you volunteer for redundancy (see p975); *or*
- because of misconduct (see p976). You can also be sanctioned if you are suspended from work for misconduct or if you resigned rather than be dismissed.[14]

For UC, you can be given a sanction on this ground even if you had no work-related requirements imposed on you at the time the event occurred because you were earning a sufficient amount (see p955 for the earnings thresholds), provided your ceasing work or losing pay means you are now subject to all the work-related requirements. However, if you currently have no work search requirement because you are still earning enough to have this requirement removed and you have not been selected for an 'in-work pilot scheme' (see p962), you cannot be sanctioned (see below).

For both UC and JSA, you can be given a sanction on this ground if you ceased the paid work or lost pay before your claim for UC (or JSA). For UC, to be given a sanction on this ground, you must be subject to all the work-related requirements when you are awarded UC (see p948). However, for both UC and JSA, no reduction in your benefit can be made if the number of days between the date you ceased work or lost pay and your date of claim for UC (or JSA) is more than the sanction period that would otherwise apply.[15]

If you are self-employed, you are not sanctioned for giving up paid work or losing pay.[16] The DWP decides whether you are still gainfully self-employed, looking at all the circumstances – eg, whether a drop in income is part of your normal pattern of work.[17] If it decides that you are still self-employed, you may be treated as having more income than you actually earn (see p130). If you stop self-employment completely because of the application of this rule (the 'minimum income floor'), you should not be sanctioned.

For what may happen if you take retirement, see p977.

### Exceptions

For UC only, you cannot be given a sanction on this ground (even if you cease paid work or lose pay voluntarily or because of misconduct) if your monthly earnings (or, if you are a joint claimant, your joint monthly earnings) are still above the amount that means a work search requirement cannot be imposed on you at the present time (see p962), unless you have been selected to take part in an 'in-work pilot scheme'. If you are in an in-work pilot scheme, you can be sanctioned for ceasing work or losing pay which takes your earnings below a higher amount (see p954).[18]

For both UC and new-style JSA, you cannot be given a sanction (even if you cease paid work or lose pay voluntarily) if:[19]

- you volunteer or accept your employer's proposal for redundancy (see p975); *or*
- you are allowed to limit the number of hours you are available for work and are looking for work (see p942), you take up paid work (or more hours of paid work) for more hours than that limit and you cease that paid work (or doing the higher hours) or lose pay within a trial period. 'Trial period' is not defined in the rules, but the DWP says it is a period of 56 days starting on the 29th day and ending on the 84th day on which you took up paid work (or more hours).[20] You can argue that anything that can reasonably be described as a trial period should count; *or*
- you ceased paid work or lost pay because of a strike; *or*
- you ceased paid work as a member of the regular or reserve armed forces, or lost pay in that capacity; *or*

- you have been laid off or kept on short-time work by your employer for at least four consecutive weeks (or for six weeks in a 13-week period). You must have applied for redundancy pay within a specified time.[21]

### Leaving a job or losing pay voluntarily

If you are getting UC or new-style JSA, you can be given a high level sanction if you leave your job or lose pay 'voluntarily' without a good reason (see p991).

#### *Voluntarily*

**'Voluntarily'** is not defined in the rules, but the DWP says it means that you have brought the situation about by your own acts and of your own free will.[22] You have not left your employment (or lost pay) voluntarily if you had no choice in the matter or there is convincing evidence (eg, medical evidence from your GP) that you were not responsible for your actions. You have not lost pay voluntarily if your hours under a zero-hour contract are reduced because you worked for another employer to gain more hours.[23]

If you are thinking of reducing your hours for a good reason (eg, because of your caring responsibilities or health), speak to your work coach first and make a written record of your conversations. It is unclear whether you would be regarded as having voluntarily lost pay in this situation. You may be expected to explore other options first – eg, investigating the availability and costs of childcare, or asking your employer for flexible working arrangements.

You are likely to be treated as giving up your job voluntarily if:

- you resign giving notice. If you genuinely believed that your employer was about to end your employment or you were given the 'choice' of resignation or dismissal, you have not left your job voluntarily, but the DWP may then consider whether you lost your job through misconduct (see p976);
- your employer gives you notice to end your employment but then cancels or suspends it, but you decide not to continue in the employment, if it is clear that you have a genuine choice to remain.[24] However, the circumstances may mean you have a good reason.

You have *not* left your job voluntarily if:

- you volunteer, or accept your employer's proposal, for redundancy, even if you were offered, or could have applied for, alternative jobs with the same employer.[25] This only applies if there is a redundancy situation at your workplace – eg, if a whole factory or department is closing down or if there is a cut in the number of people needed to carry out certain tasks. **Note:** if you refuse other work, you might be sanctioned for another reason – eg, refusing employment or 'neglecting to avail' yourself of an opportunity of employment;
- your employer ends your contract of employment.[26] If you left your job because your employer imposed a change in your terms or conditions without

your agreement and the new terms are less favourable than before, you may be able to argue that you have not left voluntarily, or that you had a good reason for leaving.[27] However, a pay cut alone is not a good reason to leave if your pay remains at or above the national minimum wage (see Appendix 6).

### Misconduct

'Misconduct' is not defined in the rules. However, bear the following in mind.

- You are only guilty of misconduct if your actions or omissions are 'blameworthy'. You do not have to have done anything dishonest or deliberately wrong; serious carelessness or negligence may be enough.[28]
- Everyone makes mistakes or is inefficient from time to time. So, for example, if you are a naturally slow worker who, despite making every effort, cannot produce the output your employer requires, you are not guilty of misconduct, even if the poor performance may justify your dismissal.
- The misconduct must have some connection with your employment but it does not have to occur during working hours to count. However, a sanction cannot be imposed if the actions or omissions took place before your employment began – eg, you gave inaccurate information about yourself when applying for the job.[29]

Some behaviour is clearly misconduct – eg, dishonesty (whether or not connected with your work) if it causes your employer to dismiss you because it no longer trusts you.[30] However, some behaviour is not necessarily misconduct.

- A refusal to carry out a reasonable instruction by an employer is not misconduct if you had a good reason or you refused because of a genuine misunderstanding.[31]
- You should not be treated as losing a job because of misconduct if you are dismissed for 'whistleblowing' – ie, for disclosing wrongful behaviour which was in the public interest to disclose. However, you might be guilty of misconduct if you have not reported the matter through the proper channels.[32]
- Bad timekeeping and failing to report in time that you are sick might amount to misconduct – eg, if you were persistently late or failed to report that you were sick on a number of occasions.
- Breaking the rules about personal conduct might be misconduct, depending on the seriousness of the breach. A breach of a trivial rule might not be misconduct.[33]
- Refusing to work overtime is misconduct if you were under a duty to work overtime when required and the request to do it was reasonable.

Although evidence from your employer is considered, the fact that it did not describe your actions as 'misconduct' does not guarantee that you will not be given a sanction.

If there is medical evidence that you had a mental illness and you were not responsible for your actions at the time of the alleged misconduct, the DWP decision maker should not impose a sanction.[34]

### Whether misconduct caused the loss of employment or pay

Your misconduct need not be the only cause of the loss of your employment or pay, but it must be an immediate and substantial reason.[35] If your misconduct was not the real reason for your dismissal (eg, your employer used this as an excuse but really only wanted to reduce staff numbers), you should not be sanctioned.

If you believe your dismissal was unreasonable or an overreaction on your employer's part, get advice to see whether you might have a case for unfair dismissal at an employment tribunal. You should tell the DWP if you are seeking advice and/or taking action against your employer.

If there was misconduct, the exact way you lost your employment is not important. You may be summarily dismissed, be dismissed with notice or resign as an alternative to possible dismissal.[36]



### Relationship with unfair dismissal and other proceedings

Sometimes the same facts have to be considered by other bodies such as employment tribunals and the criminal courts. The questions and legal tests that other bodies use may not be the same as those which apply to benefits.

DWP decision makers, the First-tier Tribunal and employment tribunals are independent of each other; decisions made by one are not binding on the other. This means:

- a finding by an employment tribunal that a dismissal was fair does not prevent the DWP decision maker or the First-tier Tribunal from concluding that you did not lose your job through misconduct;[37]
- although the First-tier Tribunal normally accepts a criminal conviction as proof that you have done what is alleged, it must go on to consider whether this was connected with your employment, whether it amounts to misconduct and whether the misconduct was the reason why you lost your employment;
- the DWP decision maker or the tribunal does not have to wait for the outcome of other proceedings before making a decision, but they are more likely to do so if there is a conflict of evidence.

### Taking retirement

If you take retirement, you might be treated as having left your job voluntarily.[38] Under employment law, your employer cannot usually make you retire at any particular age, so taking retirement is your own choice. However, you might be able to show you have a good reason – eg, if you can show that the work was getting too much for you because of your age or your health. If you have retired early due to ill health, you may need to submit fit notes at the beginning of your claim while you are waiting for a work capability assessment (see p959).

Employers sometimes have special early retirement schemes allowing you to take your occupational pension at an earlier age than normal, often to deal with a redundancy situation. In this case, you come under the special rules about redundancy (see p975). Employers often try to avoid using the word 'redundancy' and you may have to prove that a redundancy situation existed.

If you take early retirement under some other special scheme, you cannot show you have a good reason merely because your action was in your employer's interest.[39]

## Medium level sanctions

If you are getting UC or new-style JSA, you can be given a medium level sanction if you have a work search and/or work availability requirement (see p959) and, without a good reason, you:[40]

- do not take all reasonable action to get paid work, more paid work or better paid work (see p941); *or*
- are not available for work (see p945).

You should keep detailed records of your work search and be able to prove what you have done to look for work (see p943). If there are particular reasons why you cannot take your expected steps to seek work (eg, because of illness or caring responsibilities), or you think your work-related responsibilities are unreasonable for your circumstances, make sure you tell the DWP as soon as possible and keep a record of this. For more tactics to avoid sanctions, see p970.

## Low level sanctions

If you are getting UC, new-style JSA or new-style ESA, you can be given a low level sanction if, without a good reason, you:[41]

- fail to meet a work-focused interview requirement (see p939). **Note:** for UC and ESA, this does not apply if you are *only* required to meet a work-focused interview requirement and have no other work-related requirements. In this case, you can be given a lowest level sanction instead (see p979); *or*
- fail to meet a requirement to participate in interviews, provide information or evidence, confirm your compliance (eg, by completing a task on your online 'to do' list) or report a change in your circumstances that is relevant to whether work-related requirements can be imposed on you or to your compliance with a work-related requirement; *or*
- fail to meet a work preparation requirement (see p940) – eg, you refuse to do a community work placement or to go on a training scheme or employment programme. Failure to participate, even if you attend a work preparation activity, could also be a failure to meet a work preparation requirement – eg, if you fail to confirm your identity without a good reason, this could be a failure to participate;[42] *or*

- for UC and JSA only, fail to take any particular action specified by the DWP to get paid work, more paid work or better paid work (see p941).

For ESA, to be given a low level sanction, you must be required to meet a work preparation requirement *and* a work-focused interview requirement (see p957). For UC, you must be required to meet all the work-related requirements, or meet a work preparation requirement and a work-focused interview requirement.

A low level sanction should not be applied unless you have been notified clearly about what you must do and the consequences of not complying.[43] Details of the specific appointment for a work-focused interview and its purpose (ie, the type of interview), including the date, time and place, as well as the consequences of failing to attend, must have been given to you.[44]

***How quickly do you have to contact the DWP?***

The rules do not specify when you must contact the DWP to explain your reasons if you have failed to do any of the above. However, to avoid a sanction decision being made, you should contact the DWP as soon as possible and provide as much information as you can to show you had a good reason. The DWP may contact you (this may be via your journal if you are on UC) and ask for additional information (see p995), which you should provide if possible. If it was unclear what your work-related requirements were (eg, you did not realise you had to participate in an interview), state this and consider making a complaint.

### Lowest level sanctions

If you are getting UC or new-style ESA, you can be given a lowest level sanction if you can only be required to meet a work-focused interview requirement (see p956) and you fail to participate in a work-focused interview without a good reason.[45] Details of the interview and the consequences of failing to attend must have been given to you. If you fail to attend or to participate, contact the DWP as soon as possible to explain.

## 2. How your benefit is reduced

If you are given a sanction, your benefit is paid at a reduced (or nil) rate until the sanction period (see p983) ends. The reduction for each universal credit (UC) assessment period or each benefit week for new-style jobseeker's allowance (JSA) and new-style employment and support allowance (ESA) is calculated as follows.[46]

- **Step 1:** take the number of days in the assessment period or benefit week (or, if lower, the total number of outstanding days in the sanction period). Deduct any days in the assessment period/benefit week for which the sanction period

has been suspended because you have also been given a sanction for a benefit offence (see p982).
- **Step 2:** multiply the number of days in Step 1 by the relevant daily reduction rate. See below for UC, p982 for JSA and p981 for ESA.

For UC, the amount in Step 2 is adjusted so that it is not more than your standard allowance (see p67) or, if you are a joint claimant and only one of you has been sanctioned, so that it is not more than 50 per cent of your standard allowance. The reduction in your UC is made after the benefit cap has been applied, if relevant (see p1025).

## Universal credit

For UC, the daily reduction rate is normally the amount of standard allowance that applies to you multiplied by 12 and divided by 365 (the 'high rate').[47] However, the daily reduction is 40 per cent of this amount (the 'low rate') if, at the end of the assessment period for which the reduction is being calculated:[48]
- you do not have to meet any work-related requirements (see p950) because you:
  - are the responsible carer or responsible foster parent of a child under one;
  - are pregnant and there are 11 weeks or less before the week your baby is due;
  - had a baby not more than 15 weeks ago (including if the baby was stillborn);
  - are adopting a child and it is no more than 52 weeks since the child was placed with you; *or*
- you can only be required to meet a work-focused interview requirement (see p956); *or*
- you are 16- or 17-years-old.

If you are in a couple and are a joint claimant, the daily rate using the calculation above is divided by two.[49] If your partner is also given a sanction, the daily reduction rate that applies to them is divided by two. The chart below shows the daily reduction rate for a couple if only one of you has been sanctioned.

The daily reduction rate is nil if, at the end of the assessment period for which the reduction is being calculated, you do not have to meet any work-related requirements because you have limited capability for work and work-related activity (see p954).[50]

The daily reduction rates are rounded down to the nearest 10 pence.[51]

*Daily reduction rates*

| | *High rate* *£ per day* | *Low rate* *£ per day* |
|---|---|---|
| **Single** | | |
| Under 25 | 10.40 | 4.10 |
| 25 or over | 13.10 | 5.20 |
| **Couple** | | |
| Both under 25 | 8.10 | 3.20 |
| Either 25 or over | 10.30 | 4.10 |

**Note:** you may still be entitled to some UC during the assessment period – ie, if you qualify for elements for children or any other elements, such as for childcare or housing costs. However, any deductions from benefit still apply (see p1033).

*Example*

Marcel and his partner are both aged 35 and are getting UC as joint claimants. They live in rented accommodation. Marcel was given a 182-day high level sanction. There are 150 days outstanding in Marcel's sanction period. This month is a 30-day assessment period. His partner was not given a sanction.

**Step 1:** the relevant number of days is 30, as this is lower than the number of outstanding days in Marcel's sanction period.

**Step 2:** the daily rate is £10.30. The reduction is therefore 30 x £10.30 = £309

50 per cent of Marcel's standard allowance is £314.05 (£628.10 ÷ 2). This is higher than the reduction.

Marcel and his partner's UC is therefore reduced by £309 over the assessment period. They continue to get the amount to which they are entitled that exceeds £309, including the help they get with their rent.

## Employment and support allowance

For new-style ESA, the daily reduction rate is normally the weekly amount of ESA to which you are entitled (not including any component) multiplied by 52 and divided by 365, rounded down to the nearest 10 pence (the 'high rate').[52]

*Daily reduction rates*

| | *High rate* *£ per day* | *Low rate* *£ per day* |
|---|---|---|
| Entitled to main phase ESA | 13.10 | 5.24 |
| Under 25, not entitled to main phase ESA | 10.30 | 4.12 |
| 25 or over, not entitled to main phase ESA | 13.10 | 5.24 |

In practice, sanctions in ESA are now very uncommon. For more details, including when the daily reduction rate is applied at a lower rate, see Chapter 47 of the 2022/23 edition of this *Handbook*.

## Jobseeker's allowance

For new-style JSA, the daily reduction rate is the weekly amount of JSA to which you are entitled multiplied by 52 and divided by 365, rounded down to the nearest 10 pence.[53]

The daily reduction rates are as follows. If you are:

- under 25: £10.30;
- 25 or over: £13.10.

In practice, sanctions in JSA are now very uncommon. For more details, see Chapter 47 of the 2022/23 edition of this *Handbook*.

6

## If your benefits change

- If you are given a UC sanction, your UC is being paid at a reduced rate when your entitlement ends, you still come under the UC system and you are entitled to new-style JSA or new-style ESA, the reduction is then made to your JSA or ESA.[54] The reduction is calculated as for JSA (see above) or ESA (see p981) and is made for the remainder of the UC sanction period. Any days between the day your entitlement to UC ends and the day your entitlement to JSA or ESA starts are deducted from the period.
- If you are given a JSA or ESA sanction under the UC system and you become entitled to UC, the reduction is made to your UC instead of your JSA or ESA.[55] It is calculated as for UC (see p980) and is made for the remainder of the JSA or ESA sanction period. Any days between the day your entitlement to JSA or ESA ends and the day your UC starts are deducted from the period.

Special rules apply if you were given a sanction while entitled to old-style JSA (or old-style ESA) before you came under the UC system. In this case, if you are now entitled to:

- JSA (or ESA) under the UC system, but not UC, you are treated as if you were given a JSA (or ESA) sanction under the UC system;[56]
- UC, you are treated as if you were given a UC sanction.[57]

In both cases, the reduction is made for the remainder of the former JSA (or ESA) sanction period, minus any days between the day your former JSA (or ESA) entitlement ended (if relevant) and your current UC, JSA or ESA entitlement starts.

# 3. The sanction period

## Length of the sanction period

Sanctions can be given for various periods, depending on your work-related requirements and what you have done or failed to do. A sanction period may be longer if you have previously been sanctioned at the same level.

| *Sanction* | *Sanction period* |
|---|---|
| **High level sanctions (UC and JSA only)** | 91 or 182 days |
| Failing to apply for or to accept paid work | |
| Ceasing paid work or losing pay for specified reasons | |
| **Medium level sanctions (UC and JSA only)** | 28 or 91 days |
| Failing to be available for paid work or to take all reasonable action to get paid work | |
| **Low level sanctions (UC, JSA and ESA)** | 'Open-ended' – until you comply with a requirement, plus a fixed period of seven, 14 or 28 days |
| Failing to meet a work-focused interview requirement (where other requirements also apply) | |
| Failing to meet a requirement connected to a work-related requirement | |
| Failing to meet a work preparation requirement | |
| Failing to take a particular action to get paid work (UC and JSA only) | |
| **Lowest level sanctions (UC and ESA only)** | 'Open-ended' – until you comply with a requirement |
| Failing to meet a work-related interview requirement (where no other requirements apply) | |

### High level sanctions

If you are given a high level sanction, it is usually imposed for 91 days. However, it is imposed for 182 days if you have previously had a 91-day high level sanction (see below).[58]

If you are given a high level UC sanction and you are 16 or 17 years old, a fixed sanction period is imposed for:[59]

- 14 days; *or*
- 28 days, if you have previously had a 14- or 28-day high level sanction.

**Longer sanction periods if you have previously been sanctioned**

You can be given a longer sanction period of 182 days (28 days if you are 16/17 years old) if you have previously had a high level sanction. For the longer sanction period to apply, your previous sanctionable action must have occurred at least 14 days, but less than 365 days, before your current sanctionable action. If you already haved more than one high level sanction, only the most recent one is considered when deciding the length of a new sanction.

The 365 days run from the date of the previous sanctionable action, not from the date of the decision imposing the previous sanction, which could be some time later. If the previous sanctionable action was within 14 days of the current one, the new sanction period is the same as the previous one. If it was 365 days or more before the current one, the length of the new sanction period is the same as if you were given a sanction for the first time.

For JSA, a high level UC sanction, and for UC, a high level JSA sanction which has been applied to your UC, also counts for these purposes.[60]

Sanctions you received when you were getting JSA but not under the UC system also count.

**Note:** if you are given a longer sanction period, but later a previous sanction is removed (eg, by the First-tier Tribunal), ask the DWP decision maker to reduce the sanction period if relevant.[61] Appeal if they fail to do so. If you have already appealed against the later sanction, the tribunal should consider this and ensure that if it upholds the later sanction decision, the sanction period is for 91 (or 28) days.[62]

**Reduced sanction periods**

If you are given a high level sanction because you failed to accept paid work, ceased paid work or lost pay voluntarily or because of misconduct before the date of your claim, your sanction period is reduced to take account of days when you did not claim UC (or new-style JSA). It is calculated as follows and is the shorter of the following.[63]

- **Step 1:** if the job was only due to last for a limited period, work out the number of days starting with the day after the date of your current sanctionable action and ending on the day the paid work would have ended. 'Limited period' is not defined.
- **Step 2:** in any other case, work out the sanction period that would normally apply.
- **Step 3:** reduce the amount in **Step 1** or 2, as relevant, by the number of days between the date of your current sanctionable action and your date of claim (see p47 and p621).

In practical terms, this means that if you claim UC (or JSA) after the job would have ended, or you delay your claim for UC (or JSA) long enough, your benefit is not paid at a reduced (or nil) rate.[64]

*Example*

Leslie quits her job on 7 October. It was only due to last until 3 November. She claims UC on 17 November. She is given a high level sanction for the first time, so a 91-day sanction period would normally apply. However, her job was only due to last for a limited period. The number of days from 8 October to 3 November is 27 days. The number of days between 7 October and 17 November is 40 days. Leslie's sanction period is therefore reduced to nil and her UC is not paid at a reduced rate.

## Medium level sanctions

Medium level sanctions are usually imposed for 28 days. However, a medium level sanction is imposed for 91 days if you have previously had a 28-day or 91-day medium level sanction.[65]

If you are given a medium level UC sanction and you are 16 or 17 years old, a fixed sanction period applies of:[66]

- seven days; *or*
- 14 days, if you have previously had a seven- or 14-day medium level sanction.

### Longer sanction periods if you have previously been sanctioned

You can be given a longer sanction period of 91 days (14 days if you are 16 or 17 years old) if you have previously had a medium level sanction.

For the longer sanction periods to apply, the previous sanctionable action must have occurred at least 14 days, but less than 365 days, before your current sanctionable action. The 365 days run from the date of the previous sanctionable action, not from the date of the decision imposing the previous sanction, which could be some time later. If you have already had more than one medium level sanction, only the most recent one is considered when deciding on the length of a new sanction.

If the previous sanctionable action was within 14 days of the current one, the length of the new sanction period is the same as the previous one. If it was 365 days or more before the current one, the length of the new sanction period is the same as if you were given a sanction for the first time.

If you are given a sanction but later a previous sanction is removed (eg, by the First-tier Tribunal), ask the DWP decision maker to reduce the sanction period if relevant. Appeal if they fail to do so. If you have already appealed against the later sanction, the tribunal should take the removal of the previous sanction into account and ensure that if it upholds the later sanction decision, the sanction period is for 28 (or 14) days.

## Low level sanctions

If you are given a low level UC, new-style JSA or new-style ESA sanction, it is 'open-ended' – ie, imposed for a period made up of the period until you comply with the work-related requirement plus a fixed period.

**Step 1:** work out the number of days, starting on the date your sanctionable action took place and ending on the earliest of the following:[67]

- the day before the date you meet a 'compliance condition' (see below) specified by the DWP; *or*
- for UC and ESA, the day before the date you come into a category in which you no longer have to meet any work-related requirements (see p950); *or*
- the day before the date you are no longer required to take particular action specified in a work preparation requirement; *or*
- the date your entitlement to UC (or JSA or ESA) ends. For UC, this does not apply if this is because you cease to be, or become, a member of a couple.

6

*Compliance condition*

A **'compliance condition'** is:[68]

– a condition that you stop a sanctionable action – eg, if you failed to participate in an employment programme, a condition that you must participate in the programme; *or*

– a condition relating to your future compliance with a work-related requirement (or a requirement connected to one) – eg, if you failed to attend an interview about your work-related requirements, a condition that you must attend and participate in such an interview. Official guidance says that if you get in contact to arrange a new interview date as soon as reasonably possible and then attend that interview, you will have met the compliance condition on the day that you got in touch to arrange the interview.[69]

The DWP should inform you immediately of the consequences of not meeting the condition.

**Step 2:** work out the fixed sanction period.

- For UC, if you are at least 18 years old, and for JSA or ESA, this is usually for seven days. However, the period is:[70]
  - 14 days, if you have previously had a seven-day low level sanction; *or*
  - 28 days, if you have previously had a 14-day or 28-day low level sanction.
- For UC, if you are 16 or 17 years old, this is for seven days, but only if you have been given a low level sanction previously (see p987).[71] If you have not been given a low level sanction previously (or it is not taken into account – see p987), there is no fixed period and your sanction lasts only until you meet the compliance condition.

**Step 3:** add the number of days in Steps 1 and 2 together. This is your low level sanction period.

### *What can you do to limit the length of a low level sanction period?*

If the DWP does not make a decision to give you a sanction until some time after your sanctionable action, you might not have a compliance condition to meet until you are given the sanction. The DWP is still likely to say that your indefinite sanction period starts from when your sanctionable action occurred. Try to argue that you have already complied with the condition before you were given the sanction – eg, if you are given a sanction because you failed to provide your CV on a specified date, but you provided one later. Provide any relevant information and evidence to prove you have already complied. You could also complain about the time the DWP took to decide to give you a sanction (see Chapter 55). If there was any confusion about what you were required to do at the time of the sanctionable action and in the period before the DWP accepts that you complied with the condition, explain this when challenging the sanction and/or complaining.

## Longer sanction periods if you have previously been sanctioned

You can be given a longer sanction period if you have previously had a low level sanction. For the longer sanction periods to apply, the previous sanctionable action must have occurred at least 14 days, but less than 365 days, before your current sanctionable action. If you have already had more than one low level sanction, only the most recent one is considered when deciding the length of a new sanction.

The 365 days run from the date of the previous sanctionable action, not from the date of the decision imposing the previous sanction, which could be some time later. If the previous sanctionable action was within 14 days of the current one, the length of the new sanction period is the same as the previous one. If it was 365 days or more before the current one, the length of the new sanction period is the same as if you were given a sanction for the first time.

**Note:** if you are given a sanction but later a previous sanction is removed (eg, by the First-tier Tribunal), ask the DWP decision maker to reduce the sanction period if relevant.[72] Appeal if they fail to do so. If you have already appealed against the later sanction, the tribunal should take the removal of the previous sanction into account.[73]

## Lowest level sanctions

If you are given a lowest level sanction, it can be 'open-ended' – ie, imposed indefinitely. It is imposed for the number of days starting on the date your sanctionable action took place and only ends on the earliest of:[74]

- the day before the date you meet a 'compliance condition' specified by the DWP (see p986 for the meaning). If it was not made clear to you what you had to do, or it was difficult to rearrange the work-focused interview, you should include that in your good reason when challenging the length of the sanction, and complain; *or*

- the day before the date you come into a category in which you no longer have to meet any work-related requirements (see p950); *or*
- the date your entitlement to UC (or ESA) ends. For UC, this does not apply if this is because you cease to be, or become, a member of a couple.

## When the sanction period starts and ends

For all levels of sanction, the sanction period starts:[75]

- for UC, on the first day of the assessment period in which the decision is made to give you a sanction or, if your UC was not reduced for the sanction during that period, from the first day of the next assessment period;
- for new-style JSA and new-style ESA, if you have not been paid or the benefit week in which the sanctionable action took place, on the first day of that benefit week, or if you have been paid for that week, the first day of the benefit week after the last benefit week for which you were paid.



However, if your benefit is already being paid at a reduced rate because of a previous sanction, it is not reduced for a new sanction until the previous reduction ends.

Once a sanction period has begun, it continues unbroken until the sanction period comes to an end.[76] This means, for example, that if you take a job for a short period but then claim UC (or JSA or ESA) again during the period of the sanction, although you are still caught by the sanction, this is only for any days still outstanding in the sanction period.

If your UC (or JSA or ESA) entitlement ends before the DWP decision maker has decided to give you a sanction, but the decision to do so is made when you are again entitled to the benefit, the decision is treated as having been made on the day before your previous entitlement ended.[77] So, in practice, the number of days between the two awards of benefit are deducted from the sanction period.

A sanction is suspended for any period during which you are sanctioned for a benefit offence (see p1111).[78]

## If you have more than one sanction at the same time

Your sanction period is worked out for each sanction you are given. If more than one decision to sanction you is made at the same time, or you are sanctioned when your benefit is already reduced because of a sanction, the sanction periods run consecutively. If your benefit is already being paid at a reduced rate because of a previous sanction, it is not reduced for a new sanction until the previous reduction ends.[79]

The maximum outstanding sanction period for all sanctions is 1,095 days. So, if a new sanction is imposed when you already have an existing sanction, the sanction period is adjusted to ensure the outstanding period for all your sanctions will not exceed the 1,095-day limit.[80]

### When a sanction is terminated

All sanctions terminate and your benefit is no longer paid at a reduced (or nil) rate if, since the date of the most recent sanctionable action, you have been in paid work for (or for periods that total) at least six months (for UC) or 26 weeks (for JSA or ESA).[81] You count as being in paid work if:

- for UC, your monthly earnings during the six months are at least the amount of your individual earnings threshold (see p955). This includes if you are treated as having a minimum level of self-employed earnings under the rules described on p130;
- for UC, you do not have to satisfy any work-related requirements for any of the reasons listed on p950 and p956 (other situations) and your monthly earnings during the six months are at least 16 times the minimum wage for a person of your age multiplied by 52 and divided by 12;
- for JSA, your weekly earnings are at least what you would earn for the number of hours you are expected to work (see p942) at the minimum wage for a person of your age;
- for ESA, your weekly earnings are at least 16 times the minimum wage for a person your age.



## 4. Good reasons for your actions

In a number of situations, a sanction cannot be imposed if you have a good reason for your actions. **'Good reason'** is not defined in the rules, but both universal credit (UC) caselaw on 'good reason' and older caselaw on 'good cause' in the benefit system can be applied.[82] In addition, what may count as good reason is set out in guidance.[83] If you appeal against the sanction decision, the guidance is not binding on the First-tier Tribunal. It must make up its own mind about what counts as a good reason.

It is up to you to show you have a good reason, but the DWP decision maker should consider all all the circumstances.

***How much time are you given to explain your good reasons?***

You should always be given the opportunity to provide your reasons for what you did or did not do. You should be given sufficient time to explain your reasons and to provide relevant evidence. There are no specified time limits, but the DWP says you should be given at least five working days if the information is requested by post. You may be given less time than this if you can be contacted by phone, in person or by electronic means. The DWP says that you should be given more time if you have to get information or evidence from someone else, you have a representative, or you have a health condition or there are other temporary circumstances (eg, caring responsibilities) that prevent you from replying.[84] The time you are given should reflect your circumstances. If the time you are given seems unreasonable, you should mention this when you challenge the sanction decision and/or complain.

For ideas about what might count as a good reason, see below.

## Circumstances that should be taken into account

The DWP decision maker should take all your circumstances into account when deciding whether you have a good reason for any sanctionable action. This should include the following.

- Any restrictions or limitations you have been allowed to place on your availability for work, including reductions to your expected hours of work (see p942), or restrictions which should have been made if your circumstances had been fully taken into account.[85] You may have taken all 'reasonable action' given your circumstances at the time (see p941).
- Any condition you have or any personal circumstances that suggest that a particular job or activity would be likely to cause you unreasonable physical or mental stress or significant harm to your health.
- A disease or physical/mental disability that affects your ability to work or to meet your work-related requirements, or which means your health (or the health of others) would have been at risk.
- You misunderstood what you had to do because of language, learning or literacy difficulties, or because you were misled by the DWP. Instructions about work preparation and work-related activity must be clear.[86] There must be notification of the work-related requirement and an explanation of the consequences of non-compliance.[87] Ignorance of the law may sometimes mean that you have a good reason, but you are expected to make reasonable enquiries of your work coach if you do not understand what you have to do.[88] If you do not know about a requirement (eg, you do not receive notification of a work-focused interview), you have good reason for not complying with it.[89] However, you are expected to check your UC online account, including messages on your journal, where reasonable. If you were unable to do this, you should explain why.
- You (or someone for whom you care) were attending a medical, dental or other important appointment which it would have been unreasonable to rearrange.
- You have experienced domestic abuse, bullying or harassment.
- You have a sincerely held religious or conscientious objection.[90]
- Caring responsibilities that make it unreasonable for you to meet your work-related requirements or continue in work, including whether suitable childcare would have been (or was) reasonably available.[91] You are expected to consider available childcare options and give reasons if they are not suitable.

- You are homeless.[92] You may also be able to argue that your work coach should have suspended your work-related requirements during a period of homelessness.
- Any transport difficulties.
- Excessive travelling time involved, including where this is excessive because of your health or caring responsibilities (but see below for when this does not count as a good reason).
- Unreasonably high work expenses (eg, for childcare or travel) that were (or would be) unavoidable.[93]

Account should also be taken of any other factor that appears relevant. See, in particular, p995 for when the terms of a job on offer break the law on minimum working conditions.

**Note:** there are situations where the work search requirement for UC (and jobseeker's allowance) should be suspended temporarily (see p963). If this should have applied to you, you may not have to argue that you had a good reason for your actions. Instead, you should show why your work-related requirements were not reasonable at the time. You may still have been required to take part in work preparation (see p940), but you may be able to argue that you have a good reason for failing to do so because of the same temporary circumstances.

6

***When might you not have a good reason?***

You may find it difficult to show that you have a good reason for failing to apply for, or accept, paid work on the grounds of distance if your travel time is shorter than 90 minutes. This is because you have to be available for work and to look for work in locations that are up to 90 minutes from your home.[94] However, there could be other factors such as childcare or high travelling expenses, which can be considered when deciding whether you had a good reason, and in some cases the DWP should consider whether a shorter travel to work time should be allowed (see p947). Although not specified, it is probable that travel time of up to 90 minutes to attend work-related activity or an interview would also not be seen as a good reason, but all the other relevant factors (including childcare, expenses and the effect on your health) should be taken into account.

## Leaving a job or reducing your hours

You may be able to show you have a good reason for leaving a job or reducing your hours in the following situations.

- Your chances of getting other employment, including self-employment, were good, there were strong reasons for leaving your job and you acted reasonably in doing so.[95]
- You genuinely did not know or were mistaken about the conditions of the job (eg, it was beyond your physical or mental capacity, or was harmful to your

health), you gave it a fair trial before leaving and it was reasonable for you to leave when you did.[96]

- You left your job or reduced your hours for personal or domestic reasons – eg, to look after a sick relative.[97] Explain why you left your job before looking for, or getting, alternative employment. It could be helpful to show that you tried to negotiate an arrangement with your employer to resolve the problem – eg, for a reduction in your hours or time off work.
- You left your job to move with your partner who has taken a job elsewhere.[98] Relevant factors may include how important it was to your partner's career to move and your chances of finding work in the new area.
- Your employer changed the terms and conditions of your employment in a way that does not amount to your contract of employment ending. You are expected to use any grievance procedure first. In some situations (eg, with a zero-hour contract), a reduction in hours may be part of your contract of employment because your hours are not guaranteed. You should not be sanctioned if the reduction in hours is not voluntary (see p975).
  If you leave your job because your employer cuts your wages unilaterally, you might not be able to show you have a good reason. The DWP does not consider a wage cut a good reason unless it takes you below the national minimum wage (see Appendix 6), but a cut in wages may be a good reason if, for example, you are not given proper notice of an imposed change to your pay, or your work-related expenses are now an unreasonably high proportion of your pay. If you stay in your job, a cut in wages is a reduction in pay, but may not be voluntary (see p975).
- You left your job because of a firm offer of alternative employment, but claimed benefit because the offer fell through. However, the DWP may say you do not have a good reason if the offer was cancelled before you left your previous employment or you changed your mind and did not take the new job and you could have stayed in the existing employment, or you did not ask your employer if you could stay.

The DWP decision maker should take into account:

- any caring responsibilities you have which made it unreasonable for you to stay in your job and whether suitable childcare was (or could have been) available; *and*
- any childcare expenses you had to pay as a result of being in the job, if they were an unreasonably high proportion of the income you received.

***What should you do before you give up a job or reduce your hours?***

1. Do everything possible to resolve problems before you give up your job. If the conditions of a job are poor, try to sort out any problems (eg, by raising them with your employer or using any grievance procedure) rather than leaving immediately, and look for another job

seriously before giving one up. Keep a record of your negotiations with your employer. You may have difficulty showing you have a good reason if you do not do so.
2. Employers must provide certain minimum working conditions and pay the minimum wage. These could help to show that you have a good reason for giving up work. Point out that the Working Time Regulations 1998 intend to protect workers' health and safety, so conditions that do not comply with them should be regarded as unacceptable. Your employer should also comply with the Equality Act 2010 and make reasonable adjustments if you are disabled.
3. If you need to reduce your hours because of your health or caring responsibilities or other reasons, make sure that you have a record of your request to your employer and any other adjustments you have asked for before the reduction in hours. If possible, negotiate with your employer rather than leaving the job. Seek employment advice about your rights to flexible working.
4. You are likely to have difficulty showing you have a good reason for leaving a job or reducing your hours just because the pay is low (although your work-related expenses should be taken into account).[99] However, you can argue that this does not apply if you left your job because your employer refused to pay the national minimum wage.[100]



## Leaving or failing to participate in work preparation or work-related activity

You should be given clear instructions about where to attend for work-related activity and the consequences of failing to participate. For example, if it is not clear that the activity is mandatory, or you do not understand what you are supposed to do and when, you may have a good reason for failing to participate. You may not have a good reason simply because you consider that the work preparation or work related activity is not useful or relevant to your needs, but you could consider complaining. You are unlikely to have a good reason for failing to participate if you refuse to confirm your identity because of data protection concerns and you do not offer another acceptable form of evidence of identity.[101]

You may be able to show you have a good reason for leaving a particular work related activity (eg, a training scheme or employment programme) or for failing to participate in work preparation or work-related activity (see p990). The DWP decision maker should consider the following.

- Your continued participation would have put your health and safety, or that of others, at risk.
- The travelling time to or from the scheme or programme was excessive (although not listed as a good reason in guidance, this could relate to other good reasons such as your health).
- You had caring responsibilities, no one else was available to provide the care, and it was not practical to make other arrangements.

- Temporary circumstances made it difficult for you to participate – eg, you were attending court as a party to the proceedings, a witness or a juror, you were crewing or launching a lifeboat, or you were on duty as a part-time member of a fire brigade.
- You were arranging or attending the funeral of a close relative or a close friend.
- You had to deal with a domestic emergency.
- You were having structured alcohol or drug dependency treatment.

**Note:** there are temporary circumstances in which the work search requirement in UC should be lifted[102] and you may not be expected to be available for work (see p964). However, you may still have been required to take part in work preparation. If this applied to you, you may be able to argue that your good reason relates to the same temporary circumstances, and/or that the temporary circumstances should have been taken into account in limiting the work preparation you were required to do.

6

## Refusing or failing to apply for a job

You may be able to show you have a good reason for refusing a job – eg:

- if the travelling time to or from the job was more than 90 minutes or more than the maximum travelling time agreed with your work coach;
- if you are within your four-week 'permitted period' in which you can make limitations on the type of work and/or rate of pay for which you are available (see p946), these limitations have been agreed and you refuse a job that does not meet them;
- if you have been laid off or are on short-time working, have been accepted as available only for casual employment and you refuse to take some other type of work;[103]
- if you come under the rules that exempt you from having to be able to start work immediately, and you refuse to take a job which you would have to start immediately (see p945).

You can be sanctioned for refusing to accept a job which does not have guaranteed hours (a zero-hour contract), but you should not be sanctioned if:[104]

- your employer reduces your hours because you have taken work with another employer to gain more hours of work (or arguably, because you look for other work); *or*
- the hours offered by your employer would restrict the opportunity for you to increase your paid work with other employers.

**Note:** you cannot be given a sanction if you refuse a job because it is vacant due to a trade dispute.[105]

***What should you do before refusing or failing to apply for a job?***

Employers are required to provide certain minimum working conditions and pay the minimum wage (see Appendix 6). Try to argue that you have a good reason for not applying for any job where the terms do not comply with the legal requirements. Make sure that this is the case, particularly where the Working Time Regulations 1998 are concerned, as there are many exceptions and opt-outs that might apply. If the terms offered break the rules about the limit on the number of hours in the average working week, the DWP may suggest that you agree to an 'individual opt-out'. Argue that this would be unreasonable, as the working time rules are intended to protect the health and safety of workers. The DWP accepts that you have a good reason for refusing a job if you do so because it does not pay at least the national minimum wage that applies to you.[106] However, you are unlikely to have a good reason simply because you are unsure of the effect of work and pay on your benefits.[107] You may not have a good reason for not applying for a job simply because you believe you are unlikely to be successful. You should ask your work coach to reconsider, explaining why you think you will not get the job and suggesting other actions you could take. You are especially unlikely to have a good reason if you have previously agreed to apply for the job and did not attempt to negotiate with your work coach.[108]



## 5. Sanction decisions

A sanction can only be imposed on you when a decision has been made to do so. Sanction decisions can be challenged (see p997).

A DWP decision maker decides whether you should be given a sanction, often some time after the sanctionable action took place. Do not assume that because you have not yet been informed of any sanction, the DWP has decided not to sanction you.

You should be given notice telling you that you have been given a sanction.[109] This information should either be posted on your universal credit online journal or sent in a letter.

However, you may not realise that you have been given a sanction until your benefit is paid at a reduced (or nil) rate. You should contact the DWP as soon as you are aware of the reduction in your benefit to find out what sanctionable action is involved, give a good reason, if possible, and comply with your work-related requirements if applicable. For example, with a low level sanction (which runs until you comply with the requirement), you must be given formal notification of the decision and then, in theory, you could comply on the same day – eg, if you fail to attend an appointment, you could phone and remake the appointment on the same day – but only if you then attend and participate.

If the sanction decision is made some time after the sanctionable action, you could complain as well as challenge the sanction decision. Your 'good reason' may be affected by whether your work-related requirements were made clear to you at the time of the sanctionable action. Any compliance condition you need to meet to stop a sanction period from increasing must also be made clear to you. This may be a different requirement if the original is no longer appropriate – eg, if you failed to attend a training day which is no longer available. If your work-related requirements or the compliance condition (see p986) were not made clear, you should complain as well as challenge the sanction decision.

If you have complex needs (see below), before the sanction decision is made, you should be contacted by phone (or another method which is accessible to you) about what led to the sanction and any good reason you may have.

Only a DWP decision maker can decide whether you have a good reason for the sanctionable action and whether a sanction should be applied. However, if an employment or training scheme provider requires you to do something on behalf of the DWP,[110] failure to comply may result in a sanction. If a provider alerts the DWP about a possible sanctionable action, the DWP should ask you, in writing, for your version of events and if you have a good reason for what happened.

6

## People with complex needs

If you have complex needs, special procedures apply before your case is referred for a sanction decision. Complex needs procedures may apply if you are considered to be 'vulnerable'. This may be if you have a serious mental health condition, but can also apply if there is a language barrier, you have an addiction or you are homeless. These procedures involve extra checks before you are given a sanction, to make sure you understand your work-related requirements and to gather any reasons for what you did or did not do.

If you think that you are vulnerable because of your condition or situation, but have been given a sanction, ask whether the 'complex needs' procedures were considered, and seek advice. If you have a disability and the DWP does not follow these procedures (eg, it does ensure that you were able to comply with your work-related requirements without your health being affected), this could be a breach of the Equality Act 2010 and be a ground for judicial review of the decision for discrimination (see p1241). If you have failed to comply with a work-related requirement, the DWP should check whether you have complex needs before referring your case for a sanction decision.[111] If you have complex needs or a health condition which affects your ability to understand your work-related requirements, at least two attempts should be made to make a home visit, and a sanction referral should not be considered unless the home visit and all other attempts to contact you have failed.[112] Also, if there is a risk of harm or abuse, a case conference should be held before any further action is taken. If the sanction decision is passed to a decision maker and the evidence shows the requirements were unreasonable at the time of your sanctionable action, the decision maker should accept that you had a good reason and return the case to the DWP for your requirements to be reduced.[113]

## 6. Challenging a sanction decision

It is very often worth challenging a sanction decision. You can challenge:

- the decision to give you a sanction, including:
  - whether you have lawfully been required to do something: whether you have been properly notified of any requirements and the consequences of not complying – eg, to attend an interview or participate in work-related activity. Your work-related requirements must have been made clear to you,[114] and you should also make it clear if you considered your requirements to be unreasonable given your circumstances;
  - whether you failed to do something, or did something, as alleged by the DWP;
  - whether you have a good reason (see p989) for what you did or did not do;
- the length of the sanction period – eg, if there is a dispute about the number of times you have been sanctioned, or you are challenging a previous decision to give you a sanction.

6

You can apply for a revision or appeal against a sanction decision in the usual way (see Chapters 50 and 51).

You should also consider complaining if the actions of the DWP contributed to the sanction and/or the sanction length – eg, if your work-related requirements were not made clear to you, or you did not get notification until some time after the sanctionable action, which made it difficult for you to comply and end the sanction period.

If you have been given a sanction more than once, you should challenge *all* the decisions if possible. Apply for a mandatory reconsideration of all the sanction decisions. If you are not sure about the number or length of the sanctions, ask the DWP to clarify what decisions have been made.

If a previous sanction is removed (eg, by a decision maker or the First-tier Tribunal), the sanction period for a later sanction of the same type can be reduced.[115] If you have appealed against the later sanction, the tribunal should take the removal of the previous sanction into account.[116]

You must apply for a mandatory reconsideration before you can appeal. You can ask for a sanction decision to be revised, even if it was made a long time ago, as it can be revised at any time (see p1136).

You must be given written notice of the sanction decision, setting out your appeal rights.[117] Although notification of sanction decisions is meant to happen automatically when the sanction is applied to your benefit, this does not always happen. If you were given a sanction but did not receive written notice of the decision, get advice. You may still be able to ask for a mandatory reconsideration and then appeal, even if the decision was made a long time ago.

If you have received a decision letter with a postal address, you can send your request for a mandatory reconsideration to the address on the letter and/or hand it in to the job centre (if possible, do both). You can state that you want a mandatory reconsideration on your online universal credit journal. However, it is advisable to follow this up by phone and in writing if possible – eg, you may not be able to upload all the evidence you want to send via your journal. Ensure that your request for a mandatory reconsideration is acknowledged and keep a copy of your application (including a screenshot if you request it via your journal). Even if you post it on your journal, provide a copy to the job centre as soon as possible, making a note of the date and time you do so. If you do not have an online journal, you can request a mandatory reconsideration by phone or in writing. Make it clear that you are formally requesting a mandatory reconsideration and keep proof of your request.

6

You should apply for a revision of *all* outstanding sanction decisions made against you, including those which will not be applied until your existing sanction period is over. If you decide to appeal once you have a mandatory reconsideration notice (see p1168), you can ask for related sanction decisions to be considered in the same appeal hearing.

***How can you increase your chances of getting a decision changed?***

1. An appeal to the First-tier Tribunal gives you a chance to challenge the DWP's version of events, including the evidence it is using from your former employer or a work-related activity scheme provider. You should ask the DWP for all the information and documents that were used to make the sanction decision. If the DWP does not provide these, the tribunal can be asked to direct it to do so (see p1188). As you must usually request a mandatory reconsideration first, any information you can supply to the DWP at that point is useful, in case you can get the decision changed quickly. If a mandatory reconsideration is refused, you can still use the same arguments at an appeal.

2. Ask for a hearing and attend it if you can. Explain your case fully and, if relevant, the good reasons for what you did or failed to do (see p989), including any factors relating to your own situation and/or how the sanction was notified to you.

3. Provide as much evidence as you can to support your case – eg, evidence about your caring responsibilities. The tribunal can allow witnesses (eg, family members or former work colleagues) to give evidence on your behalf.

**Note:** if you do not attend the appeal hearing and the DWP submits further evidence or information about you, the tribunal should consider an adjournment to allow you to attend, or to respond to the information/evidence.

# Notes

1. **When you can be sanctioned**
   1 **UC** Reg 100(1) UC Regs
   **JSA** Reg 17 JSA Regs 2013
   **ESA** Reg 50 ESA Regs 2013
   2 **UC** s26 WRA 2012; reg 114 UC Regs
   **JSA** s6J JSA 1995; reg 29 JSA Regs 2013
   3 **UC** s26(2)(b) and (c) and (4)(a) WRA 2012
   **JSA** s6J(2)(b) and (c) and (3)(a) JSA 1995
   4 **UC** Reg 113(1)(a) UC Regs
   **JSA** Reg 28(1)(a) JSA Regs 2013
   5 **UC** Reg 113(1)(e) UC Regs
   **JSA** Reg 28(1)(c) JSA Regs 2013
   6 R(IS) 5/95
   7 para K3057 ADM
   8 *S v SSWP* [2017] UKUT 477 (AAC)
   9 **UC** Reg 97(3) UC Regs
   **JSA** Reg 14(2) JSA Regs 2013
   10 paras K3271-75 ADM
   11 s27A Small Business, Enterprise and Employment Act 2015
   12 para K2301 ADM
   13 **UC** s26(2)(d), (3) and (4) WRA 2012
   **JSA** s6J(2)(d) and (3) JSA 1995
   14 R(U) 10/71; R(U) 2/76; official guidance in para K3188 ADM
   15 **UC** Reg 113(1)(e) UC Regs
   **JSA** Reg 28(1)(c) JSA Regs 2013
   16 para K2224 ADM
   17 para H4055 ADM
   18 Reg 113(1)(g) UC Regs
   19 **UC** Reg 113(1)(b)-(d) and (f) and (2) UC Regs
   **JSA** Reg 28(1)(b) and (d)-(f) and (2) JSA Regs 2013
   20 para K3213 ADM
   21 s148 Employment Rights Act 1996
   22 para K3203 ADM
   23 para K2303 ADM
   24 para K3236 ADM
   25 **UC** Reg 113(1)(f) UC Regs
   **JSA** Reg 28(1)(f) and (2) JSA Regs 2013
   26 R(U) 25/52
   27 para K2241 ADM
   28 R(U) 8/57, para 6; official guidance in para K3069 ADM
   29 R(U) 26/56; R(U) 1/58; official guidance in para K3106 ADM
   30 R(U) 10/53; official guidance in para K3181 ADM
   31 R(U) 14/56; official guidance in para K3111 ADM
   32 *AA v SSWP (JSA)* [2012] UKUT 100 (AAC), reported as [2012] AACR 42
   33 R(U) 24/56; official guidance in para K3112 ADM
   34 K3073 ADM
   35 R(U) 1/57; official guidance in para K3191 ADM
   36 R(U) 2/76
   37 R(U) 2/74
   38 R(U) 1/81; official guidance in paras K2261-64 ADM
   39 R(U) 3/81
   40 **UC** s27 WRA 2012; reg 103(1) UC Regs
   **JSA** s6K JSA 1995; reg 17 JSA Regs 2013
   41 **UC** s27 WRA 2012; reg 104(1) UC Regs
   **JSA** s6K JSA 1995; reg 17 JSA Regs 2013
   **ESA** s11J WRA 2007; reg 50 ESA Regs 2013
   42 *CS v SSWP (JSA)* [2019] UKUT 218 (AAC)
   43 *JB v SSWP (UC)* [2018] UKUT 360 (AAC)
   44 paras K1181-82 ADM
   45 **UC** s27 WRA 2012; reg 105 UC Regs
   **ESA** s11J WRA 2007; reg 50 ESA Regs 2013

2. **How your benefit is reduced**
   46 **UC** Regs 101(5) and 110 UC Regs
   **JSA** Regs 17 and 26 JSA Regs 2013
   **ESA** Regs 50 and 58 ESA Regs 2013
   47 Reg 111(1) UC Regs
   48 Reg 111(2) UC Regs
   49 Reg 111(5) UC Regs
   50 Reg 111(3) UC Regs
   51 Reg 111(4) UC Regs
   52 Reg 59 ESA Regs 2013
   53 Reg 27 JSA Regs 2013
   54 **JSA** Reg 30 JSA Regs 2013
   **ESA** Reg 61 ESA Regs 2013
   55 **UC** Reg 112 and Sch 11 paras 1 and 2 UC Regs
   **JSA** Reg 6 JSA Regs 2013
   **ESA** Reg 43 ESA Regs 2013
   56 Arts 14, 15, 17 and 18 WRA(No.9)O
   57 Regs 30 and 32 UC(TP) Regs

3. **The sanction period**
   58 Reg 102(2)(a) UC Regs
   59 Reg 102(2)(b) UC Regs

60 **UC** Sch 11 para 3 UC Regs
**JSA** Reg 19 JSA Regs 2013
61 Reg 14 UC,PIP,JSA&ESA(DA) Regs
62 CJSA/2375/2000
63 **UC** Reg 102(4) and (5) UC Regs
**JSA** Regs 17 and 19(3) JSA Regs 2013
64 **UC** Reg 113(1)(e) UC Regs
**JSA** Reg 28(1)(c) JSA Regs 2013
65 **UC** Regs 103(2)(a) and 112 and Sch 11 para 3 UC Regs
**JSA** Reg 20 JSA Regs 2013
66 Reg 103(2)(b) UC Regs
67 **UC** Reg 104(2)(a) and (3)(a) UC Regs
**JSA** Reg 21(2) JSA Regs 2013
**ESA** Reg 52(a) ESA Regs 2013
68 **UC** s27(6) and (7) WRA 2012
**JSA** s6K(6) and (7) JSA 1995
**ESA** s11J(5) and (6) WRA 2007
69 paras K1046-8 (and examples) ADM
70 **UC** Regs 104(2)(b) and 112 and Sch 11 para 3 UC Regs
**JSA** Reg 21(3) JSA Regs 2013
**ESA** Reg 52(b) ESA Regs 2013
71 Reg 104(3)(b) UC Regs
72 Reg 14 UC,PIP,JSA&ESA(DA) Regs
73 CJSA/2375/2000
74 **UC** Reg 105(2) UC Regs
**ESA** Reg 53 ESA Regs 2013
75 **UC** Reg 106 UC Regs
**JSA** Reg 22 JSA Regs 2013
**ESA** Reg 54 ESA Regs 2013
76 **UC** Reg 107(1) UC Regs
**JSA** Reg 23(1) JSA Regs 2013
**ESA** Reg 55(1) ESA Regs 2013
77 **UC** Reg 107(2) UC Regs
**JSA** Reg 23(2) and (3) JSA Regs 2013
**ESA** Reg 55(2) and (3) ESA Regs 2013
78 **UC** Reg 108 UC Regs
**JSA** Reg 24 JSA Regs 2013
**ESA** Reg 56 ESA Regs 2013
79 **UC** Reg 106(c) UC Regs
**JSA** Reg 22(c) JSA Regs 2013
**ESA** Reg 54(c) ESA Regs 2013
80 **UC** Reg 101(1)-(3) UC Regs
**JSA** Reg 18(1)-(3) JSA Regs 2013
**ESA** Reg 51(1)-(3) ESA Regs 2013
81 **UC** Reg 109 UC Regs
**JSA** Reg 25 JSA Regs 2013
**ESA** Reg 57 ESA Regs 2013

4. **Good reasons for your actions**

82 *S v SSWP (UC)* [2017] UKUT 477 (AAC)
83 Ch K2 ADM
84 paras K2011-14 ADM
85 *RR v SSWP* [2017] UKUT 459 (AAC)
86 *SSWP v DC (JSA)* [2017] UKUT 464 (AAC)
87 *JB v SSWP* [2018] UKUT 360 (AAC)
88 *S v SSWP* [2017] UKUT 477 (AAC)
89 *SP v SSWP* [2018] UKUT 227 (AAC)
90 R(JSA) 7/03 discusses the meaning of 'conscientious objection' in this context
91 para K2142 ADM
92 paras K2091-95 ADM
93 para K2157 ADM
94 **UC** Reg 97(3) UC Regs
**JSA** Reg 14(2) JSA Regs 2013
95 R(U) 4/73; official guidance in para K2291 ADM
96 R(U) 3/73; official guidance in para K2286 ADM
97 R(U) 14/52; official guidance in para K2286 ADM
98 R(U) 19/52; R(U) 4/87; CJSA/2507/2005
99 para K2157 ADM
100 para K2238 ADM
101 *CS v SSWP (JSA)* [2019] UKUT 218 (AAC)
102 Reg 99(3) UC Regs
103 paras K2175-76 ADM
104 para K2301 ADM
105 **UC** Reg 113(1)(a) UC Regs
**JSA** reg 28(1)(a) JSA Regs 2013
106 para K2213 ADM
107 *S v SSWP* [2017] UKUT 477 (AAC)
108 *KB v SSWP (UC)* [2019] UKUT 408 (AAC)

5. **Sanction decisions**

109 Reg 51 UC,PIP,JSA&ESA(DA) Regs
110 s29 WRA 2012
111 para J3257 ADM
112 DWP, *Universal Credit Guidance,* 'Home visits', v14.0, House of Commons library deposited papers, rightsnet.org.uk/resources/universal-credit-guidance
113 paras K2054-58 ADM

6. **Challenging a sanction decision**

114 *JB v SSWP (UC)* [2018] UKUT 360 (AAC)
115 Reg 14 UC,PIP,JSA&ESA(DA) Regs
116 CJSA/2375/2000
117 Reg 51 UC,PIP,JSA&ESA(DA) Regs

# Part 7

# Claiming benefits and getting paid

# Chapter 44

# Claims

**This chapter covers:**


1. Making a claim (below)
2. Who should claim (p1005)
3. Information to support your claim (p1006)
4. The date of your claim (p1011)


This chapter covers general rules on claims and backdating. See the chapter about the benefit you are claiming for the specific rules for that benefit. This chapter does not cover rules for Scottish benefits (see Chapter 68), statutory sick pay (see Chapter 35), statutory payments (see Chapter 34), social fund budgeting loans (see p701), health benefits (see Chapter 27), the other payments in Chapter 36 or discretionary housing payments (see Chapter 25). Generally, rules for housing benefit (HB) are not covered (see Chapter 10), although the national insurance number requirement described in this chapter also applies to HB.

7

### Key facts

- To be entitled to a benefit, you must usually make a claim for it.
- Depending on the benefit, you may be able to claim online, on a paper claim form, by telephone or in person.
- You must usually provide your national insurance number and any other evidence considered reasonable.
- Once you make a valid claim, a decision maker at the DWP or HMRC must make a decision on it (see Chapter 49).

## 1. Making a claim

In most cases, to be entitled to benefit, you must make a claim for it.[1] If you cannot make a claim yourself, an 'appointee' can claim on your behalf (see p1005).

**Note:** you cannot make new claims for income-related employment and support allowance (ESA). See p183 for the limited circumstances when you can make a new claim for housing benefit (HB). New claims for new-style jobseeker's allowance (JSA) and ESA under the universal credit (UC) system can still be made (see p24).

## How to make a claim

Each benefit has its own rules for making claims. See the chapter in this *Handbook* about the benefit you want to claim. You may be able to claim in writing, including online, or by telephone. You may also have to attend an interview to complete your claim, or be sent a written statement to sign and return.

***Is making a claim impractical or impossible for you?***

If starting a claim is difficult for you, explain this to the DWP or HMRC and ask to claim in a different way. For example:

- if speaking in English is difficult, an interpreter can be arranged;
- another person may be able to telephone for you, especially if you are there with them;
- if you cannot claim online, you may be able to claim by telephone;
- if you cannot claim online or by telephone, an in-person interview could take place at a local Jobcentre Plus office or a home visit arranged;
- you may be able to claim in person at an 'alternative office' (see below);
- except for UC, a paper claim form could be completed and sent.



### Alternative offices

If the DWP has made arrangements, you can get help claiming some benefits at an 'alternative office'. You can claim carer's allowance, disability living allowance, ESA, pension credit and retirement pension, and if you are over pension age (see p690) also attendance allowance and winter fuel payment, at an alternative office.[2]

***Alternative offices***[3]

'**Alternative offices**' may include some DWP offices, local authority HB offices and English county council offices. Also included are some local advice centres. If you want to claim at an alternative office, ask whether it has been designated to accept your claim.

## Amending or withdrawing your claim

You can amend your claim at any time before a decision is made by contacting the office handling it.[4] In some circumstances, your claim is amended from the date it was originally made. For example, if you claimed ESA but did not request that it be backdated (see p1011), you can amend your claim to include this request and it should be treated as made at the date of your claim. However, if you amend your claim to say that your circumstances have changed *since* you claimed (eg, a partner has moved in with you), this amendment only takes effect from the date the change happened (in this example, the date they moved in).

You can withdraw your claim at any time before a decision is made by contacting the office handling it.[5] Notice to withdraw your claim takes effect from the day it is received.

You can also amend or withdraw your claim online if you do so in an approved way.[6]

**Note:** a claim for UC affects any existing awards you have for the benefits which UC replaces (see p19). Withdrawing your claim for UC before a decision is made on it will not enable you to continue getting the benefits you were previously awarded. Get advice before claiming UC if you already receive benefits.

You can also withdraw your claim by telephoning the DWP or HMRC office handling it.

In practice, if a claim has already been decided and an award made, you can ask for the award to end (sometimes called 'withdrawing an award'). Your award should then be superseded and brought to an end (see p1143), as you should not be forced to continue receiving benefit when you have indicated that you no longer wish to do so.[7]



## 2. Who should claim

The general rule is that you, the claimant, must make the claim. For means-tested benefits other than universal credit, although you usually receive an extra amount if you have a partner, your partner is not a claimant and does not make the claim with you. The chapters on individual benefits explain who must make the claim for each benefit.

### Appointees

Someone aged 18 or over (eg, a friend or relative, or a solicitor or the representative of an organisation) can be authorised to act on your behalf if you cannot claim or manage benefits for yourself – eg, you have a severe mental health problem or a learning disability.[8] This person is called an 'appointee'. The appointee takes on your rights and responsibilities as a claimant – eg, they can make claims for benefit on your behalf and must notify changes in your circumstances. They sign claim forms and other statements on your behalf, and if they receive the benefit for you must spend it in your best interests. If benefit is overpaid, the appointee may be responsible for repaying it (see Chapter 47). Usually, the appointeeship applies from the date of the appointment, but if someone acts on your behalf and later becomes your appointee, these actions can be validated in retrospect.[9]

**Note:** if someone is already legally appointed to take care of your finances (eg, a deputy or somebody who has lasting power of attorney), you are unlikely to need an appointee.

To apply to be an appointee, the person should contact the helpline for the benefit in question – eg, for attendance allowance (AA), the AA helpline. The DWP arranges a visit to assess whether an appointee is needed, and to make sure the potential appointee is suitable. An application form (Form BF56) can be completed by the visiting officer during the assessment. If the DWP agrees with the application, it sends Form BF57 to the appointee, confirming their appointment. The appointment is effective from this time.

Only one person at any one time can be an appointee for your DWP benefits.

The appointment continues until you are clearly able to manage your benefit or the appointee no longer wishes, or is no longer able, to act for you (they should contact the DWP straight away and inform it of this). It can also be stopped if the appointee is not acting properly.

If you are an appointee for a claimant who dies, you should reapply for appointee status to settle any outstanding benefit matters.[10] An executor of a will can pursue an outstanding claim or appeal on behalf of a claimant who has died, even if the decision was made before probate is granted.[11]

If someone is your appointee for housing benefit purposes, the DWP can make them an appointee for other benefits without a written application if they agree to this.[12]



If no one has been appointed to act for you and another person makes a claim on your behalf because you cannot act, then that claim may still be valid and can be awarded.[13]

## 3. Information to support your claim

When you claim benefit, you must:

- satisfy the national insurance (NI) number requirement (see p1007); *and*
- prove your identity, if required (see p1007); *and*
- complete the claim in a way that ensures it is valid (see p1008).

If you claim correctly (see p1004) and satisfy the above criteria, you have made a 'valid claim'. You must make a valid claim as it affects your 'date of claim' (see p1011).

If your claim is accepted as valid, it is referred to a decision maker to decide whether you are entitled to benefit (see Chapter 49).

**Note:** even if your claim is valid, you can be asked for additional information and evidence before a decision is made on it (see p1009).

If your claim is not accepted as valid, you should get a decision saying so. You can ask for a mandatory reconsideration of the decision, and then appeal if the decision is not changed (see p1168).[14]

## The national insurance number requirement

To be entitled to benefit, you must usually satisfy the NI number requirement by:[15]

- providing an NI number and information or evidence showing it is yours;[16] *or*
- providing evidence or information to enable your NI number to be traced if you do not know it; *or*
- applying for an NI number if you do not have one and providing sufficient information and evidence so that one is allocated to you.

If you claim a means-tested benefit, your partner must usually also satisfy the NI number requirement (but see below for who is exempt).[17] This also applies if you are getting benefit and your partner starts living with you and so your award must be superseded.[18]

**Note:**

- If you do not need to make a claim for the benefit (eg, in some circumstances for retirement pension), the NI number requirement should not apply.
- If you cannot satisfy the NI number requirement straight away, you may be able to ask for a short-term advance of benefit (see p1023).
- If you are refused benefit because you do not satisfy the NI number requirement, you can ask for a mandatory reconsideration of the decision and then appeal if the decision is not changed (see p1168).[19]

7

### Who is exempt

You are exempt from the NI number requirement if the benefit is:

- disability living allowance (DLA) and you are under 16;[20] *or*
- housing benefit (HB) and you live in a hostel;[21] *or*
- (from 7 April 2025) child benefit and you are under 16.[22]

A child (including a qualifying young person – see p488) included in your universal credit (UC) or HB is exempt from the NI number requirement.[23] While not exempt, in practice you are not asked to provide an NI number for a child included in your pension credit (PC) claim. If you are claiming a means-tested benefit as a couple and your partner is a 'person subject to immigration control', they could be exempt from the NI number requirement in some situations (see p1288).

## Proof of identity

You may be asked to produce documents or evidence that prove your identity. If you are claiming for your partner, you may also need to prove their identity.

You can provide various documents to prove your identity including a current passport, a European Economic Area state identity card, a certificate of naturalisation as a British citizen or a letter from the Home Office. You could also produce your full birth certificate, driving licence, local council rent card, student identity card or utility bills.

You should not be refused benefit simply because you do not have a particular document, especially if it is unreasonable for you to have or get it. If you do not have a document that is asked for, explain to the decision maker why you cannot provide it, ask what they would accept instead and/or offer any other documents or evidence you have that may help prove your identity. Provide details of other people who can confirm what you have stated – eg, your solicitor, other legal representative or official organisation. If the decision maker refuses to accept what you have offered, ask that they make a decision on your claim. Failure to provide information or evidence requested by the DWP is not in itself a reason to refuse a benefit claim.[24] Failure to verify your identity does not in itself mean you are not who you say you are.[25] If your claim is refused, you can ask for a mandatory reconsideration of the decision, and then appeal if the decision is not changed (see p1168).

Some claimants may have particular difficulty getting evidence. Ask for an explanation of precisely what is required and why. Complain if you consider any requests for information are unreasonable (see Chapter 55). If you think you have experienced discrimination, get advice – eg, from a law centre or the Equality Advisory and Support Service.[26]



## Completing a valid claim

To make a valid claim, you must make it in a way that is allowed for that benefit and provide sufficient information to ensure it is valid.

You must usually attend an interview for a jobseeker's allowance (JSA) claim to be valid (see p620). For other benefits, or for JSA if you do not have to attend an interview, see below if you claimed by telephone. If you claimed in writing or online, see p1009.

**Note:** if you claim UC, you may be required to agree your claimant commitment at an interview (see p936).

### Claims by telephone

If you are allowed to claim by telephone, it is valid if you provide all the information needed during the call. If you do not, your claim is 'defective'. You are given a chance to remedy the defect.[27] For employment and support allowance (ESA) and PC only, you must also approve a written statement of your circumstances if asked to.[28]

If you supply the necessary information within a month of the date you are first notified of a defect, your claim is treated as made when you first notified your intention to claim. The decision maker can extend this one-month period if they think it is reasonable.[29]

**Note**: you usually have to claim UC online (see p1009) and can only make a telephone claim in limited circumstances if the DWP allows it (see p44).

## Claims in writing or online

If you initially claim in writing or online on the approved form, it is valid if completed in accordance with the instructions on the form. If you do not do this, your claim is defective. You should be given a chance to remedy any defect.[30] If you correct any defect within one month of the date you are first notified of it, your claim is treated as made when it was first received. The decision maker can extend this one-month period if they think it is reasonable.[31]

If you claim online, you may not be allowed to submit a claim if essential information is not entered on the system. It is generally impossible to claim UC online without the required information, as the system will not accept it. If your UC claim is not accepted, you should complete your claim the same day if possible to avoid losing benefit. In limited circumstances, the DWP may accept a telephone claim for UC instead (see p44). For other benefits, you should try to claim in another way as soon as you can, otherwise you may lose benefit.[32]

To be valid, written claims for JSA, ESA and personal independence payment (PIP) *must* be made on an approved form.[33] UC claims cannot be made on paper forms, only online or, if permitted, by telephone.[34] For other benefits, any letter or other written communication *may* be treated as a valid claim for benefit.[35] In practice, if you make a written claim that is not on the approved form, you are likely to be sent one to complete. If you correctly complete and return the form within one month (or longer, if the decision maker considers it reasonable) of its being sent to you, you count as making a valid claim on the date of your first letter or other written communication.[36]

If you cannot complete the form, tell the office handling your claim as soon as possible. Ideally, explain your circumstances on the claim form or by telephoning the office. You can provide supporting letters – eg, from a social worker or a solicitor. The DWP may:

- help you to fill in the form or give you longer to complete it; *or*
- collect evidence or information on your behalf.

## Further information to support your claim

Even if your claim is accepted as valid, you may still be required to provide additional documentation and evidence.[37] Provided your claim is valid, your date of claim should not be affected if you fail to do so.[38]

You must provide any information or evidence within one month of a request, or within seven days of a request for JSA. A decision maker can allow longer than this if it is reasonable. If you do not provide the information, adverse conclusions are likely to be drawn and your claim decided on that basis. In some circumstances, decisions must be made in a certain way if the required information is not available (see p1119).

It is best to send evidence and documents to the office handling your claim. For some benefits, an 'alternative office' (see p1004) may also accept evidence and documents. If a local authority used information on your claim for HB and passed it to the DWP because it is relevant to your claim for another benefit, in most cases the DWP must use that information without checking it further.[39] If you must travel to provide evidence, you may be able to claim your travelling expenses.[40]

If you are asked to provide evidence you do not have, ask what other evidence would be acceptable. Ask what is required and why, and complain (see Chapter 55) if you think any requests for information are unreasonable. Ask for a decision to be made on your claim. You can challenge this decision, usually by requesting a mandatory reconsideration first and then appeal if it is not changed (see p1168).[41]

### *Contacting the benefit office*

1. Writing to the DWP or HMRC is the best way to have your case dealt with. It ensures there is a record of what you said and enables you to cover all the points you want to make. If you are claiming UC, you can contact the DWP via your UC journal.
2. Always keep a copy of the letters, forms and other documents you send, as well as copies of those sent to you. Take screenshots of correspondence on your UC journal. This may help you or your adviser to challenge decisions.
3. It is often necessary to telephone the DWP or HMRC. If you do this, note the date, the name and location of the person you spoke with and what is said. If the information is important, follow up the call with a letter or UC journal entry confirming what was said.
4. If you need to visit an office (eg, because your case cannot be dealt with by telephone) and you cannot get there (eg, because of your age, health or disability), an officer may be able to make a home visit. If you are refused a visit and are not satisfied with the reason you are given, ask to speak to a supervisor or the customer services manager. If you remain unsatisfied, you can complain (see Chapter 55).

If your claim involves medical issues, you may have to provide evidence in the form of a questionnaire. In most cases, the decision maker can refer you to a 'healthcare professional' or, for PIP only, a 'health professional' for an examination and/or a report. If you fail to have an examination and are not accepted as having 'good cause' or 'good reason', your claim will be decided against you.[42] See the chapter in this *Handbook* about the benefit that you have claimed for more details.

### *Healthcare and health professionals*

A **'healthcare professional'** is a registered medical practitioner (eg, a doctor), registered nurse, or registered occupational therapist or physiotherapist, or for DLA mobility component for a severe visual impairment only, a registered optometrist or orthoptist.[43]
The rules for who counts as a **'health professional'** for PIP are not set out in regulations. Guidance states that paramedics and pharmacists are included, along with doctors, registered nurses, occupational therapists and physiotherapists.[44]

# 4. The date of your claim

Usually, your 'date of claim' is the date the DWP or HMRC receives a 'valid claim' (see p1008). Once a decision is made that you are entitled to benefit, the date from when it is awarded and from when you are paid is determined by the date of claim. Check the relevant chapter for the specific rules about the date of claim for that benefit and the date from when you are paid.

The date of claim is earlier than the date a valid claim is made if:

- your claim is 'backdated' (see below); *or*
- the claim you made for one benefit is treated as a claim for a different benefit instead (see p1013).

In some situations, you may be able to claim in advance. See the relevant chapter for the specific rules on the benefit you want to claim.

## Backdating your claim

In general, you should submit a valid claim as soon as you think you qualify. There are strict time limits in which to complete your claim.[45] If you miss the time limit, you may be able to backdate your claim. If you want to backdate your claim, you should ask for this to happen, otherwise (except for bereavement support payment) it is not considered (but for universal credit (UC) claims, see p49). If you satisfy the conditions for getting the benefit, it should be paid from your date of claim, even if backdating is refused. If backdating is refused, you can ask for a mandatory reconsideration of the decision, and then appeal if it is not changed (see p1168). Payment should not be held up because you are challenging a decision on backdating.

If you have not asked for backdating, but want it to be considered, you should ask for your claim to be amended to include backdating *before* a decision on it is made (see p1004). If a decision has been made on your claim, the DWP or HMRC may say that to consider a request for backdating, you must make a new claim for the past period and that your request for backdating runs from when you make this new claim (but for UC claims, see p49).

The backdating rules differ depending on your circumstances and the benefit you claim.

- For the UC backdating rules, see p48.
- Claims for attendance allowance (AA), disability living allowance (DLA) and personal independence payment (PIP) can never be backdated.[46]
- Claims for some benefits can be backdated without special reasons (see p1012).
- Claims for jobseeker's allowance (JSA) can only be backdated in limited circumstances (see p622).

- The backdating period is longer for some benefits if you reclaim following an award of a 'qualifying benefit' (see p1012).

If you are prevented from receiving backdated benefit because of an error by or misadvice from the DWP (or HMRC, in child benefit and guardian's allowance cases), complain and request compensation (see p1261). The intervention of an MP or the Ombudsman (see p1266) may help.

## Benefits that can be backdated without special reasons

Claims for some benefits can be backdated for up to three months, regardless of why you did not claim earlier. State pension can be backdated for up to 12 months without special reasons. If you want benefit for a period before the date you make your claim, you must show that you would have qualified for the benefit had you claimed at the time. The benefits that can be backdated without special reasons are:[47]

- bereavement support payment (see p464);
- carer's allowance (CA) (see p481);
- child benefit and guardian's allowance (see p503);
- employment and support allowance (ESA) (see p568);
- industrial injuries benefits (see p604);
- maternity allowance (MA) (see p640);
- pension credit (PC) (see p248);
- state pension (see p697).

7

There are exceptions to the rules.

- The time limit for claiming bereavement support payment can be extended in some cases – eg, when you did not know your partner had died (see p464).
- If you are claiming backdated child benefit or guardian's allowance after receiving refugee status, see p1291.
- If you miss the time limit to claim industrial injuries disablement benefit for occupational deafness or occupational asthma (see p593), you may lose your right to benefit altogether.

## Backdating after an award of a qualifying benefit

If your claim for benefit is refused, it can be backdated if you reclaim it after an award of a qualifying benefit.

**Note:**

- More generous rules apply for CA (see p481).
- Different rules apply for Sure Start maternity grants and funeral expenses payments (see p707).
- This rule does not apply to backdating claims for new-style JSA, or to claims for UC and ESA.

*Qualifying benefit*

A **'qualifying benefit'** is any benefit (except PIP and carer support payment (CSP)) awarded to you or someone else, which entitles you to another benefit, or makes another benefit payable at a higher rate. PIP is only a qualifying benefit for backdating entitlement to CA.[48] If you *only* qualify for a means-tested benefit if awarded PIP or CSP, you should claim it immediately and ask the DWP not to decide your claim until your PIP or CSP claim is decided. You should also get specialist advice.

You can get backdating if:[49]

- your original claim (eg, for PC) is refused; *and*
- you, or your partner or dependent child, claimed a qualifying benefit (eg, AA for your partner) no later than 10 working days after your original claim; *and*
- the qualifying benefit is awarded; *and*
- you make a further claim (eg, for PC) within three months of the decision awarding the qualifying benefit and are now entitled to the award of the original benefit.

In these circumstances, benefit is backdated to the date of your original claim or the date on which the qualifying benefit was first paid, whichever is later.

**Note:**

- The qualifying benefit rule also applies if the qualifying benefit claim was originally refused, but later awarded after a revision, supersession or appeal.[50]
- If you lost entitlement to benefit (eg, CA), or payment of it stopped because the award of a qualifying benefit (eg, DLA) was terminated or reduced, your benefit is backdated if you reclaim within three months of the reinstatement of the qualifying benefit.[51]
- If you lost entitlement to your benefit because AA, DLA, adult disability payment (ADP), child disability payment (CDP) or pension age disability payment (PADP) stopped being paid because the person entitled was in hospital, a care home or other special accommodation, your benefit is backdated if you reclaim it within three months of payment of AA, DLA, ADP, CDP or PADP restarting.[52] **Note:** this rule does not apply when PIP stops in these circumstances.

If you are already entitled to UC, ESA, PC or housing benefit, you may get a higher rate once you, a family member or a non-dependant qualifies for another benefit. See p1157 for backdating additional benefit in this situation.

## If you claim the wrong benefit

If you claim one benefit when you are entitled to another, your claim can sometimes be treated as a claim for that other benefit. This can be a way round the strict rules about your date of claim and backdating, as your claim for the benefit you should have claimed is treated as made on the date you claimed the wrong benefit.

A claim for:[53]

- ESA can be treated as a claim for MA and vice versa;
- bereavement benefits (but not bereavement support payment) can be treated as a claim for state pension and vice versa;
- bereavement support payment can be treated as a claim for other bereavement benefits and vice versa;
- AA, DLA or an increase in disablement pension for constant attendance (see p600) can be treated as a claim for any of the others;
- PIP can be treated as a claim for either DLA or AA and vice versa, but only if it appears that you are not entitled to the benefit that you actually claimed;
- child benefit can be treated as a claim for guardian's allowance and vice versa.

Note:

- The decision maker does not have to accept your claim for one benefit as a claim for another. You cannot appeal if this is refused. You can request a revision (see p1130) but your only legal remedy if the decision maker refuses to change the decision is judicial review (see p1236).[54]
- For all benefits, except UC, JSA, ESA and PIP, there is a general power to treat any written document as a claim for benefit (see p1009), which could arguably include if you filled in the wrong claim form.[55]
- For some benefits, although you cannot be treated as having claimed the right benefit, there are special rules about the date your claim is treated as made if you first claimed the wrong benefit and later claim the right one when your claim is refused. For more details, see 'The date of your claim' in the chapter of this *Handbook* about the benefit you should have claimed.
- If you claimed the wrong benefit due to incorrect information given to you by an employee of the DWP or HMRC and the above rules cannot help you, see p1261 for information about how to ask for compensation.

# Notes

1. **Making a claim**
   1 s1(1) SSAA 1992
   2 Regs 4(6A)-(6CC), 4D and 4H SS(C&P) Regs
   3 Regs 4(6B), 4D(3A) and (4) and 4H(3) SS(C&P) Regs

4 **UC/PIP/new-style JSA&ESA** Reg 30 UC,PIP,JSA&ESA(C&P) Regs
**CB/GA** Reg 8 CB&GA(Admin) Regs
**Other benefits** Reg 5(1) and (1A) SS(C&P) Regs
5 **UC/PIP/new-style JSA&ESA** Reg 31 UC,PIP,JSA&ESA(C&P) Regs
**CB/GA** Reg 9 CB&GA(Admin) Regs
**Other benefits** Reg 5(2) SS(C&P) Regs
6 **UC/PIP/new-style JSA&ESA** Reg 2 and Sch 2 UC,PIP,JSA&ESA(C&P) Regs
**CB/GA** Reg 2 and Sch 2 CB&GA(Admin) Regs
**Other benefits** Reg 4ZC and Sch 9ZC SS(C&P) Regs
7 CJSA/3979/1999; CJSA/1332/2001; CDLA/1589/2005

2. **Who should claim**

8 **UC/PIP/new-style JSA&ESA** Reg 57 UC,PIP,JSA&ESA(C&P) Regs
**CB/GA** Reg 28 CB&GA(Admin) Regs
**Other benefits** Reg 33 SS(C&P) Regs
9 R(SB) 5/90
10 CIS/642/1994
11 CIS/379/1992
12 **UC/PIP/new-style JSA&ESA** Reg 57(6) UC,PIP,JSA&ESA(C&P) Regs
**Other benefits** Reg 33(1A) SS(C&P) Regs
13 R(SB) 9/84(T)

3. **Information to support your claim**

14 Sch 2 SS&CS(DA) Regs, Sch 3 UC,PIP,JSA&ESA(DA) Regs and Sch 2 CB&GA(DA) Regs do not include such decisions in the list of decisions against which there is no right of appeal
15 **CB/GA** s13(1A) and (1B) SSAA 1992
**Other benefits** s1(1A) and (1B) SSAA 1992
16 *PHC v SSWP (UC)* [2024] UKUT 340 (AAC)
17 s1(1A) SSAA 1992
18 *SSWP v Wilson* [2006] EWCA Civ 882, reported as R(H) 7/06
19 CH/1231/2004; CH/4085/2007
20 Reg 1A SS(DLA) Regs
21 Reg 4(a) HB Regs; reg 4(a) HB(SPC) Regs
22 Child Benefit and Guardian's Allowance (Miscellaneous Amendments) Regulations 2025 No.207
23 **UC** Reg 5 UC,PIP,JSA&ESA(C&P) Regs
**HB** Reg 4(b) HB Regs; reg 4(b) HB(SPC) Regs
24 *PHC v SSWP (UC)* [2024] UKUT 340 (AAC)
25 *RA v SSWP (UC)* [2024] UKUT 207 (AAC)
26 www.equalityadvisoryservice.com; telephone 0808 800 0082
27 **UC/PIP/new-style JSA&ESA** Regs 8(4) and (5), 11(4) and (5), 13 and 23 UC,PIP,JSA&ESA(C&P) Regs
**Other benefits** Regs 4(11)-(13), 4D(6A)-(6E) and 4G SS(C&P) Regs
28 **New-style ESA** Reg 13(2) UC,PIP,JSA&ESA(C&P) Regs
**Other benefits** Regs 4D(6B) and 4G(2) SS(C&P) Regs
29 **UC/PIP/new-style JSA&ESA** Regs 8(6), 11(6), 13(5) and 23 (4) UC,PIP,JSA&ESA(C&P) Regs
**Other benefits** Regs 4(13), 4D(6E) and 4G(5) SS(C&P) Regs
30 **UC/PIP/new-style JSA&ESA** Regs 8(5), 11(5), 15(3) and 21(4) UC,PIP,JSA&ESA(C&P) Regs
**CB/GA** Reg 10 CB&GA(Admin) Regs
**Other benefits** Regs 4(7), (7A) and (7B), 4D(10) and 4H(6) SS(C&P) Regs
31 **UC/PIP/new-style JSA&ESA** Regs 8(6), 11(6), 15(4) and 21(5) UC,PIP,JSA&ESA(C&P) Regs
**CB/GA** Reg 10(2)(b)(ii) CB&GA(Admin) Regs
**Other benefits** Regs 4(7)(b), 4D(11), and 4H(7) SS(C&P) Regs
32 *CW v SSWP (JSA)* [2016] UKUT 114 (AAC)
33 **UC/PIP/new-style JSA&ESA** Regs 11(1)(a), 15(1) and 21(1) UC,PIP,JSA&ESA(C&P) Regs
34 Reg 8 UC,PIP,JSA&ESA(C&P) Regs
35 **CB/GA** Reg 5 CB&GA(Admin) Regs
**Other benefits** Regs 4(1) and 4D(2) SS(C&P) Regs
36 **CB/GA** Reg 10 CB&GA(Admin) Regs
**Other benefits** Regs 4(7ZA) and 4F(3) SS(C&P) Regs
37 **UC/PIP/new-style ESA** Reg 37 UC,PIP,JSA&ESA(C&P) Regs
**JSA** Reg 31 JSA Regs 2013
**CB/GA** Reg 7 CB&GA(Admin) Regs
**Other benefits** Reg 7 SS(C&P) Regs
38 R(IS) 4/93; CIS/51/2007; *MS v SSWP (JSA)* [2016] UKUT 206 (AAC)
39 The Social Security (Claims and Information) Regulations 2007 No.2911
40 ss180 and 180A SSAA 1992
41 CIS/51/2007
42 **PIP** s80 WRA 2012
**ESA** ss8-9 WRA 2007
**IIDB** Reg 12(3) SS&CS(DA) Regs; s19 SSA 1998
**Other benefits** s19 SSA 1998

43 s39(1) SSA 1998; reg 3 SS(DLA)A Regs
44 PIP AG, 25 November 2024, para 3.1.1

4. **The date of your claim**

45 **UC/PIP/new-style JSA&ESA** Regs 26-29 UC,PIP,JSA&ESA(C&P) Regs
**CB/GA** Reg 6 CB&GA(Admin) Regs
**Other benefits** Reg 19 and Sch 4 SS(C&P) Regs
46 ss65(4) and 76 SSCBA 1992; reg 27 UC,PIP,JSA&ESA(C&P) Regs
47 **New-style ESA** Reg 28 UC,PIP,JSA&ESA(C&P) Regs
**CB/GA** Reg 6 CB&GA(Admin) Regs
**Other benefits** Reg 19(1)-(3B) and Sch 4 SS(C&P) Regs
48 Reg 6(22) SS(C&P) Regs. PIP and CSP do not count for the general rule, as they are not defined as 'qualifying benefits' or 'relevant benefits' for the purpose of this regulation
49 Reg 6(16)-(26) SS(C&P) Regs
50 Reg 6(26) SS(C&P) Regs
51 Reg 6(19) SS(C&P) Regs
52 Reg 6(19)-(21A) SS(C&P) Regs
53 **UC/PIP/new-style JSA&ESA** Reg 25 UC,PIP,JSA&ESA(C&P) Regs
**CB/GA** Reg 11 CB&GA(Admin) Regs
**Other benefits** Reg 9 and Sch 1 SS(C&P) Regs
54 **UC/PIP/new-style JSA&ESA** Sch 3 para 1(b) UC,PIP,JSA&ESA(DA) Regs
**CB/GA** Sch 2 para 6(d) CB&GA(DA) Regs
**Other benefits** Sch 2 para 5(g) SS&CS(DA) Regs
See also R(A) 3/81
55 **CB/GA** Reg 5(1)(b) CB&GA(Admin) Regs
**Other benefits** Regs 4(1) and 4D(2) SS(C&P) Regs

# Chapter 45

# Getting paid

**This chapter covers:**


1. Who is paid (p1018)
2. How and when you are paid (p1018)
3. Overlapping benefits (p1021)
4. Advance payments (p1023)
5. The benefit cap (p1025)
6. Change of circumstances after you claim (p1030)
7. When payments can be suspended (p1031)
8. When your entitlement is terminated (p1033)
9. Deductions and payments to third parties (p1033)
10. Recovery of benefits from compensation payments (p1043)


This chapter covers the general rules. See the chapter about the benefit you are getting for the specific rules about that benefit. This chapter does not cover the rules for Scottish benefits (see Chapter 68 and the chapter about the benefit you are claiming), statutory sick pay (see Chapter 35), statutory parental payments (see Chapter 34), social fund payments (see Chapter 33), the health benefits in Chapter 27, the other types of financial help in Chapter 36 or discretionary housing payments (see Chapter 25).

## Key facts

- The DWP, local authority or HMRC decides how benefit is paid to you. There is no right of appeal.
- You are usually paid by direct credit transfer into a bank or similar account.
- If a decision on your claim or payment of your benefit is delayed, you may be able to get an advance payment.
- The benefit cap may restrict the total amount of benefit you receive.
- You must report certain changes in your circumstances.
- Deductions can be made from your benefit. In certain circumstances, payment of your benefit can be suspended. In addition, your benefit may not be paid, or may be paid at a reduced rate, as a result of a sanction or a penalty.

## 1. Who is paid

Payment is usually made direct to you, the claimant, but there are some circumstances when payments can be made to other people or organisations on your behalf.

- If you cannot manage your own money, your benefit is paid to a person appointed to act on your behalf – called an 'appointee' (see p1005).[1]
- You can choose to have universal credit (UC), child benefit or guardian's allowance paid to your partner.
- Your benefit (except housing benefit (HB) or new-style employment and support allowance (ESA) and jobseeker's allowance (JSA)) can be paid to someone else if it is in the interests of you or your partner, or any children for whom you are getting benefit.[2] This includes paying your UC housing costs for rent to someone who then pays your landlord.
- Your HB can be paid direct to your landlord (or the person you pay rent to) on your behalf in certain circumstances (see p222). Your UC housing costs for rent are not paid direct to your landlord, unless the DWP thinks the 'alternative payment arrangements' should apply. If you live in Scotland, you can request direct payment (see p51).
- Deductions can be made from certain benefits (usually UC, income-related ESA or pension credit) for certain payments to someone else on your behalf (see p1033).[3]

7

## 2. How and when you are paid

The DWP or HMRC decides how and when your benefit is paid. There is no right of appeal about this. For how and when housing benefit (HB) is paid, see p221.

**Note:**

- You are usually paid by direct credit transfer into a bank or similar account.
- If you cannot open or manage an account, payment can sometimes be made by the payment exception service (see p1019). Child benefit and guardian's allowance can be paid by a payment voucher (see p1020).
- You can check your universal credit (UC) payments online. If you cannot do this, ask the DWP for help in accessing your online journal. It may be possible to do this by telephone, or in person at a Jobcentre Plus office.
- If you are entitled to arrears of benefit, but it is considered necessary to pay them in instalments to protect your interests, then if you (in a joint claim for UC, both you and your partner) agree, you are paid your arrears in instalments.[4]

## Direct payment

You are usually paid by direct credit transfer into a bank or similar account (including some credit union accounts). This is called 'direct payment'. If this is not suitable for you, you may be able to get your DWP benefit paid by the payment exception service or your child benefit or guardian's allowance paid by voucher (see below). If you change your account, contact the office that pays you the benefit.

Your benefit is paid into an account nominated by you or by your 'appointee'.[5]

If you experience difficulty accessing your money due to these arrangements, complain to the DWP or HMRC (see Chapter 55). You could also contact your MP (see p1266).

### If someone collects your benefit for you

It should be possible, if necessary, to arrange for someone else to access your account to collect your benefit for you. Ask your bank about this.

### If you lose your card or forget your PIN

If you lose your bank card or forget your PIN, contact the bank and ask for a replacement card or new PIN to be issued as soon as possible.

If you cannot access your benefit while waiting for a new card or PIN, contact the office that pays your benefit for advice.

If all else fails, you may be able to get a payment from your local authority while the problem is sorted out (see p770). Get advice if you cannot access your benefit, and the DWP or HMRC refuses to remedy the situation.

## Payment by the payment exception service or voucher

If you cannot open or manage an account, your DWP benefits are paid by the government's payment exception service (telephone 0800 015 2902). You can collect your benefit at a PayPoint outlet or Post Office (see gov.uk/payment-exception-service for links to PayPoints and Post Offices near you). To withdraw your benefit, you must produce your payment service card or voucher code from the payment exception service and proof of your identity – eg, recent benefit letter, recent council tax or fuel bill, passport or driving licence. The voucher is valid for 90 days. If you do not use it in time, ask the DWP office that pays your benefit to reissue it. If someone regularly gets your benefit for you, they can be issued with a payment service card.

If you lose your payment service card, contact the office that pays your benefit. Your card will be blocked, and you will be sent a new one. You may be sent a voucher or text message to get your benefit in the meantime. In an emergency, you may be given a telephone number to call for a reference number which will enable you to get your benefit.

If you cannot open or manage an account, HMRC may pay your child benefit or guardian's allowance by issuing you with a Post Office Payout voucher. This can be cashed at a post office, using a code and reference number which HMRC sends you. The local authority may arrange to pay your HB by another method, including by cheque.

## When you are paid

When and how often your benefit is paid depends on the benefit you have claimed.[6] You are sometimes paid in advance and sometimes in arrears. Some benefits have specific paydays. For others, the day you are paid depends on your national insurance (NI) number. See the chapter for the benefit you are claiming.

| *Last two numbers of your NI number* | *Day of payment* |
|---|---|
| 00–19 | Monday |
| 20–39 | Tuesday |
| 40–59 | Wednesday |
| 60–79 | Thursday |
| 80–99 | Friday |

## Missing payments

If you are entitled to benefit, you must be paid it.[7] If your benefit is not paid into your account, your payment service card does not allow you to collect your benefit or you are not issued with a voucher, the DWP or HMRC must rectify this.

If there is a long delay, the DWP or HMRC may say that your entitlement to payment is lost 12 months after the date it was due to be paid into your account. However, this should not apply if you have not been paid.[8]

## Emergencies

If you have lost all your money or there has been a crisis, it is possible to get help at any time. Your local police station may have a contact number for DWP staff on call outside normal office hours.

If you cannot contact the DWP, or it does not help, you may be able to get a payment from your local authority in a crisis (see p770). The police station may have a contact number.

If you need money urgently, you should provide as much information as possible to support your claim. It may help to get an advice agency or third party (eg, a health visitor, social worker, doctor or MP) to support you.

# 3. Overlapping benefits

Sometimes, you cannot be paid more than one non-means-tested benefit in full at the same time. This is because of the overlapping benefit rules. These may also apply if:

- more than one person is claiming an increase for the same child or adult (see p1022);
- you are getting child benefit, guardian's allowance or an increase in your non-means-tested benefit for your child (see p1023);
- you are entitled to an increase in your non-means-tested benefit for an adult who is getting one or more of certain benefits themself (see p1022).

Disability living allowance (DLA) care component, the daily living component of personal independence payment (PIP)/adult disability payment (ADP), attendance allowance (AA), pension age disability payment (PADP) and armed forces independence payment all overlap with (ie, are reduced by) constant attendance allowance.[9] **Note:** for ADP only, the overlap does not apply to constant attendance allowance paid with a war pension. However, war pension rules provide for the deduction of ADP from war pensions – seek advice about the impact of ADP on your war pension.

Otherwise, AA, PADP, DLA, PIP, industrial injuries disablement benefit (see p599), reduced earnings allowance (see p601) and retirement allowance (see p602) can be received in addition to any of the other benefits described in this *Handbook* – eg, you can receive employment and support allowance (ESA), both components of PIP and disablement benefit at the same time.

## Earnings-replacement benefits

You cannot usually receive more than one of the following 'earnings-replacement benefits' at the same time – eg, you cannot receive retirement pension and carer's allowance (CA) or carer support payment (CSP) at the same time.

- Contributory benefits:
  - new-style jobseeker's allowance;
  - contributory ESA;
  - maternity allowance (which counts as contributory for this rule);
  - retirement pension;
  - widow's pension;
  - widowed parent's allowance.
- Non-contributory benefits:
  - severe disablement allowance;
  - CA or CSP.

If more than one of the earnings-replacement benefits listed above is payable to you, the following applies.[10]

- A contributory benefit is paid in preference to a non-contributory benefit – eg, retirement pension is paid instead of CA or CSP. This is then topped up by any balance of a non-contributory benefit due.
- If the above bullet point does not apply, weekly benefits are paid and topped up by any balance of a daily benefit (unless you apply to receive the daily benefit in full). See the chapter in this *Handbook* about the benefit you are claiming to see if it is a daily or a weekly benefit.
- If neither of the above bullet points apply, the highest rate benefit is paid or, if the rates are the same, one benefit is paid.

## Retirement pensions

You cannot usually get more than one retirement pension at a time.[11] However, there are special rules if you are married or in a civil partnership and at least one of you reached pension age after 6 April 1979, or you are a surviving spouse or civil partner entitled to both an old category A and an old category B retirement pension (see Chapter 36 of the 2015/16 edition of this *Handbook*), and your category A pension would be paid at a reduced rate because you have not paid sufficient contributions (see p879). In this situation, your basic category A pension is increased by whichever is less:[12]

7

- the amount of the shortfall between your actual category A pension and the full category A pension of £176.45; *or*
- the amount of your category B pension.

You are also entitled to an additional pension on your own contribution record and one on that of your spouse or civil partner up to the maximum additional pension a person could theoretically receive on one contribution record.[13]

Additional pensions under the old additional state pension scheme and graduated retirement benefit do not overlap with non-means-tested benefits. However, special rules apply if they are payable with two or more such benefits: see Chapter 36 of the 2015/16 edition of this *Handbook*.

Also, an additional pension paid with widow's pension (see p461) overlaps with the state pension (see p688).[14]

An age addition paid with retirement pension overlaps with another age addition.[15]

## Increases in non-means-tested benefits for adults

An increase in a non-means-tested benefit for an adult overlaps with certain earnings-replacement benefits (see p1021) which are payable to that adult – eg, an increase of retirement pension for your partner is not paid if your partner is being paid CA in their own right.[16] If the increase is less than or equal to the benefit payable to the adult, the increase is not paid. If the increase is greater than the basic benefit, you get the difference. There is no overlap if the adult is not residing with you and is employed by you to care for a child.

### Increases in non-means-tested benefits for children

Only one person can receive child benefit or an increase in a non-means-tested benefit for the same child.

The standard rate of child benefit (see p499) does not overlap with any other benefit. However, if you receive the higher amount payable for your eldest child (see p499), any other non-means-tested benefit for the same child (except DLA, child disability payment, PIP, ADP and guardian's allowance) or increase paid for the same child is reduced by £5.15.[17] All increases for children overlap with guardian's allowance and are reduced by the amount of guardian's allowance you get for the child.[18]

## 4. Advance payments

You may be able to get an advance loan of your benefit if you are waiting for a decision on your claim or you are waiting to be paid and you are in financial need.[19] This is called a 'short-term advance' of benefit or, for universal credit (UC), a 'universal credit advance'. For UC, to get an advance you must have been allocated a national insurance (NI) number. You must repay the advance by deductions from future payments of your benefit, but you are not charged interest.

*Financial need*

'**Financial need**' means that because you have not received your benefit, there is a serious risk of damage to your health or safety or that of a member of your family. '**Family**' means your partner and any children for whom you or your partner are responsible (see p492).[20]

You may be in financial need in various circumstances – eg, if you have no money for food or for your gas or electricity meter, or during a 'waiting period' that applies before you are entitled to benefit, or while you are waiting for an increase in benefit after a change in your circumstances. For UC, if you have transferred from any of the legacy benefits (see p19) in the last month, the DWP treats you as in financial need.[21]

If you are in financial need because you are waiting for a decision on your claim, you may be able to get an advance payment if the decision maker considers it likely that you are entitled to the benefit and:

- you have made a claim, but the claim has not yet been decided; *or*
- you are not required to make a claim for the benefit, but you have not yet been awarded it.

If you are in financial need because you are waiting to be paid, you may be able to get an advance payment if you have been awarded the benefit and:

- you are waiting for your first payment; *or*
- you have received your first payment, but it was for a shorter period than subsequent payments will be paid for, and you are waiting for your next payment; *or*
- you have had a change of circumstances which increases your entitlement, but your benefit has not yet been increased and paid to you; *or*
- you are entitled to a payment, but it is 'impracticable' to pay all or some of it on the date it is due.

**Note:**

- You can request an advance payment at your local Jobcentre Plus office or use the telephone number for the specific benefit at gov.uk/short-term-benefit-advance. For UC, see gov.uk/universal-credit/get-an-advance-first-payment: the DWP encourages you to apply using your online journal or via your Jobcentre Plus work coach. If you need help, telephone the UC helpline on 0800 328 5644 (textphone: 0800 328 1344; Welsh language 0800 328 1744; Relay UK and British Sign Language services are available). There are no rules on how much a short-term advance should be. The DWP considers how much you have asked for, how much you can afford to repay and what your benefit entitlement will be. For UC, you can get up to 100 per cent of your estimated award within five days of requesting an advance – but in urgent cases, payment can be made faster, including on the same day.The DWP says that you must ask for a UC advance no later than three working days before the end of your monthly assessment period (see p39), unless you are claiming within a month of coming off a legacy benefit.You are usually contacted about your application on the day you apply or early the next day. If you are to be offered an advance payment, you are asked to accept the amount and the repayment terms. You should explain any problems with this. If you do not accept the offer, you are not given the advance.
- There is no right of appeal against a refusal to award an advance payment.[22] You can ask the DWP to reconsider the decision, but after that, the only legal remedy is judicial review (see Chapter 53). You could ask your MP to help to get the decision reconsidered (see p1266). You may be able to get help in a crisis from your local authority (see p770).
- You must be notified of your liability to repay the advance.[23] Advances of benefit paid outside the UC system are recovered by deductions from subsequent payments of your benefit. Usually, the DWP wants to recover the advance within 12 weeks, at no more than 25 per cent of your benefit. If you need longer to repay, tell the DWP and explain why. You can ask the DWP to reconsider the decision about repayment, and (for benefits other than UC) if you remain unhappy, you can appeal.[24]
- The DWP usually wants to recover a UC advance within 24 months. You are told what you monthly repayment rate will be. If you tell the DWP that you

will refuse to repay at the specified rate, it may decide not to offer you an advance in the first place, and you will not be able to appeal. If you need longer to repay, tell the DWP and explain why.
- You cannot appeal against the decision about the repayment of an advance of UC, including the rate of recovery. You can ask the DWP to reconsider the decision, but after that, the only legal remedy is judicial review.[25]

### Benefits for which you cannot get an advance

You cannot get a short-term advance of:[26]
- housing benefit (HB). If your HB is delayed and you are a private or housing association tenant, you may be able to get a 'payment on account' (see p228);
- attendance allowance, disability living allowance and personal independence payment;
- child benefit or guardian's allowance (but see p505);
- statutory sick, maternity, adoption, paternity, shared parental, parental bereavement or neonatal care pay.



## 5. The benefit cap

The benefit cap may limit the total amount of benefit you can be paid.[27] If the total amount of your benefits is capped, the cap is applied:
- by reducing the amount of your universal credit (UC) (see p1028); *or*
- by reducing the amount of your working-age housing benefit (HB) (see p1028). The cap is not applied through your HB if you are the HB claimant and you are also getting UC.[28]

See p1028 and p1029 for the specified benefits that are taken into account when deciding whether the cap applies.

There are situations when the benefit cap does not apply, or when it is not applied immediately (see below).

If the benefit cap has been applied to you but you think it should not have been or that it has been calculated incorrectly, you can challenge the decision on the amount of UC or HB that you have been left with. For HB you can appeal straight away, although for UC you must usually first have the decision looked at again in a 'mandatory reconsideration' (see Chapter 51).

### When the benefit cap does not apply

The benefit cap does not apply if:
- you are not getting UC or not getting working-age HB (see p197); *or*
- you or your partner (or, in some cases, your child) are entitled to one of the disability or carer benefits listed on p1027; *or*

- it would be applied through your UC, you and/or your partner work and your combined earnings are high enough (see below).

**Note:** the benefit cap did not apply where you or your partner were entitled to working tax credit (WTC). WTC has now been replaced by UC, but if you (and your partner) were of pension age and transferred to UC under the managed migration process, the benefit cap will still not apply in your UC (see p21).

In addition, if you or your partner have been working recently, there may be a 'grace period' during which the cap does not apply.

## Work-related exceptions

If the benefit cap can be applied through your UC, it is not applied if:[29]

- you or your partner have net monthly earnings from employed or self-employed work of at least £846.56 in your UC monthly assessment period (see p125 for what counts as earnings. Note that earnings you are treated as having under the 'minimum income floor' rules (p130) do not count for this. See p145 if the only reason you do not earn enough to meet this rule is because you are paid four-weekly or otherwise not on a monthly basis). Your partner's earnings are added to yours; *or*
- you are within a nine-month grace period.



### Grace period for universal credit

The benefit cap is not applied through your UC for a grace period of nine consecutive months, if:[30]

- during your current period of entitlement to UC, your earnings (or your and your partner's combined earnings) from employed or self-employed work drop to less than £846 a month (ie, the adult national minimum wage for 16 hours a week converted to a monthly amount) but, immediately before the first day on which this applies, they had been at least £846 a month (or, if different, the adult national minimum wage for a 16-hour week that applied at that time, converted to a monthly amount) in each of the preceding 12 months – in 2024/25, it was £793; *or*
- before your current period of entitlement to UC, you stopped paid employed or self-employed work and, before you stopped work, your earnings (or your and your partner's combined earnings) had been at least £846 a month (or, if different, the adult national minimum wage for a 16-hour week that applied at that time, converted to a monthly amount) in each of the preceding 12 months – in 2024/25, it was £793.

The grace period begins on the most recent day on which either condition applies. It does not matter if you are no longer part of a couple with your then partner – your now ex-partner's earnings in the grace period should be taken into account.

For how earnings from work are calculated for UC, see Chapter 7.

### Grace period for housing benefit

If the benefit cap should be applied through your working-age HB, it is not applied if:[31]

- you are within a 39-week grace period after finishing work.

**Note**: the cap was not applied through your working-age HB if you (or your partner) were entitled to WTC, but that has now been replaced by UC (see p21). At the time of writing, no similar rule had been replaced for UC. See CPAG's *Welfare Rights Bulletin* or the online version of this *Handbook* for updates.

The benefit cap is not applied through your working-age HB for a grace period of 39 weeks if:[32]

- you or your partner were previously in work (either employed or self-employed) for at least 50 weeks out of the 52 weeks before the last day of work; *and*
- in that 50 weeks, the person in work was not entitled to income support (IS), jobseeker's allowance (JSA) or employment and support allowance (ESA).

The grace period begins on the day after the last day of work. Note that it does not matter if you are no longer part of a couple with your then partner – your now ex-partner's earnings in the grace period should be taken into account.

You count as still in work while on maternity, adoption, paternity or other parental leave, or while receiving SSP.[33]

## Benefits for disabled people and carers

The benefit cap does not apply if you or your partner get:[34]

- UC that includes the limited capability for work-related activity element; *or*
- ESA that includes the support component; *or*
- carer's allowance, carer support payment, guardian's allowance or UC that includes the carer element; *or*
- attendance allowance or pension age disability payment (including if it is not paid because of being in hospital or a care home); *or*
- disability living allowance, Scottish adult disability living allowance, child disability payment, personal independence payment, adult disability payment or armed forces independence payment. This exemption also applies if the person entitled is a child for whom you or your partner are responsible. The exemption continues if the person entitled is not paid benefit while they are in hospital or a care home; *or*
- industrial injuries disablement benefit, reduced earnings allowance or retirement allowance; *or*
- a war pension, or a guaranteed income payment or survivor's guaranteed income payment under the Armed Forces Compensation Scheme (including if it is not paid because of being in hospital or a care home).

## When the benefit cap applies

The benefit cap only applies if:

- you get UC or you get working-age HB (see p197); *and*
- none of the exceptions apply (see p1025); *and*
- the total amount of certain specified benefits you (and your partner, if you are a member of a couple) receive is above a certain level.

When calculating the amount of benefit you receive, the general rule is that your full benefit entitlement is taken into account. Deductions for repayment of overpayments, payments to third parties, council tax debts, fines and sanctions are generally ignored (but see p1029 for some exceptions if the cap is applied through your HB and you get widowed parent's allowance).[35]

### If you get universal credit

The cap applies once your (and, if you are in a couple, your partner's) monthly entitlement to specified benefits exceeds a certain amount. The amount is:

- if you live outside Greater London: £1,229.42 a month (£283.71 a week) if you are single without children, or £1,835.00 a month (£423.46 a week) if you are a couple or a lone parent; *or*
- if you live in Greater London: £1,413.92 a month (£326.29 a week) if you are single without children, or £2,110.25 a month (£486.98 a week) if you are a couple or a lone parent.

7

Your benefit payments are converted into monthly amounts for this calculation.

***Specified benefits for universal credit***

If you get UC, the **'specified benefits'** taken into account for the benefit cap are:[36]

- UC;
- JSA;
- ESA if neither you nor your partner are in the support group (ESA is not taken into account while you are disqualified from receiving it);
- child benefit;
- incapacity benefit;
- maternity allowance (MA);
- severe disablement allowance;
- widowed parent's allowance;
- widow's pension.

### If you get housing benefit

The cap applies once your (and, if you are in a couple, your partner's) weekly entitlement to specified benefits exceeds a certain amount. The amount is:

- if you live outside Greater London: £283.71 a week if you are single without children, or £423.46 a week if you are a couple or a lone parent; *or*
- if you live in Greater London: £326.29 a week if you are single without children, or £486.98 a week if you are a couple or a lone parent.

*Specified benefits for housing benefit*

If you get working-age HB, the '**specified benefits**' taken into account for the benefit cap are:[37]

– IS;
– JSA;
– ESA, if neither you nor your partner are in the support group (ESA is not taken into account while you are disqualified from receiving it);
– HB, except for 'specified accommodation'. This means: 'exempt accommodation' (see p326) or accommodation provided by a housing association, charity, voluntary organisation or English county council to meet your need for care, support or supervision; temporary accommodation provided by one of these bodies or a local authority because you have left home because of domestic abuse; or a local authority hostel where you get care, support or supervision;
– child benefit;
– incapacity benefit;
MA;
– severe disablement allowance;
– widowed parent's allowance (after the £15 disregard);
– widow's pension;

**Note:** child tax credit also used to be taken into account, but that has now been replaced by UC (see p21).

The local authority does not have to decide whether or not to apply the cap, unless it is told by the DWP that it may apply in your case or that you have had a change in your benefit entitlement. However, it can decide to apply the cap on the basis of information or evidence suggesting that it should do so.[38]

## How the benefit cap is applied

If the cap is applied through your UC, the DWP reduces your UC by the amount by which the total amount of the specified benefits you receive exceeds the cap. However, if you are entitled to the childcare costs element in your UC (see p76) and this is more than the amount by which your specified benefits exceed the cap (the 'excess'), your UC is not reduced. If it is not more than the excess, your UC is reduced, but the excess is reduced by your childcare costs element before the reduction is applied.[39]

If the cap is applied through your HB, the local authority reduces your HB by the amount by which the total amount of the specified benefits you receive exceeds the cap. You must be left with at least 50 pence a week HB, so you can still access discretionary housing payments (see Chapter 25) and other passported payments.[40]

## 6. Change of circumstances after you claim

You have a duty to report certain changes in your circumstances. The DWP or HMRC should inform you of the main kinds of changes you must report but may not list them all. It is also your duty to report *any* change in your circumstances that you may reasonably be expected to know may affect your right to, the amount of, or the payment of, your benefit.[41] For the changes of circumstances that apply to housing benefit, see p228.

You must notify changes promptly to the DWP or HMRC office handling your claim. Check the information sent to you about your benefit award, but get advice if you are in doubt. The rules say that the office handling your claim for child benefit or guardian's allowance includes the HMRC Child Benefit Office or any office specified by HMRC.[42]

7

You must notify the changes in writing or by telephone.[43] It is best to notify changes in writing so that you have a record of what you have reported. If you report a change by telephone, note the time and date of your call, the name of the person you spoke with, and confirm what was said in writing. Keep copies of any letters you send and take screenshots if reporting online. If you give the original to an officer, ask them to confirm receipt of the original.

There are additional ways you can report a change of circumstances.

- For child benefit and guardian's allowance, you may be able to report the change in person,[44] either at the HMRC Child Benefit Office or at another office specified by HMRC. However, it is always better to do so in writing.
- If the change is a death, there is a special rule (sometimes called 'Tell Us Once'). For information, see gov.uk/after-a-death/organisations-you-need-to-contact-and-tell-us-once. You can also report a birth or a death in person at a local authority (and, in England, a county council) office specified for that purpose. If the change is a death, you can notify it by telephone to the DWP if a number has been specified for that purpose.[45]

**Note:**

- If you do not promptly report a change which you have a duty to notify, any resulting overpayment may be recoverable from you (see Chapter 47).
- If you are considered to have acted 'knowingly' or dishonestly, you may also be guilty of an offence, which may lead to prosecution or a benefit penalty.

Even if you have not committed an offence, a civil penalty may be applied (see Chapter 48).

# 7. When payments can be suspended

Payment of part or all of your benefit can be suspended in certain circumstances. This means that the suspended benefit is not paid to you. In practice, suspensions are common in universal credit (UC) when it is considered that a doubt has arisen about entitlement or that an overpayment may have occurred (see p1032).

## Suspension while an appeal is pending

Your benefit can be suspended if the DWP, the local authority or HMRC is appealing (or considering whether to appeal) against:[46]

- a decision of the First-tier Tribunal, Upper Tribunal or court to award you benefit; *or*
- a decision of the Upper Tribunal or court about someone else's case if the issue in the appeal could affect your claim.



The DWP, the local authority or HMRC must give you written notice that it intends to request the statement of reasons from the First-tier Tribunal, or that it intends to apply for leave to appeal, or to appeal. It must do this as soon as is 'reasonably practicable'.[47]

The decision maker must then do one of these things within the usual time limits (see Chapters 51 and 52). If the decision maker does not, the suspended benefit must be paid to you.[48] The suspended benefit must also be paid to you if the decision maker withdraws an application for leave to appeal, withdraws the appeal or is refused leave to appeal and cannot renew the application for leave to appeal.

## Suspension for not providing information and evidence

You can be required to supply information or evidence if the decision maker needs this to determine whether your award of benefit should be revised or superseded (see p1130 and p1143).[49]

Payment of your benefit can be suspended if you do not provide the information and evidence.[50] **Note**: there is no rule under which your benefit can be terminated for not providing information or evidence unless it has been suspended first. In practice, some UC awards have been terminated for this reason without being suspended first, but that is wrong.

You must be notified in writing if the decision maker wants you to provide information or evidence. Within 14 days, or seven days for new-style jobseeker's allowance (JSA), or one month for child benefit, guardian's allowance and housing benefit, of being sent the request, you must:

- supply the information or evidence.[51] You can be given more time than this if you satisfy the decision maker that this is necessary; *or*
- satisfy the decision maker that the information does not exist or you cannot obtain it.[52]

If the decision maker has not already done so, your benefit can be suspended if you do not provide the information or evidence within the relevant time limit.[53] See p1033 for whether your entitlement to benefit can be terminated.

## Suspension for not taking part in a medical examination

Most benefits can be suspended if you do not take part in a medical examination on two consecutive occasions without 'good cause'.[54] This applies if:

- the decision maker is looking at whether you should still be getting a benefit (or whether you are getting it at the correct rate); *or*
- you apply for a revision or a supersession and the decision maker thinks a medical examination is necessary to make a decision.



This rule does not apply if the issue is whether you have limited capability for work. For information on these medicals and the consequences of failing to take part in them, see p921. It also does not apply to personal independence payment. However, if you do not take part in a medical, the DWP may still suspend your benefit because of a doubt about your entitlement.

## Suspension in other circumstances

Your benefit can also be suspended in various other circumstances, including if:[55]

- a question has arisen about your entitlement, or if the DWP, HMRC or the local authority thinks you are being, or have been, overpaid (in practice, this is becoming increasingly common in UC under risk review investigations);[56]
- for child benefit and guardian's allowance, you have failed to provide details of a bank account or similar account, having been requested to do so.[57]

## Challenging decisions to suspend benefit

You cannot appeal to the First-tier Tribunal against the decision to suspend your benefit. The only ways to change the decision are to negotiate to get your benefit reinstated or to challenge the decision by judicial review (see Chapter 53). You could also ask for an advance payment of benefit (see p1023). Get advice.

The decision maker may be willing to continue to pay your benefit, or at least some of it, if you can show that you will experience hardship otherwise. If you receive a letter telling you that your benefit has been suspended, reply and explain how the suspension affects you and ask for it to be reconsidered. It may be wise to get advice first (see Appendix 1).

## 8. When your entitlement is terminated

Your entitlement to benefit can be terminated if:

- your benefit was suspended in full, you are then required to provide information or evidence to determine whether the decision awarding you benefit should be revised or superseded, and you fail to do so within one month of the request;[58] *or*
- your benefit was suspended in full because you did not provide the information or evidence required to determine whether the decision awarding you benefit should be revised or superseded and it is more than one month since your benefit was suspended.[59]

The termination of your entitlement to benefit takes effect from the date payment was suspended (or an earlier date if you ceased to be entitled for another reason).[60]

Your entitlement to most benefits may also be terminated if you do not take part in a medical examination and it has been more than one month since your benefit was suspended on this ground.[61]

If you disagree with a decision to terminate your benefit, you can ask for a revision (see p1130) and then appeal (see Chapter 51).



## 9. Deductions and payments to third parties

Your benefit is usually paid direct to you, but there are some circumstances when money can be deducted and paid to another person (a third party) on your behalf.

### What deductions can be made

Amounts can be deducted from your benefit to pay third parties for:[62]

- housing costs (see p1035); *and*
- rent arrears (see p1035); *and*
- fuel (see p1036); *and*
- water charges (see p1037); *and*
- council tax arrears (see p1038); *and*
- child support maintenance (see p1038); *and*
- other payments – eg, loan repayments, fines and other charges (see p1039).

**Note:** in addition to the above deductions to third parties, you may also have deductions to the DWP or HMRC made to recover budgeting loans from the social fund (see p704), overpayments (see p1072) or regarding fraud and penalties (see Chapter 48). Your benefit may also be reduced if you have been sanctioned (see Chapter 43) or because the DWP is recovering a hardship payment (see Chapter 46).

## From which benefits can deductions be made

Deductions for payments to third parties are usually made from universal credit (UC), or otherwise from income-related employment and support allowance (ESA) or pension credit (PC). They can also be made from new-style jobseeker's allowance (JSA) and contributory ESA for council tax arrears, eliglble loans and fines, and from contributory ESA instead of income-related ESA in some circumstances (see below).

Deductions can only be made from other benefits to repay eligible loans (see p1039) and child support maintenance that you owe (see p1038).

**Note:** deductions could also be made from income support and income-based JSA, but most such awards had been replaced by UC by April 2025 (see p21).

7

### Deductions from contributory employment and support allowance

If deductions would be made from your income-related ESA but you also get contributory ESA, then the deductions can be made from that if your income-related ESA is insufficient or you have an 'underlying entitlement' to income-related ESA – ie, if you were not entitled to contributory ESA, you would be entitled to income-related ESA at the same rate.[63]

## When deductions can be made

Deductions and direct payments to third parties can only be made if you or your partner are liable to make the payments.[64] Deductions should only be made if there is evidence that you are liable – eg, the bill is in your or your partner's name.

Your consent is required before direct payments (including for arrears) are made for fuel costs and water charges from your UC if the total amount deducted for these payments exceeds 25 per cent of your UC standard allowance and child elements (see Chapter 5).[65] Otherwise, the DWP can make deductions from your UC without your consent.

Your written consent is required before deductions for tax credit overpayments and self-assessment tax debts can be made from your income-related ESA or PC (but not UC). Your consent is also required before deductions are made from these benefits for rent arrears, service charges for fuel and water, fuel costs (including arrears), water charges (including arrears) and repayment of integration loans in certain circumstances: see the 2023/24 edition of this *Handbook*.[66]

The DWP can make deductions from these benefits without your consent if they are made for:

- council tax arrears;

- fines;
- current housing costs;
- nursing home charges or hostel charges not included in housing benefit (HB).

## The deductions

Deductions to third parties are made before you receive your regular benefit payment. If you want to have deductions made to help you clear any arrears or debts, ask the DWP office dealing with your claim. If you disagree with a decision about deductions, you can challenge it by applying for a revision (see p1130) and then appealing (see Chapter 51).

### Housing costs

Deductions for rent payments cannot be made. However, deductions can be made for rent arrears (see below). If you are on UC and entitled to the housing element for your rent, in some circumstances that can be paid direct to your landlord under separate rules (see p51), and if you are on HB then again in some circumstances that can be paid direct to your landlord under separate rules (see p222). Deductions can be made for other housing costs that can be included in your benefit. For these housing costs, see p118 for UC (ie, just service charges), and p287 for other benefits. For the amount of the deductions, see p1040.[67]

You must be in arrears with your service charges to have deductions made from your UC. Your earnings (or if you are claiming jointly with your partner, your combined earnings) must also be below the UC work allowance that applies to you (see p41). If your earnings (or combined earnings) are equal to, or exceed, the work allowance for three monthly assessment periods, the deduction must stop.

If your income-related ESA or PC includes amounts for housing costs and you are in arrears (excluding payments for ground rent or rent charge payments, unless paid with your service charges or for a tent[68]), deductions can be made from your ESA or PC to clear the debt and to meet current payments. Deductions are made if it would be 'in the interests' of you or your family to do so. In England and Wales, if collection of your arrears is suspended under a breathing space debt respite scheme, deductions for payment of current costs can still be made.[69]

You only qualify for direct deductions from income-related ESA and PC if you owe more than half of the annual total of the relevant housing cost. This condition can be waived if it is in the 'overriding interests' of you or your family that deductions start as soon as possible – eg, repossession of your home is imminent.[70]

### Rent arrears

Deductions can be made from your UC for rent arrears if you are in debt with your rent (including water, service and other charges included in it) if:[71]

- you are entitled to UC housing costs for rent payments or occupy 'exempt accommodation' and get HB for that (p326); *and*
- you occupy the accommodation to which the rent applies; *and*
- your earnings (or if you make a joint claim with your partner, your combined earnings) for the previous UC monthly assessment period (see p39) are below the level of the work allowance that applies to you (see p41). If your earnings (or joint earnings) equal or exceed the work allowance for three monthly assessment periods, the deduction must stop.

The DWP can make a monthly deduction from your UC equivalent to between 10 and 20 per cent of the standard allowance (see p67) that applies in your case and pay it to your landlord, although in practice the maximum deduction will be 15 per cent. The DWP should take your circumstances into account in deciding how much the deduction will be. **Note:** a recent court decision has held that it is unlawful for these deductions to be introduced without your first having been given a chance to comment (eg, to object), although your consent is not required.[72] This decision may be appealed further. See CPAG's *Welfare Rights Bulletin* or the online version of this *Handbook* for updates.

If you are in arrears with your rent while on **HB**, or are £100 or more in arrears of hostel payments, an amount can be deducted from your **income-related ESA or PC** and paid direct to your landlord. This can also apply if (in England and Wales) you are in approved premises under section 13 of the Offender Management Act 2007 and have built up arrears of service charges rather than rent arrears.[73] For the amount of the deductions, see p1040.

Deductions can cover any water or service charges payable with your rent that are not met by HB. Fuel charges included in your rent cannot be covered by direct deductions if they change more than twice a year.

Except for UC, to qualify for direct deductions for rent arrears, your arrears must equal at least four times your full weekly rent. If you have not paid your full rent for eight weeks or more, direct deductions can be made automatically if your landlord asks the DWP to make them.[74] If your arrears relate to a shorter period, deductions can only be made if it is in the overriding interests of your family to do so.[75] Once your arrears are paid off, direct payments can continue for any fuel and water charges included in your rent.[76]

## Fuel

If you are in debt with your mains gas or electricity, the DWP can make deductions from your benefit and pay them to the supplier. This is sometimes called 'Fuel Direct'. Deductions can be for reducing the debt and for ongoing costs. However, a deduction for ongoing costs can only start, or an existing one be increased, with your consent. Deductions for debt can still start or be increased following an application from your fuel supplier.[77]

**For UC**, the DWP can deduct a monthly amount equal to 5 per cent of your standard allowance (see p67) for the debt, plus an additional amount for no more than your estimated average monthly fuel costs for ongoing costs, except if you are paying for that by other means – eg, a prepayment meter.[78] Arguably, although your consent is not required for deductions for debt, you should be asked for views and/or relevant information, although the rules do not specifically require that.[79]

If you are in debt for any gas or electricity (including reconnection or disconnection charges) and have earnings, deductions can only start to be made from your UC if your earnings (or, if you are claiming jointly with your partner, your combined earnings) for the previous monthly UC assessment period (see p39) are below the level of the work allowance that applies in your case (see p41).[80] If your earnings equal or exceed the work allowance for three monthly assessment periods, the deduction must stop.

**For income-related ESA and PC**, an amount can be deducted each week and paid to the fuel company in instalments – usually once a quarter.[81] Although your consent is not required, you should be asked for views and/or relevant information.[82] For the amount of the deductions, see p1040. Deductions can be made if:[83]

- the amount you owe is £92.05 or more (including reconnection or disconnection charges if you have been disconnected); *and*
- you continue to need the fuel supply; *and*
- it is in your, or your family's, interests to have deductions made.

In England and Wales, if collection of your arrears is suspended under a breathing space debt respite scheme, deductions for payment of current costs can still be made.[84]

For full details of the deductions for income-related ESA and PC, see the 2023/24 edition of this *Handbook*.

See CPAG's *Fuel Rights Handbook* for help if you have fuel debts.

## Water charges

If you are in debt with charges for water and sewerage (including reconnection charges), deductions may be made from your **UC** if your earnings (or, if you are claiming jointly with your partner, your combined earnings) for the previous monthly UC assessment period (see p39) are below the level of the work allowance that applies in your case (see p41).[85] If your earnings equal or exceed the work allowance for three monthly assessment periods, the deduction must stop.

The DWP can make a deduction from your UC and pay it to the water company. It can deduct a monthly amount equal to 5 per cent of your standard allowance (see p67), plus an additional amount that the DWP considers necessary to meet your continuing monthly water costs. Arguably, although your consent is not required for these deductions, you should be asked for your views and/or relevant information, although the rules do not specifically require that.[86]

If you are in debt with charges for water and sewerage, direct deductions can be made from your **income-related ESA and PC**.[87] Although your consent is not required, you should be asked for your views and/or relevant information.[88] Debt includes any disconnection, reconnection and legal charges. For the amount of the deductions, see p1040. If you pay your landlord for water with your rent, deductions are made under the arrangements for rent arrears (see p1035).[89] In England and Wales, if collection of your arrears is suspended under a breathing space debt respite scheme, deductions for payment of current costs can still be made.[90] For full details, see the 2023/24 edition of this *Handbook*.

## Council tax arrears

Deductions for council tax arrears can be made from **UC, new-style JSA, income-related or contributory ESA or PC** if the local authority gets a liability order from a magistrates' court (in Scotland, a summary warrant or decree from a sheriff court) and applies to the DWP for recovery to be made in this way.[91] Deductions can be made for arrears and any unpaid costs or penalties imposed. For the amount of the deductions, see p1040. See CPAG's *Council Tax Handbook* for help with council tax arrears.

7

## Child support maintenance

Some child support maintenance is paid under the official child support scheme operated by the DWP through the Child Maintenance Service, whereby deductions from a non-resident parent's benefit can be made to enforce payment. For full details of child support maintenance, see CPAG's *Child Support Handbook*.

If you are liable to pay child support maintenance under the official scheme at the flat rate, a deduction of £8.40 a week (this includes the addition of the DWP 'collect and pay' service) can be made from your:[92]

- UC (at a rate of £36.40 a month), income-related ESA or PC, including if your partner is liable;
- carer's allowance (CA);
- contributory ESA;
- industrial injuries benefit;
- new-style JSA;
- retirement pension;
- war widow's or war disablement pension;
- widowed parent's allowance;
- widow's pension;
- training allowance.

If more than one partner in a couple or polygamous marriage is liable to pay child support maintenance at the flat rate, it is deducted from any UC, income-related

ESA or PC they jointly receive, with the deduction paid equally. So, for example, if both partners in a couple are liable for child support at a flat rate of £8.40, they each pay £4.20.

A deduction of £8.40 a week can also be made from any of the above benefits for any child support arrears, but only if there is no ongoing child support liability. This means that when ongoing liability ends, a deduction of £8.40 can continue to be made towards any arrears due.

If you come under the UC system (see p20), a deduction for arrears can be made from your UC or new-style JSA or ESA. The deduction for arrears in all cases is £8.40 a week (£36.40 a month).[93]

## Other deductions

Other deductions can be made from your benefit for the following.

- **Court fines.** Magistrates' courts (any court in Scotland) can apply to the DWP for a fine, costs or compensation order to be deducted from your UC, new-style JSA, income-related or contributory ESA or PC.[94]
- **Eligible loans.** Deductions can be made from your UC, new-style JSA, income-related or contributory ESA or PC and (if necessary) your retirement pension or CA towards repaying 'eligible' loans if you have not kept up with the repayments.[95] **'Eligible loans'** are loans made by certain not-for profit lenders, such as community development financial institutions, credit unions and charities, but do not include business loans.
- **Integration loans.** Deductions can be made to repay an integration loan – ie, loans paid to refugees and people granted humanitarian protection and their dependants. Deductions can be made from your UC, income-related ESA or PC.[96]
- **Tax credit overpayments and self-assessment tax debts.** Deductions can be made from your income-related ESA or PC to repay these. The deduction is paid to HMRC. Your written consent is required.[97] Deductions can also be made from your UC (or new-style ESA or new-style JSA). The overpayment is treated as a UC overpayment. Your consent is not required.[98]
- **Residential accommodation charges.** Deductions can be made from your income-related ESA or PC (not UC) to meet your accommodation charges (eg, for PC, in a care home or independent hospital) if you have failed to budget for them and it is considered to be in your interests for deductions to be made.[99]
- **Hostel payments.** If you (or your partner) live in a hostel or (in England and Wales) approved premises under section 13 of the Offender Management Act 2007, you have claimed HB to meet your accommodation costs and your payments cover fuel, meals, water charges, laundry and/or cleaning of your room, part of your income-related ESA or PC (not UC) can be paid direct to the hostel for these items.[100]

**Note:** in the above bullet points, rules that refer to income-related ESA or PC are also used in general to apply to awards of income support and income-based JSA, but most of those had been replaced by UC by April 2025 – see p21.

# How much can be deducted

## Deductions from universal credit

If deductions to third parties are made from your **UC**, they are usually made at a fixed rate of 5 per cent of your standard allowance (see p67), with the following exceptions.

- Deductions for child support maintenance are made at a flat rate of £8.40 a week (£36.40 a month) for ongoing liability or £8.40 a week (£36.40 a month) for arrears.
- Deductions for rent arrears are made at a rate of at least 10 per cent and not more than 20 per cent (but in practice not more than 15 per cent) of your standard allowance.

In practice, deductions of any kind from your UC do not usually exceed 15 per cent of your standard allowance (see p67). If you have more than one deduction, see p1041 for how this limit applies. Third-party deductions cannot leave you with less than one pence of UC.[101]

## Deductions from other means-tested benefits

If deductions to third parties are made from your **income-related ESA or PC**, the maximum deductions are shown below. **Note**: these amounts also applied to deductions to third parties from awards of income support and income-based JSA, but most of those had been replaced by UC by April 2025 (see p21).

| *Type of arrears* | *Deduction for arrears* | *Deduction for ongoing cost* |
|---|---|---|
| Housing costs | £4.65 for each housing debt (maximum of £13.95) | Current weekly cost |
| Rent arrears and hostel payments | £4.65 | Nil (met by UC or HB) |
| Residential accommodation charges | Nil | The accommodation allowance (for those in local authority homes); all but £32.30 of your ESA or PC (for those in private or voluntary homes) |
| Hostel payments | Nil | Weekly amount assessed by local authority |

| | | |
|---|---|---|
| Fuel | £4.65 for each fuel debt (maximum of £9.30 payable) | Estimated amount of current consumption |
| Water charges | £4.65 (adjusted every 26 weeks) | Estimated costs |
| Council tax arrears | £4.65 | Nil |
| Fines | Nil | £5 (lower amount £4.65) |
| Repayment of eligible loans | Nil | £4.65 |
| Repayment of integration loans | Nil | £4.65 |
| Child support maintenance | £8.40 | £8.40 |
| Repayment of tax credit overpayments and self-assessment tax debts | Nil | Maximum £13.95 |

## More than one deduction

More than one deduction can be made from your UC. No more than three of the following deductions for third parties may be made from UC at any one time,[102] and you must be left with at least one pence of UC:[103]

- housing costs;
- rent arrears;
- fuel;
- water charges;
- repayment of eligible loans;
- repayment of integration loans;
- council tax arrears;
- fines, costs and compensation orders.

Without your consent, the total amount payable for fuel and water charges combined cannot exceed an amount equal to 25 per cent of your standard allowance plus any child elements to which you are entitled (see Chapter 5).[104]

In practice, the DWP does not usually deduct more than 15 per cent of your standard allowance (see p67).[105] This maximum applies to the total of most deductions from your UC, not just those for third parties. The total includes all those mentioned in the priority between deductions rules (see p1042), as well as those for sanctions (see Chapter 43), benefit offences (p1111) and to recover most overpayments of UC, JSA or ESA and advances of UC. If the total deductions would exceed 15 per cent of your standard allowance, the deductions are made in the order given in the priority rules – see p1042. However, deductions for ongoing costs (as opposed to arrears) of fuel or water charges are ignored when calculating the total. Deductions of more than the limit may still be made for housing costs, rent arrears or fuel debts, if the DWP considers it would be in your best interests.[106]

More than one third-party deduction can be made from your **income-related ESA and PC**. You must be left with at least 10 pence of benefit.[107] For full details, see the 2023/24 edition of this *Handbook*.

## Priority between deductions

**For UC**, an order of priority applies if your UC is 'insufficient' to meet all the deductions. Your award of UC is **'insufficient'** if the total amount of deductions made from your UC would be more than 40 per cent of the standard allowance that applies to you (see p67). In practice, if your UC is being reduced due to a sanction (see Chapter 43), then because of that limit the deductions below will not be made. The following deductions are paid in the following order of priority:[108]

- housing costs;
- rent arrears (and related charges), if the amount of the deduction is 10 per cent of your standard allowance;
- fuel;
- council tax arrears;
- fines;
- water charges;
- repayment of social fund payments;
- recovery of hardship payments;
- penalties instead of prosecution for benefit offences;
- recovery of overpayments of benefits or tax credits caused by fraud;
- civil penalties;
- recovery of overpayments of benefits or tax credits not caused by fraud;
- repayment of integration loans;
- repayment of eligible loans;
- rent arrears (and related charges), if the amount of the deduction is more than 10 per cent of your standard allowance.

**For income-related ESA and PC**, if you have more debts or current charges than can be met from your benefit (see p1040), deductions are made in a similar order to those for UC (the first three in the list are the same as for UC).[109] See the 2023/24 edition of this *Handbook* for the full list.

Deductions for child support are always payable.

If you owe both gas and electricity arrears, the DWP chooses which one to pay first, depending on your circumstances.[110]

If you have been overpaid benefit or given a social fund loan, you may also have to repay these through deductions from your benefit.[111] Argue that these deductions should take a lower priority than those above.

## 10. Recovery of benefits from compensation payments

If you are seeking compensation from someone (the 'defendant') through the courts (eg, because you have been unfairly dismissed or because you have had a personal injury), you may be awarded damages to compensate you for your loss. However, if, as the result of a defendant's action, you have had to claim benefit, the amount of damages awarded is reduced by the amount of benefit you received.

### Employment cases

In an employment case such as wrongful or unfair dismissal, your claim for compensation for loss of earnings may be reduced by the amount of benefit (eg, universal credit (UC) or jobseeker's allowance (JSA)) you receive.[112] Get specialist employment law advice. Also, the DWP can recover payments of UC, JSA, income support (IS) or income-related employment and support allowance (ESA) from your employer by deductions from your compensation if it is an unfair dismissal or protective award case dealt with in an employment tribunal. In such cases, the DWP sends a 'recoupment notice' to the employer and a copy to you, setting out the benefit to be deducted before the compensation is paid to you. You may notify the DWP that you do not accept the amount recouped within 21 days of the recoupment notice (or longer if allowed) and can appeal to the First-tier Tribunal against the decision that the DWP makes in response.[113]

### Personal injury cases

If you are paid compensation for an accident, injury or disease after 6 October 1997, those compensating you can reduce the amount paid to you if you have received benefit in respect of the same loss. They must then pay the money back to the Compensation Recovery Unit (CRU), which is part of the DWP. It does not matter whether the payment is voluntary, with or without legal proceedings, or by court order. A reduction is not made if the compensation is paid for pain and suffering because benefits are not paid for this.

The CRU can only recover the benefit in the right-hand column of the table on p1044, and only if you were paid it as a consequence of the accident, injury or disease.

**Note:** the CRU can also recover, under a similar scheme with its own rules, certain lump-sum payments made by the DWP to you or a dependant.[114] The lump-sum payments that can be recovered are those made by the DWP for lung diseases under the Pneumoconiosis etc. (Workers' Compensation) Act 1979 (or as compensation if you have had a claim under that Act rejected) or payments under the Diffuse Mesothelioma Payment Scheme.

A guide to the procedures, *Recovery of Benefits and Lump Sum Payments and NHS Charges: technical guidance*, is available at gov.uk/government/collections/cru.

## Which benefits can be recovered

All benefits paid to you 'in consequence' of the injury or disease you suffered during the 'relevant period' are recoverable.

***The relevant period***

The **'relevant period'** is usually five years from the day:[115]

- after the day of your accident or injury if you are claiming compensation for an accident or injury; *or*
- you first claimed a recoverable benefit because of the disease if you are claiming compensation in respect of a disease.

The relevant period ends if those compensating you make a final payment of compensation or an agreement is made under which compensation already paid is accepted as final payment.[116]

7

Before you are paid compensation, those compensating you must apply to the DWP for a 'certificate of recoverable benefits'.[117] This tells them which benefits are recoverable. Those compensating you become liable to pay the DWP for the total amount of recoverable benefit 14 days after the certificate is issued.[118] It is the compensator's obligation, not yours, and so if the compensator fails to pay, the CRU cannot pursue you for the money. The compensator remains liable even if it fails to apply for a certificate.[119]

## Offsetting against your compensation

Before the compensator pays your compensation, it can deduct the recoverable benefits paid during the relevant period from certain types of compensation.[120]

| *Compensation* | *Recoverable benefits* |
|---|---|
| Loss of earnings | UC, industrial injuries disablement benefit, ESA, incapacity benefit, IS, invalidity allowance, invalidity pension, JSA, reduced earnings allowance, severe disablement allowance, sickness benefit, unemployment benefit, unemployability supplement |
| Cost of care | Attendance allowance, disability living allowance (DLA) care component, disablement benefit paid for constant attendance (see p600) or exceptionally severe disablement (see p601), personal independence payment (PIP) daily living component |
| Loss of mobility | Mobility allowance, DLA mobility component, PIP mobility component |

*Example*

Aaron receives a £30,000 compensation payment consisting of £15,000 for loss of earnings, £5,000 for pain and suffering, and £10,000 for the cost of care. By the time the award was made, he had received £20,000 of UC and £5,000 of PIP daily living component. The award for loss of earnings is reduced to nil – ie, by the UC. Aaron receives the full award for pain and suffering, but his award for the cost of care is reduced by £5,000 (ie, by the PIP), leaving £5,000 for that. The compensator is liable to pay the DWP recoverable benefits of £20,000, and pay Aaron a net award of £10,000 (£5,000 for pain and suffering, plus £5,000 for care).

Any compensation reduced by this method is treated as being paid to you. Those compensating you must give you a statement showing how the payment has been calculated, even if the recovery of benefits reduces a particular type of compensation to nil. If the recoverable benefit exceeds the compensation paid to you for a particular loss, those compensating you still have to pay the balance to the DWP.

## Exempt payments

The recovery rules apply to all claims, no matter how small. However, certain compensation payments are exempt.[121] These include:

- contractual sick pay and redundancy payments;
- payments under the Fatal Accidents Act 1976, the Vaccine Damage Payments Act 1979 and the NHS industrial injury scheme;
- payments under the Pneumoconiosis Compensation Scheme and certain payments for loss of hearing;
- criminal injuries compensation and certain disaster/emergency relief funds – eg, the London Bombings Relief Charitable Fund;
- payments from insurance companies from policies agreed before the accident;
- payments from certain trusts – eg, an approved infected blood scheme.

## Challenging a recovery decision

A decision maker may look at a certificate of recoverable benefit again (this is called a review) if they are satisfied that there was an error in its preparation, that it recovers too much benefit, or that the person who applied for the certificate supplied incorrect or insufficient information, as a result of which the amount of benefit recovered is less than it should be.[122] You and those compensating you can both appeal to the First-tier Tribunal (see Chapter 51) against the certificate, but not until the compensation payment has been made and the benefit paid back to the DWP.[123] Also, the person appealing must apply for a review before they can appeal. It is best to apply for a review as soon as possible, but there is no absolute time limit.[124] Further appeals can be made to the Upper Tribunal in the usual way (see Chapter 52).[125]

# Notes

**1. Who is paid**

1 **UC/PIP/new-style JSA&ESA** Regs 57 and 58 UC,PIP,JSA&ESA(C&P) Regs
**HB** Reg 94(2) HB Regs; reg 75(2) HB(SPC) Regs
**CB/GA** Regs 27 and 28 CB&GA(Admin) Regs
**Other benefits** Regs 30, 33 and 34 SS(C&P) Regs

2 **UC/PIP/new-style JSA&ESA** Reg 58 UC,PIP,JSA&ESA(C&P) Regs
**CB/GA** Reg 34 CB&GA(Admin) Regs
**Other benefits** Reg 34(1) and (2) SS(C&P) Regs

3 **UC/PIP/new-style JSA&ESA** Reg 60 UC,PIP,JSA&ESA(C&P) Regs
**Other benefits** Reg 35 SS(C&P) Regs

**2. How and when you are paid**

4 Reg 21ZA SS(C&P) Regs; regs 47(6A), 48, 51 and 52 UC,PIP,JSA&ESA(C&P) Regs

5 **UC/PIP/new-style JSA&ESA** Reg 46 UC,PIP,JSA&ESA(C&P) Regs
**CB/GA** Reg 16 CB&GA(Admin) Regs
**Other benefits** Reg 21 SS(C&P) Regs

6 **UC/PIP/new-style JSA&ESA** Regs 47-52 UC,PIP,JSA&ESA(C&P) Regs
**CB/GA** Reg 18 CB&GA(Admin) Regs
**Other benefits** Regs 22-26C SS(C&P) Regs

7 **UC/PIP/new-style JSA&ESA** Reg 45 UC,PIP,JSA&ESA(C&P) Regs
**HB** Reg 91 HB Regs; reg 72 HB(SPC) Regs
**CB/GA** Reg 18 CB&GA(Admin) Regs
**Other benefits** Reg 20 SS(C&P) Regs

8 **UC/PIP/new-style JSA&ESA** Reg 55 UC,PIP,JSA&ESA(C&P) Regs
**CB/GA** Reg 26 CB&GA(Admin) Regs
**Other benefits** Reg 38 SS(C&P) Regs
**All** CDLA/2609/2002 commented on the way a similar rule applied to payment by giro/order book

**3. Overlapping benefits**

9 Reg 6 SS(OB) Regs; for ADP, reg 34(4) DAWAP(S) Regs

10 Reg 4(5) SS(OB) Regs; reg 16 CA(CSP)(S) Regs

11 s43(1) SSCBA 1992; s1 PA 2014; reg 4(5) SS(OB) Regs

12 ss51A and 52(2) SSCBA 1992

13 s16(1), (2) and (6) SSCBA 1992; reg 2 SS(MAP) Regs

14 Reg 4(4A) SS(OB) Regs

15 Reg 4(3) SS(OB) Regs

16 Reg 10 SS(OB) Regs

17 Reg 8 SS(OB) Regs

18 Reg 7 SS(OB) Regs

**4. Advance payments**

19 Regs 5 and 6 SS(PAB) Regs

20 Reg 7 SS(PAB) Regs

21 Reg 17 UC(TP) Regs does not refer to 'financial need' in this situation

22 **UC/PIP/new-style JSA&ESA** Sch 3 para 14 UC,PIP,JSA&ESA(DA) Regs
**Other benefits** Sch 2 para 20A SS&CS(DA) Regs

23 Reg 8 SS(PAB) Regs

24 Advances under the UC system are recovered under regs 3, 10 and 11 SS(OR) Regs, and there is no right of appeal about recovery under those rules. For other advances, Sch 2 para 20A SS&CS(DA) Regs allows a right of appeal against decisions on deductions under reg 10 SS(PAB) Regs.

25 Advances under the UC system are recovered under regs 3, 10 and 11 SS(OR) Regs, and there is no right of appeal about recovery under those rules.

26 Reg 3, definition of 'benefit', SS(PAB) Regs

**5. The benefit cap**

27 ss96 and 97 WRA 2012

28 Reg 75F(1)(g) HB Regs

29 Reg 82(1) UC Regs

30 Reg 82(2) UC Regs

31 Reg 75E HB Regs; HB Circular A15/2013

32 Reg 75E(3) HB Regs

33 Reg 75E(4) HB Regs

34 Reg 75F HB Regs; reg 83 UC Regs

35 Reg 75C HB Regs; reg 80 UC Regs

36 s96(5A) and (10) WRA 2012; regs 79 and 80 UC Regs; reg 8B UC(TP) Regs

37 s96(5A) WRA 2012; regs 75A, 75C and 75G HB Regs
38 Reg 75B HB Regs
39 Reg 81 UC Regs
40 Reg 75D HB Regs

6. **Change of circumstances after you claim**

41 **UC/PIP/new-style JSA&ESA** Reg 38 UC,PIP,JSA&ESA(C&P) Regs
**CB/GA** Reg 23 CB&GA(Admin) Regs
**Other benefits** Reg 32 SS(C&P) Regs
42 Regs 2 and 28 CB&GA(Admin) Regs
43 **UC/PIP/new-style JSA&ESA** Reg 38(5) UC,PIP,JSA&ESA(C&P) Regs
**Other benefits** Reg 32(1B) SS(C&P) Regs; regs 2, 3 and 5 SS(NCC) Regs, which apply for fraud, allow notification by phone (unless it is specifically required to be in writing)
44 Reg 23(5) CB&GA(Admin) Regs
45 **UC/PIP/new-style JSA&ESA** Reg 39 UC,PIP,JSA&ESA(C&P) Regs
**Other benefits** Reg 32ZZA SS(C&P) Regs

7. **When payments can be suspended**

46 **UC/PIP/new-style JSA&ESA** Reg 44(2)(b) and (c) UC,PIP,JSA&ESA(DA) Regs
**HB** Reg 11(2)(b) HB&CTB(DA) Regs
**CB/GA** Sch 7 para 13(2) CSPSSA 2000
**Other benefits** s21(2)(c) and (d) SSA 1998; reg 16(3)(b) SS&CS(DA) Regs
47 **UC/PIP/new-style JSA&ESA** Reg 44(5) UC,PIP,JSA&ESA(DA) Regs
**HB** Reg 11(3) HB&CTB(DA) Regs
**CB/GA** Reg 18(4) and (5) CB&GA(DA) Regs
**Other benefits** Reg 16(4) SS&CS(DA) Regs
48 **UC/PIP/new-style JSA&ESA** Reg 46(c) UC,PIP,JSA&ESA(DA) Regs
**HB** Reg 12(1)(b) HB&CTB(DA) Regs
**CB/GA** Reg 21 CB&GA(DA) Regs
**Other benefits** Reg 20(2) and (3) SS&CS(DA) Regs
49 **UC/PIP/new-style JSA&ESA** Reg 38(2) UC,PIP,JSA&ESA(C&P) Regs; reg 45 UC,PIP,JSA&ESA(DA) Regs
**HB** Reg 86(1) HB Regs; reg 67(1) HB(SPC) Regs
**CB/GA** Reg 23 CB&GA(Admin) Regs
**Other benefits** Reg 32(1) SS(C&P) Regs
50 **UC/PIP/new-style JSA&ESA** Reg 45(6) UC,PIP,JSA&ESA(DA) Regs
**HB** Reg 13 HB&CTB(DA) Regs
**CB/GA** Reg 19 CB&GA(DA) Regs
**Other benefits** Reg 17(5) SS&CS(DA) Regs
51 **UC/PIP/new-style JSA&ESA** Reg 45(4)(a) UC,PIP,JSA&ESA(DA) Regs
**HB** Reg 13(4)(a) HB&CTB(DA) Regs
**CB/GA** Reg 19(2) CB&GA(DA) Regs
**Other benefits** Reg 17(4)(a) SS&CS(DA) Regs
52 **UC/PIP/new-style JSA&ESA** Reg 45(4)(b) UC,PIP,JSA&ESA(DA) Regs
**HB** Reg 13(4)(b) HB&CTB(DA) Regs
**CB/GA** Reg 19(2)(b) CB&GA(DA) Regs
**Other benefits** Reg 17(4)(b) SS&CS(DA) Regs
53 **UC/PIP/new-style JSA&ESA** Reg 45(6) UC,PIP,JSA&ESA(DA) Regs
**HB** Reg 13(1) and (4) HB&CTB(DA) Regs
**CB/GA** Reg 19(5) CB&GA(DA) Regs
**Other benefits** Reg 17(5) SS&CS(DA) Regs
54 s24 SSA 1998; reg 19(2) SS&CS(DA) Regs
55 **HB** Sch 7 para 13(2)(a) CSPSSA 2000
**CB/GA** Reg 18(2) CB&GA(DA) Regs
**Other benefits** ss21(2)(a) and (b), 22 and 24 SSA 1998
56 **UC/PIP/new-style JSA&ESA** Reg 44(2)(a)(i) and (iii) UC,PIP,JSA&ESA(DA) Regs
**HB** Reg 11(2)(a)(i) and (c) HB&CTB(DA) Regs
**CB/GA** Reg 18(2)(a) and (c) CB&GA(DA) Regs
**Other benefits** Reg 16(3)(a)(i) and (iii) SS&CS(DA) Regs
57 Reg 18(2)(f) CB&GA(DA) Regs

8. **When your entitlement is terminated**

58 **UC/PIP/new-style JSA&ESA** Reg 47(1)(a) UC,PIP,JSA&ESA(DA) Regs
**HB** Reg 14(1)(a) HB&CTB(DA) Regs
**CB/GA** Reg 20(1)(a) CB&GA(DA) Regs
**Other benefits** Reg 18(1)(a), (2) and (4) SS&CS(DA) Regs
59 **UC/PIP/new-style JSA&ESA** Reg 47(1)(b) UC,PIP,JSA&ESA(DA) Regs
**HB** Reg 14(1)(b) HB&CTB(DA) Regs
**CB/GA** Reg 20(1)(b) CB&GA(DA) Regs
**Other benefits** Reg 18(1)(b), (3) and (4) SS&CS(DA) Regs

60 **UC/PIP/new-style JSA&ESA** Reg 47(2) UC,PIP,JSA&ESA(DA) Regs
**HB** Reg 14(1) HB&CTB(DA) Regs
**CB/GA** Reg 20(2) CB&GA(DA) Regs
**Other benefits** Reg 18(1) SS&CS(DA) Regs
61 Reg 19(3) and (4) SS&CS(DA) Regs

9. **Deductions and payments to third parties**
62 **UC/PIP/new-style JSA&ESA** Reg 60 and Schs 6 and 7 UC,PIP,JSA&ESA(C&P) Regs
**Other benefits** Reg 35 and Sch 9 SS(C&P) Regs; CC(DIS) Regs; CT(DIS) Regs; F(DIS) Regs
63 Sch 9 para 1(2) and (3) SS(C&P) Regs
64 Sch 9 para 2(1) SS(C&P) Regs; Sch 6 para 2(1) UC,PIP,JSA&ESA(C&P) Regs
65 Sch 6 para 3(3) UC,PIP,JSA&ESA(C&P) Regs
66 Sch 9 para 8(2) and (4) SS(C&P) Regs
67 **UC/PIP/new-style JSA&ESA** Sch 6 para 6 UC,PIP,JSA&ESA(C&P) Regs
**Other benefits** Sch 9 para 3(5) SS(C&P) Regs
68 Sch 9 para 1, definition of 'housing costs', SS(C&P) Regs
69 Sch 9 para 3(2)(b) SS(C&P) Regs
70 Sch 9 para 3(4) SS(C&P) Regs
71 Sch 6 para 7 UC,PIP,JSA&ESA(C&P) Regs
72 *Roberts v Secretary of State for Work and Pensions and Guinness Partnership Trust Ltd* [2025] EWHC 51 (Admin) (16 January 2025)
73 Sch 9 para 5 SS(C&P) Regs
74 Sch 9 para 5(1)(c)(i) SS(C&P) Regs
75 Sch 9 para 5(1)(c)(ii) SS(C&P) Regs
76 Sch 9 para 5(7) SS(C&P) Regs
77 **UC** Sch 6 para 8 UC,PIP,JSA&ESA(C&P) Regs
**Income-related ESA/PC** Sch 9 para 6 SS(C&P) Regs
78 Sch 6 para 8 UC,PIP,JSA&ESA(C&P) Regs
79 The principle is set out in *Timson, R (On the application of) v SSWP* [2022] EWHC 2392 (Admin), upheld by the Court of Appeal in *Timson, R (On the Application Of) v* SSWP[2023] EWCA Civ 656, but that was not about the UC rules
80 Sch 6 para 8 UC,PIP,JSA&ESA(C&P) Regs
81 Sch 9 para 6 SS(C&P) Regs
82 *Timson, R (On the application of) v SSWP* [2022] EWHC 2392 (Admin), upheld by the Court of Appeal in *Timson, R (On the Application Of) v SSWP* [2023] EWCA Civ 656 (9 June 2023)
83 Sch 9 para 6(1) SS(C&P) Regs
84 Sch 9 para 3(2)(b) SS(C&P) Regs
85 Sch 6 para 9 UC,PIP,JSA&ESA(C&P) Regs
86 The principle is set out in *Timson, R (On the application of) v SSWP* [2022] EWHC 2392 (Admin), upheld by the Court of Appeal in *Timson, R (On the Application Of) v SSWP* [2023] EWCA Civ 656, but that was not about the UC rules
87 Sch 9 paras 1 and 7 SS(C&P) Regs
88 *Timson, R (On the application of) v SSWP* [2022] EWHC 2392 (Admin) upheld by the Court of Appeal in *Timson, R (On the Application Of) v SSWP* [2023] EWCA Civ 656
89 Sch 9 para 7(6) SS(C&P) Regs
90 Sch 9 para 3(2)(b) SS(C&P) Regs
91 CC(DIS) Regs; CT(DIS) Regs; CIS/11861/1996
92 **UC/PIP/new-style JSA&ESA** Sch 7 paras 1 and 2 UC,PIP,JSA&ESA(C&P) Regs
**Other benefits** Sch 9B para 2 SS(C&P) Regs
93 **UC/PIP/new-style JSA&ESA** Sch 7 para 3 UC,PIP,JSA&ESA(C&P) Regs
**Other benefits** Sch 9B para 3 SS(C&P) Regs
94 Reg 4 F(DIS) Regs
95 **UC/PIP/new-style JSA&ESA** Sch 6 para 11 UC,PIP,JSA&ESA(C&P) Regs
**Other benefits** Sch 9 para 7C SS(C&P) Regs
96 **UC/PIP/new-style JSA&ESA** Sch 6 para 12 UC,PIP,JSA&ESA(C&P) Regs
**Other benefits** Sch 9 para 7D SS(C&P) Regs; reg 9 ILRFO Regs
97 Sch 9 para 7E SS(C&P) Regs
98 Reg 12 UC(TP) Regs; The Tax Credits (Exercise of Functions) Order 2014 No.3280
99 Sch 9 para 4 SS(C&P) Regs
100 Sch 9 para 4A SS(C&P) Regs
101 Sch 6 para 3(1)(a) UC,PIP,JSA&ESA(C&P) Regs
102 Sch 6 para 3(1)(b) UC,PIP,JSA&ESA(C&P) Regs
103 Sch 6 para 3(1)(a) UC,PIP,JSA&ESA(C&P) Regs
104 Sch 6 para 3(3) UC,PIP,JSA&ESA(C&P) Regs

105 The legal limit is actually 40 per cent. Sch 6 para 4 UC,PIP,JSA&ESA(C&P) Regs; a limit of 15 per cent, down from 25 per cent, was made in the Autumn 2024 Budget; official guidance in *Universal credit: debt and deductions that can be taken from payment*, DWP guidance, at gov.uk/guidance/find-out-about-money-taken-off-your-universal-credit-payment.
106 Sch 6 para 4 UC,PIP,JSA&ESA(C&P) Regs
107 Sch 9 para 2(2) SS(C&P) Regs
108 Sch 6 para 5 UC,PIP,JSA&ESA(C&P) Regs
109 Sch 9 para 9 SS(C&P) Regs
110 Reg 4 CC(DIS) Regs; reg 8 CT(DIS) Regs
111 Regs 15 and 16 SS(PAOR) Regs; reg 3 SF(RDB) Regs

10. **Recovery of benefits from compensation payments**
112 *Nabi v British Leyland (UK) Ltd* [1980] 1 WLR 529 (CA)
113 The Employment Protection (Recoupment of Jobseeker's Allowance and Income Support) Regulations 1996 No.2349
114 The Social Security (Recovery of Benefits) (Lump Sum Payments) Regulations 2008 No.1596
115 s3 SS(RB)A 1997
116 s3(4) SS(RB)A 1997
117 s4 SS(RB)A 1997
118 s6(4) SS(RB)A 1997
119 s7 SS(RB)A 1997
120 s8 and Sch 2 SS(RB)A 1997
121 s1 and Sch 1 SS(RB)A 1997; reg 2 SS(RB) Regs
122 s10 SS(RB)A 1997; reg 9 SS&CS(DA) Regs
123 ss11 and 12 SS(RB)A 1997
124 s11(2A) SS(RB)A 1997; reg 9ZB SS&CS(DA) Regs. Neither provide a time limit for review. See the official guidance at gov.uk/government/publications/repaying-compensation-to-dwp-what-to-do-if-you-think-our-decision-is-wrong.
125 s13 SS(RB)A 1997; reg 13 SS(RB)App Regs

# Chapter 46

# Hardship payments

**This chapter covers:**


1. Hardship payments of universal credit (below)
2. Hardship payments of employment and support allowance (p1053)
3. Deciding hardship (p1054)
4. Applying for hardship payments (p1055)
5. Getting paid (p1056)
6. Challenging a hardship payment decision (p1056)
7. Tax, other benefits and the benefit cap (p1056)




## Key facts

- Hardship payments are reduced-rate payments of universal credit (UC) and employment and support allowance (ESA) that are made in limited circumstances, if you have been sanctioned or you have committed a benefit offence.
- You or your partner or children must be experiencing hardship to be able to get a hardship payment.
- You must apply for hardship payments. For UC, you must make a new application for each assessment period in which your UC is paid at a reduced or nil rate.
- You usually have to pay back hardship payments of UC. You do not have to pay back hardship payments of ESA.

## 1. Hardship payments of universal credit

You may be able to get hardship payments of universal credit (UC) if your UC is being paid at a reduced or nil rate because you have been given a sanction or because you have committed a benefit offence. You usually have to pay back hardship payments of UC (see p1053). You must apply for hardship payments of UC as they are not made automatically (see p1055).

**Note:** if your new-style jobseeker's allowance (JSA) or contributory employment and support allowance (ESA) is paid at a reduced or nil rate and you experience hardship, you may qualify for hardship payments of UC.

**Note:** income-based JSA has now been replaced by UC (see p21). For an explanation of the rules about hardship payments and income-based JSA, see the 2024/25 edition of this *Handbook*.

## When you can get hardship payments

### Universal credit reduced because of a sanction

If your UC has been reduced because of a sanction, you can get hardship payments of UC if:[1]

- you (or your partner – whoever has been sanctioned) are 18 or over; *and*
- your UC is being paid at a reduced or nil rate using the 'high rate' daily reduction (see p980); *and*
- you (or your partner) apply in an approved way and provide any information or evidence required by the DWP; *and*
- you (and your partner) accept that the hardship payments are recoverable. **Note:** this does not prevent you from later asking the DWP not to recover your hardship payments (see p1053); *and*
- the DWP is satisfied that you (and your partner) have met all the work-related requirements that were in force in the seven days before you applied for hardship payments; *and*
- the DWP is satisfied that you (and your partner) are experiencing hardship (see p1055); *and*
- for low level sanctions only, you (and your partner) have complied with any condition specified by the DWP – eg, you have now taken part in a work-focused interview or have agreed to attend training.

7

### Universal credit reduced because of a benefit offence

If your UC has been reduced because of a benefit offence (see p1111), you can get hardship payments of UC if:[2]

- you (and your partner) meet all the conditions of entitlement to UC; *and*
- you (and your partner) apply in an approved way and provide any information or evidence required by the DWP; *and*
- you (and your partner) accept that the hardship payments are recoverable. **Note:** this does not prevent you from later asking the DWP not to recover your hardship payments (see p1053); *and*
- the DWP is satisfied that you (and your partner) are experiencing hardship (see p1055).

**Note:** you can qualify under the benefit offences rules even if you (or your partner) are aged 16 or 17.

## Hardship payment periods

Each hardship payment is paid at a daily rate for a period described as the 'hardship period'. This starts on the date you satisfy all the conditions for getting a hardship payment, including having made an application. Guidance suggests that this start date can be no earlier than the first payday when your UC is reduced or nil.[3] Backdating is not available. The hardship payment normally ends the day before your next usual UC payday. If this would make the hardship period less than eight days long, it ends on the payday for the following assessment period or, if sooner, the last day in respect of which your UC is paid at a reduced or nil rate.[4]

***How do you ensure you get maximum hardship payments?***

You must reapply for hardship payments of UC in each assessment period you need one. To ensure you get the maximum amount, make your first application on the first payday when you receive a reduced amount of UC, and submit a new application every payday until your UC is no longer being reduced. Try not to miss these dates, as backdating is not available.

## The amount of hardship payments

7

The amount of hardship payments is worked out as follows.[5]

- **Step 1:** determine the amount of the reduction made from your UC for the sanction (see p980) or the benefit offence (see p1112) in the assessment period before the one in which you apply for hardship payments. Note that the reduction takes effect from the first day of the assessment period in which the sanction or benefit offence decision was made (see p988).
- **Step 2:** multiply the amount in Step 1 by 12 and divide by 365. Take 60 per cent of this amount, rounding to the nearest penny.
- **Step 3:** multiply the amount in Step 2 by the number of days for which hardship payments can be made to you.

***Example***

Calvin is a single claimant aged 40. His usual UC payday is the 3rd of the month. He was given a 91-day medium level sanction on 17 September, in a 30-day assessment period. When his UC starts to be paid at a reduced rate, he applies and qualifies for a hardship payment on 7 October. He therefore gets a hardship payment for the period starting on 7 October and ending on 2 November (27 days).

**Step 1**: the relevant amount is £393 (£13.10 daily reduction x 30 days).

**Step 2**: £393 x 12 ÷ 365 x 60% = £7.75

**Step 3**: Calvin can be paid hardship payments for 27 days.

£7.75 x 27 days = £209.25

Calvin's hardship payment for that assessment period is £209.25. He gets this in addition to any UC he can be paid – eg, if he qualifies for a housing costs element.

If still experiencing hardship, Calvin should apply for another hardship payment on the day he gets his next reduced UC payment – ie, 3 November.

### Recovery of hardship payments

You usually have to pay back hardship payments of UC.[6] However:

- the DWP *has a discretion not to recover* all or part of a hardship payment.[7] This is not affected by the fact that, at the application stage, you were required to accept that the payment was recoverable. You can ask the DWP not to recover your hardship payment – eg, if this would cause you to be in hardship again. Advice about the DWP's discretion not to recover hardship payments is similar to that for recovery of overpayments (see p1072); *and*
- hardship payments are *not* recoverable during any assessment period in which you have sufficient monthly earnings (see below); *and*
- hardship payments *stop* being recoverable (ie, are 'written off') if, since the last day on which your UC was paid at a reduced or nil rate, you have had sufficient monthly earnings (combined earnings, if you are a joint claimant) for a single period of, or periods that total, six months.[8]

You are classed as having sufficient monthly earnings if you (or, if you are a joint claimant, you and your partner) do not have to meet any work-related requirements:

- because your earnings (your combined earnings if you are a joint claimant) are the same as, or above, your earnings threshold (see p955); *or*
- for any of the other reasons listed on p950 and p956 (other situations).
  In this case, your monthly earnings (your combined monthly earnings if you are a joint claimant) must be at least 16 times the minimum hourly wage for a person of your age (or your partner's age if they are younger than you) multiplied by 52 and divided by 12.[9]

Hardship payments can normally only be recovered from the person they were paid to. However, if you are a joint claimant, an amount paid to your partner can be treated as paid to you, and vice versa.[10]

All the methods used to recover overpayments described on p1073 can be used to recover hardship payments.[11] Recovery rates for hardship payments from ongoing UC are the same as for the recovery of overpayments of UC (see p1074). These are the maximum rates of recovery, which can be reduced if you can show that you cannot afford them.

## 2. Hardship payments of employment and support allowance

You may be able to get hardship payments of **income-related** employment and support allowance (ESA) if you are already getting income-related ESA and it is being paid at a reduced or nil rate because you have been given a sanction or because you have committed a benefit offence.[12] Before you can get a hardship payment, the DWP must be satisfied that you will otherwise suffer hardship due to your ESA being reduced.[13] The weekly amount of hardship payments is a percentage of the personal allowance for main-phase ESA.[14] You do not have to pay these hardship payments back. You must apply for hardship payments of ESA as they are not made automatically (see p1055). For more detail about the rules for hardship payments of income-related ESA, see the 2021/22 edition of this *Handbook*.

If you get **'new-style' contributory** ESA, you may be able to claim a hardship payment of universal credit (see p1050).

**Note:** different hardship rules apply if you could be disqualified from getting ESA (eg, because you have limited capability for work through your own misconduct, or you have failed to accept treatment without 'good cause'), but you are experiencing hardship (see p557).

# 3. Deciding hardship

7

When you apply for hardship payments, explain anything causing you hardship or which makes it more likely you will experience hardship – eg, health, disability, pregnancy and any needs you, your partner and children have.

***Hardship***

'**Hardship**' is not defined in the rules.

For universal credit (UC), hardship should be decided by considering whether you can cover your immediate, basic and essential needs for accommodation, heating, food and hygiene. The DWP says that '**immediate**' means at the point of application. Although if you have children, it will be interpreted to mean within the next seven days.[15]

For employment and support allowance (ESA), the DWP says it means 'severe suffering' or 'a lack of the necessities of life'.[16]

## General rules

When deciding whether or not you are experiencing hardship, the DWP must consider certain things. For UC, see p1055; for JSA, see the 2024/25 edition of this *Handbook*; and for ESA, see the 2021/22 edition of this *Handbook*.

In all cases, the DWP looks at the resources available to you.

**Note:**

- The DWP usually takes into account income and capital that is disregarded when calculating your benefit – eg, personal independence payment, adult disability payment, disability living allowance and savings below £6,000.

- You should only be treated as having resources likely to be actually available to you. For example, if you have savings in a bank account but they are subject to a notice period for withdrawal, you should not be treated as having this capital until you can access it. You may be expected to ask your family for help and investigate sources of free help, but you are not expected to rely on charity.
- You should not be treated as having resources if these are only available on credit or if you would have to sell any of your possessions.

### Universal credit

The DWP only considers you to be in hardship if both of the following apply.[17]

- You (and your partner) cannot meet your immediate and most basic and essential needs, or those of a child or qualifying young person you (or your partner) are responsible for, because your UC has been reduced by a sanction using the 'high rate' daily reduction or because you committed a benefit offence. **'Needs'** means needs for accommodation, heating, food and hygiene – eg, products to keep you and your home clean, or nappies for your baby. In considering whether you can meet these needs, the DWP looks at the other resources available to you – it does not include child benefit.[18]
- You (and your partner) have made every effort to get alternative sources of financial support (eg, from your family) and to stop incurring expenditure not related to your basic and essential needs. The DWP says this does not mean you must stop spending money on things you need to help you look for work, such as a phone and internet access, or to maintain your children's access to education.[19] The DWP must consider what is reasonable in your case. You should not be required to sell or pawn anything (other than stocks and shares), find cheaper accommodation, take out credit or incur certain financial penalties – eg, for cancelling a gym membership.[20] The DWP should not force you to request or accept help from charities if you choose not to, but may expect you to investigate and consider what help may be available.[21]

The DWP recognises some people are more likely to suffer hardship – eg, parents, carers, disabled people and people who are seriously ill.[22]

## 4. Applying for hardship payments

You must apply for hardship payments as they are not made automatically. You can ask in your universal credit (UC) journal, at the job centre or by calling the relevant benefit helpline. You must provide information and evidence if the DWP says it is required.[23]

Although you cannot get employment and support allowance hardship payments until you have made your application, there is no general rule to prevent you from getting these backdated. You cannot get a UC hardship payment backdated.

**Note:** for UC, you must make a new application for hardship payments in each assessment period. See p1051 for when you can apply and how to ensure maximum payments.

## 5. **Getting paid**

The general rules on getting paid are covered in Chapter 45.

Hardship payments of universal credit should be made as quickly as possible, once the application has been allowed. If practical, this should be on the day the application is accepted.[24]

Hardship payments of employment and support allowance (ESA) are made on the day your ESA is usually paid.

## 6. **Challenging a hardship payment decision**

If you are refused hardship payments, you can ask for a mandatory reconsideration of the decision, and then appeal if you remain unhappy with the outcome (see Chapter 51). When (or before) you make a mandatory reconsideration request, ask for a written statement of reasons for the decision if this has not already been provided (see p1125). Remember to tell the DWP if your circumstances worsen while you are applying for a mandatory reconsideration or appealing. Ask it to consider whether hardship payments can now be paid based on your new circumstances.

If you are unhappy with a decision about the recovery of a universal credit hardship payment, see p1053.

## 7. **Tax, other benefits and the benefit cap**

### Tax

Hardship payments of universal credit (UC) and employment and support allowance (ESA) are not taxable.

### The benefit cap

Hardship payments of UC and ESA count towards the benefit cap, although in ESA cases the benefit cap only applies if you are getting housing benefit (HB). See p1025 for further information.

## Passported benefits

Hardship payments are a type of UC and income-related ESA, so while getting hardship payments, you are still entitled to passported benefits (eg, help with health costs) in the usual way.

Payment of HB should not be affected if you have been given a sanction, whether or not you are getting hardship payments. If it is, contact the local authority immediately.

# Notes

1. **Hardship payments of universal credit**
   1 s28 WRA 2012; reg 116(1) UC Regs
   2 Regs 16D(1) and (2)(a) and 16E(a)-(c) SS(LB) Regs
   3 Reg 117(1)(a) UC Regs; reg 16F(a)(i) SS(LB) Regs; paras L1142 and L1146 ADM; DWP, Universal Credit Guidance, *Recoverable hardship payments*, v11.0, House of Commons library deposited papers, available at rightsnet.org.uk/resources/universal-credit guidance. Note that the calculations in regs 118 UC Regs and 16G SS(LB) Regs are based on 'the amount of the reduction...for the assessment period *preceding* the assessment period in which an application is submitted'.
   4 Reg 117(1)(b) and (2) UC Regs; reg 16F(a)(ii) and (b) SS(LB) Regs
   5 Regs 6 and 118 UC Regs; reg 16G SS(LB) Regs
   6 s71ZH(1)(a) and (e) SSAA 1992; s28(2)(f) WRA 2012; reg 119 UC Regs; reg 16H SS(LB) Regs
   7 s71ZH(1)(a) SSAA 1992; DWP, *Benefit Overpayment Recovery Guide*, paras 5.45-47
   8 Reg 119 UC Regs
   9 Reg 119(2)(c) UC Regs
   10 s71ZH(4) SSAA 1992
   11 s71ZH(5) SSAA 1992

2. **Hardship payments of employment and support allowance**
   12 Regs 2(1), definition of 'hardship payment', 64A(a)-(c) and 64B ESA Regs; reg 16A(1) SS(LB) Regs
   13 Reg 64C ESA Regs; reg 16A SS(LB) Regs
   14 Reg 64D ESA Regs; reg 16C SS(LB) Regs

3. **Deciding hardship**
   15 paras L1002-03 and L1047 ADM
   16 para 35155 DMG
   17 Reg 116(2) and (3) UC Regs; reg 16D(2)(b)-(d) and (3) SS(LB) Regs; Ch L1 ADM
   18 para L1124 ADM
   19 paras L1099 and L1100 ADM
   20 paras L1087 and L1096-L1103 ADM
   21 paras L1084-93 ADM
   22 para L1051 ADM

4. **Applying for hardship payments**
   23 **UC** Reg 116(1)(c) and (d) UC Regs; reg 16E(a) and (b) SS(LB) Regs; paras L1031 and L1036 ADM
   **ESA** Reg 64A(d) and (e) ESA Regs; reg 16B SS(LB) Regs

5. **Getting paid**
   24 DWP, Universal Credit Guidance, *Recoverable hardship payments*, v11.0, House of Commons library deposited papers, available at rightsnet.org.uk/resources/universal-credit-guidance

7

# Chapter 47

# Overpayments

**This chapter covers:**


1. Introduction (below)
2. Benefit overpayments that are always recoverable (p1060)
3. Benefit overpayments that are sometimes recoverable (p1063)
4. Recovery of overpaid benefit (p1072)
5. Overpayments of housing benefit (p1078)
6. Overpayments of tax credits (p1088)


For overpayments of Scottish benefits, see Chapter 68.

7

## Key facts

- If you are paid more benefit than you are entitled to, this is called an overpayment.
- If you are overpaid universal credit (UC), new-style jobseeker's allowance or new-style employment and support allowance, you can always be required to repay it, regardless of how it was caused.
- All overpayments of housing benefit are recoverable, except those caused by 'official error' which you could not have reasonably known were overpayments.
- For other benefits, including the legacy benefits that have now been replaced by UC, the general rule is that you can be required to repay the overpayment if it arose because you did not disclose something or you misrepresented something, regardless of whether this was your fault.
- Overpayments of tax credits that occurred before the ending of the tax credit scheme in April 2025 are always recoverable, however caused.
- The DWP, HMRC and local authorities have the discretion not to recover an overpayment.

## 1. Introduction

An 'overpayment' of benefit occurs when you are paid more than you should have been paid. If you are told that you must repay an overpayment of benefit, do the following.

- Use the relevant chapters in this *Handbook* to check whether or not you were entitled to some or all of the amount that the DWP, HMRC or local authority says is an overpayment. If you were entitled to some or all of the amount, you should challenge the decision about your entitlement.
- If some or all of the amount should not have been paid, check whether:
  - for benefits other than housing benefit (HB), the overpayment is always recoverable (see p1060);
  - for benefits other than HB, the overpayment is sometimes recoverable, depending on the circumstances. Check whether all three conditions that allow the overpayment to be recovered are met, and also whether the overpayment can be reduced under the rules described on p1069;
  - the overpayment of HB is recoverable (see p1078). If so, check whether it can be recovered from you (p1082) and whether any amount can be offset against the sum claimed (see p1081).
- If you are not the person whose benefit was overpaid, check whether the overpayment can be recovered from you (see p1070 and p1082).
- Consider whether it is worth asking for the overpayment not to be recovered. For benefits, see p1072. For tax credits, see p1090.
- If you must repay an overpayment, check that the method of recovery used is correct. For overpayments of HB, see p1082, and for other benefits, see p1072.

7

Note:
- The tax credit system has now closed and you cannot have an award of tax credits now. However, it is still possible that you were overpaid tax credits in the past (see p1088).
- If you are overpaid benefit because you made an incorrect statement or failed to provide information, you may also have to pay a penalty (see p1101). If it is considered that an overpayment was made because of fraud, in addition to the overpayment being recovered, you may be prosecuted or given the option of paying a penalty instead of going to court. See Chapter 54 for further information.
- In England or Wales, if an overpayment has been included in a debt relief order, it cannot be recovered.[1] Also, if you are subject to a bankruptcy order, any overpayment that is notified to you as recoverable before the order was made is not recoverable. However, once the order ceases to have effect, any overpayment caused by fraud becomes recoverable.
- In England or Wales, recovery of your benefit overpayment is suspended for 60 days if you are accepted on a breathing space debt respite scheme. You must get debt advice from and apply via a professional debt adviser authorised by the Financial Conduct Authority, or a local authority which provides debt advice to residents.[2]

# 2. Benefit overpayments that are always recoverable

Benefit overpayments can always be recovered in the following situations.

- You have been paid too much universal credit (UC), new-style jobseeker's allowance (JSA) or new-style employment and support allowance (ESA).
- You have been paid too much income-related ESA or pension credit (PC) because you were owed income that you have now received (see p1062 – this also applies to older awards of income support (IS) and income-based JSA, although these have now been replaced by UC).
- Too much mortgage interest was paid direct to your lender (see p1063).
- Too much benefit has been paid into your bank account by mistake (see p1063).

You may still be able to argue that you have not been overpaid, or that the overpayment has been calculated incorrectly. The decision maker at the DWP or HMRC also has the discretion not to recover in certain circumstances (see p1072).

For recovery of overpayments of housing benefit, see p1078.

7

## Overpayments under the universal credit system

If you are overpaid UC, new-style JSA or new-style ESA, the DWP can (but does not have to) recover any amount of overpaid benefit, regardless of the cause of the overpayment.[3] See p1072 for how the overpayment can be recovered.

**Note:**

- The DWP must first change the decision awarding you benefit before it can decide whether the overpayment can be recovered (see p1068).[4]
- You can appeal against a decision that you have been overpaid, or about the amount of an overpayment. You must request a mandatory reconsideration before you can appeal (see p1167). You cannot appeal against a decision to recover an overpayment.[5]
- You can ask the DWP to use its discretion not to recover (ie, to 'waive') the overpayment (see p1072).

### The amount recovered

The amount recovered is the difference between what you received and how much you were entitled to after the decision awarding you benefit has been changed.[6] This amount can be reduced in the following circumstances.

#### Offsetting universal credit

If you were overpaid JSA or ESA, the amount may be reduced by the amount of any UC you could have received. For this to happen, you must have claimed UC. The overpaid amount is reduced by the amount of UC you would have got:[7]

- had you notified any change of circumstances that affected your JSA or ESA entitlement (other than a change of address) to the DWP at the time it occurred; *or*
- had you not misrepresented or failed to disclose something before the award of JSA or ESA; *or*
- had a mistake by the decision maker not occurred.

**You are overpaid universal credit because of a mistake about your capital**

If you are overpaid UC because of a mistake about your savings for more than three months, the amount to be recovered is reduced to take into account the fact that you would have been spending your capital had you not been receiving UC.

At the end of each three-month period for which you have been overpaid, the amount of capital you are regarded as having is reduced by the amount of UC that you were overpaid in those three months.[8] The overpayment for the next three months is then calculated as if you had this reduced amount of capital.

**You are overpaid because you moved home**

If you are overpaid the housing element of UC because you moved home, but payments continued being made for your previous home, the decision maker may reduce the amount to be recovered by an amount equal to what you would have received in respect of your new home.[9]

The decision maker can only do this if the payments for your previous home are made to the same person as those for your new home.[10] If the decision maker reduces the amount to be recovered in this way, the reduction in the overpaid amount is treated as if it were paid in respect of your new home.[11]

## From whom can an overpayment be recovered

An overpayment of UC, new-style JSA or new-style ESA is usually recoverable from the person it was paid to. However, it can be recovered from someone else in the following circumstances.[12]

- If the overpaid amount was paid to an appointee or to someone other than you because it was not in your interest to pay you directly (see p1018), the overpayment can also be recovered from you, the claimant.
- If an overpaid amount was paid to a third party under the rules about deductions and payments to third parties (see p1033), the amount is recoverable from you, the claimant. However, amounts paid to the third party in excess of the amounts allowed by those rules are only recoverable from the third party.
- If the overpaid amount includes an amount for housing costs paid to another person (eg, your landlord) and:
  - the overpayment occurred because someone failed to disclose or misrepresented a material fact (see p1064 and p1068), it is recoverable from that person, not the person to whom it was paid;

- the overpayment occurred because you moved home, it is recoverable from you, as well as from the person to whom it was paid;
- the overpayment occurred because the payment exceeded the housing costs for which you are liable (eg, it was more than your rent), it is recoverable from the person to whom it was paid – eg, your landlord;
- the overpayment did not occur for any of the above three reasons, it is recoverable from you, the claimant, not the person to whom it was paid.

## You were owed income that you have now received

For UC, if you are paid income late, and that income would have reduced your UC had it been paid on time, the UC you would not have been paid at the time is an overpayment which can be recovered from you (see Chapter 7 for what income is taken into account for UC).[13] This does not apply regarding late paid earnings, as the rule for UC is that earnings only count in the assessment period when they are actually received (see p145). However, it could apply to other income which is paid late, such as arrears of benefit. **Note:** arrears of some benefits, when they would count as capital (eg, having been ignored as income), can be ignored as capital for 52 weeks or sometimes longer (see p158).

7

A similar rule applies if you are paid income late (including earnings) which would have reduced your income-related ESA or PC and you are overpaid as a result.[14] **Note:** this also applies if the income would have reduced your IS or income-based JSA, although that will have been in an older award as these have now been replaced by UC (see p21).

If you are owed arrears of certain benefits (state pension, personal independence payment, adult disability payment, child benefit, widowed parents allowance and old-style contributory ESA), the DWP can reduce (or 'abate') those arrears before they are paid to you, to avoid an overpayment of UC, income-related ESA or PC. If the arrears are not reduced and you are overpaid, the DWP can recover the overpayment from you.[15] However, this reduction does not apply to arrears of new-style ESA or new-style JSA. So, if these are paid, you will then have been overpaid UC. In practice, the DWP may still offer to 'voluntarily abate' such arrears before you are paid them, so that you are not then overpaid UC, but this offer is at the DWP's discretion.

You can appeal about whether an overpayment has occurred and how it has been calculated.[16] You must apply for a mandatory reconsideration before you can appeal (see p1168). You cannot appeal against the decision to recover any overpayment that has occurred, but you can ask the DWP to use its discretion not to recover it (see p1072).

See p1072 for how the overpayment can be recovered.

## Too much mortgage interest has been paid to your lender

If you have a mortgage and are entitled to UC, income-related ESA or PC, the DWP may offer you loan payments to help with the interest payments (see p764).

If it is decided that you were overpaid mortgage interest included in your benefit from before April 2018, see p1239 of the 2018/19 edition of this *Handbook* for when it is recoverable.

## Too much benefit has been credited to your account

Your benefit is usually paid by direct credit transfer into a bank account. If you are credited with too much money because of the direct credit transfer system itself, the overpayment can only be recovered if:[17]

- you were notified in writing before you agreed to your benefit being paid into a bank or other account that any excess benefit could be recovered; *and*
- it has been certified that you were paid excess benefit because of the direct credit transfer system.

If the excess benefit cannot be recovered under the rules described above, it may be recoverable under the rules described below, or those for recovery following late payment of income (see p1062).

You can ask for a mandatory reconsideration of the decision to recover excess benefit credited to your bank account, and then appeal if you remain unhappy with the outcome (see p1168).[18]

Even if the overpayment is recoverable, you can ask the DWP or HMRC to use its discretion not to recover it (see p1072).

# 3. Benefit overpayments that are sometimes recoverable

Except for the overpayments described on p1060 and overpayments of housing benefit (HB) (see p1078), some benefit overpayments can only be recovered if:[19]

- you failed to disclose, or you misrepresented, a relevant 'material fact' (see p1064) and this caused the overpayment (see p1068); *and*
- the decision to award you benefit has been changed (see p1068).

If you have been overpaid and neither of the above conditions apply to the whole of the overpayment, only the part of the overpayment to which they both apply is recoverable from you. For example, if you were paid too much benefit over a two-year period, but you told the DWP about all the relevant facts after the first year, the overpayment made after this was not caused by your failure to disclose and is not recoverable from you. However, note that this does not apply to overpayments of universal credit (UC) or new-style employment and support allowance (ESA) or jobseeker's allowance (JSA).

*Example*
Lochlan was receiving income support (IS) as a carer during 2024. The person he was caring for stopped getting personal independence payment (PIP) in early 2024. Lochlan informed the DWP of this in July 2024 but the DWP continued to pay Lochlan his IS until March 2025. From July 2024 onwards, this overpayment is not recoverable.

Note:
- Even if an overpayment can be recovered, in some situations amounts must be deducted from the recoverable sum (see p1069).
- This type of overpayment can sometimes be recovered from you, even if you are not the claimant (see p1070).
- You can ask for a mandatory reconsideration of the decision that the overpayment is recoverable from you and then appeal if you remain unhappy with the outcome (see p1071).
- Even if an overpayment is recoverable, you can ask the DWP or HMRC to use its discretion not to recover it (see p1072).

7

## You failed to disclose, or you misrepresented, a material fact

For an overpayment to be recoverable, you must have:
- failed to disclose a relevant material fact (see below); *or*
- misrepresented a relevant material fact (see p1067).

### A material fact

A **'material fact'** influences how much benefit you should be paid.[20] Sometimes, your honest opinion and a material fact can differ.[21] For example, a statement about the distance you can walk should be taken as your honest opinion of your ability rather than as a statement of fact.[22] If the decision maker comes to a different conclusion about the facts, you can argue that an overpayment should not be recovered.[23]

| *Facts* | *Conclusions about the facts* |
|---|---|
| You have arthritis | You have limited capability for work |
| A friend is sharing your flat | You are living together as spouses or civil partners |
| You have a bad back | Your mobility is severely restricted most of the time |

### Failure to disclose

You count as having failed to disclose a relevant material fact if:[24]
- you knew about a fact; *and*

- you had a legal duty to disclose that fact; *and*
- you did not comply with that legal duty.

### Knowledge of a fact

If you did not know about a fact, including if it was a change in your circumstances, you have not failed to disclose it.[25] You cannot fail to disclose something you did not know about unless:

- there was a reason why you should have been aware of it;[26] *or*
- it was reasonable for you to make enquiries, which would have revealed the information to you;[27] *or*
- you had been aware of it but simply forgot.[28]

### Legal duty to disclose

You have two different legal duties to disclose facts: a specific duty and a general duty.

You have a **specific duty** to disclose a fact that you know about and which is a type of fact you have clearly been told by the DWP or HMRC that you must disclose – eg, in your benefit award letter or in the notes accompanying it.[29]

You do not have a specific legal duty to disclose something unless the instruction is clear and there is no room for doubt about whether or not you are required to report it.[30]

If you were not clearly told that you must report a certain fact, this specific duty to disclose does not apply. If, despite there being a clear instruction to disclose a particular fact in a letter or accompanying notes, you are subsequently told by an officer of the DWP that you do not need to disclose this type of fact, this can mean that you no longer have a duty to disclose it.[31]

You also have a **general duty** to disclose any change in your circumstances since the decision awarding you benefit was made if you could reasonably be expected to know that your benefit may be affected.[32]

What you can reasonably be expected to know depends on the details of your case. For example, if you were told by the DWP or a lawyer that your benefit would not be affected, or if you were too ill to have realised that it might be, it is arguable that you could not reasonably have been expected to have known that your benefit could be affected.[33] If there is no obvious connection between the fact and the overpaid benefit, argue that it was not reasonable for you to have known that your benefit might be affected.

### Complying with your duty to disclose

Generally, to make a valid disclosure, you must tell the 'relevant office' in sufficiently clear terms so that the effect on your claim can be examined.

- **If you have a specific duty to disclose**, the relevant office is the one that handles the benefit you are claiming.[34] In general, you must tell that office. You cannot assume that one office of the DWP already knows about information from other offices within the DWP. It has been suggested in some recent caselaw that you may be able to argue that this could be assumed, if there was a computer interface for sending information to the relevant office. This is particularly so if there is evidence that the relevant office accessed the information and so it knew about it.[35] However, this is not the current law and the basic rule is that you must disclose to the office handling your claim.

If, however, the relevant office for your benefit already knew about the fact, *and* you were aware it knew, it is strongly arguable that you have not failed to disclose.[36] Even if you were not aware of that, it may be possible to argue that its knowledge means that any failure on your part did not actually cause the overpayment (see p1068). This is especially so if the office would not have acted any differently, even if you had reported the fact to it.[37]

- **If you have just a general duty to disclose,** in theory, the relevant office is any DWP office or, in JSA cases, a specified DWP office. However, it is always best to tell the office handling your claim. For child benefit and guardian's allowance, you can disclose changes in your circumstances to the Child Benefit Office, or any office specified to you by HMRC.[38] Again, it is best to ensure that you tell the Child Benefit Office, as it administers your claim. You only count as having failed to disclose once the time by when it was reasonably practicable for you to have done so has passed – eg, if it was impossible for you to make the disclosure earlier than you did, you have not failed to comply with the general duty to disclose.

7

You can usually notify changes in writing or by phone, but it is best to do so in writing.[39]

If you completed a form while giving information, whether you count as having failed to disclose depends not just on what you said on the form, but also on whether you gave the necessary information in another way.[40] If you do not complete a form correctly and give the relevant information in the wrong place, you have disclosed the facts.[41]

If you made a statement in person or by phone, but the decision maker says there is no record of this, you should appeal and give as much information as possible about the circumstances in which the disclosure was made – eg, when you called, who you spoke to and what was said. A record of the phone number called, if you have it, is likely to be helpful.

You should usually make the disclosure yourself, unless an appointee is acting for you (see p1005).[42] If someone else discloses the fact on your behalf, it must be made to the correct office with your knowledge, and you must believe there is no need to repeat it yourself. If someone else makes the disclosure to an office not handling your claim, but they reasonably believe that the information will be passed to the correct office, this may count as disclosure.[43]

Once you have made a proper disclosure to the office handling your claim, you are not expected to repeat it.[44] However, if you give the information to a different office and subsequently become aware that it has not been acted on, you must take further steps to make a proper disclosure.[45] A short time may elapse before you can reasonably be expected to realise that the original information has not been acted on.[46]

## Misrepresentation

Misrepresentation occurs if you have provided information that is inaccurate – eg, you gave a wrong answer to a specific question on the claim form. It does not apply if you have not given information, unless this was deliberately intended to mislead.[47] The following apply.

- It does not matter whether a reasonable person would also have given inaccurate information. No failure on your part needs to be shown.[48]
- It does not matter if you honestly believed that the information you gave was correct – once it is shown to be incorrect, you have misrepresented it. However, you have not misrepresented if you added the phrase 'not to my knowledge' to your statement.[49]
- A written statement may be qualified by an oral one. If you fill in a form incorrectly but explain the situation to an officer when handing in the form, your explanation must be taken into account when deciding whether what is stated on the form is misrepresentation.[50] Similarly, if you give incorrect information in one document but correct information in another, there may not be a misrepresentation.[51] However, if you have declared a fact on a previous claim, but inadvertently give incorrect information on a later claim, you have misrepresented it. The decision maker is not required to check the information you gave on the earlier claim for you.[52]
- If you are incapable of managing your benefits, but nevertheless sign a claim form which is incorrectly completed, you cannot argue later that you were not capable of making a true representation of your circumstances.[53] However, it is arguable that benefit cannot be recovered from you if you:[54]
  - have a disability or you cannot read or write English very well; *and*
  - thought you were signing something different, or you did not understand the effect of your signature; *and*
  - took precautions to understand what you were signing – eg, you checked the form for accuracy before you signed it.[55]
- If you sign a declaration on a claim form that states, 'I declare that the information I have given is correct and complete', but you left out relevant information because you were unaware of it, this is not misrepresentation unless you knew (or ought reasonably to have known) the information was incomplete.[56]

**Note:**

- If you did not declare a fact because you were unaware of it, signing the declaration does not amount to a misrepresentation because all you are

7

declaring is that you have correctly disclosed those facts *which were known to you.*[57]

- If you were told by the DWP or HMRC that certain facts are irrelevant to your claim, signing the declaration cannot be a misrepresentation if you fail to disclose these facts.[58]
- If someone else disclosed a fact to an office not handling your claim but they reasonably believed it would be passed to the correct office, it may be that disclosure has been made, and therefore your signing the declaration does not amount to a misrepresentation.[59]

## Your failure to disclose, or your misrepresentation, has caused the overpayment

An overpayment is only recoverable if it was caused by your failure to disclose (see p1064), or your misrepresenting (see p1067), a material fact (see p1064). **Note:** it is possible that if you have a duty to disclose a fact in respect of one benefit and you fail to do so, this could be regarded as the cause of an overpayment of another benefit.[60]



You may be able to argue that the overpayment was not caused by your failure to disclose or your misrepresentation.

- If the relevant office has been told about changes in your circumstances by another DWP office but not acted on that, older caselaw says that the overpayment will still have been caused by your failure to disclose.[61] However, more recent caselaw says that, depending on the facts of the case (eg, if the relevant office had actually seen clear information indicating an overpayment), it may instead be right as a matter of common sense to regard the failure of the relevant office to act as the real cause of the overpayment.[62]
- If the relevant office has obtained information from another source that leads it to think you may be being overpaid but it does not suspend your benefit while it makes enquiries to establish this for certain, it is still possible that the cause of the overpayment is your failure to disclose or your misrepresentation.[63]
- If you have not disclosed a relevant fact to the relevant office and you then sign a declaration that you have reported the relevant facts (eg, when you sign on), this is a misrepresentation.
- If what you say on your claim form is obviously incorrect and the decision maker does not check this, the overpayment is caused by 'official error', not your misrepresentation, and it is not recoverable.[64]

## The decision awarding you benefit has been changed

If the decision to award you benefit is considered to be incorrect, it must be changed before any overpayment can be recovered.[65] The only exception is when the circumstances of the overpayment mean that there is no decision that needs to be revised for an overpayment to exist – ie, if you were actually paid more than the amount the original decision awarded to you.[66]

A decision to change your benefit award is made by a decision maker, who then carries out a revision or a supersession (see p1130 and p1143). The new decision should state the new amount payable (if any).[67]

During the period when you were overpaid, there may have been more than one decision on your benefit award. Unless *all* these decisions are changed, *all* of the overpayment cannot be recovered.[68]

**Note:** in practice, there are therefore two decisions that must be made before an overpayment can be recovered from you: the decision that changes a previous decision about your benefit, and the decision that the overpayment is recoverable.[69] Both decisions may be included in one decision letter, but it must be clear that both have been made.[70] It is also possible that your benefit award has been changed, but you are not notified about this until you are also notified that the overpayment is recoverable.[71]

If the decision(s) about your benefit has not been changed and/or the new decision(s) has not been notified to you (or it appears that it may not have been), you can ask for a mandatory reconsideration, and then appeal to the First-tier Tribunal (see p1166) against the decision that the overpayment is recoverable.



## The amount that is recovered

The amount of the overpayment is the difference between what you were paid and what you should have been paid.[72] Check that the amount is correct by:

- checking the period of the overpayment; *and*
- working out the total amount of benefit you were paid over the period; *and*
- establishing the correct amount of benefit you should have received during the period; *and*
- deducting this from the total amount of benefit you were paid.

No interest charges can be added to the amount of the overpayment.

The decision maker works out what you should have been paid using the information you originally gave, plus any facts you misrepresented or did not disclose.

If you have been overpaid, the decision maker should deduct from the overpayment any UC, income-related ESA or pension credit (PC) (or IS or income-based JSA, in older cases) to which you or your partner would have been entitled had benefit been paid correctly.[73]

If additional facts are needed to prove you were underpaid UC, ESA or PC (or IS or income-based JSA, in older cases), you cannot offset the underpayment of these benefits against the overpayment.[74] However, if you have been getting one of these benefits, you can ask the DWP to revise or supersede your award (see p1130 and p1143). It could then withhold any arrears owed to you to reduce the overpayment.

If you were overpaid UC for three months or more, or income-related ESA or PC (or IS or income-based JSA, in older cases) for 13 weeks or more because you had too much capital, the overpayment is calculated taking into account the fact that, had you received no benefit, you would have had to use your capital to meet everyday expenses. For each three-month or 13-week period, the DWP assumes your capital is reduced by the amount of overpaid benefit.[75] This is known as the 'diminishing capital' rule. Any subsequent overpayment is not recoverable if your capital goes below the capital limit. However, if there are any increases or decreases in your actual capital during the overpayment period, these are also taken into account.[76]

***Example***

Julia received UC of £400.14 a month for three months. She had capital of £7,000 that was not disclosed, so there was an overpayment because of the assumed (or 'tariff') income rules (see p149). The overpayment was £17.40 a month (due to assumed income of 4 x £4.35 a month). After three months, the diminishing capital rule means that her capital is to be treated as reduced by 3 x £17.40 = £52.20, and her capital is deemed to be £6,947.80. After a further three months, that is again reduced by £52.20, so that after six months her capital is deemed to be £6,895.60.

After six months, Julia paid £5,000 towards her credit card arrears after the company threatened her with court proceedings. As long as it is accepted that Julia was paying off debts and so she is not treated as having 'notional capital' for UC (see p162), her capital is now deemed to be £1,0895.60.

If you were overpaid a benefit which overlaps with another benefit you claimed but were not paid (see p1021), ask for a revision or supersession of that benefit and ask for it to be paid instead (see p1130).

If you were overpaid a benefit but, in fact, were entitled to another, check whether the claim for the benefit you were overpaid can be treated as a claim for the other (see p1013).

## From whom can an overpayment be recovered

An overpayment can be recovered from you if it was caused by your failing to disclose or your misrepresenting a material fact (see p1064).[77] The DWP or HMRC may argue that it can recover the overpayment from you, even if you are not the claimant or you were not paid the benefit. However, it is arguable that only a claimant, an appointee or a person with power of attorney to whom the benefit was paid can fail to disclose a material fact.[78]

**If you are an appointee** (see p1005), the overpayment can be recovered from you or the claimant (or both of you), depending on your circumstances and the facts of the case – ie, which one of you misrepresented or failed to disclose a material fact. The DWP or HMRC should issue a decision that deals with both your liabilities.[79] However:

- if the overpaid benefit has not been given to the claimant, the overpayment cannot be recovered from them, unless they contributed to the misrepresentation or did not disclose a material fact;
- the overpayment cannot be recovered from you if you used 'due care and diligence' in making any statements that led to the overpayment.

**If you have power of attorney**, whether the overpayment can be recovered from you depends on whether the benefit was paid to you. If benefit was paid to you on behalf of the claimant, the overpayment is recoverable from you in the same way as from appointees.[80] If benefit was not paid to you, it cannot be recovered from you.[81]

If a claimant dies, an overpayment can be recovered from their estate.[82] Recovery can only begin after either probate or letters of administration have been granted.[83]

## Challenging an overpayment decision

If you disagree that an overpayment has been made, or that an overpayment can be recovered (ie, because the required conditions are not met) or with the amount to be recovered (ie, because you were entitled to some, or all, of the payments), you can ask for a mandatory reconsideration, and then appeal if the decision is not changed.

If you have missed the time limit for a mandatory reconsideration (remember that you can make a late request on any grounds as long as that is within the absolute time limit – see p1132), you can apply for a supersession and then appeal against any refusal to supersede.[84]

The First-tier Tribunal can consider whether you were entitled to some, or all, of the money (the amount of the overpayment), as well as whether the overpayment is recoverable from you on the basis that it was caused by your failure to disclose or misrepresentation. Both issues can also be considered, even if you have only challenged the decision about whether the overpayment is recoverable (and not the decision about your entitlement to benefit during the period of overpayment).[85]

Do not pay back any of the money until your appeal has been decided. Write to the DWP or HMRC and explain that you do not intend to repay any of the money until your appeal has been decided. Official guidance says that, except for overpayments of UC, recovery of overpaid benefit should be suspended while you are challenging the decision about the overpayment.[86] If the DWP or HMRC is already making deductions from your benefit (see p1074 and p1075), ask it to stop straight away.

If you have paid back money and then successfully appealled, the DWP or HMRC should reimburse you. If it does not, you may be entitled to recover the money in court proceedings because you repaid the money on the basis of a mistake.

**Note:** even if the tribunal decides that an overpayment is recoverable, the decision maker has the discretion not to recover, so it can still be worth asking for it not to be recovered.

## 4. Recovery of overpaid benefit

**Note:** this section does *not* apply to recovery of overpayments of housing benefit (HB) (see p1078).

If an overpayment can be recovered, the DWP or HMRC must decide whether to recover it and, if so, the method to use. The recovery method depends on the type of overpayment. If you have been overpaid universal credit (UC), new-style jobseeker's allowance (JSA) or new-style employment and support allowance (ESA), see p1073. For all other overpayments, see p1075.

**Note:** except when seeking to recover overpaid benefit through the courts, there is no time limit within which the DWP or HMRC must begin recovery action. See CPAG's *Debt Advice Handbook* and *Debt Advice Handbook Scotland* for more information about recovery and enforcement methods. In England and Wales, recovery of your overpayment can be suspended for 60 days under the breathing space scheme (see p1059).

***Future changes***

At some point in the future, two new methods of recovering a benefit overpayment may be introduced.[87] These would apply if you are no longer getting benefit, it is not possible recover the overpayment by deductions from your earnings and you have not otherwise made satisfactory arrangements to repay. They are:

– direct deductions from your bank account made by the DWP; *or*

– a court order providing that you will be disqualified from holding a driving licence.

At the time of writing, the details had not been finalised and it was not known if and when the changes would be introduced. See CPAG's *Welfare Rights Bulletin* or the online version of this *Handbook* for updates.

### The discretion not to recover

Even if an overpayment is recoverable, the DWP and HMRC have the discretion not to recover (ie, to 'waive') all or part of it. This is especially important if you have been overpaid UC, as all UC overpayments are recoverable. (Alternatively, the amount recovered can be reduced or recovery paused for a while.)

The DWP's policy on waiving recovery of an overpayment (including a UC overpayment) says that this will be done only in 'exceptional circumstances' and that there need to be 'very specific and compelling grounds' for doing so.[88] In practice, recovery is pursued in the vast majority of cases. There is no complete list of situations in which waiver will be granted, and if you request that recovery be waived, all relevant facts in your case must be taken into account. The guidance does list some of the factors that should be considered. Those include:

- your financial circumstances;
- the impact of recovery of the overpayment on your health or the health of someone in your family;
- your conduct (eg, if you acted in good faith and did all you could) and that of the DWP (eg, was there an 'official error' or unclear or confusing advice);
- whether you relied on the money overpaid to you so that recovery now leaves you in a detrimental situation;
- whether in all the circumstances, recovery would be in the public interest.

If you want recovery to be waived, you need to request this, usually by writing to the DWP or HMRC debt management section given on the letters sent to you about the overpayment. Set out the reasons for your request – eg, the hardship recovery will cause you (provide full details of your income and expenditure), your concerns about the effect of recovery on your health and that of your family, your belief that the overpayment was caused by official error or misleading advice. It may be helpful to get the help of your MP.

A court has held that the DWP policy is not unlawful, but in the case concerned, the decision to refuse the request for a waiver had wrongly ignored things like repeated official errors in causing the overpayment, the claimant acting in good faith and having relied on the overpayment to her detriment, and whether recovery in this case was in the public interest.[89]

If you were overpaid due to official error, had previously queried with the DWP or HMRC whether your entitlement was correct and had been told that it was correct, it may be that recovery of the overpayment would be unlawful, as you had a 'legitimate expectation' that the benefit paid to you had been paid correctly. This was the finding in one court decision in which the claimant had twice queried the accuracy of her UC payments.[90] Much depends on the facts of your case.

If the DWP or HMRC refuses to waive recovery, you cannot appeal against this decision. Your only legal recourse is judicial review (see Chapter 53). For information about judicial review, see cpag.org.uk/jr. The First-tier Tribunal cannot 'write off' part of the overpayment, even if there are mitigating circumstances. It can only decide whether it is recoverable and, if so, how much is repayable.

## Methods of recovery: universal credit system

This section applies to the recovery of overpayments of UC, and of new-style' JSA or ESA (see p1060).

**Note:** the methods of recovery described in this section are also used to recover overpayments of tax credits where the overpayment has been transferred to the DWP (see p1088).[91]

Also, if you have an overpayment of a legacy benefit (eg, income-related ESA or, in an older case, income support (IS)) but you now get UC instead, the overpayment can be recovered by deductions from your UC.[92] Again, the overpayment will be recovered in the same way as would an overpayment of UC.[93]

The methods used in this section can also be used to collect or recover court costs incurred in recovering overpayments, advance payments of UC (see p1023), budgeting advances of UC (see p52), hardship payments of UC (see p1050), financial penalties for benefit offences (see p1109) and civil penalties for incorrect statements (see p1101).

## Deductions from benefit

Overpayments of UC, and new-style JSA or ESA, are usually recovered by deductions from UC. However, they can also be recovered through deductions from all the benefits in this *Handbook* except HB, social fund payments, child benefit and guardian's allowance.[94]



### Maximum deductions from universal credit

The maximum amounts below apply to *all* overpayments being recovered by deductions from your UC – eg, so that they also apply to an overpayment of tax credits or of income-related ESA (or in an older case, IS) that occurred before you came under the UC system.[95]

In practice, deductions from your UC are made at 15 per cent of the appropriate UC standard allowance.[96] This means that usually the maximum monthly deduction is:

- £47.55 if you are single and under 25;
- £60.02 if you are single and 25 or over;
- £74.63 if you and your partner are both under 25;
- £94.22 if you or your partner are 25 or over.

You must be left with at least one penny of UC each month after the deduction.[97]

The above maximum amounts do not apply if:

- you are being paid arrears of UC (other than if they are as a result of payments being restored following a suspension of your benefit), so the whole of the arrears can be used to recover an overpayment;[98] *or*
- the overpayment is of UC housing costs to cover rent and it is being recovered from someone else – eg, your landlord.[99]

### Maximum deductions from jobseeker's allowance or employment and support allowance

The maximum weekly deduction that can be made to recover an overpayment from your new-style JSA is an amount equal to 40 per cent of your JSA.[100]

The maximum weekly deduction that can be made to recover an overpayment from your new-style ESA is 40 per cent of the basic allowance that applies to you (see p558).[101]

In both cases, if the 40 per cent figure is not a multiple of five pence, the amount is rounded up to the next highest multiple of five pence.

### Maximum deductions from pension credit

The maximum weekly amount that can be deducted from pension credit (PC) to repay an overpayment under these rules (ie, if you were overpaid under the UC system but are now getting PC) is:[102]

- £37.20 if the overpayment is one for which you were found guilty of an offence, you were cautioned or you agreed to pay a penalty as an alternative to prosecution; *or*
- £13.95 in all other cases.

After any deductions, you must be left with at least 10 pence of PC.

7

## Deductions from earnings

Overpayments can be recovered by your employer deducting amounts from your wages or salary.[103] The rules are the same as those outlined on p1076.

## Recovery through the courts

The rules for recovering overpayments through the courts are similar to those for the recovery of HB (see p1085).[104]

# Methods of recovery: other benefits

This section applies to all recoverable overpayments, except overpayments of UC and new-style JSA or ESA. For these, see p1073.

## Deductions from benefit

If you have a recoverable overpayment of benefit (eg, income-related ESA or, in an older case, IS) but you are now getting UC, the overpayment can recovered by deductions from your UC.[105] It will be recovered in the same way that an overpayment of UC is recovered. (see p1073).

Otherwise, recoverable overpayments can usually be repaid through deductions from most of the benefits in this *Handbook*. There are some exceptions.

- Overpayments of child benefit and guardian's allowance can be recovered by deductions from either of these benefits,[106] but overpayments of other benefits cannot be deducted from them.[107]

- No deductions can be made from HB, except for HB overpayments.[108]

Deductions can only be made from the benefit of the person who must repay the overpayment. However, if you are a member of a couple, overpayments of income-related ESA and PC (or in an older case of IS or income-based JSA) can be recovered from benefits either of you receive, provided you are still a couple at the date of the deduction.[109]

Overpayments can also be recovered from arrears of benefit you are owed, except arrears of a benefit that has been suspended (see p1031).[110]

If an overpayment of income-related ESA or PC occurred because of a duplication of payment, the DWP usually deducts it from the arrears owing to you.[111] However, if it does not do so, you can still be asked to repay it even if you have spent the money.

### Maximum deductions

The maximum weekly amounts that can be deducted from **income-related ESA, old-style contributory ESA** (if you would be entitled to income-related ESA at the same rate) and **PC** are:[112]

- £37.20 if you have agreed to pay a penalty (see p1109), admitted fraud or been found guilty of fraud; *or*
- £13.95 in any other case.

The deduction can be increased by half of any:[113]

- £5, £10 or £20 earnings disregard (see p347); *or*
- charitable income paid on a regular basis subject to a disregard (see p357); *or*
- benefit subject to a £10 disregard (see p347).

The above amounts are maximum amounts. You may be able to persuade the DWP to deduct less. If other deductions are also being made from your benefit, see p1041 for the total maximum amount that can be deducted.

**If an overpayment is being recovered from a benefit other than income-related ESA or PC**, the rules limiting the maximum payment that can be deducted do not apply. See p1074 if the overpayment is being recovered from your UC.[114] The DWP usually wants to deduct one-third of your weekly benefit. However, you can argue that your rate of repayment should be less.

## Deductions from earnings

If you work for an organisation with 10 or more employees, an overpayment can be recovered by your employer deducting amounts from your earnings.[115] If this happens, you and your employer should be sent a notice setting out that deductions from your earnings are to be made and the rules for calculating how much to deduct.[116] You must inform the DWP if you leave your employment and provide details of any new employment.[117] Failure to notify the DWP of these is a criminal offence.[118] Your employer should inform you, in writing, of how much the deductions are and how they were calculated no later than the day on which you are given a payment which has had a deduction made from it (or, if that is impractical, no later than the following payday).[119]

The maximum that can be deducted each week is worked out as a percentage of your net earnings – ie, earnings after income tax, class 1 national insurance contributions and pension contributions have been deducted.[120] The maximum is higher if you have been found guilty of an offence.[121]

***Maximum deductions from earnings***

| *Net monthly earnings (if paid monthly)* | *Net weekly earnings (if paid weekly)* | *Deduction* | *Deduction if found guilty of an offence* |
|---|---|---|---|
| Less than £430 | £100 or less | Nil | 5% |
| £430.01 to £690 | £100.01 to £160 | 3% | 6% |
| £690.01 to £950 | £160.01 to £220 | 5% | 10% |
| £950.01 to £1,160 | £220.01 to £270 | 7% | 14% |
| £1,160.01 to £1,615 | £270.01 to £375 | 11% | 22% |
| £1,615.01 to £2,240 | £375.01 to £520 | 15% | 30% |
| £2,240.01 or over | £520.01 or over | 20% | 40% |

If you would be left with less than 60 per cent of your net earnings after the deductions (eg, because amounts are being deducted from your wages or salary for other things), the deduction should be reduced so that you are left with 60 per cent of your net earnings.[122] There are rules on the order of priority in which deductions should be made (see p1042).[123] **Note:** the decision maker can reduce the amount to be deducted below the above percentages by issuing a new notice to your employer with the reduced amount.[124]

## Recovery through the courts

Recoverable overpayments of benefit may be recovered by enforcement proceedings in the county court in England or Wales or the sheriff court in Scotland (but see below regarding use of the common law).[125] The DWP or HMRC may use these proceedings to recover a recoverable overpayment if you no longer claim benefit.

Once there is a decision from a decision maker, the First-tier Tribunal or Upper Tribunal, the court must enforce it, unless you persuade it to delay enforcement (known as a 'stay of execution') while you appeal against the relevant decision. If you are in this situation, get advice.

**Note**: recovery action through the courts in England and Wales must be taken within six years of the decision to recover or, if later, any written acknowledgement of the overpayment or voluntary repayment.[126] In Scotland, the DWP regards the time limit as being 20 years from the date of the decision to recover (or, if there was no such decision, five years from the decision that there was an overpayment).[127] Get advice about how these limits apply to you.

***Can the DWP rely on common law?***

The DWP cannot recover benefit overpayments using the 'common law'. This means that if an overpayment is not recoverable under the rules described in this chapter (see p1063) because, for example, it was an overpayment of a legacy benefit and not caused by misrepresentation or a failure to disclose, then it cannot instead reclaim it (using the common law) through the courts.[128]

## 5. Overpayments of housing benefit

An 'overpayment' is an amount of housing benefit (HB) which has been paid and that the local authority decides you were not entitled to under the HB rules.[129] Being 'paid' includes payment to you, your landlord or someone else, including HB credited to your local authority rent account (see p221).[130]

7

If you have been overpaid income-related employment and support allowance (ESA) (or, in an older claim, income support (IS) or income-based jobseeker's allowance (JSA)), you may also have been overpaid HB. This is because your automatic passport to maximum HB ceases when you are no longer entitled to these benefits. If you are in this situation, inform the local authority. Although it cannot change the decision about your other benefit, the local authority should still go on to make its own decision on your entitlement to HB.

### Overpayments that are always recoverable

An overpayment of HB is always recoverable if:

- it is the result of the local authority's overestimating your HB when making a payment on account (see p228). When the local authority decides how much HB you should get, it must recover any excess you were paid from future HB payments.[131] However, if you stop getting HB before the local authority decides, the overpayment can only be recovered under the other rules (see below); *or*
- it is a future payment that has been credited to your rent account. In this case, the overpayment can be recovered even if it was made due to an 'official error'.[132] If an overpayment of HB caused by an official error has been credited to your account for a *past* period, see p1079.

### Overpayments that are not recoverable

An overpayment that is not covered by either of the bullet points above is not recoverable if you can show that:[133]

- it was caused by an 'official error' (see below); *and*
- no 'relevant person' contributed to making the official error (see p1080); *and*
- no 'relevant person' could reasonably have been expected to realise that an overpayment was being made (see p1080).

Overpayments to which all these criteria apply are sometimes referred to as 'official error' overpayments.

## Was the overpayment caused by an official error?

For the overpayment not to be recoverable, it must have been caused by an 'official error'. **Note:** the official error does not have to be the sole cause of the overpayment, but if the substantial cause of the overpayment was something that you did or failed to do, the overpayment is likely to be recoverable.[134]

An 'official error' is a mistake (either an act or an omission) by:[135]

- the local authority responsible for HB; *or*
- an officer of the authority; *or*
- a person acting for that authority – eg, an employee of a contractor providing HB services; *or*
- an officer of the DWP or HMRC acting as such.

7

Examples of 'official error' include the following.

- A mistake made by the local authority in calculating your entitlement.
- A failure by the local authority to reduce your HB when you inform it of a change of circumstances. It is always best to notify changes in writing to the office you have been told to report changes to, and keep a copy. If you have reported a move into work to the DWP by telephone under the arrangements in which it passes this on to the local authority (see p228) and have provided all the information and evidence needed, any overpayment that occurs is due to official error. However, if you did not provide all that was needed, the local authority does not treat any overpayment as official error.[136]
- Using a claim form that does not ask a question relevant to your entitlement. Whether or not this counts as an official error depends on the particular facts of your case. Leaving out a particular question is more likely to be an official error if the information omitted is likely to be relevant in a large number of cases, and if it is reasonable for the question to have been asked.[137]
- A failure by another local authority department to pass on details of a change of circumstances when it promised to do so. This is an official error because the definition does not require the mistake to be made by the HB office. If you have not been given a particular office to report a change to, you may have fulfilled your duty by reporting the change to any local authority office, and there may be an official error if that office fails to pass it to the HB office.[138]
- A mistake made by the DWP in calculating your entitlement to income-related ESA (or, in an older claim, IS or income-based JSA) which results in an incorrect

calculation of your entitlement to HB. However, it is not an official error if the local authority failed to check your entitlement with the DWP, unless it has information that shows the award is wrong or fraudulent.[139]
- A failure by the DWP to pass on information to the local authority.[140]
- Incorrect advice given to you by an officer of the local authority, the DWP or HMRC, provided they acted as an officer at the time (rather than as a friend giving you informal advice).

The list above is not exhaustive.

## Did a relevant person contribute to making the official error?

Even if an official error caused the overpayment, if a 'relevant person' contributed to that mistake being made, the overpayment can still be recovered.

***Relevant person***

A **'relevant person'** is:
- the HB claimant; *or*
- a person acting on the claimant's behalf, either because the claimant is unable to deal with their affairs or because the claimant has asked the authority in writing to deal with the other person on their behalf; *or*
- a person to whom the payment was made, including a different person acting on the claimant's behalf or a landlord.

The relevant person must have caused the *error*, not the overpayment.[141]

The local authority may say it only needs to show that *any* relevant person caused the official error, but it does not have to pursue that person for the overpayment.[142] If a relevant person caused the official error, the overpayment is recoverable. However, you may still be able to argue that it is not recoverable from you – eg, it was caused by a failure to disclose a relevant fact, but it was not you who failed to disclose. See p1082 for who overpayments can be recovered from.

## Did a relevant person realise that an overpayment was being made?

Even if the official error was not caused by a relevant person, an overpayment is still recoverable if any relevant person knew, or ought reasonably to have known, that an overpayment had been made. The test is whether or not you could reasonably have been expected to *know* (not merely suspect) that an overpayment had occurred. Much depends on what could reasonably have been expected of you given the information available to you, particularly the extent to which the local authority advised you about the scheme, your duties and obligations (especially your duty to notify changes of circumstances).[143] For example, in one case, it was held that although the local authority's letter about entitlement showed that an official error had been made, the complexity of the letter and the claimant's circumstances were such that he could not reasonably be expected to have known that he was being overpaid.[144]

If you or another relevant person could only have realised that there was an overpayment at some point during the period of the overpayment, the overpayment is only recoverable from that date.

## The amount that is recovered

Check the amount of an overpayment to ensure the local authority has calculated it correctly. The local authority should distinguish between recoverable parts of an overpayment and those that are not. To calculate the amount of the overpayment, it should:

- determine the period over which you have been paid too much benefit; *and*
- identify the period(s) over which it is entitled to recover; *and*
- work out the total amount of HB you were paid over the period(s) during which it can be recovered; *and*
- work out the correct amount of HB you should have received during the period(s) of the overpayment. The local authority must award you the amount of HB you (or your partner) would have received if it had been aware of your true circumstances. If necessary, it should ask you for any required information or evidence to do this. However, the local authority does not include a change of your address when doing this;[145] *and*
- deduct the HB you should have been paid from what you were paid.[146]

The local authority must not add any interest charges to the overpayment amount.[147]

## Deductions from the overpayment

As well as any amount of HB that you should have been paid, the local authority must consider deducting other amounts from the overpayment (this is known as 'offsetting'). These are:

- if you are a council tenant, extra rent paid into your rent account. If you have been getting HB during the overpayment period and, for some reason, have paid more into your rent account than you should have paid according to your original (incorrect) benefit assessment, the extra rent you have paid can be deducted from any overpayment made during that period. The local authority may not apply this rule if you paid extra rent to repay rent arrears;[148]
- reductions under the 'diminishing capital rule'.

No other amounts can be deducted.

If you were overpaid HB because you had too much capital, the overpayment is calculated taking into account the fact that, had you received no HB, you would have used your capital. This is known as the **'diminishing capital rule'**. It only applies if you were overpaid for more than 13 weeks and either:[149]

- the overpayment was caused by a misrepresentation of, or a failure to disclose, the amount of your capital (see p1064); *or*
- the overpayment was caused by an error (other than an 'official error' – see p1079) about your capital (or that of a member of your family).

For each 13-week period, the local authority assumes that your capital is reduced by the amount of overpaid HB.[150]

## From whom can an overpayment be recovered

The general rule is that a recoverable overpayment can be recovered from the person it was paid to – eg, a landlord.[151] However, this does not apply if someone else misrepresented or failed to disclose a 'material fact', or if someone else should have realised that there was an overpayment at the time.

An overpayment can be recovered from someone other than the person to whom it was paid, including the claimant, if:[152]

- the overpayment was caused by misrepresentation or failure to disclose a material fact (see p1063). In this case, it can be recovered from the person who misrepresented or failed to disclose the fact, but not the person to whom the payment was made; *or*
- the overpayment was caused by an official error (see p1078) and the claimant (or someone acting on the claimant's behalf) or any other person to whom the HB was paid could reasonably have been expected to realise that there was an overpayment at the time. In this case, it can be recovered from whoever should have realised, but not the person to whom it was paid; *or*
- neither of the above two bullet points apply, in which case the overpayment is also recoverable from the claimant. If you are the claimant, the overpayment may be recovered from you, as well as the person to whom it was paid.

If you are the claimant and the overpayment is recoverable from you, no matter how it was caused, the local authority can also recover the overpayment by deducting any HB paid to your partner, provided you were a couple both at the time of the overpayment and when the deduction is made.[153]

If you think you have been wrongly chosen under these rules (eg, because you did not fail to disclose a material fact), you can appeal to the First-tier Tribunal. However, if the overpayment can be recovered from you under these rules, you cannot appeal simply because you think the local authority should recover from another person instead.[154]

If the person from whom recovery is being sought dies, the local authority may consider recovering any outstanding overpayment from their estate.[155]

## Methods of recovery

A local authority can decide how much, if any, of a recoverable overpayment it will recover (but see p228 if the overpayment was of a payment on account).[156]

This is similar to the discretion that the DWP and HMRC have to recover overpayments (see p1072).

If the local authority decides to recover, it can ask for the whole amount or recover it by instalments. When an overpayment is recovered from your landlord, note how this affects your liability to pay rent (see p1087). Overpayments of HB can be recovered:

- from payments of HB (see below);
- from other benefits (see p1084);
- by adjusting your rent account if you are a local authority tenant (see p1085);
- by your employer deducting amounts from your wages or salary (see p1085);
- through the courts (see p1085).

The methods used and the rates of recovery should be consistent between groups of claimants. For example, council tenants should not be required to repay an overpayment in a lump sum if private tenants can repay by instalments.

**Note:** except when seeking to recover overpaid benefit through the courts, there is no time limit within which a local authority must begin recovery action.



## Deductions from housing benefit

A local authority can recover an overpayment by deducting amounts from HB payable to any person from whom an overpayment can be recovered (see p1070).[157] As well as yourself, this could be your partner or your landlord. Deductions can be made from both future payments of HB and any arrears that are owing.

If you have moved home, the local authority may be able to recover an overpayment of HB from your previous home by adjusting the HB paid at your new home. It can decide to do this if:[158]

- the overpayment occurred after you moved, and occurred because you were no longer living at your previous home; *and*
- the same local authority that paid you the overpayment is paying your HB at your new home.

In these circumstances, the local authority can deduct all the weekly HB owing to you for your new home to recover the overpayment, for however many weeks you were overpaid at your previous home.

### Deductions from your partner's housing benefit

If you were the claimant and the overpayment, no matter how it was caused, is recoverable from you, the local authority can also recover it by deductions from any HB later awarded to your partner, provided you were a couple at both the time of the overpayment and when the deduction is made.[159]

### Deductions from your landlord's housing benefit

The local authority may recover the overpayment from:

- HB paid to your landlord if the landlord is claiming HB themself;[160] *or*
- HB paid direct to your landlord on your behalf.[161] The notification of the overpayment (see p1086) should make it clear from whom the authority is recovering; *or*
- HB paid direct to your landlord on behalf of other claimants.[162]

When HB is recovered from a landlord in this way, there are special rules on how this affects your liability to pay rent (see p1087).

### Maximum deductions

The maximum weekly amount that can be deducted is £23.25 if you have agreed to pay a penalty (see p1109), admitted fraud or been found guilty of fraud, or £13.95 in any other case.[163]

The recovery rate can be increased by up to half of any amount of earned income which is disregarded as income in the calculation of your HB (see p347 and p382).[164] Amounts of income disregarded for childcare costs cannot be used to increase the recovery rate in this way.

However, you can argue that the rate will cause you hardship and a lesser amount should be recovered instead. You must be left with at least 50 pence of HB a week.[165]

## Deductions from other benefits

The local authority can ask the DWP to recover an overpayment of HB by making deductions from most of the benefits in this *Handbook* (except guardian's allowance and, arguably, child benefit).[166] If the overpayment is recoverable from your partner (see p1082), it can be recovered by deductions from their universal credit (UC), income-related ESA, pension credit or personal independence payment.

An overpayment can also be recovered from any benefits paid to your landlord in their own right.[167]

Deductions can only be made if:[168]

- a recoverable overpayment has been made as a result of a misrepresentation of, or failure to disclose (see p1064), a material fact by you, on your behalf or by or on behalf of another person to whom HB has been paid; *and*
- the local authority is unable to recover that overpayment from any HB; *and*
- the person who is to repay the overpayment is receiving a sufficient amount of at least one of the relevant benefits to allow deductions to be made.

Except for UC (see p1074), there are no rules limiting the maximum amount that can be deducted. However, you can argue that your rate of repayment should be reasonable. If you are on income-related ESA, argue that the weekly maximum for that should apply (see p1076). Ask the DWP to use its discretion to reduce the amounts if the deductions will cause you hardship.

If deductions stop because you are no longer entitled to a particular benefit, or the amount to which you are entitled is insufficient for deductions to be made, the DWP notifies the local authority which, once again, becomes responsible for any further recovery action.

### Adjusting your rent account

If you are a local authority tenant, the local authority can recover an overpayment by adding it as a debt to your rent account. The overpayment should be separately identified and you should be informed that the amount being recovered does not represent rent arrears.[169]

Get advice if the local authority wants to evict you because you have rent arrears. It cannot argue you owe it rent arrears if you have only been overpaid HB. Local authorities are reminded in DWP guidance that overpayments of HB paid to their own tenants are not rent arrears and should not be treated as such.[170]

An overpayment cannot be recovered in this way if you have a private or housing association landlord. However, an overpayment can be recovered from your landlord (see p1083). If the local authority recovers from your landlord, you may count as being in rent arrears (see p1067).



### Deductions from earnings

The local authority can order your employer to deduct amounts from your (but not your partner's) wages or salary to recover the overpayment.[171] The rules for this are explained on p1076.

### Court action

If a local authority cannot use any of the methods of recovery listed on p1082 and you cannot agree on repayments, it can try to recover the money you owe through the county court (sheriff court in Scotland) if it thinks you can afford to make repayments. It should not start proceedings until your time for challenging the decision has passed.

A local authority should not use court proceedings to recover an overpayment if it has not followed the correct procedure (see p1077) – eg, if it has not issued the correct notification.[172]

A local authority can:

- sue you for the debt created by the overpayment. If the correct procedure has not been followed, you can use this as a defence.[173] You may also be able to claim compensation in certain circumstances. However, you cannot say that you should have received more HB;[174] *or*
- use the special rules to register the overpayment as a debt which can then be recovered using a court procedure.[175] Get advice if you think the local authority is not entitled to do this.

**Note:** recovery action through the courts in England and Wales must be taken within six years of the decision to recover or, if later, any written acknowledgement of the overpayment or voluntary repayment.[176] In Scotland, the DWP regards the time limit as being 20 years from the date of the decision to recover (or, if there was no such decision, five years from the decision that there was an overpayment). Get advice about how these limits apply to your case.[177]

You may have to pay legal costs and interest, as well as the overpayment if the local authority's case is successful. Remember that court procedures often require you to take action within a very short time. Get advice if the local authority is threatening to use court proceedings.

## Notification of an overpayment

If the local authority decides that a recoverable overpayment has occurred, it must write to the person from whom repayment is being sought (see p1082) within 14 days if possible, notifying them of this.[178]

This notification must state:[179]

- that there is an overpayment which is legally recoverable; *and*
- the reason why there is a recoverable overpayment; *and*
- the amount of the recoverable overpayment; *and*
- how the amount of the overpayment was calculated; *and*
- the benefit weeks to which the overpayment relates; *and*
- if recovery is to be made from future benefit, the amount of the deductions; *and*
- if recovery is to be made from your landlord by deductions from someone else's HB, your identity and the claimant from whose HB the deduction will be made;[180] *and*
- your right to ask for a further written explanation of any of the decisions the local authority has made about the overpayment, how you can do this and the time limit for doing so; *and*
- that you have a right to ask the local authority to reconsider any of the decisions it has made about the overpayment, how you can do this and the time limit for doing so.

It may also include any other relevant matters.

Guidance states that the local authority should issue a single notification to all relevant parties (eg, landlord and tenant) saying from whom the overpayment is recoverable and from whom it is not.[181]

Write and ask the local authority for a more detailed written explanation of any of the decisions it has made about an overpayment. It must send you this within 14 days or, if this is not reasonably practicable, as soon as possible.[182]

If a notification sent to you is a clear decision that there is an overpayment that is recoverable from you, but does not contain all the matters above, it is only valid if the omissions do not put you at a disadvantage.[183] If, for example, it does not set out your right to apply for a revision so that you do not do so until it is too late, you have been put at a disadvantage and so can argue that the overpayment is not recoverable. However, if the decision is not about recoverability and is only about the fact that you have been overpaid, you can argue that there is no decision saying that you must repay the overpayment.[184]

No recovery should be sought until after you have been notified, and the one-month period for asking for a revision or appeal has passed.[185]

## The effect of recovery from your landlord

If you are a private or housing association tenant, an overpayment of HB recovered from your landlord (see p1083) could mean that your landlord tries to obtain money from you. They could argue that you are in rent arrears and could seek possession of your home.

Whether or not HB was paid direct to your landlord, they may still try to argue that, even if you owe no rent, you nevertheless owe a debt under common law. This is probably not correct. If they threaten to sue you, get advice straight away.

If you are a local authority tenant, these rules do not apply. However, the local authority can recover an overpayment of HB by making deductions from your rent account (see p1084).



If overpaid HB was paid direct to your landlord, the following rules apply.

- If the local authority recovers the overpayment from your landlord by making deductions from direct payments of other tenants' HB (see p1083), the other tenants are treated as having paid the deduction amount towards their rent.[186]
- If the local authority recovers the overpayment from your landlord by making deductions from direct payments of your HB, you are treated as having paid the amount of the deduction towards your rent if your landlord is convicted of an offence or agrees to pay a penalty (see p1109) in relation to that overpayment.[187] If the local authority decides to recover under this rule, it must notify both your landlord and you that you are to be treated as having paid your rent.[188]

In these situations, your landlord cannot argue that you are in rent arrears. It is also much easier to argue that your landlord cannot sue you under common law for a debt.

## Challenging an overpayment decision

You can apply for a revision or appeal (see Chapters 50 and 51) if you want to dispute:

- the decision that you have been overpaid HB;
- the amount of the overpayment;
- the decision that it can be recovered;

- that the overpayment is to be recovered from you under the rules on p1082.

Do not pay back any of the money until your challenge has been dealt with. Local authority guidance states that overpayments should not be recovered while under appeal.[189] If the local authority is already making deductions from your HB (see p1081) or from your other benefits (see p1084), ask it to stop this immediately.

# 6. Overpayments of tax credits

## Introduction

The tax credits scheme closed in April 2025. You cannot now make a new claim or have a current award of tax credits. Therefore, you cannot be overpaid tax credits after April 2025. If you still had an award before April 2025, your entitlement will have been ended and, in most cases, you will have been invited to claim universal credit (UC) under the managed migration scheme (see p21).

7

It is possible that you could be considered to have been overpaid tax credits in a previous year – ie, in 2024/2025 or before. All overpayments of tax credits are legally recoverable, including those caused by official error. In most cases, HMRC still requires repayment of overpaid tax credits from past tax years. If you are required to repay an overpayment and you are now on UC, the overpayment will have been transferred to the DWP so that it can be repaid by deductions from your UC. If you are not on UC, HMRC will still recover the overpayment – eg, by direct payment or deductions from your pay. See p1093 for more about the recovery of overpayments.

## What is an overpayment of tax credits

If you (and your partner if you had a joint claim) were paid more tax credits for a tax year than you were entitled to, the extra amount is regarded as an overpayment.[190] HMRC may have decided that you have been overpaid either at the end of the tax year, or during the tax year concerned, after you claimed UC. For more on these 'finalised overpayments', see Chapter 65 of the 2024/25 edition of this *Handbook*.

The amount of the overpayment is usually just the amount you were paid but were not entitled to. In some cases, HMRC may add interest where it considers that the overpayment was due to 'fraud or neglect' on the part of you or your partner. You must be notified of a decision to add interest to the overpayment, including of your right to request a review. You can request a review or appeal against the decision to add interest (eg, because you consider that you did not act fraudulently or negligently), but time limits apply (see p1089).

## Causes of the overpayment

The most likely causes of you having been overpaid are:

- your income fell or rose by more than the threshold £2,500 in the tax year concerned, compared with the previous tax year;
- you did not tell the Tax Credit Office in time about a change in your circumstances that reduced your entitlement, or you did but the change was not acted on;
- the information you gave the Tax Credit Office was incorrect or inaccurately recorded;
- when you claimed UC, your tax credits were not stopped immediately but continued for a time (usually up to a month) until the DWP had verified your UC claim. This may be an especially common cause of overpayments during the 2024/25 tax year when tax credit claimants were being invited to claim UC under the managed migration process.

## What you can do

In practice, there may be only limited options as to what you can do if you still have an overpayment of tax credits. In general, you can:

- repay the overpayment as required; *or*
- challenge the overpayment on review or appeal if you do not accept that you have been overpaid *and* you are still within the time allowed (see below); *or*
- dispute the decision that you must repay the overpayment, if you are within the time allowed, or ask that the repayment arrangements be changed because you cannot afford to repay due to financial hardship.

## Challenging an overpayment on review or appeal

HMRC must have notified you of the overpayment by changing the decision on your entitlement and writing to you about that.[191] The decision carried rights of review (by HMRC) and appeal (to a First-tier Tribunal). If you did not request a review or appeal at the time, but now believe that the changed decision on your entitlement was wrong, so that you were in fact not overpaid or the overpayment has been calculated incorrectly, it may still be possible to challenge the decision by requesting a review or an appeal. However, time limits apply to both reviews and appeals.

For a **review**, your request must be in writing and received within 30 days of the date given on the decision.[192] HMRC may accept a late request within 13 months of the date of the decision, but must be satisfied that special circumstances meant you could not have met the time limit, and that it is reasonable to accept the late request. In practice, the later your request, the more likely it is that HMRC will refuse to accept it. For more on reviews, see Chapter 67 of the 2024/25 edition of this *Handbook*.

For an **appeal**, it is not required that you had already requested a review (although HMRC may have told you that it was), so you can appeal either after a review by HMRC or directly against the decision. Appeals should be made on Form SSCS5 (Notice of Appeal Against a Decision of HM Revenue and Customs), although they can be accepted in other written forms. Your appeal must be received by HM Courts and Tribunals Service within one month of the date of the decision you wish to appeal against.[193] A late appeal can be accepted where made within 13 months of that date (in a very exceptional case, where you could not have appealed any earlier than you did, the tribunal has a discretion to accept an appeal made later than that, but in practice, this will be rare). For more on appeals, see Chapter 67 of the 2024/25 edition of this *Handbook*.

**Note:** if you accept that you were overpaid and the overpayment has been calculated correctly, or otherwise do not wish to challenge the changed decision on your entitlement, you can still dispute recovery of the overpayment with HMRC (see below). Note that because all tax credit overpayments are recoverable, you cannot request a review or appeal against a decision to recover the overpayment.

## If you have claimed universal credit

If you have claimed UC, your tax credit entitlement will have been finalised *during* the tax year in which you claimed UC rather than waiting until the end of the tax year. The final decision may have been that you were not entitled to some or all of the tax credits you received up to the date of your UC claim – ie, that you have been overpaid tax credits.

You may still be able to request a review or appeal against the decision about entitlement (see p1089), and/or to dispute recovery (see below) if you do not think you should have to repay. Unless there is already an ongoing review, appeal or dispute about the overpayment, HMRC will usually have transferred the debt to the DWP. The DWP will then recover the overpayment from your UC.

After the overpayment has been transferred to the DWP, you can still contact HMRC about how and why the overpayment arose, and pursue a review or appeal the entitlement decision, or pursue a dispute or complaint about recovery. However, if you are late, you will need to give reasons why you did not do so within the time limit. HMRC has confirmed it will continue to deal with outstanding issues such as these.

If you are on UC and wish to discuss the level of repayment or if it is causing you hardship, contact the DWP Debt Management helpline on 0800 916 0647 (textphone 0800 916 0651).

## Disputing recovery

You cannot request a review by HMRC or appeal to the First-tier Tribunal against the decision to recover the overpayment. However, if you do not think you should be required to repay the overpayment (eg, because you did not cause it), you can ask HMRC to look at its decision again and use its discretion. This is referred to as a 'dispute'. Separately, if you cannot afford to repay, you can ask for the rate of recovery to be reduced or for recovery to be written off altogether on financial hardship grounds. If the overpayment has been transferred to the DWP (see above), you must ask the DWP to do this. If HMRC is still dealing with the overpayment, you must ask HMRC to do it.

HMRC's policy on using its discretion in recovering overpayments is set out in its leaflet *What happens if We've Paid You Too Much Tax Credits? (COP 26)*. For more on all these matters, in particular on the arrangements that applied before April 2025, see Chapter 65 of the 2024/25 edition of this *Handbook*.

You can dispute recovery if you accept that you received more tax credits than you were correctly entitled to, but you do not think you should have to pay back the money. To dispute recovery with HMRC, complete Form TC846, which can be completed online or downloaded at gov.uk/government/publications/tax-credits-overpayment-tc846 (or contact the Tax Credit Helpline for a copy) or write to the Tax Credit Office. Recovery of the overpayment usually begins immediately and is not suspended during the dispute, although if your dispute is successful, the amount already recovered is refunded to you.[194] There is no legal time limit for disputing recovery, but HMRC expects you to do so within three months of notification of the overpayment or of the outcome of a review or an appeal deciding that you have been overpaid.[195] HMRC says it will consider exceptions if you could not reasonably have been expected to act within three months – eg, if you were in hospital. Arguably, a late dispute should also be allowed if you have been waiting for an explanation of the overpayment. HMRC has discretion on this, but if it applies the time limit too rigidly, this may be unlawful. In considering a dispute, HMRC takes account of whether you met your 'responsibilities' (eg, to correctly report your circumstances) and whether HMRC met its responsibilities (eg, to give you the correct advice and to take account of what you have told them).

If you cannot afford to repay, you can ask for the rate of recovery to be reduced or for the overpayment to be written off altogether. In practice, it is rare for HMRC to agree to this. Form TC846, which is used for making a dispute, does not provide for you to make such a request, so raise this separately via the Tax Credit Helpline or contact HMRC using the address on your notice to pay. Hardship is not defined, but HMRC leaflet *What happens if We've Paid You Too Much Tax Credits? (COP 26)* refers to it in terms of family circumstances that lead to extra living costs, such as looking after someone who is ill or disabled, and an inability to pay for essential living expenses such as rent, gas or electricity. Other HMRC guidance states that if you have a mental health problem, HMRC should deal with your case carefully and sympathetically.[196]

HMRC may also use its discretion to reduce ('offset') the overpayment amount by the amount of any tax credit to which you would have been entitled had you claimed correctly – ie, by your 'notional entitlement'. This process is referred to in HMRC guidance as 'offsetting notional entitlement' and is applied if the overpayment was caused by:[197]

- continuing to claim as a single person after failing to report becoming a couple (you need details of your partner's income); *or*
- continuing to claim as a couple after failing to report a separation.

HMRC says that you must request 'offsetting' within three months of being notified of the overpayment.[198]

### Taking your dispute further

If HMRC has considered your dispute and you still think you should not have to pay back an overpayment, you can ask HMRC to review its decision, provided you give new information within 30 days (or later in exceptional circumstances). HMRC says that you can only do this once.[199]

The only legal way to challenge a decision on recovering an overpayment (ie, either after a dispute or an attempt to negotiate repayment) is by judicial review in the courts. Usually, this is only possible in extreme cases – eg, if HMRC insists on your repaying an overpayment that was clearly caused by an error or failure on its part, you met all your responsibilities and it is urgent that HMRC changes its decision. For more about judicial review, see Chapter 53.

The only other way of persuading HMRC to change its mind is by making a complaint (see Chapter 55). You first need to use HMRC's own complaints procedure. If you remain dissatisfied, you can complain to the Adjudicator's Office and then to the Parliamentary and Health Service Ombudsman via your MP. Both can recommend action and order financial compensation, but are likely to take time to complete their investigations. You may wish to involve your MP earlier in your complaint, as this can produce quicker results.

## Recovery of overpayments

HMRC can recover all or part of any overpayment.[200] It usually recovers the overpayment by:

- transferring the debt to the DWP to recover from you, in particular where you now get UC; *or*
- requiring you to repay the overpayment.

**Note:** although all overpayments are legally recoverable, HMRC can use its discretion not to recover and, if still within the time allowed, you can dispute recovery or ask for the rate of recovery to be reduced or for recovery to get written off altogether on grounds of hardship.

You must be given notice that you must repay a finalised overpayment. The notice must also say how much the overpayment is and how it is to be recovered from you.[201]

HMRC usually begins recovery immediately after it notifies you of the overpayment. It does not ask you whether recovering an overpayment will cause you hardship or if you think it should not be recovered from you. Recovery is not suspended during the dispute process, but if the dispute is found in your favour, the amount already recovered is refunded to you.[202]

**Note:** if you disagree that you have been overpaid, you may still be able to request a review by HMRC of the decision about your entitlement or appeal to the First-tier Tribunal, but time limits apply (see p1088). Recovery is suspended during the review and appeal process.[203]

## From whom can an overpayment be recovered

A finalised overpayment can be recovered from the person(s) to whom the tax credit award was made. This means:[204]

- if you made a claim as a single person, the overpayment can be recovered from you; *or*
- if you made a joint claim with your partner, the overpayment can be recovered from one or both of you. If you have separated from your partner, HMRC's practice is first to ask you both to repay the overpayment equally. You and your ex-partner may agree to pay different amounts if you wish. Although HMRC has the power to ask one person to repay the whole amount, guidance states that usually each person is asked to repay a maximum of half the overpayment, unless one partner has acted fraudulently or negligently and the other is seen to be an 'innocent partner'.[205]

## How the overpayment is recovered

You must be notified of the new decision on your entitlement.[206] HMRC must notify you (and your partner, if it is a joint overpayment) of the amount to be repaid, and how the overpayment is to be repaid.[207] Tax credit overpayments are treated as unpaid tax debts. If the debt is transferred to the DWP, all methods of recovery used by the DWP may apply.[208]

HMRC can require you to repay:[209]

- direct to HMRC. You should receive a notice showing the full amount to be repaid. You are offered a standard repayment period of 12 monthly instalments, although up to 10 years may be negotiated;
- by transferring the debt to the DWP to make deductions from UC or certain other benefits (see p1073 – your overpayment is treated as an overpayment of UC). This can happen without your agreement, but you must be notified. The debt should not be transferred to the DWP while there is an outstanding dispute about recovery, ongoing review or appeal about the decision that gave rise to the overpayment. See also p1094;[210]
- with your agreement, by deductions from certain benefits paid by the DWP (see p1039). Note that if HMRC transfers the debt to the DWP to recover, this method can be used without your agreement;[211]

- with your agreement, via pay as you earn (PAYE) by altering your tax code to allow deductions from your wages. Note that if HMRC transfers the debt to the DWP to recover, this method can be used without your agreement;[212]
- by deduction from your bank account, in some cases, or court action (see p1095).[213]

### Direct payment to HMRC

If your overpayment has not been transferred to the DWP (eg, because you do not get UC or other DWP benefits), or you were overpaid as part of a couple and have now separated, you must repay your overpayment by direct payment to HMRC. The notice to pay (Form TC610) asks you to contact HMRC to pay in full or negotiate repayment. If the overpayment has not been repaid and you have not contacted HMRC within 42 days, a reminder letter is sent, followed by a more strongly worded warning letter. If you fail to respond to this letter, HMRC may use a debt collection agency or start legal proceedings to recover the debt.

### Transfer of overpayments to DWP

7

HMRC may transfer a tax credits overpayment to the DWP to recover as if it were an overpayment of UC (or new-style ESA/JSA). This can be recovered without your consent through deductions from UC or other benefits, or by any means of recovery available to the DWP (see p1073).[214] This usually happens if you have claimed UC, but it may also happen even if you have not claimed or are not entitled to UC.

You must be notified that the overpayment is being recovered in this way.[215] If you have claimed UC, you are sent a TC1131 letter setting out the amount.

Once the debt has gone to the DWP, HMRC cannot affect the recovery amount per month, but it can write off the debt or send a new debt amount to the DWP if the award changes after the transfer, or if it agrees to write off all or part of an overpayment.[216]

HMRC has stated that you should have received an annual reminder about any historic overpayments with outstanding debt, even if you no longer receive tax credits.[217] The Adjudicator found in 2022 that in one case where there was no contact from HMRC for nearly 10 years, it was unreasonable to pass the responsibility for resolving the complaint to the DWP, and HMRC agreed to recall and waive the debt.[218]

### Other methods of recovery

HMRC usually transfers tax credits debt to the DWP to recover as if it were an overpayment of UC or new-style JSA or ESA, which can be recovered without your consent. HMRC may recover tax credit overpayments from your wages via PAYE, but only with your agreement.[219]

HMRC may recover tax credit debts direct from bank and building society accounts and individual savings accounts (ISAs). In England and Wales, it can only do so if the debt is £1,000 or more, and you must usually be left with a minimum of £5,000 in your account or accounts.[220] HMRC guidance includes safeguards, including a guaranteed face-to-face visit, before this method is used, and there is a right of appeal to the county court.[221] In Scotland, it can apply for bank arrestment under a 'summary warrant'.

If HMRC cannot recover by any other methods, or you do not respond to requests for recovery, it may consider taking legal action. Further action will follow if HMRC considers that you are refusing to repay or neglecting to keep to an agreement to repay. All the circumstances are taken into account before taking such action, but HMRC may:

- take enforcement proceedings to take control of your goods (England and Wales) or seize and sell your possessions (Scotland). Unless you let HMRC officials or agents into your property, they cannot enter your home and take control of/seize your personal possessions without a warrant from the court; *or*
- take court action against you, including bankruptcy proceedings.

**Note:** recovery action through the courts in England and Wales must be taken within six years of the decision that there has been an overpayment or, if later, any written acknowledgement of the overpayment or voluntary repayment.[222] In Scotland, HMRC regards the time limit for court action as five years from the last effective action.[223]

For more on the recovery of debts, see CPAG's *Debt Advice Handbook* and *Debt Advice Handbook Scotland*.



# Notes

1. **Introduction**

1 *SSWP v Payne and Another* [2011] UKSC 60

2 Official advice at gov.uk/government/publications/debt-respite-scheme-breathing-space-guidance

2. **Benefit overpayments that are always recoverable**

3 s71ZB(1) SSAA 1992; art 5(3A) WRA(No.8)O

4 s71ZB(3) SSAA 1992

5 s12(1)(a) and (b) and Sch 3 paras 5-6B SSA 98; *LP v SSWP* [2018] UKUT 332 (AAC)

6 Reg 16 SS(OR) Regs

7 Reg 8(3) SS(OR) Regs

8 Reg 7 SS(OR) Regs

9 Reg 9(1)(a) and (b) and (2) SS(OR) Regs

10 Reg 9(1)(c) SS(OR) Regs

11 Reg 9(3) SS(OR) Regs

12 Reg 4 SS(OR) Regs

13 s71ZB SSAA 1992; reg 6 SS(OR) Regs

14 s74 SSAA 1992; reg 7 SS(PAOR) Regs

15 s74(2) and (4) SSAA 1992; reg 8 SS(PAOR) Regs

16 See, for example, the appeals in R(SB) 28/85 and R(IS) 6/02

17 s71(4) SSAA 1992; reg 11 SS(PAOR) Regs; reg 35 CB&GA(Admin) Regs
18 Sch 2 para 20(d) SS&CS(DA) Regs

3. **Benefit overpayments that are sometimes recoverable**
19 s71(1) and (5A) SSAA 1992
20 R(SB) 2/92
21 CDLA/5803/1999
22 CDLA/1823/2004
23 R(S) 4/86; R(I) 3/75
24 *B v SSWP* [2005] EWCA Civ 929, reported as R(IS) 9/06. The effect of the decision is that recovery is under reg 32 SS(C&P) Regs and, presumably, under the equivalent rules in reg 24 JSA Regs and reg 23 CB&GA(Admin) Regs.
25 R(SB) 21/82
26 R(SB) 54/83; CSB/296/1985
27 CG/160/1999
28 R(SB) 21/82
29 Reg 32(1A) SS(C&P) Regs; reg 24(1)-(5A) JSA Regs; reg 38(3) UC,PIP,JSA&ESA(C&P) Regs
30 *Hooper v SSWP* [2007] EWCA Civ 495, reported as R(IB) 4/07. See also official guidance in Memo DMG 26/07.
31 R(A) 2/06
32 Reg 32(1B) SS(C&P) Regs; reg 24(7) JSA Regs; reg 38(4) UC,PIP,JSA&ESA(C&P) Regs
33 *DG v SSWP* [2009] UKUT 120 (AAC)
34 R(SB) 15/87; *Hinchy v SSWP* [2005] UKHL 16, reported as R(IS) 7/05
35 *SK v Department for Communities (ESA)* [2020] NICom 73. This Northern Ireland Commissioners decision found that developments in the computerisation of DWP administration mean that the decision of the House of Lords in *Hinchy v SSWP* [2005] UKHL 16 should no longer be followed. The decision is not binding authority in Great Britain, but may be persuasive: see *MW v SSWP (ESA)* [2023] UKUT 50 (AAC). See also 'Legacy overpayments – a change in the weather?', *Welfare Rights Bulletin* 295, August 2023, p7.
36 *LH v SSWP (RP)* [2017] UKUT 249 (AAC)
37 CG/5631/1999; CIS/1887/2002; *WA v SSWP* [2009] UKUT 132 (AAC); *GJ v SSWP (IS)* [2010] UKUT 107 (AAC)
38 Reg 23(5) CB&GA(Admin) Regs
39 Reg 32(1B) SS(C&P) Regs requires notification in writing or by phone, unless the DWP specifically requires otherwise
40 R(SB) 18/85
41 CWSB/2/1985
42 R(SB) 15/87
43 CDLA/6336/1999
44 R(SB) 15/87; CIS/3529/2008
45 R(SB) 54/83
46 CSB/393/1985
47 CIS/5117/1998
48 R(SB) 9/85
49 *Jones and Sharples v CAO* [1994] 1 All ER 225 (CA); R(SB) 9/85
50 R(SB) 18/85
51 R(SB) 2/91
52 R(SB) 3/90
53 *Sheriff v CAO* [1995] (CA), reported as R(IS) 14/96
54 CG/4494/1999 suggests the principle may apply in social security; R(IS) 4/06 is more doubtful, but does not rule it out
55 CIS/3846/2001
56 *Jones and Sharples v CAO* [1994] 1 All ER 225 (CA); *Franklin v CAO* [1995] (CA); CIS/674/1994; CIS/583/1994; CIS/674/1994
57 *Franklin v CAO* [1995] (CA)
58 CIS/583/1994
59 CDLA/6336/1999
60 *TM v SSWP (ESA)* [2015] UKUT 109 (AAC)
61 *Duggan v CAO* [1989] (CA); CG/662/1998; CG/4494/1999; *Hinchy v SSWP* [2003] EWCA Civ 138
62 *WS v SSWP* [2023] UKUT 81 (AAC), citing *SSWP v SS (SPC)* [2013] UKUT 272 (AAC)
63 *JM v SSWP (IS)* [2011] UKUT 15 (AAC)
64 CIS/222/1991
65 s71(5A) SSAA 1992; CIS/3228/2003; R(IS) 13/05. See CPC/3743/2006 for when not all the overpayment period has been covered by the change of the award.
66 Reg 12 SS(PAOR) Regs
67 CIS/3228/2003
68 CSIS/45/1990
69 R(SB) 7/91
70 *LL v SSWP* [2013] UKUT 208 (AAC)
71 This was the case in *Hamilton v Department for Social Development* [2010] NICA 46, but it is clear from *SSWP v AD (IS)* [2011] UKUT 184 (AAC) that whether this is the case depends on the specific decision-making history in your case
72 R(SB) 20/84; R(SB) 24/87
73 Reg 13(1)(b) and (1A) SS(PAOR) Regs
74 *Commock v CAO*, reported as an appendix to R(SB) 6/90; CSIS/8/1995

75 **UC** Reg 7 SS(OR) Regs
**Income-related ESA & PC** Reg 14 SS(PAOR) Regs
76 CIS/5825/1999
77 s71(3) SSAA 1992
78 *B v SSWP* [2005] EWCA Civ 929, reported as R(IS) 9/06, which says that overpayments for failure to disclose are recoverable because of a breach of duty by a claimant of reg 32 SS(C&P) Regs; CIS/1996/2006; CIS/2125/2006; *PA v SSWP (DLA)* [2016] UKUT 428 (AAC)
79 R(IS) 5/03. This tribunal of commissioners' decision was intended to resolve the conflict between the earlier CIS/332/1993 and R(IS) 5/00, and preferred the latter.
80 *PA v SSWP (DLA)* [2016] UKUT 428 (AAC)
81 CA/1014/1999; CSDLA/1282/2001
82 *Secretary of State for Social Services v Solly* [1974] 3 All ER 922; R(SB) 21/82
83 CIS/1423/1997
84 *PA v SSWP (DLA)* [2016] UKUT 428 (AAC)
85 *MC v SSWP (IS)* [2015] UKUT 600 (AAC)
86 DWP, *Benefit Overpayment Recovery Guide*, November 2024, Ch 4

4. **Recovery of overpaid benefit**
87 Public Authorities (Fraud, Error and Recovery) Bill 2024-25
88 DWP, *Benefit Overpayment Recovery Guide*, November 2024
89 *K, R (on the application of) v SSWP* [2023] EWHC 233 (Admin)
90 *K, R (on the application of) v SSWP* [2023] EWHC 233 (Admin)
91 The tax credit overpayment is treated as if it were an overpayment of UC: art 5 The Tax Credits (Exercise of Functions) Order 2024 No.3280
92 Reg 15 SS(PAOR) Regs
93 The recovery rules apply as they do to an overpayment of UC: reg 16(7A) and (7B) SS(PAOR) Regs
94 Reg 10 SS(OR) Regs
95 Reg 16(7A) and (7B) SS(PAOR) Regs
96 DWP, *Benefit Overpayment Recovery Guide*, November 2024; maximum deduction rate of 15 per cent of the standard allowance was announced in the Autumn 2024 Budget; reg 11 SS(OR) Regs actually permits recovery at a maximum of 40 per cent
97 Reg 11(7) SS(OR) Regs
98 Reg 11(8) SS(OR) Regs
99 Reg 11(9) SS(OR) Regs
100 Reg 12 SS(OR) Regs
101 Reg 13 SS(OR) Regs
102 Reg 14 SS(OR) Regs. The maximum recoverable weekly amounts stated in this rule are calculated as percentages of a monthly figure of UC. It is assumed that these are converted to weekly figures.
103 Reg 29A SS(PAOR) Regs
104 s71ZE SSAA 1992
105 Reg 15(2) SS(PAOR) Regs
106 Reg 42A CB&GA(Admin) Regs
107 Reg 16(1) and (2) SS(PAOR) Regs
108 Regs 15 and 16 SS(PAOR) Regs
109 Reg 17 SS(PAOR) Regs
110 Reg 16(3) SS(PAOR) Regs
111 s74(2)(b) SSAA 1992
112 Reg 16(4), (4A), (5) and (6) SS(PAOR) Regs
113 Reg 16(6) SS(PAOR) Regs
114 Reg 16(7A) and (7B) SS(PAOR) Regs
115 Reg 18 SS(OR) Regs
116 Reg 19 SS(OR) Regs
117 Reg 23 SS(OR) Regs
118 Reg 30 SS(OR) Regs
119 Reg 21 SS(OR) Regs
120 Reg 20(3) SS(OR) Regs
121 Reg 20(3A)-(3B) SS(OR) Regs
122 Regs 17(1) and 20(7) SS(OR) Regs
123 Reg 29 SS(OR) Regs
124 Reg 25 SS(OR) Regs
125 s71(10) SSAA 1992
126 s9(1) Limitation Act 1980
127 DWP, *Benefit Overpayment Recovery Guide*, based on the provisions of the Prescription and Limitation (Scotland) Act 1973, available at gov.uk
128 *CPAG v SSWP* [2010] UKSC 54, upholding the decision of the Court of Appeal in *CPAG, R (on the application of) v SSWP* [2009] EWCA Civ 1058. The DWP's *Benefit Overpayment Recovery Guide* still states that it can use common law principles for recovering 'overprovisioning' overpayments – this is not in accordance with the law.

5. **Overpayments of housing benefit**
129 Reg 99 HB Regs; reg 80 HB(SPC) Regs
130 Reg 99 HB Regs; reg 80 HB(SPC) Regs
131 Reg 93(3) HB Regs; reg 74(3) HB(SPC) Regs
132 Reg 100(4) HB Regs; reg 81(4) HB(SPC) Regs
133 Reg 100(2) HB Regs; reg 81(2) HB(SPC) Regs

134 *Duggan v CAO* [1989] (CA); *R on the application of Sier v Cambridge CC* [2001] EWCA Civ 1523; CH/571/2003; CH/3761/2005
135 Reg 100(3) HB Regs; reg 81(3) HB(SPC) Regs
136 HB/CTB Circular A23/2009
137 *MB v Christchurch BC (HB)* [2014] UKUT 201 (AAC), reported as [2014] AACR 39
138 CH/2567/2007; HB/CTB Circular A15/2009
139 CH/571/2003; CH/5485/2002
140 CH/939/2004; see also *R on the application of Sier v Cambridge CC* [2001] EWCA Civ 1523; CH/3761/2005
141 *R on the application of Sier v Cambridge CC* [2001] EWCA Civ 1523
142 *Warwick DC v Freeman* [1994] 27 HLR 616 (CA); CH/4918/2003
143 *R v Liverpool City Council ex parte Griffiths* [1990] 22 HLR 312; CH/2554/2002; CH/2567/2007
144 *DP v East Dorset DC (HB)* [2020] UKUT 270 (AAC)
145 Reg 104 HB Regs; reg 85 HB(SPC) Regs; *Adan v LB Hounslow and SSWP* [2004] EWCA Civ 101, reported as R(H) 5/04; CH/4943/2001; HB/CTB Circular A13/2006; *JM v LB Tower Hamlets* [2015] UKUT 460 (AAC)
146 Reg 104(1) HB Regs; reg 85 HB(SPC) Regs
147 *R v Kensington and Chelsea RBC ex parte Brandt* [1995] 28 HLR 528 (QBD), at 537
148 Reg 104(3) HB Regs; reg 85(3) HB(SPC) Regs
149 Reg 103 HB Regs; reg 84 HB(SPC) Regs
150 Reg 103(1)(a) and (b) HB Regs; reg 84(1)(a) and (b) HB(SPC) Regs
151 s75(3)(a) SSAA 1992
152 Reg 101(2) HB Regs; reg 82(2) HB(SPC) Regs
153 Reg 102(1ZA) HB Regs; reg 83(1ZA) HB(SPC) Regs
154 R(H) 6/06
155 DWP, *Housing Benefit Overpayments Guide,* paras 4.43(k) and 4.210-89; *NSP v Stoke on Trent City Council and AT* [2020] UKUT 311 (AAC). This makes clear that a claimant is always a second respondent in an appeal made by a landlord.
156 s75(1) SSAA 1992
157 Reg 102 HB Regs; reg 83 HB(SPC) Regs; s75 SSAA 1992
158 Reg 104A HB Regs; reg 85A HB(SPC) Regs
159 Reg 102(1ZA) HB Regs; reg 83(1ZA) HB(SPC) Regs
160 s75(5)(a) SSAA 1992; reg 106 HB Regs; reg 87 HB(SPC) Regs
161 s75(5)(b) SSAA 1992; reg 106 HB Regs; reg 87 HB(SPC) Regs
162 s75(5)(c) SSAA 1992; reg 106 HB Regs; reg 87 HB(SPC) Regs
163 Reg 102 HB Regs; reg 83 HB(SPC) Regs; HB/CTB Circular A42/00
164 Reg 102(4) HB Regs; reg 83(4) HB(SPC) Regs
165 Reg 102(5) HB Regs; reg 83(5) HB(SPC) Regs
166 Reg 105(1)(a) HB Regs
167 s75(5)(a) SSAA 1992; reg 106 HB Regs; reg 87 HB(SPC) Regs
168 Regs 102 and 105 HB Regs; regs 83 and 86 HB(SPC) Regs
169 *R v Haringey LBC ex parte Azad Ayub* [1992] 25 HLR 566 (QBD)
170 DWP, *Housing Benefit Overpayments Guide,* para 4.90
171 Reg 106A HB Regs; reg 87A HB(SPC) Regs; *LA Welfare Direct Bulletin* 9/2019
172 *Warwick DC v Freeman* [1994] 27 HLR 616 (CA)
173 *Warwick DC v Freeman* [1994] 27 HLR 616 (CA)
174 *Plymouth City Council v Gigg* [1997] 30 HLR 284 (CA)
175 s75(7) SSAA 1992
176 s9(1) Limitation Act 1980
177 DWP, *Benefit Overpayment Recovery Guide,* based on the provisions of the Prescription and Limitation (Scotland) Act 1973, available at gov.uk
178 Reg 90(1)(b) HB Regs; reg 71(1)(b) HB(SPC) Regs
179 Sch 9 paras 2, 3, 6 and 15 HB Regs; Sch 8 paras 2, 3, 6 and 15 HB(SPC) Regs; para A7.222 GM
180 Sch 9 para 15(2) HB Regs; Sch 8 para 15(2) HB(SPC) Regs
181 HB/CTB Circular A13/2006
182 Reg 90(4) HB Regs; reg 71(4) HB(SPC) Regs
183 *Haringey LBC v Awaritefe* [1999] 32 HLR 517 (CA)
184 CH/1395/2006
185 DWP, *Housing Benefit Overpayments Guide,* Part 4, paras 4.240-42
186 s75(6) SSAA 1992
187 s75(6) SSAA 1992; reg 107 HB Regs; reg 88 HB(SPC) Regs

188 Reg 107(3) HB Regs; reg 88(3) HB(SPC) Regs
189 DWP, *Housing Benefit Overpayments Guide*, Part 4, paras 4.240-42

6. **Overpayments of tax credits**
190 s28 TCA 2002
191 s23 TCA 2002
192 ss23(2) and 39(1) TCA 2002
193 r22(2)(d)(I) TP(FT) Rules
194 HMRC leaflet COP26, *What Happens If We've Paid You Too Much Tax Credits?*
195 HMRC leaflet COP26, *What Happens If We've Paid You Too Much Tax Credits?*
196 HMRC, *Debt Management and Banking Manual*, DmBm 555600
197 TCM 0228220; HMRC leaflet COP26, *What Happens If We've Paid You Too Much Tax Credits?*
198 Tax Credits Consultation Forum minutes, 23 January 2025, gov.uk/government/groups/taxcredit-consultation-forum
199 HMRC leaflet COP26, *What Happens If We've Paid You Too Much Tax Credits?*
200 s28(1) TCA 2002
201 ss28(1) and 29 TCA 2002
202 HMRC leaflet COP26, *What Happens If We've Paid You Too Much Tax Credits?*
203 HMRC leaflet COP26, *What Happens If We've Paid You Too Much Tax Credits?*
204 s28(3) and (4) TCA 2002
205 HMRC leaflet COP 26, *What Happens If We've Paid You Too Much Tax Credits?*; CCM 8290
206 s23 TCA 2002
207 s29 TCA 2002
208 The Tax Credits (Exercise of Functions) Order 2014 No.3280; The Tax Credits (Exercise of Functions in relation to Northern Ireland and Notices for Recovery of Tax Credit Overpayments) Order 2017 No.781
209 s29(3)-(5) TCA 2002
210 s28(1)(b) TCA 2002; reg 12 UC(TP) Regs; The Tax Credits (Exercise of Functions in relation to Northern Ireland and Notices for Recovery of Tax Credit Overpayments) Order 2017 No.781; *Government Response to the Public Accounts Committee*, Cm 9596, March 2018, para 7.4
211 Sch 9(7E) SS(C&P) Regs
212 s29(5) TCA 2002
213 Sch 8 Finance (No.2) Act 2015
214 s28(1)(b) TCA 2002; reg 12 UC(TP) Regs; The Tax Credits (Exercise of Functions) Order 2014 No.3280; The Tax Credits (Exercise of Functions in relation to Northern Ireland and Notices for Recovery of Tax Credit Overpayments) Order 2017 No.781
215 s29(2) TCA 2002
216 Tax Credits Consultation Forum minutes, 8 July 2021, p8, gov.uk/government/groups/tax-credit-consultation-forum
217 Tax Credits Consultation Forum minutes, 26 October 2021, p4, gov.uk/government/groups/tax-credit-consultation-forum
218 Adjudicator's Office Annual Report 2022, HMRC update and case studies
219 Reg 4 The Income Tax (Pay As You Earn) (Amendment No.4) Regulations 2014 No.2689
220 Sch 8 Finance (No.2) Act 2015
221 *Autumn Statement 2014*, para 2.165
222 s9(1) Limitation Act 1980
223 HMRC, *Debt Management and Banking Manual*, DmBm 595080

# Chapter 48

# Fraud and penalties

**This chapter covers:**

1. Civil penalties (p1101)
2. Investigations (p1102)
3. Prosecution of offences (p1106)
4. Administrative penalties for benefit offences (p1109)
5. Sanctions for benefit offences (p1111)

7

This chapter covers rules on fraud for benefits administered by the DWP, housing benefit, child benefit and guardian's allowance. Income support (IS), income-based jobseekers' allowance (JSA) and tax credits have now mostly been replaced by universal credit (see p21). For information about IS or income-based JSA and fraud, and about tax credits and fraud, see the 2024/25 edition of this *Handbook*. For the rules on the Scottish benefits and fraud, see Chapter 68. This chapter does not cover the rules for statutory sick, maternity, adoption, paternity, shared parental, parental bereavement and neonatal care pay.

## Key facts

- When you claim benefit, you must give correct and complete information to the DWP, HMRC or the local authority. You may commit an offence if you deliberately mislead the agency dealing with your claim.
- You must report changes in your circumstances that could affect your entitlement. You may commit an offence if you do not notify the relevant office of changes promptly.
- Even if you are not suspected of an offence, you may get a fine (known as a 'civil penalty') if you provide incorrect information and you are considered to have acted negligently, or if you have not notified a change of circumstances promptly and do not have a reasonable excuse.
- If it is believed that you have committed fraud, you may be prosecuted. Alternatively, you may be given the option of paying an administrative penalty. Your benefits could be suspended or sanctioned, even if you are not prosecuted.

- If you are suspected or accused of fraud, get advice before taking any action or making any statements.

*Future changes*

The Public Authorities (Fraud, Error and Recovery) Bill may affect some of the information in this chapter once its measures come into force. This is likely to include changes to the DWP's powers of investigation, including entry, search and seizure, which would allow it to require banks and financial insitutions to inform the DWP about data that affects eligibility. Measures in the Bill would also increase recovery enforcement, including possible disqualification from driving where debt is not repaid, and extend offences and the civil penalties system to cover non-benefit payments such as grants.

## 1. Civil penalties

Even if you are not considered to have acted fraudulently, you can be given a civil penalty if you, or someone acting on your behalf, acted carelessly in relation to your claim or award.

Civil penalties are different from the 'administrative penalties' imposed for benefit offences (see p1109). You cannot be given a civil penalty if you have been charged in connection with, accepted a formal caution for, or have received a notice about an administrative penalty for, the same offence.

A civil penalty of £50 can be given if, in connection with a claim for or an award of a benefit:[1]

- you 'negligently' make an incorrect statement or representation, or negligently give incorrect information or evidence, and you do not take 'reasonable steps' to correct the error; *or*
- you fail to provide information or evidence, or you fail to notify a 'relevant change of circumstances', and you do not have a 'reasonable excuse'; *and*
- your negligence or failure results in your being overpaid benefit of *more than* £65.[2] The overpayment period must start on or after 1 October 2012.

Even if it is decided you fit the criteria above, a civil penalty is *discretionary*. Both your circumstances and those that led to the overpayment should be considered before one is imposed.[3]

*Definitions*

A **'relevant change of circumstances'** is one that affects entitlement to benefit.[4]

**'Reasonable excuse'** means something that would cause a reasonable person of a similar age and experience to act as you did.[5] Your state of health and the information you received or might have obtained may be relevant, as may any advice you have received.[6]

Other terms used are not defined in the legislation but the DWP has produced guidance on the meaning of the following.[7]

**'Negligently'** is acting carelessly, not paying attention to, or disregarding the importance of, anything that needs to be done in relation to your entitlement. It is more than a simple mistake.

**'Reasonable steps'** is doing something which is sensible or practicable to correct an error.

The penalty is added to the overpayment and recovered in the same way (see p1073 for overpayments under the universal credit system, p1082 for housing benefit overpayments and p1075 for all other overpayments).[8] If a penalty is imposed on you for a benefit you were awarded jointly with your partner, it can be recovered from your partner instead, unless they were not (and could not reasonably be expected to be) aware of the error or failure.

You can ask for a mandatory reconsideration of the decision to impose a civil penalty, and then appeal if the decision is not changed (see Chapter 51)[9] – eg, you can argue you did not behave negligently or you had a reasonable excuse for not declaring a change in your circumstances. **Note:** you may also want to challenge the overpayment decision (see Chapter 47).



## 2. Investigations

Investigation of suspected benefit fraud covered by this chapter is carried out by DWP fraud and error staff. The DWP does not have to tell you why it is making enquiries. It usually waits until it has collected more information and then asks you to attend an interview.

### Collecting information

There are special rules allowing the release of information to the DWP from:

- HMRC;[10]
- government departments – eg, on issues about passports, immigration, emigration, nationality and prisoners;[11]
- the registration service – eg, about age, death, marriage and civil partnership;[12]
- local authorities.[13]

Local authorities can also be supplied with information held by the DWP or HMRC, and share information with other local authorities.[14]

Local authorities, HMRC and the DWP can require information about redirected post and have undelivered social security post returned to them.[15]

Information acquired is confidential to the bodies administering benefits, including private companies contracted to carry out such functions. Unauthorised disclosure of this information is a criminal offence.[16]

***Are you unhappy about the use of your personal information?***

The Data Protection Act 2018 restricts the use of personal data held about you. If a local authority, the DWP or HMRC makes a request for information which you think is inappropriate or unreasonable, refer the matter to the Information Commissioner (see ico.org.uk).

## Powers of investigation

As 'authorised officers', fraud investigators have certain powers to obtain information.[17] **'Authorised officers'** can be:

- officials of any government department (not just the DWP); *or*
- employees of local authorities carrying out housing benefit (HB) functions; *or*
- employees of organisations that perform contracted-out HB functions.



Authorised officers should use a code of practice when obtaining information.[18] Information that is the subject of 'legal privilege' (ie, confidential communication between a legal adviser and their client) cannot be requested.[19]

Authorised officers have powers to enter, at any reasonable time, premises which they have reasonable grounds for suspecting are:[20]

- a person's place of employment; *or*
- where a trade or business is carried out or documents relating to it are kept; *or*
- where a personal or occupational pension scheme is administered or documents relating to it are kept; *or*
- where someone operating a compensatory scheme for an industrial accident or disease may be found; *or*
- where a person on whose behalf a compensatory payment for an industrial accident or disease has been made may be found.

The above can include someone's home. Each authorised officer has a certificate of appointment which must be shown when requesting information.[21] They can question anyone on the premises and require, if reasonable, any documents or copies of documents.

Authorised officers cannot come into your home without your permission (except if you run a business from your home) and cannot detain you. They cannot make you give information or answer questions in such a way as to confess that you, or your spouse or civil partner, are guilty of an offence.[22]

Authorised officers may access certain electronic records, including those kept by:[23]

- any bank or person whose business is providing credit to the public – eg, credit card companies and building societies;
- the Director of National Savings and Investments;
- any insurer;
- any credit reference agency;
- any money transfer service;
- any utility or telephone company;
- any educational institution;
- the Student Loans Company.

All fraud investigators can use surveillance to investigate social security fraud – eg, observing people entering or leaving premises. Any surveillance must be authorised by an officer of the appropriate level.

Fraud investigators in England and Wales are bound by codes of practice under the Police and Criminal Evidence Act 1984.[24] In Scotland, fraud investigators must work to the common law principle of the 'test of fairness'. If the codes of practice or common law principle of fairness are breached, this may restrict the use of evidence they have obtained.[25] If you think the officers have acted unfairly, get advice.



## Interviews under caution

If you are suspected of fraud, fraud investigators should carry out a formal interview, known as an 'interview under caution'. You should receive reasonable advance notification in writing (uploaded to your journal if you are claiming universal credit) informing you *specifically* that you have been invited to attend an interview under caution. Note that an interview under caution is not the same as other types of interviews conducted by the DWP, such as 'compliance interviews', which are not fraud related.

You should always be cautioned before the interview. If the fraud officer fails to do so, the interview may not be admissible in court. If you do not understand the caution, the fraud officer should explain its meaning to you. If you appear unable to understand the significance of the interview or the questions being put to you (eg, due to incapacity or a learning disability), you should be asked if you want someone to assist or attend with you (such as a relative, other 'appropriate adult' or solicitor) and the interview may be suspended if needed.[26]

You do not have to answer any questions, but not answering might be taken as a sign of guilt. If you decide not to answer questions, you could instead prepare a written statement.

If you are not informed of the purpose of the interview, it may be inadmissible as evidence in court.

The interview is normally recorded and you can request a copy. A transcript is produced for use at any trial or appeal hearing.

If you have extra travel costs to attend the interview, these should be reimbursed. If you need someone to accompany you because you are vulnerable (eg, you are under 18, have a learning disability or other complex needs), their travel expenses can also be reimbursed.

***Are you suspected of fraud?***

1. If you think fraud officers may interview you, get advice before you attend the interview. Free legal advice may be available from a solicitor.
2. Take someone (eg, a solicitor, adviser or friend) to the interview with you. Although they cannot speak for you, they can support you and take notes. A solicitor can advise you during the interview, ask for clarification of questions and challenge improper questioning.
3. Try to remain calm and listen carefully to the questions you are asked. If you do not understand anything, ask for clarification. You must answer the questions yourself. Think carefully about the implications of the answers you give.
4. If you think you can explain why the situation has arisen, you should mention it at the interview, as any explanation you give later is less likely to be believed if you are prosecuted.[27] If you can explain matters, your benefit is less likely to be taken away.
5. Do not confess to something that you did not do just to finish the interview or to prevent your benefit stopping.
6. Complain (see Chapter 55) if you feel the interview was not conducted fairly or you were treated in a way which failed to take into account issues such as disability.

7

## The effect of a fraud investigation on your benefit

If the DWP, HMRC or local authority has doubts about your entitlement to benefit, other processes can be applied at the same time as a fraud investigation.

- Your benefit can be suspended (see p1031) – eg, if there are doubts about your entitlement or if there is a possibility that you are being overpaid.
- You can be asked to provide additional information and evidence. If you do not do so within a specified time limit, your award can be terminated (see p1033). If you believe that you are still entitled to benefit, make a new claim.

If a fraud investigation is taking a long time to complete, your benefit may be suspended for a long time. However, the benefit authority should not withhold your benefit indefinitely without making a decision on whether or not you are entitled. Complain if you think an investigation is taking too long (see Chapter 55). If that brings no results, seek legal advice about forcing the benefit authority to make a decision (see p1268).

The decision on whether you should be prosecuted for fraud is separate from any decision to recover any overpayment of benefit (see Chapter 47). The two processes are independent and have different tests. Therefore:

- a decision or appeal about your benefit does not have to be delayed while you wait for the outcome of a criminal prosecution;[28]

- a court fine does not prevent recovery of an overpayment. However, if you have to make payments under a compensation order made by a court to the benefit authority, it cannot also recover that amount as an overpayment.[29]

Acquittal in a fraud case does not necessarily mean that the decision on your benefit entitlement was wrong. Whatever the result of an investigation or prosecution, it may take longer to assess future claims or changes to awards because your circumstances may be checked more thoroughly. Complain if it takes too long. You should not be prevented from making a new claim during a fraud investigation if your circumstances change. You can also apply for an advance payment (see p1023) or help from a local welfare assistance scheme (see p770).

## 3. **Prosecution of offences**



Benefit offences can broadly be divided into two categories, based on the severity of the penalty you can be given.

- Making *false representations* to get benefit is the *less serious* of the benefit offences (see below).
- Making *dishonest representations* to get benefit is the *more serious* benefit offence (see p1108).

In the most serious cases in England and Wales, you can instead be charged with the criminal offences of theft or fraud, and in Scotland, with common law offences.[30] These offences carry more severe penalties.

If found guilty, you can be fined or imprisoned, or both. Any fine that you have to pay is in addition to any recoverable overpayment (see Chapter 47). Your benefits can also be sanctioned (stopped or reduced) for a period (see p1111).

In England and Wales, DWP and HMRC prosecutions are carried out by the Crown Prosecution Service, which also conducts prosecutions on behalf of many local authorities. In Scotland, prosecutions are conducted by the Crown Office and Procurator Fiscal Service.

### False representations

You commit the offence of making false representations if you:[31]

- make a statement or give information or produce documents that *you know to be false* (or '*knowingly*' cause or allow someone else to do so) to claim a benefit or payment for yourself or someone else, or for any other purpose relating to the benefit rules. It does not have to be shown that you intended to get benefit to which you were not entitled;[32] *or*
- fail to notify the DWP, HMRC or local authority *promptly* of a change of circumstances which *you know* affects your entitlement to benefit or another

payment. This also applies to appointees and other third parties receiving benefit on your behalf, and landlords receiving direct payments of housing benefit or universal credit. You count as notifying a change promptly if you do so as soon as reasonably practicable after the change occurs; *or*

- *cause or allow* another person to fail to notify a change of circumstances to the DWP, HMRC or local authority *promptly,* which *you know* affects their entitlement to benefit or other payment.

For an offence to have been committed, you must have acted 'knowingly'. You do not 'know' something if you are merely careless about whether or not something is true, or if you fail to find out.[33] You have not committed an offence if you do not notify a change of circumstances that did not affect your entitlement to benefit or if there was already no entitlement to benefit.[34] To have acted 'knowingly', you must have been made aware of where any change must be reported and the manner in which it must be reported.[35]

The maximum penalty for these offences is a fine or three months in prison, or both.[36]

7

## Duty to report a change in circumstances

The rules on fraud and your duty to report a change of circumstances are different to those outlined on p1030. For fraud purposes, you only commit an offence if you do not report *promptly* a change that *you know* affects your benefit. However, to avoid potential allegations of fraud or prosecution, you should report *all* changes promptly. It is always advisable to report the change in a way that allows you to show that you have done so – eg, if in writing, date and retain a copy or get a receipt or proof of posting, keep records of telephone calls and take screenshots if reporting online. For more information about reporting changes of circumstances, see p1030.

## Duties of advisers and other third parties

If you are an adviser, you are not under a duty to notify the DWP, HMRC or local authority about a claimant's change of circumstances, provided you have fully advised them of the law and the requirement for them to notify changes in their circumstances and provide truthful information. In order to commit an offence of *allowing or causing* someone to fail to notify a change of circumstances, or *knowingly allowing or causing* someone to give false information, there must be some sort of implied permission given to the person to not report the change or to give false information.[37] You do not 'allow' someone to do something unless you can stop them doing it.[38] You should do nothing to help facilitate a misrepresentation or failure to notify a change of circumstances – eg, help to complete a claim or review form which you know is inaccurate. If you – as an adviser – know that a claimant is being overpaid, you should make sure you advise them of their duty to notify the relevant benefit authority of the overpayment and you should do nothing that facilitates the overpayment continuing.

## Dishonest representations

You commit the offence of making dishonest representations if you make any of the false representations on p1106, with a view to obtaining benefit, and you act 'dishonestly' ('knowingly' in Scotland) in doing so.[39] This means that you did something that most people would consider dishonest and that you must have known it was dishonest.[40]

The maximum penalty if you are convicted in a magistrates' court (sheriff court in Scotland) is a fine or six months in prison (12 months in Scotland), or both.[41] If you are convicted in the Crown Court (High Court in Scotland), you can receive an unlimited fine or up to seven years in prison, or both.[42]

## Prosecutions

Not all cases in which there is evidence to justify a prosecution are taken to court. Instead, you may be given the chance to pay an 'administrative penalty' (see p1109). In some cases, no action is taken at all. The factors taken into account include the strength of the evidence, the amount of benefit involved, whether an offence was planned and your personal circumstances. The decision about whether or not to prosecute is taken by the Crown Prosecution Service or Crown Office and Procurator Fiscal Service, not the fraud investigators. **Note:** your benefits can be sanctioned (stopped or reduced) even if you are not prosecuted (see p1111).

There are time limits for bringing a prosecution for making false representations in order to get benefit (see p1106). A prosecution must be started either within three months of the date the benefit authority (or, in Scotland, the Crown Office and Procurator Fiscal Service) thinks it has sufficient evidence to prosecute you, or within 12 months of the date you committed the offence, whichever is later.[43]

There are no time limits for bringing a prosecution for making dishonest representations in order to get benefit (see above).

### *Are you being prosecuted?*

If you are being prosecuted, get advice. You may be entitled to free legal help from a solicitor and representation in court. Check carefully that the DWP is able to prove all the parts of the offence with which you are charged. Do not plead guilty until you have obtained advice. Also get specialist welfare rights advice about challenging any overpayment decision separately, as the solicitor helping with any fraud allegations may not be a welfare rights specialist.

# 4. Administrative penalties for benefit offences

The DWP can offer you the option of paying an administrative penalty under civil law instead of being prosecuted for a benefit offence under criminal law. Administrative penalties are not the same as civil penalties described on p1101. Your benefits can still be sanctioned (stopped or reduced) if you accept an administrative penalty (see p1111).

The amount of the penalty depends on when the offence was committed.

- For offences committed wholly after 7 May 2012, the penalty is 50 per cent of any amount overpaid, subject to a minimum of £350 even if you were not actually overpaid, and:[44]
  - a maximum of £2,000 if committed partly or wholly before 1 April 2015; *or*
  - a maximum of £5,000 if committed wholly after 31 March 2015.
- For offences committed partly or wholly before 8 May 2012, the amount of the penalty is 30 per cent of the overpayment.



The overpayment must have been caused by an offence you committed on or after 18 December 1997.[45]

The penalty is added to any overpayment of benefit and is recoverable in the same way (see p1073 for overpayments under the universal credit system, p1082 for housing benefit overpayments and p1075 for all other overpayments).[46]

## The option of paying a penalty

You can be offered the option of paying a penalty if:[47]

- an overpayment is recoverable from you, or, for offences committed wholly after 7 May 2012, would have been if an award had been made. The benefit authority must have revised or superseded your award of benefit and issued a decision that any overpayment is recoverable (see Chapter 47); *and*
- the overpayment was due to an act or omission on your part. This must have occurred on or after 18 December 1997;[48] *and*
- there are grounds for prosecuting you for an offence relating to the overpayment.

The DWP issues you with a notice setting out how the scheme works, how to agree to pay a penalty and how to withdraw your agreement.[49] If you are not issued with a proper notice, it may not be possible to enforce the penalty.

***What happens if you accept a penalty?***[50]

1. If you agree to pay a penalty, you cannot be prosecuted for any offence relating to the same overpayment. However, you can still be prosecuted in the future if you commit another offence or one relating to a different overpayment.

2. If it is found on revision, supersession or appeal that the overpayment is not due or not recoverable, any penalty you have paid must be repaid to you. This does not change the fact that you agreed to pay a penalty in exchange for immunity from prosecution, so you still cannot be prosecuted for the offence.
3. If the amount of the overpayment is changed following a revision, supersession or appeal, the agreement is cancelled, so you lose immunity from prosecution, and any penalty you have paid must be repaid to you. However, if you make a fresh agreement to accept a penalty, you are again immune from prosecution and the amount of penalty you have already paid can be offset against the new penalty rather than being repaid to you.

If you do not accept the penalty, the DWP may pass the case to the Crown Prosecution Service or Crown Office and Procurator Fiscal Service to consider whether to prosecute you.

## Changing your mind

If you agree to pay a penalty, you can change your mind, provided you notify the DWP within 14 days (28 days for offences committed partly or wholly before 8 May 2012) in the way it specifies.[51] If you change your mind after the end of this period, you have no right of appeal against the imposition of the penalty, but you can complain (see Chapter 55) if you think you should not have been offered a penalty – eg, if it turns out there was insufficient evidence to prosecute you. If you decide not to accept the penalty, you lose immunity from prosecution. If you have already paid any part of it, this must be refunded to you.

***Should you agree to pay a penalty?***

1. Get advice and consider your options carefully.
2. If you are not prosecuted, your case does not go to court and you cannot go to prison.
3. If you accept a penalty, your benefits can still be sanctioned (stopped or reduced).
4. You may be invited to pay a penalty when there is insufficient evidence to prosecute you. The DWP can only recommend that your case be considered for prosecution. The Crown Prosecution Service, Crown Office and Procurator Fiscal Service or local authority legal department decides whether or not to prosecute (see p1106). You are not automatically prosecuted if you refuse to accept a penalty.
5. If prosecuted and found guilty, the court may offer you a caution or community service rather than a fine. On the other hand, you could get a large court fine or even a prison sentence.
6. A penalty may be a substantial amount of money. For minor offences, the amount of a fine imposed by the court could be less.

## 5. Sanctions for benefit offences

If you get certain benefits, known as 'sanctionable benefits' (see p1112), your benefits can be sanctioned if:[52]

- you are convicted of one or more benefit offences in a set of proceedings; *or*
- you agree to pay an administrative penalty (see p1109).

If your benefit is sanctioned, it is not paid or paid at a reduced rate (see p1112).

**Note:** these sanctions are different to those imposed for failing to comply with work-related requirements described in Chapter 43.

Under what is sometimes called the 'one-strike rule' (as it can apply after just one offence), a conviction is not always required as your benefit can be sanctioned by just accepting an administrative penalty.

If you are convicted of a benefit offence and have already committed an earlier offence(s), a longer sanction can be imposed under the 'two-strikes rule' instead. This applies if:[53]

- you are convicted of one or more benefit offences in the current set of proceedings; *and*
- within five years of the date you committed any of the *current* offences, you committed an *earlier* benefit offence, including an offence for which you accepted an administrative penalty or caution; *and*
- in relation to any previous reduction under the two-strikes rule of either your benefits, or a joint claim for jobseeker's allowance (JSA) or a family member's benefits, the current offence had not been treated as a current offence, and the earlier offence had not been treated as an earlier offence.

**Note:** the DWP no longer offers cautions for offences committed wholly or partly after 1 April 2012. The DWP may offer administrative penalties instead. For details about DWP cautions, see the 2012/13 edition of this *Handbook*. However, an 'administrative caution' may still be recommended in exceptional circumstances by the Crown Prosecution Service or Crown Office and Procurator Fiscal Service as an alternative to prosecution.

The benefit offence(s) must have been committed on or after 1 April 2010 (for the one-strike rule) or on or after 1 April 2002 (for the two-strikes rule) and be:[54]

- in connection with a 'disqualifying' benefit (see below); *or*
- to attempt, conspire or aid the committing of a benefit offence.

***Disqualifying benefits***[55]

All social security benefits are **'disqualifying benefits'** for the purposes listed above, except statutory sick pay, statutory maternity pay, statutory adoption pay, statutory paternity pay and maternity allowance.

## Sanctionable benefits

'Sanctionable benefits' are:[56]

- universal credit (UC);
- employment and support allowance (ESA);
- housing benefit (HB);
- JSA
- pension credit (PC);
- bereavement benefits (except bereavement support payment);
- carer's allowance;
- industrial injuries benefits (except constant attendance and exceptionally severe disablement allowance);
- war pensions (except constant attendance allowance, exceptionally severe disablement allowance and mobility supplement).

Under separate rules, before tax credits were abolished, you could be disqualified from receiving working tax credit, but not child tax credit, if you had committed a benefit offence after 5 April 2021. For details, see the 2024/25 edition of this *Handbook*.

7

Payment of any other benefits cannot be stopped or reduced under these rules.

## The sanctions

Usually, sanctionable benefits are not paid during a sanction period (see p1113). In some cases, however, your benefit may be paid at a reduced rate.

- UC is usually reduced by the full rate of your UC standard allowance calculated on a daily basis (see p980).[57] This is called the 'high rate' reduction. However, the 'low rate' of 40 per cent of your standard allowance on a daily basis applies if you are a responsible carer or foster parent for a child under the age of one, an adopter or are pregnant. The 'high rate' still applies if you have been found to have limited capability for work-related activity. Only half of the applicable rate is applied to individual joint claimants.
  If your UC is reduced under these rules, you can get hardship payments in the same way as when sanctioned for not meeting your claimant responsibilities, except that 16/17-year-olds *can* get hardship payments in these circumstances (see p1050).[58]
- **PC and HB** are usually reduced by 40 per cent of the appropriate personal allowance for a single person of your age (see p266), or 20 per cent if you or a member of your family are pregnant or seriously ill.[59] However, HB is unaffected if you or a member of your family are entitled to income-related ESA or PC during the sanction period.[60]
- **Income-related ESA** is reduced by 100 per cent of the appropriate personal allowance for a single person of your age (see p266), 40 per cent if you or a member of your family are subject to no work-related requirements, or 20 per

cent if you or a member of your family are pregnant or seriously ill.[61] You may be able to get hardship payments (see p1053).

## The sanction period

For benefit offences committed wholly after 31 March 2013, the following sanction periods apply.[62]

The sanction period is **three years** if:

- you are convicted for serious fraud or conspiracy to defraud; *or*
- the overpayment is at least £50,000; *or*
- you are given a sentence of at least a year; *or*
- the offence is committed over a period of at least two years.

In cases where the three-year period above does not apply, the sanction period under the one-strike rule (see p1111) if convicted is **13 weeks** or, if you opt to pay an administrative penalty (see p1109), **four weeks.** Under the two-strikes rule (see p1111) where the above does not apply, the sanction period is **three years** if the earlier offence is within five years of a previous one or **26 weeks** where it is not.

The sanction period starts at least 28 days after the determination that a restriction on payment of benefits should apply.[63]

**Note:** sanctions under these rules prevent *payment* of a benefit during the sanction period, not *entitlement*, which ensures the link between benefits and other entitlements (eg, free school lunches and, in England, free prescriptions) remains.[64] However, a minimum 10 pence a week payment to PC and income-related ESA remains in place while these benefits are sanctioned.[65]

7

# Notes

1. **Civil penalties**

1 ss115C-115D SSAA 1992; SS(CP) Regs
2 para 09420 DMG; para D1271 ADM
3 *VT v SSWP (IS)* [2016] UKUT 178 (AAC), reported as [2016] AACR 42; *CT v SSWP (ESA)* [2021] UKUT 6 (AAC); *MW v SSWP (ESA)* [2023] UKUT 50 (AAC); *Secretary of State for Work and Pensions v NS* [2024] UKUT 5 (AAC)
4 s115D(6) SSAA 1992
5 *VT v SSWP (IS)* [2016] UKUT 178 (AAC), reported as [2016] AACR 42; *MW v SSWP (ESA)* [2023] UKUT 50 (AAC)
6 *JP v SSWP* [2017] UKUT 505 (AAC); *CT v SSWP (ESA)* [2021] UKUT 6 (AAC)
7 paras 09425-29 DMG; paras D1276-80 ADM
8 Reg 15 SS(PAOR) Regs; reg 3 SS(OR) Regs
9 *VT v SSWP (IS)* [2016] UKUT 178 (AAC), reported as [2016] AACR 42

2. **Investigations**

10 s127 WRA 2012
11 s122B SSAA 1992
12 ss124, 124A, 124B and 125 SSAA 1992

13 ss122D and 122E SSAA 1992
14 ss122C and 122E SSAA 1992
15 ss182A and 182B SSAA 1992
16 s123 and Sch 4 SSAA 1992
17 ss109A, 109B and 109C SSAA 1992
18 s3 SSFA 2001; DWP, *Code of Practice on Obtaining Information: Social Security Fraud Act 2001*, November 2016, available at gov.uk
19 s109B(5)(b) SSAA 1992
20 s109C SSAA 1992
21 s109A(4)(a) SSAA 1992; DWP, *Code of Practice on Obtaining Information: Social Security Fraud Act 2001*, November 2016, available at gov.uk
22 ss109B(5) and 109C(6) SSAA 1992
23 ss109BA and 109B(2A) SSAA 1992
24 s67(9) PACEA 1984
25 In England and Wales, s78(1) PACEA 1984
26 Police and Criminal Evidence Act (PACE) Code C, Home Office; 'Prosecuting Welfare and Health Fraud Cases' guidance, Crown Prosecution Service
27 s34 CJPOA 1994
28 *Mote v SSWP and Chichester DC* [2007] EWCA Civ 1324, reported as R(IS) 4/08
29 CIS/683/1994; *KP v RB of Kensington and Chelsea* [2014] UKUT 393 (AAC)

3. **Prosecution of offences**

30 *Osinuga v Director of Public Prosecutions* [1997] 30 HLR 853
31 s112(1)-(1F) SSAA 1992
32 *Clear v Smith* [1981] 1 WLR 399
33 *Taylor's Central Garages v Roper* [1951] 115 JPR 445
34 *R v Passmore* [2007] EWCA Crim 2053; *R v Laku* [2008] EWCA Crim 1745
35 *Coventry City Council v Vassell* [2011] EWHC 1542 (Admin)
36 s112(2) SSAA 1992
37 *R v Chainey* [1914] 1 KB 137 at 142 (DC)
38 *R v Tilley* [2009] EWCA Crim 1426
39 s111A SSAA 1992
40 *R v Ghosh* [1982] EWCA Crim 2
41 s111A(3)(a) SSAA 1992; s45 Criminal Proceedings etc. (Reform) (Scotland) Act 2007
42 s111A(3)(b) SSAA 1992
43 s116(2), (2A) and (7) SSAA 1992; *Bennett v SSWP* [2012] EWHC 371 (Admin)

4. **Administrative penalties for benefit offences**

44 s115A(3)-(3A) SSAA 1992
45 s25(7) SSA(F)A 1997; Art 2(1)(b) SSA(F)AO No.5
46 s115A(4)(a) SSAA 1992
47 s115A(1)-(1A) SSAA 1992
48 s25(7) SSA(F)A 1997; Art 2(1)(b) SSA(F)AO No.5
49 s115A(2) SSAA 1992
50 s115A(4)(b), (6) and (7) SSAA 1992
51 s115A(5) SSAA 1992

5. **Sanctions for benefit offences**

52 s6B(1) SSFA 2001
53 s7(1) SSFA 2001
54 ss6B(13) and 7(8), definition of 'benefit offence', SSFA 2001
55 s6A(1), definition of 'disqualifying benefit', SSFA 2001; reg 19A, definition of 'disqualifying benefit', SS(LB) Regs
56 s6A(1), definition of 'sanctionable benefit', SSFA 2001; reg 19 SS(LB) Regs
57 Reg 3ZB SS(LB) Regs
58 Regs 16D-16H SS(LB) Regs
59 ss6B, 7 and 9 SSFA 2001; regs 3ZA, 3A, 5, 9-10 and 16A-16C, 17 and 18 SS(LB) Regs
60 Reg 18 SS(LB) Regs
61 Reg 3ZA SS(LB) Regs
62 ss6B(11A), (13) and (14), and 7(1A), (6A) and (8) SSFA 2001; paras B2002 and B2201 ADM
63 ss6B(11) and 7(6) SSFA 2001; reg 1A and 2 SS(LB) Regs
64 ss6B(4) and (5) and 7(1) and (2) SSFA 2001
65 Regs 3(2), 3ZA(4) and 3A(3) SS(LB) Regs

Part 8

# Getting a benefit decision changed

# Chapter 49

# Decisions

**This chapter covers:**

1. When a decision must be made (below)
2. Decisions on claims (p1122)
3. Delays in getting a decision (p1123)
4. Information about decisions (p1124)

This chapter covers the rules for decisions about benefits (including housing benefit), the social fund payments in Chapter 33 (except budgeting loans) and decisions about DWP loans for mortgage interest (see p764). It does not cover the rules for Scottish benefits (see Chapter 69), statutory payments (see Chapter 54) or the health benefits in Chapter 27.

References in this chapter to HMRC only apply to decisions about child benefit and guardian's allowance.

8

## Key facts

- The benefits system is a 'decision-based system', so decisions about your benefit must be made and notified to you in many situations.
- Decisions are needed to create awards of benefit and set the amounts and dates of those awards.
- Decisions are also needed to decide if you have been overpaid.
- Decisions should be made within a reasonable time.
- You should be notified of decisions which carry a right of appeal.

## 1. When a decision must be made

The benefits system is a 'decision-based system'.[1] This means that there must be a formal and identifiable decision on questions such as:

- whether and when a valid claim for benefit has been made;
- when you submit a valid claim for benefit, whether or not you are entitled to an award of that benefit;
- the date from which your award should start;
- the amount you should be awarded;

- whether amounts to which you are entitled can be paid;
- whether an award of benefit to you should now be changed, and if so in what way (these decisions are revisions or supersessions – see Chapter 50);
- whether you have been overpaid and whether you need to repay an overpayment.

Decisions are made by decision makers in the agency that deals with that particular benefit (see below). To make a decision, the decision maker must first determine the facts of your case and then establish which rules apply to someone in your situation (see below). This may involve deciding other issues as part of coming to a full decision. Sometimes, the decision maker is bound to accept the ruling of another body on a particular issue (see p1121). There can only ever be a single decision in respect of your entitlement to benefit on a particular day (see p1120). In making initial decisions, the decision maker must consider the situation at the time of their decision (see p1123).

## Who makes decisions

Decisions about most benefits are made by officers of the DWP. Decisions about child benefit and guardian's allowance are made by officers of HMRC. Decisions about housing benefit (HB) are made by officers at the local authority. This *Handbook* refers to all these officers as **'decision makers'**. The DWP refers to some decision makers as 'case managers', although their role is the same.

8

The DWP makes decisions about whether you have limited capability for work or are terminally ill for benefit purposes, even if the main benefit decision is made by another authority – eg, the local authority for your HB.[2]

You may have to attend your local Jobcentre Plus office to discuss your jobseeking conditions or claimant responsibilities (see Chapter 42). In practice, the person you meet is extremely unlikely to be a decision maker, although they may make recommendations to the decision maker – eg, about whether your benefit should be sanctioned.

## How decisions are made

To make a decision about your benefit, a decision maker first needs to know the facts of your case. To do this, they should consider the evidence and decide what that evidence shows is more likely to be the situation than not. The decision maker then decides your entitlement to benefit under the relevant rules.

A decision maker can take account of what you say and accept that as evidence, even if you do not have other evidence confirming that is the case. If there is a range of evidence about a particular point which could lead to different conclusions, the decision maker has to weigh the evidence and decide what facts it establishes overall.

It is helpful to think about a decision as made up of a number of building blocks (sometimes called 'determinations'). For example, a decision that you are entitled to universal credit (UC) could be based on determinations that:

- you made a valid claim for UC on a particular date; *and*
- you are in Great Britain because you are habitually resident and have a right to reside; *and*
- you are aged 35; *and*
- you are not subject to immigration control; *and*
- you are not in education; *and*
- you do not have too much income or capital.

These determinations do not have legal force and do not affect your entitlement to UC until they are incorporated into a decision about whether or not you are entitled to UC. As your right to challenge a decision (see p1122) attaches to a decision and not a determination, if you disagree with the individual determinations, you can challenge them when they are incorporated into a decision notified to you.[3]

***Guidance used by decision makers***

A decision maker may look at official guidance. The guidance is not the law itself but simply the government's view of the law. The following are the most commonly used sources of official guidance.

– *Decision Makers' Guide: staff guide.*[4] For DWP decision makers on all DWP benefits except in the UC system, covered by the *Advice for Decision Making: staff guide.*

– *Advice for Decision Making: staff guide.* For DWP decision makers in the UC system – ie, on UC, personal independence payment (PIP), new-style jobseeker's allowance (JSA) and new-style employment and support allowance (ESA).[5]

– *Universal Credit Guidance.* Operational guidance for DWP decision makers on all aspects of UC.[6]

– *Personal Independence Payment Assessment Guide.* This is for assessment providers[7] and comes in several parts. It should be read with the assessment provider's own guidance, if it exists.[8] See also the *Personal Independence Payment Handbook*, aimed at claimants and advisers.[9]

– *Work Capability Assessment Handbook.* For healthcare professionals who carry out work capability assessments.[10]

– *Housing Benefit Guidance Manual.*[11] See also HB bulletins, urgent bulletins and the *Discretionary Housing Payment Guidance Manual.*[12] Local authorities also have their own guidance.

## Decisions made with limited information

The decision maker can make a decision in certain circumstances, even if they are waiting for you to provide more evidence or information.

A decision is always made on the basis that the evidence or information needed is adverse to you if, for income-related ESA, pension credit (PC) and social fund payments only, it is needed to decide whether you are entitled to a severe disability premium (additional amount for PC), or for new-style JSA, whether you are treated as receiving education.[13]

In such cases, if you request an 'any grounds' revision (see p1131) and provide the missing information, the decision can be revised to take account of it.

For PIP, if you are in a care home and evidence or information is required to decide whether the cost of your accommodation will be met from local or public funds, if the decision maker makes 'reasonable enquiries', they can make a decision on the evidence or information they have.[14]

For UC, if further evidence or information would be needed to decide what housing costs can be included for the purposes of the housing costs element (see Chapter 6) the decision maker can use the information that the DWP already has.[15] If you are entitled to ESA or PC, the decision maker can also make a decision on the basis of the evidence or information they already have.[16]

In all of these cases, if you request an any grounds revision (see p1131) and provide the missing information, the decision can be revised to take account of it.

## Decisions are final

8

Decisions about benefits are final, unless they are changed on revision, supersession or appeal. A decision is not changed just by making a new claim.[17]

*Example*

Jane claims PIP on 10 June. Her claim is refused on 20 August. She appeals. While she is waiting for that appeal to be dealt with, she makes a new, second claim for PIP on 7 September. On 11 October, PIP is awarded at the standard rate starting from 7 September. When the tribunal deals with Jane's appeal, it cannot award PIP for any date after 6 September as the decision on the second PIP claim is final. If Jane is not happy with the decision on her second claim, she must also challenge that decision.

This means that if you think something is wrong with your entitlement to a particular benefit on a particular day, you need to get the decision which deals with that benefit for that day changed (see p1122). Similarly, it means that if a decision maker thinks something is wrong with your entitlement on a particular day, they cannot simply make a completely new decision about this. Instead, they need to change the decision that applies to that day.

## Decisions made by a different decision maker

There are some situations in which the decision maker making the decision about a benefit you have claimed or for which you have an award is not the one who decides a particular issue. These include:

- for HB, decisions about whether you have income or capital when you get UC, income-related ESA or PC;
- for HB, decisions about limited capability for work;
- decisions about national insurance (NI) contributions.

### Housing benefit decisions on income and capital if you get certain benefits

If you get UC, income-related ESA or PC (although not if you get the savings credit of PC only), all of your income and capital is ignored when calculating HB entitlement.[18]

The HB decision maker should not therefore consider your income or capital. There are two exceptions to this rule.

- If the decision maker has evidence about your income and capital that has not already been considered by the DWP decision maker and which raises doubt about whether your benefit award is correct, they may inform the DWP. The decision maker can suspend your HB while they wait to see if the DWP makes a new decision (see p1032).
- If the decision maker has strong and clear evidence you are fraudulently concealing evidence from the DWP about your income and capital, they can make their own decision on the issue.[19]

8

### Decisions about limited capability for work

Only a DWP decision maker can decide whether you have limited capability for work, and their decision is binding for decision makers for other benefits.[20]

### Decisions about national insurance contributions

Certain questions about NI contributions and employment are dealt with by a special procedure – eg:[21]

- whether you were an 'employed earner' for the purposes of paying contributions or entitlement to industrial injuries disablement benefit; *or*
- whether you were liable to pay a particular class of contributions or have paid contributions for a particular period; *or*
- the amount of contributions you were liable to pay.

These matters are referred to HMRC for a decision, which is then binding on the decision maker.[22]

When HMRC makes a decision, you can appeal against it.[23] The appeals process is similar to appealing against an HMRC decision on your entitlement to statutory payments (see Chapter 54).

The First-tier Tribunal can also require the DWP to refer matters that are HMRC's responsibility, but which are relevant to a benefit appeal, to HMRC for a decision.[24] The DWP may revise the decision on your claim as a result. If not, the matter goes back to the tribunal.

**Note:** the decision maker can make arrangements for HMRC to decide whether you can be credited with earnings or contributions.[25] You can appeal against these decisions in the same way as against DWP decisions. You must first request a mandatory reconsideration (see p1168).

## Correcting a decision

Unless the benefit is child benefit or guardian's allowance, if the decision maker makes an accidental error in their decision (eg, a typing error or a miscalculation in the arithmetic), this can be corrected.[26] You must be sent or given written notice of the correction as soon as is practicable. To see how the time limit for applying for an 'any grounds' revision of the decision can be extended when a decision has been corrected, see p1132.

## If you disagree with a decision maker's decision

If you think a decision is wrong, you may be able to:

- apply for a revision of the decision (see p1130); *or*
- apply for a supersession of the decision (see p1143).

8

In most cases, you also have the right to appeal to the First-tier Tribunal. Usually, it is required ('mandatory') that you have first applied for the decision to be reconsidered in a revision and that a decision has been made on that – hence a revision is often also called a 'mandatory reconsideration' (see p1168).

The time limit for applying for what is known as an 'any grounds' revision is strict – normally only one month from the date on the decision letter.

Time limits apply for applying for a revision on 'any grounds' (see p1132).

# 2. Decisions on claims

Once you have made a valid claim for benefit (see p1008), your claim is referred to a decision maker to decide whether you are entitled. A decision maker must usually make a decision on the claim[27] but may sometimes withhold making a decision if there is a 'test case' pending (see p1159).

Before making a decision, the decision maker may request further information (see p1009). If there is a question about the facts of your claim that needs special expertise, the decision maker can get assistance from experts.[28]

Once a valid claim has been made, it is impossible for a decision maker to refuse to make a decision on the claim.[29] Sometimes, decision makers say that they have 'closed' a claim – eg, because after claiming universal credit (UC), you did not book or attend an interview to establish your identity. There is no power allowing them to do this – a decision to 'close' a claim is in fact a decision to say that you are not entitled, which you can challenge, and booking an interview is not a condition of entitlement to UC.[30] See p46 for more details.

## Circumstances at time of decision

When deciding a claim for benefit, the decision maker must consider your circumstances at the date they are making the decision. The decision maker cannot later change a decision to take account of new circumstances which did not exist at the time of the decision.

That means that if your claim for benefit was refused and you want to have new circumstances taken into account, you must make a new claim for benefit.[31]

*Example*

Irving had capital worth £17,750 when he claimed UC. His claim was refused on the basis that he had too much capital. He now has capital worth £12,000. He must make a new claim to allow the decision maker to take into account his new circumstances.

If your circumstances have changed between when you made your claim for benefit and when your claim is decided, the decision maker should decide whether you met the conditions of entitlement on each of the days between when you made the claim and when it is decided. For example, if you claimed contributory employment and support allowance (ESA) but you started work of over 16 hours a week before the claim was decided, you should be awarded ESA from the date of your claim to the date you started work. If you were not entitled on your date of claim but were entitled before your claim was decided, you should be awarded benefit from the date you started to be entitled.[32]

Once a decision about a claim for benefit has been made, that claim ceases to exist.[33] If the decision is that you were entitled, you will then have an award of benefit which can be changed if your circumstances change. But if no ongoing award of benefit is made, then a later change of circumstances cannot be taken into account unless you make a new claim.

# 3. Delays in getting a decision

New claims can take several weeks or more to process (or longer for claimants from abroad). All claims should be dealt with as soon as is reasonably practicable, although there is no specific time limit.[34]

*Is there a delay?*

1. If you have been waiting a long time for a decision, check that your claim has been received. If it has not, if possible send a copy or claim again, and refer to the claim you made earlier.
2. If the decision maker denies receiving your claim, claim again and ask for backdating and refer to your previous claim. If the decision maker makes a decision that your award only starts from when the second claim was received, you can challenge that decision and argue that you made the earlier claim. In an appeal, the tribunal can accept that an earlier claim was made.
3. If your claim has been received but not dealt with, ask why. Complain if you are not satisfied with the explanation for the delay (see Chapter 55). If the claim is not decided within a reasonable time, consider sending a letter before action for judicial review, which is your only legal remedy (see p1236).
4. If a decision cannot be made on your claim straight away, ask the office to make a short-term advance of benefit if this is payable for the benefit you have claimed (see p1023), or an interim payment of child benefit or guardian's allowance (see p505).
5. You may be able to claim a means-tested benefit or, for housing benefit, a payment on account while a decision is being made on your claim for a non-means-tested benefit. The amount paid may be deducted from arrears of the other benefit(s) you subsequently receive, or you may be asked to repay the amount (see p1062).
6. You may be able to get help from your local authority for any short-term needs in a crisis (see p770).



## 4. Information about decisions

You must be given written notice of a decision against which you can appeal (see p1172 for which decisions). This is usually called a **'decision notice'**. You must be informed of:[35]

- your right to appeal against the decision; *and*
- your right to a written statement of reasons for the decision, if this is not already included (see p1125).

For benefits other than housing benefit, you are also told that you must apply for a mandatory reconsideration before you can appeal against the decision (see p1168). You must be told what the time limits for the mandatory reconsideration are.[36] Arguably, if you are not told that, then the time limit has not started to run.[37]

If you have not been notified of a decision, it may not have legal effect.[38] That could mean that other decisions which depend on that decision cannot be enforced. For example, if you were not notified of a decision reducing your entitlement for a past period, then a subsequent decision that the resultant overpayment is recoverable is invalid.[39]

## Explanations

Sometimes, the decision maker may say that you must ask for an explanation before you can apply for a revision or a supersession, or to appeal. This is wrong. Although you can ask for an explanation of any decision, you do not have to do so before you challenge the decision. If you want an explanation, contact the office that made the decision.

At the end of the explanation, you should be asked whether you are happy with the decision. If you are not happy, say so. The decision maker should then advise you about your right to apply for a revision (see p1130). They may refer to this as a dispute or a mandatory reconsideration.

Explanations are usually given orally. You may also have the right to request a written statement of reasons for a decision if it is one against which you can appeal.

Time limits apply for applying for a revision on 'any grounds' (see p1132). Therefore, ensure you apply for a revision within the time limit, even if the decision has not yet been explained to you.

## Written reasons

You may want to see the reasons for a decision in writing. You only have a right to a written statement of reasons for a decision if this has not already been provided with the decision and it is a decision against which you can appeal. You must ask for a written statement of reasons within one month of the date of being notified of the decision. The decision maker must then provide the statement within 14 days, or as soon as practicable afterwards.[40]

**Note:** the time limit to apply for a revision is extended if you ask for a written statement of reasons, but only if this has not been provided (see p1132).

***Month***

'**Month**' means a complete calendar month running from the day after the day you were sent or given a decision.[41] For example, a decision sent on 22 July has a time limit that expires at the end of 22 August.

A dispute could arise about whether a decision notice already includes an explanation of the reasons for the decision. Sometimes that should be clear because the decision notice states that you can ask for a written explanation – indicating that the DWP does not think such an explanation has already been given. You may believe that a written statement of reasons has not been included with your decision or is inadequate, but the DWP, HMRC or local authority could disagree. In these cases, the decision maker is likely to argue that your time limit for applying for a revision cannot be extended.

If you are in any doubt, you should assume that the time limit for applying for a revision has *not* been extended. If you miss the time limit in this situation, argue that the rules that allow a late application for a revision apply (see p1133). You may also be able to apply for a revision if you have specific grounds (see p1135).

# Notes

1. **When a decision must be made**

1 *AW v SSWP (JSA)* [2013] UKUT 99 (AAC); CA/1020/2007
2 **UC/PIP/new-style JSA&ESA** Reg 40 UC,PIP,JSA&ESA(DA) Regs
**Other benefits** Reg 11 SS&CS(DA) Regs
3 CIB/2338/2000, paras 19-25
4 gov.uk/government/collections/decision-makers-guide-staff-guide
5 gov.uk/government/publications/advice-for-decision-making-staff-guide
6 Available at rightsnet.org.uk/resources/universal-credit-guidance
7 gov.uk/government/publications/personal-independence-payment-assessment-guide-for-assessment-providers
8 For Capita, see haas.capita.co.uk/en/pip
9 gov.uk/government/publications/personal-independence-payment-fact-sheets
10 gov.uk/government/publications/work-capability-assessment-handbook-for-healthcare-professionals
11 gov.uk/guidance/housing-benefit-information-guidance-and-good-practice-for-local-authority-staff#housing-benefit-and-council-tax-benefit-manual
12 gov.uk/government/collections/housing-benefit-for-local-authorities-bulletins; gov.uk/government/publications/housing-benefit-urgent-bulletins-2019; gov.uk/government/publications/discretionary-housing-payments-guidance-manual
13 **UC/PIP/new-style JSA&ESA** Reg 39 UC,PIP,JSA&ESA(DA) Regs
**Other benefits** Regs 13(2) and (3) and 15 SS&CS(DA) Regs
14 Reg 39(5) UC,PIP,JSA&ESA(DA) Regs
15 Reg 39(4) UC,PIP,JSA&ESA(DA) Regs
16 Reg 13(1) SS&CS(DA) Regs
17 s17 SSA 1998
18 Sch 4 para 12 and Sch 6 para 5 HB Regs; regs 25-26 HB(SPC) Regs
19 *DF v LB Waltham Forest (HB)* [2017] UKUT 161 (AAC)
20 Reg 11 SS&CS(DA) Regs; reg 40(3) UC,PIP,JSA&ESA(DA) Regs
21 s8 SSC(TF)A 1999
22 s10A SSA 1998; reg 42 UC,PIP,JSA&ESA(DA) Regs; reg 11A SS&CS(DA) Regs
23 s11 SSC(TF)A 1999
24 s24A SSA 1998; reg 43 UC,PIP,JSA&ESA(DA) Regs; reg 38A SS&CS(DA) Regs
25 s17 SSC(TF)A 1999; Sch 3 para 17 SSA 1998; National Insurance Contribution Credits (Transfer of Functions) Order 2009 No.1377
26 **UC/PIP/new-style JSA&ESA** Reg 38 UC,PIP,JSA&ESA(DA) Regs
**Other benefits** Reg 9A SS&CS(DA) Regs

2. **Decisions on claims**

27 R(SB) 29/83; CIS/807/1992; R(H) 3/05
28 s11(2) SSA 1998
29 R(H) 3/05
30 *PP v SSWP (UC)* [2020] UKUT 109 (AAC)
31 s8(2)(b) SSA 1998

32 *SSWP v KK (JSA)* [2019] UKUT 313 (AAC)
33 s8(2)(a) SSA 1998

3. **Delays in getting a decision**
34 *R (C and W) v SSWP and Zacchaeus 2000 Trust* [2015] EWHC 1607 (Admin)

4. **Information about decisions**
35 **UC/PIP/new-style JSA&ESA** Reg 51 UC,PIP,JSA&ESA(DA) Regs
**CB/GA** Reg 26(1) CB&GA(DA) Regs
**Other benefits** Reg 28(1) SS&CS(DA) Regs
36 **UC/PIP/new-style JSA&ESA** Reg 7 UC,PIP,JSA&ESA(DA) Regs
**Other benefits** Reg 3ZA SS&CS(DA) Regs
37 R(P) 1/04 (para 29) and *LC v Lambeth (HB)* [2010] UKUT 661 (AAC); [2011] AACR 27 (para 116)
38 *R (Anufrijeva) v SSHD* [2003] UKHL 26
39 *SM v SSWP (SPC)* [2017] UKUT 336 (AAC)
40 **UC/PIP/new-style JSA&ESA** Regs 3 and 51 UC,PIP,JSA&ESA(DA) Regs
**CB/GA** Regs 3 and 26(1)(b) and (2) CB&GA(DA) Regs
**Other benefits** Regs 2 and 28(1)(b) and (2) SS&CS(DA) Regs
41 R(IB) 4/02

# Chapter 50

# Revisions and supersessions

**This chapter covers:**


1. Getting a decision changed (below)
2. Revisions (p1130)
3. Supersessions (p1143)
4. Revisions and supersessions after a qualifying benefit award (p1157)
5. The 'anti-test case rule' (p1159)


This chapter covers the rules for benefits, the social fund payments in Chapter 33 (except budgeting loans) and decisions about DWP loans for mortgage interest (see p764). It does not cover the rules for Scottish benefits (see Chapter 69), statutory payments (see Chapter 54) or the health benefits in Chapter 27.



## Key facts

- If a decision is wrong or no longer correct, it can be changed by a new decision – called either a 'revision' or a 'supersession'.
- You can apply for a revision or a supersession, or the DWP, local authority or HMRC can carry out one because it wants to change your award.
- In some cases, you do not need to show any grounds for a revision, but you must ask for one within a set time limit. In other cases, you can ask for a revision at any time, but you must show there are specific grounds.
- The date on which a revision or a supersession takes effect determines the date from when you are paid arrears if you are entitled to more benefit, or the date from when you have been overpaid if you are entitled to less benefit.

## 1. Getting a decision changed

The DWP, the local authority and HMRC make many decisions about your entitlement to benefits (see Chapter 49). Once a decision has been made, it can only be changed by a further decision.[1] These further decisions are called revisions (see pp1130–43) and supersessions (see pp1143–56).

To get more information about a decision, ask for an explanation or a written statement of reasons if this has not already been provided (see p1125).

In many cases, decisions can also be changed by appealing to the First-tier Tribunal (see Chapter 51). However, you must apply for a mandatory reconsideration before you can appeal (see p1168), unless the benefit is housing benefit or, in some cases, employment and support allowance. A 'mandatory reconsideration' is simply another name for a revision – the term is used because the decision maker must have considered whether or not to revise the decision before an appeal can be made.

You can apply for a revision or a supersession of a decision you cannot appeal (see p1173 for some examples). If such a decision is not changed following your application, you may be able to apply for judicial review (see Chapter 53).

**Note:** it is important that you keep within any time limit (see p1132 for revisions and p1175 for appeals).

## Revisions and supersessions

Revisions and supersessions are both ways of changing a decision about your benefit entitlement.

- **A revision** is the way of changing a decision that was incorrect at the time it was made – ie, the decision maker incorrectly refused to award you benefit, or awarded you an incorrect amount – eg, because they thought you had savings which you did not have. A revision takes effect from the date the original decision took effect.
- **A supersession** is usually the way of changing a decision which was correct at the time it was originally made, but which has subsequently become incorrect – eg, because your circumstances have now changed and you no longer meet a condition of entitlement. A supersession does not take effect from the date the original decision took effect – it takes effect from a later date.

You can apply for a revision or a supersession and the decision maker at the DWP, local authority or HMRC can also initiate one.

**Note:** you must apply for a revision within a certain time (unless one of the specific grounds allowing revisions to be carried out at any time applies). If you miss the time limit or you do not have specific grounds, it may be possible to get a decision that was wrong when it was originally made changed via a supersession. However, as you generally get less arrears of benefit after a supersession, make sure you apply within the time allowed if you can.

In some cases, if the decision maker is reducing or removing your entitlement, it may be in your interests to argue that this can only be done by carrying out a supersession, rather than a revision.

### The risks of applying for a revision or supersession

Following a revision or a supersession, the original decision may remain the same – ie, your application for a revision or supersession is refused. It may also be revised or superseded so as to either increase *or* decrease the amount of your benefit, or to take away your entitlement altogether.

You may apply for a revision or supersession in the hope that your benefit will be increased, but the outcome could be that you get less benefit, and you could be required to repay an overpayment (see Chapter 47). This is because (although they do not have to do so) the decision maker can consider issues that are not raised in your application for a revision or supersession.[2] Therefore, before you apply for a revision or supersession, consider whether it is possible that less or no benefit could be awarded for all or some of the period in question. If the decision maker makes a decision which is less advantageous to you than the original decision, they must show that there was a specific ground to do so and that the outcome of the revision or supersession is related to that ground. However, this does not apply if the decision maker starts taking action to revise the decision within a month of the original decision having been made. In this case, they can make an 'any grounds' revision (see p1131).[3]

## 2. Revisions

If you think a decision is incorrect and want it changed, you can apply for a revision.[4] The decision maker must then look at the decision again. Your request is often referred to as a 'dispute' or a 'request for a reconsideration'.

8

***Mandatory reconsideration***

You must apply for a decision to be looked at again by way of a revision before you can appeal against it (see p1168), unless the benefit is housing benefit (HB) or employment and support allowance (ESA) and you would have a right to get ESA while appealing against the decision (see p923). This revision is called a 'mandatory reconsideration'. You do not have to use this term when applying for the decision to be looked at again, but in practice it is helpful if you do. When the DWP or HMRC deals with your application, it looks at its decision again – ie, it considers whether to carry out a revision. The rules and advice on revisions in this chapter therefore apply when you apply for a mandatory reconsideration. Once the DWP or HMRC has considered your application, it issues a mandatory reconsideration notice (see p1171). You are required to provide this notice when you appeal to the First-tier Tribunal.

### When a decision can be revised

A decision can be revised either following your request for one, or even without a request because the decision maker decides to carry one out.[5] There are two types of revision.

- 'Any grounds' revisions. You (or the decision maker) do not have to show that specific grounds apply (see below), but you (or the decision maker) must apply or start the process within a strict time limit (see p1134 for the time limit that applies to the decision maker and p1132 for the time limit that applies to you).
- 'Any time' revisions. You (or the decision maker) must show that one of the specific permitted grounds exists (see p1135). If this is the case, the decision can be revised, even if it was made a long time ago.

Decisions of the First-tier (or Upper) Tribunal cannot be revised. In some cases, these decisions can be superseded. Otherwise, they can only be changed by appealing further to the Upper Tribunal or a court (see Chapter 52).

## 'Any grounds' revisions

If action to get a decision changed is started within a specific time limit, the decision can be changed on 'any grounds'. This means it can be changed simply because a new decision maker takes a different view of the same evidence.

The time limits for getting a decision changed by a revision on 'any grounds' are different depending on whether:

- you are applying for a decision to be revised (see p1132); *or*
- the revision is started by the decision maker (see p1134).

A revision on 'any grounds' is a completely fresh look at the decision. The decision maker can do any or all of the following:

- simply form a different opinion about the same evidence – eg, the first decision maker may have decided that the money in your bank account belonged to you and so meant you had too much capital to qualify for benefit, but the new decision maker may accept your explanation that the money belonged to someone else;
- take into account any new evidence which shows what your circumstances were at the time of the original decision – eg, that you have to pay rent, or that you have a new medical report, showing that you have limited capability for work;
- take into account any omissions in the information you gave at the time – eg, if you failed to mention in your claim for universal credit (UC) that you had housing costs;
- correct any misunderstanding of the law which affected the previous decision – eg, by accepting you do not need to receive child benefit for a child to count as responsible for them for the purposes of UC.

A decision maker can only revise a decision on 'any grounds' based on your circumstances at the time:[6]

- the decision took effect; *or*
- for advance awards of benefits other than HB, the decision was made.

If the decision can be changed on 'any grounds', the reason why the decision needs to be changed does not matter.[7] For example, if the reason your UC decision was wrong is that it did not take account of the fact that you need to pay rent, if it is changed within the time limit for an 'any grounds' revision then the reason that the DWP did not know about that before is irrelevant. The DWP should not refuse to carry out the 'any grounds' revision just because it says that you did not tell it the correct facts at the time. What is important is whether or not you are within the time allowed for an 'any grounds' revision.

If, however, your circumstances have since changed, make a fresh claim if you have no current award, or ask for a supersession if you have an ongoing award (see p1143) instead.

**Note:** if you apply for an 'any grounds' revision of a decision about ESA, attendance allowance (AA), disability living allowance (DLA) or personal independence payment (PIP) because you (or the person on whose behalf you are claiming) are terminally ill, you must state this explicitly.[8] If you do not do so, the decision maker cannot revise the decision on this ground.

## Time limit for applying for an 'any grounds' revision

The basic time limit is one month. Specifically, you must apply for an 'any grounds' revision:

- in most cases:[9]
  - within one month of the date you were sent or given the decision; *or*
  - within one month and 14 days of the date you were sent or given the decision, if you requested a written statement of reasons (see p1125) and it is provided within the month; *or*
  - within 14 days of a written statement of reasons being provided, if you requested one within one month of the date you were sent or given the decision, but it is not provided within that one-month period.

But you must apply:

- **in the case of a Sure Start maternity grant or a social fund funeral expenses payment**, within one month of the date you were sent or given the decision or, if later, within the time limit for claiming the payment (see p706 and p713);[10]
- **in the case of a cold weather payment or a winter fuel payment**, within one month of the date you were notified of the decision. You are generally assumed to have been notified seven days after the decision was made, but there are exceptions;[11]
- **in the case of HB**, within one month of the date you were sent or given the decision.[12] If a written statement of reasons has not already been included with the decision, days from the date your request for the statement is received by the local authority to the date on which it is provided to you are ignored when calculating the one month;[13]

- **in the case of child benefit and guardian's allowance if HMRC has carried out a supersession because of an anticipated change in your circumstances** (see p1145), at any point between the date you are notified of the supersession decision and one month after the date it takes effect.[14]

For benefits (other than a Sure Start maternity grant or a social fund funeral expenses payment, child benefit or guardian's allowance), if an accidental error in a decision has been corrected (see p1122), any day falling before the day on which the correction is notified to you is ignored when calculating the one-month period.[15]

### Late requests

You can apply for an 'any grounds' revision outside the time limit, provided this is within an absolute time limit. In practice, for DWP benefits these applications are always admitted. For HB, if you have missed the basic one month time limit then in practice it is better to make a late appeal (see Chapter 51), as the test for having a late request for a revision accepted for HB can be more difficult to satisfy.

***The absolute time limit***

In most cases, you must apply for an 'any grounds' revision within **13 months** of the date you were notified of the decision.[16]

If you requested a written statement of reasons (see p1125):
- for HB, days from the date you requested the statement to the date on which it was provided are ignored when calculating the 13 months; *or*
- for other benefits, if the statement of reasons is provided within one month of the date you were notified of the decision, the 13 months are extended by 14 days. If it is provided during a period later than one month after that date, the 13 months are extended by 14 days, plus the number of days in that period.

In all cases, for a late request for an 'any grounds' revision to be accepted:[17]
- your application must contain:
  - sufficient details about the decision you disagree with for it to be identified. Say which benefit you disagree about and the date the DWP, the local authority or HMRC sent you the decision; *and*
  - a summary of your reasons for applying late; *and*
- you must show that:
  - it is reasonable to grant your application; *and*
  - there are special circumstances which mean that it was not practicable for you to apply for a revision within the time limit. Any special circumstances can count. The longer you have delayed applying for a revision, the more compelling these must be. These are not defined. However, in practice, the

DWP usually accepts the application as long as it is within the absolute 13-month time limit.

In addition, for child benefit, guardian's allowance and HB:[18]

- you must show that your application has merit – ie, that there is a prospect the decision can be changed if time is extended; *and*
- when deciding whether it is reasonable to grant your application, the decision maker cannot take account of the fact that:
  - a court or the Upper Tribunal has interpreted the law in a different way than previously understood and applied;
  - you (or anyone acting for you) misunderstood or were unaware of the relevant law, including the time limits for applying for a revision.

If your late request for an 'any grounds' revision is refused, you cannot appeal against that refusal.[19] However:

- for benefits other than HB, or ESA if you would have a right to payment of ESA pending appeal, you may still be able to appeal against the original decision. Under the rules on mandatory reconsiderations, you only have a right of appeal against a decision if the decision maker has considered whether to revise it. If you applied for an 'any grounds' revision within the absolute time limit, by refusing to accept that time should be extended, the decision maker *has* considered whether to revise the decision, so you can appeal.[20] If you have missed the absolute time limit for an 'any grounds' revision, you only have a right of appeal if you can show that one of the specific grounds for a revision applied. In practice, decision makers at the DWP rarely refuse to accept a late request for a revision made within the absolute time limit;
- for HB, or ESA if you would have a right to payment of ESA pending appeal, you may be able to make a late appeal against the original decision. A late appeal must be admitted if the decision maker does not object or if the First-tier Tribunal thinks it is fair and just to do so. It is more likely that you will have your request for a late appeal accepted than your request for an 'any grounds' revision accepted;
- if you are making a late application, it is also worth considering whether you can argue that some earlier contact you had with the decision maker could have been considered as a request for a revision. This may enable you to argue that your application is not late.

## Time limit for decision makers

For benefits other than HB, the decision maker can revise a decision themself on 'any grounds' provided they start action within one month of the date you are sent or given a decision.[21] For HB, a decision maker can also decide to revise a decision themself, but only if, within one month of the date you are sent or given it, they have information which shows that there was a mistake about the facts of your case or the decision was made in ignorance of relevant facts.[22]

If these conditions are not met, the decision maker can only carry out a revision if there are specific grounds.

## 'Any time' revisions

A revision can be carried out at any time (even years after the original decision was made) but only in specific situations. You can apply for an 'any time' revision, but the decision maker can decide to carry one out even if you have not applied. If a decision maker refuses to consider an 'any time' revision, see p1142.

In practice, if you apply for a revision (including a mandatory reconsideration) and it is within one month of your being sent or given the decision, the DWP, the local authority or HMRC treats your application as one for an 'any grounds' revision (see p1131). If your application is late and reasons for lateness are not accepted, the decision maker should go on to consider whether any of the specific grounds exist to allow an 'any time' revision.

There are a number of grounds for an 'any time' revision. The main ones are if there has been:

- an official error (see below);
- a sanction decision (see p1136);
- an award of a 'qualifying benefit' (see p1137);
- an appeal against a decision (see p1137);
- a mistake about or ignorance of facts (see p1138).

Some other specific grounds are summarised on p1139.

### Official error

A decision can be revised at any time if it is wrong because of official error.[23]

**For child benefit and guardian's allowance**, this means an error made by an officer of HMRC or a person employed by someone providing services to HMRC.[24]

**For benefits, other than child benefit and guardian's allowance**, this means:[25]

- an error made by an officer of the DWP or HMRC; *or*
- for HB only, errors made by the local authority or by a person authorised to carry out any function of the local authority or provide HB-related services; *or*
- other than for HB, errors made by a person employed by someone providing services to the DWP; *or*
- other than for HB, PIP, UC and, if you come under the UC system (see p20), new-style jobseeker's allowance (JSA) and new-style ESA, errors made by an employee of a local authority (or an employee of a person acting on behalf of, or providing services to, a local authority).

8

Note:

- If the error is that the decision maker got the law wrong, this does not count as an official error if this is only shown to be the case because of a later decision from the Upper Tribunal or a court.[26] If a legal mistake was made in your case that was only later shown to be a legal mistake because of a subsequent decision in another case, you could make a fresh claim (or apply for a supersession), and the 'anti-test case rule' could apply (see p1159).
- The mere fact that a decision needs to be changed does not mean that there has been an official error. For example, a decision that you have failed the work capability assessment may be changed because of new evidence, or a different view is taken of the same evidence, but that does not mean that there was an official error.
- If someone else (eg, you, your partner or your representative) caused or contributed to the error, it does not count as an official error.[27] This includes if the way your claim form was completed contributed to the error.[28]

***Official error: examples***

The following can count as official errors.

Getting the law wrong (unless this is only established by a subsequent Upper Tribunal or court decision in another case).

The decision maker (or local authority) had specific evidence which they failed to take into account, even though it was relevant. You should argue that this applies even if the evidence does not conclusively prove your entitlement, so long as it raises a strong possibility that you were entitled.

The DWP, the local authority or HMRC had documentary or other written evidence of your entitlement, but failed to give it to the decision maker dealing with your claim when the earlier decision was made.

No reasonable decision maker, having established the facts, could have made the decision.[29]

The decision maker failed to ask you about something that was relevant to the decision and which was reasonably obvious would need to be asked to be able to ensure the decision was correct.[30]

The decision maker used a procedure to make the decision which was clearly unfair – eg, you were given seven days to agree your claimant commitment for UC, but your UC was ended for not complying before that time was up.

## Sanction decisions

A decision can be revised at any time if:[31]

- for UC and new-style JSA, and, if you come under the UC system, new-style ESA, it is a decision to give you a sanction; *or*
- you do not come under the UC system and it is a decision to give you a sanction because:

- you (or in some cases your partner) failed to take part in a work-focused interview without good cause. This only applies if the decision contained an error and, for ESA only, if you did not materially contribute to the error; *or*
- for ESA, you failed to undertake work-related activity without good cause. This only applies if the decision contained an error to which you did not materially contribute.

This means that you can apply for a revision (including a mandatory reconsideration) even if the decision to give you a sanction was made a long time ago. This is useful if you did not realise you could challenge the decision at the time it was made and, for example, you can show you had good cause or a good reason for your actions or you did not do (or failed to do) what is alleged. If you have been given a sanction more than once, you should apply for a revision of all the decisions if possible and then appeal if you do not get all you want. If you are applying for a mandatory reconsideration before you can appeal (see p1168), make this clear in your application. See p997 for information about challenging a sanction decision.

## Awards of a qualifying benefit

A decision can be revised at any time if:

- you are awarded a benefit (eg, UC, income-related ESA, pension credit (PC) or HB) and, for a period which includes the date that award took effect, you (or your partner, or a child included in your claim – see p258) are awarded another benefit or an increase in its rate. This can work to your advantage if the other benefit is a 'qualifying benefit' (eg, DLA or carer's allowance – see p1157);[32] *or*
- for income-related ESA and PC only, you have a non-dependant living with you (see p275) and, since you were awarded income-related ESA or PC, your non-dependant has been awarded a qualifying benefit (see p1157) for a period that includes the date your award took effect and this means that you are now entitled to a severe disability premium (for income-related ESA) or a severe disability addition (for PC).[33]

A decision to end your entitlement to IIB because your (or your partner's or child's) qualifying benefit ceases can also be revised at any time. This only applies if the qualifying benefit is later reinstated following a revision, supersession or appeal.[34]

See p1157 for further information. If you are only entitled to a benefit once a qualifying benefit is awarded, see p219 and p1012.

## A decision that has been appealed

If you appealed against a decision, and you:

- appealed within the time limit or were allowed a late appeal (see p1175 and p1176) and the appeal has not yet been determined, a decision maker can look

8

at the decision again and revise it.[35] This includes if the First-tier Tribunal has adjourned the hearing or if the Upper Tribunal has sent a case back to the First-tier Tribunal to make a new decision. This enables the decision maker to take new information that has come to light in the appeal process into account. **Note:** your appeal could lapse if a decision maker revises the decision, even if you do not get all you want (see p1185); *or*

- make a fresh claim or request a supersession when your circumstances change (see p1203) and, as a result, a new decision about your entitlement is made, a decision maker can revise the new decision once your appeal has been decided. This only applies if you appealed against a decision to the First-tier Tribunal (or, for HB only, to the Upper Tribunal or a court) and:[36]
  - a fresh claim is decided or the decision is superseded before your appeal is determined; *and*
  - the appeal is then determined; *and*
  - the decision maker would have made their decision differently had they been aware of the appeal decision at the time their decision was made.

## Mistake about or ignorance of facts

A decision can be revised at any time if there was a mistake about the facts of your case or the decision was made in ignorance of relevant facts, provided, as a result of the mistake or ignorance about the facts, the decision was more favourable to you than it would have been – eg, you were awarded too much benefit.[37] If you have been overpaid, the decision maker may seek to recover the overpayment (see Chapter 47). Because this specific ground only arises when the decision was more generous to you than it would have been without the mistake or ignorance about a fact, in practice, this ground is only used when a decision maker wants to revise a decision. **Note:** there must have been a mistake about or ignorance of facts, not conclusions or opinions about the facts. See p1064 for some examples.

For AA, DLA and for ESA not paid under the UC system, the rules are different if there was a mistake about, or ignorance of, facts relating to a 'disability determination' or a 'limited capability for work determination'.[38] In this case, it must be shown that, at the time the decision that you were entitled to a benefit (eg, DLA or ESA) was made, you knew, or could reasonably have been expected to know, about the fact and that it was relevant to your benefit. Otherwise, a decision cannot be revised on this ground and you will not have been overpaid benefit, although there may be grounds for a supersession.

### *Disability and limited capability for work determinations*[39]

A **'disability determination'** is a decision about whether you satisfy the disability conditions for AA or DLA, are disabled, or whether the existence or extent of your disablement is sufficient for you to be entitled to industrial injuries disablement benefit or to be paid at the same rate as that paid immediately before the decision. It does *not* include decisions about PIP.

A **'limited capability for work determination'** is a decision about whether you have limited capability for work under the work capability assessment, or can be treated as having it under any of the first six bullet points in the second set of bullets on p898 or because you get the support component on the basis that you meet one of the eating and drinking descriptors in the test for limited capability for work-related activity (see Chapter 41).

If the mistake about or ignorance of facts means you should be entitled to *more* benefit:
- a decision can be superseded on this ground (see p1146);
- a decision can be revised if you are in time to apply for an 'any grounds' revision (see p1131).

## Other grounds for an 'any time' revision

There are many other circumstances in which a decision maker can carry out a revision at any time. This includes if the decision is one against which you have no right of appeal (see p1173 for which decisions).[40]

Other decisions that can be revised at any time include a decision:
- to reduce your UC or your HB under the benefit cap rules (see p1025);[41]
- to end your entitlement to contributory ESA because you have been receiving it for 365 days, but it is subsequently found that you had, or can be treated as having had, limited capability for work-related activity before your entitlement ended;[42]
- to refuse you PIP because you are resident in a care home and the costs of any qualifying services (see p827) provided for you are met by public funds, the decision was made with incomplete evidence (see p1120) and, after the decision, any of the costs of the qualifying services are recovered from you;[43]
- to treat you as not satisfying the disability conditions for the daily living component or the mobility component of PIP because you did not return your questionnaire or you failed to participate in your assessment consultation. However, this only applies if the decision was made because of an error to which you did not contribute;[44]
- to increase the amount of rent used for the housing costs element (for UC) or your maximum rent (for HB) because of a rent officer's redetermination, or because a local housing allowance rate or broad rental market area has been amended because of a rent officer's error;[45]
- about state pension (or an 'old' retirement pension), PC or HB, if you or your partner deferred claiming a pension, then changed your option from a higher pension to a lump sum (or, for state pension and retirement pension only, vice versa);[46]

- to award ESA following a period of your being treated as in an extended period of sickness for JSA of 13 weeks. This allows the component to be added to your ESA award from the date of claim.[47]

**Note:** the list above is not exhaustive. There are a number of other decisions that can be revised at any time.[48]

## How to apply for a revision

**For UC**, rules do not specify a particular way in which applications must be made. The best way is usually by requesting this in your online journal – this gives you a record you can access, proving you have made the request. If you also need to submit evidence, speak to your work coach or telephone the UC helpline and ask for a facility to enable you to upload the relevant documents. You can also telephone or send a letter by post or take a written request to the job centre. It is always worth telephoning the UC helpline after you have submitted an application, either via your journal or in writing, to confirm that it is being dealt with as a request for a revision.

**For HB**, you must apply for a revision (including a late application) in writing.[49]

**For benefits other than HB**, you do not have to apply for a revision in writing, although it is always best to do so. This ensures that the decision maker understands you are asking for one, not just seeking an explanation or complaining about the rules.

In all cases, it is worth checking that an application has been received and is being dealt with appropriately.

When establishing whether an 'any grounds' revision is made within the time limit (see p1132), your application counts as having been received on the day it arrives at an 'appropriate office'.[50] **Note:** if you are applying for a mandatory reconsideration before you can appeal, make this clear in your application (although the law does not say you must use this term, it is helpful if you do).

### *The appropriate office*

The '**appropriate office**' is the office specified on the notice of the decision with which you disagree.[51] If you are a person who is, or would be, required to attend a work-focused interview as a condition of getting benefit, the Jobcentre Plus office is also an appropriate office in respect of decisions for benefits other than child benefit, guardian's allowance, HB, PIP and, if you come under the UC system, new-style JSA, new-style ESA and UC.

A decision maker does not have to consider any issues other than those raised in your application.[52] To ensure the decision maker considers everything you want them to, you should:

- make it clear what sort of revision you are applying for. Show how you meet the specific grounds for an 'any time' revision or the time limit for an 'any grounds' revision; *and*
- set out all the points about the decision with which you disagree; *and*
- provide any information or evidence that supports your case. This includes, for example, medical evidence from a GP, consultant or other health worker if this is relevant. If the benefit is AA, DLA or PIP, evidence from your carer or a diary of your walking, supervision or care needs over a period may be useful. The decision maker may ask you for further information or evidence.

The DWP, the local authority or HMRC can treat an application for a supersession as an application for a revision and vice versa.[53] In addition, any correspondence in which you make it clear that you are unhappy with a decision and want it changed, even if you do not use the term 'revision' or 'mandatory reconsideration', should be treated as a request for a revision. For example, a claim for benefit accompanied by a request for it to be backdated to the date a previous award ended can be treated as an application for a revision of the decision to end that previous award.[54] In general, if, looking at your correspondence, the only way you could be given what you want is by a supersession or revision of a particular decision, then that correspondence should be treated as the appropriate application.[55] Although you do not have to use the correct terminology, doing so ensures that there can be no doubt about what you are asking for.



***How do you get evidence of previous decisions to support your application?***

1. If the decision you are trying to get changed was made a long time ago, it can be difficult to identify the grounds. You can obtain information held by the DWP, the local authority or HMRC by making a 'subject access request' under the Data Protection Act 2018. See the Information Commissioner's website at ico.org.uk for details.

2. In some cases, the DWP, the local authority or HMRC may say it has destroyed old papers relating to your claim. Ask whether your papers have simply been archived, rather than destroyed. You can argue that missing papers should be presumed to contain information favourable to your case. However, this is unlikely to be accepted unless you can show that the papers should have been retained because they could have been relevant to any potential appeal or they were destroyed deliberately to thwart your case.[56]

## Providing further evidence and information

The decision maker can ask you for more evidence or information if they think this is needed to consider all the issues raised by your application for a revision.[57] You must provide this within one month of the request.[58] The decision maker can allow longer. If you do not provide the information, your application is decided based on the information and evidence the decision maker already has. If this happens and as a result the decision is unfavourable to you, if you later appeal, the evidence or information should be taken into account. The DWP can also ask you to have a medical examination – eg, if the decision concerns whether you have limited capability for work.

**Note:** in some cases, if you fail to provide information in a specified time period or have a medical examination, payment of your benefit could be suspended, which may lead to your entitlement being terminated (see p1031).

Similar rules allow the decision maker to ask for evidence or information if you apply for a supersession (although in UC cases the time limit to provide the information is within 14 days).[59]

## When a revision takes effect

The date a revision takes effect is the date from when you are paid arrears if you are entitled to more benefit, or from when you have been overpaid if you are entitled to less benefit. In all cases, a revision takes effect from:

- the date the decision being revised took (or would have taken) effect[60] – eg, your date of claim if you are challenging a decision on a claim; *or*
- the correct date, if the date on which the decision being revised took effect was found to be wrong.[61]

It is important to make it clear that you want payment for the past period. You may get less backdating if the 'anti-test case rule' applies (see p1159).

**Note:** if a decision is revised on the grounds that there was a mistake about, or ignorance of, facts relating to a 'disability determination' or a 'limited capability for work determination' in the circumstances described on p1138, if the benefit is a qualifying benefit for another benefit (see p1157) and the revision means your entitlement to the other benefit is affected, the decision about the other benefit takes effect on the same date.[62]

## Challenging a revision

You must be notified in writing of whether the decision maker has revised the decision or whether they have refused to revise it. If you applied for a mandatory reconsideration (ie, a revision), the notification from the DWP or HMRC is called a 'mandatory reconsideration notice' (see p1171). If the original decision has been revised and is one against which you have a right of appeal (see p1172), you can appeal to the First-tier Tribunal, and your appeal is against that decision *as revised*. If the decision maker has refused to revise the decision, your appeal is against the original decision *as made*.

The time limit for appealing (see p1175) depends on the benefit involved and whether it was an 'any grounds' or an 'any time' revision.[63]

**For benefits other than HB**, the time limit for appealing usually runs from the date you were sent or notified of the revision/refusal to revise. The only exception to this is if the original decision was made more than 13 months ago, you were seeking an 'any time' revision of that decision, and your application for a revision is refused. In this case, you can appeal if the tribunal accepts that there was a ground for revising the decision.[64] **Note:** in this case, it is not clear whether your application needs to clearly raise a specific ground for an 'any time' revision or whether it is sufficient that a ground for an 'any time' revision was available. Get advice if this affects you.

**For HB**, the time limit for appealing runs from the date:

- you were sent or given notification of the revision or the refusal to carry out an 'any grounds' revision and your application for a revision was made within the time limit (or a late application was accepted);
- of the original decision if a decision maker has refused to do an 'any time' revision – eg, because they do not accept that an official error was made.[65]

In all cases, if the decision maker refuses to do an 'any grounds' revision because your application was late and they did not accept your reasons for why it was late, arguably the time runs from the date you are notified that the revision is not to be considered. However, it is arguable that this is wrong and the time runs from the date of the notice of the original decision. If you are in this situation, try to appeal within 13 months of the original decision.

If the time for appealing runs from the date of the original decision, you may be able to apply for judicial review (see Chapter 53) of the refusal to carry out an 'any time' revision or the refusal to accept your reasons for applying late for an 'any grounds' revision. Alternatively, you may be able to make a late appeal (see p1176). If you want to appeal against the original HB decision, the time limit runs from the date you were sent or given notice of it, so if you are outside the absolute time limit, you cannot appeal.



## 3. Supersessions

A decision that is wrong or which is no longer correct can be changed by a supersession, but there must be grounds to do so.[66] The most common ground for a supersession is that your circumstances have changed since the decision was made.

You can apply for a supersession even if the decision was made a long time ago, but the arrears of benefit you are paid can be limited (see p1148 for when a supersession takes effect). It is usually better to apply for a revision or appeal.

### When a decision can be superseded

You can ask for a decision maker's decision (and in some cases a First-tier Tribunal's or an Upper Tribunal's decision) to be superseded or the decision maker can decide to do this themself.[67] There must be grounds for a supersession. The main grounds are:

- if the decision maker has obtained a new medical report and the decision is about limited capability for work or work-related activity for universal credit (UC) or employment and support allowance (ESA), or is about the disability conditions for personal independence payment (PIP) (see below);
- a change of circumstances (see p1145);
- mistakes about or ignorance of facts (see p1146);
- if a decision is legally wrong (see p1147);
- after a qualifying benefit has been awarded (see p1147).

Some other grounds for a supersession are summarised on p1147.

**Note:** if a decision could be revised, it cannot be superseded unless there are grounds for a supersession that are not covered by the revision rules.[68]

## New medical reports from a healthcare professional and capability for work and disability conditions

A decision maker's or a tribunal's decision can be superseded if it is a decision to award you UC, ESA or national insurance (NI) credits on the basis that you have, or are treated as having, limited capability for work (see Chapter 41), or it is a decision to award you PIP on the basis that you satisfy one of the disability conditions. The decision can be superseded if:

8

- since the decision was made:[69]
  - a healthcare professional (see p1010 for who counts) or, for PIP and new-style ESA (ie, ESA under the UC system), an 'other person' approved by the Secretary of State, has provided medical evidence – eg, on your capability for work (or on whether you satisfy the disability conditions for PIP); *or*
  - the decision maker has decided that you can be treated as having limited capability for work (or, for UC, for work and work-related activity) under specified provisions.

  The rules therefore allow the decision maker to consider your entitlement to UC, ESA, NI credits or PIP without identifying a specific change of circumstances.[70] The rate of benefit may be increased or reduced, or your entitlement may end. However, your entitlement should *only* end if they decide based on the evidence that you no longer have limited capability for work, or no longer satisfy the conditions for PIP.[71]

  If you have told the decision maker that your condition has not improved since your last assessment or you have a variable condition, argue that reference should be made to earlier assessments and decisions on your claim;[72] *or*
- it is a decision to award you PIP and there has been a determination that, because you did not return your questionnaire or failed to participate in your

assessment consultation, you do not satisfy the disability conditions for the daily living component or the mobility component.[73]

## Change of circumstances

A decision maker's or a tribunal's decision can be superseded if:[74]

- your circumstances have changed since it had effect; *or*
- in the case of advance awards (other than for housing benefit (HB)), your circumstances have changed since it was made; *or*
- it is anticipated that your circumstances will change.

There must be a relevant change of circumstances (see below).

**Note:**

- The decision maker may say that a change of circumstances you have reported is a change that could not possibly result in a supersession and so refuse to consider a supersession. If this happens, see p1156.
- If there is doubt about whether a change of circumstances has occurred (eg, whether your medical condition has improved or worsened), it is necessary to compare the circumstances as they were at the time the decision took effect with the circumstances as they were at the time the supersession would take effect.[75]
- Some changes in your capability for work or the effects of your disability are dealt with under different rules (see p1144).

8

### Relevant changes of circumstances

The change must be a 'relevant change of circumstances' – ie, it must mean that the original decision (eg, to award you benefit) may no longer be correct. What is relevant can depend on the benefit. Examples include changes in your income or your medical or physical condition, moving home or being absent from home, becoming or ceasing to be a member of a couple, or having a child or a child leaving home. Bear the following in mind.

- An amendment to the law counts as a relevant change of circumstances, but a decision of a court or the Upper Tribunal that the law has been wrongly interpreted does not.[76]
- Although a new medical opinion does not count, a new medical report following an examination may provide evidence of a relevant change.[77] **Note:** a new medical report may mean there is a separate ground for a supersession (see p1144).
- If you have a fixed-term award of attendance allowance (AA), disability living allowance (DLA) or PIP, a change in how long it is likely you will continue to meet the conditions of entitlement is a change of circumstances (effectively allowing you to seek a supersession on this ground in order to say the award should be for a longer period).[78]

- Becoming terminally ill counts for UC, ESA, AA, DLA and PIP, but you or the person claiming on your behalf must state explicitly that you are terminally ill in the supersession application.[79]

### Change of circumstances after benefit is refused

If you were correctly refused benefit so that no award was made, but your circumstances are now different, you *cannot* seek a supersession on the grounds of a change of circumstances. You must instead make a fresh claim (unless you are seeking a supersession because there has been a 'recrudescence' of a prescribed disease – see p594).[80] Even if you are appealing against the decision refusing or stopping your benefit, make a fresh claim when your circumstances change and appeal if you are still refused. You could lose out if you do not do so, because the tribunal cannot take a change of circumstances into account if it happens after the decision with which you disagree (see p1203).

## Mistake about or ignorance of facts

A decision maker's or a tribunal's decision can be superseded if there was a mistake about the facts of your case or if it was made in ignorance of relevant facts. However, in the case of a decision maker's decision, this only applies if:[81]

- for housing benefit (HB), a revision on the same ground cannot be done. **Note:** the local authority can revise a decision if, within one month of your being sent or given it, it has information that shows that there was a mistake about the facts of your case or the decision was made in ignorance of relevant facts;[82] *or*
- for other benefits, the time limit for applying for an 'any grounds' revision (or any longer period allowed) has passed (see p1132) or, if the decision maker decides to do a supersession themself, it is more than one month since you were sent or given the decision.

8

In practice, this ground for supersession generally only applies if, as a result of a mistake or ignorance about the facts, a decision was less favourable to you than it would have been (eg, you were awarded too little benefit) and you have missed the time limit for applying for an 'any grounds' revision. If a decision is more favourable to you than it would have been (ie, you were being overpaid), a decision maker can initiate an 'any time' revision (see p1138).

**Note:**

- There must have been a mistake about the facts or the decision maker (or the tribunal) must not have had all the facts, but it does not matter how the mistake came about or whether you could have produced evidence sooner than you did or failed to give the information on your claim form.
- The mistake or ignorance must be in respect of facts, not conclusions or opinions about the facts.[83] See p1064 for some examples.

- Sometimes it is possible to argue that the decision maker's mistake was an 'official error' (see p1135). If so, an 'any time' revision on this ground may be possible. If superseding the decision would give you an increased award, this is the better option, as full arrears of benefit are payable.

## Decisions that are legally wrong

A decision maker's decision can be superseded if it was legally wrong (ie, based on an error of law) and:[84]

- for HB, a revision on the same basis cannot be done; *or*
- for other benefits, the time limit for seeking an 'any grounds' revision (or any longer period allowed) has passed (see p1132) or, if the decision maker decides to carry out a supersession themself, it is more than one month since you were sent or given the decision.

If there has been an error of law then an 'any time' revision based on official error (see p1135) **should always be carried out instead of a supersession, unless the error of law was only shown to be an error by a later decision.** If the new decision is to your advantage, a revision is the better option, as full arrears of benefit are payable.

**Note:** if a decision of the First-tier or Upper Tribunal is legally wrong, this is not a ground that allows it to be changed by a supersession (it can only be changed by appealing against it).



## Awards of qualifying benefits

A decision maker's or a tribunal's decision awarding benefit can be superseded if:

- you have been awarded the benefit (eg, income-related ESA or HB) but, from a later date than the entitlement began, you or your partner (or a child included in your claim – see p258) are awarded another benefit or an increase in its rate. This can work to your advantage if the other benefit is a 'qualifying benefit' (eg, DLA, PIP or carer's allowance (CA)) (see p1157);[85] *or*
- for income-related ESA and pension credit (PC) only, if you have a non-dependant living with you (see p277) and since you were awarded the benefit, your non-dependant has been awarded a qualifying benefit (see p1157) for a period beginning after the date your award took effect, and this means that you are now entitled to a severe disability premium (for income-related ESA) or a severe disability addition (for PC).[86]

See p1157 for further information. If you are only entitled to a benefit once a qualifying benefit is awarded, see p219 and p1012.

## Other grounds for supersession

There are other circumstances in which a decision can be superseded, including if the decision is one against which you have no right of appeal (see p1173).[87] Other decisions that can be superseded include those:

- concerning a decrease in the amount of rent for the purposes of the housing costs element (for UC) or your maximum rent (for HB) because of a rent officer's redetermination. **Note:** for HB, a decrease in your maximum rent because a local housing allowance rate or a broad rental market area has been amended following a rent officer's error is a change of circumstances;[88]
- which reduced your HB under the benefit cap rules (see p1025), or increased or reduced the reduction;[89]
- about PC and HB, if you or your partner deferred claiming a retirement pension or a state pension and you are paid a lump sum or repay it because you change your option to a pension increase;[90]
- of the First-tier or Upper Tribunal made if a test case was pending, if the test case is eventually decided in your favour (see p1193).[91]

The list above is not exhaustive. Other decisions can be superseded.[92]

## How to apply for a supersession

**For UC**, it is best to apply in your online journal, and if you are reporting a change in your circumstances, you should always use the 'report a change' tab in your online journal. **Otherwise, for benefits other than HB**, you do not have to apply for a supersession in writing, although it is always best to do so. This ensures that the decision maker understands that you are asking for one, not just seeking an explanation or complaining about the rules.

8

**For HB**, you must apply for a supersession in writing.[93]

The application counts as received when received at an appropriate office. This is the same as for revisions (see p1140).

A notification of a change in circumstances can be treated as an application for a supersession, so if you are reporting a change of circumstances, check that your application is received. The date of receipt is important as it can affect the date from when your benefit is changed.

When you apply for a supersession, include any information and evidence that supports your case and that may enable the decision maker to change the decision in your favour. For how to get evidence, see p1141 and for providing further information, see p1141. The issues are the same as for revisions. **Note:**

- The DWP, the local authority or HMRC can treat an application for a supersession as an application for a revision and vice versa.[94]
- A claim for benefit or a question about your entitlement can be treated as an application for a supersession.[95]

## When a supersession takes effect

The date the supersession takes effect is the date from when you are paid arrears if you are entitled to more benefit, or the date from when you have been overpaid if you are entitled to less benefit. It is important to make it clear that you want payment for a past period. For how the 'anti-test case rule' may affect the amount of backdated benefit you can receive, see p1159.

## The general rule

There is a general rule that applies in many cases. This is that if a decision is superseded, the new decision takes effect from:[96]

- the date you applied for the supersession; *or*
- if the decision maker decides to carry out a supersession on their own initiative, the date the decision is made.

There are many exceptions when the general rule does not apply. For these, the date a supersession takes effect depends on the ground for the supersession. For the exceptions, see below and the chapter in this *Handbook* about the benefit you are claiming.

## New medical reports and disability/limited capability for work decisions

If the benefit is UC, ESA or PIP and the ground for supersession is that the decision maker has received medical evidence from a healthcare professional (see p1144), the supersession takes effect as follows.

- For UC:[97]
  - if it is the first decision about whether you have limited capability for work and work-related activity and a waiting period applies (see p73), from the start of the assessment period after the waiting period;
  - in any other case, from the start of the assessment period in which the decision is made, or from the start of the assessment period in which you first asked to be reassessed.
- For ESA:
  - if it is the first decision about whether you have limited capability for work given in respect of that award, from the start of the 14th week of entitlement (or earlier if your award is linked to an earlier award – in which case the supersession takes effect from the date on which your combined entitlement has lasted 14 weeks) (see p559);[98]
  - if it is not the first decision, from the date of decision,[99] or from the date you asked to be reassessed, if the reassessment took place at your request.[100]
- For PIP, from the date of the decision.

Note that if the medical evidence shows that there has been a change in your health, the supersession could instead be on the ground of a change in your circumstances (see p1145) rather than just because of the new medical evidence. This is important as supersessions on grounds of changes in your circumstances take effect from a different date.

## Changes in your circumstances

If the ground for supersession is a change in your circumstances, when the supersession takes effect usually depends on whether or not it is advantageous to you. There are also some special rules that apply in particular situations, including the following.

- For benefits other than UC, child benefit and guardian's allowance, if there has been a change in the legislation that affects your benefit, the supersession takes effect from the date the legislation takes effect (for UC, the change takes effect from the start of the next assessment period unless the legislation took effect on the first day of an assessment period).[101]
- For income-related ESA and PC, if your carer (or your partner's carer) has stopped being paid CA, the supersession takes effect from the day after the last day for which CA was paid, provided this was to someone other than you or your partner. This means that if you are now entitled to the severe disability premium in your income-related ESA or the severe disability addition in your PC, your award can be increased from when the carer stopped getting CA for looking after you (or your partner).[102]
- For ESA and UC, if the change is that you are terminally ill (you must state this in the application for a supersession), the supersession takes effect for ESA from the date you became terminally ill and for UC from the first day of the assessment period in which you became terminally ill.[103]



### If a supersession is not advantageous

If the decision maker decides to carry out a supersession themself or you apply for a supersession and it is *not advantageous* to you, the supersession usually takes effect from:

- for UC, the start of the assessment period in which the change takes place or is expected to take place. There is an exception if the decision is one you were required to notify and is about limited capability for work;[104]
- if you come under the UC system (see p20), for new-style jobseeker's allowance (JSA) and new-style ESA, the start of the benefit week in which the change takes place or is expected to take place.[105] There is an exception if the decision is one you were required to notify and is about limited capability for work;
- for HB, the Monday after the week in which the change occurs.[106] For the exceptions to this rule, see p230;
- for PIP, the date on which the change takes place or is expected to take place.[107] There is an exception if the change is one you were required to notify and relates to the disability conditions for PIP;
- for other benefits, the date of the change of circumstances.[108] There is an exception if the change is one you were required to notify and relates to a disability or limited capability for work determination.

In some circumstances there can be a supersession that applies just for a limited period in the past. These are sometimes called 'closed period' or 'fixed-period' supersessions. This can apply where a change meant that you would have lost entitlement to your benefit, but by the time the supersession is carried out that period is past, and you are entitled again. Official guidance tells decision makers to consider this. In one case, this applied where the claimant would have lost entitlement to contributory ESA while in prison, but the supersession was not carried out until after he had left prison and would have been entitled to it again.[109] However, you should not rely on this as a reason not to report relevant changes in your circumstances when they occur (see p1030).

**Note:** if a supersession is not advantageous to you, you may have been overpaid. The DWP, the local authority or HMRC may seek to recover the overpayment.

### Disability and limited capability for work

Different rules apply if the decision is *not advantageous* to you, it concerns a change you were required to notify and it related to:

- if you come under the UC system, limited capability for work; *or*
- if you do not come under the UC system, a disability or limited capability for work determination (see p1138 for what counts); *or*
- the disability conditions for PIP.



In this case, if you (or the person being paid the benefit) failed to notify the change when you knew that you should have, or could reasonably be expected to have known that you should have, the supersession takes effect from the date you (or the person being paid the benefit) ought to have notified the change.[110] However, if you (or the person being paid) could not have reasonably been expected to know that you should have reported the change, the supersession usually takes effect from:[111]

- for UC, the start of the assessment period in which the DWP makes the decision; *or*
- for new-style ESA (ie, ESA if you come under the UC system) and PIP, the date you applied for the supersession, or if the decision maker decides to do a supersession on their own, the date the decision is made; *or*
- for other benefits, from the date on which the supersession decision is made.

So if your condition is found to have improved in the past, and you could not have been expected to report this, you will not have been overpaid or be expected to repay any overpayment.

**Note:** if you do not come under the UC system, the benefit is a 'qualifying benefit' (see p1157) and the supersession means your entitlement to another benefit is affected, the decision about the other benefit takes effect on the same date.[112]

### If a supersession is advantageous

If the supersession is *advantageous* to you, when it takes effect depends on whether the decision maker initiated the supersession or you applied for one.

If the decision maker initiated a supersession, it usually takes effect from:

- for UC, the start of the assessment period in which they first took action intending to carry out a supersession;[113]
- for HB, the Monday after the week in which the change occurs.[114] However, if the change is one you are required to notify the local authority of (other than, if you get PC and the rate of this changes as described in the first bullet point on p230), you must have notified the local authority of the change within one month of the change.[115] For when changes in circumstances take effect and exceptions to this rule, see p230;
- for AA, DLA and PIP, the date on which they first took action with a view to carrying out a supersession;[116]
- for other benefits, the start of the benefit week in which they first took action intending to carry out a supersession.[117]

If you apply for the supersession, it usually takes effect from:

- for UC, the start of the assessment period in which the change takes place or is expected to take place. You must have notified the DWP of the change within that assessment period;[118]
- for new-style JSA and ESA, the start of the benefit week in which the change takes place or is expected to take place. You must have notified the DWP of the change within one month of the change;[119]
- for HB, the Monday after the week in which the change occurs.[120] However, if the change is one you are required to notify the local authority of (other than if you get PC – see the note on p230), you must have notified the local authority of the change within one month of the change;[121]
- for PIP, the date the change occurs, or is expected to occur. You must notify the DWP of the change within one month of the change.[122] However, if the change means you are now entitled to a higher rate of benefit, the supersession takes effect from the day you satisfy the entitlement conditions for that rate (this includes the 'required period condition' – see p666).[123] In this case, you must have notified the DWP within one month of satisfying the entitlement conditions;
- for AA or DLA, if the change:[124]
  - means you are now entitled to a higher rate of benefit, the day you satisfy the conditions of entitlement to that rate (this includes the 'qualifying period condition' – see p442, p512 and p519). You must have notified the DWP of the change within one month of doing so;
  - makes a difference to whether benefit is payable to you (eg, you leave hospital or a care home), the day of the change. You must have notified the DWP of the change within one month of the change;

- for other benefits, from the date the change takes place, or is expected to take place. You must have notified the DWP (or HMRC) of the change within one month of the change.[125] There are exceptions to this rule for PC and, if you do not come under the UC system, ESA.[126]

The one-month period can be extended. If your application for an extension is refused, see below for when the supersession takes effect.

**Late notification of a change of circumstances**

If the supersession is *advantageous* to you and you fail to notify a change within the one-month periods above (or, for UC, within the assessment period), you can apply for an extension of time in limited circumstances, to a **maximum of 13 months.**[127] Your application must contain:[128]

- details of the relevant change of circumstances; *and*
- the reasons why you failed to notify the change in time. You must show that:
  - it is reasonable to grant your request; *and*
  - the change of circumstances is relevant to the decision you want changed; *and*
  - there are special circumstances that mean it was not practicable for you to notify the change within the time limit. The longer you have delayed, the more compelling the special circumstances must be.

When deciding whether it is reasonable to grant your application, the decision maker cannot take account of the fact that:[129]

- a court or the Upper Tribunal has interpreted the law in a different way than was previously understood and applied;
- you (or anyone acting for you) misunderstood or were unaware of the relevant law, including the time limits for applying for a supersession.

**If your application for an extension of time is refused**, or your application was made outside the maximum time limit, arrears are limited. The supersession takes effect:

- for UC, from the start of the assessment period in which you notified the change;[130] *or*
- for AA or DLA, from the date you applied for the supersession;[131] *or*
- for ESA and PC:[132]
  - if you are paid in arrears, from the start of the benefit week in which you notified the change; *or*
  - if you are paid in advance and you notified the change on the first day of the benefit week, from that day. Otherwise it takes effect from the start of the benefit week following the week in which you notified the change; *or*
- for HB, usually from the Monday after the date when you notified the change (see p230);[133] *or*
- for other benefits, from the date you notified the change.[134]

## Mistake about or ignorance of facts

If there has been a mistake about or ignorance of facts, the general rule on p1149 usually applies. So even if you are entitled to more benefit, arrears are limited. There are exceptions.

### Exceptions to the general rule

If the First-tier or Upper Tribunal made a decision in ignorance of relevant facts or made a mistake about the facts and, as a result, it was more *advantageous* to you than it would otherwise have been (eg, you have been overpaid benefit), the supersession takes effect:[135]

- for UC and new-style ESA (ie, ESA if you come under the UC sytem), from the start of the assessment period (for UC) or the start of the benefit week (for ESA) in which the tribunal's decision took effect; *or*
- for other benefits, from the date the tribunal's decision took effect.

However, the First-tier or Upper Tribunal decision is only superseded from this earlier date if you knew, or you could reasonably have been expected to know, the fact in question and that it was relevant to the decision and:[136]

- the decision related to a disability determination (see p1138); *or*
- it is a decision about your limited capability for work or whether you can be treated as having limited capability for work.

If you did not know (or could not be expected to know), the general rule on p1149 applies.

For HB, if a decision maker's decision was made in ignorance of facts or there was a mistake about the facts and the new decision is *advantageous* to you, the supersession takes effect from the start of the benefit week in which:[137]

- you applied for the supersession; *or*
- if you did not apply for a supersession, the local authority first had sufficient information to show that the original decision was made in ignorance of, or based on a mistake about, the facts.

The list above is not exhaustive. There are other exceptions.[138]

## Awards of qualifying benefits

If you are entitled to a benefit at a higher rate because you (or your partner, your child or a non-dependant) were awarded a qualifying benefit (see p1157), the supersession takes effect on the date of entitlement to the qualifying benefit or to an increase in its rate. For income-related ESA and PC only, if you had a non-dependant living with you while you were waiting for a decision on your claim for a qualifying benefit, your income-related ESA or PC award can be superseded to include a severe disability premium (additional amount with PC) from the date the non-dependant can be ignored (or ceased to live with you). See pp1157–59 for further information.

## Test cases

If a decision about your benefit is being superseded because of a decision by the Upper Tribunal or a court in another case (a 'test case'), the supersession is effective from the date of the tribunal's or court's decision (but not before), even if you did not realise it was relevant to your case until some time later.[139] This could help you get considerable arrears of benefit. For the special rule for the period before the date the test case is decided, see p1159.

If, while an appeal against the initial decision in a test case was pending:

- for benefits other than HB, a decision was made on your claim for benefit or to make a revision or a supersession, but your benefit was suspended, and if the test case is eventually decided against you (in whole or in part), the supersession takes effect from the date the earlier decision took effect;[140]
- you appealed to the First-tier or Upper Tribunal, it determined your appeal as if the test case had been decided in the way most unfavourable to you and the test case eventually goes in your favour (see p1193), the supersession takes effect from the date it would have taken effect had the tribunal made its decision in accordance with the decision in the test case.[141] For UC, the date is the start of the assessment period (for JSA, ESA and PC, the start of the benefit week) in which it would have taken effect had the tribunal made its decision in accordance with the decision in the test case.[142]

## Other grounds for supersession

8

There are a large number of other exceptions to the general rule on p1149. These include if:

- your rent for the purposes of the housing costs element (for UC) or your maximum rent (for HB) has decreased because of a rent officer's redetermination;[143]
- for PC and HB, you or your partner deferred claiming a retirement pension or state pension and you are paid a lump sum or change your option to a pension increase;[144]
- entitlement to a benefit depends on your NI contribution record, and the decision needs to be changed because additional contributions have been added to the record.[145]

The list above is not exhaustive. There are many other exceptions to the general rule.[146]

# Challenging a supersession

When you have applied for a supersession, or you have not but the decision maker has decided to carry one out, you should get a decision notifying you of the outcome. If you are unhappy with the decision, you can apply for a revision of the new decision. If the decision is one against which you have a right of appeal (see p1172), you can appeal to the First-tier Tribunal. Unless the benefit is HB, or is ESA and the decision is that you do not have limited capability for work and it is a case in which you would get ESA while you are appealing (see p925), you must apply for a mandatory reconsideration first (see p1168). If you have a right of appeal against the decision, you must be told about this.

If the decision maker has said there are no grounds for a supersession, you must show why there are and say what you think the new decision should be. If the decision maker has conducted a supersession, but you do not agree that they had grounds for this, you should explain why.

## If a decision maker refuses to consider a supersession

When you apply for a supersession, a decision maker must make a decision about whether to change your award. There are two possibilities.

- The decision maker agrees that there is a reason to change your award. For example, you are claiming HB and notify the decision maker that your non-dependant has moved out and so you are entitled to more benefit. In this situation, the decision maker carries out a supersession.
- The decision maker does not think there is a reason to change your award. For example, you are getting the standard rate of the PIP daily living component, feel your condition has deteriorated and want to claim the enhanced rate instead. However, the decision maker thinks you do not qualify for the enhanced rate. In this situation, the decision maker issues a decision refusing to carry out a supersession.



In either situation, you can apply for a revision of the decision maker's decision or appeal against it.[147] You must apply for a mandatory reconsideration before you can appeal (see p1168), unless the benefit is HB, or ESA where you have been found not to have limited capability for work and would be entitled to get ESA while appealing (see p923).

The only situations in which a decision maker does not have to make a decision are if an application has not been made properly and therefore cannot possibly lead to a supersession, or if an application is clearly not on a potentially relevant ground or is otherwise misconceived. In these cases, there is no decision against which you can seek a revision or appeal, but you may be able to apply for judicial review (see p1236).

## 4. Revisions and supersessions after a qualifying benefit award

Some of the rules for revisions and supersessions can help you if you (or your partner, your child or a non-dependant) become entitled to a 'qualifying benefit'.

***Qualifying benefits***

A **'qualifying benefit'** is, in general, any benefit which gives you entitlement to another benefit, or makes another benefit payable at a higher rate.

For example, the rules can help if there was a delay in assessing your entitlement to a qualifying benefit (eg, attendance allowance (AA), disability living allowance (DLA), personal independence payment (PIP), carer's allowance (CA) or child benefit) and so:

- you did not get an element in your universal credit (UC), a disability- or carer-related premium in your means-tested benefit, an additional amount in your pension credit (PC), or allowances for your children. For income-related employment and support allowance (ESA) and PC only, this includes if there are delays in assessing your non-dependant's entitlement to a qualifying benefit (see p1158); *or*
- a non-dependant deduction was made from your means-tested benefit.

**Note:** these rules can help you get arrears of benefit, even if the qualifying benefit was awarded some time ago and you did not report the change in your circumstances at the time.[148] Also, if the qualifying benefit (eg, PIP) was removed and you lost an element in your benefit as a result, but on appeal it was decided that was wrong and the qualifying benefit is reinstated, you can argue that the element should also be reinstated from the time it was removed, via a revision for official error.[149]

***Do you have to be entitled to a means-tested benefit?***

You can only apply for a revision or supersession on this ground if you are already entitled to UC, income-related ESA, PC or housing benefit (HB).[150] It is therefore essential to make a claim at the same time as the claim for a qualifying benefit (but note that new claims for income-related ESA are no longer possible and you would need to make a new claim for UC instead). If you only qualify for one of these when the qualifying benefit is awarded, see p1159.

## You or a family member are awarded a qualifying benefit or an increased rate

If you, or your partner or a child included in your claim (see p258), are awarded a qualifying benefit, or are awarded an increase in its rate (eg, you were getting the standard rate of the daily living component of PIP and are awarded the enhanced rate of that component), and arrears of the qualifying benefit are payable, your award of UC, ESA, PC or HB can be increased on revision or supersession and arrears paid for the same length of time.[151] This applies if:

- you are now entitled to more benefit – eg, an extra element of UC; *or*
- no non-dependant deduction, or for UC, a deduction for housing costs contributions, should now be made from your means-tested benefit because you or your partner are now entitled to a qualifying benefit – eg, AA, the care component of DLA or the daily living component of PIP.

**Note:** for income-related ESA and PC only, if you had a non-dependant living with you while you were waiting for a decision on your claim for a qualifying benefit, your ESA or PC award can be superseded to include the severe disability premium (or additional amount) from the date they can be ignored (or from the date they ceased to reside with you) if this is after the date from which the qualifying benefit is payable.[152]



**Example**

Jamal has been getting income-related ESA and HB. His ESA does not include any premiums and, because his uncle lives with him and his partner, Mia, a non-dependant deduction is being made from his HB. He claims PIP and Mia claims CA on 15 July. Six months later, Jamal is awarded the enhanced rate of the daily living component of PIP and Mia is awarded CA, both payable from 15 July. Jamal is now entitled to the enhanced disability and carer premiums in his ESA and a non-dependant deduction should not be made from his HB. His ESA and HB awards are superseded and he is paid arrears, backdated to 15 July.

## Your non-dependant is awarded a qualifying benefit or an increased rate

For income-related ESA and PC only, if you have a non-dependant (see p289) living with you and, but for this, a severe disability premium (or additional amount for PC) would be paid, your award of income-related ESA or PC can be increased on revision or supersession to include this premium (or additional amount) from the date the non-dependant is awarded a qualifying benefit.[153]

### You only qualify when the qualifying benefit is awarded

If you make an unsuccessful claim for a benefit, and only qualify when the qualifying benefit is awarded, you should make a second claim as soon as you hear about the qualifying benefit. See p1012 for further information.

If you only qualify for HB when the qualifying benefit is awarded, see p219. If you lose benefit because of the way the rules operate, ask the local authority for compensation.

If you only claim for the first time *after* you hear about the qualifying benefit, you can only qualify for backdated benefit under the normal backdating rules. See Chapter 50 and the chapter about the benefit you are claiming.

See p481 for a similar rule that helps you get extra backdated CA when the person for whom you care becomes entitled to a qualifying benefit.

## 5. The 'anti-test case rule'

A special rule applies when a case is going through the appeals system that will determine a point of social security law (a 'test case'), which can affect how the decision on that point in the test case is applied in your case.

The rule applies if the Upper Tribunal or a court decides in an appeal (but not a judicial review case) that a decision maker in a different case (the test case) has made an error of law (see p1216), and you make a claim, or apply for a revision or a supersession (either before or after the test case decision). In this situation, your decision maker must decide any part of your claim (or revision or supersession) which relates to the period before the test case decision as if the decision that was under appeal in the test case had been found by the tribunal or court not to have been wrong.[154] **Note:**

- The 'anti-test case rule' only applies if the test case is the first authoritative decision on the issue, and not merely a later decision confirming an earlier decision.[155]
- If the decision maker (eg, the DWP) already knew about the error of law before the decision in the test case was made, then the anti-test case rule should not apply.[156]
- The test case decision only has to be disregarded for the period before it was made if it found the decision maker to have been wrong, not if it found them to be right.

For housing benefit, you can avoid the anti-test case rule by appealing rather than seeking a revision or supersession if the rules allow you to do so.

### What happens while a test case is pending

If an appeal (a test case) is pending against a decision of the Upper Tribunal or a court, the decision maker can postpone making a decision on your claim or request for a supersession or revision.[157] The decision maker can only do this if they think that a possible result of the test case is that you will have no entitlement to benefit. This prevents you appealing until a decision is made in the test case. If the decision is postponed, once a decision has been made in the test case, the decision maker makes the decision in your case.[158]

If you would be entitled to benefit even if the test case were decided against you, the decision maker can make a decision on the assumption that the test case has been decided in the way that is most unfavourable to you.[159] However, this means that you can at least be paid something while you wait for the result of the test case. Then, if the decision in the test case is in your favour, the decision maker revises their decision. **Note:**

- If you already have a decision in your favour, the decision maker can suspend payment of your benefit (see p1031).
- If you have already appealed to the First-tier Tribunal, see p1193.

# Notes

8

1. **Getting a decision changed**

1 **HB** Sch 7 para 11 CSPSSA 2000
**Other benefits** s17 SSA 1998

2 **HB** Sch 7 paras 3(2) and 4(3) CSPSSA 2000
**Other benefits** ss9(2) and 10(2) SSA 1998

3 *Wood v SSWP* [2003] EWCA Civ 53

2. **Revisions**

4 **HB** Sch 7 para 3 CSPSSA 2000
**Other benefits** s9 SSA 1998

5 **UC/PIP/new-style JSA&ESA** s9(1) SSA 1998; regs 5 and 8 UC,PIP,JSA&ESA(DA) Regs
**HB** Sch 7 para 3(1) CSPSSA 2000; reg 4 HB&CTB(DA) Regs
**CB/GA** s9(1) SSA 1998; regs 5, 8, 10 and 11 CB&GA(DA) Regs
**Other benefits** s9(1) SSA 1998; reg 3 SS&CS(DA) Regs

6 **UC/PIP/new-style JSA&ESA** Reg 5(2)(a) UC,PIP,JSA&ESA(DA) Regs
**HB** Reg 4(10) HB&CTB(DA) Regs
**CB/GA** Reg 5(3) CB&GA(DA) Regs
**Other benefits** Reg 3(9)(a) SS&CS(DA) Regs

7 *SSWP v Miah* [2024] EWCA Civ 186; 'Not finding fault: any ground revisions', *Welfare Rights Bulletin* 301 (August 2024)

8 **UC/PIP/new-style JSA&ESA** Reg 5(2)(c) UC,PIP,JSA&ESA(DA) Regs
**Other benefits** Reg 3(9)(b) and (c) SS&CS(DA) Regs

9 **UC/PIP/new-style JSA&ESA** Regs 2, 3(2) and 5(1)(b) UC,PIP,JSA&ESA(DA) Regs
**CB/GA** Regs 3 and 5(2)(b) CB&GA(DA) Regs
**Other benefits** Regs 1(3), 2(b) and 3(1)(b) SS&CS(DA) Regs

10 Reg 3(3) SS&CS(DA) Regs

11 Regs 1(3), definition of 'date of notification', and 3(1)(b) SS&CS(DA) Regs

12 Regs 2 and 4(1)(a) HB&CTB(DA) Regs

13 Reg 4(4) HB&CTB(DA) Regs

14 Reg 5(2)(c) CB&GA(DA) Regs

15 **UC/PIP/new-style JSA&ESA** Reg 38(4) UC,PIP,JSA&ESA(DA) Regs
**HB** Reg 10A(3) HB&CTB(DA) Regs
**Other benefits** Reg 9A(3) SS&CS(DA) Regs

16 **UC/PIP/new-style JSA&ESA** Reg 6 UC,PIP,JSA&ESA(DA) Regs
**HB** Regs 4(4) and 5(3)(b) HB&CTB(DA) Regs
**CB/GA** Reg 6(3)(c) CB&GA(DA) Regs
**Other benefits** Reg 4 SS&CS(DA) Regs
17 **UC/PIP/new-style JSA&ESA** Reg 6(3)-(6) UC,PIP,JSA&ESA(DA) Regs
**HB** Reg 5(3)(a), (4) and (6) HB&CTB(DA) Regs
**CB/GA** Reg 6(3)(a) and (b), (4) and (5) CB&GA(DA) Regs
**Other benefits** Reg 4(3)(a), (4) and (5) SS&CS(DA) Regs
18 **HB** Reg 5(4)(b) and (5) HB&CTB(DA) Regs
**CB/GA** Reg 6(4)(b) and (6) CB&GA(DA) Regs
**Other benefits** Reg 4(4)(b) and (6) SS&CS(DA) Regs
19 R(TC) 1/05
20 *R(CJ) and SG v SSWP (ESA)* [2017] UKUT 324 (AAC); DMG 03013; ADM A3015
21 **UC/PIP/new-style JSA&ESA** Reg 5(1)(a) UC,PIP,JSA&ESA(DA) Regs
**CB/GA** Reg 5(2)(a) CB&GA(DA) Regs
**Other benefits** Reg 3(1)(a) SS&CS(DA) Regs
22 Reg 4(1)(b) HB&CTB(DA) Regs
23 **UC/PIP/new-style JSA&ESA** Regs 8 and 9(a) UC,PIP,JSA&ESA(DA) Regs
**HB** Reg 4(2)(a) HB&CTB(DA) Regs
**CB/GA** Reg 10(2)(a) CB&GA(DA) Regs
**Other benefits** Reg 3(5)(a) SS&CS(DA) Regs
24 Reg 10(3) CB&GA(DA) Regs
25 **UC/PIP/new-style JSA&ESA** Reg 2 UC,PIP,JSA&ESA(DA) Regs
**HB** Reg 1(2) HB&CTB(DA) Regs
**Other benefits** Reg 1(3) SS&CS(DA) Regs
26 **UC/PIP/new-style JSA&ESA** Reg 2 UC,PIP,JSA&ESA(DA) Regs
**HB** Reg 1(2) HB&CTB(DA) Regs
**CB/GA** Reg 10(3) CB&GA(DA) Regs
**Other benefits** Reg 1(3) SS&CS(DA) Regs
27 **UC/PIP/new-style JSA&ESA** Reg 2 UC,PIP,JSA&ESA(DA) Regs
**HB** Reg 1(2) HB&CTB(DA) Regs
**CB/GA** Reg 10(3) CB&GA(DA) Regs
**Other benefits** Reg 1(3) SS&CS(DA) Regs
28 CDLA/393/2006
29 CDLA/1707/2005
30 *R (Smith) v SSWP* [2018] UKUT 270 (AAC)
31 **UC/new-style JSA&ESA** Reg 14(1)(a)-(c) UC,PIP,JSA&ESA(DA) Regs
**Other benefits** Reg 3(5C), (6), (6A) and (7CD) SS&CS(DA) Regs
32 **UC/PIP/new-style JSA&ESA** Regs 8 and 12 UC,PIP,JSA&ESA(DA) Regs
**HB** Reg 4(7B) HB&CTB(DA) Regs
**CB/GA** Reg 11 CB&GA(DA) Regs
**Other benefits** Reg 3(7) SS&CS(DA) Regs
33 Reg 3(7ZA) SS&CS(DA) Regs
34 Reg 4(7C) HB&CTB(DA) Regs
35 **UC/PIP/new-style JSA&ESA** Regs 8 and 11(1) UC,PIP,JSA&ESA(DA) Regs
**HB** Reg 4(1)(c) HB&CTB(DA) Regs
**CB/GA** Reg 8(2) CB&GA(DA) Regs
**Other benefits** Reg 3(4A) SS&CS(DA) Regs
36 **UC/PIP/new-style JSA&ESA** Regs 8 and 11(2) UC,PIP,JSA&ESA(DA) Regs
**HB** Reg 4(7) HB&CTB(DA) Regs
**CB/GA** Reg 8(3) CB&GA(DA) Regs
**Other benefits** Reg 3(5A) SS&CS(DA) Regs
37 **UC/PIP/new-style JSA&ESA** Regs 8 and 9(b) UC,PIP,JSA&ESA(DA) Regs
**HB** Reg 4(2)(b) HB&CTB(DA) Regs
**CB/GA** Reg 10(2)(b) CB&GA(DA) Regs
**Other benefits** Reg 3(5)(b) and (d) SS&CS(DA) Regs
38 Regs 3(5)(c) and 7A(1) SS&CS(DA) Regs
39 Reg 7A SS&CS(DA) Regs
40 **UC/PIP/new-style JSA&ESA** Regs 8 and 10 UC,PIP,JSA&ESA(DA) Regs
**HB** Reg 4(6) HB&CTB(DA) Regs
**CB/GA** Reg 9 CB&GA(DA) Regs
**Other benefits** Reg 3(8) SS&CS(DA) Regs
41 **UC/PIP/new-style JSA&ESA** Regs 8 and 19(1) UC,PIP,JSA&ESA(DA) Regs
**HB** Reg 4(7H) HB&CTB(DA) Regs
42 **UC/PIP/new-style JSA&ESA** Reg 15(5) UC,PIP,JSA&ESA(DA) Regs
**Other benefits** Reg 3(5I) SS&CS(DA) Regs
43 Regs 8 and 18(2) UC,PIP,JSA&ESA(DA) Regs
44 Regs 8 and 18(3) UC,PIP,JSA&ESA(DA) Regs
45 **UC/PIP/new-style JSA&ESA** Regs 8 and 19(2) UC,PIP,JSA&ESA(DA) Regs
**HB** Reg 4(3) HB&CTB(DA) Regs; reg 18A(1) and (3) HB Regs; reg 18A(1) and (3) HB(SPC) Regs

46 **State pension** Reg 3(7DB) SS&CS(DA) Regs
**RP** Reg 3(7E) SS&CS(DA) Regs
**PC** Reg 3(7D) and (7DA) SS&CS(DA) Regs
**HB** Reg 4(7D) and (7DA) HB&CTB(DA) Regs
47 Reg 3(5J) SS&CS(DA) Regs; reg 15(4A) UC,PIP,JSA&ESA(DA) Regs
48 **UC/PIP/new-style JSA&ESA** Regs 8, 13, 15(2)-(4) and (4A), 16, 17 and 18(1) UC,PIP,JSA&ESA(DA) Regs
**HB** Reg 4(7A) and (7DB) HB&CTB(DA) Regs
**Other benefits** Reg 3(5D)-(5H), (7A), (7EA), (7EB), (8B)-(8K) SS&CS(DA) Regs
49 Regs 4(8) and 5(2) HB&CTB(DA) Regs
50 **UC/PIP/new-style JSA&ESA** Reg 5(1)(b) UC,PIP,JSA&ESA(DA) Regs
**CB/GA** Reg 5(1)(b) CB&GA(DA) Regs
**Other benefits** Reg 3(1)(b) SS&CS(DA) Regs
51 **UC/PIP/new-style JSA&ESA** Reg 2 UC,PIP,JSA&ESA(DA) Regs
**HB** Reg 4(8) HB&CTB(DA) Regs
**CB/GA** Reg 2(1), definition of 'appropriate office', CB&GA(DA) Regs
**Other benefits** Reg 3(11) SS&CS(DA) Regs
52 **HB** Sch 7 paras 3(2) and 4(3) CSPSSA 2000
**Other benefits** ss9(2) and 10(2) SSA 1998
53 **UC/PIP/new-style JSA&ESA** Regs 20(1) and 33(1) UC,PIP,JSA&ESA(DA) Regs
**HB** Regs 4(9) and 7(6) HB&CTB(DA) Regs
**CB/GA** Regs 7(1) and 14(1) CB&GA(DA) Regs
**Other benefits** Regs 3(10) and 6(5) SS&CS(DA) Regs
54 R(JSA) 2/04
55 *WO'C v SSWP and JW* [2020] UKUT 34 (AAC) paras 70-71 – although this concerns applications to tribunals, the same principles should apply to applications to the decision maker
56 R(IS) 11/92; *SSWP v TJ (JSA)* [2015] UKUT 56 (AAC), paras 213-15
57 **UC/PIP/new-style JSA&ESA** Regs 20(2) and (3) and 33(2) and (3) UC,PIP,JSA&ESA(DA) Regs
**HB** Regs 4(5) and 7(5) HB&CTB(DA) Regs
**CB/GA** Regs 7(2) and (3) and 14(3) CB&GA(DA) Regs
**Other benefits** Regs 3(2) and 6(4) SS&CS(DA) Regs
58 Reg 33(4) UC,PIP,JSA&ESA(DA) Regs
59 Reg 33(4) UC,PIP,JSA&ESA(DA) Regs
60 **HB** Sch 7 para 3(3) CSPSSA 2000
**Other benefits** s9(3) SSA 1998
61 **UC/PIP/new-style JSA&ESA** Reg 21 UC,PIP,JSA&ESA(DA) Regs
**HB** Reg 6 HB&CTB(DA) Regs
**CB/GA** Reg 12 CB&GA(DA) Regs
**Other benefits** Reg 5(1) SS&CS(DA) Regs
62 Reg 7A(2) SS&CS(DA) Regs
63 s9(5) SSA 1998; Sch 7 para 3(5) CSPSSA 2000; rr22(2)(d)(I) and 23 TP(FT) Rules
64 *PH & SM v SSWP (DLA) (JSA)* [2018] UKUT 404 (AAC)
65 R(IS) 15/04; *Beltekian v Westminster City Council and Another* [2004] EWCA Civ 1784, reported as R(H) 8/05; *AS v SSWP (CSM)* [2012] UKUT 448 (AAC), reported as [2013] AACR 18

3. **Supersessions**

66 **HB** Sch 7 para 4 CSPSSA 2000
**Other benefits** s10 SSA 1998
67 **UC/PIP/new-style JSA&ESA** Reg 22 UC,PIP,JSA&ESA(DA) Regs
**HB** Reg 7(2) HB&CTB(DA) Regs
**CB/GA** Reg 13(1) CB&GA(DA) Regs
**Other benefits** Reg 6(2) SS&CS(DA) Regs
68 **UC/PIP/new-style JSA&ESA** Reg 32 UC,PIP,JSA&ESA(DA) Regs
**HB** Reg 7(4) HB&CTB(DA) Regs
**CB/GA** Reg 15 CB&GA(DA) Regs
**Other benefits** Reg 6(3) SS&CS(DA) Regs
69 Reg 26(1) UC,PIP,JSA&ESA(DA) Regs; regs 6(2)(r) and 7A(1) SS&CS(DA) Regs; CIB/4033/2003; R(IB) 2/05
70 *SF v SSWP (PIP)* [2016] UKUT 481 (AAC); *DS v SSWP (PIP)* [2016] UKUT 538 (AAC), reported as [2017] AACR 19
71 CSIB/377/2003; CIB/1509/2004; R(IB) 5/05; *JB v SSWP (IB)* [2010] UKUT 246 (AAC); *ST v SSWP (ESA)* [2012] UKUT 469 (AAC)

72 CIB/1972/2000; CIB/3179/2000; CIB/3985/2001; *ST v SSWP (ESA)* [2012] UKUT 469 (AAC); *FN v SSWP (ESA)* [2015] UKUT 670 (AAC), reported as [2016] AACR 24
73 s80(5) and (6) WRA 2012; regs 8 and 9 SS(PIP) Regs; reg 26(2) UC,PIP,JSA&ESA(DA) Regs; *KB v SSWP (PIP)* [2016] UKUT 537 (AAC)
74 **UC/PIP/new-style JSA&ESA** Reg 23 UC,PIP,JSA&ESA(DA) Regs
**HB** Regs 7(2)(a) and 7A(4) HB&CTB(DA) Regs
**CB/GA** Reg 13(2)(a) CB&GA(DA) Regs
**Other benefits** Reg 6(2)(a) SS&CS(DA) Regs; Sch 2 para 25A(2) ESA(TP)(EA) (No.2) Regs
**All** *Wood v SSWP* [2003] EWCA Civ 53, reported as R(DLA) 1/03
75 CSDLA/637/2006; CSDLA/822/2006
76 *CAO v McKiernon*, 8 July 1993 (CA), reported as an attachment to R(I) 2/94
77 *Cooke v Secretary of State for Social Security* [2001] EWCA Civ 734, reported as R(DLA) 6/01; R(S) 4/86; R(IS) 2/98; CIB/7899/1996; CIS/856/1994
78 *PH v SSWP (DLA)* [2013] UKUT 268 (AAC)
79 **UC/PIP/new-style JSA&ESA** Reg 23(2) UC,PIP,JSA&ESA(DA) Regs
**Other benefits** Reg 6(6)(c) SS&CS(DA) Regs
80 **HB** Sch 7 para 2 CSPSSA 2000
**Other benefits** s8(2) SSA 1998; reg 12A SS&CS(DA) Regs
81 **UC/PIP/new-style JSA&ESA** Regs 24 and 31(a) UC,PIP,JSA&ESA(DA) Regs
**HB** Reg 7(2)(b) and (d) HB&CTB(DA) Regs
**CB/GA** Reg 13(2)(b) and (c)(i) CB&GA(DA) Regs
**Other benefits** Reg 6(2)(b) and (c) SS&CS(DA) Regs
82 Reg 4(1)(b) HB&CTB(DA) Regs
83 R(I) 3/75; CSDLA/251/2007
84 **UC/PIP/new-style JSA&ESA** Reg 24 UC,PIP,JSA&ESA(DA) Regs
**HB** Reg 7(2)(b) HB&CTB(DA) Regs
**CB/GA** Reg 13(2)(b) CB&GA(DA) Regs
**Other benefits** Reg 6(2)(b) SS&CS(DA) Regs
85 **UC/PIP/new-style JSA&ESA** Reg 23 UC,PIP,JSA&ESA(DA) Regs. For these benefits, although this counts as a change of circumstances, it takes effect differently to most such changes.
**HB** Reg 7(2)(i) HB&CTB(DA) Regs
**CB/GA** Reg 13(2)(e) CB&GA(DA) Regs
**Other benefits** Reg 6(2)(e) SS&CS(DA) Regs
86 Reg 6(2)(ee) SS&CS(DA) Regs
87 **UC/PIP/new-style JSA&ESA** Reg 25 UC,PIP,JSA&ESA(DA) Regs
**HB** Reg 7(2)(e) HB&CTB(DA) Regs
**CB/GA** Reg 13(2)(d) CB&GA(DA) Regs
**Other benefits** Reg 6(2)(d) SS&CS(DA) Regs
88 **UC** Reg 30 UC,PIP,JSA&ESA(DA) Regs
**HB** Reg 7(2)(c) HB&CTB(DA) Regs; reg 18A(2) HB Regs; reg 18A(2) HB(SPC) Regs
89 Reg 7(2)(r) HB&CTB(DA) Regs
90 **PC** Reg 6(2)(o) and (oa) SS&CS(DA) Regs
**HB** Reg 7(2)(j), (ja) and (jb) HB&CTB(DA) Regs
91 **UC/PIP/new-style JSA&ESA** Reg 31(b) UC,PIP,JSA&ESA(DA) Regs
**HB** Reg 7(2)(d)(ii) HB&CTB(DA) Regs
**CB/GA** Reg 13(2)(c)(ii) CB&GA(DA) Regs
**Other benefits** Reg 6(2)(c)(ii) SS&CS(DA) Regs
92 **UC/PIP/new-style JSA&ESA** Regs 27, 28 and 29 UC,PIP,JSA&ESA(DA) Regs
**HB** Regs 7(2)(g), (h), (q), (r) and (s) and 7A(2) and (3) HB&CTB(DA) Regs
**Other benefits** Reg 6(2)(f), (fa), (h), (j), (k), (p), (q), (s), (sa), (t) and (u) SS&CS(DA) Regs
93 Reg 7(7) HB&CTB(DA) Regs
94 **UC/PIP/new-style JSA&ESA** Regs 20(1) and 33(1) UC,PIP,JSA&ESA(DA) Regs
**HB** Regs 4(9) and 7(6) HB&CTB(DA) Regs
**CB/GA** Regs 7(1) and 14(1) CB&GA(DA) Regs
**Other benefits** Regs 3(10) and 6(5) SS&CS(DA) Regs
95 R(I) 50/56
96 **HB** Sch 7 para 4(5) CSPSSA 2000
**Other benefits** s10(5) SSA 1998
97 Reg 35(9) UC,PIP,JSA&ESA(DA) Regs
98 Reg 7(38) and (40) SS&CS(DA) Regs; reg 35(7) and (8) UC,PIP,JSA&ESA(DA) Regs
99 s10(5) SSA 1998

100 Reg 7(39) SS&CS(DA) Regs; reg 35(6) UC,PIP,JSA&ESA(DA) Regs
101 **UC/PIP/new-style JSA&ESA** Reg 35(1) and Sch 1 paras 32 and 33 UC,PIP,JSA&ESA(DA) Regs
**HB** Reg 8(10) HB&CTB(DA) Regs
**Other benefits** Reg 7(9)(a)(ii), (30) and (30A) SS&CS(DA) Regs
102 Reg 7(2)(bc) SS&CS(DA) Regs
103 **UC/PIP/new-style JSA&ESA** Reg 35(1) and Sch 1 paras 9 and 28 UC,PIP,JSA&ESA(DA) Regs
**Other benefits** Reg 7(2)(be) SS&CS(DA) Regs
104 Sch 1 para 20 UC,PIP,JSA&ESA(DA) Regs
105 Sch 1 para 1 UC,PIP,JSA&ESA(DA) Regs
106 Reg 8(2) HB&CTB(DA) Regs
107 Sch 1 para 12 UC,PIP,JSA&ESA(DA) Regs
108 **AA/DLA** Reg 7(2)(c)(iv) SS&CS(DA) Regs
**CB/GA** Reg 16(5) CB&GA(DA) Regs
**Other benefits** Reg 7(2)(c)(v) SS&CS(DA) Regs
109 Official guidance at (for example) para A4180 ADM; *SSWP v NC (ESA)* [2023] UKUT 124 (AAC)
110 **UC/PIP/new-style JSA&ESA** Sch 1 paras 7, 8, 11, 16, 17, 19, 23, 24 and 30 UC,PIP,JSA&ESA(DA) Regs
**Other benefits** Regs 7(2)(c)(ii) and 7A(1) SS&CS(DA) Regs
111 **UC/PIP/new-style JSA&ESA** s10(5) SSA 1998; Sch 1 paras 2, 13 and 25 UC,PIP,JSA&ESA(DA) Regs
**Other benefits** s10(5) SSA 1998, as none of the other heads of reg 7(2)(c) SS&CS(DA) Regs apply
112 Reg 7A(2) SS&CS(DA) Regs
113 Sch 1 para 29 UC,PIP,JSA&ESA(DA) Regs
114 Reg 8(2) HB&CTB(DA) Regs
115 Reg 8(3) HB&CTB(DA) Regs
116 **AA/DLA** Reg 7(9)(a) SS&CS(DA) Regs
**PIP** Sch 1 para 18 UC,PIP,JSA&ESA(DA) Regs
117 **New-style JSA&ESA** Sch 1 para 10 UC,PIP,JSA&ESA(DA) Regs
**CB/GA** Reg 16(4) CB&GA(DA) Regs
**Other benefits** Reg 7(2)(bb) SS&CS(DA) Regs
118 Sch 1 paras 20 and 21 UC,PIP,JSA&ESA(DA) Regs
119 Sch 1 paras 1 and 6 UC,PIP,JSA&ESA(DA) Regs
120 Reg 8(2) HB&CTB(DA) Regs
121 Reg 8(3) HB&CTB(DA) Regs
122 Sch 1 paras 12 and 14 UC,PIP,JSA&ESA(DA) Regs
123 Sch 1 para 15 UC,PIP,JSA&ESA(DA) Regs
124 Reg 7(9) SS&CS(DA) Regs; *SSWP v DA* [2009] UKUT 214 (AAC)
125 **CB/GA** Reg 16(3)(a) CB&GA(DA) Regs
**Other benefits** Reg 7(2)(a) SS&CS(DA) Regs
126 Schs 3A, 3B and 3C SS&CS(DA) Regs
127 **UC/PIP/new-style JSA&ESA** Reg 36 UC,PIP,JSA&ESA(DA) Regs
**HB** Reg 9 HB&CTB(DA) Regs
**CB/GA** Reg 17 CB&GA(DA) Regs
**Other benefits** Reg 8 SS&CS(DA) Regs
128 **UC/PIP/new-style JSA&ESA** Reg 36(3)-(7) UC,PIP,JSA&ESA(DA) Regs
**HB** Reg 9(2)-(4) HB&CTB(DA) Regs
**CB/GA** Reg 17(3)-(5) CB&GA(DA) Regs
**Other benefits** Reg 8(3)-(5) SS&CS(DA) Regs
129 **UC/PIP/new-style JSA&ESA** Reg 36(7) UC,PIP,JSA&ESA(DA) Regs
**HB** Reg 9(5) HB&CTB(DA) Regs
**CB/GA** Reg 17(6) CB&GA(DA) Regs
**Other benefits** Reg 8(6) SS&CS(DA) Regs
130 Sch 1 para 21 UC,PIP,JSA&ESA(DA) Regs
131 Reg 7(9)(d) SS&CS(DA) Regs
132 Reg 7(2)(b)(i) and (ii) SS&CS(DA) Regs; Sch 1 para 6 UC,PIP,JSA&ESA(DA) Regs
133 Reg 8(3) HB&CTB(DA) Regs; reg 79(1) HB Regs; reg 59(1) HB(SPC) Regs
134 **UC/PIP/new-style JSA&ESA** Sch 1 para 14 UC,PIP,JSA&ESA(DA) Regs
**CB/GA** Reg 16(3)(b) CB&GA(DA) Regs
**Other benefits** Reg 7(2)(b)(iii) SS&CS(DA) Regs
135 **UC/PIP/new-style JSA&ESA** Reg 37(1)-(3) UC,PIP,JSA&ESA(DA) Regs
**HB** Reg 8(7) HB&CTB(DA) Regs
**CB/GA** Reg 16(7) CB&GA(DA) Regs
**Other benefits** Reg 7(5) SS&CS(DA) Regs
136 **UC/ESA** Regs 2 and 37(1) and (3) UC,PIP,JSA&ESA(DA) Regs
**Other benefits** Reg 7(5) and Sch 3C para 8 SS&CS(DA) Regs
137 Reg 8(4) HB&CTB(DA) Regs
138 **UC/PIP/new-style JSA&ESA** Reg 35(2)-(4) UC,PIP,JSA&ESA(DA) Regs
**Other benefits** Reg 16(2) SS(C&P) Regs; Schs 3A para 12, 3B para 7, and 3C para 9 SS&CS(DA) Regs
139 **UC/PIP/new-style JSA&ESA** Reg 35(5) UC,PIP,JSA&ESA(DA) Regs
**HB** Reg 8(8) HB&CTB(DA) Regs
**CB/GA** Reg 16(9) CB&GA(DA) Regs
**Other benefits** Reg 7(6) SS&CS(DA) Regs
**All** *MP v SSWP (DLA)* [2010] UKUT 130 (AAC)

140 **UC/PIP/new-style JSA&ESA** Reg 37(5) and (6) UC,PIP,JSA&ESA(DA) Regs
**CB/GA** Reg 16(9A) CB&GA(DA) Regs
**Other benefits** Reg 7(6A) SS&CS(DA) Regs
141 **HB** Reg 8(11) HB&CTB(DA) Regs
**CB/GA** Reg 16(8) CB&GA(DA) Regs
**PIP** Reg 37(4)(a) UC,PIP,JSA&ESA(DA) Regs
**Other benefits** Reg 7(33) SS&CS(DA) Regs
142 **UC/PIP/new-style JSA&ESA** Reg 37(4)(b) and (c) UC,PIP,JSA&ESA(DA) Regs
**Other benefits** Schs 3A para 12, 3B para 7, and 3C para 8 SS&CS(DA) Regs
143 **UC** Reg 35(14) UC,PIP,JSA&ESA(DA) Regs
**HB** Reg 8(2) and (6) HB&CTB(DA) Regs
144 **PC** Reg 7(7A) SS&CS(DA) Regs
**HB** Reg 8(14A) HB&CTB(DA) Regs
145 Reg 35(13) UC,PIP,JSA&ESA(DA) Regs; reg 7(8A) SS&CS(DA) Regs
146 **UC/PIP/new-style JSA&ESA** Reg 35(10)-(12) UC,PIP,JSA&ESA(DA) Regs
**HB** Reg 8(6A), (9), (14D), (14E), (14F), (14G) and (15) HB&CTB(DA) Regs
**Other benefits** Reg 7(8), (8ZA), (11), (12A)-(12G), (24), (25), (28), (29), (29A)-(29C), (34)-(37) and (41)-(43) SS&CS(DA) Regs
147 *Wood v SSWP* [2003] EWCA Civ 53, reported as R(DLA) 1/03

4. **Revisions and supersessions after a qualifying benefit award**
148 *HR v Wakefield DC* [2009] UKUT 72 (AAC); *OL v SSWP (ESA)* [2018] UKUT 135 (AAC)
149 *DS v SSWP (CA)* (no neutral citation number available) (5 May 2023)
150 **ESA/PC/UC** s8(2) SSA 1998
**HB** Sch 7 para 2 CSPSSA 2000
151 **UC/PIP/new-style JSA&ESA** Regs 12 and 23 and Sch 1 para 31 UC,PIP,JSA&ESA(DA) Regs
**ESA/PC** Regs 3(7), 6(2)(e) and 7(7) SS&CS(DA) Regs
**HB** Regs 4(7B) and (7C), 7(2)(i) and 8(14) HB&CTB(DA) Regs; CIS/1178/2001
**All** *BB v SSWP (ESA)* [2017] UKUT 280 (AAC)
152 Reg 7(7)(b) SS&CS(DA) Regs
153 Regs 3(7ZA), 6(2)(ee) and 7(7) SS&CS(DA) Regs

5. **The 'anti-test case rule'**
154 **HB** Sch 7 para 18 CSPSSA 2000
**Other benefits** s27 SSA 1998
**All** *CAO and Another v Bate* [1996] 2 All ER 790 (HL)
155 R(FC) 3/98; R(I) 1/03
156 *R (DS) v SSWP* [2018] UKUT 270 (AAC)
157 **HB** Sch 7 para 16 CSPSSA 2000
**Other benefits** s25 SSA 1998
158 **HB** Sch 7 para 18(2) CSPSSA 2000
**Other benefits** s27(2) SSA 1998
159 **UC/PIP/new-style JSA&ESA under UC** s25(3) and (4) SSA 1998; reg 53 UC,PIP,JSA&ESA(DA) Regs
**HB** Sch 7 para 16(3) and (4) CSPSSA 2000; reg 15 HB&CTB(DA) Regs
**CB/GA** s25(3) and (4) SSA 1998; reg 22 CB&GA(DA) Regs
**Other benefits** s25(3) and (4) SSA 1998; reg 21 SS&CS(DA) Regs

Chapter 51

# Appealing to the First-tier Tribunal

**This chapter covers:**


1. Before you appeal (p1167)
2. How to appeal (p1174)
3. After you submit your appeal (p1182)
4. How the tribunal makes its decision (p1194)
5. Preparing your appeal (p1204)
6. The tribunal's decision (p1205)


This chapter covers the rules for appeals to the First-tier Tribunal about benefits, the social fund payments in Chapter 33 (except budgeting loans), decisions about DWP loans for mortgage interest (see p764) and national insurance credits. It does *not* cover the rules for statutory payments (see Chapter 54), the health benefits in Chapter 27 or the Scottish benefits (see Chapter 69).

## Key facts

- If you disagree with certain decisions made by the DWP, the local authority or HMRC, you can appeal to the First-tier Tribunal.
- For benefits other than housing benefit, you must usually apply for a mandatory reconsideration before you can appeal.
- There is a basic time limit of one month and also an absolute time limit for appealing.
- You may need to make a fresh claim for benefit or seek a supersession while you are waiting for your appeal to be heard.
- The tribunal can allow or reject your appeal, and replace the decision about which you appealed with any decision it thinks is right. This could be more or less favourable to you.
- If your appeal is unsuccessful, you may be able to appeal to the Upper Tribunal.

## 1. Before you appeal

You can appeal against some decisions of the DWP, the local authority or HMRC. Appeals are dealt with by the First-tier Tribunal. The tribunal consists of a judge and, in some cases, another one or two members of the tribunal. The administration of the work of all tribunals is the responsibility of HM Courts and Tribunals Service (HMCTS). HMCTS officials deal with the day-to-day work of the First-tier Tribunal through a network of regional offices. See p1182 for more on who may deal with your appeal.

Before you appeal, you should do the following.

- Make sure you have sufficient information about the decision you are unhappy about. You can ask for a written statement of reasons if this has not already been provided (see p1125).
- Check whether you must apply for a mandatory reconsideration before you can appeal and apply within the time limit if relevant (see p1168).
- Check whether you would be better off applying for a revision or supersession instead of appealing (see below).
- In some cases, you should get advice before you appeal. If you apply for a mandatory reconsideration, the DWP or HMRC looks at your case afresh. So does the First-tier Tribunal when you appeal. There is a risk you could lose benefit. For example, if your appeal is about a benefit that can be paid at different rates (eg, personal independence payment (PIP)), the rate could go down. If you are appealing about an overpayment, the amount could increase.

8

***Revision, supersession or appeal?***

1. You must usually apply for the decision to be looked at again, by a mandatory reconsideration, before you can appeal (see p1168), unless the benefit is housing benefit (HB). In the law, mandatory reconsiderations are called 'revisions' of your benefit decision.

2. For HB, if you are not yet sure if you want to appeal, it can be worth applying for a revision before you appeal. You get two bites at the cherry, because if your application for a revision is turned down, you can still appeal against the original decision.

3. Revisions can be carried out on 'any grounds' if they are applied for within the time limits. If you do so, you will always have the right of appeal even if your application is refused. There is no time limit for applying for 'any time' revisions but you must show specific grounds (see p1135). However, you may not be able to appeal against a refusal to do an 'any time' revision (see p1142).

4. In most cases, there is no time limit for applying for a supersession – eg, if there has been a mistake about the facts or if a test case is decided in your favour but you do not become aware of this until some time later. However, you generally get less arrears of benefit if you apply for a supersession. See pp1148–55 for when a supersession takes effect. Usually, you need to request a mandatory reconsideration against the outcome of a decision following a supersession.

5. If the 'anti-test case rule' applies to you (see p1159), and all that you did before the test case was decided was apply for a revision or a supersession, the arrears of benefit you get could be limited. This is not the case if you appealed.

## Mandatory reconsideration

Before you can appeal you must usually ask for the decision you are unhappy with to be looked at again, by applying for a revision of the decision. This is called a mandatory reconsideration. If you must apply for a mandatory reconsideration, the officer reconsidering the decision must then consider whether to revise the decision.

You do *not* have to apply for a mandatory reconsideration if:

- the benefit is HB; *or*
- your appeal concerns an employment and support allowance (ESA) decision that you do not have limited capability for work and you would qualify for payment of ESA pending an appeal against that decision (see p925). You can appeal direct to the First-tier Tribunal without having to apply for a mandatory reconsideration first.[1]

For the need for a mandatory reconsideration to apply, the decision you want to appeal against must include a written statement that you must apply for a mandatory reconsideration. If the DWP does not do that, you can appeal direct to the First-tier Tribunal without having to apply for a mandatory reconsideration.[2]

### When you must apply for a mandatory reconsideration

You must usually apply for a mandatory reconsideration before you can appeal. You can only appeal if:

- for child benefit and guardian's allowance, you have applied for a mandatory reconsideration and HMRC has decided not to revise the decision. If it revises the decision, you can appeal against the original decision, as revised;[3] *or*
- for other benefits (but not HB, or in some cases ESA – see above), you have been notified in writing that you must request a mandatory reconsideration, you have done so, and the DWP has considered your application. This includes if it refuses your application because it was late.[4] You have only been notified properly if the decision notice (see p1124) includes a statement that you only have a right of appeal if the DWP has considered an application for a revision of the decision. The notice must also inform you of the time limit for applying for an 'any grounds' revision (see p1132) and that you can ask for a statement of reasons for the decision (if one has not been included) within one month of being notified of the decision (see p1125).

It is the First-tier Tribunal that decides whether you have a right of appeal, *not* the DWP or HMRC. However, the easiest way to prove to the tribunal that you have a right of appeal is to apply for a mandatory reconsideration and send the tribunal the 'mandatory reconsideration notice' that you are given by the DWP or HMRC (see p1171).

## Mandatory reconsideration time limits

There is a basic time limit of one month for applying. However, in practice, late applications made within 13 months are usually admitted. When you apply for a mandatory reconsideration, you are applying for a revision. There are two types of revision: 'any grounds' revisions (p1131) and 'any time' revisions (see p1135). The following applies.

- It is always best to apply for an **'any grounds'** revision, as you do not have to show grounds for the revision, and this type of revision is what in practice the DWP usually regards as a mandatory reconsideration. There is a basic time limit of one month, starting with the date you were sent or given the decision (see p1132). If you can show there are special circumstances, you can make a late application outside this basic time limit, so long as you do so within the absolute time limit (usually 13 months – see p1133).
- If you have missed the time limits for an 'any grounds' revision, you need to apply for an **'any time'** revision. There is no time limit, but you must show that there are grounds for the revision (see p1135) – eg, that there has been an 'official error'. In the law, these revisions still count as a mandatory reconsideration – but the DWP may refuse to carry out one. In that case, you only have the right of appeal if your application for a mandatory reconsideration argued, or at least implied, that the decision you asked to be looked at again was wrong on the basis of an 'official error' (see p1135), and (at the time this *Handbook* was written, although this may change) it is decided that there was such an error.[5] Make it clear what official error you think occurred – note that merely thinking the decision was wrong is not enough. Even this right will only arise if the decision was one to which the mandatory reconsideration rules applied.

### If you miss the basic time limit

If you missed the one-month basic time limit for an 'any grounds' revision, but you have applied within the absolute time limit (usually, within 13 months – see p1132), then, even if the decision maker refuses your application, you have a right to appeal.[6] The DWP says that if your late application is refused, the decision maker should make a decision refusing to revise and issue you with a mandatory reconsideration notice.[7]

**Note:**[8]

- if your application for an 'any grounds' revision was made outside the absolute time limit, and the decision maker refuses to consider your application, they should go on to consider whether there are grounds for an 'any time' revision;

- if the decision maker decides there are no grounds for either an 'any grounds' or an 'any time' revision, they should consider whether to do a supersession.

If the decision maker decides not to carry out an 'any grounds' revision, and also that there are no grounds for an 'any time' revision, you only have a right of appeal if your application argued, or at least implied, that the decision you wanted looking at again was wrong based on an 'official error' (see p1135).[9] Even this right will only arise if the decision was one to which the mandatory reconsideration rules applied. Note that merely thinking that the decision was wrong will not be enough. If you think there was an official error, ask that the First-tier Tribunal decide on that and so whether you have a right of appeal.

An application for an 'any time' revision can count as an application for a mandatory reconsideration even if you apply outside the basic time limit for an 'any grounds' revision.[10] If you applied within the absolute time limit for an 'any grounds' revision, but the DWP says your application does not count, appeal to the First-tier Tribunal and point out that the DWP has considered whether to revise the decision, so you have satisfied the mandatory reconsideration rules and have a right to appeal.

## Applying for a mandatory reconsideration

8

It is best to apply for a mandatory reconsideration in writing (on a form or by letter), although you can apply by telephone. If you are applying for a mandatory reconsideration of a universal credit (UC) decision, the DWP prefers you to apply using your online journal (see the DWP information at gov.uk/mandatory-reconsideration/how-to-ask-for-mandatory-reconsideration). It is best to make it clear that you are applying for a mandatory reconsideration, although there is nothing to say you must use those words, and you could argue that it is enough that you made it clear that you wanted the decision to be looked at again.

*Forms*

For child benefit and guardian's allowance, use Form CH24A available at gov.uk/government/publications/child-benefit-and-guardians-allowance-appeal-form.

For other benefits, use Form CRMR1 available at gov.uk/government/publications/challenge-a-decision-made-by-the-department-for-work-and-pensions-dwp.

Explain why you disagree with the decision and provide any additional information and evidence that supports your case. It is important to follow up your application to ensure that it has been received.

**Note:**

- If you sent your appeal to the First-tier Tribunal when you should have applied for a mandatory reconsideration first, the tribunal may say your appeal is not

valid and return it to you to resolve the issue. If you do not do so, it can 'strike out' your appeal (see p1190).
- If you sent your appeal to the DWP or direct to the tribunal before first applying for a mandatory reconsideration, the DWP can (but does not have to) treat your appeal as an application for a mandatory reconsideration.[11] If the DWP does not do this, apply for a mandatory reconsideration as soon as possible, explaining why your application is late if relevant. Although there is no equivalent rule for child benefit and guardian's allowance, there is nothing to prevent HMRC from treating an appeal as an application for a mandatory reconsideration.

## The mandatory reconsideration notice

The DWP or HMRC gives or sends you a letter telling you about the result of your application. This is called a mandatory reconsideration notice. This notice is proof that the DWP or HMRC has accepted and considered your application. If you are still unhappy with the decision, you can then appeal to the First-tier Tribunal. The rules say that you must send a copy of the notice to the tribunal when you appeal.[12] Although the tribunal can waive this requirement, and in practice will always do so if you have appealed online via gov.uk/appeal-benefit-decision/submit-appeal, it does not have to and it may instead 'strike out' your appeal (see p1190).[13]

***What if you do not have a mandatory reconsideration notice?***

If you have applied for a mandatory reconsideration, but are not appealing online and have not been sent or given a mandatory reconsideration notice, try to provide the tribunal with as much evidence as you can that you did apply, and that the DWP or HMRC has considered your application. Provide a copy of your application along with proof you posted or delivered it, if possible. For UC, if you applied using your journal, take and provide a screenshot. Also provide copies of any correspondence, notes of telephone calls or personal contact with the DWP or HMRC since you made the application.

## Who can appeal

If you are **appealing about a benefit other than HB**, you have a right to appeal if you are:[14]
- a claimant (if the benefit is UC and you are a couple, either of you can appeal); *or*
- an appointee claiming on someone's behalf (see p1005); *or*
- claiming attendance allowance, disability living allowance or PIP on behalf of someone who is terminally ill, even if this is without their knowledge; *or*
- a person from whom an overpayment of a benefit or one of the regulated social fund payments in Chapter 33 (other than a budgeting loan) or a duplication of

payment of UC, pension credit or income-related ESA can be recovered (see Chapter 47). This is the case even if you were not the person who claimed the benefit that was overpaid;[15] *or*
- someone from whom a short-term or budgeting advance, or hardship payments, can be recovered; *or*
- the partner of a claimant, if the decision concerns whether you failed to take part in a work-focused interview without good cause;[16] *or*
- a person appointed by the DWP or HMRC to make a benefit claim for, or proceed with a claim made by, someone who has died.

If you are **appealing about HB**, you have a right to appeal if you are a person affected by the decision – ie, your rights, duties or obligations are affected by the decision, and you are:[17]
- a claimant; *or*
- someone acting for a claimant who cannot act for themself – eg, an appointee (see p214); *or*
- someone from whom the local authority decides an overpayment can be recovered (including a landlord or agent);[18] *or*
- a landlord or agent, if the decision concerns whether or not to make a direct payment of HB to you; *or*
- a person appointed by the local authority to proceed with the appeal.

8

## Decisions you can appeal

You can appeal to the First-tier Tribunal against most decisions taken by officers of the DWP, a local authority or HMRC (known as decision makers – see p1118).[19] The decision may have been an original decision or one made after a supersession – eg, following a change in your circumstances. Unless the benefit is HB, you must usually apply for a mandatory reconsideration of the decision before you can appeal (see p1168).

### *Has the decision maker refused to make a decision?*

If a decision maker refuses to make a decision on your claim, this effectively prevents you having the right to appeal. You should remind the decision maker that they *must* make a decision on every valid claim.[20] Even if the decision maker does not accept that a claim made on the correct claim form is valid, you should be given a decision saying so. You can then appeal and ask the tribunal to decide whether your claim is valid.[21] If a decision maker refuses to consider your application for a supersession, see p1156.

**Note:** a decision maker can sometimes postpone making a decision if there is a test case pending (see p1159).

You must be given a written notice (in a letter or online) of any decision that you can appeal against.[22] This written notice:

- must give you information about your right to appeal and your right to request a written statement of reasons for the decision (if this has not already been included); *and*
- normally includes information about applying for a mandatory reconsideration (except for HB, child benefit and guardian's allowance).

*Examples of decisions you can appeal*

Whether you are entitled to a benefit.

Whether an overpayment is recoverable (unless you come under the UC system and it is an overpayment of UC, new-style jobseeker's allowance or new-style ESA), and the amount of an overpayment.

Whether to impose a civil penalty (see p1101).[23]

Whether your claim has been validly made or can be backdated.

Whether benefit is payable under the overlapping benefit rules.[24]

Whether you should be given a sanction, and whether you had good cause or a good reason for your actions or your failure to take action.

Whether you have limited capability for work or limited capability for work-related activity.

Whether you satisfy the habitual residence test.

Whether you satisfy the disability conditions for benefit.

Whether you can be paid hardship payments.

Whether your award of contributory ESA should end because you have been paid it for 365 days (see p564).[25]

Whether you are available for, or actively seeking, work.

Whether a jobseeker's agreement is reasonable or you had a good reason for refusing or failing to carry out a jobseeker's direction.

8

## Decisions you cannot appeal

You cannot appeal against some decisions.[26] You *can* ask for an 'any time' revision or a supersession of a decision against which you do not have a right of appeal, whatever your reason for thinking it is wrong.[27] However, if the decision maker refuses to revise or supersede such a decision, your only legal remedy is to apply for judicial review (see Chapter 59).

*Examples of decisions you cannot appeal*

Who should be the claimant when a couple cannot decide.

Who should be entitled to child benefit when two people whose claims have equal priority cannot agree.

Whether a claim for one benefit can be treated as a claim for (or in addition to) another benefit.

Whether to demand recovery of an overpayment, and the amount of weekly deductions.

Whether to suspend payment of benefit.

Whether to appoint a person as an appointee (see p1005).
Whether to make a short-term advance, a budgeting advance or a payment on account.
How much benefits are increased (uprated) every year.[28]

## 2. How to appeal

You must appeal in writing. The usual way to do this is online, or by using the official appeal form. Your written appeal is known as a **'notice of appeal'**.

***Submitting your appeal online***

This is often the most straightforward way to submit your appeal. You can submit appeals about benefits (other than housing benefit (HB), child benefit or guardian's allowance) online at gov.uk/appeal-benefit-decision.

If you do not submit your appeal online, if possible you should use the appropriate appeal form. If you do not appeal online or use the appropriate form, your appeal must still be accepted as valid if it is in writing and includes all the information required (see p1178).

***Appeal forms***

**For HB**, use the form approved by your local authority.[29]

**For other benefits** (except child benefit and guardian's allowance), use the appeal form SSCS1.

**For child benefit and guardian's allowance**, use the appeal form SSCS5.

All the forms are available from gov.uk.

If you want the First-tier Tribunal to deal with your appeal quickly (to do what is known as expedite your appeal), make this clear when you appeal, explaining why your case is urgent. For HB, because you have to send your notice of appeal to the local authority, you could write to the tribunal, asking it to intervene. For further information, see the article 'Expediting UC appeals' on p8 of CPAG's *Welfare Rights Bulletin* 278.

### Where to send your written appeal

If you are not submitting your appeal online, you must send it:

- for HB, to the local authority office that sent you the decision.[30] It passes your appeal to the First-tier Tribunal;

- for other benefits, direct to the First-tier Tribunal at the appeal centre, sometimes referred to as 'direct lodgement'. The addresses to use are on the appeal forms. The appeal centre checks whether your appeal is valid and, if so, passes it to the appropriate regional office.[31]

## Appeal time limits

There is a basic time limit of one month. When the one month starts from depends on whether or not you had to apply for a mandatory reconsideration before you could appeal. If you miss the basic time limit, you may be able to make a late appeal (see p1176), but there is an absolute time limit within which you must appeal (see p1178).

### If you had to apply for a mandatory reconsideration

If you had to apply for a mandatory reconsideration before you could appeal (see p1168), the basic one-month time limit starts from the date you are sent the mandatory reconsideration notice. Your appeal, including all the information described on p1178, must arrive at the First-tier Tribunal appeal centre within one month after you are sent the mandatory reconsideration notice.[32]

*Month*

**'Month'** means a complete calendar month running from the day after the day you have been sent or given a decision.[33] For example, a decision sent on 23 July has an appeal time limit that expires at the end of 23 August.

When calculating time, if something has to be done by a certain day, it must be done by 5pm that day. If a time limit ends on a day other than a working day, you have until the end of the next working day to meet the time limit.[34] A 'working day' is any day other than Saturday, Sunday, Christmas Day, Good Friday or a bank holiday.

### If you did not have to apply for a mandatory reconsideration

If you did not have to apply for a mandatory reconsideration (this generally only applies to HB and in some ESA cases – see p1168), the basic one-month time limit usually starts from the date the decision was sent to you. Your appeal, including all the information described on p1178, must arrive at the relevant office (for HB, this is the office that sent you the decision and for other benefits, this is the First-tier Tribunal appeal centre) by the latest of the following:[35]

- one month after the date the written decision was sent to you; *or*
- if you ask for a written statement of reasons within one month of being given notice of the decision (if one has not already been given to you – see p1125), 14 days after the latest of:
  - the end of that month – ie, if the written statement of reasons is provided within the one-month period, you get one month plus 14 days to appeal; *or*

– the date the written statement of reasons is provided.

If you applied for a revision before you appealed and the decision maker revises the decision, but you still want to appeal because you did not get all you want, the one-month time limit runs from the date you are sent the new decision.[36] If you applied for an 'any grounds' revision and the decision maker refused to do a revision, you must appeal no later than one month after the date you are sent notice of the refusal.[37]

If the decision maker refuses to do an 'any time' revision and says you cannot appeal, you should appeal against the original decision within the time limit (if this has not already passed). If this is not possible, get advice.

## Late appeals

If you miss the basic time limit for appealing, you may still be able to appeal late, as long as, in most cases, your appeal is within the absolute 13-month time limit (see p1178). Your appeal is still treated as made in time if neither the decision maker nor any other person with a right of appeal against the decision (or anyone who has been added as a party to the appeal – eg, the other parent if you are disputing who counts as responsible for your child) does not object.[38] Usually, the DWP or HMRC does not object.

You must include the reasons why your appeal is late.[39] The tribunal can extend the time limit for appealing if this will enable it to deal with your appeal fairly and justly, so give details of any special circumstances that mean this would be the case. See p1177 for some ideas about what may be relevant.

8

**Note:**

- The First-tier Tribunal decides whether to admit your late appeal, *not* the DWP, the local authority or HMRC.
- If you miss the time limit and the First-tier Tribunal does not admit your late appeal, you can appeal to the Upper Tribunal against the First-tier Tribunal's decision.[40]

### Housing benefit appeals

A decision maker can admit your late HB appeal (ie, treat your appeal as made in time) if it is in the 'interests of justice'.[41] For these purposes, it is *not* in the interests of justice unless it was not practicable for you to appeal in time because:[42]

- your partner or a dependant died or had a serious illness; *or*
- the person who appealed died or had a serious illness; *or*
- you are not resident in the UK; *or*
- normal postal services were disrupted; *or*
- there are other special circumstances that are 'wholly exceptional'. The longer you have delayed appealing, the more compelling these must be.

When deciding whether it is in the interests of justice, account cannot be taken of the fact that:[43]

- a court or the Upper Tribunal has interpreted the law in a different way than was previously understood and applied; *or*
- you (or anyone acting for you) misunderstood or were unaware of the relevant law, including the time limits for appealing.

If the decision maker does not admit your late appeal, they must refer it to the First-tier Tribunal immediately.[44] The tribunal then decides whether to admit your late appeal.

**Why your late appeal should be admitted**

Your reasons and circumstances need to show it would be fair and just to admit your late appeal. There is no list of what reasons or circumstances count, but the following are all relevant.

- **The reasons for your delay in appealing.** Explain these as clearly and as fully as possible. Do not worry if some or all of the delay is your fault. Any explanation is better than none at all. Even if you knew the time limit, but simply ignored it, it may be possible to say something favourable. Say if things have been difficult at home or you were confused by the rules or just assumed that the DWP (or the local authority or HMRC) was the expert and had got it right until, for example, you were advised otherwise or read an article in a newspaper. Reasons for the delay could include the fact that:
  - you did not receive the decision;
  - you made a reasonable mistake in calculating the time limit;
  - you posted your appeal in time, but it went astray in the post;
  - you were ill;
  - a mistake was made by your advisers;
  - you were given wrong advice or otherwise misled by the DWP (or the local authority or HMRC) – eg, you were discouraged from appealing by a decision maker who advised you incorrectly that an appeal would be doomed to fail. If you lose money because you are refused a late appeal, consider claiming compensation (see p1261).
- **The length of the delay**. The usual approach is that time limits have to be kept to, and there has to be good reason for not doing so. Short delays are likely to be easier to justify than long delays, but a good reason is still needed.
- **The merits of your appeal**. The more likely your appeal is to succeed, the greater the injustice in refusing to admit your late appeal. A strong case is particularly useful if there has been a very long delay and a time limit is usually extended if there has been a 'clear error', which would have long-term continuing effects unless corrected.[45]
- **The amount of money at stake**. Even if there has been no clear error, a late appeal may be more likely to be admitted if there is a lot of money at stake, or the matter is otherwise very important – eg, that you might be made homeless without your universal credit (UC) housing element.[46]

- **A decision in a test case.** A decision in a test case, establishing that an earlier decision was incorrect, can be a reason to admit a late appeal, in some circumstances.[47]

#### The absolute time limit for appealing

You cannot appeal if it is more than 12 months after the date your time limit for appealing expired.[48] **Note:** in very exceptional circumstances (eg, if you did not receive notice of the decision you want to appeal), you can argue that the tribunal should waive the absolute time limit and allow you to appeal if this is absolutely necessary to protect your right to a fair hearing under human rights law.[49] However, this is unlikely to apply unless you have done all that you could to appeal in time.

For HB, if the decision maker thinks your appeal has been made outside the absolute time limit, they must refer it to the First-tier Tribunal immediately.[50] The tribunal decides whether to admit your appeal, not the local authority.

If the First-tier Tribunal decides that you cannot appeal because your appeal was made outside the absolute time limit, but you think it was made within that time, or it refuses to waive the absolute time limit, you can appeal to the Upper Tribunal against the decision.[51]

8

## Making sure your appeal is valid

The First-tier Tribunal decides whether your appeal is valid, *not* the DWP, the local authority or HMRC. For your appeal to be valid:

- you must provide all the information required. **Note:** even if you do not appeal online or use the correct appeal form, your appeal can still be valid; *and*
- if you submit your appeal other than online, you must sign your notice of appeal.[52] However, if you have provided written notice that you have appointed a representative, they can sign it on your behalf. If your solicitor signs on your behalf, it should be accepted that they are authorised to do so;[53] *and*
- your notice of appeal must be in English or Welsh.

### The information you must provide

You must provide:[54]

- your name and address and that of your representative, if you have one; *and*
- the address where documents can be sent or delivered – eg, to you or your representative; *and*
- if you are appealing about HB, details about the decision with which you disagree, sufficient for it to be identified; *and*
- if you are appealing about benefits other than HB:
  - the name and address of any other person who has a right of appeal against the decision; *and*

- where you must provide one, a copy of the mandatory reconsideration notice (see p1171) or, if you did not have to apply for a mandatory reconsideration before the appeal, a copy of the decision you want to appeal. **Note:** if you are appealing online, you are not asked to provide a copy of the mandatory reconsideration notice. Also, if you were not given written notice that you had to apply for a mandatory reconsideration before you could appeal, state this clearly on the appeal form and enclose a copy of the decision notice as proof; *and*
- any statement of reasons for the decision that you have; *and*
- any documents in support of your appeal that you have not already supplied to the decision maker; *and*

- a summary of your reasons for believing the decision is wrong (your grounds for appeal). Do not simply say you think the decision is wrong, but explain why.

***Examples of grounds for appeal***

'The decision says I have been overpaid housing benefit because I failed to disclose that my wife had started working part time, but I wrote to the local authority as soon as she started work and told it what her take home pay would be.'

'The DWP says my universal credit should be sanctioned because I failed to turn up for an interview. But I had good cause for not turning up as my child was ill, and I was late turning up rather than failed to turn up at all.'

'The decision says that I failed the work capability assessment, but I think I should have been given more points for mental health problems with coping with change and interacting with other people.'

'You say I cannot get personal independence payment daily living component. This decision is wrong because you have not taken into account the amount of help I need because of my incontinence problems.'

If you had to apply for a mandatory reconsideration before you could appeal and the DWP or HMRC only provided a mandatory reconsideration notice after a long delay, this may put you at a disadvantage – eg, if it is now difficult to obtain evidence to support your appeal. Point out if you think this affects your chances of winning your appeal. The tribunal should then consider whether it can do something to remedy the situation.[55]

#### If you are appealing about housing benefit and do not provide sufficient information

If you are appealing about HB and you do not include the information required, the local authority can ask you to provide the information you left out.[56] If you used an appeal form, this is returned to you to complete. Be sure to provide the information within the time allowed, otherwise you may not have made your appeal within the time limit.

Your time limit for appealing (see p1175) is extended by:[57]

- 14 days from the date your appeal form is returned to you for completion, if the completed form is received back within 14 days; *or*
- 14 days from the date you are asked for further information, if you provide this within 14 days of the request; *or*
- the length of time you are given to complete the form or provide information, if this is longer than 14 days.

If you do not complete the form properly or provide the information required in time, your appeal, along with any relevant documents and evidence, is forwarded to the First-tier Tribunal by the local authority. It then considers whether your appeal is valid and can go ahead.[58] **Note:** if you complete and return the form or provide the information:

- after the expiry of the time limit, but before your appeal is forwarded to the tribunal, the local authority should accept that your appeal is valid and then consider whether to object to it being treated as made in time (see p1176);[59]
- before the tribunal makes a decision, any further details you provide must be taken into account.[60]

8

If your appeal is not accepted as valid, try to make a fresh appeal, giving reasons why your appeal is late if relevant.

**If you are appealing about other benefits and do not provide sufficient information**

If you are appealing about benefits other than HB and you do not include the information or documents required (including, if required, the mandatory reconsideration notice), the tribunal clerk (or legal officer or registrar) (see p1182) can waive the requirement, or require you to provide what you left out.[61] You can ask the tribunal to reconsider that requirement. You must apply in writing within 14 days after the date you are sent notice of the decision.[62] The tribunal can give you longer, but there is no guarantee of this, so keep within the time limit wherever possible. If your appeal is struck out, it can be reinstated by the clerk – eg, if you later provide the mandatory reconsideration notice (see p1191).

If you had to (and did) apply for a mandatory reconsideration before you could appeal, but you have not been sent or given a mandatory reconsideration notice, see p1171.

## Representatives

You can have a representative to help you with your appeal and to be with you at the hearing.[63] They can explain the procedures, present your case and ensure the tribunal is aware of all the relevant issues and the law. Bear in mind that, even if you have a representative, you will probably have to answer questions from the tribunal. Your representative is not normally allowed to answer for you.

You must provide the tribunal with written notice of your representative's name and address or they can do this on your behalf – eg, on the appeal form or in a letter.[64]

This does not apply for HB if you provide this notice to the local authority before your appeal is forwarded to the tribunal. If your representative is providing the notice, unless they are a solicitor, they should also provide an authorisation signed by you.

Once you have given notice that you have a representative, they are presumed to be acting for you unless you (or your representative) give notice in writing that this is no longer the case.[65] Your representative must be sent any documents required to be sent to you. These then do not have to be sent to you.[66] However, do not presume this always happens. If you receive documents, check that your representative has also received them.

Even if you have not previously notified the tribunal that you have a representative, someone can attend the hearing with you (eg, a friend or relative) and act as one, or assist you at the hearing, if the tribunal agrees.[67]

## Meeting the costs

You do not have to pay a fee to appeal to the First-tier Tribunal, and you do not have to pay the DWP's, local authority's or HMRC's costs.[68]

Free legal help with your appeal is available in limited cases.

- In England and Wales, you cannot get free legal help to cover preparatory work, such as obtaining medical reports and writing submissions, or for representation at a hearing, except in exceptional cases. However, if you have a solicitor acting for you in an industrial injury or personal injury claim, they may have medical and other reports and evidence which you can use for your benefit appeal.
- In Scotland, you may be able to get free legal help for preparatory work.

If you are not eligible for free advice and assistance, or you want to be represented by a lawyer at a hearing, you are likely to have to pay. However, you may be able to get free help from a law centre, advice centre or Citizens Advice. There are a number of agencies that can advise you and help you prepare your case, and in some cases represent you (see Appendix 1). Remember that many non-lawyer advisers know more about social security law than do lawyers, and their advice and representation is usually free.

# 3. After you submit your appeal

For appeals about benefits other than housing benefit (HB), after you have submitted your appeal the First-tier Tribunal sends a copy to the DWP or HMRC. In all cases, the DWP, the local authority or HMRC prepares its case – known as the 'decision maker's response' (see p1183). For HB appeals, after you have submitted your appeal to the local authority, you are sent an enquiry form (see p1183) to complete and return to the tribunal. **Note:** you may find that your appeal is not dealt with if there is a test case or a lead case pending that deals with the same issues (see p1193).

***How can you track the progress of your appeal?***

If you appeal online, you are asked if you want to create an online account to manage your appeal, where you can track the progress of your appeal and also upload evidence and update your details. If you do not appeal online, you can receive email and text message updates and manage your appeal online. To ensure this happens, telephone the First-tier Tribunal enquiry line on 0300 123 1142 (England and Wales) or 0300 790 6234 (Scotland).

## Who deals with your appeal

Any of the following may be involved with your appeal at some time.

- **A judge**. Judges must have legal expertise and are usually legally qualified. As well as hearing and making the decision on your appeal, they carry out various other functions – eg, deciding whether you have made your appeal in time, and whether to extend a time limit or to issue directions.
- **A member of the First-tier Tribunal**. This could be a doctor, a person with experience of disability or an accountant. Members hear and make the decision on your appeal with the judge.
- **An expert**. If your appeal involves issues that require specialist expertise, an expert (the tribunal may call them an 'assessor') may be used.[69] If an expert provides a written report, it should be sent to every party involved in the appeal. The expert cannot take part in making the decision on your appeal.
- **A registrar** (who must be legally qualified) or **a 'legal officer' of the tribunal** (who must be appropriately trained). They can carry out any of the functions of the First-tier Tribunal, under the supervision of a judge, and can make all the decisions a judge can make other than the final decision on your appeal.[70]
- **A clerk to the First-tier Tribunal**. Clerks can carry out specified functions, including waiving a requirement for you to provide information with your notice of appeal, requiring you to provide information and in some cases 'striking out' your appeal (see p1190). Clerks attend appeal hearings in an administrative capacity – eg, to pay expenses. A clerk cannot take part in

making the decision on your appeal and should not express any views on the case.[71]

To see who hears and makes the decision on your appeal, see p1198.

**Note:** you must be given 14 days to ask a judge to reconsider a registrar's, a tribunal caseworker's or a clerk's decision.[72] You must apply in writing within 14 days after the date you are sent notice of the decision.[73] The tribunal can give you longer, but there is no guarantee of this, so keep within the time limit wherever possible.

## The enquiry form

In some cases, the First-tier Tribunal sends you a questionnaire (called an enquiry form). For appeals about:

- a benefit other than HB, you are unlikely to be sent an enquiry form if you have already provided this information online or on your appeal form. However, if you appealed in another way (eg, by letter), you *are* sent an enquiry form;
- HB, you are sent an enquiry form when the First-tier Tribunal receives your appeal papers from the local authority.

The enquiry form asks you whether you want a hearing and, if so, when you and your representative (if you have one) are available to attend. If you want a hearing, you must state this. It is always best to opt for a hearing. You should always consult your representative before completing and returning the enquiry form.

Return the enquiry form within 14 days. If you do not return it in time, then the tribunal may issue a direction (see p1188) requiring you to do so and giving you more time. A tribunal should almost certainly never strike out an appeal for failure to return the enquiry form.[74]

## The decision maker's response

The DWP, the local authority or HMRC must prepare a bundle of papers relevant to your appeal (called the 'decision maker's response') and forward this to the First-tier Tribunal:

- for HB, as soon as reasonably practicable. An ombudsman has said the local authority should forward an appeal to the First-tier Tribunal within 28 days;[75]
- for other benefits, within 28 days of receiving the notice of appeal.[76]

Both you and your representative (if you have one) are normally sent a copy.[77] However, check that your representative has also received it as this does not always happen.[78]

If the decision maker opposes your appeal, the response must include any reasons for this that are not in the documents the First-tier Tribunal has already been given.[79] It must refer to the law on which the decision was based and explain the legal basis on which the decision was made in a way that enables the tribunal to ensure that you are able to participate fully in the appeal.[80] The decision maker must also provide:[81]

- a copy of any written record of, and statement of reasons for, the decision with which you disagree, if you did not send these with your appeal form; *and*
- copies of all documents they have that may be relevant, unless the tribunal directs otherwise. The decision maker should treat as relevant anything that the tribunal may rely on to make findings about the facts, irrespective of what they consider to be relevant.[82] If the information in the documents is not in a form that can be understood by you and the tribunal (eg, screenshots that use DWP codes), the decision maker should provide an explanation or translation.[83] If the tribunal thinks that the decision maker may have other relevant evidence, it can direct them to produce this. If your appeal involves a medical issue or one about your disability:
  - any recent medical reports there have been in connection with your claim are usually included; *and*
  - if the decision you are appealing followed from a report by a healthcare professional (eg, your benefit was reduced or stopped following such a report), that report should be included; *and*
- for HB appeals only, a copy of your appeal form (or letter) along with all the documents you provided with it and, unless already provided to the First-tier Tribunal, the name and address of your representative.



Read through the whole response carefully to find out the case being made against you. Be sure to take it with you to the hearing.

***Has your appeal been held up by the decision maker?***

You cannot usually bypass the normal procedures. However, note the following.

1. Although you cannot usually expect the First-tier Tribunal to deal with your appeal before the decision maker has had a chance to prepare their response, it is free to allow matters to be handled differently if circumstances require it.[84]
2. Ask the tribunal to require the decision maker to provide documents, information and evidence by a specified date (make a direction – see p1188), or make a direction setting a hearing date.[85]
3. If you are appealing about HB and the decision maker does not forward your appeal within a reasonable period, forward a copy of it to the First-tier Tribunal yourself and proceed as above.

**Note:** in some circumstances, the tribunal can bar the decision maker from taking any further part in the appeal (see p1192), in which case your appeal could be decided without a response being made. However, it can lift the bar if the response is eventually received.

## Providing additional information

You (or your representative) are asked if you wish to make further statements or submit further evidence as a 'reply' to the decision maker's response. Make sure that everything you want to say in support of your appeal has been put in writing and that there are no other documents and evidence that you would like the tribunal to see. See p1204 for help with preparing your appeal. **Note:**

- It is always good to provide additional evidence or information to support your appeal – eg, independent medical evidence or supporting statements from witnesses. A representative may include these as part of a written submission to the tribunal, setting out your case, although you can send a written submission yourself.
- You (or your representative) must provide your reply within one month after the date you are sent the decision maker's response.[86] The tribunal can give you longer (or shorter) than one month.[87] There is no guarantee that you will be given longer, so keep within the time limit wherever possible.

***Do you intend to send a reply to the decision maker's response?***

Tribunal staff often want to fix a hearing date, or arrange for a decision to be made based on the papers only, as soon as they can after the decision maker's response has been received. As a result, they sometimes overlook the need to allow you one month to reply.[88] To avoid this happening, inform the tribunal office that you intend to send a reply as soon as possible after you receive the response.

8

Your reply and any further documents and submissions that are sent to the tribunal by you (or the DWP, local authority or HMRC) are added to the decision maker's response to form what is known as the 'appeal bundle'.

At this stage, your appeal is likely to be considered ready for a hearing or for the tribunal to make its decision based on the papers only (see p1194). The tribunal may issue directions (see p1188) requiring you (or the DWP, the local authority or HMRC) to provide a submission, further information or documents within a specific period. You (or the decision maker) can also ask it to issue directions. If you are given a direction, it is important that you comply with it. If you do not, your appeal can be struck out (see p1190).

## When your appeal can lapse

After you appeal, a decision maker may look at the decision you are appealing about again and revise it – eg, on the basis of any facts, information or evidence you provided with your appeal form. This is the case even if the decision maker had already considered a revision when you applied for a mandatory reconsideration. If the decision maker revises the decision, your appeal could lapse, even if you do not get everything you want, and you have to appeal again.[89]

Your appeal lapses if the revised decision is more advantageous to you than the original decision – eg, the decision:[90]

- awards you benefit at a higher rate or for a longer period; *or*
- lifts a refusal or disqualification of benefit or a sanction (in whole or in part); *or*
- reverses a decision to pay benefit to a third party (see p1033); *or*
- means you gain financially from the revised decision; *or*
- says an overpayment of benefit is not recoverable or that less should be recovered.

**Note:** in some cases, especially if your appeal is about personal independence payment, you may be contacted by a decision maker to see if you would still want to appeal if the decision were revised to your advantage. You should be told that you will not lose your right of appeal, whether or not you agree to the decision being revised. If you do agree to the revision, your appeal lapses but you can renew it (see below). If you do not agree to the decision, the First-tier Tribunal should regard the revision the DWP wished to make as a starting point when making its own decision.[91] You should be given enough time to decide and should *not* be put under pressure to agree to the decision being revised. If you have a representative, they should be contacted before you.

If a decision is:

- revised and is:
  - to your advantage, your appeal lapses, but you can make a fresh appeal against the revised decision – eg, if you did not get all you wanted. You do not have to apply for another mandatory reconsideration before you can appeal in this situation.[92] Your time limit for appealing (see p1175) runs from the date the revised decision is sent to you;[93]
  - not to your advantage, your appeal must go ahead, but against the decision in its revised form.[94] You have one month from the date the decision is sent or given to you to make further representations.[95] At the end of that period (or earlier if you agree in writing), your appeal proceeds unless the decision is revised again and is now more advantageous to you;[96]
- not revised, your appeal must go ahead against the original decision. If the decision maker contacted you to see if you would still want to appeal were the decision revised to your advantage, you can argue that the tribunal should take the decision maker's proposal as the starting point for its considerations.[97]

**Note:** if the First-tier Tribunal decides that your appeal has lapsed, you can appeal against that decision to the Upper Tribunal. However, it is better, if you can, to make a fresh appeal against the original decision.

## What the First-tier Tribunal can do

The First-tier Tribunal must follow procedural rules when dealing with your appeal. The 'overriding objective' of those rules is that the tribunal should proceed in a way that enables the case to be dealt with fairly and justly.[98] This includes avoiding delay (provided the issues can be considered properly), dealing with the case proportionately, avoiding unnecessary formality, seeking flexibility in the proceedings and ensuring that all the parties can participate fully. You, the DWP, the local authority and HMRC must help the First-tier Tribunal further this objective and co-operate with it. This involves ensuring, as far as possible, that your case is ready by the time of the hearing.[99]

The First-tier Tribunal can:[100]

- extend or shorten any time limits (see below); *and*
- issue directions (see p1188); *and*
- postpone or adjourn your appeal hearing (see p1189); *and*
- 'strike out' your appeal (see p1190); *and*
- bar the decision maker or another party to the appeal from taking part (see p1192); *and*
- summon witnesses to attend a hearing, answer questions or produce documents. If someone fails to comply, the First-tier Tribunal can refer the matter to the Upper Tribunal. The Upper Tribunal can punish the person for contempt of court.[101] **Note:** you cannot be required to give evidence or produce any document that you could not be compelled to give by a court;[102] *and*
- suspend the effect of its decision while any application for permission to appeal, or any appeal against or review of that decision, is outstanding.[103]

8

**Note:** the rules for what the Upper Tribunal can do are generally the same as for the First-tier Tribunal. The endnotes in this section therefore also refer to Upper Tribunal rules if relevant.

## Extending or shortening time limits

Time limits can be extended or shortened.[104] The tribunal can shorten your and the DWP's, the local authority's or HMRC's time limits if it thinks that delay should be avoided, provided the issues can be considered properly.[105] You may want to ask for the DWP's, the local authority's or HMRC's time limits (eg, to comply with a direction) to be shortened if your situation is urgent or your circumstances are exceptional.

If you know that you are going to miss (or have missed) a time limit, you should ask for it to be extended by the tribunal. Always ask in writing for a time limit to be extended and apply in advance if you can. Give the reasons why you are going to be (or are) late in meeting the time limit, as well as any special circumstances which mean your time limit should be extended so that your appeal can be dealt with fairly and justly. **Note:**

- The tribunal does not have to extend any particular time limit, so there is no guarantee that you will be given more time. Keep within the time limits wherever possible.

- For the rules about extending your time limit for appealing, so as to admit a late appeal, see p1176. For some ideas about what may count as a good reason for a late appeal, see p1177.

## Directions

In the course of your appeal, the First-tier Tribunal can issue directions. These are instructions to a party to the appeal (eg, the DWP, or you) to do something – eg, to provide a submission, further information or documents, or to attend a hearing.[106] The tribunal can decide to issue directions on its own initiative. You or the decision maker can also apply to the tribunal to ask it to issue directions. This can be useful, for example, if you are having trouble getting documents or information from the decision maker. You can apply in writing, or orally at the hearing.[107] In either case, you must give reasons for your application. For tips about making an effective application for a direction, see 'Going in the right direction', CPAG's *Welfare Rights Bulletin* 302 (October 2024).

The tribunal must send you and the decision maker (and anyone affected by the direction) notice of any direction it issues, unless it thinks there is a good reason not to do so.[108] You can challenge a direction (eg, if you think insufficient time has been given to comply with it) by applying for another direction to amend, suspend or 'set aside' the first one.[109]

8

If you are given a direction, it is important that you comply with it. If you fail to comply with a requirement or a direction, the tribunal can take any action it thinks is 'just' – eg, it can:[110]

- waive the requirement; *or*
- require you to remedy the failure; *or*
- strike out your appeal (see p1190); *or*
- conclude that any information or evidence required was adverse to you.[111] However, it should not use this as a way to punish you. It should only decide information or evidence was adverse to you if it is probable that the reason it was not provided was that it did not exist or would harm your case.[112] The tribunal should not decide information or evidence was adverse to you because you refuse your consent to disclose your medical records, but you may have more difficulty proving your case.[113]

The tribunal can also take the above action if it is the DWP, the local authority or HMRC that is given a direction. The tribunal can also bar the DWP, the local authority or HMRC from taking further part in your appeal (see p1192).

If you miss the deadline in a direction, try to provide what has been requested as soon as possible. The tribunal may still consider the information or evidence – eg, if you provide it at the hearing.[114] However, remember that it can decide *not* to consider evidence if it is late or if it would otherwise be unfair to do so.[115]

## Postponements and adjournments

The First-tier Tribunal can put off a scheduled hearing to another day (postpone it) or, once the hearing has started, pause it (adjourn it).[116] The decision must be recorded properly. **Note:** if a hearing is postponed or adjourned, this does not mean that you cannot get another postponement or adjournment if you need one – eg, if there is a good reason why the next hearing should not take place. The tribunal making the decision to postpone or adjourn should therefore not tie the hands of the next tribunal by directing it to proceed when the appeal is listed again.[117] The next tribunal must consider any further application for a postponement or adjournment on its merits, although the fact that there has been a previous one is something it can take into account.

***Postponements and adjournments***

The decision to postpone a hearing to a different date takes place before the hearing starts. The decision can be made by a judge alone. The decision to adjourn a hearing, so it is heard at a later date, takes place at the hearing. The decision must be made by the tribunal as a whole.

Remember that if you do not attend a hearing, the tribunal can decide not to adjourn the hearing and hear the appeal without you (see p1196).[118] Your appeal is less likely to succeed if you do not attend.

Your case may be postponed or adjourned if there is a test case or lead case pending which deals with the same issues as your appeal (see p1193).

### Getting a hearing postponed

If the hearing date you are given is inconvenient or you want more time to prepare your case, you can ask for the hearing to be postponed to another date. You should apply in writing to the First-tier Tribunal before the hearing date, as soon as you decide you want a postponement, giving your reasons. Make it clear that you do not want the hearing to go ahead in your absence. If you have not provided enough information about why you want your appeal to be postponed (eg, you simply say you have an appointment, but not that it is an important medical appointment), the clerk to the tribunal should ask you for more information rather than simply referring your request for a decision.[119]

Bear the following in mind.

- Do not presume that a postponement will be granted. Telephone before the hearing is due to take place to check whether it has been agreed. Be ready to attend the hearing if it goes ahead. Your representative should warn you that your application may not be successful.[120]
- The judge conducting the hearing should consider whether it should be adjourned, even if you have been refused a postponement.[121]
- The tribunal can postpone your hearing even if this is not requested.

### Getting a hearing adjourned

If a hearing is underway, or the tribunal is considering its decision on the papers only, the tribunal can adjourn (eg, if you or the DWP, the local authority or HMRC ask for an adjournment or if the First-tier Tribunal thinks this is the best course – eg, if more evidence is required or you need time to consider the law). You should consider asking for an adjournment if the tribunal says it is going to consider whether you should get a lower rate of benefit than you are getting currently, to allow you to prepare your case and make representations. If you no longer want to pursue your appeal, you may be able to withdraw it (see p1192).

The tribunal should consider the benefit of an adjournment, why you (or the DWP, the local authority or HMRC) are not ready to go ahead and what the impact would be on the other party and the tribunal system.[122] This is the case even if you have not asked for an adjournment. It should adjourn a hearing:

- if you are not there and:
  - there is doubt about whether you received notice of the hearing;[123] *or*
  - information you provided that is relevant to the decision (eg, your reply to the work capability assessment questionnaire) is missing from the appeal papers so there is not enough evidence to make your case clear;[124] *or*
- if you have advised it that you cannot attend, have a good reason for not attending and have asked for another hearing date;[125] *or*
- if you cannot attend the hearing (eg, you are in prison or hospital), but your evidence could play an important part in its reaching a decision;[126] *or*
- if you want to be represented at the hearing, but your representative is not available on the date it has been listed and has made a reasonable request for a postponement. Your representative should explain why they cannot attend and why no one else can represent you instead;[127] *or*
- if you need to get a representative – eg, because you have mental health problems or the decision with which you disagree concerns a large overpayment;[128] *or*
- to enable you to get additional evidence which you could not until then have reasonably been expected to realise was needed.[129]

### If a hearing is not postponed or adjourned

If the tribunal does not postpone or adjourn the hearing and makes a decision with which you disagree, in limited circumstances you can apply for the decision to be 'set aside' (see p1208). Alternatively, you may be able to appeal to the Upper Tribunal against the First-tier Tribunal's final decision on the grounds that its refusal to postpone or adjourn the hearing was an 'error of law'.

## When your appeal can be struck out

If you fail to comply with a direction, or in a limited number of other circumstances, your appeal can be cancelled (struck out) in whole or in part. If your appeal is struck out because you failed to comply with a direction, see p1191 for when you can get your appeal reinstated and p1192 for appealing against the decision striking your appeal out or refusing to reinstate it.

### If you fail to comply with a direction

If you fail to comply with a direction given to you by the tribunal – eg, you do not provide required information or documents:[130]

- your appeal is struck out automatically if you were notified in the direction that a failure to comply *would* lead to your appeal being struck out; *or*
- there is discretion to strike out your appeal if you were notified in the direction that a failure to comply with it *could* lead to your appeal being struck out. In this case, before deciding to do so, the tribunal should consider carefully why the direction was given and whether it can still make a fair and just decision – eg, without the information you were supposed to provide.[131]

#### *Can your appeal be reinstated?*

If your appeal is struck out because you failed to comply with a direction, you can apply for your appeal to be reinstated.[132] You must apply in writing. Your application must be received by the tribunal within one month of your being sent notice that your appeal was struck out. It can give you longer (or shorter) than one month. There is no guarantee that you will be given longer, so keep within the time limit wherever possible. Explain why you think your appeal should not have been struck out – eg, why you think you *did* comply with the direction, or why you were unable to do so or to comply in time.

8

### Other circumstances

Your appeal *must* be struck out if the tribunal does not have 'jurisdiction' to deal with it – eg, you do not have a right to appeal against the decision or you have appealed to the wrong tribunal.[133]

In addition, there is *discretion* to strike out your appeal if:[134]

- you failed to co-operate with the tribunal to such an extent that it cannot deal with your appeal fairly and justly; *or*
- the tribunal considers your appeal has no reasonable prospect of success. It should only do so if the result of the appeal is clear and incontestable. It should generally not do so if the facts of the case are in dispute.[135]

In all cases, you must be given an opportunity to comment. You should always take this opportunity and explain why you think your appeal should not be struck out – eg, why you had a good reason for failing to co-operate or why you think you have a chance of winning your appeal.

Although you cannot apply for your appeal to be reinstated, you may be able to challenge the decision to strike it out.

#### Challenging a decision to strike out your appeal

If the tribunal strikes out your appeal or refuses to reinstate your appeal after it has been struck out, you may be able to make a fresh appeal against the decision maker's decision.[136] See p1175 for the time limit for doing so. Otherwise, you can appeal to the Upper Tribunal against the decision to strike out your appeal or to refuse to reinstate it.[137]

### Being barred from taking part in an appeal

The decision maker and any person (other than you) who is taking part in the appeal can be barred from taking further part in the appeal in the same circumstances in which your appeal can be struck out.[138] In practice, this is likely to apply mainly if the decision maker (or other person with a right of appeal):

- fails to comply with a direction; *or*
- fails to co-operate with the tribunal to such an extent that it cannot deal with your appeal fairly and justly.

The decision maker (or other person) can apply for the bar to be lifted in the same circumstances in which you can apply for an appeal to be reinstated (see p1191). If the bar is not lifted, the tribunal does not have to consider any response or other submission made by them.[139] It can decide any or all of the issues against them and can deal with their case more briefly than would otherwise be required. However, the decision maker (or person) still has a right of appeal against the tribunal's decision and a right to apply for a statement of reasons for the decision.[140]

8

## Withdrawing an appeal

If you change your mind about appealing, you can withdraw your appeal.[141]

- If you are appealing about HB and your appeal has not yet been passed to the First-tier Tribunal, write to the local authority office dealing with your appeal, saying that you do not wish your appeal to go ahead. Your representative can write on your behalf.
- In any other case (ie, once your appeal is lodged with the tribunal), you can withdraw your appeal:
  - by sending or giving written notice to the tribunal. You can withdraw your appeal before the tribunal makes its decision – eg, before a hearing takes place, or if a hearing has taken place but was adjourned without the tribunal reaching a decision. The withdrawal takes effect immediately. Usually, you do not need the tribunal's agreement to withdraw in this way, but in limited cases it may notify you that you can only do so if it agrees;[142] *or*
  - at a hearing, but only if the tribunal agrees. The withdrawal takes effect when it agrees.

The tribunal must notify you and any other party that the withdrawal of the appeal has taken effect.

If you tell the tribunal that you want to withdraw your appeal before the hearing (eg, you telephone the tribunal office), but then you fail to confirm this in writing, the tribunal clerk can waive the requirement to provide written notice.[143] You can ask the tribunal to reconsider the clerk's decision – eg, if you did not send written notice because you changed your mind and no longer wanted to withdraw your appeal. You must apply in writing within 14 days after the date you are sent notice of the decision.[144] The tribunal can give you longer (or shorter) than this. There is no guarantee you will be given longer, so keep within the time limit wherever possible.

If you withdraw your appeal but then decide that you want it to go ahead, you can apply for it to be reinstated.[145] The other parties can also apply for your appeal to be reinstated. The application must be in writing and it must be received by the tribunal within one month after the earliest of the following:

- the date the applicant was sent notice that the withdrawal of your appeal had taken effect; *or*
- if your appeal was withdrawn at a hearing and the applicant was present at the hearing when this happened, the date of the hearing.

The tribunal can give you longer (or shorter) than one month. There is no guarantee that you will be given longer, so keep within the time limit wherever possible.

**Note:** you can only withdraw your appeal, or apply for the appeal to be reinstated, once – ie, if your appeal is reinstated, you cannot withdraw it again.[146]

8

## Test cases and lead cases

Sometimes appeals to the First-tier Tribunal are made by more than one person about the same issues of fact or law. When this happens, appeals dealing with the same issues may be delayed until a decision has been made in a test case or a lead case.

### Test cases

If a case is pending against a decision of the Upper Tribunal or a court that deals with issues raised in your case (a 'test case'), the DWP, the local authority or HMRC can suspend payment of your benefit (see p1031) or even postpone making a decision about your claim (see p1159), pending the outcome of the appeal in the test case. In addition, for benefits other than HB, if a test case is pending and you have already appealed to the First-tier Tribunal (your appeal is then known as a 'look alike' case), the decision maker can serve notice requiring the First-tier Tribunal in *your* appeal:[147]

- not to make a decision and to refer your case back to them; *or*
- to deal with your appeal by either:

- postponing making a decision until the test case is decided. Once a decision has been made in the test case, the decision is made on your appeal; *or*
- deciding your appeal as if the test case had been decided in the way most unfavourable to you, but only if this is in your interests. If this happens, and the test case eventually goes in your favour, the decision maker has to make a new decision superseding the tribunal's decision in the light of the decision in the test case.

### Lead cases

If appeals are made to the First-tier Tribunal by more than one person about the same issues of fact or law (eg, a number of appeals about service charges from tenants in the same block of flats), one or more of the appeals can be specified as a 'lead case'. The tribunal can then postpone making a decision on all the other related appeals.[148] In practice, specifying an appeal as a 'lead case' is rare.

## 4. How the tribunal makes its decision

8

The First-tier Tribunal makes its decision either:

- at a hearing held either in person or remotely – eg, by telephone or video call;[149] *or*
- on the papers only by looking at what you said on your appeal form, any evidence or other information you provided and the decision maker's response.

You can tell the tribunal the type of hearing you prefer on the appeal form or enquiry form, although the tribunal decides which type of hearing will take place. Your appeal *must* be dealt with at a hearing, unless:[150]

- both you and the DWP, the local authority or HMRC have consented (or both of you have not objected) to the appeal being dealt with on the papers only. **Note:** if you (or the DWP, local authority or HMRC) state you want a hearing, there must be one; *and*
- the First-tier Tribunal considers that it can decide the matter without a hearing. The tribunal must consider whether this is in the 'interests of justice', particularly if it is not clear whether you consented to your appeal being decided on the papers only.[151] It should explain this in its statement of reasons.

If you want a hearing, state this on the appeal form or the enquiry form (see p1183). Otherwise, the tribunal presumes that you do not object to your appeal being dealt with on the papers only. **Note:** if you consent to (or do not object to) your appeal being dealt with on the papers only, the tribunal should not draw adverse conclusions about your reasons for this.[152]

*Should you opt for a hearing?*

You may not want to attend a hearing – eg, because you are worried about speaking for yourself or about the cost or difficulty in attending. Get advice before you decide what to do. Bear the following in mind.

1. You are more likely to win your appeal if you attend a hearing (whether that is in person, via video or telephone call), particularly if it concerns a medical issue or your disability, or if the facts of your case are in dispute.
2. If you attend a hearing, you can explain your side of the story.
3. Unlike with hearings in a court, hearings in the First-tier Tribunal are meant to be informal. For example, you do not have to stand when the judge enters and only rarely do you have to swear an oath.
4. The tribunal must consider how to assist child, vulnerable adult and sensitive witnesses.
5. You can have a representative at the hearing (see p1180) and your chances of winning are likely to be higher if you do.[153] You can also take a friend, relative or adviser with you for support.
6. The First-tier Tribunal aims to provide a qualified interpreter if you need one.
7. You, an interpreter and any witnesses may be able to get expenses paid. You can claim for travel, meals, loss of earnings and childcare costs.[154]
8. If you or your representative cannot attend a hearing at a particular venue (eg, because of a disability), a hearing may be arranged at an alternative venue, or you may be able to participate via telephone or video call (see p1197).[155]



## Decisions based on the papers only

If there is not a hearing, the tribunal makes its decision in your absence and you are then notified of its decision.

If you want your appeal to be dealt with based on the papers only, send the tribunal your arguments about your appeal in writing and any information and evidence you can get to support it (called a 'reply') as soon as possible. See p1204 for help with preparing your appeal. Write to the tribunal to let it know you intend to send a reply and state how long it may take to do so.

You must provide your reply within one month after the date you were sent the decision maker's response.[156] If you need longer than this, ask for an extension before the month has expired. However, if a decision is made on the papers only before the month is up and you could (and would) have provided further evidence within that period, you can challenge the tribunal's decision on the ground that it made an 'error of law'.[157]

***Can there be a hearing if you do not opt for one?***

1. Even if you do not opt for a hearing, one could still take place. This could happen, for example, if the other party wants a hearing or the tribunal decides there should be one because it can only deal with your appeal fairly and justly by having one – eg, it needs to ask you questions about the facts of your case. It could also happen if, while it is considering what to decide on the papers only, it is uncertain whether or not anyone has asked for a hearing, or if the tribunal suspects that you did not opt for a hearing because of a misunderstanding.[158]
2. If you get unexpected notice of a hearing, contact the tribunal to check the reasons for this. You should attend the hearing.
3. If you do not opt for a hearing but then decide you want one, you may be able to change your mind. You must tell the tribunal before it makes its decision.

## Hearings

You must be given reasonable notice of a hearing – at least 14 days' notice, unless you agree to less notice than this or there are urgent or exceptional circumstances.[159] If your hearing takes place in person, this is at an appeal venue in your area. If you cannot attend a hearing at a venue, see p1197.

8

If you have not been given the correct notice (you can argue that this includes the decision maker's response as well as the time and date of the hearing[160]), you can object to the hearing going ahead. If the tribunal decides to proceed with the hearing, attend and explain why your case will be prejudiced (eg, you did not have adequate time to prepare it) and ask for an adjournment (see p1190).

***Can a hearing go ahead without you?***

The tribunal can go ahead with a hearing even if you are not there if:[161]

- it is satisfied that you were notified of the hearing, or that reasonable steps have been taken to notify you. However, it does not normally have to find out why you have not attended – eg, by getting the clerk to the tribunal to telephone you.[162] It *should* attempt to contact you (eg, if your case is complex or your evidence is needed to allow the tribunal to decide your appeal fairly) if this would ensure, so far as is practicable, that you are able to participate fully in the proceedings;[163] *and*
- it thinks that it is in the interests of justice. It should always consider the alternative of adjourning the hearing to give you another opportunity to attend (see p1190).

The tribunal should only go ahead with the hearing if it considers that it has sufficient evidence to decide the appeal fairly.[164] **Note:** if the panel hearing your appeal comprises more than one member, the decision whether or not to go ahead with the hearing should be made by all of the members, not just by the judge alone.[165]

If you turn up late, after the tribunal has decided to proceed in your absence, it should still consider whether to allow you to participate, and whether it should adjourn the hearing to give you another opportunity to attend.[166]

An appeal is heard in public unless the tribunal thinks it should be in private.[167] If you want your hearing to be in private, ask for this to be considered. In practice, it is extremely rare for members of the public to attend.

***Child, vulnerable adult and sensitive witnesses***

The First-tier Tribunal must consider how to assist any children under 18, vulnerable adults (eg, people aged 18 or over who are mentally or physically disabled or are appealing about personal independence payment (PIP) or the work capability assessment) and 'sensitive witnesses' to give evidence.[168] This includes allowing them to give evidence by telephone, video call or other means, appointing someone with special expertise to help the person give evidence and adopting a less robust style of questioning. You are a **'sensitive witness'** if the quality of evidence you give is likely to be diminished because of your fear or distress in connection with giving evidence. If you are a child, vulnerable adult or sensitive witness, and you need special arrangements to be made, you or your representative should let the tribunal know as soon as possible in advance of the hearing. The tribunal should make a note in its record of proceedings that it has considered how to assist you.

## Ways to participate in a hearing

The tribunal decides what sort of hearing will apply. If you cannot attend a hearing at a venue, you may still be able to participate in a 'remote hearing' via telephone or video call.[169] If you did not opt for a hearing, the tribunal should take note of any reasons that you give for this choice. If these suggest that you may be happy to give your evidence by telephone, the tribunal should consider adjourning the hearing to give you an opportunity to ask for a telephone hearing.[170]



### Alternative venues

Most appeal venues have access for disabled people, and the First-tier Tribunal may meet the cost of special transport to get there. It may also arrange the hearing at another venue – eg, a hotel meeting room near where you live. The tribunal may well order a remote hearing – ie, via telephone or video call. In very rare cases, it is possible to hold the hearing in your home (known as a 'domiciliary hearing'), although the tribunal may say this is not necessary if you can use special transport.[171] If you need a domiciliary hearing, include a letter from your doctor with your request for a domiciliary hearing, confirming that you cannot travel at all – eg, even by private ambulance. Explain why it would not be an adequate solution for you to give your evidence by telephone or video call. You can appeal against a decision to refuse you a domiciliary hearing.[172] Alternatively, if the refusal meant that the way your appeal was dealt with was unfair, you may be able to appeal to the Upper Tribunal.[173]

## At the hearing

Any of the following may be present at your appeal hearing.

- **A judge** (see p1182). They always chair the hearing.
- **A member or members of the First-tier Tribunal** (see p1182). To see which members hear and decide your appeal, see below.
- **An expert** (see p1182). They cannot take part in making the decision.
- **A tribunal clerk** (see p1182). They cannot take part in making the decision.

A **presenting officer** may be present to represent the decision maker. They explain the reasons for the decision, but are not there to defend it at all costs and may provide information which helps your case. Presenting officers often only attend if an appeal is considered complicated. The tribunal can issue a direction requiring a presenting officer to attend the hearing.

The judge and up to two other members hear and decide your appeal. A record of what is said at the hearing is kept. This is either notes made by the judge or an audio recording.

You can have a **representative** with you at the hearing (see p1180).[174] You can also be accompanied by someone at the hearing – eg, a friend or relative. The tribunal can give permission for them to act as your representative or assist you in presenting your case.[175]

8

The First-tier Tribunal aims to provide a qualified **interpreter** if you need one. If you do, tell it in advance of the hearing. If an official interpreter is not available, on rare occasions, it may allow a relative to act as your interpreter if they simply translate accurately and give your answers in your own words, without comment or explanation.[176]

### The judge and members

Those who decide a particular kind of appeal are as follows.[177]

- **A judge and a doctor and a person with experience of disability** decide attendance allowance (AA), disability living allowance (DLA) and PIP appeals (unless the appeal only concerns a 'question of law' and it has been directed that the appeal should be decided just by a judge).
- **A judge and a doctor** decide appeals:
  - about whether you have limited capability for work under the work capability assessment or have limited capability for work-related activity; *and*
  - about industrial injuries disablement benefit (IIDB) or severe disablement allowance.
- **A judge** decides all other appeals on their own.

Unless your appeal is about AA, DLA or PIP, an additional judge can be included in specified cases, an accountant may be included (if the examination of financial accounts is required) or there can be an additional doctor (if there are complex medical issues). However, there can never be more than three deciding an appeal.

If the group deciding your appeal is comprised incorrectly, you can appeal to the Upper Tribunal and argue that this was an error of law.[178]

Note:

- If your appeal is meant to be heard by two or more members but some of these are absent, the hearing can still go ahead, but only if you and the DWP, or the local authority or HMRC, agree.[179]
- If you have both a DLA (or PIP) and an employment and support allowance appeal, they should be heard completely separately, by entirely different members.[180]
- If your appeal is only partly heard by a judge and at least one member, the group deciding your appeal at a new hearing should generally be the same, or completely different.[181]

## Procedure at the hearing

At the hearing, there are no strict rules of procedure. The judge decides how it is conducted.[182] The tribunal's overriding objective is that your appeal be dealt with fairly and justly.[183] This includes ensuring that you are able to participate fully.

***What happens at a hearing?***

1. The judge should introduce everyone present.
2. The judge (and member(s)) often starts by asking you (and the presenting officer) questions. Even if you have a representative, you are usually expected to give your own evidence. Be prepared for some searching questions.
3. The presenting officer may be asked to summarise the decision maker's case.
4. You should be given the opportunity to explain your case. It is the tribunal's job to help you to say everything you want by putting you at your ease and asking the right questions. If you think there are mistakes in the papers, point them out. You can call witnesses and ask questions of the presenting officer's witnesses. If you forget to say something when it is your turn to speak, do not hesitate to add it at the end of the hearing. See p1204 for help with preparing your appeal.
5. The tribunal considers all the facts, evidence and law before it makes a decision. It should not bargain with you by 'offering' to allow part of your appeal if you agree to drop other parts – eg, by offering you one component of PIP if you agree not to argue for the other.[184]

### Appeals about disability or limited capability for work

If your appeal concerns your disability or your limited capability for work, the tribunal considers all the medical and other relevant evidence, and tries to draw out the evidence about your disabilities, listening to all you have to say with the help of questioning from the doctor member. The doctor member is there to help the tribunal understand the medical evidence and provide medical information. However, they should not give their clinical opinion.[185] The evidence may confirm the opinions expressed in medical reports with which you disagree, or it may support your view. Consider the following.

- Tell the tribunal how your disability or limited capability for work affects you at work or in your daily life at home. You should be completely straightforward, neither underplaying nor overplaying your symptoms. If you feel better on some days than others, explain how and how often, and say whether you are being seen on a good day or a bad day.
- The tribunal should not restrict itself to accepting the medical evidence about you given in written reports.[186] If there is conflict between what is said in a report and what you have said in writing (eg, on your claim form), it should not accept the evidence in the report without first listening to what you have to say about how your condition affects you.[187] Ensure that you explain any inconsistencies. The tribunal should be particularly careful not to accept automatically the findings in medical reports produced with the assistance of a computer programme.[188]

***Can the tribunal take its observations of you into account?***

The tribunal may observe your abilities and behaviour at the hearing and take these into account when making its decision (eg, if your appeal concerns your ability to walk); however, it cannot subject you to a walking test.[189] It should not attach undue weight to its observations[190] and you should usually be given the opportunity to comment on them.[191] Remind the tribunal that what it sees may only be relevant to your physical or mental condition on that day and not in general.[192] Tell it, for instance, whether you have just taken medication or have been resting for some time in the waiting area. **Note:** the tribunal can use information about walking distances it obtains itself – eg, from Google Maps. However, the evidence should be presented to you so that you can comment on or refute it.[193]

8

### Medical examination at the hearing

The tribunal cannot usually carry out physical examinations.[194] Studying x-ray evidence does not count as a physical examination, so you can ask the tribunal to consider this.[195]

It *can* carry out a physical examination if your appeal relates to the assessment of your disablement for IIDB, or whether you have a prescribed disease or injury.[196] It should let you know during the hearing if it thinks a physical examination is not necessary so you can make representations.[197]

You are examined by the medical member of the tribunal.[198] You can have someone with you as a chaperone or if, for instance, you need help undressing. Make sure you tell the medical member if you are in pain or discomfort. It is also a good idea to provide a full list of any medicines you are taking. After the examination, you should be invited to make further representations to the tribunal if you wish.

### Referral for a medical report

The tribunal can refer you to a healthcare professional approved by the DWP (see p1010) for a medical examination and report if your appeal concerns:[199]

- whether you are entitled to AA, DLA or PIP, the appropriate rate of benefit or the period for which you are entitled; *or*
- whether you have limited capability for work or for work-related activity; *or*
- the extent of your disablement for IIDB purposes; *or*
- whether you have a loss of faculty due to an industrial accident (see p595).

The tribunal can specify the type of healthcare professional to whom you should be referred.[200] The medical examination may take place in your home or at a DWP medical examination centre. **Note:** although you cannot be compelled to undergo a medical examination, the tribunal may draw negative conclusions if you refuse.

A report or medical notes may also be requested from your GP or other health professional with your permission.

The written decision to adjourn for a report should make clear why the tribunal adjourned and what sort of medical evidence is being sought.

## What the tribunal considers

The tribunal's job is to decide whether the decision you are appealing about was correct. It must look at the law and issues afresh, taking into account any new evidence or information you (and the DWP, the local authority or HMRC) provide. The tribunal considers all the evidence.[201] It should decide your appeal in an investigative way, but the members should generally not make their own enquiries into the facts of your case before the hearing.[202] **Note:**

- You (or the DWP, the local authority or HMRC) can raise an issue at the hearing.[203] However, the tribunal may then adjourn to give the other side a chance to address the point.
- The tribunal should consider an issue if it is in the appeal papers or in any representations you make, or if the evidence should lead it to believe it is relevant to your appeal, even if your representative has not made a submission on the issue.[204] It has the discretion to (ie, it does not have to) consider issues that are 'not raised by' your appeal.[205] **Note:**
  - You do not necessarily have to raise an issue with the tribunal for it to be something it should consider, even if you have a representative, but the issue must be one which in some way obviously demands attention – eg, from evidence included in the appeal papers.[206] Even if you say that you do not want an issue to be considered, the tribunal can still exercise its discretion to consider it.[207] However, the tribunal may decide not to

investigate matters that a representative does not raise on your behalf or that a representative does not want to be considered.[208]
– The tribunal can consider issues even if no one has raised them.[209] It should use its discretion fairly.

***Are you appealing about a disability benefit?***

If you are appealing because you were not awarded one component of DLA or PIP when you are in receipt of the other, or you ask for a higher rate of DLA, PIP or AA than you are already getting, the tribunal does not have to consider issues which are not the subject of your appeal. However, it may decide to consider both components of DLA or PIP, or to consider whether you should get a lower rate of DLA, PIP or AA than you are already getting. **Note:**
– You should be given warning of this, and a chance to prepare your case properly and make representations or to consider withdrawing your appeal.[210]
– Ask for the hearing to be adjourned if you need time or want someone to advise or represent you.
– If your appeal is being dealt with based on the papers only, you should be given the opportunity to attend a hearing or to withdraw your appeal.[211]
– You should be given an explanation of why the tribunal decided to use its discretion in this way in the statement of reasons for its decision.[212]



If you are concerned about what may happen in your appeal, you may be able to withdraw it (see p1192). You need permission if you ask to withdraw your appeal at the hearing, or if you are notified that you can only withdraw your appeal if the tribunal agrees. **Note:** the DWP (or the local authority or HMRC) can apply for your appeal to be reinstated (see p1193).

## Appeals involving revisions and supersessions

If your appeal involves a revision or a supersession decision, the tribunal can make any decision that the decision maker could have taken.[213] This includes if the decision maker carried out a supersession:

- but failed to state the grounds or to identify the correct grounds for doing so; *or*
- when they should have conducted a revision (and, in some cases, vice versa).

In addition, the tribunal can decide that an 'any time' revision should be done if no decision has been made on the matter by a decision maker (either to revise the decision or refuse to do so) – ie, if you are appealing because the decision maker refused to carry out a supersession.[214]

If there are errors in the decision, argue that the tribunal should correct the decision. However, it can adjourn the hearing, point out the errors to the decision maker and invite the decision maker to reconsider, rather than making any corrections itself.[215]

## Changes of circumstances after the decision under appeal

The tribunal considers whether the decision under appeal was correct for the period up to and including the date it was made. If your circumstances change after the decision (eg, your health condition changes), it cannot take this into account.[216]

Any evidence you get after the decision with which you disagree could still be relevant to your appeal. If the evidence relates to the period before the decision you are disputing was made, or to a past event that was relevant to the decision, it must be taken into account.[217] In some situations, events that happen after the date of a decision can throw light on the situation at or before that date, in which case evidence of such events may also be taken into account – eg, if the tribunal needs to decide whether an improvement in your health was likely to happen.

### What you should do if your circumstances change

As a general rule, you should consider making a fresh claim (or seeking a supersession) every time your circumstances change, and appeal if you are unhappy with the subsequent decision, particularly if your appeal is about:

- whether you have limited capability for work, have limited capability for work related activity or qualify for AA, DLA or PIP, or the rate of AA, DLA or PIP to which you are entitled and your condition has worsened; *or*
- whether you satisfy the 'habitual residence test' (see p1300); *or*
- how much income or capital you have, and this changes.

If you wait until the tribunal makes its decision and this goes against you, you could lose out. You can only get arrears from the date your circumstances changed if a fresh claim (or the effect of a supersession) can be backdated. This is only possible in limited circumstances.

***Example***

Jing has been getting PIP mobility component. A decision maker decides that Jing's condition has improved so stops his PIP. Jing appeals. While waiting for his appeal hearing, his condition deteriorates. Jing makes a fresh claim and is awarded PIP mobility component. When the tribunal hears his appeal against the original decision, it upholds the decision maker's decision. However, because Jing made a fresh claim when his circumstances changed, he has not lost out.

If you make a fresh claim (or seek a supersession), you can ask the decision maker to wait until your appeal has been determined before making a decision. However, if the decision maker decides the fresh claim (or supersession) and you disagree with the decision:

- you can appeal against the new decision. All the appeals may be heard together by the tribunal, but it may be better for them to be heard separately;[218] *or*
- whether or not you appeal against the new decision, you can ask the decision maker to revise it once your first appeal is determined (see p1137).

***Example***

Leon claims pension credit (PC) but the decision maker says he does not satisfy the habitual residence test and refuses his claim. He appeals against the decision and makes a fresh claim for PC on 8 May 2025. The new claim is refused. Leon wins his appeal. Because there has been a fresh decision on his entitlement, the tribunal can only award PC up to 8 May 2025. However, the decision maker does an 'any time' revision and awards PC from that date as well.

## 5. Preparing your appeal

There is nothing in the law about what you must or must not do to prepare your appeal. Tribunals are supposed to proceed in a relatively informal way, and to help you in taking part in your appeal. So even if you do nothing else, you could still win your appeal. However, in practice, the following steps are advisable.

- Request that your appeal is dealt with at a hearing, if you would be able to take part in one. This will ensure that the tribunal can speak to you and ask you questions. The tribunal will ask you about the facts and evidence in your case.
- If you can, get a representative (see p1180) to help you (if you do, your representative will be able to help with all of the below).
- Identify what you think the outcome of the appeal should be and why your appeal should succeed. For example, if you are appealing against a decision that you have failed the work capability assessment, try to identify the additional points that you think you should score, or why working would pose a substantial risk to your health. Ideally, use this *Handbook* to find out about the law and other matters regarding such points.
- Identify the facts that you think are relevant to your appeal and, in particular, how they mean your appeal should succeed. For example, if you think your ability to walk has been overestimated, be specific about what your walking ability is and how the decision you are unhappy about has got that wrong.
- Consider if you agree with the facts as stated by the decision maker. For example, have they drawn the wrong conclusions from the evidence, or used poor-quality evidence?
- Get evidence supporting what you say, if you can. For example, ask your doctor (or other healthcare professional who knows you well) to write a short letter

supporting what you say about how your health affects you (you may be charged for such evidence, although a copy of your medical records should be free). Ideally, such evidence would comment specifically on why your appeal should succeed – eg, on the additional points that should be applied to you in the work capability assessment.
- Consider whether someone (eg, your carer, or a family member) could provide evidence in support of your appeal (this could be by attending the tribunal hearing). Such evidence can be very useful in helping the tribunal to understand things like how your health condition affects you, or clarifying other facts in your appeal.
- Ideally, put the reasons why your appeal should succeed, and the facts and the evidence that support what you say, in a short written submission and send that to the tribunal. The submission should include a clear summary of what decision you are seeking, and say why the facts and evidence cited support your appeal. Doing a written submission is not essential (although in practice tribunals do like them), and usually is something a representative can do for you.

More details about all of these points, including on looking up the law, getting medical evidence and drawing up a written submission (with examples), are available in CPAG's *Winning Your Benefit Appeal: what you need to know*.

For what happens at the hearing, and advice about stating your case to the tribunal there, see p1199.



## 6. The tribunal's decision

You may be told the tribunal's decision at the hearing and you are given a **decision notice** confirming it. If it is not given at the hearing or you opted for a paper hearing, the decision notice is sent to you later. It may include a summary of the tribunal's reasons for its decision. You *must* be informed of:[219]
- your right to request a statement of reasons for the decision (see p1206); *and*
- the conditions for appealing to the Upper Tribunal, including the time limit for doing so.

If the tribunal cannot come to a unanimous decision, it makes a majority decision. The judge has the casting vote.[220] However, if the tribunal consists of two members and there is complete disagreement about the facts, the judge should not use their casting vote, but instead should adjourn the appeal to be heard by different tribunal members.[221]

A decision can be corrected, superseded, reviewed or set aside (see p1207). You, or the DWP, the local authority or HMRC can also appeal against it to the Upper Tribunal.

## Record of proceedings

A record of the tribunal proceedings is made by the judge that indicates the evidence taken and submissions made, as well as any procedural applications.[222] This could be a recording of the hearing or a written record.[223] If you are considering an appeal to the Upper Tribunal, it is a good idea to get a copy. If you foresee disputes about what happened at the hearing, keep your own notes.

The record is kept by the tribunal for 18 months from the date of its decision or for 18 months from various other specific dates, including the date you are sent written reasons for its decision. So, if you applied for a statement of reasons for the decision, the record of proceedings should not be destroyed until 18 months after the statement has been provided.[224]

You can request a copy of the record of proceedings. You must do so in writing within the relevant 18-month period. Bear in mind that if you request it after the 18-month period, the record may have been destroyed.

## The statement of reasons

The First-tier Tribunal may give the reasons for its decision at the hearing, or give or send you a written statement of reasons, prepared by the judge.[225] If you are not provided with a written statement of reasons, you have a right to apply for one.[226] **Note:** the judge may say that the decision notice (see p1205) is to stand as the written statement of reasons, so check it carefully.

8

You must generally have a statement of reasons if you want to appeal to the Upper Tribunal. You must show that the First-tier Tribunal made a mistake about the law (an 'error of law' – see p1216) and it may be difficult to do so without a statement of reasons.

Your request for a statement of reasons must be:[227]

- in writing; *and*
- received by the First-tier Tribunal within one month (see p1175) of your being sent or given its decision notice. It can give you longer (or shorter) than this.[228] There is no guarantee that you will be given longer, so keep within the time limit wherever possible.

The written statement of reasons must then be sent to you within one month or as soon as it is reasonably practicable after that.[229] There are, however, often long delays.

**Note:**

- If you mistakenly ask the First-tier Tribunal for permission to appeal to the Upper Tribunal instead of asking for a statement of reasons, it should treat this as a request for a statement of reasons.[230]
- If the judge refuses wrongly to provide a statement of reasons, you may have grounds for appeal to the Upper Tribunal.[231]

- If there is a long delay in getting a statement of reasons, you could apply for permission to appeal to the Upper Tribunal. The Upper Tribunal can require the First-tier Tribunal to provide reasons for its decision.[232]

The DWP, the local authority or HMRC can also ask for a statement of reasons. If this happens, it usually means it is considering appealing to the Upper Tribunal.

## If you win your appeal

If you win your appeal, the DWP, local authority or HMRC should carry out the First-tier Tribunal's decision straight away. It can do this on the basis of the decision notice (see p1205). However, if the DWP, the local authority or HMRC:

- disagrees with the decision, it may consider appealing against it to the Upper Tribunal. In this case, you are not normally paid while it decides what to do. See p1031 for what the DWP, the local authority or HMRC must do before it can suspend payment of your benefit. If the DWP, local authority or HMRC decides to appeal, you are not normally paid until the Upper Tribunal decides the case.[233] However, you can ask the DWP, the local authority or HMRC to pay you if you are in financial hardship;
- applies for permission to appeal to the Upper Tribunal, the First-tier Tribunal may be able to suspend the effect of its decision until the application is determined (by either tribunal), and then until any review of, or appeal against, the decision is determined.[234]

8

The First-tier Tribunal can also suspend the effect of its decision if *you* apply for permission to appeal to the Upper Tribunal.

## If you disagree with the tribunal's decision

If you disagree with the First tier Tribunal's decision, you cannot simply ask it to look at the decision again – eg, if you have additional evidence. However:

- if the decision contains a clerical mistake or other accidental slip or omission, this can be corrected by the tribunal. This only applies if it is a genuine error such as a typing or spelling mistake or a mathematical miscalculation, not an error of law on an important issue in your appeal. **Note:** the tribunal cannot use this rule to amend or add to its reasons for the decision, but can amend these if it reviews its decision (see p1223);[235]
- the decision can be superseded by the DWP, the local authority or HMRC, if there are grounds (see p1143), although arrears can be limited. However, if the tribunal made a mistake about the law, you must appeal to the Upper Tribunal;
- you (or the DWP, the local authority or HMRC) can appeal to the Upper Tribunal against the decision (see Chapter 52);
- if you (or the DWP, the local authority or HMRC) seek permission to appeal to the Upper Tribunal against a decision, the First-tier Tribunal can review it (see p1223);

- the decision can be set aside, which means the decision is cancelled and your appeal is heard again.

If you are considering an appeal to the Upper Tribunal, ask for the First-tier Tribunal's statement of reasons (if one has not yet been provided) within the one-month time limit (see p1206), even if you are first going to apply for the decision to be set aside.

## Setting aside a decision on procedural grounds

A First-tier Tribunal decision can only be set aside on procedural grounds if the judge thinks it is 'in the interests of justice' to do so and:[236]

- you, your representative or the DWP, the local authority or HMRC:
  - were not sent, or did not receive, appeal papers or other relevant documents at an appropriate time – eg, with sufficient time before the hearing; *or*
  - were not present at the hearing. However, if you (or they) chose not to attend, it may not be 'in the interests of justice' to set the decision aside; *or*
- the tribunal was not sent appeal papers or other relevant documents at an appropriate time – eg, with sufficient time before the hearing; *or*
- there was some other procedural irregularity.

8

The tribunal cannot set aside a decision unless an application to set aside the decision is made.[237] **Note:** this may change, so that the tribunal will be able to set a decision aside even without an application. See CPAG's *Welfare Rights Bulletin* or the online version of this *Handbook* for updates.

You must apply in writing to the First-tier Tribunal. The application must be received no later than one month after the date you are sent the decision notice (see p1205).[238] The tribunal can give you longer (or shorter) than this.[239] There is no guarantee that you will be given longer, so keep within the time limit wherever possible. The rules do not say what the time limit is if you are given the decision notice at the hearing but you should apply within the time limit above to protect your position.

**Note:**

- Applications are normally decided without a hearing.[240] Make sure you give a full explanation of your reasons when you apply.
- If you could not attend your hearing (eg, because you were ill), provide evidence of this – eg, a note from your doctor. If your application is late, explain the reasons for this.
- If the decision is set aside, your appeal is heard again and a new decision is made. You should be given the opportunity to ask for a hearing, even if your appeal was originally decided based on the papers only.[241]

- If a decision is wrongly set aside (eg, the tribunal decides to set aside the decision although no application for a set-aside has been made), any subsequent rehearing by the First-tier Tribunal is invalid.[242]

In some circumstances, a decision can also be set aside by agreement.

#### If the decision is not set aside

If the First-tier Tribunal refuses to set aside a decision, you can appeal to the Upper Tribunal against the refusal.[243] You can often argue that the circumstances you mentioned in your application for a set-aside also show that the tribunal made a mistake about the law. So it may be better to try to appeal to the Upper Tribunal against the original decision *and* the refusal. If your application for the First-tier Tribunal's decision to be set aside is refused, the time limit for applying for permission to appeal to the Upper Tribunal can run from the date you are sent notice of this.[244] However, this only applies if you applied for the decision to be set aside within the one-month time limit (or any longer period allowed by the First-tier Tribunal).

The First-tier Tribunal can treat your application for a decision to be set aside as an application for permission to appeal to the Upper Tribunal, or as an application for a correction of the decision.[245]

### Setting aside a decision by agreement

8

The First-tier Tribunal must set aside a decision if an application is made for permission to appeal against it to the Upper Tribunal, and you and the DWP, the local authority or HMRC agree that the First-tier Tribunal made a mistake about the law (an 'error of law' – see p1216).[246] Bear in mind that the First-tier Tribunal does not send copies of applications for permission to appeal to the other party. If you think that the DWP, the local authority or HMRC may agree that the tribunal made an error of law, you should send it a copy of your application. However, there is no guarantee that it will take any action on this.

## Notes

1. **Before you appeal**

1 *R (Connor) v SSWP* [2020] EWHC 1999 (Admin)

2 *PP v SSWP (UC)* [2020] UKUT 109 (AAC)

3 s12(1), (2) and (3D) SSA 1998

4 s12(2)(b) and (3A)-(3C) SSA 1998; reg 3ZA SS&CS(DA) Regs; reg 7 UC,PIP,JSA&ESA(DA) Regs

5 *PH and SM v SSWP* [2018] UKUT 404 (AAC)

6 *R (CJ) and SG v SSWP (ESA)* [2017] UKUT 324 (AAC), reported as [2018] AACR 5
7 para 03013 DMG; para A3015 ADM
8 paras 03014-35 DMG; paras A3026-3027 ADM
9 *PH and SM v SSWP* [2018] UKUT 404 (AAC)
10 *PH and SM v SSWP* [2018] UKUT 404 (AAC)
11 **UC/PIP/new-style JSA&ESA** Reg 7(5) UC,PIP,JSA&ESA(DA) Regs
**Other benefits** Reg 3ZA(5) SS&CS(DA) Regs
12 r22(4)(a) TP(FT) Rules
13 r7 TP(FT) Rules
14 **UC/PIP/new-style JSA&ESA** Reg 49 UC,PIP,JSA&ESA(DA) Regs
**CB/GA** Reg 24 CB&GA(DA) Regs
**Other benefits** Reg 25 SS&CS(DA) Regs
**All** s12 SSA 1998
15 s12(4) SSA 1998
16 Reg 14 SS(JPIP) Regs
17 Sch 7 para 6(3) and (6) CSPSSA 2000; regs 3 and 21 HB&CTB(DA) Regs; *Wirral MBC v Salisbury Independent Living Ltd* [2012] EWCA Civ 84, reported as [2012] AACR 37
18 R(H) 3/04; R(H) 10/07
19 **UC/PIP/new-style JSA&ESA** s12 and Schs 2 and 3 SSA 1998; reg 50(1) and Sch 2 UC,PIP,JSA&ESA(DA) Regs
**HB** Sch 7 para 6 CSPSSA 2000
**CB/GA** s12 and Schs 2 and 3 SSA 1998; reg 25(2) CB&GA(DA) Regs
**Other benefits** s12 and Schs 2 and 3 SSA 1998; reg 26 SS&CS(DA) Regs
20 R(SB) 29/83; R(SB) 12/89; CIS/807/1992; R(H) 3/05
21 R(IS) 6/04
22 **UC/PIP/new-style JSA&ESA** Regs 7(3) and 51 UC,PIP,JSA&ESA(DA) Regs
**HB** Reg 10 HB&CTB(DA) Regs
**CB/GA** Reg 26 CB&GA(DA) Regs
**Other benefits** Regs 3ZA and 28 SS&CS(DA) Regs
23 *VT v SSWP (IS)* [2016] UKUT 178 (AAC), reported as [2016] AACR 42
24 *SSWP v Adams* [2003] EWCA Civ 796, reported as R(G) 1/03
25 *MC and JH v SSWP (ESA)* [2014] UKUT 125 (AAC), reported as [2014] AACR 35
26 **UC/PIP/new-style JSA&ESA** Sch 2 SSA 1998; reg 50(2) and Sch 3 UC,PIP,JSA&ESA(DA) Regs
**HB** Sch 7 para 6(2) CSPSSA 2000; reg 16 and Sch HB&CTB(DA) Regs
**CB/GA** Sch 2 SSA 1998; reg 25 and Sch 2 CB&GA(DA) Regs
**Other benefits** Sch 2 SSA 1998; reg 27 and Sch 2 SS&CS(DA) Regs
27 **UC/PIP/new-style JSA&ESA** Regs 10 and 25 UC,PIP,JSA&ESA(DA) Regs
**HB** Regs 4(6) and 7(2)(e) HB&CTB(DA) Regs
**CB/GA** Regs 9 and 13(2)(d) CB&GA(DA) Regs
**Other benefits** Regs 3(8) and 6(2)(d) SS&CS(DA) Regs
28 *RL v SSWP (JSA)* [2017] UKUT 282 (AAC)

2. **How to appeal**
29 Reg 20(1) HB&CTB(DA) Regs
30 Reg 20(1) HB&CTB(DA) Regs; r23 TP(FT) Rules
31 r22 TP(FT) Rules
32 r22(2)(d)(i) TP(FT) Rules
33 R(IB) 4/02; *SSWP v SC (SF)* [2013] UKUT 607 (AAC)
34 r12 TP(FT) Rules
35 **HB** r23(2)(a)(i) and (ii) TP(FT) Rules
**Other benefits** r22(2)(d)(ii) and Sch 1 para 5(a) and (b) TP(FT) Rules
**All** r12 TP(FT) Rules
36 s9(5) SSA 1998; Sch 7 para 3(5) CSPSSA 2000
37 r23(2)(a)(iii) and Sch 1 para 5(c) TP(FT) Rules
38 rr22(8)(a) and 23(4) and (5) TP(FT) Rules
39 rr22(6) and 23(3) TP(FT) Rules
40 *LS v Lambeth LB (HB)* [2010] UKUT 461 (AAC), reported as [2011] AACR 27
41 Reg 19(5A) HB&CTB(DA) Regs
42 Reg 19(6), (7) and (8) HB&CTB(DA) Regs
43 Reg 19(9) HB&CTB(DA) Regs
44 r23(7)(a) TP(FT) Rules
45 R(M) 1/87; R(I) 5/91
46 R(M) 1/87
47 CIS/147/1995
48 rr22(8) and 23(5) and (8) TP(FT) Rules
49 *KK v Sheffield City Council (CTB)* [2015] UKUT 367 (AAC); *GJ v SSWP (PIP)* [2022] UKUT 340 (AAC)
50 r23(7)(b) TP(FT) Rules
51 *LS v Lambeth LB (HB)* [2010] UKUT 461 (AAC), reported as [2011] AACR 27
52 rr22(3) and 23(6) TP(FT) Rules

53 r11(5) TP(FT) Rules; *CO v LB Havering (HB)* [2015] UKUT 28 (AAC)
54 rr22(3), (4) and (9) and 23(6) TP(FT) Rules
55 *MM v SSWP (PIP)* [2016] UKUT 36 (AAC)
56 Reg 20(2)-(6) HB&CTB(DA) Regs
57 Reg 20(6) HB&CTB(DA) Regs
58 Reg 20(7) HB&CTB(DA) Regs
59 para C7/7.128-29 GM
60 Reg 20(8) HB&CTB(DA) Regs
61 rr4 and 7(2) TP(FT) Rules; Practice Statement: *Delegation of Functions to Staff in Relation to the Social Entitlement Chamber of the First-tier Tribunal on or after 1 October 2014*, 18 September 2014, paras 5-7
62 r4(3) TP(FT) Rules
63 r11 TP(FT) Rules; r11 TP(UT) Rules; CIB/1009/2004; CIB/2058/2004
64 r11(2) TP(FT) Rules; r11(2) TP(UT) Rules
65 r11(6)(b) TP(FT) Rules; r11(4)(b) TP(UT) Rules
66 r11(6)(a) TP(FT) Rules; r11(4)(a) TP(UT) Rules; *MP v SSWP (DLA)* [2010] UKUT 103 (AAC)
67 r11(7) and (8) TP(FT) Rules; r11(5) and (6) TP(UT) Rules
68 r10 TP(FT) Rules; s10 Legal Aid, Sentencing and Punishment of Offenders Act 2012

3. **After you submit your appeal**

69 s28 TCEA 2007
70 Practice Statement: *Delegation of Functions to Registrars First-tier Tribunal (Social Entitlement Chamber)*, 1 December 2016; Practice Statement: *Authorising Legal Officers*, 26 July 2022
71 Practice Statement: *Delegation of Functions to Staff in Relation to the Social Entitlement Chamber of the First-tier Tribunal on or after 1 October 2014*, 18 September 2014
72 *T v SSWP (ESA)* [2019] UKUT 59 (AAC)
73 r4(3) TP(FT) Rules
74 *DTM v Kettering BC (CTB)* [2013] UKUT 625 (AAC)
75 r24(1A) TP(FT) Rules; Art 6 European Convention on Human Rights; s6 HRA 1998; CH/3497/2005; *MB v Wychavon DC* [2013] UKUT 67 (AAC); Local Government Ombudsman, Complaint 01/C/13400 against Scarborough BC
76 r24(1)(c) TP(FT) Rules
77 r24(5) TP(FT) Rules
78 r11(6)(a) TP(FT) Rules
79 r24(2) TP(FT) Rules
80 *LH v SSWP (PIP)* [2018] UKUT 57 (AAC); *TM v SSWP (PIP)* [2019] UKUT 204 (AAC); *BF v SSWP (PIP)* [2020] UKUT 300 (AAC)
81 r24(4) TP(FT) Rules; *ST v SSWP (ESA)* [2012] UKUT 469 (AAC); *FN v SSWP (ESA)* [2015] UKUT 670 (AAC), reported as [2016] AACR 24
82 *FI v HMRC* [2018] UKUT 226 (AAC)
83 *RS v SSWP (ESA)* [2021] UKUT 112 (AAC)
84 R(H) 1/07
85 rr5 and 6(1)-(3) TP(FT) Rules
86 r24(6) and (7) TP(FT) Rules
87 r5(3)(a) TP(FT) Rules
88 *MP v SSWP (DLA)* [2010] UKUT 103 (AAC)
89 **HB** Sch 7 para 3(6) CSPSSA 2000
**Other benefits** s9(6) SSA 1998
90 **UC/PIP/new-style JSA&ESA** Reg 52(1) and (5) UC,PIP,JSA&ESA(DA) Regs
**HB** Reg 17(1) and (2) HB&CTB(DA) Regs
**CB/GA** Reg 27(1) and (5) CB&GA(DA) Regs
**Other benefits** Reg 30(1) and (2) SS&CS(DA) Regs
91 para 06161 DMG; para A5160 ADM; 'Latest offers – PIP appeals', *Welfare Rights Bulletin* 284, October 2021, p6; *DO v SSWP (PIP)* [2021] UKUT 161 (AAC)
92 *AI v SSWP (PIP)* [2019] UKUT 103 (AAC)
93 **HB** Sch 7 para 3(5) CSPSSA 2000; r23(2) TP(FT) Rules
**Other benefits** s9(5) SSA 1998; Sch 1 para 5 TP(FT) Rules
94 **UC/PIP/new-style JSA&ESA** Reg 52(2) UC,PIP,JSA&ESA(DA) Regs
**HB** Reg 17(3) HB&CTB(DA) Regs
**CB/GA** Reg 27(2) CB&GA(DA) Regs
**Other benefits** Reg 30(3) SS&CS(DA) Regs
95 **UC/PIP/new-style JSA&ESA** Reg 52(3) UC,PIP,JSA&ESA(DA) Regs
**HB** Reg 17(4) HB&CTB(DA) Regs
**CB/GA** Reg 27(3) CB&GA(DA) Regs
**Other benefits** Reg 30(4) SS&CS(DA) Regs
96 **UC/PIP/new-style JSA&ESA** Reg 52(4) UC,PIP,JSA&ESA(DA) Regs
**HB** Reg 17(5) HB&CTB(DA) Regs
**CB/GA** Reg 27(4) CB&GA(DA) Regs
**Other benefits** Reg 30(5) SS&CS(DA) Regs
97 *DO v SSWP (PIP)* [2021] UKUT 121 (AAC)
98 r2 TP(FT) Rules; r2 TP(UT) Rules
99 *MA v SSWP* [2009] UKUT 211 (AAC)
100 rr5, 6, 8, 15 and 16 TP(FT) Rules; rr5-7, 8, 15 and 16 TP(UT) Rules

101 s25 TCEA 2007; r7(3) TP(FT) Rules; r7(3) and (4) TP(UT) Rules; *MD v SSWP (Enforcement Reference)* [2010] UKUT 202 (AAC), reported as [2011] AACR 5; *CB v Suffolk CC (Enforcement Reference)* [2010] UKUT 413 (AAC), reported as [2011] AACR 22
102 r16(3) TP(FT) Rules; r16(3) TP(UT) Rules
103 r5(3)(l) TP(FT) Rules; r5(3)(l) and (m) TP(UT) Rules
104 r5(3)(a) TP(FT) Rules; r5(3)(a) TP(UT) Rules
105 r2(2)(e) TP(FT) Rules; r2(2)(e) TP(UT) Rules
106 rr5, 6 and 15 TP(FT) Rules; rr5, 6 and 15 TP(UT) Rules; *SR v Bristol CC* [2008] UKUT 7 (AAC)
107 r6(2) and (3) TP(FT) Rules; r6(2) and (3) TP(UT) Rules
108 r6(4) TP(FT) Rules; r5(4) TP(UT) Rules
109 r6(5) TP(FT) Rules; r6(5) TP(UT) Rules
110 r7 TP(FT) Rules; r7 TP(UT) Rules
111 R(H) 3/05; CCS/3757/2004
112 *SSWP v HS (JSA)* [2016] UKUT 272 (AAC), reported as [2017] AACR 29
113 *AP v SSWP (ESA)* [2017] UKUT 304 (AAC)
114 CIB/4253/2004
115 r15(2)(b) TP(FT) Rules; r15(2)(b) TP(UT) Rules
116 r5(3)(h) TP(FT) Rules; r5(3)(h) TP(UT) Rules; *MA v SSWP* [2009] UKUT 211 (AAC); Practice Statement: *Composition of Tribunals in Social Security and Child Support Cases in the Social Entitlement Chamber on or after 1 August 2013*, 31 July 2013, para 10
117 *LJT v SSWP (PIP)* [2019] UKUT 21 (AAC)
118 r31 TP(FT) Rules; r38 TP(UT) Rules
119 *BV v SSWP (PIP)* [2018] UKUT 444 (AAC)
120 CDLA/1290/2004
121 CDLA/3680/1997; *JC v SSWP (PIP)* [2018] UKUT 110 (AAC)
122 *MA v SSWP* [2009] UKUT 211 (AAC)
123 CDLA/5413/1999
124 *CB v SSWP (ESA)* [2020] UKUT 15 (AAC)
125 CIS/566/1991; CS/99/1993
126 CIS/2292/2000; *DC v SSWP (ESA)* [2015] UKUT 150 (AAC)
127 CIS/6002/1997; *R v Social Security Commissioner ex parte Angora Bibi* [2000] unreported (HC); CIB/1009/2004; CIB/2058/2004
128 CIS/3338/2001; *DC v SSWP* [2014] UKUT 218 (AAC)
129 *MH v Pembrokeshire CC (HB)* [2010] UKUT 28 (AAC)
130 r8(1), (3)(a) and (5) TP(FT) Rules; r8(1), (3)(a) and (5) TP(UT) Rules
131 *DTM v Kettering BC (CTB)* [2013] UKUT 625 (AAC)
132 r8(5) and (6) TP(FT) Rules; r8(5) and (6) TP(UT) Rules
133 r8(2) and (4) TP(FT) Rules; r8(2) and (4) TP(UT) Rules
134 r8(3)(b) and (c) and (4) TP(FT) Rules; r8(3)(b) TP(UT) Rules
135 *AW v IC and Blackpool CC* [2013] UKUT 30 (AAC)
136 R(IS) 5/94
137 *LS v Lambeth LB (HB)* [2010] UKUT 461 (AAC), reported as [2011] AACR 27
138 rr1(3), definition of 'respondent', and 8(7) TP(FT) Rules; rr1(3), definition of 'respondent', and 8(7) TP(UT) Rules
139 r8(8) TP(FT) Rules; r8(8) TP(UT) Rules
140 *ZB v SSWP (CSM)* [2013] UKUT 367 (AAC); *SL v SSWP and KL (CSM)* [2014] UKUT 128 (AAC); *CW v SSWP and Another (CSM)* [2014] UKUT 290 (AAC)
141 **HB** Reg 20(9) HB&CTB(DA) Regs; r17 TP(FT) Rules
**Other benefits** r17 TP(FT) Rules
**All** *WM v SSWP (DLA)* [2015] UKUT 642 (AAC)
142 *PD v SSWP (PIP)* [2021] UKUT 172 (AAC)
143 rr4 and 7(2)(a) TP(FT) Rules; Practice Statement: *Delegation of Functions to Staff in Relation to the Social Entitlement Chamber of the First-tier Tribunal on or after 1 October 2014*, 25 September 2014, paras 3 and 4
144 r4(3) TP(FT) Rules
145 r17(4) and (5) TP(FT) Rules
146 *FI v (1) SSWP (2) MC (CSM)* [2020] UKUT 173 (AAC)
147 s26 SSA 1998
148 rr5(3)(b) and 18 TP(FT) Rules

4. **How the tribunal makes its decision**
149 r1(3) TP(FT) Rules
150 r21(2) and 27(1) TP(FT) Rules; *MH v Pembrokeshire CC (HB)* [2010] UKUT 28 (AAC); *AT v SSWP (ESA)* [2010] UKUT 430 (AAC); *MM v SSWP (ESA)* [2011] UKUT 334 (AAC)
151 *RA v SSWP (II)* [2021] UKUT 148 (AAC)
152 *JS v Wirral MBC (HB)* [2021] UKUT 219 (AAC)
153 r11 TP(FT) Rules
154 r21 TP(FT) Rules
155 r1 TP(FT) Rules, definition of 'hearing'
156 r24(6) and (7) TP(FT) Rules
157 *MP v SSWP (DLA)* [2010] UKUT 103 (AAC)
158 r5(3)(f) TP(FT) Rules; *DT v SSWP (UC)* [2019] UKUT 268 (AAC)

159 r29 TP(FT) Rules
160 CH/3594/2002
161 r31 TP(FT) Rules; *WT v SSWP (DLA)* [2011] UKUT 93 (AAC)
162 *PS v SSWP (ESA)* [2017] UKUT 55 (AAC)
163 *KD v SSWP (ESA and IS) and KD v HMRC (TC)* [2020] UKUT 9 (AAC)
164 *LR v SSWP (ESA)* [2017] UKUT 412 (AAC)
165 *RK v SSWP (ESA)* [2018] UKUT 436 (AAC)
166 *AK v HMRC (TC)* [2016] UKUT 98 (AAC)
167 r30 TP(FT) Rules
168 Practice Direction: *Child, Vulnerable Adult and Sensitive Witnesses*, 30 October 2008; *SW v SSWP (DLA)* [2015] UKUT 319 (AAC); *LO'L v SSWP (ESA)* [2016] UKUT 10 (AAC), reported as [2016] AACR 31; *RT v SSWP (PIP)* [2019] UKUT 207 (AAC), reported as [2020] AACR 4; *JE v SSWP (PIP)* [2020] UKUT 17 (AAC)
169 r1(3) TP(FT) Rules, definition of 'hearing'
170 *LO'L v SSWP (ESA)* [2016] UKUT 10 (AAC), reported as [2016] AACR 31
171 *KO v SSWP (ESA)* [2013] UKUT 544 (AAC); *LS v SSWP (DLA)* [2015] UKUT 638 (AAC); *DB v SSWP (DLA)* [2016] UKUT 205 (AAC)
172 *LS v Lambeth LB (HB)* [2010] UKUT 461 (AAC), reported as [2011] AACR 27
173 CIB/2751/2002; CDLA/1350/2004
174 r11 TP(FT) Rules; CIB/1009/2004; CIB/2058/2004
175 r11(7) and (8) TP(FT) Rules
176 *ZO v SSWP (IB)* [2010] UKUT 143 (AAC); *AS v SSWP (ESA)* [2019] UKUT 261 (AAC)
177 Art 2 FTUT(CS)O; Practice Statement: *Composition of Tribunals in Social Security and Child Support Cases in the Social Entitlement Chamber on or after 1 August 2013*, 31 July 2013, updated 2 May 2024
178 *MB and Others v SSWP (ESA & DLA)* [2013] UKUT 111 (AAC), reported as [2014] AACR 1
179 Sch 4 para 15(6) TCEA 2007; *SB v SSWP (DLA)* [2013] UKUT 531 (AAC); *PF v SSWP (ESA)* [2015] UKUT 553 (AAC)
180 *PJ v SSWP (ESA)* [2011] UKUT 224 (AAC); *MB and Others v SSWP (ESA & DLA)* [2013] UKUT 111 (AAC), reported as [2014] AACR 1
181 R(U) 3/88; *JH v SSWP and MH* [2016] UKUT 158 (AAC); *SW v SSWP (ESA)* [2019] UKUT 415 (AAC)
182 Practice Statement: *Composition of Tribunals in Social Security and Child Support Cases in the Social Entitlement Chamber on or after 1 August 2013*, 31 July 2013, para 12
183 r2 TP(FT) Rules
184 CSDLA/606/2003
185 *PM v SSWP (PIP)* [2017] UKUT 154 (AAC)
186 CM/527/1992; CIB/3074/2003
187 CIB/5586/1999
188 CIB/476/2005; CIB/511/2005
189 r25(4) TP(FT) Rules
190 R(DLA) 1/95, qualified by CM/2/1994; *GL v SSWP* [2008] UKUT 36 (AAC)
191 *ID v SSWP (PIP)* [2015] UKUT 692 (AAC); *KMN v SSWP (PIP)* [2019] UKUT 42 (AAC)
192 R(DLA) 8/06
193 *HI v SSWP* [2014] UKUT 238 (AAC)
194 s20(3) SSA 1998
195 R(IB) 2/06
196 s20(3) SSA 1998; r25(2) TP(FT) Rules; R(DLA) 5/03
197 CI/3384/2006
198 Practice Statement: *Composition of Tribunals in Social Security and Child Support Cases in the Social Entitlement Chamber on or after 1 August 2013*, 31 July 2013, para 14
199 ss20(2) and 39 SSA 1998; r25(3) and Sch 2 TP(FT) Rules; *SSWP v DB (PIP)* [2016] UKUT 212 (AAC)
200 s20(2A) SSA 1998
201 CDLA/2014/2004
202 *GL v SSWP* [2008] UKUT 36 (AAC); *HI v SSWP* [2014] UKUT 238 (AAC)
203 CH/1229/2002
204 *Mongan v Department for Social Development* [2005] NICA 16, reported as R3/05 (DLA); *KN v SSWP (ESA)* [2021] UKUT 155 (AAC)
205 **HB** Sch 7 para 6(9)(a) CSPSSA 2000
**Other benefits** s12(8)(a) SSA 1998
**All** *DT v SSWP (PIP)* [2020] UKUT 156 (AAC)
206 *Mooney v SSWP* [2004] SLT 1141, reported as R(DLA) 5/04; *Mongan v Department for Social Development* [2005] NICA 16, reported as R3/05 (DLA); *SSWP v Hooper* [2007] EWCA Civ 495, reported as R(IB) 4/07; *KKL v SSWP (CPIP)* [2018] UKUT 17 (AAC)
207 *KKL v SSWP (CPIP)* [2018] UKUT 17 (AAC)
208 CSDLA/336/2000; CSIB/160/2000; R(H) 1/02
209 CH/1229/2002; R(IB) 2/04; *AP-H v SSWP (DLA)* [2010] UKUT 183 (AAC)
210 CI/531/2000; CDLA/1000/2001; CH/1229/2002; R(IB) 2/04; CDLA/884/2008; *ET v SSWP (PIP)* [2017] UKUT 478 (AAC); *LJ v SSWP (PIP)* [2017] UKUT 455 (AAC)

211 CDLA/4184/2004
212 R(IB) 2/04
213 R(IB) 2/04; CH/3009/2002
214 CDLA/1707/2005
215 R(IB) 2/04; R(IB) 7/04; CIS/1675/2004
216 **HB** Sch 7 para 6(9)(b) CSPSSA 2000
**Other benefits** s12(8)(b) SSA 1998; R(DLA) 4/05
217 R(DLA) 2/01; R(DLA) 3/01; CJSA/2375/2000; *KK v Liverpool City Council (HB)* [2020] UKUT 80 (AAC)
218 R(SB) 4/85

6. **The tribunal's decision**
219 r33 TP(FT) Rules
220 Art 8 FTUT(CS)O
221 *PF (Nigeria) v Secretary of State for the Home Department* [2015] EWCA Civ 251, reported as [2015] 1 WLR 5235
222 Practice Statement, *Record of Proceedings in Social Security and Child Support Cases in the Social Entitlement Chamber on or after 31 March 2022*, 1 April 2022, available at judiciary.uk
223 *MK v SSWP (CI)* [2014] UKUT 323 (AAC)
224 *DT v SSWP* [2015] UKUT 509 (AAC)
225 r34(2) TP(FT) Rules
226 r34(3) TP(FT) Rules; CCS/1664/2001
227 r34(4) TP(FT) Rules; CIB/3937/2000
228 r5(3)(a) TP(FT) Rules
229 r34(5) TP(FT) Rules
230 r38(7)(a) TP(FT) Rules
231 *RU v SSWP (ESA)* [2014] UKUT 532 (AAC)
232 r5(3)(n) TP(UT) Rules
233 **UC/PIP/new-style JSA&ESA** s21 SSA 1998; reg 44 UC,PIP,JSA&ESA(DA) Regs
**HB** Sch 7 para 13 CSPSSA 2000; reg 11 HB&CTB(DA) Regs
**CB/GA** s21 SSA 1998; reg 18 CB&GA(DA) Regs
**Other benefits** s21 SSA 1998; reg 16 SS&CS(DA) Regs
234 r5(3)(l) TP(FT) Rules
235 r36 TP(FT) Rules; CI/3887/1999; CSDLA/168/2008; *AS v SSWP (ESA)* [2011] UKUT 159 (AAC)
236 r37(1) and (2) TP(FT) Rules
237 *MA v SSWP (PIP)* [2020] UKUT 2 (AAC)
238 r37(3) TP(FT) Rules
239 r5(3)(a) TP(FT) Rules
240 r27(2) TP(FT) Rules; CSB/172/1990
241 CIB/4193/2003
242 CI/79/1990; CIS/373/1994; *MA v SSWP (PIP)* [2020] UKUT 2 (AAC)
243 *LS v Lambeth LB (HB)* [2010] UKUT 461 (AAC), reported as [2011] AACR 27
244 r38(3) and (4) TP(FT) Rules
245 r41 TP(FT) Rules
246 **HB** Sch 7 para 7(3) and (4) CSPSSA 2000
**Other benefits** s13(3) and (4) SSA 1998

# Chapter 52

# Appealing to the Upper Tribunal and the courts

**This chapter covers:**


1. Appealing to the Upper Tribunal (below)
2. How to appeal to the Upper Tribunal (p1219)
3. After you get permission to appeal (p1225)
4. Hearings (p1228)
5. The decision (p1229)
6. Appealing to the Court of Appeal or Court of Session (p1231)


This chapter does *not* cover the rules for appeals to the Upper Tribunal for Scotland about the Scottish benefits (see Chapter 69).

8

## Key facts

- If your appeal to the First-tier Tribunal is unsuccessful, you may be able to appeal to the Upper Tribunal, but only if the First-tier Tribunal made a legal mistake (an 'error of law'). You must first get permission to appeal from the First-tier or Upper Tribunal.
- If your Upper Tribunal appeal is unsuccessful, you may be able to appeal to the Court of Appeal or the Court of Session.
- The DWP, local authority and HMRC can also appeal to the Upper Tribunal or the courts.
- There are strict time limits for appealing. They can sometimes be extended.
- Appeals can take time. If your circumstances change while you are waiting for your appeal to be heard, you may need to make a fresh claim for benefit or request a supersession.

## 1. Appealing to the Upper Tribunal

You have a right of appeal against any First-tier Tribunal decision (except an excluded decision – see p1216) to the Administrative Appeals Chamber of the Upper Tribunal.[1] However, your right of appeal is only on a 'point of law', which usually means that you must show the decision contained an error of law. Your appeal is dealt with by a judge (or judges). HM Courts and Tribunals Service (HMCTS) is responsible for the administration of the tribunal's work.

*Excluded decisions*[2]

**'Excluded decisions'** are certain decisions taken by the First-tier Tribunal when it considers a review (see p1223) – ie, decisions:
- to review, or not to review, an earlier decision;
- to take no action, or not to take any particular action, in the light of a review of an earlier decision;
- to 'set aside' an earlier decision on review (the decision that is set aside is also excluded);
- to refer, or not to refer, a matter to the Upper Tribunal.

You can only appeal to the Upper Tribunal if the First-tier Tribunal made an 'error of law' – ie, a legal mistake (see below).[3] The mere fact that you disagree with the decision is not enough. You must first get permission to appeal. There is a strict time limit for applying (see p1222 and p1225). The DWP, the local authority and HMRC have the same appeal rights as you.

If you have evidence not known by the First-tier Tribunal, you may be able to ask the DWP, the local authority or HMRC for a supersession of the tribunal's decision on the grounds that there was a mistake about or ignorance of the facts (see p1146). You can do this while you are waiting for your appeal to be heard. Bear in mind that the amount of arrears you can get with a supersession is usually limited, so you need to continue with your appeal at the same time.

Note:

- If a decision in a test case is pending that deals with issues raised in your appeal, the Upper Tribunal may delay your appeal. For when the decision maker can serve a notice requiring the tribunal to delay your appeal, see p1193 – the rules are the same as for the First-tier Tribunal.
- Some Upper Tribunal decisions can be made by legally qualified HMCTS staff (called 'registrars').[4] You can ask an Upper Tribunal judge to reconsider a registrar's decision. You must apply in writing within 14 days after the date you are sent notice of the decision. The tribunal can give you longer (or shorter) than this. There is no guarantee you will be given longer, so keep within the time limit wherever possible.

## Error of law

An 'error of law' is a legal mistake. The error must have made a difference, or potentially made a difference, to the outcome of the appeal. The First-tier Tribunal made an error of law in the following situations.[5]

- The tribunal got the law wrong or misinterpreted it – eg, it misunderstood the particular benefit rule concerned. **Note:** if the tribunal gives the reasons for its decision in its decision notice (see p1205) and these indicate that it did not apply the law correctly, the decision notice is likely to be a more reliable statement of its reasons than a later conflicting explanation in a statement of reasons.[6]
- The tribunal gave you a physical examination when it was not permitted to do so (see p1200) and based its decision on evidence obtained from this.[7]
- There were errors due to unfairness in how the appeal was decided (see below).
- The tribunal made errors about the facts (see p1218) – ie, it failed to make proper findings of fact or did not make use of those findings correctly in coming to its decision.
- The tribunal did not provide adequate reasons for its decision (see p1219).

***What if a different tribunal would have made a different decision?***

The First-tier Tribunal has not made an error of law simply because a different First-tier Tribunal (or the Upper Tribunal) might have reached a different conclusion.[8] An appeal to the Upper Tribunal is *not* another opportunity for you to argue about the facts of the case.[9]

## Errors due to unfairness in how the appeal was decided

The First-tier Tribunal made an error of law if there were procedural or other irregularities that could make a material difference to the outcome or fairness of the proceedings. That could occur because of a breach of the principles of natural justice or a failure to follow a procedural rule, Practice Statement or Practice Direction. Examples of procedural unfairness include if:

- you have not been given the opportunity to present your case;
- there has been bias in the conduct of your case.

### Not given the opportunity to present the case

The First-tier Tribunal made an error of law if you have not been given the opportunity to present your case – eg:

- a hearing was requested, but one did not take place;[10]
- you did not get notice of the hearing through no fault of your own, and so you lost the appeal without having had a chance to put your case properly, even if you could have applied for the tribunal's decision to be set aside instead;[11]
- you did not receive the decision maker's response or did not receive it in sufficient time before the hearing, or you did not receive advance notice of documentary evidence that you had not seen before, and were not given an opportunity to read it properly;[12]
- the decision maker's response to your appeal does not make proper reference to the law used in making the decision you have appealed against, so that you have not been given adequate opportunity to make your case;[13]

- the tribunal failed to properly consider and explain why it felt it was fair to proceed to determine the appeal without a hearing, or in your absence. Even if you did not ask for a hearing, the tribunal still needs to consider whether it is fair to proceed without one;[14]
- the tribunal failed to include you as a party to the appeal when it should have been obvious that you had an interest in the outcome of the case – eg, in your child's other parent's appeal in a dispute about who should receive child benefit;[15]
- the tribunal failed to act on a request for an interpreter and, as a result, it could not understand your evidence correctly;[16]
- you were not allowed to call witnesses who were likely to be able to give relevant evidence to support you;
- the standard of interpretation was not adequate and the tribunal did not take appropriate action;[17]
- the tribunal made a decision without a hearing, based on the papers only, that was more unfavourable to you than the one you had appealed – eg, it removed your entitlement to benefit without warning you or giving you a chance to make representations.[18]

#### Bias in the conduct of the case

8

The First-tier Tribunal made an error of law if there has been bias in the conduct of your case. That is, the circumstances would lead a fair-minded and informed observer to conclude that there was a real possibility that one or more of the tribunal members regarded a party with favour or disfavour – eg:

- the person presenting the DWP case (the presenting officer) is allowed to be in the room with the tribunal members without you;[19]
- the way the tribunal conducts your case makes it look like it had already made up its mind before the hearing commenced;
- the tribunal pressurises you into giving up your right to a fair hearing – eg, it bargains with you by 'offering' you one component of personal independence payment if you agree not to argue for the other. **Note:** if you decide to carry on with the appeal and the tribunal decides not to award the component 'offered', it should warn you before the hearing ends to allow you to consider this and make representations. This should be recorded in the statement of reasons.[20]

### Errors about the facts

The First-tier Tribunal made an error of law if:

- there is no evidence to support its decision; *or*
- when making its conclusions from the facts, it took things into account which it should not have, or refused or failed to take things into account which it should have (see p1201). However, the tribunal has usually not made an error of law if it fails to take account of evidence that was not before it at the hearing – ie, evidence only produced when your appeal is before the Upper Tribunal; *or*

- the facts are inconsistent with the decision – eg, the tribunal accepted that a man and a woman live in separate households, but then decided that they are living together as a married couple;[21] *or*
- it did not give proper findings of fact. The tribunal must show there are sufficient facts to support its decision.[22] It can rely on the summary of the facts given in the decision maker's response (see p1183), provided these are not disputed and cover all the relevant issues.[23] If you and the DWP, the local authority or HMRC disagree about the facts, the tribunal must explain which version it prefers and why. It should refer to the main evidence on which it has relied. However, it is not necessarily an error of law if it does not mention every item of evidence put forward. The tribunal should give an adequate explanation of why it rejected any piece of evidence as untrue;[24] *or*
- it made a mistake about a fact that would have made a difference to the outcome of your appeal, there was unfairness as a result, and the fact could have been established by objective and uncontentious evidence. This only applies if you and your adviser were not responsible for the mistake.[25]

### Inadequate reasons for the decision

The First-tier Tribunal makes an error of law if it does not provide adequate reasons for its decision.[26] The tribunal must not simply say what its decision is; it must give sufficient reasons so that you can see why it reached the conclusion it did, even if you still disagree with the outcome. If the summary of the reasons in the decision notice is inconsistent with those in the written statement of reasons, this is an error of law.[27] If a delay in writing the reasons indicates that they are unreliable as an accurate statement of the tribunal's reasoning, you can argue that the reasons are inadequate.[28]

**Note:** the tribunal does not have to give its reasons for refusing to adjourn an appeal hearing.[29] However, a refusal to adjourn may be so obviously unfair that it constitutes an error of law.

8

## 2. How to appeal to the Upper Tribunal

You must obtain permission to appeal to the Upper Tribunal.[30] This means you must show that the First-tier Tribunal has possibly made an 'error of law' (see p1216) and you have the beginnings of a case. You must first apply to the First-tier Tribunal for permission. If it refuses (or rejects) your application, you can then apply for permission direct to the Upper Tribunal. There are strict time limits for applying for permission to appeal (see p1222 and p1225).

**Note:** because of the time you usually have to wait before your case is dealt with, you should make a fresh claim for benefit (or request a supersession) – eg, if your circumstances change. See p1203 for the advantages of doing this (the issues are similar to those for First-tier Tribunal appeals).

## Representatives

You can have a representative to help you with your appeal.[31] It is advisable to get a representative if you can. A representative can explain the procedures, check the relevant law, present your case and produce a written submission to ensure the Upper Tribunal is aware of all the relevant issues. You must send or give the tribunal written notice of your representative's name and address, or they must do this on your behalf. Unless they are a solicitor or barrister, if your representative is providing the notice, they should also provide an authorisation signed by you.

**Note:**

- You must authorise your representative to act for you in your appeal to the Upper Tribunal, even if they acted for you in your appeal to the First-tier Tribunal and you authorised them at an earlier stage. Once you have given notice that you have a representative, they are presumed to be acting for you unless you give (or they give) notice in writing that this is no longer the case. Your representative must be sent any documents that are required to be sent to you; these then do not have to be sent to you.[32] However, do not assume that this always happens. If you receive documents, check that your representative has also received them.
- If you have not previously notified the tribunal that you have a representative, someone can attend a hearing with (or for) you and act as your representative and help you present your case, if the tribunal agrees.

8

***Can your representative or adviser get help with your appeal?***

If you live in England or Wales, your representative, adviser or support worker may be able to get advice about, and assistance with, your appeal to the Upper Tribunal from CPAG's Upper Tribunal Assistance Project. This can include advice on procedure and the merits of your case, as well as help making your application for permission to appeal. In some cases, CPAG may be able to provide representation. See cpag.org.uk/upper-tribunal-assistance-project for further information and an online referral form.

## Meeting the costs of representation

Free legal help from a solicitor is available in limited cases. This is means tested. If you do not qualify, you may be able to get free help from your local Citizens Advice office, law centre, welfare rights service or advice centre.

In England or Wales, free legal help is available for advice and assistance with appealing to the Upper Tribunal, including applications for permission to appeal that are made direct to the Upper Tribunal. You only qualify for help from a lawyer to cover representation at a hearing in exceptional cases – if it is necessary to make these services available to you because a failure to do so would be a breach of your right to have legal representation as provided under human rights law or your retained enforceable European Union rights.[33]

In Scotland, free legal help is currently available for Upper Tribunal appeals, including for help preparing for appeals that will be decided at a hearing and those that will be decided on the papers only. If the Scottish Legal Aid Board approves and the Upper Tribunal is sitting in Scotland, you can get help with representation. The Board only gives approval if it is satisfied that your case is arguable, it is reasonable for representation to be made available and your case is too complex for you to present it effectively yourself in person – eg, if there is likely to be procedural difficulty or a substantial question of law, if the evidence is complex, or if you may be unable to understand the proceedings or to state your own case because of a disability, your age or your knowledge of English.[34]

If you are granted funding for legal help, you must send a copy of the funding notice (in Scotland, the legal aid certificate) to the Upper Tribunal as soon as practicable.[35] You must also let the other parties involved in your appeal know that you have been granted funding.

## Applying to the First-tier Tribunal for permission

You must first apply for permission to appeal to the First-tier Tribunal.[36] Before applying, you should obtain a statement of reasons for its decision (see p1206). If you do not have a statement of reasons, see p1222.

Your application must:[37]

- be in writing; *and*
- contain:
  - details of your grounds for appeal (ie, the error(s) of law you think the tribunal made); *and*
  - sufficient information about the decision for it to be identified; *and*
  - if you are making a late application, your reasons for this; *and*
- state the result you are seeking – eg, that permission to appeal should be given and the Upper Tribunal should send the case back to the First-tier Tribunal for a new hearing.

The person considering your application is often the same judge who decided your appeal, although this is not always the case.[38] Applications for permission to appeal are usually decided without a hearing, so make sure you fully explain your grounds for appeal when you apply.[39]

The First-tier Tribunal must send you a record of its decision on your application as soon as practicable.[40] If your application is refused, reasons must be provided, as well as notice of your right to make a fresh application to the Upper Tribunal for permission to appeal, along with information about how to apply and the time limit for doing so. You should study the First-tier Tribunal's reasons for refusal carefully.

If you, the DWP, the local authority or HMRC apply for permission to appeal to the Upper Tribunal, the First-tier Tribunal can review its decision (see p1223) or treat the application for permission to appeal as an application for the decision to be corrected or 'set aside'.[41] If you and the other party agree that the tribunal made an error of law, its decision *must* be set aside (see p1209).

## If you do not have a statement of reasons

Without a statement of reasons, you may find it difficult to show that the First-tier Tribunal made an error of law. If you do not have a statement of reasons because:[42]

- you did not apply for one, the First-tier Tribunal must treat your application for permission to appeal as an application for a statement of reasons. Once the statement of reasons is provided, unless the tribunal decides to give you permission to appeal, you must then apply for permission to appeal again;
- your application for one was refused when you missed the time limit (see p1206), the First-tier Tribunal can only allow your application for permission to appeal to go ahead ('admit' your application) if it thinks it is in the interests of justice.[43] If it admits your application, it then decides whether to give you permission. If it rejects your application (ie, refuses to admit it) or refuses to give you permission, you can apply direct to the Upper Tribunal for permission.

## Time limit for applying

8

Your application for permission to appeal must be received by the First-tier Tribunal no later than one month (see p1175) after the latest of the following dates – ie, the date you were sent:[44]

- the decision notice; *or*
- a written statement of reasons (see p1206) for the tribunal's decision; *or*
- notice that, following a review (see p1223), the reasons for the tribunal's decision were amended, or the decision was corrected; *or*
- notice that an application for the tribunal's decision to be set aside (see p1208) was unsuccessful, but only if that application was made within the time limit for applying for a set-aside (or any longer period allowed).

The tribunal can extend (or shorten) your time limit.[45] There is no absolute time limit for applying, but the longer you delay, the harder it may be to show that the time limit should be extended. There is no guarantee that you will be given longer, so keep within the one-month time limit wherever possible. See p1177 for when it may be fair and just to extend your time limit.

If your time limit is not extended, the First-tier Tribunal must reject your application.[46] If your application is rejected, you can still apply direct to the Upper Tribunal for permission. However, the Upper Tribunal can only allow your application to go ahead ('admit' your application) if it considers it is in the interests of justice to do so.[47]

## When the First-tier Tribunal can review its decision

When the First-tier Tribunal receives an application for permission to appeal to the Upper Tribunal, it must first consider whether or not to review its own decision.[48] It should not go on to consider the application until it has decided not to review its decision or decided to review it but to take no action. However, if it goes on to consider the application, that does not necessarily make its decision about permission invalid.[49] You do not have a right to apply for a review yourself, but if you do, your application can be treated as an application for permission to appeal.[50]

The First-tier Tribunal can only review a decision if it is satisfied that there is an error of law (see p1216).[51] If it decides to carry out a review, it should consider whether to give you and the decision maker an opportunity to comment. This means that if the DWP, local authority or HMRC has applied for permission to appeal, you have the chance to say why the decision should not be changed. If the tribunal *does* review the decision, it can:[52]

- correct any accidental errors in the decision or the record of the decision; *and*
- amend the reasons given for the decision – eg, if it considered matters, but inadvertently did not include them in the statement of reasons. However, the tribunal should not add reasons which were not part of its thinking at the time it made its decision;[53] *and*
- 'set aside' the decision. This means the decision is cancelled. The tribunal usually then directs a new tribunal to make a new decision. In rare circumstances, it makes a new decision itself at the same time as it reviews the decision. The tribunal also has the power to refer your appeal to the Upper Tribunal to make a decision, but this power is rarely used.

You must be notified in writing of the review's outcome and your right of appeal (if any).[54] If the First-tier Tribunal has taken any action and you were not given an opportunity to comment before the review, you must also be notified that you can apply for the action to be cancelled and for the decision to be reviewed again.

If the First-tier Tribunal decides not to review its decision or reviews it but takes no action, it must consider whether to give you permission to appeal to the Upper Tribunal against the decision.[55]

## Applying to the Upper Tribunal for permission

If the First-tier Tribunal refuses you permission to appeal or rejects your application for permission (eg, because it was late), you can make a fresh application to the Upper Tribunal.[56] You must apply in writing.

***Forms***

Use Form UT1 *Application for Permission to Appeal and Notice of Appeal from the First-tier Tribunal (Social Entitlement Chamber).* This is available at gov.uk/government/collections/

administrative-appeals-chamber-upper-tribunal-forms or from the regional office of HM Courts and Tribunals Service (HMCTS) or the Upper Tribunal Office (see gov.uk/courts-tribunals/upper-tribunal-administrative-appeals-chamber for the addresses).

Your application must include:[57]

- your name and address, the name and address of your representative (if any) and the address where documents can be sent or delivered. If you have an appointee, the appeal form asks for their details; *and*
- details of the decision you want to appeal (eg, the date of the decision) and the First-tier Tribunal reference number; *and*
- the grounds for your appeal – ie, the error(s) of law you think the First-tier Tribunal made; *and*
- if your application is late, a request for your time limit to be extended and the reasons why you are applying late; *and*
- whether you want your application to be dealt with at a hearing; *and*
- copies of the First-tier Tribunal's decision, its statement of reasons and the notice of its rejection or refusal of your application for permission. If your application to the First-tier Tribunal was rejected because it (or your application for a statement of reasons) was late, you must also include the reasons for the lateness.

8

The Upper Tribunal can waive any irregularities in your application in some cases.[58] If your application to the First-tier Tribunal for permission to appeal was rejected because it was late or your application for a statement of reasons was late, the Upper Tribunal can only allow your application for permission to appeal to go ahead ('admit' your application) if it thinks it is in the interests of justice to do so.[59] If your application is admitted, it then goes on to decide whether to give you permission to appeal.

The appeal form asks whether you want a hearing of your application.

***What if you do not have a statement of reasons?***

If you do not have a statement of reasons for the First-tier Tribunal's decision, you are not prevented from applying to the Upper Tribunal for permission to appeal. However, you must be able to show that the First-tier Tribunal made an error of law without it – eg, from what is said in the decision notice.[60] It is an error of law if the First-tier Tribunal fails to provide a statement of reasons when it has a duty to do so – eg, you apply for one in time, but the tribunal says your application was late and refuses to provide one.[61]

If you have a representative who is legally qualified (or is supervised by such a person), they must send your appeal form and any documents associated with your appeal using the Upper Tribunal's online CE-File service.[62] See gov.uk/

guidance/hmcts-e-filing-service-for-citizens-and-professionals for information about this.

If you do not have a legally qualified representative, you or your representative can still use this service if you want to. To use CE-File, you have first to register as an 'E-Filer' with the Upper Tribunal at efile.cefile-app.com/login. Or you can send your form by email or by post (or any other way which the Upper Tribunal permits you to use).[63]

The Upper Tribunal gets the file of your appeal papers from the regional HMCTS office. It considers these and what you say in your application before reaching a decision. The DWP, local authority or HMRC usually plays no part in the procedure at this stage, although the tribunal sometimes asks it to make a submission in cases of particular difficulty. If this happens, you are given an opportunity to reply. Sometimes, the Upper Tribunal may ask you if you would like a hearing (see p1228) to assist in deciding whether you should be granted permission to appeal, or may direct that one will take place.

You are sent a written notice of the tribunal's decision on your application, usually including the reasons for the decision.[64] You cannot appeal against a refusal to admit your application to appeal or to give you permission to appeal, but you may be able to apply for the decision to be set aside (see p1230) or in very rare cases to a court for judicial review (see p1247).[65]

### Time limit for applying



Your application for permission to appeal must be received by the Upper Tribunal no later than one month (see p1175) after the date the First-tier Tribunal's refusal (or rejection) was sent to you.[66] The Upper Tribunal can extend (or shorten) your time limit.[67] There is no guarantee that you will be given longer, so keep within the one-month time limit wherever possible.

The decision whether or not to allow a late appeal to the Upper Tribunal must be made bearing in mind the merits of the appeal and the consequences for you (and the DWP, the local authority or HMRC).[68] See p1177 for when it may be fair and just to extend your time limit. The issues are the same as for appeals to the First-tier Tribunal. If your time limit is not extended, the Upper Tribunal rejects your application to appeal and your appeal does not go ahead.

## 3. After you get permission to appeal

If you have been given permission to appeal by the First-tier Tribunal, you must send the Upper Tribunal:[69]

- a 'notice of appeal', so that it is received within one month after you are sent notice of the permission. You are sent Form UT1 *Application for Permission to Appeal and Notice of Appeal from the First-tier Tribunal (Social Entitlement Chamber)* on which to do this; *and*

- if you are sending the notice of appeal late, a request for an extension of time and the reasons why your notice is late; *and*
- a copy of the notice that you have been given permission to appeal; *and*
- a copy of the First-tier Tribunal's decision and its statement of reasons (if you have one); *and*
- your details; *and*
- your reasons for appealing against the decision.

The Upper Tribunal can extend (or shorten) the time limit for receipt of your notice of appeal.[70] There is no guarantee that you will be given longer, so keep within the time limit wherever possible. See p1177 for when it may be fair and just to extend your time limit. The issues are the same as for appeals to the First-tier Tribunal. If your time limit is not extended, the Upper Tribunal rejects your appeal and it does not go ahead.

**Note:** if you have applied for permission to appeal direct to the Upper Tribunal on Form UT1, unless you are told otherwise, your application is treated as a notice of appeal. In this case, you do not need to send in another.[71]

## What the Upper Tribunal can do

8

There are procedural rules that the Upper Tribunal must follow when dealing with your appeal. Whenever the Upper Tribunal is considering applying these procedural rules, it must bear in mind the 'overriding objective', which is to enable it to deal with cases fairly and justly.[72] This includes avoiding delay (provided the issues can be considered properly), avoiding unnecessary formality, allowing flexibility in the proceedings and ensuring that all the parties can participate fully. You, the DWP, the local authority and HMRC must help the tribunal further the objective and co-operate with it. This involves ensuring, as far as possible, that your case is ready by the time of any hearing.[73] The rules are generally the same as for the First-tier Tribunal, so if relevant, these are referred to below.

The Upper Tribunal can do the following:[74]

- extend or shorten any time limits (see p1187). For the rules about extending your time limit for applying for permission to appeal, see p1222; *and*
- issue directions (see p1188);
- postpone or adjourn your appeal hearing (see p1189);
- 'strike out' an appeal (see p1190). **Note:** the Upper Tribunal does *not* have the discretion to strike out your appeal on the grounds that there is no reasonable prospect of success;
- bar people from taking part in an appeal (see p1192). *You* can be barred from taking part in an appeal to the Upper Tribunal if the other party appealed;
- require the First-tier Tribunal to provide reasons for its decision, or other information or documents relating to its decision or the proceedings;[75]

- summons witnesses to attend a hearing, answer questions and produce documents. If someone fails to comply, the tribunal can punish them for contempt of court.[76] You cannot be required to give evidence or produce any document that you could not be compelled to give by a court;[77]
- suspend the effect of its decision while considering any application for permission to appeal against, or review, that decision. It can also suspend the effect of a First-tier Tribunal decision while an application for permission to appeal against the decision is being considered and pending that appeal being determined.[78]

## Withdrawing an appeal

If you change your mind about appealing, you can withdraw your appeal.[79] However, once you have been given permission to appeal, you must have the Upper Tribunal's consent. You must give notice to the tribunal that you want to withdraw your appeal in writing or at a hearing.

### Getting an appeal reinstated

If you withdraw your appeal but then decide that you want it to go ahead, you can apply for it to be reinstated.[80] You must apply in writing. Your application must be received by the Upper Tribunal within one month after the date it received written notice that you wanted to withdraw your appeal or, if you withdraw your appeal at a hearing, within one month (see p1175) of the date of the hearing. The tribunal can give you longer (or shorter) than one month.[81] There is no guarantee that you will be given longer, so keep within the time limit wherever possible.

8

## The written procedure

When permission to appeal has been given, the Upper Tribunal sends you a copy of the appeal file used by the First-tier Tribunal, and a separate file used by the Upper Tribunal. You and the DWP, local authority or HMRC are asked for a response and are told the timetable for providing one.[82]

The decision maker is usually asked to provide a response first. DWP and HMRC responses are written by specialist staff working from national centres. They often take a different view than decision makers who have been involved previously and may even support your appeal.

You are given the chance to reply to the response and are usually given one month to do so, although the tribunal may extend (or shorten) the time limit.[83] There is no guarantee that you will be given longer, so keep within the time limit wherever possible. If you know that you are going to need more time, request that as soon as possible. Tell the tribunal if you have nothing to add and do not want to reply at any stage.

If the decision maker supports your appeal, the tribunal may give its decision without reasons if you and the decision maker agree to this.[84]

***Has the decision maker been given permission to appeal?***

If you won your appeal at the First-tier Tribunal, the DWP, local authority or HMRC may have obtained permission to appeal to the Upper Tribunal. If so, you are asked to respond under the rules described above. It is crucial to provide a response. Consider the decision maker's arguments carefully and explain why you think the First-tier Tribunal did not make an error of law and its decision was correct. Bear in mind that if the decision maker wins the appeal to the Upper Tribunal, the First-tier Tribunal's decision could be overturned, and you could, for example, lose the benefit that it awarded to you, or have to repay an overpayment it said was not recoverable.

## 4. Hearings

The Upper Tribunal decides whether or not there should be a hearing of the appeal.[85] It must take your views and those of the DWP, the local authority or HMRC into account. You are asked whether you want a hearing and, if so, why. The tribunal can decide to hold a hearing, even if you have not asked for one. However, it usually only holds one if the case involves complicated issues of law that written arguments cannot easily resolve. If there is no hearing, the tribunal makes a decision based on the papers only – ie, the written responses and other documents provided.

Hearings can be in person or 'remote' hearings by telephone or video link.[86] You and your representative may be able to participate in the hearing via a video link such as the HM Courts and Tribunals Service Cloud Video Platform – eg, if your disability makes it difficult for you to travel or to avoid travel costs and time.

If the tribunal decides there should be a hearing, you must be given at least 14 days' notice, although you may get less notice than this if you agree, your appeal is urgent or there are exceptional circumstances.[87]

Hearings are held regularly in Cardiff, Edinburgh, London and Manchester, but can be held in other locations if necessary. You can claim reimbursement of your travel costs and should be given a leaflet about this. A hearing closer to your home can be arranged in exceptional circumstances – eg, if you have difficulty travelling because of a disability. A judge decides whether or not to hold a local hearing based on, for example, medical evidence and why a local hearing is needed.

Usually, one judge hears your appeal. However, if there is a 'question of law of special difficulty', an important point of principle or practice, or it is otherwise appropriate, two or three judges may hear your appeal,[88] but the procedure is the same.

**Note:**

- The tribunal will usually ask you to provide a summary of the arguments you will make (a 'skeleton argument') before the hearing. If it does, you must provide one.[89] You should do this within the time you are allowed.[90]
- The hearing is more formal than First-tier Tribunal hearings, but the judge lets you say everything you want to. Judges usually intervene a lot and ask questions, so be prepared to argue your case without your script.
- The decision maker is usually represented by a lawyer, so you should also consider obtaining representation – eg, from a solicitor, your local Citizens Advice or advice centre. See p1220 for meeting the costs of representation.

## 5. The decision

There are two stages to an Upper Tribunal decision.[91]

- **Stage one:** the tribunal decides whether the First-tier Tribunal made an 'error of law'. If it decides it did, the First-tier Tribunal's decision is normally 'set aside' and no longer has any effect. However, in some cases, the Upper Tribunal may decide that the error of law had no practical effect on the outcome of your appeal, so the decision does not have to be set aside.
- **Stage two:** if the First-tier Tribunal's decision is set aside, the Upper Tribunal decides how to deal with the case.
  - If it agrees that the First-tier Tribunal's decision was wrong, the case is often sent back to the First-tier Tribunal to hear your appeal again and make a new decision. The Upper Tribunal usually makes an order stating that the new tribunal should not include the judge or any members from the original appeal hearing and gives directions on how it should reconsider the issues. **Note:** at the new hearing, the First-tier Tribunal will not necessarily decide your appeal in your favour. However, you may be able to appeal to the Upper Tribunal again if there is another error of law.
  - If the Upper Tribunal thinks the First-tier Tribunal's statement of reasons for its decision contains all the material facts, or it has been able to make any necessary extra findings of fact, it may make the final decision. This may or may not be in your favour.

The Upper Tribunal's decision is usually given in writing, but may be given orally at the hearing.[92] You are not usually referred to by name in the decision.[93] Detailed reasons are given. You must be sent a decision notice as soon as is reasonably practicable, as well as notice of your right of appeal, how to appeal and the time limit for doing so. Decisions are often lengthy as they may need to explain complex issues of law. So it may take time for the judge to prepare the decision. You can complain to the Administrative Appeals Chamber President if there is undue delay.

## If you disagree with the Upper Tribunal's decision

If you disagree with the Upper Tribunal's decision, you cannot simply ask it to look at the decision again – eg, if you have additional points to make. However, the following may be done.

- The tribunal may correct any clerical mistake or an accidental slip or omission in a decision or record of a decision.[94]
- The tribunal may 'set aside' its decision on procedural grounds – ie, how it handled your appeal.[95] If it sets aside a decision, this means the decision is cancelled. A decision can be set aside if the tribunal thinks it is in the interests of justice and:
  - you, your representative or the DWP, the local authority or HMRC were not sent papers or other documents relating to the proceedings or did not receive them at an appropriate time, or the tribunal was not sent them at an appropriate time; *or*
  - you, your representative or the DWP, local authority or HMRC were not present at a hearing; *or*
  - there has been some other procedural irregularity in the proceedings in the Upper Tribunal.

  You must apply in writing for a decision to be set aside. Your application is dealt with by the judge who made the original decision. It must be received by the tribunal no later than one month after you were sent notice of the decision. The tribunal can extend (or shorten) this time limit. However, there is no guarantee that you will be given longer, so keep within the time limit wherever possible.[96] If you think the tribunal made a legal error, you must instead appeal to the Court of Appeal or Court of Session (see p1231) or, if relevant, apply for a judicial review (see Chapter 53). An Upper Tribunal decision to set aside the decision, or refusing to set it aside, also has the right of appeal to the Court of Appeal or Court of Session (see p1231).
- The decision can be superseded by the DWP, local authority or HMRC if there are grounds – eg, if there was a mistake about, or ignorance of, the facts (see p1143). However, if the tribunal made a mistake about the law, you must appeal to a court.
- You or the DWP, local authority or HMRC can appeal to the Court of Appeal (in Scotland, the Court of Session) – see p1231.
- If you (or the decision maker) seek permission to appeal to the Court of Appeal or Court of Session, the tribunal can review its decision (see p1232).

The Upper Tribunal can treat an application for a decision to be corrected, set aside or reviewed, or for permission to appeal against a decision, as an application for any other of these.[97]

# 6. Appealing to the Court of Appeal or Court of Session

You have a right to appeal against an Upper Tribunal decision on a point of law to the Court of Appeal or, in Scotland, the Court of Session. This applies to all Upper Tribunal decisions except an 'excluded decision'. You can only do this if the Upper Tribunal made an 'error of law' (see p1216) and you must first obtain permission to appeal.[98] The DWP, the local authority and HMRC have the same appeal rights as you.

*Excluded decisions*

**'Excluded decisions'**[99] are decisions taken by the Upper Tribunal on an application for permission to appeal against a First-tier Tribunal decision and certain decisions taken when it considers a review (see p1232) – ie, decisions:
- to review, or not to review, an earlier decision, including a decision to set aside the earlier decision on review;
- to take no action, or not to take any particular action, in the light of a review of an earlier decision.



Permission to appeal to the Court of Appeal or the Court of Session cannot be given unless the Upper Tribunal or the court considers that the appeal would raise some important point of principle or practice or there is another compelling reason to hear the appeal.[100]

These appeals often involve complex legal issues and costs, and you should obtain advice before appealing. See p1233 for information about meeting the cost of going to court. Before making any application, get advice about whether you could be liable for the other side's costs as well as your own.

The procedure in the Court of Appeal and Court of Session is strict, formal and far less flexible than the procedure before the tribunals. The DWP, local authority or HMRC is represented by a solicitor and a barrister.

**Note:** in England and Wales, if the Upper Tribunal decision involves a point of law of general public importance, in exceptional cases, it can grant you a certificate that allows you to apply for permission to appeal direct to the Supreme Court, rather than appealing to the Court of Appeal first.[101]

## Applying to the Upper Tribunal for permission

You must apply to the Upper Tribunal for permission to appeal in the first instance. Your application must:[102]
- be in writing; *and*

- contain sufficient information about the tribunal's decision for it to be identified; *and*
- state the error(s) of law you think the tribunal made. These must be identified clearly;[103] *and*
- if your application is late, include a request for an extension of time and the reasons why the application was not made in time; *and*
- state the result you are seeking – eg, what you think the tribunal's decision should have been.

You must be sent a record of the decision on your application as soon as practicable.[104] If your application is refused, you must be sent a statement of reasons for the refusal and notice of your right to apply to the Court of Appeal or Court of Session for permission to appeal, along with information about how to apply and the time limit for doing so.

### The time limit for applying

Your application must be received by the Upper Tribunal within three months after the date you were sent:[105]

- written notice of the decision; *or*
- notice that the reasons for the decision have been amended, or the decision has been corrected, following a review; *or*
- notice that an application for the tribunal's decision to be set aside was unsuccessful, but only if that application was made within the time limit for applying for a set-aside (or any longer period allowed).

8

The tribunal can extend (or shorten) your time limit for applying for permission to appeal to the Court of Appeal/Court of Session.[106] However, there is no guarantee that you will be given longer, so keep within the time limit wherever possible. If your time limit is not extended, the tribunal must refuse your application.[107]

### When the Upper Tribunal can review its decision

The Upper Tribunal can review its own decision (other than an excluded decision – see p1231) if an application has been made for permission to appeal to the Court of Appeal or Court of Session.[108] You do not have a right to apply for a review yourself, but if you do, your application can be treated as an application for permission to appeal.[109]

The tribunal can review its decision if:[110]

- when it made the decision, it overlooked a legal provision or a court or tribunal decision it was required to follow, which could have had a 'material effect' on the decision; *or*
- since the decision, a court has made a decision that the tribunal must follow. This only applies if the court's decision could have had a 'material effect' on the tribunal's decision had it been made at the time.

If the tribunal *does* review the decision, it can:[111]

- correct accidental errors in the decision or the record of the decision; *and*
- amend the reasons given for the decision; *and*
- 'set aside' the decision. If it does this, it must make a new decision.

You must be notified in writing of the review outcome and your right of appeal (if any).[112] If the tribunal has taken any action and you were not given an opportunity to comment before the review, you must also be notified that you can apply for the outcome to be set aside and for the decision to be reviewed again.

If the tribunal does not review its decision or reviews it but takes no action, it must consider whether to give you permission to appeal to the Court of Appeal or Court of Session.[113]

## Applying to the court for permission

If the Upper Tribunal refuses you permission to appeal, you can make a fresh application to the Court of Appeal or Court of Session.[114] The tribunal's statement of reasons for the refusal must specify the relevant court.[115] It tells you the time limit for applying: this is very short, so seek legal advice as soon as possible (*before* you make your application). Because the requirements and procedures are complicated, you should contact the relevant court to find out what you need to do, and when you need to serve notices on the relevant parties.

**In England and Wales**, the Court of Appeal considers your application for permission to appeal without a hearing. It can direct that there is a hearing, and must do so if it thinks your application cannot be determined fairly without one.[116] If it refuses you permission to appeal, you cannot appeal further or apply for a judicial review.

**In Scotland**, the procedure for appealing to the Court of Session is similar to that for England and Wales, but there are a number of differences. See Chapter 69 for details.

## Meeting the cost of going to court

Free legal help from a solicitor is currently available for appeals on a point of law in the Supreme Court, the Court of Appeal and the Court of Session. You should consider obtaining legal advice and representation for these. Free legal help is means tested. You usually have to pay court fees unless you are eligible for free legal help or are exempt from paying court fees – eg, because of your financial circumstances. If you want to be represented by a lawyer and do not have free legal help, you also have to pay their fees and, if you lose your case, the other side's costs. Before making *any* application to a court, get advice about the costs and how to protect yourself against having to pay the other side's costs.

# Notes

1. **Appealing to the Upper Tribunal**

1 s11 TCEA 2007; *LS v Lambeth LB (HB)* [2010] UKUT 461 (AAC), reported as [2011] AACR 27
2 s11(5)(d) and (e) TCEA 2007
3 s11 TCEA 2007
4 r4 TP(UT) Rules; Practice Statement, *Delegation of Functions to Staff on or after 3 November 2008*, 30 October 2008
5 R(A) 1/72; R(SB) 11/83; R(IS) 11/99; R(I) 2/06; *R (Iran) v Secretary of State for the Home Department* [2005] EWCA Civ 982
6 CIS/2345/2001; CH/4065/2001
7 CDLA/433/1999
8 CDLA/1456/2002; R(H) 1/03
9 *Basildon DC v AM* [2009] UKUT 113 (AAC)
10 CDLA/3224/2001
11 CS/1939/1995; CDLA/5413/1999; CIB/303/1999
12 CH/3594/2002; *RC (Dec'd) v Maldon DC (HB)* [2012] UKUT 333 (AAC)
13 *TM v SSWP (PIP)* [2019] UKUT 204 (AAC)
14 *LO'K v SSWP (ESA)* [2016] UKUT 10 (AAC), reported as [2016] AACR 31; *MS v SSWP (DLA and PIP)* [2021] UKUT 41 (AAC); *JS v Wirral MBC (HB)* [2021] UKUT 219 (AAC)
15 *GC v HMRC and DC (CHB)* [2018] UKUT 223 (AAC)
16 *DS v SSWP (ESA)* [2013] UKUT 572 (AAC)
17 CDLA/2748/2002
18 CDLA/1480/2006
19 *TA v LB of Islington (HB)* [2014] UKUT 71 (AAC)
20 CSDLA/606/2003; *KMN v SSWP (PIP)* [2019] UKUT 42 (AAC)
21 CDLA/7980/1995; CH/5221/2001; CH/396/2002; CIB/2977/2002
22 *ES v SSWP* [2009] UKUT 6 (AAC)
23 R(IS) 4/93
24 *JH v HMRC* [2015] UKUT 397 (AAC)
25 *R (Iran) v Secretary of State for the Home Department* [2005] EWCA Civ 982; *SM v SSWP (IIDB)* [2020] UKUT 287 (AAC)
26 R(DLA) 3/08; *SP v SSWP* [2009] UKUT 97 (AAC)
27 *LA v SSWP (ESA)* [2014] UKUT 482 (AAC)
28 CJSA/322/2001; R(IS) 5/04
29 *Carpenter v SSWP* [2003] EWCA Civ 33, reported as R(IB) 6/03

2. **How to appeal to the Upper Tribunal**

30 s11(3) TCEA 2007
31 r11 TP(UT) Rules; CIB/1009/2004; CIB/2058/2004
32 r11(4)(a) TP(UT) Rules; *MP v SSWP (DLA)* [2010] UKUT 103 (AAC)
33 s10 Legal Aid, Sentencing and Punishment of Offenders Act 2012
34 Regs 5A(d) and 13 The Advice and Assistance (Assistance by Way of Representation) (Scotland) Regulations 2003 No.179
35 r18 TP(UT) Rules
36 s11(4)(a) TCEA 2007; r21(2) TP(UT) Rules
37 r38(2), (5) and (6) TP(FT) Rules
38 Practice Statement, *Composition of Tribunals in Social Security and Child Support Cases in the Social Entitlement Chamber on or after 1 August 2013*, 31 July 2013, para 11
39 r27(2) TP(FT) Rules; CSB/172/1990
40 r39(3)-(5) TP(FT) Rules
41 r41 TP(FT) Rules
42 r38(7) TP(FT) Rules
43 *HP v SSWP (ESA)* [2014] UKUT 491 (AAC)
44 r38(3) and (4) TP(FT) Rules
45 r5(3)(a) TP(FT) Rules
46 r38(5) TP(FT) Rules
47 r21(7)(b) TP(UT) Rules
48 s9 TCEA 2007; r39(1) TP(FT) Rules
49 *GA v SSWP* [2017] UKUT 416 (AAC)
50 r41 TP(FT) Rules
51 r40(2) TP(FT) Rules
52 s9(4) and (5) TCEA 2007
53 *SE v SSWP* [2009] UKUT 163 (AAC); *AM v SSWP (IB)* [2009] UKUT 224 (AAC); *JS v SSWP* [2013] UKUT 100 (AAC), reported as [2013] AACR 30
54 r40(3) and (4) TP(FT) Rules; *SSWP v AM and Northumberland CC (HB)* [2015] UKUT 360 (AAC)
55 r39(2) TP(FT) Rules
56 s11(4)(a) TCEA 2007; r21(2) TP(UT) Rules

57 r21(4), (5), (6)(a) and (7) TP(UT) Rules; CSDLA/1207/2000
58 r7(1) and (2)(a) TP(UT) Rules
59 r21(7)(b) TP(UT) Rules
60 R(IS) 11/99; CDLA/5793/1997
61 CCS/1664/2001
62 judiciary.uk/guidance-and-resources/practice-direction-for-the-administrative-appeals-chamber-of-the-upper-tribunal-electronic-filing-ce-file
63 r13(1) TP(UT) Rules
64 r22(1) and (2) TP(UT) Rules
65 s13(8)(c) TCEA 2007
66 r21(3)(b) TP(UT) Rules
67 r5(3)(a) TP(UT) Rules
68 R(M) 1/87; *R (Birmingham City Council) v Birmingham County Court* [2009] EWHC 3329 (Admin), reported as [2010] 1 WLR 1287

3. **After you get permission to appeal**
69 r23 TP(UT) Rules
70 r5(3)(a) TP(UT) Rules
71 r22(2)(b) TP(UT) Rules
72 r2 TP(UT) Rules
73 *MA v SSWP* [2009] UKUT 211 (AAC)
74 rr5-7, 8, 15 and 16 TP(UT) Rules
75 r5(3)(n) TP(UT) Rules
76 s25 TCEA 2007
77 r16(3) TP(UT) Rules
78 r5(3)(l) and (m) TP(UT) Rules
79 r17 TP(UT) Rules
80 r17(4) and (5) TP(UT) Rules
81 r5(3)(a) TP(UT) Rules
82 rr24 and 25 TP(UT) Rules
83 rr5(3)(a) and 25(2) TP(UT) Rules
84 r40(3)(b) TP(UT) Rules

4. **Hearings**
85 r34 TP(UT) Rules
86 r1(3) TP(UT) Rules, definition of 'hearing'
87 r36 TP(UT) Rules
88 Art 3 FTUT(CS)O; Practice Statement, *Composition of Tribunals in Relation to Matters that Fall to be Decided by the Administrative Appeals Chamber of the Upper Tribunal on or after 26th March 2014*, 26 March 2014
89 R(I) 1/03
90 R(IS) 2/08; *NA v SSWP (ESA)* [2018] UKUT 399 (AAC)

5. **The decision**
91 s12 TCEA 2007
92 r40 TP(UT) Rules
93 *Adams v SSWP and Green (CSM)* [2017] UKUT 9 (AAC), reported as [2017] AACR 28
94 r42 TP(UT) Rules
95 r43 TP(UT) Rules; *SK v SSWP* [2016] UKUT 529 (AAC), reported as [2017] AACR 25
96 r5(3)(a) TP(UT) Rules
97 r48 TP(UT) Rules

6. **Appealing to the Court of Appeal or Court of Session**
98 s13 TCEA 2007
99 s13(8)(c)-(e) TCEA 2007
100 s13(6) and (6A) TCEA 2007; Appeals from the Upper Tribunal to the Court of Appeal Order 2008 No.2834; r41.57 Rules of the Court of Session 1994
101 ss14A-14C TCEA 2007
102 r44(1), (6)(a) and (7) TP(UT) Rules
103 *Fryer-Kelsey v SSWP* [2005] EWCA Civ 511, reported as R(IB) 6/05
104 r45(3)-(5) TP(UT) Rules
105 r44(2), (3) and (5) TP(UT) Rules
106 r5(3)(a) TP(UT) Rules
107 r44(6) TP(UT) Rules
108 r46(1) TP(UT) Rules
109 r48 TP(UT) Rules
110 s10 TCEA 2007; r45(1) TP(UT) Rules
111 s10(4) and (5) TCEA 2007
112 r46(2) and (3) TP(UT) Rules
113 r45(2) TP(UT) Rules
114 s13(3)-(5) TCEA 2007
115 s13(11)-(13) TCEA 2007; r45(4)(b) TP(UT) Rules
116 r52.5 CPR

# Chapter 53

# Applying for judicial review

**This chapter covers:**

1. The judicial review process (below)
2. Grounds for judicial review (p1239)
3. The pre-action protocol (p1242)
4. Judicial review in the High Court or Court of Session (p1245)
5. Judicial review in the Upper Tribunal (p1246)

**Key facts**

- Judicial review may be appropriate when no other effective remedy is available to you.
- Most judicial review proceedings must be started in the High Court in England and Wales or Court of Session in Scotland promptly and within three months of the decision you want to challenge.
- In England and Wales, you must usually follow a judicial review pre-action protocol before going to court. The protocol does not apply in Scotland.
- Where judicial review is appropriate, a 'letter before action' sent by your representative will often resolve the problem without going to court. You can get advice from an advice agency; your adviser should have their 'letter before action' reviewed by CPAG or a solicitor before they send it.
- If you are considering going to court, get advice from a solicitor. Legal aid is available for judicial review under a public law legal aid contract.

8

## 1. The judicial review process

Judicial review is a form of legal challenge to the lawfulness of a decision, action or a failure to act (referred to as 'decisions' in this chapter). It is generally a challenge to the *way* in which a decision has been reached, rather than to the decision itself.

A claim for judicial review can be brought by an individual with a 'sufficient interest' in the decision (you will always have a sufficient interest in a decision about your own benefit claim or award) or an organisation which has established standing in the courts – eg, CPAG.[1] A claim can only be brought against a decision of a 'public nature', which includes decisions of the DWP, HMRC or a local authority about benefit entitlement.

Judicial review is a 'remedy of last resort' and is usually only available when you do not have an alternative remedy – eg, a right of appeal (see p1238).

A claim for judicial review relating to welfare benefits is usually brought in the High Court in England and Wales or the Court of Session in Scotland (see p1245). Unlike tribunals, these courts have the power to make costs orders – ie, you can be ordered to pay the other side's costs as well as your own. If you are successful in a claim for judicial review, the court rarely substitutes its own view of the correct decision. It leaves it to the original decision maker to remake the decision, this time following the correct procedure.

In England and Wales, before you can apply for judicial review in the High Court, you must follow a 'pre-action protocol' (see p1242). This aims to avoid expensive litigation, and the majority of straightforward cases in which there has clearly been unlawfulness on the part of the decision maker are resolved at this stage. This protocol does not apply in Scotland, but it is good practice to avoid litigation and sending a 'letter before claim' can provide a way of doing so.

Judicial review can be used in exceptionally limited circumstances to challenge an Upper Tribunal decision to refuse permission to appeal against a First-tier Tribunal decision (see p1247), and occasionally to challenge First-tier Tribunal decisions in the Upper Tribunal (see p1246).

**Note:** get advice if you are considering judicial review. You are unlikely to be successful without the help of a solicitor or welfare rights adviser, and there are costs risks involved in starting a claim.

8

## Time limit

In England and Wales, you must make your claim for judicial review in the High Court promptly and, in any event, no later than three months from the date the grounds to make the claim first arose – ie, the date of the decision you want to challenge.[2] The whole pre-action stage must be completed within the three-month time limit. The High Court may extend the time limit if there are good reasons for doing so.

In Scotland, you must apply to the Court of Session within three months of the decision you want to challenge (or a longer period that it considers equitable).[3] **Note**: it is good practice to send a 'letter before claim' to try to resolve the issue without going to court.

**Note:**

- If you want to challenge a delay or failure to make a decision, your time limit does not start to run until a decision has been received.
- If it is more than three months since the date of the decision you want to challenge, seek legal advice from a solicitor as soon as possible. In some cases, you may be able to ask the decision maker to make a new decision and

challenge that decision 'promptly', to file your claim late, or to file a protective claim.

To challenge a decision of the Upper Tribunal refusing you permission to appeal against a First-tier Tribunal decision, you must apply to the court no more than 16 days from the date on which the Upper Tribunal's decision was sent (see p1246).[4] You do not need to follow a pre-action protocol.

## When to consider judicial review

Judicial review is only possible in limited circumstances.

- **If there is no right of appeal.** Judicial review is appropriate when there is no right of appeal and any other available remedies are not 'effective' (see below). There is no right of appeal against a number of benefit decisions, including most discretionary decisions (eg, discretionary housing payments) and decisions which specifically exclude a right to appeal (eg, whether to split benefit payments between members of a couple or the amount offered to you as a benefit advance).[5] In some cases you can request a review, but you cannot appeal if the review is unsuccessful – eg, refusal of a benefit advance.
- **If it is the last resort.** If there is another way of challenging a decision, you are expected to use it. This may include requesting a review, appealing to the First-tier or Upper Tribunal, complaining or using an Ombudsman service (see Chapter 55). If there is a right of appeal, or other dispute process (eg, within a local authority), you must use it. However, the alternative remedy must be both 'effective and appropriate'.[6] Using a complaints process or an Ombudsman is rarely an effective alternative if a quick decision is needed. Even if you have a right of appeal, you may still be able to start the judicial review process with a 'letter before claim' (see p1242) if the appeal will not be effective or it is not appropriate. If this applies to you, ask for a mandatory reconsideration and request a response within a specified time (eg, seven or 14 days): explain why that time is reasonable in the circumstances. If no satisfactory response is received within the time specified, send a 'letter before claim' challenging the decision maker's failure to decide within a reasonable time and your main issue.

### *Is the appeal 'effective and appropriate'?*

An appeal may not be effective and appropriate if:

- there is a need for speed. Your circumstances may mean that an appeal is not 'effective' because it will take too long – eg, if you are homeless/facing eviction for rent arrears and/or have no income for food or heating and have been refused benefits to which you are legally entitled. If you have already submitted an appeal, judicial review may not be appropriate (see p1246);
- it is a matter of public importance. If you are an adviser, you may be aware of cases in which decision makers have routinely misinterpreted or misapplied the law. Starting

judicial review proccedings with a 'letter before claim' can improve future decision making, as well as resolving the issue for an individual claimant;
- the remedy you are seeking is not available from an appeal – eg, you may want a change made to the decision makers' guidance, staff training or damages under the Human Rights Act 1998.

## 2. Grounds for judicial review

The reasons for asking for a decision to be judicially reviewed are known as 'grounds for judicial review'. Common grounds for judicial review in welfare benefit cases include the following.

### Failure to follow the law

A common ground for judicial review is a failure to apply the law. This is similar to one of the grounds for appeal (see p1216), so if there is a right of appeal, you must use it or explain why it is ineffective.

You can challenge a decision maker's failure to follow primary legislation (ie, Acts of Parliament), secondary legislation (ie, regulations) and caselaw.

### Failure to make a decision or to make a decision within a reasonable time

Decision makers have a duty to consider all benefit claims (whether new claims or revision/supersession requests) within a 'reasonable time'. What counts as 'reasonable' depends on all the circumstances, including the impact on you and the case's complexity.[7]

### Failure to exercise discretion

It is unlawful for decision makers to operate a 'blanket policy' when they have discretion.[8] Examples of blanket policies include:

- the same decision being made in all cases in your area, regardless of individual factors;
- a local authority policy with eligibility criteria for a benefit not provided for in the governing legislation,[9] or DWP guidance that purports to restrict discretion[10] and so limit a decision maker's ability to consider each application on a case-by-case basis.

### Failure to take into account relevant evidence, or taking irrelevant evidence into account

You may have grounds for judicial review if no account has been taken of relevant evidence or information (eg, medical evidence, proof of earnings or guidance) in reaching a decision. If the decision maker has made no reference to particular evidence or information you provided, and has not explained why it has not been taken into account, this may indicate no account has been taken of it. You must demonstrate how, had it been properly taken into account, a different decision would have been reached.[11]

**Note:** if the DWP or a tribunal fails to give *any* reasons for a decision (rather than failed to explain the exclusion of particular evidence), the usual remedy is to appeal. For judicial review, failure to provide reasons may indicate 'failure to take account of relevant evidence'.

You may also have grounds for judicial review if the decision maker has taken irrelevant evidence or information into account – eg, if incorrect criteria have been used (such as length of residence for council tax reduction[12]).

## Failure to make enquiries

You have a duty to provide information and evidence in connection with your benefit claim, and the DWP, HMRC and your local authority must make enquiries if information or evidence is available to them which is not available to you.[13]

*Example*

Zofia left an abusive relationship and has no contact with her estranged spouse who is a European Economic Area worker. Both have pre-settled status under the European Union Settlement Scheme. She could challenge the DWP's failure to seek information from HMRC to establish her right to reside based on her spouse's worker status.

## Failure to follow guidance, or applying unlawful guidance

There is extensive guidance for decision makers (see p1119). It is useful to identify what the guidance says, how it corresponds to the law, and whether it has been followed correctly.

- If the guidance corresponds to the law (legislation and caselaw), but has not been followed in practice, the ground for judicial review is 'failure to follow policy as demonstrated by guidance'.[14]
- If the decision maker has relied on unpublished guidance, your ground is 'unlawful reliance on unpublished policy'.[15]
- If the guidance does not correspond to the law and has been followed in preference to the law to your detriment, your ground is 'failure to follow the law'. In addition to challenging the decision affecting you, you should request that the Secretary of State change the guidance that does not reflect the law.[16]
- You can also ask for any guidance that has been relied on, and this should be provided to you under the 'duty of candour'. This duty applies at all stages of proceedings, including the pre-action stage.[17]

## Discrimination and breach of human rights

Decision makers must comply with both the Equality Act 2010 and the Human Rights Act 1998, which provide duties not to discriminate directly or indirectly.

The Equality Act can be useful if you can demonstrate that in failing to apply the law or policy (as demonstrated by guidance), the decision maker has discriminated against you because of your age, disability, gender reassignment, marriage or civil partnership, pregnancy or maternity, race, religion or belief, sex or sexual orientation – ie, the protected characteristics under the Act. Section 20 also imposes a duty on public authorities to make reasonable adjustments to avoid substantial disadvantage to disabled people; failure to make reasonable adjustments is a ground for judicial review. Equality Act arguments cannot be used in appeals before the tribunal[18] if the decision maker has breached the Equality Act when reaching a decision on your benefit entitlement. (**Note:** this does not prevent you from making a separate claim for discrimination in the county court.)

Article 14 of the European Convention on Human Rights (brought into UK law by the Human Rights Act) provides protection from discrimination in the enjoyment of the other rights set out in the Convention. Protocol 1, Article 1 provides a right to enjoy 'property' peacefully, and welfare benefits are accepted as 'property' for these purposes.[19] Article 8 provides protection for private and family life, and welfare benefits which are designed to facilitate or contribute to family life by supporting families with children are likely to fall within the ambit of Article 8 for the purposes of Article 14.[20] The Human Rights Act provides broader protection from discrimination than the Equality Act as it makes it unlawful to discriminate on a wider range of grounds. Human Rights Act arguments can also be used at the tribunal when you appeal a decision, but Human Rights Act damages cannot be awarded by the tribunal, unlike in judicial review.

**Note:**

- The Human Rights Act can be used to challenge secondary legislation (regulations);[21] the Equality Act cannot.
- The higher courts have recently been critical of the use of Human Rights discrimination arguments.[22] Equality Act arguments should therefore be made instead, if possible.

## Irrationality

Irrationality is also known as 'Wednesbury unreasonableness'. A decision is Wednesbury unreasonable if it is 'so unreasonable that no reasonable person, acting reasonably, could have made it'.[23]

Unlike other grounds for judicial review, irrationality looks at the content of a decision rather than how the decision was made. You may be able to argue irrationality if, for example, a policy's effect achieves an outcome that is opposed

8

to its stated aim or if the effect of a policy disadvantages a group it sets out to protect.[24]

# 3. The pre-action protocol

In England and Wales, before you can apply for judicial review in the High Court, you must usually comply with the pre-action protocol for judicial review.[25] In exceptional circumstances (eg, if the time limit is imminent or the matter is urgent), you do not have to comply, but you will have to explain the circumstances.

There are no court fees and no risk of having to pay the other side's costs during the pre-action stage. The only costs at this stage are any charges made by your adviser or solicitor (which may be eligible to be covered by legal help (a form of legal aid)). Failure to comply with the pre-action protocol can result in sanctions against the non-compliant party if the matter reaches the High Court, the costs of which are potentially high. The risk of costs if the matter reaches the High Court provides a strong incentive for both parties to comply with the pre-action protocol and to resolve the issue without court action.

8

The majority of cases in which there is clear unlawfulness on the part of the decision maker are resolved at the pre-action stage. Getting advice before sending a pre-action letter is important, as it is only likely to be successful if sent on your behalf by a solicitor or advice agency.

**Note:**

- If your issue is not resolved at the pre-action stage, there is no requirement to pursue the matter to the next stage (ie, actual litigation) if you do not want to go to court.
- The pre-action protocol does not apply in Scotland, but it is good practice to try to avoid litigation and sending a 'letter before claim' as described in the pre-action protocol can provide a way of doing so.
- You do not need to use the pre-action protocol if you wish to challenge a decision of the Upper Tribunal refusing you permission to appeal against a First-tier Tribunal decision (see p1247).[26]

## The letter before claim

The pre-action protocol requires you (the 'claimant') to send a 'letter before claim' to the decision maker (the 'defendant') before initiating judicial review proceedings. The letter must contain:[27]

- the name and address of the 'defendant' – ie, the legal department of the DWP, HMRC or your local authority; *and*
- your full name and address; *and*

- your reference details – this is usually your national insurance number, but could also be your housing benefit reference number or any other reference which will assist the relevant benefit authority to identify you; *and*
- the name, address and reference details of your legal advisers (if any) or welfare rights adviser; *and*
- details of the matter being challenged; *and*
- details of any interested parties who need to be sent a copy of the paperwork. An 'interested party' is 'any person (other than the claimant and defendant) who is directly affected by the claim'[28] or may be another government department – eg, HMRC (in benefit cases, there are usually no interested parties); *and*
- a brief summary of the facts and relevant legal principles; *and*
- the date and details of the decision being challenged, and why you consider it to be wrong; *and*
- details of the remedy you are seeking; *and*
- proposals for any alternative ways of resolving the dispute. Both parties should consider whether alternative dispute resolution or using a complaints procedure would be more suitable than litigation. This is unlikely to be the case, but you must demonstrate in your letter that you have considered this; *and*
- details of any information sought from the benefits authority; *and*
- details of any relevant documents; *and*
- the address to be used for all the court documents. This will usually be the address of the advice agency or legal firm assisting you; *and*
- a proposed reply date. This depends on the circumstances of your case, but within 14 days is usually a reasonable time. In urgent cases, a shorter time may be appropriate. The benefit authority should respond within 14 days, but may contact you for an extension. Failure to do so will be taken into account by the court and sanctions may be imposed if the matter proceeds to litigation.

The letter before claim should be signed, saved as a pdf and sent to:

- for DWP benefits – thetreasurysolicitor@governmentlegal.gov.uk (by email) and the address on your DWP decision letter (by post);[29] *or*
- for HMRC benefits – preactionletters@hmrc.gov.uk (by email only); *or*
- your local authority's legal department (by post and/or email).

Include 'Pre-action Correspondence' in the subject header.

If you are writing on behalf of a client, you must include your client's signed form of authority to act.

8

*'Letter before claim'*

You can use the following structure. Ensure you include all the above required information.

**Background facts**

What are your circumstances? Give relevant details of your family, health and housing.

In chronological order and including relevant dates, what has happened and what action has already been taken to try to resolve the dispute?

What has been the effect on you of the decision or action being challenged?

**Legal background**

What does the legislation say should have happened?

What does any caselaw say should have happened?

What does any guidance say should have happened?

How is this different to what, in fact, has happened – ie, to the decision/action you are challenging?

**Grounds for judicial review**

What are your reasons for requesting judicial review? These are your 'grounds for judicial review' (see p1239 and also p1216 – the grounds rules are similar to those when appealing to the Upper Tribunal).

**Alternative remedies**

If there is an alternative remedy, explain how you have exhausted it or justify not using it.

**Details of the action you expect the benefit agency to take**

Explain what you are asking for. This will depend on your grounds for judicial review. If you have challenged the decision maker's failure to do something, your request will be for it to do that and may also include a request to improve future decision making. For example, you may want to ask:

- for your claim to be decided and paid without further delay (including from the date you first made your application);
- that the decision maker takes into account all the relevant evidence you supplied and exercises its discretion. For example, you could ask it to 'waive recovery of an overpayment' or 'reduce the level of the deductions from my benefit to [amount]';
- that the decision maker follows the law and its own guidance and awards you benefit from and including [date];
- for Human Rights Act damages;
- that staff guidance be issued and staff training provided to ensure all staff are aware of the discretion available to them and the relevant regulations and guidance;
- for guidance to be amended where it does not reflect the law.

CPAG has 'letters before claim' templates available on request from jrproject@cpag.org.uk. Details of the templates are available at cpag.org.uk/jr-letters. You can use them to challenge commonly occurring benefit problems if there is no effective alternative remedy. Ask an adviser or solicitor to send the letter on your behalf and note that edits are needed if you are in Scotland. It is important that your adviser reads CPAG's guide to using the templates before they start (cpag.org.uk/using-jr-letter-templates).

If you send a letter before claim and do not receive a reply within the time requested, contact the benefit authority's legal department to request a response without further delay. Point out that 14 days is considered a reasonable time under the judicial review pre-action protocol.

If you receive a response saying that 'judicial review is not appropriate', check whether the decision has, in fact, been changed by a revision. If you are satisfied with this, no further action is needed.

If you receive a negative response that you do not think addresses your challenge and the decision has not been changed, you can:

- make further representations to the benefit authority's legal department; *or*
- drop the matter and take no further action; *or*
- refer the matter to a solicitor to issue judicial review proceedings in the High Court or Court of Session (ensuring you act promptly and within the strict time limit).

## 4. Judicial review in the High Court or Court of Session

Judicial review in the High Court in England and Wales or Court of Session in Scotland is a means of challenging a decision if there is no effective alternative means for challenging the decision and, in England and Wales, you have exhausted the pre-action stage set out on p1242 (there is no pre-action protocol in Scotland). The grounds for your challenge are those in your pre-action correspondence (see p1242).

8

You cannot usually apply to the High Court/Court of Session for judicial review if you have another way of resolving the problem (see p1238).

You are strongly advised to seek legal advice before starting an application for judicial review.

### England and Wales

To start a claim for judicial review in the High Court of England and Wales, you must submit Form N461 together with supporting documents and the court fee or a request for a fee remission. You may not have to pay some or all of your court fees if you get certain benefits or are on a low income and have little or no savings. Check eligibility and apply online or download a form at gov.uk/get-help-with-court-fees.

Once your claim has been 'issued' by the court (ie, it has been allocated a court number and stamped), send a copy of it and the supporting documents to the body whose decision you are challenging. It has 21 days to file with the court and send you an acknowledgement of service and a basic defence to the claim ('summary grounds of defence').

Once a claim for judicial review is started in the courts, the process involves two stages. First, you must get High Court permission to apply for judicial review. Your application for permission is initially decided on the papers. If refused, you have the opportunity to renew it at a hearing. If permission is refused at the hearing, you have a right of appeal to the Court of Appeal. Permission to apply for judicial review is only given if the case has reasonable prospects of success. If permission is granted (whether on the papers or at a renewed hearing), the second stage is a substantive hearing of the case.

You should always obtain legal advice from a solicitor or legal advice centre before starting judicial review proceedings as there are likely to be significant costs involved, and it is important that your claim is presented clearly and cogently, particularly as the decision maker will be legally represented. However, legal aid is available for many judicial review cases, subject to conditions. Check whether you are eligible at gov.uk/legal-aid/eligibility.

If you are looking for a solicitor to pursue judicial review in the High Court, note that legal firms and law centres that undertake judicial review work often do so under a public law legal aid contract. There is a map of legal firms that have confirmed they can consider referrals from advice agencies for judicial review litigation at cpag.org.uk/jr-court-solicitor – the majority hold public law legal aid contracts. You can search for a legal aid solicitor near to you at find-legal-advice.justice.gov.uk (search 'public law').



A judicial review claim can typically take between six and 12 months to go through all the High Court stages.

### Scotland

The procedure is similar in Scotland, except there is no pre-action protocol. Court action for judicial review starts with a document known as a 'petition'.

You must obtain 'leave' (permission) from the court to bring a judicial review action. The court may grant permission if there is 'sufficient interest' in the subject matter and the application has a real prospect of success.

If the court refuses permission, you have a right to an oral hearing before a different judge, as well as a further right of appeal to the Inner House of the Court of Session.[30]

## 5. Judicial review in the Upper Tribunal

### Challenging a decision of the First-tier Tribunal

Occasionally, you can challenge a First-tier Tribunal decision by applying for judicial review by the Upper Tribunal, although not usually if you have a right of appeal to the Upper Tribunal against the decision.

If you doubt whether you have a right of appeal against a decision you want to challenge, you can apply for both permission to appeal and judicial review and the Upper Tribunal decides which is the proper route.

If you have appealed, your appeal has been accepted by the First-tier Tribunal but not yet heard and you are in urgent need, then the appropriate remedy is to ask for your appeal to be expedited (see p1174). If your appeal is not then expedited, you can seek judicial review of the Tribunal.[31]

Get advice from a solicitor or legal advice centre before applying for judicial review; check what you have to pay – you may qualify for free legal help.

## Transferring judicial review cases to the Upper Tribunal

The High Court and the Court of Session can transfer judicial review claims to the Upper Tribunal.[32] It may be appropriate to request a transfer if you think your case would benefit from being decided by an Upper Tribunal judge experienced in social security law rather than a High Court/Court of Session judge. Your solicitor will be able to advise you on this.

## Challenging refusal of permission to appeal to the Upper Tribunal

There is no right of appeal against a decision by the Upper Tribunal to refuse permission to appeal from the First-tier Tribunal. This type of decision can only be challenged by way of judicial review in very limited circumstances. Judicial review is only available if the Upper Tribunal has acted outside the functions ascribed to it by parliament or contrary to fundamental legal principles, such as if the court was biased or corrupt. It is no longer possible to challenge the Upper Tribunal's decision to refuse permission to appeal if the proposed appeal would raise an important point of principle or there is some other compelling reason.[33]

The procedure is the same as issuing proceedings in the High Court or Court of Session (see p1245), except that the time limit is 16 days from the date the decision letter was sent,[34] and you do not need to follow the pre-action protocol.

# Notes

1. **The judicial review process**

1 **EW** s31(3) Senior Courts Act 1981
**S** s27B(2)(a) Court of Session Act 1988
2 r54.5(1) CPR
3 s27A Court of Session Act 1988
4 r54.7A(3) CPR

5 For example, Sch 3 UC, PIP, JSA&ESA (DA) Regs
6 *Glencore Energy UK Limited v Commissioners of HMRC* [2017] EWHC 1476 (Admin), para 42

2. **Grounds for judicial review**
7 *R (C and W) v SSWP* [2015] EWHC 1607 (Admin), para 61
8 *R (S) v SSHD* [2007] EWCA Civ 546, para 50
9 For example, *R (Winder & Ors) v Sandwell MBC* [2014] EWHC 2617 (Admin)
10 For example, *R (K) v SSWP* [2023] EWHC 233 (Admin)
11 For an example, request template letter JR12 by contacting jrproject@cpag.org.uk
12 *R (Winder and Ors) v Sandwell MBC* [2014] EWHC 2617 (Admin)
13 *Kerr v Department for Social Development (Northern Ireland)* [2004] UKHL 23, para 62. For an example, request template letter JR41 by contacting jrproject@cpag.org.uk.
14 *R (Lumba) v SSHD* [2011] UKSC 12, para 26
15 *R(K) v SSWP* [2023] EWHC 233 (Admin), para 115
16 For an example of a challenge to unlawful guidance, request template letter JR33 by contacting jrproject@cpag.org.uk
17 *Administrative Court Judicial Review Guide 2024*, para 15.3.2
18 *JS v SSWP (ESA)* [2014] UKUT 428 (AAC), para 56; *TS (by TS) v SSWP (DLA); EK (by MK) v SSWP (DLA)* [2020] UKUT 284 (AAC) (in relation to Public Sector Equality Duty)
19 *Stec v United Kingdom* [2006] 43 EHRR 47, para 53
20 For example, *R (SC, CB and 8 children) v SSWP* [2021] UKSC 26, para 41
21 For example, *RR v SSWP* [2019] UKSC 52, para 27
22 For example, *R (SC, CB and 8 children) v SSWP and Ors* [2021] UKSC 26, para 162
23 *Associated Provincial Picture Houses Ltd v Wednesbury Corporation* [1948] 1 KB 223
24 For example, *SSWP v Johnson, Woods, Barrett & Stewart* [2020] EWCA Civ 788

3. **The pre-action protocol**
25 gov.uk/guidance/pre-action-protocol-for-judicial-review
26 r54.7A CPR
27 Annex A of the pre-action protocol for judicial review, gov.uk/guidance/pre-action-protocol-for-judicial-review
28 r54.1(f) CPR
29 s17(3) Crown Proceedings Act 1947, with CPR Practice Direction 66 and gov.uk/government/organisations/government-legal-department

4. **Judicial review in the High Court or Court of Session**
30 ss27B-27D Court of Session Act 1988

5. **Judicial review in the Upper Tribunal**
31 For an example, see gcnchambers.co.uk/challenging-delay-in-the-first-tier-tribunal
32 s31A Senior Courts Act 1981; s20 TCEA 2007
33 s11 TCEA 2007, as amended by s2 Judicial Review and Courts Act 2022
34 r54.7A(3) CPR

Chapter 54

# Challenging decisions on statutory payments

**This chapter covers:**


1. Notification of your employer's decision (p1250)
2. Involving HMRC (p1250)
3. Appealing against a decision (p1252)
4. Appeals to the Upper Tribunal (p1256)
5. Appeals to the courts (p1257)
6. Payment if your challenge is successful (p1257)


This chapter explains the rules for challenging decisions on entitlement to statutory payments. These rules do not apply to challenging decisions on other benefits (except some decisions on national insurance contributions – see p858).

In this chapter, when the term First-tier Tribunal is used, it means the First-tier Tribunal (Tax) and when the term Upper Tribunal is used, it means the Upper Tribunal (Tax and Chancery).

## Key facts

- Your employer should make the initial decision on your entitlement to statutory sick pay, statutory maternity pay, statutory adoption pay, statutory paternity pay, statutory shared parental pay, statutory parental bereavement pay and statutory neonatal care pay.
- If you disagree with your employer's decision, or your employer has failed to make a decision, you can ask HMRC to decide whether you are entitled.
- If you disagree with HMRC's decision on your entitlement, you can ask for it to be reviewed. If you are unhappy with the outcome of the review, you can appeal to the First-tier Tribunal.
- If you disagree with the First-tier Tribunal's decision, you may be able to appeal to the Upper Tribunal. If you disagree with the Upper Tribunal's decision, you may be able to appeal to a court.

***Future changes***

The government plan to establish a Fair Work Agency which will takeover the enforcement of statutory sick pay liabilities.[1] This change is expected to take effect no earlier than 2026.[2]

## 1. Notification of your employer's decision

If you have taken the necessary steps to request statutory sick pay (SSP), statutory maternity pay (SMP), statutory adoption pay (SAP), statutory paternity pay (SPP), statutory shared parental pay (SSPP), statutory parental bereavement pay (SPBP) or statutory neonatal care pay (SNCP) from your employer (see Chapters 34 and 35), but your employer decides it is not liable (or no longer liable) to pay you, it should notify you of its decision within:[3]

- seven days for SSP or SMP (or, for SMP only, within 28 days of your giving notice of your maternity leave or your baby's birth, if this is earlier);
- 28 days for SAP, SPP, SSPP, SPBP or SNCP.

This also applies to a former employer for SMP, SAP, SPP, SSPP, SPBP and SNCP.

For SSP and SPBP, your employer should normally provide this information on Form SSP1 or SPBP1 respectively, or on its own computerised form if it contains the same information. For SMP, SAP and SPP, it is normally given on Form SMP1, SAP1 or SPP1 respectively. There is no official form for SSPP or (at the time of writing) for SNCP, but your employer must give you the reason for its refusal. If you have given your employer certain evidence to establish your entitlement, it should be returned to you – eg, Form MAT B1 for SMP.

## 2. Involving HMRC

If you disagree with your employer's decision on your entitlement to a statutory payment, or if your employer has failed to make a decision, you can request that HMRC makes a formal decision on your entitlement.[4] You must do so within six months of the earliest date for which your entitlement is in dispute.[5]

Telephone HMRC's Statutory Payment Dispute Team to initiate your request on 0300 322 9422 (textphone: 0300 200 3212). You may be sent a form to use or HMRC may suggest you write a letter. Return the form or letter to the Statutory Payment Dispute Team, PT Operations, North East England, HMRC, BX9 1AN.

On either the form or in your letter, you must provide details of the period for which your entitlement to a statutory payment is at issue and the grounds on which your employer has refused payment, if you know them.[6]

If possible, you should also send a copy of Form SSP1, SMP1, SAP1, SPP1 or SPBP1 that your employer has given you, or the information your employer has given you about its statutory shared parental pay or statutory neonatal care pay decision, and evidence of your entitlement – eg, a medical certificate (if you have been sick for more than seven days), Form MAT B1 or the 'matching certificate' from the adoption agency. However, do not delay your application if you do not have this information.

It can take some time to get a final decision on your entitlement, so consider whether there are other benefits which you can claim in the interim (see Chapter 1). However, if you claim employment and support allowance (ESA) while waiting for a decision on your entitlement to statutory sick pay (SSP), or maternity allowance (MA) while waiting for a decision on your entitlement to statutory maternity pay (SMP), the DWP does not normally make a decision on your ESA or MA claim until HMRC has made a decision on your entitlement to SSP or SMP (because you do not qualify for ESA if you are entitled to SSP, and you do not qualify for MA if you are entitled to SMP). For this reason, the DWP can request that HMRC makes a formal decision on your entitlement to SSP or SMP, if you have not already done so. If you would qualify for ESA or MA, do not delay claiming or you may lose out financially if the final decision is that you do not qualify for SSP or SMP.

**Note:** if you are thinking of challenging your employer's decision on your entitlement to a statutory payment, you should tell your employer that you intend to contact HMRC. Your employer can get advice on statutory payments from HMRC's Employers' Helpline: 0300 200 3200.



## Requests for further information

HMRC may contact you and/or your partner for information, and can also require your employer to provide information – eg, the reasons for its decision. HMRC can impose a financial penalty on your employer if it fails to provide this. If your employer fails to comply, press HMRC to make its own decision on your entitlement.

HMRC can also impose a financial penalty on you for not providing information or documents that you have been reasonably required to provide to decide your entitlement.[7] However, this is only likely to happen if HMRC believes that you have acted fraudulently or have been negligent.

## HMRC's decision

To resolve your dispute, HMRC may send both you and your employer a written opinion on your entitlement before it issues a formal decision on your application. It may give you a deadline before which both you and your employer can object to its written opinion before it issues a formal decision.

The formal decision is legally binding on your employer. If HMRC decides you are entitled to be paid by your employer (and your employer does not appeal), your employer should pay you on or before your first payday after the 30-day appeal time limit (see below) expires.[8]

### Varying or superseding a decision

HMRC can change its own decision by varying or superseding it.[9] It can **vary** its decision if it now believes that the decision was wrong at the time it was made. It must tell you and your employer of the new decision in writing. The new decision takes effect from the date that the original decision would have had effect if the reason for the variation had been known. If you or your employer have appealed against a decision, HMRC may vary that decision at any time before the appeal is determined.

HMRC can **supersede** an earlier decision if it has become incorrect for any reason – eg, if your circumstances have changed. The new decision takes effect from the date of your change of circumstances.

If HMRC varies or supersedes an earlier decision, either you or your employer can appeal against the new decision.

## 3. Appealing against a decision

Both you and your employer can appeal against a decision made by HMRC.[10]

Your appeal should be made in writing to HMRC and include your reasons for appealing.[11] Send your appeal to the Statutory Payment Dispute Team, PT Operations, North East England, HMRC, BX9 1AN. You have a choice about how your appeal is dealt with (see below).

### Time limit for appealing

Your appeal should reach HMRC within 30 days of the date on which HMRC made its formal decision.[12] This time limit may be extended by HMRC if the reason you are late is considered reasonable.[13] If HMRC does not accept your late appeal, you can apply to the First-tier Tribunal for permission to appeal late, giving reasons for lateness (see p1255). However, you cannot be certain that a late appeal will be accepted, so it is preferable to keep within the time limit.

### Choosing how your appeal is dealt with

You can choose whether you would like your appeal to be decided by the First-tier Tribunal or by HMRC conducting a review. To make this choice, in addition to sending your written appeal to HMRC, you should notify:[14]

- the tribunal in writing that you want it to consider your appeal (see p1255); *or*
- HMRC in writing that you want it to conduct a review. (If HMRC conducts a review and you disagree with its decision, you can still apply to the tribunal for a decision on your appeal, provided you apply within the time limits.)

If, having made your appeal, you do not ask either the tribunal to consider your appeal or HMRC to review its decision, HMRC should write to you, offering to review its decision (called an 'HMRC-initiated review' in this chapter). Before HMRC initiates a review, it may try to settle the appeal (see below). However, until HMRC has issued a notification offering you a review, you can still notify the tribunal that you want it to decide your appeal or inform HMRC yourself that you want it to conduct a review.

## Settling or withdrawing your appeal

HMRC can try to settle your appeal at any time before the determination of the appeal. If, before the appeal is decided, you reach an agreement with HMRC (or, if your employer has appealed, an agreement is reached between your employer and HMRC), the matter is treated as settled by agreement and the appeal lapses.[15]

You can withdraw your appeal at any time before it is decided by notifying HMRC and your employer that you wish to do so. Your employer and HMRC have 30 days to object and, if no objection is made, your appeal will lapse.[16]

## Review by HMRC

### Initial view on entitlement

8

If you have asked for your appeal to be decided by an HMRC review, or if HMRC has initiated a review, HMRC first informs you of its 'initial view on your entitlement'.

**If you have requested an HMRC review**, HMRC should send you its initial view on your entitlement within 30 days, beginning with the date it receives your written request for a review, although it can send it later than this if it is reasonable.[17] The same rules apply if it is your employer who has initiated the review.

**If HMRC has initiated the review**, HMRC should send its initial view on your entitlement with its offer of a review.[18] You then have 30 days, starting on the date of HMRC's letter, to inform in writing:[19]

- HMRC, that you want it to conduct the review (see p1254); *or*
- the First-tier Tribunal, that you want it to decide your appeal (see p1255). In some circumstances, the tribunal can consider your appeal even if you apply after the 30-day time limit (see p1255).

If HMRC has initiated the review but you neither accept the offer of a review nor notify the tribunal that you want it to consider your appeal within the above time limit, HMRC proceeds as if you have agreed to its initial view on your entitlement and treats the matter as settled by agreement. Notification of this should be sent to you and your employer, and your appeal lapses.[20]

## The review

After HMRC has issued its initial view on your entitlement (and, for HMRC-initiated reviews, provided you have accepted HMRC's offer of a review), a review is carried out by an HMRC decision maker who was not involved in making the original decision.

If you disagree with HMRC's initial view, it is important to write to explain why. The decision maker must consider any information you provide, as long as you give them a reasonable opportunity to do so.[21]

HMRC should notify you of its review decision and the reasons for it within 45 days, beginning with the date it:[22]

- notified you of its initial view of the matter, if you requested the review; *or*
- received your acceptance of its offer of a review, if HMRC initiated the review.

In either case, these time limits can be changed if you agree.

If HMRC does not notify you of its review decision within this time limit, its decision is taken to be the same as its initial view on your entitlement and HMRC must inform you of this.[23]

### If you do not agree with the review decision

If you or your employer do not agree with HMRC's review decision, you may notify the First-tier Tribunal that you want it to consider your appeal. The time limit for doing so is 30 days, beginning with the date of either:[24]

8

- HMRC's letter notifying you of its review decision; *or*
- if HMRC did not notify you of its review decision within the time limit, the date of its letter telling you it has adopted its initial view on your entitlement as its decision.

In the latter situation, you can appeal before receiving HMRC's letter, provided your appeal is made after the expiry of the time limit for making the review decision.

If you do not notify the tribunal within the time limit, your appeal can only be considered if the tribunal gives permission (see p1255).[25]

## Alternative dispute resolution

If either you or your employer have notified the First-tier Tribunal that you want it to consider your appeal, HMRC may invite you to apply for alternative dispute resolution. If alternative dispute resolution is suggested before this, do not delay notifying the tribunal of your appeal, as the time limits for notifying the tribunal are not put on hold while you consider or take part in alternative dispute resolution. If alternative dispute resolution is used, an HMRC officer who has not been involved in the decision acts as a mediator to try to resolve the dispute. If you reach an agreement, you and your employer are sent written confirmation and, if it is different from HMRC's earlier decision on your entitlement, HMRC may vary its earlier decision (see p1252). For alternative dispute resolution to be used, both you and your employer must agree to it. If you are offered alternative dispute resolution, get advice.

## Appeals to the First-tier Tribunal

You can request that the First-tier Tribunal considers your appeal if:[26]

- you have appealed against HMRC's original decision on your entitlement and want your appeal to be decided by the tribunal, rather than by an HMRC review (see p1252); *or*
- you have appealed and HMRC has initiated a review (see p1253). Rather than accept the offer of a review, you can notify the tribunal that you want it to decide your appeal. See p1253 for the time limits for notifying the tribunal, and below if you miss the time limit; *or*
- your appeal against HMRC's original decision has been decided by an HMRC review and you disagree with the decision, or HMRC has not notified you of its review decision within the time limits; *or*
- you missed the time limit for appealing against HMRC's original decision on your entitlement and HMRC does not agree to accept your late appeal (but see below).

### Notifying the First-tier Tribunal

If you want the First-tier Tribunal to consider your appeal, you must notify it in writing or submit the appeal online. See p1253 for the time limit for doing so. Your written notice must contain certain information, including the details of the decision you are appealing against, the result you want and your grounds for appealing. If you miss the time limit, you must also ask for permission to make a late application and explain why your request is late.[27]

Use Form T240 'Notice of Appeal (tax)', available from gov.uk or telephone 0300 123 1024. Alternatively, you can appeal at gov.uk/tax-tribunal/appeal-to-tribunal. You must include a copy of the written record of the decision you are appealing against and any statement giving the reasons for that decision (eg, the notification HMRC sent informing you of its decision), unless you do not have this information and cannot reasonably obtain it.

**Note**: when completing Form T240, be aware that statutory payments fall under 'direct taxes' for HMRC purposes (statutory payments are not listed but you can state which one you are appealing about in the 'other' box under the 'direct tax' heading).

### Missed time limits

If you miss the relevant time limit for notifying the First-tier Tribunal that you want it to determine your appeal or the time limit for appealing against HMRC's original decision on your entitlement (and HMRC does not agree to accept your late appeal), you can still ask the First-tier Tribunal to consider your appeal. It may give its permission for the time limit to be extended. Although there are no specific rules about when the time limit can be extended,[28] the overriding objective of the rules is to enable tribunals to deal with cases fairly and justly.[29] Whether the First-tier Tribunal extends the time limit depends on the circumstances, so give detailed reasons why your appeal is late. As you cannot be certain of success, it is essential to keep within the time limits if you can.

### How the First-tier Tribunal decides your case

The First-tier Tribunal allocates your case to be considered in one of four ways.[30] Further details of the procedures are in leaflet T242 *Making an Appeal: explanatory leaflet*, available from gov.uk.

The tribunal can confirm HMRC's decision or change it.[31] It must send you a notice informing you of its decision, which may include its full written findings and the reasons for its decision.[32] If you disagree with the tribunal's decision, you may be able to appeal against it to the Upper Tribunal (see below).

In certain circumstances, you can apply for the First-tier Tribunal's decision to be 'set aside' (there is a time limit for doing so), or the tribunal can correct its own decision.[33] The tribunal can also review its decision if you have applied for permission to appeal to the Upper Tribunal and the First-tier Tribunal considers there was an error of law in the decision.[34] If it decides to take action as the result of its review, it must notify you and your employer in writing. It may not take any action in relation to a decision without giving both you and your employer an opportunity to make representations.



## 4. Appeals to the Upper Tribunal

You and your employer can appeal to the Upper Tribunal (Tax and Chancery Chamber) against a decision of the First-tier Tribunal, but only on the grounds that the First-tier Tribunal has made a legal mistake – an 'error of law' (see p1216).[35] The rules for making an appeal are almost the same as those for making an appeal to the Upper Tribunal (Administrative Appeals Chamber) described in Chapter 52, although there are differences in the procedure for lodging an appeal and in the time limit for applying. You must first apply to the First-tier Tribunal (Tax) for permission to appeal. Your application must normally be received no later than 56 days after the latest of the dates listed on p1222 (usually the date the tribunal sent you its full written reasons for the decision). In some circumstances, the First-tier Tribunal can give permission for you to appeal later than this.[36] Use Form T247 to apply to the First-tier Tribunal for permission to appeal to the Upper Tribunal (available from gov.uk).

If you have not been sent the First-tier Tribunal's full written findings and reasons, you must obtain these before applying for permission to appeal. Write to the First-tier Tribunal to request these – your request must be received within 28 days of the date it sent you its decision notice. In some circumstances, this time limit can be extended.[37] If the First-tier Tribunal gives permission for you to appeal, you must submit a 'notice of appeal' and certain other information to the Upper Tribunal within the time limit. For details, see p1225. Use Form FTC1 available from gov.uk.

If the First-tier Tribunal refuses permission for you to appeal or only gives permission on limited grounds, you can apply to the Upper Tribunal for permission. Use Form FTC1. See p1225 for the time limits for applying.[38] If, without a hearing, the Upper Tribunal refuses you permission to appeal or to appeal late, or gives permission to appeal subject to conditions or on limited grounds, you can apply for this decision to be reconsidered at a hearing. You must apply in writing and your application must be received by the Upper Tribunal within 14 days of the date it sent you notice of its decision, although the Upper Tribunal has discretion to extend this time limit.[39] The Upper Tribunal has the power to make an order for costs (expenses in Scotland), so before making any application, get advice about whether you could be liable for costs if you lose your case.

## 5. Appeals to the courts

You and your employer can appeal against the decision of the Upper Tribunal to the Court of Appeal (the Court of Session in Scotland) if the Upper Tribunal made an 'error of law' – ie, it interpreted the law incorrectly.[40]

You must apply for permission to appeal, which is only granted if certain conditions are met (see p1231). Your application should normally be made to the Upper Tribunal within one month of the date it sent you written reasons for its decision. This time limit can be extended with the tribunal's permission.[41] See p1231 for further details on appealing to the courts.

## 6. Payment if your challenge is successful

If it is decided that your employer should pay you a statutory payment, your employer should pay you within a certain time limit. If your employer has appealed or is within the time limit for doing so, it does not have to pay you until a final decision is given on appeal, or until the time limit for the appeal or a further appeal has passed. If no appeal against the decision has been made (or if the matter has been finally determined), your employer should pay you on or before the first payday after:[42]

- the day the employer is notified that the appeal has been finally determined; *or*

- the day the employer receives notification that leave to appeal has been refused, and there is no further opportunity to apply for leave; *or*
- in any other case, the day the time limit for appeal expires.

If, because of your employer's payroll methods, it is not practical for you to be paid by that payday, your employer should pay you on or before your next payday after this date. If you are not otherwise due to be paid (eg, because you are no longer employed by that employer), then the time limits for paying you should be met by the first day on which you would have been paid (or if not practicable, by the following payday).

## If your employer does not pay

If your employer does not pay you within the time limit, HMRC should pay you (although HMRC states it will first contact your employer to try to get it to pay).[43] Write to HMRC's Statutory Payment Dispute Team (see p1250) asking for payment. This applies even if your employer is insolvent, but only for payment owed for the period before the date of insolvency. For any period that falls after the date of insolvency, HMRC, rather than your employer, is automatically liable to pay you any statutory payment for which you are eligible.[44]

8

# Notes

1 Factsheet: *Fair Work Agency in the Employment Rights Bill*, UK Government, 18 October 2024, available at gov.uk/government/publications/employment-rights-bill-factsheets
2 Factsheet: *Employment Rights Bill Overview*, UK Government, 18 October 2024, available at gov.uk/government/publications/employment-rights-bill-factsheets

1. **Notification of your employer's decision**
3 **SSP** s130 SSAA 1992; reg 15 SSP Regs
**SMP** s132 SSAA 1992; reg 25A SMP Regs
**SPP/SAP** Reg 11 SPPSAP(A) Regs
**SSPP** Regs 2(2) and 11 SSPP(A) Regs
**SPBP** Regs 2 and 11 SPBP(A) Regs
**SNCP** Reg 11 SNCP(A) Regs

2. **Involving HMRC**
4 s8 SSC(TF)A 1999
5 **SSP/SMP** Reg 3 SSP&SMP(D) Regs
**SPP/SAP** Reg 13 SPPSAP(A) Regs
**SSPP** Reg 13 SSPP(A) Regs
**SPBP** Reg 13 SPBP(A) Regs
**SNCP** Reg 13 SNCP(A) Regs
6 **SSP/SMP** Reg 3 SSP&SMP(D) Regs
**SPP/SAP** Reg 13 SPPSAP(A) Regs
**SSPP** Reg 13 SSPP(A) Regs
**SPBP** Reg 13 SPBP(A) Regs
**SNCP** Reg 13 SNCP(A) Regs
7 **SSP/SMP** s113A SSAA 1992
**SPP/SAP/SSPP/SPBP/SNCP** s11(1) and (2) Employment Act 2002

8 **SSP** Reg 9 SSP Regs
**SMP** Reg 29 SMP Regs
**SPP/SAP** Reg 42 SPPSAP(G) Regs
**SSPP** Reg 44 SSPP(G) Regs
**SPBP** Reg 24 SPBP(G) Regs
**SNCP** Reg 29 SNCP(G) Regs (draft)
9 s10 SSC(TF)A 1999; regs 5 and 6 SSC(DA) Regs

3. **Appealing against a decision**
10 s11(2)(a) SSC(TF)A 1999
11 s12 SSC(TF)A 1999
12 s12(1) SSC(TF)A 1999
13 s49 TMA 1970; reg 9 SSC(DA) Regs
14 ss49A, 49B, 49D and 49I TMA 1970; reg 7 SSC(DA) Regs
15 s49A(4) TMA 1970; reg 11 SSC(DA) Regs
16 Reg 11(5) SSC(DA) Regs
17 s49B(2) and (5) TMA 1970
18 s49C(2) TMA 1970
19 ss49C(3) and (8) and 49H TMA 1970
20 s49C(4) TMA 1970; reg 11 SSC(DA) Regs
21 s49E(4) TMA 1970
22 s49E(6) and (7) TMA 1970
23 s49E(8) and (9) TMA 1970
24 s49G TMA 1970
25 s49G(3) TMA 1970
26 ss49D, 49G and 49H TMA 1970
27 r20 TP(FT)(TC) Rules
28 s49(2)(b) TMA 1970; r20(4) TP(FT)(TC) Rules
29 r2 TP(FT)(TC) Rules
30 r23 TP(FT)(TC) Rules
31 Reg 10 SSC(DA) Regs
32 r35 TP(FT)(TC) Rules
33 rr37 and 38 TP(FT)(TC) Rules
34 r41 TP(FT)(TC) Rules

4. **Appeals to the Upper Tribunal**
35 s11 TCEA 2007; reg 12(2) SSC(DA) Regs
36 r39 TP(FT)(TC) Rules
37 rr5(3)(a) and 35(4) and (5) TP(FT)(TC) Rules
38 r21(3)(b) TP(UT) Rules
39 rr5(3)(a) and 22(3)-(5) TP(UT) Rules

5. **Appeals to the courts**
40 s13(2) TCEA 2007; reg 12(2) SSC(DA) Regs
41 r44 TP(UT) Rules

6. **Payment if your challenge is successful**
42 **SSP** Reg 9 SSP Regs
**SMP** Reg 29 SMP Regs
**SPP/SAP** Reg 42 SPPSAP(G) Regs
**SSPP** Reg 44 SSPP(G) Regs
**SPBP** Reg 24 SPBP(G) Regs
**SNCP** Reg 29 SNCP(G) Regs (draft)
43 **SSP** s151(6) SSCBA 1992; reg 9A SSP Regs
**SMP** s164(9)(b) SSCBA 1992; reg 7 SMP Regs
**SPP/SAP** ss171ZD(3) and 171ZM(3) SSCBA 1992; reg 43 SPPSAP(G) Regs
**SSPP** s171ZX(3) SSCBA 1992; reg 45 SSPP(G) Regs
**SPBP** s171ZZ8(3) SSCBA 1992; reg 25 SPBP(G) Regs
**SNCP** s171ZZ18(3) SSCBA 1992; reg 30 SNCP(G) Regs (draft)
44 **SSP** Reg 9B SSP Regs
**SMP** Reg 7(3) and (4) SMP Regs
**SPP/SAP** Reg 43(2) and (3) SPPSAP(G) Regs
**SSPP** Reg 45(3)-(5) SSPP(G) Regs
**SPBP** Reg 25 (2)-(4) SPBP(G) Regs
**SNCP** Reg 30(4)-(6) SNCP(G) Regs (draft)

8

# Chapter 55

# Complaints

**This chapter covers:**


1. Grounds for a complaint (below)
2. Compensation payments (p1261)
3. Complaining about the DWP (p1262)
4. Complaining about HMRC (p1263)
5. Complaining about a local authority (p1265)
6. Complaining about HM Courts and Tribunals Service (p1265)
7. Using your MP (p1266)
8. Complaining to an Ombudsman (p1266)
9. Legal action (p1268)


8

This chapter covers the rules for making complaints about benefits administered by the DWP and HMRC. It also covers the rules for making complaints about housing benefit and HM Courts and Tribunals Service. See p1529 for how to make a complaint about a Scottish social security benefit.

### Key facts

- You can complain about any government or local authority department, and anyone contracted to provide a service on its behalf.
- Your complaint can be about a delay in dealing with your claim, poor administration, the behaviour of staff or how a particular departmental policy or practice has affected you.
- It is best to put your complaint in writing, even if you have to start the process by phone.
- If your complaint is not resolved satisfactorily, you may be able to escalate your complaint to the Independent Case Examiner, the Adjudicator or an Ombudsman.

## 1. Grounds for a complaint

You can complain if you are unhappy with your treatment by a government or local authority department, or someone providing a service on its behalf.

Your complaint can be about any issue concerning how your claim has been handled or how you have been treated. This includes matters such as delays, discourtesy, poor administration, the behaviour of staff, bad advice or how a particular *department's* policy or practice affects you. You can also ask for compensation for any losses related to your complaint (see below).

If you disagree with a decision about your benefit *entitlement*, see Chapters 56 and 57. If you think the law or the *government's* policy discriminates against you or treats you unfairly, you may have grounds to start judicial review proceedings instead (see Chapter 53).

## 2. Compensation payments

You should expect prompt, courteous and efficient service from staff dealing with your benefit. If you are unhappy with how your benefit has been administered, you can ask for compensation. Compensation payments are discretionary.

The DWP, HMRC and local authorities sometimes pay compensation if you can show that you have lost out through their error or delay and the loss cannot be made good by a revision, supersession or appeal (see Chapters 50 and 51), or by backdating your claim (see p1011). For instance, if you did not claim carer's allowance because the DWP misled you and it cannot be backdated for more than three months, you can ask for compensation. You may also receive 'consolatory payments' if you are considered to have experienced injustice, hardship or distress.

The DWP should automatically consider whether to pay compensation if you are owed arrears of benefit, but you should still write to your local DWP office and ask. If you do not get a sympathetic response, ask your MP (see p1266) to write on your behalf or to take up your case with the social security minister.

The DWP uses a guide, *Financial Redress for Maladministration*, to help it decide when and how much compensation (known as 'extra-statutory' or ex gratia payments) should be paid.[1] HMRC's *Complaints and Remedy Guidance* sets out when it makes 'financial redress'.[2]

You should ask for a payment equal to the money you have lost. You can also ask for additional amounts to cover interest on arrears and any extra expenses you had, as well as to compensate you for any injustice, hardship or distress experienced because of the mistake. If your loss was as a clear result of incorrect advice or negligence on the part of the agency, you may be able to bring a court action for damages. Get legal advice promptly if this is the case.

# 3. Complaining about the DWP

The DWP has a complaints procedure that applies to all its agencies, including:

- the Pension Service;
- Jobcentre Plus;
- Debt Management;
- Access to Work.

The DWP does not deal with complaints about contracted providers – eg, those carrying out medical assessments on its behalf. To complain about a contracted provider, use its own internal complaints procedure. If you are still not satisfied, you can complain to the Independent Case Examiner (ICE) (see below) and then the Parliamentary and Health Service Ombudsman (see p1267).

You can find information about standards and complaints on the DWP website.[3]

For universal credit (UC) and jobseeker's allowance complaints only, the DWP has an online complaints service: makeacomplaint.dwp.gov.uk. Otherwise, start your complaint by using the contact details in any correspondence regarding the matter you want to complain about or via your online account if it is about UC. If you do not have contact details, check the 'Who to contact' section at gov.uk/government/organisations/department-for-work-pensions/about/complaints-procedure.

If you are still unhappy after you receive the DWP's initial response, you can ask that your complaint be passed to a senior manager. You should then be contacted within 15 working days by the DWP's Complaints Team to discuss your complaint and how long the investigation will take.

If you remain unhappy after getting the Complaints Team's final response, you can complain to the ICE.

## Complaining to the Independent Case Examiner

The ICE deals with complaints about DWP agencies and its contracted providers.

The ICE's role is to consider whether there has been maladministration. It cannot deal with matters of law or government policy. You can make a complaint to the ICE once you have completed the internal complaints procedure of the agency concerned. This usually means that you have had a final response to your complaint. A complaint should be made to the ICE no later than six months after the final response.

You can make a complaint to the ICE by email to ice@dwp.gov.uk, in writing to PO Box 209, Bootle L20 7WA or by phone on 0800 414 8529. Text and video relay services are also available: see gov.uk/government/organisations/independent-case-examiner. An appointed representative can act on your behalf if you provide written consent. You must provide all relevant information, including the final response to your complaint from the agency you are complaining about.

The ICE should tell you within two weeks whether it can accept your complaint. If accepted, the ICE then attempts to resolve the complaint within eight weeks by reaching an agreement between you and the agency concerned. If this fails and the ICE considers further investigation is needed, it calls for all the relevant information from the parties and allocates the case to an investigator. They will attempt to settle the complaint by agreeing actions, usually within 15 weeks of the case being allocated. If this is not possible, the investigator reports the details of the investigation to the ICE who will make a finding and any recommendations on how the complaint should be resolved within 20 weeks of the case being allocated to the investigator. If you remain unhappy, you have three months to ask the ICE to review its decision if you have new evidence or can show an error in the report, or you can ask your MP to consider referring your complaint to the Parliamentary and Health Service Ombudsman (see p1267).

If you are unhappy with how the ICE deals with your case, use its own complaints process.

***Is it worth complaining?***

The ICE's 2023/24 annual report shows that it resolved, settled or investigated 2,586 cases in 2023/24 (625 about UC), 1,081 of which were resolved or settled without investigation (299 about UC). Of the cases investigated, 50.7 per cent were partially or fully upheld (44 per cent in UC cases). ICE recommendations include apologies, corrective action and financial redress. This shows that in 2023/24, a satisfactory outcome was likely in about seven out of 10 cases (with similar numbers for UC cases). Case studies in the report include a number highlighting UC maladministration in dealing with vulnerable claimants and a case where a claimant increased their childcare, based on misinformation from the DWP, and was awarded 85 per cent of the additional costs that they had incurred as a result of this. Note that cases that were investigated but not upheld include complaints that had 'merit' but all necessary action to resolve the matter had already been taken prior to referral.

## 4. Complaining about HMRC

You can complain about how HMRC has dealt with your tax credit, child benefit or guardian's allowance claim, or with your national insurance credits or contributions. You can do this online if you have set up a Government Gateway account, by phone or in writing to HMRC (see gov.uk/complain-about-hmrc). Even though you can no longer claim tax credits, you can still dispute the recovery of a tax credit overpayment (see p1088). HMRC also has a separate process for dealing with 'serious misconduct' – eg, corruption or fraud.



8

If you are unhappy with the initial response ('first tier review'), ask HMRC to review your complaint. The review ('second tier review') should be done by a different customer service adviser, who will give you HMRC's final reply to your complaint.

If you are unhappy with HMRC's final reply, you can ask the Adjudicator to look into it.

## Complaining to the Adjudicator

The Adjudicator's Office deals with complaints about HMRC and is similar to the Independent Case Examiner (see p1262). The Adjudicator only investigates a complaint if you have completed HMRC's internal complaints procedure. You cannot complain direct to the Adjudicator about an HMRC-contracted service provider; you must complain via HMRC first. A complaint usually needs to be made within six months of the final response from HMRC.

You can make a complaint to the Adjudicator online, in writing or using the form available at gov.uk/guidance/contact-the-adjudicators-office. If you have problems, you can phone the Adjudicator's Office on 0300 057 1111. You can appoint someone to act on your behalf by completing an 'Authority to Act' form available from the Adjudicator's Office website. You must provide the final response to your complaint from HMRC.

Complaints can be made about delays, inappropriate staff behaviour, misleading advice, the application of discretion or any other form of maladministration. The Adjudicator cannot investigate disputes about matters of law or government policy. If the complaint is accepted, the Adjudicator investigates the complaint by reviewing the information you have sent, carrying out further enquiries and reaching a decision about whether HMRC did anything wrong. A formal written decision, including any recommendations, is then sent to you. Recommendations can include 'redress payments'. HMRC should follow the Adjudicator's recommendations in all but exceptional circumstances.

If you are unhappy with the Adjudicator's response, ask your MP to put your complaint to the Parliamentary and Health Service Ombudsman (see p1267). As well as looking at your complaint about HMRC, the Ombudsman may also look into the way in which the Adjudicator has investigated your complaint. There is further information about the Adjudicator at gov.uk/government/organisations/the-adjudicator-s-office.

***Is it worth complaining?***

The Adjudicator's 2024 annual report does not break down complaints by subject – eg, tax credits or other matters handled by HMRC. Of the 843 complaints about HMRC investigated in 2023/24, just under 41 per cent were partially or fully upheld. In total, the Adjudicator recommended that HMRC pay just under £103,063 in 'redress' in these cases. Case studies highlighted in the report include an example of a tax credit overpayment recovery case and a case where the complainant was a victim of fraud, where a fraudulent tax credit claim made using their name resulted in their legitimate tax credit award being terminated.

## 5. Complaining about a local authority

To complain about the actions of your local authority or someone providing services on its behalf, ask for a copy of its complaints policy. Local authorities are required to have an effective complaints procedure, which should be made available to the public. If you cannot obtain the policy, write to the supervisor of the person dealing with your case, making it clear why you are dissatisfied. Not being able to obtain a copy of the complaints procedure can form part of your complaint. If you do not receive a satisfactory reply, complain to the principal officer. Send a copy of the letter to your ward councillors and to the councillor who chairs the relevant local authority committee – local authority officers are always accountable to the councillors. If this does not produce results, or if the delay is causing you hardship, consider a complaint to the Ombudsman (see p1267) or legal action (see p1268).

Government departments also monitor local authorities, so you could contact your MP or write to the relevant minister – eg, the Secretary of State for Work and Pensions.



## 6. Complaining about HM Courts and Tribunals Service

### Complaints about the administration of your appeal

If you are dissatisfied with the administration of your appeal, complain to HM Courts and Tribunals Service (HMCTS). You can raise a complaint in person with any member of staff at the court or tribunal, or write, phone or email the court or tribunal directly (see gov.uk/find-court-tribunal), or complain online at hmcts-complaint-form-eng.form.service.justice.gov.uk. You should receive a response to your complaint within 10 working days.

If you are not satisfied with the intial response, ask that a senior manager reviews your complaint. They should respond within 10 working days. If you remain dissatisfied after the senior manager responds, you can appeal to the User Investigations Team which should respond within a further 15 working days.

If you are still dissatisfied, you can complain to the Parliamentary and Health Service Ombudsman (see p1267).

HMCTS's complaints procedure is at gov.uk/government/organisations/hm-courts-and-tribunals-service/about/complaints-procedure.

### Complaints about the conduct of tribunal members

If you are unhappy about how you were treated by a tribunal judge, tribunal member or tribunal chamber president (eg, they were rude, discourteous or racist), you can make a complaint online at complaints.judicialconduct.gov.uk/makeacomplaint. You usually need to start your complaint within three months of the incident complained about.

If you are not happy with the response to your complaint about a tribunal judge, member or president, you have 28 days to complain to the Judicial Appointments and Conduct Ombudsman (see gov.uk/guidance/judicial-conduct-complain-to-the-ombudsman). The Ombudsman's decision is final.

## 7. Using your MP

If you are not satisfied with the response from the officers you have complained to, you may wish to take up the matter with your MP. Your MP may also be able to help if you are getting no response to your complaint.

8

Your MP may want to write to the benefit authority for an explanation of what has happened. If you want to make a complaint to the Parlimentary and Health Service Ombudsman, you must usually do so through your MP.

## 8. Complaining to an Ombudsman

The role of an Ombudsman is to investigate complaints of maladministration by government departments, such as avoidable delays, failure to advise about appeal rights, refusal to answer reasonable questions or respond to correspondence, discourtesy, racism or sexism. The Parliamentary and Health Service Ombudsman (PHSO) deals with complaints about central government departments, and the Local Government and Social Care Ombudsman (in England) or the Public Services Ombudsman (in Scotland and Wales) handles complaints about local government.

***Should you ask for compensation first?***

It is probably better to pursue a compensation payment before making a complaint to an Ombudsman. This is because, if the Ombudsman does not uphold your complaint, the benefit authority is unlikely to compensate you. Wherever possible, get and keep receipts for expenses such as postage, phone calls, travel and professional advice to help prove the cost of any delay or maladministration.

An Ombudsman does not usually investigate a complaint unless you have exhausted the complained about authority's internal complaints procedure. However, if the authority is not acting on your complaint, or there are unreasonable delays, this can form part of your complaint. The time limit for lodging a complaint with an Ombudsman is normally 12 months from the date you were notified of the matter complained about. However, a delay in bringing a complaint does not necessarily prevent a complaint being investigated if there are good reasons for the delay.

An Ombudsman can look at relevant documents held by benefit authorities. You may be interviewed to check any facts. An Ombudsman can recommend financial redress if you have been unfairly treated or experienced a loss due to maladministration.

A public body, such as the DWP or a local authority, is expected to follow the recommendations of an independent complaints service, such as the Independent Case Examiner or the Adjudicator, unless there are good reasons not to. If it has failed to do so, you may have grounds to complain to an Ombudsman and, in some circumstances, may have grounds for judicial review (see p1236).

## The Parliamentary and Health Service Ombudsman

The PHSO deals with complaints about all central government departments. This includes the DWP, HMRC, HM Courts and Tribunals Service and any agencies carrying out functions on their behalf. 'Complain for change' on the PHSO website provides information to encourage people to complain about government departments, and particularly those from under-represented groups, by providing Easy Read information and some translated materials: ombudsman.org.uk/making-complaint/before-you-come-to-us/complain-change.

To make a complaint, contact your MP, who then refers the complaint to the PHSO.

## The Local Government and Social Care Ombudsman/Public Services Ombudsman

If you have complained to your local authority but you are not satisfied with the outcome, you can apply to the Local Government and Social Care Ombudsman (in England) or the Public Services Ombudsman (in Wales and Scotland). The Ombudsman can investigate any cases of maladministration by local authorities.

You usually complain to the Ombudsman by completing an online form, but you may also be able to start a complaint by post or phone.

- In England, see lgo.org.uk/make-a-complaint/how-to-register-a-complaint or phone 0300 061 0614.
- In Wales, see ombudsman.wales/how-to-complain or phone 0300 790 0203.
- In Scotland, see spso.org.uk/how-to-complain-about-public-service or phone 0800 377 7330.

The Ombudsman may take up to 12 months to complete its investigation but straightforward cases can be dealt with more quickly. A complaint may make the authority review its procedures, which could benefit others. If you are unhappy with how the Ombudsman has dealt with your complaint, you can ask that it be reviewed internally or take legal action.

## 9. Legal action

In some circumstances, you may have grounds for judicial review against a benefit authority – eg, if it refuses to process your claim or has made a decision against which you have no right of appeal. For further information, see Chapter 53.

You cannot sue a benefit authority for negligence in the way it decides your claim.[4] However, you can seek compensation through the courts if there has been:

- misadvice – ie, if an employee of a benefit authority or HM Courts and Tribunals Service gives wrong advice which leads to financial loss for you; *or*
- unpaid benefit – ie, if your benefit claim has been determined, but you have not been paid; *or*
- discrimination, victimisation or harassment under the Equality Act 2010 or a breach of human rights (see p1241).



Although it is possible to seek compensation through the courts, it should not be your first course of action and should only be considered after getting legal advice.

## Notes

2. **Compensation payments**
   1 gov.uk/government/publications/compensation-for-poor-service-a-guide-for-dwp-staff
   2 gov.uk/hmrc-internal-manuals/complaints-and-remedy-guidance

3. **Complaining about the DWP**
   3 gov.uk/government/organisations/department-for-work-pensions/about/complaints-procedure

9. **Legal action**
   4 *Jones v Department of Employment* [1989] QB 1

Part 9

# Immigration and residence rules for benefits

# Chapter 56

# Coming from abroad: immigration status

**This chapter covers:**


1. Immigration status (below)
2. Benefits affected by immigration status (p1279)
3. Partners and children (p1284)
4. National insurance numbers and contributions (p1288)
5. Asylum seekers and refugees (p1289)


The rules in this chapter can apply if you, your partner and child are *not* all British or Irish citizens. Whether or not the rules in this chapter apply, you must satisfy the residence and presence requirements in Chapter 57.

### Key facts

- Your immigration status may mean that you are not entitled to some benefits, although there are limited exceptions.
- The immigration status of your partner can affect the amount you are paid.
- If your or your partner's or child's leave in the UK is subject to a 'no recourse to public funds' condition, your claim for specific benefits could affect your or their right to remain in the UK.

9

## 1. Immigration status

It is important to know your immigration status, and that of anyone included in your claim, before making a claim for a benefit, or adding a partner or child to an existing award. This is because it can affect your right to, and amount of, benefits. Also, if your, or your partner's or child's, leave is subject to a 'no recourse to public funds' condition, receiving specific benefits can affect your or their right to remain in the UK. If you are unsure about your immigration status, you should obtain immigration advice from a local law centre, Citizens Advice or other immigration advice provider registered with the Immigration Advice Authority (previously called the Office of the Immigration Services Commissioner – OISC): gov.uk/find-an-immigration-adviser.

## Who is a 'person subject to immigration control'

Most people, apart from British citizens, are subject to immigration control. However, for benefit purposes, the term 'person subject to immigration control' has the specific meaning given below. It is this meaning that is referred to when the phrase 'person subject to immigration control' is used in this *Handbook*.

You are defined as a **'person subject to immigration control'** if you:[1]

- require leave to enter or remain in the UK, but do not have it (see p1274); *or*
- have leave to enter or remain subject to the condition that you do not have 'recourse to public funds' (see p1276); *or*
- have leave to enter or remain given as a result of a maintenance undertaking (see p1278); *or*
- have leave to enter or remain solely because you are appealing a decision to refuse to vary your previous leave (see p1279).

If you are defined as a person subject to immigration control, you are excluded from many benefits (see p1279). There are, however, some limited exempt groups – see the rules starting on p1280.

If you are a **British or Irish citizen**, you are not defined as a person subject to immigration control. British and Irish citizens do not require leave to enter or remain in the UK.

9

### Evidence of immigration status

If you have been granted leave to enter or remain in the UK of more than six months duration, you will have an electronic record of this, known as an 'eVisa'. You need a UK Visas and Immigration (UKVI) account to access your eVisa.[2]

You can view your current status online and also get a 'share code' to allow others, including your advice worker, the DWP, HMRC or a local authority, to view (and print) your status.[3]

Your online account should show any extension of your previous time-limited leave, due to you having a pending application for further leave that you made before your previous leave expired (see p1275).

Your online account should show a Certificate of Application if you have a pending valid European Union Settlement Scheme (EUSS) application for pre-settled status or, if you do not already have pre-settled status, settled status (see p1314).

The benefit authorities can check your status directly with the Home Office. However, if you are asked for evidence of your status and you cannot provide the benefit authority with a share code, or your online account has not been updated, you should provide alternative evidence – eg:

- a copy of the Home Office letter emailed or posted to you when you were granted leave; *or*
- an expired biometric residence permit (BRP) card (see below); *or*
- copies of emails when you applied for further leave; *or*
- email confirmation of your EUSS application.

Although these documents are not proof of your *current* status, the decision maker should accept them as supporting evidence and can then verify your status directly with the Home Office.

Due to the policy of replacing physical documents, such as a **BRP card**, with eVisas, BRP cards were issued with a validity end date of no later than 31 December 2024. However, this end date relates to the card and does not affect the duration of leave. Internal guidance was issued to the DWP confirming this at the end of 2024.[4] No new BRP cards have been issued since the end of October 2024. At the time of writing, DWP guidance stated that, if you do not have an eVisa, an expired BRP card can be accepted as evidence of leave (and identity).[5]

## European Union Settlement Scheme

If you have been granted leave under the EUSS (see p1314) and you are still within that period of leave, or if you have made a valid application for settled or pre-settled status that has not yet been decided, in general, you are not defined as a 'person subject to immigration control'.

If you have **settled status** (indefinite leave to enter or remain granted under the EUSS), you are not defined as a person subject to immigration control.

If you have **pre-settled status** (limited leave to enter or remain granted under the EUSS), you are not defined as a person subject to immigration control for the duration of that leave. If you have pre-settled status, note the following.

- You should apply for settled status as soon as you are eligible (in most cases, this is after residing in the UK for a continuous period of five years). For more information, including when settled status may be granted without application, see p1314.
- Get immigration advice before being absent from the UK for more than six out of any 12 months, as this could affect your eligibility to get settled status in future.
- If by the date your pre-settled status was due to expire, you have not yet been granted settled status (whether or not you have applied for it), your pre-settled status is extended by five years, and you therefore continue to *not* be a person subject to immigration control (for further details of this policy, see p1315). **Note:** if your pre-settled status is cancelled by the Home Office or is not extended beyond the date it was due to expire, you *are* defined as a person subject to immigration control because you are someone who requires leave and does not have it. Get urgent immigration advice.

- If you are claiming a benefit that requires a right to reside (see p1306), pre-settled status does not, in general, satisfy that requirement by itself, but it does mean you are in a protected group (see p1317) that can potentially have a free movement right to reside (see p1317). For the steps to follow, including limited circumstances in which pre-settled status by itself can satisfy the right to reside requirement for a means-tested benefit if you do not have a qualifying free movement right to reside, see p1307.

If you have leave to enter as the holder of an **EUSS family permit**, you are not defined as a person subject to immigration control for the duration of that leave. If you apply for settled or pre-settled status before your leave to enter expires, but this application is not decided by the date your leave would have expired, your leave is extended until your application is decided and you therefore continue to not be a person subject to immigration control (see p1275). However, if, while your leave was extended, your application for settled or pre-settled status was refused and you submitted an appeal or administrative review, the benefit authority may decide that the last bullet point of the definition of person subject to immigration control applies to you – but, arguably, this is not correct (see p1279). Leave to enter as the holder of an EUSS family permit is an excluded right to reside for those benefits that have that requirement (see p1306), but once you have made a valid application for settled or pre-settled status, you are then in a protected group (see p1317) that can potentially have a free movement right to reside (see p1317).

9

If you have made a **valid application to the EUSS** (see p1314) for pre-settled status or, if you do not currently have pre-settled status, settled status, and that application (or appeal against, or administrative review of, a refusal) has not been finally determined, withdrawn or abandoned, you are not defined as a person subject to immigration control.[6] If this is not accepted, or for further details, see the 15th edition of CPAG's *Benefits for Migrants Handbook*. While your valid EUSS application is pending, you are in a protected group (see p1317) that can potentially have a free movement right to reside (see p1317). **Note:** if you currently have leave to enter or remain that is subject to a condition that you do not have recourse to public funds and you *also* have a pending valid EUSS application, this condition (together with any other conditions attached to your leave) does not have any effect while you have a free movement right to reside under the EEA Regulations.[7]

For how to provide evidence that you have settled or pre-settled status, or a pending valid application, see p1272.

## You require leave to enter or remain but do not have it

You are a 'person subject to immigration control' if you require leave to enter or remain but do not have it,[8] *unless* you have a pending valid EUSS application for settled or pre-settled status and it has not been finally determined (see above).

You require leave to enter or remain in the UK *unless* you are:

- a British or Irish citizen or person with the right of abode; *or*
- an EEA national in the UK as a frontier worker and you hold a valid frontier worker permit (see p1342).[9]

Examples of when you require leave to enter or remain but do not have it include if you do *not* have a pending valid EUSS application (or appeal, or administrative review, against a refusal) for settled or pre-settled status and you:

- are an asylum seeker on immigration bail (see p1289);
- have overstayed your limited leave to enter or remain (but if you applied for further leave before your previous leave expired, see 'Extension of leave' below);
- have entered the UK without immigration leave, and since then have not obtained leave to remain;
- are subject to a deportation order (if you have a pending valid EUSS application, get specialist advice).

**Note:**

- If you came to live in the UK before 1973 and you are, or were, a Commonwealth citizen, or you came before August 1988 and you are now British or have a right of abode or indefinite leave, you may be entitled to compensation from the Windrush Compensation Scheme if you experienced losses, including loss of benefits, due to a lack of documentary evidence of your status.[10] Payments under this scheme have been disregarded as income or capital for all the means-tested benefits, since 1 January 2022.[11] The council tax reduction regulations also disregard these payments as income and capital.[12] If you have gaps in your national insurance contribution record, see p1288.
- There are close links between the benefit authorities and the Home Office. Making a claim for benefit could alert the immigration authorities to your presence and status in the UK. Get specialist immigration advice before claiming benefits if you are unsure about your immigration status.

### Extension of leave

If you have time-limited leave to enter or remain in the UK and you make a valid application for a further period of leave, on the same or a different basis, *before* your current leave expires, your current leave is extended from the date it was due to expire until your application is decided or withdrawn (although it can be cancelled – eg, if you breach a condition attached to the leave).[13] While your leave is extended, you continue to have the same benefit entitlements as you had previously. If you were previously entitled, you must notify the relevant benefit authority that you applied for leave before your previous leave expired, provide any evidence you have of this (see p1272), and explain that your leave has been extended under section 3C of the Immigration Act 1971 and therefore your benefit entitlements continue.[14]

## Your leave has a 'no recourse to public funds' condition

You are a 'person subject to immigration control' if you have leave to enter or remain in the UK that is subject to the condition that you do not have recourse to 'public funds'.[15]

Most people admitted to the UK with time-limited leave (such as spouses/civil partners, students or visitors) have a 'no recourse to public funds' condition attached to their leave. This condition is never attached to indefinite leave. If your leave is subject to this condition, it will be stated on the Home Office letter notifying you of your leave and on your eVisa.

### *Public funds*

**'Public funds'** are defined in the Immigration Rules as:[16]

- adult disability payment (ADP – in Scotland);
- attendance allowance;
- carer's allowance;
- carer's allowance supplement (in Scotland);
- child benefit;
- child disability payment (CDP – in Scotland);
- child tax credit;
- child winter heating payment (in Scotland);
- council tax reduction;
- disability living allowance;
- income-related employment and support allowance;
- funeral support payment (in Scotland);
- homelessness assistance and housing provided under specific provisions;
- housing benefit (HB);
- income support;
- job start payment (in Scotland);
- income-based jobseeker's allowance;
- local authority discretionary payments under section 1 of the Localism Act 2011;
- local authority welfare assistance payments in Northern Ireland;
- pension credit (PC);
- personal independence payment;
- Scottish child payment;
- Scottish Welfare Fund payments;
- severe disablement allowance;
- social fund payments;
- universal credit (UC);
- winter heating payment (in Scotland);
- working tax credit.

Only the benefits and assistance listed in the Immigration Rules (listed above) are public funds. Therefore, if you get any other benefit or other assistance, you are not in breach of any no recourse to public funds condition attached to your leave.

If you have recourse to public funds when your leave prohibits you from doing so, you have breached a condition of your leave. This may affect your right to remain in the UK. You could have your leave cancelled, be liable to be deported, have further leave refused and/or be prosecuted for committing a criminal offence.[17]

If your leave is subject to a no recourse to public funds condition, you are defined as a person subject to immigration control and, unless you are within an exempt group (see pp1280–82), the benefit rules exclude you from entitlement to all the benefits listed above *except* the following Scottish benefits: carer's allowance supplement, Scottish child payment, job start payment, child winter heating payment and winter heating payment. In most cases, you cannot receive these five benefits because being a person subject to immigration control excludes you from the qualifying benefit, but if you *are* entitled to the qualifying benefit due to being in an exempt group, receipt of one of the five benefits counts as having recourse to public funds (even though receipt of the qualifying benefit may not – see below). Get immigration advice before making a claim for the relevant benefit.

If you are within an exempt group, you can claim and receive most of the benefits listed above, and you are not regarded as having recourse to public funds under the Immigration Rules. However, this does not apply to council tax reduction, ADP, CDP or funeral support payment. If you receive one of these, you *are* regarded as having recourse to public funds under the Immigration Rules.[18] Get immigration advice before making a claim.

You are regarded as having recourse to public funds if someone else's benefit is increased because of your presence[19] – eg, if the amount of your partner's HB is greater because you are included in their claim, this breaches a no recourse to public funds condition attached to your leave. Get immigration advice before someone makes a claim that includes extra benefit for you.

For examples of circumstances in which a no recourse to public funds condition may be breached, see the 15th edition of CPAG's *Benefits for Migrants Handbook*.

**Note**: if you are, or are likely to become, destitute, get individual immigration advice about the possibility, risks and consequences of applying to the Home Office to have the no recourse to public funds condition removed.

### Domestic abuse

If you have, or last had, leave granted on the basis of your partner relationship, and that relationship has broken down due to domestic abuse, and your current immigration status means that you are not entitled to key benefits such as UC, HB and PC (eg, because you have leave subject to a no recourse to public funds condition, or because you have pre-settled status), you may be able to apply for migrant victims of domestic abuse concession (MVDAC) leave. It is essential to get immigration advice on your individual circumstances because it may not be the best immigration option for you and although, in some circumstances, you can apply for indefinite leave due to the domestic abuse, this is not an option if you have leave as the partner of a Ukrainian national under one of the Ukraine Schemes, or of a person with leave as a worker, student or graduate, and obtaining MVDAC leave can *prevent* you getting specific types of leave to remain in the UK in future.

If you are granted MVDAC leave, it replaces your previous leave (or gives you leave if you did not previously have any). While you have MVDAC leave, you are *not* defined as a person subject to immigration control, you are exempt from the habitual residence test for means-tested benefits (see p1303) and you have a right to reside that satisfies this requirement for all benefits that have it.

The MVDAC leave is granted for three months. If, before the three-month period expires, you apply for further leave (eg, indefinite leave on the basis of domestic abuse), the MVDAC leave is extended pending the outcome of your application and therefore your entitlement to benefits can continue (see p1275).

**Note:** if you have pre-settled status, for the circumstances in which this can satisfy the right to reside requirement, see, for means-tested benefits, p1307 and, for child benefit, p1310.

## Your leave was given as a result of a maintenance undertaking

9

If your leave to enter or remain was given as a result of a maintenance undertaking, you are a 'person subject to immigration control'.[20] For example, if a dependent older relative is seeking to join family in the UK, the Home Office will usually require a maintenance undertaking.

### *Maintenance undertaking*

A **'maintenance undertaking'** means a written undertaking given by another person under the Immigration Rules to be responsible for your maintenance and accommodation.[21] Specific Home Office forms are available for this. However, no official form need be used, provided the undertaking is sufficiently formal and definite.[22] The document must contain a promise or agreement that the other person will maintain and accommodate you in the future. It does not amount to an undertaking if it merely contains a statement about their present abilities and intentions.[23]

Your leave is considered to be 'as a result of a maintenance undertaking' if this was a factor in granting it. It does not need to have been the only, or even a major, factor.[24] However, if the maintenance undertaking was not relevant to your being granted leave, its existence does not make you a person subject to immigration control. If you are in doubt about whether you have leave given as a result of an undertaking, get immigration advice.

### You are appealing a refusal to vary your previous leave

If you have leave solely because you have appealed against a decision to refuse an application to vary the leave you previously had, you are a 'person subject to immigration control'.[25]

*Example*

Sayf is an Iraqi national who has been granted two and a half years' discretionary leave (without any public funds condition attached). Just before this expires, he applies for a further period of discretionary leave and his original leave is extended while that application is pending (see p1275). His application is refused and he immediately appeals against this decision. His previous discretionary leave is extended further while the appeal is pending, but he is now a person subject to immigration control.

**Note:** if the leave which has been extended pending your appeal against a refusal of further leave was leave to enter as the holder of an EUSS family permit, or if you have requested an administrative review (rather than appeal) of the refusal, it is arguable that you are *not* defined as a person subject to immigration control.[26] For details on these arguments, see CPAG's *Benefits for Migrants Handbook*. If your benefit is refused or terminated on this basis, challenge the decision and ask your adviser to contact CPAG.

9

## 2. Benefits affected by immigration status

The general rule is that if you are defined as a 'person subject to immigration control' (see p1272), you are excluded from council tax reduction[27] and the following benefits:[28]

- adult disability payment (ADP – in Scotland);[29]
- attendance allowance (AA);
- carer's allowance (CA);
- carer support payment (CSP – in Scotland);[30]
- child benefit;
- child disability payment (CDP – in Scotland);[31]
- child tax credit (CTC);
- disability living allowance (DLA);
- funeral support payment (in Scotland);[32]
- income-related employment and support allowance (ESA);
- ESA in youth;[33]

- housing benefit (HB);
- income support (IS);
- income-based jobseeker's allowance (JSA);
- pension age disability payment (PADP – in Scotland);[34]
- pension credit (PC);
- personal independence payment (PIP);
- Scottish adult disability living allowance (SADLA – in Scotland);[35]
- severe disablement allowance (SDA);
- social fund payments;
- universal credit (UC);
- working tax credit (WTC).

However, if you are defined as a person subject to immigration control, this does not exclude you from the above benefits if you are in an exempt group that can claim means-tested benefits (see below) or that can claim disability, carers' and child benefits (see p1282). **Note:** if your, or your partner's or child's, leave is subject to a no recourse to public funds condition, check the situations in which this condition could be breached (see p1276). For the exempt groups that could claim IS, income-based JSA and tax credits, see the 2024/25 edition of this *Handbook*.

A person subject to immigration control is only excluded from the above benefits and can therefore claim any other benefit. For example, if you have paid sufficient national insurance (NI) contributions, you can claim any of the contributory benefits – eg, retirement pensions, new-style JSA or new-style ESA. You can also claim benefits that depend on employment – eg, maternity allowance (MA), industrial injuries benefits or statutory payments such as statutory maternity pay.

## Exempt groups

### Means-tested benefits

If you are in any of the exempt groups below, being a 'person subject to immigration control' does not exclude you from entitlement to the following means-tested benefits:[36]

- UC;
- income-related ESA;
- PC;
- HB.

You are not excluded if:

- you have leave to enter or remain given as a result of a maintenance undertaking and have been resident in the UK for at least five years (beginning on either the date you entered the UK or when the maintenance undertaking was signed, whichever is later). If there are gaps in your residence due to you going to live for a period in another country, the periods of residence in the UK can be added together to make the five years.[37] However, depending on your circumstances, you may not have ceased to be resident during the short periods of absence, and each absence must be considered individually (see p1299);[38] *or*

- you have leave to enter or remain given as a result of a maintenance undertaking and the person (or, if more than one, all the people) who gave the undertaking has died; *or*
- you are already receiving UC (if your claim began before 1 January 2021),[39] HB (if your claim began before 3 May 2022), PC (if your claim began before 3 May 2022),[40] or income-related ESA *and* you are a national of North Macedonia, Turkey[41] or any of the European Economic Area (EEA) countries (except Bulgaria, Liechtenstein, Lithuania, Romania or Slovenia) and you are lawfully present – eg, during a period in which you have leave to enter or remain in the UK. (You are very unlikely to be assisted by this exemption if you are an asylum seeker, because although you are lawfully present, you still need a right to reside for each of these benefits – see p1306.[42]) The countries listed have each ratified either the European Convention on Social and Medical Assistance or the European Social Charter (1961). **Note: if you have leave which is subject to a 'no recourse to public funds' condition**, you are *not* regarded as having recourse if you receive a means-tested benefit because this exempt group applies to you.[43] However, if you receive Scottish child payment, winter heating payment or job start payment (due to the means-tested benefit being the necessary qualifying benefit), this *does* breach your no recourse to public funds condition. Also, if this exempt group applies, you are not excluded from council tax reduction in Scotland, but receiving this *does* breach your no recourse to public funds condition (see p1276).[44]

9

## Social fund and other payments

If you are defined as a 'person subject to immigration control', this does not exclude you from entitlement to:

- social fund payments *if* you are in any of the exempt categories for means-tested (see p1282) or disability, carers' and child benefits (see below);[45] *or*
- funeral support payment (in Scotland) *if* you are in any of the exempt categories for disability, carers' and child benefits (see p1282);[46] *or*
- children's funeral payments in England or Wales; *or*
- child winter heating payment, winter heating payment and pension age winter heating payment (in Scotland); *or*
- Best Start grants.

For each of these payments, you must meet the other conditions of entitlement, including (except for Best Start grants if you are under 20 and children's funeral payments in England or Wales) you or (except for a budgeting loan, cold weather payment, child winter heating payment or winter heating payment) your partner being in receipt of a qualifying benefit (this requirement is not expected to apply to pension age winter heating payment from winter 2025 – see p1507).

**If you have leave that is subject to a 'no recourse to public funds' condition** (see p1276), note:[47]

- receiving a social fund payment due to being in an exempt group is *not* regarded as having recourse to public funds under the Immigration Rules;
- receiving a funeral support payment as a result of being in an exempt group (see below) (and either you receive a qualifying benefit due to being in an exempt group or your partner receives a qualifying benefit) *is* regarded as having recourse to public funds under the Immigration Rules;
- receiving a child winter heating payment as a result of receiving a qualifying disability benefit due to being in an exempt group (see below) *is* regarded as having recourse to public funds under the Immigration Rules;
- receiving a winter heating payment as a result of receiving a qualifying means-tested benefit due to being in an exempt group (see p1280) *is* regarded as having recourse to public funds under the Immigration Rules;
- receiving (or if your partner receives PC, their receiving the higher rate of) a winter fuel payment due to your younger partner receiving either UC (see p1285) or PC (see p1286) is regarded as having recourse to public funds under the Immigration Rules.

Get immigration advice before claiming the relevant benefit if it would breach a no recourse to public funds condition.

9

### Disability, carers' and child benefits

If you are in any of the exempt groups below, being a 'person subject to immigration control' does not exclude you from getting the following non-means-tested, non-contributory benefits:[48]

- ADP;
- AA;
- CA;
- CSP;
- child benefit;
- CDP;
- DLA;
- ESA in youth;
- PADP;
- PIP;
- SADLA;
- SDA.

You are not excluded if:

- you have leave to enter or remain given as a result of a maintenance undertaking;
- you are a national of Albania (for child benefit only[49]), Morocco, Tunisia or Turkey (or Algeria or San Marino if you made you claim before 1 January 2021[50]) and either you are currently lawfully working (see below) in Great Britain, or you have ceased to be lawfully working in Great Britain for a reason such as pregnancy, childcare, illness or accident, or because you have reached retirement age;[51]
- you are living with a member of your family (see p1399) who is covered by the above bullet point;
- for DLA, PIP, AA and child benefit only, you are covered by a reciprocal agreement. At the time of writing, only Denmark and Germany (and, for claims made before 1 January 2021 only, Norway) had agreements in relation to AA and DLA and no agreements had been amended to include PIP. For child benefit, check whether you are covered by the agreements with Austria, Barbados, Belgium, Canada, Denmark, Finland, France, Germany, Israel, Mauritius, New Zealand, Norway (only for claims made before 1 January 2021), Portugal, Spain, Sweden, Switzerland (only for claims made before 1 November 2021) or the former Yugoslavia (Bosnia-Herzegovina, Croatia, Kosovo, North Macedonia, Montenegro, Serbia and Slovenia[52]). See p1297 for more information about reciprocal agreements.

***Lawfully working***

You should be accepted as **'lawfully working'** if you have been insured (by paying or being credited with NI contributions).[53] In practice, you are generally accepted as lawfully working if the work does not breach any conditions attached to your leave, or, if you are an asylum seeker, you have permission to work from the Home Office.

**If you have leave that is subject to a 'no recourse to public funds' condition** (see p1276), note:[54]

- receiving any of the benefits above *except* ADP or CDP due to being in the second, third or fourth exempt group is *not* regarded as having recourse to public funds under the Immigration Rules;
- receiving ADP or CDP due to being in an exempt group *is* regarded as having recourse to public funds under the Immigration Rules;
- receiving carer's allowance supplement as a result of receiving CA or CSP due to being in an exempt group, or receiving child winter heating payment as a result of receiving a qualifying disability benefit due to being in an exempt group, *is* regarded as having recourse to public funds under the Immigration Rules.

Get immigration advice before claiming the relevant benefit if it would breach a no recourse to public funds condition.

# 3. Partners and children

Some benefits have special rules that apply if any partner or child who lives with you is subject to immigration control. These rules vary, so check the rules for the relevant benefit. For the rules on how your income support, income-based jobseeker's allowance or tax credits were affected if your partner or child is subject to immigration control, see the 2024/25 edition of this *Handbook*.

## Means-tested benefits

### Universal credit

If you live with your **partner** and claim universal credit (UC), you are generally required to make a joint claim. If your partner is a 'person subject to immigration control' and is not in one of the exempt groups who can get UC (see p1280), your joint claim is *treated as* a claim for UC as a single person and:[55]

- your award is based on the maximum amount for a single person;[56] *and*
- your partner does not have to accept a claimant commitment or comply with any work-related requirements because they are not a claimant;[57] *and*
- your partner's income and capital are taken into account (see p36);[58] *and*
- your partner is not classed as a 'non-dependant' and therefore no 'housing costs contribution' (see p109) is deducted from the maximum amount of UC;[59] *and*
- if you are under 35, your partner does not prevent your rent being restricted to the one-bedroom shared accommodation rate (see p113);[60] *and*
- if you have a child, your partner does not affect your being the child's 'responsible carer' (see p952) – eg, to determine your work-related requirements;[61] *and*
- the couple rate of the earnings threshold applies for determining when no work-related requirements apply to you (see p955), and in calculating any self-employed 'minimum income floor' that may apply if you are self-employed (note that the minimum income floor does not apply to your partner if they are self-employed) (see p130).[62]

Other than in the two potential exceptions below, the awards described above do not include additional amounts for your partner. Therefore, if their leave is subject to a 'no recourse to public funds' condition, your award of UC does not breach this condition because it does not result in your receiving increased public funds as a result of their presence (see p1276). If your UC award includes a housing costs element, other than in the potential exception below, this will not be higher

9

as a result of your partner's presence, as they are not a claimant and are therefore ignored in the housing costs calculation.[63]

The first potential exception arises if you and your partner are joint tenants, as the amount of rent used to calculate your housing costs element includes your partner's share (see p111 and p116). If this results in an additional amount of UC housing costs element being paid, that breaches any no recourse to public funds condition attached to your partner's leave. The only scenario that CPAG is aware of in which this can arise is if you and your partner are joint tenants with one or more other joint tenants. The second potential exception is if you are entitled to the childcare element due to both you and your partner working (or being treated as working), and the amount of the childcare element is greater due to the amount of work done by your partner *and* not fully offset by the amount of earned income from your partner's work taken into account.[64] Obtain specialist immigration advice before claiming UC including a housing costs or childcare element if you have concerns about breaching a no recourse to public funds condition.

**Note:**

- If you have reached pension age and your partner is under pension age but is not entitled to UC because they are a person subject to immigration control, your claim is *not* treated as a single claim for UC. Instead, you must claim pension credit (PC) and housing benefit (HB) and you are treated as a single person for each of these claims (for HB, see p184).[65]
- If your partner subsequently ceases to be a person subject to immigration control before reaching pension age, provided they also satisfy the residence and presence rules for UC (see p1343), your entitlement to PC and HB ends and you can make a joint claim for UC. If your partner is receiving UC, and the claim has been treated as a single claim because you are a person subject to immigration control, and you have reached pension age, you are entitled to a winter fuel payment because your partner is receiving a qualifying benefit.[66]
- However, if you have leave which is subject to a no recourse to public funds condition, note that receiving this payment breaches this condition (see p1276). A winter fuel payment is paid automatically without the need to make a claim, but you can cancel or return a payment.[67]

You can include in your claim any **child** you are responsible for, regardless of the child's immigration status (subject to the 'two-child limit'). However, if the child's leave is subject to a no recourse to public funds condition, receiving UC amounts for them breaches that condition and could affect their right to remain in the UK (see p1276). Get immigration advice before making a claim.

## Housing benefit

If your **partner** is a 'person subject to immigration control', unless the exception below applies, they are included in your award and your applicable amount includes the couple rate of the personal allowance and any premiums to which either of you are entitled.

Similarly, if a **child** you are responsible for is a person subject to immigration control, they are included in your award and your applicable amount includes a personal allowance for each child (subject to the 'two-child limit' – see p268), together with any premiums for which they qualify.

Therefore, if your partner's and/or child's leave is subject to a 'no recourse to public funds' condition, a claim for HB can result in additional public funds being paid as a result of their presence. This can affect the right to remain in the UK of the person whose leave is subject to that condition (see p1276). Get immigration advice before making a claim.

The only **exception** is if you have reached pension age and your partner is under pension age, but you cannot make a joint claim for UC because they are a person subject to immigration control and not covered by an exempt group (see p1284). You are treated as a single person for your HB (and PC) claim (see p184).[68]

## Pension credit

If your **partner** is a 'person subject to immigration control' (whether or not they are in one of the exempt groups listed on p1280), they are treated as not being part of your household.[69] This means you are paid as a single person and your partner's income and capital do not affect your claim. It also means that if your partner is under pension age, you can claim PC and HB (rather than UC) and you are treated as a single person for both PC and HB.[70]

Your partner's presence may mean you cannot get the additional amount for severe disability, as the DWP treats them as 'normally residing with' you for this purpose, unless an exemption applies (see p275).[71]

If your partner is receiving PC as a single person because you are a person subject to immigration control, and they are aged under 80 in the qualifying week, but you are aged 80 or over in that week, they will be entitled to the higher amount of a winter fuel payment (see p716).[72] However, if you have leave which is subject to a no recourse to public funds condition, the payment of this higher amount breaches this condition (see p1276). A winter fuel payment is paid automatically without the need to make a claim, but you can cancel or return a payment.[73]

If you are entitled to PC, any **child** you are responsible for is included in your claim, regardless of the child's immigration status. However, if the child's leave is subject to a 'no recourse to public funds' condition, receipt of PC amounts for them breaches that condition and can affect their right to remain in the UK (see p1276). Get immigration advice before making a claim.

## Income-related employment and support allowance

If your **partner** is a 'person subject to immigration control' (see p1272), they are included in your claim for income-related employment and support allowance

(ESA). However, you are only paid a personal allowance at the single person's rate, unless they are in one of the exempt groups of people who can get the means-tested benefits listed on p1280, in which case you are paid at the couple rate.[74]

In all cases, your partner is still treated as part of your household and part of your claim. Therefore, their work, income and capital can all affect your benefit entitlement. Their presence may mean you are not entitled to a severe disability premium (see p275).

Premiums are payable if either you or your partner satisfy the qualifying conditions (see p270) and should be paid at the couple rate.

**Note:** if your partner's leave to enter or remain in the UK is subject to a 'no recourse to public funds' condition, receiving an additional (or a couple rate of a) premium for them can be regarded as having additional recourse to public funds and affect their right to remain in the UK (see p1276). Get immigration advice before claiming the benefit that would result in the premium being paid.

## Non-means-tested benefits

Non-means-tested benefits include both contributory benefits (based on your national insurance contribution record) and non-contributory benefits.

Your immigration status, and that of your partner or child, does not affect your entitlement to either contributory benefits (eg, contributory ESA) or benefits based on current or past employment – eg, maternity allowance and statutory payments.

Your entitlement to non-contributory benefits is affected by your immigration status if you are the claimant, but is not affected by the immigration status of any partner or child included in your claim. Therefore, for **child benefit**, if you are not a 'person subject to immigration control', or you are but you are in one of the exempt groups (see p1282), you can claim for any child for whom you are responsible, regardless of the child's immigration status. However, if the child's leave is subject to a 'no recourse to public funds' condition (see p1276), receiving child benefit for that child breaches that condition and could affect their right to remain in the UK. Get immigration advice before making a claim.

Similarly, if your child is not a person subject to immigration control, or they are but are in one of the exempt groups on p1282, they can claim **disability living allowance**, or, in Scotland, **child disability payment** (CDP), even if *you* are a person subject to immigration control. However, note that if your child has leave subject to a no recourse to public funds condition, receiving CDP due to being in an exempt group, or receiving child winter heating payment due to being in an exempt group for the qualifying disability benefit, breaches that condition and could affect their right to remain in the UK. Get immigration advice before making a claim.

# 4. National insurance numbers and contributions

## Exemption from the national insurance number requirement

In general, the national insurance (NI) number requirement (see p1007) applies, regardless of immigration status, to you and any partner included in your claim (even if you will not get any extra benefit for them because they are a 'person subject to immigration control' – see p1284).

However, if you are claiming pension credit, housing benefit, income-related employment and support allowance, bereavement benefits or retirement pension, your partner does not have to satisfy the NI number requirement if:[75]

- they are a 'person subject to immigration control' because they require leave to enter or remain in the UK, but do not have it (see p1274); *and*
- they have not previously been given an NI number.

You may still be asked for information about an NI number application for your partner, even though they are exempt, but a refusal to allocate an NI number does not prevent you from being entitled to the above benefits, or council tax reduction.

**Note:**

- This exemption is not relevant to universal credit (UC) because you do not need an NI number to *make* a claim for UC. If your partner is a 'person subject to immigration control', and you make a joint claim for UC, it is treated as a claim for UC as a single person (see p1284) and therefore your partner is not a claimant and does not need an NI number.[76]
- If you do not have an NI number when you make your claim for UC, the DWP should assist you to apply for one as part of processing your claim. However, you cannot be paid a UC advance until you have been allocated an NI number (see p1023).[77]

## National insurance contributions

If you have worked and paid insurance contributions in a European Economic Area country and you are covered by any of the European Union co-ordination rules (see p1392), your contributions can be taken into account when working out your entitlement to UK contributory benefits (under the 'aggregation principle' – see p1406). Similar rules apply if you have worked and paid insurance contributions in a country with which the UK has a reciprocal agreement (see p1297).[78] You may also be able to make up a shortfall in your contribution record by making voluntary contributions, but you should get advice to check whether this is worth doing (see p862).

If you have accepted compensation from the Windrush Compensation Scheme (see p1275) for loss of access to employment, and there is a shortfall in your contribution record due to gaps during the period you were compensated for, the Home Office can pay HMRC to fill these gaps in your contribution record if that would improve your retirement pension.[79]

Being a 'person subject to immigration control' (see p1279) does not exclude you from any of the contributory benefits.

## 5. Asylum seekers and refugees

### Asylum seekers

You are referred to as an 'asylum seeker' while you are waiting for a Home Office decision on an application for refugee status. If you are seeking asylum in the UK, you generally come within the definition of a 'person subject to immigration control' as someone who requires leave, but does not have it (see p1274). You are therefore excluded from the social security benefits listed on p1279 unless you are in one of the exempt groups on pp1280–82.

If benefit can be paid for you because, for example, you are in an exempt group or because your partner can include you in their claim, this does not affect your asylum application. You can receive any benefit defined as a 'public fund' (see p1276) because asylum seekers are *not* subject to a 'no recourse to public funds' condition.

If you are excluded from social security benefits because you are a 'person subject to immigration control', you may be entitled to alternative forms of state support. If you are destitute, you may be eligible for asylum support from the Home Office. **Note:** asylum support is not taken into account as income for universal credit (UC). It is only disregarded for income-related employment and support allowance (ESA) if it is 'income in kind'. If your partner claims housing benefit (HB), asylum support is taken into account as income unless your partner is 'passported' onto maximum HB due to receiving UC, income-related ESA or pension credit.[80]

However, any benefit your partner receives *is* taken into account as income when calculating your asylum support unless you can show it would not reasonably be available to you – eg, if your partner receives a disability benefit.

If you are not eligible for asylum support or benefits, you may be able to get assistance from your local authority under one or more of the community care provisions, particularly if you have additional needs as a result of your age, sickness or disability. If you have one or more children, or you are a child, you may be eligible for support under the Children Act 1989 or Children (Scotland)

Act 1995. Get independent legal advice about what you are entitled to, if possible before you apply, and always if you are refused.

For more about asylum support, see CPAG's *Benefits for Migrants Handbook*.

## Refugee and other leave granted after an asylum application

If, following your asylum application, you are granted leave that is not subject to a 'no recourse to public funds' condition (eg, refugee leave or humanitarian protection), you are no longer a 'person subject to immigration control'. During this period of leave, you can claim all benefits, provided you meet the usual rules of entitlement. If you are granted leave that *is* subject to a 'no recourse to public funds' condition, you *are* defined as a 'person subject to immigration control' and you are excluded from the benefits listed on p1279, unless you are in an exempt group (see pp1280–82).

When you are granted leave, the Home Office should send a letter notifying you of the leave you have been granted and the date it expires. The Home Office should create a UKVI account and send you details of how to access it within 14 days of the letter notifying you of your leave. You should be able to view your online immigration status, known as an eVisa, on your UK Visas and Immigration (UKVI) account. Your NI number should be shown on your eVisa (contact the Home Office if it is not there).

You do not need to wait until you can access your eVisa or until you have an national insurance (NI) number (see p1288) to claim benefits, but you should explain this to the benefit authority and provide all the evidence of your leave that you have.[81]

9

If you have been receiving asylum support, this stops (and if you were provided with accommodation, you are required to leave) after you are granted leave. At the time of writing, your support should continue for at least 56 days from the date you are granted leave. However, the duration of this period may change from June 2025. See the online edition of CPAG's *Benefits for Migrants Handbook* for updates.

If you are granted refugee leave or humanitarian protection, you can be joined by certain family members under the family reunion provisions. If the application is successful, the family member will be granted leave that will expire at the same time as yours (but it is not refugee leave or humanitarian protection). A family member who is given leave in the UK under these provisions is not a person subject to immigration control during their period of leave and can claim all benefits, provided they meet the usual rules of entitlement.

If you (or the family member you have joined) have refugee leave or humanitarian protection, or you have come from Afghanistan, Ukraine, Sudan, Israel, the West Bank, the Gaza Strip, East Jerusalem, the Golan Heights or Lebanon and satisfy additional conditions, you do not need to satisfy the past presence test or habitual residence requirement for the disability and carers' benefits (see p1348).

If you are granted refugee leave, humanitarian protection or leave outside the immigration rules, or you have come from Afghanistan, Ukraine, Sudan, Israel, the West Bank, the Gaza Strip, East Jerusalem, the Golan Heights or Lebanon and satisfy additional conditions, you are exempt from the habitual residence test for means-tested benefits (see p1303).

If you are granted refugee leave or humanitarian protection, or you have come from Afghanistan or Ukraine and you satisfy additional conditions (see the second and third bullet points on p1348), for Sure Start maternity or Best Start grants, any child under 16 who was a member of your family before you came to the UK is disregarded and therefore:[82]

- you are *not* excluded from a Sure Start maternity grant (see p705);
- in Scotland, you do *not* get the lower Best Start grant pregnancy and baby payment (see p1454).

## Backdating child benefit, guardian's allowance and tax credits

If you were recorded as a refugee by the Home Office before 7 April 2025, you can claim child benefit, guardian's allowance and, in limited circumstances, tax credits, backdated to the date of your asylum application.[83] If you made more than one asylum application, these benefits can be backdated to the date of the first, provided the basis of the asylum applications remained the same. If you were granted refugee leave as a result of events that only occurred after the first asylum application, these benefits will only be backdated to the date of the asylum application made after those events.[84]

You must claim backdated child benefit and guardian's allowance within three months, and tax credits within one month (but see also below), of being notified by the Home Office that you have been granted leave as a refugee.[85] If the Home Office notification is sent to a solicitor acting for you, the three- or one-month period starts from the date your solicitor receives the letter.[86]

You can only claim backdated tax credits if you applied for asylum on or before 31 January 2019 (the final day that a claim for tax credits could be made before UC was introduced). If successful, your tax credit award continues until 6 April 2025 (or the date you claimed UC, if earlier). HMRC has been working with the Home Office to invite potentially eligible refugees to claim backdated tax credits and has stated details will be accepted even if provided late.[87] However, if possible you should claim within one month of being notified of your refugee leave.

If you have received any asylum support for essential living needs, this reduces your tax credits over that period and often completely cancels out entitlement.[88] Child benefit and guardian's allowance are not reduced by any asylum support you may have received.

**Note:** there is no equivalent provision to pay backdated UC.

For further details on claiming backdated child benefit, guardian's allowance and tax credits, see CPAG's *Benefits for Migrants Handbook*.

## Integration loans

If you (or someone upon whom you are dependent) are granted refugee leave or humanitarian protection and you are aged 18 or over, you may be eligible for an integration loan.[89] This is a discretionary loan of at least £100, with a maximum of £500, or £780 for a couple, paid for expenses associated with your integration into UK society, including for employment, education and housing. Applications are made online[90] and are decided by the Home Office. For more information, see CPAG's *Benefits for Migrants Handbook*.

Before applying for, or in addition to, an integration loan, you may want to consider accessing help from your local welfare assistance scheme (see p770) or applying for other financial help (see p782).

# Notes

9

1. **Immigration status**

1 s115(9) IAA 1999
2 gov.uk/get-access-evisa; gov.uk/guidance/online-immigration-status-evisa
3 gov.uk/view-prove-immigration-status
4 Confirmed in DWP letter to The3Million, 2 December 2024, at the3million.org.uk/sites/default/files/documents/DWP-reply-t3m-MigrantsOrganise-EvisaDigitaliisation-02Dec2024.pdf
5 gov.uk/government/publications/universal-credit-and-homeless-people/universal-credit-and-homeless-people-guide-for-supporting-organisations#appendix-1
6 Arts 4, 10 and 18(3) WA 2019; Arts 4, 9 and 17(3) UK-EFTA; Arts 4, 10 and 16(3) UK-SA; ss7A-7C EU(W)A 2018; DMG Memo 14/21; ADM Memo 19/21; HB Circular A10/2021
7 Reg 43 and Sch 3 para 1 I(EEA) Regs; paras C1050 and C2012 ADM; para 070838 DMG
8 s115(9)(a) IAA 1999
9 Regs 1(2)(b) and (4), 5 and 6 CR(FW) Regs; DMG Memo 29/20, paras 45 and 49; ADM Memo 33/20, paras 45 and 49
10 gov.uk/apply-windrush-compensation-scheme
11 The Social Security (Income and Capital Disregards) (Amendment) Regulations 2021 No.1405; DMG Memo 15/21; ADM Memo 21/21
12 Regs 10(2)(f) and 19 (table 6, para 23) TC(DCI) Regs
13 s3C IA 1971
14 Vol 2 Ch7 Pt3, para 073192 DMG; paras C1385, C1679 and C2017 ADM
15 s115(9)(b) IAA 1999
16 para 6.2, 'public funds' definition, IR
17 s24(1)(b) IA 1971
18 para 6.2, note (ii) under 'public funds' definition, IR
19 para 6.2, note (i) under 'public funds' definition, IR
20 s115(9)(c) IAA 1999
21 s115(10) IAA 1999
22 *R (Begum) v Social Security Commissioner* [2003] EWHC 3380 (Admin)
23 *Ahmed v SSWP* [2005] EWCA Civ 535

24 CIS/3508/2001; see also *SJ v SSWP (SPC)* [2015] UKUT 505 (AAC), reported as [2016] AACR 17
25 s115(9)(d) IAA 1999 referred to Sch 4 para 17 IAA 1999, which was repealed by Sch 9 para 1 NIAA 2002. It has been held that the reference should be read as if to s3C(1) and (2)(b) and (c) IA 1971 (as s17(2) Interpretation Act 1978 applies) – *EE v City of Cardiff (HB)* [2018] UKUT 418 (AAC).
26 s3C(2)(ca) and (cb) IA 1971 was only inserted from 31 January 2020, and s3C(2)(d) IA 1971 from 20 October 2014, so the reasoning of *EE v City of Cardiff (HB)* [2018] UKUT 418 (AAC) does not apply

2. **Benefits affected by immigration status**
27 Reg 13 CTRS(PR)E Regs; reg 19 CTR(SPC)S Regs; reg 19 CTR(S) Regs; reg 29 CTRSPR(W) Regs; Sch para 20 CTRS(DS)W Regs
28 s115 IAA 1999; s42 TCA 2002; reg 3 TC(Imm) Regs
29 Reg 15(1)(c) DAWAP(S) Regs
30 Reg 6(1) CA(CSP)(S) Regs
31 Reg 5(1)(c) DACYP(S) Regs
32 Reg 9(5) FEA(S) Regs
33 Reg 11(1)(b) ESA Regs; reg 12(1)(b) ESA Regs 2013
34 Reg 9(1)(c) DAOP(S) Regs
35 Reg 10(1)(c) DA(SADLA) Regs
36 Reg 2(1) and Part 1 of Sch SS(IA)CA Regs; para C1060 ADM; Vol2 Ch7 Pt1, para 070835 DMG; ADM Memo 29/20, paras 36-41; DMG Memo 25/20, paras 41-46
37 R(IS) 2/02
38 CPC/1005/2005
39 Regs 1(2) and 2(2)(a) SSCBCTC(A) Regs
40 SSCTRS(A) Regs
41 Confirmed in *OD v SSWP (JSA)* [2015] UKUT 438 (AAC)
42 *Szoma v SSWP* [2005] UKHL 64, reported as R(IS) 2/06; *Yesiloz v LB Camden and Another* [2009] EWCA Civ 415. These decisions about temporary admission are likely to apply equally to immigration bail.
43 para 6.2, note (i) under 'public funds' definition, IR
44 Reg 19(2) CTR(S) Regs; reg 19(2) CTR(SPC)S Regs; para 6 CTR Regs is not included in the regulations referred to in para 6.2 note (ii) under 'public funds' definition, IR, which disregards entitlement due to exemptions
45 Reg 2 SS(IA)CA Regs
46 Reg 9(5) FEA(S) Regs
47 para 6.2 note (ii) under 'public funds' definition, IR, disregards entitlement as a result of exemptions in legislation for social fund payments but not for FSP and CWHP
48 **All** Reg 2(2), (3) and (4)(b) and Sch Part II SS(IA)CA Regs; Vol2 Ch7 Pt1, paras 070836-37 DMG; para 10140 CBTM; ADM Memo 29/20, para 41(2) and (3); DMG Memo 25/20, para 46(2) and (3)
**ADP** Reg 15(5) DAWAP(S) Regs
**AA** Reg 2(1)(a)(ib) SS(AA) Regs
**CA** Reg 9(1)(ia) SS(ICA) Regs
**CSP** Reg 6(5) CA(CSP)(S) Regs
**CDP** Reg 5(5A) DACYP(S) Regs
**DLA** Reg 2(1)(a)(ib) SS(DLA) Regs
**ESA** Reg 11(1)(b) and (3) ESA Regs; reg 12(1)(b) and (3) ESA Regs 2013
**IB** Reg 16(1)(b) and (5) SS(IB) Regs
**PADP** Reg 9(5) DAOP(S) Regs
**PIP** Reg 16(d)(ii) SS(PIP) Regs
**SADLA** Reg 10(5) DA(SADLA) Regs
**SDA** Reg 3(a)(ib) SS(SDA) Regs
49 para 10140 CBTM
50 Reg 1(3) SSCBCTC(A) Regs
51 *Krid v Caisse Nationale d'Assurance Vieillesse des Travailleurs Salariés (CNAVTS)*, C-103/94 [1995], para 26
52 The Family Allowances, National Insurance and Industrial Injuries (Yugoslavia) Order 1958 No.1263
53 *Sürül v Bundesanstalt für Arbeit*, C-262/96 [1999]
54 para 6.2 note (ii) under 'public funds' definition, IR, disregards entitlement as a result of exemptions in legislation for all the benefits except ADP, CDP, CAS and CWHP

3. **Partners and children**
55 ss3 and 4(1)(c) and (2) WRA 2012; reg 3(3) UC Regs; reg 9(1) UC,PIP,JSA&ESA(C&P) Regs
56 Regs 3(3) and 36(3) UC Regs
57 ss3 and 4(1)(e) WRA 2012; reg 3(3) UC Regs; reg 9(1) UC,PIP,JSA&ESA(C&P) Regs
58 Regs 3(3), 18(2) and 22(3) UC Regs
59 Sch 4 para 9(2)(b) UC Regs
60 Sch 4 paras 27 and 28 UC Regs

61 s19(6) WRA 2012; reg 86 UC Regs
62 s39 WRA 2012; regs 62(1), (3) and (4) and 90(3) UC Regs; para H4077 ADM
63 They must be a claimant to be defined as a joint renter or joint owner-occupier: Schs 4 para 1 and 5 para 1 UC Regs
64 Regs 32(1)(b) and 34 UC Regs
65 Art 7(1), (2)(a) and (b) and (3)(b) WRA(No.31)O; HB Circular A9/2019, paras 15-17; Vol 13 Ch 77 paras 77035 note 2, 77150-51 and 77160 DMG
66 Reg 2 SFWFP Regs
67 gov.uk/winter-fuel-payment/report-change-circumstances
68 Art 7(1), (2)(a) and (b) and (3)(b) WRA(No.31)O; HB Circular A9/2019, paras 15-17
69 Reg 5(1)(h) SPC Regs
70 Confirmed in HB Circular A9/2019, paras 15-17, and Vol13 Ch77, paras 77035 note 2, 77150-1 and 77160 DMG
71 Sch 1 paras 1(1)(a)(ii) and 2 SPC Regs; Vol13 Ch78, para 78946 DMG
72 Regs 2 and 3 SFWFP Regs
73 gov.uk/winter-fuel-payment/report-change-circumstances
74 Reg 69 and Sch 5 para 10 ESA Regs

4. **National insurance numbers and contributions**

75 **ESA** Reg 2A ESA Regs
**PC** Reg 1A SPC Regs
**HB** Reg 4(c) HB Regs; reg 4(c) HB(SPC) Regs
**Bereavement benefits and retirement pensions** Reg 1A(c) SS(WB&RP) Regs
76 paras A2153-54 ADM
77 Reg 5(1)(d) SS(PAB) Regs
78 Under orders made in powers conferred by s179 SSAA 1992
79 gov.uk/government/publications/windrush-compensation-scheme-state-pension-solution

5. **Asylum seekers and refugees**

80 **UC** Reg 66 UC Regs
**ESA** Sch 8 para 22 ESA Regs
**HB** Sch 5 para 23 HB Regs
81 gov.uk/government/publications/claiming-universal-credit-and-other-benefits-if-you-are-a-refugee
82 *SK and LL v SSWP* [2020] UKUT 145 (AAC); reg 5A(8)-(10) SFM&FE Regs; paras L2070 and L2076-79 ADM; Sch 2 para 6 EYA(BSG)(S) Regs
83 **CB/GA** Reg 6(2)(d) and (e) CB&GA(Admin) Regs; reg 2 The Child Benefit and Guardian's Allowance (Miscellaneous Amendments) Regulations 2025 No.207
**TC** Regs 3(4)-(10) and 4 TC(Imm) Regs
84 *FK v HMRC* [2009] UKUT 134 (AAC); para 10140 CBTM
85 **CB/GA** Reg 6(2)(d) and (e) CB&GA(Admin) Regs
**TC** Reg 3(5) TC(Imm) Regs
86 *Tkachuk v SSWP* [2007] EWCA Civ 515; CIS/3797/2003
87 Tax Credits Consultation Forum minutes, 13 July 2023
88 Reg 3(9) TC(Imm) Regs; CTC/3692/2008
89 s13 Asylum and Immigration (Treatment of Claimants, etc) Act 2004; The Integration Loans for Refugees and Others Regulations 2007 No.1598
90 gov.uk/refugee-integration-loan

Chapter 57

# Coming from abroad: residence rules

**This chapter covers:**

1. Introduction (below)
2. The different residence and presence tests (p1298)
3. Habitual residence (p1300)
4. Right to reside (p1306)
5. Who has a right to reside (p1312)
6. Rules for specific benefits (p1342)

This chapter describes the residence and presence rules that affect your entitlement while you are in Great Britain. If you go abroad, see Chapter 58.

If you (and your partner and child) are not a British or Irish citizen, before using this chapter check Chapter 56 to see if your (or their) immigration status means you (or they) are excluded from benefits as a 'person subject to immigration control'.

9

## Key facts

- Different types of residence conditions apply to most benefits. These are: residence, ordinary residence, right to reside and habitual residence.
- Entitlement to most benefits also depends on your being present in Great Britain or the UK or the Common Travel Area.
- Some benefits require you to have been present for a certain period of time (known as past presence).
- The rules on residence and presence vary between different benefits. If you satisfy the conditions for one, it does not mean you satisfy the conditions for another.

## 1. Introduction

Many benefits have residence and/or presence conditions. The rules vary between different benefits. Whether you meet the conditions can depend on your nationality, your immigration status, how long you have been in Great Britain (or, depending on the benefit, Scotland, the UK or common travel area – see p1300), whether you are in a protected group that can have a free movement right of residence, and whether you are covered by the European Union (EU) co-ordination rules.

Although many presence and residence rules refer to Great Britain rather than the UK, there is a reciprocal agreement between Britain and Northern Ireland, which means that, in general, you can satisfy the residence conditions if you move between Great Britain and Northern Ireland.

There are residence conditions for the following benefits:

- adult disability payment (in Scotland – see p1347);
- attendance allowance (see p1347);
- bereavement support payment (see p1345);
- Best Start grant (in Scotland – see p1356);
- carer support payment (in Scotland – see p1347)
- carer's allowance (see p1347);
- child benefit (see p1346);
- child disability payment (in Scotland – see p1347);
- child winter heating payment (in Scotland – see p1357);
- disability living allowance (see p1347);
- contributory employment and support allowance (ESA) in youth (see p1352);
- income-related ESA (see p1343);
- funeral expenses payment (see p1355);
- funeral support payment (in Scotland – see p1355);
- guardian's allowance (see p1346);
- housing benefit (see p1343);
- pension age disability payment (in Scotland – see p1347);
- pension credit (see p1343);
- personal independence payment (see p1347);
- category D retirement pension (see p1354);
- Scottish adult disability living allowance (in Scotland – see p1347);
- Scottish child payment (in Scotland – see p1346);
- severe disablement allowance (see p1347);
- Sure Start maternity grant (see p1356);
- universal credit (see p1343);
- winter fuel payment (see p1357);
- winter heating payment (in Scotland – see p1357);
- young carer grant (in Scotland – see p1347).

Council tax reduction also has residence conditions (see p1343).

For the residence and presence rules that applied to tax credits, income support and income-based JSA, see the 2024/25 edition of this *Handbook*.

Contributory benefits, such as new-style JSA, contributory ESA and retirement pensions (except category D), as well as the employment-related benefits (maternity allowance and industrial injuries benefits) do not have residence conditions. However, they have presence requirements, which mean that if you go abroad, some benefits cease and others are not increased unless exceptions apply (see Chapter 58). Industrial injuries benefits also have conditions related to your presence in Great Britain when you had your accident or contracted your disease. There are no residence or presence requirements for statutory sick pay and the statutory parental payments paid by your employer.

## Which rules apply

The UK benefits legislation contains rules about the residence and presence conditions you must satisfy to be entitled to certain benefits. These rules are set out in this chapter.

If you are covered by the **EU co-ordination rules** (see p1392), these can help you to satisfy, or disapply, residence or presence conditions and so be entitled to benefits in the UK (eg, by enabling you to count periods of residence in an EEA state to satisfy the past presence requirements – see p1298), but they can also prevent you from claiming a UK benefit – eg, if the UK is not the 'competent state' to pay that benefit (see p1404). The EU co-ordination rules are covered in Chapter 59 and the main ways they can assist with the residence and presence conditions are noted for each benefit starting on p1342.

In general, if you are covered by the EU co-ordination rules, these apply in preference to the provisions of a reciprocal agreement.

**Reciprocal agreements** exist between the UK and some other countries that can assist in similar ways to the EU co-ordination rules.

9

***Reciprocal agreements with the UK***

EEA states: Austria, Belgium, Croatia, Cyprus, Denmark, Finland, France, Germany, Iceland, Ireland, Italy, Luxembourg, Malta, Netherlands, Norway, Portugal, Slovenia, Spain and Sweden. In general, the reciprocal agreement applies if the EU co-ordination rules do not apply.

Non-EEA states: Barbados, Bermuda, Bosnia-Herzegovina, Canada, Chile, Guernsey, Isle of Man, Israel, Jamaica, Jersey, Kosova, North Macedonia, Mauritius, Montenegro, New Zealand, Philippines, Serbia, Switzerland, Turkey and the United States of America.

There are also reciprocal agreements between the UK and Gibraltar (see p1393) and between Great Britain and Northern Ireland.

There are also other agreements with Albania, Morocco, San Marino, Tunisia and Turkey and, until 1 January 2021, with Algeria.

The scope of the agreements differs greatly in terms of the people covered, the benefits covered and the provisions made. It is therefore crucial to check the individual agreement. You can find the agreements at legislation.gov.uk – search under the relevant country and check for subsequent amendments.

## 2. The different residence and presence tests

The presence and residence conditions you are required to satisfy vary between the different benefits. You may be required to satisfy tests for your:

- presence (see below);
- past presence (see below);
- residence (see p1299);
- ordinary residence (see p1299);
- habitual residence (see p1300);
- right to reside (see p1306).

### Presence

At the time you make your benefit claim, you must, in general, be present in Great Britain (England and Wales for disability living allowance (DLA), common travel area (see p1300) for child disability payment (CDP), adult disability payment (ADP), pension age disability payment (PADP), Scottish adult disability living allowance (SADLA) and carer support payment (CSP)),and continue to be present. Specific rules allow you to be treated as present during temporary absences (see Chapter 58). Also, if you are covered by the European Union (EU) co-ordination rules (see p1392), these can also mean that you do not need to be present if you are in a country to which the particular rules apply. See the specific benefit rules on the requirements starting on p1342, and on continuing to be paid when you are abroad starting on p1370.

Being present means being physically present. For the benefit authority to disqualify you because you were absent, it must show that you were absent throughout that day (see p1369).

### Past presence

The following benefits require that, in addition to being present at the time you make your claim, you must also have been present in Great Britain (common travel area for ADP, CDP, PADP, SADLA and CSP) for a period of time before you become entitled:

- ADP;
- attendance allowance;
- CSP;
- carer's allowance;
- CDP;
- DLA;

- PADP;
- personal independence payment;
- SADLA.

If you are covered by the EU co-ordination rules (see p1392), these may mean this requirement does not apply to you, or help you to satisfy it more quickly (see p1350).

For details of the past presence test, including exceptions, see p1347.

## Residence

The requirement to be simply 'resident', rather than 'ordinarily resident' or 'habitually resident', is only a condition for a category D retirement pension (see p1354), winter heating payment and child winter heating payment in Scotland (see p1357), carer's allowance supplement in Scotland (see p1347), and universal credit payment options in Scotland (see p51). However, it is a necessary part of being ordinarily resident (see below) or habitually resident (see p1300). Residence is more than just physical presence in a country and you can be resident without being present – eg, if you are away on holiday. You are usually resident in the country in which you have your home for the time being. You can remain resident during a temporary absence, depending on your circumstances, including the length of your absence, your intentions to return, your accommodation, and where your family and your personal belongings are.[1]

**Note:** you must be 'living in' England or Wales for a funeral expenses payment (see p1355) and a Sure Start maternity grant (see p1356), a phrase which is not defined and is arguably very similar to 'resident'.

## Ordinary residence

The benefits that have an ordinary residence requirement are:

- ADP (in Scotland);
- bereavement support payment;
- Best Start grant (in Scotland);
- CSP (in Scotland);
- child benefit;
- CDP (in Scotland);
- employment and support allowance in youth;
- funeral support payment (in Scotland);
- PADP (in Scotland);
- pension age winter heating payment (in Scotland);
- category D retirement pension;
- SADLA (in Scotland);
- Scottish child payment (in Scotland);
- severe disablement allowance;

- social fund funeral expenses payment;
- social fund winter fuel payment;
- young carer grant (in Scotland).

The term 'ordinary residence' is not defined in the legislation, and caselaw has confirmed that the words should have their natural and ordinary meaning.[2] You are ordinarily resident in a country if you live there for a settled purpose for the time being (whether for a short or long duration).[3] The Upper Tribunal has held that the residence must be lawful.[4] There are some exceptions to the requirement to be ordinarily resident, and if you are covered by the EU co-ordination rules, these may assist you in satisfying it (see the rules beginning on p1342). In practice, claims are rarely refused on the basis of ordinary residence.

## 3. **Habitual residence**

The requirement to be habitually resident applies to:[5]

- adult disability payment (ADP – in Scotland);
- attendance allowance (AA);
- Best Start grant (in Scotland – only in limited circumstances);
- carer support payment (CSP – in Scotland);
- carer's allowance (CA);
- child disability payment (CDP – in Scotland);
- disability living allowance (DLA);
- income-related employment and support allowance (ESA);
- housing benefit (HB);
- pension age disability payment (PADP – in Scotland);
- pension credit (PC);
- personal independence payment (PIP);
- Scottish adult disability living allowance (SADLA – in Scotland);
- universal credit (UC);
- young carer grant (in Scotland).

To be entitled to these benefits, you must be habitually resident in the **'common travel area'** (ie, the UK, Ireland, Channel Islands and the Isle of Man) or, for a Best Start grant or a young carer grant, the UK, the Channel Islands, Isle of Man or the European Economic Area (EEA), or be exempt from the requirement (see p1303).

**Note:**

- You are excluded from council tax reduction if you do not satisfy (and are not exempt from) the habitual residence test (see below).[6]
- You may be entitled to a winter fuel payment from the social fund without being ordinarily resident in England or Wales, or child winter heating payment

without being resident in Scotland, if you are habitually resident in one of the listed EEA countries (see p1357).

## The habitual residence test

To satisfy the habitual residence test for **AA, PADP, CA, CSP, DLA, CDP, SADLA, PIP and ADP**, you must be 'habitually resident in fact' in the common travel area (however, the area required is different if you are covered by the main EU co-ordination rules – see p1304).

To satisfy the habitual residence test for a **young carer grant**, you must be 'habitually resident in fact' in the UK, Channel Islands, Isle of Man or the EEA.

For a **Best Start grant**, the habitual residence test only applies if you are aged under 20 and neither you nor your partner receive a qualifying benefit. You must be 'habitually resident in fact' in the UK, Channel Islands or Isle of Man, or, if you have settled or pre-settled status under the European Union Settlement Scheme (EUSS) or a specified free movement residence right, the EEA (see p1356).

To satisfy the habitual residence test for **UC, income-related ESA, PC and HB**, you must:
- be 'habitually resident in fact' in the common travel area; *and*
- have a right to reside in the common travel area (see p1307).

For details on establishing that you are 'habitually resident in fact', see p1304.

The decision maker determines whether you satisfy the habitual residence test when you claim the benefit. To continue to be entitled, you must continue to satisfy it.

If your circumstances mean you are exempt from the habitual residence test (see p1303), your residence should not be examined further and, provided you meet the other conditions of entitlement, you are eligible for benefit. Whether or not you are exempt is not always considered, so if you might not otherwise be accepted as habitually resident (eg, if you only recently arrived in the common travel area), check whether you are exempt and, if you are, explain this to the decision maker.

The habitual residence test applies to the benefit claimant. If you are making a joint claim for UC, both you and your partner must satisfy, or be exempt from, the test. If your partner fails the test, your joint claim is treated as a claim for UC as a single person and your UC award is based on the maximum amount for a single person, but your partner's income and capital are taken into account (see p1343).[7] For other means-tested benefits, if you are the claimant and you satisfy (or are exempt from) the habitual residence test, whether or not your partner satisfies it does not affect your entitlement.

## If you fail the habitual residence test

If you fail the habitual residence test, you are not entitled to the following benefits because:

- for UC and PC, you are treated as not present in Great Britain.[8] If you are part of a couple claiming UC, see p1343;
- for income-related ESA and HB, you are classed as a 'person from abroad'. This means for income-related ESA, you have an applicable amount (see p265) of nil[9] and, for HB, you are treated as not liable for rent;[10]
- for AA, PADP, CA, CSP, DLA, CDP, SADLA, PIP and ADP, young carer grant and Best Start grant, you have failed to meet the prescribed residence requirements.[11]

***Have you failed the habitual residence test?***

1. If you are refused benefit because you have failed the habitual residence test, consider challenging this decision (see Chapters 50, 51 and 69). You may want to contact a local advice agency for help with this.
2. The decision maker must consider whether you satisfied the habitual residence test on your date of claim and, if not, on each subsequent date until the date of their decision.[12]
3. While challenging the decision, you should make a further claim. If this is refused, also challenge that decision and claim again and so on. This is because when the decision refusing your initial claim is looked at again, the decision maker (or First-tier Tribunal) cannot take account of things that have changed since the decision was made. So, if the decision maker considers that you were not habitually resident at the time benefit was originally refused, but you are now (eg, because you have now been resident for an appreciable period of time), they cannot take this into account when looking again at the original decision. However, they can take it into account if sufficient residence had been completed by the date of the decision on your second or subsequent claim. Sometimes, the benefit authorities say that you cannot make another claim while your appeal (or request to have the first decision looked at again) is pending. This is wrong and you should, with the help of an adviser if possible, insist on making a further claim.
4. Check whether you are exempt from the habitual residence test (see below).
5. Establish which part of the test the decision maker considers you have failed.
6. If you have claimed a means-tested benefit and the decision maker considers you do not have a right to reside, use the section starting on p1312 to check the circumstances in which you can have a right to reside.
7. If you made a joint claim for UC and the decision maker found that you failed the habitual residence test but your partner satisfied it, your joint claim is treated as a claim by your partner as a single person (see p1343). They can continue to be paid UC while you challenge the decision on your entitlement.
8. If you can claim HB, the local authority must make its own decision and not just follow a DWP decision that you have failed the habitual residence test.
9. Although the onus of proof is on the benefit authorities to establish that you are *not* habitually resident,[13] produce as much evidence as possible to show that you *are*. All decisions should be made on the balance of probabilities.[14]

## Who is exempt from the habitual residence test

You are exempt from the habitual residence test for **means-tested benefits** if you:[15]

- are a refugee; *or*
- have humanitarian protection; *or*
- have leave granted outside the Immigration Rules, including migrant victims of domestic abuse concession leave (see p1277) or discretionary leave; *or*
- have leave granted by virtue of the Afghan Relocations and Assistance Policy (ARAP), or the scheme for locally employed staff in Afghanistan (LES Scheme), or (for Best Start grant and young carer grant only) you have discretionary leave granted as a dependant of a person with either of the previous two types of leave or the Afghan Citizens Resettlement Scheme, or (other than for Best Start grant and young carer grant) you left Afghanistan in connection with the collapse of the Afghan government on 15 August 2021;[16] *or*
- were living in Ukraine immediately before 1 January 2022 and you left in connection with the Russian invasion of 24 February 2022, and you have leave, or a right of abode, in the UK (including if you are British), or you are Irish;[17] *or*
- were living in Sudan before 15 April 2023 and left due to the violence that escalated from that date, and you have leave, or a right of abode, in the UK (including if you are British), or you are Irish;[18] *or*
- were living in Israel, the West Bank, the Gaza Strip, East Jerusalem, the Golan Heights or Lebanon immediately before 7 October 2023 and you left in connection with the violence on or since that date, and you have leave, or a right of abode, in the UK (including if you are British), or you are Irish;[19] *or*
- have been deported, expelled or legally removed from another country to the UK and you are not a 'person subject to immigration control' (see p1272); *or*
- are an EEA national and a 'worker' (see p1322), including if you have retained this status; *or*
- are an EEA national and a 'self-employed person' (see p1324), including if you have retained this status; *or*
- are a family member (see p1329), other than an 'extended family member', of someone in either of the above two bullet points; *or*
- are an EEA national and a frontier worker (see p1342); *or*
- have pre-settled status (see p1314) and you are a family member, other than an 'extended family member', of someone in the above bullet point; *or*
- have pre-settled status, and you are a family member, other than an extended family member, of a 'relevant person of Northern Ireland' (see p1308) and they *would be* a worker or self-employed person *if* they were an EEA national; *or*
- are an EEA national with a permanent right of residence as a retired or permanently incapacitated worker or self-employed person, or you are a family member of such a person (see p1340); *or*
- (for HB only) receive income-related ESA or PC.

**For a young carer grant**, you are exempt from the requirement to be habitually resident if you are in one of the first eight bullet points listed on p1303.[20]

**For a Best Start grant**, you are exempt from the requirement to be habitually resident if you or your partner get a qualifying benefit (see p1459) or you are in one of the first eight bullet points listed on p1303.[21]

**For AA, PADP, CA, CSP, DLA, CDP, SADLA, PIP and ADP**, you are exempt from the requirement to be habitually resident (and also exempt from the past presence requirement – see p1347) if you:[22]

- have leave in the UK granted by virtue of ARAP or the LES Scheme or discretionary leave as the dependant of a person with leave under either of these two schemes, or leave granted under the Afghan Citizens Resettlement Scheme;[23] *or*
- left Ukraine and are covered by the fifth bullet point listed on p1303; *or*
- left Sudan and are covered by the sixth bullet point listed on p1303; *or*
- left Israel, the West Bank, the Gaza Strip, East Jerusalem, the Golan Heights or Lebanon and are covered by the seventh bullet on p1303; *or*
- have refugee status or humanitarian protection or have leave as the dependent family member of someone who has either leave; *or*
- are abroad in your capacity as a serving member of the armed forces (or, for CSP, CDP, ADP, PADP or SADLA, a civil servant, and immediately before the start of either employment you satisfied the residence and presence conditions), or are living with someone who is abroad as a serving member of the forces (or civil servant) and you are the spouse, civil partner (or for CSP, CDP, ADP, PADP or SADLA, living together as if married/civil partners), child, stepchild (or, for CSP, CDP or ADP, a child in the care of) or (except for CDP) parent, step-parent or parent-in-law of that person. **Note**: you are also treated as present for the purpose of the presence and past presence requirements (or for CSP, CDP, ADP, PADP and SADLA, treated as present and ordinarily resident and exempt from the past presence test) (see p1378).

## Establishing you are 'habitually resident in fact'

You must be habitually resident in the **'common travel area'** (ie, the UK, Ireland, Channel Islands and the Isle of Man) for all the benefits that have this requirement, other than the following exceptions.

- **For a young carer grant**, you must be habitually resident in the common travel area or the EEA.
- **For a Best Start grant**, if you are aged under 20 and you or your partner are not getting a qualifying benefit, you must be habitually resident in the UK, Channel Islands, Isle of Man, or, if you have leave (pre-settled or settled status) under the EUSS or a specified free movement residence right, the EEA (see p1356).

- **For the disability and carers' benefits,** if you are covered by the main EU co-ordination rules (see p1392), you must be habitually resident in:
  - Great Britain – for **AA, CA, PIP or DLA,** if you are relying on the past presence test being disapplied (and you have a genuine and sufficient link to the UK) (see p1351);
  - the UK – for **CSP, CDP, ADP, PADP and SADLA,** if you are relying on the past presence test being disapplied (see p1350);
  - (except the mobility components of PIP, ADP, DLA, CDP or SADLA) an EEA country, if you have a genuine and sufficient link to the UK (to Scotland, for CSP, CDP, ADP, PADP or SADLA) (see p1379).
- **For the disability and carers' benefits** (except the mobility components of PIP, ADP, DLA, CDP or SADLA), Gibraltar, if you are covered by the agreement with Gibraltar (see p1379).

'Habitual residence' is not defined in the legislation. However, certain principles have emerged from the caselaw on its meaning.

- There is no comprehensive list of relevant factors, so all the facts of your situation should be considered.[24]
- To be habitually resident, you must be resident (see p1299). It is not enough merely to intend to reside in the future.[25]
- You must have a settled intention to reside in the relevant area. It does not need to be permanent; it is enough if you intend to make the relevant area your home for the time being.[26] You must provide evidence of your intention, including your reasons for moving there, the strength of your ties (or your 'centre of interest') and the viability of your residence. Factors that could be relevant include arranging or seeking employment, education or training, joining and/or bringing your family, obtaining leave under the EUSS (if eligible – see p1314), arranging accommodation, bringing possessions, registering with a doctor, joining clubs and associations, and breaking ties with the place of your previous residence. The viability of your continued residence, although a relevant factor, is not an additional requirement.[27]
- In most cases, you must have an 'appreciable period' of actual residence. How long this period must be is not fixed and depends on your circumstances.[28] The DWP or local authority must not set a standard period of time for which all claimants must be resident before they can become habitually resident, and any such policy should be challenged by judicial review (see p1236). There is a large amount of caselaw on what constitutes an appreciable period of residence. Periods of between one and three months are frequently cited,[29] but no general rule can be derived from any one case and your appreciable period may be longer or shorter.[30] The stronger your settled intention to make your home in the common travel area for the time being, the shorter your period of actual residence needs to be before you can be accepted as habitually resident (and vice versa).[31]

9

You may not need an appreciable period of actual residence, or the period may be very short, if you are:
- a returning resident. This applies if you have been habitually resident in the relevant area previously, you left in circumstances which meant you ceased to be habitually resident and you then return to live in the relevant area again. The decision on how long a period of residence you must have to resume your previous habitual residence depends on the circumstances in which you left, your links with the relevant area while you were away and the circumstances of your return. You can be found to be habitually resident on the day of your return.[32] If you did not choose to go, or remain, abroad (eg, if you went abroad due to a forced marriage), you can be considered not to have ceased to be habitual resident and therefore satisfy this requirement from your date of claim when you return;[33]
- covered by the EU co-ordination rules (see p1392) and are claiming PC or the mobility component of DLA, CDP, PIP or ADP (as these are special non-contributory benefits (see p1403)). If this applies, you cannot be denied benefit solely because your period of residence is considered too short. Your period of residence is one of the factors that should be taken into account in assessing habitual residence, but it is not an absolute requirement and may be outweighed by other factors.[34]

- A temporary absence, such as a holiday, should not mean you cease to be habitually resident. This should be accepted if you have a definite date of return[35] or you are abroad for a temporary reason such as a Voluntary Service Overseas placement.[36]
- When deciding whether you are habitually resident, the decision maker must consider the whole period from your date of claim to the date the decision is made since, at some point during this period, you may have become resident for an appreciable period and your entitlement should begin from that date.[37]

9

## 4. Right to reside

The right to reside requirement applies to:
- universal credit (UC);
- income-related employment and support allowance (ESA);
- pension credit (PC);
- housing benefit (HB);
- child benefit.

You are also excluded from council tax reduction if you do not have a right to reside.[38] See CPAG's *Benefits for Migrants Handbook* for details.

## Means-tested benefits

You must have a right to reside in the **common travel area** (ie, the UK, Ireland, Channel Islands and the Isle of Man) to satisfy the habitual residence test for UC, income-related ESA, PC and HB. If you (or your partner, for UC) do not satisfy the habitual residence test because you do not have a right to reside, see p1301.

### The type of residence right you need

Any right of residence in the common travel area enables you to satisfy the right to reside requirement for each of the means-tested benefits unless your *only* right of residence is:[39]

- pre-settled status. For the circumstances in which you can satisfy the right to reside requirement if you have pre-settled status, work through the steps below; *or*
- limited leave to enter as the holder of a European Union Settlement Scheme (EUSS) family permit or travel permit (see p1315). However, once you have made a valid EUSS application for settled or pre-settled status, you are in a protected group that can potentially have a free movement right to reside while that application is pending (see p1317); *or*
- as the primary carer of a British citizen who is dependent on you and would have to leave the EU if you left the UK (known as a 'Zambrano carer' – see p1336);[40] *or*
- as an EEA jobseeker; *or*
- as a family member of an EEA jobseeker. **Note:** this exclusion does not apply if you are a former family member of a jobseeker and have retained your right to reside – eg, following the departure of the jobseeker from the UK (see p1333).[41]



For the circumstances in which you can have a right to reside, see p1312.

### Pre-settled status

The regulations for each of the means-tested benefits list pre-settled status (see p1314) as an excluded right to reside.[42] However, if you have pre-settled status, work through the steps below to check whether your other circumstances mean you have a qualifying right to reside, or that you are exempt from the habitual residence test, or the exclusion of pre-settled status must be disapplied.

**Step 1: are you an Irish citizen?** If you are, your citizenship satisfies the right to reside requirement.[43] This is not altered by your pre-settled status (see p1312).

**Step 2: do you have a free movement right to reside?** Having pre-settled status means you are in one of the protected groups (see p1317) that can potentially have one or more free movement rights to reside (see p1317). If you have such a right to reside, other than one listed above, you satisfy the right to reside requirement.

**Step 3: were you living in Ukraine, Sudan, Israel, the West Bank, the Gaza Strip, East Jerusalem, the Golan Heights or Lebanon,** and satisfy the requirements of the fifth, sixth or seventh groups exempt from the habitual residence test on p1303, or **are you a family member of an EEA frontier worker** (see p1342)? In each situation, you are exempt from the habitual residence test for each of the means-tested benefits.

**Step 4: are you a family member (other than an extended family member) of a 'relevant person of Northern Ireland'** who *would* have a free movement right to reside under the EEA Regulations, other than one listed above, *if* they were an EEA national? If this applies, the regulations for each of the means-tested benefits do not exclude you.[44]

A **'relevant person of Northern Ireland'** is defined as a British, or Irish, citizen who was born in Northern Ireland and at the time of their birth at least one of their parents was a British, or Irish, citizen, or had the right to reside in Northern Ireland without time limit.[45]

**Step 5: was your pre-settled status granted on the basis of your relationship to an EEA national, which has broken down due to domestic violence or abuse?** You may be able to apply for migrant victims of domestic abuse concession (MVDAC) leave. If granted, this leave replaces your pre-settled status and means you are exempt from the habitual residence test for each of the means-tested benefits (see p1277). See also the next step.

**Step 6: would refusing you a means-tested benefit, due to your pre-settled status being an excluded right to reside, mean you are at risk of being unable to live in dignified conditions?** If you are unable to work and unable to meet your (and your children's) most basic needs, your pre-settled status by itself can satisfy the right to reside requirement for means-tested benefits due to the caselaw referred to below.

9

The Court of Appeal[46] upheld an Upper Tribunal decision[47] that if refusing a means-tested benefit due to pre-settled status being an excluded right to reside would risk breaching the claimant's right (under the EU Charter of Fundamental Rights) to live in dignified conditions,[48] the exclusion of pre-settled status is, for that claimant, unlawful and must be disapplied to enable entitlement to the benefit. If the decision maker decides you do not have a qualifying free movement right to reside, they *must* assess whether this caselaw applies to you.[49] Dignified conditions was held to mean having sufficient resources to meet your most basic needs for adequate food, clothing, hygiene and accommodation, including heating. In assessing your risk of not living in dignified conditions, the benefit authority can take account of alternative support that is actually and currently available to you, and your ability to get paid work. To argue that this caselaw applies to your claim, you should provide details and evidence of barriers (eg, illness, disability, or caring responsibilities) that prevent you working (see also second bullet point below).[50] No assessment of your ability to work should be required if you have reached pension age.[51]

The caselaw referred to above considered the rights of an EU national with pre-settled status who was exercising a free movement right to reside in the UK on 31

December 2020, and who could not currently work. The DWP now accepts that the caselaw can also apply if you are a non-EU national granted pre-settled status because on 31 December 2020 you were a family member of an EU national who began living in the UK before that date (whether you moved to the UK before or after that date). In February 2025, the DWP revised its guidance to confirm this.[52] If your benefit was refused due to the DWP previously not accepting that the caselaw applied to non-EU national family members, you can request the decision be revised due to official error (see p1135). It is arguable that the caselaw can also apply if you:

- have pre-settled status and had exercised a free movement right to reside in the UK before, but not necessarily on, 31 December 2020.[53] This argument has been accepted by the county court in a housing case (and the local authority did not appeal),[54] and in a number of benefit appeals at the First-tier Tribunal (and the DWP, or housing benefit office, did not appeal). **Note:** if you arrived in the UK as an EU national before this date (or as the family member of such an EU national), you had an initial right to reside for the first three months (see p1321);[55] *or*
- have pre-settled status and can do *some* work, but barriers prevent you being able to work enough to enable you to live in dignified conditions or, if you are an EEA national, enough to enable you to have a right to reside as a worker (see p1322) or a self-employed person (see p1324); *or*
- have pre-settled status because you are a non-EU national who was living in the UK before the end of 2020 with a derivative right to reside (see p1336) (other than as a '*Zambrano* carer'); *or*
- have pre-settled status and you are a national of Iceland, Liechtenstein, Norway and Switzerland covered by the separation agreements between those countries and the UK (see p1319). These agreements contain broadly equivalent provisions to the Withdrawal Agreement and, arguably, the caselaw should apply in an equivalent way to nationals of these four countries; *or*
- have leave to enter as the holder of an EUSS family permit. You are within the scope of the Withdrawal Agreement and your specific type of leave is listed in the benefit regulations as an excluded right to reside in the same way as pre-settled status is; *or*
- have a pending valid application to the EUSS for settled or pre-settled status.[56]

Future caselaw is expected to clarify the scope of each group. Until such caselaw is decided, if you are in one of the above groups, make your claim on the basis that the caselaw applies. If your claim is refused, challenge the decision and ask your adviser to contact CPAG.

For further information on the caselaw, including a template arguement for the first bullet point above, see cpag.org.uk/destitutepss. See CPAG's *Welfare Rights Bulletin* and the online version of this *Handbook* for updates.

**Step 7: does refusing you a means-tested benefit, due to your pre-settled status being an excluded right to reside, amount to unlawful nationality-based discrimination under the Withdrawal Agreements?** This is a separate argument from that in Step 6 and may be arguable if you are within the personal scope of the Withdrawal Agreement but do not satisfy the other requirements of the caselaw in Step 6, or as an additional argument. The county court accepted that the equal treatment provisions of the Withdrawal Agreement required that the exclusion of pre-settled status be disapplied in a housing case (and the local authority did not appeal).[57] However, subsequently the High Court rejected this argument in a separate housing case,[58] but permission to appeal to the Court of Appeal was granted. At the time of writing, the case was due to be heard in May 2025.[59] For further details and updates, see the online version of CPAG's *Benefits for Migrants Handbook*.

**Note:** if you have pre-settled status, you should apply for settled status as soon as you become eligible. Settled status satisfies the right to reside requirement for all benefits that have it. For more details about moving from pre-settled to settled status, see p1315.

### If you have been receiving benefits since April 2004

You do not need a right to reside to be entitled to any of the means-tested benefits, except UC, if you have been receiving any combination of IS, income-based JSA, PC, HB, income-related ESA (since 31 October 2011 and including periods linked by the 12-week linking rule – see p928) or council tax benefit (until it was abolished from 1 April 2013) *continuously* since 30 April 2004. This transitional protection means you do not need a right to reside to continue receiving that benefit or if you make a new claim for HB or PC, provided the periods of entitlement have been continuous since 30 April 2004.[60] However, this transitional protection does not affect the separate requirement for each of these benefits that you must not be defined as a 'person subject to immigration control' (see p1272). For further details and an example of entitlement to PC due to these rules, see the 15th edition of CPAG's *Benefits for Migrants Handbook*.

## Child benefit

If you do not have a right to reside in the UK, you are treated as not present in Great Britain for child benefit and therefore are not entitled to it.[61]

The right to reside requirement was introduced on 1 May 2004. You do not need a right to reside to continue to receive child benefit if you have been receiving it since before this date.

### The type of residence right you need

Any right of residence in the UK enables you to satisfy the requirement for child benefit, unless your *only* right of residence is:[62]

- pre-settled status. For exceptions to this exclusion and ways to satisfy the right to reside requirement if you have pre-settled status, work through the steps below; *or*
- limited leave to enter as the holder of an EUSS family permit or travel permit (see p1315). However, once you have made a valid EUSS application for settled or pre-settled status, you are in a protected group that can potentially have a free movement right to reside while that application is pending (see p1317); *or*
- as the primary carer of a British citizen who is dependent on you and would have to leave the EU if you left the UK (known as a 'Zambrano carer' – see p1336).[63] However, you are not excluded on this basis if you are a national of Morocco, Tunisia or Turkey (or, if your claim began before 1 January 2021, Algeria or San Marino) and working in the UK, as you are covered by agreements that override this exclusion (see p1282).[64] To date, all other legal challenges to this exclusion have failed.[65]

For the circumstances in which you can have a right to reside, see p1312.

If you have **pre-settled status**, this leave by itself does not satisfy the right to reside requirement because the child benefit regulations list it as an excluded right to reside. However, work through the steps below to check whether your other circumstances mean you can either satisfy this requirement or possibly argue that the exclusion of pre-settled status must be disapplied.

**Step 1: are you an Irish citizen?** If you are, your citizenship satisfies the right to reside requirement, and this is not altered by your pre-settled status (see p1312).

**Step 2: do you have a free movement right to reside?** Having pre-settled status means you are in one of the protected groups (see p1317) that can potentially have one or more free movement rights to reside (see p1317). If you have such a right to reside, other than the one in the last bullet point above, this satisfies the right to reside requirement.

**Step 3: are you a family member** (see p1329), other than an extended family member, of a 'relevant person of Northern Ireland' (see p1308) who *would* have a free movement right to reside under the EEA Regulations (see p1317) *if* they were an EEA national? If this applies, the child benefit regulations do not exclude you on the basis of your pre-settled status.[66]

**Step 4: was your pre-settled status granted on the basis of your relationship to an EEA national, which has broken down due to domestic abuse?** You may be able to apply for migrant victims of domestic abuse concession (MVDAC) leave. If granted, this leave replaces your pre-settled status and, for its duration, gives you a qualifying right to reside (see p1277).

**Step 5: is it arguable that the exclusion of pre-settled status as a qualifying right to reside for child benefit must be disapplied?** It is unlikely the caselaw that applies to means-tested benefit (see Step 6 on p1307) can assist you to access child benefit because it is not a subsistence benefit and is unlikely to significantly affect your ability to live in dignified conditions. However, it *may* be arguable that the exclusion of pre-settled status amounts to unlawful unequal treatment, either under the Withdrawal Agreement (see Step 7 on p1307) or the main EU co-ordination rules (see p1406),[67] and therefore this exclusion must be disapplied. If your child benefit is refused due to your pre-settled status being an excluded right to reside, ask your adviser to contact CPAG's Upper Tribunal assistance project.

**Note:** if you are not entitled to child benefit for a child living with you, someone else who contributes to the cost of that child may be able to claim child benefit instead (see p493).

## 5. **Who has a right to reside**

Whether or not you have a right to reside can depend on your nationality, immigration status and the circumstances of you and your family members. You may have more than one right of residence, or you may not have any.

Any residence right is sufficient to satisfy the right to reside requirement *unless* it is specifically excluded for the benefit you want to claim (see p1307 and p1310).

### British and Irish citizens

If you are a **British citizen**, including if you also hold another nationality, you have an automatic right to reside in the UK. If you are a family member of a British citizen, see p1332. If you are the primary carer of a British citizen, see p1336.

If you are an **Irish citizen**, you have an automatic right to reside in the UK and do not require leave to enter or remain in the UK (unless you are subject to a deportation or exclusion order).[68] You are not required to obtain leave under the European Union Settlement Scheme (EUSS – see p1314), but you can if you began residing in the UK before the end of 2020 and you wish to do so.

If you are a **family member of an Irish citizen** who began living in the UK before the end of 2020, your free movement residence rights as a family member depend on the Irish citizen having a relevant right to reside in the same way as family members of other European Economic Area (EEA) nationals (see p1329). If you do not already have leave, you need to apply for leave under the EUSS.

### European and non-European nationals

Whether you are an EEA national or a non-EEA national, you have a right to reside if you are:

- a British citizen, or an Irish citizen or a Commonwealth citizen with a right of abode; *or*
- in one of the protected groups who can have a European free movement right to reside, which means you have either pre-settled status or a valid pending EUSS application (see p1317), *and* you have such a free movement right to reside (see p1317); *or*

- within a period of leave to enter or remain in the UK granted under UK immigration law. However:
  - if you have leave which is subject to a 'no recourse to public funds' condition, or leave granted as the result of a maintenance undertaking, or you have leave solely because you are appealing a decision to refuse to vary your previous leave, you are defined as a 'person subject to immigration control' (see p1272) and therefore excluded from all the benefits that require a right to reside on that basis unless you are in an exempt group (see p1279);
  - pre-settled status and limited leave to enter as the holder of a valid EUSS family permit or travel permit are listed as excluded residence rights for all benefits with that requirement. However, while you have pre-settled status, or once you have made a valid application to the EUSS for settled or pre-settled status (and while that application remains pending), you are in a protected group (see p1317) that can potentially have a free movement right to reside (see p1317). For steps to follow if you have pre-settled status, including limited circumstances in which pre-settled status by itself can satisfy the right to reside requirement, see p1307.

**Note:** for periods before the end of the transition period, you could potentially have one or more free movement rights to reside without needing to be in a protected group.

***Transition period***

The transition period (also called the 'implementation period') was the period from the UK leaving the EU at 11pm on 31 January 2020 to 11pm on 31 December 2020.[69]

During the transition period, in general, EU legislation and caselaw, and all EU-derived law (eg, the EEA Regulations, which set out free movement rights in the UK – see p1320), continued to have effect just as they did before the UK left the EU.[70] At the end of this transition period, free movement rights were, in general, ended within UK law. This included revoking the EEA Regulations. However, if you are within a protected group, these regulations continue to have effect for the purpose of claiming benefits since the end of the transition period (see p1317).

**If you are an EEA national who arrived in the UK after the end of the transition period,** unless you are joining an EEA national who was your family member on 31 December 2020 and continues to be, and who was living in the UK before that date, you are not eligible to apply for leave under the EUSS. Instead, you need to obtain leave to enter or remain in the UK under the same rules as non-EEA nationals. Your entitlement to the benefits listed on p1279 depends primarily on your immigration status, and whether you are defined as a person subject to immigration control (see p1272) and, if you are, whether you are covered by an exempt group for the benefit you want to claim (see p1280 onwards).

**If you are an EEA national who was already living in the UK by the end of the transition period**, or a family member of such an EEA national, you are, in general, required to apply for leave under the EUSS. See below for details and the relevance for claiming benefits that require a right to reside.

## European Union Settlement Scheme

The EUSS is set out in the Immigration Rules.[71]

To be eligible for leave under the EUSS, you must be an EEA national who began residing in the UK before the end of the transition period (11pm on 31 December 2020), or have been, on and since that date, a family member of such an EEA national, or have been residing in the UK with a derivative right to reside (see p1336) before that date.

Although, in general, the **deadline** for applications to the EUSS for settled or pre-settled status was 30 June 2021:[72]

- there is no deadline for applying for settled status if you already have pre-settled status. You should apply for settled status as soon as you are eligible, which in most cases is once you have resided in the UK for five years (see further information on pre-settled status on p1315);
- you can apply after the general deadline if you have 'reasonable grounds' for missing this deadline;
- the deadline can be different in specific circumstances. In particular, if you entered the UK with an EUSS family permit (see p1315), your deadline to apply to the EUSS is generally three months from your arrival. You can apply after this date if you have 'reasonable grounds' for missing this deadline.

9

If you make a 'late' EUSS application (ie, after the deadline that applies to you), the Home Office first makes a decision on whether your application is valid, including whether it accepts you have 'reasonable grounds' for not having applied by, and since, the relevant deadline. If the Home Office accepts your application as valid, it should issue a **Certificate of Application** confirming this immediately.[73] Only if your application is accepted as valid does the Home Office go on to the second stage of making an eligibility decision – ie, whether you are eligible for settled or pre-settled status. If your application is made before the deadline that applies to you, it will generally be accepted as a valid application (and you should be issued a Certificate of Application) from the date you applied.

If you are eligible to apply to the EUSS, but have not yet done so, or your previous application(s) have been rejected as not valid or refused as not eligible, get urgent immigration advice.

You may be eligible for:

- **settled status (indefinite leave under the EUSS)** if you can show you have been residing (not necessarily with a free movement right to reside) in the UK:

  - for five years as an EEA national or family member (similar to the definition on p1329) of an EEA national or with a derivative right to reside (see p1336). Certain gaps abroad are disregarded (similar to those disregarded for acquiring permanent residence – see p1339); *or*
  - for less than five years, your residence in the UK began before the end of the transition period, and you satisfy conditions that are the same as those for obtaining permanent residence in less than five years (see p1340); *or*
- **pre-settled status (limited leave for five years)** if you:
  - began residing in the UK before the end of the transition period as an EEA national, or family member of an EEA national, or with a derivative right to reside, but your residence in the UK has been less than five years; *or*
  - have come to the UK to join an EEA national who was your family member at the end of the transition period and remains your family member.

**If you have pre-settled status**, you do not need to wait until the end of the five years before you apply for settled status. You can apply as soon as you are eligible – ie, once you have resided in the UK for five years or satisfy the criteria for obtaining it in less than five years, as above. If, by the date your pre-settled status was due to expire, you have not yet been granted settled status (whether or not you have applied for it), your pre-settled status is extended by five years. Until September 2024, the duration of the extension was two years. The Home Office should confirm the extension of your pre-settled status by email shortly before the date it was due to expire. Get urgent immigration advice if your pre-settled status is not extended or if it is cancelled. Also get immigration advice before being absent from the UK for more than six out of any 12 months, as this could affect your eligibility to get settled status in future.

Since early 2025, the Home Office began implementing its policy of converting pre-settled status to settled status without an application being required if government records show you have continuously resided in the UK for five years.[74] At the time of writing, this policy only applied if you are an adult EEA national and began living in the UK before the end of 2020. If you are a non-EEA national, or you moved to the UK after the end of 2020 to join an EEA national family member already in the UK, or you are a child, the policy was instead to extend your pre-settled status by five years. However, the policy of granting settled status was due to be expanded later in 2025. **Note:** this policy does not prevent you *applying* for settled status as soon as you are eligible. See the online edition of CPAG's *Benefits for Migrants Handbook* for updates.

**If you have settled status**, note that you lose this if you are outside the UK for more than five years.

For details of benefit implications of settled and pre-settled status, see below.

If you are joining an EEA national who was living in the UK before 31 December 2020, and who was your family member on that date and continues to be, you may have entered the UK with leave to enter as a holder of an **EUSS**

**family permit.** Once in the UK, you must apply for leave under the EUSS, generally within three months (see p1314 if you miss this deadline).

If you are an Irish citizen or you have indefinite leave to remain in the UK, you do not need to obtain settled or pre-settled status, but you can do so if you are eligible.

If you are a *family member* of an Irish citizen, and you are not Irish or British and do not have leave on another basis, you need to obtain leave under the EUSS.

## Benefit entitlement

If you have **settled status**, you have a right to reside that satisfies the right to reside requirement of all benefits that have this requirement.[75] Your settled status does *not* confer a right to reside on anyone defined as your family member. However, if they have either pre-settled status or a valid pending EUSS application for settled or pre-settled status, they will be in a protected group that can potentially have a free movement right to reside (see p1317), *including* as your family member if your other circumstances mean you would have a right to reside as a qualified person or a permanent right to reside (see p1330).

If you have **pre-settled status**, this is an excluded right to reside for all benefits with that requirement. However, having pre-settled status means you are in a protected group that can have a free movement right to reside (see p1317). For steps to follow if you have pre-settled status, see p1307.

If you have **limited leave to enter as the holder of a valid EUSS family permit or travel permit**, this leave is an excluded right to reside for all benefits with that requirement. However, once you have made a valid EUSS application, the next paragraph applies to you. (It *may* be arguable that the caselaw confirming the circumstances in which pre-settled status by itself can satisfy the right to reside requirement can apply to you before you have applied to the EUSS – see Step 6 on p1307.)

If you have made a **valid EUSS application for settled or pre-settled status**, and your application (or appeal, or administrative review, against a refusal) is pending, you are in a protected group that can have a free movement right to reside (see p1317). **Note:** you are only in a protected group from the date the Home Office accept your application as valid, which, if it is a late application, includes the Home Office accepting you have 'reasonable grounds' for not having applied earlier (see p1314). (It *may* be arguable that the caselaw confirming the circumstances in which pre-settled status by itself can satisfy the right to reside requirement can apply to you while you have a pending valid application, if you do not have a qualifying free movement right to reside – see Step 6 on p1307.)

For the type of right to reside you need, see p1307 for means-tested benefits and p1310 for child benefit.

If you are in any of the above four situations (ie, you have one of the three types of EUSS leave or a pending valid EUSS application for settled or pre-settled status), you are *not* defined as a 'person subject to immigration control' (see p1272) and therefore not excluded from any benefits on this basis. See p1273 for details, including a potential exception if you have leave to enter as the holder of an EUSS family permit that was extended while you are appealing a refusal to grant you settled or pre-settled status.

For how to provide evidence that you have settled or pre-settled status or a pending valid application, see p1272.

## Protected groups who can have European free movement residence rights

Since the end of the transition period (11pm on 31 December 2020), you can only have a free movement right to reside if you are in one of the protected groups below. If you are, free movement rights remain potentially available to you, for the purpose of claiming benefits, despite these rights, in general, having been ended within UK law at the end of the transition period. For the legal basis of this, see p1319.

If you need a free movement right to reside to claim a benefit that requires you to have a right to reside, you need to check whether:

- you are in a protected group; *and*
- you have a free movement right to reside (see the checklist below), other than one that is excluded for the benefit you want to claim (see p1306).

**Since 30 June 2021, you are in a protected group while you:**

- have pre-settled status (see p1314); *or*
- have made a valid application to the EUSS for settled or pre-settled status and that application (or appeal against, or administrative review of, a refusal) has not been finally determined, withdrawn or abandoned.

For how to provide evidence that you are in either of these groups, see p1272.

In practice, while either of the above groups applies to you, the benefit authorities will generally accept that you can potentially have one or more free movement rights to reside. If this is not accepted, see the 15th edition of CPAG's *Benefits for Migrants Handbook.*

**Between the end of 2020 and 1 July 2021**, in addition to the two protected groups above, you may also have been in a protected group if you or your family member had, or were treated as having, a free movement right to reside in the UK at the end of 2020 – see pp1556–8 of the 2022/23 edition of this *Handbook.*

**Before the end of 2020**, you did not need to be in a protected group to have a free movement right to reside because free movement law continued to apply in the UK (see p1313).

## European free movement rights: checklist

Since the end of 2020, you can only have a free movement right to reside if you are in a protected group. This means you either have pre-settled status or a pending valid EUSS application for pre-settled or settled status (or pending appeal or administrative review of a refusal). For more details, see p1317.

If you *are* in a protected group (or for periods before the end of 2020), to determine whether you have (or had) one or more free movement rights to reside, check the following.

- **Option 1:** (for periods before 1 April 2021 only) were you an EEA national who began residing in the UK before 11pm on 31 December 2020, or were you a family member of such an EEA national? For details of this initial right to reside, see p1321.
- **Option 2:** are you an EEA national with a right to reside as a 'qualified person'[76] – ie, are you an EEA national in the UK as a:
  - jobseeker (see p1321);
  - worker (see p1322), including if you have retained this status (see p1325);
  - self-employed person (see p1324), including if you have retained this status (see p1325); *or*
  - self-sufficient person, including a self-sufficient student (see p1328)?
- **Option 3:** are you a 'family member' (see p1329) of an EEA national covered in Options 2 or 4? If so, you have a right to reside whether or not you are an EEA national yourself.
- **Option 4:** do you have a permanent right of residence (see p1338)? In most cases, this is acquired after five years of 'legal residence' (which can include periods with a right to reside under Options 1, 2 and 3, but *not* Option 5 (see p1339)), but can sometimes be acquired before five years (see p1340).
- **Option 5:** do you have a 'derivative right to reside' through someone else's right to reside, but not as their family member? This covers certain children and carers (see p1336).

9

**Note:**

- If you have been granted settled status (see p1314), you have a right to reside for all benefits that have this requirement, so you do not need to also show you have any free movement rights. However, note that your settled status does *not* confer a right to reside on your family members (see p1330).
- You can have more than one right to reside at a time.[77] For example, you may have pre-settled status and be a self-employed person and also a family member of someone with a permanent right of residence.
- If you only have a free movement right to reside as a jobseeker, or family member of a jobseeker, or primary carer of a dependent British citizen (known as a 'Zambrano carer'), these do not satisfy the right to reside requirement for means-tested benefits (see p1307). The latter right also does not satisfy the requirement for child benefit (see p1310).
- If you are (or are relying on the residence rights of) a Croatian, A2 or A8 national, needing to rely on past periods of residence, check whether additional restrictions applied (see p1320).

- In very limited circumstances, if you do not satisfy all the requirements for a particular free movement right to reside, it may be possible to argue that you should still have such a right by applying principles accepted in other cases – in particular, if it is necessary for someone else's rights not to be infringed or if it would be 'proportionate' in your circumstances. See CPAG's *Benefits for Migrants Handbook*.

### *Main legal sources of free movement residence rights*

Although the UK left the EU on 31 January 2020, European free movement rights continued to apply in the UK until the end of the transition period (11pm on 31 December 2020).

At the end of the transition period, EU law was converted into UK law and, together with EU-derived law, continues to apply in the UK as it did on 31 December 2020.[78] From this date, this law could be amended or revoked and, in general, the law on free movement rights, including the EEA Regulations, was revoked within UK law.[79] However, legislation to give effect to the Withdrawal Agreements provided a separate means for EU law, and EU-derived law relevant to the Agreements, including in relation to residence rights, to continue to be part of UK law.[80]

The Withdrawal Agreements that the UK made with the EU, the European Free Trade Association (EFTA) states and Switzerland provide rights and protections for EEA nationals already living in the UK, and British citizens already living in EEA states, before the end of the transition period, and the family members of each.[81] UK regulations[82] were introduced to reproduce the protections that enable the continued availability of free movement residence rights, but where they fail to do so, the Withdrawal Agreements have direct effect in the UK. If you are in one of the protected groups (see p1317), the EEA Regulations continue to be available to you and must be interpreted in accordance with not only the Withdrawal Agreements, but also EU legislation and Court of Justice of the EU (CJEU) caselaw (as of 31 December 2020), which the EEA Regulations are intended to implement (see below).[83] Only the highest courts (the Court of Appeal, Supreme Court and equivalent-level courts) may depart from CJEU caselaw.[84] The Withdrawal Agreements must also be interpreted in accordance with EU legislation, including the Treaty on the Functioning of the EU (TFEU) and caselaw.[85] Questions about the interpretation of the rights and protections provided for in Part Two ('Citizens Rights') of the Withdrawal Agreement can be referred to the CJEU for up to eight years from the end of the transition period.[86]

If you are in a protected group that can potentially have one or more free movement rights, the main EU legislation that remains relevant comes from EU treaties, in particular the **TFEU** and, for Norway, Iceland and Liechtenstein, **the EEA Agreement**. However, the details of residence rights are set out in **EU Directive 2004/38.** Swiss nationals and their family members are covered by a separate agreement, providing similar rights.[87] In addition, some derivative residence rights (see p1336) are provided by EU Regulation 492/2011 or the Withdrawal Agreements, and the Withdrawal Agreements also provide rights for dependent family members who cease to be dependent (see p1329).

The Immigration (European Economic Area) Regulations 2016 (called **'the EEA Regulations'** in this *Handbook*) apply to all EEA nationals and Swiss nationals (but not British citizens – see p1312).[88] These give similar rights of residence to those contained in the above EU Directive and should be interpreted in accordance with it and other EU legislation and caselaw on free movement residence rights. **Note:** although the EEA Regulations were, in general, revoked from the end of the transition period, they continue to be available while you are in a protected group listed on p1317.

## Croatian, A2 and A8 nationals

Your current free movement residence rights could be affected by additional restrictions that *previously* limited the circumstances in which nationals of specific 'accession' countries (listed below) could have a right to reside as a jobseeker, a worker or a person with retained worker status. The restrictions were time limited, did not apply to those in specific exempt groups, and did not apply to other residence rights – eg, as a self-employed or self-sufficient person.[89] Although Cyprus and Malta also joined the EU on 1 May 2004, no restrictions were placed on nationals of these two countries.

***Croatia, A2 and A8 states ('accession states')***

**Croatia** joined the EU on 1 July 2013 and restrictions applied from that date until 30 June 2018.

**The A2 states are:** Bulgaria and Romania. They joined the EU on 1 January 2007 and restrictions applied from then until 31 December 2013.

**The A8 states are:** Czech Republic, Estonia, Hungary, Latvia, Lithuania, Poland, Slovakia and Slovenia. They joined the EU on 1 May 2004 and restrictions applied from then until 30 April 2009.

In particular, these restrictions can be relevant if you are currently seeking to establish either:

- permanent residence and you, or your family member whose free movement residence rights you need to rely on, are a Croatian, A2 or A8 national; *or*
- a derivative right to reside as the primary carer of a child of a worker in education and the working parent was a Croatian, A2 or A8 national who worked in the UK during the period of restrictions.

For details on the restrictions, including lists of exempt groups, see the 2021/22 edition of this *Handbook* or CPAG's *Benefits for Migrants Handbook*.

## Initial right of residence

If you are an EEA national and arrived in the UK before the end of the transition period (11pm on 31 December 2020), you had an initial right of residence for the first three months of your stay in the UK, provided you had a valid identity card or passport and were not an unreasonable burden on the social assistance system of the UK.[90]

If you were a family member (see p1329) of an EEA national who had this initial right of residence (whether or not you are an EEA national), you had a right to reside, provided you had a valid passport and were not an unreasonable burden on the social assistance system of the UK.[91]

These residence rights could only apply before 1 April 2021 and did not satisfy the right to reside requirement for any of the means-tested benefits at the time. However, either can count towards meeting the five years' residence required to acquire a permanent right to reside (see p1338).[92]

## Jobseekers

You can only have a free movement right to reside, including as a jobseeker (or family member of a jobseeker), while you have either pre-settled status or a pending EUSS application. For details of these protected groups, see p1317.

While you are in one of the protected groups (or for a period before the end of 2020), you have a right to reside as a jobseeker if you are an EEA national in the UK and you provide evidence that you are seeking employment. The EEA Regulations also require you to provide evidence of having a 'genuine chance of being engaged' (see below).[93]

There is no time limit on how long you can have a right to reside as a jobseeker. It continues for as long as you satisfy the above requirements (but see below).[94]

If you are a Croatian, A2 or A8 national who was subject to restrictions, you did not have a right to reside as a jobseeker during the period of those restrictions (see p1320).[95]

The EEA Regulations contain some additional requirements that you entered the UK to seek employment, or that before seeking employment you were a worker or self-sufficient.[96] However, these are very rarely applied by the benefit authorities. Get advice if it is suggested these mean you do not have a right to reside as a jobseeker.

### Providing evidence

To have a right to reside as a jobseeker, you must provide evidence that you are seeking employment. The EEA Regulations also require you to provide evidence of having a 'genuine chance of being engaged'.[97] However, the CJEU held that this additional requirement cannot be required until after a 'reasonable period', which could be six months.[98]

The most straightforward way of demonstrating that you are a jobseeker is to sign on for new-style jobseeker's allowance (JSA) or national insurance (NI) credits on the basis of unemployment and provide evidence that you satisfy the work search and work availability requirements (see p959). There would only be a few unusual circumstances in which you would satisfy these conditions and *not* be accepted as having a genuine chance of being engaged.[99] However, it is not necessary to claim or receive JSA, or to have registered as a jobseeker with the DWP, to have a right to reside as a jobseeker if you can provide evidence that you are seeking employment and (although arguably not required until after a 'reasonable period') have a genuine chance of being engaged.[100]

Under the EEA Regulations, the evidence that you are looking for work and have a genuine chance of being engaged must be 'compelling' for you to be able to continue to have a right to reside as a jobseeker for more than 91 days. This requirement also applies from the start of the period when you have a right to reside as a jobseeker if you *previously* had a right to reside as a jobseeker for a total of 91 days, or you previously retained worker or self-employed status while involuntarily unemployed (see p1325) for at least six months.[101] The requirement for your evidence to be compelling is known as the 'genuine prospects of work test' and can only be applied to you if you have no other free movement right to reside, other than as a jobseeker. If (eg, while claiming child benefit), this requirement is applied to you, or you are told you have failed to satisfy it, check it has been applied at the right time and see CPAG's *Benefits for Migrants Handbook*.

### Benefit entitlement

9

If you have a right to reside as a jobseeker and this is your only right to reside:

- it does not satisfy the right to reside requirement for universal credit (UC), income-related employment and support allowance (ESA), pension credit (PC) or housing benefit (HB);
- it does satisfy the right to reside requirement for child benefit;
- it can count towards meeting the five years' residence required for permanent residency (see p1338).

## Workers

You can only have a free movement right to reside, including as a worker, while you have either pre-settled status or a pending EUSS application. For details of these 'protected groups', see p1317.

While you are in one of the protected groups (or for a period before the end of 2020), you have a right to reside as a 'worker' if you are an EEA national and:[102]

- you are in an employment relationship. This means you must:[103]
  - provide services; *and*
  - work in return for remuneration; *and*
  - work under the direction of another person; *and*

- your work entails activities that are 'genuine and effective', rather than 'marginal and ancillary'.

***Is your work genuine and effective?***

When deciding whether your work is genuine and effective, all relevant factors must be taken into account, including the following.

1. The duration of the employment. The longer your employment lasts, the more likely it is that you have established worker status. However, in specific cases, two weeks was held to be sufficient to establish worker status.[104]
2. The number of hours worked. There is no minimum threshold. Someone working 10 hours a week was held to be a worker,[105] as was an au pair working 13 hours a week for a modest wage plus board and lodging.[106] The European Court of Justice held that 5.5 hours' work is potentially capable of making someone a worker.[107]
3. The level of your earnings. There must be some remuneration (although it can be in kind, such as board and lodgings[108]). Voluntary work does not result in worker status.[109] Provided the work done is genuine and effective, earnings that are so low that you need to subsidise them with benefits do not prevent you from being a worker.[110]
4. The regularity of the work. The more regular and less erratic the work, the more likely it is that worker status will be established. It is possible to be a worker while on a zero-hour contract (as it depends on the work you actually do)[111] or while undertaking work through an agency[112] or working 'cash in hand' without tax and NI being deducted.[113]

Although guidance to decision makers advises that someone is *automatically* a worker if they have been earning, on average, a 'minimum income threshold' (£242 a week or £1,048 a month since 6 July 2022) for three months, it confirms that, in all other cases, an individual assessment must be made, taking the above factors into account.[114]

**Note:** if you are a Croatian, A2 or A8 national who during the period of restrictions was subject to those restrictions, you only could only have a right to reside as a 'worker' in specific circumstances (see p1320).

You only **cease to be a worker** when the employment relationship ends. While you are still under a contract of employment, you continue to be a worker. Consequently, you are still a worker if you are on maternity leave (including unpaid maternity leave),[115] on holiday leave or sick leave (including if it is unpaid),[116] or during periods when you were furloughed under the Coronavirus Job Retention Scheme.

If you have ceased to be a worker, you may retain your worker status in certain circumstances (see p1325).

If you have a right to reside as a 'worker' in the UK, this satisfies the right to reside requirement for all the benefits that have this requirement, and you are exempt from the habitual residence test (see p1303).

**Note:** if you are an EEA national and on 31 December 2020, and continuously since then, you have been working in the UK while 'not primarily resident in the UK', you may have rights as a 'frontier worker' (see p1342). These rights include being exempt from the habitual residence test for means-tested benefits (see p1303).

## Self-employed people

You can only have a free movement right to reside, including as a self-employed person, while you have either pre-settled status or a pending EUSS application. For details of these 'protected groups', see p1317.

While you are in one of the protected groups (or for a period before the end of 2020), you have a right to reside as a self-employed person if you are an EEA national and you provide services in return for remuneration, but not under the direction of another person.[117] Your work must entail activities that are 'genuine and effective' rather than 'marginal and ancillary' (see p1323).[118]

You count as being self-employed if you are established in the UK to pursue activity as a self-employed person.[119] You must provide evidence of the steps you have taken to set yourself up as self-employed.[120] It helps if you have registered with HMRC as self-employed. However, if you have not registered, this does not necessarily mean you do not have a right to reside as a self-employed person.[121]

If you are a Croatian, A2 or A8 national and during the periods of restrictions (see p1320) you were self-employed, you had the same rights as other EEA nationals; no additional restrictions applied.

9

If you stop working, you do not necessarily **cease to be self-employed**. You may be in a temporary lull, and it is accepted that you can continue to be self-employed during such times, depending on your particular circumstances and the evidence you provide – eg, the amount of work you have, any steps you are taking to develop your business or find new work, and your marketing and business administration. Account must also be taken of your motives and intentions.[122]

You can continue to be self-employed if you stop work for a period of maternity leave, but intend to return to self-employment afterwards (see p1327).[123]

If you have ceased to be self-employed, you may be able to retain your self-employed status in certain circumstances (see below).

If you have a right to reside as a 'self-employed person' in the UK, this satisfies the right to reside requirement for all the benefits that have this requirement, and you are exempt from the habitual residence test (see p1303).

**Note:** if you are an EEA national and on 31 December 2020, and continuously since then, you have been self-employed in the UK while 'not primarily resident in the UK', you may have rights as a 'frontier worker' (see p1342). These rights include being exempt from the habitual residence test for means-tested benefits (see p1303).

## Retaining worker or self-employed status

You can only have a free movement right to reside, including retained worker or self-employed status, while you have either pre-settled status or a pending EUSS application. For details of these 'protected groups', see p1317.

While you are in one of the protected groups (or for a period before the end of 2020), you can retain the status of 'worker' or 'self-employed', even though you are no longer working, if:[124]

- you are involuntarily unemployed and registered as a jobseeker (see below); *or*
- you are temporarily unable to work because of an illness or accident (see p1326); *or*
- you are undertaking vocational training (see p1326); *or*
- you are unable to work because you are in the late stages of pregnancy or have just given birth (see p1327).[125]

Before considering whether you have retained your worker or self-employed status, check whether you have ceased to be a worker (see p1323) or self-employed (see p1324). For example, if you are off work on unpaid sick leave but can return to your job when you are better, you are still a worker, so you do not need to argue that you have retained your worker status.

If you have retained worker or self-employed status, this satisfies the right to reside requirement for all the benefits that have this requirement, and you are exempt from the habitual residence test (see p1303).

**Note:** if you are a Croatian, A2 or A8 national who, during the relevant period of restrictions, was subject to those restrictions, you could only retain your worker status in the ways described in this section in specific circumstances (see p1320). There were no restrictions on retaining self-employed status.

9

### You are involuntarily unemployed and registered as a jobseeker

You retain your status as a worker or self-employed person if you:[126]

- are recorded as involuntarily unemployed (see below); *and*
- have registered yourself as a jobseeker with the relevant employment office (in the UK, the DWP); *and*
- provide evidence that you are seeking employment (or, to retain self-employed status, seeking either employment or self-employment).

In practice, you should only need to satsify the requirements above even though the EEA Regulations also contain some additional requirements (see p1579 of the 2022/23 edition of this *Handbook*).[127] In particular, note that you do not need to provide evidence of having a 'genuine chance of being engaged', and the 'genuine prospects of work' test should not be applied if you are retaining your worker or self-employed status due to involuntary unemployment.[128]

You are **'involuntarily unemployed'** if you are seeking and are available to take up employment (or self-employment, to retain your status as a self-employed person). This depends on your remaining in the labour market. The circumstances in which you left your last job, or ceased your self-employment, are just one factor in determining this, and your actions and circumstances since ceasing work must also be taken into account.[129]

The best way to **register as a jobseeker** is to claim UC and/or JSA, and show that you continue to satisfy the work search and work availability requirements, even if you are not entitled to benefit.[130] If you are claiming a benefit that does not require you to look for work, you can satisfy the requirement to register as a jobseeker (and thereby retain your worker status) if you declare to the job centre that you are looking for work before your claim is determined, and provide evidence of seeking work.[131] If there was a gap between your ceasing work and registering as a jobseeker, see p1327.

If you were employed or self-employed for less than a year, the EEA Regulations limit the period during which you can retain your worker or self-employed status while registered as a jobseeker to a maximum of six months.[132] The EU Directive allows you to retain worker status for no less than six months.[133]

If you were employed or self-employed for more than a year (not necessarily in one continuous job), you can retain your worker or self-employed status on this basis indefinitely, unless there is an event that indicates you have withdrawn from the labour market entirely.[134]

## You are temporarily unable to work because of an illness or accident

To retain your worker or self-employed status on this basis, your inability to work must be temporary. This simply means not permanent.[135] This can apply if you have a permanent health condition that fluctuates and causes temporary periods when you are unable to work.[136] You are considered to be temporarily unable to work if there is a realistic prospect of your being able to work again in the foreseeable future.[137] You do not need to have claimed ESA or another benefit on the grounds of inability to work, nor do you need to pass the test of limited capability for work. The test is a factual one of whether you are unable to do the work you were doing or, if it follows a period in which you were seeking work, the sort of work you were seeking.[138] Your inability to work must be caused by an illness or accident *you* have – eg, you are not covered if you are unable to work because you are looking after a child who is ill.[139]

If you are permanently incapable of work, you may have a permanent right to reside (see p1340).

If you are unable to work because of pregnancy, see p1327.

## You are undertaking vocational training

You retain your worker or self-employed status if you are undertaking a vocational training course and either:[140]

- the training is related to your previous employment or to retain self-employment related to your previous occupation in the UK; *or*

- you are 'involuntarily unemployed'. You should be accepted as 'involuntarily unemployed' if you have to retrain to find work that is reasonably equivalent to your former employment.[141]

## Pregnancy and childbirth

If you have established worker or self-employed status and are now not working because of the late stages of pregnancy or childbirth, you may still count as a worker or self-employed person, or you may be able to retain your worker or self-employed status.

You do not cease to be a worker while you are still under a contract of employment, so you are still a worker while on maternity leave, whether or not it is paid. This also applied to Croatian, A2 and A8 nationals who established worker status during the periods of restrictions (see p1320).[142]

You can continue to be a self-employed person if you intend to resume your self-employment after your maternity period and remain engaged in self-employed activity despite stopping work during that period.[143]

You can *retain* your worker or self-employed status if you have a pregnancy-related illness that prevents you from working (see p1326).[144]

You can *retain* worker or self-employed status if you gave up work (or seeking work, if you retained your worker or self-employed status while involuntarily unemployed – see p1325) because of the physical constraints of the late stages of pregnancy or the aftermath of childbirth, provided you intend to start work again (or start seeking work and thereby retain your worker status while involuntarily unemployed) within a 'reasonable period' after giving birth.[145] Other than in unusual cases, 52 weeks is a 'reasonable period', and the period usually starts 11 weeks before your due date (or the date you last work, if later).[146]

9

## Moving between groups and gaps

You can retain your worker or self-employed status if you are in one of the groups on p1325 and continue to do so if you move into another category.[147] For example, if you ceased work due to becoming involuntarily unemployed and you registered as a jobseeker with the DWP, then, after a few months, you became ill and were temporarily unable to work, and then you got better and started vocational training, you would retain your worker or self-employed status throughout.

If there was a gap of more than a few days between your ceasing work and registering as a jobseeker with the DWP, you should explain the reasons for the delay and provide evidence of your work search during this period. To determine whether you retain your worker or self-employed status, all your circumstances, including the reasons for the gap and what you did during it, should be considered to establish whether there was 'undue delay'[148] and whether you left the labour market during that period.[149] There is no fixed period that is considered an 'undue delay', but gaps of less than three months, throughout which there is clear evidence of work search, are generally accepted by First-tier Tribunals as not amounting to an undue delay.

Arguably, you should also be able to retain your worker or self-employed status if there is a gap between your ceasing work and being temporarily unable to work because of illness or an accident, since there is no requirement for the illness or accident to be the reason for your ceasing work.

You should also still retain your worker or self-employed status during a short gap between two different circumstances applying, provided you remain in the labour market during that time.

## Self-sufficient people and students

You can only have a free movement right to reside, including as a self-sufficient person or student, while you have either pre-settled status or a pending EUSS application. For details of these 'protected groups', see p1317.

While you are in one of the protected groups (or for a period before the end of 2020), you have a right to reside as a self-sufficient person if you are an EEA national and you, and any family members whose right to reside depends on their being your family member, have:[150]

- sufficient resources not to become an unreasonable burden on the social assistance system of the UK during your period of residence;[151] *and*
- comprehensive sickness insurance.

The UK government cannot set a fixed amount that is regarded as 'sufficient resources' and must take account of your personal situation.[152] You have **'sufficient resources'** if they:[153]

9

- exceed the maximum level you (and your family) can have to be eligible for 'social assistance' (see below); *or*
- do not exceed that level, but the decision maker considers that you still have sufficient resources, taking into account your (and your family's) personal situation.

The **'maximum level'** is the equivalent of your means-tested benefit applicable, or maximum, amount, including any premiums, elements or additions. Your resources also include your accommodation, so if your resources are more than your applicable, or maximum, amount plus your rent, or if friends or family provide you with free and stable accommodation, they should be 'sufficient'.[154]

The source of the resources does not matter.[155] However, you cannot rely on your earnings from employment in the UK to give you self-sufficient status.[156] Check instead whether the employment gives you 'worker' status (see p1322). You can, however, rely on the earnings of your non-EEA national spouse/civil partner,[157] or self-employed earnings of a British partner,[158] or if you are a child, the earnings of your non-EEA parent (even if derived from employment that is unlawful due to a lack of residence card and work permit[159]). The Court of Appeal recently upheld a decision that an EEA national could rely on the means-tested benefits paid to his British wife, which in their specific circumstances did not increase due to his presence, together with his own receipt of carer's allowance, to amount to 'sufficient resources'.[160]

You cannot automatically be regarded as *not* self-sufficient just because you make a claim for a means-tested benefit. All your circumstances, including the likely duration of your claim, must be assessed to determine whether or not your benefit claim makes you an 'unreasonable burden' on the social assistance system of the UK.[161] In two separate recent cases it was held that the additional UC paid to a couple, above the amount of the single allowance, for a duration of 23 and 27 months respectively, until the EEA national partner could obtain settled status, did not amount to an 'unreasonable burden'.[162]

The requirement to have **comprehensive sickness insurance** cover is satisfied if you have private health insurance.[163] This requirement is also satisfied by being able to use the UK's free NHS.[164]

### Students

You have a free movement right to reside as a student if you are an EEA national and you:[165]

- are enrolled as a student in a government-accredited college; *and*
- provide an assurance that you have sufficient resources, for you and any family members whose right to reside depends on their being your family member, not to become a burden on the UK social assistance system during your intended period of residence (see above); *and*
- together with any family members who do not have an independent right to reside, have comprehensive sickness insurance (see above).

9

## Family members

You can only have a free movement right to reside, including as a family member of an EEA national with a relevant free movement residence right (ie, one listed in the next paragraph), while you have either pre settled status or a pending EUSS application. For details of these 'protected groups', see p1317.

While you are in one of the protected groups (or for a period before the end of 2020), you have a right to reside if you are a 'family member' (see below) of an EEA national who has a free movement right to reside in the UK as:

- a qualified person (see p1318); *or*
- a permanent right to reside (see p1338); *or*
- an initial right to reside (see p1321).

This applies whether or not you are an EEA national yourself.

You have a right to reside for as long as you are in a protected group, the EEA national has one of the free movement rights to reside listed above and you remain their family member.

***Family members***[166]

You are a **'family member'** if you are the EEA national's:
- spouse or civil partner; *or*
- child, grandchild or great-grandchild, or the child, grandchild or great-grandchild of the EEA national's spouse/civil partner, and you are under 21; *or*
- child, grandchild or great-grandchild, or the child, grandchild or great-grandchild of the EEA national's spouse/civil partner, and you are dependent on them; *or*
- parent, grandparent or great-grandparent, or the parent, grandparent or great-grandparent of the EEA national's spouse/civil partner, and you are dependent on them.

You remain a spouse or civil partner even if you are separated. You only cease to be a spouse or civil partner on divorce or dissolution of the civil partnership.[167]

**'Dependence'** is not defined in the legislation, but caselaw has established a number of principles.[168] To be dependent, you must receive support from the other person. The support must be 'material', although not necessarily financial, and must contribute towards your basic necessities. It does not need to be your only source of support. Translation, emotional and social support do not count.[169] It is irrelevant if there are alternative sources of support available, including employment, and your dependency should be considered independently of any benefit entitlement that relies on your rights as a family member.[170]

If you had a right to reside as a family member due to being dependent on an EEA national before the end of 2020, and you have since ceased to be dependent, the Withdrawal Agreement provides for you to continue to have a right to reside as their family member.[171]

If you only became dependent on the EEA national in the UK, this does not prevent you from being classed as a family member, *unless* you are an 'extended family member' (see p1331), in which case you must have already been dependent (or a member of their household) in the country you have come from.[172]

Note:
- If you are a family member of a person with settled status, their indefinite leave does not confer a right to reside on you. However, if they are an EEA national in circumstances that mean they *would* have a right to reside in the UK as a qualified person or a permanent right to reside, other than for the fact of not being in one of the protected groups, the benefit authorities accept this *does* confer a right to reside on you, provided *you* are in a protected group.[173] If this is not accepted, challenge the refusal and get advice to argue that the Withdrawal Agreements protect your rights in this situation.
- If you have leave to enter the UK as the holder of an EUSS family permit, this leave does not satisfy the right to reside requirement for any of the benefits

that have it (see p1307 and, for child benefit, see p1310). However, once you make a valid EUSS application for settled or pre-settled status, you are then in a protected group that can potentially have one or more free movement rights, including if you are a family member of an EEA national with one of the free movement rights listed above.

- If you are not covered by the definition of family member above, check whether you can be *treated as* a family member if you are an 'extended family member' *and* you have a relevant residence document issued under the EEA Regulations (see below).
- If your only right to reside is as a family member of an EEA national who has a right to reside as a jobseeker, this does not enable you to satisfy the right to reside requirement for UC, income-related ESA, PC and HB, but does satisfy the right to reside requirement for child benefit (see p1307 and p1310).

***Are you unable to prove your right to reside?***

If you are relying on your family member for your right to reside and you cannot prove what they are, or were, doing (eg, if you have separated from your spouse and have no evidence that they are a worker), ask the DWP, HMRC or local authority to investigate this (eg, provide information about your spouse and ask the decision maker to use the NI contributions database to establish they are a worker). If the benefit authority refuses to investigate and you appeal, you can ask the First-tier Tribunal to issue a direction (see p1188) to the DWP, HMRC or local authority to make these investigations and argue that otherwise it has not shown that you do not have a right to reside.[174] Explain to the tribunal the steps you have taken to try to get the evidence and why these have failed.[175]

9

## Extended family members

If you do not come within the definition of family member, but you have a partner or relative in the UK who is an EEA national, you can be *treated as* their family member if you are defined as their 'extended family member' *and* you were issued with a residence document (an EEA family permit, a registration certificate or a residence card) under the EEA Regulaitons which remains in force.[176] Although you can no longer apply for these residence documents, if you have already have one, it should be accepted as remaining in force if it has not yet expired.

**Note:** a residence document issued under the EEA Regulations only confirms a right to reside; it does not, in itself, give you a right to reside – eg, if, due to a change in your circumstances, you no longer have that right to reside.[177]

For details of the residence documents issued under the EEA Regulations, see the 2024/25 edition of this *Handbook*.

***Extended family member***

You are an **'extended family member'** of an EEA national if they are your:[178]

- partner and you are in a durable relationship with them (or you are the child, under 18, of the partner); *or*
- non-adoptive legal guardian (under the law of the country in which the guardianship order was granted), you are under 18, dependent on them and have lived with them since they became your legal guardian; *or*
- relative; *and*
- you meet the requirements of the Immigration Rules (other than those relating to entry clearance) for indefinite leave as their dependent relative; *or*
- you have serious health problems that require their (or their spouse's or civil partner's) care; *or*
- you previously were dependent on them, or were a member of their household, in a country other than the UK, and you accompanied or joined them in the UK (or you wish to join them in the UK) and you continue to be dependent on them or to be a member of their household.[179]

## Family members of British citizens

British citizens do not generally confer free movement residence rights on their family members.

However, if you are a family member (including an extended family member with a relevant EEA Regulation residence document) of a British citizen and you have either pre-settled status or a pending EUSS application (see p1317), you have a free movement right to reside in the UK if, on or before 31 December 2020:[180]

- the British citizen was, or immediately before returning to the UK had been, residing in an EEA state with a right to reside as a worker, self-employed person, self-sufficient person or self-sufficient student, or a permanent right to reside; *and*
- you resided with the British citizen as their family member in that EEA state, your family life was created or strengthened there, and your joint residence in that EEA state was 'genuine' (see p1333).

**Note:** the British citizen can confer a right to reside on you even if they only returned to the UK after 31 December 2020, provided the above bullet points applied to you by that date. However, to obtain pre-settled (or settled) status as a family member of a British citizen on this basis, you must have made a valid application before 9 August 2023.

On returning to the UK with you, the British citizen confers free movement residence rights on you, whether or not they are working in the UK. Since 31 December 2020, under the EEA Regulations, the British person is *treated* as satisfying any requirement to be a 'qualified person' (see p1318) on their return to the UK.[181] For periods before this, you can rely on caselaw that confirms the

British person does not need to undertake economic activity on return to the UK for their family member to have a right to reside.[182]

The EEA Regulations list the following as relevant to whether your residence in the EEA state is, or was, genuine:[183]

- the length of joint residence there;
- the nature and quality of the joint accommodation there and whether it was the British citizen's principal residence;
- the degree of your and the British citizen's integration;
- whether it was your first lawful residence in the EU.

These factors go beyond the findings of the CJEU which, when considering whether residence is 'genuine', focused on whether it enabled the creation or strengthening of family life in that state and whether the conditions for the relevant residence rights were satisfied.[184]

The EEA Regulations exclude you from having a right to reside on this basis if the purpose of your residence in the EEA state was to circumvent the UK's immigration laws.[185]

### Family members of dual citizens

If you are a family member of a British citizen who also has citizenship of an EEA country, you can have a right to reside in the same circumstances as if you were a family member of an EEA national. This is the case if the British citizen moved to the UK and was residing as an EEA national with a free movement right to reside as a qualified person (see p1318), or with a permanent right to reside (see p1338) when they acquired British citizenship. If they currently have a right to reside as a qualified person, they must have had such a right continuously since acquiring British citizenship.[186]



A dual British/EEA national does not have rights under EU law if they have lived all their life in the UK and therefore you cannot derive any rights from them.[187]

## Former family members who retain their right to reside

In general, if you are a family member of an EEA national who has a right to reside, you lose your right to reside if they cease to either be your family member or have a right to reside. However, some exceptions mean you can retain your right to reside if the EEA national dies or leaves the UK or your marriage or civil partnership ends. These rights are in EU Directive 2004/38, but are not exactly reproduced in the UK's EEA Regulations. The benefit authorities accept the rights set out in the EEA Regulations (listed below), but do not always accept those in the Directive (listed on p1334). If you only have a right to reside under the Directive and are refused benefit, challenge the decision and get specialist advice.

**You retain your right to reside under the EEA Regulations** if you have pre-settled status or a pending EUSS application (see p1317) (or for periods before the end of 2020) if you are a family member of an EEA national who is a qualified person (see p1318) or a person with a permanent right to reside (see p1338) and:[188]

- the EEA national dies and you are:
  - not an EEA national, but if you were, you would be a worker, or a self-employed or self-sufficient person (or jobseeker[189]), or you are a family member of such a non-EEA national, and you resided in the UK with a right to reside under the EEA Regulations for at least a year immediately before they died; *or*
  - their child or grandchild (or the child or grandchild of their spouse or civil partner) and you were in education (see p1338) immediately before their death, and you remain in education; *or*
  - the parent with custody of a child in the previous bullet point; *or*
- the EEA national leaves the UK and you are:
  - their child or grandchild (or the child or grandchild of their spouse or civil partner) and you were in education (see p1338) immediately before they left the UK and you remain in education; *or*
  - the parent with custody of a child in the previous bullet point; *or*
- your marriage or civil partnership to the EEA national is terminated, and they were a qualified person or had a permanent right to reside at least until the termination proceedings began,[190] and you are not an EEA national, but if you were, you would be a worker, or a self-employed or self-sufficient person (or jobseeker[191]), or you are a family member of such a non-EEA national, and you were residing in the UK with a right to reside under the regulations at the date of the termination and:
  - the marriage/civil partnership had lasted for at least three years, with you both residing in the UK for at least one of those years; *or*
  - you have custody of the EEA national's child; *or*
  - you have a right of access to the EEA national's child, which a court has said must take place in the UK; *or*
  - your continued right of residence in the UK is warranted by particularly difficult circumstances, such as your (or another family member's) being subject to domestic violence during the period of the marriage/civil partnership.

You have a right to reside on this basis for as long as the conditions apply to you[192] until you can acquire a permanent right of residence (see p1338).[193]

**You should retain your right to reside under EU Directive 2004/38** if you are a family member of an EEA national who has a right to reside as a worker, as a self-employed or self-sufficient person or as a student and:

- the EEA national dies and you have lived in the UK as their family member for at least a year before their death and you are a non-EEA national;[194] *or*
- the EEA national leaves the UK and you are:[195]
  - their child or grandchild and in education; *or*

  - the parent with custody of a child in the previous bullet point in education; *or*
- your marriage or civil partnership (or that of your relative – see first bullet point in note below) to the EEA national is terminated and the EEA national had their right to reside at least until the termination proceedings began,[196] you are a non-EEA national, and:[197]
  - before the termination proceedings began (which must occur while the EEA national was in the UK[198]), the marriage/civil partnership had lasted for at least three years with you both residing in the UK for at least one of those years; *or*
  - you have custody of the EEA national's child; *or*
  - you have a right of access to the EEA national's child, which a court has said must take place in the UK; *or*
  - your continued right of residence in the UK is warranted by particularly difficult circumstances, such as your being subject to domestic violence during the period of the marriage/civil partnership. The termination proceedings must have begun while the EEA national was in the UK,[199] or arguably, within a reasonable period after they left the UK.[200]

Note:
- The last main bullet above can apply if the marriage or civil partnership that has terminated is not yours, but was a necessary element in your right to reside as a family member – eg, if you were dependent on your non-EEA national son while he was married to an EEA national with a right to reside as a worker, your son gets divorced, and one of the sub-bullet points applies to your son (or, arguably, the last sub-bullet point applies to you).[201]
- Arguably, if you are an EEA national, you can retain your right to reside in each of the three circumstances above without needing to satisfy any other conditions.[202] However, two Upper Tribunal decisions have rejected this interpretation, taking the view that the provisions in the Directive just confirm that any independent residence rights that an EEA national may have had are not affected by the above changes.[203] It is arguable that these parts of each decision are not legally binding as each case failed on other grounds, but they are persuasive until further caselaw decides the issue.
- Periods when you have retained your right to reside under the EU Directive in one of the ways above are not sufficient on their own to enable you to acquire permanent residence after five years (see p1338) because you must also show that you are a worker, or a self-employed or self-sufficient person, or you are a family member of such a person.[204]

## Derivative right to reside

You can only have a free movement right to reside, including a derivative right to reside, while you have either pre-settled status or a pending EUSS application. For details of these 'protected groups', see p1317.

While you are in one of the protected groups (or for a period before the end of 2020), you may have a right to reside based on someone else's right to reside, without necessarily being their family member. The EEA Regulations list these as 'derivative' rights of residence, but do not include all the rights listed below. Some are provided by caselaw and others by the Withdrawal Agreements. If the EEA Regulations interpret the rights more narrowly than EU caselaw, you can rely directly on the caselaw (see p1319).

You have a 'derivative' right to reside if (EEA Regulations only, you are not an 'exempt person' – see p1337 – and) you are:[205]

- the child (or stepchild[206]) of an EEA national who was a 'worker' in the UK (see p1322), or (not in EEA Regulations) a self-employed person in the UK (see p1324) while you were living in the UK, and you are currently in education (see p1337);[207] *or*
- the primary carer of a child in the above bullet point and the child would be unable to continue their education in the UK if you left the UK; *or*
- the primary carer of a self-sufficient (see p1328) child who is an EEA national, who would be unable to remain in the UK if you left the UK;[208] *or*
- the primary carer of a British citizen residing in the UK who would be unable to reside in the UK or any EEA state if you left the UK (known as a 'Zambrano carer'). (Note: if this is your only right of residence, you do not satisfy the right to reside requirement for any means-tested benefits (see p1307) and only satisfy it for child benefit if you are working in the UK and you are a national of Morocco, Tunisia, Turkey or, for claims made before 1 January 2021, Algeria or San Marino (see p1310));[209] *or*
- aged under 18 and your primary carer is covered by either the second, third or fourth bullet points above and they would be prevented from residing in the UK if you left the UK, and you do not have leave to enter or remain in the UK (other than under the EUSS – see p1314); *or*
- (not in the EEA Regulations) the primary carer of a child (or, arguably, a dependent adult) with a permanent right to reside, who would be unable to remain in the UK if you left the UK.[210]

9

You are a child's primary carer if they are dependent on you, taking into account all the circumstances, including their best interests.[211] You can have a right to reside as the primary carer if you share equally the responsibility for the child's care with someone else. If this applies, the consequences of your being required to leave the UK are considered on the basis that both you and the other carer left the UK.[212]

The EEA Regulations exclude you from having a derivative right to reside if you are defined as an **'exempt person'**. Included within this definition is if you have a right to reside under any other provision of the EEA Regulations.[213] This exclusion has been held to be unlawful.[214] If you are an EEA national and have been refused UC (or another means-tested benefit) on the basis that you have a right to reside under the EEA Regulations as a jobseeker (which does not satisfy the right to reside requirement for means-tested benefits) and are therefore an 'exempt person' who cannot have a derivative right to reside, you should challenge this decision. Firstly, if you do not have to satisfy the work search and availability requirements (see p948), argue that you are not a jobseeker. Secondly, or if you *are* required to seek work, argue that this exclusion has been held to be unlawful, citing the recent caselaw. See CPAG's *Benefits for Migrants Handbook* for further details.

**Note:** periods with any of the above derivative rights to reside do not count towards the period of residence required for acquiring a permanent right to reside.

## Child in education

For a child in education, and their primary carer, to have a right to reside, there must have been a common period when the child was in the UK and their EEA national parent (or step-parent[215]) was a worker or self-employed person in the UK. The child need not have entered education while the parent (or step-parent) was a worker or self-employed person.[216]

The EEA Regulations only provide for the child (and their primary carer) of a *worker* to have this derivative right to reside. However, the Withdrawal Agreements also provide a right to reside for the child (and their primary carer) of a *self-employed person*.[217] This is confirmed in DWP guidance.[218]

It was recently accepted that a child who came to the UK while their mother was *retaining* worker status during her maternity period (see p1327) had a right to reside once they entered education, as did their primary carer.[219] If you are refused benefit because the EEA Regulations do not provide for the child of an EEA national with retained worker (or self-employed) status to have rights,[220] challenge the decision and ask your adviser to contact CPAG.

These rights also apply if the child was in the UK while their A8, A2 or Croatian national parent (or step-parent) was employed during the period of restrictions, if additional conditions were satisfied or, for A8 nationals only, during the first month of their employment (see p1320).[221]

Your right to reside as a primary carer of a worker's child in education ends when the child reaches 18, unless they continue to need your presence and care to be able to pursue and complete their education.[222]

*Education*

**'Education'** excludes nursery or preschool education, but includes education before the compulsory school age if it is equivalent to that received at or after compulsory school age – eg, education received by a child under five in a school reception class.[223]

Caselaw has held that you do not derive a right to reside from the child if you are the primary carer of a pre-school-age child of a worker.[224]

## Permanent right to reside

You can only have a free movement right to reside, including a permanent right to reside, while you have either pre-settled status or a pending EUSS application. For details of these 'protected groups', see p1317.

While you *are* in one of the protected groups (or for a period before the end of 2020), you can have a permanent right of residence if you have 'resided legally' (see p1339) in the UK for a 'continuous period of five years' (see p1339) or in limited circumstances after a shorter period (see p1340).[225] Once you have this permanent right of residence, you satisfy the right to reside requirement for all benefits that have that requirement.[226]

Once acquired, you only lose your permanent right of residence if you are absent from the UK for more than two consecutive years (but see note below).[227] However, in exceptional circumstances, your residence rights can be revoked or cancelled on grounds of public policy, public security or public health.[228]

Note:

- Arguably, the Withdrawal Agreements provide for a permanent right to reside in the UK to only be lost if you are absent from the UK for more than *five* years (four years under the UK–Swiss Agreement).[229] However, for this to assist, you would need to be in a protected group – ie, to have pre-settled status or a valid pending EUSS application (see p1317) and either may have been affected by an absence of over two years (see next bullet point).
- Until you have been granted settled status, you should get immigration advice before being absent for more than six months in any 12-month period, as it could affect your eligibility for this leave.
- If your circumstances suggest you may have a permanent right to reside, you should check whether you can obtain settled status (see p1314), based on either five years' residence in the UK (whether or not you had a right to reside during that time), or satisfying the requirements for permanent residence in less than five years (see p1340). From the date you are granted settled status, it satisfies the right to reside requirement for all benefits that require it.

## A continuous period of five years

When calculating whether you have five years' continuous residence, temporary absences from the UK do not affect the continuity of your residence (and you can count the time spent abroad as part of your five years[230]) if:[231]

- they are not more than a total of six months a year; *or*
- they comprise one absence of up to 12 consecutive months for important reasons, such as pregnancy and childbirth, serious illness, study or vocational training, or a posting abroad; *or*
- they are for compulsory military service.

If you have a gap during which you remain in the UK but do not have a free movement right to reside, it may be possible to argue it does not break your continuity of residence. Guidance states that cumulative gaps of up to 30 days in any one year do not break your continuity of residence if they are between two periods when you have different residence rights, but not if they separate two periods when you have the same residence right.[232] Refer to this guidance if it is helpful, but remember it is not legally binding.

In most other circumstances, continuous residence during which you are 'residing legally' is required for the whole five years.[233] For how to argue that some periods of residence when you are not 'residing legally' do not interrupt your 'continuity of residence', provided the total period of 'residing legally' is at least five years, see CPAG's *Benefits for Migrants Handbook*.[234]

If you are removed from the UK or subject to a deportation or expulsion order,[235] or if you serve a sentence in prison in circumstances that mean your integration in the UK has been broken,[236] this interrupts the continuity of your residence and you cannot count this time towards your five years.

9

## What counts as 'resided legally'

You have 'resided legally' in any period during which you had a right of residence as a:

- worker (see p1322) (including if you retain your worker status – see p1325); *or*
- self-employed person (see p1324) (including if you retain your self-employed status – see p1325); *or*
- self-sufficient person or student (see p1328); *or*
- jobseeker (see p1321) since 30 April 2006 (see below); *or*
- person with an initial right of residence (see p1321) since 30 April 2006 (see below); *or*
- family member (see p1329) of any of the above.

If you have a continuous period of five years' residence on the basis of one or more of the above, you have a right of permanent residence under both the EEA Regulations and (other than an initial right of residence or as a jobseeker, or family member of either) EU Directive 2004/38.

The **EEA Regulations** require a continuous period of five years of residence 'in accordance with these regulations' (or in accordance with previous regulations), other than with a 'derivative right to reside' (see p1336).[237] This includes periods since 30 April 2006 when you had an initial right to reside or a right to reside as a jobseeker (or family member of either).[238] However, if you have pre-settled status (and are therefore in a protected group – see p1317), the EEA Regulations are amended to simply require you to have resided 'lawfully', which could include periods when you had pre-settled status but did not also have a free movement right to reside.[239]

Under **EU Directive 2004/38**, you must have 'resided legally for a continuous period of five years'.[240] This means that you must have had a residence right under the Directive or under any of the earlier EU legislation that it replaced.[241] This covers all the groups listed above, except for jobseekers and their family members.

You are not counted as having 'resided legally' during periods when your right to reside was as the primary carer of either a worker's child in education or a self-sufficient child,[242] or when your right of residence was only in accordance with UK law – eg, a period when you had leave to remain under the Immigration Rules.[243]

If you are an A8, A2 or a Croatian national, you count as having 'resided legally' during periods before your state joined the EU if you would have come into one of the groups above (other than a jobseeker), or you would have resided in accordance with the EEA Regulations were it not for the fact that you were not an EU national at that time.[244] Once your state joined the EU, the periods when you count as having resided legally are as above, except some of these rights were subject to additional restrictions during the periods when those applied (see p1320).

9

## Family members

If you are a family member (including an extended family member with a relevant EEA Regulation residence document[245]) (see p1329) of an EEA national with a permanent right of residence, you have a right to reside for as long as you continue to both be their family member and be in a protected group (see p1317) that can have free movement residence rights.[246] After five years of being a family member of an EEA national with a permanent right of residence, you acquire a permanent right of residence yourself. You can also add periods as a family member of an EEA national with a permanent right of residence to other periods when you count as 'residing legally' (see p1339) to make up your five years, and so acquire a permanent right of residence.[247]

## Permanent residence in less than five years

If you are in one of the protected groups (see p1317) or for a period before the end of 2020, you can, in the circumstances listed below, acquire a permanent right of residence before five years.[248] If so, you are exempt from the habitual residence test (see p1303).

- You were a worker (see p1322) or self-employed person (see p1324) in the UK, but have now stopped working in the UK and:
  - at the time you stopped working, you had reached pension age or (workers only) taken early retirement and:
    - your spouse or civil partner is a British citizen (or they lost that nationality by marrying you); *or*
    - you worked in the UK for the preceding year and resided (whether or not you had a right to reside[249]) in the UK continuously for more than three years; *or*
  - you stopped working as a result of a permanent incapacity (this means it is not a temporary incapacity (see p1326), but it may follow temporary incapacity – see the note below[250]) and:
    - your spouse or civil partner is a British citizen (or they lost that nationality by marrying you); *or*
    - you have resided (whether or not you had a right to reside[251]) in the UK continuously for more than two years (under the EEA Regulations only, immediately before you stopped working); *or*
    - the incapacity was because of an accident at work or occupational disease that resulted in benefit entitlement eg, industrial injuries disablement benefit; *or*
  - you are a worker or self-employed in an EEA country while residing in the UK and returning, as a rule, at least once a week, following (under the EEA Regulations only, immediately following) three years of continuous employment or self-employment and residence in the UK.
- You are a family member of a worker or self-employed person in any of the above bullet points and both of you are residing in the UK.[252] **Note**: the EEA Regulations require that you had a right to reside on the basis of being their family member at the point they ceased working.[253]
- You are a family member of a worker or self-employed person who died while still working and who did not acquire a permanent right of residence in one of the above ways and:
  - they had lived in the UK for two years; *or*
  - the death resulted from an accident at work or an occupational disease; *or*
  - you lost your UK nationality as a result of marrying them.

Note:

- You can count as periods of employment any period in which you were not working because of illness or accident, or some reason not of your own making, or periods of involuntary unemployment while registered as a jobseeker (arguably, the restriction in the EEA Regulations of this last group to workers is unlawful following the CJEU confirming that self-employed people can also retain status on this basis – see p1325).[254]

- The circumstances above which enable you to acquire a permanent right to reside in less than five years also enable you to be eligible for settled status in less than five years. See p1314 and get immigration advice to assist you to apply to the EUSS on this basis.
- The Upper Tribunal has held that no restrictions were imposed on A8 nationals (see p1320) to limit their rights to permanent residence in under five years.[255]

## Frontier workers

You may have rights as a frontier worker in the UK if you are an EEA national and on 31 December 2020, and continuously since then, you have been 'not primarily resident in the UK', and you have been either:[256]

- a worker in the UK (see p1322); *or*
- a self-employed person in the UK (see p1324); *or*
- you have retained your worker or self-employed status (see p1325).

You are treated as **'not primarily resident in the UK'** if you have either:[257]

- been present in the UK for less than 180 days in the last 12 months; *or*
- returned to your country of residence at least once in the last six months, or at least twice in the last 12 months, unless there are exceptional reasons for you not doing so.

9

The rights that you have as a frontier worker include rights to means-tested benefits without nationality-based discrimination.[258] Consequently, if you are a frontier worker, or if you have pre-settled status and are a family member of a frontier worker, you are exempt from the habitual residence test for all means-tested benefits (see p1303). **Note:** you still have to satisfy all the other entitlement conditions, including the requirement to be present in Great Britain (other than for specified temporary absences – see Chapter 58).[259]

If you are the child of a frontier worker, you and your primary carer have a right to reside in the UK in order for you to complete your education (see p1336).[260]

# 6. Rules for specific benefits

This section explains the residence and presence rules for each benefit. It includes which residence and presence tests apply and how you may be assisted by the European Union (EU) co-ordination rules. Further information on the EU co-ordination rules is in Chapter 59.

For the rules on being paid while you are abroad, see Chapter 58.

For the residence and presence rules that applied for income support, income-based JSA and tax credits, see the 2024/25 edition of this *Handbook*.

## Universal credit and other means-tested benefits

To be entitled to universal credit (UC), income-related employment and support allowance (ESA), pension credit (PC) and housing benefit (HB), you (and your partner, for UC) must:

- be present in Great Britain (although for HB, see below) (see p1298);[261] *and*
- be habitually resident (see p1300), including having a right to reside (see p1306) in the 'common travel area' – ie, the UK, Ireland, Channel Islands and the Isle of Man (unless you are exempt – see p1303).[262]

In certain circumstances, the rules treat you as being present in Great Britain during a temporary absence, so you can continue to receive these benefits while you are abroad for limited periods, or without limit in specific circumstances if you, or your partner or family member, are a Crown servant or member of the armed forces posted abroad (see p1370).

**For UC**, if your partner fails the habitual residence test, your joint claim is treated as a claim for UC as a single person (see below).

To be entitled to the carer element in your UC (see p75), you must satisfy the past presence test as it applies to carer's allowance (CA) or carer support payment (CSP) (see p1347).

Although it is no longer possible to make a new claim for **income related ESA**, if you are already receiving it, you must continue to satisfy the above requirements to remain entitled.

**For HB**, although being present in Great Britain is not a condition of entitlement, going abroad can still affect your entitlement due to the rules on occupying your home (see p1374).

**Council tax reduction** requires you to be habitually resident, including having a right to reside, in the common travel area (unless you are exempt).

**Note:** if you are moving, or have moved, to Great Britain from Northern Ireland or vice versa and are claiming income-related ESA, see p1352.

### Couples claiming universal credit

If you live with your partner and claim UC, you are generally required to make a joint claim, and you and your partner must both satisfy or be exempt from the habitual residence test. If your partner fails the habitual residence test, your joint claim is treated as a claim for UC as a single person and:[263]

- the maximum amount of UC is that for a single person;[264]
- your partner does not have to accept a claimant commitment or comply with any work-related requirements because they are not a claimant;[265]
- your partner's income and capital are taken into account (see p36);[266]

- your partner is not classed as a 'non-dependant' and therefore no 'housing costs contribution' (see p109) is deducted from the maximum amount of UC due to them living with you;[267]
- if you are under 35, your partner does not prevent your rent being restricted to the one-bedroom shared accommodation rate (see p113);[268]
- if you have a child, your partner does not affect you being the child's 'responsible carer' (see p952) to determine your work-related requirements;[269]
- the couple rate of the earnings threshold applies for determining when no work-related requirements apply to you (see p955) and in calculating any self-employed 'minimum income floor' that may apply if you are self-employed (note that the 'minimum income floor' does not apply to your partner if they are self-employed) (see p130).[270]

**Note:** if you have reached pension age and your partner is under pension age but is not entitled to UC because they fail the habitual residence test, your claim is *not* treated as a single claim for UC. Instead, you must claim PC and HB and you are treated as a single person for each of these claims.[271] If your partner subsequently satisfies the habitual residence test before reaching pension age, provided they are not defined as a 'person subject to immigration control' (see p1272), your entitlement to PC and HB ends and you can make a joint claim for UC.

## If your partner is abroad

9

If you have a partner who is abroad, you may continue to receive benefit that includes an amount for them for a limited period if you are only temporarily living apart. The rules vary between the means-tested benefits (see p1370).

If these rules do not apply, or at the end of the limited period in which they do, or before then if their absence means they are no longer habitually resident in the common travel area:

- you cease to be entitled to UC as joint claimants and must notify the DWP. To be entitled to UC, you need to make a new claim. Your award is then based on the maximum amount for a single person, but your partner's income and capital are taken into account (for details, see above) *until* you have been, or you expect to be, apart for six months (as then you cease to be treated as a couple).[272] If you have a joint award at the point you cease to be treated as a couple, you may be treated as having made a single claim (with any award depending on your circumstances – see p45),[273] but to safeguard your entitlment you should make a single claim. However, if you are of pension age, but your partner is under pension age, see p1372;
- your applicable amount for income-related ESA, PC and HB no longer includes an amount for your partner. However, your partner's capital, income and work are still taken into account when working out how much benefit you get. This is because they are still treated as being part of your household, despite

temporarily living away from you, unless you are in any of the situations listed on p257.[274]

Where questions of 'intention' are involved (eg, when deciding whether you or your partner intend to resume living with your family), the intention must be 'unqualified'. This means it must not depend on a factor over which you have no control – eg, the right of entry to the UK being granted by the Home Office,[275] or the offer of a suitable job.[276]

### If your child is abroad

If you have a child who is abroad, your benefit entitlement could be affected if they cease to be treated as part of your household (see p261).[277]

If your child is abroad, they are only included in your maximum amount for UC and PC for a limited period and their absence can also affect your HB (see Chapter 58).

## Bereavement benefits

You must be ordinarily resident (see p1299) in Great Britain on the date your spouse, civil partner or eligible cohabiting partner (see p454) died to be entitled to bereavement support payment.[278]

You do not need to satisfy any residence or presence rules to be entitled to widowed parent's allowance.

### European Union co-ordination rules

If you are covered by any of the sets of EU co-ordination rules (see p1392) and the UK is your competent state (see p1404):[279]

- you can, if necessary, rely on insurance contributions paid by your late spouse, civil partner or eligible cohabiting partner in one or more of the European Economic Area (EEA) states covered by the set of co-ordination rules you are relying on, to calculate your entitlement to bereavement benefits (under the aggregation principle – see p1406); *and*
- for bereavement support payment, the requirement to be ordinarily resident in Great Britain on the date your spouse, civil partner or eligible cohabiting partner died does not apply if you were resident in a relevant country on that date.

### Reciprocal agreements

If you are covered by a reciprocal agreement (see p1297), these can assist in similar ways to the EU co-ordination rules in respect of the relevant country. If the agreement treats you as being present in the UK while in the other country and you were ordinarily resident in that country on the date your spouse, civil partner or eligible cohabiting partner died, you are treated as ordinarily resident in Great Britain on that date.[280] Guidance lists the relevant countries.[281]

## Child benefit, Scottish child payment and guardian's allowance

### Child benefit

To be entitled to child benefit, you and your child must be present in Great Britain (see p1298).[282] To be treated as present, you (but not your child) must also:[283]

- be ordinarily resident in the UK (see p1299); *and*
- have a right to reside in the UK (see p1310), unless your current claim began before 1 May 2004.

You are treated as present if you are:[284]

- a Crown servant posted overseas and:
  - you are, or immediately before your posting abroad you were, ordinarily resident in the UK; *or*
  - immediately before your posting, you were in the UK in connection with that posting; *or*
- the partner of a Crown servant posted overseas and in the same country as them or temporarily absent from that country under the same exceptions that enable child benefit to continue during a temporary absence from Great Britain (see p1376).

You are treated as ordinarily resident if you are in the UK as a result of being deported or legally removed from another country.[285]

You and/or your child can be treated as present for limited periods during a temporary absence (see p1376).

While you are treated as present, you continue to satisfy that condition of entitlement. This means that you can continue to receive child benefit, or you can make a new claim, during your, or your child's, absence. If you, or your child, spend longer abroad than the permitted periods, you (or they) cease to satisfy the presence condition and your entitlement to child benefit ends. **Note:** if you or your child are treated as being present, you must satisfy all the other conditions of entitlement including, if your child is not living with you, contributing to the costs of that child (see p493).

### Scottish child payment

To be entitled to a Scottish child payment, you must be ordinarily resident (see p1299) in Scotland.[286]

### Guardian's allowance

Entitlement to guardian's allowance depends on entitlement to child benefit, so you must meet the conditions for child benefit above.

In addition, at least one of the child's parents must have:[287]

- been born in the UK or an EEA country; *or*

- at some time after reaching the age of 16, spent a total of 52 weeks in any two-year period in Great Britain.

To satisfy the second condition above, you are treated as being present in Great Britain during any absence abroad due to your employment as a serving member of the armed forces, an aircraft worker, mariner or continental shelf worker.

### European Union co-ordination rules

If the main EU co-ordination rules, or, for situations involving the UK and Ireland only, the UK–Ireland Convention, apply to you (see p1392), you may be able to:

- be paid child benefit and guardian's allowance for a child who is resident in an EEA country (Ireland, if relying on the Convention) without them needing to satisfy the rules on temporary absences, provided you satisfy all the other conditions of entitlement, including contributing to the costs of the child (see p493). These rules can apply, as these benefits are classed as 'family benefits' (see p1409). This does not apply to Scottish child benefit as it has been categorised as a special non-contributory benefit (see p1403);
- use time spent in one or more EEA states (Ireland, if relying on the Convention) to satisfy the requirement for guardian's allowance that one of the child's parents has spent 52 weeks in any two-year period in Great Britain (under the 'aggregation principle' – see p1406). It may also be arguable that this condition should not apply if you have a 'genuine and sufficient link to the UK' (see p1351).[288]

**Note**: the UK–EU Protocol and UK–EFTA Convention cannot assist in the above ways as they do not cover family benefits.

9

## Disability and carers' benefits

To be entitled to attendance allowance (AA), pension age disability payment (PADP), disability living allowance (DLA), child disability payment (CDP), Scottish adult disability living allowance (SADLA), personal independence payment (PIP), adult disability payment (ADP), CA and CSP you must:[289]

- be present in Great Britain (the common travel area (see p1300) for PADP, CDP, SADLA, ADP and CSP, England and Wales for DLA for a child); *and*
- satisfy the 'past presence test' (see also the exceptions below) by having been present in:
  - (PADP, CDP, SADLA, ADP and CSP only) the common travel area for at least 26 weeks in the last 52;
  - (DLA only) Great Britain for at least 26 weeks in the last 52;[290]
  - (PIP, AA and CA) Great Britain for at least 104 weeks in the last 156 – see also note on CA on p1348; *and*
- be habitually resident in the common travel area (see p1300, but also the exemptions on p1348); *and*

- (PADP, CDP, SADLA, ADP and CSP only) be ordinarily resident in Scotland.

In relation to the past presence test, note the following.

- If a DLA or CDP claim is for a **child under three**, the past presence test is reduced to 13 weeks if the claimant is a baby under six months old, and that continues to apply until the child is 12 months old. For a DLA or CDP claim when a child is aged six months to 36 months, the past presence test is 26 weeks in the last 156 weeks for DLA, or in the last 52 weeks for CDP.[291]
- (For CA only) arguably, the past presence test must be aligned with that of DLA or CDP if you are caring for a child awarded DLA or CDP after being present for 26 weeks in the last 52. See cpag.org.uk/dla-two-year-past-presence-test for template letter.
- (For **CDP, ADP or PADP** only) if you do not satisfy the past presence test (or other residence and presence requirements), but will within 13 weeks (or, for PADP only, 26 weeks), your claim may be treated as an advance claim from the date you satisfy this requirement.[292]
- (For **CSP** only) if you do not satisfy the past presence test (or other residence and presence requirements), but you will do within 13 weeks, it is expected that, from September 2025, your claim may be treated as an advance claim from that date.[293] Until then, arguably your claim may be treated as an advance claim from a future date on which you satisfy the residence and presence requirements, but the law is unclear.[294] You should therefore make a further claim once you do satisfy the requirements, and get advice if your first claim is not accepted as an advance claim.
- If you are covered by an exemption from the past presence test, you do not need to satisfy it (see below).

9

To be entitled to the **carer's allowance supplement**, you must be in receipt of CA or CSP, and resident (see p1299) in Scotland on the qualifying date (see p1475).[295]

To qualify for a **young carer grant**, on the day of your application, you must be:[296]

- ordinarily resident (see p1299) in Scotland; *and*
- habitually resident in the UK, Channel Islands, Isle of Man or the EEA (see p1301) or be exempt from this requirement (see p1303).

## When you can be treated as present

You are treated as being present during certain absences (see p1378). Any period when you are treated as present can be counted to satisfy both the presence and the past presence tests.

## Exemptions from habitual residence and past presence test

For AA, PADP, DLA, CDP, SADLA, PIP, ADP, CA and CSP, the past presence test and habitual residence requirement do not apply if you:[297]

- have refugee leave or humanitarian protection (or you have leave as the dependent family member of someone who has such leave); *or*
- have leave by virtue of the Afghan Relocations and Assistance Policy (ARAP) or the scheme for locally employed staff in Afghanistan (LES Scheme) or discretionary leave as the dependant of a person with leave under either, or leave granted under the Afghan Citizens Resettlement Scheme;[298] *or*
- were living in Ukraine immediately before 1 January 2022 and you left in connection with the Russian invasion of 24 February 2022, and have leave, or a right of abode, in the UK (including if you are British), or you are Irish;[299] *or*
- were living in Sudan before 15 April 2023 and left in connection with the violence since that date, and have leave, or a right of abode, in the UK (including if you are British), or you are Irish;[300] *or*
- were living in Israel, the West Bank, the Gaza Strip, East Jerusalem, the Golan Heights or Lebanon immediately before 7 October 2023 and you left in connection with the violence on or since that date, and have leave, or a right of abode, in the UK (including if you are British), or you are Irish;[301] *or*
- (except CA) (exemption from past presence test only) are terminally ill. For CSP, this exemption only applies if you receive a disability benefit or UC or ESA by virtue of being terminally ill; *or*
- (CSP only) are caring for a person to whom the past presence test does not apply due to the co-ordination rules on p1350; *or*
- (treated as meeting the presence and past presence conditions only) are abroad as an aircraft worker, mariner or continental shelf worker; *or*
- (AA, DLA, PIP and CA only) (exempt from the habitual residence test only, but also treated as present in Great Britain for the purpose of both the presence and past presence conditions) are abroad as a serving member of the armed forces, or are living with someone who is abroad as a serving member of the armed forces and they are your spouse, civil partner, child, stepchild, or parent, step-parent, parent-in-law; *or*
- (for PADP, ADP, CDP, SADLA and CSP only) are abroad as a serving member of the armed forces or as a civil servant, provided you satisfied the residence and presence requirements (other than the past presence test) immediately before the start of this employment outside the common travel area, or you are living with someone who is abroad as a serving member of the armed forces or civil servant, and they are your spouse, civil partner (or living together as if you were either), or child or stepchild, or child in their care or, other than for CDP, parent, step-parent or parent-in-law. You are also treated as present and ordinarily resident.

Note:

- (CSP only) the past presence test does not apply if one of the first six bullets above applies to the person you care for.[302]

- If you are prevented from making a PIP phone claim because the call handler does not accept that one of the above exemptions applies to you, see p676.

## European Union co-ordination rules

If you are covered by (see p1392) the main EU co-ordination rules or, for situations involving the UK and Ireland only, the UK–Ireland Convention, or for situations involving the UK and Gibraltar only, the agreement between the UK and Gibraltar:

- the UK must be your '**competent state**' (see the first note below) for you:[303]
  - to be entitled to PADP, AA, PIP/ADP daily living component, DLA/CDP/SADLA care component, CA or CSP;
  - while habitually resident in a member state (see p1389), to make a new claim for, or continue to be entitled to, a young carer grant or carer's allowance supplement;
- you may be entitled to AA, PADP, DLA, CDP, SADLA, PIP, ADP, CA and CSP sooner, either because the past presence test does not apply to you (see below) or because periods of residence in a member state can be used to satisfy the test – under the aggregation principle (p1406);[304]
- you may be entitled to the mobility component of PIP, ADP, DLA, SADLA or CDP, even if the UK is not your competent state, because the competent state requirement does not apply to the mobility components – ie, you may be entitled to the mobility component but not the daily living or care component. You may be entitled sooner than you would otherwise be (see the above bullet point);
- you may be able to make a new claim for AA/PADP, DLA/CDP care component, PIP/ADP daily living component, CA, CSP, young carer grant and carer's allowance supplement if you live in a member state (see p1379);
- if you have moved to the UK from a member state, you may continue to receive a sickness or invalidity benefit (or long-term care benefit, if relying on the UK–Ireland Convention) (known as 'exporting' the benefit – see p1408), if that state continues to be the competent state to pay that benefit.

Note:

- For information on 'competent state', see p1404, and note that the UK might not be your competent state if you (or your family member who brings you within the co-ordination rules) receive a contributory benefit (classed as a 'pension') paid by a member state.
- If you are only covered by the UK–EU Protocol or the UK–EFTA Convention, these do not affect your entitlement in the ways above because they do not cover disability and carers' benefits.[305]

### When the past presence test does not apply

The past presence test does not apply to AA, PADP, DLA, CDP, SADLA, PIP, ADP, CA and CSP if:[306]

- you are habitually resident in Great Britain (the UK, for CDP, ADP, PADP, SADLA and CSP); *and*
- the main co-ordination rules apply to you (or, for CDP, ADP, PADP, SADLA and CSP only, the agreement with Gibraltar) (see p1392); *and*
- (other than CDP, ADP, PADP, SADLA or CSP) you can demonstrate 'a genuine and sufficient link' to the UK (see below).

**Note:**

- For CSP only, the past presence test does not apply to you if the person you are caring for receives a qualifying disability benefit as a result of the past presence test being disapplied under the rules above.[307]
- If you are not, or no longer, covered by the Withdrawal Agreement protections (see p1393), but you are covered by the *partial* Withdrawal Agreement protections (see p1395), the second bullet point above should be accepted as applying to you. The Upper Tribunal recently focused on the word 'applies' when it accepted the DWP submission that a PIP claimant was covered by the Withdrawal Agreement protections and held the past presence test therefore did not apply.[308] However, if possible, also argue that you can aggregate periods of residence in an EEA state with periods of presence in Great Britain (or the common travel area for ADP, CDP, PADP, SADLA and CSP) and thereby satisfy the past presence test (under the 'aggregation principle' – see p1406).

***Do you have a genuine and sufficient link?***

Factors that are relevant when demonstrating that you have a 'genuine and sufficient link to the UK' (for Scottish benefits, see the note below) can include:[309]

- whether you have worked in the UK;
- whether you have spent a significant part of your life in the UK;
- whether you have been present in the UK for a reasonable period;
- whether you are receiving a UK contributory benefit;
- evidence of your motives, intentions and expectations;
- the benefit you are claiming, and if you are claiming a disability benefit, whether your carer would be entitled to CA or CSP;
- the duration of your presence in Great Britain;
- whether you are dependent on a family member who has worked in the UK and/or who receives a UK contributory benefit. 'Family member' in this context is not limited to people covered by the definition of 'member of the family' in the co-ordination rules (see p1399) and can, for example, include your sister.[310]

**Note:** the requirement to demonstrate a 'genuine and sufficient link to Scotland' for specific elements of the residence and presence requirements for CDP, ADP, PADP, SADLA and CSP, child winter heating payment, pension age winter heating payment, CA supplement and young carer grant, must be interpreted in a way that is consistent with the caselaw referred to above, but in relation to Scotland.

## Contributory employment and support allowance

To be entitled to contributory ESA, you must be in Great Britain.[311] For the rules on when you can be paid during a temporary absence, see p1373. There are no residence conditions, except for contributory ESA in youth (see the 2017/18 edition of this *Handbook* or CPAG's *Benefits for Migrants Handbook*).

### European Union co-ordination rules

If you are covered by any of the EU co-ordination rules (see p1392) and the UK is your competent state (see p1404), you can, if necessary, rely on insurance contributions paid in one or more of the EEA states covered by the set of co-ordination rules you are relying on, to entitle you to contributory ESA in the UK (under the aggregation principle – see p1406).

You may also be able to 'export' (ie, continue to receive) a 'sickness' or (unless you are only covered by the UK–EU Protocol or the UK–EFTA Convention) 'invalidity' benefit from an EEA state covered by the set of rules you are relying on to the UK (see p1408).

### Reciprocal agreements

If you have lived and worked in a country with which the UK has a reciprocal agreement (see p1297), you may be able to count periods of insurance paid in that country towards your entitlement to contributory ESA in the UK.

If you have moved from Northern Ireland to Great Britain (or vice versa), reciprocal arrangements mean your ESA (both income-related and contributory) should be paid at the same rate.[312]



## Industrial injuries benefits

To be entitled to any of the industrial injuries benefits, you must have:

- been in Great Britain when the accident at work happened;[313] *or*
- been engaged in Great Britain in the employment that caused the disease (even if you have also been engaged outside Great Britain in that employment);[314] *or*
- been paying UK class 1 or class 2 national insurance contributions when the accident at work happened or you contracted the disease. Benefit is not payable until you return to Great Britain.[315]

There are exceptions, which mean that you can qualify for benefit in respect of an accident that happens, or a disease that is contracted, outside Great Britain while you are:[316]

- employed as a mariner or aircraft worker; *or*
- employed as an apprentice pilot on board a ship or vessel; *or*
- on board an aircraft on a test flight starting in Great Britain in the course of your employment.

In these cases, there are also more generous rules for defining when accidents arise 'out of and in the course of' your employment, and for complying with time limits under benefit rules.[317]

### European Union co-ordination rules

If you are covered by any of the sets of EU co-ordination rules (see p1392) and the UK is your competent state (see p1404), you can, if necessary, rely on periods of employment and insurance contributions paid in one or more of the EEA states covered by the set of co-ordination rules you are relying on to qualify for industrial injuries benefits in the UK (under the aggregation principle – see p1406).

If you have an accident while travelling abroad in an EEA state covered by the rules you are relying on, this can be deemed to have occurred in the state liable to pay industrial injuries benefits.[318] If you have worked in two or more member states in a job that gave you a prescribed industrial disease, you get benefit from the state in which you last did work that, by its nature, is likely to cause that disease and which recognises that disease under its industrial injuries scheme.[319]

## New-style jobseeker's allowance

To be entitled to new-style JSA, you must be in Great Britain.[320] For the rules on when you can be paid during a temporary absence, see p1381. There are no residence conditions.

### European Union co-ordination rules

In most cases, if you are covered by any of the sets of EU co-ordination rules (see p1392), you may be able to count insurance contributions paid in one or more EEA states to entitle you to new-style JSA in the UK (under the 'aggregation principle'). However, this is usually only possible if your most recent period of paying, or being credited with, contributions was in the UK (see p1406).[321]

If you are covered by the main co-ordination rules, you have been working in an EEA state and are coming, or returning, to the UK to look for work, before you leave you may be able to obtain a U2 form authorising you to export your unemployment benefit from that EEA state. If you are covered by the UK–Ireland Convention and have been working in Ireland, you may be able to export your Irish unemployment benefit. In either situation, you can continue to receive that unemployment benefit for up to three months if:[322]

- you were getting it immediately before coming to the UK; *and*
- you have been registered as available for work for four weeks (or less, if that state's rules allow) in the other state; *and*
- you claim JSA within seven days after you were last registered in the other member state; *and*
- you satisfy the relevant jobseeking requirements for JSA.

The three months can be extended to a maximum of six months if the state from which you are claiming the unemployment benefit agrees.[323]

You cannot 'export' unemployment benefit under either the UK–EU Protocol or the UK–EFTA Convention.[324]

### Reciprocal agreements

If you have lived and worked in a country with which the UK has a reciprocal agreement (see p1297), you may be able to count periods of insurance paid in that country towards your entitlement to new-style JSA. If you are covered by the agreements between Great Britain and Northern Ireland, you can be treated as in Great Britain if you go to Northern Ireland (see p1381).

## Maternity allowance

Entitlement to maternity allowance (MA) is based on past employment, generally in Great Britain.[325] There are no residence requirements. However, in general you are disqualified if you are absent from Great Britain.[326] See p1382 for the rules allowing you to be paid during a temporary absence.

### European Union co-ordination rules

If any of the EU co-ordination rules apply to you (see p1392) and the UK is your competent state (see p1404), you can, if necessary, rely on periods of employment or self-employment in one or more of the EEA states covered by the set of co-ordination rules you are relying on to qualify for MA in the UK (under the aggregation principle – see p1406). You may also be able to 'export' (ie, continue to receive) a maternity or paternity benefit from a relevant EEA state (see p1408).

9

## Retirement pensions

Retirement pensions, other than category D retirement pension, do not have any residence or presence entitlement conditions. They can be paid without a time limit, whether or not you are present in Great Britain. However, going abroad can mean you are not paid the annual uprating, can be relevant to decisions on deferring your retirement and can prevent you from 'de-retiring' while you are abroad (see p1383).[327]

To be entitled to a category D retirement pension, you must have been:[328]

- resident in Great Britain for at least 10 years in any continuous period of 20 years ending on or after your 80th birthday; *and*
- ordinarily resident (see p1299) in Great Britain on either:
  - your 80th birthday; *or*
  - the date on which you claimed category D pension, if later.

### European Union co-ordination rules

If you are covered by any of the sets of EU co-ordination rules (see p1392) and the UK is your 'competent state' (see p1404), you can, if necessary, rely on insurance contributions paid, or for category D retirement pension certain periods of residence completed, in one or more of the EEA states covered by the set of co-ordination rules you are relying on to calculate your entitlement to retirement pensions in the UK (and one or more of the relevant EEA states) (under the aggregation principle – see below and p1406). You may receive pension payments from the UK and one or more member states, because your total award may be made in proportions that reflect the proportion of years of contributions paid, or periods of residence completed, in the UK and other member states, out of the total years of contributions paid or periods of residence completed in all states.[329]

Even if you are not, or no longer, covered by the Withdrawal Agreement protections:

- you may be able to rely on the aggregation principle of the main co-ordination rules if you are covered by the *partial* Withdrawal Agreement protections (see p1395);[330]
- the main co-ordination rules on aggregating insurance contributions for entitlement to, and uprating of, UK retirement pensions continue to apply even if you are not covered by the Withdrawal Agreement protections;[331]
- rules on aggregation and uprating exported old age pensions are contained in the UK–EU Protocol and the UK–EFTA Convention. Although neither applies to Switzerland, the UK has a bilateral agreement with Switzerland that covers retirement pensions.[332] Also, the main co-ordination rules may continue to apply due to the two bullet points above.

The requirement to be ordinarily resident in Great Britain for a category D retirement pension does not apply to you if, on the relevant date, you were ordinarily resident in an EEA country and were covered by any of the Withdrawal Agreements or sets of co-ordination rules.[333]

You may also be able to 'export' (ie, continue to receive) an old age pension from an EEA state (see p1408).

### Reciprocal agreements

If you have lived and worked in a country with which the UK has a reciprocal agreement (see p1297), you may be able to count periods of residence or insurance paid in that country towards your UK retirement pension entitlement.

## Social fund and other payments

### Funeral payments

To qualify for a **funeral support payment** in Scotland, you must be ordinarily resident (see p1299) in Scotland on the date you make your application.[334]

To qualify for a **funeral expenses payment** from the social fund, you must live in England or Wales.[335]

To qualify for either a **funeral expenses payment** or a **funeral support payment**:

- the person who has died must have been ordinarily resident (see p1299) in the UK at the date of death (this does not apply in Scotland if they were a stillborn child);[336] *and*
- the funeral must usually take place in the UK. However, it can take place outside the UK if there are exceptional circumstances that merit a funeral support payment, or, for either payment, in any EEA state or the UK if you or your partner:[337]
  - (funeral expenses payment only) are an EEA national with a right to reside as a worker (see p1322) or self-employed (see p1324), including if you have retained either status (see p1325), or are a family member of such an EEA national (see p1329), or have a permanent right of residence acquired in less than five years (see p1340); *or*
  - (funeral support payment only) have pre-settled status or settled status granted under the EUSS, or an outstanding valid application for either, or came to the UK to join your family member who is an EEA national who began living in the UK before the end of 2020 (see p1314), or had one of the residence rights in the above bullet point before the end of 2020; *or*
  - arguably, for funeral expenses payment, are a person with any other free movement right of residence in the UK.[338]

To qualify for a **children's funeral fund payment** in England, the funeral must take place in England for a child aged under 18 or stillborn.[339] To qualify for a **children's funeral payment** in Wales, the family home must be in Wales.[340] There are no residence (or immigration status) requirements for either payment.

9

### Maternity grant payments

To qualify for a **Sure Start maternity grant** from the social fund, you must live in England or Wales.[341]

To qualify for a **Best Start grant**, you must be ordinarily resident (see p1299) in Scotland.[342] In addition, if neither you nor your partner receive a qualifying benefit (see p1459), but you qualify for a grant because you are aged under 20 (see p1459):[343]

- you must be habitually resident (see p1300) in the UK, Channel Islands or Isle of Man; *or*
- you or your partner must be habitually resident in the EEA *and* have a right to reside in the UK either as a 'qualified person' (see p1318) or a family member (see p1329) (other than an extended family member) of a qualified person or EEA national with a permanent right to reside (see p1338), or have settled or pre-settled status under the EUSS (see p1314). **Note:** from September 2025, it is expected that these requirements will be amended so that if you or your partner are habitually resident in the EEA, you will need to have settled or pre-settled status, or a pending valid application for either, or have come to the UK within the last three months to join an EEA national who was living in the UK

by 31 December 2020, was your family member on that date and remains your family member;[344] *or*
- you must be exempt from this habitual residence test (see p1303).

## Winter fuel and heating payments

To qualify for a **winter fuel payment**, you must be ordinarily resident (see p1299) in England or Wales on any day in the qualifying week and satisfy the other rules (see p715).[345]

To qualify for a **winter heating payment,** you must be resident (see p1299) in Scotland on any day (including the last day) in the qualifying week and satisfy the other rules (see p1505).[346]

To qualify for a **pension age winter heating payment** you must be ordinarily resident in Scotland on any day in the qualifying week and satisfy the other rules (see p1507).[347]

To qualify for a **cold weather payment**, your home must be in England or Wales and you must satisfy the other rules (see p714).[348]

To qualify for **child winter heating payment**, you must, in addition to satisfying the other rules (see p1506), on any day in the qualifying week be:[349]
- resident (see p1299) in Scotland; *or*
- habitually resident (see p1300) in an EEA country (other than Cyprus, France, Greece, Malta, Portugal or Spain) *and* have a 'genuine and sufficient link' to Scotland (see p1351).

### European Union co-ordination rules

You are not required to be ordinarily resident in England or Wales to be entitled to a **winter fuel payment**, or ordinarily resident in Scotland to be entitled to a **pension age winter heating payment**, if, on any day in the qualifying week, you are:[350]
- covered by either the Withdrawal Agreement protections (see p1393) or the UK–Ireland Convention (see p1397); *and*
- habitually resident in an EEA country (other than Cyprus, France, Gibraltar, Greece, Malta, Portugal or Spain); *and*
- (or your partner is) entitled to a benefit in that EEA country that is equivalent to a qualifying benefit; *and*
- able to demonstrate a 'genuine and sufficient link' to the UK for a winter fuel payment, or to Scotland for a pension age wither heating payment; *and*
- (pension age winter heating payment only) the UK is the competent state.

Winter fuel payments are not covered by the UK–EU Protocol or the UK–EFTA Convention or, other than to overcome the requirement to be ordinarily resident in Great Britain as above, the UK–Ireland Convention.[351]

# Notes

**2. The different residence and presence tests**

1 R(IS) 6/96, para 19; CPC/1035/2005; see also *TC v SSWP (JSA)* [2017] UKUT 222 (AAC)
2 R(M) 1/85
3 *R v Barnet LBC ex parte Shah* [1983] 2 AC 309; *GC v HMRC (TC)* [2014] UKUT 251 (AAC); *Arthur v HMRC* [2017] EWCA Civ 1756, paras 16, 31 and 32
4 *MS v SSWP (DLA)* [2016] UKUT 42 (AAC)

**3. Habitual residence**

5 **UC** Reg 9 UC Regs
**ESA** Regs 69 and 70 ESA Regs
**PC** Reg 2 SPC Regs
**HB** Reg 10 HB Regs; reg 10 HB(SPC) Regs
**AA** Reg 2(1)(a)(i) SS(AA) Regs
**PIP** Reg 16(c) SS(PIP) Regs
**DLA** Reg 2(1)(a)(i) SS(DLA) Regs
**CA** Reg 9(1)(a) SS(ICA) Regs
**PADP** Reg 9(3)(a) DAOP(S) Regs
**SADLA** Reg 10(1)(b) DA(SADLA) Regs
**ADP** Reg 15(1)(b) DAWAP(S) Regs
**CDP** Reg 5(1)(b) DACYP(S) Regs
**CSP** Reg 6(1)(b) CA(CSP)(S) Regs
6 Reg 12 CTRS(PR)E Regs; reg 16 CTR(SPC)S Regs; reg 16 CTR(S) Regs; reg 28 CTRSPR(W) Regs; Sch para 19 CTRS(DS)W Regs
7 Regs 3(3), 18(2), 22(3) and 36(3) UC Regs; reg 9(1) UC,PIP,JSA&ESA(C&P) Regs
8 **UC** Reg 9 UC Regs
**PC** Reg 2 SPC Regs
9 Regs 69 and 70 and Sch 5 para 11 ESA Regs
10 Reg 10(1) HB Regs; reg 10(1) HB(SPC) Regs
11 **AA** s35(1) Social Security Act 1975; reg 2(1) SS(AA) Regs
**PADP** Regs 3 and 9(1)(b) DAOP(S) Regs
**DLA** s71(6) SSCBA 1992; reg 2(1) SS(DLA) Regs
**CDP** regs 3 and 5(1)(b) DACYP(S) Regs
**CSP** Regs 3 and 6(1)(b) CA(CSP)(S) Regs
**SADLA** Regs 3 and 10(1)(b) DA(SADLA) Regs
**PIP** s77(3) WRA 2012; reg 16 SS(PIP) Regs
**ADP** Regs 3 and 15(1)(b) DAWAP(S) Regs
**CA** s70(4) SSCBA 1992; reg 9(1) SS(ICA) Regs
**YCG** regs 3 and 8 CA(YCG)(S) Regs
**BSG** Sch 1 paras 1(c) and 4 EYA(BSG)(S) Regs
12 See, for example, *GE v SSWP (ESA)* [2017] UKUT 145 (AAC), reported as [2017] AACR 34, paras 52-58, and *SSWP v KK (JSA)* [2019] UKUT 313 (AAC), para 8
13 R(IS) 6/96
14 Confirmed in para A1340 ADM and para 01343 DMG
15 **UC** Reg 9(4) UC Regs
**ESA** Reg 70(4) ESA Regs
**PC** Reg 2(4) SPC Regs
**HB** Reg 10(3B) HB Regs
16 See also ADM Memo 14/21 and DMG Memo 11/21
17 See also ADM Memo 11/22 and DMG Memo 8/22 and HB Circular A4/2022
18 See also ADM Memo 10/23; DMG Memo 5/23; HB Circular A6/2023
19 See also ADM Memo 17/23; DMG Memo 11/23; HB Circular A7/2023
20 Reg 8(2) CA(YCG)(S) Regs
21 Sch 2 para 4(1)(b) and (2) EYA(BSG)(S) Regs

22 **AA** Regs 2(2) and (3A), and 2C SS(AA) Regs
**PADP** Regs 9(7), 11 and 15 DAOP(S) Regs
**SADLA** Regs 10(7), 12 and 17 DA(SADLA) Regs
**DLA** Regs 2(2) and (3A), and 2C SS(DLA) Regs
**CDP** Reg 5(6)-(7) and (10A)-(11) DACYP(S) Regs
**PIP** Regs 19, 20 and 23A SS(PIP) Regs
**ADP** Regs 15(7)-(8) and 17 DAWAP(S) Regs
**CA** Regs 9(3) and 9C SS(ICA) Regs
**CSP** Regs 6(6)-(9) and 8 CA(CSP)(S) Regs
23 See also ADM Memo 14/21 and DMG Memo 11/21; and confirming the narrow scope of this exempt group, see *HRA v SSWP (PIP)* [2023] UKUT 109 (AAC)
24 R(IS) 6/96, paras 17 and 20; CIS/13498/96, para 17
25 CIS/15927/1996
26 *R v Barnet LBC ex parte Shah* [1983] 2 AC 309, para 344; CIS/13498/1996
27 R(IS) 2/00; CIS/4474/2003
28 *Nessa v Chief Adjudication Officer* [1999] UKHL 41
29 CIS/4474/2003
30 CIS/1972/2003
31 CIS/1304/97; CJSA/5394/98
32 CIS/1304/1997; CJSA/5394/1998
33 HB/CTB Circular A2/2024
34 Art 70 EU Reg 883/04; Art 10a EU Reg 1408/71; *Swaddling v Adjudication Officer*, C-90/97 [1999]
35 CIS/12703/1996
36 *KS v SSWP (SPC)* [2010] UKUT 156 (AAC); see also *TC v SSWP (JSA)* [2017] UKUT 222 (AAC)
37 R(IS) 2/00; CIS/11481/1995; *SSWP v KK (JSA)* [2019] UKUT 313 (AAC), para 8

4. **Right to reside**

38 Reg 12 CTRS(PR)E Regs; reg 16 CTR(SPC)S Regs; reg 16 CTR(S) Regs; reg 28 CTRSPR(W) Regs; Sch para 19 CTRS(DS)W Regs
39 **UC** Reg 9(3) UC Regs
**ESA** Reg 70(2) and (3) ESA Regs
**PC** Reg 2(2) and (3) SPC Regs
**HB** Reg 10(3) and (3A) HB Regs; reg 10(3) and (4) HB(SPC) Regs
40 To date all legal challenges to this exclusion have failed – most recently, *R (on the application of HC) v SSWP and Others* [2017] UKSC 73
41 *Slezak v SSWP* [2017] CSIH 4, reported as [2017] AACR 21
42 **UC** Reg 9(3)(c)(i) UC Regs
**ESA** Reg 70(3A)(a) ESA Regs
**PC** Reg 2(3A)(a) SPC Regs
**HB** Reg 10(3AA)(a) HB Regs; reg 10(4ZA)(a) HB(SPC) Regs
43 s3ZA IA 1971
44 **UC** Reg 9(3A) UC Regs
**ESA** Reg 70(3B) ESA Regs
**PC** Reg 2(3B) SPC Regs
**HB** Reg 10(3AB) HB Regs; reg 10(4ZB) HB(SPC) Regs, confirmed in ADM Memo 19/20 and DMG Memo 17/20
45 Appendix EU, Annex 1, IR; see also ADM Memo 19/20, para 10, and DMG Memo 17/20, para 10
46 *SSWP v AT (Aire Centre and IMA Intervening)* [2023] EWCA Civ 1307
47 *SSWP v AT (Aire Centre and IMA Intervening)* [2022] UKUT 330 (AAC) – applying *CG v Department for Communities NI*, C-709/20 [2021], paras 84-93
48 Art 1 EU Charter of Fundamental Rights
49 *SSWP v AT (Aire Centre and IMA Intervening)* [2022] UKUT 330 (AAC), paras 126 and 127; DMG Memo 5/24, paras 11 and 13; ADM Memo 6/24, paras 12 and 15; HB Circular A10/2024, para 14
50 ADM Memo 6/24, para 14; HB Circular A10/2024, para 18
51 HB Circular A10/2024, para 24
52 DMG Memo 5/24, paras 2, 5 and 11; ADM Memo 6/24, paras 2, 5 and 12. At the time of writing, HB Circular A10/2024 had not been revised
53 Art 10 WA 2019
54 *Hynek v LB Islington (Aire Centre and The 3 Million intervening)*, claim ref K40CL206, paras 55 and 61-64
55 DMG Memo 5/24, para 11; ADM Memo 6/24, para 12; HB Circular A10/2024, para 15
56 This depends on the interpretation of Art 18(3) WA
57 *Hynek v LB Islington (Aire Centre and The 3Million intervening)*, claim ref K40CL206, paras 33-79
58 *Fertre v Vale of White Horse DC* [2024] EWHC 1754 (KB)
59 Case ref CA-2024-001773, listed for hearing 14 May 2025
60 Reg 6 SS(HR)A Regs; reg 11 SS(PA)A Regs; see also *AP v SSWP (IS)* [2018] UKUT 307 (AAC)
61 Reg 23(4) CB Regs

62 Reg 23(4) CB Regs
63 Reg 23(4) CB Regs
64 Regs 1(3) and 23(4)(b) and (4A) CB Regs; *HMRC v HEH and SSWP (TC and CHB)* [2018] UKUT 237 (AAC)
65 Most recently, *R (on the application of HC) v SSWP and others* [2017] UKSC 73
66 Regs 1(3) and 23(4B) CB Regs

67 *S v Familienkasse Niedersachsen-Bremen der Bundesagentur für Arbeit* C-411/20 [2022]; Art 4 EU Reg 883/04; Art 24 EU Dir 2004/38

5. **Who has a right to reside**
68 s3ZA IA 1971
69 Arts 2(e), 126 and 127 WA 2019; ss1A, 1B, 8A and Sch 2 Part 1A EU(W)A 2018
70 ss1A-1B EU(W)A 2018
71 Appendices EU and EU (Family Permit), IR
72 Reg 2 CR(ADTP) Regs; Art 18 WA 2019; Art 17 UK-EFTA; Art 16 UK-SA
73 Art 18(1)(b) WA 2019; Art 17(1)(b) UK-EFTA; Art 16(1)(b) UK-SA
74 gov.uk/government/publications/eu-settlement-scheme-euss-status-automation
75 Confirmed in para C1871 ADM; Vol 2, Chp7, part 3, para 073491 DMG; HB Circular A7/2019, para 9
76 Regs 6 and 14(1) I(EEA) Regs. The same groups are covered in Arts 7 and 14 EU Dir 2004/38 but the term 'qualified person' is not used in the Directive.
77 For example, see *SSWP v JB (JSA)* [2011] UKUT 96 (AAC)
78 ss2-5 EU(W)A 2018
79 s1 and Sch 1 ISSCA 2020; reg 4 ISSCA(C) Regs
80 ss7A-7C EU(W)A 2018; Art 4 WA 2019; Art 4 UK-EFTA; Art 4 UK-SA
81 Part 2 WA 2019; Part 2 UK-EFTA; UK-SA
82 ISSC Regs; CR(ADTP) Regs
83 For a helpful discussion, see *Geci (EEA Regs: transitional provisions, appeal rights) Albania* [2021] UKUT 285 (IAC)
84 s6 EU(W)A 2018; The European Union (Withdrawal) Act 2018 (Relevant Court) (Retained EU Case Law) Regulations 2020 No.1525
85 Arts 2 and 4 WA 2019; Arts 2 and 4 UK-EFTA; Art 4 UK-SA
86 Art 158 WA 2019
87 Swiss nationals: *Agreement between the European Community and its Member States, of the one part, and the Swiss Confederation, of the other, on the Free Movement of Persons*, 21 June 1999, Cmd 5639. In force from 1 June 2002.
88 Reg 2(1) I(EEA) Regs
89 **Croatia** AC(IWA) Regs
**A2** A(IWA) Regs
**A8** A(IWR) Regs; *SSWP v Gubeladze* [2019] UKSC 31
90 Reg 13(1) I(EEA) Regs; Art 6(1) EU Dir 2004/38
91 Reg 13(2) and (3) I(EEA) Regs; Art 6(2) EU Dir 2004/38
92 *GE v SSWP (ESA)* [2017] UKUT 145 (AAC), reported as [2017] AACR 34
93 Art 45 TFEU; Arts 14 and 24 EU Dir 2004/38; reg 6 I(EEA) Regs
94 *The Queen v Immigration Appeal Tribunal, ex parte Antonissen*, C-292/89 [1991]
95 **Croatia** Reg 5 AC(IWA) Regs
**A2** Reg 6 A(IWA) Regs
**A8** Regs 4(2) and (4) and 5(2) A(IWR) Regs
96 Reg 6(1) and (5) I(EEA) Regs
97 *The Queen v Immigration Appeal Tribunal, ex parte Antonissen*, C-292/89 [1991]
98 *GMA v État belge*, C-710/19 [2020]
99 R(IS) 8/08
100 *GE v SSWP (ESA)* [2017] UKUT 145 (AAC), reported as [2017] AACR 34, para 46; see also *Cardiff CC v HM (HB)* [2019] UKUT 271 (AAC), paras 6 and 18, and *SSWP v KK (JSA)* [2019] UKUT 313 (AAC), para 9
101 Reg 6(1) and (7)-(10) I(EEA) Regs
102 Regs 4(1)(a), 6(1) and 14 I(EEA) Regs; Art 45 TFEU; Arts 7(1) and 14 EU Dir 2004/38
103 *Lawrie-Blum v Land Baden-Württemberg*, C-66/85 [1986]
104 *Barry v LB Southwark* [2008] EWCA Civ 1440; *Tarola v Minister for Social Protection*, C-483/17 [2019]
105 *Rinner-Kühn v FWW Spezial-Gebäudereinigung GmbH and Co. KG*, 171/88 [1989]
106 R(IS) 12/98
107 *Genc v Land Berlin*, C-14/09 [2010]
108 *Steymann v Staatssecretaris van Justitie*, 196/87 [1988]; *Trojani v CPAS*, C-456/02 [2004]
109 CIS/1837/2006; CIS/868/2008

110 *Kempf v Staatssecretaris van Justitie,* C-139/85 [1986]; *Bettray v Staatssecretaris van Justitie,* C-344/87 [1989]; *Genc v Land Berlin,* C-14/09 [2010]
111 *Raulin v Minister van Onderwijs en Wetenschappen,* C-357/89 [1992]
112 CIS/1502/2007
113 *JA v SSWP (ESA)* [2012] UKUT 122 (AAC), cited with approval in *EP v SSWP (JSA)* [2016] UKUT 445 (AAC), para 21
114 Vol2 Ch7 Pt 3, paras 073038-40 DMG; paras C1487-89 ADM; HB A3/2014, para 15; HMRC, *Child Benefit and Child Tax Credit: right to reside establishing whether an EEA national is/was a worker or a self-employed person under EU law,* 2014, para 7; *RF v LB Lambeth* [2019] UKUT 52 (AAC)
115 CIS/4237/2007
116 *BS v SSWP* [2009] UKUT 16 (AAC)
117 Regs 4(1)(b), 6(1) and 14 I(EEA) Regs; Art 49 TFEU; Arts 7(1) and 14 EU Dir 2004/38
118 *Jany and Others v Staatssecretaris van Justitie,* C-268/99 [2001]
119 Reg 4(1)(b) I(EEA) Regs; Art 49 TFEU
120 R(IS) 6/00, para 31; *SSWP v VB (UC)* [2024] UKUT 212 (AAC), paras 13-45
121 *TG v SSWP* [2009] UKUT 58 (AAC)
122 *SSWP v JS (IS)* [2010] UKUT 240 (AAC)
123 CIS/1042/2008; *HMRC v GP* [2017] UKUT 11 (AAC)
124 Art 7(3) EU Dir 2004/38; *Gusa v Minister for Social Protection (Ireland),* C-442/16 [2017]; reg 6 I(EEA) Regs
125 *Saint Prix v SSWP,* C-507/12 [2014]; *HMRC v Dakneviciute,* C-544/18 [2019]; see also ADM Memo 21/19 and DMG Memo 17/19
126 Art 7(3)(b) and (c) EU Dir 2004/38; *Gusa v Minister for Social Protection (Ireland),* C-442/16 [2017]; Reg 6 I(EEA) Regs
127 Reg 6(2)-(10) I(EEA) Regs
128 *KH v Bury MBC and SSWP* [2020] UKUT 50 (AAC), especially paras 39-44 and 67; paras C1302 and C1403-4 ADM; DMG Memo 27/20, paras 11 and 14
129 CH/3314/2005, para 11; *SSWP v MK* [2013] UKUT 163 (AAC); *SB v SSWP (UC)* [2019] UKUT 219 (AAC), paras 8-13
130 See, for example, *SSWP v WN (rule 17)* [2018] UKUT 268 (AAC)
131 *SSWP v Elmi* [2011] EWCA Civ 1403
132 Reg 6(2)(c), (3), (4)(c), (4A), (4B), (4C), (5) and (6) I(EEA) Regs
133 Art 7(3)(c) EU Dir 2004/38; see, for example, *Tarola v Minister for Social Protection,* C-483/17 [2019] and *SB v SSWP (UC)* [2019] UKUT 219 (AAC)
134 Art 7(3)(b) EU Dir 2004/38; reg 6(2)(b), (4)(b), (4B), (4C), and (5)-(7) I(EEA) Regs; *SSWP v MM* [2015] UKUT 128 (AAC), para 54; see also *KH v Bury MBC and SSWP* [2020] UKUT 50 (AAC), paras 40-41
135 *SSHD v FB* [2010] UKUT 447 (IAC); *LM v HMRC (CHB)* [2016] UKUT 389 (AAC); *SSWP v LM (ESA) (Interim decision)* [2017] UKUT 485 (AAC), paras 31-34
136 CIS/3890/2005
137 *De Brito v SSHD* [2012] EWCA Civ 709; *Konodyba v RB of K&C* [2012] EWCA Civ 982; *Samin v SSHD* [2012] EWCA Civ 1468; *SSWP v LM (ESA) (Interim decision)* [2017] UKUT 485(AAC), paras 31-34; see also *BL v SSWP (ESA)* [2019] UKUT 364 (AAC), paras 20-23
138 CIS/4304/2007; *HK v SSWP* [2017] UKUT 421 (AAC), paras 4-6 and 8
139 CIS/3182/2005
140 Art 7(3)(d) EU Dir 2004/38; reg 6(1), (2)(d) and (e) and (4)(d) and (e) I(EEA)Regs
141 *SSWP v EM* [2009] UKUT 146 (AAC); see also *OB v SSWP (ESA)* [2017] UKUT 255 (AAC), para 32
142 CIS/4237/2007
143 CIS/1042/2008; *HMRC v GP* [2017] UKUT 11 (AAC); see also *HMRC v HD (CHB) (Second interim decision)* [2018] UKUT 148 (AAC), paras 2 and 3
144 CIS/731/2007
145 *Saint Prix v SSWP,* C-507/12 [2014]; *HMRC v Dakneviciute,* C-544/18 [2019]; *SSWP v SFF and others* [2015] UKUT 502 (AAC), reported as [2016] AACR 16
146 *SSWP v SFF and others* [2015] UKUT 502 (AAC), reported as [2016] AACR 16; *Weldemichael and Another v SSHD* [2015] UKUT 540 (IAC)
147 CIS/4304/2007; *SSWP v IR* [2009] UKUT 11 (AAC); *SSWP v SFF and others* [2015] UKUT 502 (AAC), para 40
148 *SSWP v MK* [2013] UKUT 163 (AAC); *VP v SSWP (JSA)* [2014] UKUT 32 (AAC), paras 56-61; *SSWP v MM* [2015] UKUT 128 (AAC), paras 47-52; *SSWP v LM (ESA) (Interim decision)* [2017] UKUT 485 (AAC), para 23; *SSWP v PC (UC)* [2024] UKUT 186 (AAC); *SSWP v VB (UC)* [2024] UKUT 212 (AAC), paras 100-124
149 CIS/1934/2006;*SSWP v IR* [2009] UKUT 11 (AAC)

150 Art 7(1) EU Dir 2004/38; regs 4(1)(c) and (2)-(4), 6(1) and 14(1) I(EEA) Regs
151 *Pensionsversicherungsanstalt v Brey*, C-140/12 [2013], paras 54-57
152 Art 8(4) EU Dir 2004/38
153 Reg 4(4) I(EEA) Regs
154 *SG v Tameside MBC (HB)* [2010] UKUT 243 (AAC)
155 *Commission of the European Communities v Kingdom of Belgium*, C-408/03 [2006]; *Zhu and Chen v SSHD*, C-200/02 [2004]; *Alokpa v Ministre du Travail, de l'Emploi et de l'Immigration*, C-86/12 [2013], para 27
156 *VP v SSWP (JSA)* [2014] UKUT 32 (AAC), reported as [2017] AACR 25, paras 88-97
157 *Singh and Others v Minister of Justice and Equality*, C-218/14 [2015]
158 *SSWP v VB (UC)* [2024] UKUT 212 (AAC)
159 *Bajratari v SSHD*, C-93/18 [2019]
160 *SSWP vVersnick* [2024] EWCA Civ 1454 upheld; *SSWP v WV (UC)* [2023] UKUT 112 (AAC)
161 *Pensionsversicherungsanstalt v Brey*, C-140/12 [2013]; *AMS v SSWP (PC) (Final Decision)* [2017] UKUT 381 (AAC), reported as [2018] AACR 27; *AS v SSWP (UC)* [2018] UKUT 260 (AAC), para 43
162 *SSWP v Versnick* [2024] EWCA Civ 1454; *SSWP v VB (UC)* [2024] UKUT 212 (AAC)
163 *W (China) and Another v SSHD* [2006] EWCA Civ 1494
164 *VI v HMRC*, C-247/20 [2022], paras 66-70; *WH v Powys CC and SSWP* [2022] UKUT 203 (AAC)
165 Art 7(1) EU Dir 2004/38; regs 4(1)(d) and (2)-(4), 6(1) and 14(1) I(EEA) Regs
166 Art 2(2) EU Dir 2004/38; reg 7(1) I(EEA) Regs
167 *Diatta v Land Berlin*, 267/83 [1985]
168 CIS/2100/2007, which considers the findings of *Centre Public d'Aide Sociale de Courcelles v Lebon*, C-316/85 [1987]; *Zhu and Chen v SSHD*, C-200/02 [2004]; and *Jia v Migrationsverket*, C-1/05 [2007]
169 *SSWP v MF (SPC)* [2018] UKUT 179 (AAC)
170 *Reyes v Migrationsverket*, C-423/12 [2014]; *Centre Public d'Aide Sociale de Courcelles v Lebon*, C-316/85 [1987]; *ECO v Lim (EEA dependency)* [2013] UKUT 437 (IAC); *GV v Chief Appeals Officer*, C-488/21 [2023]; *R (Ali) v SSHD* [2024] EWCA Civ 1546 – note the SSHD is seeking permission to appeal to the SC
171 Art 17(2) WA 2019; Art 16(2) UK-EFTA; *C v Oldham Council (Aire Centre and The 3Million intervening)* [2024] EWCC 1
172 *Pedro v SSWP* [2009] EWCA Civ 1358; *Jia v Migrationsverket*, C-1/05 [2007]; *SSHD v Rahman and Others*, C-83/11 [2012]; *Oboh and Others v SSHD* [2013] EWCA Civ 1525
173 Vol 2 Ch 7, para 073495 DMG; para C1875 ADM
174 *Kerr v DSDNI* [2004] UKHL 23, paras 62-69; para A1405 ADM; ADM Memo 30/20, para 42; DMG Memo 26/20, para 42; Sch 2 para 5(3) Data Protection Act 2018
175 *FN v SSWP (UC)* [2022] UKUT 77 (AAC), paras 4-8
176 Regs 7(3), 12, 17-20, 45 and Sch 6 para 2 I(EEA) Regs; Sch 3 paras 3(1)-(6) ISSC Regs; regs 3(4)-(6), 4(2) and (5)-(8) and 6(b) CR(ADTP) Regs; CPC/3588/2006; *SS v SSWP (ESA)* [2010] UKUT 8 (AAC); *SSWP v LZ (SPC)* [2014] UKUT 147 (AAC); *Macastena v SSHD* [2018] EWCA Civ 1558; *SSHD v Aibangbee* [2019] EWCA Civ 339; *MW v SSWP (UC)* [2019] UKUT 184; *AM v SSWP and CC Swansea Council* [2019] UKUT 361 (AAC), paras 19-21; para C1738 ADM; Vol2 Ch7 Pt3, para 073294 DMG
177 *SSWP v Dias*, C-325/09 [2011]; *EM and KN v SSWP* [2009] UKUT 44 (AAC); *MD v SSWP (SPC)* [2016] UKUT 319 (AAC); regs 17(8), 18(7), 19(4) and 20(5) I(EEA) Regs
178 Reg 8 I(EEA) Regs. Most of these groups are covered in Art 3 EU Dir 2004/38, but the term is not used.
179 See also *AA (Algeria) v SSHD* [2014] EWCA Civ 1741; *Dauhoo (EEA Regs – Reg 8(2)) v SSHD* [2012] UKUT 79 (IAC); *Chowdhury v SSHD* [2021] EWCA Civ 1220; *Begum v SSHD* [2021] EWCA Civ 1878
180 Regs 1, 7(4) and 9 I(EEA) Regs since 1 February 2017, and reg 4 and Sch 5 I(EEA) Regs for the prior period from 25 November 2016; Art 21(1) TFEU; *R v IAT et Surinder Singh ex parte SSHD*, C-370/90 [1992]; *O and B v Minister voor Immigratie, Integratie en Asiel*, C-456/12 [2014]; *Coman v Inspectoratul General pentru Imigrari*, C-673/16 [2018]; *SSHD v Banger*, C-89/17 [2018]
181 Reg 5(h) CR(ADTP) Regs; Sch 3 para 6(h) and Sch 4 para 4(h) ISSC Regs

182 *Minister voor Vreemdelingenzaken en Integratie v Eind*, C-291/05 [2007], para 45; *HK v SSWP (PC)* [2020] UKUT 33 (AAC); see also *FN v SSWP (UC)* [2022] UKUT 77 (AAC). For an additional summary of *Eind*, see *B v SSWP* [2017] UKUT 472 (AAC), paras 33-39. See also DMG Memo 21/20 and ADM Memo 24/20.
183 Reg 9(3) I(EEA) Regs; *ZA (Reg 9 EEA Regs; abuse of rights) Afghanistan* [2019] UKUT 281 (IAC)
184 *O and B v Minister voor Immigratie, Intergratie en Asiel*, C-456/12 [2014], especially paras 51-56; see also *ZA (Reg 9 EEA Regs; abuse of rights) Afghanistan* [2019] UKUT 281 (IAC), para 75; *VW v SSWP (PC)* [2014] UKUT 573 (AAC)
185 Reg 9(4) I(EEA) Regs
186 Regs 2(1) (see definition of 'EEA national') and 9A I(EEA) Regs; reg 3 The Immigration (European Economic Area) (Amendment) Regulations 2018 No.801; reg 5(I) CR(ADTP) Regs; Sch 4 para 4(i) ISSC Regs; *Lounes v SSHD*, C-165/16 [2017]; Art 21(1) TFEU; *AS v SSWP (UC)* [2018] UKUT 260 (AAC); *Kovacevic (British Citizen – Art 21 TFEU) Croatia* [2018] UKUT 273 (IAC); *ODS v SSWP (UC)* [2019] UKUT 192 (AAC)
187 *McCarthy v SSHD*, C-434-09 [2011]
188 Reg 10 I(EEA) Regs
189 *Gauswami v SSHD* [2018] UKUT 275 (IAC)
190 *Baigazieva v SSHD* [2018] EWCA Civ 1088
191 *Gauswami v SSHD* [2018] UKUT 275 (IAC)
192 Reg 14(3) I(EEA) Regs
193 Reg 10(8) and (9) I(EEA) Regs; *MK v SSWP (ESA)* [2020] UKUT 235 (AAC), para 11
194 Art 12 EU Dir 2004/38
195 Art 12(3) EU Dir 2004/38
196 *Baigazieva v SSHD* [2018] EWCA Civ 1088
197 Art 13 EU Dir 2004/38
198 *Singh and Others v Minister of Justice and Equality*, C-218/14 [2015]
199 *SSHD v NA*, C-115/15 [2016]
200 *X v Belgian State*, C-930/19 [2021], paras 43-45
201 *AT v LB Hillingdon and SSWP (HB)* [2023] UKUT 149 (AAC)
202 Arts 12(1) and 13(1) EU Dir 2004/38
203 *JP v SSWP (ESA)* [2018] UKUT 161 (AAC), paras 12-21; *GA v SSWP (SPC)* [2018] UKUT 172 (AAC), paras 27-44
204 Arts 12, 13 and 18 EU Dir 2004/38
205 Reg 16 I(EEA) Regs
206 *Baumbast and R v SSHD*, C-413/99 [2002], para 57; *IP v SSWP (IS)* [2015] UKUT 691 (AAC)
207 Arts 24(1)(h) and (2) and 25(1)(b) and (2) WA 2019; Arts 23(1)(h) and (2) and 24(1)(b) and (2) UK-EFTA; Vol2 Ch7 Pt3, para 073387 DMG; para C1832 ADM; see also *LB Harrow v Ibrahim and SSHD*, C-310/08 [2010]; *Teixeira v LB Lambeth and SSHD*, C-480/08 [2010]; *GBC Echternach and A Moritz v Minister van Onderwijs en Wetenschappen*, joined cases C-389/87 and C-390/87 [1989]; *Baumbast and R v SSHD*, C-413/99 [2002]
208 See also *Zhu and Chen v SSHD*, C-200/02 [2004]; *SSHD v NA*, C-115/15 [2016]
209 See also *Zambrano v ONEm*, C-34/09 [2011]; *Dereci and Others v Bundesministerium für Inneres*, C-256/11 [2011]; *DM v SSWP (PIP)* [2019] UKUT 26 (AAC)
210 *FE v HMRC (CHB)* [2022] UKUT 4 (AAC); *VI v HMRC*, C-247/20 [2022]
211 *Chavez-Vilchez v Raad van bestuur van de Sociale verzekeringsbank*, C-133/15 [2017] and caselaw cited
212 Reg 16(8)-(11) I(EEA) Regs; see also *MA v DSD (JSA)* [2011] NICom 205
213 Reg 16(7)(c) I(EEA) Regs
214 *Sandwell MBC v KK and SSWP (HB)* [2022] UKUT 123 (AAC), applying the decision of the CJEU in *JD v Jobcenter Krefeld*, C-181/19 [2020], especially paras 64, 71 and 79
215 *Baumbast and R v SSHD*, C-413/99 [2002], para 57; *IP v SSWP (IS)* [2015] UKUT 691 (AAC)
216 *Teixeira v LB Lambeth and SSHD*, C-480/08 [2010], para 74; *Bolton MBC v HY (HB)* [2018] UKUT 103 (AAC) and caselaw cited
217 Arts 24(1)(h) and (2) and 25(1)(b) and (2) WA 2019; Arts 23(1)(h) and (2) and 24(1)(b) and (2) UK-EFTA
218 Vol2 Ch7 Pt3, para 073387 DMG; para C1832 ADM
219 Consent order allowing appeal to CA in *A v Barnet* (CA-2022-000752), 14 February 2023, paras 13 and 14
220 Reg 16(7)(b) I(EEA) Regs
221 *SSWP v JS (IS)* [2010] UKUT 347 (AAC); *DJ v SSWP* [2013] UKUT 113 (AAC)
222 *Teixeira v LB Lambeth and SSHD*, C-480/08 [2010], para 87; see also *Alarape and Tijani v SSHD*, C-529/11 [2013]

**Notes**

223 Reg 16(7)(a) I(EEA) Regs; see also CIS/3960/2007; *Shabani v SSHD* [2013] UKUT 315 (IAC); *SSWP v IM (IS)* [2011] UKUT 231 (AAC), paras 17 and 28
224 *AM v SSWP and CC Swansea Council* [2019] UKUT 361 (AAC), paras 49-64
225 Arts 16 and 17 EU Dir 2004/38; regs 5 and 15 I(EEA) Regs
226 See, for example, *MW v SSWP (UC)* [2019] UKUT 184
227 Art 16(4) EU Dir 2004/38; reg 15(3) I(EEA) Regs - note that the words 'only' and 'consecutive' were removed from these regulations from 1 February 2017, but EU law has not changed and should be followed
228 Part 4 I(EEA) Regs
229 Arts 11 and 15(3) WA 2019; Arts 10 and 14(3) UK-EFTA; Art 14(2) UK-SA
230 *Idezuna v SSHD* [2011] UKUT 474 (IAC); *Babajanov v SSHD* [2013] UKUT 513 (IAC)
231 Art 16(3) EU Dir 2004/38; reg 3 I(EEA) Regs
232 Vol 2, Ch7, Pt3, paras 073433-35 DMG; paras C1812-14 ADM
233 *SSHD v Ojo* [2015] EWCA Civ 1301, para 20; *Cardiff City Council v HM (HB)* [2019] UKUT 271 (AAC)
234 *OB v SSWP (ESA)* [2017] UKUT 255 (AAC), paras 29-30 and 34; endorsed in *AP v SSWP (IS)* [2018] UKUT 307 (AAC), paras 15-18
235 Reg 3(3) I(EEA) Regs
236 Reg 3(1), (3)(a) and (4) I(EEA) Regs; Art 28(3) EU Dir 2004/38; *Onuekwere v SSHD*, C-378/12 [2014]; *SSHD v Viscu* [2019] EWCA Civ 1052 and caselaw cited
237 Reg 15(1) and (2) I(EEA) Regs; Sch 6 para 8 I(EEA) Regs
238 Regs 6(1)(a), 7, 13, 14(1) and (2), 15(1) and Sch 6 para 8 I(EEA) Regs; *GE v SSWP (ESA)* [2017] UKUT 145 (AAC), reported as [2017] AACR 34; Vol2 Ch7 Pt3, para 073428 DMG; para C1807 ADM
239 Sch 4 para 4(m) ISSC Regs
240 Art 16(1) EU Dir 2004/38
241 *SSWP v Taous Lassal*, C-162/09 [2010]; *SSWP v Dias*, C-325/09 [2011]
242 *Oakafor and Others v SSHD* [2011] EWCA Civ 499; *Alarape and Tijani v SSHD*, C-529/11 [2013]; *Bee and Another v SSHD* [2013] UKUT 83 (IAC)
243 *Ziolkowski* (C-425/10) and *Szeja* (C-425/10) *v Land Berlin* [2011]
244 *Ziolkowski* (C-425/10) and *Szeja* (C-425/10) *v Land Berlin* [2011]; Sch 6 para 8(3) I(EEA) Regs
245 See, for example, *MW v SSWP (UC)* [2019] UKUT 184 (AAC)
246 Reg 14(2) I(EEA) Regs
247 Regs 14(2) and 15(1)(a) and (b) I(EEA) Regs
248 Regs 5 and 15 I(EEA) Regs; Art 17 EU Dir 2004/38
249 *SSWP v Gubeladze* [2019] UKSC 31
250 *De Brito v SSHD* [2012] EWCA Civ 709
251 *SSWP v Gubeladze* [2019] UKSC 31; *SSWP v NZ (ESA) (Final decision)* [2019] UKUT 250 (AAC)
252 Art 17(3) EU Dir 2004/38; *PM (EEA – spouse – 'residing with') Turkey* [2011] UKUT 89 (IAC)
253 Reg 15(1)(d) I(EEA) Regs
254 Art 17(1) EU Dir 2004/38; reg 5(7) I(EEA) Regs
255 Art 17(1) EU Dir 2004/38; regs 5(7) and 6(2), and Sch 4 para 2 I(EEA) Regs, preserving regs 7A(3) and 7B(4) I(EEA) Regs 2006; *NZ v SSWP (ESA) (Third interim decision)* [2017] UKUT 360 (AAC); see also *SSWP v NZ (ESA) (Final decision)* [2019] UKUT 250 (AAC)
256 Regs 3 and 4 CR(FW) Regs; Arts 45 and 49 TFEU; Arts 24 and 25 WA 2019; Arts 23 and 24 UK-EFTA; Arts 20 and 23 UK-SA; ADM Memo 33/20; DMG Memo 29/20
257 Regs 3(3) CR(FW) Regs
258 Arts 24 and 25 WA 2019; Arts 23 and 24 UK-EFTA; Arts 20 and 23 UK-SA; Arts 45 and 49 TFEU; EU Reg 492/2011
259 ADM Memo 33/20, para 51; DMG Memo 29/20, para 51
260 Arts 24(1)(h) and (2) and 25(1)(b) and (2) WA 2019; Arts 23(1)(h) and (2) and 24(1)(b) and (2) UK-EFTA; EU Reg 492/2011; ADM Memo 33/20, para 35 and 53; DMG Memo 29/20, para 35 and 53

6. **Rules for specific benefits**

261 **UC** s4(1)(c) WRA 2012
**ESA** s1(3)(d) WRA 2007
**PC** s1(2)(a) SPCA 2002
262 **UC** Reg 9 UC Regs
**ESA** Regs 69-70 ESA Regs
**HB** Reg 10 HB Regs; reg 10 HB(SPC) Regs
**PC** Reg 2 SPC Regs
263 ss3 and 4(1)(c) and (2) WRA 2012; regs 3(3) and 9 UC Regs
264 Regs 3(3) and 36(3) UC Regs

265 ss3 and 4(1)(e) WRA 2012; reg 3(3) UC Regs; reg 9(1) UC,PIP,JSA&ESA(C&P) Regs
266 Regs 3(3), 18(2) and 22(3) UC Regs
267 Sch 4 para 9(2)(b) UC Regs
268 Sch 4 paras 27 and 28 UC Regs
269 s19(6) WRA 2012; reg 86 UC Regs
270 s39 WRA 2012; regs 62(1),(3) and (4) and 90(3) UC Regs
271 Art 7(1) and (2)(a) and (b) and (3)(b) WRA(No.31)O; HB Circular A9/2019, paras 15-17; Vol 13 Ch 77, paras 77035 note 2, 77150-51 and 77160 DMG
272 s39 WRA 2012; regs 3, 18(2), 22(3) and 36(3) UC Regs; reg 9(1) UC,PIP,JSA&ESA(C&P) Regs
273 Reg 9(6) UC,PIP,JSA&ESA(C&P) Regs
274 **ESA** Reg 156 ESA Regs
**PC** Reg 5 SPC Regs
**HB** Reg 21 HB Regs; reg 21 HB(SPC) Regs
275 CIS/508/1992; CIS/13805/1996
276 CIS/484/1993
277 **UC** Reg 4(7) UC Regs
**ESA** Reg 156 ESA Regs
**PC** Reg 5 SPC Regs
**HB** Reg 21 HB Regs; reg 21 HB(SPC) Regs
278 s30(1) PA 2014
279 Arts 5, 6, 7, 42 and 43 EU Reg 883/04; Arts 5, 6, 7 and 43 UK-IC; Arts SSC 6, 7, 8, 37 and 38 UK-EUP; Arts 9, 10, 11, 43 and 44 UK-EFTA
280 Sch 1 para 4 The Social Security (Reciprocal Agreements) Order 2017 No.159; paras 077080-83 DMG
281 Vol 2 Ch 7 Pt 6, paras 077083 and 077110-24 DMG
282 s146 SSCBA 1992
283 Reg 23 CB Regs
284 Regs 23, 30 and 31 CB Regs
285 Reg 23(3) CB Regs
286 Regs 18(d) and 19(2)(c) SCP Regs
287 Reg 9 GA(Gen) Regs
288 *Stewart v SSWP*, C-503/09 [2011]
289 **AA** Reg 2 SS(AA) Regs
**PADP** Reg 9 DAOP(S) Regs
**DLA** Reg 2 SS(DLA) Regs; see also DMG Memo 6/23
**CDP** Reg 5 DACYP(S) Regs
**SADLA** Reg 10 DA(SADLA) Regs
**PIP** Reg 16 SS(PIP) Regs
**ADP** Reg 15 DAWAP(S) Regs
**CA** Reg 9 SS(ICA) Regs
**CSP** Reg 6 CA(CSP)(S) Regs
290 *TS and EK v SSWP (DLA)* [2020] UKUT 284 (AAC), reported as [2021] AACR 4; Vol2 Ch7 Pt2, para 071721 DMG; see also gov.uk/disability-living-allowance-children/eligibility
291 **CDP** Reg 5(2) and (3) DACYP(S) Regs
**DLA** Reg 2(5)-(7) SS(DLA) Regs
292 **CDP** Regs 5(9) and 24 DACYP(S) Regs
**ADP** Reg 35 DAWAP(S) Regs
**PADP** Reg 27 DAOP(S) Regs
293 Reg 9(5)(e) SS(CPCTMA)(S) Regs inserting reg 18(3A) CA(CSP)(S) Regs
294 Regs 18(3) and 19(2) CA(CSP)(S) Regs
295 s81 SS(S)A 2018
296 Reg 8 CA(YCG)(S) Regs
297 **AA** Regs 2(2), (3) and (3A) and 2C SS(AA) Regs
**PADP** Regs 9(6)-(8), 11, 12 and 15 DAOP(S) Regs
**DLA** Regs 2(2), (3A) and (4) and 2C SS(DLA) Regs
**CDP** Reg 5(6), (7), (8), (10), (10A) and (11) DACYP(S) Regs
**SADLA** Reg 10(6)-(8), 12, 13 and 17 DA(SADLA) Regs
**PIP** Regs 19, 20, 21 and 23A SS(PIP) Regs
**ADP** Regs 15(6)-(8), 17, 18, 21 DAWAP(S) Regs
**CA** Regs 9(3) and 9C SS(ICA) Regs
**CSP** Regs 6, 8, 9 CA(CSP)(S) Regs
298 See also ADM Memo 14/21 and DMG Memo 11/21; and confirming the narrow scope of this exempt group, see *HRA v SSWP (PIP)* [2023] UKUT 109 (AAC)
299 See also ADM Memo 11/22, ADM Memo 1/23 and DMG Memo 8/22
300 See also ADM Memo 10/23 and DMG Memo 5/23
301 See also ADM Memo 17/23 and DMG Memo 11/23
302 Reg 6(6)(b) and (7) CA(CSP)(S) Regs

**Notes**

303 Art 16 UK-IC
**AA** s65(7) SSCBA 1992
**PADP** Regs 9(3)(c), 13(c)(ii), 14(2)(a)(ii) and 16 DAOP(S) Regs
**DLA** s72(7B) SSCBA 1992
**PIP** s84 WRA 2012
**ADP** Regs 15(3)(c), 19(c)(ii), 20(2)(ii) and 20A DAWAP(S) Regs
**CA** s70(4A) SSCBA 1992
**CDP** Regs 5(4)(c)(ii), 8(c)(ii), 9(2)(a)(i) and 9A DACYP(S) Regs
**SADLA** Regs 10(3)(c), 14(c)(ii), 15(2)(a)(ii) and 16 DA(SADLA) Regs
**CSP** Regs 10 and 11 CA(CSP)(S) Regs
**YCG** Reg 8(3)-(10) CA(YCG)(S) Regs
**CAS** s81(2A) and (9)-(15) SS(S)A 2018
304 Art 6 and Annex XI UK entry para 2 EU Reg 883/04; *SSWP v MM and BK v SSWP* [2016] UKUT 547 (AAC), reported as [2019] AACR 21; Art 6 UK-IC
305 Art SSC3(4) and Annex SSC-1, Parts 1 and 2 UK-EUP; Art 6(5)(a) and (d), Annex 2, Parts 1 and 2 UK-EFTA
306 **AA** Reg 2A SS(AA) Regs
**PADP** Reg 13 DAOP(S) Regs
**DLA** Reg 2A SS(DLA) Regs
**CDP** Reg 8 DACYP(S) Regs
**SADLA** Reg 14 DA(SADLA) Regs
**PIP** Reg 22 SS(PIP) Regs
**ADP** Reg 19 DAWAP(S) Regs
**CA** Reg 9A SS(ICA) Regs
**CSP** Reg 10 CA(CSP)(S) Regs
307 Reg 6(6) CA(CSP)(S) Regs
308 *ES v SSWP* [2024] UKUT 13 (AAC)
309 *Stewart v SSWP*, C-503/09 [2011]; *Kavanagh and Another v SSWP* [2019] EWCA Civ 272; *SSWP v JG (IS)* [2013] UKUT 298 (AAC); *SSWP v Garland* [2014] EWCA Civ 1550
310 *PB v SSWP (DLA)* [2016] UKUT 280 (AAC)
311 ss1(3)(d) and 18(4)(a) WRA 2007
312 SS(NIRA) Regs; SS(GBRA)NI Regs
313 s94(5) SSCBA 1992
314 Reg 14 SS(IIPD) Regs
315 Reg 10C(5) and (6) SSB(PA) Regs
316 Reg 2 SS(II)(AB) Regs; reg 2 SS(II)(MB) Regs
317 Regs 3, 4, 6 and 8 SS(II)(MB) Regs; regs 3 and 6 SS(II)(AB) Regs
318 Art 5 EU Reg 883/04; Art 5 UK-IC; Art SSC 6 UK-EUP; Art 9 UK-EFTA
319 Art 38 EU Reg 883/04; Art 36 EU Reg 987/09; *SSWP v OF (by MF) (II)* UKUT [2011] 448 (AAC); Art SSC 33 and Annex SSC-7, Art SSCI.30 UK-EUP; Arts 29 and 39 and Annex 1 UK-EFTA
320 s1(2)(i) JSA 1995
321 Art 61(2) EU Reg 883/04; Art 21(1) and (2) UK-IC; Art SSC 56 UK-EUP; Art 58 UK-EFTA
322 Art 64 EU Reg 883/04; Arts 7 and 21 UK-IC
323 Art 64(3) EU Reg 883/04; Art 21(4(c) UK-IC
324 Arts 3(1) and (4) and 8 UK-EUP; Arts 6(1)(h) and 11 UK-EFTA
325 ss2(1) and 35(1) SSCBA 1992. For exceptions, see the Social Security (Maternity Allowance) (Work Abroad) Regulations 1987 No.417; Vol2 Ch7 Pt5, paras 075570-73 DMG.
326 s113(1) SSCBA 1992
327 s113 SSCBA 1992; reg 4(1) SSB(PA) Regs
328 Reg 10(1) SS(WB&RP) Regs
329 Arts 51, 52 and 58 EU Reg 883/04; eg, paras 075771 and 076060-64 DMG; Arts 25 and 26 UK-IC; Arts SSC 45, 46 and 47 UK-EUP; Arts 49, 50, 51 UK-EFTAC
330 Art 32 WA 2019; Art 31 UK-EFTA; Art 26a UK-SA; see also DWPWAG, Ch 1 paras 43-52; DMG Memo 11/22, paras 13-15; ADM Memo, 15/22 paras 13-15
331 Regs 5 and 9 The Social Security Co-ordination (Revocation of Retained Direct EU Legislation and Related Amendments) (EU Exit) Regulations 2020 No.1508
332 UK-SCC
333 Reg 10(2) SS(WB&RP) Regs
334 Reg 9(1) FEA(S) Regs
335 Reg 7(9A) SFM&FE Regs
336 Reg 7(5) SFM&FE Regs; reg 9(2)(a) and (6) FEA(S) Regs
337 Reg 7(9) and (10) SFM&FE Regs; reg 9(2)(b) and (3)-(3B) FEA(S) Regs
338 *John O'Flynn v Adjudication Officer*, C-237/94 [1996]; R(IS) 4/98; Art 24 EU Dir 2004/38
339 The Social Fund (Children's Funeral Fund for England) Regulations 2019 No.1064
340 gov.wales/child-funeral-and-other-related-costs-information
341 Reg 5(6) SFM&FE Regs
342 Schs 2 para 4(1)(a), 3 para 3(1)(a) and 4 para 4(1)(a) EYA(BSG)(S) Regs
343 Schs 2 para 4(1)(b) and (2), 3 para 3(1)(b) and (2) and 4 para 4(1)(b) and (2) EYA(BSG)(S) Regs
344 Reg 4 SS(CPCTMA)(S) Regs
345 Reg 2 SFWFP Regs
346 Reg 4(2) WHA(LI)(S) Regs

347 Reg 8 WHA(PA)(S) Regs
348 Reg 1A(8) SFCWP Regs
349 Reg 4(1)(c) and Sch WHACYP(S) Regs
350 Reg 2 and Sch 1 SFWFP Regs; regs 7 and 8 and Sch WHA(PA)(S) Regs
351 Art SSC 3(4) UK-EUP; Art 6(5)(f) and Annex 2 Part 3 EFTA; Art 3 UK-IC

# Chapter 58

# Going abroad

**This chapter covers:**

1. Overview of the rules on getting paid abroad (below)
2. Rules for specific benefits (see p1370)

## Key facts

- Most benefits are affected if you, or your partner or child, go abroad.
- In certain circumstances, you can continue to receive benefit for a set number of weeks while you are away for a temporary period.
- You may be entitled to receive UK benefits for a longer (or indefinite) period if you go to a European Economic Area country and you are covered by European Union co-ordination rules.

9

## 1. Overview of the rules on getting paid abroad

Most benefits are affected if you, or your partner or child, go abroad. Some can always be paid abroad, some can only be paid in certain circumstances and for limited periods, and some have rules affecting the amount that can be paid if you are abroad.

Your entitlement abroad depends on:

- the benefit you are claiming (see p1370);
- the reason why you are going abroad;
- whether your absence is temporary or permanent;
- the length of time you intend to be abroad;
- the country you are going to;
- whether you are covered by any of the European Union (EU) co-ordination rules;
- whether you are covered by a reciprocal agreement.

For the rules on when income support, income-based JSA and tax credits could be paid while you, or your partner or child, were abroad, see the 2024/25 edition of this *Handbook*.

## Which rules apply

**The UK benefit legislation** contains rules about how your absence abroad affects your entitlement. If these allow your entitlement to continue when you are abroad, you do not need to check the other rules.

**The EU co-ordination rules** may apply if you, or your family member, go to a European Economic Area (EEA) country. They can allow benefits to be paid to you for longer than under UK law alone. You need to check which co-ordination rules you are covered by (see p1392). The main co-ordination rules provide the greatest protections. The UK–Ireland Convention has similar rules but only applies if you go to Ireland. The UK–EU Protocol (which only applies to EU – not all EEA – member countries) and the UK–EFTA Convention (which only applies to Iceland, Liechtenstein and Norway) have the fewest protections and cover the fewest benefits.

See p1389 for a list of EU and EEA countries, see p1370 onwards for how these rules affect individual benefits and see Chapter 59 for the co-ordination rules.

**Reciprocal agreements** exist between the UK and some other countries and can assist in similar ways to the EU co-ordination rules. In general, these only apply if the EU co-ordination rules do not assist you. Great Britain and Northern Ireland also have reciprocal agreements. See p1297 for the countries with agreements and see CPAG's *Benefits for Migrants Handbook* for more information on how they can assist.

## UK law

### Ordinary residence

You must be 'ordinarily resident' in Great Britain to receive some benefits (the UK, for child benefit, and Scotland, for most Scottish benefits) ( see p1299). If, by going abroad, you cease to be ordinarily resident, your entitlement stops. However, if your absence abroad is temporary and you intend to return to Great Britain (or the UK or Scotland), your ordinary residence is not usually affected.[1] In practice, it is very rare that ceasing to be ordinarily resident is the reason why your entitlement ends when you go abroad. It is more likely that your entitlement ends simply because you are absent (see below). If you receive a decision that your entitlement to a benefit has ended because you have ceased to be ordinarily resident, challenge the decision (see Chapter 50) and get specialist advice.

### Presence and absence

Most benefits require you to be **present** in Great Britain or, for child disability payment (CDP), adult disability payment (ADP), pension age disability payment (PADP), Scottish adult disability living allowance (SADLA) and carer support payment (CSP) (the common travel area (the UK, Ireland, Channel Islands and the Isle of Man). There are rules that allow you to be treated as present and therefore still entitled to the benefit in specified circumstances during a temporary absence. Some benefits also have a rule that disqualifies you from entitlement if you are **absent** from Great Britain. There are specified exemptions to this rule for each benefit.

**'Presence'** means being physically present in Great Britain (or the common travel area) and **'absence'** means not being physically present. You count as present on the day you arrive or return from an absence. In general, you also count as present on the day you go abroad.[2] However, for housing benefit, the day of departure counts as your first day of absence from Great Britain.[3]

### Temporary absence

In specified circumstances, you can be treated as present, and therefore entitled to benefit, for a limited period, *if* your absence counts as a 'temporary absence' (see below). For the rules on how long you can continue to be entitled during a 'temporary absence', see the rules for the specific benefit you are claiming, starting below.

***What is a 'temporary absence'?***

For attendance allowance (AA), PADP, disability living allowance (DLA), CDP, SADLA, personal independence payment (PIP), ADP, CSP and (for your, not the child's, absence) child benefit, you are defined as being temporarily absent from Great Britain (the common travel area for CDP, ADP, PADP, SADLA and CSP), if, at the beginning of the period of absence, you are unlikely to be absent for more than 52 weeks.[4]

For all other benefits, temporary absence is not defined and you must *demonstrate* that your absence will be temporary.[5] Provide full details of why you are going abroad, how long you intend to be away, and what you intend to do while abroad. **Note:** although your intentions are relevant, they are not decisive. If your circumstances change while you are abroad (eg, you go abroad for one reason and decide to stay abroad for another), your absence may no longer be regarded as temporary.[6] Although there is no set period for a temporary absence (except for child benefit, AA, PADP, DLA, CDP, SADLA, PIP, ADP and CSP), as a general rule absences of more than 12 months are not considered to be temporary unless there are exceptional circumstances.[7] If the purpose of the trip abroad is obviously temporary (eg, for a holiday, to visit friends or relatives or for a particular course of medical treatment) and you buy a return ticket, your absence should be viewed as temporary.

## 2. Rules for specific benefits

### Universal credit and other means-tested benefits

You cannot usually receive means-tested benefits when you are abroad because the rules for each benefit require you to be present in Great Britain or, for housing benefit (HB) (and council tax reduction), to occupy your home. However, you can be treated as present (or as occupying your home) in certain circumstances. The rules differ between the different means-tested benefits.

**Note:** if you are receiving income-related employment and support allowance (ESA), and it stops because you go abroad, when you return, you cannot reclaim it as new claims are no longer possible. However, you may be able to claim universal credit (UC) instead. Similarly, if your HB stops because you go abroad, you cannot reclaim it when you return, unless you have reached pension age or are in 'specified' or 'temporary' accommodation' (see p183).

## Universal credit

You cannot usually be paid UC if you (and your partner, if you are joint claimants) are not in Great Britain.[8] However, if you were entitled immediately before the period of absence and you continue to meet the other conditions of entitlement, UC can be paid when you are temporarily absent from Great Britain for:[9]

- **one month**, if your absence is not expected to exceed, and does not exceed, one month (see the first bullet point in the Note below); *or*
- **two months**, if your absence is in connection with the death of your partner or child, or a 'close relative' (see p96) of yours or your partner or child, and it would be unreasonable for you to return to Great Britain within the first month; *or*
- **six months**, if your absence is not expected to exceed, and does not exceed, six months and you are a mariner or continental shelf worker; *or*
- **six months**, if your absence is not expected to exceed, and does not exceed, six months and is solely in connection with you undergoing (or accompanying your partner or child who is undergoing):
  - treatment of an illness or impairment by, or under the supervision of, a qualified practitioner; *or*
  - medically approved care or convalescence due to an illness or impairment that you had before leaving Great Britain.

**Note:**

- You are entitled to UC for the assessment period in which you go abroad if, by the last day of that assessment period, your absence was not expected to exceed, and has not exceeded, one month. If, in the next assessment period, your situation changes and you cannot return within the month as intended (eg, due to illness), your entitlement to UC ends from the start of that next assessment period, because by the last day of *that* assessment period, your absence has exceeded one month and the supersession decision due to this change of circumstances takes effect from the start of the assessment period in which it occurred (see p1150).

- You are not required to be in Great Britain if you are a Crown servant or member of the armed forces posted abroad (or, for joint claims, you are accompanying your partner posted abroad in either capacity).[10]
- You are automatically exempt from the work search requirement and are treated as 'able and willing immediately to take up work' (see p959) during the six-month period following the death of your partner or child or while the fourth bullet point on p1371 applies.[11]
- Since 24 July 2020, periods of temporary absence in Northern Ireland are ignored due to reciprocal arrangements between Great Britain and Northern Ireland that treat periods of presence and residence (and employment) in one territory as having the same effect on UC as if it had occurred in the other territory.[12]
- To be entitled to the carer element in your UC while abroad, you must either:[13]
  - satisfy the rules for being paid carer's allowance (CA) abroad (see p1378), unless the only reason why you do not is because either you are resident (or treated as resident) in Scotland, or you are resident outside Great Britain and have a genuine and sufficient link to Scotland (see p1351); *or*
  - satisfy the rules for being paid carer support payment (CSP) abroad (see p1378).

### If your partner is abroad

If you and your partner are joint claimants and you both go abroad, UC continues to be paid while both of you meet one of the above conditions. If you both remain abroad for longer than the relevant period, your entitlement ends.

If you stay in Great Britain while your partner is abroad, their absence does not affect your entitlement during the one-, two- or six-month period if one of the above circumstances applies to them. After this time, unless your partner is in Northern Ireland (see the note above), you cease to be entitled as joint claimants. To be entitled to UC, you need to make a new claim. You can make a single claim, but if you make a joint claim, it is treated as a claim by you as a single person.[14] However, if you and your partner have been, and expect to be, apart for less than six months, although your award is based on the maximum amount for a single person, your partner's income and capital are taken into account. Therefore whether you make a single or a joint claim, you must tell the DWP about your partner's income and capital. Once you have been, or expect to be, apart for six months, you stop being treated as a couple,[15] and your entitlement as a single person is unaffected by your absent partner.

If you are of pension age, but your partner is under pension age, once their absence exceeds the periods above, your joint entitlement to UC ends. As a single person, you are not entitled to UC once you have reached pension age, but you can claim pension credit (PC) and HB and you are treated as a single person for each of these claims.[16]

For further details on couples claiming UC if one partner does not satisfy the residence or presence rules, see p1343.

### If your child is abroad

If your child is abroad, you are treated as no longer responsible for them if their absence abroad is, or is expected to be, longer than the one-, two- or six-month period allowed in the circumstances above (the circumstances must apply to your child).[17]

### European Union co-ordination rules

The DWP considers UC not to be a social security benefit under any of the EU co-ordination rules (see p1400). This means that the EU co-ordination rules cannot assist you and, if you or your partner or child go to an EEA country, you can only be paid under the UK rules above.

## Income-related employment and support allowance

You cannot usually get ESA if you are not in Great Britain.[18] However, provided you meet the other conditions of entitlement, if you were entitled to ESA immediately before leaving Great Britain and are temporarily absent, you can continue to be entitled to both income-related and contributory ESA:[19]

- **indefinitely** if:
  - your absence is for NHS treatment at a hospital or other institution outside Great Britain; *or*
  - you are living with your spouse, civil partner, child, stepchild, parent, parent-in-law or step-parent who is a serving member of the armed forces; *or*
- **for the first four weeks**, if your absence is unlikely to exceed 52 weeks; *or*
- **for the first 26 weeks**, if your absence is unlikely to exceed 52 weeks and is solely in connection with arrangements made to treat:
  - your disease or disablement which is directly related to your limited capability for work which began before you left Great Britain; *or*
  - the disease or disablement of a dependent child who you are accompanying.

'Treatment' must be carried out by, or under the supervision of, a person qualified to provide medical treatment, physiotherapy or similar treatment.

If you are going to Northern Ireland from Great Britain (or vice versa), see p1352.

**Note:** there are also rules on when you can continue to get housing costs in your income-related ESA if you are temporarily absent from your home (see p296).

### If your partner is abroad

If you are the claimant and you stay in Great Britain, your income-related ESA includes an amount for your partner for:[20]

- the first four weeks they are abroad; *or*
- the first 26 weeks if they are accompanying a child abroad for treatment in line with the 26-week rule above.

If both you and your partner are abroad, your income-related ESA includes an amount for your partner for the first 26 weeks if both of you are accompanying a child abroad for treatment in line with the 26-week rule above.[21]

After this four- or 26-week period, your benefit is reduced because your applicable amount is calculated as if you have no partner. However, your partner is still treated as being part of your household, and therefore their work, income and capital affect your income-related ESA entitlement, unless you are no longer treated as a couple (see p257).[22]

### European Union co-ordination rules

None of the co-ordination rules assist you to be paid income-related ESA abroad, and you can only be paid abroad under the UK rules on p1373.

For the circumstances in which the co-ordination rules may enable you to continue to be paid contributory ESA if you move to an EEA country, see p1380.

## Housing benefit

You cannot usually get HB if you are not in Great Britain, due to the requirements for you to occupy your home.[23] However, provided you meet the other conditions of entitlement, HB can be paid when you are temporarily absent from Great Britain for:[24]

- **up to four weeks**, if your absence is not expected to exceed this; *or*
- **up to eight weeks**, if your absence is not expected to exceed that and is in connection with the death of your partner or child who normally lives with you or your (or their) close relative (see p189) and the local authority considers it unreasonable for you to return to Great Britain within four weeks; *or*
- **up to 26 weeks**, if your absence is not expected to exceed this and it is solely in connection with your (or your partner's or child's) medical treatment, or medically approved convalescence, or you are absent from home because of domestic violence, or if you are a member of the armed forces posted overseas, a mariner or a continental shelf worker.

Note:
- The periods for which you can continue to be entitled to HB while you are absent abroad are shorter than if you were absent from your home but remain in Great Britain (see p191).
- The period of absence starts on the day you leave Great Britain.[25]
- If you are (or you are a family member of) an EEA national with a free movement right to reside in the UK and go abroad to an EEA country, it is

arguable that the shorter period for which you can be entitled while abroad is discriminatory under EU law and should not apply (see p1406).[26]

#### If your partner or child is abroad

Whether or not you have amounts included in your HB for your partner or child who is abroad depends on whether they are treated as part of your household (see p257 and p261). The amount of HB you are entitled to may also depend on whether they are treated as occupying the home (see p191).[27]

#### European Union co-ordination rules

None of the co-ordination rules assist you to be paid HB abroad, and you can only be paid HB abroad under the UK rules on p1374.

### Pension credit

You cannot usually get PC if you are not in Great Britain.[28] However, provided you meet the other conditions of entitlement, PC can be paid when you are temporarily absent from Great Britain for:[29]

- **up to four weeks**, if your absence is not expected to exceed this; *or*
- **up to eight weeks**, if your absence is not expected to exceed this and is in connection with the death of your partner or child (see p259) who normally lived with you or your (or their) close relative (see p294) and the DWP considers it unreasonable for you to return to Great Britain within four weeks; *or*
- **up to 26 weeks**, if your absence is not expected to exceed this and it is solely in connection with your (or your partner's or child's) medical treatment, or medically approved convalescence.

**Note:** there are also rules on when you can continue to receive housing costs in your PC if you are temporarily absent from your home (see p296).

#### If your partner is abroad

If you are entitled to PC and your partner is abroad, your PC only includes an amount for them if they are covered by the rules above.[30] After this, they are not treated as part of your household and you are paid as a single person. Your partner can also stop being treated as part of your household in the circumstances on p257.[31] **Note**: if your partner is under pension age and ceases to be treated as part of your household, when they return, your entitlement to PC ends but you may instead be able to claim UC, although not if, for example, they fail the habitual residence test, in which case you would continue to be entitled to PC (and HB) as a single person (see p239).

#### If your child is abroad

If your child is temporarily absent from Great Britain, you continue to be entitled to an amount in your PC for them for:[32]

- **up to four weeks**, if their absence is not expected to exceed this; *or*
- **up to eight weeks**, if their absence is not expected to exceed this and is in connection with the death of your partner or child who normally lives with you, a close relative (see p294) of theirs, yours or your partner's, and the DWP considers it unreasonable for them to return to Great Britain within four weeks; *or*
- **up to 26 weeks**, if their absence is not expected to exceed this and it is solely in connection with their or your or your partner's medical treatment, or medically approved convalescence.

### European Union co-ordination rules

None of the EU co-ordination rules assist you to be paid PC abroad, and you can only be paid PC abroad under the UK rules on p1375.

## Bereavement benefits

In general, bereavement benefits are payable while you are abroad. However, your benefit is not uprated each year if you have ceased to be ordinarily resident (see p1299) in Great Britain on the day before the annual uprating takes place,[33] unless you have gone to an EEA country and you are covered by the EU co-ordination rules or can rely on a reciprocal agreement (see p1345).

If you were abroad on the date your spouse, civil partner or eligible cohabiting partner (see p454) died, you are only entitled to a bereavement support payment if, despite your absence, you were ordinarily resident in Great Britain on that date (see p1345), or the EU co-ordination rules apply or a reciprocal agreement applies.

9

### European Union co-ordination rules

If you are covered by any of the EU co-ordination rules (see p1392) and the UK is your 'competent state' (see p1404):[34]

- if you go to stay or live in an EEA country covered by the set of co-ordination rules you are relying on, you can be paid your bereavement support payment or widowed parent's allowance for as long as you would receive it if you remained in Great Britain, including any annual uprating. See p1408 for more information on exporting benefits; *and*
- (for bereavement support payment) the requirement to be ordinarily resident in Great Britain on the date your spouse, civil partner or eligible cohabiting partner died does not apply if, on that date, you were resident in an EEA country covered by the set of co-ordination rules you are relying on.

## Child benefit, Scottish child payment and guardian's allowance

### Child benefit

You and your child can be treated as being present in Great Britain during a 'temporary absence' (see p1370).

Provided you are ordinarily resident (see p1299), *you* are treated as present, and therefore continue to be entitled to child benefit, during a temporary absence for:[35]

- **the first eight weeks**; *or*
- **the first 12 weeks** of any period of absence, or any extension to that period, which is in connection with:
  - the treatment of an illness or disability of you, your partner, a child for whom you are responsible, or another relative of you or your partner; *or*
  - the death of your partner or child for whom you or your partner are responsible, or another relative of you or your partner.

**'Relative'** means sibling, parent, grandparent, great-grandparent, child, grandchild or great-grandchild.[36]

**Your child** is treated as being present during a temporary absence for:[37]

- the first 12 weeks; *or*
- any period during which they are absent for the specific purpose of being treated for an illness or disability which began before their absence began; *or*
- any period when they are in Northern Ireland; *or*
- any period during which they are absent because they are:
  - receiving full-time education at a school or college in an EEA country; *or*
  - engaged in an educational exchange or visit made with the written approval of the school or college which they normally attend; *or*
  - a child who normally lives with a Crown servant posted overseas, who is either in the same country as the Crown servant or is absent from that country for one of the reasons in the above two bullet points.[38]

9

If a child is born outside the UK during the eight- or 12-week period in which you could be treated as being present in Great Britain, they are treated as being in the UK for up to 12 weeks from the start of your absence.[39]

While you and your child are present, or treated as present, you can continue to receive child benefit that was already in payment and can also make a fresh claim during your, or their, absence.

## Scottish child payment

You cease to be entitled to a Scottish child payment the week after you cease to be ordinarily resident in Scotland (see p1299).[40]

## Guardian's allowance

Entitlement to guardian's allowance depends on entitlement to child benefit, so you can be paid guardian's allowance abroad for the same period as child benefit.

However, your guardian's allowance is not uprated each year if you have ceased to be ordinarily resident in Great Britain on the day before the annual uprating takes place,[41] unless you have gone to an EEA country and you are covered by the EU co-ordination rules or you can rely on a reciprocal agreement.

### European Union co-ordination rules

If you are covered by the main EU co-ordination rules or the UK–Ireland Convention (see p1392):

- you can be paid child benefit and guardian's allowance for a child resident in an EEA country (Ireland, if you rely on the Convention). They do not have to be in education; *and/or*
- you can be paid child benefit and guardian's allowance, and your benefit can be uprated, if you go to stay or live in an EEA country (Ireland, if you rely on the Convention) *if* the UK continues to be your competent state (see p1404).

Child benefit and guardian's allowance are categorised under the main EU co-ordination rules, and listed under the UK–Ireland Convention, as 'family benefits' (see p1409).

Scottish child payment has been categorised as a special non-contributory benefit (see p1403), so the above rules do not apply.

The UK–EU Protocol and UK–EFTA Convention do not cover family benefits.

## Disability and carers' benefits

Provided you continue to be habitually resident, if you go abroad, you are treated as present in Great Britain (or in England and Wales for disability living allowance (DLA), or in the common travel area, for pension age disability payment (PADP), adult disability payment (ADP), child disability payment (CDP), Scottish adult disability living allowance (SADLA) and CSP). You can therefore continue to be entitled to, or make a new claim for, attendance allowance (AA), PADP, DLA, CDP, SADLA, personal independence payment (PIP), ADP, CA or CSP:[42]

- (except CA) for the first **13 weeks** of a 'temporary absence' (see p1370). For CSP, you must be abroad specifically to care for the person for whom you receive CSP; *or*
- (except CA) for the first **26 weeks** of a 'temporary absence' (see p1370), if the absence is solely in connection with medical treatment for your (or for CSP only, the person for whom you receive CSP) illness or disability that began before you (or they) left Great Britain (common travel area, for CDP, ADP, PADP, SADLA and CSP) (and for CSP, your absence is specifically to care for that person); *or*
- (for CA and CSP only) for up to **four weeks.** For CA, the absence must be, and have been when it began, for a temporary purpose and must not exceed four weeks. For CSP, you are treated as present for the first four weeks of any 'temporary absence'. If you are not accompanied by the person for whom you are caring, you must satisfy the rules that entitle you to CA or CSP during a break from caring (see p473 and p1469); *or*

9

- (for CA only) if your absence is temporary and is for the specific purpose of caring for someone who is also absent from Great Britain and who continues to receive AA, DLA/CDP care component paid at the highest or middle rate, the daily living component of PIP/ADP, armed forces independence payment (AFIP) or constant attendance allowance; *or*
- (for DLA for a child only) while you are temporarily absent from England and Wales and are present in Scotland; *or*
- if you are abroad in your capacity as an aircraft worker, mariner or continental shelf worker; *or*
- (for AA, DLA, PIP and CA) while you are a serving member of the armed forces or are living with someone who is abroad as a serving member of the armed forces and they are your spouse, civil partner, child, stepchild, parent, step-parent or parent-in-law. You are also *treated as* habitually resident; *or*
- (for ADP, CDP, PADP, SADLA and CSP) while you are a serving member of the armed forces or a civil servant, and immediately before the start of either employment outside the common travel area, you satisfied the residence and presence conditions (other than the past presence test), or you are living with someone who is abroad as a serving member of the forces or civil servant, and you are the spouse, civil partner, or living together as if you were either, or child, stepchild, or a child in the care of, or (except for CDP) the parent, step-parent or parent-in-law, of that person. You are also treated as habitually resident, ordinarily resident and are exempt from the past presence test (see p1348).

If you move from Scotland to another part of the UK or move to Scotland from another part of the UK, see p1419 for the rules about ADP, CDP, PADP, SADLA, CSP, PIP, AA, CA and DLA.

## European Union co-ordination rules

If you move to an EEA country and are covered by the main EU co-ordination rules (or, if you move from the UK to Ireland, the UK–Ireland Convention, or, if you move from the UK to Gibraltar, the agreement between the UK and Gibraltar) (see p1392), you can continue to be paid (or, except SADLA, make a new claim for) **AA/PADP, the care component of DLA/CDP/SADLA, the daily living component of PIP/ADP, CSP and CA** without having to satisfy the presence, past presence and habitual residence (and for ADP/CDP/PADP/SADLA/CSP, the ordinary residence) tests (see p1347) if:[43]

- you are habitually resident in an EEA country (Ireland if relying on the UK–Ireland Convention, or Gibraltar if relying on the agreement with Gibraltar); *and*
- you can demonstrate a 'genuine and sufficient link' to the UK (to Scotland for ADP, CDP, PADP, SADLA and CSP) (see p1351).

You can continue to be paid for as long as the UK remains your 'competent state' (see p1404).[44]

You can make a new claim for carer's allowance supplement or young carer grant without needing to be resident or ordinarily resident in Scotland if:[45]

- you have a 'genuine and sufficient link' to Scotland (see p1351); *and*
- the UK is your 'competent state' to pay this benefit; *and*
- you are either:
  - resident in an EEA state and covered by the main EU co-ordination rules (see p1396); *or*
  - resident in Ireland and covered by the UK–Ireland Convention (see p1397); *or*
  - resident in Gibraltar and covered by the agreement between the UK and Gibraltar (see p1393).

You can only be paid the **mobility components of DLA, CDP, SADLA, PIP and ADP** while you are resident in the UK, because each is classed, or treated, as a 'special non-contributory benefit' under the main co-ordination rules (see p1403). The UK–Ireland Convention does not cover mobility components.

Disability and carers' benefits are not covered by the UK–EU Protocol or the UK–EFTA Convention at all (see p1402).

If you receive CA while in the UK and the main EU co-ordination rules apply to you, you may be able to continue to be paid an addition for an adult or child who goes to stay or live in an EEA country. See p1409 for more information.

9

## Contributory employment and support allowance

You cannot usually get ESA if you are not in Great Britain.[46] However, contributory ESA can continue to be paid when you are temporarily absent from Great Britain in the same circumstances as income-related ESA (see p1373).

### European Union co-ordination rules

If you are covered by the main co-ordination rules or the UK–Ireland Convention (see p1392) and the UK is your 'competent state' (see p1404), you can, if you go to live in an EEA country (Ireland if relying on the UK–Ireland Convention), continue to be paid contributory ESA.[47] However, if you are only covered by the UK–EU Protocol or the UK–EFTA Convention, DWP guidance states that contributory ESA is not exportable because it is treated as an 'invalidity' benefit (see p1402).

If the UK continues to pay your contributory ESA while you are resident in an EEA country (or Ireland), the DWP continues to assess your limited capability for work and your limited capability for work-related activity. However, any checks and medicals take place in the state in which you live, and the reports are sent to the DWP.[48]

None of the co-ordination rules assist you to be paid income-related ESA abroad, and you can only be paid abroad under the UK rules on p1373.

## Industrial injuries benefits

Disablement benefit and retirement allowance are not affected if you go abroad.[49]

Constant attendance allowance and exceptionally severe disablement allowance are payable for the first six months of a temporary absence, or a longer period that the DWP may allow.[50]

Reduced earnings allowance (REA) can be paid while you are temporarily absent abroad for the first three months, or longer if the DWP allows, if:[51]

- your absence from Great Britain is *not* in connection with employment, trade or business; *and*
- your claim was made before you left Great Britain; *and*
- you were entitled to REA before going abroad.

**Note:** REA has now been abolished. If you break your claim, you may no longer be eligible for benefit.

### European Union co-ordination rules

Industrial injuries benefits, except retirement allowance, are classed as 'benefits for accidents at work and occupational diseases' under each of the EU co-ordination rules (see p1400). If you are covered by these rules (see p1392) and you go to stay or live in an EEA country covered by the set of co-ordination rules you are relying on, you can be paid industrial injuries benefits without any time limit and they are fully uprated each year. See p1408 for more details.

9

## New-style jobseeker's allowance

You cannot usually get new-style JSA if you are not in Great Britain.[52] However, provided you meet the other conditions of entitlement, you can continue to be entitled when you are temporarily absent:[53]

- **indefinitely**, if you are entitled to new-style JSA immediately before leaving Great Britain and your absence is for NHS treatment at a hospital or other institution outside Great Britain; *or*
- **for up to four weeks**, if you are entitled to new-style JSA immediately before leaving Great Britain and
  - your absence is unlikely to exceed 52 weeks, you continue to satisfy the conditions of entitlement and you are in Northern Ireland. **Note:** the reciprocal agreements between Great Britain and Northern Ireland can mean that after four weeks, the administration of your claim transfers to Northern Ireland – you do not need to make a new claim;[54] *or*
- **for up to eight weeks**, if you are entitled to new-style JSA immediately before leaving Great Britain and your absence is unlikely to exceed 52 weeks and is

solely in connection with arrangements made to treat a disease or disablement of a child who is a member of your family (see p258); *or*
- **for an absence of up to seven days**, if you are attending a job interview and you notified your work coach before you left (in writing if required). On your return, you must satisfy them that you attended the interview as stated; *or*
- **for an absence of up to 15 days**, to train as a member of the reserve forces.

'Treatment' must be carried out by, or under the supervision of, a person qualified to provide medical treatment, physiotherapy or similar treatment.

You are exempt from the work search requirement and are treated as 'able and willing immediately to take up work' during certain temporary absences abroad. These are similar to, but more limited than, those listed above (see p963).[55]

### European Union co-ordination rules

New-style JSA is classed as an 'unemployment benefit' under each of the EU co-ordination rules (see p1400). However, the UK–EU Protocol and the UK–EFTA Convention do not provide for unemployment benefits to be 'exported'.[56]

If you are covered by the main co-ordination rules or the UK–Ireland Convention (see p1392) and the UK is your 'competent state' (see p1404), you can continue to be paid new-style JSA for up to three months if:[57]
- you satisfied the conditions for new-style JSA for at least four weeks before you left the UK, unless the DWP authorised you to go abroad before then; *and*
- you register as unemployed in the EEA state you go to (Ireland, if relying on the UK–Ireland Convention) within seven days and comply with its procedures.

9

## Maternity allowance, incapacity benefit and severe disablement allowance

If you are temporarily absent from Great Britain, you can continue to be paid maternity allowance (MA), incapacity benefit (IB) and severe disablement allowance (SDA) if:[58]
- you are receiving AA, PADP, DLA, CDP, SADLA, PIP, ADP or AFIP (see p1378); *or*
- the DWP agrees. You can then receive the benefit for the first 26 weeks of your temporary absence; *or*
- you are the spouse, civil partner, child, stepchild, parent, step-parent or parent-in-law of a serving member of the armed forces, and you are abroad only because you are living with them.

In addition:
- when you left Great Britain, you must have been continuously incapable of work for six months and have been continuously incapable since your departure; *or*

- your absence from Great Britain must be for the specific purpose of being treated for an incapacity which began before you left Great Britain; *or*
- for IB only, the incapacity for work is the result of a personal injury caused by an accident at work (see p589) and your absence from Great Britain is for the specific purpose of receiving treatment for it.

If you are due to have a medical examination, this can be arranged abroad.

**Note:** most IB and SDA claims have been transferred to ESA (see p563). If you lose entitlement to IB or SDA by going abroad, you are not entitled to contributory ESA on your return if you do not satisfy the contribution conditions at that time.

You can continue to be paid an increase for your spouse/civil partner or dependent adult in your IB or SDA while they are abroad if you are entitled to IB/SDA and you are residing with them. You can be treated as residing together during a temporary absence from each other.[59]

### European Union co-ordination rules

If you are covered by any of the EU co-ordination rules (see p1392) and the UK is your 'competent state' for the payment of this benefit (see p1404), you can be paid **MA** if you go to stay or live in an EEA country covered by the set of co-ordination rules you are relying on, as MA is classed as a 'maternity benefit' under each set of co-ordination rules (see p1400).[60]

If you are covered by the main co-ordination rules, you can continue to be paid your **IB** and **SDA**, including any uprating, if you go to live in an EEA country, as both are classed as 'invalidity benefits' under these rules (see p1400). The UK continues to determine your incapacity for work, but any checks and medicals take place in the country where you live and the reports are then sent to the paying state.[61] If you remain in the UK, you may be able to continue to be paid an increase in your IB or SDA for an adult or child if they go to stay or live in an EEA country (see p1409).

See p1408 for more details on exporting benefits.

## Retirement pension

All retirement pensions are payable without time limit while you are abroad.[62] However, unless you have gone to an EEA country and you are covered by the EU co-ordination rules or you can rely on a reciprocal agreement, if you are not ordinarily resident (see p1299) in Great Britain:[63]

- on the day before the annual uprating takes place, your benefit is not uprated that year;[64]
- for state pension only, when you claim a pension that you have deferred, the upratings that occurred while you were abroad are ignored when calculating both the deferral increase and rate payable;
- for 'old' retirement pensions only, you cannot stop claiming your pension ('de-retire') to accrue a deferral payment.[65]

9

Although category D retirement pension is payable if you are abroad, you must meet the residence requirements on the date you claim, see p1354.

### European Union co-ordination rules

Retirement pensions are classed as 'old age benefits' under each of the EU co-ordination rules (see p1400). If you are covered by these rules (see p1392), the UK is your 'competent state' (see p1404) and you go to stay or live in an EEA country covered by the rules you are relying on:

- you can continue to be paid your retirement pension without any time limit, including your annual uprating;
- you can opt to stop claiming your pension ('de-retire') to accrue a deferral payment while living in an EEA country (Ireland, if relying on the Convention).

**Note:** if you are moving to Switzerland, see p1354.

If you are covered by the main EU co-ordination rules and you remain in the UK, you may be able to continue to be paid an increase for a child who goes to stay or live in an EEA country (see p1409).

### Reciprocal agreements

If you are covered by a reciprocal agreement (see p1297) that provides for uprating, you can be paid your pension at the same rate as if you were still in the UK, including your annual uprating. **Note:** the agreements with Canada and New Zealand, and the former agreement with Australia, do not provide for uprating.

9

## Statutory payments

There are no presence or residence rules for statutory sick pay (SSP), statutory maternity pay (SMP), statutory adoption pay (SAP), statutory paternity pay (SPP), statutory shared parental pay (SSPP), statutory parental bereavement pay (SPBP) and statutory neonatal care pay (SNCP). You remain entitled to these benefits if you go abroad, provided you meet the entitlement rules, including those relating to being an employee at the relevant time (see Chapters 34 and 35).

Although you are generally required to be employed in Great Britain to count as an 'employee', you count as an employee even while employed abroad in certain circumstances, including if:[66]

- your employer is required to pay secondary class 1 national insurance (NI) contributions for you; *or*
- you are a continental shelf worker or, in certain circumstances, an aircraft worker or mariner; *or*
- you are employed in an EEA country and, had you been employed in Great Britain, you would have been considered an employee, and the UK is the competent state under the EU co-ordination rules (see p1404).

Your employer is not required to pay you SSP, SMP, SAP, SPP, SSPP, SNCP or SPBP if:[67]

- your employer is not required by law to pay employer's class 1 NI contributions (even if those contributions are in fact made) because, at the time they become payable, your employer:
  - is not resident or present in Great Britain; *and*
  - has (or is treated as having) no place of business in Great Britain; *or*
- because of an international treaty or convention, your employer is exempt from the Social Security Acts or those Acts are not enforceable against your employer.

## European Union co-ordination rules

It has always been arguable that SSP is a 'sickness benefit' and SMP, SAP, SPP, SSPP, SNCP and SPBP are 'maternity/paternity benefits', and recent guidance lists them as such (see p1400).[68] However, the absence of residence and presence requirements for these benefits means you can generally be paid these benefits if you go abroad without needing to rely on co-ordination rules.

The UK–Ireland Convention prevents these benefits being paid at the same time as Irish sickness, invalidity, maternity or paternity benefits.[69]

# Notes



1. **Overview of the rules on getting paid abroad**

1 *R v Barnet LBC ex parte Shah* [1983] 2 AC 309 (HL), Lord Scarman at p342D; see also *GC v HMRC (TC)* [2014] UKUT 251 (AAC)
2 Vol 2 Ch 7 Pt 1 para 070642 DMG; paras C1122 and C1008 ADM
3 *Slough BC v PK* [2019] UKUT 128 (AAC)
4 **CB** Reg 24(2) CB Regs
**AA** Reg 2(3C) SS(AA) Regs
**PADP** Reg 10(2)(a) DAOP(S) Regs
**ADP** Reg 16(2) DAWAP(S) Regs
**CDP** Reg 7(2)(a) DACYP(S) Regs
**SADLA** Reg 17(2)(a) DA(SADLA) Regs
**CSP** Reg 7(2) CA(CSP)(S) Regs
**DLA** Reg 2(3C) SS(DLA) Regs
**PIP** Reg 17(2) SS(PIP) Regs
5 *Chief Adjudication Officer v Ahmed and Others*, 16 March 1994 (CA), reported as R(S) 1/96
6 R(S) 1/85; Vol 2 Ch 7 Pt 1 para 070877 DMG
7 R(U) 16/62; Vol 2 Ch 7 Pt 1 para 070864 DMG

2. **Rules for specific benefits**

8 ss3 and 4(1)(c) WRA 2012
9 Reg 11 UC Regs
10 Reg 10 UC Regs
11 Reg 99(1)-(3) UC Regs
12 Sch para 2 The Universal Credit (Northern Ireland Reciprocal Arrangements) Regulations 2020 No.677; ADM Memo 18/20, para 3
13 Regs 29 and 30 UC Regs
14 Reg 3(3) UC Regs; reg 9(1) UC,PIP,JSA&ESA(C&P) Regs
15 Regs 3, 18, 22 and 36 UC Regs

16 Art 7(1), (2)(a) and (b) and (3)(b) WRA(No.31)O; HB Circular A9/2019, paras 15-17; Vol 13 Ch 77, paras 77035 note 2, 77150-51 and 77160 DMG
17 Reg 4(7) UC Regs
18 ss1(3)(d) and 18(4)(a) WRA 2007
19 Regs 151-55 ESA Regs; regs 88-92 ESA Regs 2013
20 Reg 156 and Sch 5 paras 6 and 7 ESA Regs
21 Reg 156 and Sch 5 para 7 ESA Regs
22 Reg 156 ESA Regs
23 s130(1)(a) SSCBA 1992
24 Reg 7 HB Regs; reg 7 HB(SPC) Regs
25 *Slough BC v PK* [2019] UKUT 128 (AAC)
26 Art 18 TFEU; Art 24 EU Dir 2004/38; *O'Flynn v Adjudication Officer*, C-237/94 [1996]; R(IS) 4/98
27 Regs 7 and 21 HB Regs; regs 7 and 21 HB(SPC) Regs
28 s1(2)(a) SPCA 2002
29 Reg 3 SPC Regs
30 Reg 5 SPC Regs
31 Reg 5 SPC Regs
32 Sch IIA para 7 SPC Regs; DMG Memo 14/18, paras 21-24
33 Reg 5 SSB(PA) Regs
34 Arts 5, 7, 42 and 43 EU Reg 883/04; Arts 5, 7 and 43 UK-IC; Arts 6, 8, 37 and 38 UK-EUP; Arts 9, 11, 43 and 44 UK-EFTA
35 Reg 24 CB Regs
36 Reg 24(1) CB Regs
37 Reg 21 CB Regs
38 Reg 32 CB Regs
39 Reg 21(2) CB Regs
40 Reg 19 SCP Regs
41 Reg 5 SSB(PA) Regs
42 **AA** Reg 2(2), (3B) and (3C) SS(AA) Regs
**DLA** Regs 2(2), (2A), (3B) and (3C), 2ZA and 2ZB SS(DLA) Regs
**PIP** Regs 17-20 SS(PIP) Regs
**CA** Reg 9(2) and (3) SS(ICA) Regs
**CDP** Regs 5(6)-(8) and (10) and 7 DACYP(S) Regs
**CSP** Regs 7 and 8 CA(CSP)(S) Regs
**ADP** Regs 16-18 DAWAP(S) Regs
**PADP** Regs 10, 11 and 12 DAOP(S) Regs
**SADLA** Regs 11, 12 and 13 DA(SADLA) Regs
43 **AA** Reg 2B SS(AA) Regs
**PADP** Reg 14 DAOP(S) Regs
**DLA** Reg 2B SS(DLA) Regs
**CDP** Regs 5(4)-(5) and 9 DACYP(S) Regs
**SADLA** Reg 15 DA(SADLA) Regs
**PIP** Reg 23 SS(PIP) Regs
**ADP** Regs 15(3)-(4) and 20 DAWAP(S) Regs
**CA** Reg 9B SS(ICA) Regs
**CSP** Reg 11 CA(CSP)(S) Regs
**All** See Art 7 EU Reg 883/04; see also ADM Memos 9/20 and 17/20, and DMG Memos 12/20 and 16/20
44 **AA** s65(7) SSCBA 1992
**PADP** Regs 9(3), 14(2)(a)(ii) and 16 DAOP(S) Regs
**DLA** s72(7B) SSCBA 1992
**CDP** Regs 5(4)(c)(ii), 9(2)(a)(ii) and 9A DACYP(S) Regs
**SADLA** Regs 10(3)(c)(ii), 14(2)(a)(ii) and 15 DA(SADLA) Regs
**PIP** s84 WRA 2012
**ADP** Reg 15(3)(c)(ii), 20(2)(ii) and 20A DAWAP(S) Regs
**CA** s70(4A) SSCBA 1992
**CSP** Regs 11(a)(ii) and (4) CA(CSP)(S) Regs
45 **CAS** s81(2A) and (9)-(15) SS(S)A 2018
**YCG** Reg 8(3)-(10) CA(YCG)(S) Regs
46 ss1(3)(d) and 18(4)(a) WRA 2007
47 Confirmed in paras C4142-3 ADM
48 Arts 5, 46 and 82 EU Reg 883/04; Arts 27 and 46 EU Reg 987/2009; Art 59(7) UK-IC; Art SSC63 UK-EUP; Art 66 UK-EFTA
49 Reg 9(3) SSB(PA) Regs
50 Reg 9(4) SSB(PA) Regs
51 Reg 9(5) SSB(PA) Regs
52 s1(2)(i) JSA 1995
53 s21 and Sch 1 para 11 JSA 1995; reg 41 JSA Regs 2013
54 Sch para 2 SS(NIRA) Regs; Sch para 2 SS(GBRA)NI Regs
55 Reg 16 JSA Regs 2013
56 Arts SSC3(1) and (4) and SSC8 UK-EUP; Arts 6(1)(h) and 11 UK-EFTA
57 Art 64 EU Reg 883/04; Arts 7 and 21 UK-IC
58 Reg 2 SSB(PA) Regs
59 Reg 13 SSB(PA) Regs; reg 14 SS(IB-ID) Regs; reg 2(4) SSB(PRT) Regs
60 Arts 7 and 21 EU Reg 883/04; Art 7 UK-IC; Art SSC8 UK-EUP; Art 11 UK-EFTAC
61 Arts 5 and 46 EU Reg 883/04; Art 87 EU Reg 987/2009
62 s113 SSCBA 1992; reg 4(1) SSB(PA) Regs

63 Regs 4(3) and 5 SSB(PA) Regs; ss18 and 20 PA 2014; regs 21-23 SP Regs
64 Vol 2 Ch 7 Pt 5 paras 075780-1 and 075795 DMG
65 Reg 6 SSB(PA) Regs
66 **SSP** s163(1) SSCBA 1992; reg 16 SSP Regs; regs 5-10 SSP(MAPA) Regs
**SMP** s171(1) SSCBA 1992; regs 2, 2A, 5, 7 and 8 SMP(PAM) Regs
**SAP/SPP** ss171ZJ(2)-(3) and 171ZS(2)-(3) SSCBA 1992; regs 3, 4, 8 and 9 SPPSAP(PAM) Regs
**SSPP** s171ZZ4(2) SSCBA 1992; regs 5, 6, 7, 9, 10 SSPP(PAM) Regs
**SPBP** ss171ZZ14(2)-(3) SSCBA 1992; regs 5-10 SPBP(PAM) Regs
**SNCP** ss171ZZ24(2)-(3) SSCBA 1992; regs 5-10 SNCP(PAM) Regs
67 **SSP** Reg 16(2) SSP Regs
**SMP** Reg 3 SMP(PAM) Regs; reg 17(3) SMP Regs
**SAP/SPP** Reg 2 SPPSAP(PAM) Regs; reg 32(3) SPPSAP(G) Regs; reg 24(4) ASPP(G) Regs
**SSPP** Reg 33(5) SSPP(G) Regs; reg 4 SSPP(PAM) Regs
**SPBP** Reg 11(5) SPBP(G) Regs; reg 4 SPBP(PAM) Regs
**SNCP** Reg 14(5) SNCP(G) Regs (draft); reg 4 SNCP(PAM) Regs
68 DWPWAG, Fig 4, in contrast to Vol 2 Ch 7 Pt 1 para 070153 DMG
69 Arts 16 and 17 UK-IC

# Chapter 59

# European Union co-ordination rules

**This chapter covers:**


1. Introduction (below)
2. Who is covered (p1392)
3. Which benefits are covered (p1399)
4. Principles of co-ordination (p1404)
5. Family benefits (p1409)


## Key facts

- If your circumstances involve more than one European Economic Area (EEA) state (or the UK and an EEA state), your benefit entitlements may be affected by the European Union (EU) co-ordination rules.
- The EU co-ordination rules are most relevant when you have moved to the UK from an EEA country or vice versa.
- This *Handbook* uses the phrase 'EU co-ordination rules' to refer to five sets of co-ordination rules, which can currently apply. They provide similar social security rights and require similar conditions to be met, but differ in terms of who, which countries and which benefits each covers, and how they can affect entitlements.

9

## 1. Introduction

In this *Handbook*, the phrase 'EU co-ordination rules' refers to five different pieces, or collections, of legislation, which provide broadly similar social security rights and require broadly similar conditions to be met. However, the rules contain important differences in terms of who, which European countries and which benefits are covered by each, and the ways they affect benefit entitlements. These differences and how to determine which rules apply to you are covered in this chapter.

The co-ordination rules can affect whether you are entitled to benefits in the UK. In most cases, they make it easier to satisfy the UK rules – eg, by enabling you to count periods of residence, insurance and employment in a European

Economic Area (EEA) country to meet the conditions of entitlement for a UK benefit. However, in limited circumstances, the co-ordination rules can prevent you from claiming a UK benefit if, for example, the UK is not the 'competent state' to pay that type of benefit. For the effects on individual benefits, see the rules starting on p1342.

The co-ordination rules can also help you to be paid a UK benefit while you are abroad in an EEA country for longer than under UK law alone. For the effects on individual benefits, see the rules starting on p1370.

## Overview

The original aim of the European Union (EU) co-ordination rules was to secure and promote European free movement by co-ordinating the social security systems within the EEA to ensure that those covered do not lose out on social security protection as a result of moving to another member state.

The phrase **'member state'**, when used in the context of the co-ordination rules in this *Handbook*, means those states covered by the specific rules being referred to. The main co-ordination rules and the old co-ordination rules cover the UK and all EEA states plus Switzerland; the UK–EU Protocol covers the UK and EU states; the UK–EFTA Convention covers the UK and Iceland, Liechtenstein and Norway; and the UK–Ireland Convention is an agreement between the UK and Ireland. For disability and carers' benefits, 'member state' also includes the UK and Gibraltar, if the UK–Gibraltar Agreement applies.

### *Member states of the European Union*

| | | | |
|---|---|---|---|
| Austria | Estonia | Italy | Portugal |
| Belgium | Finland | Latvia | Romania |
| Bulgaria | France | Lithuania | Slovakia |
| Croatia | Germany | Luxembourg | Slovenia |
| Cyprus | Greece | Malta | Spain |
| Czech Republic | Hungary | The Netherlands | Sweden |
| Denmark | Ireland | Poland | |

### *Member states of the European Economic Area*

The EEA consists of the EU countries plus three of the European Free Trade Association (EFTA) countries: Iceland, Liechtenstein and Norway.

The fourth EFTA state is Switzerland, which is not part of the EEA. However, agreements with Switzerland mean that, in general, Swiss nationals are treated the same as EEA nationals. In this *Handbook*, references to EEA nationals therefore also include Swiss nationals, and references to EEA countries include Switzerland.[1] Note also the bilateral agreement between the UK and Switzerland (see p1393).

EU law, including the co-ordination rules, applies beyond the actual territory of the EEA states to territories 'for whose external relations a member state is responsible'.[2]

## The five sets of co-ordination rules

Until the UK left the EU on 31 January 2020, the main EU co-ordination rules covered most EEA nationals and their family members who moved between EEA member states. These rules, and the European caselaw which interpreted them, continued to apply during the transition period, which followed the UK leaving the EU and ended at 11pm on 31 December 2020.

From the end of the transition period, in general, the main EU co-ordination rules ceased to apply within UK law. However, the Withdrawal Agreements provide protections for people in certain situations to continue to use these co-ordination rules (see p1393).

If you are covered by the Withdrawal Agreement protections (and during the transition period), the main EU co-ordination rules continue to apply to the UK *as if* it were still an EU or EEA member state, and, if you are a British citizen, *as if* you were still an EU or EEA citizen.

If you are not covered by the Withdrawal Agreement protections, the UK–EU Protocol on Social Security or, since 1 January 2024, the UK–EFTA Convention on Social Security may apply. In addition, the UK–Ireland Convention on Social Security may apply, but only between those two countries.

This *Handbook* covers the following five sets of co-ordination rules.

- **The main co-ordination rules** – can apply if you are an EEA national or British citizen (or family member of either) covered by the Withdrawal Agreement protections (see p1393). The main co-ordination rules can also apply in limited ways if you are covered by the partial Withdrawal Agreement protections (see p1395).
- **The old co-ordination rules** – can apply in limited circumstances, mainly for non-EEA (and non-British) nationals covered by the Withdrawal Agreement protections.
- **The UK–EU Protocol on Social Security** – provides more limited social security co-ordination between the UK and EU countries for those not covered by the Withdrawal Agreement protections.
- **The UK–EFTA Convention on Social Security** – provides more limited social security co-ordination between the UK and Iceland, Liechtenstein and Norway for those not covered by the Withdrawal Agreement protections.
- **The UK–Ireland Convention on Social Security** – broadly reproduces the principles and effects of the main co-ordination rules, but only between the UK and Ireland for specified benefits.

For a summary of the co-ordination principles in each set of rules, see p1391. For who is covered by each of the five sets of rules, see p1392. For the benefits covered by each set of rules, see p1399.

Since leaving the EU, the UK has negotiated new agreements with **Switzerland** and with **Gibraltar**, which broadly reproduce some of the co-ordination principles, but only on a bilateral basis (see p1393).

## How to check if the co-ordination rules apply

To check whether and how the co-ordination rules apply to you, work through the following steps.

- **Step 1**: check which, if any, of the sets of co-ordination rules you are covered by. Follow the steps on p1392.
- **Step 2**: check whether the benefit you want to claim is covered by the relevant co-ordination rules, and into which category it falls (see p1399).
- **Step 3**: check which state is the 'competent state' to pay the benefit you are claiming (see p1404).
- **Step 4**: check the principle you want to apply. See below for a list.
- **Step 5**: check how that principle can affect your entitlement to the particular benefit:
  - while you are in the UK – see the rules starting on p1342; *or*
  - while you or a member of your family are in an EEA country – see the rules starting on p1370.

The co-ordination rules are complex and this chapter only provides an overview. For more information, see CPAG's *Benefits for Migrants Handbook*.

## The co-ordination principles

The following principles are contained in the main co-ordination rules in relation to the EEA and UK, in the UK–EU Protocol in relation to the EU and UK, in the UK–EFTA Convention in relation to Iceland, Liechtenstein and Norway and the UK, and in the UK–Ireland Convention in relation to Ireland and the UK.

- **The single-state principle**. You can generally, at any one time, only claim a particular category of benefit from one member state, referred to as the 'competent state' (see p1404).
- **Equal treatment of people.** Discrimination on nationality grounds, in terms of access to, the rate of and payment of the benefits covered, is prohibited (see p1406).
- **Equal treatment of benefits, income, facts or events.** If receipt of a benefit, or a fact or an event has a legal consequence in one member state, this must be recognised in the same way by other member states (see p1406).
- **Aggregation.** Periods of residence, insurance and employment in any member state can be used towards entitlement to benefit in another (see p1406).
- **Exportability of certain benefits**. You can continue to be paid certain benefits if you go to another member state (see p1408).
- **Administrative co-operation.** Member states undertake to co-operate in administrating the co-ordination rules.

## 2. **Who is covered**

This *Handbook* refers to you being 'covered by the co-ordination rules' if one of the five sets of rules that co-ordinate the social security systems throughout all or part of the European Economic Area (EEA – see p1389) and UK applies to you. It is important to identify which, if any, you are covered by, as some of the specific provisions differ.

Check which rules apply by working through the following steps.

- **Step 1:** are you covered by the **Withdrawal Agreement protections** (see below)? If so, you are potentially covered by the **main co-ordination rules**, so you next need to check whether you *are* covered by the main co-ordination rules (see p1396). The Withdrawal Agreement protections can also mean that you can potentially be covered by the **old co-ordination rules** (see p1396). If you are covered by the main (or the old) co-ordination rules, they apply to the UK and all the EEA countries.
- **Step 2:** are you covered by the **partial Withdrawal Agreement protections** (see p1395)? These can apply if you are not, or are no longer, covered by the Withdrawal Agreement protections. They mean you can potentially use specific provisions of the main (or old) co-ordination rules, in particular the aggregation principle, so you next need to check whether you *are* covered by these rules.
- **Step 3:** are you covered by the **UK–Ireland Convention**? This can apply if you are (or you are a member of the family of) an Irish or British citizen or a refugee and live in either Ireland or the UK. These rules only apply to the UK and Ireland. See p1397.
- **Step 4:** are you covered by the **UK–EU Protocol**? This can apply if you have only moved between the UK and the European Union (EU) since the end of 2020 and the other co-ordination rules do not apply at all or only in a limited way. These rules only apply to the UK and EU countries. See p1397.
- **Step 5:** are you covered by the **UK–EFTA Convention**? This can apply if you have only moved between the UK and three of the European Free Trade Association (EFTA) countries (Iceland, Liechtenstein and Norway) since 1 January 2024 and the other co-ordination rules do not apply at all or only in a limited way. These rules only apply to the UK and Iceland, Liechtenstein and Norway. See p1398.

**Note:**

- Whether or not you are covered by specific co-ordination rules depends on your circumstances. This is significant, as the effects of being covered can be negative (eg, if you are excluded from a disability or carer's benefit because the UK is not your 'competent state' for that type of benefit) as well as positive (eg, enabling you to be entitled to a benefit sooner than you would be under UK rules alone).

- If you are covered by the main co-ordination rules *and* another set of rules, in general, you are covered by the former.[3] However, if you are covered by both the main co-ordination rules and the UK–Ireland Convention, you can rely on whichever is the more generous.[4]
- If your situation involves the UK and **Switzerland** and you are not covered by the main co-ordination rules, note that Switzerland is not covered by the UK–EU Protocol or the UK–EFTA Convention. However, there is a new agreement between the UK and Switzerland, which broadly reproduces the co-ordination principles in a similar way to the Protocol and Convention, but just between the UK and Switzerland.[5] For details, see CPAG's *Benefits for Migrants Handbook*.
- If your situation involves the UK and **Gibraltar**, you may be covered by the UK–Gibraltar Agreement.[6] This broadly reproduces the principles and effects of the main co-ordination rules, but only between the UK and Gibraltar. It applies to anyone legally residing in and who has been 'subject to the legislation of' (see p1398) the UK or Gibraltar, and members of their families. The agreement came into force on 1 June 2024 and replaces a previous reciprocal agreement[7] (other than for claims which began before the end of 2020). In this *Handbook*, the UK–Gibraltar Agreement is only referred to in relation to disability and carers' benefits. For further details, see CPAG's *Benefits for Migrants Handbook*.

## Who is covered by Withdrawal Agreement protections



Since the end of the transition period (11pm on 31 December 2020), you can only be covered by the main co-ordination rules (or, in limited circumstances, the old co-ordination rules) if you are covered by the Withdrawal Agreement protections. **Note:** this phrase refers to the protections under each of the three Withdrawal Agreements between the UK and EU, the UK and EFTA countries (Iceland, Liechtenstein and Norway), and the UK and Switzerland.

You are covered by the Withdrawal Agreement protections if *both*:

- on 31 December 2020, one of the situations listed in the bullet points below applied to you; *and*
- since 31 December 2020, the Withdrawal Agreement protections have *continued* to apply to you (see below).

You *can be* covered by the Withdrawal Agreement protections if, on 31 December 2020, you were:[8]

- an EEA national 'subject to the legislation' (see p1398) of the UK – eg, a Polish national working in the UK; *or*
- a UK national 'subject to the legislation' of an EEA state; *or*

- an EEA national 'subject to the legislation' of an EEA state while residing in the UK – eg, a French national living in the UK receiving a French social security benefit; *or*
- a UK national 'subject to the legislation' of the UK while residing in an EEA state; *or*
- a refugee or stateless person residing in the UK or an EEA state and 'subject to the legislation' of the UK or an EEA state; *or*
- (or have become since 31 December 2020) a member of the family (see note below and p1399) or survivor of one of the above; *or*
- (other than under the EFTA or Swiss agreements) a non-EEA national covered by the old co-ordination rules (see p1396) and legally resident in, and 'subject to the legislation' of, the UK or an EEA state; *or*
- if none of the above apply, an EEA national with a European free movement right to reside in the UK (see p1317) or a UK national with an EU free movement right to reside in an EEA state. Arguably, this applies if you had such a right to reside *before* 31 December 2020, provided you continued to reside in the UK (or EEA state if you are a UK national). This issue also affects the circumstances in which pre-settled status can by itself satisfy the right to reside requirement for a means-tested benefit, and caselaw in that context is therefore relevant (see the first bullet of Step 6 on p1307);[9] *or*
- a family member (see note below and p1329) of a person in the group immediately above.

**Note:** to be covered by the sixth or last bullet above, you must currently live in the same state as the person who confers rights on you, but (unless you are relying on being an extended family member to be covered by the last bullet point) you do not need to have lived in the same state on 31 December 2020.[10]

9

If one or more of the groups listed above applies to you, the next step is to check whether these protections *continue* to apply to you (see below). If they do, then the main co-ordination rules (or, in limited circumstances, the old co-ordination rules – see p1396) can potentially apply to you. Therefore, you need to *also* check whether you are covered by the main co-ordination rules (see p1396).

The **Withdrawal Agreement protections continue to apply for as long as**:

- (if you are covered by one of the first seven bullet points above) you continue, 'without interruption', to be in one of the situations listed.[11] You can move between the situations, but there must not be an 'interruption' during which none apply. Legislation does not define 'interruption', but DWP guidance suggests that gaps of less than a month should be ignored;[12] *or*
- (if you are covered by one of the last two bullet points above) you continue to have a right to reside, or a right to work, as an EEA national in the UK, or a UK national in an EEA country, or you continue to be a family member of a person who does.[13] However, the type of right to reside you must continue to have is currently unclear. It is arguable that you do not need to continue to have a free

movement right to reside, and that it is sufficient that you continue to comply with the host country's residence scheme – eg, while you are an EEA national with pre-settled or settled status (see p1314) or a UK national complying with the residence scheme of the EEA country you have been living in (summarised on the EU Commission website[14]).[15] If you are complying with the relevant residence scheme, you may continue to have a right of residence in a country during an absence from that country.

- Absences of less than six months in a year or, in specific circumstances, up to a year are ignored under rules that are broadly the same as for absences ignored when calculating the five years to acquire a permanent right to reside (see p1339). Once you have a permanent right to reside under the Withdrawal Agreement (eg, if you are in the UK, and have obtained settled status under the EU Settlement Scheme), your right of residence only ends if you are absent for more than five years (or four years if you obtained a permanent right to reside in Switzerland).[16] This interpretation is supported by DWP guidance.[17]
- The type of right to reside you need to continue to have may be clarified by future caselaw on the circumstances in which pre-settled status can by itself satisfy the right to reside requirement for a means-tested benefit (see Steps 6 and 7 on p1307).

If you are not, or no longer, covered by the Withdrawal Agreement protections, check whether you are covered by the partial Withdrawal Agreement protections, which enable limited use of the main co-ordination rules.



## Partial Withdrawal Agreement protections

If you are not covered by the Withdrawal Agreement protections (see p1393), partial Withdrawal Agreement protections can enable you to use the 'aggregation principle' of the main co-ordination rules, or use these rules to continue to receive **family benefits** for family members living in another member state (see p1409).

The '**aggregation principle**' (see p1406) of the main co-ordination rules can potentially apply to you if you are not, or no longer, covered by the Withdrawal Agreement protections and *before* the end of the transition period (31 December 2020), you were:[18]

- an EEA national 'subject to the legislation' (see p1398) of the UK; *or*
- a UK national 'subject to the legislation' of an EEA state; *or*
- a refugee or stateless person living in an EEA state and 'subject to the legislation' of the UK or living in the UK and 'subject to the legislation' of an EEA state; *or*
- (other than under the EFTA or Swiss agreements) a non-EEA national covered by the old co-ordination rules (see p1396), 'subject to the legislation' of the UK and are currently legally resident in an EEA state, or 'subject to the legislation' of an EEA state and are currently legally resident in the UK; *or*
- a member of the family (see p1399) or a survivor of one of the above categories.

If this applies, you may be able to add together periods of residence, insurance or employment/self-employment completed in one or more EEA states or the UK to satisfy the requirements for a particular benefit, whether the periods were completed before or after the end of the transition period. If, as a result, you can potentially receive attendance allowance, pension age disability payment, carer's allowance, carer support payment, the daily living component of personal independence payment or adult disability payment, or the care component of disability living allowance or child disability payment, you are *also* subject to the requirement that the UK be the competent state to pay this benefit (see p1404).[19]

**Note:** you may also be able to *disapply* the past presence test for the disability and carers' benefits (see p1350).

## Who is covered by the main co-ordination rules

To be covered by the main co-ordination rules, you must come within the Withdrawal Agreement protections (see p1393) or the partial Withdrawal Agreement protections (see p1395) *and* come within the '**personal scope**' of the main co-ordination rules.

You are within the personal scope of the main co-ordination rules if you are:[20]

- residing in the UK or an EEA country and you have been 'subject to the legislation of' one or more of the EEA states or the UK (see p1398) and you are:
  - an EEA national; *or*
  - a British citizen; *or*
  - a refugee; *or*
  - a stateless person; *or*
- a member of the family (see p1399) or a 'survivor' of one of the above (in the UK, a widow, widower or surviving civil partner).

In addition, for the main co-ordination rules to apply, your situation must involve the UK and one or more EEA states, or at least two EEA states. This usually means that you must have moved between an EEA country and the UK (or another EEA country), or you live in one and work in another, or you live in one and are the national of another.[21]

## When the old co-ordination rules apply

This *Handbook* uses the term 'old co-ordination rules'[22] to refer to the set of rules that were succeeded by the main co-ordination rules. The old co-ordination rules can only apply to you if you are covered by the Withdrawal Agreement (or partial Withdrawal Agreement) protections (see p1393). They may apply if you are a non-EEA (and non-British) national (other than a refugee or member of the family of an EEA or British citizen who is covered by the main rules), legally resident in an EEA country or the UK. They may also continue to apply to you if you have already been relying on them to receive your benefit since before June 2012, and your 'relevant situation remains unchanged'.[23]

Very few claims are now covered by the old co-ordination rules. For when the old co-ordination rules apply, see CPAG's *Benefits for Migrants Handbook.*

## Who is covered by the UK–Ireland Convention

To be covered by the UK–Ireland Convention on Social Security, you must come within the 'personal scope' of this Convention. In addition, your situation must involve both the UK and Ireland. This generally means that you have moved between the two states, or you live in one and work in the other, or you live in one and are a national of the other.

You are within the personal scope of the UK–Ireland Convention on Social Security if you are:[24]

- residing in the UK or Ireland and you are or, have been, 'subject to the legislation of' the UK or Ireland (see p1398) and you are:
  - an Irish citizen; *or*
  - a British citizen; *or*
  - a refugee; *or*
  - a stateless person; *or*
- a member of the family (see p1399) or a survivor of someone covered in the above bullet point. 'Survivor' is defined as a surviving spouse, civil partner or child to whom a survivor's benefit or death grant is payable under Irish or (not including for a child) UK legislation.[25]

**Note:** if you are covered by both the UK–Ireland Convention and the main co-ordination rules (only possible if you are covered by the Withdrawal Agreement protections – see p1393), you can rely on whichever is the more generous.[26]

9

## Who is covered by the UK–EU Protocol

You are covered by the UK–EU Protocol if you are, or have been, 'subject to the legislation of' (see p1398) the UK or an EU state, or you are a 'member of the family' (see p1399) or survivor (not defined) of someone who has.[27] In addition, your situation must involve either the UK and one or more EU states (see p1389) or at least two EU states. This generally means that you must have moved between an EU state and the UK (or another EU state), or you live in one and work in another, or you live in one but are the national of another.[28]

**Note:**

- You can be covered by the Protocol regardless of your nationality. The Protocol simply applies to 'persons, including stateless persons and refugees' who satisfy the above requirements.[29]
- The Protocol is between the UK and the EU. Unlike the main EU co-ordinaton rules, it does not extend to Iceland, Liechtenstein, Norway and Switzerland.

However, the first three of these countries are covered by the new UK–EFTA Convention (see below) and the UK has a bilateral agreement with Switzerland (see p1393).

## Who is covered by the UK–EFTA Convention

You are covered by the UK–EFTA Convention if you are, or have been, 'subject to the legislation of' (see below) the UK or Iceland, Liechtenstein or Norway, or you are a 'member of the family' (see p1399) or survivor (not defined) of someone who has, and you are, or were, legally residing in one of those states.[30] In addition, your situation must involve the UK and one or more of the three EFTA states. This generally means that you must have moved between one of these three states and the UK, or you live in one and work in another, or you live in one but are the national of another.[31]

**Note:**

- You can be covered by the UK–EFTA Convention regardless of your nationality. The Convention simply applies to 'persons, including stateless persons and refugees' who satisfy the above requirements.[32]
- The UK–EFTA Convention is between the UK and Iceland, Liechtenstein and Norway. Unlike the main EU co-ordinaton rules, it does not extend to the EU states or Switzerland. However, the EU states are covered by the new UK–EU Protocol (see p1397) and the UK has a bilateral agreement with Switzerland (see p1393).

9

## Common terms

### Subject to the legislation of

The requirement that you (or the person you are a member of the family of) have been 'subject to the legislation of' one of the member states to which the relevant Withdrawal Agreement, or co-ordination rules, applies is essential to be covered by any of the co-ordinating rules.

***Subject to the legislation of***

You have been **'subject to the legislation of'** a state if you have worked in and paid (or should have paid) insurance contributions to, or received any 'social security' or 'special non-contributory' benefit (see p1399) from, that state. You may also be subject to the legislation if you are potentially eligible for any social security benefit or special non-contributory benefit.[33]

**'Legislation'** is defined as the legislation of each member state relating to the 'social security branches covered' (or under the UK–Ireland Convention, the benefits specified) in the relevant co-ordination rules.[34]

Recent DWP guidance may suggest that for the purpose of being covered by the Withdrawal Agreement protections or partial Withdrawal Agreement protections, you can be considered to have been 'subject to the legislation' of a state on 31 December 2020 solely on the basis of having been resident (see p1405) in that state on that date.[35]

## Member of the family

A member of the family of someone covered by the co-ordination rules can also rely on the rules that cover that person (which can vary depending on which rules they are covered by and the type of benefit claimed). **Note:** the consequences of being a member of someone's family are not always favourable – eg, if it changes which state is 'competent' to pay your benefit (see p1404).

***Members of the family***

You are a **'member of the family'** of a person covered by the co-ordination rules if you are:[36]

- someone defined or recognised as a member of the family, or designated as a member of the household, by the legislation under which benefits are provided; *or*
- if the legislation under which benefits are provided does not distinguish between members of the family and other people to whom the legislation applies, the person's spouse or child either under the age of 'majority' (18 in the UK) or older but dependent on the person covered.

If, under the legislation, you are only considered to be a member of the family or member of the household if you are living in the same household as the person, this condition is considered satisfied if you are mainly dependent on that person.

9

# 3. Which benefits are covered

The benefits to which the co-ordination rules apply are referred to as being within the 'material scope' of the rules.

Social security benefits are categorised according to the risk against which they are designed to provide financial protection.

The main co-ordination rules, the UK–EU Protocol and the UK–EFTA Convention do not list the benefits that assist with each risk within the legislation, but each member state must provide a list to the administrative committee for that set of rules.[37] The UK–Ireland Convention includes the benefits of each state that assist with each category of risk.[38] The categorisation of a benefit can be challenged, as it ultimately depends on its characteristics rather than how an individual state lists it.

The table starting on p1400 lists the benefits accepted as categorised for each risk under the main co-ordination rules, and the benefits listed in the UK–Ireland Convention. Under the UK–EU Protocol and the UK–EFTA Convention, benefit categorisation should follow that of the main co-ordination rules, unless the Protocol or Convention specifically provides otherwise.[39]

The UK–EU Protocol and the UK–EFTA Convention list benefits that are *not* covered. These sets of rules do not apply to:[40]

- family benefits (see p1409); *and*
- long-term care benefits. These are listed as attendance allowance (AA), disability living allowance (DLA) care component, personal independence payment (PIP) daily living component, carer's allowance (CA), carer's allowance supplement, young carer grant and (UK–EFTA Convention only) child disability payment (CDP) care component and child winter heating payment.[41] Although adult disability payment (ADP) daily living component, pension age disability payment (PADP), Scottish adult disability allowance (SADLA) care component, carer support payment (CSP) and, under the UK–EU Protocol, CDP care component and child winter heating payment are not listed, they are treated as long-term care benefits; *and*
- winter fuel or cold weather payments; *and*
- special non-contributory benefits (see p1403); *and*
- social and medical assistance (see p1403).

## Social security benefits

| *Risk* | *UK benefits listed under main co-ordination rules* | *UK benefits listed under UK–Ireland Convention* |
|---|---|---|
| Sickness | AA/PADP<br>CA/CSP<br>Carer's allowance supplement<br>Young carer grant<br>Child winter heating payment<br>DLA/CDP/SADLA care component<br>PIP/ADP daily living component<br>Statutory sick pay<br>Contributory employment and support allowance (ESA) in the assessment phase or for the first 365 days (see p1402) | Contributory ESA in the assessment phase |

9

| | | |
|---|---|---|
| Long-term care benefits | Treated as sickness benefits[42] | AA<br>DLA care component<br>PIP daily living component<br>CA<br>(CSP, PADP, CDP/SADLA care component and ADP daily living component are treated as long-term care benefits) |
| Maternity and paternity | Maternity allowance (MA)<br>Statutory maternity, adoption, paternity,<br>shared parental, neonatal care and parental bereavement pay (see p1385) | MA |
| Invalidity | AA, DLA care and mobility component and CA if you were in receipt of benefit before 1 June 1992<br>Long-term incapacity benefit<br>Severe disablement allowance<br>Contributory ESA after the assessment phase or after first 365 days (or arguably before – see p1402) | Contributory ESA after the assessment phase |
| Old age | State pension<br>Category A, B and D retirement pensions<br>Additional pension<br>Graduated retirement benefit<br>Pension age winter heating payment<br>Winter fuel payment<br>Increments – eg, to pensions<br>Age addition in pensions | State retirement pension |
| Pre-retirement | None | None |
| Survivors | Bereavement benefits | Widowed mother's allowance<br>Widow's pension<br>Widowed parent's allowance |
| Death grants | Bereavement support payment | Bereavement support payment |

| | | |
|---|---|---|
| Accidents at work and occupational diseases | Industrial injuries disablement benefit<br>Constant attendance allowance<br>Exceptionally severe disablement allowance<br>Reduced earnings allowance | Industrial injuries benefits |
| Unemployment | New-style jobseeker's allowance (JSA) | New-style JSA |
| Family benefits (see p1409) | Child benefit<br>Increases in other benefits for an adult or a child<br>Guardian's allowance | Child benefit<br>Guardian's allowance |

Note:

- **Contributory ESA** under the main co-ordination rules is classed initially as a sickness benefit during either the 91-day 'assessment phase' (older guidance[43]) or the first 365 days (recent guidance[44]) and then as an invalidity benefit thereafter. Under the UK–EU Protocol and the UK–EFTA Convention, the recent guidance states it is treated as an invalidity benefit from the outset. This is significant as invalidity benefits cannot be exported under either the UK–EU Protocol or the UK–EFTA Convention (see p1408).[45]
- The DWP considers **universal credit** (UC) to be neither a social security benefit nor a special non-contributory benefit.[46] The Court of Appeal recently upheld the decision of the Upper Tribunal[47] that the child element of UC is not a family benefit under the main co-ordination rules, and further held those rules do not provide for the child element to be severed from the whole of UC, which is a generalised, composite benefit outside the scope of those rules.[48] UC is listed as 'social assistance' in the UK–Ireland Convention (see p1403).
- For how income support, income-based JSA and tax credits were categorised under each of the co-ordination rules, see the 2024/25 edition of this *Handbook*.

9

## Disability and carers' benefits

Under **the main co-ordination rules**, AA/PADP, DLA/CDP/SADLA care component, PIP/ADP daily living component, CA, CSP, carer's allowance supplement and young carer grant are categorised, or treated, as sickness benefits.[49]

The mobility components of DLA, CDP, SADLA, PIP and ADP are categorised, or treated, as special non-contributory benefits (see below).

The **UK–Ireland Convention** categorises AA, DLA care component, PIP daily living component and CA as long-term care benefits, but then treats them in broadly the same way as sickness benefits are treated under the main co-ordination rules.[50] Although not listed under the Convention, the regulations for

CDP, ADP, PADP, CSP, young carer grant and carer's allowance supplement enable you to make a new claim for these benefits while resident in Ireland in certain circumstances if you are covered by the Convention (see p1379).[51]

The **UK–EU Protocol** and **UK–EFTA Convention** do not cover AA, PADP, CA, CSP, carer's allowance supplement and young carer grant or either component of PIP, ADP, SADLA, DLA or CDP.[52]

## Special non-contributory benefits

Under the **main EU co-ordination rules**, the UK government has only listed pension credit (PC), income-related ESA and DLA mobility component as special non-contributory benefits.[53] However, the mobility component of PIP is also accepted as a special non-contributory benefit,[54] and the mobility components of CDP, SADLA and ADP are also treated as such.[55] Scottish child payment, funeral support payment, Best Start grants and Best Start food payments have also been categorised as special non-contributory benefits.

Special non-contributory benefits can only be paid by, and under the legislation of, the state in which you reside.[56] See p1405 for how residence is determined. However, although you cannot 'export' special non-contributory benefits, all the other co-ordination principles apply.[57]

Under the **UK–EU Protocol** and the **UK–EFTA Convention**, all the above benefits are listed or treated as special non-contributory benefits. The Protocol and Convention state they do not apply at all to these benefits.[58]

The **UK–Ireland Convention** does not refer to special non-contributory benefits but defines the two means-tested benefits above as 'social assistance' (see below) and does not refer to the others.

9

## Social and medical assistance

Under the **main co-ordination rules**, the **UK–EU Protocol** and the **UK–EFTA Convention**, benefits that are neither social security nor special non-contributory benefits are considered to be social assistance and are excluded from the co-ordination rules.[59] The UK does not specify which benefits it considers to be social assistance under any of these sets of rules. The Scottish government has categorised job start payment as social assistance.

Under the **UK–Ireland Convention**, 'social assistance' is defined in relation to UK benefits as UC, PC and income-related ESA.[60] The only provisions made by the Convention for 'social assistance' relate to the recovery of overpayments from benefit paid by the other state.[61]

# 4. **Principles of co-ordination**

## The single competent state

In general, under each set of co-ordination rules, you can only claim a particular category of benefit from one member state, and are only liable to pay insurance contributions to one member state, at any one time. This is expressed as the general principle that you can only be subject to the legislation of a single member state.[62]

**Note:** the UK–Ireland Convention refers to 'competent party' rather than 'competent state', but the same principle applies.

The **'competent state'** is the one responsible for paying your benefit and to which you are liable to pay insurance contributions.[63] In general, it is the state in which you are:[64]

- employed or self-employed (even if you are not currently earning enough to pay insurance contributions[65]); *or*
- a civil servant; *or*
- (other than for the UK–EU Protocol or UK–EFTA Convention) resident while receiving an unemployment benefit under specific provisions;[66] *or*
- (other than for the UK–EU Protocol) a conscripted member of the armed forces or doing compulsory civilian service.

If none of the above apply, the competent state is the state in which you are 'resident' (see p1405).[67]

9

You are treated as still employed or self-employed if, as a result of that activity, you are receiving cash benefits (other than for the risks of old age, accidents at work, occupational diseases, or except under the UK–Ireland Convention, invalidity, sickness or being a survivor).[68]

There are **exceptions** to this general rule. For example, under the main co-ordination rules or the UK–Ireland Convention, for attendance allowance (AA), pension age disability payment (PADP), disability living allowance (DLA)/child disability payment/Scottish adult disability living allowance (SADLA) care component, personal independence payment/adult disability payment daily living component, carer's allowance (CA) and carer support payment (CSP), if you are not working and you receive a 'pension' (which includes most contribution-based state benefits, not only retirement pensions) from a European Economic Area (EEA) state *other than* the one in which you live (from Ireland or the UK, if you are covered by the UK–Ireland Convention), then the competent state will generally be the state that pays the pension.[69] Recent caselaw held that if you are entitled to one of these benefits, because the UK is your compentent state due to you residing in the UK, your entitlement is not affected by a member of your family working in an EEA state.[70] The reasoning of this caselaw had, at the time of writing, just been applied by the Upper Tribunal in a decision that held that a claimant's entitlement to CA while residing in the UK was not displaced by her husband receiving a 'pension' from Switzerland.[71] Howerver, the DWP has applied for permission to appeal. Arguably, this reasoning could also apply to mean your entitlement to one of these benefits, because the UK is your competent state due to you residing in the UK, is not displaced by *you* receiving a 'pension' from an EEA state. If you need to rely on this argument, ask your adviser to contact CPAG.

**'Residence'** means habitual residence.[72] If there is a difference of views between two states or institutions about where you are 'resident', they must agree where your centre of interest is, taking into account all your circumstances. If there is still a dispute, your intentions, especially your reasons for moving, will be decisive in establishing where you are resident.[73]

If the state in which you claim benefit decides it is not the competent state to pay that category of benefit, it must pass your claim to the state it considers competent without delay. The date you submitted a claim (or appeal) to a state that is not competent is treated as your date of claim (or appeal) by the state that is competent.[74]

If two or more states take a different view on which is competent to pay a benefit, you can get provisional payments from your state of residence (or, for family benefits under the UK–Ireland Convention, the child's state of residence[75]) or (other than under the UK–Ireland Convention), if you are not resident in any, the state to which you first applied, while the issue is resolved.[76]

## When the competent state changes

If you are subject to the legislation of a member state, it continues to be your competent state until a change makes another state competent. The main changes are:[77]

- you start to work in another member state;[78] *or*
- in some circumstances, you move to an EEA state and become resident there (see below).

**Note:** these general rules can be supplemented by other rules specific to the category of benefit being paid.[79] For example, if you are covered by the main co-ordination rules or the UK–Ireland Convention, and you start receiving a pension from an EEA state (or Ireland if you are covered by that Convention), this generally means that state becomes competent to pay most disability and carers' benefits (see above) and family benefits.

Whether the competent state changes if you move to an EEA state can be affected by the category of benefit being claimed, which co-ordination rules you are covered by and other circumstances, including if you work or receive any pensions. For example, the Court of Appeal held that, under the main co-ordination rules, the UK ceased to be the competent state for child benefit when the claimant moved with her child to reside in Spain. Consequently, entitlement to child benefit ceased and this was not altered by the UK continuing to be the competent state for the child's DLA care component, which is a different category of benefit.[80]

In general, under each set of co-ordination rules, if you continue to be entitled to a UK benefit when you move to an EEA state, the UK remains the competent state for paying that benefit until either you become employed/self-employed in the other state or, in certain circumstances, you start to receive a benefit from it.[81]

## Equal treatment

If you are covered by any of the sets of co-ordination rules, you are entitled to the same benefits under the legislation of the competent state (see p1404) as a national of that state.[82] Equal treatment is one of the fundamental rights of European Union (EU) law,[83] and the principle of non-discrimination prohibits discrimination based on your nationality. Both direct discrimination and, if it cannot be justified as proportionate and in pursuit of a legitimate aim, indirect discrimination based on your nationality are prohibited.

The legal effects of facts or events, including receipt of a particular benefit or income, must also be treated equally.[84] A benefit paid by a member state is 'equivalent' to a benefit paid by another if they are comparable, taking account of the aim of each benefit and the legislation under which they are established. For example, a Polish benefit was accepted in one case as equivalent to the middle or higher rate of DLA care component and therefore entitled the claimant's carer to CA, and in a separate case as equivalent to AA and therefore entitled the claimant to a severe disability addition within her pension credit (PC).[85]

**Note:**

9

- The universal credit and PC regulations treat a benefit paid by another state in the same way as a UK benefit that counts as unearned income if the foreign benefit is 'analogous to' (or, for PC, 'similar to') the UK benefit or is a state retirement pension.[86]
- Trguably, the exclusion of pre-settled status as a qualifying right to reside is unlawfully discriminatory under the equal treatment provisions of the Withdrawal Agreements (see p1310).

## Aggregation

The principle of **'aggregation'** is a key co-ordinating principle in each of the sets of co-ordination rules. It enables you to add together periods of insurance, residence or employment/self-employment completed under the legislation of one or more member states to satisfy the requirements of a benefit.[87] This may be necessary if your entitlement to benefit depends on your fulfilling a certain period of residence, employment or insurance. For example, if you want to claim a UK contribution-based benefit, such as new-style employment and support allowance, but you have not paid sufficient national insurance contributions in the UK, you can rely on periods of insurance in one or more member states to satisfy the UK contribution rules. The competent institution for the benefit you are claiming (eg, in the UK, the DWP and HMRC) must contact the institutions in the relevant state(s) to determine the periods completed under their legislation.[88] What constitutes a period of residence, employment or insurance is determined by the legislation of the state under which it took place.[89]

*Example*

Sancha is a Portuguese national who was granted settled status in 2021. In July 2022, she moved to take up employment in Portugal. She left her job in Portugal one month ago and moved back to the UK. She worked in the UK for two weeks before being made redundant. Sancha is expecting a baby in two months and claims maternity allowance (MA). She can be entitled to MA because the UK is her competent state, and she can add her period of employment in Portugal to her employment in the UK to satisfy the employment condition of having worked for 26 out of the last 66 weeks. **Note**: as Sancha was out of the UK for less than five years, and therefore continues to have settled status, she should be accepted as having Withdrawal Protections and can rely on the aggregation principle of the main co-ordination rules (see p1393). If she only had partial Withdrawal Agreement protections, she could still use the aggregation principle of the main co-ordination rules (see p1395). If Sancha had arrived in the UK for the first time a month ago (and was not joining any EEA national family members in the UK), the main co-ordination rules would not apply to her, but she would be covered by the UK–EU Protocol. The aggregation principle would apply as above in each of these scenarios (but in the latter scenario, whether she had a right to work would depend on what immigration leave she has).

**Note:**

- **For unemployment benefits**, your periods of insurance (or, if required, for entitlement, employment or self-employment) can only be aggregated if you were last insured (or worked) in the state from which you claim. However, under the main co-ordination rules and the UK–Ireland Convention, this additional condition does not apply if, during your last period of work, you resided in a state other than your competent state (eg, because you worked in another state) *and* you claim in that state where you still reside or have returned to.[90]
- **For retirement pensions**, you claim in the country where you are living (or where you last worked, if that was not where you are living), but your total pension may be made up of pensions paid by more than one of the EEA, and UK, states where you have worked. If you claim in the UK, contact the International Pension Centre and see p1354. **Note:** differing retirement ages can affect when a state pays its proportion of your pension.
- **For disability and carers' benefits**, if you need to rely on aggregating past periods of residence to satisfy the past presence test note:

- the UK–EU Protocol and UK–EFTA Convention do not cover disability and carers' benefits;
- to rely on the main co-ordination rules you need to be covered by the Withdrawal Agreement protections (see p1393). However, if you are not, or no longer, covered by these, you can use the aggregation principle of the main co-ordination rules if you are covered by the *partial* Withdrawal Agreement protections (see p1395). Also check whether the past presence test can be *disapplied* (see p1350);
- if your situation only involves the UK and Ireland, to rely on the aggregation principle of the UK–Ireland Convention, you need to be covered by this Convention (see p1397);
- the Upper Tribunal held that 'mere residence' (which the DWP interprets as residence when you have not worked) in an EEA country cannot be aggregated under the main co-ordination rules to satisfy the past presence test for disability and carers' benefits.[91] However, check whether the past presence test can be disapplied (see p1350). Similarly, the UK–Ireland Convention (and the UK–Gibraltar Agreement) requires you to have been 'insured' during periods of aggregated residence used to satisfy the past presence test to be entitled to the disability or carers' benefits that can be paid by the UK while you reside in Ireland (or Gibraltar) (see p1350).[92]

## Exporting benefits

9

Each set of co-ordination rules allow you to 'export' certain benefits from one member state to another if you cease to be resident in the state in which your entitlement arose.

This means that certain benefits may not be reduced, modified, suspended, withdrawn or confiscated just because you go to live in a different member state.[93] The rules for exporting vary according to the benefit concerned: some are fully exportable, some may be exportable temporarily and some are not exportable at all. The rules also vary between the different sets of co-ordination rules and the main co-ordination rules are the most generous.

Check the individual benefit rules starting on p1370 to see whether the benefit can be exported under the co-ordination rules that apply to you. If it can, contact the office that pays your benefit well in advance so that arrangements can be made to pay you in the country you are going to.

Under the **main co-ordination rules** and the **UK–Ireland Convention**, all benefits categorised as social security benefits are exportable, provided the UK remains the competent state for paying that benefit (see p1404). However, the **UK–EU Protocol** and the **UK–EFTA Convention** exclude invalidity and unemployment benefits from export provisions and do not cover disability or carers' benefits (classed as long-term care benefits or special non-contributory benefits) or family benefits at all.[94] See p1400 for how UK benefits are categorised.

The following benefits can be exported indefinitely:

- old age benefits; *and*
- survivors' cash benefits; *and*
- pensions for accidents at work or occupational diseases; *and*
- (not under the UK–EU Protocol or UK–EFTA Convention) invalidity benefits; *and*
- (not under the UK–EU Protocol or UK–EFTA Convention) family benefits (see below); *and*
- death grants.

The following benefits can be exported for a limited period or subject to certain restrictions:

- (not under UK–EU Protocol or UK–EFTA Convention) unemployment benefits;
- sickness, maternity and paternity benefits (although, in most cases, these are exportable in a similar way to the fully exportable benefits).

Special non-contributory benefits (see p1403) cannot be exported under any of the sets of co-ordination rules. Either the rules do not cover these benefits or, under the main co-ordination rules, they can only be paid in the country in which you reside.[95]

## Overlapping benefit rules

A general principle of each set of co-ordination rules is that you should not use one period of compulsory insurance to obtain more than one benefit.[96] In general, you are only insured in one member state for any one period, so you cannot use insurance from that period to obtain entitlement to benefits of the same kind from two states. Usually, benefits are adjusted to ensure that either only one state pays the benefit, taking into account periods of insurance in other countries, or that the benefit is paid pro rata according to the lengths of the periods of insurance in different member countries.

In certain cases, however, you may be paid both the full level of a UK benefit and a proportion of a benefit from one or more member states, accrued due to having been insured in that state for a sufficient period. Under the main co-ordination rules, member states cannot apply provisions preventing the overlapping of their own benefits with those of other member states if it would reduce what you would have received from your years of contributions in the first state alone.[97]

# 5. Family benefits

Under the **main co-ordination rules**, family benefits in the UK include child benefit, guardian's allowance and child dependants' additions in other benefits.

Scottish child payment has been categorised as a special non-contributory benefit (see p1403), so the rules below do not apply to it. The child element of universal credit has been held not to be a family benefit under the main co-ordination rules (see p1402).

Under the **UK–Ireland Convention**, family benefits are listed as child benefit and guardian's allowance.[98]

The **UK–EU Protocol** and **UK–EFTA Convention** do not apply to family benefits.[99]

If you are covered by the **main co-ordination rules** (or, for situations involving only the UK and Ireland, you are covered by the **UK–Ireland Convention**), you can export family benefits and they are uprated in the normal way, without any time limit, *provided* the competent state to pay your family benefits has not changed (see p1405).[100] You can also be paid for members of your family (see p1399) living in a European Economic Area (EEA) state (under the UK–Ireland Convention, Ireland).[101] However, you must satisfy the other conditions for that benefit, including, for child benefit, if the child is not living with you that you are contributing to the costs of that child at least the amount of child benefit that would be payable (see p493).[102]

**Note:** in general, to rely on the main co-ordination rules, you need to be covered by the Withdrawal Agreement protections (see p1393).[103] However, if these do not, or no longer, apply to you, you can continue to receive a family benefit that you were entitled to, as a result of the main co-ordination rules, on 31 December 2020 for a family member living in:[104]

- an EEA country while you were 'subject to the legislation of' (see p1398) the UK if you are a British citizen (or refugee, or stateless person or non-EEA national legally resident in the UK); *or*
- the UK while you were 'subject to the legislation of' an EEA country if you are an EEA national (or refugee, stateless person or non-EEA national legally resident in that EEA country).

This is referred to in this *Handbook* as having *partial* Withdrawal Agreement protection (see p1395). If you cease to be entitled to the family benefit, or your entitlement ceases to be as a result of the main co-ordination rules, this partial Withdrawal Agreement protection ends.[105]

In general, the competent state to pay your family benefits is determined in the usual way (see p1404).[106] However, if you are receiving a 'pension' (see p1404), you claim family benefits from the state that is the competent state for paying your pension.[107]

To ensure that equivalent family benefits are not paid by more than one state in respect of the same family member for the same period, there are detailed rules to determine which state has priority to pay.[108] **Note:** these priority rules only need to be considered if there is an actual overlap of entitlement because claims have been made in more than one state (unless entitlement does not require a claim).[109] If the state with priority pays family benefits at a lower rate than a state with lower priority, the latter pays a 'top-up' to supplement the amount paid by the priority state. However, this top-up need not be paid for children residing in another state where entitlement to the family benefit is based on residence only (rather than on employment or receipt of a pension).[110] For further information on family benefits, see CPAG's *Benefits for Migrants Handbook*.

# Notes

1. **Introduction**

1 *The Agreement between the European Community and its Member States, of the one part, and the Swiss Confederation, of the other, on the Free Movement of Persons*, Luxembourg, 21 June 1999, Cmd 5639 (in force 1 June 2002); UK-SA

2 Art 355(3) TFEU; Vol 2 Ch 7 Pt 1 para 070040 DMG; para C1005 ADM

2. **Who is covered**

3 ADM Memo 8/24; DMG Memo 7/24

4 Art 3(4) UK-IC, DWPWAG, Ch 1 para 5

5 UK-SCC

6 *Agreement on Social Security between the UK and Gibraltar*, reproduced as Schedule to The Social Security (Gibraltar) Order 2024 No.149

7 The Family Allowances, National Insurance and Industrial Injuries (Gibraltar) Order 1974 No.555

8 Title III WA 2019; Title III UK-EFTA; Part 3 UK-SA; ss7A and 7B EU(WA) 2018

9 Arts 10 and 30(3) WA 2019; Arts 9 and 29(3) UK-EFTA; Arts 10 and 25(3) UK-SA

10 Confirmed in DWPWAG, Fig 3 and Ch 2 para 64

11 Art 30(2) WA 2019; Art 29(2) UK-EFTA; Art 25(2) UK-SA

12 Ch 1 paras 28, 53, 61 and 62 DWPWAG; DMG Memo 11/22, para 6; ADM Memo 15/22, para 6

13 Arts 9, 10, 13, 24, 25 and 30(3)-(5) WA 2019; Arts 9, 12, 23, 24, 29(3)-(5) UK-EFTA; Arts 10, 12, 19, 20 and 25(3)-(5) UK-SA

14 commission.europa.eu/strategy-and-policy/relations-non-eu-countries/relations-united-kingdom/eu-uk-withdrawal-agreement/citizens-rights/information-about-national-residence-schemes-each-eu-country

15 See discussion of who is covered by Art 13 WA 2019 in *SSWP v AT (Aire Centre and IMA Intervening)* [2023] EWCA Civ 1307 and *IMA v SSHD* [2022] EWHC 3274 (Admin)

16 Arts 11, 13 and 15 WA 2019; Arts 10, 12 and 14 UK-EFTA; Arts 10, 11 and 14 UK-SA

17 DWPWAG Ch 1 paras 25-27 and 39 – example (d) and Ch 2 paras 54 and 63; DMG Memo 11/22, paras 7 and 10 (inc examples); ADM Memo 15/22, paras 7 and 10 (inc examples)

18 Art 32 WA 2019; Art 31 UK-EFTA; Art 26a UK-SA; DWPWAG Ch 1 paras 43-52; DMG Memo 11/22, paras 13-15; ADM Memo 15/22, paras 13-15

19 Art 32(2) WA 2019; Art 31(2) UK-EFTA; Art 26a(2) UK-SA; Ch 1, Title III EU Reg 883/04; DMG Memo 11/22, para 16; ADM Memo 15/22, para 16

20 Art 2 EU Reg 883/04

21 *Petit v Office National de Pensions*, C-153/91 [1992]

22 EU Reg 1408/71

23 Art 87(8) EU Reg 883/04; Recital (2), Decision H1 of 12 June 2009 of the Administrative Commission for the Co-ordination of Social Security Systems [2010] OJ C-106/13; *SSWP v PW (CA)* [2013] UKUT 296 (AAC); *KG v SSWP (DLA)* [2015] UKUT 146 (AAC); *SSWP v SO* [2019] UKUT 55 (AAC); *KR v SSWP (DLA)* [2019] UKUT 85 (AAC), reported as [2019] ACCR 22, paras 10-12; *SSWP v MC (DLA)* [2019] UKUT 84 (AAC), paras 6 and 21
24 Art 2 UK-IC
25 Art 1 UK-IC
26 Art 3(4) UK-IC; DWPWAG, Ch 1 para 5
27 Art SSC2 UK-EUP
28 *Petit v Office National de Pensions*, C-153/91 [1992]
29 Art SSC2 UK-EUP
30 Arts 2 and 3 UK-EFTAC
31 Arts 4 and 5 UK-EFTAC; see also *Petit v Office National de Pensions*, C-153/91 [1992]
32 Art 2 UK-EFTAC
33 See also Vol 2 Ch 7 Pt 1 Appendix, para 5 DMG
34 Arts 1(l) and 3 EU Reg 883/04; Art 1 and 3 UK-IC; Arts SSC1(q) and SSC3 UK-EUP; Arts 1(y) and 6 UK-EFTAC
35 para 2, example 3, of both DMG Memo 11/22 and ADM Memo 15/22; see also DWPWAG, Ch 2, para 53
36 Arts 1(i) and 2 EU Reg 883/04; Art 1(1) UK-IC; Arts 30(5) and 31(2) WA; Arts 29(5) and 30(2) UK-EFTA; Arts 25(5) and 26(2) UK-SA; DMG Memo 11/22, para 9; ADM Memo 15/22, para 9; Art SSC1(s) UK-EUP; Art 1(aa) UK-EFTAC; *PB v SSWP (DLA)* [2016] UKUT 280 (AAC), paras 8-10

3. **Which benefits are covered**

37 Arts 1(l), 3 and 9 EU Reg 883/04; Art SSC1(q) and SSC3 UK-EUP; Arts 1(y) and 6 UK-EFTAC
38 Art 3 UK-IC
39 See, for example, DWPWAG, Fig 4
40 Art SSC 3(4) UK-EUP; Art 6(5) UK-EFTAC
41 Annex SSC-1 Part 2(i) UK-EUP; Annex 2 Part 2 UK-EFTAC
42 Confirmed in Art 34 EU Reg 883/04
43 Vol 2 Ch 7 Pt 1, paras 070152, 070280 and 070401 and Appendix para 18 DMG; paras C4142-3 ADM
44 DWPWAG, Fig 4
45 DWPWAG, Fig 4; ADM 8/24 para 14(3); Arts SSC3(1) and SSC8 UK-EUP; Arts 6(1) and 11 UK-EFTAC
46 SSAC, *Universal Credit and Related Regulations Report and Government Response*, December 2012
47 *SSWP v MS (UC)* [2023] UKUT 44 (AAC)
48 *Simkova v SSWP* [2024] EWCA Civ 419
49 *Commission of the European Communities v European Parliament and Council of the EU*, C-299/05 [2007]; *SSWP v Tolley*, C-430/15 [2017]
50 Arts 3, 16, 19, 20 UK-IC
51 **CDP** Reg 5(4)-(5) DACYP(S) Regs
**ADP** Reg 15(3)-(4) DAWAP(S) Regs
**PADP** Reg 9(3)-(4) DAOP(S) Regs
**SADLA** Reg 16(3)-(4) DA(SADLA) Regs
**CSP** Reg 6(3)-(4) CA(CSP)(S) Regs
**CAS** s81(2A) and (13) SS(S)A 2018
**YCG** Reg 8(3) and (6) CA(YCG)(S) Regs
52 Art SSC3(4)(a) and (d), and Annex SSC-1, Part 1(i)(c) and (d), and Part 2(i) UK-EUP; Art 6(5)(a) and (d), and Annex 2, Parts 1 and 2 UK-EFTAC
53 Art 70 and Annex X EU Reg 883/04
54 Ch C2, para C2097 and Appendix para 4 ADM; *Bartlett and Others v SSWP*, C-537/09 [2011]; *SSWP v DS* [2019] UKUT 238 (AAC)
55 p13 DMG ADP(R and P); s10 DMG CDP(R and P)
56 Art 70 EU Reg 883/04; *Swaddling v AO*, C-90/97 [1999]
57 Art 3(3) EU Reg 883/04; *Dano v Jobcenter Leipzig*, C-333/13 [2014], paras 46-55
58 Art SSC3(4)(a) and Annex SSC-1 Part 1(i) UK-EUP; Art 6(5)(a) and Annex 2, Part 1 UK-EFTAC
59 Art 3(5) EU Reg 883/04; Art SSC3(4)(b) UK-EUP; Art 6(5)(b) UK-EFTAC
60 Art1(1) UK-IC
61 Art 47 UK-IC

4. **Principles of co-ordination**

62 Art 11 EU Reg 883/04; Art 9 UK-IC; Art SSC10 UK-EUP; Art 13 UK-EFTAC
63 Art 1(q) and (s) EU Reg 883/04; Art SSC1(h) and (i) UK-EUP; Art 1(j) and (k) UK-EFTAC
64 Art 11 EU Reg 883/04; Art 9 UK-IC; Art SSC10 UK-EUP; Art 13 UK-EFTAC
65 *JS v SSWP* [2019] UKUT 239 (AAC); ADM Memo 1/20; DMG Memo 3/20
66 Art 65 EU Reg 883/04; Art 22 UK-IC
67 Art 11(3)(e) EU Reg 883/04; Art 9(4)(e) UK-IC; Art SSC10(3)(c) UK-EUP; Art 13(3)(d) UK-EFTAC
68 Art 11(2) EU Reg 883/04; Art 9(2) and (3) UK-IC; Art SSC10(2) UK-EUP; Art 13(2) UK-EFTAC

69 Arts 23-32 EU Reg 883/04; Vol 2 Ch 7 Pt 2 Appendix 3 DMG; Ch C2 Appendix 1 ADM; DMG Memo 16/20; ADM Memo 17/20; Art 20 UK-IC
70 *Harrington v SSWP* [2023] EWCA Civ 433; see also ADM Memo 7/24 and DMG Memo 6/24
71 *SE v SSWP* [2024] UKUT 405 (AAC)
72 Art 1(j) EU Reg 883/04; Art 1(1) UK-IC; Art SSC1(aa) UK-EUP; Art 1(jj) UK-EFTAC
73 Art 11 EU Reg 987/2009; Annex SSC-7, Art SSCI.10 UK-EUP; Annex 1, Art 10 UK-EFTAC
74 **Main rules** Art 81 EU Reg 883/04; Art 2 EU Reg 987/2009; *SSWP v AK (AA)* [2015] UKUT 110 (AAC), reported as [2015] AACR 27; see also *MGL v SSWP (ESA)* [2018] UKUT 352 (AAC); Vol 2 Ch 7 Pt 2 Appendix 4 DMG; Ch C2 Appendix 2 ADM
**UK-IC** Art 60
**UK-EUP** Art SSC62
**UK-EFTAC** Art 65
75 Art 40(2) UK-IC
76 Art 6(2) and (3) EU Reg 987/2009; *SSWP v HR (AA)* [2014] UKUT 571 (AAC); *SSWP v Fileccia* [2017] EWCA Civ 1907; Vol 2 Ch 7 Pt 2 Appendix 4 DMG; Ch C2 Appendix 2 ADM; Art 63(2) UK-IC; Annex SSC-7, Art SSCI.6 UK-EUP; Annex 1, Art 6 UK-EFTAC
77 Arts 11-16 EU Reg 883/04; Arts 9-13 UK-IC; Arts SSC 10-13 UK-EUP; Arts 13-18 UK-EFTAC
78 See, for example, *SSWP v MC (DLA)* [2019] UKUT 84 (AAC)
79 See, for example, Title III EU Reg 883/04
80 *Carrington v HMRC and SSWP* [2021] EWCA Civ 1724
81 See, for example, *Kuusijärvi v Riksförsäkringsverket*, C-275/96 [1998]; *HB v HMRC (CHB)* [2014] UKUT 554 (AAC); *SSWP v Tolley*, C-430/15 [2017]; see also *KR v SSWP (DLA)* [2019] UKUT 85 (AAC), reported as [2019] AACR 22
82 Art 4 EU Reg 883/04; Art 4 UK-IC; Art SSC 5 UK-EUP; Art 8 UK-EFTAC
83 Art 18 TFEU; Art 24 EU Dir 2004/38; Art 7 EU Reg 492/2011
84 Art 5 EU Reg 883/04; Art 5 UK-IC; Art SSC 6 UK-EUP; Art 9 UK-EFTAC
85 CG/1346/2018; *HT v SSWP* [2020] UKUT 57 (AAC); Vol 10 Ch 60 para 60033 point 8 DMG (also referred to by para F6013 ADM)
86 Regs 66(1)(c) and (da) and (2)(a) and 83(2)(d) UC Regs; for example, see *LR v SSWP (UC)* [2022] UKUT 65 (AAC); reg 15(2) SPC Regs
87 Art 6 EU Reg 883/04; Art 6 UK-IC; Art SSC 7 UK-EUP; Art 10 UK-EFTAC
88 Art 12 EU Reg 987/2009; Annex SSC-7, Art SSCI 11 UK-EUP; Annex 1, Art 11 UK-EFTAC
89 Arts 1(t)(u) and (v) and 6 EU Reg 883/04; *Decision H6 of 16 December 2010 of the Administrative Commission for the Co-ordination of Social Security Systems* [2011] OJ C-45/04; Art 6(2) UK-IC; Art SSC 7 UK-EUP; Art 10 UK-EFTAC
90 Arts 61 and 65(5)(a) EU Reg 883/04; Arts 21(1) and (2) and 22(4)(a) UK-IC; Art SSC 56 UK-EUP; Art 58 UK-EFTAC
91 *SSWP v MM and BK v SSWP* [2016] UKUT 547 (AAC), reported as [2019] AACR 21 - note that the appeal against this part of the decision was not pursued when it went to the Court of Appeal – *Kavanagh and Another v SSWP* [2019] EWCA Civ 272
92 Arts 6 and 19 UK-IC; Arts 6 and 19 Agreement on Social Security between the UK and Gibraltar, reproduced as Schedule to The Social Security (Gibraltar) Order 2024 No.149
93 Art 7 EU Reg 883/04; Art 7 UK-IC; Art SSC8 UK-EUP; Art 11 UK-EFTAC
94 Arts SSC3(1) and (4) and SSC8 and Annex SSC1, Part 2 UK-EUP; Arts 6(1) and (5) and 11 and Annex 2 Part 2 UK-EFTAC
95 Art 70 EU Reg 883/04
96 Art 10 EU Reg 883/04; Arts 8 and 31-33 UK-IC; Arts SSC9 and SSC48-50 UK-EUP; Arts 12 and 52-54 UK-EFTAC
97 *Teresa and Silvana Petroni v Office National des Pensions Pour Travailleurs Salariés (ONPTS), Bruxelles* C-24/75 [1975]

5. **Family benefits**

98 Art 3(x) UK-IC
99 Art SSC3(4)(g) UK-EUP; Art 6(5)(g) UK-EFTAC
100 Arts 7 and 67 EU Reg 883/04; *HB v HMRC (CHB)* [2014] UKUT 554 (AAC); *HMRC v Carrington* [2021] EWCA Civ 1724; see also *GL v HMRC* [2023] UKUT 100 (AAC)
101 Art 67 EU Reg 883/04; *HMRC v Ruas* [2010] EWCA Civ 291; *JL v HMRC (CHB)* [2017] UKUT 193 (AAC); Art 38 UK-IC

102 s143(1)(b) SSCBA 1992; *RI v HMRC (TC)* [2019] UKUT 306 (AAC); *RK v HMRC (CHB)* [2015] UKUT 357 (AAC), reported as [2016] AACR 4; *JL v HMRC (CHB)* [2017] UKUT 193 (AAC), paras 30-32 and 49; *MZ v HMRC* [2020] UKUT 65 (AAC)
103 Confirmed in para 10015 CBTM
104 Art 32(1)(d) WA 2019; Art 31(1)(d) UK-EFTA; Art 26a(1)(d) UK-SA; see also DWPWAG, Ch 1 paras 87-95
105 DWPWAG, Ch 1 para 91
106 *Bogatu v Minister for Social Protection*, C-322/17 [2019]
107 Art 67 EU Reg 883/04, second sentence; Art 38(2) UK-IC
108 Art 68 EU Reg 883/04; Art 39 UK-IC
109 *Bundesagentur für Arbeit – Familienkasse Sachsen v Trapkowski*, C-378/14 [2015]; *JL v HMRC (CHB)* [2017] UKUT 193 (AAC); see also *WC v HMRC (CF)* [2019] UKUT 289 (AAC) in paras 1, 8 and 9, but note this decision was set aside on other grounds in *Carrington v HMRC and SSWP* [2021] EWCA Civ 1724
110 Art 68(2) EU Reg 833/04; Art 39(4) UK-IC

Part 10

# Scottish social security benefits

# Chapter 60

# The Scottish social security system

**This chapter covers:**


1. Overview of the Scottish social security system (below)
2. Moving to or from Scotland (p1419)
3. Scottish adult disability living allowance (p1420)
4. How this part of the *Handbook* is organised (p1425)


## 1. Overview of the Scottish social security system

Responsibility for some benefits is devolved to the Scottish government. Several different benefits are delivered by Social Security Scotland (SSS), an executive agency of the Scottish government.

### The Scottish benefits

10

The law refers to most of the benefits administered by SSS as coming under the 'Scottish social security system'.[1] In this *Handbook*, we refer to them as 'Scottish benefits'. There are common rules for most Scottish benefits about:[2]

- claims, payments and appointees;
- how a determination of entitlement is made and challenged;
- when and how overpayments are recovered;
- criminal offences.

The Scottish benefits that have already been introduced are:

- four Scottish disability benefits:
  - adult disability payment (ADP), which has replaced personal independence payment (PIP) (see Chapter 61);
  - child disability payment (CDP), which has replaced disability living allowance (DLA) for children (see Chapter 64);

  - pension age disability payment (PADP), which replaces attendance allowance (AA) for new claims in all areas from 22 April 2025 (see Chapter 67); *and*
  - Scottish adult disability living allowance (SADLA), which started to replace DLA for those adults in Scotland who still get it from 21 March 2025 (see p1420);
- Scottish child payment and three Best Start grants (see Chapter 62);
- carer support payment (CSP) and young carer grant (see Chapter 63);
- funeral support payment (see Chapter 65);
- three annual heating payments (see Chapter 66).

At the time of writing, the following transfers of people getting DWP benefits and living in Scotland to Scottish benefits were ongoing.

- If you get carer's allowance (CA) you will transfer to CSP – although this process is expected to be complete by spring 2025 (see p1474).
- If you get PIP, you will transfer to ADP (see p1444).
- If you get AA, you will transfer to PADP (see p1518).
- If you get DLA and are 18 or over, you will transfer to SADLA (see p1422).

**Note:** until 21 March 2025, you could instead be transferred from DLA to ADP, and this process may not be complete in some cases (see p1446).

Some other benefits are also administered by SSS or local authorities and have different rules in Scotland, but *do not* come under the Scottish social security system.

10

***Future changes***

- Industrial injuries benefits will be replaced by employment injury assistance (and existing claimants in Scotland transferred to the new benefit), but not until 2026 at the earliest.[3] The common rules described in this part of the *Handbook* will apply to the new benefit.[4]
- A new care-experience assistance may be introduced (at the time of writing, it is not clear whether the common rules in this part will apply to it).[5]
- Changes will be made to CSP to introduce new higher amounts for people caring for more than one disabled person, and to replace the current CA supplement (see p1467).[6]

See CPAG's *Welfare Rights Bulletin* or the online version of this *Handbook* for updates.

## Benefits *not* under the Scottish social security system

Some payments made by SSS, and payments made by local authorities, are *not* part of the Scottish social security system. The common rules described in this part of the *Handbook* do *not* cover:[7]

- CA supplement (*unless* you live outside Scotland – see p1476);

- Best Start foods (see p1455);
- Job Start Payment (see below);
- payments delivered by local authorities, including:
  - discretionary housing payments (see Chapter 25);
  - the Scottish Welfare Fund (see p770);
  - council tax reduction (see p761).

### Job Start Payment

You can get a Job Start Payment if you are resident in Scotland and are offered a job averaging at least 12 hours a week over a four-week period.[8] You must be either aged 16 to 24 and have been out of work and claiming universal credit or income-related employment and support allowance for six months, or a care leaver aged 16 to 25, out of work and getting one of those benefits when you are offered the job.[9]

Job Start Payment is a one-off grant of £319.80, or £511.65 if you are responsible for a child. You cannot receive another Job Start Payment within two years of getting one. Job Start Payment is administered by SSS.

See mygov.scot/job-start-payment for more information and how to claim online, by telephone or using a paper claim form.

## 2. Moving to or from Scotland

Special rules apply if you get disability living allowance (DLA), personal independence payment (PIP), attendance allowance (AA) or carer's allowance (CA) when you move to Scotland (see below). If you get adult disability payment (ADP), child disability payment (CDP), pension age disability payment (PADP), Scottish adult disability living allowance (SADLA), carer support payment (CSP) or Scottish child payment and you move elsewhere in the UK, see p1420. 10

### If you move to Scotland

If you move to Scotland and are entitled to DLA, PIP, AA or CA when you move, you should notify the DWP of your change of address. The DWP should tell Social Security Scotland (SSS), which at the time of writing transfers you to the equivalent Scottish benefit (see p1417) without a claim being required.[10] For details of the transfer process, see p1444 for ADP, p541 for CDP p1518 for PADP, p1422 for SADLA and p1474 for CSP.

DLA (for most adults), PIP, AA or CA continue until a decision is made on your entitlement to the equivalent Scottish benefit. DLA for children and some limited groups of adults ends around 13 weeks after the move, and CDP will be awarded from the day after DLA stops.[11]

**Note:** at the time of writing, it is expected that these rules will change and you will need to claim ADP, CDP, PADP or CSP when you move to Scotland (perhaps from September 2025).[12] The rules about these DWP benefits may also be amended to end your entitlement if you move to Scotland. See CPAG's *Welfare Rights Bulletin* or the online version of this *Handbook* for updates.

### If you move elsewhere in the UK

If you move from Scotland to elsewhere in the UK, you will no longer be entitled to Scottish benefits if you are no longer 'ordinarily resident' in Scotland (see p1299). **Note:** for ADP, CDP, PADP and SADLA, your entitlement does *not* end (but your payment may be affected) if you go into hospital, residential care or prison elsewhere in the UK.[13] For how your payment is affected, see Chapter 38.

If you move elsewhere in the UK:[14]

- your Scottish child payment ends on the date you are no longer ordinarily resident;
- your ADP, PADP, SADLA or CSP entitlement ends 13 weeks after you stop being ordinarily resident, no matter when you inform SSS; *and*
- your CDP entitlement ends:
  - 13 weeks after you tell SSS about the move, if you tell SSS less than 13 weeks after you stop being ordinarily resident; or
  - 13 weeks after you moved, if you tell SSS either before moving or 13 weeks or more after you stop being ordinarily resident.

For how your benefit is affected if you move out of the UK, see p1378.

10

## 3. Scottish adult disability living allowance

Scottish adult disability living allowance (SADLA) is a benefit introduced on 21 March 2025, which only people who still have an award of disabilty living allowance (DLA) and are aged at least 18 can get.[15] If you are in this situation and live in Scotland, you will be transferred to SADLA (see p1422) without needing to claim. It is not possible to make a new claim for SADLA, but if you had an award of either DLA or SADLA that ended less than one year ago, you can ask to be awarded SADLA (see p1423). SADLA is administered and paid by Social Security Scotland (SSS).

SADLA has a care component and a mobility component. Both are paid at the same weekly rates as those for child disability payment (CDP) (see p1489).[16] You normally get the highest rate of both components if you are terminally ill (see p1436).

The SADLA residence rules (including if you are a 'person subject to immigration control') are the same as those for pension age disability payment (PADP) (see p1512).[17]

Once you get SADLA, you can choose to claim adult disability payment (ADP), but only if you were born after 8 April 1948. If you do, ADP replaces your SADLA (see p1425).

**Note:** you cannot normally get SADLA for a period during which you were entitled to DLA, ADP, personal independence payment (PIP), PADP, attendance allowance (AA) or armed forces independence payment.[18] For exceptions to this rule if you transfer from DLA:

- see p1437 if you are terminally ill; *or*
- see p1423 if you reported a change before being transferred from DLA or have a severe visual impairment.

If you are entitled to SADLA and in hospital or a hospice, living in a care home or other similar accommodation, or in prison or legal detention, see Chapter 38.

## The disability conditions for the care component

If you are **over pension age**, the disability conditions for the middle and highest rate care component of SADLA are mostly the same as those for PADP (see p1513). Your needs must have lasted for 26 weeks before you can qualify for a particular rate. You can only get the lowest rate care component if you got that rate of DLA before moving to SADLA, or have satisfied the conditions for the lowest rate since before you reached pension age.[19]

If you are **under pension age**, the disability conditions to get the care component are the same as those for CDP (see p1484), except that you *do not* have to satisfy the 'additional requirement' condition (comparing your needs to those of someone else your age) to qualify, and you can *only* get the middle rate care component if you get renal dialysis – the rules are the same as for AA (see p444). Your needs must have lasted for at least 13 weeks before an award at a particular rate begins, and be likely to last for a further 26 weeks after that date.[20]

10

## The disability conditions for the mobility component

If you are **under pension age**, the disability conditions for the mobility component of SADLA are mostly the same as those for DLA (see p512).

To qualify for a particular rate, your needs must have lasted for at least 13 weeks before the award would begin, and be likely to last for a further 26 weeks after that date.[21]

The differences in the qualifying conditions for the higher rate mobility component are as follows.[22]

- You are 'blind' if you have a 'total loss of vision'.
- Someone needing to intervene to prevent your disruptive behaviour causing damage to property does *not* help you to qualify via the 'severe mental impairment' route.
- You also qualify for the higher rate if:

- your visual impairment was assessed using a test that is equivalent to the Snellen scale; *or*
- you have 'been certified as severely sight impaired or blind by a consultant ophthalmologist', *and* have insufficient vision to enable you to be 'independently mobile in familiar places outdoors'.

The only difference in the disability condition for the lower rate mobility component is that you need not satisfy the 'additional requirement' condition (comparing your needs to those of someone else your age) to qualify.[23]

If you have **reached pension age**, the differences from the DLA rules above still apply. You can continue to get your existing rate of the mobility component for as long as you meet the normal conditions to get it. However, if there is a determination due to a change that happened after you reached pension age, entitlement is restricted in broadly the same way as the ADP mobility component (see p1435).[24] The restrictions also apply if you transfer from DLA to SADLA following a change of circumstances that happened after you reached pension age.[25]

## Transfers to Scottish adult disability living allowance

**Note:** at the time of writing, the rules in this section are expected to change, requiring you to request SADLA if you move to Scotland.[26] See CPAG's *Welfare Rights Bulletin* or the online version of this *Handbook* for updates.

If you get DLA, are aged at least 18 and live in Scotland (or an EEA state and have a 'genuine and sufficient' link to Scotland – see p1350), you will transfer to SADLA without having to claim it.

10

If you have not yet transferred to SADLA, continue to report any changes (particularly to your care or mobility needs) to the DWP. If you do this, any increased entitlement will start sooner than if you wait to transfer.[27] Get advice if you are unsure whether a change is relevant to your DLA, or how your entitlement might change.

SSS notifies you in writing that you will transfer to SADLA, including how long the process will take and that your DLA will end when your SADLA starts.[28] If SSS later realises that you were wrongly sent a transfer notification or wants to extend the transfer period, it sends you another notification.[29]

Unless you are terminally ill (see p1436), you are initially awarded the same rate of SADLA as your previous DLA award.[30] If you disagree with the initial SADLA determination, you can request a redetermination. However, if you have already reported a change of circumstances to the DWP, it is better *not* to request a redetermination as you may get more benefit if you wait for your award to be reviewed (see p1423). Get advice if you are unsure.

Once you have been awarded SADLA, SSS reviews your entitlement if you have reported a change of circumstances, or have a severe visual impairment (see p1423).

### Review determinations

If you report a change of circumstances in relation to your DLA that the DWP does not take into account, SSS must carry out a 'review determination' after you transfer to SADLA.[31] It must also do so if you have a severe visual impairment but did not get the DLA higher rate mobility component. If you want your entitlement to be reviewed, you should report a change to the DWP *before* your SADLA entitlement is determined.

In the situations above, and unless you request a redetermination of your initial SADLA award, SSS makes a review determination of your entitlement after you transfer.

The review determination takes effect:[32]

- if you have a 'severe visual impairment' for SADLA but did *not* for DLA (see p1421), from the *latest* of:
  - the date you were first unable to be mobile in familiar places outdoors due to insufficient vision; *or*
  - one year before the review determination; *or*
- if it increases your award for any other reason, from:
  - the date of the change (ie, that you meet the disability conditions for a different rate of SADLA) if you reported it within one month (or up to 13 months if you had a good reason for reporting the change late); *or*
  - the date you reported the change, if the above bullet point does not apply; *or*
- if it does not change or decreases your SADLA award, from the date it is made.

If your award is higher, you can be awarded SADLA for a period during which you got DLA under the rule above (although your entitlement can *never* begin before 21 March 2025).[33] You are paid the difference between your DLA award and the SADLA award.[34]

**Note:** if the change happened or you first had a severe visual impairment after you reached pension age, your entitlement to the mobility component is restricted (see p1422).

## Requesting Scottish adult disability living allowance

You can request that your SADLA entitlement is determined if:[35]

- you previously had an award of DLA or SADLA; *and*
- your entitlement ended less than one year before you make the request; *and*
- you have *not* been entitled to ADP, PADP or PIP since your award ended; *and*
- you are not challenging the ending of your previous award.

**Note:** if your DLA ended as you lived in England or Wales and were refused PIP, you cannot get SADLA.[36]

Your request must be made in the way required and accompanied by any required evidence (this may include providing supporting evidence like that for an ADP claim – see p1440). These requirements are likely to be explained on mygov.scot.

If you are entitled to SADLA, your award starts from the date you requested it, and the following restrictions apply to it.[37]

- You can only be awarded a component if you were previously entitled to it, and due to substantially the same condition(s). However, if you are awarded SADLA you can then report a change of circumstances and get the other component if you meet the disability conditions for it (see p1421).
- If your previous award ended after you reached pension age, you can only ever get the mobility component if it was included in your previous award, and can only get the higher rate if you were previously entitled to it.

## Getting paid, tax and other benefits

SADLA is usually paid four-weekly in arrears. If you are terminally ill or were previously paid DLA weekly, you are paid weekly in advance.[38] The other rules about payments and overpayments are the same as for ADP (see p1443).[39]

The rules about changes of circumstances, reviews and providing further information during an award are the same as for ADP (see p1443 and p1444).[40] **Note:** if you are under pension age, a change of circumstances can include that your needs are no longer expected to last for 26 weeks at the same level, as you will no longer meet the disability conditions (see p1421).

At the time of writing, it is expected that you may be able to report a change by phone, on a form you can download from mygov.scot or online. Check your most recent determination carefully, as it should tell you how you must report a change.

SADLA is **not taxable.**[41]

SADLA interacts with **means-tested benefits** in the same way as DLA does (see p541).

10

The rules on how SADLA interacts with **non-means-tested benefits** are the same as for ADP, except that you must be getting the middle or highest rate care component for a carer to be able to claim benefits for looking after you (see p1447).[42]

The rules about the **benefit cap** are the same as for ADP (see p1447). The benefit cap does not apply if you or your partner get SADLA (even it is not paid because you are in hospital or a care home).

**Passports and other sources of help** are expected to be the same as for DLA (see p543). If you get the higher rate of the SADLA mobility component and have 12 months or more left until your award is due to be reviewed, you may be able to access the Motability scheme (see p1447).[43]

## Moving to adult disability payment

If you are entitled to SADLA and were born after 8 April 1948, you can choose to claim ADP.[44] This replaces your SADLA, and you will not be able to move back to SADLA once you have been awarded ADP.[45]

**Note:** instead of claiming ADP, you can report a change of circumstances to SSS and it will determine your entitlement to SADLA again. Get advice about which option is likely to leave you better off.

***Should you claim ADP?***

You should get specialist advice to help you decide whether to claim ADP. If you get the SADLA highest rate care component and higher rate mobility component, there is nothing to gain from claiming ADP. The entitlement conditions for ADP are completely different, and you may not qualify for ADP at all or may qualify for a lower award. If you claim ADP, your SADLA will end and you cannot later get it back. In that case, you can request a redetermination of the ADP determination (see p1535).

In some circumstances, you may be better off claiming ADP – eg, if you do not have any night-time care needs but would score enough points to be entitled to the enhanced rate of ADP daily living component. If you claim ADP before 1 January 2028, there are no restrictions on your entitlement to the ADP mobility component if you are over pension age. You can use the information in Chapter 61 to work out your likely ADP entitlement, and compare this to your SADLA award.

You claim ADP in the same way as for any other new claim (see p1439). Unless you are now terminally ill (see p1436), you are awarded ADP at the same rate as your SADLA under an interim determination (the SADLA low rate care component is replaced by a transitional ADP rate of £29.20 a week).[46] Your SADLA ends on the date your ADP begins.[47] You can request a redetermination of the interim determination, but you may be better off if you wait for a review determination.

Unless you have requested a redetermination, SSS then makes a review determination, applying the usual ADP disability conditions (except that if you claim ADP before 1 January 2028, there are no restrictions to your entitlement to the mobility component if you are over pension age). If your new entitlement is higher, it begins from the date your ADP would have started were you not entitled to SADLA when you claimed it (see p1442), and the SADLA you received since that date is deducted from your ADP award.[48] If your new entitlement is lower, it takes effect from the date of the determination.[49]

## 4. How this part of the *Handbook* is organised

For detailed information about how to use this *Handbook*, see Chapter 1. This part contains information about individual benefits delivered by Social Security

Scotland and the common rules for benefits that are part of the Scottish social security system (see p1417 for the benefits covered by the common rules). For the common rules, see:

- Chapter 68 for claims, getting paid, overpayments, fraud and complaints;
- Chapter 69 for determinations of entitlement and how to challenge them, including appeals to the First-tier Tribunal.

# Notes

1. **Overview of the Scottish social security system**

1 s23 SS(S)A 2018
2 **SCP** Parts 3 and 4 SS(S)A 2018; SCP Regs
**Other benefits** Parts 2 and 4 SS(S)A 2018
3 Scottish government, *Employment Injury Assistance delivery – next steps: response to consultation*
4 s33 and Sch 7 SS(S)A 2018
5 s2 SS(A)(S)A 2025
6 The Carer's Assistance (Young Carer Grant and Carer Support Payment) (Miscellaneous Amendment and Saving Provision) (Scotland) Regulations 2025 (draft)
7 s23 SS(S)A 2018
8 There are no Job Start Payment regulations, except the restrictions on when payments can be made in SA(TFSM)O. Guidance for decision makers is at socialsecurity.gov.scot/guidance-resources and information for claimants is at mygov.scot/job-start-payment.
9 For Job Start Payment, you are a 'care leaver' if you were looked after by a local authority on or after your 16th birthday but are no longer looked after by a local authority: see art 2(4)(b) SA(TFSM)O

2. **Moving to or from Scotland**

10 **ADP** Reg 52 and Sch 2 Part 3 DAWAP(S) Regs
**CDP** Reg 35 and Sch Part 3 DACYP(S) Regs
**CSP** Reg 41 and Sch 1 Part 2 CA(CSP)(S) Regs
**PADP** Reg 44 and Sch Part 3 Sch DAOP(S) Regs
**SADLA** Reg 47 and Sch 1 part 2 DA(SADLA)(S) Regs
11 **AA** s64 SSCBA 1992
**CA** s70 SSCBA 1992
**CDP** Reg 35(2) DACYP(S) Regs
**DLA** Regs 1, 1ZA, 2, 2ZA and 2ZB SS(DLA) Regs; DMG Memo 6/23
**PIP** s77 WRA 2012
12 SS(CPCTMA)(S) Regs (draft)
13 **ADP** Reg 53(2) DAWAP(S) Regs
**CDP** Reg 36(2) DACYP(S) Regs
**PADP** Reg 45(2) DAOP(S) Regs
**SADLA** Reg 48(2) DA(SADLA) Regs
14 **ADP** Reg 53(4) DAWAP(S) Regs
**CDP** Reg 36(4) DACYP(S) Regs
**CSP** Reg 42(4) CA(CSP)(S) Regs
**PADP** Reg 45(4) DAOP(S) Regs
**SADLA** Reg 48(4) DA(SADLA) Regs
**SCP** Reg 18(d) and Sch para 10(1)(a) SCP Regs

3. **Scottish adult disability living allowance**

15 s31 and Sch 5 SS(S)A 2018; regs 3 and 4 DA(SADLA) Regs
16 Reg 29 DA(SADLA) Regs

17 Regs 10-17 DA(SADLA) Regs. At the time of writing, SADLA had not yet been added to the list of public funds in the Immigration Rules.
18 Reg 5 DA(SADLA) Regs
19 Regs 6, 20 and 21 DA(SADLA) Regs
20 Regs 6, 20 and 21 DA(SADLA) Regs
21 Regs 7, 8 and 20 DA(SADLA) Regs
22 Reg 8 DA(SADLA) Regs
23 Reg 7 DA(SADLA) Regs
24 Reg 19 DA(SADLA) Regs. Unlike ADP, if the new determination is due to ignorance of a material fact, that fact must relate to *your circumstances* after you reached pension age.
25 Sch 1 para 10(8)-(10) DA(SADLA) Regs
26 SS(CPCTMA)(S) Regs (draft)
27 Sch 1 para 10(4) and (5) DA(SADLA) Regs
28 Sch 1 paras 5 and 6 DA(SADLA) Regs
29 Sch 1 paras 6(3) and (4) and 7(6)(c) DA(SADLA) Regs
30 Sch 1 para 7(5) DA(SADLA) Regs
31 Sch 1 para 10(1) DA(SADLA) Regs
32 Sch 1 para 10(1)-(7) DA(SADLA) Regs
33 Sch 1 para 10(4)(c) DA(SADLA) Regs
34 Sch 1 para 10(5) DA(SADLA) Regs
35 Sch 1 paras 12 and 13 DA(SADLA) Regs
36 Sch 1 para 13(5)(c) DA(SADLA) Regs
37 Sch 1 paras 12(4) and (7)-(10) and 13(4) and(7)-(10) DA(SADLA) Regs
38 Reg 31 DA(SADLA) Regs
39 Regs 28(1), 29(3), 50 and 51 DA(SADLA) Regs
40 Reg 42 DA(SADLA) Regs
41 s677(1) IT(EP)A 2003
42 Reg 29(4)-(6) DA(SADLA) Regs
43 Regs 50 and 51 DA(SADLA) Regs
44 Reg 24(e) and Sch 2 para 15A(1) DAWAP(S) Regs
45 Sch 1 paras 12(5)(c)(i) and 13(5)(d)(i) DA(SADLA) Regs
46 Sch 2 paras 15A-15C DAWAP(S) Regs
47 Sch 2 para 15D DAWAP(S) Regs
48 Sch 2 paras 15F and 15H DAWAP(S) Regs
49 Sch 2 para 15I DAWAP(S) Regs

# Chapter 61

# Adult disability payment

**This chapter covers:**

1. Who can get adult disability payment (below)
2. The rules about your age (p1434)
3. The amount of benefit (p1435)
4. Special benefit rules (p1436)
5. Claims and getting paid (p1439)
6. Tax, other benefits and the benefit cap (p1446)


**Key facts**

- Adult disability payment (ADP) is a benefit for adults with a disability or long-term health condition who live in Scotland.
- ADP has a daily living component and a mobility component. You can qualify for one or both components. Each component has two rates.
- ADP is a non-means-tested benefit.
- You do not need to have paid national insurance contributions to get ADP.
- ADP is disregarded as income for means-tested benefits and can be paid in addition to most other benefits.
- Social Security Scotland administers and pays ADP.
- If you disagree with a determination about ADP, you can request a redetermination and then appeal against it (see Chapter 69).



## 1. Who can get adult disability payment

You can get adult disability payment (ADP) if:[1]

- you meet the age rules (see p1434); *and*
- you are 'ordinarily resident' in Scotland (see p1299); *and*
- you meet the other residence conditions (see p1347); *and*
- you are not a 'person subject to immigration control' (see p1272). **Note:** if your leave is subject to a 'no recourse to public funds' condition, see p1282 and get immigration advice *before* claiming ADP; *and*
- you are either terminally ill (see p1436), or you:
  - meet the disability conditions for the daily living component, the mobility component or both (see p1429); *and*
  - meet the required period condition (see p1433).

You cannot normally get ADP for a period during which you were entitled to child disability payment (CDP), disability living allowance (DLA), personal independence payment (PIP), pension age disability payment, Scottish adult disability living allowance (SADLA), attendance allowance or armed forces independence payment.[2] The following situations are exceptions to this rule.

- If you get CDP and can claim ADP from 13 weeks before your 16th birthday, see p1489.
- If you get PIP and are transferring to ADP (or you get 'working-age' DLA and your transfer to ADP began by 21 March 2025), see p1444.
- If you get SADLA and claim ADP, see p1425.
- If you are terminally ill, see p1437.

## The disability conditions

**Note:** the ADP disability conditions are mostly the same as those for PIP. This section sets out the main ADP disability conditions and refers you to the information about PIP in Chapter 31 where the rules are the same.

A points-based test looks at how your physical or mental condition (see p646) affects your ability to manage specific daily living activities and mobility activities.[3] Each activity has a list of statements ('descriptors') describing different difficulties with the activity or help you may need to do it.

Each descriptor has a points score. You get points for one descriptor in each activity – the one which best describes the difficulties you have with it. If your difficulties with an activity fluctuate, or more than one descriptor in an activity applies to you, see p1431.

The points you score for each activity relevant to a component are added together. You qualify for a component at:[4]

- the standard rate if you score eight points or more; *or*
- the enhanced rate if you score 12 points or more.

### How the disability conditions are different

The following differences from PIP apply to every activity in the ADP assessment. In practice, your entitlement should normally be the same as it would be if you had claimed PIP, as almost all of the changes either reflect existing PIP caselaw before ADP was introduced, or clarify the meaning of the regulations.

- There is a definition of 'needs' in the regulations to ensure that you are assessed as needing a type of help if you reasonably require it, even if it is not available or provided to you.[5]
- Where the PIP rules refer to 'C' or a 'claimant', the ADP regulations use 'individual'. This does not change how the assessment works.

***PIP caselaw and ADP***

The different wording of some ADP rules is intended to incorporate some of the PIP caselaw (decisions made by the Upper Tribunal and the courts which say how the law must be applied) into the regulations. In one case, the Upper Tribunal for Scotland has held that a tribunal may err in law if it does not follow PIP caselaw from before ADP was introduced if the descriptors are worded identically, even though that caselaw is not formally binding.[6] However, it remains unclear whether decision makers and tribunals are normally required to follow the PIP caselaw decided *after* the introduction of ADP. Get advice if you need to challenge an ADP determination and either the PIP caselaw referenced in Chapter 31 has not been followed, or it has and you want to argue that it should not have been.

### Aids and appliances

For ADP, 'aid or appliance':[7]

'(a) means any object or device which—

(i) the individual needs to be able to perform an activity, *and*

(ii) improves, provides or replaces the individual's impaired physical or mental function,

(b) includes an object or device which a person without a disability might choose to use for the same function,

(c) in relation to managing toilet needs includes the use of incontinence pads, *and*

(d) includes a prosthesis.'

10

This definition ensures that to score points for using an aid or appliance you must *need to* use it (rather than choosing to). Aids and appliances can include things which are not designed for disabled people.

Incontinence pads are *only* an aid or appliance for the managing toilet needs activity, and *not* for other activities. In other respects, the assessment of your ability to use an aid or appliance should be the same as for PIP (see p648).

### Can you carry out an activity?

To be awarded a descriptor (rather than a higher scoring one), you must be able to carry out the activity in that way safely, to an acceptable standard, repeatedly and within a reasonable time period.[8] This is assessed in the same way as for PIP (see p663), but the rules are worded slightly differently.[9]

- In deciding whether you can manage an activity 'safely', both the likelihood and severity of any harm must be considered.
- In deciding whether you can manage an activity 'to an acceptable standard', the impact of carrying out the activity on you must be considered.

### Fluctuating conditions

For ADP, you satisfy a descriptor if it applies during some part of the day (midnight to midnight) unless you do so only for a 'minimal or fleeting' time.[10] To qualify, your needs must be expected to last for over 52 weeks at a particular level. Your needs are assessed over a past period of 13 weeks (which can begin before you claim ADP) and a future period of 39 weeks.[11] If you have a previous award of ADP, CDP, SADLA, DLA or PIP, the past period can sometimes be the last 13 weeks of that award (see p1433).

Other than these rules, how your entitlement is assessed if the effect of your condition fluctuates is the same as for PIP (see p664).

## Differences in the wording of the daily living and mobility activities

Other than the differences from PIP that affect the whole assessment (see p1429), there are *no* differences in the wording of the descriptors in the following ADP daily living activities.[12]

- Activity 1: preparing food (see p649).
- Activity 5: managing toilet needs or incontinence (see p654 – but note the slightly different defintion of 'aid or appliance' on p1430).
- Activity 8: reading and understanding signs, symbols and words (see p657).
- Activity 10: making budgeting decisions (see p659).

The following sections explain the differences in wording from the PIP rules in the other ADP activities.[13]

### Daily living activity 2: taking nutrition

The points awarded for this activity should be the same as for PIP (see p650). The definition of 'take nutrition' uses the words '*ingest* nutrition using a therapeutic source', whereas the PIP assessment uses '*take* nutrition...'.



### Daily living activity 3: managing therapy or monitoring a health condition

The definitions of 'manage medication' and 'manage therapy' include medication or therapy 'which improves the individual's symptoms or health', as well as preventing deterioration. The definitions of 'medication', 'monitor a health condition' and 'therapy' use 'medical practitioner' where PIP uses 'doctor'. In practice, this should make no difference.

'Medication' for ADP can be prescribed or recommended by any 'health professional registered by the Health and Care Professions Council' (*not* just a doctor, nurse or pharmacist). There is a list of professions on the Council's website.[14] Only descriptor 3b differs from PIP – and even then, only if the professional prescribes or recommends 'medication' (rather than 'therapy').

In all other cases, the points you score for this activity should be the same as for PIP (see p651).

### Daily living activity 4: washing and bathing

The points awarded for this activity should be the same as for PIP (see p653). The wording of descriptor 4e is 'Needs assistance to be able to get in or out of *an unadapted* bath or shower.'

### Daily living activity 6: dressing and undressing

The points awarded for this activity should be the same as for PIP (see p655). ADP has separate definitions of 'dress' and 'undress' (which are combined for PIP):

- 'dress' includes put on socks and shoes; *and*
- 'undress' includes take off socks and shoes.

### Daily living activity 7: communicating verbally

The points for this activity should be the same as for PIP (see p656). The ADP version of descriptor 7a includes extra words. It is: 'Can express and understand *basic and complex* verbal information unaided.' The ADP definitions of 'basic verbal information' and 'complex verbal information' also contain extra words. Both add that the definition 'excludes information that is not communicated orally or received aurally' – eg, writing. Your ability to lip read should never be taken into account for this activity.[15]

The definition of 'communication support' also contains extra words. A person providing support can be 'trained or experienced in communicating with *people in general, or the individual in particular…*'.

### Daily living activity 9: engaging socially with other people face to face

The points for this activity should be the same as for PIP (see p658).

10

For ADP, the title of the activity and all of the descriptors have an extra word inserted. In each case, they refer to your ability to 'engage *socially* with other people'. The definition of 'social support' also contains extra words. The person providing support can be 'trained or experienced in assisting *people in general, or the individual in particular…*'.

### Mobility activity 1: planning and following journeys

The points awarded for this activity should be the same as for PIP (see p660). The Upper Tribunal for Scotland has held that the approach taken to descriptors 1d and 1f must be that set out in previous PIP Upper Tribunal decisions described there.[16]

The ADP regulations contain an extra definition: '"Follow the route of a journey" means for an individual to navigate and make their way along a planned route to a planned destination.'

Descriptor 1b contains extra words. It reads: 'Needs *the prompting of another person* to be able to undertake any journey to avoid overwhelming psychological distress to the individual.'

### Mobility activity 2: moving around

The points awarded for this activity should be the same as for PIP (see p662). Descriptors 2c and 2d contain extra words. To satisfy them, you must only be able to move 'no more than 50 metres *either aided or unaided*'.

## The required period condition

You meet the required period condition to be awarded a component if you have satisfied the disability conditions throughout the past 13 weeks (which can be before you claim ADP), and are likely to continue to satisfy them for at least a further 39 weeks.[17] If you do not satisfy the required period condition when you claim, you can be awarded ADP if you will satisfy it within 13 weeks of the date you complete your claim (see p1443).[18] In effect, you must have a level of needs that qualify for ADP by the day you complete a new claim (normally when SSS receives 'Part 2' of your claim), but you do not need to wait until your needs have lasted for more than 13 weeks before claiming.

Note:

- If you previously got a disability benefit, the 13-week part of the required period condition may be different (see below).
- To continue to satisfy the required period condition once you get ADP, your needs must be expected to last for at least a further 39 weeks.[19]
- If your needs change, you qualify for a new rate of ADP 13 weeks later if the new level of needs is expected to last for at least a further 39 weeks after that date.

*Examples*

Cameron was involved in a serious road traffic accident on 14 June. Before this, he had no difficulty with daily living or mobility activities. As he already knew about ADP, he claimed it two weeks later. The decision maker accepts that his needs are likely to last for over a year and awards him ADP from 13 September.

Tilly gets ADP and her mobility has worsened. She reports this on 15 October. The decision maker decides that her mobility needs increased around 10 September, and the new level of needs is expected to last for over a year. Her ADP award is increased from 10 December.

### The required period condition if you previously got a disability benefit

You can be awarded ADP without having met the disability conditions for 13 weeks if:[20]

- you previously had an award of ADP, CDP, SADLA, PIP or DLA; *and*
- that award ended less than two years (one year, if you are over pension age) before you *complete* your new claim for ADP;[21] *and*
- that award was of the same component(s) as your new award is (for this rule, the DLA/CDP/PIP mobility component counts as the ADP mobility component

and the DLA/CDP care component/PIP daily living component counts as the ADP daily living component);[22] *and*
- that award was based on the same condition(s) as your new award, or a new condition that developed due to the previous one.

In this situation, the 13-week part of the required period condition is the last 13 weeks of your previous award. Your needs must also be expected to last for at least 39 weeks when you make your new ADP claim.[23]

## 2. The rules about your age

You must be aged 16 or over to get adult disability payment (ADP).[24] You can claim child disability payment (CDP) for a child under 16 (see Chapter 64).

The upper age limit to *complete* a new claim for ADP is normally the day before you reach pension age.[25]

The upper age limit will increase as pension age rises between 2026 and 2028 (see p690).

If you have reached pension age and do not get a disability benefit, you can instead claim pension age disability payment (see Chapter 67). However, you can instead be awarded ADP after reaching pension age if you:[26]
- *completed* your ADP claim (including providing any required evidence – see p1440)[27] before reaching pension age; *or*
- had a previous award of ADP, Scottish adult disability living allowance (SADLA), disability living allowance (DLA) or personal independence payment (PIP) that ended less than a year before you *complete* your ADP claim, and you meet the other conditions on p1433 about your previous award; *or*
- were born after 8 April 1948 and are entitled to SADLA when you claim ADP (see p1425); *or*
- transfer to ADP from PIP or DLA ( see p1444).

If you have an award of ADP when you reach pension age, it continues. However, if your ADP entitlement is determined after you reach pension age, your rate of the mobility component may be restricted.

### Mobility component for older people

If you are entitled to the mobility component when you reach pension age, you continue to get it, provided you still meet the entitlement conditions. If your award later changes, see p1435.

#### New claims after you reach pension age

If you can make a new ADP claim after reaching pension age, your entitlement to the mobility component is restricted. You can get:[28]

- the enhanced rate if you meet the entitlement conditions for it *and* you got the ADP/PIP enhanced rate/DLA higher rate mobility component[29] in an award which ended less than one year before you complete your new claim; *or*
- the standard rate if you meet the entitlement conditions for it and you got the ADP/PIP/DLA mobility component in an award that ended less than one year before you complete your new claim.

**Note:** these restrictions do *not* apply if you completed your claim before reaching pension age, or claim ADP before 1 January 2028 whilst entitled to SADLA (see p1425).

### If your award changes after you reach pension age

There are restrictions if your ADP entitlement is determined again due to:[30]

- a change of circumstances (see p1541) that happens after you reach pension age; *or*
- ignorance of a material fact (see p1543) that Social Security Scotland (SSS) become aware of after you reached pension age; *or*
- receipt of medical evidence by SSS after you reach pension age, except evidence that you were terminally ill (see p1436) before reaching pension age.

In these situations, to be entitled to the mobility component at its previous rate, your entitlement must be due to substantially the same condition(s) as your previous award. You can move from the enhanced rate to the standard rate (even if your mobility needs result from a new condition). You cannot move from the standard rate to the enhanced rate or qualify for the first time.[31]

Note:

- There may be other reasons why your award is changed (see p1540). Only if your award changes for one of the reasons above is your entitlement to the mobility component restricted.
- If there is a gap of less than a year since you had an award of the ADP, PIP, SADLA or DLA mobility component, you can get the same rate back under these rules.[32]
- There are no restrictions on entitlement to the mobility component due to your age if your entitlement is being reviewed for the first time after you transferred from DLA to ADP (see p1446).[33]



## 3. The amount of benefit

The daily living component of adult disability payment (ADP) is paid at one of two weekly rates:[34]

- the standard rate is £73.90;
- the enhanced rate is £110.40.

The mobility component of ADP is paid at one of two weekly rates:[35]

- the standard rate is £29.20;
- the enhanced rate is £77.05.

## 4. Special benefit rules

Special rules may apply if you:

- are terminally ill (see below);
- are subject to immigration control (see p1272);
- have come from or are going abroad (see Chapters 57, 58 and 59);
- are in hospital or a hospice, living in a care home or other similar accommodation, or in prison or legal detention (see Chapter 38).

### Terminal illness

You are terminally ill for Scottish disability benefits if it is the judgement of a doctor or nurse involved in your care or diagnosis, and acting in a professional capacity, that you have a progressive disease that can reasonably be expected to cause your death. The person making this judgement must do so taking account of guidance published by the Chief Medical Officer for Scotland.[36]

If you are terminally ill, you are normally entitled to the highest possible rate of a Scottish disability benefit, unless your age means your entitlement to the mobility component is restricted. If you are terminally ill, you are awarded:[37]

- the enhanced rate of both components of adult disability payment (ADP) (but if you become terminally ill or transfer from personal independence payment (PIP) to ADP after reaching pension age, your entitlement to the mobility component may be restricted) (see p1434);
- the higher rate of pension age disability payment (PADP);
- the highest rate care component and higher rate mobility component of Scottish adult disability living allowance (SADLA) (but if you become terminally ill or transfer from disability living allowance (DLA) to SADLA after reaching pension age, your entitlement to the mobility component may be restricted) (see p1422).

If a child is terminally ill, they are entitled to the highest rate of the care component of child disability payment (CDP), and the higher rate of the mobility component from their third birthday (or the date they become terminally ill, if later).[38]

In the rest of this section, 'you' includes a child you claim CDP for. 'Scottish disability benefit' is used to refer to *all* of the benefits above.

## Claims if you are terminally ill

The process of claiming ADP, CDP and PADP is different if you are terminally ill. You must provide a judgement that you are terminally ill – either a Benefits Assessment under Special Rules in Scotland (BASRiS) form or a DWP SR1 or DS1500 form (see p671) completed by a doctor or nurse.[39] You should get this as soon as possible, claim immediately and declare to Social Security Scotland (SSS) that you are terminally ill as part of the claim. When you do these things affects when your entitlement can begin (see below).

You can start your claim online at mygov.scot/terminal-illness or by calling 0800 182 2222 (including requesting a paper form). You should also be able to start a claim via Contact Scotland BSL.[40] If you declare that you are terminally ill, you do not have to provide extra information about your care and mobility needs. You can be asked to provide additional evidence and should do so within the time given, or contact SSS to request more time or explain why you cannot provide it.

However, if you have a progressive disease but cannot get one of the forms listed above signed, you do *not* meet the definition of being terminally ill. You can still be awarded benefit if you meet the normal disability conditions (see p1429 for ADP, p1483 for CDP and p1513 for PADP). For how to claim if you are not accepted as terminally ill, see p1439 for ADP, p1490 for CDP and p1515 for PADP.

**Note:**

- If you are not sure if you will be accepted as terminally ill, then you should assume that you will *not* be and make a claim as if you are not terminally ill as soon as possible. This is particularly important if you are close to the upper age limit to make a claim (for ADP see p1434, and for CDP see p1488).
- If you are terminally ill, someone else can claim on your behalf, if they:
  - are your parent and you are under 16; *or*
  - are your appointee (see p1522); *or*
  - inform you that they are going to claim and you give consent for them to do so (or, if you are under 16, your parent gives consent).[41]

## When your entitlement starts if you are terminally ill

**Note:**

- If you get PIP, DLA or attendance allowance (AA) and are now terminally ill, see p1438.
- Your entitlement to PADP under the rules below *cannot* begin before it was first introduced (21 October 2024).
- You cannot make a new claim for SADLA, but you can be entitled under these rules if you get SADLA and tell SSS that you are terminally ill. However, your entitlement to SADLA under the rules below *cannot* begin before it was first introduced (21 March 2025).

If you are terminally ill, your Scottish disability benefit entitlement can begin before you claim it or tell SSS that you are terminally ill. Your entitlement under the terminal illness rules starts on the *earliest* of:[42]

- (*except for* SADLA) the day SSS receives your completed claim; *or*
- the day you inform SSS that you are terminally ill (if you already get a Scottish disability benefit); *or*
- the date of the judgement that you are terminally ill (which may be earlier than the date the form was signed),[43] if this is *less than* 26 weeks before SSS receives your completed claim or you tell SSS you are terminally ill.

If the judgement that you are terminally ill was made *more than* 26 weeks before the date SSS receives your completed claim (*except for* SADLA), or you tell SSS you are terminally ill, a doctor or nurse must confirm you are still terminally ill. Your entitlement then starts 26 weeks before the earlier of the date SSS received your completed claim, or you first told SSS you were terminally ill.[44]

**When entitlement starts if you are terminally ill and transfer from another benefit**

**Note:** at the time of writing, the rules in this section are expected to no longer apply when you have to claim ADP, CDP or PADP if you move to Scotland (perhaps from September 2025).[45] See CPAG's *Welfare Rights Bulletin* or the online version of this *Handbook* for updates.

If you transfer from PIP to ADP, from AA to PADP, from DLA to SADLA and either you were already terminally ill under the DWP rules (see p669) or you provide an SR1, DS1500 or BASRiS form before you are transferred, your entitlement to ADP, PADP or SADLA begins on the *latest* of:[46]

- the date of the judgement that you are terminally ill; *or*
- one year before your ADP, PADP or SADLA entitlement was determined; *or*
- the date on which the revelant regulations came into force (21 October 2024 for PADP and 21 March 2025 for SADLA).



A similar rule to that above applies if you transfer from DLA to ADP and the transfer began before 21 March 2025.[47]

If you are now terminally ill, you can be awarded ADP, PADP or SADLA for a period during which you previously got PIP, DLA, AA or armed forces independence payment. Your entitlement for any period you got another benefit is the difference between your old award and your new award.[48]

If a terminally ill child transfers from DLA to CDP, similar rules to those above allow them to be awarded CDP for a period during which they previously got DLA. CDP entitlement can begin up to 26 weeks before they were transferred to CDP.[49]

***Moving from CDP to ADP if you are terminally ill***

If you get CDP on the basis that you are terminally ill, the upper age limit at which your entitlement ends does not apply.[50] In practice, you should be invited to move to ADP before you turn 18, and transferred automatically unless you want to stay on CDP.[51] You can choose to move to ADP at any time after turning 16.

If you transfer, you are treated as terminally ill (so your ADP award is the same as your CDP). ADP starts and CDP ends when your ADP entitlement is determined.[52]

While you do not have to transfer to ADP, it may be advisable to do so. If you remain on CDP and your condition later improves so that you are no longer terminally ill after turning 18, your CDP will end immediately and you will have to claim ADP.

However, you may wish to stay on CDP after turning 18 as your ADP payment can be affected if you later go into hospital (see p816), while CDP cannot. Also, CDP (but *not* ADP) is paid at a higher rate for the last eight weeks of someone's life (see p1494).

## 5. Claims and getting paid

The general rules on claims and getting paid are covered in Chapter 68. This section explains the specific rules for adult disability payment (ADP).

### Making a claim

Note:

- The information in this section does *not* apply if you claim ADP and are terminally ill (see p1437).
- If you get another Scottish disability benefit, for information to help you decide whether to claim ADP:
  - see p1489 if you are 15–17 and entitled to child disability payment (CDP); *or*
  - see p1425 if you are entitled to Scottish adult disability living allowance.
- If you are entitled to personal independence payment (PIP), you do not currently need to claim ADP (see p1444, but these rules may change in the future).

10

You can start a claim for ADP:

- online at mygov.scot/adult-disability-payment/how-to-apply; *or*
- by phoning 0800 182 2222 to request a paper claim form; *or*
- if you use British Sign Language, via Contact Scotland BSL.

*Forms*

If you want to claim on a paper form, phone Social Security Scotland (SSS) and ask for the form to be sent to you. Send your completed form to the address on the first page. You should be sent a prepaid envelope with the form.

There is a separate form for organisations helping someone to claim ADP, which can be completed electronically. It can be downloaded from socialsecurity.gov.scot/guidance-resources/resources/adult-disability-payment-organisation-form. If you want to claim ADP with help from an organisation using this form, phone SSS and explain this. Ask them to record your details so your ADP can begin from the date of your call.

Your claim is made in two parts. If you appear to meet the entitlement conditions *other than the disability conditions* (see p1428), you must then complete 'Part 2' of the claim. You have eight weeks to complete it from the date you started your claim.

**Note:** you have *not* made a claim for ADP until SSS receives all of the required parts of your claim, and any required evidence.

### When you do not need to make a claim

If you get PIP, you do not need to claim ADP, as you will be transferred to it (see p1444).

If you were refused ADP due to an 'official error', your entitlement must be determined again without you making a further claim (see p1540). In practice, you should also make a new claim, as you cannot be sure that SSS will accept that there was an official error.

## Who should claim

You must normally claim ADP yourself. In some situations, another person can claim ADP for you as your 'appointee' (see p1522).

## Information to support your claim

To start your claim, you must provide SSS with your full name and date of birth. In practice, you are also asked questions about the residence and presence conditions at this point. SSS calls this 'Part 1' of your ADP claim.

You then have eight weeks to complete your claim by providing the rest of the required information ('Part 2'). This eight-week period can be extended if there is 'good reason' for the delay.[53]

You should contact SSS and ask for an extension as soon as possible if you need more time to complete your claim. If SSS does not extend the period, your award may begin later (see p1442) or your entitlement to ADP may not be determined at all (see p1534).

### The required information

The information you are required to provide as Part 2 of your claim relates to your ability to manage the different daily living and mobility activities. You can provide this online if you started your claim online, or on a paper claim form. You can ask SSS to help you complete the claim by calling 0800 182 2222.

The information requested is similar to a PIP questionnaire but with more detailed questions about each daily living and mobility activity. You should complete Part 2 in the same way as a PIP questionnaire (see p672).

You may need to prove your identity. You are also asked to provide supporting evidence with your ADP claim, in the form of a confirmation of your condition(s) or needs from a professional.[54] You should be able to ask SSS for help to get any required supporting evidence – including asking it to do so on your behalf.[55] However, you must give permission for this to happen. So, if you do not give permission, or if SSS asks you to, you must provide supporting evidence yourself. Your claim can be refused if you fail to do so, or you may be referred for a consultation (see below).

You can choose to provide more than one piece of evidence. If you are unsure how useful a piece of supporting evidence is, check how closely it relates to the disability conditions (see p1429). Evidence confirming the severity of your condition (eg, details of your visual or hearing impairment), may also be useful.

Even if you have already provided supporting evidence, SSS can ask you for further information (including by calling you to discuss your needs) if it thinks this is needed to determine your entitlement.

### If you fail to provide supporting evidence or information

If you do not provide any required supporting evidence or information within the time allowed, you can be given a determination that you are not entitled to ADP.[56]

If you are sent a determination that you are not entitled to ADP for failing to provide evidence, you can request a redetermination (see p1535). You should try to provide the requested evidence as well. A decision maker carrying out a redetermination or a First-tier Tribunal at appeal can make any determination that the original decision maker *could* have made.[57] This arguably includes ignoring any failure to provide evidence and determining entitlement under the normal rules.[58] You should consider making a new claim for ADP as well, in case your challenge is unsuccessful. 10

**Note:** if you start a claim for ADP but fail to provide something required by SSS (particularly if you do not complete Part 2 of the claim on time), it may not make a determination of your entitlement at all (see p1534).

## Assessment consultations

If SSS believes it is needed to determine your entitlement, you can be asked to take part in an assessment, referred to as a 'consultation'.[59] Usually, a consultation takes place by telephone.[60] You should be asked how you would prefer to be assessed (eg, by video call or in person) and your views should be taken into account.[61] A supporter (eg, a family member or adviser) can take part, including speaking on your behalf, unless SSS considers this unreasonable.[62]

The advice about what to do at a consultation is similar to that for PIP (see p674). However, ADP consultations do not include any physical examination and may not cover all of the daily living and mobility activities.

Your consultation is recorded unless you ask for it not to be. Ask not to be recorded in advance by calling 0800 182 2222. The consultation may need to be rearranged if you do not give advance notice.[63]

**If you do not take part in a consultation**

If you cannot take part in a consultation, explain this to SSS as soon as possible and ask for it to be rearranged. If you do not take part in a consultation, a determination is normally made based on the information that SSS has about you.[64] However, the law also allows for a determination that you are not entitled to ADP because you did not take part.[65] If this happens, see p1441 (the advice is the same as if you are refused ADP for failing to provide supporting evidence).

## The date of your claim

When ADP is paid from is normally determined by the date you begin your claim. It is important to claim as soon as possible as ADP cannot begin before you started your claim, unless you are terminally ill (see p1437).

Your entitlement to ADP can begin on the date you submit your full name and date of birth to SSS, as long as it receives the rest of the required information to complete your claim within the time allowed, normally eight weeks (see p1440). If you do not provide all of the required information within the time allowed, your entitlement begins on the date you eventually provide it.[66]

Note:

- Your complete claim *must* be received by SSS before you reach pension age, otherwise you cannot be entitled to ADP (this may mean you have less than eight weeks to complete it).
- You should try to complete all of Part 1 of your ADP claim immediately, as otherwise the date on which your entitlement can begin may not be registered. If you cannot do this, provide at least your full name and date of birth. You can then request a redetermination if your award starts later than the date you gave this information.[67]
- If you do not meet the entitlement conditions when you claim, you can claim in advance (see p1443).
- If you claimed the wrong benefit, see p1443.
- There are different rules about when your ADP begins if you claim ADP while you get CDP (see p1489) or SADLA (see p1425); or you get PIP or DLA and are transferring to ADP (see p1444).
- If your ADP claim was refused due to an 'official error', your entitlement must be determined again (see p1540). In this situation, your ADP starts from when it would have begun if your previous claim had been successful.

### Backdating your claim

You cannot backdate a claim for ADP unless you are terminally ill (see p1437).

If you might have qualified for ADP sooner but did not claim because you were given the wrong information or misled by SSS, you could complain and ask for compensation (see p1529).

### If you claim the wrong benefit

SSS says that it will accept a claim for another Scottish disability benefit or PIP as being a claim for ADP, so long as you have provided your name and date of birth.[68] You are likely to be asked to provide further information if this happens.

If you realise that you have claimed the wrong benefit, contact SSS as soon as possible and explain the situation. Ask if it is treating your claim as being for ADP. Unless it is, you should immediately claim ADP.

### Claiming in advance

You can complete your ADP claim up to 13 weeks before you satisfy:[69]

- the required period condition (see p1433); *or*
- the residence rules (see p1347); *or*
- the age rules (see p1434).

Your entitlement begins on the date you meet all of the entitlement conditions (including the required period condition).

## Getting paid

ADP is usually paid four weekly in arrears. If you are terminally ill, you are paid weekly in advance.[70] You are paid into the account you choose when you claim.

If appropriate, SSS can pay your ADP to another person for your benefit.[71]

If you are entitled to ADP and home from a care home or residential school for less than a week, you are paid at a daily rate.[72]

- For when your ADP payments can be suspended, see p1525.
- For when a deduction can be made to recover an overpayment, see p1527.
- For when your ADP mobility component can be paid to Motability, see p1447.
- If you are overpaid ADP, you may have to repay it (see p1526).

### Change of circumstances

You must report any change you have been told to report to SSS.[73] A change of circumstances can include that your needs are no longer expected to last for 39 weeks at the same level, as you will no longer meet the required period condition (see p1433).

You should report any changes in your circumstances as soon as possible. You can report a change by phone or on the form you can download from mygov.scot/adult-disability-payment-changes. Many changes can also be reported online at this address. Check your most recent determination carefully, as it tells you how you must report a change.[74]

If you report a change that may affect the amount of your ADP, SSS makes a new determination. For when the new determination takes effect, see p1541.

Before making a determination, SSS can ask you to provide further information.

**Note:** if you get ADP and move elsewhere in the UK, see p1420.

### Reviews of adult disability payment awards

If your determination of entitlement specifies a period after which your ADP award must be reviewed, a further determination must be made at the end of this period.[75] The length of time between reviews depends on how likely your condition is to change. Your award should not be reviewed if you are terminally ill (see p1436), or entitled to the enhanced rate of both components and the effects of your condition are very unlikely to change.[76]

For when the new determination following a review takes effect, see p1541.

If your award is being reviewed or your circumstances may have changed, SSS can ask you to provide evidence or other information. You can be asked for any evidence that may be required when you make a new claim (see p1440), or to take part in a consultation (see p1441).[77]

If you do not provide information within the time allowed, your ADP payments can be suspended (see p1525). If you need more time to provide information, contact SSS as soon as possible to request an extension.

## Transfers to adult disability payment

If you get PIP and live in Scotland, you will transfer to ADP (see above).

**Note:**

- The rules in this section *do not* apply if you must claim ADP. If you get CDP see p1489, and if you get SADLA see p1425.
- If you get DLA and your transfer to ADP started before 21 March 2025, see p1446.

10

### Moving from personal independence payment to adult disability payment

**Note:** at the time of writing, the rules in this section are expected to change, requiring you to claim ADP if you move to Scotland from September 2025.[78] See CPAG's *Welfare Rights Bulletin* or the online version of this *Handbook* for updates.

If you get PIP and live in Scotland (or in a European Economic Area (EEA) state and have a 'genuine and sufficient' link to Scotland – see p1350), you will be transferred to ADP without having to claim it. It is likely that this process will be completed before the end of 2025. If you live in Scotland and are entitled to PIP and you have not been told that you are being transferred to ADP, contact SSS and ask when you will be transferred.

If you have not transferred to ADP, continue to report any changes (particularly to your daily living or mobility needs) to the DWP. Any increased entitlement to ADP will start sooner than if you wait to be transferred (see below).[79] Get advice if you are unsure whether a change is relevant to your PIP award, or how your entitlement might change.

You are notified in writing that you will be transferred to ADP, including how long the process will take and that your PIP will end when your ADP starts.[80] If SSS later realises that you were wrongly sent a transfer notification or wants to extend the transfer period, you are sent another notification.[81] If the transfer process has started but you have not yet been awarded ADP, continue to report any changes of circumstances to the DWP.[82]

Unless you are terminally ill (see p1436), you are initially awarded the same rate of ADP as your previous PIP award.[83]

***Should you challenge a transfer determination?***

If you disagree with the initial determination of your ADP entitlement, you can request a redetermination. However, if you have already reported a change of circumstances to the DWP, it may be better *not* to request a redetermination as you may get more benefit if you wait for a review determination. Get advice if you are unsure.

**Review determinations if you reported a change of circumstances**

If, before being awarded ADP, you reported a change of circumstances that the DWP did not take into account for your PIP award, SSS makes a 'review determination' as soon as possible after you transfer to ADP. A review determination *cannot* be made if you request a redetermination of the ADP transfer determination (so it is probably better *not* to do this).[84]

The review determination takes effect:[85]

- if it increases your award, from:
  - the date of the change (ie, that you meet the disability conditions for a different rate of ADP, including the required period condition – see p1433) if you reported it within one month (or up to 13 months if you had a good reason for reporting the change late); *or*
  - the date you reported the change, if the above bullet point does not apply; *or*
- if it does not change or decreases your ADP award, from the date it is made.

If your award is higher, you can be awarded ADP for a period during which you got PIP under the rule above. You are paid the difference between your PIP award and the ADP award.[86]

**Note:** if the change happened after you reached pension age, your entitlement to the mobility component may be restricted (see p1435).

## Moving from disability living allowance to adult disability payment

Until 21 March 2025, you could also be transferred to ADP if you were entitled to DLA, aged 16–64 on 8 April 2013, and either lived in Scotland or in an EEA country and with a 'genuine and sufficient link' to Scotland (see p1350).[87] Since that date, if you still get DLA and are 18 or over you will be transferred to SADLA instead (see p1422).

The process of the transfer from DLA to ADP was similar to the transfer from PIP to ADP (see p1444).[88] It may still be underway in some cases.

When you are transferred, your DLA award is converted to an ADP award. Unless you are terminally ill (see p1438), you are initially awarded ADP at the same rate as your DLA (so the lower rate DLA care component converts to a 'transitional rate' of the daily living component of £29.20 a week).[89] Unless you request a redetermination, your ADP award is then reviewed (see below).

While you can request a redetermination of the determination awarding you ADP, it may be better not to do so, as you could be better off if you wait for your award to be reviewed. Get advice if you are unsure.

### Reviews after you transfer from disability living allowance to adult disability payment

If you transfer from DLA to ADP, are not terminally ill and have not requested a redetermination, your award of ADP must be reviewed within 12 months of the transfer. Your ADP entitlement is determined applying the usual disability conditions (see p1429).[90] Any changes that you reported to the DWP before being transferred that were not taken into account for your DLA award are also considered.[91]

If your new entitlement to ADP is higher than your award on transfer from DLA, that higher entitlement starts from your date of transfer.[92] If your new entitlement is lower, the change takes effect from the date of the new determination.[93]



# 6. Tax, other benefits and the benefit cap

## Tax

Adult disability payment (ADP) is not taxable.[94]

## Other benefits

ADP interacts with means-tested benefits in the same way as personal independence payment (PIP) does (see p679). Note that if you move to ADP from PIP, disability living allowance or Scottish adult disability living allowance, you may need to tell the DWP and the local authority about your ADP award to ensure that any extra amounts continue to be paid.

## Non-means-tested benefits

ADP is paid in addition to most other non-means-tested benefits. You cannot be entitled to both ADP and one of the benefits listed on p1429. Your payment of ADP may be reduced if you also get constant attendance allowance under the industrial injuries scheme (see p600), or a constant attendance allowance or mobility supplement as part of a war pension (see p779).[95]

If you get the daily living component of ADP and someone regularly looks after you, they may be able to claim carer support payment (see p1468) and the carer element of universal credit (UC) (see p75). However, any severe disability premium/addition that you get stops if they get one of these, so always get advice.

If you get the daily living component, a young person may be able to get a young carer grant for looking after you (see p1476).

## The benefit cap

ADP is *not* one of the specified benefits for the benefit cap. The benefit cap does not apply if you, your partner or child get ADP (even it is not paid because the person is in hospital or a care home). In other cases, it only applies if you are getting UC or housing benefit. See p1025 for further information.

## Passports and other sources of help

These are the same as for PIP (see p681).

### Motability

Motability is a scheme to help you lease or buy a car, scooter or powered wheelchair. You are eligible if you get the enhanced rate of the ADP mobility component and have over 12 months left until your award is due to be reviewed (see p1444).[96] Social Security Scotland refers to it as the 'Accessible Vehicles and Equipment' scheme.

If you use the scheme, your ADP mobility component is paid to Motability.[97] You may also have to make extra payments. For further information, phone 0300 456 4566 or see motability.co.uk. If you use British Sign Language, see motability.co.uk/get-support/bsl-video-relay-service.

# Notes

1. **Who can get adult disability payment**

1 s31 and Sch 5 SS(S)A 2018; reg 3 DAWAP(S) Regs
2 Reg 4 DAWAP(S) Regs; *SSS v IR* [2024] UT 69
3 Regs 5-10 and Sch 1 DAWAP(S) Regs
4 Regs 8 and 9 DAWAP(S) Regs
5 Reg 2 DAWAP(S) Regs
6 *SSS v AH, AS, SS and GA* [2024] UT 63, which held that the Scottish Parliament must be taken to have intended to incorporate PIP caselaw when legislating for ADP unless the contrary can be shown
7 Reg 2 DAWAP(S) Regs
8 Reg 7(2)(b) DAWAP(S) Regs
9 Reg 7(3) DAWAP(S) Regs
10 Reg 10(2) DAWAP(S) Regs
11 Regs 10, 13 and 14 DAWAP(S) Regs
12 Sch 1 DAWAP(S) Regs
13 Sch 1 DAWAP(S) Regs
14 hcpc-uk.org/about-us/who-we-regulate/the-professions
15 The definitions are not clear that lip-reading cannot be taken into account (this is information that is 'communicated orally' (using the mouth), even though it is not 'received aurally'). If necessary you can argue that the decision in *SSS v AH, AS, SS and GA* [2024] UT 63 means that *P v SSWP (PIP)* [2018] UKUT 376 (AAC) requires that lip reading is ignored for ADP as well.
16 *SSS v AH, AS, SS and GA* [2024] UT 63, although the relevance of PIP UT decisions after ADP was introduced remains unclear
17 Regs 10(3), 11, 12 and 13 DAWAP(S) Regs; *SSS v FK* [2024] UT 23
18 Reg 35(2) DAWAP(S) Regs
19 Reg 10(3)(b) DAWAP(S) Regs
20 Regs 10(3), 14 and 23 DAWAP(S) Regs
21 You must complete your claim (providing any information and evidence required) within the required time after your award ended: reg 35 DAWAP(S) Regs
22 Regs 14(5) and 23(7) DAWAP(S) Regs. While only the care component of SADLA counts as the daily living component of ADP, and then only if you are over pension age, this should not cause problems at present (as arguably you can rely on your award of DLA before your SADLA started instead).
23 Regs 10(3), 14(3) and (4) and 23(3) and (4) DAWAP(S) Regs

2. **The rules about your age**

24 Reg 22(1)(a) DAWAP(S) Regs
25 Reg 22(1)(b) and (2) DAWAP(S) Regs
26 Regs 23 and 24 DAWAP(S) Regs
27 s38(1) SS(S)A 2018; reg 35(1)(a) DAWAP(S) Regs – nothing elsewhere in reg 35 treats a claim as made on the date you start your claim, it rather allows entitlement to begin from an earlier date than the claim was made
28 Reg 23(2), (5) and (6) DAWAP(S) Regs
29 While it is not clear from the regulations that the DLA higher rate mobility component is treated as the enhanced rate mobility component, this is understood to be the policy intention
30 Reg 25 DAWAP(S) Regs
31 Reg 25(3) DAWAP(S) Regs
32 Reg 25(4) DAWAP(S) Regs. While it is unclear from the regulations that the SADLA and DLA higher rate mobility component is treated as the enhanced rate mobility component, this is understood to be the policy intention.
33 This determination is made under reg 12 DAWAP(TPMA)(S) Regs, and so reg 25 DAWAP(S) Regs cannot restrict your entitlement to the mobility component

3. **The amount of benefit**

34 Reg 34(1) DAWAP(S) Regs
35 Reg 34(2) DAWAP(S) Regs

**4. Special benefit rules**

36 **ADP** Reg 26(7), (8) and (10) DAWAP(S) Regs
**CDP** Reg 15(6), (7) and (9) DACYP(S) Regs
**PADP** Reg 18(6), (7) and (9) DAOP(S) Regs
**SADLA** Reg 20(8), (9) and (11) DA(SADLA) Regs
**All** s31(1)(b) and Sch 5 para 1 SS(S)A 2018; SSS, *Chief Medical Officer's Guidance for Clinicians Completing a BASRiS Form*
37 **ADP** Reg 26(1) and Sch 2 para 11(1A) and (1B) DAWAP(S) Regs
**PADP** Reg 18(1) DAOP(S) Regs
**SADLA** Reg 20(1) and (2) and Sch 1 para 9(2) and (3) DA(SADLA) Regs
38 Reg 15(1) DACYP(S) Regs
39 SSS, *Special Rules for Terminal Illness: frequently asked questions*
40 **ADP** mygov.scot/adult-disability-payment/how-to-apply
**CDP** mygov.scot/child-disability-payment/how-to-apply
**PADP** mygov.scot/pension-age-disability-payment/how-to-apply
41 mygov.scot/terminal-illness/who-can-apply
42 **ADP** Reg 26(4) and (5) DAWAP(S) Regs
**CDP** Reg 15(3) and (4) DACYP(S) Regs
**PADP** Reg 18(3) and (4) DAOP(S) Regs
**SADLA** Reg 20(5) and (6) DA(SADLA) Regs
43 SSS, *Chief Medical Officer's Guidance for Clinicians Completing a BASRiS Form*
44 **ADP** Reg 26(6) DAWAP(S) Regs
**CDP** Reg 15(5) DACYP(S) Regs
**PADP** Reg 18(5) DAOP(S) Regs
**SADLA** Reg 20(7) DA(SADLA) Regs
45 SS(CPCTMA)(S) Regs (draft)
46 **AA to PADP** Reg 1 and Sch para 11(2)(b) DAOP(S) Regs
**DLA to SADLA** Reg 1 and Sch 1 para 9(4)(b) DA(SADLA) Regs
**PIP to ADP** Sch 2 para 11(2) DAWAP(S) Regs
47 Reg 9(2) DAWAP(TPMA)(S) Regs
48 **ADP** Regs 26(11) and (12), 45(3) and (4) and Sch 2 para 14(c) and (d) DAWAP(S) Regs.
**PADP** Regs 18(10) and (11), 37(3) and (4) and Sch paras 12(b) and (f) DAOP(S) Regs
**SADLA** Regs 20(12)-(14), 40(3) and (4) and Sch 1 para 9(4)(b) and (6) DA(SADLA) Regs
49 Sch paras 11 and 13(zb) DACYP(S) Regs
50 Reg 4(1B)(a) DACYP(S) Regs
51 Reg 59(1)(b) DAWAP(S) Regs; SSS DMG: *Special rules for terminal illness for adult disability payment*
52 Reg 59 DAWAP(S) Regs

**5. Claims and getting paid**

53 Reg 35(4)-(6) DAWAP(S) Regs
54 s54(1) SS(S)A 2018; SSS DMG: *Gathering supporting information for adult disability payment*
55 mygov.scot/supporting-information-disability-benefits
56 s54(2) SS(S)A 2018
57 This was the approach taken by SSS and the tribunal in *KW v SSS* [2024] UT 65
58 ss43 and 49 SS(S)A 2018. As there has been a determination of your entitlement, any redetermination or appeal determination replaces it completely, and so arguably must still consider all of the entitlement conditions.
59 s14(a) SS(S)A 2018
60 SSS DMG: *Consultations for adult disability payment*
61 s14(b) SS(S)A 2018
62 s59 SS(S)A 2018
63 mygov.scot/adult-disability-payment-consultations
64 SSS DMG, *Consultations for adult disability payment*
65 s54(3) SS(S)A 2018
66 Reg 35(1) and (5) DAWAP(S) Regs
67 Reg 35(4) DAWAP(S) Regs. You can argue that by phoning SSS or providing this information online and saving your claim, you have 'submitted' it.
68 SSS DMG, *Applying for adult disability payment*
69 Reg 35(2) DAWAP(S) Regs
70 Reg 36 DAWAP(S) Regs
71 Reg 33(1) DAWAP(S) Regs
72 Reg 34(3) DAWAP(S) Regs
73 s56 SS(S)A 2018
74 s56(2)(b) SS(S)A 2018
75 Reg 47 DAWAP(S) Regs
76 SSS DMG, *Choosing an appropriate review period for adult disability payment*
77 SSS DMG, *Relevant considerations when making a determination for an award review – adult disability payment*
78 SS(CPCTMA)(S) Regs (draft)
79 Sch 2 para 12(4) DAWAP(S) Regs
80 Sch 2 paras 7 and 8 DAWAP(S) Regs
81 Sch 2 paras 8(3) and (4) and 9(6)(c) DAWAP(S) Regs

82 SSS, *Case Transfer Guide: PIP to adult disability payment*
83 Sch 2 para 9(5) DAWAP(S) Regs
84 Sch 2 para 12(1) DAWAP(S) Regs
85 Sch 2 para 12(1)-(5) DAWAP(S) Regs
86 Sch 2 para 12(6) DAWAP(S) Regs
87 Reg 22 Disability Assistance (Scottish Adult Disability Living Allowance) (Consequential Amendment, Revocation and Saving Provision) Regulations 2024 No.311
88 Regs 2-4 DAWAP(TPMA)(S) Regs; SSS, *Case Transfer Guide: working age disability living allowance to adult disability payment*
89 Regs 5 and 6 DAWAP(TPMA)(S) Regs
90 Reg 12 DAWAP(TPMA)(S) Regs
91 Reg 14 DAWAP(TPMA)(S) Regs
92 Reg 15 DAWAP(TPMA)(S) Regs
93 Reg 16 DAWAP(TPMA)(S) Regs

6. **Tax, other benefits and the benefit cap**
94 s677(1) IT(EP)A 2003
95 Reg 34(4)-(6) DAWAP(S) Regs
96 mygov.scot/lease-accessible-vehicles
97 Regs 55 and 56 DAWAP(S) Regs

# Chapter 62

# Scottish child payment, Best Start grants and Best Start foods

**This chapter covers:**


1. Scottish child payment (p1452)
2. Best Start grant (p1452)
3. Best Start foods (p1455)
4. Responsibility for a child (p1457)
5. Qualifying benefits (p1459)
6. The rules about your age (p1459)
7. Claims and getting paid (p1460)
8. Tax, other benefits and the benefit cap (p1464)


## Key facts

- Scottish child payment is a top-up benefit for lower-income families in Scotland responsible for a child under the age of 16.
- Best Start grants include a payment for women who are pregnant or who have recently given birth – called a **pregnancy and baby payment** – and amounts to help with the costs of young children – called an **early learning payment** and a **school-age payment**.
- Best Start foods provide a payment card for pregnant women and people responsible for a child under three to spend on milk, fruit and vegetables.
- You must usually receive a means-tested benefit to qualify for these payments, but some young people can qualify for Best Start grants and Best Start foods without a qualifying benefit.
- You do not need to have paid national insurance contributions to qualify for these payments.
- Scottish child payment and Best Start are administered and paid by Social Security Scotland.
- If you disagree with a determination about Scottish child payment or Best Start grant, you can request a redetermination and then appeal against it (see Chapter 69). The process to challenge a Best Start foods decision is different.

# 1. Scottish child payment

You qualify for Scottish child payment if:[1]

- you are responsible (see p1457) for a child under the age of 16; *and*
- you are entitled to a qualifying benefit (see p1459); *and*
- you are ordinarily resident in Scotland (see p1299).

You must usually meet all the qualifying conditions on the date your claim is received.

In some circumstances, such as if you or the child are in hospital or detention or go abroad, your entitlement to Scottish child payment depends on whether you still count as responsible for the child and whether you are still entitled to a qualifying benefit.

## The amount of Scottish child payment

Scottish child payment is paid at a weekly rate of £27.15 for each child you are responsible for.

If the child for whom you are getting Scottish child payment dies, the weekly rate is doubled for the period of 12 weeks ending with the death of the child.[2]

## Change of circumstances

10

If you no longer meet the qualifying conditions, your entitlement to Scottish child payment ends from the week following the date on which you no longer qualify.[3] Your entitlement can be determined again following a change of circumstances relating to the qualifying conditions – ie, responsibility for the child, ordinary residence in Scotland and entitlement to qualifying benefits.[4] A new determination following a change of circumstances takes effect from the date of the change, or if this is not known, the date Social Security Scotland (SSS) became aware of the change. A new determination can be made on your Scottish child payment if SSS decides to pay it to someone else for the child instead, with effect from the date the other person's claim is determined.[5]

Your Scottish child payment ends from the week after the week in which the child's 16th birthday falls.[6]

# 2. Best Start grant

You qualify for a Best Start grant if:[7]

- you or your partner are receiving a qualifying benefit (see p1459); *or*
- you are aged under 18, or aged 18 or 19 and a dependant (see p1457), *and*

- you or your partner are pregnant or responsible for a child and meet the conditions for the pregnancy and baby payment (see below), the early learning payment (see below) or the school-age payment (see p1454).

For when you count as responsible for a child and the meaning of dependant, see p1457.

You must also:

- be ordinarily resident in Scotland (see p1299); *and*
- be 'habitually resident' in the UK, Channel Islands or Isle of Man or, if you have leave under the European Union Settlement Scheme or a specified free movement residence right, the European Economic Area. You do not need to meet this condition if you are receiving a qualifying benefit or you are exempt from it (see p1303); *and*
- unless payment is made automatically because you are getting Scottish child payment, claim within the time limit (see p1462).

## Who can get a pregnancy and baby payment

In addition to the basic rules for a Best Start grant on p1452, to qualify for the pregnancy and baby payment:[8]

- either:
  - you (or your partner or dependant) must be (or have been) more than 24 weeks' pregnant, or you gave birth to a child before or during the 24th week of pregnancy and the application is within six months of the birth; *or*
  - you (or your partner) have become responsible for a baby under the age of one and you (or your partner) are not the child's mother; *and*
- you have not received, and are not due to receive, a Sure Start maternity grant (see p705) for the same child; *and*
- no other person has received, and is not due to receive, a Best Start grant pregnancy and baby payment or a Sure Start maternity grant for the same child, unless:
  - you are responsible for the child on the date of your claim; *and*
  - you have not been that person's partner or dependant, and they have not been your or your partner's dependant, since that person claimed a payment or grant; *and*
  - the child does not normally live with the person who has already received a payment or grant.

If your child dies or is stillborn after the 24th week of pregnancy, you are still entitled to the pregnancy and baby payment and do not have to pay it back.

## Who can get an early learning payment

In addition to the basic rules for a Best Start grant on p1452, you qualify for the early learning payment if:[9]

- you or your partner are responsible for the child (see p1457) on the day you claim, which must be within the period from the child's second birthday to six months after the child's third birthday; *and*
- no other person has received, or is due to receive, an early learning payment for the child, unless:
  - you are responsible for the child on the date of your claim; *and*
  - you have not been that person's partner at any time since they applied for an early learning payment for the child; *and*
  - the child does not normally live with the person who has already received an early learning payment.

You can qualify for an early learning payment whether or not you have received a pregnancy and baby payment for the child. It does not matter whether your child is actually in early learning (eg, nursery, childcare or with a childminder) or not.

## Who can get a school-age payment

In addition to the basic rules for a Best Start grant on p1452, you qualify for the school-age payment if:[10]

- you or your partner are responsible for a child born between 1 March 2020 and 28 February 2021 inclusive, and you claim from 1 June 2025 to 28 February 2026; *and*
- no other person has received, or is due to receive, a school-age payment for the child unless:
  - you are responsible for the child on the date of your claim; *and*
  - you have not been that person's partner at any time since they claimed a school-age payment for the child; *and*
  - the child does not normally live with the person who has already received a school-age payment.

10

You can qualify for a school-age payment whether or not you have received a pregnancy and baby payment or an early learning payment for the child. It does not matter whether your child has actually started school or not.

## The amount of Best Start grant

The pregnancy and baby payment is £767.50 if there are no other children aged under 16 living in your household, or £383.75 if there is another child aged under 16 living in your household. You still get the £767.50 payment if the only other child(ren) in your household is:[11]

- a parent of the child for whom a Best Start grant is being made; *or*
- a sibling of a parent of the child; *or*
- a child for whom you or your partner are not responsible; *or*

- a child who is not your or your partner's child, and you became responsible for the child when they were aged 12 months or older; *or*
- a child with whom you have left your home due to domestic abuse; *or*
- a child who was born before you arrived in the UK, and you have refugee status, humanitarian protection, or you have come to the UK under the Afghan Citizens Resettlement Scheme or from Ukraine and are covered by the rule exempting you from the habitual residence test (see p1303); *or*
- a sibling born as a result of the same birth, but this only applies to one payment of £767.50 (see example below).

There is one multiple pregnancy supplement of £383.75 if more than one child is born or is to be born as a result of the same pregnancy.

***Example***

Rebekah is pregnant with triplets. She has no other children living in her household. She is entitled to £767.50 for one child, £383.75 each for the other two children, and a multiple pregnancy supplement of £383.75. Her total Best Start grant is £1,918.75.

The early learning payment is £319.80 for each child.

The school-age payment is £319.80 for each child.

## 3. Best Start foods

The Best Start foods payment card has replaced the Healthy Start scheme in Scotland.[12] If you qualify, you get £5.40 a week for yourself if you are pregnant, £10.80 a week for a child aged under one and £5.40 a week for each child aged one or two. Payments are made by credits to a payment card. 10

Best Start foods are administered by Social Security Scotland (SSS). Best Start foods include cow's milk, first infant formula milk, fresh, frozen or tinned fruit and vegetables, fresh or tinned pulses and fresh eggs.

You qualify for Best Start foods if:[13]

- you are pregnant, aged at least 18 and you or your partner are receiving a qualifying benefit; *or*
- you are responsible for a child under three, and you or your partner are receiving a qualifying benefit; *or*
- you are pregnant and aged under 18, or you are aged 18 or 19 and a dependant. If you turn 18, or are no longer a dependent 18/19-year-old, you remain entitled until the end of your pregnancy; *or*
- you are responsible for a child under one, and you are aged under 18, or you are aged 18 or 19 and a dependant, or were previously entitled to Best Start

foods during pregnancy because you or your partner were under 18 or aged 18 or 19 and a dependant. If you turn 18, or are no longer a dependent 18/19-year-old, you remain entitled until either the child's first birthday or the first anniversary of their due date, whichever is later; *or*
- you are responsible for a child aged one or two, and you are aged under 18, or you are aged 18 or 19 and a dependant. You are no longer entitled if you turn 18 or are no longer a dependent 18/19-year-old; *or*
- your partner is pregnant and you are receiving a qualifying benefit, and using the Best Start foods payment card for your partner's benefit; *or*
- your partner is pregnant and you are aged under 18, or are aged 18 or 19 and a dependant, and using the Best Start foods payment card for your partner's benefit. This means you could qualify even if your pregnant partner is aged 20 or over and would not qualify in her own right. If you turn 18, or are no longer a dependent 18/19-year-old, you remain entitled until the end of your partner's pregnancy; *or*
- your or your partner's dependant is pregnant and under 18, or aged 18 or 19. You remain entitled until the end of her pregnancy if she is no longer your dependant.

For when you count as responsible for a child and the meaning of dependant, see p1457. For the qualifying benefits, see p1459.

Someone counts as your partner if you would be a couple for universal credit (see p58).[14]

If you are pregnant and both you and another person apply for Best Start foods for you during pregnancy, you have priority.[15]

When the child is born, it is the child who is entitled to Best Start foods, and the person responsible for the child acts on their behalf.[16]

10

You must also:
- make an application for Best Start foods during pregnancy and for a child; *and*
- be ordinarily resident in Scotland (see p1299); *and*
- be 'habitually resident' in the UK, Channel Islands or Isle of Man or, if you have leave under the European Union Settlement Scheme or a specified free movement residence right, the European Economic Area. You do not need to meet this condition if you are receiving a qualifying benefit or you are exempt from it (see p1303).

If you are pregnant, you can apply from the start of your pregnancy. You are not usually asked for evidence if you register for the 'baby box' when you are around 24 weeks' pregnant. You must report the child's birth within four months to get the payment from the date of birth.[17]

You are still entitled to Best Start foods for a child even if a child element is not payable in the qualifying benefit because of the 'two-child limit'.

You continue to be entitled to Best Start foods for eight weeks after your qualifying benefit ends.[18]

If you were previously entitled to Best Start foods within 12 weeks, and you think you are eligible again, you can contact SSS and become entitled again without making a new claim.[19]

You can also receive Best Start foods on an ex-gratia basis if you are responsible for a child aged under three, you have no recourse to public funds due to your immigration status (see p1276) and your income after tax is no more than £1,763.18 a month as a single person or £2,086.00 as a couple.[20] Best Start foods is not listed as public funds.

## 4. Responsibility for a child

For Scottish child payment, Best Start grant and Best Start foods, you count as responsible for a child if the child is your dependant or you are a kinship carer for the child.[21]

### *Dependants*

A child is your dependant if:

- you are getting child benefit for them; *or*
- you are getting universal credit (UC) and they are included in your award (it does not matter if a child element is not payable because of the 'two-child limit'); *or*
- you are getting a child amount for them in your pension credit (PC).

If you are under 20, you are a dependant in someone else's claim if any of the points above apply to them getting the benefit for you.

### *Kinship carers*

You are a kinship carer if:

- you are not the child's parent, and not a foster carer or foster parent for the child; *and*
- you are related to the child by blood, marriage or civil partnership, or you are a friend or acquaintance of a relative of the child, or you are known to the child and have a pre-existing relationship with the child, *and*
- the child lives with you (exclusively or predominantly) under the terms of a kinship care order under section 72(1) of the Children and Young People (Scotland) Act 2014, or any other order under section 11(1) of the Children (Scotland) Act 1995, or under an agreement between you or your partner and a local authority in the UK for a looked-after child.

You can qualify for Scottish child payment, Best Start grant and Best Start foods if you or your partner are responsible for a child.[22] Someone counts as your partner if you would be a couple for UC (see p58).[23]

For Best Start grant and Best Start foods, you also count as responsible for a child if you meet any of the following conditions:[24]

- You are under 20, the child's parent, you normally live with them, and you are a dependant in someone else's child benefit, UC or PC award.
- You have been granted a parental order following a surrogate pregnancy.
- You have adopted the child under Scottish law or the law of any other country or jurisdiction recognised under Scottish law.
- The child has been placed with you for adoption by an approved adoption agency in the UK.
- You are the child's appointed guardian.

## Competing claims

If you and another person(s) claim Scottish child payment or a Best Start grant for the same child at the same time, Social Security Scotland (SSS) decides entitlement according to the following rules.[25]

- If only one person is responsible for the child for UC or PC, they are usually entitled.
- If more than one person is responsible for the child for UC or PC, it depends on the child's circumstances. This may happen if the competing claimants are members of the same couple, or if the DWP is paying more than one person for the same child (even if this is by mistake).
- If one person is responsible for the child for UC or PC and the other competing claimant is an approved kinship carer (see p1457) for the child, it depends on the circumstances of the child.
- If no one is responsible for the child for UC or PC, the person getting child benefit is usually entitled, unless the other competing claimant is an approved kinship carer for the child.
- If the competing claimants are both kinship carers and neither is responsible for the child for UC, PC or child benefit, the person whose claim is determined first is entitled.



If none of these apply, SSS must decide who has responsibility for the child, taking into account the child's circumstances.

If there are competing claims for Best Start foods during pregnancy, the pregnant woman has priority and SSS must stop paying anyone else.[26] If there are competing claims for Best Start foods for a child or for any other reason it considers appropriate, SSS may decide to change who receives payment for the child.[27]

## 5. Qualifying benefits

The qualifying benefits for Scottish child payment, Best Start grant and Best Start foods are:[28]

- universal credit (UC); *or*
- income-related employment and support allowance; *or*
- pension credit (PC); *or*
- for Best Start grant and Best Start foods only, housing benefit.

For Scottish child payment, *you* must be entitled to the qualifying benefit, not solely your partner. If you have a joint claim for UC, either one of you can apply for Scottish child payment.

For Best Start grant and Best Start foods, it can be you or your partner who is entitled to the qualifying benefit.

For Best Start grant, you must have been awarded UC in the assessment period that includes the date of your claim, or the assessment period before that.[29] For Best Start foods, you are entitled if you are getting UC in the current or previous assessment period. For Scottish child payment, you must be getting the benefit on the date of your claim.

If you stop getting a qualifying benefit, you continue to be entitled to Best Start foods for eight weeks after the qualifying benefit ends.[30] There is no run-on of Scottish child payment after a qualifying benefit ends.

If you are refused Scottish child payment, Best Start grant or Best Start foods, but you are later awarded a qualifying benefit to include the date of your application, you can be awarded payment without making a new claim. See p1462 for when your claim is made or can be treated as made.

You must be getting one of the above qualifying benefits at a rate of more than £0 before any third-party deductions or sanctions are applied. You do not count as getting a qualifying benefit if it was paid in error, including an official error.[31] 10

You do not need to be getting a qualifying benefit to qualify for a Best Start grant or Best Start foods if you are aged under 18, or 18/19 in certain circumstances.

## 6. The rules about your age

For Scottish child payment, you must be aged at least 16 to qualify, because you must be aged at least 16 to get any of the qualifying benefits. If you are responsible for a dependent child who has a child, you should also claim Scottish child payment for your dependant's child.

For Best Start grant and Best Start foods, there are no age limits and you can be entitled without a qualifying benefit if you are aged under 18, or are aged 18 or 19 and a dependant of another person (see p1457).[32]

# 7. Claims and getting paid

The general rules on claims and getting paid are covered in Chapter 68. This section explains the specific rules that apply to Scottish child payment, Best Start grants and Best Start foods.

## Making a claim

You can claim Scottish child payment, Best Start grant and Best Start foods:

- online at mygov.scot/scottish-child-payment/how-to-apply and mygov.scot/best-start-grant-best-start-foods/how-to-apply; *or*
- by phone on 0800 182 2222; *or*
- in writing on the approved form; *or*
- if you use British Sign Language, via Contact Scotland BSL.

***Forms***

You can download the form from mygov.scot or request it by phone. There is a single form for Scottish child payment, a combined form for Best Start grant and Best Start foods, and another combined form for Scottish child payment, Best Start grant and Best Start foods. Send your completed form to PO Box 10300, Dundee DD1 9FU. A prepaid envelope is available on request.

You can claim all three at the same time, but remember that you may qualify for Best Start foods from the start of pregnancy, Best Start grant pregnancy and baby payment from the 24th week of pregnancy and Scottish child payment from the child's birth, so you may need to apply at different times to make sure you do not miss out on any of these payments.



## When you do not have to make a claim

If you are already getting Scottish child payment for one child and you tell Social Security Scotland (SSS) that you are responsible for another child, your entitlement for that child can be determined without a new claim. Your entitlement starts on the date you notify SSS that you are responsible for the child, or up to four weeks earlier if you were responsible for the child for the purposes of universal credit (UC) or pension credit (PC).[33]

You can be awarded Scottish child payment without making a new claim if you were getting it within the last 12 weeks, your entitlement ended due to a break in responsibility for the child or receipt of a qualifying benefit, and you have since become entitled again.[34] It is important to give the date on which you met the qualifying conditions again, so that your new entitlement starts on the date on which the change occurred. If the date of the change is not known, your claim is treated as made on the date SSS became aware of the change.

If you are getting Scottish child payment, you can be awarded a Best Start grant early learning payment or school-age payment for the same child without applying. But if you would rather claim at a time of your choosing, you can request that it is not awarded without an application.[35] You still need to apply for the pregnancy and baby payment or Best Start foods even if you are getting Scottish child payment.

If you have claimed one type of Best Start grant payment (eg, a pregnancy and baby payment) and SSS finds that you will be entitled to a payment for another child (eg, a school-age payment for an older child) within 10 days, it can decide your entitlement without your having to make a claim.[36]

If you were previously entitled to Best Start foods within the last 12 weeks, and you think you are eligible again, you can contact SSS and become entitled again without making a new claim.[37]

## Information to support your claim

### Scottish child payment

For Scottish child payment, you do not usually need to provide any further information to support your claim if you are getting UC, PC or child benefit for the child. SSS checks with the DWP/HMRC that you are getting a qualifying benefit at an address in Scotland and you are responsible for the child. If you do not get a benefit for the child, you must provide evidence that you are a kinship carer to show that you are responsible for them. This could be a legal order or a letter from your local authority. Your claim may be refused if the evidence requested is not provided.[38]

### Best Start grant

For Best Start grant, you do not need to send any evidence with your claim for a pregnancy and baby payment if you are getting a qualifying benefit and you have received a 'baby box' from the Scottish government. If you are aged 18 or 19 and not getting a qualifying benefit in your own right, you must usually send a letter from your school or college confirming the course you are on. If you have responsibility for a child under a legal order but the child is not included as your dependant in a benefit claim, you may be asked to send a copy of the legal order.

You do not need to send any other evidence with your claim for early education payment or school-age payment, but it may be requested.

### Best Start foods

For Best Start foods, you do not need to send any evidence with your claim. You can apply from the start of your pregnancy. You are not usually asked for evidence if you register for the 'baby box' when you are around 24 weeks' pregnant. You must report the child's birth within four months to get the payment from the child's date of birth.[39]

## The date of your claim

### Scottish child payment

For Scottish child payment, your date of claim is usually the day SSS receives it, provided it is properly completed.[40] If you have claimed Scottish child payment and you are waiting to hear about a qualifying benefit, or a benefit showing you have responsibility for the child, the determination may be delayed until the outcome is known. If you do not meet all the qualifying conditions on the date of your claim, but it is expected that you will meet them within 14 days, your claim can be treated as made up to 14 days later.[41]

Scottish child payment cannot usually be backdated. The date your claim is received is usually the date your award starts, and it cannot be treated as made on an earlier date.[42] If you are refused Scottish child payment and you are later awarded a qualifying benefit, or a benefit showing you have responsibility for the child, which is backdated to include the date of the determination on your claim for Scottish child payment, your entitlement can be determined without making a new claim. Scottish child payment can be awarded in this case from the date of your original claim, or up to 14 days later.[43]

If you have previously been turned down for Scottish child payment due to an official error (see p1540), your entitlement can be determined again.[44]

### Best Start grants

For Best Start grant, you must usually claim within a time limit (known as the 'application window'). This is:

- for the pregnancy and baby payment, between being 24 weeks pregnant and six months after the birth if you (or your partner or dependant) have been pregnant with the child, or if you have become responsible for a child in other circumstances, the day before their first birthday;[45]
- for the early learning payment, from the child's second birthday to six months after their third birthday;[46]
- for the school-age payment, from 1 June in the calendar year in which the child's fifth birthday falls (or if the child is born in January or February, the calendar year in which their fourth birthday falls), to the last day in February in the following year.[47]

Your date of claim is usually the date SSS receives it. If you are not eligible on that date, but would be eligible within 10 days, your claim can be treated as having been made up to 10 days later.[48] If you are waiting for a backdated award of a qualifying benefit and apply for a Best Start grant within 20 working days after the end of the application window, your claim can be treated as having been made on a day that falls within the application window.[49] If you were previously turned down for a Best Start grant but are awarded a qualifying benefit on appeal, which is backdated to include the date of the determination of your Best Start grant claim, a Best Start grant can be awarded without a new claim.[50]

### Best Start foods

For Best Start foods, your date of claim is usually the date SSS receives it.[51] If you are not eligible on that date but would be eligible within 10 days, your claim can be treated as having been made up to 10 days later.[52] Best Start foods cannot be backdated. If you are refused Best Start foods and you are later awarded a qualifying benefit or a benefit showing you have responsibility for a child, which is backdated to include the date of the determination of your Best Start foods claim, you can be entitled to Best Start foods without making a new claim. Best Start foods can be awarded in this case from the date of your original claim, or up to 10 days later.[53]

If you were getting Best Start foods during pregnancy and notify SSS within four months of the birth that you are responsible for the child, payment continues from the child's date of birth.[54]

## Getting paid

Scottish child payment and Best Start grants are usually paid into the account you nominate when you claim. Best Start foods is usually paid on a payment card.

Payment of Scottish child payment starts on the day your claim is received or the date it is treated as made if you will be entitled within 14 days.[55] Payments are made every four weeks, in arrears, during the last week of the four-week period, into your nominated account.[56] If you already get Scottish child payment for one child and become entitled to a payment for another child, the payment cycles are aligned so that you receive payments for all children at the same time.[57] The first payment for another child includes arrears for each week, or part of a week, from the date you are treated as claiming, up to the payment date.

Your Scottish child payment may be reduced if you have an outstanding overpayment of a Scottish benefit (see p1527).[58] You can request a redetermination of the reduced amount (see p1527). Your Scottish child payment may be suspended in some circumstances (see p1525). If SSS considers that the original determination was made incorrectly, resulting in an overpayment (see p1526), a new determination can be made, with effect from the date of your original claim.[59]

Some or all of a Best Start grant payment can be made in a form other than money (eg, a voucher) if you accept an offer from SSS to receive it in this way. If you withdraw your agreement before the grant is given, it must be paid as money.[60]

Best Start foods payment cards are credited every four weeks. The payment card must be activated before it can be used. Credits do not have to be used within a specified period of time. The payment card can be used anywhere that sells Best Start foods and accepts Mastercard.

Best Start foods can be paid in a form other than a payment card if SSS considers it appropriate.[61]

If you are overpaid Scottish child payment due to an official error, see p1543.

If you disagree with a determination about Scottish child payment or Best Start grant, you can request a redetermination and appeal (see Chapter 69).

If you disagree with a decision about Best Start foods, you can ask SSS to review its decision, but you do not have a right of appeal to a tribunal.

# 8. Tax, other benefits and the benefit cap

## Tax

Scottish child payment, Best Start grants and Best Start foods are *not* taxable.[62]

## Means-tested benefits

Scottish child payment, Best Start grants and Best Start foods do not count as income for means-tested benefits.[63]

Arrears of Scottish child payment are disregarded as capital for 12 months for universal credit (UC) and means-tested benefits.[64] A Best Start grant is disregarded as capital for 12 months for UC and pension credit and indefinitely for other means-tested benefits.[65]

Any arrears or unused credit on a Best Start foods payment card is disregarded as capital for 12 months for UC and arguably should not count as capital for other means-tested benefits, but is not specifically disregarded.[66]

You cannot get a Best Start grant pregnancy and baby payment as well as Sure Start maternity grant for the same child.[67]

You cannot get Best Start foods as well as Healthy Start foods for the same child for the same period.[68]

10

## The benefit cap

Scottish child payment, Best Start grants and Best Start foods are *not* specified benefits for the benefit cap.

## Passports and other sources of help

If you are entitled to Scottish child payment, you may also be entitled to:

- health benefits (see Chapter 27);
- education benefits, such as a clothing grant (see p774);
- council tax reduction (see p761).

If you are pregnant, you are entitled to free vitamins during pregnancy, regardless of income.[69] If you are breastfeeding, you are entitled to free vitamin D supplements, and children under three are entitled to free vitamin D drops, regardless of income.[70]

# Notes

1. **Scottish child payment**
   1 Reg 18 SCP Regs
   2 Reg 20(5) SCP Regs
   3 Reg 19 SCP Regs
   4 Sch para 10 SCP Regs
   5 Sch para 10 SCP Regs
   6 Reg 19(2)(b) SCP Regs

2. **Best Start grant**
   7 Schs 2, 3 and 4 EYA(BSG)(S) Regs
   8 Sch 2 EYA(BSG)(S) Regs
   9 Sch 3 EYA(BSG)(S) Regs
   10 Sch 4 EYA(BSG)(S) Regs
   11 Sch 2(6) EYA(BSG) Regs

3. **Best Start foods**
   12 WF(BSF)(S) Regs
   13 Regs 6, 7, 7A, 7B and 8 WF(BSF)(S) Regs
   14 Reg 3 WF(BSF)(S) Regs
   15 Reg 11(1B) WF(BSF)(S) Regs
   16 Reg 11(4) WF(BSF)(S) Regs
   17 Reg 11 WF(BSF)(S) Regs
   18 Reg 6(3) and (4) WF(BSF)(S) Regs
   19 Reg 11 WF(BSF)(S) Regs
   20 mygov.scot/best-start-grant-best-start-foods/public-funds-access

4. **Responsibility for a child**
   21 **SCP** Regs 9, 11 and 12 SCP Regs
   **BSG** Regs 9 and 10 EYA(BSG)(S) Regs;
   **BSF** Regs 4, 5 and 5A WF(BSF)(S) Regs
   22 **SCP** Reg 9 SCP Regs
   **BSG** Sch 2 para 1(d)(iv) EYA BSG(S) Regs
   **BSF** Reg 11(4) WF(BSF)(S) Regs
   23 **SCP** Reg 10 SCP Regs
   **BSG** Reg 8 EYA(BSG)(S) Regs
   **BSF** Reg 3 WF(BSF)(S) Regs
   24 **BSG** Reg 9 EYA(BSG)(S) Regs
   **BSF** Reg 4 WF(BSF)(S) Regs
   25 **SCP** Sch para 5 SCP Regs
   **BSG** Sch 1(6) EYA(BSG)(S) Regs
   26 Reg 11(1A) WF(BSF)(S) Regs
   27 Reg 11(5) and (6) WF(BSF)(S) Regs

5. **Qualifying benefits**
   28 **SCP** Reg 14 SCP Regs
   **BSG** Regs 11 and 12 and Schs 2(1)(e), 3(1)(f) and 4(1)(f) EYA(BSG)(S) Regs
   **BSF** Reg 10 WF(BSF)(S) Regs
   29 Schs 2(1)(e) (ii), 3(1)(f)(ii) and 4(1)(f)(ii) EYA BSG Regs
   30 Reg 6(3) and (4) WF(BSF)(S) Regs
   31 **SCP** Reg 15 SCP Regs
   **BSG** Reg 12 EYA(BSG)(S) Regs
   **BSF** Reg 10(2A) WF(BSF)(S) Regs

6. **The rules about your age**
   32 **BSG** Schs 2 para 1(e)(iii) and (iv), 3 para 1(f)(iii) and (iv) and 4 para 1(f)(iii) and (iv) EYA(BSG)(S) Regs
   **BSF** Regs 7(1)(b), 7A(1)(b), 8(1)(b) WF(BSF)Regs

7. **Claims and getting paid**
   33 Sch para 11 SCP Regs
   34 Sch para 12 SCP Regs
   35 Sch para 5A EYA(BSG)(S) Regs
   36 Sch 1(3) EYA(BSG)(S) Regs
   37 Reg 11(3) WF(BSF)(S) Regs
   38 Sch para 25 SCP Regs
   39 Reg 11 WF(BSF)(S) Regs
   40 Reg 5 and Sch para 1(3) SCP Regs
   41 Sch para 1(2) SCP Regs
   42 Sch para 35 SCP Regs
   43 Sch para 8 SCP Regs
   44 Sch para 6 SCP Regs
   45 Sch 2 para 2(2) EYA(BSG)(S) Regs
   46 Sch 3 para 1(b) EYA(BSG)(S) Regs
   47 Sch 4 para 2 EYA(BSG)(S) Regs
   48 Reg 4(3) EYA(BSG)(S) Regs
   49 Regs 4 and 5 EYA(BSG)(S) Regs
   50 Sch 1(5) EYA(BSG)(S) Regs
   51 Reg 18A(1) WF(BSF)(S) Regs
   52 Reg 18A(2) WF(BSF)(S) Regs
   53 Reg 18B WF(BSF)(S) Regss
   54 Reg 11(2) WF(BSF)(S) Regs
   55 Reg 18A SCP Regs
   56 Reg 21 SCP Regs
   57 Reg 21(3) and (4) SCP Regs
   58 Sch para 13 SCP Regs
   59 Sch para 7 SCP Regs
   60 Sch 2 para 8, Sch 3 para 5 and Sch 4 para 6 EYA(BSG)(S) Regs
   61 Reg 14(2) WF(BSF)(S) Regs

8. **Tax, other benefits and the benefit cap**
   62 Table B – Parts 1 (BSG) and 2 (SCP) s677 IT(EP)A 2003
   63 **UC** Reg 66 (not included as unearned income) UC Regs
   **ESA** Sch 8 paras 46, 70 and 72 ESA Regs
   **PC** Reg 15(1)(rb)(rd) SPC Regs

64 **UC** Sch 10 para 18 UC Regs
**ESA** Sch 9 para 11(1)(a) ESA Regs
**PC** Sch 5, para 20(2)(u) SPC Regs
65 **UC** Sch 10 para 21 UC Regs
**ESA** Sch 9 para 63 ESA Regs
**PC** Sch 5 para 20(2)(r) SPC Regs
66 Sch 10 para 18 UC Regs (other benefits refer to 'any early years assistance given in accordance with' s32 SSA 2018, but Best Start foods is made under different powers)
67 Reg 3A SFM&FE(G) Regs
68 Reg 3A HSS&WF(A) Regs
69 gov.scot/policies/maternal-and-child-health/free-vitamins-for-all-pregnant-women
70 gov.scot/publications/vitamin-d-advice-for-parents

# Chapter 63

# Carers' payments

**This chapter covers:**


1. Carer support payment (below)
2. Carer's allowance supplement (p1475)
3. Young carer grant (p1476)


## Key facts

- Carer support payment (CSP) is paid for people in Scotland with 'regular and substantial' caring responsibilities for a disabled person.
- CSP has replaced carer's allowance (CA) for new claims in Scotland.
- CA supplement is paid twice a year if you live in Scotland and get CA or CSP.
- A young carer grant is an annual payment for young people in Scotland aged 16 to 18 who care, or have been caring, for one or more disabled people.
- None of these payments are means tested.
- You can qualify for these payments whether you are in or out of work, but CSP has an earnings limit.
- You do not need to have paid national insurance contributions to qualify.
- These payments are administered and paid by Social Security Scotland.
- If you disagree with a determination about CSP or a young carer grant you can request a redetermination and then appeal against it (see Chapter 69).

10

## 1. Carer support payment

***Future changes***

These changes are expected by late 2025.[1]

– Carer support payment (CSP) will be paid for 12 weeks (rather than eight) following the death of a cared-for person.

– A new carer additional person payment will provide extra income for those on CSP who care for more than one disabled person.

– Scottish carer supplement will replace carer's allowance (CA) supplement and will be paid alongside CSP, rather than in two lump sums a year.

## Who can get carer support payment

You qualify for carer support payment (CSP) if:[2]

- you care for someone who gets a qualifying disability benefit (see below); *and*
- the care you give is 'regular and substantial' (see below); *and*
- you meet the age rules (see p1470); *and*
- if you are under 20, you are not in certain kinds of education (see p805); *and*
- you are not 'gainfully employed' (see p1469); *and*
- you are not a 'person subject to immigration control' (see p1272). **Note:** if your leave is subject to a 'no recourse to public funds' condition, see p1282 and get immigration advice *before* claiming CSP; *and*
- you meet the residence conditions (see p1347).

Note:

- If you are entitled to CA, you cannot qualify for CSP as well. You will be transferred to CSP if you live in Scotland (see p1474).
- Only one person can qualify for CSP, CA and/or the carer element of universal credit (UC) for caring for the same disabled person (see p1469).
- Even if you care for more than one disabled person, you can only qualify for one award of CSP.
- Most CSP rules are the same as those for CA. This section refers to the CA rules in Chapter 22 where they are the same. However, note that caselaw (decisions of the Upper Tribunal or the courts) about CA is likely to be persuasive but does *not* have to be followed by CSP decision makers in every case.

### Qualifying benefits

10

The person you care for must be *paid* a qualifying disability benefit. The qualifying benefits are:[3]

- pension age disability payment;
- attendance allowance (AA);
- either rate of the daily living component of adult disability payment;
- either rate of the daily living component of personal independence payment;
- the highest or middle rate of child disability payment care component;
- the highest or middle rate of disability living allowance care component;
- armed forces independence payment;
- constant attendance allowance of £90.20 a week or more in respect of an industrial injury (see p600) or war disablement (see p780).

### Regularly and substantially caring

To qualify for CSP, you must be 'regularly and substantially' caring for someone who gets a qualifying benefit. You satisfy this requirement during any week in which you are (or are likely to be) caring for them for 35 hours or more.[4] A week runs from Sunday to Saturday.[5] For what may be accepted as hours spent caring, see p473. You must not be paid for the hours you spend caring, or provide the care as voluntary work.[6]

**Note:**

- You cannot average the hours of care you provide. You must normally be caring for at least 35 hours in each week of your award (but see p473 if you have a break in caring – the rules are the same as for CA).[7]
- If you are caring for two or more people, you only qualify for CSP if you care for one of them for 35 hours or more a week.
- If the person you care for dies, see p1473.

### If someone else cares for the same person

Only one person can qualify for CSP, CA and/or the carer element of UC for caring for the same disabled person.[8] If you and another person claim in respect of the same person and both meet the entitlement conditions, you can agree who should be entitled. You should inform Social Security Scotland (SSS) of your decision in writing (signed by you both).[9] If you cannot agree, SSS decides who is entitled (consulting the DWP if either of you have claimed UC or live outside Scotland and have claimed CA), and taking into account:[10]

- the best interests of the person you care for; *and*
- whether you and the other person who claimed:
  - are related to the person your care for; *and*
  - live with or near them; *and*
  - get any benefits on behalf of or in respect of them; *and*
- any other relevant information.

If you get a determination that you are not entitled to CSP under these rules, you can request a redetermination (see p1535).

10

## Gainfully employed

You cannot qualify for CSP for a week if you are 'gainfully employed'. You count as gainfully employed in a week if your earnings from employment and/or self-employment in that week are more than £196.[11] Your earnings are ignored if you work during a period you are on a break from caring (see p473 – the rules are the same as for CA).[12]

The rules about what counts as 'earnings' and what amounts can be disregarded are the same as for CA (see p473).[13] However, note the following differences.

- The CA caselaw referenced may be persuasive, but is not binding on CSP decision makers.
- SSS has an additional discretion about how to average your earnings over a period of up to 26 weeks, if they vary in different weeks and you have provided payslips.[14]

- If you are an employee, SSS should normally be able to get information about your earnings from HMRC.[15] However, you should not rely on this and should tell SSS if your earnings increase, as otherwise you may be overpaid (see p1473).

## The rules about your age

You must be aged 16 or over to be entitled to CSP. **Note:** to get CSP while you are still at school, you must meet the rules on p805.

## The amount of benefit

CSP is paid at a weekly rate of £83.30.[16]

If you are paid CSP, you can get a CA supplement (see p1475).

## Special benefit rules

Special rules may apply if:

- you are subject to immigration control (see p1272);
- you have come from or are going abroad (see Chapters 57, 58 and 59);
- you or the person you are caring for are in hospital or prison, or the person you are caring for is in a care home or similar accommodation (see Chapter 38).

## Claims and getting paid

For the general rules on claims and getting paid, see Chapter 68. This section explains the specific rules that apply to CSP.

### Making a claim

You can claim CSP:

- online at mygov.scot/carer-support-payment/how-to-apply; *or*
- by phone on 0800 182 2222; *or*
- in writing on the approved form; *or*
- if you use British Sign Language, via Contact Scotland BSL.

**Note:** if you want to request backdating of your claim for more than 13 weeks, you should claim by phone. See p1472 for when this is possible.

***Forms***

You can download the CSP form from mygov.scot/carer-support-payment-application-form or request one by phone. Send your completed form to Carer Support Payment, PO Box 10328, Dundee DD1 9HE.

### When you do not need to make a claim

If you are already entitled to CA, you do not need to claim CSP and will be transferred to it (see p1474).

If you were previously refused CSP due to an 'official error', your entitlement must be determined again without you making a further claim (see p1540). In practice, you should usually also make a new claim, as you cannot be sure that SSS will accept that there was an official error.

If you were entitled to CSP but your entitlement ended less than 26 weeks ago, see below for when you do not need to make a further claim if you become entitled again.

**Temporary gaps in entitlement**

If your CSP ends but you become entitled again within 26 weeks of it ending, your entitlement can be determined again without you needing to make another claim. These rules only apply if your CSP ends because:[17]

- you earn above the earnings limit (see p1469) *and* no one else has been awarded CSP, CA or the carer element of UC for the person that you care for; *or*
- you have a break in caring that is too long for you to continue to get CSP (see p473 – the rules are the same as for CA) *and* no-one else has been awarded CSP, CA or the carer element of UC for the person that you care for; *or*
- the person you care for:
  - gives up their disability benefit award voluntarily *and* no one else has been awarded CSP, CA or the carer element of UC for caring for them; *or*
  - has their disability benefit payment stopped as they are in residential care, hospital or prison (see Chapter 38); *or*
  - has their disability benefit payment suspended.

In all cases, you should tell SSS as soon as you satisfy the entitlement conditions again. In most of the above cases, if you do so within 13 weeks, your entitlement begins again on the date you first requalify for CSP. Later requests can be allowed if you have a good reason.[18]

**Note:** if you are reporting that you satisfy the entitlement conditions again more than 13 weeks after you do, it appears that you should also make a new claim and request backdating, as you cannot be sure that your reasons for lateness will be accepted.

## Who should claim

You must normally claim CSP yourself. In some situations, another person can claim for you as your 'appointee' (see p1522).

## Information to support your claim

You are asked to confirm that the person you care for is aware that you are applying for CSP and gives their permission for SSS to contact them or use their personal data. SSS may also ask you for evidence of your identity and where you live, and for CSP, details of your earnings or expenses if you are employed or self-employed.[19] If you claim using the paper form, you can send this evidence, if you have it, with the form.

You can be asked to provide other information or evidence if SSS requires this and must provide it within the time allowed.[20] If the information does not exist or you need more time, contact SSS as soon as possible and explain the situation. If SSS does not extend the time to provide the information, your date of claim may be delayed (see below) or your entitlement may not be determined (see p1534).

## The date of your claim

Your claim is normally treated as made on the day it is received by SSS, provided it is properly completed.[21] Unless you request backdating, your award begins on the Sunday before you claimed (or if you claimed on a Sunday, that day).[22] Advance claims for CSP are expected to be possible from late 2025.[23]

### Backdating your claim

It is important to claim in time. A claim for CSP can usually only be backdated for a maximum of 13 weeks.[24] You must ask for backdating and satisfy the qualifying conditions over that period. You do not have to show any reasons why your claim was late.

Your claim can be backdated for more than 13 weeks if you claim within 13 weeks of the person you care for being awarded a disability benefit. Your entitlement can begin on the date you first qualified for CSP.[25] If your entitlement under this rule would begin before CSP was introduced (19 November 2023), you can be treated as claiming CA for the earlier period and be paid CSP.[26]



You may be able to get further backdating if you are in full-time education, or have lived in the UK for less than two years. In most cases, this rule will only apply if you would have been entitled but could not claim CSP sooner in the area in which you live (because of the gradual rollout across the country), and you claim within 13 weeks of CSP being introduced in your area. It is now more than 13 weeks since CSP was rolled out in all parts of Scotland, so if you are trying to use this rule, your application will be late. If you have good reason for lateness, you may still be able to get extra backdating.[27]

If you might have qualified for CSP sooner but did not claim because you were given the wrong information or misled by SSS, you could complain and ask for compensation (see p1529).

## Getting paid

CSP is paid into the bank or other account you nominate when you make your claim. If you do not have access to a bank account, SSS should contact you after you claim to discuss payment options.

Payment of CSP is made either four-weekly in arrears or weekly in advance if you or the person you care for is terminally ill or, in some cases, if you transfer from CA to CSP.[28]

- For when your payments can be suspended, see p1525.
- For when a deduction can be made to recover an overpayment, see p1527.
- If you are overpaid CSP, you may have to repay it (see p1526).

## Change of circumstances

You must report any change you have been told to report to SSS.[29]

You should report any changes in your circumstances as soon as possible. You can report a change online, in writing on the form you can download from mygov.scot/carer-support-payment/if-your-circumstances-change, or by phone. Check your most recent determination of entitlement carefully, as it should tell you how you must report a change.[30]

If you report a change that may affect the amount of your CSP, SSS makes a new determination. For when the new determination takes effect (including if you move from Scotland to another part of the UK), see below.

Before making a determination, SSS can ask you to provide further information.

### When a determination following a change of circumstances takes effect

**Note:** different rules apply if the change:

- is that you are no longer ordinarily resident in Scotland (see p1420); *or*
- is that the person you care for has died. Your CSP award continues for eight weeks (expected to change to 12 weeks later in 2025) starting from the Sunday after they died, as long as you continue to meet the other entitlement conditions.[31]

If your CSP increases following a change, the new determination takes effect:[32]

- if you reported the change:
  - within 13 weeks of it happening, from the Sunday before you met the conditions for a higher rate of benefit; *or*
  - outside the time limit above, but have a good reason for reporting it late, from the Sunday before you met the conditions for a higher rate of benefit; *or*
  - if the rules above do not apply, from the Sunday before you reported the change; *or*
- if you did not report the change, from the Sunday after the new determination is made.

If your CSP decreases or ends, the new determination takes effect:[33]

- if you knowingly fail to report a change that you had been told you had to report, or fail to report it as soon as is reasonably practicable, from the Sunday after you should have reported the change (see p1542); *or*
- from the Sunday after the new determination is made.

**Note:** an earlier date for your CSP increasing or a later date for it decreasing or stopping can be set if it would be 'unjust' not to do so (see p1541).

### Reviews of carer suppport payment awards

If your determination of entitlement specifies a period after which your CSP award must be reviewed, a further determination must be made at the end of this period.[34] At the time of writing, it is understood that SSS will normally only specify a review period if it cannot get full details of your earnings from HMRC – eg, if you are self-employed.[35]

For when the new determination following a review takes effect, see p1473.

If SSS is reviewing your award, or thinks your circumstances may have changed, it can ask you to provide further information. If you do not provide the information within the time allowed, your payments can be suspended (see p1525). If you need more time to provide the information, contact SSS as soon as possible to request an extension.

### Transfers to carer support payment

If you get CA and live in Scotland, you will transfer to CSP.

Case transfers to CSP are expected to be complete by spring 2025. If you are being transferred to CSP, SSS will notify you in writing. The notification tells you how long the process will take and that your CA will end when your CSP starts.[36] If SSS later realises that you were wrongly sent a transfer notification, it wants to extend the transfer period, you move out of Scotland or the person you care for dies, it sends you another notification about this.[37]

You are awarded the same amount of CSP as your CA.[38]

If you move to Scotland from elsewhere in the UK and are getting CA, you will be transferred to CSP while case transfers from CA are still happening. After that, if you move to Scotland and get CA, you will need to make an application for CSP.[39]

10

**Note:** if you get CSP and you move from Scotland to elsewhere in the UK, CSP can continue for up to 13 weeks. You should apply for CA.

## Tax, other benefits and the benefit cap

### Tax

CSP is taxable.[40]

### Other benefits

CSP interacts with means-tested benefits in the same way as CA does (see p483). Note that if you are transferred to CSP from CA you may need to tell the DWP, HMRC and the local authority about your award to ensure that any extra amounts continue to be paid.

**Note:** if the person you care for has a severe disability premium/amount included in their income-related employment and support allowance (ESA), pension credit or housing benefit, their entitlement to that premium/amount can be affected if you claim CSP (see p279).

### Non-means-tested benefits

If you and another person would be entitled to CSP, CA and/or the carer element of UC for the same disabled person, see p1469.

If you would be entitled to CSP and a young carer grant, see p1480.

If you get one of the following 'overlapping benefits', you may not be paid any CSP even if you are entitled to it. The overlapping benefits are:[41]

- state pension and retirement pension (see Chapter 32); *and*
- new-style JSA (see Chapter 29); *and*
- contributory ESA (see Chapter 26); *and*
- bereavement benefits except bereavement support payment (see Chapter 21); *and*
- maternity allowance (see Chapter 30); *and*
- war widow's or widower's pension; *and*
- unemployability supplement paid with industrial injuries disablement benefit (see Chapter 28) or a war pension (see p779); *and*
- industrial death benefit, incapacity benefit or severe disablement allowance (if you still get them); *and*
- certain types of training allowance

If you are entitled to one of these benefits, your CSP is reduced by the amount of the other benefit. If the other benefit is higher, you are not paid CSP.[42]

### The benefit cap

CSP is *not* one of the specified benefits for the benefit cap. If you are entitled to CSP, you are exempt from the cap. See p1025 for further information.

10

### Passports and other sources of help

If you are entitled to CSP, you get a Christmas bonus (see p783).

You may be able to get help, support and services from your local authority – ask for a carer's assessment. If you have a low income, you may be entitled to council tax reduction (see p761).

## 2. Carer's allowance supplement

Carer's allowance (CA) supplement is paid to people resident in Scotland or with a close link to Scotland (see p1476) who are in receipt of CA or carer support payment (CSP).[43]

**Note:** Scottish carer supplement will replace CA supplement from late 2025, and will be paid alongside CSP.

CA supplement is paid in two lump-sum payments each year. The payments in 2025 are made in June and December at £293.50 each.

To qualify for an automatic payment, you must be resident in Scotland and receive CA or CSP on the qualifying date. The qualifying dates in 2025 are 14 April and 13 October. If you are not getting one of these benefits on the qualifying date, but later get a backdated payment that includes that date, you still get a payment. You do not get CA supplement if you do not receive CA or CSP – eg, if you have an entitlement but do not get a payment, or only get the carer element of universal credit (UC). If you get a carer element in your UC, you should claim one of these benefits in order to qualify for the supplement if you can.

You do not need to get a benefit for the whole of a six-month period to qualify. It is enough to receive the benefit on the qualifying date. You should not need to make a separate claim for the supplement if you are resident in Scotland. Social Security Scotland (SSS) should pay you automatically (if you get CA, using information shared by the DWP). If you have problems with the payment, call SSS on 0800 182 2222.

CA supplement is disregarded as income for means-tested benefits. It is taxable income.

### Carer's allowance supplement if you live abroad

If you get CA or CSP, live in a European Economic Area state and have a 'genuine and sufficient link' to Scotland (see p1380), you are eligible for CA supplement payments but must make a claim to get them. You can claim by calling +44 (0) 1382 931 000 or using a form that you can download from mygov.scot/carers-allowance-supplement-paper-form.

While the common rules in this part of the *Handbook* do not apply to CA supplement if you are resident in Scotland, if you must make a claim because you live abroad, the common rules in this part *do* apply.[44]



## 3. Young carer grant

### Who can get a young carer grant

**Note:** young carer grant is expected to be extended to include 19-year-olds in late 2025.[45]

You qualify for a young carer grant if:[46]

- you are aged at least 16 and under 19 on the date you claim (but see p1478); *and*
- you have been caring for at least one person who gets a qualifying disability benefit (see p1477); *and*
- you spent sufficient hours caring during the 13-week 'qualifying period' (see p1468); *and*

- you are not entitled to carer's allowance (CA) or carer support payment (CSP) during the qualifying period, and have not claimed either of them (unless the claim has been refused) when you claim a young carer grant (but see p1480); *and*
- you meet the residence conditions (see p1347).

Note:
- You can get a young carer grant once a year. If you have previously received a young carer grant, claim again one year after the date of your last claim.[47]
- You can only get three young carer grants in total (changing to four in late 2025).[48]
- You cannot normally get a young carer grant if someone else has received one for someone that you care for within the past year (but see p1480).
- You should claim a young carer grant if you would meet all of the above conditions, but a person you care for claimed a disability benefit more than 13 weeks ago and has not yet been awarded it. Your claim may be refused, but if the disability benefit is later awarded, you can still get a young carer grant.
- Getting a young carer grant does not affect any benefits that a person you care for gets.

## Qualifying benefits

The person or people you care for must get a qualifying disability benefit *throughout* the 13-week qualifying period (see p1468), *and* on the date you claim a young carer grant. The qualifying benefits are the same as for CSP (see p1468).[49]

If the benefit is not paid for someone that you care for during part of the qualifying period (eg, if they are in a care home, hospital or prison), you cannot count hours spent caring for them.[50] See Chapter 38 for how their payment is affected.

**Note:** if your claim for a young carer grant was refused because a person you care for was not receiving a qualifying disability benefit throughout the qualifying period, see p1479.

## The care you must provide

During the 13 weeks before your date of claim (see p1479) (the 'qualifying period'), you must have provided care for at least 208 hours, during at least 10 of those weeks.[51] You cannot have been entitled to CA or CSP during the qualifying period.[52]

If you care every week during the qualifying period, this is an average of 16 hours a week. The care you provide must involve activity that promotes the physical, mental or emotional wellbeing of the person you care for.[53] The rules do not define this, but guidance suggests that it could include activities like keeping someone company, helping with personal care, bills or shopping.[54]

You can add together hours you spend caring for up to three people, so long as they all got a qualifying benefit (see p1468) throughout the qualifying period. You must not be paid for the hours you spend caring, or provide the care as voluntary work.[55]

*Example*

Alba, 17, cares for her grandmother (who gets attendance alowance) for about 20 hours a week. She has done so for the past year. Alba also volunteers at a youth club for people with learning disabilities. Even though Alba cannot count her voluntary work as hours of care, she can still get a young carer grant, as she spends enough time caring for her grandmother.

## The rules about your age

You can get a young carer grant if you are aged at least 16 and are under 19 on the date of your claim (see p1479).[56]

## The amount of benefit

A young carer grant is a single annual payment of £390.25.[57] The amount normally increases every year, and depends on your date of claim (see p1479).

## Special benefit rules

Special rules may apply if you have come from abroad (see p1347).

10

## Claims and getting paid

For the general rules on claims and getting paid, see Chapter 68. This section explains the specific rules that apply to young carer grants.

### Making a claim

If you live in Scotland, you can claim a young carer grant:

- online at mygov.scot/young-carer-grant/how-to-apply; *or*
- by phone on 0800 182 2222; *or*
- in writing on the approved form; *or*
- if you use British Sign Language, via Contact Scotland BSL.

Note:

- If you do not have a bank account or you are claiming as someone else's appointee (see p1522), you cannot claim online.[58]

- If you live outside Scotland, you must either claim in writing on the approved form, by calling +44(0)1382 931 000 or, if you use British Sign Language, via Contact Scotland BSL.[59]

*Forms*

You can download the appropriate young carer grant form from mygov.scot/young-carer-grant-paper-form or request one by phone. Send your completed form to Social Security Scotland, PO Box 10314, Dundee DD1 9GN.

#### When you do not need to make a claim

If you previously claimed a young carer grant and your claim was refused as someone you care for did not get a qualifying benefit (see p1477), your entitlement must be determined again without you having to make another claim if they are later awarded a qualifying benefit *and* no one else has been awarded a young carer grant for caring for them since you originally claimed.[60] If your entitlement is determined again, the date of your claim is the same as it was for your original claim.

### Who should claim

You must normally claim a young carer grant yourself. In some situations, another person can claim for you as your 'appointee' (see p1522).

### Information to support your claim

The information you are asked to provide in support of your claim is similar to that for CSP (see p1471). You are also asked for evidence of your address after you have claimed.[61]

### The date of your claim

Your claim is normally treated as made on the day Social Security Scotland (SSS) receives it, provided it is properly completed.[62] Your claim for a young carer grant cannot be backdated and you cannot be treated as claiming in advance.

If you live outside the UK and meet the conditions on p1379, your young carer grant claim can be treated as having been made on any date between 22 July 2019 and 24 December 2020. There is no time limit to claim under this rule.[63]

### Getting paid

A young carer grant is paid into the bank or other account you nominate when you make your claim. If you do not have access to a bank account, you should claim by phone and discuss how you want to receive your grant.

Some, or all, of a payment can be made in a form other than money (eg, a voucher) if you accept an offer from SSS to receive it in this way.[64] If you withdraw your agreement before you get the grant, it must be paid as money.

### If someone else has claimed a young carer grant

If you and someone else care for the same person and you both claim a young carer grant, SSS decides which of you is entitled. The claim that was received first must be determined first.[65]

If someone else has received a young carer grant in respect of a person you care for within one year of the date of your claim (see p1479), you cannot get a young carer grant for caring for that person unless:[66]

- the other claimant has died; *or*
- SSS has decided that they should not have been paid a young carer grant.

## Tax, other benefits and the benefit cap

### Tax

Young carer grants are not taxable.[67]

### Other benefits

Young carer grants do not count as income or capital for means-tested benefits.[68]

You cannot qualify for a young carer grant if you are entitled to CA or CSP on the date of your claim or at any point in the 13-week qualifying period. You also cannot qualify if you have claimed either benefit, unless your claim has been refused.[69]

***Young carer grants and carer's allowance or carer support payment***

- It does not matter if someone else gets CA, CSP or the carer element of UC for looking after someone that you care for. You can still get a young carer grant.
- If you care 35 hours a week or more for one person, you may be eligible for both CA or CSP *and* a young carer grant. Get advice about which to claim, and before requesting backdating of a CA or CSP claim to cover a date for which you have already been awarded a young carer grant.[70]
- If your CA or CSP stops (eg, if you start to earn too much), check whether you can get a young carer grant. You must wait 13 weeks to claim, as the days you got CA or CSP cannot count as part of the qualifying period for a young carer grant (see p1477).

### The benefit cap

A young carer grant is *not* a specified benefit for the benefit cap.

### Passports and other sources of help

If you are a young carer living in Scotland, you can get a package of support (whether or not you can get a young carer grant) from Young Scot. There is more information at young.scot.

You may be able to get help, support and services from your local authority – ask for a young carer's assessment.

If you are 18 or over and have a low income, you may be entitled to council tax reduction (see p761).

# Notes

1. **Carer support payment**

1 The Carer's Assistance (Young Carer Grant and Carer Support Payment) (Miscellaneous Amendment and Saving Provision) (Scotland) Regulations 2025 (draft)
2 s28 and Sch 2 SS(S)A 2018; Part 3 CA(CSP)(S) Regs
3 Regs 2 and 5(1) CA(CSP)(S) Regs
4 Reg 5(1) and (2) CA(CSP)(S) Regs
5 Reg 2 CA(CSP)(S) Regs
6 Reg 5(4) CA(CSP)(S) Regs; reg 2 The Carers (Scotland) Act 2016 (Agreements of a Specified Kind) Regulations 2017 No.257, which ensures that kinship care payments from the local authority are not treated as payments for work
7 Reg 40 CA(CSP)(S) Regs
8 Regs 5(3) and 12 CA(CSP)(S) Regs
9 Reg 24(2)(a), (3)(a), (4)(a) and (5) CA(CSP)(S) Regs
10 Reg 24(4)(b) and (6) CA(CSP)(S) Regs
11 Reg 14(1) CA(CSP)(S) Regs
12 Reg 40(2) CA(CSP)(S) Regs
13 Reg 14 and Sch 2 CA(CSP)(S) Regs
14 Sch 2 para 7(3)(b) CA(CSP)(S) Regs, which has no equivalent in the CA rules
15 Scottish government, *Carer Support Payment: if you work*, available at mygov.scot/carer-support-payment/if-you-work
16 Reg 16(1) CA(CSP)(S) Regs
17 Reg 23 CA(CSP)(S) Regs
18 Reg 23(9)-(10) CA(CSP)(S) Regs
19 Scottish government, *Carer Support Payment: How to apply for Carer Support Payment*, available at mygov.scot/carer-support-payment/how-to-apply
20 s54 SS(S)A 2018
21 Reg 18(1) CA(CSP)(S) Regs
22 Reg 18(2)(a) CA(CSP)(S) Regs
23 SS(CPCTMA)(S) Regs (draft)
24 Reg 18(2)(b) CA(CSP)(S) Regs
25 Reg 19 CA(CSP)(S) Regs
26 Reg 20 CA(CSP)(S) Regs
27 Regs 18A and 18B and Sch 1 tables 1 and 2 CA(CS)(S) Regs
28 Reg 22 and Sch 1 para 7 CA(CSP)(S) Regs; Scottish government, *Carer Support Payment: how carer support payment works*, available at mygov.scot/carer-support-payment
29 s56 SS(S)A 2018
30 s56(2)(b) SS(S)A 2018
31 Reg 16(4) CA(CSP)(S) Regs
32 Regs 2 and 28(1)(a) and (c) CA(CSP)(S) Regs
33 Regs 2 and 27(1)(a) and (c) CA(CSP)(S) Regs
34 Reg 35 CA(CSP)(S) Regs
35 Scottish government, *Carer Support Payment: if you work*, available at mygov.scot/carer-support-payment/if-you-work
36 Sch 1 paras 3 and 4 CA(CSP)(S) Regs
37 Sch 1 para 4(3) and (4) CA(CSP)(S) Regs
38 Sch 1 para 5 CA(CSP)(S) Regs
39 Reg 41 CA(CSP)(S) Regs; SS(CPCTMA)(S) Regs (draft)
40 ss660 and 661 IT(EP)A 2003
41 Reg 16 CA(CSP)(S) Regs
42 Reg 16(2) CA(CSP)(S) Regs

2. **Carer's allowance supplement**

43 s81 SS(S)A 2018
44 s81 SS(S)A 2018; Part 2 and Sch 2 CASYCG(RRPP) Regs

3. **Young carer grant**

45 The Carer's Assistance (Young Carer Grant and Carer Support Payment) (Miscellaneous Amendment and Saving Provision) (Scotland) Regulations 2025 (draft)
46 s28 and Sch 2 SS(S)A 2018; Part 2 CA(YCG)(S) Regs

**Notes**

47 Reg 7(3) CA(YCG)(S) Regs
48 Reg 7(6) CA(YCG)(S) Regs
49 Reg 6 CA(YCG)(S) Regs
50 Reg 6(1) CA(YCG)(S) Regs
51 Reg 5(2) CA(YCG)(S) Regs
52 Reg 7(1) CA(YCG)(S) Regs
53 Reg 5(3) CA(YCG)(S) Regs
54 Social Security Scotland, *Eligibility for Young Carer Grant*, available at socialsecurity.gov.scot/guidance-resources/guidance/eligibility-for-young-carer-grant
55 Reg 5(4) CA(YCG)(S) Regs; reg 2 The Carers (Scotland) Act 2016 (Agreements of a Specified Kind) Regulations 2017 No.257, which ensures that kinship care payments from the local authority are not treated as payments for work
56 Reg 4(1) CA(YCG)(S) Regs
57 Reg 12(1) CA(YCG)(S) Regs
58 SSS, *Overview of Young Carer Grant*, available at socialsecurity.gov.scot/guidance-resources/guidance/overview-of-young-carer-grant
59 Scottish government, *Young Carer Grant: applying outside of Scotland*, available at mygov.scot/young-carer-grant/applying-outside-of-Scotland
60 Reg 11 CA(YCG)(S) Regs
61 Scottish government, *After you've applied for Young Carer Grant*, 1 April 2021, available at mygov.scot/after-youve-applied-for-young-carer-grant
62 Reg 4(3) CA(YCG)(S) Regs
63 Reg 4(7) CA(YCG)(S) Regs
64 Reg 12(3) CA(YCG)(S) Regs
65 Reg 10 CA(YCG)(S) Regs
66 Reg 7(4) and (5) CA(YCG)(S) Regs
67 s677 IT(EP)A 2003
68 **UC** Sch 10 para 23 UC Regs (but note that a YCG counts as capital if it is not spent within 52 weeks of receiving it)
**ESA** Sch 9 para 65 ESA Regs
**HB** Sch 6 para 67 HB Regs; reg 29(1)(j)(xviif) and Sch 6 paras 21(2)(u) and 26J HB(SPC) Regs
**PC** Reg 15(1)(re) and Sch 5 para 20(2)(v) SPC Regs
69 Reg 7(1) and (2) CA(YCG)(S) Regs
70 It is understood that the Scottish government's view is that if you are later awarded CSP or CA for the date of your YCG claim, you will have been overpaid the YCG. But it is unclear whether any overpayment would be recoverable.

# Chapter 64

# Child disability payment

**This chapter covers:**


1. Who can get child disability payment (below)
2. The rules about your age (p1488)
3. The amount of benefit (p1489)
4. Special benefit rules (p1490)
5. Claims and getting paid (p1490)
6. Tax, other benefits and the benefit cap (p1494)


## Key facts

- Child disability payment (CDP) is a benefit for children and young people with disabilities or long-term health problems who live in Scotland.
- CDP has a care component and a mobility component. You can qualify for one or both components. Each component has different rates.
- CDP is a non-means-tested benefit.
- You do not need to have paid national insurance contributions to get CDP.
- CDP is disregarded as income for means-tested benefits and can also lead to increases in those benefits.
- CDP is administered and paid by Social Security Scotland.
- If you disagree with a determination about CDP, you can request a redetermination and then appeal it (see Chapter 69).

10

## 1. Who can get child disability payment

Child disability payment (CDP) is a benefit for children and young people in Scotland with a disability or long-term health problem. It has replaced disability living allowance (DLA) for children living in Scotland. As most of the rules are the same, this chapter refers to the information about DLA in Chapter 24.

In this chapter, the term 'child' refers to both a child under 16 for whom you are claiming and a young person aged between 16 and 18 years old who may get CDP in their own right (see p1488). You can get CDP for a child if they:[1]

- meet the age rules (see p1488); *and*

- are not a 'person subject to immigration control' (see p1272). **Note**: if a child's leave is subject to a no recourse to public funds condition (see p1276) get specialist immigration advice *before* claiming CDP; *and*
- are 'ordinarily resident' in Scotland (see p1299); *and*
- meet the other residence conditions (see p1347); *and*
- are not entitled to disability living allowance (DLA), personal independence payment (PIP), adult disability payment (ADP) or armed forces independence payment, but see p1489 if they are moving from CDP to ADP; *and*
- unless terminally ill (see p1436), the child:
  - meets the disability conditions for the care component (see below), the mobility component (see p1486) or both; *and*
  - has met those conditions for 13 weeks immediately before the award would begin and is likely to continue to satisfy them for the next 26 weeks.[2]

## Disability conditions for the care component

The care component is paid at one of three rates: lowest, middle or highest.

- A child can get the **lowest rate** care component if they are 'so severely disabled physically or mentally' that:[3]
  - they require attention from another person for a significant portion of the day in connection with their bodily functions; *or*
  - they are 16 or over and cannot prepare a cooked main meal for themself if they have the ingredients.
- A child can get the **middle rate** care component if they satisfy one of the daytime conditions *or* one of the night-time conditions.[4]
- A child can get the **highest rate** care component if they satisfy one of the daytime conditions *and* one of the night-time conditions.[5]

10

A child under 16 must also satisfy the 'additional requirement' condition (see p1485).

A child can also get the care component if they are terminally ill (see p1436) or having renal dialysis in certain circumstances (see p1490).

See p1485 for definitions of the terms used in these rules.

### The daytime and night-time conditions

The **daytime conditions** are that the child is 'so severely disabled physically or mentally' that they require:[6]

- frequent attention throughout the day in connection with their bodily functions; *or*
- continual supervision throughout the day in order to avoid substantial danger to the child or others.

There may be circumstances where a child needs frequent attention throughout the day and that amounts to a significant portion of the day. If so, they could be entitled to the middle rate of the care component.[7]

The **night-time conditions** are that the child is 'so severely disabled physically or mentally' that they require:[8]

- prolonged or repeated attention from another person at night in connection with their bodily functions; *or*
- another person to be awake for a prolonged period or at frequent intervals at night to watch over the child in order to avoid substantial danger to the child or others.

When daytime begins and ends depends on the household's routine rather than the child's.[9] For example, help given after the child goes to bed but before the adults usually go to bed does not count towards satisfying the night-time conditions.

See p525 for the similar test in DLA.

## The additional requirement condition

In addition to needing attention, guidance or supervision, this must also be:[10]

- substantially in excess of the normal requirements of a child the same age; *or*
- of a kind that a younger child may have, but which a child of the same age without a physical or mental disability would not.

All young children need lots of help throughout the day. If a child needs substantially more help, or a different type of help, compared to the help normally required by a child of the same age, they should qualify. This extra test does not apply to a child aged 16 or over. For a similar test in DLA, see p520.

10

### *Definitions for the CDP care component*

Some of the terms are defined in the rules. Others have been explained in caselaw for DLA. It is expected that these terms mean the same for CDP. Decision makers and tribunals in Scotland are not bound to follow the DLA caselaw but it can provide guidance and may be followed.[11] See p1430 about adult disability payment (ADP) caselaw. The same approach is likely to be taken with DLA caselaw and CDP decisions. In time, decision makers and Scottish tribunals may interpret the rules differently.

**'Attention'** means 'the provision of personal care, prompting or motivation in relation to bodily functions or assistance with communication needs'.[12] For a similar test in DLA, see p521.

**'Bodily function'** means 'the normal actions of any organ of the body, including the brain, or of a number of organs acting together'.[13] For a similar test in DLA, see p522.

**'Frequent attention'** is not defined. For a similar test in DLA, see p524.

**'Frequent intervals'** and **'watching over'** are not defined. For a similar test in DLA, see p526.

**'Severely disabled, physically or mentally'** is not defined. For DLA, this does not mean that the child must be diagnosised with a specific medical condition (see p520). The same applies to CDP. There is no need to wait for a diagnosis before claiming.

**'Prolonged'** and **'repeated'** are not defined. For a similar test in DLA, see p525.

**'Require'** means 'reasonably require'.[14] For a similar test in DLA, see p521.

**'Significant portion of the day'** can be a single period or several periods during the day.[15] For DLA, a 'significant portion of the day' means about an hour, but a shorter period could qualify (see p523).

**'Substantial danger'** and **'continual supervision'** are not defined. For a similar test in DLA, see p524.

**'Supervision'** means 'the precautionary or anticipatory presence of another person to monitor an individual's physical, mental or emotional health including monitoring for obstacles or dangerous places or situations'.[16] For a similar test in DLA, see p522.

## Disability conditions for the mobility component

The mobility component is paid at one of two rates: higher or lower.

**Note:** a child cannot qualify for either rate of the mobility component unless they are usually 'able, from time to time, to benefit from assistance for movement'.[17] For a similar test in DLA, see p512.

### The higher rate mobility component

A child aged three or over can get the higher rate mobility component if:[18]

- they are unable, or virtually unable, to walk (see below); *or*
- the exertion required to walk would lead to a danger to the child's life or a serious deterioration in their health (for a similar test in DLA, see p514); *or*
- they have no legs or feet (regardless of the use of artificial limbs); *or*
- they are both blind and deaf (see p1487); *or*
- they have a severe visual impairment (see p1487); *or*
- they are terminally ill (see p1436); *or*
- they qualify for the highest rate of the CDP care component and have a severe mental impairment and severe behavioural difficulties (see p1487).

10

#### Unable or virtually unable to walk

A child's inability or virtual inability to walk must be assessed taking account of their physical condition as a whole, without regard to where they live.[19] For DLA, there is no need for a diagnosed medical condition and it does not matter if the original cause was mental, provided a current physical impairment affects the child's walking (see p513). Guidance confirms the same approach.[20]

A child should be considered **unable to walk** if they cannot move their body along by alternate, weight-bearing steps of the feet. See p513 for a similar test in DLA.

A child may be **virtually unable to walk** if their ability to walk outdoors is limited in terms of the distance, speed, length of time or the manner in which they can make progress on foot without severe discomfort.[21] See p513 for the similar test in DLA.

A child's ability to walk should be considered taking into account any prosthesis or artificial aid they use or that would be suitable for them to use.[22]

### Both blind and deaf

A child is both blind and deaf if:[23]

- they have total loss of vision; *and*
- they have at least 80 per cent hearing loss, even with an artificial aid which they use, or would be suitable to use; *and*
- the effect of these means they cannot get to any intended or required destination outdoors without assistance from another person.

See p515 for a similar test in DLA.

### Severe visual impairment

A child has a severe visual impairment if they meet the Visual Impairment Network for Children and Young People (VINCYP) definition of 'severe visual impairment'.[24] In practice, the child may have, or be able to get, a letter from their ophthalmologist confirming that they meet that definition.[25]

**Note:** if a child's visual impairment is not severe, they may be entitled to the lower rate mobility component (see p1488).

### Severe mental impairment and severe behavioural difficulties

A child has a 'severe mental impairment' if they have a severe impairment of intelligence and social functioning. This must result from:[26]

- a state of arrested development due to a failure of the brain to grow or develop in the way normally expected; *or*
- a deficiency in the brain's functionality due to its incomplete physical development.

'Severe impairment of intelligence and social functioning' is not defined for CDP. See p516 for a similar test in DLA.

A child has severe behavioural difficulties if they exhibit disruptive behaviour which:[27]

- is extreme; *and*
- regularly requires another person to intervene to prevent physical injury to the child or another person; *and*
- is so unpredictable that another person needs to be awake and watching over the child while they are awake.

The disruptive behaviour does not need to be constant but should be regular. The child may exhibit severe behavioural difficulties if they show aggression, destructive behaviour or behave in a way that could be dangerous for themself or another person. The intervention must be related 'to the provision of care and support of, or treatment provided to' the child.[28]

**Note:** the child must also be getting the highest rate care component to qualify for the higher rate mobility component on this basis.

### The lower rate mobility component

A child aged five or over can get the lower rate mobility component if, due to a physical or mental impairment, they cannot move around outside, on unfamiliar routes, without requiring supervision or guidance from another person most of the time.[29]

If the child is under 16 when an award of the mobility component begins, the guidance or supervision needed must meet the additional requirement condition (see p1485).[30]

***Definitions for the lower rate mobility component***

**'Supervision'** means 'the precautionary or anticipatory presence of another person to monitor an individual's physical, mental or emotional health including monitoring for obstacles or dangerous places or situations'.[31] For a similar test in DLA, see p518.

**'Guidance'** means 'direction or leading by physical means or verbal suggestion or persuasion'.[32] For a similar test for DLA, see p518.

## 2. The rules about your age



Child disability payment (CDP) entitlement can begin from:[33]

- age three months for the care component (from birth if the child is terminally ill);
- age three for the higher rate mobility component;
- age five for the lower rate mobility component.

Payment can begin as soon as the child reaches this age if the disability conditions are met for 13 weeks beforehand and CDP was claimed during that time.[34]

The upper age limit for a claim for CDP to begin is the day before the child's 16th birthday. You must complete both parts of the claim before the child turns 16 (see p1491).[35]

If the child cannot get CDP, they can claim adult disability payment (ADP) from age 16 (see p1428).

Once in payment, CDP entitlement can normally only continue until the child turns 18.[36]

It can continue until their 19th birthday if they claimed ADP before turning 18, but entitlement to ADP has not yet been determined.[37] You must complete both parts of the ADP claim before the child's 18th birthday otherwise CDP will end.

**Note:** a child can stay on CDP indefinitely if terminally ill or move to ADP when they are 18 (see p1438).

## Moving to adult disability payment

A child can choose to claim ADP from as early as 13 weeks before turning 16. Social Security Scotland (SSS) should write to the parent or appointee of a young person when they are 15 years and 8 months old to advise them that they can manage their own claim when they reach 16. Payments will then be made into the child's account. If they cannot manage their own claim, SSS will consider if an appointee is needed (see p1522).[38] If your child is terminally ill, see p1438.

***Should you claim ADP early?***

You should get specialist advice to help you and your child decide whether to claim ADP early. If they get CDP highest rate care component and higher rate mobility component, there is nothing to gain from claiming ADP sooner than necessary. The entitlement conditions for ADP are completely different, and the child may not qualify for ADP at all or may qualify for a lower award. If ADP is awarded, the child's CDP will end even if the ADP is less.[39] In that case, you can request a redetermination of the ADP award (see p1535).

In some circumstances, a child may be better off claiming ADP – eg, if they do not have any night-time care needs but would score enough points to be entitled to the enhanced rate of ADP daily living component. You can use the information in Chapter 61 to work out the likely ADP entitlement and compare this with their CDP award.

If ADP is awarded, entitlement normally starts after the next payment of CDP.[40] If the ADP award is higher than the CDP award, the first payment is increased by the amount that would have been paid if entitlement had started from the date of the ADP claim (see p1442).[41] If the ADP claim is refused, CDP entitlement continues until the child's 18th birthday (and they can try to claim ADP again later).[42]

10

# 3. The amount of benefit

Child disability payment (CDP) mobility component is paid at one of two weekly rates:[43]

- the lower rate is £29.20;
- the higher rate is £77.05 .

CDP care component is paid at one of three weekly rates:[44]

- the lowest rate is £29.20;
- the middle rate is £73.90;
- the highest rate is £110.40.

# 4. Special benefit rules

Special rules may apply to children who:

- are having renal dialysis (see below);
- are terminally ill (see p1436);
- are subject to immigration control (see p1272);
- have come from or are going abroad (see Chapters 57, 58, and 59);
- are living in a care home or similar accommodation, including some residential schools, or in a young offenders' institution or other form of detention (see Chapter 38).

## Renal dialysis

Special rules may allow a child having renal dialysis to get the child disability payment care component.[45] The child must have dialysis at least twice a week and it must be a type that requires the attendance or supervision of another person, or the child's circumstances make it necessary to have another person there to provide the specific attention or supervision the child requires. It makes no difference whether the dialysis takes place in hospital or at home.

If the renal dialysis takes place both by day *and* at night, the child is entitled to the highest rate care component. If the renal dialysis takes place *either* by day *or* at night, the child is entitled to the middle rate care component.[46]

10

To qualify under these rules, the child must have been getting the treatment for 13 weeks before the date the award would begin and it must be expected to continue for a further 26 weeks.[47]

# 5. Claims and getting paid

The general rules on claims and getting paid are covered in Chapter 68. This section explains the specific rules that apply to child disability payment (CDP).

## Making a claim

**Note:** if the child is terminally ill, there is a different claim process (see 1437).

You can start a claim for CDP:[48]

- online at mygov.scot/child-disability-payment/how-to-apply; *or*
- by phone on 0800 182 2222; *or*

- if you use British Sign Language, via Contact Scotland BSL.

Claims for CDP are made in two parts.

- **Part 1** registers the claim. You can do this by phone or online. You must provide the name and date of birth of the child.[49] In practice, Social Security Scotland (SSS) also asks for contact details, the name of the adult responsible for the child, where you live and bank details. If you do this by phone, you are sent a paper form to complete.
- **Part 2** asks about the child's disability or health condition and how it affects them.

**Note**: a claim is only made when both parts are submitted. It is important to return Part 2 before the child's 16th birthday (see p1488).

You should return the paper form (see below), or complete Part 2 if you claimed online, within six weeks of the date you completed Part 1 to protect the date your entitlement begins (see p1492).

SSS's Local Delivery Team can help with claims. You can book an appointment with a client support adviser in your area by calling 0800 182 2222.

*Forms*

You can request a paper form and prepaid envelope by phoning SSS on 0800 182 2222. You should return the form in the prepaid envelope provided.

Advisers can download an interactive form at socialsecurity.gov.scot/guidance-resources/resources/child-disability-payment-organisation-form. If you want to claim CDP with help from an organisation using this form you, phone SSS to ask that the claim be registered so that your award can start from the date of the call (see p1492).

## When you do not need to make a claim

If a child moves to Scotland from another part of the UK and was getting DLA immediately before moving, entitlement to CDP may be determined without the need for a new claim (see p541). At the time of writing, it is expected that this will change from September 2025.[50] See CPAG's *Welfare Rights Bulletin* or the online version of this *Handbook* for updates.

If you were refused CDP due to an 'official error', your entitlement should be determined again without the need for a new claim (see p1540). In practice, you should make a claim, as SSS may not accept that there was an official error.

## Who should claim

You can make a claim for CDP if you are a child's parent or someone with authority to act on the child's behalf (see p1523).

When they turn 16, a young person is normally expected to manage their own CDP award. If they are unable to, see p1522.

If a child is terminally ill, anyone can apply on their behalf if they have consent to do so from the parent or appointee.[51]

## Information to support your claim

You normally have six weeks from starting a claim to complete the application process by providing Part 2 with details of the child's care and mobility needs, but if a child is almost 16, you may have less time (see p1490). If the child is terminally ill, the required information is different (see p1437).

In most cases, SSS expects at least one piece of supporting information from a professional – eg, a letter from the child's school, GP or other health professional. If you cannot provide this yourself, SSS can gather it on your behalf. You must consent to this and are asked about this when completing Part 2. If you ask SSS to obtain this supporting information, it may take longer to get a decision on the claim. Further supporting information from family or friends can be provided to show how the disability affects the child's care and mobility needs.

If you prefer to provide this information yourself, do not delay submitting Part 2 while gathering it. It can be provided later by post or online at mygov.scot/uploading-your-documents.

If SSS asks for further information and you do not provide it within the period allowed, you may get a determination that you are not entitled to CDP.[52] It may reject your application and not make a determination at all (see p1534).[53] Let SSS know if you have difficulty getting supporting information. If you get a determination that you are not entitled to CDP because you failed to provide supporting information, you can ask for a redetermination (see p1535). You should also try to provide the requested information. If you ask for a redetermination or go on to appeal, a decision maker or the First-tier Tribunal can arguably make a new determination of entitlement (see p1441). If your application is rejected, you can appeal that 'process decision' (see p1561). In both cases, you should claim again in case your challenge is unsuccessful.

10

## The date of your claim

CDP is usually paid from the date you provide SSS with the child's full name and date of birth (ie, Part 1 of the claim) so long as you complete your claim by providing Part 2 within six weeks of that date. The six-week period can be extended if you can show there is 'good reason' for the delay.[54] Good reason could include such things as the child's or adult's health issues, hospitalisation or recent bereavement. If anything prevents you from submitting Part 2 on time, ask for more time as soon as possible.

If you do not provide this information within six weeks and do not have a good reason, entitlement begins on the date it is received,[55] or the application may be rejected (see p1534).

### Backdating your claim

CDP cannot be backdated unless your child is terminally ill (see p1437).

### Claiming in advance

A claim for CDP can be made before a child has satisfied the qualifying conditions (see p1483), provided they will meet all of the conditions within 13 weeks of completing the claim. Entitlement begins on the date the conditions are met.[56]

## Getting paid

CDP is usually paid four-weekly in arrears. If the child is terminally ill, you are paid weekly in advance.[57] If a child is paid CDP while on leave from a care home or residential school, you are paid at a daily rate.[58]

Payment is made to the parent or person with parental responsibilities who claimed on behalf of the child, or a person that SSS has appointed to act on the child's behalf (see p1522). If there is a dispute between two people with parental responsibilities, SSS decides who should act on the child's behalf.[59] When the child is 16, payment can be made direct to the child unless an appointee is needed (see p1522).

- For when CDP payments can be suspended, see p1525.
- For when a deduction can be made from CDP to recover an overpayment, see p1527.
- CDP higher rate mobility component can be paid to Motability – see similar rules for ADP on p1447.
- If you are overpaid CDP, you may have to repay it (see p1526).
- For when you can be paid short-term assistance, see p1558.

### Change of circumstances

You must tell SSS about any changes that you have been told to report.[60] The determination notice should tell you what you need to report. It is advisable to report any changes, even if you are unsure if they are relevant.

You can report a change of circumstances by telephone on 0800 182 2222 or you can download a paper form or report the change online at mygov.scot. If you do not report a change that affects your entitlement, you may miss out on extra payments or be overpaid and have to pay it back (see p1541).

**Note**: if a child gets CDP and moves elsewhere in the UK, see p1420.

### Reviews of child disability payment awards

Once awarded, CDP continues to be paid until a new determination is made about entitlement. The award has no end date but the determination notice is likely to specify a review date when SSS will look at the award again and make a new determination.[61] SSS calls this a 'scheduled review'.[62]

If a new determination reduces or ends your CDP, you may be entitled to short-term assistance if you are challenging that determination (see p1558).

For the review, SSS may request further supporting information to decide whether the child's award is correct. Failure to respond to such requests for information could lead to the benefit being suspended and SSS may then make a determination to end entitlement if the information is still not provided (see p1525).

### If a child dies

If a child dies, a lump sum payment of up to eight weeks entitlement of CDP can be paid based on their weekly award in the eight week-period up to the date of their death. This applies even if the benefit is not in payment – eg, if they are in prison or a care home.[63] In practice, any payments of CDP already made for a period after the date of death will be deducted from the lump sum due.[64]

## 6. Tax, other benefits and the benefit cap

### Tax

Child disability payment (CDP) is not taxable.[65]

### Other benefits

CDP interacts with means-tested and non-means-tested benefits, and passports you to the same sources of help, as disability living allowance (DLA) (see p541).

### Non-means-tested benefits

CDP can be paid in addition to other non-means-tested benefits. You cannot normally get CDP while you are entitled to DLA, personal independence payment (PIP), adult disability payment (ADP) or armed forces independence payment,[66] but see p1489 if your child is moving from CDP to ADP.

The amount of the care component of CDP can be reduced if the child gets constant attendance allowance under the industrial injuries scheme (see p600).[67]

If you are regularly caring for a child who gets CDP middle or highest rate care component, you may be entitled to carer support payment (CSP) (see p1467), and the carer element of universal credit (UC) (see p75).

A young person aged 16, 17 or 18 living in Scotland may be able to get a young carer grant for looking after a child who gets CDP middle or highest rate care component (see p1476).

### The benefit cap

CDP is *not* one of the specified benefits for the benefit cap. The benefit cap does not apply if you, your partner or child get CDP (even it is not paid because the person entitled is in a care home[68]). In other cases, it only applies if you are getting UC or housing benefit. See p1025 for further information.

## Passports and other sources of help

If you are not entitled to CSP, you may still be credited with class 3 national insurance contributions if you are caring for a child for at least 20 hours a week who gets CDP middle or highest rate care component (see p868).

You qualify for a Christmas bonus if you or your child get CDP at any rate. You may be entitled to council tax reduction if you have a low income.

If you get CDP mobility component, other sources of help are the same as those for DLA (see p543).

If you are in receipt of a means-tested benefit and your child gets CDP, you are entitled to a winter heating payment (see p1505).

A child who gets the CDP highest rate care component gets a child winter heating payment (see p1506).

# Notes

1. **Who can get child disability payment**

1 s31 and Sch 5 SS(S)A 2018; reg 3 DACYP(S) Regs
2 Regs 11(3), 12(6) and 13(10) DACYP(S) Regs
3 Regs 11(1)(a) and (b) and 11(5)(c) DACYP(S) Regs
4 Reg 11(5)(b) DACYP(S) Regs
5 Reg 11(5)(a) DACYP(S) Regs
6 Reg 11(1)(c) DACYP(S) Regs
7 *LK v SSS* [2025] UT 11
8 Reg 11(1)(d) DACYP(S) Regs
9 Reg 11(6)(a) DACYP(S) Regs
10 Reg 11(2) and (4) DACYP(S) Regs
11 *NB v SSS* [2023] UT 35
12 Reg 11(6)(b) DACYP(S) Regs
13 Reg 2 DACYP(S) Regs
14 Reg 11(8) DACYP(S) Regs
15 Reg 11(1)(a) DACYP(S) Regs
16 Reg 11(7) DACYP(S) Regs
17 Reg 14 DACYP(S) Regs
18 Reg 13 DACYP(S) Regs
19 Reg 13(2)(a) DACYP(S) Regs
20 SSS DMG, *The individual's physical condition as a whole*
21 Reg 13(2)(a)(ii) DACYP(S) Regs
22 Reg 13(3) DACYP(S) Regs
23 Reg 13(6) DACYP(S) Regs
24 Reg 13(2)(c) and (5) DACYP(S) Regs;
25 SSS DMG, *Severe visual disability*; nn.nhs.scot/vincyp
26 Reg 13(7) DACYP(S) Regs
27 Reg 13(8) DACYP(S) Regs
28 Reg 13(8)(b) and (9) DACYP(S) Regs
29 Reg 12 DACYP(S) Regs
30 Reg 12(3) and (4) DACYP(S) Regs
31 Reg 11(7) DACYP(S) Regs
32 Reg 12(7) DACYP(S) Regs

2. **The rules about your age**

33 Regs 4(1), 12(1) and 13(1) DACYP(S) Regs
34 Reg 24(2) DACYP(S) Regs
35 Reg 4(2) DACYP(S) Regs
36 Reg 4(1) DACYP(S) Regs
37 Reg 4(1B)(d) DACYP(S) Regs
38 s85B(3) SS(S)A 2018; SSS DMG, *CDP clients aged 16 years and older*
39 Regs 10 and 29(1)(b)(ia) DACYP(S) Regs
40 Reg 58(2) DAWAP(S) Regs

10

41 Reg 58(3) DAWAP(S) Regs
42 Reg 4(1) DACYP(S) Regs – being refused ADP does not affect your award of CDP

3. **The amount of benefit**
43 Reg 23(2) DACYP(S) Regs
44 Reg 23(1) DACYP(S) Regs

4. **Special benefit rules**
45 Reg 16(1) and (2) DACYP(S) Regs
46 Reg 16(3) and (4) DACYP(S) Regs
47 Reg 16(5) DACYP(S) Regs

5. **Claims and getting paid**
48 mygov.scot/child-disability-payment/how-to-apply
49 Reg 24(4) DACYP(S) Regs
50 SS(CPCTMA)(S) Regs (draft)
51 mygov.scot/child-disability-payment/applicants
52 s54(1) and (2) SS(S)A 2018
53 s38(1) SS(S)A 2018
54 Reg 24(4) and (6) DACYP(S) Regs
55 Reg 24(5) DACYP (S) Regs; s38 SS(S)A 2018
56 Reg 24(2) DACYP(S) Regs
57 Reg 25 DACYP(S) Regs
58 Reg 23(3) DACYP(S) Regs
59 SSS DMG, *Resolving disputes about who should act on behalf of a child*
60 s56 SS(S)A 2018
61 Reg 30 DACYP(S) Regs
62 SSS DMG, *Scheduled reviews*
63 Reg 23(7) DACYP(S) Regs
64 SSS DMG, *Overpayments of CDP after the death of an individual*



6. **Tax, other benefits and the benefit cap**
65 s677(1) IT(EP)A 2003
66 Reg 10 DACYP(S) Regs
67 Reg 23(4) and (5) DACYP(S) Regs
68 Reg 75F HB Regs; reg 83 UC Regs

# Chapter 65

# Funeral support payment

**This chapter covers:**


1. Who can get a funeral support payment (below)
2. The rules about your age (p1500)
3. The amount of benefit (p1501)
4. Claims and getting paid (p1502)
5. Tax, other benefits and the benefit cap (p1503)


### Key facts

- A funeral support payment is a one-off payment to help with the costs of a funeral.
- A funeral support payment is not means tested, but you must receive a qualifying benefit to qualify.
- You do not need to have paid national insurance contributions to qualify.
- Funeral support payments are administered and paid by Social Security Scotland.
- If you disagree with a determination about a funeral support payment, you can request a redetermination and then appeal against it (see Chapter 69). You must request a redetermination before you can appeal.

10

## 1. **Who can get a funeral support payment**

You qualify for a funeral support payment if:[1]

- you are ordinarily resident in Scotland (see p1299);[2] *and*
- on the date of your claim, you or your partner get a qualifying benefit (see p1498);[3] *and*
- you or your partner have accepted responsibility for the funeral and it is reasonable for you to do so (see p1498);[4] *and*
- the funeral takes place in the UK or, in certain circumstances, any European Economic Area (EEA) country or Switzerland (see p1500). In exceptional circumstances, it is possible to get a funeral support payment for a funeral which takes place outside the UK, where SSS considers that assistance is merited. Guidance suggests that this could be when the funeral takes place

outside the UK because, for example, of the disruption of war or disruption to air travel due to volcanic eruption;[5] *and*

- a funeral support payment or a social fund funeral expenses payment (see p707) has not already been paid in respect of the person who has died;[6] *and*
- the person who has died was ordinarily resident in the UK (see p1299);[7] *and*
- you are not a 'person subject to immigration control' (there are exceptions to this rule) – see p1272 and p1281. If you or your partner's leave is subject to a 'no recourse to public funds' condition, get specialist immigration advice *before* claiming a funeral support payment;[8] *and*
- you claim within the time limit (see p1502).[9]

It may be the funeral of a stillborn child, which means that the stillbirth occurs after the 24th week of pregnancy.[10]

## Qualifying benefits

To qualify for a funeral support payment, you or your partner must get one of the following:[11]

- universal credit (UC); *or*
- income-related employment and support allowance; *or*
- housing benefit; *or*
- pension credit.

10 You must be getting UC in the assessment period that includes the date of your claim for a funeral support payment, or in the previous assessment period.[12] For the other benefits, you must be getting the benefit on the date of your claim for a funeral support payment. See p1502 for when your claim is made, or can be treated as having been made.

The qualifying benefits must be paid at a rate of more than £0, before any third-party deductions or sanctions are applied.[13] You do not count as getting a qualifying benefit if it was paid in error, including an official error.[14]

## Responsible for the funeral expenses

To qualify for a funeral support payment, you or your partner must have accepted responsibility for the costs of the funeral and it must be reasonable that you or your partner have accepted responsibility.[15]

In assessing whether it is reasonable that you or your partner have accepted responsibility, Social Security Scotland (SSS) must take into account whether the person who has died had a closer relative than you or your partner and any other relevant factors. The following 'table of hierarchy' is used to decide whether there is a closer relative.[16]

| *Adult death* | *Child death* |
|---|---|
| Spouse or civil partner | Parent or a person who had parental rights and parental responsibilities for the child (but not a local authority) |
| Someone neither married to nor in a civil partnership with the person who died, but who had been living with them as if they were married for at least six months (or if the person who died was in hospital immediately before their death, for at least six months before they were admitted to hospital) | Sister or brother |
| Child | Grandparent |
| Parent | Aunt or uncle |
| Sister or brother | Cousin |
| Grandparent | Niece or nephew |
| Aunt or uncle | A long-standing friend |
| Cousin | |
| Niece or nephew | |
| A long-standing friend | |

Often, it is reasonable for the person who has the closest family relationship to the person who has died to take responsibility for the funeral expenses, but there are other circumstances, such as estrangement, which may be relevant and may mean that you are entitled even if there is a closer family member. SSS guidance suggests that a spouse or civil partner should not be considered to be the closest relative where the couple were permanently separated, either by court order, verbal or written agreement or by desertion.[17] The guidance also highlights situations where couples may have been living apart but were not permanently separated and should therefore still be considered the closest relative. The examples provided include couples living apart due to drug or alcohol misuse, work arrangements and care arrangements.

The guidance suggests that it *may* be reasonable for you to accept responsibility for the funeral even though there is a closer relative where:

- you were the carer of the person who has died;
- you lived with the person who has died;
- you had a close relationship with the person who has died;
- you had looked after the person who has died since their childhood;
- you had power of attorney for the person who has died, or were their legal guardian or appointee;

10

- you are the parent, sibling, relative or friend of the person who has died;
- no one else has accepted responsibility for the funeral.

The guidance also provides examples of reasons why the person who is the closest relative *may* not have been able to take responsibility for the funeral. These include:

- being estranged from, or having had a grievance with, the person who has died;
- drug or alcohol misuse;
- being too young or being in higher education;
- not being financially or emotionally capable of arranging the funeral;
- not being capable due to health, lifestyle or mental capacity;
- living too far away;
- currently serving in the armed forces;
- being under suspicion in the death of the person who has died.

If SSS decides that it was not reasonable for you to have accepted responsibility for the funeral, you can challenge this decision (see Chapter 69). At an appeal, the First-tier Tribunal can take its own view and is not bound by the guidance.

If there is another family member at the same level in the hierarchy, but no one above you, SSS should accept that it is reasonable for you to accept responsibility without looking at that other person's circumstances.[18]

If more than one person claims a funeral support payment, the application of the person who is the closest relative is considered first. If that person is entitled, the other cannot be entitled.[19] If more than one person applies, they are equally close relatives to the person who died and they cannot decide whose claim should proceed, SSS decides which to consider first.[20]



### Funerals that take place in the European Economic Area

In certain circumstances, you may be able to get a funeral support payment for a funeral that takes place in the EEA. See p1355 for details. You must satisfy all the other rules for getting a funeral support payment.

## 2. The rules about your age

There are no age limits for funeral support payment. However, because you or your partner must be getting a qualifying benefit, this means that you or your partner must be aged 16 or over.

## 3. The amount of benefit

You are entitled to a funeral support payment to cover the cost of:[21]

- a burial plot;
- necessary burial fees and fees of digging a grave;
- cremation fees, including the cost of removing a pacemaker (restricted to £25.80 if not carried out by a doctor);
- disposal by way of alkaline hydrolysis;
- any medical references and medical certificates, if required;
- documentation for the release of the assets of the person who has died;
- transport for the portion of journeys in excess of 80 kilometres, undertaken to:
  - transport the body within the UK to a funeral director's premises or to a place of rest;
  - transport the coffin and bearers in a hearse and the mourners in another vehicle from the funeral director's premises or place of rest to the funeral;
- one return journey to make arrangements for the funeral, which does not exceed the cost of a return journey from your home to the place of the funeral.

In addition, you can get £1,279.15 towards any other funeral expenses, or £156.10 if the person was aged 18 or over when they died and had a prepaid funeral plan which was paid in full.

If the funeral takes place outside the UK and the cost of the funeral, including transport costs, are more than what the costs would otherwise have been, the funeral support payment does not cover the excess.[22]

### Deductions from awards

If the following are available to help meet the funeral costs, they are deducted from the amount of the funeral support payment:[23]

- any assets of the person who died; *and*
- an insurance policy, occupational pension scheme, burial club or similar arrangement; *and*
- a funeral grant paid by the government if the person who died was receiving a war disablement pension; *and*
- any amount available from a pre-paid funeral plan. Where the plan has not been paid in full before the person died, any sum payable under the plan is deducted. Where the plan has been paid in full, the amount payable in respect of the types of costs covered by a funeral support payment is deducted.



Note:

- No deduction is made if the person who died was under 18.[24]
- No deduction is made in respect of arrears of social security benefits paid to the deceased's estate.[25]

# 4. Claims and getting paid

The general rules on claims and getting paid are covered in Chapter 68. This section explains the specific rules that apply to funeral support payment.

## Making a claim

You can claim a funeral support payment:

- online at mygov.scot/funeral-support-payment; *or*
- by phone on 0800 182 2222; *or*
- in writing on the approved form; *or*
- if you use British Sign Language, via Contact Scotland BSL.

***Forms***

Download the form from mygov.scot/funeral-support-payment or request by phone. Send your completed form to Social Security Scotland, PO Box 10311, Dundee DD1 9GH.

## Information to support your claim

You need to provide details of the funeral director, if you are using one, and details of any travel receipts or funeral bills you have already had. You are asked if you give permission for Social Security Scotland (SSS) to contact the funeral director to get further information.

## The date of your claim

10

You can claim at any time from the date the person died until six months after the date of the funeral. SSS calls this the 'period for applications'. If you are refused a funeral support payment because you are not getting a qualifying benefit and you later become entitled to a qualifying benefit, you can claim again, provided you are still within this period. If you are waiting for a backdated award of a qualifying benefit, the benefit is awarded for at least one day that falls within the period for applications and you claim within 20 days after the end of the period for applications, your claim can be treated as having been made on a day in the period for applications.[26] If you were previously turned down for a funeral support payment but are awarded a qualifying benefit on appeal, which is backdated to include the date on which your previous claim was refused, a funeral support payment can be considered again without having to make a new claim.[27]

## Getting paid

Usually, payment is made direct to the funeral director if the bill is still outstanding. If the bill has been paid, payment is usually made to you.

A funeral support payment can be recovered from the estate of the person who died.[28]

## 5. Tax, other benefits and the benefit cap

### Tax and benefits

Funeral support payments are not taxable.[29]

They are not counted as income or capital for other means-tested benefits.

You cannot get a funeral support payment if you or anyone else has been awarded a social fund funeral expenses payment in respect of the person who died.[30]

### The benefit cap

A funeral support payment is *not* a specified benefit for the benefit cap.

## Notes

1. **Who can get a funeral support payment**
1 Reg 3 FEA(S) Regs
2 Reg 9(1) FEA(S) Regs
3 Reg 10 FEA(S) Regs
4 Reg 7 FEA(S) Regs
5 Reg 9(2)(b), (3) and (3B) FEA(S) Regs; SSS guidance at socialsecurity.gov.scot/guidance-resources/guidance/exceptional-circumstances-for-funerals-outside-the-uk
6 Reg 8(4) and (5) FEA(S) Regs
7 Reg 9(2)(a) FEA(S) Regs
8 Reg 9(5) FEA(S) Regs
9 Reg 5 FEA(S) Regs
10 Reg 2 FEA(S) Regs
11 Reg 10 FEA(S) Regs
12 Reg 10(4) FEA(S) Regs
13 Reg 10(2)(b) FEA(S) Regs
14 Reg 10(2)(a) FEA(S) Regs
15 Reg 7 FEA(S) Regs
16 Reg 7(2)(a) and (3) FEA(S) Regs
17 SSS guidance at socialsecurity.gov.scot/guidance-resources/guidance/eligibility-for-funeral-support-payment
18 Reg 7(2)(a) FEA(S) Regs; Scottish government, *Funeral Expense Assistance Regulations: consultation*, May 2018; SSS guidance at socialsecurity.gov.scot/guidance-resources/guidance/eligibility-for-funeral-support-payment
19 Reg 8(1), (2) and (4) FEA(S) Regs
20 Reg 8(3) FEA(S) Regs

3. **The amount of benefit**
21 Reg 13 FEA(S) Regs
22 Reg 13(5) FEA(S) Regs
23 Reg 14 FEA(S) Regs
24 Reg 14(2) FEA(S) Regs
25 Reg 14(3) FEA(S) Regs

4. **Claims and getting paid**

26 Reg 5(5) FEA(S) Regs
27 Reg 4(2) FEA(S) Regs
28 s70 SS(S)A 2018

5. **Tax, other benefits and the benefit cap**

29 s660 IT(EP)A 2003, as amended by s12 Finance Act 2009
30 Reg 8(5) FEA(S) Regs

# Chapter 66

# Heating payments

**This chapter covers:**


1. Who can get winter heating payment (below)
2. Who can get child winter heating payment (p1506)
3. Who can get pension age winter heating payment (p1507)
4. The rules about your age (p1507)
5. The amount of benefit (p1508)
6. Claims and getting paid (p1508)
7. Tax, other benefits and the benefit cap (p1510)


### Key facts

- You may get **winter heating payment** if you get a means-tested benefit and meet other conditions. It replaces cold weather payments in Scotland.
- A child or young person may get **child winter heating payment** if they get a high rate of a disability benefit.
- If you are over pension age, you may get **pension age winter heating payment**. It replaces winter fuel payments in Scotland.
- All three are single, annual payments. To qualify, you or a child must meet the entitlement conditions on a qualifying date.
- Payments are normally made automatically with no need to claim them.
- Payments are disregarded as income for means-tested benefits and can be paid in addition to most other benefits.
- Payments are administered and paid by Social Security Scotland.
- If you disagree with a determination, you can request a redetermination and then appeal against it (see Chapter 69).

## 1. Who can get winter heating payment

You get a winter heating payment if on at least one day during the 'qualifying week', which starts on the first Monday in November (in 2025, 3–9 November):[1]

- you get a qualifying benefit (see p1506); *and*
- you are resident in Scotland (see p1299).

## Qualifying benefits

You get a winter heating payment if, on at least one day during the qualifying week, you have been awarded:[2]

- universal credit (UC) and:
  - your award includes a disabled child addition (see p68); *or*
  - you are 'responsible for' a child under five and you are not in employment or 'gainful self-employment' (see p132); *or*
  - you have limited capability for work or limited capability for work and work-related activity (see Chapter 41), and you are not in employment or gainful self-employment; *or*
- pension credit (PC) – either guarantee or savings credit; *or*
- income-related employment and support allowance (ESA) and:
  - your award includes a severe disability premium (see p275), enhanced disability premium (see p273) or pensioner premium (see p274); *or*
  - you have limited capability for work or limited capability for work and work-related activity.

**Note:**

- You are usually treated as if you had been awarded PC or income-related ESA if you get a DWP loan for help with your mortgage interest (see p765).[3] However, if you are treated as getting income-related ESA, you do not qualify if *only* the final bullet point in the list above applies.[4]
- You can also qualify if you get income-related ESA and are responsible for a child under five, but in practice this is extremely unlikely to apply.[5] In this case, you are likely to be better off if you claim UC instead – get advice.
- The rules still include income support and income-based jobseeker's allowance (now replaced by UC) as qualifying benefits in some situations. See p1721 of the 2024/25 edition of this *Handbook* for details.



# 2. Who can get child winter heating payment

A child gets a child winter heating payment if on at least one day during the 'qualifying week' – which starts on the third Monday in September (in 2025, 15–21 September) – they are:[6]

- under 19; *and*
- entitled to (unless the entitlement is not paid because they are in prison that week – see p837):
  - the highest rate care component of child disability payment (CDP) or disability living allowance (DLA); *or*
  - the enhanced rate daily living component of or adult disability payment (ADP) or personal independence payment (PIP); *and*

- either resident in Scotland or habitually resident in a specific European Economic Area country and satisfy other requirements (see p1357).

Someone (usually a parent) claims these benefits on behalf of a child under 16, and also for some young people who are 16 or over as an appointee (see p1005 for DLA and PIP, and p1522 for CDP and ADP). Other young people are responsible for these benefits themselves once they turn 16. In this chapter, 'the child' also refers to you if you are 16 or over and claim one of the qualifying disability benefits yourself.

## 3. Who can get pension age winter heating payment

At the time of writing, the rules for pension age winter heating payments in winter 2025 had not yet been finalised. See CPAG's *Welfare Rights Bulletin* or the online version of this *Handbook* for updates.

In winter 2024, to get a pension age winter heating payment, you had to get a qualifying benefit, although the Scottish government plans to remove this rule. The rules were similar to those for the DWP winter fuel payment (see p715).[7]

From winter 2025, it is expected that you will get a pension age winter heating payment if at the end of the 'qualifying week' – which starts on the third Monday in September (in 2025, 15–21 September):[8]

- you have reached pension age (see p690); *and*
- you are 'ordinarily resident' in Scotland, or satisfy the rules to be paid in an EEA country (see p1357); *and*
- you are not excluded from entitlement (see below).

### Who cannot get a pension age winter heating payment

You may be excluded from entitlement if throughout the qualifying week:[9]

- you live with a partner who got a pension age winter heating payment; *or*
- you are detained in legal custody under a sentence imposed by a court; *or*
- you have been receiving free inpatient treatment for more than 52 weeks in a hospital or similar institution (see p817); *or*
- you get pension credit, universal credit or income-related employment and support allowance, and have lived in residential care (see p716) for at least 12 weeks.

## 4. The rules about your age

Winter heating payment has no age rules. However, you must meet the age rules for the qualifying benefit (see p1506).

You can only get child winter heating payment for a child who is under 19 during the qualifying week (see p1506).[10]

You can only get pension age winter heating payment if you reach pension age by the end of the qualifying week.[11] Your payment may be higher if you are over 80 in that week.

## 5. The amount of benefit

Winter heating payment is a single annual payment of £59.75.[12]

Child winter heating payment is a single annual payment of £255.80.[13]

It is expected that pension age winter heating payment will usually be a single annual payment of:[14]

- £100 if you do not get a qualifying benefit (but see below); *or*
- £50 if you are in residential care or independent hospital, or live with someone (other than a partner) who gets a pension age winter heating payment; *or*
- £203.40 if you get a qualifying benefit and you and any partner(s) are *all* aged under 80 in the qualifying week; *or*
- £305.10 if you get a qualifying benefit and you or any partner are aged 80 or over in the qualifying week.

The qualifying benefits for a higher pension age winter fuel payment are likely to be pension credit, universal credit and income-related employment and support allowance. See CPAG's *Welfare Rights Bulletin* or the online version of this *Handbook* for updates.



## 6. Claims and getting paid

The general rules on claims and getting paid are covered in Chapter 68. This section explains the specific rules for heating payments.

### Making a claim

Usually, you do not need to make a claim.

If you need to make a claim for child winter heating payment (for a child who is not resident in the UK), you can claim:

- by phone on +44(0)1382 931 000; *or*
- in writing on the approved form. You can download the form from mygov.scot/child-winter-heating-payment-for-children-who-no-longer-live-in-scotland. Send it to Social Security Scotland, Child Winter Heating Payment, PO Box 10317, Dundee DD1 9GR.

If you do not get a DWP benefit, live abroad or get universal credit, you may need to claim pension age winter heating payment. See CPAG's *Welfare Rights Bulletin* or the online version of this *Handbook* for updates.

## When you do not need to make a claim

If you are resident in Scotland and meet the qualifying conditions, you or a child should usually be paid automatically without making a claim. If you or a child become entitled to a qualifying benefit, you are then entitled for any qualifying weeks (including in the past) covered by the award without making a claim.[15]

This does *not* apply to child winter heating payment if the child lives outside the UK (see p1508), or pension age winter payment in some cases.

***If you are awarded a qualifying benefit for a past period***

If you or a child are awarded a qualifying benefit for a qualifying week that has already passed, contact Social Security Scotland (SSS) and explain the situation. Ask for a determination of your entitlement for any previous years you or the child now qualify for a payment.

If you think you have missed out on a winter heating payment, you can ask for a determination using the form at mygov.scot/winter-heating-payment-request-form, by calling 0800 182 2222 or via Contact Scotland BSL.[16]

If entitlement is not determined, you can complain (see p1529) or apply for judicial review (see Chapter 53).[17]

If you have a previous determination, your entitlement must be determined again if you were refused:[18]

- child winter heating payment and the child is later awarded a qualifying disability benefit (see p1506) following an appeal; *or*
- any heating payment and this was due to an 'official error' (see p1540).

## Information to support your claim

If you need to claim child winter heating payment, you are asked to provide information about the child's identity and link to Scotland (see p1351).

You can also be asked to provide any other information that SSS needs to determine your entitlement (even if you did not have to make a claim).[19] If you fail to provide such evidence within the time limit, a determination can be made that you are not entitled.[20] Try to provide any evidence that you are asked for if you can, or explain why this is not possible.

## Getting paid

Winter heating payment is normally paid between December and February, into the same bank account as your qualifying benefit.[21] It is expected that pension age winter heating payment will be paid in a similar way.

Child winter heating payment is normally paid from the end of November onwards. If you do not have to claim, it is paid in the same way as the child's disability benefit. If you have to make a claim, it is paid into the account you nominate when you claim.

If SSS realises that it wrongly paid you a heating payment due to an error or mistake, it makes a further determination, creating an overpayment.[22] For when the overpayment is recoverable, see p1526.

## 7. Tax, other benefits and the benefit cap

### Tax

Winter heating payment, pension age winter heating payment and child winter heating payment are not taxable.[23]

### Other benefits

Winter heating payment, pension age winter heating payment and child winter heating payment are not counted as income or capital (in some cases, for 52 weeks from the date you receive the payment) for means-tested benefits.[24]

### The benefit cap

Winter heating payment, pension age winter heating payment and child winter heating payment are *not* specified benefits for the benefit cap.

### Other sources of help

If you have a low income, you may be entitled to council tax reduction (see p761).

If you are struggling with your fuel bills, see mygov.scot/cost-of-living-support and CPAG's *Fuel Rights Handbook*.

# Notes

1. **Who can get winter heating payment**
   1 s30 and Sch 4 SS(S)A 2018; regs 2 and 4 WHA(LI)(S) Regs
   2 Reg 4 WHA(LI)(S) Regs. Being 'responsible for' a child is defined in the same way as for income support. See p303 of the 2024/25 edition of this *Handbook* for details.
   3 Reg 4(2)(a)(vi) and (vii) WHA(LI)(S) Regs
   4 Reg 4(3)(g)(iii) WHA(LI)(S) Regs
   5 Reg 4(3)(a) WHA(LI)(S) Regs

2. **Who can get child winter heating payment**
   6 s30 and Sch 4 SS(S)A 2018; regs 2 and 4 WHACYP(S) Regs

3. **Who can get pension age winter heating payment**
   7 Regs 2 and 7 WHA(PA)(S) Regs, as amended by the Winter Heating Assistance (Pension Age) (Scotland) Amendment Regulations 2025 (draft); Scottish Parliament, *Official Report*, 28 November 2024, col 62
   8 Reg 2 and Part 3 WHA(PA)(S) Regs, as amended by the Winter Heating Assistance (Pension Age) (Scotland) Amendment Regulations 2025 (draft)
   9 Reg 9 WHA(PA)(S) Regs, as amended by the Winter Heating Assistance (Pension Age) (Scotland) Amendment Regulations 2025 (draft)

4. **The rules about your age**
   10 Regs 2 and 4(1)(a) WHACYP(S) Regs
   11 Regs 2 and 6 WHA(PA)(S) Regs

5. **The amount of benefit**
   12 Reg 9(1) WHA(LI)(S) Regs
   13 Reg 10(1) WHACYP(S) Regs
   14 Reg 10 WHA(PA)(S) Regs, as amended by the Winter Heating Assistance (Pension Age) (Scotland) Amendment Regulations 2025 (draft)

6. **Claims and getting paid**
   15 **CWHP** Reg 5 WHACYP(S) Regs
   **PAWHP** Reg 11 WHA(PA)(S) Regs
   **WHP** Reg 5 WHA(LI)(S) Regs
   16 mygov.scot/winter-heating-payment/make-request
   17 s41(1) SS(S)A 2018 – you can only request a redetermination of a determination, not of a failure to make a determination
   18 **CWHP** Regs 6 and 8 WHACYP(S) Regs
   **PAWHP** Reg 12 WHA(PA)(S) Regs
   **WHP** Reg 6 WHA(LI)(S) Regs
   19 s54(1) SS(S)A 2018
   20 s54 SS(S)A 2018
   21 mygov.scot/winter-heating-payment
   22 **CWHP** Reg 7 WHACYP(S) Regs – while this refers to an 'official error', those words are defined broadly enough (see reg 7(2)) to include errors that you have contributed to as well
   **PAWHP** Reg 13 WHA(PA)(S) Regs
   **WHP** Reg 7 WHA(LI)(S) Regs

7. **Tax, other benefits and the benefit cap**
   23 s677(1) IT(EP)A 2003
   24 **UC** Reg 66 and Sch 10 para 24 UC Regs
   **ESA** Sch 9 para 66 ESA Regs
   **HB** Sch 6 para 68 HB Regs; reg 29(1)(j)(xviih) and Sch 6 paras 21(2)(w) and 26K HB(SPC) Regs
   **PC** Reg 15 (1)(rg) and Sch 5 para 20(2)(x) SPC Regs
   While payments are not explicitly disregarded as income other than earnings for income-related ESA and HB, the Explanatory Memorandum to SI 2020 No.989 makes clear the draftsperson's view that they do not count as income

# Chapter 67

# Pension age disability payment

This chapter covers:

1. Who can get pension age disability payment (below)
2. The rules about your age (p1514)
3. The amount of benefit (p1515)
4. Special benefit rules (p1515)
5. Claims and getting paid (p1515)
6. Tax, other benefits and the benefits cap (p1519)

10

## Key facts

- Pension age disability payment (PADP) is a benefit for pension-age adults with a disability or long-term health condition who live in Scotland.
- Attendance allowance claimants living in Scotland are being transferred to PADP.
- PADP is paid at one of two rates, depending on your level of difficulty/needs.
- PADP is a non-means-tested benefit.
- You do not have to have paid national insurance contributions to qualify.
- You can get PADP whether or not you work.
- PADP is paid in addition to most other benefits and is disregarded as income for means-tested benefits.
- PADP is administered and paid by Social Security Scotland.
- If you disagree with a determination about PADP, you can request a redetermination and then appeal against it (see Chapter 69).

## 1. Who can get pension age disability payment

You can get pension age disability payment (PADP) if:[1]

- you meet the age rules (see p1514); *and*
- you are normally resident in Scotland (see p1299); *and*
- you meet the other residence conditions (see p1347); *and*

- you are not a 'person subject to immigration control' (see p1272), although there are exceptions to this (see p1272); *and*
- you satisfy the disability conditions (see below); *and*
- unless terminally ill, you have satisfied the disability conditions for at least 26 weeks (the required period condition), but see p1514 if you had a previous award of PADP or attendance allowance (AA); *and*
- you are not entitled to AA, adult disability payment (ADP), personal independence payment (PIP), disability living allowance (DLA) or armed forces independence payment. There is an exception if you are transferred from AA to PADP and an increased award of PADP is backdated because you are terminally ill (see p1438).

## The disability conditions

PADP is paid at a lower or higher rate depending on your attention and supervision needs.[2] You get the lower rate of PADP if you satisfy at least one of the daytime disability conditions *or* at least one of the night-time disability conditions.[3] You may also get the lower rate of PADP if you get renal dialysis (see p444 as the rules are the same as for AA).[4] You get the higher rate of PADP if you satisfy at least one of the daytime disability conditions *and* at least one of the night-time disability conditions.[5] You also get the higher rate of PADP if you are terminally ill (see p1515).

The daytime disability conditions are that you are so severely disabled, physically or mentally, that throughout the day you reasonably require:[6]

- frequent attention from another person in connection with bodily functions; *or*
- continual supervision in order to avoid substantial danger to yourself or others.

10

The night-time disability conditions are that you are so severely disabled physically or mentally, that at night you reasonably require:[7]

- prolonged or repeated attention from another person in connection with your bodily functions; *or*
- another person to be awake for a prolonged period or at frequent intervals to watch over you in order to avoid substantial danger to yourself or others.

'Attention' means the provision of personal care, prompting or motivation in relation to bodily functions or assistance with communication needs. It is only relevant if the attention is required to be given in your physical presence.[8]

'Supervision' means the continual presence of another person for the purpose of reducing real risk of harm to you and/or to others.[9]

'Bodily functions' means the normal actions of any organ of the body, including the brain, or of a number of organs acting together.[10]

The daytime and night-time disability conditions are the same as those for AA (see p442) and for the middle and highest rate of care component of disability DLA (see p519).

Decision makers and tribunals in Scotland are not bound by AA/DLA caselaw, but it can provide guidance and may be followed.[11] See p1430 about ADP caselaw. The same approach is likely to be taken with AA/DLA caselaw and PADP decisions. In time, Scottish tribunals and decision makers may interpret the rules differently.

### Required period condition

You meet the required period condition to be awarded PADP if you have satisfied the disability conditions throughout the past 26 weeks.[12] If you do not satisfy the required period condition when you claim, you can be awarded PADP if you will satisfy them within 26 weeks of your claim. Your award will start once the required period condition is satisfied.[13]

If you claim PADP within two years of a previous award to PADP or an award of AA ending, you do not have to satisfy the required period condition providing the new award is at the same level or less than the previous award.[14] If you were previously entitled to the lower rate of PADP or AA, you have to satisfy the required period condition in order to be entitled to the higher rate.

## 2. The rules about your age

You can only claim pension age disability payment (PADP) if you have reached pension age.[15] Pension age is currently 66. Between 2026 and 2028, it will rise to 67 (see p690).

10

If you are approaching pension age and have problems with daily living activities or mobility, it may be better to claim adult disability payment (ADP) now rather than waiting to claim PADP. ADP can be more generous as it has a mobility component in addition to a daily living component (see p1442).

### If you are getting another disability benefit and reach pension age

If you are getting ADP, Scottish adult disability living allowance (SADLA), personal independence payment (PIP) or disability living allowance (DLA) when you reach pension age, you can continue getting that benefit and do not need to claim PADP instead. You can renew or change your award of ADP or SADLA (or PIP or DLA) after you reach pension age. See p1434 for ADP and p1420 for SADLA. If you had an award of ADP or SADLA within the last 12 months, you may be able to get that benefit again rather than claim PADP. See p1434 for ADP and p1423 for SADLA.

## 3. The amount of benefit

Pension age disability payment is paid at one of two weekly rates.[16]

- The lower rate is £110.40.
- The higher rate is £73.90.

## 4. Special benefit rules

Special rules may apply if you:

- get renal dialysis (see below);
- are classed as terminally ill (see below);
- are subject to immigration control (see p1272);
- have come from or are going abroad (see Chapters 57 and 58);
- are in hospital or a hospice, living in a care home or other similar accommodation, or who are in prison or legal detention (see Chapter 38).

### Renal dialysis

You may qualify for the lower rate of pension age disability payment (PADP) if you get renal dialysis. The rules are the same as for attendance allowance (see p444).[17]

### Terminal illness

If you are accepted as terminally ill, you qualify for the higher rate of PADP (see p1436).

10

## 5. Claims and getting paid

The general rules on claims and getting paid are covered in Chapter 68. This section explains the specific rules for pension age disability payment (PADP).

### Making a claim

Note:

- The information in this section does not apply if you claim PADP on the basis that you are terminally ill (see p1437).
- If you are entitled to attendance allowance (AA) and you live in Scotland, you do not need to claim PADP and will be transferred to it (see p1518).

You can start a claim for PADP:

- online at mygov.scot/pension-age-disability-payment/how-to-apply; *or*

- by phoning 0800 182 2222 to request a paper form; *or*
- if you use British Sign Language, via Contact Scotland BSL.

*Forms*

If you want to claim on a paper form, telephone Social Security Scotland (SSS) and ask for the form to be sent to you. Send your completed form to the address on the first page. You should be sent a prepaid envelope with the form. There is a separate form for organisations helping someone to claim PADP, which can be completed electronically. It can be downloaded at socialsecurity.gov.scot/guidance-resources/resources/pension-age-disability-payment-organisation-form. If you want to claim PADP with the help of an organisation using this form, telephone SSS and explain this. Ask them to record your date of call.

The claim form has two parts. If you appear to meet the entitlement *conditions other than the disability conditions* (see p1513), you must then complete 'Part 2' of the claim. You have eight weeks to complete it from the date you started your claim.

**Note:** you have *not* made a claim to PADP until SSS receives all of the required parts of your claim and any required evidence.

### When you do not need to make a claim

If you get AA, you do not need to claim PADP, as you will be transferred to it (see p1518).

If you were refused PADP due to an 'official error', your entitlement must be determined again without you making a further claim (see p1540). In practice, you should probably also make a new claim, as you cannot be sure that SSS will accept that there was an official error.

10

## Who should claim

You must normally claim PADP yourself. In some situations, another person can claim PADP for you as your appointee (see p1522).

## Information to support your claim

To start your claim, you must provide SSS with your full name and date of birth. In practice, you are also asked questions about residence and presence conditions at this point. SSS call this 'Part 1' of your PADP claim.

You then have eight weeks to complete your claim by providing the rest of the required information ('Part 2'). This eightweek period can be extended if there is 'good reason' for the delay.[18] You may be asked to provide supporting information or confirmation from a professional or other person if you can.[19]

You should contact SSS and ask for an extension as soon as possible if you need more time to complete your claim. If SSS does not extend the period, your PADP may start later or your entitlement to PADP may not be determined (see p1534).

## The date of your claim

When PADP is paid from is determined by the date you began your claim. It is important to claim as soon as you can, as PADP cannot be backdated unless you are terminally ill (see p1436).

Your entitlement to PADP can begin on the date you 'submit' your full name and date of birth to SSS, as long as you then provide the rest of the required information to complete your claim within the time allowed, which is normally eight weeks (see p1516). If you do not provide all of the required information within the time allowed, your entitlement begins on the date you eventually provide it.[20]

### Backdating your claim

You cannot backdate a claim for PADP unless you are terminally ill (see p1436).

### If you claim the wrong benefit

SSS says that it can accept a claim for PADP made on an AA, ADP or child disability payment claim form.[21] It is likely you will be asked to provide further information in this situation.

If you realise that you have claimed the wrong benefit, contact SSS as soon as possible and explain the situation. Ask whether it is treating your claim as a claim for PADP. Unless it is, you should claim PADP as soon as possible.

### Claiming in advance

You can make a claim for PADP up to 26 weeks before you satisfy:[22]

- the required period condition (see p1514); *or*
- the condition relating to renal dialysis; *or*
- the residence rules (see p1347); *or*
- the age rules (see p1514).

Your entitlement begins on the date you meet all the requirements.

## Getting paid

PADP is usually paid four weekly in arrears. If you are terminally ill, you are paid weekly in advance.[23] Payment is made into the bank account you nominate when you claim.

SSS can pay your PADP to another person for your benefit, if it considers this is appropriate.[24]

If you are entitled to PADP and on leave from a care home or hospital, you can be paid at a daily rate.[25]

- For when PADP can be suspended, see p1525.
- If you are overpaid PADP, you may have to repay it (see p1526).
- For when a deduction can be made from your PADP to recover an overpayment, see p1527.

### Changes of circumstances

You must report any changes you have been told to report to SSS.[26] You should report any change in your circumstances as soon as possible. You can report a change by phone or on the form you can download from mygov.scot/pension-age-disability-payment-changes/letting-social-security-scotland-know-about-a-change.

If you report a change that may affect the amount of your PADP, SSS makes a new determination. For when the new determination takes effect (including if you move from Scotland to another part of the UK), see p1541.

Before making a determination, SSS can ask you to provide further information.

### Reviews of pension age disability payment awards

If your determination of PADP specifies a period after which your award must be reviewed, a further determination must be made at the end of this period.[27] Whether a review date is set depends on whether your condition is likely to change in the future. Many people will not have a review date set and will, in effect, have an indefinite award of PADP.[28]

For when a new determination following a review takes effect, see p1541.

## Transfers to pension age disability payment

10

If you live in Scotland (or in a European Economic Area state and have a 'genuine and sufficient' link to Scotland – see p1350) and you get AA, you will transfer to PADP. This is expected to happen during 2025. You will be notified in writing that you are being transferred to PADP, including how long the process will take and that your AA will end when your PADP starts.[29] If SSS later realises that you were wrongly sent a transfer notification, or wants to extend the transfer period, you are sent another notification.[30] Unless you are terminally ill (see p1436), you are awarded the same rate of PADP as your previous award of AA.[31]

Before you are transferred to PADP, you should continue to report any changes in your circumstances to the DWP.

# 6. Tax, other benefits and the benefits cap

## Tax

Pension age disability payment (PADP) is not taxable.[32]

## Means-tested benefits

PADP interacts with means-tested benefits in the same way as attendance allowance (AA) does (see p450). Note that if you are transferred from AA to PADP, you may need to tell the DWP and the local authority about your PADP award to ensure that any extra amounts continue to be paid.

## Non-means-tested benefits

PADP interacts with non-mean-tested benefits in the same way as AA does (see p451).

## The benefit cap

PADP is *not* one of the specified benefits for the benefit cap. The benefit cap does not apply to you if you or your partner get PADP, including if payment has stopped because the person entitled is in hospital or a care home. The benefits cap also does not apply to you if you do not get PADP, but you (and your partner, if you have one) are over pension age. See p1025 for further information.

## Passports and other sources of help

These are the same as for AA (see p451).

10

# Notes

1. **Who can get pension age disability payment**
   1 s31 and Sch 5 SS(S)A 2018; reg 3 DAOP(S) Regs
   2 Reg 6(1) DAOP(S) Regs
   3 Reg 6(2) DAOP(S) Regs
   4 Reg 7 DAOP(S) Regs
   5 Reg 6(3) DAOP(S) Regs
   6 Reg 5(2) DAOP(S) Regs
   7 Reg 5(3) DAOP(S) Regs
   8 Reg 5(4) and (5) DAOP(S) Regs
   9 Reg 5(5) DAOP(S) Regs
   10 Reg 5(86) DAOP(S) Regs
   11 *NB v SSS* [2023] UT 35
   12 Reg 5(6) DAOP(S) Regs
   13 Reg 27(2) DAOP(S) Regs
   14 Reg 8 DAOP(S) Regs

2. **The rules about your age**
   15 Reg 17 DAOP(S) Regs

**3. The amount of benefit**

16 Reg 26(1) DAOP(S) Regs

**4. Special benefit rules**

17 Reg 7 DAOP(S) Regs

**5. Claims and getting paid**

18 Reg 27(4)-(6) DAOP(S) Regs
19 socialsecurity.gov.scot/asset-storage/production/downloads/Supporting-Information-including-the-statement-of-support.pdf
20 Reg 27(1) DAOP(S) Regs
21 SSS, *Applying for Pension Age Disability Payment*, socialsecurity.gov.scot/asset-storage/production/downloads/Applying-for-Pension-Age-Disability-Payment.pdf, paras 35 and 36
22 Reg 27(2) DAOP(S) Regs
23 Reg 28 DAOP(S) Regs
24 Reg 25 DAOP(S) Regs
25 Reg 26(2) DAOP(S) Regs
26 s56 SS(S)A 2018
27 Reg 39 DAOP(S) Regs
28 SSS, *Decision Making Guide: choosing an appropriate review period for pension age disability payment*, available at socialsecurity.gov.scot/guidance-resources/guidance/decision-making-guide
29 Sch para 8 DAOP(S) Regs
30 Schs para 8(3) and (4) and 9(5)(c) DAOP(S) regs
31 Sch para 9(4) DAOP(S) Regs

**6. Tax, other benefits and the benefits cap**

32 s677 IT(EP)A 2003

# Chapter 68

# Claiming Scottish benefits and getting paid

**This chapter covers:**

1. Claims (below)
2. Getting paid (p1524)
3. Overpayments (p1526)
4. Fraud (p1528)
5. Complaints (p1529)

## Key facts

- Scottish benefits are administered and paid by Social Security Scotland (SSS).
- To be entitled to a Scottish benefit, you must usually make a claim for it.
- Decisions on entitlement to Scottish benefits are called 'determinations'.
- You must give correct and complete information when you make your claim, and report any changes that could affect your entitlement.
- Some overpayments, called 'assistance given in error', are recoverable.
- If you are unhappy about the way you have been treated by SSS, you can complain

10

## 1. Claims

In most cases, to be entitled to a Scottish benefit, you must make a claim for it.[1] Social Security Scotland (SSS) refers to claims as 'applications'. If you cannot claim for yourself, an appointee (see p1522) can claim on your behalf.[2]

### How to make a claim

Each Scottish benefit has its own rules for how to make a claim. See the chapter in this part of the *Handbook* about the benefit you want to claim. You may be able to claim in writing, online or by phone.

If you do not claim in the correct way, SSS may reject your application. You have a right of appeal in this situation. This is called an 'appeal against a process decision' (see p1561).[3]

You may be asked to provide further information before a decision (known as a 'determination') is made on your claim. You should be given a specific period of time to respond to the request for more information. Try to provide any evidence that you are asked for if you can, or explain why this is not possible. If you fail to provide the required information within the time you are given to do so, SSS may determine that you are not entitled to the benefit you have claimed.[4] If this happens, you can ask for a redetermination of the decision that you are not entitled to the benefit you have claimed (see p1535).

SSS local delivery teams can help with claims for Scottish benefits. You can book an appointment with a local adviser by calling SSS on 0800 182 2222.

## Withdrawing a claim

Once you have made a claim for a Scottish benefit, you can withdraw your claim at any point before the determination is made, provided you do so in the way you are told to by SSS.[5]

## Appointees

Someone aged 16 or over (eg, a relative or friend) can be authorised to act on your behalf if you cannot claim for yourself – eg, if you have a mental illness or a learning disability or if you are a child claiming a benefit such as child disability payment (CDP).[6] They are called an 'appointee'. The appointee takes on your rights and responsibilities as a claimant and receives payment of benefit.

If someone has died and there is no executor appointed to deal with the estate, another person can be appointed to deal with social security issues.[7]

It is planned that you will be able to ask the First-tier Tribunal to review certain decisions about appointeeship.[8]

10

### Appointees for adults

If you are aged 16 or over, you may have an appointee if you are incapable within the meaning of the Adults with Incapacity (Scotland) Act 2000, with no guardian acting or appointed under that Act and no other person who has the power to act on your behalf and willing to do so.[9] In appointing someone to act on your behalf, SSS must, if possible, take account of your wishes and feelings and the views of anyone else who appears to have an interest in your welfare or financial affairs.

It is planned that you may also have an appointee if you are *not* incapable within the meaning of the Adults with Incapacity (Scotland) Act 2000, you have agreed to the appointment, and:

- you understand the effect of it; *and*
- you have not been subject to any undue influence in agreeing to the appointment; *and*
- the proposed appointee is suitable to act as an appointee.[10]

It is planned that where an appointee uses any of the person's benefit without their authority, in breach of any duty or responsibility arising from the appointeeship or after the appointeeship has ended, the appointee is liable to repay the benefit to the claimant. The appointee or former appointee is not liable where they acted reasonably and in good faith, or failed to act but that failure was reasonable and in good faith.[11]

## Appointees for children

If a child is claiming a benefit, such as CDP, a person aged 16 or over can be appointed to act on behalf of the child if there is no one who:[12]

- already has the authority to act on behalf of the child; *and*
- lives with, and has responsibility for, the child; *and*
- is willing to act on the child's behalf.

When deciding whether and who to appoint, SSS must, if practicable, take account of the child's views and also the views of any person who has parental rights or parental responsibilities for the child and anyone else who appears to have an interest in the child's welfare or financial affairs.[13]

It is planned that where an appointee uses any of the child's benefit without their authority, in breach of any duty or responsibility arising from the appointeeship or after the appointeeship has ended, the appointee is liable to repay the benefit to the child.[14] The appointee or former appointee is not liable where they acted reasonably and in good faith, or failed to act but that failure was reasonable and in good faith.

## Ending an appointeeship

An appointeeship may be ended at any time by SSS.[15]

Where the appointeeship relates to a child, the following people may request that it ends:[16]

- the child; *or*
- anyone with parental rights or parental responsibilities for the child; *or*
- anyone who has an interest in the child's welfare or financial affairs.

When making a decision about ending a child appointeeship, and where it is practical to do so, SSS must take into account the views of the people in the bullet points above.[17]

Where the appointeeship relates to an adult who is *not* incapable under the Adults with Incapacity (Scotland) Act 2000, SSS must end the appointeeship if you withdraw your agreement to it and must consider ending it if a request to do so is made by someone who appears to have an interest in your welfare or financial affairs.[18] **Note:** at the time of writing, it was not yet possible to have an appointee in this situation.

Where the appointeeship relates to an adult who *is* incapable under the Adults with Incapacity (Scotland) Act 2000, SSS must consider ending the appointeeship if a request to do so is made by you or by someone who has authority to act on your behalf or by someone who appears to have an interest in your welfare or financial affairs.[19] When making a decision about ending an appointeeship for an adult in this situation, SSS must, where it is practical to do so, take into account your wishes and feelings and the views of anyone who appears to have an interest in your welfare or financial affairs.[20]

### Right to support

During the claim and assessment process, you can have someone with you to support you – eg, a support worker or advice worker. This includes during any discussions with SSS and during any assessment you are asked to undertake. A supporter is allowed to make representations to SSS on your behalf. You have the right to support unless SSS considers it unreasonable.[21]

### Right to advocacy

If you or your child have any kind of disability, you have a right to be assisted by an independent advocate in any part of the claim or assessment process.[22] If you want to get help from an advocate, phone SSS on 0800 182 2222 (Relay UK available or, if you use British Sign Language, via Contact Scotland BSL) and ask to be referred to the independent advocacy service. Although the Scottish government funds this service, it is independent of the government and of SSS. The independent advocacy service must follow service standards set out by the Scottish government.[23] You can have someone to support you (see above) as well as having an independent advocate.[24]

10

## 2. Getting paid

Once Social Security Scotland (SSS) has made a determination that you are entitled to benefit, you must be paid.[25] For details of how you are paid, see the chapter in this part of the *Handbook* about the benefit you have claimed.

Once you are receiving a Scottish benefit, you can ask for it to be stopped at any time.[26]

If you have an ongoing entitlement to a Scottish benefit, SSS informs you about your responsibility to report any changes in your circumstances. You must be told what changes you need to report and how to report them.[27] In some situations, failing to report a change of circumstances can constitute an offence (see p1528).[28]

## Suspension of payments

### When payment can be suspended

Payment of Scottish benefits which are paid on an ongoing basis can be suspended in certain circumstances. Scottish child payment, child disability payment (CDP), adult disability payment (ADP), pension age disability payment (PADP), Scottish adult disability living allowance (SADLA) and carer support payment (CSP) may be suspended if:[29]

- SSS has asked you to provide information relating to your ongoing entitlement and you have failed to provide it within the time allowed; *or*
- you have an appointee and either:
  - the appointee can no longer continue in that role; *or*
  - SSS suspects that you are at risk of financial abuse; *or*
- for CDP, you have reached 16 and SSS still has to make arrangements to pay CDP to you, as an adult, or to an appointee.

SSS must consider your financial circumstances before making a decision to suspend payment of your Scottish child payment, CDP, ADP, PADP, SADLA or CSP.[30]

You must be notified of the decision to suspend your benefit, told the reasons for the suspension and what steps you can take that may end the suspension.[31]

### Right to review

If your Scottish child payment, CDP, ADP, PADP, SADLA or CSP is suspended, you can ask SSS to look again at its decision. This is called a 'review'. SSS must complete the review within 31 days of receiving your request and must inform you of the outcome and the reasons for that outcome.[32]

### When the suspension ends

Suspension of payment ends if:[33]

- you provide the information that SSS requires and SSS decides that your award of benefit can continue unchanged; *or*
- you do *not* provide the information that SSS requires and a determination is made to end your entitlement; *or*
- if you have an appointee, that person is able to continue in that role, another person is appointed instead or SSS no longer has concerns that you are at risk of financial abuse; *or*
- SSS makes a 'determination without application' (see p1538) that:
  - you have been underpaid as a result of official error; *or*
  - you have been overpaid; *or*
  - you are no longer entitled to the benefit due to a change of circumstances; *or*
  - your benefit should be reduced to recover an overpayment, or a deduction should stop; *or*
  - you are owed a backdated award of Scottish child payment; *or*

  - you are entitled to Scottish child payment for another child; *or*
  - another person is entitled to Scottish child payment for the child instead of you; *or*
  - for CDP/ADP/PADP/SADLA/CSP, a specified period of entitlement (see p1493, p1444, p1518, p1424 and p1474) has resulted in a determination that you are no longer entitled to CDP/ADP/PADP/SADLA/CSP; *or*
- SSS decides that it is appropriate to end the suspension. This includes having regard to your financial circumstances.

### Payment after a benefit is suspended

If, when the suspension of benefit ends, you are still entitled to the benefit, SSS should immediately pay you the benefit that you have not received during the suspension period.[34]

## 3. Overpayments

If you are paid a Scottish benefit by mistake or you are paid more than you should have been, Social Security Scotland (SSS) calls this overpayment 'assistance given in error'. You may have to repay an overpayment, but only in certain circumstances.[35]

***Future changes***

Some of the rules about overpayments and recovery of overpayments may change during 2025/26, and some of the footnote references in this section may change.[36] See CPAG's *Welfare Rights Bulletin* or the online version of this *Handbook* for updates.

10

### Overpayments that may be recoverable

Overpayments of Scottish benefits can be recovered from you if you were paid in error and the error was caused, or contributed to, by you:[37]

- providing false or misleading information; *or*
- failing to report a change of circumstances which you were told you should report; *or*
- causing someone else to do either of the above.

An overpayment can also be recovered from you if you could reasonably have been expected to notice the error.[38] When assessing this, the following are examples of what should be taken into account:[39]

- the amount of benefit paid to you, compared with your actual entitlement;
- any information given to you by SSS that might have alerted you to the fact that the award was wrong.

Other relevant matters can also be taken into account.

It is planned that you are only liable if you have benefited from the overpaid benefit, although SSS will assume that you have benefited unless it is aware that this is not the case.[40] It is planned that where SSS decides that an individual who has died would have been liable for an overpayment which arose before their death, then SSS may decide that person's estate is liable.[41]

## Recovery of overpayments

The amount recoverable is the amount of benefit you received less your actual entitlement (if any) if the error had not happened.[42]

Even if the overpayment is recoverable, SSS has the discretion not to recover it from you (eg, if recovery would cause you financial hardship) and should also use its discretion when considering the method of recovery.[43]

If an overpayment of a Scottish benefit is recoverable, SSS can recover it by making deductions from ongoing payments of Scottish benefits. This currently applies to Scottish child payment, child disability payment (CDP), adult disability payment (ADP), pension age disability payment (PADP), Scottish adult disability living allowance (SADLA) and carer support payment (CSP).[44]

The level of deductions should be reasonable, taking into account your financial circumstances.[45] If you are unhappy with a determination about deductions for an overpayment from a Scottish benefit, you can challenge this by asking for a redetermination and, if necessary, by appealing (see Chapter 69).[46]

## Challenging an overpayment recoverability determination

It is planned that if you disagree with a decision that you are liable to repay an overpayment, you can ask for a review. If you are still unhappy following the review, you can appeal (see p1544).[47]

**Note**: if you want to challenge a recoverability decision before the review and appeal process is introduced, get advice and consider making a complaint, involving your MSP and/or considering judicial review (see Chapter 53).

### Reviews

It is planned that if SSS decides that you are liable to repay an overpayment, you can ask for a review of that decision. You must use the correct form and ask for a review within the specified time limit.[48] If you ask for a review outside the specified time limit, but within one year of being informed that you are liable, your review can be accepted if you have good reason for failing to ask for a review sooner.[49] If your review request is made after one year, it can be accepted if there are exceptional circumstances justifying why you did not request the review sooner.[50] If a late review request is refused, or your request is refused because it is not made in the correct form, you must be notified of SSS's decision and you can challenge the decision by making a 'process appeal' (see p1561).[51]

SSS must carry out the review within a specified time limit.[52] If SSS fails to carry out the review within this time limit, it must inform you and you then have the right to appeal (see below). Alternatively, you can wait for SSS to carry out the review.[53]

### Appeals

It is planned that if you are unhappy with the outcome of the review, or SSS has not carried out the review within the specified time limit, you can appeal to the First-tier Tribunal. You should use the form provided and send it to SSS. [54] The appeal should be made within 31 days of you being informed of SSS's review decision, or you being informed that SSS has not carried out the review within the specified timescale.[55] If you appeal outside the 31-day time limit, but within one year, the First-tier Tribunal can admit your appeal if there is good reason why you failed to appeal sooner.[56] If your appeal is made after more than one year, the First-tier Tribunal can admit your appeal if there are exceptional circumstances justifying why you did not appeal earlier.[57]

## 4. Fraud

The following are offences under the Social Security (Scotland) Act 2018.[58]

- Trying to obtain assistance by deceit. This means that you provide, or cause someone else to provide, misleading or false information with the intention of obtaining a Scottish benefit to which you would not otherwise be entitled.
- Without reasonable excuse, failing to notify a change of circumstances as soon as reasonably practicable. This must be a change that you have a duty to notify and that you ought to have known would result in your entitlement stopping or being reduced. It is also an offence to cause another person to fail to notify a change of circumstances.



The possible penalties if you are convicted of fraud include a fine and/or imprisonment.[59]

### Powers of investigation

An 'authorised officer' is authorised by Social Security Scotland (SSS) to carry out certain investigations into suspected fraud.[60] An authorised officer can require a person or body to provide information (including electronic records[61]) relevant to the fraud investigation.

The following organisations cannot be required to provide information unless the information relates to the employment of a person by that organisation or to the nature of services provided by an individual to the organisation:[62]

- those whose main purpose is providing free advice or information on social security, housing or debt;

- law centres;
- voluntary organisations providing accommodation, support or advocacy services to people who have experienced domestic abuse;
- certain advocacy services.

Authorised officers can request permission to enter premises, but not if the premises are solely occupied as someone's home.[63] They can only enter and search premises with the permission of the occupier or, if the premises are not occupied, of the owner.[64]

In the context of a fraud investigation, it is an offence to:[65]

- intentionally delay an authorised officer in their investigation;
- fail to comply with any requirement without good reason;
- knowingly provide false or misleading material;
- destroy information with the intention of avoiding compliance.

The possible penalty for this type of offence is a fine.[66]

### Interviews under caution

If you are suspected of fraud, SSS may invite you to take part in a formal interview, called an 'interview under caution'. Taking part in this interview is voluntary.[67] You should be sent a letter inviting you to attend, and SSS should be flexible about where and when the interview takes place, taking account of any particular needs you have.[68] You should be cautioned before the interview starts. This means you should be told that you do not need to say anything and that anything you do say during the interview can be used as evidence in court if there is a criminal prosecution. The interview will be recorded and you are entitled to ask for a copy of the recording.[69] You can have someone with you at the interview for support – eg, a friend, relative, advocate, welfare rights worker or solicitor.[70] If it appears that, because of a disability, you are unable to understand the process or you are unable to communicate effectively, SSS must make arrangements to have a suitable person present at the interview to provide support.[71]

## 5. Complaints

If you are unhappy about the way you have been treated by Social Security Scotland (SSS), you can complain. Your complaint can be about any issue concerning how your claim has been handled or how you have been treated. This includes matters such as delays, discourtesy, poor administration, the behaviour of staff and bad advice.

You should complain by contacting SSS by phone (0800 182 2222; Relay UK service available; if you are a British Sign Language user, via Contact Scotland

BSL); in writing (Social Security Scotland, PO Box 10304, Dundee DD1 9FZ); online at socialsecurity.gov.scot/contact/feedback/how-to-make-a-complaint or via webchat at chat.socialsecurity.gov.scot. SSS states that you should normally make your complaint within six months of the event you wish to complain about or of finding out that you have reason to complain.

SSS's complaints procedure has two stages.[72] In stage one, called 'frontline response', SSS states that it will give you a response within one to five working days unless there are exceptional circumstances. If you are unhappy with the response after stage one, you can ask for your complaint to be dealt with at stage two, which is called an 'investigation'. You should make your request for a stage two investigation within:

- six months of the event you wish to complain about; *or*
- two months of the stage one response, if this is later.

If your complaint requires investigation, it can be dealt with directly at stage two, without going through the initial stage one process. You can also request that your complaint be dealt with directly at stage two level. At stage two, SSS should acknowledge your complaint within three working days. SSS should attempt to resolve your complaint and, where it cannot resolve it, provide you with a full response, normally within 20 working days. If it takes longer than 20 working days, SSS should update you on how long it will take.

The SSS charter states that staff will listen to complaints, learn and improve the service.[73]

If you are still unhappy after SSS has considered your complaint, you can complain to the Scottish Public Services Ombudsman. Usually, you must complain to the Ombudsman within 12 months of the event you are complaining about. Use the online complaint form at forms.spso.org.uk/spso/form/start or phone 0800 377 7330.

10

# Notes

1. **Claims**

1 **SCP** Sch para 1 SCP Regs
**Other benefits** ss37 and 38 SS(S)A 2018

2 ss85A and 85B SS(S)A 2018

3 **SCP** Sch para 1(4) SCP Regs
**Other benefits** s38(5) SS(S)A 2018

4 **SCP** Sch para 25(1) and (4) SCP Regs
**Other benefits** s54(1) and (2) SS(S)A 2018

5 **SCP** Sch para 2 SCP Regs
**Other benefits** s39 SS(S)A 2018

6 ss85A and 85B SS(S)A 2018

7 s85B(6) SS(S)A 2018

8 s85D SS(S)A 2018 (not commenced at time of writing)
9 s85B(3)(b) and (7) SS(S)A 2018
10 s85B(3)(a) and (4) SS(S)A 2018 (not commenced at time of writing)
11 s85G(1) and (2) SS(S)A 2018 (not commenced at time of writing)
12 s85A SS(S)A 2018
13 s85A(5C) SS(S)A 2018
14 s85G(1) and (2) SS(S)A 2018 (not commenced at time of writing)
15 ss85A(6) and 85B(11) SS(S)A 2018
16 s85A(5A) SS(S)A 2018
17 s85A(5C) SS(S)A 2018
18 s85B(12) SS(S)A 2018
19 s85B(14) SS(S)A 2018
20 s85B(16) SS(S)A 2018
21 **SCP** Sch para 28 SCP Regs
**Other benefits** s59 SS(S)A 2018
22 s10 SS(S)A 2018
23 Reg 2 SS(ASS)(S) Regs; *Social Security Advocacy Service Standards*, gov.scot/publications/social-security-advocacy-service-standards
24 *Social Security Advocacy Service Standards*, para 8

2. **Getting paid**
25 **SCP** Reg 17 SCP Regs
**Other benefits** s24 SS(S)A 2018
26 **SCP** Reg 22 SCP Regs
**Other benefits** s26 SS(S)A 2018
27 **SCP** Sch para 26 SCP Regs
**Other benefits** s56 SS(S)A 2018
28 **SCP** Sch para 26(2)(c) SCP Regs
**Other benefits** s56(2)(c) SS(S)A 2018
29 **SCP** Reg 19A SCP Regs
**CDP** Reg 26A DACYP(S) Regs
**ADP** Reg 38 DAWAP(S)Regs
**CSP** Reg 29 CA(CSP)(S) Regs
**PADP** Reg 30 DAOP(S) Regs
**SADLA** Reg 33 DA(SADLA) Regs
30 **SCP** Reg 19B SCP Regs
**CDP** Reg 26B DACYP(S) Regs
**ADP** Reg 39 DAWAP(S) Regs
**PADP** Reg 31 DAOP(S) Regs
**SADLA** Reg 34 DA(SADLA) Regs
**CSP** Reg 30 CA(CSP)(S) Regs
31 **SCP** Reg 19C SCP Regs
**CDP** Reg 26C DACYP(S) Regs
**ADP** Reg 40 DAWAP(S) Regs
**PADP** Reg 32 DAOP(S) Regs
**SADLA** Reg 35 DA(SADLA) Regs
**CSP** Reg 31 CA(CSP)(S) Regs
32 **SCP** Reg 19D SCP Regs
**CDP** Reg 26D DACYP(S) Regs
**ADP** Reg 41 DAWAP(S) Regs
**PADP** Reg 33 DAOP(S) Regs
**SADLA** Reg 36 DA(SADLA) Regs
**CSP** Reg 32 CA(CSP) Regs
33 **SCP** Reg 19E SCP Regs
**CDP** Reg 26E DACYP(S) Regs
**ADP** Reg 42 DAWAP(S) Regs
**CSP** Reg 33 CA(CSP)(S) Regs
34 **SCP** Reg 19F SCP Regs
**CDP** Reg 26F DACYP(S) Regs
**ADP** Reg 43 DAWAP(S) Regs
**PADP** Reg 35 DAOP(S) Regs
**SADLA** Reg 38 DA(SADLA) Regs
**CSP** Reg 34 CA(CSP)(S) Regs

3. **Overpayments**
35 **SCP** Sch paras 29 and 30 SCP Regs
**Other benefits** ss63 and 64 SS(S)A 2018
36 Social Security (Amendment) (Scotland) Act 2025
37 **SCP** Sch para 30(2) SCP Regs
**Other benefits** s64(2) SS(S)A 2018
38 **SCP** Sch para 30(1)(b) SCP Regs
**Other benefits** s64(1)(b) SS(S)A 2018
39 **SCP** Sch para 30(3) SCP Regs
**Other benefits** s64(3) SS(S)A 2018
40 ss63(1A)(b)(i) and (9) SS(S)A 2018 (not commenced at time of writing)
41 s63(10) and (11) SS(S)A 2018 (not commenced at time of writing)
42 **SCP** Sch para 29(2) SCP Regs
**Other benefits** s63A(2) SS(S)A 2018
43 **SCP** Sch para 31(2) SCP Regs
**Other benefits** s65 SS(S)A 2018
44 **SCP** Reg 20(3) SCP Regs
**CDP** Reg 27 DACYP(S) Regs
**ADP** Reg 44 DAWAP(S) Regs
**PADP** Reg 36 DAOP(S) Regs
**SADLA** Reg 39 DA(SADLA) Regs
**CSP** Reg 26 CA(CSP)(S) Regs
45 **SCP** Reg 20(3) and (4) SCP Regs
**CDP** Reg 27(2) DACYP(S) Regs
**ADP** Reg 44(2) DAWAP(S) Regs
**PADP** Reg 36(2) DAOP(S) Regs
**SADLA** 39(20 DA(SADLA) Regs
**CSP** Reg 26(2) CA(CSP)(S) Regs
46 **SCP** Sch paras 13, 14 and 19 SCP Regs
**CDP** ss25, 41 and 45 SS(S)A 2018; reg 34 DACYP(S) Regs
**ADP** ss25, 41 and 45 SS(S)A 2018; reg 51 DAWAP(S) Regs
**PADP** ss25, 41 and 45 SS(S)A 2018; reg 43 DAOP(S) Regs
**CSP** ss25, 41 and 45 SS(S)A 2018; reg 39 CA(CSP)(S) Regs

47 ss69A and 69F SS(S)A 2018 (not commenced at time of writing)
48 s69A(1)-(5) SS(S)A 2018 (not commenced at time of writing)
49 s69A(5)(b)(i) SS(S)A 2018 (not commenced at time of writing)
50 s69A (5)(b)(ii) SS(S)A 2018 (not commenced at time of writing)
51 s69J(1) SS(S)A 2018 (not commenced at time of writing)
52 s69C SS(S)A 2018 (not commenced at time of writing)
53 s69C(4) SS(S)A 2018 (not commenced at time of writing)
54 ss69F and 69G SS(S)A 2018 (not commenced at time of writing)
55 s69H(1)(a) SS(S)A 2018 (not commenced at time of writing)
56 s69H((1)(b) and (3) SS(S)A 2018 (not commenced at time of writing)
57 s69H(1)(c) and (4) SS(S)A 2018 (not commenced at time of writing)

4. **Fraud**
58 ss71-73 and 80A SS(S)A 2018
59 ss71(3), 72(4), 73(4) and 80 SS(S)A 2018
60 Regs 2 and 3 SSA(IO)(S) Regs
61 Regs 4 and 7 SSA(IO)(S) Regs
62 Regs 5 and 7 SSA(IO)(S) Regs
63 Reg 8(2) SSA(IO)(S) Regs
64 Reg 8(1) SSA(IO)(S) Regs
65 Reg 9 SSA(IO)(S) Regs
66 Reg 9 SSA(IO)(S) Regs
67 SSS, *Code of Practice for Investigations*, para 71, socialsecurity.gov.scot/asset-storage/production/downloads/Code-of-Practice-for-Investigations-February-2020.pdf
68 SSS, *Code of Practice for Investigations*, para 72
69 SSS, *Code of Practice for Investigations*, para 74
70 SSS, *Code of Practice for Investigations*, para 76
71 SSS, *Code of Practice for Investigations*, para 78

5. **Complaints**
72 SSS, *Complaints Process*, August 2022, mygov.scot/complain-social-security-Scotland/complaints-process
73 SSS, *Our Charter*, p12, socialsecurity.gov.scot/asset-storage/production/downloads/Our-Charter_1.pdf

# Chapter 69

# Determinations, redeterminations and appeals

**This chapter covers:**


1. Determinations of entitlement (p1534)
2. Redeterminations (p1535)
3. Other ways to get a determination changed (p1538)
4. Appealing to the First-tier Tribunal for Scotland (p1544)
5. Appeals to the Upper Tribunal for Scotland and the Court of Session (p1554)
6. Short-term assistance (p1558)
7. Appealing about process decisions (p1561)


This chapter applies to the Scottish benefits listed on p1417. The information in this chapter also applies to carer's allowance supplement, but only if you have to claim it because you live outside the UK (see p1476).[1]

## Key facts

- If you claim a Scottish benefit correctly, you get a 'determination' of entitlement.
- In some situations, a determination must be made *without* you making a claim – eg, if you get a benefit and your circumstances change.
- If you disagree with a determination, you can ask for a 'redetermination'.
- If you disagree with a redetermination, you can appeal to the First-tier Tribunal for Scotland Social Security Chamber.
- If the First-tier Tribunal gets the law wrong, you can appeal to the Upper Tribunal for Scotland.
- If you challenge a determination reducing a Scottish disability benefit, you may be able to get short-term assistance.
- You can make a different kind of appeal against a 'process decision' that your claim or redetermination request was made in the wrong way.
- There are strict time limits to request a redetermination and appeal.

10

***Future changes***

Some of the rules about redeterminations and appeals are likely to change during 2025, and the footnote references in this chapter referring to Scottish child payment may change (although the rules are expected to remain the same).[2] See CPAG's *Welfare Rights Bulletin* or the online version of this *Handbook* for updates.

## 1. Determinations of entitlement

If you claim a Scottish benefit correctly and provide any required evidence (see p1521), Social Security Scotland (SSS) must make a 'determination' of your entitlement and notify you of this in a way that gives you a record of it – eg, by letter.[3] The determination notice must tell you what the determination is, the reasons for it and about your right to challenge it by requesting a redetermination.

The determination notice must also tell you of your right to request a copy of any adult disability payment assessment consultation report.[4]

If you do not get a determination after making a claim, see below.

**Note:** some Scottish benefits can be awarded without you having to claim them. See the chapter of this *Handbook* about the benefit to see whether it can be awarded without a claim.

***Determinations of entitlement***

A determination of your entitlement includes decisions about:[5]

- whether you are eligible for the benefit; *and*
- if you are eligible, what you will be paid (this may include reducing payment to recover an overpayment – see p1527); *and*
- for ongoing benefits, what your entitlement will be in the future; *and*
- whether you claimed a one-off payment for an event (eg, a funeral) too soon – if so, you must also be told that you can make another claim.

10

If you disagree with a determination, you can challenge it by requesting a redetermination (see p1535). There is a time limit to do so. You must request a redetermination before you can appeal.

There are also situations in which SSS must determine your entitlement again, even if you are now too late to request a redetermination (see p1538).

### If you do not get a determination after you make a claim

If there is a delay in getting a determination, check that SSS has received your claim. Make sure that you do not need to provide anything else to get a determination. If your claim was properly made and there is a long delay, you can make a complaint (see p1529).

If you claim in the wrong way, or do not provide evidence SSS requires, you may not get a determination.[6] You must be told if your entitlement will not be determined and of your right to appeal against this 'process decision' (see p1561).[7] If this happens, make another claim as soon as you can.[8] There may be a time limit to claim. See the chapter of this *Handbook* about the benefit for how to claim and any time limits.

## 2. Redeterminations

Any determination of your entitlement to a Scottish benefit (see p1534) can be challenged by requesting a 'redetermination' if you disagree with it.[9]

If you request a redetermination, every aspect of the determination is considered again. If you have been awarded some benefit, it could be reduced as a result. You can say exactly what you disagree with, but there is no guarantee that other aspects of the determination will not be changed. Get advice if you have been awarded a benefit and are considering asking for a redetermination.

***Has something changed since the date of the determination?***

**Note:** the information in this box does *not* apply if something changes and you have been *awarded* an ongoing benefit. For adult disability payment (ADP), child disability payment (CDP), pension age disability payment (PADP), carer support payment (CSP), Scottish adult disability living allowance (SADLA), see p1541, and for Scottish child payment, see p1452. If you have an award and ask for a redetermination, Social Security Scotland (SSS) must both carry out the redetermination and also take account of any changes in your circumstances since the original determination that you reported in the request.[10]

When SSS is redetermining your entitlement (or the First-tier Tribunal decides an appeal), the law currently does not explicitly prevent it from taking into account changes that happened after the previous determination.[11] However, this rule will change.[12] Until the law changes, it is unclear how the Upper Tribunal and the courts will interpret the rules However, official guidance states that any changes after the date of the determination cannot be considered if your claim was refused.[13]

If you have *not* been awarded a benefit and something changes, contact SSS as soon as possible and explain the situation, even if you have already requested a redetermination or appealed. Check whether SSS is required to make a new determination (see p1538).

For grants and one-off payments, any changes must be to your circumstances *at the time you originally claimed.*

You should make another claim if you are told that you need to, even if you have already requested a redetermination or appealed. However, for ongoing benefits, making a new claim may limit the effect of a tribunal's decision if you later win your appeal.[14]

Until the law changes, if you are now too late to make a new claim (or a new claim or increased award cannot be backdated), you can argue that the tribunal can still make an award, even if the determination was correct when it was made. Get expert advice about how to present your case.

## Who can request a redetermination

You can request a redetermination if you claimed a Scottish benefit, are claiming as someone else's appointee (see p1522) or have legal authority to act for someone – eg, as a guardian, judicial factor or the executor of someone who has died.

## How to request a redetermination

You can request a redetermination by:[15]

- completing the form sent to you with the determination. You can also download a copy from mygov.scot/request-redetermination-paper-form. Contact SSS if you need a large print, braille or audio form, or one in a different language; *or*
- phoning 0800 182 2222; *or*
- if you have hearing or speech difficulties, using text relay (18001 then 0300 244 4000); *or*
- if you use British Sigh Language, via Contact Scotland BSL; *or*
- for ADP, CDP, PADP and CSP only, online at mygov.scot/disagree-decision/request-redetermination-or-appeal.

10

Note:

- If your ADP, CDP, PADP or SADLA has been reduced, you may be able to get short-term assistance if you request a redetermination (see p1558).
- If you agree with some parts of the determination, say so. However, any aspect of a determination can be changed by a redetermination.

If you request a redetermination in the wrong way, SSS must inform you of this (and will not redetermine your entitlement).[16] You can appeal against this 'process decision' (see p1561). If you are still in time to do so, request a redetermination correctly as well – you cannot be sure of winning your appeal.

### Time limits to request a redetermination

For ADP, CDP, PADP, SADLA, CSP, child winter heating payment or short-term assistance, or, it is expected from later in 2025, pension age winter heating payment SSS must receive your redetermination request within 42 days of you being notified of the determination.[17] For other Scottish benefits, the time limit is

31 days.[18] You are normally treated as being notified of the determination two days after it is sent to you.[19]

*Example*

Rowan is refused a young carer grant. The determination letter is dated 1 July. They are treated as receiving it on 3 July. SSS must receive Rowan's redetermination request on or before 2 August.

### If you miss the time limit

If you request a redetermination late, but your request is received within one year of you being notified of the determination, your entitlement is still redetermined if you have 'good reason' for not making the request sooner.[20]

The one-year time limit can currently be extended if your good reason is related to coronavirus.[21] However, this rule will be replaced to allow the time limit to be extended in *any* 'exceptional circumstances'.[22]

You should explain why your request is late.

*Good reason*

**'Good reason'** is not defined in the law. If you think your request may be late, explain why you did not make it sooner. Your reasons might include that:
– you were away from home and did not receive the determination;
– you did not understand the determination or what you had to do next;
– you were affected by illness (of yourself or someone you had to look after);
– you were waiting for further evidence (do not wait until you get evidence before requesting a redetermination if you might miss the time limit or have already missed it);
– you have a condition that makes it hard for you to deal with letters.
Any other reasons that apply in your case may also be relevant, so include them as well.

The law does not define 'exceptional circumstances'. This could include things like severe mental illness, domestic abuse or detainment.

If SSS does not accept your reasons for missing the time limit, it does not do a redetermination. You must be informed of this, and can then appeal against the 'process decision' not to redetermine your entitlement (see p1561).[23]

## After you request a redetermination

If you have requested a redetermination correctly, SSS must redetermine your entitlement.[24] If you have evidence that shows the determination was wrong, send it to SSS. If something has changed since the determination, tell SSS and see p1535.

**Note:** the rules will change to allow you to withdraw a redetermination request if you later change your mind.[25] You must do so in the way required, which is likely to be explained on mygov.scot.

### Time limit for a redetermination to be carried out

There is a time limit for SSS to redetermine your entitlement.[26] The time limit normally runs from the day SSS receives your redetermination request. However, it runs from the date SSS (or if you had to appeal, the First-tier Tribunal) decides to accept your request if you requested a redetermination late or in the wrong way.

- For ADP, CDP, CSP, PADP, pension age winter heating payment, SADLA and short-term assistance, the time limit is 56 *calendar* days (or if you request a redetermination immediately after transferring from disability living allowance to ADP, 182 days).[27]
- For the other Scottish benefits, the time limit is 16 *working* days (any day other than a weekend or bank holiday).[28]

If your entitlement is redetermined within the time limit, you must be:[29]

- notified of the redetermination outcome; *and*
- given the reasons for it; *and*
- told that you can appeal if you disagree with it (see p1544); *and*
- sent an appeal form.

If a redetermination is not done within the time limit, you must be informed of this.[30] You can then appeal against the original determination (see p1544).[31]

**Note:** if you are notified that you can appeal because a redetermination has not been done in time, SSS can still redetermine your entitlement later, but currently does not have to.[32] However, the rules will change to always require a redetermination unless you appeal.[33]

Until the rule is changed, if you are told that you can wait for a redetermination, you should still appeal within the 31-day time limit to do so. The time limit usually runs from two days after the notification that you have the right of appeal is sent.[34]

## 3. Other ways to get a determination changed

A 'determination without application' is the legal term for when your entitlement to a Scottish benefit must be determined *without* you making a claim. These determinations are similar to some types of 'revisions' and all 'supersessions' for other benefits (see Chapter 50).

Your entitlement must be determined again if your award was too low (or no award was made) and:

- *except for* young carer grants, this was due to an 'official error' (see p1540); *or*

- for some benefits you have (or for young carer grant, someone you care for has) now been awarded a 'qualifying benefit' that means you are now entitled to it (see the chapter of this *Handbook* about the benefit you were refused).

Your entitlement must also be determined again if you have an ongoing award of adult disability payment (ADP), child disability payment (CDP), carer support payment (CSP), pension age disability payment (PADP), Scottish adult disability living allowance (SADLA) or Scottish child payment and:
- your award may no longer be correct (for ADP, CDP, CSP, PADP and SADLA see p1540; and for Scottish child payment, see p1452); *or*
- Social Security Scotland (SSS) makes or amends a deduction to recover an overpayment (see p1527).

If you get Scottish child payment, CSP or SADLA and stop meeting the entitlement conditions for a short period, in some situations your entitlement must be determined again when you requalify. For Scottish child payment, see p1460. For CSP, see p1471. For SADLA, you must ask for your entitlement to be determined again (see p1423).

Your entitlement must be determined again if you have been overpaid a heating payment (see p1510).

If you disagree with a determination made under these rules, you can request a redetermination (see p1535).

Note:
- If your entitlement must be determined again, there is no time limit to ask for this. However, in some situations, your entitlement cannot be determined again if you have requested a redetermination or appealed. See the information relevant to your situation for whether this restriction applies.
- For ongoing benefits, there are limits to when a change to your award can take effect from. Explain the situation to SSS as soon as possible. For Scottish child payment, see p1452. For ADP, CDP, PADP, SADLA and CSP, see p1540.
- If you have an award of benefit, any further determination will completely replace a previous one if it is made for the same period or event.[35] So your benefit could decrease, even if you think it should increase. Get advice if you are unsure what effect asking for another determination will have.
- See the chapter of this *Handbook* about the benefit for when you do not have to make a claim to get a determination.

## If you do not get a determination

SSS must normally make a new determination if one of the situations on p1538 applies. If you have asked for a determination or reported a change and there is a delay, check if SSS will make a new determination. If SSS does not make a new determination, you *cannot* request a redetermination.[36] Your only options are a complaint (see p1529) or judicial review (see Chapter 53).

## If there was an official error

If you were refused a Scottish benefit (except a young carer grant) or your award was too low due to an 'official error', SSS must make another determination.[37] The new determination usually takes effect from the same date as the previous determination (but for ADP, CDP, PADP, SADLA or CSP, an earlier date can be set if it would be 'unjust' not to – see p1541).[38]

A new determination *cannot* be made under these rules (*except* for heating payments) if you have requested a redetermination and your request is being considered, or have appealed against the determination. If you have already requested a redetermination or appealed, tell SSS or the First-tier Tribunal what the error was.

**Note:** the law will change to allow SSS to make a new determination if you have appealed and you agree to this (see p1549).

***Official error***

**'Official error'** is a legal mistake made by someone acting on behalf of the Scottish Ministers (SSS or another part of the Scottish government) or on behalf of a Minister of the Crown – eg, the DWP or HMRC. However, a mistake is not an official error if it was 'materially contributed to' by anyone else. So, if you or someone helping you made a mistake, there is no official error, even if SSS also made a mistake.

In practice, this is similar to the definition for other benefits (see p1135). However, an incorrect determination can arguably be due to an official error, even if it was only shown to be wrong by a later Upper Tribunal or court decision.[39]

If you realise there has been an official error and it is too late to request a redetermination (see p1537), tell SSS and ask for a determination. If SSS does not make a determination and you cannot make a new claim, see p1539.



## If your award may no longer be correct

If you are entitled to ADP, CDP, PADP, SADLA or CSP, a further determination must be made if:

- there is a 'scheduled review' of your award (see p1541); *or*
- your award was too low due to an official error (see above); *or*
- a change in your circumstances may affect your award (see p1541); *or*
- you are now terminally ill (see p1437); *or*
- you have moved out of Scotland (see p1420); *or*
- your award was too high due to an 'error' – including Scottish child payment (see p1543); *or*
- a determination was made in ignorance of a 'material fact' (see p1543); *or*
- the benefit award you had immediately before your ADP, CDP, PADP, SADLA or CSP award began changes (see p1543).

If you think one of these situations applies, ask SSS for a determination.

A further determination could increase or decrease your award. Get advice if you are unsure of the risks. See the section about your situation for the date your award changes from.

If SSS does not make a determination when you ask it to, see p1539.

***Flexibility of when changes to your award take effect***

If you get ADP, CDP, PADP, SADLA or CSP, SSS can usually increase your entitlement from earlier than the date in the rules, or decrease or stop it from a later date. This only applies if it would be 'unjust' not to do so.[40] When requesting a determination, make clear if you think that the normal rules are unfair, and ask for a different date to be set.

However, if SSS has already used this flexibility and you request a redetermination or appeal because you want your entitlement to change from a more generous date, SSS or the First-tier Tribunal can do the opposite and set a *less* favourable date. Get advice about the risks if you want to challenge the effective date of a determination.

## If your award is being reviewed

Your entitlement to ADP, CDP, PADP, SADLA or CSP must be determined again at the end of the period (if any) specified in a determination notice.[41] SSS calls this a scheduled review. For how reviews work, see p1444 for ADP, p1493 for CDP, p1518 for PADP, p1424 for SADLA and p1474 for CSP.

If your award changes, the effective date of the change depends on whether it increases or decreases (for ADP, CDP, PADP and SADLA see below, and for CSP see p1473). If your award is not changed, the new determination takes effect from the date it is made, or for CSP the following Sunday.[42]

## Changes of circumstances

When you are awarded a Scottish benefit, SSS will tell you what changes you need to report. If you are unsure if a change is relevant, you should report it anyway. If you do not report a change that affects your benefit, you may miss out if your award should increase or be overpaid if your award should decrease.

If you report a change that might affect your award, SSS must make a determination. The effective date of any change depends on whether it increases or decreases your award. If your award is not changed but you get a determination notice, you can request a redetermination.

If you do not get a determination after reporting a change, see p1539.

### When a determination following a change of circumstances takes effect

**Note:** different rules set when a change takes effect if it:

- is to your CSP award (see p1473);
- is that you are no longer ordinarily resident in Scotland (see p1420);
- is that you are now terminally ill (see p1437);

- is that you claimed ADP while entitled to CDP (see p1489) or SADLA (see p1425);
- was reported to the DWP before you transferred from PIP or DLA to ADP (see p1444), or from DLA to SADLA (see p1422).

If the change is that **your payment increases as you leave residential care, prison or hospital**, it takes effect from the date you left (no matter when you report the change). In this situation, an earlier date *cannot* be set for ADP or CDP, but *can* be set for PADP or SADLA.[43]

**If the claimant dies**, entitlement ends on the date of the death. In this situation, a later date *cannot* be set, *except* for PADP.[44] Note that if a child entitled to CDP dies, an extra payment is made for the eight weeks before the death (see p1494).

In **other situations, if your benefit increases**, the new determination takes effect:[45]

- if you reported the change:
  - within one month of it happening, from the date you met the conditions for a higher rate of benefit; *or*
  - outside the time limit above but within 13 months of the change, and you have a good reason for reporting it late, from the date you met the conditions for a higher rate of benefit; *or*
  - if the rules above do not apply, from the date you reported the change; *or*
- if you did not report the change, from the date the new determination is made.

In **other situations, if your benefit decreases or ends**, the new determination takes effect:[46]

- if you knowingly fail to report a change that you had been told you had to report or fail to report it as soon as is reasonably practicable, from the date on which you should have reported the change (see below); *or*
- from the date on which the new determination is made.

10

**Note:** except where explained above, an earlier date for your benefit increasing or a later date for it decreasing or stopping can be set if it would be unjust not to do so (see p1541).

***When should you have reported a change that reduces your entitlement?***

You should report a change as soon as you realise that your benefit might be affected. If SSS decides that you have been overpaid due to reporting a change late, check any letters from SSS to see what you ought to have reported. If the instructions were unclear, you may be able to argue that you did not need to report it immediately (and so your entitlement decreases from a later date). This depends on the wording of the letters and exactly what has changed.

Even if this does not apply, in some situations, you can argue that it would be unjust not to decrease your entitlement from a later date (see p1541).

### If your award was too high due to an error

If your award was too high due to an 'error', a new determination is made.[47] An error means that the previous determination was wrong or based on incorrect information or an incorrect assumption (including if SSS failed to correct your award straight away when it discovered an error).

The new determination usually takes effect from the same date as the previous determination.[48] *Except for* Scottish child payment, a later date can be set if it would be unjust not to (see p1541).

For whether any resulting overpayment is recoverable from you, see p1526.

**Note:** a new determination *cannot* be made under these rules if you have requested a redetermination or appealed against the previous determination. SSS can instead reduce your award in a redetermination or argue that the First-tier Tribunal should do so.

### If the previous determination was made in ignorance of a material fact

If your award of benefit was made in ignorance of a 'material fact' which might have affected your entitlement, a new determination must be made.[49] A material fact is likely to mean the same as for other benefits (see p1146).

A determination under this rule usually takes effect:[50]

- for ADP, CDP, PADP or SADLA, from the date the determination is made; *or*
- for CSP, from the Sunday before the determination is made if it increases your award, or the Sunday after it is made if it decreases your award.

An earlier or later date can be set if it would be unjust not to do so (see p1541).

**Note:**

- This rule will rarely apply if your award is too high, as there is very likely to have also been an 'error' creating an overpayment (see above).
- If your award is too low and are not too late to do so, request a redetermination (see p1535). If you are too late to do that, consider if there was an official error (see p1540). Both would increase your award from an earlier date.
- If it is too late to request a redetermination and there was no official error, consider whether there has been a change in your circumstances that may increase your award from an earlier date (see p1541).

10

### If your previous benefit award changes

The DWP may change your previous personal independence payment, disability living allowance, attendance allowance or carer's allowance award after you have transferred to ADP, CDP, SADLA, PADP or CSP. For example, you might have appealed against a DWP decision and win your appeal after being transferred to a Scottish benefit. Or your previous award might be reduced, resulting in an overpayment.

If your previous award alters, your entitlement to ADP, CDP, PADP, SADLA or CSP must be determined again.[51] Your new award will *not* necessarily be the same as the amended DWP award. SSS may ask you for further information and evidence to help it decide how much benefit to award you.

*Except for* SADLA if your entitlement *decreases* and CSP, a determination under this rule *always* takes effect from the day after your previous DWP benefit ended, and you *cannot* argue that a different date should apply instead.[52] A CSP determination under this rule currently takes effect from the Sunday after the determination is made.[53] An earlier date for an increase or a later date for a decrease to your award can currently be set if it would be unjust not to do so (see p1541). At the time of writing, the Scottish government intended to change this rule so that the new determination *always* takes effect from when your CSP began.[54]

## 4. Appealing to the First-tier Tribunal for Scotland

You can only appeal against a Scottish benefit determination after requesting a redetermination (see p1535). You do not have to request a redetermination before appealing a 'process decision', and how you appeal is different (see p1561).

Appeals about Scottish benefits are decided by the Social Security Chamber of the First-tier Tribunal for Scotland, part of the Scottish Courts and Tribunals Service. Some appeal rules for Scottish benefits are different from the rules for other benefits, and some terms used in the Scottish and UK tribunal rules are different but have the same meaning.

| *UK tribunal rules* | *Scottish tribunal rules* |
|---|---|
| Direction | Order |
| Strike out a case | Dismiss a case |
| Stay proceedings | Sist proceedings |
| Summons | Citation |
| Judge | Legal member |

### Who can appeal

If you can request a redetermination (see p1536), you can make an appeal.

**Note:** for Scottish benefits, the rules do not explicitly allow your representative to make an appeal for you, so you should appeal yourself, even if you have a representative helping you.[55]

## How to appeal

You must appeal in the way Social Security Scotland (SSS) requires. It sends you an appeal form with your redetermination notice or notice that the redetermination time limit has been missed.[56] You can also download the appeal form from mygov.scot/make-appeal-paper-form. Contact SSS if you need a large print, braille or audio form, or one in a different language. The form must be returned to SSS.[57]

SSS also allows an appeal to be submitted:[58]

- by phone (0800 182 2222); *or*
- if you have hearing or speech difficulties, via text relay (18001 then 0300 244 4000); *or*
- if you use British Sign Language, via Contact Scotland BSL; *or*
- for some Scottish benefits, online at mygov.scot/disagree-decision/request-redetermination-or-appeal.

If you appeal against a reduction of ADP, CDP, PADP or SADLA, you may be able to get short-term assistance (see p1558).

## Making sure your appeal is valid

To be valid, your appeal must give:[59]

- your name and address; *and*
- the name and address of your representative, if you have one (see p1180 – the rules are the same as for other benefits except that you must still be sent all relevant documents, even if you have a representative);[60] *and*
- a postal or email address where documents can be sent to you; *and*
- the determination you are challenging; *and*
- why you disagree with the determination; *and*
- if your appeal is late, the reasons why you did not appeal sooner.

If you cannot provide some of this information, you should still submit your appeal as soon as possible, and explain why it is incomplete. The First-tier Tribunal can waive these requirements,[61] but for the purposes of deciding whether your appeal is late, you have not appealed until you provide all the above information (or the tribunal waives the requirement).[62]

## Time limit to appeal

SSS must usually receive your appeal within **31 days** of you being notified of the redetermination (or that the redetermination time limit was missed).[63] You are normally treated as receiving a notification two days after it was sent.[64]

### If you miss the time limit

If you miss the time limit, but your appeal is received within one year of you being notified of the redetermination (or that the redetermination time limit was missed), it can still be admitted if there is a good reason it was late.[65]

The one-year time limit can currently only be extended if your good reason is 'related to' coronavirus.[66] However, this rule will be changed and it will be possible to extend the time limit in *any* 'exceptional circumstances'.[67]

You must explain why your appeal is late. If the First-tier Tribunal accepts that you have a good reason, your appeal goes ahead, unless (at the time of writing) your good reason is *not* related to coronavirus and you have missed the one-year time limit. For what may count as a good reason, see p1537.

## After you appeal

When it receives an appeal (even if you have missed the time limit), SSS must send it to the First-tier Tribunal, along with a copy of the determination, information used to make it and any claim form, and tell you it has done so.[68] If your appeal is late or incomplete, the tribunal may ask for more information.

### The response

Once the First-tier Tribunal decides that your appeal is valid, it informs you and SSS of this in writing.[69] SSS then has 31 days to produce a response to the appeal, and send it to the tribunal.[70] The response includes the decision maker's view on your appeal and any relevant documents not already sent to the tribunal. The tribunal sends the response to you, and any representative you have.[71]

When you are sent the response, you are also asked if you would like a hearing of your appeal. This is usually a good idea. See p1195, as the considerations are the same as for other benefits.[72]

10

*Form of appeal hearings*

It is understood that you can choose between a telephone, video or in-person hearing. If you (or your representative) have special requirements for a hearing (eg, an interpreter) or days when you are unavailable, you should explain this.

### Providing additional information

You (or your representative) can make written comments or submit evidence in reply to the SSS response. You must do so within 31 days of receiving it. You are treated as receiving the response two days after it was sent.[73] You can ask for this time limit to be extended.[74] Your request should be made in writing, explaining why you need more time to reply. See p1185 – the considerations are the same as for appeals about other benefits.

## What the First-tier Tribunal can do

The powers of the First-tier Tribunal are similar to those for appeals about other benefits. Most of the information on pp1182–205 also applies to appeals about Scottish benefits. See, in particular, the information about what the First-tier Tribunal can do on p1186 – the powers are similar, although the terms used are sometimes different (see p1544).[75] The most important differences for appeals about Scottish benefits are the following.

- At the time of writing, SSS *cannot* make a new determination because it now thinks you should be awarded the benefit and end your appeal. However, this rule will change (see p1549).
- The rules about tribunal decisions and what you can do if you disagree with a decision are different for Scottish benefits.
- The First-tier Tribunal *cannot* dispose of your appeal with a consent order.[76]
- If you fail to attend a hearing as a witness or produce a document when ordered to do so by the tribunal, this is potentially a criminal offence, but it is dealt with by the courts, not the Upper Tribunal.[77]
- The First-tier Tribunal cannot designate a 'lead case' (although it can join your appeal with another one if it raises the same issues).[78]
- There are no special rules about 'test cases',[79] but note that the First-tier Tribunal could 'sist' (delay) your case if it decides to wait for the outcome of another appeal.

### Sisting appeals

The tribunal can make an order sisting your appeal.[80] This means that it is not decided straight away. This power might be used, for example, to wait for the Upper Tribunal or a court to decide another case that raises similar issues to yours.

You can ask the First-tier Tribunal to make another order to cancel the order sisting your case.[81] You must apply in writing and give reasons. For example, it might be urgent that your appeal is heard quickly, or the issues in your case may be different to those in the other case. However, it can be advantageous to wait for another decision, so get advice.

10

### When your appeal can be dismissed

**Note:** 'dismissing' an appeal about a Scottish benefit means the same as 'striking out' an appeal about another benefit. If the First-tier Tribunal dismisses your appeal, it does not decide whether the determination was correct.[82]

The only situation in which the First-tier Tribunal *must* dismiss your appeal is if it does not have jurisdiction to decide it.[83] It can transfer your case to another court or tribunal with jurisdiction. You must be given a chance to argue that the appeal should not be dismissed.

The First-tier Tribunal *may* dismiss all or part of an appeal if:[84]

- you fail to comply with an order which warned you that your appeal could be dismissed if you did not comply; *or*

- there is no possibility of you meeting the conditions of entitlement; *or*
- you have failed to cooperate with the First-tier Tribunal to the extent that it cannot deal with your case fairly (in this case, you must be given a chance to argue that your appeal should not be dismissed).

You must be notified in writing that your appeal has been dismissed.[85]

The rules also allow the First-tier Tribunal to bar SSS from taking any further part in the appeal if it fails to cooperate or to comply with an order. See p1192 – the rules are the same as for other benefits.[86]

**Note:** in addition to requesting that your appeal be reinstated (see below), it is arguable that you can request a statement of reasons for the decision dismissing your appeal, and then appeal against it (see p1551).[87] Requesting a reinstatement does not stop the time limits to take these actions from running.

### Reinstating an appeal that was dismissed for failing to comply with an order

If your appeal was dismissed for failing to comply with an order, you can request that it is reinstated. You must request reinstatement in writing, giving reasons why the appeal should be reinstated. Your request must be received by the First-tier Tribunal within 31 days of you being notified of the dismissal. You are usually treated as being notified two days after a notice is sent.[88] The First-tier Tribunal can change this deadline (including shortening it).[89] Check the dismissal notice carefully, and request reinstatement within the time limit.

Your appeal is only reinstated if the First-tier Tribunal accepts you have 'good reason' for not complying with the order.[90] Good reason is not defined. You should explain in detail why you did not comply with the order.

10

## Withdrawing an appeal

You can withdraw your appeal. See p1192 for how to withdraw an appeal, including when you need the First-tier Tribunal's permission, and reinstating an appeal. The rules are similar to those for other benefits (although you must always withdraw an appeal in writing unless you do so at a hearing).[91] However, if you (or SSS) ask for an appeal to be reinstated:

- the time limit to do so is different; *and*
- the appeal is only reinstated if there is good reason to do so (see p1549).

Your application for reinstatement must be received by the First-tier Tribunal within 31 days of the notification that your appeal was withdrawn. You are treated as being notified:[92]

- if you withdrew your appeal at a hearing in person, on that day; *or*
- if the withdrawal was notified in writing, two days after it was sent to you.

The First-tier Tribunal can change this deadline (including shortening it), so check the notice carefully and request a reinstatement within the time limit.[93]

***Good reason***

The First-tier Tribunal only reinstates your appeal if it is satisfied that you have 'good reason'. Good reason is not defined. Some examples might be if:

- you did not realise that even though you have been awarded some benefit, you did not get everything you could have got if you had won your appeal;
- you thought you had no chance of success, but have since received expert advice and realised that you have a good case for your appeal;
- you now have evidence showing that you meet the entitlement conditions (if so, send a copy of it with your request).

You should mention any other reasons why you think your appeal should be reinstated.

## New determinations after you appeal

Sometimes, SSS must determine your entitlement again after you have already appealed – eg, for some Scottish benefits, if you are later awarded a 'qualifying benefit' following an appeal (see the chapter of this *Handbook* about the benefit that you claimed for details). If this happens, tell the First-tier Tribunal. Your appeal currently continues unless you withdraw it.[94]

If you claimed the same benefit again as well as appealing and this is successful before your appeal is decided, your appeal currently continues unless you withdraw it.

If you are in one of these situations, get advice about whether to withdraw your appeal. See p1548 for how to withdraw an appeal.

The above rules will change to allow SSS to determine your entitlement again *and* end your appeal if the new determination would be more favourable and you agree to it being made.[95] 10

## How your appeal is decided

The rules about when your appeal is decided at a hearing and what you should do to prove your case are similar to those for other benefits.[96] See pp1194–1205 for details. If you need to request a postponement or adjournment of a hearing, see p1189. You can contact the tribunal by phone (0141 302 5858) or email (sscadmin@scotcourtstribunals.gov.uk).

The following aspects of appeal hearings are different for Scottish benefits.

- You are asked if you want an appeal hearing when the tribunal sends you the SSS response to your appeal (see p1546).
- The First-tier Tribunal can determine your entitlement, so may consider things which were not raised by your appeal, or make a less favourable decision than the determination you are challenging.[97]

- While hearings must be recorded, or a written record produced if the equipment fails, you are not given a copy of the recording.[98] Contact the tribunal if you need to listen to the hearing again.
- The First-tier Tribunal cannot carry out a medical examination at a hearing.[99]
- In appeals about the impact of 'physical condition or mental health' on ADP, CDP, PADP or SADLA entitlement, the First-tier Tribunal includes a legal member, doctor and disability expert. In other cases, there is only a legal member.[100]
- As well as a representative, you can also bring a 'supporter'.[101] If they want to give evidence as a witness, tell the tribunal before the hearing. The tribunal can exclude a supporter from the hearing until they give evidence.[102] If this happens, you can ask for them to be present – eg, if it is harder for you to give evidence without them.[103]

**Note**: caselaw about DWP benefits may be persuasive,[104] or even binding on the First-tier Tribunal if it was decided before the Scottish benefit was introduced and the wording of the relevant rule is the same.[105] Get advice if you are unsure about how relevant caselaw is to your situation.

***The Scottish social security principles and tribunal decisions***

The law sets out eight 'principles' that underpin the Scottish social security system. While you cannot challenge a decision based on the principles alone (eg, if you have a very low income but do not meet the entitlement conditions for any Scottish benefits), a tribunal can take them into account in making a decision.[106] In one case, the Upper Tribunal for Scotland used the principles to extend the time limit to claim a benefit where SSS or the First-tier Tribunal had the discretion to do so.[107] The principles are:[108]

(a) social security is an investment in the people of Scotland,

(b) social security is itself a human right and essential to the realisation of other human rights,

(c) the delivery of social security is a public service,

(d) respect for the dignity of individuals is to be at the heart of the Scottish social security system,

(e) the Scottish social security system is to contribute to reducing poverty in Scotland,

(f) the Scottish social security system is to be designed with the people of Scotland on the basis of evidence,

(g) opportunities are to be sought to continuously improve the Scottish social security system in ways which –

 (i) put the needs of those who require assistance first, and

 (ii) advance equality and non-discrimination,

(h) the Scottish social security system is to be efficient and deliver value for money.

## The tribunal's decision

The First-tier Tribunal's decision can either uphold the determination (and so refuse your appeal), or determine your entitlement itself (including awarding you less benefit than the determination you challenged did).[109]

The tribunal can give its decision orally at a hearing, but must always also give you a written decision notice. This must tell you:[110]

- the decision; *and*
- how to ask for a statement of reasons, unless one is included (see below); *and*
- how to request permission to appeal to the Upper Tribunal once you have a statement of reasons or written summary of the decision (see below).

### The statement of reasons

It is understood that most decision notices include a full written statement of reasons, but check yours carefully. It must tell you if you can request a full statement of reasons.[111] If you want to challenge the decision, having more information will make it easier to find a legal mistake.

If the decision notice includes a written summary of the decision, you do not have to request a statement of reasons to request permission to appeal to the Upper Tribunal.[112] However, it is usually best to request a statement of reasons anyway.[113]

If you need to request a written statement of reasons, your request must be received by the First-tier Tribunal within 31 days of you being notified of the decision.[114] The tribunal can amend the time limit (including shortening it), so check your decision notice.[115] You are treated as being notified:[116]

- at the hearing if you are given the decision (orally or in writing) that day; *or*
- two days after the date it was sent to you.

## If you disagree with the tribunal's decision

If you disagree with the First-tier Tribunal's decision, you can challenge it on a point of law.

***Points of law***

While a 'point of law' is largely the same as an 'error of law' for other benefits (see p1216), Scottish tribunals are a separate jurisdiction. To successfully challenge a First-tier Tribunal decision, the Upper Tribunal for Scotland has suggested framing your challenge in terms of one or more of the following points of law:[117]

'(i) the [tribunal] decision contains a material error of law going to the root of the question for determination;

(ii) the [tribunal] entertained the wrong issue;

(iii) the [tribunal] took into account irrelevant considerations;

(iv) the [tribunal] failed to take into account relevant and material considerations which it ought to have taken into account;

(v) the [tribunal] decision was made where there was no proper basis in fact to support it and it is one for which a factual basis is required; and
(vi) the [tribunal] decision is so unreasonable that no reasonable tribunal, aware of the law and the whole facts and circumstances of the case before it and acting reasonably thereon could have reached or imposed it.'

There are two ways to challenge a decision. You can:

- ask the First-tier Tribunal to review its decision (see above); *or*
- apply straight away for permission to appeal to the Upper Tribunal (see p1554).

***Should you request a review or permission to appeal to the Upper Tribunal?***

It is usually better to request a review if you can, as this is also treated as a request for permission to appeal to the Upper Tribunal, unless you ask for this not to happen. You are later given an opportunity to change your mind before that application proceeds.

A review may be quicker and less formal than appealing to the Upper Tribunal. However, the time limit to apply for a review is shorter. While the First-tier Tribunal can extend the time limit, this is at its discretion.[118] Consider applying for permission to appeal to the Upper Tribunal if your review request is being made late.

**Note:**

- The First-tier Tribunal can correct any accidental errors or omissions in its decision.[119] This does not affect the time limit to challenge the decision.
- The tribunal can suspend its decision if you (or SSS) are challenging it.[120]
- SSS can apply for a review of, or permission to appeal against, a First-tier Tribunal decision. If SSS requests a review and you also disagree with a decision, consider requesting permission to appeal to the Upper Tribunal (see p1553).
- Decisions in appeals against 'process decisions' cannot be reviewed or appealed to the Upper Tribunal.

10

## Requesting a review

If you think the First-tier Tribunal has made an error on a point of law, you can ask for a review. Your review request must:[121]

- be made in writing; *and*
- be received by the First-tier Tribunal within 14 days of the date of the decision (or the date the written statement of reasons was sent to you, if later); *and*
- identify the error(s) on a point of law the tribunal has made (see p1216).

**Note:** unless you ask for it not to be, your review request is also treated as a request for permission to appeal to the Upper Tribunal.[122] This means that after the review decision, you may still be able to appeal to the Upper Tribunal.

Once the review is decided, you are asked if you want to continue with a request for permission to appeal.[123] You should do so unless you now think that the First-tier Tribunal's decision is correct.

### If Social Security Scotland requests a review

If SSS requests a review of a First-tier Tribunal decision, consider requesting permission to appeal to the Upper Tribunal (see p1554) if you also disagree with it. The time limit for requesting permission to appeal continues to run during a review.[124] If the review does not change the First-tier Tribunal's decision, you cannot challenge the review decision,[125] so you may lose the opportunity to challenge the original decision by waiting. You can ask the First-tier Tribunal to extend the time limit to request permission to appeal, but this may be refused.[126]

### How the First-tier Tribunal carries out a review

If the First-tier Tribunal considers that a review application is 'without merit' (if it does not identify any arguable error on a point of law), it refuses it and gives its reasons for doing so.[127] Otherwise, the tribunal sends you (and SSS) a notice:[128]

- setting a time limit for you or SSS to respond to the review request; *and*
- asking for views about whether a hearing of the review is needed; *and*
- (if it considers it appropriate) giving its initial views on the request.

Even if you requested the review, you can respond to this notice if you want a hearing, if you have comments on any provisional views the First-tier Tribunal has given, or if you can give more detail of the points of law you raised.

The First-tier Tribunal must arrange a hearing of the review, unless it decides this is not needed in the interests of justice.[129] **Note:** even if both you and SSS want a hearing, the tribunal does not have to agree to this. See p1195 for whether to request a hearing.

If it is practicable, the legal member of the tribunal who originally decided your appeal also carries out the review.[130]

**Note:** the First-tier Tribunal can review its decision even if neither party has requested a review.[131] The rules are unclear on the procedure for reviews in this situation. The First-tier Tribunal may either follow a procedure like that above, or simply decide the review straight away.

### The review decision

The review decision must be sent to both you and SSS.[132] The tribunal can:[133]

- take no action; *or*
- correct any minor errors in the decision; *or*
- 'set aside' (cancel) the decision, and:
  - redecide the matter again itself; *or*
  - refer your case to the Upper Tribunal, which can redecide the matter; *or*
  - make an order – eg, for your case to be heard again by a different tribunal.

In redeciding your appeal, the First-tier Tribunal or Upper Tribunal can make further findings about the facts of your case. If you attend a review hearing, be prepared to argue what new decision the tribunal should make.

### If you disagree with a review decision

If you disagree with a review decision, you cannot request a further review, unless the First-tier Tribunal has 'set aside' (cancelled) its original decision.[134] If the original decision was not set aside, you cannot challenge the review decision (but your review request may be treated as a request for permission to appeal to the Upper Tribunal – see p1552). You may still be in time to apply for permission to appeal against the First-tier Tribunal's original decision if you have not done so.

If the decision is set aside and remade, and you disagree with the new decision, you can request permission to appeal to the Upper Tribunal or request another review.[135] However, you cannot request a written statement of reasons.[136]

## 5. Appeals to the Upper Tribunal for Scotland and the Court of Session

You can appeal to the Upper Tribunal for Scotland against a decision of the First-tier Tribunal on a 'point of law' (see p1551). The rules for appeals about Scottish benefits are similar to other benefits, but some important differences are explained in this section.

### How to appeal to the Upper Tribunal for Scotland

10

Before you can appeal to the Upper Tribunal, you must request permission to appeal from the First-tier Tribunal. If the First-tier Tribunal refuses you permission, you can request permission from the Upper Tribunal (see p1555).

The rules about how to appeal to the Upper Tribunal are similar to those for other benefits. See p1219 for those rules.[137] There are differences in:

- the time limit to take action – this is generally 30 days, not one month;
- how the First-tier Tribunal can respond to your application for permission to appeal;
- the form you can use to apply to the Upper Tribunal (see p1556);
- what you can do if the Upper Tribunal refuses you permission to appeal without a hearing (see p1556).

### Applying to the First-tier Tribunal for permission

What must be included in your application for permission to appeal, and the information you must be given if your application is refused, are the same as for other benefits (see p1221).[138] However, note that:

- the First-tier Tribunal does not have to consider reviewing its decision if you apply for permission to appeal (but can choose to do so).[139] If you want the First-tier Tribunal to review its decision, you should ask it to (see p1552);
- the First-tier Tribunal does not treat your application as being for a written statement of reasons.[140] Check the tribunal decision notice, and ask for a statement of reasons if you want to challenge it, if it does not include full written reasons (see p1551).

You must apply for permission to appeal within 30 days of:[141]
- the date the decision was sent or given to you, if:
  - a full statement of reasons was included in the decision notice; *or*
  - you have not requested a written statement of reasons; *or*
  - you were given the decision orally at a hearing and you requested a statement of reasons more than 14 days later;[142] *or*
- the date a statement of reasons was sent to you (but see above); *or*
- if the decision was 'set aside' following a review, the date it was set aside.

This time limit can be extended by the First-tier Tribunal.[143] Keep within the time limit if possible and, if your application might be late, explain why. Unless the tribunal extends the time limit, it must 'refuse to admit' a late application.[144] It appears that you then *cannot* apply for permission to appeal to the Upper Tribunal, so your only option is to apply for judicial review of the failure to extend the time limit (see Chapter 53).[145] Get specialist advice if your application for permission to appeal is not admitted.

**If the First-tier Tribunal gives you permission to appeal**

If the First-tier Tribunal gives you permission to appeal, you must appeal to the Upper Tribunal (you can use Form UTS-1 for this). Your appeal must be received within 30 days of you being notified that you have permission to appeal. You are treated as receiving the notification two days after it was sent to you. Your notice of appeal must:[146]
- identify the First-tier Tribunal decision you are challenging; *and*
- identify the points of law in relation to the decision; *and*
- state whether you want a hearing of your appeal or not.

You must send any written decision and statement of reasons from the First-tier Tribunal with your appeal, as well as the notice of permission to appeal. If your appeal is late, you must request an extension of time. Explain why it is late and why extending the time limit is in the interests of justice. Unless the Upper Tribunal extends the time limit, it cannot consider your appeal.[147]

## Applying to the Upper Tribunal for Scotland for permission

The rules about applying for permission to appeal to the Upper Tribunal are mostly the same as those set out on p1223,[148] except that the time limit to do so is

30 days rather than one month.[149] The time limit runs from the date on which the First-tier Tribunal sent you its refusal of permission to appeal.

The Upper Tribunal can extend this time limit.[150] If your request is late, you must request an extension of time. Explain why it is late and why it is in the interests of justice to extend the time limit. Unless the Upper Tribunal extends the time limit, it cannot admit your application.[151]

***Forms***

You can download the Upper Tribunal for Scotland appeal form UTS-1 from scotcourts.gov.uk. Post or deliver it to: Upper Tribunal for Scotland, Glasgow Tribunals Centre, 20 York Street, Glasgow G2 8GT.

You can email the form to uppertribunalforscotland@scotcourtstribunals.gov.uk.

If you are refused permission to appeal by the Upper Tribunal, you cannot request a review of this decision or appeal against it to the Court of Session.[152]

However, if the Upper Tribunal refuses permission to appeal (or gives permission on limited grounds) without a hearing, you can ask for a hearing to reconsider that decision. The Upper Tribunal must receive your written application within 14 days of you being notified of the decision (you are treated as receiving the notification two days after it was sent). A different member of the Upper Tribunal then decides at a hearing whether to give you permission to appeal.[153]

If the Upper Tribunal gives you permission to appeal, your application is treated as a notice of appeal.[154]

10

## What the Upper Tribunal for Scotland can do

The Upper Tribunal for Scotland's powers when dealing with an appeal about a Scottish benefit are similar to those the Upper Tribunal has for other benefits (see pp1226–28)[155] but with the following differences.

- The time limits for responses and replies are usually 30 days and run from two days after a document is sent.[156]
- Some of the terms used in the rules are different (see p1544).
- The Upper Tribunal has the same powers as the First-tier Tribunal to dismiss appeals (but an appeal cannot be dismissed as you cannot meet the entitlement rules) and to reinstate them (see p1547).[157]
- The rules on withdrawing appeals are similar to those for the First-tier Tribunal (see p1548), but you normally need permission to withdraw an appeal, and can ask to withdraw only part of your case.[158]
- If you fail to attend a hearing as a witness or produce a document when ordered to do so, this is potentially a criminal offence, but is dealt with by the courts, not the Upper Tribunal.[159]

- The Upper Tribunal can specify 'lead cases' if several cases raise common or related issues. The other (non-lead) cases are 'sisted' (ie, delayed) until the common issues have been decided, although you can apply for an order allowing your appeal to continue (see p1547).[160]

## Upper Tribunal for Scotland hearings

The rules are similar to those for other benefits (see p1228).[161]

## Upper Tribunal for Scotland decisions

Upper Tribunal decisions are made in a similar way for Scottish benefits as for other benefits (see p1229).[162] If you disagree with the Upper Tribunal's decision, you can request a review or request permission to appeal against it.

### Reviews of Upper Tribunal for Scotland decisions

The Upper Tribunal can review its decision on its own initiative or if you or SSS ask for a review. You must request a review in writing within 14 days of the decision date, and give your reasons.[163]

The review must be decided by the same Upper Tribunal member(s) who made the decision if possible. The review decision must be sent to both you and SSS. The Upper Tribunal can decide to:[164]

- take no action; *or*
- correct any minor errors in the decision; *or*
- set aside (ie, cancel) the decision and:
  - decide the matter itself (and make further findings of fact if needed);[165] *or*
  - make an order – eg, that there will be a hearing of your case.

If the Upper Tribunal makes a new decision, you can request permission to appeal to the Court of Session against the review decision. If the Upper Tribunal does not set aside its decision, you can request permission to appeal against the original decision.[166] See below for how to appeal to the Court of Session.

If the Upper Tribunal does not set aside its decision, the deadline to request permission to appeal is extended by the time between the review application (or the Upper Tribunal deciding to review the decision) and the date you receive the review decision.[167]

## Appeals to the Court of Session

You can appeal against an Upper Tribunal for Scotland decision to the Court of Session. You can only appeal with permission, on a 'point of law', and if the case also raises an important point of principle or practice (or there are other compelling reasons for the appeal to go ahead).[168] See p1231 for details – the rules are similar to those for other benefits,[169] with the following exceptions.

- The time limit to request permission to appeal from the Upper Tribunal is 30 days. It usually runs from the date the Upper Tribunal's decision was sent to you (or, if later, the date a written statement of reasons was sent to you – but note that Upper Tribunal decisions usually include full written reasons).[170]
- Your application for permission to appeal must explain the important point of principle or practice your appeal would raise, or what other compelling reason there is to give you permission to appeal.[171]

## 6. Short-term assistance

If you challenge a determination reducing or stopping your entitlement to adult disability payment (ADP), child disability payment (CDP), pension age disability payment (PADP) or Scottish adult disability living allowance (SADLA), you may be able to get short-term assistance.[172] In this section, 'Scottish disability benefit' is used to refer to all of these benefits.

**Note:** short-term assistance is *not* a qualifying benefit to allow someone who cares for you to get carer support payment, the carer element of universal credit or a young carer grant. It is understood that the Scottish government has been assured by the DWP that getting short-term assistance should not prevent your carer from getting DWP benefits they then qualify for if you are later awarded a rate of a Scottish disability benefit that allows this as a result of your challenge,[173] and that Social Security Scotland (SSS) will take the same approach.

However, the law says that if you do not still get the relevant component (or PADP) while challenging the determination *and* the amount of short-term assistance you get is the same as or more than the benefit you are later awarded, you are not paid the ADP/CDP/SADLA component or PADP for that period. This seems to be required for your carer to qualify for any benefits.[174] Get advice before claiming short-term assistance if this may affect you.

Your entitlement to some disability premiums or elements in means-tested benefits may also be affected (as short-term assistance does not allow you to qualify for them).

### Who can get short-term assistance

You can get short-term assistance if:[175]

- you were entitled to a Scottish disability benefit; *and*
- a further determination reduced or removed that entitlement; *and*
- the further determination is 'under review'.

A determination is 'under review' if:[176]

- you have requested a redetermination and Social Security Scotland (SSS) is yet to redetermine your entitlement; *or*

- you have appealed against the determination (including a late appeal while the First-tier Tribunal considers whether to admit it); *or*
- a First-tier Tribunal's decision about your appeal has been set aside after a review (see p1552), and the tribunal will make a further determination.

You are not eligible for short-term assistance if:[177]
- the claimant has died; *or*
- the determination is that you are now too old to get CDP (see p1488); *or*
- the determination ended your CDP entitlement because you now get ADP (even if your ADP award is lower than your CDP was); *or*
- you have moved to another part of the UK and are no longer entitled for that reason (see p1420 for when your benefit ends); *or*
- the determination under review is that you no longer meet the residence or presence conditions (see p1347).

If you are not paid PADP or a component of ADP/CDP/SADLA as you are living in residential care, hospital or prison (see Chapter 38), you cannot get short-term assistance to replace the component(s) that are not paid.[178]

If you are refused short-term assistance and you think the determination is wrong, you can request a redetermination (see p1535). However, you *cannot* get short-term assistance while challenging a determination that you are not entitled to short-term assistance.[179]

## The amount of benefit

The amount of short-term assistance is normally the difference between your payment prior to the determination that is under review, and your current payment (if any).[180] However, if:

1. your award increased (eg, due to a change in your needs); *and*
2. you requested a redetermination because you thought it should be higher still; *and*
3. the redetermination then reduced your award or removed it; *and*
4. you appeal,

the amount of short-term assistance paid only tops up your award to the amount it was *before* the increase (at point 1, above) happened.

## Claims

To get short-term assistance, you must claim it. Except for SADLA (which is expected to be similar at the time of writing), you can claim by ticking a box on the redetermination or appeal form saying that you want short-term assistance, or requesting it if you make your challenge another way.[181]

**Note:**

- If you do not get a determination of your entitlement after claiming short-term assistance, see p1534.
- If you do not initially claim short-term assistance but later change your mind, phone SSS to claim on 0800 182 2222.
- Even if you got short-term assistance while requesting a redetermination, you must make a further claim for it when you appeal.
- You can be awarded short-term assistance without a further claim if:[182]
  - your appeal against a 'process decision' not to accept a redetermination request (that included a claim for short-term assistance) is later allowed by the First-tier Tribunal; *or*
  - a First-tier Tribunal decision is set aside following a review (and you got short-term assistance during your appeal).

Short-term assistance begins on the date:[183]

- your redetermination request was made, if it is accepted; *or*
- your appeal against a 'process decision' not to accept your redetermination request was allowed (although this rule may change[184]); *or*
- you appealed; *or*
- the First-tier Tribunal's decision is set aside following a review.

## Getting paid, tax and other benefits

Short-term assistance is paid in the same way as your previous award was. So any deductions to recover an overpayment (see p1527) continue.

Short-term assistance ends when:[185]

- SSS redetermines your entitlement; *or*
- you tell SSS that you no longer want to receive it (or a Scottish disability benefit); *or*
- the First-tier Tribunal decides your appeal; *or*
- the First-tier Tribunal refuses to admit your late appeal; *or*
- you withdraw your appeal.

You should not have to repay short-term assistance unless it is later discovered that you claimed the benefit it replaces fraudulently.[186]

Short-term assistance is **not taxable.**[187] It is *not* a qualifying benefit for exemption from the **benefit cap**.

Short-term assistance is not taken into account as income when calculating **means-tested benefits** and is paid in addition to them. Short-term assistance does not increase your entitlement to means-tested benefits like Scottish disability benefits do. So, any amounts that you got due to your disability benefit stop if you no longer qualify. See the chapter(s) of this *Handbook* about the other benefits you get.

If your award following a redetermination or appeal is the same as or higher than your short-term assistance, any arrears are reduced by the short-term assistance (and Scottish disability benefit) that you were paid for the same period. If your award is *lower* than your short-term assistance (and any Scottish disability benefit), you are not paid any arrears for the period you got short-term assistance.[188]

Short-term assistance is *not* a qualifying benefit to allow a carer to get any benefits for looking after you (see p1558).

Any **passported benefits** from your local authority due to your entitlement to your Scottish disability benefit should continue while you get short-term assistance.

## 7. Appealing about process decisions

Social Security Scotland (SSS) may decide:[189]

- that you claimed a benefit in the wrong way or did not send some required evidence with your claim; *or*
- that you requested a redetermination in the wrong way; *or*
- not to accept your late request for a redetermination.

These decisions are called 'process decisions' and are *not* determinations of your entitlement. You can appeal against process decisions, but some rules are different.[190] You do *not* have to request a redetermination before appealing; the decision notice should explain this.

**Note:**

- If you claimed a benefit incorrectly, claim again if it is not too late to do so or provide any missing evidence. See the chapter about the benefit in this *Handbook* for the time limits to make a claim.
- If you asked for a redetermination incorrectly, make another request in the correct way (see p1536).
- In either of the above situations, you can complain that what you tried to do was not accepted (see p1529), but you should always appeal as well.

### How to appeal against a process decision

You must appeal against a process decision to the First-tier Tribunal.[191] To be valid, your appeal must be in writing and give the same information needed to appeal against a determination (see p1545).[192]

*Forms*

You can download an appeal form from socialsecuritychamber.scot/home/your-appeal/a-process-appeal. You do not have to use the form, but it will help to provide all the information needed. Email the appeal to sscadmin@scotcourtstribunals.gov.uk, or post it to Social Security Chamber, Scottish Courts and Tribunals Service, Glasgow Tribunals Centre, 20 York Street, Glasgow G2 8GT.

## The time limit for appealing

The tribunal must receive your appeal within 31 days of you being told about the decision you are appealing against.[193] You are normally treated as receiving a notification two days after it was sent.[194]

### If you miss the time limit to appeal against a process decision

If you miss the time limit, your appeal can currently only be considered if it is received within an absolute time limit of one year after you were notified of the decision that you are appealing against.[195] The First-tier Tribunal can only consider a late appeal if it accepts that you have 'good reason' for not appealing sooner.[196] For what might count as good reason, see p1537. If your appeal might arrive late, explain why this is.

This rule will change to allow appeals to be made later than the one-year time limit in 'exceptional circumstances'.[197]

## What happens after you appeal

Once your appeal is received by the First-tier Tribunal, the rules are similar to those for other appeals (see p1546). One difference is that there is no requirement for SSS to respond to your appeal, unless it is ordered to by the First-tier Tribunal.[198]

10

## Decisions about appeals against process decisions

The First-tier Tribunal cannot determine your entitlement to benefit. If it allows your appeal, it tells SSS to determine your claim (or redetermine it). SSS can ask you for further information to enable it to do this (and the rules will change to clarify that if you do not provide something requested, another 'process decision' can be made rejecting your claim or redetermination request again[199]).

If SSS makes a (re)determination, you can challenge it by either requesting a redetermination (of a determination) or appealing (against a redetermination).

The First-tier Tribunal's decision in an appeal against a process decision is final. You (or SSS) *cannot* appeal to the Upper Tribunal or ask for a review.[200] Your only option is judicial review (see Chapter 53). If you are considering this, ask for a statement of reasons unless the decision already includes one (see p1551), and get legal advice.

# Notes

1 s81(2A) and (9)-(15) SS(S)A 2018; Part 2 and Sch 2 CASYCG(RRPP) Regs; reg 2(c) and rr1, 20B and 22(1)(c) FTT(S) Rules; reg 3(c) UT(S) Rules; reg 3(2)(c) FTTS(AFSSC) Regs
2 SS(A)(S)A 2025

1. **Determinations of entitlement**
3 **SCP** Sch paras 1, 3(a) and 4 SCP Regs
**Other benefits** ss37(a), 38 and 40 SS(S)A 2018
4 ss40(1)(e) and 60 SS(S)A 2018
5 **SCP** Reg 13(3) SCP Regs
**Other benefits** s50 SS(S)A 2018
Note: in the law, the meanings of 'determination' and 'decision' are the opposite to their meaning for other benefits described in this *Handbook*
6 **SCP** Sch para 1(3) SCP Regs
**Other benefits** s38(1) SS(S)A 2018
7 **SCP** Sch para 1(4) SCP Regs
**Other benefits** s38(5) SS(S)A 2018
8 s38(3) SS(S)A 2018 cannot prevent you from claiming again as there has been no determination of your entitlement

2. **Redeterminations**
9 **SCP** Sch para 14 SCP Regs
**Other benefits** s41 SS(S)A 2018
10 *SSS v HK* [2024] UT 53
11 SS(S)A 2018 contains no provision equivalent to ss8(2)(b) and 12(8)(b) SSA 1998
12 When it is commenced, s9 SS(A)(S)A 2025 will prevent a tribunal from taking into account changes after the date of the original determination you are appealing against.
13 See, for example, SSS DMG: *Redeterminations for adult disability payment*
14 This depends on whether the determinations of entitlement are in relation to the same period – see s27 SS(S)A 2018 and reg 23 SCP Regs
15 **SCP** Sch para 14(4) SCP Regs
**Other benefits** s41(2)(a) and (3) SS(S)A 2018
**All** mygov.scot/disagree-decision/request-redetermination-or-appeal
16 **SCP** Sch para 14(5) SCP Regs
**Other benefits** s41(6) SS(S)A 2018
17 **ADP** Reg 54(1) (and Sch 2 para 1(8) for short-term assistance) DAWAP(S) Regs
**CDP** Reg 37(1) (and Sch para 1(5) for short-term assistance) DACYP(S) Regs
**CSP** Reg 43(1) CA(CSP)(S) Regs
**CWHP** Reg 9(1) WHACYP(S) Regs
**DLA to ADP** Reg 8(1) DAWAP(TPMA)(S) Regs
**PADP** Reg 46(1) (and Sch para 1(8) for short-term assistance) DAOP(S) Regs
**SADLA** Reg 49(1) (and Sch 1 para 1(8) for short-term assistance) DA(SADLA) Regs
18 **BSG** Sch 1 para 1 EYA(BSG)(S) Regs
**FSP** Reg 6(1) FEA(S) Regs
**PAWHP** Reg 14(1) WHA(PA)(S) Regs, as amended by the Winter Heating Assistance (Pension Age) (Scotland) Amendment Regulations 2025 (draft)
**SCP** Sch para 14(2) SCP Regs
**WHP** Reg 8(1) WHA(LI)(S) Regs
**YCG** Reg 9(1) CA(YCG)(S) Regs
19 **SCP** Sch para 24 SCP Regs
**Other benefits** s62 SS(S)A 2018
20 **SCP** Sch para 14(3) SCP Regs
**Other benefits** s41(4)(b) SS(S)A 2018
21 **SCP** Sch para 34(1) SCP Regs
**Other benefits** s52A(1) SS(S)A 2018
See also *CD v SSS* [2024] UT 12 for the meaning of 'related to coronavirus'
22 s4 SS(A)(S)A 2025
23 **SCP** Sch para 15 SCP Regs
**Other benefits** s42 SS(S)A 2018
24 **SCP** Sch para 16(1) SCP Regs
**Other benefits** s43(1) SS(S)A 2018
25 s6 SS(A)(S)A 2025
26 **SCP** Sch para 16 SCP Regs
**Other benefits** s43(2) and (5) SS(S)A 2018

27 **ADP** Reg 54(2) (and Sch 2 para 1(8) for short-term assistance) DAWAP(S) Regs
**CDP** Reg 37(2) (and Sch para 1(5) for short-term assistance) DACYP(S) Regs
**CSP** Reg 43(2) CA(CSP)(S) Regs
**DLA to ADP** Reg 8(2) DAWAP(TPMA)(S) Regs
**PADP** Reg 46(2) (and Sch para 1(8) for short-term assistance) DAOP(S) Regs
**PAWHP** Reg 14(2) WHA(PA)(S) Regs
**SADLA** Reg 49(2) (and Sch 1 para 1(8) for short-term assistance) DA(SADLA) Regs

28 **BSG** Sch 1 para 2(1) and (2) EYA(BSG)(S) Regs
**CWHP** Reg 9(2) and (3) WHACYP(S) Regs
**FSP** Regs 2 and 6(2) FEA(S) Regs
**SCP** Reg 6 and Sch para 16(2) SCP Regs
**WHP** Reg 8(2) and (3) WHA(LI)(S) Regs
**YCG** Reg 9(2) and (3) CA(YCG)(S) Regs
There is a list of bank holidays at mygov.scot/scotland-bank-holidays

29 **SCP** Sch para 17 SCP Regs
**Other benefits** s44 SS(S)A 2018

30 **SCP** Sch paras 16(3) and 18 SCP Regs
**Other benefits** ss43(3) and 45 SS(S)A 2018

31 **SCP** Sch para 19 SCP Regs
**Other benefits** s46 SS(S)A 2018

32 **SCP** Sch para 16(3) SCP Regs
**Other benefits** s43(3) SS(S)A 2018

33 s7 SS(A)(S)A 2025

34 **SCP** Sch para 24 SCP Regs
**Other benefits** s62 SS(S)A 2018

### 3. Other ways to get a determination changed

35 **SCP** Reg 23 SCP Regs
**Other benefits** s27 SS(S)A 2018

36 **SCP** Sch para 14(1) SCP Regs
**Other benefits** s41(1) SS(S)A 2018
You can only request a redetermination of a determination, not of a failure to make a determination

37 **ADP** Reg 49 DAWAP(S) Regs
**BSG** Sch 1 para 4 EYA(BSG)(S) Regs
**CDP** Reg 32 DACYP(S) Regs
**CSP** Reg 37 CA(CSP)(S) Regs
**CWHP** Reg 6 WHACYP(S) Regs
**FSP** Reg 4(1) FEA(S) Regs
**PADP** Reg 41 DAOP(S) Regs
**PAWHP** Reg 12 WHA(PA)(S) Regs
**SADLA** Reg 44 DA(SADLA) Regs
**SCP** Sch para 6 SCP Regs
**WHP** Reg 6 WHA(LI)(S) Regs

38 **ADP** Reg 45(1)(c) and (2) DAWAP(S) Regs
**CDP** Reg 28(1)(c) and (2) DACYP(S) Regs
**CSP** Reg 28(1)(b) and (2) CA(CSP)(S) Regs
**PADP** Reg 37(1)(c) and (2) DAOP(S) Regs
**SADLA** Reg 40(1)(c) and (2) DA(SADLA) Regs
**SCP** Sch para 6(3) SCP Regs
For one-off payments, there is no need for the rules to explicitly say this

39 For other benefits, this is specifically excluded from the definition of an 'official error' – see, for example, reg 1(3) SS&CS(DA) Regs

40 **ADP** Regs 45(2) and 46(2) DAWAP(S) Regs
**CDP** Regs 28(2) and 29(2) DACYP(S) Regs
**CSP** Reg 27(2) and 28(2) CA(CSP)(S) Regs
**PADP** Reg 37(2) and 38(2) DAOP(S) Regs
**SADLA** Reg 40(2) and 41(2) DA(SADLA) Regs

41 **ADP** Reg 47 DAWAP(S) Regs
**CDP** Reg 30 DACYP(S) Regs
**CSP** Reg 35 CA(CSP)(S) Regs
**PADP** Reg 39 DAOP(S) Regs
**SADLA** Reg 42 DA(SADLA) Regs

42 While the regulations do not actually specify a date, this is the default position for both increases and decreases

43 **ADP** Reg 45(1)(ca) and (2) DAWAP(S) Regs
**CDP** Reg 28(1)(ca) and (2) DACYP(S) Regs
**PADP** Reg 37(1)(d) and (2) DAOP(S) Regs
**SADLA** Reg 40(1)(d) and (2) DA(SADLA) Regs
Note that it is unclear why it would ever be 'unjust' not to pay you PADP or SADLA for a period during which the rules are intended to prevent payment.

44 **ADP** Reg 46(1)(aa) and (2) DAWAP(S) Regs
**CDP** Reg 29(1)(aa) and (2) DACYP(S) Regs
**PADP** Reg 38(1)(c) and (2) DAOP(S) Regs – although it is unclear why it would ever be 'unjust' not to continue the PADP award of someone who had died
**SADLA** Reg 41(1)(b) and (2) DA(SADLA) Regs

45 **ADP** Reg 45(1)(b), (1)(d), and (2) DAWAP(S) Regs
**CDP** Reg 28(1)(b), (1)(d), and (2) DACYP(S) Regs
**PADP** Reg 37(1)(b), (1)(e), and (2) DAOP(S) Regs
**SADLA** Reg 40(1)(b), (1)(e) and (2) DA(SADLA) Regs
46 **ADP** Reg 46(1)(b), (1)(d), and (2) DAWAP(S) Regs
**CDP** Reg 29(1)(b), (1)(d), and (2) DACYP(S) Regs
**PADP** Reg 38(1)(b), (1)(e), and (2) DAOP(S) Regs
**SADLA** Reg 41(1)(c), (1)(e), and (2) DA(SADLA) Regs
47 **ADP** Reg 50 DAWAP(S) Regs
**CDP** Reg 33 DACYP(S) Regs
**CSP** Reg 38 CA(CSP)(S) Regs
**PADP** Reg 42 DAOP(S) Regs
**SADLA** Reg 45 DA(SADLA) Regs
**SCP** Sch para 7 SCP Regs
48 **ADP** Reg 46(1)(c) and (2) DAWAP(S) Regs
**CDP** Reg 29(1)(c) and (2) DACYP(S) Regs
**CSP** Reg 27(1)(b) and (2) CA(CSP)(S) Regs
**PADP** Reg 38(1)(d) and (2) DAOP(S) Regs
**SADLA** Reg 41(1)(d) and (2) DA(SADLA) Regs
**SCP** Sch para 7(3) SCP Regs
49 **ADP** Reg 48(a) DAWAP(S) Regs
**CDP** Reg 31(a) DACYP(S) Regs
**CSP** Reg 36(b) CA(CSP)(S) Regs
**PADP** Reg 40(a) DAOP(S) Regs
**SADLA** Reg 43(a) DA(SADLA) Regs
50 **ADP** Regs 45(1)(b)(ii) and (2) and 46(1)(b)(ii) and (2) DAWAP(S) Regs
**CDP** Regs 28(1)(b)(ii) and (2) and 29(1)(b)(ii) and (2) DACYP(S) Regs
**CSP** Regs 27(1)(c) and (2) and 28(1)(a)(iii) and (2) CA(CSP)(S) Regs
**PADP** Reg 37(1)(b)(ii) and (2) and 38(1)(b)(ii) and (2) DAOP(S) Regs
**SADLA** Reg 40(1)(b)(ii) and (2) and 41(1)(c)(ii) and (2) DA(SADLA) Regs
51 **ADP** Reg 48(c), (d) and (e) DAWAP(S) Regs
**CDP** Reg 31(c) and (d) DACYP(S) Regs
**CSP** Reg 36(f) and (g) CA(CSP)(S) Regs
**PADP** Reg 40(c) and (d) DAOP(S) Regs
**SADLA** Reg 43(c) and (d) DA(SADLA) Regs
52 **ADP** Regs 45(1)(a) and 46(1)(a) DAWAP(S) Regs
**CDP** Regs 28(1)(a) and 29(1)(a) DACYP(S) Regs
**PADP** Regs 37(1)(a) and 38(1)(a) DAOP(S) Regs
**SADLA** Regs 40(1)(a) and 41(1)(a) and (2) DA(SADLA) Regs
53 Reg 27(1)(c) and (2) and 28(1)(c) and (2) CA(CSP)(S) Regs
54 Regs 3(14)(b) and (15)(d) CA(YCGCSP)(MA) Regs (draft)

4. **Appealing to the First-tier Tribunal for Scotland**

55 There is no equivalent to r11(5) TP(FT) Rules in r9 FTTSSSC(P) Rules
56 **SCP** Sch paras 17(1)(b) and 18(1)(b) SCP Regs
**Other benefits** ss44(1)(b) and 45(1)(b) SS(S)A 2018
57 **SCP** Sch para 20(1) SCP Regs
**Other benefits** s47(1) SS(S)A 2018
58 mygov.scot/disagree-decision/request-redetermination-or-appeal
59 **SCP** r20A(5) FTTSSSC(P) Rules
**Other benefits** r20(5) FTTSSSC(P) Rules
60 r9 FTTSSSC(P) Rules
61 r6 FTTSSSC(P) Rules
62 **SCP** Sch para 21(2)(b) SCP Regs
**Other benefits** s48(2)(b) SS(S)A 2018
Arguably, if a requirement is waived, your appeal should be treated as made on the date SSS received it
63 **SCP** Sch para 21(1) SCP Regs
**Other benefits** s48 SS(S)A 2018
64 **SCP** Sch para 24 SCP Regs
**Other benefits** s62 SS(S)A 2018
65 **SCP** Sch para 21(1) SCP Regs
**Other benefits** s48 SS(S)A 2018
66 **SCP** Sch para 34(2) and (3) SCP Regs
**Other benefits** s52A(2)-(4) SS(S)A 2018
See also *CD v SSS* [2024] UT 12 for the meaning of 'related to coronavirus'
67 s5 SS(A)(S)A 20225
68 **SCP** Sch para 20(2) and (3) SCP Regs; r20A(7), (8) and (10) FTTSSSC(P) Rules
**Other benefits** s47(2) and (3) SS(S)A 2018; r20(7), (8) and (10) FTTSSSC(P) Rules
69 r21(1) FTTSSSC(P) Rules
70 r21(2)-(4) FTTSSSC(P) Rules
71 rr9(3) and 21(5) FTTSSSC(P) Rules

72 Note that the rules about expenses for hearings are found in s64 T(S)A 2014 and reg 3 of The Social Security Appeals (Expenses and Allowances) (Scotland) Regulations 2018 No.275
73 rr1(2) and 21(6) and (7) FTTSSSC(P) Rules
74 r4(3)(a) FTTSSSC(P) Rules
75 rr4-19 FTTSSSC(P) Rules
76 The FTTSSSC(P) Rules contain no equivalent to r32 TP(FT) Rules
77 s67 T(S)A 2014; ST(ORP) Regs
78 r4(3)(b) FTTSSSC(P) Rules
79 The law about appeals for Scottish benefits contains no equivalent to s26 SSA 1998
80 r4(3)(j) FTTSSSC(P) Rules
81 r5(5) FTTSSSC(P) Rules
82 r7 FTTSSSC(P) Rules
83 r7(1) and (3) FTTSSSC(P) Rules
84 r7(2) and (3) FTTSSSC(P) Rules
85 r7(9) FTTSSSC(P) Rules
86 r7(7) and (8) FTTSSSC(P) Rules
87 The decision is not excluded from the possibility of appealing against it by T(S)A 2014, so arguably the decision in *LS v Lambeth BC (HB)* [2010] UKUT 461, reported as [2011] AACR 27, applies to the FTTSSSC(P) Rules
88 rr1(2) and 7(4)-(6) FTTSSSC(P) Rules
89 r4(3)(a) FTTSSSC(P) Rules
90 r7(4) FTTSSSC(P) Rules
91 r17 FTTSSSC(P) Rules
92 rr1(2) and 17(5) FTTSSSC(P) Rules
93 r4(3)(a) FTTSSSC(P) Rules
94 ss46 and 49 SS(S)A 2018 (for SCP, Sch para 19 and 22 SCP Regs) let the First-tier Tribunal determine your entitlement, even though there has been another determination since you appealed
95 s8 SS(A)(S)A 2025
96 rr23-27 FTTSSSC(P) Rules
97 s49 SS(S)A 2018; Sch para 22 SCP Regs; reg 4 FTTS(AFSSC) Regs
98 r19 FTTSSSC(P) Rules; see also socialsecuritychamber.scot/home/chamber-hearings
99 FTTSSSC(P) Rules contain no equivalent of r25 TP(FT) Rules
100 Regs 2-4A of The First-tier Tribunal for Scotland Social Security Chamber and Upper Tribunal for Scotland (Composition) Regulations 2018 No.351
101 r10 FTTSSSC(P) Rules
102 r26(5) FTTSSSC(P) Rules
103 r5 FTTSSSC(P) Rules – this is technically a request for another order
104 *NB v SSS* [2023] UT 35
105 *SSS v AH, AS, SS and GA* [2024] UT 63
106 s2 SS(S)A 2018
107 *CD v SSS* [2024] UT 12
108 s1 SS(S)A 2018
109 **SCP** Sch para 22 SCP Regs
**Other benefits** s49 SS(S)A 2018
110 r28 FTTSSSC(P) Rules
111 r28(3)(b) FTTSSSC(P) Rules
112 r28(3)(c) FTTSSSC(P) Rules
113 If you later apply for permission to appeal, that is not treated as a request for full reasons, as there is no equivalent of r38(7) TP(FT) Rules in the FTTSSSC(P) Rules
114 r29 FTTSSSC(P) Rules; reg 2 ST(TL) Regs
115 r4(3)(a) FTTSSSC(P) Rules
116 rr28 and 29(3) FTTSSSC(P) Rules – r1(2) of the Rules applies only to decisions sent to you by post or email
117 *Garrett v Your Place Property Management Limited* [2020] UT 34; *Advocate General for Scotland v A Decision of The Upper Tribunal, Re Assessments to Tax Made on Murray Group Holdings Ltd & Ors* [2015] ScotCS CSIH 77
118 r4(3)(a) FTTSSSC(P) Rules
119 r32 FTTSSSC(P) Rules
120 r4(1)(l) FTTSSSC(P) Rules
121 r35(2) FTTSSSC(P) Rules
122 r36(1) FTTSSSC(P) Rules
123 r36 FTTSSSC(P) Rules
124 r35(8) FTTSSSC(P) Rules
125 ss44(1)(a), 51 and 52 T(S)A 2014
126 r33(3) FTTSSSC(P) Rules. If necessary, you can argue that *Aberdeen CC v LS* [2021] UT 1 suggests that the review process should not cause a delay that means you lose the right to challenge the decision. However, it is better to request permission to appeal within the time limit if you can.
127 r35(3) FTTSSSC(P) Rules
128 r35(4) FTTSSSC(P) Rules
129 r35(5) FTTSSSC(P) Rules
130 r35(6) FTTSSSC(P) Rules
131 s43(2)(a) T(S)A 2014
132 r35(7) FTTSSSC(P) Rules
133 s44 T(S)A 2014
134 s45 T(S)A 2014
135 ss45(2)(b) and 52 T(S)A 2014
136 r29(5) FTTSSSC(P) Rules

5. **Appeals to the Upper Tribunal for Scotland and the Court of Session**

137 rr33 and 34 FTTSSSC(P) Rules; rr3 and 4 UTS(SSRP) Rules
138 rr33 and 34 FTTSSSC(P) Rules
139 s43(2)(a) T(S)A 2014
140 There is no equivalent of r38(7) TP(FT) Rules in the FTTSSSC(P) Rules
141 Reg 2 ST(TL) Regs
142 While this is unlikely in practice, if it does happen and you requested a statement of reasons more than 14 days after the hearing, make sure that you request permission to appeal within 30 days, even if you do not have the statement of reasons yet
143 r33(3) FTTSSSC(P) Rules
144 r33(3)(b) FTTSSSC(P) Rules
145 As your application has not been admitted, it appears that you will not be given the 'notice of refusal of permission to appeal' that you need to apply to the Upper Tribunal (see r3(1) and (3)(c) UTS(SSRP) Rules, which is worded differently to r21(2) TP(UT) Rules)
146 rr1 and 4 UTS(SSRP) Rules
147 r4(3) and (5) UTS(SSRP) Rules
148 r3 UTS(SSRP) Rules
149 Reg 3 ST(TL) Regs
150 Reg 3(3) ST(TL) Regs
151 r3(4) UTS(SSRP) Rules
152 s55(2) T(S)A 2014
153 rr1(2) and 3(6) and (7) UTS(SSRP) Rules
154 r3(8) UTS(SSRP) Rules
155 rr5-21 UTS(SSRP) Rules
156 rr1(2), 5(2) and 6(2) UTS(SSRP) Rules
157 r11 UTS(SSRP) Rules. While you must have good reason 'to apply for reinstatement', rather than for your failure to comply with an order, the intention appears to be the same.
158 r20 UTS(SSRP) Rules
159 s67 T(S)A 2014; ST(ORP) Regs
160 rr8(3)(c) and 9(5) UTS(SSRP) Rules
161 rr22-26 UTS(SSRP) Rules
162 s47 T(S)A 2014; r27 UTS(SSRP) Rules
163 r28(2) UTS(SSRP) Rules
164 s44(1) and (4) T(S)A 2014; r28(4) and (5) UTS(SSRP) Rules
165 s44(5) T(S)A 2014
166 ss48 and 52 T(S)A 2014 – s52 only excludes a review decision from having a right of appeal, not the original decision, if it was not set aside
167 rr1(1) and 28(6) UTS(SSRP) Rules
168 ss48 and 50 T(S)A 2014
169 ss48-55 T(S)A 2014; rr29-31 UTS(SSRP) Rules
170 Reg 2 ST(TL) Regs
171 r30(2)(c) UTS(SSRP) Rules

6. **Short-term assistance**

172 s36 and Sch 10 SS(S)A 2018
173 See *Scottish Government Response to SCoSS Scrutiny Report on Disability Assistance for Older People (Scotland) Regulations (2024)*
174 s70(2) SSCBA 1992 requires that a qualifying benefit is 'payable' to you for someone who cares for you to get CA (or the UC carer element – reg 30(1)(a) UC regs); while reg 5(1) CA(CSP)(S) Regs and reg 6(1) CA(YCG)(S) Regs require a disability benefit is 'normally payable' for CSP and YCG. Sch para 4 DACYP(S) Regs, Sch 2 para 4 DAWAP(S) Regs, Sch 1 para 4 DA(SADLA) Regs and Sch para 4 DAOP(S) Regs appear to prevent payment of the ADP/CDP/SADLA component or PADP if the short-term assistance award for the period was the same amount.
175 **ADP** Sch 2 para 1(1) DAWAP(S) Regs
**CDP** Sch para 1(1) DACYP(S) Regs
**PADP** Sch para 1(1) DAOP(S) Regs
**SADLA** Sch 1 para 1(1) DA(SADLA) Regs
176 **ADP** Sch 2 para 1(1)(c) and (2) DAWAP(S) Regs
**CDP** Sch para 1(1)(c) and (1A) DACYP(S) Regs
**PADP** Sch para 1(1)(c) and (2) DAOP(S) Regs
**SADLA** Sch 1 para 1(1)(c) and (2) DA(SADLA) Regs
**All** Sch 10 para 1(2) SS(S)A 2018
177 **ADP** Sch 2 para 1(1)(d) and (5) DAWAP(S) Regs
**CDP** Sch para 1(1)(d) and (2) DACYP(S) Regs
**PADP** Sch para 1(1)(d) and (5) DAOP(S) Regs
**SADLA** Sch 1 para 1(1)(d) and (5) DA(SADLA) Regs
178 **ADP** Sch 2 para 1(6) DAWP(S) Regs
**CDP** Sch para 1(3) DACYP(S) Regs
**PADP** Sch para 1(6) DAOP(S) Regs
**SADLA** Sch 1 para 1(6) DA(SADLA) Regs
179 Sch 10 para 1(1)(a) SS(S)A 2018
180 **ADP** Sch 2 para 2(1) DAWAP(S) Regs
**CDP** Sch para 2(1) DACYP(S) Regs
**PADP** Sch para 2(1) DAOP(S) Regs
**SADLA** Sch 1 para 2(1) DA(SADLA) Regs

181 s38(1) and (2) SS(S)A 2018; mygov.scot/short-term-assistance/apply-short-term-assistance
182 **ADP** Sch 2 para 1(3) and (4) DAWAP(S) Regs
**CDP** Sch para 1(1B) and (1C) DACYP(S) Regs
**PADP** Sch paras 1(3) and (4) DAOP(S) Regs
**SADLA** Sch 1 para 1(3) and (4) DA(SADLA) Regs
183 **ADP** Sch 2 para 1(7) DAWAP(S) Regs
**CDP** Sch para 1(4) DACYP(S) Regs
**PADP** Sch para 1(7) DAOP(S) Regs
**SADLA** Sch 1 para 1(7) DA(SADLA) Regs
184 s10 SS(A)(S)A 2025 may require changes to the relevant rules when it comes into force
185 **ADP** Sch 2 para 3 DAWAP(S) Regs
**CDP** Sch para 3 DACYP(S) Regs
**PADP** Sch para 3 DAOP(S) Regs
**SADLA** Sch 1 para 3 DA(SADLA) Regs
**All** Sch 10 para 1(2)(a) SS(S)A 2018
186 See, for example, SSS DMG: *Short-term assistance for adult disability payment*. It appears that the legal basis for this guidance is that if you had not fraudulently claimed, you would not be eligible for short-term assistance later, and so in this situation, short-term assistance has been paid 'in error' – see s63 SS(S)A 2018
187 s677(1) IT(EP)A 2003
188 **ADP** Sch 2 para 4 DAWAP(S) Regs
**CDP** Sch para 4 DACYP(S) Regs
**PADP** Sch para 4 DAOP(S) Regs
**SADLA** Sch 1 para 4 DA(SADLA) Regs

7. **Appealing about process decisions**
189 **SCP** Sch paras 1(4), 14(5) and 15 SCP Regs
**Other benefits** ss38(5), 41(6) and 42 SS(S)A 2018
190 **SCP** Sch para 23 SCP Regs
**Other benefits** s61 SS(S)A 2018
191 r22(2) FTTSSSC(P) Rules
192 r22(4) FTTSSSC(P) Rules
193 **SCP** Sch para 23(2)(a) SCP Regs
**Other benefits** s61(2)(a) SS(S)A 2018
194 **SCP** Sch para 24 SCP Regs – although note that this does not apply if your claim was not accepted
**Other benefits** s62 SS(S)A 2018
195 **SCP** Sch para 23(2)(c) SCP Regs
**Other benefits** s61(2)(c) SS(S)A 2018
196 **SCP** Sch para 23(2)(b) and (3) SCP Regs
**Other benefits** s61(2)(b) and (3) SS(S)A 2018
197 s5(6) SS(A)(S)A 2025
198 r21 FTTSSSC(P) Rules only applies to appeals against a determination of entitlement
199 s10(4) SS(A)(S)A 2025
200 **SCP** Sch para 23(4) and (5) SCP Regs
**Other benefits** s61(4) and (5) SS(S)A 2018

# Appendices

# Appendix 1

# Information and advice

## Independent advice and representation

If you want advice or information on a benefit or tax credit issue, the following may be able to assist.

- Advicelocal (advicelocal.uk) has details of advice organisations in your area.
- Citizens Advice. You can find out where your local office is from the Citizens Advice website at citizensadvice.org.uk (England and Wales) or cas.org.uk (Scotland).
- Law centres. You can find your nearest law centre at lawcentres.org.uk or mygov.scot/legal-advice.
- LawWorks (lawworks.org.uk) has details of local legal advice centres that give free advice.
- Housing association welfare rights services for tenants.
- Local authority welfare rights services.
- Local and national organisations for particular groups of claimants may offer help. For instance, there are unemployed centres, pensioners' groups and organisations for people with disabilities.

## Advice from CPAG

CPAG is unable to deal with enquiries directly from members of the public, but if you are an adviser you can phone or email for help with advising your client.

Advisers in England, Wales and Northern Ireland can call from 10am to 12pm and from 2pm to 4pm (Monday to Friday) on 020 7812 5231. Email advice is limited to enquiries that are specifically about universal credit, child benefit and tax credits. Our email address is advice@cpag.org.uk.

Advisers in Scotland can call from 10am to 4pm (Monday to Thursday) and from 10am to 12pm (Friday) on 0141 552 0552, or email advice@cpagscotland.org.uk. The Scotland service covers all benefits.

For more information on CPAG's advice service, see cpag.org.uk/advisers.

CPAG's Upper Tribunal assistance project can provide help to advisers in England and Wales helping claimants challenge tribunal decisions. See cpag.org.uk/upper-tribunal-assistance-project. We also provide training and advice to support advisers to pursue judicial review remedies. See cpag.org.uk/jrproject.

CPAG takes on a small number of test cases each year. We focus on cases that have the potential to improve the lives of families with children in poverty. If you are an adviser and would like to refer a test case to us, see cpag.org.uk/refer-test-case.

## Finding help online

You can find information about benefits, including a selection of leaflets and forms, on the gov.uk and mygov.scot websites.

CPAG Welfare Rights is a dedicated site for advisers and frontline workers: see cpag.org.uk/welfare-rights for the online version of this *Handbook* and others, updated throughout the year, plus articles, factsheets, eLearning, updates on our legal test cases, and tools to produce tailored letters and appeal submissions.

The rightsnet website (aimed at advisers) at rightsnet.org.uk provides information on new welfare rights legislation, caselaw and guidance. It also gives updates on developments in other areas of social welfare law and has a discussion forum where advisers can discuss particular cases.

## Social security legal resources

You can find most Acts and regulations at legislation.gov.uk. Search for legislation by name or statutory instrument (SI) number and select 'Latest available (Revised)', as social security legislation is regularly updated.

### Caselaw

You can find **Upper Tribunal** decisions at:

- gov.uk/administrative-appeals-tribunal-decisions (for decisions from 2016 onwards);
- administrativeappeals.decisions.tribunals.gov.uk (for pre-2016 decisions);
- scotcourts.gov.uk/judgments (for decisions from 2017 onwards);
- scotcourts.gov.uk/judgments/judgments-archive (for pre-2017 decisions).

To find **Court of Appeal** (CA) and **Supreme Court** (SC) decisions, go to bailii.org/form/search_multidatabase.html and limit your search results to decisions by the SC and CA. You can also find SC decisions at supremecourt.uk/cases.

Through **rightsnet**, you can search for recent caselaw (subscription needed). At rightsnet.org.uk/search, in the 'Where' dropdown menu select 'Welfare rights caselaw' then search using keywords. Its archive at rightsnet.org.uk/resources/case-law-archive has free-to-view older caselaw, including commissioners' decisions dating from the late 1940s onwards and some Upper Tribunal decision which are not published elsewhere.

For **more caselaw on disability benefits and universal credits**, see the following websites.

- wcainfo.net
- pipinfo.net
- disabilityrightsuk.org/case-law
- universalcreditinfo.net.

# Appendix 2

# Useful publications

## 1. Caselaw and legislation

*The Law Relating to Social Security*
All the legislation but without any commentary is available at legislation.gov.uk.

*Sweet & Maxwell's Social Security Legislation* (with commentary):
Volume I: Non-Means-Tested Benefits
Volume II: Universal Credit, State Pension Credit and the Social Fund
Volume III: Administration, Adjudication and the European Dimension
Volume IV: HMRC-administered Social Security Benefits and Scotland

*CPAG's Housing Benefit and Council Tax Reduction Legislation.* Legislation with commentary.

*CPAG's Child Support: the legislation.* Legislation with commentary.

## 2. Official guidance

*Advice for Decision Making: staff guide* (for universal credit, personal independence payment, new-style employment and support allowance and new-style jobseeker's allowance)
gov.uk/government/publications/advice-for-decision-making-staff-guide

A

*Decision Makers' Guide: staff guide* (for all other benefits)
gov.uk/government/collections/decision-makers-guide-staff-guide

*Universal Credit Guidance* (from DWP, links updated when new guidance released)
rightsnet.org.uk/resources/universal-credit-guidance

*Housing Benefit Guidance Manual*
gov.uk/government/collections/housing-benefit-claims-processing-and-good-practice-for-local-authority-staff

*Discretionary Housing Payments Guidance Manual*
gov.uk/government/publications/discretionary-housing-payments-guidance-manual

*Healthcare professionals: information from DWP*
gov.uk/government/collections/healthcare-practitioners-guidance-and-information-from-dwp

*Work Capability Assessment (WCA) Handbook: for healthcare professionals*
gov.uk/government/publications/work-capability-assessment-handbook-for-healthcare-professionals

*Child Benefit Technical Manual*

gov.uk/hmrc-internal-manuals/child-benefit-technical-manual

*Tax Credits Technical Manual*
hmrc.gov.uk/manuals/tctmanual

*Budgeting Loan Guide*
gov.uk/government/publications/budgeting-loan-guide-for-decision-makers-reviewing-officers-and-further-reviewing-officers

*Personal Independence Payment (PIP) Assessment Guide for Assessment Providers*
gov.uk/government/publications/personal-independence-payment-assessment-guide-for-assessment-providers

*Benefit overpayment recovery guide*
gov.uk/government/publications/benefit-overpayment-recovery-staff-guide/benefit-overpayment-recovery-guide

*Suspension and termination of benefits: staff guide*
gov.uk/government/publications/suspension-and-termination-of-benefits-staff-guide

## 3. Leaflets

The DWP publishes many leaflets, available free from your local DWP or Jobcentre Plus office. To order DWP leaflets, download the order form at gov.uk/government/publications/dwp-leaflets-order-form then email your completed form to dwp@hhglobal.com or fax it to 0300 373 0125. Your local council will have leaflets on housing benefit.

## 4. Periodicals

*Welfare Rights Bulletin* (CPAG, bi-monthly)
Available in print or online, this covers developments in social security law and updates this *Handbook* between editions. For more information, see cpag.org.uk/subscriptions.

You can also find articles on social security in *Legal Action* (Legal Action Group), *Adviser* (Citizens Advice, available at medium.com/adviser) and the *Journal of Social Security Law* (Sweet & Maxwell).

## 5. Other publications

Online access to the full content of CPAG's *Welfare Benefits Handbook* and *Benefits for Migrants Handbook*, both updated throughout the year. See cpag.org.uk/subscriptions for details.

**Digital+**
CPAG's full digital package, which includes the full content of the *Welfare Benefits Handbook* and the *Benefits for Migrants Handbook* updated throughout the year, the *Welfare Rights Bulletin*, *Poverty* journal and decision-making tools and appeal letter generators. See cpag.org.uk/subscriptions for details.

**CPAG guides**
*Universal Credit: what you need to know*
*Financial Help for Families: what you need to know*
*Personal Independence Payment: what you need to know*
*Winning Your Benefit Appeal: what you need to know*

**Other CPAG handbooks**
*Benefits for Migrants Handbook* (subscription available at CPAG Welfare Rights: see cpag.org.uk/welfare-rights)
*Child Support Handbook*
*Council Tax Handbook*
*Debt Advice Handbook* (available free at CPAG Welfare Rights)
*Debt Advice Scotland Handbook* (available free at CPAG Welfare Rights)
*Fuel Rights Handbook* (available free at CPAG Welfare Rights)
*Mental Health and Benefits Handbook* (available free at CPAG Welfare Rights)
*Benefits for Students in Scotland Handbook* (available free at CPAG Welfare Rights)
*Children's Handbook Scotland* (available free at CPAG Welfare Rights)

**Books from other publishers**

*Disability Rights Handbook,* Disability Rights UK (subscription available at CPAG Welfare Rights)

*Help with Housing Costs: Advising on housing benefit, universal credit and pension credit,* Shelter

*Defending Possession Proceedings: a practitioner's guide,* LAG

*Housing Possession Duty Desk,* LAG

*Employment Law: an adviser's handbook,* LAG

*Housing Conditions,* LAG

*Community Care and the Law,* LAG

*Tribunal Practice and Procedure,* LAG

*Migrant Support,* LAG

*Employment Handbook,* Tolley

*The Guide to Grants for Individuals in Need,* DSC

**CPAG membership**

Being a member gives discounts on CPAG publications, training and events. For more information, see cpag.org.uk/membership.

*Individual membership (print)* includes a subscription to a print version of *Poverty*?journal, published three times per year; 15 per cent discount on books and subscriptions; 20 per cent discount on training and events; and the opportunity to attend and vote at the CPAG AGM.

*Individual membership (online)* includes a subscription to the online version of *Poverty* journal; 15 per cent discount on books and subscriptions; 20 per cent discount on training and events; and the opportunity to attend and vote at the CPAG AGM.

*Organisational membership* is offered for small organisations (up to 10 named members of staff) and large organisations (up to 30 named members of staff). It includes one subscription to the print version of *Poverty* journal; access for up to 10 /30 named members of staff to the online version of *Poverty* journal; 15 per cent discount on books and subscriptions (for up to 10/30 named members of staff); 20 per cent discount on training and events (for up to 10/30 named members of staff); and the opportunity to attend and vote at the CPAG AGM (one representative per organisation).

**For CPAG publications and most of those in Sections 1 and 5 contact:**

CPAG, 30 Micawber Street, London N1 7TB (tel: 020 7837 7979, email: bookorders@cpag.org.uk). Order from cpag.org.uk/shop.

# Appendix 3

# Disability which puts a person at a disadvantage in getting a job

## Schedule 1 Regulation 9(1) to the Working Tax Credit (Entitlement and Maximum Rate) Regulations 2002 No.2005

### PART 1

1. When standing he cannot keep his balance unless he continually holds onto something.

2. Using any crutches, walking frame, walking stick, prosthesis or similar walking aid which he habitually uses, he cannot walk a continuous distance of 100 metres along level ground without stopping or without suffering severe pain.

3. He can use neither of his hands behind his back as in the process of putting on a jacket or of tucking a shirt into trousers.

4. He can extend neither of his arms in front of him so as to shake hands with another person without difficulty.

5. He can put neither of his hands up to his head without difficulty so as to put on a hat.

6. Due to lack of manual dexterity he cannot, with one hand, pick up a coin which is not more than 2½ centimetres in diameter.

7. He is not able to use his hands or arms to pick up a full jug of 1 litre capacity and pour from it into a cup, without difficulty.

8. He can turn neither of his hands sideways through 180 degrees.

9. He is certified as severely sight impaired or blind by a consultant ophthalmologist.

10. He cannot see to read 16 point print at a distance greater than 20 centimetres, if appropriate, wearing the glasses he normally uses.

**11.** He cannot hear a telephone ring when he is in the same room as the telephone, if appropriate, using a hearing aid he normally uses.

**12.** In a quiet room he has difficulty in hearing what someone talking in a loud voice at a distance of 2 metres says, if appropriate, using a hearing aid he normally uses.

**13.** People who know him well have difficulty in understanding what he says.

**14.** When a person he knows well speaks to him, he has difficulty in understanding what that person says.

**15.** At least once a year during waking hours he is in a coma or has a fit in which he loses consciousness.

**16.** He has a mental illness for which he receives regular treatment under the supervision of a medically qualified person.

**17.** Due to mental disability he is often confused or forgetful.

**18.** He cannot do the simplest addition and subtraction.

**19.** Due to mental disability he strikes people or damages property or is unable to form normal social relationships.

**20.** He cannot normally sustain an eight hour working day or a five day working week due to a medical condition or intermittent or continuous severe pain.

PART 2 (INITIAL CLAIMS ONLY)

**21.** As a result of an illness or accident he is undergoing a period of habilitation or rehabilitation.

# Appendix 4

# Prescribed degrees of disablement

## Schedule 2 to the Social Security (General Benefit) Regulations 1982 No.1408

| *Description of injury* | *Degree of disablement %* |
|---|---|
| 1 Loss of both hands or amputation at higher sites | 100 |
| 2 Loss of a hand and a foot | 100 |
| 3 Double amputation through leg or thigh, or amputation through leg or thigh on one side and loss of other foot | 100 |
| 4 Loss of sight to such an extent as to render the claimant unable to perform any work for which eyesight is essential | 100 |
| 5 Very severe facial disfiguration | 100 |
| 6 Absolute deafness | 100 |
| 7 Forequarter or hindquarter amputation | 100 |
| **Amputation cases – upper limbs (either arm)** | |
| 8 Amputation through shoulder joint | 90 |
| 9 Amputation below shoulder with stump less than 20.5 cm from tip of acromion | 80 |
| 10 Amputation from 20.5 cm from tip of acromion to less than 11.5 cm below tip of olecranon | 70 |
| 11 Loss of a hand or of the thumb and 4 fingers of 1 hand or amputation from 11.5 cm below tip of olecranon | 60 |
| 12 Loss of thumb | 30 |
| 13 Loss of thumb and its metacarpal bone | 40 |

A

| | |
|---|---|
| 14 Loss of 4 fingers of 1 hand | 50 |
| 15 Loss of 3 fingers of 1 hand | 30 |
| 16 Loss of 2 fingers of 1 hand | 20 |
| 17 Loss of terminal phalanx of thumb | 20 |
| **Amputation cases – lower limbs** | |
| 18 Amputation of both feet resulting in end-bearing stumps | 90 |
| 19 Amputation through both feet proximal to the metatarso-phalangeal joint | 80 |
| 20 Loss of all toes to both feet through the metatarso-phalangeal joint | 40 |
| 21 Loss of all toes of both feet proximal to the proximal inter-phalangeal joint | 30 |
| 22 Loss of all toes of both feet distal to the proximal inter-phalangeal joint | 20 |
| 23 Amputation at hip | 90 |
| 24 Amputation below hip with stump not exceeding 13 cm in length measured from tip of great trochanter | 80 |
| 25 Amputation below hip and above knee with stump exceeding 13 cm in length measured from tip of great trochanter, or at knee not resulting in end-bearing stump | 70 |
| 26 Amputation at knee resulting in end-bearing stump or below knee with stump not exceeding 9 cm | 60 |
| 27 Amputation below knee with stump exceeding 9 cm but not exceeding 13 cm | 50 |
| 28 Amputation below knee with stump exceeding 13 cm | 40 |
| 29 Amputation of 1 foot resulting in end-bearing stump | 30 |
| 30 Amputation through 1 foot proximal to the metatarso-phalangeal joint | 30 |
| 31 Loss of all toes of 1 foot through the metatarso-phalangeal joint | 20 |
| **Other injuries** | |
| 32 Loss of 1 eye, without complications, the other being normal | 40 |
| 33 Loss of vision of 1 eye, without complications or disfigurement of the eyeball, the other being normal | 30 |
| **Loss of fingers of right or left hand** | |
| *Index finger:* | |
| 34 Whole | 14 |
| 35 2 phalanges | 11 |

| | |
|---|---|
| 36 1 phalanx | 9 |
| 37 Guillotine amputation of tip without loss of bone | 5 |
| *Middle finger:* | |
| 38 Whole | 12 |
| 39 2 phalanges | 9 |
| 40 1 phalanx | 7 |
| 41 Guillotine amputation of tip without loss of bone | 4 |
| *Ring or little finger:* | |
| 42 Whole | 7 |
| 43 2 phalanges | 6 |
| 44 1 phalanx | 5 |
| 45 Guillotine amputation of tip without loss of bone | 2 |
| **Loss of toes of right or left foot** | |
| *Great toe:* | |
| 46 Through metatarso-phalangeal joint | 14 |
| 47 Part, with some loss of bone | 3 |
| *Any other toe:* | |
| 48 Through metatarso-phalangeal joint | 3 |
| 49 Part, with some loss of bone | 1 |
| *2 toes of 1 foot, excluding great toe:* | |
| 50 Through metatarso-phalangeal joint | 5 |
| 51 Part, with some loss of bone | 2 |
| *3 toes of 1 foot, excluding great toe:* | |
| 52 Through metatarso-phalangeal joint | 6 |
| 53 Part, with some loss of bone | 3 |
| *4 toes of 1 foot, excluding great toe:* | |
| 54 Through metatarso-phalangeal joint | 9 |
| 55 Part, with some loss of bone | 3 |

The degree of disablement due to occupational deafness is assessed using tables and a formula to be found in reg 34 and Sch 3 Social Security (Industrial Injuries) (Prescribed Diseases) Regulations 1985, as amended.

# Appendix 5

# Upper and lower earnings limits

| *Year* | *Lower earnings limit £* | *Primary threshold £* | *Upper earnings limit £* |
|---|---|---|---|
| 1992/93 | 54 | | 405 |
| 1993/94 | 56 | | 420 |
| 1994/95 | 57 | | 430 |
| 1995/96 | 58 | | 440 |
| 1996/97 | 61 | | 455 |
| 1997/98 | 62 | | 465 |
| 1998/99 | 64 | | 485 |
| 1999/00 | 66 | | 500 |
| 2000/01 | 67 | 76 | 535 |
| 2001/02 | 72 | 87 | 575 |
| 2002/03 | 75 | 89 | 585 |
| 2003/04 | 77 | 89 | 595 |
| 2004/05 | 79 | 91 | 610 |
| 2005/06 | 82 | 94 | 630 |
| 2006/07 | 84 | 97 | 645 |
| 2007/08 | 87 | 100 | 670 |
| 2008/09 | 90 | 105 | 770 |
| 2009/10 | 95 | 110 | 844 |
| 2010/11 | 97 | 110 | 844 |
| 2011/12 | 102 | 139 | 817 |
| 2012/13 | 107 | 146 | 817 |
| 2013/14 | 109 | 149 | 797 |
| 2014/15 | 111 | 153 | 805 |
| 2015/16 | 112 | 155 | 815 |
| 2016/17 | 112 | 155 | 827 |
| 2017/18 | 113 | 157 | 866 |
| 2018/19 | 116 | 162 | 892 |
| 2019/20 | 118 | 166 | 962 |
| 2020/21 | 120 | 183 | 962 |
| 2021/22 | 120 | 184 | 967 |
| 2022/23 | 123 | 190 (242 from July 2022) | 967 |
| 2023/24 | 123 | 242 | 967 |
| 2024/25 | 123 | 242 | 967 |
| 2025/26 | 125 | 242 | 967 |

# Appendix 6

# Minimum working conditions

Employers are required to provide certain minimum working conditions. These rules are relevant to the universal credit and jobseeker's allowance rules about sanctions and being available for and looking for work. A brief summary of the rules follows.

## The Working Time Regulations 1998 No.1833

These regulations are designed to protect the health and safety of workers. The main rules are:

- a limit on the hours in the average working week;
- minimum annual holiday entitlement;
- entitlement to breaks from work (both daily breaks and a longer break once a week) and to rest periods while at work;
- special protection for night workers.

This *Handbook* cannot cover the detailed rules nor the complicated system of exceptions to them. Get specialist advice if you think your employer is breaking these rules.

## The National Minimum Wage Act 1998

This Act provides that the minimum hourly rate of pay in any job should be:

- if you are aged 21 or over, £12.21. The government calls this the 'national living wage';
- if you are aged 18–20, £10.00;
- if you are aged 16 or 17, £7.55;
- if you are in the first year of employment or are under 19, and you are employed under a contract of apprenticeship (or treated as if you are), £7.55.

# Appendix 7

# Abbreviations used in the notes

| | |
|---|---|
| AAC | Administrative Appeals Chamber |
| AACR | Administrative Appeals Chamber Reports |
| AC | Appeal Cases |
| Admin | Administrative Court |
| ADP | Adult disability payment |
| All ER | All England Law Reports |
| App | Appendix |
| Art(s) | Article(s) |
| BC | Borough Council |
| BSG | Best Start grant |
| CA | Court of Appeal |
| CAS | carer's allowance supplement |
| CC | County Council |
| CCLR | Community Care Law Reports |
| CDP | child disability payment |
| Ch | chapter |
| CJEU | Court of Justice of the European Union |
| CLY | Current Law Year Book |
| col | column |
| CPR | Civil Procedure Rules |
| CS | Court of Session |
| CSIH | Court of Session, Inner House |
| CSOH | Court of Session, Outer House |
| CSP | carer support payment |
| CWHP | child winter heating payment |
| DC | Divisional Court |
| DHP | discretionary housing payment |
| Dir | Directive |
| E | England |
| EEA | European Economic Area |
| EU | European Union |
| EWCA Civ | England and Wales Court of Appeal (Civil Division) |
| EWCA Crim | England and Wales Court of Appeal (Criminal Division) |
| EWHC | England and Wales High Court |
| FLR | Family Law Reports |
| FSP | funeral support payment |
| HC | High Court |
| HL | House of Lords |
| HLR | Housing Law Reports |
| IAC | Immigration and Asylum Chamber |
| ICR | Industrial Cases Reports |
| IR | Immigration Rules |
| JPR | Justice of the Peace Reports |
| KB | King's Bench |
| LB | London Borough |
| LC | Lands Chamber |
| MBC | Metropolitan Borough Council |

| | |
|---|---|
| NICA | Northern Ireland Court of Appeal |
| NICom | Northern Ireland Social Security Commissioner |
| OJ | Official Journal of the European Union |
| para(s) | paragraph(s) |
| QB | Queen's Bench Reports |
| QBD | Queen's Bench Division |
| r(r) | rule(s) |
| Reg(s) | Regulation(s) |
| s(s) | section(s) |
| SC | Supreme Court |
| Sch(s) | Schedule(s) |
| SCLR | Scottish Civil Law Reports |
| ScotCS | Scottish Court of Session |
| SCP | Scottish child payment |
| SDHP | Scottish discretionary housing payment |
| SLT | Scots Law Times |
| SSAC | Social Security Advisory Committee |
| SSWP | Secretary of State for Work and Pensions |
| TCC | Tax and Chancery Chamber |
| UKHL | United Kingdom House of Lords |
| UKSC | United Kingdom Supreme Court |
| UKUT | United Kingdom Upper Tribunal |
| UT | Upper Tribunal for Scotland |
| Vol | volume |
| W | Wales |
| WHP | winter heating payment |
| WLR | Weekly Law Reports |
| YCG | young carer grant |

## Acts of Parliament

| | |
|---|---|
| C(LC)A 2000 | Children (Leaving Care) Act 2000 |
| CJPOA 1994 | Criminal Justice and Public Order Act 1994 |
| CMOPA 2008 | Child Maintenance and Other Payments Act 2008 |
| CSPSSA 2000 | Child Support, Pensions and Social Security Act 2000 |
| ETA 1973 | Employment and Training Act 1973 |
| EU(W)A 2018 | European Union (Withdrawal) Act 2018 |
| GRA 2004 | Gender Recognition Act 2004 |
| HRA 1998 | Human Rights Act 1998 |
| IA 1971 | Immigration Act 1971 |
| IA 1988 | Immigration Act 1988 |
| IAA 1999 | Immigration and Asylum Act 1999 |
| IT(EP)A 2003 | Income Tax (Earnings and Pensions) Act 2003 |
| JSA 1995 | Jobseekers Act 1995 |
| LGFA 1992 | Local Government Finance Act 1992 |
| M(SSC)A 2013 | Marriage (Same Sex Couples) Act 2013 |
| MCA 1973 | Matrimonial Causes Act 1973 |
| NHSA 2006 | National Health Service Act 2006 |
| NHS(S)A 1978 | National Health Service (Scotland) Act 1978 |
| NHS(W)A 2006 | National Health Service (Wales) Act 2006 |
| NIAA 2002 | Nationality, Immigration and Asylum Act 2002 |

| | |
|---|---|
| PA 1995 | Pensions Act 1995 |
| PA 2014 | Pensions Act 2014 |
| PACEA 1984 | Police and Criminal Evidence Act 1984 |
| SA 2016 | Scotland Act 2016 |
| SPCA 2002 | State Pension Credit Act 2002 |
| SS(AP)A 2023 | Social Security (Additional Payments) Act 2023 |
| SS(RB)A 1997 | Social Security (Recovery of Benefits) Act 1997 |
| SS(A)(S)A 2025 | Social Security (Amendment) (Scotland) Act 2025 |
| SS(AP)A 2023 | Social Security (Additional Payments) Act 2023 |
| SS(S)A 2018 | Social Security (Scotland) Act 2018 |
| SSA 1998 | Social Security Act 1998 |
| SSA(F)A 1997 | Social Security Administration (Fraud) Act 1997 |
| SSAA 1992 | Social Security Administration Act 1992 |
| SSC(TF)A 1999 | Social Security Contributions (Transfer of Functions etc) Act 1999 |
| SSCBA 1992 | Social Security Contributions and Benefits Act 1992 |
| SSFA 2001 | Social Security Fraud Act 2001 |
| T(S)A 2014 | Tribunals (Scotland) Act 2014 |
| TCA 2002 | Tax Credits Act 2002 |
| TCEA 2007 | Tribunals, Courts and Enforcement Act 2007 |
| TMA 1970 | Taxes Management Act 1970 |
| WRA 2007 | Welfare Reform Act 2007 |
| WRA 2012 | Welfare Reform Act 2012 |
| WRWA 2016 | Welfare Reform and Work Act 2016 |

## Regulations and other statutory instruments

Each set of regulations has a statutory instrument (SI) number and a date. You can find them all at legislation.gov.uk.

| | |
|---|---|
| A(IWA) Regs | The Accession (Immigration and Worker Authorisation) Regulations 2006 No.3317 |
| A(IWR) Regs | The Accession (Immigration and Worker Registration) Regulations 2004 No.1219 |
| AC(IWA) Regs | The Accession of Croatia (Immigration and Worker Authorisation) Regulations 2013 No.1460 |
| ASPP(G) Regs | The Additional Statutory Paternity Pay (General) Regulations 2010 No.1056 |
| BB(R)O | The Bereavement Benefits (Remedial) Order 2023 No.134 |
| BSP Regs | The Bereavement Support Payment Regulations 2017 No.410 |

A

| | |
|---|---|
| C(LC)SSB(S) Regs | The Children (Leaving Care) Social Security Benefits (Scotland) Regulations 2004 No.747 |
| C(LC)(W) Regs | The Children (Leaving Care) (Wales) Regulations 2001 No.2189 |
| CA(CSP)(S) Regs | The Carer's Assistance (Carer Support Payment) (Scotland) Regulations 2023 No.302 |
| CA(YCG)(S) Regs | The Carer's Assistance (Young Carer Grants) (Scotland) Regulations 2019 No.324 |
| CA(YCGCSP)(MA) Regs | The Carer's Assistance (Young Carer Grant and Carer Support Payment) (Miscellaneous Amendment and Saving Provision) (Scotland) Regulations 2025 (draft) |
| CASYCG(RRPP) Regs | The Carer's Allowance Supplement and Young Carer Grants (Residence Requirements and Procedural Provisions) (EU Exit) (Scotland) Regulations 2020 No.475 |
| CB Regs | The Child Benefit (General) Regulations 2006 No.223 |
| CB(R) Regs | The Child Benefit (Rates) Regulations 2006 No.965 |
| CB&GA(AA) Regs | The Child Benefit and Guardian's Allowance (Administrative Arrangements) Regulations 2003 No.494 |
| CB&GA(Admin) Regs | The Child Benefit and Guardian's Allowance (Administration) Regulations 2003 No.492 |
| CB&GA(DA) Regs | The Child Benefit and Guardian's Allowance (Decisions and Appeals) Regulations 2003 No.916 |
| CC(DIS) Regs | The Community Charges (Deductions from Income Support) (No.2) Regulations 1990 No.545 |
| CL(E) Regs | The Care Leavers (England) Regulations 2010 No.2571 |
| CR(ADTP) Regs | The Citizens' Rights (Application Deadline and Temporary Protection) (EU Exit) Regulations 2020 No.1209 |
| CR(FW) Regs | The Citizens' Rights (Frontier Workers) (EU Exit) Regulations 2020 No.1213 |
| CT(DIS) Regs | The Council Tax (Deductions from Income Support) Regulations 1993 No.494 |
| CTC Regs | The Child Tax Credit Regulations 2002 No.2007 |
| CTR(S) Regs | The Council Tax Reduction (Scotland) Regulations 2021 No.249 |
| CTR(SPC)S Regs | The Council Tax Reduction (State Pension Credit) (Scotland) Regulations 2012 No.319 |
| CTRS(DS)E Regs | The Council Tax Reduction Schemes (Default Scheme) (England) Regulations 2012 No.2886 |
| CTRS(DS)W Regs | The Council Tax Reduction Schemes (Default Scheme) (Wales) Regulations 2013 No.3035 |

A

| | |
|---|---|
| CTRS(PR)E Regs | The Council Tax Reduction Schemes (Prescribed Requirements) (England) Regulations 2012 No.2885 |
| CTRSPR(W) Regs | The Council Tax Reduction Schemes and Prescribed Requirements (Wales) Regulations 2013 No.3029 |
| DACYP(S) Regs | The Disability Assistance for Children and Young People (Scotland) Regulations 2021 No.174 |
| DAOP(S) Regs | The Disability Assistance for Older People (Scotland) Regulations 2024 No.166 |
| DA(SADLA) Regs | The Disability Assistance (Scottish Adult Disability Living Allowance) Regulations 2025 No.3 |
| DAWAP(S) Regs | The Disability Assistance for Working Age People (Scotland) Regulations 2022 No.54 |
| DAWAP(TPMA)(S) Regs | The Disability Assistance for Working Age People (Transitional Provisions and Miscellaneous Amendment) (Scotland) Regulations 2022 No.217 |
| DFA Regs | The Discretionary Financial Assistance Regulations 2001 No.1167 |
| ESA Regs | The Employment and Support Allowance Regulations 2008 No.794 |
| ESA Regs 2013 | The Employment and Support Allowance Regulations 2013 No.379 |
| ESA(TP)(EA)(No.2) Regs | The Employment and Support Allowance (Transitional Provisions, Housing Benefit and Council Tax Benefit) (Existing Awards) (No.2) Regulations 2010 No.1907 |
| ESA(WRA) Regs | The Employment and Support Allowance (Work-Related Activity) Regulations 2011 No.1349 |
| ESAUC(MA) Regs | The Employment and Support Allowance and Universal Credit (Miscellaneous Amendments and Transitional and Savings Provisions) Regulations 2017 No.204 |
| EYA(BSG)(S) Regs | The Early Years Assistance (Best Start Grants) (Scotland) Regulations 2018 No.370 |
| F(DIS) Regs | The Fines (Deductions from Income Support) Regulations 1992 No.2182 |
| FEA(S) Regs | The Funeral Expense Assistance (Scotland) Regulations 2019 No.292 |
| FTTS(AFSSC) Regs | The First-tier Tribunal for Scotland (Allocation of Functions to the Social Security Chamber) Regulations 2018 No.350 |
| FTTSSSC(P) Rules | The First-tier Tribunal for Scotland Social Security Chamber (Procedure) Regulations 2018 No.273 |
| FTUT(CS)O | The First-tier Tribunal and Upper Tribunal (Composition of Tribunal) Order 2008 No.2835 |

| | |
|---|---|
| GA(Gen) Regs | The Guardian's Allowance (General) Regulations 2003 No.495 |
| HB Regs | The Housing Benefit Regulations 2006 No.213 |
| HB(SPC) Regs | The Housing Benefit (Persons who have Attained the Qualifying Age for State Pension Credit) Regulations 2006 No.214 |
| HB&CTB(CP) Regs | The Housing Benefit and Council Tax Benefit (Consquential Provisions) Regulations 2006 No.217 |
| HB&CTB(DA) Regs | The Housing Benefit and Council Tax Benefit (Decisions and Appeals) Regulations 2001 No.1002 |
| HB&CTB(WPD) Regs | The Housing Benefit and Council Tax Benefit (War Pension Disregards) Regulations 2007 No.1619 |
| HSS(DHSF)(W) Regs | The Healthy Start Scheme (Description of Healthy Start Food) (Wales) Regulations 2006 No.3108 |
| HSS&WF(A) Regs | The Healthy Start Scheme and Welfare Food (Amendment) Regulations 2005 No.3262 |
| I(EEA) Regs | The Immigration (European Economic Area) Regulations 2016 No.1052 |
| I(EEA) Regs 2006 | The Immigration (European Economic Area) Regulations 2006 No.1003 |
| IIB(ETSC) Regs | The Industrial Injuries Benefit (Employment Training Schemes and Courses) Regulations 2013 No.2540 |
| ILRFO Regs | The Integration Loans for Refugees and Others Regulations 2007 No.1598 |
| IS Regs | The Income Support (General) Regulations 1987 No.1967 |
| ISSC Regs | The Immigration and Social Security Co-ordination (EU Withdrawal) Act 2020 (Consequential, Saving, Transitional and Transitory Provisions) (EU Exit) Regulations 2020 No.1309 |
| JSA Regs | The Jobseeker's Allowance Regulations 1996 No.207 |
| JSA Regs 2013 | The Jobseeker's Allowance Regulations 2013 No.378 |
| JSA(SAPOE) Regs | The Jobseeker's Allowance (Schemes for Assisting Persons to Obtain Employment) Regulations 2013 No.276 |
| LMI Regs | The Loans for Mortgage Interest Regulations 2017 No.725 |
| MA(C) Regs | The Maternity Allowance (Curtailment) Regulations 2014 No.3053 |
| NHS(CDA) Regs | The National Health Service (Charges for Drugs and Appliances) Regulations 2015 No.570 |
| NHS(DC) Regs | The National Health Service (Dental Charges) Regulations 2005 No.3477 |

| | |
|---|---|
| NHS(DC)(S) Regs | The National Health Service (Dental Charges) (Scotland) Regulations 2003 No.158 |
| NHS(DC)(W) Regs | The National Health Service (Dental Charges) (Wales) Regulations 2006 No.491 |
| NHS(FP&CDA)(S) Regs | The National Health Service (Free Prescriptions and Charges for Drugs and Appliances) (Scotland) Regulations 2011 No.55 |
| NHS(FP&CDA)(W) Regs | The National Health Service (Free Prescriptions and Charges for Drugs and Appliances) (Wales) Regulations 2007 No.121 |
| NHS(GOS) Regs | The National Health Service (General Ophthalmic Services) Regulations 1986 No.975 |
| NHS(OCP) Regs | The National Health Service (Optical Charges and Payments) Regulations 1997 No.818 |
| NHS(OCP) Regs 2013 | The National Health Service (Optical Charges and Payments) Regulations 2013 No.461 |
| NHS(OCP)(S) Regs | The National Health Service (Optical Charges and Payments) (Scotland) Regulations 1998 No.642 |
| NHS(TERC) Regs | The National Health Service (Travelling Expenses and Remission of Charges) Regulations 2003 No.2382 |
| NHS(TERC)(S) Regs | The National Health Service (Travelling Expenses and Remission of Charges) (Scotland) (No.2) Regulations 2003 No.460 |
| NHS(TERC)(W) Regs | The National Health Service (Travelling Expenses and Remission of Charges Regulations) (Wales) 2007 No.1104 |
| PIP(TP) Regs | The Personal Independence Payment (Transitional Provisions) Regulations 2013 No.387 |
| POS Regs | The Primary Ophthalmic Services Regulations 2008 No.1186 |
| RO(HBF)O | The Rent Officers (Housing Benefit Functions) Order 1997 No.1984 |
| RO(HBF)(S)O | The Rent Officers (Housing Benefit Functions) (Scotland) Order 1997 No.144 |
| RO(UCF)O | The Rent Officers (Universal Credit Functions) Order 2013 No.382 |
| SA(TFSM)O | The Scotland Act 1998 (Transfer of Functions to the Scottish Ministers etc.) Order 2020 No.276 |
| SCP Regs | The Scottish Child Payment Regulations 2020 No.351 |
| SF(AM) Regs | The Social Fund (Budgeting Loans) (Applications and Miscellaneous Provisions) Regulations 2015 No.1411 |
| SF(AR) Regs | The Social Fund (Application for Review) Regulations 1988 No.34 |

A

| | |
|---|---|
| SF(RDB) Regs | The Social Fund (Recovery by Deductions from Benefits) Regulations 1988 No.35 |
| SFCWP Regs | The Social Fund Cold Weather Payments (General) Regulations 1988 No.1724 |
| SFM&FE Regs | The Social Fund Maternity and Funeral Expenses (General) Regulations 2005 No.3061 |
| SFWFP Regs | The Social Fund Winter Fuel Payment Regulations 2024 No.869 |
| SMP Regs | The Statutory Maternity Pay (General) Regulations 1986 No.1960 |
| SMP(PAM) Regs | The Statutory Maternity Pay (Persons Abroad and Mariners) Regulations 1987 No.418 |
| SMP&SAP(C) Regs | The Statutory Maternity Pay and Statutory Adoption Pay (Curtailment) Regulations 2014 No.3054 |
| SNCP(A) Regs | The Statutory Neonatal Care Pay (Administration) Regulations 2025 No.206 |
| SNCP(G) Regs | The Statutory Neonatal Care Pay (General) Regulations 2025 (draft) |
| SNCP(PAM) Regs | The Statutory Neonatal Care Pay (Persons Abroad and Mariners) Regulations 2025 No.202 |
| SP Regs | The State Pension Regulations 2015 No.173 |
| SPBP(A) Regs | The Statutory Parental Bereavement Pay (Administration) Regulations 2020 No.246 |
| SPBP(G) Regs | The Statutory Parental Bereavement Pay (General) Regulations 2020 No.233 |
| SPBP(PAM) Regs | The Statutory Parental Bereavement Pay (Persons Abroad and Mariners) Regulations 2020 No.252 |
| SPC Regs | The State Pension Credit Regulations 2002 No.1792 |
| SPC(CTMP) Regs | The State Pension Credit (Consequential, Transitional and Miscellaneous Provisions) Regulations 2002 No.3019 |
| SPP(A)&SAP(AO)(No.2) Regs | The Statutory Paternity Pay (Adoption) and Statutory Adoption Pay (Adoptions from Overseas) (No.2) Regulations 2003 No.1192 |
| SPPSAP(A) Regs | The Statutory Paternity Pay and Statutory Adoption Pay (Administration) Regulations 2002 No.2820 |
| SPPSAP(G) Regs | The Statutory Paternity Pay and Statutory Adoption Pay (General) Regulations 2002 No.2822 |
| SPPSAP(PAM) Regs | The Statutory Paternity Pay and Statutory Adoption Pay (Persons Abroad and Mariners) Regulations 2002 No.2821 |

| | |
|---|---|
| SPPSAP(POPA) Regs | The Statutory Paternity Pay and Statutory Adoption Pay (Parental Orders and Prospective Adopters) Regulations 2014 No.2934 |
| SS(AA) Regs | The Social Security (Attendance Allowance) Regulations 1991 No.2740 |
| SS(ASS)(S) Regs | The Social Security (Advocacy Service Standards) (Scotland) Regulations 2020 No.115 |
| SS(CatE) Regs | The Social Security (Categorisation of Earners) Regulations 1978 No.1689 |
| SS(CCPC) Regs | The Social Security (Contribution Credits for Parents and Carers) Regulations 2010 No.19 |
| SS(Con) Regs | The Social Security (Contributions) Regulations 2001 No.1004 |
| SS(C&P) Regs | The Social Security (Claims and Payments) Regulations 1987 No.1968 |
| SS(CP) Regs | The Social Security (Civil Penalties) Regulations 2012 No.1990 |
| SS(CPCTMA)(S) Regs (draft) | The Social Security (Cross-border Provision, Case Transfer and Miscellaneous Amendment) (Scotland) Regulations 2025 (draft and subject to change) |
| SS(Cr) Regs | The Social Security (Credits) Regulations 1975 No.556 |
| SS(CTCNIN) Regs | The Social Security (Crediting and Treatment of Contributions, and National Insurance Numbers) Regulations 2001 No.769 |
| SS(DLA) Regs | The Social Security (Disability Living Allowance) Regulations 1991 No.2890 |
| SS(DLA)A Regs | The Social Security (Disability Living Allowance) (Amendment) Regulations 2010 No.1651 |
| SS(EEEIIP) Regs | The Social Security (Employed Earners' Employment for Industrial Injuries Purposes) Regulations 1975 No.467 |
| SS(GB) Regs | The Social Security (General Benefits) Regulations 1982 No.1408 |
| SS(GBRA)NI Regs | The Social Security (Great Britain Reciprocal Arrangements) Regulations (Northern Ireland) 2016 No.149 |
| SS(HIP) Regs | The Social Security (Hospital In-Patients) Regulations 2005 No.3360 |
| SS(HR)A Regs | The Social Security (Habitual Residence) Amendment Regulations 2004 No.1232 |
| SS(IA)CA Regs | The Social Security (Immigration and Asylum) Consequential Amendments Regulations 2000 No.636 |
| SS(IB) Regs | The Social Security (Incapacity Benefit) Regulations 1994 No.2946 |

| | |
|---|---|
| SS(IB)(T) Regs | The Social Security (Incapacity Benefit) (Transitional) Regulations 1995 No.310 |
| SS(IB-ID) Regs | The Social Security (Incapacity Benefit – Increases for Dependants) Regulations 1994 No.2945 |
| SS(IBWFI) Regs | The Social Security (Incapacity Benefit Work-focused Interviews) Regulations 2008 No.2928 |
| SS(ICA) Regs | The Social Security (Invalid Care Allowance) Regulations 1976 No.409 |
| SS(II)(AB) Regs | The Social Security (Industrial Injuries) (Airmen's Benefits) Regulations 1975 No.469 |
| SS(II)(MB) Regs | The Social Security (Industrial Injuries) (Mariners' Benefits) Regulations 1975 No.470 |
| SS(II)(REA) Regs | The Social Security (Industrial Injuries) (Reduced Earnings Allowance and Transitional) Regulations 1987 No.415 |
| SS(II&D)MP Regs | The Social Security (Industrial Injuries and Diseases) Miscellaneous Provisions Regulations 1986 No.1561 |
| SS(IIPD) Regs | The Social Security (Industrial Injuries) (Prescribed Diseases) Regulations 1985 No.967 |
| SS(IIPD)(A) Regs | The Social Security (Industrial Injuries) (Prescribed Diseases) Amendment Regulations 2017 No.232 |
| SS(JPI) Regs | The Social Security (Jobcentre Plus Interviews) Regulations 2002 No.1703 |
| SS(JPIP) Regs | The Social Security (Jobcentre Plus Interviews for Partners) Regulations 2003 No.1886 |
| SS(LB) Regs | The Social Security (Loss of Benefit) Regulations 2001 No.4022 |
| SS(MAP) Regs | The Social Security (Maximum Additional Pension) Regulations 1978 No.949 |
| SS(MatA) Regs | The Social Security (Maternity Allowance) Regulations 1987 No.416 |
| SS(MatA)(E) Regs | The Social Security (Maternity Allowance) (Earnings) Regulations 2000 No.688 |
| SS(MatA)(WA) Regs | The Social Security (Maternity Allowance) (Work Abroad) Regulations 1987 No.417 |
| SS(ME) Regs | The Social Security (Medical Evidence) Regulations 1976 No.615 |
| SS(NCC) Regs | The Social Security (Notification of Change of Circumstances) Regulations 2001 No.3252 |
| SS(NIRA) Regs | The Social Security (Northern Ireland Reciprocal Arrangements) Regulations 2016 No.287 |
| SS(OB) Regs | The Social Security (Overlapping Benefits) Regulations 1979 No.597 |

A

| | |
|---|---|
| SS(OR) Regs | The Social Security (Overpayments and Recovery) Regulations 2013 No.384 |
| SS(PA)A Regs | The Social Security (Persons from Abroad) Amendment Regulations 2006 No.1026 |
| SS(PAB) Regs | The Social Security (Payments on Account of Benefit) Regulations 2013 No.383 |
| SS(PAOR) Regs | The Social Security (Payments on Account, Overpayments and Recovery) Regulations 1988 No.664 |
| SS(PIP) Regs | The Social Security (Personal Independence Payment) Regulations 2013 No.377 |
| SS(RB) Regs | The Social Security (Recovery of Benefits) Regulations 1997 No.2205 |
| SS(RB)App Regs | The Social Security (Recovery of Benefits) (Appeals) Regulations 1997 No.2237 |
| SS(SDA) Regs | The Social Security (Severe Disablement Allowances) Regulations 1984 No.1303 |
| SS(SPAC)(A) Regs | The Social Security (State Pension Age Claimants: Closure of Tax Credits) (Amendment) Regulations 2024 No.611 |
| SS(WB&RP) Regs | The Social Security (Widow's Benefit and Retirement Pensions) Regulations 1979 No.642 |
| SS(WFILP) Regs | The Social Security (Work-focused Interviews for Lone Parents) and Miscellaneous Amendments Regulations 2000 No.1926 |
| SS(WTCCTC)(CA) Regs | The Social Security (Working Tax Credit and Child Tax Credit) (Consequential Amendments) Regulations 2003 No.455 |
| SSA(F)AO No.5 | The Social Security Administration (Fraud) Act 1997 (Commencement No.5) Order 1997 No.2766 |
| SSA(IO)(S)Regs | The Social Security Assistance (Investigation of Offences) (Scotland) Regulations 2020 No.11 |
| SSB(CE) Regs | The Social Security Benefit (Computation of Earnings) Regulations 1996 No.2745 |
| SSB(Dep) Regs | The Social Security Benefit (Dependency) Regulations 1977 No.343 |
| SSB(MW&WSP) Regs | The Social Security (Benefit) (Married Women and Widows Special Provisions) Regulations 1974 No.2010 |
| SSB(PA) Regs | The Social Security Benefit (Persons Abroad) Regulations 1975 No.563 |
| SSB(PRT) Regs | The Social Security Benefit (Persons Residing Together) Regulations 1977 No.956 |
| SSC(DA) Regs | The Social Security Contributions (Decisions and Appeals) Regulations 1999 No.1027 |

| | |
|---|---|
| SSCBA(AAO) Regs | The Social Security Contributions and Benefits Act 1992 (Application of Parts 12ZA and 12ZB to Adoptions from Overseas) Regulations 2003 No.499 |
| SSCBA(APOC) Regs | The Social Security Contributions and Benefits Act 1992 (Application of Parts 12ZA, 12ZB and 12ZC to Parental Order Cases) Regulations 2014 No.2866 |
| SSCBCTC(A) Regs | The Social Security, Child Benefit and Child Tax Credit (Amendment) (EU Exit) Regulations 2020 No.1505 |
| SSCTRS(A) Regs | The Social Security and Council Tax Reduction Schemes (Amendment) Regulations 2022 No.449 |
| SS&CS(DA) Regs | The Social Security and Child Support (Decisions and Appeals) Regulations 1999 No.991 |
| SSFA(PM) Regs | The Social Security and Family Allowances (Polygamous Marriages) Regulations 1975 No.561 |
| SSP Regs | The Statutory Sick Pay (General) Regulations 1982 No.894 |
| SSP(MAPA) Regs | The Statutory Sick Pay (Mariners, Airmen and Persons Abroad) Regulations 1982 No.1349 |
| SSP(ME) Regs | The Statutory Sick Pay (Medical Evidence) Regulations 1985 No.1604 |
| SSPP(A) Regs | The Statutory Shared Parental Pay (Administration) Regulations 2014 No.2929 |
| SSPP(G) Regs | The Statutory Shared Parental Pay (General) Regulations 2014 No.3051 |
| SSPP(PAM) Regs | The Statutory Shared Parental Pay (Persons Abroad and Mariners) Regulations 2014 No.3134 |
| SSPP(POC) Regs | The Statutory Shared Parental Pay (Parental Order Cases) Regulations 2014 No.3097 |
| SSP&SMP(D) Regs | The Statutory Sick Pay and Statutory Maternity Pay (Decisions) Regulations 1999 No.776 |
| ST(ORP) Regs | The Scottish Tribunals (Offences in Relation to Proceedings) Regulations 2016 No.342 |
| ST(TL) Regs | The Scottish Tribunals (Time Limits) Regulations 2016 No.231 |
| TC(DCI) Regs | The Tax Credits (Definition and Calculation of Income) Regulations 2002 No.2006 |
| TC(Imm) Regs | The Tax Credits (Immigration) Regulations 2003 No.653 |
| TP(FT) Rules | The Tribunal Procedure (First-tier Tribunal) (Social Entitlement Chamber) Rules 2008 No.2685 |
| TP(FT)(TC) Rules | The Tribunal Procedure (First-tier Tribunal) (Tax Chamber) Rules 2009 No.273 |

| | |
|---|---|
| TP(UT) Rules | The Tribunal Procedure (Upper Tribunal) Rules 2008 No.2698 |
| UC Regs | The Universal Credit Regulations 2013 No.376 |
| UC(MMP&MA) Regs | The Universal Credit (Managed Migration Pilot and Miscellaneous Amendments) Regulations 2019 No.1152 |
| UC(TP) Regs | The Universal Credit (Transitional Provisions) Regulations 2014 No.1230 |
| UC(TP)(A) Regs | The Universal Credit (Transitional Provisions) (Amendment) Regulations 2014 No.1626 |
| UC(TP)(SDP)A Regs | The Universal Credit (Transitional Provisions) (Claimants previously entitled to a severe disability premium) Amendment Regulations 2021 No.4 |
| UC,PIP,JSA&ESA(C&P) Regs | The Universal Credit, Personal Independence Payment, Jobseeker's Allowance and Employment and Support Allowance (Claims and Payments) Regulations 2013 No.380 |
| UC,PIP,JSA&ESA(DA) Regs | The Universal Credit, Personal Independence Payment, Jobseeker's Allowance and Employment and Support Allowance (Decisions and Appeals) Regulations 2013 No.381 |
| UTS(SSRP) Rules | The Upper Tribunal for Scotland (Social Security Rules of Procedure) Regulations 2018 No. 274 |
| VP Regs | The Victims' Payments Regulations 2020 No.103 |
| WF Regs | The Welfare Food Regulations 1996 No.1434 |
| WF(BSF)(S) Regs | The Welfare Foods (Best Start Foods) (Scotland) Regulations 2019 No.193 |
| WHACYP(S) Regs | The Winter Heating Assistance for Children and Young People (Scotland) Regulations 2020 No.352 |
| WHA(LI)(S) Regs | The Winter Heating Assistance (Low Income) (Scotland) Regulations 2023 No.16 |
| WHA(PA)(S) Regs | The Winter Heating Assistance (Pension Age) (Scotland) Regulations 2024 No.351 |
| WRA(No.8)O | The Welfare Reform Act 2012 (Commencement No.8 and Savings and Transitional Provisions) Order 2013 No.358 |
| WRA(No.9)O | The Welfare Reform Act 2012 (Commencement No.9 and Transitional and Transitory Provisions and Commencement No.8 and Savings and Transitional Provisions (Amendment)) Order 2013 No.983 |
| WRA(No.21)O | The Welfare Reform Act 2012 (Commencement and Transitional and Transitory Provisions) Order 2015 No.33 |

| | |
|---|---|
| WRA(No.23)O | The Welfare Reform Act 2012 (Commencement No.23 and Transitional and Transitory Provisions) Order 2015 No.634 |
| WRA(No.31)O | The Welfare Reform Act 2012 (Commencement No.31 and Savings and Transitional Provisions and Commencement No.21 and 23 and Transitional and Transitory Provisions (Amendment)) Order 2019 No.37 |
| WRA(No.32)O | The Welfare Reform Act (Commencement No.32 and Savings and Transitional Provisions) Order 2019 No.167 |
| WTC(EMR) Regs | The Working Tax Credit (Entitlement and Maximum Rate) Regulations 2002 No.2005 |

## Other information

| | |
|---|---|
| ADM | *Advice for Decision Making*, vols A1-V8 |
| BLG | *Social Fund Budgeting Loan Guide* |
| CBTM | *Child Benefit Technical Manual* |
| CCM | *Claimant Compliance Manual* (HMRC guidance on investigation of tax credit claims) |
| DMG | *Decision Makers' Guide*, vols 1-14 |
| DWPWAG | *Guidance relating to the UK's operational implementation of the social security coordination provisions of Part 2 of the EU Withdrawal Agreement: Citizens' Rights* |
| GM | *Housing Benefit/Council Tax Benefit Guidance Manual* |
| PIP AG | *PIP Assessment Guide for Assessment Providers* |
| SF Dir | Social Fund Directive |
| SSS DMG | Social Security Scotland, *Decision Making Guide* |
| TCM | *Tax Credits Manual* |
| TCTM | *Tax Credits Technical Manual* |
| TFEU | The Treaty on the Functioning of the European Union |
| UK-EFTA | Agreement on arrangements between Iceland, Liechtenstein, Norway and the UK following the withdrawal of the UK from the EU, the EEA Agreement and other agreements |
| UK-EFTAC | Convention on Social Security Coordination between Iceland, Liechtenstein, Norway and the UK |

| | |
|---|---|
| UK-EUP | Trade and cooperation agreement between the EU and (1) the European Atomic Energy Community and (2) the UK |
| UK-IC | Convention on Social Security between the UK and Ireland |
| UK-SA | Agreement between the UK and the Swiss Confederation on Citizens' Rights following the withdrawal of the UK from the EU and the Free Movement of Persons Agreement |
| UK-SCC | Convention on Social Security Coordination between the UK and the Swiss Confederation |
| WA 2019 | Agreement on the withdrawal of the United Kingdom of Great Britain and Northern Ireland from the European Union and the European Atomic Energy Community |

# Index

**How to use this Index**

Because the *Handbook* is divided into separate sections covering the different benefits, many entries in the index have several references, each to a different section. Where this occurs, we use the following abbreviations to show to which benefit each reference relates.

| | |
|---|---|
| AA | Attendance allowance |
| ADP | Adult disability payment |
| CA | Carer's allowance |
| CDP | Child disability payment |
| C-ESA | Contributory employment and support allowance |
| C-JSA | Contribution-based jobseeker's allowance |
| CSP | carer support payment |
| DLA | Disability living allowance |
| ESA | Employment and support allowance |
| HB | Housing benefit |
| IB | Incapacity benefit |
| IIDB | Industrial injuries disablement benefit |
| IS | Income support |
| I-ESA | Income-related employment and support allowance |
| I-JSA | Income-based jobseeker's allowance |
| JSA | Jobseeker's allowance |
| MA | Maternity allowance |
| NI | National insurance |
| PADP | Pension age disability payment |
| PC | Pension credit |
| PIP | Personal independence payment |
| SADLA | Scottish adult disability living allowance |
| SAP | Statutory adoption pay |
| SDA | Severe disablement allowance |
| SMP | Statutory maternity pay |
| SPBP | Statutory parental bereavement pay |
| SPP | Statutory paternity pay |
| SSP | Statutory sick pay |
| SSPP | Statutory shared parental pay |
| UC | Universal credit |

Entries against the bold headings direct you to the general information on the subject, or where the subject is covered most fully. Sub-entries are listed alphabetically and direct you to specific aspects of the subject.


**1**

**16 to 19 bursaries** 776
- treatment of payments 364

**16 to 24-year-olds**
- work preparation
  - UC 940

**16/17-year-olds**
- approved training 490
- care leavers 846
- child benefit 488
- child benefit extension period 490
- free dental treatment 580
- free prescriptions 578
- free sight tests 580
- HB 186
- leaving custody 847
- liable to pay rent 186
- NI starting credits 871
- non-dependant deduction
  - HB 209
  - I-ESA/PC 291
  - UC 109
- personal allowance rates 267
- UC 37
- vouchers for glasses and contact lenses 580
- *see also: young people*

**2**

**21-year-olds**
- no non-dependant deductions aged under 21
  - UC 109

**3**

**35-year-olds**
- one-bedroom shared accommodation aged under 35

HB 310
UC 113
rent restrictions aged under 35
HB 328

## A

**A2 nationals** 1320
jobseekers 1321
member states 1320
pregnancy 1327
resided legally 1340
residence rights 1320
restrictions 1320
self-employment 1324
workers 1322
**A8 nationals** 1320
jobseekers 1321
member states 1320
pregnancy 1327
resided legally 1340
residence rights 1320
restrictions 1320
self-employment 1324
workers 1322
**abroad**
absence abroad 1369
AA/DLA 1378
ADP 1378
bereavement benefits 1376
CA 1378
CDP 1378
child benefit 1376
CSP 1378
ESA 1373, 1380
guardian's allowance 1377
HB 194, 1374
IB 1382
industrial injuries benefits 1381
MA 1382
new-style JSA 1381
PAPD 1378
PC 1375
PIP 1378
SADLA 1378
Scottish child payment 1377
SDA 1382
state pension 695, 1383
UC 1371
adoption
SAP/SPP/SSPP/SNCP 736
benefit entitlement 1368
capital abroad
means-tested benefits under pension age 420
UC 166
children abroad 1345
new-style JSA 1381
PC 1375
UC 1373
coming to UK from abroad 1269
earnings from abroad
CA 479
means-tested benefits over pension age 390
means-tested benefits under pension age 342, 364
exporting benefits 1408
funeral expenses payments 711
funeral support payments 1500
medical treatment
child benefit 1377
I-ESA 262
new-style JSA 963
UC 963
medical treatment, housing costs
I-ESA/PC 297
UC 108
medical treatment, travel costs 582
NI contributions 863
partner abroad 1344
ESA 1373
HB 1375
PC 1375
UC 1372
temporary absence 1370
HB 194
working abroad
EU co-ordination rules 1404
MA 638
NI contributions 863
SMP/SAP/SPP/SSPP/SPBP/SNCP 1384
SSP 1384
**absence from home**
child benefit
child absent 492, 499
parent absent 492, 495
children
means-tested benefits 261
couple living apart
means-tested benefits 257
UC 61
guardian's allowance
child absent 499
housing costs during temporary absence
HB 191
I-ESA/PC 296
UC 100, 107
students
HB 802
**absence from work**
continuous employment
SMP/SAP/SPP/SSPP/SPBP/SNCP 728
**academic year** 810
**access fund payments**
instalments 813
lump-sum payment 812

payments in advance of the course 813
treatment as income 812
**accidents**
EEA worker and self-employed status 1326
EU co-ordination of benefits 1402
industrial accidents 589
industrial accidents while travelling 591
recovery of benefits from compensation 1043
**accommodation**
definition for homeless people 849
provided as part of job
UC 127
rented from educational establishment
HB 803
size criteria
local housing allowance for HB 309
pre-Jan '96 rules 323
rent officer determination related rent 320
social sector tenants for HB 316
UC 104
specified accommodation
HB 183
UC 91
suitable alternative accommodation
pre-Jan '96 rules 324
**actively seeking work**
appealing a decision 1173
EEA jobseekers 1321
sanctions for not complying 978
work search requirement 941
**adaptations to home**
moving home
HB 190
I-ESA/PC 295
UC 98
**addiction treatment**
work search requirement 963
**Addison's disease**
free prescriptions 579
**additional state pension** 691
overlapping benefits 1022
**additional statutory paternity pay**
NI credits 873
**Adjudicator**
complaints 1264
**administration of benefits**
complaints 1260
Scottish benefits 1529
**Administrative Appeals Chamber of the Upper Tribunal** 1215
**administrative earnings threshold** 955
**administrative penalties**
benefits 1109
**adoption**
additional bedroom
HB 333
local housing allowance for HB 330
rent officer determined rent for HB 320
social sector tenants for HB 316
UC 106
allowances
means-tested benefits over pension age 391
means-tested benefits under pension age 357
UC 142
child benefit 500
claiming for children
means-tested benefits 262
foster parent approved as adopter
SAP/SPP/SSPP/SPBP/SNCP 736
guardian's allowance 498
overseas 736
SPP 721
SSPP 722
Sure Start maternity grant 706
two-child limit
means-tested benefits 269
UC 70
work-related requirements 952
*see also: statutory adoption pay*
**adoption leave**
childcare costs
HB 351
treated as not in full-time work
HB 889
new-style JSA/I-ESA 885
PC 889
**adoption pay period**
curtailment notice 723
definition 720
working during period 731
**adult disability payment** 1428
absence abroad 1378
age rules 1434
aids and appliances 1430
amount 1435
appeals 1544
assessment consultation 1441
assessment of activities 1429
benefit cap 1447
care homes 826
change of circumstances 1443, 1541
child winter heating payment 1506
claims 1439
components 1428
daily living activities 1431
daily living component 1428, 1435
date of claim 1442
descriptors 1429
disability conditions 1429

disability premium 272
enhanced disability premium 273
entitlement to other benefits
means-tested benefits 1446
non-means-tested benefits 1447
EU co-ordination rules 1350, 1379
failure to provide supporting evidence/ information 1441
failure to take part in consultation 1442
fluctuating conditions 1431
fraud 1528
habitual residence test 1300
hospital patients 818
incorrect award of ADP 1540
information to support claim 1440
managing an activity 1430
mobility activities 1431
mobility component 1428, 1436
upper age limit 1434
Motability 1447
moving from Scotland 1420
no non-dependant deduction
HB 208
I-ESA/PC 291
UC 109
overpayments 1526
passport to other benefits 1447
payment 1439, 1443
person subject to immigration control 1279
prisoners 837
public funds 1276
redetermination 1535
required information 1440
required period condition 1433
residence rules 1347
reviews 1444
short-term assistance 1558
tax 1446
terminal illness 1436
transferring to ADP 1444
from CDP 1489
from DLA 1446
from PIP 1444
from SADLA 1425
treatment as income
means-tested benefits over pension age 385
means-tested benefits under pension age 353
UC 137
who can get ADP 1428
**adult placement schemes** 833
**advance claims**
AA 447
ADP 1443
bereavement benefits 465
Best Start foods 1463
Best Start grants 1462
C-ESA 568
CA 482
CDP 1493
child benefit 504
DLA 533
guardian's allowance 504
HB 218
industrial injuries benefits 604
MA 641
new-style JSA 624
PADP 1517
PC 249
PIP 676
Scottish child payment 1462
state pension 698
UC 49
**advanced education** 489
UC 792
**advisers**
committing fraud 1107
**advocacy**
Scottish benefits 1524
**Afghanistan relocation and resettlement schemes**
benefit entitlement 1290
habitual residence test 1303
**after-school clubs**
childcare allowance
HB 351
**age**
pension age 689
proof of age 697
**age rules**
AA 443
ADP 1434
bereavement support payment 455
Best Start foods 1459
Best Start grants 1459
CA 479
CDP 1488
child benefit 498
child winter heating payment 1507
CSP 1470
discretionary housing payments 560
DLA 526
ESA
C-ESA 558
I-ESA 173
funeral support payment 1500
guardian's allowance 498
hardship payments
UC 1051
HB 196
IIDB 599
MA 636
new-style JSA 615
NI contributions 859

PADP 1514
PC 239
pension age winter heating payment 1507
PIP 667
retirement allowance 602
SADLA 1420
Scottish child payment 1459
single room rent 328
SMP/SAP/SPP/SSPP/SPBP/SNCP 733
SSP 752
state pension 689
UC 37
widowed parent's allowance 457
winter fuel payments 715
winter heating payment 1507
young carer grant 1478
**age-related additions**
retirement pensions before 6 April 2016 690
**agent**
payment of benefit to agent
HB 222
**aggregation** 1406
**aids and appliances**
ADP 1430
PIP 648
**Albania**
child benefit 1282
reciprocal agreements 1297
**alcohol dependency**
PIP 646
**Algeria**
benefit entitlement 1282
reciprocal agreements 1297
**almshouses**
HB 185
UC 91
**alternative dispute resolution**
SSP/SMP/SAP/SPP/SSPP/SPBP/SNCP 1254
**alternative payment arrangements**
UC 51
**amending a claim** 1004
HB 213
**amount of benefit**
AA 444
ADP 1435
bereavement support payment 455
Best Start grants 1454
budgeting loans 703
CA 479
CDP 1489
child benefit 499
child element
UC 69
child winter heating payment 1508
cold weather payments 714
CSP 1470
discretionary housing payments 551
DLA 529
early learning payment 1455
ESA
C-ESA 558
I-ESA 174
extended payments
HB 226
funeral expenses payments 711
funeral support payment 1501
guardian's allowance 499
hardship payments
ESA 1054
UC 1052
HB 199
Healthy Start food 772
housing costs run-on 300
IIDB 599
MA 637
new-style JSA 616
PADP 1515
PC 241
pension age winter heating payment 1508
PIP 669
pregnancy and baby payment 1454
reduced earnings allowance 602
retirement allowance 603
SADLA 1420
school-age payment 1455
Scottish child payment 1452
short-term assistance 1559
SMP/SAP/SPP/SSPP/SPBP/SNCP 733
SSP 752
state pension 690
Sure Start maternity grant 706
UC 39, 67
widowed parent's allowance 458
winter fuel payments 716
winter heating payment 1508
young carer grant 1478
**amputees**
DLA mobility component 515
**annuities**
future payments 408
surrender value
means-tested benefits over pension age 431
means-tested benefits under pension age 407
UC 158
treatment as income
means tested benefits over pension age 389
means-tested benefits under pension age 360, 361
UC 139
**annulment of marriage**
bereavement benefits 459

**appeals** 1166, 1544
adjournments 1189
advice/representation 1181
after appeal submitted
benefits 1182
Scottish benefits 1546, 1562
alternative dispute resolution
SSP/SMP/SAP/SPP/SSPP/SPBP/SNCP 1254
attendance at hearing 1197, 1228
barred from taking part 1192
before appeal 1167
carrying out decision of First-tier Tribunal 1207
complaints about HM Courts and Tribunals Service 1265
court costs 1233
decision maker's response 1183
Scottish benefits 1546
decision of First-tier Tribunal 1198
decisions which can be appealed 1172
decisions which cannot be appealed 1173
determination after appeal made
Scottish benefits 1549
disability 1199
dismissing an appeal
Scottish benefits 1547
domiciliary hearings 1197
enquiry form 1183
error of law by First-tier Tribunal 1216
First-tier Tribunal 1166
Scottish benefits 1544
hardship payments 1056
hearings 1194, 1196, 1228
Scottish benefits 1546, 1549, 1557
how to appeal 1174
Scottish benefits 1545, 1561
information required
benefits 1178, 1185
Scottish benefits 1545, 1546
lapsed appeals 1185
late appeals 1176
Scottish benefits 1546, 1562
lead cases 1193
limited capability for work 1199
mandatory reconsideration before appeal 1168
NI contributions 858
online submissions 1174
overpayments 1071
HB 1087
Scottish benefits 1528
tax credits 1089
paper-based decisions 1194, 1195, 1228
Scottish benefits 1549
penalties
benefits 1102
postponements 1189
preparing a case 1204
process decisions
Scottish benefits 1561
redetermination before appeal
Scottish benefits 1544
reinstating an appeal 1191, 1193, 1227
Scottish benefits 1548
remote hearings 1197, 1228
revision after appeal made 1137, 1185
sanctions 997
setting aside a First-tier Tribunal decision 1208
Scottish benefits 1553, 1554
setting aside an Upper Tribunal decision 1230
settling an appeal
SSP/SMP/SAP/SPP/SSPP/SPBP/SNCP 1253
sisting appeals
Scottish benefits 1547
SSP/SMP/SAP/SPP/SSPP/SPBP/SNCP 1252, 1255
striking out an appeal 1190
suspension of benefit, appeal pending 1031
test case pending 1193
time limits 1175, 1187
Scottish benefits 1545, 1562
to the courts 1231
Scottish benefits 1557
SSP/SMP/SAP/SPP/SSPP/SPBP/SNCP 1257
Upper Tribunal 1215
Scottish benefits 1554
valid appeals 1178
Scottish benefits 1545
who can appeal 1171
HB 1172
Scottish benefits 1544
who deals with appeals 1182
withdrawing an appeal to First-tier Tribunal 1192
Scottish benefits 1548
withdrawing an appeal to HMRC
SSP/SMP/SAP/SPP/SSPP/SPBP/SNCP 1253
withdrawing an appeal to Upper Tribunal 1227
**applicable amounts** 265
definition 265
HB 281
I-ESA 175, 281
personal allowances 266
**appointees** 1005
appeals 1171, 1172
bereavement benefits 463
C-ESA 566
CA 480

child benefit 502
collection of benefit 1019
DLA 539
guardian's allowance 502
HB 214, 222
hospital patients 816
PC 247
recovery of overpayments 1070
Scottish benefits 1522
SMP/SAP/SSP/SSPP/SPBP/SNCP 738
state pension 697
UC 46, 50
**apportionment**
of deductions for fuel
HB 204
of non-dependant deduction
HB 210
of rent
HB 203
**apprenticeships**
child benefit 490
**appropriate minimum guarantee**
PC 241
reductions 243
**approved training** 490
UC 63
**armed forces**
ESA after discharge 570
NI credits for service families 874
non-dependant deductions
HB 209
UC 110
payments for ill health and disability 779
size criteria for families with members in the armed forces
HB 329
UC 108
**Armed Forces Compensation Scheme** 780
treatment of payments
means-tested benefits over pension age 385, 386
means-tested benefits under pension age 353, 354
UC 138
**armed forces independence payment** 780
disability premium 272
enhanced disability premium 273
no non-dependant deduction
I-ESA/PC 291
UC 109
overlapping benefits 1021
treatment as income
means-tested benefits over pension age 385
means-tested benefits under pension age 353
UC 137
**arrears**
benefit arrears leading to overpayments 1062
benefit arrears, treatment as capital
means-tested benefits over pension age 432
means-tested benefits under pension age 408
UC 158
benefit arrears, treatment as income
means-tested benefits over pension age 387
means-tested benefits under pension age 355
child maintenance arrears, treatment as income
means-tested benefits under pension age 355
following imprisonment on remand 838
following revision 1142
following supersession 1148
rent arrears 1035
**assistance**
PIP assessments 647
**asthma**
occupational 593
**asylum seekers** 1289
asylum support 1289
benefit entitlement 1289
claiming health benefits 583
Healthy Start food vouchers 772
means-tested benefits 1281
NHS charges, exemption 574
recourse to public funds 1289
**attendance allowance** 439
absence abroad 1378
advance claims 447
age rules 443
amount 444
appeals 1166
backdating 447, 1011
benefit cap 451
care homes 826
change of circumstances 449
claims 445
date of claim 447
daytime conditions 442
decisions 448, 1115
delays 1123
dialysis 444
disability conditions 442
disability premium 272
entitlement to other benefits
means-tested benefits 450
non-means-tested benefits 451
EU co-ordination rules 1350, 1379
fraud 1100
habitual residence test 1300

I

hospital patients 818
information to support claim 446
interchange of claims 1014
length of award 449
medical examination 448
moving to Scotland 1419
night-time conditions 442
no non-dependant deduction
HB 208
I-ESA/PC 291
UC 109
overlapping benefits 451, 1021
overpayments 1058
passport to other benefits 451
payment 449
person subject to immigration control 1279
prisoners 837
public funds 1276
renewal claims 448
residence rules 1347
revisions 1128, 1130
severe disability premium 276
supersessions 1128, 1143
tax 450
terminal illness 444
transferring to PADP 1518
treatment as income 450
means-tested benefits over pension age 385
means-tested benefits under pension age 353
UC 137
who can get AA 442
**attention condition**
DLA care component 521, 523, 524
**autistic spectrum disorder** 516
**available for work** *see: work availability requirement*

**B**
**backdating** 1011
AA 447
ADP 1443
bereavement benefits 464
Best Start foods 1463
C-ESA 568
CA 481
CDP 1493
child benefit 503
components 283
CSP 1472
DLA 533
following award of qualifying benefit 1012
guardian's allowance 503
HB 216
industrial injuries benefits 604
MA 640
new-style JSA 622
one month's backdating
HB 217
new-style JSA 623
PADP 1517
pay rises
SMP/SAP/SPP/SSPP/SPBP/SNCP 730
PC 248
PIP 676
premiums 280
qualifying benefit
Best Start foods 1463
Best Start grants 1462
budgeting loans 702
funeral expenses payments 707
funeral support payment 1502
premiums 280
Scottish child payment 1462
Sure Start maternity grant 705
refugees 1291
Scottish child payment 1462
SSP 756
state pension 697
three months' backdating
HB 217
new-style JSA 623
UC 48
**bail**
HB 190, 842
hostels
HB 306
UC 91
housing costs
I-ESA/PC 297, 842
means-tested benefits 840, 842
non-means-tested benefits 836
UC 842
**bank and building society accounts**
forgotten PIN numbers 1019
lost bank cards 1019
payment of benefits 1019
treatment of money in account
means-tested benefits over pension age 427
means-tested benefits under pension age 400
UC 151
**bankruptcy**
deprivation of capital
means-tested benefits under pension age 415
UC 162
recovery of overpayments
tax credits 1095
**bedroom tax**
definition of bedroom
HB 330

discretionary housing payments in
Scotland 549
HB 313
UC 117
**bedrooms**
additional bedrooms
means-tested benefits 329
UC 105
children who cannot share a bedroom
HB 332
couples who cannot share bedroom
HB 331
UC 106
definition
HB 330
UC 108
maximum number of bedrooms
local housing allowance for HB 309
social sector rules for HB 316
UC 104
one-bedroom self-contained
accommodation
UC 114
one-bedroom shared accommodation
UC 113
two or more bedrooms
UC 114
**behavioural difficulties**
CDP mobility component 1487
DLA mobility component 516
**benefit cap** 1025
AA 451
ADP 1447
bereavement benefits 468
Best Start foods 1464
Best Start grants 1464
CA 485
CDP 1494
child benefit 508
child winter heating payment 1510
CSP 1475
discretionary housing payments 553
DLA 543
ESA
C-ESA 571
I-ESA 179
funeral support payment 1503
grace period
HB 1027
UC 1026
guardian's allowance 508
hardship payments 1056
HB 231, 1028
how the cap is applied 1029
industrial injuries benefits 606
MA 643
new-style JSA 627
PADP 1519
PC 252
pension age winter heating payment 1510
PIP 681
revisions 1139
SADLA 1424
Scottish child payment 1464
SMP/SAP/SPP/SSPP/SPBP/SNCP 741
social fund loans and payments 716
specified benefits
HB 1029
UC 1028
SSP 759
state pension 699
supersessions 1148
UC 56, 1028
when benefit cap applies 1028
when benefit cap does not apply 1025
winter heating payment 1510
young carer grant 1480
**benefit offences** 1106
administrative penalties 1109
change in circumstances 1107
dishonest representation 1108
disqualifying benefits 1111
false representation 1106
hardship payments
ESA 1054
UC 1051
loss of benefits 1111
one-strike rule 1111
prosecution or administrative penalty
1108, 1109
sanctionable benefits 1112
sanctions 1111, 1112
two-strikes rule 1111
**benefit offices**
contacting 1010
**benefit system**
decisions 1117
overview 7
Scottish social security system 1415
**benefit week**
CA 476
HB 203
I-ESA 369
PC 394
student loans 810
**bereavement**
EU co-ordination of benefits 1401
rent restriction delayed
HB 333
UC 105
work search requirement 961
**bereavement allowance**
late claim
delay finding out/uncertainty about
death 465
NI credits 873

**bereavement benefits** 453
absence abroad 1376
advance claims 465
appeals 1166
appointees 463
Bereavement Service 462
bereavement support payment 454
change of circumstances 467
claims 462
cohabiting partners
death before February 2023 453, 462
definition 458, 461
date of claim 464
decisions 1115
delay finding out/uncertainty about death 464
delay getting decision 1123
entitlement to other benefits
means-tested benefits 467
non-means-tested benefits 468
EU co-ordination rules 1345
fraud 1100
gender reassignment 462
industrial accidents/diseases 461
information to support claim 463
interchange of claims 1014
overpayment 1058
passport to other benefits 468
payment 465
polygamous marriages 460
priority between claimants 466
prisoners 837
reciprocal agreements 1345
residence rules 1345
revisions 1128, 1130
statutory parental bereavement pay 724
supersessions 1128, 1143
tax 467
voluntary class 3 NI contributions 862
widowed before April 2001 461
widowed parent's allowance 456
**bereavement payment**
late claim
delay finding out/uncertainty about death 465
NI credits 873
**bereavement support payment** 454
absence abroad 1376
age rules 455
amount 455
backdating 1012
benefit cap 468
claims 462
entitlement to other benefits
means-tested benefits 467
non-means-tested benefits 468
EU co-ordination rules 1345, 1376
interchange of benefits 1014
new relationship 456
NI contribution conditions 878
people included in the claim 455
reciprocal agreements 1345
residence rules 1345
sanctionable benefits 466
tax 467
time limits for claiming 454
treatment as capital
means-tested benefits under pension age 409
means-tmeans-tested benefits over pension age 433
UC 159
treatment as income 467
means-tested benefits over pension age 385
means-tested benefits under pension age 353
UC 137
who can get bereavement support payment 454
**Best Start foods** 1451, 1455
advance claims 1463
age rules 1459
backdating 1463
benefit cap 1464
claims 1460
date of claim 1463
entitlement to other benefits 1464
information to support claim 1461
more than one claimant 1458
payment 1463
payment card 1455
qualifying benefits 1459
responsibility for a child 1457
tax 1464
treatment as income 1464
vitamins 1464
who can qualify 1455
**Best Start grants** 1451
advance claims 1462
age rules 1459
amounts 1454
appeals 1544
benefit cap 1464
change of circumstances 1535
claims 1460
date of claim 1462
early learning payment 1453
entitlement to other benefits 1464
fraud 1528
habitual residence test 1300
information to support claim 1461
more than one claimant 1458
overpayments 1526
payment 1463

person subject to immigration control 1281
pregnancy and baby payment 1453
qualifying benefits 1459
redeterminations 1535
residence rules 1356
responsibility for a child 1457
school-age payment 1454
tax 1464
time limits for claiming 1462
trade disputes 893
treatment as capital
means-tested benefits over pension age 432
means-tested benefits under pension age 409
UC 159
treatment as income 1464
means-tested benefits over pension age 385
means-tested benefits under pension age 353
UC 137
who can qualify 1452
**biometric residence permits** 1272
**bitcoin**
treatment as capital
UC 152
**blindness**
ADP 1431
CDP mobility component 1487
disability premium 272
disabled child premium 271
disregarded earnings
HB over pension age 384
PC 383
DLA care component 522
DLA mobility component 515
free sight tests 580
no non-dependant deduction
HB 208
I-ESA/PC 291
UC 109
PIP 657
severe disability premium 275
**Blue Badge parking scheme**
DLA 543
PIP 681
**boarders**
not a non-dependant
HB 208
UC 104
rent restrictions
HB 317
treatment of payment from 479
means-tested benefits over pension age 388
means-tested benefits under pension age 358
**boarding school**
child benefit 492
**bonus of wages**
treatment as earnings
CA 474
means-tested benefits over pension age 379
means-tested benefits under pension age 341
UC 126
**breathing space debt respite scheme**
overpayments 1059
**Brexit** 1390
EEA nationals' residence rights 1312
end of transition period 1393
EU co-ordination rules 1390
transition period 1313, 1319, 1390
Withdrawal Agreements 1319, 1393
**British citizens**
dual British and EEA nationals 1333
EU co-ordination of benefits rules 1388
EU law 1389
family members' residence rights 1332
residence rights 1312
right to reside 1312
UK-Ireland Convention 1397
**budgeting advances of UC** 52
**budgeting decisions**
ADP 1431
PIP 659
**budgeting loans** 701
amount 703
applying 703
payment 703
person subject to immigration control 702
repayment 704
who can claim 701
**Bulgaria** 1320
**business**
treatment of assets
means-tested benefits over pension age 430
means-tested benefits under pension age 403, 406
UC 134, 157
use of home
HB 202
**business partners**
earnings
CA 477
**byssinosis** 600, 606

**C**
**caecostomy**
free prescriptions 579

**calculations**
net earnings from employment
CA 475
means-tested benefits over pension age 380
means-tested benefits under pension age 342
UC 127
net earnings from self-employment
means-tested benefits over pension age 381
means-tested benefits under pension age 346
UC 128
UC housing costs element 101
weekly income
means-tested benefits over pension age 394
means-tested benefits under pension age 368
weekly self-employed earnings
CA 477
means-tested benefits over pension age 382
means-tested benefits under pension age 346
**campsite fees**
HB 185
I-ESA/PC 287
**cancer treatment**
free prescriptions 579
limited capability for work
ESA 899
UC 897
limited capability for work-related activity 918
**capital**
arrears of benefits
means-tested benefits over pension age 432
means-tested benefits under pension age 408
UC 158
assumed income from capital 140
budgeting loans 702
capital limits
means-tested benefits over pension age 426
means-tested benefits under pension age 399
UC 149
capital treated as income
means-tested benefits under pension age 360
UC 125
care home residents
means-tested benefits under pension age 399
child's
means-tested benefits under pension age 399
UC 151
council tax reduction schemes
pension age or over 762
under pension age 763, 764
definition
means-tested benefits over pension age 427
means-tested benefits under pension age 400
UC 151
deprivation of capital
means-tested benefits over pension age 435
means-tested benefits under pension age 413
UC 161
difference between capital and income 340
diminishing capital rule 1070
means-tested benefits under pension age 415
UC 163
disregards
means-tested benefits over pension age 428
means-tested benefits under pension age 403
UC 154
expenses of sale
means-tested benefits under pension age 418
UC 164
hardship payments 1054
income from capital
means-tested benefits over pension age 388
means-tested benefits under pension age 359
UC 140
income treated as capital
means-tested benefits under pension age 402
UC 153
instalments
means-tested benefits 360
UC 125
investments
means-tested benefits over pension age 427
means-tested benefits under pension age 400
UC 152
jointly owned
means-tested benefits under pension age 419

UC 164
loans
means-tested benefits over pension age 427
means-tested benefits under pension age 400
UC 152
matrimonial assets
means-tested benefits under pension age 419
UC 165
means-tested benefits
over pension age 425
under pension age 398
non-dependants
HB 211
notional capital
means-tested benefits over pension age 435
means-tested benefits under pension age 413
UC 161
overpayments arising from amount of capital
HB 1082
means-tested benefits 1070
partner's
means-tested benefits over pension age 427
means-tested benefits under pension age 399
UC 151
property
means-tested benefits over pension age 427
means-tested benefits under pension age 400, 403
UC 152, 154
savings
means-tested benefits over pension age 427
means-tested benefits under pension age 400
UC 151
spending capital to increase benefit
means-tested benefits over pension age 435
means-tested benefits under pension age 413
UC 161
students
ESA 801
HB 804
tariff income
means-tested benefits over pension age 388
means-tested benefits under pension age 360
UC 140
third-party payments
means-tested benefits under pension age 416
transitional capital disregard
UC 150
trusts
means-tested benefits over pension age 428
means-tested benefits under pension age 401
UC 153
UC 149
valuation
means-tested benefits over pension age 436
means-tested benefits under pension age 418
UC 164
**care homes** 826
AA/ADP/CDP/DLA/PIP/PADP 826
CA 830
capital limits
means-tested benefits under pension age 399
child in care home 833
child benefit 492, 499
UC 832
costs for usual home 834
HB 835
I-ESA/PC 297, 835
UC 98, 831, 835
CSP 830
deferred payment of charges 829
definition
means-tested benefits 831
ESA 832
fees paid by local authority
I-ESA 363
free dental treatment 580
free prescriptions 578
HB 187, 832
health benefits 577
linking rules
AA/ADP/CDP/DLA/PIP/PADP 829
mortgage interest loan 831, 835
moving house
HB 191
nursing care needs 817
AA/DLA/PIP 828
paid by deductions from benefit 1039
partner in care home 833
UC 831
PC 832
qualifying services 827
self-funding
AA/ADP/CDP/DLA/PIP/PADP 829
severe disability premium 276

social fund payments 834
tariff income 833
means-tested benefits under pension age 399
temporary residents
HB 193
trial period
HB 194
I-ESA/PC 297
UC 91, 831
**care leavers** 846
eligibility to claim UC 847
local authority payments
treatment as capital 411
treatment as income 363
UC 161
UC housing costs element 90
**care-experience assistance** 1418
**carer premium** 279
earnings disregard 348
rate 280
**carer support payment** 1467
absence abroad 1378
age rules 1470
amount 1470
appeals 1544
backdating 1472
benefit cap 1475
care homes 830
carer premium 279
change of circumstances 1473, 1541
claims 1470
date of claim 1472
death of cared-for person 1473
employment 1469
entitlement to other benefits 279, 1474
EU co-ordination rules 1350
fraud 1528
future changes 1467
habitual residence test 1300
hospital patients 819
hours of caring 1468
incorrect award of CSP 1540
information to support claim 1471
linked periods
new-style JSA 612
NI credits 871
overpayments 1526
passport to other benefits 1475
payment 1472
person subject to immigration control 1279
prisoners 839
qualifying benefits 1468
redeterminations 1535
residence rules 1347
reviews 1474
students 805
tax 1474
transferring from CA 1474
treatment as income
means-tested benefits over pension age 385
means-tested benefits under pension age 353
UC 137
two people care for same person 1469
who can get CSP 1468
young carer grant 1480
**carer's allowance** 471
absence abroad 1378
advance claims 482
age rules 479
amount 479
appeals 1166
backdating 481, 1012
benefit cap 485
breaks from caring 473
CA supplement 1475
care homes 830
carer premium 279
change of circumstances 483
claims 480
date of claim 481
death of cared-for person 473
decisions 1115
deductions from earnings for care costs 478
delays 1123
dependants 479
earnings 473
employment 473
entitlement to other benefits 279
means-tested benefits 483
non-means-tested benefits 485
EU co-ordination rules 1350, 1379
fraud 1100
habitual residence test 1300
holidays for carers 473
hospital patients 473, 819
hours of caring 473
information to support claim 481
late claims 481
linked periods
new-style JSA 612
moving to Scotland 1419
NI credits 871
overlapping benefits 485, 1021
overpayments 1058
passport to other benefits 485
payment 482
person subject to immigration control 1279
prisoners 837
public funds 1276
qualifying benefits 482

residence rules 1347
revisions 1128, 1130
Scotland 471
students 804
supersessions 1128, 1143
tax 483
treatment as income 484
means-tested benefits over pension age 385
means-tested benefits under pension age 353
UC 137
who can get CA 472
young carer grant 1480
**carer's allowance supplement** 1475
amount 1476
living abroad 1476
public funds 1276
residence rules 1348
Scottish carer supplement 1475
treatment as income
means-tested benefits over pension age 386
means-tested benefits under pension age 353
UC 137
who can get CA supplement 1476
**carers**
additional bedroom
local housing allowance for HB 329
rent officer determined rent for HB 320
social sector tenants for HB 316
UC 105
adult placement scheme 833
available for work requirement 945
benefit entitlement 483
better-off benefit decisions 483
breaks from caring
CA 473
CA 472
carer addition
PC 242, 279
carer element 75
carer premium 279
costs of care deducted from earnings 478
CSP 1467
EEA nationals' derivative rights 1336
friend or family carer 957
good reason for not attending training 993
good reason for refusing a job 990
housing costs when absent from home
I-ESA/PC 297
NI credits 868, 871
non-dependant deductions
HB 208
I-ESA/PC 290
UC 110
regularly and substantially caring 473
shared lives carers 142
treated as not in work
new-style JSA/I-ESA 885
UC 75
unpaid work 367
work-related requirements 952
working during limited capability for work 929
young carer grant 1476
young people
UC 38
**carpal tunnel syndrome** 594
**cataracts** 593
**cautions**
DWP formal cautions 1111
fraud interview 1104
**certificate of recoverable benefits** 1044
**challenging a decision** 1128, 1533
appeals 1166
Scottish benefits 1544
budgeting loans 703
cohabitation
means-tested benefits 258
UC 62
decision maker's decision 1122
First-tier Tribunal decisions 1207
Scottish benefits 1551, 1554
hardship payments 1056
limited capability for work 923
mandatory reconsideration 1168
overpayments 1071
HB 1087
Scottish benefits 1527
tax credits 1090
recovery of benefits from compensation 1045
redeterminations
Scottish benefits 1535
rent restrictions
HB 334
revisions 1129, 1130
sanctions 997
SSP/SMP/SAP/SPP/SSPP/SPBP/SNCP 1249
supersessions 1129, 1143
suspension of benefit 1032
termination of benefit 1033
Upper Tribunal decision 1230
Scottish benefits 1557
**change of circumstances**
AA 449
ADP 1443
after appeal made 1203
benefit entitlement changes 1128
HB 230
bereavement benefits 467
CA 483

CDP 1493
child benefit 506
CSP 1473
date of change
HB 230
date of new decision following supersession 1150
death of family member
UC 67
DLA 540
duty to report 1030, 1107
ESA
C-ESA 569
I-ESA 178
guardian's allowance 506
HB 228
hours of work
means-tested benefits 885
industrial injuries benefits 605
late notification 1153
MA 641
making a new claim 1203
medical condition worsens 927
new-style JSA 626
PADP 1518
PC 229, 250
penalties for failing to report 1106
PIP 679
redeterminations 1535
SADLA 1424
Scottish benefits 1524
SMP/SAP/SPP/SSPP/SPBP/SNCP 739
SSP 757
state pension 699
supersession 1143, 1145, 1150
transferring to UC 25
UC 32, 53
**charitable payments**
treatment as capital
means-tested benefits over pension age 434
means-tested benefits under pension age 410
treatment as income
means-tested benefits over pension age 391
means-tested benefits under pension age 357
UC 142
**charities**
financial help and assistance 783
**chemotherapy**
free prescriptions 579
limited capability for work
ESA 899
UC 897
limited capability for work-related activity 918
**child abuse**
treatment of payments for historic abuse
means-tested benefits over pension age 434
means-tested benefits under pension age 411
UC 160
**child arrangements order allowance**
means-tested benefits over pension age 391
means-tested benefits under pension age 357
UC 142
**child benefit** 487
absence abroad 1376, 1409
absence from home 492
adoption 500
advance claims 504
age rules 498
amount 499
appeals 1166
approved training 490
backdating 503, 1012
benefit cap 508
boarding school 492
care homes 492
change of circumstances 506
children with no entitlement 495
claims 501
contributing to supporting child 493
date of claim 503
decisions 1115
definition of child 488
delays 1123
entitlement to other benefits
means-tested benefits 508
non-means-tested benefits 508
EU co-ordination rules 1347, 1378
extension period 490
fostering 500
fraud 1100
full-time education 489
guardian's allowance 496
high-income child benefit charge 507
higher rate 499
hospital patients 492, 824
information to support claim 502
interchange of claims 1014
interim payments 505
interruption of education 491
kinship care 500
late claims 503
living apart 492
looked after by local authority 496, 499
non-advanced education 489
overlapping benefits 1023
overpayments 1058, 1075

partner subject to immigration control 1287
payment 504
person subject to immigration control 1279
priority of claimants 493
prisoners 838
child in prison 496, 499
public funds 1276
qualifying young person 488
refugees 1291
relevant education 488
residence rules 1310, 1346
residing together 495
responsibility for a child 492
revisions 1128, 1130
shared care 494
supersessions 1128, 1143
tax 507
terminal date 491
treatment as income 508
means-tested benefits over pension age 386
means-tested benefits under pension age 353
UC 137
who can get child benefit 488
who should claim 502
working child 496
**child benefit extension period** 490
**child disability payment** 1483
absence abroad 1378
advance claims 1493
age rules 1488
amount 1489
appeals 1544
backdating 1493
benefit cap 1494
care component conditions 1484
additional requirement 1485
daytime conditions 1484
definitions 1485
highest rate 1484
lowest rate 1484
middle rate 1484
night-time conditions 1485
care homes 826
change of circumstances 1493, 1541
child winter heating payment 1506
claims 1490
date of claim 1492
dialysis 1490
entitlement to other benefits 1494
non-means-tested benefits 1494
EU co-ordination rules 1350, 1379
fraud 1528
habitual residence test 1300
hospices 819, 828
hospital patients 818
incorrect award of CDP 1540
information to suppport claim 1492
mobility component conditions 1486
higher rate 1486
lower rate 1488
moving from Scotland 1420
moving to ADP 1489
no non-dependant deductions
HB 208
I-ESA 291
UC 109
overpayments 1526
partner subject to immigration control 1287
passport to other benefits 1495
payment 1493
person subject to immigration control 1279
prisoners 837
public funds 1276
redeterminations 1535
residence rules 1347
reviews 1493
short-term assistance 1558
tax 1494
terminal illness 1436
treatment as capital
means-tested benefits over pension age 432
means-tested benefits under pension age 408
treatment as income
means-tested benefits over pension age 386
means-tested benefits under pension age 353
UC 137
who can get CDP 1483
**child element**
two-child limit
UC 69
UC 68
**child maintenance**
deductions from benefit 1038
definition 355
flat-rate benefit deductions 1038
treatment as income
means-tested benefits over pension age 387
means-tested benefits under pension age 355
UC 138
**Child Migrants Trust**
treatment of compensation payments
means-tested benefits over pension age 434

means-tested benefits under pension age 411
UC 160
**child tax credit** *see: tax credits*
**child winter heating payment** 1505
age rules 1507
amount 1508
appeals 1544
benefit cap 1510
care home residents 834
change of circumstances 1535
claims 1508
information to support claim 1509
payment 1509
public funds 1276
qualifying benefits 1506
redeterminations 1535
residence rules 1357
tax 1510
treatment as capital
means-tested benefits over pension age 432
means-tested benefits under pension age 409
UC 159
treatment as income 1510
means-tested benefits over pension age 386
UC 137
who can get child winter heating payment 1506
**childcare**
calculating childcare costs
HB 352
childcare costs element
UC 76
costs, disregarded
CA 478
HB over pension age 384
HB under pension age 350
deductions from earnings
HB over pension age 384
HB under pension age 350
disabled parents, DLA care component 523
family members
NI credits 870
free early education and childcare 777
free milk 775
friend or family carer 957
home responsibilities protection 870
NI credits 868
relevant childcare
UC 77
tax-free childcare scheme 779
vouchers
UC 127
work search requirement 942
work-focused interviews 956
work-related requirements 952
**childminders**
childcare allowance
HB 351
free milk for children 775
self-employed 347
treatment of earnings
CA 477
means-tested benefits over pension age 382
means-tested benefits under pension age 347
**children**
absence from home
means-tested benefits 261
Best Start foods 1451, 1455
Best Start grants 1451, 1452
capital
means-tested benefits under pension age 399
UC 151
care home
housing costs 835
means-tested benefits 833
UC 832
CDP 1483
child element
UC 68
claiming for children
means-tested benefits 258
UC 62
definition
child benefit 488
guardian's allowance 496
UC 63
widowed parent's allowance 456
disabled child premium 271
DLA 511
care component 519
completing claim form 534
mobility component 512
payment of benefit 538
EEA workers with child in education 1336
family premium 271
free dental treatment 580
free early education and childcare 777
free prescriptions 578
free sight tests 580
funeral expenses payments 708
guardian's allowance 497
Healthy Start food and vitamins 771
hospital patient 823
CDP/DLA 818
child benefit 824
housing costs 825
I-ESA 262
Scottish child payment 824

UC 821
income
means-tested benefits over pension age 378
means-tested benefits under pension age 339
UC 124
living with child 492
medical treatment abroad
I-ESA 262
NI number requirement for child 1007
not non-dependants
HB 208
UC 104
personal allowances 268
rates 269
premiums 270
prisoner
housing costs 845
means-tested benefits 840
UC 839
responsibility for a child
Best Start foods 1457
Best Start grants 1457
child benefit 492
means-tested benefits 260
Scottish child payment 1457
UC 64
responsibility for landlord's child
HB 188
Scottish child payment 1451
shared care
child benefit 494
means-tested benefits 261
UC 64
SNCP 725
SPBP 724
supporting a child
child benefit 493
two-child limit
means-tested benefits 268
UC 69
vouchers for glasses and contact lenses 580
work allowance
UC 41
**children in care**
*see: looked-after children*
**children's funeral fund payment** 708
**Christmas bonus** 353, 386, 783
**civil partners**
bereavement benefits 453
bereavement support payment 454
claiming as a couple
means-tested benefits 255
UC 58
surviving partner
definition 458
state pension 693
void/voidable partnerships 459
widowed parent's allowance 456
**civil penalties** 1101
**claim-related rent** 320
**claimant commitment** 934
accepting commitment 936
closure of claim for not attending commitments meeting 937
reviewing commitment 937
work-related requirements 938
**claims** 1001
AA 445
ADP 1439
amending a claim 1004
backdating 1011
bereavement benefits 462
Best Start foods 1460
Best Start grants 1460
CA 480
CDP 1490
child benefit 501
child winter heating payment 1508
claiming as a couple
means-tested benefits 254
UC 38, 58
claiming for a family
means-tested benefits 254
UC 38, 58
claiming on behalf of someone else 1005
claiming the wrong benefit 1013
cold weather payments 714
CSP 1470
date of claim 1011
discretionary housing payments 552
DLA 530
ESA
C-ESA 565
I-ESA 178
funeral expenses payments 713
funeral support payment 1502
guardian's allowance 501
hardship payments 1055
HB 211
health benefits 582
Healthy Start vouchers 773
how to claim 1004
Scottish benefits 1521
industrial injuries benefits 603
information to support a claim 1006, 1009
Scottish benefits 1522
interchange of claims 1013
investigation of claims 1102
MA 638
new-style JSA 619
PADP 1515
PC 246
pension age winter heating payment 1508

PIP 670
renewing a claim
AA 448
DLA 533, 540
PIP 678
SADLA 1420
Scottish child payment 1460
short-term assistance 1559
SMP/SAP/SPP/SSPP/SPBP/SNCP 737
SSP 754
state pension 695
Sure Start maternity grant 706
UC 44
valid claims 1006, 1008
attending interview 1008
by telephone 1008
claim not valid 1006
in writing 1009
online 1009
where to claim
HB 213
who should claim 1005
winter fuel payments 716
winter heating payment 1508
withdrawing a claim 1004
Scottish benefits 1522
written claims
HB 211
young carer grant 1478
*see also: date of claim*
**close relatives**
funeral expenses payments 709
funeral support payment 1498
HB 187, 189
I-ESA/PC 294
severe disability premium 278
treatment of home
means-tested benefits over pension age 430
means-tested benefits under pension age 405
UC 156
UC 96
**clothing**
budgeting loans 702
grants for school clothes 775
**co-ownership scheme**
HB 186
I-ESA/PC 287
**coal**
concessionary coal, treatment as income 364
UC 127
**coastguard**
payments treated as capital
means-tested benefits under pension age 403
payments treatment as income
CA 479
means-tested benefits over pension age 383, 384
means-tested benefits under pension age 349
treated as not in full-time work
new-style JSA/I-ESA 885
**cohabiting partners**
bereavement benefits 453, 461
bereavement support payment 454
challenging a cohabiting decision
means-tested benefits 258
UC 62
means-tested benefits 255
surviving partner
definition 458
UC 59
widowed parent's allowance 456
**cold weather payments** 714
amount 714
appeals 1166
care home residents 834
claims 714
payment 714
person subject to immigration control 714
qualifying benefits 714
residence rules 1357
revisions 1130
**colostomy**
free prescriptions 579
**commission**
treatment as earnings
CA 474
means-tested benefits over pension age 379
means-tested benefits under pension age 341
UC 126
**common travel area** 1300
**Commonwealth citizens**
right to reside 1312
Windrush generation 1275
**communal areas**
fuel
HB 205
service charges
HB 205
UC 93
**communicating**
engaging with others
ADP 1432
PIP 658
speech and hearing
ADP 1432
PIP 656

**community care payments**
treatment as capital
means-tested benefits over pension age 435
means-tested benefits under pension age 411
UC 161
treatment as income
means-tested benefits under pension age 363
**community dental service**
free dental treatment 580
**community sentences** 841
**compensation**
delays in payment of benefit 1261
legal action 1268
loss of employment/unfair dismissal
CA 474, 475
means-tested benefits under pension age 342
offical errors 1261
payments exempt from recovery of benefits 1045
personal injuries
UC 140
recovery of benefits from compensation 1043
special compensation schemes
means-tested benefits over pension age 434
means-tested benefits under pension age 410
UC 159
**Compensation Recovery Unit** 1043
**compensation schemes**
treatment of payments
means-tested benefits over pension age 434
means-tested benefits under pension age 410
UC 159
**competent state** 1404
**complaints** 1260
about DWP 1262
about HM Courts and Tribunals Service 1265
about HMRC 1263
about local authority administration
HB 1265
about Social Security Scotland 1529
grounds 1260
to councillor
HB 1265
to Independent Case Examiner 1262
to MP 1266
to Ombudsman 1266
HB 1267
**complex needs**
sanctions 996
**components** 281
ADP 1428
hospital patients 823
PIP 646
rates 283
support component
C-ESA 560
HB 282
I-ESA 282
work-related activity component 282
ESA 561
**comprehensive sickness insurance** 1329
**conscientious objection**
good reason for refusing a job 990
**constant attendance allowance** 600
armed services 780
interchange of claims 1014
overlapping benefits 1021
treatment as income
means-tested benefits over pension age 386
means-tested benefits under pension age 353
**contact lenses**
vouchers 580
**continuous employment**
SMP/SAP/SPP/SSPP/SPBP/SNCP 727
**contributory benefits** 857
contribution conditions 874
**cooking test**
ADP 1431
PIP 649
**cost of living payments**
treatment as capital
means-tested benefits over pension age 433
means-tested benefits under pension age 410
UC 159
**council tax**
arrears paid by deductions from benefit 1038
discretionary housing payments 550
discretionary reduction of bill 761
**council tax reduction schemes** 761
entitlement conditions 762
pension age or over 762
under pension age 763
habitual residence 1300
payments treatment as income
means-tested benefits under pension age 354
person subject to immigration control 1279
public funds 1276
residence rules 1306

**councillors**
treated as not in full-time work
new-style JSA/I-ESA 885
treatment as earnings
C-ESA 563
means-tested benefits over pension age 380
means-tested benefits under pension age 342
working during limited capability for work 929
**counselling services**
HB 206
**couples**
16/17-year-olds, personal allowance rates
I-ESA 268
capital
means-tested benefits over pension age 427
means-tested benefits under pension age 399
UC 151
change of partner claiming
HB 214
PC 247
child benefit 495
Christmas bonus 784
civil partners
means-tested benefits 255
UC 58
claiming as a couple
C-ESA 558
HB 198, 214
I-ESA 174
means-tested benefits 254
new-style JSA 615
PC 240
UC 38, 58
cohabitation
means-tested benefits 255
UC 59
disregard of partner's home
means-tested benefits over pension age 430
means-tested benefits under pension age 405
UC 156
funeral expenses payment 708
joint claims
UC 45
liability for rent
HB 186, 189
UC 95
living apart
means-tested benefits 257
UC 61
married couples
means-tested benefits 255
UC 58
mixed-age couples
HB 184, 197
PC 240
UC 37
NI number requirement for partner 1007
non-dependant couples
HB 210
I-ESA/PC 293
not non-dependants
HB 208
I-ESA/PC 290
partner fails habitual residence test
UC 1343
partner in care home
housing costs 835
means-tested benefits 833
UC 831
partner in hospital
housing costs 825
means-tested benefits 823
UC 821
partner in prison
housing costs 845
means-tested benefits 840
UC 839
partner subject to immigration control 1284
pensioner premium 274
personal allowances
rates 266
recourse to public funds
HB 1286
I-ESA 1287
UC 1284
recovery of overpayments
HB 1083
IS/I-JSA/I-ESA/PC 1076
severe disability premium 276
PC 276
sharing a bedroom
HB 331
UC 106
students
HB 802, 803
UC 793
UC 33, 36
whose income counts
means-tested benefits over pension age 377
UC 124
**Court of Appeal**
appealing Upper Tribunal decisions
benefits 1231
SSP/SMP/SAP/SPP/SSPP/SPBP/SNCP 1257

**Court of Session**
appealing Upper Tribunal decisions
benefits 1231
Scottish benefits 1557
SSP/SMP/SAP/SPP/SSPP/SPBP/SNCP 1257
**courts**
appealing Upper Tribunal decisions
benefits 1231
Scottish benefits 1557
compensation 1268
permission to appeal to courts 1233
recovery of overpayments 1077
HB 1085
UC/new-style JSA/new-style ESA 1075
**credit sale agreements**
HB 186
**Criminal Injuries Compensation Scheme**
treatment of payments
means-tested benefits over pension age 434
means-tested benefits under pension age 411
UC 160
**Croatia** 1320
jobseekers 1321
pregnancy 1327
resided legally 1340
residence rights 1320
restrictions 1320
self-employment 1324
workers 1322
**croft land**
HB 185
treatment as capital
means-tested benefits over pension age 428
means-tested benefits under pension age 403
UC 154
**Crown servants**
child benefit 1346
**Crown tenants**
HB 186
rent met by I-ESA/PC 287
**currency**
payments in non-UK currencies
CA 479
means-tested benefits over pension age 390
means-tested benefits under pension age 364
**Czech Republic** 1320

**D**
**daily living activities**
ADP 1431
PIP 647
**Data Protection Act**
access to personal information 1103
**date of claim**
AA 447
ADP 1442
bereavement benefits 464
Best Start foods 1463
Best Start grants 1462
CA 481
CDP 1492
child benefit 503
CSP 1472
DLA 532
ESA
C-ESA 567
funeral expenses payments 713
funeral support payment 1502
guardian's allowance 503
HB 215
industrial injuries benefits 604
MA 640
new-style JSA 621
PC 248
PIP 676
Scottish child payment 1462
state pension 697
Sure Start maternity grant 707
UC 47
young carer grant 1479
**daytime attention/supervision**
CDP 1484
DLA 523, 524
**deafness**
CDP mobility component 1487
DLA care component 522
DLA mobility component 515
occupational 593, 598
students
HB 802
**death**
children's funeral fund payment 708
claimant's death
HB 222
delayed claims for bereavement benefits 464
EU co-ordination of benefits 1401
funeral expenses payments 707
funeral support payments 1497
of child
CDP 1494
child benefit 506
disabled child premium 271
guardian's allowance 506
SPBP 724
UC 67
of family member
UC 67
of person receiving care

CA 473
parents
guardian's allowance 497
presumption of death for bereavement benefits 464
recovery of funeral expenses payments 713
recovery of overpayments from estate 1071
HB 1082
rent restriction delayed
HB 333
UC 105
reporting 1030
right to reside after death of EEA family member 1333
Tell Us Once scheme 1030
treatment of pension payments
new-style JSA 617
work search requirement following bereavement 961

**debt**
deductions from benefit 1033
deprivation of capital
means-tested benefits under pension age 415
UC 162
more than one debt 1041
priority for payment by deductions from benefit 1042
self-assessment tax debts 1039
valuation of capital
means-tested benefits under pension age 418
UC 164

**debt relief order**
overpayments 1059

**decision makers**
benefits 1118
guidance 1119
making decisions 1118
response to First-tier Tribunal
benefits 1183
Scottish benefits 1546
Scottish benefits 1534
wrong decisions
benefits 1122

**decisions** 1115
AA 448
anti-test case rule 1159
budgeting loans 703
can be appealed 1172
cannot be appealed 1173
changing a decision 1128
circumstances on date decision made 1123
correcting 1122
date of new decision following supersession 1148
decision makers 1118
decision notices 1124
delay getting decision 1123
HB 228
DLA 538
explanation 1125
final decisions 1120
First-tier Tribunal
benefits 1198, 1205
Scottish benefits 1551
HB 219, 1121
HMRC decisions
SSP/SMP/SAP/SPP/SSPP/SPBP/SNCP 1251
how decisions are made 1118
incorrect decision leading to overpayment 1068
limited capability for work 923, 1121
limited information decision 1119
NI contributions 858, 1121
notification of decision
HB 219
process decisions
Scottish benefits 1561
sanctions 995
Scottish benefits 1417
statement of reasons 1206
Scottish benefits 1551
test case pending 1159
Upper Tribunal 1229
Scottish benefits 1557
valid claim 1122
who makes decisions 1118
written reasons for a decision 1125
wrong decisions 1122
*see also: challenging a decision*

**deductions from benefits** 1033
amount of deduction 1040
I-ESA/PC 1040
UC 1040
budgeting advance repayments 53
budgeting loan repayments 704
child support maintenance payments 1038
civil penalties 1074
consent for deductions 1034
fuel debts 1036
funeral expenses payments 712
funeral support payments 1501
hardship payments recovery 1053
housing costs 1035
housing costs contributions
UC 109
means-tested benefits 1034
more than one deduction 1041
non-dependant deductions

HB 207
I-ESA/PC 289
UC 109
non-means-tested benefits 1034
priority between debts 1042
recovery of overpayments 1075
child benefit 1075
guardian's allowance 1075
HB 1083, 1084
I-ESA/PC 1075
PC 1075
Scottish benefits 1527
UC/new-style JSA/new-style ESA 1074
rent arrears 1035
sanctions 979
I-ESA 177
new-style ESA 981
new-style JSA 982
UC 980
short-term advance recovery 1024
treatment as income
means-tested benefits over pension age 387
means-tested benefits under pension age 355
what deductions can be made for 1033
when deductions can be made 1034
**deductions from eligible rent**
charges for meals
HB 206
HB 203
service charges
HB 206
**deemed income**
treatment as income
means-tested benefits over pension age 388
**deferring**
state pension 688
**degree of disablement** 596
**delays**
advance payments 1023
benefits due but not paid 366
compensation 1261
decisions 1123
HB 228
health benefits 584
moving home
HB 190
UC 98
**dental treatment**
free 579
reduced-cost treatment 575
**Department for Work and Pensions**
alternative offices 1004
collecting information 1102
complaints 1262
contacting benefit offices 1010
discretion to recover overpayments 1072
**deprivation of resources**
capital
means-tested benefits over pension age 435
means-tested benefits under pension age 413
UC 161
diminishing capital rule
means-tested benefits under pension age 415
UC 163
income
means-tested benefits over pension age 392
means-tested benefits under pension age 365
UC 143
**dermatitis** 594
**detention centres**
child benefit 499
**determinations** 1534
ADP/CDP/CSP/PADP/SADLA awards 1540
change of circumstances 1535
changing a determination 1533
determination not made 1534, 1539
notice 1534
official error 1540
without a claim 1538
**diabetes**
free prescriptions 579
free sight tests 580
**dialysis** *see: renal dialysis*
**diffuse mesothelioma** 600, 606, 607
**diffuse pleural thickening** 606
**diminishing capital rule**
means-tested benefits over pension age 435
means-tested benefits under pension age 415
UC 163
**direct credit transfer**
overpayments 1063
payment of benefits 1019
**direct payments** 1033
housing costs 1035
payment of benefits 1019
rent arrears 1035
to landlord
HB 222
**disability**
adaptations to home 288
additional amounts
PC 242
additional bedroom
HB 331
UC 106

ADP 1428
appeals 1199
appeals held at home 1197
armed forces, payments to former members 779
CDP 1483
childcare costs disregarded
CA 478
HB 351
couple who cannot share a bedroom
HB 331
UC 106
descriptors
ADP 1429
PIP 646
UC/ESA 903
direct payments
treatment as income 363
disability conditions
AA 442
ADP 1429
DLA 512
PADP 1513
PIP 646
disability determination 1138
disability premium 272
DLA 511
enhanced disability premium 273
EU co-ordination of benefits 1401
financial help with costs of disability 783
fluctuating conditions
ADP 1431
ESA 903
PIP 664
free prescriptions 579
good reason for not attending training 990
health benefits 573
industrial injuries/disease 595
limited capability for work 895
PIP 645
points for mental disabilities test 909
points for physical disabilities test 903
severe disability addition
PC 275
severe disability premium 275
transferring to UC 27
UC 27
work capability assessment 896
work preparation requirement 940
work search requirement 959
work-related requirements 954
**disability living allowance** 511
absence abroad 1378
advance claims 533
age rules 526
appeals 1166
backdating 533, 1011
benefit cap 543
change of circumstances 540
child reaches 16 527
child winter heating payment 1506
claim forms
guidance on completing 534
claims 530
date of claim 532
decisions 538, 1115
delays 1123
disability premium 272
disabled child premium 271
entitlement to other benefits
means-tested benefits 541
non-means-tested benefits 542
EU co-ordination rules 1350, 1379
fraud 1100
habitual residence test 1300
hospital patients 818
information to support claim 532
interchange of claims 1014
length of award 539
medical examination 538
moving to Scotland 1419
moving to/from Scotland 541
no non-dependant deduction
HB 208
I-ESA/PC 291
UC 109
overlapping benefits 542
overpayments 1058
passport to other benefits 543
payment 538
person subject to immigration control 1279
prisoners 837
public funds 1276
renewal claims 533, 540
residence rules 1347
revisions 1130
severe disability premium 276
supersessions 1143
tax 541
terminal illness 530, 531
transferring to ADP 1446
transferring to PIP 527, 528
transferring to SADLA 1422
treatment as income 541
means-tested benefits over pension age 386
means-tested benefits under pension age 353
UC 137
**disability living allowance care component** 519
additional requirements test 520
age rules 526
amount 530

attention condition 521, 523, 524
bodily functions 522
care homes 826
daytime disability conditions 520
dialysis 530
disability conditions highest rate 519
disability conditions lowest rate 519
disability conditions middle rate 519
domestic duties 523
enhanced disability premium 273
night-time disability conditions 520
overlapping benefits 1021
supervision condition 521, 522, 524
terminal illness 530
who can get the component 519
**disability living allowance mobility component** 512
additional requirements test 517
age rules 526
amount 529
care homes 827
disability conditions higher rate 512
disability conditions lower rate 517
guidance 518
hospital patients 819
Motability 543
supervision 518
terminal illness 530
who can get the component 512
**disability premium** 272
earnings disregard 348
qualifying benefits 272
rate 280
training 272
transferring to UC 28
**disabled child addition**
UC 68
**disabled child premium** 271
rate 280
transferring to UC 28
**disabled children**
additional bedroom
HB 332
UC 106
CDP 1483
childcare costs
HB 350
disabled child addition
UC 68
disabled child premium 271
DLA 511
completing claim form 534
enhanced disability premium 273
**disabled students**
disabled students' allowance
disregards for grant income 808
ESA 797
HB 802
**disablement**
assessment 595
definition 595
disablement questions 595
industrial injury/disease 595
physical and mental disablement 518
prescribed degrees of disablement 596
**discharge grant**
I-ESA 403
**Discretionary Assistance Fund for Wales** 770
**discretionary housing payments** 548
age rules 550
amounts 551
benefit cap 553
challenging a decision 553
claims 552
entitlement to other benefits 553
extended payments of HB 226
tax 553
treatment as income
means-tested benefits under pension age 364
who can get discretionary housing payments 548
**discretionary leave**
benefit entitlement 1290
**discrimination**
EU co-ordination rules 1406
**dishonesty**
penalties for fraud 1108
**dismissal**
sanctions
new-style JSA 973
UC 973
SMP/SAP/SPP/SSPP/SPBP/SNCP 734
SSP 747
**disqualification**
C-ESA 557
I-ESA 173
IIDB 599
MA 635
widowed parent's allowance 458
**disqualifying benefits** 1111
**disregards**
benefits
means-tested benefits over pension age 385
means-tested benefits under pension age 353
capital
means-tested benefits over pension age 428
means-tested benefits under pension age 403
UC 154
charitable/voluntary payments 357
childcare costs
CA 478

HB over pension age 384
HB under pension age 350
discretionary local schemes
HB over pension age 387
HB under pension age 354
earnings
CA 478
HB over pension age 383
HB under pension age 349
I-ESA 347
means-tested benefits over pension age 380, 382
means-tested benefits under pension age 342, 347, 348
new-style JSA 616
UC 127
income
means-tested benefits over pension age 391
means-tested benefits under pension age 364
income from capital
means-tested benefits over pension age 388
means-tested benefits under pension age 359
self-employed earnings
means-tested benefits under pension age 348
UC 129
student grant income 808
student loans 809
tax/NI contributions changes
HB 343
**dissolution of civil partnerships**
bereavement benefits 459
right to reside after end of civil partnership to EEA national 1333
**divorce**
bereavement benefits 459
right to reside after divorce from EEA national 1333
**domestic duties**
DLA care component 523
**domestic violence and abuse**
definition
HB 328
I-ESA/PC 298
UC 951
exempt from bedroom tax
UC 118
good reason for refusing a job 990
housing costs for two homes
HB 193, 196
I-ESA/PC 298
UC 99
migrant victims of domestic abuse concession 1277, 1303
refuge housing costs
HB 183
UC 91
sanctuary scheme housing 313
work search requirement 961
work-related requirements 951
**domiciliary hearings** 1197
**dressing**
ADP 1432
PIP 655
**driving licence**
DLA 543
**drug dependency**
PIP 646
**dual citizens**
British and EEA nationals 1333

**E**

**early learning payment** 1453
amount 1455
**early retirement**
payments, treatment as income
UC 139
sanctions for voluntary unemployment
new-style JSA 977
UC 977
**earnings**
administrative earnings threshold 955
advance of earnings, treatment as capital 403
advance of earnings, treatment as income
CA 479
CA 474
calculating net employed earnings
CA 475
means-tested benefits over pension age 380
means-tested benefits under pension age 342
UC 127
calculating net self-employed earnings
CA 477
means-tested benefits over pension age 381
means-tested benefits under pension age 345
UC 128
childcare costs, disregarded
CA 478
means-tested benefits over pension age 384
means-tested benefits under pension age 350
deductions to recover overpayments 1076
HB 1085
UC/new-style JSA/new-style ESA 1075
disregarded

CA 478
means-tested benefits over pension age 380, 382
means-tested benefits under pension age 342, 347, 348
new-style JSA 616
UC 127
earnings thresholds 955
fluctuating
HB 370
I-ESA 369
gross earnings
means-tested benefits over pension age 381
means-tested benefits under pension age 342
MA 632
means-tested benefits
over pension age 379
under pension age 340
minimum income floor for self-employed earnings
UC 130
monthly earned income
UC 145
new-style JSA 616
notional earnings
CA 478
part weeks
I-ESA 370
payments on leaving a job
CA 475
means-tested benefits over pension age 381
means-tested benefits under pension age 343
UC 127
period covered by earnings 476
prescribed amount
new-style JSA 617
SMP/SAP/SPP/SSPP/SPBP/SNCP 729
SSP 750
surplus earnings
UC 135
two wage payments in one assessment period
UC 145
UC 126, 128
work allowance 41
**earnings condition**
budgeting advance 53
MA 632
**earnings limits**
NI contributions 1583
**earnings replacement benefits** 1021
**earnings rule**
CA 473
new-style JSA 616
state pension 688
**East Jerusalem**
benefit entitlement 1290
habitual residence test 1303
**eating**
ADP 1431
PIP 650
**education**
advanced education
UC 792
EEA nationals, child in education 1337
interruption of education
child benefit 491
NI credits 872
non-advanced
child benefit 489
receiving education
UC 37, 792
terminal date 491
*see also: full-time education, part-time students*
**education benefits** 774
**education maintenance allowance** 776
disregarded as income
means-tested benefits 364
**education, health and care plans**
payments, treatment as income
means-tested benefits under pension age 363
**elements** 68
carer element 75
child element 68
childcare costs element 76
housing costs element 78, 88
limited capability for work element 71
limited capability for work-related activity element 73
transitional element 78
transitional SDP element 27, 78
**eligible rent**
deductions 203
definition 202
fuel charges 204
HB 202
housing costs element 90
local authority discretion to reduce HB 307
maximum eligible rent
local housing allowance for HB 308
pre-Jan '96 rules 323
rent officer determination related rent 317
social sector tenants 314
UC housing costs element 112

restrictions
HB 303
UC 112
**emergencies**
advance payments 1023
alarm system
HB 206
good reason for not attending training 994
local authority welfare assistance 770
payment of benefits 1020
work search requirement 943
**emergency services**
payments, treatment as income
means-tested benefits over pension age 383
means-tested benefits under pension age 349
**employed earners**
decisions about NI contributions 1121
definition
NI contributions 859
disregarded earnings
CA 478
means-tested benefits under pension age 347
UC 127
earnings
CA 474
ESA/JSA/HB under pension age 340
MA 632
means-tested benefits over pension age 379
SMP/SAP/SPP/SSPP/SPBP/SNCP 729
SSP 750
UC 126
industrial injuries benefits 588
MA 631
SMP/SAP/SPP/SSPP/SPBP/SNCP 727
SSP 747
work search requirement 962
work-related requirements 954
**employers**
deductions from earnings 1076
HB 1085
UC/new-style JSA/new-style ESA 1075
notification of decisions
SSP/SMP/SAP/SPP/SSPP/SPBP/SNCP 1250
SSP 755
**employment and support allowance** 169, 555
absence abroad 565, 1373, 1380
advance claims
C-ESA 568
age rules
C-ESA 558
I-ESA 173
amount
C-ESA 558
I-ESA 174
appeal pending on limited capability for work 899, 925
appeals 1166
applicable amount
I-ESA 175, 265
assessment phase 559
backdating
C-ESA 568, 1012
basic allowance 560
benefit cap
C-ESA 571
I-ESA 179
benefit week 369
calculation
C-ESA 560
I-ESA 174
capital 398
capital limits 399
care homes 832
child's income 339
children
C-ESA 558
I-ESA 258
claimant commitment
new-style ESA 934
claims
C-ESA 565
I-ESA 178
components 281
contributory ESA 555
couples
C-ESA 558
I-ESA 174, 254
date of claim
C-ESA 567
decisions 1115
deductions from benefit
C-ESA 1034
I-ESA 1034
delays 1123
disqualification
C-ESA 557
I-ESA 173
disregarded earnings
I-ESA 347
earnings
C-ESA 930
entitlement to other benefits based on C-ESA
means-tested benefits 570
non-means-tested benefits 570
entitlement to other benefits based on I-ESA
means-tested benefits 179
non-means-tested benefits 179
EU co-ordination rules 1352, 1374, 1380

families
  I-ESA 254
fraud 1100
habitual residence test 1300
hardship payments 1053
homeless
  I-ESA 849
hospital patients 821, 822, 824
how long is it paid for
  C-ESA 564
income
  C-ESA 562
  I-ESA 339
income-related ESA 169
information to support claim
  C-ESA 567
interchange of claims 1014
leaseholder charges 286
limited capability for work 895, 898
limited capability for work-related activity
  913
maximum deductions 1040
mortgage interest loan 764
new claims 20
  C-ESA 24
  I-ESA 23
new-style ESA 24, 556
NHS charges, exemption
  I-ESA 574
NI contribution conditions 875
NI credits 867
old-style ESA 556
overlapping benefits
  C-ESA 570, 1021
overpayments 1058
  new-style ESA 1060
paid work 884
partner subject to immigration control
  1286
partner's income 339
passport to other benefits
  C-ESA 571
  I-ESA 179
payment
  C-ESA 568
  I-ESA 178
pension payments
  C-ESA 562
periods of limited capability for work 928
permitted work 347, 930
person subject to immigration control
  C-ESA 1280
  I-ESA 1279
personal allowances
  I-ESA 266
premiums
  I-ESA 270
prisoners
  C-ESA 837
  I-ESA 840
public funds 1276
reciprocal agreements 1352
replaced by UC 23
residence rules
  C-ESA 1352
  I-ESA 1307, 1343
revisions 1128, 1130
  following award of qualifying benefit
    1157
run-on
  I-ESA 138, 178
sanctions
  benefit offences 1112
  work-related requirements 177, 970
SMP/SAP/SPP/SSPP/SNCP 740
SSP 566, 758
starting work
  I-ESA 180
students 797
supersessions 1128, 1143
support component
  C-ESA 560
  I-ESA 282
tax
  C-ESA 570
  I-ESA 179
trade disputes 891
transferring to PC 242
transferring to UC 25
transfers from incapacity benefits 563
treated as claim for MA 640
treatment as income
  means-tested benefits over pension
    age 385
  means-tested benefits under pension
    age 353, 354
  UC 137
who can get ESA
  C-ESA 556
  I-ESA 172
work 888, 928
  I-ESA 884
work capability assessment 896
work preparation requirement
  new-style ESA 940
work-focused interviews
  new-style ESA 939
work-related activity 176
work-related activity component
  C-ESA 561
  I-ESA 282
work-related requirements
  new-style ESA 938, 959
  old-style ESA 176
young people 557

**employment injury assistance** 1418
**employment programmes**
good reason for leaving 993
payments, treatment as capital
means-tested benfits under pension age 412
payments, treatment as income
means-tested benefits under pension age 360
UC 138
sanctions for failure to participate 978
**energy efficiency grants** 782
**enhanced disability premium** 273
rate 280
transferring to UC 28
**epilepsy**
free prescriptions 579
**equal pay settlements**
treatment as earnings
CA 474
UC 126
treatment as income 340
**equal treatment** 1406
CA 479
EU co-ordination rules 1406
**equity release schemes**
treatment as income
means-tested benefits 389
UC 139
**errors**
claimant error
HB 1080
error of law by First-tier Tribunal 1216
official error 1136
HB 1078
NI credits 866
Scottish benefits 1540
on claim form
HB 213
revision due to factual error 1138
revision due to official error 1135
supersession due to error of law 1147
supersession due to factual error 1146, 1154
**estate**
recovery of funeral payments 713
recovery of overpayment 1071
HB 1082
**Estonia** 1320
**estrangement from parents**
definition
UC 793
UC 38
**European Economic Area**
member states 1389
**European Economic Area nationals**
benefit entitlement
means-tested benefits 1280
Brexit 1312
checklist of free movement rights 1317
child in education 1337
comprehensive sickness insurance 1329
covered by co-ordination rules 1392
derivative right to reside 1336
discrimination 1406
EU co-ordination of benefits rules 1388
EU Settlement Scheme 1314
exporting benefits 1408
family members 1329, 1399
free movement rights 1317
frontier workers 1342
funeral payments in EEA states
funeral expenses payments 711
funeral support payments 1500
habitual residence test 1303
initial right of residence 1321
jobseekers 1321
NI contributions 863
permanent right of residence 1338
person subject to immigration control 1273
pre-settled status 1315
pregnancy 1327
protected groups 1317
qualified person 1318
resided legally 1339
residence documents 1331
residence rights 1312
right to reside 1317
self-employment 1324
self-sufficient people 1328
settled status 1314
students 1329
transition period 1313
unemployed people 1325
workers 1322
**European free movement rights** 1317
A2 nationals 1320
A8 nationals 1320
Croatian nationals 1320
family members of British citizens 1332
family members of EEA nationals 1329
jobseekers 1321
legal sources of rights 1319
protected groups 1317
right to reside 1312
self-employed 1324
self-sufficient people 1328
students 1328
workers 1322
**European Free Trade Association** 1389
**European Union**
law 1389
member states 1389

**European Union co-ordination rules** 1388
aggregation 1406
benefits covered 1399
Brexit 1390
equal treatment 1406
exporting benefits 1408
old co-ordination rules 1396
overlapping benefits 1409
partial Withdrawal Agreement protections 1395
principles 1391, 1404
single competent state 1404
transition period 1390
using the rules 1391
who is covered 1392
Withdrawal Agreement protections 1393
**European Union Settlement Scheme** 1273, 1314
family permits 1274
late applications 1314
**evidence**
age 697
death for bereavement benefits 463
preparing a case at appeal 1204
required to support claims 1009, 1031
ADP 1441
child winter heating payment 1509
new-style JSA 620
pension age winter heating payment 1509
UC 46
winter heating payment 1509
*see also: medical evidence*
**eVisa** 1272
**exceptionally severe disablement allowance** 601
treatment as income
means-tested benefits over pension age 386
means-tested benefits under pension age 353
**excluded tenancies**
HB 306
**exempt accommodation** 326
**expected week of childbirth**
definition 631
**expenses**
councillors' expenses 342, 380
medical assessments 921
sale of capital
means-tested benefits under pension age 418
UC 164
voluntary work
treatment as income 364
**exporting benefits** 1408
**extended benefit unit** 103
**extended payments**
amount
HB 226
council tax reduction 761
HB 224
**extra-statutory payments**
administrative errors 1261
HB 217
new-style JSA 622
treatment as income
means-tested benefits under pension age 354

**F**
**failure to**
apply for capital
means-tested benefits under pension age 416
apply for income
means-tested benefits over pension age 392
means-tested benefits under pension age 365
UC 143
apply for job
new-style JSA 972
UC 972
attend interview
new-style JSA 622
UC 978
attend medical examination 922
complete claim
new-style JSA 622
disclose a material fact 1064, 1068
HB 1082
participate in assessment process
PIP 675
participate in consultation
ADP 1442
PIP 675
report change of circumstances 1030
HB 228
return questionnaire
PIP 675
take up job
new-style JSA 972
UC 972
**false statements**
penalties 1106
**families**
British citizens 1332
claiming for a family
C-ESA 558
HB 198, 254
I-ESA 174, 254
new-style JSA 615

PC 254
UC 58
dual British and EEA nationals 1333
EEA nationals 1329
EU co-ordination of benefits 1402
extended benefit unit 103
extended family members of EEA nationals 1331
family benefits 1409
former family members of EEA nationals 1333
permanent right of residence 1340
person subject to immigration control 1284
premiums 270
providing childcare
NI credits 870
**family premium** 270
rate 280
**family reunion** 1290
**Financial Assistance Scheme**
treatment as income
means-tested benefits 389
UC 139
**financial need**
advance payments 1023
discretionary housing payments 548
**Find a Job service** 944
**fines**
paid by deductions from benefit 1039
**firefighters**
payments treated as capital
means-tested benefits under pension age 403
payments treatment as income
CA 479
means-tested benefits over pension age 383, 384
means-tested benefits under pension age 349
treated as not full-time work
new-style JSA/I-ESA 885
work search requirement 963
**First-tier Tribunal** 1166, 1544
attendance at hearing 1197
carrying out a decision 1207
challenging a tribunal decision 1207
Scottish benefits 1551
complaints about HM Courts and Tribunals Service 1265
decisions 1205
Scottish benefits 1551, 1562
directions 1188
domiciliary hearings 1197
error of law 1209, 1216
inadequate reasons for decision 1219
relating to facts 1218
unfairness 1217
evidence at hearing
help for child/vulnerable adult/sensitive witness 1197
hearings
benefits 1196, 1199
Scottish benefits 1546, 1549
issues which must be considered 1201
judicial review of decisions 1246
late appeals 1176
Scottish benefits 1546, 1562
medical examinations 1200
Scottish benefits 1550
membership 1198
paper-based decisions 1195
Scottish benefits 1549
permission to appeal to Upper Tribunal 1221
Scottish benefits 1554
point of law
Scottish benefits 1551
preparing a case 1204
record of proceedings 1206
remote hearings 1194
representatives 1180
reviewing a tribunal decision 1223
Scottish benefits 1552
setting aside a decision 1208, 1209
Scottish benefits 1553, 1554
SSP/SMP/SAP/SPP/SSPP/SPBP/SNCP 1255
statement of reasons 1206
Scottish benefits 1551
striking out an appeal 1190
tribunal procedures 1198
what the tribunal can do 1186
Scottish benefits 1547
**fistula, permanent**
free prescriptions 579
**fit notes**
fitness for work 756
SSP 756
**fixed-term investments**
means-tested benefits over pension age 427
means-tested benefits under pension age 400
UC 152
**Flexible Support Fund** 781
**fluctuating hours of work**
means-tested benefits 885
term-time work
means-tested benefits 886
**fluctuating income**
CA 475
HB 370
I-ESA 369
means-tested benefits over pension age 394

**food banks** 782
**footwear**
budgeting loans 702
**foster care**
additional bedroom
HB 333
local housing allowance for HB 330
rent officer determined rent for HB 320
social sector tenants for HB 316
UC 106
allowances
CA 479
means-tested benefits over pension age 391
means-tested benefits under pension age 357
UC 142
child benefit 500
claiming for children
means-tested benefits 262
UC 64
foster parent approved as adopter
SAP/SPP/SSPP/SPBP/SNCP 736
lone foster carers who are students
HB 802
NI credits 869
treated as not in full-time work
new-style JSA/I-ESA 885
work-focused interviews 956
work-related requirements 952
**foster parent condition** 106
**fraud** 1100
advisers committing an offence 1107
convicted of fraud 1110
disqualifying benefits 1111
formal cautions 1111
fraud investigators 1103
future changes 1101
health benefits 584
imprisonment 1110
interviews under caution 1104
Scottish benefits 1529
landlords
HB 223
loss of benefits 1111
penalties 1109
powers of authorised officers 1103
Scottish benefits 1528
prosecution of offences 1106
prosecution or penalty 1109
sanctionable benefits 1112
Scottish benefits 1528
suspending/withholding benefit 1105
who can be required to give evidence 1102
**free school lunches** 774
**frequency of payment**
HB 221
UC 51
**frontier worker**
habitual residence test 1303
right to reside 1342
**fuel costs**
communal areas
HB 205
debts paid by deductions from benefit 1036
ineligible charges
HB 204
I-ESA/PC 287
**Fuel Direct** 1036
**full-time education**
advanced education
UC 792
CA 804
CSP 805
ESA
C-ESA 797
I-ESA 798
full-time courses 798
Scotland 799
HB 802
modular courses 793, 800
NI credits 872
non-advanced education
child benefit 489
sandwich courses 799
UC 792
*see also: education*
**full-time work**
extended payments
HB 224
financial help seeking or starting work 781
HB
over pension-age 384
under pension-age 349
housing costs run-on 299
new-style JSA 613
treatment of work
HB 889
I-ESA 884, 888
new-style JSA 884, 887
PC 888
*see also: work*
**funeral expenses payment** 707
amount 711
appeals 1166
claim form 713
deductions from award 712
EEA nationals 711
eligibility 708
excluded people 709
payment 713

person subject to immigration control 708
qualifying benefits 707
recovery from the estate 713
residence rules 1355
revisions 1130
time limits for claiming 713
**funeral support payment** 1497
age rules 1500
amount 1501
appeals 1544
benefit cap 1503
change of circumstances 1535
claims 1502
date of claim 1502
deductions from awards 1501
EEA nationals 1500
entitlement to other benefits 1503
fraud 1528
information to support claim 1502
overpayments 1526
payment 1502
person subject to immigration control 1279
public funds 1276
qualifying benefits 1498
recovery from the estate 1503
redeterminations 1535
residence rules 1355
responsible for funeral expenses 1498
tax 1503
time limit for claiming 1502
treatment as income 1503
means-tested benefits over pension age 386
means-tested benefits under pension age 353
UC 137
who can get funeral support payments 1497
**funerals**
abroad
funeral expenses payments 711
funeral support payments 1500
budgeting loans 702
funeral plan payments
means-tested benefits over pension age 434
UC 160
good reason for not attending training 994
responsibility for costs
funeral expenses payments 711
funeral support payment 1498
**furniture**
budgeting loans 702
**future interest in property**
means-tested benefits over pension age 431
means-tested benefits under pension age 408
**future payments**
means-tested benefits over pension age 431
means-tested benefits under pension age 408
UC 166

**G**
**garages**
HB 185
**Gaza**
benefit entitlement 1290
habitual residence test 1303
**gender recognition certificate**
bereavement benefits 462
**George Cross payments**
treatment as income
means-tested benefits under pension age 364
UC 161
**Gibraltar**
UK-Gibraltar agreement 1393
**glasses**
vouchers 580
**glaucoma**
free sight tests 580
**Golan Heights**
benefit entitlement 1290
habitual residence test 1303
**good reason**
failure to attend consultation
PIP 675
failure to attend medical examination 922
failure to return questionnaire
PIP 675
late claim
HB 218
new-style JSA 622
leaving a job 991
leaving a training scheme 993
refusing a job 994
refusing to attend training 993
sanctions 989
**graduated retirement benefit** 691
overlapping benefits 1022
**Grenfell Tower**
treatment of compensation payments
means-tested benefits over pension age 434
means-tested benefits under pension age 411
UC 160
**ground rent**
HB 185
I-ESA/PC 287
UC 91

**guarantee payments**
treatment as earnings
CA 474
means-tested benefits 344
**guardian's allowance** 487
absence abroad 1377, 1409
adoption 498
advance claims 504
age rules 498
amount 499
appeals 1166
backdating 503, 1012
benefit cap 508
change of circumstances 506
claims 501
contributing to cost of child 498
date of claim 503
decisions 1115
delays 1123
eligible child 497
entitlement to child benefit 496
entitlement to other benefits
means-tested benefits 508
non-means-tested benefits 508
EU co-ordination rules 1347, 1378
fraud 1100
information to support claim 502
interchange of claims 1014
interim payments 505
late claims 503
looked after by local authority 499
missing parents 497
overlapping benefits 1023
overpayments 1058, 1075
payment 504
prisoners 497, 838
child in prison 499
qualifying children 496
qualifying young person 496
refugees 1291
residence rules 1346
revisions 1128, 1130
supersessions 1128, 1143
tax 507
treated as entitled to child benefit 496
treatment as income 508
means-tested benefits over pension age 386
means-tested benefits under pension age 353
UC 138
who can get guardian's allowance 496
who should claim 502
**guidance**
CDP mobility component 1488
DLA mobility component 518
**guided learning**
definition of full-time education
I-ESA 798

H
**habitual residence** 1300
benefits affected 1300
definition 1304
exempt from habitual residence test 1303
failing the habitual residence test 1301
habitual residence test 1301
returning residents 1306
**halls of residence**
HB 803
**hardship**
definition 1054
recovery of overpayments
tax credits 1091
**hardship payments** 1050
age rules
UC 1051
amounts
ESA 1054
UC 1052
benefit cap 1056
challenging a decision 1056
claims 1055
deciding hardship 1054
UC 1055
ESA 1053
JSA 1050
length of payment
UC 1051
payment 1056
recovery of payments
UC 1053
sanctions
ESA 1053
UC 1051
tax 1056
UC 1050
who can get hardship payments
UC 1051
**health and safety**
working hours 1584
**health benefits** 573
Best Start foods 1455
calculating income 577
calculating requirements 576
certificates 583
claims 582
delays 584
exemptions from charges 574
fraud 584
Healthy Start food and vitamins 771
low income scheme 575
overpayments 584
prescriptions 578

refunds 584
who can get health benefits 573
**health condition**
ADP 1431
PIP 651
**healthcare professionals** 1010
consultations
PIP 674
**Healthy Start** 771
amount 772
claims 773
payment card 771
qualifying benefits 772
vitamins 773
who can claim 771
**heating payments**
Scotland 1505
**Help to Save scheme** 782
**high-income child benefit charge** 507
**hire purchase agreement**
HB 186
**HM Courts and Tribunals Service** 1167, 1216
complaints 1265
**HM Revenue and Customs**
complaints 1263, 1264
decisions on statutory payments 1250
NI contributions decisions 858, 1121
recovery of overpayments
benefits 1072
tax credits 1092
**holiday pay**
treatment as capital
means-tested benefits under pension age 403
treatment as earnings
CA 474
means-tested benefits over pension age 380
means-tested benefits under pension age 341
UC 126
**holidays**
available for work requirement 946
carers
CA 473
work search requirement 946
**home**
definition 295
occupation
HB 190
mortgage interest loan 767
UC 97
treatment as capital
means-tested benefits over pension age 428
means-tested benefits under pension age 403
UC 154
treatment of relative's home
means-tested benefits over pension age 430
means-tested benefits under pension age 405
UC 156
**home detention curfew**
means-tested benefits 840
HB 844
**home improvements**
budgeting loans 702
interest on DWP loans
I-ESA/PC 289, 766
local authority grants 782
**home responsibilities protection**
NI credits 870
**home visits** 1010
**homeless** 847
good reason for refusing a job 991
hostel costs
UC 113
jobseeking conditions 848
recourse to public funds 1276
UC 848
work-related requirements 848
**hospices**
benefit entitlement
AA/DLA/PIP 819, 828
ADP/PADP 819, 828
CDP 819, 828
SADLA 819
**hospital** 816
AA 818
ADP/CDP/DLA/PIP/PADP/SADLA 818
benefit entitlement 816
CA 819
child benefit 492, 824
child in hospital 823
means-tested benefits 262
UC 821
childcare costs allowance
HB 350
costs for usual home 825
HB 825
I-ESA/PC 297
UC 98, 820, 825
CSP 819
definition 817
ESA 821, 822, 824
fares to hospital 581
HB 193, 821, 822
independent hospital
HB 187
limited capability for work
ESA 899
UC 897
linking rules 819
lone parents 823

mentally ill prisoners
means-tested benefits 841
non-means-tested benefits 841
UC 841
mortgage interest loan 820, 825
moving home
HB 191
new-style JSA 824
NHS charges, exemption 574
non-dependant deductions
HB 209
I-ESA/PC 291
partner in 823
UC 821
patient definition 817
PC 821, 822
private patients 817
Scottish child payment 824
UC 820
winter fuel payments 715
**hostels**
paid by deductions from benefit 1039
rent restrictions
HB 317
specified accommodation
HB 183
UC 91
**hours of work**
calculating hours of work
new-style JSA/I-ESA 885
expected hours of work 942
fluctuating hours of work
means-tested benefits 885
full-time work
means-tested benefits 884
increased hours, extended payments
HB 224
increased hours, financial help 781
increased hours, housing costs run-on
I-ESA/PC 299
limits to working week 1584
normal hours of work
means-tested benefits 885
**house sale**
proceeds on separation
means-tested benefits over pension age 429
means-tested benefits under pension age 404
UC 154
**houseboats**
excluded tenancies 306
HB 185
rent restrictions
HB 317
UC 90
**household equipment**
budgeting loans 702
**household support fund payments**
treatment as capital
means-tested benefits over pension age 435
means-tested benefits under pension age 412
UC 161
treatment as income
means-tested benefits income over pension age 391
means-tested benefits income under pension age 363
UC 142
**households**
children treated as member of household
means-tested benefits 261
means-tested benefits 262
separate households 263
UC 60
**housing associations**
deposits
means-tested benefits under pension age 405
UC 155
excluded tenancies 306
local housing allowance
HB 307
registered housing associations 306
rent restrictions
HB 305, 327
UC 115
**housing benefit** 181
16/17-year-olds 186
absence abroad 1374
additional earnings disregard
over pension age 384
age rules 196
amount 199
appeals 1166, 1176
applicable amount 265
backdating a claim 216
benefit cap 231, 1025, 1028
benefit week 203
calculation
not receiving means-tested benefits 200
receiving means-tested benefits 200
capital
over pension age 425
under pension age 398
capital limits
over pension age 426
under pension age 399
care homes 187, 832, 835
care leavers 846
change of circumstances 228
charges for meals 206
children 198, 258

claims 183, 211
components 281
continuing payments 224
PC 224
couples 214, 254
date of claim 215
death 222
decisions 219
deductions from eligible rent 203
deductions to recover overpayments 1083
delays 228
discretionary housing payments 548
disregarded earnings
over pension age 382
under pension age 347, 349
earnings 370
eligible rent 202
entitlement to other benefits
means-tested benefits 231
non-means-tested benefits 231
EU co-ordination rules 1375
extended payment on return to work 224
families 254
financial help on starting work 232
fraud 1100
fuel charges 204
good cause for late claim 218
grace period for benefit cap 1027
habitual residence test 1300
hospital patients 193, 821, 822, 825
income
over pension age 377, 378
under pension age 339
increase following award of qualifying benefit 219
interim payments 228
joint occupiers 189
maximum rent
local housing allowance 308
pre-Jan '96 rules 323
rent officer determination related rent 317
social sector tenants 314
moving house 218
new claims 183
working age HB 23
non-commercial agreements 188
non-dependants 207
overpayments 1078
paid work 889
partner subject to immigration control 1285
partner's income
under pension age 339
passport to other benefits 232
payments 221
payments on account 228
pension-age HB 197
permitted work disregard
HB over pension age 383
HB under pension age 349
person subject to immigration control 1279
personal allowances 266
premiums 270
prisoners 840, 844
public funds 1276
rent 202
rent restrictions 303
rent-free periods 203
replaced by UC 24
residence rules 1307, 1343
revisions 1128, 1130
following award of qualifying benefit 1157
run-on 227
sanctions for benefit offences 1112
service charges 205
shared accommodation 190
specified accommodation 183
start of entitlement 220
students 187, 801
supersessions 1128, 1143
support component 282
taking advantage of HB 189
tapers 201
tax 231
temporary accommodation 183, 196
trade disputes 891
transferring to UC 25
treatment as income
means-tested benefits over pension age 386
means-tested benefits under pension age 353
two homes 190, 195
violence 195, 196
waiving of rent during repairs 187
weekly income 370
who can get HB 182
work 884
work-related activity component 282
working-age HB 197
**housing costs element** 88
16/17 year old care leavers 90
accommodation not covered 90
amount 101
cap rent 112
contrived agreements 96
core rent 110
death of family member 105
eligible payments 89
families 103
housing costs contributions 109
liability condition 93

non-dependant deductions 109
non-dependants 103
occupation condition 97
one-bedroom shared accommodation 113
overpayments 1061
owner-occupiers 89, 90
payment 50
payment condition 90
private tenants 110
service charges 92, 118
size criteria 104
social sector tenants 115
specified accommodation 91
two homes 97, 98, 102
waiting period 119
who can get 89
**housing costs run-on**
I-ESA/PC 299
**housing repair grants** 782
**humanitarian protection**
benefit entitlement 1290
family reunion 1290
integration loans 1292
**Hungary** 1320
**hypoadrenalism**
free prescriptions 579
**hypoparathyroidism**
free prescriptions 579
**hypopituitarism**
free prescriptions 579

**I**
**Iceland**
EFTA nationals 1389
**ileostomy**
free prescriptions 579
**immigration status** 1271
evidence of status 1272
**in-work conditionality** 959
**incapacitated**
means-tested benefits 352
**incapacity benefit** 556
absence abroad 1382
appeals 1166
EU co-ordination rules 1383
overpayments 1058
residence rules 1347
revisions 1128, 1130
supersessions 1128, 1143
transfers to ESA 563
**incapacity for work**
continuous employment
SMP/SAP/SPP/SSPP/SPBP/SNCP 728
disability premium 272
EEA worker and self-employed status 1326
evidence
SSP 756
linked periods
new-style JSA 612
NI credits 867
period of incapacity
SSP 748
SSP 747
students
HB 802
treated as incapable of work
SSP 748
**income**
assessed income period
PC 251
assumed income
UC 140
benefits not treated as income
means-tested benefits under pension age 353
benefits treated as income
means-tested benefits over pension age 385
means-tested benefits under pension age 353
UC 137
calculating net employed earnings
CA 475
means-tested benefits over pension age 380
means-tested benefits under pension age 342
calculating net self-employed earnings
means-tested benefits over pension age 381
means-tested benefits under pension age 346
capital treated as income
means-tested benefits under pension age 360
UC 125
child's
means-tested benefits over pension age 378
means-tested benefits under pension age 339
UC 124
deemed income 389
definition
HB over pension age 378
means-tested benefits under pension age 340
PC 378
UC 125
deprivation of income
means-tested benefits over pension age 392
means-tested benefits under pension age 365

UC 143
difference between income and capital 340
failure to apply for income
means-tested benefits over pension age 392
means-tested benefits under pension age 365
UC 143
hardship payments 1054
health benefits 577
income from capital
means-tested benefits over pension age 388
means-tested benefits under pension age 359
UC 42, 140
income treated as capital
means-tested benefits under pension age 402
UC 153
means-tested benefits
over pension age 377
under pension age 339
monthly amount
UC 144, 146
non-dependants
HB 210, 211
I-ESA/PC 292
non-means-tested benefits
CA 474
new-style JSA 616
notional income
means-tested benefits over pension age 391
means-tested benefits under pension age 365
UC 142
part weeks
I-ESA 370
partner's
means-tested benefits over pension age 377
means-tested benefits under pension age 339
UC 124
period covered by income
new-style JSA/I-ESA 368
strike pay
new-style JSA 891
UC 891
students 806
ESA 801
HB 804
UC 795
UC 124, 136
weekly amount
HB under pension age 370
means-tested benefits over pension age 379, 393, 394
means-tested benefits under pension age 368

**income support**
absence abroad 1368
overpayments 1062
recovery 1074
person subject to immigration control 1279
personal allowances 266
public funds 1276
replaced by UC 21, 23
run-on 138
transferring to PC 242
transferring to UC 29

**income tax**
AA 450
ADP 1446
bereavement benefits 467
Best Start foods 1464
Best Start grants 1464
CA 483
CDP 1494
changes ignored
HB 343
child benefit 507
child winter heating payment 1510
Christmas bonus 784
CSP 1474
discretionary housing payments 553
DLA 541
ESA
C-ESA 570
I-ESA 179
funeral support payment 1503
guardian's allowance 507
hardship payments 1056
HB 231
industrial injuries benefits 606
JSA 626
MA 642
PADP 1519
PC 251
pension age winter heating payment 1510
PIP 679
refunds treatment as capital
means-tested benefits under pension age 403
refunds treatment as income
CA 479
means-tested benefits under pension age 360
UC 126
SADLA 1424
Scottish child payment 1464
short-term assistance for ADP/CDP/PADP/SADLA 1560

SMP/SAP/SPP/SSPP/SPBP/SNCP 739
social fund loans and payments 716
SSP 758
state pension 699
UC 55
winter heating payment 1510
young carer grant 1480

**increases for dependants**
adult dependants
bereavement support payment 455
SSP 752
children
bereavement support payment 455
widowed parent's allowance 457
overlapping benefits 1022

**indefinite leave to enter or remain**
EEA nationals 1314

**Independent Case Examiner** 1262

**industrial accidents/diseases**
accidents 589
assessing disablement 595
bereavement benefits 461
causation 593
in the course of employment 590
legal action 588
loss of faculty 595
more than one cause of disability 596
one-off lump-sum payment 606
onset 594
out of employment 592
period of assessment 598
personal injury definition 589
prescribed industrial diseases 593
prescribed occupations 593
recrudescence 594
time limits 593
travel to work 591
two or more accidents/diseases 597

**industrial injuries benefits** 587
absence abroad 1381
advance claims 604
appeals 1166
backdating 604, 1012
benefit cap 606
change of circumstances 605
claims 603
date of claim 604
employed earner definition 588
entitlement to other benefits
means-tested benefits 606
non-means-tested benefits 606
EU co-ordination rules 1353, 1381
IIDB 599
in the course of employment 590
industrial injury condition 587
information to support claim 604
late claims 604
misconduct 592
NI contribution conditions 588
overlapping benefits 606
payment of benefit 605
person subject to immigration control 1280
personal injury definition 589
reduced earnings allowance 601
renewal claims 605
residence rules 1352
retirement allowance 602
self-employed 588
tax 606
treatment as income 606
means-tested benefits over pension age 385
means-tested benefits under pension age 353
UC 137
who can get industrial injuries benefits 587

**industrial injuries disablement benefit** 599
absence abroad 1381
age rules 599
amount 599
disqualification 599
EU co-ordination rules 1353, 1381
increases of benefit 600
overlapping benefits 1021
prisoners 838
residence rules 1352
who can get IIDB 599

**infected blood schemes**
treatment of compensation payments
means-tested benefits over pension age 434
means-tested benefits under pension age 411
UC 160

**infectious disease**
limited capability for work
ESA 899
UC 897

**information**
about decision 1124
HB 220
required by employer
SAP 720
SMP 719
SNCP 727
SPBP 725
SPP 721
SSPP 723
required by HMRC
SSP/SMP/SAP/SPP/SSPP/SPBP/SNCP 1251
required to prevent fraud 1102
to make a decision 1118
to support an appeal 1178, 1185

Scottish benefits 1545, 1546
to support claim 1009, 1031
AA 446
ADP 1440
bereavement benefits 463
Best Start foods 1461
Best Start grants 1461
C-ESA 567
CA 481
CDP 1492
child benefit 502
child winter heating payment 1509
CSP 1471
DLA 532
funeral support payment 1502
guardian's allowance 502
HB 212, 215
industrial injuries benefits 604
MA 639
new-style JSA 620
PADP 1516
PC 247
pension age winter heating payment 1509
PIP 671
Scottish child payment 1461
SSP 755
state pension 697
UC 46
winter heating payment 1509
young carer grant 1479
to support revision 1141
to support supersession 1148
written reasons for a decision
benefits 1125
**insurance payments**
treatment as income
C-ESA 563
means-tested benefits 362
UC 139
**insurance policies**
surrender value
means-tested benefits over pension age 431
means-tested benefits under pension age 407
UC 158
**integration loans** 1292
repayment 1039
**interest**
on mortgage interest loans 767
on overpayments 1069
HB 1081
on savings, treatment as capital
means-tested benefits under pension age 402
UC 153
on savings, treatment as income
UC 141
**interim payments**
child benefit 505, 1124
guardian's allowance 505, 1124
**interviews**
failure to attend
new-style JSA 622
UC 978
fraud 1104
initial interviews
new-style JSA 620
work-focused interviews 939
work-related requirements 948
**investigation of claims** 1102
authorised officers 1103
interviews under caution 1104
**Irish citizens**
right to reside 1312
UK-Ireland Convention 1397
**ISA**
treatment as capital
UC 151
**Israel**
benefit entitlement 1290
habitual residence test 1303

J
**Job Start Payment** 781, 1419
public funds 1276
**Jobcentre Plus travel discount card** 781
**jobseeker's agreement**
appealing a decision 1173
**jobseeker's allowance, income-based**
absence abroad 1368
overpayments 1062
person subject to immigration control 1279
personal allowances 266
public funds 1276
replaced by UC 21, 23
run-on 138
transferring to UC 29
*see also: new-style jobseeker's allowance*
**jobseekers from the EEA**
A2 nationals 1321
A8 nationals 1321
benefit entitlement 1322
Croatia 1321
genuine chance of employment 1321
genuine prospects of work test 1322
right to reside 1321
**jobseeking periods**
linked periods 612
new-style JSA 611
**joint tenants**
deductions for fuel charges
HB 204

HB 189
not a non-dependant
HB 208
I-ESA/PC 290
UC 104
UC 111, 116
**judicial review** 1236
grounds for review 1239
in High Court/Court of Session 1245
in Upper Tribunal 1246
letter before claim 1242
pre-action protocol 1242
process 1236
time limits 1237
transferring cases to Upper Tribunal 1247
when to use judicial review 1238
**jury service**
allowances 413
NI credits 873
work search requirement 963

**K**
**keeping in touch days** 731
**kidney dialysis** *see: renal dialysis*
**kinship carers**
additional bedroom
HB 333
local housing allowance for HB 330
rent officer determined rent for HB 320
social sector tenants for HB 316
UC 106
child benefit 500
definition 1457
NI credits 869
payments, treatment as income
means-tested benefits over pension age 391
means-tested benefits under pension age 357
UC 142
treated as not in full-time work
new-style JSA/I-ESA 885
two-child limit
UC 70

**L**
**land** 152, 400, 427
**landlord**
close relative
HB 187
UC 96
direct payments for rent arrears 1035
HB fraud 223
not a non-dependant
HB 208
UC 104
payment of benefit direct to a landlord
HB 221, 222
UC 50
recovery of overpayments
HB 1083, 1087
responsibility for landlord's child
HB 188
**laryngostomy**
free prescriptions 579
**late claims** 1011
bereavement benefits
delay finding out/uncertainty about death 464
CA 481
child benefit 503
good cause 218
guardian's allowance 503
HB 216
industrial injuries benefits 604
new-style JSA 622
SSP 756
state pension 697
**Latvia** 1320
**laundry facilities**
HB 205
UC 92
**LEAP reviews**
PIP 678
**learner support funds** 812
**leaseholder charges** 118, 286
amount of charges
I-ESA/PC 289
charges paid after return to work
I-ESA/PC 299
ground rent
I-ESA/PC 287
UC 91
liability for charges 294
non-dependant deductions 289
service charges
I-ESA/PC 288
UC 92
waiting period for charges
UC 119
who can get help with charges 287
**leave to enter or remain** 1274
appealing refusal of application to vary leave 1279
domestic violence and abuse concessionary leave 1277
extension of leave to remain 1275
indefinite leave under EU Settlement Scheme 1314
means-tested benefits 1280
non-means-tested benefits 1282
right to reside during a period of leave 1313
**leaving a job**
good reason 991
misconduct

new-style JSA 973
UC 973
payments
CA 475
means-tested benefits over pension age 381
means-tested benefits under pension age 343
UC 127
voluntarily
new-style JSA 973
UC 973
**Lebanon**
benefit entitlement 1290
habitual residence test 1303
**legacy benefits** 9, 19
recovery of overpayments 1074
who can still claim 21
**legal aid**
court costs for appeals 1233
representation at appeals 1181, 1220
**legal fees**
court costs for appeals 1233
First-tier Tribunal appeals 1181
Upper Tribunal appeals 1220
**LGBT Financial Recognition Scheme**
treatment as capital
means-tested benefits under pension age 411
UC 160
**liable for rent**
16/17-year-olds 186
before moving in
HB 190
UC 97
definition
UC 93
HB 186
joint liability
HB 189
UC 111
separation
UC 95
treated as liable to pay rent
HB 187
UC 94
treated as not liable to pay rent
HB 187
UC 95
UC 94
**liable relatives**
definition 355
payments 355
**licensees**
HB 185
not a non-dependant
I-ESA/PC 290
UC 90
**Liechtenstein**
EFTA nationals 1389
**life insurance**
surrender value
means-tested benefits over pension age 431
means-tested benefits under pension age 407
UC 158
**life interest** 408
**life rent** 408
**lifeboat crew**
payments treated as capital
means-tested benefits under pension age 403
payments treated as income
CA 479
means-tested benefits over pension age 383, 384
means-tested benefits under pension age 349
treated as not full-time work
new-style JSA/I-ESA 885
work search requirement 963
**limited capability for work** 895
appeal pending 924
ESA 925
new-style JSA 927
UC 927
appeals 923, 1199
challenging a decision 923
condition worsens 927
decision 923, 1121
descriptors 903
determinations 923, 1138
disability premium 273
element 71
ESA
C-ESA 556
I-ESA 172
fluctuating condition 903
future changes 895
linking rules 928
mandatory reconsiderations 923
medical assessments 921
new-style JSA 613
NI credits 867
period of limited capability for work 928
permitted work 930
points for mental disabilities test 909
points for physical disabilities test 903
pregnancy 643
ESA 899
UC 897
questionnaire 920
self-employment 133
SMP/SAP/SPP/SSPP/SNCP 740
students

UC 793
supersessions 1144, 1149
transferring to UC from ESA 72, 898
treated as having limited capability for work 900
ESA 898
UC 896
treated as not having limited capability for work
ESA 902
new-style JSA 613
UC 901
UC 71
work allowance
UC 41
work capability assessment 896
work preparation 940
work-related activity component 282
work-related requirements 954, 957, 959
working during limited capability for work period 928
young people
ESA 557
UC 37
**limited capability for work-related activity** 913
assessments 914
descriptors 914
element 73
ESA support component 560
future changes 895
questionnaire 914
transferring to UC from ESA 74, 919
treated as having limited capability for work-related activity 917
UC 73
work-related requirements 954, 959
**limited leave to remain**
EEA nationals 1315
**linking rules**
C-ESA 568
care home residents
AA/ADP/CDP/DLA/PIP/PADP 829
hospital patients 819
limited capability for work 928
new-style JSA 612
SSP 748, 749, 753
**Lithuania** 1320
**living together as a couple**
means-tested benefits 255
UC 59
**loans**
home repair/improvement
I-ESA/PC 289, 405, 766
UC 155
repaid by deductions from benefit 1039
treatment as capital
means-tested benefits over pension age 427
means-tested benefits under pension age 400
UC 152
**loan for mortgage interest**
*see: mortgage interest loan*
**local authorities**
complaints about benefit administration
HB 1265
council tax help 761
education benefits 774
local welfare assistance 770
rent restrictions for tenants
HB 305, 327
social care payments
treatment as capital 411
treatment as income 363
UC 161
support for care leavers 846
**Local Government and Social Care Ombudsman** 1267
**local housing allowance** 307
broad rental market area
HB 311
UC 114
cap rent
HB 308
UC 112
challenging a rent restriction
HB 334
change in circumstances
HB 312
delaying a rent restriction after a death
HB 333
direct payment to landlord 223
ineligible charges 203
maximum rent
HB 308
occupiers
HB 329
one-bedroom self-contained accommodation
HB 310
one-bedroom shared accommodation
HB 310
rates
HB 311
UC 114
size criteria
HB 309
UC 104
two or more bedrooms
HB 311
UC housing costs element 112
**local welfare assistance** 770
Discretionary Assistance Fund for Wales 770

recourse to public funds 1276
Scottish Welfare Fund 770
treatment as capital
means-tested benefits over pension age 435
means-tested benefits under pension age 411
UC 161
treatment as income
means-tested benefits over pension age 391
means-tested benefits under pension age 363
UC 142
**lodgers**
treatment of income from 479
means-tested benefits under pension age 358
**lone parents**
childcare costs disregarded
CA 478
earnings disregard
HB over pension age 383
HB under pension age 348
PC 382
HB 214
hospital patients 823
personal allowance rates 266
students
HB 802
work-focused interviews 956
work-related requirements 177, 952
**long lease**
excluded from HB 185
**looked-after children** 846
ADP/CDP/DLA/PIP 828
child benefit 499
disabled child premium 271
eligibility to claim UC 847
excluded from UC 846
family premium 271
guardian's allowance 499
HB 846
health benefits 574
leaving local authority care
UC 113
local authority payments
treatment as capital 411
treatment as income 363
UC 161
treatment as member of household
means-tested benefits 262
UC 64
UC 846
**loss of faculty** 595
**low income**
Help to Save scheme 782
ineligible for SSP 750
low-paid work, notional income
UC 143
minimum income floor for self-employed earnings
UC 130
NHS charges 575
**lower earnings limit**
NI contributions 860
SMP/SAP/SPP/SSPP/SPBP/SNCP 730
SSP 750

**M**
**maintenance**
liable relative payments 355
treatment as income
means-tested benefits over pension age 387
means-tested benefits under pension age 355
UC 138
**maintenance undertaking** 1278
death of sponsor 1281
means-tested benefits 1280
non-means-tested benefits 1282
**managed migration**
transferring to UC 29
transitional element 78
**mandatory reconsideration**
applying 1170
before appeal 1130, 1168
benefits 1168
claiming benefits while request is considered 924
hardship payments 1056
late requests 1169, 1171
time limits 1169
**mandatory reconsideration notice** 1130, 1171
**market value**
capital 164, 418
**marriage**
NI reduced liability for married women 862
void/voidable marriage 459
*see also: couples*
**married women**
reduced liability for NI contributions 862
**maternity**
Best Start foods 1455
budgeting loans 702
EEA worker and self-employed status 1327
EU co-ordination of benefits 1401
free dental treatment 580
free prescriptions 578
Healthy Start 771
limited capability for work
ESA 898

maternity pay and benefits 629, 718
pregnancy and baby payment 1453
Sure Start maternity grant 705
work-related requirements 952
**maternity allowance** 629
absence abroad 638, 1382
age rules 636
amount 637
appeals 1166
backdating 640, 1012
benefit cap 643
calculating average earnings 637
change of circumstances 641
choosing SSPP 722
claims 638
curtailment notification 634
date of claim 640
decisions 1115
delays 1123
disqualification 635
earnings condition 632
employed earner 630
employment condition 631
entitlement to other benefits
means-tested benefits 642
non-means-tested benefits 642
EU co-ordination rules 1354, 1383
evidence of expected date of birth 639
failure to attend medical examination 636
fraud 1100
interchange of claims 1014
limited capability for work 643
linked periods
new-style JSA 612
MA period 633
miscarriages 638
more than one job 631
neonatal deaths 638
NI contributions 862
NI credits 867
overlapping benefits 642, 1021
overpayments 1058
passport to other benefits 643
payment 641
period of payment 633, 634
person subject to immigration control 1280
prisoners 837
qualifying period 634
reducing MA period 634
residence rules 1354
revisions 1128, 1130
self-employed earner 630
spouse/civil partner self-employed 630
SSP 754
stillbirths 638
supersessions 1128, 1143
tax 642
test period 631
treatment as income 642
means-tested benefits over pension age 385
means-tested benefits under pension age 353
UC 137
who can get MA 630
working 635
**maternity grants**
*see: Sure Start maternity grant, Best Grant*
**maternity leave**
childcare costs
HB 351
EEA workers 1323
treated as not in full-time work
HB 889
new-style JSA/I-ESA 885
PC 889
**maternity pay period**
curtailment notice 723
definition 719
working during period 731
**maximum amount of UC** 66
calculation 40
elements 68
standard allowance 67
**maximum benefit**
HB 201
**maximum rent** 304
local housing allowance
HB 308
pre-Jan '96 rules 323
rent officer determination related rent 317
social sector tenants 314
UC housing costs element 112
**meals**
deductions from benefit
HB 206
**medical assessments**
DLA 538
failure to take part in 922
limited capability for work 921
work capability assessments 921
**medical certificates**
SSP 756
**medical evidence**
ADP 1441
appeals 1200
DLA 537
limited capability for work 924
C-ESA 567
PIP 674
SSP 756
**medical examinations**
AA 448
appeals 1200

DLA 538
expenses 921
failure to attend 922, 1032
AA 448
DLA 538
MA 636
healthcare professional 1010
limited capability for work 921
PIP 674
**medical treatment**
absence from home
HB 193
child abroad
I-ESA 262
excluded from HB 206
housing costs
I-ESA/PC 297
**medication**
ADP 1431
PIP 651
**Member of Parliament**
complaints to MP 1266
**mental illness**
ADP 1429
appointees 1005
PIP 646
prisoners detained in hospital
means-tested benefits 841
non-means-tested benefits 841
UC 841
sanctions 996
work capabilty assessment 909
**mental stress**
good reason for refusing a job 990
**mesne profits**
HB 185
UC 91
**migrant victims of domestic abuse concession** 1277
**migration notice** 30
**milk**
Best Start foods 1455
free milk for children 775
Healthy Start food and vitamins 771
milk tokens 364
**minimum benefit**
HB 221
new-style JSA 625
PC 241
**minimum wage** 1584
availability for work 947
good reason for refusing a job 995
**misconduct**
dismissal from work
new-style JSA 621
industrial injuries benefits 592
sanctions 976
new-style JSA 973
UC 973
**misrepresentation**
overpayments 1067, 1068
HB 1082
**missing persons**
presumption of death 464
**mobile homes**
excluded tenancies 306
HB 185
rent restrictions
HB 317
UC 90
**mobility activities**
ADP 1431
PIP 660
**mobility supplement**
armed services 780
disability premium 272
treatment as income 354
**modern slavery**
housing costs
UC 113
**modular courses**
ESA 800
UC 793
**Morocco**
benefit entitlement 1282
reciprocal agreements 1297
**mortgage insurance policy**
treatment as income 362
UC 139
**mortgage interest loan** 764
amount 767
care homes 835
challenging a decision 765
entitlement ends 768
hospital patients 825
independent financial advice 765
liability for mortgage interest payments 766
mortgage interest run-on 769
payments 764, 768
prisoners 844
qualifying loans 766
repayment 769
who can claim 765
**mortgage interest run-on** 769
**Motability**
ADP 1447
DLA 543
PIP 681
SADLA 1424
**moving home**
advance claims
HB 218
UC 97
extended payment of HB 226

liability for rent or service charges before moving in
HB 190
I-ESA/PC 295
UC 97
two homes
HB 190, 195
I-ESA/PC 298
UC 97
value of home disregarded
means-tested benefits over pension age 429
means-tested benefits under pension age 404
UC 155
**multiple births**
SMP/SAP/SPP/SSPP/SPBP 735
two-child limit
means-tested benefits 269
UC 70
**myalgic encephalomyelitis (ME)** 513
**myasthenia gravis**
free prescriptions 579
**myxoedema**
free prescriptions 579

**N**
**National Emergencies Trust**
treatment of compensation payments
means-tested benefits over pension age 434
means-tested benefits under pension age 411
UC 160
**national insurance contribution conditions** 874
bereavement support payment 878
ESA 875
JSA 875
state pension 879
widowed parent's allowance 458, 879
**national insurance contributions** 855
age rules 859
aggregating contributions 1406
appeals 858
changes ignored
HB 343
class 1 860
class 2 861
rates 861
class 3 862
rates 862
class 3A 862
classes 858
credited contributions 865
decisions 858, 1121
earnings limits 1583
EEA nationals 863
EU co-ordination rules 863
late payment 864
more than one job 860
non-payment 864
person subject to immigration control 1288
primary threshold 860
reduced liability 862
residence/presence conditions 863
voluntary contributions 862, 864
**national insurance credits** 865
CA 871
carers 868
education 872
family members providing childcare 870
home responsibilities protection 870
incapacity for work 867
jury service 873
limited capability for work 867
new-style JSA 620
parents 868
service families 874
SMP/SAP/SPP/SSPP/SPBP/SNCP 873
starting credits 871
state pension 866
students 806
tax credits 873
training 872
UC 868
unemployment 866
widowers 873
widows 873
**national insurance number**
NI number requirement 1007
DLA 532
HB 215
person subject to immigration control 1288
proof of identity 1007
**natural migration**
transferring to UC 25
**negligence**
civil penalties 1101
**neonatal care pay period**
working during period 731
**net profit**
self-employed earnings over pension age 381
self-employed earnings under pension age 346
**new-style jobseeker's allowance** 610
absence abroad 1381
advance claims 624
age rules 615
amount 616
appeal pending on limited capability for work 927
appeals 1166

backdating 622
benefit cap 627
change of circumstances 626
children 615
claimant commitment 934
claims 619
couples 615
date of claim 621
decisions 1115
deductions from benefit 1034
delays 1123
disregarded earnings 616
duration 618
earnings 616
entitlement to other benefits
  means-tested benefits 627
  non-means-tested benefits 627
EU co-ordination rules 1353, 1382
fraud 1100
full-time paid work 613
hardship payments 1050
hospital patients 824
income 616
new claims 20, 24
NI contribution conditions 875
NI credits 866
overlapping benefits 1021
overpayments 1058, 1060
paid work 884
passport to other benefits 627
payment 625
pension payments 617
person subject to immigration control 1280
prescribed amount 617
reciprocal agreements 1354
relevant education 805
residence rules 1353
revisions 1128, 1130
sanctions
  work-related requirements 970
starting work 627
students 805
supersessions 1128, 1143
tax 626
trade disputes 891
transferring to PC 242
treatment as income 627
  means-tested benefits over pension age 385
  means-tested benefits under pension age 353
  UC 137
who can get new-style JSA 611
who should claim 620
work 884
work availability 945
work preparation requirement 940
work search requirement 941
work-focused interview 939
work-related requirements 938, 959

**NHS mobility scooter**
  disability premium 272

**night-time attention/supervision**
  CDP 1485
  DLA 525, 526

**non-advanced education** 489
  child benefit 489
  UC 63, 793

**non-dependants**
  amount of deductions
    HB 209
    I-ESA/PC 292
    UC 110
  capital
    HB 211
  couples
    HB 210
  deductions for housing costs
    I-ESA/PC 289
    UC 109
  HB 207
  income
    HB 210, 211
    I-ESA/PC 292
  loan for mortgage interest 768
  no deductions made
    HB 208
    I-ESA/PC 291
    UC 109
  not non-dependant
    HB 208
    I-ESA/PC 290
    UC 104
  qualifying benefits 1158
  severe disability premium 277
  trade disputes 892
  UC 103

**North Macedonia**
  benefit entitlement 1281

**Northern Ireland** 4
  reciprocal agreements 1296

**Northern Ireland Troubles-related incident**
  treatment of payments
    means-tested benefits over pension age 434
    means-tested benefits under pension age 411
    UC 160

**Norway**
  EFTA nationals 1389

**notice**
  to employer
    SAP 720
    SMP 719
    SNCP 726

SPBP 725
SPP 721
SSPP 723
**notification**
decision
HB 219
overpayment
HB 1086
**notional capital**
deprivation of capital
means-tested benefits over pension age 435
means-tested benefits under pension age 413
UC 161
failure to apply for capital
means-tested benefits under pension age 416
means-tested benefits over pension age 435
means-tested benefits under pension age 413
third-party payments
means-tested benefits under pension age 416
**notional income**
CA 478
deferring retirement pension 392
UC 143
means-tested benefits over pension age 391
means-tested benefits under pension age 365
UC 142
**nurseries**
free milk 775
**nursing care**
care homes
AA/DLA/PIP 828
HB 206
**nursing homes**
*see: care homes*

O
**occupational pensions**
future payments 366, 408
payments treated as income
C-ESA 562
CA 475
means-tested benefits over pension age 380, 389, 393
means-tested benefits under pension age 342, 361
new-style JSA 617
UC 139, 144
treatment as capital
UC 157
treatment of contributions
CA 475
**occupiers**
local housing allowance for HB 329
rent officer determined rent for HB 329
social sector tenants for HB 329
**office-holders** 859
**older claimants**
EU co-ordination of benefits 1401
pension credit 239
pensioner premium 274
winter fuel payments 715
**Ombudsman**
complaining to 1266
HB 1267
**one bedroom**
self-contained accommodation
HB 310
UC 114
shared accommodation
HB 310
UC 113
single room rent 328
**one-strike rule** 1111
**online claims** 1004, 1009
ADP 1439
Best Start foods 1460
Best Start grants 1460
budgeting loan 703
C-ESA 566
CA 480
CDP 1490
child benefit 501
CSP 1470
funeral support payment 1502
guardian's allowance 501
housing benefit 212
new-style JSA 619
PC 246
PIP 670
Scottish child payment 1460
state pension 696
UC 44
young carer grant 1478
**ordinary residence** 1299
benefits affected 1299
**orphans**
guardian's allowance 497
UC 38
**overlapping benefits** 1021
earnings-replacement benefits 1021
EU co-ordination rules 1409
increases for dependants 1022
non-means-tested benefits 1021
**overnight care**
additional bedroom
local housing allowance for HB 329
rent officer determined rent for HB 320

social sector tenants for HB 316
UC 105
definition of person requiring overnight care
HB 332
**overpayments** 1058
administrative penalty 1109
benefit arrears 1062
calculating the overpayment 1069
HB 1081
Scottish benefits 1527
causes
tax credits 1089
challenging
benefits 1071
HB 1087
Scottish benefits 1527
tax credits 1090
civil penalties 1101
claimant error
HB 1080
definition 1058
HB 1078
tax credits 1088
diminishing capital rule
HB 1081
means-tested benefits 1070
direct credit transfer 1063
discretion to recover 1072
HB 1083
failure to disclose material fact 1064, 1068
HB 1078
health benefits 584
interest charges 1069
HB 1081
tax credits 1088
late receipt of other income 1062
misrepresentation 1067, 1068
mortgage interest payments 1063
notification
HB 1086
official error
HB 1078
payments on account
HB 228
prosecution or administrative penalty 1109
recoverable overpayments 1060, 1063
HB 1078
Scottish benefits 1526
tax credits 1088
reducing the overpayment
HB 1081
tax credits 1091
UC/new-style JSA/new-style ESA 1060
Scottish benefits 1526
SMP/SAP/SPP/SSPP/SPBP/SNCP 739
SSP 757
tax credits 1088
treatment as income
means-tested benefits under pension age 355
UC 137
**overseas assets**
means-tested benefits under pension age 420
UC 166
**overtime pay**
treatment as earnings
UC 126
**owner-occupiers**
amount of leaseholder/service charges
I-ESA/PC 289
leaseholder charges
means-tested benefits 286, 287
UC 118
leaseholder service charges paid after return to work
I-ESA/PC 299
leaseholder service charges waiting period
UC 119
liability for leaseholder/service charges 294
loan for mortgage interest 764
service charges
I-ESA/PC 288
UC 92, 118
who can get help with leaseholder/service charges 287

**P**

**parental bereavement leave**
childcare costs
HB 351
treated as not in full-time work
HB 889
new-style JSA/I-ESA 885
PC 889
**parental bereavement pay period**
working during period 731
**parental contribution** 807, 809
HB over pension age 391
HB under pension age 364
**parental order**
Sure Start maternity grant 706
**parents**
16/17 year olds unsupported by parents
UC 38
EU co-ordination of benefits 1401
guardian's allowance 498
missing parents
guardian's allowance 497
NI credits 868
work allowance
UC 41

work-focused interview requirement 956
work-related requirements 952
*see also: step-parents*
**Parliamentary and Health Service Ombudsman** 1267
**partners**
*see: couples*
**part-time students**
ESA
C-ESA 797
I-ESA 801
HB 803
UC 795
**partially sighted**
free sight tests 580
**passported benefits**
AA 451
ADP 1447
bereavement benefits 468
CA 485
CDP 1495
child benefit 508
CSP 1475
DLA 543
ESA
C-ESA 571
I-ESA 179
guardian's allowance 508
hardship payments 1057
HB 232
industrial injuries benefits 606
maternity benefits 643
new-style JSA 627
PC 252
PIP 681
SADLA 1424
Scottish child payment 1464
state pension 700
UC 56
young carer grant 1480
**past presence requirement** 1298
benefits affected 1298
when the test does not apply 1350
**paternity leave**
childcare costs
HB 351
treated as not in full-time work
HB 889
new-style JSA/I ESA 885
PC 889
**paternity pay period**
definition 722
working during period 731
**pay in lieu of notice**
treatment as income
CA 475
means-tested benefits over pension age 380
means-tested benefits under pension age 342
UC 127
**payment cards**
benefits 1019
Healthy Start 771
**payment in kind** 884
treatment as income
means-tested benefits over pension age 380
means-tested benefits under pension age 342
**payment of benefit** 1017
AA 449
abroad 1368
ADP 1439, 1443
advance payments 1023
alternative payment arrangements
UC 51
bereavement benefits 465
Best Start foods 1463
Best Start grants 1463
budgeting loans 703
CA 482
CDP 1493
child benefit 504
child winter heating payment 1509
cold weather payments 714
compensation payments 1261
CSP 1472
delays in payment
HB 228
direct credit transfer 1019
DLA 538
emergencies 1020
ESA
C-ESA 568
I-ESA 178
funeral expenses payments 713
funeral support payment 1502
guardian's allowance 504
hardship payments 1056
HB 221
housing costs element 50
in advance/arrears
HB 221
industrial injuries benefits 605
lost payments 1020
HB 222
MA 641
missing payments 1020
HB 222
new-style JSA 625
overlapping benefit rules 1021
PADP 1517
payment exception service 1019
payment service card 1019
payment to other people 1018

payments on account
HB 228
PC 249
pension age winter heating payment 1509
PIP 677
Post Office Payout vouchers 1020
SADLA 1424
Scottish benefits 1524
Scottish child payment 1463
short-term assistance 1560
SMP/SAP/SPP/SSPP/SPBP/SNCP 738
SSP 757
state pension 698
students
HB 804
suspension of payment 1031
Scottish benefits 1525
to appointee
HB 222
to landlord
HB 221, 222
UC 50
UC 49
vouchers 1019
when benefit is paid 1020
winter fuel payments 716
winter heating payment 1509
young carer grant 1479
**penalties** 1100
administrative penalties 1109
challenging 1102
civil penalties 1101
consequences of paying a penalty 1109
fraud offences 1109
prosecution or penalty 1109
**pension age** 689
bereavement support payment 455
council tax reduction scheme 762
free prescriptions 578
free sight tests 580
future changes 690
NI contributions 859
pension-age HB 197
proof of age 697
widowed parent's allowance 457
**pension age disability payment** 1512
absence abroad 1378
advance claims 1517
age rules 1514
amount 1515
appeals 1544
attention 1513
backdating 1517
benefit cap 1519
care homes 826
change of circumstances 1518, 1541
claims 1515
date of claim 1517
daytime conditions 1513
dialysis 1515
disability conditions 1513
disability premium 272
entitlement to other benefits
means-tested benefits 1519
non-means-tested benefits 1519
EU co-ordination rules 1350, 1379
habitual residence 1300
hospital patients 818
incorrect award of PADP 1540
information to support claim 1516
moving from Scotland 1420
night-time conditions 1513
no non-dependant deductions
HB 208
I-ESA/PC 291
UC 109
overlapping benefits 1021
payment 1517
prisoners 837
redeterminations 1535
required period condition 1514
residence rules 1347
reviews 1518
supervision 1513
tax 1519
terminal illness 1436, 1515
transferring from AA 1518
treatment as capital
means-tested benefits under pension age 409
treatment as income
means-tested benefits over pension age 386
means-tested benefits under pension age 354
UC 138
who can get PADP 1512
**pension age winter heating payment** 1505
age rules 1507
amount 1508
benefit cap 1510
claims 1508
hospital patients 824
information to support claim 1509
payment 1509
redeterminations 1535
residence rules 1357
tax 1510
treatment as capital
means-tested benefits inder pension age 409
means-tested benefits over pension age 432
UC 159
treatment as income 1510

means-tested benefits over pension age 386
UC 138
who can get pension age winter heating payment 1507
who cannot get pension age winter heating payment 1507
**pension credit** 238
absence abroad 1375
additional amounts 241
advance claims 249
age rules 239
amount 241
appeals 1166
appropriate minimum guarantee 241
assessed income period 251
backdating 248, 1012
benefit cap 252
benefit week 394
calculation
guarantee credit 244
capital 425
capital limits 426
care homes 832
carer addition 241, 279
change of circumstances 250
HB 229
children 258
claims 246
continuing payments
HB 224
council tax reduction scheme 762
couples 240, 254
decisions 1115
deductions from benefit 1034
delays 1123
disregarded earnings 382
entitlement to other benefits
means-tested benefits 251
non-means-tested benefits 252
EU co-ordination rules 1376
families 254
fraud 1100
guarantee credit 239, 241
habitual residence test 1300
HB 251
hospital patients 821, 822
housing costs 241, 242
income 377, 378
savings credit 245
leaseholder charges 286
maximum deductions 1040
maximum savings credit 245
mixed-age couples 240
UC 24
mortgage interest loan 764
NHS charges, exemption 574
overpayments 1058
paid work 888
partner subject to immigration control 1286
passport to other benefits 252
payment 249
person subject to immigration control 1279
prisoners 840
public funds 1276
qualifying young person 259
residence rules 1307, 1343
retirement provision 251
revisions 1128, 1130
following award of qualifying benefit 1157
sanctions for benefit offences 1112
savings credit 239, 245
threshold 245
severe disability addition 241, 275
standard minimum guarantee 241
supersessions 1128, 1143
tax 251
tax credits and PC 21
trade disputes 891
transitional amount 242
who can get PC 239
who should claim 247
work 884
**Pension Protection Fund**
treatment as income
C-ESA 563
means-tested benefits 389
UC 139
**pensioner premium** 274
qualifying benefits 274
rate 280
**period of cold weather** 714
**period of incapacity**
SSP 748
**period of limited capability for work** 928
**period of study** 807
**period products**
free 776
**permanent right of residence** 1338
EEA family members 1340
permanently incapacitated people 1340
retired people 1340
**permitted work**
earnings limit
HB over pension age 383
HB under pension age 349
supported work 930
transferring to UC from ESA 902
working hours
ESA 930
working with limited capability for work 930

**person subject to immigration control**
benefit entitlement 1279
disability, carers and child benefits 1282
means-tested benefits 1280
children 1284
definition 1272
EEA nationals 1273
maintenance undertaking 1278
NI contributions 1288
NI number 1288
partners 1284
HB 1285
I-ESA 1286
non-means-tested benefits 1287
PC 1286
UC 1284
recourse to public funds 1276
requiring leave to enter or remain 1274
right to reside 1313
**personal allowances** 266
16/17-year-olds 267
children 268
health benefits 576
rates 266
**personal independence payment** 645
absence abroad 1378
administrative practices reviews (LEAP) 678
age rules 667
amount 669
appeals 1166
assessment 671
backdating 1011
benefit cap 681
care homes 826
change of circumstances 679
child winter heating payment 1506
claims 670
components 646
consultation 674
daily living activities 647
daily living component 646, 669
date of claim 676
descriptors 648
disability conditions 646
disability premium 272
disabled child premium 271
enhanced daily living component 273
entitlement to other benefits
means-tested benefits 679
non-means-tested benefits 680
EU co-ordination rules 1350, 1379
fluctuating conditions 664
fraud 1100
habitual residence test 1300
hospital patients 818
housing costs contribution
UC 109
information to support claim 671
interchange of claims 1014
length of awards 677
managing an activity 663
mobility activities 660
mobility component 646, 669
upper age limit 667
Motability 681
moving to Scotland 1419
negative determination 675
no non-dependant deduction
HB 208
I-ESA/PC 291
overlapping benefits 680, 1021
overpayments 1058
passport to other benefits 681
payment 677
person subject to immigration control 1279
prisoners 837
public funds 1276
questionnaire 672
renewing a claim 678
required period condition 666
residence rules 1347
revisions 1130
severe disability premium 276
supersessions 1143, 1144, 1149
tax 679
terminal illness 669, 671
transferring to ADP 1444
transfers from DLA 527
treatment as income 679
means-tested benefits over pension age 386
means-tested benefits under pension age 354
UC 138
who can get PIP 646
**personal injuries**
definition 411
definition for industrial injuries benefits 589
**personal injury payments**
recovery of benefits from compensation 1043
special compensation schemes
means-tested benefits over pension age 434
means-tested benefits under pension age 411
UC 160
treatment as capital
means-tested benefits over pension age 434
means-tested benefits under pension age 410

UC 159
treatment as income
means-tested benefits over pension age 388
means-tested benefits under pension age 358, 360
UC 140
**personal pensions**
future payments 408
payments treated as income
C-ESA 562
CA 475
means-tested benefits over pension age 389, 393
means-tested benefits under pension age 361
new-style JSA 617
UC 139, 144
treatment as capital
means-tested benefits under pension age 407
UC 157
treatment of contributions
CA 475
treatment of premiums
means-tested benefits over pension age 382
means-tested benefits under pension age 346
**personal possessions**
treatment as capital
means-tested benefits over pension age 430
means-tested benefits under pension age 406
UC 156
**physical stress**
good reason for refusing a job 990
**planning and undertaking a journey**
ADP 1432
PIP 660
**plasmapheresis**
limited capability for work
ESA 899
UC 897
**pneumoconiosis** 594, 598, 600, 606
**Poland** 1320
**polygamous marriages**
bereavement benefits 460
means-tested benefits 255
non-dependants
HB 210
personal allowances 266
UC 37, 59
**Post Office Horizon compensation scheme**
treatment of payments
means-tested benefits over pension age 434
means-tested benefits under pension age 411
UC 160
**Post Office Payout vouchers** 1020
**power of attorney**
HB 214
recovery of overpayments 1071
**powers to enter**
investigating claims 1103
**pre-settled status for EEA nationals** 1273, 1315
benefit entitlement 1316
child benefit 1310
means-tested benefits 1307
derivative right to reside 1336
evidence of status 1272
extension of pre-settled status 1315
family members 1329
habitual residence test 1303
jobseekers 1321
permanent right of residence 1338
right to reside 1312
self-employed 1324
self-sufficient people 1328
students 1328
unemployed 1325
workers 1322
**pre-tenancy determination** 322
**pregnancy**
16/17 year olds
UC 38
Best Start foods 1455
claiming health benefits 582
dismissal
SMP 734
EEA worker and self-employed status 1327
expected week of childbirth 631
free dental treatment 580
free presciptions 578
free vitamins 773
Healthy Start food and vitamin vouchers 771
limited capability for work 643
ESA 899
UC 897
limited capability for work-related activity 918
MA 630
maternity pay and benefits 629, 718
pregnancy and baby payment 1453
pregnancy-related illness 740
sickness during maternity pay period 754
SMP 719
Sure Start maternity grant 705
work-related requirements 952
**pregnancy and baby payment** 1453
amount 1454

**premiums** 270
backdating 280
carer premium 279
definition 270
disability premium 272
disabled child premium 271
enhanced disability premium 273
family premium 270
health benefits 577
hospital patients 823
pensioner premium 274
rates 280
severe disability premium 275
**prescribed amount of earnings**
new-style JSA 617
**prescribed degrees of disablement** 596
**prescribed industrial diseases** 593
causation 593
**prescribed occupations** 593
**prescriptions** 578
free 578
pre-payment certificates 579
**presence** 1295
benefits affected by presence conditions 1295
definition 1298, 1369
past presence 1298
tests 1298
**prisoners** 836
ADP 837
CDP 837
child benefit 838
child in custody
child benefit 496, 499, 838
guardian's allowance 499
means-tested benefits 262, 840
UC 839
childcare costs allowance
HB 350
costs for usual home 844
HB 844
I-ESA/PC 297, 844
UC 839, 844
definition
means-tested benefits 840
non-means-tested benefits 836
UC 839
discharge grant treated as capital
I-ESA 403
ESA
C-ESA 837
I-ESA 840
free dental treatment 580
free prescriptions 578
guardian's allowance 497, 838
HB 840, 844
home detention curfew
means-tested benefits 840
hospital patients
means-tested benefits 841
non-means-tested benefits 841
UC 841
IIDB 838
mortgage interest loan 844
non-dependant deductions
HB 209
I-ESA/PC 291
UC 110
non-means-tested benefits 836
PADP 837
partner in custody
I-ESA/PC 840
UC 839
PC 840
PIP 837
quashed conviction
arrears of benefits 838
NI credits 873
released from prison 843
remand prisoners 193, 838
SADLA 837
social fund 841
SSP/SMP/SAP/SPP/SSPP/SPBP/SNCP 837
suspended benefits 838
temporary release 843, 845
HB 190, 193
UC 100
UC 839, 844
visits 364, 843
winter fuel payments 715
work search requirement 963
**private rented sector tenants**
contrived tenancies
HB 189
UC 96
excluded tenancies 306
local housing allowance
HB 307
UC 110
maximum number of bedrooms
UC 105
rent restrictions
HB 305
UC 112
size criteria
HB 309
UC 104
UC housing costs element 110
**probation**
hostels
HB 190, 306, 842
housing costs
I-ESA/PC 842
means-tested benefits 840, 842
non-means-tested benefits 836
UC 842

**prompting**
PIP assessments 647
**proof of age** 697
**proof of identity**
acceptable documents 1007
NI number required 1007
**property**
future interest
means-tested benefits under pension age 408
means-tested benefits over pension age 427
means-tested benefits under pension age 400
UC 152
**proprietary estoppel** 153, 401
**prosecution**
fraud offences 1106
prosecution or penalty 1109
**protected groups of EEA nationals** 1317
**protected tenancy** 306
**Public Lending Right scheme** 347, 381, 390
**Public Services Ombudsman for Wales** 1267

**Q**
**qualifying benefits** 1013
award of benefit 1158
backdating claims 1012, 1159
Best Start foods 1459
Best Start grants 1459
budgeting loans 701
CA 482
child winter heating payment 1506
cold weather payments 714
CSP 1468
disability premium 272
free school lunches 774
funeral expenses payments 707
funeral support payment 1498
HB 219
NI credits for carers and parents 869
pensioner premiums 274
revision due to award of qualifying benefit 1137, 1157
Scottish child payment 1459
supersession due to award of qualifying benefit 1147, 1154, 1157
Sure Start maternity grant 705
winter fuel payments 715
winter heating payment 1506
young carer grant 1477
**qualifying days**
SSP 751
**qualifying parent or carer**
additional bedroom
HB 333
**qualifying young person**
child benefit 488
guardian's allowance 496
PC 259
UC 792
widowed parent's allowance 456

**R**
**rape**
two-child limit
means-tested benefits 269
UC 70
**reading**
ADP 1431
PIP 657
**reciprocal agreements** 1297
bereavement benefits 1345
C-ESA 1352
N. Ireland 1296
new-style JSA 1354
state pension 1355, 1384
**recourse to public funds** 1276
asylum seekers 1289
definition of public funds 1276
domestic abuse and violence 1277
**recovery of benefits**
budgeting advances 53
budgeting loans 704
from compensation payments 1043
funeral expenses payment from estate 713
hardship payments
UC 1053
short-term advances 1024
**recovery of overpayments** 1072
challenging
tax credits 1090
common law 1078
deductions from benefits 1075
HB 1083
Scottish benefits 1527
UC/new-style JSA/new-style ESA 1074
deductions from earnings 1076
HB 1085
UC/new-style JSA/new-style ESA 1075
direct payments to HMRC 1094
discretion to recover 1072
HB 1078
from whom can overpayments be recovered 1070
HB 1082
tax credits 1093
UC/new-style JSA/new-style ESA 1061
maximum deductions from benefit 1076
HB 1084
new-style JSA/new-style ESA 1075
UC 1074
methods of recovery 1075

future changes to recovery methods 1072
HB 1082
tax credits 1093
UC/new-style JSA/new-style ESA 1073
notification
HB 1086
offsetting
HB 1081
new-style JSA/new-style ESA 1060
tax credits 1091
recoverable overpayments 1060, 1063
HB 1078
Scottish benefits 1526
recovery through the courts 1077
HB 1085
tax credits 1095
UC/new-style JSA/new-style ESA 1075
Scottish benefits 1527
tax credit debt transferred to DWP 1094
tax credits 1092
**redeterminations** 1535
before appeal 1544
late request 1537
requesting redetermination 1536
time limits
to carry out redetermination 1538
to request redetermination 1536
who can request redetermination 1536
**reduced earnings allowance** 601
amount 602
overlapping benefits 1021
prisoners 837
who can get REA 601
**reduced liability for national insurance contributions** 862
**reductions in benefit**
sanctions
new-style ESA 981
new-style JSA 982
old-style ESA 177
UC 980
widowed parent's allowance 458
**redundancy**
sanctions
new-style JSA 974
UC 974
treatment as earnings
CA 475
means-tested benefits over pension age 381
means-tested benefits under pension age 345
UC 127
**refugees**
backdated benefit payments 1291
tax credits 21
benefit entitlement 1290
eVisa 1290
family reunion 1290
habitual residence test 1303
integration loans 1039, 1292
pregnancy and baby payment 1455
Sure Start maternity grant 706
**refunds**
health benefits 584
**refusal of job offer**
good reason 994
sanctions
new-style JSA 972
UC 972
**registered housing associations** 306
**regulated tenancy** 306
**relative**
disregard of relative's home
means-tested benefits over pension age 430
means-tested benefits under pension age 405
UC 156
**relevant education**
child benefit 488
new-style JSA 805
**religion**
religious objections to job 990
**religious orders**
HB 187
PC 244
**remand**
housing costs
HB 193
I-ESA/PC 297
non-means-tested benefits 838
**remarriage**
bereavement support payment 456
widowed parent's allowance 458
**removal of spare room subsidy** 313
**remunerative work**
means-tested benefits 884
**renal dialysis**
AA 444
CDP 1490
DLA 530
PADP 1515
**renewing a claim**
AA 448
industrial injuries benefits 605
**rent**
advance payments
budgeting loans 702
apportionment
HB 203
cap rent
HB 308
UC housing costs element 112
core rent

UC housing costs element 110
eligible rent
HB 202
UC 90
ineligible charges
HB 203
UC 91
liability to pay rent
HB 186
UC 93, 94
non-commercial agreements
HB 187
UC 93
payments treated as rent
HB 185
rent officer determination related rent 317
service charges excluded from
HB 206
single room rent 328
size criteria
local housing allowance for HB 309
pre-Jan '96 rules 323
rent officer determination related rent 320
social sector tenants for HB 316
UC 104
treatment of rental income
means-tested benefits over pension age 388
means-tested benefits under pension age 359
UC 142
UC housing costs element 101
unreasonably high rent
pre-Jan '96 rules 324
**rent allowance** 221
**rent arrears**
discretionary housing payments 550
payment direct to landlord
HB 222
payments excluded from HB 202
recovery of overpayments
HB 1085, 1087
repaid by deductions from benefit 1035
**rent direct**
HB 222
**rent increases**
pre-Jan '96 rules 327
**rent officer determination related rent** 317
broad rental market area 321
challenging a rent restriction 334
claim-related rent 320
exceptionally high rent determination 320
local reference rent 321
maximum rent 317
occupiers 329
pre-April '08 rules 317
pre-tenancy determinations 322
rent officer determinations 319
service charges 321
significantly high rent determination 320
size criteria 320
size-related determination 320
**rent officers**
rent officer determination related rent 319
**rent rebate**
HB 221
**rent restrictions** 303
cap rent
HB 308
UC housing costs element 112
challenging a rent restriction
HB 334
delaying a rent restriction
HB 333
discretionary housing payments 548
discretionary reductions
HB 307
excluded tenancies
HB 306
exempt accommodation pre-Jan '96 rules 326
exempt claimants pre-Jan '96 rules 326
housing association tenants
HB 305
UC 115
local housing allowance 307
local reference rent 317
pre-Jan '96 rules 322
private tenants
HB 305
UC 110, 112
rent restriction schemes 304
revisions 1139
size criteria
local housing allowance for HB 309
pre-Jan '96 rules 323
rent officer determination related rent 320
social sector tenants 316
UC 104
social sector tenants
HB 305, 313
UC 115
suitable alternative accommodation
pre-Jan '96 rules 324
supersessions 1148
unreasonably high rent
pre-Jan '96 rules 324
which HB restrictions apply 303
**rent-free period**
HB 187, 203
UC 101

**rental income**
treatment as income
means-tested benefits over pension age 387
means-tested benefits under pension age 358
UC 141, 142
**rental purchase**
HB 185
**rentcharge payments**
I-ESA/PC 287
**repairs**
help with repairs 782
interest on loans
I-ESA/PC 766
service charges for leaseholders 288
two homes during repair work
HB 196
I-ESA/PC 297
UC 99
waiver of housing costs during repair work
HB 187
**representation**
First-tier Tribunal appeals 1180
Upper Tribunal appeals 1220
**reserve forces**
payments treated as capital
means-tested benefits under pension age 403
payments treated as income
means-tested benefits over pension age 383, 384
means-tested benefits under pension age 349
treated as not in full-time work
new-style JSA/I-ESA 885
**residence** 1295
A2/A8 nationals 1320
benefits affected by residence conditions 1295
continuous residence 1339
Croatians 1320
definition 1299
documents for EEA nationals 1331
EEA jobseekers 1321
EEA nationals 1312
EEA self-employed people 1324
EEA self-sufficient people 1328
EEA students 1329
EEA workers 1322
European free movement rights 1317
family members
EEA nationals 1329
frontier workers 1342
habitual residence 1300
initial right of residence 1321
NI contributions 863
ordinary residence 1299, 1369
permanent residence 1338
presence 1298, 1369
registration certificate 1331
resided legally 1339
residence card 1331
right to reside 1306
settled status for EEA Nationals 1314
tests 1298
**residential care**
*see: care homes*
**respite care**
temporary care home resident 193
**responsibility for a child**
Best Start foods 1457
Best Start grants 1457
child benefit 492
means-tested benefits 260
NI credits 868
Scottish child payment 1457
student couples
HB 802
UC 793
UC 64, 953
young person in relevant education
ESA 801
**retainer fee**
treatment as earnings
CA 474, 475
means-tested benefits over pension age 380
means-tested benefits under pension age 342
**retirement**
EEA workers' rights 1340
sanctions for voluntary unemployment
new-style JSA 977
UC 977
**retirement allowance** 602
overlapping benefits 1021
prisoners 837
**retirement pension**
see: state pensions
**reviews**
ADP 1444
CDP 1493
claimant commitment 937
CSP 1474
discretionary housing payments 553
First-tier Tribunal decisions
Scottish benefits 1552
overpayments
Scottish benefits 1527
tax credits 1089
PADP 1518
PIP 678
SSP/SMP/SAP/SPP/SSPP/SPBP/SNCP 1253

I

suspension of benefit
Scottish benefits 1525
Upper Tribunal decisions
Scottish benefits 1557
**revisions** 1128
after appeal made 1137, 1185, 1202
anti-test case rule 1159
any grounds revision 1131
any time revision 1135
applying 1140
arrears following revision 1142
before appeal 1130, 1168
challenging 1142
date revision takes effect 1142
factual error 1138
information required for a revision 1141
mandatory reconsideration 1130, 1168
official error 1135
overpayments
HB 1087
qualifying benefit awarded 1137, 1157
risks 1129
sanction decision 1136
time limits 1132, 1134
when to seek a revision 1128, 1130
**right to reside**
benefits affected 1306
Brexit 1312
British citizens 1312
carer of child in education 1336
Commonwealth citizens 1312
derivative rights 1336
EEA jobseekers 1321
EEA nationals 1317
EEA self-employed people 1324
EEA self-sufficient people 1328
EEA students 1329
EEA workers 1322
European free movement rights 1317
family members
EEA nationals 1329, 1333
frontier workers 1342
Irish citizens 1312
leave to enter or remain 1313
means-tested benefits 1307
permanent right of residence 1338
pre-settled status for EEA nationals
means-tested benefits 1307
qualified person 1318
resided legally 1339
who has a right to reside 1312
**road tax**
exemptions
DLA 543
PIP 681
**Romania** 1320
**rough sleepers** 849

**S**

**San Marino**
benefit entitlement 1282
reciprocal agreements 1297
**sanctionable benefits** 1112
**sanctions** 969
avoiding sanctions 970
benefit offences 1111, 1112
benefit reductions 979
I-ESA 177
new-style ESA 981
new-style JSA 982
UC 980
benefits which can be sanctioned 1112
challenging a decision 997
circumstances that should be taken into account 990
complex needs 996
decisions 995
discretionary housing payments 550
employment programmes 978
ESA
old-style ESA 177
good reason 989
hardship payments
ESA 1053
UC 1051
high level
new-style JSA 972, 983
UC 972, 983
length of sanction period
benefit offences 1113
I-ESA 177
new-style ESA 983, 988
new-style JSA 983, 988
UC 983, 988
work availability sanctions 985
work preparation sanctions 986
low level
new-style ESA 978, 986
new-style JSA 978, 986
UC 978, 986
lowest level 979, 987
medium level 978, 985
misconduct at work
new-style JSA 973
UC 973
more than one sanction at once 988
moving to another benefit 982
NI credits 867
open-ended sanctions 986
reduced sanction periods
new-style JSA 984
UC 984
refusing to take up job

new-style JSA 972
UC 972
revisions 1136
termination of sanctions 989
training schemes 978
voluntary unemployment
new-style JSA 973
UC 973
vulnerable people 996
work-focused interview
new-style ESA 978, 979
new-style JSA 978
UC 978, 979
work-related activity
old-style ESA 177
work-related requirements
old-style ESA 177
UC 970
zero-hour contracts 973
**sanctuary scheme** 313
bedroom tax
UC 118
local housing allowance for HB 330
social sector tenants 313
**sandwich courses** 799
grant income 807
**savings**
Help to Save scheme 782
means-tested benefits over pension age 427
means-tested benefits under pension age 400
UC 151
**school activities and equipment** 775
**school holidays**
calculating hours of work
means-tested benefits 886
**school leavers**
child benefit 488
NI starting credits 871
**school lunches**
free school lunches 774
**school transport** 775
**school uniform**
grants for school clothes 775
**school-age payment** 1454
amount 1455
**Scotland** 4
**Scottish adult disability living allowance** 1420
absence abroad 1378
age rules 1420
amount 1420
appeals 1544
benefit cap 1424
care component conditons 1421
change of circumstances 1424, 1541
claims 1420
entitlement to other benefits
means-tested benefits 1424
non-means-tested benefits 1424
EU co-ordination rules 1350, 1379
habitual residence 1300
hospital patients 818
incorrect award of SADLA 1540
mobility component conditions 1421
Motability 1424
moving from Scotland 1420
moving to ADP 1425
no non-dependant deductions
I-ESA/PC 291
UC 109
passport to other benefits 1424
payment 1424
prisioners 837
redeterminations 1535
requesting determination of entitlement 1423
residence rules 1347
reviews 1424
tax 1424
terminal illness 1420, 1436
transfers from DLA 1422
treatment as income
means-tested benefits over pension age 386
means-tested benefits under pension age 354
UC 138
**Scottish benefits** 1417
appeals 1544
appointees 1522
claims 1521
complaints 1529
determinations 1534
fraud 1528
future changes 1418
moving to/from Scotland 1419
overpayments 1526
payment 1524
redeterminations 1535
right to advocacy 1524
right to support 1524
suspension of payments 1525
**Scottish carer supplement** 1475
**Scottish child payment** 1451
absence abroad 1377, 1409
advance claims 1462
age rules 1459
amount 1452
appeals 1544
backdating 1462
benefit cap 1464
care home residents 834
change of circumstances 1452
claims 1460

date of claim 1462
entitlement to other benefits 1464
EU co-ordination rules 1347, 1378
fraud 1528
hospital patients 824
information to support claim 1461
more than one claimant 1458
overpayments 1526
passport to other benefits 1464
payment 1463
public funds 1276
qualifying benefits 1459
redeterminations 1535
residence rules 1346
responsibility for a child 1457
tax 1464
treatment as capital
means-tested benefits over pension age 433
means-tested benefits under pension age 409
treatment as income 1464
means-tested benefits over pension age 386
means-tested benefits under pension age 354
UC 138
who can qualify 1452
**Scottish Public Services Ombudsman** 1267, 1530
**Scottish social security system** 1415
benefits not under Scottish system 1418
benefits under Scottish system 1417
future changes 1418
overview 1417
**Scottish Welfare Fund** 770
public funds 1276
**second adult rebate**
council tax reduction schemes 761
**Second World War**
treatment of compensation payments
means-tested benefits over pension age 386
means-tested benefits under pension age 354
**self-contained accommodation**
local housing allowance
HB 310
**self-employed EEA nationals** 1324
gaps between jobs 1327
pregnancy 1327
registered as a jobseeker 1325
retaining self-employed status 1325
sickness or injury 1326
unemployed 1325
**self-employment**
business assets
means-tested benefits over pension age 430
means-tested benefits under pension age 403, 406
UC 157
calculation of weekly earnings
means-tested benefits over pension age 382
means-tested benefits under pension age 346
UC 128
class 2 NI contributions 861
class 4 NI contributions 859
definition of self-employed earner
NI contributions 859
disregarded earnings
CA 478
means-tested benefits over pension age 382
means-tested benefits under pension age 347
earnings
CA 477
MA 632
means-tested benefits over pension age 381
means-tested benefits under pension age 345
UC 128
EEA nationals 1324
gainful self-employment 128
industrial injuries benefits 588
limited capability for work 133
minimum income floor 130
offsetting losses 130
paid work 884
proof of earnings 128
sickness 133
small profits exception 861
sole traders
means-tested benefits over pension age 430
means-tested benefits under pension age 407
UC 134
start-up period 133
work expenses
means-tested benefits under pension age 346
UC 129
**self-sufficient people**
EEA nationals 1328
**separation**
bereavement benefits 459
child benefit 494
continuing to live under the same roof

means-tested benefits 263
UC 61
house sale, proceeds
means-tested benefits over pension age 429
means-tested benefits under pension age 404, 419
UC 154, 165
liability for housing costs following separation
UC 95
means-tested benefits 257
renting former joint home from ex-partner
HB 188
right to reside after separation from EEA national 1333
UC 61
**service charges**
apportionment of ineligible service charges
HB 203
discretionary housing payments 550
eligible service charges
HB 205
I-ESA/PC 288
UC 92
HB 205
ineligible service charges
HB 206
I-ESA/PC 288
UC 92
leaseholders
I-ESA/PC 288
UC 92
non-dependant deductions 289
owner-occupiers
I-ESA/PC 288
UC 92, 118
rent officer determination related rent
HB 321
social rented sector tenants
UC 92
supported accommodation 206
UC 92
waiting period for charges
UC 119
**service user expenses**
employed earners, treatment as income
UC 127
**settled status for EEA nationals** 1273, 1314
benefit entitlement 1316
evidence of status 1272
**severe disability premium** 275
claiming UC 27
non-dependants 277
qualifying benefits 276
rate 280
transferring to UC 27
transitional SDP element 27, 78
**severe disablement allowance** 556
absence abroad 1382
disability premium 272
EU co-ordination rules 1383
overlapping benefits 1021
prisoners 837
residence rules 1347
transfers to ESA 563
treatment as income
means-tested benefits over pension age 385
means-tested benefits under pension age 353
**severe mental impairment**
CDP mobility component 1487
DLA care component 520
DLA mobility component 516
**sexual relationship**
proof of cohabitation
means-tested benefits 256
UC 59
**share fishermen** 477, 861
**shared accommodation**
apportionment of rent
HB 203
HB 203
local housing allowance
HB 310
with landlord
HB 187
UC 95
**shared lives carers**
treatment of payments as income
UC 142
**shared ownership schemes**
bedroom tax
UC 118
HB 185, 306
UC 89, 119
**shared parental leave**
childcare costs
HB 351
treated as not in full-time work
HB 889
new-style JSA/I-ESA 885
PC 889
**shared parental pay period**
definition 724
working during period 731
**shares**
treatment as capital
means-tested benefits over pension age 427
means-tested benefits under pension age 400, 402
UC 134, 151, 153

valuation
means-tested benefits under pension age 420
UC 166
**short-term advances** 1023, 1124
**short-term assistance** 1558
amount 1559
benefit cap 1560
change of circumstances 1535
claims 1559
entitlement to other benefits
means-tested benefits 1560
passport to other benefits 1561
payment 1560
redeterminations 1535
treatment as income
means-tested benefits over pension age 386
means-tested benefits under pension age 354
UC 138
who can get short-term assistance 1558
**sick leave**
EEA workers 1323
treated as not in full-time work
HB 889
new-style JSA/I-ESA 885
PC 889
**sick pay**
payment 757
treatment as earnings
CA 474, 475
means-tested benefits over pension age 380
means-tested benefits under pension age 341
UC 126
**sickness**
armed forces, payments to former members 779
childcare costs disregarded
HB 351
continuous employment
SMP/SAP/SPP/SSPP/SPBP/SNCP 728
disability premium 272
EEA worker and self-employed status 1326
ESA 169
EU co-ordination of benefits 1400
financial help with costs of sickness 783
health benefits 573
limited capability for work 895
short periods of sickness
new-style JSA 613
SSP 747
work search requirement 959
work-related requirements 954
**sight tests** 580
free sight tests 580
reduced-cost treatment 575
**signing on**
EEA nationals 1325
NI credits 866
**single room rent** 328
local housing allowance
HB 310
rent officer determination related rent 321
**size criteria**
local housing allowance
HB 309
UC 104
pre-Jan '96 rules 323
rent officer determined rent for HB 320
social sector tenants for HB 316
temporary absence of family member
UC 107
UC housing costs element 104
**Slovakia** 1320
**Slovenia** 1320
**social and medical assistance** 1403
**social care payments**
treatment as capital 411
UC 161
treatment as income 363
**social fund** 701
benefit cap 716
budgeting loans 701
children's funeral fund payment 708
cold weather payments 714
entitlement to other benefits 716
funeral expenses payments 707
person subject to immigration control 1281
prisoners 841
public funds 1276
Sure Start maternity grant 705
tax 716
trade disputes 892
treatment as capital
means-tested benefits over pension age 433
means-tested benefits under pension age 409
UC 159
treatment as income
means-tested benefits over pension age 386
means-tested benefits under pension age 354
UC 138
winter fuel payments 715
**social media**
income from online activity
UC 128

**social sector tenants**
bedroom tax
HB 313
UC 117
delaying a rent restriction after a death
HB 333
joint liability
HB 315
UC 116
maximum rent 314
occupiers
HB 329
overnight care required
HB 330
rent restrictions
HB 305, 313
UC 115
service charges
UC 92
size criteria
HB 316
sole liability
UC housing costs element 115
UC housing costs element 115
**Social Security Scotland** 1417
complaints 1529
**social services**
support for care leavers 846
**solicitors**
money held by solicitors
means-tested benefits over pension age 428
means-tested benefits under pension age 402
UC 153
**special guardianship allowance**
treatment as income
means-tested benefits under pension age 357
**special non-contributory benefits** 1403
**specified accommodation**
HB 183
UC housing costs element 91
**sports award**
disregarded capital 413
treated as not in work
HB 890
new-style JSA/I-ESA 885
PC 889
treatment as income
means-tested benefits under pension age 364
UC 141
**sports facilities**
HB 206
**standard allowance** 67
**starting credits** 871
**starting work**
assessment of earnings
HB 370
extended payments
HB 224
financial help 781
C-ESA 571
HB 232
I-ESA 180
new-style JSA 627
**state pensions** 687
absence abroad 695, 1383
additional state pension 691
advance claims 698
age rules 689
amount 690
appeals 1166
backdating 697, 1012
benefit cap 699
bereavement benefits 465
category A pension 688
amount 690
category B pension 688
amount 690
category D pension 688
amount 690
changes of circumstance 699
civil partners
surviving partner 693
claiming for others 690
claims 695
class 3 NI contributions 862
date of claim 697
decisions 1115
deferring retirement 688
pension age before 6 April 2016 688
pension treated as income 143, 392, 688
delays 1123
earnings 688
EEA nationals 695
entitlement to other benefits
means-tested benefits 699
non-means-tested benefits 699
EU co-ordination rules 1354, 1384, 1401
fraud 1100
graduated retirement benefit 691, 695
information to support claim 697
interchange of claims 1014
late claims 697
NI contribution conditions 879
NI credits 866
NI credits for parents and carers 868
overlapping benefits 699, 1021, 1022
overpayments 1058
passport to other benefits 700

payment 698
pension age before 6 April 2016 687, 688
amount 690
person subject to immigration control 1280
prisoners 837
proof of age 697
protected payment 692
reciprocal agreements 1355
residence rules 1354
retirement 688
revisions 1128, 1130, 1139
supersessions 1128, 1143
tax 699
transitional rate 691, 880
treatment as income
means-tested benefits over pension age 385
means-tested benefits under pension age 353
UC 137
who can get state pension 688
widowers 693
widows 693, 696
women who paid reduced rate contributions 692

**statutory adoption pay** 718
absence abroad 1384
age rules 733
amount 733
appeals 1252, 1255
arrears, treatment as income
means-tested benefits under pension age 344
asking for an HMRC decision 1250
benefit cap 741
challenging a decision 1249
change of circumstances 739
choosing SSPP 722
claims 737
continuous employment 727
curtailment of SAP 723
dismissal 734
earnings 729
employed earner 727
employers' decisions 1250
entitlement to other benefits
means-tested benefits 739
non-means-tested benefits 740
EU co-ordination rules 1385
insolvent employer 1258
limited capability for work 740
lower earnings limit 730
more than one employer 731
multiple births 735
NI credits 873
notice to employer 720
overpayments 739
overseas adoption 736
pay rise 730
payment 738
payment following appeal 1257
period of payment 720
person subject to immigration control 1280
prisoners 837
surrogacy 736
tax 739
time limits 737
trade disputes 892
treatment as earnings
CA 474, 475
means-tested benefits over pension age 380, 385
means-tested benefits under pension age 341, 353
UC 126, 137
who can get SAP 720
working 731

**statutory maternity pay** 718
absence abroad 1384
age rules 733
amount 733
appeals 1252, 1255
arrears, treatment as income
means-tested benefits under pension age 344
asking for an HMRC decision 1250
benefit cap 741
challenging a decision 1249
change of circumstances 739
choosing SSPP 722
claim refused, claiming MA 640
claims 737
continuous employment 727
curtailment of SMP 723
dismissal 734
earnings 729
employed earner 727
employers' decisions 1250
entitlement to other benefits
means-tested benefits 739
non-means-tested benefits 740
EU co-ordination rules 1385
insolvent employer 1258
limited capability for work 740
lower earnings limit 730
more than one employer 731
multiple births 735
NI credits 873
notice to employer 719
overpayments 739
pay rise 730
payment 738
payment following appeal 1257
period of payment 719

person subject to immigration control 1280
prisoners 837
SSP 754
stillbirths 735
tax 739
time limits 737
trade disputes 892
treatment as earnings
CA 474, 475
means-tested benefits over pension age 380, 385
means-tested benefits under pension age 341, 353
UC 126, 137
who can get SMP 719
working 731
**statutory neonatal care pay** 718
absence abroad 1384
age rules 733
amount 734
appeals 1252, 1255
asking for an HMRC decision 1250
benefit cap 741
challenging a decision 1249
change of circumstances 739
claims 737
continuous employment 727
death of child 736
dismissal 734
earnings 729
employed earner 727
employers' decisions 1250
entitlement to other benefits
means-tested benefits 739
non-means-tested benefits 740
EU co-ordination rules 1385
insolvent employer 1258
limited capability for work 740
lower earnings limit 730
more than one employer 731
notice to employer 726
overpayments 739
overseas adoption 736
pay rise 730
payment 738
payment following appeal 1257
period of payment 726
surrogacy 736
tax 739
time limits 737
treatment as earnings
CA 474, 475
means-tested benefits over pension age 380, 385
means-tested benefits under pension age 341, 353
UC 126, 137
who can get SNCP 725
working 731
**statutory parental bereavement pay** 718
absence abroad 1384
age rules 733
amount 733
appeals 1252, 1255
arrears, treatment as income
means-tested benefits under pension age 344
asking for an HMRC decision 1250
benefit cap 741
bereaved parent 725
challenging a decision 1249
change of circumstances 739
claims 737
continuous employment 727
dismissal 734
earnings 729
employed earner 727
employers' decisions 1250
entitlement to other benefits
means-tested benefits 739
non-means-tested benefits 740
EU co-ordination rules 1385
insolvent employer 1258
lower earnings limit 730
more than one employer 731
NI credits 873
notice to employer 725
overpayments 739
pay rise 730
payment 738
payment following appeal 1257
period of payment 725
person subject to immigration control 1280
prisoners 837
stillbirths 735
surrogacy 736
tax 739
time limits 737
trade disputes 892
treatment as earnings
CA 474, 475
means-tested benefits over pension age 380, 385
means-tested benefits under pension age 341, 353
UC 126, 137
who can get SPBP 724
working 731
**statutory paternity pay** 718
absence abroad 1384
age rules 733
amount 733
appeals 1252, 1255
arrears, treatment as income

means-tested benefits under pension age 344
asking for an HMRC decision 1250
benefit cap 741
challenging a decision 1249
change of circumstances 739
claims 737
continuous employment 727
dismissal 734
earnings 729
employed earner 727
employers' decisions 1250
entitlement to other benefits
means-tested benefits 739
non-means-tested benefits 740
EU co-ordination rules 1385
insolvent employer 1258
limited capability for work 740
lower earnings limit 730
more than one employer 731
multiple births 735
notice to employer 721
overpayments 739
overseas adoption 736
pay rise 730
payment 738
payment following appeal 1257
period of payment 722
person subject to immigration control 1280
prisoners 837
stillbirths 735
surrogacy 736
tax 739
time limits 737
trade disputes 892
treatment as earnings
CA 474, 475
means-tested benefits over pension age 380, 385
means-tested benefits under pension age 341, 353
UC 126, 137
who can get SPP 721
working 731
**statutory shared parental pay** 718
absence abroad 1384
age rules 733
amount 733
appeals 1252, 1255
arrears, treatment as income
means-tested benefits under pension age 344
asking for an HMRC decision 1250
benefit cap 741
challenging decisions 1249
change of circumstances 739
claims 737
continuous employment 727
curtailment of SMP/SAP/MA 723
dismissal 734
earnings 729
employed earner 727
employers' decisions 1250
entitlement to other benefits
means-tested benefits 739
non-means-tested benefits 740
EU co-ordination rules 1385
insolvent employer 1258
limited capability for work 740
lower earnings limit 730
more than one employer 731
multiple births 735
NI credits 873
notice to employer 723
overpayments 739
overseas adoption 736
pay rise 730
payment 738
payment following appeal 1257
period of payment 724
person subject to immigration control 1280
prisoners 837
reducing MA period 634
surrogacy 736
tax 739
time limits 737
trade disputes 892
treatment as earnings
CA 474, 475
means-tested benefits over pension age 380, 385
means-tested benefits under pension age 341, 353
UC 126, 137
who can get SSPP 722
working 731
**statutory sick pay** 746
absence abroad 1384
age rules 752
amount 752
appeals 1252, 1255
arrears, treatment as income
means-tested benefits under pension age 344
asking for an HMRC decision 1250
backdating 756
benefit cap 759
challenging decisions 1249
change of circumstances 757
claiming ESA 756, 757
claims 754
dismissal 747
employees 747
employers' decisions 1250

end of entitlement 749
entitlement to other benefits
means-tested benefits 758
non-means-tested benefts 758
ESA 566, 758
EU co-ordination rules 1385
incapable of work 747
information to support claim 755
insolvent employer 1258
late claim 756
linking rules 748, 749, 753
low earnings 750
maximum entitlement 753
medical evidence 756
more than one job 753
NI contributions 758
NI credits 867
not yet started work 751
notification of sickness 755
overpayments 757
payment 757
payment following appeal 1257
period of entitlement 749
period of incapacity 748
person subject to immigration control 1280
pregnancy 754
prisoners 837
qualifying days 751
refusal of SSP 756
residence/presence test for employers 747
stillbirth 754
tax 758
trade disputes 892
treatment as earnings
CA 474, 475
means-tested benefits over pension age 380, 385
means-tested benefits under pension age 341, 353
UC 126, 137
waiting days 752
who can get SSP 747
who does not qualify 749
**step-parents**
guardian's allowance 498
two-child limit
UC 71
**stillborn baby**
funeral expenses payment 709
funeral support payment 1498
pregnancy and baby payment 1453
SMP/SPP/SPBP 735
SSP 754
Sure Start maternity grant 705
**stockpiling claims**
HB 219
**stocks**
treatment as capital
means-tested benefits over pension age 427
**student grants** 806
calculating income 806, 807
disregarded income 391, 808
treatment as income
means-tested benefits 806
UC 795
**student loans** 809
academic year 810
benefit weeks 810
calculating income 806, 809, 812
completing a course 813
disregarded income 391, 809
final year of course 811
treatment as income
means-tested benefits 806, 809
UC 795
**students** 789
absence from home
HB 802
I-ESA/PC 298
accommodation rented from educational establishment
HB 803
availability for work 794
CA 804
capital
ESA 801
HB 804
care home resident
DLA/PIP 828
couples
HB 802
UC 793
CSP 805
disabled students
ESA 797
HB 802
EEA nationals 1329
ESA 797
final year of course 811
financial support 806, 813
full-time students
C-ESA 797
HB 802
I-ESA 798
UC 792
giving up a course
UC 797
grants 806
HB 187, 193, 801
health benefits 578
income
ESA 801
HB 804

UC 795
limited capability for work 793
loans 809
lone parents
HB 802
modular courses 793, 800
new-style JSA 805
NI credits 806
non-dependant deductions
HB 209
I-ESA/PC 291
part-time students
C-ESA 797
HB 803
I-ESA 801
UC 795
partner liable for rent
HB 187
period of study 807
time out from course
UC 797
treated as not being in full-time work
new-style JSA/I-ESA 885
two homes
HB 196, 803
I-ESA/PC 298
UC 792
work-related requirements 794, 956
**sub-tenants**
not non-dependants
I-ESA/PC 290
**subject to the legislation** 1398
**Sudan**
benefit entitlement 1290
habitual residence test 1303
**sufficient resources** 1328
sickness insurance 1329
**supersessions** 1128, 1143
after appeal made 1202
anti-test case rule 1159
applying 1148
arrears following supersession 1148
capability for work decisions 1144, 1149, 1151
challenging 1155
change of circumstances 1145, 1150
closed-period supersessions 1151
date new decision takes effect 1148
decision is advantageous 1152
decision not advantageous 1150
decision of First-tier Tribunal 1207
decision of Upper Tribunal 1230
disability conditions for PIP 1144, 1149, 1151
error of law 1147
factual error 1146, 1154
grounds for supersession 1143
HMRC decisions on SSP/SMP/SAP/SPP/SSPP/SPBP/SNCP 1252
information required 1148
qualifying benefit awarded 1147, 1154, 1157
refusal to consider 1156
risks 1129
test cases 1155
when to seek a supersession 1128, 1143
**supervised study** 805
**supervision**
CDP mobility component 1488
DLA care component 521, 522, 524
DLA mobility component 518
PIP assessments 647
**support component**
backdating 283
ESA
C-ESA 560
I-ESA 282
HB 282
rate 283
transferring to UC 74
**supported accommodation**
HB 183, 206
UC housing costs element 91
**supported work**
working during limited capability for work period 930
**Supporting People programme** 363, 412
**Sure Start maternity grant** 705
amount 706
appeals 1166
claim form 706
person subject to immigration control 706
qualifying benefits 705
residence rules 1356
revisions 1130
time limits for claiming 707
trade disputes 893
**surrogacy**
SPP/SAP/SSPP/SPBP/SNCP 736
Sure Start maternity grant 706
**surveillance**
investigating claims 1104
**suspension of benefit** 1031
challenging a decision 1032
discretionary housing payments 550
failure to attend medical examinations 1032
failure to supply information 1031
fraud 1105
prisoners
non-means-tested benefits 838
Scottish benefits 1525
test case pending 1159
widowed parent's allowance 458

**Switzerland**
right to reside 1319
treated as EEA nationals 1389
UK-Switzerland agreement 1393

**T**
**tapers**
HB 201
UC 41
**tariff income**
diminishing capital rule 415
treatment as income
means-tested benefits over pension age 388
means-tested benefits under pension age 360
UC 42, 140
**tax credits**
absence abroad 1368
complaints about HMRC 1263
complaints to the Adjudicator 1264
NI credits 873
overpayments 1090
person subject to immigration control 1279
public funds 1276
refugees 21, 1291
replaced by UC 21, 23
**tax-free childcare scheme** 779
**telephone claims** 1004, 1008
ADP 1439
bereavement benefits 462
Best Start foods 1460
Best Start grants 1460
CDP 1490
CSP 1470
ESA
C-ESA 566
funeral support payment 1502
HB 212
new-style JSA 619
PC 247
PIP 670
Scottish child payment 1460
UC 44
young carer grant 1478
**Tell Us Once** 1030
**temporary accommodation**
HB 183
two homes during repair work
HB 196
I-ESA/PC 297
UC 99
UC housing costs element 91
**tenants**
treatment of income from
means-tested benefits over pension age 387
means-tested benefits under pension age 358
UC 142
**tents**
HB 185
I-ESA/PC 287
UC 91
**term-time accommodation**
HB 803
I-ESA/PC 299
**term-time work**
means-tested benefits 886
**terminal date** 491
**terminal illness**
AA 444
ADP 1436
start of entitlement 1437
CDP 1436
start of entitlement 1437
claimant commitment 935
claims under special rules
AA 446
ADP 1437
CDP 1437
DLA 531
PADP 1437
PIP 671
DLA care component 520, 530
DLA mobility component 530
ESA 562, 569
hospice care
AA/DLA/PIP 819, 828
ADP/PADP 819, 828
limited capability for work 900
ESA 899
UC 897
limited capability for work-related activity 917
PADP 1436
start of entitlement 1437
PIP 669
SADLA 1436
start of entitlement 1437
UC 897
**termination of entitlement** 1033
**test case**
anti-test case rule 1159
appeals while test case pending 1193
supersession while test case pending 1155, 1159
**therapy**
ADP 1431
PIP 651
**third-party payments** 1033
capital
means-tested benefits under pension age 416
income 393

means-tested benefits under pension age 366
UC 142
**tied accommodation**
UC 127
**time limits**
any grounds revision 1132
appealing HMRC decisions
SSP/SMP/SAP/SPP/SSPP/SPBP/SNCP 1252
appealing to First-tier Tribunal
benefits 1175, 1187
Scottish benefits 1545, 1562
SSP/SMP/SAP/SPP/SSPP/SPBP/SNCP 1255
appealing to the courts 1232
appealing to Upper Tribunal 1222, 1225
Scottish benefits 1555
SSP/SMP/SAP/SPP/SSPP/SPBP/SNCP 1256
Best Start grants 1462
decisions
HB 228
funeral expenses payments 713
funeral support payment 1502
industrial diseases 593
late appeals
benefits 1176
Scottish benefits 1546, 1562
mandatory reconsiderations
benefits 1169
notification of overpayment
HB 1086
notification of sickness
SSP 755
payments on appeals
SSP/SMP/SAP/SPP/SSPP/SPBP/SNCP 1257
prosecution of offences 1108
setting aside a First-tier Tribunal decision 1208
Sure Start maternity grant 707
**tips**
treatment as earnings
CA 474
means-tested benefits over pension age 379
means-tested benefits under pension age 341
UC 126
**toilet needs**
ADP 1431
PIP 654
**trade disputes** 891
continuous employment
SSP/SMP/SAP/SPP/SSPP/SPBP/SNCP 892
earnings
HB 371
good reason for refusing job 994
HB 891
I-ESA 891
new-style JSA 891
NI credits 867
PC 891
SMP/SAP/SPP/SSPP/SPBP/SNCP 892
social fund payments 892
SSP 892
strike pay
UC 142
Sure Start maternity grant 706
UC 891
**training**
approved training
child benefit 490
disability premium 272
EEA worker and self-employed status 1326
HB 193
housing costs
I-ESA/PC 297
NI credits 872
**training allowance**
disability premium 272
linked periods
new-style JSA 612
non-dependant deductions
I-ESA/PC 291
treated as not in work
new-style JSA/I-ESA 885
**training schemes**
good reason for leaving 993
industrial injuries benefits 588
payments, treatment as income
means-tested benefits under pension age 360
UC 138
sanctions for failure to participate 978
treated as not in full-time work
new-style JSA/I-ESA 885
**transitional element of UC** 78
calculating 81
challenging a decision 84
reduction of transitional element 83
**transitional protection**
transferring to UC under managed migration 43, 78
transferring to UC under natural migration 26
**transitional SDP element** 27, 78
**transport to school**
free school transport 775
**travel distance**
acceptable distance to training 993
acceptable distance to work 991

**travel expenses**
budgeting loans 702
medical assessments 921
NHS treatment 581
prison visits 843
student grants 808
treatment as earnings
CA 474
means-tested benefits over pension age 380
means-tested benefits under pension age 341
UC 127
**trusts**
capital
means tested benefits under pension age 401
means-tested benefits over pension age 428
UC 153
renting accommodation from a trustee
HB 188
UC 96
treatment of payments from
means-tested benefits under pension age 401
UC 140
**tuberculosis** 594
**Tunisia**
benefit entitlement 1282
reciprocal agreements 1297
**Turkey**
benefit entitlement 1281, 1282
reciprocal agreements 1297
**two homes**
essential repairs
HB 196
I-ESA/PC 297
UC 99
extended payments
HB 226
fear of violence
HB 193, 196
I-ESA/PC 298
UC 99
HB 190, 195
housing costs for home owners
I-ESA/PC 294, 298
students
HB 196, 803
I-ESA/PC 298
UC 97, 98, 102
**two-child limit**
means-tested benefits 268
UC 69
**two-strikes rule** 1111

**U**
**UK-EFTA Convention** 1398
**UK-EU Protocol** 1397
**UK-Ireland Convention** 1397
**Ukraine**
benefit entitlement 1290
habitual residence 1303
Homes for Ukraine Scheme payments
means-tested benefits over pension age 435
means-tested benefits under pension age 363, 412
UC 142, 161
**under-occupation charge** 313
**underpayments**
offset against overpayment
HB 1081
**unemployment**
EEA workers 1325
EU co-ordination of benefits 1402
NI credits for signing on 866
**unfair dismissal**
compensation
means-tested benefits over pension age 380
means-tested benefits under pension age 344
recovery of benefits from compensation 1043
**unit trusts**
treatment as capital
means-tested benefits over pension age 427
means-tested benefits under pension age 400
UC 151
valuation
means-tested benefits under pension age 420
UC 166
**universal credit** 35
16/17-year-olds 37
absence abroad 1371
advance payment 1023
age rules 37
amount 39, 67
appeal pending on limited capability for work 927
appeals 1166
assessment period 39, 50
basic conditions 36
benefit cap 56, 1025, 1028
budgeting advances 52
calculation 40
capital 149
capital limits 149

care homes 831
care leavers 846
carer element 75
change of circumstances 32, 53
child element 68
childcare costs 76
children 62
claimant commitment 934
claims 44
closure of claim 937
couples 38, 58
death of family member 67
decisions 1115
deductions from benefit 1034
delays 50, 1123
discretionary housing payments 548
earnings 125
earnings thresholds 955
elements 68
entitlement to other benefits
means-tested benefits 55
non-means-tested benefits 55
EU co-ordination rules 1373
failed claim 47
families 58
financial conditions 36
following award of qualifying benefit 1157
fraud 1100
full-time paid work 883
grace period for benefit cap 1026
habitual residence test 1300
hardship payments 1050
HB run-on 227
homeless 848
hospital patients 820
housing costs element 78, 88
income 124, 136
indicative UC amount 80
introduction of UC 17
legacy benefits 19
light touch regime 955
limited capability for work 895
limited capability for work element 71
limited capability for work-related activity 913
limited capability for work-related activity element 73
managed migration 29
maximum amount 40, 66
maximum deductions 1040
means-tested benefits 23
monthly income 144
mortgage interest loan 764
natural migration 25
NHS charges 574
NI credits 868
overpayments 1058, 1060
partner subject to immigration control 1284
passport to other benefits 56
payment 49
person subject to immigration control 1279
prisoners 839
public funds 1276
receiving education 792
residence rules 1307, 1343
revisions 1128, 1130
sanctions 969
benefit offences 1112
work-related requirements 970
Scottish choices payment scheme 51
severe disability 27
standard allowance 67
students 792
supersessions 1128, 1143
tax 55
tax credits 1090
trade disputes 891
transitional protection 43
treatment as income
means-tested benefits over pension age 386
two wages payments in one assessment period 145
two-child limit 69
when you come under UC system 20
who can get UC 36
who should claim 45
work 883, 886
work allowance 41
work availability requirement 945
work capability assessment 896
work preparation requirement 940
work search requirement 941
work-focused interviews 939
work-related requirements 938, 959
working out your UC 40
**untidy tenancy** 111
**upper earnings limit**
NI contributions 860
**Upper Tribunal**
appealing a First-tier Tribunal decision 1207
Scottish benefits 1554
appealing an Upper Tribunal decision 1231
Scottish benefits 1557
appeals 1215
Scottish benefits 1554
attendance at hearing 1228
challenging an Upper Tribunal decision 1230
Scottish benefits 1557

decision maker appeals to Upper Tribunal 1228
decisions 1229
Scottish benefits 1557
decisions that cannot be appealed 1216
hearings 1228
Scottish benefits 1557
how to appeal to Upper Tribunal 1219
Scottish benefits 1554
judicial review 1246
notice of appeal 1225
permission to appeal to the courts 1231
permission to appeal to Upper Tribunal 1223
Scottish benefits 1555
reinstating an appeal 1227
remote hearings 1228
representatives 1220
reviewing an Upper Tribunal decision 1232
Scottish benefits 1557
setting aside a decision
Scottish benefits 1557
SSP/SMP/SAP/SPP/SSPP/SPBP/SNCP 1256
what the Upper Tribunal can do 1226
Scottish benefits 1556
withdrawing an appeal 1227
written procedure 1227

V

**Vaccine Damage Payment Scheme**
treatment of payments
means-tested benefits over pension age 434
means-tested benefits under pension age 411
UC 160
**valuation of capital**
means-tested benefits over pension age 436
means-tested benefits under pension age 418
UC 164
**Victims of Overseas Terrorism Compensation Scheme**
treatment of payments
means-tested benefits over pension age 391
means-tested benefits under pension age 411
UC 160
**Victoria Cross payments**
treatment as income
means-tested benefits under pension age 364
UC 161
**violence**
*see: domestic violence and abuse*
**visits**
prisoners 843
**visual impairment**
CDP mobility component 1487
*see also: blindness*
**vitamins** 364, 771
free vitamins 773, 1464
**voluntary contributions** 862
**voluntary unemployment**
definition 975
sanctions
new-style JSA 973
UC 973
**voluntary work**
available for work requirement 945
expenses 364
treated as not in work
new-style JSA/ESA 885
unpaid work, notional income
means-tested benefits 367
UC 143
work search requirement 943
working during limited capability for work 929
**volunteer development worker** 861, 863
**vouchers**
food banks 782
glasses and contact lenses 580
payment of benefits 1019
treatment as earnings
means-tested benefits over pension age 380
means-tested benefits under pension age 342
**vulnerable groups**
sanctions 996

W

**wages**
minimum wage 1584
pay rises
SMP/SAP/SPP/SSPP/SPBP/SNCP 730
unpaid 366
**waiting days**
ESA 569
new-style JSA 626
SSP 752
**waiting period**
service charge payments
UC 119
**walking**
ADP 1433
CDP 1486
DLA 513, 537
PIP 662

**war pension disablement benefits** 779
claiming health benefits 583
NHS charges, exemption 574
treatment as income
means-tested benefits over pension age 386
means-tested benefits under pension age 354
UC 138
**war pensions**
treatment as income
means-tested benefits over pension age 386
means-tested benefits under pension age 354
UC 138
**Warm Home Discount** 781
**washing**
ADP 1432
PIP 653
**water charges**
debts paid by deductions from benefit 1037
HB 204
**West Bank**
benefit entitlement 1290
habitual residence test 1303
**widow's pension**
overlapping benefits 1021
treatment as income
means-tested benefits over pension age 385
means-tested benefits under pension age 353
UC 137
**widowed mother's allowance** 461
**widowed parent's allowance** 456
absence abroad 1376
age rules 457
amount 458
backdating 464
benefit cap 468
claims 462
disqualification 458
eligible child 456
entitlement to other benefits
means-tested benefits 467
non-means-tested benefits 468
EU co-ordination rules 1345, 1376
increases for dependent children 457
new relationship 458
NI contribution conditions 879
NI credits 873
NI credits for parents and carers 868
overlapping benefits 468, 1021
payment of benefit 465
people included in the claim 457
reciprocal agreements 1345
reduced rate 458
residence rules 1345
sanctionable benefits 466
suspension 458
tax 467
time limits for claiming 457
treatment as income 467
means-tested benefits over pension age 386
means-tested benefits under pension age 354
UC 137
who can get widowed parent's allowance 456
**widowers**
bereavement benefits 453
bereavement support payment 454
definition 458
NI credits 873
state pension 693
widowed parent's allowance 456
**widows**
bereavement benefits 453
bereavement support payment 454
definition 458
husband died before April 2001 461
NI credits 873
reduced liability for NI contributions 862
state pension 693, 696
widowed parent's allowance 456
**wigs and fabric supports** 581
**Windrush generation** 1275
treatment of Compensation Scheme payments
means-tested benefits over pension age 434
means-tested benefits under pension age 411
UC 160
**winter fuel payments** 715
age rules 715
amount 716
appeals 1166
care home residents 834
claims 716
EU co-ordination rules 1357
hospital patients 824
payment 716
person subject to immigration control 716
prisoners 841
qualifying benefits 715
residence rules 1357
revisions 1130
**winter heating payment** 1505
age rules 1507
amount 1508
appeals 1544
benefit cap 1510

care home residents 834
change of circumstances 1535
claims 1508
information to support claim 1509
payment 1509
public funds 1276
qualifying benefits 1506
redeterminations 1535
residence rules 1357
tax 1510
treatment as capital
means-tested benefits over pension age 433
means-tested benefits under pension age 410
UC 159
treatment as income 1510
means-tested benefits over pension age 386
UC 138
who can get a winter heating payment 1505
**Withdrawal Agreement**
partial Withdrawal Agreement protections 1395
protections 1390, 1393
who is covered 1396
**withdrawing a claim** 1004
HB 213
Scottish benefits 1522
**withholding benefit**
fraud 1105
**witnesses**
allowances 364, 413
work search requirement 963
**work** 883
CA 473
calculating hours of work
new-style JSA/I-ESA 885
during period of SMP/SAP/SPP/SSPP/SPBP/SNCP 731
ESA 928
financial help seeking or starting work 781
full-time paid work
means-tested benefits 884
genuine and effective 1323
in-work conditionality 959
means-tested benefits 884
new-style JSA 884
non-means-tested benefits 890
paid work
means-tested benefits 884
sanctionable actions
new-style JSA 972
UC 972
seasonal work
means-tested benefits 886
term-time work
means-tested benefits 886
treated as being in full-time paid work
I-ESA 888
new-style JSA 887
treated as not being in full-time paid work
HB 889
new-style JSA/I-ESA 884
UC 883, 886
work search requirement 962
work-related requirements 954
**work allowance**
effect on earnings 126
UC 41
**work availabilty requirement** 945
appealing a decision 1173
disabled 959
EEA jobseekers 1321
holidays 946
homeless 848
limitations on availability 946
location of work 947
new-style JSA 945
no work availability requirement 959
prisoners 838
sanctions for not complying 978
sick 959
students 794
type of work and rate of pay 946
willing and able to work 945
working hours restrictions 946
**work capability assessment** 896
appealing against a decision
ESA 899
assessment process 919
descriptors 903, 914
failing work capability assessment
ESA 902
UC 901
fluctuating condition 903
limited capability for work assessment 896
limited capability for work-related activity assessment 913
medical assessments 919, 921
mental disabilities test 909
questionnaire 920
reassessments 920
scoring points 902
treated as having limited capability for work 900
ESA 898
UC 896
waiting for an assessment
ESA 899
**work coaches** 935
**work expenses**
budgeting loans 702
employed earners, treatment as earnings

CA 474
means-tested benefits over pension age 380
means-tested benefits under pension age 341, 342
UC 127
good reason for refusing a job 991
self-employed, treatment as earnings
means-tested benefits over pension age 382
means-tested benefits under pension age 346
UC 129
**work preparation requirement** 940, 957
sanctions 978
**work search requirement** 941
all reasonable action 941
holidays 946
homeless 848
no work search requirement 959
permitted limitations 946
proving you are searching for work 943
rate of pay 946
sanctions 978
type of work 946
voluntary work 943
**work-focused interview** 939
lone parents 956
sanctions
new-style ESA 978, 979
new-style JSA 978
UC 978, 979
work-focused interview requirement
old-style ESA 176
UC 939, 956, 957
**work-related activity**
exemptions
old-style ESA 177
limited capability 914
sanctions
old-style ESA 177
work-related activity requirement 176
**work-related activity component**
backdating 283
ESA
C-ESA 561
I-ESA 282
HB 282
rate 283
transferring to UC 72
**work-related activity group** 561
**work-related requirements** 934, 938
availability for work 945, 959
earnings threshold 955
exemptions 950
in-work conditionality 959
interviews 948
levels of sanction 971
prisoners 838
sanctions 970
sickness and disability 954
students 794
which requirements apply 948
work preparation 940, 957
work search requirement 941, 959
work-focused interviews 939, 956
**workers from the EEA**
A2 nationals 1323
A8 nationals 1323
child in education 1336
Croatians 1323
definition 1322
gaps between jobs 1327
genuine and effective work 1323
habitual residence test 1303
permanently incapacitated 1340
pregnancy 1327
registered as a jobseeker 1325
retaining worker status 1325
A2 nationals 1325
A8 nationals 1325
Croatians 1325
retirement 1340
right to reside 1322
self-employed 1324
sickness or injury 1326
unemployed 1325
**working tax credit** *see: tax credits*
**Working Time Regulations** 1584
**wrong/misleading advice**
late claim
new-style JSA 622, 623

Y

**young carer grant** 1476
age rules 1478
amount 1478
appeals 1544
benefit cap 1480
CA 1480
change of circumstances 1535
claims 1478
CSP 1480
date of claim 1479
entitlement to other benefits 1480
EU co-ordination rules 1350, 1379
fraud 1528
habitual residence test 1300
hours of caring 1477
information to support claim 1479
overpayments 1526
passport to other benefits 1480
payment 1479
qualifying benefits 1477
redeterminations 1535
residence rules 1347

tax 1480
treatment as capital
means-tested benefits over pension age 433
means-tested benefits under pension age 410
UC 159
treatment as income 1480
means-tested benefits over pension age 386
UC 138
two people care for same person 1480
who can get young carer grant 1476
**young individual**
single room rent 328
**young people**
16/17-year-olds
UC 37
approved training
child benefit 490
estrangement from parents
UC 38, 793
free dental treatment 580
free period products 776
free prescriptions 578
free sight tests 580
limited capability for work
ESA 557
local authority payments
treatment as capital 411
treatment as income 363
UC 161
non-dependant deductions
HB 209
qualifying young person
child benefit 488
guardian's allowance 496
PC 259
UC 792
single room rent 328
vouchers for glasses and contact lenses 580
*see also: 16/17-year-olds, 18 to 24-year-olds*
**youth custody**
leaving custody 847
young person in custody
child benefit 496, 499
guardian's allowance 499
I-ESA 262

**Z**
**Zambrano carer** 1336
**zero-hour contract**
available for work 947
reduced hours 975
sanctions 973